THE JOHNS HOPKINS

COMPLETE HOME GUIDE TO

PILLS & MEDICINES

THE JOHNS HOPKINS

COMPLETE HOME GUIDE TO

PILLS & MEDICINES

- 3,000 Prescription and Over-the-Counter Medications
- Easy-to-Use A to Z Format
- 600 Color Photos
- Drug and Food Interactions

Medical Editor
Simeon Margolis, M.D., Ph.D.

Prepared by the Editors of *The Johns Hopkins Medical Letter: Health After 50*

BLACK DOG
& LEVENTHAL
PUBLISHERS
NEW YORK

For information about permission to reproduce selections from this book, write to Permissions, Medletter Associates, Inc., 325 Redding Road, Redding, CT 06896.

This book is not intended as a substitute for the advice and expertise of a physician or a pharmacist. Readers who suspect they may have specific medical problems should consult a physician about any suggestions made in this book.

For updated information on drugs, visit the Johns Hopkins Health After 50 web site: www.HopkinsAfter50.com

Published by
Black Dog & Leventhal Publishers, Inc.
151 West 19th Street
New York, NY 10011

Distributed by
Workman Publishing Company
708 Broadway
New York, NY 10003

ISBN-13: 978-1-57912-359-8
ISBN-10: 1-57912-359-7

g f e d c b

Library of Congress Cataloging-in-Publication Data is on file at Black Dog & Leventhal Publishers, Inc.

Cover design by Christina Gaugler

Manufactured in China

The Johns Hopkins
Consumer Guide to Drugs

RODNEY FRIEDMAN
Publisher

THOMAS DICKEY
Executive Editor

JEREMY D. BIRCH
Managing Editor

CARNEY W. MIMMS III
Production Database Designer

JOHN VASILIADIS
Production Database Programmer

TIMOTHY JEFFS
Art Director

ROBERT DUCKWALL
Medical Illustrator

Johns Hopkins Medical Books are published
under the auspices of The Johns Hopkins
Medical Letter HEALTH AFTER 50

RODNEY FRIEDMAN
Editor and Publisher

THOMAS DICKEY
Executive Editor

MAUREEN O'SULLIVAN
Senior Writer

JOAN MULLALLY
Business Development and Licensing

BARBARA MAXWELL O'NEILL
Associate Publisher

Special Acknowledgments

GIGA COMMUNICATIONS, INC.
Digital Production

**DEBORAH WIBLE AND THE STAFF OF
THE DEPARTMENT OF PHARMACY,
BETH ISRAEL MEDICAL CENTER, NEW YORK, NY
MT. SINAI HOSPITAL MEDICAL CENTER, CHICAGO, IL**
Pharmacological Resources

HOW TO USE THIS BOOK

The Johns Hopkins Consumer Guide to Drugs contains the most essential information regarding nearly every major medication available for consumers—both prescription and over-the-counter (OTC) drugs. It presents the facts about medications in plain, easy-to-understand language so that everyone, and particularly older adults (the largest group of people using medications), can achieve the maximum therapeutic benefit from taking drugs, while keeping side effects and adverse reactions to a minimum.

Each drug is covered in a succinct one- or two-page profile. These profiles appear in alphabetical order according to the generic name of the drug (e.g., acetaminophen). If you do not know the generic name, you can look up the drug's brand name (e.g., Tylenol) in the general index starting on page 862, and it will guide you to the appropriate page. You can also look up a specific ailment in the disorder index (see page 16) and find the various drugs used to treat it.

Following the drug profiles are two additional sections. The first is devoted to color photographs of many of the pills described in the book. The second section is an overview of herbs and other dietary supplements, which are widely used to self-treat health problems. The overview focuses on issues of efficacy and safety concerning supplements, including their potential for interactions with conventional medications. Following the overview are profiles of 10 of the most popular supplements.

Important Note Regarding the Color Pill Photographs in This Book: The physical appearance of a particular drug may vary considerably from one manufacturer to another, or from one dosage strength to another even when made by the same manufacturer. The pictures that appear with the drug profiles (and in the color pill section on pages 842-859) of this book represent but one dosage strength of one brand of a drug made by one manufacturer. If the pill you take looks different from the one you see in the photograph, do not be alarmed. However, if you have any doubts, concerns, or questions whatsoever about the medication you take, consult your doctor or pharmacist.

DRUGS AND AGING

If you're over 50, chances are you're taking more kinds of medications and in greater quantities than you ever did in previous decades. Indeed, people between the ages of 55 and 64 are given an average of eight different prescriptions during the course of a year. And those over age 70 take an average of 6.5 medications per day. It's only logical that the more medications you take concurrently, the more likely it is that an adverse drug reaction could occur. And for older people, such risks are further compounded by physiological changes that make the body more sensitive to the effects of drugs (see below). Consequently, adverse reactions to drugs are seven times more common in older people than younger ones and account for approximately 20 percent of all hospitalizations among older adults. If you fall into this age group, knowledge about the medications you take can help ensure that your drug therapy is effective—and as safe as possible.

HOW AGING AFFECTS THE BODY'S RESPONSE TO DRUGS

Beginning sometime during our middle thirties and continuing throughout life, measurements of functional capacity of most major organ systems show a gradual decline. Such changes, which are natural and inevitable, do not necessarily have any noticeable effect on one's quality of life. But they can affect the way that our bodies respond to drugs, and make us more susceptible to untoward reactions and side effects. For one thing, there is an overall decrease in body fluid volume. This results in proportionally higher concentrations of drugs or other substances in the bloodstream, thus increasing the risk of toxicity. This effect may be further compounded by an age-related decline in liver and kidney function. These organs are primarily responsible for metabolizing drugs and eliminating toxins. Therefore, a decrease in their function means chemical substances remain in the body longer and are more likely to build up to potentially hazardous levels. Conversely, a sluggish digestive system can slow the rate that drugs are absorbed into the bloodstream, meaning that less of the drug is available to produce the desired therapeutic effect.

Diminished blood flow to the brain may boost the likelihood that certain drugs will cause dizziness, fainting, loss of coordination, forgetfulness, confusion, or other signs of cognitive impairment. In some people the heart functions less efficiently with age, which in turn may deprive other organs of an adequate blood supply, causing further disruptions in how drugs are distributed in the body.

SOME WAYS THE BODY CHANGES WITH AGE

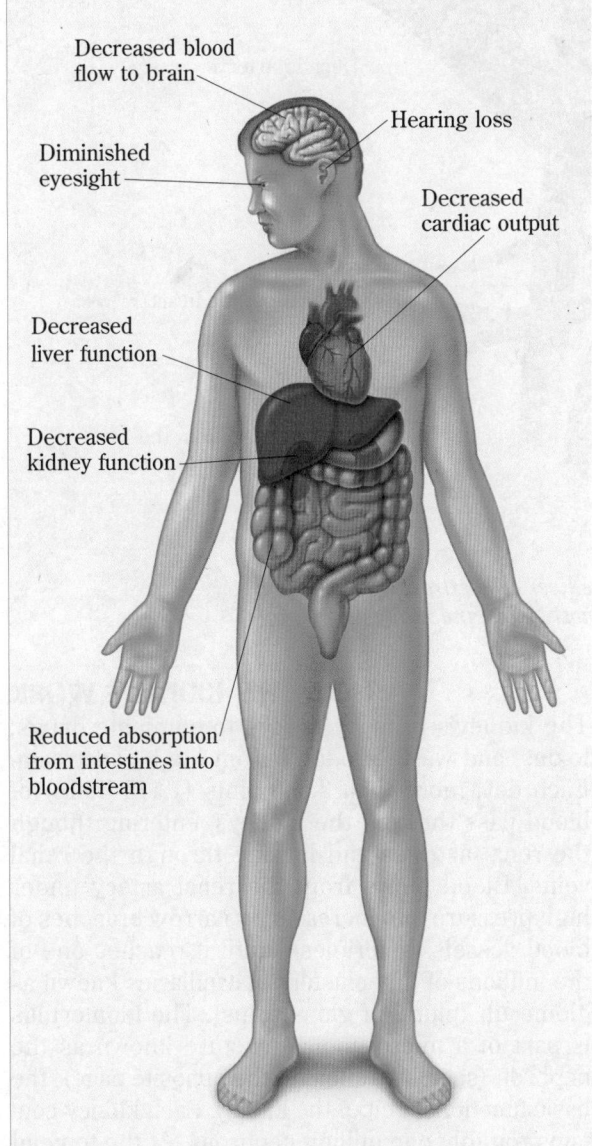

Decreased blood flow to brain

Hearing loss

Diminished eyesight

Decreased cardiac output

Decreased liver function

Decreased kidney function

Reduced absorption from intestines into bloodstream

The physiological changes that occur with age can affect the way our bodies react to drugs.

Finally, age-associated decrements in vision, hearing, and memory may affect an older person's ability to properly understand prescription labels, package inserts, or doctors' instructions. Bear in mind, however, that chronological age alone is not necessarily a good predictor of the degree of functional decline; there is considerable variability from one person to another in the rate at which such changes occur. For example, approximately one-third of healthy elderly people exhibit no significant decrease in kidney function.

DRUGS AND THE DIGESTIVE SYSTEM

Drugs are absorbed primarily in the stomach and small intestine. As we age, these organs may not absorb food and medications as well as they once did, resulting in reduced therapeutic levels of the drug in the bloodstream. A larger dose may be needed to compensate for this phenomenon. A more common problem is that some drugs are not metabolized as efficiently as we age. As a result, greater amounts of the drug circulate in the bloodstream for longer periods of time; thus smaller dosages may be warranted for older patients.

HOW THE LIVER BREAKS DOWN DRUGS AND TOXINS

One of the primary functions of the liver is to cleanse and detoxify the blood of drugs (including alcohol) and poisonous substances that would otherwise build up in the bloodstream. How does it do this? First, nutrient-rich blood passes from the stomach and small intestine through the portal vein into the liver (see illustration, page 10). This blood is then exposed to the many thousands of cells (hepatocytes) within the liver. Here, the nutrients are extracted and chemically broken down (metabolized) into their smallest useful components, and then either stored in the liver for future use or returned to the bloodstream via the hepatic vein to become available for use by cells throughout the body. Many drugs and toxins are also chemically modified (most often inactivated) in the liver. Most of the byproducts of the metabolism of nutrients, toxins, and drugs are also returned to the bloodstream and travel to the kidneys where they are eliminated in the urine. The substances that cannot

THE ROUTE OF BLOOD THROUGH THE LIVER

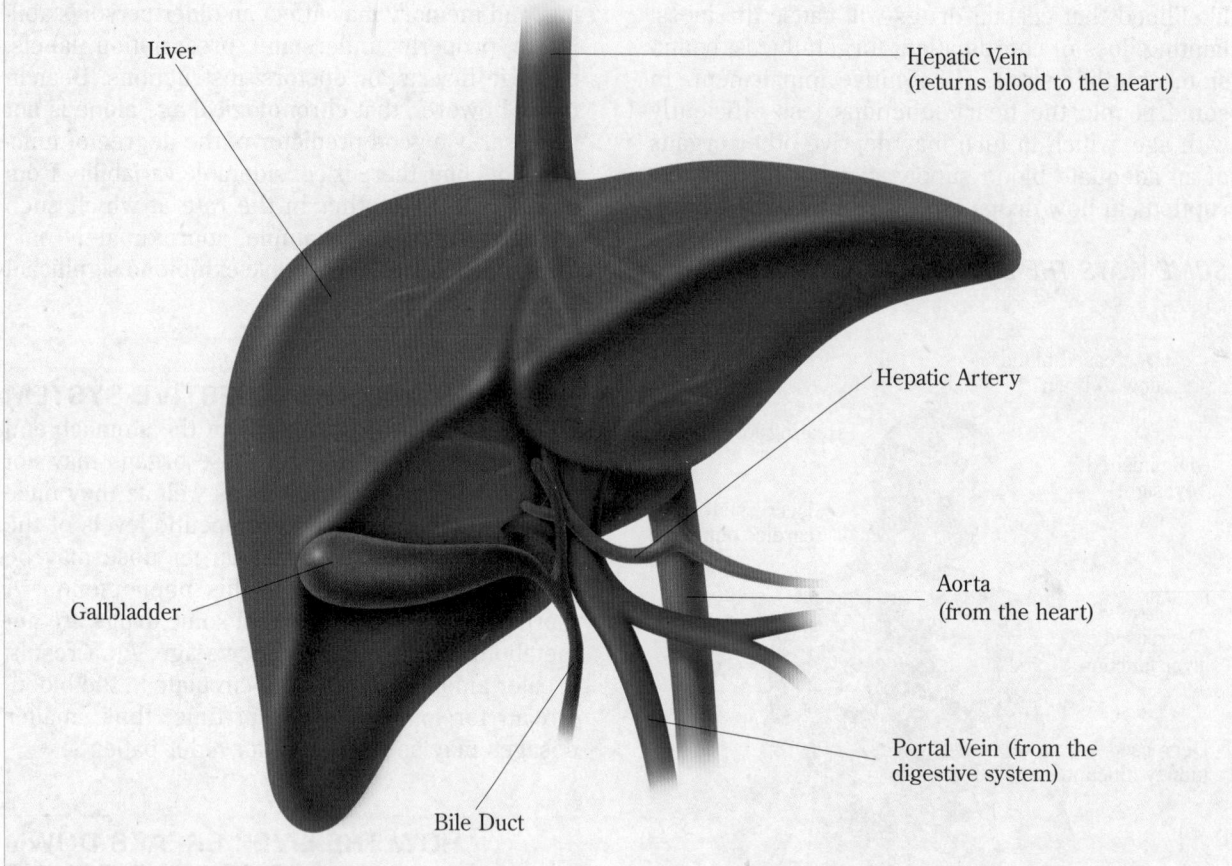

Liver

Hepatic Vein
(returns blood to the heart)

Hepatic Artery

Aorta
(from the heart)

Portal Vein (from the
digestive system)

Gallbladder

Bile Duct

Blood passes through the spongelike channels of the liver, where liver cells extract nutrients and metabolize them for use by the rest of the body and neutralize most toxins and many drugs.

be eliminated by the kidneys are incorporated into the bile, a digestive fluid produced by liver cells and stored in the gallbladder. Bile is released via the common bile duct to help absorb fats in the small intestine, and its constituents are mostly excreted in the feces. Liver cells themselves are nourished by fresh blood coming in through the hepatic artery, a branch of the aorta—the heart's primary artery.

The liver is composed of 50,000 to 100,000 individual clusters of cells known as lobules. At the core of each lobule is a centrilobar vein, from which radiate hundreds of hepatocytes. Each lobule is served by a network of minuscule branches of the bile ducts, the hepatic artery, and the portal vein. This structure is suggestive of a liver lobule's function as a minuscule chemical processing plant.

HOW THE KIDNEYS WORK

The kidney's primary task is to eliminate drugs, toxins, and waste products from the bloodstream. Each day, more than 2,500 pints (1,175 liters) of blood pass through the kidneys, entering though the renal arteries and leaving through the renal veins. Blood pours from the renal artery under high pressure into increasingly narrow branches of blood vessels (arterioles), until it reaches one of the millions of tiny clusters of capillaries known as glomeruli (plural of glomerulus). The glomerulus is part of a microscopic structure known as the nephron (see illustration on the opposite page), the basic functional unit of the kidney. Each kidney contains roughly one million nephrons. At the top end of the nephron is Bowman's capsule, which surrounds the glomerulus. Water, salts, wastes, and

THE KIDNEYS

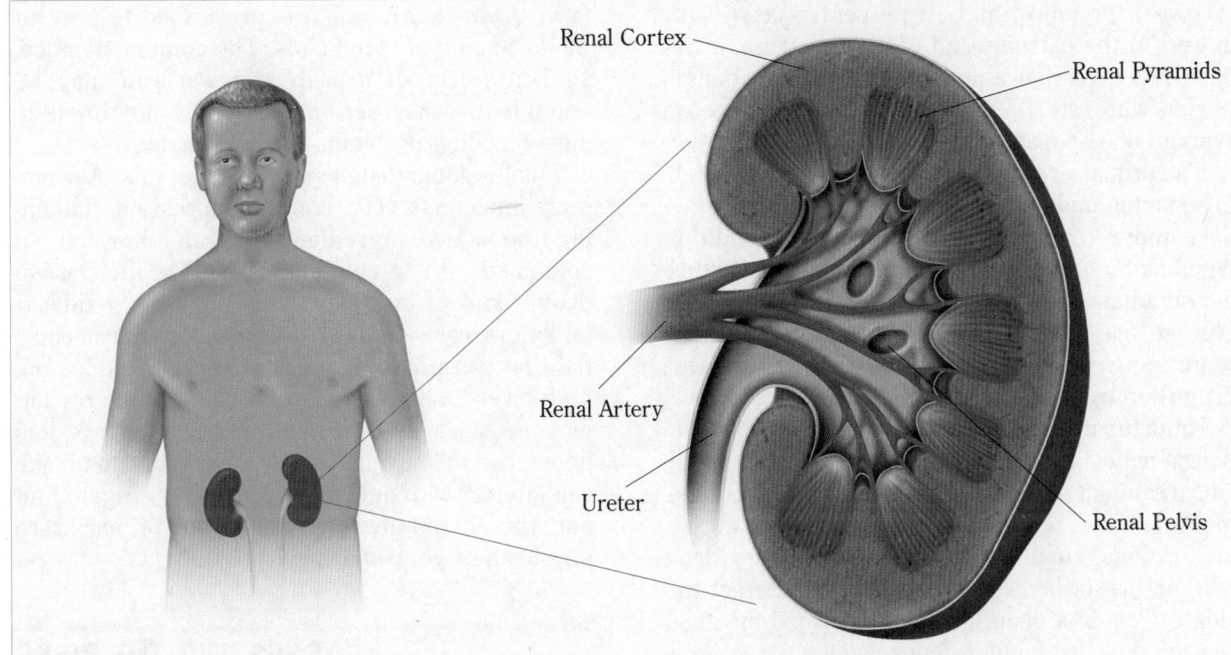

Renal Cortex

Renal Pyramids

Renal Artery

Ureter

Renal Pelvis

In conjunction with the liver, the kidney is responsible for cleansing the blood of drugs and toxins.

toxins filter through the tiny blood vessels of the glomerulus and enter Bowman's capsule. This filtrate, which will become urine, passes from Bowman's capsule through the nephron's convoluted tubule, which has a hairpin turn known as the loop of Henle (the structure affected by so-called loop diuretics). Next it travels back out to the renal cortex (the outer region of the kidney), down through the collecting tubule, and out the renal pelvis, where it flows into the ureter, the conduit through which urine reaches the bladder. Meanwhile, the purified portion of the filtrate (containing almost all the salts and water entering the kidney) is conserved and returned to the bloodstream via the renal vein. Indeed, for all of the many quarts of fluid the kidney processes per day, only one quart or so is eliminated as urine.

AGING AND THE RISKS OF MULTIPLE DRUG USE

Two-thirds of all people over 65 take medications on a daily basis, and many of those in this population take more than one medication at a time. Among persons ages 65 to 84, 61 percent receive 3

A NEPHRON

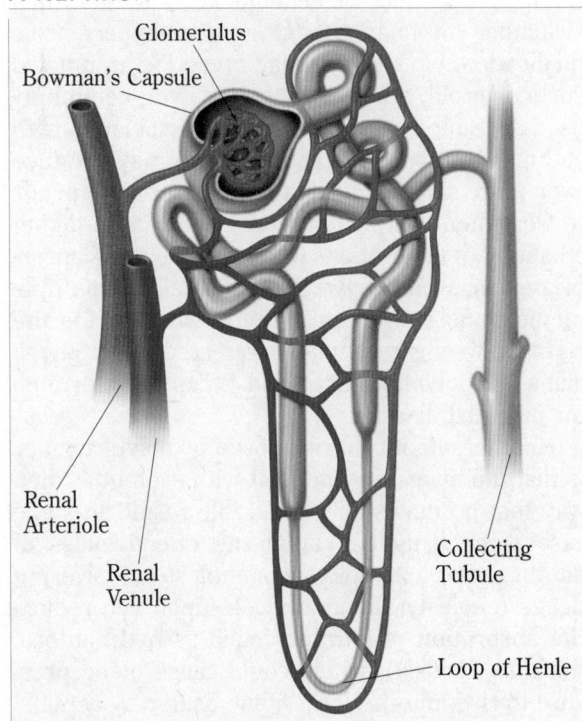

Glomerulus

Bowman's Capsule

Renal Arteriole

Renal Venule

Collecting Tubule

Loop of Henle

In the tiny capillaries of the nephron, wastes are filtered out of the blood to be excreted in the urine.

11

or more different drugs in a year; 37 percent receive 5 or more; and 19 percent receive 7 or more. (At the extreme end of the spectrum, it has been reported that a portion of Medicare beneficiaries who rate their health as poor receive an average of 31 separate prescriptions per year.)

The primary reason older people are more likely to be taking multiple drugs is simply that they often have more than one chronic medical condition (such as high blood pressure, glaucoma, or arthritis) simultaneously. In fact, elderly people have, on average, five separate coexisting medical conditions requiring treatment, which almost always involves drug therapy.

Unfortunately, in some instances relief from the typical aches and pains of aging—rather than specific treatment of illness or restoration of function—motivates the use of multiple prescription and OTC medications. Or oftentimes, an unnecessary drug may be prescribed merely to help counteract the side effects of a drug initially prescribed for good reason. For example, suppose you take a beta-blocker (such as propranolol) for high blood pressure and you begin to experience wheezing, a known side effect of beta-blockers. Rather than switching you to another class of antihypertensive medication, your doctor may prescribe an inhaled corticosteroid, a powerful type of drug commonly used to suppress the wheezing associated with asthma. In turn, the corticosteroid may produce even more side effects that require yet more drugs to treat them. Ultimately, you may wind up taking a handful of medications when a single more appropriate one would have sufficed. Taking multiple medications at the same time—whether for the right or wrong reasons—is referred to by physicians as "polypharmacy," and it can be a formula for potential disaster.

Another significant risk posed by polypharmacy is that the drugs may interact with each other in a way that produces an undesirable result. In some cases, one drug can blunt the effectiveness of another. For example, two cholesterol-lowering drugs (cholestyramine and colestipol) can reduce the absorption of diuretics such as hydrochlorothiazide (Esidrix), which could cause blood pressure to rise. In other cases, one drug may actually enhance the effects of another drug so that dangerous adverse effects may occur, as when aspirin, which has an anticlotting effect, is taken with warfarin (Coumadin), which is prescribed to prevent the formation of blood clots. The combined anticoagulant effect of aspirin and warfarin may be enough to cause serious—possibly life-threatening—bleeding problems (hemorrhaging).

Finally, some drugs simply do not mix. A seemingly innocuous OTC cough suppressant containing the active ingredient dextromethorphan, if combined with an antidepressant from the class of drugs known as MAO (monoamine oxidase) inhibitors, can result in a dangerous chemical cocktail that can produce extreme nervous excitation, high fever, a sharp increase in blood pressure, and in some cases, death. In light of such dangers, it is imperative to know if any new drug you plan to take can interact with one you are already using; to find out, you should always consult your primary-care physician or your pharmacist.

ASSESSING THE RISKS

Broadly defined as any unwanted response to a drug, adverse drug reactions (ADRs) occur with considerable frequency in persons over the age of 60. At least 17 percent—but as many as 30 percent by some estimates—of all hospital admissions and one in a thousand hospital deaths of older Americans are a direct result of drug toxicity or ADRs. The Inspector General of the U.S. Department of Health and Human Services estimates that 32,000 hip fractures, 163,000 cases of mental impairment, and 61,000 cases of drug-induced parkinsonism occur annually as a result of ADRs in the elderly. Women are generally at greater risk for ADRs because more drugs are prescribed for them on average than for men; and women lose significantly more muscle mass as they age, which increases their sensitivity to drugs. Yet the single most important contributing factor to ADRs is the number of medications taken. Susceptibility to ADRs increases with each drug added to the therapeutic regimen. Recent findings indicate that the presence of coexisting disease is equally important in determining the risk of ADRs. Individual health status, rather than chronological age alone, becomes a key predictor in assessing risk for ADRs.

It must be noted, however, that not all multiple drug combinations are undesirable or unnecessary.

Appropriate drug therapy can be vastly beneficial for older persons by providing symptom relief, improved functional capacities, pain management, reduced complications of chronic disease, and even prolongation of life. Naturally, every drug has the potential for adverse effects. But minor or irritating side effects, or even more problematic ones, must be weighed against benefits that could make a pronounced difference in terms of the quality and length of a person's life

PREVENTING ADVERSE DRUG REACTIONS

Considering the age-related physiological changes that can affect the body's response to drugs, as well as the alarming statistics regarding polypharmacy and adverse drug reactions, the message is clear that extra caution is in order when older people take medications. The first step is simply to put all of your medicines into a paper bag and bring them to your doctor for a review of everything you are currently taking. Include all of your over-the-

Drugs That Don't Mix with Grapefruit Juice

While doctors, pharmacists, and the package inserts that come with medications provide clear warnings against adverse interactions between one drug and another, patients are considerably less likely to be warned of potential bad reactions caused by taking a drug with a particular food. In recent years it has come to light that grapefruit may cause potentially serious interactions when taken with a number of drugs. A compound found in grapefruit (but not other citrus fruits) can block an enzyme in the small intestine which helps to metabolize certain drugs. As a result, more of the drug is absorbed and the level of the drug is increased in the bloodstream.However, this enhancement of the drug occurs only if the drug and grapefruit juice are taken close together.

In some situations, the effect may be beneficial. Those taking a calcium channel blocker such as felodipine (Plendil) for hypertension may suddenly acquire better, more stable control of their blood pressure, or be able to

take a lower—and thus safer—dose while obtaining the same therapeutic benefit. On the other hand, for some patients, excessive quantities of felodipine may build up in the blood and cause blood pressure to drop precipitously and cause dizziness or fainting. (Interestingly, medical researchers are currently looking for ways to harness the natural effect of grapefruit juice on drug metabolism, so that one day it could be incorporated into the formulation of certain medications to achieve optimal results while using less of the primary active ingredient. Because individual responses vary so widely, however, many experts are skeptical that such an approach would work reliably from patient to patient.)

The following is a list of the medications known to interact adversely with grapefruit juice. If you take any of these drugs and you also regularly eat grapefruit or drink its juice, you don't need to suddenly change your dietary habits. Rather, you should consult your doctor for advice.

- **Calcium channel blockers**, especially felodipine (Plendil), nifedipine (Adalat, Procardia), and nimodipine (Nimotop). Also affects verapamil (Calan, Isoptin, Verelan), but to a lesser degree. No apparent affect on diltiazem (Cardizem, Dilacor, Tiazac).
- **Cilostazol** (Pletal).
- **Cyclosporine** (Sandimmune).
- **Tacrolimus** (Prograf).
- **Midazolam** (a short-acting benzodiazepine marketed only in injectable form in the US). Grapefruit juice may also increase elimination times of other benzodiazepine tranquilizers, such as alprazolam (Xanax) and triazolam (Halcion).
- **Statins**, such as atorvastatin (Lipitor)and simvastatin(Zocor).
- **Estrogens**.
- **Caffeine**.
- **Saquinavir** (Invirase), an antiviral drug used against HIV. (Curiously, grapefruit juice actually decreases elimination times for indinavir, a similar drug.)

counter medicines as well. Your doctor can evaluate whether any of the drugs might interact badly with one another, or determine which ones may not be appropriate at all for you (see box below, for example). Repeat this "brown-bag review" once every year. In addition, the following tips can help you use your medications more safely.

YOU AND YOUR MEDICATIONS
▶ Keep a record of all your medications. Note the

name of the drug, the doctor who prescribed it, the amount you take, and the times of day you take it, along with comments on any allergies or other reactions you have had to medications. If for some reason you need to see a new doctor, take your medication record with you, so the new doctor can see the drugs you are currently taking. If your pharmacist does not keep a medications record for you, take your record to the drugstore each time you purchase a medication.

Drugs Not Recommended for Older Patients

According to a report published several years ago in the *Journal of the American Medical Association* by a panel of experts in the field of geriatrics and pharmacology, 24 drugs commonly prescribed to older adults may be potentially inappropriate for them. These drugs are regarded as either ineffective in older people or generally more toxic than equally effective alternatives. Some of these drugs have a strong anticholinergic effect, meaning they block the neurotransmitter acetylcholine, which in turn blocks the transmission of certain nerve impulses. Since the amount of acetylcholine in the body decreases with age, older people are especially sensitive to the effects of anticholinergic agents and are prone to experiencing side effects from them. These include daytime drowsiness, mental confusion, dizziness, and loss of coordination. Such effects may precipitate falls or traffic accidents. A conservative estimate indicates that 25 percent of patients over the age of 65 are prescribed one or more of these inappropriate and potentially dangerous drugs.

It is important to point out, however, that just because a drug

appears on this list does not completely rule out its use by older patients. While some drugs such as chlorpropamide and phenylbutazone should probably always be avoided, others—particularly the antihypertensives—can and have been used successfully by many patients for years with no adverse consequences. There's no reason such patients should change their drug regimens. If you are alarmed because one of the medications you take is cited in the list here, talk to your doctor. There may be good reasons why the drug is needed. On the other hand, perhaps another drug that has a similar therapeutic effect, but is safer to use in older people, can be prescribed instead. Above all, you should never stop taking any prescription drug without first consulting your doctor. Many medications need to be tapered off gradually; dangerous reactions could occur if they are discontinued abruptly.

Sedative or Hypnotic Drugs
Chlordiazepoxide (Librium)
Diazepam (Valium)
Flurazepam (Dalmane)
Meprobamate (Equanil, Miltown)
Pentobarbital (Nembutal)
Secobarbital (Seconal)

Antidepressants
Amitriptyline (Elavil)
Amitriptyline + Perfenazine (Trilafon, Etrafon)

Nonsteroidal Anti-inflammatory Drugs (NSAIDs)
Indomethacin (Indocin)
Phenylbutazone (Butazolidin)

Oral Antidiabetics
Chlorpropamide (Diabinese)

Dementia Treatments
Cyclandelate (Cyclospasmol)
Isoxsuprine (Vasodilan)

Platelet Inhibitors
Dipyridamole (Persantine)

Muscle Relaxants/ Antispasmodics
Carisoprodol (Rela, Soma)
Cyclobenzaprine (Flexeril)
Methocarbamol (Robaxin)
Orphenadrine Citrate (Norflex)

Antiemetic (Antinausea) Drugs
Trimethobenzamide (Tigan)

Antihypertensives
Methyldopa (Aldomet)
Propranolol (Inderal)
Reserpine (Serpasil)

Analgesics
Pentazocine (Talwin)
Propoxyphene (Darvon)

- Know what each drug is intended to treat.
- Know what side effects to expect, and which ones warrant medical treatment. Virtually all drugs can produce side effects in addition to their desired therapeutic effects, even when taken exactly as prescribed. You can find this information in the drug profiles in this book. Although the profiles for most drugs carry a long list of possible side effects, any one or more of these reactions usually affect only a small number of the patients taking the medication. Any unfavorable change that occurs after you begin taking a new medication—whether listed in the drug profile or not—should be reported to your physician.
- Do not stop taking a prescribed drug without first consulting your doctor.
- If you take a drug at night, turn on a light, and if you need glasses for reading, put them on to make certain you are taking the right medicine.
- If you transfer your medication from its original container to another bottle, make sure you label the new bottle thoroughly and accurately.
- Never take drugs prescribed for someone else or share your prescription medications with others.
- Store your medication in a cool, dry place—not in the bathroom medicine cabinet where steam might affect it.
- Discard any drugs that have become discolored or begun to give off an unusual odor, or whose expiration dates have passed. Do not save medication (such as antibiotics) with the intent to treat or ward off future illnesses.

YOU AND YOUR PHARMACIST

- Try to use one pharmacy for all your drug purchases. When buying any new drug, ask the pharmacist how it might interact with other drugs you take, including over-the-counter drugs, and if there are any special instructions about when or how it should be taken. Be sure to read any written instructions included with your prescription.
- Generic formulations of drugs are often much cheaper than their brand-name counterparts. Ask your doctor or pharmacist if a generic version is available for any brand-name prescription drug that you take—but also ask if switching to a generic drug would be safe in your case. By law,

a generic drug must have the same effectiveness and safety as its brand-name counterpart. However, some generic drugs may not be exactly equivalent, and these differences may be important for a few drugs that have a narrow therapeutic index—a small difference between an unsafe and safe dose. Some examples are the bloodthinner warfarin (Coumadin), the heart failure drug digoxin (Lanoxin), and the antiseizure drug carbamazepine (Tegretol). So it's important to check with your doctor before making the switch. Once you do switch, be alert for any new side effects or changes in your response.

- When buying over-the-counter drugs, selecting generics also makes sense. Widely used generics, such as the pain reliever ibuprofen or the acid blocker famotidine, cost about 50% less than Motrin or Pepcid, their brand-name counterparts. And aspirin is aspirin is aspirin.
- Many pharmacies can provide labels in foreign languages. If it would help you to have a label in another language, ask your pharmacist.
- If you have trouble opening a medicine's bottle or container, ask your pharmacist for an easy-to-open container.

AVOIDING INTERACTIONS

- Know which foods or drugs to avoid while taking your medication. For example, grapefruit is dangerous when taken with various types of medication (see box, page 13), while patients taking monoamine oxidase (MAO) inhibitors for depression must avoid foods containing tyramines (aged cheeses; sauerkraut; organ meats; pickled or smoked meat, poultry, or fish; and processed meats such as bologna and salami). Likewise, people taking anticoagulants such as warfarin (Coumadin) should avoid liver, green leafy vegetables, and other foods high in vitamin K, which can counteract the effect of the drug.
- Do not drink alcoholic beverages while taking a medication unless your physician okays it. According to the FDA, "of the 100 medicines most commonly prescribed, over half contain at least one substance that reacts badly with alcohol."

This section is designed to help guide you to information about the drugs that appear in this book as they are classified for use to treat specific disorders. Beneath each major category (for example, the Heart and Blood Vessels), you will find the various disorders (such as hypertension) that belong to that category, followed by a list of the drugs used to treat that disorder. (If you want to find information about a particular drug directly, look it up in the general index in the back of the book, page 862, or, if you know the drug's generic name, you can find it simply by flipping through the book, which is organized in alphabetical order by generic drug name.) The disorders featured in this index are grouped under the following general categories:

1. Cancer
2. The Blood
3. The Brain and Nervous System
4. Dental and Oral Disorders
5. The Digestive System
6. The Ears, Nose, and Throat
7. The Endocrine System
8. The Eyes
9. The Heart and Blood Vessels
10. The Genitourinary Tract
11. The Lungs and Respiratory System
12. The Muscles and Bones
13. Infectious Disease
14. The Skin
15. Health Concerns of Men
16. Health Concerns of Women
17. Mental Health

1
Cancer

BRAIN TUMOR (MALIGNANT)
Carmustine

BREAST CANCER
Anastrozole
Cyclophosphamide
Diethylstilbestrol (DES)
Estradiol
Estropipate
Ethinyl Estradiol
Exemestane
Fluoxymesterone
Goserelin Acetate
Letrozole
Megestrol Acetate
Paclitaxel Injection
Tamoxifen Citrate
Testolactone
Toremifene Citrate

COLORECTAL CANCER
Leucovorin Calcium
Levamisole Hydrochloride

HODGKIN'S DISEASE
Carmustine
Chlorambucil
Cyclophosphamide
Dacarbazine
Etoposide
Lomustine
Procarbazine Hydrochloride
Uracil Mustard

LEUKEMIA
Busulfan
Chlorambucil
Hydroxyurea
Imatinib Mesylate
Interferon Alfa-2a
Interferon Alfa-2b
Interferon Alfa-n1

Mercaptopurine
Mitoxantrone
Thioguanine

LIVER CANCER
Carmustine

LUNG CANCER
Paclitaxel Injection

MALIGNANT MELANOMA
Dacarbazine
Hydroxyurea
Interferon Alfa-2b
Paclitaxel Injection

MULTIPLE MYELOMA
Cyclophosphamide
Melphalan

NON-HODGKIN'S LYMPHOMAS
Carmustine
Cyclophosphamide
Etoposide
Uracil Mustard

OVARIAN CANCER
Altretamine
Cyclophosphamide
Hydroxyurea
Melphalan
Paclitaxel Injection

PANCREATIC CANCER
Diazoxide

PROSTATE CANCER
Chlorotrianisene
Diethylstilbestrol (DES)
Estradiol
Estramustine Phosphate Sodium
Estrogens, Conjugated
Estropipate
Ethinyl Estradiol
Flutamide
Goserelin Acetate
Leuprolide Acetate

Nilutamide

STOMACH CANCER
Carmustine

UTERINE CANCER
Megestrol Acetate

2
The Blood

BLEEDING/HEMOPHILIA
Desmopressin Acetate
Vitamin K

CLOTTING DISORDERS
Aminocaproic Acid
Aspirin
Dalteparin Sodium
Dipyridamole
Enoxaparin Sodium Injection
Warfarin

VITAMIN AND MINERAL DEFICIENCY/ANEMIAS
Calcium
Ferrous Salts
Folic Acid
Magnesium Sulfate
Potassium Chloride
Vitamin B_6 (Pyridoxine)
Vitamin B_{12} (Cyanocobalamin)
Vitamin C (Ascorbic Acid)
Vitamin D
Vitamin E (Tocopherol)
Vitamin K
Zinc Sulfate Systemic

3
The Brain and Nervous System

ALZHEIMER'S DISEASE
Donepezil
Galantamine Hydrobromide
Memantine Hydrochloride
Rivastigmine Tartrate
Tacrine

CHRONIC OR MODERATE TO SEVERE PAIN
Acetaminophen with Codeine Phosphate
Amitriptyline Hydrochloride
Bromfenac Sodium
Butorphanol Tartrate
Clomipramine Hydrochloride
Codeine
Diclofenac Systemic
Diflunisal
Fentanyl Transdermal
Fentanyl Transmucosal
Fluoxetine Hydrochloride
Hydrocodone Bitartrate/ Acetaminophen
Hydrocodone Bitartrate/Ibuprofen
Hydromorphone Hydrochloride
Ketorolac Tromethamine Systemic
Meperidine Hydrochloride
Methadone Hydrochloride
Morphine
Nalbuphine Hydrochloride
Nortriptyline Hydrochloride
Oxycodone Hydrochloride
Oxycodone/Acetaminophen
Oxycodone/Aspirin
Pentazocine
Propoxyphene
Propoxyphene/Acetaminophen
Tramadol Hydrochloride

DEMENTIA
Ergoloid Mesylates

DIZZINESS/MOTION SICKNESS
Dimenhydrinate
Diphenhydramine Hydrochloride
Meclizine
Promethazine Hydrochloride
Scopolamine Systemic
Trimethobenzamide Hydrochloride

EPILEPSY/SEIZURE DISORDER
Carbamazepine
Clonazepam
Diazepam
Ethosuximide
Felbamate
Gabapentin
Lamotrigine
Levetiracetam
Mephenytoin
Oxcarbazine
Pentobarbital Sodium
Phenobarbital
Phenytoin
Primidone
Tiagabine Hydrochloride
Topiramate
Valproic Acid

HEADACHE/MIGRAINE
Acetaminophen
Acetaminophen/Aspirin/Caffeine
Almotriptan Malate
Butalbital/Acetaminophen/ Caffeine
Butalbital/Acetaminophen/ Caffeine/Codeine
Butalbital/Aspirin/Caffeine
Butalbital/Aspirin/Caffeine/ Codeine Phosphate
Butorphanol Tartrate
Diclofenac Systemic
Diflunisal

Dihydroergotamine Mesylate
Eletriptan Hydrobromide
Ergotamine/Belladonna Alkaloids/Phenobarbital
Etodolac
Fenoprofen Calcium
Flurbiprofen Oral
Ibuprofen
Indomethacin
Ketoprofen
Meclofenamate Sodium
Mefenamic Acid
Methysergide Maleate
Nabumetone
Naproxen
Naratriptan Hydrochloride
Oxaprozin
Piroxicam
Propranolol Hydrochloride
Rizatriptan Benzoate
Sulindac
Sumatriptan Succinate
Timolol Maleate Oral
Tolmetin Sodium
Zolmitriptan

MULTIPLE SCLEROSIS
Betamethasone Systemic
Cortisone Oral
Dexamethasone Systemic
Glatiramer Acetate (Copolymer-1)
Hydrocortisone Systemic
Interferon Beta-1a
Interferon Beta-1b (rIFN-B)
Methylprednisolone
Prednisolone Systemic
Prednisone
Tizanidine Hydrochloride
Triamcinolone Systemic

PARKINSON'S DISEASE
Amantadine Hydrochloride
Benztropine Mesylate
Biperiden

Bromocriptine Mesylate
Diphenhydramine Hydrochloride
Entacapone
Levodopa
Levodopa/Carbidopa
Orphenadrine Citrate
Pergolide Mesylate
Pramipexole Dihydrochloride
Procyclidine
Ropinirole Hydrochloride
Selegiline Hydrochloride
   (L-Deprenyl)
Tolcapone
Trihexyphenidyl Hydrochloride

SHINGLES
Acyclovir
Amitriptyline Hydrochloride
Capsaicin
Famciclovir
Valacyclovir Hydrochloride

TOURETTE'S SYNDROME
Haloperidol

TREMOR
Trihexyphenidyl Hydrochloride
Propranolol Hydrochloride

4
Dental and Oral Disorders

CANKER SORES AND COLD SORES
Amlexanox
Benzocaine
Lidocaine Hydrochloride Topical
Penciclovir

PERIODONTAL DISEASE
Chlorhexidine Gluconate

TOOTHACHE/DENTAL PAIN
Benzocaine

5
The Digestive System

CIRRHOSIS OF THE LIVER
Ethacrynic Acid
Furosemide
Torsemide
Triamterene

CONSTIPATION
Bisacodyl
Castor Oil
Docusate
Glycerin Rectal
Lactulose
Magnesium Citrate
Milk of Magnesia
Psyllium
Senna
Sodium Phosphate/Sodium
   Biphosphate

DIARRHEA
Attapulgite
Bismuth Subsalicylate
Charcoal, Activated
Diphenoxylate Hydrochloride/
   Atropine Sulfate
Kaolin with Pectin
Loperamide Hydrochloride
Loperamide/Simethicone
Psyllium
Trimethoprim/Sulfamethoxazole

ESOPHAGITIS
Aluminum Salts
Cimetidine
Esomeprazole Magnesium
Magaldrate

Omeprazole
Pantoprazole
Rabeprazole
Ranitidine

FLATULENCE/GAS
Charcoal, Activated
Simethicone

GALLSTONES
Ursodiol

GASTROESOPHAGEAL REFLUX DISEASE
Aluminum Salts
Cimetidine
Esomeprazole Magnesium
Famotidine
Lansoprazole
Magaldrate
Nizatidine
Omeprazole
Ranitidine

HEARTBURN/INDIGESTION
Aluminum Salts
Bismuth Subsalicylate
Famotidine
Magaldrate
Magnesium Oxide
Metoclopramide Hydrochloride
Milk of Magnesia
Nizatidine
Ranitidine
Simethicone
Sodium Bicarbonate

HEMORRHOIDS
Benzocaine
Hydrocortisone Topical

IRRITABLE BOWEL SYNDROME
Atropine Sulfate Oral
Atropine Sulfate/Scopolamine
   Hydrobromide/ Hyoscyamine
   Sulfate/Phenobarbital

Dicyclomine Hydrochloride
Tegaserod Maleate

PANCREATIC ENZYME DEFICIENCY
Pancrelipase

ULCERATIVE COLITIS
Mesalamine
Olsalazine Sodium
Sulfasalazine

ULCERS, STOMACH AND DUODENAL
Aluminum Salts
Bismuth Subsalicylate
Cimetidine
Clarithromycin
Esomeprazole Magnesium
Famotidine
Glycopyrrolate
Lansoprazole
Magaldrate
Magnesium Oxide
Milk of Magnesia
Misoprostol
Nizatidine
Omeprazole
Propantheline Bromide
Rabeprazole
Ranitidine
Ranitidine Bismuth Citrate
Sucralfate

VIRAL HEPATITIS
Adefovir Dipivoxil
Interferon Alfacon-1

6
The Ears, Nose, and Throat

EAR INFECTION
Azithromycin
Bacampicillin Hydrochloride
Cefepime
Cefpodoxime Proxetil
Cefprozil
Cefuroxime
Cephalexin
Cephradine
Chloramphenicol Otic
Clarithromycin
Colistin/Neomycin/Hydrocortisone
Neomycin/Polymyxin B/
    Hydrocortisone Otic
Ofloxacin Otic
Penicillin G
Penicillin V
Phenylephrine Hydrochloride
    Systemic
Sulfisoxazole Systemic
Trimethoprim/Sulfamethoxazole

NASAL CONGESTION
Ephedrine
Epinephrine Hydrochloride
Oxymetazoline Nasal
Phenylephrine Hydrochloride
Phenylpropanolamine
    Hydrochloride
Phenylpropanolamine
    Hydrochloride/Guaifenesin
Pseudoephedrine
Pseudoephedrine/Guaifenesin

SINUSITIS
Amoxicillin/Potassium Clavulanate
Ampicillin
Azithromycin
Phenylephrine Hydrochloride
    Systemic

Phenylpropanolamine
    Hydrochloride/Guaifenesin
Pseudoephedrine

THROAT INFECTION
Amoxicillin
Cefaclor
Cefadroxil
Cefamandole Nafate
Cefepime
Cefpodoxime Proxetil
Cefprozil
Cefuroxime
Cephalexin
Cephradine
Dirithromycin
Loracarbef
Penicillin G
Penicillin V
Phenylpropanolamine
    Hydrochloride/Guaifenesin

7
The Endocrine System

DIABETES MELLITUS
Acarbose
Acetohexamide
Chlorpropamide
Glimepiride
Glipizide
Glipizide/Metformin
Glucagon
Glyburide
Glyburide/Metformin
Insulin
Insulin Glargine (rDNA origin)
Metformin
Miglitol
Nateglinide
Pioglitazone

Sotalol Hydrochloride
Verapamil Hydrochloride

Congestive Heart Failure
Benazepril Hydrochloride
Captopril
Carvedilol
Chlorothiazide
Chlorthalidone
Digitoxin
Digoxin
Enalapril Maleate
Enalapril/Hydrochlorothiazide
Ethacrynic Acid
Fosinopril Sodium
Furosemide
Hydralazine Hydrochloride
Hydrochlorothiazide
Hydrochlorothiazide/Triamterene
Indapamide
Lisinopril
Metolazone
Moexipril Hydrochloride
Quinapril Hydrochloride
Ramipril
Spironolactone/
  Hydrochlorothiazide
Torsemide
Trandolapril

High Cholesterol
Amlodipine/Atorvastatin
Atorvastatin
Cholestyramine
Colesevelam Hydrochloride
Colestipol Hydrochloride
Ezetimibe
Fluvastatin
Lovastatin
Niacin
Pravastatin
Rosuvastatin
Simvastatin

High Triglycerides
Atorvastatin
Fenofibrate
Gemfibrozil
Simvastatin

Hypertension
Acebutolol Hydrochloride
Amlodipine/Benazepril
Atenolol
Atenolol/Chlorthalidone
Benazepril Hydrochloride
Betaxolol Oral
Bisoprolol Fumarate
Bisoprolol Fumarate/
  Hydrochlorothiazide
Capecitabine
Captopril
Carteolol Hydrochloride Oral
Carvedilol
Chlorothiazide
Chlorthalidone
Clonidine Hydrochloride
Diltiazem Hydrochloride
Doxazosin Mesylate
Enalapril
Enalapril/Diltiazem
Enalapril/Felodipine
Enalapril/Hydrochlorothiazide
Eplerenone
Eprosartan Mesylate
Felodipine
Fosinopril Sodium
Furosemide
Guanabenz Acetate
Guanadrel Sulfate
Guanethidine Monosulfate
Guanfacine Hydrochloride
Hydralazine Hydrochloride
Hydrochlorothiazide
Hydrochlorothiazide/Triamterene
Irbesartan

Isradipine
Labetalol Hydrochloride
Lisinopril
Lisinopril/Hydrochlorothiazide
Losartan Potassium
Methyldopa
Metoprolol
Mibefradil Dihydrochloride
Minoxidil Oral
Moexipril Hydrochloride
Moexipril Hydrochloride/
  Hydrochlorothiazide
Nadolol
Nicardipine Hydrochloride Oral
Nifedipine
Olmesartan Medoxomil
Penbutolol Sulfate
Perindopril Erbumine
Pindolol
Polythiazide
Prazosin
Propranolol Hydrochloride
Propranolol/Hydrochlorothiazide
Quinapril Hydrochloride
Quinapril Hydrochloride/
  Hydrochlorothiazide
Ramipril
Spironolactone/
  Hydrochlorothiazide
Telmisartan
Terazosin
Timolol Maleate Oral
Torsemide
Trandolapril
Trandolapril/Verapamil
  Hydrochloride
Valsartan
Valsartan/Hydrochlorothiazide
Verapamil Hydrochloride

Peripheral Vascular Disease
Cilostazol

Nasal

Dexamethasone Inhalant and Nasal

Dyphylline

Ephedrine

Epinephrine Hydrochloride

Flunisolide

Fluticasone

Fluticasone/Salmeterol

Hydrocortisone Systemic

Ipratropium Bromide

Isoetharine

Isoproterenol

Metaproterenol Sulfate

Methylprednisolone

Montelukast

Nedocromil Sodium

Pirbuterol Acetate

Prednisolone Systemic

Prednisone

Salmeterol Xinafoate

Terbutaline Sulfate

Theophylline

Triamcinolone Inhalant and Nasal

Triamcinolone Systemic

Zafirlukast

Zileuton

BRONCHITIS, ACUTE

Azithromycin

Clarithromycin

Loracarbef

Tobramycin

Trovafloxacin

COUGH/COLD

Codeine

Dextromethorphan

Diphenhydramine Hydrochloride

Guaifenesin

Phenylephrine Hydrochloride Systemic

Pseudoephedrine

Pseudoephedrine/Guaifenesin

CHRONIC OBSTRUCTIVE PULMONARY DISEASE (EMPHYSEMA; CHRONIC BRONCHITIS)

Acetylcysteine

Albuterol

Aminophylline

Bitolterol Mesylate

Dyphylline

Epinephrine Hydrochloride

Fluticasone/Salmeterol

Gemifloxacin Mesylate

Ipratropium Bromide

Isoetharine

Isoproterenol

Levofloxacin

Metaproterenol Sulfate

Pirbuterol Acetate

Salmeterol Xinafoate

Sparfloxacin

Terbutaline Sulfate

Theophylline

Trimethoprim/Sulfamethoxazole

INFLUENZA

Amantadine Hydrochloride

Aspirin

Ibuprofen

Influenza Virus Vaccine

Oseltamivir Phosphate

Pseudoephedrine/Guaifenesin

Rimantadine Hydrochloride

Zanamivir

PNEUMONIA

Acetylcysteine

Atovaquone

Azithromycin

Clarithromycin

Dirithromycin

Erythromycin Systemic

Gemifloxacin Mesylate

Levofloxacin

Linezolid

Loracarbef

Metronidazole

Pentamidine Isethionate

Pneumococcal Vaccine

Sparfloxacin

Trimethoprim/Sulfamethoxazole

Trovafloxacin

12

The Muscles and Bones

BURSITIS

Acetaminophen

Aspirin

Diclofenac Systemic

Diflunisal

Etodolac

Fenoprofen Calcium

Flurbiprofen Oral

Ibuprofen

Indomethacin

Ketoprofen

Meclofenamate Sodium

Mefenamic Acid

Nabumetone

Naproxen

Oxaprozin

Piroxicam

Sulindac

Tolmetin Sodium

GOUT

Allopurinol

Colchicine

Diclofenac Systemic

Flurbiprofen Oral

Indomethacin

Meclofenamate Sodium

Mefenamic Acid

Nabumetone
Naproxen
Oxaprozin
Piroxicam
Probenecid
Sulfinpyrazone
Sulindac
Tolmetin Sodium

MUSCLE SPASMS

Baclofen
Carisoprodol
Chlordiazepoxide
Chlorzoxazone
Cyclobenzaprine
Dantrolene Sodium
Diazepam
Methocarbamol
Orphenadrine Citrate

OSTEOARTHRITIS

Acetaminophen/Aspirin/Caffeine
Aspirin
Aspirin/Caffeine
Betamethasone Systemic
Capsaicin
Celecoxib
Cortisone Oral
Dexamethasone Systemic
Diclofenac Systemic
Diclofenac/Misoprostol
Diflunisal
Etodolac
Fenoprofen Calcium
Flurbiprofen Oral
Hydrocortisone Systemic
Ibuprofen
Indomethacin
Ketoprofen
Meclofenamate Sodium
Mefenamic Acid
Meloxicam
Methylprednisolone

Nabumetone
Naproxen
Oxaprozin
Piroxicam
Prednisolone Systemic
Prednisone
Salsalate
Sulindac
Tolmetin Sodium
Triamcinolone Systemic
Valdecoxib

OSTEOPOROSIS

Alendronate Sodium
Calcitonin — Salmon
Calcium
Etidronate Disodium
Raloxifene Hydrochloride
Teriparatide
Vitamin D

PAGET'S DISEASE

Alendronate Sodium
Calcitonin — Salmon
Calcium
Etidronate Disodium
Risedronate Sodium
Tiludronate Disodium
Vitamin D

RHEUMATOID ARTHRITIS

Adalimumab
Auranofin
Azathioprine
Celecoxib
Diclofenac/Misoprostol
Etanercept
Gold Sodium Thiomalate
Indomethacin
Infliximab
Leflunomide
Methotrexate
Penicillamine

Salsalate
Valdecoxib

TENDINITIS

Acetaminophen
Aspirin
Diclofenac Systemic
Diflunisal
Etodolac
Fenoprofen Calcium
Flurbiprofen Oral
Ibuprofen
Indomethacin
Ketoprofen
Meclofenamate Sodium
Mefenamic Acid
Nabumetone
Naproxen
Oxaprozin
Piroxicam
Sulindac
Tolmetin Sodium

13
Infectious Disease

AIDS/HIV

Abacavir Sulfate
Abacavir/Lamivudine/Zidovudine
Amprenavir
Atazanavir Sulfate
Delavirdine
Didanosine (ddI)
Efavirenz
Emtricitabine
Enfuvirtide
Fosamprenavir Calcium
Indinavir
Lamivudine (3TC)
Lamivudine/Zidovudine

14
The Skin

Oxybutynin Chloride

YEAST INFECTION
Butoconazole Nitrate
Clotrimazole
Fluconazole
Nystatin
Terconazole
Tioconazole

17
Mental Health

ALCOHOLISM
Chlordiazepoxide
Disulfiram
Hydroxyzine
Naltrexone
Oxazepam

ANXIETY DISORDERS
Alprazolam
Buspirone Hydrochloride
Chlordiazepoxide
Chlordiazepoxide/Amitriptyline
Clomipramine Hydrochloride
Clonazepam
Clorazepate Dipotassium
Diazepam
Fluoxetine Hydrochloride
Lorazepam
Nortriptyline Hydrochloride
Oxazepam
Sertraline Hydrochloride

BIPOLAR (MANIC-DEPRESSIVE) DISORDER
Lithium
Olanzapine/Fluoxetine
Valproic Acid
Ziprasidone Mesylate

DEPRESSION
Amitriptyline Hydrochloride
Amoxapine
Bupropion Hydrochloride
Citalopram
Clomipramine Hydrochloride
Desipramine Hydrochloride
Doxepin Hydrochloride
Escitalopram Oxalate
Fluoxetine Hydrochloride
Imipramine
Maprotiline Hydrochloride
Mirtazapine
Nortriptyline Hydrochloride
Paroxetine Hydrochloride
Phenelzine Sulfate
Protriptyline Hydrochloride
Sertraline Hydrochloride
Tranylcypromine Sulfate
Trazodone
Venlafaxine

NARCOLEPSY/ATTENTION-DEFICIT HYPERACTIVITY DISORDER (ADHD)
Amphetamine
Amphetamine/ Dextroamphetamine
Atomoxetine Hydrochloride
Dextroamphetamine Sulfate
Methamphetamine Hydrochloride
Methylphenidate Hydrochloride

OBSESSIVE-COMPULSIVE DISORDER
Fluvoxamine Maleate

SCHIZOPHRENIA/PSYCHOSIS
Aripiprazole
Chlorpromazine Hydrochloride
Clozapine
Fluphenazine
Haloperidol
Loxapine
Molindone
Olanzapine
Perphenazine
Quetiapine Fumarate
Risperidone
Thioridazine Hydrochloride
Thiothixene
Trifluoperazine Hydrochloride
Ziprasidone Mesylate

SLEEP DISORDERS/INSOMNIA
Chloral Hydrate
Diphenhydramine Hydrochloride
Estazolam
Ethchlorvynol
Flurazepam Hydrochloride
Hydroxyzine
Lorazepam
Quazepam
Temazepam
Triazolam
Zaleplon
Zolpidem

SMOKING CESSATION
Bupropion Hydrochloride
Nicotine

A to Z
Drug Profiles

Abacavir

BRAND NAME
Ziagen

▶ Drug Class: Antiviral/reverse transcriptase inhibitor

▶ Available in: Tablets, oral solution

▶ Available OTC? No

▶ As Generic? No

Side Effects

SERIOUS
Uncommon (in approximately 5% of patients) and possibly fatal hypersensitivity reactions have been reported. Symptoms may include fever, skin rash, fatigue, nausea, vomiting, diarrhea, abdominal pain, weakness, lethargy, muscle and joint pain, swelling, shortness of breath, numbness, tingling, or prickling sensations, conjunctivitis, and mouth sores. Stop taking the drug and call your doctor immediately. Rarely, abacavir can also cause lactic acidosis (which is often fatal) and a greatly enlarged liver.

COMMON
Nausea, vomiting, weakness, fatigue, headache, loss of appetite, and diarrhea.

LESS COMMON
Insomnia and other sleep disorders.

PRINCIPAL USES
To treat human immunodeficiency virus (HIV) infection in combination with other drugs. While not a cure for HIV, such drugs may suppress the replication of the virus and delay the progression of the disease.

HOW THE DRUG WORKS
Abacavir prevents HIV from reproducing in two ways. A metabolite of the drug inhibits the activity of an enzyme needed for the replication of DNA in viral cells. The metabolite is also incorporated into viral DNA and terminates the formation of the complete DNA.

DOSAGE
Adults: To start, 300 mg 2 times a day. The drug must be taken in combination with other drugs for HIV to delay the development of resistant strains of the virus. Children 3 months to 16 years: 8 mg per 2.2 lbs (1 kg) of body weight 2 times a day in combination with other drugs for HIV. Children should take no more than 300 mg twice a day.

ONSET OF EFFECT
Unknown. With most antiretroviral drugs, an early response can be seen within the first few days of therapy, but the maximum effect may take 12 to 16 weeks.

DURATION OF ACTION
Unknown. Effects of the drug may be prolonged when abacavir is used in combination with other effective drugs and the virus is maximally suppressed.

DIETARY ADVICE
Abacavir can be taken with or without food.

STORAGE
Store at room temperature in a tightly sealed container away from heat, moisture, and direct light. The oral solution may be refrigerated, but should not be allowed to freeze.

IF YOU MISS A DOSE
Take it as soon as you remember. If it is near the time for the next dose, skip the missed dose and resume your regular dosage schedule. Do not double the next dose. It is especially important to take abacavir on schedule, to assure constant, proper blood levels of the drug.

STOPPING THE DRUG
The decision to stop taking the drug should be made in consultation with your physician.

PROLONGED USE
See your doctor regularly for tests and examinations.

PRECAUTIONS
Over 60: It is not known whether abacavir causes different or more severe side effects in older patients.

Driving and Hazardous Work: Do not drive or engage in hazardous work until you determine how the medicine affects you.

Alcohol: Alcohol may raise the blood concentration of the drug.

Pregnancy: Abacavir has been shown to cause birth defects in animals. Human studies have not been done. This medication should be given during pregnancy only if potential benefits outweigh the risks to the unborn child.

Breast Feeding: Women infected with HIV should not breast feed, to avoid transmitting the virus to an uninfected child.

Infants and Children: Your pediatrician will determine the appropriate dosage based on your child's weight. Call your doctor immediately if you notice rash or any other side effects while your child is taking abacavir. The drug has not been tested in infants less than 3 months of age.

Special Concerns: If, while taking abacavir, you have a skin rash or two or more of the following sets of symptoms, you may be having a serious, possibly fatal, allergic reaction: fever; nausea, vomiting, diarrhea, or abdominal pain; severe tiredness, achiness, or general feeling of illness; sore throat, shortness of breath, or cough. Use of abacavir does not eliminate the risk of passing the AIDS virus to other persons. You should take appropriate preventive measures.

OVERDOSE
Symptoms: No cases of overdose have been reported.

What to Do: If you suspect an overdose or if someone takes a much larger dose than prescribed, call your doctor, emergency medical services (EMS), or the nearest poison control center immediately.

DRUG INTERACTIONS
Currently, there are no clinically significant drug interactions. Further studies are being conducted.

FOOD INTERACTIONS
No known food interactions.

DISEASE INTERACTIONS
Currently, there are no clinically significant disease interactions. Further studies are being conducted.

Abacavir/Lamivudine/Zidovudine

BRAND NAME
Trizivir

▶ Drug Class: Antiviral

▶ Available in: Tablets

▶ Available OTC? No

▶ As Generic? No

Side Effects

SERIOUS
Severe stomach or abdominal pain; anemia (low red blood cell count) causing paleness, fatigue, or shortness of breath; fever; chills; sore throat. Also numbness, burning, tingling, or pain in the hands, arms, legs or feet, breathing difficulty, itching, hives, skin rash, swelling of the face, mouth, lips, throat, or tongue. Call your doctor immediately. Trizivir contains abacavir, which has caused serious allergic reactions resulting in death. If you develop fever, skin rash, stomach pain, cough, shortness of breath, talk to your doctor immediately.

COMMON
Headaches, nausea and vomiting, insomnia, stomach upset, loss of appetite, diarrhea, dizziness, cough.

LESS COMMON
Mild to moderate abdominal pain or cramping, muscle aches and pain, hepatitis (liver inflammation, which may cause yellowish discoloration of skin and eyes), joint pain, loss of hair.

PRINCIPAL USES
To treat HIV (human immunodeficiency virus) infection. While not a cure for HIV, this combination of abacavir, lamivudine (3TC), and zidovudine (AZT) may suppress the replication of the virus and delay the progression of the disease.

HOW THE DRUG WORKS
This drug combination interferes with the activity of enzymes needed for the replication of DNA in HIV-infected cells, thus preventing HIV from reproducing.

DOSAGE
Adults and teenagers: 1 tablet (containing 300 mg of abacavir, 150 mg of lamivudine, and 300 mg of zidovudine) twice a day. Children: Should not be taken by children because it is a fixed-dose combination that cannot be adjusted.

ONSET OF EFFECT
Unknown. With most antiretroviral drugs, an early response can be seen within the first few days of therapy, but the maximum effect may take at least 16 weeks.

DURATION OF ACTION
Unknown. Effects of the drug combination may be prolonged if the virus is maximally suppressed.

DIETARY ADVICE
Can be taken with or without food. Be sure to drink plenty of fluids.

STORAGE
Store in a tightly sealed container away from heat, moisture, and direct light.

IF YOU MISS A DOSE
Take it as soon as you remember. If it is near the time for the next dose, skip the missed dose and resume your regular dosage schedule. Do not double the next dose. It is especially important to take this medication on schedule, to assure constant, proper blood levels of the drug.

STOPPING THE DRUG
The decision to stop taking the drug should be made in consultation with your physician.

PROLONGED USE
See your doctor regularly for tests and examinations as long as you take this medication.

PRECAUTIONS
Over 60: No special studies have been done on older patients. A different medication may be warranted, especially if liver or kidney function is impaired.

Driving and Hazardous Work: Use of this drug combination should not diminish your ability to perform such tasks safely.

Alcohol: Avoid alcohol if liver function is impaired.

Pregnancy: Adequate human studies have not been done. Discuss with your doctor the relative risks and benefits of using this drug while pregnant.

Breast Feeding: Women infected with HIV should not breast-feed, so as to avoid transmitting the virus to an uninfected child.

Infants and Children: Not recommended for children under the age of 12.

Special Concerns: Use of this drug combination does not eliminate the risk of passing the AIDS virus (HIV) to other persons. Be sure to take all appropriate preventive measures. This medication should not be used in patients with low body weight.

OVERDOSE
Symptoms: No cases of overdose with this combination have been reported. However, cases of overdose have been reported for zidovudine taken alone (see Zidovudine).

What to Do: If you suspect an overdose or if someone takes a much larger dose than prescribed, call your doctor, emergency medical services (EMS), or the nearest poison control center immediately.

DRUG INTERACTIONS
Consult your doctor for specific advice if you are taking amphotericin B (by injection), anticancer agents, thyroid drugs, azathioprine, chloramphenicol, colchicine, cyclophosphamide, flucytosine, ganciclovir, interferon, mercaptopurine, methotrexate, plicamycin, clarithromycin, or probenecid. Also consult your doctor for specific advice if you are taking any other prescription or over-the-counter medication.

FOOD INTERACTIONS
No known food interactions.

DISEASE INTERACTIONS
Caution is advised when taking this drug combination. Consult your doctor if you have anemia or another blood problem. Use of this drug is not recommended in patients with impaired kidney function or risk factors for liver disease.

Acarbose

BRAND NAME
Precose

Precose 50 mg
(BAYER)

▶ Drug Class: Antidiabetic agent

▶ Available in: Tablets

▶ Available OTC? No

▶ As Generic? No

Side Effects

SERIOUS
There are no serious side effects associated with acarbose.

COMMON
Feelings of bloating, gas, abdominal discomfort, diarrhea. These symptoms tend to decrease over time.

LESS COMMON
Rise in liver enzymes, causing yellowish tinge to eyes or skin (jaundice), when maximal dose is exceeded. When used in combination with sulfonylureas, may cause symptoms of low blood sugar, which include sweating, tremor, anxiety, hunger, confusion, seizures, rapid heartbeat, vision changes, dizziness, headache, loss of consciousness. Hypoglycemia must be treated by ingestion of glucose (dextrose). Sucrose (table sugar) and foods or drinks containing sugars or starches are ineffective because acarbose prevents their breakdown and absorption.

PRINCIPAL USES
As an adjunct (supplemental) therapy in patients with diabetes who do not require insulin injections yet are unable to control their blood glucose levels with diet alone or with other medications.

HOW THE DRUG WORKS
Acarbose inhibits the activity of enzymes required to break carbohydrates down into simple sugars within the intestine. This effect delays the digestion of carbohydrates and thus reduces the rise in blood sugar that typically occurs after meals.

DOSAGE
Initially, 25 mg, 1 to 3 times a day. The dose may be increased (at 4- to 8-week intervals) to a maximum of 100 mg, 3 times daily.

ONSET OF EFFECT
Within 1 hour.

DURATION OF ACTION
Up to 2 hours.

DIETARY ADVICE
This medicine should be taken with the first bite of breakfast, lunch, and dinner. Follow your doctor's advice regarding diet, weight loss, and exercise.

STORAGE
Keep in a tightly sealed container away from heat and direct light.

IF YOU MISS A DOSE
If you have finished a meal without taking the medication, skip the missed dose and resume your regular dosing schedule with the next meal. Do not double the next dose.

STOPPING THE DRUG
Take it as prescribed for the full treatment period.

PROLONGED USE
Since non-insulin-dependent diabetes is a chronic condition, use of acarbose will be ongoing. Blood glucose levels should be checked regularly during treatment so that the dosage may be adjusted if necessary.

PRECAUTIONS
Over 60: No special precautions required.

Driving and Hazardous Work: Acarbose should not impair your ability to perform such tasks safely.

Alcohol: Drink only in moderation when taking acarbose.

Pregnancy: Consult your doctor for advice. Insulin is usually the treatment of choice for pregnant diabetic patients.

Breast Feeding: Trace amounts of acarbose can be found in breast milk; however, adverse effects in infants have not been documented. Consult your doctor for advice.

Infants and Children: Safety and effectiveness have not been established for patients under 18 years of age. Consult your doctor for specific advice.

Special Concerns: You should not take acarbose if you've had an allergic reaction to it previously or if you are taking, or took within the past 14 days, a monoamine oxidase (MAO) inhibitor (a class of antidepressant drugs).

OVERDOSE
Symptoms: Increased gas, diarrhea, and stomach pain.

What to Do: These symptoms usually subside on their own within a short period of time. If not, consult your doctor for advice. Symptoms of hypoglycemia should not occur when taking acarbose alone, but may occur if a patient is also taking sulfonylurea or insulin for diabetes.

DRUG INTERACTIONS
Do not take acarbose if you are taking, or took within the past 14 days, an MAO inhibitor. Consult your doctor for specific advice if you are taking any of the following drugs that may interact with acarbose: digestive enzyme preparations containing amylase or pancreatin, intestinal absorbents (such as charcoal), insulin, or sulfonylureas (oral antidiabetic agents).

FOOD INTERACTIONS
Avoid foods that contain large amounts of sugar (for example, cake, cookies, candy, acidic fruits). Closely follow the diet your doctor has prescribed.

DISEASE INTERACTIONS
This drug should not be taken by patients with a history of diabetic ketoacidosis, intestinal disorders (including malabsorption or obstruction), inflammatory bowel disease (for example, Crohn's disease or ulcerative colitis), liver or kidney disease, or gastric ulcers.

Acebutolol Hydrochloride

Sectral 200 mg
(WYETH-AYERST)

▶ Drug Class: Beta-blocker

▶ Available in: Capsules

▶ Available OTC? No

▶ As Generic? Yes

Side Effects

SERIOUS
Severe shortness of breath and rapid heartbeat (symptoms of congestive heart failure), worsening of asthma, severe allergic reaction (skin rash, itching, wheezing, swelling of lips, tongue, and throat). If any of these symptoms develop, seek medical attention immediately.

COMMON
Cough, diarrhea, decreased sexual ability, depression, drowsiness, dizziness, fatigue, frequent urination, gas, indigestion, nausea, trouble sleeping, cold hands and feet, numbness or tingling in fingers or toes.

LESS COMMON
Fever, sore throat, abdominal pain, headache, anxiety, joint or back pain, dry or burning eyes, unusual bleeding or bruising, dark urine, nightmares or unusually vivid dreams.

PRINCIPAL USES
To treat mild to moderate high blood pressure; also used to prevent or control heartbeat irregularities (cardiac arrhythmias).

HOW THE DRUG WORKS
Acebutolol slows the rate and force of contraction of the heart by blocking certain nerve impulses, thus reducing blood pressure. By modifying nerve impulses to the heart, the drug also helps to stabilize heart rhythm.

DOSAGE
Adults: Initially, 400 mg a day, either as a single dose in the morning or as two 200 mg doses taken in the morning and evening (12 hours apart). Maximum daily dose is 1,200 mg; for those over 65, daily dose should not exceed 800 mg.

ONSET OF EFFECT
1 to 1 ½ hours.

DURATION OF ACTION
Up to 24 hours.

DIETARY ADVICE
Follow your doctor's dietary recommendations to improve control over high blood pressure and heart disease.

STORAGE
Store away from heat, moisture, and direct light.

IF YOU MISS A DOSE
Take it as soon as you remember. If it is within 4 hours of the next scheduled dose, skip the missed dose and resume your regular dosage schedule. Do not double the next dose.

STOPPING THE DRUG
Suddenly stopping acebutolol may cause blood pressure to rise (rebound) to high or even dangerous levels, possibly triggering angina or a heart attack in patients with advanced heart disease. Slow reduction of the dose over a period of 2 to 3 weeks is advised, under careful supervision by your doctor.

PROLONGED USE
Regular visits to your doctor are needed to evaluate the drug's ongoing, long-term effectiveness.

PRECAUTIONS
Over 60: Many elderly patients are more sensitive to the drug than younger persons. Smaller doses and frequent blood pressure checks may be advised.

Driving and Hazardous Work: Use caution until you determine how the medication affects you.

Alcohol: Drink in careful moderation, if at all. Alcohol may interact with the drug and cause a dangerous drop in blood pressure.

Pregnancy: Discuss with your doctor the relative risks and benefits of using this drug while pregnant.

Breast Feeding: Trace amounts of this drug can be found in breast milk, though adverse effects in infants have not been documented. Consult your doctor for advice.

Infants and Children: Not recommended.

Special Concerns: Use of the drug should be considered but one element of a comprehensive therapeutic program that includes weight control, smoking cessation, regular exercise, and a healthy low-salt, low-fat diet.

OVERDOSE
Symptoms: Unusually slow or rapid heartbeat, severe dizziness or fainting, poor circulation in the hands (bluish skin), breathing difficulty, seizures.

What to Do: Contact your doctor immediately.

DRUG INTERACTIONS
Consult your doctor for specific advice if you are taking amphetamines, oral antidiabetic agents, asthma medication (such as aminophylline or theophylline), calcium channel blockers, clonidine, guanabenz, halothane, allergy shots, insulin, MAO inhibitors, reserpine, or other beta-blockers.

FOOD INTERACTIONS
None reported.

DISEASE INTERACTIONS
Acebutolol should be used with caution in people with diabetes, especially insulin-dependent diabetes, since the drug may mask symptoms of hypoglycemia. Consult your doctor for specific advice if you have a history of allergies or asthma, heart or blood vessel disease (including congestive heart failure and peripheral vascular disease), hyperthyroidism, irregular (slow) heartbeat, myasthenia gravis, psoriasis, respiratory problems such as bronchitis or emphysema, kidney or liver disease, or mental depression.

Acetaminophen

BRAND NAMES
Aceta, Actamin, Anacin-3, Apacet, Aspirin Free Anacin, Atasol, Banesin, Dapa, Datril Extra-Strength, Feverall, Genapap, Genebs, Liquiprin, Neopap, Oraphen-PD, Panadol, Phenaphen, Redutemp, Snaplets-FR, Suppap, Tapanol, Tylenol, Valorin

Tylenol Regular Strength 325 mg
(MᶜNᴇɪʟ)

Additional photographs

▶ Drug Class: Analgesic; antipyretic (fever reducer)

▶ Available in: Capsules, caplets, tablets, powder, liquid, suppositories

▶ Available OTC? Yes

▶ As Generic? Yes

Side Effects

SERIOUS
Allergic reaction causing rash, itching, hives, swelling, or breathing difficulty; yellow-tinged skin and eyes (indicating liver damage). Seek medical assistance immediately.

COMMON
No common side effects have been reported.

LESS COMMON
Sore throat and fever (not present before treatment and not caused by the condition being treated), extreme fatigue or weakness, unexplained bleeding or bruising, blood in urine, painful, decreased, or frequent urination.

PRINCIPAL USES
To treat mild to moderate pain and fever, including simple headaches, muscle aches, and mild forms of arthritis. Acetaminophen is useful for patients who cannot take aspirin, such as those taking anticoagulants or suffering from gastrointestinal ulcers or bleeding disorders.

HOW THE DRUG WORKS
Acetaminophen appears to interfere with the action of prostaglandins, substances in the body that cause inflammation and make nerves more sensitive to pain impulses. It also relieves fever, probably by acting on the heat-regulating center of the brain.

DOSAGE
For adults and teenagers: 325 to 650 mg every 4 to 6 hours, or 1 g, 3 to 4 times a day, as needed. Extended-release caplets: Take 2 every 8 hours. Maximum dosage with short-term therapy should not exceed 4 g a day; with long-term therapy it should not exceed 2.6 g a day unless otherwise prescribed by your doctor. For children 12 years and under: Consult a pediatrician for proper dose. Liquid form may be recommended for young children.

ONSET OF EFFECT
Within 15 to 30 minutes.

DURATION OF ACTION
3 to 4 hours; 8 hours for extended-release form.

DIETARY ADVICE
Take it with water 30 minutes before or 2 hours after meals. It may be taken with milk to minimize stomach upset. If you are on a salt-restricted diet, be sure to account for the sodium present in the powder form of acetaminophen.

STORAGE
Store in a tightly sealed container away from heat and direct light. Refrigerate liquid forms (to make them more palatable) and rectal suppositories. Do not allow the medication to freeze.

IF YOU MISS A DOSE
Take it as soon as you remember. If it is near the time for the next dose, skip the missed dose and resume your regular dosage schedule. Do not double the next dose.

STOPPING THE DRUG
Unless directed otherwise by your doctor, limit use to 5 days for children under 12 and 10 days for adults.

PROLONGED USE
Prolonged use may lead to liver problems, kidney problems, or anemia in some patients. Talk to your doctor about the need for periodic physical examinations and laboratory tests.

PRECAUTIONS
Over 60: Adverse reactions may be more likely and more severe in older patients; lower doses may be warranted.

Driving and Hazardous Work: No problems are expected.

Alcohol: Avoid alcohol; combining the two can cause serious liver problems. Patients with a history of alcohol abuse should not use acetaminophen except under close supervision by a doctor.

Pregnancy: No problems have been reported. Consult your doctor if you are or plan to become pregnant.

Breast Feeding: No problems have been reported.

Infants and Children: No problems are expected; however, some formulations are sweetened with aspartame, which should not be consumed by children with phenylketonuria.

OVERDOSE
Symptoms: Nausea, vomiting, appetite loss, abdominal pain, excessive sweating, confusion, drowsiness or exhaustion, stomach tenderness, heartbeat irregularities, yellowing of the skin and eyes.

What to Do: If you suspect an overdose, seek medical aid immediately, even if no symptoms are present. Steps must be taken promptly to avoid potentially fatal liver damage.

DRUG INTERACTIONS
Consult your doctor for specific advice if you are taking anticoagulants (such as warfarin), aspirin, an NSAID, barbiturates, carbamazepine, hydantoins, rifampin, sulfinpyrazone, isoniazid, nicotine, or zidovudine.

FOOD INTERACTIONS
No known food interactions.

DISEASE INTERACTIONS
Consult your doctor if you have liver or kidney disease, diabetes mellitus, phenylketonuria, or a history of alcohol abuse.

Acetaminophen with Codeine Phosphate

Tylenol With Codeine 300/60 mg
(McNEIL)

Additional photographs

▶ Drug Class: Opioid (narcotic)
analgesic/antipyretic

▶ Available in: Capsules,
tablets, oral solution, oral
suspension

▶ Available OTC? No

▶ As Generic? Yes

Side Effects

SERIOUS
See Overdose and
Special Concerns.

COMMON
Dizziness, lightheaded-
ness, nausea or vomiting,
drowsiness, constipation,
unusual fatigue.

LESS COMMON
Stomach pain, allergic
reaction, false sense of
well-being (euphoria),
depression, loss of
appetite, blurring or
change in vision, night-
mares or unusual
dreams, dry mouth, gen-
eral feeling of illness,
headache, nervousness,
insomnia.

PRINCIPAL USES
To relieve mild to severe
pain when nonprescription
pain relievers prove inadequate. A narcotic analgesic
such as codeine, in combination with acetaminophen,
may provide better pain
relief than either medicine
used alone. Used together,
pain relief may be achieved
at lower doses of the two
medications.

HOW THE DRUG WORKS
Acetaminophen appears to
interfere with the action of
prostaglandins, naturally
occurring substances in the
body that cause inflamma-
tion and make nerves more
sensitive to pain impulses.
It also relieves fever, probably by acting on the heat-
regulating center of the
brain. Unlike aspirin, however, acetaminophen does
not reduce inflammation.
Codeine, a narcotic anal-
gesic, is believed to relieve
pain by acting on specific
areas in the spinal cord and
brain that process pain
signals from nerves
throughout the body.

DOSAGE
Adults— Capsules or
tablets: 1 or 2 capsules containing 15 or 30 mg of
codeine with acetaminophen
or 1 capsule containing 60
mg of codeine with aceta-
minophen, every 4 hours as
needed. Oral solution or
suspension: 1 tablespoon
every 4 hours as needed.
Children— Oral solution or
suspension: Ages 3 to 6: 1
teaspoon 3 or 4 times a day
as needed. Ages 7 to 12: 2
teaspoons 3 or 4 times a day
as needed.

ONSET OF EFFECT
Acetaminophen: Rapid.
Codeine: Within 2 hours.

DURATION OF ACTION
Up to 4 hours.

DIETARY ADVICE
Take it with meals or milk
to avoid stomach upset,
unless doctor directs you to
do otherwise.

STORAGE
Store in a tightly sealed container away from heat, moisture, and direct light. Keep
liquid forms from freezing.

IF YOU MISS A DOSE
If you are taking aceta-
minophen with codeine on a
fixed schedule, take it as
soon as you remember. If it
is near the time for the next
dose, skip the missed dose
and resume your regular
dosage schedule. Do not
double the next dose.

STOPPING THE DRUG
You should take the medication as prescribed for the
full treatment period, but
you may stop taking it if
you are feeling better before
the scheduled end of therapy. This drug should never
be stopped abruptly after
long-term regular use.

PROLONGED USE
Narcotic drugs such as
codeine may cause physical
dependence. Taking too
much acetaminophen may
cause liver damage. Ther-
apy with acetaminophen and
codeine should not continue
for more than 2 weeks and
may actually cease to be
effective before then.

PRECAUTIONS
Over 60: Adverse reactions
may be more likely and
more severe in older
patients.

**Driving and Hazardous
Work:** Acetaminophen with
codeine can cause dizziness
or drowsiness; proceed with
caution.

Alcohol: Avoid alcohol.
The combination of alcohol
and this drug may increase
the depressant effects of the
medicine. Drinking alcohol-
containing beverages while
taking acetaminophen
greatly increases the risk
of liver damage.

Pregnancy: Use of this
drug during pregnancy can
cause fetal addiction and
may cause breathing prob-
lems in the newborn infant
if taken during or just
before delivery. Consult
your doctor for specific
guidelines and advice and
discuss the relative risks
and benefits of using this
drug while pregnant.

Breast Feeding: Acetaminophen with codeine
passes into breast milk;
avoid or discontinue nursing
while taking this drug.

Infants and Children:
This medicine should not
be given to infants. The
drug may be used by chil-
dren over the age of 3, but
only with extreme caution
and under the careful supervision of your doctor. Children are generally
prescribed the oral solution
or suspension instead of the
capsule or tablet.

Special Concerns: Taking
a narcotic such as codeine
for an extended period of
time can lead to physical
dependence. When discon-
tinuing the drug after using
it for an extended period, it
is important to decrease the
dosage gradually under the
supervision of your doctor
to reduce the risk of suffering from withdrawal symp-
toms. Call your doctor if
you notice these symptoms
after discontinuing the
drug: shivering or trem-
bling; insomnia; gooseflesh;
nausea or vomiting; body
aches; loss of appetite;
stomach cramps; weakness;
diarrhea; restlessness, nervousness, or irritability;

Acetaminophen with Codeine Phosphate (continued)

rapid heartbeat; runny nose, sneezing, or fever; increased yawning; or increased sweating. Overuse of acetaminophen with codeine may also lead to anemia, liver problems, or central nervous system disorders. Contact your doctor as soon as possible if you experience any of the following symptoms during or after the use of this drug: bloody, dark, or cloudy urine; severe pain in the lower back or side; frequent urge to urinate; painful or difficult urination; sudden decrease in urine output; pale or black, tarry stools; yellow discoloration of the eyes or skin (jaundice); hal-

lucinations; unusual bleeding or bruising; skin rash, hives, or itching; pinpoint red spots on skin; sore throat and fever; unusual excitability; trembling or uncontrolled muscle movements; redness, flushing, or swelling of the face.

OVERDOSE

Symptoms: Severe dizziness or drowsiness; cold, clammy skin; difficult or slow breathing or shortness of breath; severe confusion; seizures; stomach cramps or pain; diarrhea; low blood pressure; increased sweating; constricted pupils; nausea or vomiting; irregular heartbeat; severe weakness.

What to Do: Call your doctor, emergency medical services (EMS), or the nearest poison control center immediately.

DRUG INTERACTIONS

Some drugs may interact with acetaminophen and codeine. Consult your doctor for specific advice if you are taking any prescription or over-the-counter drugs, especially if they contain acetaminophen; central nervous system depressants such as antihistamines or medicine for hay fever, allergies, or colds; barbiturates; seizure medicine; muscle relaxants; anesthetics; or

tranquilizers, sedatives, or sleep medications.

FOOD INTERACTIONS

No significant food interactions have been reported.

DISEASE INTERACTIONS

Consult your doctor if you have a head injury or brain disease, an underactive thyroid, an enlarged prostate, seizures, kidney or liver disease, gallbladder problems, a blood disorder, or a history of alcohol or drug abuse. These conditions may increase the likelihood of side effects from acetaminophen and codeine.

Acetaminophen/Aspirin/Caffeine

▶ Drug Class: Analgesic

▶ Available in: Tablets, caplets, oral powder

▶ Available OTC? Yes

▶ As Generic? Yes

Side Effects

SERIOUS
Difficulty swallowing; dizziness, lightheadedness, or fainting; flushing, redness, or change in color of skin; difficulty breathing, shortness of breath, tightness in the chest, or wheezing; sudden decrease in urine output; swelling of face, eyelids, or lips; black or tarry stools; unusual bleeding or bruising; yellow discoloration of the skin and eyes (indicating liver damage). Call your doctor immediately.

COMMON
Indigestion, nausea and vomiting, stomach pain.

LESS COMMON
Sleeping difficulty, nervousness, irritability.

PRINCIPAL USES
For the temporary relief of mild to moderate pain associated with arthritis or migraine headache.

HOW THE DRUG WORKS
Acetaminophen and aspirin both appear to interfere with the production of prostaglandins, naturally occurring substances in the body that cause inflammation and make nerves more sensitive to pain impulses. Caffeine is believed to enhance the effectiveness of pain relievers.

DOSAGE
Because the amount of each of the components varies with different brands, consult your doctor for the appropriate dose. The following are general guidelines. Adults and teenagers— Tablets and caplets: 1 to 2 tablets or caplets every 3 to 6 hours, as needed and depending on the strength of the product. Do not take more than 8 pills in a 24-hour period. If migraine pain persists for more than 48 hours or joint pain lasts for more than 10 days, stop taking the medication and call your doctor. Oral powder: 1 packet of powder followed immediately by a full glass of water every 6 hours. Children— Generally not recommended for children.

ONSET OF EFFECT
Unknown.

DURATION OF ACTION
Unknown.

DIETARY ADVICE
Should be taken with food or a full glass of water to minimize stomach upset.

STORAGE
Store in a tightly sealed container away from heat, moisture, and direct light.

IF YOU MISS A DOSE
Skip the missed dose and then resume your regular dosage schedule. Do not double the next dose.

STOPPING THE DRUG
You may stop taking the drug whenever you choose.

PROLONGED USE
This combination is indicated for short-term use only. Side effects are more likely with prolonged use.

PRECAUTIONS
Over 60: Adverse reactions may be more likely and more severe.

Driving and Hazardous Work: May cause drowsiness or vision difficulties.

Alcohol: Do not consume more than 2 alcohol-containing beverages a day.

Pregnancy: Discuss with your doctor the relative risks and benefits of using this drug while pregnant. This drug should not be used during the last 3 months of pregnancy.

Breast Feeding: This drug may pass into breast milk; consult your doctor for specific advice.

Infants and Children: Consult your pediatrician. This drug is not recommended for children under 16, since the aspirin component may cause a rare but life-threatening condition known as Reye's syndrome.

Special Concerns: Be sure your doctor knows you are taking this medication; it can interfere with the results of some blood and urine tests. Patients allergic to aspirin should not take this medication.

OVERDOSE
Symptoms: Nausea and vomiting, disorientation, seizures, rapid breathing, ringing or buzzing in the ears, fever, appetite loss, abdominal pain, excessive sweating, drowsiness or exhaustion, stomach tenderness, heartbeat irregularities, yellow discoloration of the skin and eyes, agitation, anxiety, excitement, restlessness, delirium.

What to Do: Call your doctor, emergency medical services (EMS), or the nearest poison control center immediately.

DRUG INTERACTIONS
Consult your doctor before taking this drug if you are currently taking any of the following: blood pressure medication, gout or arthritis drugs, anticoagulants such as warfarin, antidiabetic agents, steroids, seizure medication, NSAIDs, barbiturates, nicotine, zidovudine (AZT), isoniazid, any central nervous system stimulant, a MAO inhibitor, amantadine, over-the-counter cold and allergy medications, or asthma medicine.

FOOD INTERACTIONS
Do not drink large amounts of caffeine-containing beverages like coffee, tea, cola, cocoa, or chocolate milk.

DISEASE INTERACTIONS
Consult your doctor if you have liver or kidney disease, diabetes mellitus, phenylketonuria, a history of alcohol abuse, asthma, a bleeding disorder, congestive heart failure, gout, hemophilia, high blood pressure, thyroid disease, a peptic ulcer, anxiety, panic attacks, agoraphobia, or insomnia.

Acetazolamide

Diamox 500 mg
(STORZ)

Additional photographs

▶ Drug Class: Carbonic anhydrase inhibitor; anticonvulsant

▶ Available in: Tablets, extended-release capsules, injection

▶ Available OTC? No

▶ As Generic? Yes

Side Effects

SERIOUS
Breathing difficulty, seizures, serious allergic reaction (hives, itching, swelling of eyes, lips, and throat).

COMMON
Unusual fatigue; diarrhea; increase in volume and frequency of urination; loss of appetite and weight; metallic taste in mouth; numbness, tingling, or prickling sensations in hands, feet, fingers, toes, lips, and elsewhere.

LESS COMMON
Worsening nearsightedness, dark or bloody urine, painful urination, depression, lower back or flank pain, sudden decrease in urine output, unusual bruising or bleeding, bloody, black, pale, or tarry stools, confusion, clumsiness.

PRINCIPAL USES
To treat glaucoma, seizures, familial periodic paralysis; to prevent or treat mountain (altitude) sickness; to prevent one type of kidney stones.

HOW THE DRUG WORKS
For glaucoma: Blocks the enzyme carbonic anhydrase, thus decreasing the normal secretion of fluid inside the eyeball. For seizures: Appears to reduce the firing of neurons in the brain. For paralysis: Stabilizes muscle membranes. For mountain sickness: Stimulates greater oxygen intake, improves blood flow to the brain, and improves release of oxygen from red blood cells. For kidney stones: Increases alkalinity of urine, which reduces stone formation.

DOSAGE
Tablets— For glaucoma: Adults: 250 mg, 1 to 4 times a day. Children: 4.5 to 6.8 mg per lb of body weight per day in divided doses. For seizures: 4.5 mg per lb daily in divided doses. For altitude sickness: 250 mg, 2 to 4 times a day. Extended-release capsules— For glaucoma: 500 mg twice a day (morning and evening). For altitude sickness: 500 mg, 1 to 2 times a day. Injection— For glaucoma: Adults: 500 mg once a day. Children: 2.3 to 4.5 mg per lb every 6 hours.

ONSET OF EFFECT
Tablets: Within 60 to 90 minutes. Extended release capsules: 2 hours. Injection: 2 minutes.

DURATION OF ACTION
Tablets: 8 to 12 hours. Extended-release capsules: 18 to 24 hours. Injection: 4 to 5 hours.

DIETARY ADVICE
Take oral acetazolamide with food or milk to avoid stomach upset. Tablets can be crushed and mixed with sweet foods to cover taste. (Do not crush extended-release capsules.) Eat foods high in potassium.

STORAGE
Store in a tightly sealed container away from heat, moisture, and direct light.

IF YOU MISS A DOSE
Take it as soon as you remember. If it is near the time for the next dose, skip the missed dose and resume your regular dosage schedule. Do not double the next dose.

STOPPING THE DRUG
The decision to stop taking the drug should be made by your doctor. Do not stop taking the drug abruptly.

PROLONGED USE
Prolonged use of this drug may require increased potassium intake.

PRECAUTIONS
Over 60: Adverse reactions may be more likely and more severe in older patients.

Driving and Hazardous Work: Do not drive or engage in hazardous work until you determine how the medicine affects you.

Alcohol: Alcohol may interfere with seizure control.

Pregnancy: Adequate studies have not been done; discuss the relative risks and benefits with your doctor.

Breast Feeding: It may be necessary to switch medications or discontinue breast feeding.

Infants and Children: No problems are expected.

Special Concerns: May increase urine output, especially at first, as your body adapts to the drug. To keep this condition from disrupting sleep, take a single dose after breakfast if possible; if you take multiple daily doses, take the last one before 6 pm, unless your doctor instructs otherwise.

OVERDOSE
Symptoms: Drowsiness, numbness, nausea, thirst, vomiting, seizures, coma.

What to Do: Call your doctor, emergency medical services (EMS), or the nearest poison control center immediately.

DRUG INTERACTIONS
Do not take acetazolamide with high doses of aspirin or amphetamines, as this may be toxic. Do not take it if you are allergic to sulfa-type drugs. Consult your doctor if you are taking mecamylamine, quinidine, lithium, methenamine, or oral hypoglycemia agents.

FOOD INTERACTIONS
Avoid black licorice. Include high-potassium foods such as bananas and citrus fruits in your diet.

DISEASE INTERACTIONS
Do not take acetazolamide if you have serious liver or kidney disease, Addison's disease, low blood levels of potassium or sodium, or diabetes mellitus. Consult your doctor if you have gout or a lung disease such as emphysema, or a history of kidney stones.

Acetohexamide

Side Effects

SERIOUS
Hypoglycemia (blood sugar levels that are too low), resulting in shakiness, headache, cold sweats, anxiety, and changes in mental state. Stop taking the drug and seek medical help immediately. Severe diarrhea, bleeding, bruising, chills, fever, stomach pain, or heartburn may also occur; stop taking the drug and notify your doctor. Other serious but less-common side effects include bone marrow suppression, hemolytic anemia, and elevation of liver-associated enzymes; these problems can be detected by your doctor.

COMMON
Increased skin sensitivity to sunlight.

LESS COMMON
Fatigue, itchy skin, sore throat, ringing in ears, weakness.

PRINCIPAL USES
Used as an adjunct (supplemental) therapy to dietary modification to help control sugar levels in patients with non-insulin-dependent (type 2) diabetes mellitus.

HOW THE DRUG WORKS
It stimulates the pancreas to produce more insulin. Increased insulin levels reduce blood glucose levels and promote the transport of glucose into muscle cells and other tissues, where it is burned for energy.

DOSAGE
Starting at 250 mg once a day, increased as needed to a maximum of 1.5 g per day. In patients receiving less than 1 g per day, sugar levels can usually be controlled with a once-a-day dose; for those receiving between 1 and 1.5 g, the drug is given in two daily doses, morning and evening.

ONSET OF EFFECT
Within 1 hour.

DURATION OF ACTION
12 to 24 hours.

DIETARY ADVICE
Take it with food or liquid to minimize stomach upset.

STORAGE
Store in a tightly sealed container away from heat, moisture, and direct light.

IF YOU MISS A DOSE
If you miss a dose, take it as soon as you remember unless it is almost time for the next dose. In that case, skip the missed dose and return to your regular schedule. Do not double the next dose.

STOPPING THE DRUG
Do not stop taking acetohexamide without consulting your doctor.

PROLONGED USE
The dosage may need to be adjusted with prolonged use. Over time, many patients become resistant to the effects of the medication and may require treatment with insulin instead.

PRECAUTIONS
Over 60: A smaller dosage is usually warranted for older patients.

Driving and Hazardous Work: No problems are expected.

Alcohol: Drink in moderation only. Small amounts of alcohol at mealtimes usually cause no problems with blood sugar; however, alcohol may cause unpleasant flushing in the face, arms, and neck, up to 12 hours after ingestion.

Pregnancy: Acetohexamide is not usually given during pregnancy. Insulin is generally the treatment of choice for pregnant diabetic patients.

Breast Feeding: Acetohexamide may pass into breast milk; caution is advised. Consult your doctor if you are considering breast feeding.

Infants and Children: Safety and effectiveness have not been established for young patients.

Special Concerns: Follow your doctor's advice about diet, exercise, and weight control carefully. These aspects of treatment are just as essential to the proper control of diabetes as taking the medication. Be sure to carry at all times some form of medical identification that indicates you have diabetes and that lists all of the drugs you are taking.

OVERDOSE
Symptoms: Excessive hunger, nausea, anxiety, cold sweats, drowsiness, rapid heartbeat, weakness, changes in mental state, loss of consciousness (indications of hypoglycemia). Overdose is most likely to occur after you have delayed or missed a meal, have exercised more than usual, or have consumed more than a small amount of alcohol.

What to Do: Call your doctor, emergency medical services (EMS), or local hospital immediately.

DRUG INTERACTIONS
The effects of acetohexamide can be altered by anticoagulants, antidepressants, aspirin, over-the-counter cold preparations containing aspirin, some diuretics, glucagon, beta-blockers, steroids, phenylbutazone, probenecid, rifampin, nonprescription drugs for colds, hay fever, and appetite control, and sulfa-containing antibiotics.

FOOD INTERACTIONS
A special diet is essential for proper control of blood glucose levels. Avoid foods high in sugar.

DISEASE INTERACTIONS
Liver disease, overactive or underactive thyroid, and kidney disease can affect the activity of the drug.

Acetylcysteine

BRAND NAMES
Mucomyst, Mucosil

▶ Drug Class: Decongestant/cough drug

▶ Available in: Inhalant solution

▶ Available OTC? No

▶ As Generic? Yes

Side Effects

SERIOUS
Wheezing, tightness in the chest, and breathing difficulty (especially among patients with asthma); spitting up of blood. Contact your doctor immediately if any such symptoms arise.

COMMON
Acetylcysteine does not commonly cause side effects.

LESS COMMON
Clammy skin, fever, increased mucus production in the lungs, pain or irritation around the mouth or throat, nausea and vomiting, runny nose, drowsiness. Such symptoms are likely to diminish as your body adjusts to the medication.

PRINCIPAL USES
To relieve congestion and make breathing easier in lung conditions associated with the production of large amounts of thick mucus, such as bronchiectasis (irreversible destruction of the bronchial walls), bronchitis, pneumonia, and cystic fibrosis. It may also be used in patients who have undergone tracheostomy (surgical opening in the neck to establish an airway when the throat is obstructed), or who have a collapsed lobe of the lung due to a plug of mucus blocking an airway.

HOW THE DRUG WORKS
Acetylcysteine liquefies and thins mucus so that it may be coughed up (or removed with suction if necessary).

DOSAGE
3 to 5 ml of 20% solution, or 6 to 10 ml of 10% solution by nebulizer every 2 to 6 hours. (The medicine may be inhaled through a face mask, mouthpiece, or via tracheostomy.) Or, 1 to 2 ml of 10% or 20% solution placed directly into the trachea via catheter every hour. The dosage differs from patient to patient; follow your doctor's directions carefully.

ONSET OF EFFECT
Within 1 minute.

DURATION OF ACTION
Up to several hours.

DIETARY ADVICE
This drug should not be taken with meals. Be sure to drink plenty of fluids.

STORAGE
Before opening, store container away from heat and direct light. After opening, store it in the refrigerator, but do not allow it to freeze. Discard the container 96 hours after opening.

IF YOU MISS A DOSE
Take it as soon as you remember. Take the rest of the day's doses at evenly spaced intervals.

STOPPING THE DRUG
The decision to stop taking the drug should be made by your doctor.

PROLONGED USE
No special problems are expected.

PRECAUTIONS
Over 60: No special problems are expected.

Driving and Hazardous Work: Be cautious if acetylcysteine makes you drowsy.

Alcohol: Alcohol intake should be limited.

Pregnancy: The effects of acetylcysteine on the human fetus have not been documented; consult your doctor or OB/GYN for specific advice if your are pregnant or plan to become pregnant.

Breast Feeding: It is not known whether acetylcysteine passes into breast milk; problems have not been documented. Consult your doctor for specific advice before deciding to nurse while using this drug.

Infants and Children: No special problems are expected.

Special Concerns: Be sure to tell your doctor if you have ever had any unusual or allergic reaction to acetylcysteine, or if you are allergic to any other substances including foods, preservatives, latex, or dyes. If you use a nebulizer to administer the medication, it should be cleaned immediately after use, since residues of the medicine can be sticky and may clog the apparatus. Nebulized solution may be inhaled directly from the nebulizer, or the nebulizer may be fitted with a plastic face mask or mouthpiece. When acetylcysteine is used by patients with asthma or other types of hypersensitivity of the airways, a bronchodilator should be administered first to prevent bronchospasm.

OVERDOSE
Symptoms: Unusual breathing difficulties.

What to Do: Call your doctor, emergency medical services (EMS), or local hospital immediately.

DRUG INTERACTIONS
Simultaneous use of acetylcysteine with tetracycline, erythromycin, lactobionate, amphotericin B, ampicillin, chymotrypsin, or hydrogen peroxide in the same solution should be avoided. Such medications should be taken at another time.

FOOD INTERACTIONS
No known food interactions.

DISEASE INTERACTIONS
Acetylcysteine can aggravate asthma or other respiratory diseases.

Acitretin

Side Effects

SERIOUS
Severe headache, liver damage, eye lesions, joint pain, abnormal spinal bone growth, rigidity, violent shivering associated with chills and fever. Call your doctor as soon as possible.

COMMON
Dry mouth, dryness and cracking of the lips, runny nose, nosebleeds, skin peeling, hair loss, dry skin, nail problems, itching, rash, increased sensitivity to touch, numbness or tingling, inflammation of fingers or toes, sticky skin, dry eyes, irritation of eyes, loss of eyebrows and eyelashes.

LESS COMMON
Bleeding gums, increased saliva, thirst, inflammation of the mouth, abnormal skin odor, blisters, cold and clammy skin, increased sweating, skin infection, ulcerations, sunburn, abnormal or blurred vision, reduced night vision, joint pain, back pain, muscle pain, mild headache, abdominal pain, diarrhea, nausea, odd taste in mouth, ringing in ears, depression, insomnia.

PRINCIPAL USES
To treat severe psoriasis. Acitretin is used only when other medications to treat psoriasis prove ineffective.

HOW THE DRUG WORKS
The exact mechanism of action of acitretin is unknown. It appears to establish a more normal pattern of growth and shedding of skin cells.

DOSAGE
To start, 25 mg once a day. A maintenance dose, given after the initial response to therapy, is 25 to 50 mg once a day. If the response to the drug is unsatisfactory after 4 weeks and there are minimal side effects, the dose may be increased by your doctor, depending on your condition and body weight.

ONSET OF EFFECT
It may take 2 or 3 months to attain the full therapeutic benefit of acitretin.

DURATION OF ACTION
Unknown.

DIETARY ADVICE
Acitretin is best taken with the main meal of the day.

STORAGE
Store in a tightly sealed container away from heat, moisture, and direct light.

IF YOU MISS A DOSE
Take it as soon as you remember. If it is near the time for the next dose, skip the missed dose and resume your regular dosage schedule. Do not double the next dose.

STOPPING THE DRUG
You should take it as prescribed for the full treatment period, but you may stop taking the drug before the scheduled end of therapy if the symptoms have sufficiently resolved. Consult your doctor.

PROLONGED USE
Acitretin is generally prescribed for 1-month periods. See your doctor regularly for tests and examinations to assess the effectiveness and safety of the drug.

PRECAUTIONS
Over 60: Adverse reactions may be more likely and more severe in older patients.

Driving and Hazardous Work: Do not drive or engage in hazardous work until you determine how the medicine affects you.

Alcohol: Avoid alcohol during and for two months after completing therapy.

Pregnancy: Acitretin can cause serious birth defects. Before your doctor will prescribe it, you must sign a waiver agreeing to use contraceptive measures for one month prior to therapy and three years afterward. You must receive a negative result on a pregnancy test within one week of beginning treatment.

Breast Feeding: Acitretin may pass into breast milk and cause serious harm. Do not nurse while taking this medication.

Infants and Children: No studies have been done with children, although it is believed that acitretin could adversely affect growth.

Special Concerns: You may experience increased sensitivity to contact lenses while taking acitretin. If it causes increased sensitivity to sunlight, wear protective clothing, use a sun block, and try to avoid exposure to sunlight. Do not donate blood while you take acitretin and for three years afterward. Many patients will experience a relapse and require further treatment after they stop taking acitretin.

OVERDOSE
Symptoms: No cases of overdose have been reported.

What to Do: An overdose of acitretin is unlikely to be life-threatening. However, if someone takes a much larger dose than prescribed, call your doctor, emergency medical services (EMS), or the nearest poison control center immediately.

DRUG INTERACTIONS
Other drugs may interact with acitretin. Consult your doctor if you are taking vitamin A, any other retinoid, or methotrexate. Also tell your doctor if you are taking any other prescription or over-the-counter drug.

FOOD INTERACTIONS
No known food interactions.

DISEASE INTERACTIONS
Consult your doctor for advice if you have diabetes mellitus, liver disease, or any other medical condition.

Acyclovir

Zovirax 200 mg
(GLAXO WELLCOME)

▶ Drug Class: Antiviral

▶ Available in: Capsules, tablets, liquid, ointment, injection

▶ Available OTC? No

▶ As Generic? Yes

Side Effects

SERIOUS
No known serious side effects are associated with the use of acyclovir.

COMMON
Rash, nausea and vomiting. Ointment can cause pain, burning, or itching at the site where it is applied. Should such adverse symptoms persist, notify your doctor. Injection can cause inflammation of the vein (phlebitis); call your doctor if this occurs.

LESS COMMON
Diarrhea, stomach pain, lightheadedness, dizziness, confusion, tremor. In rare cases kidney function may be altered when the drug is given by injection, causing such symptoms as decreased urine output.

PRINCIPAL USES
To treat herpes virus infections such as genital herpes, shingles, herpes simplex, and chicken pox.

HOW THE DRUG WORKS
Acyclovir interferes with the activity of enzymes needed for the replication of viral DNA in cells. This prevents the virus from multiplying.

DOSAGE
Oral forms— For genital herpes: Up to 1,200 mg a day in evenly distributed doses, every 4 or 8 hours. For shingles: Up to 4,000 mg a day in evenly distributed doses every 4 hours. For chicken pox: Up to 800 mg, 4 times a day, not to exceed 3,200 mg a day. Topical form— To relieve herpes symptoms: Apply a small amount to lesions every 3 hours (6 times a day) for 7 days. Use a glove or finger cot when applying medication.

ONSET OF EFFECT
2 hours or more.

DURATION OF ACTION
Up to 5 hours following the final dose.

DIETARY ADVICE
Capsule, tablet, and liquid forms should all be taken with food and with a full (8 oz) glass of water.

STORAGE
Store in a dry place at room temperature, away from direct sunlight. Refrigerate any liquid form of acyclovir, but do not allow it to freeze.

IF YOU MISS A DOSE
If you miss a tablet, capsule, or liquid dose, take it as soon as you remember, up to 2 hours late. If more than 2 hours, wait for the next scheduled dose. Do not double the next dose. For ointment, apply dose as soon as you remember, then return to your regular dosing schedule.

STOPPING THE DRUG
Take the drug as prescribed for the full treatment period, even if you begin to feel better before the scheduled end of therapy, but do not take it for longer than the recommended period.

PROLONGED USE
Women with genital herpes are at increased risk of developing cervical cancer; annual Pap smears are recommended for these patients.

PRECAUTIONS
Over 60: Adverse reactions and side effects may be more common in older persons. Such effects can be minimized by drinking at least 2 to 3 quarts of liquid per day.

Driving and Hazardous Work: The use of acyclovir should not impair your ability to perform such tasks safely.

Alcohol: Alcohol may accentuate the side effects of lightheadedness and dizziness.

Pregnancy: Acyclovir has been used by pregnant women and no birth defects or other related problems have been reported; however, studies in humans have been limited and inconclusive. Consult your doctor about using acyclovir if you are pregnant or plan to become pregnant.

Breast Feeding: Acyclovir may pass into breast milk. Breast feeding should be avoided while taking any oral form of the drug. No problems are expected with the topical form.

Infants and Children: Acyclovir should not be used for children under 2 years of age. Its use for children under 12 should be carefully supervised by a physician.

Special Concerns: Be sure to tell your doctor if you have ever had any unusual or allergic reaction to acyclovir. It is important to remember that the use of acyclovir is not a cure and will not help prevent you from spreading herpes infections to others.

OVERDOSE
Symptoms: No specific ones have been reported.

What to Do: An overdose of acyclovir is unlikely to be life-threatening. However, if someone takes a much larger dose than prescribed, call your doctor, emergency medical services (EMS), or the nearest poison control center right away for advice. Prolonged overdose may lead to kidney damage.

DRUG INTERACTIONS
Consult your doctor for specific advice if you are taking cyclosporine, probenecid, meperidine, or zidovudine.

FOOD INTERACTIONS
No significant food interactions have been reported.

DISEASE INTERACTIONS
Use of acyclovir may cause complications in patients with liver or kidney disease, since these organs work together to remove the medication from the body.

Adalimumab

BRAND NAME
Humira

▶ Drug Class: Biologic response modifier

▶ Available in: Injection

▶ Available OTC? No

▶ As Generic? No

Side Effects

SERIOUS
Serious side effects are rare, but may include serious infections (such as tuberculosis), nervous system diseases (symptoms may include numbness or tingling, vision problems, weakness in the legs, dizziness), lupus-like symptoms.

COMMON
Itching, redness, pain, or swelling at the site of injection.

LESS COMMON
Upper respiratory infection, headache, nausea.

PRINCIPAL USES
To reduce the signs and symptoms of moderate to severe active rheumatoid arthritis. Adalimumab is prescribed for patients who have not responded adequately to one or more antirheumatic medications. It may also be used in combination with methotrexate in patients who have not responded adequately to methotrexate alone.

HOW THE DRUG WORKS
Adalimumab works by binding with tumor necrosis factor (TNF), a key protein involved in the inflammatory process. Adalimumab reduces inflammation by blocking the interaction of TNF with its receptors on cells.

DOSAGE
Adults: 1 syringe (40 mg) every other week as a subcutaneous (under the skin) injection.

ONSET OF EFFECT
Within 1 to 2 weeks.

DURATION OF ACTION
Unknown.

DIETARY ADVICE
May be taken without regard to diet.

STORAGE
Keep adalimumab refrigerated, but do not allow it to freeze. Keep away from direct light.

IF YOU MISS A DOSE
Take it as soon as you remember and resume your regular dosage schedule.

STOPPING THE DRUG
The decision to stop taking the medication should be made in consultation with your doctor.

PROLONGED USE
No special problems are expected.

PRECAUTIONS
Over 60: No special problems are expected.

Driving and Hazardous Work: No special precautions.

Alcohol: Alcohol may accentuate the side effect of dizziness.

Pregnancy: Adequate human studies have not been done. Before taking adalimumab, tell your doctor if you are pregnant or plan to become pregnant.

Breast Feeding: Adalimumab may pass into breast milk; caution is advised. Consult your doctor for advice on whether to discontinue nursing or discontinue the drug.

Infants and Children: Safety and effectiveness in children have not been determined.

Special Concerns: Prior to starting therapy, you should have a tuberculosis skin test (PPD) placed and read. Your doctor should instruct you on how to prepare and administer the injection of adalimumab before you attempt to do it yourself. Follow your doctor's instructions about selecting and rotating injection sites. Sites for self-injection are the arms, stomach, and thighs. The first injection should be administered under the supervision of your doctor. Other antirheumatic medications may be continued during treatment with adalimumab. Consult your doctor for advice.

OVERDOSE
Symptoms: No cases of overdose have been reported.

What to Do: An overdose with adalimumab is unlikely. If someone takes a much larger dose than prescribed, call your doctor.

DRUG INTERACTIONS
Avoid live-virus vaccines. Adequate studies involving interactions with other drugs have not been done. Consult your doctor for specific advice.

FOOD INTERACTIONS
No known food interactions.

DISEASE INTERACTIONS
Adalimumab should be used with caution in patients with any active infection, including chronic or localized infections, or who are immunosuppressed.

Adapalene

▶ Drug Class: Acne drug

▶ Available in: Topical gel

▶ Available OTC? No

▶ As Generic? No

Side Effects

SERIOUS
No serious side effects are associated with adapalene.

COMMON
Redness, dryness, and scaling of skin; itching or burning immediately after application.

LESS COMMON
Skin irritation, sunburn, flareups of acne. These usually occur during the first month of treatment and then decrease in severity and frequency.

PRINCIPAL USES
To treat acne.

HOW THE DRUG WORKS
Its exact mechanism of action is unclear, but adapalene appears to bind with specific receptors in skin cells in a way that encourages the formation of normal skin cells and discourages the formation of acne lesions.

DOSAGE
After washing affected areas, apply a thin film of adapalene once a day to affected skin areas before bedtime.

ONSET OF EFFECT
Becomes noticeable after 8 to 12 weeks. During the first few weeks of therapy, acne may actually get worse before it begins to get better. This is because the drug is affecting previously unseen lesions, and it should not be considered a reason to stop using the medication.

DURATION OF ACTION
Unknown.

DIETARY ADVICE
Adapalene can be used without regard to diet.

STORAGE
Store in a tightly sealed container away from heat and direct light.

IF YOU MISS A DOSE
Apply it as soon as you remember. If it is near the time for the next dose, skip the missed dose and resume your regular dosage schedule. Do not double the next dose.

STOPPING THE DRUG
The decision to stop using the drug should be made by your doctor.

PROLONGED USE
No problems are expected with prolonged use.

PRECAUTIONS
Over 60: No special precautions are required.

Driving and Hazardous Work: No special precautions are required.

Alcohol: No special precautions are required.

Pregnancy: In some tests, large doses of adapalene caused minor birth defects (an excess number of ribs) in animals, and theoretically could cause major birth defects. Human tests have not been done. Generally, adapalene should not be used during pregnancy. Consult your doctor for specific advice.

Breast Feeding: Adapalene may pass into breast milk; caution is advised. Consult your doctor for specific advice.

Infants and Children: The safety and effectiveness of adapalene in children under the age of 12 have not been established.

Special Concerns: Anyone with a history of allergy to adapalene or any ingredients in the gel should not use this medication. Acne may appear to worsen temporarily during the first weeks of adapalene therapy; cosmetic improvement should become apparent after 8 to 12 weeks. The medicine should be kept away from the eyes, lips, nostrils, and mucous membranes. It should not be applied to cuts, abrasions, scaly or flaky skin, or patches of sunburned skin. The extremes of winter weather, including high winds and cold temperatures, can cause extra skin irritation and dryness. In sunny conditions, protect the treated area with sunscreen products (with a minimum sun protection factor, or SPF, of 15) and adequate clothing; keep exposure to sunlight to a minimum. If you get a sunburn, adapalene therapy should be stopped or delayed until the sunburned areas return to normal. Use of skin products containing alcohol, astringents, spices, or lime should be avoided.

OVERDOSE
Symptoms: Excessive application of adapalene may lead to redness, pain, and peeling of the skin.

What to Do: Discontinue the drug and consult your doctor. If accidentally ingested, seek emergency medical aid right away.

DRUG INTERACTIONS
Some drugs may interact with adapalene. Consult your doctor for specific advice if you are taking other products that can irritate the skin, such as medicated or abrasive soaps and cleansers and products containing sulfur, resorcinol, or salicylic acid. They generally should not be used during adapalene therapy unless otherwise recommended by your doctor.

FOOD INTERACTIONS
No food interactions have been documented.

DISEASE INTERACTIONS
Caution is advised when using adapalene. Consult your doctor if you have any other skin condition.

Adefovir Dipivoxil

BRAND NAME
Hepsera

▶ Drug Class: Antiviral

▶ Available in: Tablets

▶ Available OTC? No

▶ As Generic? No

Side Effects

SERIOUS
Kidney damage, causing decreased or increased urination, thirst, and shortness of breath. In rare cases, adefovir may lead to lactic acidosis, an abnormal and potentially life-threatening buildup of lactic acid in the blood. Symptoms include rapid, shallow breathing, unusual sleepiness or weakness, muscle pain, and abdominal distress. Some people who have taken medicines like adefovir have developed serious liver problems called hepatotoxicity, with liver enlargement (hepatomegaly), and fat in the liver (steatosis). Symptoms include yellowish tinge to your eyes or skin (jaundice), dark urine, light-colored bowel movements, decreased appetite, nausea, and abdominal pain. Call your doctor immediately.

COMMON
Weakness, headache, stomach pain, nausea.

LESS COMMON
Indigestion.

PRINCIPAL USES
To treat chronic hepatitis B infection in people age 18 and older.

HOW THE DRUG WORKS
Adefovir dipivoxil interferes with the activity of enzymes required for the replication of viral DNA in cells, thus preventing the virus from multiplying.

DOSAGE
10 mg once a day.

ONSET OF EFFECT
Unknown.

DURATION OF ACTION
Unknown.

DIETARY ADVICE
No special restrictions.

STORAGE
Store in a tightly sealed container away from heat, moisture, and direct light.

IF YOU MISS A DOSE
Take it as soon as you remember that day. If it is near the time for the next dose, skip the missed dose and resume your regular dosage schedule. Do not double the next dose. Call your doctor if you are unsure of what to do.

STOPPING THE DRUG
The decision to stop using this medication should be made in consultation with your doctor. Your hepatitis may get worse if you change doses or stop.

PROLONGED USE
See your doctor regularly for tests and examinations if you must use this medicine for a prolonged period.

PRECAUTIONS
Over 60: No special studies have been done on older patients. A different medication may be warranted, especially if liver or kidney function is impaired.

Driving and Hazardous Work: Do not drive or engage in hazardous work until you determine how the medication affects you.

Alcohol: It is advisable to abstain from alcohol when you have hepatitis B.

Pregnancy: Adequate human studies have not been done. Discuss with your doctor the relative risks and benefits of using this drug while pregnant.

Breast Feeding: Adefovir may pass into breast milk. Do not use this drug while nursing.

Infants and Children: The safety and effectiveness of adefovir have not been established for children under 18 years of age.

Special Concerns: To help prevent the spread of hepatitis B, do not share razors or toothbrushes; cover any cuts or wounds; dispose of wound dressings in a sealed bag in the trash; keep used syringes for injecting interferon, insulin, or other medications capped and in a needle disposal container; use a condom and dental dam if you have sex; and do not donate blood. It is safe to have close non-sexual contact with others, to dispose of facial tissues normally, and to share dinnerware. People you have had sexual contact with should receive the hepatitis B vaccine.

OVERDOSE
Symptoms: Few cases of overdose have been reported. In clinical studies, excessive doses appear to result in gastrointestinal side effects.

What to Do: If you suspect an overdose or if someone takes a much larger dose than prescribed, call your doctor, emergency medical services (EMS), or the nearest poison control center immediately.

DRUG INTERACTIONS
Consult your doctor for specific advice if you are taking any other prescription or over-the-counter medication.

FOOD INTERACTIONS
No known food interactions.

DISEASE INTERACTIONS
Use of this drug may cause complications in patients with kidney disease, since this organ works to remove the medication from the body. Consult your doctor if you have HIV, hepatitis C, or have had a liver transplant.

Albendazole

▸ Drug Class: Anthelmintic

▸ Available in: Tablets

▸ Available OTC? No

▸ As Generic? No

Side Effects

SERIOUS
Neutropenia (low white blood cell count), thrombocytopenia (low platelet count), and hepatitis can occur during prolonged therapy, but are reversible by discontinuing the drug. If fever, sore throat, abdominal pain, loss of appetite, unusual fatigue, skin rash, or itching occur, call your doctor immediately.

COMMON
No common side effects are associated with albendazole.

LESS COMMON
Nausea, vomiting, dizziness, stomach upset, diarrhea, headache. Alopecia (thinning or loss of hair), a rare side effect, can occur, but is reversible by stopping the drug.

PRINCIPAL USES
To treat hydatid disease and neurocysticercosis. Hydatid disease is a parasitic infection, usually of the liver, caused by echinococcus (dog tapeworm) larvae. Humans can become infected through ingestion of tapeworm eggs in dog feces. Neurocysticercosis is a parasitic infection of the nervous system, caused by taenia solium (pork tapeworm) larvae. It can be contracted by ingesting egg-containing feces from an infected person, owing to food mishandling. Albendazole may be used to treat a variety of other roundworm infections and may be useful in treating a type of intestinal protozoan common in AIDS patients, but it is not licensed for such uses in the United States.

HOW THE DRUG WORKS
Albendazole interferes with various energy-producing processes of helminths (worms), including impairing the uptake of glucose (sugar) for energy.

DOSAGE
For hydatid disease—
Patients weighing more than 132 lbs (60 kg): 1 cycle consisting of 400 mg twice a day for 28 days followed by a 14-day albendazole-free period; repeat for at least 3 cycles. Patients weighing less than 132 lbs (60 kg): 1 cycle consisting of 7.5 mg per 2.2 lbs (1 kg) of body weight twice a day for 28 days followed by a 14-day albendazole-free period; repeat for at least 3 cycles. For neurocysticercosis—
Patients weighing more than 132 lbs (60 kg): 400 mg twice a day for 8 to 30 days. Patients weighing less than 132 lbs (60 kg): 7.5 mg per 2.2 lbs twice a day for 8 to 30 days. Corticosteroids are often administered con-currently for therapy of neurocysticercosis to control the inflammation caused by dying larvae.

ONSET OF EFFECT
Unknown.

DURATION OF ACTION
Unknown.

DIETARY ADVICE
Take it with meals high in fat content to help the body better absorb the drug.

STORAGE
Store in a tightly sealed container away from heat, moisture, and direct light.

IF YOU MISS A DOSE
Take it as soon as you remember. If it is near the time for the next dose, skip the missed dose and resume your regular dosage schedule. Do not double the next dose.

STOPPING THE DRUG
Take it as prescribed for the full treatment period even if you begin to feel better before the scheduled end of therapy. The decision to stop taking the drug should be made by your doctor.

PROLONGED USE
See your doctor regularly for tests and examinations every 2 weeks if you must take this medicine for a prolonged period of time.

PRECAUTIONS
Over 60: No studies have been done specifically on older patients; adverse reactions may be more likely or more severe.

Driving and Hazardous Work: Do not drive or engage in hazardous work until you determine how the medicine affects you.

Alcohol: No special precautions are necessary.

Pregnancy: Pregnant women should not use albendazole except when no other alternative is available. Discuss with your doctor the relative risks and benefits of using this drug while pregnant.

Breast Feeding: Albendazole may pass into breast milk; caution is advised. Consult your doctor for specific advice.

Infants and Children: No special problems are expected.

OVERDOSE
Symptoms: No cases of overdose have been reported.

What to Do: If someone takes a much larger dose than prescribed, call your doctor, emergency medical services (EMS), or the nearest poison control center right away.

DRUG INTERACTIONS
Other drugs may interact with albendazole. Consult your doctor for specific advice if you are taking dexamethasone, praziquantel, cimetidine, theophylline, or any other prescription or over-the-counter medication.

FOOD INTERACTIONS
No known food interactions.

DISEASE INTERACTIONS
Dosage may need to be adjusted in patients with cirrhosis. Consult your doctor for specific advice if you have any other medical condition.

Albuterol

Generic 2 mg
(BIOCRAFT)

▶ Drug Class: Bronchodilator/sympathomimetic

▶ Available in: Inhaler, solution, capsules, tablets, syrup

▶ Available OTC? No

▶ As Generic? Yes

Side Effects

SERIOUS
Inhaled form: May become ineffective if used too often, resulting in more-severe breathing difficulty that does not improve. Signs include persistent wheezing, coughing, or shortness of breath; confusion; bluish color to lips or fingernails; inability to speak. Ingested form: Chest pain or heaviness; irregular, racing, fluttering, or pounding heartbeat; lightheadedness; fainting; severe weakness; severe headache.

COMMON
Nervousness, tremor, dizziness, headache, insomnia.

LESS COMMON
Dryness and irritation of the nose, mouth, and throat; heartburn; nausea; muscle cramps.

PRINCIPAL USES
To dilate air passages in the lungs that have become narrowed as a result of disease or inflammation. It is used in the treatment of asthma and chronic obstructive pulmonary disease (COPD).

HOW THE DRUG WORKS
Albuterol widens constricted airways by relaxing the smooth muscles that surround the bronchial passages in the lungs.

DOSAGE
Use it when needed to relieve breathing difficulty. For bronchospasm: 1 to 2 puffs of aerosol inhaler every 4 to 6 hours; or 2.5 mg of solution delivered via nebulizer 3 to 4 times a day; or 200 micrograms (mcg) of capsules for inhalation using Rotahaler every 4 to 6 hours; or 2 to 4 mg of tablets 3 or 4 times a day, not to exceed 32 mg per day. Children may require a smaller dose, and the syrup form of the drug may be preferable to young patients. For prevention of exercise-induced asthma: 1 or 2 inhalations (at least 1 full minute apart), 15 minutes prior to exercise.

ONSET OF EFFECT
Inhalant: Within 5 minutes. Oral forms: Within 15 to 30 minutes.

DURATION OF ACTION
Inhalant: 3 to 6 hours. Oral forms: 8 hours.

DIETARY ADVICE
Albuterol can be taken on an empty stomach or with food or milk.

STORAGE
Contents of aerosol canisters are under pressure; do not puncture. Store canister away from heat, open flame, and direct light.

IF YOU MISS A DOSE
Skip the missed dose and resume your regular dosage schedule. Do not double the next dose.

STOPPING THE DRUG
It may not be necessary to finish the recommended course of therapy. Consult your doctor.

PROLONGED USE
Therapy may require months or years. Excessive use may result in temporary loss of effectiveness.

PRECAUTIONS
Over 60: Adverse reactions may be more likely and more severe.

Driving and Hazardous Work: Avoid such activities until you determine how the medicine affects you.

Alcohol: No special precautions are necessary.

Pregnancy: Studies have indicated that albuterol may cause birth defects in mice when given in extremely large doses; effects from normal doses have not been established. Consult your doctor for advice.

Breast Feeding: Albuterol may pass into breast milk; caution is advised. Consult your doctor for advice.

Infants and Children: Not recommended for use by children under age 2.

Special Concerns: Be sure to tell your doctor if you have ever had any unusual or allergic reaction to albuterol. The inhaler should be primed prior to the first use and in cases when it has not been used for more than four days. Prime it by releasing four test sprays in the air away from the face. You should wash your rotahaler (once every two weeks) and inhaler (once a week) to prevent medication build-up and blockage. Wash the two halves of the rotahaler or the mouthpiece of the inhaler (with the canister removed) with warm water and shake to remove excess water. Both the rotahaler and the inhaler should be air-dried thoroughly.

OVERDOSE
Symptoms: Confusion, delirium, severe anxiety, seizures, nervousness, headache, nausea, dry mouth, dizziness, insomnia, chest pain, muscle tremors, profound weakness, rapid and irregular pulse.

What to Do: Call your doctor, emergency medical services (EMS), or your local hospital immediately.

DRUG INTERACTIONS
Albuterol should not be used within 14 days of using an MAO inhibitor or tricyclic antidepressants. Consult your doctor for specific advice if you are taking beta-blockers, loop or thiazide diuretics, high blood pressure medication, digitalis drugs, epinephrine, ergot, finasteride, furazolidone, guanadrel, guanethidine, maprotiline, methyldopa, any nitrate, a phenothiazine, pseudoephedrine-containing products, rauwolfia alkaloids, terazosin, theophylline or other asthma medications, or thyroid hormone.

FOOD INTERACTIONS
No known food interactions.

DISEASE INTERACTIONS
Consult your doctor if you have an overactive thyroid, diabetes mellitus, a history of seizures, heart problems, high blood pressure, or blood vessel disease.

Alclometasone

BRAND NAME
Aclovate

- ▶ Drug Class: Topical corticosteroid
- ▶ Available in: Cream, ointment
- ▶ Available OTC? No
- ▶ As Generic? No

Side Effects

SERIOUS
Failure of skin to heal; severe burning and continued itching of skin. Seek medical assistance immediately.

COMMON
Burning, itching, irritation, redness, dryness, acne, stinging and cracking of skin.

LESS COMMON
Prolonged use, especially in covered areas, may produce blistering and pus near hair follicles, unusual bleeding or easy bruising, darkening or prominence of small surface veins, or increased susceptibility to infection.

PRINCIPAL USES
To relieve swelling, itching, redness, and other kinds of discomfort associated with certain skin conditions.

HOW THE DRUG WORKS
Alclometasone appears to interfere with the formation of natural substances within the body that are directly responsible for the process of inflammation, which produces swelling, redness, and itching.

DOSAGE
Apply sparingly (as a thin film), 2 or 3 times a day, only to the specific areas of skin where it is needed. Prior to application, wash or soak the affected area and allow it to dry; this may improve the absorption of the medication.

ONSET OF EFFECT
Rapid, but may take 24 to 48 hours to see the effect.

DURATION OF ACTION
Unknown.

DIETARY ADVICE
No special precautions.

STORAGE
Store in a tightly sealed container away from heat and direct light.

IF YOU MISS A DOSE
Apply it as soon as you remember. If it is close to the next application, skip the missed dose and resume your regular dosage schedule as prescribed.

STOPPING THE DRUG
Take it as prescribed for the full treatment period, even if you begin to feel better before the scheduled end of therapy. For some conditions, you may be directed to taper off the medication if symptoms and rash abate.

PROLONGED USE
See your doctor regularly for tests and examinations if you must use this drug for a prolonged period; use of this drug for more than 14 days is generally not recommended unless your doctor advises otherwise. Avoid prolonged use, particularly near the eyes, on the face in general, on genital or rectal areas, or in the folds of the skin.

PRECAUTIONS
Over 60: Side effects may be more likely and more severe in elderly patients; therapy with topical corticosteroids should therefore be brief and infrequent.

Driving and Hazardous Work: Use of alclometasone should not impair your ability to perform such tasks safely.

Alcohol: No special precautions are necessary.

Pregnancy: Should not be used for prolonged periods by pregnant women or by women trying to become pregnant.

Breast Feeding: Although problems have not been documented, caution is advised. Do not apply to breasts prior to nursing.

Infants and Children: Should not be used for more than 2 weeks on children and adolescents, unless otherwise directed by your doctor. Do not use tight-fitting diapers or plastic pants on children when treating skin irritation in the diaper area.

Special Concerns: Do not use alclometasone longer or more frequently than recommended by your doctor. Do not use it for other skin problems without a doctor's approval. Do not bandage or otherwise wrap the skin unless directed by your doctor. Wash the skin gently and allow it to dry and cool before applying. Be careful not to get the medicine in your eyes; if you do, flush your eyes with water. Wash hands after applying it with your fingers. Do not apply it to the face, mucous membranes, armpits, groin, or under breasts unless your doctor so directs. When treating a hairy site, part the hair and apply directly to the lesion.

OVERDOSE
Symptoms: No cases of overdose have been reported.

What to Do: An overdose of alclometasone is unlikely. However, in the event of accidental ingestion, call your doctor, emergency medical services (EMS), or the nearest poison control center immediately.

DRUG INTERACTIONS
Do not mix topical alclometasone with other products, especially alcohol-containing preparations (which include colognes, aftershave, and many moisturizer lotions), since this may cause dryness and irritation, or increase the risk of an allergic reaction. Consult your doctor if you are taking antifungal agents or antibiotics.

FOOD INTERACTIONS
No known food interactions.

DISEASE INTERACTIONS
Consult your doctor if you have cataracts; diabetes mellitus; glaucoma; infection, sores, or ulcerations of the skin; infection elsewhere in your body; or tuberculosis.

Alendronate Sodium

Fosamax 10 mg
(MERCK)

▶ Drug Class: Bisphosphonate inhibitor of bone resorption

▶ Available in: Tablets

▶ Available OTC? No

▶ As Generic? No

Side Effects

SERIOUS
No serious side effects have been reported in association with alendronate.

COMMON
Abdominal pain or bloating (persistent abdominal pain should be reported to your doctor), indigestion, heartburn, nausea.

LESS COMMON
Headache, constipation, diarrhea, gas, swallowing difficulty, throat irritation, abdominal swelling or tightness, muscle or bone pain, changes in taste perception.

PRINCIPAL USES
To prevent and treat osteoporosis by increasing bone mass. Alendronate also treats glucocorticoid-induced osteoporosis in those receiving corticosteroids. Also used to treat Paget's disease, a disorder characterized by rapid breakdown and reformation of bone, which can lead to fragility and malformation of bones.

HOW THE DRUG WORKS
Healthy bones are continuously remodeled (broken down and then reformed); the minerals and other components of bones are reabsorbed by one set of cells (osteoclasts) and replaced by another set of cells to form new bone. Alendronate suppresses the activity of osteoclasts; consequently, the breakdown of bone tissue occurs more slowly than the laying down of new bone. This action preserves bone density and strength.

DOSAGE
For prevention of osteoporosis: 5 mg once a day or 35 mg once a week. For treatment of osteoporosis: 10 mg once a day or 70 mg once a week. For glucocorticoid-induced osteoporosis in men and women: 5 mg once a day; postmenopausal women not receiving estrogen should take 10 mg once a day. For Paget's disease: 40 mg once a day. The dose is taken in the morning. Swallow tablets whole; do not suck or chew them. Do not lie down for 30 minutes following your dosage. The tablet must be taken with an 8 oz glass of water at least 30 minutes before any food or other medication.

ONSET OF EFFECT
Within 2 hours.

DURATION OF ACTION
24 hours to 7 days.

DIETARY ADVICE
Take alendronate at least 30 minutes before your first food or beverage of the day, with a full glass of water. Some patients may be advised to take calcium or vitamin D supplements to aid in the formation of new bone tissue.

STORAGE
Store in a tightly sealed container away from heat, moisture, and direct light.

IF YOU MISS A DOSE
Take it as soon as you remember. If it is near the time for the next dose, skip the missed dose and resume your regular dosage schedule. Do not double the next dose.

STOPPING THE DRUG
The decision to stop taking the drug should be made by your doctor. In most cases, patients with Paget's disease are treated for 6 months; the drug is then stopped. Retreatment may be necessary if such patients show signs of relapse after a subsequent 6-month observation period.

PROLONGED USE
No special precautions.

PRECAUTIONS
Over 60: No special problems are expected.

Driving and Hazardous Work: No special warnings.

Alcohol: Alcohol should be restricted in high-risk women because it is a risk factor for osteoporosis.

Pregnancy: Alendronate is normally not used in premenopausal women. The drug should not be given to pregnant women because animal studies have shown adverse effects in the fetus.

Breast Feeding: Alendronate may pass into breast milk; consult your doctor for specific advice.

Infants and Children: Not recommended.

Special Concerns: Patients taking alendronate are encouraged to engage in regular weight-bearing exercise and should avoid cigarettes and limit alcohol, which inhibit healthy bone production.

OVERDOSE
Symptoms: Severe heartburn, stomach cramps, or throat irritation might occur if an overdose disturbs the body's normal mineral (electrolyte) balance.

What to Do: Few alendronate overdoses have been reported. However, if someone takes a much larger dose than prescribed, call your doctor or the nearest poison control center.

DRUG INTERACTIONS
Consult your doctor for specific advice if you are taking antacids, calcium supplements, aspirin or other nonsteroidal anti-inflammatory drugs (NSAIDs), or hormone replacement therapy. Wait at least 30 minutes after taking alendronate before taking any other drugs.

FOOD INTERACTIONS
Any food eaten within 30 minutes of taking alendronate decreases its effect. Mineral water, coffee, tea, and fruit juice can interfere with the drug's absorption.

DISEASE INTERACTIONS
Kidney impairment or a gastrointestinal disease may increase the risk of side effects. Low blood calcium levels and vitamin D deficiency must be treated before using alendronate.

Alfuzosin Hydrochloride

▶ Drug Class: BPH therapy agent

▶ Available in: Tablets

▶ Available OTC? No

▶ As Generic? No

Side Effects

SERIOUS
No serious side effects have been reported.

COMMON
Dizziness, headache, fatigue.

LESS COMMON
Chest pain; lightheadedness or fainting, especially when getting up quickly from a seated or lying position. Such symptoms are typically more common when you first take the medication, and generally diminish over time.

PRINCIPAL USES
To ease urinary tract symptoms due to benign prostatic hyperplasia (BPH)—that is, noncancerous enlargement of the prostate gland, which is extremely common among men over the age of 50.

HOW THE DRUG WORKS
Alfuzosin helps relax the muscles in the prostate gland and the opening of the bladder, improving the passage of urine.

DOSAGE
10 mg a day.

ONSET OF EFFECT
Unknown.

DURATION OF ACTION
Unknown.

DIETARY ADVICE
Take immediately following the same meal every day. Do not take on an empty stomach.

STORAGE
Store in a tightly sealed container away from heat, moisture, and direct light.

IF YOU MISS A DOSE
Take it as soon as possible the same day. If it is the next day, skip the missed dose. Do not double the dose. Resume your regular dosage schedule.

STOPPING THE DRUG
Take it as prescribed for the full treatment period, even if you feel better before the scheduled end of therapy.

PROLONGED USE
Consult your doctor about the need for follow-up medical examinations and laboratory studies if you must take alfuzosin for a prolonged period.

PRECAUTIONS
Over 60: Older persons are generally more sensitive to alfuzosin and more likely to experience adverse side effects, especially when getting up from a lying or seated position. Rise slowly to minimize symptoms.

Driving and Hazardous Work: Alfuzosin may impair mental ability, causing drowsiness, lightheadedness, or dizziness, especially when you take the medication for the first time. Caution is advised; for 24 hours after the initial dose, avoid driving or other activities requiring mental alertness. Effects should diminish after several doses.

Alcohol: May increase effects of dizziness or fainting; drink in strict moderation, if at all.

Pregnancy: Alfuzosin is not indicated for use in women.

Breast Feeding: Alfuzosin is not indicated for use in women.

Infants and Children: Alfuzosin is not indicated for use in children.

Special Concerns: Do not crush, split, or chew tablets.

OVERDOSE
Symptoms: Extremely low blood pressure (hypotension), with accompanying fatigue, weakness, headache, palpitations, fainting, or dizziness.

What to Do: Call your doctor, emergency medical services (EMS), or the nearest poison control center immediately.

DRUG INTERACTIONS
Do not take alfuzosin if you are taking antifungal drugs like ketoconazole or HIV drugs called protease inhibitors.

FOOD INTERACTIONS
None are expected.

DISEASE INTERACTIONS
Do not take alfuzosin if you have liver dysfunction. Alfuzosin may aggravate kidney disease, severe heart disease, or chest pain caused by angina. Consult your physician if you have any of these conditions.

Alitretinoin

BRAND NAME
Panretin

▶ Drug Class: Retinoid

▶ Available in: Topical gel

▶ Available OTC? No

▶ As Generic? No

Side Effects

SERIOUS
No serious side effects are associated with alitretinoin.

COMMON
Redness, rash, itching, numbness and tingling, skin cracking, scabbing, swelling, burning sensation, and pain at application site.

LESS COMMON
No less common side effects are associated with alitretinoin.

PRINCIPAL USES
To treat skin lesions topically in patients with AIDS-related Kaposi's sarcoma (a type of skin cancer that commonly affects immuno-compromised patients). Not for use when systemic anti-Kaposi's sarcoma therapy is required.

HOW THE DRUG WORKS
Alitretinoin, a vitamin A-related retinoid found naturally in the body, inhibits the growth of Kaposi's sarcoma cells.

DOSAGE
To start, apply a generous layer of gel to the skin lesions twice a day. Frequency of application may be gradually increased by your doctor to 3 to 4 times a day.

ONSET OF EFFECT
A response to the gel may be seen as soon as 2 weeks after the initiation of therapy. However, some patients require up to 14 weeks of therapy before a response is noted.

DURATION OF ACTION
Unknown.

DIETARY ADVICE
No special restrictions.

STORAGE
Store in a tightly sealed container away from heat, moisture, and direct light.

IF YOU MISS A DOSE
If you fail to apply the medication on one day, return to your regular schedule the next day; do not apply an extra amount in an attempt to compensate for the missed dose.

STOPPING THE DRUG
Use of alitretinoin should be continued as long as its benefit persists. Consult your doctor before discontinuing treatment.

PROLONGED USE
Long-term therapy with this medication is often required.

PRECAUTIONS
Over 60: Information is inadequate, but no special problems are expected.

Driving and Hazardous Work: The use of alitretinoin should not impair your ability to perform such tasks safely.

Alcohol: No special precautions are necessary.

Pregnancy: Alitretinoin should not be used if you are pregnant or plan to become pregnant. Adequate birth-control methods should be practiced when alitretinoin is used in women of child-bearing age.

Breast Feeding: Alitretinoin may pass into breast milk. However, women infected with HIV should not breast-feed, so as to avoid transmitting the virus to an uninfected child.

Infants and Children: Not recommended for use by children.

Special Concerns: Avoid applying the gel to unaffected skin, as skin irritation may result. Allow the gel to dry for 3 to 5 minutes before covering with clothing. Do not apply near mucous membranes such as the nose, eyes, and mouth. Patients with cutaneous T-cell lymphoma are less tolerant to the drug.

OVERDOSE
Symptoms: Excessive use of alitretinoin may lead to skin redness, peeling, or discomfort.

What to Do: An overdose is unlikely to occur. If someone accidentally ingests alitretinoin, call your doctor.

DRUG INTERACTIONS
If you are using alitretinoin, do not use any products containing DEET, a common ingredient in some insect repellents.

FOOD INTERACTIONS
No known food interactions.

DISEASE INTERACTIONS
Consult your doctor if you have any other skin condition before using alitretinoin.

Allopurinol

Generic 300 mg
(PAR)

Additional photographs

▶ Drug Class: Antigout drug

▶ Available in: Tablets

▶ Available OTC? No

▶ As Generic? Yes

Side Effects

SERIOUS
Anemia or other blood or bone marrow disorders that may produce fatigue, bleeding, or bruising; yellowish tinge to eyes or skin (signifying hepatitis or liver damage); severe skin reactions (marked by rashes, skin ulcers, hives, intense itching); chest tightness; weakness. Call your doctor right away if such symptoms arise.

COMMON
Mild rash, drowsiness, nausea, diarrhea. The frequency of gout attacks may increase during the first weeks of use.

LESS COMMON
Headache, abdominal pain, boils on face, chills or fever, vomiting, hair loss.

PRINCIPAL USES
To treat chronic gout or excessive uric acid buildup caused by kidney disorders, cancer, or the use of chemotherapy drugs for cancer. Also prescribed to prevent recurrence of uric acid kidney stones. Allopurinol should not be used for treating acute gout attacks in progress.

HOW THE DRUG WORKS
Allopurinol blocks the enzyme xanthine oxidase, which is required for the production of uric acid, thus reducing blood levels of uric acid.

DOSAGE
Adults: Initially 100 mg per day, increased by 100 mg per week to a maximum of 800 mg per day. 100 mg doses are administered once a day; doses of 300 mg or more are taken in 2 or 3 evenly divided portions throughout the day. Children ages 6 to 10: 300 mg per day for certain types of cancer. Children age 6 and under: 50 mg per day in 3 evenly divided portions.

ONSET OF EFFECT
Reduces uric acid levels in 2 to 3 days; may take 6 months for full effect to occur.

DURATION OF ACTION
1 to 2 weeks.

DIETARY ADVICE
Take it with food or milk to avoid stomach irritation. Drink 10 to 12 glasses (8 oz each) of water a day.

STORAGE
Store in a tightly sealed container away from heat and direct light.

IF YOU MISS A DOSE
Take it as soon as you remember. However, if it is near the time for the next dose, skip the missed dose and resume your regular dosage schedule. Do not double the next dose.

STOPPING THE DRUG
Take allopurinol as prescribed for the full treatment period, even if you begin to feel better before the scheduled end of therapy.

PROLONGED USE
Consult your doctor about the need for tests of liver function, kidney function, blood counts, and blood and urine levels of uric acid.

PRECAUTIONS
Over 60: Adverse reactions may be more likely and more severe in older patients.

Driving and Hazardous Work: Allopurinol may cause drowsiness. If possible, avoid driving and hazardous work.

Alcohol: No special precautions are necessary.

Pregnancy: Caution is advised; consult your doctor about whether the benefits outweigh potential risks to the unborn child.

Breast Feeding: Allopurinol passes into breast milk; avoid or discontinue use while nursing.

Infants and Children: Follow your doctor's instructions carefully for children.

OVERDOSE
Symptoms: No specific symptoms have been reported.

What to Do: An overdose of allopurinol is unlikely to be life-threatening. However, if someone takes a much larger dose than prescribed, contact your doctor, poison control center, or local emergency room for instructions.

DRUG INTERACTIONS
Consult your doctor for specific advice if you are taking an antibiotic (such as amoxicillin, ampicillin, or bacampicillin), an anticoagulant (warfarin, dicumarol), an anticancer (chemotherapy) drug, chlorpropamide, a diuretic, or theophylline.

FOOD INTERACTIONS
None are likely, but a low-purine diet is recommended to reduce the risk of gout attacks. Foods high in purines include anchovies, sardines, legumes, poultry, sweetbreads, liver, kidneys, and other organ meats.

DISEASE INTERACTIONS
Caution is advised when taking allopurinol. Consult your doctor if you have high blood pressure, diabetes mellitus, kidney disease, or impaired iron metabolism.

Almotriptan Malate

BRAND NAME
Axert

▶ Drug Class: Antimigraine/ antiheadache drug

▶ Available in: Tablets

▶ Available OTC? No

▶ As Generic? No

Side Effects

SERIOUS
Serious side effects with almotriptan are rare. However, almotriptan may cause a heart attack, chest pain or tightness, sudden or severe abdominal pain, shortness of breath, wheezing, heartbeat irregularities, swelling of eyelids, face, or lips, skin rash, or hives. Seek emergency medical assistance immediately.

COMMON
Nausea, drowsiness, prickling or tingling sensations, dry mouth, headache.

LESS COMMON
Many less common side effects can occur; consult your doctor if you are concerned about any adverse or unusual reactions you experience while taking this drug.

PRINCIPAL USES
To treat severe, acute migraine headaches. Almotriptan is not intended as a migraine preventive or for use against any other kinds of pain or headache, including basilar and hemiplegic migraines.

HOW THE DRUG WORKS
The exact mechanism of almotriptan's action is unknown. However, it is believed that almotriptan may reduce the swelling of blood vessels in the brain that are associated with the pain of migraine, block the release of substances from nerve endings that cause more pain and other symptoms of migraine, and interrupt the transmission of specific pain signals from the brain.

DOSAGE
A single dose ranging from 6.25 to 12.5 mg is generally effective. If the migraine returns or there is only partial relief, the dose may be repeated once after 2 hours, but no more than 25 mg should be taken in a 24-hour period. Since individual response to almotriptan may vary, your doctor will determine the appropriate dosage. A general recommendation is to take one 6.25 mg tablet as the initial dose.

ONSET OF EFFECT
Within 2 hours.

DURATION OF ACTION
Unknown.

DIETARY ADVICE
The medication can be taken with or without food.

STORAGE
Store in a tightly sealed container away from heat, moisture, and direct light.

IF YOU MISS A DOSE
Not applicable, since the drug is taken only when necessary.

STOPPING THE DRUG
Consult your doctor before discontinuing almotriptan.

PROLONGED USE
No special problems are expected.

PRECAUTIONS
Over 60: This drug should not be used unless coronary heart disease has been ruled out through appropriate diagnostic tests.

Driving and Hazardous Work: Some people feel drowsy or dizzy during or following a migraine attack or after taking almotriptan. Avoid driving or other tasks requiring concentration if you have such symptoms.

Alcohol: No special warnings, although alcohol may trigger or exacerbate migraine headaches.

Pregnancy: Adequate human studies have not been done. Discuss with your doctor the relative risks and benefits of using almotriptan while pregnant.

Breast Feeding: Almotriptan may pass into breast milk; consult your doctor for specific advice.

Infants and Children: Safety and effectiveness have not been established for children under age 18.

Special Concerns: Serious, but rare, heart-related problems may occur after taking almotriptan. Almotriptan should not be used by anyone with any symptoms of coronary artery disease (chest pain or tightness, shortness of breath). Anyone at risk for unrecognized CAD—such as postmenopausal women, men over the age of 40, or those with known risk factors for heart disease (hypertension, high blood cholesterol levels, obesity, diabetes, strong family history of heart disease, or cigarette smoking)—should have the first dose of almotriptan administered in a doctor's office, and then only after tests show they are probably free of coronary artery disease.

OVERDOSE
Symptoms: No overdoses have been reported.

What to Do: Although overdose is unlikely, if you take a much larger dose than prescribed, seek medical attention immediately.

DRUG INTERACTIONS
Do not take almotriptan within 24 hours of taking naratriptan, rizatriptan, sumatriptan, zolmitriptan, ergotamine-containing medication, dihydroergotamine mesylate, or methysergide mesylate. Almotriptan and MAO inhibitors such as phenelzine, tranylcypromine, procarbazine, and selegiline should not be used within 14 days of each other. Do not take almotriptan within one week of using ketoconazole, itraconazole, or erythromycin.

FOOD INTERACTIONS
No known food interactions.

DISEASE INTERACTIONS
You should not take almotriptan if you have a history of angina, heart disease, stroke, uncontrolled hypertension, heartbeat irregularities, or peripheral vascular disease. Almotriptan should be used with caution in patients with liver disease or severely impaired kidney function.

Alprazolam

Generic 0.25 mg
(GENEVA)

▶ Drug Class: Benzodiazepine tranquilizer; antianxiety agent

▶ Available in: Tablets, oral solution

▶ Available OTC? No

▶ As Generic? Yes

Side Effects

SERIOUS
Difficulty concentrating, outbursts of anger, other behavior problems, depression, hallucinations, low blood pressure (causing faintness or confusion), memory impairment, muscle weakness, skin rash or itching, sore throat, fever and chills, sores or ulcers in throat or mouth, unusual bruising or bleeding, extreme fatigue, yellowish tinge to eyes or skin. Call your doctor immediately.

COMMON
Drowsiness, loss of coordination, unsteady gait, dizziness, lightheadedness, slurred speech.

LESS COMMON
Change in sexual desire or ability, constipation, false sense of well-being, nausea and vomiting, urinary problems, unusual fatigue.

PRINCIPAL USES
To treat anxiety and panic disorder.

HOW THE DRUG WORKS
In general, alprazolam produces mild sedation by depressing activity in the central nervous system. In particular, alprazolam appears to enhance the effect of gamma-aminobutyric acid (GABA), a natural chemical that inhibits the firing of neurons and dampens the transmission of nerve signals, thus decreasing nervous excitation.

DOSAGE
Adults: Initial dose is 1.5 mg a day, taken in 3 divided doses; may be gradually increased to a maximum dose of 4 mg a day. Older adults: Initial dose is 0.5 to 0.75 mg per day, taken in 2 or 3 divided doses; may be gradually increased to a maximum dose of 2 mg a day. Children: Not usually prescribed.

ONSET OF EFFECT
2 hours.

DURATION OF ACTION
Up to 6 hours.

DIETARY ADVICE
Alprazolam can be taken on an empty stomach or with food or milk.

STORAGE
Store in a tightly sealed container away from heat and direct light.

IF YOU MISS A DOSE
If you miss a dose, take it if you remember within 1 hour. Otherwise, skip the missed dose and take the next one at the regular time. Do not double the next dose.

STOPPING THE DRUG
Never stop taking the drug abruptly, as this can cause withdrawal symptoms (seizures, sleep disruption, nervousness, irritability, diarrhea, abdominal cramps, muscle aches, memory impairment). Dosage should be reduced gradually as directed by your doctor.

PROLONGED USE
Short-term therapy (8 weeks or less) is typical; do not take it for a longer period unless so advised by your doctor.

PRECAUTIONS
Over 60: Use with caution; side effects such as drowsiness and dizziness may be more pronounced in older patients.

Driving and Hazardous Work: Alprazolam can impair mental alertness and physical coordination. Adjust your activities accordingly.

Alcohol: Alcohol intake should be extremely moderate or stopped altogether while taking alprazolam.

Pregnancy: Use of this drug during pregnancy should be avoided if possible. Be sure to tell your doctor if you are pregnant or plan to become pregnant.

Breast Feeding: Alprazolam passes into breast milk; do not take it while nursing.

Infants and Children: Safety and effectiveness have not been established for children under age 18.

Special Concerns: Use of this drug can lead to psychological or physical dependence. Short-term therapy (8 weeks or less) is typical; patients should not take the drug for a longer period unless so advised by their doctor. Never take more than the prescribed daily dose.

OVERDOSE
Symptoms: Extreme drowsiness, confusion, slurred speech, slow reflexes, poor coordination, staggering gait, tremor, slowed breathing, loss of consciousness.

What to Do: Call your doctor, emergency medical services (EMS), or the nearest poison control center immediately.

DRUG INTERACTIONS
Other drugs may interact with alprazolam. Consult your doctor for specific advice if you are taking any drugs that depress the central nervous system; these include antihistamines, antidepressants (including nefazodone) or other psychiatric medications, barbiturates, sedatives, cough medicines, decongestants, and painkillers. Be sure your doctor knows about any over-the-counter medication you may take.

FOOD INTERACTIONS
None reported.

DISEASE INTERACTIONS
Consult your doctor if you have a history of alcohol or drug abuse, stroke or other brain disease, any chronic lung disease, hyperactivity, depression or other mental illness, myasthenia gravis, sleep apnea, epilepsy, porphyria, kidney disease, or liver disease.

Alprostadil Injection

BRAND NAMES
Caverject, Edex, Prostin
VR Pediatric

▶ Drug Class: Vasodilator

▶ Available in: Injection

▶ Available OTC? No

▶ As Generic? Yes

Side Effects

SERIOUS
Painful or prolonged
erection (lasting more
than 4 hours), usually as
a result of excessive
dosage. If erection does
not resolve on its own in
a reasonable amount of
time, seek medical help
promptly. If erection does
resolve on its own, sub-
sequent doses should be
reduced; consult your
doctor for specific guidelines.

COMMON
Pain, itching, or burning
at site of injection.

LESS COMMON
Bruising or bleeding at
site of injection.

PRINCIPAL USES
To treat erectile dysfunction (impotence) in men; also, to
help maintain adequate
blood flow in infants during
heart surgery.

HOW THE DRUG WORKS
Alprostadil causes dilation
of blood vessels, thereby
increasing blood flow to the
tissues supplied by the vessels affected by the drug.
When injected into the
penis, alprostadil causes the
penile arteries to dilate,
thus promoting erection.

DOSAGE
For adult men: Injection of
0.001 to 0.04 mg, self-administered at the base of the
penis as needed. It should
not be administered more
than once a day. For infants:
Injection of 0.005 to 0.01 mg
before surgery.

ONSET OF EFFECT
5 to 10 minutes.

DURATION OF ACTION
30 minutes to 3 hours.

DIETARY ADVICE
Diet is not significant in
alprostadil therapy.

STORAGE
Keep the liquid form of
alprostadil refrigerated, but
do not allow it to freeze.

IF YOU MISS A DOSE
Not applicable; the drug is
taken only when the patient
chooses.

STOPPING THE DRUG
Consult your doctor if you
wish to discontinue therapy
or if you feel alprostadil is
losing its effectiveness.

PROLONGED USE
Alprostadil should not be
used more frequently than a
physician recommends,
which is generally not more
than 3 times a week, with at
least 24 hours between each

dose. Patients who self-
administer alprostadil
should visit their doctor
every 3 months for evaluation; dosage adjustments or
the decision to stop using
the drug will be made at
these times. Never increase
the dosage without consulting your doctor.

PRECAUTIONS
Over 60: Information about
use specifically in older persons is not available, though
elderly patients are more
likely to suffer from circulatory problems and thus may
be less responsive to the
drug than their younger
counterparts. Your doctor
may need to adjust the
dosage.

**Driving and Hazardous
Work:** No special precautions are necessary.

Alcohol: No special precautions are necessary.

Pregnancy: Not applicable;
the drug is used only in
men and infants. No prob-
lems have been reported in
women who became preg-
nant by partners using
alprostadil.

Breast Feeding: Not
applicable; the drug is used
only by men or in infants.

Infants and Children:
Prostin VR Pediatric should
be used for infants only in a
hospital setting.

Special Concerns: Your
doctor should instruct you
on how to administer the
injection of alprostadil
before you attempt to do it
yourself. Only men who
have been diagnosed with
and are being medically
treated for erectile dysfunction should use this drug as
a sexual aid.

OVERDOSE
Symptoms: Painful erection or an erection that persists for more than 4 hours.

What to Do: Call your
doctor, emergency medical
services (EMS), or your
local hospital right away.
Prolonged erection may
result in permanent damage
to the tissues of the penis
and the inability to achieve
subsequent erections.

DRUG INTERACTIONS
None reported in infants.
Adults should notify their
doctor if they are taking any
other drugs.

FOOD INTERACTIONS
No significant interactions
have been reported.

DISEASE INTERACTIONS
An adult who has a blood
coagulation defect, liver disease, sickle cell disease, or
a history of priapism (erections lasting more than 4
hours) should inform his
physician before using
alprostadil.

Altretamine

BRAND NAME
Hexalen

Hexalen 50 mg
(US Bioscience)

▶ Drug Class: Antineoplastic (anticancer) agent

▶ Available in: Capsules

▶ Available OTC? No

▶ As Generic? No

Side Effects

SERIOUS
Anemia or other blood problems that cause fatigue, bleeding, bruising, fever, and chills; anxiety, confusion, dizziness, weakness, and loss of balance or coordination; numbness or tingling in the arms and legs. Call your doctor right away.

COMMON
Dizziness, drowsiness, mood changes, nausea, vomiting.

LESS COMMON
Diarrhea, loss of appetite, abdominal cramps, skin rash, temporary hair loss.

PRINCIPAL USES
To treat persistent or recurrent ovarian cancer. This drug is generally used following first-line treatment with other chemotherapy agents.

HOW THE DRUG WORKS
The exact mechanism of action of altretamine is not known, but the drug appears to interfere with the synthesis of genetic material within cells, thereby inhibiting the growth of cancer cells.

DOSAGE
260 mg per square meter of body size, in 4 equally divided doses per day (at mealtimes and at bedtime), generally given 14 or 21 consecutive days out of a 28-day cycle. The actual dose will depend on how much toxicity has occurred in previous cycles of chemotherapy.

ONSET OF EFFECT
Peak blood levels are achieved within 3 hours.

DURATION OF ACTION
Up to 10 hours.

DIETARY ADVICE
Take it after meals to minimize nausea and vomiting. Maintain adequate intake of food and fluids.

STORAGE
Store in a tightly sealed container away from heat and direct light.

IF YOU MISS A DOSE
Take it as soon as you remember, unless it is almost time for the next dose. In that case, skip the missed dose and take the next one. If you miss more than one dose, call your doctor.

STOPPING THE DRUG
The decision to stop taking the drug should be made in consultation with your physician.

PROLONGED USE
Prolonged use can increase the incidence of nausea and vomiting, which can be treated by antiemetic drugs. Blood tests should be taken every 2 to 4 weeks and prior to the beginning of each new course of therapy with altretamine. Neurological exams should be performed regularly as well to determine whether altretamine is causing any nerve damage.

PRECAUTIONS
Over 60: No special problems are expected.

Driving and Hazardous Work: This drug may produce side effects such as dizziness or nausea; avoid any potentially dangerous activities until you determine how the medication affects you.

Alcohol: Alcohol intake should be limited; drink only in moderation while taking this drug.

Pregnancy: Altretamine should not be used during pregnancy because it may cause birth defects. When using this drug, a reliable method of birth control is recommended.

Breast Feeding: Breast feeding is not recommended; altretamine passes into breast milk and may harm the nursing child.

Infants and Children: No specific information on use in children is available.

Special Concerns: This drug may affect your ability to resist infections. If possible, avoid others who are sick with any sort of infection. Be careful when using a toothbrush, dental floss, or a toothpick, and check with your doctor before having any dental work done. Avoid touching your eyes, nose, or mouth, unless your hands are very clean. Be careful not to cut yourself with objects such as razors or nail clippers, and avoid contact sports or any other activities that could result in injuries.

OVERDOSE
Symptoms: The symptoms of an altretamine overdose have not been well-defined, but an overdose may be life-threatening.

What to Do: If someone takes a much larger dose than prescribed, call emergency medical services (EMS) immediately to receive evaluation and treatment in the closest emergency facility.

DRUG INTERACTIONS
Consult your doctor if you are taking amphotericin B (by injection), antithyroid drugs, azathioprine, chlorambucil, colchicine, flucytosine, ganciclovir, interferon, plicamycin, zidovudine, or an MAO inhibitor (a class of antidepressants). Do not get vaccinated against bacteria or viruses while you are taking altretamine.

FOOD INTERACTIONS
None expected.

DISEASE INTERACTIONS
Caution is advised when taking altretamine. Consult your doctor if you have any of the following conditions: bone marrow depression, chicken pox, shingles, any infection, or reduced kidney function.

Aluminum Salts

Amphojel 600 mg
(WYETH-AYERST)

▶ Drug Class: Antacid

▶ Available in: Tablets, capsules, oral suspension, gel

▶ Available OTC? Yes

▶ As Generic? Yes

Side Effects

SERIOUS
Severe and continuing constipation, dizziness, lightheadedness, and heartbeat irregularities. Bone loss may occur, especially with prolonged use in dialysis patients. Hypophosphatemia (too little phosphate in the blood) may occur with prolonged use and a low-phosphate diet; symptoms include bone pain, fractures, muscle weakness, loss of appetite, mood changes, a general feeling of discomfort, swelling of the wrists and ankles, unusual weight loss, and anemia (decreased number of red blood cells; symptoms include weakness and fatigue).

COMMON
Chalky taste.

LESS COMMON
Mild constipation, stomach cramps, speckling or whitish coloration of stools, increased thirst, nausea and vomiting.

PRINCIPAL USES
To treat heartburn, acid indigestion, sour stomach, peptic ulcers, gastritis, esophagitis, and gastro-esophageal reflux. May also be used to treat or prevent excess phosphate in the blood or to prevent urinary phosphate stones.

HOW THE DRUG WORKS
Aluminum salts neutralize stomach acid and reduce the action of pepsin, a digestive enzyme. This provides symptomatic relief from excess stomach acid.

DOSAGE
1 to 2 tablets or capsules or 5 to 30 ml suspension or gel as often as every 2 hours, up to 12 times per day. Take the dose between meals unless your doctor directs otherwise. When used as sole treatment of peptic ulcer or esophagitis, take it 1 and 3 hours after meals and at bedtime. Tablets should be chewed.

ONSET OF EFFECT
Within minutes.

DURATION OF ACTION
20 minutes to 3 hours.

DIETARY ADVICE
Avoid a low-phosphate diet during prolonged use, unless your doctor directs otherwise. Some recommended high-phosphate foods include red meat, poultry, fish, eggs, dark green leafy vegetables, dairy products, and nuts.

STORAGE
Store in a tightly sealed container away from heat, moisture, and direct light. Keep liquid forms refrigerated.

IF YOU MISS A DOSE
Take it as soon as you remember. Do not double the next dose.

STOPPING THE DRUG
Take as directed.

PROLONGED USE
Do not take it for more than 2 weeks unless your doctor recommends otherwise.

PRECAUTIONS
Over 60: Constipation or intestinal trouble is more common in older persons. Older patients who have or who are at high risk for osteoporosis or other bone disorders should avoid frequent use of this medicine.

Driving and Hazardous Work: No special precautions are necessary.

Alcohol: Alcohol decreases the effect of antacids.

Pregnancy: Consult your doctor before taking aluminum salts while pregnant.

Breast Feeding: Aluminum-containing antacids pass into breast milk. It is unknown whether this poses any risk to nursing infants. Consult your doctor for advice.

Infants and Children: Antacids should not be dispensed to children under age 6 unless otherwise instructed by a physician.

Special Concerns: Use over-the-counter antacids only occasionally unless otherwise directed by your doctor. Persistent heartburn not readily relieved by antacids may be signaling a heart attack or another serious disorder. In such cases, seek medical help promptly.

OVERDOSE
Symptoms: Shallow breathing, dry mouth, constipation or diarrhea, confusion, headache, weakness or fatigue, bone pain, stupor.

What to Do: Seek medical assistance immediately.

DRUG INTERACTIONS
Other medications may lose their effectiveness when taken within 1 hour of antacids. Consult your doctor for specific advice if you are taking amphetamines, bisacodyl, citrates, chenodiol, digoxin, enteric-coated medications, iron salts, isoniazid, ketoconazole, mecamylamine, methenamine, penicillamine, phosphates, nitrofurantoin, quinidine, salicylates, or tetracyclines.

FOOD INTERACTIONS
Taking an aluminum salt with food can decrease its activity. Wait at least 60 minutes after eating before taking it.

DISEASE INTERACTIONS
Do not take aluminum salts if you have any symptoms of appendicitis or an inflamed bowel (abdominal pain, cramps, soreness, bloating, nausea, vomiting). Aluminum salts are not recommended for Alzheimer's patients. Consult your doctor if you have chronic constipation, colitis, ileostomy, colostomy, intestinal or stomach blockage, bone fractures, diarrhea, kidney disease, hypophosphatemia, heart disease, liver disease, edema, stomach bleeding, intestinal bleeding.

Amantadine Hydrochloride

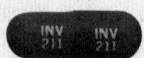

Generic 100 mg
(INVAMED)

▶ Drug Class: Antiviral/
antiparkinsonism agent

▶ Available in: Tablets, syrup

▶ Available OTC? No

▶ As Generic? Yes

Side Effects

SERIOUS
Skin rash, confusion, seizures, hallucinations, swollen feet or arms, difficulty breathing. Call your doctor at once.

COMMON
Dizziness, irritability, distractibility, difficulty sleeping. Consult your doctor if such symptoms persist.

LESS COMMON
Mild skin rash, weakness, depression, fatigue, anxiety, headache, lightheadedness, loss of appetite, nausea, constipation, dry mouth. Consult your doctor if such symptoms persist.

PRINCIPAL USES
To prevent or treat type A influenza; to treat Parkinson's disease. It may also be used to minimize stiffness and shaking caused by certain other drugs prescribed for treating nervous, mental, or emotional disorders.

HOW THE DRUG WORKS
The exact mechanism of action is unknown, though amantadine appears to prevent the influenza A virus from penetrating and entering healthy cells. In Parkinsonism, it increases the release and activity of dopamine, which plays a key role in the control of muscle movement. The increased availability of dopamine in the brain helps compensate for the reduction in the natural supply caused by the disease, and so eases symptoms of Parkinsonism.

DOSAGE
For treatment or prevention of influenza— Adults: 100 to 200 mg a day in 1 or 2 doses for 5 days. Children: Up to 150 mg once a day. For Parkinsonism— Adults: 100 mg, 2 times a day. In some cases the maximum dose may be increased to 400 mg a day. Older patients and those with a history of seizure disorders are usually given reduced doses, generally 100 mg a day.

ONSET OF EFFECT
For influenza A: 2 hours. For Parkinsonism: 48 hours.

DURATION OF ACTION
Up to 12 hours.

DIETARY ADVICE
Take it with or after meals.

STORAGE
Store in a tightly sealed container away from heat and direct light.

IF YOU MISS A DOSE
If you miss a dose, take it as soon as you remember unless it is almost time for your next dose. In that case, skip the missed dose and return to your regular schedule. Do not double the next dose.

STOPPING THE DRUG
Influenza: For prevention, take amantadine for the full treatment period as recommended by your doctor; for treatment, do not stop taking amantadine without consulting your doctor. Parkinsonism: Doses must be decreased gradually according to your doctor's instructions.

PROLONGED USE
Prolonged use requires periodic checks by your doctor.

PRECAUTIONS
Over 60: Older persons are generally more sensitive to amantadine and more likely to experience adverse side effects. Smaller doses may be warranted.

Driving and Hazardous Work: Amantadine can cause drowsiness, dizziness, blurred vision, or confusion. Avoid driving and hazardous work until you determine how the medicine affects you.

Alcohol: Avoid alcohol since it may increase side effects such as dizziness and blurred vision.

Pregnancy: In some animal studies, amantadine has been shown to cause birth defects, though human studies have not been done. Accordingly, the drug should be avoided during the first 3 months of pregnancy. Notify your doctor if you are pregnant or plan to become pregnant.

Breast Feeding: Amantadine passes into breast milk and should not be taken while breast feeding.

Infants and Children: Safety for children under the age of 1 has not been established.

Special Concerns: Individuals with kidney disease must take reduced dosages and be closely monitored.

OVERDOSE
Symptoms: Hyperactivity, disorientation, confusion, visual hallucinations, seizures, drop in blood pressure, palpitations or heart rhythm disturbances.

What to Do: Call your doctor, emergency medical services (EMS), or the nearest poison control center immediately.

DRUG INTERACTIONS
The effects of amantadine can be altered by amphetamines, diet pills, asthma and cold medicines, methylphenidate, nabilone, and pemoline. Anticholinergic drugs can increase the side effects of amantadine.

FOOD INTERACTIONS
None are expected.

DISEASE INTERACTIONS
Caution is advised when taking this medication. Consult your doctor if you have eczema, epilepsy, heart disease, circulation problems, kidney disease, or an emotional disorder.

Amiloride Hydrochloride

BRAND NAME
Midamor

Midamor 5 mg
(MERCK)

▶ Drug Class: Potassium-sparing diuretic

▶ Available in: Capsules, tablets

▶ Available OTC? No

▶ As Generic? Yes

Side Effects

SERIOUS
Heartbeat irregularities, lightheadedness (caused by high blood potassium levels). Notify your doctor at once.

COMMON
There are no common side effects associated with the use of amiloride.

LESS COMMON
Headache, nausea, loss of appetite, weight loss, diarrhea, vomiting, weakness, dizziness, drowsiness, abdominal pain, constipation, impotence, increased skin sensitivity to sunlight, nervousness, irregular heartbeat, shortness of breath, tingling in hands, feet, or lips.

PRINCIPAL USES
As adjunctive (supplementary) treatment with other diuretics to increase excretion of sodium and water in the urine, while conserving potassium.

HOW THE DRUG WORKS
Amiloride promotes loss of sodium and water from the body by altering kidney enzymes that control urine production. Unlike other types of diuretics, amiloride belongs to a class that promotes excretion of excess water but does not deplete normal levels of potassium. In conjunction with thiazide or loop diuretics, amiloride reduces the overall fluid volume in the body and helps to control symptoms of heart disease, kidney disease, and liver disease.

DOSAGE
In most cases, 5 mg a day, increased to 10 mg a day if necessary. Maximum dose is 20 mg a day. The drug is usually taken in one daily dose, preferably in the morning.

ONSET OF EFFECT
2 to 4 hours.

DURATION OF ACTION
Up to 24 hours.

DIETARY ADVICE
Amiloride can be taken with liquid or food to lessen stomach irritation. Avoid large quantities of high-potassium foods (see Food Interactions).

STORAGE
Store in a tightly sealed container away from heat and direct light.

IF YOU MISS A DOSE
Take it as soon as you remember. If it is near the time for the next dose, skip the missed dose and resume your regular dosage schedule. Do not double the next dose.

STOPPING THE DRUG
The decision to stop taking the drug should be made by your doctor.

PROLONGED USE
No apparent problems.

PRECAUTIONS
Over 60: No special precautions are warranted.

Driving and Hazardous Work: No special precautions are necessary.

Alcohol: No special precautions are necessary.

Pregnancy: Animal studies have not shown birth defects. Adequate human studies have not been done. Consult your doctor about taking amiloride during pregnancy.

Breast Feeding: It is not known whether amiloride passes into breast milk. Consult your doctor about its use while nursing.

Infants and Children: A small dose (0.625 mg per day) may be used in young children.

OVERDOSE
Symptoms: Rapid, irregular heartbeat, shortness of breath, nervousness, confusion, weakness, stupor.

What to Do: Call your doctor, emergency medical services (EMS), or the nearest poison control center immediately.

DRUG INTERACTIONS
Tell your doctor if you are taking other medications, especially ACE inhibitors, nonsteroidal anti-inflammatory drugs (NSAIDs), digoxin, lithium, potassium supplements, another diuretic, cyclosporine, or tacrolimus.

FOOD INTERACTIONS
Avoid consuming large servings of high-potassium foods, which include bananas, citrus fruits and juices, melons, prunes, (and most fruits in general), avocados, potatoes, nuts, baked beans, brussels sprouts, and skim milk.

DISEASE INTERACTIONS
Caution is advised when taking amiloride. Consult your doctor if you have any of the following: diabetes mellitus, gout, kidney stones, liver disease, or kidney disease.

Aminocaproic Acid

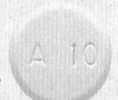

Amicar 500 mg
(IMMUNEX)

▶ Drug Class: Antifibrolytic (bleeding prevention) agent

▶ Available in: Tablets, syrup, injection

▶ Available OTC? No

▶ As Generic? Yes

Side Effects

SERIOUS
Shortness of breath; weakness or numbness of arm or leg; slurred speech; severe and sudden headache; sharp pain in the chest, upper arm, or legs; vision changes. Although the frequency is rare, such symptoms may be signaling a stroke or heart attack. Other rare, but serious side effects include: bleeding problems, seizures, and hallucinations. Discontinue the medication and seek emergency medical treatment immediately.

COMMON
Nausea, diarrhea, severe menstrual cramps, muscle cramps and aches, vomiting. Notify your doctor if such symptoms persist.

LESS COMMON
Dizziness, headache, muscle weakness and fatigue, ringing in the ears, skin rash, abdominal pain, rapid weight gain, swelling in the feet, face, and legs, nasal congestion, delirium, confusion.

PRINCIPAL USES
To treat serious bleeding that occurs after surgery or dental work or to prevent potentially life-threatening bleeding during surgery in patients with hemophilia, low blood platelet counts, or other medical problems.

HOW THE DRUG WORKS
Aminocaproic acid inhibits certain biochemical reactions that involve enzymes, including the activation of plasminogen, a natural enzyme that dissolves blood clots. As a result, blood becomes more prone to clotting, which helps to stanch episodes of uncontrolled bleeding.

DOSAGE
Adults: Initial dose is 5 g, then 1 or 1.25 g per hour, 3 or 4 times a day after the initial dose. The maximum daily dose is 30 g per day. It may be taken by mouth or intravenously. Children: Initial dose is 45.5 mg per lb of body weight, followed by 15.1 mg per lb, 3 or 4 times a day, for 2 to 8 days.

ONSET OF EFFECT
Within 1 hour.

DURATION OF ACTION
3 to 4 hours.

DIETARY ADVICE
Tablet or syrup forms may be taken with food to prevent stomach irritation.

STORAGE
Store in a tightly sealed container away from heat and direct light.

IF YOU MISS A DOSE
Take the missed dose as soon as you remember, unless it is almost time for the next dose. In that case, double the next dose. Then resume your regular dosage schedule.

STOPPING THE DRUG
Do not stop taking aminocaproic acid without your doctor's consent, unless a serious problem occurs, at which time discontinue the drug immediately. Gradual reduction of the dosage may be necessary if you have taken the drug for a long time. Consult your doctor for specific guidelines. Never take more than 30 g per day.

PROLONGED USE
Ask your doctor about the need for medical examinations or laboratory studies with prolonged use.

PRECAUTIONS
Over 60: No special problems are expected.

Driving and Hazardous Work: Do not drive or engage in hazardous work until you determine how the drug affects you.

Alcohol: Alcohol should be avoided because it decreases the therapeutic effect of aminocaproic acid.

Pregnancy: It is not known whether aminocaproic acid can cause fetal harm. It should be used during pregnancy only if clearly necessary, after a detailed discussion with your doctor.

Breast Feeding: Aminocaproic acid passes into breast milk, although it has not been reported to cause health problems in nursing infants. Consult your doctor or pediatrician for specific advice.

Infants and Children: Safety and effectiveness in young patients have not been established; this drug should be used in children only under a doctor's careful supervision.

OVERDOSE
Symptoms: Few cases of overdose have been reported. However, symptoms following high doses of injectable aminocaproic acid may include dizziness, confusion, slow heartbeat, fainting, sluggishness, fatigue, confusion, seizures, increased urination, gastrointestinal bleeding.

What to Do: Discontinue the medication and call your doctor, emergency medical services (EMS), or local hospital immediately.

DRUG INTERACTIONS
Oral contraceptives and estrogens boost the the clot-promoting effect of aminocaproic acid, which may therefore increase the risk of potentially dangerous blood clot formation. Thrombolytic (blood-clot-dissolving) agents such as streptokinase decrease the effect of aminocaproic acid.

FOOD INTERACTIONS
No significant food interactions have been reported.

DISEASE INTERACTIONS
Patients with a history of disseminated intravascular coagulation (also known as DIC, a rare disorder marked by excessive and hazardous blood coagulation) should not take aminocaproic acid. If you are pregnant or have heart disease, kidney disease, or liver disease, you may be at increased risk for side effects.

Aminophylline

BRAND NAMES
Aminophyllin,
Phyllocontin, Truphylline

Generic 100 mg
(WEST-WARD)

▶ Drug Class: Bronchodilator/
xanthine

▶ Available in: Tablets, liquid,
injection, suppositories

▶ Available OTC? No

▶ As Generic? Yes

Side Effects

SERIOUS
Although very rare,
aminophylline may lead
to heartbeat irregularities,
seizures, or extreme
breathing difficulty. Seek
emergency medical assis-
tance immediately.

COMMON
Headache, irritability, nervousness, nausea, vomit-
ing, rapid breathing or
heartbeat, restlessness,
insomnia, stomach pain,
increased urine output.

LESS COMMON
Hives or skin rash, diar-
rhea, dizziness, lightheadedness, loss of appetite,
fatigue.

PRINCIPAL USES
To widen the airways (bronchodilation) and so prevent
the wheezing and constriction of the airways associated with asthma and other
breathing disorders, such as
chronic bronchitis, emphysema, and chronic obstructive pulmonary disease
(COPD).

HOW THE DRUG WORKS
An asthma attack occurs
when the smooth muscles
in the bronchial passages of
the lungs go into a spasm
(bronchospasm). Amino-
phylline relaxes these muscles, thus helping to widen
the constricted airways and
restore normal breathing.

DOSAGE
Adults: 6 to 8 mg per day
per 2.2 lbs (1 kg) of body
weight. Children: 18 mg per
day per 2.2 lbs of body
weight. The dosage must be
adjusted for each person.
Higher doses are warranted
during an acute asthma
attack and taken as needed.
Maintenance dose is taken
every 6 to 8 hours.

ONSET OF EFFECT
15 to 60 minutes.

DURATION OF ACTION
Several hours, depending
on dosage and form.

DIETARY ADVICE
Best taken 1 hour before or
2 hours after eating. Can be
taken with meals to lessen
any stomach upset.

STORAGE
Keep in a tightly sealed container away from heat, moisture, and direct light.

IF YOU MISS A DOSE
If you miss a dose, take it
as soon as you remember
up to 2 hours late. If more
than 2 hours, wait for the
next scheduled dose. Do
not double the next dose.

STOPPING THE DRUG
Take it as long as your doctor advises. See your doctor
for regular checkups.

PROLONGED USE
If used properly, amino-
phylline can be taken safely
for a lifetime; no specific
problems are expected.

PRECAUTIONS
Over 60: Adverse reactions
may be more likely and
more severe in older
patients.

**Driving and Hazardous
Work:** Do not engage in
such activities until you
determine how the drug
affects you. If you experience side effects such as
dizziness and lightheadedness, proceed with caution.

Alcohol: No special precautions are necessary.

Pregnancy: It is unclear
whether aminophylline
causes fetal harm; discuss
the risks with your doctor.
Generally, this drug should
be used only if necessary
and if a substitute cannot be
prescribed.

Breast Feeding: Aminophylline passes into breast
milk and may be toxic to
nursing infants; avoid the
drug or discontinue breast
feeding.

Infants and Children:
Be alert for side effects
such as agitation, irritability,
fever, lethargy, rapid heartbeat and breathing, or
seizures. The liquid form of
aminophylline is often recommended for children to
make it easier to use and
ensure a more accurate
dosage.

Special Concerns: Aminophylline should not be used
by patients who have had
prior allergic reactions to it

or its components (including ethylenediamine).

OVERDOSE
Symptoms: Acute restlessness, irritability, confusion,
breathing difficulties, heart
rhythm irregularities, delirium, seizures.

What to Do: Stop taking
the drug and contact your
doctor, emergency medical
services (EMS), or the
nearest poison control center immediately.

DRUG INTERACTIONS
Consult your doctor for specific advice if you are taking
allopurinol, cimetidine,
ciprofloxacin, erythromycin,
troleandomycin, lithium,
oral contraceptives, phenytoin, propranolol, or
rifampin.

FOOD INTERACTIONS
Avoid excessive use of caffeine-containing beverages.
High-carbohydrate and
high-fat meals can decrease
the effect of aminophylline.

DISEASE INTERACTIONS
You should not take aminophylline if you have active
peptic ulcer disease or an
underlying disorder that
causes seizures (unless you
are also taking appropriate
anticonvulsant medication).
The suppository form
should not be used by people with inflammation or
infection of the rectum or
lower colon. Use caution
when taking aminophylline
if you have heart disease,
liver disease, or an underactive thyroid (hypothy-
roidism). Consult your
doctor in such cases.

Aminosalicylate Sodium

▶ Drug Class: Anti-infective/ antitubercular agent

▶ Available in: Tablets

▶ Available OTC? No

▶ As Generic? No

Side Effects

SERIOUS
Joint pain, fever, unusual fatigue, skin rash or itching, lower back pain, yellow discoloration of the eyes or skin, severe abdominal pain, sore throat, pale skin, headache, pain or burning while urinating. Call your doctor immediately.

COMMON
Abdominal discomfort, nausea and vomiting, diarrhea, loss of weight and appetite.

LESS COMMON
Peptic ulcer disease, intestinal bleeding, lowered white and red blood cell counts.

PRINCIPAL USES
To treat active tuberculosis; must be used in conjunction with other antitubercular agents, such as isoniazid, streptomycin, and rifampin.

HOW THE DRUG WORKS
Aminosalicylate kills tuberculosis bacteria by preventing them from utilizing folic acid, a vitamin necessary for cell growth and reproduction.

DOSAGE
Adults and teenagers: 4 to 6 grams every 12 hours; usually not more than 68 to 91 mg per lb of body weight a day. Children age 12 and under: 23 to 34 mg per lb of body weight every 12 hours. Aminosalicylate is taken in conjunction with other antitubercular agents.

ONSET OF EFFECT
Unknown.

DURATION OF ACTION
Unknown.

DIETARY ADVICE
Take it with or after meals or with an antacid to minimize stomach irritation.

STORAGE
Store in a tightly sealed container away from heat, moisture, and direct light.

IF YOU MISS A DOSE
Take it as soon as you remember. This will help keep a constant level of medication in your system. If it is near the time for the next dose, skip the missed dose and resume your regular dosage schedule. Do not double the next dose.

STOPPING THE DRUG
Take it as prescribed for the full treatment period, even if you begin to feel better before the scheduled end of therapy. Treatment may continue for months or years. The decision to stop taking the drug should be made by your doctor.

PROLONGED USE
Prolonged use with high doses may cause swelling in the front of the neck, menstrual changes in women, decreased sexual ability in men, unusual weight gain, and dry, puffy skin. Consult your doctor about the need for periodic medical examinations and laboratory tests if you take this medication for a prolonged period.

PRECAUTIONS
Over 60: Adverse reactions may be more likely and more severe in older patients.

Driving and Hazardous Work: Do not drive or engage in hazardous work until you determine how the medicine affects you.

Alcohol: No special precautions are necessary.

Pregnancy: Adequate studies of aminosalicylate use during pregnancy have not been done. Consult your doctor for specific advice if you are pregnant or plan to become pregnant.

Breast Feeding: Aminosalicylate passes into breast milk, but no problems have been documented.

Infants and Children: No special warnings; children may tolerate the drug better than adults.

Special Concerns: Do not take tablets that are brown or purple in color.

OVERDOSE
Symptoms: An overdose with aminosalicylate is unlikely.

What to Do: Emergency instructions not applicable.

DRUG INTERACTIONS
Do not take rifampin within 6 hours of taking aminosalicylate. Other drugs may interact with aminosalicylate. Consult your doctor if you are taking aminobenzoates or other over-the-counter or prescription medications.

FOOD INTERACTIONS
None are anticipated, although aminosalicylate can interfere with the absorption of vitamin B12 and other nutrients; vitamin supplementation may be necessary.

DISEASE INTERACTIONS
Caution is advised when taking aminosalicylate. Consult your doctor if you have any of the following: gastric ulcers, epilepsy, heart disease, cancer, an overactive thyroid, or adrenal insufficiency. Use of aminosalicylate may cause complications in patients with liver or kidney disease, since these organs work together to remove the medication from the body.

Amiodarone

Cordarone 200 mg
(WYETH-AYERST)

▶ Drug Class: Antiarrhythmic

▶ Available in: Tablets

▶ Available OTC? No

▶ As Generic? Yes

Side Effects

SERIOUS
Cough, shortness of breath, increased palpitations, loss of voice (rare). Seek medical assistance immediately. Nausea, vomiting, and yellow-tinged skin or eyes (jaundice) may occur as an indication of serious liver problems; notify your doctor right away if such symptoms arise.

COMMON
Stomach upset, nausea, vomiting, constipation, loss of appetite, low-grade fever, heightened skin sensitivity to sun, resulting in greater predisposition to sunburn, numbness or tingling in the fingers or toes, trembling or shaking, unsteadiness when walking, headache.

LESS COMMON
Bitter or metallic taste in the mouth, blue-gray discoloration of skin, vision disturbances, dry eyes, dry, puffy skin, coldness or chills, dizziness, nervousness or restlessness, diminished sex drive in males, scrotal pain and swelling, slow heartbeat, unusual or profuse sweating, insomnia, fatigue, unexpected gain or loss of weight.

PRINCIPAL USES
To prevent and treat heartbeat irregularities, including atrial fibrillation and ventricular tachycardia. The relative risks of using this drug must be weighed carefully against its benefits, since amiodarone can be toxic, especially when taken at high doses or for long periods of time.

HOW THE DRUG WORKS
Amiodarone slows and helps regulate nerve impulses in the heart, and acts directly on the tissue of the heart, making heart muscle less responsive to abnormal stimuli.

DOSAGE
Adults: 800 to 2,400 mg per day in 3 or 4 equally divided doses at first; then 600 to 800 mg per day for one month; then 200 to 400 mg per day. Children: Dosage schedule varies according to the severity of the arrhythmia and often according to individual physician preferences.

ONSET OF EFFECT
2 or 3 days to 2 to 3 weeks.

DURATION OF ACTION
10 days to several months depending on total amount of time the drug has been prescribed and total quantity consumed.

DIETARY ADVICE
Amiodarone be taken with liquid or food to minimize the risk of stomach upset.

STORAGE
Store in a tightly sealed container away from heat, moisture, and direct light.

IF YOU MISS A DOSE
Skip the missed dose and return to your regular schedule. Do not double next dose.

STOPPING THE DRUG
The decision to stop taking the drug should be made by your doctor. Be sure to report any unusual symptoms after you discontinue the medication.

PROLONGED USE
Dosage is typically reduced (to 100 to 200 mg daily) with prolonged use.

PRECAUTIONS
Over 60: Side effects may be more likely and more severe. Thyroid problems (both hypo- and hyperthyroidism) as well as walking difficulty, and numbness, tingling, trembling, or weakness in the hands and feet are likely to develop.

Driving and Hazardous Work: Proceed with caution until you determine how the drug affects you.

Alcohol: Drink only in strict moderation if at all.

Pregnancy: Studies have indicated that amiodarone may cause thyroid and heart problems in unborn children. Nonetheless, the drug may be needed if a history of serious cardiac arrhythmia is a threat to the mother's life. Discuss the relative risks and benefits with your doctor.

Breast Feeding: Amiodarone passes into breast milk; consult your doctor for advice. If you are taking this medication, discontinue nursing.

Infants and Children: Amiodarone can be used in children who have symptomatic or life-threatening arrhythmias. Discuss relative risks and benefits with your doctor.

Special Concerns: To screen for early signs of side effects, most patients should have regular blood tests for liver, thyroid, and pulmonary function, and have eye exams at least annually. Before dental work, emergency treatment, or surgery requiring general anesthesia, be sure to tell the attending doctor or dentist that you are taking amiodarone.

OVERDOSE
Symptoms: Seizures, irregular or very slow heartbeat, loss of consciousness.

What to Do: Call your doctor, emergency medical services (EMS), or the nearest poison control center immediately.

DRUG INTERACTIONS
Consult your doctor for specific advice if you are taking anticoagulants, other heart medications, theophylline, or phenytoin. The blood-thinning effect of warfarin may be drastically enhanced within days of starting amiodarone. Usually the dose of warfarin is reduced once amiodarone is prescribed; prothrombin time is monitored carefully.

FOOD INTERACTIONS
None are expected.

DISEASE INTERACTIONS
Consult your doctor if you have liver or kidney disease, or a thyroid disorder.

Amitriptyline Hydrochloride

Generic 50 mg
(SIDMAK)

Additional photographs

▶ Drug Class: Tricyclic antidepressant; antimanic agent

▶ Available in: Tablets

▶ Available OTC? No

▶ As Generic? Yes

Side Effects

SERIOUS
Confusion, heartbeat
irregularities, hallucinations, seizures, extreme
fatigue or drowsiness,
blurred or altered vision,
breathing difficulty, constipation, impaired con-
centration, difficult
urination, fever, extreme
and persistent restless-
ness, loss of coordination
and balance, difficulty
swallowing or speaking,
dilated pupils, eye pain,
fainting. Also trembling,
shaking, weakness, and
stiffness in the extremi-
ties; shuffling gait. Call
your doctor immediately.

COMMON
Drowsiness, dizziness,
or lightheadedness;
headache, dry mouth or
unpleasant taste, fatigue,
heightened sensitivity to
light, unusual weight
gain, increased appetite,
nausea.

LESS COMMON
Heartburn, insomnia,
diarrhea, increased
sweating, vomiting.

PRINCIPAL USES
To relieve symptoms of
major depression and
chronic pain.

HOW THE DRUG WORKS
Amitriptyline affects levels
of specific brain chemicals
(serotonin, norepinephrine,
and acetylcholine) that are
thought to be linked to
mood, emotions, and
mental state.

DOSAGE
Adults: To start, 25 mg, 2 to
4 times a day; may be
increased to 150 mg a day.
Teenagers: 10 mg, 3 times a
day, and 20 mg at bedtime.
Children ages 6 to 12: 10 to
30 mg a day. Older adults:
To start, 25 mg a day at
bedtime; may be increased
to 100 mg a day.

ONSET OF EFFECT
1 to 6 weeks.

DURATION OF ACTION
Unknown.

DIETARY ADVICE
To lessen stomach upset,
take with food, unless your
doctor instructs otherwise.
Increase intake of fiber
and fluids.

STORAGE
Store in a tightly sealed container away from heat, moisture, and direct light.

IF YOU MISS A DOSE
If you take a one-time daily
bedtime dose, do not take
the missed dose in the
morning; it may cause
drowsiness. Call your doctor. If you take more than 1
dose a day, take it as soon
as you remember. If it is
near the time for the next
dose, skip the missed dose
and resume your regular
dosage schedule. Do not
double the next dose.

STOPPING THE DRUG
Take it as prescribed for the
full treatment period, even if
you feel better before the
scheduled end of therapy.
The decision to stop taking
the drug should be made in
consultation with your doctor. The dosage should be
gradually tapered over 5 to
7 days when stopping.

PROLONGED USE
The usual course of therapy
lasts 6 months to 1 year;
some patients may benefit
from additional therapy.

PRECAUTIONS
Over 60: Adverse reactions
are more likely and more
severe in older patients.
Amitriptyline is generally
not recommended, as there
are safer alternatives for
older patients. A lower dose
may be warranted.

**Driving and Hazardous
Work:** Use caution when
driving and engaging in hazardous work until you determine how the medicine
affects you. Drowsiness or
lightheadedness can occur.

Alcohol: Avoid alcohol.

Pregnancy: Adequate
human studies have not
been done in pregnant
women. Consult your doctor
for advice.

Breast Feeding:
Amitriptyline passes into
breast milk; do not use it
while nursing.

Infants and Children:
Not prescribed for children
under the age of 6. Antidepressants increase the risk
of suicidal thinking and
behavior (suicidality) in
children with major depression and other psychiatric
disorders. Discuss with
your doctor this risk versus
the benefits of using this
drug. Use only under close
medical supervision.

Special Concerns: This
is a potentially dangerous
drug, especially if taken in
excess. It should not be
within easy reach of suicidal
patients. If dry mouth
occurs, use sugarless gum
or candy.

OVERDOSE
Symptoms: Breathing difficulty, fever, severe fatigue,
impaired concentration,
mental confusion, hallucinations, dilated pupils, irregular heartbeat or palpitations,
and seizures.

What to Do: Call your
doctor, emergency medical
services (EMS), or the
nearest poison control center immediately.

DRUG INTERACTIONS
Consult your doctor if you
are taking antithyroid
agents, cimetidine, clonidine, guanadrel, guanethidine, metrizamide, appetite
suppressants, isoproterenol,
ephedrine, epinephrine,
amphetamines, phenyl-
ephrine, antipsychotic drugs,
pimozide, methyldopa, metyrosine, metoclopramide,
pemoline, promethazine,
trimeprazine, rauwolfia alkaloids, MAO inhibitors, or
any drugs that depress the
central nervous system.

FOOD INTERACTIONS
No known food interactions.

DISEASE INTERACTIONS
Consult your doctor if you
have any of the following:
a history of alcohol abuse,
difficulty urinating, asthma,
bipolar disorder, high blood
pressure, stomach or intestinal problems, glaucoma,
overactive thyroid, enlarged
prostate, schizophrenia,
seizures, a blood disorder,
or kidney, heart, or liver
disease.

Amlexanox

▶ Drug Class: Antiaphthous ulcer drug

▶ Available in: Adhesive oral paste

▶ Available OTC? No

▶ As Generic? No

Side Effects

SERIOUS
No serious side effects are associated with amlexanox.

COMMON
Transient pain, stinging, or burning at site of application.

LESS COMMON
Nausea, diarrhea, inflammation of the mucous membranes.

PRINCIPAL USES
To help heal aphthous ulcers (canker sores) of the mouth. Amlexanox works best if it is taken as soon as such ulcers are diagnosed.

HOW THE DRUG WORKS
The exact way in which amlexanox works is unknown. Studies have suggested that it inhibits the formation and release of substances in the body associated with allergic reactions and inflammation.

DOSAGE
Apply ¼ inch of paste on each lesion (mouth ulcer), 4 times a day.

ONSET OF EFFECT
Unknown.

DURATION OF ACTION
Unknown.

DIETARY ADVICE
The paste is best applied after each meal and at bedtime.

STORAGE
Store in a tightly sealed container away from heat and direct light.

IF YOU MISS A DOSE
Apply it as soon as you remember. If it is near the time for the next dose, skip the missed dose and resume your regular dosage schedule. Do not double the next dose.

STOPPING THE DRUG
Use this drug as prescribed for the full treatment period, even if you begin to feel better before the scheduled end of therapy.

PROLONGED USE
You should see your doctor regularly for tests and examinations if you take this medicine for a prolonged period. If ulcers have not healed significantly or pain has not been reduced after 10 days, consult your doctor.

PRECAUTIONS
Over 60: It is not known whether amlexanox causes side effects in older patients different from or more severe than those in younger persons.

Driving and Hazardous Work: No special warnings.

Alcohol: No special precautions are necessary.

Pregnancy: In animal studies, amlexanox has not caused birth defects or other problems. Human studies have not been done. Before you take amlexanox, tell your doctor if you are pregnant or plan to become pregnant.

Breast Feeding: Amlexanox may pass into breast milk; caution is advised. Consult your doctor for specific advice.

Infants and Children: The safety and effectiveness of amlexanox in children have not been established.

Special Concerns: Wash your hands immediately after applying amlexanox. Flush your eyes with water promptly if they come in contact with the paste. If a rash or inflammation of the mucous membranes develops, discontinue use of amlexanox and contact your doctor.

OVERDOSE
Symptoms: None have been reported.

What to Do: An overdose of amlexanox is very unlikely to occur. Emergency instructions are not applicable.

DRUG INTERACTIONS
Consult your doctor for specific advice if you are taking any other prescription or over-the-counter drug.

FOOD INTERACTIONS
No known food interactions.

DISEASE INTERACTIONS
Caution is advised when taking amlexanox. Consult your doctor for specific advice if you have any other medical condition, especially a weakened immune system, which is prevalent in people receiving immunosuppressant drugs or chemotherapy, as well as those with acquired immunodeficiency syndrome (AIDS). The safety and effectiveness of amlexanox in persons with a weakened immune system have not been established. In addition, amlexanox should not be used by anyone who has had a previous allergic reaction to the medication or any other ingredient in the formulation.

Amlodipine

Norvasc 10 mg
(PFIZER)

829

Additional photographs

▶ Drug Class: Calcium channel blocker

▶ Available in: Tablets, capsules

▶ Available OTC? No

▶ As Generic? No

Side Effects

SERIOUS
Increased angina attacks, dizziness upon arising from a sitting or lying position, shortness of breath, weakness, very slow heartbeat. Call your doctor immediately.

COMMON
Headache; flushing in the face and body; water retention causing decreased urination, swelling of the feet and ankles, weight gain.

LESS COMMON
Fatigue, dizziness, drowsiness, palpitations, nausea, abdominal pain.

PRINCIPAL USES
To relieve angina (chest pain associated with heart disease) and to treat hypertension.

HOW THE DRUG WORKS
Amlodipine interferes with the movement of calcium into heart muscle cells and the smooth muscle cells in the walls of the arteries. This action relaxes blood vessels (causing them to widen), which lowers blood pressure, increases the blood supply to the heart, and decreases the heart's overall workload.

DOSAGE
2.5 to 10 mg per day in one daily dose (usually in the morning, with breakfast).

ONSET OF EFFECT
1 to 2 hours.

DURATION OF ACTION
24 hours.

DIETARY ADVICE
It can be taken with or after meals to minimize stomach irritation. Be sure to follow a low-sodium, low-fat diet if your doctor so advises.

STORAGE
Store in a tightly sealed container away from heat and direct light.

IF YOU MISS A DOSE
If you miss a dose, take it as soon as you remember, unless the next dose is less than 4 hours away. In that case, skip the missed dose and go back to your regular schedule. Do not double the next dose.

STOPPING THE DRUG
Take as prescribed for the full treatment period. Do not stop taking this drug suddenly, as this may cause potentially serious health problems. If therapy is to be discontinued, dosage should be reduced gradually, according to doctor's instructions.

PROLONGED USE
In some cases amlodipine therapy may be required for years or even a lifetime. Consult your doctor about the need for medical or laboratory tests of heart activity, blood pressure, kidney function, and liver function.

PRECAUTIONS
Over 60: Adverse reactions may be more likely and more severe in older patients. Smaller doses (2.5 mg per day) are generally prescribed.

Driving and Hazardous Work: Avoid driving or engaging in hazardous work until you determine how this medication affects you. Be cautious if it causes dizziness.

Alcohol: Alcohol should be used with caution because it may increase the effect of the drug and cause an excessive drop in blood pressure.

Pregnancy: Amlodipine should not be taken during the first 3 months of pregnancy and should be used in the last 6 months only if your doctor so advises.

Breast Feeding: Amlodipine should not be taken by nursing mothers.

Infants and Children: Amlodipine is not usually prescribed for patients under the age of 6.

Special Concerns: Amlodipine should not be taken by anyone who has had a prior adverse reaction to it. When taking amlodipine, avoid sudden changes in position, especially standing up quickly after sitting or lying down; such movements may cause dizziness.

OVERDOSE
Symptoms: Severe drop in blood pressure resulting in weakness, dizziness, drowsiness, confusion, or slurred speech.

What to Do: Call your doctor, emergency medical services (EMS), or your local hospital immediately.

DRUG INTERACTIONS
Other heart drugs taken with amlodipine can cause heart rate and rhythm problems. In general, consult your doctor if you are taking any other prescription or nonprescription drugs.

FOOD INTERACTIONS
Avoid excessive intake of foods high in sodium.

DISEASE INTERACTIONS
Consult your doctor if you have kidney disease, liver disease, high blood pressure, or any heart disease other than coronary artery disease.

Amlodipine/Atorvastatin

▶ Drug Class: Calcium channel blocker/antilipidemic combination

▶ Available in: Tablets

▶ Available OTC? No

▶ As Generic? No

Side Effects

SERIOUS
Increased angina attacks, dizziness upon arising from a sitting or lying position, shortness of breath, weakness, very slow heartbeat, fever, chest pain, unusual or unexplained muscle aches and tenderness. Call your doctor immediately if any of thes occur.

COMMON
Headache; flushing in the face and body; water retention causing decreased urination, swelling of the feet and ankles, weight gain; constipation or diarrhea; dizziness or lightheadedness; bloating or gas; heartburn; nausea; allergic reaction; stomach pain; rise in liver enzymes.

LESS COMMON
Fatigue, drowsiness, palpitations, sleeping difficulty, skin rash.

PRINCIPAL USES
Amlodipine is used to relieve angina and to treat hypertension. Atorvastatin is prescribed to reduce blood levels of total and low-density lipoprotein (LDL) cholesterol.

HOW THE DRUG WORKS
Amlodipine blocks the movement of calcium into heart muscle cells and the smooth muscle cells in arterial walls. This action causes blood vessels to widen, which lowers blood pressure, increases the blood supply to the heart, and decreases the heart's overall workload. Atorvastatin inhibits the key enzyme involved in cholesterol formation, thereby reducing its production. By lowering cholesterol levels in the liver cells, atorvastatin increases the formation of liver receptors for LDL, which reduces blood levels of total and LDL cholesterol. Atorvastatin also modestly lowers triglyceride levels and raises HDL (so-called "good") cholesterol.

DOSAGE
5 to 10 mg amlodipine and 10 to 80 mg atorvastatin once a day. Your doctor will determine the appropriate dose.

ONSET OF EFFECT
1 to 2 hours for relief of angina and hypertensive effect. 2 to 4 weeks for cholesterol-lowering effects.

DURATION OF ACTION
Angina and hypertension: 24 hours. Cholesterol-lowering persists for the duration of therapy.

DIETARY ADVICE
It can be taken with or after meals to minimize stomach irritation.

STORAGE
Store in a tightly sealed container away from heat, moisture, and direct light.

IF YOU MISS A DOSE
Take it as soon as you remember. Take your next scheduled dose at the proper time and resume your regular dosage schedule. Do not double your next dose.

STOPPING THE DRUG
Stopping this drug suddenly may cause potentially serious health problems. If therapy is discontinued, dosage should be reduced gradually, according to doctor's instructions. Once the medication is discontinued, blood cholesterol will return to original levels.

PROLONGED USE
In some cases amlodipine and atorvastatin therapy may be required for years or even a lifetime. Consult your doctor about the need for medical or laboratory tests of heart activity, blood pressure, kidney function, and liver function.

PRECAUTIONS
Over 60: No special problems are expected in older patients.

Driving and Hazardous Work: Avoid driving or engaging in hazardous work until you determine how this medication affects you. Be cautious if it causes dizziness.

Alcohol: Use with caution because it may increase the effect of amloipine and cause an excessive drop in blood pressure.

Pregnancy: Should not be used during pregnancy or by women who plan to become pregnant in the near future.

Breast Feeding: Not recommended for women who are nursing.

Infants and Children: Safety and effectiveness are not known; this medication is rarely used in children. Consult your pediatrician.

Special Concerns: Avoid sudden changes in position, standing up quickly after sitting or lying down may cause dizziness.

OVERDOSE
Symptoms: Severe drop in blood pressure resulting in weakness, dizziness, drowsiness, confusion, or slurred speech.

What to Do: Call your doctor, emergency medical services (EMS), or your local hospital immediately.

DRUG INTERACTIONS
Other heart drugs taken with amlodipine can cause heart rate and rhythm problems. Cyclosporine, gemfibrozil, niacin, antibiotics, especially erythromycin, or medications for fungus infections may increase the risk of myositis (muscle inflammation) when taken with atorvastatin and may lead to kidney failure.

FOOD INTERACTIONS
Avoid excessive intake of foods high in sodium.

DISEASE INTERACTIONS
Consult your doctor if you have liver, kidney, or muscle disease, a medical history involving organ transplant or recent surgery, or any heart disease other than coronary artery disease.

Amlodipine/Benazepril Hydrochloride

BRAND NAME
Lotrel

▶ Drug Class: Calcium channel blocker/ACE inhibitor combination

▶ Available in: Capsules

▶ Available OTC? No

▶ As Generic? No

Side Effects

SERIOUS
Serious side effects are very rare; they include fever and chills, sore throat and hoarseness, sudden difficulty breathing or swallowing, swelling of the face, mouth, or extremities, worsening kidney function (ankle swelling, decreased urination), confusion, jaundice (yellowish tinge to eyes or skin, indicating liver problems), intense itching, chest pain or heart palpitations, abdominal pain, irregular or slow heartbeat, low blood pressure (causing dizziness or faintness). Call your doctor immediately.

COMMON
Swelling, mild headache, dizziness, dry cough.

LESS COMMON
Dizziness or fainting, skin rash, numbness or tingling in the hands, feet, or lips, unusual fatigue or muscle weakness, nausea, drowsiness, loss of taste, palpitations, headache.

PRINCIPAL USES
This combination pill is prescribed for people whose blood pressure is not adequately controlled by either amlodipine or benazepril alone. It is also prescribed for people who take both drugs separately and want to reduce the number of pills.

HOW THE DRUG WORKS
Amlodipine, a calcium channel blocker, interferes with the movement of calcium into heart muscle cells and the smooth muscle cells in the walls of the arteries. This action relaxes blood vessels (causing them to widen), which lowers blood pressure, increases the blood supply to the heart, and decreases the heart's overall workload. Angiotensin-converting enzyme inhibitors like benazepril block an enzyme that produces angiotensin, a naturally occurring substance that causes blood vessels to constrict and stimulates production of the adrenal hormone, aldosterone, which promotes sodium retention in the body. As a result, ACE inhibitors relax blood vessels (causing them to widen) and reduce sodium retention, which lowers blood pressure.

DOSAGE
From 2.5 to 10 mg of amlodipine and 10 to 20 mg of benazepril per day. Capsules containing both ingredients are taken once a day.

ONSET OF EFFECT
Unknown.

DURATION OF ACTION
Unknown.

DIETARY ADVICE
It can be taken with or after meals to minimize stomach irritation. Be sure to follow a low-sodium, low-fat diet unless your doctor prescribes otherwise.

STORAGE
Store in a tightly sealed container away from heat, moisture, and direct light.

IF YOU MISS A DOSE
If you miss a dose on one day, do not double the dose the next day.

STOPPING THE DRUG
Take it as prescribed for the full treatment period. The decision to stop taking the drug should be made in consultation with your physician.

PROLONGED USE
See your doctor regularly for tests and examinations.

PRECAUTIONS
Over 60: No special problems are expected.

Driving and Hazardous Work: Exercise caution until you determine how the medicine affects you.

Alcohol: Consume alcohol only in moderation since it may increase the effect of the medication and cause an excessive drop in blood pressure.

Pregnancy: This medication should not be used during pregnancy and is especially dangerous to the unborn child during the final 6 months (second and third trimesters). Before taking this drug, tell your doctor if you are pregnant or plan to become pregnant.

Breast Feeding: Amlodipine with benazepril may pass into breast milk; avoid use while nursing or discontinue breast feeding.

Infants and Children: The safety and effectiveness for use by children has not been established.

Special Concerns: Amlodipine with benazepril is not recommended as the first line of therapy when high blood pressure is diagnosed. It may be prescribed after other medications have proved unsatisfactory. Before you undergo surgery, tell the doctor or dentist in charge that you are taking this drug.

OVERDOSE
Symptoms: No cases of overdose have been reported. Symptoms might include extreme dizziness, fainting, or confusion.

What to Do: If someone takes a much larger dose than prescribed, seek medical assistance right away.

DRUG INTERACTIONS
Other heart drugs taken with amlodipine can cause heart rate and rhythm problems. In general, consult your doctor if you are taking any other medications.

FOOD INTERACTIONS
Avoid excessive intake of foods high in sodium. Also avoid salt substitutes. Many of these products contain high amounts of potassium.

DISEASE INTERACTIONS
Consult your doctor if you have kidney disease, liver disease, high blood pressure, any heart disease other than coronary artery disease, systemic lupus erythematosus, or if you have had a prior allergic reaction to ACE inhibitors. This medication should be used with caution by patients with severe kidney disease or renal artery stenosis (narrowing of one or both of the arteries that supply blood to the kidneys).

Amobarbital/Secobarbital

▶ Drug Class: Barbiturate; central nervous system depressant

▶ Available in: Capsules

▶ Available OTC? No

▶ As Generic? No

Side Effects

SERIOUS
Extreme confusion, severe drowsiness, shortness of breath, wheezing or difficulty breathing, fever, bleeding, rash, hives, hallucinations. Stop taking the drug and call your doctor immediately if you experience any of these side effects.

COMMON
Clumsiness or unsteadiness; dizziness or lightheadedness; drowsiness; hangover-like feelings.

LESS COMMON
Nausea, vomiting, constipation, headache, irritability, sleep disturbances including nightmares and difficulty falling asleep.

PRINCIPAL USES
Amobarbital/secobarbital was previously used for the short-term treatment of insomnia. It is now prescribed only rarely by doctors, usually for the purpose of sedation.

HOW THE DRUG WORKS
This medication is actually two barbiturates, amobarbital and secobarbital, in combination. These drugs act on the central nervous system as a powerful sedative.

DOSAGE
100 or 200 mg at bedtime.

ONSET OF EFFECT
Within 15 minutes.

DURATION OF ACTION
From 3 to 8 hours.

DIETARY ADVICE
The capsules may be crushed and taken with food or liquids.

STORAGE
Store in a tightly sealed container away from heat, moisture, and direct light.

IF YOU MISS A DOSE
Amobarbital/secobarbital is prescribed for once-daily use at bedtime only. If you are unable to take this medication on a particular night, resume only your regularly scheduled dose the following night. Do not double the next dose.

STOPPING THE DRUG
Never stop taking the drug abruptly, as this can cause withdrawal symptoms (seizures, sleep disruption, nervousness, irritability, diarrhea, abdominal cramps, muscle aches, memory impairment). Dosage should be reduced gradually, as directed by your doctor.

PROLONGED USE
Barbiturates are habit-forming. Prolonged use of amobarbital/secobarbital increases the risk of dependency. Amobarbital/secobarbital should not be prescribed for long-term therapy because safer and more effective drugs are available.

PRECAUTIONS
Over 60: Adverse reactions may be more likely and more severe in older patients.

Driving and Hazardous Work: The use of amobarbital/secobarbital may impair your ability to perform such tasks safely.

Alcohol: Avoid alcohol completely; the combination of alcohol and barbiturates is potentially lethal.

Pregnancy: Discuss with your doctor the relative risks and benefits of using this drug while pregnant.

Breast Feeding: Do not use this drug while nursing.

Infants and Children: This drug is not recommended for children.

Special Concerns: Amobarbital/secobarbital is a potentially dangerous drug. Barbiturates should not be used for the treatment of anxiety or stress.

OVERDOSE
Symptoms: Lethargy, excessive sleepiness, slurred speech, severe clumsiness, difficulty walking, confusion, extremely slow, noisy breathing, loss of consciousness. Some patients may become agitated and unusually excited (paradoxical excitation). Pupils may become very tiny, although with severe overdose the pupils may become very dilated.

What to Do: Contact emergency medical services (EMS) immediately.

DRUG INTERACTIONS
The risk of an undesirable interaction is increased when amobarbital/secobarbital is used with any or all of the following drugs: alcohol-containing medicines, antihistamines, allergy medications, sedatives, anti-seizure medications, pain medications (especially prescription pain relievers and narcotics), muscle relaxants, and antidepressants. Use of amobarbital/secobarbital may cause the following to be less effective: blood thinners, birth control pills, and medications similar to cortisone.

FOOD INTERACTIONS
No known food interactions.

DISEASE INTERACTIONS
Patients with kidney or liver disease should avoid amobarbital/secobarbital. The drug may make the following conditions worse: asthma, emphysema, and other respiratory diseases; mental depression; porphyria; and diabetes mellitus.

Amoxapine

Asendin 50 mg
(LEDERLE)

▶ Drug Class: Tricyclic antidepressant

▶ Available in: Tablets

▶ Available OTC? No

▶ As Generic? Yes

Side Effects

SERIOUS
Confusion; sexual dysfunction; heartbeat irregularities; hallucinations; seizures; extreme fatigue or drowsiness; blurred or altered vision; breathing difficulty; constipation; staring and absence of facial expression; impaired concentration; difficult urination; fever; extreme and persistent restlessness; loss of coordination and balance; difficulty swallowing or speaking; dilated pupils; eye pain; fainting; trembling, shaking, weakness, and stiffness in the extremities; shuffling gait; persistent, uncontrolled chewing, lip-smacking, or tongue movements; uncontrolled movements, including tics, twitching, twisting movements, and muscle spasms in the face, arms hands, and legs. Call your doctor immediately.

COMMON
Drowsiness or dizziness, headache, dry mouth or unpleasant taste, fatigue, heightened sensitivity to light, nausea, weight gain, increased appetite.

LESS COMMON
Heartburn, insomnia, diarrhea, sweating, vomiting.

PRINCIPAL USES
To relieve symptoms of major depression.

HOW THE DRUG WORKS
Amoxapine affects levels of norepinephrine, a brain chemical that is thought to be linked to mood, emotions, and mental state.

DOSAGE
Adults: To start, 50 mg, 2 to 3 times a day. Older adults: To start, 25 mg, 2 to 3 times a day. Dosages may be gradually increased, as determined by your doctor.

ONSET OF EFFECT
1 to 6 weeks.

DURATION OF ACTION
Unknown.

DIETARY ADVICE
To lessen stomach upset, take with food, unless your doctor instructs otherwise. Increase intake of fiber and fluids.

STORAGE
Store in a tightly sealed container away from heat, moisture, and direct light.

IF YOU MISS A DOSE
If you take a one-time daily bedtime dose, do not take a missed dose in the morning because it may cause drowsiness. Call your doctor. If you take more than 1 dose a day, take it as soon as you remember. If it is near the time for the next dose, skip the missed dose and resume your regular dosage schedule. Do not double the next dose.

STOPPING THE DRUG
Take it as prescribed for the full treatment period, even if you feel better before the scheduled end of therapy. The decision to stop taking the drug should be made in consultation with your doctor. The dosage should be gradually tapered over several days when stopping.

PROLONGED USE
The usual course of therapy lasts 6 months to 1 year; some patients may benefit from additional therapy. There is increased risk of movement disorders with prolonged use.

PRECAUTIONS
Over 60: Adverse reactions may be more likely and more severe in older patients. A lower dose may be warranted.

Driving and Hazardous Work: Use caution when driving or engaging in hazardous work until you determine how the medication affects you. Drowsiness and lightheadedness can occur.

Alcohol: Avoid alcohol.

Pregnancy: Adequate human studies have not been done. Consult your doctor.

Breast Feeding: Amoxapine passes into breast milk; do not use it while nursing.

Infants and Children: Not prescribed for children under the age of 6. Antidepressants increase the risk of suicidal thinking and behavior (suicidality) in children with major depression and other psychiatric disorders. Discuss with your doctor this risk versus the benefits of using this drug. Children should be observed closely for worsening of symptoms, suicidality, or unusual changes in behavior at the onset of therapy and when making changes in dosage.

Special Concerns: This is a potentially dangerous drug, especially if taken in excess. Tricyclic antidepressants should not be within easy reach of suicidal patients. If dry mouth occurs, use sugarless gum or candy for relief.

OVERDOSE
Symptoms: Difficulty breathing, severe fatigue, seizures, confusion, hallucinations, dilated pupils, irregular heartbeat, heart palpitations, fever, difficulty concentrating.

What to Do: Call your doctor, emergency medical services (EMS), or the nearest poison control center immediately.

DRUG INTERACTIONS
Consult your doctor for specific advice if you are taking antithyroid agents, cimetidine, clonidine, guanadrel, guanethidine, metrizamide, appetite suppressants, isoproterenol, ephedrine, epinephrine, amphetamines, phenylephrine, antipsychotic drugs, pimozide, methyldopa, metyrosine, metoclopramide, pemoline, promethazine, trimeprazine, rauwolfia alkaloids, MAO inhibitors, or central nervous system depressants.

FOOD INTERACTIONS
No known food interactions.

DISEASE INTERACTIONS
Consult your doctor if you have any of the following: a history of alcohol abuse, difficulty urinating, asthma, bipolar disorder, high blood pressure, stomach or intestinal problems, glaucoma, overactive thyroid, enlarged prostate, schizophrenia, seizures, a blood disorder, or kidney, heart, or liver disease.

Amoxicillin

BRAND NAMES
Amoxil, Larotid, Moxlin, Polymox, Trimox, Wymox

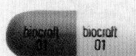

Generic 250 mg
(BIOCRAFT)

829

Additional photographs

▶ Drug Class: Penicillin antibiotic

▶ Available in: Capsules, oral suspension, chewable tablets, liquid drops

▶ Available OTC? No

▶ As Generic? Yes

Side Effects

SERIOUS
Irregular, rapid, or labored breathing, light-headedness or sudden fainting, joint pain, fever, severe abdominal pain and cramping with watery or bloody stools, severe allergic reaction (marked by sudden swelling of the lips, tongue, face, or throat; breathing difficulty; skin rash, itching, or hives), unusual bleeding or bruising, yellowish tinge to eyes or skin. Call your doctor immediately.

COMMON
Rash, mild diarrhea, nausea, vomiting, headache, vaginal discharge and itching, pain or white patches in the mouth or on the tongue.

LESS COMMON
Diminished urine output, chills, weakness, fatigue.

PRINCIPAL USES
To treat bacterial infections of the ear, nose, and throat, genitourinary tract, skin and soft tissues, and the lower respiratory tract. It is used, often with other drugs, to treat uncomplicated gonorrhea. It is also prescribed preventively before surgery or dental work to patients at risk for endocarditis (infection of the interior lining of the heart). It is also used to treat some stages of Lyme disease and, along with other drugs, to treat *H. pylori* infection (the cause of stomach ulcers). Amoxicillin is also approved for prophylactic use following known exposure to anthrax bacteria and for treating anthrax infections.

HOW THE DRUG WORKS
Amoxicillin blocks the formation of bacterial cell walls, rendering bacteria unable to multiply and spread.

DOSAGE
For infections— Adults: 250 to 500 mg every 8 hours (3 doses per day). Children: 3 to 6 mg per lb of body weight every 8 hours (3 doses per day). To treat gonorrhea— 3 g in a single oral dose.

ONSET OF EFFECT
Rapid; within 2 hours.

DURATION OF ACTION
8 hours.

DIETARY ADVICE
Best taken on an empty stomach, but may be taken with food to minimize stomach irritation or diarrhea.

STORAGE
Store in a tightly sealed container away from heat and direct light. Keep any liquid form refrigerated, but do not allow it to freeze, and discard after 14 days.

IF YOU MISS A DOSE
Take it as soon as you remember. If it is near the time for the next dose, skip the missed dose and resume your regular dosage schedule. Do not double the next dose.

STOPPING THE DRUG
Take as prescribed for the full treatment period, even if you begin to feel better before the scheduled end of therapy. Stopping the drug prematurely may slow your recovery or lead to a rebound infection, also known as superinfection, in which the heartier strains of bacteria survive and multiply, leading to a more serious and drug-resistant infection.

PROLONGED USE
Prolonged use of any antibiotic increases the risk of superinfection; caution is advised.

PRECAUTIONS
Over 60: No special problems are expected.

Driving and Hazardous Work: The use of amoxicillin should not impair your ability to perform such tasks safely.

Alcohol: No special precautions are necessary.

Pregnancy: Adequate studies of the use of this drug during pregnancy have not been done; however, no problems have been reported.

Breast Feeding: Amoxicillin passes into breast milk and may cause diarrhea, fungal infections, and allergic reactions in nursing infants; avoid use while nursing.

Infants and Children: No special problems are expected.

Special Concerns: Amoxicillin can cause false results on some urine sugar tests for diabetics. Those who are prone to asthma, hay fever, hives, or allergies may be more likely to have an allergic reaction to a penicillin antibiotic. Oral contraceptives may not be effective while you are taking amoxicillin; use other methods of contraception to avoid unplanned pregnancy.

OVERDOSE
Symptoms: Severe nausea, vomiting, diarrhea, muscle spasticity, seizures.

What to Do: Call your doctor, emergency medical services (EMS), or the nearest poison control center immediately.

DRUG INTERACTIONS
Consult your doctor for specific advice if you are taking: aminoglycosides, ACE inhibitors, diuretics, potassium supplements or potassium-containing medications, anticoagulants or other anticlotting drugs, nonsteroidal anti-inflammatory drugs (NSAIDS), sulfinpyrazone, cholestyramine, colestipol, oral contraceptives, methotrexate, probenecid, allopurinol, or rifampin.

FOOD INTERACTIONS
No known food interactions.

DISEASE INTERACTIONS
Consult your doctor if you have a history of allergies, asthma, congestive heart failure, gastrointestinal disorders (especially colitis associated with the use of antibiotics), or impaired kidney function.

Amoxicillin/Potassium Clavulanate

Augmentin 500/125 mg
(SMITHKLINE BEECHAM)

▶ Drug Class: Penicillin antibiotic combination

▶ Available in: Tablets, chewable tablets, oral suspension

▶ Available OTC? No

▶ As Generic? Yes

Side Effects

SERIOUS
Irregular, rapid, or labored breathing, light-headedness or sudden fainting, seizures, joint pain, fever, severe abdominal pain and cramping with watery or bloody stools, severe allergic reaction (marked by sudden swelling of the lips, tongue, face, or throat; breathing difficulty; skin rash, itching, or hives), unusual bleeding or bruising, yellowish tinge to eyes or skin. Call your doctor immediately.

COMMON
Rash, mild diarrhea, nausea, vomiting, headache, vaginal discharge and itching, pain or white patches in the mouth or on the tongue.

LESS COMMON
Weakness, fatigue.

PRINCIPAL USES
To treat a variety of bacterial infections, including those of the sinuses and middle ear, skin and soft tissues, genitourinary tract, and the respiratory tract. The medication is effective only against infections caused by bacteria, not against those caused by viruses, fungi, or other microorganisms.

HOW THE DRUG WORKS
Amoxicillin blocks the formation of bacterial cell walls, rendering bacteria unable to multiply and spread. Clavulanate enhances the effectiveness of amoxicillin by inhibiting the activity of a specific enzyme (beta-lactamase) produced by certain drug-resistant strains of bacteria.

DOSAGE
Tablets— Adults and children more than 88 lbs: 250 to 500 mg of amoxicillin with 125 mg of clavulanate every 8 hours. Children up to 88 lbs: 6.7 to 13.3 mg of amoxicillin with 1.7 to 3.3 mg of clavulanate per 2.2 lbs (1 kg) of body weight every 8 hours. Chewable tablets and oral suspension— Adults and children more than 88 lbs: 250 to 500 mg of amoxicillin with 62.5 to 125 mg of clavulanate every 8 hours. Children up to 88 lbs: 6.7 to 13.3 mg of amoxicillin with 1.7 to 3.3 mg of clavulanate per 2.2 lbs (1 kg) of body weight every 8 hours. Newer dosage for adults: 875 mg of amoxicillin with 125 mg of clavulanate twice a day.

ONSET OF EFFECT
1 to 2 hours.

DURATION OF ACTION
6 to 8 hours.

DIETARY ADVICE
Best taken on an empty stomach, but may be taken with food to minimize stomach irritation or diarrhea.

STORAGE
Store in a tightly sealed container away from heat and direct light. Keep the liquid form refrigerated, but do not allow it to freeze.

IF YOU MISS A DOSE
Take it as soon as you remember unless it is almost time for the next dose. In that case, skip the missed dose and take the next one. Do not double the next dose.

STOPPING THE DRUG
Take this medication as prescribed for the full treatment period, even if you begin to feel better before the scheduled end of therapy.

PROLONGED USE
Prolonged use can make you more susceptible to bacterial or fungal infections (such as yeast infections).

PRECAUTIONS
Over 60: No special problems are expected.

Driving and Hazardous Work: Do not drive or engage in hazardous work until you determine how the medicine affects you.

Alcohol: No special precautions are necessary.

Pregnancy: Limited studies have found no evidence of birth defects. Consult your doctor if you are pregnant or plan to become pregnant.

Breast Feeding: Amoxicillin/clavulanate may pass into breast milk and cause problems in the nursing infant; avoid use while breast feeding.

Infants and Children: No special problems are expected.

Special Concerns: Those who are prone to asthma, hay fever, hives, or allergies may be more likely to have an allergic reaction to a penicillin antibiotic. If severe diarrhea occurs as a side effect of this drug, do not take antidiarrheal medications; call your doctor for advice instead. This drug can cause false results on some urine sugar tests for patients who have diabetes.

OVERDOSE
Symptoms: Severe diarrhea, nausea, unusual excitability, seizures, or vomiting.

What to Do: Call your doctor, emergency medical services (EMS), or the nearest poison control center immediately.

DRUG INTERACTIONS
Consult your doctor for advice if you are taking erythromycins, disulfiram, anticoagulants, tetracyclines, oral contraceptives, or gout drugs.

FOOD INTERACTIONS
None expected.

DISEASE INTERACTIONS
Consult your doctor if you have a history of allergies, asthma, congestive heart failure, gastrointestinal disorders (especially colitis associated with the use of antibiotics), or impaired kidney function.

Amphetamine

▶ Drug Class: Central nervous system stimulant/amphetamine

▶ Available in: Tablets

▶ Available OTC? No

▶ As Generic? Yes

Side Effects

SERIOUS
Irregular heartbeat, chest pain, increased blood pressure, skin rash, uncontrollable movements of arms and legs, mental changes, unusual weakness, very high fever. Call your doctor immediately.

COMMON
Mood changes, insomnia, drowsiness, restlessness.

LESS COMMON
Blurred vision, constipation, diarrhea, loss of appetite, headache, increased sweating, stomach cramps or pain, nausea or vomiting, changes in sexual desire or decreased sexual ability.

PRINCIPAL USES
To treat narcolepsy and attention-deficit hyperactivity disorder (ADHD) in children and adults.

HOW THE DRUG WORKS
Amphetamine activates nerve cells in the brain and spinal cord to increase motor activity and alertness and lessen drowsiness and fatigue.

DOSAGE
For narcolepsy— Adults: 5 to 60 mg a day, 1 to 3 times a day; not to exceed 60 mg a day. Teenagers: 5 mg twice a day. Children ages 6 to 12: 2.5 mg twice a day. For ADHD— Adults and children age 6 and older: 5 to 40 mg a day, 1 to 3 times a day; not to exceed 40 mg a day. Children ages 3 to 6: 2.5 mg once a day.

ONSET OF EFFECT
Variable.

DURATION OF ACTION
Variable.

DIETARY ADVICE
Swallow with liquid. May be taken with or without food. Avoid caffeine-containing beverages like tea, coffee, and some carbonated colas. Avoid acidic foods rich in vitamin C, such as fruit juices and other citrus products. Avoid vitamin C tablets.

STORAGE
Store in a tightly sealed container away from heat, moisture, and direct light.

IF YOU MISS A DOSE
If dosage is once daily, take your missed dose as soon as you remember, unless your bedtime is within the next 6 hours. If so, do not take the missed dose. Take your next dose at the proper time and resume your regular schedule. Do not double the next dose. If dosage is more than once daily, take your missed dose as soon as you remember, unless the time for your next scheduled dose is within the next 2 hours. If so, do not take the missed dose. Take your next dose at the proper time and resume your regular schedule. Do not double the next dose.

STOPPING THE DRUG
Take amphetamine as prescribed for the full treatment period, even if you begin to feel better before the scheduled end of therapy. The decision to stop taking the drug should be made by your doctor. The doctor may decrease your dosage gradually to reduce the possibility of withdrawal symptoms.

PROLONGED USE
Amphetamines may be habit-forming, and prolonged use may increase the risk of dependency.

PRECAUTIONS
Over 60: Adverse reactions may be more likely and more severe in older patients.

Driving and Hazardous Work: Do not drive or engage in hazardous work until you determine how the medicine affects you.

Alcohol: Avoid alcohol.

Pregnancy: Amphetamine taken during pregnancy may cause premature delivery, low birth weight, and birth defects. Discuss with your doctor the relative risks and benefits of using this drug while pregnant.

Breast Feeding: Amphetamine passes into breast milk; avoid or discontinue use while nursing. Consult your doctor for specific advice.

Infants and Children: Long-term amphetamine use by children can affect behavior and growth. Discuss the use of the drug and its relative risks and benefits with your doctor.

OVERDOSE
Symptoms: Extreme degrees of restlessness, agitation, bizarre behavior; panic; rapid breathing; confusion; high fever; hallucinations; seizures; coma.

What to Do: Call your doctor, emergency medical services (EMS), or the nearest poison control center immediately.

DRUG INTERACTIONS
The following drugs may interact with amphetamine. Consult your doctor for specific advice if you are taking tricyclic antidepressants, caffeine, beta-blockers, digitalis drugs, central nervous system stimulants, meperidine, MAO inhibitors, sympathomimetic agents, or thyroid hormones.

FOOD INTERACTIONS
Citrus juices and caffeinated beverages and foods may interact with amphetamine.

DISEASE INTERACTIONS
Caution is advised when taking amphetamine. Consult your doctor if you have any of the following: advanced blood vessel disease, heart disease, hyperthyroidism, high blood pressure, severe anxiety, Tourette's syndrome, glaucoma, or a history of drug abuse.

Amphetamine/Dextroamphetamine

▶ Drug Class: Central nervous system stimulant/ amphetamine

▶ Available in: Tablets

▶ Available OTC? No

▶ As Generic? No

Side Effects

SERIOUS
Irregular heartbeat, chest pain, increased blood pressure, skin rash, uncontrollable movements of arms and legs, mental changes, unusual weakness, very high fever. Call your doctor immediately.

COMMON
Mood changes, insomnia, drowsiness, restlessness.

LESS COMMON
Blurred vision, constipation, diarrhea, loss of appetite, headache, increased sweating, stomach cramps or pain, nausea or vomiting, changes in sexual desire or decreased sexual ability.

PRINCIPAL USES
To treat narcolepsy and attention-deficit hyperactivity disorder (ADHD) in children and adults.

HOW THE DRUG WORKS
Amphetamine and dextroamphetamine activate nerve cells in the brain and spinal cord to increase motor activity and alertness and lessen drowsiness and fatigue. In hyperactivity disorders and narcolepsy, amphetamines improve mental focus and the ability to stay awake or concentrate.

DOSAGE
For narcolepsy— Adults: 5 to 60 mg a day, 1 to 3 times a day; not to exceed 60 mg a day. Teenagers: To start, 10 mg a day. Children ages 6 to 12: To start, 5 mg a day. To treat ADHD— Children age 6 and older: To start, 5 mg, 1 or 2 times a day. Children ages 3 to 6: To start, 2.5 mg a day.

ONSET OF EFFECT
Within 30 to 45 minutes.

DURATION OF ACTION
Adults: 8 to 12 hours. Children: 6 to 10 hours.

DIETARY ADVICE
Take it with liquid 30 to 45 minutes before meals. Avoid caffeine-containing beverages like tea, coffee, and some carbonated colas. Avoid acidic foods rich in vitamin C, such as fruit juices and other citrus products. Avoid vitamin C tablets.

STORAGE
Store in a tightly sealed container away from heat, moisture, and direct light.

IF YOU MISS A DOSE
If dosage is once daily, take your missed dose as soon as you remember, unless your bedtime is within the next 6 hours. If so, do not take the missed dose. Take your next dose at the proper time and resume your regular schedule. Do not double the next dose. If dosage is more than once daily, take your missed dose as soon as you remember, unless the time for your next scheduled dose is within the next 2 hours. If so, do not take the missed dose. Take your next dose at the proper time and resume your regular schedule. Do not double the next dose.

STOPPING THE DRUG
The decision to stop taking the drug should be made in consultation with your doctor. The doctor may decrease your dosage gradually to reduce the possibility of withdrawal symptoms.

PROLONGED USE
Amphetamines may be habit-forming, and prolonged use may increase the risk of dependency.

PRECAUTIONS
Over 60: Adverse reactions may be more likely and more severe.

Driving and Hazardous Work: Do not drive or engage in hazardous work until you determine how the medicine affects you.

Alcohol: Avoid alcohol.

Pregnancy: Amphetamines taken during pregnancy may cause premature delivery, low birth weight, and birth defects. Discuss with your doctor the relative risks and benefits of using this drug while pregnant.

Breast Feeding: Amphetamine passes into breast milk; avoid or discontinue use while nursing.

Infants and Children: Not recommended for use by children under age 3.

Special Concerns: Take only as directed and do not increase the dose on your own. Remember that fatigue, excessive drowsiness, sleepiness, or depression while taking stimulants may mean an emergency situation is developing. Difficulty sleeping may be improved by taking the last scheduled dose several hours before bedtime.

OVERDOSE
Symptoms: Extreme restlessness, agitation, or bizarre behavior; panic; rapid breathing; confusion; high fever; hallucinations; seizures; coma.

What to Do: Call your doctor, emergency medical services (EMS), or the nearest poison control center immediately.

DRUG INTERACTIONS
The following drugs may interact with amphetamines. Consult your doctor for specific advice if you are taking tricyclic antidepressants, caffeine, beta-blockers, digitalis drugs, central nervous system stimulants, meperidine, MAO inhibitors, sympathomimetic agents (such as ephedrine, phenylephrine, and diethylpropion), or thyroid hormones.

FOOD INTERACTIONS
Citrus juices and caffeinated beverages and foods may interact with this drug.

DISEASE INTERACTIONS
Consult your doctor if you have any of the following: advanced blood vessel disease, heart disease, hyperthyroidism, high blood pressure, severe anxiety, Tourette's syndrome, glaucoma, or a history of drug abuse.

Amphotericin B

BRAND NAMES
Abelcet, AmBisome,
Amphocin, Fungizone,
Fungizone Intravenous

▸ Drug Class: Antifungal

▸ Available in: Cream, lotion,
ointment, injection

▸ Available OTC? No

▸ As Generic? Yes

Side Effects

SERIOUS
Topical: Redness, burning, itching, or irritation not present prior to therapy. Injection into a vein: Headache, fever, muscle pain or cramps, fatigue, chills, heartbeat irregularities, seizures, increased or decreased urine output, nausea, vomiting, pain at site of injection, change in or blurred vision, skin rash or itching, breathing difficulties, tightness in chest, unusual bleeding or bruising, sore throat. Injection into the spinal column: Urination difficulties, change in or blurred vision, numbness, tingling, fatigue, or weakness.

COMMON
Topical: None reported. Injection: Mild headache, diarrhea, indigestion, stomach pain, loss of appetite, mild nausea or vomiting.

LESS COMMON
Topical (cream only): Dry skin. Injection into the spinal column: Severe nausea or vomiting, dizziness or lightheadedness, headache, pain in the back, leg, or neck.

PRINCIPAL USES
To treat serious and potentially life-threatening fungal infections.

HOW THE DRUG WORKS
Amphotericin B prevents fungal organisms from producing vital substances required for growth and function. This drug is effective only for infections caused by fungal organisms. It will not work for bacterial or viral infections.

DOSAGE
Topical forms: Apply a liberal amount to the affected area 2 to 4 times a day, according to doctor's instructions. It should be applied externally only. Injection: Dose is determined by your doctor based on many factors.

ONSET OF EFFECT
Topical: Not applicable. Injection: Immediate.

DURATION OF ACTION
Injection and topical: Unknown.

DIETARY ADVICE
Increase fluid intake to 2 to 3 quarts a day.

STORAGE
Can be stored at room temperature for 24 hours or in the refrigerator for 7 days in a tightly sealed container away from heat, moisture, and direct light. Keep it from freezing.

IF YOU MISS A DOSE
Tell your doctor if you miss an injected dose. If you miss a topical dose, apply it as soon as you remember, then resume your regular dosage schedule.

STOPPING THE DRUG
Take it as prescribed for the full treatment period, even if you begin to feel better before the scheduled end of therapy. The decision to stop taking the drug should be made by your doctor.

PROLONGED USE
Topical forms are generally prescribed for short-term therapy (1 to 4 weeks). Consult your doctor if your condition does not improve, or worsens, within 1 to 2 weeks. The injection may be prescribed for up to 12 months. Your doctor will determine the proper length of therapy.

PRECAUTIONS
Over 60: Adverse reactions may be more likely and more severe in older patients.

Driving and Hazardous Work: Avoid such activities until you determine how the medicine affects you.

Alcohol: Avoid alcohol.

Pregnancy: Adequate studies of the use of amphotericin B use during pregnancy have not been done. Consult your doctor for specific advice if you are pregnant or plan to become pregnant.

Breast Feeding: Amphotericin B may pass into breast milk; caution is advised. Consult your doctor for advice.

Infants and Children: No special problems are expected.

Special Concerns: Use gloves when applying the topical form of amphotericin B, as it can stain or discolor skin and clothing. The stain may be removed by hand washing with warm water and soap. Do not use an airtight dressing to cover the topical form, since this may increase the risk of infection.

OVERDOSE
Symptoms: Heartbeat irregularities; breathing difficulty.

What to Do: Treatment should be discontinued. Call your doctor, emergency medical services (EMS), or the nearest poison control center immediately.

DRUG INTERACTIONS
Consult your doctor for specific advice if you are taking corticosteroids, corticotropin, digitalis drugs, potassium-sparing diuretics, bone marrow depressants, nephrotoxic medications, or other topical prescription or over-the-counter medications. Also consult your doctor if you are undergoing radiation therapy.

FOOD INTERACTIONS
No known food interactions.

DISEASE INTERACTIONS
Caution is advised when taking amphotericin B. Consult your doctor if you have any other medical problem, especially kidney disease.

Ampicillin

▶ Drug Class: Penicillin antibiotic

▶ Available in: Capsules, oral suspension, injection (available only in hospitals)

▶ Available OTC? No

▶ As Generic? Yes

Side Effects

SERIOUS
Irregular, rapid, or labored breathing, lightheadedness or sudden fainting, joint pain, fever, severe abdominal pain and cramping with watery or bloody stools, severe allergic reaction (marked by sudden swelling of the lips, tongue, face, or throat; breathing difficulty; skin rash, itching, or hives), unusual bleeding or bruising, yellowish tinge to eyes or skin. Call your doctor immediately.

COMMON
Mild rash, mild diarrhea, nausea, vomiting, headache, vaginal discharge and itching, pain or white patches in the mouth or on the tongue.

LESS COMMON
Diminished urine output, chills, weakness, fatigue, seizures.

PRINCIPAL USES
Oral ampicillin is used to treat infections of the skin, urinary tract, and respiratory tract (sinuses, tonsils, and lung) caused by certain bacteria known to be susceptible to this antibiotic. Injectable ampicillin is used to treat more serious infections in hospitalized patients.

HOW THE DRUG WORKS
Ampicillin blocks the formation of bacterial cell walls, rendering bacteria unable to multiply and spread.

DOSAGE
Adults or children weighing more than 44 lbs (20 kg): 250 to 500 mg, 4 times a day. The dosage for smaller children must be adjusted according to weight.

ONSET OF EFFECT
Within 2 hours of oral dose.

DURATION OF ACTION
6 to 8 hours with oral dose.

DIETARY ADVICE
Should be taken on an empty stomach with plenty of water.

STORAGE
Store in a tightly sealed container away from heat and direct light. Keep the suspension refrigerated, but do not allow it to freeze.

IF YOU MISS A DOSE
Take it as soon as you remember. If it is within 60 to 90 minutes of the next dose, skip the missed dose and resume your regular dosage schedule. Do not double the next dose.

STOPPING THE DRUG
Take it as prescribed for the full treatment period, even if you begin to feel better before the scheduled end of therapy. Stopping the drug prematurely may slow your recovery or lead to a rebound infection, also known as superinfection, in which the heartier strains of bacteria survive and multiply, leading to a more serious and drug-resistant infection.

PROLONGED USE
Therapy with ampicillin is usually completed within 7 to 10 days. Prolonged use may promote infection by bacteria resistant to the medication's effects (superinfection).

PRECAUTIONS
Over 60: No special problems are expected.

Driving and Hazardous Work: No problems are expected.

Alcohol: No interactions are expected, but alcohol may dampen the immune system's response against infection and may increase the risk of stomach upset when taking this drug.

Pregnancy: Ampicillin may be used during pregnancy under certain conditions. Consult your doctor for guidelines.

Breast Feeding: Ampicillin may pass into breast milk and cause problems in the nursing infant; avoid use while nursing.

Infants and Children: No special problems are expected.

Special Concerns: If severe diarrhea occurs as a side effect of this drug, do not take antidiarrheal medications; call your doctor. Oral contraceptives may not be effective while you are taking ampicillin; consider other methods of birth control. Those who are prone to asthma, hay fever, hives, or allergies may be more likely to have an allergic reaction to a penicillin antibiotic.

OVERDOSE
Symptoms: Severe nausea, vomiting, diarrhea, muscle spasticity, seizures.

What to Do: Call your doctor, emergency medical services (EMS), or the nearest poison control center immediately.

DRUG INTERACTIONS
Consult your doctor for specific advice if you are taking aminoglycosides, ACE inhibitors, diuretics, potassium supplements or potassium-containing medications, anticoagulants or other anticlotting drugs, nonsteroidal anti-inflammatory drugs, sulfinpyrazone, cholestyramine, colestipol, oral contraceptives, methotrexate, probenecid, allopurinol, or rifampin.

FOOD INTERACTIONS
Acidic fruits or juices can interfere with this drug's therapeutic effect.

DISEASE INTERACTIONS
Consult your doctor if you have a history of allergies, asthma, congestive heart failure, gastrointestinal disorders (especially colitis associated with the use of antibiotics), infectious mononucleosis, or impaired kidney function.

Ampicillin Sodium/Sulbactam Sodium

Unasyn

▶ Drug Class: Penicillin antibiotic

▶ Available in: Injection (available primarily in hospitals and nursing facilities)

▶ Available OTC? No

▶ As Generic? No

Side Effects

SERIOUS
Irregular, rapid, or labored breathing, lightheadedness or sudden fainting, joint pain, fever, severe abdominal pain and cramping with watery or bloody stools, severe allergic reaction (marked by sudden swelling of the lips, tongue, face, or throat; breathing difficulty; skin rash, itching, or hives), unusual bleeding or bruising, yellowish tinge to eyes or skin. Call your doctor immediately.

COMMON
Mild rash, mild diarrhea, nausea, vomiting, headache, vaginal discharge and itching, pain or white patches in the mouth or on the tongue, pain at the site of injection.

LESS COMMON
Diminished urine output, chills, weakness, fatigue.

PRINCIPAL USES
Ampicillin sodium/sulbactam sodium is used to treat moderately severe bacterial infections requiring hospitalization. These infections are frequently caused by bacteria that are likely to be resistant to penicillin and not treatable with oral antibiotics alone.

HOW THE DRUG WORKS
Ampicillin blocks the formation of bacterial cell walls, rendering bacteria unable to multiply and spread; sulbactam is added to protect ampicillin from the effects of a destructive enzyme (betalactamase) produced by certain drug-resistant strains of bacteria.

DOSAGE
Adults: 1.5 to 3 g injected into a muscle or vein every 6 hours. Children age 1 and older: 300 mg per 2.2 lbs (1 kg) of body weight per day into a vein in divided doses every 6 hours.

ONSET OF EFFECT
Immediate with intravenous injection; unknown for intramuscular injection.

DURATION OF ACTION
Unknown.

DIETARY ADVICE
No special restrictions.

STORAGE
Not applicable.

IF YOU MISS A DOSE
Not applicable; the dosage schedule is determined by a doctor or other health care professional.

STOPPING THE DRUG
The decision to stop treatment with this drug will be made by your doctor.

PROLONGED USE
Therapy with ampicillin sodium/sulbactam sodium is usually completed within 7 to 14 days. Infections in hospitalized patients may be more serious and can respond unpredictably to treatment. But treatment may also result in rapid improvement, and your doctor may stop intravenous or intramuscular ampicillin sodium/sulbactam sodium earlier than 7 to 14 days and begin oral therapy with another appropriate antibiotic in preparation for your discharge.

PRECAUTIONS
Over 60: Adverse reactions may be more likely and more severe in older patients.

Driving and Hazardous Work: Not applicable; therapy with this drug generally requires hospitalization.

Alcohol: Avoid alcohol.

Pregnancy: Adequate studies of the use of penicillin antibiotics during pregnancy have not been done. Consult your doctor concerning the use of ampicillin sodium/sulbactam sodium if you are pregnant.

Breast Feeding: Avoid or discontinue the use of ampicillin sodium/sulbactam sodium while nursing.

Infants and Children: This drug is not recommended for infants and children under age 1.

Special Concerns: Anyone who has had a prior allergic reaction to penicillin or any penicillin antibiotic should not take this drug. Those who are prone to asthma, hay fever, hives, or allergies are at increased risk of having an allergic reaction to it.

OVERDOSE
Symptoms: Seizures may occur with very high doses; overdose is nonetheless unlikely.

What to Do: Call your doctor or emergency medical services (EMS) immediately if you suspect an overdose.

DRUG INTERACTIONS
Consult your doctor for specific advice if you are taking aminoglycosides, ACE inhibitors, diuretics, potassium supplements or potassium-containing medications, anticoagulants or other anticlotting drugs, nonsteroidal anti-inflammatory drugs, sulfinpyrazone, cholestyramine, colestipol, oral contraceptives, methotrexate, probenecid, allopurinol, or rifampin.

FOOD INTERACTIONS
No known food interactions.

DISEASE INTERACTIONS
Consult your doctor if you have a history of allergies, asthma, bleeding disorders (such as hemophilia), congestive heart failure, gastrointestinal disorders (especially colitis associated with the use of antibiotics), infectious mononucleosis, or impaired kidney function.

Amprenavir

- ▶ Drug Class: Antiviral/protease inhibitor
- ▶ Available in: Capsules, oral solution
- ▶ Available OTC? No
- ▶ As Generic? No

Side Effects

SERIOUS
Severe rash or moderate rash with other symptoms. Call your doctor immediately. High blood sugar (diabetes) has occurred in patients taking drugs of this class, although a cause-and-effect relationship has not been established. Call your doctor if you develop increased thirst or excessive urination.

COMMON
Nausea, vomiting, abdominal pain, rash, diarrhea.

LESS COMMON
Taste disorders, numbness, tingling, prickling sensation, depression.

PRINCIPAL USES
To treat advanced HIV (human immunodeficiency virus) infection and AIDS (acquired immunodeficiency syndrome), usually in combination with other drugs. While not a cure for HIV infection, this drug may suppress the replication of the virus and delay the progression of the disease.

HOW THE DRUG WORKS
Amprenavir blocks the activity of a viral protease, an enzyme that is needed by HIV to reproduce. Blocking the protease causes HIV to make copies that cannot infect new cells.

DOSAGE
Capsules— Adults and children age 13 to 16: 1200 mg (8 capsules) 2 times a day, in combination with other antiretroviral drugs. Oral solution— Recommended for children age 4 and older: Consult pediatrician for appropriate dosage. The capsules and the oral solution are not interchangeable. Do not change forms without consulting your doctor.

ONSET OF EFFECT
Unknown. With most antiretroviral drugs, an early response can be seen within the first few days of therapy, but the maximum effect may take 12 to 16 weeks.

DURATION OF ACTION
Unknown.

DIETARY ADVICE
Amprenavir can be taken with or without food. However, taking it with a meal high in fat could reduce the absorption of the drug from the intestine.

STORAGE
Store in a tightly sealed container away from heat, moisture, and direct light. Do not refrigerate.

IF YOU MISS A DOSE
If you miss a dose, take it as soon as you remember up to 4 hours late. If more than 4 hours, wait for the next scheduled dose. Do not double the next dose.

STOPPING THE DRUG
The decision to stop taking the drug should be made in consultation with your physician.

PROLONGED USE
See your doctor regularly for tests and examinations.

PRECAUTIONS
Over 60: It is not known whether amprenavir causes different or more severe side effects in older patients.

Driving and Hazardous Work: Do not drive or engage in hazardous work until you determine how the medicine affects you.

Alcohol: Avoid alcohol if liver function is impaired.

Pregnancy: Adequate studies of amprenavir use during pregnancy have not been done. There is no evidence that the drug will reduce the risk of transmitting the virus from the mother to the fetus.

Breast Feeding: It is unknown whether amprenavir passes into breast milk; however, to avoid transmitting the virus to an uninfected child, women infected with HIV should not breast feed.

Infants and Children: The safety and effectiveness of amprenavir have not been established for children under 4 years of age.

Special Concerns: Do not switch between the capsules and solution without consulting your doctor; the body absorbs them at different rates. Taking amprenavir does not eliminate the risk of passing the AIDS virus to other persons. Take appropriate preventive measures.

OVERDOSE
Symptoms: No overdoses have been reported.

What to Do: If you suspect an overdose or if someone takes a much larger dose than prescribed, seek medical attention immediately.

DRUG INTERACTIONS
Amprenavir should not be used at the same time as astemizole, bepridil, dihydroergotamine, ergotamine, midazolam, triazolam, rifampin, oral contraceptives, and vitamin E supplements. Use extreme caution if you are taking amiodarone, systemic lidocaine, tricyclic antidepressants, quinidine, warfarin, sildenafil, tadalafil, vardenafil, phenobarbital, phenytoin, carbamazepine, statin (cholesterol-lowering) drugs, and the herb St. John's wort. Patients taking antacids or didanosine should take them at least one hour before or after amprenavir. Rifabutin dosage may have to be adjusted by your doctor. Consult your doctor if you are taking any other medications.

FOOD INTERACTIONS
Meals high in fat could reduce the absorption of amprenavir.

DISEASE INTERACTIONS
Consult your doctor for advice if you have any other medical condition, especially hemophilia. Use of amprenavir can cause complications in patients with diseases of the liver, which works to remove the drug from the body.

Amyl Nitrite

Side Effects

SERIOUS
Shortness of breath, extreme dizziness or fainting, bluish appearance of lips, fingernails, and palms of hands, irregular heartbeat.

COMMON
Dizziness or lightheadedness, especially upon arising from a seated or lying position, rapid heartbeat and pulse, headache, restlessness, flushing in the face and neck. Such side effects tend to occur less frequently as your body adjusts to the medication. Contact your doctor if such symptoms do not subside quickly or if they interfere with your daily activities.

LESS COMMON
Unusual tiredness or weakness, skin rash.

PRINCIPAL USES
To prevent or relieve attacks of angina (chest pain associated with heart disease).

HOW THE DRUG WORKS
Amyl nitrite relaxes the smooth muscle of the blood vessels and increases the supply of blood and oxygen to the heart. It also reduces the heart's workload and demand for oxygen.

DOSAGE
No fixed schedule; take as needed. When angina attack occurs, break the protective cloth-covered glass capsule between your fingers and inhale 1 to 6 times while seated. If inhaling 2 capsules in 10 minutes does not bring relief, seek medical assistance immediately. When inhaling 2 capsules, wait 3 to 5 minutes between capsules.

ONSET OF EFFECT
30 seconds to 5 minutes.

DURATION OF ACTION
3 to 5 minutes.

DIETARY ADVICE
Amyl nitrite can be taken without regard to diet.

STORAGE
Store away from direct light and heat. Heat may cause the medicine to break down. Do not store it in the kitchen, because amyl nitrite is flammable. Keep refrigerated, but do not allow it to freeze.

IF YOU MISS A DOSE
Not applicable.

STOPPING THE DRUG
Consult your doctor before stopping use.

PROLONGED USE
Prolonged, too-frequent use can lead to tolerance of the drug, reducing its effectiveness. Notify your doctor if you experience an increase in angina attacks.

PRECAUTIONS
Over 60: Adverse reactions and side effects may be more common and severe in older persons.

Driving and Hazardous Work: The use of amyl nitrite may impair your ability to perform such tasks safely.

Alcohol: Alcohol can increase the lightheadedness caused by amyl nitrite and may cause a serious drop in blood pressure. Consult your doctor for specific advice.

Pregnancy: Use is not recommended during pregnancy because of the danger to the unborn baby.

Breast Feeding: Amyl nitrite may pass into breast milk; caution is advised. Consult your doctor for advice.

Infants and Children: Safety and effectiveness have not been determined. Consult your pediatrician.

Special Concerns: Before use, extinguish all tobacco products and stay away from open flames, since amyl nitrite is highly flammable. Since dizziness is common after taking amyl nitrite, it is advisable to sit or lie down rather than remain standing while taking the medication. For relief of headache (very common following use of amyl nitrate), take acetaminophen.

OVERDOSE
Symptoms: Blue lips, palms of hands, or fingernails; extreme dizziness, extreme headache or feeling of intense pressure in the head; fainting; shortness of breath; unusual weakness; weak and rapid heartbeat.

What to Do: Call your doctor, emergency medical services (EMS), or the nearest poison control center immediately.

DRUG INTERACTIONS
Consult your doctor for specific advice if you are taking drugs for high blood pressure, norepinephrine, or sympathomimetic drugs (such as ephedrine, phenylephrine, or epinephrine).

FOOD INTERACTIONS
No known food interactions.

DISEASE INTERACTIONS
Caution is advised when taking amyl nitrite. Consult your doctor if you have any of the following: severe anemia, recent head trauma, recent heart attack or brain hemorrhage, glaucoma, hyperthyroidism, or prior allergic reaction to nitrates.

Anastrozole

BRAND NAME
Arimidex

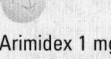

Arimidex 1 mg
(**AstraZeneca**)

▶ Drug Class: Antiestrogen; antineoplastic (anticancer) agent

▶ Available in: Tablets

▶ Available OTC? No

▶ As Generic? No

Side Effects

SERIOUS
No serious side effects from therapy with anastrozole have been reported.

COMMON
Headache, diarrhea, nausea, hot flashes, back pain, weakness, and a feeling of reduced energy (asthenia).

LESS COMMON
Dizziness; chest pain; tingling or numbness in the extremities (paresthesia); weight gain; abdominal pain; vaginal itching, dryness, and occasionally bleeding; swelling of fingers and skin around the eyes; rash; formation of blood clots.

PRINCIPAL USES
Anastrozole is given for breast cancer chemotherapy.

HOW THE DRUG WORKS
The growth of some breast tumors is stimulated by estradiol, a hormone that is produced by adult females. Anastrozole is not directly toxic to cancer cells but rather reduces blood levels of estradiol in the body and thus inhibits the growth of such tumors.

DOSAGE
1 mg once a day.

ONSET OF EFFECT
Unknown.

DURATION OF ACTION
Unknown.

DIETARY ADVICE
Maintain adequate food and fluid intake. Calorie, protein, and vitamin needs increase in patients with cancer. Good nutrition is essential to cope with the demands of chemotherapy.

STORAGE
Store safely and securely away from heat and light.

IF YOU MISS A DOSE
Anastrozole is prescribed for once-daily use only. If you are unable to take this medication on a particular day, skip the missed dose and resume your regularly scheduled dose the following day. Do not double the next dose.

STOPPING THE DRUG
This medication is used to treat a chronic condition. You may need to remain on this medication for an extended period, and you should take the drug exactly as prescribed throughout the course of treatment. The decision to stop the drug must be made in consultation with your doctor. Do not stop taking anastrozole on your own, even if you are feeling better. Contact your doctor if you have any questions about the way you feel while taking anastrozole, or if you think that you are experiencing a side effect that would require discontinuation of the drug.

PROLONGED USE
There is no standard duration of therapy with anastrozole, although you can expect to remain on it for several weeks in order to determine if it is effective. Your doctor will determine whether your response to the drug is satisfactory or not, and will recommend the continuation or discontinuation of therapy.

PRECAUTIONS
Over 60: Adverse reactions may be more likely and more severe in older patients.

Driving and Hazardous Work: The use of anastrozole may impair your ability to drive or operate machinery safely or perform hazardous work.

Alcohol: Avoid alcohol while taking this drug.

Pregnancy: Anastrozole must not be used in pregnant women. Although anastrozole is not generally prescribed for premenopausal women, it is important that patients be sure they are not pregnant before starting treatment with this drug.

Breast Feeding: Use of this drug is not recommended while breast feeding; the benefits must clearly outweigh potential risks. Consult your doctor for advice.

Infants and Children: Use of anastrozole is not approved for infants and children.

Special Concerns: Patients with cancer are very often weakened by their illness, by poor nutrition, and by the effects of chemotherapy, radiation, and surgery. Such patients are more likely to experience undesirable side effects of a medication. In addition, these side effects may be more pronounced. Follow all medication directions carefully.

OVERDOSE
Symptoms: No cases of overdose with anastrozole have been reported.

What to Do: An overdose is unlikely; however, if you have any reason to suspect that one has occurred, call emergency medical services (EMS) to receive evaluation and treatment in the closest emergency facility.

DRUG INTERACTIONS
No significant interactions.

FOOD INTERACTIONS
No significant interactions.

DISEASE INTERACTIONS
No significant interactions.

Aripiprazole

BRAND NAME
Abilify

▶ Drug Class: Antipsychotic

▶ Available in: Tablets

▶ Available OTC? No

▶ As Generic? No

Side Effects

SERIOUS
Tardive dyskinesia (involuntary movements of the jaw, lips, and tongue), amnesia, psychosis, hallucinations, paranoia, delusions, manic episodes, suicidal impulses, catatonic reaction, stroke, shortness of breath, asthma, paralysis of one side of the body. Call your doctor immediately. Neuroleptic malignant syndrome, characterized by high fever, muscle rigidity, altered mental status, and heart rhythm abnormalities, is a potentially fatal condition.

COMMON
Headache, nausea, vomiting, constipation, anxiety, insomnia, lightheadedness, drowsiness.

LESS COMMON
Fatigue, fever, tremor, runny nose, cough, rash, blurred vision.

PRINCIPAL USES
To treat psychotic conditions such as schizophrenia.

HOW THE DRUG WORKS
While the exact mechanism of action of aripiprazole is unknown, it appears to interfere with receptors for certain critical natural substances (neurotransmitters) in the brain to produce a tranquilizing and antipsychotic effect.

DOSAGE
Usual adult dose: Initially, 10 to 15 mg once a day. Your doctor may increase the dose if necessary (and if side effects are tolerated) up to a maximum of 30 mg a day.

ONSET OF EFFECT
Unknown.

DURATION OF ACTION
Unknown.

DIETARY ADVICE
Aripiprazole can be taken without regard to food intake.

STORAGE
Store in a tightly sealed container away from heat, moisture, and direct light.

IF YOU MISS A DOSE
Take it as soon as you remember. If it is near the time for the next dose, skip the missed dose and resume your regular dosage schedule. Do not double the next dose.

STOPPING THE DRUG
Take it as prescribed for the full treatment period. The decision to stop taking the drug should be made in consultation with your physician.

PROLONGED USE
Consult your doctor about the need for follow-up evaluations and tests if you must take this drug for an extended period. Because aripiprazole is a recently released drug, its risk of inducing potentially irreversible tardive dyskinesia (involuntary movements of the jaw, lips, tongue, and body) is unknown.

PRECAUTIONS
Over 60: Adverse reactions are more likely and more severe in older patients.

Driving and Hazardous Work: The use of aripiprazole may impair your ability to perform such tasks safely. Do not drive or engage in hazardous work until you determine how the medicine affects you.

Alcohol: Avoid alcohol.

Pregnancy: Discuss with your doctor the relative risks and benefits of taking this drug if you are, or plan to become, pregnant.

Breast Feeding: Aripiprazole may pass into breast milk; avoid use while breast feeding.

Infants and Children: Not recommended for use by children under age 18.

Special Concerns: Avoid prolonged exposure to high temperatures or hot climates. Drink plenty of fluids and stay cool in the summertime.

OVERDOSE
Symptoms: Few cases of overdose have been reported. In clinical studies, excessive doses appear to result in extreme drowsiness and vomiting.

What to Do: Call your doctor, emergency medical services (EMS), or the nearest poison control center immediately.

DRUG INTERACTIONS
Consult your doctor for specific advice if you are taking fluoxetine, paroxetine, quinidine, ketoconazole, itraconazole, fluconazole, antihypertensives, carbamazepine, central nervous system depressants, or any other prescription or over-the-counter drug.

FOOD INTERACTIONS
No known food interactions.

DISEASE INTERACTIONS
Caution is advised when taking aripiprazole if you have a history of symptomatic reactions to low blood pressure (dizziness, lightheadedness, or fainting, especially when rising from a sitting or lying position), heart disease, stroke, seizures, or diabetes.

Aspirin

Generic 325 mg
(LNK)

829

Additional photographs

▶ Drug Class: Nonsteroidal anti-inflammatory drug (NSAID); analgesic; anticoagulant

▶ Available in: Tablets, capsules

▶ Available OTC? Yes

▶ As Generic? Yes

Side Effects

SERIOUS
Vomiting, agitation, extreme fatigue, confusion; allergic reaction causing troubled breathing, redness of face, itching, swelling of face, lips, or eyelids. These are symptoms of Reye's syndrome, a rare but serious disorder that is most likely to affect patients under the age of 16. Seek emergency medical attention immediately.

COMMON
Stomach upset, rash, nausea, ringing in the ears.

LESS COMMON
Insomnia.

PRINCIPAL USES
For mild to moderate everyday pain and inflammation; to reduce fever; to prevent the formation of blood clots, a primary cause of heart attack, stroke, and other circulatory problems; to ease the inflammation, joint pain, and stiffness associated with arthritis.

HOW THE DRUG WORKS
Nonsteroidal anti-inflammatory drugs (NSAIDs) such as aspirin inhibit the release of chemicals in the body called prostaglandins, which play a role in inflammation, though it is unknown exactly how they exert their pain-relieving, fever-reducing, and anti-inflammatory effects.

DOSAGE
For pain or fever: 325 to 650 mg every 4 hours as needed. For prevention of blood clots: 80 to 100 mg daily or every other day. For arthritis: 3,600 to 5,400 mg daily in divided doses.

ONSET OF EFFECT
30 minutes.

DURATION OF ACTION
For pain relief, up to 4 hours.

DIETARY ADVICE
Swallow aspirin with food or a full glass of water to lessen stomach irritation.

STORAGE
Store in a tightly sealed container away from heat and direct light.

IF YOU MISS A DOSE
For pain and fever, take a missed dose as soon as you remember, then wait 4 hours for your next dose. For arthritis, take the aspirin as soon as you remember up to 2 hours late, then return to your regular schedule.

STOPPING THE DRUG
For pain and fever, stop when relief is achieved. For arthritis and blood clotting, consult your doctor about stopping.

PROLONGED USE
Talk to your doctor about the need for medical examinations or laboratory tests if you must take aspirin regularly for a prolonged period.

PRECAUTIONS
Over 60: Gastrointestinal bleeding and irritation are more likely to occur in older persons.

Driving and Hazardous Work: The use of aspirin should not impair your ability to perform such tasks safely.

Alcohol: Alcohol intake should be limited because it increases the risk of stomach irritation and bleeding.

Pregnancy: Do not use aspirin during the last 3 months of pregnancy unless prescribed by your doctor.

Breast Feeding: Aspirin passes into breast milk. Avoid it or do not nurse.

Infants and Children: Do not give aspirin to children under age 16 unless your doctor instructs otherwise, since it may cause a very rare but life-threatening condition known as Reye's syndrome.

OVERDOSE
Symptoms: Nausea, disorientation, seizures, vomiting, rapid breathing, fever.

What to Do: Call your doctor, emergency medical services (EMS), or the nearest poison control center immediately.

DRUG INTERACTIONS
Consult your doctor before taking aspirin if you currently take a blood pressure medication, a medication for gout, an arthritis drug, an anticoagulant such as warfarin, a diabetes medication, a steroid, or an antiseizure medication.

FOOD INTERACTIONS
No known adverse food interactions. Taking aspirin with caffeine-containing foods or beverages may actually enhance the medicine's pain-relieving effects.

DISEASE INTERACTIONS
Consult your doctor about taking aspirin if you have asthma, a bleeding disorder, congestive heart failure, diabetes mellitus, gout, hemophilia, high blood pressure, kidney disease, liver disease, thyroid disease, or a peptic ulcer.

Aspirin/Caffeine

Side Effects

SERIOUS
Vomiting, agitation,
extreme fatigue, confu-
sion; allergic reaction
causing troubled breath-
ing, redness of face, itching, swelling of face, lips,
or eyelids. These are
symptoms of Reye's syn-
drome, a rare but serious
disorder that is most
likely to affect patients
under the age of 16. Seek
emergency medical atten-
tion immediately.

COMMON
Stomach upset, rash,
nausea, ringing in the
ears.

LESS COMMON
Insomnia.

PRINCIPAL USES
For mild to moderate everyday pain and inflammation;
to reduce fever; to ease the
inflammation, joint pain, and
stiffness associated with
arthritis.

HOW THE DRUG WORKS
Aspirin appears to interfere
with the production of
prostaglandins, naturally
occurring substances in
the body that cause inflammation and make nerves
more sensitive to pain
impulses. Caffeine may
enhance the effectiveness
of pain relievers.

DOSAGE
Adults— For pain or fever:
325 to 650 mg every 4
hours as needed. For arthritis: 3,600 to 5,400 mg daily
in divided doses. Children
9 years of age and older—
For pain or fever: 325 to
400 mg every 4 hours as
needed. For arthritis: 80 to
100 mg per 2.2 lbs (1 kg)
of body weight a day in
divided doses.

ONSET OF EFFECT
For pain, inflammation, or
fever: within 30 minutes.
For arthritis: May take 2 to
3 weeks to achieve maxi-
mum effect.

DURATION OF ACTION
For pain relief, up to 4
hours.

DIETARY ADVICE
Take with food or a full
glass of water to lessen
stomach irritation.

STORAGE
Store in a tightly sealed container away from heat, moisture, and direct light.

IF YOU MISS A DOSE
For pain and fever, take a
missed dose as soon as you
remember, then wait 4
hours for your next dose.
For arthritis, take as soon

as you remember up to 2
hours late, then return to
your regular schedule.

STOPPING THE DRUG
For pain and fever, stop
when relief is achieved. For
arthritis, consult your doctor about stopping.

PROLONGED USE
Talk to your doctor about
the need for medical examinations or laboratory tests if
you must take this medication regularly for a pro-
longed period.

PRECAUTIONS
Over 60: Gastrointestinal
bleeding and irritation are
more likely to occur in
older persons.

**Driving and Hazardous
Work:** No special precautions are necessary.

Alcohol: Alcohol intake
should be limited because it
increases the risk of stomach irritation and bleeding.

Pregnancy: Do not use
this drug during the last 3
months of pregnancy unless
prescribed by your doctor.

Breast Feeding: Aspirin
passes into breast milk.
Avoid it or do not nurse.

Infants and Children:
Do not give products that
contain aspirin to children
under age 16 unless your
doctor instructs otherwise,
since it may cause a very
rare but life-threatening
condition known as Reye's
syndrome.

OVERDOSE
Symptoms: Nausea, disorientation, seizures, vomiting,
rapid breathing, fever.

What to Do: Call your
doctor, emergency medical
services (EMS), or the

nearest poison control center immediately.

DRUG INTERACTIONS
Consult your doctor before
taking this drug if you currently take a blood pressure
medication, a medication for
gout, an arthritis drug, an
anticoagulant such as warfarin, a diabetes medication,
a steroid, or an antiseizure
medication.

FOOD INTERACTIONS
No known interactions.

DISEASE INTERACTIONS
Consult your doctor about
taking this drug if you have
asthma, a bleeding disorder,
congestive heart failure, diabetes mellitus, gout, hemophilia, high blood pressure,
kidney disease, liver disease, thyroid disease, or a
peptic ulcer.

Atazanavir

Side Effects

SERIOUS
Yellow-tinged eyes or skin (jaundice), heart rhythm abnormalities; call your doctor immediately. High levels of blood sugar (diabetes) have occurred in patients taking drugs of this class, although a cause-and-effect relationship has not been established. Call your doctor if you develop increased thirst or excessive urination.

COMMON
Nausea, headache, rash, stomach pain, vomiting, diarrhea, fever, increased cough, dizziness, depression, insomnia, drowsiness, pain, back pain, numbness, tingling, or burning of hands or feet, joint pain.

LESS COMMON
Fatigue, unusual distribution of fat.

PRINCIPAL USES
To treat HIV (human immunodeficiency virus) infection in combination with other drugs. While not a cure for HIV infection, atazanavir may suppress the replication of the virus and delay progression of the disease. Unlike other protease inhibitors, atazanavir appears to have minimal effect on cholesterol and triglyceride levels.

HOW THE DRUG WORKS
Atazanavir blocks the activity of a viral protease, an enzyme that is needed by HIV to replicate. Blocking the protease causes HIV to make copies that cannot infect new cells.

DOSAGE
Adults: 400 mg once a day. When taken with efavirenz, it is recommended that 300 mg atazanavir and 100 mg ritonavir be given with 600 mg efavirenz (all as a single daily dose with food). Atazanavir without ritonavir should not be taken with efavirenz. When taken with didanosine buffered formulations, atazanavir should be given (with food) 2 hours before or 1 hour after didanosine.

ONSET OF EFFECT
Unknown. With most antiretroviral drugs, an early response can be seen within the first few days of therapy, but the maximum effect may take at least 16 weeks.

DURATION OF ACTION
Unknown. Effects of the drug may be prolonged if atazanavir is used in combination with other effective drugs and the virus is maximally suppressed.

DIETARY ADVICE
Atazanavir should be taken with a light meal or snack.

STORAGE
Store in a tightly sealed container away from heat, moisture, and direct light.

IF YOU MISS A DOSE
Take it as soon as you remember. If it is within 6 hours of the next dose, skip the missed dose and resume your regular dosage schedule. Do not double the next dose.

STOPPING THE DRUG
The decision to stop taking the drug should be made in consultation with your physician.

PROLONGED USE
See your doctor regularly for tests and examinations.

PRECAUTIONS
Over 60: No special studies have been done on older patients.

Driving and Hazardous Work: Do not drive or engage in hazardous work until you determine how the medicine affects you.

Alcohol: Avoid alcohol if liver function is impaired.

Pregnancy: Adequate studies of use during pregnancy have not been done; consult your doctor about whether the benefits outweigh potential risks to the unborn child. There is no evidence that the drug will reduce the risk of transmitting the virus from the mother to the fetus.

Breast Feeding: It is unknown whether atazanavir passes into breast milk; however, to avoid transmitting the virus to an uninfected child, women infected with HIV should not breast feed.

Infants and Children: The safety and effectiveness of atazanavir in children under the age of 16 have not been established.

Special Concerns: Taking this drug does not eliminate the risk of passing the AIDS virus to other persons. Take preventive measures.

OVERDOSE
Symptoms: Few cases of overdose have been reported.

What to Do: If you suspect an overdose or if someone has taken a much larger dose than prescribed, seek medical help right away.

DRUG INTERACTIONS
Atazanavir should not be used at the same time as rifampin, triazolam, midazolam, calcium channel blockers, cholesterol-lowering statins, ergot drugs, pimozide, indinavir, proton-pump inhibitors, or the herb St. John's wort. Consult your doctor for specific advice if you are taking any other prescription or over-the-counter medication, especially sildenafil, tadalafil, or vardenafil. Some drugs, such as efavirenz and ritonavir, are used in combination with atazanavir because they increase its blood levels and, possibly, its effectiveness.

FOOD INTERACTIONS
Food improves the absorption of atazanavir.

DISEASE INTERACTIONS
Consult your doctor if you have any other medical condition, especially hemophilia, infection with hepatitis B or C virus, diabetes, or heart problems. Use of atazanavir can cause complications in patients with diseases of the liver, which works to remove the drug from the body.

Atenolol

Side Effects

SERIOUS
Depression, shortness of breath, wheezing, slow heartbeat (especially less than 50 beats per minute), chest pain or tightness, swelling of the ankles, feet, and lower legs. If you experience such symptoms, stop taking atenolol and call your doctor immediately.

COMMON
Decreased sexual ability; decreased ability to engage in usual physical activities or exercise; dizziness or lightheadedness, especially when rising suddenly from a sitting or lying position; drowsiness, fatigue, or weakness; insomnia.

LESS COMMON
Anxiety, irritability; constipation; diarrhea; dry eyes; itching; nausea or vomiting; nightmares or intensely vivid dreams; numbness, tingling, or other unusual sensations in the fingers and toes; abdominal pain; nasal congestion.

PRINCIPAL USES
To treat mild to moderate high blood pressure and to treat angina; also used to prevent or control heartbeat irregularities (cardiac arrhythmias). The injectable form is used in hospitals to treat heart attack.

HOW THE DRUG WORKS
Atenolol slows the rate and force of contraction of the heart by blocking certain nerve impulses, thus reducing blood pressure. By modifying nerve impulses to the heart, the drug also helps to stabilize heart rhythm.

DOSAGE
50 to 100 mg, once a day. Smaller doses may be recommended for elderly patients or for those with impaired kidney function.

ONSET OF EFFECT
Oral: 1 to 2 hours; the full therapeutic effect may take 1 to 2 weeks. Injectable: Within 10 minutes.

DURATION OF ACTION
Up to 24 hours.

DIETARY ADVICE
Take atenolol on an empty stomach. Avoid alcohol and caffeine.

STORAGE
Store in a tightly sealed container away from heat and direct light.

IF YOU MISS A DOSE
Take it as soon as you remember. If it is within 4 hours of the next scheduled dose, skip the missed dose and resume your regular schedule. Do not double the next dose.

STOPPING THE DRUG
Suddenly stopping atenolol may cause serious health problems. Slow reduction of the dose over a period of 2 to 3 weeks is advised, under doctor's careful supervision.

PROLONGED USE
Therapy with atenolol may be lifelong; prolonged use may be associated with an increased risk of side effects.

PRECAUTIONS
Over 60: Adverse reactions may be more likely and more severe in older patients; a reduction in dosage may be warranted.

Driving and Hazardous Work: In rare cases atenolol may impair your ability to drive or operate machinery safely or perform hazardous work. Use caution, especially soon after beginning therapy.

Alcohol: Drink in careful moderation if at all. Alcohol may interact with the drug and cause a dangerous drop in blood pressure.

Pregnancy: Discuss with your doctor the relative risks and benefits of using this drug while pregnant.

Breast Feeding: Avoid or discontinue the use of atenolol while nursing.

Infants and Children: Proper dose will be determined by pediatrician.

Special Concerns: Use of the drug should be considered but one element of a comprehensive therapeutic program that includes weight control, smoking cessation, regular exercise, and a healthy low-salt, low-fat diet.

OVERDOSE
Symptoms: Slow heartbeat; severe dizziness, lightheadedness or fainting; rapid or irregular heartbeat; difficulty breathing; extreme weakness; seizures; confusion; coma.

What to Do: Call your doctor, emergency medical services (EMS), or the nearest poison control center immediately.

DRUG INTERACTIONS
Consult your doctor if you are taking amphetamines, oral antidiabetic agents, asthma medication (such as aminophylline or theophylline), calcium channel blockers, clonidine, guanabenz, halothane, allergy shots, insulin, MAO inhibitors, reserpine, or other beta-blockers.

FOOD INTERACTIONS
None known.

DISEASE INTERACTIONS
Atenolol should be used with caution in people with diabetes, especially insulin-dependent diabetes, since the drug may mask symptoms of hypoglycemia. Consult your doctor for specific advice if you have allergies or asthma, heart or blood vessel disease (including congestive heart failure and peripheral vascular disease), irregular (slow) heartbeat, hyperthyroidism, myasthenia gravis, psoriasis, respiratory problems such as bronchitis or emphysema, kidney or liver disease, or a history of mental depression.

Atenolol/Chlorthalidone

▶ Drug Class: Beta-blocker/diuretic

▶ Available in: Tablets

▶ Available OTC? No

▶ As Generic? Yes

Side Effects

SERIOUS
Mental depression; shortness of breath, wheezing; slow heartbeat (especially less than 50 beats per minute); chest pain or tightness; swelling of the ankles, feet, and lower legs. If you experience such symptoms, stop taking this drug and call your doctor immediately.

COMMON
Decreased sexual ability; decreased ability to engage in usual physical activities or exercise; dizziness or lightheadedness, especially when rising suddenly from a sitting or lying position; drowsiness, fatigue, or weakness; insomnia.

LESS COMMON
Anxiety, irritability; constipation; diarrhea; dry eyes; itching; nausea or vomiting; nightmares or intensely vivid dreams; numbness, tingling, or other unusual sensations in the fingers and toes; abdominal pain; visual disturbances.

PRINCIPAL USES
To treat high blood pressure with or without concurrent angina.

HOW THE DRUG WORKS
Atenolol slows the rate and force of contraction of the heart by blocking certain nerve impulses, thus reducing blood pressure. Chlorthalidone (a diuretic) increases the elimination of urine from the body. By reducing the overall fluid volume and excess sodium in the body, diuretics reduce blood volume and so reduce pressure within the blood vessels.

DOSAGE
Initial dose is 1 tablet a day (each tablet contains 50 mg atenolol and 25 mg chlorthalidone). The dose can be increased to 2 tablets a day.

ONSET OF EFFECT
Within 1 hour.

DURATION OF ACTION
24 hours.

DIETARY ADVICE
This drug can be taken with or without food, as instructed by your doctor.

STORAGE
Store in a tightly sealed container away from heat and direct light.

IF YOU MISS A DOSE
If you miss a dose, take it as soon as you remember unless the next dose is less than 8 hours away. In that case, skip the missed dose and go back to your regular schedule. Do not double the next dose.

STOPPING THE DRUG
Suddenly stopping this drug may cause blood pressure to rise dangerously high, possibly triggering angina or heart attack in patients with advanced heart disease. Slow reduction of the dose over a period of 2 to 3 weeks is advised, under careful supervision by your doctor.

PROLONGED USE
No special problems are expected, although prolonged use may increase the chance of side effects. Regular visits to your doctor are needed to evaluate the drug's ongoing, long-term effectiveness.

PRECAUTIONS
Over 60: Older persons with reduced kidney function may require a lower dosage.

Driving and Hazardous Work: Be cautious about any activity that requires acuity since this medication may cause drowsiness and impaired alertness.

Alcohol: Drink in careful moderation if at all. Alcohol may interact with the drug and cause a dangerous drop in blood pressure.

Pregnancy: This drug may harm the developing child. Inform your doctor if you are pregnant or plan to become pregnant.

Breast Feeding: This drug passes into breast milk; avoid breast feeding while taking it.

Infants and Children: Not usually prescribed for infants or children.

Special Concerns: Use of the drug should be considered but one element of a comprehensive therapeutic program that includes weight control, smoking cessation, regular exercise, and a healthy low-salt, low-fat diet.

OVERDOSE
Symptoms: Breathing difficulties, slow heartbeat, sluggishness, extremely low blood pressure.

What to Do: Call your doctor, emergency medical services (EMS), or the nearest poison control center immediately.

DRUG INTERACTIONS
Consult your doctor for specific advice if you are taking amphetamines, oral antidiabetic agents, asthma medication (such as aminophylline or theophylline), calcium channel blockers, clonidine, guanabenz, halothane, allergy shots, insulin, MAO inhibitors, reserpine, or other beta-blockers.

FOOD INTERACTIONS
None expected.

DISEASE INTERACTIONS
Atenolol/chlorthalidone should be used with caution in people with diabetes, especially insulin-dependent diabetes, since atenolol can mask the symptoms of hypoglycemia. Consult your doctor if you have allergies or asthma, heart or blood vessel disease (including congestive heart failure and peripheral vascular disease), irregular (slow) heartbeat, hyperthyroidism, myasthenia gravis, psoriasis, respiratory problems such as bronchitis or emphysema, kidney or liver disease, or a history of mental depression.

Atomoxetine Hydrochloride

BRAND NAME
Strattera

▶ Drug Class: Selective norepinephrine reuptake inhibitor
(SNRI)

▶ Available in: Capsules

▶ Available OTC? No

▶ As Generic? No

Side Effects

SERIOUS
No serious side effects
are associated with the
use of atomoxetine.

COMMON
Indigestion, nausea, vom-
iting, fatigue, decreased
appetite, headache, mood
swings.

LESS COMMON
Constipation, dizziness,
headache, drowsiness,
irritability, cough.

PRINCIPAL USES
To treat attention-deficit
hyperactivity disorder
(ADHD).

HOW THE DRUG WORKS
The exact mechanism of
action is unknown, but ato-
moxatine is thought to
affect levels of norepinephrine, a natural hormone that
promotes the transmission
of nerve impulses in the
brain.

DOSAGE
Children at least 6 years of
age and up to 70 kg (144
lbs): To start, 0.5 mg per kg
(2.2 lbs) a day. After 3 days,
dose may be adjusted by
your doctor to 1.2 mg per
2.2 lbs either as a single
dose in the morning or in
divided doses in the morning and late afternoon/early
evening. The maximum
daily dose should not
exceed 1.4 mg per 2.2 lbs or
100 mg, whichever is less.
Children and teenagers over
70 kg and adults: To start,
40 mg a day. After 3 days,
dose may be adjusted by
your doctor to 80 mg either
as a single dose in the
morning or in divided doses
in the morning and late
afternoon/early evening.
The maximum daily dose
should not exceed 100 mg.

ONSET OF EFFECT
Unknown.

DURATION OF ACTION
Unknown.

DIETARY ADVICE
Can be taken with or without food.

STORAGE
Store in a tightly sealed container away from heat, moisture, and direct light.

IF YOU MISS A DOSE
Take it as soon as you
remember. However, if it is
near the time for the next
dose, skip the missed dose
and resume your regular
dosage schedule. Do not
double the next dose. If you
miss a dose on one day, do
not double the dose the
next day.

STOPPING THE DRUG
The decision to stop taking
the drug should be made in
consultation with your
physician.

PROLONGED USE
See your doctor regularly
for tests and examinations.

PRECAUTIONS
Over 60: No special problems are expected, but the
safety and efficacy of atomoxetine in this age group
has not been systematically
studied.

**Driving and Hazardous
Work:** This drug may
cause drowsiness or dizziness. Do not drive or
engage in hazardous work
until you determine how the
medicine affects you.

Alcohol: No special problems are expected.

Pregnancy: Adequate
human studies have not
been done. Discuss with
your doctor the relative
risks and benefits of using
this drug while pregnant.

Breast Feeding: Atomoxetine may pass into breast
milk; caution is advised.
Consult your doctor for
advice on whether to dis-
continue nursing or discontinue the drug.

Infants and Children:
Not recommended for use
by children under age 6.

OVERDOSE
Symptoms: No cases of
overdose have been
reported.

What to Do: If someone
takes a much larger dose
than prescribed, call your
doctor, emergency medical
services (EMS), or the
nearest poison control center immediately.

DRUG INTERACTIONS
Atomoxetine and MAO
inhibitors should not be
used within 14 days of each
other. Very serious side
effects such as myoclonus
(uncontrolled muscle
spasms), hyperthermia
(excessive rise in body temperature), and extreme stiffness may result. The
following drugs may also
interact with atomoxetine;
consult your doctor for
advice if you are taking
blood pressure drugs,
albuterol, paroxetine, or fluoxetine.

FOOD INTERACTIONS
No known food interactions.

DISEASE INTERACTIONS
Do not use if you have glaucoma, especially narrow-
angle glaucoma, without
consulting your doctor. Consult your doctor if you have
heart disease or a history of
heart rhythm irregularities.

Atorvastatin

Lipitor 20 mg
(PARKE-DAVIS)

▶ Drug Class: Antilipidemic (cholesterol-lowering agent)

▶ Available in: Tablets

▶ Available OTC? No

▶ As Generic? No

Side Effects

SERIOUS
Fever, chest pain, unusual or unexplained muscle aches and tenderness. Call your doctor right away.

COMMON
Side effects occur in only 1% to 2% of patients. These include constipation or diarrhea, dizziness or lightheadedness, bloating or gas, heartburn, nausea, allergic reaction, stomach pain, rise in liver enzymes.

LESS COMMON
Sleeping difficulty, skin rash.

PRINCIPAL USES
To treat high cholesterol. Usually prescribed after the first lines of treatment— including diet changes, weight loss, and exercise— fail to reduce to acceptable levels the amounts of total and low-density lipoprotein (LDL) cholesterol in the blood.

HOW THE DRUG WORKS
Atorvastatin blocks the action of an enzyme required for the manufacture of cholesterol, thereby interfering with its formation. By lowering the amount of cholesterol in the liver cells, atorvastatin increases the formation of receptors for LDL, and thereby reduces blood levels of total and LDL cholesterol. In addition to lowering LDL cholesterol, atorvastatin also modestly reduces triglyceride levels and raises HDL (the so-called "good") cholesterol.

DOSAGE
Initial dose is 10 mg a day, taken once daily. It may be increased by your doctor as needed up to a maximum dose of 80 mg per day. Unlike other "-statin" cholesterol-lowering drugs, atorvastatin does not have to be taken in the evening to be maximally effective.

ONSET OF EFFECT
2 to 4 weeks.

DURATION OF ACTION
The effect persists for the duration of therapy.

DIETARY ADVICE
Cholesterol-lowering drugs are only one part of a total program that should include regular exercise and a healthy diet. The American Heart Association publishes a "Healthy Heart" diet, which is recommended.

STORAGE
Store in a tightly sealed container in a dry place away from heat and direct light.

IF YOU MISS A DOSE
Take it as soon as you remember. Take your next scheduled dose at the proper time and resume your regular dosage schedule. Do not double your next dose.

STOPPING THE DRUG
The decision to stop taking the drug should be made in consultation with your doctor. Once the medication is discontinued, blood cholesterol is likely to return to original elevated levels.

PROLONGED USE
Side effects are more likely with prolonged use. As you continue with atorvastatin, your doctor will periodically order blood tests to evaluate liver function.

PRECAUTIONS
Over 60: No special problems are expected in older patients.

Driving and Hazardous Work: The use of atorvastatin should not impair your ability to perform such tasks safely.

Alcohol: No special precautions are necessary.

Pregnancy: Should not be used during pregnancy or by women who plan to become pregnant in the near future.

Breast Feeding: This drug is not recommended for women who are nursing.

Infants and Children: Safety and effectiveness are not known; this drug is rarely used in children. Consult your pediatrician.

Special Concerns: Important elements of treatment for high cholesterol include proper diet, weight loss, regular moderate exercise, and avoidance of certain medications that may increase cholesterol levels. Because atorvastatin has potential side effects, it is important that you maintain a recommended healthy diet and cooperate with other treatments your doctor may suggest.

OVERDOSE
Symptoms: An overdose of atorvastatin is unlikely.

What to Do: Emergency instructions not applicable.

DRUG INTERACTIONS
Consult your doctor if you are taking cyclosporine, gemfibrozil, niacin, antibiotics, especially erythromycin, or medications for fungus infections. All of these drugs may increase the risk of myositis (muscle inflammation) when taken with atorvastatin and may lead to kidney failure.

FOOD INTERACTIONS
No known food interactions.

DISEASE INTERACTIONS
Consult your doctor if you have any of the following problems: liver, kidney, or muscle disease, or a medical history involving organ transplant or recent surgery.

Atovaquone

▶ Drug Class: Anti-infective/antiprotozoal

▶ Available in: Oral suspension, tablets

▶ Available OTC? No

▶ As Generic? No

Side Effects

SERIOUS
Skin rash, fever. Call your doctor immediately.

COMMON
Insomnia, diarrhea, cough, headache, nausea or vomiting.

LESS COMMON
Lack of energy, fatigue, itching, stomach upset or abdominal pain, constipation, dizziness.

PRINCIPAL USES
To treat mild to moderately severe *Pneumocystis carinii* pneumonia (PCP) in patients who cannot take the antibiotic trimethoprim/sulfamethoxazole (the standard therapy for PCP). This serious type of pneumonia is prevalent among patients with AIDS.

HOW THE DRUG WORKS
Atovaquone prevents infecting cells from manufacturing DNA and other substances necessary for growth and reproduction.

DOSAGE
Adults and teenagers— Oral suspension: 750 mg twice a day, with meals, for 21 days. Tablets: 750 mg, 3 times a day, with meals, for 21 days.

ONSET OF EFFECT
Unknown.

DURATION OF ACTION
Unknown.

DIETARY ADVICE
Take it with meals high in fat content to help the body absorb the medication.

STORAGE
Store in a tightly sealed container away from heat, moisture, and direct light. Do not allow to freeze. Keep away from extreme temperatures.

IF YOU MISS A DOSE
Take it as soon as you remember. This will help keep a constant level of medication in your system. However, if it is near the time for the next dose, skip the missed dose and resume your regular dosage schedule. Do not double the next dose.

STOPPING THE DRUG
Take it as prescribed for the full treatment period, even if you begin to feel better before the scheduled end of therapy. The decision to stop taking the drug should be made in consultation with your doctor. Stopping the drug prematurely may slow your recovery or lead to a rebound infection.

PROLONGED USE
Therapy with atovaquone requires 21 days. Prolonged use of atovaquone beyond this period may be associated with an increased chance of side effects.

PRECAUTIONS
Over 60: No studies have been done specifically on older patients; adverse reactions may be more likely or more severe.

Driving and Hazardous Work: Do not drive or engage in hazardous work until you determine how the medicine affects you.

Alcohol: No special precautions are necessary.

Pregnancy: Adequate human studies on the use of this drug in pregnant women have not been done. Before taking atovaquone, tell your doctor if you are pregnant or plan to become pregnant. Discuss with your doctor the relative risks and benefits of using this drug while pregnant.

Breast Feeding: Atovaquone may pass into breast milk; caution is advised. Consult your doctor for advice.

Infants and Children: Adequate studies of the use of atovaquone in children have not been done. Consult your pediatrician for advice.

Special Concerns: A regular teaspoon may not hold the correct amount of medication. Use a specially marked measuring spoon or other device to dispense each dose.

OVERDOSE
Symptoms: No cases of atovaquone overdose have been reported.

What to Do: If someone takes a much larger dose than prescribed, call your doctor, emergency medical services (EMS), or the nearest poison control center as soon as possible.

DRUG INTERACTIONS
Other drugs may interact with atovaquone. Consult your doctor for specific advice if you are taking rifampin, rifabutin, sulfamethoxazole and trimethoprim combination, or zidovudine.

FOOD INTERACTIONS
No known food interactions.

DISEASE INTERACTIONS
Atovaquone may not work properly in patients with a stomach or an intestinal condition (such as colitis) that limits drug absorption. Consult your doctor for more information.

Atropine Sulfate Ophthalmic

BRAND NAMES
Atropair, Atropine Sulfate
S.O.P., Atropine-Care,
Atropisol, Atrosulf,
I-Tropine, Isopto Atropine,
Ocu-Tropine

▶ Drug Class: Eye muscle relaxant, pupil enlarger

▶ Available in: Ophthalmic solution, ointment

▶ Available OTC? No

▶ As Generic? Yes

Side Effects

SERIOUS
Hallucinations, confusion, extreme sleepiness, heart palpitations. Call your doctor immediately.

COMMON
Blurred vision, increased sensitivity of eyes to light.

LESS COMMON
Eye crusting or drainage, itching and redness of the eye, swelling within the eye, eye pain, dry eyes, dry skin, dry mouth, irritability, agitation, flushing, fever.

PRINCIPAL USES
Used for eye examinations, before and after eye surgery, and to treat certain types of eye conditions, including uveitis (inflammation of the uvea, or the central portion of the eye) and posterior synechiae (a potentially blinding eye disorder). May also be used to help determine the proper prescription for eyeglasses in young children.

HOW THE DRUG WORKS
Atropine sulfate relaxes the ciliary muscle, which controls the shape of the eye's lens as it focuses, and another eye muscle called the sphincter, which controls the narrowing and widening of the pupil. Relaxation of these muscles prevents the lens from focusing and widens the pupil. This allows the doctor to view the interior structures of the eye during an ophthalmologic procedure. And, by immobilizing the tiny structures within the eye, the drug prevents scarring of eye tissue and may also alleviate pain somewhat.

DOSAGE
For eye examination—
Adults: Dose to be determined by your doctor. Children: Ophthalmic solution: 1 drop in the eye twice a day for 2 days before the examination. Ointment: A thin strip of ointment applied to the eye 3 times a day for up to 3 days before the examination. For uveitis— Adults: 1 drop in the eye or a thin strip of ointment applied to the eye 1 to 4 times a day. Children: 1 drop in the eye or a thin strip of ointment applied to the eye up to 3 times a day.

ONSET OF EFFECT
Unknown.

DURATION OF ACTION
From 6 to 12 days. The drug's effect on the lens's ability to focus may last longer than its effect on the size of the pupil.

DIETARY ADVICE
No special restrictions.

STORAGE
Store in a tightly sealed container away from heat, moisture, and direct light.

IF YOU MISS A DOSE
If you miss a dose, apply the missed dose as soon as possible unless it is almost time for the next dose. In that case, skip the missed dose and go back to your regular schedule. Do not double the next dose.

STOPPING THE DRUG
The decision to stop using the drug should be made by your doctor.

PROLONGED USE
Call your doctor if symptoms persist for more than 14 days.

PRECAUTIONS
Over 60: Sleepiness and agitation are more likely.

Driving and Hazardous Work: Avoid such activities until temporary blurring of vision goes away.

Alcohol: No special precautions are necessary.

Pregnancy: Adequate human studies have not been done. Tell your doctor if you are pregnant or are planning a pregnancy.

Breast Feeding: Small amounts of this drug may pass into breast milk; extreme caution is advised. Infants exposed to atropine may exhibit a rapid pulse, fever, or dry skin.

Infants and Children: Infants, young children, and children with blond hair or blue eyes may be more sensitive to the effects of this drug and may have an increased risk of side effects. Use with extreme caution in these groups.

Special Concerns: Before administering the drug, wash your hands. Tilt your head back. Gently apply pressure to the inside corner of the eyelid and pull downward on the lower eyelid to make a space. Drop the medicine or put about ⅓ inch of ointment into this space and close your eye. Apply pressure for 1 or 2 minutes while the eye is closed. Wash your hands again. Make sure the tip of the applicator does not touch any other surface.

OVERDOSE
Symptoms: Impaired vision, extreme sensitivity to light, confusion, clumsiness, dizziness, hallucinations, irregular heartbeat, extreme drowsiness or weakness, unusual dry skin or mouth.

What to Do: Call your doctor, emergency medical services (EMS), or the nearest poison control center immediately.

DRUG INTERACTIONS
Consult your doctor if you use tranquilizers, drugs for glaucoma or myasthenia gravis, or any other eye drops or medications.

FOOD INTERACTIONS
None expected.

DISEASE INTERACTIONS
Do not use if you have glaucoma, especially closed-angle glaucoma, without consulting your doctor. The drug may increase abdominal pain in gastrointestinal disorders.

Atropine Sulfate Oral

Generic 0.4 mg
(LILLY)

▸ Drug Class: Anticholinergic; antispasmodic

▸ Available in: Tablets

▸ Available OTC? No

▸ As Generic? Yes

Side Effects

SERIOUS
Blurring or changes in vision; large, dilated pupils; eye pain; hot, dry, or flushed skin; high fever; heartbeat irregularities; seizures; fainting; coma; unusual agitation; bizarre behavior; hallucinations. Call your doctor immediately.

COMMON
Dry mouth, nose, throat, or skin; constipation; decreased sweating.

LESS COMMON
Difficult urination, decreased breast milk production, difficulty swallowing, headache, memory loss, increased sensitivity of eyes to light, nausea or vomiting, unusual fatigue.

PRINCIPAL USES
To relieve painful cramps and spasms due to irritable bowel syndrome. It is also used in rare cases to treat stomach ulcers in conjunction with other drugs such as cimetidine, and as an antidote to poisoning with certain pesticides.

HOW THE DRUG WORKS
Nerve impulses are transmitted to muscles and glands throughout the body by the action of specialized, naturally occurring chemicals known as neurotransmitters. Atropine blocks the ability of the neurotransmitter acetylcholine to stimulate certain muscles and glands. This produces effects ranging from drying of secretions (saliva, perspiration) to changing the size of the pupils and relief of intestinal muscle spasms.

DOSAGE
Adults and teenagers: 300 to 1,200 micrograms (mcg) every 4 to 6 hours. Children: 4.5 mcg per lb of body weight every 4 to 6 hours, not exceeding 400 mcg per dose.

ONSET OF EFFECT
Within 30 to 60 minutes.

DURATION OF ACTION
From 4 to 6 hours.

DIETARY ADVICE
Take it 30 to 60 minutes before meals and at bedtime.

STORAGE
Store in a tightly sealed container away from heat, moisture, and direct light.

IF YOU MISS A DOSE
Take it as soon as you remember. However, if it is near the time for the next dose, skip the missed dose and resume your regular dosage schedule. Do not double the next dose.

STOPPING THE DRUG
Take it as prescribed for the full treatment period, even if you feel better before the scheduled end of therapy.

PROLONGED USE
Therapy with this medication may require a period of several days to weeks. Prolonged use may increase the risk of an undesirable side effect.

PRECAUTIONS
Over 60: Common side effects may be more likely and more severe in older patients, who may also develop confusion and drowsiness.

Driving and Hazardous Work: The use of atropine may impair your ability to perform such tasks safely.

Alcohol: Use alcohol only in moderation.

Pregnancy: Although studies have been limited, atropine crosses the placenta and is not recommended during pregnancy. Before taking atropine, tell your doctor if you are pregnant or plan to become pregnant.

Breast Feeding: Atropine passes into breast milk and should not be used during breast feeding. This medication may also inhibit milk formation.

Infants and Children: Not recommended for use by children unless under close medical supervision. Infants and very young children are very susceptible to the effects of atropine.

Special Concerns: Atropine must be used with care; it is potentially a very dangerous drug. Use caution when exercising, especially when physical activity is sustained or carried out in hot weather. By inhibiting perspiration, atropine may impair your ability to cool down; heat stroke may result.

OVERDOSE
Symptoms: Blurred or altered vision, dilated pupils, eye pain, hot, dry, or flushed skin, high fever, heartbeat irregularities, seizures, unusual agitation, bizarre behavior, hallucinations, fainting, coma.

What to Do: Call your doctor, emergency medical services (EMS), or the nearest poison control center immediately.

DRUG INTERACTIONS
Consult your doctor for specific advice if you are taking antacids or diarrhea medication; decongestants, antihistamines, and other medications for allergies or colds; ketoconazole; medicines that cause drowsiness, such as barbiturates, sedatives, and cough medicines; psychiatric medications, including antidepressants; alcohol-containing medicines; or painkillers.

FOOD INTERACTIONS
No known food interactions.

DISEASE INTERACTIONS
Consult your doctor if you have heart disease or a history of heart rhythm irregularities, pacemaker usage, or fainting; esophagitis or hiatal hernia; glaucoma; a history of intestinal obstruction, intestinal inflammation (colitis), or other gastrointestinal problems; myasthenia gravis; prostate enlargement or other urinary problems.

Atropine Sulfate/Scopolamine Hydrobromide/ Hyoscyamine Sulfate/Phenobarbital

▶ Drug Class: Anticholinergic; antispasmodic

▶ Available in: Tablets, elixir, capsules, extended-release tablets

▶ Available OTC? No

▶ As Generic? Yes

Side Effects

SERIOUS
Yellow-tinged eyes or skin, skin rash or hives, eye pain, unusual bruising or bleeding, sore throat and fever. Call your doctor immediately.

COMMON
Constipation; dry mouth, nose, skin, or throat; decreased sweating; dizziness; drowsiness.

LESS COMMON
Loss of memory, difficult urination, blurred vision, nausea or vomiting, bloated feeling, unusual weakness or tiredness, difficulty swallowing, decreased flow of breast milk.

PRINCIPAL USES
To relieve symptoms of irritable bowel syndrome, peptic and duodenal ulcers, and gastrointestinal cramps.

HOW THE DRUG WORKS
Acetylcholine is a naturally occurring chemical in the body that is involved in the activity of nerves, muscles, glands, and other physiological processes. This drug interferes with the action of acetylcholine, leading to a variety of effects including the drying of secretions (saliva, perspiration), relief of muscle spasms in the intestines, and changing the size of the pupils.

DOSAGE
Capsules or tablets— Adults and teenagers: 1 or 2 capsules, 2 to 4 times a day. Children ages 2 to 12: ½ to 1 chewable tablet, 3 or 4 times a day. Elixir— Adults: 5 to 10 ml, 3 to 4 times a day. Children: 0.5 to 7.5 ml every 4 to 6 hours. Extended-release tablets— Adults and teenagers: 1 tablet every 8 to 12 hours. Children: Not recommended for use in patients under the age of 13.

ONSET OF EFFECT
Unknown.

DURATION OF ACTION
Unknown.

DIETARY ADVICE
Take this medication 30 to 60 minutes before meals unless your doctor orders otherwise.

STORAGE
Store in a tightly sealed container away from heat, moisture, and direct light. Keep the liquid form refrigerated, but do not allow it to freeze.

IF YOU MISS A DOSE
Take it as soon as you remember. If it is near the time for the next dose, skip the missed dose and resume your regular dosage schedule. Do not double the next dose.

STOPPING THE DRUG
The decision to stop taking the drug should be made by your doctor.

PROLONGED USE
No special problems are expected.

PRECAUTIONS
Over 60: Adverse reactions may be more likely and more severe in older patients.

Driving and Hazardous Work: Do not drive or engage in hazardous work until you determine how the medicine affects you.

Alcohol: Avoid alcohol when using this medication.

Pregnancy: Tell your doctor if you are pregnant or plan to become pregnant before taking this medicine.

Breast Feeding: This drug may pass into breast milk; caution is advised. Consult your doctor for advice.

Infants and Children: The drug should not be prescribed for children under age 2. Adverse reactions may be more likely and more severe in infants and young children, especially those suffering from brain damage or spastic paralysis.

OVERDOSE
Symptoms: Nausea, vomiting, headache, blurred vision, dilated pupils, weak pulse, fever, hallucinations, seizures, unconsciousness, confusion, dry skin and mouth.

What to Do: Call your doctor, emergency medical services (EMS), or the nearest poison control center immediately.

DRUG INTERACTIONS
Other drugs may interact with this medication. Consult your doctor for specific advice if you are taking an anticholinergic (such as belladonna), an adrenocorticoid, an antacid, an antidiarrheal medicine containing kaolin or attapulgite, ketoconazole, an anticoagulant (blood thinner), central nervous system depressants (such as antihistamines, cold medicines, sleep aids, or tranquilizers), an MAO inhibitor, haloperidol, or potassium chloride.

FOOD INTERACTIONS
No known food interactions.

DISEASE INTERACTIONS
Caution is advised when taking this drug. Consult your doctor if you have any of the following: a nerve disorder, asthma or other lung problems, an enlarged prostate, severe and continuing dry mouth, liver disease, kidney disease, Down's syndrome, intestinal blockage or other intestinal problems, an overactive thyroid gland, heart disease, high blood pressure, glaucoma, or ulcerative colitis.

Attapulgite

Donnagel 600 mg
(WYETH-AYERST)

▶ Drug Class: Antidiarrheal

▶ Available in: Oral suspension, tablets, chewable tablets

▶ Available OTC? Yes

▶ As Generic? Yes

Side Effects

SERIOUS
No serious side effects are associated with attapulgite. However, loss of body water due to diarrhea can cause dry mouth, increased thirst, dizziness, lightheadedness, decreased urination, and wrinkling of skin. Call your doctor immediately.

COMMON
Constipation.

LESS COMMON
There are no less-common side effects associated with the use of attapulgite.

PRINCIPAL USES
To treat diarrhea.

HOW THE DRUG WORKS
Attapulgite is believed to bind to and remove large volumes of bacteria and toxins from the digestive tract. It may also reduce the fluidity of the stool associated with diarrhea. There is some debate regarding attapulgite's effectiveness.

DOSAGE
Adults and teenagers— Suspension and tablets: 1,200 to 1,500 mg taken after each loose bowel movement; take no more than 9,000 mg in 24 hours. Chewable tablets: 1,200 mg after each loose bowel movement; take no more than 8,400 mg in 24 hours. Children ages 6 to 12— Suspension and chewable tablets: 600 mg after each loose bowel movement; take no more than 4,200 mg in 24 hours. Tablets: 750 mg after each loose bowel movement; take no more than 4,500 mg in 24 hours. Children ages 3 to 6— Suspension and chewable tablets: 300 mg after each loose bowel movement; take no more than 2,100 mg in 24 hours. Tablets: Should not be taken by children in this age group.

ONSET OF EFFECT
Unknown.

DURATION OF ACTION
Unknown.

DIETARY ADVICE
A mild diet is recommended when recovering from diarrhea. Bananas, rice, applesauce, and plain toast are good choices. Be sure to get plenty of fluids.

STORAGE
Store in a tightly sealed container away from heat, moisture, and direct light.

IF YOU MISS A DOSE
Take it as soon as you remember. However, if it is near the time for the next dose, skip the missed dose and resume your regular dosage schedule. Do not double the next dose.

STOPPING THE DRUG
You may stop taking the drug if you feel better before the scheduled end of therapy.

PROLONGED USE
If diarrhea has not improved or has gotten worse in 2 days, or if you develop a fever, call your doctor.

PRECAUTIONS
Over 60: Older persons are more likely to experience excessive loss of body fluid and therefore are advised to increase fluid intake accordingly.

Driving and Hazardous Work: The use of attapulgite should not impair your ability to perform such tasks safely.

Alcohol: Avoid alcohol.

Pregnancy: Attapulgite is not absorbed by the body and is not expected to cause problems during pregnancy.

Breast Feeding: Attapulgite is not absorbed by the body and is not expected to cause problems while nursing.

Infants and Children: Should not be given to children under the age of 3 without consulting your doctor. Be sure your child drinks a sufficient amount of fluids.

Special Concerns: In addition to taking attapulgite, it is important to replace the body fluids lost because of diarrhea. During the first day you should drink ample amounts of clear liquids, like decaffeinated colas, ginger ale, and decaffeinated tea, and eat gelatin. On the following day you should continue your fluid intake and eat bland foods, such as applesauce, cooked cereals, and bread. Do not take attapulgite if your diarrhea is accompanied by blood or mucus in the stools.

OVERDOSE
Symptoms: No cases of overdose have been reported.

What to Do: An overdose of attapulgite is unlikely to be life-threatening. However, if someone takes a much larger dose than prescribed, seek medical assistance immediately.

DRUG INTERACTIONS
Other drugs may interact with attapulgite. If you are taking any other medication, do not take it within 2 to 3 hours before or after taking attapulgite.

FOOD INTERACTIONS
Eating fried or spicy foods, bran, fruits, vegetables, or drinking caffeinated or alcoholic beverages can make diarrhea worse.

DISEASE INTERACTIONS
Consult your doctor if you have dysentery or any other medical condition.

Auranofin

Side Effects

SERIOUS
Severe abdominal pain, widespread rash, neurological disturbances causing confusion or seizures.

COMMON
Itching, hives, sores or spots in mouth or throat, poor appetite, diarrhea, nausea, vomiting, rashes, fever, stomach pains, indigestion, heartburn, constipation.

LESS COMMON
Coughing, hoarseness, breathing difficulty, or wheezing; dark urine or reduced urine output; impaired vision; difficulty swallowing; sore throat; fever and chills; hair loss; hallucinations; painful urination; low back pain or flank pain; red, painful, itching eyes; unusual bleeding or bruising; red, thickened, or scaly patches on skin; swelling of face, legs, or feet; swollen or painful glands; excessive fatigue or weakness; yellow discoloration of the eyes or skin (jaundice).

PRINCIPAL USES
To treat rheumatoid arthritis. Because of the risk of highly unpleasant side effects, auranofin is generally prescribed for patients who have not responded adequately to other more conservative arthritis treatments, such as non-steroidal anti-inflammatory drugs, corticosteroids, and aspirin. (Auranofin is not appropriate for the treatment of osteoarthritis, which is much more common.)

HOW THE DRUG WORKS
Auranofin contains gold. It is not precisely known how gold compounds work, but evidently they reduce some of the painful joint inflammation associated with arthritis. Auranofin can halt the progress of severe rheumatoid arthritis, preventing further joint damage, and in some cases it may bring about a remission from the disease.

DOSAGE
Adults: 6 mg once a day, or 3 mg twice a day. After 6 months of therapy, your doctor may increase the dose to 3 mg, 3 times a day. Children: Consult your pediatrician for proper dosage.

ONSET OF EFFECT
Within 3 to 4 months.

DURATION OF ACTION
Unknown.

DIETARY ADVICE
Maintain your usual food and fluid intake.

STORAGE
Store in a tightly sealed container away from heat and direct light.

IF YOU MISS A DOSE
Take the missed dose as soon as you remember. If you are within 2 hours of your next scheduled dose, skip the missed dose. Take your next scheduled dose at the proper time, then resume your regular dosage schedule. Do not double the next dose.

STOPPING THE DRUG
This medication should be taken as prescribed for the full treatment period. Do not stop taking it on your own if you are feeling better before the scheduled end of drug therapy unless you are experiencing a serious side effect.

PROLONGED USE
Several months of therapy may be necessary to determine whether this medication is helping you. Prolonged use of auranofin may increase the risk of side effects.

PRECAUTIONS
Over 60: Adverse reactions may be more likely and more severe in older patients.

Driving and Hazardous Work: The use of auranofin may impair your ability to perform such tasks safely.

Alcohol: Avoid alcohol while taking this drug.

Pregnancy: Do not use this drug during pregnancy.

Breast Feeding: Auranofin passes into breast milk; avoid or discontinue use while nursing.

Infants and Children: Not recommended.

Special Concerns: Gold compounds may have many adverse effects resulting from gold toxicity. Your doctor will order periodic blood tests to determine if you are having any undesirable reactions to auranofin, such as anemia or low white blood cell count. Always contact your doctor if you have any concerns about the way you feel while taking auranofin. Auranofin may cause heightened sensitivity to sunlight. Avoid direct sunlight during peak hours, and wear protective clothing. Use sunscreens if possible.

OVERDOSE
Symptoms: No cases of overdose have been reported.

What to Do: If you are concerned about the possibility of an overdose, contact your doctor, emergency medical services (EMS), or the nearest poison control center immediately.

DRUG INTERACTIONS
Consult your doctor for specific advice if you are taking penicillamine.

FOOD INTERACTIONS
No known food interactions.

DISEASE INTERACTIONS
Consult your doctor if you have anemia or any other blood disease, skin disease, colitis or any other intestinal disease, ulcers or heartburn, kidney disease, or systemic lupus erythematosus (SLE).

Azathioprine

Generic 50 mg
(ROXANE)

▸ Drug Class: Immunosuppressant

▸ Available in: Tablets, injection

▸ Available OTC? No

▸ As Generic? Yes

Side Effects

SERIOUS
Rapid heartbeat; sudden fever or chills; back, side, muscle, or joint pain; unusual tiredness or weakness; cough or hoarseness; shortness of breath; black, tarry stools; blood in urine or stools; difficult or painful urination; severe or sudden stomach pain with nausea, vomiting, or diarrhea; red spots, red patches, or blisters on skin; unusual bleeding or bruising; abrupt or sudden, unusual feeling of discomfort or illness. These may be signs of serious infection, bleeding emergencies, or gastrointestinal problems. Seek immediate medical assistance.

COMMON
Moderate nausea and vomiting; loss of appetite.

LESS COMMON
Liver problems, skin rash, sores in mouth, stomach pain, swelling of feet or lower legs, shortness of breath.

PRINCIPAL USES
To slow down or reduce the natural tendency of the immune system to reject organ transplants, and to treat rheumatoid arthritis and other conditions.

HOW THE DRUG WORKS
Azathioprine prevents the immune system from attacking transplanted organs and slows down immune cells that cause inflammation in joints and elsewhere.

DOSAGE
For transplant rejection—Tablet and injection: Initially, 3 to 5 mg per 2.2 lbs (1 kg) of body weight daily. With improvement the dose may be reduced to 1 to 2 mg per 2.2 lbs daily. For rheumatoid arthritis—Tablet: 1 mg per 2.2 lbs daily. This may be increased to not more than 2.5 mg per 2.2 lbs daily.

ONSET OF EFFECT
4 to 8 weeks.

DURATION OF ACTION
Suppression of the immune system may persist long after the drug is completely eliminated.

DIETARY ADVICE
Take it with food or immediately following a meal to reduce stomach irritation.

STORAGE
Store in a tightly sealed container in a dry place away from heat and direct light. Keep liquid form refrigerated, but do not allow it to freeze.

IF YOU MISS A DOSE
For once-daily schedules: Do not take the missed dose. Take your next scheduled dose at the proper time and resume your regular dosage schedule. Do not double the next dose. For multiple-dose daily schedules: Take your missed dose as soon as you remember. If it is time for your next scheduled dose, take the two doses together and resume your regular dosage schedule. If you miss more than one dose in a day, call your doctor.

STOPPING THE DRUG
Take this drug as prescribed for the full length of treatment, even if you begin to feel better before the scheduled end of therapy.

PROLONGED USE
Prolonged use increases the risk of side effects and the possibility of cancer.

PRECAUTIONS
Over 60: Adverse reactions may be more likely and more severe in older patients.

Driving and Hazardous Work: The use of azathioprine may impair your ability to perform such tasks safely.

Alcohol: Avoid alcohol.

Pregnancy: Do not use this drug if you are pregnant. It should not be used by either the male or the female partners if you are trying to become pregnant.

Breast Feeding: Azathioprine passes into breast milk; avoid or discontinue use while nursing.

Infants and Children: Azathioprine has not been shown to affect children differently than adults. Consult your pediatrician for advice.

Special Concerns: Infection is a great threat to people with suppressed immune systems. Azathioprine may lower your ability to resist infection by lowering the number of white blood cells in the blood. Do not receive any vaccinations without approval from your doctor. Avoid people with infections. Azathioprine may also suppress platelets (the blood components that control blood coagulation), and thus cause bleeding problems. Use care with scissors, nail clippers, nail files, razors, toothbrushes, dental floss, or toothpicks. Inform your dentist that you are taking azathioprine.

OVERDOSE
Symptoms: Unusual bleeding, increased susceptibility to infection.

What to Do: Call your doctor, emergency medical services (EMS), or the nearest poison control center immediately.

DRUG INTERACTIONS
Inform your doctor if you are taking allopurinol, ACE inhibitors, chlorambucil, corticosteroids, cotrimoxazole, cyclophosphamide, cyclosporine, mercaptopurine, or muromonab-CD3.

FOOD INTERACTIONS
No known food interactions.

DISEASE INTERACTIONS
Caution is advised when taking azathioprine. Consult your doctor if you have any of the following: chicken pox, shingles, gout, infection, kidney or liver disease, or pancreatitis.

Azelastine

- ▶ Drug Class: Histamine (H1) blocker
- ▶ Available in: Nasal spray
- ▶ Available OTC? No
- ▶ As Generic? No

Side Effects

SERIOUS
No serious side effects are associated with the use of azelastine.

COMMON
Bitter taste in the mouth, drowsiness, headache, unexpected weight gain.

LESS COMMON
Nasal burning, sore throat, dry mouth, sneezing, nausea, fatigue, dizziness, nosebleeds.

PRINCIPAL USES
To treat or relieve symptoms of hay fever (allergic rhinitis) and chronic nasal inflammation and obstruction (vasomotor rhinitis).

HOW THE DRUG WORKS
Azelastine blocks the effects of histamine, a naturally occurring substance within the body that causes swelling, itching, sneezing, watery eyes, hives, and other symptoms of allergic reaction.

DOSAGE
Adults and teenagers: 2 sprays per nostril, not to exceed 2 times per day. Children ages 5 to 11 (allergic rhinitis only): 1 spray per nostril twice a day.

ONSET OF EFFECT
Within 1 to 3 hours.

DURATION OF ACTION
12 hours.

DIETARY ADVICE
No special restrictions.

STORAGE
Store upright in a tightly sealed container away from heat, moisture, and direct light. Do not allow the medication to freeze.

IF YOU MISS A DOSE
Take it as soon as you remember. If it is near the time for the next dose, skip the missed dose and resume your regular dosage schedule. Do not double the next dose.

STOPPING THE DRUG
Take it as prescribed for the full treatment period, even if you start to feel better before the scheduled end of therapy.

PROLONGED USE
Safety and effectiveness during prolonged use have yet to be established.

PRECAUTIONS

Over 60: No special problems are expected.

Driving and Hazardous Work: Azelastine may cause drowsiness. Do not drive or engage in hazardous work until you determine how the medication affects you.

Alcohol: No specific restrictions, though alcohol may increase the drug's sedative effects in some patients.

Pregnancy: Adequate studies of azelastine use during pregnancy have not been done. Before taking it, tell your doctor if you are pregnant or plan to become pregnant. Discuss with your doctor the relative risks and benefits of using this drug.

Breast Feeding: Azelastine may pass into breast milk; caution is advised. Consult your doctor for specific advice.

Infants and Children: The safety and effectiveness of azelastine use by children under the age of 5 have not been determined.

Special Concerns: If the pump has not been used for 3 days or more, it should be reprimed with at least 2 sprays or until a fine mist appears. To avoid the possible spread of infection, this medicine should be used by one person only. Before using this medication, blow your nose gently. When inhaling the nasal spray, keep your head upright and sniff briskly while spraying.

OVERDOSE
Symptoms: No cases of overdose have been reported.

What to Do: An overdose of azelastine is unlikely to occur or to be life-threatening. However, if someone takes a much larger dose than prescribed or accidentally ingests the medication, you should seek medical assistance immediately.

DRUG INTERACTIONS
No drug interactions have been reported. Azelastine may, however, increase the depressant effects of alcohol, sedatives, tranquilizers, pain-killers, barbiturates, or other antihistamines on the central nervous system. Consult your doctor for specific advice.

FOOD INTERACTIONS
No food interactions have been reported.

DISEASE INTERACTIONS
No disease interactions have been reported.

Azithromycin

Zithromax 600 mg
(**PFIZER**)

▶ Drug Class: Azalide antibiotic

▶ Available in: Capsules, tablets, powder, injection

▶ Available OTC? No

▶ As Generic? No

Side Effects

SERIOUS
Breathing difficulty, fever, hives, itching, skin rash, swelling of face, mouth, lips, throat, or tongue, sweating, yellowish discoloration of the eyes or skin. These may be signs of a rare but potentially serious allergic reaction. Seek medical assistance immediately.

COMMON
No common side effects are associated with the use of azithromycin.

LESS COMMON
Nausea and vomiting, abdominal discomfort, diarrhea (generally mild), headache, dizziness.

PRINCIPAL USES
To treat various bacterial infections, particularly of the sinuses, throat, and respiratory tract (such as bronchitis and pneumonia); infections of the ear; venereal disease due to chlamydial and chancroid infection; skin infections; and diarrhea associated with campylobacter and other bacteria that cause food poisoning. Also used to prevent and treat a tuberculosis-like disease known as Mycobacterium avium complex (MAC), which is common in people with advanced AIDS.

HOW THE DRUG WORKS
Azithromycin prevents bacterial cells from manufacturing specific proteins necessary for their survival.

DOSAGE
For bronchitis, strep throat, pneumonia, and skin infections: 500 mg (2 pills) taken in a single dose on the first day of treatment; then, 250 mg (1 pill) per day on days 2 through 5. For chlamydia and chancroid: 1,000 mg (4 pills) taken in a single one-time dose. To prevent MAC: 1,200 mg weekly. To treat MAC: 500 mg, twice a day.

ONSET OF EFFECT
Unknown.

DURATION OF ACTION
Unknown.

DIETARY ADVICE
Take capsules on an empty stomach, at least 1 hour before or 2 hours after eating. Tablets may be taken with or without food. Drink plenty of fluids (at least 2 to 3 quarts of water per day).

STORAGE
Store in a tightly sealed container away from heat and direct light.

IF YOU MISS A DOSE
Take it as soon as you remember. If you miss a day entirely, skip the missed dose and resume your regular dosage schedule the next day. Do not double the next dose.

STOPPING THE DRUG
It is very important to take this drug as prescribed for the full treatment period, even if you begin to feel better before the scheduled end of therapy.

PROLONGED USE
For acute infections, treatment is usually complete after 5 days with capsules, and 1 day with the powdered form. For MAC prevention and treatment, therapy may be lifelong. Prolonged use may be associated with an increased risk of side effects.

PRECAUTIONS
Over 60: Adverse reactions may be more likely and more severe.

Driving and Hazardous Work: The use of azithromycin should not impair your ability to perform such tasks safely.

Alcohol: Avoid alcohol while taking this drug.

Pregnancy: Adequate studies of the use of azithromycin during pregnancy have not been done; consult your doctor for advice.

Breast Feeding: It is not known if azithromycin passes into breast milk; consult your doctor for advice.

Infants and Children: The safety and effectiveness of azithromycin use in patients under 16 years of age have not been established, although no special problems are expected.

Special Concerns: Before taking any antibiotic, make sure you tell your doctor about allergies that you might have. If you are allergic to erythromycin, you are likely to be allergic to azithromycin. Azithromycin is useful only against bacteria that are susceptible to its effects. Therefore, it is important to tell your doctor if your condition has not improved, or instead has worsened, within a few days of starting the drug. The particular bacteria causing your illness may be resistant to azithromycin.

OVERDOSE
Symptoms: No cases of overdose have been reported.

What to Do: Emergency instructions not applicable.

DRUG INTERACTIONS
Other drugs may interact with azithromycin. Consult your doctor for specific advice if you are taking anticoagulants (such as warfarin), anticonvulsants (such as phenytoin and carbamazepine), antihistamines (especially terfenadine), and theophylline. Antacids that contain aluminum or magnesium can interfere with the absorption of azithromycin; separate the use of azithromycin and an antacid by at least 2 hours.

FOOD INTERACTIONS
Azithromycin capsules should be taken on an empty stomach.

DISEASE INTERACTIONS
Consult your doctor if you have a medical history that includes liver disease.

Bacampicillin Hydrochloride

▶ Drug Class: Penicillin antibiotic

▶ Available in: Capsules, oral suspension

▶ Available OTC? No

▶ As Generic? No

Side Effects

SERIOUS
Irregular, rapid, or labored breathing, light-headedness or sudden fainting, joint pain, fever, severe abdominal pain and cramping with watery or bloody stools, severe allergic reaction (marked by sudden swelling of the lips, tongue, face, or throat; breathing difficulty; severe rash, itching, or hives), unusual bleeding or bruising, yellowish tinge to eyes or skin. Call your doctor immediately.

COMMON
Rash, mild diarrhea, headache, sore tongue, sore mouth, vaginal discharge and itching, white patches in mouth.

LESS COMMON
Diminished urine output, chills, weakness, fatigue.

PRINCIPAL USES
To treat a variety of bacterial infections, including those of the respiratory tract, gastrointestinal tract, urinary tract, and middle ear. Bacampicillin is effective only against infections caused by bacteria; it is ineffective against those caused by viruses, fungi, or other microorganisms.

HOW THE DRUG WORKS
Bacampicillin blocks the formation of bacterial cell walls, rendering bacteria unable to multiply and spread.

DOSAGE
Adults and children weighing 55 lbs or more: 400 to 800 mg every 12 hours (2 times a day). Children weighing less than 55 lbs: 5.7 to 11.4 mg per lb of body weight every 12 hours.

ONSET OF EFFECT
Unknown.

DURATION OF ACTION
Unknown.

DIETARY ADVICE
Tablets can be taken with or without food. The oral suspension should be taken on an empty stomach, at least 1 hour before or 2 hours after meals, with plenty of water.

STORAGE
Store in a tightly sealed container away from heat and direct light. The suspension can be refrigerated but should not be frozen.

IF YOU MISS A DOSE
Take it as soon as you remember. If it is near the time for the next dose, skip the missed dose and resume your regular dosage schedule. Do not double the next dose.

STOPPING THE DRUG
Take it as prescribed for the full treatment period, even if you begin to feel better before the scheduled end of therapy. Stopping the drug prematurely may slow your recovery or lead to a rebound infection, also known as superinfection, in which the heartier strains of bacteria survive and multiply, leading to a more serious and drug-resistant infection.

PROLONGED USE
The prolonged use of any antibiotic will increase the risk of superinfection; caution is advised.

PRECAUTIONS
Over 60: No special problems are expected.

Driving and Hazardous Work: Do not drive or engage in hazardous work until you determine how the medicine affects you.

Alcohol: No special precautions are necessary.

Pregnancy: Adequate studies of the use of penicillin antibiotics during pregnancy have not been done; however, no problems have been reported.

Breast Feeding: Bacampicillin may pass into breast milk and cause problems in the nursing infant; avoid use of this drug while nursing.

Infants and Children: No special problems are expected.

Special Concerns: Bacampicillin can cause false results on some urine sugar tests for patients with diabetes. Those who are prone to asthma, hay fever, hives, or allergies may be more likely to have an allergic reaction to a penicillin antibiotic. If severe diarrhea occurs as a side effect of this drug, do not take antidiarrheal medications; call your doctor.

OVERDOSE
Symptoms: Severe nausea, vomiting, diarrhea, muscle spasticity, seizures.

What to Do: Call your doctor, emergency medical services (EMS), or the nearest poison control center immediately.

DRUG INTERACTIONS
Consult your doctor for specific advice if you are taking aminoglycosides, ACE inhibitors, diuretics, potassium supplements or potassium-containing drugs, anticoagulants or other anti-clotting drugs, nonsteroidal anti-inflammatory drugs, sulfinpyrazone, cholestyramine, colestipol, oral contraceptives, methotrexate, probenecid, allopurinol, or disulfiram.

FOOD INTERACTIONS
No known food interactions.

DISEASE INTERACTIONS
Consult your doctor if you have a history of allergies, asthma, congestive heart failure, gastrointestinal disorders (especially colitis associated with the use of antibiotics), infectious mononucleosis, or impaired kidney function.

Bacitracin

▶ Drug Class: Antibiotic

▶ Available in: Ophthalmic ointment and solution; dermatologic (skin) ointment

▶ Available OTC? Yes

▶ As Generic? Yes

Side Effects

SERIOUS
Dermatologic and ophthalmic ointment: Rare severe allergic reaction that may cause hives, breathing difficulty, or at the extreme, total closure of the airways with potentially fatal anaphylactic shock. Contact emergency medical services (EMS) immediately. Ophthalmic preparations only: Severe eye pain, headache, rapid change in vision, sudden appearance of floating spots, acute redness of eye, pain on exposure to light, double vision, itching, burning, inflammation. Call your doctor or ophthalmologist immediately.

COMMON
No common side effects have been reported.

LESS COMMON
Dermatologic ointment: Irritation or skin allergy at the site of application, marked by redness, burning, itching, or the development of a rash.

PRINCIPAL USES
Dermatologic (skin) ointment is available over the counter for application to minor cuts and abrasions to prevent infection. Ophthalmic preparations are prescribed by a doctor for application to the eyelids or into the eye to treat early minor bacterial infections of the eyelids or conjunctiva (the mucous membranes that line the inner surface of the eyelids).

HOW THE DRUG WORKS
Hinders the ability of bacteria to manufacture cell walls, which causes cell death.

DOSAGE
Dermatologic ointment: Apply to a small cut or abrasion 2 times daily. Ophthalmic preparations: Apply to the eye 1 or more times daily.

ONSET OF EFFECT
Unknown.

DURATION OF ACTION
Unknown.

DIETARY ADVICE
No special restrictions.

STORAGE
Store in a tightly sealed container away from heat and direct light.

IF YOU MISS A DOSE
Apply it as soon as you remember and resume your regular dosage schedule.

STOPPING THE DRUG
You can stop using the dermatologic ointment as soon as the cut or abrasion is sufficiently healed. The decision to stop using the ophthalmic preparation should be made by your doctor.

PROLONGED USE
Ongoing observation is needed when the ointment is used, to detect any possible overgrowth of bacterial organisms that are not susceptible to the drug (known as superinfection).

PRECAUTIONS
Over 60: No special problems are expected.

Driving and Hazardous Work: Ophthalmic ointment may cloud vision; caution is advised.

Alcohol: No special precautions required.

Pregnancy: Before using bacitracin, tell your doctor if you are pregnant or plan to become pregnant.

Breast Feeding: Bacitracin may pass into breast milk. Consult your doctor for specific advice.

Infants and Children: No special problems are expected.

Special Concerns: Bacitracin preparations should not be used if you have a history of sensitivity or allergy to bacitracin or any of the other components in the ointment. To use the eye drops or the ointment, first wash your hands. Tilt your head back. Gently apply pressure to the inside corner of the eyelid and with the index finger of the same hand, pull downward on the lower eyelid to make a space. Drop the medicine or put a short strip of ointment (about ⅓ inch long) into this space and close your eye. Apply gentle pressure for 1 or 2 minutes while keeping the eye closed without blinking. Then wash your hands again. Make sure the tip of the dropper or the applicator does not touch your eye, finger, or any other surface. If your symptoms do not improve in a few days or if they become worse, check with your doctor.

OVERDOSE
Symptoms: Severe eye pain, headache, rapid change in vision, sudden appearance of floating spots, acute redness of eye, pain on exposure to light, double vision, itching, burning, inflammation.

What to Do: Call your doctor, emergency medical services (EMS), or the nearest poison control center immediately.

DRUG INTERACTIONS
No other drugs should be applied topically when using bacitracin unless otherwise instructed by your doctor. Bacitracin has not been shown to have any significant interactions with orally taken medications.

FOOD INTERACTIONS
No known food interactions.

DISEASE INTERACTIONS
Caution is advised when using bacitracin. Consult your doctor if superinfection (see Prolonged Use) with nonsusceptible bacteria occurs during therapy, so appropriate treatment can be started immediately.

Baclofen

Generic 10 mg
(ZENITH)

▶ Drug Class: Muscle relaxant

▶ Available in: Tablets

▶ Available OTC? No

▶ As Generic? Yes

Side Effects

SERIOUS
Chest pain, bloody or dark urine, skin rash or itching, hallucinations, fainting, depression or changes in mood, ringing or buzzing in the ears. Call your doctor.

COMMON
Dizziness, drowsiness, weakness (especially muscle weakness), fatigue, nausea, headache, insomnia.

LESS COMMON
Muscle or joint pain; numbness or tingling in hands or feet; unsteadiness, clumsiness, trembling, or other muscle control problems; stomach pain or discomfort; diarrhea; constipation; false sense of well-being (euphoria); loss of appetite; sexual problems in males; swelling of ankles; frequent urge to urinate or uncontrolled urination; difficult or painful urination or decreased urine output; unexpected weight gain; unusual excitability.

PRINCIPAL USES
To relax muscles and relieve the pain of muscle spasms and cramping. Chronic muscle spasms may be associated with disorders such as multiple sclerosis or spinal injuries. Baclofen has also been shown to improve urinary or fecal incontinence in patients with spinal cord injuries.

HOW THE DRUG WORKS
Baclofen appears to reduce the transmission of nerve impulses from the spinal cord to muscle tissue.

DOSAGE
To start, 5 mg, 3 times a day for 3 days. The dose may then increase 5 mg every 3 days until the desired response is attained. The maximum dose is 80 mg a day.

ONSET OF EFFECT
Varies from hours to weeks.

DURATION OF ACTION
Unknown.

DIETARY ADVICE
Take it with milk or food to reduce stomach upset.

STORAGE
Store in a tightly sealed container away from heat, moisture, and direct light.

IF YOU MISS A DOSE
Take it as soon as you remember if it is within an hour of the scheduled dose. If more than an hour has passed, do not take the missed dose. Take your next scheduled dose at the proper time, and resume your regular dosage schedule. Do not double the next dose.

STOPPING THE DRUG
Do not stop taking this medication suddenly. Consult your doctor about reducing the doses gradually to avoid suffering from withdrawal symptoms such as hallucinations or seizures.

PROLONGED USE
Consult your doctor about reducing doses gradually after prolonged use.

PRECAUTIONS
Over 60: Central nervous system side effects such as confusion, dizziness, and drowsiness are more likely in older persons.

Driving and Hazardous Work: This drug may cause drowsiness; avoid driving or engaging in hazardous work until you determine how the medicine affects you.

Alcohol: Avoid alcohol while taking this drug.

Pregnancy: Some animal studies have found that very large doses of baclofen can cause birth defects. Human studies have not been done. Before taking baclofen, tell your doctor if you are pregnant or are planning to become pregnant.

Breast Feeding: Baclofen passes into breast milk; caution is advised. Consult your doctor for specific advice.

Infants and Children: The safety and effectiveness of baclofen in children under age 12 have not been determined.

Special Concerns: Baclofen may cause dizziness, lightheadedness, or faintness when you rise from a sitting or lying position; avoid any sudden position changes. Some side effects may appear after stopping baclofen; if any of the following develop, call your doctor immediately: hallucinations; seizures; confusion or changes in mental state; increase in muscle spasms, cramping, or tightness; unusual restlessness or nervousness.

OVERDOSE
Symptoms: Blurred or loss of vision, drowsiness, loss of consciousness, muscle weakness, twitching, seizures, slowed breathing, vomiting.

What to Do: Call your doctor, emergency medical services (EMS), or the nearest poison control center immediately.

DRUG INTERACTIONS
Consult your doctor for specific advice if you are taking an antidepressant, an MAO inhibitor, a tranquilizer, a sedative, a barbiturate, another muscle relaxant, or a narcotic pain reliever.

FOOD INTERACTIONS
No known food interactions.

DISEASE INTERACTIONS
Caution is advised when taking baclofen. Consult your doctor if you have a history of any of the following: stroke, diabetes mellitus, a mental or emotional problem, epilepsy, or kidney disease.

Becaplermin

BRAND NAME
Regranex

▶ Drug Class: Topical recombinant human growth factor

▶ Available in: Topical gel

▶ Available OTC? No

▶ As Generic? No

Side Effects

SERIOUS
No serious side effects are associated with the use of becaplermin.

COMMON
Irritation at the site of application.

LESS COMMON
No less-common side effects are associated with becaplermin.

PRINCIPAL USES
To treat diabetic ulcers that develop on the lower legs.

HOW THE DRUG WORKS
Becaplermin is a genetically engineered form of a naturally occurring human platelet-derived growth factor. It helps heal ulcers by attracting and promoting the growth of cells involved in wound repair and the formation of new tissue.

DOSAGE
Apply a thin, continuous layer (approximately 1/16th of an inch in thickness) of becaplermin, as directed by your doctor, to the affected area once a day. Cover the treated area with a saline-moistened dressing and leave in place for 12 hours. The dressing should then be removed and the area rinsed with water or saline to remove any residual gel. Cover the area again with a second saline-moistened dressing (without the gel) for the rest of the day. Your doctor will tell you how much becaplermin to apply to the affected area and how to apply it.

ONSET OF EFFECT
Unknown.

DURATION OF ACTION
Unknown.

DIETARY ADVICE
Becaplermin can be applied without regard to meals.

STORAGE
Keep refrigerated, but do not allow it to freeze. Discard unused portions after the expiration date.

IF YOU MISS A DOSE
If you miss a dose on one day, resume your regular treatment regimen the next day, following your doctor's instructions on the amount of gel to apply.

STOPPING THE DRUG
The decision to stop taking the drug should be made in consultation with your physician.

PROLONGED USE
Consult your doctor if the ulcer does not shrink in size by 30% after 10 weeks or complete healing has not occurred after 20 weeks.

PRECAUTIONS
Over 60: No special problems are expected.

Driving and Hazardous Work: The use of becaplermin should not impair your ability to perform such tasks safely.

Alcohol: No special precautions are necessary.

Pregnancy: Adequate human studies have not been done. Before using becaplermin, tell your doctor if you are pregnant or plan to become pregnant.

Breast Feeding: Becaplermin may be absorbed into the bloodstream and pass into breast milk; caution is advised. Consult your doctor for specific advice.

Infants and Children: Not recommended for use by children under age 16.

Special Concerns: Wash your hands thoroughly before and after applying becaplermin. Do not allow the tip of the tube to touch the ulcer, your finger, or any other surface. Becaplermin should be applied in a carefully measured quantity each day. Your doctor will teach you how to determine the correct amount based on the size of the ulcer area. The calculated amount of gel should be squeezed onto a clean measuring surface (for example, wax paper). Becaplermin should then be transferred to the affected area using an applicator such as a clean cotton swab or a tongue depressor. The amount of becaplermin to be applied should be recalculated at weekly or biweekly intervals by your doctor. Becaplermin should be used together with a good ulcer-care program, including a strict non-weight-bearing program.

OVERDOSE
Symptoms: No cases of overdose have been reported.

What to Do: An overdose with becaplermin is unlikely. If someone applies a much larger dose than prescribed or accidentally ingests the gel, call your doctor.

DRUG INTERACTIONS
Consult your doctor if you are applying any other topical medication to the affected area.

FOOD INTERACTIONS
No known food interactions.

DISEASE INTERACTIONS
You should not apply becaplermin if you have any cancerous or other unusual growths at the affected area. Consult your doctor for specific advice.

Beclomethasone Inhalant and Nasal

BRAND NAMES
Beclovent, Beconase AQ
Nasal Spray, Beconase
Nasal Inhaler, Vancenase
AQ Nasal Spray,
Vancenase Nasal Inhaler,
Vanceril

▶ Drug Class: Respiratory
corticosteroid

▶ Available in: Nasal inhaler,
oral inhalation

▶ Available OTC? No

▶ As Generic? No

Side Effects

SERIOUS
No serious side effects
are associated with
beclomethasone.

COMMON
Nasal form: Nosebleeds
or bloody nasal secre-
tions, nasal burning or
irritation, sore throat.
Oral inhalation: Sore
throat, white patches in
the mouth or throat,
hoarseness.

LESS COMMON
Eye pain, watering eyes,
gradual decrease of
vision, stomach pain and
digestive disturbances.

PRINCIPAL USES
To treat bronchial asthma;
to treat allergic rhinitis (seasonal and perennial allergies such as hay fever); to
prevent recurrence of nasal
polyps after they have been
removed surgically.

HOW THE DRUG WORKS
Respiratory corticosteroids
such as beclomethasone primarily reduce or prevent
inflammation of the lining of
the airways (the underlying
cause of asthma), reduce
the allergic response to
inhaled allergens, and
inhibit secretion of mucus
within airways.

DOSAGE
Adults and teenagers—
Nasal inhaler: 1 or 2 inhalations in each nostril, 1 or 2
times a day. Oral inhalation:
2 inhalations, 3 or 4 times a
day. For severe asthma: 12
to 16 inhalations daily (maximum of 20 inhalations per
day). Children ages 6 to
12— Nasal inhaler: 1 inhalation in each nostril, 1 to 3
times a day. Oral inhalation:
1 to 2 inhalations, 3 or 4
times a day. Maximum of 10
inhalations per day.

ONSET OF EFFECT
Within 5 to 7 days; it may
take 3 weeks for the full
effect to occur.

DURATION OF ACTION
6 hours or more.

DIETARY ADVICE
Use it before or after meals.

STORAGE
Store away from fire and
direct light.

IF YOU MISS A DOSE
Take it as soon as you
remember. However, if it is
near the time for the next
dose, skip the missed dose
and resume your regular
dosage schedule. Do not
double the next dose.

STOPPING THE DRUG
Take it as prescribed for the
full treatment period, even if
you begin to feel better
before the scheduled end of
the therapy.

PROLONGED USE
Consult your doctor about
the need for periodic medical examinations and laboratory tests if you must take
this drug for a prolonged
period.

PRECAUTIONS
Over 60: No special problems are expected.

**Driving and Hazardous
Work:** The use of
beclomethasone should not
impair your ability to perform such tasks safely.

Alcohol: No special precautions are necessary.

Pregnancy: Nasal or
inhaled steroids have not
been reported to cause
birth defects if taken during
pregnancy. Before using
such drugs, tell your doctor
if you are pregnant or plan
to become pregnant.

Breast Feeding:
Beclomethasone may pass
into breast milk; caution is
advised. Consult your doctor for advice.

Infants and Children: It
has not been established
whether beclomethasone is
safe and effective in young
children.

Special Concerns:
Inhaled steroids will not
help an asthma attack in
progress. Inhaled steroids
can lower resistance to
yeast infections of the
mouth, throat, or voice box.
To prevent yeast infections,
gargle or rinse your mouth
with water after each use;
do not swallow the water.
Know how to use the

inhaler effectively; read and
follow the directions that
come with the device.
Before you have surgery,
tell the doctor or dentist
that you are using a steroid.

OVERDOSE
Symptoms: No specific
ones have been reported.

What to Do: An overdose
of beclomethasone is
unlikely to be life-threatening. However, if someone
takes a much larger dose
than prescribed, call your
doctor, emergency medical
services (EMS), or the
nearest poison control center immediately.

DRUG INTERACTIONS
Consult your doctor for
specific advice if you are
taking systemic cortico-
steroids, other inhaled
corticosteroids, or any
drugs that suppress the
immune system.

FOOD INTERACTIONS
No known food interactions.

DISEASE INTERACTIONS
Consult your doctor if you
have any of the following: a
lung disease such as tuberculosis; an infection of the
mouth, nose, sinuses,
throat, or lungs; a herpes
infection of the eye; or any
other untreated infection.

Benazepril Hydrochloride

Lotensin 20 mg
(**Novartis**)

▶ Drug Class: Angiotensin-converting enzyme (ACE) inhibitor

▶ Available in: Tablets

▶ Available OTC? No

▶ As Generic? Yes

Side Effects

SERIOUS
Fever and chills, sore throat and hoarseness, sudden difficulty breathing or swallowing, swelling of the face, mouth, or extremities, impaired kidney function (ankle swelling, decreased urination), confusion, yellow discoloration of the eyes or skin (indicating liver disorder), intense itching, chest pain or palpitations, abdominal pain. Serious side effects are very rare; contact your doctor immediately.

COMMON
Dry, persistent cough.

LESS COMMON
Dizziness or fainting, skin rash, numbness or tingling in the hands, feet, or lips, unusual fatigue or muscle weakness, nausea, drowsiness, loss of taste, headache.

PRINCIPAL USES
To control high blood pressure; to treat congestive heart failure; to treat patients with left ventricular dysfunction (damage to the pumping chamber of the heart); and to minimize further kidney damage in diabetics with mild kidney disease.

HOW THE DRUG WORKS
Angiotensin-converting enzyme (ACE) inhibitors block an enzyme that produces angiotensin, a naturally occurring substance that causes blood vessels to constrict and stimulates production of the adrenal hormone, aldosterone, which promotes sodium retention in the body. As a result, ACE inhibitors relax blood vessels (causing them to widen) and reduces sodium retention, which lowers blood pressure and so decreases the workload of the heart.

DOSAGE
If you are not also taking a diuretic (water pill), 10 mg once a day to start, increased to 20 to 80 mg a day in 1 or 2 doses. If you are taking a diuretic, 5 mg per day.

ONSET OF EFFECT
60 to 90 minutes.

DURATION OF ACTION
Up to 24 hours.

DIETARY ADVICE
Take it on an empty stomach, about 1 hour before mealtime. Follow your doctor's dietary advice to improve control over high blood pressure and heart disease. Avoid high-potassium foods like bananas and citrus fruits and juices, unless you are also taking medications, such as diuretics, that lower potassium levels.

STORAGE
Store in a tightly sealed container away from heat and direct light.

IF YOU MISS A DOSE
Take it as soon as you remember. If it is near the time for the next dose, skip the missed dose and resume your regular dosage schedule. Do not double the next dose.

STOPPING THE DRUG
Do not stop taking this drug abruptly, as this may cause potentially serious health problems. Dosage should be reduced gradually, according to your doctor's instructions.

PROLONGED USE
See your doctor regularly for examinations and tests if you must take this medicine for a prolonged period. Remember that benazepril helps control high blood pressure but does not cure it. Lifelong therapy may be necessary.

PRECAUTIONS
Over 60: Adverse reactions may be more likely and more severe in older patients.

Driving and Hazardous Work: Avoid such activities until you determine how the medication affects you.

Alcohol: Consume alcohol only in moderation since it may increase the effect of the drug and cause an excessive drop in blood pressure.

Pregnancy: Tell your doctor before taking this medication if you are pregnant or plan to become pregnant. Use of this drug during the last 6 months of pregnancy may cause severe defects, even death, in the fetus.

Breast Feeding: Benazepril passes into breast milk; if possible, avoid using the drug while nursing.

Infants and Children: Benazepril is generally not prescribed for children; benefits must be weighed against risks. Consult your pediatrician for specific advice.

OVERDOSE
Symptoms: None reported.

What to Do: While overdose is unlikely, call your doctor, emergency medical services (EMS), or the nearest poison control center immediately if you suspect that someone has taken a much larger dose than prescribed.

DRUG INTERACTIONS
Consult your doctor if you are taking diuretics (especially potassium-sparing diuretics), potassium supplements or drugs containing potassium (check ingredient labels), lithium, anticoagulants (such as warfarin), indomethacin or other anti-inflammatory drugs, or any over-the-counter drugs (especially cold remedies and diet pills).

FOOD INTERACTIONS
Avoid low-salt milk and salt substitutes. Many of these products contain potassium.

DISEASE INTERACTIONS
Consult your doctor if you have systemic lupus erythematosus or if you have had a prior allergic reaction to ACE inhibitors. This medication should be used with caution by patients with severe kidney disease or renal artery stenosis (narrowing of one or both of the arteries that supply blood to the kidneys).

Benzocaine

▶ Drug Class: Anesthetic

▶ Available in: Cream, ointment, aerosol spray, dental paste, lozenges, solution

▶ Available OTC? Yes

▶ As Generic? Yes

Side Effects

SERIOUS
Skin: Severe allergic reaction, producing large, red, hive-like swellings on the skin. Dental use: Large swellings in the mouth or throat. Call your doctor immediately.

COMMON
No common side effects are associated with the skin product or the dental product.

LESS COMMON
Contact dermatitis (skin irritation), causing mild burning, stinging, swelling, itching, redness, or tenderness not present before treatment; hives in or around the mouth.

PRINCIPAL USES
To relieve minor pain and itching of the skin caused by mild burns, bites, cuts, abrasions, and contact dermatitis (skin inflammation caused by contact with an irritant such as poison ivy, or by an allergic response to certain metals or other substances). Dental forms of benzocaine are used to treat pain caused by toothache, teething, cold sores, canker sores, dentures, or other dental appliances.

HOW THE DRUG WORKS
Benzocaine interferes with the ability of certain nerves to conduct electrical signals, which blocks the transmission of nerve impulses that carry pain messages.

DOSAGE
Skin cream, ointment, aerosol spray: Apply to affected area 3 or 4 times a day as needed. Dental paste: Apply as needed. Lozenges: 1 lozenge dissolved in the mouth every 2 hours as needed. Aerosol dental solution: 1 or 2 sprays of at least 1 second each, taken as needed.

ONSET OF EFFECT
Within minutes.

DURATION OF ACTION
Unknown.

DIETARY ADVICE
Forms applied to skin: Can be taken without regard to diet. Oral and dental forms: Do not eat or drink anything for 1 hour after using medicine.

STORAGE
Store in a tightly sealed container away from heat and direct light.

IF YOU MISS A DOSE
Take it as soon as you remember. If it is near the time for the next dose, skip the missed dose and resume your regular dosage schedule. Do not double the next dose.

STOPPING THE DRUG
It is advisable to take the medication as prescribed for the full treatment period. However, you may stop taking the drug before the scheduled end of therapy if you are feeling better.

PROLONGED USE
For skin pain or discomfort: Check with your doctor if the condition does not improve within 7 days. For dental pain: If used temporarily for a toothache, arrange for proper dental treatment as soon as possible. For sore throat: Check with your doctor if pain lasts more than 2 days.

PRECAUTIONS
Over 60: Skin: No information is available. Dental use: Adverse reactions may be more likely and more severe in older patients.

Driving and Hazardous Work: No special precautions are necessary.

Alcohol: No special precautions are necessary.

Pregnancy: Benzocaine has not been reported to cause problems during pregnancy.

Breast Feeding: No problems are expected.

Infants and Children: Dental paste can be used in teething babies 4 months and older. Use of other forms of benzocaine is not recommended for children under 2 unless prescribed by your doctor.

Special Concerns: Do not swallow the dental form unless your doctor has instructed you to do so.

OVERDOSE
Symptoms: Both skin and dental forms: Blurred or double vision; confusion; convulsions; dizziness or lightheadedness; drowsiness; feeling hot, cold, or numb; headache; increased sweating; ringing or buzzing in ears; shivering or trembling; slow or irregular heartbeat; trouble breathing; anxiety, nervousness, or restlessness; pale skin; unusual fatigue.

What to Do: Call your doctor, emergency medical services (EMS), or the nearest poison control center immediately.

DRUG INTERACTIONS
With dental benzocaine, consult your doctor for specific advice if you are taking cholinesterase inhibitors or sulfonamides.

FOOD INTERACTIONS
No known food interactions.

DISEASE INTERACTIONS
Consult your doctor if you have any other condition affecting the mouth or skin.

Benzoyl Peroxide

BRAND NAMES
Benzac W, Benzagel, BenzaShave, Clear By Design, Clearasil, Cuticura Acne Cream, Del-Aqua, Desquam, Fostex, Neutrogena Acne Mask, Noxzema Clear-ups, Oxy 10, Oxy 5, PanOxyl, Stri-Dex Maximum Strength, Theroxide

▶ Drug Class: Acne drug

▶ Available in: Lotion, cream, gel, pads, cleansing bar, facial mask, stick

▶ Available OTC? Yes

▶ As Generic? Yes

Side Effects

SERIOUS
Allergic reaction causing burning, blistering, crusting, itching, severe redness, and swelling of skin. Contact your doctor right away.

COMMON
Mild dryness and peeling of skin.

LESS COMMON
Excessive dryness, unusual feeling of warmth or heat, mild stinging, redness, irritation. This medicine may cause a rash or intensify sunburn in areas of the skin exposed to sunlight or ultraviolet light; avoid excessive sun exposure and tell your doctor if a skin reaction occurs.

PRINCIPAL USES

To treat mild to moderate acne. In more severe cases benzoyl peroxide may be used in conjunction with other acne treatments, such as antibiotics, retinoic acid preparations, and sulfur- or salicylic-acid-containing medications. It may also be used to treat pressure sores and other skin disorders.

HOW THE DRUG WORKS

Benzoyl peroxide slowly releases oxygen, which has an antibacterial effect (bacteria are a primary cause of acne). It also causes peeling and drying of skin, which helps to eliminate blackheads and whiteheads.

DOSAGE

For the cream, gel, lotion or stick form of benzoyl, first wash the affected area of skin with medicated soap and water. Pat dry gently with a towel; apply enough medicine to cover the affected area and rub in gently once or twice a day. For the shave cream form, wet the area to be shaved, apply a small amount of the cream, rub over the entire area, shave, then rinse the area and pat it dry. Check with your doctor about using aftershave lotions. If you have a fair complexion, start with a single daily application at bedtime. Keep the medicine away from eyes, nose, and mouth.

ONSET OF EFFECT

1 to several weeks.

DURATION OF ACTION

Up to 24 hours.

DIETARY ADVICE

This medication may be used without regard to diet.

STORAGE

Store in a tightly sealed container away from heat and direct light.

IF YOU MISS A DOSE

If you miss an application, apply it as soon as you remember.

STOPPING THE DRUG

Although benzoyl peroxide can be discontinued when acne improves, stopping usually leads to a recurrence of acne.

PROLONGED USE

Check with your doctor if you do not see improvement within 4 to 6 weeks. Other medications may be necessary to control acne and to prevent permanent scarring.

PRECAUTIONS

Over 60: No special problems are expected.

Driving and Hazardous Work: No special precautions are necessary.

Alcohol: No special precautions are necessary.

Pregnancy: Problems in pregnancy have not been documented, but the manufacturer recommends that the medicine should not be used by pregnant women unless it is considered essential.

Breast Feeding: Benzoyl peroxide may pass into breast milk. Ask your doctor about its use during breast feeding.

Infants and Children: Studies on this medicine have been done only with teenagers and adults, so there is no specific information about its use with other age groups. Nonetheless, no special side effects or problems are expected in children over 12. No studies have been done in children under 12. Use and dose must be determined by a doctor.

OVERDOSE

Symptoms: Overapplication to the skin may cause burning, itching, scaling, swelling, or redness.

What to Do: Discontinue the drug and consult your doctor. If this drug is accidentally ingested, call your doctor, emergency medical services (EMS), or the nearest poison control center immediately.

DRUG INTERACTIONS

Use of this medicine with skin-peeling agents such as salicylic acid, sulfur, tretinoin, or resorcinol can cause excessive skin irritation. Consult your doctor if you take an oral contraceptive, or if you are using any other prescription or nonprescription medication for acne, or if you use medicated cosmetics or abrasive skin cleaners.

FOOD INTERACTIONS

See below.

DISEASE INTERACTIONS

A history of allergy to cinnamon and foods containing benzoic acid increases the chances of developing an allergic skin rash to benzoyl peroxide. Be sure to notify your doctor if you have either of these allergies. Consult your doctor if you have any skin condition other than acne before using benzoyl peroxide.

Benzphetamine

▶ Drug Class: Appetite
   suppressant

▶ Available in: Tablets

▶ Available OTC? No

▶ As Generic? Yes

Side Effects

SERIOUS
Mental depression, nausea or vomiting, abdominal pain, trembling, overactivity, rapid heartbeat, confusion, hallucinations, convulsions, coma, highly elevated blood pressure. Call your doctor at once.

COMMON
Irritability, nervousness, insomnia, mood changes including elation, euphoria, or a false sense of well-being.

LESS COMMON
Irregular or pounding heartbeat, difficulties with urination; call your doctor at once. Blurred vision, dry mouth, unpleasant or metallic taste in the mouth, decreased sexual ability, increased sweating, diarrhea, headache. Notify your doctor if such symptoms persist.

PRINCIPAL USES
For short-term use in a weight reduction program.

HOW THE DRUG WORKS
Benzphetamine reduces appetite by acting on the satiety center in the brain.

DOSAGE
To start, 25 to 50 mg once a day. Usually taken in midmorning or midafternoon. The dose can be increased up to 150 mg per day, taken in 3 doses, if necessary and if the patient can tolerate this dosage without severe side effects. The magnitude of the increased weight loss associated with benzphetamine is a fraction of a pound a week, with the weight loss greatest in the first weeks of therapy.

ONSET OF EFFECT
Within 1 to 2 hours.

DURATION OF ACTION
Up to 4 hours.

DIETARY ADVICE
Take the drug 1 hour before or 2 hours after meals, in midmorning or midafternoon. The last dose should be taken at least 4 to 6 hours before bedtime, since this medicine may cause insomnia.

STORAGE
Store in a tightly sealed container away from heat, moisture, and direct light.

IF YOU MISS A DOSE
If you miss a dose, take it if you remember within 2 hours. However, if more than 2 hours have passed, skip the missed dose and return to your regular schedule. Do not double the next dose.

STOPPING THE DRUG
Take it as prescribed for the full treatment period. The decision to stop taking the drug should be made in consultation with your physician.

PROLONGED USE
The dose should be reduced with prolonged use. Prolonged use may cause drug dependence. The maximum recommended duration of therapy is 8 to 12 weeks.

PRECAUTIONS
Over 60: Adverse reactions and side effects may be more common in older persons.

Driving and Hazardous Work: Don't drive or engage in hazardous work until you determine how the medicine affects you. It may cause dizziness or blurred vision.

Alcohol: Drink in strict moderation if at all while using this drug.

Pregnancy: Benzphetamine should not be taken during pregnancy because it may harm the fetus. A reliable form of birth control should be used while taking this medicine.

Breast Feeding: Benzphetamine passes into breast milk. It should not be taken while breast feeding.

Infants and Children: Benzphetamine should not be used in children under the age of 12.

OVERDOSE
Symptoms: Overactivity, irritability, trembling, insomnia, rapid heartbeat, confusion, hallucinations, convulsions, coma.

What to Do: Call your doctor, emergency medical services (EMS), or the nearest poison control center immediately.

DRUG INTERACTIONS
Benzphetamine should not be used with any other central nervous stimulant drug. It may decrease the effect of drugs for high blood pressure and increase the effect of antidepressants. Caution is necessary when urinary acidifiers or alkalizers are taken with benzphetamine. Avoid MAO inhibitors. Vitamin C supplements increase excretion and therefore decrease the effectiveness of this drug.

FOOD INTERACTIONS
Avoid beverages containing caffeine since they may increase the drug's effect of stimulating the central nervous system.

DISEASE INTERACTIONS
This medicine should not be taken by persons with advanced arteriosclerosis, moderate to severe high blood pressure, hyperthyroidism, or glaucoma. It should not be given to persons with a history of drug abuse. For people with diabetes, taking this medicine may affect the amount of insulin or oral antidiabetic medicines that must be taken.

Benztropine Mesylate

Generic 2 mg
(PAR)

Additional photographs

▶ Drug Class: Antiparkinsonism drug

▶ Available in: Capsules, injection

▶ Available OTC? No

▶ As Generic? Yes

Side Effects

SERIOUS
Unusually rapid or slow heartbeat, heart palpitations, abnormal behavior, confusion, bowel obstruction. Call your doctor immediately.

COMMON
Constipation. It can be reduced by drinking more fluids and eating high-fiber foods.

LESS COMMON
Restlessness, irritability, disorientation, headache, sleepiness, depression, muscle weakness, eye sensitivity to light, dry mouth, heartburn, nausea, vomiting, difficulty swallowing, increased body temperature, decreased sweating.

PRINCIPAL USES
To treat Parkinson's disease or the adverse effects of some central nervous system drugs, which produce Parkinson-like symptoms or affect muscle control.

HOW THE DRUG WORKS
The exact mechanism of action is unknown, but it is believed to help increase the release of certain neurological chemicals that improve control over muscle movement.

DOSAGE
For Parkinson's disease: 0.5 to 6 mg per day in 1 dose at bedtime. For drug-induced Parkinson reactions: 1 to 4 mg per day either in 1 dose or 2 to 3 doses. For drug-induced nervous system effects: 1 to 4 mg per day in 1 to 3 doses.

ONSET OF EFFECT
Within 1 to 2 hours.

DURATION OF ACTION
Up to 24 hours.

DIETARY ADVICE
Benztropine can be taken with food to reduce stomach irritation.

STORAGE
Store this medicine in a tightly sealed container away from heat and direct light.

IF YOU MISS A DOSE
If you miss a dose, take it as soon as you remember unless the next scheduled dose is to be taken within 2 hours. In that case, skip the missed dose and resume your normal schedule. Do not double the next dose.

STOPPING THE DRUG
Do not stop taking benztropine suddenly. If therapy is to be discontinued, dosage should be reduced gradually, according to your doctor's instructions.

PROLONGED USE
Prolonged use of this drug may increase pressure in the eye and thus increase the risk of glaucoma, especially in older persons.

PRECAUTIONS
Over 60: Side effects may be more common in older persons. Smaller starting doses are advisable.

Driving and Hazardous Work: Avoid driving and hazardous work until you determine if the drug causes drowsiness.

Alcohol: Alcohol should be avoided or used with caution because it may increase the sedative effects of this medication.

Pregnancy: Benztropine may affect the unborn child's intestinal tract. Do not use the drug while pregnant.

Breast Feeding: It is not known whether benztropine passes into breast milk. Do not use the drug while breast feeding.

Infants and Children: Not generally prescribed for children under the age of 3. Your doctor must determine the exact dosage for older children.

Special Concerns: Eye pressure should be measured regularly because of the risk of glaucoma. Limit physical activity in hot weather.

OVERDOSE
Symptoms: Clumsiness, drowsiness, fast or slow heartbeat, flushed skin, breathing difficulty, seizures, loss of consciousness, muscle weakness, inability to sweat, uncoordinated movement.

What to Do: Call your doctor, emergency medical services (EMS), or the nearest poison control center immediately.

DRUG INTERACTIONS
The activity of benztropine can affect or be affected by many drugs. Talk to your doctor about any drug you are taking, especially phenothiazines, tricyclic antidepressants, and amantadine.

FOOD INTERACTIONS
None are expected.

DISEASE INTERACTIONS
Consult your doctor if you have glaucoma, high blood pressure, heart disease, impaired liver function, kidney disease, or myasthenia gravis.

Beta-Carotene

BRAND NAMES
Max-Caro, Provatene, Solatene

▶ Drug Class: Dietary supplement

▶ Available in: Capsules, tablets

▶ Available OTC? Yes

▶ As Generic? Yes

Side Effects

SERIOUS
No serious side effects are associated with beta-carotene.

COMMON
Yellowing of the palms, hands, or soles of feet, and, in some cases, the face.

LESS COMMON
No less common side effects are associated with the use of beta-carotene.

PRINCIPAL USES
Beta-carotene is a natural source of vitamin A. While most Americans get sufficient amounts of vitamin A in their diet, beta-carotene may be prescribed as a dietary supplement for people with certain medical conditions that increase the need for the vitamin. Such conditions include cystic fibrosis, long-term chronic illness, chronic diarrhea, and intestinal malabsorption. A profound deficiency of vitamin A (which occurs very rarely) can lead to night blindness. It may also lead to skin problems, dry eyes and eye infections, and slowed growth. Beta-carotene may also be prescribed in larger doses to reduce the severity of photosensitive reactions (heightened sensitivity to sunlight) that occur in patients with a rare inherited disorder known as erythopoietic protoporphyria. Beta-carotene is an antioxidant that has been prescribed to prevent atherosclerosis and coronary heart disease, but beta-carotene supplements did not reduce the incidence of heart attacks in three large clinical trials.

HOW THE DRUG WORKS
Approximately half of ingested beta-carotene is converted to vitamin A in the intestine. The rest is absorbed unchanged and is stored in various tissues, especially fat.

DOSAGE
As a dietary supplement—Adults and teenagers: 6 to 15 mg a day. Children: 3 to 6 mg a day. To treat erythopoietic porphyria— 30 to 300 mg a day.

ONSET OF EFFECT
Unknown.

DURATION OF ACTION
Unknown.

DIETARY ADVICE
It is best taken with meals.

STORAGE
Store in a tightly sealed container away from heat, moisture, and direct light. Do not refrigerate beta-carotene, and keep it from freezing.

IF YOU MISS A DOSE
There is no danger in doubling the next dose if you miss a scheduled dose.

STOPPING THE DRUG
Take it as prescribed. If beta-carotene is prescribed for a specific medical condition, the decision to stop taking it should be made in consultation with your physician.

PROLONGED USE
No known problems.

PRECAUTIONS
Over 60: No special precautions are warranted.

Driving and Hazardous Work: No precautions are necessary.

Alcohol: No special precautions are necessary.

Pregnancy: Beta-carotene has not been studied in pregnant women, but no problems with fertility or pregnancy have been reported in women taking up to 30 mg of beta-carotene a day. The effects of higher daily doses are unknown.

Breast Feeding: Beta-carotene may pass into breast milk, although problems have not been documented with the intake of normal recommended amounts. Consult your doctor for advice.

Infants and Children: No problems have been reported with the intake of recommended amounts of beta-carotene.

Special Concerns: Beta-carotene is found in carrots, dark-green leafy vegetables such as spinach and lettuce, tomatoes, sweet potatoes, broccoli, cantaloupe, and winter squash. Be sure to eat a proper, balanced diet to obtain adequate amounts of beta-carotene from foods. Some fat is needed so that the body can absorb beta-carotene. Beta-carotene is safer than vitamin A because high doses of vitamin A can be harmful. If high levels of vitamin A are present, less beta-carotene is converted to vitamin A by the body.

OVERDOSE
Symptoms: None have been reported.

What to Do: An overdose of beta-carotene is unlikely to be dangerous. Emergency instructions do not apply.

DRUG INTERACTIONS
Consult your doctor for specific advice if you are taking cholestyramine or colestipol (cholesterol-lowering drugs), mineral oil, neomycin (an antibiotic), or vitamin E.

FOOD INTERACTIONS
No known food interactions.

DISEASE INTERACTIONS
If you have any medical problems, consult your doctor before taking beta-carotene. Large doses of beta-carotene may cause complications in patients with liver disease or kidney disease.

Betamethasone Systemic

▶ Drug Class: Corticosteroid

▶ Available in: Syrup, tablets, extended-release tablets, injection, rectal solution

▶ Available OTC? No

▶ As Generic? Yes

Side Effects

SERIOUS
Vision problems, frequent urination, increased thirst, rectal bleeding, blistering skin, confusion, hallucinations, paranoia, euphoria, depression, mood swings, redness and swelling at injection site. Call your doctor immediately.

COMMON
Increased appetite, indigestion, nervousness, insomnia, greater susceptibility to infections, increased blood pressure, slowed healing of wounds, unusual weight gain, easy bruising, fluid retention.

LESS COMMON
Change in skin color, dizziness, headache, increased sweating, unusual growth of body or facial hair, increased blood sugar, peptic ulcers, adrenal insufficiency, muscle weakness, cataracts, glaucoma, osteoporosis.

PRINCIPAL USES
To treat numerous conditions that involve inflammation (a response by body tissues, producing redness, warmth, swelling, and pain). Such conditions include arthritis, allergic reactions, asthma, some skin diseases, multiple sclerosis flare-ups, and other autoimmune diseases. Also prescribed to treat deficiency of natural steroid hormones.

HOW THE DRUG WORKS
Betamethasone mimics the effects of the body's corticosteroids. It depresses the synthesis, release, and activity of inflammation-producing chemicals. It also suppresses immune system activity.

DOSAGE
Adults— Syrup or tablets: 600 micrograms (mcg) to 7.2 mg a day, as a single dose or in divided doses. Extended-release tablets: 2 to 6 mg a day to start, then as ordered by your doctor. Injection: Up to 9 mg a day. Rectal solution: 5 mg, given as an enema at night. Consult pediatrician for children's dosage.

ONSET OF EFFECT
Within 1 hour. It may take 2 to 4 days for full effect.

DURATION OF ACTION
More than 3 days for oral forms; 24 hours or more for other forms.

DIETARY ADVICE
Take it with food or milk to minimize stomach upset. Your doctor may recommend a special diet.

STORAGE
Store in a tightly sealed container away from heat, moisture, and direct light.

IF YOU MISS A DOSE
Take it as soon as you remember. If you take several doses a day and it is close to the next dose, double the next dose. If you take 1 dose a day and you do not remember until the next day, skip the missed dose and do not double the next dose.

STOPPING THE DRUG
With long-term therapy, do not stop taking the drug abruptly; the dosage should be decreased gradually.

PROLONGED USE
See your doctor regularly for tests and examinations. Long-term use may lead to cataracts, diabetes, hypertension, or osteoporosis.

PRECAUTIONS
Over 60: Adverse reactions may be more likely and more severe in older patients.

Driving and Hazardous Work: Do not drive or engage in hazardous work until you determine how the medicine affects you.

Alcohol: May cause stomach problems; avoid alcohol unless your doctor approves occasional moderate drinking.

Pregnancy: Overuse during pregnancy can retard the child's growth and cause other developmental problems. Consult your physician.

Breast Feeding: Do not use while nursing.

Infants and Children: Betamethasone may retard the normal growth and development of bone and other tissues. Consult your doctor for advice.

Special Concerns: Avoid immunizations with live vaccines if possible. This drug can lower your resistance to infection. Patients undergoing long-term therapy should wear a medical-alert bracelet. Call your doctor if you develop a fever.

OVERDOSE
Symptoms: Fever, muscle or joint pain, nausea, dizziness, fainting, difficulty breathing. Prolonged overuse: Moonface, obesity, unusual hair growth, acne, loss of sexual function, muscle wasting.

What to Do: Seek medical assistance immediately.

DRUG INTERACTIONS
Consult your doctor for specific advice if you are taking aminoglutethimide, antacids, barbiturates, carbamazepine, griseofulvin, mitotane, phenylbutazone, phenytoin, primidone, rifampin, injectable amphotericin B, oral antidiabetes agents, insulin, digitalis drugs, diuretics, or medications that contain potassium or sodium.

FOOD INTERACTIONS
Avoid excess sodium.

DISEASE INTERACTIONS
Consult your doctor if you have a history of bone disease, chicken pox, measles, gastrointestinal disorders, diabetes, recent serious infection, tuberculosis, glaucoma, heart disease, hypertension, liver or kidney disorders, high blood cholesterol, overactive or underactive thyroid, myasthenia gravis, or lupus.

Betamethasone Topical

▶ Drug Class: Topical
corticosteroid

▶ Available in: Cream, gel,
lotion, ointment, aerosol,
foam

▶ Available OTC? No

▶ As Generic? Yes

Side Effects

SERIOUS
Serious side effects from
the use of topical beta-
methasone are rare.

COMMON
Burning, itching, irrita-
tion, redness, dryness,
acne, stinging and crack-
ing of skin, numbness or
tingling in the extremities
in 0.5% to 1% of patients.
Risk of such reactions is
higher with lotion and
gel and lower in oint-
ment and cream. (Prod-
ucts vary in potency from
one brand to another;
higher-potency products
are more likely to cause
side effects.)

LESS COMMON
Blistering and pus near
hair follicles, unusual
bleeding or easy bruis-
ing, darkening or promi-
nence of small surface
veins, increased susceptibility to infection.

PRINCIPAL USES
To treat skin rashes and
inflammation.

HOW THE DRUG WORKS
Topical betamethasone
appears to interfere with the
formation of natural sub-
stances within the body that
are directly responsible for
the process of inflammation,
which produces swelling,
redness, and itching.

DOSAGE
Apply sparingly as a thin
film, 2 (sometimes 3) times
a day, only to the specific
areas of skin where needed.
Wash or soak the affected
area prior to application, as
this may improve the
absorption of the drug.
Foam is for use on the
scalp.

ONSET OF EFFECT
Rapid, but may take 24 to
48 hours to see effect.

DURATION OF ACTION
Unknown.

DIETARY ADVICE
No special restrictions.

STORAGE
Store in a tightly sealed container away from heat and
direct light.

IF YOU MISS A DOSE
Apply it as soon as you
remember. If it is near the
time for the next dose, skip
the missed dose and
resume your regular dosage
schedule as prescribed.

STOPPING THE DRUG
Take as prescribed for the
full treatment period, even if
you begin to feel better
before the scheduled end of
therapy.

PROLONGED USE
Avoid prolonged use, particularly near the eyes, on the
face in general, on the genital or rectal regions, or in
the folds of the skin (for
example, underneath the
breasts).

PRECAUTIONS
Over 60: Side effects may
be more likely and more
severe; therapy with topical
corticosteroids should be
limited.

**Driving and Hazardous
Work:** The use of topical
betamethasone should not
impair your ability to perform such tasks safely.

Alcohol: No special precautions are necessary.

Pregnancy: Should not be
used for prolonged periods
in pregnant women or in
women trying to become
pregnant.

Breast Feeding: Although
problems have not been
documented, caution is
advised. Do not apply to
breasts prior to nursing.
Consult your doctor for
specific advice.

Infants and Children: It
should not be used for more
than 2 weeks on children
and adolescents, unless otherwise directed by your doctor. Do not use tight-fitting
diapers or plastic pants on
children when treating skin
irritation in the diaper area.

Special Concerns: Wash
your hands thoroughly after
application. Do not wrap the
treated area with bandages
or tight-fitting clothing
unless otherwise instructed
by your doctor. Doing so
may cause skin infections to
worsen; corticosteroid treatment may need to be dis-
continued to treat
infections, then resumed
later. Note that topical
betamethasone is not a
treatment for acne, burns,
infections, or disorders of
pigmentation.

OVERDOSE
Symptoms: No specific
ones have been reported.

What to Do: An overdose
of a topical corticosteroid is
unlikely to be life-threatening. However, in the event
of accidental ingestion or an
apparent overdose, call a
doctor, emergency medical
services (EMS), or the
nearest poison control center right away.

DRUG INTERACTIONS
Do not mix topical
betamethasone with other
products, especially alcohol-
containing preparations
(which include colognes,
aftershave, and many moisturizer lotions), since this
may cause dryness and irritation, or increase the risk
of an allergic reaction.

FOOD INTERACTIONS
Potassium supplements may
decrease this drug's effects.
Avoid foods high in sodium.

DISEASE INTERACTIONS
Caution is advised when
taking this drug. Consult
your doctor if you have any
of the following: cataracts;
diabetes mellitus; glaucoma;
infection, sores, or ulcerations of the skin; infection at
another site in your body;
or tuberculosis.

Betamethasone/Clotrimazole

BRAND NAME
Lotrisone

▶ Drug Class: Topical antifungal

▶ Available in: Cream

▶ Available OTC? No

▶ As Generic? Yes

Side Effects

SERIOUS
Blistering or ulceration of the skin; blistering of the lips, nose, and mouth.

COMMON
Brief burning or irritation after application; peeling.

LESS COMMON
Severe burning, itching, swelling, increased redness, or any increased discomfort developing at the application site that was not present prior to therapy; dry skin; pus or inflammation at base of hair follicles; change in skin color at site of application; acne.

PRINCIPAL USES
To treat fungal infections of the skin.

HOW THE DRUG WORKS
Clotrimazole prevents fungal organisms from manufacturing the vital proteins they require for growth and function. Betamethasone dipropionate is a steroid; it interferes with the formation of natural substances within the body that are directly responsible for the process of inflammation, which produces swelling, redness, and pain. The use of these two effective medications in combination for skin infections appears to hasten recovery sooner than use of clotrimazole alone. This medication is only effective for infections caused by fungal organisms. It will not work for bacterial or viral infections.

DOSAGE
Adults and children older than 12 years of age: Apply and massage a sufficient amount of cream to the affected site twice daily for 2 to 4 weeks. This combination drug contains a high-potency topical steroid that should not be used in skin creases or with bandages (occlusive dressing) unless closely supervised by your doctor.

ONSET OF EFFECT
Clotrimazole begins killing susceptible fungi shortly after contact. The effects may not be noticeable for several days or weeks.

DURATION OF ACTION
Unknown.

DIETARY ADVICE
Drink plenty of fluids.

STORAGE
Store in a tightly sealed container away from heat and direct light. Keep away from moisture and extremes in temperature.

IF YOU MISS A DOSE
Apply it as soon as you remember. If it is near the time for the next dose, skip the missed dose and resume your regular dosage schedule. Do not double the next dose or apply an excessively thick film of topical medication to compensate for a missed dose.

STOPPING THE DRUG
Apply as prescribed for the full treatment period, even if the fungal infection appears to be eradicated before the scheduled end of therapy. Unfortunately, it can be difficult to assess when the drug has achieved its desired effect since it suppresses redness and inflammation of the skin before the infection is completely clear; recurrence of fungal infection owing to inadequate length of therapy is a significant risk.

PROLONGED USE
Therapy with this medication should not exceed 4 weeks.

PRECAUTIONS
Over 60: Adverse reactions may be more likely and more severe in older patients.

Driving and Hazardous Work: No special precautions are necessary.

Alcohol: No special precautions are necessary.

Pregnancy: Not recommended during pregnancy.

Breast Feeding: Betamethasone dipropionate/clotrimazole may pass into breast milk; caution is advised. Consult your doctor for advice.

Infants and Children: Not recommended for use by children under age 12.

Special Concerns: Avoid contact with eyes. Wash hands thoroughly after application. Tell your doctor if your condition has not improved within a few days of starting the medication. As with any other antifungal, betamethasone dipropionate/clotrimazole is useful only against organisms that are vulnerable to its effects. Therefore, it is important to tell your doctor if your condition has not improved—or has worsened—within a few days of starting betamethasone dipropionate/clotrimazole. The particular organism causing your illness may be resistant to this medication.

OVERDOSE
Symptoms: No specific ones have been reported.

What to Do: An overdose is unlikely to be life-threatening. However, if someone applies a much larger dose than prescribed or ingests the medication, call your doctor, emergency medical services (EMS), or the nearest poison control center immediately.

DRUG INTERACTIONS
No specific drug interactions have been documented.

FOOD INTERACTIONS
No known food interactions.

DISEASE INTERACTIONS
Consult your physician if you have ever experienced an allergic reaction to any topical medication, or undesirable reactions to any steroid or steroid-containing preparation.

Betaxolol Ophthalmic

BRAND NAMES
Betoptic, Betoptic Pilo,
Betoptic S

▶ Drug Class: Antiglaucoma
drug; ophthalmic beta-blocker

▶ Available in: Ophthalmic
solution, suspension

▶ Available OTC? No

▶ As Generic? No

Side Effects

SERIOUS
Palpitations, trouble
breathing, dizziness and
weakness caused by low
blood pressure. Call your
doctor right away.

COMMON
Temporary eye irritation,
tearing, eye inflamma-
tion, burning, swelling.

LESS COMMON
Blurred vision, poor night
vision, and increased
sensitivity to light;
headache; insomnia;
sinus irritation; odd or
bitter taste in the mouth.

PRINCIPAL USES
To treat glaucoma.

HOW THE DRUG WORKS
Glaucoma, a sight-threatening disorder, occurs when
aqueous humor (the fluid
inside the eye) cannot drain
properly, resulting in an
increase in pressure within
the eyeball (known as
intraocular pressure).
Increased intraocular pressure can damage the optic
nerve and lead to a gradually progressive loss of
vision. Betaxolol decreases
the production of aqueous
humor, thereby reducing
intraocular pressure.

DOSAGE
1 or 2 drops of 0.5% solution
or 0.25% suspension twice
a day.

ONSET OF EFFECT
30 minutes.

DURATION OF ACTION
12 hours or more.

DIETARY ADVICE
No special restrictions or
recommendations.

STORAGE
Store in a tightly sealed container away from heat, moisture, and direct light. Do
not allow the medicine to
freeze.

IF YOU MISS A DOSE
Apply the missed dose as
soon as you remember. If it
is near the time for the next
dose, skip the missed dose
and resume your regular
dosage schedule. Do not
double the next dose.

STOPPING THE DRUG
The decision to stop taking
the drug should be made by
your doctor. Gradual discontinuation rather than a sudden stop may be required.

PROLONGED USE
Consult your doctor about
the need for periodic oph-
thalmological examinations
to check intraocular pressure (the pressure within
the eyeball).

PRECAUTIONS
Over 60: Adverse reactions
may be more likely and
more severe in older
patients.

**Driving and Hazardous
Work:** Exercise caution
until you determine how the
drug affects your vision.

Alcohol: Alcohol should be
used with caution.

Pregnancy: Ophthalmic
betaxolol has not been
shown to cause birth
defects in animals; human
studies have not been done.
Before taking it, tell your
doctor if you are pregnant
or planning a pregnancy.

Breast Feeding: Oph-
thalmic betaxolol may pass
into breast milk; caution is
advised. Consult your doctor for specific advice.

Infants and Children:
Not recommended for use
by children under age 12.

Special Concerns: To use
the eye drops, first wash
your hands. Tilt your head
back. Gently apply pressure
to the inside corner of the
eyelid and with the index
finger of the same hand,
pull downward on the lower
eyelid to make a space.
Drop the medicine into this
space and close your eye.
Apply pressure for 1 or 2
minutes while keeping the
eye closed without blinking.
Then wash your hands
again. Make sure the tip of
the dropper does not touch
your eye, finger, or any
other surface. Betaxolol
may make your eyes more

sensitive to sunlight. If this
occurs, wear sunglasses or
avoid bright light as necessary. Shake the suspension
well before using.

OVERDOSE
Symptoms: Double vision,
slow pulse, dizziness and
weakness caused by low
blood pressure, unusual
fatigue, drowsiness,
seizures, hallucinations,
loss of consciousness.

What to Do: An overdose
of this drug is unlikely to be
life-threatening. If a large
volume of the medicine
enters the eyes, flush with
water. If someone accidentally ingests it, seek medical
assistance immediately.

DRUG INTERACTIONS
It is not recommended to
use two ophthalmic beta-
blockers at the same time.
Special concern is war-
ranted in people taking
antidiabetic drugs, since
ophthalmic betaxolol may
mask symptoms of low
blood sugar. Other drugs
may interact with oph-
thalmic betaxolol. Tell your
doctor if you are using any
other prescription or over-
the-counter medication.

FOOD INTERACTIONS
No known food interactions.

DISEASE INTERACTIONS
Caution is advised when
taking ophthalmic betaxolol.
Consult your doctor if you
have any of the following
conditions: diabetes, hypoglycemia, heart disease,
high blood pressure, lung
disorders, irregular heartbeat, or an overactive thyroid gland.

Betaxolol Oral

▶ Drug Class: Beta-blocker

▶ Available in: Tablets

▶ Available OTC? No

▶ As Generic? No

Side Effects

SERIOUS
Shortness of breath, wheezing; irregular or slow heartbeat (50 beats per minute or less); pain or feelings of tightness or pressure in the chest; swelling of the ankles, feet, and lower legs; mental depression. If you experience such symptoms, stop taking betaxolol and call your doctor immediately.

COMMON
Dizziness or lightheadedness, especially when rising suddenly to a standing position, rapid heartbeat or palpitations, decreased sexual ability, frequent headaches.

LESS COMMON
Anxiety, irritability, nervousness; constipation; diarrhea; dry, sore eyes; itching; nausea or vomiting; nightmares or intensely vivid dreams; numbness, tingling, or other unusual sensations in the fingers, toes, or scalp.

PRINCIPAL USES
To treat high blood pressure (hypertension).

HOW THE DRUG WORKS
Betaxolol slows the rate and force of contraction of the heart by blocking certain nerve impulses, thus reducing blood pressure.

DOSAGE
To start, 10 mg, once a day. Dose may be increased to a maximum of 20 mg per day.

ONSET OF EFFECT
Within 1 hour.

DURATION OF ACTION
24 hours or more.

DIETARY ADVICE
This medication can be used without regard to diet.

STORAGE
Store in a tightly sealed container away from heat and direct light.

IF YOU MISS A DOSE
Take the missed dose as soon as possible. If it is within 8 hours of the next dose, skip the missed dose and resume your regular dosage schedule. Do not double the next dose.

STOPPING THE DRUG
Take it as prescribed for the full treatment period even if you begin to feel better before the scheduled end of therapy. Lifelong therapy with betaxolol may be necessary. Do not stop taking the medication suddenly, as this may result in potentially serious medical consequences. Dose must be tapered gradually.

PROLONGED USE
Consult your doctor about the need for periodic examinations or laboratory studies to check blood pressure, heart function, kidney function, and blood sugar levels.

PRECAUTIONS
Over 60: Adverse reactions may be more likely and more severe in older patients. Lower doses may be warranted, and frequent measurement of blood pressure is important.

Driving and Hazardous Work: Use caution when driving or engaging in hazardous work until you determine how the medication affects you.

Alcohol: Drink in careful moderation if at all. Alcohol may interact with the drug and cause a dangerous drop in blood pressure.

Pregnancy: Betaxolol has caused birth defects in animals; adequate human studies have not been done. Use of this drug should be avoided during the first three months of pregnancy if possible, and during labor and delivery, because of possible damaging effects on the newborn baby.

Breast Feeding: Betaxolol may pass into breast milk; caution is advised. Consult your doctor for advice.

Infants and Children: The safety and effectiveness of this drug for children under the age of 12 have not been established. If it is used, the child should have periodic tests for low blood glucose (sugar) levels.

OVERDOSE
Symptoms: Double vision, unusually slow or rapid heartbeat, severe dizziness or fainting, poor circulation in the hands (bluish skin), breathing difficulty, seizures.

What to Do: Call your doctor, emergency medical services (EMS), or the nearest poison control center immediately.

DRUG INTERACTIONS
Consult your doctor for specific advice if you are taking calcium channel blockers, ACE inhibitors, insulin or any other diabetes drug, antihistamines, other drugs for high blood pressure, nonsteroidal anti-inflammatory drugs, barbiturates, or clonidine.

FOOD INTERACTIONS
No known food interactions.

DISEASE INTERACTIONS
Betaxolol should be used with caution in people with diabetes, especially insulin-dependent diabetes, since the drug may mask symptoms of hypoglycemia. Consult your doctor if you have any of the following: heart disease, hay fever, asthma, chronic bronchitis, hypoglycemia, an overactive thyroid gland, impaired liver function, or impaired kidney function.

Bethanechol Chloride

BRAND NAMES
Duvoid, Urabeth,
Urecholine

Generic 5 mg
(SIDMAK)

▶ Drug Class: Cholinergic

▶ Available in: Tablets, injection

▶ Available OTC? No

▶ As Generic? Yes

Side Effects

SERIOUS
Difficulty breathing, wheezing, severe or persistent abdominal cramps, diarrhea. Call your doctor at once.

COMMON
Dizziness or lightheadedness. This can be minimized by getting up slowly from a sitting or lying position.

LESS COMMON
Headache, blurred vision, nausea, stomach discomfort, excessive urge to urinate.

PRINCIPAL USES
To treat bladder or urinary tract disorders that make urination difficult. To help initiate urination after surgery.

HOW THE DRUG WORKS
Bethanechol strengthens the ability of bladder muscles to contract, facilitating urination.

DOSAGE
Tablets— Adults: 10 to 50 mg, 3 or 4 times a day. Children: 0.6 mg per 2.2 lbs (1 kg) of body weight, in 3 to 4 doses a day. Injection— Adults: 2.5 to 5 mg injected under the skin 3 or 4 times a day. Children: 0.2 mg per 2.2 lbs of body weight per day, injected 3 to 4 times a day, as determined by your pediatrician.

ONSET OF EFFECT
30 to 90 minutes.

DURATION OF ACTION
Up to 6 hours.

DIETARY ADVICE
Take this medicine on an empty stomach with liquid 1 hour before or 2 hours after meals to avoid nausea and vomiting.

STORAGE
Store in a tightly sealed container away from heat and direct light.

IF YOU MISS A DOSE
Take it as soon as you remember. If it is near the time for the next dose, skip the missed dose and resume your regular dosage schedule. Do not double the next dose.

STOPPING THE DRUG
It may not be necessary to take this drug for the entire prescribed course of treatment. Follow your doctor's instructions about discontinuing the medicine.

PROLONGED USE
No problems expected.

PRECAUTIONS
Over 60: Adverse reactions and side effects may be more severe in older persons.

Driving and Hazardous Work: Determine if the drug causes dizziness, lightheadedness or blurred vision before driving or doing hazardous work. Danger increases if you drink alcohol or take a medicine that affects alertness, such as an antihistamine, a tranquilizer, a pain medicine, a sedative, or a narcotic.

Alcohol: Alcohol intake should be limited to 1 or 2 drinks a day because it can add to the diminished alertness caused by this medicine. Consult your doctor about the exact amount of alcohol you can consume.

Pregnancy: Animal and human studies have not been done. Consult your doctor about taking bethanechol if you are pregnant or plan to become pregnant.

Breast Feeding: It is not known whether bethanechol passes into breast milk. Consult your doctor about taking it if you are nursing.

Infants and Children: Use of bethanechol by infants and children requires close medical supervision.

Special Concerns: Bethanechol interferes with diagnostic laboratory studies of pancreas and liver function. While undergoing treatment with this drug, be cautious when standing up suddenly, as dizziness and lightheadedness are common side effects.

OVERDOSE
Symptoms: Abdominal discomfort, salivation, flushing of the skin, sweating, nausea, vomiting.

What to Do: Call your doctor, emergency medical services (EMS), or the nearest poison control center immediately.

DRUG INTERACTIONS
Consult your doctor if you are taking bethanechol at the same time that you are taking any prescription or nonprescription drugs, especially anticholinergics, ganglionic blockers, nitrates, procainamide, quinidine, or other cholinergic drugs.

FOOD INTERACTIONS
None expected.

DISEASE INTERACTIONS
Consult your doctor if you have low blood pressure, any blood vessel problem, a weakened bladder wall, any urinary tract problem, any digestive problem, an overactive thyroid (hyperthyroidism), asthma, seizures, or Parkinson's disease.

Biperiden

Akineton 2 mg
(KNOLL)

▶ Drug Class: Antiparkinsonism drug

▶ Available in: Tablets, injection

▶ Available OTC? No

▶ As Generic? Yes

Side Effects

SERIOUS
Retention of urine (decreased urine output), confusion, disorientation.

COMMON
Blurred vision, drowsiness, agitation, dry mouth, constipation, urine retention. Constipation can be avoided by increasing the intake of fluids and high-fiber foods. Dry mouth can be relieved by cool drinks, sugarless gum, or hard candy.

LESS COMMON
Restlessness, irritability or unusual feeling of well-being, dizziness, tremor, stomach upset, nausea.

PRINCIPAL USES
To treat Parkinson's disease or the side effects of certain drugs that act on the central nervous system and produce Parkinson-like symptoms, including slowed movement, stiffness, and loss of balance.

HOW THE DRUG WORKS
The exact mechanism of action is unknown, but biperiden is believed to help increase the release of certain neurological chemicals that improve control over movement.

DOSAGE
Tablets: For Parkinson's disease, 2 mg, 3 or 4 times per day, to a maximum of 16 mg per day. For side effects of other drugs, 2 mg, 1 to 3 times per day. If you have difficulty swallowing the tablet, it can be crushed. Injection: 2 mg up to 4 times per day, injected into a muscle or vein. The maximum dose should not exceed 10 mg per day.

ONSET OF EFFECT
Within 1 hour.

DURATION OF ACTION
6 to 12 hours with tablets; 1 to 8 hours after injection.

DIETARY ADVICE
Take this medicine with or immediately after meals unless your doctor orders otherwise.

STORAGE
Store in a tightly sealed container away from heat and direct light.

IF YOU MISS A DOSE
If you miss a dose, take it as soon as you remember unless it is within 2 hours of the next dose. In that case, skip the missed dose and return to your regular schedule. Do not double the next dose.

STOPPING THE DRUG
Do not stop taking the drug suddenly. If therapy is to be discontinued, the dosage should be reduced gradually, according to your doctor's instructions, to avoid a withdrawal reaction.

PROLONGED USE
Your doctor should test your progress regularly so that the dose can be adjusted if necessary.

PRECAUTIONS
Over 60: Side effects may be more common in older persons. A reduced dose may be necessary. This medicine can aggravate symptoms of an enlarged prostate gland and cause impaired thinking, hallucinations, and nightmares in older persons.

Driving and Hazardous Work: Determine how this medicine affects you before driving or engaging in hazardous work.

Alcohol: Alcohol intake should be avoided because this medicine increases its effects.

Pregnancy: Do not use this drug while pregnant.

Breast Feeding: Do not use this drug while breast feeding.

Infants and Children: Safety and effectiveness have not been established for infants and children.

Special Concerns: Pay careful attention to dental hygiene, since biperiden tends to decrease salivation, which can promote the development of cavities and other dental problems.

OVERDOSE
Symptoms: Agitation, anxiety, restlessness, disorientation, hallucinations, blurred vision, fast pulse, difficulty swallowing, and difficulty urinating.

What to Do: Call your doctor, emergency medical services (EMS), or the nearest poison control center immediately.

DRUG INTERACTIONS
Tell your doctor about any other drugs you are taking, especially amantadine, digoxin, any drug for mental illness, antidepressants, or antacids. This medicine can decrease the activity of phenothiazines (mood-altering drugs used in the treatment of psychiatric disorders).

FOOD INTERACTIONS
No known food interactions.

DISEASE INTERACTIONS
Glaucoma, seizures, an irregular pulse, a bowel obstruction, or an enlarged prostate may make it impossible for you to take this medicine.

Bisacodyl

Correctol 5 mg
(SCHERING-PLOUGH)

Additional photographs

▶ Drug Class: Stimulant laxative

▶ Available in: Tablets, powder, suppositories

▶ Available OTC? Yes

▶ As Generic? Yes

Side Effects

SERIOUS
Severe stomach pain, laxative dependence. Call your doctor immediately.

COMMON
Abdominal cramping, burning sensation in the rectum (with suppository), diarrhea.

LESS COMMON
Nausea; vomiting; muscle weakness; rectal pain, bleeding, burning, or itching. If you have a sudden change in bowel habits that lasts longer than 2 weeks, consult your doctor.

PRINCIPAL USES
To relieve short-term constipation or to clear the bowel before rectal or bowel examination, surgery, or childbirth.

HOW THE DRUG WORKS
Bisacodyl increases the volume of fluid in the intestines to stimulate passage of the stool. It also acts on the smooth muscle of the intestine to increase contractions.

DOSAGE
For constipation— Adults and teenagers: Tablets: 10 to 15 mg at bedtime. Children age 6 and older: 5 mg before breakfast. Swallow tablets whole; do not chew. For medical examination— Adults and teenagers: Up to 30 mg orally, or 10 mg given rectally before examination. Children age 6 and older: 5 mg orally or rectally, before breakfast.

ONSET OF EFFECT
Tablets: Within 6 to 12 hours. Suppositories: Within 15 to 60 minutes.

DURATION OF ACTION
Variable.

DIETARY ADVICE
Take the tablet on an empty stomach for rapid effect. Increase intake of fluids and dietary fiber.

STORAGE
Store in a tightly sealed container away from heat, moisture, and direct light.

IF YOU MISS A DOSE
Take the missed dose as soon as you remember, unless it is almost time for your next dose. In that case, skip the missed dose and resume your regular dosage schedule. Do not double the next dose.

STOPPING THE DRUG
Take it as prescribed for the full treatment period. However, you may stop taking the drug if you are feeling better before the scheduled end of the therapy.

PROLONGED USE
Do not use this medicine for more than one week unless your doctor prescribes it.

PRECAUTIONS
Over 60: Excessive use of this drug by an older person can cause loss of body fluid leading to weakness and lack of coordination.

Driving and Hazardous Work: Do not drive or engage in hazardous work until you determine how the medicine affects you.

Alcohol: Avoid alcohol while taking this drug.

Pregnancy: Bisacodyl is not usually used during pregnancy, except immediately before delivery. Consult your doctor for advice.

Breast Feeding: Bisacodyl may pass into breast milk. Consult your doctor for specific advice.

Infants and Children: Do not give this medicine to a child under 6 without your doctor's approval. Do not give this medicine to a child who refuses to have a bowel movement. It may result in a painful bowel movement, which will make the child resist even more.

Special Concerns: Remember that chronic use of bisacodyl or any laxative can lead to laxative dependence. You should consume adequate amounts of fiber in your diet, sources of which include bran or whole-grain cereals, fruit, and vegetables.

OVERDOSE
Symptoms: Weakness, increased sweating, lower abdominal pain, muscle cramps, irregular heartbeat.

What to Do: An overdose of bisacodyl is unlikely to be life-threatening. However, if someone takes a much larger dose than prescribed, seek medical assistance immediately.

DRUG INTERACTIONS
Be sure to tell your doctor about any other drugs you are taking, especially antacids. Do not take an antacid within 2 hours of taking this drug.

FOOD INTERACTIONS
Do not drink milk within 2 hours of taking this drug.

DISEASE INTERACTIONS
Caution is advised when taking bisacodyl. Consult your doctor if you have very severe constipation, severe pain in the stomach or lower abdomen, cramping, bloating, nausea, or unexplained rectal bleeding. Failure to produce a bowel movement or the presence of rectal bleeding may indicate a serious medical condition.

Bismuth Subsalicylate

Pepto-Bismol Caplets 262 mg
(PROCTER & GAMBLE)

Additional photographs

▶ Drug Class: Antidiarrheal/
antacid

▶ Available in: Tablets, oral
suspension

▶ Available OTC? Yes

▶ As Generic? Yes

Side Effects

SERIOUS
Ringing in the ears. Call
your doctor immediately.

COMMON
Black stools, darkening of
the tongue.

LESS COMMON
Nausea, vomiting (with
high doses), abdominal
pain, increased sweating,
muscle weakness, hear-
ing loss, thirst, confusion,
dizziness, vision prob-
lems, trouble breathing.
Discontinue the medicine
and call your physician
right away.

PRINCIPAL USES
To treat heartburn, acid
indigestion, diarrhea, and
duodenal ulcers, and to help
prevent traveler's diarrhea.

HOW THE DRUG WORKS
Bismuth subsalicylate stimulates the passage of fluid
and electrolytes across the
wall of the intestinal tract,
and binds or neutralizes the
toxins of some bacteria, rendering them nontoxic. It
decreases intestinal inflammation and increases the
activity of intestinal muscles
and lining.

DOSAGE
Adults— For acid indiges-
tion or mild diarrhea: 2
tablets or 2 tablespoons of
liquid every 30 to 60 minutes, to a maximum of 16
doses daily of the regular-
strength drug for no more
than 2 days. Children ages
9 to 12— 1 tablet or 1 tablespoon every 30 to 60 min-
utes, to a maximum of 8
doses daily of the regular-
strength drug for no more
than 2 days. Children ages
6 to 9— 2 teaspoons every
30 to 60 minutes, to a maximum of 16 doses daily of
the regular-strength drug
for no more than 2 days.
Children under age 3—
Consult your pediatrician.
Tablets are not recom-
mended for children under
the age of 9.

ONSET OF EFFECT
Within 30 to 60 minutes.

DURATION OF ACTION
Unknown.

DIETARY ADVICE
A mild diet is recommended
when recovering from diarrhea. Bananas, rice, applesauce, and plain toast are
good choices. Be sure to
get plenty of fluids.

STORAGE
Store in a tightly sealed container away from heat and
direct light. Keep liquid
forms of bismuth subsalicylate refrigerated, but do not
allow the medicine to
freeze.

IF YOU MISS A DOSE
Take it as soon as you
remember. If it is near the
time for the next dose, skip
the missed dose and
resume your regular dosage
schedule. Do not double the
next dose.

STOPPING THE DRUG
Take it as prescribed for the
full treatment period. However, you may stop taking
the drug if you are feeling
better before the scheduled
end of the therapy.

PROLONGED USE
Prolonged use of this medicine may cause constipation.
Consult your physician if
relief is not achieved within
two days.

PRECAUTIONS
Over 60: Adverse reactions
may be more likely and
more severe in older
patients.

**Driving and Hazardous
Work:** Do not drive or
engage in hazardous work
until you determine how
this medicine affects you.

Alcohol: Alcohol intake
should be limited.

Pregnancy: Regular use of
this medicine late in pregnancy may harm the fetus
or cause delivery problems.
Consult your doctor about
taking it if you are pregnant
or plan to become pregnant.

Breast Feeding: Bismuth
subsalicylate passes into
breast milk; avoid or discontinue use while nursing.

Infants and Children:
Consult your doctor before
giving this medicine to a
child or teenager who has
or is recovering from
chicken pox or flu.

Special Concerns: Do not
take bismuth subsalicylate if
you are allergic to aspirin or
another salicylate, an anticoagulant, or a medicine for
diabetes or gout. Do not
swallow tablets whole. They
should be crushed, chewed,
or allowed to dissolve in the
mouth.

OVERDOSE
Symptoms: Seizures, confusion, rapid or deep breathing, hearing loss or ringing
or buzzing in the ears,
severe excitability or nervousness, severe drowsi-
ness, loss of consciousness.

What to Do: Call your
doctor, emergency medical
services (EMS), or the
nearest poison control center immediately.

DRUG INTERACTIONS
Consult your doctor for specific advice if you are taking
anticoagulants, aspirin and
other salicylates, oral diabetes medicine, heparin, probenecid, thrombolytic
agents, oral tetracycline,
or sulfinpyrazone.

FOOD INTERACTIONS
No known food interactions.

DISEASE INTERACTIONS
Caution is advised when
using bismuth subsalicylate.
Before taking this drug, tell
your doctor if you have a
history of allergies, diabetes, kidney disease, dehydration, stomach ulcers,
dysentery, gout, or a bleeding problem.

Bisoprolol Fumarate

BRAND NAME
Zebeta

Zebeta 5 mg
(LEDERLE)

▶ Drug Class: Beta-blocker

▶ Available in: Tablets

▶ Available OTC? No

▶ As Generic? Yes

Side Effects

SERIOUS
Shortness of breath, wheezing; irregular or slow heartbeat (50 beats per minute or less); pain or feelings of tightness or pressure in the chest; swelling of the ankles, feet, and lower legs; mental depression. If you experience such symptoms, stop taking bisoprolol and call your doctor immediately.

COMMON
Dizziness or lightheadedness, especially when rising suddenly to a standing position; rapid heartbeat or palpitations; decreased sexual ability; unusual fatigue, weakness, or drowsiness; insomnia.

LESS COMMON
Anxiety, irritability, nervousness; constipation; diarrhea; dry, sore eyes; itching; nausea or vomiting; nightmares or intensely vivid dreams; numbness, tingling, or other unusual sensations in the fingers, toes, or scalp.

PRINCIPAL USES
To control hypertension (high blood pressure).

HOW THE DRUG WORKS
Bisoprolol slows the rate and force of contraction of the heart by blocking certain nerve impulses, thus reducing blood pressure.

DOSAGE
Starting dose is 5 mg once a day, or 2.5 mg once a day for those with kidney or liver problems. If necessary, it may be increased gradually to 20 mg once a day. Maximum dose is 20 mg per day.

ONSET OF EFFECT
Within 1 to 4 hours.

DURATION OF ACTION
24 hours.

DIETARY ADVICE
Take this drug at mealtime or immediately afterward.

STORAGE
Store in a tightly sealed container away from heat and direct light.

IF YOU MISS A DOSE
If you miss a dose, take it as soon as you remember unless it is almost time for your next dose. In that case, skip the missed dose and return to your regular schedule. Do not double the next dose.

STOPPING THE DRUG
Do not stop taking this drug without consulting your doctor. It may be necessary to reduce the dosage gradually to prevent adverse effects.

PROLONGED USE
Ask your doctor about the need for medical examinations or laboratory studies of your heart, blood pressure, kidney function, and blood sugar. Monitor your blood pressure often.

PRECAUTIONS
Over 60: Adverse reactions and side effects may be more common in older persons.

Driving and Hazardous Work: Determine how bisoprolol affects you before driving or engaging in any hazardous activities.

Alcohol: Drink in careful moderation if at all. Alcohol may interact with the drug and cause a dangerous drop in blood pressure.

Pregnancy: Be sure to notify your doctor promptly if you are pregnant or plan to become pregnant. Use bisoprolol during pregnancy only if the expected benefits outweigh the possible risks.

Breast Feeding: Bisoprolol passes into breast milk. Do not use it while you are breast feeding.

Infants and Children: Your pediatrician must determine the correct dose for a child.

Special Concerns: Prior to any dental or medical procedure or test, be sure to tell the doctor or dentist that you are taking bisoprolol. This drug may mask exercise-induced chest pain (angina). Ask your doctor for advice on a safe exercise program. Dress warmly in cold weather.

OVERDOSE
Symptoms: Asthmalike attacks (wheezing, breathlessness), very slow pulse, extreme shortness of breath associated with congestive heart failure.

What to Do: Call your doctor, emergency medical services (EMS), or the nearest poison control center immediately.

DRUG INTERACTIONS
Consult your doctor if you are taking any other blood pressure drug or beta-blocker. Be sure to check with your doctor before taking any over-the-counter medication, especially diet aids or cold preparations, as these may contain ingredients that can interact adversely with bisoprolol.

FOOD INTERACTIONS
None are expected, unless you are allergic to certain foods, as this medicine may cause allergic reactions to be more severe.

DISEASE INTERACTIONS
Bisoprolol should be used with caution in people with diabetes, especially insulin-dependent diabetes, since the drug may mask symptoms of hypoglycemia. Consult your doctor if you have a medical history of heart disease, asthma, blood vessel (vascular) disease, or thyroid disease. Diabetic patients must monitor their blood glucose (sugar) levels closely.

Bisoprolol Fumarate/Hydrochlorothiazide

BRAND NAME
Ziac

▶ Drug Class: Beta-blocker/ thiazide diuretic

▶ Available in: Tablets

▶ Available OTC? No

▶ As Generic? Yes

Side Effects

SERIOUS
Slow heartbeat, difficulty breathing, mental depression, cold hands and feet, swelling of ankles, feet, or lower legs. Call your doctor immediately.

COMMON
Dizziness or lightheadedness, decreased sexual ability, drowsiness, insomnia, fatigue, diarrhea.

LESS COMMON
Anxiety, loss of appetite, upset stomach, nervousness or excitability, constipation, numbness and tingling in the fingers and toes, stuffy nose.

PRINCIPAL USES
To control hypertension (high blood pressure).

HOW THE DRUG WORKS
Bisoprolol, a beta-blocker, blocks certain nerve impulses to various parts of the body, which accounts for its many effects. For example, it reduces the rate and force of the heart's contractions (which helps to lower blood pressure), decreases the heart's oxygen requirement (which helps prevent angina) and helps stabilize heart rhythm. Hydrochlorothiazide (HCTZ), a diuretic, increases the excretion of salt and water in the urine. By reducing the overall amount of fluid in the body, diuretics reduce pressure within the blood vessels.

DOSAGE
Tablets contain 6.25 mg HCTZ and 2.5, 5, or 10 mg bisoprolol. Therapy is initiated with the lowest dose and may be increased at 1 week intervals to 2 tablets with 10 mg bisoprolol once a day.

ONSET OF EFFECT
Within 1 to 4 hours.

DURATION OF ACTION
Up to 24 hours.

DIETARY ADVICE
No special restrictions.

STORAGE
Store in a tightly sealed container away from heat, moisture, and direct light.

IF YOU MISS A DOSE
If you miss a dose on one day, resume your regular dosage schedule the next day. Do not double the next dose.

STOPPING THE DRUG
The decision to stop taking the drug should be made in consultation with your physician. Do not stop taking this drug abruptly; your doctor will gradually decrease your dose before stopping completely.

PROLONGED USE
Bisoprolol/hydrochlorothiazide can control high blood pressure, but cannot cure it. Lifelong therapy may be necessary. See your doctor regularly for tests and examinations if you must take this drug for a prolonged period of time.

PRECAUTIONS
Over 60: Adverse reactions, especially dizziness, lightheadedness, and reduced tolerance to cold, may be more likely and more severe in older patients.

Driving and Hazardous Work: Do not drive or engage in hazardous work until you determine how the medicine affects you.

Alcohol: Drink in careful moderation if at all. Alcohol may interact with the bisoprolol component and cause a dangerous drop in blood pressure.

Pregnancy: Beta-blockers and thiazide diuretics may cause problems during pregnancy. Before taking this medication, tell your doctor if you are pregnant or plan to become pregnant.

Breast Feeding: This drug passes into breast milk; caution is advised. Consult your doctor for specific advice.

Infants and Children: Adequate studies have not been done on the use of this drug in children. No special problems are expected. Consult your pediatrician for advice.

Special Concerns: In addition to taking this medicine, follow your doctor's instructions on weight control and diet for reduction of blood pressure.

OVERDOSE
Symptoms: Slow heartbeat, severe dizziness or fainting, difficulty breathing, bluish-colored fingernails or palms of hands, seizures.

What to Do: Call your doctor, emergency medical services (EMS), or the nearest poison control center immediately.

DRUG INTERACTIONS
Do not take with other beta-blockers. Consult your doctor for specific advice if you are taking any other antihypertensive medications, oral diabetes medications, insulin, digitalis drugs, cholestyramine, colestipol, clonidine, lithium, nonsteroidal anti-inflammatory drugs, MAO inhibitors, rifampin, narcotic analgesics, or skeletal muscle relaxants.

FOOD INTERACTIONS
Avoid foods high in sodium.

DISEASE INTERACTIONS
Do not use if you have a history of bronchospasm. Consult your doctor if you have any of the following: bronchial asthma, emphysema, slow heartbeat, heart or blood vessel disease, diabetes mellitus, congestive heart failure, gout, kidney disease, liver disease, depression, parathyroid disease, or an overactive thyroid (hyperthyroidism).

Bitolterol Mesylate

BRAND NAME
Tornalate

▶ Drug Class: Bronchodilator/ sympathomimetic

▶ Available in: Aerosol inhaler

▶ Available OTC? No

▶ As Generic? No

Side Effects

SERIOUS
This drug may become ineffective if used too often, resulting in more-severe breathing difficulty that does not improve. Signs include persistent wheezing, coughing, or shortness of breath; confusion; bluish color to lips or fingernails; inability to speak. Other side effects include chest pain or heaviness; irregular, racing, fluttering, or pounding heartbeat; lightheadedness; fainting; severe weakness; severe headache.

COMMON
Changes in blood pressure causing headache, blurred vision, weakness.

LESS COMMON
Nervousness, throat irritation, nausea.

PRINCIPAL USES
Bitolterol is used to dilate air passages in the lungs that have become narrowed as a result of disease or inflammation. It is used in the treatment of asthma and chronic obstructive pulmonary disease (COPD).

HOW THE DRUG WORKS
Bitolterol widens constricted airways in the lungs by relaxing the smooth muscles that surround the bronchial passages.

DOSAGE
To treat bronchial asthma and bronchospasm; use it when needed to relieve breathing difficulty: 1 or 2 inhalations at an interval of 1 to 3 minutes, with a third inhalation 2 to 3 minutes later if needed. To prevent bronchospasm: Usually 2 inhalations every 8 hours, with a maximum dose of 2 inhalations every 4 hours or 3 inhalations every 6 hours; actual dosage and administration schedule must be determined by a doctor for each patient. Specific written directions from your doctor should be followed carefully. Rinse your mouth after each dose. Rinse and dry inhaler after each use.

ONSET OF EFFECT
Within 5 minutes.

DURATION OF ACTION
From 5 to 8 hours.

DIETARY ADVICE
Excessive intake of coffee or other caffeine-containing beverages should be avoided.

STORAGE
Store in a tightly sealed container away from heat and direct light.

IF YOU MISS A DOSE
Skip the missed dose and resume your regular dosage schedule. Do not double the next dose.

STOPPING THE DRUG
It may not be necessary to finish the recommended course of therapy. Consult your doctor.

PROLONGED USE
Therapy may require months or years. Excessive use may result in temporary loss of effectiveness.

PRECAUTIONS
Over 60: Adverse reactions may be more likely and more severe in older patients.

Driving and Hazardous Work: Be cautious about driving or doing hazardous work until you determine if excessive nervousness or dizziness occurs.

Alcohol: No special precautions are necessary.

Pregnancy: Adequate studies have not been done; the benefits must be weighed against potential risks. Consult your doctor for specific advice.

Breast Feeding: Bitolterol can pass into breast milk; breast feeding should be avoided while taking bitolterol.

Infants and Children: Safety and effectiveness of bitolterol for children under the age of 12 have not been established.

Special Concerns: Call your doctor if you cannot breathe properly 1 hour after using bitolterol or if your breathing problem worsens. Do not let the spray from the inhaler get in your eyes. Discontinue use and contact your doctor if you notice an unusual smell or taste when using this product. Use of this medicine is a disqualification for piloting an aircraft.

OVERDOSE
Symptoms: Tremor, nausea, vomiting, rapid or irregular pulse.

What to Do: Call your doctor immediately.

DRUG INTERACTIONS
Use of MAO inhibitors may cause an excessive increase in blood pressure and heart stimulation. If you are also using a steroid inhaler, take bitolterol first and then wait about 15 minutes before using the steroid inhaler. This allows bitolterol to open air passages, increasing the effectiveness of the steroid.

FOOD INTERACTIONS
Excessive intake of coffee or other caffeine-containing beverages should be avoided.

DISEASE INTERACTIONS
Before taking bitolterol, consult your doctor if you have a circulatory disorder, heart disease, diabetes mellitus, epilepsy, or an overactive thyroid.

Brimonidine Tartrate

BRAND NAME
Alphagan

▶ Drug Class: Antiglaucoma agent

▶ Available in: Ophthalmic solution

▶ Available OTC? No

▶ As Generic? No

Side Effects

SERIOUS
Fainting. Call your doctor immediately.

COMMON
Burning or stinging of the eyes, fatigue, dry mouth, eye discomfort, drowsiness.

LESS COMMON
Excess tear production, redness of eyes or inner lining of the eyelids, headache, swelling of eye or eyelid, eye ache or pain, blurring or other changes in vision, dizziness, mental depression, insomnia, muscle pain or weakness, nausea, increased blood pressure, vomiting, anxiety, pounding heartbeat, change in taste, crusting in corner of eye or on eyelid, discoloration of eyeball, paleness of inner lining of eyelid, dry eyes, sensitivity of eyes to light.

PRINCIPAL USES
To treat glaucoma.

HOW THE DRUG WORKS
Glaucoma, a sight-threatening disorder, occurs when aqueous humor (fluid inside the eye) cannot drain properly, causing increased pressure within the eyeball (intraocular pressure). Increased eye pressure can damage the optic nerve and lead to a gradually progressive loss of vision. Brimonidine decreases the production of aqueous humor and promotes its outflow, thereby reducing intraocular pressure.

DOSAGE
1 drop of brimonidine in each eye 3 times a day at 8-hour intervals.

ONSET OF EFFECT
Within 60 minutes.

DURATION OF ACTION
8 hours or more.

DIETARY ADVICE
No special restrictions.

STORAGE
Store in a tightly sealed container away from heat, moisture, and direct light. Do not allow the medicine to freeze.

IF YOU MISS A DOSE
Apply it as soon as you remember. If it is near the time for the next dose, skip the missed dose and resume your regular dosage schedule. Do not double the next dose.

STOPPING THE DRUG
The decision to stop using the drug should be made by your doctor.

PROLONGED USE
You should see your doctor regularly for tests and examinations as part of glaucoma follow-up if you take this drug for a prolonged period.

PRECAUTIONS
Over 60: Adverse reactions may be more likely and more severe in older patients.

Driving and Hazardous Work: Do not drive or engage in hazardous work until you determine how the drug affects your vision.

Alcohol: Use alcohol with caution.

Pregnancy: In animal studies, brimonidine caused impaired fetal circulation. Human studies have not been done. Before you take brimonidine, tell your doctor if you are pregnant or are planning to become pregnant.

Breast Feeding: Brimonidine may pass into breast milk; caution is advised. Consult your doctor for specific advice.

Infants and Children: The safety and effectiveness of brimonidine in infants and children under two have not been established.

Special Concerns: To use the eye drops, first wash your hands. Tilt your head back. Gently apply pressure to the inside corner of the eyelid and with the index finger of the same hand, pull downward on the lower eyelid to make a space. Drop the medicine into this space and close your eye. Apply pressure for 1 or 2 minutes while keeping the eye closed without blinking. Then wash your hands again. Make sure the tip of the dropper does not touch your eye, finger, or any other surface. Bromonidine may make your eyes more sensitive to sunlight. If this occurs, wear sunglasses or avoid bright light as comfort dictates.

OVERDOSE
Symptoms: No specific ones have been reported.

What to Do: An overdose of brimonidine is unlikely to be life-threatening. However, if someone takes a much larger dose than prescribed or accidentally ingests the medicine, call your doctor, emergency medical services (EMS), or the nearest poison control center immediately.

DRUG INTERACTIONS
Consult your doctor for advice if you are taking MAO inhibitors, tricyclic antidepressants, central nervous system depressants, beta-blockers, antihypertensives, or digitalis drugs (such as digoxin).

FOOD INTERACTIONS
No known food interactions.

DISEASE INTERACTIONS
Caution is advised when taking brimonidine. Consult your doctor if you have cardiovascular disease, kidney disease, liver disease, depression, cerebral or coronary insufficiency, Raynaud's phenomenon, orthostatic hypotension, or thromboangiitis obliterans.

Brinzolamide

▸ Drug Class: Antiglaucoma agent; carbonic anhydrase inhibitor

▸ Available in: Ophthalmic suspension

▸ Available OTC? No

▸ As Generic? No

Side Effects

SERIOUS
Severe generalized reactions involving the skin, liver, and blood cells. Discontinue using the medication and call your doctor immediately if signs of serious reaction occur.

COMMON
Burning, stinging, or discomfort in the eye or blurred vision when drug is administered; bitter taste in mouth.

LESS COMMON
Eye pain, severe or continued tearing, nausea.

PRINCIPAL USES
To treat glaucoma or ocular hypertension (a glaucoma-like condition).

HOW THE DRUG WORKS
Glaucoma and ocular hypertension, both sight-threatening disorders, occur when poor drainage of aqueous humor (the fluid inside the front part of the eye) increases the pressure within the eyeball (known as intraocular pressure). Increased intraocular pressure can damage the optic nerve and lead to a gradual loss of vision. By inhibiting the activity of the enzyme carbonic anhydrase, brinzolamide decreases the production of aqueous humor, and reduces intraocular pressure.

DOSAGE
Adults and teenagers:
1 drop in affected eye(s) 3 times per day.

ONSET OF EFFECT
Unknown.

DURATION OF ACTION
Unknown.

DIETARY ADVICE
No special restrictions.

STORAGE
Store in a tightly sealed container away from heat, moisture, and direct light. Do not refrigerate or allow it to freeze.

IF YOU MISS A DOSE
Apply it as soon as you remember. If it is near the time for the next dose, skip the missed dose and resume your regular dosage schedule. Do not double the next dose.

STOPPING THE DRUG
The decision to stop using the drug should be made by your doctor.

PROLONGED USE
Schedule regular eye examinations with your doctor to be sure the drug is controlling the glaucoma or ocular hypertension.

PRECAUTIONS
Over 60: No special problems are expected.

Driving and Hazardous Work: Do not drive or engage in hazardous work until you determine how the medicine affects your vision.

Alcohol: No special precautions are necessary.

Pregnancy: One animal study found that very high doses of this drug caused birth defects. Human studies have not been done. Before using this medicine, tell your doctor if you are pregnant or plan to become pregnant.

Breast Feeding: It is not known whether brinzolamide passes into breast milk; caution is advised. Consult your doctor for specific advice about whether to use a different medicine or to stop breast feeding.

Infants and Children: Safety and dosage guidelines for children have not been established. Brinzolamide should be given to infants and children only under close medical supervision.

Special Concerns: To use the eye drops, first wash your hands. Tilt your head back. Gently apply pressure to the inside corner of the eyelid and with the index finger of the same hand, pull downward on the lower eyelid to make a space. Drop the medicine into this space and close your eye. Apply pressure for 1 or 2 minutes while keeping the eye closed without blinking. Then wash your hands again. Make sure that the tip of the dropper does not touch your eye, finger, or any other surface.

OVERDOSE
Symptoms: No specific ones have been reported.

What to Do: An overdose of brinzolamide is unlikely to be life-threatening. If a large volume enters the eye, flush with water. If someone accidentally ingests the medicine, call your doctor, emergency medical services (EMS), or the nearest poison control center.

DRUG INTERACTIONS
Wait 10 minutes before administering any other eye medicine. Brinzolamide should not be used in conjunction with oral carbonic anhydrase inhibitors. People allergic to sulfa-type drugs should not use brinzolamide.

FOOD INTERACTIONS
No known food interactions.

DISEASE INTERACTIONS
Do not use if you have severe kidney impairment. Use with caution if you have liver disease.

Bromocriptine Mesylate

Parlodel 2.5 mg
(**NOVARTIS**)

▶ Drug Class: Ergot alkaloid

▶ Available in: Tablets, capsules

▶ Available OTC? No

▶ As Generic? Yes

Side Effects

SERIOUS
Seizures, chest pain, severe nausea and vomiting, headache and blurred vision caused by high blood pressure, wet cough and shortness of breath caused by fluid in the lungs. Consult your doctor immediately.

COMMON
Dizziness, weakness, and fainting caused by low blood pressure; nasal congestion and headache; abdominal cramping or pain.

LESS COMMON
Confusion, fatigue, nervousness, depression, ringing in the ears, dry mouth, blurred vision, hallucinations, hair loss, anemia, impotence, constipation, or diarrhea.

PRINCIPAL USES
To treat hyperprolactinemia, a disorder caused by overproduction of the hormone prolactin. Hyperprolactinemia may occur by itself or in association with a tumor (prolactinoma) in the pituitary gland. The disorder causes abnormal production and persistent leakage of breast milk (in either men or women), infertility and cessation of menstrual periods in women, and testicular shrinkage and impotence in men. In some cases bromocriptine may be used to treat acromegaly (overproduction of growth hormone, causing enlargement of the hands, feet, jawbone, and internal organs). It is also used to treat Parkinson's disease.

HOW THE DRUG WORKS
Bromocriptine blocks the pituitary from releasing the hormone prolactin, which is involved in the regulation of the menstrual cycle, reproduction, and milk production. Similarly, it blocks the pituitary from releasing growth hormone. The drug activates certain chemical receptor sites in brain cells to reduce Parkinson's symptoms.

DOSAGE
For hyperprolactinemia: Starting with 1.25 to 2.5 mg a day, the dose is increased by 1.25 mg a day at 3- to 7-day intervals until the desired therapeutic effect is achieved. Maintenance dose is 1.25 to 15 mg in divided doses, 2 or 3 times a day. For acromegaly: 1.25 to 30 mg a day in divided doses, 2 or 3 times a day. For Parkinson's disease: Starting with 1.25 to 2.5 mg a day, the dose is increased by 2.5 mg a day at 14- to 28-day intervals, to a maximum of 100 mg a day in divided doses, 2 or 3 times a day.

ONSET OF EFFECT
From 30 to 90 minutes. Full effects become apparent after a few weeks of therapy.

DURATION OF ACTION
For hyperprolactinemia and acromegaly: 8 hours. For Parkinson's disease: 12 to 18 hours.

DIETARY ADVICE
For best results, bromocriptine should be taken with food or milk.

STORAGE
Store in a dry place away from heat and direct light. Discard the medicine if it becomes outdated.

IF YOU MISS A DOSE
If you miss a dose, take it if you remember within 2 hours. After that, wait for the next dose and return to your regular schedule. Do not double the next dose.

STOPPING THE DRUG
Complete the prescribed dose even though symptoms diminish or disappear. Consult your doctor before discontinuing this drug.

PROLONGED USE
Prolonged use at doses greater than 50 mg per day may cause uncontrolled movements of face, mouth, tongue, arms, or legs (a condition known as tardive dyskinesia). Consult your doctor if such symptoms occur.

PRECAUTIONS
Over 60: Adverse reactions and side effects may be more common in older persons.

Driving and Hazardous Work: Do not drive or engage in hazardous work until you determine how bromocriptine affects you.

Alcohol: Bromocriptine reduces the body's tolerance to alcohol.

Pregnancy: If you are pregnant or plan to become pregnant, tell your doctor before taking this drug.

Breast Feeding: Bromocriptine should not be used when nursing because it reduces breast milk production.

Infants and Children: Not recommended for anyone under the age of 15.

OVERDOSE
Symptoms: Severe dizziness and weakness, nausea, and vomiting.

What to Do: Call your doctor immediately.

DRUG INTERACTIONS
Consult your doctor for specific advice if you are taking any of the following drugs that may interact with bromocriptine: blood pressure medication, an oral contraceptive, erythromycin, a phenothiazine, an MAO inhibitor, progestin, levodopa, or a rauwolfia alkaloid.

FOOD INTERACTIONS
None are expected.

DISEASE INTERACTIONS
Consult your doctor if you have any of the following: diabetes, epilepsy, heart disease, lung disease, a peptic ulcer, or high blood pressure. Also tell your doctor if you plan to have surgery, including dental surgery, within 2 months.

Brompheniramine Maleate

BRAND NAMES
Bromphen, Dimetane,
Nasahist B

- Drug Class: Antihistamine

- Available in: Capsules,
  tablets, extended-release
  tablets, elixir, injection

- Available OTC? Yes

- As Generic? Yes

Side Effects

SERIOUS
Bleeding problems;
small, red pinpoints on
the skin; fever; extreme
fatigue; bleeding ulcers
in the rectum, mouth,
and vagina; reduced
white blood cell count
(rare).

COMMON
Drowsiness; unusual
excitability; dry mouth,
nose, or throat. Symp-
toms of drowsiness tend
to subside after a few
days' use as your body
adjusts to the drug.

LESS COMMON
Vision changes, loss of
appetite, dizziness,
painful or difficult urination, less tolerance for
contact lenses.

PRINCIPAL USES
To prevent or relieve symptoms of hay fever, other
allergies, itching skin, or
hives.

HOW THE DRUG WORKS
Brompheniramine blocks
the effects of histamine, a
substance in the body that
causes swelling, itching,
sneezing, watery eyes,
hives, and other symptoms
of allergic reaction.

DOSAGE
Capsules, tablets, elixir—
Adults and teenagers: 4 mg
every 4 to 6 hours. Children
ages 6 to 12: 2 mg every
4 to 6 hours. Children ages
2 to 6: 1 mg every 4 to 6
hours. Extended-release
tablets— Adults: 8 mg
every 8 to 12 hours, or
12 mg every 12 hours.
Children age 6 and older:
8 or 12 mg every 12 hours.
Injection— Adults and
teenagers: 10 mg under the
skin or into a vein or muscle every 8 to 12 hours.
Children younger than age
12: 0.125 mg per 2.2 lbs (1
kg) of body weight, under
the skin or into a vein or
muscle 3 or 4 times a day.

ONSET OF EFFECT
15 to 60 minutes.

DURATION OF ACTION
3 to 6 hours for regular
form; 8 to 12 for extended-
release tablets.

DIETARY ADVICE
Take it with food or milk to
minimize stomach upset.

STORAGE
Store in a tightly sealed container away from heat and
direct light.

IF YOU MISS A DOSE
Take it as soon as you
remember. If it is near the
time for the next dose, skip
the missed dose and
resume your regular dosage

schedule. Do not double the
next dose.

STOPPING THE DRUG
You should take it as prescribed for the full treatment period, but you may
stop if you feel better before
the scheduled end of therapy. It may be taken as
needed.

PROLONGED USE
No special concerns.

PRECAUTIONS
Over 60: Older persons
are more sensitive to
antihistamine side effects,
particularly confusion,
dizziness, drowsiness,
restlessness, irritability,
nightmares, and dry
mouth, nose, and throat.

**Driving and Hazardous
Work:** Brompheniramine
can make you feel tired and
lessen your concentration.
Do not drive or engage in
hazardous work until you
determine how the drug
affects you.

Alcohol: Alcohol increases
the likelihood and the
severity of side effects like
drowsiness and confusion.

Pregnancy: Studies in
animals suggest that
brompheniramine has no
adverse effect on fetal
development, but human
studies have not been done.
Before taking this drug, tell
your doctor if you are pregnant or are planning to
become pregnant.

Breast Feeding:
Brompheniramine passes
into breast milk; avoid or
discontinue use while breast
feeding.

Infants and Children:
Brompheniramine should
be given to children age 6
and under only as directed
by a doctor.

Special Concerns: Do not
break, crush, or chew the
capsules or the extended-
release tablets.

OVERDOSE
Symptoms: Seizures, loss
of consciousness, hallucinations, severe drowsiness.

What to Do: The patient
should be made to vomit
immediately, using ipecac
syrup. If he or she is unconscious, the patient should
be taken to a hospital emergency room immediately.

DRUG INTERACTIONS
MAO inhibitors can
increase the sedative effects
of brompheniramine. Cen-
tral nervous system depressants such as alcohol,
sedatives, or narcotics
should be taken only if
approved by a doctor.

FOOD INTERACTIONS
No known food interactions.

DISEASE INTERACTIONS
Before taking brompheni-
ramine, consult your doctor
if you wear contact lenses
or you have glaucoma,
prostate enlargement, difficulty with urination, or dryness of the mouth or eyes.

BRAND NAMES
Pulmicort Turbuhaler,
Rhinocort Aqua,
Rhinocort Turbuhaler

▶ Drug Class: Respiratory corticosteroid

▶ Available in: Nasal inhalant, oral inhalation, inhalation powder

▶ Available OTC? No

▶ As Generic? No

Side Effects

SERIOUS
No serious side effects are associated with budesonide.

COMMON
Nasal inhalant: Nosebleeds or bloody nasal secretions, burning or irritation of the nasal passages, sore throat. Oral inhalation: Sore throat, white patches in mouth or throat, hoarseness.

LESS COMMON
Eye pain, watering eyes, gradual decrease of vision, stomach pain and digestive disturbances.

PRINCIPAL USES
To treat the symptoms of allergic rhinitis (seasonal and perennial allergies such as hay fever) and to prevent recurrence of nasal polyps after surgical removal.

HOW THE DRUG WORKS
Respiratory corticosteroids such as budesonide primarily reduce or prevent inflammation of the lining of the airways, reduce the allergic response to inhaled allergens, and inhibit the secretion of mucus within the airways.

DOSAGE
Nasal inhalant: 2 sprays (32 micrograms [mcg] each) in each nostril in the morning and evening or 4 sprays in each nostril in the morning. Oral inhalation: 200 to 800 mcg (1 to 4 inhalations), 2 times a day. Highest dose for children is 400 mcg (2 inhalations), 2 times a day. The dose may be increased or decreased as determined by your doctor, based on the patient's response.

ONSET OF EFFECT
Usually within several days; it may take 3 weeks for the full effect to occur.

DURATION OF ACTION
Up to 12 hours.

DIETARY ADVICE
Budesonide can be taken without regard to diet.

STORAGE
Store in a dry place away from heat and light, out of the reach of children.

IF YOU MISS A DOSE
Take the missed dose if you remember within an hour. Otherwise, skip the missed dose and return to your regular schedule. Do not double the next dose.

STOPPING THE DRUG
Nasal inhalant: No problems expected. Oral inhalation: Do not discontinue without consulting your doctor. Gradual reduction in dosage may be required.

PROLONGED USE
Consult with your doctor about the need for periodic physical examinations and laboratory tests.

PRECAUTIONS
Over 60: No special problems are expected.

Driving and Hazardous Work: Budesonide should not affect your ability to perform such tasks safely.

Alcohol: No special precautions are necessary.

Pregnancy: Nasal or inhaled steroids have not been reported to cause birth defects if taken during pregnancy. Before using such drugs, tell your doctor if you are pregnant or plan to become pregnant.

Breast Feeding: This drug may pass into breast milk. Consult your doctor about use of either form during breast feeding.

Infants and Children: Nasal form: Should be used only under close medical supervision. Oral form: Large doses may make children more susceptible to infectious disease. Long-term use may affect the adrenal glands.

Special Concerns: Inhaled steroids will not help an asthma attack in progress. Inhaled steroids can lower resistance to yeast infections of the mouth, throat, or voice box. To prevent yeast infections, gargle or rinse your mouth with water after each use;

do not swallow the water. Know how to use the inhalant properly; read and follow the directions that come with the device. Before you have surgery, tell the doctor or dentist that you are using a steroid.

OVERDOSE
Symptoms: No specific symptoms.

What to Do: Call your doctor, emergency medical services (EMS), or the nearest poison control center if you have any reason to suspect an overdose.

DRUG INTERACTIONS
Consult your doctor for specific advice if you are taking systemic corticosteroids, other inhaled corticosteroids, or any medications that suppress the immune system.

FOOD INTERACTIONS
No known food interactions.

DISEASE INTERACTIONS
Consult your doctor if you have any other medical problem, particularly glaucoma, a herpes infection of the eye, a history of tuberculosis, liver disease, an underactive thyroid, or osteoporosis.

Bumetanide

Generic 0.5 mg
(ZENITH)

▶ Drug Class: Loop diuretic

▶ Available in: Tablets, injection

▶ Available OTC? No

▶ As Generic? Yes

Side Effects

SERIOUS
Rapid or irregular heartbeat, dry mouth, increased thirst, mood or mental changes, muscle cramps or pain, nausea or vomiting, unusual fatigue, black and tarry stools, buzzing or ringing in ears, hearing loss, skin rash. Call your doctor immediately.

COMMON
Muscle cramps. Fluid depletion can cause dizziness when the patient rises from a sitting or lying position, as well as thirst and constipation. Minor potassium depletion can cause mild weakness, and rapid or irregular heartbeat.

LESS COMMON
Gout, increased blood sugar (glucose) levels, hearing loss.

PRINCIPAL USES
To reduce the accumulation of fluid (containing salts and water) that leads to edema (swelling) and breathlessness in patients with heart disease, cirrhosis of the liver, and kidney disease. Bumetanide may also be used to help control high blood levels of potassium.

HOW THE DRUG WORKS
Loop diuretics work on a specific portion of the kidney (the loop of Henle) to increase the excretion of both water and sodium in the urine.

DOSAGE
0.5 to 6 mg per day, usually taken in the morning; may be increased to 2 to 3 doses a day, as needed.

ONSET OF EFFECT
This drug begins eliminating excess water within 1 to 2 hours.

DURATION OF ACTION
Up to 4 hours.

DIETARY ADVICE
Bumetanide can be taken with or after meals to reduce stomach irritation.

STORAGE
Store in a tightly sealed container away from heat and direct light.

IF YOU MISS A DOSE
If you miss a dose, take it as soon as you remember unless it is almost time for the next dose. In that case, skip the missed dose and return to your regular schedule. Do not double the next dose.

STOPPING THE DRUG
Take it as prescribed for the full treatment period, even if you begin to feel better before the scheduled end of therapy. The decision to stop taking the drug should be made by your doctor.

PROLONGED USE
Prolonged use of bumetanide requires regular examinations by your doctor, since it may lead to imbalances of sodium, potassium, magnesium, and body fluid.

PRECAUTIONS
Over 60: No special problems are expected.

Driving and Hazardous Work: No special precautions are necessary.

Alcohol: No special precautions are necessary.

Pregnancy: Adequate studies of using this drug during pregnancy have not been done. Before taking this drug, tell your doctor if you are pregnant or plan to become pregnant. If diuretic treatment is warranted, other drugs are preferred.

Breast Feeding: This drug may pass into breast milk. Consult your doctor about its use while nursing.

Infants and Children: This drug is not generally prescribed for children. Its safety and effectiveness for anyone under the age of 18 have not been established.

Special Concerns: You may have to take a potassium supplement or consume foods or fluids high in potassium while taking this drug. To prevent disruption of sleep, avoid taking this drug in the evening.

OVERDOSE
Symptoms: Severe fatigue, weakness, lethargy, confusion, muscle cramps, nausea, vomiting, weak and rapid pulse, loss of consciousness.

What to Do: Call your doctor, emergency medical services (EMS), or the nearest poison control center immediately.

DRUG INTERACTIONS
Consult your doctor about any other drugs you are taking, particularly antibiotics, other blood pressure medications (especially ACE inhibitors), analgesics (pain relievers), lithium, cortisone-related drugs, digitalis drugs, or any nonsteroidal anti-inflammatory drug (NSAID).

FOOD INTERACTIONS
No food interactions have been documented.

DISEASE INTERACTIONS
Caution is advised when taking bumetanide. Consult your doctor if you have any of the following: diabetes, gout, a hearing problem, or a recent heart attack.

Bupropion Hydrochloride

Wellbutrin 100 mg
(GLAXO WELLCOME)

▶ Drug Class: Antidepressant/
smoking deterrent

▶ Available in: Tablets,
extended-release tablets

▶ Available OTC? No

▶ As Generic? Yes

Side Effects

SERIOUS
When treating depression: Hallucinations, heartbeat irregularities, confusion, skin rash, insomnia, severe headache, excitement or agitation, seizures. Call your doctor immediately. Smoking cessation: None reported.

COMMON
When treating depression: Nausea or vomiting, constipation, unusual weight loss, dry mouth, loss of appetite, dizziness, increased sweating, trembling or shaking. Smoking cessation: Dry mouth, insomnia.

LESS COMMON
When treating depression: Fever or chills, concentration difficulties, drowsiness, fatigue, change in or blurred vision, unusual feeling of euphoria, hostility or anger. Smoking cessation: Mild rash, tremor.

PRINCIPAL USES
To relieve symptoms of major depression. Bupropion is also used as a nonnicotine aid to smoking cessation. It should be used as a part of a comprehensive smoking cessation program carried out under the supervision of your doctor.

HOW THE DRUG WORKS
While the exact mechanism of action of bupropion is not known, it appears to help balance the levels of brain chemicals that are thought to be linked to mood, emotions, and mental state. Unlike other smoking cessation medications, bupropion does not contain nicotine. It is believed that bupropion's effects on brain chemistry help to curb the desire for nicotine and enhance the patient's ability to abstain from smoking.

DOSAGE
Depression (Wellbutrin)— Adults: To start, 100 mg twice a day. Dosage may be increased to 450 mg a day. No more than 150 mg should be taken within 4 hours. Older adults: To start, 75 or 100 mg twice a day. Children: Dosages must be determined by your doctor. Smoking cessation (Zyban)— Adults: For the first 3 days of treatment, 150 mg a day. Dosage may then be increased to 150 mg, 2 times a day. The doses should be taken at least 8 hours apart. Do not take more than 300 mg per day. You should not stop smoking until you have been taking Zyban for 1 week. Treatment generally lasts 7 to 12 weeks.

ONSET OF EFFECT
1 to 3 weeks.

DURATION OF ACTION
Unknown.

DIETARY ADVICE
Bupropion can be taken with food to reduce stomach irritation. The tablet should be swallowed whole, because it has a bitter taste and can produce an unpleasant numbing sensation inside of the mouth.

STORAGE
Store in a tightly sealed container away from heat, moisture, and direct light.

IF YOU MISS A DOSE
Take it as soon as you remember, unless your next scheduled dose is within the next 4 hours (8 hours for smoking cessation). If so, do not take the missed dose. Take your next scheduled dose at the proper time and resume your regular dosage schedule. Do not double the next dose.

STOPPING THE DRUG
Depression: Take it as prescribed for the full treatment period, even if you begin to feel better before the scheduled end of therapy. Discontinuing the drug abruptly may produce unpleasant withdrawal symptoms. Dosage should be reduced gradually according to your doctor's instructions. The decision to stop taking the drug should be made in consultation with your doctor. Smoking cessation: If you have not made significant progress toward abstinence by the end of the seventh week of treatment, consult your doctor. Treatment should probably be discontinued. You do not need to gradually decrease the dose before stopping.

PROLONGED USE
Depression: The usual course of therapy lasts 6 months to 1 year; some patients benefit from additional therapy. Smoking cessation: Treatment generally lasts 7 to 12 weeks.

PRECAUTIONS
Over 60: Dosage may be decreased because of age-related decline in liver or kidney function.

Driving and Hazardous Work: Use caution until you determine how the medication affects you. Drowsiness or lightheadedness can occur.

Alcohol: Alcohol increases the risk of seizures. It is recommended to abstain from alcohol or to drink very little while taking bupropion. If you regularly drink a lot of alcohol and then suddenly stop, this may also increase your chance of having a seizure; gradual tapering of alcohol is recommended.

Pregnancy: Bupropion has not caused birth defects in animals. Adequate human studies have not been done. Bupropion is not recommended while you are pregnant. Before taking it, tell your doctor if you are pregnant or plan to become pregnant.

Breast Feeding: Bupropion passes into breast milk; avoid or discontinue using it while nursing.

Infants and Children: Adequate studies in children have not been done. Bupropion is not recommended for use by children under age 18. Antidepressants increase the risk of suicidal thinking and behavior (suicidality) in children with major depression and other psychiatric disorders. Discuss with your doctor this risk versus the benefits of using this drug. A child taking bupropion should be observed closely for wors-

Bupropion Hydrochloride (continued)

ening of symptoms, suicidality, or unusual changes in behavior at the onset of therapy and when making changes in dosage.

Special Concerns: This is a potentially dangerous drug, especially if taken in excess. Antidepressants should not be within easy reach of suicidal patients. To prevent insomnia, take the last dose several hours before bedtime. When taking bupropion for smoking cessation, it is advised to continue smoking through the first week of treatment. Set a target date to stop smoking no later than the second week of therapy. Continuing to smoke beyond the designated date reduces your chances of successfully quitting. You may use a nicotine transdermal patch (see Nicotine) while taking Zyban, but consult your doctor before initiating such therapy. The combination of nicotine and bupropion increases the risk of hypertension; blood pressure should be monitored regularly throughout treatment. Zyban should be regarded as but one part of a comprehensive treatment program that includes counseling, social support, and regular contact with your doctor. The goal of therapy with Zyban is complete abstinence from cigarettes. Do not chew, divide, or crush the tablets or extended-release tablets.

OVERDOSE

Symptoms: Hallucinations, seizures, rapid heartbeat, chest pain, breathing difficulty, loss of consciousness.

Few cases of overdose associated with treatment for smoking cessation have been reported. Some of the symptoms experienced include: vomiting, blurred vision, lightheadedness, confusion, lethargy, nausea, jitteriness, hallucinations, drowsiness, and seizures.

What to Do: Call your doctor, emergency medical services (EMS), or the nearest poison control center immediately.

DRUG INTERACTIONS

Bupropion should not be taken if you are taking other medicines containing bupropion or within 14 days of taking an MAO inhibitor. Consult your doctor for advice if you are taking loxapine, tricyclic antidepressants, phenothiazines, clozapine, molindone, fluoxetine, thioxanthenes, haloperidol, lithium, trazodone, maprotiline, levodopa, or theophylline.

FOOD INTERACTIONS

No known food interactions.

DISEASE INTERACTIONS

Bupropion should not be taken if you have a history of seizures, anorexia nervosa, or bulimia. Caution is advised when taking bupropion. Consult your doctor if you have any of the following: a tumor of the brain or spinal cord, heart disease, or head injury. Since the liver and kidneys work together to remove bupropion from the body, a lower dose may be prescribed for patients with impaired liver or kidney function.

Buspirone Hydrochloride

BRAND NAME
BuSpar

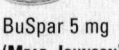

BuSpar 5 mg
(MEAD JOHNSON)

▶ Drug Class: Antianxiety drug

▶ Available in: Tablets

▶ Available OTC? No

▶ As Generic? Yes

Side Effects

SERIOUS
No serious side effects have been directly associated with the use of buspirone.

COMMON
Dizziness or lightheadedness, nausea, paradoxical increase in nervousness or excitability, restlessness, headache.

LESS COMMON
Blurred vision, impaired ability to concentrate, drowsiness, dry mouth, difficulty sleeping, muscle cramps or spasms, fatigue or weakness, ringing in the ears, dreams that are unusual, disturbing, or vivid.

PRINCIPAL USES
To treat anxiety.

HOW THE DRUG WORKS
Buspirone affects the activity of specific brain chemicals (dopamine and especially serotonin) that are profoundly linked to mood, emotions, and mental state. Unlike many other medications used to treat anxiety disorders, buspirone has no muscle relaxant or sedative effects, and does not appear to lead to physical dependence.

DOSAGE
To start, 5 mg, 3 times per day (for a total of 15 mg a day). Can be increased to 60 mg a day, taken in divided doses every 6 to 8 hours.

ONSET OF EFFECT
May take 1 to 2 weeks to attain the full therapeutic benefit of buspirone.

DURATION OF ACTION
8 hours or more.

DIETARY ADVICE
No special restrictions.

STORAGE
Store in a tightly sealed container away from heat, moisture, and direct light.

IF YOU MISS A DOSE
If you miss a dose, take it as soon as you remember. If it is near the time for your next dose, skip the missed dose and resume your regular dosage schedule. Do not double the next dose.

STOPPING THE DRUG
The decision to stop taking buspirone should be made in consultation with your physician.

PROLONGED USE
No known problems.

PRECAUTIONS
Over 60: Adverse side effects and reactions may be more common and more severe in older patients.

Driving and Hazardous Work: The use of buspirone may impair your ability to drive or perform hazardous tasks safely. The danger increases if you drink alcohol or take other medications that can affect alertness, such as antihistamines, painkillers, or mind-altering drugs.

Alcohol: Avoid alcohol while using this medication.

Pregnancy: No problems are expected, but adequate studies of buspirone use during pregnancy have not been done. Consult your doctor if you are pregnant or plan to become pregnant.

Breast Feeding: Buspirone can pass into breast milk. Avoid taking it if possible or refrain from breast feeding.

Infants and Children: The safety and effectiveness of buspirone have not been established for anyone under the age of 18.

Special Concerns: Before you undergo surgery requiring anesthesia, be sure to notify the surgeon that you take buspirone.

OVERDOSE
Symptoms: Severe drowsiness, dizziness, nausea and vomiting, constricted (pinpoint) pupils.

What to Do: Call your doctor, emergency medical services (EMS), or the nearest poison control center immediately.

DRUG INTERACTIONS
Other drugs may interact with buspirone. Consult your doctor for specific advice if you take any of the following: antihistamines, barbiturates, MAO inhibitors, muscle relaxants, narcotics, sedatives, or other tranquilizers.

FOOD INTERACTIONS
None expected.

DISEASE INTERACTIONS
Use of buspirone may cause complications in patients with liver or kidney disease, since these organs work together to remove the medication from the body.

Busulfan

BRAND NAME
Myleran

Myleran 2 mg
(GLAXO WELLCOME)

▶ Drug Class: Alkylating agent

▶ Available in: Tablets

▶ Available OTC? No

▶ As Generic? No

Side Effects

SERIOUS
Signs of unusual bleeding, including black, tarry, or bloody stools; blood in the urine; bright red, pinpointlike dots on the skin; unusual bruising; excessive gum bleeding; uncontrolled bleeding. Seizures are associated with higher doses. Consult your doctor at once.

COMMON
Increased pigmentation (darkening) of the skin; menstrual irregularities or absent periods.

LESS COMMON
Joint pain, shortness of breath, dizziness, sudden, unexpected loss of weight or appetite, lip or mouth sores, swelling in legs, ankles, and feet, nausea and vomiting, diarrhea, unusual fatigue or weakness.

PRINCIPAL USES
To treat certain forms of chronic leukemia (myeloid, myelocytic, and granulocytic leukemias). Busulfan slows the progress of these cancers, eases symptoms, and generally improves the condition of the patient, but it does not cure the disease. It is also used in conjunction with the transplanting of bone marrow to treat other forms of cancer.

HOW THE DRUG WORKS
Leukemia, in its many varieties, is a cancer marked by overproduction and abnormal formation of white blood cells, which are made in the bone marrow. Busulfan interferes with the growth and function of all cells, including the cells of the bone marrow. By interfering with bone marrow function, busulfan slows the production of the abnormal white blood cells.

DOSAGE
From 4 to 8 mg a day, as ordered by your doctor, until the desired response occurs.

ONSET OF EFFECT
Begins to take effect in 1 to 2 weeks.

DURATION OF ACTION
Up to 24 hours.

DIETARY ADVICE
Swallow tablet with liquid after a light meal. Avoid sweet or fatty foods. Do not drink fluids with meals. Drink extra fluids between meals.

STORAGE
Store in a tightly sealed container away from heat and direct light.

IF YOU MISS A DOSE
Take it as soon as you remember. If it is near the time for the next dose, skip the missed dose and resume your regular dosage schedule. Do not double the next dose.

STOPPING THE DRUG
Stop taking this medicine only on your doctor's advice

PROLONGED USE
Careful, continuous patient monitoring is needed during prolonged use.

PRECAUTIONS
Over 60: No special precautions are warranted.

Driving and Hazardous Work: Determine whether this drug affects your alertness and physical abilities before you drive or engage in hazardous activities.

Alcohol: Do not consume alcohol while you take this medicine.

Pregnancy: Busulfan may cause birth defects; it is best to use some method of birth control while you are taking this medicine. Inform your doctor at once if you become pregnant during therapy.

Breast Feeding: It is not known whether this medicine passes into breast milk. Breast feeding is generally not recommended while taking busulfan.

Infants and Children: This medicine is not expected to cause problems or side effects in children that are different from those it causes in adults.

Special Concerns: Busulfan can increase the risk of infection because it reduces the number of white blood cells in your body. Try to avoid contact with people who have infections. The medicine can also reduce blood levels of platelets, cells that are necessary for clotting. Be careful when using a toothbrush, dental floss, or toothpick, and be careful to avoid cutting yourself when you use a knife, razor, or other sharp instrument.

OVERDOSE
Symptoms: Bleeding, chills, fever, collapse, loss of consciousness.

What to Do: Seek emergency medical assistance immediately; call emergency medical services (EMS) or go to a hospital emergency room.

DRUG INTERACTIONS
Avoid any OTC product that contains aspirin, since it increases the danger of bleeding; carefully read ingredient labels of nonprescription drugs. Tell your doctor about any other drug you are taking, including an anticoagulant, any other anticancer drug, antithyroid medication, antibiotics, and antiviral medication.

FOOD INTERACTIONS
Avoid sweet or fatty foods.

DISEASE INTERACTIONS
Consult your doctor if you have any other medical problem, such as a history of seizures, chicken pox (or recent exposure to someone with chicken pox), shingles, gout, kidney stones, any head injury, or any infection.

Butalbital/Acetaminophen/Caffeine

Fioricet 50/325/40 mg
(NOVARTIS)

▶ Drug Class: Nonnarcotic analgesic

▶ Available in: Capsules, tablets

▶ Available OTC? No

▶ As Generic? Yes

Side Effects

SERIOUS
Shallow breathing, dizziness, weakness, confusion, blood in urine or stools, unusual bleeding or bruising, bleeding or crusting sores on lips, hives, muscle cramps, chest pain, white spots on the tongue, sore throat, pinpoint red spots on skin, fever, itchiness, rash, persistent or recurrent pain before next scheduled dose, swollen or painful glands, vomiting, yellow discoloration of skin or gums. Also swelling of the eyelids, lips, tongue, or face; red, thickened, or scaly skin. Call your physician immediately.

COMMON
Abdominal pain, dizziness, nausea or vomiting, mild stomach pain, lightheadedness, drowsiness.

LESS COMMON
Mental depression.

PRINCIPAL USES
To treat headaches when nonprescription pain relievers are ineffective.

HOW THE DRUG WORKS
Butalbital, a barbiturate, acts on the central nervous system to cause sedation. Acetaminophen (APAP) appears to interfere with the action of prostaglandins, naturally occurring substances in the body that cause inflammation and make nerves more sensitive to pain impulses. Caffeine, a stimulant, is believed to enhance the effectiveness of pain relievers.

DOSAGE
1 or 2 tablets every 4 hours as needed. If your medication contains 325 or 500 mg of acetaminophen per capsule or tablet, do not take more than 6 pills a day. If your medication contains 650 mg of acetaminophen per capsule or tablet, do not take more than 4 pills a day.

ONSET OF EFFECT
Unknown.

DURATION OF ACTION
Up to 4 hours.

DIETARY ADVICE
Take this medicine with milk or meals to minimize stomach upset.

STORAGE
Store in a tightly sealed container away from heat, moisture, and direct light.

IF YOU MISS A DOSE
If your doctor has directed you to take this medication on a regular schedule, take it as soon as you remember. If it is near the time for the next dose, skip the missed dose and resume your regular dosage schedule. Do not double the next dose.

STOPPING THE DRUG
You should take it as prescribed for the full treatment period, but you may stop taking the drug if you are feeling better before the scheduled end of therapy. This medication should never be stopped abruptly after long-term regular use.

PROLONGED USE
Barbiturates such as butalbital can cause physical dependence. Taking too much acetaminophen may cause liver damage.

PRECAUTIONS
Over 60: Adverse reactions may be more likely and more severe in older patients.

Driving and Hazardous Work: The use of this medicine may impair your ability to perform such tasks safely.

Alcohol: Avoid alcohol.

Pregnancy: Before taking this medicine, tell your doctor if you are pregnant or plan to become pregnant.

Breast Feeding: This medicine passes into breast milk; do not use while breast feeding.

Infants and Children: Not recommended for use by children under age 12.

Special Concerns: The medicine works best if you take it at the first sign of a headache. Do not take the medicine if it has a strong vinegary odor. If you do not feel better 1 hour after taking this medication, call your doctor. Do not take a larger dose.

OVERDOSE
Symptoms: Difficulty breathing, excessive perspiration, impaired mental state, loss of consciousness, agitation or nervousness.

What to Do: Call your doctor, emergency medical services (EMS), or the nearest poison control center immediately.

DRUG INTERACTIONS
Consult your doctor for specific advice if you are taking antihistamines, antidepressants, antipsychotic drugs, muscle relaxants, other narcotic pain relievers, sleep medications, tranquilizers, or anticoagulants.

FOOD INTERACTIONS
No known food interactions.

DISEASE INTERACTIONS
Consult your doctor if you have any of the following: asthma, mental depression, heart disease, a blood disorder, an overactive thyroid gland, a kidney or liver disorder, or a history of alcoholism or drug abuse.

Butalbital/Acetaminophen/Caffeine/Codeine

BRAND NAMES
Amaphen with Codeine #3, Fioricet with Codeine

▶ Drug Class: Opioid (narcotic) analgesic

▶ Available in: Capsules, tablets

▶ Available OTC? No

▶ As Generic? Yes

Side Effects

SERIOUS
Chest pains, muscle or joint pain, sores or ulcers in mouth, swelling of face, lips, or eyelids, yellow discoloration of eyes or skin, sore throat with or without fever. Call your doctor immediately.

COMMON
Drowsiness, dizziness, shortness of breath, light-headedness, constipation, confusion, nausea, and vomiting.

LESS COMMON
Skin rash or hives.

PRINCIPAL USES
To treat tension headaches when nonprescription pain relievers prove ineffective.

HOW THE DRUG WORKS
Butalbital, a barbiturate, acts on the central nervous system to cause sedation. Acetaminophen (APAP) appears to interfere with the action of prostaglandins, naturally occurring substances in the body that cause inflammation and make nerves more sensitive to pain impulses. Caffeine, a stimulant, is believed to enhance the effectiveness of pain relievers. Codeine, a narcotic, is believed to block pain signals to the brain and spinal cord.

DOSAGE
1 or 2 tablets or capsules every 4 hours. Do not take more than 6 pills a day.

ONSET OF EFFECT
Unknown.

DURATION OF ACTION
Unknown.

DIETARY ADVICE
This medication should be taken with food or water.

STORAGE
Store in a tightly sealed container away from heat, moisture, and direct light.

IF YOU MISS A DOSE
If your doctor has directed you to take this drug on a regular schedule, take it as soon as you remember. If it is near the time for the next dose, skip the missed dose and resume your regular dosage schedule. Do not double the next dose.

STOPPING THE DRUG
Take it as prescribed for the full treatment period, but you may stop taking the drug if you are feeling better before the scheduled end of therapy. This medicine should never be stopped abruptly after long-term regular use.

PROLONGED USE
Narcotic drugs, such as codeine, and barbiturates, such as butalbital, can cause physical dependence. Taking too much acetaminophen may cause liver damage.

PRECAUTIONS
Over 60: Adverse reactions may be more likely and more severe in older patients.

Driving and Hazardous Work: Do not drive or engage in hazardous work until you determine how the medicine affects you.

Alcohol: Avoid alcohol.

Pregnancy: Components of this medication have caused birth defects in animals. Taking the drug late in pregnancy may cause drug dependence in the unborn child. Tell your doctor if you are pregnant or plan to become pregnant before you take this drug.

Breast Feeding: Components of this medicine pass into breast milk; avoid or discontinue use while breast feeding.

Infants and Children: Not recommended for use by children under age 12.

Special Concerns: Tell any doctor or dentist whom you consult that you are taking this medicine. It works best if taken at the first sign of a headache. Tell your doctor if you begin having headaches more frequently than before you started using this drug. Check with your doctor if the medicine stops working as well as it did at the outset of therapy. This may be a sign of drug dependence. Do not increase the dose to attain better pain relief.

OVERDOSE
Symptoms: Drowsiness, confusion, nausea, vomiting, abnormal heartbeat, insomnia, slowed or suppressed breathing, trembling, loss of consciousness.

What to Do: Call your doctor, emergency medical services (EMS), or the nearest poison control center immediately.

DRUG INTERACTIONS
Consult your doctor for specific advice if you are taking beta-blockers, estrogens, felodipine, griseofulvin, nifedipine, theophylline, warfarin, carbamazepine, sulfinpyrazone, tranquilizers, sedatives, or tricyclic antidepressants.

FOOD INTERACTIONS
No known food interactions. A high-fiber diet is recommended because the medicine may cause constipation.

DISEASE INTERACTIONS
Consult your doctor if you have any of the following: asthma, liver disease, kidney disease, diabetes, mental depression, an overactive thyroid, porphyria, heart disease, or a history of alcohol or drug abuse.

Butalbital/Aspirin/Caffeine

▶ Drug Class: Nonnarcotic analgesic

▶ Available in: Capsules, tablets

▶ Available OTC? No

▶ As Generic? Yes

Side Effects

SERIOUS
Difficulty breathing, tightness in chest, coughing, or wheezing; sores or white spots in mouth; bluish discoloration, flushing, or redness of skin; stuffy nose; pinpoint pupils; fever; swollen eyelids, face, lips, or tongue; difficulty swallowing; crusting or bleeding sores on lips; sore throat; burning, tenderness, or peeling of skin. Call your physician immediately.

COMMON
Drowsiness, dizziness, heartburn.

LESS COMMON
Insomnia, nightmares, headache, constipation, increased sweating, unusual fatigue.

PRINCIPAL USES
To treat headaches or migraines.

HOW THE DRUG WORKS
Butalbital, a barbiturate, acts on the central nervous system to cause sedation. Aspirin appears to interfere with the action of prostaglandins, naturally occurring substances in the body that cause inflammation and make nerves more sensitive to pain impulses. Caffeine is believed to enhance the effectiveness of pain relievers.

DOSAGE
1 or 2 capsules or tablets every 4 hours. Do not take more than 6 pills a day.

ONSET OF EFFECT
Within 1 hour.

DURATION OF ACTION
4 hours.

DIETARY ADVICE
Take this drug with food or a full glass of water to avoid stomach irritation.

STORAGE
Store in a tightly sealed container away from heat, moisture, and direct light.

IF YOU MISS A DOSE
If your doctor has directed you to take this drug on a regular schedule, take it as soon as you remember. If it is near the time for the next dose, skip the missed dose and resume your regular dosage schedule. Do not double the next dose.

STOPPING THE DRUG
Take it as prescribed for the full treatment period, but you may stop taking the drug if you are feeling better before the scheduled end of therapy. This drug should never be stopped abruptly after long-term regular use.

PROLONGED USE
Prolonged use may result in physical dependence and may cause kidney damage. Periodic kidney function tests are recommended. Prolonged use may make exposure to cold weather more hazardous.

PRECAUTIONS
Over 60: Adverse reactions may be more likely and more severe in older patients.

Driving and Hazardous Work: Do not drive or engage in hazardous work until you determine how the medicine affects you.

Alcohol: Avoid alcohol.

Pregnancy: Taking this medicine late in pregnancy may cause drug dependence in the unborn child. Before you take it, tell your doctor if you are pregnant or are planning to become pregnant.

Breast Feeding: Butalbital and aspirin pass into breast milk; avoid or discontinue use while nursing.

Infants and Children: Consult your doctor before giving this medicine to anyone under age 18 who has a viral illness, especially chicken pox or influenza. The aspirin may cause a serious illness called Reye's syndrome.

Special Concerns: Tell any doctor or dentist whom you consult that you are taking this medicine. It works best if taken at the first sign of a headache. Tell your doctor if you begin having headaches more frequently than before you started using it, or if the drug stops working as well as it did at the outset of therapy. This may be a sign of drug dependence. Do not try to get better pain relief by increasing the dose. Do not take the drug if it has a strong vinegary odor.

OVERDOSE
Symptoms: Deep sleep, weak pulse, ringing in ears, nausea, vomiting, dizziness, deep and rapid breathing, convulsions, loss of consciousness.

What to Do: Call your doctor, emergency medical services (EMS), or the nearest poison control center immediately.

DRUG INTERACTIONS
Consult your doctor for advice if you are taking acetazolamide, gout medicines, beta-blockers, anticoagulants, methotrexate, narcotic pain relievers, nonsteroidal anti-inflammatory drugs, oral contraceptives, oral diabetes medicines, steroid medicines, tranquilizers, or valproic acid.

FOOD INTERACTIONS
No known food interactions.

DISEASE INTERACTIONS
Consult your doctor if you have any of the following: stomach or duodenal ulcers, asthma, epilepsy, anemia, gout, or a history of alcohol or drug abuse. Use of this drug may cause complications in patients with liver or kidney disease, since these organs work together to remove the medication from the body.

▶ Drug Class: Opioid (narcotic) analgesic

▶ Available in: Capsules, tablets

▶ Available OTC? No

▶ As Generic? Yes

Side Effects

SERIOUS
Wheezing, tightness in chest, pinpoint pupils, yellowish discoloration of the skin and eyes, easy bruising, vomiting blood, sore throat, fever, mouth sores, difficult urination, hearing loss, blood in urine. Call your doctor immediately.

COMMON
Drowsiness, dizziness, lightheadedness, flushed face, depression, increased urination.

LESS COMMON
Insomnia, nightmares, headache, constipation, increased sweating, unusual fatigue.

PRINCIPAL USES
To treat tension headaches or migraines.

HOW THE DRUG WORKS
Butalbital, a barbiturate, acts on the central nervous system to relieve pain. Aspirin appears to interfere with the action of prostaglandins, naturally occurring substances in the body that cause inflammation and make nerves more sensitive to pain impulses. Caffeine is believed to enhance the effectiveness of pain relievers. Codeine, a narcotic, is believed to block pain signals to the brain.

DOSAGE
1 or 2 capsules or tablets every 4 hours. Do not take more than 6 pills a day.

ONSET OF EFFECT
Within 1 hour.

DURATION OF ACTION
4 hours.

DIETARY ADVICE
This medicine should be taken with food or water to minimize stomach irritation.

STORAGE
Store in a tightly sealed container away from heat, moisture, and direct light.

IF YOU MISS A DOSE
Take it as soon as you remember. If it is near the time for the next dose, skip the missed dose and resume your regular dosage schedule. Do not double the next dose.

STOPPING THE DRUG
You should take this medication as prescribed for the full treatment period, but you may stop taking it if you are feeling better before the scheduled end of therapy. This drug should never be stopped abruptly after long-term regular use.

PROLONGED USE
Narcotic drugs, such as codeine, and barbiturates, such as butalbital, can cause physical dependence. Prolonged use can cause kidney dysfunction.

PRECAUTIONS
Over 60: Adverse reactions may be more likely and more severe in older patients.

Driving and Hazardous Work: Do not drive or engage in hazardous work until you determine how the medicine affects you.

Alcohol: Avoid alcohol.

Pregnancy: Taking the medicine late in pregnancy may cause drug dependence in the unborn child. Before you take this medicine, tell your doctor if you are pregnant or plan to become pregnant.

Breast Feeding: Do not use while nursing.

Infants and Children: This medicine is generally not prescribed for children under age 12. Consult your doctor before giving it to anyone under age 18 who has a viral illness, especially chicken pox or influenza. The aspirin may cause a serious illness called Reye's syndrome.

Special Concerns: Tell any doctor or dentist whom you consult that you are taking this medicine. The drug works best if taken at the first sign of a headache. Tell your doctor if you begin having headaches more frequently than before you started using this medicine. Check with your doctor if the medicine stops working as well as it did at the outset of therapy. Do not try to get better pain relief by increasing the dose. Do not take this drug if it has a strong, vinegary odor.

OVERDOSE
Symptoms: Ringing in ears, slow and weak pulse, deep sleep, dizziness, nausea, vomiting, hallucinations, deep and rapid breathing, convulsions, loss of consciousness.

What to Do: Call your doctor, emergency medical services (EMS), or the nearest poison control center immediately.

DRUG INTERACTIONS
Consult your doctor for specific advice if you are taking acetazolamide, gout medicines, beta-blockers, anticoagulants, methotrexate, narcotic pain relievers, nonsteroidal anti-inflammatory drugs, oral contraceptives, oral diabetes medicines, steroid medicines, tranquilizers, or valproic acid.

FOOD INTERACTIONS
No known food interactions.

DISEASE INTERACTIONS
Consult your doctor if you have any of the following: stomach or duodenal ulcers, asthma, epilepsy, anemia, gout, or a history of alcohol or drug abuse. Use of this drug may cause complications in patients with liver or kidney disease, since these organs work together to remove the medication from the body.

Butenafine Hydrochloride

BRAND NAME
Mentax, Lotrimin Ultra

▶ Drug Class: Topical antifungal

▶ Available in: Cream

▶ Available OTC? Yes

▶ As Generic? No

Side Effects

SERIOUS
No serious side effects are associated with the use of butenafine.

COMMON
Burning, stinging, irritation, itching, redness, swelling, or blistering at the site of application.

LESS COMMON
There are no less-common side effects associated with the use of butenafine.

PRINCIPAL USES
To treat tinea pedis (athlete's foot), a fungal infection.

HOW THE DRUG WORKS
Butenafine prevents fungal organisms from producing vital substances required for their growth and function. This drug is effective only for infections caused by fungal organisms. It will not work for bacterial or viral infections.

DOSAGE
Apply it to the affected area either twice a day for 7 days or once a day for 4 weeks, in accordance with your doctor's instructions.

ONSET OF EFFECT
Unknown.

DURATION OF ACTION
Unknown.

DIETARY ADVICE
No special restrictions.

STORAGE
Store in a tightly sealed container away from heat, moisture, and direct light. Do not allow the cream to freeze.

IF YOU MISS A DOSE
Apply butenafine as soon as you remember. If it is near the time for the next dose, skip the missed dose and resume your regular dosage schedule. Do not double the next dose or apply an excessively thick film of topical medication to compensate for a missed dose.

STOPPING THE DRUG
Apply as prescribed for the full treatment period, even if the fungal infection appears to be eradicated before the scheduled end of therapy. Unfortunately, it can be difficult to assess when the drug has achieved its desired effect since it suppresses redness and inflammation of the skin before the infection is completely clear; recurrence of fungal infection owing to inadequate length of therapy is a significant risk.

PROLONGED USE
If your skin problem does not improve or instead becomes worse after 4 weeks of treatment, consult your doctor.

PRECAUTIONS
Over 60: No special problems are expected.

Driving and Hazardous Work: The use of butenafine should not impair your ability to perform such tasks safely.

Alcohol: No special precautions are necessary.

Pregnancy: Adequate human studies have not been done. Before taking butenafine, tell your physician if you are pregnant or plan to become pregnant.

Breast Feeding: It is not known whether butenafine passes into breast milk; caution is advised. Consult your doctor for specific advice.

Infants and Children: The safety and effectiveness of butenafine use by children below the age of 12 have not been determined. Use of the medication in patients 12 to 16 years of age has not caused any problems and has been effective.

Special Concerns: Butenafine is intended for external use only. Wash your hands after butenafine is applied to the affected area. Contact with the eyes, nose, and mouth should be avoided. If you apply butenafine after bathing or showering, dry the affected area thoroughly first. Do not use a tight-fitting dressing unless your physician tells you to do so. Do not use butenafine for any condition other than the one for which it was prescribed. As with any antifungal, butenafine is useful only against organisms that are vulnerable to its effects. Therefore, it is important to tell your doctor if your condition has not improved—or instead has worsened—within a few days of starting butenafine. The particular organism causing your illness may be resistant to this drug.

OVERDOSE
Symptoms: No cases of overdose have been reported.

What to Do: An overdose of butenafine is unlikely to be life-threatening. However, if someone uses a much larger dose than prescribed or ingests the medicine, seek medical assistance immediately.

DRUG INTERACTIONS
Consult your doctor for specific advice if you are taking allylamine antifungal drugs. Also tell your doctor if you are taking any other prescription or over-the-counter medications.

FOOD INTERACTIONS
No known food interactions.

DISEASE INTERACTIONS
Caution is advised when taking butenafine. Consult your doctor if you have any other medical condition.

Butoconazole Nitrate

BRAND NAME
Femstat 3

▶ Drug Class: Antifungal

▶ Available in: Vaginal cream

▶ Available OTC? Yes

▶ As Generic? No

Side Effects

SERIOUS
Vaginal itching, burning, discharge, or irritation not present prior to treatment. Call your doctor as soon as possible.

COMMON
No common side effects are associated with the use of butoconazole.

LESS COMMON
Headache, stomach cramps or pain, irritation or burning of sexual partner's penis.

PRINCIPAL USES
To treat fungal (yeast) infections of the vagina.

HOW THE DRUG WORKS
Butoconazole prevents fungal organisms from producing vital substances required for growth and function. This drug is effective only for infections caused by fungal organisms. It will not work for bacterial or viral infections.

DOSAGE
Nonpregnant women and teenagers: 5 g (1 applicatorful) of cream inserted with an applicator into the vagina at bedtime for 3 consecutive days. Pregnant women and teenagers: After third month, 5 g (1 applicatorful) of cream inserted with an applicator into the vagina at bedtime for 6 consecutive days.

ONSET OF EFFECT
Unknown.

DURATION OF ACTION
Unknown.

DIETARY ADVICE
Butoconazole can be applied without regard to diet.

STORAGE
Store in a tightly sealed container away from heat, moisture, and direct light. Do not allow it to freeze.

IF YOU MISS A DOSE
Insert it as soon as you remember. If it is near the time for the next dose, skip the missed dose and resume your regular dosage schedule.

STOPPING THE DRUG
Take the medicine as directed for the full treatment period, even if you begin to feel better before the scheduled end of therapy. Recurrence of the infection is likely if you stop before the full treatment period is complete.

PROLONGED USE
Butoconazole is generally prescribed for short-term therapy (3 to 6 days).

PRECAUTIONS
Over 60: No special problems are expected.

Driving and Hazardous Work: The use of butoconazole should not impair your ability to perform such tasks safely.

Alcohol: No special precautions are necessary.

Pregnancy: Studies on the use of butoconazole during the first 3 months (trimester) of pregnancy have not been done. No adverse effects while using it during the second or third trimesters have been reported.

Breast Feeding: No problems are expected. Consult your doctor about using this medicine while nursing.

Infants and Children: Studies on the use of butoconazole in children have not been done. Consult your pediatrician for specific advice.

Special Concerns: The drug may be used with oral contraceptives and antibiotic therapy. Sanitary napkins should be used to prevent staining of clothing. The affected area should be kept cool and dry. The patient should wear loose-fitting cotton clothing and freshly laundered cotton underwear or pantyhose with a cotton crotch. Avoid underwear made from nonventilating materials. Do not sit for a long time in a wet bathing suit. Avoid feminine hygiene sprays. Wash daily with unscented soap and dry thoroughly with a clean towel. Tampons should not be used during therapy. The patient's sexual partner should wear a condom during intercourse and should consult a doctor if penile redness, itching, or discomfort occurs. Do not stop using this medicine during your menstrual period. After urination or a bowel movement, cleanse by wiping the area from front to back to prevent reinfection.

OVERDOSE
Symptoms: An overdose with butoconazole is unlikely.

What to Do: If someone should swallow a large amount of the medicine, call your doctor, emergency medical services (EMS), or the nearest poison control center immediately.

DRUG INTERACTIONS
Tell your doctor if you are using any other vaginal prescription or over-the-counter medication.

FOOD INTERACTIONS
No food interactions have been reported.

DISEASE INTERACTIONS
No disease interactions have been reported.

Butorphanol Tartrate

BRAND NAME
Stadol NS

▶ Drug Class: Opioid (narcotic) analgesic

▶ Available in: Nasal spray

▶ Available OTC? No

▶ As Generic? No

Side Effects

SERIOUS
Shallow or slow breathing, sinus congestion, changes in mental state, nosebleeds, fever, sneezing, runny nose, blurred or distorted vision, ear pain, bronchitis, itching, hallucinations, difficulty urinating, skin rash, fainting. Call your doctor immediately.

COMMON
Headache, sedation, dizziness, insomnia, nose irritation, confusion, dry mouth, nausea, vomiting, constipation, loss of appetite, clammy skin, unpleasant taste in mouth.

LESS COMMON
Nervousness, unusual dreams, sluggishness, agitation, euphoria, floating sensation, trembling, stomach pain.

PRINCIPAL USES
To relieve headaches, post-operative pain, or other pain for which a narcotic analgesic is necessary.

HOW THE DRUG WORKS
Butorphanol blocks pain impulses at specific sites in the brain and spinal cord.

DOSAGE
Spray once into one nostril only. Do not spray into both nostrils unless directed by physician. Dose may be repeated in 60 to 90 minutes, and every 4 to 6 hours if needed.

ONSET OF EFFECT
Within 15 minutes.

DURATION OF ACTION
4 to 5 hours.

DIETARY ADVICE
No special restrictions.

STORAGE
Store in a tightly sealed container away from heat, moisture, and direct light.

IF YOU MISS A DOSE
Not applicable; butorphanol should not be taken on a routine schedule.

STOPPING THE DRUG
You may stop taking the drug if you are feeling better, but butorphanol should never be stopped abruptly after long-term regular use.

PROLONGED USE
The effects of long-term use are unknown. This drug could be habit-forming. Consult your doctor regularly during prolonged use.

PRECAUTIONS
Over 60: Adverse reactions and side effects, particularly dizziness, may be more likely and more severe in older persons.

Driving and Hazardous Work: Do not drive or engage in hazardous work until you determine how the medicine affects you.

Alcohol: Avoid alcohol because it can further dull alertness and slow reflexes.

Pregnancy: Before taking butorphanol, discuss with your doctor the relative risks and benefits of using this drug while pregnant.

Breast Feeding: Butorphanol may pass into breast milk; caution is advised. Consult your doctor for specific advice.

Infants and Children: Butorphanol is not recommended for use by children under the age of 18.

Special Concerns: When you first use this medicine, get up slowly from a sitting or lying position to avoid dizziness. Tell any doctor or dentist whom you consult that you are using butorphanol. Do not increase or decrease the dosage without consulting your doctor. When using a new bottle of butorphanol, point the bottle away from you and pump about 3 times to start the pump. Each time you use the spray, wipe the tip with a clean tissue or cloth. Every 3 or 4 days, rinse the tip with warm water and wipe the tip for about 15 seconds, then dry. To administer a dose of butorphanol, first blow your nose gently. Hold your head forward a little, put the spray tip in the nostril, and aim for the back. Close the other nostril by pressing with one finger. After the spray, tilt your head back for a few seconds. Do not blow your nose.

OVERDOSE
Symptoms: Irregular heartbeat; difficulty breathing; seizures; cold, clammy skin; loss of consciousness; pinpoint pupils of eyes; severe drowsiness, restlessness, weakness, dizziness, or nervousness.

What to Do: Call your doctor, emergency medical services (EMS), or the nearest poison control center immediately.

DRUG INTERACTIONS
The following drugs may interact with butorphanol: tranquilizers, sleeping pills, barbiturates, antihistamines, heart drugs, oral diabetes drugs, and antidepressants. Consult your doctor for specific advice about any drug you are taking.

FOOD INTERACTIONS
None expected.

DISEASE INTERACTIONS
Tell your doctor if you have had a heart attack or a head injury or if you have heart disease, a respiratory disease, a kidney problem, a liver problem, or a history of alcohol or drug abuse.

Caffeine

Vivarin 200 mg
(SMITHKLINE BEECHAM)

Additional photographs

▶ Drug Class: Central nervous system stimulant

▶ Available in: Tablets, extended-release capsules

▶ Available OTC? Yes

▶ As Generic? Yes

Side Effects

SERIOUS
Diarrhea, insomnia, dizziness, rapid heartbeat, severe nausea, vomiting, irritability, unusual agitation, tremors. Call your doctor immediately.

COMMON
Mild nausea or jitters.

LESS COMMON
There are no less-common side effects associated with the use of caffeine.

PRINCIPAL USES
To restore mental alertness.

HOW THE DRUG WORKS
Caffeine acts as a stimulant to all levels of the central nervous system.

DOSAGE
Tablets: 100 to 200 mg; repeat after 3 or 4 hours if needed. Extended-release capsules: 200 to 250 mg; can be repeated after 3 or 4 hours if needed. Citrated caffeine: 65 to 325 mg, 3 times a day as needed. Take no more than 1,000 mg a day.

ONSET OF EFFECT
Unknown.

DURATION OF ACTION
Unknown.

DIETARY ADVICE
Take it with food to minimize stomach upset.

STORAGE
Store in a tightly sealed container away from heat and direct light. Keep away from moisture and extremes in temperature.

IF YOU MISS A DOSE
Take it as soon as you remember. If it is near the time for the next dose, skip the missed dose and resume your regular dosage schedule. Do not double the next dose.

STOPPING THE DRUG
The decision to stop taking the drug should be made by your doctor.

PROLONGED USE
Caffeine is not intended for prolonged use.

PRECAUTIONS
Over 60: No special problems are expected.

Driving and Hazardous Work: The use of caffeine should not impair your ability to perform such tasks safely.

Alcohol: No special precautions are necessary.

Pregnancy: Large doses can cause miscarriage, delay the growth of the fetus, or cause problems with the heart rhythm of the fetus. No more than 300 mg of caffeine (the amount in 3 cups of coffee) should be consumed daily during pregnancy.

Breast Feeding: Caffeine passes into breast milk; caution is advised. Consult your doctor for specific advice.

Infants and Children: Caffeine is not recommended for use by children under the age of 12.

Special Concerns: To prevent insomnia, do not take caffeine or caffeine-containing beverages too close to bedtime. After you stop taking caffeine, you may experience anxiety, dizziness, headache, irritability, muscle tension, nausea, nervousness, stuffy nose, and unusual fatigue. Consult your doctor if you suffer from any of these symptoms.

OVERDOSE
Symptoms: Stomach or abdominal pains, agitation, anxiety, excitement, restlessness, confusion, delirium, seizures. A very large overdose can cause an irregular heartbeat; seeing zig-zag flashes of light; frequent urination; increased sensitivity to touch; muscle twitching; nausea and vomiting, sometimes with blood; insomnia; and ringing in the ears.

What to Do: An overdose of caffeine is unlikely to be life-threatening. However, if someone takes a much larger dose than directed, call your doctor, emergency medical services (EMS), or the nearest poison control center right away.

DRUG INTERACTIONS
Call your doctor for specific advice if you are taking central nervous system stimulants; MAO inhibitors; amantadine; ciprofloxacin and norfloxacin (antibiotics); cold, sinus, hay fever, or allergy medications; asthma medicine; pemoline; amphetamines; nabilone; methylphenidate; or chlophedianol.

FOOD INTERACTIONS
Do not drink large amounts of caffeine-containing beverages like coffee, tea, soft drinks, cocoa, or chocolate milk.

DISEASE INTERACTIONS
Caution is advised when taking caffeine. Consult your doctor if you have any of the following: anxiety, panic attacks, heart disease, high blood pressure, agoraphobia (fear of open places), or insomnia. Use of caffeine may cause complications in patients with liver disease, since this organ works to remove the medication from the body.

Calamine

BRAND NAME
Calamox

▶ Drug Class: Topical anti-itching agent; astringent

▶ Available in: Lotion, ointment

▶ Available OTC? Yes

▶ As Generic? Yes

Side Effects

SERIOUS
No serious side effects are associated with calamine.

COMMON
No common side effects are associated with calamine.

LESS COMMON
Rash, irritation, or sensitivity of the treated area that was not present prior to beginning therapy. Call your doctor promptly if such symptoms persist.

PRINCIPAL USES
To relieve the itching, pain, and discomfort of skin irritations, such as those caused by poison ivy, poison oak, and poison sumac. Calamine will also dry the oozing and weeping of skin eruptions caused by poison ivy, poison oak, and poison sumac.

HOW THE DRUG WORKS
The exact mechanism of action is unknown; calamine appears to have natural soothing properties.

DOSAGE
Apply calamine to the affected area of skin as often as needed. To use the lotion, shake it well to start. Then moisten a wad of cotton with the lotion and use the cotton to apply the lotion to the affected area of skin. Allow the lotion to dry on the skin. To use the ointment, gently rub just enough ointment into the skin to lightly cover the affected area.

ONSET OF EFFECT
Within 1 hour.

DURATION OF ACTION
Unknown.

DIETARY ADVICE
Calamine can be used without regard to diet.

STORAGE
Store in a tightly sealed container away from heat and direct light. Do not refrigerate or allow medication to freeze.

IF YOU MISS A DOSE
If you are using calamine on a fixed schedule, apply the missed dose as soon as you remember. If it is close to the next dose, skip the missed dose and resume your regular dosage schedule. Do not use more lotion or ointment than necessary.

STOPPING THE DRUG
Take it as prescribed for the full treatment period. However, you may stop taking the drug if you are feeling better before the scheduled end of therapy.

PROLONGED USE
Call your doctor if your condition does not improve or gets worse after 7 days of treatment.

PRECAUTIONS
Over 60: No special problems have been documented in older patients.

Driving and Hazardous Work: Use of calamine should not impair your ability to perform such tasks safely.

Alcohol: No special precautions are necessary.

Pregnancy: No problems during pregnancy have been documented.

Breast Feeding: Calamine may be used safely while nursing; no problems that affect the baby during breast feeding have been documented.

Infants and Children: Studies on the use of calamine on infants and children have not been done; however, no pediatric-specific problems have been documented.

Special Concerns: Calamine is for external use only. Do not swallow it. Do not use calamine on the eyes or mucous membranes, such as the inside of the mouth, nose, genitals, or anal area. Ingestion of calamine has been reported to cause gastritis (inflammation of the stomach lining) and vomiting. Milk or antacids may be used to treat gastritis.

OVERDOSE
Symptoms: None.

What to Do: No emergency instructions are applicable, since no cases of overdose have been reported. However, if someone accidentally ingests calamine, seek medical assistance right away.

DRUG INTERACTIONS
No drug interactions with calamine have been reported. However, you should tell your doctor if you are using any other prescription or over-the-counter medication to treat the same area of skin as calamine.

FOOD INTERACTIONS
No known food interactions.

DISEASE INTERACTIONS
No disease interactions with calamine have been documented. However, tell your doctor if you have any other skin condition.

Calcipotriene

BRAND NAME
Dovonex

▶ Drug Class: Vitamin D analog

▶ Available in: Cream, ointment, scalp solution

▶ Available OTC? No

▶ As Generic? No

Side Effects

SERIOUS
No serious side effects have been reported in association with the use of calcipotriene.

COMMON
Temporary burning, tingling, and stinging; rash; peeling. Consult your doctor if these symptoms persist.

LESS COMMON
Skin irritation, dry skin, worsening of psoriasis, thinning of the skin, darkening of the skin.

PRINCIPAL USES
Cream and ointment are used to treat mild to moderate psoriasis in adults. Scalp solution is used to treat chronic, moderately severe psoriasis of the scalp.

HOW THE DRUG WORKS
Calcipotriene is a synthetic form of vitamin D. It appears to slow excessive growth of skin cells; however, the exact mechanism of action is unknown.

DOSAGE
Cream and ointment: Apply a thin layer to the affected area once or twice daily and rub in evenly. Do not apply to the face. Scalp solution: Comb through the hair to remove scaly debris. Apply calcipotriene only to the lesions and rub in evenly. Do not allow the solution to spread to the forehead or other unaffected areas. Wash hands thoroughly after use.

ONSET OF EFFECT
Within 24 hours.

DURATION OF ACTION
Unknown.

DIETARY ADVICE
Calcipotriene can be used without regard to diet.

STORAGE
Store in a tightly sealed container away from heat, moisture, and direct light. Do not allow it to freeze. Keep the scalp solution away from open flame.

IF YOU MISS A DOSE
Apply it as soon as you remember.

STOPPING THE DRUG
The decision to stop taking the drug should be made in consultation with your physician.

PROLONGED USE
Treatment periods, depending on the severity of the psoriasis, generally last 8 weeks but have been approved to continue for up to 1 year.

PRECAUTIONS
Over 60: Adverse reactions may be more likely and more severe in older patients.

Driving and Hazardous Work: The use of calcipotriene should not impair your ability to perform such tasks safely.

Alcohol: No special precautions are necessary.

Pregnancy: Adequate human studies have not been done. Before taking calcipotriene, tell your doctor if you are pregnant or plan to become pregnant.

Breast Feeding: Calcipotriene may pass into breast milk; caution is advised. Consult your doctor for specific advice.

Infants and Children: Not recommended for use by children under age 12.

OVERDOSE
Symptoms: Small amounts of the medication are absorbed through the skin. Symptoms of an overdose are due to elevated levels of blood calcium (hypercalcemia). Early symptoms of hypercalcemia: Constipation (especially in children), diarrhea, dry mouth, increased thirst and frequency of urination, persistent headache, loss of appetite, metallic taste, nausea and vomiting, unusual fatigue. Advanced symptoms: Bone and muscle pain, irregular heartbeat, persistent itching, extreme drowsiness, mental changes. Severe calcium toxicity may be fatal.

What to Do: Call your doctor, emergency medical services (EMS), or the nearest poison control center immediately.

DRUG INTERACTIONS
No known drug interactions.

FOOD INTERACTIONS
No known food interactions.

DISEASE INTERACTIONS
You should not take calcipotriene if you have high blood levels of calcium (hypercalcemia) or evidence of vitamin D toxicity.

Calcitonin — Salmon

▶ Drug Class: Hormone/bone resorption inhibitor

▶ Available in: Injection, nasal spray

▶ Available OTC? No

▶ As Generic? No

Side Effects

SERIOUS
Skin rash or hives. Call your doctor immediately.

COMMON
Diarrhea, loss of appetite, nausea or vomiting, stomach pain, pain and redness at injection site, flushing or redness of face, ears, hands, or feet.

LESS COMMON
Increased output of urine, headache, dizziness, pressure in the chest, breathing difficulty, stuffy nose, nasal bleeding or crusting, tingling of hands or feet, weakness, back pain, joint pain, chills.

PRINCIPAL USES
To treat Paget's disease, a disorder in which bone tissue is broken down and restored too rapidly, resulting in bone fragility and in some cases malformation; to prevent bone loss in women with postmenopausal osteoporosis; to treat abnormally high blood calcium levels; to treat osteoporosis resulting from hormonal disturbances, drug therapy, and immobilization; to relieve compression of nerves that may occur with Paget's disease of bone.

HOW THE DRUG WORKS
Calcitonin blocks the bone-mineral-absorbing activity of the osteoclasts (bone cells), increases calcium excretion by the kidneys, and slows bone resorption (the speed at which bone is broken down before it is replaced).

DOSAGE
Injection— For Paget's disease: 100 international units (IU) injected under the skin once a day to start. The dosage may be reduced depending on results. To prevent postmenopausal bone loss: 100 IU injected into muscle or under the skin once a day, once every other day, or 3 times a week. For excessive blood calcium: 1.8 IU per lb of body weight injected every 12 hours to start. Dose may be increased or decreased by your doctor. Nasal spray— 200 IU (1 spray) a day delivered in alternating nostrils, 1 spray a day.

ONSET OF EFFECT
Within 15 minutes.

DURATION OF ACTION
8 to 24 hours.

DIETARY ADVICE
If you are using this drug to lower blood calcium, your doctor may want you to follow a low-calcium diet. An injection is best administered at bedtime.

STORAGE
Store in a tightly sealed container away from heat and direct light.

IF YOU MISS A DOSE
If you take 2 doses a day: Take the missed dose if you remember within 2 hours. If not, skip the missed dose and resume your regular dosage schedule. If you take 1 dose a day: Take the missed dose if you remember it the same day, then resume your regular dosage schedule. If you remember the next day, skip the missed dose and resume your regular dosage schedule. If you take one dose every other day: Take the missed dose if you remember the same day. Otherwise, take the dose the next day, skip a day and resume your regular dosage schedule. If you take 1 dose 3 times a week: Take the missed dose the next day, set each dose back a day for the rest of the week, then resume your regular dosage schedule. In no cases should you double the next dose.

STOPPING THE DRUG
The decision to stop taking the drug should be made by your doctor.

PROLONGED USE
Development of antibodies to the medicine may diminish its effectiveness with prolonged use.

PRECAUTIONS
Over 60: Fluid balance should be monitored if the drug is given to reduce blood levels of calcium.

Driving and Hazardous Work: The use of calcitonin should not impair your ability to perform such tasks safely.

Alcohol: Avoid alcohol.

Pregnancy: In animal studies, large doses of calcitonin reduced birth weight. Before you take calcitonin, tell your doctor if you are pregnant or plan to become pregnant.

Breast Feeding: Calcitonin may pass into breast milk; caution is advised. Consult your doctor for specific advice.

Infants and Children: Studies of calcitonin use in infants and children have not been done. Consult your doctor for specific advice.

Special Concerns: You should not take calcitonin if you have a recently healed bone fracture.

OVERDOSE
Symptoms: No specific ones have been reported.

What to Do: An overdose of calcitonin is unlikely to be life-threatening. However, if someone takes a much larger dose than prescribed, call your doctor, emergency medical services (EMS), or the nearest poison control center.

DRUG INTERACTIONS
There are no known drug interactions.

FOOD INTERACTIONS
No known food interactions.

DISEASE INTERACTIONS
Caution is advised when taking calcitonin. Consult your doctor for specific advice if you have a kidney problem or a history of allergies.

Calcitriol

Rocaltrol 0.25 mcg
(ROCHE)

▶ Drug Class: Vitamin D analog

▶ Available in: Capsules, oral solution

▶ Available OTC? No

▶ As Generic? No

Side Effects

SERIOUS
Fatigue, headache, loss of appetite, metallic taste in mouth, nausea, vomiting, abdominal cramps, constipation or diarrhea, dizziness, drowsiness, dry mouth, ringing in ears, muscle pains, joint pains, irritability. Call your doctor immediately.

COMMON
No common side effects are associated with the use of calcitriol.

LESS COMMON
No less-common side effects are associated with calcitriol.

PRINCIPAL USES
To treat abnormally low blood levels of calcium (hypocalcemia) in those with chronic kidney failure who are undergoing dialysis or who have other conditions resulting in low blood calcium, such as hypoparathyroidism (underactive parathyroid gland).

HOW THE DRUG WORKS
Vitamin D must be modified by both the liver and kidneys before it is fully active. Calcitriol, a synthetic form of active vitamin D, promotes the absorption and utilization of calcium and phosphorus in the body. This ensures that blood levels of these minerals are high enough to support the constant turnover of bone and to supply cells with the calcium needed to perform essential functions.

DOSAGE
Frequent blood tests to measure levels of calcium and phosphorus are required when calcitriol is first taken to determine the proper dose. For hypocalcemia in dialysis patients: Adults and children age 6 and over start at 0.25 micrograms (mcg) once a day. Dose may be gradually increased every 4 to 8 weeks to no more than 1 mcg a day. Maintenance dose is usually 0.25 mcg every other day up to 1.25 mcg daily. Children ages 1 to 5: 0.25 to 2 mcg once a day. For hypoparathyroidism: Adults and children age 6 and over start at 0.25 mcg once a day. Dose may be gradually increased every 2 to 4 weeks to no more than 0.5 to 2 mcg a day. Children ages 1 to 5: 0.25 to 0.75 mcg per 2.2 lbs (1 kg) once a day.

ONSET OF EFFECT
2 to 6 hours.

DURATION OF ACTION
3 to 5 days.

DIETARY ADVICE
No special advice.

STORAGE
Store in a tightly sealed container away from heat, moisture, and direct light.

IF YOU MISS A DOSE
Take it as soon as you remember. If it is near the time for the next dose, skip the missed dose and resume your regular dosage schedule. Do not double the next dose.

STOPPING THE DRUG
The decision to stop taking the drug should be made by your doctor.

PROLONGED USE
See your doctor regularly for tests and examinations.

PRECAUTIONS
Over 60: Adverse reactions may be more likely and more severe in older patients.

Driving and Hazardous Work: Do not drive or engage in hazardous work until you determine how the medicine affects you.

Alcohol: Avoid excessive amounts of alcohol.

Pregnancy: No problems have been reported with the recommended daily dose. However, during pregnancy, calcitriol may cause problems in the unborn child when taken in excess of the recommended dosage, especially if the mother develops hypercalcemia (high blood levels of calcium). Before taking it, tell your doctor if you are pregnant or plan to become pregnant.

Breast Feeding: Calcitriol may pass into breast milk; extreme caution is advised. Some experts recommend that the mother not nurse while taking calcitriol. Consult your doctor.

Infants and Children: Calcitriol is not recommended for use by children under the age of 1. Consult your doctor.

OVERDOSE
Symptoms: Symptoms are due to the resulting hypercalcemia. Early symptoms: Constipation (especially in children), diarrhea, dry mouth, increased thirst and frequency of urination, persistent headache, loss of appetite, metallic taste, nausea and vomiting, unusual fatigue. Advanced symptoms: Bone and muscle pain, irregular heartbeat, persistent itching, extreme drowsiness, mental changes.

What to Do: Call your doctor if such symptoms occur. If someone accidentally ingests an extremely large dose, seek medical assistance right away.

DRUG INTERACTIONS
Consult your doctor for specific advice if you are taking antacids, cardiac glycosides, cholestyramine, colestipol, mineral oil, phenobarbital, phenytoin, primidone, thiazide diuretics, other forms of vitamin D, or calcium.

FOOD INTERACTIONS
No known food interactions.

DISEASE INTERACTIONS
Consult your doctor if you have blood vessel disease, heart disease, hypercalcemia, hypervitaminosis D, hypoparathyroidism, kidney disease, hyperphosphatemia, or sarcoidosis.

Calcium

BRAND NAMES
Alka-Mints, Amitone, BioCal, Cal-Plus, Calcarb 600, Calci-Chew, Calci-Mix, Calciday 667, Calcilac, Calcionate, Calcium 600, Calglycine, Calphosan, Caltrate 600, Chooz, Citracal, Dicarbosil, Gencalc 600, Liqui-Cal, Liquid Cal-600, Maalox Antacid Caplets, Mallamint, Neo-Calglucon, Nephro-Calci, Os-Cal 500, Oysco, Oyst-Cal 500, Oyster Shell Calcium-500, Posture, Rolaids Calcium Rich, Titralac, Tums, Tums 500

Caltrate 600 600 mg
(LEDERLE)

Additional photographs

▶ Drug Class: Antihypocalcemic; dietary supplement; antacid

▶ Available in: Capsules, oral suspension, tablets, chewable tablets, liquid

▶ Available OTC? Yes

▶ As Generic? Yes

Side Effects

SERIOUS
Serious side effects are associated with excessively high doses (see Overdose).

COMMON
No common side effects with recommended doses of calcium.

LESS COMMON
Constipation, diarrhea, drowsiness, loss of appetite, dry mouth, and muscle weakness are some of the symptoms that could result if blood levels of calcium are too high (hypercalcemia).

PRINCIPAL USES
To ensure adequate calcium intake in those who do not get sufficient amounts by diet alone. Calcium is essential to many body functions, including the transmission of nerve impulses, the regulation of muscle contraction and relaxation (including of the heart), blood clotting, and various metabolic activities. Calcium is also necessary for maintaining strong bones and is commonly prescribed to prevent and treat postmenopausal osteoporosis (bone thinning). Vitamin D, which aids in the absorption of calcium from the intestine, is often prescribed along with calcium supplements to prevent or treat osteoporosis. (Indeed, some calcium supplement tablets contain vitamin D.) Calcium is also prescribed for individuals with persistently low blood calcium levels (hypocalcemia) caused, for example, by low levels of parathyroid hormone (hypoparathyroidism).

HOW THE DRUG WORKS
Calcium supplements compensate for inadequate dietary intake of this essential mineral. Forms of supplements available include calcium carbonate (the most common and inexpensive), calcium citrate (the best absorbed, but relatively expensive), calcium phosphate, calcium lactate, and calcium gluconate. Because calcium carbonate and phosphate supplements are difficult to absorb, other calcium products are preferable for individuals with low gastric (stomach) acid secretion.

DOSAGE
Optimal daily calcium intakes— Ages 0 to 6 months: 210 mg. Ages 6 months to 1 year: 270 mg. Ages 1 to 3 years: 500 mg.

Ages 4 to 8 years: 800 mg. Ages 9 to 18 years: 1,300 mg. Ages 19 to 50 years: 1,000 mg. Age 51 and older: 1,200. For pregnant or breast-feeding women, under 19 years: 1,300 mg; ages 19 to 50 years: 1,000 mg. Be sure to include dietary calcium as well as the supplements in your total daily intake. It is important to realize that calcium itself constitutes only a fraction of any calcium-containing pill. For example, calcium accounts for only 40% of the weight of a calcium carbonate tablet. Thus, a 500 mg tablet of calcium carbonate provides only 200 mg of calcium.

ONSET OF EFFECT
Unknown.

DURATION OF ACTION
For as long as the supplement is taken.

DIETARY ADVICE
Calcium carbonate and calcium phosphate supplements are best absorbed if taken 60 to 90 minutes after meals. Take with 1 full glass (8 oz) of water or juice. Follow all special dietary guidelines as recommended by your doctor.

STORAGE
Store in a tightly sealed container away from heat, moisture, and direct light.

IF YOU MISS A DOSE
If you are taking calcium supplements on a regular basis and miss a dose, take it as soon as you remember, then resume your regular dosage schedule.

STOPPING THE DRUG
The decision to stop taking calcium supplements should be made in consultation with your doctor.

PROLONGED USE
Adverse effects are more likely to occur if supplements are taken in doses greater than 2,000 to 2,500 mg a day for a long period of time. Your doctor should regularly check your blood calcium levels if you are taking calcium supplements to treat low blood calcium (hypocalcemia).

PRECAUTIONS
Over 60: No special problems are expected.

Driving and Hazardous Work: Calcium supplements should have no effect on your ability to perform such tasks safely.

Alcohol: To ensure proper absorption of calcium, consume alcohol in moderation only (no more than 2 drinks per day).

Pregnancy: It is crucial to receive enough calcium during pregnancy and to maintain those levels throughout pregnancy, preferably through diet alone. However, excessive calcium intake during pregnancy may be harmful to the mother or fetus and should be avoided.

Breast Feeding: Excessive amounts of this supplement taken while nursing may be harmful to the mother or infant and should be avoided.

Infants and Children: No special problems expected.

OVERDOSE
Symptoms: Early symptoms: Constipation (especially in children), diarrhea, dry mouth, increased thirst and frequency of urination, persistent headache, loss of appetite, metallic taste, nausea and vomiting, unusual

Calcium (continued)

fatigue. Advanced symptoms: Bone and muscle pain, irregular heartbeat, persistent itching, extreme drowsiness, mental changes. Severe calcium toxicity may be fatal.

What to Do: Call your doctor, emergency medical services (EMS), or the nearest poison control center immediately.

DRUG INTERACTIONS

Consult your doctor for specific advice if you are taking other calcium-containing preparations, cellulose sodium phosphate, digitalis drugs, etidronate, gallium nitrate, phenytoin, or tetracycline antibiotics. Combined use of calcium supplements with thiazide diuretics or vitamin D may lead to excessively high calcium levels.

FOOD INTERACTIONS

Excessive protein consumption can increase the excretion of calcium in the urine. In meals preceding calcium consumption, avoid spinach and rhubarb (high in oxalic acid), and bran andwhole cereals (high in phytic acid), since these substances may interfere with calcium absorption.

DISEASE INTERACTIONS

Consult your doctor if you have frequent episodes of diarrhea, any stomach or intestinal problems, heart disease, sarcoidosis, kidney disease, or kidney stones.

Candesartan Cilexetil

▶ Drug Class: Antihypertensive/ angiotensin II antagonist

▶ Available in: Tablets

▶ Available OTC? No

▶ As Generic? No

Side Effects

SERIOUS
No serious side effects are associated with the use of candesartan. (In clinical trials, the incidence of adverse effects was not significantly greater with the medication than with a placebo.)

COMMON
No common side effects are associated with the use of candesartan.

LESS COMMON
Headache, dizziness, back pain, upper respiratory tract infection, sore throat, and nasal congestion.

PRINCIPAL USES
To control high blood pressure. This drug appears to have the same benefits as the class of antihypertensive drugs known as ACE inhibitors, without producing the common side effect (experienced by as many as 30% of patients) of a dry cough. Candesartan may be used by itself or in conjunction with other antihypertensive medications.

HOW THE DRUG WORKS
Candesartan blocks the effects of angiotensin II, a naturally occurring substance that causes blood vessels to narrow. Candesartan causes the blood vessels to dilate, thereby lowering blood pressure and decreasing the workload of the heart.

DOSAGE
To start, 16 mg once a day when used as the only drug to treat hypertension. Usual maintenance dose is 8 to 32 mg daily, taken once a day or divided into 2 doses.

ONSET OF EFFECT
Within 2 weeks.

DURATION OF ACTION
Up to 24 hours.

DIETARY ADVICE
No special restrictions, unless your doctor has advised a low-sodium diet or other dietary modifications to help you control your blood pressure.

STORAGE
Store in a tightly sealed container away from heat, moisture, and direct light.

IF YOU MISS A DOSE
Take it as soon as you remember. If it is near the time for the next dose, skip the missed dose and resume your regular dosage schedule. Do not double the next dose.

STOPPING THE DRUG
Take it as prescribed for the full treatment period. The decision to stop taking the drug should be made in consultation with your physician.

PROLONGED USE
Lifelong therapy may be necessary. However, if you do change certain health habits (for example, increasing exercise or losing weight), a reduced dose may be possible under a doctor's supervision.

PRECAUTIONS
Over 60: No special problems are expected.

Driving and Hazardous Work: Do not drive or engage in hazardous work until you determine how the medicine affects you.

Alcohol: No special precautions are necessary.

Pregnancy: Candesartan should not be used by pregnant women. Discontinue taking the drug as soon as possible when pregnancy is detected and discuss treatment alternatives with your doctor.

Breast Feeding: Candesartan may pass into breast milk; caution is advised. Consult your doctor for advice.

Infants and Children: The safety and effectiveness of use in children have not been established.

Special Concerns: Candesartan may cause excessively low blood pressure with dizziness or lightheadedness, which is most noticeable when you change position. This may lead to fainting, falls, and injury. Sit or lie down immediately if you feel dizzy or lightheaded. This side effect may be worsened by alcohol, hot weather, dehydration, salt depletion from diuretic use, fever, prolonged standing, prolonged sitting, or exercise.

OVERDOSE
Symptoms: Few cases of overdose have been reported. However, if you take a much larger dose than prescribed, you may experience fainting, dizziness, weak pulse that might be very slow or very fast.

What to Do: Call your doctor, emergency medical services (EMS), or the nearest poison control center immediately.

DRUG INTERACTIONS
No drug interactions have yet been observed with candesartan. Consult your doctor for specific advice if you are taking any other medication, especially other drugs for high blood pressure. Candesartan can be taken together with diuretics or other medications for high blood pressure, if your doctor approves.

FOOD INTERACTIONS
No known food interactions.

DISEASE INTERACTIONS
Patients with moderate to severe liver or kidney disease are advised to exercise caution when taking candesartan.

Capecitabine

BRAND NAME
Xeloda

▶ Drug Class: Antineoplastic (anticancer) agent

▶ Available in: Tablets

▶ Available OTC? No

▶ As Generic? No

Side Effects

SERIOUS
Fever greater than 100.5°F; severe diarrhea, nausea, and vomiting; loss of or decreased appetite; pain, redness, swelling and sores in the mouth and throat; pain, numbness, tingling, swelling, and redness of the palms of the hands or soles of the feet (hand-and-foot syndrome). Stop taking the drug and call your oncologist immediately.

COMMON
Abdominal pain, constipation, dehydration, rash, dry or itchy skin, weakness, headache, drowsiness, dizziness, mild fever.

LESS COMMON
Numerous less common side effects can occur; consult your doctor if you are concerned about any adverse or unusual reactions you experience while taking this drug.

PRINCIPAL USES
To treat advanced (metastatic) breast cancer. Capecitabine is used for secondary treatment when other therapies have not produced adequate results. Your oncologist will determine if capecitabine is appropriate for your condition.

HOW THE DRUG WORKS
By interfering with essential phases of cell division in cancer cells, capecitabine prevents them from multiplying. The drug may cause side effects by affecting other kinds of cells in the body.

DOSAGE
2,500 mg per square meter of body surface in 2 divided doses (12 hours apart) a day. Capecitabine is taken in 3-week cycles: 2 weeks on and 1 week off. Your oncologist will determine the proper dosage and how many cycles of treatment are needed.

ONSET OF EFFECT
Unknown.

DURATION OF ACTION
Unknown.

DIETARY ADVICE
Take with water within 30 minutes after the end of a meal (breakfast and dinner).

STORAGE
Store at room temperature in a tightly sealed container away from heat, moisture, and direct light.

IF YOU MISS A DOSE
It is imperative to try not to miss a dose of capecitabine. If you do miss a dose, skip the missed dose and resume your regular dosage schedule. Do not double the next dose. If you miss more than one dose, contact your oncologist.

STOPPING THE DRUG
Take it as prescribed for the full treatment period. The decision to stop taking the drug should be made by your oncologist.

PROLONGED USE
See your oncologist regularly if you must take this drug for a prolonged period.

PRECAUTIONS
Over 60: Severe gastrointestinal side effects may be more likely and more severe in patients 80 years of age and older.

Driving and Hazardous Work: Do not drive or engage in hazardous work until you determine how the medicine affects you.

Alcohol: No special precautions are necessary.

Pregnancy: Avoid becoming pregnant while taking this drug. Tell your doctor at once if you become pregnant while taking capecitabine.

Breast Feeding: Capecitabine may pass into breast milk; avoid nursing while taking this drug.

Infants and Children: The safety and effectiveness of the use of capecitabine in children under the age of 18 have not been determined.

Special Concerns: Take the medication in the combination prescribed by your oncologist for the morning and evening doses.

OVERDOSE
Symptoms: Nausea, vomiting, diarrhea, stomach irritation and bleeding, fatigue, and paleness.

What to Do: Call your oncologist, emergency medical services (EMS), or the nearest poison control center immediately.

DRUG INTERACTIONS
Do not take leucovorin or fluorouracil if you are taking capecitabine. Consult your oncologist for advice if you are taking folic acid or anticoagulants (such as warfarin).

FOOD INTERACTIONS
No known food interactions.

DISEASE INTERACTIONS
Patients with severe kidney impairment should not take capecitabine. Consult your oncologist if you have a history of heart disease. Patients with liver or kidney disease should be carefully monitored by their doctor while taking capecitabine.

Capsaicin

- Drug Class: Analgesic
- Available in: Cream
- Available OTC? Yes
- As Generic? Yes

Side Effects

SERIOUS
No serious side effects are associated with the use of capsaicin.

COMMON
Stinging or burning sensation when cream is applied. This should subside with regular use, as your body adjusts to the medication.

LESS COMMON
Skin redness; coughing, sneezing, or shortness of breath if dried residues of the drug are inhaled.

PRINCIPAL USES
To relieve neuralgia—pain in the nerve endings near the surface of the skin. Capsaicin is commonly prescribed for neuralgia associated with shingles, an acutely painful condition caused by infection with the varicella zoster virus, the same organism that causes chicken pox. Capsaicin is also used to relieve mild to moderate arthritis, diabetic neuropathy (pain caused by nerve cell damage that occurs as a complication of diabetes), and postoperative pain.

HOW THE DRUG WORKS
When applied topically, capsaicin (a derivative of hot peppers) appears to reduce the amount of a natural chemical known as substance P, which is present in painful joints. Substance P is believed to be involved in two processes central to arthritis: the release of enzymes that produce inflammation and the transmission of pain impulses from the joints to the central nervous system. By blocking the production and release of substance P, capsaicin can reduce the pain associated with arthritis as well as dampen the transmission of pain messages to the brain.

DOSAGE
Apply a small amount to the affected area up to 4 times a day. Do not apply to broken or irritated skin. If the use of a bandage is recommended, do not apply it too tightly.

ONSET OF EFFECT
Therapeutic pain response is usually achieved in 1 to 2 weeks but may take as long as 4 weeks.

DURATION OF ACTION
Up to 6 hours.

DIETARY ADVICE
This medication can be used without regard to diet.

STORAGE
Store in a tightly sealed container away from heat and direct light.

IF YOU MISS A DOSE
Apply it as soon as you remember. If it is near the time for the next dose, skip the missed dose and resume your regular dosage schedule. Do not double the next dose.

STOPPING THE DRUG
Pain relief will last only as long as capsaicin is used regularly. If you discontinue using the medication and the pain returns, it is safe to resume treatment.

PROLONGED USE
No special problems are expected. Burning and stinging sensations upon application frequently subside with prolonged use. If your condition worsens or does not improve after 1 month, discontinue using capsaicin and consult your doctor.

PRECAUTIONS
Over 60: No special problems are expected.

Driving and Hazardous Work: No problems are expected.

Alcohol: No special precautions are necessary.

Pregnancy: No problems have been reported.

Breast Feeding: No problems are expected.

Infants and Children: Not recommended for use on children under the age of 2. No problems are expected in older children.

Special Concerns: You may not be able to use capsaicin if you are allergic to it or if you have ever had an allergic reaction to hot peppers. Wash your hands thoroughly after applying the cream; if you are using it for arthritis of the hands, wait 30 minutes before washing. It can cause a burning sensation if even small amounts get into the eyes or on other sensitive areas of the body. If you wear contact lenses, be especially cautious. If it does get into your eyes, flush them with water. On other sensitive areas of the body, wash the area with warm (but not hot) soapy water. After applying capsaicin cream, avoid contact with children and pets until you have thoroughly washed your hands.

OVERDOSE
Symptoms: No cases of overdose have been reported.

What to Do: An overdose is unlikely to be life-threatening. However, if someone applies a much larger dose than prescribed, suffers adverse side effects, or accidentally ingests it, call your doctor or the nearest poison control center for advice.

DRUG INTERACTIONS
Capsaicin may alter the action of some drugs or trigger unwanted side effects. Consult your doctor about any other drugs that you take, including over-the-counter medications.

FOOD INTERACTIONS
None are known.

DISEASE INTERACTIONS
Consult your doctor if you have broken or irritated skin, or conditions that may result in broken skin, on the area to be treated.

Captopril

BRAND NAME
Capoten

Capoten 100 mg
(Bristol-Myers Squibb)

Additional photographs

▶ Drug Class: Angiotensin-converting enzyme (ACE) inhibitor

▶ Available in: Tablets

▶ Available OTC? No

▶ As Generic? Yes

Side Effects

SERIOUS
Fever and chills, sore throat and hoarseness, sudden difficulty breathing or swallowing, swelling of the face, mouth, or extremities, impaired kidney function (ankle swelling, decreased urination), confusion, yellow discoloration of the eyes or skin (indicating liver disorder), intense itching, chest pain or palpitations, abdominal pain. Serious side effects are very rare; contact your doctor immediately.

COMMON
Dry, persistent cough.

LESS COMMON
Dizziness or fainting, skin rash, numbness or tingling in the hands, feet, or lips, unusual fatigue or muscle weakness, nausea, drowsiness, loss of taste, headache.

PRINCIPAL USES
To control high blood pressure; to treat congestive heart failure (CHF); to treat patients with left ventricular dysfunction (damage to the pumping chamber of the heart); and to minimize further kidney damage in diabetics with mild kidney disease.

HOW THE DRUG WORKS
Angiotensin-converting enzyme (ACE) inhibitors block an enzyme that produces angiotensin, a naturally occurring substance that causes blood vessels to constrict and stimulates production of the adrenal hormone, aldosterone, which promotes sodium retention in the body. As a result, ACE inhibitors relax blood vessels (causing them to widen) and reduces sodium retention, which lowers blood pressure and so decreases the workload of the heart.

DOSAGE
Adults— For high blood pressure: 12.5 to 150 mg, 2 or 3 times a day. For CHF: 6.25 to 100 mg, 2 or 3 times a day. For left ventricular dysfunction: 6.25 to 50 mg, 3 times a day. For kidney problems associated with diabetes: 25 mg, 3 times a day. Children— Consult your pediatrician.

ONSET OF EFFECT
15 to 60 minutes.

DURATION OF ACTION
6 to 12 hours.

DIETARY ADVICE
Take it on an empty stomach, about 1 hour before mealtime. Follow your doctor's dietary advice (such as low-salt or low-cholesterol restrictions) to improve control over high blood pressure and heart disease. Avoid high-potassium foods like bananas and citrus fruits and juices, unless you are also taking medications, such as diuretics, that lower potassium levels.

STORAGE
Store in a tightly sealed container away from heat and direct light.

IF YOU MISS A DOSE
Take it as soon as you remember. If it is near the time for the next dose, skip the missed dose and resume your regular dosage schedule. Do not double the next dose.

STOPPING THE DRUG
Do not stop taking this drug abruptly, as this may cause potentially serious health problems. Dosage should be reduced gradually, according to your doctor's instructions.

PROLONGED USE
See your doctor regularly for examinations and tests if you must take this medicine for a prolonged period. Remember that captopril helps control high blood pressure but does not cure it. Lifelong therapy may be necessary.

PRECAUTIONS
Over 60: Adverse reactions may be more likely and more severe.

Driving and Hazardous Work: Avoid such activities until you determine how the medication affects you.

Alcohol: Consume alcohol only in moderation since it may increase the effect of the drug and cause an excessive drop in blood pressure.

Pregnancy: Captopril should not be used during the final 6 months of pregnancy. Notify your doctor right away if you become pregnant.

Breast Feeding: If possible, avoid using captopril while nursing.

Infants and Children: Captopril is only prescribed for children when other means of controlling hypertension fail; benefits must be weighed against risks. Consult your pediatrician for advice.

OVERDOSE
Symptoms: Dizziness or fainting; weak, rapid pulse; nausea, vomiting; chest pain.

What to Do: Call your doctor, emergency medical services (EMS), or the nearest poison control center immediately.

DRUG INTERACTIONS
Consult your doctor if you are taking diuretics (especially potassium-sparing diuretics), potassium supplements or drugs containing potassium (check ingredient labels), lithium, anticoagulants (such as warfarin), indomethacin or other anti-inflammatory drugs, or any over-the-counter drugs (especially cold remedies and diet pills).

FOOD INTERACTIONS
Avoid low-salt milk and salt substitutes. Many of these products contain potassium.

DISEASE INTERACTIONS
Consult your doctor if you have systemic lupus erythematosus or if you have had a prior allergic reaction to ACE inhibitors. This medication should be used with caution by patients with severe kidney disease or renal artery stenosis (narrowing of one or both of the arteries that supply blood to the kidneys).

Carbamazepine

Tegretol 200 mg
(BASEL)

Additional photographs

▶ Drug Class: Anticonvulsant/
analgesic

▶ Available in: Oral suspension,
tablets, extended-release
tablets and capsules

▶ Available OTC? No

▶ As Generic? Yes

Side Effects

SERIOUS
Fever, sore throat,
swollen glands, point-like
rash, blistering or peel-
ing, easy bruising, pallor,
weakness, confusion,
lethargy, or seizures may
be a sign of a potentially
fatal blood reaction
(aplastic anemia). Call
your doctor at once.

COMMON
Drowsiness, rash, itching,
increased sensitivity of
the skin to sunlight, dizziness, blurred vision, incoordination, nausea,
vomiting, stomach pain
or upset, diarrhea, constipation, loss of appetite,
dry or inflamed mouth.

LESS COMMON
Impaired speech, involun-
tary movements of the
face, limbs, or tongue,
tingling or numbness in
the extremities, depres-
sion, agitation, psychosis,
talkativeness, abnormal
eye movements, ringing
in the ears, heart rhythm
abnormalities, impotence,
hair loss, or excessive
hair growth. There are
numerous additional
potential side effects.

PRINCIPAL USES
To control certain types of
seizures due to epilepsy.
Also to treat facial pain in
those with trigeminal neuralgia (tic douloureux).

HOW THE DRUG WORKS
Carbamazepine appears to
inhibit neurons from firing
repeatedly and uncontrol-
lably (which causes
seizures).

DOSAGE
Adults: 600 to 2,000 mg a
day, in 3 or 4 divided doses.
Children: 9 to 18 mg per lb
of body weight, in 3 or 4
divided doses. Some
patients require higher
doses. A low dose should be
used initially, then gradually
increased if needed. The
extended-release forms may
be given twice a day.

ONSET OF EFFECT
Several hours or longer.

DURATION OF ACTION
Maximum effectiveness: 12
hours or longer; effectiveness then gradually
decreases.

DIETARY ADVICE
Take with food to lessen the
chance of stomach upset.

STORAGE
Store in a tightly sealed container away from heat, moisture, and direct light.

IF YOU MISS A DOSE
Take it as soon as you
remember. If it is near the
time for the next dose, skip
the missed dose and
resume your regular dosage
schedule. Do not double the
next dose, unless advised to
do so by your doctor. Call
your doctor if you miss
more than a full day's worth
of doses.

STOPPING THE DRUG
Never stop this drug
abruptly; seizures may

occur. Your doctor will taper
the dose over many weeks.

PROLONGED USE
Therapy may last several
years or longer. Some side
effects may diminish after a
few weeks of therapy.

PRECAUTIONS
Over 60: Older patients
may require lower doses to
minimize side effects.

**Driving and Hazardous
Work:** Avoid such tasks
until you determine how the
medication affects you.

Alcohol: May contribute to
excessive drowsiness.

Pregnancy: This drug
increases the risk of birth
defects. However, seizures
during pregnancy also
increase the risks to the
fetus. Discuss potential
risks and benefits with your
doctor. Folate supplementation is advised starting 1 to
2 months before conception
and continuing throughout
pregnancy. Vitamin K1 may
be needed during the last 4
weeks of pregnancy.

Breast Feeding: This
drug passes into breast
milk, although at low levels.
Consult your doctor for
specific advice.

Infants and Children:
Behavioral side effects are
more likely to be seen in
children.

Special Concerns: The
generic form is not recommended. Do not change the
brand you are taking without consulting your doctor.
Your doctor may suggest
you carry an ID card or
bracelet saying that you
take this drug.

OVERDOSE
Symptoms: Confusion,
double vision, seizures,

extreme drowsiness, loss of
consciousness, poor muscle
control, spasms, tremors,
walking difficulty, abnormal
heartbeat, slow or irregular
breathing.

What to Do: Seek medical
assistance immediately.

DRUG INTERACTIONS
Carbamazepine may interact
with many drugs, including
other anticonvulsants (clonazepam, ethosuximide,
primidone, valproic acid,
phenytoin, and phenobarbital), anticoagulants, certain
anti-infectives (erythro-
mycin, doxycycline, troleandomycin, isoniazid), oral
contraceptives, cimetidine,
corticosteroids, danazol,
diltiazem, lithium, nicotinamide, propoxyphene,
theophylline, thyroid hormones, verapamil.

FOOD INTERACTIONS
No known food interactions.

DISEASE INTERACTIONS
Special caution is advised in
those with lupus; heart, kidney, or liver disease; diabetes; or glaucoma.

Carbenicillin Indanyl Sodium

BRAND NAMES
Geocillin, Geopen

Geocillin 382 mg
(ROERIG)

▶ Drug Class: Penicillin antibiotic

▶ Available in: Tablets, injection

▶ Available OTC? No

▶ As Generic? Yes

Side Effects

SERIOUS
Irregular, rapid, or labored breathing, light-headedness or sudden fainting, joint pain, fever, severe abdominal pain and cramping with watery or bloody stools, severe allergic reaction (marked by sudden swelling of the lips, tongue, face, or throat; breathing difficulty; skin rash, itching, or hives), unusual bleeding or bruising, yellowish tinge to eyes or skin. Call your doctor immediately.

COMMON
Mild rash, mild diarrhea, nausea, vomiting, headache, vaginal discharge and itching, pain or white patches in the mouth or on the tongue.

LESS COMMON
Diminished urine output, chills, weakness, fatigue.

PRINCIPAL USES
To treat bacterial infections, especially those of the prostate and urinary tract. Carbenicillin is effective only against infections caused by bacteria; it is ineffective against those caused by viruses, fungi, or other microorganisms.

HOW THE DRUG WORKS
Carbenicillin blocks the formation of bacterial cell walls, rendering bacteria unable to multiply and spread.

DOSAGE
Tablets— Adults and teenagers: 382 to 764 mg every 6 hours. Children: Consult your pediatrician. Injection— The dose is determined by your doctor based on patient's body weight and other variables.

ONSET OF EFFECT
Unknown.

DURATION OF ACTION
Unknown.

DIETARY ADVICE
Carbenicillin should be taken on an empty stomach, at least 1 hour before or 2 hours after meals, with plenty of water. Patients with high blood pressure who follow a sodium-restricted diet should be aware that carbenicillin tablets contain a significant amount of salt.

STORAGE
Store in a tightly sealed container away from heat and direct light.

IF YOU MISS A DOSE
Take it as soon as you remember. If it is within 2 hours of the next dose, skip the missed dose and resume your regular dosage schedule. Do not double the next dose.

STOPPING THE DRUG
Take it as prescribed for the full treatment period, even if you begin to feel better before the scheduled end of therapy. Stopping the drug prematurely may slow your recovery or lead to a rebound infection, also known as superinfection, in which the heartier strains of bacteria survive and multiply, leading to a more serious and drug-resistant infection.

PROLONGED USE
Prolonged use of any antibiotic increases the risk of superinfection; caution is advised.

PRECAUTIONS
Over 60: No special problems are expected.

Driving and Hazardous Work: Do not drive or engage in hazardous work until you determine how the medicine affects you.

Alcohol: No special precautions are necessary.

Pregnancy: Adequate studies of the use of penicillin antibiotics during pregnancy have not been done; however, no problems have been reported.

Breast Feeding: Carbenicillin may pass into breast milk and cause problems in the nursing infant; avoid use while nursing.

Infants and Children: No special problems are expected.

Special Concerns: Carbenicillin can cause false results on some urine sugar tests for patients with diabetes. Those who are prone to asthma, hay fever, hives, or allergies may be more likely to have an allergic reaction to a penicillin antibiotic. If severe diarrhea occurs as a side effect of this drug, do not take antidiarrheal medications; call your doctor.

OVERDOSE
Symptoms: Seizures may occur with very high doses; overdose is nonetheless unlikely.

What to Do: If you have reason to suspect an overdose, seek medical assistance immediately.

DRUG INTERACTIONS
Consult your doctor for specific advice if you are taking aminoglycosides, ACE inhibitors, diuretics, potassium supplements or potassium-containing medications, anticoagulants or other anticlotting drugs, nonsteroidal anti-inflammatory drugs, sulfinpyrazone, cholestyramine, colestipol, oral contraceptives, methotrexate, or probenecid.

FOOD INTERACTIONS
No known food interactions.

DISEASE INTERACTIONS
Consult your doctor if you have a history of allergies, asthma, bleeding disorders (such as hemophilia), congestive heart failure, gastrointestinal disorders (especially colitis associated with the use of antibiotics), high blood pressure, or impaired kidney function.

Carisoprodol

Generic 350 mg
(SCHEIN/DANBURY)

▶ Drug Class: Muscle relaxant

▶ Available in: Tablets

▶ Available OTC? No

▶ As Generic? Yes

Side Effects

SERIOUS
Fainting; palpitations or rapid heartbeat; fever; hives or severe swelling of face, lips, or tongue along with shortness of breath, chest tightness, or wheezing (indicating a potentially life-threatening allergic reaction); depression. Seek medical help immediately.

COMMON
Drowsiness, dizziness, dry mouth.

LESS COMMON
Inability to pass urine; sores on lips, ulcers in mouth; abdominal cramps or pain; clumsiness; unsteady gait; confusion; constipation; diarrhea; excitability, nervousness, restlessness, or irritability; flushing or redness of face; headache; heartburn; hiccups; muscle weakness; nausea and vomiting; trembling; insomnia or fitful sleep; burning, red eyes; stuffy nose.

PRINCIPAL USES
Skeletal muscle relaxants are used to relieve stiffness and discomfort caused by severe sprains and strains, muscle spasms, or other muscle problems. They may be prescribed in conjunction with other treatment methods, such as physical therapy.

HOW THE DRUG WORKS
Muscle relaxants such as carisoprodol depress activity in the central nervous system, which in turn interferes with the transmission of nerve impulses from the spinal cord to the muscles.

DOSAGE
Adults and teenagers: 350 mg, 3 to 4 times a day. Children ages 5 to 12: 6.25 mg per 2.2 lbs (1 kg) of body weight 4 times a day.

ONSET OF EFFECT
30 minutes.

DURATION OF ACTION
4 to 6 hours.

DIETARY ADVICE
Be sure to eat a well-balanced diet; the healing of injured tissue increases the body's protein and calorie requirements. To avoid dry mouth, maintain adequate fluid intake and suck on ice chips.

STORAGE
Store in a tightly sealed container in a dry place away from heat and direct light.

IF YOU MISS A DOSE
Take it as soon as you remember. If it is within 2 hours of the next dose, skip the missed dose and resume your regular dosage schedule. Do not double the next dose.

STOPPING THE DRUG
This medication should be taken as prescribed for the full treatment period. Do not stop taking carisoprodol abruptly.

PROLONGED USE
Therapy with carisoprodol ranges from several days to weeks. Prolonged use may be associated with an increased risk of side effects.

PRECAUTIONS
Over 60: Adverse reactions to medications such as carisoprodol may be more likely and more severe in older patients.

Driving and Hazardous Work: Carisoprodol may impair your ability to drive or perform hazardous work.

Alcohol: Avoid alcohol while taking this medication because it may compound the sedative effect and may cause liver damage.

Pregnancy: Adequate studies of carisoprodol during pregnancy have not been done; discuss the relative risks and benefits with your doctor.

Breast Feeding: Breast feeding is not recommended during therapy.

Infants and Children: No special problems have been documented; consult your pediatrician for advice.

Special Concerns: Carisoprodol will intensify the effect that alcohol, sedatives, and other central nervous system depressants have on the brain. It is not a substitute for other safe, nonmedical therapies for muscle stiffness, including rest, gentle guided exercise, and physical therapy.

OVERDOSE
Symptoms: Excessive drowsiness or difficulty awakening, even when being shaken or pinched; confusion; weakness; slowed breathing; coma.

What to Do: Call emergency medical services (EMS) or the nearest poison control center immediately.

DRUG INTERACTIONS
Consult your doctor for specific advice if you are taking antihistamines and decongestants, antidepressants, sedatives, tranquilizers, sleep aids, pain medication, barbiturates, or seizure medication.

FOOD INTERACTIONS
No known food interactions.

DISEASE INTERACTIONS
Caution is advised when taking carisoprodol. Consult your doctor if you have a history of any of the following: allergies, drug abuse or dependence, kidney disease, liver disease, porphyria, epilepsy, or any other seizure disorder.

Carmustine

BRAND NAMES
BCNU, BiCNU

▶ Drug Class: Alkylating agent

▶ Available in: Injection

▶ Available OTC? No

▶ As Generic? Yes

Side Effects

SERIOUS
Black or tarry stools; blood-tinged (pink or maroon) urine or stools; cough or shortness of breath; fever and chills; lower back pain or pain in flanks; painful, difficult urination; small, red spots on the skin; bleeding from gums, nose, or other unusual places; easy bruising. These side effects may mean that normal blood cells and special blood-clotting cells have been affected, or that normal immune cells have been affected and an infection is developing somewhere in your body. See your doctor right away if any of these symptoms occur.

COMMON
Nausea and vomiting, weakness, fatigue, loss of appetite, pain or redness at injection site (tell your nurse immediately if this happens while the drug is being administered).

LESS COMMON
Decreased urination, edema (swelling) of the feet and ankles, diarrhea, dizziness, skin discoloration at injection site, skin rash or itching, difficulty swallowing, difficulty walking, hair loss.

PRINCIPAL USES
To treat brain, liver, and gastrointestinal cancers, in addition to lymphomas (cancers of the lymphatic system).

HOW THE DRUG WORKS
Carmustine interferes with the growth of cancer cells by preventing them from reproducing. The drug may also affect the growth and development of normal cells in the body, resulting in unpleasant side effects.

DOSAGE
Adults and children: The dose of carmustine depends on the type of tumor, the patient's body weight, and whether other chemotherapy drugs are being used. Your oncologist (cancer specialist) will determine the proper dose.

ONSET OF EFFECT
Almost immediately following injection.

DURATION OF ACTION
Unknown.

DIETARY ADVICE
Maintain optimal food and fluid intake. Calorie, protein, and vitamin needs increase in patients with cancer. Good nutrition is essential to cope with the demands of chemotherapy.

STORAGE
Refrigerate.

IF YOU MISS A DOSE
Inform your oncologist as soon as possible.

STOPPING THE DRUG
The decision to stop administering carmustine must be made by your doctor.

PROLONGED USE
Use beyond 1 to 2 days is not recommended.

PRECAUTIONS
Over 60: Adverse reactions may be more likely and more severe.

Driving and Hazardous Work: The use of this medication may impair your ability to drive or operate machinery safely, or perform hazardous work.

Alcohol: Avoid alcohol.

Pregnancy: Carmustine may cause birth defects. Persons of childbearing years should take steps to prevent pregnancy during therapy.

Breast Feeding: Not recommended during therapy.

Infants and Children: Consult your pediatrician.

Special Concerns: Patients with cancer are very often weakened by their illness, by poor nutrition, and by the effects of chemotherapy, radiation, and surgery. These patients are more likely to experience undesirable side effects of a medication. In addition, these side effects may be more pronounced. Follow directions very carefully for all medication that you are taking. Read and understand all potential side effects and drug interactions. Infection is the single greatest threat to people receiving chemotherapy. Carmustine may lower your ability to resist infection by lowering the number of white blood cells in the blood. Therefore, do not receive any vaccinations without your doctor's approval. Avoid people with infections. Inform your doctor immediately if you have fever, chills, diarrhea, or a cough. Shortness of breath may develop many years after initial treatment in children or adolescents who receive higher doses.

OVERDOSE
Symptoms: No cases of overdose have been reported.

What to Do: Although not likely to occur, if you are concerned about the possibility of an overdose of carmustine, contact your doctor.

DRUG INTERACTIONS
Consult your doctor for specific advice if you are taking amphotericin B, thyroid medications, azathioprine, chloramphenicol, colchicine, flucytosine, ganciclovir, interferon, plicamycin, or zidovudine (AZT).

FOOD INTERACTIONS
None are known.

DISEASE INTERACTIONS
Consult your doctor if you have any of the following: chicken pox (or recent exposure to someone with it), shingles, an infection, kidney disease, liver disease, or lung disease.

Carteolol Hydrochloride Ophthalmic

BRAND NAME
Ocupress

▶ Drug Class: Antiglaucoma drug; ophthalmic beta-blocker

▶ Available in: Ophthalmic solution

▶ Available OTC? No

▶ As Generic? No

Side Effects

SERIOUS
Palpitations, breathing difficulty, dizziness and weakness caused by low blood pressure. Call your doctor right away.

COMMON
Temporary eye irritation, tearing, eye inflammation, burning, swelling.

LESS COMMON
Blurred vision, poor night vision, and increased sensitivity to light; headache; insomnia; sinus irritation; odd or bitter taste in the mouth.

PRINCIPAL USES
To treat glaucoma.

HOW THE DRUG WORKS
Glaucoma, a sight-threatening disorder, occurs when aqueous humor (the fluid inside the eye) cannot drain properly, causing an increase in pressure within the eyeball (known as intraocular pressure). Increased intraocular pressure can damage the optic nerve and lead to a gradually progressive loss of vision. Carteolol decreases the production of aqueous humor, thereby reducing intraocular pressure.

DOSAGE
1 drop inside the lower eyelid twice a day.

ONSET OF EFFECT
30 to 60 minutes.

DURATION OF ACTION
From 6 to 8 hours.

DIETARY ADVICE
Can be applied without regard to dietary habits or schedule.

STORAGE
Store in a tightly sealed container away from heat, moisture, and direct light.

IF YOU MISS A DOSE
Apply it as soon as you remember. If it is near the time for the next dose, skip the missed dose and resume your regular dosage schedule. Do not double the next dose.

STOPPING THE DRUG
The decision to stop using the drug should be made by your doctor.

PROLONGED USE
Eye examinations should be done regularly as part of glaucoma follow-up.

PRECAUTIONS
Over 60: Adverse reactions may be more likely and more severe in older patients.

Driving and Hazardous Work: Do not drive or engage in hazardous work until you determine how the medicine affects your vision.

Alcohol: Use with caution.

Pregnancy: Adequate human studies have not been completed. Before taking ophthalmic carteolol, tell your doctor if you are pregnant or plan to become pregnant.

Breast Feeding: Ophthalmic carteolol may pass into breast milk; caution is advised. Consult your doctor for advice.

Infants and Children: Adverse reactions may be more likely and more severe in children.

Special Concerns: To use the eye drops, first wash your hands. Tilt your head back. Gently apply pressure to the inside corner of the eyelid and with the index finger of the same hand, pull downward on the lower eyelid to make a space. Drop the medicine into this space and close your eye. Apply pressure for 1 or 2 minutes while keeping the eye closed without blinking. Then wash your hands again. Make sure the tip of the dropper does not touch your eye, finger, or any other surface. Carteolol may make your eyes more sensitive to sunlight. If this occurs, wear sunglasses or avoid bright light as comfort dictates. Before you have any kind of surgery, emergency treatment, or dental treatment, tell the doctor or dentist that you are taking ophthalmic carteolol.

OVERDOSE
Symptoms: Nervousness, chest pain, confusion, hallucinations, coughing, wheezing, drowsiness, dizziness, irregular or pounding heartbeat, insomnia, fatigue.

What to Do: If a large volume of the drug enters the eyes, flush with water. If the medication is accidentally ingested, seek medical assistance right away.

DRUG INTERACTIONS
It is not recommended to use two ophthalmic beta-blockers at the same time. Special caution is warranted in people taking antidiabetic drugs, since ophthalmic carteolol may mask symptoms of low blood sugar. Other drugs may interact with ophthalmic carteolol. Tell your doctor if you are using any other prescription or over-the-counter medication.

FOOD INTERACTIONS
No known food interactions.

DISEASE INTERACTIONS
Do not use ophthalmic carteolol if you have asthma, chronic obstructive pulmonary disease (COPD), or heart rhythm irregularities. Caution is advised when taking ophthalmic carteolol. Consult your doctor if you have any of the following: hay fever, chronic bronchitis, diabetes, low blood sugar, heart disease, blood vessel disease, myasthenia gravis, or an overactive thyroid. Use of this drug may cause complications in patients with liver or kidney disease, since these organs work together to remove the medication from the body.

Carteolol Hydrochloride Oral

BRAND NAME
Cartrol

Cartrol 5 mg
(**Abbott**)

▸ Drug Class: Beta-blocker

▸ Available in: Tablets

▸ Available OTC? No

▸ As Generic? No

Side Effects

SERIOUS
Shortness of breath, wheezing; irregular or slow heartbeat (50 beats per minute or less); pain or feelings of tightness or pressure in the chest; swelling of the ankles, feet, and lower legs; mental depression. Call your doctor right away.

COMMON
Dizziness or lightheadedness, especially when rising rapidly to a standing position; rapid heartbeat or palpitations; decreased sexual ability; unusual fatigue, weakness, or drowsiness; muscle cramps; insomnia.

LESS COMMON
Anxiety, irritability, nervousness; constipation; diarrhea; dry, sore eyes; itching; nausea or vomiting; nightmares or intensely vivid dreams; numbness, tingling, or other unusual sensations in the fingers, toes, or scalp.

PRINCIPAL USES
To treat high blood pressure (hypertension).

HOW THE DRUG WORKS
By blocking actions of the sympathetic nervous system, carteolol reduces the rate and force of the heartbeat, thus lowering blood pressure.

DOSAGE
To treat high blood pressure: 2.5 mg once a day, increased to 5 to 10 mg per day if needed. (Dosage schedule for persons with impaired kidney function: 2.5 mg once every 1, 2, or 3 days as needed.)

ONSET OF EFFECT
Three weeks of therapy may be needed for the full effect of the drug to occur.

DURATION OF ACTION
24 hours.

DIETARY ADVICE
Most effective when taken at least 1 hour before or 2 hours after eating.

STORAGE
Store in a tightly sealed container away from heat and direct light.

IF YOU MISS A DOSE
Take it as soon as you remember. If it is within 8 hours of the next dose, skip the missed dose and resume your regular dosage schedule. Do not double the next dose.

STOPPING THE DRUG
The decision to stop taking the drug should be made in consultation with your doctor. Gradual reduction of the dose over 2 to 3 weeks is generally necessary; stopping the drug abruptly may cause potentially serious medical consequences.

PROLONGED USE
Prolonged use may weaken the heart.

PRECAUTIONS
Over 60: Adverse reactions may be more likely and more severe in older patients. Treatment usually begins with small doses that are increased gradually to avoid an excessive reduction in blood pressure.

Driving and Hazardous Work: Do not drive or engage in hazardous work until you determine how the medicine affects you.

Alcohol: Drink in careful moderation if at all. Alcohol may interact with the drug and cause a dangerous drop in blood pressure.

Pregnancy: No birth defects were found in animal studies. Adequate studies in pregnant human patients have not been done. Before taking carteolol, notify your doctor if you are pregnant or plan to become pregnant.

Breast Feeding: Carteolol may pass into breast milk; caution is advised. Consult your doctor for advice.

Infants and Children: The safety and effectiveness of carteolol use in children under 12 have not been determined. It should be used only under close medical supervision.

Special Concerns: Be cautious about exposure to very hot or very cold weather conditions. Heavy exercise or exertion can cause excessive fatigue, muscle cramping, or dangerous increases in your blood pressure.

OVERDOSE
Symptoms: Slow heartbeat, severe dizziness, fainting, fast or irregular heartbeat, difficulty breathing, bluish-colored fingernails or palms, seizures.

What to Do: Call your doctor, emergency medical services (EMS), or the nearest poison control center immediately.

DRUG INTERACTIONS
Consult your doctor for specific advice if you are taking other drugs for high blood pressure, reserpine, theophylline, amiodarone, clonidine, diltiazem, epinephrine, ergot preparations, fluvoxamine, insulin, nifedipine, oral antidiabetic agents, phenothiazines, nonsteroidal anti-inflammatory drugs, or indomethacin.

FOOD INTERACTIONS
No known food interactions.

DISEASE INTERACTIONS
Use of carteolol may cause complications in patients with liver or kidney disease, since these organs work together to remove the medication from the body. Carteolol should be used with caution in people with diabetes, especially insulin-dependent diabetes, since the drug may mask the symptoms of hypoglycemia. Also consult your doctor if you have any of the following disorders: congestive heart failure, coronary artery disease, allergic rhinitis (seasonal allergies), asthma, chronic bronchitis, hyperthyroidism, myasthenia gravis, or blood vessel (vascular) disease.

Carvedilol

▶ Drug Class: Beta-blocker

▶ Available in: Tablets

▶ Available OTC? No

▶ As Generic? No

Side Effects

SERIOUS
Shortness of breath, wheezing; irregular or slow heartbeat (50 beats per minute or less); pain or feelings of tightness or pressure in the chest; swelling of the ankles, feet, and lower legs; mental depression. If you experience such symptoms, call your doctor immediately.

COMMON
Dizziness or lightheadedness, especially when rising suddenly to a standing position; decreased sexual ability; unusual fatigue, weakness, or drowsiness; insomnia; diarrhea; nausea or vomiting.

LESS COMMON
Anxiety, irritability, nervousness; constipation; dry, sore eyes; itching; nightmares or intensely vivid dreams; numbness, tingling, or other unusual sensations in the fingers, toes, or scalp.

PRINCIPAL USES
To treat mild to severe congestive heart failure (CHF) in conjunction with digitalis, diuretics, or ACE inhibitors. Also used to treat high blood pressure.

HOW THE DRUG WORKS
It is not known how carvedilol improves CHF and lowers blood pressure.

DOSAGE
Dosages must be tailored individually to each patient, using the following guidelines as starting points. For CHF: Initially, 3.125 mg twice a day for 2 weeks. If the dose is tolerated, it may be increased to 6.25 mg twice a day. Dosing should then be doubled every 2 weeks to the highest level tolerated by the patient. For patients weighing less than 187 lbs, maximum daily dose is 25 mg twice a day. For patients weighing more than 187 lbs, maximum daily dose is 50 mg twice a day. For high blood pressure: Initially, 6.25 mg twice a day for 7 to 14 days. Dose may then be increased to 12.5 mg twice a day for 7 to 14 days, as needed. Dose may be further increased to 25 mg twice a day for 7 to 14 days, if tolerated and needed. Maximum daily dose is 50 mg.

ONSET OF EFFECT
Within 1 to 2 hours.

DURATION OF ACTION
Unknown.

DIETARY ADVICE
Take it with food to reduce the risk of potentially dangerous drop in blood pressure. Follow your doctor's dietary guidelines.

STORAGE
Store in a tightly sealed container away from heat, moisture, and direct light.

IF YOU MISS A DOSE
Take it as soon as you remember. If it is within 4 hours of the next scheduled dose, skip the missed dose and resume your regular dosage schedule. Do not double the next dose.

STOPPING THE DRUG
This drug should not be stopped suddenly, as this may lead to angina and possibly a heart attack in patients with advanced heart disease. Slow reduction of dosage over a period of 1 to 2 weeks is advised.

PROLONGED USE
Regular visits to your doctor are needed to evaluate the drug's ongoing, long-term effectiveness.

PRECAUTIONS
Over 60: Many elderly patients are more sensitive to the drug than younger persons. Smaller doses and frequent blood pressure checks may be warranted.

Driving and Hazardous Work: Use caution in such activities until you determine how the medication affects you.

Alcohol: Drink in careful moderation if at all. Alcohol may interact with the drug and cause a dangerous drop in blood pressure.

Pregnancy: Discuss with your doctor the relative risks and benefits of using this drug while pregnant.

Breast Feeding: Trace amounts of this drug can be found in breast milk; however, adverse effects in infants have not been documented. Consult your doctor for specific advice.

Infants and Children: Not recommended.

Special Concerns: Use of the drug should be considered but one element of a comprehensive therapeutic program that includes weight control, smoking cessation, regular exercise, and a healthy (low-salt, low-fat) diet.

OVERDOSE
Symptoms: Unusually slow heartbeat, severe dizziness or fainting, vomiting, breathing difficulty, seizures.

What to Do: Call your doctor, emergency medical services (EMS), or the nearest poison control center immediately.

DRUG INTERACTIONS
The following drugs may interact with carvedilol. Inform your doctor if you are taking amphetamines, oral antidiabetic agents, insulin, asthma medication (such as aminophylline or theophylline), calcium channel blockers, clonidine, guanabenz, immunotherapy for allergies (allergy shots), MAO inhibitors, reserpine, cyclosporine, other beta-blockers, or any over-the-counter medicine.

FOOD INTERACTIONS
None reported.

DISEASE INTERACTIONS
Carvedilol should be used with caution by people with diabetes, especially insulin-dependent diabetes, since the drug may mask symptoms of hypoglycemia. Consult your doctor for specific advice if you have allergies or asthma; heart or blood vessel disease (including peripheral vascular disease); hyperthyroidism; irregular (slow) heartbeat; a history of mental depression; myasthenia gravis; psoriasis; respiratory problems such as bronchitis or emphysema; or kidney or liver disease.

Castor Oil

Side Effects

SERIOUS
Confusion, irregular
heartbeat, muscle
cramps. Call your doctor
immediately.

COMMON
Laxative dependence,
skin rashes, stomach
cramps, belching,
diarrhea, nausea.

LESS COMMON
Fatigue or weakness.

PRINCIPAL USES
For short-term relief of constipation.

HOW THE DRUG WORKS
Castor oil stimulates muscle
contractions in the wall of
the bowel. These contrac-
tions promote the passage
of stool.

DOSAGE
The dose will be different
for different products. A typical dose is 15 to 60 ml for
adults and teenagers. Castor
oil should be taken early in
the day because the laxative
effect is unpredictable and
might otherwise interfere
with a full night's sleep.

ONSET OF EFFECT
Within 2 to 6 hours.

DURATION OF ACTION
Variable.

DIETARY ADVICE
Laxatives may contain a
large amount of sodium or
sugar. Regular bowel movements are more likely with
a diet that contains an adequate amount of liquid (6 to
8 full 8-oz glasses per day),
whole-grain products and
bran, fruit, and vegetables.

STORAGE
Store in a tightly sealed container away from heat, moisture, and direct light. Keep
the liquid form refrigerated,
but do not allow it to freeze.

IF YOU MISS A DOSE
If you are on a prescribed
dosage schedule, take a
missed dose as soon as you
remember, unless the time
for your next scheduled
dose is within the next 2
hours. If so, do not take the
missed dose. Take your
next scheduled dose at the
proper time, and resume
your regular dosage
schedule. Do not double the
next dose.

STOPPING THE DRUG
Take it as prescribed for the
full treatment period. However, you may stop taking
the drug if you are feeling
better before the scheduled
end of the therapy.

PROLONGED USE
Do not use castor oil for
more than 3 to 5 days without informing your physi-
cian. Prolonged, excessive
use of castor oil may be
associated with an increased
risk of side effects, including laxative dependence.

PRECAUTIONS
Over 60: Adverse reactions
may be more likely and
more severe in older
patients.

**Driving and Hazardous
Work:** Do not drive or
engage in hazardous work
until you determine how the
medicine affects you.

Alcohol: Avoid alcohol
when using this medication.

Pregnancy: Castor oil may
cause premature contrac-
tions and so should be
avoided in pregnant women.

Breast Feeding: Castor oil
may be used by nursing
mothers.

Infants and Children:
Do not give laxatives to children under 6 years of age
unless prescribed by a
physician.

Special Concerns: Occasional missed bowel move-
ments do not constitute
constipation; do not use castor oil under such circumstances. Persistent
constipation or difficulty in
passing stool is serious and
requires evaluation.

OVERDOSE
Symptoms: No cases of
overdose with castor oil
have been reported.

What to Do: An overdose
of castor oil is unlikely to be
life-threatening. However, if
someone takes a much
larger dose than prescribed,
contact a physician.

DRUG INTERACTIONS
Do not take a prescription
medication within 2 hours
of taking a laxative (either
before or after), since this
may diminish the effects of
the prescription drug. Consult your doctor for specific
advice if you are taking digitalis drugs or a diuretic.

FOOD INTERACTIONS
No known food interactions.

DISEASE INTERACTIONS
Caution is advised when
taking castor oil. Do not use
any laxative if you have any
of the following: stomach or
abdominal pain, especially if
accompanied by fever;
cramping; abdominal
swelling or bloating; nausea
or vomiting. Consult your
doctor if you have any of
the following problems:
abdominal pain and fever,
rectal bleeding, ostomy (an
artificial surgical opening in
the body to allow the
release of urine or feces),
diabetes mellitus, heart or
kidney disease, or high
blood pressure.

Cefaclor

Generic 500 mg
(**MYLAN**)

▶ Drug Class: Cephalosporin antibiotic

▶ Available in: Capsules, oral suspension

▶ Available OTC? No

▶ As Generic? Yes

Side Effects

SERIOUS
Severe allergic reaction (breathing difficulties, confusion, hives, itching, swelling of the face or throat, sweating, and lightheadedness), severe stomach pain and cramps, fever, severe, sometimes bloody diarrhea. Call your doctor immediately.

COMMON
Mild diarrhea or stomach cramps, sore mouth or tongue, nausea and vomiting.

LESS COMMON
Vaginal itching or unusual discharge, anemia, rash, decreased white blood cell count causing increased susceptibility to infection.

PRINCIPAL USES
To treat a variety of bacterial infections, including those of the nose, tonsils, and throat, skin and soft tissues, genitourinary tract, and the respiratory tract. Cefaclor is effective only against infections caused by bacteria; it is ineffective against those caused by viruses, fungi, or other microorganisms.

HOW THE DRUG WORKS
Cefaclor prevents bacteria from forming cell walls.

DOSAGE
Adults and teenagers: 250 to 500 mg every 8 hours. Children 1 month to 12 years: 20 mg per 2.2 lbs (1 kg) of body weight a day in divided doses every 8 hours. It can be given every 12 hours for ear infection or sore throat.

ONSET OF EFFECT
30 to 60 minutes.

DURATION OF ACTION
1 to 2 hours.

DIETARY ADVICE
Cefaclor may be taken on a full or empty stomach, but taking it with food will reduce stomach irritation.

STORAGE
Store in a tightly sealed container away from heat, moisture, and direct light. Keep liquid form refrigerated, but do not allow it to freeze.

IF YOU MISS A DOSE
Take it as soon as you remember. This will help keep a constant level of medication in your system. If it is near the time for the next dose, skip the missed dose and resume your regular dosage schedule. Do not double the next dose.

STOPPING THE DRUG
Take it as prescribed for the full treatment period, even if you begin to feel better before the scheduled end of therapy. Stopping cefaclor prematurely may slow your recovery or lead to a rebound infection, also known as superinfection, in which the heartier strains of bacteria survive and multiply, leading to a more serious and drug-resistant infection. When taking this drug to treat a streptococcal (strep) infection, it is particularly important to take it for the entire treatment period. Serious heart and kidney problems can develop later if the drug is discontinued prematurely.

PROLONGED USE
Cefaclor is generally prescribed for short-term therapy (10 to 14 days). Use of cefaclor beyond this period increases the risk of adverse effects and superinfection.

PRECAUTIONS
Over 60: Adverse reactions may be more likely and more severe in older patients.

Driving and Hazardous Work: Do not drive or engage in hazardous work until you determine how the medicine affects you.

Alcohol: Avoid alcohol.

Pregnancy: Adequate studies of cephalosporin use in pregnant women have not been done. Before taking cefaclor, tell your physician if you are pregnant or are planning to become pregnant.

Breast Feeding: Cefaclor passes into breast milk; caution is advised. Consult your doctor for specific advice.

Infants and Children: This drug may be used by children 1 month and older. Consult your pediatrician for advice.

Special Concerns: People who are allergic to penicillin may have equally serious allergic reactions to cephalosporin antibiotics such as cefaclor. This drug is useful only against bacteria that are susceptible to its effects, not against colds, flu, or other viral infections. If your condition has not improved within a few days of starting cefaclor, or instead has worsened, tell your doctor.

OVERDOSE
Symptoms: Seizures, severe abdominal pain, bloody diarrhea, vomiting.

What to Do: Call your doctor, emergency medical services (EMS), or the nearest poison control center immediately.

DRUG INTERACTIONS
Consult your doctor for specific advice if you are taking carbenicillin injection, heparin, divalproex, anticoagulants, sulfinpyrazone, dipyridamole, pentoxifylline, plicamycin, ticarcillin, probenecid, or valproic acid.

FOOD INTERACTIONS
No known food interactions.

DISEASE INTERACTIONS
Caution is advised when taking cefaclor. Consult your doctor if you have a history of kidney disease or colitis.

Cefadroxil

Duricef 500 mg
(BRISTOL-MYERS SQUIBB)

▶ Drug Class: Cephalosporin antibiotic

▶ Available in: Capsules, tablets, oral suspension

▶ Available OTC? No

▶ As Generic? Yes

Side Effects

SERIOUS
Severe allergic reaction (breathing difficulties, confusion, hives, itching, swelling of the face or throat, sweating, and lightheadedness), severe stomach pain and cramps, fever, severe, sometimes bloody diarrhea. Call your doctor immediately.

COMMON
Mild diarrhea or stomach cramps, sore mouth or tongue, nausea and vomiting.

LESS COMMON
Vaginal itching or discharge, anemia, rash, decreased white blood cell count causing increased susceptibility to infection, decreased blood platelets causing increased risk of bleeding problems.

PRINCIPAL USES
To treat a variety of bacterial infections, including those of the throat, skin and soft tissues, and the genitourinary tract. Cefadroxil is effective only against infections caused by bacteria; it is ineffective against those caused by viruses, fungi, or other microorganisms.

HOW THE DRUG WORKS
Cefadroxil prevents bacteria from forming protective cell walls necessary for survival.

DOSAGE
Adults and teenagers: 500 mg every 12 hours, or 1 to 2 g once a day. Children: 15 mg per 2.2 lbs (1 kg) of body weight every 12 hours, or 30 mg per 2.2 lbs once a day.

ONSET OF EFFECT
12 hours.

DURATION OF ACTION
20 to 22 hours.

DIETARY ADVICE
Cefadroxil may be taken on a full or empty stomach, but taking it with food will reduce stomach irritation.

STORAGE
Store in a tightly sealed container away from heat, moisture, and direct light. Keep liquid form refrigerated, but do not allow it to freeze.

IF YOU MISS A DOSE
Take it as soon as you remember. This will help keep a constant level of medication in your system. If it is near the time for the next dose, skip the missed dose and resume your regular dosage schedule. Do not double the next dose.

STOPPING THE DRUG
Take it as prescribed for the full treatment period, even if you begin to feel better before the scheduled end of therapy. Stopping cefadroxil prematurely may slow your recovery or lead to a rebound infection, also known as superinfection, in which the heartier strains of bacteria survive and multiply, leading to a more serious and drug-resistant infection. When taking this drug to treat a streptococcal (strep) infection, it is particularly important to take it for the entire treatment period. Serious heart and kidney problems can develop later if the drug is discontinued prematurely.

PROLONGED USE
Cefadroxil is generally prescribed for short-term therapy (10 to 14 days). Use of cefadroxil beyond this period increases the risk of adverse effects and superinfection.

PRECAUTIONS
Over 60: Adverse reactions may be more likely and more severe in older patients.

Driving and Hazardous Work: Do not drive or engage in hazardous work until you determine how the medicine affects you.

Alcohol: Avoid alcohol.

Pregnancy: Adequate studies of cephalosporin use in pregnant women have not been done. Before taking cefadroxil, tell your doctor if you are or plan to become pregnant.

Breast Feeding: Cefadroxil passes into breast milk; caution is advised. Consult your doctor for specific advice.

Infants and Children: This drug may be used by children age 1 and older. Consult your pediatrician for advice.

Special Concerns: People who are allergic to penicillin may have equally serious allergic reactions to cephalosporin antibiotics such as cefadroxil. This drug is useful only against bacteria that are susceptible to its effects, not against colds, flu, or other viral infections. If your condition has not improved within a few days of starting cefadroxil, or instead has worsened, tell your doctor.

OVERDOSE
Symptoms: Seizures, severe abdominal pain, bloody diarrhea, vomiting.

What to Do: Call your doctor, emergency medical services (EMS), or the nearest poison control center immediately.

DRUG INTERACTIONS
Consult your doctor for specific advice if you are taking carbenicillin injection, heparin, divalproex, anticoagulants, sulfinpyrazone, dipyridamole, pentoxifylline, plicamycin, ticarcillin, probenecid, or valproic acid.

FOOD INTERACTIONS
No known food interactions.

DISEASE INTERACTIONS
Caution is advised when taking cefadroxil. Consult your doctor if you have a history of kidney disease or colitis.

Cefamandole Nafate

▶ Drug Class: Cephalosporin antibiotic

▶ Available in: Injection

▶ Available OTC? No

▶ As Generic? Yes

Side Effects

SERIOUS
Severe allergic reaction (breathing difficulties, confusion, hives, swelling of the face or throat, sweating, and lightheadedness), severe stomach pain and cramps, fever, severe, sometimes bloody diarrhea, unusual bleeding or bruising. Call your doctor immediately.

COMMON
Mild diarrhea or stomach cramps, sore mouth or tongue, nausea and vomiting.

LESS COMMON
Vaginal itching or discharge, pain at site of injection, rash, decreased white blood cell count causing increased susceptibility to infection, decreased blood platelets causing increased risk of bleeding problems.

PRINCIPAL USES
To treat a variety of serious bacterial infections, including those of the lung, genitourinary tract, blood, bones, joints, skin, and other organs. Cefamandole nafate is effective only against infections caused by bacteria; it is ineffective against those caused by viruses, fungi, or other microorganisms. Cephalosporins such as cefamandole nafate are prescribed when other antibiotics are not sufficient to treat the infection.

HOW THE DRUG WORKS
Cefamandole nafate prevents bacteria from forming protective cell walls.

DOSAGE
Adults and teenagers: 500 to 1,000 mg (2,000 mg for life-threatening infections) every 4 to 8 hours, injected into a vein or muscle. Children 1 month to 12 years: 8.3 to 33.3 mg per 2.2 lbs (1 kg) of body weight every 4 to 8 hours into a vein or muscle.

ONSET OF EFFECT
Into a vein: Immediate. Into a muscle: 30 to 120 minutes.

DURATION OF ACTION
Into a vein: 1 hour. Into a muscle: 2 hours.

DIETARY ADVICE
Eat 4 oz of yogurt or drink 4 oz of buttermilk a day to protect against intestinal superinfection. Drink plenty of fluids.

STORAGE
Not applicable; the dose is administered only at a health care facility.

IF YOU MISS A DOSE
Not applicable; the dose is administered by a health care professional.

STOPPING THE DRUG
The decision to stop taking cefamandole nafate should be made by your doctor.

PROLONGED USE
Cefamandole nafate is generally prescribed for short-term therapy (10 to 14 days). Use beyond this period increases the risk of adverse effects and superinfection, a subsequent infection caused by heartier, drug-resistant strains of bacteria.

PRECAUTIONS
Over 60: Adverse reactions may be more likely and more severe in older patients.

Driving and Hazardous Work: Not applicable; the dose is administered only in a health care institution.

Alcohol: Avoid alcohol.

Pregnancy: Adequate studies of cephalosporin use in pregnant women have not been done. Before taking cefamandole nafate, tell your doctor if you are pregnant or plan to become pregnant.

Breast Feeding: Cefamandole nafate passes into breast milk; caution is advised. Consult your doctor for advice.

Infants and Children: This drug may be used by children 1 month and older. Consult your pediatrician for advice.

Special Concerns: People who are allergic to penicillin may have equally serious allergic reactions to cephalosporin antibiotics such as cefamandole nafate. This drug is useful only against bacteria that are susceptible to its effects, not against colds, flu, or other viral infections. If your condition has not improved within a few days of starting cefamandole nafate, or instead has worsened, tell your doctor.

OVERDOSE
Symptoms: An overdose of cefamandole nafate is unlikely to occur.

What to Do: Emergency instructions not applicable.

DRUG INTERACTIONS
Consult your doctor for specific advice if you are taking carbenicillin injection, heparin, divalproex, anticoagulants, sulfinpyrazone, dipyridamole, pentoxifylline, plicamycin, ticarcillin, probenecid, medications containing alcohol, or valproic acid.

FOOD INTERACTIONS
No known food interactions.

DISEASE INTERACTIONS
Caution is advised when taking cefamandole nafate. Consult your doctor if you have a history of kidney disease, bleeding disorders, or colitis.

Cefazolin Sodium

BRAND NAMES
Ancef, Kefzol, Zolicef

▶ Drug Class: Cephalosporin antibiotic

▶ Available in: Injection

▶ Available OTC? No

▶ As Generic? Yes

Side Effects

SERIOUS
Severe allergic reaction (breathing difficulties, confusion, itching, hives, swelling of the face or throat, sweating, and lightheadedness), severe stomach pain and cramps, fever, severe, sometimes bloody diarrhea. Call your doctor immediately.

COMMON
Mild diarrhea or stomach cramps, sore mouth or tongue, nausea and vomiting.

LESS COMMON
Vaginal itching or unusual discharge, pain or itching at the site of injection.

PRINCIPAL USES

To treat a variety of moderately severe bacterial infections, including those of the heart, lung, genitourinary tract, bones, joints, skin and soft tissue, and blood. Cefazolin sodium is effective only against infections caused by bacteria; it is ineffective against those caused by viruses, fungi, or other microorganisms. Cephalosporins such as cefazolin sodium are prescribed when other antibiotics are not sufficient to treat the infection. It is also used prior to some surgeries to prevent infection.

HOW THE DRUG WORKS

Cefazolin sodium prevents bacteria from forming protective cell walls.

DOSAGE

Adults and teenagers: 250 to 1,500 mg every 6 to 8 hours into a vein. Children 1 month to 12 years: 6.25 to 25 mg per 2.2 lbs (1 kg) of body weight every 6 hours, or 8.3 to 33.3 mg per 2.2 lbs every 8 hours into a vein.

ONSET OF EFFECT

Immediate.

DURATION OF ACTION

4 hours.

DIETARY ADVICE

Eat 4 oz of yogurt or drink 4 oz of buttermilk a day to protect against intestinal superinfection. Drink plenty of fluids.

STORAGE

Not applicable; the dose is administered only at a health care facility.

IF YOU MISS A DOSE

Not applicable; the dose is administered by a health care professional.

STOPPING THE DRUG

The decision to stop taking the drug should be made by your doctor.

PROLONGED USE

Cefazolin sodium is generally prescribed for short-term therapy (10 to 14 days). Use beyond this period increases the risk of adverse effects and superinfection, a subsequent infection caused by heartier, drug-resistant strains of bacteria.

PRECAUTIONS

Over 60: Adverse reactions may be more likely and more severe in older patients.

Driving and Hazardous Work: Not applicable; the dose is administered only in a health care institution.

Alcohol: Avoid alcohol.

Pregnancy: Adequate studies of cephalosporin use in pregnant women have not been done. Before taking cefazolin sodium, tell your doctor if you are pregnant or plan to become pregnant.

Breast Feeding: Cefazolin sodium passes into breast milk; caution is advised. Consult your doctor for specific advice.

Infants and Children: This drug may be used by children 1 month and older. Consult your pediatrician for advice.

Special Concerns: People who are allergic to penicillin may have equally serious allergic reactions to cephalosporin antibiotics. Cefazolin sodium is useful only against bacteria that are susceptible to its effects and will not work against colds, flu, or other viral infections. If your condition has not improved within a few days of starting cefazolin sodium, or instead has worsened, tell your doctor.

OVERDOSE

Symptoms: An overdose of cefazolin sodium is unlikely.

What to Do: Emergency instructions not applicable.

DRUG INTERACTIONS

Consult your doctor for specific advice if you are taking carbenicillin injection, heparin, divalproex, anticoagulants, sulfinpyrazone, dipyridamole, pentoxifylline, plicamycin, ticarcillin, probenecid, or valproic acid.

FOOD INTERACTIONS

No known food interactions.

DISEASE INTERACTIONS

Caution is advised when taking cefazolin. Consult your doctor if you have a history of kidney disease or colitis.

Cefepime

▶ Drug Class: Cephalosporin antibiotic

▶ Available in: Injection

▶ Available OTC? No

▶ As Generic? No

Side Effects

SERIOUS
Severe allergic reaction (breathing difficulties, confusion, hives, swelling of the face or throat, sweating, and lightheadedness), severe stomach pain and cramps, fever, severe, sometimes bloody diarrhea, unusual bleeding or bruising. Call your doctor immediately.

COMMON
Mild diarrhea or stomach cramps, sore mouth or tongue, nausea and vomiting.

LESS COMMON
Vaginal itching or unusual discharge, pain at the site of injection, itching.

PRINCIPAL USES
To treat a variety of moderate to serious bacterial infections, including those of the ear, nose, tonsils, and throat, skin and soft tissues, genitourinary tract, and the respiratory tract. Cefepime is effective only against infections caused by bacteria; it is ineffective against those caused by viruses, fungi, or other microorganisms. Cephalosporins such as cefepime are prescribed when other antibiotics are not sufficient to treat the infection.

HOW THE DRUG WORKS
Cefepime prevents bacteria from forming cell walls.

DOSAGE
Adults and teenagers—
Mild to moderate urinary tract infections: 500 to 1,000 mg every 12 hours. Severe urinary tract infections: 2,000 mg every 12 hours. Moderate to severe pneumonia: 1,000 to 2,000 mg every 12 hours. Moderate to severe skin infections: 2,000 mg every 12 hours. Injections are usually into a vein. For mild to moderate urinary tract infections, cefepime may be administered into a muscle. Children age 2 months to 16 years and weighing less than 40 kg: 50 mg per 2.2 lbs (1 kg) of body weight every 12 hours. The dose should not exceed the recommended adult dose.

ONSET OF EFFECT
Immediate.

DURATION OF ACTION
Unknown.

DIETARY ADVICE
Eat 4 oz of yogurt or drink 4 oz of buttermilk a day to protect against intestinal superinfection. Drink plenty of fluids.

STORAGE
Not applicable; the dose is administered only at a health care facility.

IF YOU MISS A DOSE
Not applicable; the dose is administered by a health care professional.

STOPPING THE DRUG
The decision to stop taking the drug should be made by your doctor.

PROLONGED USE
Cefepime is generally prescribed for short-term therapy (10 to 14 days). Use of cefepime beyond this period increases the risk of adverse effects and superinfection, a subsequent infection caused by heartier, drug-resistant bacteria.

PRECAUTIONS
Over 60: Adverse reactions may be more likely and more severe in older patients.

Driving and Hazardous Work: Not applicable; the dose is administered only in a health care institution.

Alcohol: Avoid alcohol.

Pregnancy: Adequate studies of cephalosporin use in pregnant women have not been done. Before taking cefepime, tell your doctor if you are pregnant or plan to become pregnant.

Breast Feeding: Cefepime passes into breast milk; caution is advised. Consult your doctor for specific advice.

Infants and Children: This drug is not recommended for use by children under 2 months of age.

Special Concerns: People who are allergic to penicillin may have equally serious allergic reactions to cephalosporin antibiotics such as cefepime. This drug is useful only against bacteria that are susceptible to its effects. Cephalosporins will not work against colds, flu, or other viral infections. If your condition has not improved within a few days of starting cefepime, or instead has worsened, tell your doctor.

OVERDOSE
Symptoms: An overdose of cefepime is unlikely.

What to Do: Emergency instructions not applicable.

DRUG INTERACTIONS
Consult your doctor for specific advice if you are taking carbenicillin injection, heparin, divalproex, anticoagulants, sulfinpyrazone, dipyridamole, pentoxifylline, plicamycin, ticarcillin, probenecid, or valproic acid.

FOOD INTERACTIONS
No known food interactions.

DISEASE INTERACTIONS
Consult your doctor if you have a history of kidney disease, bleeding disorders, or colitis.

Cefixime

Suprax 400 mg
(LEDERLE)

▶ Drug Class: Cephalosporin antibiotic

▶ Available in: Tablets, oral suspension

▶ Available OTC? No

▶ As Generic? No

Side Effects

SERIOUS
Severe allergic reaction (breathing difficulties, confusion, hives, itching, swelling of the face or throat, sweating, and lightheadedness), severe stomach pain and cramps, fever, severe, sometimes bloody diarrhea. Call your doctor immediately.

COMMON
Mild diarrhea or stomach cramps, sore mouth or tongue, nausea and vomiting.

LESS COMMON
Vaginal itching or unusual discharge, decreased white blood cell count causing increased susceptibility to infection, decreased blood platelets causing increased risk of bleeding problems, itching.

PRINCIPAL USES
To treat a variety of bacterial infections, including those of the ear, nose, tonsils, and throat, skin and soft tissues, genitourinary tract, and the respiratory tract. Cefixime is also used to treat gonorrhea. It is effective only against infections caused by bacteria; it is ineffective against those caused by viruses, fungi, or other microorganisms.

HOW THE DRUG WORKS
Cefixime prevents bacteria from forming protective cell walls necessary for survival.

DOSAGE
Adults and teenagers: 200 mg every 12 hours, or 400 mg once a day. Uncomplicated gonorrhea is treated with 400 mg, given in a one-time dose. Children 6 months to 12 years: 4 mg per 2.2 lbs (1 kg) of body weight every 12 hours, or 8 mg per 2.2 lbs once a day.

ONSET OF EFFECT
2 to 4 hours.

DURATION OF ACTION
6 to 18 hours.

DIETARY ADVICE
It may be taken with food to reduce stomach irritation.

STORAGE
Store in a tightly sealed container away from heat, moisture, and direct light. Oral suspension does not need to be refrigerated.

IF YOU MISS A DOSE
Take it as soon as you remember. If it is near the time for the next dose, skip the missed dose and resume your regular dosage schedule. Do not double the next dose.

STOPPING THE DRUG
Take it as prescribed for the full treatment period, even if you begin to feel better before the scheduled end of therapy. Stopping cefixime prematurely may slow your recovery or lead to a rebound infection, also known as superinfection, in which the heartier strains of bacteria survive and multiply, leading to a more serious and drug-resistant infection. When taking this drug to treat a streptococcal (strep) infection, it is particularly important to take it for the entire treatment period. Serious heart and kidney problems can develop later if the drug is discontinued prematurely.

PROLONGED USE
Cefixime, when taken to treat gonorrhea, is prescribed as a one-time dose. For other bacterial infections, cefixime is generally prescribed for short-term therapy (10 to 14 days). Use of cefixime beyond this period increases the risk of adverse effects and superinfection.

PRECAUTIONS
Over 60: Adverse reactions may be more likely and more severe in older patients.

Driving and Hazardous Work: Do not drive or engage in hazardous work until you determine how the medicine affects you.

Alcohol: Avoid alcohol.

Pregnancy: Adequate studies of cephalosporin use in pregnant women have not been done. Before taking cefixime, tell your doctor if you are pregnant or are planning to become pregnant.

Breast Feeding: Cefixime passes into breast milk; caution is advised. Consult your doctor for specific advice.

Infants and Children: May be used by children 6 months and older. Consult your pediatrician for specific advice.

Special Concerns: Those allergic to penicillin may have equally serious allergic reactions to cephalosporin antibiotics such as cefixime. It is useful only against bacteria that are susceptible to its effects, not against colds, flu, or other viral infections. If your condition has not improved within a few days of starting cefixime, or instead has worsened, tell your doctor.

OVERDOSE
Symptoms: Seizures, severe abdominal pain, bloody diarrhea, vomiting.

What to Do: Call your doctor, emergency medical services (EMS), or the nearest poison control center immediately.

DRUG INTERACTIONS
Consult your doctor for specific advice if you are taking carbenicillin injection, heparin, divalproex, anticoagulants, sulfinpyrazone, dipyridamole, pentoxifylline, plicamycin, ticarcillin, probenecid, or valproic acid.

FOOD INTERACTIONS
No known food interactions.

DISEASE INTERACTIONS
Consult your doctor if you have a history of kidney disease or colitis.

Cefotetan Disodium

▶ Drug Class: Cephalosporin antibiotic

▶ Available in: Injection

▶ Available OTC? No

▶ As Generic? No

Side Effects

SERIOUS
Severe allergic reaction (breathing difficulties, confusion, hives, swelling of the face or throat, sweating, and lightheadedness), severe stomach pain and cramps, fever, severe, sometimes bloody diarrhea, unusual bleeding or bruising. Call your doctor immediately.

COMMON
Mild diarrhea or stomach cramps, sore mouth or tongue, nausea and vomiting.

LESS COMMON
Vaginal discharge or itching, pain at site of injection, rash, decreased white blood cell count causing increased susceptibility to infection, decreased blood platelets causing increased risk of bleeding problems.

PRINCIPAL USES
To treat a variety of serious bacterial infections, including those of the lung, genitourinary tract, blood, bones, joints, skin and soft tissues, and other organs. Cefotetan disodium is also used to treat gonorrhea. It is effective only against infections caused by certain strains of bacteria; it is ineffective against those caused by viruses, fungi, or other microorganisms. Cephalosporins such as cefotetan disodium are prescribed when other antibiotics are not sufficient to treat the infection. Cefotetan disodium is also used in some cases prior to certain major surgical procedures in order to minimize the risk of infection.

HOW THE DRUG WORKS
Cefotetan disodium prevents bacteria from forming protective cell walls necessary for their survival.

DOSAGE
1 to 3 g into a vein or muscle every 12 hours.

ONSET OF EFFECT
Into a vein: Immediate. Into a muscle: 1 hour.

DURATION OF ACTION
6 to 9 hours.

DIETARY ADVICE
Eat 4 oz of yogurt or drink 4 oz of buttermilk a day to protect against intestinal superinfection. Drink plenty of fluids.

STORAGE
Not applicable; the dose is administered only at a health care facility.

IF YOU MISS A DOSE
Not applicable; the dose is administered by a health care professional.

STOPPING THE DRUG
The decision to stop taking the drug should be made by your doctor.

PROLONGED USE
Cefotetan disodium is generally prescribed for short-term therapy (10 to 14 days). Use beyond this period increases the likelihood of adverse effects and superinfection, a subsequent infection caused by heartier, drug-resistant strains of bacteria.

PRECAUTIONS
Over 60: Adverse reactions may be more likely and more severe in older patients.

Driving and Hazardous Work: Not applicable; the dose is administered only in a health care institution.

Alcohol: Avoid alcohol.

Pregnancy: Adequate studies of cephalosporin use in pregnant women have not been done. Before taking cefotetan disodium, tell your doctor if you are pregnant or plan to become pregnant.

Breast Feeding: Cefotetan disodium passes into breast milk; caution is advised. Consult your doctor for specific advice.

Infants and Children: This drug is not recommended for use by children under the age of 12.

Special Concerns: People who are allergic to penicillin may have equally serious allergic reactions to cephalosporin antibiotics such as cefotetan disodium. This drug is useful only against bacteria that are susceptible to its effects, not against colds, flu, or other viral infections. If your condition has not improved within a few days of starting cefotetan disodium, or instead has worsened, tell your doctor.

OVERDOSE
Symptoms: An overdose of cefotetan disodium is unlikely.

What to Do: Emergency instructions not applicable.

DRUG INTERACTIONS
Consult your doctor for specific advice if you are taking carbenicillin injection, heparin, divalproex, anticoagulants, sulfinpyrazone, dipyridamole, pentoxifylline, plicamycin, ticarcillin, probenecid, medications containing alcohol, or valproic acid.

FOOD INTERACTIONS
No known food interactions.

DISEASE INTERACTIONS
Caution is advised when taking cefotetan disodium. Consult your doctor if you have a history of kidney disease, bleeding disorders, or colitis.

Cefpodoxime Proxetil

Vantin 100 mg
(UPJOHN)

▶ Drug Class: Cephalosporin antibiotic

▶ Available in: Oral suspension, tablets

▶ Available OTC? No

▶ As Generic? No

Side Effects

SERIOUS
Severe allergic reaction (breathing difficulties, itching, hives, swelling of the face or throat, and sweating), severe stomach pain and cramps, fever, severe, sometimes bloody diarrhea. Call your doctor immediately.

COMMON
Mild diarrhea or stomach cramps, sore mouth or tongue, nausea and vomiting.

LESS COMMON
Vaginal itching or unusual discharge, rash, decreased white blood cell count causing increased susceptibility to infection, decreased blood platelets causing increased risk of bleeding problems.

PRINCIPAL USES
To treat a variety of bacterial infections, including those of the ear, nose, and throat, skin and soft tissues, genitourinary tract, respiratory tract, and other organs. Cefpodoxime is also used to treat gonorrhea. It is effective only against infections caused by bacteria; it is ineffective against those caused by viruses, fungi, or other microorganisms.

HOW THE DRUG WORKS
Cefpodoxime prevents bacteria from forming protective cell walls.

DOSAGE
Adults and teenagers: 100 to 400 mg every 12 hours. Gonorrhea is treated with 200 mg, given in a one-time dose. Children 6 months to 12 years: 5 mg per 2.2 lbs (1 kg) of body weight every 12 hours.

ONSET OF EFFECT
Unknown.

DURATION OF ACTION
Approximately 6 hours.

DIETARY ADVICE
Take it with food to increase the absorption of the drug by the body.

STORAGE
Store in a tightly sealed container away from heat, moisture, and direct light. Keep liquid form refrigerated, but do not allow it to freeze.

IF YOU MISS A DOSE
Take it as soon as you remember. This will help keep a constant level of medication in your system. If it is near the time for the next dose, skip the missed dose and resume your regular schedule. Do not double the next dose.

STOPPING THE DRUG
Take it as prescribed for the full treatment period, even if you begin to feel better before the scheduled end of therapy. Stopping the drug prematurely may slow your recovery or lead to a rebound infection, also known as superinfection, in which the heartier strains of bacteria survive and multiply, leading to a more serious and drug-resistant infection. When taking this drug to treat a streptococcal (strep) infection, it is particularly important to take it for the entire treatment period. Serious heart and kidney problems can develop later if it is discontinued prematurely.

PROLONGED USE
Cefpodoxime is generally prescribed for short-term therapy (10 to 14 days). Use of cefpodoxime beyond this period increases the risk of adverse effects and superinfection.

PRECAUTIONS
Over 60: Adverse reactions may be more likely and more severe.

Driving and Hazardous Work: Avoid such activities until you determine how the medicine affects you.

Alcohol: Avoid alcohol.

Pregnancy: Adequate studies of cephalosporin use in pregnant women have not been done. Before taking cefpodoxime proxetil, tell your doctor if you are pregnant or plan to become pregnant.

Breast Feeding: Cefpodoxime proxetil passes into breast milk and may be hazardous to the nursing infant; caution is advised. Consult your doctor for advice.

Infants and Children: May be used in children 6 months and older. Consult your pediatrician for advice.

Special Concerns: People who are allergic to penicillin may have equally serious allergic reactions to cephalosporin antibiotics. Cefpodoxime is useful only against bacteria that are susceptible to its effects, not against colds, flu, or other viral infections. If your condition has not improved within a few days of starting the drug, or instead has worsened, notify your physician.

OVERDOSE
Symptoms: Seizures, severe abdominal pain, bloody diarrhea, vomiting.

What to Do: Call your doctor, emergency medical services (EMS), or the nearest poison control center immediately.

DRUG INTERACTIONS
Consult your doctor for specific advice if you are taking carbenicillin injection, heparin, divalproex, anticoagulants, sulfinpyrazone, dipyridamole, pentoxifylline, plicamycin, ticarcillin, probenecid, or valproic acid.

FOOD INTERACTIONS
No known food interactions.

DISEASE INTERACTIONS
Caution is advised when taking cefpodoxime proxetil. Consult your doctor if you have a history of kidney disease or colitis.

Cefprozil

BRAND NAME
Cefzil

Cefzil 250 mg
(BRISTOL-MYERS SQUIBB)

▶ Drug Class: Cephalosporin antibiotic

▶ Available in: Oral suspension, tablets

▶ Available OTC? No

▶ As Generic? No

Side Effects

SERIOUS
Severe allergic reaction (breathing difficulties, confusion, lightheadedness, itching, hives, swelling of the face or throat, and unusual sweating), severe stomach pain and cramps, fever, severe, sometimes bloody diarrhea. Call your doctor immediately.

COMMON
Mild diarrhea or stomach cramps, sore mouth or tongue, nausea and vomiting.

LESS COMMON
Vaginal itching or unusual discharge, decreased white blood cell count causing increased susceptibility to infection, decreased blood platelets causing increased risk of bleeding problems.

PRINCIPAL USES
To treat a variety of bacterial infections, including those of the ear, nose, tonsils, and throat, skin and soft tissues, and the respiratory tract. Cefprozil is effective only against infections caused by bacteria; it is ineffective against those caused by viruses, fungi, or other microorganisms.

HOW THE DRUG WORKS
Cefprozil prevents bacteria from forming protective cell walls necessary for survival.

DOSAGE
Adults and teenagers: 250 to 500 mg every 12 to 24 hours. Children ages 2 to 12: 7.5 mg per 2.2 lbs (1 kg) of body weight every 12 hours. Children 6 months to 12 years: 15 mg per 2.2 lbs every 12 hours.

ONSET OF EFFECT
Approximately 90 minutes.

DURATION OF ACTION
Unknown.

DIETARY ADVICE
It may be taken with food to reduce stomach irritation.

STORAGE
Store in a tightly sealed container away from heat, moisture, and direct light. Keep liquid form refrigerated, but do not allow it to freeze.

IF YOU MISS A DOSE
Take it as soon as you remember. This will help keep a constant level of medication in your system. If it is near the time for the next dose, skip the missed dose and resume your regular dosage schedule. Do not double the next dose.

STOPPING THE DRUG
Take it as prescribed for the full treatment period, even if you begin to feel better before the scheduled end of therapy. Stopping cefprozil prematurely may slow your recovery or lead to a rebound infection, also known as superinfection, in which the heartier strains of bacteria survive and multiply, leading to a more serious and drug-resistant infection. When taking this drug to treat a streptococcal (strep) infection, it is particularly important to take it for the entire treatment period. Serious heart and kidney problems can develop later if it is discontinued prematurely.

PROLONGED USE
Cefprozil is generally prescribed for short-term therapy (10 to 14 days). Use of cefprozil beyond this period increases risks of adverse effects and superinfection.

PRECAUTIONS
Over 60: Adverse reactions may be more likely and more severe in older patients.

Driving and Hazardous Work: Do not drive or engage in hazardous work until you determine how the medicine affects you.

Alcohol: Avoid alcohol.

Pregnancy: Adequate studies of cephalosporin use in pregnant women have not been done. Before taking cefprozil, tell your doctor if you are pregnant or are planning to become pregnant.

Breast Feeding: Cefprozil passes into breast milk; caution is advised. Consult your doctor for specific advice.

Infants and Children: Cefprozil may be used by children 6 months and older. Consult your pediatrician for specific advice.

Special Concerns: People who are allergic to penicillin may have equally serious allergic reactions to cephalosporin antibiotics such as cefprozil. This drug is useful only against bacteria that are susceptible to its effects, not against colds, flu, or other viral infections. If your condition has not improved within a few days of starting cefprozil, or instead has worsened, tell your doctor.

OVERDOSE
Symptoms: Seizures, severe abdominal pain, bloody diarrhea, vomiting.

What to Do: Call your doctor, emergency medical services (EMS), or the nearest poison control center immediately.

DRUG INTERACTIONS
Consult your doctor for specific advice if you are taking carbenicillin injection, heparin, divalproex, anticoagulants, sulfinpyrazone, dipyridamole, pentoxifylline, plicamycin, ticarcillin, probenecid, or valproic acid.

FOOD INTERACTIONS
No known food interactions.

DISEASE INTERACTIONS
Caution is advised when taking cefprozil. Consult your doctor if you have a history of kidney disease, phenylketonuria, or colitis.

Cefuroxime

Ceftin 500 mg
(GLAXO WELLCOME)

▶ Drug Class: Cephalosporin antibiotic

▶ Available in: Tablets, injection, oral suspension

▶ Available OTC? No

▶ As Generic? Yes

Side Effects

SERIOUS
Severe allergic reaction (breathing difficulties, confusion, hives, swelling of the face or throat, and lightheadedness), severe stomach pain and cramps, fever, severe, sometimes bloody diarrhea. Call your doctor immediately.

COMMON
Mild diarrhea or stomach cramps, sore mouth or tongue, nausea and vomiting.

LESS COMMON
Vaginal itching or discharge, pain at site of injection, rash, decreased white blood cell count causing increased susceptibility to infection, decreased blood platelets causing increased risk of bleeding problems.

PRINCIPAL USES
To treat a variety of bacterial infections, including those of the brain, ear, nose, tonsils, and throat, skin and soft tissues, genitourinary tract, respiratory tract, blood, bones, joints, and other organs. Cefuroxime also is used to treat gonorrhea and is given prior to some surgeries to prevent infection. It is effective only against susceptible infections caused by bacteria; it is ineffective against those caused by viruses, fungi, or other microorganisms.

HOW THE DRUG WORKS
Cefuroxime prevents bacteria from forming cell walls.

DOSAGE
Adults and teenagers—Tablets: 125 to 500 mg every 12 hours for 5 to 10 days. Injection: 750 to 1,500 mg every 6 to 8 hours into a vein or muscle. Children 3 months to 12 years—Tablets: 125 mg every 12 hours for 10 days. Injection: 16.7 to 33.3 mg per 2.2 lbs (1 kg) of body weight every 8 hours into a vein or muscle. Oral suspension: 10 to 15 mg per 2.2 lbs every 12 hours for 10 days. Special note— Gonorrhea is treated with a one-time tablet dose of 1,000 mg or a one-time injected dose of 1,500 mg into a muscle. The injected dose is divided and administered at 2 separate sites on the body, along with a single 1,000 mg oral dose of probenecid.

ONSET OF EFFECT
Into a vein: Immediate. Into a muscle: 15 to 60 minutes. Oral forms: Unknown.

DURATION OF ACTION
5 to 8 hours.

DIETARY ADVICE
Tablets can be taken without regard to meals. Take oral suspension with food to increase the absorption of the drug by the body. Maintain normal fluid intake.

STORAGE
Store in a tightly sealed container away from heat, moisture, and direct light. Keep liquid form refrigerated, but do not allow it to freeze.

IF YOU MISS A DOSE
Take it as soon as you remember. If it is near the time for the next dose, skip the missed dose and resume your regular dosage schedule. Do not double the next dose.

STOPPING THE DRUG
Take it as prescribed for the full treatment period, even if you begin to feel better before the scheduled end of therapy. Stopping prematurely may slow your recovery or lead to a rebound infection, also known as superinfection, in which the heartier strains of bacteria survive and multiply, leading to a more serious and drug-resistant infection. When taking this drug to treat a streptococcal (strep) infection, it is particularly important to take it for the entire treatment period. Serious heart and kidney problems can develop later if the drug is discontinued prematurely.

PROLONGED USE
Cefuroxime is generally prescribed for short-term therapy (5 to 10 days). Use beyond this period increases risks of adverse effects and superinfection.

PRECAUTIONS
Over 60: Adverse reactions may be more likely and more severe in older patients.

Driving and Hazardous Work: Do not drive or engage in hazardous work until you determine how the medicine affects you.

Alcohol: Avoid alcohol.

Pregnancy: Adequate studies of use during pregnancy have not been done. Consult your doctor for advice.

Breast Feeding: Cefuroxime passes into breast milk; caution is advised. Consult your doctor for advice.

Infants and Children: May be used by children 3 months and older. Consult your pediatrician for advice.

Special Concerns: Those who are allergic to penicillin may have equally serious allergic reactions to cephalosporin antibiotics. If your condition has not improved within a few days, or instead has worsened, tell your doctor. The tablets and the oral suspension can not be equally substituted for each other.

OVERDOSE
Symptoms: Seizures, severe abdominal pain, bloody diarrhea, vomiting.

What to Do: Seek medical assistance immediately.

DRUG INTERACTIONS
Consult your doctor for specific advice if you are taking carbenicillin injection, heparin, divalproex, anticoagulants, sulfinpyrazone, dipyridamole, pentoxifylline, plicamycin, ticarcillin, probenecid, or valproic acid.

FOOD INTERACTIONS
No known food interactions.

DISEASE INTERACTIONS
Consult your doctor if you have a history of kidney disease or colitis.

BRAND NAME
Celebrex

▶ Drug Class: Nonsteroidal anti-inflammatory drug (NSAID)/COX-2 inhibitor

▶ Available in: Capsules

▶ Available OTC? No

▶ As Generic? No

Side Effects

SERIOUS
Stomach ulcers. Black, tarry stools may signal stomach bleeding. Symptoms of liver disease (nausea, fatigue, lethargy, itching, yellowish discoloration of the eyes or skin, fluid retention). Call your doctor immediately.

COMMON
Indigestion, diarrhea, and mild abdominal pain.

LESS COMMON
Flatulence, mild swelling, sore throat, and upper respiratory tract infection.

PRINCIPAL USES
To relieve the pain, inflammation, and stiffness of osteoarthritis and rheumatoid arthritis. To relieve acute pain and menstrual pain. Because celecoxib may be associated with an increased risk of stroke and heart attack, use of this drug may be limited to patients who cannot take other pain medications or who have a history of gastrointestinal bleeding.

HOW THE DRUG WORKS
By inhibiting the activity of the enzyme cyclooxygenase-2 (COX-2), celecoxib reduces the synthesis of prostaglandins that play a role in causing arthritis pain and inflammation. It does not inhibit the activity of COX-1, the enzyme involved in the synthesis of prostaglandins that help protect against stomach ulcers and other health problems.

DOSAGE
For osteoarthritis: 200 mg a day, either as one single dose or 100 mg twice a day. For rheumatoid arthritis: 100 to 200 mg twice a day. To minimize potential gastrointestinal side effects, the lowest effective dose should be used for the shortest possible time. For acute or menstrual pain: To start, 400 mg; a second dose of 200 mg may be taken if needed on the first day. On subsequent days, 200 mg as needed.

ONSET OF EFFECT
Within 24 to 48 hours.

DURATION OF ACTION
Unknown.

DIETARY ADVICE
Celecoxib may be taken with or without food.

STORAGE
Store in a tightly sealed container away from heat, moisture, and direct light.

IF YOU MISS A DOSE
Take it as soon as you remember. If it is near the time for the next dose, skip the missed dose and resume your regular dosage schedule. Do not double the next dose.

STOPPING THE DRUG
The decision to stop taking the drug should be made in consultation with your physician.

PROLONGED USE
The risk of gastrointestinal side effects may be increased with extended use.

PRECAUTIONS
Over 60: Adverse reactions may be more likely and more severe in older patients.

Driving and Hazardous Work: No special problems are expected.

Alcohol: Avoid alcohol when using this medication because it increases the risk of stomach irritation.

Pregnancy: Discuss with your doctor the relative risks and benefits of using this drug while pregnant. Do not use celecoxib during the last trimester.

Breast Feeding: Celecoxib may pass into breast milk; caution is advised. Consult your doctor for advice on whether to discontinue nursing or discontinue the drug.

Infants and Children: The safety and effectiveness of this drug have not been established for children under the age of 18.

Special Concerns: The risk of cardiovascular events may be increased in patients taking celecoxib. Discuss these risks with your doctor before using this drug.

OVERDOSE
Symptoms: No cases of overdose have been reported. Symptoms may include lethargy, drowsiness, nausea, vomiting, abdominal pain, black, tarry stools, breathing difficulty, and coma.

What to Do: If you suspect an overdose or if someone takes a much larger dose than prescribed, call your doctor, emergency medical services (EMS), or the nearest poison control center immediately.

DRUG INTERACTIONS
Do not take this drug with aspirin or any other NSAIDs without your doctor's approval. In addition, consult your doctor if you are taking furosemide, ACE inhibitors, fluconazole, lithium, or warfarin.

FOOD INTERACTIONS
No known food interactions.

DISEASE INTERACTIONS
Celecoxib should not be taken by people who have experienced asthma, hives, or allergic-type reactions after taking aspirin or other NSAIDs. Consult your doctor if you have any of the following: bleeding problems, inflammation or ulcers of the stomach and intestines, asthma, high blood pressure, or heart failure. Use of celecoxib may cause complications in patients with liver or kidney disease, since these organs work together to remove the medication from the body.

Cephalexin

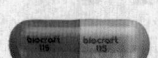

Generic 250 mg
(BIOCRAFT)

Additional photographs

▶ Drug Class: Cephalosporin antibiotic

▶ Available in: Capsules, oral suspension, tablets

▶ Available OTC? No

▶ As Generic? Yes

Side Effects

SERIOUS
Severe allergic reaction (breathing difficulties, confusion, hives, itching, swelling of the face or throat, unusual sweating, and lightheadedness), severe stomach pain and cramps, fever, severe, sometimes bloody diarrhea. Call your doctor immediately.

COMMON
Mild diarrhea or stomach cramps, sore mouth or tongue, nausea and vomiting.

LESS COMMON
Vaginal itching or unusual discharge, rash, decreased white blood cell count causing increased susceptibility to infection, decreased blood platelets causing increased risk of bleeding problems.

PRINCIPAL USES
To treat a variety of bacterial infections, including those of the ear, nose, tonsils, and throat, bones, joints, skin and soft tissues, genitourinary tract, and respiratory tract. It is effective only against infections caused by bacteria; it is ineffective against those caused by viruses, fungi, or other microorganisms.

HOW THE DRUG WORKS
Cephalexin prevents bacteria from forming cell walls.

DOSAGE
Adults and teenagers: 250 to 500 mg every 6 to 12 hours. Children: 6.25 to 25 mg per 2.2 lbs (1 kg) of body weight every 6 hours, or 12.5 to 50 mg per 2.2 lbs every 12 hours.

ONSET OF EFFECT
1 hour.

DURATION OF ACTION
Unknown.

DIETARY ADVICE
Cephalexin may be taken on a full or empty stomach, but taking it with food will reduce stomach irritation.

STORAGE
Store in a tightly sealed container away from heat, moisture, and direct light. Keep liquid form refrigerated, but do not allow it to freeze.

IF YOU MISS A DOSE
Take it as soon as you remember. This will help keep a constant level of medication in your system. If it is near the time for the next dose, skip the missed dose and resume your regular dosage schedule. Do not double the next dose.

STOPPING THE DRUG
Take it as prescribed for the full treatment period, even if you begin to feel better before the scheduled end of therapy. Stopping cephalexin prematurely may slow your recovery or lead to a rebound infection, also known as superinfection, in which the heartier strains of bacteria survive and multiply, leading to a more serious and drug-resistant infection. When taking this drug to treat a streptococcal (strep) infection, it is particularly important to take it for the entire treatment period. Serious heart and kidney problems can develop later if it is discontinued prematurely.

PROLONGED USE
Cephalexin is generally prescribed for short-term therapy (10 to 14 days). Further use increases the risk of adverse effects and superinfection.

PRECAUTIONS
Over 60: Adverse reactions may be more likely and more severe in older patients.

Driving and Hazardous Work: Do not drive or engage in hazardous work until you determine how the medicine affects you.

Alcohol: Avoid alcohol.

Pregnancy: Adequate studies of cephalosporin use in pregnant women have not been done. Before taking cephalexin, tell your doctor if you are pregnant or plan to become pregnant.

Breast Feeding: Cephalexin passes into breast milk; caution is advised. Consult your doctor for specific advice.

Infants and Children: Adequate studies of cephalexin use in children have not been done. Consult your pediatrician.

Special Concerns: People who are allergic to penicillin may have equally serious allergic reactions to cephalosporin antibiotics such as cephalexin. This drug is useful only against bacteria that are susceptible to its effects, not against colds, flu, or other viral infections. If your condition has not improved within a few days of starting cephalexin, or instead has worsened, tell your doctor.

OVERDOSE
Symptoms: Seizures, severe abdominal pain, bloody diarrhea, vomiting.

What to Do: Call your doctor, emergency medical services (EMS), or the nearest poison control center immediately.

DRUG INTERACTIONS
Consult your doctor for specific advice if you are taking carbenicillin injection, heparin, divalproex, anticoagulants, sulfinpyrazone, dipyridamole, pentoxifylline, plicamycin, ticarcillin, probenecid, or valproic acid.

FOOD INTERACTIONS
No known food interactions.

DISEASE INTERACTIONS
Caution is advised when taking cephalexin. Consult your doctor if you have a history of kidney disease or colitis.

Cephradine

Generic 250 mg
(Biocraft)

▶ Drug Class: Cephalosporin antibiotic

▶ Available in: Oral suspension, capsules

▶ Available OTC? No

▶ As Generic? Yes

Side Effects

SERIOUS
Severe allergic reaction (breathing difficulties, confusion, hives, itching, swelling of the face or throat, sweating, and lightheadedness), severe stomach pain and cramps, fever, severe, sometimes bloody diarrhea. Call your doctor immediately.

COMMON
Mild diarrhea or stomach cramps, sore mouth or tongue, nausea and vomiting.

LESS COMMON
Vaginal itching or discharge.

PRINCIPAL USES
To treat a variety of bacterial infections, including those of the ear, nose, tonsils, and throat, skin and soft tissues, genitourinary tract, and the respiratory tract. Cephradine is effective only against infections caused by bacteria; it is ineffective against those caused by viruses, fungi, or other microorganisms.

HOW THE DRUG WORKS
Cephradine prevents bacteria from forming cell walls.

DOSAGE
Oral suspension and capsules— Adults and teenagers: 250 to 500 mg every 6 hours, or 500 to 1,000 mg every 12 hours. Children: 6.25 to 25 mg every 6 hours.

ONSET OF EFFECT
1 hour.

DURATION OF ACTION
Unknown.

DIETARY ADVICE
Cephradine may be taken on a full or empty stomach, but taking it with food will reduce stomach irritation.

STORAGE
Store in a tightly sealed container away from heat, moisture, and direct light. Keep liquid form refrigerated, but do not allow it to freeze.

IF YOU MISS A DOSE
Take it as soon as you remember. This will help keep a constant level of medication in your system. If it is near the time for the next dose, skip the missed dose and resume your regular dosage schedule. Do not double the next dose.

STOPPING THE DRUG
Take it as prescribed for the full treatment period, even if you begin to feel better before the scheduled end of therapy. Stopping cephradine prematurely may slow your recovery or lead to a rebound infection, also known as superinfection, in which the heartier strains of bacteria survive and multiply, leading to a more serious and drug-resistant infection. When taking this drug to treat a streptococcal (strep) infection, it is particularly important to take it for the entire treatment period. Serious heart and kidney problems can develop later if it is discontinued prematurely.

PROLONGED USE
Cephradine is generally prescribed for short-term therapy (10 to 14 days). Use of cephradine beyond this period increases the risk of adverse effects and superinfection.

PRECAUTIONS
Over 60: Adverse reactions may be more likely and more severe in older patients.

Driving and Hazardous Work: Do not drive or engage in hazardous work until you determine how the medicine affects you.

Alcohol: Avoid alcohol.

Pregnancy: Adequate studies of cephalosporin use during pregnancy have not been done. Consult your doctor for specific advice.

Breast Feeding: Cephradine passes into breast milk; caution is advised. Consult your doctor for specific advice.

Infants and Children: Cephradine may be used by children age 1 and older. Consult your pediatrician for specific advice.

Special Concerns: People who are allergic to penicillin may have equally serious allergic reactions to cephalosporin antibiotics such as cephradine. This drug is useful only against bacteria that are susceptible to its effects, not against colds, flu, or other viral infections. If your condition has not improved within a few days of starting cephradine, or instead has worsened, tell your doctor.

OVERDOSE
Symptoms: Seizures, severe abdominal pain, bloody diarrhea, vomiting.

What to Do: Call your doctor, emergency medical services (EMS), or the nearest poison control center immediately.

DRUG INTERACTIONS
Consult your doctor for specific advice if you are taking carbenicillin injection, heparin, divalproex, anticoagulants, sulfinpyrazone, dipyridamole, pentoxifylline, plicamycin, ticarcillin, probenecid, or valproic acid.

FOOD INTERACTIONS
No known food interactions.

DISEASE INTERACTIONS
Caution is advised when taking cephradine. Consult your doctor if you have a history of kidney disease or colitis.

Cetirizine

Zyrtec 10 mg
(PFIZER)

▶ Drug Class: Histamine (H1) blocker

▶ Available in: Tablets, syrup

▶ Available OTC? No

▶ As Generic? No

Side Effects

SERIOUS
No serious side effects are associated with the use of cetirizine.

COMMON
Drowsiness, fatigue, headache, dry mouth.

LESS COMMON
Nausea and vomiting.

PRINCIPAL USES
For symptomatic relief of perennial and seasonal allergies (including hay fever), itchy skin, and chronic hives.

HOW THE DRUG WORKS
Cetirizine blocks the effects of histamine, a naturally occurring substance within the body that causes swelling, itching, sneezing, watery eyes, hives, and other symptoms of allergic reaction.

DOSAGE
Adults and children over age 12: 5 to 10 mg once a day. Do not increase the dose to obtain quicker relief of symptoms. A lower dose (no more than 5 mg a day) is recommended for patients with impaired kidney or liver function.

ONSET OF EFFECT
Within 20 to 40 minutes.

DURATION OF ACTION
Approximately 24 hours.

DIETARY ADVICE
Cetirizine can be taken without regard to diet.

STORAGE
Store in a tightly sealed container away from heat, moisture, and direct light. Do not allow the syrup to freeze.

IF YOU MISS A DOSE
This drug is prescribed to be taken once a day. If you miss a day, skip the missed dose and resume your regular dosage schedule. Do not double the next dose.

STOPPING THE DRUG
Take it as prescribed for the full treatment period, even if you feel better before the scheduled end of therapy.

PROLONGED USE
Safety and effectiveness during prolonged use have yet to be established.

PRECAUTIONS
Over 60: The dosage may need to be reduced in elderly patients, especially for those in whom kidney function is impaired.

Driving and Hazardous Work: Do not drive or engage in hazardous work until you determine how the medication affects you.

Alcohol: Avoid alcohol while taking this medication, since it can magnify side effects such as drowsiness and fatigue.

Pregnancy: Adequate human studies of the use of this drug during pregnancy have not been done; caution is advised. Before taking cetirizine, tell your doctor if you are pregnant or plan to become pregnant.

Breast Feeding: Cetirizine passes into breast milk; avoid or discontinue use while nursing.

Infants and Children: The safety and effectiveness of cetirizine use by children under the age of 12 have not been established.

Special Concerns: If cetirizine causes dry mouth as a side effect, use sugarless gum, sugarless sour hard candy, or ice chips for relief.

OVERDOSE
Symptoms: No cases of overdose have been reported.

What to Do: An overdose of cetirizine is unlikely to be life-threatening. However, if someone takes a much larger dose than prescribed, call your doctor, emergency medical services (EMS), or the nearest poison control center immediately.

DRUG INTERACTIONS
No significant drug interactions have been reported. Cetirizine may, however, increase the depressant effects of alcohol, sedatives, tranquilizers, painkillers, barbiturates, or other antihistamines on the central nervous system. Consult your doctor for specific advice.

FOOD INTERACTIONS
No food interactions have been reported.

DISEASE INTERACTIONS
Cetirizine blood levels may increase in patients with liver or kidney disease, since these organs work together to remove the medication from the body. Reduced doses may be required for such persons.

Cevimeline Hydrochloride

BRAND NAME
Evoxac

▶ Drug Class: Cholinergic (muscarinic) agonist

▶ Available in: Capsules

▶ Available OTC? No

▶ As Generic? No

Side Effects

SERIOUS
Serious side effects are rare, but may include: heartbeat irregularities, chest pain, increased bronchial secretions. Some of these side effects may be relevant only to those who have a history of heart problems or respiratory conditions (see Disease Interactions).

COMMON
Excessive sweating, nausea, runny nose.

LESS COMMON
Excessive salivation, weakness, sinusitis, upper respiratory infection, abdominal pain, urinary tract infection, coughing, vomiting, back pain, conjunctivitis, bronchitis, joint pain, fatigue, pain, insomnia, hot flushes.

PRINCIPAL USES
To treat symptoms of dry mouth in patients with Sjogren's syndrome.

HOW THE DRUG WORKS
Cevimeline stimulates the secretion of glands such as salivary and sweat glands and increases the tone of smooth muscle in the gastrointestinal and urinary tracts.

DOSAGE
Adults: 30 mg 3 times a day.

ONSET OF EFFECT
Unknown.

DURATION OF ACTION
Unknown.

DIETARY ADVICE
Cevimeline may be taken with or without food.

STORAGE
Store in a tightly sealed container away from heat, moisture, and direct light.

IF YOU MISS A DOSE
Take it as soon as you remember. If it is near the time for the next dose, skip the missed dose and resume your regular dosage schedule. Do not double the next dose.

STOPPING THE DRUG
The decision to stop taking the drug should be made in consultation with your physician.

PROLONGED USE
See your doctor regularly for tests and examinations if you must take this drug for a prolonged period.

PRECAUTIONS
Over 60: Adverse reactions may be more likely and more severe.

Driving and Hazardous Work: This drug can cause visual blurring, which may affect depth perception, night vision, and general vision. Do not drive or engage in hazardous work until you determine how the medicine affects you.

Alcohol: Avoid alcohol while taking this medication, as the diuretic effect of alcohol may aggravate your condition.

Pregnancy: No human tests have been done. However, discuss with your doctor the relative risks and benefits of using this drug while pregnant.

Breast Feeding: Cevimeline may pass into breast milk; caution is advised. Consult your doctor for advice on whether to discontinue nursing or discontinue the drug.

Infants and Children: The safety and effectiveness of this drug have not been established for children under the age of 18.

Special Concerns: Dehydration may result if you sweat excessively while taking cevimeline. Drink extra water and consult your physician.

OVERDOSE
Symptoms: No cases of overdose have been reported.

What to Do: If you suspect an overdose or if someone takes a much larger dose than prescribed, call your doctor, emergency medical services (EMS), or the nearest poison control center immediately.

DRUG INTERACTIONS
Consult your doctor for specific advice if you are taking a beta-blocker.

FOOD INTERACTIONS
No known interactions.

DISEASE INTERACTIONS
Do not take cevimeline if you have uncontrolled asthma or if you have an eye condition, such as acute iritis or narrow-angle glaucoma, which may be aggravated by the drug's tendency to cause the pupil's to constrict. The drug should be used with caution in people with a history of kidney or gallbladder stones.

Charcoal, Activated

BRAND NAMES
Actidose-Aqua, CharcoAid 2000, Charcocaps, Insta-Char Aqueous, Liqui-Char, Pediatric Aqueous Insta-Char, Superchar

▶ Drug Class: Antidote

▶ Available in: Oral suspension, powder, tablets, capsules

▶ Available OTC? Yes

▶ As Generic? Yes

Side Effects

SERIOUS
Swelling or pain in stomach. If this symptom persists, call your doctor immediately.

COMMON
Black, tarry stools.

LESS COMMON
Nausea, constipation. Notify your doctor if any common or less-common side effects persist.

PRINCIPAL USES
Used as an emergency antidote for treatment of poisonings by most drugs and chemicals; also used to relieve diarrhea or excess gas.

HOW THE DRUG WORKS
Activated charcoal prevents the absorption of certain kinds of drugs and chemicals by the body.

DOSAGE
For treatment of poisoning— Oral suspension and powder: Adults and teenagers: 25 to 100 grams (g). Children: 1 g per 2.2 lbs (1 kg) of body weight, or 25 to 50 g. Mix powder with water. Take 1 time only. For treatment of diarrhea— Capsules: Adults and children age 3 and older: 520 mg every 30 to 60 minutes, as needed. Do not take more than 4.16 g per day. For treatment of excess gas— Tablets and capsules: Adults and teenagers: 975 mg to 3.9 g, 3 times a day.

ONSET OF EFFECT
Immediate.

DURATION OF ACTION
Not applicable. Activated charcoal is not absorbed by the body.

DIETARY ADVICE
As an antidote: No special restrictions. To treat diarrhea: It is important to replace the fluid lost by your body and to eat a proper diet. During the first 24 hours, drink plenty of caffeine-free clear liquids like water, broth, ginger ale, and decaffeinated tea. During the second 24 hours you may eat bland foods such as applesauce, bread, crackers, and oatmeal. Avoid caffeine, fried or spicy foods, bran, candy, fruits, and vegetables. These may worsen your condition.

STORAGE
Store in a tightly sealed container away from heat, moisture, and direct light. Premixed suspension can be stored for up to 1 year. Do not allow the liquid form of activated charcoal to freeze.

IF YOU MISS A DOSE
As an antidote: Not applicable. To treat diarrhea or excess gas: Take it as soon as you remember. If it is near the time for the next dose, skip the missed dose and resume your regular dosage schedule. Do not double the next dose.

STOPPING THE DRUG
As an antidote: Not applicable. To treat diarrhea or excess gas: Take as prescribed for the full treatment period. However, you may stop taking the drug if you are feeling better before the scheduled end of therapy.

PROLONGED USE
As an antidote: Not applicable. To treat diarrhea: If diarrhea has not improved or if you have developed a fever after 2 days, call your doctor. To treat excess gas: If your condition has not improved after 3 to 4 days, call your doctor.

PRECAUTIONS
Over 60: No special problems are expected.

Driving and Hazardous Work: The use of activated charcoal should not impair your ability to perform such tasks safely.

Alcohol: No special precautions are necessary.

Pregnancy: Activated charcoal has not been reported to cause problems in an unborn child. Consult your doctor for specific advice.

Breast Feeding: No problems have been reported.

Infants and Children: May be used in infants and children only under strict supervision by a doctor.

Special Concerns: Call your doctor, emergency medical services (EMS), or the nearest poison control center before administering activated charcoal. Charcoal will not be effective if you have been poisoned by swallowing alkalies (lye), petroleum products, strong acids, ethyl or methyl alcohol, iron, boric acid, or lithium. Activated charcoal will not prevent these poisons from being absorbed by the body. If inducing vomiting with ipecac syrup, do so 1 to 2 hours before administering activated charcoal.

OVERDOSE
Symptoms: None expected.

What to Do: Emergency procedures not applicable.

DRUG INTERACTIONS
Activated charcoal may decrease the absorption of any medicine taken within 2 hours of administration. Acetylcysteine and ipecac syrup can decrease the effectiveness of activated charcoal.

FOOD INTERACTIONS
Do not eat chocolate syrup, ice cream, or sherbet with activated charcoal. They will decrease the amount of poison the charcoal can absorb.

DISEASE INTERACTIONS
Caution is advised when taking activated charcoal if you also suffer from dysentery or dehydration.

Chloral Hydrate

Generic 500 mg
(SCHEIN)

▶ Drug Class: Sedative/hypnotic

▶ Available in: Capsules, syrup

▶ Available OTC? No

▶ As Generic? Yes

Side Effects

SERIOUS
Hallucinations, confusion, excitability, skin rash, hives. Stop taking the drug and call your doctor immediately.

COMMON
Nausea, vomiting, stomach pain or abdominal discomfort, hangover-like symptoms, drowsiness.

LESS COMMON
Diarrhea, loss of coordination, dizziness or lightheadedness.

PRINCIPAL USES
For the short-term treatment of insomnia. Chloral hydrate is being replaced by safer, more effective drugs for this purpose.

HOW THE DRUG WORKS
Drugs such as chloral hydrate depress activity in the central nervous system (brain and spinal cord), producing a mild sedative effect.

DOSAGE
Adults: 250 to 1,500 mg, 30 minutes before bedtime.

ONSET OF EFFECT
Within 30 minutes.

DURATION OF ACTION
From 4 to 8 hours.

DIETARY ADVICE
Both oral forms of chloral hydrate should be taken shortly after meals. They may be taken with a full glass of a liquid such as water, fruit juice, or ginger ale to improve flavor and minimize stomach upset.

STORAGE
Store in a tightly sealed container away from heat, moisture, and direct light. Avoid extremes in temperature.

IF YOU MISS A DOSE
If it is near the time for the next dose, skip the missed dose and resume your regular dosage schedule. Do not double the next dose.

STOPPING THE DRUG
The dosage will be gradually reduced to prevent withdrawal effects.

PROLONGED USE
Chloral hydrate may be habit-forming. Prolonged use increases the risk of drug dependency.

PRECAUTIONS
Over 60: Adverse reactions may be more likely and more severe in older patients.

Driving and Hazardous Work: Avoid such activities until you determine how this medication affects you.

Alcohol: Avoid alcohol while taking this drug.

Pregnancy: Adequate studies of the use of chloral hydrate during pregnancy have not been done. Before taking chloral hydrate, tell your doctor if you are pregnant or plan to become pregnant.

Breast Feeding: Chloral hydrate passes into breast milk; caution is advised. Consult your doctor for advice.

Infants and Children: Chloral hydrate should be used by children only under a doctor's supervision.

Special Concerns: Swallow the capsules whole. Do not chew them, since chloral hydrate has an unpleasant taste. Make sure your doctor has specifically indicated to your pharmacist both how many milligrams and how many capsules or teaspoonfuls you or your child should receive in a single dose.

OVERDOSE
Symptoms: Severe nausea, vomiting, or stomach pain; difficulty swallowing; severe drowsiness; continuing confusion; seizures; low body temperature; difficulty breathing or shortness of breath; irregular heartbeat; severe weakness; staggering; slurred speech.

What to Do: Call your doctor, emergency medical services (EMS), or the nearest poison control center immediately.

DRUG INTERACTIONS
The following drugs may interact with chloral hydrate. Consult your doctor for specific advice if you are taking anticoagulants, tricyclic antidepressants, or central nervous system depressants.

FOOD INTERACTIONS
No food interactions have been reported.

DISEASE INTERACTIONS
Caution is advised when taking chloral hydrate. Consult your doctor if you have any of the following: kidney or liver problems, ulcers or other intestinal problems, esophagitis, or sleep apnea.

Chlorambucil

BRAND NAME
Leukeran

Leukeran 2 mg
(GLAXO WELLCOME)

▶ Drug Class: Alkylating agent

▶ Available in: Tablets

▶ Available OTC? No

▶ As Generic? No

Side Effects

SERIOUS
Black or tarry stools; blood-tinged (pink or maroon) urine or stools; cough or hoarseness; fever; chills; lower back pain or pain in flanks; painful, difficult urination; small, red spots on the skin; bleeding from gums, nose, or other unusual places; easy bruising; shortness of breath. These side effects may mean that normal blood cells and special blood-clotting cells have been affected, or that normal immune cells have been affected and an infection is developing somewhere in your body. See your doctor right away if any of these occur.

COMMON
Nausea and vomiting.

LESS COMMON
Painful joints, rash, itching, swelling of feet or lower legs (edema), changes in menstruation.

PRINCIPAL USES
To treat some types of cancer, especially leukemia and lymphoma (cancer of the lymphatic system). More specifically, chlorambucil is used to treat chronic lymphocytic leukemia (a type of leukemia caused by overproduction and abnormal formation of certain white blood cells important in the body's immune system) and Hodgkin's disease (a type of cancer affecting the lymphatic system, characterized by painless swelling of the lymph nodes).

HOW THE DRUG WORKS
Chlorambucil kills cancer cells by interfering with the activity of their genetic material, thus preventing the cells from reproducing. The drug may also affect the growth and development of normal cells in the body, resulting in unpleasant side effects.

DOSAGE
Initial dose: 0.1 to 0.2 mg per 2.2 lbs (1 kg) of body weight daily (approximately 4 to 10 mg per day) for 3 to 6 weeks. Maintenance dose will depend on white blood cell counts.

ONSET OF EFFECT
Within 3 to 4 weeks.

DURATION OF ACTION
Unknown.

DIETARY ADVICE
Swallow with liquid 2 hours after a light meal. Drink plenty of fluids between meals.

STORAGE
Store in a tightly sealed container away from heat and direct light.

IF YOU MISS A DOSE
Take it as soon as you remember. If it is near the time for the next dose, skip the missed dose and resume your regular dosage schedule. Do not double the next dose.

STOPPING THE DRUG
The decision to stop taking chlorambucil should be made by your doctor.

PROLONGED USE
Consult with your doctor about the need for periodic medical exams and blood tests, since adverse reactions are more likely the longer the drug is used.

PRECAUTIONS
Over 60: Adverse reactions may be more likely and severe in elderly patients.

Driving and Hazardous Work: Should not interfere with any activities requiring mental alertness.

Alcohol: Avoid alcohol.

Pregnancy: Chlorambucil may cause birth defects. Persons of childbearing years should take steps to prevent pregnancy when being treated with this medication.

Breast Feeding: Not recommended during therapy.

Infants and Children: No special problems are expected, although children with impaired kidney function may be at greater risk of having seizures while taking chlorambucil.

Special Concerns: Infection is the single greatest threat to people receiving chemotherapy. Chlorambucil may lower your ability to resist infection by lowering the number of white blood cells in the blood. Therefore, do not receive any vaccinations without doctor's approval. Avoid people with infections. Inform your doctor immediately if you have fever, chills, diarrhea, or a cough.

OVERDOSE
Symptoms: Fever, chills, unusual bleeding, seizures, agitation.

What to Do: Call your doctor, emergency medical services (EMS), or the nearest poison control center immediately.

DRUG INTERACTIONS
Consult your doctor for specific advice if you are taking amphotericin B (by injection), other antineoplastic (anticancer) drugs, antithyroid medications, chloramphenicol, colchicine or other antigout drugs, corticosteroid drugs, or immunosuppressant drugs (such as azathioprine, cyclosporine, ganciclovir, and interferon).

FOOD INTERACTIONS
Avoid consuming excess quantities of foods high in fat or sugar.

DISEASE INTERACTIONS
Caution is advised. Consult your doctor if you have any of the following: gout; a history of kidney stones; an active infection; recent exposure to chicken pox or shingles; liver or kidney problems.

Chloramphenicol Ophthalmic and Otic

▶ Drug Class: Antibiotic

▶ Available in: Ophthalmic solution and ointment, otic solution

▶ Available OTC? No

▶ As Generic? Yes

Side Effects

SERIOUS
Bone marrow depression is a rare complication of chloramphenicol use. Other serious side effects include pale skin, sore throat and fever, unusual bleeding or bruising, unusual fatigue, itching, redness, swelling, skin rash, and skin irritation. Stop using the medication and call your doctor immediately.

COMMON
No common side effects are associated with otic chloramphenicol. Ophthalmic chloramphenicol may delay healing of the surface layer of the cornea.

LESS COMMON
Stinging or burning sensation.

PRINCIPAL USES
To treat infections of the eye or of the ear canal.

HOW THE DRUG WORKS
Chloramphenicol inhibits the spread of bacteria by interfering with protein synthesis in bacterial cells, preventing them from multiplying.

DOSAGE
Ophthalmic solution: 1 drop every 1 to 4 hours. Ophthalmic ointment: Apply every 3 hours. Otic solution: 2 or 3 drops every 6 to 8 hours.

ONSET OF EFFECT
Unknown.

DURATION OF ACTION
Unknown.

DIETARY ADVICE
This drug can be used without regard to diet.

STORAGE
Store in a tightly sealed container away from heat, moisture, and direct light. Do not allow the medicine to freeze. You may refrigerate the otic solution.

IF YOU MISS A DOSE
Apply it as soon as you remember. If it is near the time for the next dose, skip the missed dose and resume your regular dosage schedule. Do not double the next dose.

STOPPING THE DRUG
Use this drug as prescribed for the full treatment period, even if you begin to feel better before the scheduled end of therapy.

PROLONGED USE
You should see your doctor regularly for tests and examinations if you take this drug for a prolonged period.

PRECAUTIONS
Over 60: No special problems are expected.

Driving and Hazardous Work: Do not drive or engage in hazardous work until you determine how the drug affects your vision.

Alcohol: Avoid alcohol.

Pregnancy: Caution is advised; consult your doctor about whether the benefits outweigh potential risks to the unborn child.

Breast Feeding: Chloramphenicol may pass into breast milk; caution is advised. Consult your doctor if you are considering breast feeding.

Infants and Children: Do not use this drug on infants or children unless specifically directed by your physician.

Special Concerns: To use the eye drops or the ointment, first wash your hands. Tilt your head back. Gently apply pressure to the inside corner of the eyelid and with the index finger of the same hand, pull downward on the lower eyelid to make a space. Drop the medicine or put a short strip of ointment (about ⅓ inch long) into this space and close your eye. Apply pressure for 1 or 2 minutes while keeping the eye closed without blinking. To use the ear drops, lie down or tilt your head so the infected ear faces up. Gently pull the earlobe up and back for adults (down and back for children) to straighten the ear canal. Drop the medicine into the ear. Keep the ear facing upward for 1 to 2 minutes after inserting the drops to allow the medicine to reach the infection. You may insert a cotton ball to prevent the medicine from leaking out. Make sure the applicator for eye or ear drops does not touch your eye, ear, finger, or any other surface.

OVERDOSE
Symptoms: No specific symptoms have been reported.

What to Do: An overdose of ophthalmic or otic chloramphenicol is unlikely to be life-threatening. If a large volume enters the eye, flush with water. If a large volume enters the ear or someone accidentally ingests the medication, call your physician, emergency medical services (EMS), or the nearest poison control center immediately.

DRUG INTERACTIONS
Other drugs may interact with ophthalmic or otic chloramphenicol. Consult your doctor for specific advice if you are taking any other prescription or over-the-counter medication.

FOOD INTERACTIONS
No known food interactions.

DISEASE INTERACTIONS
Caution is advised when taking ophthalmic or otic chloramphenicol. Consult your doctor if you have a perforated eardrum (for otic solution) or any other medical condition.

Chloramphenicol Oral and Topical

BRAND NAME
Chloromycetin

▶ Drug Class: Antibiotic

▶ Available in: Capsules, oral suspension, injection, cream

▶ Available OTC? No

▶ As Generic? Yes

Side Effects

SERIOUS
Pale or sickly appearance, sore throat, fever, unusual bruising or bleeding, unusual fatigue, confusion, delirium, headache, eye pain, blurring or loss of vision, weakness, numbness, tingling, or pain in hands or feet, skin rash, breathing difficulty. Call your doctor immediately.

COMMON
No common side effects are associated with the use of chloramphenicol.

LESS COMMON
Diarrhea, nausea, and vomiting.

PRINCIPAL USES
To treat serious infections caused by bacteria. Because of the risk of dangerous side effects, it is prescribed only when other less toxic antibiotics cannot be used.

HOW THE DRUG WORKS
Chloramphenicol works by killing bacteria or inhibiting their growth.

DOSAGE
Oral forms and injection—Adults and teenagers: 5.7 mg per lb of body weight, 4 times a day. Children: 5.7 mg per lb of body weight, 4 times a day, or 11.4 mg per lb, 2 times a day. Infants under 2 weeks: 2.8 mg per lb, 4 times a day. Cream—Apply to infected area of skin 3 or 4 times a day.

ONSET OF EFFECT
Unknown.

DURATION OF ACTION
Unknown.

DIETARY ADVICE
Oral forms work best when taken on an empty stomach, at least 1 hour before or 2 hours after meals, with a full glass of water.

STORAGE
Store in a tightly sealed container away from heat and direct light. Do not allow liquid forms to freeze.

IF YOU MISS A DOSE
Take it as soon as you remember. If it is near the time for the next dose, skip the missed dose and resume your regular dosage schedule. Do not double the next dose.

STOPPING THE DRUG
Take the medicine as prescribed for the full treatment period, even if you begin to feel better before the scheduled end of therapy.

PROLONGED USE
You should see your doctor regularly for tests and examinations if you must take this medicine for a prolonged period of time.

PRECAUTIONS
Over 60: In older patients it is not known whether chloramphenicol causes side effects different from or more severe than those in younger persons.

Driving and Hazardous Work: Do not drive or engage in hazardous work until you determine how the medicine affects you.

Alcohol: It is advisable to abstain from alcohol when fighting an infection.

Pregnancy: Chloramphenicol has not been shown to cause birth defects in humans. However, its use is not recommended in the weeks immediately before delivery because it can cause temporary adverse side effects in the newborn child. Consult your doctor before using this drug during pregnancy.

Breast Feeding: Chloramphenicol passes into breast milk; avoid or discontinue use while nursing.

Infants and Children: Adverse reactions may be more likely and more severe in newborn babies.

Special Concerns: Chloramphenicol may cause anemia, which may increase the risk of infections and other problems in the gums. Blood must be monitored frequently while using this medicine. Be careful when brushing and flossing. Delay dental work, if possible, until you have stopped taking chloramphenicol. Chloramphenicol may cause false results on blood sugar tests for diabetics. Use of chloramphenicol while you are receiving x-ray treatment can increase the risk of blood problems.

OVERDOSE
Symptoms: Nausea, vomiting, unpleasant taste in the mouth, diarrhea.

What to Do: An overdose of chloramphenicol is unlikely to be life-threatening, Nonetheless, call your doctor, emergency medical services (EMS), or the nearest poison control center immediately.

DRUG INTERACTIONS
Consult your doctor for specific advice if you are taking alfentanil, amphotericin B, antithyroid agents, azathioprine, chemotherapy drugs for cancer, colchicine, clindamycin, cyclophosphamide, ethotoin, erythromycins, oral antidiabetic agents, flucytosine, ganciclovir, interferon, mephenytoin, mercaptopurine, methotrexate, phenytoin, plicamycin, or zidovudine (AZT).

FOOD INTERACTIONS
No known food interactions.

DISEASE INTERACTIONS
Caution is advised when taking chloramphenicol. Consult your doctor if you have anemia or another blood disorder, liver disease, or if you are undergoing radiation therapy.

Chlordiazepoxide

Generic 10 mg
(BARR)

▶ Drug Class: Benzodiazepine tranquilizer; antianxiety agent

▶ Available in: Capsules, tablets, injection

▶ Available OTC? No

▶ As Generic? Yes

Side Effects

SERIOUS
Difficulty concentrating, outbursts of anger, other behavior problems, depression, hallucinations, confusion, memory impairment, faintness, muscle weakness, skin rash or itching, sore throat, fever and chills, sores or ulcers in throat or mouth, unusual bruising or bleeding, extreme fatigue, yellow discoloration of the eyes or skin. Call your doctor immediately.

COMMON
Drowsiness, loss of coordination, unsteady gait, dizziness, lightheadedness, slurred speech.

LESS COMMON
Change in sexual desire or ability, constipation, false sense of well-being, nausea and vomiting, urinary problems, unusual fatigue.

PRINCIPAL USES
To treat anxiety, muscle spasms, and alcohol withdrawal symptoms.

HOW THE DRUG WORKS
In general, chlordiazepoxide produces mild sedation by depressing activity in the central nervous system. In particular, the drug appears to enhance the effect of gamma-aminobutyric acid (GABA), a natural chemical that inhibits the firing of neurons and dampens the transmission of nerve signals, thus decreasing nervous excitation.

DOSAGE
For anxiety— Adults: 5 to 25 mg, 3 or 4 times per day. Patients older than 60 or those who have a chronic illness: Initial dose of 5 to 10 mg, 2 to 4 times per day. Dose may be increased by your doctor to a maximum of 25 mg, 2 to 3 times per day. For alcohol withdrawal— Initial dose is 50 to 100 mg, repeated as recommended by your doctor. Some patients will require up to 300 mg per day in the early stages of alcohol withdrawal. Your doctor will determine a daily maintenance dose once the early stages of withdrawal have passed.

ONSET OF EFFECT
Within 1 to 2 hours.

DURATION OF ACTION
Up to 48 hours.

DIETARY ADVICE
No special restrictions.

STORAGE
Store in a tightly sealed container away from heat, moisture, and direct light.

IF YOU MISS A DOSE
Take it as soon as you remember. If it is near the time for the next dose, skip the missed dose and resume your regular dosage schedule. Do not double the next dose.

STOPPING THE DRUG
Do not stop taking the drug abruptly or without your doctor's approval. Dosage should be reduced gradually to prevent withdrawal symptoms, including seizures.

PROLONGED USE
This medication may slowly lose its effectiveness with prolonged use. You should see your doctor for periodic evaluation if you must take it for an extended time.

PRECAUTIONS
Over 60: Adverse reactions may be more likely and more severe in older patients.

Driving and Hazardous Work: The use of this drug may impair your ability to perform such tasks safely.

Alcohol: Alcohol intake should be extremely moderate or stopped altogether while taking this drug.

Pregnancy: Use during pregnancy should be avoided if possible. Be sure to tell your doctor if you are pregnant or plan to become pregnant.

Breast Feeding: This drug passes into breast milk; do not take it while nursing.

Infants and Children: This drug is not recommended for use by children under the age of 6.

Special Concerns: Chlordiazepoxide use can lead to psychological or physical dependence. Never take more than the prescribed daily dose.

OVERDOSE
Symptoms: Extreme drowsiness, confusion, slurred speech, slow reflexes, poor coordination, staggering gait, tremor, slowed breathing, loss of consciousness.

What to Do: Call your doctor, emergency medical services (EMS), or the nearest poison control center immediately.

DRUG INTERACTIONS
Consult your doctor for specific advice if you are taking any drugs that depress the central nervous system; these include antihistamines, antidepressants or other psychiatric medications, barbiturates, sedatives, cough medicines, decongestants, and painkillers. Be sure your doctor knows about any over-the-counter medication you may take.

FOOD INTERACTIONS
None reported.

DISEASE INTERACTIONS
Consult your doctor if you have a history of alcohol or drug abuse, stroke or other brain disease, any chronic lung disease, hyperactivity, depression or other mental illness, myasthenia gravis, sleep apnea, epilepsy, porphyria, kidney disease, or liver disease.

Chlordiazepoxide/Amitriptyline

BRAND NAMES
Limbitrol, Limbitrol DS

Generic 10\25 mg
(**MYLAN**)

▶ Drug Class: Benzodiazepine tranquilizer; antianxiety agent/antidepressant

▶ Available in: Tablets

▶ Available OTC? No

▶ As Generic? Yes

Side Effects

SERIOUS
Blurred vision, confusion, difficulty speaking or swallowing, eye pain, fainting, rapid or uneven heartbeat, hallucinations, poor balance, nervousness or restlessness, problems urinating, shakiness or trembling, shuffling walk, slowed movements, stiffness in the arms and legs.

COMMON
Dizziness, drowsiness, loss of coordination, poor balance, dry mouth, headache, increased appetite, nausea, fatigue or mild weakness, unpleasant taste in mouth or of food, unexpected weight gain.

LESS COMMON
Diarrhea, heartburn, increased sweating, vomiting, increased sensitivity to sunlight.

PRINCIPAL USES
Chlordiazepoxide/amitriptyline is used to treat anxiety occurring simultaneously with depression.

HOW THE DRUG WORKS
Chlordiazepoxide depresses activity in the central nervous system, producing a mild sedative effect. Amitriptyline affects the activity of certain brain chemicals (serotonin and norepinephrine) that are linked to mood, emotions, and mental state.

DOSAGE
Adults: Initial dose is 5 mg of chlordiazepoxide and 12.5 mg of amitriptyline, or 10 mg of chlordiazepoxide and 25 mg of amitriptyline, 3 to 4 times daily. Some patients require higher doses, while some do well with lower doses. Your doctor will determine the correct dose.

ONSET OF EFFECT
The antianxiety and sedation effects occur within the first week of therapy. The antidepressant effect may require several weeks.

DURATION OF ACTION
Unknown.

DIETARY ADVICE
No special restrictions.

STORAGE
Store in a tightly sealed container away from heat, moisture, and direct light.

IF YOU MISS A DOSE
Take it as soon as you remember. If it is near the time for the next dose, skip the missed dose and resume your regular dosage schedule. Do not double the next dose.

STOPPING THE DRUG
Discontinuing the drug abruptly may produce withdrawal symptoms. Dosage should be reduced gradually according to your doctor's instructions.

PROLONGED USE
Short-term therapy (8 weeks or less) is typical; do not take it for a longer period unless so advised by your doctor.

PRECAUTIONS
Over 60: Adverse reactions may be more likely and more severe in older patients.

Driving and Hazardous Work: This drug can impair mental alertness and physical coordination. Adjust your activities accordingly.

Alcohol: Avoid alcohol while using this medication.

Pregnancy: Use during pregnancy should be avoided if possible. Be sure to tell your doctor if you are pregnant or plan to become pregnant.

Breast Feeding: Avoid or discontinue use while breast feeding.

Infants and Children: This drug combination is not recommended for use by infants and children. Antidepressant drugs increase the risk of suicidal thinking and behavior (suicidality) in children with major depression and other psychiatric disorders. If you are considering use of this drug, discuss with your doctor the risk of suicidality versus the benefits of using the drug. Children should be observed closely for worsening of symptoms, suicidality, or unusual changes in behavior at the onset of therapy and when making changes in dosage.

Special Concerns: Use of this medication can lead to physical dependence. Never take more than the prescribed daily dose.

OVERDOSE
Symptoms: Confusion; convulsions; poor concentration; severe drowsiness, fatigue, or weakness (some patients will become unusually restless or agitated); dilated pupils; rapid or irregular heartbeat; rapid, shallow breathing, shortness of breath, or other breathing trouble; fever; hallucinations.

What to Do: Call your doctor, emergency medical services (EMS), or the nearest poison control center immediately.

DRUG INTERACTIONS
Consult your doctor for specific advice if you are taking sedatives, tranquilizers, or other medications that cause drowsiness; amphetamines or diet pills; asthma medication; prescription or nonprescription decongestants; prescription or nonprescription medicine for colds, sinus problems, allergies, and hay fever; high blood pressure medication; thyroid medicine; or MAO inhibitors.

FOOD INTERACTIONS
None reported.

DISEASE INTERACTIONS
Consult your doctor if you have a history of alcohol or drug abuse, stroke or other brain disease, any chronic lung disease, glaucoma, hyperactivity, depression or other mental illness, myasthenia gravis, sleep apnea, epilepsy, porphyria, kidney disease, or liver disease.

Chlorhexidine Gluconate

▶ Drug Class: Topical antiseptic;
anti-infective

▶ Available in: Skin cleanser,
wound cleanser, oral rinse

▶ Available OTC? No

▶ As Generic? No

Side Effects

SERIOUS
Rare severe allergic
reaction with swelling,
breathing difficulty, and
even complete closure of
the airways with poten-
tially fatal anaphylactic
shock. Seek medical
assistance immediately.

COMMON
Staining (sometimes
heavy) of the teeth,
gums, dental fillings,
dentures, and other oral
surfaces (staining may be
more pronounced in
patients with greater preexisting plaque accumu-
lation); alteration in taste
perception (taste percep-
tion returns to normal
when medicine is discon-
tinued); paradoxical
increase in plaque
buildup on the teeth.

LESS COMMON
Irritation or allergy of the
skin, gums, tongue, or
other mouth surfaces
with redness, burning,
stinging, or rash; swollen
glands in the neck or
sides of the face.

PRINCIPAL USES
Skin or wound cleanser: To
prevent infection. Oral
rinse: To treat gingivitis
(inflammation of the gums,
marked by redness, tenderness, swelling, and bleeding
of gum tissue).

HOW THE DRUG WORKS
On the skin, it reduces surface bacteria to prevent
infection. In the mouth,
chlorhexidine kills the bacteria that cause dental
plaque and gingivitis. However, it cannot prevent
plaque from forming, nor
does it remove plaque that
has already formed. Scrupu-
lous brushing and flossing
and regular visits to a dentist are still necessary.

DOSAGE
Skin cleanser: 5 ml (1 teaspoon) lathered for 30 seconds to 3 minutes and
rinsed. Oral rinse: average
adult dose (individual dose
may vary): 15 ml (1 capful),
used as a mouthwash for 30
seconds, twice a day, after
brushing and flossing teeth.
Do not dilute the drug with
water. Rinse your mouth
thoroughly before use and
be careful not to swallow
any of the product. Do not
rinse with water after using
the medication.

ONSET OF EFFECT
Within 1 hour.

DURATION OF ACTION
Unknown.

DIETARY ADVICE
Do not eat or drink for 2 to
3 hours following treatment.

STORAGE
Store in a tightly sealed container away from heat and
direct light. Do not allow
the medication to freeze.

IF YOU MISS A DOSE
Use as soon as you remem-
ber. If it is near the time for

the next dose, skip the
missed dose and resume
your regular dosing schedule following the next
brushing. Do not double the
next dose.

STOPPING THE DRUG
Use for the full treatment
period, unless directed otherwise by your doctor or
dentist.

PROLONGED USE
See your doctor as recom-
mended; see your dentist
every 6 months for professional cleaning and evaluation of the progress of
therapy.

PRECAUTIONS
Over 60: No precautions.

**Driving and Hazardous
Work:** No special precautions are necessary.

Alcohol: No special restrictions. Persons with a history of alcoholism, however,
should not use chlorhexi-
dine oral rinse since it contains a relatively high
percentage of alcohol,
which may trigger a relapse
of alcohol abuse.

Pregnancy: Adequate
human studies have not
been done; consult your
doctor.

Breast Feeding: No problems have been docu-
mented, but be sure your
doctor knows if you are
breast feeding.

Infants and Children: It
is not commonly prescribed
for patients under 18 years
old; children may be most
susceptible to side effects,
especially those related to
alcohol intoxication (oral
rinse contains more than
10% alcohol).

Special Concerns: If the
skin or wound being

scrubbed with chlorhexi-
dene appears to become
infected, notify your doctor
immediately. Do not allow
the medication to come in
contact with eyes or ears,
since it may cause perma-
nent injury. Do not use
chlorhexidine if you have
had a prior allergic reaction
to it. Cosmetic dentistry
may be needed to treat discoloration of teeth.

OVERDOSE
Symptoms: Slurred
speech, staggering, drowsiness or stupor, stomach
upset, nausea (overdose is
most likely to affect young
or underweight patients).

What to Do: Call your
doctor or EMS right away if
anyone—especially a
child—accidentally ingests
more than 4 oz of chlorhexidine or exhibits the above
symptoms.

DRUG INTERACTIONS
Do not use any other pre-
scription or nonprescription
medications for the area of
the skin being treated or for
the mouth without checking
with your doctor or dentist.

FOOD INTERACTIONS
No known food interactions.

DISEASE INTERACTIONS
Do not take chlorhexidine
gluconate if you have periodontal disease (various disorders of the bones of the
jaw and other tissues surrounding and supporting
the teeth).

Chloroquine

A 77

Aralen Phosphate 500 mg
(SANOFI WINTHROP)

▶ Drug Class: Anti-infective/
antimalarial

▶ Available in: Tablets, injection

▶ Available OTC? No

▶ As Generic? Yes

Side Effects

SERIOUS
Blurred or altered vision;
blood problems including
low white blood cell
count (sore throat, fever),
anemia (fatigue, weak-
ness), and low platelet
count (easy bleeding and
bruising). Such side
effects are extremely
rare; call your doctor
immediately if they
occur.

COMMON
No common side effects
are associated with
chloroquine.

LESS COMMON
Diarrhea, loss of appetite,
headache, stomach
cramps or pain, nausea
or vomiting, itching, dizziness, fatigue, confusion,
loss or bleaching of hair,
skin rash. Also blue-black
discoloration of skin,
inside of mouth, or

PRINCIPAL USES
To prevent and treat malaria
caused by specific strains of
plasmodia (the parasite that
causes malaria) that are susceptible to chloroquine.
(The drug is ineffective
against other strains.) It is
also used with another drug
as a second line of therapy
for hard-to-treat amebic
(parasitic) liver abscess.

HOW THE DRUG WORKS
Chloroquine is poisonous to
the malarial parasite.

DOSAGE
Tablets— For malaria pre-
vention: 500 mg (300 mg
base) once a week. For
treatment of malaria: To
start, 1,000 mg (600 mg
base). Then, 500 mg (300
mg base), 6 to 8 hours after
the first dose, and 500 mg
once a day on the second
and third days of treatment.
To treat amebic liver
abscess: To start, 250 mg
(150 mg base), 4 times a
day for 2 days. Then, 250
mg twice a day for at least 2
to 3 weeks. Injection— For
treatment of malaria: 200 to
250 mg (160 to 200 mg
base). If needed, the dose
may be repeated after 6
hours, not to exceed 1,000
mg (800 mg base) in the
first 24 hours. To treat amebic liver abscess: 200 to 250
mg a day for 10 to 12 days.
(Note: All dosages are for
adults and adolescents.
Consult your pediatrician
for children's doses, which
are based on body weight
and should not exceed
adult doses.)

ONSET OF EFFECT
Unknown.

DURATION OF ACTION
Unknown.

DIETARY ADVICE
Take it with food or milk to
reduce stomach upset.

STORAGE
Store in a tightly sealed container away from heat, moisture, and direct light.

IF YOU MISS A DOSE
If taking 1 or more doses a
day, take it as soon as you
remember. If it is near the
time for the next dose, skip
the missed dose and
resume your regular dosage
schedule. Do not double the
next dose. If taking 1
weekly dose, take it as soon
as possible, then resume
regular schedule.

STOPPING THE DRUG
Take it as prescribed for the
full treatment period.

PROLONGED USE
If you are taking this drug
as a preventive, your doctor
may want you to begin 1 to
2 weeks before you travel to
an area where malaria is
prevalent. Keep taking
chloroquine while you are
in the area and for 4 weeks
after you leave.

PRECAUTIONS
Over 60: Adverse reactions
may be more likely and
more severe.

**Driving and Hazardous
Work:** Do not drive or
engage in hazardous work
until you determine how the
medicine affects you.

Alcohol: No special precautions are necessary.

Pregnancy: The use of
chloroquine is discouraged
during pregnancy because
of the risks it poses to the
unborn child. However, in
some cases it may be pre-
scribed to prevent or treat
malaria or amebic liver
abscess, since the risks of
these diseases are poten-
tially more serious than
those posed by the drug.
Consult your doctor for
advice.

Breast Feeding: Chloroquine passes into breast
milk; extreme caution is
advised. Consult your physician for specific advice.

Infants and Children:
Extreme caution is neces-
sary when used by children.

Special Concerns: If you
take chloroquine once a
week, take it on the same
day every week. Malaria is
spread by mosquitoes. Take
appropriate precautions,
such as using mosquito netting, to guard against being
bitten by malaria-carrying
mosquitoes.

OVERDOSE
Symptoms: Increased
excitability, headache,
drowsiness, seizures, vision
changes, heartbeat irregularities, low blood pressure
(causing dizziness or fainting), respiratory and cardiac arrest.

What to Do: Seek medical
assistance immediately.

DRUG INTERACTIONS
Consult your doctor for specific advice if you are taking
magnesium salts, antacids,
cimetidine, or penicillamine.
The intradermal rabies vaccine may not be effective if
chloroquine is being used at
the time of vaccination.

FOOD INTERACTIONS
No known food interactions.

DISEASE INTERACTIONS
Consult your doctor for specific advice if you have a
severe blood disorder, any
eye disorder, liver disease, a
severe nervous system disorder, G6PD deficiency, porphyria, or psoriasis.

Chlorothiazide

BRAND NAMES
Diurigen, Diuril

Generic 250 mg
(WEST POINT)

▶ Drug Class: Thiazide diuretic

▶ Available in: Tablets, oral suspension, injection

▶ Available OTC? No

▶ As Generic? Yes

Side Effects

SERIOUS
Skin rash, hives, intense itching, swelling of the mouth and throat, breathing difficulty, serious heartbeat irregularities or palpitations, lightheadedness or dizziness, unusual bleeding or bruising. Call your doctor immediately.

COMMON
Potassium depletion may lead to heart palpitations and weakness. Fluid depletion may lead to dizziness, especially upon arising from a sitting or lying position.

LESS COMMON
Decreased sexual ability, increased sensitivity to sunlight, loss of appetite, gout, increased blood sugar (a problem for patients with diabetes).

PRINCIPAL USES
To treat high blood pressure and conditions causing edema (swelling of body tissues resulting from excess salt and water retention).

HOW THE DRUG WORKS
Diuretics increase the excretion of salt and water in the urine. By reducing the overall fluid volume in the body, these drugs reduce blood volume and so reduce pressure within the blood vessels.

DOSAGE
Adults— For high blood pressure: 250 mg once a day. To reduce edema: 250 to 500 mg once a day, or 2 or 3 days a week.

ONSET OF EFFECT
2 hours after oral dose; 15 minutes after injection.

DURATION OF ACTION
6 to 12 hours.

DIETARY ADVICE
Tablets should be taken with food.

STORAGE
Store in a tightly sealed container away from heat and direct light. Keep the liquid form from freezing.

IF YOU MISS A DOSE
Take it as soon as you remember. If it is near the time for the next dose, skip the missed dose and resume your regular dosage schedule. Do not double the next dose.

STOPPING THE DRUG
The decision to stop taking the drug should be made by your doctor.

PROLONGED USE
See your doctor regularly for examinations and tests if you must take this medicine for an extended period.

PRECAUTIONS
Over 60: No special problems are expected.

Driving and Hazardous Work: No special precautions are necessary.

Alcohol: No special precautions are necessary.

Pregnancy: Chlorothiazide has caused birth defects in animals. Human studies have not been done. This medicine should not be taken during pregnancy unless recommended by your doctor. Other diuretics are preferred in pregnant women.

Breast Feeding: Chlorothiazide passes into breast milk; avoid or discontinue use during the first month of nursing.

Infants and Children: This drug generally is not prescribed for children.

Special Concerns: Chlorothiazide is usually taken once a day. To prevent it from interfering with sleep, take it in the morning (unless otherwise prescribed by your doctor). If you are taking it for high blood pressure, follow the diet and weight control measures recommended by your doctor. Avoid exposure to sunlight, use a sunblock, or wear protective clothing. This medicine may cause your body to lose potassium. Follow your doctor's instructions about eating potassium-rich foods or taking a potassium supplement.

OVERDOSE
Symptoms: Lethargy, dizziness, drowsiness, muscle weakness, cramps, heartbeat irregularities, fainting.

What to Do: Call your doctor, emergency medical services (EMS), or the nearest poison control center immediately.

DRUG INTERACTIONS
Consult your doctor for specific advice if you are taking anticoagulants, cholestyramine, colestipol, drugs for diabetes, nonsteroidal anti-inflammatory drugs, digitalis drugs, or lithium.

FOOD INTERACTIONS
No known food interactions.

DISEASE INTERACTIONS
Caution is advised when taking chlorothiazide. Consult your doctor if you have any of the following: diabetes, gout, lupus erythematosus, pancreatitis, heart disease, blood vessel disease, liver disease, or kidney disease.

Chlorotrianisene

▶ Drug Class: Female sex hormone

▶ Available in: Capsules

▶ Available OTC? No

▶ As Generic? Yes

Side Effects

SERIOUS
Profuse or abnormal vaginal bleeding, blood clots (pain, redness, swelling in arm, leg, or buttock), stroke (slurred speech, loss of sensation, blurry vision), chest pain, shortness of breath. Call your doctor immediately.

COMMON
Nausea, diarrhea, stomach cramps, loss of appetite, breast pain or tenderness. In men: Breast enlargement, reduction in the size of the testicles, diminished sex drive.

LESS COMMON
Rash, joint pain, lumps in breast, depression, dizziness, migraine headaches.

PRINCIPAL USES
To relieve the symptoms of inoperable prostate cancer and ease some of the symptoms of menopause (hot flashes, sweating, chills, faintness). Chlorotrianisene may also be used to prevent breast engorgement following childbirth.

HOW THE DRUG WORKS
In women, chlorotrianisene supplements deficient natural levels of estrogen in the body. In men, the drug inhibits growth of cells in the prostate gland.

DOSAGE
For prostate cancer: 12 to 25 mg a day. For menopausal symptoms: 12 to 25 mg a day for 30 days or a cyclic regimen that requires 3 weeks on and 1 week off.

ONSET OF EFFECT
Unknown.

DURATION OF ACTION
24 hours.

DIETARY ADVICE
Take chlorotrianisene with or immediately following a meal to reduce nausea. If you have difficulty swallowing the capsule whole, open it and take it with liquid or food. Follow a low-sodium diet, since sodium causes your body to retain excess water.

STORAGE
Store in a tightly sealed container away from heat, moisture, and direct light.

IF YOU MISS A DOSE
Take it as soon as you remember, unless the time for your next scheduled dose is within the next 12 hours. If so, skip the missed dose and resume your regular dosage schedule. Do not double the next dose.

STOPPING THE DRUG
Take it as prescribed for the full treatment period, even if you begin to feel better before the scheduled end of therapy. The decision to stop taking the drug should be made in consultation with your doctor.

PROLONGED USE
Prolonged use of chlorotrianisene may lead to an increased risk of uterine or breast cancer and growth of fibroid tumors of the uterus (a common benign tumor). Talk to your doctor about the need for follow-up medical examinations or laboratory tests including Pap smear, mammogram, and liver function tests.

PRECAUTIONS

Over 60: Adverse reactions may be more likely and more severe in elderly patients.

Driving and Hazardous Work: This drug does not interfere with your ability to engage in such activities.

Alcohol: No special precautions are necessary.

Pregnancy: You should not use chlorotrianisene if you are pregnant or plan to become pregnant.

Breast Feeding: Chlorotrianisene is used to prevent breast engorgement and milk production following pregnancy; it should not be used by women wishing to nurse.

Infants and Children: Not prescribed for children.

Special Concerns: If you are on cyclic therapy (3 weeks on, 1 week off) for menopausal symptoms, some minor vaginal bleeding may occur during the week you are not taking the drug. This symptom is common and should diminish at the start of the next treatment cycle.

OVERDOSE

Symptoms: Nausea, vomiting, fluid retention, breast enlargement, abnormal vaginal bleeding.

What to Do: Call your doctor, emergency medical services (EMS), or the nearest poison control center immediately.

DRUG INTERACTIONS
Consult your doctor for specific advice if you are taking antidepressants, aspirin, barbiturates, bromocriptine, calcium supplements, corticosteroids, corticotropin, cyclosporine, dantrolene, nicotine, somatropin, tamoxifen, or warfarin.

FOOD INTERACTIONS
No known food interactions.

DISEASE INTERACTIONS
Caution is advised when taking chlorotrianisene. Consult your doctor if you have any of the following: a history of cancer of the breast or reproductive organs; a family history of breast cancer; breast lumps; heart or blood vessel disease; asthma; bone disease; gallbladder disease; liver or kidney problems; migraines; seizures; or phlebitis.

Chlorpheniramine Maleate Oral

Chlor-Trimeton Allergy 8 Hr. 8 mg
(SCHERING-PLOUGH)

Additional photographs

▶ Drug Class: Antihistamine

▶ Available in: Tablets, sustained-release capsules, syrup

▶ Available OTC? Yes

▶ As Generic? Yes

Side Effects

SERIOUS
Bleeding problems; small red pinpoints on the skin; fever; extreme fatigue; bleeding ulcers in the rectum, mouth, and vagina; reduced count of white blood cells (rare).

COMMON
Drowsiness; unusual excitability; dry mouth, nose, or throat. Symptoms of drowsiness tend to subside after a few days' use as your body adjusts to the drug.

LESS COMMON
Vision changes, loss of appetite, dizziness, painful or difficult urination, less tolerance for contact lenses.

PRINCIPAL USES
To relieve the symptoms of hay fever and other allergies, and for itching skin and hives.

HOW THE DRUG WORKS
Chlorpheniramine maleate works by blocking the effects of histamine, a naturally occurring substance that causes swelling, itching, sneezing, watery eyes, hives, and other symptoms of allergic reaction.

DOSAGE
Tablets— Adults: 4 mg, 3 to 4 times per day as needed, for a maximum dose of 24 mg a day. Sustained-release capsules— 8 mg every 8 hours, or 12 mg every 12 hours, as needed. Syrup— Children ages 6 to 12: 2 mg, 3 to 4 times a day, not exceeding 12 mg a day. Children ages 2 to 6: 1 mg every 6 hours.

ONSET OF EFFECT
15 to 60 minutes.

DURATION OF ACTION
3 to 6 hours for regular form, 8 to 12 hours for sustained-release capsules.

DIETARY ADVICE
Chlorpheniramine maleate may be taken with food or milk to reduce stomach upset. Use sugarless gum, sugarless sour hard candy, or ice chips to ease dry mouth.

STORAGE
Store in a tightly sealed container away from heat and direct light.

IF YOU MISS A DOSE
Take it as soon as you remember, up to 2 hours late. If it is more than 2 hours late, skip the missed dose and resume your regular dosage schedule. Do not double the next dose.

STOPPING THE DRUG
You should take it as prescribed for the full treatment period, but you may stop if you are feeling better before the scheduled end of therapy. Chlorpheniramine may be taken as needed.

PROLONGED USE
No special concerns.

PRECAUTIONS
Over 60: Older persons are more sensitive to antihistamine side effects, particularly confusion, dizziness, drowsiness, restlessness, irritability, nightmares, and dry mouth, nose, and throat.

Driving and Hazardous Work: Do not drive or engage in hazardous work until you determine how the medicine affects you. Use of this drug is a disqualification for piloting aircraft.

Alcohol: Alcohol increases the likelihood and the severity of side effects like drowsiness and confusion.

Pregnancy: In animal studies, no birth defects have been reported. Studies of pregnant women have not been undertaken. Before taking this drug, tell your doctor if you are pregnant or are planning to become pregnant.

Breast Feeding: Chlorpheniramine passes into breast milk; avoid or discontinue use while nursing.

Infants and Children: This drug is not recommended for children under the age of 2.

Special Concerns: Do not break, crush, or chew sustained-release capsules.

OVERDOSE
Symptoms: Marked drowsiness, dilated and sluggish pupils, combativeness, excessive excitability, confusion, loss of coordination, weak pulse, seizures, loss of consciousness.

What to Do: Patient should be made to vomit immediately, using ipecac syrup. If the patient is unconscious, he or she should be taken to the nearest hospital emergency room right away.

DRUG INTERACTIONS
Consult your doctor for specific advice if you are taking anticholinergics, bepridil, medications containing alcohol, or MAO inhibitors.

FOOD INTERACTIONS
No known food interactions.

DISEASE INTERACTIONS
Before taking chlorpheniramine, consult your doctor if you wear contact lenses or if you have glaucoma, prostate enlargement, difficulty with urination, or dry mouth or eyes.

Chlorpromazine Hydrochloride

Generic 10 mg
(GENEVA)

▶ Drug Class: Neuroleptic; antipsychotic

▶ Available in: Capsules, tablets, liquid concentrate, syrup, suppositories

▶ Available OTC? No

▶ As Generic? Yes

Side Effects

SERIOUS
Extreme and persistent restlessness; uncontrolled movements, including tics, twitching, twisting movements, and muscle spasms in the face, neck, and back; loss of coordination and balance; shuffling gait; trembling, weakness, or stiffness in the extremities; difficulty swallowing or speaking; persistent, uncontrolled chewing, lip-smacking, or tongue movements; staring and absence of facial expression; fainting; difficulty urinating; increased skin sensitivity to the sun; skin rash; yellow discoloration of the eyes or skin (indicating a liver disorder).

COMMON
Constipation, decreased sweating, lightheadedness, dizziness or faintness, drowsiness, dry mouth.

LESS COMMON
Menstrual irregularities; sexual dysfunction; breast pain, swelling, or secretion; weight gain; blurred vision.

PRINCIPAL USES
To treat psychotic conditions such as schizophrenia. It can also be used to ease severe nausea and vomiting, and persistent hiccups.

HOW THE DRUG WORKS
Chlorpromazine inhibits activity of the brain chemical dopamine, thereby helping to prevent the overstimulation of specific nerve centers believed to be responsible for certain psychiatric disorders. The drug also suppresses activity in the trigger zones of the brain and gastrointestinal tract that govern the vomiting reflex and hiccupping.

DOSAGE
Dose, dosage form, and dosing schedule vary based on many factors, including patient's age, medical condition, body weight, tolerance of side effects, and overall response to the drug. Usual adult dose: Initially, 10 to 25 mg, 3 or 4 times a day. Your doctor may increase it as needed and tolerated; maximum dose may reach 200 mg a day for many, or even 800 mg a day for severely psychotic patients. Children: Consult your pediatrician.

ONSET OF EFFECT
For psychotic conditions: 4 to 6 weeks. For nausea and vomiting: 1 hour or less.

DURATION OF ACTION
Unknown.

DIETARY ADVICE
Take it with meals in order to reduce stomach upset.

STORAGE
Store in a tightly sealed container away from heat, moisture, and direct light.

IF YOU MISS A DOSE
Take it as soon as you remember. However, if it is near the time for the next dose, skip the missed dose and resume your regular dosage schedule. Do not double the next dose.

STOPPING THE DRUG
Do not stop taking the drug abruptly or without your doctor's approval. Dosage should be reduced gradually by your doctor to prevent withdrawal symptoms.

PROLONGED USE
Prolonged use may lead to tardive dyskinesia (involuntary movements of the jaw, lips, and tongue). Consult your doctor about the need for follow-up evaluations and tests if you must take this drug for an extended period.

PRECAUTIONS
Over 60: Adverse reactions, especially drowsiness and low blood pressure, are more common in elderly patients. A lower dose may be warranted.

Driving and Hazardous Work: The use of this drug may impair your ability to perform such tasks safely.

Alcohol: Avoid alcohol.

Pregnancy: Avoid using this drug if you are pregnant or plan to become pregnant.

Breast Feeding: Either avoid taking the drug if possible or refrain from breast feeding.

Infants and Children: This drug should not be used by infants and children younger than 2 years old. For older children, use it only under the care of your pediatrician.

OVERDOSE
Symptoms: Extreme drowsiness, heart rhythm irregularities, dry mouth, restlessness or agitation, seizures, unconsciousness.

What to Do: Call your doctor, emergency medical services (EMS), or the nearest poison control center immediately.

DRUG INTERACTIONS
Consult your doctor for specific advice if you are taking amantadine, high blood pressure medication, bromocriptine, deferoxamine, diuretics, levobunolol, heart medication, metoprolol, nabilone, other psychiatric drugs, pentamidine, pimozide, promethazine, trimeprazine, a thyroid agent, central nervous system depressants, epinephrine, lithium, levodopa, methyldopa, metoclopramide, metyrosine, pemoline, a rauwolfia alkaloid, or metrizamide.

FOOD INTERACTIONS
No known food interactions.

DISEASE INTERACTIONS
Consult your doctor if you have a history of alcohol abuse, any blood disorder, breast cancer, benign prostatic hyperplasia (BPH), epilepsy or seizures, glaucoma, heart, lung, or blood vessel disease, liver disease, Parkinson's disease, peptic ulcer, or urinary difficulty.

Chlorpropamide

BRAND NAMES
Chlorabetic, Diabinese, Glucamide, Insulase

Generic 100 mg
(SIDMAK)

▸ Drug Class: Antidiabetic agent/sulfonylurea

▸ Available in: Tablets

▸ Available OTC? No

▸ As Generic? Yes

Side Effects

SERIOUS
Low blood sugar; perspiration or a cold sweat; restlessness; rapid pulse; anxious feeling; nausea; difficulty breathing; feelings of dizziness, weakness, or lightheadedness; poor coordination, slurred speech, confusion; sleepiness; seizures or convulsions; weakness of an arm, leg, or an entire side of the body; fainting. Contact your doctor immediately. Administer sugar-containing substances only if the patient is conscious and alert.

COMMON
Mild dizziness, diarrhea, frequent or unusual hunger, nausea, heartburn, itching, changes in taste, constipation, fluid retention, rash.

LESS COMMON
Fatigue, heightened skin sensitivity to light, yellowish tinge to skin and eyes, ringing in the ears.

PRINCIPAL USES
To help control mild to moderate non-insulin-dependent (type 2) diabetes mellitus in patients whose blood sugar cannot be adequately controlled by diet, weight loss, and exercise.

HOW THE DRUG WORKS
Chlorpropamide stimulates the release of additional insulin from the pancreas and makes the tissues of the body more responsive to insulin.

DOSAGE
Initially, 250 mg once a day. After 5 to 7 days, dose can be increased by 50 to 125 mg. It may be increased every 3 to 5 days, if needed, to a maximum dose of 750 mg a day. Adults over age 65: 100 to 125 mg each day, increased as described above.

ONSET OF EFFECT
Within 1 hour.

DURATION OF ACTION
Up to 60 hours.

DIETARY ADVICE
Take 1 dose daily, 30 minutes before breakfast; if stomach upset occurs, divide the daily amount into two equal doses and take them before your morning and evening meals. The tablet may be crushed. Follow the dietary guidelines given to you by your doctor, and restrict intake of sugar-containing snacks.

STORAGE
Store in a tightly sealed container away from heat and direct light.

IF YOU MISS A DOSE
Take it as soon as you remember. If it is near the time for the next dose, skip the missed dose and resume your regular dosage schedule. Do not double the next dose.

STOPPING THE DRUG
Do not stop taking the drug without your doctor's approval. Take it as prescribed for the full treatment period, even if you begin to feel better.

PROLONGED USE
Prolonged use increases the risk of adverse effects. Periodic physical examinations and laboratory tests (blood and urine tests to monitor sugar levels) are needed.

PRECAUTIONS
Over 60: Adverse reactions may be more likely and more severe in elderly patients.

Driving and Hazardous Work: Do not drive or engage in hazardous work until you determine how this medication affects you.

Alcohol: Avoid alcohol. Patients who consume alcohol while taking chlorpropamide are at risk for a severe reaction that may include nausea, vomiting, flushing, lightheadedness, headache, and shortness of breath.

Pregnancy: Avoid using chlorpropamide if you are pregnant or are planning to become pregnant.

Breast Feeding: Chlorpropamide passes into breast milk and may be harmful; avoid or discontinue use while nursing.

Infants and Children: Chlorpropamide is not recommended for infants and children.

OVERDOSE
Symptoms: Excessive hunger, nausea, anxiety, cool skin, cold sweats, drowsiness, rapid heartbeat, tingling of lips and tongue, weakness, unconsciousness, confusion, seizures.

What to Do: Call your doctor, emergency medical services (EMS), or the nearest poison control center immediately.

DRUG INTERACTIONS
Consult your doctor for specific advice if you are taking anabolic steroids or corticosteroids, allopurinol, anticoagulants, aspirin and aspirin-containing cough, cold, and appetite-control drugs, barbiturates, beta-blockers, calcium channel blockers, cimetidine, ranitidine, pentamidine, chloramphenicol, ciprofloxacin, cyclosporine, estrogens, ethanol, thiazide diuretics, fenfluramine, oral miconazole or ketoconazole, lithium, MAO inhibitors, probenecid, rifampin, selegiline or procarbazine, sulfinpyrazone, quinidine.

FOOD INTERACTIONS
No known food interactions.

DISEASE INTERACTIONS
Do not take chlorpropamide if you have type 1 diabetes. Caution is advised when taking chlorpropamide. Consult your doctor if you have any of the following: malnutrition, heart problems, liver or kidney disease, thyroid disease, a severe infection, fever, or an underactive pituitary or adrenal gland.

Chlorthalidone

Generic 50 mg
(**Mylan**)

Additional photographs

▶ Drug Class: Thiazide-like diuretic

▶ Available in: Tablets

▶ Available OTC? No

▶ As Generic? Yes

Side Effects

SERIOUS
Skin rash, hives, intense itching, swelling of the mouth and throat, breathing difficulty, serious heartbeat irregularities or palpitations, lightheadedness or dizziness, unusual bleeding or bruising. Call your doctor immediately.

COMMON
Potassium depletion may lead to heart palpitations and weakness. Fluid depletion may lead to dizziness, especially upon arising from a sitting or lying position.

LESS COMMON
Decreased sexual ability, increased sensitivity to sunlight, loss of appetite, gout, increased blood sugar (a problem for patients with diabetes).

PRINCIPAL USES
To treat high blood pressure (hypertension) and conditions that cause edema (swelling of body tissues resulting from excess salt and water retention).

HOW THE DRUG WORKS
Diuretics increase the excretion of salt and water in the urine. By reducing the overall fluid volume in the body, these drugs reduce blood volume and so reduce pressure within the blood vessels.

DOSAGE
Adults: 25 to 100 mg once a day or every other day.

ONSET OF EFFECT
2 to 3 hours.

DURATION OF ACTION
2 to 3 days.

DIETARY ADVICE
Take it with food to avoid stomach upset.

STORAGE
Store in a tightly sealed container away from heat and direct light.

IF YOU MISS A DOSE
Take it as soon as you remember. However, if it is near the time for the next dose, skip the missed dose and resume your regular dosage schedule. Do not double the next dose.

STOPPING THE DRUG
Unless directed otherwise by your doctor, take this medication as prescribed for the full treatment period, even if you begin to feel better before the scheduled end of therapy.

PROLONGED USE
See your doctor regularly for examinations and tests, if you must take this medicine for an extended period.

PRECAUTIONS
Over 60: Adverse reactions may be more likely and severe in older patients.

Driving and Hazardous Work: No special precautions are warranted.

Alcohol: Avoid alcohol while taking this drug.

Pregnancy: This medicine should not be taken during pregnancy unless recommended by your doctor.

Breast Feeding: Chlorthalidone passes into breast milk; avoid or discontinue use while nursing.

Infants and Children: Although chlorthalidone is rarely prescribed for children, no unusual side effects are expected. The dose must be determined by a pediatrician.

Special Concerns: Chlorthalidone is usually taken once a day. To prevent it from interfering with sleep, take it in the morning. If you are taking it for high blood pressure, follow the diet and weight control measures recommended by your doctor. Avoid exposure to sunlight, use a sunblock, or wear protective clothing. This medicine may cause your body to lose potassium. Follow your doctor's instructions about eating potassium-rich foods or taking a potassium supplement.

OVERDOSE
Symptoms: Fainting, lethargy, dizziness, drowsiness, confusion, gastrointestinal irritation.

What to Do: Call your doctor, emergency medical services (EMS), or the nearest poison control center immediately.

DRUG INTERACTIONS
Consult your doctor for specific advice if you are taking anticoagulants, cholestyramine, colestipol, drugs for diabetes, nonsteroidal anti-inflammatory drugs, digitalis drugs, or lithium.

FOOD INTERACTIONS
No significant food interactions have been reported.

DISEASE INTERACTIONS
Caution is advised when taking chlorthalidone. Consult your doctor if you have any of the following: diabetes, gout, lupus erythematosus, pancreatitis, diabetes, heart disease, blood vessel disease, liver disease, or kidney disease.

Chlorzoxazone

BRAND NAMES
EZE-DS, Paraflex, Parafon
Forte DSC, Relax-Ds,
Relaxazone, Remular,
Strifon Forte DSC

Generic 500 mg
(**Barr**)

▶ Drug Class: Muscle relaxant

▶ Available in: Caplets, tablets

▶ Available OTC? No

▶ As Generic? Yes

Side Effects

SERIOUS
Fainting; palpitations or
rapid heartbeat; fever;
hives or severe swelling
of face, lips, or tongue
along with shortness of
breath, chest tightness,
or wheezing (indicating a
potentially life-threatening allergic reaction);
mental depression; tem-
porary loss of vision. Call
your doctor right away.

COMMON
Drowsiness, dizziness,
dry mouth.

LESS COMMON
Bruises, feeling of illness,
excitability, stomach
upset, discolored urine,
bloody or black stools,
hiccups.

PRINCIPAL USES
Muscle relaxants are used
to relieve stiffness and discomfort caused by severe
sprains and strains, muscle
spasms, or other muscle
problems. They may be prescribed in conjunction with
other treatment methods,
such as physical therapy.

HOW THE DRUG WORKS
Muscle relaxants such as
chlorzoxazone depress
activity in the central nervous system, which in turn
interferes with the transmission of nerve impulses from
the spinal cord to the skeletal muscles.

DOSAGE
Adults: 250 to 750 mg, 3 or
4 times a day. The dosage
can be reduced as improvement occurs.

ONSET OF EFFECT
15 to 30 minutes.

DURATION OF ACTION
Up to 4 hours.

DIETARY ADVICE
Take it with meals to lessen
stomach upset. Be sure to
eat a well-balanced diet; the
healing of injured tissue
increases the body's protein
and calorie requirements.
To avoid dry mouth, main-
tain adequate fluid intake
and suck on ice chips if
desired.

STORAGE
Store in a tightly sealed container away from heat, moisture, and direct light.

IF YOU MISS A DOSE
Take it as soon as you
remember. If it is near the
time for the next dose, skip
the missed dose and
resume your regular dosage
schedule. Do not double the
next dose.

STOPPING THE DRUG
The decision to stop taking
the drug should be made by
your doctor. Gradual reduction of the dose may be necessary if you have taken the
drug for a long time.

PROLONGED USE
Adult use should generally
be limited to 10 days. Consult your doctor about the
need for follow-up medical
examinations or laboratory
studies. Periodic liver tests
are recommended during
therapy.

PRECAUTIONS
Over 60: Adverse reactions
may be more likely and
more severe in older
patients.

**Driving and Hazardous
Work:** Do not drive or
engage in hazardous work
until you determine how the
medicine affects you.

Alcohol: Avoid alcohol
while taking this drug
because it may compound
the sedative effect and may
cause liver damage.

Pregnancy: Before taking
chlorzoxazone, be sure to
tell your doctor if you are
pregnant or are planning to
become pregnant.

Breast Feeding: Chlorzoxazone passes into breast
milk; avoid or discontinue
use while nursing.

Infants and Children:
Not recommended for use
by children under age 12.

Special Concerns: If your
symptoms do not improve
after 2 days of use, call your
doctor. Use of chlorzoxa-
zone should be accompa-
nied by bed rest, physical
therapy, and other measures
to relieve discomfort. Do
not take this drug if you are

allergic to any skeletal muscle relaxant.

OVERDOSE
Symptoms: Nausea, vomiting, diarrhea, loss of
appetite, headache, severe
weakness, unusual increase
in sweating, fainting, breathing difficulties, irritability,
convulsions, feeling of paralysis, loss of consciousness.

What to Do: An overdose
of chlorzoxazone is unlikely
to be life-threatening, However, if someone takes a
much larger dose than prescribed, seek medical assistance immediately.

DRUG INTERACTIONS
Tell your doctor if you are
taking oral anticoagulants,
antidepressants, antihistamines, clozapine, dronabinol, any mind-altering
medication, MAO inhibitors,
other muscle relaxants, any
narcotic, phenobarbital, sertraline, sleeping pills, or a
tetracycline antibiotic.

FOOD INTERACTIONS
No known food interactions.

DISEASE INTERACTIONS
Use of this drug may cause
complications in patients
with liver or kidney disease,
since these organs work
together to remove the
medication from the body.

Cholestyramine

▶ Drug Class: Antilipidemic (cholesterol-lowering agent)

▶ Available in: Powder

▶ Available OTC? No

▶ As Generic? Yes

Side Effects

SERIOUS
Severe abdominal pain (a very rare reaction, indicating intestinal obstruction). Stop taking the drug and contact your doctor immediately.

COMMON
Constipation, heartburn, bloating, belching, abdominal discomfort, irritation of the anal area.

LESS COMMON
Hives, rash, gas, diarrhea, nausea, vomiting, gallstones.

PRINCIPAL USES
To reduce cholesterol in people with high blood levels of low-density lipoprotein (LDL), as part of a comprehensive treatment program that includes exercise and special diet. The drug is also used to relieve itching caused by high levels of bile acids in the blood, a problem associated with blockage of the bile ducts. Cholestyramine may also be used to prevent some types of diarrhea or to serve as an antidote to poisoning from or overdose of digitalis drugs.

HOW THE DRUG WORKS
Cholestyramine binds with bile acids in the intestine, forming an insoluble complex that is excreted in the feces. This process reduces the bile acids in the blood. In response to the lower levels of bile acids, the liver converts more cholesterol to bile acids. Consequently, the amount of cholesterol in liver cells declines, and the liver makes more LDL receptors. The resulting increased removal of LDL from the blood lowers LDL cholesterol.

DOSAGE
Initial dose is 4 g, 1 or 2 times a day. Maintenance dose is 8 to 24 g per day in 2 equally divided doses. Always mix the powder thoroughly with appropriate liquid (water or fruit juice; do not use carbonated beverages), and wait 10 to 15 minutes after mixing before drinking. Dosages are increased or decreased according to the individual's response.

ONSET OF EFFECT
Within 1 to 3 weeks.

DURATION OF ACTION
Cholestyramine's effects persist for 2 to 4 weeks after final dose.

DIETARY ADVICE
Follow all special dietary restrictions and guidelines as directed by your doctor.

STORAGE
Store in a tightly sealed container away from heat and direct light. Keep away from moisture.

IF YOU MISS A DOSE
Take it as soon as you remember. However, if it is near the time for the next dose, skip the missed dose and resume your regular dosage schedule. Do not double the next dose.

STOPPING THE DRUG
The drug may be stopped after 1 to 3 months if the therapeutic effect is not adequate. The decision to stop taking the drug should be made by your doctor.

PROLONGED USE
Cholestyramine may be used safely for years; however, periodic evaluation of the drug's effectiveness is necessary.

PRECAUTIONS
Over 60: Adverse reactions (particularly constipation) are more likely and more severe in older patients.

Driving and Hazardous Work: No special precautions are necessary.

Alcohol: No special precautions are necessary.

Pregnancy: The effects on a fetus are unknown. Consult your doctor if you become or plan to become pregnant.

Breast Feeding: At very high doses cholestyramine may interfere with the absorption of vitamins A, D, E, and K, which may affect the nutritional intake of the nursing infant. Consult your doctor for specific advice.

Infants and Children: Prescribed for children only in rare circumstances. Follow doctor's instructions and dosage guidelines carefully in such cases.

Special Concerns: At very high doses cholestyramine may interfere with the absorption of fats and fat-soluble vitamins (vitamins A, D, E, and K); vitamin supplementation may be advised.

OVERDOSE
Symptoms: None reported.

What to Do: Emergency instructions not applicable.

DRUG INTERACTIONS
Cholestyramine may bind with other drugs and hinder their absorption. Therefore, take all other drugs 1 to 2 hours before or 4 hours after taking cholestyramine.

FOOD INTERACTIONS
No known food interactions.

DISEASE INTERACTIONS
Do not take this drug if you have had a prior allergic reaction to it. Do not take Questran Light if you have phenylketonuria. Use of cholestyramine may make the following conditions worse: gallstones, peptic ulcer, intestinal bleeding disorders, hemorrhoids, malabsorption, constipation.

Cidofovir Intravenous

▶ Drug Class: Antiviral

▶ Available in: Intravenous injection

▶ Available OTC? No

▶ As Generic? No

Side Effects

SERIOUS
Kidney damage, causing decreased or increased urination, thirst, and shortness of breath. Impaired vision or other changes in vision may also develop. If such symptoms occur, call your doctor right away.

COMMON
Probenecid, which is given with cidofovir, may cause fever, chills, headache, rash, nausea, or vomiting.

LESS COMMON
Persistent weakness and fatigue or general loss of strength.

PRINCIPAL USES
To treat cytomegalovirus (CMV) retinitis (an eye infection) or other forms of CMV disease in patients with human immunodeficiency virus (HIV) infection. Cidofovir is given in combination with probenecid, a drug that enhances the effectiveness of antimicrobial medications.

HOW THE DRUG WORKS
Cidofovir interferes with the activity of enzymes needed for the replication of DNA in viral cells, thus preventing CMV from reproducing.

DOSAGE
For patients with normal kidney function: Initially, 5 mg per 2.2 lbs (1 kg) of body weight infused intravenously over a period of 60 minutes, once a week, for 2 consecutive weeks. Probenecid is also given at a dose of 2 g, 3 hours before infusion, followed by 1 g, 2 hours later, then again 8 hours later. Maintenance dose of cidofovir: 5 mg per 2.2 lbs of body weight once every 2 weeks. For patients with impaired kidney function: A reduced dose is necessary, as determined by your doctor.

ONSET OF EFFECT
Unknown.

DURATION OF ACTION
Unknown.

DIETARY ADVICE
Cidofovir can be given without regard to diet. Probenecid should be given after food intake. Drink plenty of fluids.

STORAGE
Not applicable; the dose is administered at a health care facility or by a home nurse.

IF YOU MISS A DOSE
If you miss a dose for any reason, contact your doctor and arrange to receive treatment as soon as possible.

STOPPING THE DRUG
The decision to stop taking the drug should be made in consultation with your physician.

PROLONGED USE
See your doctor regularly for tests and examinations if you must take this medication for a prolonged period. See an ophthalmologist regularly for eye examinations.

PRECAUTIONS
Over 60: Older patients are more likely to have impaired kidney function requiring an adjustment in dosage.

Driving and Hazardous Work: Do not drive or engage in hazardous work until you determine how the medicine affects you.

Alcohol: Avoid alcohol if liver function is impaired.

Pregnancy: Cidofovir has been shown to cause birth defects in animals. Human studies have not been done. This medication should be given during pregnancy only if potential benefits outweigh the risks to the unborn child.

Breast Feeding: It is unknown whether cidofovir passes into breast milk; however, women infected with HIV should not nurse, to avoid transmitting the virus to an uninfected child.

Infants and Children: The safety and effectiveness of cidofovir in infants and children have not been established.

Special Concerns: The risk of severe nausea when probenecid is given can be reduced by taking an anti-nausea medication, such as diphenhydramine hydrochloride.

OVERDOSE
Symptoms: No cases of overdose have been reported.

What to Do: An overdose of cidofovir is unlikely to occur. Nonetheless, if you have any reason to suspect an overdose, call your physician, emergency medical services (EMS), or the nearest poison control center immediately.

DRUG INTERACTIONS
Other drugs may interact with cidofovir. Consult your doctor for specific advice if you are taking any other drug that can cause kidney damage, such as aminoglycosides, amphotericin B, foscarnet, nonsteroidal anti-inflammatory drugs, pentamidine, vancomycin, and zidovudine. A seven-day waiting period after use of such drugs is recommended before beginning therapy with cidofovir.

FOOD INTERACTIONS
No known food interactions, but side effects of probenecid are decreased when it is taken with food.

DISEASE INTERACTIONS
Consult your doctor if you have any condition that impairs kidney function.

Cilostazol

BRAND NAME
Pletal

▶ Drug Class: Phosphodiesterase type 3 inhibitor

▶ Available in: Tablets

▶ Available OTC? No

▶ As Generic? No

Side Effects

SERIOUS
No serious side effects have been reported.

COMMON
Headache, heart palpitations, diarrhea, increased risk of infection.

LESS COMMON
Rapid heartbeat, abdominal pain, indigestion, flatulence, nausea, swelling of the extremities, dizziness, sore throat, runny nose.

PRINCIPAL USES
To reduce symptoms of intermittent claudication (leg pain that is induced by walking and which subsides after rest).

HOW THE DRUG WORKS
Intermittent claudication results from impaired blood supply to the legs. Although its precise mechanism of action is not clear, cilostazol appears to improve circulation by dilating blood vessels, especially those supplying the legs. It also appears to inhibit the aggregation (clumping) of platelets and this reduces the formation of blood clots which can block arterial blood flow.

DOSAGE
100 mg 2 times a day.

ONSET OF EFFECT
From 2 to 12 weeks.

DURATION OF ACTION
Unknown.

DIETARY ADVICE
Take on an empty stomach at least 30 minutes before or 2 hours after a meal.

STORAGE
Store in a tightly sealed container away from heat, moisture, and direct light.

IF YOU MISS A DOSE
Take it as soon as you remember. If it is near the time for the next dose, skip the missed dose and resume your regular dosage schedule. Do not double the next dose.

STOPPING THE DRUG
The decision to stop taking the drug should be made in consultation with your physician.

PROLONGED USE
The safety and effectiveness of cilostazol have not been determined beyond 24 weeks of use.

PRECAUTIONS
Over 60: No special problems are expected.

Driving and Hazardous Work: Use caution when driving or engaging in hazardous work until you determine how the medicine affects you.

Alcohol: No special precautions are necessary.

Pregnancy: Adequate human studies have not been done. Before taking cilostazol, tell your doctor if you are pregnant or plan to become pregnant.

Breast Feeding: Cilostazol may pass into breast milk; caution is advised. Consult your doctor for advice on whether to discontinue nursing or discontinue the drug.

Infants and Children: Safety and effectiveness have not been established for children under age 18.

OVERDOSE
Symptoms: Few cases of overdose have been reported. However, if you take a much larger dose than prescribed, you may experience severe headache, diarrhea, dizziness or fainting, and heartbeat irregularities.

What to Do: Call your doctor, emergency medical services (EMS), or the nearest poison control center immediately.

DRUG INTERACTIONS
The following drugs may interact with cilostazol. Consult your doctor for specific advice if you are taking ketoconazole, itraconazole, fluconazole, miconazole, fluvoxamine, fluoxetine, nefazodone, sertraline, erythromycin and other macrolide antibiotics, omeprazole, diltiazem, or clopidogrel.

FOOD INTERACTIONS
Do not take cilostazol with grapefruit juice.

DISEASE INTERACTIONS
Do not take cilostazol if you have congestive heart failure of any severity.

Cimetidine

BRAND NAMES
Tagamet, Tagamet HB,
Tagamet HB 200

Tagamet 300mg
(SMITHKLINE BEECHAM)

Additional photographs

▶ Drug Class: Histamine (H2) blocker

▶ Available in: Tablets, oral solution, oral suspension

▶ Available OTC? Yes

▶ As Generic? Yes

Side Effects

SERIOUS
Irregular heart rhythm (palpitations), slowed heartbeat, severe blood problems resulting in unusual bleeding, bruising, fever, chills, and increased susceptibility to infection. Call your doctor immediately.

COMMON
Headache, fatigue, drowsiness, dizziness, nausea, vomiting, abdominal pain, diarrhea.

LESS COMMON
Blurred vision, decreased sexual desire or function, swelling of breasts in males or females, temporary hair loss, hallucinations, depression, insomnia, skin rash, hives, or redness.

PRINCIPAL USES
To treat ulcers of the stomach and duodenum, as well as other conditions, such as esophagitis (chronic inflammation of the esophagus), and gastroesophageal reflux (backwash of stomach acid into the esophagus, resulting in heartburn).

HOW THE DRUG WORKS
Cimetidine blocks the action of histamine (a compound produced in the body's cells), which in turn decreases the stomach's secretion of hydrochloric acid. Once stomach acid production is decreased, the body is better able to heal itself.

DOSAGE
For treatment of acute (symptomatic, bothersome) duodenal or gastric ulcers—Adults and teenagers: Various dosage schedules are used, including 300 mg, 4 times a day, with meals and at bedtime; 400 or 600 mg, 2 times a day; or 800 mg taken once daily at bedtime. For prevention of duodenal ulcers— Adults and teenagers: Usual dose is 300 mg, 2 times a day; another common dosage schedule is 400 mg taken once daily at bedtime. For treatment as needed of heartburn and acid indigestion— Adults and teenagers: 200 mg with water when symptoms start; another 200 mg may be taken within the next 24 hours, for a maximum of 400 mg in a 24-hour period. For treatment of gastroesophageal reflux disease— Adults: 800 to 1,600 mg a day, in 2 to 4 divided doses, for approximately 12 weeks.

ONSET OF EFFECT
Within 1 hour.

DURATION OF ACTION
At least 4 to 5 hours.

DIETARY ADVICE
Avoid foods that cause stomach irritation.

STORAGE
Store away from heat and direct light. Keep the liquid form from freezing.

IF YOU MISS A DOSE
Take it as soon as you remember. If it is near the time for the next dose, skip the missed dose and resume your regular dosage schedule. Do not double the next dose.

STOPPING THE DRUG
Prescription-strength: Take it for the full treatment period, even if you begin to feel better before the scheduled end of therapy. Nonprescription-strength: Take as needed.

PROLONGED USE
Do not take nonprescription-strength cimetidine for more than 2 weeks unless instructed to do so by your physician.

PRECAUTIONS
Over 60: Adverse reactions may be more likely and more severe in older patients.

Driving and Hazardous Work: Do not drive or engage in hazardous work until you determine how the medicine affects you.

Alcohol: Avoid alcohol.

Pregnancy: Avoid or discontinue use if you are pregnant or trying to become pregnant.

Breast Feeding: Cimetidine passes into breast milk; avoid or discontinue use while nursing.

Infants and Children: Not recommended for use by children under the age of 16 years old.

Special Concerns: Avoid cigarette smoking because it may increase stomach acid secretion and thus worsen the disease. Do not take cimetidine if you have ever had an allergic reaction to a histamine (H2) blocker. If stomach pain becomes worse while you are using the drug, tell your doctor right away.

OVERDOSE
Symptoms: No symptoms have been reported.

What to Do: An overdose is unlikely to be life-threatening. However, if someone takes a much larger dose than directed, seek medical assistance right away.

DRUG INTERACTIONS
Consult your doctor for specific advice if you are taking aminophylline, anticoagulants, caffeine, metoprolol, oxtriphylline, phenytoin, propranolol, theophylline, tricyclic antidepressants, itraconazole, ketoconazole, metronidazole.

FOOD INTERACTIONS
Carbonated drinks, citrus fruits and juices, caffeine-containing beverages, and other acidic foods or liquids may irritate the stomach or interfere with the therapeutic action of cimetidine.

DISEASE INTERACTIONS
Patients with kidney or liver disease or weakened immune systems should not use cimetidine or should use it in smaller, limited doses under careful medical supervision.

Ciprofloxacin Ophthalmic

▶ Drug Class: Fluoroquinolone antibiotic

▶ Available in: Ophthalmic solution

▶ Available OTC? No

▶ As Generic? Yes

Side Effects

SERIOUS
Nausea, blurry or decreased vision, skin rash, severe irritation or redness of the eye. Stop using the drug and call your doctor immediately.

COMMON
Burning or crusting in the eye or eyelid.

LESS COMMON
Redness of the edge of the eyelids, bad taste in mouth, tearing or itching of the eye, swelling of the eyelid, sensation of a foreign body in the eye, increased sensitivity of eyes to bright light.

PRINCIPAL USES

To treat or prevent bacterial infections of the eye, such as conjunctivitis or keratitis (infection of the cornea). Often used to prevent infection while a corneal abrasion is healing.

HOW THE DRUG WORKS

Ciprofloxacin interferes with the action of certain enzymes necessary for bacteria to grow and multiply.

DOSAGE

Exact dosing depends on the nature of the infection and its response to treatment. Follow your doctor's instructions precisely. The following is an example of a typical dose for conjunctivitis. Adults and teenagers: 1 drop in eye every 2 hours for 2 days, then 1 drop every 4 hours for the next 5 days (doses administered during waking hours only).

ONSET OF EFFECT

Unknown.

DURATION OF ACTION

Unknown.

DIETARY ADVICE

No special restrictions.

STORAGE

Store in a tightly sealed container away from heat, moisture, and direct light. Do not refrigerate or allow the solution to freeze.

IF YOU MISS A DOSE

Apply it as soon as you remember. If it is near the time for the next dose, skip the missed dose and resume your regular dosage schedule. Do not double the next dose.

STOPPING THE DRUG

Use this drug as prescribed for the full treatment period, even if you begin to feel better before the scheduled end of therapy.

PROLONGED USE

Prolonged use, as directed by your doctor, may be necessary for severe cases of infection. See your doctor regularly for tests and examinations if you take this drug for a prolonged period.

PRECAUTIONS

Over 60: Adverse reactions may be more likely and more severe in older patients.

Driving and Hazardous Work: Do not drive or engage in hazardous work until you determine how the medicine affects your vision.

Alcohol: No special precautions are necessary.

Pregnancy: Adequate human studies have not been done. Before taking ophthalmic ciprofloxacin, tell your doctor if you are pregnant or plan to become pregnant.

Breast Feeding: Ophthalmic ciprofloxacin may pass into breast milk; caution is advised. Ciprofloxacin taken orally has been found in trace amounts in breast milk. Consult your doctor for advice.

Infants and Children: This medication is not recommended for use by children under the age of 12.

Special Concerns: To use the eye drops, first wash your hands. Tilt your head back. Gently apply pressure to the inside corner of the eyelid and with the index finger of the same hand, pull downward on the lower eyelid to make a space. Drop the medicine into this space and close your eye. Apply pressure for 1 or 2 minutes while keeping the eye closed without blinking. Then wash your hands again. Make sure the tip of the dropper does not touch your eye, finger, or any other surface. If your symptoms do not improve or if they become worse, check with your doctor. You should not share your medication, towels, or washcloths with other people. Call your doctor if anyone else close to you develops similar symptoms.

OVERDOSE

Symptoms: No specific ones have been reported.

What to Do: An overdose of ophthalmic ciprofloxacin is unlikely to be life-threatening. However, if someone takes a much larger dose of the drug than prescribed or accidentally ingests the medicine, seek medical assistance right away.

DRUG INTERACTIONS

Other drugs may interact with ophthalmic ciprofloxacin. Consult your doctor for specific advice if you are taking any other prescription or over-the-counter medication.

FOOD INTERACTIONS

No known food interactions.

DISEASE INTERACTIONS

Caution is advised when taking ophthalmic ciprofloxacin. Consult your doctor if you have ever had an allergic reaction to ciprofloxacin or other fluoroquinolone antibiotics.

Ciprofloxacin Systemic

Cipro 750 mg
(BAYER)

831
Additional photographs

▶ Drug Class: Fluoroquinolone antibiotic

▶ Available in: Tablets, oral suspension

▶ Available OTC? No

▶ As Generic? Yes

Side Effects

SERIOUS
Serious reactions to ciprofloxacin are rare and include seizures, mental confusion, hallucinations, agitation, nightmares, depression, shortness of breath, unusual swelling in the face or extremities, and loss of consciousness. Also skin burning, redness, blisters, rash, or itching on exposure to sunlight. Call your doctor immediately.

COMMON
Increased sensitivity to sunlight (and increased risk of sunburn) for days following therapy.

LESS COMMON
Diarrhea, nausea and vomiting, stomach pain and upset, gas, headache, dizziness, insomnia, changes in taste perception, drowsiness, itching, dry mouth, unusual body aches or pains.

PRINCIPAL USES
To treat mild to severe bacterial infections, including those of the urinary tract, lower respiratory tract, bones and joints, and the skin. It is also used to treat certain sexually transmitted diseases (such as chancroid and gonorrhea), and diarrhea caused by bacterial infection. Ciprofloxacin is also approved for prophylactic use following known exposure to anthrax bacteria and for treating anthrax infections.

HOW THE DRUG WORKS
Ciprofloxacin inhibits the activity of a bacterial enzyme (gyrase) that is necessary for proper DNA formation and replication. This fights infection by preventing bacteria cells from reproducing.

DOSAGE
250 to 750 mg every 12 hours (2 times a day), for 5 to 14 days, depending on kidney function and the infection being treated. Gonorrhea is usually treated with a one-time dose of 250 mg.

ONSET OF EFFECT
Varies depending on the infection being treated.

DURATION OF ACTION
Unknown.

DIETARY ADVICE
Be sure to drink plenty of fluids, but avoid milk and dairy derivatives.

STORAGE
Store in a tightly sealed container away from heat and direct light.

IF YOU MISS A DOSE
Take it as soon as you remember. If it is near the time for the next dose, skip the missed dose and resume your regular dosage schedule. Do not double the next dose.

STOPPING THE DRUG
Take it as prescribed for the full treatment period, even if you begin to feel better before the scheduled end of therapy.

PROLONGED USE
See your doctor regularly for tests and examinations if you must take this medicine for a prolonged period.

PRECAUTIONS
Over 60: No special problems are expected.

Driving and Hazardous Work: Do not drive or engage in hazardous work until you determine how the medicine affects you.

Alcohol: It is advisable to abstain from alcohol when fighting an infection.

Pregnancy: In some animal tests, ciprofloxacin has caused birth defects. Adequate studies in humans have not been done. It should be used during pregnancy only if potential benefits clearly justify the risks. Before you take ciprofloxacin, tell your doctor if you are pregnant or plan to become pregnant.

Breast Feeding: Ciprofloxacin passes into breast milk and may cause serious side effects in the nursing infant; use of the drug is discouraged when nursing.

Infants and Children: Ciprofloxacin is not recommended for use by persons under the age of 18, as it has been shown to interfere with bone development.

Special Concerns: If ciprofloxacin causes sensitivity to sunlight, stop taking the drug and try to avoid exposure to sunlight for the next 5 days; also wear protective clothing and use a sunblock. Ciprofloxacin should not be taken by patients whose work makes it impossible to avoid exposure to sunlight. It is important to drink plenty of fluids while taking this drug.

OVERDOSE
Symptoms: No specific ones have been reported.

What to Do: If you have any reason to suspect an overdose, call your doctor, emergency medical services (EMS), or the nearest poison control center.

DRUG INTERACTIONS
Consult your doctor for specific advice if you are taking aminophylline, antacids, didanosine, iron supplements, oxtriphylline, sucralfate, theophylline, warfarin, or zinc salts. Also tell your doctor if you are taking any other prescription or over-the-counter medication.

FOOD INTERACTIONS
The effects of caffeine may be magnified by this drug. Milk and dairy products can reduce blood levels of ciprofloxacin by as much as half.

DISEASE INTERACTIONS
Caution is advised when taking ciprofloxacin. Consult your doctor if you have any other medical condition. Use of ciprofloxacin can cause complications in patients with kidney disease, since this organ works to remove the medication from the body.

Citalopram Hydrobromide

BRAND NAME
Celexa

▶ Drug Class: Selective serotonin reuptake inhibitor (SSRI) antidepressant

▶ Available in: Tablet, oral solution

▶ Available OTC? No

▶ As Generic? No

Side Effects

SERIOUS
Chest pain, rapid or irregular heartbeat, lightheadedness or fainting. Call your doctor immediately.

COMMON
Delayed ejaculation (males), dry mouth, increased sweating, nausea, trembling, diarrhea, drowsiness, numbness, tingling, or prickling sensations.

LESS COMMON
Fatigue, fever, loss of appetite, agitation, nasal congestion, sinus infection, erectile dysfunction.

PRINCIPAL USES
To treat symptoms of major depression.

HOW THE DRUG WORKS
Citalopram increases brain levels of serotonin, a chemical that is thought to be linked to mood, emotions, and mental state.

DOSAGE
To start, 20 mg once a day, taken in the morning or evening; dose may be gradually increased by your doctor to 40 mg a day.

ONSET OF EFFECT
Unknown.

DURATION OF ACTION
Unknown.

DIETARY ADVICE
No special restrictions.

STORAGE
Store in a tightly sealed container away from heat, moisture, and direct light.

IF YOU MISS A DOSE
If you miss a dose on one day, do not double the dose the next day.

STOPPING THE DRUG
Take it as prescribed for the full treatment period even if you notice improvement. When it is time to stop therapy, your dosage will be tapered gradually by your doctor.

PROLONGED USE
Usual course of therapy for depression lasts 6 months to 1 year; some patients may benefit from additional therapy.

PRECAUTIONS
Over 60: Adverse reactions may be more likely and more severe in older patients. A lower dose may be warranted.

Driving and Hazardous Work: Use caution when driving or engaging in hazardous work until you determine how the medicine affects you.

Alcohol: Avoid alcohol.

Pregnancy: Citalopram should be used during pregnancy only if the potential benefit justifies the potential risk to the fetus. Before you take this medicine, tell your doctor if you are pregnant or plan to become pregnant.

Breast Feeding: Citalopram passes into breast milk; caution is advised. Consult your doctor for specific advice.

Infants and Children: The safety and effectiveness of the use of citalopram in children have not been established. Antidepressants increase the risk of suicidal thinking and behavior (suicidality) in children with major depression and other psychiatric disorders. Discuss with your doctor this risk versus the benefits of using this drug. Children should be observed closely for worsening of symptoms, suicidality, or unusual changes in behavior at the onset of therapy and when making changes in dosage.

OVERDOSE
Symptoms: Dizziness, sweating, nausea, vomiting, trembling, drowsiness, rapid heartbeat.

What to Do: Call your doctor, emergency medical services (EMS), or the nearest poison control center immediately.

DRUG INTERACTIONS
Citalopram and MAO inhibitors should not be used within 14 days of each other. Very serious side effects such as myoclonus (uncontrolled muscle spasms), hyperthermia (excessive rise in body temperature), and extreme stiffness may result. The following drugs may also interact with citalopram; consult your doctor for advice if you are taking cimetidine, warfarin, lithium, carbamazepine, antifungals (such as ketoconazole, itraconazole, and fluconazole), erythromycin antibiotics, omeprazole, tricyclic antidepressants, NSAIDs, aspirin, or any prescription or over-the-counter drugs that depress the central nervous system (including antihistamines, barbiturates, sedatives, cough medicines, and decongestants).

FOOD INTERACTIONS
No known food interactions.

DISEASE INTERACTIONS
Caution is advised when taking citalopram, especially if you have heart disease or a seizure disorder. Use of citalopram may cause complications in patients with liver or kidney disease.

Clarithromycin

Biaxin 500 mg
(ABBOTT)

831

Additional photographs

▶ Drug Class: Macrolide antibiotic

▶ Available in: Tablets, oral suspension

▶ Available OTC? No

▶ As Generic? No

Side Effects

SERIOUS
Colitis (inflammation of the lower gastrointestinal tract, with symptoms including severe abdominal pain, watery or bloody stools, severe diarrhea, fever); liver toxicity (causing fever, nausea, vomiting, yellowish tinge to eyes or skin); allergic reaction (swelling of the lips, tongue, face, and throat, breathing difficulty, skin rash or hives); blood clotting disorders (causing unusual bleeding and bruising); confusion or change in behavior; heartbeat irregularities in patients with predisposing heart conditions. Such side effects are rare, but if they do occur, stop taking the drug and seek medical assistance immediately.

COMMON
No common side effects.

LESS COMMON
Changes in taste perception; mild abdominal pain or discomfort; mild diarrhea; mild nausea or vomiting; headache; oral thrush (fungal infections of the mouth or throat).

PRINCIPAL USES
To treat various bacterial infections, including those of the sinuses, tonsils, and respiratory tract (such as bronchitis and pneumonia); infections of the ear; and venereal disease due to chlamydial infection. Clarithromycin may also be used to treat certain skin infections, Legionnaires' disease, Lyme disease, and peptic ulcers caused by the bacterium H. pylori. Also used to prevent and, when taken with other drugs, treat a tuberculosis-like disease known as Mycobacterium avium complex (MAC), which is common in people with advanced acquired immunodeficiency syndrome (AIDS).

HOW THE DRUG WORKS
Clarithromycin prevents bacterial cells from manufacturing specific proteins necessary for their survival.

DOSAGE
For bacterial infections—Usual adult dose: 250 to 500 mg every 12 hours, for 7 to 14 days. Children 6 months of age or older: 3.4 mg per lb of body weight, up to 500 mg every 12 hours for 10 days. To prevent MAC—500 mg, 2 times a day. To treat MAC— 500 mg, 2 times a day in combination with other drugs.

ONSET OF EFFECT
Within 2 hours; full effect may occur in 2 to 5 days.

DURATION OF ACTION
Unknown.

DIETARY ADVICE
Clarithromycin may be taken with or without food. Drink plenty of liquids.

STORAGE
Store in a tightly sealed container away from heat, moisture, and direct light.

IF YOU MISS A DOSE
Take it as soon as you remember. If it is near the time for the next dose, skip the missed dose and resume your regular dosing schedule. Do not double the next dose. If you are taking 2 doses a day, wait 5 to 6 hours before taking the next dose.

STOPPING THE DRUG
For acute infections, take it exactly as prescribed for the full treatment period, even if you feel better before the scheduled end of therapy. Therapy for prevention of MAC should be lifelong.

PROLONGED USE
You may become susceptible to infections caused by germs that are not responsive to clarithromycin. Also, severe drug-induced gastrointestinal problems may result from long-term use.

PRECAUTIONS
Over 60: Older patients, especially those with kidney disease, may require a decrease in dose.

Driving and Hazardous Work: No special precautions are necessary.

Alcohol: No special precautions are necessary.

Pregnancy: Adequate studies of the use of this drug during pregnancy have not been done; discuss potential risks and benefits with your doctor.

Breast Feeding: It is not known if clarithromycin passes into breast milk; consult your doctor for advice.

Infants and Children: No special problems are expected.

OVERDOSE
Symptoms: Severe nausea, vomiting, diarrhea, abdominal discomfort.

What to Do: Call your doctor, emergency medical services (EMS), or the nearest poison control center immediately.

DRUG INTERACTIONS
This drug should not be taken by patients known to have had prior allergic reactions to erythromycins or other macrolide antibiotics. Do not take clarithromycin if you are taking astemizole, or pimozide. Also, alert your doctor if you are taking any of the following drugs: carbamazepine, digoxin, theophylline, warfarin, rifabutin, rifampin, or zidovudine.

FOOD INTERACTIONS
No known food interactions.

DISEASE INTERACTIONS
Consult your doctor if you have a history of a blood disorder, liver disease, or any allergy.

Clemastine Fumarate

Tavist-1 12 Hour 1.34 mg
(**NOVARTIS**)

▶ Drug Class: Antihistamine

▶ Available in: Tablets, syrup,
extended-release tablets
and caplets

▶ Available OTC? Yes

▶ As Generic? Yes

Side Effects

SERIOUS
Confusion, hallucinations,
convulsions, blurred
vision, difficulty urinating
(urinary obstruction).

COMMON
Drowsiness; nausea;
thickening of mucus; dry
mouth, nose, and throat;
dizziness; disturbed coordination.

LESS COMMON
Chills, headache, fatigue,
vomiting, restlessness,
irritability, nasal congestion, profuse sweating,
diarrhea, constipation.

PRINCIPAL USES
To prevent or relieve symptoms of hay fever and other
allergies, and for itching
skin and hives.

HOW THE DRUG WORKS
Clemastine blocks the
effects of histamine, a naturally occurring substance
within the body that causes
swelling, itching, sneezing,
watery eyes, hives, and
other symptoms of allergic
reactions.

DOSAGE
Adults and teenagers: 1.34
mg, 2 times a day (for hay
fever), or 2.68 mg, 1 to 3
times a day (for hay fever
or hives). Children ages 6
to 12: 0.67 mg (syrup) to
1.34 mg, 2 times a day.

ONSET OF EFFECT
15 minutes to 60 minutes.

DURATION OF ACTION
At least 12 hours.

DIETARY ADVICE
Take it with food, water, or
milk to avoid stomach irritation. Drinking coffee or tea
will help reduce drowsiness.
Use sugarless gum, sugar-
less sour hard candy, or ice
chips to ease dry mouth.

STORAGE
Store in a tightly sealed container away from heat and
direct light.

IF YOU MISS A DOSE
Take it as soon as you
remember. If it is near the
time for the next dose, skip
the missed dose and
resume your regular dosage
schedule. Do not double the
next dose.

STOPPING THE DRUG
You should take it as prescribed for the full treatment period, but you may
stop if you are feeling better
before the scheduled end of
therapy. It may be taken as
needed.

PROLONGED USE
No special problems are
expected.

PRECAUTIONS
Over 60: Adverse reactions
may be more likely and
more severe in older
patients.

**Driving and Hazardous
Work:** The use of clemastine may impair your ability
to perform such tasks
safely. Do not drive or
engage in hazardous work
until you determine how the
medicine affects you.

Alcohol: Alcohol increases
the likelihood and the severity of side effects like
drowsiness and confusion.

Pregnancy: Animal studies
with high doses of clemastine have found no birth
defects. Human studies
have not been done.
Because the studies cannot
rule out potential harm, the
drug should be used during
pregnancy only if it is
clearly needed.

Breast Feeding: Clemastine passes into breast milk;
do not use it while nursing.

Infants and Children:
Children tend to be more
sensitive to the effects of
antihistamines. Symptoms
of excitability, restlessness,
and nightmares may occur.

OVERDOSE
Symptoms: Hallucinations,
seizures, drowsiness,
lethargy, coma.

What to Do: Call your
doctor, emergency medical
services (EMS), or the
nearest poison control center immediately. A con-
scious patient should be
induced to vomit using
ipecac syrup.

DRUG INTERACTIONS
Sleeping pills, sedatives,
tranquilizers, MAO
inhibitors, and antidepressants can increase the sedative effects of clemastine.
Anticholinergics may fur-
ther increase the likelihood
that drying of the mucous
membranes and urinary
obstruction will occur as
side effects.

FOOD INTERACTIONS
No known food interactions.

DISEASE INTERACTIONS
Consult your doctor if you
have any of the following:
asthma, enlarged prostate,
difficult urination, glaucoma, sleep apnea, or dry
mouth or eyes.

Clindamycin

Generic 150 mg
(BIOCRAFT)

▶ Drug Class: Antibiotic

▶ Available in: Capsules, oral solution, injection, gel, topical solution, suspension, cream, vaginal suppositories

▶ Available OTC? No

▶ As Generic? Yes

Side Effects

SERIOUS
For oral forms, injection, gel, solution, and suspension: Severe stomach or abdominal pains and cramps, weight loss, severe diarrhea, fever, sore throat; skin rash, itching, and redness, unusual bleeding or bruising. For vaginal cream and suppositories: Itching of genital area, pain during intercourse, whitish vaginal discharge, diarrhea, dizziness, headache, nausea, vomiting, stomach cramps or pain. Call your doctor right away.

COMMON
For oral forms: Mild diarrhea, nausea, vomiting, stomach pain. For topical forms: Dry, peeling, or scaly skin.

LESS COMMON
For oral forms: Itching of rectal or genital regions. For topical forms: Stomach pain, mild diarrhea, irritated or oily skin, stinging or burning skin, dizziness (cream and suppository), headache (cream and suppository).

PRINCIPAL USES
Orally and by injection, clindamycin is used to treat serious bacterial infections. Topically, it is used to treat acne and vaginal infections.

HOW THE DRUG WORKS
Clindamycin inhibits the synthesis of protein in bacterial organisms.

DOSAGE
For systemic infections, using oral forms— Adults and teenagers: 150 to 300 mg, 4 times a day. For systemic infections, using injection— Adults and teenagers: 300 to 600 mg, 3 or 4 times a day, or 900 mg, 3 times a day. For acne, using gel, solution, or suspension— Adults and teenagers: Apply 2 times a day. Use and dose for children under 12 must be determined by your doctor. For vaginal infections, using vaginal cream— Non-pregnant adults and teenagers: 100 mg inserted in vagina once daily at bedtime for 3 or 7 days (7-day therapy is prescribed for pregnant patients). Dose for children must be determined by your doctor. For bacterial vaginal infections, using vaginal suppositories— Non-pregnant adults and teenagers: 1 suppository (containing 100 mg clindamycin) inserted in vagina once daily at bedtime for 3 days.

ONSET OF EFFECT
Unknown.

DURATION OF ACTION
Unknown.

DIETARY ADVICE
Take the oral forms with food to minimize stomach upset. Take the capsule with a glass of water.

STORAGE
Store in a tightly sealed container away from heat, mois-ture, and direct light. Do not refrigerate the liquid forms, cream, or suppositories.

IF YOU MISS A DOSE
Take it as soon as you remember. If it is near the time for the next dose, skip the missed dose and resume your regular dosage schedule. Do not double the next dose.

STOPPING THE DRUG
Take it as prescribed for the full treatment period, even if you feel better before the scheduled end of therapy.

PROLONGED USE
See your doctor regularly for tests and examinations if you must take this medicine for a prolonged period.

PRECAUTIONS
Over 60: It is not known whether this drug causes side effects in older patients different from or more severe than those in younger persons.

Driving and Hazardous Work: The use of clindamycin should not impair your ability to perform such tasks safely.

Alcohol: It is advisable to abstain from alcohol when fighting an infection.

Pregnancy: Clindamycin has not been reported to cause birth defects in humans; consult your doctor before taking it during pregnancy.

Breast Feeding: Clindamycin may pass into breast milk; consult your doctor for specific advice.

Infants and Children: Adequate studies of clindamycin use by children have not been done, although no special problems are expected.

Special Concerns: Wash and dry the skin thoroughly before applying the gel, topical solution, or suspension. When using the vaginal cream or suppository, sexual intercourse should be avoided. Clindamycin may weaken latex or rubber products such as condoms and vaginal contraceptive diaphragms; use of such products is not recommended within 72 hours of the application of clindamycin cream or suppositories. Do not use other vaginal products such as tampons or douches when using the vaginal suppositories. Before having surgery with a general anesthetic, tell the doctor or dentist in charge that you are taking clindamycin.

OVERDOSE
Symptoms: No specific ones have been reported.

What to Do: If you have any reason to suspect an overdose, call your doctor, emergency medical services (EMS), or the nearest poison control center.

DRUG INTERACTIONS
Consult your doctor for advice if you are taking chloramphenicol, erythromycin, or any diarrhea medicine containing kaopectate or attapulgite.

FOOD INTERACTIONS
No known food interactions.

DISEASE INTERACTIONS
Consult your doctor if you have a history of kidney disease, liver disease, or intestinal or stomach disease, especially colitis. The vaginal suppositories should not be used if you have a history of enteritis, ulcerative colitis, or "antibiotic-associated" colitis.

Clomiphene Citrate

Generic 50 mg
(LEMMON)

▶ Drug Class: Antiestrogen

▶ Available in: Tablets

▶ Available OTC? No

▶ As Generic? Yes

Side Effects

SERIOUS
Bloating, stomach or pelvic pain, changes in vision or unusual sensitivity to light, yellow discoloration of the eyes or skin (jaundice). Serious side effects with clomiphene are unusual. If any of these side effects develop, call your doctor immediately.

COMMON
Hot flashes, premenstrual syndrome (PMS). Multiple pregnancies (especially twin pregnancies) are more likely in women who use this drug.

LESS COMMON
Swelling, tenderness, or discomfort in the breasts; dizziness; headache; heavy menstrual periods or unexpected bleeding from the vagina; depression; nausea and vomiting; nervousness; restlessness; fatigue; insomnia.

PRINCIPAL USES
To stimulate the release of eggs by the ovaries (ovulation) in women who wish to become pregnant.

HOW THE DRUG WORKS
Clomiphene causes an increase in the level of the hormones that stimulate the ovary to release eggs.

DOSAGE
The usual dose is 50 mg once daily for 5 days, starting on the fifth day of the menstrual period. Women who do not have menstrual cycles can begin taking it on any convenient day. The dose may be increased gradually, up to a maximum of 250 mg a day. Clomiphene is usually prescribed for 3 to 4 menstrual cycles and is stopped if pregnancy is achieved during that time.

ONSET OF EFFECT
Ovulation occurs 7 to 10 days after the last day of clomiphene treatment. There may be considerable individual variation in this number, depending on the patient's sensitivity to clomiphene.

DURATION OF ACTION
Unknown.

DIETARY ADVICE
No special restrictions.

STORAGE
Store in a tightly sealed container away from heat and direct light.

IF YOU MISS A DOSE
Take the missed dose as soon as you remember, unless the time for your next scheduled dose is within the next 2 hours. If so, take a double dose at the proper time, and resume your regular dosage schedule. Inform your doctor if you miss more than 1 day of treatment.

STOPPING THE DRUG
To be effective, this medication should be taken as prescribed for the full treatment period. Do not stop taking clomiphene on your own.

PROLONGED USE
Do not take clomiphene for more than 5 days in each cycle unless otherwise instructed by your doctor. Clomiphene is usually prescribed for no more than 3 to 4 cycles; do not take it for more than 3 to 4 cycles without your doctor's approval.

PRECAUTIONS
Over 60: Clomiphene is usually prescribed only for women of childbearing age.

Driving and Hazardous Work: Do not drive or engage in hazardous work until you determine how the medicine affects you.

Alcohol: Drink in strict moderation if at all.

Pregnancy: Clomiphene must not be used during pregnancy; discontinue use immediately if you become pregnant.

Breast Feeding: Clomiphene interferes with the production of breast milk and should not be used while nursing.

Infants and Children: Clomiphene should not be used by children.

Special Concerns: Use some means of monitoring ovulation (for example, by recording body temperature changes or by using a home urine ovulation test kit), as it is crucial to discontinue use of this drug when pregnancy occurs. See your doctor with each cycle and be examined before resuming clomiphene therapy. There are many important aspects to the treatment of infertility; clomiphene is one of them. Remember to follow instructions concerning the frequency and timing of intercourse with your partner. Try to take clomiphene at the same time every day. Maintain a strict dosing schedule and try not to miss any doses. Remember that doses of clomiphene can be doubled if you miss one day.

OVERDOSE
Symptoms: No cases of overdose have been reported.

What to Do: If you are concerned about the possibility of an overdose of clomiphene, call your doctor, emergency medical services (EMS), or the nearest poison control center.

DRUG INTERACTIONS
None reported.

FOOD INTERACTIONS
No known food interactions.

DISEASE INTERACTIONS
Consult your doctor if you have any of the following conditions: large ovary; cyst on ovary; endometriosis or excessively painful menstrual periods; fibroids (growths on the uterus); phlebitis (painful inflammation of the veins, usually in the leg); liver disease; depression; or unusual vaginal bleeding.

Clomipramine Hydrochloride

▶ Drug Class: Tricyclic antidepressant

▶ Available in: Capsules

▶ Available OTC? No

▶ As Generic? Yes

Side Effects

SERIOUS
Confusion, sexual dysfunction, heartbeat irregularities, hallucinations, seizures, extreme fatigue or drowsiness, vision problems, breathing difficulty; constipation, staring and absence of facial expression, impaired concentration, difficult urination, fever, extreme and persistent restlessness, loss of coordination and balance, difficulty swallowing or speaking, dilated pupils, eye pain, fainting. Also trembling, weakness, and stiffness in the extremities; shuffling gait. Call your doctor as soon as possible.

COMMON
Drowsiness or dizziness, headache, dry mouth or unpleasant taste, fatigue, heightened sensitivity to light, weight gain, nausea, increased appetite.

LESS COMMON
Heartburn, insomnia, diarrhea, sweating, vomiting.

PRINCIPAL USES
To treat obsessive-compulsive disorder, depression, panic disorder, and chronic pain.

HOW THE DRUG WORKS
Clomipramine affects levels of a specific brain chemical (serotonin) that is thought to be linked to mood, emotions, and mental state.

DOSAGE
Adults: To start, 25 mg once a day; may be increased to 250 mg a day. Children age 10 and older: To start, 25 mg once a day; may be increased to 200 mg a day. Older adults: To start, 25 mg a day; may be increased gradually by your doctor.

ONSET OF EFFECT
1 to 6 weeks.

DURATION OF ACTION
Unknown.

DIETARY ADVICE
To lessen stomach upset, take with food, unless your doctor instructs otherwise. Increase intake of fiber and fluids.

STORAGE
Store in a tightly sealed container away from heat, moisture, and direct light.

IF YOU MISS A DOSE
If you take a one-time daily bedtime dose, do not take a missed dose in the morning because it may cause drowsiness. Call your doctor. If you take more than 1 dose a day, take it as soon as you remember. If it is near the time for the next dose, skip the missed dose and resume your regular dosage schedule. Do not double the next dose.

STOPPING THE DRUG
Take as prescribed for the full treatment period, even if you begin to feel better before the scheduled end of therapy. The decision to stop taking the drug should be made in consultation with your doctor. The dosage should be gradually tapered when stopping.

PROLONGED USE
Usual course of therapy for depression lasts 6 months to 1 year; some patients may benefit from additional therapy. Usual course of therapy for obsessive-compulsive disorder lasts 1 year or more.

PRECAUTIONS
Over 60: Adverse reactions, especially confusion, are more likely and more severe in older patients. A lower dose may be warranted.

Driving and Hazardous Work: Exercise caution until you determine how the medication affects you. Drowsiness, lightheadedness, or confusion can occur.

Alcohol: Avoid alcohol.

Pregnancy: Adequate human studies have not been done. Consult your doctor.

Breast Feeding: Do not use clomipramine while nursing.

Infants and Children: Not prescribed for children under the age of 10. Antidepressants increase the risk of suicidal thinking and behavior (suicidality) in children with major depression and other psychiatric disorders. Discuss with your doctor this risk versus the benefits of using this drug. Children should be observed closely for worsening of symptoms at the outset of therapy and when making changes in dosage.

Special Concerns: This is a potentially dangerous drug, especially if taken in excess. Tricyclic antidepressants should not be within easy reach of suicidal patients. If dry mouth occurs, use sugarless gum or candy.

OVERDOSE
Symptoms: Difficulty breathing, severe fatigue, seizures, confusion, hallucinations, distractibility, dilated pupils, irregular heartbeat, fever.

What to Do: Call your doctor, emergency medical services (EMS), or the nearest poison control center immediately.

DRUG INTERACTIONS
Consult your doctor for specific advice if you are taking antithyroid agents, cimetidine, clonidine, guanadrel, guanethidine, metrizamide, SSRI antidepressants, appetite suppressants, isoproterenol, ephedrine, epinephrine, amphetamines, phenylephrine, antipsychotic drugs, pimozide, methyldopa, metyrosine, metoclopramide, pemoline, promethazine, trimeprazine, rauwolfia alkaloids, MAO inhibitors, or any drugs that depress the central nervous system.

FOOD INTERACTIONS
No known food interactions.

DISEASE INTERACTIONS
Consult your doctor if you have any of the following: a history of alcohol abuse, difficulty urinating, asthma, bipolar disorder, high blood pressure, stomach or intestinal problems, glaucoma, overactive thyroid, enlarged prostate, schizophrenia, seizures, a blood disorder, or kidney, heart, or liver disease.

Clonazepam

BRAND NAME
Klonopin

Klonopin 0.5 mg
(ROCHE)

▶ Drug Class: Benzodiazepine tranquilizer; antianxiety agent

▶ Available in: Tablets, wafer

▶ Available OTC? No

▶ As Generic? Yes

Side Effects

SERIOUS
Difficulty concentrating, outbursts of anger, other behavior problems, depression, hallucinations, low blood pressure (causing faintness or confusion), memory impairment, muscle weakness, skin rash or itching, sore throat, fever and chills, sores or ulcers in throat or mouth, unusual bruising or bleeding, extreme fatigue, yellowish tinge to eyes or skin. Call your doctor immediately.

COMMON
Drowsiness, loss of coordination, unsteady gait, dizziness, lightheadedness, slurred speech.

LESS COMMON
Change in sexual desire or ability, constipation, false sense of well-being, nausea and vomiting, urinary problems, unusual fatigue.

PRINCIPAL USES
To control seizures; for relief of anxiety and panic attacks.

HOW THE DRUG WORKS
In general, clonazepam produces mild sedation by depressing activity in the central nervous system (the brain and spinal cord). In particular, clonazepam appears to enhance the effect of gamma-aminobutyric acid (GABA), a natural chemical that inhibits the firing of neurons and dampens the transmission of nerve signals, thus decreasing nervous excitation.

DOSAGE
Adults: Initial dose of 0.5 mg, 3 times a day. Patients with seizures may require significantly higher doses. Your doctor will determine the optimal dose. Maximum dose rarely exceeds 20 mg a day. Children: Dose is based on age and body weight.

ONSET OF EFFECT
Within 1 to 2 hours.

DURATION OF ACTION
Less than 24 hours.

DIETARY ADVICE
No special restrictions.

STORAGE
Store in a tightly sealed container away from heat, moisture, and direct light.

IF YOU MISS A DOSE
Take it as soon as you remember, unless your next scheduled dose is within the next 2 hours. If so, do not take the missed dose. Take your next scheduled dose at the proper time and resume your regular dosage schedule. Do not double the next dose.

STOPPING THE DRUG
Discontinuing the drug abruptly may produce withdrawal symptoms (sleep disruption, nervousness, irritability, diarrhea, abdominal cramps, muscle aches, memory impairment). Dosage should be reduced gradually according to your doctor's instructions.

PROLONGED USE
Short-term therapy (8 weeks or less) is typical; do not take it for a longer period unless so advised by your doctor.

PRECAUTIONS
Over 60: Adverse reactions are more likely and more severe in older patients.

Driving and Hazardous Work: Clonazepam can impair mental alertness and physical coordination. Adjust your activities accordingly.

Alcohol: Alcohol must be avoided while taking this medication.

Pregnancy: Taking clonazepam during pregnancy is not recommended.

Breast Feeding: Clonazepam passes into breast milk and may be harmful to the infant; do not take it while nursing.

Infants and Children: This drug is rarely prescribed for young patients.

Special Concerns: Clonazepam use can lead to psychological or physical dependence. Never take more than the prescribed daily dose.

OVERDOSE
Symptoms: Extreme drowsiness, confusion, slurred speech, slow reflexes, poor coordination, staggering gait, tremor, slowed breathing, loss of consciousness.

What to Do: Call your doctor, emergency medical services (EMS), or the nearest poison control center immediately.

DRUG INTERACTIONS
Other drugs may interact with clonazepam. Consult your doctor for specific advice if you are taking any drugs that depress the central nervous system; these include antihistamines, antidepressants or other psychiatric medications, barbiturates, sedatives, cough medicines, decongestants, and painkillers. Be sure your doctor knows about any over-the-counter medication you may take.

FOOD INTERACTIONS
None reported.

DISEASE INTERACTIONS
Caution is advised when taking clonazepam. Consult your doctor if you have a history of alcohol or drug abuse, stroke or other brain disease, any chronic lung disease, hyperactivity, depression or other mental illness, myasthenia gravis, sleep apnea, epilepsy, porphyria, kidney disease, or liver disease.

Clonidine Hydrochloride

Generic 0.2 mg
(MYLAN)

Additional photographs

▸ Drug Class: Centrally acting antihypertensive

▸ Available in: Tablets, skin patch

▸ Available OTC? No

▸ As Generic? Yes

Side Effects

SERIOUS
Serious side effects are less likely when clonidine is used as directed.

COMMON
Dry mouth, reduced saliva, drowsiness, dizziness, constipation. Also itching or skin irritation (with skin patch only).

LESS COMMON
Mental depression, swelling of feet and lower legs, pale or cold fingertips and toes, vivid dreams or nightmares. Also darkening of skin (skin patch only).

PRINCIPAL USES
To treat high blood pressure (hypertension).

HOW THE DRUG WORKS
Clonidine acts upon certain areas of the central nervous system (the brain and spinal cord) that regulate the activity of the heart and the smooth muscle tissue surrounding the arteries. It causes the blood vessels to relax and widen, which lowers blood pressure.

DOSAGE
Tablets–– Adults: Initial dose is 0.1 mg, 2 times per day. Your doctor may increase this to 0.3 mg, 2 times per day. Most patients achieve adequate blood pressure control with 1 mg or less per day; maximum daily dose is 2.4 mg. Children: Pediatrician will determine proper dosage. Skin patch— The starting dose is one TTS-1 patch per week. Doses above two TTS-3 patches per week are usually not effective. The patch should be applied to a hairless area of skin, ideally on the chest or upper arm. The skin must be free of rashes, blisters, or any form of skin disease.

ONSET OF EFFECT
Tablets: 30 to 60 minutes. Skin patch: 2 to 3 days.

DURATION OF ACTION
Tablets: Up to 8 hours. Skin patch: 7 days per patch, if patch is left in place as directed; otherwise, up to 8 hours from the time the patch is removed.

DIETARY ADVICE
Follow a healthy diet (low-salt, low-fat, low-cholesterol) as advised by your doctor to help control blood pressure and prevent heart disease.

STORAGE
Store in a tightly sealed container away from heat, moisture, and direct light.

IF YOU MISS A DOSE
Take your missed dose as soon as you remember, unless the time for your next scheduled dose is within the next 2 hours. If so, do not take the missed dose. Take your next dose at the proper time and resume your regular dosage schedule. Do not take a double dose. If you miss more than 1 day of clonidine, inform your doctor.

STOPPING THE DRUG
Stopping clonidine abruptly can lead to a dangerous increase in blood pressure. Do not stop taking clonidine on your own, even if you are feeling better. Your doctor will gradually decrease your dose if necessary.

PROLONGED USE
Long-term use may be necessary and may lead to an increased risk of side effects.

PRECAUTIONS
Over 60: Adverse reactions may be more likely and more severe in older patients.

Driving and Hazardous Work: This medication may cause dizziness and drowsiness; avoid potentially dangerous activities until you know how it affects you.

Alcohol: Avoid alcohol while taking this drug.

Pregnancy: Clonidine use is not recommended during pregnancy.

Breast Feeding: Clonidine passes into breast milk; consult your doctor for advice.

Infants and Children: This drug is not recommended for young patients.

Special Concerns: Blood pressure may rise significantly after missing a few doses. Signs of dangerously high blood pressure are chest pain, dizziness, headache, blurred vision, confusion, restlessness, trembling of hands and fingers, anxiety, stomach pains, nausea, and vomiting. Make sure you have enough clonidine to last through weekends, vacations, or extended trips. Apply each skin patch to a different area of the chest or upper arm.

OVERDOSE
Symptoms: Low blood pressure, slow heartbeat, difficulty breathing, severe dizziness, confusion, weakness or faintness, tiny, constricted pupils.

What to Do: Call your doctor, emergency medical services (EMS), or the nearest poison control center immediately.

DRUG INTERACTIONS
Consult your doctor if you are taking beta-blockers or tricyclic antidepressants.

FOOD INTERACTIONS
No known food interactions.

DISEASE INTERACTIONS
Tell your doctor if you have any of the following problems: heart or blood vessel disease, including strokes and cardiac arrhythmias; skin disease, such as scleroderma (a concern with the skin patch only); kidney disease; mental depression; Raynaud's syndrome; or systemic lupus erythematosus.

Clopidogrel Bisulfate

BRAND NAME
Plavix

▶ Drug Class: Antiplatelet drug

▶ Available in: Tablets

▶ Available OTC? No

▶ As Generic? No

Side Effects

SERIOUS
Gastrointestinal bleeding, fainting, palpitations, extreme fatigue, shortness of breath, chest pain. Call your doctor immediately. In rare instances the drug can block production of white blood cells (a major component of the immune system), leading to potentially severe infections. Seek medical attention promptly at the first signs of infection, especially a high fever.

COMMON
Stomach pain, indigestion, diarrhea, skin rash, itching, flu-like symptoms, body aches or pain, headache, dizziness, joint pain, back pain, increased risk of upper respiratory infection.

LESS COMMON
General weakness, hernia, leg cramps, tingling and numbness in the limbs, vomiting, gout, arthritis, anxiety, insomnia, anemia, dermatitis and skin eruptions, bladder infection, cataract, conjunctivitis.

PRINCIPAL USES
To reduce the risk of recurrence of heart attack or stroke in patients diagnosed with severe arterial disease (atherosclerosis).

HOW THE DRUG WORKS
Heart attacks and strokes occur when a blood clot that forms in a narrowed portion of an artery blocks blood flow and thus cuts off the supply of oxygen and nutrients to the tissue that lies beyond the site of the clot. Clopidogrel can prevent heart attacks and strokes by preventing the aggregation (clumping) of platelets, a type of blood cell that initiates clot formation.

DOSAGE
75 mg once a day.

ONSET OF EFFECT
2 hours or more.

DURATION OF ACTION
Unknown.

DIETARY ADVICE
Clopidogrel can be taken with or without food.

STORAGE
Store in a tightly sealed container away from heat, moisture, and direct light.

IF YOU MISS A DOSE
If you miss a dose on one day, do not double the dose the next day. Resume your regular dosage schedule.

STOPPING THE DRUG
Take it as prescribed for the full treatment period.

PROLONGED USE
Side effects are more likely with prolonged use.

PRECAUTIONS
Over 60: No special problems are expected.

Driving and Hazardous Work: The use of this drug should not impair your ability to perform such tasks safely.

Alcohol: No special precautions are necessary.

Pregnancy: Adequate human studies have not been done. Before taking clopidogrel, tell your doctor if you are pregnant or plan to become pregnant.

Breast Feeding: Clopidogrel passes into breast milk; extreme caution is advised. Consult your doctor for specific advice.

Infants and Children: The safety and effectiveness of clopidogrel use in infants and children have not been established.

Special Concerns: Before you schedule surgery, tell the surgeon or dentist that you are taking this drug.

OVERDOSE
Symptoms: No overdose symptoms have been reported.

What to Do: However, if a greatly excessive dose is taken, call your doctor, emergency medical services (EMS), or the nearest poison control center.

DRUG INTERACTIONS
Consult your doctor for specific advice if you are taking any of the following drugs that may interact with clopidogrel: aspirin or any other nonsteroidal anti-inflammatory drugs (NSAIDs), phenytoin, tamoxifen, tolbutamide, torsemide, fluvastatin, or warfarin.

FOOD INTERACTIONS
No known food interactions.

DISEASE INTERACTIONS
This drug should not be used if you have a peptic ulcer or a history of brain hemorrhage. Caution is advised when taking clopidogrel. Consult your doctor if you have a history of bleeding problems or if you develop bleeding problems while taking this drug. Use of clopidogrel may cause complications in patients with liver disease, since the liver inactivates the drug.

202

Clorazepate Dipotassium

BRAND NAME
Tranxene

▶ Drug Class: Benzodiazepine tranquilizer; antianxiety agent

▶ Available in: Tablets

▶ Available OTC? No

▶ As Generic? Yes

Side Effects

SERIOUS
Difficulty concentrating, outbursts of anger, other behavior problems, depression, hallucinations, low blood pressure (causing faintness or confusion), memory impairment, muscle weakness, skin rash or itching, sore throat, fever and chills, sores or ulcers in throat or mouth, unusual bruising or bleeding, extreme fatigue, yellowish tinge to eyes or skin. Call your doctor immediately.

COMMON
Drowsiness, loss of coordination, unsteady gait, dizziness, lightheadedness, slurred speech.

LESS COMMON
Change in sexual desire or ability, constipation, false sense of well-being, nausea and vomiting, urinary problems, unusual fatigue.

PRINCIPAL USES
For relief of anxiety and panic attacks.

HOW THE DRUG WORKS
In general, clorazepate produces mild sedation by depressing activity in the central nervous system. In particular, clorazepate appears to enhance the effect of gamma-aminobutyric acid (GABA), a natural chemical that inhibits the firing of neurons and dampens the transmission of nerve signals, thus decreasing nervous excitation.

DOSAGE
For anxiety: Usual dose is 7.5 to 15 mg, 2 to 4 times a day. The dosage may be increased or decreased depending on an individual's response. Older adults are usually started at a total dose of 7.5 to 15 mg a day.

ONSET OF EFFECT
Within 1 to 2 hours.

DURATION OF ACTION
Less than 48 hours.

DIETARY ADVICE
No special restrictions.

STORAGE
Store in a tightly sealed container away from heat, moisture, and direct light.

IF YOU MISS A DOSE
Take it as soon as you remember, unless the time for your next scheduled dose is within 2 hours. If so, skip the missed dose and resume your regular dosage schedule. Do not double the next dose.

STOPPING THE DRUG
Do not stop taking the drug abruptly, as this can cause withdrawal symptoms (seizures, sleep disruption, nervousness, irritability, diarrhea, abdominal cramps, muscle aches, memory impairment). Dosage should be reduced gradually as directed by your doctor.

PROLONGED USE
Clorazepate may slowly lose its effectiveness with prolonged use. See your doctor for periodic evaluation if you must take this drug for an extended time.

PRECAUTIONS
Over 60: Adverse reactions may be more likely and more severe in older patients.

Driving and Hazardous Work: The use of clorazepate may impair your ability to perform such tasks safely.

Alcohol: Avoid alcohol.

Pregnancy: Avoid or discontinue use of this drug during pregnancy.

Breast Feeding: Do not take this drug while breast feeding.

Infants and Children: Not recommended for children under 9 years of age.

Special Concerns: Use of this drug can lead to psychological or physical dependence. Never take more than the prescribed daily dose.

OVERDOSE
Symptoms: Extreme drowsiness, confusion, slurred speech, slow reflexes, poor coordination, staggering gait, tremor, slowed breathing, loss of consciousness.

What to Do: Call your doctor, emergency medical services (EMS), or the nearest poison control center immediately.

DRUG INTERACTIONS
Consult your doctor for specific advice if you are taking any drugs that depress the central nervous system; these include antihistamines, antidepressants or other psychiatric medications, barbiturates, sedatives, cough medicines, decongestants, and painkillers. Be sure your doctor knows about any over-the-counter medication you may take.

FOOD INTERACTIONS
None are known.

DISEASE INTERACTIONS
Consult your doctor if you have a history of alcohol or drug abuse, stroke or other brain disease, any chronic lung disease, hyperactivity, depression or other mental illness, myasthenia gravis, sleep apnea, epilepsy, porphyria, kidney disease, or liver disease.

Clotrimazole

▶ Drug Class: Antifungal

▶ Available in: Topical cream, lotion, solution, oral lozenges, vaginal cream, tablets

▶ Available OTC? Yes

▶ As Generic? Yes

Side Effects

SERIOUS
Topical: Hives, skin rash, itching, burning, peeling, stinging, redness, or other skin irritation not present prior to treatment. Lozenge and vaginal: None reported.

COMMON
Topical: None reported. Lozenge (when swallowed): Diarrhea, stomach cramping or pain, nausea or vomiting. Vaginal: Vaginal burning, itching, discharge, or other irritation not present prior to treatment.

LESS COMMON
Topical and lozenge: None reported. Vaginal: Headache, stomach cramps or pain, irritation or burning of sexual partner's penis.

PRINCIPAL USES
To treat fungal infections of the mouth and throat (thrush), vaginal area (yeast infection), and the skin, such as tinea corporis (ringworm), tinea cruris (jock itch), tinea pedis (athlete's foot), and pityriasis versicolor ("sun fungus," a fungal skin condition characterized by fine scaly patches of varying shapes, sizes, and colors).

HOW THE DRUG WORKS
Clotrimazole prevents fungal organisms from producing vital substances required for growth and function.

DOSAGE
Topical cream, lotion, solution (for skin infections)— Adults and children: Apply twice a day, in the morning and in the evening. Oral lozenges (to treat thrush)— Adults and children age 5 and older: Dissolve one 10 mg lozenge in mouth 5 times a day for 14 days. To prevent thrush: Adults and children age 5 and older: Dissolve one 10 mg lozenge in mouth 3 times a day. Vaginal cream (for yeast infections)— Adults and teenagers: At bedtime, insert vaginally with an applicator 50 mg of 1% cream for 6 to 14 nights, or 100 mg of 2% cream for 3 nights, or 500 mg of 10% cream for 1 night only. Vaginal tablets (for yeast infections)— Nonpregnant women and teenagers: At bedtime, insert one 100 mg tablet for 6 to 7 nights, or one 200 mg tablet for 3 nights, or one 500 mg tablet for 1 night only. Pregnant women and teenagers: At bedtime, insert one 100 mg tablet for 7 nights.

ONSET OF EFFECT
Unknown.

DURATION OF ACTION
Lozenges: 3 hours. Other forms: Unknown.

DIETARY ADVICE
No special restrictions.

STORAGE
Store in a tightly sealed container away from heat, moisture, and direct light. Do not allow it to freeze.

IF YOU MISS A DOSE
Take it as soon as you remember. If it is near the time for the next dose, skip the missed dose and resume your regular dosage schedule. Do not double the next dose.

STOPPING THE DRUG
If you are using this drug by prescription, take it as prescribed for the full treatment period, even if you begin to feel better before the scheduled end of therapy. Recurrence of the infection is likely if you stop before the full treatment period is complete.

PROLONGED USE
Clotrimazole is generally prescribed for short-term therapy (1 to 14 days). Consult your doctor for further information.

PRECAUTIONS
Over 60: No special problems are expected.

Driving and Hazardous Work: No special precautions are necessary.

Alcohol: No special precautions are necessary.

Pregnancy: Adequate studies on the use of clotrimazole during pregnancy have not been done; however, no problems have been reported. Consult your doctor for specific advice.

Breast Feeding: Clotrimazole may pass into breast milk; caution is advised. Consult your doctor for advice.

Infants and Children: Topical forms: No special warnings. Lozenges are not recommended for children younger than age 5. Vaginal forms: Not commonly prescribed for children under the age of 12.

Special Concerns: Do not chew or swallow lozenges. Clotrimazole lozenges may take 15 to 30 minutes to dissolve completely and are useless if swallowed.

OVERDOSE
Symptoms: An overdose with clotrimazole is unlikely.

What to Do: If someone should swallow a large amount of the medicine, call your doctor, emergency medical services (EMS), or the nearest poison control center immediately.

DRUG INTERACTIONS
No drug interactions have been reported.

FOOD INTERACTIONS
No food interactions have been reported.

DISEASE INTERACTIONS
No disease interactions have been reported.

Clozapine

BRAND NAME
Clozaril

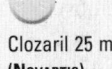

Clozaril 25 mg
(NOVARTIS)

▶ Drug Class: Neuroleptic; antipsychotic

▶ Available in: Tablets

▶ Available OTC? No

▶ As Generic? Yes

Side Effects

SERIOUS
Signs of serious infection including high fever, chills, and sweating, sores or ulcers in the mouth, unusual bruising or bleeding, severe fatigue or weakness. Other serious side effects include seizures, yellow discoloration of the eyes or skin, rapid or irregular heartbeat, severe dizziness, severe low blood pressure (which may cause lightheadedness and fainting, especially when getting up suddenly from sitting or lying positions), and hyperglycemia (elevated blood glucose levels), with symptoms including increased thirst, hunger, and urination. If you experience such symptoms, contact your doctor immediately.

COMMON
Increased salivation, dizziness, drowsiness, mild headache, constipation, nausea or vomiting, weight gain.

LESS COMMON
Abdominal pain, heartburn, sore throat, diarrhea, muscle aches, spasms, or weakness, loss of coordination.

PRINCIPAL USES
Clozapine is used to treat schizophrenia after other standard medications have proved inadequate.

HOW THE DRUG WORKS
Clozapine inhibits activity of the brain chemical dopamine, thereby helping to prevent the overstimulation of specific nerve centers in the brain believed to be responsible for certain psychiatric disorders.

DOSAGE
Adults: 12.5 mg, 1 to 2 times daily; may be increased gradually by your doctor to as much as 900 mg a day. Children: Consult your pediatrician.

ONSET OF EFFECT
Within 2 to 4 weeks. Full effect may not be seen until after 3 months of therapy.

DURATION OF ACTION
Unknown.

DIETARY ADVICE
No special restrictions.

STORAGE
Store in a tightly sealed container away from heat and direct light.

IF YOU MISS A DOSE
Take it as soon as you remember, unless the time for the next scheduled dose is within the next 2 hours. If so, skip the missed dose and resume your regular dosage schedule with the next dose. Do not double the next dose.

STOPPING THE DRUG
Do not stop taking the drug abruptly or without your doctor's approval. Dose must be reduced gradually to prevent withdrawal symptoms from occurring.

PROLONGED USE
The risk of side effects may increase with long-term use of clozapine.

PRECAUTIONS
Over 60: Adverse reactions may be more likely and more severe in older patients.

Driving and Hazardous Work: The use of clozapine may impair your ability to perform such tasks safely.

Alcohol: Avoid alcohol.

Pregnancy: Adequate studies on the use of clozapine during pregnancy have not been done. Consult your doctor for specific advice.

Breast Feeding: Clozapine passes into breast milk; do not use it while nursing.

Infants and Children: Safety and effectiveness of the use of clozapine in children under the age of 16 have not been established.

Special Concerns: Frequent blood tests are required while taking clozapine. This medication can cause a marked decrease in the level of white blood cells in the body. Clozapine prescriptions are sometimes filled only one week at a time, on the condition that the patient be given a blood test to check white cell count before the following week's medication is dispensed. Report symptoms of fever, chills, nausea, vomiting, diarrhea, painful urination, or cough to your doctor when taking this medication.

OVERDOSE
Symptoms: Confusion, restlessness, nervousness, severe drowsiness, hallucinations, fainting, unconsciousness, coma; unusual excitement or agitation; slow, deep breathing or rapid, shallow breathing, or breathing difficulty; increased salivation; rapid or irregular pulse.

What to Do: Call your doctor, emergency medical services (EMS), or the nearest poison control center immediately.

DRUG INTERACTIONS
Other drugs may interact with clozapine. Consult your doctor for specific advice if you are taking sleeping pills or sedatives, antidepressants, amphotericin B, anticancer drugs, thyroid medications, azathioprine, chlorambucil, chloramphenicol, colchicine, cyclophosphamide, flucytosine, haloperidol, interferon, lithium, mercaptopurine, methotrexate, plicamycin, zidovudine (AZT), cimetidine, or erythromycin.

FOOD INTERACTIONS
None reported.

DISEASE INTERACTIONS
Consult your doctor if you have a history of any type of blood disorder, enlarged prostate, difficult urination, stomach or intestinal disorder, heart or blood vessel disease, epilepsy or other seizure disorder, kidney disease, or liver disease.

Coal Tar

▶ Drug Class: Antipsoriasis drug

▶ Available in: Cleansing bar, cream, gel, lotion, ointment, shampoo, liquid

▶ Available OTC? Yes

▶ As Generic? Yes

Side Effects

SERIOUS
Skin irritation or rash not present before use of coal tar. Call your doctor immediately.

COMMON
Mild stinging, increased sensitivity to sunlight.

LESS COMMON
There are no less-common side effects associated with the use of coal tar.

PRINCIPAL USES
To treat skin conditions including dandruff, eczema, seborrheic dermatitis, and psoriasis.

HOW THE DRUG WORKS
Coal tar promotes softening, dissolution, and peeling of hard, scaly, roughened, or irregular surface skin. It also has antiseptic properties and fights fungal, bacterial, and parasitic organisms.

DOSAGE
Cleansing bar: Use 1 or 2 times a day as directed by your doctor. Cream: Apply to affected areas up to 4 times a day. Gel: Apply to affected areas 1 or 2 times a day. Lotion: Apply to affected areas as needed. Ointment: Apply to affected areas 2 or 3 times a day. Shampoo: Use once a day, once a week, or as directed by your doctor. Topical solution: Apply to skin or scalp or use in the bath, depending on product. Topical bath solution: Add appropriate amount to bath water; immerse yourself in the bath for 20 minutes. If you have any questions about its use, consult your doctor.

ONSET OF EFFECT
Unknown.

DURATION OF ACTION
Unknown.

DIETARY ADVICE
Coal tar can be used without regard to diet.

STORAGE
Store in a tightly sealed container away from heat and direct light. Do not allow liquid forms to freeze.

IF YOU MISS A DOSE
Apply it as soon as you remember. If it is near the time for the next dose, skip the missed dose and resume your regular dosage schedule. Do not apply a double dose.

STOPPING THE DRUG
If you are applying coal tar by prescription, the decision to stop using it should be made by your doctor. If you are using the drug without a prescription, you may stop treatment whenever you choose.

PROLONGED USE
Do not use coal tar for longer than your physician prescribes.

PRECAUTIONS
Over 60: Coal tar is not expected to cause different side effects or problems in older patients than it does in younger persons.

Driving and Hazardous Work: The use of coal tar should not impair your ability to perform such tasks safely.

Alcohol: No special restrictions apply.

Pregnancy: Studies of coal tar use during pregnancy have not been done in animals or humans. Before you use coal tar, tell your doctor if you are pregnant or plan to become pregnant.

Breast Feeding: It is not known if coal tar passes into breast milk. Consult your doctor for specific advice.

Infants and Children: Use and dose in infants and children must be determined by your doctor.

Special Concerns: For external use only. Keep coal tar away from the eyes. If you accidentally get some of the medicine in your eyes, flush them thoroughly with water. After applying coal tar, protect the treated area from sunlight for 72 hours, and be sure to remove all coal tar before being exposed to sunlight or using a sunlamp . Do not apply coal tar to infected, blistered, raw, or oozing areas of the skin.

OVERDOSE
Symptoms: None reported.

What to Do: Emergency instructions not applicable.

DRUG INTERACTIONS
Consult your doctor for specific advice if you are using tetracyclines, psoralens, or retinoids. Also tell your doctor if you are using any other prescription or over-the-counter medication.

FOOD INTERACTIONS
No known food interactions.

DISEASE INTERACTIONS
You should not use coal tar if you have had a prior allergic reaction to it.

Codeine

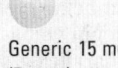

Generic 15 mg
(ROXANE)

Additional photographs

▶ Drug Class: Opioid (narcotic) analgesic

▶ Available in: Tablets, oral solution

▶ Available OTC? No

▶ As Generic? Yes

Side Effects

SERIOUS
Serious side effects of codeine are indistinguishable from those of overdose: Confusion; sleepiness; slurred speech; unconsciousness; small, pinpoint pupils; cold, clammy skin; slow breathing; seizures; severe drowsiness, weakness, or dizziness.

COMMON
Mild dizziness or lightheadedness, nausea or vomiting, constipation, drowsiness, itching.

LESS COMMON
Headache, sweating, false sense of well-being (euphoria).

PRINCIPAL USES
To treat mild to moderate pain or to control a severe cough.

HOW THE DRUG WORKS
Narcotics such as codeine relieve pain by acting on specific areas of the spinal cord and brain that process pain signals from nerves throughout the body. Codeine dulls the cough reflex, which is why it may be used to treat certain coughs.

DOSAGE
Adults— For pain: 15 to 60 mg every 3 to 6 hours as needed. Usual dose is 30 mg. For cough: 10 to 20 mg every 3 to 6 hours as needed. Children— Oral solution: For pain: 0.5 mg per 2.2 lbs (1 kg) of body weight every 4 to 6 hours as needed. For cough: Age 2: 3 mg every 4 to 6 hours. Take no more than 12 mg a day. Age 3: 3.5 mg every 4 to 6 hours. Take no more than 14 mg a day. Age 4: 4 mg every 4 to 6 hours. Take no more than 16 mg a day. Age 5: 4.5 mg every 4 to 6 hours. Take no more than 18 mg a day. Ages 6 to 12: 5 to 10 mg every 4 to 6 hours. Take no more than 60 mg per day.

ONSET OF EFFECT
30 to 45 minutes.

DURATION OF ACTION
4 to 6 hours.

DIETARY ADVICE
Codeine is constipating; make sure your diet contains adequate amounts of fiber and vegetables.

STORAGE
Store in a tightly sealed container away from heat, moisture, and direct light.

IF YOU MISS A DOSE
Take it as soon as you remember. If it is near the time for the next dose, skip the missed dose and resume your regular dosage schedule. Do not double the next dose.

STOPPING THE DRUG
You should take it as prescribed for the full treatment period, but you may stop taking the drug if you are feeling better before the scheduled end of therapy.

PROLONGED USE
Therapy varies, depending on the cause of the pain. Some patients require long-term narcotic therapy. Side effects may be more likely with prolonged use.

PRECAUTIONS
Over 60: Adverse reactions may be more likely and more severe in older patients.

Driving and Hazardous Work: The use of codeine may impair your ability to perform such tasks safely.

Alcohol: Avoid alcohol.

Pregnancy: Adequate human studies have not been completed. Before taking codeine, tell your physician if you are pregnant or plan to become pregnant.

Breast Feeding: Codeine passes into breast milk; caution is advised. Consult your doctor for specific advice.

Infants and Children: Adverse reactions may be more likely and more severe in children.

Special Concerns: Codeine can cause physical dependence. Some patients may experience withdrawal symptoms when the medication is discontinued. These may include body aches, abdominal pain, stomach cramps, diarrhea, runny nose, gooseflesh, nervousness, agitation, sweating, yawning, loss of appetite, shivering, insomnia, dilated pupils, and weakness. Do not exceed recommended doses or increase the dose on your own.

OVERDOSE
Symptoms: Confusion; sleepiness; slurred speech; unconsciousness; small, pinpoint pupils; cold, clammy skin; slow breathing; seizures; severe drowsiness, weakness, or dizziness.

What to Do: Call your doctor, emergency medical services (EMS), or the nearest poison control center immediately.

DRUG INTERACTIONS
Consult your doctor for specific advice if you are taking carbamazepine or other medicine for seizures, barbiturates, sedatives, cough medicines, decongestants, antidepressants, other prescription pain medications, MAO inhibitors, naltrexone, rifampin, or zidovudine.

FOOD INTERACTIONS
None known.

DISEASE INTERACTIONS
Consult your doctor if you have any of the following: emotional illness; brain disorders or head injury; seizures; lung disease; prostate problems or other problems with urination; gallstones; colitis; heart, kidney, liver, or thyroid disease; or a history of alcohol or drug abuse.

Colchicine

BRAND NAME
Colsalide Improved

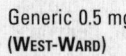

Generic 0.5 mg
(WEST-WARD)

▸ Drug Class: Antigout drug

▸ Available in: Tablets, injection

▸ Available OTC? No

▸ As Generic? Yes

Side Effects

SERIOUS
Allergic reactions, causing rash or hives, swelling of face, lips, tongue, eyelids, and throat; such reactions may interfere with breathing—seek medical help immediately. Unusual or persistent fevers, fatigue, chills, sore throat, bruising, or bleeding; these may be signs of serious anemia or suppression of the immune system.

COMMON
Diarrhea, vomiting, nausea, stomach pain.

LESS COMMON
Muscle weakness; numbness, tingling, or prickling in the hands and feet.

PRINCIPAL USES
To treat painful attacks of gout, as well as to prevent or reduce the frequency of such attacks. Oral colchicine is used for moderate attacks. Injectable colchicine is used for serious attacks or in patients who cannot take the tablets.

HOW THE DRUG WORKS
In gout, crystals of a chemical called monosodium urate are deposited in joints, where they cause inflammation and lead to the sharp, excruciating pain of a gout attack. Colchicine prevents inflammation that may result from the accumulation of monosodium urate crystals.

DOSAGE
For an acute attack: 0.5 to 1.2 mg immediately; then 0.5 or 0.6 mg every 1 or 2 hours, or 1 to 1.2 mg every 2 hours, to a maximum of 6 mg. Stop as soon as you achieve relief. For chronic gout or to prevent attacks: 0.5 or 0.6 mg, usually once a day. Not all patients require daily doses; some may take colchicine periodically. Consult your doctor.

ONSET OF EFFECT
6 to 12 hours.

DURATION OF ACTION
Unknown.

DIETARY ADVICE
No special restrictions.

STORAGE
Store in a tightly sealed container away from heat and direct light. Keep it away from moisture and extremes in temperature.

IF YOU MISS A DOSE
Take it as soon as you remember. If it is near the time for the next dose, skip the missed dose and resume your regular dosage schedule. Do not double the next dose.

STOPPING THE DRUG
You may stop taking the drug if you are feeling better before the scheduled end of therapy. If it was prescribed for long-term use, however, do not stop without first consulting your doctor.

PROLONGED USE
Therapy for a severe attack is usually completed within 1 day. Do not take colchicine for a longer period without your doctor's approval.

PRECAUTIONS
Over 60: Adverse reactions may be more likely and more severe in older patients.

Driving and Hazardous Work: Do not drive or engage in hazardous work until you determine how the medicine affects you.

Alcohol: Avoid alcohol.

Pregnancy: Avoid or discontinue this medication if you are pregnant or trying to become pregnant.

Breast Feeding: Colchicine passes into breast milk; avoid or discontinue use while nursing.

Infants and Children: Not recommended.

Special Concerns: Make sure you understand how to take this drug; colchicine treatments vary. Dosing schedules for an acute attack can be confusing. Read your label carefully; make sure you understand how many tablets constitute the correct dose. Many patients find it helpful to write the dosing plan on an index card and to carry a copy in a wallet or handbag.

Do not continue taking colchicine during an acute gout attack if you begin feeling nauseated, begin vomiting, or develop diarrhea. Call your doctor. Do not continue taking colchicine during an acute attack once you have taken 6 mg; if you still have not achieved relief after reaching this limit, call your doctor.

OVERDOSE
Symptoms: Fever; convulsions; confusion, disorientation, delirium; rapid or irregular breathing; sharp, burning pain in stomach; diarrhea, which may be bloody.

What to Do: Call emergency medical services (EMS), your doctor, or the nearest poison control center immediately.

DRUG INTERACTIONS
Consult your doctor for ad-vice if you are taking phenylbutazone or drugs that may affect your bone marrow including anticonvulsants, certain antibiotics, and chemotherapy drugs for cancer.

FOOD INTERACTIONS
None are likely, but a low-purine diet is recommended to reduce the risk of gout attacks. Foods high in purines include anchovies, sardines, legumes, poultry, sweetbreads, liver, kidneys, and other organ meats.

DISEASE INTERACTIONS
Consult your doctor if you have heart, liver, or kidney disease; blood disorders; or gastrointestinal disorders, such as ulcers, colitis, and intestinal malabsorption.

Colesevelam Hydrochloride

BRAND NAME
WelChol

▶ Drug Class: Antilipidemic
(cholesterol-lowering agent)

▶ Available in: Tablets

▶ Available OTC? No

▶ As Generic? No

Side Effects

SERIOUS
No serious side effects
have been reported in
association with the use
of colesevelam.

COMMON
Constipation, heartburn.

LESS COMMON
No less common side
effects have been
reported in association
with colesevelam.

PRINCIPAL USES
To reduce cholesterol in
people with high blood levels of low-density lipoprotein (LDL), as part of a
comprehensive treatment
program that includes exercise and special diet. May
also be taken in conjunction
with another cholesterol
drugs called "statins" (such
as simvastatin, lovastatin,
fluvastatin, pravastatin, or
atorvastatin).

HOW THE DRUG WORKS
Colesevelam binds bile
acids in the intestine, forming an insoluble complex
that is excreted in the feces.
This process reduces the
amount of bile acids in the
blood. In response to the
lower levels of bile acids,
the liver converts more
cholesterol to bile acids.
As a consequence, the
amount of cholesterol in
liver cells declines, and the
liver makes more receptors
for LDL. The resulting
increased removal of LDL
from the blood lowers
LDL cholesterol.

DOSAGE
3 tablets (625 mg each)
twice a day with meals or
6 tablets once a day with a
meal, either alone or in
combination with a statin.
The dose may be increased
by your doctor to 7 tablets
a day.

ONSET OF EFFECT
Within 2 weeks.

DURATION OF ACTION
For as long as the drug is
continued.

DIETARY ADVICE
Follow all special dietary
restrictions and guidelines
as directed by your doctor.
Take colesevelam with a liquid and a meal.

STORAGE
Store in a tightly sealed container away from heat and
moisture.

IF YOU MISS A DOSE
Take as soon as you
remember. However, if it is
near the time for the next
dose, skip the missed dose
and resume your regular
dosage schedule. Do not
double the next dose.

STOPPING THE DRUG
The decision to stop taking
the drug should be made
in consultation with your
physician.

PROLONGED USE
Colesevelam may be used
safely for years; however,
periodic evaluation of the
drug's effectiveness and
its effects on the liver is
necessary.

PRECAUTIONS
Over 60: No special problems are expected.

**Driving and Hazardous
Work:** No special precautions are necessary.

Alcohol: No special precautions are necessary.

Pregnancy: The effects
on a fetus are unknown.
Consult your doctor if you
become or plan to become
pregnant.

Breast Feeding: No
special precautions are
necessary.

Infants and Children:
Safety and effectiveness
have not been established
for patients under 18 years
of age. Consult your doctor
for specific advice.

Special Concerns: At
very high doses, colesevelam may interfere with the
absorption of fats and fat-
soluble vitamins (vitamins

A, D, E, and K); vitamin
supplementation may be
advised.

OVERDOSE
Symptoms: None
reported.

What to Do: Emergency
instructions not applicable.

DRUG INTERACTIONS
No known drug interac-
tions.

FOOD INTERACTIONS
No known food interactions.

DISEASE INTERACTIONS
Colesevelam must be used
cautiously in patients with
blood triglycerides greater
than 300 mg/dL and in
those with a history of
swallowing difficulties,
severe abnormalities of
gastrointestinal motility, or
major gastrointestinal tract
surgery.

Colestipol Hydrochloride

BRAND NAME
Colestid

▶ Drug Class: Antilipidemic (cholesterol-lowering agent)

▶ Available in: Powder, tablets

▶ Available OTC? No

▶ As Generic? No

Side Effects

SERIOUS
Severe abdominal pain (a very rare reaction, indicating intestinal obstruction). Stop taking the drug and contact your doctor immediately.

COMMON
Constipation, heartburn, bloating, belching, abdominal discomfort, irritation of the anal area.

LESS COMMON
Hives, rash, gas, diarrhea, nausea, vomiting, gallstones.

PRINCIPAL USES
To reduce cholesterol in people with high blood levels of low-density lipoprotein (LDL), as part of a comprehensive treatment program that includes exercise and special diet. The drug is also used to relieve itching caused by high levels of bile acids in the blood, a problem associated with blockage of the bile ducts. It may also be used to prevent some types of diarrhea or serve as an antidote to poisoning from or overdose of digitalis drugs.

HOW THE DRUG WORKS
Colestipol binds with bile acids in the intestine, forming an insoluble complex that is excreted in the feces. This process reduces the amount of bile acids in the blood. In response to the lower levels of bile acids, the liver converts more cholesterol to bile acids. As a consequence, the amount of cholesterol in liver cells declines, and the liver makes more receptors for LDL. The resulting increased removal of LDL from the blood lowers LDL cholesterol.

DOSAGE
Initial dose is 5 g, 1 or 2 times a day. Maintenance dose is 10 to 30 g, given in 2 equally divided doses. Always mix the powder thoroughly with appropriate liquid (water or fruit juice; do not use carbonated beverages) and wait 10 to 15 minutes after mixing before drinking. Doses are increased or decreased according to the individual's response.

ONSET OF EFFECT
Within 1 to 3 weeks.

DURATION OF ACTION
The drug's effects persist for 2 to 4 weeks after the final dose.

DIETARY ADVICE
Follow all special dietary restrictions and guidelines as directed by your doctor.

STORAGE
Store in a tightly sealed container away from heat and direct light. Keep away from moisture.

IF YOU MISS A DOSE
Take as soon as you remember. However, if it is near the time for the next dose, skip the missed dose and resume your regular dosage schedule. Do not double the next dose.

STOPPING THE DRUG
The drug may be stopped after 1 to 3 months if the therapeutic effect is not adequate. The decision to stop taking the drug should be made by your doctor.

PROLONGED USE
Colestipol may be used safely for years; periodic evaluation of the drug's effectiveness is necessary.

PRECAUTIONS
Over 60: Adverse reactions (particularly constipation) are more likely and more severe in older patients.

Driving and Hazardous Work: Colestipol should not impair your ability to perform such tasks safely.

Alcohol: No special precautions are necessary.

Pregnancy: Consult your doctor if you become or plan to become pregnant.

Breast Feeding: At very high doses colestipol may interfere with the absorption of vitamins A, D, E, and K, which may affect the nutritional intake of the nursing infant. Consult your doctor for specific advice.

Infants and Children: Prescribed for children only in rare circumstances. Follow doctor's instructions and dosage guidelines carefully in such cases.

Special Concerns: At very high doses, colestipol may interfere with the absorption of fats and fat-soluble vitamins (vitamins A, D, E, and K); vitamin supplementation may be advised.

OVERDOSE
Symptoms: None reported.

What to Do: Emergency instructions not applicable.

DRUG INTERACTIONS
Colestipol may bind with other drugs and hinder their absorption. Therefore, take all other drugs 1 to 2 hours before or 4 hours after taking colestipol.

FOOD INTERACTIONS
No known food interactions.

DISEASE INTERACTIONS
Do not take this drug if you have had a prior allergic reaction to it. Use of colestipol may make the following conditions worse: gallstones, peptic ulcer, intestinal bleeding disorders, hemorrhoids, malabsorption, constipation.

Colistin/Neomycin/Hydrocortisone

▶ Drug Class: Antibiotic combination drug

▶ Available in: Otic suspension

▶ Available OTC? No

▶ As Generic? No

Side Effects

SERIOUS
Skin rash, itching, redness, swelling, or other signs of irritation that were not present before therapy. Call your doctor immediately.

COMMON
No common side effects are associated with this drug.

LESS COMMON
There are no less-common side effects associated with the use of this drug.

PRINCIPAL USES
To treat infections of the ear canal and other types of ear problems.

HOW THE DRUG WORKS
This drug is a combination of three active ingredients. Colistin and neomycin are both antibiotics that destroy infection-causing bacteria. Hydrocortisone is a steroid hormone that mimics the effects of the body's natural corticosteroids to help reduce redness and pain associated with specific ear problems.

DOSAGE
Adults: 4 drops in the affected ear, 3 or 4 times a day. Children: Up to 3 drops in the affected ear, 3 or 4 times a day.

ONSET OF EFFECT
Unknown.

DURATION OF ACTION
Unknown.

DIETARY ADVICE
No special restrictions.

STORAGE
Store in a tightly sealed container away from heat, moisture, and direct light. Do not allow it to freeze.

IF YOU MISS A DOSE
Apply it as soon as you remember. If it is near the time for the next dose, skip the missed dose and resume your regular dosage schedule. Do not double the next dose.

STOPPING THE DRUG
Use it as prescribed for the full treatment period, even if you feel better before the scheduled end of therapy.

PROLONGED USE
Do not use this medication for more than 10 days unless directed otherwise by your doctor.

PRECAUTIONS
Over 60: No special problems are expected.

Driving and Hazardous Work: The use of this medication should not impair your ability to perform such tasks safely.

Alcohol: No special problems are expected, although it is generally advisable to abstain from alcohol when fighting an infection.

Pregnancy: Problems related to the use of this preparation during pregnancy have not been reported. Consult your doctor before using this medication during pregnancy

Breast Feeding: When used as directed, this medication does not pass into breast milk. Consult your doctor for specific advice.

Infants and Children: No studies on the use of this medication by children have been done. No special problems are expected.

Special Concerns: Before applying this medication, clean the ear canal thoroughly and dry it with a sterile wipe. Tilt the head so that the affected ear is up. Adults should gently pull the earlobe up and back; for children, pull down and back. After the medicine is dropped into the ear canal, keep the ear facing up for 5 minutes (or 1 to 2 minutes for restless children). Your doctor may have further instructions on how to apply the medication.

OVERDOSE
Symptoms: No cases of overdose have been reported.

What to Do: An overdose of this medication is unlikely to be life-threatening. However, if someone takes a much larger dose than prescribed or accidentally ingests the medication, call your doctor, emergency medical services (EMS), or the nearest poison control center immediately.

DRUG INTERACTIONS
It is possible that other drugs may interact with colistin, neomycin, and hydrocortisone. Before you use this medication, tell your doctor if you are taking any other prescription or over-the-counter medication, especially any other kinds of ear drops.

FOOD INTERACTIONS
No known food interactions.

DISEASE INTERACTIONS
Caution is advised when taking this drug. Consult your doctor if you have herpes simplex infection or any other ear problem.

▶ Drug Class: Progestin
(hormone)

▶ Available in: Tablets, injection

▶ Available OTC? No

▶ As Generic? No

Side Effects

SERIOUS
Changes in or cessation of menstrual bleeding, unexpected or increased flow of breast milk, mental depression, skin rash, loss of or change in speech, impaired coordination or vision, severe and sudden shortness of breath. Call your doctor immediately.

COMMON
Stomach pain, swelling of face, ankles, or feet, mild headache, mood changes, unusual fatigue, weight gain, pain or irritation at site of injection.

LESS COMMON
Acne, breast pain or tenderness, hot flashes, insomnia, loss of sexual desire, loss or gain of scalp hair or body hair, brown spots on skin.

PRINCIPAL USES
To prevent pregnancy.

HOW THE DRUG WORKS
Progestin prevents a woman's egg from developing fully; it also causes changes in the uterine lining and the cervical secretions, making it difficult for sperm to reach the egg.

DOSAGE
Tablets: 75 micrograms (mcg) (Ovrette) or 350 mcg (Nor-QD, Miconor) every day beginning on the first day of the menstrual cycle. Injection (Depo-Provera): 150 mg injected into the upper arm or buttock every 13 weeks.

ONSET OF EFFECT
Tablets: Protection begins 3 weeks after first taking the medication. Injection: Immediate if the injection is given within 5 days of the menstrual period.

DURATION OF ACTION
Tablets: 24 hours. Injection: 13 weeks.

DIETARY ADVICE
Tablets can be taken with meals to prevent gastrointestinal upset.

STORAGE
Store in a tightly sealed container away from heat and direct light.

IF YOU MISS A DOSE
Take the missed dose of the tablet as soon as you remember, resume your regular dosage, and use another birth control method for 2 days.

STOPPING THE DRUG
You may stop at any time you choose. This will naturally increase the likelihood of pregnancy unless another birth control method is employed.

PROLONGED USE
You should see your doctor for periodic examinations and laboratory tests if you use these contraceptives for a prolonged period.

PRECAUTIONS
Over 60: Generally not used by older patients.

Driving and Hazardous Work: No special precautions are necessary.

Alcohol: No special precautions are necessary.

Pregnancy: Low-dose progestins for contraception have not been shown to cause problems later if pregnancy occurs.

Breast Feeding: Progestins pass into breast milk but have not been shown to cause problems. They are recommended for nursing mothers who wish to practice contraception.

Infants and Children: Progestin contraceptives have not caused problems in teenagers. Birth control methods that protect against sexually transmitted diseases are also recommended for them.

Special Concerns: No contraceptive method is perfect. If you suspect a pregnancy, call your doctor immediately. If you have any laboratory test, tell the health professional that you are using these contraceptives. Cigarette smoking or alcohol abuse can increase the risk of osteoporosis and may increase the risk of blood clots.

OVERDOSE
Symptoms: No specific ones have been reported.

What to Do: An overdose of these contraceptives is unlikely to be life-threatening. However, if someone takes a much larger dose than prescribed, call your doctor, emergency medical services (EMS), or the nearest poison control center immediately.

DRUG INTERACTIONS
The following drugs may interact with these contraceptives. Consult your doctor for specific advice if you are taking aminoglutethimide, carbamazepine, phenytoin, rifabutin, or rifampin.

FOOD INTERACTIONS
No known food interactions.

DISEASE INTERACTIONS
Caution is advised when taking these contraceptives. Consult your doctor if you have any of the following: asthma, epilepsy, heart problems, circulation problems, kidney disease, liver disease, migraine headaches, breast disease, bleeding problems, diabetes, high blood cholesterol, or central nervous system disorders such as depression.

Contraceptives, Oral (Combination Products)

▶ Drug Class: Hormones, estrogen with progestins

▶ Available in: Tablets

▶ Available OTC? No

▶ As Generic? Yes

Side Effects

SERIOUS

Sudden, severe, or continuing stomach pain; sudden or severe headache or migraine; loss of coordination; loss of or change in vision; pains in chest, groin, or leg; sudden slurring of speech; weakness, numbness, or pain in an arm or leg; changes in uterine bleeding pattern; prolonged bleeding at menses; vaginal infection. Call your doctor immediately.

COMMON

Abdominal cramps or bloating; acne; breast pain, tenderness, or swelling; dizziness; nausea; swelling of ankles or feet; unusual fatigue; vomiting; absence of normal menstruation. Call your doctor if you do not have your period at the end of the cycle and before you start a new cycle.

LESS COMMON

Blotchy spots on skin, gain or loss of hair, increased sensitivity to sunlight, changes in sexual interest.

PRINCIPAL USES

To prevent pregnancy.

HOW THE DRUG WORKS

Such products stop a woman's egg from fully developing each month.

DOSAGE

For 21-day cycle: 1 tablet a day for 21 days. Skip 7 days; repeat the cycle. For 28-day cycle: 1 tablet a day for 28 days. Repeat cycle. Each package of pills consists of 21 active tablets only, or 21 active tablets and 7 placebos. During the 7 days of taking placebos or no tablets, menstruation should occur.

ONSET OF EFFECT

At least 7 days.

DURATION OF ACTION

As long as tablets are taken.

DIETARY ADVICE

Take it with food if stomach upset occurs.

STORAGE

Store in a tightly sealed container away from heat and direct light.

IF YOU MISS A DOSE

If you miss the first tablet of a new cycle or 1 tablet during the cycle, take the missed tablet as soon as you remember and take the next tablet at the usual time. If you miss 2 tablets in a row in the first or second week, take 2 tablets the day you remember and 2 the next day, then resume normal dosage schedule and use another birth control method until the next cycle begins. If you miss 2 tablets during the third week or 3 tablets at any time, begin a new cycle on its scheduled starting day, but use another birth control method for 7 days into the new cycle.

STOPPING THE DRUG

You may stop at any time you choose after completing a full 21-day cycle of tablets.

PROLONGED USE

See your doctor at least every 6 months.

PRECAUTIONS

Over 60: Generally not used by older persons.

Driving and Hazardous Work: No special precautions are necessary.

Alcohol: No special precautions are necessary.

Pregnancy: Discontinue use if you become pregnant or suspect that you might be pregnant.

Breast Feeding: Oral contraceptive hormones pass into breast milk; avoid or discontinue use while breast feeding.

Infants and Children: No special problems have been found in teenagers who use oral contraception.

Special Concerns: Limit your exposure to sunlight until you determine how this medication affects you. Smoking can reduce the effectiveness of oral contraceptives and increase the risk of potentially dangerous blood clots.

OVERDOSE

Symptoms: Unexplained vaginal bleeding.

What to Do: An overdose of oral contraceptives is unlikely to be life-threatening. However, if someone takes a much larger dose than prescribed, call your doctor, emergency medical services (EMS), or the nearest poison control center immediately.

DRUG INTERACTIONS

Consult your doctor for specific advice if you are taking: amiodarone, anabolic steroids, androgens, anti-infectives, barbiturates, carbamazepine, carmustine, dantrolene, daunorubicin, disulfiram, divalproex, estrogens, etretinate, gold salts, griseofulvin, hydroxychloroquine, mercaptopurine, methotrexate, naltrexone, phenothiazines, phenylbutazone, phenytoin, plicamycin, primidone, rifabutin, rifampin, troleandomycin, corticosteroids, theophylline, cyclosporine, or ritonavir.

FOOD INTERACTIONS

No known food interactions.

DISEASE INTERACTIONS

Consult your doctor if you have any of the following: endometriosis, fibroid tumors of the uterus, heart or circulation disease, a history of stroke, breast disease, cancer, gallbladder disease, high blood cholesterol, liver disease, mental depression, diabetes, epilepsy, or migraines.

BRAND NAME
Cortone Acetate

Generic 25 mg
(RUGBY)

831

Additional photographs

▶ Drug Class: Corticosteroid

▶ Available in: Tablets

▶ Available OTC? No

▶ As Generic? Yes

Side Effects

SERIOUS
Vision problems, frequent urination, increased thirst, rectal bleeding, blistering skin, confusion, hallucinations, paranoia, euphoria, depression, mood swings, redness and swelling at injection site. Call your doctor immediately.

COMMON
Increased appetite, indigestion, nervousness, insomnia, greater susceptibility to infections, increased blood pressure, slow healing of wounds, weight gain, easy bruising, fluid retention.

LESS COMMON
Change in skin color, dizziness, headache, increased sweating, unusual growth of body or facial hair, increased blood sugar, peptic ulcers, adrenal insufficiency, muscle weakness, cataracts, glaucoma, osteoporosis.

PRINCIPAL USES
To treat numerous conditions that involve inflammation (a response by body tissues, producing redness, warmth, swelling, and pain). Such conditions include arthritis, allergic reactions, asthma, some skin diseases, multiple sclerosis flare-ups, and other autoimmune diseases. Also prescribed to treat deficiency of natural steroid hormones.

HOW THE DRUG WORKS
This hormone mimics the effects of the body's natural corticosteroids. It depresses the synthesis, release, and activity of inflammation-producing body chemicals. It also suppresses the activity of the immune system.

DOSAGE
Adults and teenagers: 25 to 300 mg a day, in 1 or several doses. Doses are individualized, depending on the condition being treated. The dose for children depends on body weight or size and must be determined by your doctor.

ONSET OF EFFECT
Variable.

DURATION OF ACTION
Variable.

DIETARY ADVICE
It can be taken with food or milk to minimize stomach upset. Your doctor may recommend a low-salt, high-potassium, high-protein diet.

STORAGE
Store in a tightly sealed container away from heat, moisture, and direct light.

IF YOU MISS A DOSE
Take it as soon as you remember. If you take several doses a day and it is close to the next dose, double the next dose. If you take 1 dose a day and you do not remember until the next day, skip the missed dose and do not double the next dose.

STOPPING THE DRUG
With long-term therapy, do not stop taking the drug abruptly; the dosage should be decreased gradually.

PROLONGED USE
See your doctor regularly for tests and examinations. Long-term use may lead to cataracts, diabetes, hypertension, or osteoporosis.

PRECAUTIONS
Over 60: Adverse reactions may be more likely and more severe.

Driving and Hazardous Work: Do not drive or engage in hazardous work until you determine how the medicine affects you.

Alcohol: May cause stomach problems; avoid unless your doctor approves occasional moderate drinking.

Pregnancy: Overuse during pregnancy can retard the child's growth and cause other developmental problems. Consult your physician.

Breast Feeding: Do not use while nursing.

Infants and Children: Cortisone may retard the normal growth and development of bone and other tissues. Consult your doctor for advice.

Special Concerns: Avoid immunizations with live vaccines if possible. Remember that this drug can lower your resistance to infection. Patients undergoing long-term therapy should wear a medical-alert bracelet. Call your doctor if you develop a fever.

OVERDOSE
Symptoms: Fever, muscle or joint pain, nausea, dizziness, fainting, breathing difficulty. Prolonged overuse: Moonface, obesity, unusual hair growth, acne, loss of sexual function, muscle wasting.

What to Do: Call your doctor, emergency medical services (EMS), or the nearest poison control center immediately.

DRUG INTERACTIONS
Consult your doctor for specific advice if you are taking aminoglutethimide, antacids, barbiturates, carbamazepine, griseofulvin, mitotane, phenylbutazone, phenytoin, primidone, rifampin, injectable amphotericin B, oral antidiabetes agents, insulin, digitalis drugs, diuretics, or medications containing potassium or sodium.

FOOD INTERACTIONS
Avoid excess sodium.

DISEASE INTERACTIONS
Consult your doctor if you have a history of bone disease, chicken pox, measles, stomach or intestinal disorders, diabetes mellitus, recent serious infection, tuberculosis, glaucoma, heart disease, hypertension, liver or kidney disorders, high blood cholesterol, overactive or underactive thyroid, myasthenia gravis, or lupus.

Cosyntropin

BRAND NAME
Cortrosyn

▶ Drug Class: Hormone; diagnostic agent

▶ Available in: Injection

▶ Available OTC? No

▶ As Generic? No

Side Effects

SERIOUS
No serious side effects are associated with cosyntropin.

COMMON
No common side effects are associated with cosyntropin, especially since it is used for diagnostic rather than therapeutic purposes.

LESS COMMON
It has not been established whether cosyntropin produces any minor or rare side effects. In an extremely few number of instances, it has been shown to cause mild allergy-like reactions (mild fever, nausea, vomiting, or skin irritation and redness at the site of injection).

PRINCIPAL USES
The adrenal glands manufacture steroids and other substances that are vital for overall health and well-being. Cosyntropin is used for diagnostic purposes when the adrenal gland is suspected of not working properly. The injection of cosyntropin forms the basis of a very simple, safe, and reliable test, taking 30 to 60 minutes, that measures adrenal gland function.

HOW THE DRUG WORKS
Cosyntropin is a synthetic form of corticotropin, a naturally occurring substance that stimulates the adrenal gland to release the hormone cortisol. After the injection of cosyntropin, blood tests will be performed to measure whether or not your adrenal gland was properly stimulated to produce cortisol.

DOSAGE
Adults: 0.25 mg injected into a vein or into a muscle. Children 2 years of age or less: 0.125 mg injected into a vein or muscle.

ONSET OF EFFECT
Within 30 minutes.

DURATION OF ACTION
Several hours at most.

DIETARY ADVICE
You may be given special dietary instructions for the period prior to diagnostic testing. If not, maintain your usual food and fluid intake. Follow other dietary restrictions, if any, as recommended by your doctor.

STORAGE
Not applicable.

IF YOU MISS A DOSE
Not applicable.

STOPPING THE DRUG
This medication is designed to be administered only once. Your doctor will determine if further injections are needed at a later date.

PROLONGED USE
Cosyntropin is never used for extended periods; it is generally administered on a one-time only basis.

PRECAUTIONS
Over 60: Adverse reactions are not anticipated in older patients.

Driving and Hazardous Work: The use of cosyntropin should not impair your ability to perform such tasks safely.

Alcohol: Alcohol should be avoided during the day or two before diagnostic testing is scheduled.

Pregnancy: Cosyntropin may be used during pregnancy; consult your physician for specific recommendations.

Breast Feeding: It is not known if cosyntropin passes into breast milk. However, no serious problems have been documented.

Infants and Children: Cosyntropin may be used safely in children.

OVERDOSE
Symptoms: No specific ones have been reported.

What to Do: An overdose of cosyntropin is unlikely, since it is administered under the close supervision of your doctor. No cases of overdose have been documented.

DRUG INTERACTIONS
None known.

FOOD INTERACTIONS
None known.

DISEASE INTERACTIONS
None known.

▶ Drug Class: Respiratory inhalant

▶ Available in: Inhalation aerosol, inhalation solution, nasal solution

▶ Available OTC? Yes

▶ As Generic? Yes

Side Effects

SERIOUS
Difficulty swallowing; hives; itching; swelling of face, lips, or eyelids; rash; nosebleeds. Call your doctor immediately.

COMMON
Inhalation: Throat irritation or dryness. Nasal: Increased sneezing; burning, stinging, or irritation in nose.

LESS COMMON
Nasal: Cough, headache, postnasal drip, unpleasant taste.

PRINCIPAL USES
To control, through regular use, chronic bronchial asthma; or it may be used preventively just prior to exposure to certain conditions or substances (allergens such as pollen and dust mites, as well as cold air, chemicals, exercise, or air pollution) that can trigger an acute asthma attack (bronchospasm).

HOW THE DRUG WORKS
Cromolyn sodium inhibits the release of histamine, a naturally occurring substance that causes swelling, itching, sneezing, watery eyes, hives, and other symptoms of allergic reaction, including those that occur in association with an asthma attack.

DOSAGE
Inhalation aerosol— To prevent asthma symptoms: Adults and children age 5 and older: 2 inhalations 4 times a day, 4 to 6 hours apart. To prevent bronchospasm: Adults and children age 5 and older: 2 inhalations at least 10 to 15 minutes before exercise or exposure. Inhalation solution— To prevent asthma symptoms: Adults and children 2 and older: 20 mg, 4 times a day, 4 to 6 hours apart. Nasal solution— For hay fever: Adults and children age 6 and older: 1 spray in each nostril 3 to 6 times a day.

ONSET OF EFFECT
Inhalation: Up to 4 weeks. Nasal: Unknown.

DURATION OF ACTION
Unknown.

DIETARY ADVICE
This medication should be taken 30 minutes before meals.

STORAGE
Store in a tightly sealed container away from heat and direct light.

IF YOU MISS A DOSE
Take it as soon as you remember. If it is near the time for the next dose, skip the missed dose and resume your regular dosage schedule. Do not double the next dose.

STOPPING THE DRUG
The decision to stop taking cromolyn sodium should be made in consultation with your doctor.

PROLONGED USE
If your symptoms do not improve after 4 weeks, consult your doctor.

PRECAUTIONS
Over 60: No studies have been done, but no special problems are expected in older patients.

Driving and Hazardous Work: No special problems are expected.

Alcohol: No special precautions are necessary.

Pregnancy: In animal studies, large doses of cromolyn sodium have caused a decrease in successful pregnancies and a decrease in fetal weight. Human studies have not been done. Before taking cromolyn sodium, tell your doctor if you are currently pregnant or plan to become pregnant.

Breast Feeding: It is not known whether cromolyn sodium passes into breast milk. Mothers who wish to breast feed while taking this drug should discuss the matter with their doctor.

Infants and Children: The inhalation form of cromolyn sodium has not been shown to cause special problems in children. The nasal form has not been studied in children. Consult your pediatrician for advice.

Special Concerns: Clean the inhaler and other devices at least once a week.

OVERDOSE
Symptoms: None reported.

What to Do: An overdose of cromolyn sodium is unlikely to be life-threatening. However, if someone takes a much larger dose than prescribed, call your doctor, emergency medical services (EMS), or the nearest poison control center immediately.

DRUG INTERACTIONS
Before taking cromolyn sodium, check with your doctor if you are using any other prescription or over-the-counter drug.

FOOD INTERACTIONS
No known food interactions.

DISEASE INTERACTIONS
Before taking cromolyn sodium, consult your physician if you are undergoing treatment for any medical condition.

Cromolyn Sodium Ophthalmic

▶ Drug Class: Antiallergy agent

▶ Available in: Ophthalmic solution

▶ Available OTC? No

▶ As Generic? No

Side Effects

SERIOUS
Rarely, ophthalmic cromolyn sodium causes a rash or redness around the eyes, swelling of the membrane covering the whites of the eyes, red or bloodshot eyes, or other eye irritation. Call your doctor immediately.

COMMON
Mild and temporary burning or stinging of the eyes.

LESS COMMON
Increased watering or itching of the eyes, dryness or puffiness around the eyes.

PRINCIPAL USES
To treat eye disorders associated with seasonal allergies. Such disorders include conjunctivitis (inflammation of the mucous membranes that line the inner surface of the eyelids and whites of the eyes) and keratitis (inflammation of the cornea).

HOW THE DRUG WORKS
Cromolyn inhibits the body's release of certain allergy-related chemicals including histamine, a naturally occurring substance that causes swelling, itching, sneezing, watery eyes, hives, and other symptoms of an allergic reaction.

DOSAGE
Adults and children age 4 and older: 1 drop 4 to 6 times a day in regularly spaced intervals. Children up to 4 years of age: Use and dosage must be determined by your doctor.

ONSET OF EFFECT
The effect might not be felt for several days or possibly several weeks.

DURATION OF ACTION
Unknown.

DIETARY ADVICE
This drug can be used without regard to diet.

STORAGE
Store in a tightly sealed container away from heat, moisture, and direct light. Do not allow it to freeze.

IF YOU MISS A DOSE
Apply it as soon as you remember. If it is near the time for the next dose, skip the missed dose and resume your regular dosage schedule. Do not double the next dose.

STOPPING THE DRUG
Use this drug as prescribed for the full treatment period, even if you begin to feel better before the scheduled end of therapy.

PROLONGED USE
You should see your doctor regularly for tests and examinations if you take this drug for a prolonged period. The therapy may last for as long as 6 weeks.

PRECAUTIONS
Over 60: No special problems are expected.

Driving and Hazardous Work: The use of ophthalmic cromolyn should not impair your ability to perform such tasks safely.

Alcohol: No special precautions are necessary.

Pregnancy: Adequate human studies have not been completed. Before taking ophthalmic cromolyn, tell your doctor if you are pregnant or plan to become pregnant.

Breast Feeding: Ophthalmic cromolyn may pass into breast milk; caution is advised. Consult your doctor for specific advice.

Infants and Children: Use and dosage for infants and children under the age of 4 years must be determined by your doctor.

Special Concerns: To use the eye drops, first wash your hands. Tilt your head back. Gently apply pressure to the inside corner of the eyelid and with the index finger of the same hand, pull downward on the lower eyelid to make a space. Drop the medicine into this space and close your eye. Apply pressure for 1 or 2 minutes while keeping the eye closed without blinking. Then wash your hands again. Make sure the tip of the dropper does not touch your eye, finger, or any other surface. If your symptoms do not improve or if they become worse, check with your doctor.

OVERDOSE
Symptoms: No specific ones have been reported.

What to Do: An overdose of ophthalmic cromolyn is unlikely to be life-threatening. However, if someone takes a much larger dose of the drug than prescribed or accidentally ingests the medicine, call your doctor, emergency medical services (EMS), or the nearest poison control center.

DRUG INTERACTIONS
Other drugs may interact with ophthalmic cromolyn. Consult your doctor for specific advice if you are taking any other prescription or over-the-counter medication.

FOOD INTERACTIONS
No known food interactions.

DISEASE INTERACTIONS
Caution is advised when taking ophthalmic cromolyn. Consult your doctor if you have any other medical condition.

Cyclobenzaprine

Generic 10 mg
(**M**YLAN)

▶ Drug Class: Muscle relaxant

▶ Available in: Tablets

▶ Available OTC? No

▶ As Generic? Yes

Side Effects

SERIOUS
Unusual heartbeat (racing, pounding, or fluttering), confusion, seizures, hallucinations.

COMMON
Drowsiness, dry mouth, dizziness.

LESS COMMON
Fatigue or excessive tiredness, weakness, nausea, constipation, heartburn, unpleasant bitter or metallic taste in mouth, vision problems, headache, restlessness, nervousness, difficulty urinating, unusual bleeding or bruising.

PRINCIPAL USES
To relieve painful, temporary muscle stiffness and spasms. It is not used for stiffness and spasms due to serious, chronic illnesses of the nervous system and muscles, such as spinal cord injury or cerebral palsy.

HOW THE DRUG WORKS
Cyclobenzaprine appears to work by decreasing nerve impulses from the brain and spinal cord that lead to tensing or tightening of muscle fibers.

DOSAGE
Adults and teenagers 15 years of age and older: Usual dose is 10 mg, 3 times a day, which may be increased by your doctor to a maximum total dose of no more than 60 mg per day. Children and teenagers up to 15 years of age: Consult pediatrician.

ONSET OF EFFECT
Within 1 hour. The maximum effect may require 1 to 2 weeks of therapy.

DURATION OF ACTION
12 to 24 hours following a single dose.

DIETARY ADVICE
Dry mouth is a common complaint with muscle relaxants; maintain adequate fluid intake and suck on ice chips if desired.

STORAGE
Store in a tightly sealed container away from heat and direct light. Keep it away from moisture and extremes in temperature.

IF YOU MISS A DOSE
Take it as soon as you remember. If it is near the time for the next dose, skip the missed dose and resume your regular dosage schedule. Do not double the next dose.

STOPPING THE DRUG
You should take it as prescribed for the full treatment period, but you may stop if you are feeling better before the scheduled end of therapy.

PROLONGED USE
Therapy with cyclobenzaprine is usually completed within 14 to 21 days. Do not take cyclobenzaprine for a longer period without your doctor's approval. Muscle pain and stiffness that does not improve within 14 to 21 days may require a more thorough evaluation.

PRECAUTIONS
Over 60: Adverse reactions may be more likely and more severe in older patients.

Driving and Hazardous Work: The use of cyclobenzaprine may impair your ability to perform such tasks safely; use caution.

Alcohol: Avoid alcohol.

Pregnancy: Adequate studies of cyclobenzaprine use during pregnancy have not been done; discuss the relative risks and benefits with your doctor.

Breast Feeding: Cyclobenzaprine may pass into breast milk; caution is advised. Consult your doctor for advice.

Infants and Children: Cyclobenzaprine is not recommended for use by children under the age of 15.

Special Concerns: Cyclobenzaprine is not meant to be used as the only treatment for sore or stiff muscles. It should be accompanied by bed rest, physical therapy, and other measures to relieve discomfort, such as the application of heat or ice packs (as suggested by your physician).

OVERDOSE
Symptoms: Severe mental confusion, agitation, impaired concentration, difficulty walking or standing, dilated pupils, severe drowsiness, coma.

What to Do: Call emergency medical services (EMS), your doctor, or the nearest poison control center immediately.

DRUG INTERACTIONS
Consult your doctor for specific advice if you are taking sedatives, tranquilizers, or other medications that cause drowsiness (including alcohol); tricyclic antidepressants; or MAO inhibitors.

FOOD INTERACTIONS
No known food interactions.

DISEASE INTERACTIONS
Consult your doctor if you have a history of any of the following: glaucoma, difficult urination, prostate problems, heart disease, or overactive thyroid.

Cyclopentolate

BRAND NAMES
Ak-Pentolate, Cyclogyl,
Cylate, I-Pentolate,
Ocu-Pentolate, Pentolair,
Spectro-Pentolate

▶ Drug Class: Eye muscle
relaxant, pupil enlarger

▶ Available in: Ophthalmic
solution

▶ Available OTC? No

▶ As Generic? No

Side Effects

SERIOUS
If absorbed into the
bloodstream: Clumsiness or unsteadiness,
confusion or changes in
behavior, hallucinations,
slurred speech, rapid or
irregular pulse, flushing,
fever, unusual fatigue,
dizziness, unusually dry
skin, skin rash, dry
mouth; in infants,
abdominal swelling.
Seek medical assistance immediately.

COMMON
Eye irritation and redness
not present prior to treatment, swelling of the
eyelids, blurred vision,
increased sensitivity to
bright light.

LESS COMMON
There are no less-common side effects
associated with the
use of cyclopentolate.

PRINCIPAL USES
To dilate the pupils and
temporarily paralyze certain
structures within the eye.
This is useful in eye examinations to help determine
the proper prescription for
eyeglasses or for other diagnostic procedures involving
the eyes. It may also be
needed before or after eye
surgery.

HOW THE DRUG WORKS
Cyclopentolate relaxes the
ciliary muscle, which controls the shape of the eye's
lens as it focuses, and
another eye muscle called
the sphincter, which controls the narrowing and
widening of the pupil. Relaxation of these muscles prevents the lens from focusing
and widens the pupil. This
allows the doctor to view
the interior structures of
the eye during an ophthalmologic procedure. And, by
immobilizing the tiny structures within the eye, the
drug prevents scarring of
eye tissue and may alleviate
eye pain.

DOSAGE
1 to 2 drops, applied 3 times
a day or as needed as determined by your eye doctor.

ONSET OF EFFECT
Maximum effect occurs
within 25 to 75 minutes.

DURATION OF ACTION
8 hours, although some
effects may persist for up to
several days.

DIETARY ADVICE
No special restrictions.

STORAGE
Store in a tightly sealed container away from heat, moisture, and direct light. Do
not allow it to freeze.

IF YOU MISS A DOSE
Apply it as soon as you
remember. If it is near the
time for the next dose, skip
the missed dose and
resume your regular dosage
schedule. Do not double the
next dose.

STOPPING THE DRUG
The decision to stop taking
the drug should be made by
your ophthalmologist.

PROLONGED USE
Not recommended for long-term therapy.

PRECAUTIONS
Over 60: Adverse reactions
may be more likely and
more severe in older
patients.

**Driving and Hazardous
Work:** Do not drive or
engage in hazardous work
until you determine how the
medicine affects your
vision. Extreme caution
should be observed for
activities requiring sharp
vision for close objects (less
than an arm's length away).

Alcohol: No special precautions are necessary.

Pregnancy: Adequate studies have not been done.
Inform your doctor if you
are pregnant or are planning to become pregnant.

Breast Feeding: It is not
known if cyclopentolate
passes into breast milk; caution is advised. Consult your
doctor for specific advice.

Infants and Children:
Young children with blond
hair or blue eyes may be
more sensitive to the drug
and may have an increased
risk of side effects. Use
with extreme caution.
Infants should not eat for 4
hours following application
of drops.

Special Concerns: To use
the eye drops, first wash
your hands. Tilt your head
back. Gently apply pressure
to the inside corner of the
eyelid and with the index
finger of the same hand,
pull downward on the lower
eyelid to make a space.
Drop the medicine into this
space and close your eye.
Apply pressure for 1 or 2
minutes while keeping the
eye closed without blinking.
Then wash your hands
again. Make sure that the
tip of the dropper does not
touch your eye, finger, or
any other surface.

OVERDOSE
Symptoms: Drowsiness,
hallucinations, memory
problems, dry mouth, dry
skin, restlessness, palpitations, dizziness and disorientation, delirium.

What to Do: Call your
doctor, emergency medical
services (EMS), or the
nearest poison control center immediately.

DRUG INTERACTIONS
Consult your physician if
you are taking any other
prescription or over-the-counter drugs, especially
those designed for use in
the eyes.

FOOD INTERACTIONS
No known food interactions.

DISEASE INTERACTIONS
Consult your doctor if you
have a history of glaucoma,
Down's syndrome, or spastic paralysis.

Cyclophosphamide

Cytoxan 25 mg
(BRISTOL-MYERS SQUIBB)

▶ Drug Class: Antineoplastic (anticancer) agent; immuno-suppressant

▶ Available in: Tablets, liquid for injection

▶ Available OTC? No

▶ As Generic? No

Side Effects

SERIOUS
Shortness of breath, chest tightness, chest or abdominal pain, persistent cough or hoarseness, fever and chills, pain in the lower back or sides, painful or difficult urination, tiny bright red dots on the skin, unusual bleeding or bruising, breathing difficulty, blood in the urine or stool. Call your doctor immediately should any of these occur.

COMMON
Nausea and vomiting, loss of appetite and weight, temporary hair loss, increased susceptibility to infections, loss of hearing or ringing in the ears, sterility in men (usually temporary), unusual fatigue, increased pigmentation in skin and fingernails, dizziness, confusion.

LESS COMMON
Diarrhea, stomach upset, flushing, skin rash, itching, or hives, rapid heartbeat, swelling in the feet or lower legs.

PRINCIPAL USES
To treat a number of cancers, including malignant lymphoma, multiple myeloma, sarcoma, retinoblastoma, leukemia, breast cancer, and ovarian cancer. Cyclophosphamide is sometimes prescribed for other, noncancerous conditions, although this is done with extreme caution in light of the potentially serious side effects associated with this drug.

HOW THE DRUG WORKS
Cyclophosphamide kills cancer cells by interfering with the synthesis of their genetic material, which prevents the malignant cells from multiplying.

DOSAGE
Adults— Oral dose for cancer: 1 to 5 mg for every 2.2 lbs (1 kg) of body weight, once a day, for 5 to 7 days every month. Injection: 40 to 60 mg a day, in divided doses, for 2 to 5 days, depending on the type of cancer treated. This drug should never be administered intravenously without additional intravenous fluids. The dosage may vary considerably, depending on the patient, the disease, and whether any other drugs are being taken. Children— Consult your pediatric oncologist.

ONSET OF EFFECT
2 to 3 hours.

DURATION OF ACTION
Unknown.

DIETARY ADVICE
Take it on an empty stomach; may be taken with small amounts of food or milk if stomach irritation occurs. Be sure to drink plenty of fluids.

STORAGE
Store the tablets in a tightly sealed container away from heat and light.

IF YOU MISS A DOSE
Skip the missed dose and resume your regular dosage schedule. Do not double the next dose.

STOPPING THE DRUG
Continue taking this drug as prescribed, even if you experience side effects such as nausea and vomiting. The decision to stop taking the medication should be made by your doctor.

PROLONGED USE
Prolonged use is associated with an increased risk of adverse effects. Consult your doctor about the need for periodic medical tests and examinations.

PRECAUTIONS
Over 60: Side effects more common in older patients.

Driving and Hazardous Work: Avoid such activities until you determine how the medicine affects you.

Alcohol: Limit alcohol to moderate intake only.

Pregnancy: This drug can cause serious birth defects when taken by the mother or father. Use reliable birth control while taking this drug and for 4 months after therapy.

Breast Feeding: Use is not recommended while nursing.

Infants and Children: Cyclophosphamide can be used in children under close medical supervision.

Special Concerns: Watch for signs of infection, such as fever, sore throat, and fatigue. If your temperature rises above 100°F, call your doctor. To avoid urinary problems, drink a minimum of 3 quarts of water a day. Do not get vaccinated against bacteria or viruses while taking this drug.

OVERDOSE
Symptoms: Shortness of breath, palpitations, chest pain or discomfort, bloody urine, water retention, unusual weight gain, severe infection.

What to Do: Call emergency medical services (EMS) to receive evaluation and treatment in the closest emergency facility.

DRUG INTERACTIONS
Consult your doctor for specific advice if you are taking allopurinol or other gout medications, oral hypoglycemia drugs, clozapine, cyclosporine, digoxin or other antiarrhythmic drugs, other immunosuppressants, insulin, levamisole, lovastatin, phenobarbital, probenecid, sulfinpyrazone, or tiopronin.

FOOD INTERACTIONS
No known food interactions.

DISEASE INTERACTIONS
Consult your doctor if you have a recent history of chicken pox, shingles, gout, kidney stones, or infections. Use of this drug may cause complications in patients with liver or kidney disease, since these organs work together to remove the medication from the body.

Cycloserine

Seromycin 250 mg
(DURA)

▶ Drug Class: Anti-infective /antitubercular agent

▶ Available in: Capsules

▶ Available OTC? No

▶ As Generic? No

Side Effects

SERIOUS
Dizziness, drowsiness, changes in mental state, depression, anxiety, suicidal thoughts, psychosis, confusion, nightmares, speech difficulties, increased irritability, muscle twitches, increased restlessness, skin rash, seizures. Call your doctor immediately.

COMMON
Headache; numbness, burning pain, prickling, tingling, or weakness in the hands or feet.

LESS COMMON
Abnormal heart rhythm, liver disease (hepatitis).

PRINCIPAL USES
To treat active tuberculosis; used in conjunction with other antitubercular agents after use of the primary antitubercular agents, such as isoniazid, rifampin, ethambutol, pyrazinamide, and streptomycin, have proven ineffective.

HOW THE DRUG WORKS
Cycloserine kills tuberculosis bacteria by interfering with specific enzymes needed for the manufacture of cell walls.

DOSAGE
Adults and teenagers: To start, 250 mg every 12 hours for 2 weeks. If needed, your doctor may increase the dose to 250 mg every 6 to 8 hours; usually not more than 750 to 1,000 mg (6.8 mg per lb of body weight) a day. Children under age 12: 4.5 to 9 mg per lb per day. Cycloserine is taken in conjunction with other antitubercular agents. Vitamin B6 (pyridoxine) should also be taken (at least 100 mg a day) to prevent nerve damage.

ONSET OF EFFECT
Unknown.

DURATION OF ACTION
Unknown.

DIETARY ADVICE
This medication may be taken with liquid or food to minimize stomach irritation.

STORAGE
Store in a tightly sealed container away from heat, moisture, and direct light.

IF YOU MISS A DOSE
Take the drug as soon as you remember. This will help keep a constant level of medication in your system. If it is near the time for the next dose, skip the missed dose and resume your regular dosage schedule. Do not double the next dose.

STOPPING THE DRUG
Take it as prescribed for the full treatment period, even if you begin to feel better before the scheduled end of therapy. Treatment may continue for months or years. The decision to stop taking the drug should be made by your doctor.

PROLONGED USE
Consult your doctor about the need for having periodic medical examinations and laboratory tests.

PRECAUTIONS
Over 60: Adverse reactions may be more likely and more severe in older patients. Smaller doses for shorter treatment periods may be warranted.

Driving and Hazardous Work: Do not drive or engage in hazardous work until you determine how the medicine affects you.

Alcohol: Avoid alcohol.

Pregnancy: No problems have been reported. In any case, tell your doctor if you are pregnant or plan to become pregnant before taking cycloserine.

Breast Feeding: Cycloserine may pass into breast milk; caution is advised. Consult your doctor for specific advice.

Infants and Children: Adequate studies of the use of cycloserine by children have not been done. Consult your pediatrician for specific advice.

Special Concerns: Before taking cycloserine, tell your doctor if you are depressed or have severe anxiety. Persons with a seizure disorder should not take cycloserine.

OVERDOSE
Symptoms: Seizures, drowsiness, confusion, dizziness, headache, extreme irritability, joint pain, psychosis, numbness, tingling, or prickling sensation in the hands or feet.

What to Do: Call your doctor, emergency medical services (EMS), or the nearest poison control center immediately.

DRUG INTERACTIONS
Ethionamide may interact with cycloserine. Consult your doctor for specific advice if you are taking it. Also tell your doctor if you are taking any other prescription or over-the-counter medication.

FOOD INTERACTIONS
No known food interactions.

DISEASE INTERACTIONS
Use of cycloserine may cause complications in patients with kidney disease, since the kidneys play a major role in removing the medication from the body. Caution is advised when taking cycloserine. Consult your doctor if you have any of the following: a seizure disorder such as epilepsy; a history of alcohol abuse; mental depression; psychosis; or severe anxiety.

Cyclosporine

BRAND NAMES
Ciclosporin, Neoral,
Sandimmune

Sandimmune 25 mg
(**NOVARTIS**)

Additional photographs

▶ Drug Class: Immunosuppressant

▶ Available in: Capsules, oral solution, injection

▶ Available OTC? No

▶ As Generic? No

Side Effects

SERIOUS
Frequent urge to urinate; fever or chills; yellow-tinged eyes and skin caused by liver problems; abnormal bleeding; fatigue; high blood pressure. Call your doctor immediately. Psoriasis patients formerly treated with other types of therapy (for example, ultraviolet light or methotrexate) are at increased risk of skin cancer; report any new skin lesion to your doctor immediately.

COMMON
Headache, tremor, unusual hair growth on body and face, swelling or bleeding of gums.

LESS COMMON
Nausea, vomiting, diarrhea, acne or oily skin, sinus inflammation or infection, leg cramps, enlargement and tenderness of the breasts in males (gynecomastia).

PRINCIPAL USES
To slow down or reduce the natural tendency of the immune system to reject organ transplants. Also to treat severe rheumatoid arthritis or severe psoriasis that has not responded to other drug therapy.

HOW THE DRUG WORKS
Cyclosporine suppresses the functioning of the body's immune system. In this way it prevents the normal reaction against foreign substances or tissue that would otherwise cause the body to reject donor organs. Cyclosporine is also used to manage rheumatoid arthritis and psoriasis, as these disorders are classified as autoimmune diseases, that is, those in which the immune system inappropriately attacks healthy tissue.

DOSAGE
Your doctor will determine the correct dose based on a number of individual factors. During therapy, doses may be adjusted according to drug levels in the blood. The various brands of cyclosporine are not interchangeable; any changes in brand or dose should be made only by your doctor.

ONSET OF EFFECT
Unknown.

DURATION OF ACTION
Unknown.

DIETARY ADVICE
Cyclosporine can be taken with food to avoid stomach upset. The oral solution can be taken with orange juice in a glass container, served at room temperature. Do not take cyclosporine with grapefruit juice.

STORAGE
Store in a tightly sealed container away from heat and direct light. Do not store the oral solution in the refrigerator. Injection: Not applicable; injections are administered only at a health care facility.

IF YOU MISS A DOSE
Take it as soon as you remember, up to 12 hours late. However, if more than 12 hours have elapsed since the time for the missed dose, skip the missed dose and resume your regular dosage schedule. Do not double the next dose.

STOPPING THE DRUG
The decision to stop taking cyclosporine should be made by your doctor.

PROLONGED USE
Prolonged use of cyclosporine may impair kidney function. Periodic examinations and laboratory tests are required.

PRECAUTIONS
Over 60: The dose must be adjusted for a possible decline in kidney function in older patients.

Driving and Hazardous Work: Do not drive or engage in hazardous work until you determine how the medicine affects you.

Alcohol: Avoid alcohol.

Pregnancy: Cyclosporine has been shown to cause serious birth defects in animals. Adequate human studies have not been done. Avoid this drug during pregnancy unless it is clearly needed.

Breast Feeding: Cyclosporine passes into breast milk; avoid or discontinue use while nursing.

Infants and Children: Cyclosporine has not been shown to affect children differently than adults.

Special Concerns: Avoid any immunizations except those approved by your doctor. Do not use plastic or wax-lined cups to take this medicine. Maintain good dental hygiene; this medication can cause gum problems. Cyclosporine can make you more sensitive to sunlight. Limit exposure until you determine how the drug affects you.

OVERDOSE
Symptoms: Yellowish tinge to the skin or eyes (jaundice), lethargy, confusion, swelling of body tissues.

What to Do: Call your doctor, emergency medical services (EMS), or the nearest poison control center immediately.

DRUG INTERACTIONS
Do not take cyclosporine with the herb St. John's wort. Consult your doctor if you are taking androgens, cimetidine, danazol, diltiazem, diuretics, erythromycin, estrogens, other immunosuppressants, ketoconazole, statin (cholesterol-lowering) drugs, or virus vaccines. Many other drugs interact with cyclosporine. Consult your doctor before taking any new medicines, whether by prescription or over the counter.

FOOD INTERACTIONS
Do not take cyclosporine with grapefruit juice.

DISEASE INTERACTIONS
Consult your doctor if you have any of the following: chicken pox, shingles, high blood pressure, infection, a chronic gastrointestinal disorder, or a blood cell disorder. Use of cyclosporine may cause complications in patients with liver or kidney disease, since these organs work together to remove the drug from the body.

Cyclosporine Ophthalmic

BRAND NAME
Restasis

▶ Drug Class: Immunomodulator

▶ Available in: Ophthalmic emulsion in single-use vials

▶ Available OTC? No

▶ As Generic? No

Side Effects

SERIOUS
No serious side effects have been reported.

COMMON
Eye burning.

LESS COMMON
Increased redness of the eye, eye discharge, tearing, eye pain, foreign-body sensation, itching, stinging, and visual disturbance (most often blurring).

PRINCIPAL USES
To increase tear production in patients whose tear production is believed to be suppressed due to ocular inflammation associated with keratoconjunctivitis sicca surface—also known as Dry Eye Disease.

HOW THE DRUG WORKS
The exact mechanism of action is unknown, but it is believed to treat inflammation.

DOSAGE
One drop in each eye twice daily.

ONSET OF EFFECT
Unknown. No immediate improvement of symptoms should be expected.

DURATION OF ACTION
Unknown.

DIETARY ADVICE
No special restrictions.

STORAGE
Store at room temperature away from direct light. Do not store in refrigerator.

IF YOU MISS A DOSE
Apply the next dose as needed; do not double the next dose.

STOPPING THE DRUG
Consult your doctor.

PROLONGED USE
You should see your doctor regularly for tests and examinations if you take this drug for a prolonged period.

PRECAUTIONS
Over 60: No special problems are expected.

Driving and Hazardous Work: Do not drive or engage in hazardous work until you determine how the medicine affects your vision.

Alcohol: No special precautions.

Pregnancy: No problems are expected, but studies of effects in pregnancy have not been done in humans. Consult your physician.

Breast Feeding: It is not known whether cyclosporine passes into breast milk; caution is advised. Consult your doctor for specific advice about whether to use a different medicine or to stop breast feeding.

Infants and Children: Safety and effectiveness have not been established for children under 16 years of age.

Special Concerns: To use the eye drops, first wash your hands. Tilt your head back. Gently apply pressure to the inside corner of the eyelid and with the index finger of the same hand, pull downward on the lower eyelid to make a space. Drop the medicine into this space and close your eye. Then wash your hands again. Make sure the tip of the dropper does not touch your eye, finger, or any other surface. Wearing contact lenses is not recommended. Do not use opened vials.

OVERDOSE
Symptoms: No cases of overdose have been reported.

What to Do: An overdose is unlikely to occur; in case of accidental ingestion, call your doctor, emergency medical services (EMS), or the nearest poison control center right away.

DRUG INTERACTIONS
No drug interactions have been reported. Nonetheless, it is wise to consult your doctor before taking any other prescription or over-the-counter eye medication.

FOOD INTERACTIONS
No known food interactions.

DISEASE INTERACTIONS
Do not take cyclosporine if you have an active eye infection.

Cyproheptadine Hydrochloride

Generic 4 mg
(SIDMAK)

▶ Drug Class: Antihistamine; serotonin blocker

▶ Available in: Syrup, tablets

▶ Available OTC? No

▶ As Generic? Yes

Side Effects

SERIOUS
Confusion, hallucinations, convulsions, restlessness, blurred vision, fainting, unusual or irregular pulse, wheezing.

COMMON
Dry mouth, dry nose, drowsiness (often transient).

LESS COMMON
Difficult urination, dizziness, increased sensitivity to sunlight, rash, weight gain, unusual excitement, irritability, euphoria, or restlessness.

PRINCIPAL USES
To prevent or relieve symptoms of rhinitis (inflammation of the mucous membranes of the nasal passages, often associated with hay fever and other seasonal allergies); skin itching and hives; and tissue swelling (angioedema). Cyproheptadine is also used as an appetite stimulant in patients with anorexia nervosa and to treat vascular headaches.

HOW THE DRUG WORKS
Cyproheptadine blocks the effects of histamine, a naturally occurring substance within the body that causes swelling, itching, sneezing, watery eyes, hives, and other symptoms of allergic reaction. It also blocks the brain chemical serotonin, and so may stimulate appetite and relieve the symptoms of vascular headaches.

DOSAGE
Adults and children over age 14: 4 mg every 8 hours. The dose may gradually be increased by your doctor. Children ages 2 to 6: 2 mg every 8 to 12 hours. Children ages 6 to 14: 4 mg every 8 to 12 hours.

ONSET OF EFFECT
15 to 60 minutes.

DURATION OF ACTION
8 hours.

DIETARY ADVICE
Maintain your usual food and fluid intake. Increase fluid intake during persistent attacks, or if you have a fever or diarrhea.

STORAGE
Store in a tightly sealed container away from heat and direct light. Keep it away from moisture and extremes in temperature. Keep the liquid form of cyproheptadine refrigerated, but do not allow it to freeze.

IF YOU MISS A DOSE
Take it as soon as you remember. However, if it is near the time for the next dose, skip the missed dose and resume your regular dosage schedule. Do not double the next dose.

STOPPING THE DRUG
Take it as prescribed for the full treatment period, but you may stop if you are feeling better before the scheduled end of therapy.

PROLONGED USE
Therapy with cyproheptadine may require days or weeks, depending on the severity of your allergies. Side effects may be more likely with prolonged use.

PRECAUTIONS
Over 60: Adverse reactions may be more likely and more severe in older patients.

Driving and Hazardous Work: Because cyproheptadine may cause drowsiness, its use may impair your ability to perform hazardous tasks safely.

Alcohol: Avoid alcohol.

Pregnancy: Animal studies with high doses of cyproheptadine have found no birth defects. Human studies have not been done. Because the studies cannot rule out harm, the drug should be used during pregnancy only if it is clearly needed.

Breast Feeding: Cyproheptadine may pass into breast milk; caution is advised. Consult your doctor for advice.

Infants and Children: This drug is not recommended for use by children under 2 years of age.

Special Concerns: Children should be observed carefully for signs of side effects; they are more likely to develop serious complications from these medications, and younger children are often unable to describe changes in the way that they are feeling.

OVERDOSE
Symptoms: Hallucinations; convulsions; excitability or severe sedation; blurred vision; flushing or redness of skin; very dry, warm skin; wide, dilated pupils.

What to Do: Call your doctor, emergency medical services (EMS), or the nearest poison control center immediately.

DRUG INTERACTIONS
Consult your doctor for specific advice if you are taking medications containing alcohol or medications that may cause drowsiness such as barbiturates, sedatives, cough medicines, other antihistamines, psychiatric medications (especially MAO inhibitors), and prescription pain medications.

FOOD INTERACTIONS
No known food interactions.

DISEASE INTERACTIONS
Consult your doctor if you have glaucoma or other visual disorders, prostate problems, or other problems urinating.

Cysteamine Bitartrate

▶ Drug Class: Nephropathic cystinosis therapeutic agent

▶ Available in: Capsules

▶ Available OTC? No

▶ As Generic? No

Side Effects

SERIOUS

Loss of appetite, fever, abdominal pain, nausea or vomiting, drowsiness, diarrhea, skin rash, confusion, dizziness, sore throat, mental depression, trembling, headache. Call your doctor as soon as possible. Side effects are most common when cysteamine is first started. Symptoms may improve when the drug is temporarily stopped or the dose is reduced.

COMMON

No common side effects are associated with the use of cysteamine.

LESS COMMON

Constipation, bad breath.

PRINCIPAL USES

To treat the kidney-damaging form of cystinosis. People born without the ability to metabolize the amino acid cystine suffer from cystinosis, a rare inherited disorder characterized by the deposition and accumulation of cystine crystals throughout the body. These crystals cause considerable damage, particularly in the kidney. Kidney failure can occur by the age of 10 in untreated patients. Cysteamine prevents the accumulation of cystine crystals and is prescribed to prevent further kidney damage.

HOW THE DRUG WORKS

Cysteamine helps to convert cystine into less harmful chemical forms that can be removed from cells.

DOSAGE

Adults and teenagers weighing more than 110 pounds: To start, 500 mg a day. Over a period of 4 to 6 weeks, your doctor will gradually increase the dose to a total of 2,000 mg per day, taken in 4 divided doses. Children up to age 12: Dose depends on weight and body surface area. White blood cell counts and cystine levels should be measured every 3 months until the proper dose is determined.

ONSET OF EFFECT

Unknown.

DURATION OF ACTION

As long as it is taken.

DIETARY ADVICE

Children or people who have difficulty swallowing the capsules may open them and sprinkle the contents onto food. Your doctor will recommend dietary and nutritional adjustments should kidney failure develop.

STORAGE

Store in a tightly sealed container away from heat, moisture, and direct light.

IF YOU MISS A DOSE

Take it as soon as you remember, unless the time for your next scheduled dose is within the next 2 hours. If so, skip the missed dose and resume your regular dosage schedule. Do not double the next dose.

STOPPING THE DRUG

Continue to take the medicine as prescribed unless your doctor recommends that the dose be reduced or the drug be discontinued.

PROLONGED USE

Lifelong therapy with cysteamine bitartrate may be necessary.

PRECAUTIONS

Over 60: No studies specifically on older patients have been done.

Driving and Hazardous Work: Do not drive or engage in hazardous work until you determine how the medicine affects you.

Alcohol: Avoid alcohol.

Pregnancy: Adequate human studies have not been done. Before taking cysteamine, tell your physician if you are pregnant or are planning to become pregnant.

Breast Feeding: It is not known whether cysteamine passes into breast milk; caution is advised. Consult your doctor for specific advice.

Infants and Children: Treatment should be started as soon as diagnosis of cystinosis is made. Your pediatrician will determine the size and frequency of the dose.

Special Concerns: If you vomit your dose of cysteamine within 20 minutes of taking it, take the dose again. If you vomit again, do not repeat the dose. Wait until your next scheduled dose. If you vomit 20 minutes after taking the dose, do not repeat the dose.

OVERDOSE

Symptoms: An overdose is unlikely to occur or to be life-threatening.

What to Do: If you have any reason to suspect an overdose, call your doctor, emergency medical services (EMS), or the nearest poison control center.

DRUG INTERACTIONS

No drug interactions have been reported.

FOOD INTERACTIONS

No known food interactions.

DISEASE INTERACTIONS

The dose of cysteamine may need to be adjusted for patients with a medical history of seizures, blood problems, or any form of kidney disease.

Dacarbazine

BRAND NAME
DTIC-Dome

▶ Drug Class: Antineoplastic (anticancer) agent

▶ Available in: Injection

▶ Available OTC? No

▶ As Generic? Yes

Side Effects

SERIOUS
Black, tarry, or bloody stools; blood-tinged (pink or maroon) urine; cough or hoarseness; fever; chills; lower back pain or pain in flanks; painful, difficult urination; tiny bright red spots on skin; bleeding from gums, nose, or other unusual places; easy bruising; shortness of breath. These side effects may mean that normal blood cells and special blood-clotting cells have been affected, or that normal immune cells have been affected and an infection is developing somewhere in your body. Contact your doctor immediately if any of these occur.

COMMON
Nausea, vomiting, weakness, loss of appetite. If pain or redness occurs at the injection site while dacarbazine is being administered, tell your physician or nurse immediately.

LESS COMMON
Flushing; unusual numbness or tingling of the face; flu-like symptoms (including muscle aches, fever, and joint pain) usually occurring about 7 days after treatment begins.

PRINCIPAL USES
Dacarbazine is used for treatment of malignant melanoma (a type of skin cancer), Hodgkin's disease (a type of lymph node cancer), and occasionally sarcomas (uncommon cancers of the soft tissues).

HOW THE DRUG WORKS
Dacarbazine kills cancer cells by interfering with the synthesis of their genetic material, which prevents the cells from reproducing.

DOSAGE
The dose of dacarbazine depends on the type of tumor, patient weight, and whether other chemotherapy medicines are being used. Your oncologist (cancer specialist) will determine the proper dose.

ONSET OF EFFECT
Immediately after injection.

DURATION OF ACTION
Unknown.

DIETARY ADVICE
Maintain optimal food and fluid intake. Calorie, protein, and vitamin needs increase in patients with cancer. Good nutrition is essential to cope with the demands of chemotherapy.

STORAGE
Refrigerate, but do not allow it to freeze.

IF YOU MISS A DOSE
Inform your oncologist if you miss a dose. Adjustments will be made depending on the other chemotherapy you receive.

STOPPING THE DRUG
The decision to stop dacarbazine must be made in consultation with your physician.

PROLONGED USE
Use beyond 5 to 10 days out of every 28 days in a chemotherapy cycle is not recommended.

PRECAUTIONS
Over 60: Adverse reactions may be more likely and more severe in older patients.

Driving and Hazardous Work: The use of dacarbazine with other chemotherapy agents may impair your ability to perform such tasks safely.

Alcohol: Limit alcohol to moderate intake only.

Pregnancy: The use of chemotherapy during pregnancy could cause birth defects or fetal death. A reliable method of contraception is recommended while using this drug.

Breast Feeding: Dacarbazine passes into breast milk; you should avoid or discontinue use while breast feeding.

Infants and Children: Consult your pediatric oncologist.

Special Concerns: Dacarbazine may lower your ability to resist infection by reducing the number of white blood cells in the blood. Therefore, do not get vaccinated against bacteria or viruses without your doctor's approval. Avoid people with infections. Use care when shaving, trimming nails, or using sharp objects. Inform your doctor immediately if you have fever, chills, unusual bleeding or bruising, diarrhea, or a cough.

OVERDOSE
Symptoms: No specific information is available.

What to Do: If you are concerned about the possibility of an overdose of dacarbazine, call emergency medical services (EMS) to receive evaluation and treatment in the closest emergency facility.

DRUG INTERACTIONS
Consult your doctor if you are taking aspirin, ibuprofen, phenobarbital, phenytoin, amphotericin B, thyroid medications, azathioprine, chloramphenicol, colchicine, flucytosine, ganciclovir, interferon, plicamycin, or zidovudine.

FOOD INTERACTIONS
No known food interactions.

DISEASE INTERACTIONS
Consult your doctor if you have any of the following problems: chicken pox (or possible recent exposure to it), shingles, other infections elsewhere in your body, or kidney, liver, or lung disease.

Dalteparin Sodium

▶ Drug Class: Anticoagulant

▶ Available in: Injection

▶ Available OTC? No

▶ As Generic? No

Side Effects

SERIOUS
Easy or unusual bruising or bleeding, especially from the nose and gums, passage of black and tarry stools, vomiting or coughing of bright red blood, unusual weakness, dizziness.

COMMON
Pain or bruising at site of needle injection.

LESS COMMON
Shortness of breath, wheezing, breathing difficulty, confusion, hives, itching, rash, abdominal pain, facial swelling, sweating, weakness, lightheadedness (symptoms of anaphylaxis, a severe allergic reaction).

PRINCIPAL USES
To prevent or inhibit the formation of potentially dangerous blood clots within a blood vessel. Dalteparin is usually prescribed before major surgery, especially for prolonged operations that require general anesthesia. Those most likely to require the drug include patients who are over 40 years old, obese, immobile, suffering from a chronic debilitating disease, or who have had problems in the past with blood clots or who have a history of cancer.

HOW THE DRUG WORKS
Blood clotting (coagulation) is controlled by the interaction of many specialized proteins called coagulation factors. Dalteparin interferes with the normal functioning of several coagulation factors, thereby reducing the risk that a clot will form within a blood vessel. Anticoagulants such as dalteparin are often referred to as blood thinners.

DOSAGE
Adults: 2,500 international units injected under the skin once daily, beginning 1 to 2 hours prior to surgery, and continuing for 5 to 10 days afterward.

ONSET OF EFFECT
Rapid; within minutes.

DURATION OF ACTION
Therapeutic effect will persist for approximately 24 hours.

DIETARY ADVICE
Follow all of your doctor's dietary recommendations and other instructions carefully. Patients recovering from surgery require increased quantities of carbohydrates and proteins.

STORAGE
Not applicable; the dose is administered only at a health care facility.

IF YOU MISS A DOSE
Hospital personnel will ensure that you are administered this medication on schedule, once daily.

STOPPING THE DRUG
The decision to stop taking the drug should be made by your doctor.

PROLONGED USE
Therapy with this medication is usually concluded within 5 to 10 days. Prolonged use may increase the risk of undesirable side effects.

PRECAUTIONS
Over 60: Adverse reactions may be more likely and more severe in older patients.

Driving and Hazardous Work: Consult your doctor regarding the advisability of driving and performing hazardous work while taking an anticoagulant.

Alcohol: No special precautions are necessary.

Pregnancy: Adequate studies of the use of dalteparin during pregnancy have not been done; the drug should be used only if it is determined that benefits clearly outweigh potential risks. One form of dalteparin contains benzyl alcohol; this should not be used in pregnant women.

Breast Feeding: Dalteparin may pass into breast milk; caution is advised. Consult your doctor for specific advice.

Infants and Children: This drug is not recommended for use by children.

Special Concerns: Used properly, dalteparin prevents undesirable blood clots without seriously disrupting your ability to stop bleeding following minor injuries, scrapes, and bruises. Before taking this medication, be sure to inform your doctor if you have had any problem with unusual bleeding in the past. Occasionally, bleeding may occur internally and not be visible; primary symptoms are dizziness or weakness, especially when moving about or changing position. Keep in mind that such symptoms may occur following surgery for many reasons (use of pain medications or other drugs, or prolonged bed rest). It is important to tell your doctor about any changes in the way you are feeling during recovery period.

OVERDOSE
Symptoms: Unusual or uncontrolled bleeding, unusual bruising, weakness, or dizziness.

What to Do: Discontinue use and inform hospital personnel immediately.

DRUG INTERACTIONS
Consult your doctor if you are taking aspirin or other blood thinners.

FOOD INTERACTIONS
No known food interactions.

DISEASE INTERACTIONS
Caution is advised when taking dalteparin. Consult your doctor if you have allergies to pork or pork products, unusual bleeding or bruising, peptic ulcer, or high blood pressure, or if you have had recent surgery.

Danazol

Danocrine 200 mg
(SANOFI WINTHROP)

▶ Drug Class: Gonadotropin inhibitor

▶ Available in: Capsules

▶ Available OTC? No

▶ As Generic? Yes

Side Effects

SERIOUS
Yellow tinge in the eyes or skin (jaundice); headache, which may be accompanied by nausea, vomiting, and changes in vision; severe abdominal pain; fatigue; skin rashes, which may be extensive and involve the inside of the mouth and nose; unusual nosebleeds, vaginal bleeding, bleeding from gums, or other bruising and bleeding.

COMMON
Cessation of menstruation, irregular or unpredictable vaginal bleeding or spotting, decreased breast size, weight gain, edema (swelling due to fluid retention), flushing, sweating, vaginal dryness, acne.

LESS COMMON
Cataracts; pain or tingling in fingers; increased sensitivity to sunlight; increase in body hair; enlargement of clitoris; hoarseness, sore throat, or deepening of voice.

PRINCIPAL USES
Danazol is used to treat endometriosis, fibrocystic breast disease, and an uncommon condition called hereditary angioedema, which causes abnormal swelling of body tissues.

HOW THE DRUG WORKS
Danazol blocks the production of the hormone estrogen by the ovaries. Without estrogen, endometrial tissue (the uterine lining) shrinks and becomes inactive. Subsequently, menstrual cycles cease, as do the hormone-related flare-ups of endometriosis and fibrocystic breast disease.

DOSAGE
Endometriosis: 100 to 400 mg, 2 times a day, beginning on the first day of menstrual flow. Treatment may take up to 6 months. Fibrocystic breast disease: 50 to 200 mg, 2 times a day, beginning on the first day of menstrual flow. Angioedema: 200 mg, 2 or 3 times a day. Increase in dosage may be necessary depending on results.

ONSET OF EFFECT
The full effect of danazol may take months to occur.

DURATION OF ACTION
Menstrual cycles return within 60 to 90 days after stopping danazol; breast discomfort due to fibrocystic disease may return within one year.

DIETARY ADVICE
Maintain your usual food and fluid intake. Increase fluids if you have a fever or diarrhea.

STORAGE
Store in a tightly sealed container away from heat and direct light. Keep away from moisture and extremes in temperature.

IF YOU MISS A DOSE
Take it as soon as you remember. If it is near the time for the next dose, skip the missed dose and resume your regular dosage schedule. Do not double the next dose.

STOPPING THE DRUG
Take danazol as prescribed for the full treatment period, even if you begin to feel better before the scheduled end of therapy.

PROLONGED USE
Therapy with danazol is usually completed within 3 to 6 months, although it may be extended to 9 months if necessary. Prolonged use may be associated with an increased risk of side effects.

PRECAUTIONS
Over 60: Adverse reactions may be more likely and more severe in older patients.

Driving and Hazardous Work: Do not drive or engage in hazardous work until you determine how the medicine affects you.

Alcohol: Drink alcohol only in moderation.

Pregnancy: Do not use danazol if you are pregnant.

Breast Feeding: Danazol must be avoided by women who are nursing.

Infants and Children: Danazol is not recommended for use by children.

Special Concerns: An effective method of contraception other than birth control pills (such as condoms or other barrier methods) should be used while taking danazol. Exposure of a fetus to danazol may lead to severe deformities. Be sure to report any unusual headache or change in vision to your physician. Some patients are treated successfully with one course of danazol; others require further treatments.

OVERDOSE
Symptoms: No specific ones have been reported.

What to Do: An overdose of danazol is unlikely to be life-threatening. However, if someone takes a much larger dose than prescribed, call your doctor, emergency medical services (EMS), or the nearest poison control center immediately.

DRUG INTERACTIONS
Consult your doctor for advice if you are taking anticoagulants (blood thinners).

FOOD INTERACTIONS
No known food interactions.

DISEASE INTERACTIONS
Consult your doctor if you have any of the following: heart or kidney disease; epilepsy or other seizure disorders; headaches, especially migraines; or any unexplained vaginal bleeding. Such conditions must be evaluated before starting danazol.

Dantrolene Sodium

Dantrium 100 mg
(P&GP)

▶ Drug Class: Muscle relaxant

▶ Available in: Capsules, injection

▶ Available OTC? No

▶ As Generic? No

Side Effects

—SERIOUS
Seizures, yellowish tinge to eyes and skin (indicating serious liver inflammation), difficulty breathing caused by fluid in the lungs, unusual bleeding, blood in urine or stools, fever, severe diarrhea, weakness, rash, itching, hives. Call your doctor immediately.

—COMMON
Muscle weakness, drowsiness, dizziness, headaches.

—LESS COMMON
Nervousness, confusion, insomnia, hallucinations, rapid or irregular heartbeat, watery eyes, blood pressure changes, double vision, weight loss, constipation, cramps, difficulty swallowing, frequent urination, sensitivity to sunlight, sweating, unusual hair growth, muscle pain, chills.

PRINCIPAL USES
To control recurrent muscle spasms and cramps, which may occur in association with multiple sclerosis, cerebral palsy, stroke, spinal cord injury, and other conditions. Dantrolene is sometimes used to prevent or control extremely high body temperature (malignant hyperthermia).

HOW THE DRUG WORKS
Calcium is necessary for muscle contraction; dantrolene directly interferes with the release of calcium in skeletal muscle tissue and thereby inhibits muscle cramping and spasms.

DOSAGE
For muscle spasms—
Adults: 25 mg once a day to start, increased in 25 mg increments to 100 mg, 2 to 4 times a day, to a maximum of 400 mg a day. Children: 0.5 mg for each 2.2 lbs (1 kg) of body weight, 2 times a day to start; may be increased to a maximum of 100 mg, 4 times a day. For malignant hyperthermia: 4 to 8 mg for each 2.2 lbs of body weight in 3 or 4 doses a day.

ONSET OF EFFECT
1 to 2 weeks.

DURATION OF ACTION
Up to 24 hours.

DIETARY ADVICE
Capsules should be swallowed with milk or meals to prevent stomach upset.

STORAGE
Store in a tightly sealed container in a dry place away from heat and direct light.

IF YOU MISS A DOSE
Take it if you remember within 2 hours. Otherwise, skip the missed dose and resume your regular dosage schedule. Do not double the next dose.

STOPPING THE DRUG
The decision to stop taking the drug should be made by your doctor. Gradual reduction of the dose may be necessary if you have taken the drug for a long time.

PROLONGED USE
Tests that should be conducted periodically during prolonged use include blood counts, liver function studies, and G6PD tests.

PRECAUTIONS
Over 60: Adverse reactions may be more likely and more severe.

Driving and Hazardous Work: Avoid such activites until you determine how the medicine affects you.

Alcohol: Avoid alcohol while taking this drug.

Pregnancy: Dantrolene has not been shown to cause birth defects in humans. Consult your doctor about its use during pregnancy.

Breast Feeding: Dantrolene passes into breast milk; avoid or discontinue use while nursing.

Infants and Children: This drug should be used in children only under close medical supervision.

Special Concerns: You may have trouble swallowing while taking dantrolene; take care to avoid choking. Follow your doctor's advice regarding rest and physical therapy.

OVERDOSE
Symptoms: Bloody urine, chest pains, shortness of breath, convulsions, loss of consciousness.

What to Do: Call your doctor, emergency medical services (EMS), or the nearest poison control center immediately.

DRUG INTERACTIONS
Consult your doctor for specific advice if you are taking acetaminophen, amiodarone, anabolic steroids, androgens, medicines for infections, antithyroid agents, calcium channel blockers (verapamil in particular), carbamazepine, central nervous system depressants, chloroquine, daunorubicin, disulfiram, divalproex, estrogens, etretinate, gold salts, hydroxychloroquine, mercaptopurine, methotrexate, methyldopa, naltrexone, oral contraceptives, phenothiazines, phenytoin, plicamycin, tricyclic antidepressants, or valproic acid.

FOOD INTERACTIONS
No known food interactions.

DISEASE INTERACTIONS
Caution is advised when taking dantrolene. Consult your doctor if you have any of the following: emphysema, asthma, bronchitis, another chronic lung disease, heart disease, or liver disease.

Delavirdine

BRAND NAME
Rescriptor

▶ Drug Class: Antiviral

▶ Available in: Tablets

▶ Available OTC? No

▶ As Generic? No

Side Effects

SERIOUS
Severe skin rash, fever, blistering, mouth sores, muscle or joint aches. Stop taking the medication and call your doctor immediately.

COMMON
Skin rash.

LESS COMMON
Abdominal cramps or pain, back or chest pain, chills, fatigue, lethargy, stiff neck, rapid breathing, migraine headache, fainting, loss of appetite, unusual gain or loss of weight, blood in stools, constipation or diarrhea, loss of appetite, gas, increased thirst, swollen or ulcerated tongue, leg cramps, swollen arms or legs, loss of coordination, amnesia, anxiety, decreased sexual function, depression, disorientation, dizziness, hallucinations, impaired concentration, insomnia, nightmares, restlessness, tremor, cough, breathing difficulty, hair loss, dry eyes, ear pain, ringing in ears, flank pain, blood in urine.

PRINCIPAL USES
To treat HIV infection in combination with other drugs. While not a cure for HIV, it may suppress the replication of the virus and delay the progression of the disease.

HOW THE DRUG WORKS
Delavirdine interferes with the activity of enzymes needed for the replication of DNA in viral cells, thus preventing the human immunodeficiency virus (HIV) from reproducing.

DOSAGE
400 mg, 3 times a day. The tablets can be dissolved in water before being administered. Rinse the glass and drink the rinse water to be sure that the entire dose has been taken.

ONSET OF EFFECT
Unknown. With most antiretroviral drugs, an early response can be seen within the first few days of therapy, but the maximum effect may take 12 to 16 weeks.

DURATION OF ACTION
Unknown. Effects of the drug may be prolonged if delavirdine is used in combination with other effective drugs and the virus is maximally suppressed.

DIETARY ADVICE
No special restrictions.

STORAGE
Store in a tightly sealed container away from heat and direct light.

IF YOU MISS A DOSE
Take it as soon as you remember. If it is near the time for the next dose, skip the missed dose and resume your regular dosage schedule. Do not double the next dose.

STOPPING THE DRUG
Take delavirdine every day, as prescribed. The decision to stop taking the drug should be made in consultation with your doctor.

PROLONGED USE
See your doctor regularly for tests and examinations for the duration of therapy.

PRECAUTIONS
Over 60: A lower dose may be advised for older patients.

Driving and Hazardous Work: Do not drive or engage in hazardous work until you determine how the medicine affects you.

Alcohol: Avoid alcohol if liver function is impaired.

Pregnancy: Delavirdine has been shown to cause birth defects in animals. Nevertheless, it is increasingly being used with other antiretroviral drugs to treat pregnant HIV-infected women.

Breast Feeding: It is not known whether delavirdine passes into breast milk; however, women infected with HIV should not breast-feed, to avoid transmitting the virus to an uninfected child.

Infants and Children: Safety and effectiveness of the use of this drug in children under 16 have not been established.

Special Concerns: Use of delavirdine does not eliminate the risk of passing the AIDS virus to other persons. Be sure to take appropriate preventive measures.

OVERDOSE
Symptoms: No cases of overdose have been reported.

What to Do: An overdose is unlikely to occur. Nonetheless, if you have any reason to suspect an overdose, seek medical assistance right away.

DRUG INTERACTIONS
Some drugs, when combined with delavirdine, may cause severe liver damage and so should not be taken. These drugs include certain nonsedating antihistamines, sedative hypnotic drugs, calcium channel blockers, ergot alkaloid preparations, and amphetamines. Other drugs may interact with delavirdine, requiring changes in your drug regimen; consult your doctor for specific advice if you are taking any other prescription or over-the-counter medication, especially antacids, clarithromycin, fluoxetine, ketoconazole, phenytoin, phenobarbital, carbamazepine, rifabutin, rifampin, cimetidine, famotidine, nizatidine, ranitidine, didanosine, indinavir, ritonavir, nelfinavir, or saquinavir.

FOOD INTERACTIONS
No known food interactions.

DISEASE INTERACTIONS
No disease interactions have been reported.

Desipramine Hydrochloride

SL

Generic 25 mg
(SIDMAK)

Additional photographs

▶ Drug Class: Tricyclic antidepressant

▶ Available in: Tablets

▶ Available OTC? No

▶ As Generic? Yes

Side Effects

SERIOUS
Confusion, heartbeat irregularities, hallucinations, seizures, extreme fatigue or drowsiness, blurred or altered vision, breathing difficulty, constipation, impaired concentration, difficult urination, fever, extreme and persistent restlessness, loss of coordination and balance, difficulty swallowing or speaking, dilated pupils, eye pain, fainting. Also trembling, shaking, weakness, and stiffness in the extremities; shuffling gait. Call your doctor immediately.

COMMON
Drowsiness or dizziness, headache, dry mouth or unpleasant taste, fatigue, heightened sensitivity to light, weight gain, nausea, increased appetite.

LESS COMMON
Heartburn, difficulty sleeping, diarrhea, sweating, vomiting.

PRINCIPAL USES
To relieve symptoms of major depression.

HOW THE DRUG WORKS
Desipramine affects levels of norepinephrine, a brain chemical that is thought to be linked to mood, emotions, and mental state.

DOSAGE
Adults: 100 to 200 mg once a day; may be increased to 300 mg a day. Older adults: 25 to 50 mg a day; may be increased to 150 mg a day.

ONSET OF EFFECT
1 to 6 weeks.

DURATION OF ACTION
Unknown.

DIETARY ADVICE
To lessen stomach upset, take with food, unless your doctor instructs otherwise. Increase your intake of fiber and fluids.

STORAGE
Store in a tightly sealed container away from heat, moisture, and direct light.

IF YOU MISS A DOSE
If you take a one-time daily bedtime dose, do not take the missed dose in the morning because it may cause drowsiness. Call your doctor. If you take more than 1 dose a day, take it as soon as you remember. If it is near the time for the next dose, skip the missed dose and resume your regular dosage schedule. Do not double the next dose.

STOPPING THE DRUG
Take it as prescribed for the full treatment period, even if you begin to feel better before the scheduled end of therapy. The decision to stop taking desipramine should be made in consultation with your doctor. The dosage should be tapered gradually over a period of 5 to 7 days when stopping treatment.

PROLONGED USE
Usual course of therapy lasts 6 months to 1 year; some patients may benefit from additional therapy.

PRECAUTIONS
Over 60: Adverse reactions may be more likely and more severe in older patients. A lower dose may be warranted.

Driving and Hazardous Work: Use caution when driving or engaging in hazardous work until you determine how the medication affects you. Drowsiness or lightheadedness can occur.

Alcohol: Avoid alcohol.

Pregnancy: Adequate studies have not been done. Consult your doctor for specific advice.

Breast Feeding: Desipramine passes into breast milk; do not use it while nursing.

Infants and Children: Not prescribed for children under age 16. Should not be prescribed for children, as unexplained deaths have occurred.

Special Concerns: This is a potentially dangerous drug, especially if taken in excess. Tricyclic antidepressants should not be within easy reach of suicidal patients.

OVERDOSE
Symptoms: Difficulty breathing, severe fatigue, seizures, confusion, hallucinations, distractibility, dilated pupils, irregular heartbeat, fever.

What to Do: Call your doctor, emergency medical services (EMS), or the nearest poison control center immediately.

DRUG INTERACTIONS
Consult your doctor for specific advice if you are taking antithyroid agents, cimetidine, clonidine, guanadrel, guanethidine, metrizamide, appetite suppressants, isoproterenol, ephedrine, epinephrine, amphetamines, phenylephrine, antipsychotic drugs, pimozide, methyldopa, metyrosine, metoclopramide, pemoline, promethazine, trimeprazine, rauwolfia alkaloids, MAO inhibitors, or any drugs that depress the central nervous system.

FOOD INTERACTIONS
No known food interactions.

DISEASE INTERACTIONS
Consult your doctor if you have any of the following: a history of alcohol abuse, difficulty urinating, asthma, bipolar disorder, high blood pressure, stomach or intestinal problems, glaucoma, overactive thyroid, enlarged prostate, schizophrenia, seizures, a blood disorder, or kidney, heart, or liver disease.

Desloratadine

BRAND NAME
Clarinex

- ▶ Drug Class: Antihistamine
- ▶ Available in: Tablets, sublinguinal tablets
- ▶ Available OTC? No
- ▶ As Generic? No

Side Effects

SERIOUS
No serious side effects are associated with the use of desloratadine.

COMMON
No common side effects are associated with the use of desloratadine.

LESS COMMON
In rare cases adverse reactions have been reported in persons taking desloratadine, but none of these reactions is clearly linked to use of the drug.

PRINCIPAL USES
To prevent or relieve symptoms of hay fever and other allergies, such as watery or itchy eyes, runny nose, sneezing, or itchy skin. Desloratadine is also used sometimes to treat chronic (persistent) hives.

HOW THE DRUG WORKS
Desloratadine blocks the effects of histamine, a naturally occurring substance that causes swelling, itching, sneezing, watery eyes, hives, and other symptoms of allergic reaction.

DOSAGE
Adults and children age 12 and older: 5 mg once a day. Do not increase the dose in an attempt to achieve quicker relief of symptoms.

ONSET OF EFFECT
Within 1 hour.

DURATION OF ACTION
24 hours or more.

DIETARY ADVICE
Desloratadine can be taken without regard to diet.

STORAGE
Store in a tightly sealed container at room temperature, away from heat, moisture, and direct light. Reditabs should be placed on the tongue immediately after opening blister pack.

IF YOU MISS A DOSE
Take it as soon as you remember. However, if it is near the time for the next dose, skip the missed dose and resume your regular dosage schedule. Do not double the next dose.

STOPPING THE DRUG
The decision to stop taking the drug should be made in consultation with your physician.

PROLONGED USE
Desloratadine can be taken safely for prolonged periods. Long-term use is not associated with decreased effectiveness of the drug (a problem with certain allergy medications and other drugs).

PRECAUTIONS
Over 60: Adverse reactions may be more likely and more severe in older patients.

Driving and Hazardous Work: The use of desloratadine, at recommended doses, should not impair your ability to perform such tasks safely.

Alcohol: No special precautions are necessary.

Pregnancy: Before you take desloratadine, tell your doctor if you are pregnant or plan to become pregnant.

Breast Feeding: Desloratadine passes into breast milk; avoid or discontinue use while nursing.

Infants and Children: Adverse reactions may be more likely and more severe in children.

Special Concerns: Stop taking desloratadine 4 to 7 days before you have an allergy skin test.

OVERDOSE
Symptoms: Rapid heartbeat, headache, drowsiness.

What to Do: An overdose of desloratadine is unlikely to be life-threatening. However, if someone takes a much larger dose than prescribed, call your doctor, emergency medical services (EMS), or the nearest poison control center.

DRUG INTERACTIONS
Consult your doctor for advice if you are taking clarithromycin, erythromycin, troleandomycin, itraconazole, or ketoconazole.

FOOD INTERACTIONS
There are no known interactions between desloratadine and specific foods.

DISEASE INTERACTIONS
There are no known disease interactions.

Desmopressin Acetate

BRAND NAMES
DDAVP, Stimate

▶ Drug Class: Antidiuretic; antihemorrhagic

▶ Available in: Injection, nasal solution, tablets

▶ Available OTC? No

▶ As Generic? Yes

Side Effects

SERIOUS
Rare severe allergic reaction (skin rash, itching, wheezing, swelling of lips, tongue, and throat). In some cases water intoxication may occur, causing lethargy, nausea, vomiting, mental impairment, and in severe cases seizures or coma. Seek medical attention immediately.

COMMON
No common side effects are associated with the use of desmopressin.

LESS COMMON
Headache, flushing, nausea, abdominal cramps, and slight rise in blood pressure. Such symptoms are generally associated with excessive doses.

PRINCIPAL USES
To treat diabetes insipidus, a relatively rare disorder characterized by excessive loss of water in the urine. Desmopressin is also used to help manage nighttime bedwetting. It may also be used to increase blood plasma levels of factor VIII, a crucial protein needed for clot formation. A deficiency of factor VIII may result in uncontrolled bleeding, the primary feature of hemophilia and a related disorder known as von Willebrand's disease type 1.

HOW THE DRUG WORKS
Desmopressin simulates the action of the hormone vasopressin, which helps the kidneys reabsorb water from urine, thus maintaining proper fluid balance. It also helps to boost plasma levels of factor VIII.

DOSAGE
For diabetes insipidus— Injection: 2 to 4 mg, 1 or 2 times a day. Nasal solution: 1 to 2 sprays per day. Tablets: 0.1 to 0.8 mg, 2 times a day in divided doses. For bedwetting in patients age 6 and over— Tablets: 0.2 mg at bedtime. May be increased to 0.6 mg. For von Willebrand's type 1— Injection: 0.3 mg per 2.2 lbs (1 kg) of body weight per day, administered over 15 to 30 minutes. Lowest effective dose will be determined by the doctor based on the patient's response to the drug.

ONSET OF EFFECT
Within 1 hour.

DURATION OF ACTION
Injection or nasal spray: 12 to 24 hours. Tablets: Approximately 8 hours.

DIETARY ADVICE
Take it with or between meals.

STORAGE
Keep nasal or injectable forms refrigerated, but do not allow them to freeze. When traveling, these forms remain stable at room temperature for up to 3 weeks. Keep tablets at room temperature, away from heat and direct light.

IF YOU MISS A DOSE
Take it as soon as you remember. If it is near the time for the next dose, skip the missed dose and resume your regular dosage schedule. Do not double the next dose.

STOPPING THE DRUG
The decision to stop taking the drug should be made by your doctor.

PROLONGED USE
No apparent problems with prolonged use of this drug.

PRECAUTIONS
Over 60: Adverse reactions may be more likely and more severe in older patients.

Driving and Hazardous Work: Do not drive or engage in hazardous work until you determine how the medication affects you.

Alcohol: Drink alcohol only in moderation.

Pregnancy: Desmopressin has not been shown to cause birth defects in animals. While no adequate studies have been done in humans, the drug is presumed to be safe.

Breast Feeding: Desmopressin has not been shown to cause problems in nursing babies. Consult your doctor about its use if you are breast feeding.

Infants and Children: Adverse reactions may be more likely and more severe in children under the age of 18.

Special Concerns: Periodic laboratory tests are needed to check your fluid status. Desmopressin tablets used for bedwetting may be taken alone or in conjunction with other kinds of non-medical therapy such as behavioral conditioning.

OVERDOSE
Symptoms: Drowsiness, listlessness, headache, confusion, inability to urinate, unexpected weight gain or fluid retention.

What to Do: An overdose of desmopressin is unlikely to be life-threatening but can cause water intoxication (leading to symptoms above) and spasm of the blood vessels. If someone takes a much larger dose than prescribed, call your doctor, emergency medical services (EMS), or poison control center immediately.

DRUG INTERACTIONS
Large doses of desmopressin should be used with other "pressor" agents only with careful monitoring. Consult your physician for specific advice if you are taking carbamazepine, chlorpropamide, demeclocycline, ethanol, fludrocortisone, heparin, lithium, norepinephrine, or tricyclic antidepressants.

FOOD INTERACTIONS
No known food interactions.

DISEASE INTERACTIONS
Consult your doctor if you have any of the following: seizures, migraine headaches, asthma, heart disease, blood vessel disease, congestive heart failure, or kidney disease.

Dexamethasone Inhalant and Nasal

▶ Drug Class: Respiratory
corticosteroid

▶ Available in: Oral inhalation,
nasal spray

▶ Available OTC? No

▶ As Generic? No

Side Effects

SERIOUS
No serious side effects
are associated with this
drug.

COMMON
Nosebleeds or bloody
nasal secretions, nasal
burning or irritation, sore
throat.

LESS COMMON
Eye pain, watering eyes,
gradual decrease of
vision, stomach pain and
digestive disturbances.

PRINCIPAL USES
To treat bronchial asthma;
to treat allergic rhinitis (seasonal allergies such as hay fever); to prevent recurrence of nasal polyps after they have been removed surgically.

HOW THE DRUG WORKS
Respiratory corticosteroids such as dexamethasone primarily reduce or prevent inflammation of the lining of the airways, reduce the allergic response to inhaled allergens, and inhibit the secretion of mucus within the airways.

DOSAGE
Oral inhalation— Adults: To start, 3 inhalations 3 or 4 times a day; decreased as needed. Most patients respond to 2 inhalations 2 times a day. Children: 2 inhalations 3 or 4 times a day; decreased as needed. Most patients respond to 2 inhalations 2 times a day. Nasal spray— 2 sprays each nostril 3 times a day; decreased as needed.

ONSET OF EFFECT
Usually within 1 week; it may take 3 weeks for the full effect to occur.

DURATION OF ACTION
Unknown.

DIETARY ADVICE
No special restrictions.

STORAGE
Store in a tightly sealed container away from heat and direct light. Keep from getting cold; the medicine is less effective when cold.

IF YOU MISS A DOSE
Take it as soon as you remember. However, if it is near the time for the next dose, skip the missed dose and resume your regular dosage schedule. Do not double the next dose.

STOPPING THE DRUG
The decision to stop taking the drug should be made by your doctor.

PROLONGED USE
Consult your doctor about the need for regular medical tests and examinations if you must take this drug for a prolonged period of time.

PRECAUTIONS
Over 60: No special problems are expected.

Driving and Hazardous Work: The use of dexamethasone should not impair your ability to perform such tasks safely.

Alcohol: No special precautions are necessary.

Pregnancy: Nasal or inhaled steroids have not been reported to cause birth defects if taken during pregnancy. Before using such drugs, tell your doctor if you are pregnant or plan to become pregnant.

Breast Feeding: Dexamethasone may pass into breast milk; caution is advised. Consult your doctor for advice.

Infants and Children: Inhalation corticosteroids like dexamethasone have not been shown to cause different side effects or problems in children than they do in adults. Consult your doctor for specific advice.

Special Concerns: Inhaled steroids will not help an asthma attack in progress. Inhaled steroids can lower resistance to yeast infections of the mouth, throat, or voice box. To prevent yeast infections, gargle or rinse your mouth with water after each use; do not swallow the water.

Know how to use the spray properly; read and follow the directions that come with the device. Before you have surgery, tell the doctor or dentist that you are using a steroid.

OVERDOSE
Symptoms: No specific ones have been reported.

What to Do: Call your doctor, emergency medical services (EMS), or the nearest poison control center if you have any reason to suspect an overdose.

DRUG INTERACTIONS
Consult your doctor for specific advice if you are taking systemic corticosteroids, other inhaled corticosteroids, or any medications that suppress the immune system.

FOOD INTERACTIONS
No known food interactions.

DISEASE INTERACTIONS
Caution is advised when taking dexamethasone. Consult your doctor if you have osteoporosis or a history of tuberculosis.

Dexamethasone Ophthalmic

▶ Drug Class: Corticosteroid

▶ Available in: Ophthalmic
  solution, suspension

▶ Available OTC? No

▶ As Generic? Yes

Side Effects

SERIOUS
Decreased vision or
blurring of vision (from
cataract); eye pain,
nausea, vomiting (from
increased eye pressure);
pain, redness, sensitivity
to bright light, discharge
(from eye infection). Call
your doctor immediately
if you experience any of
these signs or symptoms.
This drug may trigger a
recurrence of herpes
infection of the eye; mention any previous herpes
infection to your doctor.

COMMON
No common side effects
are associated with the
use of ophthalmic dex-
amethasone.

LESS COMMON
Burning, stinging, red-
ness, or watering of eyes.

PRINCIPAL USES
To control inflammation and
prevent potentially permanent damage that may
result from conditions that
involve inflammation in the
eye tissues.

HOW THE DRUG WORKS
Dexamethasone inhibits the
release of natural sub-
stances that stimulate an
inflammatory reaction.

DOSAGE
Solution or suspension: 1 or
2 drops in each eye up to 16
times a day.

ONSET OF EFFECT
Unknown.

DURATION OF ACTION
Unknown.

DIETARY ADVICE
This drug can be used without regard to diet.

STORAGE
Store in a tightly sealed container away from heat, moisture, and direct light. Do
not allow it to freeze.

IF YOU MISS A DOSE
Administer it as soon as you
remember. If it is near the
time for the next dose, skip
the missed dose and
resume your regular dosage
schedule. Do not double the
next dose.

STOPPING THE DRUG
Use this drug as prescribed
for the full treatment period,
even if symptoms improve
before the scheduled end of
the therapy.

PROLONGED USE
See your doctor regularly
for tests and examinations if
you must take this drug for
a prolonged period.

PRECAUTIONS
Over 60: No special problems are expected.

**Driving and Hazardous
Work:** Avoid such activities
until you determine how the
medicine affects your
vision.

Alcohol: No special precautions are necessary.

Pregnancy: Ophthalmic
dexamethasone has caused
birth defects in animals.
Reliable human studies
have not been done, but no
human birth defects have
been documented. Before
you use this drug, tell your
doctor if you are pregnant
or plan to become pregnant.

Breast Feeding: This
drug has not been reported
to cause problems in nursing babies. Consult your
doctor for specific advice.

Infants and Children:
Children under age 2 may
be especially sensitive to
the effects of this drug.

Special Concerns: To use
the eye drops, first wash
your hands. Tilt your head
back. Gently apply pressure
to the inside corner of the
eyelid and with the index
finger of the same hand,
pull downward on the lower
eyelid to make a space.
Drop the medicine into this
space and close your eye.
Apply pressure for 1 or 2
minutes while keeping the
eye closed without blinking.
Then wash your hands
again. Make sure the tip of
the dropper does not touch
your eye, finger, or any
other surface. If your symptoms do not improve in 5 to
7 days or if they become
worse, check with your doctor. Wearing contact lenses
while using this medication
may increase the risk of
infection. Your doctor may
tell you not to wear contact
lenses during and for a day
or two after treatment.

OVERDOSE
Symptoms: When applied
topically, an overdose of
ophthalmic dexamethasone
is very unlikely. Inadvertent
oral ingestion, however,
may cause fever, muscle
weakness, nausea, loss of
appetite, dizziness, fainting,
or difficulty breathing.

What to Do: An overdose
of this drug is unlikely to be
life-threatening. However, if
someone takes a much
larger dose than prescribed
or accidentally ingests the
medicine, call your doctor,
emergency medical services
(EMS), or the nearest poison control center.

DRUG INTERACTIONS
Other drugs may interact
with ophthalmic dexamethasone. Consult your doctor
for specific advice if you are
taking any other prescription or over-the-counter
medication.

FOOD INTERACTIONS
No known food interactions.

DISEASE INTERACTIONS
Caution is advised when
taking ophthalmic dexam-
ethasone. Consult your doctor if you have any of the
following: diabetes, herpes
infection of the eye, glaucoma, cataracts, tuberculosis of the eye, or any other
eye infection.

Dexamethasone Systemic

▶ Drug Class: Corticosteroid

▶ Available in: Elixir, oral
solution, tablets, injection

▶ Available OTC? No

▶ As Generic? Yes

Side Effects

SERIOUS
Vision problems, frequent
urination, increased
thirst, rectal bleeding,
blistering skin, confusion,
hallucinations, paranoia,
euphoria, depression,
mood swings, redness
and swelling at injection
site. Call your doctor
immediately.

COMMON
Increased appetite, indi-
gestion, nervousness,
insomnia, greater suscep-
tibility to infections,
increased blood pressure,
slow healing of wounds,
weight gain, easy bruis-
ing, fluid retention.

LESS COMMON
Change in skin color,
dizziness, headache,
increased sweating,
unusual growth of body
or facial hair, increased
blood sugar, peptic
ulcers, adrenal insuffi-
ciency, muscle weakness,
cataracts, glaucoma,
osteoporosis.

PRINCIPAL USES
To treat numerous condi-
tions that involve inflammation (a response by body
tissues, producing redness,
warmth, swelling, and pain).
Such conditions include
arthritis, allergic reactions,
asthma, some skin diseases,
multiple sclerosis flare-ups,
and other autoimmune dis-
eases. Also prescribed to
treat deficiency of natural
steroid hormones.

HOW THE DRUG WORKS
This hormone mimics the
effects of the body's natural
corticosteroids. It depresses
the synthesis, release, and
activity of inflammation-
producing body chemicals.
It also suppresses the activity of the immune system.

DOSAGE
Adults and teenagers— Oral
dosage: 25 to 300 mg a day,
depending on condition, in 1
or several doses. Injection:
20 to 300 mg once a day,
depending on condition.
Children— Consult your
pediatrician.

ONSET OF EFFECT
Within 2 hours of oral form,
1 hour of injection.

DURATION OF ACTION
More than 2 days for oral
form; 6 days after injection.

DIETARY ADVICE
It can be taken with food or
milk to minimize stomach
upset. Your doctor may recommend a low-salt, high-
potassium, high-protein diet.

STORAGE
Store in a tightly sealed container away from heat, moisture, and direct light.

IF YOU MISS A DOSE
Take it as soon as you
remember. If you take several doses a day and it is
close to the next dose, double the next dose. If you

take 1 dose a day and you
do not remember until the
next day, skip the missed
dose and do not double the
next dose.

STOPPING THE DRUG
With long-term therapy, do
not stop taking the drug
abruptly; the dosage should
be decreased gradually.

PROLONGED USE
See your doctor regularly
for tests and examinations.
Long-term use may lead to
cataracts, diabetes, hypertension, or osteoporosis.

PRECAUTIONS
Over 60: Adverse reactions
may be more likely and
more severe in older
patients.

**Driving and Hazardous
Work:** Do not drive or
engage in hazardous work
until you determine how the
medicine affects you.

Alcohol: May cause stomach problems; avoid it
unless your physician
approves occasional moderate drinking.

Pregnancy: Overuse during pregnancy can retard
the child's growth and
cause other developmental
problems. Consult your
physician.

Breast Feeding: Do not
use while nursing.

Infants and Children:
Dexamethasone may retard
the normal growth and
development of bone and
other tissues. Consult your
doctor.

Special Concerns: Avoid
immunizations with live vaccines if possible. Remember
that this drug can lower
your resistance to infection.
Patients undergoing long-
term therapy should wear a

medical-alert bracelet. Call
your doctor if you develop a
fever.

OVERDOSE
Symptoms: Fever, muscle
or joint pain, nausea, dizziness, fainting, difficulty
breathing. Prolonged
overuse: Moonface, obesity,
unusual hair growth, acne,
loss of sexual function, muscle wasting.

What to Do: Call your
doctor, emergency medical
services (EMS), or the
nearest poison control center immediately.

DRUG INTERACTIONS
Consult your doctor for specific advice if you are taking
aminoglutethimide,
antacids, barbiturates, carbamazepine, griseofulvin,
mitotane, phenylbutazone,
phenytoin, primidone,
rifampin, injectable amphotericin B, oral antidiabetes
agents, insulin, digitalis
drugs, diuretics, or medications containing potassium
or sodium.

FOOD INTERACTIONS
Avoid excess sodium.

DISEASE INTERACTIONS
Consult your doctor if you
have a history of bone disease, chicken pox, measles,
gastrointestinal disorders,
diabetes, recent serious
infection, tuberculosis, glaucoma, heart disease, hypertension, liver or kidney
disorders, high blood cholesterol, overactive or
underactive thyroid, myasthenia gravis, or lupus.

Dexamethasone Topical

▶ Drug Class: Topical
corticosteroid

▶ Available in: Gel, aerosol
solution, cream

▶ Available OTC? No

▶ As Generic? Yes

Side Effects

SERIOUS
No serious side effects
are associated with topi-
cal dexamethasone.

COMMON
Burning, itching, irrita-
tion, redness, dryness,
acne, stinging and crack-
ing of skin, numbness or
tingling in the extremi-
ties. Such side effects are
unlikely to occur except
when topical dexametha-
sone is used with ban-
dages or other occlusive
dressings.

LESS COMMON
With prolonged use: Blis-
tering and pus near hair
follicles, unusual bleed-
ing or bruising, darken-
ing or prominence of
small surface veins,
increased susceptibility
to infection.

PRINCIPAL USES
To treat skin rash and
inflammation. Topical
steroids come in many
strengths; dexamethasone
is a lower-strength steroid,
which is safest and most
appropriate for certain
minor skin conditions.

HOW THE DRUG WORKS
Topical dexamethasone
appears to interfere with the
formation of natural sub-
stances within the body that
are directly responsible for
the process of inflammation,
which produces swelling,
redness, and pain.

DOSAGE
Gel (0.1% strength)—
Apply 2 or 3 times daily.
Aerosol (0.01% and 0.04%
strength)— Adults: Apply 2
to 4 times daily. Children: 1
or 2 times daily. Cream
(0.1% strength)— Adults:
Apply 3 or 4 times daily.
Children: once daily.

ONSET OF EFFECT
Soon after application. However, recognizable changes
in your condition may take
several days or more to
develop.

DURATION OF ACTION
Unknown.

DIETARY ADVICE
No special restrictions.

STORAGE
Store in a tightly sealed container away from heat and
direct light.

IF YOU MISS A DOSE
Apply it as soon as you
remember. If it is near the
time for the next dose, skip
the missed dose and
resume your regular dosage
schedule.

STOPPING THE DRUG
Take as prescribed for the
full treatment period, even if
you begin to feel better
before the scheduled end of
therapy.

PROLONGED USE
Avoid prolonged use, particularly near the eyes, on the
face, genital, or rectal areas,
or in the folds of the skin.

PRECAUTIONS
Over 60: Side effects may
be more likely and more
severe in elderly patients;
therapy with topical corticosteroids should therefore
be brief and infrequent.

**Driving and Hazardous
Work:** The use of topical
dexamethasone should not
impair your ability to perform such tasks safely.

Alcohol: No special precautions are necessary.

Pregnancy: This drug
should not be used for prolonged periods by pregnant
women or women trying to
become pregnant.

Breast Feeding: Although
problems have not been
documented, caution is
advised. Do not apply to
breasts prior to nursing.
Consult your doctor for specific advice.

Infants and Children: It
should not be used for more
than 2 weeks on children
and teenagers, unless otherwise directed by your doctor. Do not use tight-fitting
diapers or plastic pants on
children when treating skin
irritation in the diaper area.

Special Concerns: Take
care to avoid use of this
medication around the eyes.
Take care to apply only to
the affected area. Note that
dexamethasone is not a
treatment for acne, burns,
infections, or disorders of
pigmentation. Do not ban-
dage or wrap the medicated
area of skin with any special
dressings or coverings
unless specifically told to do
so by your doctor. Applying
special coverings may
increase the chance of an
undesirable interaction or
side effect.

OVERDOSE
Symptoms: None known.

What to Do: An overdose
of a topical corticosteroid is
unlikely to be life-threatening. However, in the event
of accidental ingestion or an
apparent overdose, call your
doctor, emergency medical
services (EMS), or the
nearest poison control
center right away.

DRUG INTERACTIONS
Do not mix topical dexam-
ethasone with other prod-
ucts, especially alcohol-
containing preparations
(which include colognes,
aftershave, and many moisturizer lotions), since this
may cause dryness and irritation, or increase the risk
of an allergic reaction.

FOOD INTERACTIONS
Potassium supplements may
decrease this drug's effects.
Avoid foods high in sodium.

DISEASE INTERACTIONS
Consult your doctor if you
have any of the following:
cataracts; diabetes mellitus;
glaucoma; infection, sores,
or ulcerations of the skin;
infection elsewhere in your
body; or tuberculosis.

Dextroamphetamine Sulfate

BRAND NAMES
Dexedrine, Dexedrine
Spansule, DextroStat

Generic 5 mg
(SMITHKLINE BEECHAM)

▶ Drug Class: Central nervous system stimulant/amphetamine

▶ Available in: Extended-release capsules, tablets

▶ Available OTC? No

▶ As Generic? No

Side Effects

SERIOUS
Irregular heartbeat, chest pain, increased blood pressure, skin rash, uncontrollable movements of arms and legs, mental changes, unusual weakness, very high fever. Call your doctor immediately.

COMMON
Mood changes, insomnia, drowsiness, restlessness.

LESS COMMON
Blurred vision, constipation, diarrhea, loss of appetite, headache, increased sweating, stomach cramps or pain, nausea or vomiting, changes in sexual desire or decreased sexual ability.

PRINCIPAL USES
To treat attention-deficit hyperactivity disorder, sometimes referred to as ADHD or simply hyperactivity. It is also used to treat narcolepsy (uncontrolled onset of sleep).

HOW THE DRUG WORKS
Dextroamphetamine activates nerve cells in the brain and spinal cord to increase motor activity and alertness and lessen drowsiness and fatigue. In hyperactivity disorders and narcolepsy, amphetamines improve mental focus and the ability to stay awake or concentrate.

DOSAGE
To treat ADHD— Adults: 5 to 60 mg a day. Children age 6 and older: To start, 5 mg, 1 or 2 times a day. Children ages 3 to 6: To start, 2.5 mg a day. To treat narcolepsy— Adults: 5 to 60 mg a day. Teenagers: To start, 10 mg once a day. Children ages 6 to 12: To start, 5 mg once a day.

ONSET OF EFFECT
Usually within 30 to 45 minutes for tablets, and somewhat later for extended-release capsules.

DURATION OF ACTION
In adults, 8 to 12 hours; in children, 6 to 10 hours. Extended-release capsules have a somewhat longer duration of action.

DIETARY ADVICE
Take it with liquid 30 to 45 minutes before meals. Avoid caffeinated beverages like tea, coffee, and some colas. Avoid vitamin C pills and acidic foods rich in vitamin C, such as fruit juices and other citrus products.

STORAGE
Store in a tightly sealed container away from heat, moisture, and direct light.

IF YOU MISS A DOSE
Take it as soon as you remember. If it is near the time for the next dose, skip the missed dose and resume your regular dosage schedule. Do not double the next dose.

STOPPING THE DRUG
Take it as prescribed for the full treatment period, even if you begin to feel better before the scheduled end of therapy. The decision to stop taking the drug should be made by your doctor. The doctor may decrease your dosage gradually to reduce the possibility of withdrawal symptoms.

PROLONGED USE
Amphetamines can be habit-forming, and prolonged use may increase the risk of dependency.

PRECAUTIONS
Over 60: Adverse reactions may be more likely and more severe in older patients.

Driving and Hazardous Work: Do not drive or engage in hazardous work until you determine how the medicine affects you.

Alcohol: Avoid alcohol.

Pregnancy: Adequate human studies have not been completed. Before taking dextroamphetamine, tell your doctor if you are pregnant or plan to become pregnant.

Breast Feeding: Dextroamphetamine passes into breast milk; caution is advised. Consult your doctor for advice.

Infants and Children: Not recommended for use by children under age 3.

Special Concerns: Take only as directed and do not increase the dose on your own. Remember that fatigue, excessive drowsiness, sleepiness, or depression while taking stimulants may mean an emergency situation is developing. Difficulty sleeping may be improved by taking the last scheduled dose several hours before bedtime.

OVERDOSE
Symptoms: Extreme restlessness, agitation, or bizarre behavior; panic; rapid breathing; confusion; high fever; hallucinations; seizures; coma.

What to Do: Call your doctor, emergency medical services (EMS), or the nearest poison control center immediately.

DRUG INTERACTIONS
Consult your doctor for specific advice if you are taking tricyclic antidepressants, caffeine, beta-blockers, digitalis drugs, central nervous system stimulants, meperidine, MAO inhibitors, sympathomimetic agents, or thyroid hormones.

FOOD INTERACTIONS
Citrus juices and caffeinated beverages and foods may interact with this drug.

DISEASE INTERACTIONS
Consult your doctor if you have any of the following: advanced blood vessel disease, heart disease, hyperthyroidism, hypertension, severe anxiety, Tourette's syndrome, glaucoma, or a history of drug abuse.

Dextromethorphan

▶ Drug Class: Cough
suppressant

▶ Available in: Capsules,
lozenges, tablets, oral
suspension, syrup

▶ Available OTC? Yes

▶ As Generic? Yes

Side Effects

SERIOUS
Serious side effects occur
only in cases of overdose
(see Overdose).

COMMON
No common side effects
are associated with the
use of this drug.

LESS COMMON
Mild dizziness or seda-
tion, nausea or vomiting,
abdominal pain. Such
symptoms are more
likely to occur at the
beginning of therapy and
tend to diminish as your
body becomes accus-
tomed to taking the drug.
Consult your doctor if
they persist or interfere
with daily activities.

PRINCIPAL USES
To relieve a dry or mini-
mally productive cough
(that is, a mild cough that
rids the lungs of modest
amounts of phlegm or
mucus), commonly associ-
ated with allergies, colds,
influenza, and certain lung
disorders. This medicine is
ideally useful when a mild
or hacking cough would
otherwise interrupt sleep
or interfere with your daily
activities.

HOW THE DRUG WORKS
Dextromethorphan works
by directly reducing the
sensitivity of the cough center—the part of the brain
that responds to stimuli in
the lower respiratory passages that irritate and trigger the cough reflex.

DOSAGE
Adults: 10 to 20 mg every
4 hours or 30 mg every 6 to
8 hours; 30 to 60 mg of
extended-release liquid
twice a day. Children 6 to
12: 5 to 10 mg every 4
hours or 30 mg of extended-
release liquid twice a day.
Children 2 to 6: 2.5 to 5 mg
every 4 hours, or 7.5 mg
every 6 to 8 hours, or 15
mg of the extended-release
liquid twice a day. Children
under 2: Dosage must be
individualized.

ONSET OF EFFECT
15 to 30 minutes.

DURATION OF ACTION
Up to 6 hours.

DIETARY ADVICE
No special restrictions.

STORAGE
Store in a tightly sealed container away from heat, moisture, and direct light.

IF YOU MISS A DOSE
Take it as soon as you
remember. However, if it is
near the time for the next
dose, skip the missed dose
and resume your regular
dosage schedule. Do not
double the next dose.

STOPPING THE DRUG
Take it as prescribed for the
full treatment period. However, you may stop taking
the drug if you are feeling
better before the scheduled
end of therapy. If the cough
does not improve after 7
days, consult your doctor.

PROLONGED USE
No problems are expected.

PRECAUTIONS
Over 60: Side effects
may be more frequent and
severe than in younger persons. Smaller doses for
shorter periods may be
needed. If this drug is used
to control coughing, other
treatment measures may be
needed to liquefy any accumulation of thick mucus
that may form in the
bronchial tubes.

**Driving and Hazardous
Work:** Determine if dex-
tromethorphan causes
drowsiness or dizziness
before you drive or engage
in hazardous work.

Alcohol: Avoid alcohol
while using this drug; it
may increase the risk of
sedation.

Pregnancy: Ask your doctor whether the benefits of
the drug justify the possible
risk to the fetus.

Breast Feeding: Dextromethorphan may pass into
breast milk; caution is
advised. Consult your doctor for specific advice about
taking dextromethorphan
while you are nursing.

Infants and Children:
Doses for children under 2
must be individualized; consult your pediatrician.

Special Concerns: Do not
take dextromethorphan to
relieve a cough caused by
asthma, emphysema, or
smoking.

OVERDOSE
Symptoms: Nausea, vomiting, extreme drowsiness or
dizziness, nervousness and
agitation, extreme irritability or mood changes, hallucinations, blurred vision,
uncontrollable eye move-
ment, inability to urinate,
confusion, loss of consciousness, or coma.

What to Do: Call your
doctor, emergency medical
services (EMS), or the
nearest poison control center immediately.

DRUG INTERACTIONS
Taking a sedative or other
depressant can increase the
sedative effects of both
drugs. Using doxepin
increases the toxic effects
of both drugs. Taking an
MAO inhibitor can cause a
high fever, disorientation, or
loss of consciousness. Using
quinidine increases the risk
of experiencing side effects
with dextromethorphan.

FOOD INTERACTIONS
No known food interactions.

DISEASE INTERACTIONS
Caution is advised when
taking dextromethorphan.
Consult your doctor if you
have a history of asthma or
impaired liver function.

Diazepam

Generic 2 mg
(PUREPAC)

▶ Drug Class: Benzodiazepine
tranquilizer; antianxiety
agent/muscle relaxant

▶ Available in: Tablets, capsules, injection, rectal gel

▶ Available OTC? No

▶ As Generic? Yes

Side Effects

SERIOUS
Difficulty concentrating,
outbursts of anger, other
behavior problems,
depression, hallucina-
tions, low blood pressure
(causing faintness or confusion), memory impair-
ment, muscle weakness,
skin rash or itching, sore
throat, fever and chills,
sores or ulcers in throat
or mouth, unusual bruis-
ing or bleeding, extreme
fatigue, yellowish tinge to
eyes or skin. Call your
doctor immediately.

COMMON
Drowsiness, loss of coor-
dination, unsteady gait,
dizziness, lightheaded-
ness, slurred speech.

LESS COMMON
Change in sexual desire
or ability, constipation,
false sense of well-being,
nausea and vomiting, uri-
nary problems, unusual
fatigue.

PRINCIPAL USES
To treat anxiety, panic
attacks, and muscle spasms.
It is also used in the acute
treatment of seizures.

HOW THE DRUG WORKS
In general, diazepam pro-
duces mild sedation by
depressing activity in the
central nervous system. In
particular, diazepam appears
to enhance the effect of
gamma-aminobutyric acid
(GABA), a natural chemical
that inhibits the firing of
neurons and dampens the
transmission of nerve signals, thus decreasing nervous excitation.

DOSAGE
For anxiety— Adults: 2 to
10 mg, 4 times a day. Children: 1 to 2.5 mg, 3 or 4
times a day. For muscle
spasms— 2 to 10 mg, 2 to 4
times a day. For treatment
of seizures— Injection: The
dose is determined and
administered by your doc-
tor. Rectal gel: The recommended dose is 0.2 to 0.5
mg per 2.2 lbs (1 kg) of
body weight depending on
age. Your doctor will determine the correct dosage.

ONSET OF EFFECT
30 minutes.

DURATION OF ACTION
Up to 48 hours.

DIETARY ADVICE
No special restrictions.

STORAGE
Store in a tightly sealed container away from heat, moisture, and direct light.

IF YOU MISS A DOSE
Take the missed dose if you
remember within 2 hours. If
more than 2 hours, skip the
missed dose and return to
your regular schedule. Do
not double the next dose.

STOPPING THE DRUG
Discontinuing the drug
abruptly may produce withdrawal symptoms (seizures,
sleep disruption, nervousness, irritability, diarrhea,
abdominal cramps, muscle
aches, memory impair-
ment). Dosage should be
reduced gradually accord-
ing to your physician's
instructions.

PROLONGED USE
Diazepam may slowly lose
its effectiveness with prolonged use. You should see
your doctor for periodic
evaluation if you must take
it for an extended time.

PRECAUTIONS
Over 60: Dosage is often
reduced because adverse
reactions are more likely
and may be more severe in
older patients.

**Driving and Hazardous
Work:** Diazepam can
impair mental alertness
and physical coordination.
Adjust your activities
accordingly.

Alcohol: Alcohol intake
should be extremely moderate or stopped altogether
while taking this drug.

Pregnancy: Use during
pregnancy should be
avoided if possible. Be sure
to tell your doctor if you are
pregnant or plan to become
pregnant.

Breast Feeding:
Diazepam passes into breast
milk; do not take it while
nursing.

Infants and Children:
Diazepam should be used
by children only under
close medical supervision.

Special Concerns:
Diazepam use can lead to
psychological or physical
dependence. Never take

more than the prescribed
daily dose. Your physician
will teach you how to determine when it is appropriate
and how to properly administer the rectal gel.

OVERDOSE
Symptoms: Extreme
drowsiness, confusion,
slurred speech, slow
reflexes, poor coordination,
staggering gait, tremor,
slowed breathing, loss of
consciousness.

What to Do: Call your
doctor, emergency medical
services (EMS), or the
nearest poison control center immediately.

DRUG INTERACTIONS
Other drugs may interact
with diazepam. Consult your
doctor for specific advice if
you are taking any drugs
that depress the central nervous system; these include
antihistamines, antidepressants or other psychiatric
medications, barbiturates,
sedatives, cough medicines,
decongestants, and
painkillers. Be sure your
doctor knows about any
over-the-counter medication
you may take.

FOOD INTERACTIONS
None reported.

DISEASE INTERACTIONS
Do not take diazepam if you
have acute narrow angle
glaucoma. Consult your
doctor if you have a history
of alcohol or drug abuse,
stroke or other brain
disease, any chronic lung
disease, hyperactivity,
depression or other mental
illness, myasthenia gravis,
sleep apnea, epilepsy, porphyria, kidney disease, or
liver disease.

Diazoxide

BRAND NAME
Proglycem

▶ Drug Class: Glucose-elevating agent (capsules); antihypertensive (injection)

▶ Available in: Capsules, injectable solution

▶ Available OTC? No

▶ As Generic? Yes

Side Effects

SERIOUS
Excess sodium and water retention (edema), resulting in decreased urination, rapid weight gain (or bloating), swelling of feet or lower legs. In some cases this condition, if unchecked, may lead to congestive heart failure; call your doctor at once. A diuretic may be prescribed to counteract the edema, but the combination of diazoxide with a thiazide diuretic may further raise blood glucose levels. Attacks of gout may occur since diazoxide can raise uric acid levels.

COMMON
Rapid heartbeat.

LESS COMMON
Fever, rash, stiffness of arms or legs, unusual bleeding or bruising, constipation, loss of appetite, stomach pain, nausea and vomiting. With long-term use: growth of hair on forehead, back, arms, and legs.

PRINCIPAL USES
To correct low blood glucose levels (hypoglycemia) resulting from overproduction of insulin by the pancreas, which may occur when an insulin-producing pancreatic tumor cannot be removed by surgery or when a malignant insulin-producing tumor has spread.

HOW THE DRUG WORKS
Insulin, a hormone produced by the beta cells of the pancreas, lowers blood glucose (sugar) levels by increasing the uptake of glucose by muscles and reducing its release from the liver. Too much insulin causes blood glucose to drop to low levels. Diazoxide inhibits the release of insulin from the pancreas and thus helps to prevent blood glucose from falling to low levels.

DOSAGE
The dose is based on body weight and should be determined by your doctor. Adults, teenagers, and children: Starting at 1 mg per 2.2 lbs (1 kg) of body weight every 8 hours. Can be increased to 3 to 8 mg per 2.2 lbs in 2 or 3 doses a day. Newborn babies and infants: Starting at 3.3 mg per 2.2 lbs of body weight every 8 hours. Can be increased to 8 to 15 mg per 2.2 lbs (3.6 to 6.8 mg per lb) in 2 or 3 doses a day.

ONSET OF EFFECT
1 hour.

DURATION OF ACTION
8 hours.

DIETARY ADVICE
Can be taken with or between meals. A diet rich in carbohydrates may help to raise and maintain blood glucose levels.

STORAGE
Store in a dry place away from heat and light. Keep the solution from freezing.

IF YOU MISS A DOSE
Take it as soon as you remember. If it is near the time for the next dose, skip the missed dose and go back to your regular dosage schedule. Do not double the next dose.

STOPPING THE DRUG
Do not stop taking diazoxide without first consulting your doctor.

PROLONGED USE
Close monitoring of blood sugar levels is necessary. Long-term side effects of diazoxide may include stiffening of limbs; shaking and trembling of hands and fingers; increased hair growth on forehead, back, arms, and legs.

PRECAUTIONS
Over 60: Older persons are more likely to suffer from impaired kidney function and may therefore require a reduced dose.

Driving and Hazardous Work: Do not drive or engage in hazardous work until you determine how diazoxide affects you.

Alcohol: Follow your physician's instructions about alcohol use while taking this drug.

Pregnancy: Use of diazoxide during pregnancy may have adverse effects on the fetus. Consult your doctor if you are pregnant or plan to become pregnant.

Breast Feeding: It is not known whether diazoxide passes into breast milk. Consult your doctor about the drug's relative risks and benefits if you are breast feeding.

Infants and Children: Careful monitoring is required.

Special Concerns: Follow the special diet that your doctor gives you, and be sure to call your doctor if you experience edema (swelling, especially in the lower extremities), excessive rise in your blood glucose levels, or a drop in blood pressure.

OVERDOSE
Symptoms: An excessive rise in blood glucose can cause drowsiness, flushed skin, dry skin, increased urination, or unusual thirst (symptoms of diabetic ketoacidosis or hyperosmolar coma).

What to Do: Call your doctor immediately.

DRUG INTERACTIONS
Drugs that can affect or be affected by diazoxide include alpha- and beta-blockers, anticoagulants, antigout drugs, anticonvulsants, and thiazide diuretics.

FOOD INTERACTIONS
No known food interactions.

DISEASE INTERACTIONS
Your doctor must be aware of any other medical problems, especially angina, gout, heart disease, blood vessel disease, kidney disease, liver disease, or a recent stroke.

Diclofenac Ophthalmic

BRAND NAME
Voltaren Ophthalmic

▶ Drug Class: Nonsteroidal anti-inflammatory drug (NSAID)

▶ Available in: Ophthalmic solution

▶ Available OTC? No

▶ As Generic? No

Side Effects

SERIOUS
Rarely, ophthalmic diclofenac will cause bleeding in the eye, redness or swelling of the eye or eyelid not present before the start of therapy, or tearing or itching of the eye. Call your doctor immediately.

COMMON
Mild and temporary burning or stinging of eyes after application.

LESS COMMON
No less-common side effects are associated with the use of ophthalmic diclofenac.

PRINCIPAL USES
To treat inflammation and eye problems that occur after cataract removal surgery. Also used to control eye pain after corneal refractive surgery (such as the increasingly popular radial keratotomy to correct nearsightedness).

HOW THE DRUG WORKS
Ophthalmic diclofenac inhibits the release of natural substances that stimulate inflammation and can cause pain in eye tissues.

DOSAGE
Adults: 1 drop in each affected eye 4 times a day, beginning 24 hours after surgery and continuing for the next 2 weeks. Children: Use and dosage must be determined by your doctor.

ONSET OF EFFECT
Unknown.

DURATION OF ACTION
Unknown.

DIETARY ADVICE
This medication can be used without regard to diet.

STORAGE
Store in a tightly sealed container away from heat and direct light. Do not refrigerate or allow to freeze.

IF YOU MISS A DOSE
Apply it as soon as you remember. If it is near the time for the next dose, skip the missed dose and resume your regular dosage schedule. Do not double the next dose.

STOPPING THE DRUG
Use this drug as prescribed for the full treatment period, even if you begin to feel better before the scheduled end of therapy.

PROLONGED USE
You should see your doctor regularly for tests and examinations if you take this drug for a prolonged period.

PRECAUTIONS
Over 60: No special problems are expected.

Driving and Hazardous Work: The use of ophthalmic diclofenac should not impair your ability to perform such tasks safely.

Alcohol: No special precautions are necessary.

Pregnancy: Adequate human studies have not been completed. Before taking ophthalmic diclofenac, tell your doctor if you are pregnant or plan to become pregnant.

Breast Feeding: Ophthalmic diclofenac may pass into breast milk; caution is advised. Consult your doctor for specific advice.

Infants and Children: Use and dosage for infants and children must be determined by your doctor.

Special Concerns: To use the eye drops, first wash your hands. Tilt your head back. Gently apply pressure to the inside corner of the eyelid and with the index finger of the same hand, pull downward on the lower eyelid to make a space. Drop the medicine into this space and close your eye. Apply pressure for 1 or 2 minutes while keeping the eye closed without blinking. Then wash your hands again. Make sure the tip of the dropper does not touch your eye, finger, or any other surface. If your symptoms do not improve or if they become worse, check with your doctor. Ophthalmic diclofenac has caused severe eye irritation in some persons wearing soft contact lenses. Do not wear soft contact lenses while using this medication.

OVERDOSE
Symptoms: No specific ones have been reported.

What to Do: An overdose of ophthalmic diclofenac is unlikely to be life-threatening. However, if someone takes a much larger dose of the drug than prescribed or accidentally ingests the medicine, call your doctor, emergency medical services (EMS), or the nearest poison control center.

DRUG INTERACTIONS
Consult your doctor for advice if you are taking aspirin or another salicylate, diflunisal, etodolac, fenoprofen, floctafenine, flurbiprofen, ibuprofen, indomethacin, ketoprofen, ketorolac, meclofenamate, mefenamic acid, nabumetone, naproxen, oxyphenbutazone, phenylbutazone, piroxicam, sulindac, suprofen, tenoxicam, tiaprofenic acid, tolmetin, or zomepirac.

FOOD INTERACTIONS
No known food interactions.

DISEASE INTERACTIONS
Caution is advised when using ophthalmic diclofenac. Consult your doctor if you have hemophilia or any other bleeding problem.

Diclofenac Systemic

▶ Drug Class: Nonsteroidal anti-inflammatory drug (NSAID)

▶ Available in: Tablets, delayed-release tablets, suppositories

▶ Available OTC? No

▶ As Generic? Yes

Side Effects

SERIOUS
Shortness of breath or wheezing, with or without swelling of legs or other signs of heart failure; chest pain; peptic ulcer disease with vomiting of blood; black, tarry stools; decreasing kidney function. Call your doctor immediately.

COMMON
Nausea, vomiting, heartburn, diarrhea, constipation, headache, dizziness, sleepiness.

LESS COMMON
Ulcers or sores in mouth, depression, rashes or blistering of skin, ringing sound in the ears, unusual tingling or numbness of the hands or feet, seizures, blurred vision. Also elevated potassium levels, decreased blood counts; such problems can be detected by your doctor.

PRINCIPAL USES
To treat mild to moderate pain and inflammation caused by tendinitis, arthritis, bursitis, gout, soft tissue injuries, migraine and other vascular headaches, menstrual cramps, and other conditions. When patients fail to respond to one NSAID, another may be tried. The greatest effectiveness often requires trial and error of several different NSAIDs.

HOW THE DRUG WORKS
NSAIDs work by interfering with the formation of prostaglandins, substances that cause inflammation and make nerves more sensitive to pain impulses. NSAIDs also have other modes of action that are less well understood.

DOSAGE
Adults— For osteoarthritis and rheumatoid arthritis: 50 mg, 2 or 3 times a day. Ankylosing spondylitis: 25 mg, 4 times a day, with another 25 mg at bedtime if needed. Menstrual pain: 50 mg, 3 times a day; an initial dose of 100 mg may be given.

ONSET OF EFFECT
Within 30 minutes.

DURATION OF ACTION
Up to 8 hours.

DIETARY ADVICE
Take it with food.

STORAGE
Store in a tightly sealed container away from heat, moisture, and direct light.

IF YOU MISS A DOSE
Take it as soon as you remember. If it is near the time for the next dose, skip the missed dose and resume your regular dosage schedule. Do not double the next dose.

STOPPING THE DRUG
The decision to stop taking the drug should be made in consultation with your physician.

PROLONGED USE
Prolonged use can cause gastrointestinal problems, including ulceration and bleeding, kidney dysfunction, and liver inflammation. Consult your physician about the need for medical examinations and laboratory studies.

PRECAUTIONS
Over 60: Because of the potentially greater consequences of gastrointestinal side effects, the dose of NSAIDs for older patients, especially those over age 70, is often cut in half.

Driving and Hazardous Work: Do not drive or engage in hazardous work until you determine how the medicine affects you.

Alcohol: Avoid alcohol when using this medication because it increases the risk of stomach irritation.

Pregnancy: Avoid or discontinue this drug if you are pregnant or plan to become pregnant.

Breast Feeding: Diclofenac passes into breast milk; avoid or discontinue use while nursing.

Infants and Children: Diclofenac may be used in exceptional circumstances; consult your pediatrician for specific advice.

Special Concerns: Because NSAIDs can inhibit blood coagulation, this drug should be discontinued at least 3 days prior to any surgery. Do not crush or chew the tablets.

OVERDOSE
Symptoms: Nausea, vomiting, severe headache, confusion, seizures.

What to Do: Call your doctor, emergency medical services (EMS), or the nearest poison control center immediately.

DRUG INTERACTIONS
Do not take this drug with aspirin or any other NSAIDs without your doctor's approval. In addition, consult your doctor if you are taking antihypertensives, steroids, anticoagulants, antibiotics, itraconazole or ketoconazole, plicamycin, penicillamine, valproic acid, phenytoin, cyclosporine, digitalis drugs, lithium, methotrexate, probenecid, triamterene, or zidovudine.

FOOD INTERACTIONS
No known food interactions.

DISEASE INTERACTIONS
Consult your doctor if you have any of the following: bleeding problems, inflammation or ulcers of the stomach and intestines, diabetes mellitus, systemic lupus erythematosus (SLE, lupus), anemia, asthma, epilepsy, Parkinson's disease, kidney stones, or a history of heart disease or alcohol abuse. Use of diclofenac may cause complications in patients with liver or kidney disease, since these organs work together to remove the medication from the body.

Diclofenac/Misoprostol

▶ Drug Class: Antirheumatic

▶ Available in: Tablets

▶ Available OTC? No

▶ As Generic? No

Side Effects

SERIOUS
Irregular heartbeat, fainting, coma, seizures, yellowish tinge to eyes or skin, or pain or tenderness in the upper-right abdomen. Call your doctor immediately.

COMMON
Stomach pain or upset, diarrhea, indigestion, nausea, flatulence.

LESS COMMON
Fatigue, weakness, fever, tremor, dizziness, loss of appetite, dry mouth, gastroesophageal reflux (backwash of stomach acid into the esophagus, resulting in heartburn), breathing difficulty, persistent but unproductive urge to urinate or defecate, hemorrhoids, breast pain, painful menstruation, menstrual irregularities, hives, impotence, unexpected changes in weight, muscle and joint pain, confusion, mental depression, sleeping difficulty, nightmares or unusually vivid dreams, hallucinations, irritability, nervousness, paranoia, bruising, skin rash, blurred or abnormal vision.

PRINCIPAL USES
To relieve the symptoms of osteoarthritis or rheumatoid arthritis in patients at high risk of developing peptic ulcers as a result of therapy with NSAIDs.

HOW THE DRUG WORKS
Diclofenac, a nonsteroidal anti-inflammatory drug (NSAID), works by interfering with the formation of prostaglandins, substances that cause inflammation and make nerves more sensitive to pain impulses. Ongoing therapy with NSAIDs can irritate and damage the stomach lining, increasing the risk of peptic ulcers. Misoprostol, a synthetic prostaglandin, helps prevent ulcers and enhances the stomach's natural healing ability by increasing the production of protective mucus and inhibiting the secretion of stomach acid.

DOSAGE
Osteoarthritis: 1 tablet of Arthrotec 50 (50 mg diclofenac/200 micrograms [mcg] misoprostol), 3 times a day. Rheumatoid arthritis: 1 tablet of Arthrotec 75 (75 mg diclofenac/200 mcg misoprostol), 3 to 4 times a day. Different doses may be warranted in some patients. Consult your doctor.

ONSET OF EFFECT
Unknown.

DURATION OF ACTION
Unknown.

DIETARY ADVICE
The drug should be taken with food to minimize stomach upset and diarrhea.

STORAGE
Store in a tightly sealed container away from heat, moisture, and direct light.

IF YOU MISS A DOSE
Take it as soon as you remember. If it is near the time for the next dose, skip the missed dose and resume your regular dosage schedule. Do not double the next dose.

STOPPING THE DRUG
Take it as prescribed for the full treatment period.

PROLONGED USE
Since side effects are more likely with prolonged use, regular follow-up visits with your doctor are important. To minimize the chance of an adverse effect, the lowest effective dose should be used for the shortest possible duration (misoprostol is generally not prescribed for longer than 4 weeks).

PRECAUTIONS
Over 60: No special problems are expected.

Driving and Hazardous Work: Do not drive or engage in hazardous work until you determine how the medicine affects you.

Alcohol: Avoid alcohol, as it may increase the risk of stomach irritation.

Pregnancy: This drug combination should not be used during pregnancy. The misoprostol component can cause miscarriage and induce abortion. Before it can be prescribed, female patients are required to have had a negative pregnancy test within the previous 2 weeks. Therapy then begins only on the second or third day of the following menstrual period. An effective method of birth control should be used while taking this drug. If you suspect you are pregnant, stop taking the drug immediately and consult your doctor.

Breast Feeding: This drug passes into breast milk and may be harmful; avoid use while nursing.

Infants and Children: Not recommended for use by children under 18.

OVERDOSE
Symptoms: Nausea, vomiting, severe headache, confusion, seizures, tremors, sleepiness, difficulty breathing, stomach pain, severe diarrhea, fever, palpitations, extremely low blood pressure causing dizziness or fainting, slow heartbeat.

What to Do: Call your doctor, emergency medical services (EMS), or the nearest poison control center immediately.

DRUG INTERACTIONS
The following drugs may interact with this drug: aspirin, digoxin, blood pressure medication, warfarin, methotrexate, cyclosporine, oral diabetes drugs, lithium, antacids, diuretics, or any over-the-counter drugs. Consult your doctor. To minimize the risk of diarrhea, avoid the use of magnesium-containing antacids.

FOOD INTERACTIONS
No known food interactions.

DISEASE INTERACTIONS
You should not take this medication if you have ever experienced breathing difficulty, hives, swelling of the face, tongue, or throat, or any other allergic reactions after taking aspirin or other NSAIDs. Caution is advised if you have a history of high blood pressure or asthma. Use of this drug combination may cause complications in patients with liver or kidney disease, since these organs work together to remove the medications from the body.

Dicloxacillin Sodium

Generic 250 mg
(BIOCRAFT)

Additional photographs

▶ Drug Class: Penicillin antibiotic

▶ Available in: Capsules, liquid

▶ Available OTC? No

▶ As Generic? Yes

Side Effects

SERIOUS
Irregular, rapid, or labored breathing, light-headedness or sudden fainting, joint pain, fever, severe abdominal pain and cramping with watery or bloody stools, severe allergic reaction (marked by sudden swelling of the lips, tongue, face, or throat; breathing difficulty; skin rash, itching, or hives), unusual bleeding or bruising, yellowish tinge to eyes or skin. Call your doctor immediately.

COMMON
Mild rash, mild diarrhea, nausea, vomiting, headache, vaginal discharge and itching, pain or white patches in the mouth or on the tongue.

LESS COMMON
Diminished urine output, chills, weakness, fatigue.

PRINCIPAL USES
To treat bacterial infections, especially those of the skin or bone caused by penicillin-resistant staphylococcus bacteria. Dicloxacillin is ineffective against infections caused by viruses, fungi, or other microorganisms.

HOW THE DRUG WORKS
Dicloxacillin blocks the formation of bacterial cell walls, rendering bacteria unable to multiply and spread. Unlike other penicillin antibiotics, dicloxacillin is resistant to bacterial enzymes that chemically inactivate penicillins.

DOSAGE
Adults and children over 88 lbs: 125 to 250 mg every 6 hours, for a total dosage of 500 to 1,000 mg a day. Children under 88 lbs: Dose is determined by doctor, based on several factors. Usual dose is 1.4 to 2.8 mg per lb of body weight every 6 hours.

ONSET OF EFFECT
Unknown.

DURATION OF ACTION
Up to 6 hours.

DIETARY ADVICE
Take dicloxacillin on an empty stomach, 1 to 2 hours before or 2 to 3 hours after a meal, with a full glass of water.

STORAGE
Store capsules in a dry place away from heat and light. Keep the liquid form refrigerated, but do not allow it to freeze.

IF YOU MISS A DOSE
Take it as soon as you remember. If you take 2 doses a day, take the next dose 5 to 6 hours later and go back to your regular schedule. If you take 3 or more doses a day, take the next dose 2 to 4 hours later, then go back to your regular schedule. Do not double the next dose.

STOPPING THE DRUG
Take it as prescribed for the full treatment period, even if you begin to feel better before the scheduled end of therapy. Stopping the drug prematurely may slow your recovery or lead to a rebound infection, also known as superinfection, in which the heartier strains of bacteria survive and multiply, leading to a more serious and drug-resistant infection.

PROLONGED USE
Prolonged use may make you more susceptible to infections that are resistant to penicillin; caution is advised.

PRECAUTIONS
Over 60: No special problems are expected.

Driving and Hazardous Work: Usually not dangerous, since most hazardous reactions occur a few minutes after the drug is taken.

Alcohol: Alcohol may increase stomach irritation.

Pregnancy: Adequate studies of the use of penicillin antibiotics during pregnancy have not been done; however, no problems have been reported.

Breast Feeding: Dicloxacillin passes into breast milk and may cause diarrhea, fungal infections, and allergic reactions in nursing infants; avoid use while nursing.

Infants and Children: No special problems are expected.

Special Concerns: Dicloxacillin can cause false results on some urine sugar tests for patients with diabetes. Those who are prone to asthma, hay fever, hives, or allergies may be more likely to have an allergic reaction to a penicillin antibiotic. If severe diarrhea occurs as a side effect of this drug, do not take antidiarrheal medications; call your doctor.

OVERDOSE
Symptoms: Severe diarrhea, nausea, vomiting, seizures.

What to Do: Call your doctor, emergency medical services (EMS), or the nearest poison control center immediately.

DRUG INTERACTIONS
Consult your doctor for specific advice if you are taking aminoglycosides, ACE inhibitors, diuretics, potassium supplements or potassium-containing drugs, anticoagulants or other anticlotting drugs, nonsteroidal anti-inflammatory drugs, sulfinpyrazone, cholestyramine, colestipol, oral contraceptives, methotrexate, probenecid, or rifampin.

FOOD INTERACTIONS
No known food interactions.

DISEASE INTERACTIONS
Consult your doctor if you have a history of allergies, asthma, congestive heart failure, gastrointestinal disorders (especially colitis associated with the use of antibiotics), or impaired kidney function.

Dicyclomine Hydrochloride

▶ Drug Class: Antidiarrheal/antispasmodic

▶ Available in: Tablets, syrup, capsules, injection

▶ Available OTC? No

▶ As Generic? Yes

Side Effects

SERIOUS
No serious side effects are associated with dicyclomine.

COMMON
Headache; dizziness; constipation; dry mouth, nose, throat, or skin; difficulty urinating; heart palpitations.

LESS COMMON
Drowsiness, decreased sweating, confusion, nervousness, rapid pulse, blurred vision, nausea, vomiting.

PRINCIPAL USES
To treat irritable bowel syndrome, and to reduce spasms of the digestive system, bladder, and urethra.

HOW THE DRUG WORKS
Dicyclomine slows bowel action and reduces production of stomach acid.

DOSAGE
Oral forms— Adults and teenagers: 10 to 20 mg, 3 or 4 times a day. Children age 2 and older: 5 to 10 mg, 3 or 4 times a day. Children ages 6 months to 2 years: 5 to 10 mg of the syrup 3 or 4 times a day. Injection— Adults and teenagers: 20 mg into a muscle every 4 to 6 hours. Children: Consult a pediatrician for advice.

ONSET OF EFFECT
Unknown.

DURATION OF ACTION
Unknown.

DIETARY ADVICE
Take this medicine 30 to 60 minutes before meals and bedtime unless your doctor directs otherwise. Bedtime dose should be given at least 2 hours after the last meal of the day.

STORAGE
Store in a tightly sealed container away from heat, moisture, and direct light. Keep liquid forms of the drug refrigerated, but do not allow them to freeze.

IF YOU MISS A DOSE
Take it as soon as you remember, unless the time for your next scheduled dose is within the next 2 hours. If so, skip the missed dose and resume your regular dosage schedule. Do not double the next dose.

STOPPING THE DRUG
Take it as prescribed for the full treatment period. However, you may stop taking the drug if you are feeling better before the scheduled end of therapy. The doctor may want you to reduce the amount you take gradually.

PROLONGED USE
Prolonged use can cause chronic constipation and fecal impaction. Consult your doctor immediately.

PRECAUTIONS
Over 60: Adverse reactions may be more likely and more severe in older patients.

Driving and Hazardous Work: Do not drive or engage in hazardous work until you determine how the drug affects you. The use of dicyclomine disqualifies you from piloting an aircraft.

Alcohol: No special precautions are necessary.

Pregnancy: Consult your doctor about taking dicyclomine if you are pregnant or plan to become pregnant.

Breast Feeding: Dicyclomine passes into breast milk and decreases milk production. Avoid taking this medicine or discontinue breast feeding while you take it. Consult your doctor about maintaining milk flow if you breast feed.

Infants and Children: Give dicyclomine to infants and children only under close medical supervision.

Special Concerns: Tell any other doctor or dentist whom you consult that you take dicyclomine. Strenuous exercise, hot baths, or saunas while you take this medicine can make you dizzy or faint.

OVERDOSE
Symptoms: Blurred vision; dilated pupils; dizziness; rapid pulse; hot, dry skin; slurred speech; confusion; nausea; headache; loss of consciousness.

What to Do: Call your doctor, emergency medical services (EMS), or the nearest poison control center immediately.

DRUG INTERACTIONS
Consult your doctor about any other medicines you are taking, especially antacids, antihistamines, narcotic pain relievers, antiarrhythmic drugs, drugs for Parkinson's disease, antidepressants, or antipsychotic drugs (such as phenothiazines). Large doses of vitamin C can reduce the effect of dicyclomine. Potassium supplements can increase the risk of an intestinal ulcer. Nitrates and nitrites can increase internal pressure of the eye.

FOOD INTERACTIONS
No known food interactions.

DISEASE INTERACTIONS
You may not be able to take dicyclomine if you have intestinal problems, heart disease, bleeding problems, glaucoma, chronic bronchitis, an enlarged prostate, a hernia, liver disease, kidney disease, a fever, brain damage (in children), an overactive thyroid, or urinary problems.

Didanosine (Dideoxyinosine; ddI)

Videx 100 mg
(BRISTOL-MYERS SQUIBB)

▶ Drug Class: Antiviral

▶ Available in: Tablets, powder for solution

▶ Available OTC? No

▶ As Generic? No

Side Effects

SERIOUS
Nerve damage causing numbness, tingling, prickling, or pain in the hands and feet; pancreatitis (inflammation of the pancreas) causing abdominal pain, nausea, and vomiting. Call your doctor immediately.

COMMON
Temporary toxicity of the central nervous system causing headache, anxiety, irritability, restlessness, or sleep disruption; gastrointestinal disturbances, including stomach pain, gas, nausea, vomiting, and diarrhea; dry mouth.

LESS COMMON
Swollen hands or legs, shortness of breath, yellow discoloration of the eyes or skin, rash, itch, weakness, vision problems, muscle aches or spasms, muscle wasting, pain, pneumonia, cough, hair loss.

PRINCIPAL USES
To treat HIV infection. While not a cure for HIV, this drug may suppress the replication of the virus and delay the progression of the disease.

HOW THE DRUG WORKS
Didanosine (also known as dideoxyinosine or ddI) interferes with the activity of enzymes needed for the replication of DNA in viral cells.

DOSAGE
Tablets— Adults and teenagers weighing 132 lbs or more: 200 mg every 12 hours. Adults and teenagers weighing less than 132 lbs: 125 mg every 12 hours. Children: Dose may range from 25 to 100 mg every 8 to 12 hours. Tablets must be chewed or dissolved in water or apple juice. Always take 2 tablets at the same time; there is not enough medicine in a single tablet to ensure adequate absorption. Powder (dissolved in water)— Adults and teenagers weighing 132 lbs or more: 250 mg every 12 hours. Adults and teenagers weighing less than 132 lbs: 167 mg every 12 hours. Children (a special pediatric formulation is used): Dose may range from 31 to 125 mg every 8 to 12 hours. Didanosine is sometimes given once a day, using the full dose (400 mg in adults).

ONSET OF EFFECT
Unknown.

DURATION OF ACTION
Unknown.

DIETARY ADVICE
Didanosine should be taken on an empty stomach, at least 1 hour before or 2 hours after eating. If you are on a low-salt diet, be aware that this drug contains high quantities of sodium.

STORAGE
Store tablets in a dry place away from heat and direct light. The mixed solution may be refrigerated, but do not allow it to freeze.

IF YOU MISS A DOSE
If it is near the time for the next dose, skip the missed dose and resume your regular dosage schedule. Do not double the next dose.

STOPPING THE DRUG
The decision to stop taking the drug should be made in consultation with your physician.

PROLONGED USE
See your doctor regularly for tests and examinations.

PRECAUTIONS
Over 60: No special problems are expected.

Driving and Hazardous Work: Do not drive or engage in hazardous work until you determine how the medicine affects you.

Alcohol: Avoid alcohol if liver function is impaired. Heavy alcohol use can increase the risk of pancreatitis, an uncommon side effect of didanosine.

Pregnancy: While didanosine has been shown to cause birth defects in animals, it is nonetheless increasingly being used in combination with other antiretroviral drugs to treat pregnant HIV-infected women. The combination of didanosine and stavudine should be used with caution during pregnancy and is recommended only if potential benefits outweigh potential risks.

Breast Feeding: Women infected with HIV should not breast-feed.

Infants and Children: Safety and effectiveness for children under 6 months have not been established.

Special Concerns: Use of didanosine does not eliminate the risk of passing the AIDS virus to other persons. Be sure to take appropriate preventive measures.

OVERDOSE
Symptoms: Seizures, severe nausea and vomiting, extreme fatigue or weakness, unusual bleeding or bruising, clumsiness, involuntary eye movement.

What to Do: Seek medical assistance immediately.

DRUG INTERACTIONS
Consult your doctor for specific advice if you are taking antibiotic or anti-infective drugs, antidepressants, antifungals, antimalarial drugs, antiparkinson's agents, blood pressure medication, cancer drugs, diuretics, estrogens, lithium, nitrous oxide, phenytoin, stavudine, or zalcitabine.

FOOD INTERACTIONS
Food can interfere with the absorption of didanosine.

DISEASE INTERACTIONS
You may not be able to take didanosine if you have had pancreatitis (inflammation of the pancreas), hepatitis (liver inflammation), other liver or kidney problems, high blood pressure, blood disorders, gout, swollen ankles, or numbness and tingling in the hands or feet.

Diethylpropion Hydrochloride

▶ Drug Class: Sympatho-mimetic; central nervous system stimulant

▶ Available in: Tablets, extended-release tablets

▶ Available OTC? No

▶ As Generic? Yes

Side Effects

SERIOUS
Chest pain; severe dizziness; headache (especially if associated with nausea or vomiting); convulsions; rash; racing, pounding, or fluttering heartbeat.

COMMON
Lightheadedness; irritability or nervousness, difficulty falling asleep, exaggerated feelings of well-being or confidence (euphoria), increased heartbeat, palpitations, increased blood pressure.

LESS COMMON
Persistent or unusual fever, chills, sore throat, or cough; persistent or unusual bruising or bleeding; gastrointestinal problems.

PRINCIPAL USES
Diethylpropion is used to suppress appetite in obese patients. It is used in conjunction with a strict diet, and should never be prescribed as the sole method of achieving weight loss. Diethylpropion is indicated for patients with an initial body mass index (BMI) of 30 or greater (see Special Concerns for information on BMI calculation).

HOW THE DRUG WORKS
It is believed that the appetite-control center for the body may be found in a part of the brain called the hypothalamus. Diethylpropion probably affects the transmission of nerve impulses in this region.

DOSAGE
Oral tablet: 25 mg, 3 times per day before meals. Oral extended-release tablet: 75 mg, once a day, taken at midmorning.

ONSET OF EFFECT
Within a few hours after ingestion.

DURATION OF ACTION
Regular tablets: 4 hours. Extended-release: 12 hours.

DIETARY ADVICE
Take this medication one hour before meals. Significant weight loss will not occur without carefully adhering to a strict diet as outlined by your physician or nutritionist.

STORAGE
Store in a tightly sealed container away from heat and direct light. Keep away from moisture and extremes in temperature.

IF YOU MISS A DOSE
Take it as soon as you remember. If it is near the time for the next dose, skip the missed dose and resume your regular dosage schedule. Do not double the next dose.

STOPPING THE DRUG
Take as prescribed for the full treatment period. Your dose may need to be reduced gradually to prevent withdrawal effects or a rebound increase in appetite.

PROLONGED USE
This drug is usually prescribed for several weeks. Side effects may become more likely over this period of time. Prolonged use may result in mental or physical dependence.

PRECAUTIONS
Over 60: Adverse reactions may be more likely and more severe in older patients, especially with drugs that act on the central nervous system.

Driving and Hazardous Work: Do not drive or engage in hazardous activities until you determine how the drug affects you.

Alcohol: Avoid alcohol.

Pregnancy: Avoid or discontinue diethylpropion if you are pregnant or trying to become pregnant.

Breast Feeding: Diethylpropion passes into breast milk; avoid or discontinue usage while nursing.

Infants and Children: Not recommended for use by children under age 12.

Special Concerns: The appetite suppressant effect of this medication may diminish after a few weeks. This is known as drug tolerance, and you should inform your physician. Do not increase the dose. The BMI can be calculated by dividing your weight in pounds by your height in inches squared, and then multiplying by 705.

OVERDOSE
Symptoms: Extreme restlessness; tremor or shaking of the hands, muscles of the face, or other areas of the body; confusion; hallucinations; extreme fear or panic; rapid breathing; violent behavior; nausea; vomiting; fainting; coma.

What to Do: Call emergency medical services (EMS), your doctor, or the nearest poison control center immediately.

DRUG INTERACTIONS
Consult your doctor for specific advice if you are taking amantadine; amphetamines, medications for hyperactivity, or other drugs for appetite control; caffeine; chlophedianol; asthma medication; prescription and nonprescription decongestants or medicine for colds, sinus problems, or seasonal allergies such as hay fever (including nose drops or sprays); methylphenidate; nabilone; pemoline; or an MAO inhibitor.

FOOD INTERACTIONS
Avoid food or beverages containing caffeine.

DISEASE INTERACTIONS
Consult your doctor if you have a history of alcohol or drug abuse; diabetes mellitus; glaucoma; heart disease; blood vessel disease, especially of the arteries; strokes or "mini strokes" (transient ischemic attacks); high blood pressure; mental illness; or thyroid or kidney disease. An increased frequency of seizures has been reported in patients with epilepsy.

Diethylstilbestrol (DES)

BRAND NAMES
Stilbestrol, Stilbetin

Generic 5 mg
(LILLY)

832

Additional photographs

▶ Drug Class: Antineoplastic (anticancer) agent; hormone treatment

▶ Available in: Tablets, injection

▶ Available OTC? No

▶ As Generic? Yes

Side Effects

SERIOUS
Breast pain or increased breast size (in both men and women), swelling of feet and lower legs, rapid weight gain, irregular vaginal bleeding, painful menstrual periods, breast lumps, pain in stomach, side, or abdomen, jerky muscle movements, yellowish tinge to eyes or skin (jaundice), sudden or severe headache, loss of coordination, loss of or change in vision, pain in chest, groin, or leg, sudden shortness of breath, slurred speech, weakness or numbness in arm or leg. Notify your doctor promptly.

COMMON
Bloating of or cramps in stomach, loss of appetite, nausea, rash, freckles on the face.

LESS COMMON
Abnormal hair loss or growth, joint pain, depression, dizziness, headache, problems with contact lenses, change in level of sexual desire, vomiting, diarrhea.

PRINCIPAL USES
To slow the progress of advanced breast and prostate cancers.

HOW THE DRUG WORKS
Diethylstilbestrol is a form of the hormone estrogen. It can block the action of certain other hormones that promote tumor growth; this in turn will slow the progress of the cancer.

DOSAGE
Tablet— For breast cancer: 15 mg once a day. For prostate cancer: 1 to 3 mg a day; dose may be decreased to 1 mg a day. Injection— 500 mg a day. The dose may be increased to 1 g per day, then lowered to 250 to 500 mg once a week.

ONSET OF EFFECT
Unknown.

DURATION OF ACTION
Unknown.

DIETARY ADVICE
Drink plenty of fluids.

STORAGE
Store in a tightly sealed container away from heat and direct light.

IF YOU MISS A DOSE
Take it as soon as you remember. If it is close to the time for the next dose, skip the missed dose and resume your regular dosage schedule. Do not double the next dose.

STOPPING THE DRUG
The decision to stop taking diethylstilbestrol should be made in consultation with your doctor.

PROLONGED USE
You should see your doctor regularly for tests and examinations if you take this drug for a prolonged period.

PRECAUTIONS
Over 60: No extra problems or side effects are expected in older patients as compared with younger persons.

Driving and Hazardous Work: Do not drive or engage in hazardous work until you determine how the medicine affects you.

Alcohol: Avoid alcohol.

Pregnancy: Diethylstilbestrol can cause birth defects and should never be taken during pregnancy.

Breast Feeding: Not recommended while taking diethylstilbestrol.

Infants and Children: Diethylstilbestrol is not recommended for use in infants and children.

Special Concerns: Diethylstilbestrol may cause tenderness, swelling, or bleeding of the gums. Brush and floss your teeth regularly and see your dentist regularly. Patients who take DES may be at increased risk for cancer.

OVERDOSE
Symptoms: Loss of appetite, nausea, vomiting, abdominal cramps, diarrhea, vaginal bleeding.

What to Do: Call your doctor, emergency medical services (EMS), or the nearest poison control center immediately.

DRUG INTERACTIONS
Consult your doctor for specific advice if you are taking acetaminophen, amiodarone, anabolic steroids, androgens, anti-infective medications, antithyroid agents, carbamazepine, carmustine, chloroquine, dantrolene, daunorubicin, disulfiram, divalproex, etretinate, gold salts, hydroxychloroquine, mercaptopurine, methotrexate, methyldopa, naltrexone, oral contraceptives, phenothiazines, phenytoin, plicamycin, tamoxifen, valproic acid, bromocriptine, or cyclosporine.

FOOD INTERACTIONS
No known food interactions.

DISEASE INTERACTIONS
Caution is advised when taking diethylstilbestrol. Consult your doctor if you have a history of blood clots, changes in vaginal bleeding, endometriosis, fibroid tumors of the uterus, gallbladder disease or gallstones, jaundice, liver disease, porphyria, blood clots, heart or circulatory disease, stroke, high blood pressure, diabetes mellitus, asthma, kidney disease, liver disease, or depression.

Diflunisal

▶ Drug Class: Nonsteroidal anti-inflammatory drug (NSAID)

▶ Available in: Tablets

▶ Available OTC? No

▶ As Generic? Yes

Side Effects

SERIOUS
Shortness of breath or wheezing, with or without swelling of legs or other signs of heart failure; chest pain; peptic ulcer disease with vomiting of blood; black, tarry stools; decreasing kidney function. Call your doctor immediately.

COMMON
Nausea, vomiting, heartburn, diarrhea, constipation, headache, dizziness, sleepiness.

LESS COMMON
Ulcers or sores in mouth, depression, rashes or blistering of skin, ringing sound in the ears, unusual tingling or numbness of the hands or feet, seizures, blurred vision. Also elevated potassium levels, decreased blood counts; such problems can be detected by your doctor.

PRINCIPAL USES
To treat mild to moderate pain and inflammation caused by tendinitis, arthritis, bursitis, gout, soft tissue injuries, migraine and other vascular headaches, menstrual cramps, and other conditions. When patients fail to respond to one NSAID, another may be tried. The greatest effectiveness often requires trial and error of several different NSAIDs.

HOW THE DRUG WORKS
NSAIDs work by interfering with the formation of prostaglandins, naturally occurring substances in the body that cause inflammation and make nerves more sensitive to pain impulses. NSAIDs also have other modes of action that are less well understood.

DOSAGE
Adults and teenagers: 500 to 1,000 mg a day in 2 divided doses. Adults over age 65: 250 to 500 mg a day in 2 divided doses.

ONSET OF EFFECT
Within 1 hour; 3 weeks of regular use may be required for maximum effect.

DURATION OF ACTION
8 to 12 hours.

DIETARY ADVICE
Take with food; maintain your usual food and fluid intake.

STORAGE
Store in a tightly sealed container away from heat, moisture, and direct light.

IF YOU MISS A DOSE
Take it as soon as you remember. If it is near the time for the next dose, skip the missed dose and resume your regular dosage schedule. Do not double the next dose.

STOPPING THE DRUG
The decision to stop taking the drug should be made in consultation with your physician.

PROLONGED USE
Prolonged use can cause gastrointestinal problems, including ulceration and bleeding, kidney dysfunction, and liver inflammation. Consult your physician about the need for medical examinations and laboratory studies.

PRECAUTIONS
Over 60: Because of the potentially greater consequences of gastrointestinal side effects, the dose of NSAIDs for older patients, especially those over age 70, is often cut in half.

Driving and Hazardous Work: Do not drive or engage in hazardous work until you determine how this drug affects you.

Alcohol: Avoid alcohol when using this medication because it increases the risk of stomach irritation.

Pregnancy: Avoid or discontinue this drug if you are pregnant or plan to become pregnant.

Breast Feeding: Diflunisal passes into breast milk; avoid or discontinue use while nursing.

Infants and Children: Diflunisal is not generally prescribed for children under the age of 12, but may be used in exceptional circumstances; consult your pediatrician.

Special Concerns: Because NSAIDs can interfere with blood coagulation, this drug should be stopped at least 3 days prior to any surgery.

OVERDOSE
Symptoms: Nausea, vomiting, severe headache, confusion, seizures.

What to Do: Call your doctor, emergency medical services (EMS), or the nearest poison control center immediately.

DRUG INTERACTIONS
Do not take this drug with aspirin or any other NSAIDs without your doctor's approval. In addition, consult your doctor if you are taking antihypertensives, steroids, anticoagulants, antibiotics, itraconazole or ketoconazole, plicamycin, penicillamine, valproic acid, phenytoin, cyclosporine, digitalis drugs, lithium, methotrexate, probenecid, triamterene, or zidovudine.

FOOD INTERACTIONS
No known food interactions.

DISEASE INTERACTIONS
Caution is advised when taking diflunisal. Consult your doctor if you have any of the following: bleeding problems, inflammation or ulcers of the stomach and intestines, diabetes mellitus, systemic lupus erythematosus (SLE, lupus), anemia, asthma, epilepsy, Parkinson's disease, kidney stones, or a history of heart disease or alcohol abuse. Use of diflunisal may cause complications in patients with liver or kidney disease, since these organs work together to remove the medication from the body.

Digitoxin

BRAND NAME
Crystodigin

Generic 0.1 mg
(LILLY)

▶ Drug Class: Digitalis drug (cardiac glycoside)

▶ Available in: Tablets

▶ Available OTC? No

▶ As Generic? Yes

Side Effects

SERIOUS
Heartbeat irregularities that may be life-threatening and cause dizziness, palpitations, shortness of breath, sweating, or fainting. Other serious side effects include hallucinations, confusion, and mental changes; extreme drowsiness; and visual disturbances such as double vision or seeing colored halos around objects. Call your doctor right away.

COMMON
Weakness, fatigue, blurred vision, nausea, agitation, erectile dysfunction, male breast enlargement.

LESS COMMON
Headache, vertigo, numbness or tingling sensation, overall feeling of illness, increased sensitivity of eyes to light, diarrhea, vomiting.

PRINCIPAL USES
To treat congestive heart failure and atrial arrhythmias (heart rhythm irregularities). Because this drug carries potentially serious risks, it is seldom prescribed in current medical practice.

HOW THE DRUG WORKS
Digitalis drugs such as digitoxin enhance and strengthen the force of the heart's contractions, and thus help to regulate the rate and the rhythm of the heartbeat.

DOSAGE
Adults: Initial dose is 0.2 mg, 2 times a day for 4 days. Maintenance dosage ranges from 0.05 to 0.3 mg, taken once a day. Children: Dosage must be determined by your pediatrician. Dosages for all patients must be closely regulated by frequently checking drug levels in the blood.

ONSET OF EFFECT
30 minutes to 2 hours.

DURATION OF ACTION
3 to 4 days.

DIETARY ADVICE
Take it on an empty stomach at the same time every day. Taking digitoxin with food can decrease the absorption rate and peak concentration.

STORAGE
Store in a tightly sealed container away from heat, moisture, and direct light.

IF YOU MISS A DOSE
Take it as soon as you remember. However, if it is within 12 hours of the next scheduled dose, skip the missed dose and resume your regular dosage schedule. Do not double the next dose.

STOPPING THE DRUG
Many patients must take digitoxin for extended periods. Do not stop taking digitoxin unless your doctor advises you to do so.

PROLONGED USE
Prolonged use requires your doctor's careful supervision and periodic assessments of the continued need to take the drug. Blood levels of digitoxin must be measured at regular intervals to ensure proper dosing.

PRECAUTIONS
Over 60: Underweight or frail older persons may require a lower maintenance dose.

Driving and Hazardous Work: Digitoxin may cause drowsiness or vision changes. Do not drive or engage in hazardous work until you determine how it affects you.

Alcohol: No interactions are expected.

Pregnancy: Human studies have not been done. In animal studies, no birth defects have been reported. Digitoxin should be used during pregnancy only if your doctor says it is clearly needed.

Breast Feeding: Digitoxin passes into breast milk. The nursing infant should be monitored carefully. Stop using the drug or discontinue breast feeding if adverse effects develop.

Infants and Children: The dosage for infants and children must be determined by your pediatrician.

Special Concerns: You should carry a card that says you are taking digitoxin. Do not take over-the-counter antacids or cold or allergy remedies without consulting your doctor. Digitoxin causes impotence and enlarged breasts in a third of the men who take it. Mental changes induced by the drug may be mistaken for psychosis or senility.

OVERDOSE
Symptoms: Heart palpitations, abdominal pain, diarrhea, nausea, vomiting, very slow pulse.

What to Do: Call your doctor, emergency medical services (EMS), or the nearest poison control center immediately.

DRUG INTERACTIONS
Numerous drugs interact with digitoxin and may alter blood levels of the drug, leading to toxicity. Consult your doctor for specific advice if you are taking any drug, especially airway-opening drugs (bronchodilators), antacids, antibiotics such as neomycin or tetracycline, anticholinergic drugs such as atropine, cholesterol-lowering drugs, diuretics, steroids, indomethacin, or any other heart drug.

FOOD INTERACTIONS
Ask your doctor about the advisability of eating high-potassium foods.

DISEASE INTERACTIONS
Consult your doctor if you have any other medical condition, especially lung disease, kidney disease, or poor thyroid function.

Digoxin

Lanoxin 0.125 mg
(GLAXO WELLCOME)

Additional photographs

▶ Drug Class: Digitalis drug
(cardiac glycoside)

▶ Available in: Tablets,
capsules, elixir

▶ Available OTC? No

▶ As Generic? Yes

Side Effects

SERIOUS
Heartbeat irregularities
causing dizziness, palpitations, shortness of
breath, sweating, or fainting. Other serious side
effects include hallucinations, confusion, and
mental changes; extreme
drowsiness; visual disturbances such as double
vision or seeing colored
halos around objects;
weakness, fatigue,
blurred vision; nausea;
or agitation. Call your
doctor immediately.

COMMON
Erectile dysfunction,
male breast enlargement.
Notify your doctor if
such symptoms occur.

LESS COMMON
Headache, vertigo, numb-
ness or tingling sensa-
tion, overall feeling of
illness, sensitivity of eyes
to light, diarrhea, vomiting. Call your doctor if
such symptoms persist.

PRINCIPAL USES
To treat congestive heart
failure (CHF) and atrial
arrhythmias (heart rhythm
irregularities).

HOW THE DRUG WORKS
Digitalis drugs such as
digoxin enhance and
strengthen the force of the
heart's contractions, and
help to regulate the rate and
the rhythm of the heartbeat.

DOSAGE
Adults: Initial dose is 0.5
mg. Maintenance dosage,
starting the next day,
ranges from 0.125 to 0.25
mg a day (rarely more)
taken once a day. Periodic
blood tests are necessary to
determine the proper dose.
Children: Dosage is determined by your doctor.

ONSET OF EFFECT
30 minutes to 2 hours.

DURATION OF ACTION
3 to 4 days.

DIETARY ADVICE
Take it on an empty stom-
ach, at the same time every
day. Taking digoxin with
food can decrease the
absorption rate and the
peak concentration.

STORAGE
Store in a tightly sealed container away from heat, moisture, and direct light.

IF YOU MISS A DOSE
Take it as soon as you
remember. If it is within 12
hours of the next scheduled
dose, skip the missed dose
and resume your regular
dosage schedule. Do not
double the next dose.

STOPPING THE DRUG
Do not stop taking it unless
your doctor advises otherwise. Abrupt discontinuation
can cause serious heart
problems. Most patients
take digoxin for an

extended period or for the
rest of their lives.

PROLONGED USE
Prolonged use requires
your doctor's supervision
and periodic assessments of
the continued need to take
the drug. Blood levels of
digoxin must be measured
at regular intervals to
ensure proper dosing.

PRECAUTIONS
Over 60: Underweight or
frail older persons may
require a lower mainte-
nance dose.

**Driving and Hazardous
Work:** Digoxin may cause
drowsiness or vision
changes. Do not drive or
engage in hazardous work
until you determine how it
affects you.

Alcohol: No interactions
are expected.

Pregnancy: Human studies have not been done. In
animal studies, no birth
defects have been reported.
Digoxin should be used during pregnancy only if your
doctor decides it is clearly
needed.

Breast Feeding: Digoxin
passes into breast milk. The
nursing infant should be
monitored carefully. Stop
using the drug or discon-
tinue breast feeding if
adverse effects develop.

Infants and Children:
The dosage for infants and
children must be deter-
mined by your pediatrician.

Special Concerns: You
should carry a card that
says you are taking
digoxin. Do not take over-
the-counter antacids or cold
or allergy remedies without
consulting your doctor.
Digoxin causes impotence
and enlarged breasts in a

third of the men who take
it. Mental changes induced
by the drug may be mis-
taken for psychosis or senility.

OVERDOSE
Symptoms: Heart palpitations, abdominal pain, diarrhea, nausea, vomiting, very
slow pulse.

What to Do: Call your
doctor, emergency medical
services (EMS), or the
nearest poison control center immediately.

DRUG INTERACTIONS
Numerous drugs interact
with digoxin and may alter
blood levels of the drug,
leading to toxicity. Consult
your doctor for specific
advice if you are taking
any medications, especially
antiarrhythmic drugs,
such as quinidine or pro-
cainamide, airway-opening
drugs (bronchodilators),
antacids, antibiotics such
as neomycin or tetracycline,
anticholinergic drugs such
as atropine, cholesterol-
lowering drugs, diuretics
(water pills), steroids,
indomethacin, or any
other heart drug.

FOOD INTERACTIONS
Ask your doctor about the
advisability of eating high-
potassium foods.

DISEASE INTERACTIONS
Tell your doctor if you have
any other medical condition,
especially lung disease, kidney disease, or poor thyroid
function.

Dihydroergotamine Mesylate

BRAND NAMES
D.H.E. 45, Migranal

▶ Drug Class: Antimigraine/ antiheadache drug

▶ Available in: Injection, nasal spray

▶ Available OTC? No

▶ As Generic? No

Side Effects

SERIOUS
Blurred vision, headaches, chest pain, pale, cold, bluish-colored hands or feet, numbness or tingling in fingers and toes, gangrene. Such symptoms may indicate inadequate blood circulation owing to excessive blood vessel constriction. Other serious side effects include: rapid or slow heartbeat, itching, weakness in legs, muscle pain, severe anxiety or confusion, and excess water retention. Seek medical attention immediately.

COMMON
Constipation, reduced sweating, dizziness or lightheadedness, drowsiness.

LESS COMMON
Nausea, vomiting.

PRINCIPAL USES
To treat migraine headaches. This drug is ineffective against other kinds of pain or headaches, and because of its potential for serious side effects, it is prescribed only when other treatments prove ineffective.

HOW THE DRUG WORKS
It reduces throbbing pain by constricting the walls of the blood vessels that carry blood in the brain. It may also depress activity in certain areas in the brain, directly suppressing headache pain. Because this drug may cause constriction of blood vessels throughout the body, serious side effects may result from lack of sufficient blood supply to various organ systems.

DOSAGE
Injection: 1 mg per injection, up to 2 mg per attack, with at least 1 or 2 hours between injections. Maximum weekly dosage is 6 mg. Lie down in a quiet, dark room after the injection. Nasal spray: 1 spray (0.5 mg) in each nostril. Fifteen minutes later, an additional 1 spray should be administered in each nostril for a total of 4 sprays (2 mg). Maximum daily dosage is 3 mg; maximum weekly dosage is 4 mg. Do not sniff following administration. The nasal spray should stay in the nose so that it can be absorbed into the bloodstream through the lining of the nose. This drug works best when taken at the first sign of a migraine headache; dihydroergotamine should not be taken preventively.

ONSET OF EFFECT
Injection: Intravenous: Within 5 minutes. Intramuscular: Within 15 to 30 minutes. Nasal spray: Unknown

DURATION OF ACTION
Injection: About 8 hours. Nasal spray: Unknown.

DIETARY ADVICE
Do not fast or skip meals; this may trigger a migraine. Try to eat at least three meals a day, at the same times each day. Avoid foods that contain preservatives (such as nitrates and nitrites), monosodium glutamate (MSG), and large amounts of caffeine or salt.

STORAGE
Store in a tightly sealed container away from moisture, heat, and direct light. Do not refrigerate or freeze the nasal spray.

IF YOU MISS A DOSE
Not applicable. This drug is only taken as needed.

STOPPING THE DRUG
Headaches may get worse if you stop using this drug. Consult your doctor.

PROLONGED USE
Prolonged use can lead to addiction or tolerance to this medicine. Consult your doctor if the usual dose fails to relieve headaches or if the frequency or severity of headaches increases.

PRECAUTIONS
Over 60: Side effects are more likely and may be more severe.

Driving and Hazardous Work: Exercise caution until you determine how this drug affects you.

Alcohol: Limit intake of alcohol, as it may increase the constriction of blood vessels caused by this drug.

Pregnancy: This medicine should not be used during pregnancy because it can cause a miscarriage or serious damage to the fetus.

Breast Feeding: This drug passes into breast milk and can cause vomiting, diarrhea, convulsions, or other untoward effects in nursing infants.

Infants and Children: Consult your pediatrician about giving the injection to children age 6 and older. Adequate studies of the use of the nasal spray have not been done.

OVERDOSE
Symptoms: Seizures, nausea, vomiting, stomach pain or bloating, unusually rapid or slow heartbeat, severe headache, dizziness, drowsiness, constipation, shortness of breath, excitability.

What to Do: Call your doctor, emergency medical services (EMS), or the nearest poison control center immediately.

DRUG INTERACTIONS
Do not take dihydroergotamine within 24 hours of taking naratriptan, sumatriptan, or zolmitriptan. Do not take this medication if you are taking ritonavir, nelfinavir, indinavir, erythromycin, clarithromycin, troleandromycin, ketoconazole, itraconazole, or any allergy or cold remedies. Consult your doctor if you are taking any other drugs, especially, nicotine, insulin, or beta-blockers.

FOOD INTERACTIONS
Caffeine and salt intake should be limited.

DISEASE INTERACTIONS
Tell your doctor if you are overly sensitive to this drug or other ergot derivatives or if you have any other condition, especially high blood pressure, a blood vessel condition, any infection, a liver problem, a heart problem, or a kidney problem.

Diltiazem Hydrochloride

Side Effects

SERIOUS
Irregular or slow heartbeat, shortness of breath, and fatigue caused by heart failure. Call a doctor immediately.

COMMON
Headache, drowsiness, swelling of feet and ankles, constipation, nausea, sudden weight gain, fatigue.

LESS COMMON
Dizziness, weakness, depression, nervousness, insomnia, confusion, slow pulse, vomiting, diarrhea, excessive urination, itch, sensitivity to sunlight, yellowish tinge to eyes or skin due to liver failure, skin rash, overgrowth of the gums.

PRINCIPAL USES
To relieve and control angina (chest pain associated with heart disease), to reduce high blood pressure, and to correct heartbeat irregularities (cardiac arrhythmia).

HOW THE DRUG WORKS
Diltiazem interferes with the movement of calcium into heart muscle cells and the smooth muscle cells in the walls of the arteries. This action relaxes blood vessels (causing them to widen), which lowers blood pressure, increases the blood supply to the heart, and decreases the heart's overall workload.

DOSAGE
Tablets (for chest pain)—30 mg, 3 or 4 times a day to start, increased to 40 to 60 mg, 3 or 4 times a day. Extended-release capsules (for high blood pressure)—120 to 240 mg a day taken in 1 or 2 divided doses. (For heartbeat irregularities, diltiazem is administered by injection by a health care professional.)

ONSET OF EFFECT
Tablets: 30 to 60 minutes. Extended-release capsules: 2 to 3 hours.

DURATION OF ACTION
Tablets: 6 to 8 hours. Extended-release capsules: 10 to 14 hours.

DIETARY ADVICE
Diltiazem is best taken before meals or at bedtime.

STORAGE
Store tablets and capsules in a tightly sealed container away from heat, moisture, and direct light.

IF YOU MISS A DOSE
Take it as soon as you remember. However, if it is near the time for the next dose, skip the missed dose and resume your regular dosage schedule. Do not double the next dose.

STOPPING THE DRUG
Do not stop taking this drug suddenly, as this may cause potentially serious health problems. If therapy is to be discontinued, dosage should be reduced gradually, according to doctor's instructions.

PROLONGED USE
No unusual side effects are expected with prolonged therapy.

PRECAUTIONS
Over 60: Weakness, dizziness, and fainting are more likely in older persons.

Driving and Hazardous Work: Diltiazem can cause dizziness or drowsiness. Do not drive or engage in hazardous work until you determine how the medicine affects you.

Alcohol: Use alcohol with caution because it may increase the effect of the drug and cause an excessive drop in blood pressure.

Pregnancy: Birth defects have occurred in animal studies. Adequate human studies have not been done. Avoid this drug during the first 3 months of pregnancy and take it during the last 6 months only if your doctor says it is clearly needed.

Breast Feeding: Diltiazem passes into breast milk; avoid or discontinue use while breast feeding.

Infants and Children: Usually not prescribed; the safety and effectiveness of diltiazem for children under the age of 12 have not been established.

Special Concerns: It is important to brush and floss your teeth and see your dentist regularly, since using diltiazem may promote dental problems. This drug may make you sensitive to sunlight.

OVERDOSE
Symptoms: Heart block causing unusual shortness of breath; fatigue, excessive dizziness, fainting.

What to Do: Call your doctor, emergency medical services (EMS) or the nearest poison control center immediately.

DRUG INTERACTIONS
Consult your doctor for specific advice if you are taking aspirin, beta-blockers, digitalis preparations, carbamazepine, cyclosporine, digoxin, lithium, oral diabetes agents, phenytoin, rifampin, cimetidine, fluvoxamine, or ranitidine.

FOOD INTERACTIONS
Avoid excessive salt intake.

DISEASE INTERACTIONS
Consult your doctor if you have any of the following: kidney disease, liver disease, high blood pressure, or any kind of heart or blood vessel disease.

Dimenhydrinate

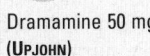

Dramamine 50 mg
(UPJOHN)

Additional photographs

▶ Drug Class: Antihistamine

▶ Available in: Capsules,
tablets, elixir, syrup, injection,
suppositories

▶ Available OTC? Yes

▶ As Generic? Yes

Side Effects

SERIOUS
No serious side effects
are associated with this
drug.

COMMON
Drowsiness.

LESS COMMON
Headache, blurred vision,
palpitations, loss of coordination, dry mouth, low
blood pressure causing
dizziness and weakness,
ringing in ears.

PRINCIPAL USES
To relieve nausea and vomiting and to treat or prevent
motion sickness.

HOW THE DRUG WORKS
Dimenhydrinate directly
inhibits the stimulation of
certain nerves in the brain
and inner ear to suppress
nausea, vomiting, dizziness,
and vertigo.

DOSAGE
Capsules, tablets, liquids—
Adults: 50 to 100 mg every
4 to 6 hours. Children ages
6 to 12: 25 to 50 mg every 6
to 8 hours. Children ages 2
to 6: 12.5 to 25 mg every 6
to 8 hours. Injection—
Adults: 50 mg into a vein
every 4 hours. Children:
1.25 mg per 2.2 lbs (1 kg)
of body weight into a vein
or muscle every 6 hours.
Suppositories— Adults: 50
to 100 mg every 6 to 8
hours. Children over age
12: 50 mg every 8 to 12
hours. Children ages 8 to
12: 25 to 50 mg every 8 to
12 hours. Children ages 6 to
8: 12.5 to 25 mg every 8 to
12 hours. To prevent motion
sickness, take this drug at
least 30 minutes, and preferably 1 to 2 hours, before
traveling.

ONSET OF EFFECT
Oral: Within 20 to 30 minutes. Injection: 2 to 20 minutes. Suppositories: 30 to 45
minutes.

DURATION OF ACTION
3 to 6 hours.

DIETARY ADVICE
This drug can be taken with
food or milk to minimize
gastrointestinal distress.

STORAGE
Store in a tightly sealed container in a dry place away
from heat and direct light.

IF YOU MISS A DOSE
Take it as soon as you
remember. However, if it is
near the time for the next
dose, skip the missed dose
and resume your regular
dosage schedule. Do not
double the next dose.

STOPPING THE DRUG
You should take it as prescribed for the full treatment period, but you may
stop if you are feeling better
before the scheduled end of
therapy.

PROLONGED USE
Take this drug only as long
as it is needed.

PRECAUTIONS
Over 60: Older persons
are more sensitive to the
effects of dimenhydrinate.
Dizziness, drowsiness, confusion, difficult or painful
urination, and other side
effects are more likely to
occur.

**Driving and Hazardous
Work:** Do not drive or
engage in hazardous work
until you determine how the
medicine affects you.

Alcohol: Avoid alcohol.

Pregnancy: Animal studies
with high doses of dimenhydrinate have found no birth
defects. Human studies
have not been done.
Because the studies cannot
rule out harm, the drug
should be used during pregnancy only if it is clearly
needed.

Breast Feeding: Dimenhydrinate may pass into breast
milk; caution is advised;
avoid or discontinue use
while nursing.

Infants and Children:
The safety and efficacy of
this drug in children under
2 years of age (age 6 for the
suppository form) have not

been established. Older
children are especially
sensitive to the drug's
side effects.

Special Concerns: Children should be observed
carefully for signs of side
effects; they are more likely
to develop serious complications from these medica-
tions, and younger children
are often unable to describe
changes in the way that
they are feeling.

OVERDOSE
Symptoms: Seizures, hallucinations, drowsiness, difficulty breathing,
unconsciousness.

What to Do: An overdose
of dimenhydrinate is
unlikely to be life-threatening. However, if someone
takes a much larger dose
than prescribed, call your
doctor, emergency medical
services (EMS), or the
nearest poison control center immediately.

DRUG INTERACTIONS
Consult your doctor for
specific advice if you are
taking any narcotic pain
relievers, sedatives, tranquilizers, antidepressants,
antibiotics, aspirin, barbiturates, cisplatin, diuretics,
or theophylline.

FOOD INTERACTIONS
No known food interactions.

DISEASE INTERACTIONS
Caution is advised when
taking dimenhydrinate.
Consult your doctor if you
have glaucoma or an
enlarged prostate.

Diphenhydramine Hydrochloride

BRAND NAMES
Benadryl, Benahist,
Benylin Cough, Compoz,
Diphenhist, Nytol,
Phendry, Sleep-Eze 3,
Sominex Formula 2,
Unisom SleepGels
Maximum Strength

Benadryl Allergy 25 mg
(PARKE-DAVIS)

Additional photographs

▶ Drug Class: Antihistamine

▶ Available in: Capsules, elixir,
syrup, tablets, injection

▶ Available OTC? Yes

▶ As Generic? Yes

Side Effects

SERIOUS
No serious side effects
are associated with this
drug.

COMMON
Drowsiness, dry mouth,
nausea, thickening of
mucus.

LESS COMMON
Confusion, difficult urination, blurred vision.

PRINCIPAL USES
To relieve hay fever symptoms, itching skin and
hives, motion sickness, non-
productive cough due to
cold or hay fever, and sleeping difficulty; also used to
treat symptoms of Parkin-
son's disease.

HOW THE DRUG WORKS
It blocks the effects of histamine, a naturally occurring
substance that causes
swelling, itching, sneezing,
and watery eyes. In patients
with Parkinson's disease, it
decreases tremors and
muscle stiffness.

DOSAGE
For hay fever symptoms—
Capsules, elixir, syrup,
tablets: Adults and
teenagers: 25 to 50 mg
every 4 to 6 hours. Children
younger than age 6: 6.25 to
12.5 mg every 4 to 6 hours.
Children ages 6 to 12: 12.5
to 25 mg every 4 to 6 hours.
Injection: Adults: 10 to 50
mg into a vein or muscle.
Children: 1.25 mg per 2.2
lbs (1 kg) of body weight
into a muscle 4 times a day.
For nausea, vomiting and
dizziness— Capsules, elixir,
syrup, tablets: Adults: 25 to
50 mg every 4 to 6 hours.
Children: 1 to 1.5 mg per
2.2 lbs every 4 to 6 hours.
Injection: Adults: 10 mg into
a vein or muscle. May be
increased to 25 to 50 mg
every 2 to 3 hours. Chil-
dren: 1 to 1.5 mg per 2.2 lbs
every 6 hours. For Parkinson's disease— Capsules,
elixir, syrup, tablets: Adults:
25 mg, 3 times a day. Doctor may gradually in-crease
dose. Injection: Adults: 10 to
50 mg into a vein or muscle.
Children: 1.25 mg per 2.2
lbs into a muscle, 4 times a
day. As a sedative— Cap-
sules, elixir, syrup, tablets:
Adults: 50 mg 20 to 30 minutes before bedtime. For
cough— Liquid: Adults and
teenagers: 25 mg every 4 to
6 hours. Children ages 2 to
6: 6.25 mg (½ teaspoon)
every 4 to 6 hours. Children
ages 6 to 12: 12.5 mg (1 teaspoon) every 4 to 6 hours.

ONSET OF EFFECT
After capsules, elixir, syrup,
or tablets: 15 minutes. Injection: unknown.

DURATION OF ACTION
6 to 8 hours.

DIETARY ADVICE
Take diphenhydramine with
food or milk to reduce gastrointestinal distress.

STORAGE
Store in a dry place away
from heat and direct light.
Prevent liquid forms from
freezing.

IF YOU MISS A DOSE
Take it as soon as you
remember. If it is near the
time for the next dose, skip
the missed dose and
resume your regular dosage
schedule. Do not double the
next dose.

STOPPING THE DRUG
Stop taking this drug and
call your doctor if it is not
effective after 5 days.

PROLONGED USE
No special problems have
been reported.

PRECAUTIONS
Over 60: Adverse reactions
may be more likely and
more severe.

**Driving and Hazardous
Work:** Do not drive or
engage in hazardous work
until you determine how the
medicine affects you. Use of
this drug is a disqualification for piloting aircraft.

Alcohol: Alcohol may
increase the likelihood and
severity of side effects such
as drowsiness and mental
confusion.

Pregnancy: No birth
defects have been reported
in animals. Studies of pregnant women have found no
significant increase in birth
defects.

Breast Feeding: Diphenhydramine passes into
breast milk; avoid or discontinue use while nursing.

Infants and Children:
This drug is not recom-
mended for children under
the age of 2.

Special Concerns: Children should be observed
carefully for signs of side
effects; they are more likely
to develop serious complications, and younger children
are often unable to describe
changes in the way that
they are feeling.

OVERDOSE
Symptoms: Marked
drowsiness, dilated and
unreactive pupils, fever,
excitability, breathing interruptions, combativeness,
confusion, loss of coordination, weak pulse, seizures,
loss of consciousness.

What to Do: Call your
doctor, emergency medical
services (EMS), or the
nearest poison control center immediately.

DRUG INTERACTIONS
Consult your doctor for specific advice if you are taking
anticholinergics, alcohol,
disopyramide, central nervous system depressants,
or MAO inhibitors.

FOOD INTERACTIONS
No known food interactions.

DISEASE INTERACTIONS
Consult your doctor if you
have a history of severe respiratory disease, glaucoma,
urinary obstruction, or
prostate enlargement.

Diphenoxylate Hydrochloride/Atropine Sulfate

Lonox 2.5/0.025 mg
(GENEVA)

▶ Drug Class: Antidiarrheal

▶ Available in: Liquid, tablet

▶ Available OTC? No

▶ As Generic? Yes

Side Effects

SERIOUS
Swelling of the hands, feet, face, lips or throat; severe stomach pain accompanied by nausea and vomiting. Call your doctor immediately.

COMMON
Dizziness, dry mouth, sedation.

LESS COMMON
Drowsiness, lethargy, headache, restlessness, mental depression, fast pulse, enlarged pupils, nausea, vomiting, abdominal discomfort, loss of appetite, slowed breathing, rash, itching, inability to urinate.

PRINCIPAL USES
To relieve severe diarrhea and intestinal cramps.

HOW THE DRUG WORKS
This medication blocks nerve activity in the intestinal tract, which reduces propulsive contractions (peristalsis) and diminishes intestinal secretions.

DOSAGE
Adults and teenagers: 5 mg (2 tablets or 2 teaspoons), 3 or 4 times a day. Your doctor may reduce the dose when diarrhea starts to be controlled. Children: Consult your pediatrician.

ONSET OF EFFECT
Within 45 to 60 minutes.

DURATION OF ACTION
3 to 4 hours.

DIETARY ADVICE
The tablet should be taken with liquid or food to reduce stomach irritation. A mild diet is recommended when recovering from diarrhea. Bananas, rice, applesauce, and plain toast are good choices. Be sure to get plenty of fluids.

STORAGE
Store in a tightly sealed container in a dry place away from heat, moisture, and direct light. Keep the liquid form from freezing.

IF YOU MISS A DOSE
Take it as soon as you remember. If it is near the time for the next dose, skip the missed dose and resume your regular dosage schedule. Do not double the next dose.

STOPPING THE DRUG
Continue taking the medicine until at least 24 to 36 hours after diarrhea has stopped. Consult with your doctor if the diarrhea does not stop after 2 days or if you develop a fever.

PROLONGED USE
Diphenoxylate and atropine may be habit-forming if larger doses are taken for a long time. Ask your doctor about the need for follow-up medical examinations or laboratory studies to check liver function if you must take this medication for a prolonged period of time.

PRECAUTIONS
Over 60: Adverse reactions may be more likely and more severe in older patients.

Driving and Hazardous Work: Do not drive or engage in hazardous work until you determine how the medicine affects you.

Alcohol: Avoid alcohol while taking this medicine.

Pregnancy: If you are pregnant or plan to become pregnant, consult your doctor; discuss whether the benefits justify the possible risks to the unborn child.

Breast Feeding: This drug passes into breast milk; caution is advised. Consult your doctor for specific advice.

Infants and Children: Not recommended for use by children under the age of 2. For children over 2, use the drug only under a doctor's supervision.

Special Concerns: During the first 24 hours, drink plenty of caffeine-free clear liquids such as broth, ginger ale, and decaffeinated tea. During the second 24 hours you may eat bland foods such as applesauce, bread, toast, crackers, rice, and oatmeal. Avoid caffeine, fried or spicy foods, bran, candy, fruits, and vegetables. They can make your condition worse.

OVERDOSE
Symptoms: Drowsiness, dizziness, and weakness caused by low blood pressure; seizures; slow or arrested breathing; blurred vision; reddened face; dryness of the mouth; unusual behavior.

What to Do: Call your doctor, emergency medical services (EMS), or the nearest poison control center immediately.

DRUG INTERACTIONS
The following drugs may interact with the combination of diphenoxylate and atropine. Consult your doctor for specific advice if you are taking antibiotics; central nervous system depressants; MAO inhibitors; naltrexone; or anticholinergic medicines to reduce stomach acid, spasms, or cramps.

FOOD INTERACTIONS
No known food interactions.

DISEASE INTERACTIONS
Caution is advised when taking this drug. Before starting, consult your doctor if you have liver problems, Down's syndrome, ulcerative colitis, Crohn's disease, glaucoma, chronic lung disease (such as emphysema), heart disease, a history of alcohol or drug abuse, an enlarged prostate, gallbladder disease or gallstones, high blood pressure, an underactive or overactive thyroid, kidney disease, dysentery, myasthenia gravis, or intestinal or urinary tract blockage.

Diphtheria, Tetanus Toxoids, and Pertussis Vaccine (DTP)

BRAND NAMES
Acel-Immune, Certiva, DTP Adsorbed, Tri-Immunol, Tripedia

▶ Drug Class: Vaccine

▶ Available in: Injection

▶ Available OTC? No

▶ As Generic? Yes

Side Effects

SERIOUS
Fever of 105°F or more, seizures, collapse, difficulty breathing or swallowing, hives, unusual irritability, temporary loss of consciousness or awareness. Call your doctor as soon as possible.

COMMON
Fever between 100.4°F and 102.2°F, sometimes accompanied by loss of appetite, drowsiness, vomiting, and fretfulness; redness, swelling, lump, pain, or tenderness at the site of the injection.

LESS COMMON
Fever between 102.2°F and 104°F and skin rash.

PRINCIPAL USES

The DTP vaccine is used as a combination immunizing agent to prevent three serious childhood diseases—diphtheria, tetanus, and pertussis. Diphtheria can cause difficulty breathing, pneumonia, nerve damage, heart problems, and possibly death. Tetanus (lockjaw) can cause severe muscle spasms. Pertussis (whooping cough) causes severe bouts of coughing that can interfere with breathing. Pertussis can also cause long-lasting bronchitis, pneumonia, seizures, and brain damage, and can lead to death.

HOW THE DRUG WORKS

The DTP vaccine stimulates the body's immune system to produce protective antibodies against diphtheria, tetanus, and pertussis.

DOSAGE

Children 2 months to 7 years: 0.5 ml injected into muscle 4 to 8 weeks apart for 3 doses, followed by a fourth 0.5 ml dose injected into a muscle 1 year later, usually at 15 to 18 months of age. A fifth dose (booster) may be administered at 4 to 6 years of age. Persons over 7 years of age should not receive the whole-cell pertussis vaccine.

ONSET OF EFFECT

Unknown.

DURATION OF ACTION

Up to 10 years.

DIETARY ADVICE

The vaccine can be administered without regard to diet.

STORAGE

Not applicable; the dose is administered only at a health care facility.

IF YOU MISS A DOSE

If your child misses a scheduled vaccination, contact your pediatrician.

STOPPING THE DRUG

The full schedule of injections should be followed unless a medical problem intervenes.

PROLONGED USE

No special problems are expected.

PRECAUTIONS

Over 60: This vaccine is not intended for use by older persons.

Driving and Hazardous Work: Not applicable.

Alcohol: Not applicable.

Pregnancy: This vaccine is not intended for women of childbearing age.

Breast Feeding: This vaccine is not intended for women of childbearing age.

Infants and Children: Not recommended for use by children over age 7.

Special Concerns: Anyone over the age of 7 should receive a vaccine that contains tetanus and diphtheria toxoids, but not whole-cell pertussis vaccine. Older persons should receive the diphtheria and tetanus booster injections every 10 years for life. Your doctor may want the child to take 1 or more doses of acetaminophen or another medicine that helps prevent fever after receiving the DTP injection. Consult your doctor for specific advice. DTP should not be given to a child who has had a previous serious adverse reaction to a DTP vaccination.

OVERDOSE

Symptoms: Not applicable.

What to Do: No cases of overdose have been reported.

DRUG INTERACTIONS

The following drugs may interact with DTP. Consult your doctor for specific advice if your child is taking an anticoagulant or a drug that suppresses the immune system. DTP can be given with vaccines for other diseases, but should not be given within 3 days of influenza vaccine.

FOOD INTERACTIONS

No known food interactions.

DISEASE INTERACTIONS

Consult your doctor if your child has any of the following: a brain disease, a central nervous system disorder, epilepsy, a fever, muscle spasms, or seizures.

258

Dipivefrin

BRAND NAME
Propine

▶ Drug Class: Antiglaucoma agent

▶ Available in: Ophthalmic solution

▶ Available OTC? No

▶ As Generic? Yes

Side Effects

SERIOUS
Fast or irregular heartbeat. Call your doctor immediately.

COMMON
In people who have had prior cataract surgery, this drug may cause swelling at the center of the retina that can lead to (in most cases) reversible vision impairment.

LESS COMMON
Increased sensitivity of eyes to light; burning, stinging, or other eye irritation.

PRINCIPAL USES
To treat glaucoma.

HOW THE DRUG WORKS
Glaucoma, a sight-threatening disorder, occurs when the aqueous humor (the fluid inside the eye) cannot drain properly, causing an increase in pressure within the eyeball (intraocular pressure). The increased eye pressure can damage the optic nerve and lead to a gradually progressive loss of vision. Dipivefrin is converted in the eye to epinephrine, which decreases the production of aqueous humor and increases its outflow.

DOSAGE
To start, 1 drop in each eye every 12 hours. The dose may be changed based on patient's response.

ONSET OF EFFECT
Within 30 minutes.

DURATION OF ACTION
12 hours or more.

DIETARY ADVICE
No special restrictions.

STORAGE
Store in a tightly sealed container away from heat, moisture, and direct light. Do not allow the medicine to freeze.

IF YOU MISS A DOSE
Apply it as soon as you remember. If it is near the time for the next dose, skip the missed dose and resume your regular dosage schedule. Do not double the next dose.

STOPPING THE DRUG
The decision to stop using the drug should be made by your doctor.

PROLONGED USE
See your doctor regularly for tests and examinations if you must take this drug for a prolonged period.

PRECAUTIONS
Over 60: No special problems are expected.

Driving and Hazardous Work: The use of dipivefrin should not impair your ability to perform such tasks safely.

Alcohol: No special precautions are necessary.

Pregnancy: Dipivefrin has not caused birth defects in animals. Human studies have not been done. Before you take dipivefrin, tell your doctor if you are pregnant or plan to become pregnant.

Breast Feeding: Dipivefrin may pass into breast milk; caution is advised. Consult your doctor for specific advice.

Infants and Children: No special precautions.

Special Concerns: Dipivefrin should not be used by people with closed-angle glaucoma. To use the eye drops, first wash your hands. Tilt your head back. Gently apply pressure to the inside corner of the eyelid and with the index finger of the same hand, pull downward on the lower eyelid to make a space. Drop the medicine into this space and close your eye. Apply pressure for 1 or 2 minutes while keeping the eye closed without blinking. Then wash your hands again. Make sure the tip of the dropper does not touch your eye, finger, or any other surface. If you are taking the medicine with the compliance cap (C Cap), make sure that the number 1 or the correct day of the week appears in the window of the cap before using the eye drops for the first time. After every dose, rotate the bottle until the cap clicks to the position that tells you the next dose.

OVERDOSE
Symptoms: Rapid or irregular heartbeat.

What to Do: An overdose of dipivefrin is unlikely to be life-threatening. If a large volume enters the eyes, flush with water. If someone accidentally ingests the medicine, call your doctor, emergency medical services (EMS), or the nearest poison control center.

DRUG INTERACTIONS
Other drugs may interact with dipivefrin. Consult your doctor for specific advice if you are taking tricyclic antidepressants, maprotiline, nomifensine, ophthalmic beta-blockers, digitalis drugs, or systemic sympathomimetics.

FOOD INTERACTIONS
No known food interactions.

DISEASE INTERACTIONS
Caution is advised when taking dipivefrin. Consult your doctor if you have closed-angle glaucoma or aphakia (absence of part or all of the lens of the eye).

Dipyridamole

Side Effects

SERIOUS
Dizziness and weakness caused by low blood pressure (hypotension). Call your doctor.

COMMON
Headache, nausea, rash.

LESS COMMON
Vomiting, diarrhea, flushing, itching, chest pain, liver problems causing nausea, vomiting, yellow-tinged eyes and skin, swelling, bloating.

PRINCIPAL USES
To prevent blood clots during recovery from heart valve replacement surgery; to reduce frequency and intensity of angina attacks (chest pain associated with heart disease).

HOW THE DRUG WORKS
Dipyridamole is believed to increase blood levels of adenosine, a metabolic product that causes blood vessels to expand and prevents platelets, a type of blood cell, from adhering to one another to form a clot.

DOSAGE
Tablets: 75 to 100 mg, 4 times a day, given with an anticoagulant such as warfarin, to prevent blood clots. If at all possible, when dipyridamole is taken with warfarin, the injectable form of dipyridamole should be avoided; injection (when necessary) is administered under doctor's supervision. Aspirin may also be used with dipyridamole, as the two drugs have a synergistic anticoagulant effect.

ONSET OF EFFECT
About 10 minutes; 3 months of continual use is needed for the full effect to occur.

DURATION OF ACTION
About 6 hours.

DIETARY ADVICE
Take this medication 1 hour before or 2 hours after meals. Swallow the tablet with 6 to 8 ounces of water.

STORAGE
Store in a tightly sealed container in a dry place away from heat and direct light.

IF YOU MISS A DOSE
Take it as soon as you remember. However, if it is near the time for the next dose, skip the missed dose and resume your regular dosage schedule as prescribed. Do not double the next dose.

STOPPING THE DRUG
Take as prescribed for the full treatment period.

PROLONGED USE
If you must use dipyridamole for a prolonged period, consult your doctor about the possible need for follow-up medical examinations or laboratory studies.

PRECAUTIONS
Over 60: Older patients should start with smaller doses. Otherwise, no special problems are expected.

Driving and Hazardous Work: Dipyridamole may cause dizziness. Do not drive or engage in hazardous work until you determine how the medicine affects you.

Alcohol: Avoid alcohol while taking this medication because it may lower blood pressure excessively.

Pregnancy: Dipyridamole has not been reported to cause birth defects. Consult your doctor about its use during pregnancy.

Breast Feeding: While dipyridamole passes into breast milk, it has not been reported to cause problems in nursing babies. Consult your doctor for specific advice about its use while nursing.

Infants and Children: Dipyridamole is not recommended for use by children under the age of 12.

Special Concerns: If your doctor tells you to take dipyridamole with aspirin, take only the amount of aspirin that is prescribed. Tell any doctor or dentist whom you consult that you are taking dipyridamole.

OVERDOSE
Symptoms: Dizziness and weakness caused by extremely low blood pressure (hypotension).

What to Do: Discontinue taking the drug. An overdose of dipyridamole is unlikely to be life-threatening; however, if someone takes a much larger dose than prescribed, call your doctor, emergency medical services (EMS), or the nearest poison control center immediately.

DRUG INTERACTIONS
Consult your doctor for specific advice if you are taking anticoagulants (such as warfarin, aspirin, and ticlopidine), valproic acid, or any nonsteroidal anti-inflammatory drug (NSAID) such as indomethacin.

FOOD INTERACTIONS
Taking dipyridamole within 1 hour of eating will decrease the body's absorption of the drug. When possible, take dipyridamole on an empty stomach.

DISEASE INTERACTIONS
Caution is advised when taking dipyridamole. Consult your doctor if you have low blood pressure or liver disease or if you are recovering from a heart attack.

Dirithromycin

DYNABAC
UC5364

Dynabac 250 mg
(Bock)

▶ Drug Class: Macrolide antibiotic

▶ Available in: Tablets

▶ Available OTC? No

▶ As Generic? No

Side Effects

SERIOUS
Colitis (inflammation of the lower gastrointestinal tract, with symptoms including severe abdominal pain or cramping, watery or bloody stools, severe diarrhea, fever); liver toxicity (causing fever, nausea, vomiting, yellowish tinge to eyes or skin); allergic reaction (swelling of the lips, tongue, face, and throat, breathing difficulty, skin rash or hives); blood clotting disorders (causing unusual bleeding, bruising, and tiny bright red spots on the skin). Such side effects are rare, but if they do occur, stop taking dirithromycin and seek medical assistance immediately.

COMMON
No common side effects are associated with the use of dirithromycin.

LESS COMMON
Dizziness, stomach upset or discomfort, mild diarrhea, mild nausea and vomiting, headache, unusual fatigue.

PRINCIPAL USES
To treat bronchitis, some types of pneumonia such as Legionnaires' disease, skin infections, and tonsillitis or other throat infections such as strep throat. Dirithromycin is effective only against infections caused by bacteria; it is ineffective against those caused by viruses (for example, colds and flu), fungi, or other microorganisms.

HOW THE DRUG WORKS
Dirithromycin prevents bacterial cells from manufacturing specific proteins necessary for their survival.

DOSAGE
Adults and children age 12 and over: 500 mg, once a day for 5 to 14 days (depending on the condition being treated). It is recommended that this medication be taken at the same time every day.

ONSET OF EFFECT
Within 2 hours; full effect may occur in 2 to 5 days.

DURATION OF ACTION
From 30 to 50 hours.

DIETARY ADVICE
Take this medicine with food or within 1 hour of eating. Drink plenty of fluids.

STORAGE
Store in a tightly sealed container away from moisture, heat, and direct light.

IF YOU MISS A DOSE
Take it as soon as you remember, up to 12 hours late. However, if more than 12 hours have passed, skip the missed dose and resume your regular dosage schedule. Do not double the next dose.

STOPPING THE DRUG
Take this drug for the full treatment period, even if you begin to feel better before the scheduled end of therapy.

PROLONGED USE
Prolonged use is not recommended. Your doctor will discontinue the medicine once the infection is cured. Unnecessary or prolonged use of any antibiotic may promote infection by microorganisms that are resistant to the drug's effects. This is known as superinfection.

PRECAUTIONS
Over 60: No special problems are expected.

Driving and Hazardous Work: Do not drive or engage in hazardous work until you determine how dirithromycin affects you.

Alcohol: No special precautions are necessary.

Pregnancy: Adequate studies of the use of dirithromycin during pregnancy have not been done; discuss the potential risks and benefits with your doctor.

Breast Feeding: It is not known if dirithromycin passes into breast milk; consult your doctor for advice.

Infants and Children: Dirithromycin should be given to children under 12 only under close medical supervision.

Special Concerns: Tell any doctor or dentist you consult that you are taking this medicine. Before taking dirithromycin, tell your doctor if you are allergic to any other drug, especially an antibiotic.

OVERDOSE
Symptoms: No cases of dirithromycin overdose have been reported. Symptoms would most likely include diarrhea, nausea, vomiting, and heartburn.

What to Do: An overdose of dirithromycin is unlikely to be life-threatening. However, if someone takes a much larger dose than prescribed, contact a doctor or the nearest poison control center for advice.

DRUG INTERACTIONS
This drug should not be taken by patients known to have had prior allergic reactions to erythromycins or other macrolide antibiotics. Also, consult your doctor for specific advice if you are taking any other drugs, especially allergy drugs, antacids or histamine (H2) blockers, anticoagulants, antiarrhythmics, seizure drugs, cholesterol-lowering drugs, digitalis drugs, ergotamine, bromocriptine, cyclosporine, or valproate.

FOOD INTERACTIONS
No known food interactions.

DISEASE INTERACTIONS
Consult your doctor if you have a blood or liver disorder or any allergy.

Disopyramide

BRAND NAMES
Norpace, Norpace CR

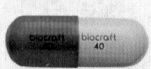

Generic 100 mg
(BIOCRAFT)

▶ Drug Class: Antiarrhythmic

▶ Available in: Capsules, extended-release capsules, tablets

▶ Available OTC? No

▶ As Generic? Yes

Side Effects

SERIOUS
Chest pain, shortness of breath, irregular or rapid heartbeat (palpitations), fainting, sudden weight gain, swelling of fingers or ankles, anxiety. Call your doctor immediately if such symptoms arise.

COMMON
Dizziness, faintness, weakness caused by low blood pressure, blurred vision, constipation, dry eyes, dry nose, dry mouth. Consult your doctor if such symptoms persist.

LESS COMMON
Depression, agitation, fatigue, muscle weakness, decreased urination, nausea, vomiting, severe loss of appetite and weight, abdominal pain, difficulty urinating, yellow-tinged eyes and skin, low blood sugar causing drowsiness, headache, cold sweats, nervousness, confusion, skin rash.

PRINCIPAL USES
To control abnormal or irregular heart rhythms (cardiac arrhythmias).

HOW THE DRUG WORKS
It slows the activity of the heart's natural pacemaker and delays the transmission of electrical impulses through the heart muscle, thus stabilizing heartbeat.

DOSAGE
Adults weighing more than 110 lbs: 150 mg capsules every 6 hours; 300 mg extended-release capsules every 12 hours. Dosage must be individualized for adults weighing less than 110 lbs. Children age 12 to 18: 6 to 15 mg for every 2.2 lbs (1 kg) of body weight daily; ages 4 to 12: 10 to 15 mg per 2.2 lbs daily; ages 1 to 4: 10 to 20 mg per 2.2 lbs of body weight daily; under 1 year: 10 to 30 mg per 2.2 lbs daily. Doses are divided into equal amounts and taken every 6 hours. Initial doses should be smaller in patients suffering from impaired left ventricular function.

ONSET OF EFFECT
30 minutes to 3.5 hours.

DURATION OF ACTION
Up to 8.5 hours (longer in patients with impaired kidney function).

DIETARY ADVICE
Can be taken with or between meals.

STORAGE
Store in a tightly sealed container in a dry place away from heat and direct light.

IF YOU MISS A DOSE
Take it as soon as you remember. However, if it is within 4 hours of the next dose, skip the missed dose and return to your regular dosage schedule as pre-

scribed. Do not double the next dose.

STOPPING THE DRUG
The decision to stop taking the drug should be made by your doctor.

PROLONGED USE
Prolonged use requires supervision and periodic evaluation by your doctor.

PRECAUTIONS
Over 60: Adverse reactions (especially dry mouth and difficulty urinating) may be more likely and more severe in older patients. Dosage reduction may be required.

Driving and Hazardous Work: Avoid such activities until you determine how the medicine affects you.

Alcohol: Avoid alcohol.

Pregnancy: Before taking this medicine, tell your doctor if you are pregnant or plan to become pregnant. Discuss with your doctor whether the benefits of taking disopyramide justify the possible risk to the unborn child.

Breast Feeding: Disopyramide passes into breast milk; avoid or discontinue use while nursing.

Infants and Children: Children using this drug should do so only under close medical supervision.

Special Concerns: Try to take disopyramide exactly at the times prescribed. An alarm clock may be needed for nighttime doses. Tell your doctor if you have had an unfavorable reaction to any other antiarrhythmic medication.

OVERDOSE
Symptoms: Heartbeat irregularities, severe drop in blood pressure, loss of consciousness, breathing difficulty.

What to Do: Call your doctor, emergency medical services (EMS), or the nearest poison control center immediately.

DRUG INTERACTIONS
Consult your doctor if you are taking other antiarrhythmics, anticholinergics, anticoagulants, insulin, drugs for high blood pressure, nimodipine, phenobarbital, phenytoin, pimozide, propafenone, or rifampin.

FOOD INTERACTIONS
No known food interactions.

DISEASE INTERACTIONS
Caution is advised when taking disopyramide. Consult your doctor if you have any of the following: heart disease or heart block, diabetes mellitus, enlarged prostate, glaucoma, myasthenia gravis, kidney or liver disease.

Disulfiram

BRAND NAME
Antabuse

Generic 250 mg
(SIDMAK)

▶ Drug Class: Alcoholism control drug

▶ Available in: Tablets

▶ Available OTC? No

▶ As Generic? Yes

Side Effects

SERIOUS
Confusion and disorientation, severe skin rash, seizures, neuritis (nerve inflammation causing pain, numbness, or paralysis), low thyroid function, decrease or increase in blood pressure, carpal tunnel syndrome. Call your doctor if such symptoms arise.

COMMON
Drowsiness.

LESS COMMON
Eye pain, vision changes, abdominal discomfort, throbbing headache, mood change, numbness in hands and feet, decreased sexual ability in men, unpleasant taste in mouth, offensive breath and body odor.

PRINCIPAL USES
To help treat chronic alcoholism.

HOW THE DRUG WORKS
Disulfiram interferes with the activity of the liver enzyme that processes and metabolizes alcohol, causing an accumulation of a chemical known as acetaldehyde. A buildup of acetaldehyde in the body leads to a severely unpleasant reaction, including nausea and vomiting. Thus, while not a cure for alcoholism, disulfiram is a deterrent to alcohol consumption.

DOSAGE
Initial dose: 250 to 500 mg a day in a single dose in the morning or evening. Maintenance dose: 125 to 500 mg once a day. Treatment with disulfiram should not start until at least 12 hours after consumption of an alcoholic beverage.

ONSET OF EFFECT
1 to 2 hours.

DURATION OF ACTION
Effects usually last 3 to 4 days but may persist for up to 2 weeks.

DIETARY ADVICE
Take it with or following meals to decrease stomach irritation.

STORAGE
Store in a tightly sealed container in a dry place away from heat and direct light.

IF YOU MISS A DOSE
Take it as soon as you remember. If it is within 12 hours of the next dose, skip the missed dose and return to your normal dosage schedule. Do not double the next dose.

STOPPING THE DRUG
The decision to stop taking the drug should be made in consultation with your physician.

PROLONGED USE
Use of disulfiram on a regular schedule for several months is needed to see if alcohol consumption is deterred. Use should continue until permanent self-control is achieved. Periodic tests of liver function should be done. Gradual reduction of doses may be required when disulfiram has been taken for a prolonged period of time.

PRECAUTIONS
Over 60: Adverse reactions may be more likely and more severe in older patients.

Driving and Hazardous Work: Do not drive or engage in hazardous work until you determine how the medication affects you.

Alcohol: This medication should never be taken by anyone with alcohol in the bloodstream.

Pregnancy: Studies have indicated that disulfiram may lead to birth defects; however, alcohol abuse may lead to births defects as well. Ask your doctor if the possible benefits justify the risk to the unborn baby.

Breast Feeding: It is not known whether disulfiram passes into breast milk. Consult your doctor for advice.

Infants and Children: Not recommended for use by children under age 12.

Special Concerns: Check all liquids that you drink or rub on your skin for the presence of alcohol. Disulfiram may interfere with sexual performance in men. Tell your doctor if you plan to have surgery under general anesthesia while taking disulfiram.

OVERDOSE
Symptoms: Loss of memory, behavior disturbances, confusion, headaches, lethargy, increased blood pressure, nausea, vomiting, stomach pain, diarrhea, unsteady walk, temporary paralysis.

What to Do: Call your doctor, emergency medical services (EMS), or the nearest poison control center immediately.

DRUG INTERACTIONS
Other drugs may interact with disulfiram. Consult your doctor if you are taking anticoagulants, anticonvulsants, antidepressants (especially amitriptyline), barbiturates, cephalosporin antibiotics, clozapine, fluoxetine, guanethidine, guanfacine, isoniazid, leucovorin, methyprion, metronidazole, paraldehyde, sedatives, or sertraline.

FOOD INTERACTIONS
Any food prepared with alcohol, including sauces, fermented vinegar, marinades, or desserts, can produce the unpleasant reaction characteristic of disulfiram.

DISEASE INTERACTIONS
Caution is advised when taking disulfiram. Consult your doctor if you have any of the following: diabetes, epilepsy, kidney disease, liver disease, low thyroid function, lung disease, or a history of psychosis.

Docusate

Colace 100 mg
(ROBERTS)

Additional photographs

▶ Drug Class: Stool softener

▶ Available in: Capsules, tablets, liquid, syrup

▶ Available OTC? Yes

▶ As Generic? Yes

Side Effects

SERIOUS
Severe cramping. Stop taking the drug and call your doctor immediately.

COMMON
Diarrhea, mild abdominal cramps.

LESS COMMON
Throat irritation, laxative dependence. Consult your doctor if you cannot maintain normal bowel habits without docusate for more than 2 weeks.

PRINCIPAL USES
To prevent constipation (but not to treat existing constipation). Recommended for persons who should not strain during defecation, such as those recovering from rectal or heart surgery, or women who experience constipation after childbirth.

HOW THE DRUG WORKS
Docusate promotes easier bowel movements by drawing liquid into stools, forming a softer mass.

DOSAGE
Adults and teenagers: 50 to 500 mg once a day until bowel movements return to normal. Children ages 6 to 12: 40 to 140 mg once a day. Liquid forms should be mixed with milk or fruit juice.

ONSET OF EFFECT
Within 24 to 72 hours.

DURATION OF ACTION
Up to 72 hours.

DIETARY ADVICE
Add high-fiber foods like bran and fresh fruits and vegetables to your diet. Drink at least 6 glasses (8 oz each) of water or other liquids a day to help soften stools.

STORAGE
Store in a tightly sealed container away from heat, moisture, and direct light.

IF YOU MISS A DOSE
Take it as soon as you remember. If it is near the time for the next dose, skip the missed dose and resume your regular dosage schedule. Do not double the next dose.

STOPPING THE DRUG
Take it as prescribed for the full treatment period. However, you may stop taking the drug if you are feeling better and normal bowel function has returned before the scheduled end of therapy.

PROLONGED USE
Docusate should not be taken for more than 1 week unless you are under your doctor's supervision. Be aware that overuse can make you dependent on it and may cause damage to the nerves, muscles, and other tissues of the bowel and lead to vitamin and mineral deficiency.

PRECAUTIONS

Over 60: No special problems are expected.

Driving and Hazardous Work: The use of docusate should not impair your ability to perform such tasks safely.

Alcohol: No special precautions are necessary.

Pregnancy: Before taking docusate, tell your doctor if you are pregnant or plan to become pregnant.

Breast Feeding: No special problems are expected if you take docusate while nursing.

Infants and Children: Do not give docusate to children under age 6 unless it is prescribed by your doctor.

Special Concerns: Do not take mineral oil while you are taking docusate.

OVERDOSE
Symptoms: Weakness, sweating, muscle cramps, irregular heartbeat.

What to Do: An overdose of docusate is unlikely to be life-threatening. However, if someone takes a much larger dose than prescribed, call your doctor, emergency medical services (EMS), or the nearest poison control center immediately.

DRUG INTERACTIONS
A number of drugs may interact with docusate if they are ingested at or near the time it is taken. Consult your doctor for specific advice if you are taking any other oral drug within 2 hours before or after taking docusate.

FOOD INTERACTIONS
No known food interactions.

DISEASE INTERACTIONS
This drug cannot be used by people with intestinal obstruction or appendicitis. Symptoms of these conditions include vomiting, abdominal rigidity and tenderness, and fever. Call your doctor or emergency medical services (EMS) immediately if you suspect you may be suffering from intestinal obstruction or appendicitis.

BRAND NAME
Aricept

Aricept 5 mg
(EISAI)

▶ Drug Class: Acetylcholinesterase inhibitor

▶ Available in: Tablets

▶ Available OTC? No

▶ As Generic? No

Side Effects

SERIOUS
No serious side effects
are associated with the
use of donepezil.

COMMON
Nausea, vomiting, diar-
rhea, headache, dizziness,
fatigue, insomnia.

LESS COMMON
Vivid or unusual dreams,
drowsiness, depression,
loss of appetite, unusual
bleeding or bruising,
fainting, muscle cramps,
frequent urination, joint
pain, stiffness, or
swelling.

PRINCIPAL USES
To treat mild to moderate
Alzheimer's disease.

HOW THE DRUG WORKS
Donepezil prevents the
breakdown of acetylcholine,
a brain chemical crucial to
memory. Acetylcholine deficiency is thought to result
in memory loss associated
with Alzheimer's disease.

DOSAGE
To start, 5 mg at bedtime.
The dose may be increased
after 4 to 6 weeks to 10 mg
at bedtime.

ONSET OF EFFECT
Unknown.

DURATION OF ACTION
Unknown.

DIETARY ADVICE
No special restrictions.

STORAGE
Store in a tightly sealed container away from heat, moisture, and direct light.

IF YOU MISS A DOSE
Skip the missed dose and
resume your regular dosage
schedule. Do not double the
next dose.

STOPPING THE DRUG
The decision to stop taking
the drug should be made by
your doctor.

PROLONGED USE
No problems are expected
with long-term use.

PRECAUTIONS
Over 60: No special problems are expected.

**Driving and Hazardous
Work:** Do not drive or
engage in hazardous work
until you determine how the
medicine affects you.

Alcohol: Avoid alcohol
while using this medication.

Pregnancy: In some animal studies, large doses of
donepezil were shown to
cause problems. Before you
take donepezil, tell your
doctor if you are pregnant
or plan to become pregnant.

Breast Feeding: It is not
known whether donepezil
passes into breast milk; caution is advised. Consult your
doctor for specific advice.

Infants and Children:
Donepezil is not intended
for use in children.

Special Concerns: Before
you have any surgery or
dental or emergency treatment, tell the doctor or dentist in charge that you are
taking donepezil. Donepezil
will not cure Alzheimer's
disease and will not stop the
disease from getting worse,
but it will improve cognitive
ability of some patients.

OVERDOSE
Symptoms: Seizures,
severe nausea, slow heartbeat, increased muscle
weakness, vomiting, greatly
increased sweating, greatly
increased watering of the
mouth, weak pulse, irregular breathing, enlargement
of the pupils of the eyes.

What to Do: Call your
doctor, emergency medical
services (EMS), or the
nearest poison control center immediately.

DRUG INTERACTIONS
The following drugs may
interact with donepezil. Consult your doctor for specific
advice if you are taking carbamazepine, dexametha-
sone, ketoconazole,
phenobarbital, phenytoin,
quinidine, or rifampin. Also
tell your doctor if you are
taking any other prescription or over-the-counter
medication.

FOOD INTERACTIONS
No known food interactions.

DISEASE INTERACTIONS
Caution is advised when
taking donepezil. Consult
your doctor if you have any
of the following: asthma,
chronic obstructive pul-
monary disease, urinary difficulties, heart disease, liver
disease, a seizure disorder,
stomach ulcers, or blockage
of the urinary tract.

Dornase Alfa

▶ Drug Class: Cystic fibrosis drug

▶ Available in: Inhalation solution

▶ Available OTC? No

▶ As Generic? No

Side Effects

SERIOUS
Chest pain. Call your doctor immediately.

COMMON
Sore throat, voice changes, such as hoarseness.

LESS COMMON
Skin rash; redness, itching, swelling, pain, or other symptoms of eye irritation.

PRINCIPAL USES
To make breathing easier and help prevent lung infections in patients with cystic fibrosis. It is used in conjunction with other cystic fibrosis drugs such as antibiotics, bronchodilators, and anti-inflammatory agents.

HOW THE DRUG WORKS
The mucus in the lungs of people with cystic fibrosis contains large amounts of DNA; this makes the mucus much thicker than normal. Dornase alfa breaks down the DNA, making the mucus less sticky and easier to cough up.

DOSAGE
Adults and children age 5 and older: 2.5 mg in a nebulizer once a day. Selected patients may require 2 daily doses. Use only the following nebulizers and compressors: Hudson T Up-draft II disposable jet nebulizer with the Pulmo-Aide compressor, Marquest Acorn II disposable jet nebulizer with the Pulmo-Aide compressor, or the PARI LC Jet+ nebulizer with the PARI PRONEB compressor.

ONSET OF EFFECT
Lung function tests improve significantly within 3 days to 1 week. Reduction in respiratory tract infections may occur over the course of weeks to months.

DURATION OF ACTION
The drug is effective only when it is used daily.

DIETARY ADVICE
No special restrictions.

STORAGE
Refrigerate the drug in its protective foil pouch, away from heat, moisture, and direct light. Do not allow it to freeze. Discard the drug if it is cloudy or discolored.

IF YOU MISS A DOSE
Take it as soon as you remember. If it is near the time for the next dose, skip the missed dose and resume your regular dosage schedule. Do not double the next dose.

STOPPING THE DRUG
Take it as prescribed for the full treatment period, even if you begin to feel better before the scheduled end of therapy. The decision to stop taking the drug should be made in conjunction with your doctor.

PROLONGED USE
Prolonged use requires periodic evaluation of response and possible dose adjustment by your doctor. It is expected that dornase alfa will be used for a prolonged period.

PRECAUTIONS
Over 60: No special problems are expected.

Driving and Hazardous Work: The use of this medication should not impair your ability to perform such tasks safely.

Alcohol: No special precautions are necessary.

Pregnancy: Adequate human studies have not been done. Before taking dornase alfa, tell your doctor if you are pregnant or plan to become pregnant.

Breast Feeding: Dornase alfa may pass into breast milk; caution is advised. Consult your doctor for specific advice concerning the relative risks and benefits of using this drug while breast feeding.

Infants and Children: Dornase alfa is not recommended for use by children under the age of 5.

Special Concerns:
Breathe only through the mouth while using the nebulizer. A nose clip can help. Use the mouthpiece provided with the nebulizer. Do not use a face mask because less medicine will get into the lungs. If you begin coughing during treatment, turn off the nebulizer taking care not to spill the drug. You can resume treatment when coughing stops. Do not dilute dornase alfa or use other medicines in the nebulizer.

OVERDOSE
Symptoms: An overdose of dornase alfa is unlikely to occur and unlikely to be life-threatening.

What to Do: If you have any reason to suspect an overdose, call your doctor, emergency medical services (EMS), or the nearest poison control center.

DRUG INTERACTIONS
Do not use this medication if you are allergic to Chinese hamster ovary cells. No other drug interactions are known.

FOOD INTERACTIONS
No known food interactions.

DISEASE INTERACTIONS
No disease interactions have been reported.

Dorzolamide Hydrochloride

BRAND NAME
Trusopt

▶ Drug Class: Antiglaucoma agent; carbonic anhydrase inhibitor

▶ Available in: Ophthalmic solution

▶ Available OTC? No

▶ As Generic? No

Side Effects

SERIOUS
Allergic reaction causing redness, itching, and swelling of the eyelid; continued or severe sensitivity to light; feeling that something is in the eye; detachment of the choroid (a thin membrane within the eye) following filtration surgery. Call your doctor immediately.

COMMON
Burning, stinging, or discomfort in the eye when drug is administered; bitter taste in mouth.

LESS COMMON
Eye pain, severe or continued tearing, nausea or vomiting, blood in urine.

PRINCIPAL USES
To treat glaucoma.

HOW THE DRUG WORKS
Glaucoma, a sight-threatening disorder, occurs when aqueous humor (the fluid inside the eye) cannot drain properly, resulting in an increase in pressure within the eyeball (known as intraocular pressure). Increased intraocular pressure can damage the optic nerve and lead to a gradually progressive loss of vision. Dorzolamide inhibits the activity of the enzyme carbonic anhydrase, which is needed in the production of aqueous humor. In this way the drug reduces intraocular pressure.

DOSAGE
Adults and teenagers: 1 drop in each eye 3 times per day.

ONSET OF EFFECT
Unknown.

DURATION OF ACTION
8 hours.

DIETARY ADVICE
No special restrictions.

STORAGE
Store in a tightly sealed container away from heat, moisture, and direct light. Do not refrigerate or allow it to freeze.

IF YOU MISS A DOSE
Apply it as soon as you remember. If it is near the time for the next dose, skip the missed dose and resume your regular dosage schedule. Do not double the next dose.

STOPPING THE DRUG
The decision to stop using the drug should be made by your doctor.

PROLONGED USE
Schedule regular eye examinations with your doctor to be sure the drug is controlling the glaucoma.

PRECAUTIONS
Over 60: No special problems are expected.

Driving and Hazardous Work: Do not drive or engage in hazardous work until you determine how the medicine affects your vision.

Alcohol: No special precautions are necessary.

Pregnancy: One animal study found that very high doses of this drug caused birth defects. Human studies have not been done. Before using this medicine, tell your doctor if you are pregnant or plan to become pregnant.

Breast Feeding: Dorzolamide may pass into breast milk; caution is advised. Consult your doctor for specific advice about whether to use a different medicine or to stop breast feeding.

Infants and Children: Safety and dosage for children have not been established. Dorzolamide should be given to infants and children only under close medical supervision.

Special Concerns: To use the eye drops, first wash your hands. Tilt your head back. Gently apply pressure to the inside corner of the eyelid and with the index finger of the same hand, pull downward on the lower eyelid to make a space. Drop the medicine into this space and close your eye. Apply pressure for 1 or 2 minutes while keeping the eye closed without blinking. Then wash your hands

again. Make sure that the tip of the dropper does not touch your eye, finger, or any other surface.

OVERDOSE
Symptoms: No specific ones have been reported.

What to Do: An overdose of dorzolamide is unlikely to be life-threatening. If a large volume enters the eye, flush with water. If someone accidentally ingests the medicine, call your doctor, emergency medical services (EMS), or the nearest poison control center.

DRUG INTERACTIONS
Wait 10 minutes before administering any other eye medicine. Dorzolamide should not be used in conjunction with eye medications containing silver, such as silver nitrate. People allergic to sulfa-type drugs should not use dorzolamide

FOOD INTERACTIONS
No known food interactions.

DISEASE INTERACTIONS
Use of dorzolamide may cause complications in patients with liver disease or kidney disease, since these organs work together to remove the medication from the body.

Doxazosin Mesylate

BRAND NAME
Cardura

Cardura 4 mg
(**Roerig**)

▶ Drug Class: Antihypertensive; BPH therapy agent

▶ Available in: Tablets

▶ Available OTC? No

▶ As Generic? Yes

Side Effects

SERIOUS
Irregular heartbeat. Call your doctor immediately. Another serious but rare side effect is priapism, a condition characterized by a prolonged or painful erection (lasting more than 4 hours).

COMMON
Dizziness, drowsiness.

LESS COMMON
Headache, weakness, palpitations, rapid pulse, pain and tingling sensations in the fingers or toes, diarrhea or constipation, runny nose, rash or itchy skin, muscle or joint pain, headache, mental depression.

PRINCIPAL USES
To treat mild to moderate high blood pressure; to ease urinary tract symptoms due to benign prostatic hyperplasia (BPH)—that is, noncancerous enlargement of the prostate gland, which is extremely common among men over the age of 50. Note: Findings from a major clinical trial indicate that doxazosin is associated with an unacceptably high incidence of cardiovascular complications. The American Academy of Cardiology has since recommended that physicians reconsider the use of doxazosin in the treatment of their hypertensive patients on a case-by-case basis.

HOW THE DRUG WORKS
For high blood pressure, the drug relaxes and widens blood vessels so blood passes through them more easily. For prostate enlargement, it relaxes muscles in the prostate and the opening of the bladder. Note that doxazosin will not shrink the prostate; symptoms may worsen and surgery may eventually be required.

DOSAGE
For high blood pressure, initial dose is 1 mg taken once a day. It can be increased gradually to a maximum of 16 mg a day. For prostate enlargement, initial dose is 1 mg taken once a day, which may be gradually increased to a maximum of 12 mg a day.

ONSET OF EFFECT
For high blood pressure: 1 to 2 hours. For prostate enlargement: 1 to 2 weeks.

DURATION OF ACTION
For high blood pressure: 24 hours. For prostate enlargement: Unknown.

DIETARY ADVICE
No special restrictions.

STORAGE
Store in a tightly sealed container in a dry place away from heat and direct light.

IF YOU MISS A DOSE
Take it as soon as you remember. If it is near the time for the next dose, skip the missed dose and resume your regular dosage schedule. Do not double the next dose.

STOPPING THE DRUG
Take it as prescribed for the full treatment period, even if you feel better before the scheduled end of therapy.

PROLONGED USE
Consult your doctor about the need for follow-up medical examinations and laboratory studies if you must take doxazosin for a prolonged period.

PRECAUTIONS
Over 60: Adverse reactions may be more likely and more severe in older patients. Dose should be increased slowly in patients over 60.

Driving and Hazardous Work: Do not drive or engage in hazardous work until you determine how the medicine affects you.

Alcohol: Alcohol should be avoided while taking this medicine because it may cause an excessive drop in blood pressure.

Pregnancy: In animal studies, very high doses of doxazosin damaged the fetus. Before taking this medicine, tell your doctor if you are pregnant or plan to become pregnant.

Breast Feeding: Doxazosin may pass into breast milk; caution is advised. Consult your doctor for specific advice.

Infants and Children: This drug is not recommended for use by children.

Special Concerns: The first dose is likely to cause dizziness or lightheadedness. Take the drug at night and get out of bed slowly the next day. Be cautious while exercising and during hot weather. Tell your doctor whether you will have surgery requiring general anesthesia, including dental surgery, within the next 2 months.

OVERDOSE
Symptoms: Cold, sweaty skin, rapid pulse, weakness, loss of consciousness.

What to Do: Call your doctor, emergency medical services (EMS), or the nearest poison control center immediately.

DRUG INTERACTIONS
Consult your doctor for specific advice if you are taking amphetamines, other antihypertensive drugs, nonsteroidal anti-inflammatory drugs (NSAIDs), estrogen, or sympathomimetic drugs.

FOOD INTERACTIONS
No known food interactions.

DISEASE INTERACTIONS
Use of doxazosin may cause complications in patients with liver or kidney disease, since these organs work together to remove the medication from the body. Also, consult your doctor if you have coronary artery disease, impaired blood circulation to the brain, or mental depression.

268

Doxepin Hydrochloride

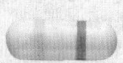

Generic 25 mg
(GENEVA)

Additional photographs

▶ Drug Class: Tricyclic antidepressant

▶ Available in: Capsules, oral solution

▶ Available OTC? No

▶ As Generic? Yes

Side Effects

SERIOUS
Confusion, heartbeat irregularities, hallucinations, seizures, extreme fatigue or drowsiness, blurred or altered vision, breathing difficulty, constipation, impaired concentration, difficult urination, fever, extreme and persistent restlessness, loss of coordination and balance, difficulty swallowing or speaking, dilated pupils, eye pain, fainting. Also trembling, shaking, weakness, and stiffness in the extremities; shuffling gait. Call your doctor immediately.

COMMON
Drowsiness or dizziness, headache, dry mouth or unpleasant taste, fatigue, heightened sensitivity to light, weight gain, nausea, increased appetite.

LESS COMMON
Heartburn, sleeping difficulty, diarrhea, increased sweating, vomiting.

PRINCIPAL USES
To relieve symptoms of major depression.

HOW THE DRUG WORKS
Doxepin affects levels of serotonin, norepinephrine, and acetylcholine, brain chemicals that are thought to be linked to mood, emotions, and mental state.

DOSAGE
Adults: To start, 25 mg, 3 times a day; may be increased to 150 mg a day. Older adults: To start, 25 to 50 mg a day; the dose may be increased gradually by your doctor.

ONSET OF EFFECT
1 to 6 weeks.

DURATION OF ACTION
Unknown.

DIETARY ADVICE
To lessen stomach upset, take it with food, unless your doctor instructs otherwise. Increase intake of fiber and fluids. When taking the oral solution, dilute doxepin in half a glass of water, milk, or fruit juice, but not grapefruit juice. Do not take this drug with a carbonated beverage.

STORAGE
Store in a tightly sealed container away from heat, moisture, and direct light. Do not allow liquid form to freeze.

IF YOU MISS A DOSE
If you take a one-time daily bedtime dose, do not take a missed dose in the morning because it may cause drowsiness. Call your doctor. If you take more than 1 dose a day, take it as soon as you remember. If it is near the time for the next dose, skip the missed dose and resume your regular dosage schedule. Do not double the next dose.

STOPPING THE DRUG
Take as prescribed for the full treatment period, even if you begin to feel better before the scheduled end of therapy. The decision to stop taking the drug should be made with your doctor.

PROLONGED USE
The usual course of therapy lasts 6 months to 1 year; some patients benefit from additional therapy.

PRECAUTIONS

Over 60: Adverse reactions, especially confusion and urination difficulty, may be more likely and more severe in older patients. Your doctor may prescribe a lower dose.

Driving and Hazardous Work: Drowsiness or light-headedness can occur, so use caution when driving or doing hazardous work.

Alcohol: Avoid alcohol.

Pregnancy: Adequate human studies have not been done. Consult your doctor for specific advice.

Breast Feeding: Doxepin passes into breast milk; do not use it while nursing. Doxepin has been found to cause drowsiness in infants.

Infants and Children: This drug is not prescribed for children under age 6. Antidepressants increase the risk of suicidal thinking and behavior (suicidality) in children with major depression and other psychiatric disorders. Discuss with your doctor this risk versus the benefits of using this drug. Children should be observed closely for worsening of symptoms, suicidality, or unusual changes in behavior at the onset of therapy and when making changes in dosage.

Special Concerns: This is a potentially dangerous drug, especially if taken in excess. Tricyclic antidepressants should not be within easy reach of suicidal patients. If dry mouth occurs, use sugarless gum or candy.

OVERDOSE

Symptoms: Difficulty breathing, severe fatigue, seizures, confusion, hallucinations, dilated pupils, irregular heartbeat, fever, impaired concentration.

What to Do: Call your doctor, emergency medical services (EMS), or the nearest poison control center immediately.

DRUG INTERACTIONS
Consult your doctor for specific advice if you are taking antithyroid agents, cimetidine, clonidine, guanadrel, guanethidine, metrizamide, appetite suppressants, isoproterenol, ephedrine, epinephrine, amphetamines, phenylephrine, antipsychotic drugs, pimozide, methyldopa, metyrosine, metoclopramide, pemoline, promethazine, trimeprazine, rauwolfia alkaloids, MAO inhibitors, or any drugs that depress the central nervous system.

FOOD INTERACTIONS
No known food interactions.

DISEASE INTERACTIONS
Consult your doctor if you have any of the following: a history of alcohol abuse, difficulty urinating, asthma, bipolar disorder, high blood pressure, stomach or intestinal problems, glaucoma, overactive thyroid, enlarged prostate, schizophrenia, seizures, a blood disorder, or kidney, heart, or liver disease.

Doxycycline

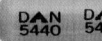

Generic 100 mg
(Schein/Danbury)

Additional photographs

▶ Drug Class: Tetracycline
antibiotic

▶ Available in: Capsules,
delayed-release capsules,
liquid, tablets

▶ Available OTC? No

▶ As Generic? Yes

Side Effects

SERIOUS
Chest pain; increased pressure in the head, causing confusion, sleepiness, and headache; allergic reaction causing severe headache, vision changes, itching, swelling, wheezing, or difficulty breathing; severe rash; severe abdominal pain and diarrhea. Call your doctor immediately.

COMMON
Stomach upset, nausea, mild diarrhea, increased sensitivity to sunlight, increased skin pigmentation, vaginal yeast infection, thrush (oral fungal infection).

LESS COMMON
Sore throat, tongue irritation, loss of appetite, colitis, inflamed anus or genitals, tooth discoloration, pain and swelling of legs.

PRINCIPAL USES
To treat infections caused by bacteria or protozoa (tiny single-celled organisms), including certain sexually transmitted diseases (such as chlamydia, gonorrhea, and syphilis), urinary tract infections, and Lyme disease. Also used to prevent and treat malaria and to treat acne. Doxycycline is also approved for prophylactic use following known exposure to anthrax bacteria and for treating anthrax infections.

HOW THE DRUG WORKS
Doxycycline kills bacteria and protozoa by inhibiting their manufacture of proteins they need for survival.

DOSAGE
For bacterial or protozoal infections— Adults and children over 100 lbs: 100 mg every 12 hours (twice a day) on the first day of therapy, followed by 100 to 200 mg a day. Usual dose for children under 99 lbs: 1 mg per lb of body weight in 2 doses on first day, followed by 1 to 2 mg per lb per day in 1 single or 2 divided doses. For gonorrhea— Adults and children over 100 lbs: 200 mg to start, then 100 mg, 2 times a day for 3 days. For prevention of malaria— Adults and teenagers: 100 mg once a day, starting 1 or 2 days prior to travel, and for 4 weeks after return from a high-risk area. Children ages 8 to 12: 0.9 mg per lb with the same dosage schedule as adults.

ONSET OF EFFECT
Up to 5 days for infection.

DURATION OF ACTION
Several days.

DIETARY ADVICE
Take with a full (8 oz) glass of water.

STORAGE
Store in a tightly sealed container away from heat, moisture, and direct light.

IF YOU MISS A DOSE
Take it as soon as you remember. If it is near the time for the next dose, skip the missed dose and resume your regular dosage schedule. Do not double the next dose.

STOPPING THE DRUG
Take it as prescribed for the full treatment period even if you feel better before the scheduled end of therapy.

PROLONGED USE
Prolonged use may make you more susceptible to infections caused by microorganisms resistant to this antibiotic. Some patients will need periodic monitoring of blood, liver, and kidney function.

PRECAUTIONS
Over 60: Itching in the genital and anal areas may be more common among patients over 60.

Driving and Hazardous Work: No special precautions are necessary.

Alcohol: Avoid alcohol when fighting an infection.

Pregnancy: Studies of pregnant women indicate that this drug can cause discoloration and impaired development of teeth as well as other birth defects. Avoid using doxycycline during pregnancy.

Breast Feeding: Not recommended during therapy.

Infants and Children: Doxycycline should not be used in children younger than 8 years old since it can cause permanent tooth staining.

Special Concerns: To avoid heartburn, do not take capsules or tablets within 1 hour of bedtime. If you take the liquid form, use a specially marked spoon to measure the dose accurately. Do not take outdated capsules or tablets. If this drug causes increased sensitivity to sunlight, use sunscreen when outdoors to prevent sunburn.

OVERDOSE
Symptoms: Nausea and vomiting, diarrhea, difficulty swallowing.

What to Do: An overdose is unlikely to be life-threatening. However, if someone takes a much larger dose than prescribed, call your doctor, emergency medical services (EMS), or the nearest poison control center immediately.

DRUG INTERACTIONS
Consult your doctor for specific advice if you are taking any other antibiotics, antacids, warfarin, antiviral drugs, bismuth salicylate, calcium supplements, cefixime, cholestyramine, oral contraceptives, desmopressin, digitalis drugs, etretinate, lithium, mineral supplements, sodium bicarbonate, or tiopronin.

FOOD INTERACTIONS
Dairy products can decrease absorption of this drug. Take it 2 hours after or 1 hour before consuming milk or another dairy product. Avoid meats and iron-fortified cereals for 2 hours before and after taking doxycycline.

DISEASE INTERACTIONS
Consult your doctor if you have a history of kidney disease, liver disease, lupus, or myasthenia gravis.

Dronabinol

RL

Marinol 2.5 mg
(ROXANE)

▶ Drug Class: Antiemetic; appetite stimulant

▶ Available in: Capsules

▶ Available OTC? No

▶ As Generic? No

Side Effects

SERIOUS
Hallucinations, severe mood changes, irritability, euphoria.

COMMON
Dizziness, drowsiness, poor coordination, trouble thinking.

LESS COMMON
Depression, anxiety, nervousness, headache, hallucinations, blurred vision, rapid heartbeat, frequent or difficult urination, convulsions, dry mouth.

PRINCIPAL USES
To prevent nausea and vomiting caused by cancer drugs, and to stimulate the appetite of AIDS patients.

HOW THE DRUG WORKS
The exact mechanism of action is unknown. Dronabinol may inhibit the centers of the brain that govern the vomiting reflex.

DOSAGE
For nausea and vomiting: 5 mg per square meter of body surface, 1 to 3 hours before chemotherapy is given. The same dose can be taken every 2 to 4 hours after chemotherapy for 4 to 6 doses a day. To stimulate appetite: 2.5 mg twice a day, before lunch and dinner. The dose can be reduced to 2.5 mg taken once in the evening. Maximum dose (if necessary) is up to 20 mg a day, taken in divided doses.

ONSET OF EFFECT
Unknown.

DURATION OF ACTION
From 4 to 6 hours. Appetite stimulation may last 24 hours or longer.

DIETARY ADVICE
For nausea and vomiting control, take it between meals. As an appetite stimulant, take it before lunch and before dinner.

STORAGE
Store in a tightly sealed container away from heat, moisture, and direct light. Keep the medication refrigerated, but do not allow it to freeze.

IF YOU MISS A DOSE
Take it as soon as you remember. If it is near the time for the next dose, skip the missed dose and resume your regular dosage schedule. Do not double the next dose.

STOPPING THE DRUG
The decision to stop taking the drug should be made by your doctor. Withdrawal effects such as insomnia, irritability, sweating, loss of appetite, and hot flashes may follow abrupt termination. These effects will dissipate over the subsequent 24 hours.

PROLONGED USE
Prolonged use increases the risk of side effects and drug dependence.

PRECAUTIONS
Over 60: Adverse reactions may be more likely and more severe in older patients. Older patients should be watched carefully when they take this medicine because of dronabinol's effects on the mind. Changes in mental state due to dronabinol use should not be mistaken for those caused by conditions such as Alzheimer's disease.

Driving and Hazardous Work: Do not drive or engage in hazardous work until you determine how the medicine affects you.

Alcohol: Avoid alcohol.

Pregnancy: Adequate human studies have not been completed. Before taking dronabinol, tell your doctor if you are pregnant or plan to become pregnant.

Breast Feeding: Dronabinol passes into breast milk; avoid or discontinue its use while nursing.

Infants and Children: Dronabinol is not recommended for use by children under age 12 or children with AIDS cachexia.

Special Concerns: Be aware that dronabinol is a derivative of the principal active substance in marijuana and has a high potential for abuse. Prior allergic reaction to marijuana, marijuana by-products, or sesame oil may rule out use of dronabinol.

OVERDOSE
Symptoms: Confusion, slurred speech, red eyes, hallucinations, change in perceptions of taste, sound, touch, smell, or sight, drastic mood changes, rapid, pounding heartbeat, difficulty urinating, nervousness, dry mouth, loss of coordination, fainting, or dizziness.

What to Do: If someone takes a much larger dose of dronabinol than prescribed, call your doctor, emergency medical services (EMS), or the nearest poison control center right away.

DRUG INTERACTIONS
Other drugs may interact with dronabinol. Consult your doctor for specific advice if you are taking anticonvulsants, antidepressants, antihistamines, clozapine, ethinamate, fluoxetine, leucovorin, narcotics, theophylline, muscle relaxants, or any central nervous system depressant.

FOOD INTERACTIONS
No known food interactions.

DISEASE INTERACTIONS
Caution is advised when taking dronabinol. Consult your doctor if you have any of the following: heart disease, high blood pressure, a history of alcohol or drug abuse, schizophrenia, or manic depression (bipolar disorder).

Dutasteride

BRAND NAME
Avodart

- ▶ Drug Class: 5-alpha reductase inhibitor
- ▶ Available in: Softgel capsules
- ▶ Available OTC? No
- ▶ As Generic? No

Side Effects

SERIOUS
No serious side effects are associated with the use of dutasteride.

COMMON
No common side effects are associated with the use of dutasteride.

LESS COMMON
Reduced sex drive, erectile dysfunction (impotence), decreased quantity of ejaculate. It should be noted that this decrease is not a sign of reduced fertility.

PRINCIPAL USES
To treat benign prostatic hyperplasia (BPH)—that is, noncancerous enlargement of the prostate gland, which is extremely common among men over 50.

HOW THE DRUG WORKS
Dutasteride halts or reverses enlargement of the prostate by blocking the action of the enzyme 5-alpha reductase, which the body needs to produce dihydrotestosterone (DHT), a chemical involved in the mechanism that enlarges the prostate.

DOSAGE
0.5 mg once a day.

ONSET OF EFFECT
Unknown.

DURATION OF ACTION
Unknown.

DIETARY ADVICE
Dutasteride can be taken without regard to diet.

STORAGE
Store in a tightly sealed container away from heat, moisture, and direct light.

IF YOU MISS A DOSE
If you miss a dose on one day, do not double the dose the next day.

STOPPING THE DRUG
The decision to stop taking the drug should be made by your doctor.

PROLONGED USE
If you take this drug for a prolonged period for BPH, see your doctor regularly so that changes in prostate size can be monitored.

PRECAUTIONS
Over 60: No special problems are expected.

Driving and Hazardous Work: The use of dutasteride should not impair your ability to perform such tasks safely.

Alcohol: No special precautions are necessary.

Pregnancy: Although dutasteride is not prescribed for women, those who are pregnant or planning to become pregnant should not handle the medication, especially if it is crushed or broken open, because it can have an adverse effect on a male fetus. Men who take dutasteride should use a barrier method of birth control (such as a condom), which prevents the female sexual partner from being exposed to small quantities of the drug present in semen.

Breast Feeding: Women who are nursing should avoid contact with dutasteride or the sperm of a man who is taking the drug.

Infants and Children: Dutasteride is not prescribed for children.

Special Concerns: Before taking this medicine for BPH, you should have a digital rectal examination and other tests for prostate cancer. Note that dutasteride may affect the results of the prostate-specific antigen (PSA) test for prostate cancer; be sure any doctor you see for treatment, including your dentist, knows that you are taking this drug. Men treated with dutasteride should not donate blood until at least 6 months after their final dose to prevent giving dutastreide to a pregnant female through a blood transfusion.

OVERDOSE
Symptoms: No specific ones have been reported.

What to Do: An overdose of dutasteride is unlikely to be life-threatening. However, if someone takes a much larger dose than prescribed, call your doctor, emergency medical services (EMS), or the nearest poison control center.

DRUG INTERACTIONS
Consult your doctor for specific advice if you are taking ritonavir, ketoconazole, verapamil, diltiazem, cimetidine, or ciprofloxacin.

FOOD INTERACTIONS
No known food interactions.

DISEASE INTERACTIONS
Caution is advised when taking dutasteride. Before you start, consult your doctor if you have liver disease, which may magnify the effects of dutasteride.

Dyphylline

BRAND NAMES
Dilor, Lufyllin, Neothylline

▶ Drug Class: Bronchodilator/
  xanthine

▶ Available in: Elixir, tablets

▶ Available OTC? No

▶ As Generic? No

Side Effects

SERIOUS
No serious side effects
are associated with
dyphylline when used at
recommended doses (see
Overdose).

COMMON
No common side effects
are associated with
dyphylline.

LESS COMMON
Heartburn, nausea, vom-
iting, rapid heartbeat,
headache, increased
urine output, nervous-
ness, trembling, difficulty.

PRINCIPAL USES
To prevent or treat acute
bronchial asthma or
episodes of breathing difficulty associated with
chronic bronchitis and
emphysema.

HOW THE DRUG WORKS
Dyphylline is a mild bronchodilator, similar in effect
to drugs like theophylline
and aminophylline. It
relaxes the smooth muscle
tissue surrounding the
bronchial passages, helping
to widen the airways and
aid breathing.

DOSAGE
Adults: Dose is based on
individual body weight, usually 15 mg per 2.2 lbs (1
kg), or 6.8 mg per lb, up to
4 times a day. Children:
Consult pediatrician for
appropriate dose.

ONSET OF EFFECT
Rapid.

DURATION OF ACTION
Unknown.

DIETARY ADVICE
Best when taken on an
empty stomach at least 1
hour before or 2 hours after
eating. However, it may be
taken with meals to mini-
mize the incidence of stomach irritation or upset.

STORAGE
Store in a tightly sealed container away from heat and
direct light.

IF YOU MISS A DOSE
Take it as soon as you
remember. However, if it is
near the time for the next
dose, skip the missed dose
and resume your regular
dosage schedule. Do not
double the next dose.

STOPPING THE DRUG
The decision to stop taking
the drug should be made in

consultation with your
physician.

PROLONGED USE
Therapy with this medica-
tion may require months or
years. See your doctor regularly for tests and examinations if you must take the
medication for a prolonged
period.

PRECAUTIONS
Over 60: Adverse reactions
may be more likely and
more severe in older
patients.

**Driving and Hazardous
Work:** Do not drive or
engage in hazardous work
until you determine how the
medicine affects you.

Alcohol: No special precautions are necessary.

Pregnancy: Adequate studies of the use of dyphylline
during pregnancy have not
been done. Discuss the relative risks and benefits with
your doctor.

Breast Feeding:
Dyphylline passes into
breast milk, although no
adverse consequences have
been reported. Consult your
doctor for specific advice.

Infants and Children:
The safety and effectiveness
of dyphylline use by children have not been estab-
lished; other medications
are generally preferred.

OVERDOSE
Symptoms: Persistent and
severe abdominal pain, confusion or changes in mental
state, seizures, dark or
bloody vomit, rapid or irregular heartbeat, nervousness,
restlessness, trembling.

What to Do: Call your
doctor, emergency medical
services (EMS), or the

nearest poison control center immediately.

DRUG INTERACTIONS
Other drugs may interact
with dyphylline. Consult
your doctor for specific
advice if you are taking
beta-blockers (including
ophthalmic beta-blocker
preparations used to treat
glaucoma), probenecid, or
other xanthine-derivative
medications such as theo-
phylline or aminophylline.

FOOD INTERACTIONS
Your doctor may suggest
that you restrict your consumption of foods and beverages containing caffeine
(including chocolate), since
caffeine may heighten
dyphylline's stimulating
effects to the central nervous system.

DISEASE INTERACTIONS
You should not use
dyphylline if you have had a
prior allergic reaction to
xanthine-derivative drugs
such as theophylline or
aminophylline. Consult your
doctor if you have active
gastritis (inflammation of
the stomach lining) or a
history of peptic ulcer or
impaired kidney function.

Econazole Nitrate

BRAND NAME
Spectazole

▶ Drug Class: Antifungal

▶ Available in: Cream

▶ Available OTC? No

▶ As Generic? Yes

Side Effects

SERIOUS
No serious side effects are associated with econazole.

COMMON
No common side effects are associated with econazole.

LESS COMMON
Itching, burning, stinging, skin redness, or other irritation not present prior to treatment.

PRINCIPAL USES
To treat fungal infections of the skin, such as tinea corporis (ringworm), tinea cruris (jock itch), tinea pedis (athlete's foot), and pityriasis versicolor ("sun fungus," a skin condition characterized by fine scaly patches of varying shapes, sizes, and colors).

HOW THE DRUG WORKS
Econazole prevents fungal organisms from producing vital substances required for growth and function. This drug is effective only for infections caused by fungal organisms. Econazole will not work for bacterial or viral infections.

DOSAGE
Apply to affected area 1 to 2 times a day. When twice a day, apply it in the morning and the evening. Athlete's foot is usually treated for 1 month; jock itch, ringworm, and sun fungus, for 2 weeks.

ONSET OF EFFECT
Unknown.

DURATION OF ACTION
Unknown.

DIETARY ADVICE
Econazole can be applied without regard to diet.

STORAGE
Store in a tightly sealed container away from heat, moisture, and direct light. Do not allow it to freeze.

IF YOU MISS A DOSE
Apply it as soon as you remember. However, if it is near the time for the next application, skip the missed dose and resume your regular dosage schedule.

STOPPING THE DRUG
Use it as prescribed for the full treatment period, even if you begin to feel better before the scheduled end of therapy. Recurrence of the infection is likely if you stop before the full treatment period is complete.

PROLONGED USE
Notify your doctor if no improvement occurs after 2 weeks of treatment for jock itch, ringworm, and sun fungus, or after 4 weeks of treatment for athlete's foot.

PRECAUTIONS

Over 60: No special problems are expected.

Driving and Hazardous Work: The use of econazole should not impair your ability to perform such tasks safely.

Alcohol: No special precautions are necessary.

Pregnancy: Before using econazole, tell your doctor if you are pregnant or plan to become pregnant. Econazole should be used in the first trimester only if the doctor says it is essential to your health, and it should be used in the last two trimesters only if it is clearly needed.

Breast Feeding: Econazole may pass into breast milk; caution is advised. Consult your doctor for specific advice.

Infants and Children: Special problems that would limit the usefulness of this medicine in children are not expected. Consult your pediatrician for specific advice.

Special Concerns: Avoid allowing econazole to come into contact with the eyes. If using the medication for jock itch, do not wear underwear that is tight or made from synthetic materials; wear loose-fitting cotton underwear. If using econazole for athlete's foot, dry your feet carefully after bathing and wear clean cotton socks with sandals or well-ventilated shoes. Before applying the medication, wash the affected area with soap and warm water and dry thoroughly. Econazole may stain your clothing.

OVERDOSE
Symptoms: An overdose of econazole is unlikely.

What to Do: If someone should swallow a large amount of econazole, call your doctor, emergency medical services (EMS), or the nearest poison control center immediately.

DRUG INTERACTIONS
Consult your doctor for specific advice if you are taking topical corticosteroids. They may inhibit the antifungal effect of econazole.

FOOD INTERACTIONS
No food interactions have been reported.

DISEASE INTERACTIONS
No disease interactions have been reported.

Efalizumab

▶ Drug Class: Immuno-suppressant agent

▶ Available in: Injection

▶ Available OTC? No

▶ As Generic? No

Side Effects

SERIOUS
Increased risk of infection and reactivation of latent, chronic infections; bleeding disorders; worsening of psoriasis. Psoriasis patients formerly treated with other types of therapy (for example, ultraviolet light or methotrexate) are at increased risk of skin cancer; report any new skin lesion to your doctor immediately.

COMMON
Headache, chills, fever, nausea, and muscle aches.

LESS COMMON
Flu-like symptoms, back pain, acne.

PRINCIPAL USES
To treat chronic moderate to severe plaque psoriasis in adult patients who are candidates for systemic therapy or phototherapy.

HOW THE DRUG WORKS
Efalizumab targets the cells that cause psoriasis and controls their activity without destroying them. It can be used for continuous control. Efalizumab works under the skin and prevents the cells that cause psoriasis from becoming activated and entering the skin. As it starts working in the body and plaque formation is slowed, psoriasis symptoms start to clear.

DOSAGE
Adults: To start, a single 0.7 mg per kilogram (2.2 lbs) subcutaneous (under the skin) injection followed by weekly subcutaneous doses of 1 mg per 2.2 lbs (maximum single dose not to exceed a total of 200 mg).

ONSET OF EFFECT
Within 4 to 12 weeks.

DURATION OF ACTION
Unknown.

DIETARY ADVICE
No special restrictions.

STORAGE
Keep efalizumab refrigerated, but do not allow it to freeze. If not administered immediately after preparing (reconstituting), it may be stored in the vial at room temperature for up to 8 hours.

IF YOU MISS A DOSE
Use efalizumab the same day each week. If you miss your dose, contact your healthcare provider to find out when to take your next dose and what schedule to follow after that.

STOPPING THE DRUG
The decision to stop taking the drug should be made in consultation with your physician.

PROLONGED USE
See your doctor regularly for tests and examinations.

PRECAUTIONS
Over 60: Adverse reactions may be more likely and more severe in older patients.

Driving and Hazardous Work: The use of efalizumab should not impair your ability to perform such tasks safely.

Alcohol: Avoid alcohol.

Pregnancy: Adequate human studies have not been done. Before taking efalizumab, tell your doctor if you are pregnant or plan to become pregnant.

Breast Feeding: It is not known whether efalizumab passes into breast milk. Consult your doctor about the drug's relative risks and benefits if you are breast feeding.

Infants and Children: Safety and effectiveness have not been established for children under age 18.

Special Concerns: Efalizumab may lower your resistance to infection by reducing the number of white blood cells in the blood. Do not have any immunizations without your doctor's approval. Avoid people with infections. Use care when shaving, trimming nails, or using sharp objects. Inform your doctor immediately if you have fever, chills, unusual bleeding or bruising, diarrhea, or a cough.

OVERDOSE
Symptoms: No cases of overdose have been reported.

What to Do: If you have any reason to suspect an overdose, contact your doctor or seek medical assistance right away.

DRUG INTERACTIONS
Avoid vaccines. No other medications should be added to solutions containing efalizumab. Adequate studies involving interactions with other drugs have not been done. Tell your doctor about all the medications you take, including prescription and nonprescription medicines, as well as any vitamins and herbal supplements. Consult your doctor for specific advice.

FOOD INTERACTIONS
No known food interactions.

DISEASE INTERACTIONS
Efalizumab should be used with caution in patients with any active infection, including chronic or localized infections, or who are immunosuppressed.

Efavirenz

- Drug Class: Antiviral/reverse transcriptase inhibitor
- Available in: Capsules
- Available OTC? No
- As Generic? No

Side Effects

SERIOUS
Severe depression, mood changes, confusion. Call your doctor immediately.

COMMON
Dizziness, difficulty sleeping, fatigue, impaired concentration, unusual dreams, stomach upset, fever, cough, vomiting, diarrhea. Rash is also common; although the rash usually goes away without a change in treatment, sometimes it may be serious. If you develop a rash, call your doctor immediately.

LESS COMMON
Numerous less common side effects can occur; consult your doctor if you are concerned about any adverse or unusual reactions you experience while taking this drug.

PRINCIPAL USES
To treat human immunodeficiency virus (HIV) infection in combination with other drugs. While not a cure for HIV, such drugs may suppress the replication of the virus and delay the progression of the disease.

HOW THE DRUG WORKS
Efavirenz prevents HIV from reproducing in two ways. A metabolite of the drug inhibits the activity of an enzyme needed for the replication of DNA in viral cells. The metabolite is also incorporated into viral DNA and terminates the formation of the complete DNA.

DOSAGE
Adults: To start, 600 mg once a day. The drug must be taken in combination with other drugs for HIV to delay the development of resistant strains of the virus. For the first two to four weeks of therapy, take the daily dose at bedtime to improve tolerability of certain side effects (such as dizziness, drowsiness, and impaired concentration). Children: The dose may be lower. Consult your doctor.

ONSET OF EFFECT
Unknown. With most antiretroviral drugs, an early response can be seen within the first few days of therapy, but the maximum effect may take 12 to 16 weeks.

DURATION OF ACTION
Unknown. Effects of the drug may be prolonged when efavirenz is used in combination with other effective drugs and the virus is maximally suppressed.

DIETARY ADVICE
Efavirenz should be taken with plenty of water or other liquid. It may also be taken with a meal, but not one high in fat.

STORAGE
Store at room temperature in a tightly sealed container away from heat, moisture, and direct light.

IF YOU MISS A DOSE
Take it as soon as you remember. If it is near the time for the next dose, skip the missed dose and resume your regular dosage schedule. Do not double the next dose. It is especially important to take efavirenz on schedule, to assure constant, proper blood levels of the drug.

STOPPING THE DRUG
The decision to stop taking the drug should be made in consultation with your physician.

PROLONGED USE
See your doctor regularly for tests and examinations.

PRECAUTIONS
Over 60: It is not known whether efavirenz causes different or more severe side effects in older patients.

Driving and Hazardous Work: Do not drive or engage in hazardous work until you determine how the medicine affects you.

Alcohol: Alcohol may raise the blood concentration of the drug.

Pregnancy: Efavirenz has been shown to cause birth defects in animals. Human studies have not been done. This medication should be given during pregnancy only if potential benefits outweigh the risks to the unborn child.

Breast Feeding: Women infected with HIV should not breast feed, to avoid transmitting the virus to an uninfected child.

Infants and Children: Your pediatrician will determine the appropriate dosage based on your child's weight. Call your doctor immediately if you notice rash or any other side effects while your child is taking efavirenz.

Special Concerns: Use of efavirenz does not eliminate the risk of passing the AIDS virus to other persons. You should take appropriate preventive measures. Taking efavirenz with the herbal supplement St. John's wort is not recommended.

OVERDOSE
Symptoms: Increased severity of common side effects.

What to Do: Call your doctor, emergency medical services (EMS), or the nearest poison control center immediately.

DRUG INTERACTIONS
Do not take efavirenz with astemizole, midazolam, triazolam, or ergot medications (migraine drugs). Dose adjustments may be necessary if taking indinavir, saquinavir, or clarithromycin. Consult your doctor before taking with warfarin, rifampin, rifabutin, or oral contraceptives.

FOOD INTERACTIONS
Do not take efavirenz with high-fat meals.

DISEASE INTERACTIONS
Caution is advised when taking efavirenz. Consult your doctor if you have a history of mental illness or drug or alcohol abuse. This drug should be used with caution in patients with impaired liver function or risk factors for liver disease.

Eletriptan Hydrobromide

BRAND NAME
Relpax

▶ Drug Class:
Antimigraine/antiheadache
drug

▶ Available in: Tablets

▶ Available OTC? No

▶ As Generic? No

Side Effects

SERIOUS
Serious side effects with
eletriptan are rare. How-
ever, eletriptan may
cause a heart attack,
chest pain or tightness,
sudden or severe abdom-
inal pain, shortness of
breath, wheezing, heart-
beat irregularities,
swelling of eyelids, face,
or lips, skin rash, or
hives. Seek emergency
medical assistance imme-
diately.

COMMON
Dizziness, nausea, weak-
ness, tiredness.

LESS COMMON
Many less common side
effects can occur; consult
your doctor if you are
concerned about any
adverse or unusual reac-
tions you experience
while taking this drug.

PRINCIPAL USES
To treat severe, acute
migraine headaches. Eletriptan is not intended as a
migraine preventive or for
use against any other kinds
of pain or headache, including basilar and hemiplegic
migraines. Your doctor will
determine whether this
medication is appropriate in
your particular case.

HOW THE DRUG WORKS
It is believed that eletriptan
may reduce the swelling of
blood vessels in the brain
that are associated with the
pain of migraine, block the
release of substances from
nerve endings that cause
more pain and other symp-
toms of migraine, and interrupt transmission of specific
pain signals from the brain.

DOSAGE
A single dose ranging from
20 to 40 mg is generally
effective. If the migraine
returns or there is only partial relief, the dose may be
repeated once after 2 hours,
but no more than 80 mg
should be taken in a 24-
hour period. If there is no
relief, do not take a second
dose without talking to your
doctor. Since individual
response to eletriptan may
vary, your doctor will determine the appropriate
dosage. A general recom-
mendation is to take one 40
mg tablet as the initial dose.

ONSET OF EFFECT
Within 30 minutes to 2
hours.

DURATION OF ACTION
Unknown.

DIETARY ADVICE
The medication can be
taken with or without food.

STORAGE
Store in a tightly sealed container away from heat, moisture, and direct light.

IF YOU MISS A DOSE
Not applicable, since the
drug is taken only when
necessary.

STOPPING THE DRUG
Consult your doctor before
discontinuing eletriptan.

PROLONGED USE
No special problems are
expected. Patients at risk
for heart disease should
undergo periodic evaluation.

PRECAUTIONS
Over 60: This drug should
not be used unless the presence of coronary heart disease has been ruled out
through appropriate diag-
nostic tests.

**Driving and Hazardous
Work:** Some people feel
drowsy or dizzy during or
following a migraine attack
or after taking eletriptan.
Avoid driving or other tasks
requiring concentration if
you have such symptoms.

Alcohol: No special warnings, although alcohol may
trigger or exacerbate
migraine headaches.

Pregnancy: Adequate
human studies have not
been done. Discuss with
your doctor the relative
risks and benefits of using
eletriptan while pregnant.

Breast Feeding: Eletriptan
may pass into breast milk;
caution is advised. Consult
your doctor for advice.

Infants and Children:
Safety and effectiveness
have not been established
for children under age 18.

Special Concerns: Serious, but rare, heart-related
problems may occur after
taking eletriptan. Eletriptan
should not be used by anyone with any symptoms of
coronary artery disease

(chest pain or tightness,
shortness of breath). Anyone at risk for unrecognized
CAD—such as post-
menopausal women, men
over the age of 40, or those
with known risk factors for
heart disease—should have
the first dose of eletriptan
administered in a doctor's
office, and then only after
tests show they are probably free of CAD.

OVERDOSE
Symptoms: No overdoses
have been reported.

What to Do: Although
overdose is unlikely, if you
take a much larger dose
than prescribed, call your
doctor, emergency medical
services (EMS), or the
nearest poison control center immediately.

DRUG INTERACTIONS
Do not take eletriptan
within 24 hours of taking
naratriptan, rizatriptan,
sumatriptan, zolmitriptan,
almotriptan, ergotamine-containing medication, dihy-
droergotamine mesylate, or
methysergide mesylate.
Eletriptan and MAO
inhibitors such as
phenelzine and tranyl-
cypromine should not be
used within 14 days of each
other. Do not take eletriptan
within 72 hours of using
ketoconazole, itraconazole,
or clarithromycin.

FOOD INTERACTIONS
No known food interactions.

DISEASE INTERACTIONS
You should not take eletriptan if you have a history of
angina, heart disease,
stroke, uncontrolled hypertension, heartbeat irregularities, or peripheral vascular
disease. Eletriptan should
be used with caution in
patients with liver disease
or severely impaired kidney
function.

277

Emedastine Difumarate

BRAND NAME
Emadine

▶ Drug Class: Histamine (H1) blocker

▶ Available in: Ophthalmic solution

▶ Available OTC? No

▶ As Generic? No

Side Effects

SERIOUS
No serious side effects are associated with emedastine.

COMMON
Headache.

LESS COMMON
Bad taste in the mouth, abnormal dreams, eye dryness, blurred vision, burning or stinging of the eye, tearing, runny nose, skin rash, weakness.

PRINCIPAL USES
For short-term therapy of eye itching caused by seasonal allergic conjunctivitis (inflammation of the mucous membranes that line the inner surface of the eyelids and whites of the eyes).

HOW THE DRUG WORKS
Emedastine blocks the effects of histamine, a naturally occurring substance within the body that causes swelling, itching, sneezing, watery eyes, hives, and other symptoms associated with allergic reactions.

DOSAGE
Instill 1 drop in the affected eye(s) up to 4 times a day.

ONSET OF EFFECT
Unknown.

DURATION OF ACTION
Unknown.

DIETARY ADVICE
Emedastine can be used without regard to diet.

STORAGE
Store in a tightly sealed container away from heat, moisture, and direct light. Do not allow it to freeze.

IF YOU MISS A DOSE
Apply it as soon as you remember. If it is near the time for the next dose, skip the missed dose and resume your regular dosage schedule. Do not double the next dose.

STOPPING THE DRUG
You may stop using emedastine whenever you choose.

PROLONGED USE
Emedastine is prescribed for short-term use only.

PRECAUTIONS
Over 60: No special problems are expected.

Driving and Hazardous Work: Do not drive or engage in hazardous work until you determine how the medicine affects you.

Alcohol: No special precautions are necessary.

Pregnancy: No adequate human studies have been done. Before taking emedastine, tell your doctor if you are pregnant or plan to become pregnant.

Breast Feeding: Emedastine may pass into breast milk; caution is advised. Consult your doctor for specific advice.

Infants and Children: Not recommended for use by children under the age of 3 years.

Special Concerns: To use the eye drops, first wash your hands. Tilt your head back. Gently apply pressure to the inside corner of the eyelid and with the index finger of the same hand, pull downward on the lower eyelid to make a space. Drop the medicine into this space and close your eye. Apply pressure for 1 or 2 minutes while keeping the eye closed without blinking. Then wash your hands again. Make sure the tip of the dropper does not touch your eye, finger, or any other surface. You should not wear a contact lens if your eye is red. Emedastine should not be used to treat contact-lens-related irritation. If you wear soft contact lenses and your eyes are not red, wait at least 10 minutes after instilling the drops before inserting your contact lenses.

OVERDOSE
Symptoms: Drowsiness and general feelings of illness have been reported following unintentional oral intake of the drug.

What to Do: An overdose with emedastine is unlikely to be life-threatening. However, if someone accidentally ingests the medicine, seek emergency medical attention immediately.

DRUG INTERACTIONS
None reported.

FOOD INTERACTIONS
None reported.

DISEASE INTERACTIONS
None reported.

Emtricitabine

- ▶ Drug Class: Antiviral/reverse transcriptase inhibitor
- ▶ Available in: Capsules
- ▶ Available OTC? No
- ▶ As Generic? No

Side Effects

SERIOUS
Rarely, emtricitabine can cause lactic acidosis and severe liver abnormalities, including liver enlargement and fatty liver. These side effects may result in death.

COMMON
Headache, nausea, diarrhea, rash, increased cough, runny nose, and skin discoloration of palms and/or soles.

LESS COMMON
Indigestion, joint pain, muscle pain, abnormal dreams, dizziness, insomnia, numbness, prickling, or tingling in the hands or feet.

PRINCIPAL USES
To treat human immunodeficiency virus (HIV) infection in combination with other drugs. While not a cure for HIV, emtricitabine may suppress the replication of the virus and delay progression of the disease.

HOW THE DRUG WORKS
Emtricitabine prevents HIV from reproducing in two ways. A metabolite of the drug inhibits the activity of an enzyme needed for the replication of DNA in HIV-infected cells. The metabolite is also incorporated into viral DNA and terminates the formation of the complete DNA.

DOSAGE
Adults: 200 mg once a day. The drug must be taken in combination with other drugs for HIV to prevent the development of resistant strains of the virus.

ONSET OF EFFECT
Unknown. With most antiretroviral drugs, an early response can be seen within the first few days of therapy, but the maximum effect may take at least 16 weeks.

DURATION OF ACTION
Unknown. Effects of this drug may be prolonged when it is used in combination with other effective drugs and the virus is maximally suppressed.

DIETARY ADVICE
Emtricitabine can be taken with or without food.

STORAGE
Store at room temperature in a tightly sealed container away from heat, moisture, and direct light.

IF YOU MISS A DOSE
Take it as soon as you remember. If you miss a dose on one day, skip the missed dose and resume your regular dosage schedule. Do not double the next dose. It is especially important to take emtricitabine on schedule, to assure constant, proper blood levels of the drug.

STOPPING THE DRUG
The decision to stop taking the drug should be made in consultation with your physician.

PROLONGED USE
See your doctor regularly for tests and examinations.

PRECAUTIONS
Over 60: It is not known whether emtricitabine causes different or more severe side effects in older patients.

Driving and Hazardous Work: Do not drive or engage in hazardous work until you determine how the medicine affects you.

Alcohol: No special precautions are required.

Pregnancy: Human studies have not been done. This medication should be given during pregnancy only if potential benefits outweigh the risks to the unborn child.

Breast Feeding: Women infected with HIV should not breast feed to avoid transmitting the virus to an uninfected child.

Infants and Children: Safety and effectiveness in children have not been determined.

Special Concerns: If you are infected with HIV and hepatitis B, you may experience worsening of hepatitis after discontinuation of emtricitabine; careful clinical and laboratory followup is recommended for several months after stopping treatment. Use of emtricitabine does not eliminate the risk of passing the AIDS virus to other persons. Take appropriate preventive measures.

OVERDOSE
Symptoms: No cases of overdose have been reported.

What to Do: If you suspect an overdose or if someone takes a much larger dose than prescribed, call your doctor, emergency medical services (EMS), or the nearest poison control center immediately.

DRUG INTERACTIONS
Currently, there are no clinically significant drug interactions. Further studies are being conducted.

FOOD INTERACTIONS
No known food interactions.

DISEASE INTERACTIONS
This drug should be used with caution in patients with impaired kidney function or with risk factors for kidney disease.

Enalapril Maleate

Vasotec 10 mg
(MERCK)

Additional photographs

▶ Drug Class: Angiotensin-converting enzyme (ACE) inhibitor

▶ Available in: Tablets

▶ Available OTC? No

▶ As Generic? Yes

Side Effects

SERIOUS
Fever and chills, sore throat and hoarseness, sudden difficulty breathing or swallowing, swelling of the face, mouth, or extremities, impaired kidney function (ankle swelling, decreased urination), confusion, yellow discoloration of the eyes or skin (indicating liver disorder), intense itching, chest pain or palpitations, abdominal pain. Serious side effects are very rare; contact your doctor immediately.

COMMON
Dry, persistent cough.

LESS COMMON
Dizziness or fainting, skin rash, numbness or tingling in the hands, feet, or lips, unusual fatigue or muscle weakness, nausea, drowsiness, loss of taste, headache, unusual dreams.

PRINCIPAL USES
To control high blood pressure; to treat congestive heart failure; to treat patients with left ventricular dysfunction (damage to the pumping chamber of the heart); and to minimize further kidney damage in diabetic patients with mild kidney disease.

HOW THE DRUG WORKS
Angiotensin-converting enzyme (ACE) inhibitors block an enzyme that produces angiotensin, a naturally occurring substance that causes blood vessels to constrict. As a result, ACE inhibitors relax blood vessels (causing them to widen), which lowers blood pressure and so decreases the workload of the heart.

DOSAGE
Adults: 2.5 to 40 mg a day, taken 1 or 2 times a day. Children ages 1 month to 16 years (for high blood pressure): To start, 0.08 mg per kg (2.2 lbs) once a day, up to 5 mg a day. Your pediatrician may gradually raise the dose up to 40 mg a day, depending upon response to the drug.

ONSET OF EFFECT
Within 1 hour.

DURATION OF ACTION
Up to 24 hours.

DIETARY ADVICE
Take enalapril on an empty stomach, about 1 hour before mealtime. Follow your doctor's dietary advice (such as low-salt or low-cholesterol restrictions) to improve control over high blood pressure and heart disease. Avoid high-potassium foods like bananas and citrus fruits and juices, unless you are also taking medications, such as diuretics, that lower potassium levels.

STORAGE
Keep in a tightly sealed container in a cool, dry place.

IF YOU MISS A DOSE
Take it as soon as you remember. If it is near the time for the next dose, skip the missed dose and resume your regular dosage schedule. Do not double the next dose.

STOPPING THE DRUG
Do not stop taking this drug abruptly, as this may cause potentially serious health problems. Dosage should be reduced gradually, according to your doctor's instructions.

PROLONGED USE
See your doctor regularly for examinations and tests if you must take this medicine for a prolonged period. Remember that enalapril helps control high blood pressure but does not cure it. Lifelong therapy may be necessary.

PRECAUTIONS
Over 60: Some elderly patients may be more sensitive to the effects of this drug; smaller doses may be warranted.

Driving and Hazardous Work: Do not drive or engage in hazardous work until you determine how the medicine affects you.

Alcohol: Consume alcohol only in moderation since it may increase the effect of the drug and cause an excessive drop in blood pressure. Consult your doctor for advice.

Pregnancy: Enalapril use is not recommended, especially during the final 6 months of pregnancy. If you become pregnant, notify your doctor as soon as possible.

Breast Feeding: Trace amounts of enalapril can be found in breast milk; however, adverse effects in infants have not been documented. Consult your doctor for advice.

Infants and Children: Benefits of enalapril use by children must be weighed against risks. Consult your pediatrician for advice.

OVERDOSE
Symptoms: No specific ones have been reported.

What to Do: While overdose is unlikely, call your doctor, emergency medical services (EMS), or the nearest poison control center immediately if you suspect that someone has taken a much larger dose than prescribed.

DRUG INTERACTIONS
Consult your doctor if you are taking diuretics (especially potassium-sparing diuretics), potassium supplements or drugs containing potassium (check ingredient labels), lithium, anticoagulants, anti-inflammatory drugs, or any over-the-counter drugs (especially cold remedies and diet pills).

FOOD INTERACTIONS
Avoid low-salt milk and salt substitutes. Many of these products contain potassium.

DISEASE INTERACTIONS
Consult your doctor if you have systemic lupus erythematosus or if you have had a prior allergic reaction to ACE inhibitors. This medication should be used with caution by patients with severe kidney disease or renal artery stenosis (narrowing of one or both of the arteries that supply blood to the kidneys).

Enalapril Maleate/Diltiazem Malate

▶ Drug Class: ACE inhibitor/ calcium channel blocker combination

▶ Available in: Extended-release tablets

▶ Available OTC? No

▶ As Generic? No

Side Effects

SERIOUS
Fever and chills; sore throat and hoarseness; sudden difficulty breathing or swallowing; swelling of the face, mouth, or extremities; impaired kidney function (ankle swelling, decreased urination); confusion; yellow discoloration of the eyes or skin (indicating liver disorder); intense itching; chest pain or palpitations; irregular or slow heartbeat, shortness of breath, and fatigue caused by heart failure; abdominal pain. Serious side effects are very rare; contact your doctor immediately.

COMMON
Headache, drowsiness, swelling of feet and ankles, constipation, nausea, sudden weight gain, fatigue, dry, persistent cough.

LESS COMMON
Dizziness or fainting, weakness, depression, nervousness, insomnia, vomiting, diarrhea, excessive urination, skin rash, sensitivity to sunlight, overgrowth of the gums, numbness or tingling in the hands, feet, or lips, unusual muscle weakness, loss of taste.

PRINCIPAL USES
As a secondary treatment for high blood pressure. It is prescribed for people whose blood pressure is not adequately controlled by either enalapril or diltiazem alone and for those taking both drugs separately.

HOW THE DRUG WORKS
Angiotensin-converting enzyme (ACE) inhibitors such as enalapril maleate block an enzyme that produces angiotensin, a naturally occurring substance that causes blood vessels to constrict. Diltiazem, a calcium channel blocker, interferes with the movement of calcium into heart muscle cells and smooth muscle cells in the walls of the arteries. The combined action of enalapril and diltiazem causes blood vessels to relax (causing them to widen), which lowers blood pressure and decreases the workload of the heart.

DOSAGE
Adults: 1 to 4 tablets, each containing 5 mg enalapril and 180 mg diltiazem, in a single dose per day.

ONSET OF EFFECT
Unknown.

DURATION OF ACTION
Unknown.

DIETARY ADVICE
Take enalapril/diltiazem on an empty stomach, about 1 hour before mealtime. Avoid high-potassium foods like bananas and citrus fruits and juices, unless you are also taking medications, such as diuretics, that lower potassium levels.

STORAGE
Store in a tightly sealed container away from heat, moisture, and direct light.

IF YOU MISS A DOSE
If you miss a dose on one day, do not double the dose the next day.

STOPPING THE DRUG
Do not stop taking this drug abruptly, as this may cause potentially serious health problems. Dosage should be reduced gradually.

PROLONGED USE
See your doctor regularly for tests and examinations.

PRECAUTIONS
Over 60: Adverse reactions may be more likely and more severe.

Driving and Hazardous Work: Exercise caution until you determine how the medicine affects you.

Alcohol: Use alcohol with caution because it may increase the effect of the drug and cause an excessive drop in blood pressure.

Pregnancy: This drug can cause injury and even death in the developing fetus. See your doctor and discontinue using the medication as soon as possible when pregnancy is detected.

Breast Feeding: Diltiazem passes into breast milk; avoid use while nursing.

Infants and Children: Safety and effectiveness have not been established for children under 12.

Special Concerns: Brush and floss your teeth and see your dentist regularly, since the diltiazem component may promote dental problems. This drug may make you sensitive to sunlight.

OVERDOSE
Symptoms: None reported. However, heart block (causing shortness of breath), fatigue, excessive dizziness, fainting, and low blood pressure have been attributed to enalapril and diltiazem when taken alone.

What to Do: If someone takes a much larger dose than prescribed, seek medical assistance right away.

DRUG INTERACTIONS
Consult your doctor if you are taking aspirin, beta-blockers, digitalis drugs, carbamazepine, cyclosporine, lithium, oral antidiabetic agents, phenytoin, rifampin, cimetidine, fluvoxamine, ranitidine, diuretics (especially potassium-sparing diuretics), potassium supplements or drugs containing potassium (check ingredient labels), anticoagulants, anti-inflammatory drugs, or any nonprescription drugs (especially cold remedies and diet pills).

FOOD INTERACTIONS
Avoid excessive salt intake. Avoid low-salt milk and salt substitutes. Many of these products contain potassium.

DISEASE INTERACTIONS
Consult your doctor for advice if you have systemic lupus erythematosus or if you have had a prior allergic reaction to ACE inhibitors. This medication should not be used by patients with sick sinus syndrome or heart block (unless a pacemaker is in place), or by those with low blood pressure (hypotension) or history of acute heart attack with lung congestion. This medication should be used with caution by patients with congestive heart failure, liver disease, severe kidney disease, or renal artery stenosis (narrowing of one or both of the arteries that supply blood to the kidneys).

Enalapril Maleate/Felodipine

BRAND NAME
Lexxel

▶ Drug Class: ACE inhibitor/
calcium channel blocker
combination

▶ Available in: Tablets

▶ Available OTC? No

▶ As Generic? No

Side Effects

SERIOUS
Serious side effects are
very rare; they include
fever and chills, sore
throat and hoarseness,
sudden difficulty breath-
ing or swallowing,
swelling of the face,
mouth, or extremities,
worsening kidney func-
tion (ankle swelling,
decreased urination),
confusion, jaundice (yel-
lowish tinge to eyes or
skin, indicating liver
problems), intense itch-
ing, chest pain or heart
palpitations, abdominal
pain, irregular or slow
heartbeats, low blood
pressure (causing dizzi-
ness or faintness). Call
your doctor immediately.

COMMON
Mild swelling of arms
and legs, fatigue, mild
headache, dizziness,
cough, flushed skin.

LESS COMMON
Fainting, dry mouth, con-
stipation or diarrhea, gas,
nausea, vomiting, rectal
pain, gout, neck pain,
joint swelling, nervous-
ness, insomnia, sleepi-
ness, skin rash, increased
eye pressure, impotence,
hot flashes.

PRINCIPAL USES
To control hypertension
(high blood pressure).

HOW THE DRUG WORKS
Angiotensin-converting
enzyme (ACE) inhibitors
such as enalapril maleate
block an enzyme that pro-
duces angiotensin, a naturally occurring substance
that causes blood vessels to
constrict and stimulates production of the adrenal hormone, aldosterone, which
promotes sodium retention
in the body. As a result,
ACE inhibitors relax blood
vessels (causing them to
widen) and reduces sodium
retention. Felodipine, a calcium channel blocker, interferes with the movement of
calcium into heart muscle
cells and the smooth mus-
cle cells in the walls of the
arteries. As a result of the
combined action of enalapril
maleate and felodipine,
blood vessels relax (causing
them to widen), which lowers blood pressure and
thereby decreases the workload of the heart.

DOSAGE
To start, 5 mg once a day.
The dose may be increased
or decreased gradually by
your doctor to 2.5 to 10 mg
once a day, as needed. The
recommended initial dose
for older patients is 2.5 mg
a day.

ONSET OF EFFECT
Unknown.

DURATION OF ACTION
Unknown.

DIETARY ADVICE
Enalapril maleate/felodipine
is best taken without food.
The drug can, however, be
taken with grapefruit juice.

STORAGE
Store in a tightly sealed container away from heat, moisture, and direct light.

IF YOU MISS A DOSE
Take it as soon as you
remember. If it is near the
time for the next dose, skip
the missed dose and
resume your regular dosage
schedule. Do not double the
next dose.

STOPPING THE DRUG
The decision to stop taking
the drug should be made by
your doctor.

PROLONGED USE
See your doctor periodically
for tests and examinations.

PRECAUTIONS
Over 60: No special problems are expected.

**Driving and Hazardous
Work:** Avoid such activities
until you determine how
this medication affects you.

Alcohol: Consume alcohol
only in moderation since it
may increase the effect of
the drug and cause an
excessive drop in blood
pressure. Consult your
doctor for advice.

Pregnancy: Adequate studies have not been done.
Before taking enalapril with
felodipine, tell your doctor if
you are pregnant or plan to
become pregnant.

Breast Feeding: This
drug passes into breast
milk. Discuss with your
doctor the relative risks
and benefits of using it
while nursing.

Infants and Children:
The safety and effectiveness
of enalapril with felodipine
use by infants and children
have not been established.

Special Concerns:
Enalapril with felodipine is
not recommended as the
first treatment when high
blood pressure is diag-
nosed. It may be prescribed

after other medications have
proved unsatisfactory.
Before you undergo
surgery, tell the doctor or
dentist in charge that you
are taking this drug.

OVERDOSE
Symptoms: No cases of
overdose have been
reported.

What to Do: If someone
takes a much larger dose
than prescribed, call your
doctor, emergency medical
services (EMS), or the
nearest poison control center right away.

DRUG INTERACTIONS
Consult your doctor for specific advice if you are taking
diuretics, antihypertensives,
lithium, cimetidine, anticonvulsants, or other over-the-
counter or prescription
medications.

FOOD INTERACTIONS
No known food interactions.

DISEASE INTERACTIONS
Caution is advised when
taking enalapril with felodipine. Consult your doctor if
you have congestive heart
failure (CHF) or any other
medical condition. Use of
this drug may cause complications in patients with liver
or kidney disease, since
these organs work together
to remove the medication
from the body.

Enalapril/Hydrochlorothiazide (HCTZ)

Vaseretic 5/12.5 mg
(MERCK)

▶ Drug Class: Angiotensin-converting enzyme (ACE) inhibitor/diuretic

▶ Available in: Tablets

▶ Available OTC? No

▶ As Generic? Yes

Side Effects

SERIOUS
Fever and chills, sore throat and hoarseness, sudden difficulty breathing or swallowing, swelling of the face, mouth, or extremities, impaired kidney function (ankle swelling, decreased urination), confusion, yellow discoloration of the eyes or skin (indicating liver disorder), intense itching, chest pain or palpitations, abdominal pain. Serious side effects are very rare; contact your doctor immediately.

COMMON
Dry, persistent cough.

LESS COMMON
Dizziness or fainting, skin rash, numbness or tingling in the hands, feet, or lips, change in color of the hands from white to blue to red (Raynaud's phenomenon) in cold weather, unusual fatigue or muscle weakness, nausea, drowsiness, loss of taste, headache, unusual dreams.

PRINCIPAL USES
To control high blood pressure; to treat congestive heart failure (CHF); to treat patients with left ventricular dysfunction (damage to the pumping chamber of the heart); and to minimize further kidney damage in diabetics with mild kidney disease.

HOW THE DRUG WORKS
Angiotensin-converting enzyme (ACE) inhibitors such as enalapril block an enzyme that produces angiotensin, a naturally occurring substance that causes blood vessels to constrict and stimulates production of the adrenal hormone, aldosterone, which promotes sodium retention in the body. As a result, ACE inhibitors relax blood vessels (causing them to widen) and reduces sodium retention, which lowers blood pressure and so decreases the workload of the heart. Hydrochlorothiazide (HCTZ), a diuretic, increases sodium and water in the urine output. By reducing the overall fluid volume in the body, diuretics reduce blood volume and so reduce blood pressure.

DOSAGE
Adults: 1 to 2 tablets containing 10 mg enalapril and 25 mg hydrochlorothiazide once a day.

ONSET OF EFFECT
Within 1 hour.

DURATION OF ACTION
24 hours.

DIETARY ADVICE
Take on an empty stomach, about 1 hour before mealtime. Follow your doctor's dietary advice (such as low-salt or low-cholesterol restrictions) to improve control over high blood pressure and heart disease.

STORAGE
Store in a tightly sealed container away from heat and direct light.

IF YOU MISS A DOSE
Take it as soon as you remember. If it is near the time for the next dose, skip the missed dose and resume your regular dosage schedule. Do not double the next dose.

STOPPING THE DRUG
Do not stop taking this drug abruptly, as this may cause potentially serious health problems. Dosage should be reduced gradually, according to your doctor's instructions.

PROLONGED USE
See your doctor regularly for examinations and tests if you must take this medication for a prolonged period. Lifelong therapy may be necessary.

PRECAUTIONS
Over 60: Adverse reactions may be more likely and more severe in older patients.

Driving and Hazardous Work: Do not drive or engage in hazardous work until you determine how the medicine affects you.

Alcohol: Consume alcohol only in moderation since it may increase the effect of the drug and cause an excessive drop in blood pressure. Consult your doctor for advice.

Pregnancy: Before taking this medication, tell your doctor if you are pregnant or plan to become pregnant. Use of this drug during the last 6 months of pregnancy may cause severe defects, even death, in the fetus.

Breast Feeding: Enalapril may pass into breast milk; caution is advised. Consult your doctor for specific advice.

Infants and Children: Children may be especially sensitive to the effects of enalapril. Consult your pediatrician about the relative risks and benefits.

OVERDOSE
Symptoms: Overdose has not been reported; symptoms might include dizziness, faintness, or confusion.

What to Do: While overdose is unlikely, call your doctor, emergency medical services (EMS), or the nearest poison control center immediately if you suspect that someone has taken a much larger dose than prescribed.

DRUG INTERACTIONS
Consult your doctor for specific advice if you are taking cholestyramine, colestipol, digitalis drugs, lithium, potassium-containing medicines or supplements, or any over-the-counter drug (especially cold remedies and diet pills).

FOOD INTERACTIONS
Avoid low-salt milk and salt substitutes. Many of these products contain potassium.

DISEASE INTERACTIONS
Consult your doctor if you have systemic lupus erythematosus or if you have had a prior allergic reaction to ACE inhibitors. This medication should be used with caution by patients with severe kidney disease or renal artery stenosis (narrowing of one or both of the arteries that supply blood to the kidneys).

▶ Drug Class: HIV fusion inhibitor

▶ Available in: Injection

▶ Available OTC? No

▶ As Generic? No

Side Effects

SERIOUS
Cough, fever, difficulty breathing, vomiting, blood in urine, and swelling of the feet. Call your doctor immediately.

COMMON
Injection site reactions (itching, swelling, redness, pain or tenderness, hardend skin, bumps), pain and numbness in feet or legs, insomnia, depression, decreased appetite, weakness, muscle pain, diarrhea, nausea, and fatigue.

LESS COMMON
Change in sense of taste, anxiety, sinusitis, decreased weight, flu-like symptoms, constipation.

PRINCIPAL USES
To treat HIV (human immunodeficiency virus) infection in combination with other drugs. While not a cure for HIV, such drugs may suppress the replication of the virus and delay the progression of the disease.

HOW THE DRUG WORKS
Enfuvirtide block's HIV's ability to infect healthy CD4 cells (a type of white blood cell). When used with other anti-HIV medicines, this drug can reduce the amount of HIV in the blood and increase the number of CD4 cells. This may keep your immune system healthy, so it can help fight infection.

DOSAGE
Adults: 90 mg twice a day injected under the skin of the upper arm, thigh, or abdomen. Children ages 6 to 16: 2 mg per kg (2.2 lbs) twice a day, up to a maximum of 90 mg twice a day, injected under the skin of the upper arm, thigh, or abdomen. Each injection should be given at a site different from the previous injection site. Enfuvirtide should not be injected into moles, scar tissue, bruises, or the navel.

ONSET OF EFFECT
Unknown.

DURATION OF ACTION
Unknown.

DIETARY ADVICE
Can be taken with or without food.

STORAGE
Powder for injection should be stored in a tightly sealed container away from heat, moisture, and direct light. When reconstituted, refrigerate, but do not allow to freeze, for up to 24 hours.

IF YOU MISS A DOSE
Take it as soon as you remember. If it is near the time for the next dose, skip the missed dose and resume your regular dosage schedule. Do not double the next dose. It is especially important to take this medication on schedule, to assure constant, proper blood levels of the drug.

STOPPING THE DRUG
The decision to stop taking the drug should be made in consultation with your physician.

PROLONGED USE
See your doctor regularly for tests and examinations as long as you take this medication.

PRECAUTIONS

Over 60: No special studies have been done on older patients.

Driving and Hazardous Work: Do not drive or engage in hazardous work until you determine how the medicine affects you.

Alcohol: Avoid alcohol if liver function is impaired.

Pregnancy: Adequate human studies have not been done. Discuss with your doctor the relative risks and benefits of using this drug while pregnant.

Breast Feeding: Women infected with HIV should not breast feed, so as to avoid transmitting the virus to an uninfected child.

Infants and Children: The safety and effectiveness of enfuvirtide have not been established for children under 6 years of age.

Special Concerns: Use of enfuvirtide does not eliminate the risk of passing HIV to other persons. You should take appropriate preventive measures. Consult your doctor for step-by-step instructions about how to inject enfuvirtide.

OVERDOSE
Symptoms: No cases of overdose have been reported.

What to Do: If you suspect an overdose or if someone takes a much larger dose than prescribed, call your doctor, emergency medical services (EMS), or the nearest poison control center immediately.

DRUG INTERACTIONS
None reported.

FOOD INTERACTIONS
No known food interactions.

DISEASE INTERACTIONS
None reported.

Enoxacin

BRAND NAME
Penetrex

Generic 400 mg
(RHONE-POULENC RORER)

▶ Drug Class: Fluoroquinolone
antibiotic

▶ Available in: Tablets

▶ Available OTC? No

▶ As Generic? No

Side Effects

SERIOUS
Serious reactions are rare
and include seizures,
confusion, hallucinations,
agitation, nightmares,
depression, shortness of
breath, unusual swelling
in the face or extremities,
decreased urine output,
and loss of conscious-
ness. Also skin burning,
redness, blisters, rash, or
itching on exposure to
sunlight. Call your doctor
immediately.

COMMON
Increased sensitivity to
sunlight (and increased
risk of sunburn) for days
following therapy.

LESS COMMON
Diarrhea, nausea and
vomiting, stomach pain
and upset, gas, headache,
dizziness, restlessness,
insomnia, changes in
taste perception, drowsi-
ness, itching, dry mouth,
unusual body aches or
pains.

PRINCIPAL USES
To treat bacterial urinary
tract infections, including
gonorrhea.

HOW THE DRUG WORKS
Enoxacin inhibits the activity of a bacterial enzyme
(gyrase) that is necessary
for proper DNA formation
and replication. This prevents bacteria cells from
reproducing.

DOSAGE
For uncomplicated urinary
tract infections: 200 mg
every 12 hours for 7 days.
For severe or complicated
urinary tract infections: 400
mg every 12 hours for 14
days. For gonorrhea: 400
mg in a one-time dose. For
persons with kidney impairment, doses may be
decreased by half.

ONSET OF EFFECT
Varies depending on the
infection being treated.

DURATION OF ACTION
Unknown.

DIETARY ADVICE
Take with a full glass of
water on an empty stomach,
1 hour before or 2 hours
after a meal. Drink plenty of
fluids.

STORAGE
Store in a tightly sealed container away from heat, moisture, and direct light.

IF YOU MISS A DOSE
Take it as soon as you
remember. If it is near the
time for the next dose, skip
the missed dose and
resume your regular dosage
schedule. Do not double the
next dose.

STOPPING THE DRUG
Take it as prescribed for the
full treatment period, even if
you begin to feel better
before the scheduled end of
therapy.

PROLONGED USE
There are no documented
problems with prolonged
use, but if you must take
this drug for an extended
period, see your physician
regularly.

PRECAUTIONS
Over 60: No special problems are expected.

**Driving and Hazardous
Work:** Do not drive or
engage in hazardous work
until you determine how the
medicine affects you.

Alcohol: It is advisable to
abstain from alcohol when
fighting an infection.

Pregnancy: In some animal tests, enoxacin has
caused birth defects. Adequate studies in humans
have not been done. It
should be used during pregnancy only if potential benefits clearly justify the risks.
Before you take enoxacin,
tell your doctor if you are
pregnant or plan to become
pregnant.

Breast Feeding: Enoxacin
passes into breast milk and
may cause serious side
effects in the nursing infant;
use of the drug is discouraged when nursing.

Infants and Children:
Not recommended for use
by persons under age 18, as
it has been shown to interfere with bone development.

Special Concerns: If
enoxacin causes sensitivity
to sunlight, stop taking the
drug and try to avoid exposure to sunlight for the next
5 days; also wear protective
clothing and use a sun-
block. Enoxacin should not
be taken by patients whose
work makes it impossible to
stay out of the sun. Avoid
smoking. Do not take this
medicine if you are allergic

to any quinolone antibiotic.
You should avoid people
who have an active infec-
tion. Refrain from strenuous
physical activity while taking this medicine. Be sure
to drink at least 8 glasses of
water a day while taking
enoxacin.

OVERDOSE
Symptoms: No specific
ones have been reported.

What to Do: If you have
any reason to suspect an
overdose, call your doctor,
emergency medical services
(EMS), or the nearest poison control center.

DRUG INTERACTIONS
Consult your doctor for specific advice if you are taking
aminophylline, antacids,
didanosine, iron supple-
ments, oxtriphylline, sucralfate, theophylline, warfarin,
or zinc salts. Also tell your
doctor if you are taking any
other prescription or over-
the-counter medication.

FOOD INTERACTIONS
The effects of caffeine may
be magnified by this drug.

DISEASE INTERACTIONS
Do not use enoxacin if you
have a history of hypersensitivity, tendinitis, or tendon
rupture associated with the
use of enoxacin or any
other quinolone antibiotic.
Consult your doctor if you
have any other medical condition. Use of enoxacin can
cause complications in
patients with kidney dis-
ease, since this organ works
to remove the medication
from the body.

Enoxaparin Sodium Injection

Side Effects

SERIOUS
Extreme fatigue; abnormal bleeding; bleeding gums; arm or leg bruises; purple or red spots on skin; nosebleeds; black, tarry stools; blood in urine; vomiting of blood. Seek medical assistance immediately.

COMMON
There are no common side effects associated with the enoxaparin use.

LESS COMMON
Nausea, fever, increased menstrual bleeding, confusion, swelling, pain or redness at injection site.

PRINCIPAL USES
To prevent blood clots in the legs after hip or knee replacement surgery, or for other conditions where blood clots could pose a problem.

HOW THE DRUG WORKS
Enoxaparin forms a complex with certain natural body chemicals that prevent clot formation; it also decreases the activity of chemicals that cause clot formation. The combined effect reduces the speed at which blood may coagulate and thus prevents blood clots from developing.

DOSAGE
The appropriate dose will be determined by your doctor and your condition. The usual dosage is 30 mg every 12 hours or 40 mg once a day injected under the skin for 7 to 10 days. It must not be administered intramuscularly or intravenously. Rotate the site of injections from abdomen to thighs to upper arms. After injection, do not massage the site of the injection. Watch for signs of bruising or bleeding at injection sites. Children: Consult your pediatrician for proper dosage.

ONSET OF EFFECT
Within 30 minutes to 3 hours.

DURATION OF ACTION
Up to 24 hours.

DIETARY ADVICE
Injections can be delivered regardless of diet or meal schedule.

STORAGE
Store in a tightly sealed container away from heat and direct light. Do not refrigerate or allow to freeze (for instance, in the trunk of a car during wintertime).

IF YOU MISS A DOSE
Take it as soon as you remember. If it is near the time for the next dose, skip the missed dose and resume your regular dosage schedule. Do not double the next dose.

STOPPING THE DRUG
The decision to stop taking the drug should be made by your doctor.

PROLONGED USE
Enoxaparin should be used only for the period recommended by your doctor.

PRECAUTIONS
Over 60: Older patients may be more susceptible to bleeding during therapy.

Driving and Hazardous Work: Do not drive or engage in hazardous work until you determine how the medicine affects you.

Alcohol: Alcohol should be avoided while taking this medicine.

Pregnancy: Enoxaparin does not appear to cross the placenta. No birth defects have been found in animal studies. Human studies have not been conducted.

Breast Feeding: It is not known if enoxaparin passes into breast milk. Use caution. Consult your doctor for specific advice.

Infants and Children: There is no information about the safety and efficacy of enoxaparin in infants and children. Consult your doctor for specific advice.

Special Concerns: Place used syringes in a disposable, puncture-proof container or follow your doctor's instructions on discarding them. Be sure to tell all doctors and dentists whom you consult that you are using enoxaparin. Before taking enoxaparin, tell your doctor if you have recently given birth, injured your head or body, or had surgery, including dental surgery. Tell your doctor if you are allergic to substances such as pork, preservatives, or dyes.

OVERDOSE
Symptoms: Bleeding complications (such as uncontrolled hemorrhaging).

What to Do: Stop taking enoxaparin, and call your doctor, emergency medical services (EMS), or the nearest poison control center immediately.

DRUG INTERACTIONS
Consult your doctor for specific advice if you are taking aspirin or any other salicylate; inflammation or pain medicine; or drugs that lower blood platelet count, such as famotidine, plicamycin, sulfinpyrazone, ticlopidine, valproic acid, anagrelide, or any other anticoagulant.

FOOD INTERACTIONS
No known food interactions.

DISEASE INTERACTIONS
Caution is advised when taking enoxaparin. Consult your doctor if you have any of the following: blood disease, heart disease, high blood pressure, kidney disease, liver disease, a heart infection, an ulce, or a prosthetic heart valve.

Entacapone

▶ Drug Class: Antiparkinsonism drug/COMT inhibitor

▶ Available in: Tablets

▶ Available OTC? No

▶ As Generic? No

Side Effects

SERIOUS
Dizziness, lightheadedness, or fainting, especially when rising from a sitting or lying position, owing to a sudden drop in blood pressure (orthostatic hypotension). Such symptoms, in addition to nausea, are more common at the beginning of therapy. Hallucinations may also occur and require discontinuation of therapy.

COMMON
Slowed movement, nausea, quirky involuntary muscle movements that may contort the body, discolored urine, abdominal pain, diarrhea.

LESS COMMON
Increased sweating, back pain, anxiety, agitation, drowsiness, vomiting, constipation, dry mouth, indigestion, flatulence, shortness of breath, fatigue, weakness.

PRINCIPAL USES
To treat Parkinson's disease, in conjunction with standard levodopa/carbidopa therapy, in patients who have begun to be less responsive to levodopa and experience worsening symptoms between doses, a phenomenon known as end-of-dose wearing-off.

HOW THE DRUG WORKS
When used with levodopa/carbidopa, entacapone sustains higher levels of levodopa in the blood. Entacapone increases blood levels of levodopa by blocking the action of catechol-O-methyltransferase (COMT), one of the enzymes responsible for breaking down levodopa, before it reaches its receptors in the brain. Levodopa raises the amount of dopamine available in the brain; dopamine plays an essential role in smooth movement of muscles and is deficient in patients with Parkinson's disease.

DOSAGE
Adults: 200 mg in conjunction with each levodopa/carbidopa dose, up to a maximum of 8 times a day (1600 mg a day). Entacapone must be administered with levodopa/carbidopa as entacapone has no antiparkinsonian effect of its own. Patients may require a decrease in their daily dosage of levodopa upon beginning entacapone therapy.

ONSET OF EFFECT
Unknown.

DURATION OF ACTION
Unknown.

DIETARY ADVICE
Entacapone can be taken without regard to meals.

STORAGE
Store in a tightly sealed container away from heat, moisture, and direct light.

IF YOU MISS A DOSE
Take it as soon as you remember. If it is near the time for the next dose, skip the missed dose and resume your regular dosage schedule. Do not double the next dose.

STOPPING THE DRUG
Take it as prescribed for the full treatment period. The decision to stop taking the drug should be made in consultation with your physician. Abrupt discontinuation of entacapone, without a gradual reduction in dose, may increase the risk of adverse effects.

PROLONGED USE
Since Parkinson's disease is a chronic condition, lifelong therapy with entacapone may be required. No special problems are expected.

PRECAUTIONS
Over 60: No specific problems for older people have been reported.

Driving and Hazardous Work: Avoid such activities until you determine how the medicine affects you.

Alcohol: No special precautions are necessary.

Pregnancy: Adequate human studies have not been done. Before taking entacapone, tell your doctor if you are or are planning to become pregnant. Discuss with your doctor the relative risks and benefits of using this drug while pregnant.

Breast Feeding: Entacapone may pass into breast milk; caution is advised. Consult your doctor for specific advice.

Infants and Children: Not applicable. No potential use for entacapone has been identified in children.

Special Concerns: Entacapone may be combined with either the immediate or sustained-release forms of levodopa/carbidopa.

OVERDOSE
Symptoms: An overdose with entacapone is unlikely. However, diarrhea and abdominal pain may occur with an excessive dose.

What to Do: If someone takes a much larger dose than prescribed, call your doctor, emergency medical services (EMS), or the nearest poison control center immediately.

DRUG INTERACTIONS
Consult your doctor for specific advice if you are taking any of the following drugs, which may interact with entacapone: MAO inhibitor antidepressants (such as phenelzine sulfate or tranylcypromine sulfate, but not selegiline), isoproterenol, epinephrine, norepinephrine, dopamine, dobutamine, bitolterol, probenecid, cholestyramine, and some antibiotics (erythromycin, rifampicin, ampicillin, and chloramphenicol).

FOOD INTERACTIONS
No known food interactions.

DISEASE INTERACTIONS
Entacapone should be used with caution in people with liver disease, bile duct obstruction, or low blood pressure.

Ephedrine

BRAND NAMES
Ephedrine Sulfate,
Kondon's Nasal, Pretz-D,
Vicks Vatronol

▶ Drug Class: Adrenergic bronchodilator

▶ Available in: Capsules, injection

▶ Available OTC? Yes

▶ As Generic? Yes

Side Effects

SERIOUS
Irregular heartbeats; hallucinations with high doses; shortness of breath. Call your doctor.

COMMON
Nervousness, rapid heartbeat, paleness, insomnia.

LESS COMMON
Dizziness, loss of appetite, nausea, vomiting, muscle cramps, headache, difficult or painful urination.

PRINCIPAL USES
To relieve bronchial asthma, to decrease nasal and lower respiratory congestion, and to suppress allergic reactions. Ephedrine commonly appears in combination with other drugs in such brand name products as Broncholate, Bronkotuss Expectorant, Quelidrine Cough Formula, and Rynatuss.

HOW THE DRUG WORKS
Ephedrine prevents cells from releasing histamine, a naturally occurring substance that causes swelling, itching, sneezing, watery eyes, hives, and other symptoms of allergic reaction. It also relaxes the smooth muscle surrounding the bronchial tubes, widening the airways, and causes constriction of blood vessels in the nose, which helps to open the nasal passages.

DOSAGE
Capsules— Adults: 25 to 50 mg every 3 or 4 hours, if needed. Children: 3 mg per 2.2 lbs (1 kg) of body weight per day, in 4 to 6 divided doses. Injection— Adults: 1 dose of 12.5 to 25 mg injected into a muscle, a vein, or under the skin. A second dose may be administered if approved by your doctor. Children: 3 mg per 2.2 lbs of body weight a day, in 4 to 6 divided doses.

ONSET OF EFFECT
Capsules: 15 to 60 minutes. Injection: 10 to 20 minutes.

DURATION OF ACTION
Capsules: 3 to 5 hours. Injection: 30 minutes to 1 hour after 25 to 50 mg dose.

DIETARY ADVICE
Swallow capsules with water and drink plenty of fluids.

STORAGE
Store in a dry place in a tightly sealed container away from heat and direct light. Keep injection form refrigerated, but do not allow it to freeze. Do not use injection if the liquid is cloudy or unclear.

IF YOU MISS A DOSE
Take it if you remember within 2 hours. If not, skip the missed dose and resume your normal dosage schedule. Do not double the next dose.

STOPPING THE DRUG
You may stop taking this drug at your own discretion. Consult your doctor.

PROLONGED USE
This drug may lose its effectiveness if taken on a continuous basis for 3 to 4 days. Men with an enlarged prostate gland may have difficulty urinating.

PRECAUTIONS
Over 60: Adverse reactions may be more likely and more severe. Small doses are advisable until individual response to the drug has been evaluated.

Driving and Hazardous Work: Ephedrine may cause dizziness. Do not drive or engage in hazardous work until you determine how it affects you.

Alcohol: No special precautions are necessary.

Pregnancy: Consult your doctor; benefits must clearly outweigh risks.

Breast Feeding: Ephedrine passes into breast milk and may be harmful to the child; do not use it while nursing.

Infants and Children: Use caution. Ask your doctor if the benefits of ephedrine justify possible risk to the child.

Special Concerns: Ephedrine can cause insomnia. Take the last dose at least 2 hours before bedtime. Before you take ephedrine, tell your doctor if you will have surgery requiring general anesthesia, including dental surgery, within 2 months.

OVERDOSE
Symptoms: Severe anxiety, convulsions, trouble breathing, coma, confusion, delirium, rapid and irregular pulse, muscle tremors.

What to Do: Call your doctor, emergency medical services (EMS), or the nearest poison control center immediately.

DRUG INTERACTIONS
Consult your doctor for specific advice if you are taking tricyclic antidepressants, high blood pressure medication, beta-blockers, dextrothyroxine, digitalis drugs, ergot-containing preparations, furazolidone, guanadrel, guanethidine, heart medication, methyldopa, MAO inhibitors, nitrates, phenothiazines, pseudoephedrine, rauwolfia alkaloids, sympathomimetic drugs, terazosin, theophylline, or any nonprescription drug for a cough, cold, allergy, or asthma.

FOOD INTERACTIONS
No known food interactions.

DISEASE INTERACTIONS
Caution is advised when taking ephedrine. Consult your doctor if you have any of the following: enlarged prostate, high blood pressure, history of seizures, diabetes, Parkinson's disease, or an overactive thyroid gland.

Epinastine Hydrochloride Ophthalmic

BRAND NAME
Elestat

▶ Drug Class: Antihistamine

▶ Available in: Ophthalmic solution

▶ Available OTC? No

▶ As Generic? No

Side Effects

SERIOUS
No serious side effects are associated with epinastine.

COMMON
Temporary burning and stinging of the eye.

LESS COMMON
Inflammation of the eyelashes, tearing, itching, dryness of the surface of the eye.

PRINCIPAL USES
For temporary relief of itching of the eye due to allergic conjunctivitis (an inflammation of the mucous membranes that line the inner surface of the eyelids and whites of the eyes).

HOW THE DRUG WORKS
Epinastine inhibits the release and blocks the effects of histamine, a substance that causes swelling, itching, sneezing, watery eyes, hives, and other symptoms of allergy.

DOSAGE
1 drop in each affected eye twice a day.

ONSET OF EFFECT
Within 3 minutes.

DURATION OF ACTION
Up to 8 hours.

DIETARY ADVICE
No special restrictions.

STORAGE
Store in a tightly sealed container away from heat, moisture, and direct light. Do not allow it to freeze.

IF YOU MISS A DOSE
Apply the next dose as needed; do not double the next dose.

STOPPING THE DRUG
This medication is to be used throughout the period of exposure (the duration of the pollen season or until the cause of the conjunctivitis is no longer present).

PROLONGED USE
See your doctor regularly for tests and examinations if you must take this drug for a prolonged period.

PRECAUTIONS
Over 60: No special problems are expected.

Driving and Hazardous Work: Do not drive or engage in hazardous work until you determine how the medicine affects your vision.

Alcohol: No special precautions are necessary.

Pregnancy: In animal studies, large doses of epinastine did not cause birth defects. Human studies have not been done. Epinastine should be used by pregnant women only if the potential benefit to the mother justifies the potential risk to the embryo or fetus. Consult your doctor for specific advice.

Breast Feeding: Epinastine may pass into breast milk; caution is advised. Consult your doctor for advice.

Infants and Children: The safety and effectiveness of epinastine in infants and children under the age of 3 have not been established.

Special Concerns: To use the eye drops, first wash your hands. Tilt your head back. Gently apply pressure to the inside corner of the eyelid and with the index finger of the same hand, pull downward on the lower eyelid to make a space. Drop the medicine into this space and close your eye. Then wash your hands again. Make sure the tip of the dropper does not touch your eye, finger, or any other surface. If you use contact lenses, do not wear them while administering epinastine.

OVERDOSE
Symptoms: No specific ones have been reported.

What to Do: An overdose of epinastine is unlikely to be life-threatening. However, if someone applies a much larger dose than prescribed or accidentally ingests the medicine, call your doctor, emergency medical services (EMS), or the nearest poison control center immediately.

DRUG INTERACTIONS
None reported.

FOOD INTERACTIONS
No known food interactions.

DISEASE INTERACTIONS
Consult your doctor if you have any medical condition, especially one affecting the eyes.

Epinephrine Hydrochloride

▶ Drug Class: Bronchodilator/
sympathomimetic;
antiglaucoma agent

▶ Available in: Inhalation
aerosols and solutions,
injection, eye drops

▶ Available OTC? Yes

▶ As Generic? Yes

Side Effects

SERIOUS
Bluish color of skin,
severe dizziness, flushing,
and difficulty breathing
may indicate an allergic
reaction to sulfites in the
medication. Contact your
doctor immediately.

COMMON
Dry mouth and throat;
trembling; headaches.
Check with your doctor if
these symptoms continue
or become bothersome.

LESS COMMON
Eye pain or headache
from using eye drops.

PRINCIPAL USES
To treat bronchial asthma,
emphysema, and other lung
diseases. Epinephrine is
also a primary treatment for
anaphylaxis; that is, a hypersensitive (allergic) reaction
to drugs or other sub-
stances. It may also be used
to treat nasal congestion, to
prolong the action of anesthetics, and to treat cardiac
arrest. The ophthalmic form
of the drug is used to treat
glaucoma.

HOW THE DRUG WORKS
Epinephrine widens con-
stricted airways in the lungs
by relaxing smooth muscles
that surround bronchial passages. It also raises blood
pressure by constricting
small blood vessels,
increases the heart rate and
strength of heart contractions, and decreases fluid
pressure in the eye.

DOSAGE
It may be used when
needed to relieve breathing
difficulty. For adults and
children 4 years of age or
older with asthma— Inhaled
aerosol: 200 micrograms
(mcg) to 275 mcg (1 puff),
repeated if needed after 1 or
2 minutes, with doses taken
at least 3 hours apart.
Inhalation solution: 1 puff
of 1% solution repeated after
1 or 2 minutes, if needed.
Injection: 0.2 to 1 mg,
increased if needed. For
open-angle glaucoma— 1 or
2 drops of 1% or 2% solution,
once or twice daily.

ONSET OF EFFECT
Inhalation: Within 5 minutes.
Injection: 1 to 5 minutes.

DURATION OF ACTION
Inhalation: 1 to 3 hours.
Injection: 1 to 4 hours.

DIETARY ADVICE
No special concerns.

STORAGE
Store in a tightly sealed container, away from heat,
moisture, and direct light.

IF YOU MISS A DOSE
Take your missed dose as
soon as you remember,
unless the time for your
next scheduled dose is
within the next 2 hours, in
which case skip the missed
dose. Take your next scheduled dose at the proper time
and resume your regular
dosage schedule. Do not
take a double dose.

STOPPING THE DRUG
Take the drug exactly as
prescribed. Contact your
doctor if you do not respond
to the strength of the
dosage you have been
given.

PROLONGED USE
Tolerance to epinephrine
may develop with prolonged
use.

PRECAUTIONS
Over 60: Adverse reactions
may be more likely and
more severe in older
patients.

**Driving and Hazardous
Work:** Do not drive or
engage in hazardous work
until you determine how the
medicine affects you.

Alcohol: It may increase
the excretion of epinephrine
in the urine.

Pregnancy: Benefits of
taking the drug must out-
weigh the potential risks;
consult your doctor for
specific advice.

Breast Feeding: Epinephrine passes into the breast
milk. Consult your doctor
for specific advice.

Infants and Children:
They may be especially sensitive to epinephrine; faint-

ing by children with asthma
taking the drug has been
reported.

Special Concerns: Do not
use without a prescription,
unless your problem has
been diagnosed as asthma.
Take aerosol doses exactly
as directed; overuse has
caused sudden death. Keep
the injectable form ready
for use at all times, along
with phone numbers of your
physician and the local
emergency room.

OVERDOSE
Symptoms: Chest discomfort, chills or fever, seizures,
dizziness, irregular heartbeat, trouble breathing.

What to Do: Call your
doctor, emergency medical
services (EMS), or the
nearest poison control center immediately.

DRUG INTERACTIONS
Consult your doctor for specific advice if you are taking
anesthetics, tricyclic antidepressants, antidiabetic
agents, antihypertensives or
diuretics, beta-blockers, digitalis drugs, ergoloid mesylates, maprotiline, ergotamine, or MAO inhibitors.

FOOD INTERACTIONS
Avoid any foods that have
previously triggered an
allergic reaction or asthma
attack.

DISEASE INTERACTIONS
The benefits of taking the
drug need to be weighed
against the potential risks if
you have any of the following conditions: organic
brain damage, diabetes mellitus, Parkinson's disease,
heart or blood vessel disease, or overactive thyroid.

Eplerenone

▶ Drug Class: Antihypertensive/aldosterone-blocker

▶ Available in: Tablets

▶ Available OTC? No

▶ As Generic? No

Side Effects

SERIOUS
Heartbeat irregularities, lightheadedness (caused by high blood potassium levels). Notify your doctor at once.

COMMON
No common side effects are associated with the use of eplerenone.

LESS COMMON
Diarrhea, abdominal pain, cough, dizziness, fatigue, flu-like symptoms.

PRINCIPAL USES
To treat high blood pressure (hypertension).

HOW THE DRUG WORKS
Eplerenone blocks the effect of the adrenal hormone aldosterone by binding to the mineralocorticoid receptor.

DOSAGE
50 mg once a day. May be taken alone or in combination with other antihypertensive agents. The dose may be increased by your doctor up to 50 mg twice a day, if needed.

ONSET OF EFFECT
The full therapeutic effect may take 4 weeks.

DURATION OF ACTION
Unknown.

DIETARY ADVICE
Follow your doctor's dietary advice (such as low-salt or low-cholesterol restrictions) to improve control over high blood pressure and prevent heart disease.

STORAGE
Store in a tightly sealed container away from heat, moisture, and direct light.

IF YOU MISS A DOSE
Once a day dose: If you do not remember until the next day, skip the missed dose and resume your regular dosage schedule. Do not double the next dose. Twice a day dose: Take it as soon as you remember. If it is near the time for the next dose, skip the missed dose and resume your regular dosage schedule. Do not double the next dose.

STOPPING THE DRUG
Take it as prescribed for the full treatment period. The decision to stop taking the drug should be made in consultation with your physician.

PROLONGED USE
See your doctor regularly for evaluation if you must take this medicine for a prolonged period. Lifelong therapy may be necessary.

PRECAUTIONS
Over 60: Adverse reactions may be more likely and more severe in older patients.

Driving and Hazardous Work: Do not drive or engage in hazardous work until you determine how the medicine affects you.

Alcohol: No special precautions are necessary.

Pregnancy: Adequate human studies have not been done. Before taking eplerenone, tell your doctor if you are or are planning to become pregnant. Discuss with your doctor the relative risks and benefits of using this drug while pregnant.

Breast Feeding: Eplerenone may pass into breast milk; caution is advised. Consult your doctor for advice on whether to discontinue nursing or discontinue the drug.

Infants and Children: Safety and effectiveness have not been established for patients under age 18.

Special Concerns: Use of the drug should be considered but one element of a comprehensive therapeutic program that includes weight control, smoking cessation, regular exercise, and a healthy low-salt, low-fat diet.

OVERDOSE
Symptoms: No cases of overdose have been reported. However, if you take a much larger dose than prescribed, you may experience dizziness, fainting, and confusion.

What to Do: Call your doctor, emergency medical services (EMS), or the nearest poison control center immediately if you suspect that someone has taken a much larger dose than prescribed.

DRUG INTERACTIONS
Do not take with potassium supplements, potassium-sparing diuretics (such as amiloride, spironolactone, or triamterene), ketoconazole, or itraconazole. Consult your doctor for specific advice if you are taking erythromycin, verapamil, saquinavir, fluconazole, an ACE inhibitor, an angiotensin II receptor antagonist, lithium, or an NSAID.

FOOD INTERACTIONS
Avoid salt substitutes. Many of these products contain high amounts of potassium.

DISEASE INTERACTIONS
Consult your doctor if you have any other medical condition. Eplerenone can increase blood triglycerides and worsen the control of blood sugar in people with diabetes.

Epoetin Alfa

BRAND NAMES
Epogen, Procrit

▶ Drug Class: Antianemia drug

▶ Available in: Injection

▶ Available OTC? No

▶ As Generic? No

Side Effects

SERIOUS
Chest pain, convulsions, shortness of breath, rapid heartbeat, headache, swelling in the face, hands, and lower extremities, vision problems, unexplained weight gain. Such symptoms are due to an inappropriate elevation of the number of red cells; check with your doctor immediately if such symptoms occur.

COMMON
Influenza-like symptoms, bone pain, burning at the injection site, fatigue. Such symptoms tend to occur at the beginning of therapy but usually diminish as your body adjusts to the medicine. Notify your doctor if such side effects persist or interfere with normal activities.

LESS COMMON
Skin rash, hives.

PRINCIPAL USES
For treating severe anemia due to impaired production of erythropoietin (a hormone that stimulates the bone marrow to produce red blood cells), which may occur with chronic kidney disease, in anemic cancer patients receiving chemotherapy, and anemic HIV-infected patients taking zidovudine.

HOW THE DRUG WORKS
Epoetin alfa stimulates the production of red blood cells in the bone marrow, replacing the hormone erythropoietin, which is depleted in patients suffering from renal (kidney) failure, or who have diseases or take medications that suppress the body's natural erythropoietin production.

DOSAGE
Average dosage range for adults and teenagers: 23 to 68 units per lb of body weight, 3 times a week. May be increased by 11 units per lb every 4 weeks or more, up to 90 units per lb, to produce the desired effect. Once that has been achieved, the dose should be adjusted downward at 4-week intervals to achieve the lowest effective maintenance dose.

ONSET OF EFFECT
Within 2 to 6 weeks.

DURATION OF ACTION
In the presence of impaired erythropoietin production, the drug must be given at least several times per week to maintain its effect.

DIETARY ADVICE
Patients may require iron supplements, but these should be taken only on the advice of a doctor; other vitamins may also be recommended to aid in the manufacture of red blood cells. Patients with kidney problems or high blood pressure are often on restricted diets, which need to be reinforced with vitamin supplementation.

STORAGE
Keep epoetin alfa refrigerated, but do not allow it to freeze.

IF YOU MISS A DOSE
Take it as soon as you remember. If it is near the time for the next dose, skip the missed dose and resume your regular dosage schedule. Do not double the next dose.

STOPPING THE DRUG
Take the drug as prescribed for the full treatment period, in accordance with your doctor's instructions.

PROLONGED USE
Comply with schedules for proper dosage and administration, dialysis, blood tests, and blood pressure tests set by your doctor. If you are performing dialysis at home and self-administering epoetin alfa, follow your doctor's orders carefully and report changes outside of guidelines the doctor has given to you.

PRECAUTIONS
Over 60: Adverse reactions may be more likely and more severe in older patients.

Driving and Hazardous Work: Avoid such activities in the first 90 days of treatment when seizures are most likely to occur.

Alcohol: No special problems are expected.

Pregnancy: Consult your doctor about whether benefits outweigh the potential risk to the unborn child.

Breast Feeding: Epoetin alfa may pass into breast milk; caution is advised. Consult your doctor for specific advice.

Infants and Children: Epoetin alfa is safe for use in children.

Special Concerns: Be sure to follow you doctor's advice, including dietary recommendations and dialysis prescriptions, even if you begin to feel better while taking the drug. Epoetin alfa will correct only anemia, not kidney disease or other medical problems that may be present.

OVERDOSE
Symptoms: Headache, weakness, flushing, dizziness, seizures, chest pain.

What to Do: Call your doctor, emergency medical services (EMS), or the nearest poison control center immediately.

DRUG INTERACTIONS
No known drug interactions.

FOOD INTERACTIONS
No known food interactions.

DISEASE INTERACTIONS
High blood pressure (hypertension) must be controlled before this drug is used. Also, advise your doctor if you have a history of blood clotting disorders, heart or blood vessel disease, blood disorders such as sickle cell anemia, or bone problems.

Eprosartan Mesylate

▶ Drug Class: Antihypertensive/
angiotensin II antagonist

▶ Available in: Tablets

▶ Available OTC? No

▶ As Generic? No

Side Effects

SERIOUS
No serious side effects are associated with the use of eprosartan. (In clinical trials, the incidence of adverse effects was not significantly greater with the medication than with a placebo.)

COMMON
No common side effects are associated with the use of eprosartan.

LESS COMMON
Viral infection, fatigue, abdominal pain, increased blood triglyceride levels, joint pain, depression, upper respiratory tract infection, runny nose, throat infection, cough, urinary tract infection.

PRINCIPAL USES
To control high blood pressure. This drug appears to have the same benefits as the class of antihypertensive drugs known as ACE inhibitors, without producing the common side effect (experienced by as many as 30% of patients) of a dry cough. Eprosartan may be used by itself or in conjunction with other antihypertensive medications.

HOW THE DRUG WORKS
Eprosartan blocks the effects of angiotensin II, a naturally occurring substance that causes blood vessels to narrow. Eprosartan causes the blood vessels to dilate, thereby lowering blood pressure and decreasing the workload of the heart.

DOSAGE
To start, 600 mg once a day when used as the only drug to treat hypertension. Usual maintenance dose is 400 to 800 mg daily.

ONSET OF EFFECT
Within 2 to 3 weeks.

DURATION OF ACTION
Unknown.

DIETARY ADVICE
No special restrictions.

STORAGE
Store in a tightly sealed container away from heat, moisture, and direct light.

IF YOU MISS A DOSE
Take it as soon as you remember. If it is near the time for the next dose, skip the missed dose and resume your regular dosage schedule. Do not double the next dose.

STOPPING THE DRUG
Take it as prescribed for the full treatment period. The decision to stop taking the drug should be made in consultation with your physician.

PROLONGED USE
Lifelong therapy may be necessary. However, if you do change certain health habits (for example, increasing exercise or losing weight), a reduced dose may be possible under a doctor's supervision.

PRECAUTIONS
Over 60: No special problems are expected.

Driving and Hazardous Work: Do not drive or engage in hazardous work until you determine how the medicine affects you.

Alcohol: No special precautions are necessary.

Pregnancy: Eprosartan should not be used by pregnant women. Discontinue taking the drug as soon as possible when pregnancy is detected and discuss treatment alternatives with your doctor.

Breast Feeding: Eprosartan may pass into breast milk; caution is advised. Consult your doctor for specific advice.

Infants and Children: The safety and effectiveness of use in children have not been established.

Special Concerns: Eprosartan may cause excessively low blood pressure with dizziness or lightheadedness, which is most noticeable when you change position. This may lead to fainting, falls, and injury. Sit or lie down immediately if you feel dizzy or lightheaded. This side effect may be worsened by alcohol, hot weather, dehydration, salt depletion from diuretic use, fever, prolonged standing, prolonged sitting, or exercise.

OVERDOSE
Symptoms: Few cases of overdose have been reported. However, if you take a much larger dose than prescribed, you may experience fainting, dizziness, weak pulse that might be very slow or very fast.

What to Do: Call your doctor, emergency medical services (EMS), or the nearest poison control center immediately.

DRUG INTERACTIONS
No drug interactions have yet been observed with eprosartan. Consult your doctor for specific advice if you are taking any other medication, especially potassium supplements or potassium-sparing diuretics. Eprosartan can be taken together with diuretics or other medications for high blood pressure, if your doctor approves.

FOOD INTERACTIONS
No known food interactions.

DISEASE INTERACTIONS
Tell your doctor if you have liver or kidney disease before taking eprosartan.

Ergoloid Mesylates

BRAND NAMES
Alkergot, Gerimal,
Hydergine, Hydergine LC,
Niloric

▶ Drug Class: Psychotherapeutic agent

▶ Available in: Capsules, sublingual tablets, oral solution

▶ Available OTC? No

▶ As Generic? Yes

Side Effects

SERIOUS
No serious side effects are associated with the recommended dosage of ergoloid mesylates.

COMMON
There are no common side effects.

LESS COMMON
At the recommended dosage, side effects are usually rare and remit when therapy is discontinued. Check with your doctor if the following symptoms appear: drowsiness, slow heartbeat, dizziness or lightheadedness when getting up from a sitting or lying position (orthostatic hypotension), skin rash, stomach pain, sensitivity of eyes to sunlight, soreness under the tongue (from sublingual tablet) that does not go away.

PRINCIPAL USES
To treat decline in mental capacity due to dementia (progressive breakdown of mental function).

HOW THE DRUG WORKS
The exact way in which ergoloid mesylates work has not been established.

DOSAGE
1 to 2 mg, 3 times a day. Maximum dose: 12 mg daily.

ONSET OF EFFECT
Unknown.

DURATION OF ACTION
Unknown.

DIETARY ADVICE
When taking the sublingual form of the medication, do not eat, drink, or smoke while the tablet is dissolving under your tongue; do not chew, swallow, or crush it either.

STORAGE
Store in a tightly sealed container away from heat, moisture, and direct light. Keep the oral solution form of the drug refrigerated, but do not allow it to freeze.

IF YOU MISS A DOSE
Take it as soon as you remember. However, if it is near the time for the next dose, skip the missed dose and resume your regular dosage schedule. Do not double the next dose.

STOPPING THE DRUG
The decision to stop taking ergoloid mesylates should be made in consultation with your doctor.

PROLONGED USE
Regular evaluation by your doctor is necessary to determine whether or not there are initial and continuing therapeutic benefits from taking ergoloid mesylates; the medication's effectiveness may not be apparent for several weeks or even months.

PRECAUTIONS
Over 60: No special precautions are necessary.

Driving and Hazardous Work: Do not drive or engage in hazardous work until you determine how the medicine affects you.

Alcohol: Avoid alcohol. Be aware that some over-the-counter cough, cold, and allergy medications contain alcohol; check ingredient labels carefully.

Pregnancy: Studies of the use of ergoloid mesylates during pregnancy have not been done. Consult your doctor for specific advice.

Breast Feeding: Studies of the use of ergoloid mesylates in breast-feeding women have not been done. Consult your doctor for specific advice.

Infants and Children: Ergoloid mesylates are not prescribed for children.

Special Concerns: The therapeutic benefit of ergoloid mesylates in treating dementia is a matter of controversy. Some doctors believe it may be helpful; others do not.

OVERDOSE
Symptoms: Headache, blurred vision, dizziness, fainting, nausea or vomiting, stomach cramps, flushing, nasal congestion.

What to Do: Call your doctor, emergency medical services (EMS), or the nearest poison control center immediately.

DRUG INTERACTIONS
Other drugs may interact with ergoloid mesylates. Consult your doctor for specific advice if you are taking any other prescription or over-the-counter medication.

FOOD INTERACTIONS
No known food interactions.

DISEASE INTERACTIONS
The benefits of the drug should be weighed against possible risks for patients with the following conditions: bradycardia (slow heartbeat), low blood pressure, or liver disease. Ergoloid mesylates are not used to treat acute or chronic psychosis.

Ergotamine/Belladonna Alkaloids/Phenobarbital

BRAND NAME
Bellergal-S

▶ Drug Class: Antimigraine/antiheadache drug

▶ Available in: Extended-release tablets

▶ Available OTC? No

▶ As Generic? No

Side Effects

SERIOUS
Severe anxiety or confusion; change in vision; chest pain; pale, cold, bluish-colored hands or feet; pain in arms, legs, or lower back; red blisters on hands or feet; gangrene. Seek medical attention immediately.

COMMON
Constipation; swelling of face, fingers, feet, or lower legs; reduced sweating; dizziness or lightheadedness; drowsiness; dry mouth, nose, throat, or skin.

LESS COMMON
Blurred vision; unusual weakness; increased sensitivity of eyes to bright light; diarrhea, nausea, or vomiting; skin rash or itching of skin; sore throat and fever; unusual bruising or bleeding; weakness in legs; yellow discoloration of the eyes or skin; difficulty urinating; difficulty in swallowing; unusual excitability; loss of memory.

PRINCIPAL USES
Used to prevent vascular headaches (those involving the blood vessels to the brain), such as migraines and cluster headaches. Also used to ease symptoms of menopause, such as hot flashes, sweating, restlessness, and insomnia, usually in women for whom estrogen replacement therapy has been ruled out.

HOW THE DRUG WORKS
The above conditions are believed to be caused, in part, by overactivity in the autonomic nervous system, the part that controls involuntary body functions like heart rate, sweating, and digestion. The combination of ergotamine, belladonna alkaloids, and phenobarbital helps to balance and calm this part of the nervous system, thus reducing various kinds of physical distress.

DOSAGE
Adults: 1 tablet in the morning and 1 in the evening. Children: Consult pediatrician. Tablet must be taken whole.

ONSET OF EFFECT
Unknown.

DURATION OF ACTION
Unknown.

DIETARY ADVICE
No special concerns.

STORAGE
Store in a tightly sealed container, away from heat, moisture, and direct light.

IF YOU MISS A DOSE
Skip the missed dose and then resume your regular dosage schedule. Do not double the next dose.

STOPPING THE DRUG
The decision to stop taking the drug should be made by your doctor. Discontinue the drug in gradually diminishing doses, according to your doctor's instructions, to minimize the risk of withdrawal symptoms.

PROLONGED USE
Prolonged use at high doses may produce some degree of physical dependence due to the barbiturate, phenobarbital, and may increase the risk of blood circulation problems.

PRECAUTIONS
Over 60: Adverse reactions may be more likely and more severe in older patients.

Driving and Hazardous Work: Do not drive or engage in hazardous work until you determine how the drug affects you.

Alcohol: Avoid alcohol.

Pregnancy: Do not take the drug combination during pregnancy. Consult your doctor if you become or plan to become pregnant.

Breast Feeding: The drug combination passes into breast milk; avoid or discontinue use while nursing.

Infants and Children: Adverse reactions may be more likely and more severe.

Special Concerns: Avoid smoking, since it may increase the risk of side effects associated with impaired blood circulation. Dress warmly if you have blood circulation problems (most common among elderly patients).

OVERDOSE
Symptoms: Convulsions; severe diarrhea, nausea, vomiting, or stomach pain or bloating; severe dizziness, drowsiness, or weakness; rapid or slow heartbeat; shortness of breath; unusual excitement.

What to Do: Call your doctor, emergency medical services (EMS), or the nearest poison control center immediately.

DRUG INTERACTIONS
Do not take this drug if you are taking naratriptan, sumatriptan, or zolmitriptan. Consult your doctor for specific advice if you are taking antacids, anticoagulants, anticholinergics, carbamazepine, central nervous system depressants, diarrhea medication, digitalis drugs, ketoconazole, MAO inhibitors, other ergot medications, oral contraceptives, potassium chloride, or tricyclic antidepressants.

FOOD INTERACTIONS
No known food interactions.

DISEASE INTERACTIONS
Consult your doctor if you have any of the following: chronic lung disease such as asthma or emphysema, difficult urination, urinary tract blockage, Down's syndrome, enlarged prostate, heart, kidney, or liver disease, blood vessel disease or recent surgery on blood vessels, severe high blood pressure, infection, intestinal conditions, overactive thyroid, porphyria, glaucoma, severe dry mouth, severe itching. In children: brain damage, hyperactivity, spastic paralysis.

Erythromycin Ethylsuccinate/Sulfisoxazole

▶ Drug Class: Erythromycin antibiotic

▶ Available in: Oral suspension

▶ Available OTC? No

▶ As Generic? Yes

Side Effects

SERIOUS
Skin rash, itching, aching joints and muscles, difficulty swallowing, pale skin or red, blistered, peeling, or loose skin, sore throat and fever, unusual bleeding or bruising, unusual fatigue, yellowish tinge to the eyes or skin, blood in urine, darkened urine, pain in lower back, pain while urinating, pale stools, stomach pain, swollen neck, increased sensitivity to sunlight. Call your doctor immediately.

COMMON
Stomach or abdominal discomfort and cramps, diarrhea, loss of appetite, nausea, vomiting.

LESS COMMON
Sore tongue or mouth.

PRINCIPAL USES
To treat middle ear infections in children.

HOW THE DRUG WORKS
Erythromycin prevents bacterial cells from manufacturing specific proteins necessary for their survival; sulfisoxazole prevents bacteria from utilizing folic acid, a vitamin essential to both cell growth and reproduction.

DOSAGE
Children weighing more than 100 lbs: 2 teaspoons (10 ml) 4 times a day for 10 days. Children weighing 53 to 100 lbs: 1½ tsps (7.5 ml) 4 times a day for 10 days. Children weighing 35 to 53 lbs: 1 tsp (5 ml) 4 times a day for 10 days. Children weighing 18 to 35 lbs: ½ tsp (2.5 ml) 4 times a day for 10 days. Children under 18 lbs: The dose must be determined by your pediatrician.

ONSET OF EFFECT
Unknown.

DURATION OF ACTION
Unknown.

DIETARY ADVICE
Give it 1 hour before or 2 hours after meals with a full glass of water. If it causes stomach upset, it can be taken with milk or food. Increase patient's fluid intake.

STORAGE
Store in a tightly sealed container away from heat and direct light. Refrigerate but do not freeze.

IF YOU MISS A DOSE
Give it as soon as you remember. If it is close to the time for the next dose, skip the missed dose and resume the regular dosage schedule. Do not double the next dose.

STOPPING THE DRUG
Give the medicine as prescribed for the full treatment period, even if the child begins to feel better before the scheduled end of therapy.

PROLONGED USE
Your child should see a doctor regularly for tests and examinations if this medicine is prescribed for a prolonged period. Bacteria that are resistant to this medication may develop with long-term use.

PRECAUTIONS
Over 60: This medication is not intended for use by older persons.

Driving and Hazardous Work: This medication should not impair mental alertness or physical coordination.

Alcohol: Not applicable; this drug is for children.

Pregnancy: Adequate studies of the use of this drug during pregnancy have not been done; consult your doctor for specific advice if there is any chance that the patient could become pregnant.

Breast Feeding: Not applicable; the drug is for children.

Infants and Children: This medicine is not recommended for children under 2 months of age.

Special Concerns: If the medicine causes sensitivity to sunlight, take preventive measures: patients should use sunscreens, wear protective clothing, and avoid exposure to sunlight.

OVERDOSE
Symptoms: Severe nausea, vomiting, diarrhea, dizziness, headache, drowsiness, fever, loss of consciousness.

What to Do: Overdose is not likely, but if symptoms occur, call your doctor, emergency medical services (EMS), or the nearest poison control center immediately.

DRUG INTERACTIONS
This drug may interact with acetaminophen, acetohydroxamic acid, alfentanil, amiodarone, aminophylline, oral antidiabetics, carbamazepine, carmustine, chloramphenicol, chloroquine, cholesterol-lowering drugs, dantrolene, dapsone, daunorubicin, divalproex, estrogens, ethotoin, etretinate, gold salts, hydroxychloroquine, lincomycin, methenamine, mephenytoin, methotrexate, mercaptopurine, methyldopa, naltrexone, nitrofurantoin, oral contraceptives, phenytoin, plicamycin, primaquine, procainamide, quinidine, quinine, sulfoxone, or vitamin K. Consult your doctor for specific advice.

FOOD INTERACTIONS
Avoid caffeinated beverages or food.

DISEASE INTERACTIONS
Consult your doctor if the patient has any of the following: anemia or another blood problem, G6PD deficiency, kidney disease, liver disease, hearing loss, or porphyria.

Erythromycin Ophthalmic

BRAND NAME
Ilotycin

▶ Drug Class: Antibiotic

▶ Available in: Ophthalmic ointment

▶ Available OTC? No

▶ As Generic? Yes

Side Effects

SERIOUS
Eye irritation, redness, swelling, or itching that was not present before therapy. Stop using the medication and call your doctor immediately.

COMMON
Blurred vision for up to 30 minutes following application.

LESS COMMON
There are no less-common side effects associated with ophthalmic erythromycin.

PRINCIPAL USES
To treat infections of the eye; to treat inflammation of the edges of the eyelids (blepharitis); to prevent some eye infections in newborn babies (neonatal conjunctivitis and ophthalmia neonatorum).

HOW THE DRUG WORKS
Erythromycin kills bacteria by interfering with the genetic material of bacterial cells, thereby preventing them from multiplying.

DOSAGE
Adults and children— For eye infections: Apply ointment to the affected eye up to 6 times a day, as directed by your doctor. For blepharitis: Apply once a day immediately before bedtime after performing standard eyelid hygiene measures as directed by your doctor. To prevent eye infections in newborns— Ointment is applied once, shortly after birth.

ONSET OF EFFECT
Unknown.

DURATION OF ACTION
Unknown.

DIETARY ADVICE
This medication can be used without regard to diet.

STORAGE
Store in a tightly sealed container away from heat, moisture, and direct light. Do not allow it to freeze.

IF YOU MISS A DOSE
Apply it as soon as you remember. If it is near the time for the next dose, skip the missed dose and resume your regular dosage schedule. Do not double the next dose.

STOPPING THE DRUG
Use it as prescribed for the full treatment period, even if you feel better before the scheduled end of therapy.

PROLONGED USE
You should see your doctor regularly for tests and examinations if you take this drug for a prolonged period.

PRECAUTIONS
Over 60: No special problems are expected.

Driving and Hazardous Work: Do not drive or engage in hazardous work until you determine how the medicine affects your vision.

Alcohol: No special precautions are necessary.

Pregnancy: Erythromycin has not been shown to cause birth defects or other problems during pregnancy. Before using erythromycin, tell your doctor if you are pregnant or are planning to become pregnant.

Breast Feeding: Erythromycin has not been shown to cause problems in nursing babies.

Infants and Children: No special precautions.

Special Concerns: To use the ointment, first wash your hands. Tilt your head back. Gently apply pressure to the inside corner of the eyelid and with the index finger of the same hand, pull downward on the lower eyelid to make a space. Put a short strip of ointment (about ⅓ inch long) into this space and close your eye. Apply pressure for 1 or 2 minutes while keeping the eye closed without blinking. Then wash your hands again. Make sure that the tip of the applicator does not touch your eye, finger, or any other surface. If your symptoms do not improve in a few days or if they become worse, check with your doctor. Do not use this drug if you have a history of allergy to azithromycin, clarithromycin, erythromycin, or lincomycin.

OVERDOSE
Symptoms: No specific ones have been reported.

What to Do: If someone accidentally ingests the medicine, call your doctor, emergency medical services (EMS), or the nearest poison control center.

DRUG INTERACTIONS
Other drugs may interact with ophthalmic erythromycin. Consult your doctor for specific advice if you are taking any other prescription or over-the-counter medication.

FOOD INTERACTIONS
No known food interactions.

DISEASE INTERACTIONS
Caution is advised when taking ophthalmic erythromycin. Consult your doctor if you have any other medical condition.

Erythromycin Systemic

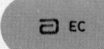

Ery-Tab 250 mg
(ABBOTT)

Additional photographs

▶ Drug Class: Erythromycin
antibiotic

▶ Available in: Capsules,
tablets, oral suspension,
injection

▶ Available OTC? No

▶ As Generic? Yes

Side Effects

SERIOUS
Fever, nausea, skin red-
dening or itching, severe
stomach pain, yellow dis-
coloration of the eyes or
skin, fainting, slow or
irregular heartbeat in
patients with predispos-
ing heart conditions,
breathing difficulty, persistent or severe diar-
rhea, abdominal pain,
temporary deafness. Also
pain, swelling, or redness
at injection site. Although
serious side effects are
rare, call your doctor
immediately.

COMMON
Stomach cramps and
abdominal discomfort,
diarrhea, nausea,
vomiting.

LESS COMMON
Soreness of mouth or
tongue, vaginal itching
or discharge.

PRINCIPAL USES
To treat bacterial infections,
including throat infections,
pneumonia, Legionnaires'
disease, chlamydia, and
diphtheria. It is also prescribed to prevent strep
infections that may damage
heart valves in susceptible
patients (for example, those
with a history of rheumatic
fever or heart valve replacement) who are allergic to
penicillin.

HOW THE DRUG WORKS
Erythromycin prevents bacterial cells from manufacturing specific proteins
necessary for their survival.

DOSAGE
To treat infections— Adults
and teenagers: 250 to 800
mg, 2 to 4 times a day. Children: 3.4 to 12.5 mg per lb
of body weight, 2 to 4 times
a day. To prevent strep
infections— Adults and
teenagers: 1 to 1.6 g before
dental appointment or
surgery; 500 to 800 mg, 6
hours later. Children: 1.7
to 11.4 mg per lb of body
weight before dental
appointment or surgery;
4.5 mg per lb of body
weight 6 hours later.

ONSET OF EFFECT
Immediate after injection;
unknown for oral forms.

DURATION OF ACTION
Unknown.

DIETARY ADVICE
This drug is best taken on
an empty stomach, at least 1
hour before or 2 hours after
meals, with a full glass of
water. If it causes stomach
upset, it can be taken with
food or milk.

STORAGE
Store in a tightly sealed container away from heat and
direct light. Refrigerate liquid form but do not freeze.

IF YOU MISS A DOSE
Take it as soon as you
remember. If it is near the
time for the next dose, skip
the missed dose and
resume your regular dosage
schedule. Do not double the
next dose.

STOPPING THE DRUG
Take it as prescribed for the
full treatment period, even
if you begin to feel better
before the scheduled end
of therapy.

PROLONGED USE
You should see your doctor
regularly for tests and
examinations, including
those to evaluate liver function, if this medicine is
taken for a prolonged
period.

PRECAUTIONS
Over 60: Older patients
may be at higher risk of
experiencing hearing loss as
a side effect.

**Driving and Hazardous
Work:** No special precautions are necessary.

Alcohol: No special precautions are necessary.

Pregnancy: Erythromycin
has been shown to cause
liver damage in some pregnant women. It has not
been shown to cause birth
defects or other problems in
babies. Before taking erythromycin, tell your doctor
if you are pregnant or plan
to become pregnant.

Breast Feeding: Ery-
thromycin passes into
breast milk; caution is
advised. Consult your doctor for specific advice.

Infants and Children:
No special problems
expected.

Special Concerns: Consult your doctor if your

symptoms do not improve,
or instead become worse,
after a few days of therapy.

OVERDOSE
Symptoms: Severe nausea,
vomiting, abdominal pain,
diarrhea, dizziness, loss of
hearing.

What to Do: Call your
doctor, emergency medical
services (EMS), or the
nearest poison control center immediately.

DRUG INTERACTIONS
Do not use erythromycin if
you are taking astemizole or
pimozide. Consult your doctor for specific advice if you
are taking acetaminophen,
amiodarone, anabolic
steroids, androgens,
antibiotics, azithromycin,
carbamazepine, carmustine,
chloramphenicol, chloro-
quine, clarithromycin,
cyclosporine, dantrolene,
daunorubicin, disulfiram,
divalproex, estrogens, etretinate, gold salts, hydroxychloroquine, lincomycin,
methotrexate, mercaptop-
urine, methyldopa, naltrexone, oral contraceptives,
phenothiazines, phenytoin,
plicamycin, theophylline,
valproic acid, warfarin,
tacrolimus, disopyramide,
lovastatin, or bromocriptine.

FOOD INTERACTIONS
No known food interactions.

DISEASE INTERACTIONS
Use of this drug is not
advised in patients with a
history of heart rhythm disorders, kidney disease, liver
disease, or hearing prob-
lems. Consult your doctor.

298

Escitalopram Oxalate

▶ Drug Class: Selective serotonin reuptake inhibitor (SSRI) antidepressant

▶ Available in: Tablets, oral solution

▶ Available OTC? No

▶ As Generic? No

Side Effects

SERIOUS
Chest pain, rapid or irregular heartbeat, lightheadedness or fainting. Activation of mania/hypomania. Call your doctor immediately. May also be associated with decreased salt levels in the body.

COMMON
Delayed ejaculation (males), dry mouth, increased sweating, nausea, trembling, diarrhea, drowsiness, insomnia, numbness, tingling, or prickling sensations.

LESS COMMON
Fatigue, fever, loss of appetite, agitation, nasal congestion, sinus infection, erectile dysfunction.

PRINCIPAL USES
To treat symptoms of major depression.

HOW THE DRUG WORKS
Escitalopram increases brain levels of serotonin, a chemical that is thought to be linked to mood, emotions, and mental state.

DOSAGE
To start, 10 mg once a day, taken in the morning or evening; dose may be gradually increased by your doctor to 20 mg a day.

ONSET OF EFFECT
Unknown.

DURATION OF ACTION
Unknown.

DIETARY ADVICE
No special restrictions.

STORAGE
Store in a tightly sealed container away from heat, moisture, and direct light.

IF YOU MISS A DOSE
If you miss a dose on one day, do not double the dose the next day.

STOPPING THE DRUG
Take it as prescribed for the full treatment period even if you notice improvement. When it is time to stop therapy, your dosage will be tapered gradually by your doctor.

PROLONGED USE
Usual course of therapy for depression lasts 6 months to 1 year; some patients may benefit from additional therapy.

PRECAUTIONS
Over 60: Adverse reactions may be more likely and more severe in older patients. A lower dose may be warranted.

Driving and Hazardous Work: Use caution when driving or engaging in hazardous work until you determine how the medicine affects you.

Alcohol: Avoid alcohol.

Pregnancy: Escitalopram should be used during pregnancy only if the potential benefit justifies the potential risk to the fetus. Before you take this medicine, tell your doctor if you are pregnant or plan to become pregnant.

Breast Feeding: Escitalopram passes into breast milk; caution is advised. Consult your doctor for specific advice.

Infants and Children: The safety and effectiveness of escitalopram in children have not been established. Antidepressants increase the risk of suicidal thinking and behavior (suicidality) in children with major depression and other psychiatric disorders. Discuss with your doctor this risk versus the benefits of using this drug. Children should be observed closely for worsening of symptoms, suicidality, or unusual changes in behavior at the onset of therapy and when making changes in dosage.

OVERDOSE
Symptoms: Dizziness, sweating, nausea, vomiting, trembling, drowsiness, rapid heartbeat.

What to Do: Call your doctor, emergency medical services (EMS), or the nearest poison control center immediately.

DRUG INTERACTIONS
Escitalopram and MAO inhibitors should not be used within 14 days of each other. Very serious side effects such as myoclonus (uncontrolled muscle spasms), hyperthermia (excessive rise in body temperature), and extreme stiffness may result. The following drugs may also interact with escitalopram; consult your doctor for advice if you are taking cimetidine, warfarin, metoprolol, lithium, carbamazepine, antifungals (such as ketoconazole, itraconazole, and fluconazole), erythromycin antibiotics, omeprazole, tricyclic antidepressants, NSAIDs, aspirin, or any prescription or over-the-counter drugs that depress the central nervous system (including antihistamines, barbiturates, sedatives, cough medicines, and decongestants).

FOOD INTERACTIONS
No known food interactions.

DISEASE INTERACTIONS
Caution is advised when taking escitalopram, especially if you have heart disease or a seizure disorder. Use of escitalopram may cause complications in patients with liver or kidney disease. Consult your doctor if you have any of these conditions.

Esomeprazole Magnesium

▶ Drug Class: Antacid/proton pump inhibitor

▶ Available in: Delayed-release capsules

▶ Available OTC? No

▶ As Generic? No

Side Effects

SERIOUS
No serious side effects are associated with this medication.

COMMON
Headache, diarrhea, constipation, nausea, dry mouth, dizziness, stomach pain. Consult your physician if such side effects persist or interfere with daily activities.

LESS COMMON
Many less common side effects can occur; consult your doctor if you are concerned about any adverse or unusual reactions you experience while taking this drug.

PRINCIPAL USES

To treat erosive esophagitis (severe, chronic inflammation of the esophagus) and gastroesophageal reflux (backwash of stomach acid into the esophagus, resulting in heartburn); in combination with amoxicillin and clarithromycin, to reduce the risk of recurrence of duodenal (intestinal) ulcers caused by the bacteria *Helicobacter pylori*.

HOW THE DRUG WORKS

Esomeprazole blocks the action of a specific enzyme in the cells that line the stomach, thereby decreasing the production of stomach acid. Reduction of stomach acid promotes healing of ulcers.

DOSAGE

To treat active erosive esophagitis: 20 or 40 mg a day for 4 to 8 weeks. Maintenance dose for esophagitis: 20 mg a day. To treat gastroesophageal reflux: 20 mg a day for 4 weeks. To reduce risk of duodenal ulcer recurrence: 40 mg esomeprazole a day for 10 days, 1,000 mg amoxicillin twice a day for 10 days, and 500 mg clarithromycin twice a day for 10 days.

ONSET OF EFFECT

Unknown.

DURATION OF ACTION

Unknown.

DIETARY ADVICE

Esomeprazole should be swallowed whole at least one hour before eating. If you have trouble swallowing the pills, mix the contents of the capsules in with food such as applesauce. The applesauce/drug mixture should be swallowed without chewing.

STORAGE

Store in a tightly sealed container away from heat and direct light.

IF YOU MISS A DOSE

Take it as soon as you remember. If it is near the time for the next dose, skip the missed dose and resume your regular dosage schedule. Do not double the next dose.

STOPPING THE DRUG

Take it as prescribed for the full treatment period, even if you begin to feel better before the scheduled end of therapy. The decision to stop taking the drug should be made by your doctor.

PROLONGED USE

Esomeprazole should not be used indefinitely as maintenance therapy for duodenal ulcer or esophagitis; it is generally taken for a limited period of 4 to 8 weeks. Do not take it for a longer period unless instructed to do so by your doctor. See your doctor regularly for tests and examinations if you must take this drug for an extended period of time.

PRECAUTIONS

Over 60: No specific problems for older people have been reported.

Driving and Hazardous Work: Do not drive or engage in hazardous activities until you determine how the drug affects you.

Alcohol: Avoid alcohol while taking this medication, as it may aggravate your condition.

Pregnancy: In animal tests, esomeprazole has not caused problems. Human tests have not been done. Before you take esomeprazole, tell your doctor if you are pregnant or plan to become pregnant.

Breast Feeding: Esomeprazole may pass into breast milk; caution is advised. Consult your doctor for advice.

Infants and Children: Safety and effectiveness have not been established for patients under 18 years of age.

Special Concerns: Tell any doctor or dentist whom you see for treatment that you are taking esomeprazole. If your doctor directs, you may take an antacid along with esomeprazole.

OVERDOSE

Symptoms: No cases of overdose have been reported. However, symptoms may include: blurred vision, confusion, profuse sweating, drowsiness, dry mouth, flushing of the face, headache, nausea, palpitations or unusually rapid heartbeat.

What to Do: Call your doctor, emergency medical services (EMS), or the nearest poison control center immediately.

DRUG INTERACTIONS

Consult your doctor for specific advice if you are taking: ampicillin, sucralfate, iron salts or supplements, cyclosporine, diazepam, disulfiram, ketoconazole, digoxin, or theophylline.

FOOD INTERACTIONS

No significant food interactions have been reported.

DISEASE INTERACTIONS

Caution is advised when taking esomeprazole. Consult your doctor if you have severe liver disease, since it may increase the risk of side effects.

Estazolam

ProSom 1 mg
(ABBOTT)

▶ Drug Class: Benzodiazepine tranquilizer

▶ Available in: Tablets

▶ Available OTC? No

▶ As Generic? Yes

Side Effects

SERIOUS
Difficulty concentrating, outbursts of anger, other behavior problems, depression, seizures, hallucinations, low blood pressure (causing faintness or confusion), memory impairment, muscle weakness, skin rash or itching, sore throat, fever and chills, sores or ulcers in throat or mouth, unusual bruising or bleeding, extreme fatigue, yellowish tinge to eyes or skin. Call your doctor immediately.

COMMON
Drowsiness, loss of coordination, unsteady gait, dizziness, lightheadedness, slurred speech.

LESS COMMON
Change in sexual desire or ability, constipation, false sense of well-being, nausea and vomiting, urinary problems, unusual fatigue.

PRINCIPAL USES
To treat insomnia.

HOW THE DRUG WORKS
In general, estazolam produces a mild sedative effect by depressing activity in the central nervous system (the brain and spinal cord). In particular, estazolam appears to enhance the effect of gamma-aminobutyric acid (GABA), a natural chemical that inhibits the firing of neurons and dampens the transmission of nerve signals, thus decreasing nervous excitation.

DOSAGE
Adults: 1 or 2 mg taken at bedtime.

ONSET OF EFFECT
Unknown.

DURATION OF ACTION
Unknown.

DIETARY ADVICE
No special restrictions.

STORAGE
Store in a tightly sealed container away from heat and direct light.

IF YOU MISS A DOSE
Take it as soon as you remember, unless it is late at night. Do not take the medicine unless your schedule permits a full night's sleep.

STOPPING THE DRUG
The decision to stop taking the drug should be made in consultation with your doctor. Stopping it abruptly may cause withdrawal symptoms.

PROLONGED USE
Estazolam can lead to psychological or physical dependence. Short-term therapy (8 weeks or less) is typical; do not take it for a longer period unless so advised by your doctor.

Never take more than the prescribed daily dose.

PRECAUTIONS
Over 60: Adverse reactions are more likely and more severe. A lower dose may be warranted.

Driving and Hazardous Work: Estazolam can impair mental alertness and physical coordination. Adjust your activities accordingly.

Alcohol: Avoid alcohol.

Pregnancy: Estazolam should not be used during the first 3 months (first trimester) of pregnancy and only with great caution and close medical supervision later in pregnancy. Overuse of estazolam during pregnancy may cause drug dependence in the unborn child.

Breast Feeding: Estazolam passes into breast milk; do not take it while nursing.

Infants and Children: Safety and effectiveness have not been determined for children under age 18.

Special Concerns: Estazolam use can lead to psychological or physical dependence.

OVERDOSE
Symptoms: Extreme drowsiness, confusion, slurred speech, slow reflexes, poor coordination, staggering gait, tremor, slowed breathing, loss of consciousness.

What to Do: Call your doctor, emergency medical services (EMS), or the nearest poison control center immediately.

DRUG INTERACTIONS
Other drugs may interact with estazolam. Consult your doctor for specific advice if you are taking any drugs that depress the central nervous system; these include antihistamines, antidepressants or other psychiatric medications, barbiturates, sedatives, cough medicines, decongestants, and painkillers. Be sure your doctor knows about any over-the-counter medication you may take.

FOOD INTERACTIONS
None reported.

DISEASE INTERACTIONS
Caution is advised when taking estazolam. Consult your doctor if you have a history of alcohol or drug abuse, stroke or other brain disease, any chronic lung disease, hyperactivity, depression or other mental illness, myasthenia gravis, sleep apnea, epilepsy, porphyria, kidney disease, or liver disease.

Estradiol

▶ Drug Class: Female sex hormone

▶ Available in: Tablets, skin patch, vaginal cream, injection

▶ Available OTC? No

▶ As Generic? Yes

Side Effects

SERIOUS
For men being treated for prostate cancer: Sudden or severe headache, loss of coordination, sudden changes in vision, pains in chest, groin, or leg, shortness of breath, slurring of speech, weakness or numbness in arm or leg. For women: Breast pain or enlargement, swelling of legs and feet, rapid weight gain. Call your doctor immediately.

COMMON
Abdominal bloating, stomach cramps, loss of appetite, skin irritation at site of patch.

LESS COMMON
Diarrhea, dizziness, headaches, discomfort when wearing contact lenses, decreased sexual desire in men, increased sexual desire in women, vomiting.

PRINCIPAL USES
To provide estrogen when the body does not produce enough; to treat carefully selected cases of advanced breast cancer; to reduce risk of osteoporosis after menopause; to ease unpleasant symptoms of menopause, including vaginal dryness; to prevent breast engorgement following childbirth; to ease symptoms of advanced prostate cancer.

HOW THE DRUG WORKS
In women, estradiol replaces deficient natural levels of estrogen in the body. In men, the hormone inhibits growth of cells in the prostate gland.

DOSAGE
To treat breast cancer: 10 mg, 3 times a day. For postmenopausal vaginal dryness or prevention of osteoporosis: 1 to 2 mg a day of oral form, or 10 to 20 mg injected every 4 weeks, or 1 Estraderm, Alora, or Vivelle patch (0.05 mg) 2 times a week or 1 Climara patch weekly. A progestin should also be taken for 10 to 14 days in each month of use, except in women who have had a hysterectomy. To relieve postmenopausal vaginal dryness using intravaginal estrogen creams: To start, ½ to 1 applicatorful daily and tapered to 1 applicatorful 1 to 3 times weekly. To treat menopausal symptoms: 1 to 5 mg injected every 3 to 4 weeks. To prevent breast engorgement after childbirth: 10 to 25 mg injected in a muscle at the time of delivery. To treat prostate cancer: 1 to 2 mg, 3 times daily.

ONSET OF EFFECT
Within 1 hour.

DURATION OF ACTION
Up to 24 hours.

DIETARY ADVICE
No special restrictions.

STORAGE
Keep in a tightly sealed container away from heat and direct light.

IF YOU MISS A DOSE
Take the missed dose as soon as you remember. If it is near time for the next dose, skip the missed dose and resume your regular dosage schedule. Do not double the next dose.

STOPPING THE DRUG
The decision to stop taking the drug should be made in consultation with your physician.

PROLONGED USE
May increase the risk of endometrial cancer and perhaps breast cancer. Consult your doctor about periodic examinations and other measures to help prevent these diseases.

PRECAUTIONS
Over 60: No special problems are expected.

Driving and Hazardous Work: Do not drive or engage in hazardous work until you determine how the medicine affects you.

Alcohol: No special precautions are necessary.

Pregnancy: Not recommended during pregnancy; estrogens have been shown to cause birth defects in animals and humans.

Breast Feeding: Do not use estradiol while nursing.

Infants and Children: Estradiol is not recommended for use by young patients in whom bone growth is not complete.

Special Concerns: Swelling or bleeding of the gums may occur; see your dentist regularly. Do not apply a patch to the same site more than once a week.

OVERDOSE
Symptoms: Nausea, unexpected vaginal bleeding.

What to Do: An overdose of estradiol is unlikely to occur. However, if someone takes a much larger dose than prescribed, seek medical assistance immediately.

DRUG INTERACTIONS
Consult your doctor for specific advice if you are taking acetaminophen, amiodarone, anticonvulsants, anti-infective drugs, antithyroid agents, carmustine, chloroquine, dantrolene, daunorubicin, gold salts, divalproex, etretinate, hydroxychloroquine, mercaptopurine, methotrexate, oral contraceptives, methyldopa, naltrexone, phenothiazines, plicamycin, steroids, bromocriptine or cyclosporine.

FOOD INTERACTIONS
No known food interactions.

DISEASE INTERACTIONS
You should not take estradiol if you have breast cancer, any hormone-dependent cancer, abnormal genital bleeding, thrombophlebitis, or thromboembolitis. Consult your doctor if you have any of the following: a history of liver disease, heart attack, stroke, a blood clotting disorder, gallbladder disease or gallstones, or if you smoke tobacco heavily.

Estramustine Phosphate Sodium

BRAND NAME
Emcyt

▶ Drug Class: Antineoplastic (anticancer) agent

▶ Available in: Capsules

▶ Available OTC? No

▶ As Generic? No

Side Effects

SERIOUS
Black, tarry stools, blood in urine or stools, cough or hoarseness, fever or chills, severe or sudden headaches, sudden loss of coordination, pain in lower back or side, pain in chest, groin, or leg, painful urination, red spots on skin, sudden shortness of breath, sudden slurred speech, unusual bleeding or bruising, sudden changes in vision, weakness or numbness in arm or leg, skin rash, or fever. Call your doctor or emergency medical services (EMS) immediately.

COMMON
Breast tenderness or enlargement, swelling of feet or lower legs, decreased sexual desire, diarrhea, nausea, general weakness.

LESS COMMON
Insomnia, vomiting.

PRINCIPAL USES
To treat some types of prostate cancer.

HOW THE DRUG WORKS
Estramustine is a combination of two drugs: a form of estrogen (estradiol) and mechlorethamine (nitrogen mustard). It is uncertain precisely how the drug works, but it appears to kill cancer cells by interfering with the synthesis of their genetic material and blocking the activity of hormones and proteins that certain types of prostate tumors need in order to grow.

DOSAGE
10 to 16 mg per 2.2 lbs (1 kg) of body weight daily in 3 or 4 doses.

ONSET OF EFFECT
Unknown.

DURATION OF ACTION
Unknown.

DIETARY ADVICE
Best taken with water 1 hour before or 2 hours after meals. Milk, milk products, or calcium-rich foods should not be taken simultaneously.

STORAGE
Store in a tightly sealed container away from heat and direct light.

IF YOU MISS A DOSE
Take it as soon as you remember. If it is near the time for the next dose, skip the missed dose and resume your regular dosage schedule. Do not double the next dose.

STOPPING THE DRUG
The decision to stop taking the drug should be made in consultation with your physician.

PROLONGED USE
You should see your doctor regularly for tests and examinations if you take this drug for a prolonged period.

PRECAUTIONS
Over 60: Side effects tend to occur more commonly in patients over 60.

Driving and Hazardous Work: Do not drive or engage in hazardous work until you determine how the medicine affects you.

Alcohol: Avoid alcohol while taking this drug.

Pregnancy: Estramustine can cause birth defects if the father is taking it at the time of conception. Before taking estramustine, tell your doctor if you intend to have children; while taking it, a reliable barrier method of birth control is advised.

Breast Feeding: Not applicable for this drug.

Infants and Children: Estramustine is not intended for use in infants and children.

Special Concerns: If you vomit shortly after taking a dose of estramustine, ask your doctor if you should take the dose again or wait for the next scheduled dose. During and after treatment with estramustine, do not get immunized against bacteria or viruses without your doctor's approval. Avoid persons who have recently taken oral polio vaccine. If you must be close to them, consider wearing a protective mask that covers both the nose and mouth.

OVERDOSE
Symptoms: Severe and exaggerated side effects (see Side Effects).

What to Do: Call your doctor, emergency medical services (EMS), or the nearest poison control center immediately.

DRUG INTERACTIONS
Consult your doctor for specific advice if you are taking acetaminophen, amiodarone, anabolic steroids, androgens, antibiotics, antithyroid agents, carbamazepine, carmustine, chloroquine, dantrolene, disulfiram, divalproex, estrogens, etretinate, gold salts, hydrochloroquine, mercaptopurine, methyldopa, naltrexone, phenothiazines, phenytoin, plicamycin, or valproic acid.

FOOD INTERACTIONS
See dietary advice.

DISEASE INTERACTIONS
Caution is advised when taking estramustine. Consult your doctor if you have any of the following: asthma, epilepsy, mental depression, migraine headaches, kidney disease, history of blood clots, history of stroke, a recent heart attack, shingles, diabetes, gallbladder disease, heart or blood vessel disease, liver disease, or a stomach ulcer.

Estrogens, Conjugated

Premarin 1.25 mg
(WYETH-AYERST)

833

Additional photographs

▶ Drug Class: Female sex hormone

▶ Available in: Tablets, injection, vaginal cream

▶ Available OTC? No

▶ As Generic? Yes

Side Effects

SERIOUS
Women: Breast pain or enlargement; swelling of legs and feet; rapid weight gain. Men being treated for prostate cancer: Sudden or severe headache; loss of coordination; sudden changes in vision; pains in chest, groin, or leg; sudden shortness of breath; slurred speech; weakness or numbness in arm or leg. Call your doctor immediately.

COMMON
Abdominal bloating or cramps, loss of appetite, breast tenderness.

LESS COMMON
Diarrhea, dizziness, headaches, discomfort when wearing contact lenses, decreased sexual desire in men, increased sexual desire in women, vomiting.

PRINCIPAL USES
To provide estrogen after the menopause, when the body produces too little; to treat carefully selected cases of advanced breast cancer; to reduce risk of osteoporosis after menopause; to ease unpleasant symptoms of menopause, including vaginal dryness; to prevent breast engorgement following childbirth; or to ease symptoms of advanced prostate cancer.

HOW THE DRUG WORKS
In women, conjugated estrogens replace deficient natural levels of estrogen in the body. In men, estrogens inhibit growth of cells in the prostate gland.

DOSAGE
Usual adult dose is taken in cycles, with no dosing on certain days of the month. Women must also take a progestin 10 to 14 days in each month of use, except those who have had a hysterectomy (these women may take estrogen daily). To treat breast cancer in men or postmenopausal women: 10 mg, 3 times a day for 3 months or more. To prevent bone loss from osteoporosis: 0.3 to 1.25 mg a day. To ease symptoms of menopause: 0.625 to 1.25 mg a day. To treat prostate cancer: 1.25 to 2.5 mg a day.

ONSET OF EFFECT
Unknown.

DURATION OF ACTION
Unknown.

DIETARY ADVICE
Conjugated estrogens may be taken with food to reduce stomach upset.

STORAGE
Store in a tightly sealed container away from heat, moisture, and direct light. Keep it away from extremes in temperature. Keep the liquid form refrigerated, but do not allow it to freeze.

IF YOU MISS A DOSE
Take it as soon as you remember. If it is near the time for the next dose, skip the missed dose and resume your regular dosage schedule. Do not double the next dose.

STOPPING THE DRUG
The decision to stop taking the drug should be made by your doctor.

PROLONGED USE
Prolonged use of estrogens has been reported to increase the risk of endometrial cancer and perhaps of breast cancer. Consult your doctor about the need for periodic examinations and other measures to screen for these diseases.

PRECAUTIONS
Over 60: No special problems are expected.

Driving and Hazardous Work: Use of this hormone should not impair your ability to perform such tasks safely.

Alcohol: No special precautions are necessary.

Pregnancy: Do not use if you are pregnant. Estrogen use in pregnant women has been associated with birth defects.

Breast Feeding: Talk to your doctor about whether the benefits of the therapy outweigh the potential harm to the nursing infant.

Infants and Children: Should be used with caution by children, as the drug may interfere with bone growth.

OVERDOSE
Symptoms: Nausea, unexpected vaginal bleeding.

What to Do: An overdose of estrogen is unlikely to be life-threatening. However, if someone takes a much larger dose than prescribed, call your doctor, emergency medical services (EMS), or the nearest poison control center immediately.

DRUG INTERACTIONS
Other drugs may interact with estrogens. Consult your doctor if you are taking anticoagulants, anticonvulsants, antidiabetic drugs, thyroid hormones, tricyclic antidepressants, barbiturates, tranquilizers, cyclosporine, corticosteroids, corticotropin, tamoxifen, rifampin, carbamazepine, or bromocriptine.

FOOD INTERACTIONS
Calcium supplements used with estrogen may increase calcium absorption. Vitamin C may increase the effects of estrogen.

DISEASE INTERACTIONS
You should not take conjugated estrogens if you have thrombophlebitis, thromboembolitis, breast cancer, any hormone-dependent cancer, or abnormal genital bleeding. Consult your doctor if you have any of the following: a history of liver disease, heart attack, stroke, a blood clotting disorder, gallbladder disease or gallstones, or if you smoke tobacco heavily.

Estrogens, Conjugated/Medroxyprogesterone Acetate

▶ Drug Class: Female sex hormones

▶ Available in: Tablets

▶ Available OTC? No

▶ As Generic? No

Side Effects

SERIOUS
The most serious side effect is a modest increase in the incidence of breast cancer among women taking estrogen, especially for a long time (10 years or longer). Other side effects requiring your doctor's attention include swelling of legs and feet, rapid weight gain, abnormal menstrual bleeding, mental depression, and skin rash.

COMMON
Nausea, breast tenderness, headache, abdominal pain.

LESS COMMON
Change in appetite, vomiting, stomach cramps or bloating, change in blood pressure, dizziness, nervousness, insomnia, sleepiness, increase or decrease in weight, fatigue, backache.

PRINCIPAL USES
To provide estrogen after the menopause, when the body produces too little; to reduce the risk of osteoporosis; to ease unpleasant symptoms of menopause, including hot flashes and vaginal dryness; and to treat atrophy (wasting) of the vulva or vagina. Estrogen also protects women against coronary artery disease.

HOW THE DRUG WORKS
Estrogen protects against osteoporosis by diminishing the loss of bone that results from estrogen deficiency. Conjugated estrogens replace deficient levels of natural estrogen in women. When given alone to menopausal women, estrogen increases the risk of excessive growth of the uterine lining, which can lead to endometrial cancer. Medroxyprogesterone (a type of progestin) given in conjunction with estrogen nearly eliminates this risk.

DOSAGE
1 tablet, taken once a day. Prempro contains 0.625 mg of estrogen (Premarin) and 2.5 mg of medroxyprogesterone (MPA). Premphase contains 0.625 mg Premarin and 5 mg of MPA.

ONSET OF EFFECT
Unknown.

DURATION OF ACTION
As long as the product is taken.

DIETARY ADVICE
Take it with food to reduce stomach upset.

STORAGE
Store in a tightly sealed container away from heat, moisture, and direct light.

IF YOU MISS A DOSE
If you miss a dose on one day, do not double the dose the next day. Resume your regular dosage schedule.

STOPPING THE DRUG
The decision to stop taking this hormone combination should be made in consultation with your doctor.

PROLONGED USE
You should be reevaluated at 3-month to 6-month intervals to determine whether or not continued treatment is necessary.

PRECAUTIONS
Over 60: No special problems are expected.

Driving and Hazardous Work: Use of this hormone combination should not impair your ability to perform such tasks safely.

Alcohol: No special precautions are necessary.

Pregnancy: Do not use this hormone combination if you are or are planning to become pregnant. Estrogen use in pregnant women has been associated with birth defects.

Breast Feeding: Do not use this hormone combination if you are nursing.

Infants and Children: Not recommended for use by children.

Special Concerns: When this hormone combination is being used in the management or prevention of osteoporosis, regular weight-bearing exercise and good nutrition are important.

OVERDOSE
Symptoms: No serious ill effects have been reported following an overdose. However, nausea, vomiting, and withdrawal bleeding may occur when extremely large doses are ingested.

What to Do: An overdose is unlikely. However, if someone takes a much larger dose than prescribed, seek medical attention.

DRUG INTERACTIONS
Other drugs may interact with this hormone combination. Consult your doctor if you are taking anticoagulants, anticonvulsants, antidiabetic drugs, thyroid hormones, tricyclic antidepressants, barbiturates, tranquilizers, cyclosporine, corticosteroids, corticotropin, tamoxifen, rifampin, carbamazepine, or bromocriptine.

FOOD INTERACTIONS
Estrogen may increase calcium absorption from calcium supplements. Vitamin C may increase the effects of estrogen.

DISEASE INTERACTIONS
You should not take this hormone combination if you have thrombophlebitis, breast cancer, any hormone-dependent cancer, or abnormal vaginal bleeding. Consult your doctor if you have a history of any of the following: liver disease, heart attack, diabetes mellitus, stroke, a blood clotting disorder, thromboembolic disease, gallbladder disease or gallstones, liver disease, or if you smoke cigarettes heavily.

Estropipate

BRAND NAMES
Ogen, Ortho-Est

Generic 0.75 mg
(WATSON)

▶ Drug Class: Female sex hormone

▶ Available in: Tablets, vaginal cream

▶ Available OTC? No

▶ As Generic? Yes

Side Effects

SERIOUS
Breast pain or enlargement, swelling of legs and feet, rapid weight gain. Call your doctor immediately.

COMMON
Stomach bloating, lower abdominal cramps, loss of appetite.

LESS COMMON
Diarrhea, dizziness, headaches, discomfort when wearing contact lenses, increased sexual desire in women, vomiting, unusual sensitivity to sunlight.

PRINCIPAL USES
To provide estrogen when the body does not produce enough; to treat selected cases of advanced breast cancer; to reduce risk of osteoporosis after menopause; to ease unpleasant symptoms of menopause, including vaginal dryness; to ease symptoms of advanced prostate cancer.

HOW THE DRUG WORKS
In women, estropipate replaces deficient natural levels of estrogen in the body. In men, it inhibits the growth of cells in the prostate gland.

DOSAGE
For vaginal skin conditions: 0.625 to 5 mg a day of oral form or 2 to 4 grams a day of vaginal cream. For treating menopausal symptoms: 1.25 to 2.5 mg a day of oral form, 3 weeks on, 1 week off. To prevent osteoporosis: 0.625 mg of oral form daily for 25 days of a 31-day cycle. A progestin must also be taken for 10 to 14 days in each month of use, except in women who have had a hysterectomy.

ONSET OF EFFECT
Within 1 hour.

DURATION OF ACTION
Up to 24 hours.

DIETARY ADVICE
This medicine can be taken without regard to meals.

STORAGE
Keep in a tightly sealed container away from heat and direct light.

IF YOU MISS A DOSE
Take the missed dose as soon as you remember. If it is near time for the next dose, skip the missed dose and resume your regular dosage schedule. Do not double the next dose.

STOPPING THE DRUG
The decision to stop taking the drug should be made by your doctor.

PROLONGED USE
Prolonged use of estrogens has been reported to increase the risk of endometrial cancer and perhaps breast cancer. Endometrial cancer is largely prevented by using estropipate in sequence with a progestin. Consult your doctor about the need for periodic examinations and other measures to help detect and prevent these diseases.

PRECAUTIONS
Over 60: No special problems are expected.

Driving and Hazardous Work: Do not drive or engage in hazardous work until you determine how the medicine affects you.

Alcohol: No special precautions are necessary.

Pregnancy: Estrogens have been shown to cause birth defects in animals and humans. Before taking estropipate, be sure to tell your doctor if you are pregnant or plan to become pregnant.

Breast Feeding: Estropipate passes into breast milk; avoid using it while nursing.

Infants and Children: This medicine is not recommended for use by children in whom bone growth is not complete.

Special Concerns: Swelling or bleeding of the gums may occur. See your dentist regularly. You should have a Pap test every 6 to 12 months while taking estropipate. Avoid excessive exposure to sun-light until you determine how the drug affects you.

OVERDOSE
Symptoms: Nausea, unexpected vaginal bleeding.

What to Do: An overdose of estropipate is unlikely to be life-threatening. However, if someone takes a much larger dose than prescribed, call your doctor, emergency medical services (EMS), or the nearest poison control center.

DRUG INTERACTIONS
Consult your doctor for specific advice if you are taking acetaminophen, amiodarone, anabolic steroids, androgens, anti-infective drugs, antithyroid agents, bromocriptine, carbamazepine, carmustine, chloroquine, cyclosporine, dantrolene, daunorubicin, disulfiram, divalproex, etretinate, gold salts, hydroxychloroquine, mercaptopurine, methotrexate, methyldopa, naltrexone, oral contraceptives, phenothiazines, phenytoin, plicamycin, or valproic acid.

FOOD INTERACTIONS
No known food interactions.

DISEASE INTERACTIONS
You should not take estropipate if you have thrombophlebitis, thromboembolitis, a history of breast cancer, any hormone-dependent cancer, or abnormal genital bleeding.

Etanercept

- ▶ Drug Class: Biologic response modifier

- ▶ Available in: Injection

- ▶ Available OTC? No

- ▶ As Generic? No

Side Effects

SERIOUS
There are no serious side effects associated with the use of etanercept.

COMMON
Itching, redness, pain, or swelling at the site of injection; upper respiratory infection.

LESS COMMON
Headache, nasal congestion, dizziness, sore throat, cough, general weakness, abdominal discomfort, rash, runny nose.

PRINCIPAL USES
To reduce the signs and symptoms of moderate to severe active rheumatoid arthritis. Etanercept is prescribed for patients who have not responded adequately to one or more antirheumatic medications. It may also be used in combination with methotrexate in patients who have not responded adequately to methotrexate alone.

HOW THE DRUG WORKS
Etanercept works by binding with tumor necrosis factor (TNF), a key protein involved in the inflammatory process. Etanercept reduces inflammation by blocking the interaction of TNF with its receptors on cells.

DOSAGE
Adults: 25 mg, twice a week as a subcutaneous (under the skin) injection. Children: See your pediatrician for the appropriate dosage.

ONSET OF EFFECT
Within 1 to 2 weeks.

DURATION OF ACTION
As long as the drug is taken, but studies have only lasted for 6 months.

DIETARY ADVICE
May be taken without regard to diet.

STORAGE
Keep etanercept refrigerated, but do not allow it to freeze. If not administered immediately after preparing (reconstituting), etanercept may be stored in the vial in the refrigerator for up to 6 hours.

IF YOU MISS A DOSE
Take it as soon as you remember. If it is near the time for the next dose, skip the missed dose and resume your regular dosage schedule. Do not double the next dose.

STOPPING THE DRUG
The decision to stop taking the medication should be made in consultation with your doctor.

PROLONGED USE
No special problems are expected.

PRECAUTIONS
Over 60: No special problems are expected.

Driving and Hazardous Work: The use of etanercept should not impair your ability to perform such tasks safely.

Alcohol: Alcohol may accentuate the side effect of dizziness.

Pregnancy: Adequate human studies have not been done. Before taking etanercept, tell your doctor if you are pregnant or plan to become pregnant.

Breast Feeding: Etanercept may pass into breast milk; caution is advised. Consult your doctor for advice on whether to discontinue nursing or discontinue the drug.

Infants and Children: Not recommended for use by children under age 4.

Special Concerns: Your doctor should instruct you on how to prepare and administer the injection of etanercept before you attempt to do it yourself. Follow your doctor's instructions about selecting and rotating injection sites. Sites for self-injection are the arms, stomach, and thighs. The first injection should be administered under the supervision of your doctor. Other antirheumatic medications may be continued during treatment with etanercept. Consult your doctor for advice.

OVERDOSE
Symptoms: No cases of overdose have been reported.

What to Do: An overdose with etanercept is unlikely. If someone takes a much larger dose than prescribed, call your doctor.

DRUG INTERACTIONS
Avoid live-virus vaccines. No other medications should be added to solutions containing etanercept. Adequate studies involving interactions with other drugs have not been done. Consult your doctor for specific advice.

FOOD INTERACTIONS
No known food interactions.

DISEASE INTERACTIONS
Etanercept should be used with caution in patients with any active infection, including chronic or localized infections, or who are immunosuppressed.

Ethacrynic Acid (Ethacrynate)

BRAND NAMES
Edecrin, Edecrin Sodium

Edecrin 25 mg
(MERCK)

▶ Drug Class: Loop diuretic

▶ Available in: Tablets, injection

▶ Available OTC? No

▶ As Generic? No

Side Effects

SERIOUS
Mood or mental changes, nausea or vomiting, unusual fatigue, black and tarry stools, skin rash. Call your doctor immediately.

COMMON
Muscle cramps or pain. Potassium depletion may lead to heart palpitations and weakness. Fluid depletion may lead to dizziness, especially upon arising from a sitting or lying position, as well as thirst, dry mouth, and constipation.

LESS COMMON
Buzzing or ringing in ears, loss of hearing (particularly after intravenous treatment), diarrhea, loss of appetite, gout, increased blood sugar (a problem for diabetic patients).

PRINCIPAL USES
To reduce fluid (salt and water) accumulation that leads to edema (swelling) and breathlessness in patients who have heart disease, cirrhosis of the liver, and kidney disease.

HOW THE DRUG WORKS
Loop diuretics work on a specific portion of the kidney (the loop of Henle) to increase the excretion of water and salts (including potassium) in urine.

DOSAGE
Adults— Ethacrynic acid (oral dose): 50 to 200 mg a day. Ethacrynate sodium (injection): 50 mg injected into a vein every 2 to 6 hours as needed.

ONSET OF EFFECT
Within 30 minutes after an oral dose; within 5 minutes after intravenous injection.

DURATION OF ACTION
Oral dose lasts 6 to 8 hours; intravenous, 2 hours.

DIETARY ADVICE
Ethacrynic acid may cause depletion of potassium; your doctor may want you to eat high-potassium foods (such as bananas, tomatoes, and citrus fruits) or take potassium supplements. Take the drug with food or milk to minimize stomach upset.

STORAGE
Store in a tightly sealed container away from heat, moisture, and direct light.

IF YOU MISS A DOSE
Take it as soon as you remember. If it is near the time for the next dose, skip the missed dose and resume your regular dosage schedule. Do not double the next dose.

STOPPING THE DRUG
Take it as prescribed for the full treatment period, even if you begin to feel better before the scheduled end of therapy.

PROLONGED USE
Your doctor will schedule regular checkups to determine the medication's effect on your body, and adjust the dosage and dosing frequency. After a maintenance dose is established, diuretic therapy may continue for intermittent periods alternating with periods not using the drug.

PRECAUTIONS
Over 60: No special precautions are warranted.

Driving and Hazardous Work: No special precautions are warranted.

Alcohol: Alcohol should be avoided or used with caution because it may increase the effect of antihypertensive drugs and cause an excessive drop in blood pressure.

Pregnancy: This drug is not usually prescribed during pregnancy. Other diuretics are preferred.

Breast Feeding: It is not known whether the drug is excreted in milk; consult your doctor for specific advice.

Infants and Children: Although ethacrynic acid is rarely prescribed for children, no unusual side effects are expected. The dose must be determined by a pediatrician.

Special Concerns: To prevent sleep disruption, avoid taking this medicine in the evening. You may be advised to in-crease potassium in your diet or take a potassium supplement while taking a diuretic.

OVERDOSE
Symptoms: Weakness, lethargy, dizziness, nausea, vomiting, leg muscle cramps.

What to Do: Call your doctor, emergency medical services (EMS), or the nearest poison control center immediately.

DRUG INTERACTIONS
Consult your doctor if you are taking any of the following: ACE inhibitors, aminoglycosides, cisplatin, digitalis drugs, lithium, nonsteroidal anti-inflammatory drugs, salicylates, or thiazide diuretics.

FOOD INTERACTIONS
No known food interactions.

DISEASE INTERACTIONS
Consult your doctor if you have any of the following conditions: diabetes mellitus, gout, hearing problems, pancreatitis, recent heart attack, kidney or liver disease, or systemic lupus erythematosus.

Ethchlorvynol

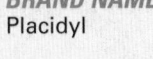

Placidyl 500 mg
(ABBOTT)

Additional photographs

▶ Drug Class: Sedative

▶ Available in: Capsules

▶ Available OTC? No

▶ As Generic? Yes

Side Effects

SERIOUS
Unusual bleeding or bruising; unusual excitement, nervousness, or restlessness; skin rash or hives; yellowish tinge to eyes or skin (jaundice); itching; darkening of urine; pale stools. Call your doctor immediately.

COMMON
Blurred vision, nausea or vomiting, indigestion, bitter or unusual aftertaste, numbness in the face, abdominal pain, dizziness or lightheadedness, unusual fatigue or weakness.

LESS COMMON
Unsteady gait or loss of coordination; confusion; daytime sleepiness. Check with your doctor promptly if such symptoms persist.

PRINCIPAL USES
Used as short-term therapy for insomnia; however, other medications are generally preferred.

HOW THE DRUG WORKS
The exact mechanism of action is unknown; ethchlorvynol appears to depress the central nervous system in a manner similar to that of barbiturates.

DOSAGE
Adults: 500 to 1,000 mg at bedtime.

ONSET OF EFFECT
30 to 60 minutes.

DURATION OF ACTION
5 hours.

DIETARY ADVICE
Take ethchlorvynol with milk or food to minimize temporary dizziness or unsteadiness that may result from the body's rapid absorption of the drug.

STORAGE
Store in a tightly sealed container away from heat, moisture, and direct light.

IF YOU MISS A DOSE
Ethchlorvynol is generally prescribed for once-daily use at bedtime. If you are unable to take it on a particular night, resume your regular scheduled dose the following night.

STOPPING THE DRUG
The decision to stop taking the drug should be made in consultation with your doctor. Generally, therapy lasts no more than 1 week.

PROLONGED USE
Ethchlorvynol should not be prescribed for a period exceeding 1 week, as the body will build up tolerance to the drug, and physical and psychological dependence may develop. Patients abruptly stopping the drug after prolonged use may experience withdrawal symptoms (seizures, delirium, perceptual distortions, agitation, tremors) as late as 9 days after ending therapy. A gradual, progressive reduction of dosage over a period of days or weeks is recommended for patients who have become dependent on ethchlorvynol.

PRECAUTIONS
Over 60: Older patients may be more sensitive to the effects of ethchlorvynol and so should take the smallest effective dose.

Driving and Hazardous Work: The use of this drug may impair your ability to perform such tasks safely.

Alcohol: Avoid alcohol.

Pregnancy: Ethchlorvynol should not be used during the first 2 trimesters (6 months) of pregnancy. Discuss with your doctor the relative risks and benefits of using this drug during the final 3 months (third trimester) of pregnancy.

Breast Feeding: Ethchlorvynol may pass into breast milk. Consult your doctor for specific advice.

Infants and Children: Not recommended for persons under the age of 18.

Special Concerns: Ethchlorvynol may become habit forming. Use only as directed by your doctor. Never take more than the prescribed dose and do not use the drug for a longer period than prescribed.

OVERDOSE
Symptoms: Severe nausea, vomiting, or stomach pain; difficulty swallowing; severe drowsiness; continuing confusion; seizures; low body temperature; difficulty breathing or shortness of breath; irregular heartbeat; severe weakness; staggering; slurred speech.

What to Do: Call your doctor, emergency medical services (EMS), or the nearest poison control center immediately.

DRUG INTERACTIONS
Consult your doctor for specific advice if you are taking barbiturates or other central nervous system depressants, tricyclic antidepressants, MAO inhibitors, or anticoagulants.

FOOD INTERACTIONS
No known food interactions.

DISEASE INTERACTIONS
Your physician should know if you have any of the following conditions: impaired kidney or liver function, a history of alcohol or drug abuse, mental depression, or porphyria.

Ethinyl Estradiol

BRAND NAMES
Estinyl, Feminone

Estinyl 0.05 mg
(SCHERING-PLOUGH)

▶ Drug Class: Anticancer estrogen

▶ Available in: Tablets

▶ Available OTC? No

▶ As Generic? Yes

Side Effects

SERIOUS
Breast pain or enlargement, swelling of feet and lower legs, rapid weight gain, changes in vaginal bleeding, lumps in or discharge from the breast, visual disturbances, sharp pains in stomach, side, or abdomen, uncontrolled muscle movements, yellowish tinge of eyes or skin (jaundice). Call your doctor immediately.

COMMON
Stomach bloating, lower abdominal cramping and discomfort, loss of appetite.

LESS COMMON
Dizziness, diarrhea, headaches, unusual increase in sexual desire, vomiting, problems with contact lenses.

PRINCIPAL USES
To provide estrogen when the body does not produce enough (hypogonadism); to treat carefully selected cases of advanced breast cancer; to reduce risk of osteoporosis after menopause; to ease unpleasant symptoms of menopause, including vaginal dryness; to ease symptoms of advanced prostate cancer.

HOW THE DRUG WORKS
In women, ethinyl estradiol replaces deficient natural levels of estrogen in the body. In men, it inhibits the growth of cells in the prostate gland.

DOSAGE
For female hypogonadism: 0.05 mg, 1 to 3 times a day for 25 days per month (in conjunction with 10 to 14 days of a progestin, except in women who have had a hysterectomy), for 3 to 6 months. For breast cancer: 1 mg, 3 times a day. For menopausal symptoms: 0.02 to 0.05 mg a day. For prostate cancer: 0.15 to 2 mg a day.

ONSET OF EFFECT
Within 8 hours.

DURATION OF ACTION
Up to 24 hours.

DIETARY ADVICE
This drug can be taken with or immediately after meals to reduce nausea.

STORAGE
Store in a tightly sealed container away from heat and direct light.

IF YOU MISS A DOSE
Take it as soon as you remember. However, if it is near the time for the next dose, skip the missed dose and resume your regular dosage schedule. Do not double the next dose.

STOPPING THE DRUG
The decision to stop taking the drug should be made by your doctor.

PROLONGED USE
Women who take ethinyl estradiol for more than 5 years to treat menopausal symptoms may be at increased risk for endometrial cancer. Consult your physician about the need for discontinuing the drug temporarily. Although the drug may cause menstrual bleeding, it does not restore fertility.

PRECAUTIONS

Over 60: No special problems are expected.

Driving and Hazardous Work: The use of ethinyl estradiol may impair your ability to perform such tasks safely. Do not drive or engage in hazardous work until you determine how the medication affects you.

Alcohol: No special precautions are necessary.

Pregnancy: Drugs of this class have caused serious birth defects in animals and humans. Ethinyl estradiol should not be taken if you are pregnant or are planning to become pregnant.

Breast Feeding: Ethinyl estradiol passes into breast milk; avoid or discontinue use while nursing.

Infants and Children: Not recommended for use by children and adolescents whose bone growth is not complete.

Special Concerns: Ethinyl estradiol may cause dental bleeding and excessive gingival (gum) growth. See your dentist regularly. Nausea may occur in the first weeks after you start taking this drug.

OVERDOSE

Symptoms: Nausea and abnormal vaginal bleeding.

What to Do: An overdose of ethinyl estradiol is unlikely to be life-threatening. However, if someone takes a much larger dose than prescribed, call your doctor, emergency medical services (EMS), or local poison control center.

DRUG INTERACTIONS
Consult your doctor for specific advice if you are taking acetaminophen, amiodarone, anabolic steroids, androgens, anti-infective drugs, antithyroid drugs, carbamazepine, carmustine, chloroquine, dantrolene, daunorubicin, disulfiram, divalproex, etretinate, gold salts, hydroxychloroquine, mercaptopurine, naltrexone, oral contraceptives, phenothiazines, phenytoin, valproic acid, bromocriptine, or cyclosporine.

FOOD INTERACTIONS
No known food interactions.

DISEASE INTERACTIONS
Caution is advised when taking ethinyl estradiol. Consult your doctor if you have any of the following: a history of blood clots while taking estrogens, breast cancer, endometriosis, fibroid tumors of the uterus, gallbladder disease or gallstones, jaundice, liver disease, or porphyria.

Ethosuximide

Zarontin 250 mg
(PARKE-DAVIS)

▶ Drug Class: Anticonvulsant/
succinimide

▶ Available in: Capsules, syrup

▶ Available OTC? No

▶ As Generic? Yes

Side Effects

SERIOUS
Sore throat, fever, swollen glands, red or purple point-like rash on the skin or mucous membranes, blistering or peeling skin lesions, mouth sores, easy bruising, paleness, weakness, confusion, lethargy, muscle pain, or seizures may be a sign of a potentially fatal blood reaction or other complication. Call your doctor immediately.

COMMON
Nausea and vomiting, loss of appetite, stomach upset, gastrointestinal cramps, weight loss, diarrhea, sedation, mild sensory nerve impairment.

LESS COMMON
Irritability, headache, dizziness, sleep disturbances. There are numerous additional side effects associated with the use of this drug; consult your physician if you are concerned about any adverse or unusual reactions.

PRINCIPAL USES
To control seizures in patients with certain types of epilepsy.

HOW THE DRUG WORKS
Ethosuximide acts on the central nervous system to control the number and severity of seizures. It is thought to depress the activity of certain parts of the brain and suppress the abnormal transmission of nerve impulses that causes absence seizures.

DOSAGE
Adults: 750 to 1,500 mg a day, in 2 divided doses. A higher dose may be required. Children: 4 to 5 mg a day, in 2 divided doses. A low dose is used to start, and is gradually increased by your doctor.

ONSET OF EFFECT
Several hours.

DURATION OF ACTION
The drug is most effective for 24 hours or longer. After this time, effectiveness gradually decreases.

DIETARY ADVICE
Take it with food to minimize the risk of stomach upset.

STORAGE
Store in a tightly sealed container away from heat and direct light. Do not refrigerate or freeze the syrup.

IF YOU MISS A DOSE
Take it as soon as you remember, unless your next scheduled dose is within the next 4 hours. If so, skip the missed dose. Take your next dose at the proper time, and resume your regular dosage schedule. Do not double the next dose, unless advised to do so by your doctor.

STOPPING THE DRUG
The decision to stop taking the drug should be made by your doctor. Ethosuximide should never be stopped abruptly, since this may cause seizures. The dose is typically tapered over a period of weeks to months.

PROLONGED USE
Ethosuximide can be taken on a long-term basis. Some side effects that are prominent in the first few weeks of therapy usually diminish over time.

PRECAUTIONS
Over 60: Older patients may require lower doses to minimize side effects.

Driving and Hazardous Work: Ethosuximide may cause drowsiness and impair your ability to perform such tasks safely. Do not drive or engage in hazardous work until you determine how the medicine affects you.

Alcohol: May contribute to excessive drowsiness.

Pregnancy: Use of anticonvulsants is associated with an increased risk of birth defects, although studies with ethosuximide are incomplete. However, seizures during pregnancy can also increase risks to the fetus. Discuss with your doctor the potential risks and benefits of using this drug during pregnancy. Folate supplementation is recommended 1 to 2 months prior to conception, and continuing throughout pregnancy.

Breast Feeding: Ethosuximide passes into breast milk, although at low levels. Consult your doctor for specific advice if you are breast feeding.

Infants and Children: No special problems are expected.

Special Concerns: The generic form is not recommended. Your doctor may want you to wear a medical bracelet or carry an identification card saying that you are taking this drug.

OVERDOSE
Symptoms: Severe nausea and vomiting, difficulty breathing, severe drowsiness, coma.

What to Do: Call your doctor, emergency medical services (EMS), or the nearest poison control center immediately.

DRUG INTERACTIONS
Ethosuximide may be affected by other drugs or alter the blood levels of other medications, including other anticonvulsants (carbamazepine, phenacemide, phenobarbital, phenytoin, primidone, valproic acid) and certain psychiatric drugs (tricyclic antidepressants, MAO inhibitors, haloperidol).

FOOD INTERACTIONS
No known food interactions.

DISEASE INTERACTIONS
Special caution is advised if you have liver disease, kidney disease, a blood disorder, or intermittent porphyria.

Etidronate Disodium

Side Effects

SERIOUS
Bone fractures—especially in the long bones of the limbs—may occur, usually in patients on high doses or those taking the drug continuously for longer than 6 months.

COMMON
Bone pain or tenderness, often developing 4 to 6 weeks after treatment begins; it may persist, get worse, or sporadically ease and then return in patients with Paget's disease. Nausea and diarrhea may occur with higher doses. Headache, stomach upset, leg cramps, and joint pain may also occur.

LESS COMMON
Hives, skin rash, itching, swelling of the arms, legs, face, lips, tongue, or throat. The injectable form may cause loss of taste or metallic taste in the mouth.

PRINCIPAL USES

To treat Paget's disease, a disorder characterized by rapid breakdown and reformation of bone, which can lead to fragility and malformation of bones. May also be used to treat elevated blood levels of calcium (hypercalcemia) caused by cancer; to treat and prevent calcium and bone deposits around artificial joint replacements (especially hip replacements) or around an area of spinal cord injury. Etidronate is also commonly used to treat postmenopausal osteoporosis.

HOW THE DRUG WORKS

Etidronate slows bone resorption (the speed at which bone is broken down before it is replaced), promoting the formation of healthy bone. It prevents the bone pain, deformity, and fractures associated with Paget's disease. In cancer-related hypercalcemia, this drug slows bone resorption and thus the flow of calcium from bone into the blood. Etidronate slows the progression of abnormal bone deposition after hip replacement and spinal cord injury. In osteoporosis, it helps to slow the breakdown of bone tissue.

DOSAGE

Usual adult oral dosage for Paget's disease: 2.3 mg per lb of body weight per day, or 2.7 to 4.6 mg per lb, in alternating 6 month courses of treatment and abstention. Or: 5 to 9.1 mg per lb per day for not more than 3 months at a time. For hypercalcemia related to cancer: 9 mg per lb of body weight for 30 to 90 days. For prevention of calcium deposits, with hip replacement: 9 mg per lb for 1 month before and 3 months after surgery; for spinal cord injury: 9 mg per lb for

2 weeks, then 4.5 mg per lb for 10 weeks.

ONSET OF EFFECT

May be observed after 1 month of treatment.

DURATION OF ACTION

Possibly up to a year or more after therapy is stopped.

DIETARY ADVICE

Take the tablets with water on an empty stomach at least 2 hours before or after eating. Eat a well-balanced diet with adequate calcium and vitamin D intake.

STORAGE

Store in a tightly sealed container away from direct light, moisture, and extremes in temperature.

IF YOU MISS A DOSE

Take it as soon as possible. However, if it is near the time for the next dose, skip the missed dose, and resume the normal dosage schedule. Do not double the next dose.

STOPPING THE DRUG

Do not stop taking the drug on your own. Etidronate may take up to 3 months for the full effect to occur.

PROLONGED USE

Regular visits to your doctor are necessary—even between treatments—to evaluate the drug's effect.

PRECAUTIONS

Over 60: Elderly patients may be more prone to excess fluid retention (overhydration) when treated with injected etidronate in conjunction with hydration therapy. Careful monitoring of fluid and electrolyte levels is important.

Driving and Hazardous Work: No special precautions are required.

Alcohol: Alcohol should be restricted in high risk women because it is a risk factor for osteoporosis.

Pregnancy: Consult your doctor about whether the benefits of taking the medicine outweigh the potential risks to the unborn child.

Breast Feeding: It is not known if etidronate passes into breast milk.

Infants and Children: Safety and effectiveness have not been established.

OVERDOSE

Symptoms: Vomiting or diarrhea; palpitations; numbness or tingling in the hands, feet, lips, and tongue; facial pain.

What to Do: Call your doctor, emergency medical services (EMS), or the nearest poison control center immediately.

DRUG INTERACTIONS

Antacids or other medications containing calcium, magnesium, or aluminum may interfere with your body's absorption of oral etidronate. Warfarin may also interact with etidronate; consult your doctor for advice.

FOOD INTERACTIONS

Foods containing large amounts of calcium, such as milk or other dairy products, and mineral supplements containing calcium, iron, magnesium, or aluminum should not be consumed within 2 hours of taking etidronate.

DISEASE INTERACTIONS

Consult your doctor for advice if you have a bone fracture, intestinal or bowel disease, kidney disease, or a heart condition.

Etodolac

Lodine 200 mg
(WYETH-AYERST)

▶ Drug Class: Nonsteroidal anti-inflammatory drug (NSAID)

▶ Available in: Capsule, tablet, extended-release tablets

▶ Available OTC? No

▶ As Generic? Yes

Side Effects

SERIOUS
Shortness of breath or wheezing, with or without swelling of legs or other signs of heart failure; chest pain; peptic ulcer disease with vomiting of blood; black, tarry stools; decreasing kidney function. Call your doctor immediately.

COMMON
Nausea, vomiting, heartburn, diarrhea, constipation, headache, dizziness, sleepiness.

LESS COMMON
Ulcers or sores in mouth, depression, rashes or blistering of skin, ringing sound in the ears, unusual tingling or numbness of the hands or feet, seizures, blurred vision. Also elevated potassium levels, decreased blood counts; such problems can be detected by your doctor.

PRINCIPAL USES
To treat mild to moderate pain and inflammation caused by tendinitis, arthritis, bursitis, gout, soft tissue injuries, migraine and other vascular headaches, menstrual cramps, and other conditions. When patients fail to respond to one NSAID, another may be tried. The greatest effectiveness often requires trial and error of several different NSAIDs.

HOW THE DRUG WORKS
NSAIDs work by interfering with the formation of prostaglandins, substances in the body that cause inflammation and make nerves more sensitive to pain impulses. NSAIDs have other modes of action that are less well understood.

DOSAGE
For osteoarthritis— Adults: To start, 400 mg, 2 or 3 times a day, or 300 mg, 3 or 4 times a day. For pain— Adults: To start, 400 mg. Then, 200 to 400 mg every 6 to 8 hours as needed. Consult your pediatrician for children's dose.

ONSET OF EFFECT
Within 30 minutes.

DURATION OF ACTION
4 to 6 hours.

DIETARY ADVICE
Take with food; maintain your usual food and fluid intake.

STORAGE
Store in a tightly sealed container away from heat, moisture, and direct light.

IF YOU MISS A DOSE
Take it as soon as you remember. If it is near the time for the next dose, skip the missed dose and resume your regular dosage schedule. Do not double the next dose.

STOPPING THE DRUG
The decision to stop taking the drug should be made in consultation with your physician.

PROLONGED USE
Prolonged use can cause gastrointestinal problems, including ulceration and bleeding, kidney dysfunction, and liver inflammation. See your doctor for regular evaluation.

PRECAUTIONS
Over 60: Because of the potentially greater consequences of gastrointestinal side effects, the dose of NSAIDs for older patients, especially those over age 70, is often cut in half.

Driving and Hazardous Work: Do not drive or engage in hazardous work until you determine how the medicine affects you.

Alcohol: Avoid alcohol when using this medication because it increases the risk of stomach irritation.

Pregnancy: Avoid or discontinue this drug if you are pregnant or are planning to become pregnant.

Breast Feeding: Etodolac passes into breast milk; avoid use while nursing.

Infants and Children: Etodolac may be used in exceptional circumstances; consult your doctor.

Special Concerns: Because NSAIDs can interfere with blood coagulation, this drug should be stopped at least 3 days prior to any surgery.

OVERDOSE
Symptoms: Nausea, vomiting, severe headache, confusion, seizures.

What to Do: Call your doctor, emergency medical services (EMS), or the nearest poison control center immediately.

DRUG INTERACTIONS
Do not take this drug with aspirin or any other NSAIDs without your doctor's approval. In addition, consult your doctor if you are taking antihypertensives, steroids, anticoagulants, antibiotics, itraconazole or ketoconazole, plicamycin, penicillamine, valproic acid, phenytoin, cyclosporine, digitalis drugs, lithium, methotrexate, probenecid, triamterene, or zidovudine.

FOOD INTERACTIONS
No known food interactions.

DISEASE INTERACTIONS
Caution is advised when taking etodolac. Consult your doctor if you have any of the following: bleeding problems, inflammation or ulcers of the stomach and intestines, diabetes mellitus, systemic lupus erythematosus (SLE, lupus), anemia, asthma, epilepsy, Parkinson's disease, kidney stones, or a history of heart disease or alcohol abuse. Use of etodolac may cause complications in patients with liver or kidney disease, since these organs work together to remove the medication from the body.

Etoposide

BRAND NAME
VePesid

▸ Drug Class: Antineoplastic (anticancer) agent

▸ Available in: Capsules, injection

▸ Available OTC? No

▸ As Generic? Yes

Side Effects

SERIOUS
Bone marrow suppression (myelosuppression) causing fatigue, bleeding, bruising, fever, sore throat, chills. Severe gastrointestinal upset. Contact your doctor immediately if such symptoms appear.

COMMON
Loss of appetite, mild to moderate nausea, vomiting. Check with your doctor if these symptoms continue. Hair loss, sometimes progressing to total baldness, is generally temporary; hair will usually begin to grow back when the therapy is discontinued.

LESS COMMON
Allergic reactions, diarrhea, fatigue. Temporary drop in blood pressure (hypotension) causing dizziness and lightheadedness may occur with intravenous infusion.

PRINCIPAL USES
To treat recurrent or persistent testicular cancer or lymphoma (cancer of the lymph nodes). It is also used to treat certain types of lung cancer.

HOW THE DRUG WORKS
Etoposide kills cancer cells by interfering with the activity of their genetic material, which prevents the cells from dividing normally and multiplying. The drug may also affect the growth and development of other kinds of cells in the body, which may cause unpleasant side effects.

DOSAGE
Usual adult dose by intravenous infusion for testicular carcinoma: 50 to 100 mg per square meter of body surface for 5 days to 100 mg per square meter on days 1, 3, and 5. Usual adult oral dose for small-cell lung cancer: 70 mg per square meter of body surface per day for 4 days to 100 mg per square meter per day for 5 days. Both regimens are repeated every 3 to 4 weeks, depending on the severity of any side effects.

ONSET OF EFFECT
Variable.

DURATION OF ACTION
Unknown.

DIETARY ADVICE
No special concerns.

STORAGE
Keep liquid forms of the drug refrigerated, but do not allow them to freeze.

IF YOU MISS A DOSE
Skip the missed dose and continue your normal dosage schedule; do not double the next dose. Notify your doctor about the missed dose right away.

STOPPING THE DRUG
Continue to take the medicine exactly as prescribed by your doctor, even if you begin to feel ill. Certain side effects such as stomach upset and vomiting are common. Notify your doctor if vomiting occurs shortly after dosing.

PROLONGED USE
Follow the treatment schedule determined by your doctor. Periodic evaluation of the drug's effect and blood tests are an important part of treatment; blood cell counts need to be closely monitored.

PRECAUTIONS
Over 60: Adverse reactions may be more likely and more severe in older patients.

Driving and Hazardous Work: Check with your doctor before engaging in activities where you are at risk for bruising or injury.

Alcohol: Limit alcohol to moderate intake.

Pregnancy: Birth defects may result if etoposide is used at the time of conception or during pregnancy. Sterility is another potential side effect. Tell your doctor before taking the drug if you are pregnant; use birth control while taking etoposide, and notify your doctor immediately if you think you have become pregnant while taking the drug.

Breast Feeding: Etoposide is distributed into breast milk and may cause serious side effects; consult your doctor for advice.

Infants and Children: Consult your pediatric oncologist.

Special Concerns: Advise your doctor if you or a family member plans to receive a vaccination; there is a danger you might get the infection the immunization is meant to prevent. Patients with low blood counts should avoid crowds and people with infections, and should be alert for signs of infection and bleeding. Exercise caution when cleaning your teeth, and check with your doctor before having any dental work done.

OVERDOSE
Symptoms: Increased severity of nausea or vomiting, rapid pulse, shortness of breath, fainting.

What to Do: Call your doctor, emergency medical services (EMS), or the nearest poison control center immediately.

DRUG INTERACTIONS
Any or all of the following drugs may cause undesirable effects when taken together with etoposide: bone marrow depressants, antivirals, antifungals, anticoagulants, cyclosporine, or aspirin.

FOOD INTERACTIONS
No known food interactions.

DISEASE INTERACTIONS
Advise your doctor if you have any of the following conditions: chicken pox, shingles, infection, or kidney or liver disease.

Exemestane

BRAND NAME
Aromasin

▶ Drug Class: Antineoplastic (anticancer) agent

▶ Available in: Tablets

▶ Available OTC? No

▶ As Generic? No

Side Effects

SERIOUS
No serious side effects have been reported.

COMMON
Hot flashes, nausea, fatigue, pain, depression, insomnia, anxiety, shortness of breath.

LESS COMMON
Sweating, flulike symptoms, swelling, dizziness, headache, vomiting, abdominal pain, loss of appetite, constipation, diarrhea, increased appetite, weight gain, cough.

PRINCIPAL USES
To treat advanced breast cancer in postmenopausal women whose tumors stop responding to tamoxifen therapy.

HOW THE DRUG WORKS
The growth of some breast cancers is stimulated by the hormone estrogen. The estrogen in postmenopausal women arises primarily from the conversion by the enzyme aromatase of male hormones (androgens) made in the adrenal and ovaries. Exemestane inactivates aromatase, thus preventing the natural synthesis of estrogen and inhibiting the growth of estrogen-dependent tumors.

DOSAGE
25 mg a day following a meal.

ONSET OF EFFECT
Unknown.

DURATION OF ACTION
Unknown.

DIETARY ADVICE
It is recommended that exemestane be taken after a meal.

STORAGE
Store in a tightly sealed container away from heat, moisture, and direct light.

IF YOU MISS A DOSE
Exemestane is prescribed for once-daily use only. If you are unable to take the medication on a particular day, simply resume your regular dosage schedule the following day. Do not double the next dose.

STOPPING THE DRUG
The decision to stop the drug must be made in consultation with your doctor. Do not stop taking exemestane on your own.

PROLONGED USE
There is no standard duration of therapy with exemestane, although you can expect to remain on it for at least several weeks in order to determine if it is effective. Your doctor will determine whether your response to the drug is satisfactory or not, and will recommend continuation or discontinuation of therapy.

PRECAUTIONS
Over 60: No special problems are expected.

Driving and Hazardous Work: Do not drive or engage in hazardous work until you determine how the medicine affects you.

Alcohol: No special problems are expected, but you should consult your doctor about drinking alcohol while taking exemestane.

Pregnancy: Exemestane must not be used in pregnant women. Although exemestane is only prescribed for postmenopausal women, it is important that patients be sure they are not pregnant before starting treatment with this drug.

Breast Feeding: Not applicable; this drug is prescribed only for postmenopausal women.

Infants and Children: Not applicable.

Special Concerns: Exemestane often lowers blood levels of lymphocytes (a type of infection-fighting white blood cell), but no increase in infections was seen during clinical trials.

OVERDOSE
Symptoms: No cases of overdose have been reported.

What to Do: An overdose is unlikely; however, if you have any reason to suspect that one has occurred, call emergency medical services (EMS) to receive evaluation and treatment at the closest emergency facility.

DRUG INTERACTIONS
None reported.

FOOD INTERACTIONS
None reported.

DISEASE INTERACTIONS
None reported.

Ezetimibe

▶ Drug Class: Antilipidemic (cholesterol-lowering agent)

▶ Available in: Tablets

▶ Available OTC? No

▶ As Generic? No

Side Effects

SERIOUS
No serious side effects have been reported in association with the use of ezetimibe.

COMMON
None.

LESS COMMON
Fatigue, diarrhea.

PRINCIPAL USES
To reduce cholesterol in people with high blood levels of total and low-density lipoprotein (LDL), as part of a comprehensive treatment program that includes exercise and special diet. May also be taken in conjunction with another cholesterol-lowering drug in the class called "statins" (such as simvastatin, lovastatin, fluvastatin, pravastatin, rosuvastatin or atorvastatin).

HOW THE DRUG WORKS
Ezetimibe reduces bood cholesterol by inhibiting the absorption of cholesterol from the small intestine.

DOSAGE
10 mg once a day.

ONSET OF EFFECT
2 to 4 weeks.

DURATION OF ACTION
Persists as long as treatment continues.

DIETARY ADVICE
Cholesterol-lowering drugs are only one part of a total program that should include regular exercise and a healthy diet. The American Heart Association publishes a recommended "Healthy Heart" diet.

STORAGE
Store in a tightly sealed container away from heat, moisture, and direct light.

IF YOU MISS A DOSE
Take as soon as you remember. However, if it is near the time for the next dose, skip the missed dose and resume your regular dosage schedule. Do not double the next dose.

STOPPING THE DRUG
The decision to stop taking the drug should be made in consultation with your doctor. Once the medication is discontinued, blood cholesterol is likely to return to original elevated levels.

PROLONGED USE
Side effects are more likely with prolonged use. If you take ezetimibe along with a statin drug, your doctor will periodically order blood tests to evaluate your liver function.

PRECAUTIONS
Over 60: No special problems are expected.

Driving and Hazardous Work: No special precautions are necessary.

Alcohol: No special precautions are necessary.

Pregnancy: The effects on a fetus are unknown. Consult your doctor if you become or plan to become pregnant. If you are pregnant, do not take ezetimibe while taking a statin.

Breast Feeding: Adequate studies have not been done. If you are breast feeding, do not take ezetimibe while taking a statin.

Infants and Children: Safety and effectiveness have not been established for patients under 10 years of age. Consult your doctor for specific advice.

Special Concerns: Important elements of treatment for high cholesterol include proper diet, weight loss, regular moderate exercise, and avoidance of certain medications that may increase cholesterol levels. It is important that you maintain a recommended healthy diet and cooperate with other treatments your doctor may suggest.

OVERDOSE
Symptoms: No specific ones have been reported; overdose is unlikely.

What to Do: Emergency instructions not applicable.

DRUG INTERACTIONS
No known drug interactions.

FOOD INTERACTIONS
No known food interactions.

DISEASE INTERACTIONS
Consult your doctor if you have liver disease. Patients with liver disease should not take ezetimibe while taking a statin.

Famciclovir

BRAND NAME
Famvir

Famvir 500 mg
(SMITHKLINE BEECHAM)

▶ Drug Class: Antiviral

▶ Available in: Tablets

▶ Available OTC? No

▶ As Generic? No

Side Effects

SERIOUS
Extreme drowsiness. Call your doctor immediately.

COMMON
Headache, nausea.

LESS COMMON
Fatigue, vomiting, diarrhea, itchiness, rash, hallucinations, confusion, sore throat, back or joint pain, sinus infection, fever, shivering.

PRINCIPAL USES
To treat shingles (herpes zoster) and recurrent genital herpes.

HOW THE DRUG WORKS
Famciclovir interferes with the activity of specific enzymes needed for the replication of DNA in viral cells, thus preventing the virus from multiplying.

DOSAGE
For shingles (herpes zoster): 500 mg every 8 hours for 7 days. The effectiveness of famciclovir in treating herpes zoster is usually determined after 2 days of regular use. The best effect is achieved if the medicine is prescribed immediately after the diagnosis is made. For recurrent genital herpes: 250 mg twice a day for up to 1 year. It should be taken at the first sign of recurrence.

ONSET OF EFFECT
Within 1 hour.

DURATION OF ACTION
Unknown.

DIETARY ADVICE
No special restrictions.

STORAGE
Store in a tightly sealed container away from heat, moisture, and direct light.

IF YOU MISS A DOSE
Take it as soon as you remember. If it is near the time for the next dose, skip the missed dose and resume your regular dosage schedule. Do not double the next dose.

STOPPING THE DRUG
Take it as prescribed for the full treatment period, even if you feel better before the end of therapy. The decision to stop taking the drug should be made by your doctor.

PROLONGED USE
This drug is not intended for prolonged use, but under some circumstances it may be used for an extended period for the suppression of a chronic herpesvirus infection.

PRECAUTIONS
Over 60: No special problems expected except for older persons with impaired kidney or liver function.

Driving and Hazardous Work: Famciclovir may cause dizziness and fatigue. Do not drive or engage in hazardous work until you determine how the medicine affects you.

Alcohol: No special precautions are necessary.

Pregnancy: Studies of the use of famciclovir in pregnant women have not been done. Consult your doctor about the risk of taking famciclovir during pregnancy.

Breast Feeding: Famciclovir may pass into breast milk; avoid or discontinue use while nursing.

Infants and Children: The safety and effectiveness of famciclovir for anyone under 18 have not been established. It should be used only under close medical supervision.

Special Concerns: This medicine is not recommended for use if you have had a bone marrow transplant or a kidney transplant. Before taking famciclovir, tell the doctor if your immune system is compromised. Do not take famciclovir if you have had an allergic response to it previously. Keep the affected area of skin clean and dry; wear loose-fitting clothing. Your doctor may periodi-

cally wish to take blood tests to evaluate your kidney function.

OVERDOSE
Symptoms: No cases of overdose have been reported.

What to Do: An overdose is unlikely to occur. However, if you have any reason to suspect an overdose, call your doctor, emergency medical services (EMS), or the nearest poison control center immediately.

DRUG INTERACTIONS
Other drugs may interact with famciclovir. Consult your doctor for specific advice if you are taking probenecid or any other prescription or over-the-counter drug.

FOOD INTERACTIONS
No known food interactions.

DISEASE INTERACTIONS
Consult your doctor if you have any disorder or condition associated with a weakened immune system, such as HIV infection or AIDS. Use of famciclovir may cause complications in patients with impaired liver or kidney function, since these organs work together to remove the medication from the body.

Famotidine

Pepcid 20 mg
(MERCK)

Additional photographs

▶ Drug Class: Histamine (H2) blocker

▶ Available in: Tablets, powder for suspension, orally disintegrating tablets, chewable tablets

▶ Available OTC? Yes

▶ As Generic? Yes

Side Effects

SERIOUS
Irregular heart rhythm (palpitations), slowed heartbeat, severe blood problems resulting in unusual bleeding, bruising, fever, chills, and increased susceptibility to infection. Call your doctor immediately.

COMMON
Headache, fatigue, drowsiness, dizziness, nausea, vomiting, abdominal pain, diarrhea, constipation.

LESS COMMON
Blurred vision, decreased sexual desire or function, temporary hair loss, hallucinations, depression, insomnia, skin rash, hives, or redness.

PRINCIPAL USES
To treat heartburn, ulcers of the stomach and duodenum, conditions that cause excess production of stomach acid (such as Zollinger-Ellison syndrome), and gastroesophageal reflux (backwash of stomach acid into the esophagus, resulting in heartburn). Chewable tablets are taken for prevention or treatment of heartburn.

HOW THE DRUG WORKS
Famotidine blocks the action of histamine (a compound produced in the body's cells), which in turn decreases the stomach's secretion of hydrochloric acid. Once the production of stomach acid is decreased, the body is better able to heal itself.

DOSAGE
To prevent heartburn: 10 mg, 1 hour before meals. For excess stomach acid: 20 to 160 mg every 6 hours. For acid reflux disease: 20 mg twice a day for up to 6 weeks. For stomach ulcers: 40 mg once a day for 8 weeks. For duodenal ulcers: To start, 40 mg once a day at bedtime or 20 mg twice a day; later, 20 mg once a day. Chewable tablets— For treatment of heartburn: Chew one tablet (10 mg). For prevention of heartburn: Chew one tablet 15 to 60 minutes before eating.

ONSET OF EFFECT
Prescription form: Within 30 minutes. The lower dosage in the nonprescription form may take 45 minutes to relieve heartburn.

DURATION OF ACTION
Up to 12 hours.

DIETARY ADVICE
Take it after meals or with milk to minimize stomach irritation. Avoid foods that cause stomach irritation. Take chewable tablet with a glass of water.

STORAGE
Store tablets in a tightly sealed container away from heat, moisture, and direct light. After powder vials are reconstituted, store the medicine in the refrigerator, but keep it from freezing. Discard after 30 days.

IF YOU MISS A DOSE
Take it as soon as you remember. If it is near the time for the next dose, skip the missed dose and resume your regular dosage schedule. Do not double the next dose.

STOPPING THE DRUG
The decision to stop taking the prescription drug should be made in consultation with your doctor.

PROLONGED USE
Do not take the prescription drug for more than 8 weeks unless your doctor orders it. Do not take the over-the-counter drug for more than 2 weeks unless otherwise instructed by your doctor.

PRECAUTIONS
Over 60: Adverse reactions may be more likely and more severe in older patients.

Driving and Hazardous Work: Do not drive or engage in hazardous work until you determine how the medicine affects you.

Alcohol: Avoid alcohol while taking this drug; it may slow recovery. Also, this drug increases blood alcohol levels.

Pregnancy: Risks vary, depending on patient and dosage. Consult your physician for advice.

Breast Feeding: Famotidine passes into breast milk; you should avoid or discontinue use while breast feeding.

Infants and Children: Famotidine is not generally prescribed for infants and children.

Special Concerns: If necessary, famotidine may be given with antacids. Avoid cigarette smoking because it may increase secretion of stomach acid and thus worsen the disease.

OVERDOSE
Symptoms: Confusion, slurred speech, rapid heartbeat, difficulty breathing, delirium.

What to Do: Call your doctor, emergency medical services (EMS), or the nearest poison control center immediately.

DRUG INTERACTIONS
None reported.

FOOD INTERACTIONS
Carbonated drinks, citrus fruits and juices, caffeine-containing beverages, and other acidic foods or liquids may irritate the stomach or interfere with the therapeutic action of famotidine.

DISEASE INTERACTIONS
Patients with kidney disease should use famotidine in smaller, limited doses under careful supervision by a physician.

Felbamate

Felbatol 400 mg
(WALLACE)

▶ Drug Class: Anticonvulsant

▶ Available in: Oral suspension, tablets

▶ Available OTC? No

▶ As Generic? No

Side Effects

SERIOUS
Fever, weakness, sore throat, swollen glands, purple or red point-like spots on the skin, easy bruising, skin blistering, or yellowing of the eyes or skin may be signs of aplastic anemia, liver failure, or other potentially fatal complications. Call your doctor at once.

COMMON
Headache, nausea and vomiting, loss of appetite, stomach upset, constipation, sleepiness, insomnia, dizziness, anxiety, nervousness, tremor, muscle incoordination, runny nose and upper respiratory tract infection.

LESS COMMON
Blurred or double vision, coughing, diarrhea, abdominal pain, dry mouth. There are numerous additional side effects; consult your doctor if you are concerned about any adverse or unusual reactions.

PRINCIPAL USES
To control certain types of seizures due to epilepsy or other disorders. Because felbamate has a relatively high rate of potentially fatal side effects (including a serious blood disorder called aplastic anemia as well as liver disease), it is used only when other drugs have failed to control seizures. It may be used alone or combined with other anticonvulsants.

HOW THE DRUG WORKS
Felbamate is thought to depress the activity of certain parts of the brain and suppress the abnormal firing of neurons that causes seizures.

DOSAGE
Adults: 1,800 to 3,600 mg a day, in 3 or 4 divided doses. Children: 7 to 20 mg per lb of body weight, in 3 or 4 divided doses. Some patients may require higher doses. Low doses are used to start; the dose is gradually increased by your doctor to achieve the maximum therapeutic benefit. When switching to felbamate from other anticonvulsants, doses of the other drugs should be reduced gradually.

ONSET OF EFFECT
1 to 4 hours.

DURATION OF ACTION
Maximum effect persists for 18 to 24 hours or longer; effectiveness then gradually decreases.

DIETARY ADVICE
Take with food to minimize stomach upset.

STORAGE
Store in a tightly sealed container away from heat, moisture, and direct light.

IF YOU MISS A DOSE
Take it as soon as you remember. If it is near the time for the next dose, skip the missed dose and resume regular dosage schedule. Do not double the next dose, unless so advised by your doctor.

STOPPING THE DRUG
Never stop it abruptly; this may cause seizures. Your doctor will taper the dose over a period of weeks.

PROLONGED USE
Periodic examinations or laboratory tests to check blood counts and liver function may be needed.

PRECAUTIONS
Over 60: Older patients may require lower doses to minimize side effects.

Driving and Hazardous Work: Felbamate may cause drowsiness or dizziness. Do not drive or engage in hazardous work until you determine how the drug affects you.

Alcohol: May contribute to excessive drowsiness.

Pregnancy: Adequate studies of felbamate use during pregnancy have not been done, but many anticonvulsants are associated with an increased rate of birth defects. However, seizures during pregnancy can also increase the risks to the fetus. Discuss with your doctor the potential risks and benefits of using this drug while pregnant. Folate supplementation is recommended beginning 1 to 2 months before conception and throughout pregnancy.

Breast Feeding: Felbamate passes into breast milk, although at low levels. Consult your doctor for advice.

Infants and Children: Close medical supervision is advised for such patients.

Special Concerns: Your doctor may want you to wear a medical bracelet or carry an identification card saying that you are taking this drug.

OVERDOSE
Symptoms: Unknown; reports of felbamate overdose are very rare.

What to Do: If an excessive dose is taken, call your doctor, emergency medical services (EMS), or poison control center immediately.

DRUG INTERACTIONS
Felbamate can increase blood levels of certain anticonvulsants (phenytoin, valproic acid) and decrease blood levels of others (carbamazepine). Phenytoin and carbamazepine can decrease blood levels of felbamate. Patients sensitive to chemically related drugs, such as meprobamate or carisoprodol, may also be sensitive to felbamate.

FOOD INTERACTIONS
No known food interactions.

DISEASE INTERACTIONS
Special caution is advised if you have a history of any blood disorder, bone marrow depression (causing anemia), or liver disease.

Felodipine

Plendil 5 mg
(ASTRA MERCK)

▶ Drug Class: Calcium channel blocker

▶ Available in: Tablets, extended-release tablets

▶ Available OTC? No

▶ As Generic? No

Side Effects

SERIOUS
Irregular or slow heartbeat, low blood pressure (causing dizziness or faintness).

COMMON
Flushing or skin rash; headache; swelling of the lower legs or feet.

LESS COMMON
Dizziness, numbness or tingling sensation, chest pain, palpitations, weakness, runny nose, rapid pulse, sore throat, abdominal discomfort, nausea, constipation or diarrhea, cough, muscle cramps, back pain, overgrowth of the gums.

PRINCIPAL USES
To control high blood pressure (hypertension).

HOW THE DRUG WORKS
Felodipine interferes with the movement of calcium into heart muscle cells and the smooth muscle cells in the walls of the arteries. This action relaxes blood vessels (causing them to widen), which lowers blood pressure, increases the blood supply to the heart, and decreases the heart's overall workload.

DOSAGE
To start, 5 to 10 mg once a day. The dose may be increased if necessary to a maximum of 20 mg once a day. For patients over 65, starting dose is 2.5 mg per day, to a maximum dose of 10 mg per day.

ONSET OF EFFECT
Within 2 to 5 hours.

DURATION OF ACTION
24 hours.

DIETARY ADVICE
Felodipine should be taken either on an empty stomach or with a light meal. Do not crush or chew tablets.

STORAGE
Store in a tightly sealed container away from heat, moisture, and direct light.

IF YOU MISS A DOSE
Take it as soon as you remember. However, if it is near the time for the next dose, skip the missed dose and resume your regular dosage schedule. Do not double the next dose.

STOPPING THE DRUG
Do not stop taking felodipine suddenly, as this may cause potentially serious health problems. If therapy is to be discontinued, the dosage should be reduced gradually, according to your doctor's instructions.

PROLONGED USE
Consult your doctor about the need for medical examinations or laboratory studies to check liver function, kidney function, and heart function.

PRECAUTIONS
Over 60: Older patients are prescribed lower starting doses, which may be gradually increased until the doctor determines the appropriate individual maintenance dose.

Driving and Hazardous Work: Do not drive or engage in hazardous work until you determine how felodipine affects you.

Alcohol: Avoid alcohol while taking this medication as it may cause an excessive drop in blood pressure.

Pregnancy: Consult your physician to determine whether the benefits of felodipine outweigh its possible risks while pregnant.

Breast Feeding: Felodipine may pass into breast milk; caution is advised. Consult your doctor for specific advice.

Infants and Children: Felodipine is generally not prescribed for children.

Special Concerns: Tell all your health care providers that you are taking felodipine and carry a note that says you take this medicine. Felodipine can cause erectile dysfunction in some men. Nicotine can reduce the effectiveness of the medicine. Hot environments can exaggerate the blood-pressure-lowering effect of felodipine.

OVERDOSE
Symptoms: Weakness, light-headedness, rapid pulse, shortness of breath, tremors, flushed skin, fainting, slurred speech.

What to Do: Call your doctor, emergency medical services (EMS), or the nearest poison control center immediately.

DRUG INTERACTIONS
Consult your doctor for advice if you are taking anticonvulsants, beta-blockers, digitalis drugs, carbamazepine, cyclosporine, digoxin, disopyramide, magnesium, phenobarbital, phenytoin, quinidine, rifampin, cimetidine, or erythromycin.

FOOD INTERACTIONS
Grapefruit juice should be avoided because it can amplify the effect of the drug and cause a serious drop in blood pressure. Avoid excessive salt intake.

DISEASE INTERACTIONS
Caution is advised when taking felodipine. Consult your doctor if you have any of the following: congestive heart failure, a history of heart attack or stroke, heart rhythm disturbances, or impaired liver or kidney function.

Fenofibrate

▶ Drug Class: Antilipidemic
 (triglyceride-lowering agent)

▶ Available in: Capsules

▶ Available OTC? No

▶ As Generic? No

Side Effects

SERIOUS
Fever, unusual or unexplained muscle aches and tenderness. Call your doctor right away.

COMMON
Skin rash, infection, flu-like symptoms.

LESS COMMON
Fatigue, general feeling of pain, headache, belching, flatulence, nausea, vomiting, constipation, decreased libido, dizziness, nasal congestion, itching, visual disturbances, eye irritation.

PRINCIPAL USES
To treat high levels of blood triglyceride. Usually prescribed after other treatments—including diet, weight loss, exercise, and control of diabetes (when present)—fail to lower triglyceride levels adequately.

HOW THE DRUG WORKS
Fenofibrate speeds the removal of triglycerides from the lipoprotein known as very low density lipoprotein (VLDL), which is converted to low density lipoprotein (LDL). In some people total and LDL cholesterol levels may rise while triglycerides fall.

DOSAGE
Adults: 67 mg (1 capsule) once a day. The dose may be increased by your doctor to no more than 201 mg (3 capsules) a day.

ONSET OF EFFECT
Unknown.

DURATION OF ACTION
Unknown.

DIETARY ADVICE
Follow your doctor's dietary advice to improve control over high blood pressure and help prevent heart disease. The American Heart Association publishes a "Healthy Heart" diet; discuss this with your doctor. Limit intake of alcohol, which can raise triglyceride levels.

STORAGE
Store in a tightly sealed container away from heat, moisture, and direct light.

IF YOU MISS A DOSE
If you miss a dose on one day, do not double the dose the next day.

STOPPING THE DRUG
Do not stop taking fenofibrate on your own; the level of triglycerides in your blood will increase.

PROLONGED USE
During therapy, your doctor will conduct periodic tests to measure triglyceride levels. Therapy should be discontinued if there is an inadequate response to the medication following two months of therapy at the maximum dose of 3 capsules per day.

PRECAUTIONS
Over 60: No special problems are expected.

Driving and Hazardous Work: The use of fenofibrate should not impair your ability to perform such tasks safely.

Alcohol: Alcohol intake should be limited because it can raise triglyceride levels.

Pregnancy: Do not take fenofibrate while pregnant unless your doctor indicates that the risks of stopping the drug are too great. Triglycerides increase substantially during pregnancy and extremely high triglycerides can trigger an attack of acute pancreatitis.

Breast Feeding: Avoid or discontinue use while nursing.

Infants and Children: Safety and effectiveness have not been established for children under age 18.

Special Concerns: The most important treatment for high levels of blood triglycerides is a proper diet, weight loss, regular moderate exercise, the avoidance of certain medications, and control of diabetes. Because fenofibrate has potential side effects, it is important that you maintain a healthy diet and cooperate with other treatment strategies your physician may suggest. Fenofibrate may increase the chances of gallbladder, liver, and pancreas problems; your physician will order periodic blood tests.

OVERDOSE
Symptoms: No specific ones have been reported.

What to Do: If someone takes a much larger dose than prescribed, call your doctor, emergency medical services (EMS), or the nearest poison control center immediately.

DRUG INTERACTIONS
Certain drugs may interact adversely with fenofibrate, particularly anticoagulants such as warfarin, niacin, and any of the group of cholesterol-lowering drugs referred to as "statins." It is usually necessary to reduce the dose of warfarin to prevent bleeding. The combination of fenofibrate with either niacin or a statin drug can cause severe myositis (muscle inflammation), which can release a protein that damages the kidneys. Consult your doctor for specific advice.

FOOD INTERACTIONS
No known food interactions.

DISEASE INTERACTIONS
Inform your doctor if you have any of the following problems: gallstones, stomach or intestinal ulcer, kidney disease, muscle disease, or liver disease. The dose of fenofibrate must be reduced in those with significant kidney damage.

Fenoprofen Calcium

Nalfon 300 mg
(DISTA)

▶ Drug Class: Nonsteroidal anti-inflammatory drug (NSAID)

▶ Available in: Capsules, tablets

▶ Available OTC? No

▶ As Generic? Yes

Side Effects

SERIOUS
Shortness of breath or wheezing, with or without swelling of legs or other signs of heart failure; chest pain; peptic ulcer disease with vomiting of blood; black, tarry stools; decreasing kidney function. Call your doctor immediately.

COMMON
Nausea, vomiting, heartburn, diarrhea, constipation, headache, dizziness, sleepiness.

LESS COMMON
Ulcers or sores in mouth, depression, rashes or blistering of skin, ringing sound in the ears, unusual tingling or numbness of the hands or feet, seizures, blurred vision. Also elevated potassium levels, decreased blood counts; such problems can be detected by your doctor.

PRINCIPAL USES
To treat mild to moderate pain and inflammation caused by tendinitis, arthritis, bursitis, gout, soft tissue injuries, migraine and other vascular headaches, menstrual cramps, and other conditions. When patients fail to respond to one NSAID, another may be tried. The greatest effectiveness often requires trial and error of several different NSAIDs.

HOW THE DRUG WORKS
NSAIDs work by interfering with the formation of prostaglandins, naturally occurring substances in the body that cause inflammation and make nerves more sensitive to pain impulses. NSAIDs also have other modes of action that are less well understood.

DOSAGE
Adults— For arthritis: 300 to 600 mg, 3 or 4 times a day, to a maximum of 3,200 mg a day. Full effect may take 2 to 4 weeks to begin. For mild to moderate pain: 200 mg every 4 to 6 hours.

ONSET OF EFFECT
15 to 30 minutes.

DURATION OF ACTION
4 to 6 hours.

DIETARY ADVICE
Take with food; maintain your usual food and fluid intake.

STORAGE
Store in a tightly sealed container away from heat, moisture, and direct light.

IF YOU MISS A DOSE
Take it as soon as you remember. If it is near the time for the next dose, skip the missed dose and resume your regular dosage schedule. Do not double the next dose.

STOPPING THE DRUG
The decision to stop taking the drug should be made in consultation with your physician.

PROLONGED USE
Prolonged use can cause gastrointestinal problems, including ulceration and bleeding, kidney dysfunction, and liver inflammation. See your doctor for regular evaluation.

PRECAUTIONS
Over 60: Because of the potentially greater consequences of gastrointestinal side effects, the dose of NSAIDs for older patients, especially those over age 70, is often cut in half.

Driving and Hazardous Work: Do not drive or engage in hazardous work until you determine how the medicine affects you.

Alcohol: Avoid alcohol when using this medication because it increases the risk of stomach irritation.

Pregnancy: Avoid or discontinue this drug if you are pregnant or are planning to become pregnant.

Breast Feeding: Fenoprofen passes into breast milk; avoid or discontinue use while nursing.

Infants and Children: May be used in exceptional circumstances; consult your doctor.

Special Concerns: Because NSAIDs can interfere with blood coagulation, this drug should be stopped at least 3 days prior to any surgery.

OVERDOSE
Symptoms: Nausea, vomiting, severe headache, confusion, seizures.

What to Do: Call your doctor, emergency medical services (EMS), or the nearest poison control center immediately.

DRUG INTERACTIONS
Do not take this drug with aspirin or any other NSAID without your doctor's approval. In addition, consult your doctor if you are taking antihypertensives, steroids, anticoagulants, antibiotics, itraconazole or ketoconazole, plicamycin, penicillamine, valproic acid, phenytoin, cyclosporine, digitalis drugs, lithium, methotrexate, probenecid, triamterene, or zidovudine.

FOOD INTERACTIONS
No known food interactions

DISEASE INTERACTIONS
Caution is advised when taking fenoprofen. Consult your doctor if you have any of the following: bleeding problems, inflammation or ulcers of the stomach and intestines, diabetes mellitus systemic lupus erythematosus (SLE, lupus), anemia, asthma, epilepsy, Parkinson's disease, kidney stones, or a history of heart disease or alcohol abuse. Use of fenoprofen may cause complications in patients with liver or kidney disease, since these organs work together to remove the drug from the body.

Fentanyl Transdermal

BRAND NAME
Duragesic

▶ Drug Class: Opioid (narcotic) analgesic

▶ Available in: Transdermal (skin) patch

▶ Available OTC? No

▶ As Generic? No

Side Effects

SERIOUS
Seizures, severe drowsiness, hallucinations, slow heartbeat, very slow or weak breathing, cold, clammy skin, pinpoint pupils of eyes. Call your doctor immediately.

COMMON
Dizziness, nausea or vomiting, constipation, drowsiness, urine retention, itching.

LESS COMMON
Sweating, skin reaction at patch site, rigid muscles, fainting, jerking body movements (myoclonus).

PRINCIPAL USES
To control severe chronic pain.

HOW THE DRUG WORKS
Fentanyl, a narcotic, relieves pain by acting on specific areas of the spinal cord and brain that process pain signals from nerves throughout the body.

DOSAGE
Attach the patch to the skin using the dose recommended by your doctor. Replace the patch every 72 hours or as your doctor directs. To apply, remove the patch from its protective pouch and remove the liner from the sticky side of the patch. Place the patch on a site that is hairless and dry, and hold it in place for 10 to 30 seconds to ensure adhesion. Wash the area with water if necessary, but do not use soap, lotion, alcohol, or other substances that may irritate the skin. Do not apply it in the same place more than once within a 3-day period. Avoid any area that is burned, irritated, or excessively oily. Wash your hands after applying a new patch. Remove an old patch after 72 hours (3 days), fold it onto itself and dispose of it in the toilet. Fentanyl transdermal patches are available in the following concentrations: 25 micrograms per hour (mcg/hr); 50 mcg/hr; 75 mcg/hr; 100 mcg/hr.

ONSET OF EFFECT
12 to 24 hours.

DURATION OF ACTION
Up to 72 hours.

DIETARY ADVICE
The patch can be applied without regard to diet.

STORAGE
Store the patch in its protective pouch away from heat, moisture, and direct light.

IF YOU MISS A DOSE
Apply a new patch as soon as you remember. Do not apply more than one patch at a time, unless directed to do otherwise by your doctor. Remove the patch 3 days after applying it.

STOPPING THE DRUG
The decision to stop using the drug should be made by your doctor. It may be necessary to reduce the dose gradually if the medication is used for a long time, to decrease the risk of suffering withdrawal symptoms.

PROLONGED USE
Prolonged use may result in physical dependence.

PRECAUTIONS
Over 60: Adverse reactions may be more likely and more severe in older patients. The smallest-dose patch is generally used at the beginning of therapy.

Driving and Hazardous Work: The use of fentanyl may impair your ability to perform such tasks safely.

Alcohol: Avoid alcohol.

Pregnancy: Adequate human studies have not been done. Before taking fentanyl, discuss with your doctor the relative risks and benefits of using this drug while pregnant.

Breast Feeding: This drug passes into breast milk; avoid or discontinue using it while nursing.

Infants and Children: This drug should not be used by patients under age 18 who weigh less than 110 pounds. Safety and effectiveness for children under the age of 12 have not been determined.

Special Concerns: Do not alter your dose or suddenly stop using this drug without consulting your doctor. Abruptly stopping its use may cause withdrawal symptoms. Heat can cause fentanyl to be absorbed more rapidly. Avoid heating pads, sunbathing, or long showers or baths in hot water. Not recommended for postoperative pain.

OVERDOSE
Symptoms: Seizures, severe drowsiness, hallucinations, slow heartbeat, very slow or weak breathing, cold, clammy skin, pinpoint pupils of eyes.

What to Do: Call your doctor, emergency medical services (EMS), or the nearest poison control center immediately.

DRUG INTERACTIONS
Consult your doctor for specific advice if you are taking benzodiazepines; central nervous system depressants such as opiates, barbiturates, and tranquilizers; or antidepressants, amiodarone, clonidine, or MAO inhibitors.

FOOD INTERACTIONS
No known food interactions.

DISEASE INTERACTIONS
Consult your doctor if you have any of the following: liver disease, kidney disease, prostate problems, gallbladder disease, intestinal problems such as colitis, underactive thyroid, brain tumor, any heart disease, anemia, or a history of alcohol or drug abuse. Fever may increase the rate at which the drug is absorbed by the body, thus increasing risk of overdose.

Fentanyl Transmucosal

BRAND NAME
Actiq

▶ Drug Class: Opioid (narcotic) analgesic

▶ Available in: Oral transmucosal (inside the mouth) lozenge

▶ Available OTC? No

▶ As Generic? No

Side Effects

SERIOUS
Seizures, severe drowsiness, hallucinations, slow heartbeat, very slow or weak breathing, cold, clammy skin, pinpoint pupils of eyes. Call your doctor immediately.

COMMON
Dizziness, nausea or vomiting, constipation, drowsiness, urine retention, itching.

LESS COMMON
Sweating, skin reaction at patch site, rigid muscles, fainting, jerking body movements (myoclonus).

PRINCIPAL USES
To manage flare-ups of cancer pain in people who are already receiving and who are tolerant to narcotic (opioid) therapy for underlying cancer pain. People considered opioid tolerant are those taking at least 60 mg of morphine a day, 50 mcg of transdermal fentanyl per hour, or an equivalent dose of another narcotic for a week or longer. Fentanyl lozenges are not for short-term pain, including pain from injuries or surgery.

HOW THE DRUG WORKS
Fentanyl, a narcotic, relieves pain by acting on specific areas of the spinal cord and brain that process pain signals from nerves throughout the body.

DOSAGE
Your oncologist or physician will determine the appropriate dosage. Dosage will be individually adjusted to provide adequate pain relief with minimal side effects. Do not consume more than 4 lozenges per day (no more than 2 per flare-up); if you are not getting adequate pain relief, consult your doctor.

ONSET OF EFFECT
Within 15 to 45 minutes.

DURATION OF ACTION
Unknown.

DIETARY ADVICE
You may drink water before using the drug. Do not eat or drink anything while using it.

STORAGE
Store the lozenge in its protective package away from heat, moisture, and direct light in a child-resistant locked storage space. Do not freeze or refrigerate.

IF YOU MISS A DOSE
Not applicable. This drug is used as needed for breakthrough cancer pain that is not successfully controlled by regularly prescribed pain medication.

STOPPING THE DRUG
The lozenges are used on an as needed basis. However, because fentanyl can be addictive, it may be necessary to reduce the dose gradually if the medication is used for a long time, to decrease the risk of withdrawal symptoms.

PROLONGED USE
Prolonged use may result in physical dependence.

PRECAUTIONS
Over 60: Adverse reactions may be more likely and more severe in older patients. The smallest-dose lozenge is generally used at the beginning of therapy.

Driving and Hazardous Work: The use of fentanyl may impair your ability to perform such tasks safely.

Alcohol: Avoid alcohol.

Pregnancy: Adequate human studies have not been done. Before taking fentanyl, discuss with your doctor the relative risks and benefits of using this drug while pregnant.

Breast Feeding: This drug passes into breast milk; avoid or discontinue using it while nursing.

Infants and Children: Safety and effectiveness for children under the age of 16 have not been determined. The lozenges contain a high concentration of fentanyl which can be fatal to a child.

Special Concerns: You must be opioid tolerant to use this form of fentanyl. The lozenges contain a high concentration of the drug and can cause serious, possibly fatal side effects in those not already taking narcotic pain relievers. If you do not finish the lozenge within 15 minutes, dispose of the remainder appropriately. Your doctor or health care provider will teach you how to do so.

OVERDOSE
Symptoms: Seizures, severe drowsiness, hallucinations, slow heartbeat, very slow or weak breathing, cold, clammy skin, pinpoint pupils of eyes.

What to Do: Call your doctor, emergency medical services (EMS), or the nearest poison control center immediately.

DRUG INTERACTIONS
Consult your doctor for specific advice if you are taking benzodiazepines; central nervous system depressants such as barbiturates, and tranquilizers; or antidepressants, amiodarone, clonidine, or MAO inhibitors.

FOOD INTERACTIONS
No known food interactions.

DISEASE INTERACTIONS
Consult your doctor if you have any of the following: liver disease, kidney disease, prostate problems, gallbladder disease, intestinal problems such as colitis, underactive thyroid, brain tumor, any heart disease, anemia, chronic obstructive pulmonary disease or other respiratory illnesses, or a history of alcohol or drug abuse. Fever may increase the rate at which the drug is absorbed by the body, thus increasing risk of overdose.

BRAND NAMES
Feosol, Fer-In-Sol, Fer-Iron, Fero-Gradumet, Ferospace, Ferra-TD, Ferralyn Lanacaps

Generic 300 mg
(UPSHER-SMITH)

833

Additional photographs

▶ Drug Class: Dietary supplement

▶ Available in: Capsules, drops, elixir, solution, tablets

▶ Available OTC? Yes

▶ As Generic? Yes

Side Effects

SERIOUS
No serious side effects are associated with ferrous salts, except for iron overload due to prolonged, inappropriate use of the mineral.

COMMON
Nausea, constipation, black stools.

LESS COMMON
Stained teeth (with liquid forms), stomach pain, vomiting, diarrhea.

PRINCIPAL USES
To help increase the body's stores of iron, a mineral essential to the manufacture of red blood cells. An insufficient number of red blood cells results in anemia.

HOW THE DRUG WORKS
Ferrous salts are required for the production of hemoglobin in developing red blood cells. Hemoglobin is a complex iron-based protein in the red cell that carries oxygen to the body's tissues and carries carbon dioxide gas away from the tissues to be exhaled by the lungs.

DOSAGE
For iron deficiency, 325 mg, 3 times a day. Children: 5 to 10 mg for every 2.2 lbs (1 kg) of body weight 3 times a day.

ONSET OF EFFECT
From 5 to 7 days. Depending on the extent of the iron deficiency, more than 3 months of therapy may be needed for maximum benefit to be realized.

DURATION OF ACTION
Depends on the body's ability to utilize it.

DIETARY ADVICE
Take 1 hour before or 2 hours after eating.

STORAGE
Store in a tightly sealed container away from heat and direct light. Keep the liquid form from freezing.

IF YOU MISS A DOSE
Take it as soon as you remember. If it is near the time for the next dose, skip the missed dose and resume your regular dosage schedule. Do not double the next dose.

STOPPING THE DRUG
If the medication was prescribed, the decision to stop taking this supplement should be made by your physician.

PROLONGED USE
Prolonged use may result in the accumulation of iron in the tissues, the effects of which can include liver damage, heart problems, diabetes, erectile dysfunction, and unusually bronzed skin. Do not take iron supplements without consulting your doctor.

PRECAUTIONS
Over 60: Problems in older adults have not been reported with intake of normal daily recommended amounts.

Driving and Hazardous Work: No problems are expected.

Alcohol: Avoid alcohol while taking this medication because it may cause excess absorption of iron.

Pregnancy: This medication should be taken during pregnancy only if your doctor so advises.

Breast Feeding: No problems are expected during breast feeding; however, consult your doctor before taking ferrous salts.

Infants and Children: No unusual problems reported in infants and children. Close medical supervision is nonetheless recommended, and iron tablets should be stored out of reach of small children to avoid accidental ingestion, which can be severely toxic.

Special Concerns: The genetic disorder hemochromatosis, in which iron absorption is excessive, is very common. Iron deficiency may also be the first indication of a gastrointestinal malignancy. Therefore, iron should only be taken on the advice of a physician. Liquid forms of iron can stain the teeth. To prevent stains, mix each dose in water, fruit juice, or tomato juice and drink it through a straw. When using a dropper, place the dose on the back of the tongue and drink a glass of water or juice. Tooth stains can be removed by brushing with baking soda or 3% hydrogen peroxide.

OVERDOSE
Symptoms: Lethargy, nausea, vomiting, weak and rapid pulse, dehydration, loss of consciousness.

What to Do: Call your doctor, emergency medical services (EMS), or the nearest poison control center immediately.

DRUG INTERACTIONS
The following drugs may interact with ferrous salts and prevent their absorption: antacids, antibiotics, fluoroquinalones, levodopa, cholestyramine, or vitamin E. Consult your doctor for specific advice.

FOOD INTERACTIONS
Some foods can reduce the effect of this drug. The following foods should be avoided or taken in small amounts for at least 1 hour before and 2 hours after iron is taken: Eggs, milk, spinach, cheese, yogurt, tea, coffee, whole-grain bread, cereal, and bran.

DISEASE INTERACTIONS
Consult your doctor if you have any of the following: a history of alcoholism; kidney disease; liver disease; porphyria; rheumatoid arthritis; asthma; allergies; heart disease; or a stomach ulcer, colitis, or another intestinal problem.

Fexofenadine

BRAND NAME
Allegra

Allegra 60 mg
(HOECHST MARION ROUSSEL)

▶ Drug Class: Antihistamine

▶ Available in: Capsules

▶ Available OTC? No

▶ As Generic? No

Side Effects

SERIOUS
No serious side effects are associated with the use of fexofenadine.

COMMON
No common side effects are associated with the use of fexofenadine.

LESS COMMON
Drowsiness, fatigue, stomach upset, painful menstrual bleeding.

PRINCIPAL USES
To prevent or relieve symptoms of hay fever and other allergies, and to treat itchy skin and hives.

HOW THE DRUG WORKS
Fexofenadine blocks the effects of histamine, a naturally occurring substance within the body that causes swelling, itching, sneezing, watery eyes, hives, and other symptoms of allergic reaction.

DOSAGE
For adults and children age 12 and over: 60 mg, 2 times a day, or 180 mg once a day. For patients with decreased kidney function, a starting dose of 60 mg once a day is recommended. Children under age 12: Safety and effectiveness of fexofenadine in this age group have not been established.

ONSET OF EFFECT
Within 1 to 2 hours.

DURATION OF ACTION
12 hours or longer.

DIETARY ADVICE
This drug can be taken without regard to food or drink.

STORAGE
Store in a tightly sealed container in a dry place away from heat and direct light at room temperature.

IF YOU MISS A DOSE
Take it as soon as you remember. If it is near the time for the next dose, skip the missed dose and resume your regular dosage schedule. Do not double the next dose.

STOPPING THE DRUG
You should take it as prescribed for the full treatment period, but you may stop if you are feeling better before the scheduled end of therapy. Fexofenadine can be used as needed to relieve symptoms of hay fever or other allergies.

PROLONGED USE
Tolerance, or decreased responsiveness to the drug, generally does not develop with prolonged use of fexofenadine; if it does, consult your physician. No special problems are expected with long-term use.

PRECAUTIONS
Over 60: No special problems are expected.

Driving and Hazardous Work: In rare cases fexofenadine may cause drowsiness and fatigue. Do not drive or engage in hazardous work until you determine how the medicine affects you.

Alcohol: No special precautions are necessary.

Pregnancy: In animal studies, fexofenadine did not cause birth defects. Adequate, well-controlled studies in humans have not been done. Consult your doctor about taking fexofenadine if you are pregnant or are planning to become pregnant.

Breast Feeding: Fexofenadine may pass into breast milk; caution is advised. Consult your doctor for specific advice about the use of fexofenadine while nursing.

Infants and Children: Side effects are not expected to be any different in children ages 12 to 18 than those in patients 18 and older. The safety and effectiveness of fexofenadine for children up to 12 years of age have not been established.

OVERDOSE
Symptoms: Extreme drowsiness or fatigue.

What to Do: An overdose of fexofenadine is unlikely to be life-threatening. However, if someone takes a much larger dose than prescribed, call your doctor, emergency medical services (EMS), or local poison control center right away.

DRUG INTERACTIONS
There are no known interactions between fexofenadine and other drugs.

FOOD INTERACTIONS
No known food interactions.

DISEASE INTERACTIONS
Consult your physician if you have impaired kidney function.

Fexofenadine/Pseudoephedrine

▶ Drug Class: Antihistamine/ decongestant

▶ Available in: Extended-release tablets

▶ Available OTC? No

▶ As Generic? No

Side Effects

SERIOUS
Palpitations, shortness of breath, breathing difficulty. Stop taking the medication and call your doctor right away.

COMMON
Headache, insomnia, nausea.

LESS COMMON
Dry mouth, indigestion, throat irritation, dizziness, agitation, back pain, anxiety, nervousness, stomach pain, upper respiratory infection.

PRINCIPAL USES
To prevent or relieve symptoms of seasonal allergies such as hay fever.

HOW THE DRUG WORKS
Fexofenadine blocks the effects of histamine, a naturally occurring substance within the body that causes swelling, itching, sneezing, watery eyes, hives, and other symptoms of allergic reaction. Pseudoephedrine narrows and constricts blood vessels to decrease the blood flow to swollen nasal passages and other tissues, which in turn reduces nasal secretions, shrinks swollen nasal mucous membranes, and improves airflow in nasal passages.

DOSAGE
Adults and teenagers: 1 tablet (60 mg fexofenadine/120 mg pseudoephedrine) twice a day.

ONSET OF EFFECT
Within 1 to 2 hours.

DURATION OF ACTION
12 hours or longer.

DIETARY ADVICE
This medication should be taken at least 1 hour before or 2 hours after a meal. Taking it with food delays the onset of the drug's effects. The tablet should be swallowed whole.

STORAGE
Store in a tightly sealed container away from heat, moisture, and direct light.

IF YOU MISS A DOSE
Take it as soon as you remember. If it is near the time for the next dose, skip the missed dose and resume your regular dosage schedule. Do not double the next dose.

STOPPING THE DRUG
You may stop taking the drug before the scheduled end of therapy if you are feeling better.

PROLONGED USE
Consult your doctor about taking this drug for more than 5 to 7 days.

PRECAUTIONS
Over 60: Adverse reactions may be more likely and more severe in older patients.

Driving and Hazardous Work: Do not drive or engage in hazardous work until you determine how the medicine affects you.

Alcohol: No special precautions are necessary.

Pregnancy: Adequate human studies have not been done. Before taking this drug, tell your doctor if you are or are planning to become pregnant. Discuss with your doctor the relative risks and benefits of using this drug while pregnant.

Breast Feeding: The pseudoephedrine component of this drug passes into breast milk; avoid or discontinue taking this drug while breast feeding.

Infants and Children: Not recommended for use by children under age 12.

Special Concerns: If your symptoms do not improve within 7 days, check with your doctor. To help prevent insomnia, take the last dose at least 2 hours before your bedtime.

OVERDOSE
Symptoms: No cases of overdose with this drug have been reported.

What to Do: An overdose is unlikely; however, if you have reason to suspect one has occurred, call emergency medical services (EMS) to receive evaluation and treatment.

DRUG INTERACTIONS
This drug and MAO inhibitors should not be used within 14 days of each other. Consult your doctor for specific advice if you are taking antihypertensives or digitalis drugs.

FOOD INTERACTIONS
No known food interactions.

DISEASE INTERACTIONS
You should not take this drug if you have a history of narrow-angle glaucoma, urinary retention, severe high blood pressure, or severe coronary artery disease. Caution is advised if you have mild to moderate high blood pressure, diabetes mellitus, a history of angina or heart attack, an overactive thyroid gland, impaired kidney function, or an enlarged prostate.

Finasteride

BRAND NAMES
Propecia, Proscar

Proscar 5 mg
(MERCK)

▶ Drug Class: 5-alpha reductase inhibitor

▶ Available in: Tablets

▶ Available OTC? No

▶ As Generic? No

Side Effects

SERIOUS
No serious side effects are associated with the use of finasteride.

COMMON
No common side effects are associated with the use of finasteride.

LESS COMMON
Reduced sex drive, erectile dysfunction (impotence), decreased quantity of ejaculate. It should be noted that this decrease is not a sign of reduced fertility.

PRINCIPAL USES
To treat benign prostatic hyperplasia (BPH)—that is, noncancerous enlargement of the prostate gland, which is extremely common among men over 50. Also used to treat male pattern hair loss.

HOW THE DRUG WORKS
Finasteride halts or reverses enlargement of the prostate by blocking the action of the enzyme 5-alpha reductase, which the body needs to produce dihydrotestosterone (DHT), a chemical involved in the mechanism that enlarges the prostate. DHT is also integral to the processs of male pattern hair loss; by decreasing DHT concentrations in the scalp, finasteride may slow or reverse this process.

DOSAGE
For BPH: 5 mg once a day. For male pattern hair loss: 1 mg once a day.

ONSET OF EFFECT
Unknown.

DURATION OF ACTION
For BPH: 24 hours for a single dose; up to 2 weeks after standard therapy is ended. For hair loss: New hair resulting from finasteride treatments will likely regress following discontinuation of the medication.

DIETARY ADVICE
Finasteride can be taken without regard to diet. If you have trouble swallowing the tablet whole, you can crush it and take it with liquid or food.

STORAGE
Store in a tightly sealed container away from heat, moisture, and direct light.

IF YOU MISS A DOSE
If you miss a dose on one day, do not double the dose the next day.

STOPPING THE DRUG
The decision to stop taking the drug should be made by your doctor.

PROLONGED USE
If you take this drug for a prolonged period for BPH, see your doctor regularly so that changes in prostate size can be monitored. For hair loss, continued use is recommended to sustain the drug's benefits.

PRECAUTIONS
Over 60: No special problems are expected.

Driving and Hazardous Work: The use of finasteride should not impair your ability to perform such tasks safely.

Alcohol: No special precautions are necessary.

Pregnancy: Although finasteride is not prescribed for women, those who are pregnant or planning to become pregnant should not handle the medication, especially if it is crushed or broken, because it can have an adverse effect on a male fetus. Men who take finasteride should use a barrier method of birth control (such as a condom), which prevents the female sexual partner from being exposed to small quantities of the drug present in semen.

Breast Feeding: Women who are nursing should avoid contact with finasteride or the sperm of a man who is taking the drug.

Infants and Children: Finasteride is not prescribed for children.

Special Concerns: Before taking this medicine for BPH, you should have a digital rectal examination and other tests for prostate cancer. Note that finasteride may affect the results of the prostate-specific antigen (PSA) test for prostate cancer; be sure any doctor you see for treatment, including your dentist, knows that you are taking this drug.

OVERDOSE
Symptoms: No specific ones have been reported.

What to Do: An overdose of finasteride is unlikely to be life-threatening. However, if someone takes a much larger dose than prescribed, call your doctor, emergency medical services (EMS), or the nearest poison control center.

DRUG INTERACTIONS
Consult your doctor for specific advice if you are taking amantadine, amphetamines, antihistamines, antidepressants, antidyskinetics (medications for Parkinson's disease or similar conditions), antipsychotics, appetite suppressants, anticholinergics (medications for stomach spasms or cramps), bronchodilators, decongestants, ephedrine, or pseudoephedrine.

FOOD INTERACTIONS
No known food interactions.

DISEASE INTERACTIONS
Caution is advised when taking finasteride. Before you start, consult your doctor if you have liver disease, which may magnify the effects of finasteride.

Flavoxate

Urispas 100 mg
(SmithKline Beecham)

▶ Drug Class: Urinary tract antispasmodic

▶ Available in: Tablets

▶ Available OTC? No

▶ As Generic? No

Side Effects

SERIOUS
Rash, fever, rapid pulse. Call your doctor right away.

COMMON
Confusion, dry mouth and throat, blurred vision, heightened sensitivity of the eyes to light (photophobia), decreased ability to sweat.

LESS COMMON
Dizziness, headache, nervousness, drowsiness, difficulty concentrating, abdominal pain, difficulty focusing the eyes, constipation, nausea, vomiting, hives, fever.

PRINCIPAL USES
To relieve the symptoms of urinary tract spasms, which may include chronic urinary urgency, frequent urination, pain, and incontinence.

HOW THE DRUG WORKS
Flavoxate blocks nerve impulses to the smooth muscles of the urinary tract, preventing muscle contraction in the bladder.

DOSAGE
Adults and children over 12: 100 to 200 mg, 3 or 4 times a day.

ONSET OF EFFECT
45 to 60 minutes.

DURATION OF ACTION
Unknown.

DIETARY ADVICE
Take flavoxate with water 30 minutes before meals unless your physician advises otherwise. If it causes stomach upset, ask your physician if you can take it with food or milk.

STORAGE
Store in a tightly sealed container away from heat, moisture, and direct light.

IF YOU MISS A DOSE
Take it as soon as you remember. If it is near the time for the next dose, skip the missed dose and resume your regular dosage schedule. Do not double the next dose.

STOPPING THE DRUG
Take as prescribed for the full treatment period, even if you begin to feel better before the scheduled end of therapy.

PROLONGED USE
Tell your doctor if symptoms do not improve after prolonged use of this drug.

PRECAUTIONS
Over 60: Adverse reactions, especially confusion, may be more likely and more severe in older patients.

Driving and Hazardous Work: Do not drive or engage in hazardous work until you determine how the medicine affects you.

Alcohol: No special precautions are necessary.

Pregnancy: Flavoxate has not been shown to cause birth defects in animals. Adequate human studies have not been done. Before you take the medicine, tell your doctor if you are pregnant or plan to become pregnant; you must weigh the drug's benefits against the risks.

Breast Feeding: Flavoxate may pass into breast milk; caution is advised. Consult your doctor for advice.

Infants and Children: Not generally recommended for use by children under the age of 12. If flavoxate is prescribed for children, the dose should be determined by your pediatrician, and it should be given under close medical supervision.

Special Concerns: Limit exposure to sunlight and wear sunglasses in bright light. Avoid overexertion, since flavoxate interferes with the ability to sweat, which may lead to heatstroke. Use sugarless gum, candy, or ice chips to relieve dry mouth. Contact your doctor 2 months prior to having any surgery (including dental surgery) that will require general or spinal anesthesia. Tell your doctor if you experience abdominal bloating or difficulty emptying your bladder completely.

OVERDOSE
Symptoms: Rapid pulse and breathing, dilated pupils, dizziness, fever, hallucinations, slurred speech, confusion, agitation, unusual excitability, flushed face, convulsions, loss of consciousness.

What to Do: Call your doctor, emergency medical services (EMS), or the nearest poison control center immediately.

DRUG INTERACTIONS
Certain drugs may interact adversely with flavoxate or interfere with its action. Consult your doctor if you are taking cholinergic drugs. Also, tell your doctor if you are taking any other prescription or over-the-counter medicine before you take flavoxate.

FOOD INTERACTIONS
No known food interactions.

DISEASE INTERACTIONS
Caution is advised when taking flavoxate. Consult your doctor if you have any of the following: severe bleeding, narrow-angle glaucoma, angina, intestinal obstruction, urinary tract blockage, hiatal hernia, an enlarged prostate, myasthenia gravis, or a peptic ulcer.

Flecainide Acetate

Tambocor 100 mg
(3M)

▶ Drug Class: Antiarrhythmic

▶ Available in: Tablets

▶ Available OTC? No

▶ As Generic? No

Side Effects

SERIOUS
Shortness of breath, chest pain, irregular or rapid heartbeat, fainting, swollen feet or lower extremities, shaking or trembling. Call your doctor immediately.

COMMON
Headache; dizziness or lightheadedness; blurred vision or other visual disturbances, such as seeing spots.

LESS COMMON
Nausea, constipation, tremor, fatigue, abdominal pain, swollen hands, skin rash, anxiety, mental depression.

PRINCIPAL USES
To stabilize irregular heartbeats (cardiac arrhythmias).

HOW THE DRUG WORKS
Flecainide slows nerve impulses in the heart and makes heart tissue less sensitive to nerve impulses, thus stabilizing heartbeat.

DOSAGE
For paroxysmal supraventricular tachycardia or paroxysmal atrial fibrillation, or flutter, in persons without structural heart disease: Starting with 50 mg every 12 hours, increased by 50 mg every 4 days if necessary to a maximum of 150 mg every 12 hours. For life-threatening heart arrhythmias: Starting with 100 mg every 12 hours, increased by 50 mg every 4 days if necessary to a maximum of 200 mg every 12 hours. Initial dose should be lower in patients who have impaired heart or kidney function.

ONSET OF EFFECT
1 to 6 hours. May require daily doses for 3 to 5 days for full effect to occur.

DURATION OF ACTION
12 to 27 hours (longer in patients with impaired heart or kidney function).

DIETARY ADVICE
Take tablet with liquid. May be taken with or between meals.

STORAGE
Store in a tightly sealed container in a dry place away from heat and direct light.

IF YOU MISS A DOSE
Take it as soon as you remember, up to 6 hours late. If more than 6 hours, skip the missed dose and resume your regular dosage schedule as prescribed. Do not double the next dose.

STOPPING THE DRUG
Take as prescribed for the full treatment period, even if you begin to feel better before the scheduled end of therapy. The decision to stop taking the drug should be made by your doctor.

PROLONGED USE
Lifelong therapy may be necessary. See your doctor regularly for examinations and diagnostic tests if you must take this medicine for a prolonged period.

PRECAUTIONS
Over 60: Adverse reactions, especially heartbeat irregularities, may be more common and more severe in older patients.

Driving and Hazardous Work: Do not drive or engage in hazardous work until you determine how the medicine affects you.

Alcohol: Alcohol should be avoided while taking this medicine because it may further depress normal heart function.

Pregnancy: In animal studies large doses of flecainide have been shown to cause birth defects. Human studies have not been done. Before taking flecainide, tell your doctor if you are pregnant or plan to become pregnant.

Breast Feeding: Flecainide passes into breast milk and may cause harm to the infant; avoid or discontinue use while nursing.

Infants and Children: Not recommended for use by patients under age 18.

Special Concerns: Before you have any surgery (including dental surgery) or receive emergency medical care, be sure to tell the doctor or dentist that you are using flecainide. If you have a pacemaker, its function should be assessed shortly after starting therapy with flecainide.

OVERDOSE
Symptoms: Dizziness or faintness, rapid or irregular heartbeat, tremor, unusual or profuse sweating, drowsiness, loss of consciousness.

What to Do: Call your doctor, emergency medical services (EMS), or the nearest poison control center immediately.

DRUG INTERACTIONS
The following drugs may interact with flecainide. Consult your doctor if you are taking antacids, amiodarone or other antiarrhythmic drugs, beta-blockers, calcium channel blockers, bone marrow depressants, carbonic anhydrase inhibitors, carbamazepine, cimetidine, digitalis drugs, doxepin, nicotine, phenobarbital, or phenytoin.

FOOD INTERACTIONS
Caffeine-containing beverages can decrease flecainide activity. No other food interactions are expected.

DISEASE INTERACTIONS
Use of flecainide may cause complications in patients with heart disease, heart block, or slow heart rates, and may cause complications in patients with liver or kidney disease, since these organs work together to remove the medication from the body.

Fluconazole

BRAND NAME
Diflucan

Diflucan 200 mg
(ROERIG)

Additional photographs

▶ Drug Class: Antifungal

▶ Available in: Tablets, oral suspension, injection

▶ Available OTC? No

▶ As Generic? Yes

Side Effects

SERIOUS
Skin rash or itching, fever or chills. Call your doctor right away.

COMMON
No common side effects have been reported with the use of fluconazole.

LESS COMMON
Diarrhea, nausea, vomiting, constipation, dizziness, headache, redness or flushing of skin.

PRINCIPAL USES
To treat fungal infections of the mouth and throat (thrush), of the vagina (yeast infection), or throughout the body, as well as meningitis (inflammation of the protective membranes surrounding the brain). Often used to treat AIDS-related fungal infections. May also be used to prevent recurring fungal infections in susceptible patients weakened by AIDS or by chemotherapy or radiation treatment.

HOW THE DRUG WORKS
Fluconazole prevents fungal organisms from manufacturing vital substances required for their growth and function. This drug is effective only for infections caused by fungal organisms. It will not work for bacterial or viral infections.

DOSAGE
Adults and teenagers— For fungal infections: 200 to 400 mg on the first day, then 100 to 400 mg once a day, using oral forms or injection. Injections are into a vein. For vaginal yeast infection: 1 dose of 150 mg, tablet or oral suspension.

ONSET OF EFFECT
Oral forms: Unknown.
Injection: Immediate.

DURATION OF ACTION
Unknown.

DIETARY ADVICE
Swallow tablets with liquid. Oral suspension should be shaken and carefully measured out before you take it. This drug can be taken without regard to diet.

STORAGE
Store in a tightly sealed container away from heat, moisture, and direct light. Keep any liquid form refrigerated, but do not allow it to freeze.

IF YOU MISS A DOSE
Take it as soon as you remember. This will help keep a constant level of medication in your system. If it is near the time for the next dose, skip the missed dose and resume your regular dosage schedule. Do not double the next dose.

STOPPING THE DRUG
Take it as prescribed for the full treatment period, even if you begin to feel better before the scheduled end of therapy. The decision to stop taking the drug should be made by your doctor. Gradual reduction of the dose may be necessary if you have been taking this medicine for a long time.

PROLONGED USE
Notify your doctor if your condition does not improve, or instead becomes worse, within a few weeks.

PRECAUTIONS
Over 60: Dosage may need to be reduced in older patients with impaired kidney function.

Driving and Hazardous Work: The use of fluconazole should not impair your ability to perform such tasks safely.

Alcohol: No special precautions are necessary.

Pregnancy: Adequate studies of fluconazole use during pregnancy have not been done. Consult your doctor for specific advice if you are currently pregnant or plan to become pregnant.

Breast Feeding: Fluconazole may pass into breast milk; caution is advised. Consult your doctor for specific advice.

Infants and Children: Fluconazole is not generally prescribed for children under 14.

Special Concerns: Your doctor should monitor your kidney function while you take fluconazole. Tell any doctor or dentist whom you consult that you are taking this medicine. Be sure to shake the oral suspension well before taking it.

OVERDOSE
Symptoms: An overdose with fluconazole is unlikely.

What to Do: Emergency instructions not applicable.

DRUG INTERACTIONS
Consult your doctor for specific advice if you are taking oral antidiabetic drugs, cyclosporine, rifampin, phenytoin, rifabutin, tacrolimus, astemizole, or warfarin.

FOOD INTERACTIONS
No food interactions have been reported.

DISEASE INTERACTIONS
Caution is advised when taking fluconazole. Consult your doctor if you have a history of alcohol abuse (and associated liver problems), or any type of liver or kidney disease, since these organs work together to remove the medication from the body.

BRAND NAME
Ancobon

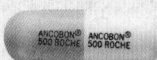

Ancobon 500 mg
(ROCHE)

▶ Drug Class: Antifungal

▶ Available in: Capsules

▶ Available OTC? No

▶ As Generic? No

Side Effects

SERIOUS
Unusual fatigue, yellow eyes or skin, unusual bleeding or bruising, skin rash, redness, or itching, sore throat, fever, increased sensitivity of eyes to sunlight, confusion, hallucinations. Call your doctor immediately.

COMMON
Loss of appetite, abdominal pain, stomach upset, nausea and vomiting, diarrhea.

LESS COMMON
Dizziness or lightheadedness, headache, unusual drowsiness.

PRINCIPAL USES
To treat general fungal infections and severe fungal infections of the bone and bone marrow (osteomyelitis), the protective layers of tissue surrounding the brain (meningitis), the respiratory tract (pneumonia), the blood (septicemia), and the genitourinary tract (particularly those infections associated with AIDS).

HOW THE DRUG WORKS
Flucytosine kills infectious microorganisms by preventing them from synthesizing genetic material (RNA and DNA), thereby preventing the cells from reproducing.

DOSAGE
Adults and children: Usual dose is 12.5 to 37.5 mg per 2.2 lbs (1 kg) of body weight every 6 hours.

ONSET OF EFFECT
Unknown.

DURATION OF ACTION
Unknown.

DIETARY ADVICE
Flucytosine can be taken without regard to diet. You should take a few capsules at a time, over a 15-minute period, with food to reduce stomach distress.

STORAGE
Store in a tightly sealed container away from heat, moisture, and direct light.

IF YOU MISS A DOSE
Take it as soon as you remember. If it is near the time for the next dose, skip the missed dose and resume your regular dosage schedule. Do not double the next dose.

STOPPING THE DRUG
Take it as prescribed for the full treatment period, even if you begin to feel better before the scheduled end of therapy. The decision to stop taking the drug should be made by your doctor.

PROLONGED USE
Prolonged use may cause or aggravate bone marrow depression (reduced bone marrow function), liver damage, or kidney damage. Consult your doctor about the need for periodic blood cell counts and liver and kidney function tests.

PRECAUTIONS
Over 60: Dosage must be reduced in older patients who have impaired kidney function.

Driving and Hazardous Work: Do not drive or engage in hazardous work until you determine how the medicine affects you. Use of this drug may be a disqualification for piloting aircraft.

Alcohol: No special precautions are necessary.

Pregnancy: Adequate studies of flucytosine use during pregnancy have not been done. Consult your doctor for specific advice if you are pregnant or are planning to become pregnant.

Breast Feeding: Flucytosine may pass into breast milk; it is unclear if this poses any risks to the nursing infant. Consult your doctor for specific advice.

Infants and Children: No special problems are expected in young patients.

Special Concerns: Stay out of direct sunlight, especially between 10 am and 3 pm. Wear protective clothing, including a hat, and sunglasses. Apply a sun block with a sun protection factor (SPF) of at least 15. This medicine is generally given in conjunction with amphotericin B to avoid development of drug resistance. Flucytosine may cause infection of the gums. Be careful when using a toothbrush, toothpick, or dental floss. Avoid dental work while taking this drug.

OVERDOSE
Symptoms: Severe nausea, vomiting, abdominal pain, diarrhea, mental confusion.

What to Do: An overdose of flucytosine is unlikely to be life-threatening. However, if someone takes a much larger dose than prescribed, call your doctor, emergency medical services (EMS), or nearest poison control center immediately.

DRUG INTERACTIONS
Other drugs may interact with flucytosine. Consult your doctor for advice if you are taking amphotericin B injection, cytosine, or bone marrow depressants, or if you are undergoing radiation therapy.

FOOD INTERACTIONS
No known food interactions.

DISEASE INTERACTIONS
Caution is advised when taking flucytosine. Consult your doctor if you have bone marrow depression or liver or kidney disease. Use of flucytosine may cause complications in patients with liver or kidney disease, since these organs work together to remove the medication from the body.

Fluodrocortisone

Florinef Acetate 0.1 mg
(APOTHECON)

▶ Drug Class: Corticosteroid

▶ Available in: Tablets

▶ Available OTC? No

▶ As Generic? No

Side Effects

SERIOUS
Headache and blurred vision caused by high blood pressure; low body potassium levels, causing cramps, weakness, and heart palpitations. Call your doctor immediately.

COMMON
Mild swelling of hands and feet.

LESS COMMON
Dizziness, difficulty swallowing, headache, hives, itchiness, rash, cough, vomiting, sudden weight gain, retention of sodium and water in the body.

PRINCIPAL USES
To supplement inadequate production of a specific salt-retaining corticosteroid hormone in the body, which leads to conditions known as adrenocortical insufficiency and adrenogenital syndrome. Untreated, these disorders can cause premature puberty in boys, masculinization in females, and even death.

HOW THE DRUG WORKS
Fluodrocortisone performs the same functions as one of the body's normal corticosteroid hormones called aldosterone.

DOSAGE
For adrenocortical insufficiency— Adults: 50 to 200 micrograms (mcg) once a day. Children: 50 to 100 mcg once a day. For adrenogenital syndrome— Adults: 100 to 200 mcg once a day.

ONSET OF EFFECT
Variable.

DURATION OF ACTION
1 to 2 days.

DIETARY ADVICE
Can be taken with or between meals. Best taken with a full glass of water. Carefully monitor the amount of sodium in your diet. Excess sodium will increase potassium loss. Eat foods rich in potassium.

STORAGE
Store in a tightly sealed container in a dry place away from heat and direct light.

IF YOU MISS A DOSE
Take it as soon as you remember. If it is near the time for the next dose, skip the missed dose and resume your regular dosage schedule. Do not double the next dose. Notify your physician if more than one dose is missed or a dose cannot be taken due to vomiting or nausea.

STOPPING THE DRUG
The decision to stop taking the drug should be made by your doctor.

PROLONGED USE
Your doctor may need to monitor your blood pressure, blood serum electrolyte (mineral salt) concentration, and other variables if you must take this medicine for a prolonged period.

PRECAUTIONS
Over 60: Adverse reactions may be more likely and more severe in older patients.

Driving and Hazardous Work: Do not drive or engage in hazardous work until you determine how the medicine affects you.

Alcohol: No special precautions are necessary.

Pregnancy: Studies on birth defects in animals and humans have not been done. Before you take fluodrocortisone, tell your doctor if you are pregnant or plan to become pregnant, to determine whether benefits outweigh potential risks.

Breast Feeding: Fluodrocortisone passes into breast milk; consult your doctor.

Infants and Children: It can be used safely when needed; consult your pediatrician for guidelines.

Special Concerns: Your doctor may ask you to follow a diet that is low in sodium and high in potassium and protein to avoid high blood pressure and excessive accumulation of water in the body. You should drink lots of water every day, unless your doctor directs otherwise.

OVERDOSE
Symptoms: Dizziness, weakness, swelling of the hands and feet, excessive weight gain.

What to Do: Call your doctor, emergency medical services (EMS), or the nearest poison control center immediately.

DRUG INTERACTIONS
Consult your doctor for specific advice if you are taking acetazolamide, amphotericin B, capreomycin, carbenicillin, corticotropin (ACTH), dichlorphenamide, a diuretic, an antiglaucoma drug, insulin or oral antidiabetic agents, laxatives, methazolamide, mezlocillin, piperacillin, a salicylate, aspirin, sodium bicarbonate, ticarcillin, vitamin B, vitamin D, a barbiturate, carbamazepine, griseofulvin, phenylbutazone, phenytoin, primidone, rifampin, digitalis drugs, another steroid, or any medication that contains sodium.

FOOD INTERACTIONS
High-sodium foods should be avoided.

DISEASE INTERACTIONS
Caution is advised if you have any of the following: bone disease, edema (swelling due to fluid retention), heart disease, high blood pressure, kidney disease, liver disease, or thyroid disease. Use of fluodrocortisone may cause complications in patients with liver or kidney disease, since these organs work together to remove the medication from the body.

Flunisolide

BRAND NAMES
AeroBid, AeroBid-M,
Nasalide, Nasarel

▶ Drug Class: Respiratory corticosteroid

▶ Available in: Oral inhalation, nasal spray

▶ Available OTC? No

▶ As Generic? No

Side Effects

SERIOUS
No serious side effects are associated with the use of flunisolide.

COMMON
Oral inhalation: Sore throat, white patches in mouth or throat, hoarseness. Nasal spray: Nosebleeds or bloody nasal secretions, nasal burning or irritation, sore throat.

LESS COMMON
Eye pain, watering eyes, gradual decrease of vision, stomach pain and digestive disturbances.

PRINCIPAL USES
To treat bronchial asthma; to treat allergic rhinitis (seasonal allergies such as hay fever); to prevent recurrence of nasal polyps after they have been removed surgically.

HOW THE DRUG WORKS
Respiratory corticosteroids such as flunisolide primarily reduce or prevent inflammation of the lining of the airways (the underlying cause of asthma), reduce the allergic response to inhaled allergens, and inhibit the secretion of mucus within the airways.

DOSAGE
Oral inhalation— Adults: 2 inhalations of 250 micrograms (mcg) each twice a day, morning and evening. Maximum dose is 4 inhalations twice a day. Children: Do not exceed 2 inhalations twice a day. Nasal spray— Adults and teenagers 15 and older: 2 sprays of 25 mcg in each nostril twice a day. Maximum dose is 8 sprays in each nostril a day. Children ages 6 to 14: One spray of 25 mcg in each nostril 3 times a day, or 2 sprays in each nostril twice a day. Maximum dose is 4 sprays in each nostril a day.

ONSET OF EFFECT
Usually within 1 week; it may take 3 weeks for the full effect to occur.

DURATION OF ACTION
Unknown.

DIETARY ADVICE
No special restrictions.

STORAGE
Store the inhaler in a dry place away from heat and direct light.

IF YOU MISS A DOSE
Take it as soon as you remember. If it is near the time for the next dose, skip the missed dose and resume your regular dosage schedule. Do not double the next dose.

STOPPING THE DRUG
If you have been using flunisolide for a long period, do not stop taking it suddenly. Consult your doctor about how to stop.

PROLONGED USE
Consult your doctor about the need for continuing medical examinations or laboratory tests.

PRECAUTIONS
Over 60: No special problems are expected with older patients.

Driving and Hazardous Work: Do not drive or engage in hazardous work until you determine how the medicine affects you.

Alcohol: No special precautions are necessary.

Pregnancy: Flunisolide has not been reported to cause birth defects if taken during pregnancy. Before using this drug, tell your doctor if you are pregnant or plan to become pregnant.

Breast Feeding: Flunisolide may pass into breast milk; caution is advised. Consult your doctor for advice.

Infants and Children: Not recommended for children under the age of 6. The drug may inhibit growth and make children more susceptible to infection. If a younger person takes this medicine, be careful to avoid exposure to chicken pox and measles.

Special Concerns: Inhaled steroids will not help an asthma attack in progress. They can lower resistance to yeast infections of the mouth, throat, or voice box. To prevent yeast infections, gargle or rinse your mouth with water after each use; do not swallow the water. Know how to use the spray; read and follow the directions that come with the device. Before you have surgery, tell the doctor or dentist that you are using a steroid.

OVERDOSE
Symptoms: No specific ones have been reported.

What to Do: An overdose of flunisolide is unlikely to be life-threatening. However, if someone takes a much larger dose than prescribed, or if you have any reason to suspect an overdose, call your doctor, emergency medical services (EMS), or the nearest poison control center.

DRUG INTERACTIONS
Consult your doctor for specific advice if you are taking systemic corticosteroids, other inhaled corticosteroids, or drugs that suppress the immune system.

FOOD INTERACTIONS
No known food interactions.

DISEASE INTERACTIONS
Consult your doctor if you have a history of tuberculosis, herpes simplex infection of the eye, chicken pox, chronic bronchitis or bronchiectasis, osteoporosis, underactive thyroid, liver disease, glaucoma, measles, recent injury to the nose or nose surgery, or any active infection.

Fluorometholone

▶ Drug Class: Corticosteroid

▶ Available in: Ophthalmic ointment, suspension

▶ Available OTC? No

▶ As Generic? No

Side Effects

SERIOUS
Decreased or blurred vision (from cataract); eye pain, nausea, vomiting (from increased eye pressure); pain, redness, sensitivity to bright light, discharge (from eye infection). Call your doctor immediately if you experience any of these signs or symptoms.

COMMON
Increased eye pressure; this is usually reversed once the drug is stopped.

LESS COMMON
Burning, stinging, redness, or watering of eyes.

PRINCIPAL USES
To control inflammation and prevent potentially permanent damage that may result from various conditions involving inflammation in the tissues of the eye.

HOW THE DRUG WORKS
Fluorometholone inhibits the release of substances that stimulate an inflammatory reaction and pain in eye tissues.

DOSAGE
Ointment: Apply to eye 1 to 3 times a day, according to doctor's instructions. Suspension: 1 or 2 drops, 2 to 4 times a day. For severe conditions, more frequent application of either form may be recommended initially; the dosage will be decreased as inflammation subsides.

ONSET OF EFFECT
Unknown.

DURATION OF ACTION
Unknown.

DIETARY ADVICE
No special restrictions.

STORAGE
Store in a tightly sealed container away from heat, moisture, and direct light. Do not allow it to freeze.

IF YOU MISS A DOSE
Apply it as soon as you remember. If it is near the time for the next dose, skip the missed dose and resume your regular dosage schedule. Do not double the next dose.

STOPPING THE DRUG
It is very important to take this drug as prescribed for the full treatment period, even if symptoms improve before the scheduled end of therapy.

PROLONGED USE
See your doctor regularly for tests and examinations if you must take this drug for a prolonged period.

PRECAUTIONS
Over 60: No special problems are expected.

Driving and Hazardous Work: Do not drive or engage in hazardous work until you determine how the medicine affects your vision.

Alcohol: No special precautions are necessary.

Pregnancy: Adequate human studies have not been done, although there have been no reports of birth defects. Before taking fluorometholone, tell your doctor if you are pregnant or are planning to become pregnant.

Breast Feeding: This medicine has not been reported to cause problems in nursing babies. Consult your doctor for specific advice.

Infants and Children: Safety and effectiveness have not been established for children under 2 years of age.

Special Concerns: To use the eye drops or the ointment, first wash your hands. Tilt your head back. Gently apply pressure to the inside corner of the eyelid and with the index finger of the same hand, pull downward on the lower eyelid to make a space. Drop the medicine or put a short strip of ointment (about ⅓ inch long) into this space and close your eye. Apply pressure for 1 or 2 minutes while keeping the eye closed without blinking. Then wash your hands again. Make sure the tip of the dropper or the applicator does not touch your eye, finger, or any other surface. If your symptoms do not improve in 5 to 7 days or if they become worse, check with your doctor. Wearing contact lenses while using this medication may increase the risk of infection. Your doctor may tell you not to wear contact lenses during treatment and for a day or two afterward.

OVERDOSE
Symptoms: When used topically, an overdose of fluorometholone is very unlikely. Inadvertent oral ingestion, however, may cause fever, muscle pain, loss of appetite, dizziness, fainting, and difficulty breathing.

What to Do: In case of accidental ingestion, call your doctor, emergency medical services (EMS), or the nearest poison control center right away.

DRUG INTERACTIONS
Other medications may interact with fluorometholone. Consult your doctor for specific advice if you are taking any other prescription or over-the-counter medication, especially any preparation designed for use in the eyes.

FOOD INTERACTIONS
No known food interactions.

DISEASE INTERACTIONS
Consult your doctor if you have a history of cataracts, diabetes mellitus, glaucoma, herpes infection of the eye, fungal infection of the eye, or any other eye infection.

Fluorouracil (5-Fluorouracil; 5-FU)

BRAND NAMES
Efudex, Fluoroplex

▶ Drug Class: Antimetabolite

▶ Available in: Cream, topical solution

▶ Available OTC? No

▶ As Generic? Yes

Side Effects

SERIOUS
Severe redness, swelling, and tenderness of otherwise healthy regions of skin.

COMMON
Burning sensation where medicine is applied, increased sensitivity of skin to sunlight, redness, swelling, itching, rash, tenderness, pain, or oozing and crusting of the skin.

LESS COMMON
Hyperpigmentation (darkening) of skin, scaling, scarring, watery eyes.

PRINCIPAL USES
To treat actinic keratosis (a type of precancerous skin lesion). The drug is prescribed generally for multiple lesions or when limited access to a lesion makes other methods of removal difficult.

HOW THE DRUG WORKS
Topical fluorouracil kills precancerous cells by interfering with the activity of their genetic material, thus preventing the cells from reproducing. The drug selectively destroys cells that multiply rapidly, as many malignant cells do.

DOSAGE
For precancerous skin lesions— Adults: Apply 1% cream or 5% solution to the affected area 1 or 2 times a day. The 5% cream is sometimes prescribed. Children: Use and dose must be determined by your pediatrician.

ONSET OF EFFECT
From 2 to 7 days. The complete effect may require 2 to 6 weeks, or even 12 weeks for some patients. Complete healing may require 1 or 2 months after the drug has been stopped.

DURATION OF ACTION
Up to 24 hours.

DIETARY ADVICE
Fluorouracil may be applied without regard to diet.

STORAGE
Store in a tightly sealed container away from heat and direct light.

IF YOU MISS A DOSE
Apply it as soon as you remember. If it is near the time for the next application, skip the missed dose and resume your regular dosage schedule. Do not double the next dose.

STOPPING THE DRUG
Apply fluorouracil for the entire duration of therapy, as prescribed. The decision to stop the drug should be made by your doctor.

PROLONGED USE
No problems are expected with prolonged use, but check regularly with your physician. Treatment usually lasts 2 to 8 weeks for precancerous lesions. Your physician may order a biopsy if the condition does not clear up.

PRECAUTIONS
Over 60: No special problems are expected.

Driving and Hazardous Work: The use of fluorouracil should not impair your ability to perform such tasks safely.

Alcohol: No special precautions are necessary.

Pregnancy: Some fluorouracil is absorbed through the skin and may affect the unborn child. Before using fluorouracil, tell your doctor if you are pregnant or plan to become pregnant.

Breast Feeding: Fluorouracil passes into breast milk; avoid or discontinue usage while nursing.

Infants and Children: Fluorouracil is generally not prescribed for infants and children, but you should consult your doctor about its use for young patients.

Special Concerns: While you use fluorouracil, and for 1 or 2 months afterward, your skin may become much more sensitive to sunlight, and sunlight may increase the effect of the drug. During this period, stay out of direct sunlight, especially between 10 am and 3 pm. Wear protective clothing, including a hat and sunglasses. Apply a sun block that has a sun protection factor (SPF) of at least 15. When applying fluorouracil, wash the area with soap and water and use a cotton-tipped applicator or your fingertips to apply the drug. Wash your hands immediately to prevent any of the medicine from accidentally getting into your eyes or mouth.

OVERDOSE
Symptoms: No specific ones have been reported.

What to Do: An overdose is unlikely. However, if topical fluorouracil is accidentally swallowed, call your doctor, emergency medical services (EMS), or nearest poison control center.

DRUG INTERACTIONS
None known.

FOOD INTERACTIONS
No known food interactions.

DISEASE INTERACTIONS
Caution is advised when taking fluorouracil. Consult your doctor if you have any other skin problem.

Fluoxetine Hydrochloride

BRAND NAMES
Prozac, Sarafem

Prozac 20 mg
(DISTA)

▶ Drug Class: Selective
serotonin reuptake inhibitor
(SSRI) antidepressant

▶ Available in: Capsules, oral
solution

▶ Available OTC? No

▶ As Generic? Yes

Side Effects

SERIOUS
Agitation, shaking, difficulty breathing, rash, hives, itching, joint or muscle pain, chills or fever. If such symptoms occur, call your doctor immediately.

COMMON
Nervousness, drowsiness, anxiety, insomnia, headache, diarrhea, excessive sweating, nausea, decreased appetite, decreased initiative.

LESS COMMON
Nasal congestion, unusual or vivid dreams, cough, increased appetite, chest pain, constipation, vision disturbances, abdominal pain, stomach gas, constipation, vomiting, frequent urination, difficulty concentrating, sexual dysfunction, heartbeat irregularities, trembling, fatigue, dizziness, change in taste, flushing of the skin on the face and neck, dry mouth, menstrual pain.

PRINCIPAL USES
To treat major depression, obsessive-compulsive disorder, panic disorder, chronic pain, and premenstrual dysphoric disorder (PMDD).

HOW THE DRUG WORKS
Fluoxetine affects levels of serotonin, a brain chemical that is thought to be linked to mood, emotions, and mental state.

DOSAGE
To start, 20 mg a day, taken in the morning. Your doctor may increase the dose gradually to a maximum of 80 mg a day. Older adults: To start, 10 to 20 mg a day. It may be increased gradually by your doctor to a maximum of 40 to 60 mg a day.

ONSET OF EFFECT
1 to 4 weeks.

DURATION OF ACTION
Unknown.

DIETARY ADVICE
Taking the drug with liquid or food can lessen stomach irritation. Capsules may be opened and mixed with food or juice if the patient has difficulty swallowing them.

STORAGE
Store in a tightly sealed container away from heat, moisture, and direct light. Keep the liquid form refrigerated, but do not allow it to freeze.

IF YOU MISS A DOSE
Take it as soon as you remember. If it is near the time for the next dose, skip the missed dose and resume your regular dosage schedule. Do not double the next dose.

STOPPING THE DRUG
Take it as prescribed for the full treatment period, even if you begin to feel better before the scheduled end of therapy. Discontinuing the drug abruptly may produce unpleasant withdrawal symptoms. Dosage should be reduced gradually according to your doctor's instructions.

PROLONGED USE
The usual course of therapy lasts 6 months to 1 year; some patients benefit from additional therapy. The usual course of therapy for obsessive-compulsive disorder lasts 1 year or more.

PRECAUTIONS
Over 60: Adverse reactions may be more likely and more severe in older patients, since their metabolism is slower. A lower dose may be warranted.

Driving and Hazardous Work: Use caution when driving or engaging in hazardous work until you determine how the medicine affects you.

Alcohol: Avoid alcohol.

Pregnancy: Fluoxetine should be used during pregnancy only if the potential benefit justifies the potential risk to the fetus. Before you take this medicine, tell your doctor if you are pregnant or plan to become pregnant.

Breast Feeding: Fluoxetine may pass into breast milk; caution is advised. Consult your doctor for specific advice.

Infants and Children: Not recommended for use by children under age 12. Antidepressants increase the risk of suicidal thinking and behavior (suicidality) in children with major depression and other psychiatric disorders. Discuss with your doctor this risk versus the benefits of using this drug. Children should be observed closely for worsening of symptoms, suicidality, or unusual changes in behavior at the onset of therapy and when making changes in dosage.

Special Concerns: Take it at least 6 hours before bedtime to prevent insomnia, unless the drug causes drowsiness.

OVERDOSE
Symptoms: Agitation, excitement, severe nausea and vomiting, seizures.

What to Do: Call your doctor, emergency medical services (EMS), or the nearest poison control center immediately.

DRUG INTERACTIONS
Fluoxetine should not be used within 5 weeks of taking MAO inhibitors or thioridazine. The following drugs may interact with fluoxetine. Consult your doctor for specific advice if you are taking nortriptyline, caffeine, oral anticoagulants, central nervous system depressants, digitalis preparations, lithium, loratadine, dextromethorphan, ketorolac, buspirone, phenytoin, trazodone, tryptophan, sumatriptan, naratriptan, or zolmitriptan.

FOOD INTERACTIONS
No known food interactions.

DISEASE INTERACTIONS
Use of fluoxetine may cause complications in patients with liver or kidney disease, since these organs work together to remove the medication from the body. Use of the drug may make diabetes or seizures worse.

Fluoxymesterone

BRAND NAMES
Android-F, Halotestin

Halotestin 5 mg
(UPJOHN)

▶ Drug Class: Hormone treatment (androgen); antineoplastic (anticancer) agent

▶ Available in: Tablets

▶ Available OTC? No

▶ As Generic? Yes

Side Effects

SERIOUS
Itching of skin, yellowish tinge to eyes or skin. Call your doctor immediately.

COMMON
Women: Acne or oily skin, decreased breast size, hoarseness or deepening of voice, irregular menstrual periods, male-type baldness, excessive hair growth. Men: Enlarged or sore breasts, frequent or prolonged erections, frequent urination, temporary infertility. Notify your doctor if any of these symptoms occur.

LESS COMMON
Changes in skin coloration, confusion, constipation, dizziness, frequent headaches, increased thirst and urination, depression, nausea, vomiting, swelling of feet or lower legs, unusual bleeding, unusual fatigue, rapid weight gain, diarrhea, increased risk of infection, insomnia, increase or decrease in sexual desire. Men only: Testicular shrinkage, erectile dysfunction, skin irritation of the scrotum. Boys only: Acne, early growth of pubic hair, penis enlargement, increased frequency of erections.

PRINCIPAL USES
For hormone replacement in men; to treat delayed sexual development in boys; to treat certain types of breast cancer in women.

HOW THE DRUG WORKS
Fluoxymesterone replaces natural testosterone in men deficient of the hormone. Fluoxymesterone also blocks the action of certain other hormones that promote the growth of some types of breast tumors.

DOSAGE
For hormone replacement in men: 5 to 20 mg daily, in single or divided doses. For treatment of delayed sexual development in boys: 2.5 to 10 mg a day for 4 to 6 months. For treatment of breast cancer in women: 10 to 40 mg daily, in divided doses.

ONSET OF EFFECT
1 month.

DURATION OF ACTION
Unknown.

DIETARY ADVICE
It can be taken with food to prevent stomach upset.

STORAGE
Store in a tightly sealed container away from heat and direct light.

IF YOU MISS A DOSE
Take it as soon as you remember. If it is near the time for the next dose, skip the missed dose and resume your regular dosage schedule. Do not double the next dose.

STOPPING THE DRUG
The decision to stop taking the drug should be made by your doctor.

PROLONGED USE
You should see your doctor regularly for tests and examinations if you must take this drug for a prolonged period.

PRECAUTIONS
Over 60: An increased risk of prostate enlargement or prostate cancer is found in older men.

Driving and Hazardous Work: Use of this drug should not impair your ability to perform such tasks safely.

Alcohol: No special precautions are necessary.

Pregnancy: Fluoxymesterone can affect both male and female fetuses; it should not be used during pregnancy.

Breast Feeding: Fluoxymesterone passes into breast milk; avoid or discontinue use while nursing.

Infants and Children: Fluoxymesterone can profoundly affect the growth and sexual development of infants and children. Risks must be weighed against benefits; consult your pediatrician for advice.

Special Concerns: This drug contains the dye tartrazine, which may cause allergic reactions in some people. The risk of some cancers is increased with long-term, high-dose use. In some cases this drug can pass to a sexual partner and cause side effects. A non-hormonal (barrier) method of contraception is advised during therapy.

OVERDOSE
Symptoms: No specific ones have been reported.

What to Do: An overdose is unlikely to be life-threatening. However, if someone takes a much larger dose than prescribed, call your doctor, emergency medical services (EMS), or the nearest poison control center immediately.

DRUG INTERACTIONS
Consult your doctor for specific advice if you are taking acetaminophen, amiodarone, anabolic steroids, anticoagulants, anti-infective drugs, antithyroid agents, carbamazepine, carmustine, chloroquine, cyclosporine, dantrolene, daunorubicin, disulfiram, divalproex, estrogens, etretinate, gold salts, hydroxychloroquine, insulin, mercaptopurine, methotrexate, methyldopa, naltrexone, oral contraceptives, phenothiazines, phenytoin, plicamycin, or valproic acid.

FOOD INTERACTIONS
No known food interactions.

DISEASE INTERACTIONS
Consult your doctor if you have a history of prostate cancer, diabetes, edema (swelling owing to excess fluid retention), kidney disease, liver disease, enlarged prostate, heart disease, or blood vessel disease.

Fluphenazine

BRAND NAMES
Permitil, Prolixin

Generic 10 mg
(GENEVA)

Additional photographs

▶ Drug Class: Antipsychotic; phenothiazine

▶ Available in: Tablets, oral concentrate, elixir, injection

▶ Available OTC? No

▶ As Generic? Yes

Side Effects

SERIOUS
Extreme and persistent restlessness; uncontrolled movements, including tics, twitching, twisting movements, and muscle spasms in the face, neck, and back; loss of coordination and balance; trembling, weakness, and stiffness in the extremities; difficulty swallowing or speaking; persistent, uncontrolled chewing, lip-smacking, or tongue movements; staring and absence of facial expression; fainting; increased skin sensitivity to the sun; skin rash; yellowish tinge to eyes or skin.

COMMON
Constipation, decreased sweating, dizziness or faintness, drowsiness, dry mouth, shaking, mild stiffness, shuffling gait, restlessness, blurred vision.

LESS COMMON
Menstrual irregularities, sexual dysfunction, unusual milk secretion, breast pain or swelling, unexpected weight gain, difficulty urinating.

PRINCIPAL USES
To treat psychotic conditions such as schizophrenia.

HOW THE DRUG WORKS
Fluphenazine inhibits the activity of the brain chemical dopamine, thereby helping to prevent the overstimulation of specific nerve centers in the brain that are thought to be responsible for certain psychiatric disorders.

DOSAGE
Oral forms— Adults: To start, 2.5 to 10 mg a day, taken in divided doses every 6 to 8 hours; may be increased to a maximum of 20 mg a day. Maintenance dose is 1 to 20 mg a day. Children: 0.25 to 0.75 mg, 1 to 4 times a day. Older adults: 1 to 2.5 mg a day. Injection— 12.5 to 50 mg every 2 to 4 weeks.

ONSET OF EFFECT
Within 1 hour for oral forms; 24 to 72 hours for injection. Full therapeutic effect may take several weeks.

DURATION OF ACTION
From 6 to 8 hours with oral forms; 1 to 6 weeks with injection.

DIETARY ADVICE
It can be taken with liquid or food to minimize stomach upset. If your medicine comes with a dropper bottle, dilute your dose in half a glass of grapefruit or orange juice or water.

STORAGE
Store in a tightly sealed container in a dry place away from heat and direct light. Do not refrigerate, and keep liquid forms from freezing.

IF YOU MISS A DOSE
Take it as soon as you remember. However, if it is more than 2 hours late, skip the missed dose and resume your regular dosage schedule. Do not double the next dose.

STOPPING THE DRUG
Do not stop taking the drug abruptly or without your doctor's approval. Dosage should be reduced gradually by your doctor to prevent withdrawal symptoms.

PROLONGED USE
Prolonged use may lead to tardive dyskinesia (involuntary movements of the jaw, lips, and tongue). Consult your doctor about the need for follow-up evaluations and tests if you must take this drug for an extended period.

PRECAUTIONS
Over 60: Adverse reactions, especially shuffling gait, shaking, stiffness, and constipation, are more common in older patients.

Driving and Hazardous Work: Do not drive or engage in hazardous work until you determine how the medicine affects you.

Alcohol: Avoid alcohol.

Pregnancy: Discuss with your doctor the relative risks and benefits of taking this drug if you are, or plan to become, pregnant.

Breast Feeding: Either avoid taking the drug if possible or refrain from breast feeding.

Infants and Children: Not for use by children under age 12.

Special Concerns: Avoid getting overheated or chilled. Avoid getting the liquid form of the medicine on the skin, because it can cause irritation or a rash.

OVERDOSE
Symptoms: Extreme drowsiness, heartbeat irregularities, dry mouth, paradoxical restlessness or agitation, seizures, loss of consciousness.

What to Do: Call your doctor, emergency medical services (EMS), or the nearest poison control center immediately.

DRUG INTERACTIONS
The following drugs may interact with fluphenazine. Consult your doctor for specific advice if you are taking anticholinergics, antidepressants, antihistamines, antihypertensives, barbiturates, anesthetics, beta-blockers, diuretics, thyroid drugs, appetite suppressants, epinephrine, bupropion, or calcium supplements.

FOOD INTERACTIONS
Avoid caffeinated beverages, apple juice, and tea.

DISEASE INTERACTIONS
Consult your doctor if you have a history of alcohol abuse, any blood disorder, breast cancer, enlarged prostate, epilepsy or a seizure disorder, glaucoma, lung disease, heart or blood vessel disease, liver disease, Parkinson's disease, peptic ulcer, or urinary difficulty.

Flurazepam Hydrochloride

Generic 15 mg
(MYLAN)

▶ Drug Class: Benzodiazepine tranquilizer; sedative/hypnotic

▶ Available in: Capsules

▶ Available OTC? No

▶ As Generic? Yes

Side Effects

SERIOUS
Difficulty concentrating, outbursts of anger, other behavior problems, depression, hallucinations, low blood pressure (causing faintness or confusion), memory impairment, muscle weakness, skin rash or itching, sore throat, fever and chills, sores or ulcers in throat or mouth, unusual bruising or bleeding, extreme fatigue, yellowish tinge to eyes or skin. Call your doctor immediately.

COMMON
Daytime drowsiness, dizziness, lightheadedness, loss of coordination, headaches, slurred speech.

LESS COMMON
Stomach cramps or pain, vision disturbances, change in sexual desire or ability, constipation, false sense of well-being, nausea and vomiting, urinary problems, unusual weakness or fatigue.

PRINCIPAL USES
For the short-term treatment of insomnia.

HOW THE DRUG WORKS
In general, flurazepam produces a mild sedative effect by depressing activity in the central nervous system (the brain and spinal cord). In particular, flurazepam appears to enhance the effect of gamma-aminobutyric acid (GABA), a natural chemical that inhibits the firing of neurons and dampens the transmission of nerve signals, thus decreasing nervous excitation.

DOSAGE
15 or 30 mg, taken in a single dose at bedtime.

ONSET OF EFFECT
From 30 to 60 minutes.

DURATION OF ACTION
Unknown.

DIETARY ADVICE
Limit your intake of caffeine-containing foods and beverages while taking this medication.

STORAGE
Store in a tightly sealed container away from heat, moisture, and direct light.

IF YOU MISS A DOSE
Take it as soon as you remember, unless it is late at night. Do not take the medicine unless your schedule permits a full night's sleep.

STOPPING THE DRUG
Discontinuing the drug abruptly may produce withdrawal symptoms (sleep disruption, nervousness, irritability, diarrhea, abdominal cramps, muscle aches, memory impairment). The dosage should be reduced gradually according to your doctor's instructions.

PROLONGED USE
Do not use flurazepam for more than 8 weeks without consulting your doctor.

PRECAUTIONS
Over 60: Adverse reactions are more likely and more severe. A lower dose may be warranted.

Driving and Hazardous Work: Flurazepam can impair mental alertness and physical coordination. Adjust your activities accordingly.

Alcohol: Avoid alcohol.

Pregnancy: Use during pregnancy should be avoided if possible. Be sure to tell your doctor if you are pregnant or plan to become pregnant.

Breast Feeding: Flurazepam passes into breast milk; do not take it while nursing.

Infants and Children: Flurazepam is not recommended for use by children under the age of 6 months, and it is not generally prescribed for children under age 15. It should be used by older children only under close medical supervision.

Special Concerns: Use of this drug can lead to psychological or physical dependence.

OVERDOSE
Symptoms: Extreme drowsiness, confusion, slurred speech, slow reflexes, poor coordination, staggering gait, tremor, slowed breathing, loss of consciousness.

What to Do: Call your doctor, emergency medical services (EMS), or the nearest poison control center immediately.

DRUG INTERACTIONS
Other drugs may interact with flurazepam. Consult your doctor for specific advice if you are taking any drugs that depress the central nervous system; these include antihistamines, antidepressants or other psychiatric medications, barbiturates, sedatives, cough medicines, decongestants, and painkillers. Be sure your doctor knows about any over-the-counter medication you may take.

FOOD INTERACTIONS
None reported.

DISEASE INTERACTIONS
Caution is advised when taking flurazepam. Consult your doctor if you have a history of alcohol or drug abuse, stroke or other brain disease, any chronic lung disease, hyperactivity, depression or other mental illness, myasthenia gravis, sleep apnea, epilepsy, porphyria, kidney disease, or liver disease.

Flurbiprofen Ophthalmic

▶ Drug Class: Nonsteroidal anti-inflammatory drug (NSAID)

▶ Available in: Ophthalmic solution

▶ Available OTC? No

▶ As Generic? No

Side Effects

SERIOUS
Rarely, ophthalmic flurbiprofen will cause bleeding in the eye, redness or swelling of the eye or eyelid not present before the start of therapy, itching of the eye, or excessive tear production. Call your doctor immediately.

COMMON
Mild and temporary burning or stinging of eyes after application.

LESS COMMON
There are no less-common side effects associated with ophthalmic flurbiprofen.

PRINCIPAL USES
To treat some eye conditions and problems that occur during or after eye surgery.

HOW THE DRUG WORKS
Ophthalmic flurbiprofen inhibits the release of substances that stimulate inflammation and cause pain in eye tissues.

DOSAGE
Adults: 1 drop in each eye every 4 hours. Children: Consult your pediatrician.

ONSET OF EFFECT
Unknown.

DURATION OF ACTION
Unknown.

DIETARY ADVICE
No special restrictions.

STORAGE
Store in a tightly sealed container away from heat, moisture, and direct light. Do not allow it to freeze.

IF YOU MISS A DOSE
Apply it as soon as you remember. If it is near the time for the next dose, skip the missed dose and resume your regular dosage schedule. Do not double the next dose.

STOPPING THE DRUG
Use it as prescribed for the full treatment period, even if you feel better before the scheduled end of therapy.

PROLONGED USE
See your doctor regularly for tests and examinations if you must use this drug for a prolonged period.

PRECAUTIONS
Over 60: No special problems are expected.

Driving and Hazardous Work: The use of ophthalmic flurbiprofen should not impair your ability to perform such tasks safely.

Alcohol: No special precautions are necessary.

Pregnancy: Adequate human studies have not been completed. Before taking ophthalmic flurbiprofen, tell your doctor if you are pregnant or plan to become pregnant.

Breast Feeding: Ophthalmic flurbiprofen may pass into breast milk; caution is advised. Consult your doctor for specific advice.

Infants and Children: Use and dosage for infants and children must be determined by your doctor.

Special Concerns: To use the eye drops, first wash your hands. Tilt your head back. Gently apply pressure to the inside corner of the eyelid and with the index finger of the same hand, pull downward on the lower eyelid to make a space. Drop the medicine into this space and close your eye. Apply pressure for 1 or 2 minutes while keeping the eye closed without blinking. Then wash your hands again. Make sure the tip of the dropper does not touch your eye, finger, or any other surface. If your symptoms do not improve or if they become worse, check with your doctor. Ophthalmic flurbiprofen may cause problems in patients who wear soft contact lenses. Your doctor may want you to stop wearing the lenses while you take it.

OVERDOSE
Symptoms: No specific ones have been reported.

What to Do: An overdose of ophthalmic flurbiprofen is unlikely to be life-threatening. However, if someone takes a much larger dose of the drug than prescribed or accidentally ingests the medicine, call your doctor, emergency medical services (EMS), or the nearest poison control center.

DRUG INTERACTIONS
Consult your doctor for specific advice if you are taking aspirin or another salicylate, difunisal, etodolac, fenoprofen, floctafenine, oral flurbiprofen, ibuprofen, indomethacin, ketoprofen, ketorolac, meclofenamate, mefanamic acid, nabumetone, naproxen, oxyphenbutazone, phenylbutazone, piroxicam, sulindac, suprofen, tenoxicam, tiaprofenic acid, tolmetin, or zomepirac. Ophthalmic flurbiprofen reduces the effectivness of acetylcholine or carbachol, two drugs used to treat glaucoma. These drugs are rarely used today, but if you take them, be sure to let your doctor know.

FOOD INTERACTIONS
No known food interactions.

DISEASE INTERACTIONS
Caution is advised when taking ophthalmic flurbiprofen. Consult your doctor if you have hemophilia or any other bleeding problem.

Flurbiprofen Oral

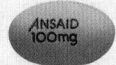

Ansaid 100 mg
(UPJOHN)

▶ Drug Class: Nonsteroidal
anti-inflammatory drug
(NSAID)

▶ Available in: Tablets,
extended-release capsules

▶ Available OTC? No

▶ As Generic? Yes

Side Effects

SERIOUS
Shortness of breath or
wheezing, with or with-
out swelling of legs or
other signs of heart failure; chest pain; peptic
ulcer disease with vomit-
ing of blood; black, tarry
stools; decreasing kidney
function. Call your doctor
immediately.

COMMON
Nausea, vomiting, heart-
burn, diarrhea, constipa-
tion, headache, dizziness,
sleepiness.

LESS COMMON
Ulcers or sores in mouth,
depression, rashes or
blistering of skin, ringing
sound in the ears,
unusual tingling or
numbness of the hands
or feet, seizures, blurred
vision. Also elevated
potassium levels,
decreased blood counts;
such problems can be
detected by your doctor.

PRINCIPAL USES
To treat mild to moderate
pain and inflammation
caused by tendinitis, arthritis, bursitis, gout, soft tissue
injuries, migraine and other
vascular headaches, men-
strual cramps, and other
conditions. When patients
fail to respond to one
NSAID, another may be
tried. The greatest effectiveness often requires trial and
error of several different
NSAIDs.

HOW THE DRUG WORKS
NSAIDs work by interfering
with the formation of
prostaglandins, substances
that cause inflammation and
make nerves more sensitive
to pain impulses. NSAIDs
also have other modes of
action that are less well
understood.

DOSAGE
Adults: Tablets: 50 mg, 4
times daily or 100 mg, 2
times daily. Extended-
release capsules: 200 mg
once a day. Maximum dose
is 300 mg a day. For children's dose, consult your
pediatrician.

ONSET OF EFFECT
Several hours.

DURATION OF ACTION
Varies; some patients
require daily maintenance
doses to control pain.

DIETARY ADVICE
Take flurbiprofen with food.

STORAGE
Store in a tightly sealed container away from heat, moisture, and direct light.

IF YOU MISS A DOSE
Take it as soon as you
remember. If it is near the
time for the next dose, skip
the missed dose and
resume your regular dosage
schedule. Do not double the
next dose.

STOPPING THE DRUG
The decision to stop taking
the drug should be made in
consultation with your
physician.

PROLONGED USE
Prolonged use can cause
gastrointestinal problems,
including ulceration and
bleeding, kidney dysfunc-
tion, and liver inflammation.
Consult your doctor about
the need for medical examinations and laboratory tests.

PRECAUTIONS
Over 60: Because of the
potentially greater consequences of gastrointestinal
side effects, the dose of
NSAIDs for older patients,
especially those over age
70, is often cut in half.

**Driving and Hazardous
Work:** Do not drive or
engage in hazardous work
until you determine how the
medicine affects you.

Alcohol: Avoid alcohol
when using this medication
because it increases the risk
of stomach irritation.

Pregnancy: Do not use
this drug during pregnancy.

Breast Feeding: Flur-
biprofen passes into breast
milk; avoid use while breast
feeding.

Infants and Children:
Flurbiprofen may be used in
exceptional circumstances;
consult your doctor.

Special Concerns:
Because NSAIDs can inter-
fere with blood coagulation,
this drug should be stopped
at least 3 days prior to any
surgery.

OVERDOSE
Symptoms: Severe nausea,
vomiting, headache, confusion, seizures.

What to Do: Call your
doctor, emergency medical
services (EMS), or the
nearest poison control center immediately.

DRUG INTERACTIONS
Do not take this drug with
aspirin or any other NSAIDs
without your doctor's
approval. In addition, consult your doctor if you are
taking antihypertensives,
steroids, anticoagulants,
antibiotics, itraconazole or
ketoconazole, plicamycin,
penicillamine, valproic acid,
phenytoin, cyclosporine,
digitalis drugs, lithium,
methotrexate, probenecid,
triamterene, or zidovudine.

FOOD INTERACTIONS
No known food interactions.

DISEASE INTERACTIONS
Caution is advised when
taking flurbiprofen. Consult
your doctor if you have any
of the following: bleeding
problems, inflammation or
ulcers of the stomach and
intestines, diabetes mellitus,
systemic lupus erythematosus (SLE, lupus), anemia,
asthma, epilepsy, Parkin-
son's disease, kidney
stones, or a history of heart
disease or alcohol abuse.
Use of flurbiprofen may
cause complications in
patients with liver or kidney
disease, since these organs
work together to remove
the drug from the body.

Flutamide

Eulexin 125 mg
(Schering-Plough)

▶ Drug Class: Antiandrogen

▶ Available in: Capsules

▶ Available OTC? No

▶ As Generic? No

Side Effects

SERIOUS
Bluish coloring of lips, fingernails, or palms of hands (a sign of inadequate blood and oxygen supply to body tissues), dark urine, extreme dizziness or fainting, feeling of extreme pressure in the head, itching, loss of appetite, nausea or vomiting, pain in the right flank, shortness of breath, weak and rapid heartbeat, yellow discoloration of the skin or eyes (jaundice). Call your doctor immediately.

COMMON
Diarrhea, erectile dysfunction (impotence) or loss of sexual desire, sudden sweating and feeling of warmth.

LESS COMMON
Loss of appetite, tingling or numbness of hands or feet, swollen and tender breasts, swelling of feet or lower legs.

PRINCIPAL USES
To treat cancer of the prostate gland.

HOW THE DRUG WORKS
The growth of some types of prostate tumors is stimulated by the hormone testosterone. Flutamide interferes with the activity of testosterone, thus slowing or halting the growth of such tumors.

DOSAGE
250 mg every 8 hours, in conjunction with leuprolide, a synthetic form of luteinizing hormone-releasing hormone (LHRH), a hormone that also blocks the release of testosterone.

ONSET OF EFFECT
Unknown.

DURATION OF ACTION
Unknown.

DIETARY ADVICE
Take with or without food. Be sure to drink plenty of fluids.

STORAGE
Store in a tightly sealed container away from heat and direct light.

IF YOU MISS A DOSE
Take it as soon as you remember. If it is near the time for the next dose, skip the missed dose and resume your regular dosage schedule. Do not double the next dose.

STOPPING THE DRUG
The decision to stop taking the drug should be made in consultation with your physician.

PROLONGED USE
You should see your doctor regularly for tests and examinations if you take this drug for a prolonged period.

PRECAUTIONS
Over 60: The dosage may be reduced, because the medication takes longer to be eliminated from the body in older patients, but flutamide is not otherwise expected to cause different side effects or problems in older persons than it does in younger people.

Driving and Hazardous Work: Use of flutamide should not impair your ability to perform such tasks safely.

Alcohol: Limit alcohol to moderate intake only.

Pregnancy: Flutamide lowers sperm count, and the medication taken with it causes sterility that may be permanent. If you intend to have children, consult your doctor before you begin to take this medication to discuss utilizing a sperm bank.

Breast Feeding: Not applicable, since flutamide is not given to women.

Infants and Children: Flutamide is not recommended for children.

Special Concerns: If an anticoagulant is taken in combination with flutamide, close monitoring of blood clotting time is necessary, so that the dose of the anticoagulant can be adjusted if needed.

OVERDOSE
Symptoms: Dramatically slowed movement and activity, slow respiration, loss of muscle coordination, excessive tear production (weeping), loss of appetite, breast tenderness, gooseflesh, and vomiting.

What to Do: An overdose of flutamide is unlikely to be life-threatening. However, if someone takes a much larger dose than prescribed, call your doctor, emergency medical services (EMS), or the nearest poison control center immediately.

DRUG INTERACTIONS
The activity of an anticoagulant such as warfarin may be increased by flutamide. Consult your doctor for advice if you are taking an anticoagulant. Also consult your doctor if you are taking cholestyramine, cyclosporine, erythromycin, gemfibrozil, digoxin, cimetidine, ranitidine, omeprazole, or rifampin.

FOOD INTERACTIONS
No known food interactions.

DISEASE INTERACTIONS
You should not take flutamide if you have severe liver impairment. Consult your doctor if you have any other medical condition.

Fluticasone

BRAND NAMES
Flonase, Flovent

▶ Drug Class: Respiratory corticosteroid

▶ Available in: Oral inhalation, nasal spray

▶ Available OTC? No

▶ As Generic? No

Side Effects

SERIOUS
No serious side effects are associated with the use of fluticasone.

COMMON
Oral inhalation: Sore throat, white patches in mouth or throat, hoarseness. Nasal spray: Nosebleeds or bloody nasal secretions, nasal burning or irritation, sore throat.

LESS COMMON
Eye pain, watering eyes, gradual decrease of vision, stomach pain and digestive disturbances.

PRINCIPAL USES
To preventively treat bronchial asthma, and to treat allergic rhinitis (seasonal or perennial allergies such as hay fever).

HOW THE DRUG WORKS
Respiratory corticosteroids such as fluticasone primarily reduce or prevent inflammation of the lining of the airways (the underlying cause of asthma), reduce the allergic response to inhaled allergens, and inhibit the secretion of mucus within the airways.

DOSAGE
For asthma— Oral inhalation: 88 to 220 micrograms (mcg) a day, 2 times per day; not to exceed 440 mcg a day. For patients previously treated with oral corticosteroids: 880 mcg, 2 times a day. Dosage may gradually be reduced after 1 week of therapy. For allergic rhinitis— Nasal spray: Adults: 2 sprays (50 micrograms each) in each nostril once per day, or 1 spray in each nostril twice a day (in the morning and at night). Children ages 4 to 17: One spray in each nostril once a day. Dose, if needed, may be increased to 2 sprays in each nostril once a day. Maximum daily dose should not exceed 200 micrograms. After relief is achieved, the dose may be reduced to 1 spray per day.

ONSET OF EFFECT
Usually within 1 week; it may take 3 weeks for the full effect to occur.

DURATION OF ACTION
Unknown.

DIETARY ADVICE
No special restrictions.

STORAGE
Store the inhaler in a dry place away from heat and direct light.

IF YOU MISS A DOSE
Take it as soon as you remember. If it is near the time for the next dose, skip the missed dose and resume your regular dosage schedule. Do not double the next dose.

STOPPING THE DRUG
If you have been using fluticasone for a long period, do not stop taking it suddenly. Consult your doctor about how to stop.

PROLONGED USE
Consult your doctor about the need for regular medical tests and examinations if you must take this drug for a prolonged period of time.

PRECAUTIONS
Over 60: No special problems are expected.

Driving and Hazardous Work: The use of fluticasone should not impair your ability to perform such tasks safely.

Alcohol: No special precautions are necessary.

Pregnancy: Well-controlled studies of fluticasone use during pregnancy have not been done; it is generally not recommended unless the benefits clearly outweigh the risks. Consult your doctor.

Breast Feeding: Fluticasone may pass into breast milk; caution is advised. Consult your doctor for specific advice.

Infants and Children: Safety and effectiveness have not been established for children under age 4.

Special Concerns:
Inhaled steroids will not help an asthma attack in progress. Inhaled steroids can lower resistance to yeast infections of the mouth, throat, or voice box. To prevent yeast infections, gargle or rinse your mouth with water after each use; do not swallow the water. Know how to use the spray properly; read and follow the directions that come with the device. Before you have surgery, tell the doctor or dentist that you are using a steroid.

OVERDOSE
Symptoms: No cases of overdose have been reported.

What to Do: An overdose of fluticasone is unlikely. If you have any reason to suspect an overdose, contact your doctor or seek medical assistance right away.

DRUG INTERACTIONS
Consult your doctor for specific advice if you are taking systemic corticosteroids, other inhaled corticosteroids, or drugs that suppress the immune system.

FOOD INTERACTIONS
No known food interactions.

DISEASE INTERACTIONS
Caution is advised when taking fluticasone. Consult your doctor if you have any of the following: a lung disease such as tuberculosis; a herpes infection of the eye; nasal ulcers or recent nose surgery or injury; or any bacterial, viral, or fungal infection. If you are exposed to chicken pox or measles, tell your doctor at once.

Fluticasone/Salmeterol

BRAND NAME
Advair

- ▶ Drug Class:
  Bronchodilator/respiratory corticosteroid

- ▶ Available in: Inhalation powder

- ▶ Available OTC? No

- ▶ As Generic? No

Side Effects

SERIOUS
No serious side effects are associated with the use of fluticasone. Salmeterol may become ineffective if used too often, resulting in more-severe breathing difficulty that does not improve. Signs include persistent wheezing, coughing, or shortness of breath; confusion; bluish color to lips or fingernails; inability to speak. Other side effects include chest pain or heaviness; irregular, racing, fluttering, or pounding heartbeat; lightheadedness; fainting; severe weakness; severe headache.

COMMON
Headache, sore throat, runny or stuffy nose, white patches in mouth or throat, hoarseness.

LESS COMMON
Abdominal pain, diarrhea, nausea, cough, muscle aches, eye pain, watering eyes, gradual decrease of vision.

PRINCIPAL USES
To dilate air passages in the lungs that have become narrowed as a result of disease or inflammation. It is used in in treating asthma and chronic obstructive pulmonary disease (COPD) associated with chronic bronchitis.

HOW THE DRUG WORKS
Respiratory corticosteroids such as fluticasone primarily reduce or prevent inflammation of the lining of the airways (the underlying cause of asthma), reduce the allergic response to inhaled allergens, and inhibit the secretion of mucus within the airways. Salmeterol widens constricted airways in the lungs by relaxing the smooth muscles that surround the bronchial passages.

DOSAGE
COPD (adults) and asthma (adults and teenagers): 1 inhalation twice a day, 12 hours apart.

ONSET OF EFFECT
Within 30 minutes; it may take 1 to 3 weeks for the full effect to occur.

DURATION OF ACTION
Up to 12 hours.

DIETARY ADVICE
Maintain your usual food and fluid intake. Increase fluids if you have a fever or diarrhea, in hot weather, or during exercise.

STORAGE
Store the inhaler in a dry place away from heat and direct light.

IF YOU MISS A DOSE
Take it as soon as you remember. If it is near the time for the next dose, skip the missed dose and resume your regular dosage schedule. Do not double the next dose.

STOPPING THE DRUG
If you have been using this medication for a long period, do not stop taking it suddenly. Consult your doctor about how to stop.

PROLONGED USE
Consult your doctor about the need for regular medical tests and examinations if you must take this drug for a prolonged period of time.

PRECAUTIONS
Over 60: Adverse reactions may be more likely and more severe in older patients.

Driving and Hazardous Work: Do not drive or engage in hazardous work until you determine how the medicine affects you.

Alcohol: No special precautions are necessary.

Pregnancy: It is generally not recommended unless the benefits clearly outweigh the risks. Consult your doctor.

Breast Feeding: It is not known if this medication passes into breast milk. Consult your doctor.

Infants and Children: Use of this medication for COPD/bronchitis is not recommended in children younger than 12. For asthma, use is approved for children from the age of 4.

Special Concerns: Do not use this medication for acute or sudden attacks, or for worsening asthma. Pay heed to any asthma attack or other breathing difficulty that does not improve after your usual rescue treatment. Seek help immediately if you feel your lungs are persistently constricted, if you are using more than the recommended number of treatments or puffs per day, or if you feel a recent attack is somehow different from others. Keep the device dry. To prevent yeast infections, gargle or rinse your mouth with water after each use; do not swallow the water. Before surgery, tell the doctor or dentist that you are using a steroid.

OVERDOSE
Symptoms: Few cases have been reported. However, symptoms associated with overdose of the salmeterol component include chest pain or heaviness; irregular, racing, fluttering, or pounding heartbeat; dizziness; lightheadedness; severe weakness; fainting; severe headache; muscle tremors or shaking.

What to Do: If you suspect an overdose, contact your doctor or seek medical assistance right away.

DRUG INTERACTIONS
Consult your doctor if you are taking systemic corticosteroids, other inhaled corticosteroids, beta-blockers, or drugs that suppress the immune system.

FOOD INTERACTIONS
No known food interactions.

DISEASE INTERACTIONS
Consult your doctor if you have a history of any of the following: heart disease or heartbeat irregularities; high blood pressure; anxiety disorders; a thyroid condition; a lung disease such as tuberculosis; a herpes infection of the eye; nasal ulcers or recent nose surgery or injury; or any bacterial, viral, or fungal infection. If you are exposed to chicken pox or measles, tell your doctor at once.

Fluvastatin

BRAND NAME
Lescol

Lescol 20 mg
(NOVARTIS)

▶ Drug Class: Antilipidemic (cholesterol-lowering agent)

▶ Available in: Capsules

▶ Available OTC? No

▶ As Generic? No

Side Effects

SERIOUS
Fever, unusual or unexplained muscle aches and tenderness. Call your doctor right away.

COMMON
Side effects occur in only 1% to 2% of patients. These include constipation or diarrhea, dizziness or lightheadedness, bloating or gas, heartburn, nausea, skin rash, stomach pain, rise in liver enzymes.

LESS COMMON
Sleeping difficulty.

PRINCIPAL USES
To treat high cholesterol. Usually prescribed after first lines of treatment—including diet, weight loss, and exercise—fail to reduce total and low-density lipoprotein (LDL) cholesterol to acceptable levels.

HOW THE DRUG WORKS
Fluvastatin blocks the action of an enzyme required for the manufacture of cholesterol, thereby interfering with its formation. By lowering the amount of cholesterol in the liver cells, fluvastatin increases the formation of receptors for LDL, and thereby reduces blood levels of total and LDL cholesterol. In addition to lowering LDL cholesterol, fluvastatin also modestly reduces triglyceride levels and raises HDL (the so-called "good" cholesterol) levels.

DOSAGE
Initial dose is 20 mg, taken once a day in the evening. Dose may be increased by your doctor to 40 mg, taken once a day in the evening.

ONSET OF EFFECT
Within 2 to 4 weeks after starting therapy.

DURATION OF ACTION
The effect persists for the duration of therapy.

DIETARY ADVICE
Cholesterol-lowering drugs are only one part of a total program that should include regular exercise and a healthy diet. The American Heart Association publishes a "Healthy Heart" diet, which is recommended.

STORAGE
Store in a tightly sealed container away from heat and direct light. Keep away from moisture and extremes in temperature.

IF YOU MISS A DOSE
Take it as soon as you remember. Take your next dose at the proper time and resume your regular dosage schedule. Do not double the next dose.

STOPPING THE DRUG
The decision to stop taking the drug should be made in consultation with your doctor. Once the medication is discontinued, blood cholesterol is likely to return to original elevated levels.

PROLONGED USE
Side effects are more likely with prolonged use. As you continue with fluvastatin, your doctor will periodically order blood tests to evaluate liver function.

PRECAUTIONS
Over 60: No special problems are expected in older patients.

Driving and Hazardous Work: The use of fluvastatin should not impair your ability to perform such tasks safely.

Alcohol: No special precautions are necessary.

Pregnancy: Should not be used during pregnancy or by women who plan to become pregnant in the near future.

Breast Feeding: Fluvastatin passes into breast milk and is not recommended while breast feeding.

Infants and Children: Rarely used in children.

Special Concerns: Important elements of treatment for high cholesterol include proper diet, weight loss, regular moderate exercise, and the avoidance of certain medications that may increase cholesterol levels.

Because fluvastatin has potential side effects, it is important that you maintain a recommended healthy diet and cooperate with other treatments your physician may suggest.

OVERDOSE
Symptoms: An overdose of fluvastatin is unlikely.

What to Do: Emergency instructions not applicable.

DRUG INTERACTIONS
Consult your doctor if you are taking cyclosporine, gemfibrozil, niacin, antibiotics, especially erythromycin, or medications for fungus infections. All of these drugs may increase the risk of myositis (muscle inflammation) when taken with fluvastatin and may lead to kidney failure.

FOOD INTERACTIONS
No known food interactions.

DISEASE INTERACTIONS
Consult your doctor if you have any of the following problems: liver, kidney, or muscle disease, or a medical history involving organ transplant or recent surgery.

Fluvoxamine Maleate

▶ Drug Class: Selective
serotonin reuptake inhibitor
(SSRI) antidepressant/anti-
obsessive-compulsive agent

▶ Available in: Tablets

▶ Available OTC? No

▶ As Generic? Yes

Side Effects

SERIOUS
Decreased libido, sexual
dysfunction, diarrhea,
dizziness, rapid heartbeat,
difficulty breathing,
seizures, trembling, vom-
iting, difficulty swallowing, fainting, psychotic
reaction. Call your doctor
immediately.

COMMON
Insomnia, decreased
appetite, constipation,
dry mouth, drowsiness,
heartburn, runny nose,
unexpected weight loss,
headache, frequent urina-
tion, increased sweating,
change in taste, yawning.

LESS COMMON
Swelling of the feet or
lower legs, chills, gas,
weight gain.

PRINCIPAL USES
To treat obsessive-compulsive disorder.

HOW THE DRUG WORKS
Fluvoxamine affects levels
of serotonin, a brain chemical that is thought to be
linked to mood, emotions,
and mental state.

DOSAGE
Adults: To start, 50 mg
taken at bedtime; may be
increased gradually by your
doctor to 300 mg a day.
Doses greater than 100 mg
a day may be taken in 2
divided doses. Children
ages 8 to 17: To start, 25
mg taken at bedtime; may
be increased gradually by
your doctor to 200 mg a
day. Doses greater than 50
mg a day may be taken in
2 divided doses.

ONSET OF EFFECT
Unknown.

DURATION OF ACTION
Unknown.

DIETARY ADVICE
Fluvoxamine can be taken
without regard to diet. Do
not chew the tablet.

STORAGE
Store in a tightly sealed container away from heat, moisture, and direct light.

IF YOU MISS A DOSE
Take it as soon as you
remember. If it is near the
time for the next dose, skip
the missed dose and
resume your regular dosage
schedule. Do not double the
next dose.

STOPPING THE DRUG
Take it as prescribed for the
full treatment period, even if
you begin to feel better
before the scheduled end of
therapy. Discontinuing the
drug abruptly may produce
unpleasant withdrawal
symptoms. Dosage should
be reduced gradually
according to your doctor's
instructions.

PROLONGED USE
Consult your doctor about
the need for follow-up evaluation and tests if you must
take this drug for an
extended period.

PRECAUTIONS
Over 60: Adverse reactions
may be more likely and
more severe in older
patients. A lower dose
may be warranted.

**Driving and Hazardous
Work:** Use caution when
driving or engaging in hazardous work until you determine how the medication
affects you.

Alcohol: Avoid alcohol.

Pregnancy: Adequate
human studies have not
been done. Before taking
fluvoxamine, tell your doctor if you are pregnant or
plan to become pregnant.
Discuss with your doctor
the relative risks and benefits of using this drug while
pregnant.

Breast Feeding: Fluvoxamine passes into breast
milk; avoid or discontinue
use while nursing.

Infants and Children:
Not recommended for use
by children under age 8.
Antidepressants used for
any indication increase the
risk of suicidal thinking and
behavior (suicidality) in
children with major depression and other psychiatric
disorders. Discuss with
your doctor this risk versus
the benefits of using this
drug. Children should be
observed closely for worsening of symptoms, suicidality, or unusual changes in
behavior at the onset of
therapy and when making
changes in dosage.

OVERDOSE
Symptoms: Severe diarrhea; extreme dizziness,
drowsiness, difficulty awakening, or coma; rapid or
slow heartbeat; seizures; or
severe vomiting.

What to Do: Call your
doctor, emergency medical
services (EMS), or the
nearest poison control center immediately.

DRUG INTERACTIONS
You should not take fluvoxamine if you are taking terfenadine or astemizole.
Fluvoxamine and MAO
inhibitors should not be
used within 14 days of each
other. Very serious side
effects such as myoclonus
(uncontrolled muscle
jerking), hyperthermia
(excessive rise in body
temperature), and extreme
stiffness may result.
Consult your doctor for
specific advice if you are
taking or have recently
taken alprazolam, diazepam,
midazolam, triazolam,
beta-blockers, tricyclic antidepressants, carbamazepine,
clozapine, theophylline,
tryptophan, lithium, war-
farin, or methadone. Also
consult your doctor if you
smoke tobacco.

FOOD INTERACTIONS
No known food interactions.

DISEASE INTERACTIONS
Caution is advised when
taking fluvoxamine. Consult
your doctor if you have a
history of alcohol or drug
abuse, mania, or seizures.

Folic Acid (Folacin; Folate)

Side Effects

SERIOUS
Wheezing, breathing difficulty, chest pain, swelling, tightness in throat or chest, dizziness, rash, itching. Such symptoms may indicate a serious allergic reaction, although this is extremely rare.

COMMON
The are no known common side effects associated with the use of folic acid.

LESS COMMON
Mild allergic reactions.

PRINCIPAL USES
The vitamin folic acid (also known as folacin and folate) is prescribed for treatment or prevention of certain types of anemia that result from folic acid deficiency. Such deficiencies may occur due to insufficient intake of folic acid (a result of poor diet or malnutrition), an inability to absorb the vitamin (as occurs in gastrointestinal disease), impaired ability to utilize the vitamin (due to excessive alcohol intake or phenytoin use), or as a result of conditions requiring increased amounts of folic acid (as occurs with pregnancy, breast feeding, hemodialysis, hemolytic anemia, and bone marrow failure).

HOW THE DRUG WORKS
Folic acid enhances chemical reactions that contribute to the production of red blood cells, the manufacture of DNA needed for cell replication, and the metabolism of amino acids (compounds necessary for the manufacture of proteins).

DOSAGE
For severe deficiency—Adults and children, regardless of age: 1 mg daily. For recommended dietary allowances (RDAs)— Adults and adolescents: 400 micrograms (mcg).During pregnancy: 600 mcg, once daily. While breast feeding: 500 mcg, once daily. Children, newborn to 3 years of age: 65 to 250 mcg, once daily; children 4 to 8 years of age: 200 mcg, once daily; children 9 to 13 years of age: 300 mcg, once daily.

ONSET OF EFFECT
Folic acid is used immediately by the body for a number of vital chemical functions.

DURATION OF ACTION
Folic acid is required by your body on a daily basis throughout a lifetime.

DIETARY ADVICE
Maintain your usual food and fluid intake. Increase fluids if you have a fever or diarrhea, in hot weather, or during exercise. Follow your doctor's dietary advice (such as low-fat, low-salt, or low-cholesterol restrictions) to improve control over high blood pressure and heart disease.

STORAGE
Store in a tightly sealed container away from heat and direct light. Keep away from moisture and extremes in temperature.

IF YOU MISS A DOSE
Take it as soon as you remember. If it is near the time for the next dose, skip the missed dose and resume your regular dosage schedule. Do not double the next dose.

STOPPING THE DRUG
The decision to stop taking the drug should be made by your doctor.

PROLONGED USE
Therapy with folacin may require weeks or months.

PRECAUTIONS
Over 60: No special problems are expected in older patients.

Driving and Hazardous Work: The use of folic acid should not impair your ability to perform such tasks safely.

Alcohol: Alcohol impairs the body's utilization of folic acid; avoid it completely if you are taking folic acid.

Pregnancy: Folic acid supplementation is recommended during pregnancy.

Breast Feeding: Folic acid supplementation is recommended while nursing.

Infants and Children: Folic acid may be used regardless of age.

Special Concerns: Folic acid ingestion can mask vitamin B_{12} deficiency and lead to irreversible neurological damage; therefore, folic acid should be taken only upon the recommendation of your doctor. Folic acid deficiency should not occur, and supplementation is not necessary, in healthy individuals who consume a normal balanced diet. However, women who are capable of becoming pregnant are advised to take 400 mcg of supplemental folic acid on a daily basis to prevent certain birth defects.

OVERDOSE
Symptoms: No specific ones have been reported.

What to Do: An overdose of folic acid is not life-threatening. No emergency procedures are warranted.

DRUG INTERACTIONS
Consult your doctor for specific advice if you are taking analgesics (pain relievers), antibiotics, anticonvulsants, epoetin, estrogens, oral contraceptives, methotrexate, pyrimethamine, triamterene, sulfasalazine, or zinc supplements.

FOOD INTERACTIONS
No known food interactions.

DISEASE INTERACTIONS
Consult your doctor if you have pernicious anemia.

Fosamprenavir Calcium

▶ Drug Class: Antiviral/protease inhibitor

▶ Available in: Tablets

▶ Available OTC? No

▶ As Generic? No

Side Effects

SERIOUS
Severe rash or moderate rash with other symptoms. Call your doctor immediately. High blood sugar (diabetes) has occurred in patients taking drugs of this class, although a cause-and-effect relationship has not been established. Call your doctor if you develop increased thirst or excessive urination.

COMMON
Nausea, vomiting, diarrhea.

LESS COMMON
Taste disorders, numbness, tingling, prickling sensation, abdominal pain, rash, depression.

PRINCIPAL USES
To treat HIV (human immunodeficiency virus) infection in combination with other drugs. While not a cure for HIV infection, fosamprenavir may suppress the replication of the virus and delay progression of the disease.

HOW THE DRUG WORKS
Fosamprenavir blocks the activity of a viral protease, an enzyme that is needed by HIV to replicate. Blocking the protease causes HIV to make copies that cannot infect new cells.

DOSAGE
Adults: 1,400 mg fosamprenavir is taken with 200 mg ritonavir daily in one or two divided doses.

ONSET OF EFFECT
Unknown. With most antiretroviral drugs, an early response can be seen within the first few days of therapy, but the maximum effect may take at least 16 weeks.

DURATION OF ACTION
Unknown. Effects of the drug may be prolonged if this drug is used in combination with other effective drugs and the virus is maximally suppressed.

DIETARY ADVICE
Fosamprenavir can be taken with or without food.

STORAGE
Store in a tightly sealed container away from heat, moisture, and direct light.

IF YOU MISS A DOSE
If you miss a dose, take it as soon as you remember up to 4 hours late. If more than 4 hours, wait for the next scheduled dose. Do not double the next dose.

STOPPING THE DRUG
The decision to stop taking the drug should be made in consultation with your physician.

PROLONGED USE
See your doctor regularly for tests and examinations.

PRECAUTIONS
Over 60: No special studies have been done on older patients.

Driving and Hazardous Work: Do not drive or engage in hazardous work until you determine how the medicine affects you.

Alcohol: Avoid alcohol if liver function is impaired.

Pregnancy: Adequate studies of use during pregnancy have not been done; consult your doctor about whether the benefits outweigh potential risks to the unborn child. There is no evidence that the drug will reduce the risk of transmitting the virus from the mother to the fetus.

Breast Feeding: It is unknown whether fosamprenavir passes into breast milk; however, to avoid transmitting the virus to an uninfected child, women infected with HIV should not breast feed.

Infants and Children: Safety and effectiveness of fosamprenavir for children under the age of 18 have not been established.

Special Concerns: Do not take fosamprenavir with the herbal supplement St. John's wort because it may lead to drug resistance. Taking fosamprenavir does not eliminate the risk of passing the AIDS virus to other persons. Take appropriate preventive measures.

OVERDOSE
Symptoms: No cases of overdose have been reported.

What to Do: If you suspect an overdose or if someone takes a much larger dose than prescribed, immediately call your doctor or seek emergency medical help.

DRUG INTERACTIONS
Fosamprenavir should not be used at the same time as astemizole, dihydroergotamine, ergotamine, midazolam, triazolam, rifampin, the herb St. John's wort, lovastatin, simvastatin, pimozide, or cisapride. Use extreme caution if you are taking amiodarone, systemic lidocaine, tricyclic antidepressants, bepridil, quinidine, warfarin, sildenafil, tadalafil, vardenafil, phenobarbital, phenytoin, carbamazepine, or statin drugs (cholesterol-lowering). Fosamprenavir may alter hormonal levels of oral contraceptives; therefore, nonhormonal methods are recommended. Patients taking antacids or didanosine should take them at least one hour before or after fosamprenavir. If you are taking rifabutin, the dosage may have to be adjusted by your doctor. Consult your doctor if you are taking any other prescription or over-the-counter medications.

FOOD INTERACTIONS
No known interactions.

DISEASE INTERACTIONS
Consult your doctor for advice if you have any other medical condition, especially hemophilia. Use of fosamprenavir can cause complications in patients with diseases of the liver, which works to remove the drug from the body.

Foscarnet Sodium (Phosphonoformic Acid)

BRAND NAME
Foscavir

▶ Drug Class: Antiviral

▶ Available in: Injection

▶ Available OTC? No

▶ As Generic? No

Side Effects

SERIOUS
Kidney damage, causing symptoms such as increased or decreased urine output, increased or decreased urge to urinate, and increased thirst; toxicity of the nervous system, causing twitching or seizures, or numbness, tingling, or prickling in the extremities; fever and chills; pain at injection site; extreme fatigue. Call your doctor right away.

COMMON
Headache, abdominal pain or upset, nausea and vomiting, loss of weight or appetite, nervousness, anxiety, restlessness, mental confusion, lightheadedness, unusual fatigue.

LESS COMMON
Sores on the mouth, throat, penis, or vulva.

PRINCIPAL USES
To treat the eye disorder cytomegalovirus (CMV) retinitis in patients with acquired immunodeficiency syndrome (AIDS). Sometimes prescribed for other viral infections.

HOW THE DRUG WORKS
Foscarnet interferes with the activity of enzymes needed for the replication of viral DNA in cells, thus preventing CMV from multiplying.

DOSAGE
60 mg for every 2.2 lbs (1 kg) of body weight, injected into a vein every 8 hours for 2 to 3 weeks, followed by a maintenance dose of 90 to 120 mg for every 2.2 lbs, injected daily.

ONSET OF EFFECT
Immediate.

DURATION OF ACTION
24 hours.

DIETARY ADVICE
No special restrictions.

STORAGE
Not applicable, since this drug is administered exclusively in a health care facility or by a home intravenous (I.V.) infusion team.

IF YOU MISS A DOSE
Consult your doctor.

STOPPING THE DRUG
The decision to stop taking the drug should be made by your doctor.

PROLONGED USE
Your doctor should check your progress periodically.

PRECAUTIONS
Over 60: Adverse reactions may be more likely and more severe in older patients.

Driving and Hazardous Work: Do not drive or engage in hazardous work until you determine how the medicine affects you.

Alcohol: Avoid alcohol.

Pregnancy: In animal studies, foscarnet has been shown to cause birth defects. Human studies have not been done. Before taking this drug, tell your doctor if you are pregnant or are planning to become pregnant.

Breast Feeding: Foscarnet may pass into breast milk; caution is advised. Consult your doctor for specific advice.

Infants and Children: There is no specific information about the use of foscarnet by infants and children. Consult your doctor about the possible risks and benefits.

Special Concerns: Drink several glasses of water every day unless your doctor advises otherwise. While taking foscarnet, your doctor may conduct periodic tests on the function of your kidneys. Anemia caused by foscarnet may be severe enough to require blood transfusions. If you are receiving the drug as therapy for CMV retinitis, you should periodically receive eye examinations by an ophthalmologist to check for signs of vision loss. Foscarnet may cause sores on the genital organs. Washing the genitals after urinating may decrease the likelihood of this problem.

OVERDOSE
Symptoms: Sudden or severe onset of serious side effects.

What to Do: Call your doctor, emergency medical services (EMS), or the nearest poison control center immediately.

DRUG INTERACTIONS
Other drugs may interact with foscarnet. Consult your doctor for specific advice if you are taking amphotericin B, carmustine, cisplatin, combination pain medicines containing acetaminophen or aspirin, cyclosporine, deferoxamine, gentamicin, gold salts, any pain medicine, lithium, methotrexate, pentamidine, penicillamine, plicamycin, streptozocin, or tiopronin.

FOOD INTERACTIONS
No known food interactions.

DISEASE INTERACTIONS
Caution is advised when taking foscarnet. Consult your doctor if you have anemia, kidney disease, or dehydration.

Fosfomycin Tromethamine

▶ Drug Class: Antibiotic

▶ Available in: Powder for solution

▶ Available OTC? No

▶ As Generic? No

Side Effects

SERIOUS
No serious side effects are associated with the use of fosfomycin.

COMMON
Diarrhea, headache, vaginal itching, nausea, runny nose, back pain, painful menstruation, throat irritation, dizziness, abdominal pain, generalized pain, weakness, skin rash, indigestion or stomach upset. Call your doctor if such symptoms persist or interfere with daily activities.

LESS COMMON
Abnormal stools, loss of appetite, constipation, dry mouth, failure to urinate, ear disorders, fever, gas, flu-like symptoms, blood in urine, infection, insomnia, swollen lymph glands, nerve pain, nervousness, burning sensation, sleepiness, vomiting.

PRINCIPAL USES
To treat uncomplicated urinary tract infections (acute cystitis) in women.

HOW THE DRUG WORKS
Fosfomycin interferes with the formation of bacterial cell walls, rendering bacteria unable to multiply and spread.

DOSAGE
Adult and teenage females: 3 g in a single dose, given orally.

ONSET OF EFFECT
Within 3 hours.

DURATION OF ACTION
Unknown.

DIETARY ADVICE
No special dietary recommendations. Mix the powder with half a glass of water. (Do not use hot water.)

STORAGE
Store in a tightly sealed container away from heat, moisture, and direct light.

IF YOU MISS A DOSE
Not applicable. Fosfomycin is intended for one-time use.

STOPPING THE DRUG
Not applicable. Fosfomycin is intended for one-time use.

PROLONGED USE
Fosfomycin is intended for one-time use only. Repeated doses increase the likelihood of adverse side effects. Call your doctor if the infection has not improved, or has worsened, within 2 to 3 days.

PRECAUTIONS
Over 60: No special problems are expected.

Driving and Hazardous Work: Do not drive or engage in hazardous work until you determine how the medicine affects you.

Alcohol: No special precautions are necessary.

Pregnancy: Adequate studies of the use of this drug during pregnancy have not been done. Before taking fosfomycin, tell your doctor if you are pregnant or plan to become pregnant; discuss the relative risks and benefits of using the drug, and weigh them carefully.

Breast Feeding: It is not known whether fosfomycin passes into breast milk; caution is advised. Consult your doctor for specific advice.

Infants and Children: Not recommended for use by children under age 12.

Special Concerns: Urine tests to determine the type of bacteria causing the infection and its susceptibility to treatment should be done before and after the completion of therapy with fosfomycin.

OVERDOSE
Symptoms: An overdose with fosfomycin is unlikely to occur; no cases of overdose have been reported.

What to Do: Emergency instructions not applicable.

DRUG INTERACTIONS
Consult your doctor for specific advice if you are concurrently taking metoclopramide. Before taking fosfomycin, tell your doctor if you are taking any other prescription or over-the-counter medication.

FOOD INTERACTIONS
No known food interactions.

DISEASE INTERACTIONS
Caution is advised when taking fosfomycin. Consult your doctor if you have kidney disease or any other medical condition. Use of fosfomycin may cause complications in patients with kidney disease, since this organ works to remove the medication from the body.

Fosinopril Sodium

Monopril 10 mg
(BRISTOL-MYERS SQUIBB)

834

Additional photographs

▶ Drug Class: Angiotensin-converting enzyme (ACE) inhibitor

▶ Available in: Tablets

▶ Available OTC? No

▶ As Generic? Yes

Side Effects

SERIOUS
Fever and chills, sore throat and hoarseness, sudden difficulty breathing or swallowing, swelling of the face, mouth, or extremities, impaired kidney function (ankle swelling, decreased urination), confusion, yellow discoloration of the eyes or skin (indicating liver disorder), intense itching, chest pain or palpitations, abdominal pain. Serious side effects are very rare; contact your doctor immediately.

COMMON
Dry, persistent cough.

LESS COMMON
Dizziness or fainting, skin rash, numbness or tingling in the hands, feet, or lips, unusual fatigue or muscle weakness, nausea, drowsiness, loss of taste, headache.

PRINCIPAL USES
To control high blood pressure; to treat congestive heart failure; to treat patients with left ventricular dysfunction (damage to the pumping chamber of the heart); and to minimize further kidney damage in diabetics with mild kidney disease.

HOW THE DRUG WORKS
Angiotensin-converting enzyme (ACE) inhibitors block an enzyme that produces angiotensin, a naturally occurring substance that causes blood vessels to constrict and stimulates production of the adrenal hormone, aldosterone, which promotes sodium retention in the body. As a result, ACE inhibitors relax blood vessels (causing them to widen) and reduces sodium retention, which lowers blood pressure and so decreases the workload of the heart.

DOSAGE
Initial dose: 10 mg once a day. Maintenance dose: 20 to 80 mg a day, in 1 or 2 doses.

ONSET OF EFFECT
Within 1 hour.

DURATION OF ACTION
24 hours.

DIETARY ADVICE
Take fosinopril on an empty stomach, about 1 hour before mealtime. Follow your doctor's dietary advice (such as low-salt or low-cholesterol restrictions) to improve control over high blood pressure and heart disease. Avoid high-potassium foods like bananas and citrus fruits and juices, unless you are also taking medications, such as diuretics, that lower potassium levels.

STORAGE
Store in a tightly sealed container away from heat and direct light. Keep away from moisture and extremes in temperature.

IF YOU MISS A DOSE
Take it as soon as you remember. If it is near the time for the next dose, skip the missed dose and resume your regular dosage schedule. Do not double the next dose.

STOPPING THE DRUG
Do not stop taking this drug abruptly, as this may cause potentially serious health problems. Dosage should be reduced gradually, according to your doctor's instructions.

PROLONGED USE
Therapy with this medication may require months or years. Prolonged use may increase the risk of adverse effects.

PRECAUTIONS
Over 60: Adverse reactions may be more likely and more severe.

Driving and Hazardous Work: Avoid such activities until you determine how this medication affects you.

Alcohol: Consume alcohol only in moderation since it may increase the effect of the drug and cause an excessive drop in blood pressure. Consult your doctor for advice.

Pregnancy: Do not use fosinopril if you are pregnant or trying to become pregnant. Use of this drug during the last 6 months of pregnancy may cause severe defects, even death, in the fetus.

Breast Feeding: Fosinopril passes into breast milk and may be harmful to the infant; avoid using the drug while nursing.

Infants and Children: Fosinopril is generally not recommended for children.

OVERDOSE
Symptoms: No specific ones have been reported.

What to Do: While overdose is unlikely, call your doctor, emergency medical services (EMS), or the nearest poison control center immediately if you suspect that someone has taken a much larger dose than prescribed.

DRUG INTERACTIONS
Consult your doctor if you are taking diuretics (especially potassium-sparing diuretics), potassium supplements or drugs containing potassium (check ingredient labels), lithium, anticoagulants (such as warfarin), indomethacin or other anti-inflammatory drugs, antacids, allopurinol, or any over-the-counter medications (especially cold remedies and diet pills).

FOOD INTERACTIONS
Avoid low-salt milk and salt substitutes. Many brands contain high amounts of potassium. Avoid high-potassium foods like bananas and citrus fruits and juices.

DISEASE INTERACTIONS
Consult your doctor if you have systemic lupus erythematosus or if you have had a prior allergic reaction to ACE inhibitors. This medication should be used with caution by patients with severe kidney disease or renal artery stenosis (narrowing of one or both of the arteries that supply blood to the kidneys).

Furosemide

Generic 20 mg
(ROXANE)

834
Additional photographs

▶ Drug Class: Loop diuretic

▶ Available in: Tablets, oral
solution, injection

▶ Available OTC? No

▶ As Generic? Yes

Side Effects

SERIOUS
Skin rash, hives, intense
itching, swelling of the
mouth and throat, breath-
ing difficulty, mood or
mental changes, nausea
and vomiting, unusual
fatigue, black or tarry
stools. Call your doctor
immediately.

COMMON
Muscle cramps or pain.
Potassium depletion may
lead to heart palpitations
and weakness. Fluid
depletion may lead to
dizziness, especially upon
arising from a sitting or
lying position, as well as
thirst, dry mouth, and
constipation.

LESS COMMON
Buzzing or ringing in
ears, loss of hearing (particularly after intravenous
treatment), diarrhea, loss
of appetite, gout,
increased blood sugar (a
problem for diabetic
patients).

PRINCIPAL USES
To reduce fluid (salt and
water) accumulation that
leads to edema (swelling)
and breathlessness in
patients with heart disease,
cirrhosis of the liver, and
kidney disease. Furosemide
is also sometimes used to
help control high blood
pressure.

HOW THE DRUG WORKS
Loop diuretics work on a
specific portion of the kidney (the loop of Henle) to
increase the excretion of
water and sodium in urine.

DOSAGE
20 to 600 mg a day. Tablets
and solution: dosage is
given in 1, 2, or 3 divided
doses daily. Injection (given
in a hospital setting only):
dosage given in divided
doses every 2 to 3 hours or
as a continuous infusion.

ONSET OF EFFECT
20 to 60 minutes.

DURATION OF ACTION
Tablets and solution: 6 to 8
hours. Injection: 2 hours.

DIETARY ADVICE
Take with food to reduce
stomach irritation.

STORAGE
Keep in refrigerator, in a
light-resistant container. Do
not allow liquid forms to
freeze.

IF YOU MISS A DOSE
Take it as soon as you
remember. If it is near the
time for the next dose, skip
the missed dose and
resume your regular dosage
schedule. Do not double the
next dose.

STOPPING THE DRUG
The decision to stop taking
the drug should be made by
your doctor.

PROLONGED USE
No apparent problems. Regular examinations by your
doctor are advised.

PRECAUTIONS
Over 60: No special problems are expected.

**Driving and Hazardous
Work:** No special precautions are required.

Alcohol: No special precautions are required.

Pregnancy: Diuretics are
not useful for the normal
fluid retention that occurs
with pregnancy. In patients
who do need diuretic therapy, furosemide is generally
preferred, but should be
taken only after careful consultation with your primary
care doctor or OB/GYN
specialist.

Breast Feeding:
Furosemide passes into
breast milk; avoid or discontinue use while nursing.

Infants and Children:
Use furosemide only under
careful supervision by a
pediatrician.

Special Concerns: To
prevent sleep disruption,
avoid taking furosemide in
the evening. You may have
to take a potassium supplement or consume foods or
fluids high in potassium
while taking this drug.
Diabetic patients should
monitor their blood sugar
levels carefully.

OVERDOSE
Symptoms: Weakness,
lethargy, mental confusion,
muscle cramps.

What to Do: Call your
doctor, emergency medical
services (EMS), or the
nearest poison control center immediately.

DRUG INTERACTIONS
Consult your doctor about
any other drugs you are
taking, especially antibiotics, other blood pressure
drugs, any ACE inhibitor,
any pain reliever, lithium,
cortisone-related drugs,
digitalis-related drugs, or
any nonsteroidal anti-
inflammatory drug.

FOOD INTERACTIONS
None reported.

DISEASE INTERACTIONS
Caution is advised when
taking this medication. Consult your doctor if you have
diabetes, gout, or a hearing
problem, or have had a
recent heart attack.

Gabapentin

BRAND NAME
Neurontin

Neurontin 100 mg
(PARKE-DAVIS)

▶ Drug Class: Anticonvulsant

▶ Available in: Capsules, tablets

▶ Available OTC? No

▶ As Generic? Yes

Side Effects

SERIOUS
Fever, sore throat, swollen glands, red or purple point-like rash on the skin or mucous membranes, blistering or peeling skin lesions, mouth sores, easy bruising, paleness, weakness, confusion, lethargy, or seizures may be a sign of a potentially fatal blood disorder (aplastic anemia) or other complication. Call your physician immediately.

COMMON
Fatigue, dizziness, sedation, clumsiness or unsteadiness, unusual eye movements, blurred or altered vision, nausea, vomiting, tremor.

LESS COMMON
Diarrhea, muscle aches or weakness, dry mouth, headache, sleep disturbances, irritability, slurred speech. There are numerous additional side effects associated with the use of this drug; consult your doctor if you are concerned about any adverse or unusual reactions.

PRINCIPAL USES
To control certain kinds of seizures in the treatment of epilepsy. Gabapentin is often prescribed in combination with another anticonvulsant medication.

HOW THE DRUG WORKS
The mechanism of action is not well understood. It is believed that gabapentin inhibits activity in certain parts of the brain and suppresses the abnormal firing of neurons that causes seizures.

DOSAGE
Adults and teenagers: 900 to 3,600 mg a day, in 3 or 4 divided doses. Some patients require higher doses. The dose is started low and then gradually increased by your doctor to achieve maximum therapeutic benefit with a minimum of side effects. Children ages 3 to 12: To start, 10 to 15 mg per 2.2 lbs (1 kg), in 3 divided doses. The dose is started low and then gradually increased by your doctor to achieve maximum therapeutic benefit with a minimum of side effects.

ONSET OF EFFECT
Several hours.

DURATION OF ACTION
Maximum effectiveness lasts 5 to 8 hours or longer; effectiveness then gradually decreases.

DIETARY ADVICE
No special restrictions.

STORAGE
Store in a tightly sealed container away from heat, moisture, and direct light. Refrigerate the oral solution, but do not allow it to freeze.

IF YOU MISS A DOSE
Take it as soon as you remember. If your next dose is scheduled within the next 2 hours, take the missed dose, and take the next dose 1 to 2 hours later. Resume your regular dosage schedule. Do not double the next dose unless advised to do so by your doctor. Do not wait more than 12 hours between doses.

STOPPING THE DRUG
The decision to stop taking the drug should be made by your doctor. Never stop this drug abruptly because this may cause seizures. The dose is typically tapered over a period of weeks.

PROLONGED USE
Therapy with gabapentin may be required for months or years. Some side effects that are prominent during the first few weeks of therapy may subsequently diminish.

PRECAUTIONS
Over 60: Older persons may require lower doses to minimize side effects.

Driving and Hazardous Work: Avoid such activities until you determine how the medication affects you.

Alcohol: May contribute to excessive drowsiness.

Pregnancy: Adequate human studies of gabapentin during pregnancy have not been done, but the use of other anticonvulsants is associated with an increased risk of birth defects. However, seizures during pregnancy can also increase the risks to the unborn child. Discuss with your doctor the potential risks and benefits of using gabapentin during pregnancy. Folate supplementation is recommended beginning 1 to 2 months before conception and throughout pregnancy.

Breast Feeding: Gabapentin may pass into breast milk, although at low levels. Consult your doctor for specific advice if you are nursing.

Infants and Children: There are few published studies regarding the use of gabapentin in children age 12 and younger, but effectiveness should be similar to that seen in older patients. Safety and effectiveness have not been established for children under the age of 3.

Special Concerns: Your doctor may want you to wear a medical bracelet or carry an identification card saying that you are taking this drug.

OVERDOSE
Symptoms: There have been few reports of gabapentin overdose. Symptoms include double vision, slurred speech, drowsiness, lethargy, and diarrhea.

What to Do: Call your doctor, emergency medical services (EMS), or the nearest poison control center immediately.

DRUG INTERACTIONS
Gabapentin has no significant drug interactions.

FOOD INTERACTIONS
No known food interactions.

DISEASE INTERACTIONS
The dose of gabapentin may need to be lower in patients with kidney disease.

Galantamine Hydrobromide

BRAND NAME
Reminyl

▶ Drug Class: Reversible cholinesterase inhibitor

▶ Available in: Tablets

▶ Available OTC? No

▶ As Generic? No

Side Effects

SERIOUS
No serious side effects are associated with the use of galantamine.

COMMON
Nausea, vomiting, diarrhea, loss of appetite, and weight loss.

LESS COMMON
Fatigue, lightheadedness, dizziness, tremor, headache, abdominal pain, heartburn, depression, insomnia, drowsiness, runny nose, urinary tract infection, blood in the urine.

PRINCIPAL USES
To treat mild to moderate Alzheimer's disease.

HOW THE DRUG WORKS
The exact mechanism of action is unknown. However, galantamine is believed to work by inhibiting acetylcholinesterase enzymes, which reduces the breakdown of acetylcholine, a brain chemical crucial to memory. Acetylcholine deficiency is thought to result in memory loss associated with Alzheimer's disease.

DOSAGE
To start, 4 mg twice a day. After a minimum of four weeks of treatment, your doctor may increase the dose to 8 mg twice a day. The dose may be further increased after no less than a 4-week interval to 12 mg twice a day, if tolerated. People with moderate liver or kidney impairment should not take more than 16 mg a day.

ONSET OF EFFECT
Unknown.

DURATION OF ACTION
Unknown,

DIETARY ADVICE
Rivastigmine should be taken with food in the morning and evening.

STORAGE
Store in a tightly sealed container away from heat, moisture, and direct light.

IF YOU MISS A DOSE
Take it as soon as you remember. If it is near the time for the next dose, skip the missed dose and resume your regular dosage schedule. Do not double the next dose. If therapy has been interrupted for several days or longer, consult your doctor.

STOPPING THE DRUG
The decision to stop taking the drug should be made in consultation with your physician.

PROLONGED USE
No problems are expected with long-term use.

PRECAUTIONS
Over 60: No special problems are expected.

Driving and Hazardous Work: Do not drive or engage in hazardous work until you determine how the medicine affects you.

Alcohol: Avoid alcohol while using this medication.

Pregnancy: Adequate studies on the use of galantamine during pregnancy have not been done. Discuss with your doctor the relative risks and benefits of using this drug while pregnant.

Breast Feeding: It is not known whether galantamine passes into breast milk; caution is advised. Consult your doctor for specific advice.

Infants and Children: Galantamine is not intended for use in children.

Special Concerns: Galantamine will not cure Alzheimer's disease and will not stop the disease from getting worse, but it will improve cognitive ability of some patients.

OVERDOSE
Symptoms: Severe nausea, vomiting, increased salivation, sweating, slow heartbeat, low blood pressure, irregular breathing, unconsciousness, increased muscle weakness, death.

What to Do: Call your doctor, emergency medical services (EMS), or the nearest poison control center immediately.

DRUG INTERACTIONS
The following drugs may interact with galantamine. Consult your doctor for specific advice if you are taking anticholinergic drugs or paroxetine.

FOOD INTERACTIONS
No known food interactions.

DISEASE INTERACTIONS
Do not take galantamine if you have severe liver or kidney impairment. Caution is advised when taking this drug. Consult your doctor if you have any of the following: asthma, obstructive pulmonary disease, epilepsy or a history of seizures, heart problems, intestinal blockage, stomach or duodenal ulcer, liver disease, or urinary problems.

Ganciclovir Sodium

BRAND NAME
Cytovene

Cytovene 250 mg
(ROCHE)

▶ Drug Class: Antiviral

▶ Available in: Capsules, injection, intraocular implant

▶ Available OTC? No

▶ As Generic? Yes

Side Effects

SERIOUS
Unusual or persistent fevers, chills, unusual fatigue, sore throat, bruising, or bleeding (these may be signs of serious anemia or problems with the cells of your immune system); skin rash, tremor, eye pain, or sudden change in vision (blurring or partial loss of sight), pain at the injection site. Call your doctor immediately.

COMMON
No common side effects are associated with the use of ganciclovir.

LESS COMMON
Abdominal discomfort, decreased appetite, nausea, vomiting, sweating.

PRINCIPAL USES
To treat or prevent infections caused by cytomegalovirus (CMV). CMV infection of the eyes occurs in patients with weakened immune systems and is prevalent among people with AIDS. A more widespread infection with CMV may occur in patients who have received organ or bone marrow transplants and who are being treated with medications (immunosuppressants) to prevent rejection.

HOW THE DRUG WORKS
Ganciclovir interferes with the activity of enzymes needed for the replication of viral DNA in cells, thus preventing the virus from multiplying.

DOSAGE
Adults: Capsules (for maintenance and prevention therapy only; not for treatment of active infection): 1,000 mg, 3 times a day with food, or 500 mg every 3 hours while awake, for a total of 6 consecutive doses. Patients with kidney problems may require smaller doses. An injection form is available for hospitalized patients and those in special home care situations; the dose is determined by weight. The intraocular insert must be surgically implanted in the eye and replaced every 6 months.

ONSET OF EFFECT
Unknown.

DURATION OF ACTION
About 24 to 48 hours.

DIETARY ADVICE
Take the capsules with food. Increase fluids if you have a fever or diarrhea. Patients with AIDS are often weakened and may be unable to consume adequate amounts of nutritious food. Use special liquid supplements if necessary. Your doctor may refer you to a nutritionist.

STORAGE
Store in a tightly sealed container away from heat and direct light.

IF YOU MISS A DOSE
Take it as soon as you remember. If it is near the time for the next dose, skip the missed dose and resume your regular dosage schedule. Do not double the next dose.

STOPPING THE DRUG
Take it as prescribed for the full treatment period, even if you feel better before the scheduled end of therapy.

PROLONGED USE
Your doctor should check your progress periodically during prolonged use.

PRECAUTIONS
Over 60: Adverse reactions may be more likely and more severe in older patients.

Driving and Hazardous Work: Avoid such activities until you determine how the medicine affects you.

Alcohol: Avoid alcohol.

Pregnancy: Avoid use of this drug if you are pregnant or trying to become pregnant. If you must use the drug, use a reliable birth control method (both men and women) throughout therapy and for at least 3 months afterward.

Breast Feeding: Ganciclovir passes into breast milk and may be harmful to the nursing infant; do not breast feed when taking this drug.

Infants and Children: Not recommended for infants and children.

Special Concerns: Therapy with oral ganciclovir requires many weeks or months. Relapse of eye problems is common, once the drug is stopped. Remember that infection is a great threat to people with weakened immune systems. Do not receive any vaccinations without your doctor's approval, and try to avoid people with infections. Watch for unusual bleeding, bruising, or fevers.

OVERDOSE
Symptoms: Extreme weakness and dizziness, severe diarrhea and stomach upset, shortness of breath.

What to Do: Call your doctor, emergency medical services (EMS), or the nearest poison control center immediately.

DRUG INTERACTIONS
Consult your doctor for specific advice if you are taking amphotericin B, azathioprine, carmustine, chloramphenicol, cisplatin, cyclosporine, dapsone, deferoxamine, didanosine (ddI), flucytosine, gold salts, any pain medicine, lithium, methotrexate, pentamidine, penicillamine, plicamycin, probenecid, streptozocin, tiopronin, trimethoprim/sulfamethoxazole, or zidovudine (AZT).

FOOD INTERACTIONS
No known food interactions.

DISEASE INTERACTIONS
Consult your doctor for advice if you have been diagnosed as having a low white blood cell count, low platelet count, clotting or bleeding problems, or kidney disease.

BRAND NAME
Tequin

▶ Drug Class: Fluoroquinolone antibiotic

▶ Available in: Tablets, injection

▶ Available OTC? No

▶ As Generic? No

Side Effects

SERIOUS
Serious reactions to gatifloxacin are rare and include seizures, rapid heartbeat, mental confusion, hallucinations, agitation, nightmares, depression, shortness of breath, unusual swelling in the face or extremities, and loss of consciousness. Also skin burning, redness, blisters, rash, or itching on exposure to sunlight; increased risk of tendinitis or tendon rupture. Call your doctor immediately.

COMMON
Nausea, vaginitis, diarrhea, headache, dizziness.

LESS COMMON
Chills, fever, back pain, abdominal pain, constipation, heartburn, inflammation of the tongue, mouth sores, vomiting, swelling, insomnia, numbness, shortness of breath, sore throat, sweating, abnormal vision, change in sense of taste, ringing in the ears, painful urination, blood in the urine.

PRINCIPAL USES
To treat mild to severe bacterial infections, including acute sinusitis, community-acquired pneumonia, urinary tract infections, kidney infections, acute bacterial complications due to chronic bronchitis, and gonorrhea.

HOW THE DRUG WORKS
Gatifloxacin inhibits the activity of bacterial enzymes (DNA gyrase and a topoisomerase) that are necessary for proper DNA formation and replication. This fights infection by preventing bacteria from reproducing.

DOSAGE
For most infections: 400 mg once a day for 7 to 10 days (14 days for community-acquired pneumonia). For uncomplicated urinary tract infections: 400 mg as a one-time dose or 200 mg a day for 3 days. For gonorrhea: 400 mg as a one-time dose.

ONSET OF EFFECT
Varies depending on the infection being treated.

DURATION OF ACTION
Unknown.

DIETARY ADVICE
Can be taken without regard to meals.

STORAGE
Store in a tightly sealed container away from heat, moisture, and direct light.

IF YOU MISS A DOSE
Take it as soon as you remember. If it is near the time for the next dose, skip the missed dose and resume your regular dosage schedule. Do not double the next dose.

STOPPING THE DRUG
It is very important to take this drug as prescribed for the full treatment period, even if you begin to feel better before the scheduled end of therapy.

PROLONGED USE
If your symptoms do not improve or instead become worse after a few days, consult your doctor promptly. Gatifloxacin is typically taken for no more than 14 days.

PRECAUTIONS
Over 60: No special advice.

Driving and Hazardous Work: Avoid such activities until you determine how the medicine affects you.

Alcohol: It is advisable to abstain from alcohol when fighting an infection.

Pregnancy: In some animal tests, gatifloxacin has caused birth defects. Adequate human studies have not been done. It should be used during pregnancy only if potential benefits clearly justify the risks. Before you take gatifloxacin, tell your doctor if you are pregnant or plan to become pregnant.

Breast Feeding: Gatifloxacin may pass into breast milk and cause serious side effects in the nursing infant; use of the drug is discouraged when nursing.

Infants and Children: Gatifloxacin is not recommended for use by persons under the age of 18.

Special Concerns: Do not take this medicine if you are allergic to any quinolone antibiotic, such as ciprofloxacin, or lomefloxacin.

OVERDOSE
Symptoms: An overdose is unlikely to occur. Possible symptoms after an excessive dose may include decreased activity and rate of breathing, vomiting, tremors, and seizures.

What to Do: If you have any reason to suspect an overdose, call your doctor, emergency medical services (EMS), or the nearest poison control center.

DRUG INTERACTIONS
Because gatifloxacin can affect the function of the heart, it should not be used if you are taking antiarrhythmic drugs such as amiodarone, quinidine, procainamide, or sotalol. It should be used with caution in patients taking erythromycin, antipsychotics, tricylic antidepressants, warfarin, nonsteroidal anti-inflammatory drugs (NSAIDs), antidiabetic agents, or digoxin. Gatifloxacin should be taken at least 4 hours before using ferrous sulfate (iron supplement), dietary supplements containing zinc, didanosine, or antacids containing aluminum or magnesium salts.

FOOD INTERACTIONS
No known food interactions.

DISEASE INTERACTIONS
Gatifloxacin should not be taken by people with prolongation of the QT interval on an electrocardiogram, known heart rhythm disturbances, uncorrected hypokalemia (low blood potassium levels), or those taking antiarrhythmic drugs such as amiodarone, quinidine, procainamide, or sotalol. This drug should be used with caution in people with significant bradycardia (slow heart rate), recent myocardial ischemia, diabetes who are taking oral hypoglycemic drugs with or without insulin, known or suspected nervous system disorders, or those predisposed to seizures. People with impaired kidney function may require a reduced dose. Your doctor will determine the appropriate dose.

Gemfibrozil

BRAND NAME
Lopid

℞

Generic 600 mg
(LEMMON)

▶ Drug Class: Antilipidemic
(triglyceride-lowering agent)

▶ Available in: Tablets

▶ Available OTC? No

▶ As Generic? Yes

Side Effects

SERIOUS
Muscle aches and tenderness; crampy abdominal pain, especially in the area under the ribs on the right side, with nausea and vomiting (this is an uncommon, serious side effect that may indicate gallbladder disease); decreased urine output.

COMMON
Diarrhea, nausea, gas.

LESS COMMON
Decreased sexual ability; headache; weight gain; feelings similar to the flu, with muscle aches or cramps, weakness, and unusual tiredness; inflammation of mouth and lips; heartburn.

PRINCIPAL USES
To treat high levels of blood triglyceride. Usually prescribed after other treatments—including diet, weight loss, exercise, and control of diabetes (when present)—fail to lower triglyceride levels adequately.

HOW THE DRUG WORKS
Gemfibrozil speeds the removal of triglycerides from the lipoprotein known as very-low-density lipoprotein (VLDL), which is converted to low-density lipoprotein (LDL). In some people total and LDL cholesterol levels may rise while triglycerides fall.

DOSAGE
Adults: 600 milligrams, 2 times per day. Usually taken 30 to 60 minutes before morning and evening meals.

ONSET OF EFFECT
Improvement begins in about 1 week and becomes most noticeable in about 4 weeks.

DURATION OF ACTION
Blood triglyceride levels increase within a few weeks of stopping gemfibrozil.

DIETARY ADVICE
Follow your doctor's dietary advice to improve control over high blood pressure and help prevent heart disease. The American Heart Association publishes a "Healthy Heart" diet; discuss this with your doctor. Limit intake of alcohol, which can raise triglyceride levels.

STORAGE
Store in a tightly sealed container away from heat and direct light.

IF YOU MISS A DOSE
Take your missed dose as soon as you remember, unless the time for your next scheduled dose is within the next 2 hours. If so, do not take the missed dose. Take your next scheduled dose at the proper time, and resume your regular dosage schedule. Do not double the next dose.

STOPPING THE DRUG
Do not stop taking gemfibrozil on your own; the level of triglycerides in your blood will increase.

PROLONGED USE
Gemfibrozil is often taken for long periods of time. If your blood triglycerides do not diminish, your physician may stop the medication.

PRECAUTIONS
Over 60: Adverse reactions may be more likely and more severe in older patients.

Driving and Hazardous Work: The use of gemfibrozil should not impair your ability to perform such tasks safely.

Alcohol: Alcohol intake should be limited because it can raise triglyceride levels.

Pregnancy: Do not take gemfibrozil while pregnant unless your doctor indicates that the risks of stopping the drug are too great. Triglycerides increase substantially during pregnancy and extremely high triglycerides can trigger an attack of acute pancreatitis.

Breast Feeding: Avoid or discontinue usage while nursing.

Infants and Children: Rarely used in infants and children.

Special Concerns: The most important treatment for high levels of blood triglycerides is a proper diet, weight loss, regular moderate exercise, the avoidance of certain medications, and control of diabetes. Because gemfibrozil has potential side effects, it is important that you maintain a healthy diet and cooperate with other treatment strategies your physician may suggest. Gemfibrozil may increase the chances of gallbladder, liver, and pancreas problems; your physician will order periodic blood tests.

OVERDOSE
Symptoms: No specific ones have been reported.

What to Do: Emergency instructions not applicable.

DRUG INTERACTIONS
Do not take gemfibrozil with repaglinide or any of the group of cholesterol-lowering drugs referred to as "statins." Certain drugs may interact adversely with gemfibrozil, particularly anticoagulants (blood thinners, such as warfarin) and niacin. It may be necessary to reduce the dose of warfarin to prevent bleeding. The combination of gemfibrozil with either niacin or a statin drug can cause severe myositis (muscle inflammation), which can release a protein that damages the kidneys. Consult your doctor for specific advice.

FOOD INTERACTIONS
No known food interactions.

DISEASE INTERACTIONS
Inform your doctor if you have any of the following problems: gallstones, stomach or intestinal ulcer, kidney disease, muscle disease, or liver disease. The dose of gemfibrozil must be reduced in those with significant kidney damage.

Gemifloxacin Mesylate

▶ Drug Class: Fluoroquinolone antibiotic

▶ Available in: Tablets

▶ Available OTC? No

▶ As Generic? No

Side Effects

SERIOUS
Serious reactions to gemifloxacin are rare and include seizures, rapid heartbeat, mental confusion, hallucinations, depression, agitation, unusual swelling in the face or extremities, and loss of consciousness. Also skin burning, redness, blisters, rash, or itching on exposure to sunlight; increased risk of tendinitis or tendon rupture. Call your doctor immediately.

COMMON
Diarrhea, rash, nausea, headache, vomiting, stomach pain, dizziness, change in sense of taste.

LESS COMMON
Chills, fever, back pain, abdominal pain, constipation, heartburn, inflammation of the tongue, mouth sores, swelling, insomnia, numbness, shortness of breath, sore throat, sweating, abnormal vision, ringing in the ears, painful urination, blood in the urine.

PRINCIPAL USES
To treat mild to severe bacterial infections, including community-acquired pneumonia and acute bacterial complications due to chronic bronchitis.

HOW THE DRUG WORKS
Gemifloxacin inhibits the activity of bacterial enzymes (DNA gyrase and a topoisomerase) that are necessary for proper DNA formation and replication. This fights infection by preventing bacteria from reproducing.

DOSAGE
For community-acquired pneumonia: 320 mg a day for 7 days. For those with acute bacterial complications due to chronic bronchitis: 320 mg a day for 5 days. For those with impaired kidney function: Your doctor will determine the appropriate dosage.

ONSET OF EFFECT
Unknown.

DURATION OF ACTION
Unknown.

DIETARY ADVICE
Can be taken without regard to meals. Take with plenty of liquid.

STORAGE
Store in a tightly sealed container away from heat, moisture, and direct light.

IF YOU MISS A DOSE
Take it as soon as you remember. If it is near the time for the next dose, skip the missed dose and resume your regular dosage schedule. Do not double the next dose.

STOPPING THE DRUG
It is important to take this drug for the full treatment period, even if you begin to feel better before the scheduled end of therapy.

PROLONGED USE
If your symptoms do not improve or become worse after a few days, consult your doctor promptly. Gemifloxacin is typically taken for no more than 7 days.

PRECAUTIONS
Over 60: No special problems are expected.

Driving and Hazardous Work: Do not drive or engage in hazardous work until you determine how the medicine affects you.

Alcohol: It is advisable to abstain from alcohol when fighting an infection.

Pregnancy: In some animal tests, gemifloxacin has caused birth defects. Adequate studies in humans have not been done. It should be used during pregnancy only if potential benefits clearly justify the risks. Before you take gemifloxacin, tell your doctor if you are pregnant or plan to become pregnant.

Breast Feeding: Gemifloxacin may pass into breast milk and cause serious side effects in the nursing infant; use of the drug is discouraged when nursing.

Infants and Children: Gemifloxacin is not recommended for use by persons under the age of 18.

Special Concerns: Do not take this medicine if you are allergic to any quinolone antibiotic, such as ciprofloxacin, gatifloxacin, or lomefloxacin. Protect yourself from sun exposure while you are taking this drug, plus another 5 days.

OVERDOSE
Symptoms: An overdose is unlikely. Possible symptoms after an excessive dose may include decreased rate of breathing, vomiting, tremors, and seizures.

What to Do: If you have any reason to suspect an overdose, seek emergency medical assistance.

DRUG INTERACTIONS
Because gemifloxacin can affect the function of the heart, it should not be used if you are taking antiarrhythmic drugs such as amiodarone, quinidine, procainamide, or sotalol. It should be used with caution in patients taking erythromycin, antipsychotics, tricylic antidepressants, warfarin, or nonsteroidal anti-inflammatory drugs (NSAIDs), or corticosteroids. Gemifloxacin should be taken at least 3 hours after or 2 hours before using ferrous sulfate (iron supplement), dietary supplements or multivitamins containing zinc, didanosine, or antacids containing aluminum or magnesium salts. Gemifloxacin should be taken at least 2 hours before sucralfate.

FOOD INTERACTIONS
No known food interactions.

DISEASE INTERACTIONS
Gemifloxacin should not be taken by people with prolongation of the QT interval on an electrocardiogram, known heart rhythm disturbances, uncorrected hypokalemia (low blood potassium levels), or those taking antiarrhythmic drugs. This drug should be used with caution in people with significant bradycardia (slow heart rate), recent myocardial ischemia, known or suspected nervous system disorders, or those who are predisposed to seizures. People with impaired kidney function may require a reduced dose.

Gentamicin Topical

▶ Drug Class: Antibacterial
(topical)

▶ Available in: Cream, ointment

▶ Available OTC? No

▶ As Generic? Yes

Side Effects

SERIOUS
No serious side effects
are associated with topi-
cal gentamicin when
used as directed.

COMMON
No common side effects
are associated with topi-
cal gentamicin when
used as directed.

LESS COMMON
Itching, swelling,
increased redness, or discomfort at the application
site not present prior to
therapy (as a result of
allergic reaction).

PRINCIPAL USES
To treat minor bacterial
infections of the skin,
including infected bites,
burns, abrasions, and other
wounds; infected cysts, hair
follicles, and other skin
structures; and infections
complicating rashes,
eczema, dermatitis, and
other inflammatory skin
conditions. Gentamicin is
not effective against fungal
infections or viruses.

HOW THE DRUG WORKS
Gentamicin works by pre-
venting bacterial organisms
from manufacturing the vital
proteins they require for
growth and function.

DOSAGE
Adults, teenagers, and children over 1 year of age:
Apply it to the affected site
3 or 4 times a day.

ONSET OF EFFECT
Gentamicin begins killing
susceptible bacteria shortly
after contact. The drug's
effects may not be noticeable for several days.

DURATION OF ACTION
The exact duration of action
of gentamicin is not known,
but replenishing the topical
antibiotic 3 or 4 times a day
is sufficient for treatment.

DIETARY ADVICE
No special restrictions.

STORAGE
Store in a tightly sealed container away from heat, moisture, and direct light.

IF YOU MISS A DOSE
Apply it as soon as you
remember. If it is near the
time for the next dose, skip
the missed dose and
resume your regular dosage
schedule. Do not double the
next dose or apply exces-
sive amounts of the drug to
compensate for a missed
application.

STOPPING THE DRUG
Apply the medicine as prescribed by your doctor for
the full treatment period,
even if you begin to feel better before the scheduled
end of therapy.

PROLONGED USE
Therapy with gentamicin is
usually completed within 7
to 14 days. Use of any antibiotic drug for longer than
your doctor recommends
increases your risk of infection by drug-resistant bacteria or other microorganisms
(known as superinfection).

PRECAUTIONS
Over 60: Adverse reactions
may be more likely and
more severe in older
patients.

**Driving and Hazardous
Work:** No special precautions are necessary.

Alcohol: No special precautions are necessary.

Pregnancy: Problems in
pregnant women using gen-
tamicin have not been
reported. Consult your doctor for specific advice.

Breast Feeding: Gentamicin may pass into breast
milk; caution is advised.
Consult your doctor for
specific advice.

Infants and Children:
This drug is not recom-
mended for use by children
under 1 year of age.

Special Concerns: Make
sure you tell your doctor
about allergies that you
might have before taking
any antibiotic. There is
varying opinion as to
whether or not topical
antibiotics are effective to
treat infections. Tell your
doctor if your condition has
not improved within a few
days of starting gentamicin.

As with any other antibiotic,
gentamicin is useful only
against strains of bacteria
that are susceptible to its
effects.

OVERDOSE
Symptoms: No specific
ones have been reported.

What to Do: An overdose
of gentamicin is unlikely to
be life-threatening. How-
ever, if someone takes a
much larger dose than prescribed or accidentally
ingests the cream or ointment, call your doctor,
emergency medical services
(EMS), or the nearest poison control center.

DRUG INTERACTIONS
No drug interactions have
been reported. If you are
concerned about whether a
prescription or nonprescription medication you are taking may interact with topical
gentamicin, consult your
doctor or pharmacist for
current information.

FOOD INTERACTIONS
No known food interactions.

DISEASE INTERACTIONS
Caution is advised when
using gentamicin. Consult
your doctor if you have
hearing problems, kidney
disease, any prior reactions
to a skin cream or ointment,
or any history of allergic
reaction to antibiotics.

Glatiramer Acetate (Copolymer-1)

BRAND NAME
Copaxone

▶ Drug Class: Immunomodulator

▶ Available in: Powder that is used for injection

▶ Available OTC? No

▶ As Generic? No

Side Effects

SERIOUS
Severe pain or rash at injection site immediately after injection. Call your doctor immediately.

COMMON
Flushed skin, dizziness, depression, palpitations, anxiety, difficulty breathing, throat constriction, fast heartbeat, tremor, hives, transient chest pain, enlarged blood vessels, fever, chills, infection, migraine headache, loss of appetite, gastrointestinal disorders, nausea, vomiting, swelling of arms and legs, joint pains, anxiety, muscle tension, bronchitis, nasal inflammation, itching skin, ear pain, urge to urinate frequently.

LESS COMMON
There are no less-common side effects associated with glatiramer acetate.

PRINCIPAL USES
To prevent or reduce the frequency of relapses in patients with relapsing-remitting multiple sclerosis (the most common form of MS, in which periods of active disease alternate with periods of remission or reduced severity of symptoms).

HOW THE DRUG WORKS
Nerves are insulated by a layer of fatty material known as myelin. MS is a frequently progressive, often debilitating, disorder that occurs when the protective myelin is damaged at various (multiple) sites throughout the central nervous system (brain and spinal cord) by the body's own immune system, with the subsequent development of scarlike tissue, a process referred to by doctors as sclerosis. Glatiramer acetate is believed to block the attack on the myelin sheath, slowing the progress of the disease.

DOSAGE
20 mg injected under the skin once a day.

ONSET OF EFFECT
Unknown.

DURATION OF ACTION
Unknown.

DIETARY ADVICE
No special restrictions.

STORAGE
The powder should be kept refrigerated; if refrigeration is not available, it may be stored at room temperature for up to one week. The vials of sterile water with which the powder is mixed should be stored at room temperature. The powder and water should be kept in tightly sealed containers away from direct light.

IF YOU MISS A DOSE
Take it as soon as you remember. However, if it is near the time for the next dose, skip the missed dose and resume your regular dosage schedule. Do not double the next dose.

STOPPING THE DRUG
The decision to stop taking the drug should be made by your doctor.

PROLONGED USE
You should see your doctor regularly for tests and examinations if you must take this medicine for a prolonged period of time.

PRECAUTIONS
Over 60: No special problems are expected.

Driving and Hazardous Work: Do not drive or engage in hazardous activities until you determine how the drug affects you.

Alcohol: No special precautions are necessary.

Pregnancy: Glatiramer acetate has not been shown to cause birth defects in animals. Human studies have not been done. Before you take glatiramer acetate, tell your doctor if you are pregnant or plan to become pregnant.

Breast Feeding: Glatiramer acetate may pass into breast milk; caution is advised. Consult your doctor for specific information.

Infants and Children: The safety and effectiveness of glatiramer acetate in persons under age 18 have not been established.

Special Concerns: Glatiramer acetate should be injected at a different site every day during the week; 7 sites in all. Sites for self-injection are the arms, stomach, thighs, and hips. The injection is best given at the same time every day. To prepare the medication for injection, use a sterile syringe and needle to transfer the sterile water into the glatiramer acetate vial. Swirl the vial gently and let it stand at room temperature until the solid material is completely dissolved. Discard the preparation if it contains visible sediment. Put the preparation into a sterile syringe fitted with a new 27-gauge needle and make the injection under the skin at the selected site of the day. After the injection, a cotton ball should be held against the injection site for a few seconds, but the site should not be rubbed.

OVERDOSE
Symptoms: No specific ones have been reported.

What to Do: If someone receives a much larger dose than prescribed or accidentally ingests glatiramer acetate, call the nearest poison control center immediately.

DRUG INTERACTIONS
Other drugs potentially may interact with glatiramer acetate. Consult your doctor for advice if you are taking any other prescription or over-the-counter drug.

FOOD INTERACTIONS
No known food interactions.

DISEASE INTERACTIONS
Caution is advised when taking glatiramer acetate. Consult your physician if you have any other medical condition.

Glimepiride

Amaryl 2 mg
(HOECHST MARION ROUSSEL)

▶ Drug Class: Antidiabetic agent/sulfonylurea

▶ Available in: Tablets

▶ Available OTC? No

▶ As Generic? Yes

Side Effects

SERIOUS
Serious side effects are related to hypoglycemia, or low blood sugar, whose symptoms include perspiration or a cold sweat, restlessness, rapid pulse, anxious feeling, nausea, feelings of dizziness, weakness, or lightheadedness, poor coordination, slurred speech, confusion, sleepiness, seizures or convulsions, weakness of an arm, leg, or an entire side of the body, fainting. Seek emergency assistance. Administer sugar-containing substances only if the patient is conscious and alert. Other serious but less common side effects include low white blood cell count and elevation of liver-associated enzymes; these problems can be detected by your doctor.

COMMON
Dizziness, weakness, nausea, headache.

LESS COMMON
Skin reactions, such as itching, peeling, rashes, and hives; blurred vision; edema (swelling due to fluid retention) of face or extremities; severe tiredness; abdominal pain.

PRINCIPAL USES
Glimepiride is used to treat diabetes (high blood sugar) in patients who require little or no injectable insulin. It is used in conjunction with a special diet and exercise. Some patients may fail to respond initially or gradually lose their responsiveness to glimepiride. The antidiabetic agent metformin may be used in conjunction with glimepiride to achieve the desired results.

HOW THE DRUG WORKS
Glimepiride stimulates the release of insulin from the pancreas and makes the tissues of your body more responsive to insulin.

DOSAGE
Adults: 1 to 4 mg once daily, 30 minutes before breakfast. Children: Not recommended for use by children.

ONSET OF EFFECT
2 to 3 hours.

DURATION OF ACTION
12 to 24 hours.

DIETARY ADVICE
Maintain special diets as recommended by your doctor. Restrict excessive intake of sugar-containing snacks. Read food labels carefully.

STORAGE
Keep away from direct light, moisture, and extremes in temperature.

IF YOU MISS A DOSE
Take it as soon as you remember. If it is near the time for the next dose, skip the missed dose and resume your regular dosage schedule. Do not double the next dose.

STOPPING THE DRUG
The decision to stop taking glimepiride should be made by your doctor.

PROLONGED USE
Therapy with glimepiride may require months or years. Its prolonged use may be associated with an increased risk of side effects.

PRECAUTIONS
Over 60: Adverse reactions from this drug may be more likely and more severe.

Driving and Hazardous Work: Do not drive or engage in hazardous work until you determine how the medicine affects you.

Alcohol: Use only in a moderate, responsible fashion. Consult your doctor.

Pregnancy: Glimepiride should not be used during pregnancy.

Breast Feeding: It should not be used by nursing mothers.

Infants and Children: Not recommended for use by children.

Special Concerns: Understand the symptoms of low blood sugar. Always have easy access to sources of simple sugar—juice, candy bars, energy bars, hard candy, honey, sugar cubes, sugar dissolved in water—in the event you experience symptoms of hypoglycemia (low blood sugar). Inform your physician promptly about changes in the way you are feeling, changes in your lifestyle and level of activity, medications that you may have been prescribed by other specialists, medications that you have stopped taking, unusually high or low results for any at-home tests you use to check your urine or blood, episodes of low blood sugar, and pregnancy. Wear a special medical ID bracelet. Do not miss meals. Use caution when exercising.

OVERDOSE
Symptoms: Symptoms are similar to serious side effects.

What to Do: Call emergency medical services (EMS), your doctor, or the nearest poison control center immediately.

DRUG INTERACTIONS
Consult your doctor for specific advice if you are taking steroids and nonsteroidal anti-inflammatory drugs (such as ibuprofen, aspirin, or aspirin-containing drugs), anticoagulants, certain antibiotics, especially for fungal infections, diuretics, lithium, beta-blockers, ulcer medications, ciprofloxacin, cyclosporine, guanethidine, MAO inhibitors, quinidine, quinine, chloramphenicol, estrogen, isoniazid, thyroid hormones, theophylline, pentamidine phenothiazines, or phenytoin.

FOOD INTERACTIONS
No known food interactions.

DISEASE INTERACTIONS
Consult your doctor if you have diarrhea, persistent vomiting, malabsorption disease, liver, thyroid, kidney, or adrenal gland disease, fever, or infection.

Glipizide

Generic 5 mg
(**MYLAN**)

▸ Drug Class: Antidiabetic agent/sulfonylurea

▸ Available in: Tablets, extended-release tablets

▸ Available OTC? No

▸ As Generic? Yes

Side Effects

SERIOUS
Serious side effects are related to hypoglycemia, or low blood sugar, whose symptoms include perspiration or a cold sweat, restlessness, rapid pulse, anxious feeling, nausea, feelings of dizziness, weakness, or lightheadedness, poor coordination, slurred speech, confusion, drowsiness, seizures, weakness of an arm, leg, or an entire side of the body, and fainting. Seek emergency assistance. Administer sugar-containing substances only if the patient is conscious and alert. Other serious but less common side effects include low white blood cell count and elevation of liver-associated enzymes; these problems can be detected by your doctor.

COMMON
Dizziness, constipation, nausea, heartburn, unusual or changed taste of food, or unusual taste in the mouth.

LESS COMMON
Peeling, red, bruised, or itching skin, pale skin, edema (swelling) of face or extremities, reduced ability to exercise, headache, fever.

PRINCIPAL USES
Glipizide is used to lower blood glucose (sugar) levels in patients with (type 2) diabetes who require little or no injectable insulin. It is used in conjunction with a special diet and exercise. Some patients may fail to respond initially or gradually lose their responsiveness to glipizide. Other antidiabetic agents such as metformin may be used in conjunction with glipizide to achieve the desired results.

HOW THE DRUG WORKS
Glipizide stimulates the release of insulin from special cells in the pancreas and therefore helps to lower blood glucose.

DOSAGE
Usual starting dose: 5 mg a day, taken 30 minutes before breakfast. Dosage should be adjusted by 2.5 to 5 mg per day based on blood sugar response. When greater than 15 mg a day, dosages should be divided. In the elderly or patients with liver disease, the initial dose should be 2.5 mg a day. While the maximum dose is 40 mg a day, little additional benefit is derived from more than 20 mg a day. Extended-release tablets: 5 to 10 mg, once daily, usually with breakfast.

ONSET OF EFFECT
Within 30 minutes.

DURATION OF ACTION
12 to 24 hours.

DIETARY ADVICE
Maintain special diets as recommended by your doctor, nutritionist, or the American Diabetes Association. Restrict excessive intake of sugar-laden snacks. Read labels carefully when buying food.

STORAGE
Store away from direct light, moisture, and extremes in temperature.

IF YOU MISS A DOSE
Take it as soon as you remember. If it is near the time for the next dose, skip the missed dose and resume your regular dosage schedule. Do not double the next dose.

STOPPING THE DRUG
The decision to stop taking it should be made by your doctor.

PROLONGED USE
Therapy may require months or years. Prolonged use may be associated with an increased risk of side effects.

PRECAUTIONS
Over 60: Adverse reactions from this drug may be more likely and more severe.

Driving and Hazardous Work: Do not drive or engage in hazardous work until you determine how the medication affects you.

Alcohol: Drink only in moderation.

Pregnancy: Glipizide should not be used. Insulin is the treatment of choice for pregnant diabetic women.

Breast Feeding: This drug passes into breast milk, although it is uncertain whether this is harmful to nursing infants. Consult your doctor.

Infants and Children: Not recommended for use by children.

Special Concerns: Keep simple sugars (juice, candy bars, hard candy) on hand in the event of hypoglycemia. Inform your doctor promptly of changes in how you feel, unusually high or low results for any at-home tests, episodes of low blood sugar, or pregnancy. Wear a medical ID bracelet. Do not miss meals. Use caution when exercising.

OVERDOSE
Symptoms: Symptoms similar to serious side effects.

What to Do: Call emergency medical services (EMS), your doctor, or the nearest poison control center immediately.

DRUG INTERACTIONS
Consult your doctor for specific advice if you are taking anticoagulants, antibiotics (especially sulfa-containing antibiotics or those used to treat fungal infections), steroids, diuretics, seizure medications (such as carbamazepine or phenytoin), beta-blockers (which may include eye drops for glaucoma) or other blood pressure medications, lithium, ulcer drugs, guanethidine, MAO inhibitors, quinidine, quinine, salicylates, chloramphenicol, estrogens, isoniazid, thyroid hormones, theophylline, or pentamidine.

FOOD INTERACTIONS
Food delays the absorption of immediate-release tablets.

DISEASE INTERACTIONS
Consult your doctor if you have diarrhea, persistent vomiting, malabsorption disease, liver, thyroid, kidney, or adrenal gland disease, fever, infection, or impending or recent surgery.

Glipizide/Metformin

BRAND NAME
Metaglip

▶ Drug Class: Antidiabetic agent combination

▶ Available in: Tablets

▶ Available OTC? No

▶ As Generic? No

Side Effects

SERIOUS
Serious side effects are related to hypoglycemia, or low blood sugar, whose symptoms include cold sweats, restlessness, rapid pulse, anxious feeling, dizziness, weakness, or lightheadedness, poor coordination, slurred speech, confusion, drowsiness, seizures, and fainting. Seek emergency assistance. Other serious but less common side effects of glipizide include low white blood cell count and elevation of liver-associated enzymes. In rare cases, metformin may lead to lactic acidosis, a potentially life-threatening buildup of lactic acid in the blood. Symptoms include rapid, shallow breathing, unusual sleepiness or weakness, muscle pain, and abdominal distress.

COMMON
Diarrhea, nausea, and vomiting. Usually such symptoms are mild and transient. Consult your doctor if symptoms persist or if they increase in severity.

LESS COMMON
Peeling, red, bruised, or itching skin, pale skin, edema (swelling) of face or extremities, reduced ability to exercise, headache, fever, unpleasant or metallic taste in mouth.

PRINCIPAL USES
This drug combination is used to lower blood glucose (sugar) levels in patients with (type 2) diabetes whose blood sugar levels cannot be adequately controlled by diet and exercise alone. Used as second-line therapy when diet, exercise, and initial treatment with a sulfonylurea (such as glipizide) or metformin do not adequately control blood sugar levels.

HOW THE DRUG WORKS
Glipizide stimulates the release of insulin from special cells in the pancreas and therefore helps to lower blood glucose. Metformin increases the body's sensitivity and responsiveness to its own insulin.

DOSAGE
Initial therapy: To start, 2.5 mg/250 mg (glipizide/metformin) once a day with a meal. More intensive therapy: 2.5 mg/500 mg or 5 mg/500 mg twice daily with the morning and evening meals. Maximum daily dosage should not exceed 20 mg glipizide and 2,000 mg metformin.

ONSET OF EFFECT
Within 2 to 4 weeks.

DURATION OF ACTION
Unknown.

DIETARY ADVICE
Take with meals to reduce risk of stomach upset. Tablets must be swallowed whole, not crushed or chewed.

STORAGE
Store in a tightly sealed container away from heat, moisture, and direct light.

IF YOU MISS A DOSE
Take it with food as soon as you remember. However, if it is almost time for the next dose, skip the missed dose and resume your regular dosage schedule. Do not double the next dose.

STOPPING THE DRUG
Stop taking only when your doctor advises.

PROLONGED USE
Therapy may require months or years. Prolonged use may be associated with an increased risk of side effects.

PRECAUTIONS

Over 60: Because metformin is cleared by the kidneys, extra caution is warranted in thin, elderly patients with mild renal insufficiency (not often detected by the usual tests for kidney impairment).

Driving and Hazardous Work: Do not drive or engage in hazardous work until you determine how the medication affects you.

Alcohol: Excessive amounts of alcohol can result in abnormally low blood glucose levels.

Pregnancy: Taking this drug combination is not advised during pregnancy. Consult your doctor if you become pregnant or plan to become pregnant.

Breast Feeding: The components of this drug combination pass into breast milk, although it is uncertain whether this is harmful to nursing infants. Consult your doctor.

Infants and Children: Safety and effectiveness of this drug have not been established in children.

Special Concerns: Do not take this drug if you have previously had an allergic reaction to metformin or glipizide.

OVERDOSE
Symptoms: Symptoms similar to serious side effects.

What to Do: Seek emergency medical assistance.

DRUG INTERACTIONS
Consult your doctor for specific advice if you are taking anticoagulants, antibiotics (especially sulfa-containing antibiotics or those used to treat fungal infections), steroids, diuretics, seizure medications (such as carbamazepine or phenytoin), beta-blockers (which may include eye drops for glaucoma) or other blood pressure medications, lithium, ulcer drugs, guanethidine, MAO inhibitors, cimetidine, digoxin, furosemide, morphine, procainamide, quinidine, quinine, salicylates, chloramphenicol, estrogens, isoniazid, thyroid hormones, theophylline, ranitidine, trimethoprim, triamterene, vancomycin, or pentamidine.

FOOD INTERACTIONS
None.

DISEASE INTERACTIONS
Do not take this drug if you have any condition that requires careful control of blood glucose levels, such as severe infection; any condition contributing to abnormally low blood oxygen levels, such as congestive heart failure or emphysema; metabolic acidosis (buildup of acid in the blood); a history of alcohol abuse; or kidney or liver disease. Consult your doctor if you have diarrhea, persistent vomiting, malabsorption disease, liver, thyroid, kidney, or adrenal gland disease, fever, infection, or impending or recent surgery.

Glucagon

▶ Drug Class: Hormone; antidote; antidiabetic agent

▶ Available in: Injection

▶ Available OTC? No

▶ As Generic? Yes

Side Effects

SERIOUS
No serious side effects
are associated with
glucagon.

COMMON
Nausea may be
associated with higher
dosages.

LESS COMMON
Rare allergic reactions
(wheezing, itching,
weakness); redness and
pain at site of injection.
Consult your doctor if
such side effects persist
or recur.

PRINCIPAL USES
Glucagon is an injectable
drug that is used for the
emergency treatment of low
blood sugar in diabetics
who are unable to take any
sugar-containing foods or
liquids by mouth. These
patients are usually unconscious or very confused
and sleepy.

HOW THE DRUG WORKS
Glucagon stimulates the
liver to release glucose
(sugar) into the blood-
stream.

DOSAGE
Adults and children weighing more than 45 pounds: 1
mg, by injection. Children
less than 45 pounds: 0.5 mg.
Doses may be repeated
twice, at 15 minute intervals. Glucagon emergency
kits usually contain two
vials. One is glucagon. The
other is a fluid that must
be used to dilute glucagon
before it can be drawn up
in a syringe and injected.

ONSET OF EFFECT
Within 15 minutes.

DURATION OF ACTION
The effect persists for 1 to 2
hours.

DIETARY ADVICE
Solutions containing glucose
(sugar) must be adminis-
tered following glucagon
injections for the drug to
work properly.

STORAGE
Store in a tightly sealed container away from heat and
direct light. If you prepared
glucagon for injection but
did not use it, it may be
refrigerated and kept for no
more than 48 hours.

IF YOU MISS A DOSE
Not applicable; glucagon is
used only in emergencies.

STOPPING THE DRUG
If the patient has not
responded within 15 min-
utes of the first injection,
do not stop glucagon treatments. You may administer
2 more injections at 15-
minute intervals.

PROLONGED USE
Not applicable.

PRECAUTIONS
Over 60: No unusual problems are expected.

**Driving and Hazardous
Work:** Not applicable.

Alcohol: Not applicable.

Pregnancy: Glucagon may
be administered.

Breast Feeding: It is
unlikely that glucagon is
hazardous to nursing
infants, since the drug is
used only occasionally,
although no studies have
been done to confirm this.

Infants and Children:
Not applicable.

Special Concerns:
Glucagon is effective only if
given by injection. Therefore, it is very important
that family members or
caregivers know exactly
how to prepare glucagon for
injection. The best time to
read and understand
glucagon instructions is
before an emergency
occurs. Any diabetic patient
who is confused, drowsy,
sleepy, or unconscious
should be assumed to have
low blood sugar. Do not
attempt to feed drowsy, dis-
oriented, or unconscious
individuals. Administer
glucagon promptly. If not
already notified, emergency
personnel should be con-
tacted immediately after the
first glucagon dose has
been injected. Do not wait
for further doses to be

given before calling for
emergency assistance. Do
not wait for additional 15-
minute intervals. Glucagon
is not a cure for low blood
sugar. It is an emergency
treatment that may be life-
saving, but it is only a temporary treatment that buys
time. Even after glucagon
injection, blood sugar may
fall again to dangerously
low levels. Do not assume
that the danger has passed
after successful treatment
with glucagon. Any patient
who was ill enough to
receive glucagon needs to
be evaluated fully by a
physician.

OVERDOSE
Symptoms: Nausea, vomiting, severe weakness, irregular heartbeat, hoarseness,
or cramps.

What to Do: An overdose
of glucagon is unlikely to be
life-threatening. However, if
someone receives a much
larger dose than prescribed,
call your doctor, emergency
medical services (EMS), or
the nearest poison control
center immediately.

DRUG INTERACTIONS
None known.

FOOD INTERACTIONS
No known food interactions.

DISEASE INTERACTIONS
Inform your doctor if you
have insulinoma or
pheochromocytoma. While
these conditions may com-
plicate the use of glucagon,
they do not prohibit a
patient from receiving the
drug in an emergency.

Glyburide

Generic 2.5 mg
(GENEVA)

Additional photographs

▶ Drug Class: Antidiabetic
agent/sulfonylurea

▶ Available in: Tablets

▶ Available OTC? No

▶ As Generic? Yes

Side Effects

SERIOUS
Serious side effects are
related to hypoglycemia,
or low blood sugar,
whose symptoms include
perspiration or a cold
sweat, restlessness, rapid
pulse, anxious feeling,
nausea, feelings of dizziness, weakness, or light-
headedness, poor
coordination, slurred
speech, confusion, sleepiness, seizures, weakness
of an arm, leg, or an
entire side of the body,
and fainting. Seek emer-
gency assistance. Admin-
ister sugar-containing
substances only if the
patient is conscious and
alert. Other serious but
less common side effects
include bone marrow
suppression, hemolytic
anemia, and elevation of
liver-associated enzymes;
these problems can be
detected by your doctor.

COMMON
Bloating, heartburn, nau-
sea, indigestion.

LESS COMMON
Blurred vision, changes in
taste, itching, hives, joint
or muscle pain.

PRINCIPAL USES
To help control adult-onset
(non-insulin-dependent, or
type 2) diabetes. Glyburide
is sometimes used in con-
junction with metformin
(another oral antidiabetic).

HOW THE DRUG WORKS
Glyburide stimulates the
release of insulin by the
pancreas and decreases
sugar production in the
liver.

DOSAGE
Starting dose is 2.5 to 5 mg
daily, 30 minutes before
breakfast. It can be
increased by your doctor in
increments of 2.5 mg to a
maximum of 20 mg per day,
or decreased if needed.
Elderly patients or those
with kidney or liver dysfunction should receive an initial
dose of 1.25 mg per day. If
the daily maintenance dose
is increased to 10 mg or
more, the total dose should
be divided equally between
breakfast and dinner.

ONSET OF EFFECT
1 hour.

DURATION OF ACTION
24 hours.

DIETARY ADVICE
It is usually taken 30
minutes before breakfast.

STORAGE
Store in a tightly sealed container away from heat and
direct light.

IF YOU MISS A DOSE
Take it as soon as you
remember. If it is near the
time for the next dose, skip
the missed dose and
resume your regular dosage
schedule. Do not double the
next dose.

STOPPING THE DRUG
The decision to stop taking
the drug should be made by
your doctor. You may need
to take glyburide for the
rest of your life.

PROLONGED USE
Periodic blood tests should
be done to determine how
prolonged use affects blood
sugar levels.

PRECAUTIONS
Over 60: Treatment should
start with lower doses,
which should be increased
slowly as determined by
periodic tests. Adverse
reactions may be more
likely and more severe
in older patients.

**Driving and Hazardous
Work:** Do not drive or
engage in hazardous work
until you determine how the
medication affects you.

Alcohol: Avoid alcohol.

Pregnancy: Uncontrolled
blood sugar levels during
pregnancy are associated
with an increased risk of
birth defects, so many
experts recommend a
switch to insulin during
pregnancy.

Breast Feeding: Gly-
buride may pass into breast
milk; caution is advised.
Consult your doctor for
advice.

Infants and Children:
Glyburide does not work in
juvenile-onset, insulin-
dependent diabetes.

Special Concerns: Carry
medical identification that
says you have diabetes. If
you are under stress due to
an infection, fever, an injury,
or surgery, you may need
insulin therapy in addition
to or instead of glyburide.

OVERDOSE
Symptoms: Symptoms are
similar to serious side
effects.

What to Do: An overdose
of glyburide is unlikely to
be life-threatening. How-
ever, if someone takes a
much larger dose than prescribed, call your doctor,
emergency medical services
(EMS), or the nearest poison control center.

DRUG INTERACTIONS
Consult your doctor for specific advice if you are taking
anabolic steroids, aspirin or
other salicylates, cimetidine,
gemfibrozil, fenfluramine,
MAO inhibitors, phenylbutazone, ranitidine, sulfa drugs,
beta-blockers, bumetanide,
diazoxide, ethacrynic acid,
furosemide, phenytoin,
rifampin, thiazide diuretics,
thyroid hormone, antacids,
antifungal agents, enalapril,
steroids, or warfarin.

FOOD INTERACTIONS
Glyburide is just part of the
treatment for diabetes; be
sure to follow the diet recommended by your doctor.

DISEASE INTERACTIONS
Use of this medication may
cause complications in
patients with liver or kidney
disease, since these organs
work together to remove
the drug from the body.

Glyburide/Metformin

▶ Drug Class: Antidiabetic agent combination

▶ Available in: Tablets

▶ Available OTC? No

▶ As Generic? No

Side Effects

SERIOUS
In rare cases, metformin may lead to lactic acidosis, a potentially life-threatening buildup of lactic acid in the blood. Symptoms include rapid, shallow breathing, unusual sleepiness or weakness, muscle pain, and abdominal distress. Glyburide can cause abnormally low blood glucose levels (hypoglycemia); symptoms include blurred vision, cold sweats, confusion, anxiousness, rapid heartbeat, shakiness, and nausea. Seek medical assistance immediately. Administer sugar-containing substances only if the patient is conscious and alert. Other serious but less common side effects include bone marrow suppression, hemolytic anemia, and elevation of liver enzymes; these problems can be detected by your doctor.

COMMON
Diarrhea, nausea, vomiting, abdominal bloating, gas, diminished appetite, heartburn, indigestion. Often such symptoms are mild and transient. Consult your doctor if the symptoms persist or increase in severity.

LESS COMMON
Blurred vision, changes in taste, itching, hives, joint or muscle pain.

PRINCIPAL USES
This drug combination is used to help control blood glucose levels in patients with type 2 diabetes.

HOW THE DRUG WORKS
Metformin decreases the liver's production of glucose, inhibits the absorption of glucose from the intestine, and increases the uptake and utilization of glucose by muscle and other peripheral tissues. Glyburide, a sulfonylurea, stimulates the release of insulin by the pancreas.

DOSAGE
Your doctor will determine the appropriate dosage. Starting dose is generally 1.25 to 5 mg glyburide and 250 to 500 mg metformin once or twice daily, with a meal. The dose can be decreased or increased by your doctor to a maximum of 20 mg glyburide and 2,000 mg metformin per day, if needed.

ONSET OF EFFECT
1 to 2 hours.

DURATION OF ACTION
24 hours.

DIETARY ADVICE
Take with meals to reduce risk of stomach upset. Tablets must be swallowed whole, not crushed or chewed.

STORAGE
Store in a sealed container at room temperature away from heat, moisture, and direct light.

IF YOU MISS A DOSE
Take it with food as soon as you remember. However, if it is almost time for the next dose, skip the missed dose and resume your regular dosage schedule. Do not double the next dose.

STOPPING THE DRUG
The decision to stop taking the drug should be made by your doctor. You may need to take this medication for the rest of your life.

PROLONGED USE
Periodic blood tests should be done to determine how prolonged use affects blood sugar levels.

PRECAUTIONS
Over 60: Because metformin is metabolized in the kidneys, extra caution is warranted in thin, elderly patients with mild renal insufficiency (not often detected by the usual tests for kidney impairment). Higher doses should be avoided or used with caution in elderly patients.

Driving and Hazardous Work: Do not drive or engage in hazardous work until you determine how the medication affects you.

Alcohol: Avoid alcohol.

Pregnancy: Taking this medication is not advised during pregnancy. Consult your doctor if you become pregnant or plan to become pregnant; insulin is usually the treatment of choice for pregnant diabetic women.

Breast Feeding: This medication may pass into breast milk; caution is advised. Consult your doctor for advice.

Infants and Children: This medication is not recommended for use in children under the age of 18.

Special Concerns: Carry medical identification that says you have diabetes. If you are under stress due to an infection, fever, an injury, or surgery, you may need insulin therapy in addition to or instead of this drug.

OVERDOSE
Symptoms: Symptoms of lactic acidosis or hypoglycemia (see Serious Side Effects).

What to Do: Seek emergency medical assistance right away.

DRUG INTERACTIONS
Consult your doctor for specific advice if you are taking anabolic steroids, aspirin or other salicylates, cimetidine, gemfibrozil, fenfluramine, MAO inhibitors, phenylbutazone, ranitidine, sulfa drugs, beta-blockers, bumetanide, diazoxide, ethacrynic acid, furosemide, phenytoin, rifampin, thiazide diuretics, thyroid hormone, antacids, antifungal agents, enalapril, steroids, warfarin, amiloride, calcium channel blockers, digoxin, morphine, procainamide, quinidine, quinine, trimethoprim, triamterene, or vancomycin.

FOOD INTERACTIONS
The amount and type of food you eat affect your blood glucose levels.

DISEASE INTERACTIONS
Do not take this medication if you have any condition that requires careful control of blood glucose levels, such as severe infection; any condition contributing to abnormally low blood oxygen levels, such as congestive heart failure or emphysema; metabolic acidosis (buildup of acid in the blood); a history of alcohol abuse; or kidney or liver disease.

BRAND NAMES
Glyrol, Osmoglyn

▶ Drug Class: Diuretic, antiglaucoma agent

▶ Available in: Oral solution

▶ Available OTC? No

▶ As Generic? Yes

Side Effects

SERIOUS
Confusion, heart rhythm irregularities. Call your doctor immediately.

COMMON
Headache, nausea, and vomiting.

LESS COMMON
Dizziness, diarrhea, dry mouth, increased thirst.

PRINCIPAL USES
To treat glaucoma.

HOW THE DRUG WORKS
Glaucoma, a sight-threatening disorder, occurs when aqueous humor (the fluid inside the eye) cannot drain properly, causing an increase in pressure within the eyeball (intraocular pressure). This can damage the optic nerve and lead to a gradually progressive loss of vision. Oral glycerin promotes outflow of aqueous humor, thereby reducing intraocular pressure. It is used on a short-term basis to reduce eye pressure until further medical intervention, such as other medications or surgery, can be implemented for more long-term control of glaucoma.

DOSAGE
Adults: To start, 1 dose of 1 to 2 grams (g) per 2.2 lbs (1 kg) of body weight. Additional doses of 500 mg per 2.2 lbs may be given 4 times a day if needed. Children: To start, 1 dose of 1 to 1.5 g per 2.2 lbs. Dose may be repeated in 4 to 8 hours if needed.

ONSET OF EFFECT
Within 10 minutes.

DURATION OF ACTION
About 5 hours.

DIETARY ADVICE
No special restrictions.

STORAGE
Store in a tightly sealed container away from heat and direct light. Do not allow it to freeze.

IF YOU MISS A DOSE
If this drug is prescribed beyond immediate short-term use, take the missed dose as soon as you remember. However, if it is near the time for the next dose, skip the missed dose and resume your regular dosage schedule. Do not double the next dose.

STOPPING THE DRUG
If this drug is prescribed beyond immediate short-term use, take it as prescribed for the full treatment period.

PROLONGED USE
In most cases oral glycerin is used exclusively on a short-term basis, either in a doctor's office or hospital, until other forms of treatment can be implemented.

PRECAUTIONS
Over 60: Excessive dehydration may be more likely to occur in older patients.

Driving and Hazardous Work: Do not drive or engage in hazardous work until you determine how the medicine affects you.

Alcohol: No special precautions are necessary.

Pregnancy: Adequate studies have not been done. Before taking oral glycerin, tell your doctor if you are pregnant or plan to become pregnant.

Breast Feeding: Glycerin may pass into breast milk; caution is advised. Consult your doctor for specific advice.

Infants and Children: No special problems expected.

Special Concerns: To improve the taste of glycerin, it can be mixed with a small amount of unsweetened orange, lemon, or lime juice, poured over ice, and sipped through a straw. If you experience a headache while taking glycerin, you should lie down while you take it and for a short time afterward. If your headaches continue or become severe, consult your doctor. Diabetic patients must be sure their ophthalmologist and other doctors know they have diabetes and that it is under good control. This medication may interfere with blood sugar control.

OVERDOSE
Symptoms: Severe dehydration, heart rhythm abnormalities (cardiac arrhythmias), loss of consciousness, coma.

What to Do: Call your doctor, emergency medical services (EMS), or the nearest poison control center immediately.

DRUG INTERACTIONS
Consult your doctor for specific advice if you are taking a diuretic or any other prescription or over-the-counter medication.

FOOD INTERACTIONS
No known food interactions.

DISEASE INTERACTIONS
Caution is advised when taking glycerin. Consult your doctor if you have any of the following: diabetes mellitus, heart disease, hypovolemia (insufficient fluid volume in the body, due to dehydration or other causes), hypervolemia (excess fluid volume in the body, causing circulatory problems and swelling at various sites, due to fluid retention in the tissues), or a psychological condition associated with persistent confusion. Use of glycerin may cause complications in patients with kidney disease, since this organ works to remove the medication from the body.

BRAND NAMES
Fleet Babylax, Fleet
Glycerine Laxative,
Sani-Supp

▶ Drug Class: Hyperosmotic laxative

▶ Available in: Rectal solution, rectal suppositories

▶ Available OTC? Yes

▶ As Generic? Yes

Side Effects

SERIOUS
There are no serious side effects associated with the use of glycerin rectal.

COMMON
Cramping.

LESS COMMON
Rectal pain, itching, or burning sensation. This is thought to be more common with dosage forms that require an applicator. If you notice increased pain or bleeding from the rectum after use of glycerin products, call your doctor. Weakness, sweating, and symptoms of dehydration (thirst, dizziness) also may occur.

PRINCIPAL USES
To treat constipation.

HOW THE DRUG WORKS
Glycerin attracts and retains water in the intestine, softening stools and inducing the urge to defecate.

DOSAGE
Adults and children age 6 and older: Insert one suppository or 5 to 15 ml of solution as rectal enema and retain for 15 minutes. Do not lubricate suppositories with anything other than water.

ONSET OF EFFECT
Within 15 to 60 minutes.

DURATION OF ACTION
Only while the solution or suppository is within the rectum.

DIETARY ADVICE
Maintain your usual food and fluid intake. Increase your intake of fluids if you have a fever or diarrhea, during hot weather, or during exercise.

STORAGE
Store solutions and suppositories away from heat, moisture, and direct light. Suppositories may be refrigerated, but do not allow them to freeze.

IF YOU MISS A DOSE
Laxatives are usually prescribed for use only on an as-needed basis and are not meant to be taken regularly or for a prolonged period.

STOPPING THE DRUG
Take rectal glycerin only as needed. However, you may stop using it if you are feeling better before the scheduled end of therapy.

PROLONGED USE
Prolonged, excessive use of glycerin may be associated with an increased risk of side effects, including laxative dependence. Therefore, do not use glycerin for more than 3 to 5 days unless your doctor instructs you to do otherwise.

PRECAUTIONS
Over 60: Adverse reactions may be more likely and more severe in older patients.

Driving and Hazardous Work: Do not drive or engage in hazardous work until you determine how the medicine affects you.

Alcohol: No special precautions are required.

Pregnancy: Adequate human studies have not been done. Before taking glycerin, tell your doctor if you are or are planning to become pregnant.

Breast Feeding: Glycerin suppositories may be used safely by nursing mothers.

Infants and Children: Not recommended for use by children under age 6.

Special Concerns: A single missed bowel movement does not constitute constipation; do not use glycerin under such circumstances. Prolonged constipation or persistent rectal pain and discomfort should be evaluated by your doctor. Remember that chronic use of glycerin or any laxative can lead to laxative dependence. You should be sure to consume adequate amounts of bulk in your diet; good sources include bran or other cereals, fresh fruit, and vegetables.

OVERDOSE
Symptoms: No specific ones have been reported.

What to Do: An overdose of glycerin is unlikely to be life-threatening. However, if someone takes a much larger dose than prescribed, call your doctor.

DRUG INTERACTIONS
No significant drug interactions have been reported.

FOOD INTERACTIONS
No known food interactions.

DISEASE INTERACTIONS
Caution is advised when taking glycerin laxatives. Consult your doctor if you have any of the following: abdominal pain and fever, rectal bleeding, ostomy (an artificial surgical opening in the body to allow the release of urine or feces), diabetes mellitus, heart or kidney disease, or high blood pressure.

Glycopyrrolate

▶ Drug Class: Anticholinergic, antispasmodic

▶ Available in: Tablets

▶ Available OTC? No

▶ As Generic? Yes

Side Effects

SERIOUS
Hives, rash, intense itching, faintness, or swelling soon after a dose. Call your doctor immediately.

COMMON
Enlarged pupils, blurred vision, constipation, dry mouth, difficulty urinating or inability to urinate, breathing difficulty.

LESS COMMON
Disorientation, irritability, incoherence, weakness, rapid or slow pulse, heart palpitations, unusual sensitivity of eyes to light, difficulty swallowing, nausea, vomiting, bloated abdomen, stomach upset, decreased sweating, skin problems, fever, loss of taste, impotence.

PRINCIPAL USES
To treat stomach ulcers and ease cramps and spasms of the stomach and intestines.

HOW THE DRUG WORKS
Glycopyrrolate inhibits gastrointestinal nerve receptor sites that stimulate both the secretion of stomach acid and smooth muscle activity in the digestive tract.

DOSAGE
Usually 1 to 2 mg, 2 to 3 times a day, with a maximum of 8 mg per day.

ONSET OF EFFECT
15 to 30 minutes.

DURATION OF ACTION
Up to 7 hours.

DIETARY ADVICE
Unless your doctor tells you otherwise, take glycopyrrolate 30 minutes to 1 hour before meals.

STORAGE
Store in a tightly sealed container away from heat and direct light.

IF YOU MISS A DOSE
Take it as soon as you remember. If it is near the time for the next dose, skip the missed dose and resume your regular dosage schedule. Do not double the next dose.

STOPPING THE DRUG
Take it as prescribed for the full treatment period, or stop taking it if you are feeling better before the scheduled end of therapy. Do not stop the drug suddenly; consult your doctor about reducing the dose gradually.

PROLONGED USE
Prolonged use may cause chronic constipation and fecal impaction. Consult your doctor immediately.

PRECAUTIONS
Over 60: Adverse reactions may be more likely and more severe in older patients.

Driving and Hazardous Work: Do not drive or engage in hazardous work until you determine how glycopyrrolate affects you. Use of this medicine disqualifies you from piloting aircraft.

Alcohol: No special precautions are necessary.

Pregnancy: Safety of using this drug during pregnancy has not been established. Before taking glycopyrrolate, tell your doctor if you are pregnant or plan to become pregnant and discuss whether the benefits clearly outweigh any potential risks.

Breast Feeding: Glycopyrrolate passes into breast milk; avoid or discontinue use while nursing.

Infants and Children: Smaller doses are recommended for infants and children. Glycopyrrolate should be given to young patients only under close medical supervision.

Special Concerns: Be sure that any doctor or dentist you go to knows that you are taking glycopyrrolate. To prevent heatstroke, avoid becoming overheated during exertion. Take this drug 2 to 3 hours before or after any antacids you are taking.

OVERDOSE
Symptoms: Blurred vision, dry mouth, low blood pressure, decreased breathing rate, rapid heartbeat, drowsiness, inability to urinate, flushed, hot, dry skin.

What to Do: Call your doctor, emergency medical services (EMS), or the nearest poison control center immediately.

DRUG INTERACTIONS
Consult your doctor for specific advice if you are taking antacids, other anticholinergics, tricyclic antidepressants, cyclopropane, cortisone drugs, digitalis drugs, haloperidol, ketoconazole, meperidine, methylphenidate, molindone, narcotic pain relievers, potassium chloride, quinidine, sedatives, or any central nervous system depressants.

FOOD INTERACTIONS
Avoid taking large amounts of vitamin C. No other food interactions are known.

DISEASE INTERACTIONS
Caution is advised while taking glycopyrrolate. Consult your doctor if you have any of the following: open-angle glaucoma, angina, chronic bronchitis, asthma, liver disease, hiatal hernia, enlarged prostate, myasthenia gravis, peptic ulcer, kidney disease, or thyroid disease.

Gold Sodium Thiomalate

BRAND NAME
Myochrysine

▶ Drug Class: Antirheumatic

▶ Available in: Injection

▶ Available OTC? No

▶ As Generic? Yes

Side Effects

SERIOUS
Severe abdominal pain or bloody, black, or tarry stools; confusion; seizures.

COMMON
Temporary joint pain shortly after injection, itching, skin rash, indigestion, heartburn, constipation.

LESS COMMON
Hives, bloody or cloudy urine, sore tongue, bleeding, red, sore, swollen gums; painful sores in the mouth or throat.

PRINCIPAL USES
To treat rheumatoid arthritis. Gold sodium thiomalate is generally prescribed for patients who have not responded adequately to more conservative arthritis treatments, such as aspirin, nonsteroidal anti-inflammatory drugs (NSAIDs), and corticosteroids.

HOW THE DRUG WORKS
Gold sodium thiomalate contains gold. It is not precisely known how gold compounds work, but evidently they reduce some of the painful joint inflammation associated with arthritis. This drug can halt the progress of severe rheumatoid arthritis, preventing further joint damage, and in some cases it may bring about a remission from the disease.

DOSAGE
Adults: 10 mg given once by intramuscular injection during week 1. This is followed by 25 mg given once by injection during week 2, then 25 to 50 mg given once weekly until satisfactory relief is achieved or until 1,000 mg have been administered. If a satisfactory response is achieved, your doctor will begin a maintenance dose of 25 to 50 mg given once by injection every 2 to 4 weeks. Children: 10 mg given once by injection during week 1. This is followed by 1 mg per 2.2 lbs (1 kg) of body weight (but not more than 50 mg) given once by injection during week 2. Further doses are spaced similarly to the adult schedule, with the amount of drug determined by the weight of the child.

ONSET OF EFFECT
Within 6 to 8 weeks at the earliest.

DURATION OF ACTION
Unknown.

DIETARY ADVICE
Maintain your usual food and fluid intake.

STORAGE
Not applicable.

IG YOU MISS A DOSE
Consult your physician.

STOPPING THE DRUG
Your doctor will stop this medication depending on whether you respond satisfactorily, develop side effects that make continuation impossible, or approach the maximum amount of drug that can be taken safely.

PROLONGED USE
Several months of therapy may be necessary to determine whether this medication is helping you. Prolonged use may be associated with an increased risk of side effects.

PRECAUTIONS
Over 60: Adverse reactions may be more likely and severe.

Driving and Hazardous Work: Do not drive or engage in hazardous work until you determine how the medicine affects you.

Alcohol: Avoid alcohol.

Pregnancy: Do not use this drug during pregnancy.

Breast Feeding: This drug may pass into breast milk; caution is advised. Consult your doctor for specific advice.

Infants and Children: Consult your pediatrician.

Special Concerns: Gold compounds may have many adverse effects. Your doctor may order periodic blood tests to determine if you are having any undesirable reactions, such as anemia, low white blood cell count, or protein in the urine. This drug may increase your sensitivity to sunlight. Avoid direct sunlight during peak hours; wear protective clothing and use sunscreens.

OVERDOSE
Symptoms: No specific ones have been reported.

What to Do: Not applicable; an overdose of gold sodium thiomalate is unlikely to be administered by your doctor.

DRUG INTERACTIONS
Consult your doctor for advice if you are taking penicillamine or drugs that may depress bone marrow production, such as seizure medications or chemotherapy agents to treat cancer.

FOOD INTERACTIONS
No known food interactions.

DISEASE INTERACTIONS
Consult your doctor if you have anemia or any other blood disease, skin disease, colitis or any other intestinal disease, ulcers or heartburn, kidney disease, or systemic lupus erythematosus (SLE).

Goserelin Acetate

▶ Drug Class: Antineoplastic (anticancer) agent

▶ Available in: Implant

▶ Available OTC? No

▶ As Generic? No

Side Effects

SERIOUS
Bone pain; numbness or tingling of hands or feet; difficulty urinating; muscle weakness of the arms or legs. This may occur shortly after therapy begins. Call your doctor.

COMMON
Hot flashes; change in sex drive or decreased interest in sexual activity; erectile dysfunction (impotence); pelvic pain during sex; vaginal dryness and itching.

LESS COMMON
Edema (swelling in the extremities due to fluid retention); dizziness; headache; increased appetite; nausea or vomiting; abdominal pain; pain at application site; sore throat; change in voice; itching; leg cramps; breast pain or swelling; weight gain; chest pain; joint pain; acne or skin rash; increased anxiety or irritability, mood swings, or depression; fatigue; difficulty sleeping; nausea; increase in body or facial hair (in women); decrease in breast size.

PRINCIPAL USES
To treat advanced forms of prostate cancer in men, and to treat advanced forms of breast cancer in women. It may also be used by women to relieve the pain and discomfort of endometriosis.

HOW THE DRUG WORKS
In men, goserelin decreases blood levels of testosterone. This slows the growth of cells in the prostate gland, which may lead to improvement of some of the pain and discomfort of advanced prostate cancer. In women, goserelin decreases blood levels of estrogen and thereby may relieve some of the symptoms of advanced breast cancer. In women with endometriosis, reduced blood levels of estrogen lead to shrinking of endometrial tissue (uterine lining) and thus eases the painful cyclical flare-ups of endometriosis.

DOSAGE
Goserelin implants containing 3.6 mg of medication are placed just under the skin of the upper abdominal wall once every 28 days.

ONSET OF EFFECT
Within 2 to 4 weeks.

DURATION OF ACTION
Blood levels of the hormones testosterone and estrogen remain low for the duration of therapy with goserelin.

DIETARY ADVICE
Maintain your usual food and fluid intake. Increase fluids if you have a fever or diarrhea. Patients with cancer are often weakened by their illness, medications, or other treatments, and may be unable to consume adequate quantities of nutritious food. They should use liquid nutritional supplements if necessary.

STORAGE
Not applicable.

IF YOU MISS A DOSE
Not applicable; the medication is delivered continuously in the form of an implant under the skin.

STOPPING THE DRUG
The decision to stop taking the drug should be made by your doctor.

PROLONGED USE
You should see your doctor regularly for tests and examinations while taking this medicine. Therapy with goserelin for prostate and breast cancer may be required for an indefinite period. Therapy with goserelin for endometriosis is usually completed within 6 months.

PRECAUTIONS

Over 60: Adverse reactions may be more likely and more severe in older patients.

Driving and Hazardous Work: Do not drive or engage in hazardous work until you determine how the medication affects you.

Alcohol: Use alcohol only in moderation.

Pregnancy: Avoid or immediately discontinue taking the drug if you are pregnant or trying to become pregnant.

Breast Feeding: Avoid or discontinue use while breast feeding.

Infants and Children: This drug is not recommended for use by nonmenstruating females under the age of 18.

Special Concerns: Women of childbearing age must use effective non-hormonal contraception (that is, a form other than birth control pills) during treatment with goserelin and for 12 weeks following the end of therapy. In men, goserelin will cause sterility for at least the duration of therapy.

OVERDOSE
Symptoms: No specific ones have been reported.

What to Do: An overdose of goserelin is unlikely to be life-threatening.

DRUG INTERACTIONS
No specific ones known.

FOOD INTERACTIONS
No known food interactions.

DISEASE INTERACTIONS
No specific ones known.

Griseofulvin

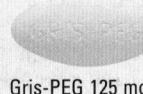

Gris-PEG 125 mg
(WYETH-AYERST)

▸ Drug Class: Antifungal

▸ Available in: Microsize
capsules, oral suspension,
tablets, ultramicrosize tablets

▸ Available OTC? No

▸ As Generic? Yes

Side Effects

SERIOUS
Irritation or soreness of
mouth or tongue; skin
rash, hives, or itching;
confusion; increased
sensitivity of eyes to
sunlight. Call your
doctor immediately.

COMMON
Headache.

LESS COMMON
Insomnia, stomach pain,
nausea or vomiting,
unusual fatigue, dizzi-
ness, diarrhea.

PRINCIPAL USES
To treat various forms of
fungal infection, including
ringworm (tinea barbae,
tinea capitis, tinea corporis),
jock itch (tinea cruris), athlete's foot (tinea pedis), and
nail fungus (tinea unguium).

HOW THE DRUG WORKS
Griseofulvin prevents fungal
organisms from manufacturing vital substances
required for reproduction.

DOSAGE
Microsize capsules, oral
suspension, tablets— Adults
and teenagers: For feet and
nails: 500 mg every 12
hours. For scalp, skin, and
groin: 250 mg every 12
hours or 500 mg once a day.
Children: 5 mg per 2.2 lbs
(1 kg) of body weight every
12 hours, or 10 mg per 2.2
lbs once a day. Ultramicrosize tablets— Adults and
teenagers: For feet and
nails: 250 to 375 mg every
12 hours. For scalp, skin,
and groin: 125 to 187.5 mg
every 12 hours, or 250 to
375 mg once a day. Children
age 2 and older: 2.75 to 3.65
mg per 2.2 lbs every 12
hours, or 5.5 to 7.3 mg per
2.2 lbs once a day.

ONSET OF EFFECT
Unknown.

DURATION OF ACTION
Unknown.

DIETARY ADVICE
Take griseofulvin with or
after meals or milk. Milk,
cheese, and other fatty
foods increase the amount
of medication absorbed
from your stomach. Check
with your physician if you
are on a low-fat diet. Otherwise, maintain your usual
food and fluid intake.

STORAGE
Store in a tightly sealed container away from heat, moisture, and direct light. Keep

the liquid form refrigerated,
but do not allow it to freeze.

IF YOU MISS A DOSE
Take it as soon as you
remember. However, if it is
near the time for the next
dose, skip the missed dose
and resume your regular
dosage schedule. Do not
double the next dose.

STOPPING THE DRUG
Take it as prescribed for the
full treatment period, even if
you begin to feel better
before the scheduled end of
therapy. Recurrence of the
infection is likely if you stop
before the full treatment
period is complete.

PROLONGED USE
Prolonged use may cause or
aggravate bone marrow
depression (reduced bone
marrow function), liver
damage, or kidney damage.
Consult your doctor about
the need for periodic blood
cell counts and liver and
kidney function tests.

PRECAUTIONS
Over 60: Adverse reactions
may be more likely and
more severe in older
patients.

**Driving and Hazardous
Work:** Do not drive or
engage in hazardous work
until you determine how the
medicine affects you.

Alcohol: Avoid alcohol.

Pregnancy: Do not use
griseofulvin if you are pregnant or trying to become
pregnant.

Breast Feeding: The drug
may pass into breast milk;
caution is advised. Consult
your doctor for advice.

Infants and Children:
Griseofulvin is not recommended for use by children
under the age of 2.

Special Concerns: Stay
out of direct sunlight, especially between 10 am and 3
pm. Wear protective clothing, including a hat, and
sunglasses. Apply a sun
block with a sun protection
factor (SPF) of at least 15.
Griseofulvin is usually used
in conjunction with a topical
antifungal to aid in the healing process and to reduce
the likelihood of relapse.

OVERDOSE
Symptoms: An overdose
with griseofulvin is unlikely.

What to Do: Emergency
instructions not applicable.

DRUG INTERACTIONS
Other drugs may interact
with griseofulvin. Consult
your doctor for advice if you
are taking anticoagulants or
oral contraceptives.

FOOD INTERACTIONS
No known food interactions.

DISEASE INTERACTIONS
Caution is advised when
taking griseofulvin. Consult
your doctor if you have
lupus, porphyria, or liver
disease.

Guaifenesin

▶ Drug Class: Expectorant

▶ Available in: Capsules, tablets, oral solution, syrup, extended-release forms

▶ Available OTC? Yes

▶ As Generic? Yes

Side Effects

SERIOUS
No serious side effects are associated with guaifenesin.

COMMON
No common side effects are associated with guaifenesin.

LESS COMMON
Diarrhea; dizziness; headache; abdominal pain, nausea, or vomiting; skin rash; itching; hives.

PRINCIPAL USES
Guaifenesin is classified as an expectorant; that is, it is designed to reduce the thickness of mucus and phlegm, making it easier to cough up and out of the lungs and so improve breathing. It is used to treat minor upper respiratory infections and related conditions, such as bronchitis, colds, and sinus or throat infections. Guaifenesin is not a cough suppressant, and despite its popularity and its FDA approval as an expectorant, there is little scientific evidence that it is truly effective at reducing the thickness of mucus.

HOW THE DRUG WORKS
Guaifenesin supposedly increases the production of fluids in the respiratory tract and helps to liquefy and thin mucus secretions.

DOSAGE
Adults— Capsules, tablets, oral solution, syrup: 200 to 400 mg every 4 hours, to a maximum of 2,400 mg a day. Extended-release capsules and tablets: 600 to 1,200 mg every 12 hours, to a maximum of 2,400 mg a day. Children 2 to 12 years of age— Consult your pediatrician.

ONSET OF EFFECT
Usually within several hours.

DURATION OF ACTION
The exact duration of action is not known.

DIETARY ADVICE
Maintain your usual food and fluid intake. Increase fluids if you have a fever or diarrhea. Coughing also increases your daily fluid requirements.

STORAGE
Store in a tightly sealed container away from heat and direct light. Keep liquid forms of guaifenesin refrigerated, but do not allow it to freeze. Keep away from moisture and extremes in temperature.

IF YOU MISS A DOSE
Take it as soon as you remember. If it is near the time for the next dose, skip the missed dose and resume your regular dosage schedule. Do not double the next dose.

STOPPING THE DRUG
You may stop taking guaifenesin before the scheduled end of therapy if you are feeling better; otherwise, take as prescribed for the full treatment period.

PROLONGED USE
Therapy with guaifenesin is usually completed within 7 to 10 days. Persistent cough may require special evaluation. Do not take nonprescription guaifenesin for more than 7 days without your doctor's approval.

PRECAUTIONS
Over 60: Adverse reactions may be more likely and more severe.

Driving and Hazardous Work: Do not drive or engage in hazardous work until you determine how the medicine affects you.

Alcohol: No special precautions are necessary.

Pregnancy: Thorough studies have not been done, although no serious problems have been reported; consult your doctor for advice.

Breast Feeding: Guaifenesin may pass into breast milk, although no problems have been documented. Consult your doctor for advice.

Infants and Children: Generally, it should not be given to children under 2 unless directed otherwise by a pediatrician; children under 12 who have a persistent cough should be examined by a doctor before they are given guaifenesin.

Special Concerns: Guaifenesin is present in numerous nonprescription cough and cold remedies, so ask your pharmacist if you are unsure whether a product you are buying contains it. Do not treat a persistent cough on your own for more than a week or so without seeking medical advice. When treating young children, avoid capsules or tablets, since it is difficult to rely on children to swallow these dosage forms in one piece. Capsules and tablets should not be chewed.

OVERDOSE
Symptoms: No specific ones have been reported.

What to Do: An overdose of guaifenesin is unlikely to be life-threatening. However, if someone takes a much larger dose than prescribed, call your doctor, emergency medical services (EMS), or the nearest poison control center.

DRUG INTERACTIONS
None reported.

FOOD INTERACTIONS
None reported.

DISEASE INTERACTIONS
None reported.

Guanabenz Acetate

Generic 4 mg
(COPLEY)

▶ Drug Class: Centrally acting antihypertensive

▶ Available in: Tablets

▶ Available OTC? No

▶ As Generic? Yes

Side Effects

SERIOUS
There are no serious side effects associated with recommended doses of guanabenz. However, serious side effects may occur from missing several doses or upon completion of therapy (see Special Concerns).

COMMON
Dizziness or lightheadedness, faintness, drowsiness, dry mouth, general weakness.

LESS COMMON
Headache, decreased sexual ability, nausea.

PRINCIPAL USES
To treat high blood pressure (hypertension).

HOW THE DRUG WORKS
Guanabenz acts upon certain areas of the central nervous system (the brain and spinal cord) that regulate the activity of the heart and the smooth muscle tissue surrounding the arteries. The drug causes the blood vessels to relax and widen, which in turn lowers blood pressure.

DOSAGE
Adults: Initially, 4 mg, 2 times a day. Your doctor will increase this dose gradually over a period of a few weeks until your blood pressure is acceptable. The usual maximum dose of guanabenz is 32 mg per day, given in divided doses.

ONSET OF EFFECT
Within 1 hour.

DURATION OF ACTION
12 hours.

DIETARY ADVICE
Follow a healthy diet (low-salt, low-fat, low-cholesterol) as advised by your doctor to help control blood pressure and prevent heart disease.

STORAGE
Store in a tightly sealed container away from heat, moisture, and direct light.

IF YOU MISS A DOSE
Take it as soon as you remember. If it is near the time for the next dose, skip the missed dose and resume your regular dosage schedule. Do not double the next dose. Call your doctor if you have missed more than one day of medication.

STOPPING THE DRUG
Do not stop taking this drug suddenly, as this may cause potentially serious health problems. If therapy is to be discontinued, dosage should be reduced gradually, according to doctor's instructions.

PROLONGED USE
Extended therapy with guanabenz may be necessary. Side effects may be more likely with prolonged use.

PRECAUTIONS
Over 60: Adverse reactions may be more likely and more severe.

Driving and Hazardous Work: The use of guanabenz may impair your ability to perform such tasks safely. Do not drive or engage in hazardous work until you determine how the medicine affects you.

Alcohol: Avoid alcohol.

Pregnancy: Avoid or discontinue the drug if you are pregnant or are planning to become pregnant.

Breast Feeding: Guanabenz may pass into breast milk; caution is advised. Consult your doctor for advice.

Infants and Children: Guanabenz is not recommended for use in children.

Special Concerns: If you miss several doses of guanabenz or upon completion of therapy, your blood pressure may return to dangerously high levels (known as rebound effect). Symptoms of rebound hypertension include: severe headache; nausea, vomiting, and abdominal pain; confusion; blurred vision; chest pain; sweating; nervousness, restlessness, anxiety, or trembling; heartbeat irregularities; trouble breathing. Call your doctor immediately. To avoid rebound hypertension, make every effort to follow your dosage schedule. Be sure to have adequate supplies of guanabenz available for vacations, travel, and holidays. Avoid nonprescription decongestants and cough, cold, and flu remedies. Drowsiness is common with guanabenz; take your last dose of the day around bedtime if possible. Remember that control of high blood pressure requires medication, diet, weight loss, and careful supervision by your physician.

OVERDOSE
Symptoms: Very low blood pressure causing faintness, extreme drowsiness, weakness, dizziness, or confusion; unusually slow heartbeat; irritability; tiny, constricted pupils.

What to Do: Call emergency medical services (EMS), your doctor, or the nearest poison control center immediately.

DRUG INTERACTIONS
Consult your doctor for specific advice if you are taking medicines that causes drowsiness, such as barbiturates, sedatives, cough medicines, or decongestants; alcohol; psychiatric medications; pain medications; anti-inflammatory drugs; beta-blockers or other medicines to lower blood pressure.

FOOD INTERACTIONS
No known food interactions.

DISEASE INTERACTIONS
Consult your doctor if you have any of the following: blood vessel disease of the brain, including a history of strokes or transient ischemic attacks (TIAs); angina or other heart disease; liver disease or kidney disease.

Guanadrel Sulfate

BRAND NAME
Hylorel

Hylorel 10 mg
(Fisons)

▶ Drug Class: Peripherally
acting antihypertensive

▶ Available in: Tablets

▶ Available OTC? No

▶ As Generic? Yes

Side Effects

SERIOUS
Excess fluid retention,
which can cause swelling
of lower legs and feet;
chest pain; shortness of
breath; fainting; repeated
episodes of dizziness or
falling, especially when
changing position.

COMMON
Drowsiness; dizziness or
lightheadedness; weight
gain. In men, impotence
and impaired ejaculation.

LESS COMMON
Diarrhea; dry mouth;
headache; muscle aches;
increased urination, especially at night.

PRINCIPAL USES
To treat high blood pres-
sure. Guanadrel is used
in conjunction with other
established treatments,
such as weight loss and
sodium restriction.

HOW THE DRUG WORKS
Guanadrel acts on special
nerve pathways that regu-
late the size of blood vessels by interfering with the
release of a natural sub-
stance called norepineph-
rine, which constricts
muscles surrounding the
vessels. The drug relaxes
these muscles, causing
blood vessels to widen,
which in turn lowers
blood pressure.

DOSAGE
Adults: To start, 5 mg, 2
times a day. Your doctor
will increase this dose as
needed over a period of
weeks until satisfactory
blood pressure is achieved.
This usually requires a dose
of 20 to 75 mg per day,
given in 2 to 4 equally
divided doses.

ONSET OF EFFECT
Within 2 hours.

DURATION OF ACTION
About 9 hours.

DIETARY ADVICE
Follow a healthy diet (low-
salt, low-fat, low-cholesterol)
as advised by your doctor to
help control blood pressure
and prevent heart disease.

STORAGE
Store in a tightly sealed container away from heat and
direct light. Keep it away
from moisture and extremes
in temperature.

IF YOU MISS A DOSE
Take it as soon as you
remember. However, if it is
near the time for the next
dose, skip the missed dose
and resume your regular
dosage schedule. Do not
double the next dose.

STOPPING THE DRUG
Take the drug as prescribed
for the full treatment period,
even if you begin to feel better before the scheduled
end of therapy.

PROLONGED USE
Lifelong therapy may be
necessary. See your doctor
regularly for examinations
and tests if you must take
this medicine for an
extended period of time.

PRECAUTIONS
Over 60: Adverse reactions
may be more likely and
more severe in older
patients.

**Driving and Hazardous
Work:** Do not drive or
engage in hazardous work
until you determine how the
medicine affects you.

Alcohol: Avoid alcohol.

Pregnancy: Before taking
guanadrel, tell your doctor
if you are pregnant or plan
to become pregnant.

Breast Feeding: Gua-
nadrel may pass into breast
milk; caution is advised.
Consult your doctor for
advice.

Infants and Children:
Guanadrel is not recom-
mended for use by children.

Special Concerns: Guanadrel frequently causes
dizziness or lightheaded-
ness, which is most noticeable when you change
position, such as rising from
a seated or lying position, or
when getting out of bed or
bending to pick up some-
thing. This may lead to
fainting, falls, and injury. Sit
or lie down immediately if
you feel dizzy or light-
headed. This side effect
may be worsened by
alcohol, hot weather, dehydration, fever, prolonged
standing, prolonged sitting,
or exercise.

OVERDOSE
Symptoms: Severe dizziness, confusion, weakness,
fainting.

What to Do: Call emergency medical services
(EMS), your doctor, or the
nearest poison control center immediately.

DRUG INTERACTIONS
Consult your doctor for specific advice if you are taking
antidepressants, appetite
suppressants, cyclobenza-
prine, haloperidol, loxapine,
maprotiline, methylpheni-
date, phenothiazines, thioxanthenes, trimeprazine,
MAO inhibitors, metaram-
inol, methoxamine, norepinephrine, or phenylephrine.

FOOD INTERACTIONS
No known food interactions.

DISEASE INTERACTIONS
Consult your doctor if you
have any of the following:
asthma; poor circulation to
the brain, with any history
of stroke, fainting, convulsions, or epilepsy; angina,
recent heart attack, problems with pulse, unusual
heart rhythms, pacemaker,
or heart failure; conditions
that lead to dehydration,
such as fever, diarrhea,
or colitis; diabetes; or
pheochromocytoma.

Guanethidine Monosulfate

▶ Drug Class: Peripherally acting antihypertensive

▶ Available in: Tablets

▶ Available OTC? No

▶ As Generic? Yes

Side Effects

SERIOUS
Excess fluid retention, which can cause swelling of lower legs and feet; chest pain; shortness of breath; fainting; dizziness or falling, especially when changing position.

COMMON
Dizziness or lightheadedness, drowsiness, weight gain, slow pulse, stuffy nose. In men, impotence and impaired ejaculation.

LESS COMMON
Diarrhea, dry mouth, headache, muscle aches, increased urination, especially at night, rash, vision problems.

PRINCIPAL USES
To help control moderate to severe high blood pressure, usually after other medications have failed to achieve satisfactory results.

HOW THE DRUG WORKS
Guanethidine interferes with the release of norepinephrine, a natural substance that constricts the muscles surrounding blood vessels. The drug relaxes these muscles, causing blood vessels to widen, thus lowering blood pressure.

DOSAGE
Adults: To start, 10 or 12.5 mg once a day. Your doctor may increase this gradually over weekly intervals until your blood pressure reaches an acceptable level. Your doctor will then prescribe a maintenance dose, usually 25 to 50 mg, taken once a day. Children: Dosage depends on age and weight of the child. Consult your pediatrician.

ONSET OF EFFECT
Blood pressure begins to drop shortly after ingestion; maximum benefits require 1 to 3 weeks.

DURATION OF ACTION
Blood pressure returns to previously high levels within 1 to 3 weeks after stopping.

DIETARY ADVICE
Increase fluids if you have a fever or diarrhea, in hot weather, or during exercise. Follow a healthy diet (low-salt, low-fat, low-cholesterol) as advised by your doctor to help control blood pressure and prevent heart disease.

STORAGE
Store in a tightly sealed container away from heat and direct light.

IF YOU MISS A DOSE
Take it as soon as you remember. However, if it is near the time for the next dose, skip the missed dose and resume your regular dosage schedule. Do not double the next dose. Inform your doctor if you miss more than a full day of medication.

STOPPING THE DRUG
The decision to stop taking the drug should be made by your doctor. Do not stop this medication abruptly.

PROLONGED USE
Lifelong therapy may be necessary. See your doctor regularly for examinations and tests if you must take this drug for an extended period.

PRECAUTIONS
Over 60: Adverse reactions may be more likely and more severe in older patients.

Driving and Hazardous Work: Do not drive or engage in hazardous work until you determine how the medicine affects you.

Alcohol: Avoid alcohol.

Pregnancy: Before taking guanethidine, tell your doctor if you are pregnant or plan to become pregnant.

Breast Feeding: Guanethidine may pass into breast milk; consult your doctor.

Infants and Children: May be used; consult your pediatrician.

Special Concerns: Guanethidine frequently causes dizziness or lightheadedness, especially when you change position. This may lead to fainting, falls, and injury. Sit or lie down immediately if you feel dizzy or lightheaded. This side effect may be worsened by alcohol, hot weather, dehydration, fever, prolonged standing or sitting or exercise.

OVERDOSE
Symptoms: Severe dizziness, confusion, weakness, or fainting; very slow pulse; severe diarrhea; severe nausea; cold, clammy skin; unresponsiveness or loss of consciousness.

What to Do: Call emergency medical services (EMS), your doctor, or the nearest poison control center immediately.

DRUG INTERACTIONS
Consult your doctor for specific advice if you are taking antidepressants, appetite suppressants, cyclobenzaprine, haloperidol, loxapine, maprotiline, methylphenidate, minoxidil, phenothiazines, thioxanthenes, trimeprazine, MAO inhibitors, metaraminol, methoxamine, norepinephrine, phenylephrine, insulin or oral medicines to control blood sugar, or anti-inflammatory drugs, especially NSAIDs.

FOOD INTERACTIONS
No known food interactions.

DISEASE INTERACTIONS
Consult your doctor if you have any of the following: asthma; poor circulation to the brain in association with history of stroke, fainting, epilepsy or other seizure disorders; angina, recent heart attack, heart rhythm irregularities, or heart failure; conditions that lead to dehydration, such as fever, diarrhea, or colitis; diabetes mellitus; pheochromocytoma; or impaired liver or kidney function.

Guanfacine Hydrochloride

BRAND NAME
Tenex

Generic 1 mg
(**WATSON**)

▶ Drug Class: Centrally acting antihypertensive

▶ Available in: Tablets

▶ Available OTC? No

▶ As Generic? Yes

Side Effects

SERIOUS
There are no serious side effects associated with recommended doses of guanfacine. However, serious side effects may occur from missing several doses or upon completion of therapy (see Special Concerns).

COMMON
Dry mouth, dizziness or lightheadedness, fatigue or drowsiness, weakness, constipation.

LESS COMMON
Headache, decreased sexual ability, depression, dry, burning eyes.

PRINCIPAL USES
To treat high blood pressure (hypertension).

HOW THE DRUG WORKS
Guanfacine acts upon certain areas of the central nervous system (the brain and spinal cord) that regulate the activity of the heart and the smooth muscle tissue surrounding the arteries. The drug causes the blood vessels to relax and widen, which in turn lowers blood pressure.

DOSAGE
Adults: To start, 1 mg once daily, at bedtime. Your doctor will increase the dose as needed over a period of 4 to 8 weeks until satisfactory blood pressure is achieved. Maintenance dose is usually 2 to 3 mg per day, taken once daily at bedtime.

ONSET OF EFFECT
Peak effect within 7 days.

DURATION OF ACTION
24 hours.

DIETARY ADVICE
Increase fluid intake in hot weather, during exercise, or if you have a fever or diarrhea. Follow a healthy diet (low-salt, low-fat, low-cholesterol) as advised by your doctor to help control blood pressure and prevent heart disease.

STORAGE
Store in a tightly sealed container away from heat and direct light.

IF YOU MISS A DOSE
Take it as soon as you remember. If it is near the time for the next dose, skip the missed dose and resume your regular dosage schedule. Do not double the next dose. Call your doctor if you have missed more than one day of medication.

STOPPING THE DRUG
Do not stop taking this drug suddenly, as this may cause potentially serious health problems. If therapy is to be discontinued, dosage should be tapered, according to a doctor's instructions.

PROLONGED USE
Extended therapy with this drug may be necessary. Side effects may be more likely with prolonged use.

PRECAUTIONS
Over 60: Adverse reactions may be more likely and more severe.

Driving and Hazardous Work: Do not drive or engage in hazardous work until you determine how the medicine affects you.

Alcohol: Avoid alcohol.

Pregnancy: Avoid or discontinue use if you are pregnant or plan to become pregnant.

Breast Feeding: Guanfacine may pass into breast milk; caution is advised. Consult your doctor.

Infants and Children: Guanfacine is not recommended for use by children.

Special Concerns: If you miss several doses of guanfacine or upon completion of therapy, your blood pressure may return to dangerously high levels (known as rebound effect). Symptoms of rebound hypertension include: severe headache; nausea, vomiting, and abdominal pain; confusion; blurred vision; chest pain; sweating; nervousness, restlessness, anxiety, or trembling; heartbeat irregularities; trouble breathing. Call your doctor immediately. To avoid rebound hypertension, make every

effort to follow your dosage schedule. Be sure to have adequate supplies of guanfacine available for vacations, travel, and holidays. Avoid nonprescription decongestants and cough, cold, and flu remedies. Drowsiness is common with guanfacine; take your last dose of the day around bedtime if possible. Remember that control of high blood pressure requires medication, diet, weight loss, and careful supervision by your physician.

OVERDOSE
Symptoms: Extreme drowsiness, weakness, dizziness, or confusion; unusually slow heartbeat; irritability; tiny, constricted pupils.

What to Do: Call emergency medical services (EMS), your doctor, or the nearest poison control center immediately.

DRUG INTERACTIONS
Many patients taking guanfacine also require treatment with a diuretic to control their blood pressure. Consult your doctor for specific advice if you are taking medicines that cause drowsiness, such as barbiturates, sedatives, cough medicines, or decongestants; alcohol; psychiatric medications; pain medications; anti-inflammatory drugs; beta-blockers or other medicines to lower blood pressure.

FOOD INTERACTIONS
No known food interactions.

DISEASE INTERACTIONS
Consult your doctor if you have any of the following: blood vessel disease of the brain, including a history of strokes or transient ischemic attacks (TIAs); angina or other heart disease; liver disease; or kidney disease.

Haloperidol

Haldol, Haldol Decanoate

Generic 5 mg
(GENEVA)

834

Additional photographs

▶ Drug Class: Neuroleptic; antipsychotic

▶ Available in: Tablets, liquid, injection

▶ Available OTC? No

▶ As Generic? Yes

Side Effects

SERIOUS
Rapid heartbeat, profuse sweating, seizures, difficulty breathing, neck stiffness, swelling of the tongue, difficulty swallowing. Also a rare condition can develop called neuroleptic malignant syndrome, characterized by stiffness or spasms of the muscles, high fever, and confusion or disorientation. Call your doctor immediately.

COMMON
Nausea, reduced sweating, dry mouth, blurred vision, drowsiness, shaking of hands, stiffness, stooped posture.

LESS COMMON
Difficult urination, menstrual irregularities, breast pain or swelling, unexpected weight gain, uncontrolled movements of the tongue, fever, chills, sore throat, unusual bruising or bleeding, heart palpitations, skin rash, itching, increased sensitivity of the skin to sunlight.

PRINCIPAL USES
To treat moderate to severe psychiatric conditions including schizophrenia, manic states, and drug-induced psychosis. It is also used to treat extreme behavior problems in children (including infantile autism), to ease the symptoms of Tourette's syndrome, and to reduce nausea and vomiting associated with chemotherapy for cancer.

HOW THE DRUG WORKS
Haloperidol blocks receptors of dopamine (a chemical that aids in the transmission of nerve impulses) in the central nervous system. Presumably, this produces a tranquilizing or antipsychotic effect.

DOSAGE
For psychotic disorders— Adults: Initial dose is 0.5 to 5 mg, 2 or 3 times a day; maximum dose is 100 mg a day. Children ages 3 to 12: 0.05 to 0.15 mg for every 2.2 lbs (1 kg) of body weight. For Tourette's syndrome— Adults: 0.5 to 5 mg, 2 or 3 times a day. Children ages 3 to 12: 0.075 mg for every 2.2 lbs daily.

ONSET OF EFFECT
Sedation may occur within minutes, but onset of antipsychotic effect may take hours to occur or may not occur until days or weeks after the beginning of therapy.

DURATION OF ACTION
12 to 24 hours, but effects may persist for several days.

DIETARY ADVICE
Take haloperidol with food or a full glass of milk or water. To prevent stomach irritation, the oral solution can be diluted in beverages such as orange, apple, or tomato juice, or cola.

STORAGE
Store in a tightly sealed container away from heat and direct light.

IF YOU MISS A DOSE
Take it as soon as you remember. Do not double the next dose. Space any remaining doses for that day at regular intervals. Return to your regular schedule the next day.

STOPPING THE DRUG
The decision to stop taking the drug should be made in consultation with your doctor. Gradual reduction of doses may be required if you have taken it for an extended period.

PROLONGED USE
Prolonged use may lead to tardive dyskinesia (involuntary movements of the jaw, lips, tongue, and, in rare cases, the arms, legs, hands, or body). Consult your doctor about the need for periodic evaluation and lab tests.

PRECAUTIONS
Over 60: Adverse reactions are more likely and more severe in older patients.

Driving and Hazardous Work: Exercise caution until you determine how the medication affects you.

Alcohol: Avoid alcohol.

Pregnancy: Before taking haloperidol, be sure to tell your doctor if you are, or plan to become, pregnant.

Breast Feeding: Haloperidol passes into breast milk and may be harmful to the child; do not use it while nursing.

Infants and Children: Not recommended for children under age 3 or those weighing less than 33 pounds.

Special Concerns: Avoid prolonged exposure to high temperatures or hot climates. Drink plenty of fluids and stay cool in the summertime. Avoid overexposure to sunlight until you determine if the drug heightens your skin's sensitivity to ultraviolet light.

OVERDOSE
Symptoms: Shallow, slow breathing, weak or rapid pulse, muscle weakness or tremor, dizziness, confusion, seizures, deep sleep, coma.

What to Do: Call your doctor, emergency medical services (EMS), or the nearest poison control center immediately.

DRUG INTERACTIONS
Consult your doctor for specific advice if you are taking anticholinergics, anticonvulsants, antidepressants, antihistamines, antihypertensives, bupropion, central nervous system depressants such as barbiturates, clozapine, dronabinol, ethinamate, fluoxetine, guanethidine, guanfacine, lithium, methyldopa, carbamazepine, rifampin, or trihexyphenidyl.

FOOD INTERACTIONS
No known food interactions.

DISEASE INTERACTIONS
Consult your doctor if you have Parkinson's disease or any movement disorder, glaucoma, epilepsy, or liver or kidney disease.

Haloprogin

BRAND NAME
Halotex

▶ Drug Class: Topical antifungal

▶ Available in: Cream, solution

▶ Available OTC? No

▶ As Generic? No

Side Effects

SERIOUS
No serious side effects have been reported.

COMMON
A mild, temporary stinging when the solution form of haloprogin is applied.

LESS COMMON
Blistering, burning, itching, or other forms of skin irritation that were not present before the start of therapy. Call your doctor immediately.

PRINCIPAL USES
To treat fungal infections of the skin, such as tinea corporis (ringworm), tinea cruris (jock itch), tinea pedis (athlete's foot), tinea manuum ("ringworm of the hand"), pityriasis versicolor ("sun fungus," a skin condition characterized by the formation of fine scaly patches of varying shapes, sizes, and colors).

HOW THE DRUG WORKS
Haloprogin prevents the growth and reproduction of fungus cells.

DOSAGE
For many conditions, rub the medicine gently into the affected area of skin 2 times a day for 2 to 4 weeks. (Note: This is simply the average dose of haloprogin. If the dose recommended by your physician is different, do not change it unless your physician advises you otherwise.)

ONSET OF EFFECT
Unknown.

DURATION OF ACTION
Unknown.

DIETARY ADVICE
Haloprogin can be used without regard to diet.

STORAGE
Store in a tightly sealed container away from heat and direct light. Do not allow the medicine to freeze.

IF YOU MISS A DOSE
Apply it as soon as you remember. If it is near the time for the next dose, skip the missed dose and resume your regular dosage schedule. Do not apply a double dose.

STOPPING THE DRUG
Use the medication as prescribed for the full treatment period, even if you begin to feel better before the scheduled end of therapy. Discontinuing the drug prematurely may lead to an even worse fungal infection later (known as a rebound infection).

PROLONGED USE
If your skin problem does not improve within 4 weeks of starting therapy or if it becomes worse, notify your doctor.

PRECAUTIONS
Over 60: Although there is no specific information comparing use of haloprogin in older patients with use in other age groups, the medicine is not expected to cause different side effects or problems in older people than in younger patients.

Driving and Hazardous Work: The use of haloprogin should not impair your ability to perform such tasks safely.

Alcohol: No special problems are expected with moderate use of alcohol.

Pregnancy: In animal studies, haloprogin has not been shown to cause birth defects or other problems. Human studies have not been done. Before you use haloprogin, be sure to tell your doctor if you are pregnant or plan to become pregnant.

Breast Feeding: It is not known whether haloprogin passes into breast milk; caution is advised. Consult your doctor for specific advice.

Infants and Children: Studies on the relationship of age to the effects of haloprogin have not been done in children. The safety and efficacy of the medicine on children have not been established. Use and dosage should be determined by your doctor.

Special Concerns: Avoid contact of the medicine with the eyes. Do not use haloprogin if you have had a prior allergic reaction to it or to any other topical antifungal medicine.

OVERDOSE
Symptoms: No specific ones have been reported.

What to Do: An overdose of haloprogin is unlikely. However, if someone accidentally ingests the drug, call your doctor, emergency medical services (EMS), or the nearest poison control center right away.

DRUG INTERACTIONS
Consult your doctor for specific advice if you are taking any other antifungal medication for the skin.

FOOD INTERACTIONS
No known food interactions.

DISEASE INTERACTIONS
Caution is advised when taking haloprogin. Consult your doctor if you have any other medical condition.

Hepatitis A Vaccine

BRAND NAMES
Havrix, VAQTA

▶ Drug Class: Vaccine

▶ Available in: Injection

▶ Available OTC? No

▶ As Generic? No

Side Effects

SERIOUS
Serious allergic reaction involving difficulty swallowing or breathing; reddened skin, especially around the ears; itching, particularly of the hands or feet; hives; unusual and severe fatigue; and swollen face, eyes, or nasal passages. Call your doctor immediately.

COMMON
Soreness at the site of injection.

LESS COMMON
Fever, general feeling of illness or discomfort, lack of appetite, headache, nausea, tenderness or warmth at site of injection, aches or pain in joints or muscles, diarrhea or stomach cramps or pain, itching, swelling of the glands in armpits or neck, vomiting, welts.

PRINCIPAL USES
To protect against infection by the hepatitis A virus in people over the age of 2. The vaccine is recommended for people traveling to Africa, Asia (except Japan), parts of the Caribbean, Central and South America, eastern Europe, the Mediterranean basin, the Middle East, and Mexico. The vaccine is also recommended for people who live in or are moving to other areas that have frequent outbreaks of hepatitis A or those who may be at increased risk of infection. These people include military personnel, Alaskan Eskimos, Native Americans, persons engaging in high-risk sexual activity, such as homosexual males; people who use illegal injectable drugs, people working in facilities for the mentally retarded, employees of and children in day-care centers, people who work with hepatitis A virus in the laboratory, people who handle primate animals, food handlers, and people with chronic liver disease.

HOW THE DRUG WORKS
Hepatitis A vaccine stimulates the body's immune system to produce protective antibodies against the disease.

DOSAGE
All doses are administered by a health care professional. Adults: 1 dose injected into a muscle in the upper arm. A booster dose is given 6 months after the first dose. Children ages 2 to 18: 1 pediatric dose injected into a muscle in the upper arm. A similar booster is given 6 to 18 months later.

ONSET OF EFFECT
Within 4 weeks.

DURATION OF ACTION
Unknown.

DIETARY ADVICE
No special restrictions.

STORAGE
Not applicable; the dose is administered only at a health care facility.

IF YOU MISS A DOSE
If you miss a scheduled vaccination, contact your doctor.

STOPPING THE DRUG
The full schedule of injections should be followed unless a medical problem intervenes. A full course of injections must be completed to ensure adequate immunization.

PROLONGED USE
Not applicable.

PRECAUTIONS
Over 60: Hepatitis A vaccine is not expected to cause different or more severe side effects in older patients than it does in younger persons. However, patients over age 50 may not develop as strong an immunity as their younger counterparts.

Driving and Hazardous Work: The vaccine should not impair your ability to perform such tasks safely.

Alcohol: No special precautions are necessary.

Pregnancy: Adequate human studies have not been done. Before taking hepatitis A vaccine, tell your physician if you are pregnant or planning to become pregnant.

Breast Feeding: No problems have been reported in nursing babies, but caution is advised. Consult your doctor.

Infants and Children: Not recommended for use by children under the age of 2. No special problems are expected in children over the age of 2.

OVERDOSE
Symptoms: Not applicable.

What to Do: No cases of overdose have been reported.

DRUG INTERACTIONS
There are no known drug interactions. Tell your doctor if you are taking any prescription or over-the-counter medication.

FOOD INTERACTIONS
No known food interactions.

DISEASE INTERACTIONS
Consult your doctor if you have a bleeding disorder, an immune deficiency condition, or any other medical condition. Vaccine injection may be postponed in persons with a fever or acute illness.

Hepatitis B Vaccine

BRAND NAMES
Engerix-B, Recombivax HB, Recombivax HB Dialysis Formulation

▶ Drug Class: Vaccine

▶ Available in: Injection

▶ Available OTC? No

▶ As Generic? No

Side Effects

SERIOUS
Serious allergic reaction involving difficulty swallowing or breathing; reddened skin, especially around the ears; itching, particularly of the hands or feet; hives; unusual and severe fatigue; and swollen face, eyes, or nasal passages. Call your doctor immediately.

COMMON
Soreness at the site of injection.

LESS COMMON
Dizziness, fever, unusual fatigue, headache. Also tenderness, warmth, hard lump, swelling, pain, itching, or purple spot at site of injection.

PRINCIPAL USES
To protect against infection by the hepatitis B virus.

HOW THE DRUG WORKS
Hepatitis B vaccine stimulates the body's immune system to produce protective antibodies against the disease.

DOSAGE
Adults age 20 and older: A first injection of 10 micrograms (mcg) (Recombivax HB) or 20 mcg (Engerix-B) into upper arm, followed by an injection 1 month later and another 6 months after the first dose, for a total of 3 doses. Adults receiving dialysis: A first injection of 40 mcg (Recombivax HD Dialysis Formulation) followed by doses 1 month and 6 months after the first dose; some patients may receive a dose at 2 months. Dialysis patients receiving 4 doses will use Engerix-B. Children ages 11 to 20: A first injection of 5 mcg (Recombivax HB) or 20 mcg (Engerix-B) into upper arm, followed by an injection 1 month later and another 6 months after the first dose, for a total of 3 doses. Infants and children up to age 11: A first dose of 2.5 mcg (Recombivax HB) or 10 mcg (Engerix-B) into the thigh, with doses 1 month and 6 months after the first dose, for a total of 3 doses.

ONSET OF EFFECT
Unknown.

DURATION OF ACTION
Unknown.

DIETARY ADVICE
No special restrictions.

STORAGE
Not applicable; the dose is administered only at a health care facility.

IF YOU MISS A DOSE
If you miss a scheduled vaccination, contact your doctor.

STOPPING THE DRUG
The full schedule of injections should be followed unless a medical problem intervenes. A full course of injections must be completed to ensure adequate immunization.

PROLONGED USE
No special problems are expected.

PRECAUTIONS
Over 60: Hepatitis B vaccine is not expected to cause different or more severe side effects in older patients than it does in younger persons. However, patients over age 50 may not develop as strong an immunity as their younger counterparts.

Driving and Hazardous Work: Hepatitis B vaccine should not impair your ability to perform such tasks safely.

Alcohol: No special precautions are necessary.

Pregnancy: Adequate human studies have not been done. However, problems during pregnancy are not expected. Before you take hepatitis B vaccine, tell your doctor if you are pregnant or plan to become pregnant.

Breast Feeding: Hepatitis B vaccine may pass into breast milk; caution is advised. Consult your doctor for more information.

Infants and Children: Hepatitis B vaccine, with recommended doses, does not cause different or more severe side effects in infants and children than it does in older persons. Studies of the vaccine strength for use by dialysis patients have only been conducted on adult subjects. Consult your pediatrician for specific advice if your child is receiving dialysis.

OVERDOSE
Symptoms: Not applicable.

What to Do: No cases of overdose have been reported.

DRUG INTERACTIONS
Other drugs may interact with hepatitis B vaccine. Tell your doctor if you are taking any prescription or over-the-counter medication.

FOOD INTERACTIONS
No known food interactions.

DISEASE INTERACTIONS
Consult your doctor if you have any of the following: severe heart or lung disease, a moderate or severe illness with or without fever, or an immune deficiency condition.

Homatropine Hydrobromide

BRAND NAMES
AK-Homatropine,
I-Homatrine, Isopto
Homatropine, Spectro-
Homatropine

▶ Drug Class: Eye muscle relaxant, pupil enlarger

▶ Available in: Ophthalmic solution

▶ Available OTC? No

▶ As Generic? Yes

Side Effects

SERIOUS
If absorbed into the bloodstream: Loss of coordination or unsteadiness, confusion or changes in behavior, hallucinations, slurred speech, rapid or irregular pulse, flushing, fever, unusual fatigue, dizziness, unusually dry skin, skin rash, dry mouth; in infants, abdominal swelling. Seek medical assistance immediately.

COMMON
Eye irritation and redness not present prior to treatment, swelling of the eyelids, blurred vision, increased sensitivity to bright light.

LESS COMMON
There are no less-common side effects associated with the use of homatropine.

PRINCIPAL USES
To protect the eye before and after surgery, and to treat certain types of eye conditions, including iritis (inflammation of the iris, the colored or pigmented portion of the eye). It may also be used in eye examinations to help determine the proper prescription for eyeglasses.

HOW THE DRUG WORKS
Homatropine relaxes the ciliary muscle, which controls the shape of the eye's lens as it focuses, and another eye muscle called the sphincter, which controls the narrowing and widening of the pupil. Relaxation of these muscles prevents the lens from focusing and widens the pupil. This allows the doctor to view the interior of the eye during an ophthalmologic procedure. And, by immobilizing the tiny structures within the eye, the drug prevents scarring of eye tissue and may also alleviate pain somewhat.

DOSAGE
To aid in ophthalmic surgery or eye examinations: 1 drop (applied by doctor) every 5 to 10 minutes as needed. For treatment of iritis: 1 drop in affected eye(s), 2 or 3 times a day, or up to every 2 or 3 hours in more severe cases.

ONSET OF EFFECT
Within 1 hour.

DURATION OF ACTION
From 24 to 72 hours.

DIETARY ADVICE
It can be taken without regard to diet.

STORAGE
Store in a tightly sealed container away from heat, moisture, and direct light. Do not allow it to freeze.

IF YOU MISS A DOSE
Apply it as soon as you remember. If it is near the time for the next dose, skip the missed dose and resume your regular dosage schedule. Do not double the next dose.

STOPPING THE DRUG
The decision to stop taking the drug should be made by your ophthalmologist.

PROLONGED USE
Not recommended.

PRECAUTIONS
Over 60: Adverse reactions may be more likely and more severe.

Driving and Hazardous Work: Do not drive or engage in hazardous work until you determine how the medicine affects your vision. Extreme caution should be observed for activities requiring sharp vision for close objects (less than an arm's length away).

Alcohol: No special precautions are necessary.

Pregnancy: Adequate studies have not been done. Inform your doctor if you are pregnant or are planning to become pregnant.

Breast Feeding: Small amounts of homatropine pass into breast milk; either discontinue breast feeding or stop taking the drug. Consult your doctor for advice.

Infants and Children: Young children, especially those with blond hair or blue eyes, may be more sensitive to the drug and may have an increased risk of side effects. Use with extreme caution. This medication should not be used at all by infants younger than 3 months old.

Special Concerns: To use the eye drops, first wash your hands. Tilt your head back. Gently apply pressure to the inside corner of the eyelid and with the index finger of the same hand, pull downward on the lower eyelid to make a space. Drop the medicine into this space and close your eye. Apply pressure for 1 or 2 minutes while keeping the eye closed without blinking. Then wash your hands again. Make sure that the tip of the dropper does not touch your eye, finger, or any other surface.

OVERDOSE
Symptoms: Drowsiness, hallucinations, memory problems, dry mouth, dry skin, restlessness, palpitations, dizziness and disorientation, delirium.

What to Do: Call your doctor, emergency medical services (EMS), or the nearest poison control center immediately.

DRUG INTERACTIONS
Consult your doctor if you are taking any other prescription or over-the-counter drugs, especially those preparations designed for use in the eyes.

FOOD INTERACTIONS
No known food interactions.

DISEASE INTERACTIONS
Consult your doctor if you have a history of glaucoma, Down's syndrome, or spastic paralysis.

Hydralazine Hydrochloride

Generic 10 mg
(PAR)

Additional photographs

▶ Drug Class: Antihypertensive
vasodilator

▶ Available in: Tablets, injection

▶ Available OTC? No

▶ As Generic? Yes

Side Effects

SERIOUS
Lupus-like syndrome causing fast pulse and palpitations, rapid or irregular heartbeat, hives, itching, or rash, swollen lymph glands, weakness and fainting when standing up, swelling of the feet or legs, and joint pain. Call your doctor immediately.

COMMON
Headache, chest pain, nausea, vomiting, diarrhea, loss of appetite, stomach pain, blood in urine or stools, fatigue.

LESS COMMON
Dizziness; numbness, tingling, and weakness in hands or feet, chills, fever, skin rash.

PRINCIPAL USES
To treat moderate to severe high blood pressure and congestive heart failure.

HOW THE DRUG WORKS
Hydralazine hydrochloride acts upon the smooth muscle tissue surrounding the blood vessels, causing them to relax. The vessels widen and blood pressure decreases.

DOSAGE
To start, 10 mg, 4 times a day for 2 to 4 days. The dose is then increased to 25 mg, 4 times a day. The dose may then be further increased to 50 mg, 4 times a day if needed. The total dose generally should not exceed 200 mg per day, but some patients may require 300 or 400 mg per day.

ONSET OF EFFECT
Within 20 to 30 minutes.

DURATION OF ACTION
3 to 8 hours.

DIETARY ADVICE
This medication should be taken with food. Follow a healthy diet (low-salt, low-fat, low-cholesterol) as advised by your doctor to help control blood pressure and prevent heart disease.

STORAGE
Store in a tightly sealed container away from heat and direct light.

IF YOU MISS A DOSE
Take it as soon as you remember. If it is near the time for the next dose, skip the missed dose and resume your regular dosage schedule. Do not double the next dose.

STOPPING THE DRUG
Take the medicine as prescribed, even if you begin to feel better before the scheduled end of therapy.

PROLONGED USE
Prolonged use may cause an arthritis-like illness similar to lupus, numbness and tingling in hands or feet, and mental effects. Consult your doctor about the need for continuing medical examinations, including blood cell counts and other laboratory studies.

PRECAUTIONS
Over 60: Adverse reactions may be more likely and more severe in older patients.

Driving and Hazardous Work: Do not drive or engage in hazardous work until you determine how the medicine affects you.

Alcohol: Alcohol should be avoided while taking this medication because it may trigger an excessive drop in blood pressure.

Pregnancy: In animal studies, hydralazine has caused birth defects. Human studies have not been done. Before taking hydralazine, tell your doctor if you are pregnant or plan to become pregnant.

Breast Feeding: Hydralazine passes into breast milk; you should avoid or discontinue its use while nursing.

Infants and Children: In children, this medicine is not expected to cause side effects different from those in adults. However, hydralazine should be given to young patients only under close medical supervision.

Special Concerns: It may be necessary to take a diuretic along with hydralazine to reduce its side effects. Several weeks may be needed to determine the effectiveness of hydralazine in reducing blood pressure.

OVERDOSE
Symptoms: Rapid and weak heartbeat, extreme weakness, loss of consciousness, cold and sweaty skin, flushing.

What to Do: Call your doctor, emergency medical services (EMS), or the nearest poison control center immediately.

DRUG INTERACTIONS
Consult your doctor for specific advice if you are taking diazoxide, MAO inhibitors, loop diuretics, beta-blockers, nitrates, or nonsteroidal anti-inflammatory agents such as indomethacin.

FOOD INTERACTIONS
No known food interactions.

DISEASE INTERACTIONS
Caution is advised when taking hydralazine. Consult your doctor if you have any of the following: rheumatic heart disease, mitral valve heart disease, lupus erythematosus, or impaired brain circulation. Use of hydralazine may cause complications in patients with liver or kidney disease, since these organs work together to remove the medication from the body.

Hydrochlorothiazide/Triamterene

Dyazide 25/37.5 mg
(SMITHKLINE BEECHAM)

▶ Drug Class: Thiazide diuretic

▶ Available in: Capsules, tablets

▶ Available OTC? No

▶ As Generic? Yes

Side Effects

SERIOUS
Skin rash, hives, intense itching, swelling of the mouth and throat, breathing difficulty, heart rhythm irregularities or palpitations, lightheadedness or dizziness, unusual bleeding or bruising. Call your doctor immediately.

COMMON
Fluid depletion may lead to dizziness, especially upon arising from a sitting or lying position, as well as thirst, dry mouth, and constipation.

LESS COMMON
Decreased sexual ability, increased sensitivity to sunlight, loss of appetite, gout, increased blood sugar (a problem for diabetic patients).

PRINCIPAL USES
To treat high blood pressure (hypertension); to treat conditions that cause edema (swelling of body tissues resulting from excess salt and water retention).

HOW THE DRUG WORKS
This drug combines a thiazide diuretic (hydrochlorothiazide) and a potassium-sparing diuretic (triamterene) that reduces excess loss of potassium in the body. Diuretics increase the excretion of salt and water in the urine. By reducing the overall fluid volume in the body, these drugs reduce blood volume and so reduce pressure within the blood vessels.

DOSAGE
Adults: 1 or 2 capsules or tablets once a day. Children: The dose must be determined by your doctor.

ONSET OF EFFECT
Within 2 hours.

DURATION OF ACTION
6 to 12 hours.

DIETARY ADVICE
This medication should be taken in the morning after breakfast.

STORAGE
Store in a tightly sealed container away from heat and direct light.

IF YOU MISS A DOSE
Take it as soon as you remember. If it is near the time for the next dose, skip the missed dose and resume your regular dosage schedule. Do not double the next dose.

STOPPING THE DRUG
The decision to stop taking the drug should be made by your doctor.

PROLONGED USE
See your doctor regularly for examinations and tests if you must take this medicine for an extended period.

PRECAUTIONS
Over 60: Adverse reactions may be more likely and more severe.

Driving and Hazardous Work: No special precautions are necessary.

Alcohol: No special precautions are necessary.

Pregnancy: This drug should not be taken during pregnancy unless recommended by your doctor. Other diuretics are generally preferred.

Breast Feeding: This drug passes into breast milk; avoid or discontinue use while nursing.

Infants and Children: No unusual side effects are expected in children. The dose must be determined by a pediatrician.

Special Concerns: To prevent hydrochlorothiazide from interfering with sleep, take it in the morning. If you are taking it for high blood pressure, follow the diet and weight control measures recommended by your doctor. Avoid exposure to sunlight, use a sunblock, or wear protective clothing. This medicine may cause a loss or increase of potassium in your body, so it's important to discuss your diet with your doctor. Follow your doctor's instructions about eating potassium-rich foods or taking a potassium supplement.

OVERDOSE
Symptoms: Dehydration, muscle weakness, cramps, heart arrhythmias.

What to Do: Call your doctor, emergency medical services (EMS), or the nearest poison control center immediately.

DRUG INTERACTIONS
Consult your doctor for specific advice if you are taking ACE inhibitors, cyclosporine, medications or dietary supplements that contain potassium, cholestyramine, colestipol, digitalis drugs, lithium, or any over-the-counter medication.

FOOD INTERACTIONS
Most patients taking this drug should avoid consuming large servings of high-potassium foods, which include bananas, citrus fruits and juices, melons, prunes, (and most fruits in general), avocados, potatoes, nuts, baked beans, brussels sprouts, and skim milk. Check with your doctor if you have questions about your diet.

DISEASE INTERACTIONS
Caution is advised when taking this medicine. Consult your doctor if you have diabetes, gout, kidney stones, lupus erythematosus, pancreatitis, heart disease, blood vessel disease, menstrual problems, liver disease, or kidney disease.

Hydrochlorothiazide (HCTZ)

Generic 25 mg
(GOLDLINE)

▶ Drug Class: Thiazide diuretic

▶ Available in: Tablets, oral suspension

▶ Available OTC? No

▶ As Generic? Yes

Side Effects

SERIOUS
Skin rash, hives, intense itching, swelling of the mouth and throat, breathing difficulty, heart rhythm irregularities, lightheadedness, unusual bleeding or bruising. Call your doctor immediately.

COMMON
Muscle cramps or pain. Potassium depletion may lead to heart palpitations and weakness. Fluid depletion may lead to dizziness, especially upon arising from a sitting or lying position, as well as thirst, dry mouth, and constipation.

LESS COMMON
Decreased sexual ability, increased sensitivity to sunlight, loss of appetite, gout, increased blood sugar (a problem for diabetic patients), pancreatitis (rare).

PRINCIPAL USES
To treat high blood pressure (hypertension); to treat conditions that cause edema (swelling of body tissues resulting from excess salt and water retention).

HOW THE DRUG WORKS
Diuretics increase the excretion of salt and water in the urine. By reducing the overall fluid volume in the body, these drugs reduce pressure within the blood vessels.

DOSAGE
Adults— To reduce excess body water: 25 to 100 mg, 1 or 2 times a day. Your doctor may change the frequency to every other day or 3 to 5 days a week. For high blood pressure: 25 to 100 mg a day. Children, to reduce body water— Ages 2 to 12: 37.5 to 100 mg a day in 2 doses. Ages 6 months to 2 years: 12.5 to 37.5 mg a day in 2 doses. Infants under 6 months: Up to 3.3 mg per 2.2 lbs (1 kg) of body weight in 2 doses.

ONSET OF EFFECT
Within 2 hours.

DURATION OF ACTION
6 to 12 hours.

DIETARY ADVICE
It can be be taken with food to avoid stomach upset.

STORAGE
Store in a tightly sealed container away from heat and direct light. Keep the liquid form from freezing.

IF YOU MISS A DOSE
Take it as soon as you remember. If it is near the time for the next dose, skip the missed dose and resume your regular dosage schedule. Do not double the next dose.

STOPPING THE DRUG
The decision to stop taking the drug should be made by your doctor.

PROLONGED USE
See your doctor regularly for examinations and tests if you must take this medicine for an extended period.

PRECAUTIONS
Over 60: Adverse reactions may be more likely and more severe in older patients.

Driving and Hazardous Work: No special precautions are necessary.

Alcohol: No special precautions are necessary.

Pregnancy: Hydrochlorothiazide has caused birth defects in animals. Human studies have not been done. This medicine should not be taken during pregnancy unless recommended by your doctor; other diuretics are generally preferred for pregnant women.

Breast Feeding: Hydrochlorothiazide passes into breast milk; avoid or discontinue use during the first month of nursing.

Infants and Children: No unusual side effects are expected in children. The dose must be determined by a pediatrician.

Special Concerns: Hydrochlorothiazide is usually prescribed once a day. To prevent it from interfering with sleep, take it in the morning. If you are taking this drug for high blood pressure, follow the diet and weight control measures recommended by your doctor. Avoid exposure to sunlight, use a sunblock, or wear protective clothing. This medicine may cause your body to lose potassium. Follow your doctor's instructions about eating potassium-rich foods or taking a potassium supplement

OVERDOSE
Symptoms: Fainting, lethargy, dizziness, drowsiness, confusion, gastrointestinal irritation.

What to Do: Call your doctor, emergency medical services (EMS), or the nearest poison control center immediately.

DRUG INTERACTIONS
Consult your doctor for specific advice if you are taking anticoagulants, cholestyramine, colestipol, drugs for diabetes, nonsteroidal anti-inflammatory drugs, digitalis drugs, or lithium.

FOOD INTERACTIONS
No known food interactions.

DISEASE INTERACTIONS
Caution is advised when taking hydrochlorothiazide. Consult your doctor if you have any of the following: diabetes, gout, lupus erythematosus, pancreatitis, heart disease, blood vessel disease, liver disease, or kidney disease.

Hydrocodone Bitartrate/Acetaminophen

▶ Drug Class: Opioid (narcotic) analgesic

▶ Available in: Capsules, oral solution, tablets

▶ Available OTC? No

▶ As Generic? Yes

Side Effects

SERIOUS
Bloody, dark, or cloudy urine; severe pain in lower back or side; pale or black, tarry stools; yellow-tinged eyes or skin; hallucinations; frequent urge to urinate; painful or difficult urination; sudden decrease in amount of urine; increased sweating; unusual bleeding or bruising; irregular heartbeat; skin rash, hives, or itching; unusual excitement; irregular breathing or wheezing; ringing or buzzing in ears; pinpoint red spots on skin; sore throat and fever; confusion; trembling or uncontrolled muscle movements; flushing or swelling of face. Call your doctor immediately.

COMMON
Dizziness, lightheadedness, nausea or vomiting, drowsiness, constipation, itching.

LESS COMMON
Stomach pain, allergic reaction, false sense of well-being, depression, loss of appetite, blurring or change in vision, feeling of illness, headache, nervousness, insomnia.

PRINCIPAL USES
To relieve moderate to severe pain, when nonprescription pain relievers prove inadequate. Hydrocodone, in combination with acetaminophen, may provide better pain relief at lower doses than either medication used alone at higher doses.

HOW THE DRUG WORKS
Hydrocodone, a narcotic, is believed to relieve pain by acting on specific areas in the spinal cord and brain that process pain signals from nerves throughout the body. Acetaminophen appears to interfere with the action of prostaglandins, substances in the body that cause inflammation and make nerves more sensitive to pain impulses.

DOSAGE
Adults— Capsules: 1 every 4 to 6 hours. Oral solution: 1 to 3 teaspoons every 4 to 6 hours. Tablets: 1 or 2 containing 2.5 mg of hydrocodone, or 1 containing 5, 7.5, or 10 mg of hydrocodone, every 4 to 6 hours.

ONSET OF EFFECT
30 to 60 minutes.

DURATION OF ACTION
4 to 6 hours.

DIETARY ADVICE
This drug can be taken without regard to diet.

STORAGE
Store in a tightly sealed container away from heat, moisture, and direct light.

IF YOU MISS A DOSE
If you are taking this drug on a fixed schedule, take it as soon as you remember. If it is near the time for the next dose, skip the missed dose and resume your regular dosage schedule. Do not double the next dose.

STOPPING THE DRUG
The decision to stop taking the drug should be made by your doctor.

PROLONGED USE
See your doctor regularly for tests and examinations if you take this medication for a prolonged period. Prolonged use can cause mental or physical dependence.

PRECAUTIONS

Over 60: Adverse reactions may be more likely and more severe in older patients.

Driving and Hazardous Work: Do not drive or engage in hazardous work until you determine how the medicine affects you.

Alcohol: Avoid alcohol.

Pregnancy: Overuse during pregnancy can cause drug dependence in the fetus.

Breast Feeding: It is not known whether this drug passes into breast milk; caution is advised. Consult your doctor for specific advice.

Infants and Children: Adverse reactions may be more likely and more severe in children.

Special Concerns: If you feel the drug is not working properly after a few weeks, do not increase the dose.

OVERDOSE
Symptoms: Severe dizziness or drowsiness; cold, clammy skin; difficult or slow breathing or shortness of breath; severe confusion; seizures; stomach cramps or pain; diarrhea; increased sweating; constricted pupils; nausea or vomiting; irregular heartbeat; severe weakness.

What to Do: Call your doctor, emergency medical services (EMS), or the nearest poison control center immediately.

DRUG INTERACTIONS
Consult your doctor for specific advice if you are taking any prescription or over-the-counter medications, especially drugs with acetaminophen or central nervous system depressants such as barbiturates, seizure medicine, muscle relaxants, anesthetics, tranquilizers, or sedatives.

FOOD INTERACTIONS
No known food interactions.

DISEASE INTERACTIONS
Consult your doctor if you have a head injury or brain disease, an underactive thyroid (hypothyroidism), an enlarged prostate, seizures, kidney or liver disease, gall bladder problems, a blood disorder, or a history of alcohol or drug abuse.

Hydrocodone Bitartrate/Ibuprofen

▶ Drug Class: Opioid (narcotic) analgesic

▶ Available in: Tablets

▶ Available OTC? No

▶ As Generic? No

Side Effects

SERIOUS
Shallow or labored breathing; bloody, dark, or cloudy urine; severe pain in lower back or side; frequent urge to urinate; painful or difficult urination; sudden decrease in urine output; unusual bleeding or bruising; irregular heartbeat; skin rash, hives, or itching; confusion; trembling or uncontrolled muscle movements. Call your doctor immediately.

COMMON
Headache, dizziness, lightheadedness, nausea, stomach upset, drowsiness, constipation.

LESS COMMON
Abdominal pain, weakness, insomnia, nervousness, diarrhea, flatulence, dry mouth, swelling of the limbs or other areas, unusual sweating.

PRINCIPAL USES
For short-term (generally less than 10 days) relief of acute pain, when nonprescription pain relievers prove inadequate. Hydrocodone, in combination with ibuprofen, may provide better pain relief at lower doses than either medicine used alone.

HOW THE DRUG WORKS
Hydrocodone, a narcotic, is believed to relieve pain by acting on specific areas in the spinal cord and brain that process pain signals from nerves throughout the body. Ibuprofen, a nonsteroidal anti-inflammatory drug (NSAID), works by interfering with the formation of prostaglandins, substances that cause inflammation and make nerves more sensitive to pain impulses. NSAIDs also have other modes of action that are less well understood.

DOSAGE
Adults and teenagers age 16 and over: 1 tablet every 4 to 6 hours, as needed. Do not take more than 5 tablets in a 24-hour period.

ONSET OF EFFECT
Unknown.

DURATION OF ACTION
Less than 10 hours.

DIETARY ADVICE
Take this drug with food.

STORAGE
Store in a tightly sealed container away from heat, moisture, and direct light.

IF YOU MISS A DOSE
If you are taking this medicine on a fixed schedule, take it as soon as you remember. If it is near the time for the next dose, skip the missed dose and resume your regular dosage schedule. Do not double the next dose.

STOPPING THE DRUG
You may stop taking this drug whenever you choose.

PROLONGED USE
Opioids may be habit-forming, and prolonged use may increase the risk of dependency. Hydrocodone is used only for short-term (10 days or less) treatment of pain.

PRECAUTIONS
Over 60: Adverse reactions may be more likely and more severe in older patients.

Driving and Hazardous Work: The use of this drug may impair your ability to perform such tasks safely.

Alcohol: Avoid alcohol. The combination of alcohol and this drug may increase the depressant effects of the medicine. Drinking alcoholic beverages while taking ibuprofen may increase the risk of stomach irritation.

Pregnancy: Avoid or discontinue this drug if you are pregnant or planning to become pregnant. Overuse during pregnancy can cause drug dependence in the fetus.

Breast Feeding: Ibuprofen passes into breast milk; avoid use while nursing.

Infants and Children: Not recommended for use by children under age 16.

Special Concerns: If you feel the drug is not working properly, do not increase your dose. Call your doctor. Because NSAIDs can interfere with blood coagulation, this drug should be stopped at least 3 days prior to any surgery.

OVERDOSE
Symptoms: Severe nausea, vomiting, difficult or slow breathing or shortness of breath, severe dizziness or drowsiness, cold, clammy or bluish skin, irregular or slow heartbeat, severe weakness, headache, confusion, loss of consciousness.

What to Do: Call your doctor, emergency medical services (EMS), or the nearest poison control center immediately.

DRUG INTERACTIONS
Consult your doctor for specific advice if you are taking any of the following medications that may interact with this drug: ACE inhibitors; anticholinergics; MAO inhibitors; tricyclic antidepressants; aspirin; central nervous system depressants such as barbiturates, seizure medicines, muscle relaxants, anesthetics, tranquilizers, or sedatives; furosemide and other diuretics; lithium; methotrexate; or warfarin.

FOOD INTERACTIONS
No known food interactions.

DISEASE INTERACTIONS
Consult your doctor if you have an underactive thyroid, Addison's disease, an enlarged prostate, urinary difficulty, asthma, any lung disease, bleeding problems, inflammation or ulcers of the stomach and intestine, systemic lupus erythematosus (SLE, lupus), anemia, high blood pressure, or a history of heart disease. Use of this drug may cause complications in patients with severely impaired liver or kidney function.

Hydrocortisone Ophthalmic

BRAND NAME
Cortamed

▶ Drug Class: Corticosteroid

▶ Available in: Ointment

▶ Available OTC? No

▶ As Generic? No

Side Effects

SERIOUS
Decreased vision or blurring of vision (from cataract); eye pain, nausea, vomiting (from increased eye pressure); pain, redness, sensitivity to bright light, discharge (from eye infection). Call your doctor immediately if you experience any of these signs or symptoms. This drug may trigger a recurrence of herpes infection of the eye; mention any previous herpes infection to your doctor.

COMMON
Mild and temporary blurred vision.

LESS COMMON
Burning, stinging, redness, or watering of eyes.

PRINCIPAL USES
To control inflammation and prevent potentially permanent damage that may result from conditions that involve inflammation in the eye tissues.

HOW THE DRUG WORKS
Hydrocortisone inhibits the release of natural substances that stimulate an inflammatory reaction.

DOSAGE
Adults and children: Ointment is applied to eye 3 or 4 times a day to start; doses are spaced further apart as therapeutic effect is achieved.

ONSET OF EFFECT
Unknown.

DURATION OF ACTION
Unknown.

DIETARY ADVICE
This medication can be used without regard to diet.

STORAGE
Store in a tightly sealed container away from heat and direct light.

IF YOU MISS A DOSE
Apply it as soon as you remember. If it is near the time for the next dose, skip the missed dose and resume your regular dosage schedule. Do not double the next dose.

STOPPING THE DRUG
It is very important to use this drug as prescribed for the full treatment period, even if symptoms improve before the scheduled end of therapy.

PROLONGED USE
You should see your doctor regularly for tests and examinations if you must use this drug for a prolonged period.

PRECAUTIONS
Over 60: While there is no information comparing use of this drug in older patients with use in younger persons, no different side effects or problems are expected.

Driving and Hazardous Work: Do not drive or engage in hazardous work until you determine how the medicine affects you.

Alcohol: No special precautions are necessary.

Pregnancy: This drug has caused birth defects in animals. Reliable human studies have not been done, but no human birth defects have been reported. Before you take ophthalmic hydrocortisone, tell your doctor if you are pregnant or plan to become pregnant.

Breast Feeding: Ophthalmic hydrocortisone has not been reported to cause problems in nursing babies. Consult your doctor for advice.

Infants and Children: Children under 2 years of age may be especially sensitive to the effects of ophthalmic hydrocortisone.

Special Concerns: To use the ointment, first wash your hands. Tilt your head back. Gently apply pressure to the inside corner of the eyelid and with the index finger of the same hand, pull downward on the lower eyelid to make a space. Put a short strip of ointment (about ⅓ inch long) into this space and close your eye. Apply pressure for 1 or 2 minutes while keeping the eye closed without blinking. Then wash your hands again. Make sure the tip of the applicator does not touch your eye, finger, or any other surface. If your symptoms do not improve in a few days or if they become worse, check with your doctor.

OVERDOSE
Symptoms: When used topically, an overdose of ophthalmic hydrocortisone is extremely unlikely. Inadvertent oral ingestion, however, may cause fever, muscle aches, general feeling of weakness and illness, loss of appetite, dizziness, fainting, trouble breathing.

What to Do: An overdose of ophthalmic hydrocortisone is unlikely to be life-threatening. However, if someone applies a much larger dose of the drug than prescribed or accidentally ingests the medicine, call your doctor, emergency medical services (EMS), or the nearest poison control center right away.

DRUG INTERACTIONS
Other drugs may interact with ophthalmic hydrocortisone. Consult your doctor for specific advice if you are taking any other prescription or over-the-counter medication.

FOOD INTERACTIONS
No known food interactions.

DISEASE INTERACTIONS
Caution is advised when taking ophthalmic hydrocortisone. Consult your doctor if you have any of the following: cataracts, diabetes mellitus, glaucoma, herpes infection of the eye, tuberculosis of the eye, or any other eye infection.

Hydrocortisone Systemic

Cortef 5 mg
(UPJOHN)

▶ Drug Class: Corticosteroid

▶ Available in: Oral suspension, tablets, injection, enema, rectal aerosol foam

▶ Available OTC? No

▶ As Generic? No

Side Effects

SERIOUS
Vision problems, frequent urination, increased thirst, rectal bleeding, blistering skin, confusion, hallucinations, paranoia, euphoria, depression, mood swings, redness and swelling at injection site. Call your doctor immediately.

COMMON
Increased appetite, indigestion, nervousness, insomnia, greater susceptibility to infections, increased blood pressure, slowed healing of wounds, rapid weight gain, easy bruising, fluid retention.

LESS COMMON
Change in skin color, dizziness, headache, increased sweating, unusual growth of body or facial hair, increased blood sugar, peptic ulcers, adrenal insufficiency, muscle weakness, cataracts, glaucoma, osteoporosis.

PRINCIPAL USES
To treat numerous conditions that involve inflammation (a response by body tissues, producing redness, warmth, swelling, and pain). Such conditions include arthritis, allergic reactions, asthma, some skin diseases, multiple sclerosis flare-ups, and other autoimmune diseases. Also prescribed to treat deficiency of natural steroid hormones.

HOW THE DRUG WORKS
This hormone mimics the effects of the body's natural corticosteroids. It depresses the synthesis, release, and activity of inflammation-producing body chemicals. It also suppresses the activity of the immune system.

DOSAGE
Oral dose: 20 to 240 mg a day, depending on condition, in 1 or several doses. Injection: 15 to 240 mg a day, injected into a muscle, or 5 to 75 mg every 2 or 3 weeks, injected into a joint or lesion, or 100 to 500 mg every 2 to 6 hours, into muscle or vein or under skin, depending on condition. Enema: 100 mg taken nightly. Rectal aerosol foam: 90 mg, 1 or 2 times a day. Consult pediatrician for children's dosage.

ONSET OF EFFECT
Varies widely depending on the form of the drug used.

DURATION OF ACTION
Variable.

DIETARY ADVICE
Can be taken with food or milk to minimize stomach upset. Your doctor may recommend a special diet.

STORAGE
Store in a tightly sealed container away from heat, moisture, and direct light.

Do not allow liquid form to freeze.

IF YOU MISS A DOSE
If you take several doses a day and it is close to the next dose, double the next dose. If you take 1 dose a day and you do not remember until the next day, skip the missed dose and do not double the next dose.

STOPPING THE DRUG
With long-term therapy, do not stop taking the drug abruptly; the dosage should be decreased gradually.

PROLONGED USE
See your doctor regularly for tests and examinations. Long-term use may lead to cataracts, diabetes, hypertension, or osteoporosis.

PRECAUTIONS
Over 60: Adverse reactions may be more likely and more severe in older patients.

Driving and Hazardous Work: Do not drive or engage in hazardous work until you determine how the medicine affects you.

Alcohol: May cause stomach problems; avoid it unless your physician approves occasional moderate drinking.

Pregnancy: Overuse during pregnancy can retard the child's growth and cause other developmental problems. Consult your doctor for advice.

Breast Feeding: Do not use this drug while nursing.

Infants and Children: Hydrocortisone may retard the normal growth and development of bone and other tissues.

Special Concerns: This drug can lower your resistance to infection. Avoid immunizations with live vaccines. Patients undergoing long-term therapy should wear a medical-alert bracelet. Call your doctor if you develop a fever.

OVERDOSE
Symptoms: Fever, muscle or joint pain, nausea, dizziness, fainting, difficulty breathing. Prolonged overuse: Moonface, obesity, unusual hair growth, acne, loss of sexual function, muscle wasting.

What to Do: Seek medical assistance immediately.

DRUG INTERACTIONS
Consult your doctor for specific advice if you are taking aminoglutethimide, antacids, barbiturates, carbamazepine, griseofulvin, mitotane, phenylbutazone, phenytoin, primidone, rifampin, injectable amphotericin B, oral antidiabetes agents, insulin, digitalis drugs, diuretics, or medications containing potassium or sodium.

FOOD INTERACTIONS
Avoid excess sodium.

DISEASE INTERACTIONS
Consult your doctor if you have a history of bone disease, chicken pox, measles, gastrointestinal disorders, diabetes, recent serious infection, tuberculosis, glaucoma, heart disease, hypertension, liver or kidney disorders, high blood cholesterol, overactive or underactive thyroid, myasthenia gravis, or lupus.

Hydrocortisone Topical

BRAND NAMES
BRAND NAMES
Acticort 100, Aeroseb-HC,
Ala-Cort, Ala-Scalp HP,
Allercort, Alphaderm,
Anusol, Anusol-HC,
Bactine, Beta HC,
CaldeCORT Anti-Itch,
Cetacort, Cort-Dome,
Cortaid, Cortifair, Cortril,
Delacort, Dermacort,
DermiCort, Dermtex HC,
Gly-Cort, Gynecort, Hi-Cor
2.5, Hydro-Tex, Hytone,
LactiCare-HC, Lanacort,
Lemoderm, Locoid, My
Cort, Nutracort, Orabase-
HCA, Pentacort, Rederm,
S-T Cort, Synacort,
Texacort, Westcort

▶ Drug Class: Topical
corticosteroid

▶ Available in: Cream, lotion,
ointment, topical solution,
dental paste

▶ Available OTC? Yes

▶ As Generic? Yes

Side Effects

SERIOUS
Serious side effects from
the use of topical hydro-
cortisone are very rare.

COMMON
Burning, itching, irrita-
tion, redness, dryness,
acne, stinging and crack-
ing of skin, numbness or
tingling in the extremities
(in 0.5% to 1% of
patients).

LESS COMMON
Blistering and pus near
hair follicles, unusual
bleeding or easy bruis-
ing, darkening or promi-
nence of small surface
veins, increased susceptibility to infection.

PRINCIPAL USES
To treat certain skin conditions that are associated
with itching, redness, scaling and peeling, pain, and
other signs of inflammation.
It is also used to treat
inflammatory conditions
within the mouth.

HOW THE DRUG WORKS
Topical hydrocortisone
appears to interfere with the
formation of natural sub-
stances within the body that
are directly responsible for
the process of inflammation,
which produces swelling,
redness, and pain.

DOSAGE
Adults using dental paste:
Apply at bedtime to affected
areas of the mouth. Adults
using cream, lotion, ointment, solution: Apply sparingly to affected areas of
the skin 1 to 2 (sometimes
3) times daily. Children:
Consult your pediatrician
for specific dosage and
other advice.

ONSET OF EFFECT
Steroids begin to exert their
effect soon after application.
However, recognizable
changes in your condition
may take several days or
more to develop.

DURATION OF ACTION
Unknown.

DIETARY ADVICE
Maintain your usual food
and fluid intake.

STORAGE
Store in a tightly sealed container away from heat and
direct light. Keep away from
moisture and extremes in
temperature.

IF YOU MISS A DOSE
Apply it as soon as you
remember. If it is near the
time for the next dose, skip
the missed dose and
resume your regular dosage
schedule. Do not double the
next dose.

STOPPING THE DRUG
Take as prescribed for the
full treatment period, even
if you begin to feel better
before the scheduled end
of therapy.

PROLONGED USE
Therapy with this medica-
tion may require weeks or
months; long-term therapy
requires monitoring by your
physician even with a low-
potency product.

PRECAUTIONS
Over 60: Adverse reactions
may be more likely and
more severe; therapy with
topical corticosteroids
should therefore be brief
and infrequent.

**Driving and Hazardous
Work:** The use of hydro-
cortisone topical preparation should not impair your
ability to perform such
tasks safely.

Alcohol: No special precautions are necessary.

Pregnancy: It should not
be used for prolonged periods in pregnant women or
in those trying to become
pregnant.

Breast Feeding: Although
problems have not been
documented, caution is
advised. Do not apply to
breasts prior to nursing.
Consult your doctor for specific advice.

Infants and Children:
Not recommended for pro-
longed use. Consult your
pediatrician.

Special Concerns: Avoid
use of this medication
around the eye. Hydrocortisone is not a treatment for
acne, burns, infections, or
disorders of pigmentation.

Do not bandage or wrap the
medicated area of skin with
any special dressings or
coverings unless specifically
told to do so by your doctor.

OVERDOSE
Symptoms: No specific
ones have been reported.

What to Do: An overdose
is unlikely to be life-threatening. However, in the
event of accidental ingestion
or an apparent overdose,
call your doctor, emergency
medical services (EMS), or
the nearest poison control
center immediately.

DRUG INTERACTIONS
None reported.

FOOD INTERACTIONS
None reported.

DISEASE INTERACTIONS
Consult your doctor if you
have any of the following:
diabetes; skin infection, or
skin sores and ulcers; infection at another site in your
body; tuberculosis; unusual
bleeding or bruising; glaucoma; or cataracts.

Hydromorphone Hydrochloride

BRAND NAMES
Dilaudid, Dilaudid-5,
Dilaudid-HP, Hydrostat IR

Generic 2 mg
(ROXANE)

▶ Drug Class: Opioid (narcotic)
analgesic

▶ Available in: Oral solution,
tablets, injection, rectal
suppositories

▶ Available OTC? No

▶ As Generic? Yes

Side Effects

SERIOUS
Serious side effects of
hydromorphone are
indistinguishable from
those of overdose: Confu-
sion; sleepiness; slurred
speech; unconsciousness;
small, pinpoint pupils;
cold, clammy skin; slow
breathing; seizures;
severe drowsiness,
weakness, or dizziness.

COMMON
Dizziness or lightheaded-
ness, nausea or vomiting,
constipation, itching.

LESS COMMON
Dry mouth, mood swings
or false sense of well-
being and euphoria, hal-
lucinations, nightmares.

PRINCIPAL USES
To treat severe pain.

HOW THE DRUG WORKS
Opioids such as hydromor-
phone relieve pain by acting
on specific areas of the
spinal cord and brain that
process pain signals from
nerves throughout the body.

DOSAGE
Adults: Oral solution or
tablets: 2 or 2.5 mg every 3
to 6 hours as needed. Injection: 1 to 2 mg into a muscle or under the skin every
3 to 6 hours as needed. Suppositories: 3 mg every 4 to
8 hours as needed. All
doses may be increased by
your physician, depending
on the severity of your pain.

ONSET OF EFFECT
Oral forms and supposito-
ries: Within 30 minutes.
Injection: Within 10 to 15
minutes.

DURATION OF ACTION
Oral forms and supposito-
ries: 4 hours. Injection: 2 to
5 hours. These times may
decrease as a tolerance to
hydromorphone develops.

DIETARY ADVICE
Take hydromorphone with
food. Maintain your usual
food and fluid intake. Narcotics cause constipation, so
make sure your diet con-
tains adequate amounts of
fiber and vegetables.

STORAGE
Store in a tightly sealed container away from heat, moisture, and direct light. Keep
the liquid form refrigerated,
but do not allow it to freeze.

IF YOU MISS A DOSE
If you are taking it on a
fixed schedule, take it as
soon as you remember. If it
is near time for the next
dose, skip the missed dose
and resume your regular

dosage schedule. Do not
double the next dose.

STOPPING THE DRUG
You should take it as prescribed for the full treatment period, but you may
stop taking the drug if you
are feeling better before the
scheduled end of therapy.

PROLONGED USE
Therapy with hydromor-
phone varies, depending
on the cause of your pain.
Some patients require long-
term narcotic therapy. Side
effects may be more likely
with prolonged use.

PRECAUTIONS
Over 60: Adverse reactions
may be more likely and
more severe in older
patients.

**Driving and Hazardous
Work:** The use of hydro-
morphone may impair your
ability to perform such
tasks safely.

Alcohol: Avoid alcohol.

Pregnancy: Adequate
human studies have not
been done. Before taking
hydromorphone, tell your
doctor if you are pregnant
or are planning to become
pregnant.

Breast Feeding: Hydromorphone passes into
breast milk; caution is
advised. Consult your doctor for advice.

Infants and Children:
This drug may be used by
young patients. Side effects
may be more likely in children under the age of 2.
Consult your pediatrician
for advice.

Special Concerns: This
medication may be habit-
forming. Do not exceed recommended doses or
increase the dose on your

own. This drug is more
effective if taken before pain
becomes too severe.

OVERDOSE
Symptoms: Confusion;
sleepiness; slurred speech;
unconsciousness; small, pinpoint pupils; cold, clammy
skin; slow breathing;
seizures; severe drowsiness,
weakness, or dizziness.

What to Do: Call your
doctor, emergency medical
services (EMS), or the
nearest poison control center immediately.

DRUG INTERACTIONS
Consult your doctor for specific advice if you are taking
carbamazepine or other
medicine for seizures, barbiturates, sedatives, cough
medicines, decongestants,
antidepressants, other prescription pain medications,
MAO inhibitors, naltrexone,
rifampin, or zidovudine.

FOOD INTERACTIONS
No known food interactions.

DISEASE INTERACTIONS
Consult your doctor if you
have any of the following:
history of alcohol or drug
abuse; emotional illness;
brain disorders or head
injury; seizures; lung disease; prostate problems or
other problems with urination; gallstones; colitis; or
heart, kidney, liver, or thyroid disease.

Hydroxychloroquine Sulfate

Generic 200 mg
(**APOTHECON**)

▶ Drug Class: Anti-infective/
antimalarial; antirheumatic

▶ Available in: Tablets

▶ Available OTC? No

▶ As Generic? Yes

Side Effects

SERIOUS
Blurred or altered vision;
blood problems including
low white blood cell
count (sore throat, fever),
anemia (fatigue, weak-
ness), and low platelet
count (easy bleeding and
bruising). Such side
effects are extremely
rare; call your doctor
immediately if they
occur.

COMMON
No common side effects
are associated with the
use of this drug.

LESS COMMON
Diarrhea, loss of appetite,
headache, stomach
cramps or pain, nausea
or vomiting, itching, dizziness, fatigue, confusion,
loss or bleaching of hair,
skin rash. Also blue-black
discoloration of the skin,
the inside of the mouth,

PRINCIPAL USES
To prevent and treat malaria
caused by specific strains of
plasmodia (the parasite that
causes malaria) that are
chloroquine-sensitive, but
when chloroquine is not
available. It is also used to
treat rheumatoid arthritis
and systemic lupus erythematosus (SLE, or lupus).

HOW THE DRUG WORKS
Hydroxychloroquine is poisonous to the malarial parasite. For rheumatoid
arthritis and lupus, it may
suppress the release of certain chemicals that cause
inflammation.

DOSAGE
All dosages are for adults
and adolescents. Consult
your pediatrician for children's doses, which are
based on body weight and
should not exceed adult
doses. To prevent malaria:
400 mg (310 mg base) once
a week. To treat malaria:
800 mg (620 mg base)
taken once; or 800 mg, followed by 400 mg (310 mg
base), 6 to 8 hours after the
first dose, then 400 mg once
a day for 2 more days. For
rheumatoid arthritis or
lupus erythematosus: 6.5
mg (5 mg base) per 2.2 lbs
(1 kg) of body weight daily.

ONSET OF EFFECT
Unknown. When taking this
drug for arthritis, it may
take up to 6 months for the
effect to occur. Consult your
physician if your condition
has not improved within
this time.

DURATION OF ACTION
Unknown.

DIETARY ADVICE
Take it with food or milk to
reduce stomach upset.

STORAGE
Store in a tightly sealed container away from heat, moisture, and direct light.

IF YOU MISS A DOSE
Take it as soon as you
remember. However, if it is
near the time for the next
dose, skip the missed dose
and resume your regular
dosage schedule. Do not
double the next dose.

STOPPING THE DRUG
Take it as prescribed for the
full treatment period, even if
you feel better before the
scheduled end of therapy.

PROLONGED USE
You may need to take this
medication for an extended
period of time. If you are
taking it to prevent malaria,
your doctor will want you to
begin 1 to 2 weeks before
you travel to an area where
malaria is prevalent. Keep
taking this medication while
you are in the area and for
4 weeks after you leave.

PRECAUTIONS
Over 60: Adverse reactions
may be more likely and
more severe in older
patients.

**Driving and Hazardous
Work:** The use of this drug
may impair your ability to
perform such tasks safely.
Exercise caution.

Alcohol: No special precautions are necessary.

Pregnancy: The use of
hydroxychloroquine is generally discouraged during
pregnancy because of the
risks it poses to the unborn
child. However, in some
cases it may be prescribed
to prevent or treat malaria,
since the risks of malaria
are potentially more serious
than those posed by the
drug. Discuss with your
doctor the relative risks

and benefits of using this
drug while pregnant.

Breast Feeding: Hydroxychloroquine passes into
breast milk; extreme cau-
tion is advised. Consult your
doctor for specific advice.

Infants and Children:
Children are extremely sensitive to toxic effects of this
drug. Use by children is
considered risky, although it
may be prescribed if benefits outweigh the potential
risks. Consult your pediatrician for advice.

Special Concerns:
Malaria is spread by mos-
quitoes. Take appropriate
precautions to guard against
being bitten by malaria-carrying mosquitoes. Note that
hydroxychloroquine is not
effective against all types of
malaria.

OVERDOSE
Symptoms: Excitability,
headache, drowsiness.

What to Do: Call your
doctor, emergency medical
services (EMS), or the
nearest poison control center immediately.

DRUG INTERACTIONS
Consult your doctor for specific advice if you are taking
magnesium or aluminum
salts, cimetidine, or digoxin.

FOOD INTERACTIONS
No known food interactions.

DISEASE INTERACTIONS
Consult your doctor if you
have any blood disorders,
including anemia, unex-
plained bleeding or bruising, porphyria, or low white
blood cells; liver, neurological, or vision disorders; or
psoriasis.

Hydroxyurea

Hydrea 500 mg
(BRISTOL-MYERS SQUIBB)

▶ Drug Class: Antimetabolite

▶ Available in: Capsules

▶ Available OTC? No

▶ As Generic? Yes

Side Effects

SERIOUS
Cough or hoarseness, fever or chills, pain in lower back or side, painful or difficult urination, black, tarry stools, blood in urine or stools, red spots on skin, unusual bleeding or bruising, sores in mouth or on lips, confusion, seizures, dizziness, hallucinations, headache, joint pain, swelling of feet or lower legs. Call your doctor immediately.

COMMON
Diarrhea, loss of appetite, nausea or vomiting.

LESS COMMON
Constipation, reddening of skin, skin rash and itching, drowsiness.

PRINCIPAL USES
To treat various types of cancer, including malignant melanoma, certain kinds of leukemia, inoperable ovarian tumors, and cancers of the head and neck.

HOW THE DRUG WORKS
Hydroxyurea prevents cancer cell growth by interfering with the synthesis of genetic material. It interferes with the synthesis of DNA in cancer cells and inhibits cell repair, thus decreasing the cell survival rate. The drug may also affect the growth and development of other kinds of cells in the body, resulting in unpleasant side effects.

DOSAGE
For intermittent therapy of solid tumors, with radiation therapy: 60 to 80 mg per 2.2 lbs (1 kg) of body weight every 3 days. For continuous therapy of solid tumors and chronic myelocytic leukemia: 500 to 2,000 mg per day, in 1 or 2 doses.

ONSET OF EFFECT
Unknown.

DURATION OF ACTION
Up to 24 hours.

DIETARY ADVICE
If you cannot swallow the capsule, empty the contents into a glass of water and consume immediately.

STORAGE
Store in a tightly sealed container away from heat and direct light.

IF YOU MISS A DOSE
Take it as soon as you remember. If it is close to the next dose, skip the missed dose and resume your regular dosage schedule. Do not double the next dose.

STOPPING THE DRUG
The decision to stop taking the drug should be made in consultation with your physician.

PROLONGED USE
Hydroxyurea should be discontinued if there is no clinical response as determined by your doctor. If there is a response, the drug may be continued indefinitely.

PRECAUTIONS
Over 60: Adverse reactions may be more likely and more severe in older patients.

Driving and Hazardous Work: Do not drive or engage in hazardous work until you determine how the medicine affects you.

Alcohol: Avoid alcohol.

Pregnancy: Hydroxyurea may cause birth defects if it is taken at the time of conception. Before taking it, tell your doctor if you are pregnant or plan a pregnancy.

Breast Feeding: Not recommended during therapy.

Infants and Children: Adverse reactions may be more likely and more severe in children.

Special Concerns: Be careful when you use a toothbrush, toothpick, or dental floss. Check with your doctor before having any dental work done. Avoid people with infections. Be careful not to cut yourself when you are using sharp objects such as a nail cutter or razor. Wash your hands regularly to decrease the likelihood of spreading bacteria or viruses. Avoid contact sports or other situations where an injury could occur. Watch closely for signs of infection, and take your temperature if you feel ill. Do not receive any immunizations without your doctor's approval. After you stop taking hydroxyurea, check with your doctor if you notice black, tarry stools, blood in urine or stools, cough or hoarseness, fever or chills, pain in lower back or side, painful or difficult urination, red spots on skin, or unusual bleeding or bruising.

OVERDOSE
Symptoms: Excessive side effects.

What to Do: Call your doctor, emergency medical services (EMS), or the nearest poison control center immediately.

DRUG INTERACTIONS
Consult your doctor for specific advice if you are taking amphotericin B, antithyroid agents, azathioprine, chloramphenicol, colchicine, flucytosine, ganciclovir, interferon, plicamycin, zidovudine, probenecid, sulfinpyrazone, didanosine, or stavudine.

FOOD INTERACTIONS
No known food interactions.

DISEASE INTERACTIONS
Caution is advised when taking hydroxyurea. Consult your doctor if you have a history of any of the following: anemia, chicken pox, shingles, gout, kidney stones, any infection, or kidney disease.

Hydroxyzine

Generic 50 mg
(ZENITH)

834

Additional photographs

▶ Drug Class: Antihistamine/ mild sedative

▶ Available in: Tablets, syrup, injection

▶ Available OTC? No

▶ As Generic? Yes

Side Effects

SERIOUS
Loss of coordination, seizures, extreme drowsiness, breathing difficulty, inability to urinate.

COMMON
Drowsiness; dryness in the mouth, nasal passages, and other mucous membranes.

LESS COMMON
Difficult urination, dizziness, rash, sore throat, fever, nightmares, restlessness, sleep disruption, irritability, increased skin sensitivity to sunlight, loss of appetite, stomach upset, decreased sexual ability in men.

PRINCIPAL USES
Hydroxyzine is used for several conditions. Its mild sedative effect is useful in treating insomnia and agitation in some patients. It is also used to treat itching, hives, and other allergy symptoms; to control nausea and vomiting; to ease the symptoms of alcohol withdrawal; and to provide mild sedation prior to a dental procedure or to the administration of general anesthesia before surgery.

HOW THE DRUG WORKS
Hydroxyzine is an antihistamine; that is, it blocks the effects of histamine, a naturally occurring substance in the body that causes swelling, itching, sneezing, watery eyes, hives, and other symptoms of allergic reactions. In addition to its antihistamine effect, hydroxyzine also has a sedative effect and appears to suppress activity in some regions of the central nervous system (the brain and spinal cord) associated with nausea and psychological distress.

DOSAGE
For sedation— Adults: 50 to 100 mg a day. For allergy symptoms— Adults: 25 to 100 mg, 3 or 4 times a day, as needed. Children age 6 and older: 12.5 to 25 mg, every 6 hours as needed. Children up to age 6: 12.5 mg every 6 hours as needed. For nausea and vomiting— Adults: 25 to 100 mg, 3 or 4 times a day. Children: 0.6 mg per 2.2 lbs of body weight per day.

ONSET OF EFFECT
15 to 30 minutes.

DURATION OF ACTION
Approximately 6 to 8 hours.

DIETARY ADVICE
Drink plenty of fluids.

STORAGE
Store in a tightly sealed container away from heat and direct light. Keep tablets away from moisture and extremes in temperature. Keep liquid forms refrigerated, but do not allow to freeze.

IF YOU MISS A DOSE
Take it as soon as you remember. If it is near the time for the next dose, skip the missed dose and resume your regular dosage schedule. Do not double the next dose.

STOPPING THE DRUG
The decision to stop taking the drug should be made in consultation with your physician.

PROLONGED USE
Therapy with hydroxyzine may require days or weeks, depending on the condition. Side effects may be more likely with prolonged use.

PRECAUTIONS
Over 60: Adverse reactions may be more likely and more severe in older patients.

Driving and Hazardous Work: Hydroxyzine may impair mental alertness; caution is advised.

Alcohol: Avoid alcohol.

Pregnancy: Adequate studies of hydroxyzine use during pregnancy have not been done; consult your doctor for specific advice.

Breast Feeding: Hydroxyzine may pass into breast milk and cause side effects in the nursing infant; do not use.

Infants and Children: Use this drug only under close supervision by your pediatrician.

Special Concerns: Antihistamines are widely available without prescription; if you are taking a prescription antihistamine, avoid other cough, cold, flu, sinus, or allergy preparations.

OVERDOSE
Symptoms: Severe dryness in mouth, nose, and throat, extreme drowsiness, loss of coordination, faintness, flushing, tremor, hallucinations, breathing difficulty.

What to Do: Call emergency medical services (EMS), your doctor, or the nearest poison control center immediately.

DRUG INTERACTIONS
Consult your doctor for specific advice if you are taking any drugs that depress the central nervous system; these include antidepressants or other psychiatric medications, other antihistamines, barbiturates, sedatives, cough medicines, decongestants, and painkillers. Be sure your doctor knows about any over-the-counter medication you may take.

FOOD INTERACTIONS
None are known.

DISEASE INTERACTIONS
Consult your doctor if you have any of the following: asthma, glaucoma or another eye disorder, thyroid disease, heart or blood vessel disease, high blood pressure, enlarged prostate, or urinary difficulty.

Ibuprofen

Advil 200 mg
(WHITEHALL)

Additional photographs

▶ Drug Class: Nonsteroidal anti-inflammatory drug (NSAID)

▶ Available in: Tablets, oral solution, chewable tablets

▶ Available OTC? Yes

▶ As Generic? Yes

Side Effects

SERIOUS
Shortness of breath or wheezing, with or without swelling of legs or other signs of heart failure; chest pain; peptic ulcer disease with vomiting of blood; black, tarry stools; decreasing kidney function. Call your doctor immediately.

COMMON
Nausea, vomiting, heartburn, diarrhea, constipation, headache, dizziness, sleepiness.

LESS COMMON
Ulcers or sores in mouth, depression, rashes or blistering of skin, ringing sound in the ears, unusual tingling or numbness of the hands or feet, seizures, blurred vision. Also: elevated potassium levels, decreased blood counts; such problems can be detected by your doctor.

PRINCIPAL USES
To treat mild to moderate pain and inflammation caused by tendinitis, arthritis, bursitis, gout, soft tissue injuries, migraine and other vascular headaches, menstrual cramps, and other conditions. It is also used to reduce fever.

HOW THE DRUG WORKS
NSAIDs work by interfering with the formation of prostaglandins, substances that cause inflammation and make nerves more sensitive to pain impulses. NSAIDs also have other modes of action that are less well understood.

DOSAGE
Adults— For mild to moderate pain, arthritis, and menstrual pain: 200 to 400 mg every 4 to 6 hours. For fever: 200 to 400 mg every 4 to 6 hours, but not more than 1,200 mg a day. Children ages 6 months to 12 years— For fevers below 102.5°F, 5 mg for every 2.2 lbs (1 kg) of body weight every 6 to 8 hours. For higher fevers, 10 mg per 2.2 lbs every 6 to 8 hours, but not more than 40 mg per 2.2 lbs a day.

ONSET OF EFFECT
For pain and fever, 30 minutes. For arthritis, up to 3 weeks.

DURATION OF ACTION
4 hours or more.

DIETARY ADVICE
Take ibuprofen with food.

STORAGE
Store in a tightly sealed container away from heat, moisture, and direct light.

IF YOU MISS A DOSE
Take it as soon as you remember. However, if it is near the time for the next dose, skip the missed dose and resume your regular dosage schedule. Do not double the next dose.

STOPPING THE DRUG
If taking this drug by prescription, do not stop without consulting your doctor.

PROLONGED USE
Prolonged use can cause gastrointestinal problems, including ulceration and bleeding, kidney dysfunction, and liver inflammation. See your doctor regularly for laboratory tests and examinations.

PRECAUTIONS
Over 60: Because of the potentially greater consequences of gastrointestinal side effects, the dose of NSAIDs for older patients, especially those over age 70, is often cut in half.

Driving and Hazardous Work: Do not drive or engage in hazardous work until you determine how the medicine affects you.

Alcohol: Avoid alcohol, as it may increase the risk of stomach irritation.

Pregnancy: Avoid or discontinue this drug if you are pregnant or are planning to become pregnant.

Breast Feeding: Ibuprofen passes into breast milk; avoid use while nursing.

Infants and Children: May be used in exceptional circumstances; consult your doctor.

Special Concerns: Because NSAIDs can interfere with blood coagulation, this drug should be stopped at least 3 days prior to any surgery.

OVERDOSE
Symptoms: Severe nausea, vomiting, headache, confusion, seizures.

What to Do: Call your doctor, emergency medical services (EMS), or the nearest poison control center immediately.

DRUG INTERACTIONS
Do not take this drug with aspirin or any other NSAIDs without your doctor's approval. In addition, consult your doctor if you are taking antihypertensives, steroids, anticoagulants, antibiotics, itraconazole or ketoconazole, plicamycin, penicillamine, valproic acid, phenytoin, cyclosporine, digitalis drugs, lithium, methotrexate, probenecid, triamterene, or zidovudine.

FOOD INTERACTIONS
No known food interactions.

DISEASE INTERACTIONS
Consult your doctor if you have any of the following: bleeding problems, inflammation or ulcers of the stomach and intestines, diabetes mellitus, systemic lupus erythematosus (SLE, lupus), anemia, asthma, epilepsy, Parkinson's disease, kidney stones, or a history of heart disease or alcohol abuse. Use of ibuprofen may cause complications in patients with liver or kidney disease, since these organs work together to remove the medication from the body.

Idoxuridine (IDU)

BRAND NAMES
Herplex Liquifilm, Stoxil

▶ Drug Class: Ophthalmic antiviral drug

▶ Available in: Drops, ointment

▶ Available OTC? No

▶ As Generic? No

Side Effects

SERIOUS
Allergic reaction causing itching, swelling, redness, pain, and constant burning; corneal ulcer causing painful sensation of having something lodged in the eye. In either case, call your doctor or ophthalmologist immediately.

COMMON
Heightened sensitivity of the eyes to bright light, stinging or burning in the eyes.

LESS COMMON
Blurred vision, excessive tear production.

PRINCIPAL USES
To treat viral infections of the eye, especially those caused by the herpes simplex virus.

HOW THE DRUG WORKS
Idoxuridine interferes with the activity of enzymes necessary for the replication of viral DNA in cells, thus preventing the virus from multiplying.

DOSAGE
The dosage may vary considerably from patient to patient, depending on a number of factors. The following guidelines represent typical doses; follow your doctor's specific dosing instruction. Eye drops: Apply 1 drop in the eye every hour during the day and every 2 hours at night. When the condition improves, apply it every 2 hours during the day and every 4 hours at night. Ointment: Apply a ⅜-inch strip of ointment every 4 hours (5 times a day), making the last application at bedtime.

ONSET OF EFFECT
Within 1 hour.

DURATION OF ACTION
Up to 6 hours.

DIETARY ADVICE
No special restrictions.

STORAGE
Keep the liquid form of idoxuridine refrigerated, but do not allow it to freeze.

IF YOU MISS A DOSE
Apply the missed dose as soon as you remember. If it is near time for the next dose, skip the missed dose and resume your regular dosage schedule. Do not double the next dose.

STOPPING THE DRUG
Take the drug as prescribed for the full treatment period, even if you begin to feel better before the scheduled end of therapy.

PROLONGED USE
Idoxuridine is not intended for prolonged use. If your symptoms do not improve in 7 days, consult your physician.

PRECAUTIONS
Over 60: No special problems are expected.

Driving and Hazardous Work: The use of idoxuridine should not impair your ability to perform such tasks safely.

Alcohol: No special precautions are necessary.

Pregnancy: Before taking idoxuridine, tell your doctor if you are pregnant or plan to become pregnant.

Breast Feeding: Idoxuridine may pass into breast milk; caution is advised. Consult your doctor for advice.

Infants and Children: Studies of the use of idoxuridine specifically in children have not been done; this drug should be used by young patients only under close medical supervision.

Special Concerns: Be sure you know how to apply idoxuridine. For the eye drops, first wash your hands. Then apply pressure to the inside corner of the eye with your middle finger. Tilt your head backward and pull the lower lid away from the eye with the index finger of the same hand. Drop the eye drops into the pouch you have created and close your eyes without blinking. Keep your eyes closed for 1 to 2 minutes. Then wash your hands. For the ointment, first wash your hands. Pull the lower lid down from the eye to form a pouch. Squeeze the tube to apply a thin strip of the ointment into the pouch. Close your eyes for 1 to 2 minutes. Then wash your hands. Do not let the applicator touch any surface, including the eye. If you accidentally touch its tip, clean it with warm water and soap. Family members should use separate washcloths and towels to prevent the spread of infection.

OVERDOSE
Symptoms: No specific ones have been reported.

What to Do: An overdose of idoxuridine is unlikely to occur. Emergency instructions are not applicable.

DRUG INTERACTIONS
Consult your doctor if you are using any eye product containing boric acid.

FOOD INTERACTIONS
No known food interactions.

DISEASE INTERACTIONS
Caution is advised when taking idoxuridine; consult your doctor if you have a history of any other eye problems.

Imatinib Mesylate

▶ Drug Class: Antineoplastic (anticancer) agent

▶ Available in: Capsules

▶ Available OTC? No

▶ As Generic? No

Side Effects

SERIOUS
Pleural effusion (excess fluid in the pleural space, which lies between the lungs and the chest wall), ascites (excess fluid in the abdomen), pulmonary edema (fluid in the lungs). Call your doctor immediately.

COMMON
Nausea, vomiting, diarrhea, swelling around the eyes and of the lower limbs, and muscle cramps.

LESS COMMON
Skin rash, headache, fatigue, joint pain, heartburn, fever, abdominal pain, and cough.

PRINCIPAL USES
To treat chronic myeloid leukemia (CML) during blast crisis, accelerated phase, or in chronic phase after failure of interferon-alpha therapy.

HOW THE DRUG WORKS
CML is caused by a genetic abnormality known as the Philadelphia chromosome, which produces a new and abnormal protein that causes the uncontrolled growth of white blood cells. By blocking the action of this protein, imatinib may lower the white blood cell count.

DOSAGE
400 mg once a day during chronic phase. 600 mg once a day during accelerated phase or blast crisis.

ONSET OF EFFECT
Unknown.

DURATION OF ACTION
Unknown.

DIETARY ADVICE
Take with a meal and a large glass of water.

STORAGE
Store in a tightly sealed container away from heat and direct light.

IF YOU MISS A DOSE
If you miss a dose, do not take the missed dose and do not double the next dose. Check with your doctor on what to do.

STOPPING THE DRUG
The decision to stop taking the drug should be made in consultation with your physician.

PROLONGED USE
You should see your doctor regularly for tests and examinations if you must take this drug for a prolonged period.

PRECAUTIONS
Over 60: No special problems are expected.

Driving and Hazardous Work: Do not drive or engage in hazardous work until you determine how the medicine affects you.

Alcohol: Avoid alcohol.

Pregnancy: Use of this drug during pregnancy should be avoided if possible. Be sure to tell your doctor if you are pregnant or plan to become pregnant.

Breast Feeding: It is not known whether this medication passes into breast milk. Breast feeding is not recommended while taking imatinib.

Infants and Children: Safety and effectiveness have not been established for patients under 18 years of age. Consult your pediatric oncologist for advice.

Special Concerns: Consult your doctor if you are taking St. John's wort. It may interact with imatinib.

OVERDOSE
Symptoms: No specific ones have been reported.

What to Do: Call your doctor or emergency medical services (EMS) immediately if you suspect an overdose.

DRUG INTERACTIONS
Consult your doctor if you are taking ketoconazole, itraconazole, erythromycin, clarithromycin, atorvastatin, fluvastatin, lovastatin, pravastatin, simvastatin, phenytoin, dexamethasone, carbamazepine, phenobarbital, cyclosporine, pimozide, benzodiazepine tranquilizers, calcium channel blockers, and warfarin.

FOOD INTERACTIONS
No known food interactions.

DISEASE INTERACTIONS
Use of this drug may cause complications in patients with liver or kidney disease, since these organs work together to remove the medication from the body.

Imipramine

▶ Drug Class: Tricyclic antidepressant

▶ Available in: Tablets, capsules

▶ Available OTC? No

▶ As Generic? Yes

Side Effects

SERIOUS
Confusion, heartbeat irregularities, hallucinations, seizures, extreme fatigue or drowsiness, blurred or altered vision, breathing difficulty, constipation, impaired concentration, difficult urination, fever, extreme and persistent restlessness, loss of coordination and balance, difficulty swallowing or speaking, dilated pupils, eye pain, fainting. Also trembling, shaking, weakness, and stiffness in the extremities; shuffling gait. Call your doctor immediately.

COMMON
Drowsiness, dizziness, or lightheadedness, headache, dry mouth or unpleasant taste, fatigue, heightened sensitivity of skin to sunlight, weight gain, increased appetite, nausea.

LESS COMMON
Heartburn, insomnia, diarrhea, increased sweating, vomiting.

PRINCIPAL USES
To relieve symptoms of major depression. Also used to treat bed-wetting in children age 6 and older and incontinence in older women.

HOW THE DRUG WORKS
Imipramine affects levels of specific brain chemicals (serotonin and norepinephrine) that are thought to be linked to mood, emotions, and mental state.

DOSAGE
For depression— Tablets: Adults: To start, 25 to 50 mg, 3 to 4 times a day; may be increased to 200 mg a day. Teenagers: 25 to 50 mg a day; may be increased to 100 mg a day. Older adults: To start, 25 mg a day at bedtime; may be increased to 100 mg a day. Children ages 6 to 12: 10 to 30 mg a day. Capsules: Adults: To start, 75 mg a day at bedtime; may be increased to 200 mg a day. For bed-wetting— Tablets: Children age 6 and older: 25 mg a day, 1 hour before bedtime. Dose may be increased based on the child's age.

ONSET OF EFFECT
1 to 6 weeks.

DURATION OF ACTION
Unknown.

DIETARY ADVICE
To lessen stomach upset, take with food, unless your doctor instructs otherwise. Increase intake of fiber and fluids.

STORAGE
Store in a tightly sealed container away from heat, moisture, and direct light.

IF YOU MISS A DOSE
If you take a one-time daily bedtime dose, do not take a missed dose in the morning because it may cause drowsiness. Call your doctor. If you take more than 1 dose a day, take it as soon as you remember. If it is near the time for the next dose, skip the missed dose and resume your regular dosage schedule. Do not double the next dose.

STOPPING THE DRUG
Take as prescribed for the full treatment period, even if you begin to feel better before the scheduled end of therapy. The decision to stop taking the drug should be made in consultation with your doctor.

PROLONGED USE
The usual course of therapy lasts 6 months to 1 year; some patients benefit from additional therapy.

PRECAUTIONS
Over 60: Adverse reactions may be more likely and more severe in older patients. A lower dose may be warranted.

Driving and Hazardous Work: Use caution until you determine how the medicine affects you. Drowsiness and lightheadedness can occur.

Alcohol: Avoid alcohol.

Pregnancy: Adequate studies have not been done. Consult your doctor.

Breast Feeding: Do not use this drug while nursing.

Infants and Children: Not prescribed for children under age 6. Antidepressants increase the risk of suicidal thinking and behavior (suicidality) in children with major depression and other psychiatric disorders. Discuss with your doctor this risk versus the benefits of using this drug. Children should be observed closely for worsening of symptoms, suicidality, or unusual changes in behavior at the onset of therapy and when making changes in dosage.

Special Concerns: This is a potentially dangerous drug, especially if taken in excess. Keep out of reach of suicidal patients.

OVERDOSE
Symptoms: Difficulty breathing, severe fatigue, seizures, confusion, hallucinations, distractibility, dilated pupils, irregular heartbeat, fever.

What to Do: Call your doctor, emergency medical services (EMS), or the nearest poison control center immediately.

DRUG INTERACTIONS
Consult your doctor for specific advice if you are taking antithyroid agents, cimetidine, clonidine, guanadrel, guanethidine, metrizamide, appetite suppressants, isoproterenol, ephedrine, epinephrine, amphetamines, phenyl-ephrine, antipsychotic drugs, pimozide, methyldopa, metyrosine, metoclopramide, pemoline, promethazine, trimeprazine, rauwolfia alkaloids, MAO inhibitors, or any drugs that depress the central nervous system.

FOOD INTERACTIONS
No known food interactions.

DISEASE INTERACTIONS
Consult your physician if you have any of the following: a history of alcohol abuse, difficulty urinating, asthma, bipolar disorder, high blood pressure, stomach or intestinal problems, glaucoma, overactive thyroid, enlarged prostate, schizophrenia, seizures a blood disorder, or kidney, heart, or liver disease.

Imiquimod

BRAND NAME
Aldara

▶ Drug Class: Immunomodulator

▶ Available in: Cream

▶ Available OTC? No.

▶ As Generic? No

Side Effects

SERIOUS
Swollen eyelids, face, or lips, wheezing, or rash may be signs of a drug allergy. Call your doctor immediately.

COMMON
Common side effects are limited to the treated area of the skin. The following have been observed: redness, thinning of the skin, flaking, swelling of the treated area.

LESS COMMON
Hardening or stiffening of the treated area, sores, scabbing, blisters.

PRINCIPAL USES
To treat external condylomata acuminata (genital and perianal warts) in adults.

HOW THE DRUG WORKS
Imiquimod's mechanism of action is unknown.

DOSAGE
Apply a thin layer to the affected area 3 times a week at bedtime. Leave it on the skin for 6 to 10 hours. The cream should then be removed by washing with mild soap and water.

ONSET OF EFFECT
Unknown.

DURATION OF ACTION
Unknown.

DIETARY ADVICE
Imiquimod can be used without regard to diet.

STORAGE
Store in a tightly sealed container away from heat, moisture, and direct light. Do not allow it to freeze.

IF YOU MISS A DOSE
If you miss a scheduled dose, skip it and resume your regular dosage schedule on the appointed day; do not apply the cream 2 days in a row.

STOPPING THE DRUG
Treatment should continue until there is total clearance of the warts or for no more than 16 weeks. If the warts do not clear up within this time, do not continue to apply imiquimod to the area; consult your doctor.

PROLONGED USE
Imiquimod is prescribed for no more than 16 weeks.

PRECAUTIONS
Over 60: No special problems are expected.

Driving and Hazardous Work: The use of imiquimod should not impair your ability to perform such tasks safely.

Alcohol: No special precautions are necessary.

Pregnancy: Adequate human studies have not been done. Before taking imiquimod, tell your doctor if you are pregnant or plan to become pregnant.

Breast Feeding: Imiquimod may pass into breast milk; caution is advised. Consult your doctor for specific advice.

Infants and Children: Not recommended for use by children under age 18.

Special Concerns: The treated area should not be covered by tight bandages or clothing. Wash your hands before and after applying imiquimod to the skin. Avoid getting the drug in your eyes. Sexual relations should be avoided while the cream is on the skin. Imiquimod cream may weaken condoms and diaphragms, compromising the protection they provide. If serious irritation of the treated area occurs, discontinue the medication for several days to allow the reaction to subside. You may then resume therapy.

OVERDOSE
Symptoms: No cases of overdose have been reported.

What to Do: An overdose with imiquimod is unlikely. If someone accidentally ingests imiquimod, call your doctor, emergency medical services (EMS), or the nearest poison control center immediately.

DRUG INTERACTIONS
None known.

FOOD INTERACTIONS
No known food interactions.

DISEASE INTERACTIONS
Imiquimod should be used with caution by anyone with a history of inflammatory skin conditions. If you have had any recent medical or surgical treatment in the genital or perianal area, therapy with imiquimod should be delayed until the affected tissue has healed.

Indapamide

Generic 2.5 mg
(RHONE-POULENC RORER)

▶ Drug Class: Thiazide diuretic

▶ Available in: Tablets

▶ Available OTC? No

▶ As Generic? Yes

Side Effects

SERIOUS
Skin rash, hives, intense itching, swelling of the mouth and throat, breathing difficulty, heart rhythm irregularities, lightheadedness, unusual bleeding or bruising. Call your doctor immediately.

COMMON
Muscle cramps or pain. Potassium depletion may lead to heart palpitations and weakness. Fluid depletion may lead to dizziness, especially upon arising from a sitting or lying position, as well as thirst, dry mouth, and constipation.

LESS COMMON
Decreased sexual ability, increased sensitivity to sunlight, loss of appetite, gout, increased blood sugar (a problem for diabetic patients).

PRINCIPAL USES
To help control high blood pressure and to treat conditions that cause edema (swelling of body tissues resulting from excess salt and water retention).

HOW THE DRUG WORKS
Diuretics increase the excretion of salt and water in the urine. By reducing the overall fluid volume in the body, these drugs reduce blood volume and so reduce pressure within the blood vessels.

DOSAGE
For high blood pressure: Initial dose is 1.5 mg once a day. It can be increased to 5 mg a day. To reduce edema: 2.5 mg once a day; it can be increased to 5 mg a day.

ONSET OF EFFECT
From 2 to 3 hours.

DURATION OF ACTION
24 hours.

DIETARY ADVICE
A single daily dose should be taken in the morning after breakfast.

STORAGE
Store in a tightly sealed container away from heat and direct light.

IF YOU MISS A DOSE
Take it as soon as you remember. If it is near the time for the next dose, skip the missed dose and resume your regular dosage schedule. Do not double the next dose.

STOPPING THE DRUG
The decision to stop taking the drug should be made by your doctor.

PROLONGED USE
See your doctor regularly for examinations and tests if you must take this medicine for an extended period.

PRECAUTIONS
Over 60: Adverse reactions may be more likely and more severe in older patients.

Driving and Hazardous Work: No special precautions are necessary.

Alcohol: No special precautions are necessary.

Pregnancy: Indapamide should not be used during pregnancy unless recommended by your doctor.

Breast Feeding: Indapamide may pass into breast milk; caution is advised. Consult your doctor for specific advice.

Infants and Children: The safety and effectiveness of indapamide for children under 12 have not been determined. Consult your doctor for specific advice.

Special Concerns: Follow your doctor's instructions about consuming potassium-rich foods or taking a potassium supplement. It may be necessary to discontinue indapamide 5 to 7 days before undergoing major surgery. If you are taking more than 1 dose a day, the last dose should be taken no later than 6 pm unless your doctor advises otherwise.

OVERDOSE
Symptoms: Stomach irritation, thirst, muscle cramps, nausea, vomiting, increased urination, lethargy, loss of consciousness.

What to Do: Call your doctor, emergency medical services (EMS), or the nearest poison control center immediately.

DRUG INTERACTIONS
Consult your doctor for specific advice if you are taking other drugs for high blood pressure, lithium, oral antidiabetic drugs, digitalis preparations, nonsteroidal anti-inflammatory drugs, cholestyramine, or colestipol.

FOOD INTERACTIONS
Follow your doctor's advice about salt use and potassium-rich foods.

DISEASE INTERACTIONS
Caution is advised when taking indapamide. Consult your doctor if you have diabetes, gout, or systemic lupus erythematosus. Use of indapamide may cause complications in patients with liver or kidney disease, since these organs work together to remove the medication from the body.

Indinavir

BRAND NAME
Crixivan

Crixivan 200 mg
(MERCK)

▶ Drug Class: Antiviral/
protease inhibitor

▶ Available in: Capsules

▶ Available OTC? No

▶ As Generic? No

Side Effects

SERIOUS
Blood in urine and sharp
back pain caused by kid-
ney stones. High blood
sugar (diabetes) has
occurred in patients tak-
ing drugs of this class,
although a cause-and-
effect relationship has
not been established.
Call your doctor if you
develop increased thirst
or excessive urination.

COMMON
Generalized weakness,
abdominal pains, diar-
rhea, nausea, vomiting,
headache, insomnia,
changes in taste, dry
skin, chapped lips.

LESS COMMON
Dizziness, drowsiness,
depression, memory
changes, abdominal
bloating, muscle wasting.

PRINCIPAL USES
To treat advanced HIV
(human immunodeficiency
virus) infection and AIDS
(acquired immunodeficiency
syndrome), usually in combination with other drugs.
While not a cure for HIV
infection, this drug may
suppress the replication of
the virus and delay the progression of the disease.

HOW THE DRUG WORKS
Indinavir blocks the activity
of a viral protease, an
enzyme that is needed by
HIV to reproduce. Blocking
the protease causes HIV to
make copies that cannot
infect new cells.

DOSAGE
800 mg every 8 hours,
alone or in combination
with other antiviral agents.
Higher or lower doses are
sometimes prescribed when
indinavir is being combined
with medications such as
nevirapine and delavirdine,
which alter indinavir blood
levels.

ONSET OF EFFECT
Unknown. With most anti-
retroviral drugs, an early
response can be seen within
the first few days of therapy,
but the maximum effect
may take 12 to 16 weeks.

DURATION OF ACTION
Unknown. Effects of the
drug may be prolonged if
indinavir is used in combination with other effective
drugs and the virus is maximally suppressed.

DIETARY ADVICE
Indinavir should be taken
with plenty of water or
other liquid, preferably at
least 1 hour before or 2
hours after a meal. It may
also be taken with a light,
nonfat snack. Drink at least
48 ounces of water per day.

STORAGE
Store in a tightly sealed container away from heat, moisture, and direct light.

IF YOU MISS A DOSE
Take it as soon as you
remember. However, if it is
near the time for the next
dose, skip the missed dose
and resume your regular
dosage schedule. Do not
double the next dose.

STOPPING THE DRUG
The decision to stop taking
the drug should be made by
your doctor.

PROLONGED USE
See your doctor regularly
for tests and examinations.

PRECAUTIONS
Over 60: No special studies have been done on older
patients.

**Driving and Hazardous
Work:** Do not drive or
engage in hazardous work
until you determine how the
medicine affects you.

Alcohol: Avoid alcohol if
liver function is impaired.

Pregnancy: Indinavir has
been shown to cause birth
defects in animals. Human
studies have not been done.
Neverthelessl, indinavir is
increasingly used in combination with other antiretroviral drugs to treat pregnant
HIV-infected women.

Breast Feeding: Women
infected with HIV should
not breast-feed, so as to
avoid transmitting the virus
to an uninfected child.

Infants and Children:
Safety and effectiveness of
indinavir for children under
the age of 16 have not been
established.

Special Concerns: Indinavir should not be taken

concurrently with the herb
St. John's wort, which can
increase blood levels of the
drug in the body and lead
to possible resistance to indinavir. It is important to drink
at least 48 ounces of water or
other liquids every 24 hours
to help prevent kidney
stones. Therapy may be
interrupted for patients who
develop kidney stones. Be
sure to tell any doctor or
dentist treating you that you
are taking indinavir. Remember that taking indinavir does
not eliminate the chance of
passing the AIDS virus to
other persons. Take appropriate preventive measures.

OVERDOSE
Symptoms: Pain in the
lower back, blood in the
urine, nausea, vomiting,
diarrhea.

What to Do: An overdose
of indinavir is unlikely to be
life-threatening. However, if
someone takes a much
larger dose than prescribed,
seek medical attention
immediately.

DRUG INTERACTIONS
Consult your doctor for specific advice if you are taking
any other drug, especially
astemizole, didanosine,
delavirenz, efavirenz, itraconazole, ketoconazole,
midazolam, triazolam, didanosine, rifabutin, rifampin,
phenobarbital, phenytoin,
carbamazepine, cholesterol-
lowering drugs, dexamethasone, sildenafil, tadalafil,
vardenafil, or calcium channel blockers.

FOOD INTERACTIONS
Food, especially fatty foods,
will decrease absorption of
the drug.

DISEASE INTERACTIONS
Use of indinavir may cause
complications in patients
with liver disease.

Generic 25 mg
(LEDERLE)

▶ Drug Class: Nonsteroidal anti-inflammatory drug (NSAID)

▶ Available in: Capsules, suspension, rectal suppositories

▶ Available OTC? No

▶ As Generic? Yes

Side Effects

SERIOUS
Wheezing or breathing difficulty, with or without swelling of the legs or other signs of heart failure; chest pain; peptic ulcers with vomiting of blood; black, tarry stools; decreased kidney function causing blood in the urine, decreased urine output, and shortness of breath. NSAIDs may cause constriction of the airways or severe allergic reactions in patients who are sensitive to aspirin, especially those with aspirin-induced nasal polyps or asthma.

COMMON
Nausea, vomiting, heartburn, diarrhea, constipation, headache, dizziness, drowsiness.

LESS COMMON
Ulcers or sores in mouth, rashes or blistering, unusual tingling or numbness of the hands and feet, depression, ringing in the ears, seizures, blurred vision. Also high blood potassium levels and decreased blood counts; such problems can be detected by your doctor.

PRINCIPAL USES
To treat mild to moderate pain and inflammation occurring in association with tendinitis, arthritis, bursitis, gout, soft tissue injuries, migraine and other types of vascular headache, menstrual cramps, and other conditions. Because of its greater risk of toxicity, indomethacin should be taken only when other NSAIDs prove ineffective.

HOW THE DRUG WORKS
NSAIDs such as indomethacin work by interfering with the formation of prostaglandins. These are naturally occurring substances in the body that cause inflammation and make nerves more sensitive to pain impulses. NSAIDs also have other modes of action that are less well understood.

DOSAGE
Adults— Capsules: For arthritis: 25 to 50 mg, 2 to 4 times daily, up to a usual maximum of 200 mg a day at first. For gout: 100 mg immediately, then 50 mg taken 3 times a day. This may be decreased gradually by your doctor. For bursitis or tendinitis: 25 mg, 3 to 4 times a day, or 50 mg, 3 times a day. Extended-release capsules: For arthritis: 75 mg, 1 to 2 times a day. Rectal suppositories: For arthritis, gout, bursitis, and tendinitis: 50 mg suppository, inserted 1 to 4 times a day. Children— Consult a pediatrician for dosage for all forms.

ONSET OF EFFECT
30 minutes to several hours.

DURATION OF ACTION
4 hours or more.

DIETARY ADVICE
Take with food; maintain your usual food and fluid intake.

STORAGE
Store in a tightly sealed container away from heat, moisture, and direct light.

IF YOU MISS A DOSE
Take it as soon as you remember. If it is near the time for the next dose, skip the missed dose and resume your regular dosage schedule. Do not double the next dose.

STOPPING THE DRUG
Take it as prescribed for the full treatment period. Ask your doctor about stopping the drug if you are feeling better before the scheduled end of therapy.

PROLONGED USE
Therapy may require weeks or months.

PRECAUTIONS
Over 60: Because of the potentially greater consequences of gastrointestinal side effects, the dose in older patients, especially those over age 70, is often cut in half.

Driving and Hazardous Work: Avoid such activities until you determine how the medicine affects you.

Alcohol: Avoid alcohol.

Pregnancy: Do not use this drug while pregnant.

Breast Feeding: Do not use indomethacin while nursing.

Infants and Children: May be used in exceptional circumstances only when other NSAIDs prove ineffective; consult a pediatrician.

Special Concerns: Because NSAIDs can interfere with blood coagulation, this drug should be stopped at least 3 days prior to any surgery.

OVERDOSE
Symptoms: Severe nausea, vomiting, headache, confusion, seizures.

What to Do: Call your doctor, emergency medical services (EMS), or the nearest poison control center immediately.

DRUG INTERACTIONS
Do not take with aspirin or other NSAIDs. Consult your doctor if you are taking anticoagulants, antibiotics, itraconazole or ketoconazole, plicamycin, penicillamine, valproic acid, phenytoin, cyclosporine, digitalis drugs, lithium, medication for high blood pressure, methotrexate, probenecid, steroids, triamterene, or zidovudine.

FOOD INTERACTIONS
No known food interactions.

DISEASE INTERACTIONS
Consult your doctor if you have a history of alcohol abuse, bleeding problems, inflammation or ulcers of the stomach and intestines, diabetes mellitus, heart, liver, or kidney disease (including kidney stones), systemic lupus erythematosus (SLE, lupus), anemia, asthma, epilepsy, or Parkinson's disease.

Infliximab

▶ Drug Class: Biologic response modifier

▶ Available in: Injection

▶ Available OTC? No

▶ As Generic? No

Side Effects

SERIOUS
Serious side effects are rare, but may include serious infections (such as tuberculosis), nervous system diseases (symptoms may include numbness or tingling, vision problems, weakness in the legs, dizziness), lupus-like symptoms.

COMMON
Respiratory infection, sore throat, coughing, stomach pain.

LESS COMMON
Itching, rash, insomnia, depression, thrush.

PRINCIPAL USES
To reduce the signs and symptoms of moderate to severe active rheumatoid arthritis and Crohn's disease. Infliximab is prescribed for patients who have not responded adequately to other treatments.

HOW THE DRUG WORKS
Infliximab works by binding with tumor necrosis factor (TNF), a key protein involved in the inflammatory process. It reduces inflammation by blocking the interaction of TNF with its receptors on cells.

DOSAGE
Infliximab is administered intravenously in a hospital or outpatient setting. Dosage will be determined by your doctor. For rheumatoid arthritis, infliximab is administered in combination with methotrexate.

ONSET OF EFFECT
Several days.

DURATION OF ACTION
Unknown.

DIETARY ADVICE
May be taken without regard to diet.

STORAGE
Not applicable; this drug is administered only in a hospital or outpatient clinic.

IF YOU MISS A DOSE
Not applicable; your doctor will decide when to administer doses.

STOPPING THE DRUG
The decision to stop taking the drug should be made in consultation with your physician.

PROLONGED USE
You should see your doctor regularly for tests and examinations while taking this medicine. Therapy may be required for an indefinite period.

PRECAUTIONS
Over 60: No special problems are expected.

Driving and Hazardous Work: No special precautions.

Alcohol: No special precautions.

Pregnancy: Adequate human studies have not been done. Before taking infliximab, tell your doctor if you are pregnant or plan to become pregnant.

Breast Feeding: Infliximab may pass into breast milk; caution is advised. Consult your doctor for advice on whether to discontinue nursing or discontinue the drug.

Infants and Children: Safety and effectiveness in children have not been determined.

Special Concerns: Prior to starting therapy, you should have a tuberculosis skin test (PPD) placed and read.

OVERDOSE
Symptoms: No cases of overdose have been reported.

What to Do: An overdose with infliximab is unlikely. If someone takes a much larger dose than prescribed, call your doctor.

DRUG INTERACTIONS
Avoid live-virus vaccines. Adequate studies involving interactions with other drugs have not been done. Consult your doctor for specific advice.

FOOD INTERACTIONS
No known food interactions.

DISEASE INTERACTIONS
Infliximab should be used with caution in patients with any active infection, including chronic or localized infections, or who are immunosuppressed.

Influenza Virus Vaccine

▶ Drug Class: Vaccine

▶ Available in: Injection

▶ Available OTC? No

▶ As Generic? No

Side Effects

SERIOUS
Serious allergic reaction involving difficulty swallowing or breathing; reddened skin, especially around the ears; itching, particularly of the hands or feet; hives; unusual and severe fatigue; and swollen face, eyes, or nasal passages. Call your doctor immediately.

COMMON
Pain, redness, or hard lump at site of injection.

LESS COMMON
Fever, muscle aches, general feeling of illness.

PRINCIPAL USES
To help prevent infection by the influenza (flu) virus.

HOW THE DRUG WORKS
The influenza vaccine is an injection that works by introducing a dead (inactive) flu virus into the body, which stimulates the immune system to produce protective antibodies against the disease. The virus used for the vaccine at any given time is similar to the one that the World Health Organization and the U.S. Public Health Service believe is likely to appear during the upcoming flu season, since the strains of influenza change from season to season and year to year.

DOSAGE
Adults and children age 9 and older: 1 injection into the upper arm annually, usually in early November. Children ages 6 months to 9 years: 1 or 2 injections into the thigh annually, usually in early November.

ONSET OF EFFECT
Most patients develop immunity within 2 to 4 weeks.

DURATION OF ACTION
Unknown. The antibodies may be available for protection against a particular strain of flu for many years following the injection, but the antibodies will only protect against a flu virus that is identical or very similar to the one that was used in the vaccine. A different strain of the flu may not be affected by the antibodies, leading to infection.

DIETARY ADVICE
No special restrictions.

STORAGE
Not applicable; the dose is administered only at a health care facility.

IF YOU MISS A DOSE
Not applicable.

STOPPING THE DRUG
Not applicable.

PROLONGED USE
Not applicable.

PRECAUTIONS
Over 60: Influenza vaccine is not expected to cause different or more severe side effects in older patients than it does in younger persons. However, older adults may not develop as strong an immunity as younger persons.

Driving and Hazardous Work: The vaccine should not impair your ability to perform such tasks safely.

Alcohol: No special precautions are necessary.

Pregnancy: The vaccine has not been shown to cause problems in pregnant women. Consult your doctor for more information.

Breast Feeding: The vaccine has not been shown to cause any problems in nursing babies. Consult your doctor for advice.

Infants and Children: Not recommended for use by children under the age of 6 months. Only the "split-virus" vaccine should be administered to children under the age of 13.

Special Concerns: If you want to decrease your chances of coming down with the flu, discuss appropriate health care measures with your doctor. Remember that the vaccine is not effective against all strains of the flu. The ability of the vaccine to stimulate your immune system is affected by your age, by the presence of other diseases, and by the use of other medications. Protection from flu infection during the flu season may be less in these circumstances. Make sure to tell your doctor if you or your child are ill on the day the injection is scheduled. Your doctor may decide to reschedule your vaccination.

OVERDOSE
Symptoms: An overdose with the influenza vaccine is unlikely.

What to Do: No cases of overdose have been reported.

DRUG INTERACTIONS
Other drugs may interact with influenza vaccine. Tell your doctor if you are taking any prescription or over-the-counter medication.

FOOD INTERACTIONS
No known food interactions.

DISEASE INTERACTIONS
Consult your doctor if you have any of the following: bronchitis, pneumonia, or other respiratory problems, seizures, allergies to eggs, or allergies to antibiotics, especially gentamicin.

405

Insulin Glargine (rDNA origin)

▶ Drug Class: Antidiabetic agent

▶ Available in: Injection

▶ Available OTC? No

▶ As Generic? No

Side Effects

SERIOUS
Symptoms of hypoglycemia can be caused by the release of adrenaline or by an inadequate supply of glucose to the brain. With severe hypoglycemia, lack of sufficient glucose to the brain may cause slurred speech, impaired concentration, confusion, seizures, coma, irreversible brain damage, and death. Mild hypoglycemia may cause restless sleep, nightmares, or a cold sweat that awakens patients at night.

COMMON
Symptoms resulting from release of adrenaline are common manifestations of mild to moderate hypoglycemia. They include cold sweats, anxiety, shakiness, hunger, rapid heartbeat, headache, and nervousness. Weight gain is common when taking insulin.

LESS COMMON
Allergic reactions, lipoatrophy (depressions in the skin due to loss of fat tissue), and lipohypertrophy (excessive accumulation of fat tissue).

PRINCIPAL USES
For long-term treatment of diabetes mellitus. All patients with type 1 diabetes require lifelong insulin treatment. Patients with type 2 diabetes may require insulin if they are unable to control their blood glucose (sugar) levels with diet and oral medications. Insulin glargine is a slightly modified form of human insulin that maintains a relatively constant glucose-lowering effect over a 24-hour period and thus permits dosing once a day.

HOW THE DRUG WORKS
Insulin, a hormone secreted by the beta cells of the pancreas, plays an essential role in controlling the metabolism and storage of carbohydrates, fat, and protein. Insulin is secreted in response to a rise in blood sugar (glucose). Insulin lowers blood glucose by increasing its uptake by body cells, especially muscle, and by reducing the release of glucose from the liver between meals.

DOSAGE
Injected under the skin (stomach, thigh, or upper arm) once a day at bedtime. Doses are determined by your doctor. The solution should be clear and colorless, without any visible particles. Insulin glargine must not be diluted or mixed with any other insulin or solution.

ONSET OF EFFECT
About 1 to 2 hours.

DURATION OF ACTION
At least 24 hours.

DIETARY ADVICE
All patients with diabetes should follow the general dietary recommendations of the American Diabetes Association. Though intake of simple sugars is not forbidden, consuming a large amount of sugary foods at one time may trigger a rapid rise in blood glucose that can increase urination and thirst. In addition, patients who take insulin must remain consistent from day to day in the timing and caloric content of their meals. Depending on the timing, dose, and types of insulin prescribed, snacks may be recommended in the late afternoon, before bedtime, or prior to unusual physical activity. Diabetic patients must always have available a juice, food, or tablets that can raise blood glucose levels rapidly to counter an episode of hypoglycemia.

STORAGE
Refrigerate insulin but do not allow it to freeze. If refrigeration is not possible, the 10 milliliter (mL) vial or 3 mL cartridge in use can be kept unrefrigerated for up to 28 days away from direct heat and light, as long as the temperature is not greater than 86°F. Unrefrigerated 10 mL vials and 3 mL cartridges must be used within the 28-day period or they must be discarded. If refrigeration is not possible, the 5 mL vial in use can be kept unrefrigerated for up to 14 days away from direct heat and light, as long as the temperature is not greater than 86°F. Unrefrigerated 5 mL vials must be used within the 14-day period or they must be discarded. If refrigerated, the 5 mL vial in use can be kept for up to 28 days. Once the 3 mL cartridge is placed into an OptiPen One, it should not be put in the refrigerator.

IF YOU MISS A DOSE
Timing of insulin doses is extremely important. The best approach is to measure blood glucose and add a dose of regular insulin if glucose levels are too high. Otherwise, wait for the next scheduled dose.

STOPPING THE DRUG
Do not stop taking insulin injections unless ordered by your doctor. Patients with diabetes are often given general instructions for modifying their insulin doses based on home blood glucose measurements.

PROLONGED USE
After many years with diabetes, some patients become insensitive to the symptoms of hypoglycemia and are at risk for serious brain complications of prolonged, unrecognized hypoglycemia.

PRECAUTIONS
Over 60: No special warnings. Some older people may, however, have vision problems that may make it difficult to draw up the correct dose of insulin.

Driving and Hazardous Work: Patients taking insulin must be very careful to avoid hypoglycemia when driving or engaging in hazardous work.

Alcohol: Moderate alcohol intake, especially when taken with large meals, does not adversely affect control of diabetes or alter the dose of insulin. However, large amounts of alcohol increase the risk of hypoglycemia.

Pregnancy: Strict metabolic control—using insulin injections in most women—must be maintained during pregnancy to reduce the risk of birth defects, fetal complications, or death at the time of delivery. In women who had diabetes before the onset of pregnancy, the dose of insulin is often smaller during the first third (trimester) of pregnancy and then higher during the final two trimesters. When women first develop diabetes during pregnancy (gestational diabetes), insulin requirements drop rapidly after delivery and most do not need to continue with insulin treatment.

Breast Feeding: Insulin requirements tend to be lower during breast feeding. Home glucose monitoring is important to avoid hypoglycemia. Insulin glargine may pass into breast milk; consult your doctor for advice.

Infants and Children: Treatment with insulin in young patients age 6 and older is the same as that in older people with diabetes. The safety and effectiveness of insulin glargine in children under the age of 6 have not been established.

Special Concerns: Inadequate amounts of insulin in type 1 diabetes may lead to the serious complication of diabetic ketoacidosis, characterized by loss of appetite, excessive thirst and urination, nausea, vomiting, deep breathing, fruity breath odor, drowsiness, confusion, and loss of consciousness. Insulin glargine is not the insulin of choice for treatment of diabetic ketoacidosis. An intravenous short-acting insulin is the preferred treatment.

OVERDOSE
Symptoms: Insulin overdose results in hypoglycemia (see Side Effects for symptoms).

What to Do: For mild to moderate hypoglycemia, ingest drinks or food containing sugar. For more severe hypoglycemia, administer injections of glucagon or call emergency medical services (EMS) immediately.

DRUG INTERACTIONS
A large number of drugs can promote either elevated blood glucose levels or hypoglycemia. Be sure that your doctor knows about all of the medications you take and is informed before you start taking any new drugs, either by prescription or over the counter. Corticosteroids in particular are likely to raise blood glucose levels and insulin requirements. Beta-blockers (commonly prescribed for hypertension) may cause either high blood glucose levels or hypoglycemia; in addition, because these medications may dampen the symptoms of hypoglycemia that are caused by adrenaline release, mild degrees of hypoglycemia may progress unnoticed to more serious hypoglycemia affecting the brain.

FOOD INTERACTIONS
Insulin requirements are increased by the ingestion of large amounts of calories, especially simple sugars and other carbohydrates.

DISEASE INTERACTIONS
Insulin requirements are increased by infections, psychological stress, or an uncontrolled overactive thyroid, and often at a time of surgery. Requirements may diminish with kidney disease or an underactive adrenal or pituitary gland.

Insulin (Intermediate-acting, NPH, Lente)

BRAND NAMES
Humulin L, Humulin N, Insulatard NPH (purified pork), Insulated NPH Human, Lente Iletin I (beef and pork), Lente Iletin II (purified beef), Lente Iletin II (purified pork), Novolin L, Novolin L Pen-Fill Cartridges, Novolin N, NPH Iletin I (beef and pork), NPH Iletin II (purified beef), NPH Iletin II (purified pork)

▶ Drug Class: Antidiabetic agent

▶ Available in: Injection

▶ Available OTC? Yes

▶ As Generic? No

Side Effects

SERIOUS
Symptoms of hypoglycemia can be caused by the release of adrenaline or by an inadequate supply of glucose to the brain. With severe hypoglycemia, lack of sufficient glucose to the brain may cause slurred speech, impaired concentration, confusion, seizures, coma, irreversible brain damage, and death. Mild hypoglycemia may cause restless sleep, nightmares, or a cold sweat that awakens patients at night.

COMMON
Symptoms resulting from the release of adrenaline are common with mild to moderate hypoglycemia. They include cold sweats, anxiety, shakiness, hunger, rapid heartbeat, and headache. Weight gain is also common when taking insulin.

LESS COMMON
Allergic reactions, lipoatrophy (depressions in the skin due to loss of fat tissue), and lipohypertrophy (excessive accumulation of fat tissue).

PRINCIPAL USES
For long-term treatment of diabetes mellitus. All patients with type 1 diabetes require lifelong insulin treatment. Patients with type 2 diabetes may require insulin if they are unable to control their blood glucose (sugar) levels with diet and oral medications.

HOW THE DRUG WORKS
Insulin, a hormone secreted by the beta cells of the pancreas, plays an essential role in controlling the metabolism and storage of carbohydrates, fat, and protein. Insulin is secreted in response to a rise in blood sugar (glucose). Insulin lowers blood glucose by increasing its uptake by body cells, especially muscle, and by reducing the release of glucose from the liver between meals.

DOSAGE
Injected 1 or 2 times a day. Doses and frequency are determined by your doctor. Intermediate-acting (NPH or Lente) insulin can be mixed in the same syringe with rapid-acting insulin; draw up the rapid-acting insulin first. Intermediate-acting insulin solutions are cloudy (insulin settles to the bottom of the bottle) and must be rolled or gently shaken to distribute the insulin evenly in the solution before drawing it up into the syringe.

ONSET OF EFFECT
Within 1 hour; peak effect occurs within 8 to 12 hours.

DURATION OF ACTION
From 12 to 18 hours.

DIETARY ADVICE
All patients with diabetes should follow the general dietary recommendations of the American Diabetes Association. Though intake of simple sugars is not forbidden, consuming a large amount of sugary foods at one time may trigger a rapid rise in blood glucose that can increase urination and thirst. In addition, patients who take insulin must remain consistent from day to day in the timing and caloric content of their meals. Depending on the timing, dose, and types of insulin prescribed, snacks may be recommended in the late afternoon, before bedtime, or prior to unusual physical activity. Diabetic patients must always have available a juice, food, or tablets that can raise blood glucose levels rapidly to counter an episode of hypoglycemia.

STORAGE
Refrigerate insulin but do not allow it to freeze. Insulin does not have to be kept refrigerated when you're traveling for short periods, but exposure to high temperatures must be avoided.

IF YOU MISS A DOSE
Timing of insulin doses is extremely important. The best approach is to measure blood glucose and add a dose of regular insulin if your glucose levels are too high. Otherwise, wait for the next scheduled dose.

STOPPING THE DRUG
Do not stop taking insulin injections unless ordered by your doctor. Patients with diabetes are often given general instructions for modifying their insulin doses based on home blood glucose measurements.

PROLONGED USE
After many years with diabetes, some patients become insensitive to the symptoms of hypoglycemia and are at risk for serious brain complications of prolonged, unrecognized hypoglycemia.

PRECAUTIONS
Over 60: No special warnings. Some older people may, however, have vision problems that may make it difficult to draw up the correct dose of insulin.

Driving and Hazardous Work: Patients taking insulin must be very careful to avoid hypoglycemia when driving or engaging in hazardous work.

Alcohol: Moderate alcohol intake, especially when taken with large meals, does not adversely affect control of diabetes or alter the dose of insulin. However, large amounts of alcohol increase the risk of hypoglycemia.

Pregnancy: Strict metabolic control—using insulin injections in most women—must be maintained during pregnancy to reduce the risk of birth defects, fetal complications, or death at the time of delivery. In women who had diabetes before the onset of pregnancy, the dose of insulin is often smaller during the first third (trimester) of pregnancy and then higher during the final two trimesters. When women first develop diabetes during pregnancy (gestational diabetes), insulin requirements drop rapidly after delivery and most do not need to continue with insulin treatment.

Breast Feeding: Insulin requirements tend to be lower during breast feeding. Home glucose monitoring is important to avoid hypoglycemia. Insulin is not present in breast milk.

Infants and Children: Treatment with insulin in children is the same as in older people with diabetes.

Special Concerns: Inadequate amounts of insulin in type 1 diabetes may lead to the serious complication of diabetic ketoacidosis, characterized by loss of appetite, excessive thirst and urination, nausea, vomiting, deep breathing, fruity breath odor, drowsiness, confusion, and loss of consciousness.

OVERDOSE

Symptoms: Insulin overdose results in hypo- glycemia (see Side Effects for symptoms).

What to Do: For mild to moderate hypoglycemia, ingest drinks or food containing sugar. For more severe hypoglycemia, administer injections of glucagon or call emergency medical services (EMS) immediately.

DRUG INTERACTIONS

A large number of drugs can promote either elevated blood glucose levels or hypoglycemia. Be sure that your doctor knows about all of the medications you take and is informed before you start taking any new drugs, either by prescription or over the counter. Corticosteroids in particular are likely to raise blood glucose levels and insulin requirements. Beta-blockers (commonly prescribed for hypertension) may cause either high blood glucose levels or hypoglycemia; in addition, because these medications may dampen the symptoms of hypoglycemia that are caused by adrenaline release, mild degrees of hypoglycemia may progress unnoticed to more serious hypoglycemia affecting the brain.

FOOD INTERACTIONS

Insulin requirements are increased when larger amounts of calories are ingested, especially simple sugars and carbohydrates.

DISEASE INTERACTIONS

Insulin requirements are increased by infections, psychological stress, or an uncontrolled overactive thyroid, and often at a time of surgery. Requirements may diminish with kidney disease or an underactive adrenal or pituitary gland.

Insulin Lispro (rDNA origin)

▶ Drug Class: Antidiabetic agent

▶ Available in: Injection

▶ Available OTC? No

▶ As Generic? No

Side Effects

SERIOUS
Symptoms of hypoglycemia can be caused by the release of adrenaline or by an inadequate supply of glucose to the brain. With severe hypoglycemia, lack of sufficient glucose to the brain may cause slurred speech, impaired concentration, confusion, seizures, coma, irreversible brain damage, and death. Mild hypoglycemia may cause restless sleep, nightmares, or a cold sweat that awakens patients at night.

COMMON
Symptoms resulting from release of adrenaline are common manifestations of mild to moderate hypoglycemia. They include cold sweats, anxiety, shakiness, hunger, rapid heartbeat, headache, and nervousness. Weight gain is common when taking insulin.

LESS COMMON
Allergic reactions, lipoatrophy (depressions in the skin due to loss of fat tissue), and lipohypertrophy (excessive accumulation of fat tissue).

PRINCIPAL USES
For long-term treatment of diabetes mellitus. All patients with type 1 diabetes require lifelong insulin treatment. Patients with type 2 diabetes may require insulin if they are unable to control their blood glucose (sugar) levels with diet and oral medications.

HOW THE DRUG WORKS
Insulin, a hormone secreted by the beta cells of the pancreas, plays an essential role in controlling the metabolism and storage of carbohydrates, fat, and protein. Insulin is secreted in response to a rise in blood sugar (glucose). Insulin lowers blood glucose by increasing its uptake by body cells, especially muscle, and by reducing the release of glucose from the liver between meals.

DOSAGE
It may be taken 1 to 4 times daily, before meals and possibly at bedtime. Doses and frequency are determined by your doctor. Rapid-acting (lispro rDNA origin) insulin should be administered 15 minutes before a meal.

ONSET OF EFFECT
Within 30 to 45 minutes; the peak effect occurs within 1 hour.

DURATION OF ACTION
From 3 to 4 hours.

DIETARY ADVICE
All patients with diabetes should follow the general dietary recommendations of the American Diabetes Association. Though intake of simple sugars is not forbidden, consuming a large amount of sugary foods at one time may trigger a rapid rise in blood glucose that can increase urination and thirst. In addition, patients who take insulin must remain consistent from day to day in the timing and caloric content of their meals. Depending on the timing, dose, and types of insulin prescribed, snacks may be recommended in the late afternoon, before bedtime, or prior to unusual physical activity. Diabetic patients must always have available a juice, food, or tablets that can raise blood glucose levels rapidly to counter an episode of hypoglycemia.

STORAGE
Refrigerate insulin but do not allow it to freeze. Insulin does not have to be kept refrigerated when you're traveling for short periods, but exposure to high temperatures must be avoided.

IF YOU MISS A DOSE
Timing of insulin doses is extremely important. The best approach is to measure blood glucose and add a dose of regular insulin if your glucose levels are too high. Otherwise, wait for the next scheduled dose.

STOPPING THE DRUG
Do not stop taking insulin injections unless ordered by your doctor. Patients with diabetes are often given general instructions for modifying their insulin doses based on home blood glucose measurements.

PROLONGED USE
After many years with diabetes, some patients become insensitive to the symptoms of hypoglycemia and are at risk for serious brain complications of prolonged, unrecognized hypoglycemia.

PRECAUTIONS
Over 60: No special warnings. Some older people may, however, have vision problems that may make it difficult to draw up the correct dose of insulin.

Driving and Hazardous Work: Patients taking insulin must be very careful to avoid hypoglycemia when driving or engaging in hazardous work.

Alcohol: Moderate alcohol intake, especially when taken with large meals, does not adversely affect control of diabetes or alter the dose of insulin. However, large amounts of alcohol increase the risk of hypoglycemia.

Pregnancy: Strict metabolic control—using insulin injections in most women—must be maintained during pregnancy to reduce the risk of birth defects, fetal complications, or death at the time of delivery. In women who had diabetes before the onset of pregnancy, the dose of insulin is often smaller during the first third (trimester) of pregnancy and then higher during the final two trimesters. When women first develop diabetes during pregnancy (gestational diabetes), insulin requirements drop rapidly after delivery and most do not need to continue with insulin treatment.

Breast Feeding: Insulin requirements tend to be lower during breast feeding. Home glucose monitoring is important to avoid hypoglycemia. Insulin is not present in breast milk.

Infants and Children: Treatment with insulin in young patients is the same as that in older people with diabetes.

Special Concerns: Inadequate amounts of insulin in type 1 diabetes may lead to

Insulin Lispro (rDNA origin) (continued)

the serious complication of diabetic ketoacidosis, characterized by loss of appetite, excessive thirst and urination, nausea, vomiting, deep breathing, fruity breath odor, drowsiness, confusion, and loss of consciousness.

OVERDOSE

Symptoms: Insulin overdose results in hypoglycemia (see Side Effects for symptoms).

What to Do: For mild to moderate hypoglycemia, ingest drinks or food containing sugar. For more severe hypoglycemia, administer injections of glucagon or call emergency medical services (EMS) immediately.

DRUG INTERACTIONS

A large number of drugs can promote either elevated blood glucose levels or hypoglycemia. Be sure that your doctor knows about all of the medications you take and is informed before you start taking any new drugs, either by prescription or over the counter. Corticosteroids in particular are likely to raise blood glucose levels and insulin requirements. Beta-blockers (commonly prescribed for hypertension) may cause either high blood glucose levels or hypoglycemia; in addition, because these medications may dampen the symptoms of hypoglycemia that are caused by adrenaline release, mild degrees of hypoglycemia may progress unnoticed to more serious hypoglycemia affecting the brain.

FOOD INTERACTIONS

Insulin requirements are increased when larger amounts of calories are ingested, especially simple sugars and carbohydrates.

DISEASE INTERACTIONS

Insulin requirements are increased by infections, psychological stress, or an uncontrolled overactive thyroid, and often at a time of surgery. Requirements may diminish with kidney disease or an underactive adrenal or pituitary gland.

BRAND NAMES
Humulin U Ultralente,
Ultralente Iletin I (beef
and pork)

Insulin (Long-acting, Ultralente)

▶ Drug Class: Antidiabetic
agent

▶ Available in: Injection

▶ Available OTC? Yes

▶ As Generic? No

Side Effects

SERIOUS
Symptoms of hypo-
glycemia can be caused
by the release of adrena-
line or by an inadequate
supply of glucose to the
brain. With severe hypo-
glycemia, lack of suffi-
cient glucose to the
brain may cause slurred
speech, impaired concen-
tration, confusion,
seizures, coma, irre-
versible brain damage,
and death. Mild hypo-
glycemia may cause rest-
less sleep, nightmares, or
a cold sweat that awak-
ens patients at night.

COMMON
Symptoms resulting from
release of adrenaline are
common manifestations
of mild to moderate
hypoglycemia. They
include cold sweats,
anxiety, shakiness,
hunger, rapid heartbeat,
headache, and nervous-
ness. Weight gain is com-
mon when taking insulin.

LESS COMMON
Allergic reactions, lipoatrophy (depressions in the
skin due to loss of fat tissue), and lipohypertrophy
(excessive accumulation
of fat tissue).

PRINCIPAL USES
For long-term treatment
of diabetes mellitus. All
patients with type 1 diabetes
require lifelong insulin treatment. Patients with type 2
diabetes may require insulin
if they are unable to control
their blood glucose (sugar)
levels with diet and oral
medications.

HOW THE DRUG WORKS
Insulin, a hormone secreted
by the beta cells of the
pancreas, plays an essential
role in controlling the
metabolism and storage of
carbohydrates, fat, and protein. Insulin is secreted in
response to a rise in blood
sugar (glucose). Insulin
lowers blood glucose by
increasing its uptake by
body cells, especially muscle, and by reducing the
release of glucose from
the liver between meals.

DOSAGE
Injected 1 or 2 times a day.
Doses and frequency are
determined by your doctor.
Long-acting (Ultralente)
insulin can be mixed in the
same syringe with rapid-
acting insulin; draw up the
rapid-acting insulin first.
Long-acting insulin solu-
tions are cloudy (insulin
settles to the bottom of the
bottle) and must be rolled
or gently shaken to distribute the insulin evenly in the
solution before drawing it
up into the syringe.

ONSET OF EFFECT
Within 6 to 8 hours; the
peak effect occurs within
10 to 20 hours.

DURATION OF ACTION
From 24 to 36 hours.

DIETARY ADVICE
All patients with diabetes
should follow the general
dietary recommendations of
the American Diabetes
Association. Though intake

of simple sugars is not forbidden, consuming a large
amount of sugary foods at
one time may trigger a
rapid rise in blood glucose
that can increase urination
and thirst. In addition,
patients who take insulin
must remain consistent
from day to day in the timing and caloric content of
their meals. Depending on
the timing, dose, and types
of insulin prescribed, snacks
may be recommended in
the late afternoon, before
bedtime, or prior to unusual
physical activity. Diabetic
patients must always have
available a juice, food, or
tablets that can raise blood
glucose levels rapidly to
counter an episode of
hypoglycemia.

STORAGE
Refrigerate insulin but do
not allow it to freeze. Insulin
does not have to be kept
refrigerated when you're
traveling for short periods,
but exposure to high tem-
peratures must be avoided.

IF YOU MISS A DOSE
Timing of insulin doses is
extremely important. The
best approach is to measure
blood glucose and add a
dose of regular insulin if
your glucose levels are too
high. Otherwise, wait for
the next scheduled dose.

STOPPING THE DRUG
Do not stop taking insulin
injections unless ordered by
your doctor. Patients with
diabetes are often given
general instructions for
modifying their insulin
doses based on home blood
glucose measurements.

PROLONGED USE
After many years with
diabetes, some patients
become insensitive to the
symptoms of hypoglycemia
and are at risk for serious
brain complications of

prolonged, unrecognized
hypoglycemia.

PRECAUTIONS
Over 60: No special warnings. Some older people
may, however, have vision
problems that may make it
difficult to draw up the correct dose of insulin.

**Driving and Hazardous
Work:** Patients taking
insulin must be very careful
to avoid hypoglycemia when
driving or engaging in hazardous work.

Alcohol: Moderate alcohol
intake, especially when
taken with large meals,
does not adversely affect
control of diabetes or alter
the dose of insulin. How-
ever, large amounts of
alcohol increase the risk
of hypoglycemia.

Pregnancy: Strict metabolic control—using insulin
injections in most women—
must be maintained during
pregnancy to reduce the
risk of birth defects, fetal
complications, or death at
the time of delivery. In
women who had diabetes
before the onset of preg-
nancy, the dose of insulin
is often smaller during the
first third (trimester) of
pregnancy and then higher
during the final two
trimesters. When women
first develop diabetes
during pregnancy (gesta-
tional diabetes), insulin
requirements drop rapidly
after delivery and most do
not need to continue with
insulin treatment.

Breast Feeding: Insulin
requirements tend to be
lower during breast feeding.
Home glucose monitoring is
important to avoid hypo-
glycemia. Insulin is not present in breast milk.

Insulin (Long-acting, Ultralente) (continued)

Infants and Children: Treatment with insulin in young patients is the same as that in older people with diabetes.

Special Concerns: Inadequate amounts of insulin in type 1 diabetes may lead to the serious complication of diabetic ketoacidosis, characterized by loss of appetite, excessive thirst and urination, nausea, vomiting, deep breathing, fruity breath odor, drowsiness, confusion, and loss of consciousness.

OVERDOSE

Symptoms: Insulin overdose results in hypoglycemia (see Side Effects for symptoms).

What to Do: For mild to moderate hypoglycemia, ingest drinks or food containing sugar. For more severe hypoglycemia, administer injections of glucagon or call emergency medical services (EMS) immediately.

DRUG INTERACTIONS

A large number of drugs can promote either elevated blood glucose levels or hypoglycemia. Be sure that your doctor knows about all of the medications you take and is informed before you start taking any new drugs, either by prescription or over the counter. Corticosteroids in particular are likely to raise blood glucose levels and insulin requirements. Beta-blockers (commonly prescribed for hypertension) may cause either high blood glucose levels or hypoglycemia; in addition, because these medications may dampen the symptoms of hypoglycemia that are caused by adrenaline release, mild degrees of hypoglycemia may progress unnoticed to more serious hypoglycemia affecting the brain.

FOOD INTERACTIONS

Insulin requirements are increased when larger amounts of calories are ingested, especially simple sugars and carbohydrates.

DISEASE INTERACTIONS

Insulin requirements are increased by infections, psychological stress, or an uncontrolled overactive thyroid, and often at a time of surgery. Requirements may diminish with kidney disease or an underactive adrenal or pituitary gland.

▶ Drug Class: Antidiabetic
agent

▶ Available in: Injection

▶ Available OTC? Yes

▶ As Generic? No

Side Effects

SERIOUS

Symptoms of hypo-
glycemia can be caused
by the release of adrena-
line or by an inadequate
supply of glucose to the
brain. With severe hypo-
glycemia, lack of suffi-
cient glucose to the
brain may cause slurred
speech, impaired concen-
tration, confusion,
seizures, coma, irre-
versible brain damage,
and death. Mild hypo-
glycemia may cause rest-
less sleep, nightmares, or
a cold sweat that awak-
ens patients at night.

COMMON

Symptoms resulting from
release of adrenaline are
common manifestations
of mild to moderate
hypoglycemia. They
include cold sweats,
anxiety, shakiness,
hunger, rapid heartbeat,
headache, and nervous-
ness. Weight gain is com-
mon when taking insulin.

LESS COMMON

Allergic reactions, lipoatrophy (depressions in the
skin due to loss of fat tissue), and lipohypertrophy
(excessive accumulation
of fat tissue).

PRINCIPAL USES

For long-term treatment
of diabetes mellitus. All
patients with type 1 diabetes
require lifelong insulin treatment. Patients with type 2
diabetes may require insulin
if they are unable to control
their blood glucose (sugar)
levels with diet and oral
medications.

HOW THE DRUG WORKS

Insulin, a hormone secreted
by the beta cells of the
pancreas, plays an essential
role in controlling the
metabolism and storage of
carbohydrates, fat, and protein. Insulin is secreted in
response to a rise in blood
sugar (glucose). Insulin
lowers blood glucose by
increasing its uptake by
body cells, especially muscle, and by reducing the
release of glucose from
the liver between meals.

DOSAGE

It may be taken 1 to 4 times
daily, before meals and possibly at bedtime. Doses and
frequency are determined
by your doctor. Regular (or
rapid-acting or semilente)
insulin should be administered 30 to 45 minutes
before a meal. It can be
mixed in the same syringe
with intermediate-acting
insulins. Draw up the regular insulin first.

ONSET OF EFFECT

Within 45 minutes; peak
effect occurs within 2 to 4
hours.

DURATION OF ACTION

From 4 to 6 hours.

DIETARY ADVICE

All patients with diabetes
should follow the general
dietary recommendations of
the American Diabetes
Association. Though intake
of simple sugars is not forbidden, consuming a large
amount of sugary foods at

one time may trigger a
rapid rise in blood glucose
that can increase urination
and thirst. In addition,
patients who take insulin
must remain consistent
from day to day in the timing and caloric content of
their meals. Depending on
the timing, dose, and types
of insulin prescribed, snacks
may be recommended in
the late afternoon, before
bedtime, or prior to unusual
physical activity. Diabetic
patients must always have
available a juice, food, or
tablets that can raise blood
glucose levels rapidly to
counter an episode of
hypoglycemia.

STORAGE

Refrigerate insulin but do
not allow it to freeze. Insulin
does not have to be kept
refrigerated when you're
traveling for short periods,
but exposure to high tem-
peratures must be avoided.

IF YOU MISS A DOSE

Timing of insulin doses is
extremely important. The
best approach is to measure
blood glucose and add a
dose of regular insulin if
glucose levels are too high.
Otherwise, wait for the next
scheduled dose.

STOPPING THE DRUG

Do not stop taking insulin
injections unless ordered by
your doctor. Patients with
diabetes are often given
general instructions for
modifying their insulin
doses based on home blood
glucose measurements.

PROLONGED USE

After many years with
diabetes, some patients
become insensitive to the
symptoms of hypoglycemia
and are at risk for serious
brain complications of
prolonged, unrecognized
hypoglycemia.

PRECAUTIONS

Over 60: No special warnings. Some older people
may, however, have vision
problems that may make it
difficult to draw up the correct dose of insulin.

**Driving and Hazardous
Work:** Patients taking
insulin must be very careful
to avoid hypoglycemia when
driving or engaging in hazardous work.

Alcohol: Moderate alcohol
intake, especially when
taken with large meals,
does not adversely affect
control of diabetes or alter
the dose of insulin. How-
ever, large amounts of
alcohol increase the risk
of hypoglycemia.

Pregnancy: Strict metabolic control—using insulin
injections in most women—
must be maintained during
pregnancy to reduce the
risk of birth defects, fetal
complications, or death at
the time of delivery. In
women who had diabetes
before the onset of preg-
nancy, the dose of insulin
is often smaller during the
first third (trimester) of
pregnancy and then higher
during the final two
trimesters. When women
first develop diabetes
during pregnancy (gesta-
tional diabetes), insulin
requirements drop rapidly
after delivery and most do
not need to continue with
insulin treatment.

Breast Feeding: Insulin
requirements tend to be
lower during breast feeding.
Home glucose monitoring is
important to avoid hypo-
glycemia. Insulin is not present in breast milk.

Infants and Children:
Treatment with insulin in
young patients is the same

...s that in older people with diabetes.

Special Concerns: Inadequate amounts of insulin in type 1 diabetes may lead to the serious complication of diabetic ketoacidosis, characterized by loss of appetite, excessive thirst and urination, nausea, vomiting, deep breathing, fruity breath odor, drowsiness, confusion, and loss of consciousness.

OVERDOSE

Symptoms: Insulin overdose results in hypo-glycemia (see Side Effects for symptoms).

What to Do: For mild to moderate hypoglycemia, ingest drinks or food containing sugar. For more severe hypoglycemia, administer injections of glucagon or call emergency medical services (EMS) immediately.

DRUG INTERACTIONS

A large number of drugs can promote either elevated blood glucose levels or hypoglycemia. Be sure that your doctor knows about all of the medications you take and is informed before you start taking any new drugs, either by prescription or over the counter. Corticosteroids in particular are likely to raise blood glucose levels and insulin requirements. Beta-blockers (commonly prescribed for hypertension) may cause either high blood glucose levels or hypoglycemia; in addition, because these medications may dampen the symptoms of hypoglycemia that are caused by adrenaline release, mild degrees of hypoglycemia may progress unnoticed to more serious hypoglycemia affecting the brain.

FOOD INTERACTIONS

Insulin requirements are increased when larger amounts of calories are ingested, especially simple sugars and carbohydrates.

DISEASE INTERACTIONS

Insulin requirements are increased by infections, psychological stress, or an uncontrolled overactive thyroid, and often at a time of surgery. Requirements may diminish with kidney disease or an underactive adrenal or pituitary gland.

BRAND NAME
Roferon-A

▶ Drug Class: Immunomodulator

▶ Available in: Injection

▶ Available OTC? No

▶ As Generic? No

Side Effects

SERIOUS
Confusion, depression, nervousness, distractibility, impaired thinking, or thoughts of suicide; numbness or tingling of fingers, toes, and face; black, tarry, or bloody stools; blood in urine; chest pain; hoarseness; fever or chills after 3 weeks of treatment; irregular heartbeat; pain in lower back or side; difficult or painful urination; red spots on skin; unusual bleeding or bruising; increased incidence of infections. Call your doctor immediately.

COMMON
Flu-like symptoms, fatigue, muscle aches, fever, or chills in first weeks of treatment; general discomfort or ill feeling; headache; loss of appetite; nausea and vomiting; odd, metallic, or altered taste; skin rash; temporary hair loss. Side effects are more common with higher doses. Tolerance to high doses may be improved by gradually increasing the doses over the first weeks of treatment.

LESS COMMON
Back pain, blurred vision, dizziness, dry mouth, dry or itching skin, profuse or unusual sweating, joint pain, leg cramps, lip or mouth sores, weight loss.

PRINCIPAL USES
To treat hairy-cell leukemia, AIDS-associated Kaposi's sarcoma, or chronic myelogenous leukemia.

HOW THE DRUG WORKS
Interferon alfa-2a acts in the same way as the body's natural interferons, which are proteins released by cells of the immune system to fight viruses and cancer cells.

DOSAGE
For hairy-cell leukemia: 3 million units daily by injection for 16 to 24 weeks. Then 3 million units 3 times a week for maintenance. For AIDS-related Kaposi's sarcoma: 36 million units daily for 10 to 12 weeks, then 36 million units 3 times a week. For Philadelphia chromosome-positive (Ph+) chronic myelogenous leukemia: 9 million units daily for the duration of treatment or as determined by your doctor.

ONSET OF EFFECT
Unknown.

DURATION OF ACTION
Unknown.

DIETARY ADVICE
Drink plenty of fluids to reduce the risk of excessively low blood pressure.

STORAGE
Keep interferon alfa-2a refrigerated but do not allow it to freeze.

IF YOU MISS A DOSE
If you miss a dose, do not take the missed dose and do not double the next dose. Check with your doctor on what to do.

STOPPING THE DRUG
The decision to stop taking the drug should be made by your doctor.

PROLONGED USE
See your doctor regularly for tests and examinations if you must take this drug for a prolonged period.

PRECAUTIONS
Over 60: Adverse reactions may be more likely and more severe in older patients.

Driving and Hazardous Work: Avoid such activities until you determine how the medicine affects you. Administering interferon at bedtime may help to minimize daytime sleepiness.

Alcohol: Avoid alcohol.

Pregnancy: Adequate studies have not been done. Consult your doctor for advice.

Breast Feeding: Interferon alfa-2a may pass into breast milk; caution is advised. Consult your doctor for advice.

Infants and Children: Severe adverse effects have been noted in some children treated with high doses of interferon. Consult your pediatrician for advice.

Special Concerns: Do not change to another brand of alfa interferon without consulting your doctor. They have different dosage schedules. Try to avoid people with infections, because this drug can lower white blood cell levels temporarily and increase susceptibility to disease. Be careful when cleaning your teeth, and avoid cutting yourself when using sharp objects such as a razor. Avoid contact sports or other situations where bruising could occur.

OVERDOSE
Symptoms: No specific ones have been reported.

What to Do: Call your doctor or emergency medical services (EMS) immediately if you suspect an overdose.

DRUG INTERACTIONS
Consult your doctor for specific advice if you are taking any prescription or over-the-counter medication, especially theophylline, or central nervous system depressants including antihistamines, alcohol, tranquilizers, or psychiatric medications.

FOOD INTERACTIONS
None are known.

DISEASE INTERACTIONS
Consult your doctor if you have a history of bleeding or clotting disorders, chicken pox, shingles, psychological or neurological disorders, seizures, diabetes, heart attack, heart disease, kidney disease, liver disease, lung disease, autoimmune disorders, or thyroid disease.

Interferon alfa-2b

▶ Drug Class: Immunomodulator

▶ Available in: Injection

▶ Available OTC? No

▶ As Generic? No

Side Effects

SERIOUS
Confusion, depression, nervousness, distractibility, or impaired thinking; numbness or tingling of fingers, toes, and face; sleeping difficulty; black, tarry, or bloody stools; blood in urine; chest pain, cough, or hoarseness; fever or chills after 3 weeks of treatment; irregular heartbeat; pain in lower back or side; difficult or painful urination; red spots on skin; unusual bleeding or bruising; increased incidence of infections. Call your doctor immediately.

COMMON
Flu-like symptoms, fatigue, muscle aches, fever, or chills in first weeks of treatment; general discomfort or ill feeling; headache; loss of appetite; nausea and vomiting; odd, metallic, or altered taste; skin rash; temporary hair loss. Side effects are more common with higher doses. Tolerance to high doses may be improved by gradually increasing the doses over the first weeks of treatment.

LESS COMMON
Back pain, blurred vision, dizziness, dry mouth, dry or itching skin, profuse or unusual sweating, joint pain, leg cramps, lip or mouth sores, weight loss.

PRINCIPAL USES
To treat hairy-cell leukemia, AIDS-associated Kaposi's sarcoma, condylomata acuminata (genital warts), and types of chronic hepatitis; also used as an adjuvant (supplemental) treatment to surgery for malignant melanoma.

HOW THE DRUG WORKS
It acts in the same way as the body's natural interferons, which are proteins released by the cells of the immune system to fight viruses and cancer cells.

DOSAGE
For hairy-cell leukemia: 2 million units per square meter of body surface 3 times a week. For AIDS-related Kaposi's sarcoma: 30 million units 3 times a week. For condylomata acuminata: 1 million units per lesion 3 times a week for 3 weeks. For chronic hepatitis: 3 million units 3 times a week for 6 months (in patients with evidence of response). For malignant melanoma: 20 million units per square meter of body surface for 5 consecutive days per week for 4 weeks, followed by maintenance with 10 million units per square meter 3 times a week for 48 weeks.

ONSET OF EFFECT
Unknown.

DURATION OF ACTION
Unknown.

DIETARY ADVICE
Drink plenty of fluids to reduce the risk of excessively low blood pressure.

STORAGE
Keep interferon alfa-2b refrigerated but do not allow it to freeze.

IF YOU MISS A DOSE
If you miss a dose, do not take the missed dose and do not double the next dose. Check with your doctor on what to do.

STOPPING THE DRUG
The decision to stop taking the drug should be made by your doctor.

PROLONGED USE
See your doctor regularly for tests and examinations if you must take this drug for a prolonged period.

PRECAUTIONS
Over 60: Adverse reactions may be more likely and more severe in older patients.

Driving and Hazardous Work: Do not drive or engage in hazardous work until you determine how the medicine affects you. Administering interferon at bedtime may help to minimize daytime sleepiness.

Alcohol: Avoid alcohol.

Pregnancy: Adequate studies have not been done. Consult your doctor for advice.

Breast Feeding: This drug may pass into breast milk; caution is advised. Consult your doctor for advice.

Infants and Children: May be used to treat chronic hepatitis B in children aged 1 and older; consult your pediatrician for advice and dosage.

Special Concerns: Do not change to another brand without consulting your doctor. They have different dosage schedules. Try to avoid people with infections, because this drug can lower white blood cell levels temporarily and increase susceptibility to disease. Be careful when cleaning your teeth, and avoid cutting yourself when using sharp objects such as a razor. Avoid contact sports or other situations where bruising could occur.

OVERDOSE
Symptoms: No specific ones have been reported.

What to Do: Call your doctor or emergency medical services (EMS) immediately if you suspect an overdose.

DRUG INTERACTIONS
Consult your doctor for specific advice if you are taking any prescription or over-the-counter medication, especially central nervous system depressants including antihistamines, alcohol, tranquilizers, or psychiatric medications.

FOOD INTERACTIONS
None are known.

DISEASE INTERACTIONS
Consult your doctor if you have a history of bleeding or clotting disorders, chicken pox, shingles, psychological or neurological disorders, diabetes, autoimmune disorders, or heart, kidney, liver, lung, or thyroid disease.

Interferon alfa-n1

BRAND NAME
Wellferon

▶ Drug Class: Immunomodulator

▶ Available in: Injection

▶ Available OTC? No

▶ As Generic? No

Side Effects

SERIOUS
Confusion, depression, nervousness, distractibility, impaired thinking, or thoughts of suicide; numbness or tingling of fingers, toes, and face; black, tarry, or bloody stools; blood in urine; chest pain; hoarseness; fever or chills after 3 weeks of treatment; irregular heartbeat; pain in lower back or side; difficult or painful urination; red spots on skin; unusual bleeding or bruising; increased incidence of infections. Call your doctor immediately.

COMMON
Flu-like symptoms, fatigue, muscle aches, fever, or chills in first weeks of treatment; general discomfort or ill feeling; headache; loss of appetite; nausea and vomiting; odd, metallic, or altered taste; skin rash; temporary hair loss. Side effects are more common with higher doses. Tolerance to high doses may be improved by gradually increasing the doses over the first weeks of treatment.

LESS COMMON
Back pain, blurred vision, dizziness, dry mouth, dry or itching skin, profuse or unusual sweating, joint pain, leg cramps, lip or mouth sores, weight loss.

PRINCIPAL USES
To treat hairy-cell leukemia, condylomata acuminata (genital warts), or juvenile laryngeal papillomatosis (abnormal growths in the voice box, occurring in children).

HOW THE DRUG WORKS
It acts in the same way as the body's natural interferons, which are proteins released by the cells of the immune system to fight viruses and cancer cells.

DOSAGE
For hairy-cell leukemia: 3 million units a day by injection for 16 to 24 weeks, then 3 million units 3 times a week. For condylomata acuminata: 1 million units per square meter of body surface 5 times a week, then the same dose 5 times a week for 2 weeks, then 3 times a week for 4 weeks, then 3 times a week for 1 month. For juvenile laryngeal papillomatosis: The dose is based on area of body surface and is given daily for 26 days, followed by maintenance dosage 3 times a week for at least 6 months.

ONSET OF EFFECT
Unknown.

DURATION OF ACTION
Unknown.

DIETARY ADVICE
Drink plenty of fluids to reduce the risk of excessively low blood pressure.

STORAGE
Keep interferon alfa-n1 refrigerated but do not allow it to freeze.

IF YOU MISS A DOSE
If you miss a dose, do not take the missed dose and do not double the next dose. Check with your doctor on what to do.

STOPPING THE DRUG
The decision to stop taking the drug should be made by your doctor.

PROLONGED USE
See your doctor regularly for tests and examinations if you must take this drug for a prolonged period.

PRECAUTIONS
Over 60: Adverse reactions may be more likely and more severe in older patients.

Driving and Hazardous Work: Do not drive or engage in hazardous work until you determine how the medicine affects you. Administering interferon at bedtime may help to minimize daytime sleepiness.

Alcohol: Avoid alcohol.

Pregnancy: Adequate studies have not been done. Consult your doctor for advice.

Breast Feeding: Interferon alfa-n1 may pass into breast milk; caution is advised. Consult your doctor for advice.

Infants and Children: No special studies have been done; consult your pediatrician.

Special Concerns: Do not change to another brand of alfa interferon without consulting your doctor. They have different dosage schedules. Try to avoid people with infections, because this drug can lower white blood cell levels temporarily and increase susceptibility to disease. Be careful when cleaning your teeth, and avoid cutting yourself when using sharp objects such as a razor. Avoid contact sports or other situations where bruising could occur.

OVERDOSE
Symptoms: No specific ones have been reported.

What to Do: Call your doctor or emergency medical services (EMS) immediately if you suspect an overdose.

DRUG INTERACTIONS
Consult your doctor for specific advice if you are taking any prescription or over-the-counter medication, especially central nervous system depressants including antihistamines, alcohol, tranquilizers, or psychiatric medications.

FOOD INTERACTIONS
None are known.

DISEASE INTERACTIONS
Consult your doctor if you have a history of bleeding or clotting disorders, chicken pox, shingles, psychological or neurological disorders, diabetes, autoimmune disorders, heart disease, kidney disease, liver disease, lung disease, or thyroid disease.

▶ Drug Class: Immunomodulator

▶ Available in: Injection

▶ Available OTC? No

▶ As Generic? No

Side Effects

SERIOUS
Confusion, depression, nervousness, distractibility, impaired thinking, or thoughts of suicide; numbness or tingling of fingers, toes, and face; black, tarry, or bloody stools; blood in urine; chest pain; hoarseness; fever or chills after 3 weeks of treatment; irregular heartbeat; pain in lower back or side; difficult or painful urination; red spots on skin; unusual bleeding or bruising; increased incidence of infections. Call your doctor immediately.

COMMON
Flu-like symptoms, fatigue, muscle aches, fever, or chills in first weeks of treatment; general discomfort or ill feeling; headache; loss of appetite; nausea and vomiting; odd, metallic, or altered taste; skin rash; temporary hair loss. Side effects are more common with higher doses. Tolerance to high doses may be improved by gradually increasing the doses over the first weeks of treatment.

LESS COMMON
Back pain, blurred vision, dizziness, dry mouth, dry or itching skin, profuse or unusual sweating, joint pain, leg cramps, lip or mouth sores, weight loss.

PRINCIPAL USES
To treat condylomata acuminata (genital or venereal warts) in patients 18 years of age or older.

HOW THE DRUG WORKS
It acts in the same way as the body's natural interferons, which are proteins released by the immune system to fight viruses, cancer cells, and other types of disease. Interferon alfa-n3 is derived from human white blood cells and has an antiviral effect.

DOSAGE
0.05 ml injected into each wart 2 times a week for up to 8 weeks. Total dose for each session should not exceed 0.5 ml (2.5 million units).

ONSET OF EFFECT
Unknown.

DURATION OF ACTION
Unknown; however, warts will continue to disappear after completion of 8 weeks of therapy and discontinuation of the drug.

DIETARY ADVICE
Drink plenty of fluids to reduce risk of excessively low blood pressure.

STORAGE
Keep interferon alfa-n3 refrigerated but do not allow it to freeze.

IF YOU MISS A DOSE
If you miss a dose, do not take the missed dose and do not double the next dose. Check with your doctor on what to do.

STOPPING THE DRUG
The decision to stop taking the drug should be made by your doctor.

PROLONGED USE
See your doctor regularly for tests and examinations if you must take this drug for a prolonged period.

PRECAUTIONS
Over 60: Adverse reactions may be more likely and more severe in older patients.

Driving and Hazardous Work: Do not drive or engage in hazardous work until you determine how the medicine affects you. Administering interferon at bedtime may help to minimize daytime sleepiness.

Alcohol: Avoid alcohol.

Pregnancy: Adequate studies have not been done. Consult your doctor for advice.

Breast Feeding: Interferon alfa-n3 may pass into breast milk; caution is advised. Consult your doctor for advice.

Infants and Children: No special studies have been done; consult your pediatrician.

Special Concerns: Do not change to another brand of alfa interferon without consulting your doctor. They have different dosage schedules. Try to avoid people with infections, because this drug can lower white blood cell levels temporarily and increase susceptibility to disease. Be careful when cleaning your teeth, and avoid cutting yourself when using sharp objects such as a razor. Avoid contact sports or other situations where bruising could occur.

OVERDOSE
Symptoms: No specific ones have been reported.

What to Do: Call your doctor or emergency medical services (EMS) immediately if you suspect an overdose.

DRUG INTERACTIONS
Consult your doctor for specific advice if you are taking any prescription or over-the-counter medication, especially central nervous system depressants including antihistamines, alcohol, tranquilizers, or psychiatric medications.

FOOD INTERACTIONS
None are known.

DISEASE INTERACTIONS
Caution is advised when taking interferon alfa-n3. Consult your doctor if you have a history of bleeding or clotting disorders, chicken pox, shingles, psychological or neurological disorders, diabetes, autoimmune disorders, heart disease, kidney disease, liver disease, lung disease, or thyroid disease.

Interferon alfacon-1

BRAND NAME
Infergen

▶ Drug Class: Immunomodulator

▶ Available in: Injection

▶ Available OTC? No

▶ As Generic? No

Side Effects

SERIOUS
Confusion, depression, nervousness, distractibility, or impaired thinking; numbness or tingling of fingers, toes, and face; sleeping difficulty; black, tarry, or bloody stools; blood in urine; chest pain, cough, or hoarseness; fever or chills after 3 weeks of treatment; irregular heartbeat; pain in lower back or side; difficult or painful urination; red spots on skin; unusual bleeding or bruising; increased incidence of infections. Call your doctor immediately.

COMMON
Flu-like symptoms, fatigue, muscle aches, fever, or chills in first weeks of treatment; general discomfort or ill feeling; headache; loss of appetite; nausea and vomiting; odd, metallic, or altered taste; skin rash; temporary hair loss. Side effects are more common with higher doses. Tolerance to high doses may be improved by gradually increasing the doses over the first weeks of treatment.

LESS COMMON
Back pain, blurred vision, dizziness, dry mouth, dry or itching skin, profuse or unusual sweating, joint pain, leg cramps, lip or mouth sores, weight loss.

PRINCIPAL USES
To treat chronic hepatitis C infection in people age 18 and older who have developed liver disease.

HOW THE DRUG WORKS
It acts in the same way as the body's natural interferons, which are proteins released by the cells of the immune system to fight viruses.

DOSAGE
For people who have never been treated with interferons: 9 micrograms (mcg) injected under the skin 3 times a week for 24 weeks, with at least 48 hours between doses. For people who have undergone previous interferon therapy and either did not respond to it or relapsed following discontinuation of therapy: 15 mcg under the skin 3 times a week for 6 months.

ONSET OF EFFECT
Unknown.

DURATION OF ACTION
Unknown.

DIETARY ADVICE
Drink plenty of fluids to reduce the risk of excessively low blood pressure.

STORAGE
Refrigerate the drug but do not allow it to freeze. Do not expose it to high temperatures or direct sunlight. Store it on a separate shelf or in a drawer, away from food. Just prior to administration, interferon alfacon-1 may be allowed to reach room temperature.

IF YOU MISS A DOSE
If you miss a dose, do not take the missed dose and do not double the next dose. Check with your doctor on what to do.

STOPPING THE DRUG
The decision to stop taking the drug should be made by your doctor.

PROLONGED USE
See your doctor regularly for tests and examinations if you take this drug for a prolonged period.

PRECAUTIONS
Over 60: Adverse reactions may be more likely and more severe in older patients.

Driving and Hazardous Work: Do not drive or engage in hazardous work until you determine how the medicine affects you.

Alcohol: No special precautions are necessary.

Pregnancy: Adequate human studies have not been done. Interferon alfacon-1 should not be used during pregnancy.

Breast Feeding: Interferon alfacon-1 may pass into breast milk; caution is advised. Consult your doctor for specific advice.

Infants and Children: Not recommended for patients under age 18.

Special Concerns: Do not shake the vial prior to administration. If the liquid in the vial is cloudy or discolored, do not use it. Discard any unused portion. Do not change to another brand of interferon without consulting your doctor. They have different dosage schedules. To help prevent the spread of hepatitis C, do not share razors or toothbrushes; cover any cuts or wounds; dispose of wound dressings in a sealed bag in the trash; keep used syringes for injecting interferon, insulin, or other medications capped and in a needle disposal container; use a condom if you have multiple sexual partners or if you have a genital herpes infection; and do not donate blood. It is safe to have close contact with others, to dispose of facial tissues normally, to share dinnerware, and to breast-feed.

OVERDOSE
Symptoms: An overdose with interferon alfacon-1 is unlikely. However, with a very high dose, you may experience some side effects more acutely, particularly loss of appetite, chills, fever, and muscle pain.

What to Do: If you take a much larger dose than prescribed, call your doctor or get emergency medical attention immediately.

DRUG INTERACTIONS
Consult your doctor for specific advice if you are taking any prescription or over-the-counter medication, especially central nervous system depressants including antihistamines, alcohol, tranquilizers, or psychiatric medications.

FOOD INTERACTIONS
No known food interactions.

DISEASE INTERACTIONS
Interferon alfacon-1 should not be taken by patients with severe depression, suicidal feelings, or a history of other severe psychiatric disorders. Those with preexisting heart disease must use this drug with special caution. Consult your doctor for specific advice if you have a history of bleeding or clotting disorders, chicken pox, shingles, psychological or neurological disorders, diabetes, autoimmune disorders, kidney disease, liver disease, lung disease, or thyroid disease.

BRAND NAME
Avonex

▶ Drug Class: Immunomodulator

▶ Available in: Powder for injection

▶ Available OTC? No

▶ As Generic? No

Side Effects

SERIOUS
Seizures, swelling and fluid retention, pelvic pain, pounding in the chest, breast pain, frequent urination, sweating, anxiety, confusion, joint pain, breathing difficulty, mental depression, suicidal thoughts or impulses. Call your physician right away.

COMMON
Pain, inflammation, or allergic reaction at injection site (most common side effect); flu-like symptoms, including headache, fever, muscle aches, general weakness, and fatigue (these symptoms tend to diminish as the body adjusts to therapy); insomnia; increased susceptibility to infection; nausea and vomiting; diarrhea; abdominal pain; temporary hair loss.

LESS COMMON
Dizziness, dry mouth, dry or itching skin, increased sweating, joint pain, changes in vision, hearing problems.

PRINCIPAL USES
To treat relapsing-remitting multiple sclerosis (the most common form of MS, in which periods of active disease alternate with periods of remission or reduced severity of symptoms).

HOW THE DRUG WORKS
It acts in the same way as the body's natural interferons, which are proteins released by the immune system to fight viruses, cancer cells, and other types of disease. The exact way in which the drug fights MS is unknown, but it appears to interfere with the immune system's attack on healthy tissue (the apparent cause of MS).

DOSAGE
6 million units once a week by injection.

ONSET OF EFFECT
Unknown.

DURATION OF ACTION
Unknown.

DIETARY ADVICE
Drink plenty of fluids to reduce the risk of excessively low blood pressure.

STORAGE
Keep liquid form of interferon beta-1a refrigerated but do not allow it to freeze.

IF YOU MISS A DOSE
If you miss a dose, do not take the missed dose and do not double the next dose. Check with your doctor on what to do.

STOPPING THE DRUG
The decision to stop taking the drug should be made by your doctor.

PROLONGED USE
See your doctor regularly for tests and examinations if you must take this drug for a prolonged period.

PRECAUTIONS
Over 60: Adverse reactions may be more likely and more severe in older patients.

Driving and Hazardous Work: Do not drive or engage in hazardous work until you determine how the medicine affects you.

Alcohol: Avoid alcohol.

Pregnancy: Adequate studies have not been done. Consult your doctor for advice.

Breast Feeding: Interferon beta-1a may pass into breast milk; caution is advised. Consult your doctor for advice.

Infants and Children: No special studies have been done on the effects of beta interferon in children.

Special Concerns: Interferon beta-1a should be used with caution in patients with a history of depression, since it has been linked to an increase in suicidal impulses. Try to avoid people with infections, because this drug can lower white blood cell levels temporarily and increase susceptibility to disease. Be careful when using a toothbrush, dental floss, or toothpick. Your doctor or dentist may recommend other ways to clean your teeth. Check with your doctor before having any dental work done. Be careful not to cut yourself when using sharp objects such as a razor. Avoid contact sports or other situations where bruising could occur. Do not touch your eyes or the inside of your mouth unless you have just washed your hands.

OVERDOSE
Symptoms: No specific ones have been reported.

What to Do: Call your doctor or emergency medical services (EMS) immediately if you suspect an overdose.

DRUG INTERACTIONS
Consult your doctor for specific advice if you are taking any prescription or over-the-counter medication.

FOOD INTERACTIONS
None are known.

DISEASE INTERACTIONS
Caution is advised when taking interferon beta-1a. Consult your doctor if you have a history of bleeding or clotting disorders, chicken pox, shingles, psychological or neurological disorders, diabetes, autoimmune disorders, heart disease, kidney disease, liver disease, lung disease, or thyroid disease.

Interferon beta-1b (rIFN-B)

▶ Drug Class: Immunomodulator

▶ Available in: Powder for injection

▶ Available OTC? No

▶ As Generic? No

Side Effects

SERIOUS
Seizures, swelling and fluid retention, pelvic pain, pounding in the chest, breast pain, frequent urination, sweating, anxiety, confusion, joint pain, breathing difficulty, mental depression, suicidal thoughts or impulses. Call your doctor right away.

COMMON
Pain, inflammation, or allergic reaction at injection site (most common side effect); flu-like symptoms, including headache, fever, muscle aches, general weakness, and fatigue (these symptoms tend to diminish as the body adjusts to therapy); insomnia; increased susceptibility to infection; nausea and vomiting; diarrhea; abdominal pain; temporary hair loss.

LESS COMMON
Dizziness, dry mouth, dry or itching skin, increased sweating, joint pain, vision or hearing problems. Tissue death at the site of injection has occurred in a few patients.

PRINCIPAL USES
To treat relapsing-remitting multiple sclerosis (the most common form of MS, in which periods of active disease alternate with periods of remission or reduced severity of symptoms).

HOW THE DRUG WORKS
It acts in the same way as the body's natural interferons, which are proteins released by the immune system to fight viruses, cancer cells, and other types of disease. The exact way in which this drug fights MS is unknown, but it appears to interfere with the immune system's attack on healthy tissue.

DOSAGE
8 million units (0.25 mg) by injection every other day.

ONSET OF EFFECT
Unknown.

DURATION OF ACTION
Unknown.

DIETARY ADVICE
Drink plenty of fluids to reduce the risk of excessively low blood pressure.

STORAGE
Keep the liquid form refrigerated but do not allow it to freeze.

IF YOU MISS A DOSE
If you miss a dose, do not take the missed dose and do not double the next dose. Notify your doctor.

STOPPING THE DRUG
The decision to stop taking the drug should be made by your doctor.

PROLONGED USE
See your doctor regularly for tests and examinations if you must take this drug for a prolonged period.

PRECAUTIONS
Over 60: Adverse reactions may be more likely and more severe in older patients.

Driving and Hazardous Work: Do not drive or engage in hazardous work until you determine how the medicine affects you.

Alcohol: Avoid alcohol.

Pregnancy: Adequate studies have not been done. Consult your doctor for advice.

Breast Feeding: Interferon beta-1b may pass into breast milk; caution is advised. Consult your doctor for specific advice.

Infants and Children: No special studies have been done on the effects of beta interferon in children.

Special Concerns: Interferon beta-1b should be used with caution in patients with a history of depression, since it has been linked to an increase in suicidal impulses. Try to avoid people with infections, because this drug can lower white blood cell levels temporarily and increase susceptibility to disease. Be careful when using a toothbrush, dental floss, or toothpick. Your doctor or dentist may recommend other ways to clean your teeth. Check with your doctor before having any dental work done. Be careful not to cut yourself when using sharp objects such as a razor. Avoid contact sports or other situations where bruising could occur. Do not touch your eyes or the inside of your mouth unless you have just washed your hands.

OVERDOSE
Symptoms: No specific ones have been reported.

What to Do: Call your doctor or emergency medical services (EMS) immediately if you suspect an overdose.

DRUG INTERACTIONS
Consult your doctor for specific advice if you are taking any prescription or over-the-counter medication.

FOOD INTERACTIONS
None are known.

DISEASE INTERACTIONS
Caution is advised when taking interferon beta-1b. Consult your doctor if you have a history of bleeding or clotting disorders, chicken pox, shingles, psychological or neurological disorders, diabetes, autoimmune disorders, heart disease, kidney disease, liver disease, lung disease, or thyroid disease.

Interferon gamma-1b

BRAND NAME
Actimmune

▶ Drug Class: Immunomodulator

▶ Available in: Injection

▶ Available OTC? No

▶ As Generic? No

Side Effects

SERIOUS
Black, tarry, or bloody stools; blood in the urine; painful or difficult urination; pain in the lower back or side; loss of balance or coordination; mental confusion and impaired thinking; mask-like facial expression; trouble walking or shuffling gait; red spots on the skin; stiffness of arms or legs; trembling and shaking of hands and fingers; trouble speaking or swallowing. Call your doctor right away.

COMMON
Muscle aches, diarrhea, fever and chills, general discomfort or feelings of illness, headache, nausea or vomiting, skin rash, unusual fatigue, increased incidence of infections, unusual bleeding or bruising.

LESS COMMON
Dizziness, joint pain, loss of appetite, weight loss, cough or hoarseness.

PRINCIPAL USES
To treat chronic granulomatous disease (an inherited disorder characterized by recurring infections and the widespread growth of lesions or tumors in the skin, lungs, and lymphatic system).

HOW THE DRUG WORKS
It acts in the same way as the body's natural interferons, which are proteins released by the immune system to fight viruses, cancer cells, and other types of disease. Of all the interferons, interferon gamma has the greatest immunomodulator properties (ability to alter the efficacy of the immune system).

DOSAGE
For adults with body surface area greater than 0.5 square meters: 1.5 million units (50 micrograms) per square meter by injection 3 times a week. For adults with body surface area less than 0.5 square meters: 1.5 micrograms per 2.2 lbs (1 kg) of body weight 3 times a week. The preferred injection sites are the deltoid (shoulder) muscle or the front thigh muscle.

ONSET OF EFFECT
Unknown.

DURATION OF ACTION
Unknown.

DIETARY ADVICE
Drink plenty of fluids to reduce the risk of excessively low blood pressure.

STORAGE
Keep interferon gamma-1b refrigerated but do not allow it to freeze.

IF YOU MISS A DOSE
If you miss a dose, do not take the missed dose and do not double the next dose. Check with your doctor on what to do.

STOPPING THE DRUG
The decision to stop taking the drug should be made by your doctor.

PROLONGED USE
See your doctor regularly for tests and examinations if you must take this drug for a prolonged period.

PRECAUTIONS
Over 60: No special problems are expected.

Driving and Hazardous Work: Do not drive or engage in hazardous work until you determine how the medicine affects you.

Alcohol: Avoid alcohol.

Pregnancy: Very large doses of interferon gamma-1b have increased fetal deaths and uterine bleeding in animals. Before you take interferon gamma-1b, tell your doctor if you are pregnant or plan to become pregnant.

Breast Feeding: Interferon gamma-1b may pass into breast milk; caution is advised. Consult your doctor for specific advice.

Infants and Children: Interferon gamma-1b is not expected to cause different side effects or problems in infants and children than it does in other age groups.

Special Concerns: Taking interferon gamma-1b at bedtime can help to minimize its flu-like side effects. Your doctor may want you to take acetaminophen before each injection to avoid such side effects. Your doctor may tell you to drink extra fluids to prevent low blood pressure caused by loss of too much water. Interferon gamma-1b may make you more sensitive to sunlight. Use sunscreen or wear protective clothing.

OVERDOSE
Symptoms: No specific ones have been reported.

What to Do: Call your doctor or emergency medical services (EMS) immediately if you have any reason to suspect an overdose.

DRUG INTERACTIONS
Consult your doctor for specific advice if you are taking any prescription or over-the-counter medication.

FOOD INTERACTIONS
No known food interactions.

DISEASE INTERACTIONS
Caution is advised when taking interferon gamma-1b. Consult your doctor if you have a history of seizures, mental or psychiatric illness, heart disease, multiple sclerosis, or systemic lupus erythematosus (which may be worsened by gamma interferon).

423

Iodine, Strong

BRAND NAMES
Lugol's Solution, Strong
Iodine (generic)

▶ Drug Class: Thyroid agent

▶ Available in: Oral solution

▶ Available OTC? No

▶ As Generic? Yes

Side Effects

SERIOUS
Fever, swollen glands, rash, joint pain. Call your doctor immediately.

COMMON
Nausea, metallic taste.

LESS COMMON
Fever, headache, inflamed salivary glands, runny nose, stained teeth, swelling around eyes, warm and reddened skin, pinkeye, stomach upset, vomiting, diarrhea, sores on mucous membranes.

PRINCIPAL USES
To treat an overactive thyroid gland (hyperthyroidism); to treat iodine deficiency; to prepare for thyroid surgery.

HOW THE DRUG WORKS
Strong iodine blocks production and release of thyroid hormone by the thyroid gland.

DOSAGE
For overactive thyroid gland, adults and children over age 10: 1 ml, 3 times a day. To prepare for thyroid surgery: 0.1 ml, 3 times a day for 10 to 14 days.

ONSET OF EFFECT
Unknown.

DURATION OF ACTION
Unknown.

DIETARY ADVICE
Take with a glass of fruit juice, milk, or broth to minimize stomach upset. Drink all of the liquid to get the full dose of the medicine.

STORAGE
Keep the solution refrigerated, but do not allow it to freeze.

IF YOU MISS A DOSE
Take it as soon as you remember. If it is near the time for the next dose, skip the missed dose and resume your regular dosage schedule. Do not double the next dose.

STOPPING THE DRUG
The decision to stop taking the drug should be made by your doctor.

PROLONGED USE
It is necessary to see your physician regularly to check the progress of treatment when taking strong iodine for a prolonged period.

PRECAUTIONS
Over 60: While no specific studies of the use of strong iodine in older persons have been done, no special problems or side effects are expected in older patients.

Driving and Hazardous Work: Use of strong iodine should not impair your ability to perform such tasks safely.

Alcohol: No special precautions are necessary.

Pregnancy: Iodine can cross the placenta and cause thyroid problems or goiter in the fetus. Before you take strong iodine, tell your doctor if you are pregnant or plan to become pregnant.

Breast Feeding: Strong iodine passes into breast milk; avoid or discontinue use while nursing.

Infants and Children: The use and dose of strong iodine in an infant or a child must be determined by your doctor.

Special Concerns: Take the oral solution by mouth even if it comes in a dropper bottle. Do not use the medicine if the solution turns reddish brown. If crystals form in the solution, they can be dissolved by warming the closed container in warm water and then shaking the container gently. Take the liquid through a straw to lessen tooth discoloration. If stomach upset continues, consult your doctor.

OVERDOSE
Symptoms: Gastrointestinal pain and diarrhea, sometimes bloody; loss of consciousness.

What to Do: Call your doctor, emergency medical services (EMS), or the nearest poison control center immediately.

DRUG INTERACTIONS
Other drugs may interact with strong iodine. Consult your doctor for specific advice if you are taking amiloride, spironolactone, triamterene, other thyroid agents, or lithium.

FOOD INTERACTIONS
This medicine contains potassium. Consult your doctor if you are on a low-potassium diet.

DISEASE INTERACTIONS
Caution is advised when taking strong iodine. Consult your doctor if you have any of the following: bronchitis or another lung condition, kidney disease, or hyperkalemia (excess potassium in the blood).

Ipratropium Bromide

BRAND NAME
Atrovent

▶ Drug Class: Respiratory inhalant

▶ Available in: Inhalation aerosol, inhalation solution

▶ Available OTC? No

▶ As Generic? Yes

Side Effects

SERIOUS
Persistent constipation; lower abdominal pain or bloating; wheezing or difficulty breathing; tightness in chest; severe eye pain; skin rash or hives; swelling of face, lips, or eyelids. Call your doctor immediately.

COMMON
Dry mouth, cough, unpleasant taste.

LESS COMMON
Blurred vision, other changes in vision, burning eyes, difficult urination, dizziness, headache, nausea, pounding heartbeat, nervousness, sweating, trembling.

PRINCIPAL USES
To control the symptoms of lung diseases, such as asthma, chronic bronchitis, and emphysema.

HOW THE DRUG WORKS
It inhibits the cough reflex by blocking the activity of acetylcholine, a chemical that, in the lungs, causes the smooth muscles surrounding the airways to constrict. Therefore, when inhaled, ipratropium bromide causes the airways to widen (bronchodilation).

DOSAGE
The drug may be used as needed to relieve respiratory symptoms. For chronic obstructive lung disease such as bronchitis or emphysema— Inhalation aerosol: Adults and children 6 and over: 2 to 4 inhalations 3 or 4 times a day at regularly spaced intervals. Some patients may need 6 to 8 inhalations a day. Inhalation solution, adults and children 12 and over: 250 to 500 micrograms in a nebulizer 3 or 4 times a day, every 6 to 8 hours.

ONSET OF EFFECT
5 to 15 minutes.

DURATION OF ACTION
3 to 4 hours.

DIETARY ADVICE
Sugarless hard candy or gum can be taken to relieve dry mouth.

STORAGE
Store in a tightly sealed container away from heat and direct light. Open bottles of the solution should be refrigerated, but do not allow the solution to freeze.

IF YOU MISS A DOSE
Take it as soon as you remember. If it is near the time for the next dose, skip the missed dose and resume your regular dosage schedule. Do not double the next dose.

STOPPING THE DRUG
It may not be necessary to continue using the medication for as long as originally prescribed; consult your doctor.

PROLONGED USE
You should see your doctor regularly if you must take this drug for a prolonged period.

PRECAUTIONS
Over 60: Ipratropium is not expected to cause different problems in older patients than in younger persons.

Driving and Hazardous Work: Do not drive or engage in hazardous work until you determine how the medicine affects you.

Alcohol: No special precautions are necessary.

Pregnancy: Ipratropium has not caused birth defects in animals. Human studies have not been done. Before you take ipratropium, tell your doctor if you are pregnant or plan to become pregnant.

Breast Feeding: It is not known whether ipratropium passes into breast milk; caution is advised. Consult your doctor for specific advice.

Infants and Children: Ipratropium has been tested in children and has not been shown to cause different effects than in adults.

Special Concerns: To test the inhaler, insert the canister into the mouthpiece, take the cap off the mouthpiece, shake the inhaler 3 or 4 times, and spray once into the air. To use the inhaler, hold it upright, with the mouthpiece end down, shake it 3 or 4 times, then breathe out. Spray into open mouth or with mouth closed over inhaler, as recommended by your doctor. Clean the inhaler, mouthpiece, and spacer at least twice a week. To take the inhalation solution, use a power-operated nebulizer with a face mask or mouthpiece. Get instructions for using the nebulizer from your doctor.

OVERDOSE
Symptoms: No specific ones have been reported.

What to Do: An overdose of ipratropium is unlikely to be life-threatening. However, if someone takes a much larger dose than prescribed, call your doctor, emergency medical services (EMS), or the nearest poison control center.

DRUG INTERACTIONS
Before you use ipratropium, tell your doctor if you are using any other prescription or over-the-counter drug.

FOOD INTERACTIONS
No known food interactions.

DISEASE INTERACTIONS
Consult your doctor if you have glaucoma or difficulty urinating.

Irbesartan

BRAND NAME
Avapro

▶ Drug Class: Antihypertensive/
angiotensin II antagonist

▶ Available in: Tablets

▶ Available OTC? No

▶ As Generic? No

Side Effects

SERIOUS
No serious side effects are associated with the use of irbesartan. (In clinical trials, the incidence of adverse effects was not significantly greater with the medication than with a placebo.)

COMMON
No common side effects are associated with the use of irbesartan.

LESS COMMON
Diarrhea, indigestion, heartburn, fatigue, muscle pain, edema, sexual dysfunction, low blood pressure.

PRINCIPAL USES
To control high blood pressure. This drug appears to have the same benefits as the class of antihypertensive drugs known as ACE inhibitors, without producing the common side effect (experienced by as many as 30% of patients) of a dry cough. Irbesartan may be used by itself or in conjunction with other antihypertensive medications.

HOW THE DRUG WORKS
Irbesartan blocks the effects of angiotensin II, a naturally occurring substance that causes blood vessels to narrow. Irbesartan causes the blood vessels to dilate, thereby lowering blood pressure and decreasing the workload of the heart.

DOSAGE
To start, 150 mg once a day. It may be increased by your doctor to a maximum dose of 300 mg per day.

ONSET OF EFFECT
Within 2 to 4 hours.

DURATION OF ACTION
More than 24 hours.

DIETARY ADVICE
No special restrictions, unless your doctor has advised a low-sodium diet or other dietary modifications to help you control your blood pressure.

STORAGE
Store in a tightly sealed container away from heat, moisture, and direct light.

IF YOU MISS A DOSE
If you miss a dose on one day, do not double the dose the next day. Resume your regular dosage schedule.

STOPPING THE DRUG
Take it as prescribed for the full treatment period. The decision to stop taking the drug should be made in consultation with your physician.

PROLONGED USE
Lifelong therapy may be necessary. However, if you do change certain health habits (for example, increasing exercise or losing weight), a reduced dose may be possible under a doctor's supervision.

PRECAUTIONS
Over 60: Adverse reactions may be more likely and more severe in older patients.

Driving and Hazardous Work: Do not drive or engage in hazardous work until you determine how the medicine affects you.

Alcohol: No special precautions are necessary.

Pregnancy: Irbesartan should not be used by pregnant women. Discontinue taking the drug as soon as possible when pregnancy is detected and discuss treatment alternatives with your doctor.

Breast Feeding: Irbesartan may pass into breast milk; caution is advised. Consult your doctor for specific advice.

Infants and Children: The safety and effectiveness of use in children have not been established.

Special Concerns: Irbesartan may cause excessively low blood pressure with dizziness or lightheadedness, which is most noticeable when you change position. This may lead to fainting, falls, and injury. Sit or lie down immediately if you feel dizzy or lightheaded. This side effect may be worsened by alcohol, hot weather, dehydration, salt depletion from diuretic use, fever, prolonged standing, prolonged sitting, or exercise.

OVERDOSE
Symptoms: No cases of overdose have been reported. However, if you take a much larger dose than prescribed, you may experience extremely low blood pressure or heartbeat irregularities.

What to Do: If you take a much larger dose than prescribed, contact your doctor.

DRUG INTERACTIONS
No drug interactions have yet been observed with irbesartan. Consult your doctor for specific advice if you are taking any other medication, including other drugs for high blood pressure. Irbesartan can be taken together with diuretics or other medications for high blood pressure, if your doctor approves.

FOOD INTERACTIONS
No known food interactions.

DISEASE INTERACTIONS
Patients with liver or kidney disease are advised to exercise caution when taking irbesartan.

Isoetharine

BRAND NAMES
Arm-a-Med Isoetharine,
Bronkometer, Bronkosol,
Dey-Lute Isoetharine S/F

▶ Drug Class: Bronchodilator/
sympathomimetic

▶ Available in: Inhalation
solution, inhalation aerosol

▶ Available OTC? No

▶ As Generic? Yes

Side Effects

SERIOUS
Isoetharine may become
ineffective if used too
often, resulting in more-
severe breathing diffi-
culty that does not
improve. Signs include
persistent wheezing,
coughing, or shortness of
breath; confusion; bluish
color to lips or finger-
nails; inability to speak.
Other side effects include
chest pain or heaviness;
irregular, racing, fluttering, or pounding heart-
beat; lightheadedness;
fainting; severe weak-
ness; severe headache.

COMMON
Trouble sleeping, dry
mouth, sore throat, ner-
vousness, restlessness.

LESS COMMON
Trembling, sweating,
headache, nausea or
vomiting, flushing or redness to cheeks or other
skin, muscle aches,
unpleasant or unusual
taste in mouth.

PRINCIPAL USES
Isoetharine is used to dilate
air passages in the lungs
that have become narrowed
as a result of disease or
inflammation. It is used in
the treatment of asthma and
chronic obstructive pul-
monary disease (COPD).

HOW THE DRUG WORKS
Isoetharine widens con-
stricted airways in the lungs
by relaxing the smooth
muscles that surround the
bronchial passages.

DOSAGE
May be used when needed
to relieve breathing difficulty. Adults, using inhalation solution for nebulizers:
Usual dose is 4 inhalations,
not to be taken more fre-
quently than every 4 hours,
for a usual maximum of 3
to 4 times a day. Note that
isoetharine for nebulizers
may or may not require
dilution with saline. Check
with your physician to
determine whether your
medication requires dilu-
tion; if so, follow directions
accordingly. Children: Consult your pediatrician.
Adults using inhalation
aerosol: A treatment con-
sists of 340 micrograms (1
puff), repeated after 1 to 2
minutes if necessary. Treatments may be repeated
every 4 hours if necessary.
Children: Not recom-
mended in children younger
than 12 years of age.

ONSET OF EFFECT
Within 5 minutes.

DURATION OF ACTION
1 to 4 hours.

DIETARY ADVICE
Maintain your usual food
and fluid intake.

STORAGE
Store in a tightly sealed container away from heat and
direct light. Do not refrigerate inhalation solutions.

IF YOU MISS A DOSE
Skip the missed dose and
resume your regular dosage
schedule. Do not double the
next dose.

STOPPING THE DRUG
It may not be necessary to
finish the recommended
course of therapy. Consult
your doctor.

PROLONGED USE
Therapy may require
months or years. Excessive
use may result in temporary
loss of effectiveness.

PRECAUTIONS
Over 60: Adverse reactions
may be more likely and
more severe in older
patients.

**Driving and Hazardous
Work:** Do not drive or
engage in hazardous work
until you determine how the
medicine affects you.

Alcohol: No special precautions are necessary.

Pregnancy: Adequate studies have not been done;
benefits must be weighed
against potential risks. Consult your doctor for specific
advice.

Breast Feeding: It is not
known if isoetharine passes
into breast milk. Mothers
who wish to breast-feed
while taking this drug
should discuss the matter
with their doctor.

Infants and Children:
Nebulized solutions may be
used to treat breathing difficulties in infants and children. Consult your
pediatrician. Use of the
inhalation aerosol is not recommended in children
younger than 12 years old.

Special Concerns: Pay
heed to any asthma attack
or other breathing problem
that does not improve after
your usual nebulizer treatment or usual number of
puffs. Seek help immedi-
ately if you feel your lungs
are persistently constricted,
if you are using more than
the recommended number
of treatments or puffs per
day, or if you feel a recent
attack is somehow different
from others.

OVERDOSE
Symptoms: See Serious
Side Effects.

What to Do: Call your
doctor, emergency medical
services (EMS), or the
nearest poison control
center immediately.

DRUG INTERACTIONS
Consult your doctor for specific advice if you are taking
a beta-blocker, ergotamine
or ergotamine-like medications, antidepressants, digitalis drugs, or an MAO
inhibitor.

FOOD INTERACTIONS
No known food interactions.

DISEASE INTERACTIONS
Consult your doctor if you
have a history of substance
abuse (especially cocaine),
seizures, brain damage,
heart disease, heartbeat
irregularities, high blood
pressure, anxiety disorders,
or a thyroid condition.

Isoniazid

BRAND NAMES
Laniazid, Nydrazid

Generic 100 mg
(BARR)

Additional photographs

▶ Drug Class: Anti-infective/antitubercular agent

▶ Available in: Syrup, tablets, injection

▶ Available OTC? No

▶ As Generic? Yes

Side Effects

SERIOUS
Numbness, pain, burning, or tingling in hands and feet, loss of appetite, stomach pain, clumsiness, yellowish tinge to the eyes or skin, nausea, vomiting, darkened urine, unusual fatigue. Call your doctor immediately.

COMMON
Diarrhea, rash, fever.

LESS COMMON
Irritability, seizures.

PRINCIPAL USES
To prevent and treat tuberculosis (TB). It may be taken alone to prevent TB, but must be used with other antitubercular agents to treat an active case of TB.

HOW THE DRUG WORKS
Isoniazid interferes with the formation of DNA and lipids, needed to manufacture the TB bacteria's cell walls.

DOSAGE
For prevention— Adults and teenagers: 300 mg once a day. Children: 4.5 to 9 mg per lb of body weight once a day (not more than 300 mg a day). For treatment— Adults and teenagers: 300 mg once a day, or 6.8 mg per lb twice a week (not more than 900 mg per dose). Children: 4.5 to 9.1 mg per lb (not more than 300 mg a day) once a day, or 9.1 to 18.2 mg per lb twice a week (not more than 900 mg per dose). Vitamin B6 may be given in a dosage of 10 to 25 mg a day to prevent nerve damage.

ONSET OF EFFECT
Unknown.

DURATION OF ACTION
Unknown.

DIETARY ADVICE
Take this medicine 1 hour before or 2 hours after meals. Taking it with food or an antacid will prevent stomach irritation but decrease the absorption of the drug. Do not take an antacid containing aluminum within 1 hour of taking isoniazid.

STORAGE
Store in a tightly sealed container away from heat, moisture, and direct light. Do not freeze the liquid forms.

IF YOU MISS A DOSE
Take it as soon as you remember, to help keep a constant level of medication in your system. If it is near the time for the next dose, skip the missed dose and resume your regular dosage schedule. Do not double the next dose.

STOPPING THE DRUG
Take it as prescribed for the full treatment period, even if you feel better before the scheduled end of therapy. Treatment may continue for months or years. The decision to stop the drug should be made by your doctor.

PROLONGED USE
See your doctor regularly for tests and examinations if you must take this medicine for a prolonged period. If your symptoms do not improve or instead become worse after 3 weeks, consult your doctor.

PRECAUTIONS
Over 60: Adverse reactions may be more likely and more severe in older patients.

Driving and Hazardous Work: Do not drive or engage in hazardous work until you determine how the medicine affects you.

Alcohol: Avoid alcohol; it may diminish isoniazid's effectiveness and may interact with the drug, increasing the risk of hepatitis (liver inflammation).

Pregnancy: In human studies, isoniazid has not caused birth defects. Tell your doctor if you are pregnant or are planning to become pregnant and discuss the relative risks and benefits of using this drug.

Breast Feeding: Isoniazid passes into breast milk; cau-

tion is advised. Consult your doctor for specific advice.

Infants and Children: No special problems are expected. Discuss with your pediatrician the relative risks and benefits of your child's using this drug.

Special Concerns: Isoniazid can cause false results on urine sugar tests for diabetics.

OVERDOSE
Symptoms: Severe seizures, nausea, vomiting, difficulty breathing, slurred speech, blurred vision, hallucinations, dizziness, loss of consciousness, stupor.

What to Do: Call your doctor, emergency medical services (EMS), or the nearest poison control center immediately.

DRUG INTERACTIONS
Consult your doctor for specific advice if you are taking narcotic pain relievers, antacids, acetaminophen, carbamazepine, disulfiram, phenytoin, rifampin, ketoconazole, itraconazole, warfarin, or diazepam. Ask your doctor if any of the medications you take are toxic to the liver; such drugs should be avoided.

FOOD INTERACTIONS
Swiss cheese, fish, chocolate, and beer can react with this medication. Consult your doctor for advice.

DISEASE INTERACTIONS
Consult your doctor if you have epilepsy or another seizure disorder, or a history of alcohol abuse. Use of isoniazid may cause complications in patients with liver or kidney disease, since these organs work together to remove the medication from the body.

Isoproterenol

▶ Drug Class: Bronchodilator/
sympathomimetic

▶ Available in: Inhalation
solution or aerosol

▶ Available OTC? No

▶ As Generic? Yes

Side Effects

SERIOUS
Isoproterenol may
become ineffective if
used too often, resulting
in more-severe breathing
difficulty that does not
improve. Signs include
persistent wheezing,
coughing, or shortness of
breath; confusion; bluish
color to lips or finger-
nails; inability to speak.
Other side effects include
chest pain or heaviness;
irregular, racing, fluttering, or pounding heart-
beat; lightheadedness;
fainting; severe weak-
ness; severe headache.

COMMON
Trouble sleeping, dry
mouth, sore throat, pink-
ish color to saliva, ner-
vousness, restlessness.

LESS COMMON
Trembling, sweating,
headache, nausea or
vomiting, flushing or redness to cheeks or other
skin surfaces.

PRINCIPAL USES
To dilate air passages in the
lungs that have become narrowed as a result of disease
or inflammation. It is used
in the treatment of asthma
and chronic obstructive pulmonary disease (COPD).

HOW THE DRUG WORKS
Isoproterenol widens con-
stricted airways in the lungs
by relaxing smooth muscles
that surround the bronchial
passages.

DOSAGE
For use when needed to
relieve wheezing or difficulty breathing— By nebu-
lizer: Adults: 6 to 12
inhalations of 0.25% solution. May be repeated if
necessary every 15 minutes
for a maximum of 3 doses.
Take no more than 8 treatments every 24 hours. Or:
5 to 10 inhalations of 0.5%
solution, or 3 to 7 inhalations of 1.0% solution,
repeated once after 5 to 10
minutes if necessary. Take
no more than 5 treatments
per day. If you are on a program of scheduled, daily
isoproterenol treatments,
do not take a treatment
more often than every 3 to
4 hours. Children: Follow
directions above for 0.25%
and 0.5% solutions. A 1.0%
solution is not used in children. By inhalation aerosol,
adults and children: 1 puff.
Wait 1 minute to assess
effect. May be repeated
after 1 to 5 minutes if
needed. This treatment
may be repeated 4 to 6
times per day. For sched-
uled, daily use— 1 puff
every 3 to 4 hours.

ONSET OF EFFECT
Within 5 minutes.

DURATION OF ACTION
From 30 to 120 minutes.

DIETARY ADVICE
Maintain your usual food
and fluid intake.

STORAGE
Store at room temperature
in a tightly sealed container
away from heat and direct
light.

IF YOU MISS A DOSE
Skip the missed dose and
resume your regular dosage
schedule. Do not double the
next dose.

STOPPING THE DRUG
It may not be necessary to
finish the recommended
course of therapy. Consult
your doctor.

PROLONGED USE
Therapy may require
months or years. Excessive
use may result in temporary
loss of effectiveness.

PRECAUTIONS
Over 60: Adverse reactions
may be more likely and
more severe in older
patients.

**Driving and Hazardous
Work:** Do not drive or
engage in hazardous work
until you determine how the
medicine affects you.

Alcohol: No special precautions are necessary.

Pregnancy: Benefits must
be weighed against potential
risks; consult your doctor.

Breast Feeding: Mothers
who wish to breast feed
while taking this drug
should discuss the matter
with their doctor.

Infants and Children:
May be used to treat
breathing difficulties in
infants and children.

Special Concerns: Pay
heed to any breathing problem that does not improve

after your usual nebulizer
treatment or usual number
of puffs. Seek help immediately if you feel your lungs
are persistently constricted,
if you are using more than
the recommended number
of treatments per day, or if
you feel a recent attack is
somehow different from
others.

OVERDOSE
Symptoms: Chest pain or
heaviness; irregular, racing,
fluttering, or pounding
heartbeat; dizziness; lightheadedness; fainting; severe
weakness; severe headache.

What to Do: Call your
doctor, emergency medical
services (EMS), or the
nearest poison control
center immediately.

DRUG INTERACTIONS
Consult your doctor for
specific advice if you are
taking a beta-blocker, ergotamine or ergotamine-like
medications, antidepres-
sants, digitalis drugs, or
an MAO inhibitor.

FOOD INTERACTIONS
No known food interactions.

DISEASE INTERACTIONS
Consult your doctor if you
have a history of substance
abuse (especially cocaine),
seizures, brain damage,
heart disease, heartbeat
irregularities, high blood
pressure, anxiety disorders,
or a thyroid condition.

Isosorbide Dinitrate

▶ Drug Class: Nitrate

▶ Available in: Capsules,
tablets, chewable tablets,
sublingual and buccal forms

▶ Available OTC? No

▶ As Generic? Yes

Side Effects

SERIOUS
Blurred vision, dry
mouth, severe or pro-
longed headache. Call
your doctor immediately.

COMMON
Dizziness or lightheaded-
ness, especially when
getting up from a seated
or lying position, flushing
of the face and neck,
unusually rapid pulse or
heartbeat, nausea and
vomiting, restlessness.

LESS COMMON
Skin rash.

PRINCIPAL USES

To prevent or relieve
attacks of angina (chest
pain associated with heart
disease).

HOW THE DRUG WORKS

Isosorbide dinitrate relaxes
the smooth muscle of the
blood vessels and increases
the supply of blood and
oxygen to the heart. It also
reduces the heart's work-
load and demand for
oxygen.

DOSAGE

To prevent angina attacks:
Extended-release capsules
or tablets, 20 to 80 mg
every 8 to 12 hours. For
short-acting capsules or
tablets, 5 to 40 mg, 4 times
a day. To treat angina
attack: When you feel an
attack of angina starting,
place a sublingual (under
tongue) or buccal (inside
the cheek) tablet in your
mouth or chew a chewable
tablet. If pain is not relieved
in 5 minutes with a sublingual tablet, take a second
tablet. A third tablet may
be used after another 5
minutes. If pain continues
to persist, call your doctor
or go to the nearest hospital
emergency room.

ONSET OF EFFECT

Chewable and sublingual
(under the tongue) tablets:
2 to 5 minutes; tablets: 15
to 40 minutes; extended-
release capsules and tablets:
30 minutes.

DURATION OF ACTION

1 to 2 hours for chewable
tablets, 4 to 6 hours for
tablets and capsules, 12
hours for extended-release
forms.

DIETARY ADVICE

Take capsules or tablets 30
minutes before or 1 to 2
hours after meals.

STORAGE

Store in a tightly sealed container away from heat and
direct light.

IF YOU MISS A DOSE

Take it as soon as you
remember. If it is near the
time for the next dose, skip
the missed dose and
resume your regular dosage
schedule as prescribed. Do
not double the next dose.

STOPPING THE DRUG

The decision to stop taking
the drug should be made by
your doctor. Do not stop
taking this medicine sud-
denly. Consult your doctor
about reducing the dose
gradually.

PROLONGED USE

You should see your doctor
regularly if you must take
this medicine for an
extended period.

PRECAUTIONS

Over 60: Adverse reactions
may be more likely and
more severe in older
patients.

**Driving and Hazardous
Work:** Do not drive or
engage in hazardous work
until you determine how the
medicine affects you.

Alcohol: Alcohol should be
avoided.

Pregnancy: Animal tests
have shown adverse effects
on the fetus. Human tests
have not been done. Before
taking isosorbide dinitrate,
tell your doctor if you are
pregnant or plan to become
pregnant.

Breast Feeding: Isosorbide dinitrate may pass
into breast milk; caution
is advised. Consult your
doctor for advice.

Infants and Children:
No studies on the use of
this medicine in children
have been done. Use and
dose should be determined
by your doctor.

Special Concerns: Use
extra care in hot weather or
during exercise, or when
standing for long periods
of time.

OVERDOSE

Symptoms: Bluish fingernails, lips, or palms;
extreme dizziness or fainting; unusual weakness,
fever, weak and rapid heartbeat, seizures.

What to Do: Call your
doctor, emergency medical
services (EMS), or the
nearest poison control center immediately.

DRUG INTERACTIONS

Do not take isosorbide
dinitrate within 24 hours
of taking sildenafil citrate.
Sildenafil can enhance the
action of nitrates (such as
isosorbide), causing potentially dangerous decreases
in blood pressure. Consult
your doctor for specific
advice if you are taking
other heart medicines,
or antihypertensives.

FOOD INTERACTIONS

No known food interactions.

DISEASE INTERACTIONS

Caution is advised when
taking isosorbide dinitrate.
Consult your doctor if you
have any of the following:
anemia, glaucoma, a recent
head injury or stroke,
hyperthyroidism, or a
recent heart attack. Use
of isosorbide dinitrate may
cause complications in
patients with severe liver or
kidney disease, since these
organs work together to
remove the medication
from the body.

Isosorbide Mononitrate

IMDUR 30 mg
(KEY)

▶ Drug Class: Nitrate

▶ Available in: Tablets, extended-release tablets

▶ Available OTC? No

▶ As Generic? Yes

Side Effects

SERIOUS
Blurred vision, dry mouth, severe or prolonged headache. Call your doctor immediately.

COMMON
Dizziness or lightheadedness, especially when rising suddenly to a standing position, flushing of the face and neck, rapid pulse or heartbeat, nausea or vomiting, restlessness.

LESS COMMON
Skin rash.

PRINCIPAL USES
To prevent or relieve attacks of angina (chest pain associated with heart disease).

HOW THE DRUG WORKS
Isosorbide relaxes the smooth muscle of the blood vessels and increases the supply of blood and oxygen to the heart. It also reduces the heart's workload and demand for oxygen.

DOSAGE
To prevent angina attacks—Tablets: 20 mg, 2 times a day, with doses 7 hours apart. Extended-release tablets: 30 to 240 mg once a day.

ONSET OF EFFECT
60 minutes.

DURATION OF ACTION
Unknown.

DIETARY ADVICE
Take tablets on an empty stomach, at least 30 minutes before or 1 to 2 hours after mealtime.

STORAGE
Store in a tightly sealed container away from heat and direct light.

IF YOU MISS A DOSE
Take it as soon as you remember. If it is near the time for the next dose, skip the missed dose and resume your regular dosage schedule as prescribed. Do not double the next dose.

STOPPING THE DRUG
The decision to stop taking the drug should be made by your doctor.

PROLONGED USE
You should see your doctor regularly if you take this medicine for an extended period.

PRECAUTIONS
Over 60: Adverse reactions may be more likely and more severe in older patients.

Driving and Hazardous Work: Avoid such activities until you determine how the medicine affects you.

Alcohol: Avoid alcohol.

Pregnancy: Animal tests have shown adverse effects on the fetus. Human tests have not been done. Before taking this drug, tell your doctor if you are pregnant or plan to become pregnant.

Breast Feeding: Isosorbide mononitrate may pass into breast milk; caution is advised. Consult your doctor for specific advice.

Infants and Children: No studies on the use of this medicine in children have been done. Use and dose should be determined by your doctor.

Special Concerns: Do not stop taking this medicine suddenly because it can cause a spasm of the blood vessels in the heart. Consult your doctor about reducing the dose gradually. Use extra care in hot weather or during exercise, or when you must stand for long periods of time. This medicine may cause headaches at the beginning of therapy. Headaches can be treated with aspirin or acetaminophen and usually stop after your body becomes accustomed to the medication. The dose may be reduced temporarily because of headaches. The effectiveness of the medicine may decrease over time; notify your doctor if this occurs.

OVERDOSE
Symptoms: Bluish fingernails, lips or palms; extreme dizziness or fainting; unusual weakness, fever, weak and fast heartbeat, seizures.

What to Do: Call your doctor, emergency medical services (EMS), or the nearest poison control c enter immediately.

DRUG INTERACTIONS
Do not take isosorbide mononitrate within 24 hours of taking sildenafil citrate. Sildenafil can enhance the action of nitrates (such as isosorbide), causing potentially dangerous decreases in blood pressure. Consult your doctor for specific advice if you are taking other heart medicines, or antihypertensives.

FOOD INTERACTIONS
No known food interactions.

DISEASE INTERACTIONS
Consult your doctor if you have any of the following: anemia, glaucoma, a recent head injury or stroke, an overactive thyroid, or a recent heart attack. Use of isosorbide mononitrate may cause complications in patients with severe liver or kidney disease, since these organs work together to remove the medication from the body.

Isotretinoin

▶ Drug Class: Acne drug

▶ Available in: Capsules

▶ Available OTC? No

▶ As Generic? No

Side Effects

SERIOUS

Severe headache that may occur in conjunction with blurred vision, nausea, and vomiting. Discontinue isotretinoin and contact your doctor immediately as this may be an indication of a very serious condition known as pseudotumor cerebri, marked by increased pressure within the skull, which may damage the brain. Severe central abdominal pain, penetrating through to the back, may indicate acute pancreatitis; call your doctor or get to an emergency room immediately. Stop taking isotretinoin and call your doctor if you become unusally irritable, angry, or aggressive.

COMMON

Dry, itching, or cracked skin or lips; easy bruising; nosebleeds; dry, red, or inflamed eyes, difficulty wearing contact lenses; increased susceptibility to sunburn; muscle or joint pain. Consult your doctor if such symptoms persist or interfere with daily activities.

LESS COMMON

Rashes, peeling of skin on palms and soles, nausea, dizziness, poor night vision, cataracts, appearance of small spots or shadows passing slowly across the line of vision, thinning hair, weight loss, swelling in the feet and ankles (edema) due to excess fluid retention in the body tissues, mental depression.

PRINCIPAL USES

Isotretinoin is used to treat severe acne that has not responded adequately to other treatments, such as oral antibiotics. Because of the risk for potentially serious side effects, isotretinoin is prescribed only as a last resort.

HOW THE DRUG WORKS

Isotretinoin decreases the size of and interferes with the functioning of structures in the skin called sebaceous glands. These tiny glands, located along hair shafts all over the body's surface, produce sebum—a thick, oily substance that serves as the skin's natural lubricant. Hormonal activity (during pregnancy, puberty, or menstruation, for example) can stimulate overproduction of sebum by the sebaceous glands so that it is secreted faster than it can exit the pores. This may lead to blockage of the hair follicle and result in the sort of skin lesion that characterizes acne. By thinning the composition of sebum and reducing sebum production (as well as causing other, only partly-understood changes), isotretinoin improves acne.

DOSAGE

Adults and teenagers: 0.5 to 1 mg per 2.2 lbs (1 kg) of body weight, in 1 or 2 doses per day, taken for a total period of 20 weeks (average) for complete treatment. Children: Not recommended. Capsules should be swallowed whole; do not open, crush, or chew them.

ONSET OF EFFECT

Variable, usually within several weeks after starting therapy.

DURATION OF ACTION

Most patients have complete and prolonged improvement of acne following therapy with isotretinoin, while others do not. Good results are usually achieved only with the appropriate dose and length of treatment.

DIETARY ADVICE

Isotretinoin should be taken with food. Maintain your usual food and fluid intake. Do not take vitamin supplements containing vitamin A while taking isotretinoin.

STORAGE

Store in a tightly sealed container away from heat and direct light. Keep away from moisture and extremes in temperature.

IF YOU MISS A DOSE

Take it as soon as you remember. If it is near the time for the next dose, skip the missed dose and resume your regular dosage schedule. Do not double the next dose.

STOPPING THE DRUG

Take it as prescribed for the full treatment period, even if your acne clears before the scheduled end of therapy. Special exception: Stop taking the medication immediately if you become pregnant or believe that there is a possibility that you are pregnant.

PROLONGED USE

Therapy with isotretinoin usually lasts 15 to 20 weeks. A second course of therapy may be initiated if the first yields less-than-satisfactory results; a period of two months without using the drug is required between the first and second course of therapy.

PRECAUTIONS

Over 60: It is possible that adverse reactions may be more likely or more severe in older patients.

Driving and Hazardous Work: The use of isotretinoin should not impair your ability to perform such tasks safely during daytime. Exercise caution at night, since the drug may impair night vision.

Alcohol: Simultaneous use of alcohol and isotretinoin may cause an unhealthy rise in triglyceride levels.

Pregnancy: Do not use this medication under any circumstances during pregnancy or within one month of intended pregnancy.

Breast Feeding: Do not use this medication while nursing.

Infants and Children: Not recommended for use by children under age 13.

Special Concerns: Isotretinoin can lead to a severely deformed infant if used during pregnancy, even if only for a very short time. Therefore, this medication should not be used by any woman of childbearing age who is not using established methods of contraception. If you are a woman starting on isotretinoin, you should first be using two reliable forms of contraception and have a pregnancy test done to exclude the possibility of pregnancy. Then, begin isotretinoin on the third day of the subsequent menstrual cycle to further ensure that you are not pregnant. You must also avoid pregnancy for 1 full month after discontinuing therapy. Your doctor may

Isotretinoin (continued)

require you to sign a consent form before prescribing this medication. Once you have started isotretinoin, expect some drying, cracking, peeling, or itching of your skin, as well as dry nasal passages and mouth. About 9 out of every 10 people taking isotretinoin experience these problems. Avoid prolonged exposure to the sun and be sure to use sunblock when spending time outdoors, since isotretinoin may increase your skin's sensitivity to ultraviolet light and thus your risk of sunburn.

OVERDOSE

Symptoms: Headache, vomiting, facial flushing, dry or cracked lips, abdominal pain, dizziness. Such symptoms usually resolve on their own in a short period of time.

What to Do: An overdose is unlikely to be life-threatening. However, if overdose symptoms occur and persist, or if someone accidentally ingests isotretinoin, call your doctor, emergency medical services (EMS), or the nearest poison control center immediately.

DRUG INTERACTIONS

Consult your doctor for specific advice if you are taking etretinate, tretinoin, vitamin A supplements, multivitamins, tetracycline, topical sulfur, or topical benzoyl peroxide.

FOOD INTERACTIONS

No known food interactions. (Isotretinoin should be taken with food.)

DISEASE INTERACTIONS

Consult your doctor if you have any of the following: a history of alcohol abuse, diabetes mellitus, pancreatitis, high blood levels of cholesterol or triglycerides, severe weight problems, vision problems, or severe headaches.

Isoxsuprine Hydrochloride

BRAND NAME
Vasodilan

Generic 20 mg
(GENEVA)

▶ Drug Class: Vasodilator

▶ Available in: Tablets

▶ Available OTC? No

▶ As Generic? No

Side Effects

SERIOUS
Chest pain, dizziness, or faintness; rapid heartbeat; skin rash; shortness of breath; continuing nausea and repeated vomiting. Such side effects are rare but potentially serious; if they do occur, call your doctor immediately.

COMMON
There are no common side effects associated with the use of isoxsuprine.

LESS COMMON
Nausea, vomiting.

PRINCIPAL USES
To treat problems resulting from poor blood circulation to the brain (cerebrovascular insufficiency) or the body (arteriosclerosis obliterans, thromboangiitis obliterans, and Raynaud's disease).

HOW THE DRUG WORKS
Isoxsuprine acts upon the smooth muscle tissue surrounding the arteries, causing it to relax, which widens the blood vessels and lowers blood pressure, as well as increasing heart output and improving blood circulation.

DOSAGE
10 to 20 mg, 3 or 4 times a day.

ONSET OF EFFECT
1 hour.

DURATION OF ACTION
Unknown.

DIETARY ADVICE
Isoxsuprine can be taken with meals or milk.

STORAGE
Store in a tightly sealed container in a dry place away from heat and direct light.

IF YOU MISS A DOSE
Take a missed dose as soon as you remember. If it is near the time for the next dose, skip the missed dose and resume your regular dosage schedule. Do not double the next dose.

STOPPING THE DRUG
Take as prescribed for the full treatment period, even if you begin to feel better before the scheduled end of therapy. The decision to stop taking the drug should be made by your doctor.

PROLONGED USE
You should see your doctor regularly for tests and examinations if you take this drug for a prolonged period.

PRECAUTIONS
Over 60: There is no specific information comparing use of isoxsuprine in older patients with use in other age groups. However, older patients may be more likely to experience an increased sensitivity to cold temperatures.

Driving and Hazardous Work: Do not drive or engage in hazardous work until you determine how the medicine affects you.

Alcohol: Alcohol should be avoided while taking this medication.

Pregnancy: Isoxsuprine has not been shown to cause birth defects. Given prior to delivery, it may cause low blood sugar, bowel problems, low blood pressure, and other problems in a newborn baby.

Breast Feeding: Isoxsuprine has not been shown to cause problems in nursing babies.

Infants and Children: Isoxsuprine is generally not prescribed for infants and children.

Special Concerns: You should avoid sudden changes in position to reduce the possibility of dizziness, lightheadedness, and falling. You should not smoke cigarettes if you take isoxsuprine. Taking blood pressure measurements in sitting, lying, and standing positions is recommended to detect the likelihood of episodes of low blood pressure in patients receiving isoxsuprine. Be sure to tell your doctor if you have had any unusual or allergic reaction to isoxsuprine in the past. Also tell your doctor if you are allergic to any other substances, such as foods, dyes, and preservatives.

OVERDOSE
Symptoms: Headache, vomiting, flushed face, abdominal pain, dizziness, loss of muscle coordination.

What to Do: Call your doctor, emergency medical services (EMS), or the nearest poison control center immediately.

DRUG INTERACTIONS
Consult your doctor for specific advice if you are taking any prescription or over-the-counter medicine. In some cases your doctor may want to change the dose or have you take other precautions.

FOOD INTERACTIONS
No known food interactions.

DISEASE INTERACTIONS
Caution is advised when taking isoxsuprine. Consult your doctor if you have any of the following: angina, bleeding problems, glaucoma, hardening of the arteries, pulmonary hypertension, low blood pressure, a recent heart attack, or a recent stroke.

Isradipine

BRAND NAME
DynaCirc

DynaCirc 5 mg
(NOVARTIS)

▶ Drug Class: Calcium channel blocker

▶ Available in: Capsules

▶ Available OTC? No

▶ As Generic? No

Side Effects

SERIOUS
Breathing difficulty, coughing, or wheezing; irregular or pounding heartbeat; chest pain; fainting. Call your doctor immediately.

COMMON
Headache, dizziness, skin flushing and feeling of warmth, swelling in the feet, ankles, or calves, palpitations.

LESS COMMON
Constipation or diarrhea, nausea, unusual fatigue and weakness, skin rash, increased urination.

PRINCIPAL USES
To treat high blood pressure (hypertension).

HOW THE DRUG WORKS
Isradipine interferes with the movement of calcium into heart muscle cells and the smooth muscle cells in the walls of the arteries. This action relaxes blood vessels (causing them to widen), which lowers blood pressure, increases the blood supply to the heart, and decreases the heart's overall workload.

DOSAGE
2.5 mg twice a day to start. The dose may be increased.

ONSET OF EFFECT
Within 20 minutes.

DURATION OF ACTION
More than 12 hours.

DIETARY ADVICE
No special restrictions.

STORAGE
Store in a tightly sealed container away from heat and direct light. Keep away from moisture and extremes in temperature.

IF YOU MISS A DOSE
Take it as soon as you remember. If it is near the time for the next dose, skip the missed dose and resume your regular dosage schedule. Do not double the next dose.

STOPPING THE DRUG
Do not stop taking this drug suddenly, as this may cause potentially serious health problems. If therapy is to be discontinued, dosage should be reduced gradually, according to doctor's instructions.

PROLONGED USE
See your doctor regularly for examinations and tests if you take this medicine for a prolonged period. Remember that isradipine controls high blood pressure but does not cure it. Lifelong therapy may be necessary.

PRECAUTIONS
Over 60: Adverse reactions may be more likely and more severe in older patients.

Driving and Hazardous Work: Do not drive or engage in hazardous work until you determine how the medicine affects you.

Alcohol: Avoid alcohol.

Pregnancy: In animal studies, large doses of isradipine have caused birth defects. Human studies have not been done. Before you take isradipine, tell your doctor if you are currently pregnant or plan to become pregnant.

Breast Feeding: Isradipine may pass into breast milk; caution is advised. Consult your doctor for specific advice.

Infants and Children: Safety and effectiveness of isradipine have not been determined for young patients.

Special Concerns: In addition to taking isradipine, be sure to follow all special instructions on weight control and diet. Your doctor will tell you which specific factors are most important for you. Check with your doctor before changing your diet.

OVERDOSE
Symptoms: Dizziness, slurred speech, nausea, weakness, drowsiness, and confusion.

What to Do: Call your doctor, emergency medical services (EMS), or the nearest poison control center immediately.

DRUG INTERACTIONS
Consult your physician for specific advice if you are taking acetazolamide, amphotericin B, corticosteroids, dichlorphenamide, diuretics, methazolamide, beta-blockers, carbamazepine, cyclosporine, procainamide, quinidine, digitalis, disopyramide or the following eye medicines: betaxolol, levobunolol, metipranolol, or timolol.

FOOD INTERACTIONS
Avoid foods high in sodium.

DISEASE INTERACTIONS
Caution is advised when taking isradipine. Consult your doctor if you have any of the following: abnormal heart rhythm (cardiac arrhythmia), or other disorders of the heart and blood vessels, mental depression, or Parkinson's disease. Use of isradipine may cause complications in patients with liver or kidney disease, since these organs work together to remove the medication from the body.

BRAND NAME
Sporanox

Sporanox 100 mg
(JANSSEN)

▸ Drug Class: Antifungal

▸ Available in: Capsules, oral solution

▸ Available OTC? No

▸ As Generic? Yes

Side Effects

SERIOUS
Skin rash or itching, fever or chills, unusual fatigue, loss of appetite, nausea, vomiting, yellow discoloration of the skin, dark urine, or pale stools. Call your doctor right away.

COMMON
No common side effects have been reported with the use of itraconazole.

LESS COMMON
Diarrhea, nausea, vomiting, constipation, dizziness, headache, redness or flushing of skin.

PRINCIPAL USES
To treat serious fungal infections in the lungs and other parts of the body. These infections may occur in patients who do not have other illnesses, although they frequently occur in patients with weakened immune systems. Itraconazole is sometimes prescribed for fungal infections that are limited only to the nails.

HOW THE DRUG WORKS
Itraconazole prevents fungal organisms from producing vital substances required for growth and function. This drug is effective only for fungal infections. It will not work against bacterial or viral infections.

DOSAGE
Capsules— Adults and teenagers 16 and older: 200 to 400 mg, taken once daily. Children under age 16: Consult your pediatrician for proper dosage. Oral solution— Adults and teenagers: 100 to 200 mg once a day for days or weeks, depending on the condition being treated. Children: Consult your pediatrician. Swish the solution vigorously in your mouth for several seconds before swallowing.

ONSET OF EFFECT
Unknown.

DURATION OF ACTION
Unknown.

DIETARY ADVICE
Take capsules with food, but do not take the oral solution with food. Maintain your usual food and fluid intake. Patients with compromised immune systems are often weakened by their illness, by medications, or by other treatments, and may be unable to consume adequate amounts of nutritious food. Use liquid supplements if necessary.

STORAGE
Store in a tightly sealed container away from heat, moisture, and direct light.

IF YOU MISS A DOSE
Take it as soon as you remember. This will help keep a constant level of medication in your system. If it is near the time for the next dose, skip the missed dose and resume your regular dosage schedule. Do not double the next dose.

STOPPING THE DRUG
Take it as prescribed for the full treatment period, even if you begin to feel better before the scheduled end of therapy. The decision to stop taking the drug should be made by your doctor. Gradual reduction of the dose may be necessary if you have been taking this medicine for a long time.

PROLONGED USE
Therapy with this medication may require months. Prolonged use may increase the risk of adverse effects.

PRECAUTIONS
Over 60: Adverse reactions may be more likely and more severe.

Driving and Hazardous Work: Avoid such activites until you determine how the medicine affects you.

Alcohol: Avoid alcohol throughout therapy and for two days afterwards.

Pregnancy: Adequate studies of itraconazole use during pregnancy have not been done. Consult your doctor for specific advice if you are or are planning to become pregnant.

Breast Feeding: Itraconazole passes into breast milk; avoid or discontinue use while nursing.

Infants and Children: Itraconazole is not recommended for use by children under the age of 16.

Special Concerns: Women should use effective contraception to prevent pregnancy while taking this medication. Continue these measures for at least 2 months following the end of therapy. The capsules and the oral solution should not be used interchangeably.

OVERDOSE
Symptoms: An overdose with itraconazole is unlikely.

What to Do: Emergency instructions not applicable.

DRUG INTERACTIONS
While taking itraconazole, do not take astemizole, oral midazolam, pimozide, quinidine, dofetilide, triazolam, statin (anti-cholesterol) drugs. You should not take medications containing alcohol, such as cough syrups, elixirs, and tonics. Consult your doctor if you are taking antacids, anticholinergics, histamine H2-blockers, omeprazole, oral antidiabetics, erythromycin, sucralfate, carbamazepine, cyclosporine, isoniazid, didanosine, digoxin, phenytoin, rifampin, or warfarin. If you are taking an antacid, take it at least 2 hours after taking itraconazole.

FOOD INTERACTIONS
No known food interactions.

DISEASE INTERACTIONS
Do not take itraconazole for onychomycosis (a fungal nail infection) if you have congestive heart failure (CHF). Consult your doctor if you have any of the following conditions: liver or kidney disease, low levels or absence of stomach acid, or a history of alcohol abuse.

Kaolin with Pectin

BRAND NAMES
K-P, Kao-Spen, Kapectolin

▶ Drug Class: Antidiarrheal

▶ Available in: Oral suspension

▶ Available OTC? Yes

▶ As Generic? Yes

Side Effects

SERIOUS
No serious side effects have been reported.

COMMON
No common side effects have been reported.

LESS COMMON
Constipation.

PRINCIPAL USES
To treat diarrhea.

HOW THE DRUG WORKS
Kaolin with pectin absorbs fluids and binds to and removes bacteria and toxins from the digestive tract.

DOSAGE
Adults: 4 to 8 tablespoons (60 to 120 ml) after each loose bowel movement. Children age 12 and older: 3 to 4 tbsp (45 to 60 ml) after each loose bowel movement. Children ages 6 to 12: 2 to 4 tbsp (30 to 60 ml) after each loose bowel movement. Children ages 3 to 6: 1 to 2 tbsp (15 to 30 ml) after each loose bowel movement.

ONSET OF EFFECT
Unknown.

DURATION OF ACTION
Unknown.

DIETARY ADVICE
A mild diet is recommended when recovering from diarrhea. Bananas, rice, applesauce, and plain toast are good choices. Be sure to get plenty of fluids.

STORAGE
Store in a tightly sealed container away from heat, moisture, and direct light.

IF YOU MISS A DOSE
Take it as soon as you remember. If it is nearly time for another dose, skip the missed dose. Do not double the next dose.

STOPPING THE DRUG
Do not use this drug for more than 2 days without consulting your doctor.

PROLONGED USE
This drug is not intended for prolonged use. Consult your doctor if diarrhea continues for more than 2 days.

PRECAUTIONS
Over 60: Adverse reactions associated with diarrhea may be more severe in older patients. They should be sure to consume enough liquids to replace body fluids lost because of diarrhea.

Driving and Hazardous Work: The use of kaolin with pectin should not impair your ability to perform such tasks safely.

Alcohol: Avoid alcohol.

Pregnancy: It is not absorbed into the body and is not expected to cause problems during pregnancy.

Breast Feeding: It is not absorbed into the body and is not expected to cause problems during breast feeding.

Infants and Children: Kaolin with pectin should be used in children under the age of 3 only under the supervision of a doctor.

Special Concerns: In addition to taking medicine for diarrhea, it is important to replace the fluid lost by your body and to eat a proper diet. During the first 24 hours, drink plenty of caffeine-free clear liquids like water, broth, ginger ale, and decaffeinated tea. During the second 24 hours you may eat bland foods such as applesauce, bread, crackers, and oatmeal. Avoid caffeine, fried or spicy foods, bran, candy, fruits, and vegetables. They can make your condition worse.

OVERDOSE
Symptoms: Constipation.

What to Do: An overdose of kaolin with pectin is unlikely to be life-threatening. However, if someone takes a much larger dose than prescribed, call your doctor, emergency medical services (EMS), or the nearest poison control center immediately.

DRUG INTERACTIONS
Consult your doctor for specific advice if you are taking anticholinergics, antidyskinetics, digitalis drugs, lincomycins, loxapine, phenothiazines, thioxanthenes, or any other oral medication. Do not take any medication within 2 to 3 hours of taking kaolin with pectin.

FOOD INTERACTIONS
Fruits, fried or spicy foods, bran, candy, and caffeine-containing beverages can make diarrhea worse.

DISEASE INTERACTIONS
Caution is advised when taking kaolin with pectin. Consult your doctor if the diarrhea is suspected to be caused by parasites or dysentery.

Ketoconazole Oral

Nizoral 200 mg
(JANSSEN)

▶ Drug Class: Antifungal

▶ Available in: Tablets

▶ Available OTC? No

▶ As Generic? No

Side Effects

SERIOUS
Skin rash, itching, fever, chills. Call your doctor right away.

COMMON
No common side effects have been reported.

LESS COMMON
Diarrhea, nausea, vomiting, constipation, dizziness, headache, redness or flushing of skin.

PRINCIPAL USES
To treat serious fungal infections occurring in the lungs and other parts of the body. Ketoconazole is used to treat fungal infections of the skin, such as tinea corporis (ringworm), tinea cruris (jock itch), tinea pedis (athlete's foot), and pityriasis versicolor ("sun fungus," a condition characterized by fine scaly patches of varying shapes, sizes, and colors), that are severe or are unresponsive to griseofulvin.

HOW THE DRUG WORKS
Ketoconazole prevents fungal organisms from producing vital substances required for growth and function. This drug is effective only for infections caused by fungal organisms. It will not work for bacterial or viral infections.

DOSAGE
Adults and teenagers: 200 to 400 mg once a day. Children over age 2: 3.3 to 6.6 mg per 2.2 lbs of body weight once a day. Treatment may last from 1 week to 6 months, depending on the type of infection being treated.

ONSET OF EFFECT
Unknown.

DURATION OF ACTION
Unknown.

DIETARY ADVICE
Take it with food to reduce stomach upset. Tablets may be crushed and mixed with a beverage or food to reduce the bitter taste.

STORAGE
Store in a tightly sealed container away from heat, moisture, and direct light.

IF YOU MISS A DOSE
Take it as soon as you remember. This will help keep a constant level of medication in your system. If it is near the time for the next dose, skip the missed dose and resume your regular dosage schedule. Do not double the next dose.

STOPPING THE DRUG
Take it as prescribed for the full treatment period, even if you begin to feel better before the scheduled end of therapy. The decision to stop taking the drug should be made by your doctor. Dose should be reduced gradually if you have used the drug for a long time.

PROLONGED USE
Months of therapy may be necessary. Prolonged use increases the risk of adverse effects and may interfere with the body's synthesis of steroid hormones, which may cause erectile dysfunction in men and cessation of menstrual periods in women.

PRECAUTIONS

Over 60: Adverse reactions may be more likely and more severe.

Driving and Hazardous Work: Avoid such activities until you determine how the medication affects you.

Alcohol: Avoid alcohol.

Pregnancy: Adequate studies of ketoconazole use during pregnancy have not been done. Consult your doctor for advice if you are pregnant or planning to become pregnant.

Breast Feeding: Ketoconazole passes into breast milk; caution is advised. Consult your doctor for specific advice.

Infants and Children: Not recommended for use by children under 2 years.

Special Concerns: Ketoconazole may make your eyes more sensitive to sunlight. If this occurs, avoid exposure to bright light and wear sunglasses. For full effectiveness, ketoconazole should be taken at the same time every day.

OVERDOSE
Symptoms: An overdose is unlikely to occur.

What to Do: Emergency instructions not applicable.

DRUG INTERACTIONS
While taking ketoconazole, do not take astemizole or terfenadine. Serious side effects involving the heart may result. Do not take medications containing alcohol, such as cough syrups, elixirs, and tonics. Consult your doctor for advice if you are taking cyclosporine, isoniazid, didanosine, phenytoin, rifampin, or warfarin. If you are taking antacids, anticholinergics, histamine H2-blockers, omeprazole, or sucralfate, take them at least 2 hours after taking ketoconazole.

FOOD INTERACTIONS
No known food interactions.

DISEASE INTERACTIONS
Caution is advised when taking ketoconazole. Consult your doctor if you have any of the following: history of alcohol abuse, decreased amount of stomach acid, liver disease, or kidney disease. Use of ketoconazole can cause complications in patients with liver or kidney disease, since these organs work together to remove the medication from the body. If you have no stomach acid or a decreased amount of stomach acid, your doctor may prescribe a special solution.

Ketoconazole Topical

▶ Drug Class: Topical antifungal

▶ Available in: Cream, shampoo

▶ Available OTC? Yes

▶ As Generic? Yes

Side Effects

SERIOUS
Blistering or ulceration of the skin; blistering of the lips, nose, and mouth.

COMMON
Brief burning, itching, or irritation after application of cream; peeling.

LESS COMMON
Severe burning, itching, swelling, increased redness, or any discomfort at the application site not present prior to therapy (as a result of allergic reaction).

PRINCIPAL USES
Ketoconazole is used to treat fungal infections of the skin. These infections include tinea pedis (athlete's foot), tinea corporis (ringworm), tinea cruris (jock itch), yeast infections of the skin, seborrheic dermatitis, and others.

HOW THE DRUG WORKS
Ketoconazole prevents fungal organisms from manufacturing vital substances required for growth and function.

DOSAGE
Adults, for tinea and yeast: Apply once daily to affected skin. Treatment generally requires 2 to 6 weeks. Adults, for seborrheic dermatitis: Apply two times a day to affected skin. Treatment generally requires 4 weeks. Children: Consult your pediatrician.

ONSET OF EFFECT
Ketoconazole begins killing susceptible fungi shortly after contact. The effects may not be noticeable for several days or weeks.

DURATION OF ACTION
Unknown.

DIETARY ADVICE
Maintain your usual food and fluid intake. Increase fluid intake in hot weather, during exercise, or if you have a fever or diarrhea.

STORAGE
Store in a tightly sealed container away from heat and direct light.

IF YOU MISS A DOSE
Apply it as soon as you remember. If it is near the time for the next dose, skip the missed dose and resume your regular dosage schedule. Do not double the next dose or apply an excessively thick film of topical medication to compensate for a missed application.

STOPPING THE DRUG
Apply ketoconazole as prescribed for the full treatment period, even if you notice marked improvement before the scheduled end of therapy.

PROLONGED USE
Therapy with this medication should not exceed 4 weeks.

PRECAUTIONS
Over 60: Adverse reactions may be more likely and more severe in older patients.

Driving and Hazardous Work: The use of ketoconazole cream should not impair your ability to perform such tasks safely.

Alcohol: No special precautions are necessary.

Pregnancy: Avoid or discontinue use of ketoconazole if you are pregnant or trying to become pregnant.

Breast Feeding: Ketoconazole may pass into breast milk; avoid or discontinue usage while nursing. Consult your doctor for specific advice.

Infants and Children: Not recommended for use by young children.

Special Concerns: Avoid contact with eyes. Wash hands thoroughly after application. Tell your doctor if your condition has not improved within a few days of starting ketoconazole. As with any other antifungal, ketoconazole is useful only against organisms that are vulnerable to its effects. Therefore, it is important to tell your doctor if your condition has not improved—or has worsened—within a few days of starting ketoconazole. The particular organism causing your illness may be resistant to this medication.

OVERDOSE
Symptoms: No specific ones have been reported.

What to Do: An overdose of ketoconazole is unlikely to be life-threatening. However, if someone applies a much larger dose than prescribed or ingests the medication, call your doctor, emergency medical services (EMS), or the nearest poison control center.

DRUG INTERACTIONS
No specific drug interactions are known as of this writing. If you are concerned whether a prescription or over-the-counter medication you are taking may interact with ketoconazole, consult your physician or pharmacist for current information.

FOOD INTERACTIONS
No known food interactions.

DISEASE INTERACTIONS
Consult your physician if you have had previous allergies or an undesirable reaction to any other topical medication.

Ketoprofen

Orudis KT Caplets 12.5 mg
(WHITEHALL-ROBINS)

Additional photographs

▶ Drug Class: Nonsteroidal
anti-inflammatory drug
(NSAID)

▶ Available in: Tablets and capsules (also extended-release
forms), rectal suppositories

▶ Available OTC? Yes

▶ As Generic? Yes

Side Effects

SERIOUS
Shortness of breath or
wheezing, with or with-
out swelling of legs or
other signs of heart failure; chest pain; peptic
ulcer disease with vomit-
ing of blood; black, tarry
stools; decreasing kidney
function. Call your doctor
immediately.

COMMON
Nausea, vomiting, heart-
burn, diarrhea, constipa-
tion, headache, dizziness,
sleepiness.

LESS COMMON
Ulcers or sores in mouth,
depression, rashes or
blistering of skin, ringing
sound in the ears,
unusual tingling or
numbness of the hands
or feet, seizures, blurred
vision. Also elevated
potassium levels,
decreased blood counts;
such problems can be
detected by your doctor.

PRINCIPAL USES
To treat mild to moderate
pain and inflammation
caused by tendinitis, arthritis, bursitis, gout, soft tissue
injuries, migraine and other
vascular headaches, men-
strual cramps, and other
conditions. When patients
fail to respond to one
NSAID, another may be
tried. The greatest effectiveness often requires trial and
error of several different
NSAIDs.

HOW THE DRUG WORKS
NSAIDs work by interfering
with the formation of
prostaglandins, naturally
occurring substances in the
body that cause inflamma-
tion and make nerves more
sensitive to pain impulses.
NSAIDs also have other
modes of action that are
less well understood.

DOSAGE
Adults— Tablets or cap-
sules: 50 mg, 4 times a day,
or 75 mg, 3 times a day.
Extended-release tablets or
capsules: 200 mg once a
day. Suppositories: 50 to 100
mg inserted twice a day
(morning and evening).
Sometimes, suppositories
may be used only at night
by people who take an oral
dose during the day. Maximum dosage for all forms
is 300 mg per day.

ONSET OF EFFECT
1 to 2 hours.

DURATION OF ACTION
3 to 4 hours.

DIETARY ADVICE
Take oral forms with food.

STORAGE
Store in a tightly sealed container away from heat, moisture, and direct light.

IF YOU MISS A DOSE
Take it as soon as you
remember. If it is near the

time for the next dose,
skip the missed dose and
resume your regular dosage
schedule. Do not double the
next dose.

STOPPING THE DRUG
If taking this drug by prescription, do not stop without consulting your doctor.

PROLONGED USE
Prolonged use can cause
gastrointestinal problems,
including ulceration and
bleeding, kidney dysfunc-
tion, and liver inflammation.
Consult your doctor about
the need for medical examinations and lab tests.

PRECAUTIONS
Over 60: Because of the
potentially greater consequences of gastrointestinal
side effects, the dose of
NSAIDs for older patients,
especially those over age
70, is often cut in half.

**Driving and Hazardous
Work:** Do not drive or
engage in hazardous work
until you determine how the
medicine affects you.

Alcohol: Avoid alcohol
when using this medication
because it increases the risk
of stomach irritation.

Pregnancy: Do not use
ketoprofen while pregnant.

Breast Feeding: Ketoprofen passes into breast milk;
avoid use while nursing.

Infants and Children:
Ketoprofen may be used in
exceptional circumstances;
consult your doctor.

Special Concerns:
Because NSAIDs can inter-
fere with blood coagulation,
this drug should be stopped
at least 3 days prior to any
surgery.

OVERDOSE
Symptoms: Severe nausea,
vomiting, headache, confusion, seizures.

What to Do: Call your
doctor, emergency medical
services (EMS), or the
nearest poison control center immediately.

DRUG INTERACTIONS
Do not take this drug with
aspirin or any other NSAIDs
without your doctor's
approval. In addition, consult your doctor if you are
taking antihypertensives,
steroids, anticoagulants,
antibiotics, itraconazole or
ketoconazole, plicamycin,
penicillamine, valproic acid,
phenytoin, cyclosporine,
digitalis drugs, lithium,
methotrexate, probenecid,
triamterene, or zidovudine.

FOOD INTERACTIONS
No known food interactions.

DISEASE INTERACTIONS
Consult your doctor if you
have any of the following:
bleeding problems, inflammation or ulcers of the
stomach and intestines,
diabetes mellitus, systemic
lupus erythematosus (SLE,
lupus), anemia, asthma,
epilepsy, Parkinson's disease, kidney stones, or a
history of heart disease or
alcohol abuse. Use of ketoprofen may cause complications in patients with liver
or kidney disease, since
these organs work together
to remove the medication
from the body.

Ketorolac Tromethamine Ophthalmic

▶ Drug Class: Nonsteroidal anti-inflammatory drug (NSAID)

▶ Available in: Ophthalmic solution

▶ Available OTC? No

▶ As Generic? No

Side Effects

SERIOUS
Rarely, ophthalmic ketorolac tromethamine will cause bleeding in the eye, redness or swelling of the eye or eyelid not present before the start of therapy, or tearing or itching of the eye. Call your doctor immediately.

COMMON
Mild and temporary burning or stinging of eyes after application; eye infection.

LESS COMMON
There are no less-common side effects associated with ophthalmic ketorolac.

PRINCIPAL USES
For short-term therapy of eye itching caused by seasonal allergic conjunctivitis. It is also used to treat inflammation and eye problems that may occur after cataract surgery.

HOW THE DRUG WORKS
Ophthalmic ketorolac inhibits the release of substances that stimulate inflammation and cause pain in eye tissues.

DOSAGE
Adults: 1 drop in each eye 4 times a day. Children: Consult your pediatrician.

ONSET OF EFFECT
Unknown.

DURATION OF ACTION
Unknown.

DIETARY ADVICE
No special restrictions.

STORAGE
Store this medication in a tightly sealed container away from heat, moisture, and direct light. Do not refrigerate or allow it to freeze.

IF YOU MISS A DOSE
Apply it as soon as you remember. If it is near the time for the next dose, skip the missed dose and resume your regular dosage schedule. Do not double the next dose.

STOPPING THE DRUG
Use it as prescribed for the full treatment period, even if you feel better before the scheduled end of therapy.

PROLONGED USE
See your doctor regularly for tests and examinations if you must use this drug for a prolonged period.

PRECAUTIONS
Over 60: Adverse reactions may be more likely and more severe.

Driving and Hazardous Work: Avoid such activities until you determine how the medicine affects your vision.

Alcohol: Avoid alcohol.

Pregnancy: Adequate human studies have not been completed. Before taking ophthalmic ketorolac, tell your doctor if you are pregnant or plan to become pregnant.

Breast Feeding: Ophthalmic ketorolac may pass into breast milk; caution is advised. Consult your doctor for specific advice.

Infants and Children: Use and dosage for infants and children must be determined by your doctor.

Special Concerns: To use the eye drops, first wash your hands. Tilt your head back. Gently apply pressure to the inside corner of the eyelid and with the index finger of the same hand, pull downward on the lower eyelid to make a space. Drop the medicine into this space and close your eye. Apply pressure for 1 or 2 minutes while keeping the eye closed without blinking. Then wash your hands again. Make sure the tip of the dropper does not touch your eye, finger, or any other surface. If your symptoms do not improve or if they become worse, check with your doctor. Ophthalmic ketorolac may cause problems in patients who wear soft contact lenses. Your physician may want you to stop wearing the lenses while you take the medicine.

OVERDOSE
Symptoms: No specific ones have been reported.

What to Do: An overdose of ophthalmic ketorolac is unlikely to be life-threatening. However, if someone applies a much larger dose of the drug than prescribed or accidentally ingests the medicine, call your doctor, emergency medical services (EMS), or the nearest poison control center.

DRUG INTERACTIONS
Consult your doctor for specific advice if you are taking aspirin or another salicylate, diflunisal, etodolac, fenoprofen, floctafenine, flurbiprofen, ibuprofen, indomethacin, ketoprofen, oral ketorolac, meclofenamate, mefenamic acid, nabumetone, naproxen, oxyphenbutazone, phenylbutazone, piroxicam, sulindac, suprofen, tenoxicam, tiaprofenic acid, tolmetin, or zomepirac.

FOOD INTERACTIONS
No known food interactions.

DISEASE INTERACTIONS
Caution is advised when taking ophthalmic ketorolac. Consult your doctor if you have hemophilia or any other bleeding problem.

Ketorolac Tromethamine Systemic

BRAND NAME
Toradol

▶ Drug Class: Nonsteroidal anti-inflammatory drug (NSAID)

▶ Available in: Tablets, injection

▶ Available OTC? No

▶ As Generic? Yes

Side Effects

SERIOUS
Gastrointestinal bleeding causing dark or bloody stools or vomiting; severe high blood pressure causing headache and blurred vision; prolonged bleeding from a cut; burnlike rash. Call your doctor immediately. This drug may cause breathing difficulty or a severe allergic reaction in persons who are sensitive to aspirin, especially those with aspirin-induced nasal polyps or asthma.

COMMON
Stomach distress.

LESS COMMON
Drowsiness, diarrhea, confusion, ringing in ears, sensitivity to sunlight, water retention, hives, headache.

PRINCIPAL USES
To treat moderate to severe pain and inflammation, usually following surgery.

HOW THE DRUG WORKS
NSAIDs work by interfering with the action of prostaglandins, naturally occurring substances that cause inflammation and make nerves more sensitive to pain impulses. NSAIDs also have other modes of action that are less well understood.

DOSAGE
For acute pain— Initial adult dose is usually by injection, which may be followed (if necessary) by injections or tablets. Injection: 30 mg into a vein every 6 hours. Some people may receive one 60 mg dose into a muscle. The dose should not exceed 120 mg per 24-hour period. Tablets: 10 mg, 4 times a day, taken every 4 to 6 hours. Your doctor may recommend a different dose, though it should not exceed 40 mg per day. For pain in children— Consult your pediatrician.

ONSET OF EFFECT
Into a vein: Immediate. Into a muscle: Within 10 minutes. Tablets: 30 to 60 minutes.

DURATION OF ACTION
6 to 8 hours.

DIETARY ADVICE
Tablets should be taken with food; maintain your usual food and fluid intake.

STORAGE
Not applicable for injection form; it is administered only at a health care facility. Store tablets in a tightly sealed container away from heat and direct light.

IF YOU MISS A DOSE
Take tablets as soon as you remember. If it is near the time for the next dose, skip the missed dose and resume your regular dosage schedule. Do not double the next dose.

STOPPING THE DRUG
Take it as prescribed for the full treatment period. Ask your doctor about stopping the drug if you are feeling better before the scheduled end of therapy.

PROLONGED USE
Therapy generally does not last more than 5 days. Use beyond that period may cause serious side effects.

PRECAUTIONS
Over 60: Because of the potentially greater consequences of gastrointestinal side effects, the dose of NSAIDs for older patients, especially those over age 70, is often cut in half.

Driving and Hazardous Work: Avoid such activities until you determine how the medicine affects you.

Alcohol: Avoid alcohol.

Pregnancy: Avoid or discontinue ketorolac if you are pregnant or are planning to become pregnant.

Breast Feeding: Ketorolac passes into breast milk; avoid use while nursing.

Infants and Children: May be used in exceptional circumstances; consult your doctor.

OVERDOSE
Symptoms: Nausea, vomiting, severe headache, confusion, seizures.

What to Do: Call your doctor, emergency medical services (EMS), or the nearest poison control center immediately.

DRUG INTERACTIONS
Do not take this drug with aspirin or any other NSAIDs. In addition, consult your doctor if you are taking acetaminophen, anticoagulants, enoxaparin, lithium, methotrexate, diuretics, beta-blockers, sulfinpyrazone, valproic acid, or warfarin.

FOOD INTERACTIONS
No known food interactions

DISEASE INTERACTIONS
Caution is advised when taking ketorolac. Consult your doctor if you have any of the following: nasal polyps, severe hives, any stomach or intestinal disorder, high blood pressure, a blood coagulation defect, or a history of heart disease. Use of ketorolac may cause complications in patients with liver or kidney disease, since these organs work together to remove the medication from the body.

Ketotifen Fumarate

▶ Drug Class: Histamine (H1) blocker

▶ Available in: Ophthalmic solution

▶ Available OTC? No

▶ As Generic? No

Side Effects

SERIOUS
No serious side effects are associated with ketotifen.

COMMON
Headache, runny nose.

LESS COMMON
Allergic reaction, burning or stinging of the eye, tearing, eye dryness, eye pain, itching, corneal inflammation, pupil dilation, light sensitivity, rash, flu-like symptoms, sore throat.

PRINCIPAL USES
For short-term therapy of eye itching caused by seasonal allergic conjunctivitis (inflammation of the mucous membranes that line the inner surface of the eyelids and whites of the eyes).

HOW THE DRUG WORKS
Ketotifen blocks the effects of histamine, a naturally occurring substance within the body that causes swelling, itching, sneezing, watery eyes, hives, and other symptoms associated with allergic reactions.

DOSAGE
Instill 1 drop in the affected eye(s) every 8 to 12 hours.

ONSET OF EFFECT
Unknown.

DURATION OF ACTION
Unknown.

DIETARY ADVICE
Ketotifen can be used without regard to diet.

STORAGE
Store in a tightly sealed container away from heat, moisture, and direct light. Do not allow it to freeze.

IF YOU MISS A DOSE
Apply it as soon as you remember. If it is near the time for the next dose, skip the missed dose and resume your regular dosage schedule. Do not double the next dose.

STOPPING THE DRUG
You may stop using ketotifen whenever you choose.

PROLONGED USE
Ketotifen is prescribed for short-term use only.

PRECAUTIONS
Over 60: No special problems are expected.

Driving and Hazardous Work: Do not drive or engage in hazardous work until you determine how the medicine affects you.

Alcohol: No special precautions are necessary.

Pregnancy: No adequate human studies have been done. Before taking ketotifen, tell your doctor if you are pregnant or plan to become pregnant.

Breast Feeding: Ketotifen may pass into breast milk; caution is advised. Consult your doctor for specific advice.

Infants and Children: Not recommended for use by children under the age of 3 years.

Special Concerns: To use the eye drops, first wash your hands. Tilt your head back. Gently apply pressure to the inside corner of the eyelid and with the index finger of the same hand, pull downward on the lower eyelid to make a space. Drop the medicine into this space and close your eye. Apply pressure for 1 or 2 minutes while keeping the eye closed without blinking. Then wash your hands again. Make sure the tip of the dropper does not touch your eye, finger, or any other surface. You should not wear a contact lens if your eye is red. Ketotifen should not be used to treat contact-lens-related irritation. If you wear soft contact lenses and your eyes are not red, wait at least 10 minutes after instilling the drops before inserting your contact lenses.

OVERDOSE
Symptoms: No specific ones have been reported.

What to Do: An overdose with ketotifen is unlikely to be life-threatening. However, if someone accidentally ingests the medicine, seek emergency medical attention immediately.

DRUG INTERACTIONS
None reported.

FOOD INTERACTIONS
None reported.

DISEASE INTERACTIONS
None reported.

Labetalol Hydrochloride

Trandate 200 mg
(GLAXO WELLCOME)

Additional photographs

▶ Drug Class: Beta-blocker

▶ Available in: Tablets (Injection is for hospital use only.)

▶ Available OTC? No

▶ As Generic? Yes

Side Effects

SERIOUS
Shortness of breath, wheezing; chest pain or tightness; swelling of the ankles, feet, and lower legs; mental depression. If you experience such symptoms, stop taking the drug and call your doctor immediately.

COMMON
Dizziness or lightheadedness, especially when rising suddenly to a standing position; decreased sexual ability; unusual fatigue, weakness, or drowsiness; insomnia; scalp tingling, especially at the beginning of treatment.

LESS COMMON
Changes in taste; itching, numbness, or tingling; vivid dreams or nightmares; nausea or vomiting; irregular or slow heartbeat (50 beats per minute or less).

PRINCIPAL USES
To treat severe high blood pressure (hypertension).

HOW THE DRUG WORKS
Labetalol hydrochloride is a beta-blocker with alpha-blocker activity. Such drugs work by preventing—or blocking—nerve impulses from exerting an accelerating or intensifying effect on specific parts of the body, especially the blood vessels and heart. Unlike other beta-blockers, this drug does not significantly slow the heart rate.

DOSAGE
Usual adult dose: 100 mg twice daily, 6 to 12 hours apart, increased to a maintenance dose of 200 to 400 mg twice daily. Maximum dose: 800 mg, 3 times daily.

ONSET OF EFFECT
Within 20 minutes.

DURATION OF ACTION
12 to 24 hours.

DIETARY ADVICE
Follow your doctor's dietary restrictions, such as a low-salt or low-fat diet, to improve control over high blood pressure and heart disease. Take the tablets with food.

STORAGE
Store in a tightly sealed container away from heat and direct light.

IF YOU MISS A DOSE
Take it as soon as you remember. If it is within 8 hours of your next dose, skip the missed dose, and go back to your regular schedule. Do not double the next dose.

STOPPING THE DRUG
Do not stop this drug suddenly, as this may lead to angina or a heart attack in patients with advanced heart disease. Slow reduction of the dose over a period of 2 to 3 weeks is advised. Do not stop taking the drug or make any changes in dosage without consulting your doctor.

PROLONGED USE
Lifelong therapy may be necessary. See your doctor regularly for examinations and tests if you must take this medication for a prolonged period.

PRECAUTIONS
Over 60: Adverse reactions may be more likely and more severe in older patients.

Driving and Hazardous Work: Do not drive or engage in hazardous work until you determine how the medicine affects you.

Alcohol: Drink in careful moderation if at all. Alcohol may interact with the drug and cause a dangerous drop in blood pressure.

Pregnancy: Discuss with your doctor the relative risks and benefits of using this drug while pregnant.

Breast Feeding: Adverse effects in infants have not been reported. Consult your doctor for specific advice.

Infants and Children: No special problems.

Special Concerns: Get up slowly from a sitting or lying position to avoid dizziness or lightheadedness, especially when you first start taking the drug or if the dosage has been increased.

OVERDOSE
Symptoms: Unusually slow or rapid heartbeat, severe dizziness or fainting, poor circulation in the hands (bluish skin), breathing difficulty, seizures.

What to Do: Call your doctor, emergency medical services (EMS), or the nearest poison control center immediately.

DRUG INTERACTIONS
Consult your physician for specific advice if you are taking amphetamines, oral antidiabetic agents, asthma medication (such as aminophylline or theophylline), calcium channel blockers, clonidine, guanabenz, halothane, allergy shots, insulin, MAO inhibitors, reserpine, other beta-blockers, any over-the-counter medicine, sodium bicarbonate injection.

FOOD INTERACTIONS
None reported.

DISEASE INTERACTIONS
Labetalol hydrochloride should be used with caution in people with diabetes, especially insulin dependent diabetes, since the drug may mask symptoms of hypoglycemia. Consult your doctor if you have allergies or asthma, heart or blood vessel disease (including congestive heart failure and peripheral vascular disease), hyperthyroidism, irregular (slow) heartbeat, myasthenia gravis, psoriasis, respiratory problems such as bronchitis or emphysema, kidney or liver disease, or a history of depression.

Lactulose

▶ Drug Class: Hyperosmotic laxative

▶ Available in: Syrup

▶ Available OTC? No

▶ As Generic? Yes

Side Effects

SERIOUS
Unusual weakness, confusion, muscle cramps, dizziness or lightheadedness, irregular heartbeat.

COMMON
Diarrhea, gas, intestinal cramps, increased thirst.

LESS COMMON
No less-common side effects are associated with lactulose.

PRINCIPAL USES
For long-term treatment of chronic constipation. It is also sometimes used for treatment of severe liver disease.

HOW THE DRUG WORKS
Lactulose draws water into the bowel to help loosen and soften the stool and stimulate bowel activity.

DOSAGE
For constipation: 15 to 30 ml once a day. The dose may be increased to 60 ml once a day, if needed. For severe liver disease: 30 to 45 ml, 3 or 4 times a day until 2 or 3 soft stools are produced daily.

ONSET OF EFFECT
24 to 48 hours.

DURATION OF ACTION
Up to 24 hours.

DIETARY ADVICE
Take it with a full glass (8 oz) of water or fruit juice, or 2 glasses of water if your doctor directs. You should not use lactulose if you are on a low-galactose diet.

STORAGE
Store in a tightly sealed container away from heat, moisture, and direct light. Do not allow to freeze.

IF YOU MISS A DOSE
Take it as soon as you remember. If it is near the time for the next dose, skip the missed dose and resume your regular dosage schedule. Do not double the next dose.

STOPPING THE DRUG
Take it as prescribed for the full treatment period. However, you may stop taking the drug if you are feeling better before the scheduled end of therapy.

PROLONGED USE
Do not take lactulose for more than 1 week unless you are under a doctor's supervision. Prolonged use may cause laxative dependence.

PRECAUTIONS
Over 60: No special problems are expected in older patients.

Driving and Hazardous Work: The use of lactulose should not impair your ability to perform such tasks safely.

Alcohol: No special precautions are necessary.

Pregnancy: Caution is advised. Discuss with your doctor the relative risks and benefits of using this drug while pregnant.

Breast Feeding: Lactulose may pass into breast milk; caution is advised. Consult your doctor for advice.

Infants and Children: Lactulose is not recommended for use by children under the age of 6 unless prescribed by your doctor.

Special Concerns: Excessive use of lactulose or any laxative in teenagers may indicate an eating disorder such as anorexia nervosa or bulimia nervosa. Consult your doctor if you observe such behavior. If you have a sudden change in bowel function or habits that lasts more than 2 weeks, consult your doctor.

OVERDOSE
Symptoms: Diarrhea, severe abdominal cramps.

What to Do: An overdose of lactulose is unlikely to be life-threatening. However, if someone takes a much larger dose than prescribed, call your doctor, emergency medical services (EMS), or the nearest poison control center.

DRUG INTERACTIONS
Consult your doctor for specific advice if you are taking other laxatives, antacids, antibiotics, anticoagulants, digitalis drugs, oral tetracyclines, sodium polystyrene sulfonate, ciprofloxacin, or potassium supplements.

FOOD INTERACTIONS
If you are on a low-calorie, low-salt, or low-sugar diet, check with your doctor before taking lactulose.

DISEASE INTERACTIONS
Caution is advised when taking lactulose. Consult your doctor if you have symptoms of appendicitis or an inflamed bowel (abdominal pain, cramps, soreness, bloating, nausea, and vomiting), diabetes mellitus, difficulty swallowing, heart disease or blood pressure disorder, intestinal problems, or kidney disease.

Lamivudine (3TC)

Epivir 150 mg
(GLAXO WELLCOME)

▶ Drug Class: Antiviral

▶ Available in: Solution, tablets

▶ Available OTC? No

▶ As Generic? No

Side Effects

SERIOUS
Severe stomach or abdominal pain, nausea, vomiting, unusual fatigue, fever, chills, sore throat, numbness, burning, tingling, or pain in hands, arms, legs or feet, breathing difficulty, itching, hives, skin rash, swelling of face, mouth, lips, throat, or tongue. Call your doctor immediately if any of these side effects arise.

COMMON
No common side effects are associated with lamivudine.

LESS COMMON
Mild to moderate abdominal pain, diarrhea, dizziness, cough, headache, mild nausea or vomiting, insomnia, loss of hair.

PRINCIPAL USES
To treat HIV (human immunodeficiency virus) infection in combination with zidovudine (AZT) or other antiretroviral agents. While not a cure for HIV infection, these drugs may suppress the replication of the virus and delay the progression of the disease. Also used to treat chronic hepatitis B.

HOW THE DRUG WORKS
Lamivudine interferes with the activity of enzymes needed for the replication of DNA in viral cells, thus preventing HIV and hepatitis B from reproducing. HIV that has become resistant to lamivudine may be less likely to become resistant to zidovudine.

DOSAGE
To treat HIV (Epivir)—Adults and teenagers weighing 110 lbs or more: 150 mg, 2 times a day. Adults weighing less than 110 lbs: 2 mg per 2.2 lbs (1 kg) of body weight 2 times a day. Children 3 months to 12 years: 4 mg per 2.2 lbs of body weight 2 times a day, up to 150 mg per dose. In all cases lamivudine should be taken with other antiretroviral agents. To treat hepatitis B (Epivir-HBV)— Adults: 100 mg once a day. Children 2 years and older: 3 mg per 2.2 lbs a day, but no more than 100 mg daily. Epivir and Epivir-HBV are not interchangeable; Epivir tablets and oral solution contain a higher dose of the same active ingredient then Epivir-HBV tablets and oral solution.

ONSET OF EFFECT
Unknown. Maximum effect may take 12 to 16 weeks.

DURATION OF ACTION
Unknown. Effects of the drug may be prolonged if lamivudine is used in combination with other effective drugs and the virus is maximally suppressed.

DIETARY ADVICE
Can be taken with or without food. Be sure to drink plenty of fluids.

STORAGE
Store in a tightly sealed container away from heat and direct light.

IF YOU MISS A DOSE
Take it as soon as you remember. If it is near the time for the next dose, skip the missed dose and resume your regular dosage schedule. Do not double the next dose. It is especially important to take lamivudine on schedule, to assure constant, proper blood levels of the drug.

STOPPING THE DRUG
Take it as prescribed for the full treatment period, even if you begin to feel better.

PROLONGED USE
See your doctor regularly if you must take this medicine for a prolonged period.

PRECAUTIONS
Over 60: No special studies have been done on older patients. A lower dose may be warranted, especially if liver or kidney function is impaired.

Driving and Hazardous Work: Do not drive or engage in hazardous work until you determine how the medicine affects you.

Alcohol: Avoid alcohol if liver function is impaired.

Pregnancy: In animal studies, lamivudine has been shown to cause birth defects. Nevertheless, lamivudine is increasingly being used in combination with other antiretroviral drugs to treat pregnant HIV-infected women.

Breast Feeding: Women infected with HIV should not breast feed, so as to avoid transmitting the virus to an uninfected child.

Infants and Children: Adverse reactions may be more likely and more severe in young patients.

Special Concerns: If you are taking the solution, use a special measuring spoon or other precisely marked scoop to dispense the proper dose. The risk of transmitting the HIV or hepatitis B to other persons is not reduced by lamivudine. Be sure to take precautionary measures.

OVERDOSE
Symptoms: No cases of overdose have been reported. The symptoms would likely include diarrhea or abdominal cramps.

What to Do: An overdose of lamivudine is unlikely to occur. Nonetheless, if you have any reason to suspect an overdose, call your doctor, emergency medical services (EMS), or the nearest poison control center as soon as possible.

DRUG INTERACTIONS
Consult your doctor if you are taking any other drug.

FOOD INTERACTIONS
No known food interactions.

DISEASE INTERACTIONS
Consult your doctor if you have any other medical condition. Use of lamivudine may cause complications in patients with impaired liver or kidney function, since these organs work together to remove the medication from the body.

Lamivudine/Zidovudine

▶ Drug Class: Antiviral

▶ Available in: Tablets

▶ Available OTC? No

▶ As Generic? No

Side Effects

SERIOUS
Severe stomach or abdominal pain; anemia (low red blood cell count) causing paleness, fatigue, or shortness of breath; fever; chills; sore throat. Also numbness, burning, tingling, or pain in the hands, arms, legs or feet, breathing difficulty, itching, hives, skin rash, swelling of the face, mouth, lips, throat, or tongue. Call your doctor immediately.

COMMON
Headaches, nausea and vomiting, insomnia, stomach upset, loss of appetite, diarrhea, dizziness, cough.

LESS COMMON
Mild to moderate abdominal pain or cramping, muscle aches and pain, hepatitis (liver inflammation, which may cause yellowish discoloration of skin and eyes), joint pain, loss of hair.

PRINCIPAL USES
To treat HIV (human immunodeficiency virus) infection. While not a cure for HIV, this combination of lamivudine (3TC) and zidovudine (AZT) may suppress the replication of the virus and delay the progression of the disease.

HOW THE DRUG WORKS
This drug combination interferes with the activity of enzymes needed for the replication of DNA in viral cells, thus preventing HIV from reproducing.

DOSAGE
Adults and teenagers: 1 tablet (containing 150 mg of lamivudine and 300 mg of zidovudine) twice a day. Children: Should not be taken by children because it is a fixed-dose combination that cannot be adjusted.

ONSET OF EFFECT
Unknown. With most antiretroviral drugs, an early response can be seen within the first few days of therapy, but the maximum effect may take 12 to 16 weeks.

DURATION OF ACTION
Unknown. Effects of the drug combination may be prolonged if the virus is maximally suppressed.

DIETARY ADVICE
Can be taken with or without food. Be sure to drink plenty of fluids.

STORAGE
Store in a tightly sealed container away from heat, moisture, and direct light.

IF YOU MISS A DOSE
Take it as soon as you remember. If it is near the time for the next dose, skip the missed dose and resume your regular dosage schedule. Do not double the next dose. It is especially important to take this medication on schedule, to assure constant, proper blood levels of the drug.

STOPPING THE DRUG
The decision to stop taking the drug should be made in consultation with your physician.

PROLONGED USE
See your doctor regularly for tests and examinations as long as you take this medication.

PRECAUTIONS
Over 60: No special studies have been done on older patients. A lower dose may be warranted, especially if liver or kidney function is impaired.

Driving and Hazardous Work: Use of this drug combination should not diminish your ability to perform such tasks safely.

Alcohol: Avoid alcohol if liver function is impaired.

Pregnancy: Adequate human studies have not been done. Discuss with your doctor the relative risks and benefits of using this drug while pregnant.

Breast Feeding: Women infected with HIV should not breast-feed, so as to avoid transmitting the virus to an uninfected child.

Infants and Children: Not recommended for children under the age of 12.

Special Concerns: Use of this drug combination does not eliminate the risk of passing the AIDS virus (HIV) to other persons. Be sure to take all appropriate preventive measures. This medication should not be used in patients with low body weight.

OVERDOSE
Symptoms: No cases of overdose with this combination have been reported. However, cases of overdose have been reported for zidovudine taken alone (see Zidovudine).

What to Do: If you suspect an overdose or if someone takes a much larger dose than prescribed, call your doctor, emergency medical services (EMS), or the nearest poison control center immediately.

DRUG INTERACTIONS
Consult your doctor for specific advice if you are taking amphotericin B (by injection), anticancer agents, thyroid drugs, azathioprine, chloramphenicol, colchicine, cyclophosphamide, flucytosine, ganciclovir, interferon, mercaptopurine, methotrexate, plicamycin, clarithromycin, or probenecid. Also consult your doctor for specific advice if you are taking any other prescription or over-the-counter medication.

FOOD INTERACTIONS
No known food interactions.

DISEASE INTERACTIONS
Caution is advised when taking this drug combination. Consult your doctor if you have anemia or another blood problem. Use of this drug is not recommended in patients with impaired kidney function or risk factors for liver disease.

Lamotrigine

Lamictal 100 mg
(GLAXO WELLCOME)

835

Additional photographs

▶ Drug Class: Anticonvulsant

▶ Available in: Tablets, chewable tablets

▶ Available OTC? No

▶ As Generic? No

Side Effects

SERIOUS
Fever, sore throat, swollen glands, red or purple point-like rash on the skin or mucous membranes, blistering or peeling skin lesion, weakness, confusion, lethargy, or seizures may be a sign of a potentially fatal blood reaction or other complication. Call your doctor immediately.

COMMON
Dizziness, blurred or double vision, clumsiness or incoordination, drowsiness, nausea, vomiting, headache.

LESS COMMON
Indigestion, runny nose, loss of strength, insomnia, depression, mood changes, trembling or shaking, slurred speech. Numerous additional side effects are associated with the use of this drug; consult your doctor if you are concerned about any adverse or unusual reactions.

PRINCIPAL USES
To control certain kinds of seizures in the treatment of epilepsy. Lamotrigine is generally taken in conjunction with other anticonvulsants.

HOW THE DRUG WORKS
Lamotrigine acts on the central nervous system to control the number and severity of seizures. It is thought to depress the activity of certain parts of the brain and suppress the abnormal firing of neurons that causes seizures.

DOSAGE
Adults: 200 to 900 mg a day, in 2 divided doses. Some patients may require higher doses. A low dose is used to start; the dose is gradually increased by your doctor. The increase in dose is very slow if you are also taking valproic acid (Depakene, Depakote). Lamotrigine is generally not recommended for use in children younger than age 16.

ONSET OF EFFECT
Several hours.

DURATION OF ACTION
Maximum effectiveness lasts 24 hours or longer; effectiveness then gradually decreases.

DIETARY ADVICE
Take it with food to minimize the likelihood of stomach upset. Chewable tablets can be taken with a small amount of water or diluted fruit juice.

STORAGE
Store in a tightly sealed container away from heat, moisture, and direct light.

IF YOU MISS A DOSE
Take it as soon as you remember. If it is near the time for the next dose, skip the missed dose and resume your regular dosage schedule. Do not double the next dose, unless advised to do so by your doctor.

STOPPING THE DRUG
Never stop taking this drug abruptly because seizures may ensue. The dose is typically tapered over a period of weeks under your doctor's supervision.

PROLONGED USE
See your doctor regularly for tests if you must take this drug for an extended period.

PRECAUTIONS
Over 60: Adverse reactions may be more likely in older patients. Lower dosages may be warranted.

Driving and Hazardous Work: This drug may cause drowsiness or dizziness. Do not drive or engage in hazardous work until you determine how it affects you.

Alcohol: May contribute to excessive drowsiness.

Pregnancy: Anticonvulsants have been associated with an increased risk of birth defects, though adequate studies of lamotrigine have not been done. However, seizures during pregnancy can also increase the risks to the fetus. Discuss with your doctor the potential risks and benefits of using this drug during pregnancy. Folate supplementation is advised beginning 1 to 2 months before conception, continuing throughout pregnancy.

Breast Feeding: Lamotrigine passes into breast milk, although at low levels. Caution is advised; consult your doctor for specific advice.

Infants and Children: Because side effects are more common and may be more severe in young patients, lamotrigine is generally not recommended.

Special Concerns: Your doctor may want you to wear a medical bracelet or carry an identification card saying that you are taking this drug.

OVERDOSE
Symptoms: Severe clumsiness and unsteadiness, severe dizziness or drowsiness, extremely slurred speech, severe, unusual, rapid, side-to-side, or rolling eye movements, rapid heart beat, loss of consciousness, dry mouth.

What to Do: Call your doctor, emergency medical services (EMS), or the nearest poison control center immediately.

DRUG INTERACTIONS
Lamotrigine can interact with many other drugs, including other anticonvulsants (carbamazepine, phenobarbital, phenytoin, primidone, valproic acid), as well as acetaminophen, methotrexate, pyrimethamine, and trimethoprim.

FOOD INTERACTIONS
No known food interactions.

DISEASE INTERACTIONS
Special caution is advised in those with kidney or liver disease or folate deficiency.

Lansoprazole

Prevacid 30 mg
(TAP)

Additional photographs

- ▶ Drug Class: Antacid/proton pump inhibitor
- ▶ Available in: Delayed-release capsules
- ▶ Available OTC? No
- ▶ As Generic? No

Side Effects

SERIOUS
No serious side effects are associated with the use of this medication.

COMMON
Diarrhea, itching or rash, headache, dizziness.

LESS COMMON
Abdominal or stomach pain, nausea, increase or decrease in appetite, anxiety, flu-like symptoms, constipation, coughing, mental depression, muscle pain.

PRINCIPAL USES

To treat stomach and duodenal (intestinal) ulcers, gastroesophageal reflux disease (chronic heartburn caused by the backwash of stomach acid into the esophagus), and conditions that cause increased stomach acid secretion, such as Zollinger-Ellison syndrome. To treat and prevent nonsteroidal anti-inflammatory drug (NSAID)-associated stomach ulcers. Lansoprazole is also prescribed in conjunction with the antibiotics amoxicillin and clarithromycin to eradicate the bacterium *H. pylori* and thus prevent the recurrence of duodenal ulcers caused by this bacterium.

HOW THE DRUG WORKS

Lansoprazole blocks the action of a specific enzyme in the cells that line the stomach, thus decreasing the production of stomach acid. Reduction of stomach acid creates a more favorable environment for the eradication of *H. pylori* and promotes the healing of ulcers.

DOSAGE

Prevacid— To treat duodenal ulcers: Initial dose is 15 mg once a day; it may later be increased. To treat gastroesophageal reflux disease: 15 mg once a day for up to 8 weeks. To treat NSAID-associated stomach ulcers: 30 mg once a day for 8 weeks. To reduce the risk of NSAID-associated stomach ulcer: 15 mg once a day for up to 12 weeks. To treat other conditions: Initial dose is 60 mg once a day; it may be increased. Treatment usually runs 4 to 8 weeks. A second course of treatment may be necessary. For Zollinger-Ellison syndrome: Initial dose is 60 mg once a day; it may be increased. Prevpac— To prevent duodenal ulcers: 30 mg lansoprazole, 1 gram amoxicillin, and 500 mg clarithromycin every 12 hours for 14 days.

ONSET OF EFFECT

1 to 3 hours.

DURATION OF ACTION

More than 24 hours.

DIETARY ADVICE

The drug is best taken 30 minutes or more before a meal, preferably breakfast.

STORAGE

Store in a tightly sealed container away from heat, moisture, and direct light.

IF YOU MISS A DOSE

Take it as soon as you remember. However, if it is near the time for the next dose, skip the missed dose and resume your regular dosage schedule. Do not double the next dose.

STOPPING THE DRUG

Take as prescribed for the full treatment period, even if your symptoms improve before the scheduled end of therapy.

PROLONGED USE

Lansoprazole should not be used indefinitely as maintenance therapy for duodenal ulcer or esophagitis; other treatments are advised.

PRECAUTIONS

Over 60: No special problems are expected.

Driving and Hazardous Work: Avoid such activities until you determine how the drug affects you.

Alcohol: Avoid alcohol throughout the duration of therapy with this drug.

Pregnancy: Adequate human studies have not been done. Before taking lansoprazole, tell your doctor if you are pregnant or plan to become pregnant.

Breast Feeding: Lansoprazole may pass into breast milk; consult your doctor for advice.

Infants and Children: Use and dose for anyone under 18 should be determined by your doctor or pediatrician.

Special Concerns: Tell any doctor or dentist whom you see for treatment that you are taking lansoprazole. Do not chew the capsules. If you have trouble swallowing them, you may open them and sprinkle the contents on one tablespoon of applesauce, cottage cheese, yogurt, or similar food. If your doctor directs, you may take an antacid along with lansoprazole.

OVERDOSE

Symptoms: No cases of overdose have been reported.

What to Do: An overdose is unlikely to be life-threatening. However, if someone takes a much larger dose than prescribed, seek medical attention immediately.

DRUG INTERACTIONS

Consult your doctor for specific advice if you are taking ampicillin, sucralfate, iron salts or supplements, cyclosporine, diazepam, disulfiram, ketoconazole, phenytoin, or theophylline.

FOOD INTERACTIONS

No significant food interactions have been reported.

DISEASE INTERACTIONS

Caution is advised when taking lansoprazole. Consult your doctor if you have liver disease, since it may increase the risk of side effects.

Latanoprost

BRAND NAME
Xalatan

▶ Drug Class: Antiglaucoma agent

▶ Available in: Ophthalmic solution

▶ Available OTC? No

▶ As Generic? No

Side Effects

SERIOUS
Chest pain, difficulty breathing. Call your doctor right away.

COMMON
Blurred vision, burning and stinging of the eye, sensation of something in the eye, increased brown pigmentation of the iris, eye redness.

LESS COMMON
Dry eye, excessive tearing, eye pain, lid crusting, swollen eyelid, eyelid pain or discomfort, sensitivity to light, upper respiratory tract infection, double vision, pain in the chest and back.

PRINCIPAL USES
To treat glaucoma.

HOW THE DRUG WORKS
Glaucoma, a sight-threatening disorder, occurs when the aqueous humor (fluid inside the eye) cannot drain properly, causing increased pressure within the eyeball (intraocular pressure). Increased eye pressure can damage the optic nerve and lead to a gradually progressive loss of vision. Latanoprost promotes outflow of aqueous humor, thereby reducing intraocular pressure.

DOSAGE
1 drop of latanoprost in each eye once daily in the evening.

ONSET OF EFFECT
3 to 4 hours.

DURATION OF ACTION
24 hours or more.

DIETARY ADVICE
This medication can be used without regard to diet.

STORAGE
Store in a tightly sealed container away from heat, moisture, and direct light. Do not allow the medicine to freeze.

IF YOU MISS A DOSE
Apply it as soon as you remember. If it is near the time for the next dose, skip the missed dose and resume your regular dosage schedule. Do not double the next dose.

STOPPING THE DRUG
The decision to stop using the drug should be made by your doctor.

PROLONGED USE
See your doctor regularly for tests and examinations if you must take this drug for a prolonged period.

PRECAUTIONS
Over 60: No special problems are expected.

Driving and Hazardous Work: Do not drive or engage in hazardous work until you determine how the medicine affects your vision.

Alcohol: No special precautions are necessary.

Pregnancy: Latanoprost has not caused birth defects in animals. Human studies have not been done. Before you take latanoprost, tell your doctor if you are pregnant or plan to become pregnant.

Breast Feeding: Latanoprost may pass into breast milk; caution is advised. Consult your doctor for advice.

Infants and Children: The safety and effectiveness of latanoprost in infants and children have not been established.

Special Concerns: To use the eye drops, first wash your hands. Tilt your head back. Gently apply pressure to the inside corner of the eyelid and with the index finger of the same hand, pull downward on the lower eyelid to make a space. Drop the medicine into this space and close your eye. Apply pressure for 1 or 2 minutes while keeping the eye closed without blinking. Then wash your hands again. Make sure the tip of the dropper does not touch your eye, finger, or any other surface. Latanoprost may make your eyes more sensitive to sunlight. If this occurs, wear sunglasses or avoid exposure to bright light as necessary. Latanoprost may change eye color, increasing the brown pigment in the iris over a period of months or years. The color change may be permanent. Latanoprost contains ingredients that may damage contact lenses. Contact lenses should be removed 15 minutes before applying the medication and reinserted 15 minutes or more afterward.

OVERDOSE
Symptoms: No specific ones have been reported.

What to Do: An overdose of latanoprost is unlikely to be life-threatening. If a large volume enters the eyes, flush with water. If someone accidentally ingests the medicine, call your doctor, emergency medical service (EMS), or the nearest poison control center.

DRUG INTERACTIONS
Other drugs may interact with latanoprost. Consult your doctor for specific advice if you are taking any other prescription or over-the-counter medication. If you are using other ophthalmic medications to reduce fluid pressure in the eye, administer them at least 5 minutes apart.

FOOD INTERACTIONS
No known food interactions.

DISEASE INTERACTIONS
Use of latanoprost may cause complications in patients with liver or kidney disease, since these organs work together to remove the drug from the body.

Leflunomide

▶ Drug Class: Antirheumatic

▶ Available in: Tablets

▶ Available OTC? No

▶ As Generic? No

Side Effects

SERIOUS
Liver toxicity may occur; it can be detected by your doctor with blood tests; it may be discerned by the patient if it causes jaundice, characterized by yellowish discoloration of the skin and eyes. Call your doctor immediately.

COMMON
Diarrhea, hair loss, rash.

LESS COMMON
Allergic reaction, back pain, bronchitis, pneumonia, nasal congestion, itching.

PRINCIPAL USES
To reduce the signs and symptoms of moderate to severe active rheumatoid arthritis. Leflunomide is prescribed for patients who have not responded adequately to one or more antirheumatic medications.

HOW THE DRUG WORKS
Leflunomide appears to suppress overactivity of the immune system, which is believed to cause rheumatoid arthritis. It also appears to reduce inflammation.

DOSAGE
Adults: To start, 100 mg a day for 3 days. Maintenance dose: 20 mg a day. Dose may be lowered by your doctor to 10 mg a day, if necessary.

ONSET OF EFFECT
Unknown.

DURATION OF ACTION
Unknown.

DIETARY ADVICE
Maintain your usual food and fluid intake.

STORAGE
Store in a tightly sealed container away from heat, moisture, and direct light.

IF YOU MISS A DOSE
If you miss a dose on one day, do not double the dose the next day.

STOPPING THE DRUG
Take it as prescribed for the full treatment period, even if you begin to feel better.

PROLONGED USE
See your doctor regularly for liver function tests while taking this medication.

PRECAUTIONS
Over 60: No special problems are expected.

Driving and Hazardous Work: The use of leflunomide should not impair your ability to perform such tasks safely.

Alcohol: Drink only in moderation.

Pregnancy: Leflunomide can cause serious birth defects. Do not take the drug if you are pregnant. Before you start taking leflunomide, you must have had a negative pregnancy test within the previous 2 weeks. An effective method of birth control should be used while you are taking leflunomide. If you suspect you are pregnant, stop taking the drug immediately and consult your doctor.

Breast Feeding: It is unknown whether leflunomide passes into breast milk. However, do not take the drug while nursing. Consult your doctor for advice.

Infants and Children: Safety and effectiveness have not been established for children under age 18.

Special Concerns: Upon completion of treatment, it is recommended that you follow a specific procedure to lower the levels of leflunomide in the blood. Take 8 grams cholestyramine 3 times a day for 11 days (does not have to be 11 consecutive days, unless there is a need to reduce levels rapidly). Your doctor will conduct two tests (each at least 2 weeks apart) to monitor blood levels of the medication. Without following this procedure, it may take up to 2 years to reach undetectable blood levels of the drug.

OVERDOSE
Symptoms: No cases of overdose have been reported.

What to Do: If someone takes a much larger dose than prescribed, call your doctor, emergency medical services (EMS), or the nearest poison control center immediately.

DRUG INTERACTIONS
The following drugs may interact with leflunomide. Consult your doctor for specific advice if you are taking: methotrexate, rifampin, cholestyramine, charcoal, or tolbutamide.

FOOD INTERACTIONS
No known food interactions.

DISEASE INTERACTIONS
Do not take leflunomide if you have liver disease. Caution is advised in patients with kidney disease. Consult your doctor for advice.

Letrozole

BRAND NAME
Femara

▶ Drug Class: Antiestrogen; antineoplastic (anticancer) agent

▶ Available in: Tablets

▶ Available OTC? No

▶ As Generic? No

Side Effects

SERIOUS
No serious side effects have been reported.

COMMON
Fatigue, nausea and vomiting, muscle and joint pain, headache, shortness of breath.

LESS COMMON
Chest pain, edema (swelling around the feet and ankles), weakness, increase in weight, high blood pressure, constipation, diarrhea, abdominal pain, loss of appetite, indigestion, viral infection, drowsiness or dizziness, cough, hot flashes, rash, itching.

PRINCIPAL USES
Letrozole is used for the treatment of advanced breast cancer in postmenopausal women. It is also prescribed for women whose breast cancer has progressed following treatment with other antiestrogens, such as tamoxifen.

HOW THE DRUG WORKS
The growth of some breast tumors is stimulated by estrogens. After the menopause, women's ovaries produce little estrogen, but androgens formed in the adrenals can be converted to estrogen. Letrozole blocks the enzyme that carries out this conversion. Thus, letrozole is not directly toxic to cancer cells but rather inhibits the growth of some breast tumors by reducing blood levels of estrogen.

DOSAGE
2.5 mg once a day.

ONSET OF EFFECT
Unknown.

DURATION OF ACTION
Unknown.

DIETARY ADVICE
Letrozole can be taken without regard to meals. Maintain adequate food and fluid intake, since calorie, protein, and vitamin needs increase in patients with cancer.

STORAGE
Store in a tightly sealed container away from heat, moisture, and direct light.

IF YOU MISS A DOSE
Letrozole is prescribed for once-daily use only. If you are unable to take this medication on a particular day, resume your regularly scheduled dose the following day. Do not double the next dose.

STOPPING THE DRUG
This medication is used to treat a chronic condition. You may need to remain on this drug for an extended period, and you should take letrozole exactly as prescribed throughout the course of treatment. The decision to stop the drug must be made in consultation with your doctor. Do not stop taking letrozole on your own.

PROLONGED USE
There is no standard duration of therapy with letrozole, although you can expect to remain on it for several weeks in order to determine if it is effective. Your doctor will decide whether your response to the drug is satisfactory or not, and will recommend continuation or discontinuation of therapy.

PRECAUTIONS
Over 60: No special problems are expected.

Driving and Hazardous Work: Use of this medication should not impair your ability to engage in such tasks safely.

Alcohol: No special precautions are necessary.

Pregnancy: Letrozole must not be used in pregnant women. Although letrozole is not generally prescribed for premenopausal women, it is important that patients be sure they are not pregnant before starting treatment with this drug.

Breast Feeding: Use of this drug is not recommended while nursing; the benefits must clearly outweigh potential risks. Consult your doctor for advice.

Infants and Children: Use of letrozole is not approved for infants and children.

Special Concerns: Patients with cancer are very often weakened by their illness, by poor nutrition, and by the effects of chemotherapy, radiation, and surgery. Such patients are more likely to experience undesirable side effects of a medication. In addition, these side effects may be more pronounced. Follow all medication directions carefully.

OVERDOSE
Symptoms: No cases of overdose have been reported.

What to Do: An overdose is unlikely; however, if you have any reason to suspect that one has occurred, call emergency medical services (EMS) to receive evaluation and treatment in the closest emergency facility.

DRUG INTERACTIONS
No significant drug interactions are associated with the use of letrozole.

FOOD INTERACTIONS
No known food interactions.

DISEASE INTERACTIONS
No significant interactions.

Leucovorin Calcium

BRAND NAME
Wellcovorin

Generic 25 mg
(BARR)

Additional photographs

▸ Drug Class: Folic acid derivative

▸ Available in: Tablets, injection

▸ Available OTC? No

▸ As Generic? Yes

Side Effects

SERIOUS
Skin rash, hives, itching, seizures. These may be signs of a serious allergic reaction; call your doctor right away.

COMMON
No common side effects have been reported.

LESS COMMON
There are no less-common side effects associated with leucovorin.

PRINCIPAL USES
To serve as an antidote to the toxic effects of high doses of methotrexate (a cancer drug) and other drugs that antagonize (block the action of) the essential nutrient folic acid. Leucovorin is also used in conjunction with another drug, fluorouracil, to treat some kinds of colon cancer. It may also be used to treat some forms of anemia.

HOW THE DRUG WORKS
Folic acid is needed by healthy cells in the body to grow, survive, and multiply. Leucovorin is a derivative of folic acid and thus prevents some of the damage done to healthy cells by therapy with methotrexate and other drugs that deplete folic acid in the body. Because leucovorin acts in the body the same way as folic acid, it is useful against anemia due to folic acid deficiency.

DOSAGE
To prevent drug side effects: 10 mg per square meter of body surface every 6 hours for 10 doses. For colon cancer, there are 3 accepted regimens: (a) 200 mg per square meter of body surface daily for 5 days; (b) 20 mg per square meter of body surface daily for 5 days; or (c) 500 mg per square meter of body surface in a single dose. In each regimen leucovorin is followed by appropriate doses of fluorouracil. The drug combination is cycled depending on the regimen. To treat megaloblastic anemia caused by congenital enzyme deficiency: 3 to 6 mg to start, then 1 mg per day. To treat folate-deficient megaloblastic anemia: Up to 1 mg of leucovorin daily; duration of treatment depends upon the response of the individual.

ONSET OF EFFECT
From 5 to 20 minutes after injection; 20 to 30 minutes after oral ingestion.

DURATION OF ACTION
From 3 to 6 hours.

DIETARY ADVICE
Leucovorin can be given between meals. The doses must be evenly spaced, day and night.

STORAGE
Store in a tightly sealed container away from heat and direct light.

IF YOU MISS A DOSE
As soon as you remember, check with your doctor to learn if you should take an extra dose. Do not take more medicine without consulting your doctor. Resume your regular dosage schedule as soon as possible.

STOPPING THE DRUG
The decision to stop taking the drug should be made by your doctor.

PROLONGED USE
See your doctor regularly for tests and examinations if you take this medication for a prolonged period.

PRECAUTIONS
Over 60: There is no specific information comparing use of leucovorin in older patients with use in younger persons.

Driving and Hazardous Work: The use of leucovorin should not impair your ability to perform such tasks safely.

Alcohol: Avoid alcohol while taking this medication, since alcohol only further depletes folic acid.

Pregnancy: Neither animal nor human studies on the effects of using leucovorin during pregnancy have been done. Before taking leucovorin, tell your doctor if you are pregnant or plan to become pregnant. It should be used during pregnancy only under the close supervision of a doctor who is experienced in antimetabolite cancer therapy.

Breast Feeding: It is not known whether leucovorin passes into breast milk. It has not been reported to cause problems in nursing infants. Consult your doctor for specific advice.

Infants and Children: In children who suffer from seizure disorders, treatment with leucovorin may increase the frequency of seizures.

Special Concerns: Inform your doctor if you cannot tolerate the oral dose and it causes vomiting. Injection therapy may be warranted.

OVERDOSE
Symptoms: No specific ones have been reported.

What to Do: An overdose of leucovorin is unlikely to be life-threatening. However, if someone takes a much larger dose than prescribed, seek medical assistance right away.

DRUG INTERACTIONS
Consult your doctor for specific advice if you are taking any other prescription or over-the-counter drugs.

FOOD INTERACTIONS
No known food interactions.

DISEASE INTERACTIONS
Caution is advised when taking leucovorin. Consult your doctor if you have kidney disease or vitamin B12 deficiency.

Leuprolide Acetate

BRAND NAMES
Lupron, Lupron Depot, Viadur

- ▶ Drug Class: Synthetic hormone
- ▶ Available in: Injection, implanted capsule
- ▶ Available OTC? No
- ▶ As Generic? No

Side Effects

SERIOUS
In men: Pain in groin or leg, chest pain. In women: Increased hair growth, deepening of voice. In men and women: Rapid or irregular heartbeat. Call your doctor immediately. Implanted capsule— If reactions such as itching and redness around the insertion site do not heal within 2 weeks contact your doctor.

COMMON
Injection— In women: Light, irregular vaginal bleeding, cessation of menstrual periods (amenorrhea), vaginal dryness. In both men and women: Sudden sweating and feelings of warmth (hot flashes). Implanted capsule— Hot flashes, lack of energy, depression, sweating, headache, bruising, and breast enlargement.

LESS COMMON
In men: Bone pain, constipation, decreased testicle size, impotence, loss of appetite, swollen and tender breasts. In women: Burning, itching, or dryness of vagina, decreased interest in sex, breast tenderness, pelvic pain, mood changes. In men and women: Blurred vision, burning or itching at injection or implant site, headache, nausea or vomiting, swollen feet or lower legs, insomnia, weight gain, numbness or tingling of the hands or feet.

PRINCIPAL USES
To ease symptoms of advanced forms of prostate cancer in men (this is the only FDA-approved use for the implanted capsule), and to relieve the pain and discomfort of endometriosis in women. It is also used by children with precocious (early onset) puberty and in certain patients with anemia owing to bleeding from fibroids.

HOW THE DRUG WORKS
In men, leuprolide decreases blood levels of testosterone. This slows the growth of cells in the prostate gland, which may lead to improvement of some of the pain and discomfort of advanced prostate cancer. In women, leuprolide decreases blood levels of estrogen. Reduced blood estrogen leads to shrinking of endometrial tissue (uterine lining) and thus eases the painful cyclical flare-ups of endometriosis. It will suppress menstrual periods and thus help to correct the anemia associated with bleeding from fibroids.

DOSAGE
Injection— Men: 1 mg injected under the skin once a day or 7.5 mg of the Depot form injected into muscle once a month. Women: 3.75 mg injected into muscle once a month for up to 6 months. Children: Consult your pediatrician. Implanted capsule— Men: 1 capsule is implanted under the skin of the upper arm. The implant contains 65 mg of leuprolide that is continuously released for 12 months. After 12 months the implant must be removed. Another implant may be inserted to continue therapy.

ONSET OF EFFECT
Injection— Men: 2 to 4 weeks. Women: 1 to 2 months. Implanted capsule— Unknown.

DURATION OF ACTION
Injection— Men: 4 to 12 weeks. Women: 60 to 90 days. Implanted capsule— 12 months.

DIETARY ADVICE
This drug can be taken without regard to diet.

STORAGE
Keep the liquid form of this medicine refrigerated until the first dose, but do not allow it to freeze. Then store it in a tightly sealed container at room temperature away from heat and direct light. Implanted capsule: Not applicable.

IF YOU MISS A DOSE
If you are taking this medicine every day, take the missed dose as soon as you remember. If you do not remember until the next day, skip the missed dose and resume your regular dosage schedule. Do not double the next dose. Implanted capsule: Not applicable.

STOPPING THE DRUG
The decision to stop taking the drug should be made by your doctor.

PROLONGED USE
Consult your doctor about the need for periodic examinations and laboratory tests if you use leuprolide for a prolonged period.

PRECAUTIONS
Over 60: No special problems are expected.

Driving and Hazardous Work: Do not drive or engage in hazardous work until you determine how the medicine affects you.

Alcohol: No special precautions are necessary.

Pregnancy: Because of a risk of birth defects, leuprolide should not be taken by women who are pregnant or may be pregnant. Call your doctor immediately if you think you are pregnant.

Breast Feeding: Leuprolide may pass into breast milk. It should not be taken when nursing. Consult your doctor for specific advice.

Infants and Children: Leuprolide (injection only) should be given to children only under close medical supervision to treat precocious puberty.

Special Concerns: Use only the syringes in the kit. Other types may not deliver the same dose. When taking leuprolide, women should use nonhormonal contraception (that is, methods other than birth control pills).

OVERDOSE
Symptoms: No specific ones have been reported.

What to Do: An overdose of leuprolide is unlikely to be life-threatening. However, if someone takes a much larger dose than prescribed, seek medical attention immediately.

DRUG INTERACTIONS
Other drugs may interact with leuprolide. Consult your doctor if you are taking any prescription or nonprescription drugs or herbal remedies.

FOOD INTERACTIONS
No known food interactions.

DISEASE INTERACTIONS
Consult your doctor if you experience vaginal bleeding of unknown cause or, in men, difficulty urinating.

Levamisole Hydrochloride

Ergamisol 50 mg
(JANSSEN)

▶ Drug Class: Immunomodulator; antineoplastic (anti-cancer) agent

▶ Available in: Tablets

▶ Available OTC? No

▶ As Generic? No

Side Effects

SERIOUS
Flu-like symptoms (such as fever or chills, body aches, general feeling of discomfort, weakness, and cough), unusual bleeding or bruising, blurred vision, trouble walking, uncontrolled movements of the arms or legs. Although such side effects are rare, they are serious; call your physician immediately if you experience such symptoms.

COMMON
Nausea, vomiting, and diarrhea.

LESS COMMON
Anxiety or nervousness, dizziness, headache, depression, nightmares, pain in joints or muscles, skin rash or itching, insomnia, unusual sleepiness or tiredness, metallic taste, sores in the mouth or on the lips.

PRINCIPAL USES
Levamisole enhances the effectiveness of fluorouracil, a drug used to treat cancer of the colon.

HOW THE DRUG WORKS
It is unknown precisely how levamisole works. It appears that it improves the responsiveness of the immune system, which is suppressed by other chemotherapy agents such as fluorouracil. Therefore it improves the patient's overall ability to fight disease. Unlike many other cancer drugs, levamisole does not directly attack malignant cells.

DOSAGE
50 mg every 8 hours for 3 days, beginning no later than 30 days after surgery. Usual maintenance dose is 50 mg for 3 days every 2 weeks for 1 year.

ONSET OF EFFECT
Unknown.

DURATION OF ACTION
Unknown.

DIETARY ADVICE
Maintain adequate food and fluid intake. Calorie, protein, and vitamin needs increase in patients with cancer. Good nutrition is essential to cope with the demands of chemotherapy.

STORAGE
Store in a tightly sealed container away from heat and direct light.

IF YOU MISS A DOSE
Take it as soon as you remember. If it is near the time for the next dose, skip the missed dose and resume your regular dosage schedule. Do not double the next dose.

STOPPING THE DRUG
The decision to stop taking the drug should be made by your doctor.

PROLONGED USE
You should see your doctor regularly for tests and examinations if you take levamisole for a prolonged period.

PRECAUTIONS
Over 60: Levamisole is not expected to cause different side effects or problems in older persons than it does in younger patients.

Driving and Hazardous Work: Do not drive or engage in hazardous work until you determine how the medicine affects you.

Alcohol: Avoid alcohol completely while taking this medication. When alcohol is consumed with the combination of levamisole and fluorouracil, severe nausea and vomiting may result.

Pregnancy: Levamisole has not been shown to cause birth defects in animals. Human studies have not been done. Consult your doctor for advice if you are pregnant or plan to become pregnant.

Breast Feeding: It is not known whether levamisole passes into breast milk; caution is advised. Consult your doctor for specific advice.

Infants and Children: There is no information comparing the use of levamisole in infants and children with use in older persons.

Special Concerns: If you vomit after taking a dose of levamisole, ask your doctor whether you should take the dose again or wait for the next dose. Avoid contact with persons who have infections. Do not receive any immunizations while you take this medication. Before you have dental work done, tell the dentist that you are taking levamisole. Rinse your mouth after eating and drinking and use a soft toothbrush and an electric razor.

OVERDOSE
Symptoms: Nausea, vomiting, infection, inflammation of the mouth.

What to Do: Call your doctor, emergency medical services (EMS), or the nearest poison control center immediately.

DRUG INTERACTIONS
Consult your doctor for specific advice if you are taking phenytoin or the anticoagulant warfarin. Side effects of levamisole may be more frequent when taken with fluorouracil.

FOOD INTERACTIONS
No known food interactions.

DISEASE INTERACTIONS
Caution is advised when taking levamisole. Consult your doctor if you have any other medical condition.

Levetiracetam

BRAND NAME
Keppra

▶ Drug Class: Anticonvulsant

▶ Available in: Tablets

▶ Available OTC? No

▶ As Generic? No

Side Effects

SERIOUS
Extreme drowsiness, psychotic symptoms. Call your doctor immediately.

COMMON
Drowsiness, fatigue, increased susceptibility to infection, dizziness.

LESS COMMON
Coordination difficulties, agitation, hostility, anxiety, nervousness, depression, hallucinations, attempted suicide, loss of appetite, amnesia, emotional instability, numbness, prickling or tingling sensations, cough, sore throat, runny nose, sinusitis, double vision.

PRINCIPAL USES
Used in combination with one or more other anticonvulsant drugs to control partial seizures (those which begin with an abnormal burst of electrical activity in a small portion of the brain, often resulting in twitching or numbness in a localized part of the body).

HOW THE DRUG WORKS
The precise mechanism of action is unknown.

DOSAGE
To start, 500 mg twice a day. Dosage may be gradually increased by your doctor (1,000 mg a day every 2 weeks) to a maximum of 3,000 mg a day. People with impaired kidney function may require an adjustment in dose.

ONSET OF EFFECT
Within 48 hours.

DURATION OF ACTION
Unknown.

DIETARY ADVICE
Can be taken without regard to meals.

STORAGE
Store in a tightly sealed container away from heat, moisture, and direct light.

IF YOU MISS A DOSE
Take it as soon as you remember. If it is near the time for the next dose, skip the missed dose and resume your regular dosage schedule. Do not double the next dose.

STOPPING THE DRUG
The decision to stop taking the drug should be made by your doctor. Never stop this drug abruptly because this may cause seizures. The dose is typically tapered over a period of weeks.

PROLONGED USE
This drug is often taken for prolonged periods. See your physician for periodic checkups.

PRECAUTIONS
Over 60: Decreased kidney function is more common in older persons. Because levetiracetam is eliminated from the body through the kidney, the risk of side effects is increased. Kidney function should be carefully monitored. A dosage adjustment may be warranted.

Driving and Hazardous Work: This drug may cause drowsiness or dizziness, particularly in the first few weeks it is used. Do not drive or engage in hazardous work until you determine how the medicine affects you.

Alcohol: Avoid alcohol; it may contribute to excessive drowsiness.

Pregnancy: Levetiracetam has caused birth defects in animal studies. Human studies with this drug have not been done, but other anticonvulsants are known to increase the risk of birth defects. However, seizures during pregnancy can also increase the risks to the fetus. Discuss with your doctor the potential risks and benefits of using this drug during pregnancy.

Breast Feeding: Levetiracetam may pass into breast milk; caution is advised. Consult your doctor for specific advice.

Infants and Children: Not recommended for use by children under age 16.

Special Concerns: See your doctor for regular check-ups to detect the onset of any serious side effects. Your doctor may advise you to carry an ID card or bracelet that says you are taking this drug.

OVERDOSE
Symptoms: Few cases of overdose have been reported. In clinical trials, the most common symptom following overdose was drowsiness.

What to Do: If an excessive dose is taken, call your doctor, emergency medical services (EMS), or poison control center immediately.

DRUG INTERACTIONS
No known drug interactions.

FOOD INTERACTIONS
No known food interactions.

DISEASE INTERACTIONS
A lower dose of levetiracetam may be needed in patients with decreased kidney function.

Levobunolol

▶ Drug Class: Antiglaucoma
drug; ophthalmic beta-blocker

▶ Available in: Ophthalmic
solution

▶ Available OTC? No

▶ As Generic? No

Side Effects

SERIOUS
Palpitations, trouble breathing, dizziness, and weakness caused by low blood pressure. Call your doctor right away.

COMMON
Burning, stinging, tearing, and irritation of the eye when medication is taken.

LESS COMMON
Eyebrow pain, itching, decreased night vision, crusted eyelashes, increased sensitivity of eye to light, dry eye.

PRINCIPAL USES
To treat glaucoma.

HOW THE DRUG WORKS
Glaucoma, a sight-threatening disorder, occurs when aqueous humor (fluid inside the eye) cannot drain properly, causing an increase in pressure within the eyeball (intraocular pressure). The increased eye pressure can damage the optic nerve and lead to a gradually progressive loss of vision. Levobunolol decreases the production of aqueous humor and promotes its outflow, thereby reducing intraocular pressure.

DOSAGE
Adults and older children: 1 drop in each affected eye, 1 or 2 times a day. Children: The dose must be determined by your doctor.

ONSET OF EFFECT
Within 60 minutes.

DURATION OF ACTION
Up to 24 hours.

DIETARY ADVICE
No special restrictions.

STORAGE
Store in a tightly sealed container away from heat, moisture, and direct light. Do not allow it to freeze.

IF YOU MISS A DOSE
Apply it as soon as you remember. If it is near the time for the next dose, skip the missed dose and resume your regular dosage schedule.

STOPPING THE DRUG
The decision to stop using the drug should be made by your doctor.

PROLONGED USE
See your doctor regularly for tests and examinations if you take this drug for a prolonged period.

PRECAUTIONS
Over 60: Adverse reactions may be more likely and more severe.

Driving and Hazardous Work: Avoid such activities until you determine how the medication affects your vision.

Alcohol: Consume alcohol in moderation only.

Pregnancy: Levobunolol has not been shown to cause birth defects in animals. Human studies have not been done. Before you take levobunolol, tell your doctor if you are pregnant or plan to become pregnant.

Breast Feeding: Levobunolol may pass into breast milk; caution is advised. Consult your doctor for advice.

Infants and Children: Adverse reactions may be more likely and more severe in young patients.

Special Concerns: To use the eye drops, first wash your hands. Tilt your head back. Gently apply pressure to the inside corner of the eyelid and with the index finger of the same hand, pull downward on the lower eyelid to make a space. Drop the medicine into this space and close your eye. Apply pressure for 1 or 2 minutes while keeping the eye closed without blinking. Then wash your hands again. Make sure the tip of the dropper does not touch your eye, finger, or any other surface. If you are taking the medicine with the compliance cap (C Cap), make sure the number 1 or the correct day of the week appears in the window of the cap before using the eye drops for the first time. After every dose, rotate the bottle until the cap clicks to the position that tells you the next dose. Before you have any kind of surgery, dental treatment, or emergency treatment, tell the person in charge that you are taking levobunolol. This medication may make you more sensitive to sunlight. If this occurs, wear sunglasses or avoid bright light as comfort dictates.

OVERDOSE
Symptoms: Nervousness, chest pain, confusion, hallucinations, coughing, wheezing, drowsiness, dizziness, nausea or vomiting, irregular or pounding heartbeat, insomnia, unusual fatigue.

What to Do: If a large volume enters the eye, flush with water. If someone accidentally ingests the drug, call your doctor, emergency medical services (EMS), or the nearest poison control center immediately.

DRUG INTERACTIONS
It is not recommended to use two ophthalmic beta-blockers at the same time. Special caution is warranted in people taking antidiabetic drugs, since levobunolol may mask symptoms of low blood sugar. Other drugs may interact with levobunolol. Tell your doctor about any other prescription or over-the-counter medication that you take.

FOOD INTERACTIONS
No known food interactions.

DISEASE INTERACTIONS
Consult your doctor if you have asthma, emphysema or other lung disease, heart disease, hyperthyroidism, or diabetes mellitus.

Levocabastine

BRAND NAME
Livostin

▶ Drug Class: Histamine (H1) blocker

▶ Available in: Ophthalmic suspension

▶ Available OTC? No

▶ As Generic? No

Side Effects

SERIOUS
Cough, breathing difficulty, swelling around the eyes, eye pain or discharge, excessive tear production, unusual fatigue, nausea, sore throat, redness or irritation not present prior to treatment, visual disturbances. Such side effects are very rare, but if they occur, stop using the drug and call your doctor immediately.

COMMON
Temporary burning or stinging in the eyes upon application of the drops.

LESS COMMON
Headache, dry eyes, dry mouth, and drowsiness. Call your doctor if such symptoms persist or begin to interfere with daily activities.

PRINCIPAL USES
For temporary symptomatic relief of itching and irritation of the eyes associated with seasonal allergies.

HOW THE DRUG WORKS
Levocabastine blocks the effects of histamine, a naturally occurring substance within the body that causes swelling, itching, sneezing, watery eyes, hives, and other symptoms associated with allergic reactions.

DOSAGE
Instill 1 drop in affected eye(s), 4 times a day, for up to 2 weeks. Shake well before using the drug.

ONSET OF EFFECT
Within 10 to 15 minutes.

DURATION OF ACTION
From 2 to 4 hours.

DIETARY ADVICE
This drug can be used without regard to diet.

STORAGE
Store in a tightly sealed container away from heat, moisture, and direct light. Do not allow it to freeze.

IF YOU MISS A DOSE
Apply it as soon as you remember. If it is near the time for the next dose, skip the missed dose and resume your regular dosage schedule. Do not double the next dose.

STOPPING THE DRUG
Take it as prescribed for the full treatment period, even if you feel better before the scheduled end of therapy.

PROLONGED USE
This medicine is for short-term symptomatic relief only; treatment should not exceed 2 weeks. Check with your doctor if symptoms do not improve, or if your condition becomes worse, after 3 days.

PRECAUTIONS
Over 60: No special problems are expected.

Driving and Hazardous Work: No problems are expected, but it is advisable not to engage in such activities until you determine how this drug affects your vision.

Alcohol: No special precautions are necessary.

Pregnancy: Adequate studies have not been done, although no problems have been reported. Before taking levocabastine, tell your doctor if you are pregnant or plan to become pregnant.

Breast Feeding: Levocabastine passes into breast milk; do not use it when nursing.

Infants and Children: The safety and effectiveness of levocabastine have not been established in children under the age of 12. This drug should not be used by patients in this age group.

Special Concerns: To use the eye drops, first wash your hands. Tilt your head back. Gently apply pressure to the inside corner of the eyelid and with the index finger of the same hand, pull downward on the lower eyelid to make a space. Drop the medicine into this space and close your eye. Apply pressure for 1 or 2 minutes while keeping the eye closed without blinking. Then wash your hands again. Make sure the tip of the dropper does not touch your eye, finger, or any other surface. The manufacturer of this drug recommends that soft contact lenses not be worn while undergoing treatment with levocabastine.

OVERDOSE
Symptoms: No cases of overdose have been reported.

What to Do: An overdose of levocabastine is unlikely to occur. In case of accidental ingestion, call your doctor, emergency medical services (EMS), or the nearest poison control center immediately.

DRUG INTERACTIONS
No drug interactions have been reported. Nonetheless, it is wise to consult your doctor before taking any other prescription or over-the-counter eye medication.

FOOD INTERACTIONS
No food interactions have been reported.

DISEASE INTERACTIONS
No disease interactions have been reported.

Levodopa

Larodopa 100 mg
(ROCHE)

▶ Drug Class: Antiparkinsonism drug

▶ Available in: Tablets, capsules

▶ Available OTC? No

▶ As Generic? Yes

Side Effects

SERIOUS
Irregular heartbeat, heart rhythm abnormalities, low blood pressure, fainting or near fainting, hallucinations.

COMMON
Nausea, confusion.

LESS COMMON
Breathing difficulty.

PRINCIPAL USES
To treat Parkinson's disease and Parkinson-like syndromes. Such syndromes can occur following injury to or infection of the central nervous system, damage to the blood vessels in the brain (for example, after a stroke), or exposure to certain toxins.

HOW THE DRUG WORKS
Levodopa replenishes the supply of dopamine in the brain. Dopamine is a chemical in the central nervous system that plays an essential role in the initiation and smooth control of voluntary muscle movement.

DOSAGE
Adults: To start, 0.5 g per day in 2 or more divided doses. The dose is increased gradually (by 0.5 to 0.75 g per day) over the course of 4 to 7 days, until the desired therapeutic response is achieved. The onset of adverse side effects may preclude the use of higher doses. The maximum beneficial dose is usually 5 to 6 g per day. Children: Smaller doses are used; consult your pediatrician for specific information.

ONSET OF EFFECT
Within 1 to 2 hours.

DURATION OF ACTION
From 4 to 5 hours.

DIETARY ADVICE
Eating food shortly after taking this medication may minimize the chance of stomach upset. Eating food before taking the medicine or at the same time may blunt levodopa's effects.

STORAGE
Store in a tightly sealed container away from heat, moisture, and direct light.

IF YOU MISS A DOSE
Take it as soon as you remember. However, if it is near the time for the next dose, skip the missed dose and resume your regular dosage schedule. Do not double the next dose.

STOPPING THE DRUG
Consult your doctor for the best approach to stopping the drug. The dose should be decreased very gradually. Abruptly stopping the drug can cause an acute (sudden-onset) adverse reaction.

PROLONGED USE
Prolonged use of levodopa can result in a less predictable therapeutic response and bothersome involuntary muscle movements.

PRECAUTIONS
Over 60: Adverse reactions to levodopa may be more likely and more severe in older patients. The dose should be increased very gradually in this age group.

Driving and Hazardous Work: Do not drive or engage in hazardous work until the full dose has been attained and you determine how the drug affects you.

Alcohol: Do not consume alcohol. Alcohol can cause pronounced confusion or delirium in patients taking this medication.

Pregnancy: Adequate human studies have not been done, and the effects of levodopa during pregnancy have not been determined. Pregnant women should therefore avoid taking levodopa.

Breast Feeding: Levodopa passes into breast milk; levodopa should not be used by nursing mothers.

Infants and Children:
Levodopa should be used with caution by infants and children. The dose should be smaller than that for adults and should be determined by your pediatrician.

Special Concerns:
Patients taking levodopa should not eat a high-protein diet, because it can reduce the medication's effectiveness.

OVERDOSE
Symptoms: The symptoms of levodopa overdose are unknown.

What to Do: If you have any reason to suspect an overdose, call your doctor, emergency medical services (EMS), or the nearest poison control center.

DRUG INTERACTIONS
Consult your doctor for specific advice if you are taking any of the following drugs that may interact with levodopa: MAO inhibitor antidepressants (such as phenelzine sulfate or tranylcypromine sulfate) or antihypertensives.

FOOD INTERACTIONS
A high-protein diet can reduce the effectiveness of levodopa. Persons taking levodopa should therefore decrease their protein intake if it is high.

DISEASE INTERACTIONS
Caution is advised when taking levodopa. Consult your doctor if you have any of the following: heart disease or heart rhythm abnormalities, bronchial asthma, glaucoma, malignant melanoma, or changes in mental state.

Levodopa/Carbidopa

Sinemet 200/50 mg
(DUPONT)

Additional photographs

▶ Drug Class: Antiparkinsonism
drug

▶ Available in: Tablets,
sustained-release tablets

▶ Available OTC? No

▶ As Generic? Yes

Side Effects

SERIOUS
Nausea, fatigue, depression, dizziness or lightheadedness when standing or sitting up suddenly (orthostatic hypotension), fainting or near fainting.

COMMON
With long-term use, quirky involuntary muscle movements, an unpredictable therapeutic response.

LESS COMMON
Confusion, delirium; dark saliva, urine, or sweat.

PRINCIPAL USES
To treat Parkinson's disease and Parkinson-like syndromes, which can occur following injury to or infection of the central nervous system, damage to the blood vessels in the brain, or exposure to certain toxins. Levodopa/carbidopa improves or alleviates such symptoms as rigidity, slowness, loss of smoothness of movement, and tremor.

HOW THE DRUG WORKS
Levodopa/carbidopa increases brain levels of dopamine, a chemical that plays an essential role in the smooth movement of muscles.

DOSAGE
Adults: To start, 1 tablet of 100/10 levodopa/carbidopa (containing 100 mg of levodopa and 10 mg of carbidopa), 3 or 4 times a day; or 1 tablet of 100/25 levodopa/carbidopa (containing 100 mg of levodopa and 25 mg of carbidopa), 3 times a day. The dose is gradually increased every 5 to 7 days until the maximum therapeutic benefit is achieved without the onset of serious side effects. The maximum dose is variable, ranging from the equivalent of 4 to 10 tablets (either 100/10 or 100/25 levodopa/carbidopa) per day. Children: Smaller doses can be used; consult your pediatrician.

ONSET OF EFFECT
Within 90 to 120 minutes.

DURATION OF ACTION
From 3 to 4 hours.

DIETARY ADVICE
Eating food shortly after taking the medication may minimize the chance of stomach upset. Eating food before taking the medicine or at the same time may blunt levodopa's effects.

STORAGE
Store in a tightly sealed container away from heat, moisture, and direct light.

IF YOU MISS A DOSE
Take it as soon as you remember, unless the time for your next scheduled dose is within the next 2 hours. If so, skip the missed dose and resume your regular dosage schedule. Do not double the next dose.

STOPPING THE DRUG
Consult your doctor before stopping the drug. The dosage should be decreased very gradually. Abruptly stopping the medication can result in an acute (sudden-onset) adverse reaction.

PROLONGED USE
Prolonged use may result in a less predictable therapeutic response as well as the onset of involuntary muscle movements.

PRECAUTIONS
Over 60: Adverse reactions may be more likely and more severe.

Driving and Hazardous Work: Avoid such activities until you determine how the medicine affects you.

Alcohol: Avoid alcohol while using this medication.

Pregnancy: This combination drug should not be used by pregnant women.

Breast Feeding: Levodopa passes into breast milk. This combination drug should not be used by nursing mothers.

Infants and Children: Levodopa/carbidopa can be used by children, with caution. The appropriate dosage will be determined by your pediatrician. Use of the sustained-release tablets in children under the age of 18 is not recommended.

Special Concerns: Levodopa/carbidopa should be used with special caution if you are also taking other antiparkinsonism drugs. Do not crush or chew the sustained-release tablets. Swallow them whole.

OVERDOSE
Symptoms: Sudden or severe confusion, delirium, hallucinations.

What to Do: Seek emergency medical attention immediately.

DRUG INTERACTIONS
Do not take levodopa/carbidopa if you are taking, or took within the past 14 days, an MAO inhibitor (such as phenelzine sulfate or tranylcypromine sulfate). Consult your doctor for specific advice if you are taking selegiline, tricyclic antidepressants, risperidone, fluphenazine, phenytoin, papaverine, iron salts, metoclopramide, or any antihypertensive drugs.

FOOD INTERACTIONS
The effectiveness of levodopa/carbidopa may be impaired by a high-protein diet. Persons taking the drug should take care to limit their protein intake.

DISEASE INTERACTIONS
You should not take levodopa/carbidopa if you have malignant melanoma, ischemic heart disease, heart rhythm abnormalities, bronchial asthma, narrow-angle glaucoma, or any changes in mental state. Levodopa/carbidopa should be used with caution in people who have kidney, liver, or endocrine disease, a history of heart attack, peptic ulcer, or chronic wide-angle glaucoma.

Levofloxacin

Levaquin 250 mg
(McNeil)

▶ Drug Class: Fluoroquinolone antibiotic

▶ Available in: Tablets, injection

▶ Available OTC? No

▶ As Generic? No

Side Effects

SERIOUS
Serious reactions to levofloxacin are rare and include seizures, mental confusion, hallucinations, agitation, nightmares, depression, shortness of breath, unusual swelling in the face or extremities, and loss of consciousness. Also skin burning, redness, blisters, rash, or itching on exposure to sunlight; increased risk of tendinitis or tendon rupture. Call your doctor immediately.

COMMON
Increased sensitivity to sunlight (and increased risk of sunburn) for days following therapy.

LESS COMMON
Diarrhea, nausea and vomiting, stomach pain and upset, gas, headache, dizziness, restlessness, insomnia, changes in taste perception, drowsiness, itching, dry mouth, unusual body aches or pains.

PRINCIPAL USES
To treat pneumonia, chronic bronchitis, and other infections caused by bacteria.

HOW THE DRUG WORKS
Levofloxacin inhibits the activity of a bacterial enzyme (gyrase) that is necessary for proper DNA formation and replication. This fights infection by preventing bacteria cells from reproducing.

DOSAGE
Adults: 250 to 500 mg once a day for 7 to 14 days. After an initial dose of 250 to 500 mg, patients with kidney problems receive 250 mg every day for 7 to 14 days.

ONSET OF EFFECT
Varies depending on the infection being treated.

DURATION OF ACTION
Unknown.

DIETARY ADVICE
Drink plenty of fluids.

STORAGE
Store in a tightly sealed container away from heat and direct light. Do not allow the injection form to freeze.

IF YOU MISS A DOSE
Take it as soon as you remember. If it is near the time for the next dose, skip the missed dose and resume your regular dosage schedule. Do not double the next dose.

STOPPING THE DRUG
It is very important to take this drug as prescribed for the full treatment period, even if you begin to feel better before the scheduled end of therapy (unless you experience intolerable side effects, including increased sensitivity to sunlight).

PROLONGED USE
See your doctor regularly for tests and examinations if you must take this medicine for a prolonged period.

PRECAUTIONS
Over 60: No special problems are expected.

Driving and Hazardous Work: Do not drive or engage in hazardous work until you determine how the medicine affects you.

Alcohol: It is advisable to abstain from alcohol when fighting an infection.

Pregnancy: In some animal tests, levofloxacin has caused birth defects. Adequate studies in humans have not been done. It should be used during pregnancy only if potential benefits clearly justify the risks. Before you take levofloxacin, tell your doctor if you are pregnant or plan to become pregnant.

Breast Feeding: Levofloxacin passes into breast milk and may cause serious side effects in the nursing infant; use of the drug is discouraged when nursing.

Infants and Children: Levofloxacin is not recommended for use by persons under the age of 18, as it has been shown to interfere with bone development.

Special Concerns: If levofloxacin causes sensitivity to sunlight, stop taking the drug and try to avoid exposure to sunlight for the next 5 days; also wear protective clothing and use a sunblock. Levofloxacin should not be taken by patients whose work makes it impossible to avoid exposure to sunlight. It is important to drink plenty of fluids while taking this drug.

OVERDOSE
Symptoms: No specific ones have been reported.

What to Do: If you have any reason to suspect an overdose, call your doctor, emergency medical services (EMS), or the nearest poison control center.

DRUG INTERACTIONS
Consult your doctor for specific advice if you are taking aminophylline, antacids, didanosine, iron supplements, sucralfate, or zinc salts. Also tell your doctor if you are taking any other prescription or over-the-counter drug.

FOOD INTERACTIONS
No known food interactions.

DISEASE INTERACTIONS
Caution is advised when taking levofloxacin. Consult your doctor if you have any other medical condition. Use of levofloxacin can cause complications in patients with kidney disease, since this organ works to remove the medication from the body.

Levomethadyl Acetate Hydrochloride

BRAND NAME
Orlaam

▶ Drug Class: Narcotic

▶ Available in: Oral solution

▶ Available OTC? No

▶ As Generic? No

Side Effects

SERIOUS
Some serious side effects of levomethadyl are indistinguishable from those of overdose: Confusion; slurred speech; severe drowsiness; small, pinpoint pupils; cold, clammy skin; slow breathing; seizures; unconsciousness. Other serious side effects are depression; enlarged pupils; swelling of fingers, feet, face, and lower legs; skin rash; diarrhea; insomnia; rapid heartbeat; nervousness; runny nose; trembling; stomach cramps; fever. Call your doctor immediately.

COMMON
Abdominal or stomach pains, nausea, and constipation.

LESS COMMON
Back pain, watering eyes, anxiety, blurred vision, flu symptoms, chills, decreased sexual desire, dizziness when getting up, headache, cough, hot flashes, muscle pain, unusual dreams.

PRINCIPAL USES
To prevent or ease withdrawal symptoms during detoxification from illegal narcotics, and to serve as maintenance therapy during narcotic addiction treatment programs.

HOW THE DRUG WORKS
Levomethadyl serves as a substitute for other narcotics that tend to produce more-pronounced effects.

DOSAGE
Addicts who have not begun treatment with methadone: To start, between 20 and 40 mg per day, 3 times a week. Addicts who have been receiving methadone: To start, the dose will be a little higher than the amount of methadone per day, but not more than 120 mg, 3 times a week. The dose will be reduced in detoxification programs, continued as long as needed in maintenance programs. Levomethadyl should not be taken daily because of the risk of overdose.

ONSET OF EFFECT
Levomethadyl may not be fully effective for several days. For this reason methadone may be the first drug used in a detoxification program, since its effect is more immediate; levomethadyl may then be used since, unlike methadone, it does not need to be taken every day.

DURATION OF ACTION
48 to 72 hours.

DIETARY ADVICE
No special restrictions.

STORAGE
Not applicable; dose may be taken only at approved treatment facilities.

IF YOU MISS A DOSE
Not applicable; the dose is administered by a health care professional specializing in addiction treatment.

STOPPING THE DRUG
The decision to stop taking levomethadyl should be made by the addiction treatment specialist.

PROLONGED USE
See your health care professional regularly for tests and examinations.

PRECAUTIONS
Over 60: Studies on older patients have not been conducted.

Driving and Hazardous Work: Do not drive or engage in hazardous work until you determine how the medicine affects you.

Alcohol: Avoid alcohol.

Pregnancy: Using this drug during pregnancy may cause withdrawal symptoms in the newborn baby. Federal law requires pregnancy tests before starting treatment and once-a-month exams during treatment.

Breast Feeding: Levomethadyl may pass into breast milk; caution is advised. Consult your doctor for advice.

Infants and Children: Federal law prohibits use of levomethadyl by persons under 18 years of age.

Special Concerns: Tell any doctor or dentist you see for treatment that you are taking levomethadyl. To prevent constipation, you may be advised to increase the fiber in your diet, drink a lot of fluids, or take laxatives.

OVERDOSE
Symptoms: See Serious Side Effects.

What to Do: Call your doctor, emergency medical services (EMS), or the nearest poison control center immediately.

DRUG INTERACTIONS
Consult your doctor for specific advice if you are taking barbiturates, buprenorphine, butorphanol, carbamazepine, central nervous system depressants, chloramphenicol, cimetidine, corticosteroids, dezocine, diltiazem, disulfiram, divalproex, erythromycin, griseofulvin, isoniazid, oral contraceptives, nalbuphine, naltrexone, pentazocine, phenylbutazone, phenytoin, primidone, quinine, rifampin, ranitidine, tricyclic antidepressants, valproic acid, or verapamil.

FOOD INTERACTIONS
No known food interactions.

DISEASE INTERACTIONS
Consult your doctor if you have any of the following: chronic lung disease, brain disease, head injury, colitis, Crohn's disease, enlarged prostate, gallbladder disease, heart disease, high blood pressure, kidney or liver disease, or an underactive thyroid.

Levonorgestrel Implants

▶ Drug Class: Progestin (hormone)

▶ Available in: Implanted capsule

▶ Available OTC? No

▶ As Generic? No

Side Effects

SERIOUS
Changes in or cessation of menstrual bleeding, unexpected or increased flow of breast milk, mental depression, skin rash, loss of or change in speech, impaired coordination or vision, severe and sudden shortness of breath. Call your doctor immediately.

COMMON
Stomach pain, swelling of face, ankles, or feet, mild headache, mood changes, unusual fatigue, weight gain, pain or irritation at site of implant.

LESS COMMON
Acne, breast pain or tenderness, hot flashes, insomnia, loss of sexual desire, loss or gain of scalp hair or body hair, brown spots on skin.

PRINCIPAL USES
As a birth control method.

HOW THE DRUG WORKS
The implant slowly releases levonorgestrel, a synthetic hormone, into the bloodstream. It prevents a woman's egg from developing fully and causes changes in the uterine lining that make it difficult for sperm to reach the egg. It may prevent ovulation in some patients.

DOSAGE
6 capsules are implanted under the skin of the upper arm. The capsules are placed in a fanlike position, 15 degrees apart. They are removed after 5 years.

ONSET OF EFFECT
Within 24 hours if implanted within 7 days of the menstrual period.

DURATION OF ACTION
Up to 5 years.

DIETARY ADVICE
No special restrictions.

STORAGE
Not applicable.

IF YOU MISS A DOSE
Not applicable; the drug is delivered continuously from the implant under the skin.

STOPPING THE DRUG
The decision to stop using the implant can be made whenever you choose, but the implants should be removed by your doctor.

PROLONGED USE
See your doctor at least once a year for periodic examinations and lab tests.

PRECAUTIONS
Over 60: Not normally prescribed for postmenopausal women.

Driving and Hazardous Work: No special precautions are necessary.

Alcohol: No special precautions are necessary.

Pregnancy: Extensive studies have shown that no special risks to mother or child are associated with pregnancies occurring prior to or shortly after implantation of levonorgestrel capsules. Nonetheless, it is advisable to have the implants removed if pregnancy occurs.

Breast Feeding: Levonorgestrel passes into breast milk but has not been shown to cause problems. It can be used by nursing mothers who desire contraception.

Infants and Children: Levonorgestrel implants have not been shown to cause problems in teenagers. However, birth control methods that protect against sexually transmitted diseases (for example, condoms) are preferred for those in this age group.

Special Concerns: Do not have this implant inserted until you are sure you are not pregnant. Call your doctor immediately if one of the capsules falls out before the skin heals over the implant. No contraceptive method is perfect: If you suspect a pregnancy, you should call your doctor immediately. If you have any laboratory test, tell the health professional that you are using these contraceptives. Cigarette smoking or alcohol abuse can increase the risk of osteoporosis and blood clot formation. Implants should be removed if you develop active thrombophlebitis (pain caused by a blot clot lodged in a blood vessel), thromboembolic disease, or jaundice (yellowish tinge to the eyes or skin), or if you will be immobilized for a significant period of time because of illness or some other factor. If you have sudden unexplained vision problems, including changes in tolerance for contact lenses, you should be evaluated by an ophthalmologist.

OVERDOSE
Symptoms: Not applicable.

What to Do: Emergency instructions not applicable.

DRUG INTERACTIONS
Consult your doctor for specific advice if you are taking aminoglutethimide, carbamazepine, phenytoin, rifabutin, or rifampin.

FOOD INTERACTIONS
No known food interactions.

DISEASE INTERACTIONS
Caution is advised when using this contraceptive. Consult your doctor if you have any of the following: asthma, epilepsy, heart or circulation problems, kidney disease, liver disease, migraine headaches, breast disease, bleeding disorders, central nervous system disorders (including depression), diabetes, or high blood cholesterol.

Levothyroxine Sodium

Levoxyl 0.1 mg
(DANIELS)

836

Additional photographs

▶ Drug Class: Hypothyroid
agent

▶ Available in: Tablets, injection

▶ Available OTC? No

▶ As Generic? Yes

Side Effects

SERIOUS
In rare instances levothyroxine may cause severe
headaches, skin rash,
hives, rapid or irregular
heartbeat, chest pain, or
shortness of breath.
These symptoms may
signal an overdose or an
allergic reaction. Seek
emergency medical assis-
tance immediately.

COMMON
No common side effects
are associated with the
use of levothyroxine.

LESS COMMON
Leg cramps, diarrhea,
changes in menstrual
cycle, changes in
appetite, sweating,
sensitivity to heat, shaking of the hands, fever,
headache, insomnia, irri-
tability, weight loss, vomiting, nervousness. These
symptoms may indicate
your dose needs adjust-
ment by your doctor.

PRINCIPAL USES
To treat patients with an
underactive thyroid gland,
goiter (enlarged thyroid
gland), and benign and
malignant (noncancerous
and cancerous) thyroid
nodules.

HOW THE DRUG WORKS
Levothyroxine acts in the
body as a substitute for
natural thyroid hormone.

DOSAGE
Tablets— Adults and
teenagers: 0.0016 mg per
2.2 lbs (1 kg) a day. Children less than 6 months
old: 0.025 to 0.05 mg once a
day. Children 6 to 12
months old: 0.05 to 0.075
mg once a day. Children
ages 1 to 5: 0.075 to 0.1 mg
once a day. Children ages 6
to 12: 0.1 to 0.15 mg a day.
Injection— Adults and
teenagers: 0.05 to 0.1 mg
into a vein or muscle once a
day. Children less than 6
months old: 0.019 to 0.038
mg once a day. Children 6
to 12 months old: 0.038 to
0.056 mg once a day. Children ages 1 to 5: 0.056 to
0.075 mg once a day. Children ages 6 to 10: 0.075 to
0.113 mg once a day. Children ages 10 to 12: 0.113
to 0.15 mg once a day.

ONSET OF EFFECT
24 hours.

DURATION OF ACTION
1 to 3 weeks.

DIETARY ADVICE
Take it before breakfast on
an empty stomach.

STORAGE
Store in a tightly sealed container away from heat, moisture, and direct light.

IF YOU MISS A DOSE
If you miss your dose on
one day, you may double
the dose on the next day. If

you miss two or more doses
in a row, call your doctor.

STOPPING THE DRUG
The decision to stop taking
the drug should be made in
consultation with your
physician.

PROLONGED USE
If you must take this drug,
it is very likely that lifelong
therapy will be necessary.
See your doctor regularly
for routine tests and examinations to evaluate your
condition.

PRECAUTIONS
Over 60: Older patients
may require modification
of dosage size.

**Driving and Hazardous
Work:** Do not drive or
engage in hazardous work
until you determine how the
medicine affects you.

Alcohol: Avoid alcohol.

Pregnancy: Using the recommended dose of levothy-
roxine has not been shown
to cause birth defects.
The dose may need to be
changed during pregnancy.
Consult your doctor for
specific advice.

Breast Feeding: Using the
recommended dose of
levothyroxine has not been
shown to cause problems
while nursing. Consult your
doctor for specific advice.

Infants and Children:
No special problems are
expected.

Special Concerns: You
should wear a medical
bracelet or carry an identification card saying that you
are taking this medication.

OVERDOSE
Symptoms: Rapid heartbeat, chest pain, shortness
of breath.

What to Do: Call your
doctor, emergency medical
services (EMS), or the
nearest poison control center immediately.

DRUG INTERACTIONS
Consult your doctor for
advice if you are taking anticoagulants, cholestyramine,
colestipol, amphetamines,
appetite suppressants,
asthma medication, or
cold, sinus, or allergy
medications.

FOOD INTERACTIONS
No known food interactions.

DISEASE INTERACTIONS
Caution is advised when
taking levothyroxine. Consult your doctor if you have
any of the following: diabetes mellitus, diabetes
insipidus, myxedema, an
overactive thyroid gland,
atherosclerosis (so-called
hardening of the arteries),
heart disease, high blood
pressure, an underactive
adrenal gland, or an underactive pituitary gland.

Lidocaine Hydrochloride Topical

BRAND NAMES
Dermaflex, Lidoderm, Xylocaine

▶ Drug Class: Topical analgesic

▶ Available in: Gel, ointment, aerosol spray, transdermal patch

▶ Available OTC? No

▶ As Generic? Yes

Side Effects

SERIOUS
Hives, itching, rash, swelling of face, mouth, lips, throat, or tongue; burning, swelling, worsening redness, or pain at site of application. These may be signs of a potentially serious allergic reaction, which is rare.

COMMON
There are no significant common side effects of topical lidocaine when used in recommended amounts.

LESS COMMON
Mild redness, blanching (whitening), or swelling of skin at application sites. If irritation or a burning sensation occurs during application of the transdermal patch, remove the patch and do not reapply until the irritation recedes.

PRINCIPAL USES
For topical therapy of certain skin conditions associated with itching or pain. Some such conditions are minor burns, including sunburn; insect stings and bites; inflammatory skin rashes associated with intense itching, like those caused by poison ivy, poison oak, or poison sumac; and minor cuts and scratches. The transdermal patch is used to relieve pain associated with post-herpetic neuralgia. Topical lidocaine is not meant to be used to relieve the pain of severe injuries, nor should it be prescribed for large or actively bleeding wounds.

HOW THE DRUG WORKS
Lidocaine interferes with the ability of certain nerves to conduct electrical signals, which blocks the transmission of nerve impulses that carry pain messages.

DOSAGE
Gel, ointment, and spray—Adults: Apply to affected area 3 to 4 times a day as needed. Children: Consult a pediatrician for advice. Transdermal patch—Adults: Apply a patch to intact skin to cover the most painful area. Up to 3 patches may be applied simultaneously, for no more than 12 hours at a time per 24-hour period.

ONSET OF EFFECT
Within minutes.

DURATION OF ACTION
Gel, ointment, and spray: About 45 minutes. Transdermal patch: Up to 12 hours.

DIETARY ADVICE
Maintain your usual food and fluid intake. Increase fluids if you have a fever or diarrhea, in hot weather, or during exercise.

STORAGE
Store in a tightly sealed container away from heat and direct light. Keep away from moisture and extremes in temperature.

IF YOU MISS A DOSE
Apply it as soon as you remember. If it is near the time for the next dose, skip the missed dose and resume your regular dosage schedule. Do not double the next dose or apply an excessively thick film of topical lidocaine to compensate for a missed application.

STOPPING THE DRUG
Apply it as prescribed for the full treatment period. However, you may stop using the drug if you are feeling better before the scheduled end of the therapy.

PROLONGED USE
Therapy with this medication is generally finished within several days. Prolonged use may increase the risk of side effects.

PRECAUTIONS
Over 60: Adverse reactions may be more likely and more severe.

Driving and Hazardous Work: No special warnings.

Alcohol: No special precautions are necessary.

Pregnancy: Lidocaine may be used during pregnancy, but first consult your physician for advice.

Breast Feeding: Lidocaine may pass into breast milk; caution is advised. Consult your doctor for advice.

Infants and Children: Not recommended for use by children under age 2. The transdermal patch is not recommended for children under the age of 18.

Special Concerns: Lidocaine has serious side effects if it is absorbed in large amounts into the blood. Therefore, do not apply excessive amounts of gel or ointment to the affected skin or wear a patch longer than 12 hours. Use only enough medication to make a thin film. Above all, never apply this medication to open wounds, deep cuts, or bleeding or ulcerated skin. Dispose of the patch to prevent access by children or pets because a significant amount of lidocaine remains in the patch following use.

OVERDOSE
Symptoms: Dizziness, slow or irregular heartbeat, confusion, seizures, shivering, unusual restlessness or agitation, hallucinations, difficulty breathing, bluish color to skin, lips, or fingertips.

What to Do: Call your doctor, emergency medical services (EMS), or the nearest poison control center immediately.

DRUG INTERACTIONS
The following drugs may interact with topical lidocaine, especially if excessive amounts of lidocaine are applied to the skin: medications to control heart rhythms, such as mexiletine or tocainide; beta-blockers; and cimetidine.

FOOD INTERACTIONS
No known food interactions.

DISEASE INTERACTIONS
Caution is advised when taking lidocaine. Consult your doctor if you have any of the following: skin infection at or close to the application site; large sores, blisters, ulcerations, or broken skin at the application site; or severe injury at the application site.

Lindane

BRAND NAMES
Bio-Well, G-Well, GBH, Kildane, Kwell, Kwildane, Scabene, Thionex

▶ Drug Class: Insecticide

▶ Available in: Cream, lotion, shampoo.

▶ Available OTC? No

▶ As Generic? Yes

Side Effects

SERIOUS
Seizures; dizziness, clumsiness, or unsteady gait; rapid heartbeat; muscle cramps; nervousness, restlessness, or irritability; vomiting. Call your doctor immediately.

COMMON
There are no common side effects associated with lindane. However, when you stop using lindane, itching may occur and persist for 1 or more weeks; notify your doctor if this continues for more than a few weeks or interferes with daily activity.

LESS COMMON
Skin rash; redness or skin irritation that was not present prior to therapy.

PRINCIPAL USES
Lindane cream and lotion are used to treat scabies infestation. The shampoo form is used to treat lice infestation.

HOW THE DRUG WORKS
Lindane is absorbed directly into the bodies of scabies and lice, where it overstimulates nerve activity, ultimately causing convulsions and death of the insect.

DOSAGE
Cream and lotion: Wash, rinse, and dry your skin thoroughly before applying. Apply enough lindane to cover the entire surface of your body from the neck down, including the soles of the feet. Rub in well. Leave it on for no more than 8 hours, then remove it by washing thoroughly. Shampoo: Rinse and dry your hair and scalp. Apply enough lindane to thoroughly wet the scalp and affected areas. Allow it to remain in place for 4 minutes, then lather. Rinse thoroughly and dry with a clean towel. Then use a fine-tooth comb to remove nits. Treatment may be repeated after 7 days if necessary.

ONSET OF EFFECT
Unknown.

DURATION OF ACTION
Unknown.

DIETARY ADVICE
Lindane can be used without regard to diet. After applying the medication, be sure to wash your hands thoroughly before eating.

STORAGE
Store in a tightly sealed container away from heat and direct light.

IF YOU MISS A DOSE
If you require a second dose of the shampoo (usually applied 7 days after the first dose) and forget it, administer it as soon as you remember.

STOPPING THE DRUG
In most cases lindane is needed only once; a second application may be necessary if living nits are found after initial treatment.

PROLONGED USE
Not applicable, since lindane is generally used only once or twice.

PRECAUTIONS
Over 60: Adverse reactions may be more likely in older patients.

Driving and Hazardous Work: Do not drive or engage in hazardous work until you determine how the medicine affects you.

Alcohol: No special precautions are necessary.

Pregnancy: Lindane is absorbed through the skin and could reach the fetus. Before you use lindane, tell your doctor if you are currently pregnant or plan to become pregnant. Do not use lindane more than twice during pregnancy.

Breast Feeding: Lindane passes into breast milk; caution is advised. You should not breast feed for 2 days after using lindane. Consult your doctor for advice.

Infants and Children: Adverse reactions may be more likely and more severe in infants and children. Do not use lindane on premature infants.

Special Concerns: Lindane is a poison that can depress the activity of the central nervous system (brain and spinal cord). Keep it away from the eyes and mouth. It may be fatal if swallowed. If you accidentally get some lindane in your eyes, wash them thoroughly with water and call your doctor. Do not use lindane on open wounds, such as cuts and sores. When applying lindane to another person, wear disposable plastic or rubber gloves, especially if you are breast feeding or pregnant. Do not keep lindane in your home any longer than needed. Be sure that any discarded lindane is out of the reach of children and pets.

OVERDOSE
Symptoms: Seizures, dizziness, vomiting.

What to Do: Call your doctor, emergency medical services (EMS), or the nearest poison control center immediately.

DRUG INTERACTIONS
Consult your doctor for specific advice if you are taking any prescription or over-the-counter medication.

FOOD INTERACTIONS
No known food interactions.

DISEASE INTERACTIONS
Caution is advised when using lindane. Consult your doctor if you have a seizure disorder, a skin rash, or any raw and broken skin.

Linezolid

▶ Drug Class: Oxazolidinone antibiotic

▶ Available in: Injection, tablets, oral suspension

▶ Available OTC? No

▶ As Generic? No

Side Effects

SERIOUS
Serious side effects are rare, but may include: thrombocytopenia (reduced blood platelet numbers, resulting in uncontrolled bleeding) and pseudomembranous colitis. Consult your doctor immediately.

COMMON
Diarrhea, headache, nausea.

LESS COMMON
Insomnia, vomiting, constipation, dizziness.

PRINCIPAL USES
To treat certain hospital- or community-acquired pneumonias and some bacterial infections of the skin and bloodstream, including vancomycin-resistant *Enterococcus faecium* infections and *Staphylococcus aureus*.

HOW THE DRUG WORKS
Linezolid inhibits the growth of bacteria by interfering with the process of translating DNA messages into proteins. Because this drug works differently from other antibiotics, the development of cross-resistance between linezolid and other classes of antibiotics is unlikely.

DOSAGE
For vancomycin-resistant *E. faecium* infections: 600 mg every 12 hours for 14 to 28 days. For pneumonia and complicated skin infections: 600 mg every 12 hours for 10 to 14 days. For uncomplicated skin infections: 400 mg every 12 hours for 10 to 14 days.

ONSET OF EFFECT
Unknown.

DURATION OF ACTION
Unknown.

DIETARY ADVICE
Linezolid may be taken with or without food.

STORAGE
Injection: Not applicable; injections are administered only at a health care facility. Tablets and oral solution: Store in a tightly sealed container away from heat, moisture, and direct light.

IF YOU MISS A DOSE
Take it as soon as you remember. If it is near the time for the next dose, skip the missed dose and resume your regular dosage schedule. Do not double the next dose.

STOPPING THE DRUG
Take it as prescribed for the full treatment period, even if your symptoms improve before the scheduled end of therapy.

PROLONGED USE
Prolonged use of any antibiotic increases the risk of superinfection (a more severe and drug-resistant infection); caution is advised. Use is generally limited to 10 to 28 days. People who are at increased risk for bleeding disorders or have low platelets should have their blood platelet counts monitored by their doctor while taking linezolid.

PRECAUTIONS
Over 60: No special problems are expected.

Driving and Hazardous Work: Avoid such activities until you determine how the medicine affects you.

Alcohol: It is advisable to abstain from alcohol when treating a serious infection.

Pregnancy: Adequate human studies have not been done. Before taking linezolid, discuss with your doctor the relative risks and benefits of using this drug while pregnant.

Breast Feeding: Linezolid may pass into breast milk; caution is advised.

Infants and Children: Safety and effectiveness have not been established for children under age 18.

Special Concerns: The oral suspension is supplied in powder form. Tap the bottle gently to loosen the powder. Add a total of 123 milliliters (mL) distilled water in two portions. After adding the first half, shake the bottle well to wet all of the powder. Add the second portion of water and shake vigorously to mix the suspension. After constitution, each 5 mL of suspension contains 100 mg linezolid. Before using, gently mix by inverting the bottle 3 to 5 times. Do not shake. Store at room temperature and use the suspension within 21 days of reconstitution.

OVERDOSE
Symptoms: No overdoses have been reported. Symptoms may include lethargy, impaired coordination, vomiting, and tremor.

What to Do: If you suspect an overdose or if someone takes a much larger dose than prescribed, seek emergency medical attention (EMS) immediately.

DRUG INTERACTIONS
Consult your doctor for specific advice if you are taking an MAO inhibitor (such as phenelzine or tranylcypromine), pseudoephedrine, dopamine, epinephrine, or SSRI antidepressants.

FOOD INTERACTIONS
Avoid tyramine-rich foods, which include aged cheeses, avocados, banana skins, bean curd, bologna and other processed lunch meats, chicken livers, chocolate, figs, canned or dried fish, pickled herring, meat extracts, pepperoni, raisins, raspberries, soy sauce, unpasteurized beer, Chianti, sherry, vermouth, and red wines in general.

DISEASE INTERACTIONS
Consult your doctor if you have a history of high blood pressure, hyperthyroidism, pheochromocytoma, carcinoid syndrome, thrombocytopenia or other bleeding disorders, diarrhea, or decreased kidney function.

Liothyronine Sodium

BRAND NAMES
Cytomel, Triostat

Cytomel 25 mcg
(SMITHKLINE BEECHAM)

▶ Drug Class: Thyroid hormone

▶ Available in: Tablets

▶ Available OTC? No

▶ As Generic? Yes

Side Effects

SERIOUS
Severe headache in children; skin rash or hives. Call your physician immediately.

COMMON
Changes in appetite, changes in menstrual period, headache, hand tremors, increased sensitivity to heat, irritability, leg cramps, nervousness, sweating, insomnia, vomiting, weight loss, clumsiness, coldness, constipation, dry skin, muscle aches, weakness, weight gain.

LESS COMMON
Diarrhea or other forms of gastrointestinal upset.

PRINCIPAL USES
Liothyronine is prescribed when the thyroid gland does not naturally produce enough thyroid hormone.

HOW THE DRUG WORKS
Liothyronine is a synthetic form of thyroid hormone. It functions in the same manner as (and so serves as a substitute for) the natural hormone when the body does not produce enough on its own.

DOSAGE
25 micrograms (mcg) per day to start. It can be increased to 50 mcg per day, taken in 2 or more daily doses.

ONSET OF EFFECT
Within 48 to 72 hours.

DURATION OF ACTION
Up to 72 hours after the drug is discontinued.

DIETARY ADVICE
Best if taken before breakfast, to minimize risk of insomnia.

STORAGE
Store in a tightly sealed container away from heat and direct light.

IF YOU MISS A DOSE
Take it as soon as you remember. If it is near the time for the next dose, skip the missed dose and resume your regular dosage schedule. Do not double the next dose.

STOPPING THE DRUG
The decision to stop taking the drug should be made by your doctor.

PROLONGED USE
No special problems are expected.

PRECAUTIONS
Over 60: A different dose may be needed for older patients. Consult your doctor about the proper dose.

Driving and Hazardous Work: The use of liothyronine should not impair your ability to perform such tasks safely.

Alcohol: Avoid alcohol.

Pregnancy: Use of proper amounts of liothyronine during pregnancy has not been shown to cause problems. Your doctor may want you to change the dose while you are pregnant. Regular visits to the doctor during pregnancy are advised.

Breast Feeding: Use of proper amounts of liothyronine in nursing women has not been shown to cause problems in their babies.

Infants and Children: The dose for infants and children must be carefully adjusted by the doctor.

Special Concerns: Before undergoing any kind of medical or dental procedure, be sure to tell the doctor or dentist in charge that you are taking liothyronine.

OVERDOSE
Symptoms: Headache, irritability, nervousness, sweating, rapid heartbeat, fever, palpitations or other heartbeat irregularities, increased bowel movements, menstrual irregularities, vomiting, seizures.

What to Do: An overdose of liothyronine is unlikely to be life-threatening. However, if someone takes a much larger dose than prescribed, call your doctor, emergency medical services (EMS), or nearest poison control center immediately.

DRUG INTERACTIONS
Consult your doctor for specific advice if you are taking amphetamines, anticoagulants, appetite suppressants, cholestyramine, colestipol, medicine for asthma or other breathing problems, or medicine for colds, sinus problems or hay fever.

FOOD INTERACTIONS
No known food interactions.

DISEASE INTERACTIONS
Caution is advised when taking liothyronine. Consult your doctor if you have any of the following: diabetes mellitus, hardening of the arteries, heart disease, high blood pressure, history of overactive thyroid, or underactive adrenal gland, underactive pituitary gland. If you have certain kinds of heart disease, this medicine may cause chest pains or shortness of breath during exertion. If these symptoms occur, consult your doctor.

Lisinopril

Prinivil 5 mg
(MERCK)

Additional photographs

▶ Drug Class: Angiotensin-converting enzyme (ACE) inhibitor

▶ Available in: Tablets

▶ Available OTC? No

▶ As Generic? Yes

Side Effects

SERIOUS
Fever and chills, sore throat and hoarseness, sudden difficulty breathing or swallowing, swelling of the face, mouth, or extremities, impaired kidney function (ankle swelling, decreased urination), confusion, yellow discoloration of the eyes or skin (indicating liver disorder), intense itching, chest pain or palpitations, abdominal pain. Serious side effects are very rare; contact your doctor immediately.

COMMON
Dry, persistent cough.

LESS COMMON
Dizziness or fainting, skin rash, numbness or tingling in the hands, feet, or lips, unusual fatigue or muscle weakness, nausea, drowsiness, loss of taste, headache.

PRINCIPAL USES
To control high blood pressure (hypertension). Also used to treat congestive heart failure (CHF) and left ventricular dysfunction (damage to the primary pumping chamber of the heart), and to minimize further kidney damage in diabetic patients with mild kidney disease.

HOW THE DRUG WORKS
Angiotensin-converting enzyme (ACE) inhibitors block an enzyme that produces angiotensin, a naturally occurring substance that causes blood vessels to constrict and stimulates production of the adrenal hormone, aldosterone, which promotes sodium retention in the body. As a result, ACE inhibitors relax blood vessels (causing them to widen) and reduces sodium retention, which lowers blood pressure and so decreases the workload of the heart.

DOSAGE
For high blood pressure: 5 to 40 mg once a day. For congestive heart failure: 2.5 to 20 mg once a day.

ONSET OF EFFECT
Within 1 hour.

DURATION OF ACTION
24 hours.

DIETARY ADVICE
Take lisinopril on an empty stomach, about 1 hour before mealtime. Follow your doctor's dietary advice (such as low-salt or low-cholesterol restrictions) to improve control over high blood pressure and heart disease. Avoid high-potassium foods like bananas and citrus fruits and juices, unless you are also taking medications, such as diuretics, that lower potassium levels.

STORAGE
Store in a tightly sealed container away from heat and direct light.

IF YOU MISS A DOSE
Take it as soon as you remember. If it is near the time for the next dose, skip the missed dose and resume your regular dosage schedule. Do not double the next dose.

STOPPING THE DRUG
Do not stop taking this drug abruptly, as this may cause potentially serious health problems. Dosage should be reduced gradually, according to your doctor's instructions.

PROLONGED USE
Lifelong therapy with lisinopril may be necessary. See your doctor regularly for examinations and tests if you must take this medicine for a prolonged period.

PRECAUTIONS
Over 60: No unusual problems are expected in older patients.

Driving and Hazardous Work: Do not drive or engage in hazardous work until you determine how the medicine affects you.

Alcohol: Consume alcohol only in moderation since it may increase the effect of the drug and cause an excessive drop in blood pressure. Consult your doctor for advice.

Pregnancy: Use of lisinopril during the last 6 months of pregnancy may cause severe defects, even death, in the fetus. The drug should be discontinued if you are pregnant or plan to become pregnant.

Breast Feeding: Lisinopril may pass into breast milk;

caution is advised. Consult your doctor for advice.

Infants and Children: Children may be especially sensitive to the effects of lisinopril. Benefits must be weighed against potential risks; consult your pediatrician for advice.

OVERDOSE
Symptoms: Dizziness, confusion, faintness.

What to Do: Call your doctor, emergency medical services (EMS), or the nearest poison control center immediately.

DRUG INTERACTIONS
Consult your doctor if you are taking diuretics (especially potassium-sparing diuretics), potassium supplements or drugs containing potassium (check ingredient labels), lithium, anticoagulants (such as warfarin), indomethacin or other anti-inflammatory drugs, or any over-the-counter medications (especially cold remedies and diet pills).

FOOD INTERACTIONS
Avoid low-salt milk and salt substitutes. Many of these products contain potassium.

DISEASE INTERACTIONS
Consult your doctor if you have systemic lupus erythematosus (SLE) or if you have had a prior allergic reaction to ACE inhibitors. Lisinopril should be used with caution by patients with severe kidney disease or renal artery stenosis (narrowing of one or both of the arteries that supply blood to the kidneys).

▶ Drug Class: Angiotensin-converting enzyme (ACE) inhibitor/diuretic

▶ Available in: Tablets

▶ Available OTC? No

▶ As Generic? Yes

Side Effects

SERIOUS
Fever and chills, sore throat and hoarseness, sudden difficulty breathing or swallowing, swelling of the face, mouth, or extremities, impaired kidney function (ankle swelling, decreased urination), confusion, yellow discoloration of the eyes or skin (indicating liver disorder), intense itching, chest pain or heartbeat irregularities, abdominal pain. Serious side effects are very rare; contact your doctor immediately.

COMMON
Dry, persistent cough.

LESS COMMON
Dizziness or fainting, skin rash, numbness or tingling in the hands, feet, or lips, change in color of the hands from white to blue to red (Raynaud's phenomenon) in cold weather, unusual fatigue or muscle weakness, nausea, drowsiness, loss of taste, headache, unusual dreams.

PRINCIPAL USES
To treat high blood pressure (hypertension). Used in patients for whom both lisinopril and hydrochlorothiazide have been prescribed.

HOW THE DRUG WORKS
Angiotensin-converting enzyme (ACE) inhibitors such as lisinopril block an enzyme that produces angiotensin, a naturally occurring substance that causes blood vessels to constrict and stimulates production of the adrenal hormone, aldosterone, which promotes sodium retention in the body. As a result, ACE inhibitors relax blood vessels (causing them to widen) and reduces sodium retention, which lowers blood pressure and so decreases the workload of the heart. Hydrochlorothiazide (HCTZ), a diuretic, increases sodium and water in the urine output. By reducing the overall fluid volume in the body, diuretics reduce blood volume and so reduce blood pressure.

DOSAGE
This combination medication comes in three strengths: lisinopril/hydrochlorothiazide 10/12.5, 20/12.5, and 20/25. The dose ranges from 10 to 40 mg of lisinopril and 12.5 to 50 mg of hydrochlorothiazide per day. 1 or 2 tablets are taken once a day in the morning after breakfast.

ONSET OF EFFECT
Within 1 hour.

DURATION OF ACTION
Unknown.

DIETARY ADVICE
Follow your doctor's dietary advice (such as low-salt or low-cholesterol restrictions) to improve control over high blood pressure and heart disease.

STORAGE
Store in a tightly sealed container away from heat, moisture, and direct light.

IF YOU MISS A DOSE
Take it as soon as you remember. If it is near the time for the next dose, skip the missed dose and resume your regular dosage schedule. Do not double the next dose.

STOPPING THE DRUG
Discontinuing this drug abruptly may cause potentially serious problems. The dosage should be reduced gradually, according to your doctor's instructions.

PROLONGED USE
See your doctor regularly for evaluation if you must take this medicine for a prolonged period. Lifelong therapy may be necessary.

PRECAUTIONS
Over 60: Adverse reactions may be more likely and more severe.

Driving and Hazardous Work: Do not drive or engage in hazardous work until you determine how the medicine affects you.

Alcohol: Consume alcohol only in moderation since it may increase the effect of the drug and cause an excessive drop in blood pressure. Consult your doctor for advice.

Pregnancy: Before taking this medication, tell your doctor if you are pregnant or plan to become pregnant. Use of this drug during the last 6 months of pregnancy may cause severe defects, even death, in the fetus.

Breast Feeding: Lisinopril may pass into breast milk; caution is advised. Consult your doctor for advice.

Infants and Children: Children may be especially sensitive to the effects of lisinopril. Consult your pediatrician about the relative risks and benefits.

OVERDOSE
Symptoms: Overdose has not been reported; symptoms might include dizziness, faintness, or confusion.

What to Do: While overdose is unlikely, call your doctor, emergency medical services (EMS), or the nearest poison control center immediately if you suspect that someone has taken a much larger dose than prescribed.

DRUG INTERACTIONS
Consult your doctor for specific advice if you are taking cholestyramine, colestipol, digitalis drugs, lithium, potassium-containing medicines or supplements, or any over-the-counter drug (especially cold remedies and diet pills).

FOOD INTERACTIONS
Avoid low-salt milk and salt substitutes. Many of these products contain potassium.

DISEASE INTERACTIONS
Consult your doctor if you have systemic lupus erythematosus or if you have had a prior allergic reaction to ACE inhibitors. This medication should be used with caution by patients with severe kidney disease or renal artery stenosis (narrowing of one or both of the arteries that supply blood to the kidneys).

Lithium

Generic 300 mg
(ROXANE)

▶ Drug Class: Antimanic agent

▶ Available in: Capsules, syrup,
tablets, extended-release
tablets

▶ Available OTC? No

▶ As Generic? Yes

Side Effects

SERIOUS
Sedation, pronounced
muscle weakness, confu-
sion or disorientation,
muscle twitching, vomit-
ing, increased urination,
slow heartbeat, fatigue,
weight gain, dizziness,
cold arms and legs, dry
and rough skin, hoarse-
ness, sensitivity to cold,
swollen feet or legs,
swollen neck. Call your
physician immediately.

COMMON
Increased thirst,
increased urination, nau-
sea, loss of appetite, diarrhea, a slight tremor in
the hands, fatigue, unex-
pected weight gain,
metallic taste in mouth.

LESS COMMON
Skin rash, acne, hair loss.

PRINCIPAL USES
To treat the manic phase
of bipolar disorder (also
known as manic-depression)
and to enhance the effect
of other antidepressant
medications in patients
with recurrent depression.

HOW THE DRUG WORKS
The exact mechanism of
action of lithium is
unknown.

DOSAGE
The dose is determined by
measuring blood levels of
lithium 12 hours after the
drug is administered. The
average adult dose is 900 to
1,800 mg a day. For older
adults, the average dose is
150 to 900 mg a day.

ONSET OF EFFECT
1 to 2 weeks for mania.
When used in conjunction
with an antidepressant,
symptoms may improve
within a few days.

DURATION OF ACTION
24 hours.

DIETARY ADVICE
Can be taken with meals to
lessen stomach upset. You
should drink 8 to 10 glasses
of water or caffeine-free
beverages every day.

STORAGE
Store in a tightly sealed container away from heat and
direct light.

IF YOU MISS A DOSE
Take it as soon as you
remember. If it is near the
time for the next dose, skip
the missed dose and
resume your regular dosage
schedule. Do not double the
next dose.

STOPPING THE DRUG
The decision to stop taking
the drug should be made in
consultation with your
physician.

PROLONGED USE
You should see your doctor
regularly for tests and
examinations if you take
this medicine. Blood levels
of lithium must be mea-
sured carefully to prevent
lithium toxicity.

PRECAUTIONS
Over 60: Adverse reactions
may be more likely and
more severe in older
patients. A lower dose may
be warranted.

**Driving and Hazardous
Work:** Avoid such activities
until you determine how the
medicine affects you.

Alcohol: No special precautions are necessary.

Pregnancy: Lithium can
cause problems in the
unborn child, especially
during the first 3 months of
pregnancy. Before you take
lithium, tell your doctor if
you are pregnant or plan to
become pregnant.

Breast Feeding: Lithium
passes into breast milk; caution is advised. Consult your
doctor for specific advice.

Infants and Children:
Lithium can weaken the
bones of infants and children. Use and dosage for
children under the age of
12 must be determined by
your pediatrician.

Special Concerns: Take
care to avoid dehydration
in hot weather and while
engaging in vigorous
activities. Be sure to drink
plenty of fluids when using
lithium. If you cannot consume enough fluids or you
develop severe diarrhea
while taking lithium, stop
taking the drug and con-
tact your doctor. Nons-
teroidal anti-inflammatory
drugs (NSAIDs) such as

ibuprofen increase blood
levels of lithium.

OVERDOSE
Symptoms: Twitching,
tremor, slurred speech,
extreme drowsiness,
disorientation, confusion,
seizures, muscle weakness,
loss of consciousness,
diarrhea, vomiting.

What to Do: Call your
doctor, emergency medical
services (EMS), or the
nearest poison control
center immediately.

DRUG INTERACTIONS
Other drugs may increase
blood levels of lithium; consult your doctor for specific
advice if you are taking
another medicine for mental
illness, a diuretic, medicine
for pain or inflammation
(especially NSAIDs),
tetracycline, metronidazole,
or ACE inhibitors. Some
drugs lower blood levels of
lithium; consult your doctor
for advice if you are taking
theophylline, caffeine, or
acetazolamide.

FOOD INTERACTIONS
Avoid drinks and foods that
contain caffeine.

DISEASE INTERACTIONS
You should not take lithium
if you have seriously
impaired kidney function,
cardiovascular disease, or a
history of leukemia. Before
taking lithium, consult your
doctor for specific advice if
you have a history of brain
disease, schizophrenia, diabetes, difficulty urinating,
any infection, epilepsy,
thyroid disease, Parkinson's
disease, psoriasis, or
leukemia.

Lomefloxacin Hydrochloride

Maxaquin 400 mg
(SEARLE)

▶ Drug Class: Fluoroquinolone antibiotic

▶ Available in: Tablets

▶ Available OTC? No

▶ As Generic? No

Side Effects

SERIOUS
Serious reactions to lomefloxacin are rare and include seizures, mental confusion, hallucinations, agitation, nightmares, depression, shortness of breath, unusual swelling in the face or extremities, and loss of consciousness. Also severe skin burning, redness, blisters, rash, or itching on exposure to sunlight. Call your doctor immediately.

COMMON
Increased sensitivity to sunlight (and increased risk of sunburn) for days following therapy.

LESS COMMON
Diarrhea, nausea and vomiting, stomach pain and upset, gas, headache, dizziness, restlessness, insomnia, changes in taste perception, drowsiness, itching, dry mouth, unusual body aches or pains.

PRINCIPAL USES
To treat bacterial infections of the lower respiratory tract and urinary tract; to prevent urinary tract infections in patients preparing to undergo transurethral surgery (such as that performed to treat an enlarged prostate).

HOW THE DRUG WORKS
Lomefloxacin inhibits the activity of a bacterial enzyme (gyrase) that is necessary for proper DNA formation and replication. This prevents bacteria cells from reproducing.

DOSAGE
To treat infection— Adults age 18 and over: 400 mg, once a day for 10 to 14 days, depending on the type of infection being treated. To prevent infections presurgically— 400 mg, 2 to 6 hours before surgery.

ONSET OF EFFECT
Varies depending on the infection being treated.

DURATION OF ACTION
Unknown.

DIETARY ADVICE
Take it without regard to meals, although the drug is absorbed faster when taken on an empty stomach. Take it with a full glass of water, and drink lots of fluids, particularly citrus or cranberry juices.

STORAGE
Store in a tightly sealed container away from heat and direct light.

IF YOU MISS A DOSE
Take it as soon as you remember. If it is near the time for the next dose, skip the missed dose and resume your regular dosage schedule. Do not double the next dose.

STOPPING THE DRUG
Take lomefloxacin as prescribed for the full treatment period, even if you begin to feel better before the scheduled end of therapy.

PROLONGED USE
See your doctor regularly for tests and examinations if you must take this medicine for a prolonged period.

PRECAUTIONS
Over 60: No special problems are expected.

Driving and Hazardous Work: Avoid such activities until you determine how the medicine affects you.

Alcohol: It is advisable to abstain from alcohol when fighting an infection.

Pregnancy: In some animal tests, lomefloxacin has caused birth defects. Adequate studies in humans have not been done. It should be used during pregnancy only if potential benefits clearly justify the risks. Before you take lomefloxacin, tell your doctor if you are pregnant or plan to become pregnant.

Breast Feeding: Lomefloxacin passes into breast milk and may cause serious side effects in the nursing infant; use of the drug is discouraged when nursing.

Infants and Children: Lomefloxacin is not recommended for use by persons under the age of 18, as it has been shown to interfere with bone development.

Special Concerns: If lomefloxacin makes you unusually sensitive to sunlight, wear protective clothing, apply a sunblock, and try to stay out of direct sunlight, particularly between 10 am and 3 pm. Do not take any antacid or vitamin 4 hours before or 2 hours after taking this drug.

OVERDOSE
Symptoms: Severely reduced urination, weight gain, confusion, dryness and flakiness of skin, trembling, seizures.

What to Do: Call your doctor, emergency medical services (EMS), or the nearest poison control center immediately.

DRUG INTERACTIONS
Other drugs may interact with lomefloxacin. Consult your doctor for specific advice if you are taking aminophylline, antacids, didanosine, iron supplements, oxtriphylline, sucralfate, theophylline, warfarin, or zinc salts.

FOOD INTERACTIONS
No known food interactions.

DISEASE INTERACTIONS
Consult your doctor if you have a brain or spinal cord condition, epilepsy, or any other condition causing seizures. Use of lomefloxacin may cause complications in patients with liver or kidney disease, since these organs work together to remove the medication from the body.

Lomustine

CeeNU 10 mg
(BRISTOL-MYERS SQUIBB)

▶ Drug Class: Alkylating agent

▶ Available in: Capsules

▶ Available OTC? No

▶ As Generic? No

Side Effects

SERIOUS
Black, tarry, or bloody stools; blood in urine; fever and chills, cough or hoarseness; pain in lower back or side; difficult, decreased, or painful urination; red spots on skin; unusual bleeding or bruising; confusion; loss of coordination; slurred speech; sores on lips or in mouth; swollen feet or lower legs; unusual fatigue; cough; shortness of breath. Call your doctor immediately.

COMMON
Loss of appetite; nausea and vomiting (for periods of less than 24 hours); temporary hair loss.

LESS COMMON
Darkened skin, diarrhea, itching or skin rash.

PRINCIPAL USES
To treat brain tumors and Hodgkin's disease (a type of cancer affecting the lymph nodes and spleen).

HOW THE DRUG WORKS
Lomustine kills cancer cells by interfering with the activity of their genetic material, thus preventing the cells from reproducing. The drug may also affect the growth and development of normal cells in the body, resulting in unpleasant side effects.

DOSAGE
130 mg per square meter of body surface once every 6 weeks. The dose may need to be lowered, based on red blood cell counts.

ONSET OF EFFECT
Unknown.

DURATION OF ACTION
Unknown.

DIETARY ADVICE
Lomustine is best taken on an empty stomach at bedtime to minimize stomach upset.

STORAGE
Store in a tightly sealed container away from heat and direct light.

IF YOU MISS A DOSE
Take it as soon as you remember. Do not double the next dose.

STOPPING THE DRUG
The decision to stop taking the drug should be made by your doctor.

PROLONGED USE
See your doctor regularly for tests and examinations if you take this medication for a prolonged period.

PRECAUTIONS
Over 60: No special precautions are necessary.

Driving and Hazardous Work: Do not drive or engage in hazardous work until you determine how the medicine affects you.

Alcohol: Avoid alcohol.

Pregnancy: Lomustine can cause birth defects if taken by either the father or the mother. Persons of childbearing years should take steps to prevent pregnancy while being treated with this drug.

Breast Feeding: Not recommended while undergoing therapy with this drug.

Infants and Children: Lomustine is expected to have the same therapeutic effect and cause the same side effects in infants and children as it does in adults.

Special Concerns: Do not receive any immunizations without your doctor's approval. Avoid persons who have recently had oral polio vaccine and those with any infection. Consult your doctor or dentist about appropriate ways to clean your teeth to avoid injury. Be careful not to cut yourself when using sharp objects such as a safety razor or nail cutters. Avoid activities and contact sports where bruising or injury could occur. If you vomit shortly after taking a dose of lomustine, check with your doctor. You may be told to take the dose again. Lomustine may have cumulative effects on bone marrow, causing low blood counts. This drug has been reported to have an effect on the lungs, causing shortness of breath up to 15 years after taking it.

OVERDOSE
Symptoms: Swelling of the abdomen or glands, weakness, nosebleed.

What to Do: Call your doctor, emergency medical services (EMS), or the nearest poison control center immediately.

DRUG INTERACTIONS
Consult your doctor for specific advice if you are taking amphotericin B, anti-thyroid agents, aspirin, azathioprine, chloramphenicol, colchicine, coumadin, flucytosine, ganciclovir, interferon, plicamycin, or zidovudine (AZT). Also consult your doctor if you are taking any over-the-counter medications.

FOOD INTERACTIONS
No known food interactions.

DISEASE INTERACTIONS
Consult your doctor if you have any of the following: shingles, chicken pox, any infection, kidney disease, or lung disease.

Loperamide Hydrochloride

Generic 2 mg
(MYLAN)

Additional photographs

▶ Drug Class: Antidiarrheal

▶ Available in: Capsules, oral solution, tablets

▶ Available OTC? Yes

▶ As Generic? Yes

Side Effects

SERIOUS
Bloating, skin rash, constipation, loss of appetite, stomach pains, nausea, vomiting. Call your doctor immediately.

COMMON
No common side effects are associated with loperamide.

LESS COMMON
Dizziness or drowsiness, dry mouth.

PRINCIPAL USES
To treat diarrhea.

HOW THE DRUG WORKS
Loperamide eases diarrhea by slowing the activity of the intestines.

DOSAGE
Capsules— Adults and teenagers: 4 mg after the first loose bowel movement, 2 mg after each subsequent loose bowel movement. Take no more than 16 mg every 24 hours. Children ages 8 to 12: 2 mg, 3 times a day. Children ages 6 to 8: 2 mg, 2 times a day. Oral solution— Adults and teenagers: 4 mg (4 teaspoons) after the first loose bowel movement, 2 mg after each subsequent loose bowel movement. No more than 8 mg every 24 hours. Children ages 9 to 11: 2 mg after the first loose bowel movement, 1 mg after each subsequent loose bowel movement. No more than 6 mg every 24 hours. Children ages 6 to 8: 2 mg after the first loose bowel movement, 1 mg after each subsequent loose bowel movement. No more than 4 mg every 24 hours. Tablets— Adults and teenagers: 4 mg after the first loose bowel movement, 1 mg after each subsequent loose bowel movement. No more than 8 mg every 24 hours. Children ages 9 to 11: 2 mg after the first loose bowel movement, 1 mg after each subsequent loose bowel movement. No more than 6 mg every 24 hours. Children ages 6 to 8: 2 mg after the first loose bowel movement, 1 mg after each subsequent loose bowel movement. No more than 4 mg every 24 hours.

ONSET OF EFFECT
Unknown.

DURATION OF ACTION
Up to 24 hours.

DIETARY ADVICE
Take it on an empty stomach (1 hour before or 2 hours after eating). A mild diet is recommended when recovering from diarrhea. Bananas, rice, applesauce, and plain toast are good choices. Be sure to drink plenty of fluids.

STORAGE
Store in a tightly sealed container away from heat, moisture, and direct light.

IF YOU MISS A DOSE
Skip the missed dose and resume your regular dosage schedule. Do not double the next dose.

STOPPING THE DRUG
You may stop taking the drug whenever you choose.

PROLONGED USE
Loperamide should not be used for more than 2 days unless directed otherwise by your doctor.

PRECAUTIONS
Over 60: Diarrhea may easily lead to dehydration, especially in older patients, and loperamide may mask the effects of dehydration. When using loperamide, older persons should be sure to get plenty of fluids.

Driving and Hazardous Work: Avoid such activities until you determine how the medicine affects you.

Alcohol: Avoid alcohol.

Pregnancy: Discuss with your doctor the relative risks and benefits of using loperamide while pregnant.

Breast Feeding: It is not known whether loperamide passes into breast milk; cau-

tion is advised. Consult your doctor for specific advice.

Infants and Children: Do not give to children under 6 years of age unless otherwise directed by your doctor.

Special Concerns: During the first 24 hours, drink plenty of caffeine-free clear liquids like water, broth, ginger ale, and decaffeinated tea. During the second 24 hours you may eat bland foods such as applesauce, bread, crackers, and oatmeal.

OVERDOSE
Symptoms: Constipation, central nervous system depression, gastrointestinal irritation.

What to Do: An overdose of loperamide is unlikely to be life-threatening. However, if someone takes a much larger dose than prescribed, call your doctor, emergency medical services (EMS), or the nearest poison control center.

DRUG INTERACTIONS
Consult your doctor for specific advice if you are taking antibiotics such as cephalosporin, erythromycin, and tetracycline; or any narcotic pain medication.

FOOD INTERACTIONS
Fruits, fried or spicy foods, bran, candy, and caffeine-containing beverages can make diarrhea worse.

DISEASE INTERACTIONS
Consult your doctor if you have any of the following: dysentery, severe colitis, or liver disease.

Loperamide/Simethicone

BRAND NAME
Imodium Advanced

▶ Drug Class: Antidiarrheal/ antigas combination

▶ Available in: Chewable tablet

▶ Available OTC? Yes

▶ As Generic? No

Side Effects

SERIOUS
Skin rash, bloating, constipation, loss of appetite, stomach pain, nausea, vomiting. Call your doctor immediately.

COMMON
Expulsion of excess gas, causing belching and flatulence.

LESS COMMON
Dizziness or drowsiness, dry mouth.

PRINCIPAL USES
To treat diarrhea and to relieve bloating, pain, pressure, and cramps caused by excess gas in the stomach and intestines.

HOW THE DRUG WORKS
Loperamide eases diarrhea by slowing the activity of the intestines. Simethicone disperses and prevents the formation of gas bubbles in the gastrointestinal tract.

DOSAGE
Adults and teenagers: Chew 2 tablets and drink a full glass of water after the first loose stool. If needed, chew 1 tablet and drink more water after the next loose stool. Take no more than 4 tablets per day. Children ages 6 to 11: Chew 1 tablet after the first loose stool. If needed, chew half a tablet after the next loose stool. Children ages 9 to 11 (or weighing 60 to 95 lbs) should take no more than 3 tablets per day. Children ages 6 to 8 (or weighing 48 to 59 lbs) should take no more than 2 tablets per day. Follow each dose with plenty of clear liquids.

ONSET OF EFFECT
Unknown.

DURATION OF ACTION
Unknown.

DIETARY ADVICE
A mild diet is recommended when recovering from diarrhea. Bananas, rice, applesauce, and plain toast are good choices. Be sure to drink plenty of fluids.

STORAGE
Store in a tightly sealed container away from heat, moisture, and direct light.

IF YOU MISS A DOSE
Not applicable, since the drug is taken only when necessary.

STOPPING THE DRUG
You may stop taking the drug whenever you choose.

PROLONGED USE
This drug should not be used for more than 2 days unless directed otherwise by your doctor.

PRECAUTIONS
Over 60: Diarrhea may easily lead to dehydration, especially in older patients, and this drug may mask the symptoms of dehydration. When using this drug, older persons should be sure to get plenty of fluids.

Driving and Hazardous Work: No special precautions are necessary.

Alcohol: Avoid alcohol, as it may irritate the lining of the gastrointestinal tract and promote dehydration.

Pregnancy: Discuss with your doctor the relative risks and benefits of using this drug while pregnant.

Breast Feeding: This drug may pass into breast milk; caution is advised. Consult your doctor for specific advice.

Infants and Children: Not recommended for use by children younger than age 6 or who weigh less than 48 lbs.

Special Concerns: Chew the tablets thoroughly before swallowing for quicker and more complete relief. You should change position frequently and walk about to help eliminate gas. During the first 24 hours, drink plenty of caffeine-free clear liquids like water, broth, ginger ale, and decaffeinated tea. During the second 24 hours you may eat bland foods such as applesauce, bread, crackers, and oatmeal. Tell your doctor if you are on a low-sodium, low-sugar or other special diet. Do not smoke before meals.

OVERDOSE
Symptoms: Constipation, gastrointestinal irritation, drowsiness, confusion.

What to Do: An overdose of this drug is unlikely to be life-threatening. However, if someone takes a much larger dose than prescribed, call your doctor.

DRUG INTERACTIONS
Consult your doctor for specific advice if you are taking antibiotics such as cephalosporin, erythromycin, and tetracycline; or any narcotic pain medication.

FOOD INTERACTIONS
Fruits, fried or spicy foods, bran, candy, and caffeine-containing beverages can make diarrhea worse. Avoid any foods that increase gas formation. Chew your food slowly and thoroughly.

DISEASE INTERACTIONS
Do not use this drug if you have a high fever (over 101°F) or stools containing blood or mucus. Consult your physician if you have dysentery, severe colitis, or liver disease.

Lopinavir/Ritonavir

▶ Drug Class: Antiviral/protease inhibitor

▶ Available in: Capsules, oral solution

▶ Available OTC? No

▶ As Generic? No

Side Effects

SERIOUS
Pancreatitis has occurred in patients taking this drug, although a cause-and-effect relationship has not been established. Contact your doctor if you develop increased nausea, vomiting, or abdominal pain.

COMMON
Diarrhea.

LESS COMMON
Abdominal pain, weakness, headache, nausea, vomiting, insomnia.

PRINCIPAL USES
To treat HIV (human immunodeficiency virus), often in combination with other drugs. While not a cure for HIV, this drug may suppress replication of the virus and delay the progression of the disease.

HOW THE DRUG WORKS
Lopinavir blocks the activity of a viral protease, an enzyme that is needed by HIV to replicate. Blocking the protease causes HIV to make copies that cannot infect new cells. Ritonavir affects the body's metabolism of lopinavir, resulting in increased levels of lopinavir in the body.

DOSAGE
Adults and teenagers: 3 capsules or 5 mL oral solution twice a day with food. When taken in combination with efavirenz or nevirapine, 4 capsules or 6.5 mL oral solution twice a day with food. Children 6 months to 12 years of age: Dosage depends on weight. Consult your pediatrician for proper dose.

ONSET OF EFFECT
Unknown. An early response can be seen within the first few days of therapy, but the maximum effect may take at least 16 weeks.

DURATION OF ACTION
Unknown. Effects of the drug may be prolonged if it is used with other drugs and the virus is maximally suppressed.

DIETARY ADVICE
Take it with food.

STORAGE
Refrigerate the capsules and oral solution in a tightly sealed container. Avoid excessive heat.

IF YOU MISS A DOSE
Take it as soon as you remember. If it is near the time for the next dose, skip the missed dose and resume your regular dosage schedule. Do not double the next dose.

STOPPING THE DRUG
The decision to stop taking the drug should be made in consultation with your physician.

PROLONGED USE
See your doctor regularly for tests and examinations.

PRECAUTIONS
Over 60: No special studies have been done on older patients.

Driving and Hazardous Work: Do not drive or engage in hazardous work until you determine how the medicine affects you.

Alcohol: Avoid alcohol if liver function is impaired.

Pregnancy: Adequate studies of use during pregnancy have not been done; consult your doctor for specific advice. There is no evidence that the drug will reduce the risk of transmitting the virus from the mother to the fetus.

Breast Feeding: Women infected with HIV should not breast feed to avoid transmitting the virus to an uninfected child.

Infants and Children: Not recommended for use by children under the age of 6 months.

Special Concerns: Taking this medication does not eliminate the risk of passing the AIDS virus to other people. Use appropriate preventive measures.

OVERDOSE
Symptoms: Few cases of overdose have been reported.

What to Do: An overdose is unlikely to occur or be life-threatening. If, however, someone takes a much larger dose than prescribed or a child accidentally ingests the oral solution, seek medical assistance right away.

DRUG INTERACTIONS
You should not take lopinavir/ritonavir with the following drugs because serious or life-threatening adverse effects such as heartbeat irregularities, breathing difficulties, or excessive sedation could occur: amiodarone, sildenafil, tadalafil, vardenafil, astemizole, bepridil, flecainide, propafenone, quinidine, terfenadine, midazolam, triazolam, pimozide, ergotamine, or dihydroergotamine. Use of lopinavir/ritonavir with the cholesterol-lowering statin drugs simvastatin, lovastatin, and atorvastatin is not recommended. Caution should be used when taking lopinavir/ritonavir with pravastatin or fluvastatin. Avoid taking lopinavir/ritonavir with the herb St. John's wort. Consult your doctor for specific advice if you are taking any other prescription or over-the-counter medication.

FOOD INTERACTIONS
Increasing the amount of fat in the diet can help to reduce side effects.

DISEASE INTERACTIONS
Consult your doctor if you have liver disease or any other medical condition.

Loracarbef

BRAND NAME
Lorabid

Lorabid 200 mg
(LILLY)

▶ Drug Class: Antibiotic

▶ Available in: Capsules, oral suspension

▶ Available OTC? No

▶ As Generic? No

Side Effects

SERIOUS
Severe diarrhea, skin rash, hives, intense itching. Call your doctor right away.

COMMON
Loss of appetite, mild diarrhea, stomach pain, nausea, vomiting. Consult your doctor.

LESS COMMON
Dizziness, drowsiness, headache, discharge from or itching of the vagina, insomnia, general nervousness. Consult your doctor if such symptoms persist.

PRINCIPAL USES
To treat bacterial infections including urinary tract infections, bronchitis, pneumonia, and strep throat (streptococcal pharyngitis).

HOW THE DRUG WORKS
Loracarbef, an antibiotic similar to those in the cephalosporin family, kills bacteria or inhibits their growth and multiplication.

DOSAGE
For infections of the urinary tract— Adults and teenagers: 200 to 400 mg, 1 or 2 times a day for 7 to 14 days. For bronchitis— Adults and teenagers: 200 to 400 mg, 2 times a day for 7 days. For pneumonia— Adults and teenagers: 400 mg, 2 times a day for 14 days. For infections of skin and soft tissue— Adults and teenagers: 200 mg, 2 times a day for 7 days. For strep throat— Adults and teenagers: 200 mg, 2 times a day for 10 days. For all conditions, use and dosage of loracarbef for children ages 6 months to 12 years must be determined by your doctor.

ONSET OF EFFECT
Unknown.

DURATION OF ACTION
Unknown.

DIETARY ADVICE
Loracarbef should be taken on an empty stomach at least 1 hour before or 2 hours after meals. Drink plenty of fluids.

STORAGE
Store in a tightly sealed container away from heat and direct light.

IF YOU MISS A DOSE
Take it as soon as you remember. If it is near the time for the next dose, skip the missed dose and resume your regular dosage schedule. Do not double the next dose.

STOPPING THE DRUG
It is very important to take antibiotics as prescribed for the full treatment period, even if you begin to feel better before the scheduled end of therapy. This is especially important when being treated for streptococcal infections.

PROLONGED USE
You should see your doctor regularly for tests and examinations if you must take this medicine for a prolonged period.

PRECAUTIONS

Over 60: In older patients, loracarbef is not expected to cause side effects different from or more severe than those in younger persons.

Driving and Hazardous Work: Do not drive or engage in hazardous work until you determine how the medicine affects you.

Alcohol: No special problems are expected, although it is generally advisable to abstain from alcohol when fighting an infection.

Pregnancy: Loracarbef has not been shown to cause birth defects in animals. Human studies have not been done. Before you take loracarbef, tell your doctor if you are pregnant or plan to become pregnant.

Breast Feeding: Loracarbef may pass into breast milk; caution is advised. Consult your doctor for advice.

Infants and Children: Consult your doctor about use of loracarbef by children 12 years or younger.

Special Concerns: It is important to maintain consistent blood levels of loracarbef. You should be very careful not to miss a dose. If you have difficulty maintaining a proper dosage schedule, consult your physician.

OVERDOSE

Symptoms: Unusually rapid or slow heartbeat, unusual drop in blood pressure (causing dizziness, lightheadedness, confusion, or fainting).

What to Do: An overdose of loracarbef is unlikely to be life-threatening. However, if someone takes a larger dose than prescribed, call your doctor, emergency medical services (EMS), or the nearest poison control center right away.

DRUG INTERACTIONS
Other drugs may interact with loracarbef. Consult your doctor for specific advice if you are taking diuretics (water pills) or probenecid. Also tell your doctor if you are taking any other prescription or over-the-counter medication.

FOOD INTERACTIONS
No known food interactions.

DISEASE INTERACTIONS
Use of loracarbef may cause complications in patients with liver or kidney disease, since these organs work together to remove the medication from the body.

477

Loratadine

Claritin 10 mg
(SCHERING-PLOUGH)

▶ Drug Class: Antihistamine

▶ Available in: Tablets, syrup

▶ Available OTC? Yes

▶ As Generic? Yes

Side Effects

SERIOUS
No serious side effects are associated with the use of loratadine.

COMMON
No common side effects are associated with the use of loratadine.

LESS COMMON
In rare cases adverse reactions have been reported in persons taking loratadine, but none of these reactions is clearly linked to use of the drug.

PRINCIPAL USES
To prevent or relieve symptoms of hay fever and other allergies, such as watery or itchy eyes, runny nose, sneezing, or itchy skin. Loratadine is also used sometimes to treat chronic (persistent) hives.

HOW THE DRUG WORKS
Loratadine blocks the effects of histamine, a naturally occurring substance that causes swelling, itching, sneezing, watery eyes, hives, and other symptoms of allergic reaction.

DOSAGE
Tablets and syrup— Adults and children age 10 and older: 10 mg once a day. Children ages 2 to 9: 5 mg once a day. Do not increase the dose in an attempt to achieve quicker relief of symptoms.

ONSET OF EFFECT
Within 1 hour.

DURATION OF ACTION
24 hours or more.

DIETARY ADVICE
Loratadine can be taken without regard to diet, but taking this medicine with food may be beneficial because it may increase absorption of the drug from the gastrointestinal tract by up to 40%.

STORAGE
Store in a tightly sealed container at room temperature, away from heat, moisture, and direct light.

IF YOU MISS A DOSE
Take it as soon as you remember. However, if it is near the time for the next dose, skip the missed dose and resume your regular dosage schedule. Do not double the next dose.

STOPPING THE DRUG
The decision to stop taking the drug should be made in consultation with your physician.

PROLONGED USE
Loratadine can be taken safely for prolonged periods. Long-term use is not associated with decreased effectiveness of the drug (a problem with certain allergy medications and other drugs).

PRECAUTIONS
Over 60: Adverse reactions may be more likely and more severe in older patients.

Driving and Hazardous Work: The use of loratadine, at recommended doses, should not impair your ability to perform such tasks safely.

Alcohol: No special precautions are necessary.

Pregnancy: Before you take loratadine, tell your doctor if you are pregnant or plan to become pregnant.

Breast Feeding: Loratadine passes into breast milk; avoid or discontinue use while nursing.

Infants and Children: Adverse reactions may be more likely and more severe in children.

Special Concerns: Stop taking loratadine 4 to 7 days before you have an allergy skin test.

OVERDOSE
Symptoms: Rapid heartbeat, headache, drowsiness.

What to Do: An overdose of loratadine is unlikely to be life-threatening. However, if someone takes a much larger dose than pre-scribed, call your doctor, emergency medical services (EMS), or the nearest poison control center.

DRUG INTERACTIONS
Consult your doctor for advice if you are taking clarithromycin, erythromycin, troleandomycin, itraconazole, or ketoconazole.

FOOD INTERACTIONS
There are no known interactions between loratadine and specific foods.

DISEASE INTERACTIONS
There are no known disease interactions.

Loratadine/Pseudoephedrine

BRAND NAME
Claritin-D

▶ Drug Class: Antihistamine/ decongestant

▶ Available in: Extended-release tablets

▶ Available OTC? Yes

▶ As Generic? Yes

Side Effects

SERIOUS
No serious side effects are associated with the use of this drug.

COMMON
Insomnia, dry mouth, drowsiness.

LESS COMMON
Nervousness, dizziness, indigestion.

PRINCIPAL USES
To relieve the symptoms of seasonal allergic rhinitis (hay fever), which include runny nose, nasal congestion, and sneezing.

HOW THE DRUG WORKS
Loratadine blocks the effects of histamine, a naturally occurring substance that causes swelling, itching, sneezing, nasal discharge and congestion, and other symptoms of an allergic reaction. Pseudoephedrine narrows and constricts blood vessels to reduce the blood flow to swollen nasal passages, which reduces nasal secretions, shrinks swollen nasal mucous membranes, and improves airflow through the nasal passages.

DOSAGE
The 12-hour formulation may be taken twice a day (every 12 hours). The 24-hour formulation should only be taken once a day. Tablets should be taken with a full glass of water.

ONSET OF EFFECT
Within 1 to 3 hours.

DURATION OF ACTION
12 to 24 hours or more.

DIETARY ADVICE
This drug can be taken without regard to meals. Take it with a full glass of water.

STORAGE
Store in a tightly sealed container away from heat, moisture, and direct light.

IF YOU MISS A DOSE
Not applicable. This drug is taken as needed.

STOPPING THE DRUG
Not applicable. This drug is taken as needed.

PROLONGED USE
This drug is prescribed for short-term (seasonal) use only.

PRECAUTIONS
Over 60: Adequate studies have not been done. However, older patients are more susceptible to the effects of the pseudoephedrine component (see Pseudoephedrine).

Driving and Hazardous Work: The use of this drug should not impair your ability to perform such tasks safely. However, exercise caution if the medication makes you drowsy.

Alcohol: No special precautions are necessary.

Pregnancy: Adequate human studies have not been done. Discuss with your doctor the relative risks and benefits of using this drug while pregnant.

Breast Feeding: Both drugs pass into breast milk. Discuss with your doctor the relative risks and benefits of using this drug while nursing.

Infants and Children: Not recommended for use by children under age 12.

Special Concerns: Do not break or chew the tablet. Patients with a history of esophageal narrowing or swallowing difficulty should not take this drug.

OVERDOSE
Symptoms: Drowsiness, heartbeat irregularities, headache, giddiness, nausea, vomiting, sweating, increased thirst, chest pain, urination difficulties, muscle weakness and tenseness, anxiety, restlessness, insomnia, hallucinations, delusions, seizures, difficulty breathing.

What to Do: Call your doctor, emergency medical services (EMS), or the nearest poison control center immediately.

DRUG INTERACTIONS
This drug and MAO inhibitors should not be used within 14 days of each other. Consult your doctor for specific advice if you are taking beta-blockers, digitalis drugs, or over-the-counter antihistamines or decongestants.

FOOD INTERACTIONS
No known food interactions.

DISEASE INTERACTIONS
You should not take this drug if you have narrow-angle glaucoma, severe hypertension, urinary retention, or severe coronary artery disease. Caution is advised when taking this drug if you have any of the following: high blood pressure, diabetes mellitus, heart disease, increased eye pressure, hyperthyroidism, or enlarged prostate. Use of this drug may cause complications in patients with liver or kidney disease, since these organs work together to remove the medication from the body.

BRAND NAME
Ativan

Generic 0.5 mg
(SCHEIN/DANBURY)

▶ Drug Class: Benzodiazepine tranquilizer; antianxiety agent

▶ Available in: Oral solution, tablets, injection

▶ Available OTC? No

▶ As Generic? Yes

Side Effects

SERIOUS
Difficulty concentrating, outbursts of anger, other behavior problems, depression, hallucinations, low blood pressure (causing faintness or confusion), memory impairment, muscle weakness, skin rash or itching, sore throat, fever and chills, sores or ulcers in throat or mouth, unusual bruising or bleeding, extreme fatigue, yellowish tinge to eyes or skin. Call your doctor immediately.

COMMON
Drowsiness, loss of coordination, unsteady gait, dizziness, lightheadedness, slurred speech.

LESS COMMON
Change in sexual desire or ability, constipation, false sense of well-being, nausea and vomiting, urinary problems, unusual fatigue.

PRINCIPAL USES
To treat anxiety and insomnia. The injection form of lorazepam, administered in a hospital setting, is used to treat a type of seizure disorder (status epilepticus) and is used before surgery to sedate patients prior to the administration of anesthesia.

HOW THE DRUG WORKS
In general, lorazepam produces mild sedation by depressing activity in the central nervous system. In particular, lorazepam appears to enhance the effect of gamma-aminobutyric acid (GABA), a natural chemical that inhibits the firing of neurons and dampens the transmission of nerve signals, thus decreasing nervous excitation.

DOSAGE
For anxiety— Adults and teenagers: 1 to 2 mg every 8 or 12 hours, up to 6 mg a day. Older adults: 0.5 mg, 2 times a day to start; the dose may be increased. For insomnia— Adults and teenagers: 1 to 2 mg taken at bedtime. Note: In all cases, use and dosage for children under 12 years of age must be determined by your doctor.

ONSET OF EFFECT
30 minutes to 2 hours for oral forms.

DURATION OF ACTION
12 to 24 hours.

DIETARY ADVICE
Can be taken with food to prevent gastrointestinal upset.

STORAGE
Store in a tightly sealed container away from heat, moisture, and direct light.

IF YOU MISS A DOSE
Take it as soon as you remember. However, if it is near the time for the next dose, skip the missed dose and resume your regular dosage schedule. Do not double the next dose. For insomnia, do not take it unless your schedule allows a full night's sleep.

STOPPING THE DRUG
Never stop taking the drug abruptly, as this can cause withdrawal symptoms (seizures, sleep disruption, nervousness, irritability, diarrhea, abdominal cramps, muscle aches, memory impairment). Dosage should be reduced gradually as directed by your doctor.

PROLONGED USE
Lorazepam may slowly lose its effectiveness with prolonged use. See your doctor for periodic evaluation if you must take this drug for an extended length of time.

PRECAUTIONS
Over 60: Adverse reactions may be more likely and more severe in older patients. A lower dose may be warranted.

Driving and Hazardous Work: Lorazepam can impair mental alertness and physical coordination. Adjust your activities accordingly.

Alcohol: Avoid alcohol.

Pregnancy: Use during pregnancy should be avoided if possible. Tell your doctor if you are pregnant or plan to become pregnant.

Breast Feeding: Lorazepam passes into breast milk; do not take it while nursing.

Infants and Children: Lorazepam should be used by children only under close medical supervision.

Special Concerns: Lorazepam use can lead to psychological or physical dependence. Short-term therapy (8 weeks or less) is typical; do not take the drug for a longer period unless so advised by your doctor. Never take more than the prescribed daily dose.

OVERDOSE
Symptoms: Extreme drowsiness, confusion, slurred speech, slow reflexes, poor coordination, staggering gait, tremor, slowed breathing, loss of consciousness.

What to Do: Call your doctor, emergency medical services (EMS), or the nearest poison control center immediately.

DRUG INTERACTIONS
Consult your doctor for specific advice if you are taking any drugs that depress the central nervous system (such as antihistamines, antidepressants or other psychiatric medications, barbiturates, sedatives, cough medicines, decongestants, and painkillers). Be sure your doctor knows about any over-the-counter drug you may take.

FOOD INTERACTIONS
None reported.

DISEASE INTERACTIONS
Consult your doctor if you have a history of alcohol or drug abuse, stroke or other brain disease, any chronic lung disease, hyperactivity, depression or other mental illness, myasthenia gravis, sleep apnea, epilepsy, porphyria, kidney disease, or liver disease.

Losartan Potassium

BRAND NAME
Cozaar

Cozaar 25 mg
(MERCK)

▶ Drug Class: Antihypertensive/ angiotensin II antagonist

▶ Available in: Tablets

▶ Available OTC? No

▶ As Generic? No

Side Effects

SERIOUS
Sudden difficulty breathing or swallowing, hoarseness, swelling of the face, mouth, hands, or throat, dizziness, cough, fever or sore throat. Call your doctor immediately.

COMMON
Headache.

LESS COMMON
Back pain, fatigue, diarrhea, nasal congestion.

PRINCIPAL USES
To control high blood pressure. This drug appears to have the same benefits as the class of antihypertensive drugs known as ACE inhibitors, without producing the common side effect (experienced by as many as 30% of patients) of a dry cough. Losartan may be used alone or in conjunction with other antihypertensive medications.

HOW THE DRUG WORKS
Losartan blocks the effects of angiotensin II, a naturally occurring substance that causes blood vessels to narrow. Losartan causes the blood vessels to dilate, thereby lowering blood pressure and decreasing the workload of the heart.

DOSAGE
Adults: To start, 25 to 50 mg once a day. Usual maintenance dose is 25 to 100 mg, taken once a day or divided into 2 doses. Children: Not recommended.

ONSET OF EFFECT
Within 1 hour.

DURATION OF ACTION
24 hours.

DIETARY ADVICE
Follow a healthy diet (low-salt, low-fat, low-cholesterol) as advised by your doctor to help control blood pressure and prevent heart disease.

STORAGE
Store in a tightly sealed container away from heat, moisture, and direct light.

IF YOU MISS A DOSE
Take it as soon as you remember. If it is near the time for the next dose, skip the missed dose and resume your regular dosage schedule. Do not double the next dose.

STOPPING THE DRUG
Take it as prescribed for the full treatment period. The decision to stop taking the drug should be made in consultation with your physician.

PROLONGED USE
Lifelong therapy may be necessary. However, if you do change certain health habits (for example, increasing exercise or losing weight), it may be possible, under your doctor's supervision, to reduce the dose.

PRECAUTIONS
Over 60: Adverse reactions may be more likely and more severe in older patients.

Driving and Hazardous Work: Do not drive or engage in hazardous work until you determine how the medicine affects you.

Alcohol: Drink only in careful moderation. (See Special Concerns.)

Pregnancy: In certain ways losartan is similar to a class of drugs that have caused damage to the unborn child when taken in the second or third trimester of pregnancy. Because safer, more effective medications can lower blood pressure during pregnancy, and because adequate studies on the use of losartan during pregnancy have not been done, women who are pregnant or planning to become pregnant should not take this drug.

Breast Feeding: Losartan passes into breast milk; avoid use while nursing.

Infants and Children: The safety and effectiveness of this drug have not been established for children.

Special Concerns: Losartan may cause dizziness or lightheadedness, which is most noticeable when you change position. This may lead to fainting, falls, and injury. Sit or lie down immediately if you feel dizzy or lightheaded. This side effect may be worsened by alcohol, hot weather, dehydration, fever, prolonged standing, prolonged sitting, or exercise.

OVERDOSE
Symptoms: Fainting, dizziness, weak pulse that might be very slow or very fast, nausea and vomiting, chest pain.

What to Do: Call your doctor, emergency medical services (EMS), or the nearest poison control center immediately.

DRUG INTERACTIONS
Consult your doctor for specific advice if you are taking diuretics, potassium-containing medicines or supplements, salt substitutes, low-salt milk, NSAIDs, allopurinol, over-the-counter medications for colds, coughs, hay fever, asthma, sinus problems, or appetite control, or other prescription drugs.

FOOD INTERACTIONS
No known food interactions.

DISEASE INTERACTIONS
Use of losartan may cause complications in patients with liver or kidney disease, since these organs work together to remove the medication from the body.

Loteprednol Etabonate

BRAND NAMES
Alrex, Lotemax

▶ Drug Class: Corticosteroid

▶ Available in: Ophthalmic suspension

▶ Available OTC? No

▶ As Generic? No

Side Effects

SERIOUS
Decreased vision or blurring of vision (from cataract); eye pain, nausea, vomiting (from increased intraocular pressure); pain, redness, sensitivity to bright light, discharge (from eye infection). Call your doctor immediately if you experience any of these signs or symptoms. The drug may trigger a recurrence of herpes infection of the eye; mention any previous herpes infection to your doctor.

COMMON
Burning, stinging, redness, or watering of eyes.

LESS COMMON
Headache, runny nose, sore throat.

PRINCIPAL USES
Alrex is prescribed for temporary relief of eye symptoms due to seasonal allergic inflammation of the conjunctiva. Lotemax is used to control inflammation and prevent potentially permanent damage that may result from eye problems such as conjunctivitis, herpes of the eye, and corneal injuries. It is also used to help relieve redness, irritation, and discomfort in the eye, and may be used after eye surgery to control any inflammatory response. Loteprednol is less potent than prednisolone but also less likely to cause adverse effects.

HOW THE DRUG WORKS
Ophthalmic loteprednol inhibits the release of natural substances that cause inflammation and pain in eye tissues.

DOSAGE
Alrex (0.2%)— To treat seasonal allergic conjunctivitis: 1 drop into the affected eye 4 times a day. Lotemax (0.5%)— 1 to 2 drops into the affected eye 4 times a day. Within the first week of treatment, dose may be increased, up to 1 drop per hour, if needed. For postoperative inflammation: 1 to 2 drops into the operated eye 4 times a day beginning 24 hours following surgery and for the next 2 weeks.

ONSET OF EFFECT
Unknown.

DURATION OF ACTION
Unknown.

DIETARY ADVICE
No special restrictions.

STORAGE
Store in a tightly sealed container away from heat, moisture, and direct light. Do not allow it to freeze.

IF YOU MISS A DOSE
Apply it as soon as you remember. If it is near the time for the next dose, skip the missed dose and resume your regular dosage schedule. Do not double the next dose.

STOPPING THE DRUG
It is very important to use this drug as prescribed for the full treatment period, even if symptoms improve before the scheduled end of therapy.

PROLONGED USE
You should see your ophthalmologist to have your eye pressure monitored if you use this drug for 10 days or longer.

PRECAUTIONS
Over 60: No special problems are expected.

Driving and Hazardous Work: Do not drive or engage in hazardous work until you determine how the medicine affects your vision.

Alcohol: No special precautions are necessary.

Pregnancy: Adequate human studies have not been done, though no birth defects have been reported. Before taking ophthalmic loteprednol, tell your doctor if you are pregnant or plan to become pregnant.

Breast Feeding: Ophthalmic loteprednol has not been reported to cause problems in nursing babies. Consult your doctor.

Infants and Children: Safety and effectiveness have not been established.

Special Concerns: Shake the bottle vigorously before administering. Wash your hands and tilt your head back. Gently apply pressure to the inside corner of the eyelid and with the index finger of the same hand, pull downward on the lower eyelid to make a space. Drop the medicine into this space and close your eye. Apply pressure for 1 or 2 minutes while keeping the eye closed without blinking. Then wash your hands again. Make sure the tip of the dropper does not touch your eye, finger, or any other surface. If your symptoms do not improve in 2 days or if they become worse, check with your doctor. Wearing contact lenses while using this medication may increase the risk of infection. Your doctor may tell you not to wear contact lenses during and for a day or two after treatment.

OVERDOSE
Symptoms: When used topically, an overdose is very unlikely. Inadvertent oral ingestion, however, may cause fever, muscle pain, loss of appetite, dizziness, fainting, and trouble breathing.

What to Do: An overdose is unlikely to be life-threatening. However, if someone accidentally ingests the medicine, call your doctor, emergency medical services (EMS), or the nearest poison control center.

DRUG INTERACTIONS
Consult your doctor for specific advice if you are taking any other medication.

FOOD INTERACTIONS
No known food interactions.

DISEASE INTERACTIONS
Consult your doctor if you have any of the following: cataracts, diabetes, glaucoma, herpes infection or tuberculosis of the eye, or any other eye infection.

Lovastatin

Mevacor 20 mg
(MERCK)

▶ Drug Class: Antilipidemic
(cholesterol-lowering agent)

▶ Available in: Tablets

▶ Available OTC? No

▶ As Generic? Yes

Side Effects

SERIOUS
Fever, unusual or unexplained muscle aches and tenderness. Call your doctor right away.

COMMON
Side effects occur in only 1% to 2% of patients. These include constipation or diarrhea, dizziness or lightheadedness, bloating or gas, heartburn, nausea, skin rash, stomach pain, rise in liver enzymes.

LESS COMMON
Sleeping difficulty.

PRINCIPAL USES
To treat high cholesterol. Usually prescribed after first lines of treatment—including diet, weight loss, and exercise—fail to reduce total and low-density lipoprotein (LDL) cholesterol to acceptable levels. Lovastatin has also been approved for the primary prevention of coronary artery disease (CAD) in persons with no symptoms of CAD, but who have average to modestly elevated levels of total and LDL cholesterol and below average HDL.

HOW THE DRUG WORKS
Lovastatin blocks the action of an enzyme required for the manufacture of cholesterol, thereby interfering with its formation. By lowering the amount of cholesterol in the liver cells, lovastatin increases the formation of receptors for LDL, and thereby reduces blood levels of total and LDL cholesterol. In addition to lowering LDL cholesterol, lovastatin also modestly reduces triglyceride levels and raises HDL (the so-called "good") cholesterol.

DOSAGE
20 to 80 mg per day, taken with meals. The 20 mg dose is taken with the evening meal; doses greater than 20 mg per day are taken in the morning and evening.

ONSET OF EFFECT
2 to 4 weeks.

DURATION OF ACTION
The effect persists for the duration of therapy.

DIETARY ADVICE
Cholesterol-lowering drugs are only one part of a total program that should include regular exercise and a healthy diet. The American Heart Association publishes a "Healthy Heart" diet, which is recommended.

STORAGE
Store in a tightly sealed container away from heat, moisture, and direct light.

IF YOU MISS A DOSE
Take your missed dose as soon as you remember. Take your next scheduled dose at the proper time, and resume your regular dosage schedule. Do not take a double dose.

STOPPING THE DRUG
The decision to stop taking the drug should be made in consultation with your doctor. Once the medication is discontinued, blood cholesterol is likely to return to original elevated levels.

PROLONGED USE
Side effects are more likely with prolonged use. As you continue with lovastatin, your doctor will periodically order blood tests to evaluate liver function.

PRECAUTIONS
Over 60: No special problems are expected in older patients.

Driving and Hazardous Work: The use of lovastatin should not impair your ability to perform such tasks safely.

Alcohol: No special precautions are necessary.

Pregnancy: Lovastatin should not be used during pregnancy nor by women who are trying to become pregnant.

Breast Feeding: This drug is not recommended for women who are nursing.

Infants and Children: The drug can be effective, but safety is not known; rarely used in children. Consult your pediatrician.

Special Concerns: Important elements of treatment for high cholesterol include proper diet, weight loss, regular moderate exercise, and the avoidance of certain medications that may increase cholesterol levels. Because lovastatin has potential side effects, it is important that you maintain a recommended healthy diet and cooperate with other treatments your physician may suggest.

OVERDOSE
Symptoms: An overdose of lovastatin is unlikely.

What to Do: Emergency instructions not applicable.

DRUG INTERACTIONS
Consult your doctor if you are taking cyclosporine, gemfibrozil, niacin, antibiotics, especially erythromycin, or medications for fungus infections. All of these drugs may increase the risk of myositis (muscle inflammation) when taken with lovastatin and may lead to kidney failure.

FOOD INTERACTIONS
None reported.

DISEASE INTERACTIONS
Consult your doctor if you have any of the following problems: liver, kidney, or muscle disease, or a medical history involving organ transplant or recent surgery.

Loxapine

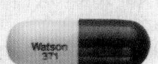

Generic 25 mg
(**WATSON**)

Additional photographs

▶ Drug Class: Neuroleptic;
antipsychotic

▶ Available in: Tablets, oral
solution, capsules, injection

▶ Available OTC? No

▶ As Generic? Yes

Side Effects

SERIOUS
Seizures, breathing difficulty, heartbeat irregularities, high fever, unusual
sweating, loss of bladder
control, lip puckering or
smacking, uncontrolled
chewing and tongue
movements, uncontrolled
limb or body movements,
difficulty speaking or
swallowing, loss of bal-
ance, trembling, muscle
spasms, severe constipa-
tion, difficulty urinating,
rash, sore throat and
fever, unusual bleeding
or bruising, jaundice. Call
your doctor immediately.

COMMON
Blurred vision, dizziness,
confusion, fainting,
drowsiness, shuffling
gait, slow movements,
staring and absence of
facial expression, dry
mouth.

LESS COMMON
Mild constipation, sexual
dysfunction, headache,
increased sensitivity of
skin to sun, nausea or
vomiting, insomnia,
menstrual irregularities,
breast swelling, unusual
milk secretion, unex-
pected weight gain.

PRINCIPAL USES
To treat moderate to severe
psychiatric conditions such
as schizophrenia.

HOW THE DRUG WORKS
Loxapine appears to block
receptors of dopamine (a
chemical that aids in the
transmission of nerve
impulses) in the central nervous system. Presumably,
this produces a tranquilizing
or antipsychotic effect.

DOSAGE
Oral forms: To start, 10 mg,
2 times a day. The dose may
be gradually increased by
your physician to a maxi-
mum of 250 mg a day. Injection: 12.5 to 50 mg, 4 to 6
times per day, injected into
a muscle.

ONSET OF EFFECT
Sedation may occur within
minutes, but onset of
antipsychotic effect may
take hours to occur or may
not occur until days or
weeks after the beginning
of therapy.

DURATION OF ACTION
12 to 24 hours.

DIETARY ADVICE
Oral solution should be
mixed with orange juice or
grapefruit juice.

STORAGE
Store in a tightly sealed container away from heat, moisture, and direct light. Do
not allow the solution or
injection forms to freeze.

IF YOU MISS A DOSE
Take it as soon as you
remember. However, if it is
near the time for the next
dose, skip the missed dose
and resume your regular
dosage schedule. Do not
double the next dose.

STOPPING THE DRUG
The decision to stop taking
the drug should be made in
consultation with your
physician.

PROLONGED USE
Prolonged use may lead to
tardive dyskinesia (involuntary movements of the jaw,
lips, tongue, and, in rare
cases, the arms, legs,
hands, or body). Consult
your doctor about the need
for follow-up evaluations and
tests if you must take this
drug for an extended
period.

PRECAUTIONS
Over 60: Adverse reactions
may be more likely and
more severe in older
patients.

**Driving and Hazardous
Work:** Do not drive or
engage in hazardous work
until you determine how the
medicine affects you.

Alcohol: Avoid alcohol.

Pregnancy: Adequate
studies have not been completed; consult your doctor
for more information.

Breast Feeding: It is not
known whether loxapine
passes into breast milk,
although no problems have
been reported.

Infants and Children:
The safety and effectiveness
of loxapine in children have
not been established. Use
and dose for children up
to age 16 should be determined by your doctor.

Special Concerns: Avoid
prolonged exposure to
high temperatures in hot
climates. Drink plenty of
fluids and stay cool in the
summertime. Avoid overex-
posure to sunlight until
you determine if the drug
heightens your skin's sensitivity to ultraviolet light.

OVERDOSE
Symptoms: Severe drowsiness, severe dizziness, muscle jerking, trembling, or
stiffness, trouble breathing,
unusual fatigue.

What to Do: Call your
doctor, emergency medical
services (EMS), or the
nearest poison control
center immediately.

DRUG INTERACTIONS
Do not take loxapine within
2 hours of taking an antacid
or an antidiarrheal medication. Consult your doctor for
specific advice if you are
taking amoxapine, methyl-
dopa, metoclopramide,
metyrosine, other drugs for
mental illness, pemoline,
pimozide, promethazine,
rauwolfia alkaloids,
trimeprazine, any medica-
tion that depresses the
central nervous system, tricyclic antidepressants, guanadrel, or guanethidine.

FOOD INTERACTIONS
None are known.

DISEASE INTERACTIONS
Consult your doctor if you
have a history of alcohol or
drug abuse, difficulty urinating, benign prostatic hyperplasia (BPH), glaucoma,
Parkinson's disease, heart
or blood vessel disease,
liver disease, or a seizure
disorder.

Lyme Disease Vaccine (Recombinant OspA)

BRAND NAME
LYMErix

▶ Drug Class: Vaccine

▶ Available in: Injection

▶ Available OTC? No

▶ As Generic? No

Side Effects

SERIOUS
No serious side effects have been reported.

COMMON
Soreness or redness at the site of injection.

LESS COMMON
Muscle pain, chills, fever, flu-like symptoms.

PRINCIPAL USES
To protect against, but not treat, Lyme disease in people ages 15 to 70. The vaccine is recommended for people who live or work in grassy or wooded areas infested with ticks infected with *Borrelia burgdorferi* (the bacteria that causes Lyme disease) as well as for people planning to travel to those areas.

HOW THE DRUG WORKS
Lyme disease vaccine stimulates the body's immune system to produce antibodies against a protein on the outer surface of the tick. When infected ticks bite vaccinated humans, the vaccine-induced antibodies enter the tick and attack the B. burgdorferi inside the gut of the tick, thereby preventing transmission of the disease.

DOSAGE
All doses are administered by a health care professional. Adults and teenagers: 1 dose injected into a muscle in the upper arm. Booster doses are given 1 month and 12 months after the first dose. All three doses are required to confer optimal protection.

ONSET OF EFFECT
Unknown.

DURATION OF ACTION
Unknown.

DIETARY ADVICE
No special restrictions.

STORAGE
Not applicable; the dose is administered only at a health care facility.

IF YOU MISS A DOSE
If you miss a scheduled vaccination, contact your doctor. According to the Centers for Disease Control and Prevention (CDC), if you miss the one-month booster, you may take it as soon as possible within the first year. All 3 injections should be completed within 1 year.

STOPPING THE DRUG
The full schedule of injections should be followed unless a medical problem intervenes. A full course of injections must be completed to ensure adequate immunization.

PROLONGED USE
Periodic booster shots may be recommended.

PRECAUTIONS
Over 60: Lyme disease vaccine is not expected to cause different or more severe side effects in older patients than in younger persons.

Driving and Hazardous Work: The vaccine should not impair your ability to perform such tasks safely.

Alcohol: No special precautions are necessary.

Pregnancy: Adequate human studies have not been done. Before taking Lyme disease vaccine, tell your physician if you are pregnant or planning to become pregnant.

Breast Feeding: Lyme disease vaccine may pass into breast milk; caution is advised. Consult your doctor for specific advice.

Infants and Children: Not recommended for use by children under the age of 15. No special problems are expected in persons over the age of 15.

Special Concerns: Previous infection with *B. burgdorferi* does not mean that you are immune to future infections of Lyme disease. As with any vaccine, Lyme disease vaccine may not protect all individuals. In clinical studies, the vaccine was effective in approximately 78% of cases after receiving all three doses. In addition to vaccination, people can decrease their chances of acquiring tick-borne infections by wearing pants and long-sleeved shirts, tucking pants into socks, spraying tick repellent on clothing, checking for ticks in a tick-infested area, and removing attached ticks.

OVERDOSE
Symptoms: Not applicable.

What to Do: No cases of overdose have been reported.

DRUG INTERACTIONS
No drug interactions have been reported. However, as with other intramuscular injections, Lyme disease vaccine should not be administered to people taking anticoagulant drugs such as warfarin unless the potential benefit outweighs the risks.

FOOD INTERACTIONS
No known food interactions.

DISEASE INTERACTIONS
No known disease interactions. However, as with other intramuscular injections, Lyme disease vaccine should not be administered to people with blood clotting disorders. The safety of the vaccine has not been tested in people with joint or neurological complications of Lyme disease, disorders associated with chronic joint swelling, and in those with a pacemaker.

Magaldrate

BRAND NAMES
Losopan, Riopan

▶ Drug Class: Antacid

▶ Available in: Oral suspension

▶ Available OTC? Yes

▶ As Generic? Yes

Side Effects

SERIOUS
Severe and continuing constipation, dizziness, lightheadedness, and heartbeat irregularities. Bone loss (osteomalacia) may occur, especially with prolonged use in dialysis patients. Hypophosphatemia (too little phosphate in the blood) may occur with prolonged use and a low-phosphate diet; symptoms include bone pain, fractures (due to bone loss), muscle weakness, loss of appetite, mood changes, a general feeling of discomfort, swelling of the wrists and ankles, unusual weight loss, and anemia (decreased number of red blood cells; symptoms include weakness and fatigue). Call your doctor immediately.

COMMON
Chalky taste.

LESS COMMON
Increased thirst, speckling or whitish color of stools, stomach cramps, diarrhea, mild constipation.

PRINCIPAL USES
To relieve symptoms of heartburn, acid indigestion, sour stomach, and gastro-esophageal reflux. Also prescribed to treat hyperacidity associated with peptic ulcers, gastritis, and esophagitis.

HOW THE DRUG WORKS
Magaldrate neutralizes stomach acid and reduces the action of pepsin, a digestive enzyme. This provides symptomatic relief from excess stomach acid.

DOSAGE
Adults: 540 to 1,080 mg (5 to 10 ml). Children: 5 to 10 mg. Take it between meals and at bedtime.

ONSET OF EFFECT
Within 20 minutes.

DURATION OF ACTION
20 to 60 minutes in fasting patients; 3 hours when taken after meals.

DIETARY ADVICE
Eat a balanced diet.

STORAGE
Store in a tightly sealed container away from heat, moisture, and direct light.

IF YOU MISS A DOSE
Take it as soon as you remember. If it is near the time for the next dose, skip the missed dose and resume your regular dosage schedule. Do not double the next dose.

STOPPING THE DRUG
Take as directed for the full treatment period.

PROLONGED USE
Do not take magaldrate for more than 2 weeks unless your doctor advises you to do otherwise.

PRECAUTIONS
Over 60: Constipation and intestinal trouble are more common in older persons. Older patients who have or who are at high risk for osteoporosis or other bone disorders should avoid frequent use of magaldrate.

Driving and Hazardous Work: No special precautions are necessary.

Alcohol: Avoid alcohol.

Pregnancy: Adequate studies have not been done. Before taking magaldrate, tell your doctor if you are pregnant or plan to become pregnant.

Breast Feeding: Magaldrate may pass into breast milk but has not been reported to cause problems in nursing babies. Consult your doctor for advice.

Infants and Children: Do not give antacids and other magnesium-containing medicines to young children unless prescribed by a physician.

Special Concerns: Use over-the-counter antacids only occasionally unless otherwise directed by your doctor. Persistent heartburn not readily relieved by antacids may be signaling a heart attack or other serious disorder. Seek medical help promptly.

OVERDOSE
Symptoms: Diarrhea, nausea, vomiting, constipation, confusion, palpitations, weakness, fatigue, bone pain, stupor.

What to Do: An overdose of magaldrate is unlikely to be life-threatening. However, if someone takes a much larger dose than prescribed, call your doctor, emergency medical services (EMS), or the nearest poison control center.

DRUG INTERACTIONS
Magaldrate and other magnesium-containing antacids may interact with vitamin D (including calcitediol and calcitriol), and may decrease the effectiveness of pancrelipase. Note that other medications may lose their effectiveness when taken within 1 hour of antacids. Consult your doctor for specific advice if you are taking amphetamines, bisacodyl, cellulose sodium phosphate, citrates, chenodiol, digoxin, enteric-coated medications, fluoroquinolones, isoniazid, ketoconazole, mecamylamine, methenamine, nitrofurantoin, penicillamine, phosphates, sodium polystyrene sulfonate resin, quinidine, or tetracyclines.

FOOD INTERACTIONS
No known food interactions.

DISEASE INTERACTIONS
Do not take magaldrate if you have any symptoms of appendicitis or an inflamed bowel (abdominal pain, cramps, soreness, bloating, nausea, and vomiting). Magaldrate is not recommended for Alzheimer's patients. Consult your doctor if you have any of the following: broken bones, colitis, diarrhea, intestinal blockage or bleeding, colostomy or ileostomy, edema, hypophosphatemia, heart disease, liver disease, toxemia of pregnancy, or kidney disease.

Magnesium Citrate

BRAND NAMES
Citrate of Magnesia,
Citro-Nesia, Citroma

▶ Drug Class: Hyperosmotic laxative

▶ Available in: Oral solution

▶ Available OTC? Yes

▶ As Generic? Yes

Side Effects

SERIOUS
Confusion, dizziness or lightheadedness, intestinal blockage, skin rash or itching, difficulty swallowing. Call your doctor immediately.

COMMON
Cramping, diarrhea, gas, increased thirst.

LESS COMMON
Sweating, weakness.

PRINCIPAL USES
To treat short-term constipation and for rapid emptying of the colon for rectal and bowel examinations.

HOW THE DRUG WORKS
Magnesium citrate attracts and retains water in the intestine, softening stools and inducing the urge to defecate.

DOSAGE
Adults and teenagers: 11 to 25 g daily in 1 or more doses. Children ages 6 to 12: 5.5 to 12.5 g daily in 1 or more doses.

ONSET OF EFFECT
30 minutes to 3 hours.

DURATION OF ACTION
Variable.

DIETARY ADVICE
Take it on an empty stomach with a full glass of cold water or juice.

STORAGE
Store in a tightly sealed container away from heat, moisture, and direct light.

IF YOU MISS A DOSE
If you are taking this drug on a fixed schedule, take the missed dose as soon as you remember. If it is near the time for the next dose, skip the missed dose and resume your regular dosage schedule. Do not double the next dose.

STOPPING THE DRUG
Take it as prescribed for the full treatment period. However, you may stop taking the drug if you are feeling better before the scheduled end of the therapy.

PROLONGED USE
Magnesium citrate is intended for short-term therapy only.

PRECAUTIONS
Over 60: No special problems are expected in older patients.

Driving and Hazardous Work: The use of magnesium citrate should not impair your ability to perform such tasks safely.

Alcohol: Avoid alcohol.

Pregnancy: Pregnant women with impaired kidney function should avoid taking magnesium citrate.

Breast Feeding: Magnesium citrate may pass into breast milk; caution is advised. Consult your doctor for advice.

Infants and Children: Do not give magnesium citrate and other laxatives to children under 6 years of age unless prescribed by a doctor.

Special Concerns: Chilling the medication or taking it with ice or following it with citrus fruit juice or citrus-flavored carbonated beverages may make it more palatable. Remember that chronic use of magnesium citrate or any laxative can lead to laxative dependence. You should consume adequate amounts of fiber in your diet, like bran, whole-grain cereals, fruit, and vegetables. Magnesium citrate should be taken on a schedule that doesn't interfere with activities or sleep, as it produces watery stools in 3 to 6 hours. It should not be taken within 2 hours of taking other medications.

OVERDOSE
Symptoms: Severe or protracted diarrhea.

What to Do: An overdose of magnesium citrate is unlikely to be life-threatening. However, if someone takes a much larger dose than prescribed, call your doctor, emergency medical services (EMS), or the nearest poison control center right away.

DRUG INTERACTIONS
Consult your doctor for specific advice if you are taking cellulose sodium phosphate; other magnesium-containing medications such as antacids; other laxatives; sodium polystyrene sulfonate; and oral tetracycline antibiotics.

FOOD INTERACTIONS
No known food interactions.

DISEASE INTERACTIONS
Caution is advised when taking magnesium citrate. Consult your doctor if you have kidney problems, symptoms of appendicitis (abdominal pain, nausea, vomiting), heart damage, intestinal obstruction or perforation, heart block, or rectal fissures.

Magnesium Oxide

BRAND NAMES
Mag-Ox 400, Maox 420,
Uro-Mag

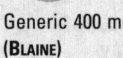

Generic 400 mg
(BLAINE)

▶ Drug Class: Antacid

▶ Available in: Capsules, tablets

▶ Available OTC? Yes

▶ As Generic? Yes

Side Effects

SERIOUS
Dizziness, lightheadedness, continuing feeling of discomfort, irregular heartbeat, loss of appetite, mental or mood changes, muscle weakness, unusual fatigue or weakness, unusual weight loss. Call your doctor immediately.

COMMON
Chalky taste, laxative effect.

LESS COMMON
Diarrhea, increased thirst, speckling or discoloration of stools, stomach cramps, nausea or vomiting, elevated magnesium in the blood (detectable by your doctor).

PRINCIPAL USES
To treat low magnesium in the blood (hypomagnesemia). Also used to replace or prevent magnesium loss resulting from other medications or conditions. It is used as an antacid to relieve heartburn, sour stomach, and acid indigestion.

HOW THE DRUG WORKS
Magnesium oxide neutralizes stomach acid and reduces the action of pepsin, a digestive enzyme. This provides symptomatic relief from excess stomach acid and heartburn.

DOSAGE
Capsules: 140 mg, 3 to 4 times a day. Tablets: 400 to 800 mg a day in evenly divided doses.

ONSET OF EFFECT
Within 20 minutes.

DURATION OF ACTION
For 20 minutes in fasting patients; 3 hours when taken after meals.

DIETARY ADVICE
Take this medication at least 1 hour after meals.

STORAGE
Store in a tightly sealed container away from heat, moisture, and direct light.

IF YOU MISS A DOSE
Take it as soon as you remember. If it is near the time for the next dose, skip the missed dose and resume your regular dosage schedule. Do not double the next dose.

STOPPING THE DRUG
Take it as prescribed for the full treatment period. However, when magnesium oxide is used as an antacid, it may be taken as needed.

PROLONGED USE
You should see your doctor regularly for tests and examinations if you must take this drug for a prolonged period.

PRECAUTIONS
Over 60: Adverse reactions may be more likely and more severe.

Driving and Hazardous Work: Do not drive or engage in hazardous work until you determine how the medicine affects you.

Alcohol: Avoid alcohol.

Pregnancy: Adequate studies have not been done. Before taking magnesium oxide, tell your doctor if you are pregnant or planning to become pregnant.

Breast Feeding: Magnesium oxide may pass into breast milk; consult your doctor for advice.

Infants and Children: Not recommended for use by children under 6 unless prescribed by a doctor.

Special Concerns: Using magnesium oxide in large amounts or for prolonged periods may have a laxative effect; the drug should not be used regularly for this purpose. In general, do not take other medicines within 2 hours of taking magnesium-containing antacids. Heartburn or upper abdominal pain not readily relieved by antacids may be signaling a heart attack or other serious disorder. In such cases, seek medical help promptly.

OVERDOSE
Symptoms: Diarrhea, bloating, change in mental state, muscle pain or twitching, slowed or shallow breathing, coma.

What to Do: An overdose of magnesium oxide is unlikely to be life-threatening. However, if someone takes a much larger dose than prescribed, call your doctor, emergency medical services (EMS), or the nearest poison control center immediately.

DRUG INTERACTIONS
Consult your doctor if you are taking fluoroquinolones, ketoconazole, methenamine, mecamylamine, sodium polystyrene sulfonate, tetracyclines, urinary acidifiers, digitalis drugs, misoprostol, pancrelipase, iron salts, phosphates, salicylates, or vitamin D (including calcifediol and calcitriol). Also, certain medications may lose their effectiveness or cause unexpected side effects when taken within 2 hours of magnesium oxide. These include enteric-coated medicines, folic acid, penicillamine, phenothiazines, and phenytoin. Take at least 2 hours apart (3 hours with phenytoin).

FOOD INTERACTIONS
No known food interactions.

DISEASE INTERACTIONS
Do not take magnesium oxide if you have any symptoms of appendicitis or an inflamed bowel (abdominal pain, cramps, soreness, bloating, nausea, and vomiting). Magnesium-containing antacids should not be taken by patients with kidney disease. Consult your doctor if you have any of the following: bone fractures, colitis, severe and continuing constipation, hemorrhoids, intestinal or rectal bleeding, a colostomy or ileostomy, persistent diarrhea, edema, heart disease, liver disease, toxemia of pregnancy, sarcoidosis, or underactive parathyroid glands.

Magnesium Sulfate

BRAND NAMES
Bilagog, Epsom Salts

▶ Drug Class: Laxative/dietary supplement

▶ Available in: Crystals, tablets

▶ Available OTC? Yes

▶ As Generic? Yes

Side Effects

SERIOUS
Abdominal cramps, nausea, diarrhea. Call your doctor immediately.

COMMON
There are no common side effects associated with the use of magnesium sulfate.

LESS COMMON
There are no less-common side effects associated with the use of magnesium sulfate.

PRINCIPAL USES
Magnesium sulfate is used to evacuate the bowel before surgery, and as a dietary supplement for people with a magnesium deficiency due to illness or as a result of the use of certain medications.

HOW THE DRUG WORKS
As a laxative, magnesium sulfate attracts and retains water in the intestine, softening stools and inducing the urge to defecate.

DOSAGE
As a laxative— Adults and teenagers: 10 to 30 g daily in 1 or more doses. Children ages 6 to 12: 5 to 10 g daily in 1 or more doses. To treat magnesium deficiency— The dose is determined by your doctor according to the severity of the deficiency.

ONSET OF EFFECT
Within 30 minutes to 3 hours.

DURATION OF ACTION
Variable.

DIETARY ADVICE
Take it on an empty stomach with a full glass of cold water or juice.

STORAGE
Store in a tightly sealed container away from heat, moisture, and direct light.

IF YOU MISS A DOSE
If you are taking this drug on a fixed schedule, take the missed dose as soon as you remember. If it is near the time for the next dose, skip the missed dose and resume your regular dosage schedule. Do not double the next dose.

STOPPING THE DRUG
You should not take magnesium sulfate for more than one week unless your physician prescribes its continued use.

PROLONGED USE
You should see your doctor regularly for tests and examinations if you must take this drug for a prolonged period.

PRECAUTIONS
Over 60: No special problems are expected.

Driving and Hazardous Work: The use of magnesium sulfate should not impair your ability to perform such tasks safely.

Alcohol: Avoid alcohol.

Pregnancy: Magnesium sulfate is used as a treatment, in the hospital only, for certain symptoms of toxemia of pregnancy. In proper amounts it can be used if necessary as a dietary supplement during pregnancy.

Breast Feeding: Magnesium sulfate passes into breast milk; caution is advised. Consult your doctor for advice.

Infants and Children: Magnesium sulfate and other laxatives should not be given to children under 6 years of age unless prescribed by your pediatrician.

Special Concerns: Taking it with ice or following it with citrus fruit juice or citrus-flavored carbonated beverages may make it more palatable. Remember that chronic use of magnesium sulfate or any laxative can lead to laxative dependence. Consume adequate amounts of fiber in your diet, such as bran, whole-grain cereals, fruit, and vegetables. Magnesium sulfate should be taken on a schedule that does not interfere with activities or sleep, as it produces watery stools within 3 to 6 hours. It should not be taken within 2 hours of taking other medications.

OVERDOSE
Symptoms: Blurred or double vision, dizziness or fainting, severe drowsiness, increased or decreased urination, slow heartbeat, trouble breathing.

What to Do: Call your doctor, emergency medical services (EMS), or the nearest poison control center immediately.

DRUG INTERACTIONS
Consult your doctor for specific advice if you are taking oral tetracycline, other magnesium-containing preparations, cellulose sodium phosphate, sodium polystyrene sulfonate, or digitalis drugs.

FOOD INTERACTIONS
No known food interactions.

DISEASE INTERACTIONS
Caution is advised when taking magnesium sulfate. Consult your doctor if you have any of the following: myasthenia gravis, severe kidney disease, heart blockage, intestinal obstruction or perforation, or any respiratory disease.

Maprotiline Hydrochloride

BRAND NAME
Ludiomil

Generic 50 mg
(**MYLAN**)

▶ Drug Class: Tetracyclic antidepressant

▶ Available in: Tablets

▶ Available OTC? No

▶ As Generic? Yes

Side Effects

SERIOUS
Severe constipation, trembling, weight loss, unusual excitability, severe dizziness or drowsiness, seizures, nausea or vomiting, palpitations or heartbeat irregularities, difficulty breathing, fever, restlessness, severe muscle stiffness or fatigue. Also skin redness, swelling, itching, or rash. Call your doctor right away.

COMMON
Dizziness, lightheadedness, drowsiness, visual disturbances, dry mouth, headache, sexual dysfunction, fatigue.

LESS COMMON
Diarrhea, constipation, heartburn, increased sensitivity to sunlight, increased sweating, weight loss, insomnia, increased appetite with weight gain.

PRINCIPAL USES
To relieve symptoms of major depression.

HOW THE DRUG WORKS
Maprotiline affects levels of norepinephrine, a brain chemical that is thought to be linked to mood, emotions, and mental state.

DOSAGE
Adults: To start, 25 mg, 1 to 3 times a day. The dose may be increased gradually by your doctor to 150 mg a day. Children: Dosage is determined by your doctor.

ONSET OF EFFECT
1 to 3 weeks.

DURATION OF ACTION
Unknown.

DIETARY ADVICE
No special restrictions.

STORAGE
Store in a tightly sealed container away from heat, moisture, and direct light.

IF YOU MISS A DOSE
If you take a one-time daily bedtime dose, do not take a missed dose in the morning because it may cause drowsiness. Call your doctor. If you take more than 1 dose a day, take it as soon as you remember. If it is near the time for the next dose, skip the missed dose and resume your regular dosage schedule. Do not double the next dose.

STOPPING THE DRUG
Take it as prescribed for the full treatment period, even if you feel better before the scheduled end of therapy. The decision to stop taking the drug should be made by your doctor.

PROLONGED USE
See your doctor regularly for tests and examinations if you must take maprotiline for a prolonged period.

PRECAUTIONS
Over 60: Adverse reactions may be more likely and more severe in older patients.

Driving and Hazardous Work: Use caution while driving or engaging in hazardous work until you determine how the medicine affects you. Drowsiness or lightheadedness can occur.

Alcohol: Avoid alcohol.

Pregnancy: In animal studies, maprotiline has not caused problems. Human studies have not been done. Before you take maprotiline, tell your doctor if you are pregnant or plan to become pregnant.

Breast Feeding: Maprotiline passes into breast milk; caution is advised. Consult your doctor for specific advice.

Infants and Children: Use and dosage for infants and children must be determined by your doctor. It is not known whether maprotiline causes different or more severe side effects in infants and children than it does in older persons. Antidepressants increase the risk of suicidal thinking and behavior (suicidality) in children with major depression and other psychiatric disorders. Discuss with your doctor this risk versus the benefits of using this drug. Children should be observed closely for worsening of symptoms, suicidality, or unusual changes in behavior at the onset of therapy and when making changes in dosage.

Special Concerns: Risk of seizures is increased if more than 150 mg is taken within a 24-hour period. If maprotiline causes dry mouth, use sugarless candy, gum, or ice chips for relief.

OVERDOSE
Symptoms: Severe dizziness or drowsiness, seizures, nausea or vomiting, heartbeat irregularities, difficulty breathing, fever, restlessness, muscle stiffness or fatigue.

What to Do: Call your doctor, emergency medical services (EMS), or the nearest poison control center immediately.

DRUG INTERACTIONS
Maprotiline and MAO inhibitors should not be used within 14 days of each other. Consult your doctor for specific advice if you are taking asthma medicine, amphetamines, cold medicine, medicines that depress the central nervous system, or appetite suppressants.

FOOD INTERACTIONS
No known food interactions.

DISEASE INTERACTIONS
Caution is advised when taking maprotiline. Consult your doctor if you have any of the following: epilepsy or another seizure disorder, gastrointestinal problems, asthma, urinary problems, glaucoma, a history of alcohol abuse, an enlarged prostate, heart disease, blood vessel disease, liver disease, or an overactive thyroid.

Masoprocol

▶ Drug Class: Topical antineoplastic (anticancer) agent

▶ Available in: Cream

▶ Available OTC? No

▶ As Generic? No

Side Effects

SERIOUS
Shortness of breath, wheezing, difficulty breathing, confusion, hives, itching, rash, abdominal pain, facial swelling, sweating, weakness, and lightheadedness (allergic reaction to sulfites or other components of the preparation).

COMMON
Redness, pain, swelling, and dry, flaking skin at the site of application.

LESS COMMON
Blistering or wet discharge at the site of application; burning or other discomfort following application; rough, wrinkled skin.

PRINCIPAL USES
Masoprocol is used for therapy of actinic keratoses (precancerous skin growths that can become malignant if left untreated).

HOW THE DRUG WORKS
It is not known exactly how masoprocol works. Laboratory experiments have shown that masoprocol prevents cells similar to the ones found in actinic keratoses from multiplying.

DOSAGE
Adults: Apply cream to lesions 2 times a day. Use sufficient cream to cover lesions entirely. Do not apply a covering bandage or dressing to the site. Children: Consult a pediatrician.

ONSET OF EFFECT
The anticancer effect of masoprocol begins as soon as the medication comes in contact with diseased skin. Significant improvement, however, may not be visible to the patient or physician until after therapy has continued for a period of time.

DURATION OF ACTION
Unknown.

DIETARY ADVICE
Maintain your usual food and fluid intake. Increase intake of fluids if you have a fever or diarrhea, in hot weather, or during exercise.

STORAGE
Store in a tightly sealed container away from heat and direct light. Keep away from moisture and extremes in temperature.

IF YOU MISS A DOSE
Apply it as soon as you remember. If it is near the time for the next dose, skip the missed dose and resume your regular dosage schedule. Do not double the next dose.

STOPPING THE DRUG
Take it as prescribed for the full treatment period, even if you begin to feel better before the scheduled end of the therapy.

PROLONGED USE
Therapy with this medication may require many weeks. The risk of an undesirable side effect increases with prolonged use.

PRECAUTIONS
Over 60: Adverse reactions may be more likely and more severe in older patients.

Driving and Hazardous Work: Masoprocol may cause dizziness and allergic reactions. Therefore, do not drive or engage in hazardous work until you determine how the medicine affects you.

Alcohol: No special precautions are necessary.

Pregnancy: The effects are unknown. Consult your physician if you are pregnant or trying to become pregnant.

Breast Feeding: Masoprocol may pass into breast milk; caution is advised. Consult your doctor for advice.

Infants and Children: Safety and effectiveness of masoprocol are unknown in young patients. Your pediatrician will weigh the risks of using it.

Special Concerns: Masoprocol contains sulfites; be sure to inform your physician if you are allergic to sulfites or sulfur-containing compounds. This medication should be kept away from your eyes and mouth. Wash your hands thoroughly immediately after

applying masoprocol to prevent accidental contact with these sensitive areas. Your skin may appear reddened and blotchy wherever masoprocol has been in contact with it. These reactions usually disappear completely within 2 weeks of stopping the medication.

OVERDOSE
Symptoms: No specific ones have been reported.

What to Do: An overdose of masoprocol is unlikely to be life-threatening. However, if someone applies a much larger dose than prescribed, call your doctor, emergency medical services (EMS), or the nearest poison control center.

DRUG INTERACTIONS
No specific interactions are known at this time. Consult your doctor or pharmacist if you are concerned whether a prescription or nonprescription medication you are using may interact with masoprocol.

FOOD INTERACTIONS
No known food interactions.

DISEASE INTERACTIONS
Caution is advised when taking masoprocol. Consult your doctor if you have allergies to sulfites or had previous allergic reactions to masoprocol.

Measles, Mumps, and Rubella Vaccine, Live

BRAND NAME
M-M-R II

▶ Drug Class: Vaccine

▶ Available in: Injection

▶ Available OTC? No

▶ As Generic? No

Side Effects

SERIOUS
Serious allergic reaction involving difficulty swallowing or breathing; reddened skin, especially around the ears; itching, particularly of the hands or feet; hives; severe fatigue; swelling of face, eyes, or nasal passages; eye pain or tenderness; or high fever. Call your doctor immediately.

COMMON
Burning or stinging at site of injection, fever, skin rash.

LESS COMMON
Mild headache, sore throat, nausea, vomiting, diarrhea. Also redness, itching, swelling, or hard lump at site of injection; general feeling of illness; aches or pain in joints.

PRINCIPAL USES
To prevent infection by the measles, mumps, and rubella (German measles) viruses.

HOW THE DRUG WORKS
The measles, mumps, and rubella vaccine is an injection that works by introducing small amounts of live strains of the viruses into the body, which stimulate the immune system to produce its own protective antibodies against these viruses.

DOSAGE
The first dose, injected under the skin, should be given at 12 to 15 months of age. A second dose should be given between either ages 4 and 6 or ages 11 and 12. Adults born before 1957 are generally considered to be immune to measles and mumps.

ONSET OF EFFECT
Most patients develop immunity within 2 to 6 weeks.

DURATION OF ACTION
Up to 11 years or more.

DIETARY ADVICE
No special restrictions.

STORAGE
Not applicable; the dose is administered only at a health care facility.

IF YOU MISS A DOSE
If your child misses a scheduled vaccination, contact your pediatrician.

STOPPING THE DRUG
The full schedule of injections should be followed unless a medical problem intervenes.

PROLONGED USE
No special problems are expected.

PRECAUTIONS
Over 60: Measles, mumps, and rubella vaccine is not expected to cause different or more severe side effects in older patients than it does in younger persons.

Driving and Hazardous Work: The use of measles, mumps, and rubella vaccine should not impair your ability to perform such tasks safely.

Alcohol: No special precautions are necessary.

Pregnancy: Generally, its use during pregnancy should be avoided. Before you have a measles, mumps, and rubella vaccination, tell your doctor if you are pregnant or plan to become pregnant. A pregnancy test should be done before the vaccine is given. Women should avoid pregnancy for 3 months following vaccination.

Breast Feeding: Components of the vaccine may pass into breast milk; caution is advised. Consult your doctor for specific advice.

Infants and Children: Measles, mumps, and rubella vaccine is not recommended for children younger than 12 months. The presence of the mother's antibodies in children under 12 months may prevent the vaccine from working. If a child is vaccinated before 12 months, another dose is recommended at 12 to 15 months of age.

Special Concerns: Applying a warm compress to the injection site can reduce redness and swelling. Do not use the vaccine within 3 months of an infusion of immunoglobulin. Immunosuppressive drugs and corticosteroids may decrease the vaccine's effect.

OVERDOSE
Symptoms: An overdose with measles, mumps, and rubella vaccine is unlikely.

What to Do: No cases of overdose have been reported.

DRUG INTERACTIONS
Other drugs may interact with measles, mumps, and rubella vaccine. Consult your doctor for specific advice if you are taking any prescription or over-the-counter medication.

FOOD INTERACTIONS
No known food interactions.

DISEASE INTERACTIONS
Consult your doctor if you have any of the following: a history of immune system deficiency, cancer, a blood disease, active tuberculosis, an allergic reaction to eggs or egg products, or an allergic reaction to neomycin.

Mebendazole

Generic 100 mg
(COPLEY)

▶ Drug Class: Anthelmintic

▶ Available in: Chewable tablets

▶ Available OTC? No

▶ As Generic? Yes

Side Effects

SERIOUS
Fever, sore throat, skin rash or itching, unusual fatigue. Call your doctor immediately.

COMMON
There are no common side effects associated with the use of this drug.

LESS COMMON
Nausea, vomiting, stomach pain or upset, diarrhea. Such symptoms tend to be short-lived and resolve on their own.

PRINCIPAL USES
To treat various intestinal roundworm infections, including ascariasis (common roundworm), hookworm infection, trichuriasis (whipworm), and enterobiasis or oxyuriasis (pinworm). It may be used to treat nonintestinal roundworm infections or more than one worm infection at a time.

HOW THE DRUG WORKS
Mebendazole interferes with the worm's energy-producing processes, including preventing the worm from absorbing glucose (sugar).

DOSAGE
For roundworms, hookworms, and whipworms—Adults and children age 2 and over: 100 mg, 2 times a day, in the morning and evening, for 3 days. Treatment may be repeated in 2 to 3 weeks. For pinworms—Adults and children age 2 and over: 100 mg for 1 day, repeated in 2 to 3 weeks. For multiple worm infections— Adults and children age 2 and over: 100 mg, 2 times a day, in the morning and evening, for 3 days. Treatment may be repeated in 2 to 3 weeks.

ONSET OF EFFECT
Unknown.

DURATION OF ACTION
Unknown.

DIETARY ADVICE
Take it with meals high in fat content to help the body better absorb the medication. If you are on a low-fat diet, consult your doctor for specific advice.

STORAGE
Store in a tightly sealed container away from heat, moisture, and direct light.

IF YOU MISS A DOSE
Take it as soon as you remember. If it is near the time for the next dose, skip the missed dose and resume your regular dosage schedule. Do not double the next dose.

STOPPING THE DRUG
Take as prescribed for the full treatment period, even if you begin to feel better before the scheduled end of therapy.

PROLONGED USE
You should see your doctor regularly for tests and examinations if you take this medicine for a prolonged period.

PRECAUTIONS
Over 60: No studies have been done specifically on older patients; adverse reactions may be more likely or more severe.

Driving and Hazardous Work: The use of mebendazole should not impair your ability to perform such tasks safely.

Alcohol: No special precautions are necessary.

Pregnancy: The use of mebendazole while pregnant is not recommended. Consult your doctor for advice.

Breast Feeding: Mebendazole may pass into breast milk; caution is advised. Consult your doctor for advice.

Infants and Children: Use and dose for children up to 2 years of age must be determined by your doctor.

Special Concerns: For pinworm infection, clothing, bedding, and towels should be washed daily. All members of the family may have to be treated to eradicate the infestation. A second treatment for all household members may be necessary after 2 or 3 weeks. All bedding and nightclothes should be washed after treatment. To prevent reinfection, you should wash the anal region daily, change your underwear and bedding every day, and wash your hands and fingernails before each meal and after bowel movements. Hookworm infection can cause anemia, and your doctor may tell you to take iron supplements during and after treatment.

OVERDOSE
Symptoms: Gastrointestinal upset lasting several hours; possible respiratory arrest or seizures.

What to Do: Call your doctor, emergency medical services (EMS), or the nearest poison control center immediately.

DRUG INTERACTIONS
Other drugs may interact with mebendazole. Consult your doctor for specific advice if you are taking carbamazepine or any other prescription or over-the-counter medication.

FOOD INTERACTIONS
No known food interactions.

DISEASE INTERACTIONS
Consult your doctor if you have liver disease, Crohn's disease, or ulcerative colitis.

Meclizine

Generic 25 mg
(PAR)

Additional photographs

▶ Drug Class: Antiemetic;
antivertigo agent

▶ Available in: Capsules,
tablets, chewable tablets

▶ Available OTC? Yes

▶ As Generic? Yes

Side Effects

SERIOUS
No serious side effects
are associated with the
use of meclizine.

COMMON
Drowsiness.

LESS COMMON
Blurred or double vision;
upset stomach; constipa-
tion or diarrhea; insom-
nia; painful or difficult
urination; dizziness; dry
mouth, nose, and throat;
headache; loss of
appetite; fast heartbeat;
nervousness; restless-
ness; skin rash.

PRINCIPAL USES
To treat and prevent nau-
sea, vomiting, and dizziness
caused by motion sickness
and vertigo (dizziness) associated with other medical
problems.

HOW THE DRUG WORKS
Meclizine acts on brain
centers that control nausea,
vomiting, and dizziness.

DOSAGE
To prevent and treat motion
sickness— Adults and teenagers: 25 to 50 mg, 1 hour
before travel; the dose may
be repeated every 24 hours.
To prevent and treat ver-
tigo— Adults and teenagers:
25 to 100 mg a day as
needed, in divided doses.

ONSET OF EFFECT
Within 1 hour.

DURATION OF ACTION
Up to 24 hours.

DIETARY ADVICE
Can be taken with food.

STORAGE
Store in a tightly sealed container away from heat, moisture, and direct light.

IF YOU MISS A DOSE
Take it as soon as you
remember. If it is near the
time for the next dose, skip
the missed dose and
resume your regular dosage
schedule. Do not double the
next dose.

STOPPING THE DRUG
Take it as prescribed for the
full treatment period. However, you may stop taking
the medication if you are
feeling better before the
scheduled end of therapy.

PROLONGED USE
See your doctor regularly
for tests and examinations if
you must use this drug for
a prolonged period.

PRECAUTIONS
Over 60: Adverse reactions
may be more likely and
more severe in older
patients.

**Driving and Hazardous
Work:** Do not drive or
engage in hazardous work
until you determine how the
medicine affects you.

Alcohol: Avoid alcohol
when using this medication.

Pregnancy: Adequate
human studies have not
been completed. Before taking meclizine, tell your doctor if you are pregnant or
plan to become pregnant.

Breast Feeding: Meclizine
may pass into breast milk
but has not been reported
to cause problems in nursing babies. It may reduce
the flow of breast milk. Consult your doctor for advice.

Infants and Children:
Meclizine is not recom-
mended for use by children
under the age of 12.

Special Concerns: If dry
mouth occurs, use sugarless
candy or gum or bits of ice
for temporary relief. If constipation occurs, a high-fiber
diet and drinking plenty of
fluids can help relieve the
problem. Meclizine can
cause false-negative results
in allergy skin testing.

OVERDOSE
Symptoms: Extreme
excitability, seizures, drowsiness, hallucinations.

What to Do: Call your
doctor, emergency medical
services (EMS), or the
nearest poison control center immediately.

DRUG INTERACTIONS
Consult your doctor for specific advice if you are taking
medications that can
depress the central nervous
system, such as antihistamines, medicines for hay
fever, tranquilizers, sleep
medications, prescription
pain medicines, or muscle
relaxants, or if you are taking any over-the-counter
medication.

FOOD INTERACTIONS
No known food interactions.

DISEASE INTERACTIONS
Caution is advised when
taking meclizine. Consult
your doctor if you have any
of the following: urinary
tract blockage, glaucoma,
asthma, bronchitis, emphysema, any other chronic
lung disease, enlarged
prostate, heart failure,
or intestinal blockage.

Meclofenamate Sodium

Generic 50 mg
(GENEVA)

▶ Drug Class: Nonsteroidal anti-inflammatory drug (NSAID)

▶ Available in: Capsules

▶ Available OTC? No

▶ As Generic? Yes

Side Effects

SERIOUS
Shortness of breath or wheezing, with or without swelling of legs or other signs of heart failure; chest pain; peptic ulcer disease with vomiting of blood; black, tarry stools; decreasing kidney function. Call your doctor immediately.

COMMON
Nausea, vomiting, heartburn, diarrhea, constipation, headache, dizziness, sleepiness.

LESS COMMON
Ulcers or sores in mouth, depression, rashes or blistering of skin, ringing sound in the ears, unusual tingling or numbness of the hands or feet, seizures, blurred vision. Also elevated potassium levels, decreased blood counts; such problems can be detected by your doctor.

PRINCIPAL USES
To treat mild to moderate pain and inflammation caused by tendinitis, arthritis, bursitis, gout, soft tissue injuries, migraine and other vascular headaches, menstrual cramps, and other conditions. When patients fail to respond to one NSAID, another may be tried. The greatest effectiveness often requires trial and error of several different NSAIDs.

HOW THE DRUG WORKS
NSAIDs work by interfering with the formation of prostaglandins, naturally occurring substances in the body that cause inflammation and make nerves more sensitive to pain impulses. NSAIDs also have other modes of action that are less well understood.

DOSAGE
Adults: 50 mg, 4 to 6 times a day. Maximum dose is 400 mg a day. Children: Consult your pediatrician.

ONSET OF EFFECT
From 30 minutes to several hours or longer.

DURATION OF ACTION
4 hours or more.

DIETARY ADVICE
Take with food; maintain your usual food and fluid intake.

STORAGE
Store in a tightly sealed container away from heat, moisture, and direct light. Keep away from extremes in temperature.

IF YOU MISS A DOSE
Take it as soon as you remember. If it is near the time for the next dose, skip the missed dose and resume your regular dosage schedule. Do not double the next dose.

STOPPING THE DRUG
The decision to stop taking the drug should be made in consultation with your physician.

PROLONGED USE
Prolonged use can cause gastrointestinal problems, including ulceration and bleeding, kidney dysfunction, and liver inflammation. See your doctor regularly for evaluation.

PRECAUTIONS
Over 60: Because of the potentially greater consequences of gastrointestinal side effects, the dose of NSAIDs for older patients, especially those over age 70, is often cut in half.

Driving and Hazardous Work: Do not drive or engage in hazardous work until you determine how the medicine affects you.

Alcohol: Avoid alcohol when using this medication because it increases the risk of stomach irritation.

Pregnancy: Avoid or discontinue this drug if you are pregnant or plan to become pregnant.

Breast Feeding: Meclofenamate passes into breast milk; avoid or discontinue use while nursing.

Infants and Children: May be used in exceptional circumstances; consult your doctor.

Special Concerns: Because NSAIDs can interfere with blood coagulation, this drug should be stopped at least 3 days prior to any surgery.

OVERDOSE
Symptoms: Severe nausea, vomiting, headache, confusion, seizures.

What to Do: Call your doctor, emergency medical services (EMS), or the nearest poison control center immediately.

DRUG INTERACTIONS
Do not take this drug with aspirin or any other NSAIDs without your doctor's approval. In addition, consult your doctor if you are taking antihypertensives, steroids, anticoagulants, antibiotics, itraconazole or ketoconazole, plicamycin, penicillamine, valproic acid, phenytoin, cyclosporine, digitalis drugs, lithium, methotrexate, probenecid, triamterene, or zidovudine.

FOOD INTERACTIONS
No known food interactions.

DISEASE INTERACTIONS
Consult your doctor if you have any of the following: bleeding problems, inflammation or ulcers of the stomach and intestines, diabetes mellitus, systemic lupus erythematosus (SLE, lupus), anemia, asthma, epilepsy, Parkinson's disease, kidney stones, or a history of heart disease or alcohol abuse. Use of meclofenamate may cause complications in patients with liver or kidney disease, since these organs work together to remove the medication from the body.

Medroxyprogesterone Acetate

Cycrin 10 mg
(ESI)

Additional photographs

▶ Drug Class: Progestin (hormone)

▶ Available in: Tablets, injection

▶ Available OTC? No

▶ As Generic? Yes

Side Effects

SERIOUS
Abnormal menstrual bleeding; unexpected or increased flow of breast milk; mental depression; skin rash; loss of or change in speech, coordination, or vision; severe and sudden shortness of breath. Call your doctor immediately.

COMMON
Stomach pain, swelling of face, ankles, or feet, mild headache, mood changes, unusual fatigue, weight gain.

LESS COMMON
Acne, breast pain or tenderness, hot flashes, insomnia, loss of sexual desire, loss or gain of scalp hair or body hair, brown spots on skin.

PRINCIPAL USES
To treat amenorrhea (cessation of menstrual periods) and abnormal uterine bleeding. It also may be used as a contraceptive.

HOW THE DRUG WORKS
Medroxyprogesterone inhibits secretion of pituitary hormones that in turn regulate menstrual and reproductive cycles. It also alters activity of uterine cells, resulting in, among other changes, thickening of the cervical mucus. These changes make it less likely for a partner's sperm to reach and fertilize an egg.

DOSAGE
For amenorrhea: Tablets, 5 to 10 mg a day for 5 to 10 days. For abnormal uterine bleeding: Tablets, 5 to 10 mg a day for 5 to 10 days beginning on the 16th or 21st day of the menstrual cycle. For contraception: 1 depo (Depo-Provera) injection (150 mg) every 3 months. For use in treating menopause: Tablets, 10 mg a day for 10 to 14 days, together with estrogen in each 25-day cycle.

ONSET OF EFFECT
Varies with mode of delivery. Protection against pregnancy can begin immediately if injection is given within 5 days of the menstrual period.

DURATION OF ACTION
Tablets: 24 hours or more. Injection: More than 3 months.

DIETARY ADVICE
Take it with meals to prevent gastrointestinal upset.

STORAGE
Store in a tightly sealed container away from heat and direct light.

IF YOU MISS A DOSE
Take a missed dose of the tablet as soon as you remember. If it is near the time for the next dose, skip the missed dose and resume your regular dosage schedule. Do not double the next dose.

STOPPING THE DRUG
The decision to stop taking the drug should be made by your doctor.

PROLONGED USE
Consult your doctor about the need for periodic examinations and laboratory tests if you use this drug for a prolonged period.

PRECAUTIONS
Over 60: No special problems are expected in older patients.

Driving and Hazardous Work: Do not drive or engage in hazardous work until you determine how the medicine affects you.

Alcohol: No special problems are expected.

Pregnancy: Before you use medroxyprogesterone, tell your doctor if you are pregnant or plan to become pregnant. This medicine must not be used during pregnancy.

Breast Feeding: Medroxyprogesterone passes into breast milk; avoid or discontinue use while nursing.

Infants and Children: This medication is not recommended for young patients.

Special Concerns: Remember that no contraceptive method is foolproof; 1% of women using the medroxyprogesterone injections have become pregnant.

OVERDOSE
Symptoms: No specific ones have been reported.

What to Do: An overdose of medroxyprogesterone is unlikely to be life-threatening. However, if someone takes a much larger dose than prescribed, call your doctor, emergency medical services (EMS), or the nearest poison control center immediately.

DRUG INTERACTIONS
Consult your doctor for specific advice if you are taking aminoglutethimide, carbamazepine, phenytoin, rifabutin, or rifampin.

FOOD INTERACTIONS
No known food interactions.

DISEASE INTERACTIONS
Do not take medroxyprogesterone if you have: known or suspected breast malignancies or tumors, acute liver disease or liver tumors, or active thrombophlebitis or thromboembolic disease. Consult your doctor if you have any of the following: asthma, epilepsy, migraine headaches, heart or circulation problems, bleeding problems, a history of thrombophlebitis or thromboembolic disease, diabetes mellitus, high blood cholesterol, kidney disease, risk factors for osteoporosis, or central nervous system disorders such as depression.

Medrysone

BRAND NAME
HMS Liquifilm

▶ Drug Class: Corticosteroid

▶ Available in: Ophthalmic suspension

▶ Available OTC? No

▶ As Generic? No

Side Effects

SERIOUS
Serious side effects are less likely than with ophthalmic dexamethasone, hydrocortisone, or prednisolone, but may include decreased vision or blurring of vision (from cataract); eye pain, nausea, vomiting (from increased eye pressure); and pain, redness, sensitivity to bright light, and discharge (from eye infection). Call your doctor immediately if you experience any of these signs or symptoms. This drug may trigger a recurrence of herpes infection of the eye; mention any previous herpes infection to your doctor.

COMMON
No common side effects are associated with medrysone.

LESS COMMON
Burning, stinging, redness, or watering of eyes.

PRINCIPAL USES
To control inflammation and prevent potentially permanent damage that may result from conditions that involve inflammation in the tissues of the eye. Also used to help relieve redness, irritation, and discomfort in the eye. Medrysone is less effective than ophthalmic dexamethasone, hydrocortisone, or prednisolone but also less likely to cause adverse effects.

HOW THE DRUG WORKS
Medrysone inhibits the release of natural substances that stimulate inflammation and pain in eye tissues.

DOSAGE
1 drop in each eye up to every 4 hours.

ONSET OF EFFECT
Unknown.

DURATION OF ACTION
Unknown.

DIETARY ADVICE
This medication can be used without regard to diet.

STORAGE
Store in a tightly sealed container away from heat, moisture, and direct light. Do not allow it to freeze.

IF YOU MISS A DOSE
Apply it as soon as you remember. If it is near the time for the next dose, skip the missed dose and resume your regular dosage schedule. Do not double the next dose.

STOPPING THE DRUG
Use it as prescribed for the full treatment period, even if your symptoms improve before the scheduled end of therapy.

PROLONGED USE
You should see your doctor regularly for tests and examinations if you take this drug for a prolonged period.

PRECAUTIONS
Over 60: No special problems are expected.

Driving and Hazardous Work: Do not drive or engage in hazardous work until you determine how the medicine affects your vision.

Alcohol: No special precautions are necessary.

Pregnancy: In animal studies, medrysone has caused problems during pregnancy. Reliable human studies have not been done, but no human birth defects have been reported. Before you take medrysone, tell your doctor if you are pregnant or plan to become pregnant.

Breast Feeding: Medrysone has not been reported to cause problems in nursing babies. Consult your doctor for specific advice.

Infants and Children: Children under 2 years of age may be especially sensitive to the effects of medrysone.

Special Concerns: To use the eye drops, first wash your hands. Tilt your head back. Gently apply pressure to the inside corner of the eyelid and with the index finger of the same hand, pull downward on the lower eyelid to make a space. Drop the medicine into this space and close your eye. Apply pressure for 1 or 2 minutes while keeping the eye closed without blinking. Then wash your hands again. Make sure the tip of the dropper does not touch your eye, finger, or any other surface. If your symptoms do not improve in 5 to 7 days or if they become worse, check with your doctor. Wearing contact lenses while using this medication may increase the risk of infection. Your doctor may tell you not to wear contact lenses during and for a day or two after treatment.

OVERDOSE
Symptoms: When used topically, an overdose of medrysone is very unlikely. Inadvertent oral ingestion, however, may cause fever, muscle pain, malaise, loss of appetite, dizziness, fainting, and breathing trouble.

What to Do: An overdose of medrysone is unlikely to be life-threatening. However, if someone applies a much larger dose than prescribed or accidentally ingests the medicine, call your doctor, emergency medical services (EMS), or the nearest poison control center immediately.

DRUG INTERACTIONS
Consult your doctor for specific advice if you are taking any other prescription or over-the-counter medication.

FOOD INTERACTIONS
No known food interactions.

DISEASE INTERACTIONS
Caution is advised when taking medrysone. Consult your doctor if you have any of the following: diabetes, tuberculosis of the eye, glaucoma, cataracts, herpes infection of the eye, or any other eye infection.

Mefenamic Acid

Ponstel 250 mg
(PARKE-DAVIS)

▶ Drug Class: Nonsteroidal anti-inflammatory drug (NSAID)

▶ Available in: Capsules

▶ Available OTC? No

▶ As Generic? No

Side Effects

SERIOUS
Shortness of breath or wheezing, with or without swelling of legs or other signs of heart failure; chest pain; peptic ulcer disease with vomiting of blood; black, tarry stools; decreasing kidney function. Call your doctor immediately.

COMMON
Nausea, vomiting, heartburn, diarrhea, constipation, headache, dizziness, sleepiness.

LESS COMMON
Ulcers or sores in mouth, depression, rashes or blistering of skin, ringing sound in the ears, unusual tingling or numbness of the hands or feet, seizures, blurred vision. Also elevated potassium levels, decreased blood counts; such problems can be detected by your doctor.

PRINCIPAL USES
To treat mild to moderate pain and inflammation caused by tendinitis, arthritis, bursitis, gout, soft tissue injuries, migraine and other vascular headaches, menstrual cramps, and other conditions. When patients fail to respond to one NSAID, another may be tried. The greatest effectiveness often requires trial and error of several different NSAIDs.

HOW THE DRUG WORKS
NSAIDs work by interfering with the formation of prostaglandins, naturally occurring substances in the body that cause inflammation and make nerves more sensitive to pain impulses. NSAIDs also have other modes of action that are less well understood.

DOSAGE
Adults: 250 mg every 6 hours. The drug should not be used for more than 7 days. For children's dose, consult your pediatrician.

ONSET OF EFFECT
Several hours to several days.

DURATION OF ACTION
4 hours or more.

DIETARY ADVICE
Take with food; maintain your usual food and fluid intake.

STORAGE
Store in a tightly sealed container away from heat, moisture, and direct light. Keep away from extremes in temperature.

IF YOU MISS A DOSE
Take it as soon as you remember. If it is near the time for the next dose, skip the missed dose and resume your regular dosage schedule. Do not double the next dose.

STOPPING THE DRUG
The decision to stop taking the drug should be made in consultation with your physician.

PROLONGED USE
Mefenamic acid is not recommended for use longer than 7 days in a course of therapy.

PRECAUTIONS
Over 60: Because of the potentially greater consequences of gastrointestinal side effects, the dose of NSAIDs for older patients, especially those over age 70, is often cut in half.

Driving and Hazardous Work: Avoid such activities until you determine how the medicine affects you.

Alcohol: Avoid alcohol when using this medication because it increases the risk of stomach irritation.

Pregnancy: Avoid or discontinue this drug if you are pregnant or plan to become pregnant.

Breast Feeding: Mefenamic acid passes into breast milk; avoid use while nursing.

Infants and Children: May be used in exceptional circumstances; consult your doctor.

Special Concerns: Because NSAIDs can interfere with blood coagulation, this drug should be stopped at least 3 days prior to any surgery.

OVERDOSE
Symptoms: Severe nausea, vomiting, headache, confusion, seizures.

What to Do: Call your doctor, emergency medical services (EMS), or the nearest poison control center immediately.

DRUG INTERACTIONS
Do not take this drug with aspirin or any other NSAIDs without your doctor's approval. In addition, consult your doctor if you are taking antihypertensives, steroids, anticoagulants, antibiotics, itraconazole or ketoconazole, plicamycin, penicillamine, valproic acid, phenytoin, cyclosporine, digitalis drugs, lithium, methotrexate, probenecid, triamterene, or zidovudine.

FOOD INTERACTIONS
No known food interactions.

DISEASE INTERACTIONS
Consult your doctor if you have any of the following: bleeding problems, inflammation or ulcers of the stomach and intestines, diabetes mellitus, systemic lupus erythematosus (SLE, lupus), anemia, asthma, epilepsy, Parkinson's disease, kidney stones, or a history of heart disease or alcohol abuse. Use of mefenamic acid may cause complications in patients with liver or kidney disease, since these organs work together to remove the medication from the body.

Mefloquine Hydrochloride

▶ Drug Class: Anti-infective/ antimalarial

▶ Available in: Tablets

▶ Available OTC? No

▶ As Generic? No

Side Effects

SERIOUS
Slowed heartbeat, seizures. Severe anxiety, depression, restlessness, or confusion during preventive therapy may be signs of more serious psychiatric problems. Call your doctor immediately.

COMMON
Treatment-related: dizziness, muscle pain, nausea, fever, headache, vomiting, chills, diarrhea, skin rash, abdominal pain, fatigue, loss of appetite, ringing in the ears. Prevention-related: vomiting, nausea.

LESS COMMON
Treatment-related: hair loss, emotional problems, itching, fatigue. Prevention-related: dizziness, lightheadedness.

PRINCIPAL USES
To treat mild to moderate acute malaria caused by strains of plasmodia (the parasite that causes malaria) that are susceptible to mefloquine—specifically, *Plasmodium falciparum* and *P. vivax*. (The drug may be ineffective against other strains.) Also used to prevent malaria caused by these strains, including chloroquine-resistant *P. falciparum*.

HOW THE DRUG WORKS
Mefloquine is poisonous to the malarial parasite.

DOSAGE
Adults— To treat: 5 tablets (1,250 mg each) taken as a single dose. Patients with acute *P. vivax* malaria are at high risk of relapse. To avoid relapse after the initial treatment, patients should take another antimalarial such as primaquine. To prevent: 250 mg once a week. Begin taking mefloquine one week prior to departure and continue taking the drug for 4 weeks upon return. Children 6 months of age and older— To treat, 20 to 25 mg per 2.2 lbs (1 kg) of body weight. Split the total dose into 2 doses 6 to 8 hours apart in order to reduce the risk and severity of side effects. To prevent: Your pediatrician will determine the appropriate dose.

ONSET OF EFFECT
Unknown.

DURATION OF ACTION
Up to 3 weeks.

DIETARY ADVICE
Do not take on an empty stomach. Take with at least 8 oz of water.

STORAGE
Store in a tightly sealed container away from heat, moisture, and direct light.

IF YOU MISS A DOSE
If taking 1 or more doses a day, take it as soon as you remember. If it is near the time for the next dose, skip the missed dose and resume your regular dosage schedule. Do not double the next dose. If taking 1 weekly dose, take it as soon as possible, then resume regular schedule.

STOPPING THE DRUG
Take it as prescribed for the full treatment period.

PROLONGED USE
If you are taking this drug as a preventive, your doctor may want you to begin at least 1 week before traveling to an area where malaria is prevalent. Keep taking mefloquine while you are in the area and for 4 weeks after you leave. Periodic liver function tests and eye exams are recommended.

PRECAUTIONS
Over 60: Adverse reactions may be more likely and more severe.

Driving and Hazardous Work: Do not drive or engage in hazardous work until you determine how the medicine affects you. Dizziness and coordination difficulties may occur after the drug is discontinued.

Alcohol: No special precautions are necessary.

Pregnancy: The use of mefloquine is discouraged during pregnancy because of the risks it poses to the unborn child. Women of child-bearing age should practice contraception during preventive therapy.

Breast Feeding: Mefloquine passes into breast milk; extreme caution is advised. Consult your physician for specific advice.

Infants and Children:
Safety and effectiveness have not been established for children under the age of 6 months. Early vomiting has been associated with mefloquine use in children and with treatment failure. If a second dose is not tolerated, alternative antimalarial measures should be considered.

Special Concerns: If you take mefloquine once a week, take it on the same day every week. Malaria is spread by mosquitoes. Take appropriate precautions, such as using mosquito netting, to guard against being bitten by malaria-carrying mosquitoes.

OVERDOSE
Symptoms: Side effects may be more pronounced. (See Side Effects.)

What to Do: If you have reason to suspect overdose, call your doctor, emergency medical services (EMS), or the nearest poison control center immediately.

DRUG INTERACTIONS
Consult your doctor for more advice if you are taking a beta-blocker, quinidine, quinine, chloroquine, antiarrhythmic drugs, calcium channel blockers, halofantrine, antihistamines, histamine (H1) blockers, tricyclic antidepressants, phenothiazines, anticonvulsants. Also, tell your physician if you are taking any other prescription or over-the-counter drug.

FOOD INTERACTIONS
No known food interactions.

DISEASE INTERACTIONS
Consult your doctor for specific advice if you have a seizure or psychiatric disorder, impaired liver function, any eye condition, or heart disease.

Megestrol Acetate

Generic 20 mg
(PAR)

Additional photographs

▶ Drug Class: Progestin (hormone treatment); antineoplastic (anticancer) agent

▶ Available in: Oral suspension, tablets

▶ Available OTC? No

▶ As Generic? Yes

Side Effects

SERIOUS
Abnormal vaginal discharge or bleeding, changes in menstrual cycle. Less frequently: High blood pressure; palpitations; heart failure; headache; loss of or change in speech, coordination, or vision; numbness or pain in chest, arm, or leg; shortness of breath; high blood sugar causing dry mouth, frequent urination, loss of appetite, and unusual thirst; depression; skin rash. Call your doctor promptly.

COMMON
Diarrhea, nausea, vomiting, impotence, diminished sex drive, abdominal cramps or pain, swollen face, ankles, or feet, mild increase in blood pressure, headache, mood changes, nervousness, fatigue, weight gain.

LESS COMMON
Acne, constipation, breast pain or tenderness, brown spots on skin, hot flashes, loss or gain of hair, insomnia, sweating.

PRINCIPAL USES
To treat cancer of the breast or uterus, and to treat loss of appetite and loss of weight (wasting) caused by AIDS (acquired immunodeficiency syndrome).

HOW THE DRUG WORKS
Megestrol, a synthetic form of the hormone progestin, interferes with the activity of certain other hormones and proteins needed for some types of cancer cells to grow. The mechanism by which megestrol increases weight is unclear. It appears to stimulate the appetite and affect metabolism, resulting in weight gain.

DOSAGE
For breast cancer: 160 mg per day in 1 or several doses for 2 or more months. For uterine cancer: 40 to 320 mg per day for 2 or more months. For loss of weight and appetite associated with AIDS: 800 mg a day for the first month; the dose may be adjusted later.

ONSET OF EFFECT
Unknown.

DURATION OF ACTION
Unknown.

DIETARY ADVICE
No special restrictions..

STORAGE
Store in a tightly sealed container away from heat and direct light.

IF YOU MISS A DOSE
Take it as soon as you remember. If it is near the time for the next dose, skip the missed dose and resume your regular dosage schedule. Do not double the next dose.

STOPPING THE DRUG
The decision to stop taking the drug should be made by your doctor.

PROLONGED USE
You should see your doctor regularly for tests and examinations if you take this drug for a prolonged period.

PRECAUTIONS
Over 60: No special problems are expected in older patients.

Driving and Hazardous Work: Do not drive or engage in hazardous work until you determine how the medicine affects you.

Alcohol: Avoid alcohol while taking this drug.

Pregnancy: Megestrol should never be taken during pregnancy. Consult your doctor immediately if you believe you have become pregnant.

Breast Feeding: Megestrol passes into breast milk; caution is advised. Consult your doctor for specific advice.

Infants and Children: Safety and effectiveness have not been established; consult your pediatrician to weigh risks against benefits.

Special Concerns: If you take any laboratory or diagnostic test, tell the clinician that you are taking megestrol. Megestrol may cause tenderness, swelling, or bleeding of the gums. Brush and floss your teeth carefully and see your dentist regularly.

OVERDOSE
Symptoms: No specific ones have been reported.

What to Do: An overdose of megestrol is unlikely to be life-threatening. However, if someone takes a much larger dose than prescribed, call your doctor, emergency medical services (EMS), or the nearest poison control center.

DRUG INTERACTIONS
Consult your doctor for specific advice if you are taking aminogluthimide, carbamazepine, phenobarbital, phenytoin, rifabutin, or rifampin.

FOOD INTERACTIONS
No known food interactions.

DISEASE INTERACTIONS
Caution is advised when taking megestrol. Consult your doctor if you have a history of asthma, epilepsy, heart or circulation problems, kidney disease, migraine headaches, bleeding disorders, blood clots, stroke, varicose veins, breast disease, mental depression, high blood cholesterol, diabetes mellitus, or liver disease.

Meloxicam

▶ Drug Class: Nonsteroidal anti-inflammatory drug (NSAID)

▶ Available in: Tablets

▶ Available OTC? No

▶ As Generic? No

Side Effects

SERIOUS
Shortness of breath or wheezing, with or without swelling of legs or other signs of congestive heart failure; chest pain; peptic ulcer disease with vomiting of blood; black, tarry stools; decreasing kidney function. Call your doctor immediately.

COMMON
Diarrhea.

LESS COMMON
Nausea, upper respiratory tract infection, sore throat, dizziness, swelling of the legs.

PRINCIPAL USES
To relieve the pain, inflammation, and stiffness of osteoarthritis.

HOW THE DRUG WORKS
NSAIDs work by interfering with the formation of prostaglandins, naturally occurring substances in the body that cause inflammation and make nerves more sensitive to pain impulses. NSAIDs also have other modes of action that are less well understood.

DOSAGE
Adults: To start, 7.5 mg a day. The dose may be adjusted later to no more than 15 mg a day.

ONSET OF EFFECT
Unknown.

DURATION OF ACTION
Unknown.

DIETARY ADVICE
Meloxicam may be taken with or without food.

STORAGE
Store in a tightly sealed container away from heat, moisture, and direct light.

IF YOU MISS A DOSE
If you do not remember until the next day, skip the missed dose and resume your regular dosage schedule. Do not double the next dose.

STOPPING THE DRUG
The decision to stop taking the drug should be made in consultation with your physician.

PROLONGED USE
The risk of gastrointestinal side effects may be increased with extended use.

PRECAUTIONS
Over 60: Caution should be exercised, as with any NSAID, in using meloxicam. Therapy should be started with the lowest recommended dose.

Driving and Hazardous Work: No special problems are expected.

Alcohol: Avoid alcohol when using this medication because it increases the risk of stomach irritation.

Pregnancy: Discuss with your doctor the relative risks and benefits of using this drug while pregnant. Do not use meloxicam during the last trimester.

Breast Feeding: Meloxicam may pass into breast milk; caution is advised. Consult your doctor for advice on whether to discontinue nursing or discontinue the drug.

Infants and Children: The safety and effectiveness of this drug have not been established for children under the age of 18.

OVERDOSE
Symptoms: Few cases of overdose have been reported. Symptoms may include lethargy, drowsiness, nausea, vomiting, abdominal pain, black, tarry stools, breathing difficulty, and coma.

What to Do: If you suspect an overdose or if someone takes a much larger dose than prescribed, call your doctor, emergency medical services (EMS), or the nearest poison control center immediately.

DRUG INTERACTIONS
Do not take this drug with aspirin or any other NSAIDs without your doctor's approval. In addition, consult your doctor if you are taking furosemide, ACE inhibitors, lithium, cholestyramine, or warfarin.

FOOD INTERACTIONS
No known food interactions.

DISEASE INTERACTIONS
Meloxicam should not be taken by people who have experienced asthma, hives, or allergic-type reactions after taking aspirin or other NSAIDs. People with a history of ulcer disease or gastrointestinal bleeding (especially if elderly or debilitated) should only take meloxicam with extreme caution. Consult your doctor if you have high blood pressure or heart failure. In patients with advanced liver or kidney disease meloxicam is not recommended, since these organs both work to remove the medication from the body.

Melphalan

BRAND NAMES
Alkeran, L-PAM,
Phenylalanine Mustard

Alkeran 2 mg
(GLAXO WELLCOME)

▶ Drug Class: Alkylating agent

▶ Available in: Tablets, injection

▶ Available OTC? No

▶ As Generic? No

Side Effects

SERIOUS
Black, tarry, or bloody stools; blood in the urine; fever and chills; cough or hoarseness; pain in lower back or side; difficult, decreased, or painful urination; red spots on skin; unusual bleeding or bruising; swollen feet or lower legs. Call your doctor immediately. Some of these side effects may recur after you stop taking melphalan. If so, consult your doctor.

COMMON
There are no common side effects associated with melphalan.

LESS COMMON
Nausea and vomiting, mouth sores, allergic reaction.

PRINCIPAL USES
To treat multiple myeloma (a cancer of the bone marrow) and ovarian cancer.

HOW THE DRUG WORKS
Melphalan kills cancer cells by interfering with the activity of their genetic material, thus preventing the cells from reproducing. The drug may also affect the growth and development of normal cells in the body, resulting in unpleasant side effects.

DOSAGE
For multiple myeloma: 6 mg (3 tablets) per day for 2 to 3 weeks; the drug is discontinued for up to 4 weeks, then resumed at a dose of 2 mg a day, depending on blood counts. For ovarian cancer: Initial dose is 0.2 mg per 2.2 lbs (1 kg) of body weight once a day for 5 days. Dosage and duration of treatment may be altered to meet the needs of each patient.

ONSET OF EFFECT
Unknown.

DURATION OF ACTION
Unknown.

DIETARY ADVICE
Melphalan is best taken with food to minimize stomach upset.

STORAGE
Store in a tightly sealed container away from heat and direct light.

IF YOU MISS A DOSE
Take it as soon as you remember. If it is near the time for the next dose, skip the missed dose and resume your regular dosage schedule. Do not double the next dose.

STOPPING THE DRUG
The decision to stop taking the drug should be made by your doctor.

PROLONGED USE
See your doctor regularly for tests and examinations if you must take this medication for a prolonged period.

PRECAUTIONS
Over 60: No special problems are expected.

Driving and Hazardous Work: The use of melphalan should not impair your ability to perform such tasks safely.

Alcohol: Avoid alcohol.

Pregnancy: Melphalan can cause birth defects if taken by either the father or the mother. Before you take it, tell your doctor if you are pregnant or plan to become pregnant.

Breast Feeding: Melphalan passes into breast milk; avoid or discontinue use while nursing.

Infants and Children: There is no specific information about the use of melphalan in children.

Special Concerns: While taking melphalan, do not receive any immunizations without your doctor's approval. Avoid persons who have recently had oral polio vaccine and those with any infection. Check with your doctor before having any dental work done. Consult your doctor or dentist about appropriate ways to clean your teeth to avoid injury. Be careful not to cut yourself when using sharp objects such as a safety razor or nail cutters. Avoid activities and contact sports where bruising or injury could occur. If you vomit shortly after taking a dose of melphalan, check with your doctor. You may be instructed to take the dose again.

OVERDOSE
Symptoms: Vomiting, mouth ulcerations, diarrhea, gastrointestinal hemorrhage (causing blood in the stool).

What to Do: Call your doctor, emergency medical services (EMS), or the nearest poison control center immediately.

DRUG INTERACTIONS
Consult your doctor for specific advice if you are taking amphotericin B, antithyroid agents, azathioprine, chloramphenicol, colchicine, flucytosine, interferon, plicamycin, probenecid, or sulfinpyrazone. Also consult your doctor if you are taking any over-the-counter medications.

FOOD INTERACTIONS
No known food interactions.

DISEASE INTERACTIONS
Consult your doctor if you have any of the following: shingles, chicken pox, any infection, kidney disease, or lung disease.

Memantine Hydrochloride

▶ Drug Class: NMDA receptor antagonist

▶ Available in: Tablets

▶ Available OTC? No

▶ As Generic? No

Side Effects

SERIOUS
No serious side effects are associated with the use of memantine.

COMMON
Dizziness, confusion, headache, constipation.

LESS COMMON
Fatigue, shortness of breath, vomiting, back pain, drowsiness, hallucinations.

PRINCIPAL USES
To treat moderate to severe Alzheimer's disease.

HOW THE DRUG WORKS
It is thought that overexcitation of NMDA receptors by the neurotransmitter glutamate, a brain chemical crucial to learning and memory, may play a role in Alzheimer's disease. The toxicity resulting from abnormal levels of glutamate is thought to be responsible for the cell death associated with Alzheimer's disease. Memantine is thought to selectively block the toxic effects of glutamate by blocking its action at the NMDA receptor.

DOSAGE
To start, 5 mg once a day. After one week of treatment, your doctor may increase the dose to 5 mg twice a day. The dose may be further increased at no less than 1-week intervals to 5 mg twice a day, 15 mg a day (5 mg and 10 mg as separate doses), and then to the maximum dose of 10 mg twice a day, if tolerated.

ONSET OF EFFECT
Unknown.

DURATION OF ACTION
Unknown.

DIETARY ADVICE
No special restrictions.

STORAGE
Store in a tightly sealed container away from heat, moisture, and direct light.

IF YOU MISS A DOSE
Take it as soon as you remember. If it is near the time for the next dose, skip the missed dose and resume your regular dosage schedule. Do not double the next dose. If therapy has been interrupted for several days or longer, consult your doctor.

STOPPING THE DRUG
The decision to stop taking the drug should be made in consultation with your physician.

PROLONGED USE
No problems are expected with long-term use.

PRECAUTIONS
Over 60: No special problems are expected.

Driving and Hazardous Work: Do not drive or engage in hazardous work until you determine how the medicine affects you.

Alcohol: Avoid alcohol.

Pregnancy: Adequate studies on the use of memantine during pregnancy have not been done. Discuss with your doctor the relative risks and benefits of using this drug while pregnant.

Breast Feeding: It is not known whether memantine passes into breast milk; caution is advised. Consult your doctor for specific advice.

Infants and Children: Memantine is not intended for use in children.

Special Concerns: Memantine will not cure Alzheimer's disease and will not stop the disease from getting worse, but it will improve cognitive ability of some patients.

OVERDOSE
Symptoms: Few cases of overdose have been reported. Symptoms may include restlessness, psychosis, drowsiness, hallucinations, stupor, loss of consciousness.

What to Do: Call your doctor, emergency medical services (EMS), or the nearest poison control center immediately.

DRUG INTERACTIONS
Consult your doctor for specific advice if you are taking sodium bicarbonate or a carbonic anhydrase inhibitor (such as acetazolamide, brinzolamide, or dorzolamide).

FOOD INTERACTIONS
No known food interactions.

DISEASE INTERACTIONS
Do not use if you have severe kidney impairment. Use with caution if you have liver disease.

Meperidine Hydrochloride

BRAND NAME
Demerol

Generic 50 mg
(WYETH-AYERST)

▶ Drug Class: Opioid (narcotic) analgesic

▶ Available in: Syrup, tablets, injection

▶ Available OTC? No

▶ As Generic? Yes

Side Effects

SERIOUS
Meperidine should not be taken for a prolonged period. Serious side effects are indistinguishable from those of overdose: Confusion; slurred speech; extreme sedation, weakness, or dizziness; small, pinpoint pupils; cold, clammy skin; slow breathing; seizures; loss of consciousness.

COMMON
Dizziness or lightheadedness, nausea or vomiting, constipation, mild drowsiness, itching.

LESS COMMON
Mood swings or false sense of well-being (euphoria), redness or flushing of face.

PRINCIPAL USES
To treat moderate to severe pain.

HOW THE DRUG WORKS
Narcotics such as meperidine relieve pain by acting on specific areas of the spinal cord and brain that process pain signals from nerves throughout the body.

DOSAGE
Adults— Syrup or tablets: 50 to 150 mg every 3 or 4 hours as needed. Injection: 50 to 150 mg into a muscle or under the skin every 3 or 4 hours as needed. Children— Syrup, tablet, or injection into a muscle or under the skin: 1.1 to 1.76 mg per 2.2 lbs (1 kg) of body weight every 3 or 4 hours as needed.

ONSET OF EFFECT
Oral forms: 15 minutes. Injection: 10 to 15 minutes.

DURATION OF ACTION
2 to 4 hours.

DIETARY ADVICE
Tablets can be taken with food to lessen stomach upset. Syrup should be taken with a half glass of water.

STORAGE
Store the drug in a tightly sealed container away from heat, moisture, and direct light. Do not allow the liquid form to freeze.

IF YOU MISS A DOSE
If you are taking meperidine on a fixed schedule, take it as soon as you remember. If it is near the time for the next dose, skip the missed dose and resume your regular dosage schedule. Do not double the next dose.

STOPPING THE DRUG
The decision to stop taking the drug should be made by your doctor.

PROLONGED USE
Meperidine should not be taken for a prolonged period. Prolonged use can cause nerve damage and physical dependence. Do not abruptly stop taking meperidine without consulting your doctor.

PRECAUTIONS
Over 60: Adverse reactions may be more likely and more severe in older patients.

Driving and Hazardous Work: Do not drive or engage in hazardous work until you determine how the medicine affects you.

Alcohol: Avoid alcohol.

Pregnancy: Before you use this medication, tell your doctor if you are pregnant or plan to become pregnant. Overuse during pregnancy can cause physical dependence in the unborn baby. Meperidine use just before delivery can cause breathing problems in the newborn.

Breast Feeding: Meperidine passes into breast milk; caution is advised. Consult your doctor for specific advice.

Infants and Children: Adverse reactions may be more likely and more severe in infants and children. Consult your pediatrician for specific advice.

Special Concerns: If you feel the medication is not working properly after a few weeks, do not increase the dose. Consult your doctor. Before having any surgery, tell the doctor or dentist in charge that you are taking meperidine.

OVERDOSE
Symptoms: Confusion; slurred speech; extreme sedation, weakness, or dizziness; small, pinpoint pupils; cold, clammy skin; slow breathing; seizures; loss of consciousness.

What to Do: Call your doctor, emergency medical services (EMS), or the nearest poison control center immediately.

DRUG INTERACTIONS
Consult your doctor for specific advice if you are taking carbamazepine or other medicine for seizures, barbiturates, sedatives, cough medicines, decongestants, antidepressants, other prescription pain medications, MAO inhibitors, naltrexone, rifampin, or zidovudine.

FOOD INTERACTIONS
No known food interactions.

DISEASE INTERACTIONS
Consult your doctor if you have any of the following: history of alcohol or drug abuse; emotional illness; brain disorders or head injury; seizures; lung disease; prostate problems or other problems with urination; gallstones; colitis; heart, kidney, liver, or thyroid disease.

Mephenytoin

▸ Drug Class: Hydantoin anticonvulsant

▸ Available in: Tablets

▸ Available OTC? No

▸ As Generic? No

Side Effects

SERIOUS
Fever, sore throat, swollen glands, red or purple point-like rash on the skin or mucous membranes, blistering or peeling skin lesions, mouth sores or bleeding, easy bruising, paleness, weakness, confusion, lethargy, or seizures may be a sign of a potentially fatal blood disorder or other complication. Call your doctor immediately.

COMMON
Dizziness, drowsiness, fatigue, clumsiness or unsteadiness, double vision, nervousness, nausea, vomiting, insomnia

LESS COMMON
Hair loss, weight gain, swelling, depression, disorientation. Numerous additional side effects are associated with the use of this drug; consult your doctor if you are concerned about any unusual reactions.

PRINCIPAL USES
To control certain kinds of seizures due to epilepsy. It is often given along with another anticonvulsant, such as phenytoin, phenobarbital, or primidone.

HOW THE DRUG WORKS
Mephenytoin is thought to depress the activity of certain parts of the brain and suppress the abnormal firing of neurons that causes seizures.

DOSAGE
Adults: 200 to 800 mg a day, in 3 divided doses. Children: 100 to 400 mg a day, in 3 divided doses. Some patients require higher doses. A low dose is used to start; it may then be gradually increased by your physician.

ONSET OF EFFECT
30 minutes.

DURATION OF ACTION
Maximum effectiveness lasts 24 to 48 hours; effectiveness then gradually decreases.

DIETARY ADVICE
Take with food to minimize stomach upset.

STORAGE
Store in a tightly sealed container away from heat, moisture, and direct light.

IF YOU MISS A DOSE
Take it as soon as you remember. However, if it is near the time for the next dose, skip the missed dose and resume you regular dosage schedule. Do not double the next dose unless advised to do so by your doctor.

STOPPING THE DRUG
Never stop taking this drug abruptly; seizures may ensue. The dose should be tapered gradually over a period of weeks under the supervision of your doctor.

PROLONGED USE
This drug is typically used on a long-term basis. If so, see your doctor regularly for tests and examinations.

PRECAUTIONS
Over 60: Adverse reactions may be more likely and more severe in older patients. A lower dose may be used.

Driving and Hazardous Work: This drug may cause drowsiness or dizziness, particularly in the first few weeks it is used. Do not drive or engage in hazardous work until you determine how the medicine affects you.

Alcohol: Avoid alcohol; it may contribute to excessive drowsiness.

Pregnancy: Anticonvulsants are associated with an increased risk of birth defects, although studies with this drug are incomplete. However, seizures during pregnancy can also increase the risks to the fetus. Discuss with your doctor the potential risks and benefits of using this drug during pregnancy. Folate supplementation is advised starting 1 to 2 months before conception and throughout pregnancy.

Breast Feeding: Mephenytoin may pass into breast milk, although at low levels. Consult your doctor for advice.

Infants and Children: Adverse reactions may be more frequent and more severe in infants and children. Not generally recommended in those younger than age 16.

Special Concerns: See your doctor for regular check-ups to detect the onset of any serious side effects. Your doctor may advise you to carry an ID card or bracelet that says you are taking this drug.

OVERDOSE
Symptoms: Blurred or double vision, difficulty walking, extreme clumsiness or unsteadiness, severe confusion, dizziness or drowsiness.

What to Do: Call your doctor, emergency medical services (EMS), or the nearest poison control center immediately.

DRUG INTERACTIONS
Mephenytoin can interact with many other drugs, including central nervous system depressants, xanthines, amiodarone, antacids, medicines containing calcium, anticoagulants, chloramphenicol, cimetidine, disulfiram, isoniazid, fluconazole, phenylbutazone, sulfonamides, corticosteroids, estrogens or oral contraceptives, corticotropin, oral diazoxide, lidocaine, methadone, phenacemide, rifampin, streptozocin, sucralfate, or other anticonvulsants (such as valproic acid).

FOOD INTERACTIONS
No known food interactions.

DISEASE INTERACTIONS
Special caution is advised in those with a blood disease, porphyria, lupus, coronary artery disease, kidney disease, or liver disease.

Mercaptopurine

Purinethol 50 mg
(GLAXO WELLCOME)

▶ Drug Class: Antimetabolite

▶ Available in: Tablets

▶ Available OTC? No

▶ As Generic? Yes

Side Effects

SERIOUS
Black or tarry stools; blood-tinged urine or stools; cough or hoarseness; fever; chills; lower back pain or pain in flanks; painful, difficult urination; small, red spots on the skin; bleeding from gums, nose, or other unusual places; easy bruising; shortness of breath. See your doctor right away if any of these occur. Other serious side effects include low white blood cell and platelet counts, anemia, and liver damage. Such problems can be detected by your doctor.

COMMON
Unusual fatigue, yellowish tinge to skin and eyes (jaundice). Notify your doctor.

LESS COMMON
Nausea, vomiting, abdominal pain or bloating, mouth sores, darkening of skin, diarrhea, headaches, skin rash and itching, weakness.

PRINCIPAL USES
To treat certain types of leukemia.

HOW THE DRUG WORKS
Mercaptopurine kills cancer cells by interfering with the synthesis of their genetic material, which prevents the cells from reproducing. The drug may also affect the growth and development of other kinds of cells in the body, resulting in unpleasant side effects.

DOSAGE
A variety of dosage schedules and regimens for mercaptopurine, with and without other antitumor drugs, is used. For acute myeloblastic leukemia, acute lymphocytic leukemia, and chronic myelocytic leukemia, the initial dose is 80 to 100 mg per square meter of body surface, once a day. Maintenance dose is 50 to 100 mg per square meter of body surface a day.

ONSET OF EFFECT
2 hours.

DURATION OF ACTION
Variable.

DIETARY ADVICE
Drink plenty of fluids.

STORAGE
Store in a tightly sealed container away from heat and direct light.

IF YOU MISS A DOSE
Take it as soon as you remember. However, if it is near the time for the next dose, skip the missed dose and resume your regular dosage schedule. Do not double the next dose.

STOPPING THE DRUG
The decision to stop taking the drug should be made by your doctor.

PROLONGED USE
See your doctor regularly for tests and examinations if you must take this drug for a prolonged period.

PRECAUTIONS
Over 60: No special problems are expected.

Driving and Hazardous Work: Avoid such activities until you determine how the medicine affects you.

Alcohol: Avoid alcohol.

Pregnancy: Mercaptopurine may cause birth defects if either the father or the mother is taking it at the time of conception. Persons of childbearing years should take steps to prevent pregnancy when taking this medication.

Breast Feeding: Not recommended during therapy.

Infants and Children: No special warnings.

Special Concerns: Your doctor will want to check blood work (liver, kidney, and blood cell function) weekly or monthly while you are taking this medicine. If you vomit after taking a dose, call your doctor to learn if you should take the dose again or wait for the next dose. Do not receive any immunizations while you are taking mercaptopurine, and avoid people with infections. Be careful when brushing your teeth and check with your doctor before having dental work done. Take care not to cut yourself when using sharp objects such as a safety razor. Avoid contact sports.

OVERDOSE
Symptoms: Loss of appetite, nausea, vomiting, diarrhea, gastrointestinal upset.

What to Do: Call your doctor, emergency medical services (EMS), or the nearest poison control center immediately.

DRUG INTERACTIONS
Consult your doctor for specific advice if you are taking acetaminophen, amiodarone, anabolic steroids, androgens, antibiotics, carbamazepine, chloroquine, dantrolene, disulfiram, divalproex, estrogens, etretinate, gold salts, hydroxychloroquine, methyldopa, naltrexone, oral contraceptives, phenothiazines, phenytoin, plicamycin, valproic acid, azathioprine, corticosteroids, cyclosporine, monoclonal antibodies, allopurinol, amphotericin B, antithyroid agents, chloramphenicol, colchicine, flucytosine, ganciclovir, interferon, zidovudine, probenecid, or sulfinpyrazone.

FOOD INTERACTIONS
No known food interactions.

DISEASE INTERACTIONS
Consult your doctor if you have a history of chicken pox, shingles, gout, kidney stones, any infection, kidney disease, or liver disease.

Mesalamine

Asacol 400 mg
(P&GP)

▶ Drug Class: Gastrointestinal anti-inflammatory

▶ Available in: Extended-release capsules, delayed-release tablets, enema

▶ Available OTC? No

▶ As Generic? No

Side Effects

SERIOUS
Severe abdominal pains or cramps; bloody diarrhea; fever; severe headache; skin rash and itching; blue or pale skin; severe back or stomach pain, possibly moving to the left arm, neck, or shoulder; chills; rapid heartbeat; nausea or vomiting; shortness of breath; swollen stomach; unusual fatigue; yellow eyes or skin; rectal irritation (with enema). Call your doctor immediately.

COMMON
Mild abdominal cramping, mild diarrhea, dizziness, headache, runny or stuffy nose, sneezing.

LESS COMMON
Acne, back or joint pain, gas or flatulence, loss of appetite, loss of hair.

PRINCIPAL USES
To treat inflammatory bowel diseases such as ulcerative colitis.

HOW THE DRUG WORKS
The exact mechanism of action is uncertain, although it appears that mesalamine inhibits the production of substances known as metabolites of arachidonic acid (leukotrienes and prostaglandins), which produce inflammation in the digestive tract.

DOSAGE
Dosage can differ for different brands. Extended-release capsules— Adults: 1 g, 4 times a day for up to 8 weeks. Delayed-release tablets— Adults: Asacol: 800 mg, 3 times a day for 6 weeks. Enema— 4 g (1 unit) used every night for 3 to 6 weeks.

ONSET OF EFFECT
Unknown.

DURATION OF ACTION
Unknown.

DIETARY ADVICE
Take the oral forms before meals and at bedtime with a full glass of water unless you are directed otherwise by your doctor.

STORAGE
Store in a tightly sealed container away from heat and direct light.

IF YOU MISS A DOSE
Take the oral forms as soon as you remember. If it is near the time for the next dose, skip the missed dose and resume your regular dosage schedule. If you miss a dose of mesalamine enema, take it if you remember the same night. Otherwise, skip the missed dose and resume your regular dosage schedule. In all cases, do not double the next dose.

STOPPING THE DRUG
Take as prescribed for the full treatment period, even if you begin to feel better before the scheduled end of therapy.

PROLONGED USE
You should see your doctor regularly for tests and examinations if you take this drug for a prolonged period.

PRECAUTIONS
Over 60: There is no information comparing the use of mesalamine by older patients with use by other age groups.

Driving and Hazardous Work: Do not drive or engage in hazardous work until you determine how the medicine affects you.

Alcohol: Avoid alcohol.

Pregnancy: Mesalamine has not caused birth defects in animals. Human studies have not been done. Before you take mesalamine, tell your doctor if you are pregnant or plan to become pregnant.

Breast Feeding: Mesalamine may pass into breast milk; caution is advised. Consult your doctor for advice.

Infants and Children: There is no specific information comparing use of mesalamine in infants and children with use in other age groups. Use and dose must be determined by your doctor.

Special Concerns: Do not change to another brand without consulting your doctor. The enema may stain clothing, fabrics, or any surface that it touches.

OVERDOSE
Symptoms: Confusion, severe diarrhea, dizziness or lightheadedness, drowsiness, severe headache, hearing loss, buzzing or ringing in ear, continuing nausea or vomiting.

What to Do: An overdose of mesalamine is unlikely to be life-threatening. However, if someone takes a much larger dose than prescribed, call your doctor, emergency medical services (EMS), or the nearest poison control center.

DRUG INTERACTIONS
Be sure to consult your doctor if you are taking any other prescription or over-the-counter medication.

FOOD INTERACTIONS
No known food interactions.

DISEASE INTERACTIONS
Those with kidney disease should not take mesalamine, as it may make the condition worse. Patients with hypertension should be monitored closely.

Metaproterenol

Generic 10 mg
(PAR)

▶ Drug Class: Bronchodilator/
sympathomimetic

▶ Available in: Inhalation
aerosol or solution, syrup,
tablets

▶ Available OTC? No

▶ As Generic? Yes

Side Effects

SERIOUS
Inhaled form: May
become ineffective if
used too often, resulting
in more-severe breathing
difficulty that does not
improve. Signs include
persistent wheezing,
coughing, or shortness of
breath; confusion; bluish
color to lips or finger-
nails; inability to speak.
Ingested form: Chest pain
or heaviness; irregular,
racing, fluttering, or
pounding heartbeat;
lightheadedness; fainting;
severe weakness; severe
headache.

COMMON
Trouble sleeping, dry
mouth, sore throat, ner-
vousness, restlessness.

LESS COMMON
Trembling, sweating,
headache, nausea or
vomiting, flushing or redness to cheeks or other
skin, muscle aches,
unpleasant or unusual
taste in mouth.

PRINCIPAL USES
To dilate air passages in the
lungs that have become narrowed as a result of disease
or inflammation. It is used
in the treatment of asthma
and chronic obstructive pulmonary disease (COPD).

HOW THE DRUG WORKS
Metaproterenol widens
constricted airways by
relaxing the smooth mus-
cles that surround the
bronchial passages.

DOSAGE
Use when needed to relieve
breathing difficulty. Inhalation solution for nebulizers— Adults and children
over 12 years of age: Usual
dose is 10 inhalations, not
to be taken more frequently
than every 3 to 4 hours, for
a usual maximum of 3 to 4
times a day. Infants and children under 12 years of age:
Consult a pediatrician.
Inhalation aerosol— Adults
and children 12 years and
older: 2 to 3 puffs every 3
to 4 hours. Do not exceed
more than 12 puffs per day.
Infants and children under
12 years of age: Not recommended. Syrup and
tablets— Adults and chil-
dren 9 years of age and
older: 20 mg, 3 or 4 times
a day. Infants and children
under 9 years of age:
Consult a pediatrician.

ONSET OF EFFECT
Inhalation: Within 5 min-
utes. Oral: 15 to 30 minutes.

DURATION OF ACTION
Inhalation: 1 to 5 hours.
Oral: Up to 4 hours.

DIETARY ADVICE
Maintain your usual food
and fluid intake.

STORAGE
Store in a tightly sealed container away from heat and
direct light. Do not refrigerate inhalation solutions.

IF YOU MISS A DOSE
Skip the missed dose and
resume your regular dosage
schedule. Do not double the
next dose.

STOPPING THE DRUG
It may not be necessary to
finish the recommended
course of therapy. Consult
your doctor.

PROLONGED USE
Therapy may require
months or years. Excessive
use may result in temporary
loss of effectiveness.

PRECAUTIONS
Over 60: Adverse reactions
may be more likely and
more severe in older
patients.

**Driving and Hazardous
Work:** Avoid such activities
until you determine how the
medicine affects you.

Alcohol: No special precautions are necessary.

Pregnancy: Adequate studies have not been done; the
benefits must be weighed
against potential risks. Consult your doctor for specific
advice.

Breast Feeding: Mothers
who wish to breast feed
while taking this drug
should discuss the matter
with their doctor.

Infants and Children:
Use of the inhalation
aerosol is not recommended
in children younger than 12.

Special Concerns: Pay
heed to any breathing problem that does not improve
after your usual nebulizer
treatment or usual number
of puffs. Seek help immediately if you feel your lungs
are persistently constricted,
if you are using more than
the recommended number
of treatments per day, or if
you feel a recent attack is
somehow different from
others.

OVERDOSE
Symptoms: Chest pain or
heaviness; irregular, racing,
fluttering, or pounding
heartbeat; dizziness; lightheadedness; fainting; severe
weakness; severe headache

What to Do: Call your
doctor, emergency medical
services (EMS), or the
nearest poison control center immediately.

DRUG INTERACTIONS
Consult your doctor for specific advice if you are taking
a beta-blocker, ergotamine
or ergotamine-like medications, antidepressants, digitalis drugs, or an MAO
inhibitor.

FOOD INTERACTIONS
No known food interactions.

DISEASE INTERACTIONS
Consult your doctor if you
have a history of substance
abuse (especially cocaine),
seizures, brain damage,
heart disease, heartbeat
irregularities, high blood
pressure, anxiety disorders,
or a thyroid condition.

Metformin

Glucophage 850 mg
(BRISTOL-MYERS SQUIBB)

▶ Drug Class: Antidiabetic
  agent/biguanide

▶ Available in: Tablets,
  extended-release tablets

▶ Available OTC? No

▶ As Generic? No

Side Effects

SERIOUS
In rare cases, metformin may lead to lactic acidosis, an abnormal and potentially life-threatening buildup of lactic acid in the blood. Symptoms include rapid, shallow breathing, unusual sleepiness or weakness, muscle pain, and abdominal distress. Metformin also occasionally causes abnormally low blood glucose levels (hypoglycemia); symptoms include blurred vision, cold sweats, confusion, anxiousness, rapid heartbeat, shakiness, and nausea. Seek medical assistance immediately.

COMMON
Diarrhea, nausea, vomiting, abdominal bloating, gas, diminished appetite. Usually such symptoms are mild and transient. Consult your doctor if the symptoms persist or increase in severity.

LESS COMMON
Unpleasant or metallic taste in mouth.

PRINCIPAL USES
Used to lower abnormally high blood glucose (sugar) levels in patients with non-insulin-dependent (type 2) diabetes whose blood sugar levels cannot be adequately controlled by diet or exercise alone. The drug may be used alone or in conjunction with sulfonylurea drugs or insulin.

HOW THE DRUG WORKS
Metformin decreases the liver's production of glucose, inhibits the breakdown of fatty acids used to produce glucose, and increases the removal of glucose from muscle, the liver, and other body tissues where it is stored.

DOSAGE
Available in 500 mg, 850 mg, or 1,000 mg tablets; extended-release tablets are available in 500-mg strength only and should not be used by patients under the age of 17. Initial dose: 500 mg a day, taken with dinner. If tolerated, a second dose can be added, taken with breakfast. The dose may be slowly increased (1 tablet every 1 or 2 weeks) to a maximum of 2,500 mg a day. Alternatively, 850 mg daily, increased by 850 mg every other week to a maximum of 2,550 mg per day.

ONSET OF EFFECT
Within 2 hours.

DURATION OF ACTION
From 12 to 15 hours.

DIETARY ADVICE
Take with meals to reduce risk of stomach upset. Tablets must be swallowed whole, not crushed or chewed.

STORAGE
Store in a sealed container at room temperature away from heat and direct light.

IF YOU MISS A DOSE
Take it with food as soon as you remember. However, if it is almost time for the next dose, skip the missed dose and resume your regular dosage schedule. Do not double the next dose.

STOPPING THE DRUG
Stop taking metformin only when your doctor advises.

PROLONGED USE
Because metformin helps to manage diabetes but does not cure the disease, its use will be ongoing as long as your blood glucose levels are being adequately controlled. If not, the metformin dosage may be adjusted or a different treatment prescribed.

PRECAUTIONS
Over 60: Because metformin is metabolized in the kidneys, extra caution is warranted in thin, elderly patients with mild adrenal insufficiency (not often detected by the usual tests for kidney impairment).

Driving and Hazardous Work: No special precautions are necessary.

Alcohol: Excessive amounts of alcohol can increase the effect of metformin, possibly resulting in abnormally low blood glucose levels.

Pregnancy: Taking metformin is not advised during pregnancy. Consult your doctor if you become pregnant or plan to become pregnant; insulin is usually the treatment of choice for pregnant diabetic women.

Breast Feeding: Metformin passes into breast milk, although it has not been shown to cause harm to nursing infants. Consult your doctor for advice.

Infants and Children: Glucophage may be used in children 10 years of age and older; Glucophage XR may be used in children 17 years of age and older.

Special Concerns: Do not take metformin if you have previously had an allergic reaction to it.

OVERDOSE
Symptoms: Symptoms of lactic acidosis or hypoglycemia (see Serious Side Effects).

What to Do: Seek emergency medical assistance right away.

DRUG INTERACTIONS
Consult your doctor if you are taking any of the following: amiloride, calcium channel blockers, cimetidine, digoxin, furosemide, morphine, procainamide, quinidine, quinine, ranitidine, trimethoprim, triamterene, or vancomycin.

FOOD INTERACTIONS
The amount and type of food you eat affect your blood glucose levels and must be taken into account while you receive metformin therapy.

DISEASE INTERACTIONS
Do not take metformin if you have any condition that requires careful control of blood glucose levels, such as severe infection; any condition contributing to abnormally low blood oxygen levels, such as congestive heart failure or emphysema; metabolic acidosis (buildup of acid in the blood); a history of alcohol abuse; or kidney or liver disease.

Methadone Hydrochloride

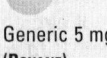

Generic 5 mg
(ROXANE)

▶ Drug Class: Opioid (narcotic) analgesic

▶ Available in: Oral concentrate, oral solution, tablets, injection

▶ Available OTC? No

▶ As Generic? Yes

Side Effects

SERIOUS
Serious side effects of methadone are indistinguishable from those of overdose: Confusion; severe drowsiness, weakness, or dizziness; slurred speech; small, pinpoint pupils; cold, clammy skin; slow breathing; seizures; loss of consciousness.

COMMON
Dizziness or lightheadedness, nausea or vomiting, constipation, drowsiness, itching.

LESS COMMON
Sweating, swelling of the feet and ankles, redness or flushing of face.

PRINCIPAL USES
To relieve severe pain. It is also used to prevent or ease withdrawal symptoms during detoxification from illegal narcotics, and to serve as maintenance therapy during narcotic addiction treatment programs.

HOW THE DRUG WORKS
Methadone is a long-acting opioid. It binds with natural opiate receptors throughout the central nervous system, thereby altering the perception of and emotional response to pain.

DOSAGE
For pain— Oral solution: 5 to 20 mg every 6 to 8 hours. Tablets: 5 to 10 mg every 6 to 8 hours. For narcotic addiction maintenance therapy— Oral solution or tablets: Up to 120 mg a day, depending on individual needs. Children: Dosages must be determined by your doctor. The injectable form is administered only when patients are unable to take methadone orally.

ONSET OF EFFECT
Oral forms: 30 minutes to 1 hour.

DURATION OF ACTION
Oral forms: 4 to 8 hours.

DIETARY ADVICE
Oral forms can be taken with food to lessen stomach upset. Dispersible tablets should be stirred into water or juice before taking.

STORAGE
Store the medication in a tightly sealed container away from heat, moisture, and direct light. Do not freeze the liquid forms.

IF YOU MISS A DOSE
If you are taking methadone on a fixed schedule, take as soon as you remember. If it is near the time for the next dose, skip the missed dose and resume your regular dosage schedule. Do not double the next dose.

STOPPING THE DRUG
The decision to stop taking the drug should be made by your doctor.

PROLONGED USE
Prolonged use can cause physical dependence.

PRECAUTIONS
Over 60: Adverse reactions may be more likely and more severe in older patients.

Driving and Hazardous Work: Avoid such activities until you determine how the medicine affects you.

Alcohol: Avoid alcohol.

Pregnancy: Adequate human studies have not been done. Before taking methadone, tell your doctor if you are pregnant or plan to become pregnant, and discuss the relative risks and benefits of methadone use during pregnancy.

Breast Feeding: Methadone passes into breast milk; caution is advised. Taking large doses in a maintenance program can cause physical dependence in the baby. Consult your doctor for advice.

Infants and Children: Adverse reactions may be more likely and more severe in children. Consult your doctor for advice.

Special Concerns: If you feel the medication is not working properly after a few weeks, do not increase the dose. Consult your doctor. Before having any surgery, tell the doctor or dentist in charge that you are taking methadone.

OVERDOSE
Symptoms: Confusion; slurred speech; extreme sedation, weakness, or dizziness; small, pinpoint pupils; cold, clammy skin; slow breathing; seizures; loss of consciousness.

What to Do: Call your doctor, emergency medical services (EMS), or the nearest poison control center immediately.

DRUG INTERACTIONS
Consult your doctor for specific advice if you are taking carbamazepine or other medicine for seizures, barbiturates, sedatives, cough medicines, decongestants, antidepressants, other prescription pain medications, MAO inhibitors, naltrexone, rifampin, or zidovudine.

FOOD INTERACTIONS
None are known.

DISEASE INTERACTIONS
Consult your doctor if you have any of the following: history of alcohol or drug abuse; emotional illness; brain disorders or head injury; seizures; lung disease; prostate problems or other problems with urination; gallstones; colitis; heart, kidney, liver, or thyroid disease.

Methamphetamine Hydrochloride

BRAND NAMES
Desoxyn, Desoxyn
Gradumet

▶ Drug Class: Central
nervous system stimulant/
amphetamine

▶ Available in: Tablets,
extended-release tablets

▶ Available OTC? No

▶ As Generic? No

Side Effects

SERIOUS
Irregular heartbeat, chest
pain, increased blood
pressure, skin rash,
uncontrollable move-
ments of arms and legs,
mental changes, unusual
weakness, very high
fever. Call your doctor
immediately.

COMMON
Mood changes, insomnia,
drowsiness, restlessness.

LESS COMMON
Blurred vision, constipa-
tion, diarrhea, loss of
appetite, headache,
increased sweating,
stomach cramps or
abdominal pain, nausea
or vomiting, changes
in sexual desire or
decreased sexual ability.

PRINCIPAL USES
To treat narcolepsy and
attention-deficit hyperactivity disorder (ADHD) in children and adults.

HOW THE DRUG WORKS
Methamphetamine activates
nerve cells in the brain and
spinal cord to increase
motor activity and alertness,
and lessen drowsiness and
fatigue. In hyperactivity disorders and narcolepsy,
amphetamines improve the
ability to pay attention.

DOSAGE
Children age 6 and older—
To start, regular tablets are
used, 5 mg, 1 or 2 times a
day. The dose is gradually
increased to 20 to 25 mg a
day, either as regular tablets
(in 2 or 3 divided doses) or
extended-release tablets
(once a day). Adults—
Tablets: To start, 5 mg, 2
or 3 times a day. Extended-
release tablets: To start, 10
mg, 1 or 2 times a day. The
dosage may be increased to
a total of 60 mg a day, in 2
or 3 divided doses.

ONSET OF EFFECT
Variable.

DURATION OF ACTION
Variable.

DIETARY ADVICE
This drug can be taken
without regard to food.
Avoid caffeine-containing
beverages like tea, coffee,
and some carbonated colas.
Avoid acidic foods that are
rich in vitamin C, such as
fruit juices and other citrus
products. Avoid vitamin C
tablets.

STORAGE
Store in a tightly sealed container away from heat, moisture, and direct light.

IF YOU MISS A DOSE
Take the missed dose as
soon as you remember. If it
is close to the next dose or
within 6 hours of bedtime,
skip the missed dose and
resume your regular dosage
schedule. Do not double the
next dose.

STOPPING THE DRUG
Take it as prescribed for the
full treatment period, even
if you begin to feel better
before the scheduled end
of therapy. The decision to
stop taking the drug should
be made by your doctor.
The doctor may decrease
your dosage gradually to
reduce the possibility of
withdrawal symptoms.

PROLONGED USE
Amphetamines can be habit-
forming, and prolonged use
may increase the risk of
dependency.

PRECAUTIONS
Over 60: There is no specific information comparing
use of methamphetamine in
older patients with use in
younger persons.

**Driving and Hazardous
Work:** Do not drive or
engage in hazardous work
until you determine how the
medicine affects you.

Alcohol: Avoid alcohol.

Pregnancy: Adequate
human studies have not
been completed. Before taking methamphetamine, tell
your doctor if you are pregnant or plan to become
pregnant.

Breast Feeding: Methamphetamine passes into
breast milk; do not use
it while nursing.

Infants and Children:
This drug is not recom-
mended for use by children
under age 6.

Special Concerns: Take
methamphetamine only as
directed and do not
increase the dose on your
own. Remember that
fatigue, excessive drowsiness, or depression while
taking stimulants may mean
an emergency situation is
developing. Difficulty sleeping may be improved by
taking the last scheduled
dose several hours before
bedtime.

OVERDOSE
Symptoms: Extreme
degrees of restlessness,
agitation, bizarre behavior;
panic; rapid breathing; confusion; high fever; hallucinations; seizures; coma.

What to Do: Call your
doctor, emergency medical
services (EMS), or the
nearest poison control
center immediately.

DRUG INTERACTIONS
Consult your doctor for specific advice if you are taking
tricyclic antidepressants,
caffeine, beta-blockers, digitalis drugs, central nervous
system stimulants, meperidine, MAO inhibitors, sympathomimetic agents, or
thyroid hormones.

FOOD INTERACTIONS
Citrus juices and caffeinated
beverages and foods may
interact with this drug.

DISEASE INTERACTIONS
Consult your doctor if you
have any of the following:
advanced blood vessel disease, heart disease, hyperthyroidism, hypertension,
severe anxiety, Tourette's
syndrome, glaucoma, or a
history of drug abuse.

Methenamine and Methenamine Salts

BRAND NAMES
Hiprex, Mandelamine, Urex

Generic 500 mg
(JEROME STEVENS)

▶ Drug Class: Anti-infective

▶ Available in: Tablets, enteric-coated tablets, oral suspension, granules for solution

▶ Available OTC? No

▶ As Generic? Yes

Side Effects

SERIOUS
Skin rash, blood in urine, lower back pain, burning or pain while urinating. Call your physician immediately.

COMMON
No common side effects are associated with the use of methenamine.

LESS COMMON
Nausea or vomiting may occur. Contact your doctor if such symptoms persist.

PRINCIPAL USES
To prevent and treat urinary tract infections.

HOW THE DRUG WORKS
Methenamine and methenamine salts kill bacteria in the urinary tract by forming ammonia and formaldehyde, chemicals that are toxic to the microorganisms that cause infection.

DOSAGE
For prevention of infection— Adults and teenagers: 1,000 mg, 2 times a day. Children ages 6 to 12: 500 mg to 1,000 mg, 2 times a day. For treatment of infection— Adults and teenagers: 1,000 mg, 4 times a day. Children ages 6 to 12: 500 mg, 4 times a day. Children up to age 6: 8.3 mg per lb of body weight, 4 times a day.

ONSET OF EFFECT
Within 1 hour.

DURATION OF ACTION
Up to 8 hours.

DIETARY ADVICE
Take it after meals and at bedtime. Drink plenty of liquids, ensuring that your fluid intake is at least 2 quarts a day. This drug works best in highly acidic urine. Maintain a protein-rich diet and consume liberal amounts of cranberries or cranberry juice, plums, or prunes to ensure sufficiently acidic urine. If this cannot be achieved through diet alone, take vitamin C supplements. Avoid citrus fruits and juices.

STORAGE
Store in a tightly sealed container away from heat and direct light.

IF YOU MISS A DOSE
Take it as soon as you remember. However, if it is near the time for the next dose, skip the missed dose and resume your regular dosage schedule. Do not double the next dose.

STOPPING THE DRUG
Take as prescribed for the full treatment period, even if you begin to feel better before the scheduled end of therapy.

PROLONGED USE
Consult your doctor about the need for liver function tests and other tests during prolonged therapy.

PRECAUTIONS
Over 60: Adverse reactions may be more likely and more severe in older patients.

Driving and Hazardous Work: Avoid such activities until you determine how the medication affects you.

Alcohol: No special precautions are necessary.

Pregnancy: It is not known whether methenamine is harmful during pregnancy. Discuss with your physician the relative risks and benefits.

Breast Feeding: Methenamine passes into breast milk but has not been reported to cause problems in nursing babies. Consult your doctor about its use during nursing.

Infants and Children: No special problems are expected.

Special Concerns: If you take the dry granule form of methenamine, dissolve the contents of each packet in 2 to 4 ounces of water and stir well before drinking it. Avoid use of antacids while taking this medicine. Urine pH should be monitored before starting and throughout therapy.

OVERDOSE
Symptoms: No specific ones have been reported.

What to Do: An overdose of methenamine is unlikely to be life-threatening. However, if someone takes a much larger dose than prescribed, call your doctor, emergency medical services (EMS), or the nearest poison control center.

DRUG INTERACTIONS
Consult your doctor for advice if you are taking thiazide diuretics, sodium bicarbonate, methazolamide, sulfamethoxazole, or urinary alkalizers such as acetazolamide.

FOOD INTERACTIONS
While taking methenamine, avoid milk products, citrus fruits and juices, and alkaline foods like vegetables and peanuts.

DISEASE INTERACTIONS
Use of methenamine may cause complications in patients with liver or kidney disease, since these organs work together to remove the medication from the body. Before you take methenamine, tell your doctor if you have ever experienced severe dehydration.

Methimazole

Tapazole 5 mg
(LILLY)

▶ Drug Class: Antithyroid agent

▶ Available in: Tablets

▶ Available OTC? No

▶ As Generic? No

Side Effects

SERIOUS
Cough, continuing or severe fever or chills, hoarseness, mouth sores, pain, swelling, or redness in joints, throat infection, yellow discoloration of the skin or eyes, general feeling of illness. Call your doctor immediately.

COMMON
Mild and temporary fever; rash or itching.

LESS COMMON
Backache; black and tarry stools; blood in urine or stools; shortness of breath; increased or decreased urination; swelling of feet or lower legs; swollen lymph or salivary glands; numbness or tingling of face, fingers, or toes; dizziness; nausea; stomach pain; vomiting.

PRINCIPAL USES
To treat conditions in which the thyroid gland produces too much thyroid hormone.

HOW THE DRUG WORKS
Methimazole interferes with the body's ability to use iodine in the manufacture of thyroid hormone.

DOSAGE
Adults: 15 to 60 mg a day in 1 daily dose or in 2 divided daily doses. Usual maintenance dose is 5 to 15 mg a day. Children: 0.2 mg per 2.2 lbs (1 kg) of body weight a day in 1 daily dose or in 2 divided daily doses. To treat a thyroid crisis: 12 to 20 mg every 4 hours.

ONSET OF EFFECT
5 days or more.

DURATION OF ACTION
Unknown.

DIETARY ADVICE
Methimazole can be taken with or without food. It should be taken consistently in the same way, either with or between meals.

STORAGE
Store in a tightly sealed container away from heat and direct light.

IF YOU MISS A DOSE
Take it as soon as you remember. However, if it is near the time for the next dose, skip the missed dose and resume your regular dosage schedule. Do not double the next dose.

STOPPING THE DRUG
Take it as prescribed for the full treatment period, even if you begin to feel better before the scheduled end of therapy.

PROLONGED USE
No special problems are expected. It may be necessary to take this medication for several years.

PRECAUTIONS

Over 60: Adverse reactions may be more common and more severe in older patients.

Driving and Hazardous Work: The use of this medication should not impair your ability to perform such tasks safely.

Alcohol: Consult your doctor about using alcohol while taking methimazole.

Pregnancy: Too large a dose during pregnancy may cause problems in the fetus. Use of the prescribed dose, with careful monitoring, is not likely to cause problems.

Breast Feeding: Methimazole passes into breast milk, but your doctor may allow you to continue to nurse if the dose is low and the infant is checked regularly.

Infants and Children: No special problems are expected.

Special Concerns: Before undergoing any kind of medical or dental procedure, tell the doctor or dentist in charge that you are taking methimazole. During and after treatment with methimazole, do not receive any immunizations without your doctor's approval, and avoid persons who have taken oral polio vaccine recently.

OVERDOSE
Symptoms: Nausea, vomiting, coldness, constipation, changes in menstrual period, dry and puffy skin, headache, listlessness, swollen neck, sleepiness, muscle aches, unusual weight gain.

What to Do: An overdose of methimazole is unlikely to be life-threatening. However, if someone takes a much larger dose than prescribed, call your doctor, emergency medical services (EMS), or the local poison control center right away.

DRUG INTERACTIONS
Consult your doctor for specific advice if you are taking amiodarone, iodinated glycerol, potassium iodide, anticoagulants, beta-blockers, theophylline, or digitalis drugs.

FOOD INTERACTIONS
Consult your doctor about a special low-iodine diet.

DISEASE INTERACTIONS
Use of methimazole may cause complications in patients with liver disease, since this organ works to remove the medication from the body.

Methocarbamol

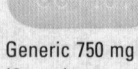

Generic 750 mg
(GENEVA)

▶ Drug Class: Muscle relaxant

▶ Available in: Tablets, injection

▶ Available OTC? No

▶ As Generic? Yes

Side Effects

SERIOUS
Fainting; palpitations or rapid heartbeat; fever; hives or severe swelling of face, lips, or tongue along with shortness of breath, chest tightness, or wheezing (indicating a potentially life-threatening allergic reaction); seizures; mental depression. Seek medical help immediately.

COMMON
Blurred, double, or altered vision, dizziness or lightheadedness, drowsiness, dry mouth.

LESS COMMON
Inability to pass urine; sores on lips, ulcers in mouth; abdominal cramps or pain; clumsiness; unsteady gait; confusion; constipation; diarrhea; excitability, nervousness, restlessness, or irritability; flushing or redness of face; headache; heartburn; hiccups; muscle weakness; nausea and vomiting; trembling; insomnia or fitful sleep; burning, red eyes; stuffy nose.

PRINCIPAL USES
Muscle relaxants are used to relieve stiffness and discomfort caused by severe sprains and strains, muscle spasms, or other muscle problems. They may be prescribed in conjunction with other treatment methods, such as physical therapy.

HOW THE DRUG WORKS
Muscle relaxants such as methocarbamol depress activity in the central nervous system (brain and spinal cord), which in turn interferes with the transmission of nerve impulses from the spinal cord to the skeletal muscles.

DOSAGE
Adults and teenagers— Tablets: 1,500 mg, 4 times a day to start, then the dose may be reduced. Injection: 1 to 3 g a day, in 1 or several doses. Children— Consult your pediatrician.

ONSET OF EFFECT
Immediate after injection; within 30 minutes after oral administration.

DURATION OF ACTION
Unknown.

DIETARY ADVICE
Take the tablets with food to reduce stomach irritation.

STORAGE
Store in a tightly sealed container away from heat and direct light.

IF YOU MISS A DOSE
Take it as soon as you remember. However, if it is near the time for the next dose, skip the missed dose and resume your regular dosage schedule. Do not double the next dose.

STOPPING THE DRUG
The decision to stop taking the drug should be made by your doctor.

PROLONGED USE
You should see your doctor regularly for tests and examinations if you take this drug for a prolonged period.

PRECAUTIONS
Over 60: No special problems are expected.

Driving and Hazardous Work: Do not drive or engage in hazardous work until you determine how the medicine affects you.

Alcohol: Avoid alcohol while taking this drug because it may compound the sedative effect and may cause liver damage.

Pregnancy: Adequate studies of methocarbamol during pregnancy have not been done; discuss relative risks and benefits with your doctor.

Breast Feeding: Methocarbamol may pass into breast milk; caution is advised. Consult your doctor for advice.

Infants and Children: No special problems have been documented; consult your pediatrician for advice.

Special Concerns: Methocarbamol can cause false results in tests of sugar levels for diabetic patients. This drug will intensify the effect that alcohol, sedatives, and other central nervous system depressants have on the brain. Do not take methocarbamol if you are allergic to any skeletal muscle relaxant. Use of this drug should be accompanied by bed rest, physical therapy, and other measures to relieve discomfort.

OVERDOSE
Symptoms: Nausea, vomiting, diarrhea, loss of appetite, headache, severe weakness, fainting, breathing difficulties, irritability, seizures, feeling of paralysis, profuse sweating, loss of consciousness.

What to Do: Call your doctor, emergency medical services (EMS), or the nearest poison control center immediately.

DRUG INTERACTIONS
Consult your doctor for specific advice if you are taking any drug that depresses the central nervous system or any tricyclic antidepressant.

FOOD INTERACTIONS
No known food interactions

DISEASE INTERACTIONS
Caution is advised when taking methocarbamol. Consult your doctor if you have a history of any of the following: alcohol or drug abuse, allergies, a blood disease caused by an allergy or another medication, kidney disease, liver disease, porphyria, or epilepsy.

Methotrexate

BRAND NAMES
Folex, Folex PFS, Mexate, Mexate-AQ, Rheumatrex

Generic 2.5 mg
(**MYLAN**)

▶ Drug Class: Antineoplastic agent/antimetabolite; anti-psoriatic; antirheumatic

▶ Available in: Tablets, injection

▶ Available OTC? No

▶ As Generic? Yes

Side Effects

SERIOUS
Black, tarry stools, bloody vomit, diarrhea, flushing or redness of skin, sores in mouth and on lips, stomach pain, blood in urine or stools, confusion, seizures, cough or hoarseness, fever or chills, pain in lower back or side, painful or difficult urination, red spots on skin, shortness of breath, swollen feet or lower legs, unusual bleeding or bruising, back pain, dark urine, drowsiness, dizziness, headache, joint pain, unusual fatigue, yellow-tinged eyes or skin. Call your doctor immediately.

COMMON
Loss of appetite, nausea and vomiting, minor mouth ulcers.

LESS COMMON
Acne, boils, pale skin, skin rash, or itching.

PRINCIPAL USES
To treat certain kinds of cancer, psoriasis, and rheumatoid arthritis.

HOW THE DRUG WORKS
Methotrexate interferes with the activity of an enzyme needed for the maintenance and replication of cells, especially those that divide and proliferate rapidly. Such cells include many types of cancer cells, as well as those that compose the bone marrow and the cells that line the mouth, intestine, and bladder. Consequently, in addition to its cancer-fighting effects, methotrexate may also harm healthy tissues in the body, causing unpleasant or serious side effects. It is unknown how methotrexate works to ease rheumatoid arthritis, but it appears to modify the function of the immune system, whose activity is believed to play a role in the progression of the disease.

DOSAGE
For psoriasis or rheumatoid arthritis— Tablets: 2.5 to 5 mg every 12 hours for 3 doses in 1 week; or 7.5 to 10 mg once a week. Injection: 10 mg, once a week. For cancer— Use and dose depends on type and stage of disease. Your doctor may alter dosage as needed. Consult pediatrician for children's dose.

ONSET OF EFFECT
Unknown.

DURATION OF ACTION
Unknown.

DIETARY ADVICE
This drug is best taken 1 to 2 hours before meals.

STORAGE
Store in a tightly sealed container away from heat, moisture, and direct light.

IF YOU MISS A DOSE
If you miss a dose, do not take the missed dose and do not double the next dose. Resume your regular schedule and check with your doctor.

STOPPING THE DRUG
The decision to stop taking the drug should be made by your doctor.

PROLONGED USE
See your doctor regularly for tests and examinations.

PRECAUTIONS
Over 60: Adverse reactions may be more likely and more severe in older patients.

Driving and Hazardous Work: Avoid such activities until you determine how the medicine affects you.

Alcohol: Avoid alcohol.

Pregnancy: Methotrexate can cause birth defects and other problems; avoid use during pregnancy.

Breast Feeding: Methotrexate passes into breast milk and may cause serious side effects in the nursing infant; it should not be used during breast feeding.

Infants and Children: Infants are more sensitive to the effects of methotrexate. No special problems are expected in older children.

Special Concerns: Methotrexate may lower your resistance to infection by reducing the number of white blood cells in the blood. Do not have any immunizations without your doctor's approval. Avoid people with infections. Use care when shaving, trimming nails, or using sharp objects. Inform your doctor immediately if you have fever, chills, unusual bleeding or bruising, diarrhea, or a cough. Methotrexate may increase skin sensitivity to sunlight. Limit sun exposure until you see how the medicine affects you. After you stop taking methotrexate, you may experience back pain, blurred vision, confusion, seizures, dizziness, fever, or unusual fatigue; consult your doctor immediately.

OVERDOSE
Symptoms: Severe damage to the liver, kidneys, stomach, intestines, bone marrow, and lungs, causing a wide array of symptoms.

What to Do: If you suspect an overdose, seek medical assistance immediately.

DRUG INTERACTIONS
A number of drugs may interact with methotrexate. Consult your doctor for specific advice if you are taking any drugs that may affect the liver such as azathioprine, retinoids, and sulfasalazine; or any other prescription or over-the-counter medication.

FOOD INTERACTIONS
No known food interactions.

DISEASE INTERACTIONS
Consult your doctor if you have any of the following: a history of alcohol abuse, chicken pox, shingles, colitis, any disease of the immune system, kidney stones, any infection, intestinal blockage, kidney disease, liver disease, mouth sores or inflammation, or stomach ulcers.

Methyldopa

Generic 250 mg
(LEDERLE)

Additional photographs

▶ Drug Class: Centrally acting antihypertensive

▶ Available in: Oral suspension, tablets, injection

▶ Available OTC? No

▶ As Generic? Yes

Side Effects

SERIOUS
Fever shortly after starting to take this medicine, swelling of feet or lower legs, mental depression or anxiety, nightmares, dark or amber urine, stomach cramps, chills, troubled breathing, fast heartbeat, general feeling of discomfort, joint pain, skin rash or itching, yellowish tinge to eyes or skin, continued fatigue, pale stools, nausea and vomiting. Call your doctor immediately.

COMMON
Drowsiness, dry mouth, headache.

LESS COMMON
Diarrhea, dizziness or lightheadedness when getting up, decreased sexual performance, slow heartbeat, stuffy nose, swelling of breasts, unusual milk production, tingling, pain, or weakness in hands or feet.

PRINCIPAL USES
To treat high blood pressure (hypertension).

HOW THE DRUG WORKS
Methyldopa acts upon certain areas of the central nervous system (the brain and spinal cord) that regulate the activity of the heart and the smooth muscle tissue surrounding the arteries. The drug causes blood vessels to relax and widen, which in turn lowers blood pressure.

DOSAGE
Suspension or tablets—Adults: 250 mg to 2 g a day in 2 to 4 doses. Children: 10 mg per 2.2 lbs (1 kg) of body weight in 2 to 4 doses. Injection— Adults: 250 to 500 mg injected into a vein every 6 hours. Children: 20 to 40 mg per 2.2 lbs injected every 6 hours.

ONSET OF EFFECT
Unknown.

DURATION OF ACTION
12 to 24 hours after single oral dose, 24 to 48 hours after multiple oral doses; 10 to 16 hours after injection.

DIETARY ADVICE
Methyldopa can be taken without regard to the timing of meals. Follow a healthy diet (low-salt, low-fat, low-cholesterol) as advised by your doctor to help control blood pressure and prevent heart disease.

STORAGE
Store tablets and injection in a tightly sealed container away from heat, moisture, and direct light. Keep oral suspension refrigerated, but do not allow it to freeze.

IF YOU MISS A DOSE
Take it as soon as you remember. However, if it is near the time for the next dose, skip the missed dose and resume your regular dosage schedule. Do not double the next dose.

STOPPING THE DRUG
Do not stop taking this drug suddenly, as this may cause potentially serious health problems. If therapy is to be discontinued, dosage should be reduced gradually, according to a doctor's instructions.

PROLONGED USE
Lifelong therapy may be required. See your doctor regularly for tests and examinations if you take this medicine for a prolonged period.

PRECAUTIONS
Over 60: Adverse reactions may be more likely and more severe in older patients.

Driving and Hazardous Work: Do not drive or engage in hazardous work until you determine how the medicine affects you.

Alcohol: Avoid alcohol.

Pregnancy: Methyldopa is one of the few antihypertensive medications that can be used by pregnant women. It effectively reduces high blood pressure and has been found in several studies to be safe for both the mother and the unborn child.

Breast Feeding: Methyldopa may pass into breast milk; caution is advised. Consult your doctor for advice.

Infants and Children: No special problems are expected.

Special Concerns: Check your weight frequently and tell your doctor if you gain 5 pounds or more.

OVERDOSE
Symptoms: Weakness, fast heartbeat, dizziness, light-headedness, constipation or diarrhea, nausea, vomiting, loss of consciousness.

What to Do: Call your doctor, emergency medical services (EMS), or the nearest poison control center immediately.

DRUG INTERACTIONS
Certain drugs may interact with methyldopa. Consult your doctor for specific advice if you are taking an MAO inhibitor.

FOOD INTERACTIONS
No known food interactions

DISEASE INTERACTIONS
Caution is advised when taking methyldopa. Consult your doctor if you have any of the following: angina, Parkinson's disease, mental depression, or pheochromocytoma. Use of methyldopa may cause complications in patients with kidney disease or liver disease, since these organs work together to remove the medication from the body.

Methylphenidate Hydrochloride

Side Effects

SERIOUS
Fast heartbeat, unusual
bleeding or bruising,
chest pain, fever, joint
pain, increased heartbeat,
skin rash or hives, uncontrolled body movements,
blurred vision or other
vision changes, seizures,
sore throat and fever,
unusual fatigue, weight
loss, mood or mental
changes. Call your doctor
immediately.

COMMON
Loss of appetite, insom-
nia, nervousness.

LESS COMMON
Dizziness, stomach pain,
drowsiness, nausea,
headache.

PRINCIPAL USES
To treat attention-deficit
hyperactivity disorder
(ADHD). It is also used
to treat narcolepsy.

HOW THE DRUG WORKS
Methylphenidate is thought
to stimulate the release of
norepinephrine, a natural
hormone that promotes the
transmission of nerve
impulses in the brain. It
works by decreasing rest-
lessness and increasing
attention in adults and children who cannot concen-
trate for very long, are
easily distracted, or are
unusually impulsive.

DOSAGE
For ADHD— Tablets:
Adults and teenagers: 5 to
20 mg, 2 to 3 times a day,
taken with or after meals.
Children ages 6 to 12: To
start, 5 mg, 2 times a day.
If needed, your doctor may
increase the dose by 5 to
10 mg a week. Extended-
release tablets: Adults,
teenagers and children ages
6 to 12: 20 mg, 1 to 3 times
a day, every 8 hours. For
narcolepsy— Tablets:
Adults and teenagers: 5 to
20 mg, 3 or 4 times a day,
taken with or after meals.
Extended-release tablets:
Adults and teenagers: 20
mg, 2 to 3 times a day.

ONSET OF EFFECT
Tablets: Usually within 30
minutes. Extended-release
tablets: Usually between 30
and 60 minutes.

DURATION OF ACTION
Tablets: 4 to 6 hours.
Extended-release tablets: 6
hours or longer.

DIETARY ADVICE
For ADHD, this medicine
should be taken with or
after meals. For narcolepsy,
it should be taken 30 to 45
minutes before meals.

STORAGE
Store in a tightly sealed container away from heat, moisture, and direct light.

IF YOU MISS A DOSE
Take it as soon as you
remember. If it is near the
time for the next dose, skip
the missed dose and
resume your regular dosage
schedule. Do not double the
next dose.

STOPPING THE DRUG
The decision to stop taking
the drug should be made by
your doctor.

PROLONGED USE
See your doctor regularly
for tests and examinations.

PRECAUTIONS
Over 60: No special problems are expected.

**Driving and Hazardous
Work:** Do not drive or
engage in hazardous work
until you determine how the
medicine affects you.

Alcohol: Avoid alcohol.

Pregnancy: Adequate
human studies have not
been completed. Before taking methylphenidate, tell
your doctor if you are pregnant or plan to become
pregnant.

Breast Feeding: It is not
known whether methyl-
phenidate passes into breast
milk; caution is advised.
Consult your doctor for
advice.

Infants and Children:
This drug is not recom-
mended for use by children
under the age of 6. Older
children may be especially
likely to experience side
effects such as loss of
appetite, stomach pain, and
weight loss.

Special Concerns: To
prevent insomnia, do not
take methylphenidate too
close to bedtime. Your prescription cannot be refilled,
so you must get a new one
from your doctor to obtain
more medication.

OVERDOSE
Symptoms: Agitation, confusion, delirium, seizures,
dry mouth, false sense of
well-being, rapid, pounding,
or irregular heartbeat, fever,
sweating, severe headache,
increased blood pressure,
muscle twitching, trembling
or tremors, vomiting.

What to Do: Call your
doctor, emergency medical
services (EMS), or the
nearest poison control center immediately.

DRUG INTERACTIONS
Do not take methylphen-
idate if you are taking, or
took within the past 14
days, an MAO inhibitor. Call
your doctor for specific
advice if you are taking caffeine, amantadine, appetite
suppressants, tricyclic antidepressants, chlophedianol,
pemoline, asthma medicine,
amphetamines, medicine for
colds or sinus problems or
allergies, nabilone, or
pimozide.

FOOD INTERACTIONS
Do not drink large amounts
of caffeinated beverages
like coffee, tea, soft drinks,
cocoa, or chocolate milk.

DISEASE INTERACTIONS
Consult your doctor if you
have Tourette's syndrome
or other tics, glaucoma,
epilepsy or another seizure
disorder, high blood pressure, psychosis, severe anxiety, depression, or a history
of alcohol or drug abuse.

Methylprednisolone

Medrol 2 mg
(UPJOHN)

Additional photographs

▶ Drug Class: Corticosteroid

▶ Available in: Tablets,
injection, enema

▶ Available OTC? No

▶ As Generic? Yes

Side Effects

SERIOUS
Vision problems, frequent
urination, increased
thirst, rectal bleeding,
blistering skin, confusion,
hallucinations, paranoia,
euphoria, depression,
mood swings, redness
and swelling at injection
site. Call your doctor
immediately.

COMMON
Increased appetite, indi-
gestion, nervousness,
insomnia, greater suscep-
tibility to infections,
increased blood pressure,
slowed wound healing,
weight gain, easy bruis-
ing, fluid retention.

LESS COMMON
Change in skin color,
dizziness, headache,
increased sweating,
unusual growth of body
or facial hair, increased
blood sugar, peptic
ulcers, adrenal insuffi-
ciency, muscle weakness,
cataracts, glaucoma,
osteoporosis.

PRINCIPAL USES
To treat numerous condi-
tions that involve inflammation (a response by body
tissues, producing redness,
warmth, swelling, and pain).
Such conditions include
arthritis, allergic reactions,
asthma, some skin diseases,
multiple sclerosis flare-ups,
and other autoimmune dis-
eases. Also prescribed to
treat deficiency of natural
steroid hormones.

HOW THE DRUG WORKS
This hormone mimics the
effects of the body's natural
corticosteroids. It depresses
the synthesis, release, and
activity of inflammation-producing body chemicals. It
also suppresses the activity
of the immune system.

DOSAGE
Tablets: 4 to 160 mg a day,
depending on condition, in 1
or more doses. Injection: 10
to 160 mg a day injected
into a muscle or vein, or 4
to 120 mg as needed,
injected into a muscle, joint,
or lesion. Enema: 40 mg, 3
to 7 times a week. Consult
your pediatrician for children's dose.

ONSET OF EFFECT
Varies widely depending on
form used.

DURATION OF ACTION
30 to 36 hours with tablets;
1 to 4 weeks after muscle
injection; 1 to 5 weeks after
other injections.

DIETARY ADVICE
Take it with food or milk to
minimize stomach upset.
Your doctor may recom-
mend a low-salt, high-potassium, high-protein diet.

STORAGE
Store in a tightly sealed container away from heat, moisture, and direct light. Do
not freeze the liquid form.

IF YOU MISS A DOSE
If you take several doses a
day and it is close to the
next dose, double the next
dose. If you take 1 dose a
day and you do not remem-
ber until the next day, skip
the missed dose and do not
double the next dose.

STOPPING THE DRUG
With long-term therapy, do
not stop taking the drug
abruptly; the dosage should
be decreased gradually.

PROLONGED USE
Long-term use may lead to
cataracts, diabetes, hypertension, or osteoporosis; see
your physician for regular
visits.

PRECAUTIONS
Over 60: Adverse reactions
may be more likely and
more severe in older
patients.

**Driving and Hazardous
Work:** Avoid such activities
until you determine how the
medicine affects you.

Alcohol: May cause stomach problems; avoid it
unless your physician
approves occasional
moderate drinking.

Pregnancy: Overuse during pregnancy can impair
growth and development
of the child.

Breast Feeding: Do not
use this drug while nursing.

Infants and Children:
Methylprednisolone may
retard the development of
bone and other tissues.

Special Concerns: This
drug can lower your resistance to infection. Avoid
immunizations with live vaccines. Patients undergoing
long-term therapy should
wear a medical-alert
bracelet. Call your doctor if
you develop a fever.

OVERDOSE
Symptoms: Fever, muscle
or joint pain, nausea, dizziness, fainting, difficulty
breathing. Prolonged
overuse: Moonface, obesity,
unusual hair growth, acne,
loss of sexual function, mus
cle wasting.

What to Do: Seek medical
assistance immediately.

DRUG INTERACTIONS
Consult your doctor for specific advice if you are taking
aminoglutethimide,
antacids, barbiturates, carbamazepine, griseofulvin,
mitotane, phenylbutazone,
phenytoin, primidone,
rifampin, injectable amphotericin B, oral antidiabetes
agents, insulin, digitalis
drugs, diuretics, or medications containing potassium
or sodium.

FOOD INTERACTIONS
Avoid excess sodium.

DISEASE INTERACTIONS
Consult your doctor if you
have a history of bone disease, chicken pox, measles,
gastrointestinal disorders,
diabetes, recent serious
infection, glaucoma, heart
disease, hypertension, liver
or kidney disorders, high
blood cholesterol, thyroid
problems, myasthenia
gravis, or lupus.

Methysergide Maleate

▶ Drug Class: Antimigraine/
antiheadache drug

▶ Available in: Tablets

▶ Available OTC? No

▶ As Generic? No

Side Effects

SERIOUS
Chest pain or tightness; shortness of breath; extreme dizziness; difficult or painful urination; large increase or decrease in urine output; pain in the arms, legs, groin, lower back, or side; swelling of hands, ankles, feet, or lower legs; fever or chills; pale or cold hands or feet; hallucinations. Call your doctor immediately. Contact your doctor as soon as possible if you experience abdominal pain, itching, numbness or tingling of fingers, toes, or face, or weakness in the legs.

COMMON
Diarrhea; mild dizziness or lightheadedness, particularly upon arising from a lying or sitting position; drowsiness; nausea; vomiting.

LESS COMMON
Vision changes, loss of coordination, rapid or slow heartbeat, cough or hoarseness, loss of appetite or weight, raised red spots on your skin, redness or flushing of the face, skin rash.

PRINCIPAL USES
Used to prevent vascular headaches (those that occur in response to changes in normal blood flow within the blood vessels in the brain), such as migraines and cluster headaches. Because of the possible risk of serious, irreversible side effects, methysergide is prescribed only as a last resort for patients with frequent or disabling headaches who are unresponsive to other treatments. This medication is not useful against tension headaches or a vascular headache that has already started.

HOW THE DRUG WORKS
The exact mechanism of action is unknown, although it appears that methysergide eases vascular headaches by causing constriction of the blood vessels in the brain. It is also believed to block the effects of serotonin, a chemical messenger in the nervous system associated with vascular headaches.

DOSAGE
One 2 mg tablet, 2 or 3 times a day, with meals or milk. Do not crush methysergide tablets before taking them.

ONSET OF EFFECT
Within 1 to 2 days.

DURATION OF ACTION
From 1 to 2 days.

DIETARY ADVICE
Take methysergide with meals or milk to prevent stomach upset. A low-salt diet is advised.

STORAGE
Store in a tightly sealed container, away from direct light, moisture, and extremes in temperature.

IF YOU MISS A DOSE
Take it as soon as you remember. However, if it is almost time for the next dose, skip the missed dose and resume your regular dosage schedule. Do not double the next dose.

STOPPING THE DRUG
Stop taking methysergide only when your doctor advises. Methysergide is usually discontinued gradually over 2 to 3 weeks to prevent rebound headaches, which may occur if the drug is discontinued abruptly.

PROLONGED USE
To reduce the risk of serious side effects, after every 4-month course of methysergide therapy, discontinue the drug for 4 weeks before starting the next course.

PRECAUTIONS
Over 60: Adverse reactions may be more likely and more severe in older patients.

Driving and Hazardous Work: Do not drive or engage in hazardous work until you determine how the drug affects you.

Alcohol: Avoid alcohol, which can trigger or exacerbate vascular headaches.

Pregnancy: Avoid use during pregnancy. Consult your doctor if you become or plan to become pregnant.

Breast Feeding: Do not use methysergide while breast feeding.

Infants and Children: Methysergide is not recommended for this age group because of the potential adverse reactions associated with its long-term use.

Special Concerns: Avoid smoking, since it may increase the risk of side effects associated with decreased blood circulation.

OVERDOSE
Symptoms: Cold and pale hands or feet, severe dizziness, excitability.

What to Do: Seek emergency medical assistance right away.

DRUG INTERACTIONS
Consult your physician if you are using or plan to use any other drugs, particularly other types of ergot alkaloids, epinephrine, metaraminol, methoxamine, norepinephrine, phenylephrine, local anesthesia, or tobacco products.

FOOD INTERACTIONS
No known food interactions.

DISEASE INTERACTIONS
Tell your doctor if you have or have had any other medical problems, including arthritis, heart or blood vessel disease, high blood pressure, kidney, liver, or lung disease, stomach ulcer, severe infection, or severe itching.

Metoclopramide Hydrochloride

BRAND NAMES
Clopra, Octamide,
Octamide PFS,
Reclomide, Reglan

Generic 10 mg
(SCHEIN)

▶ Drug Class: Gastrointestinal
   stimulant

▶ Available in: Tablets, syrup,
   injection

▶ Available OTC? No

▶ As Generic? Yes

Side Effects

SERIOUS
Muscle spasms, aching
or crawling sensation in
lower legs, stiffness or
uncontrolled movements
of arms or legs, panicky
feeling, unusual nervous-
ness, restlessness,
irritability, difficulty
speaking or swallowing,
dizziness or fainting, fast
or irregular heartbeat,
general fatigue, shaking
of hands and fingers,
uncontrolled chewing
movements, lip smacking
or puckering, loss of balance, severe headache,
unusual tongue move-
ments, difficulty walking
or shuffling walk. Call
your doctor immediately.

COMMON
Diarrhea, restlessness,
drowsiness.

LESS COMMON
Breast tenderness and
swelling, increased flow
of breast milk, menstrual
changes, depression, con-
stipation, nausea, skin
rash, insomnia, dryness
of mouth.

PRINCIPAL USES
To prevent nausea and vomiting caused by anticancer
medicines or to treat
impaired emptying of food
from the stomach (gastro-
paresis) as a complication
of diabetes. Also used as a
short-term treatment for
heartburn (gastroesopha-
geal reflux, a backflow of
stomach acid into the
esophagus).

HOW THE DRUG WORKS
Metoclopramide increases
the contractions or move-
ments of the stomach and
small intestine. It decreases
nausea by blocking the
effect of the chemical
dopamine in the vomiting
center of the brain.

DOSAGE
Tablets or syrup— To treat
diabetic gastroparesis:
Adults and teenagers: 10
mg, 30 minutes before
symptoms are likely to
begin or before each meal
and at bedtime, up to 4
times a day. For heartburn:
Adults and teenagers: 10 to
15 mg, 30 minutes before
symptoms are likely to
begin or before each meal
and bedtime. To increase
movements of stomach and
intestine: Children ages 5 to
14: 2.5 to 5 mg, 3 times a
day, 30 minutes before
meals. Injection— To
increase movements of
stomach and intestine:
Adults and teenagers: 10
mg into a vein. Children:
0.45 mg per lb of body
weight into a vein. Dose
may be repeated after 60
minutes. To prevent vomiting and nausea caused by
cancer medicines: Adults
and teenagers: 1 to 2 mg
per 2.2 lbs (1 kg) into a vein
30 minutes before taking
cancer medicine. Children:
1 mg per 2.2 lbs (1 kg) into
a vein.

ONSET OF EFFECT
Within 3 minutes of intravenous injection; 10 to 15
minutes of intramuscular
injection; 30 to 60 minutes
after tablets or syrup.

DURATION OF ACTION
1 to 2 hours.

DIETARY ADVICE
Take the drug 30 minutes
before meals unless your
doctor directs otherwise.

STORAGE
Store in a tightly sealed container away from heat, moisture, and direct light.

IF YOU MISS A DOSE
Take it as soon as you
remember. If it is near the
time for the next dose, skip
the missed dose and
resume your regular dosage
schedule. Do not double the
next dose.

STOPPING THE DRUG
The decision to stop taking
the drug should be made by
your doctor.

PROLONGED USE
You should see your doctor
regularly for tests and
examinations if you take
this drug for a prolonged
period.

PRECAUTIONS
Over 60: Adverse reactions
may be more likely and
more severe in older
patients.

**Driving and Hazardous
Work:** Do not drive or
engage in hazardous work
until you determine how the
medicine affects you.

Alcohol: Avoid alcohol.

Pregnancy: Adequate
human studies have not
been completed. Before taking metoclopramide, tell
your doctor if you are pregnant or plan to become
pregnant.

Breast Feeding: Metoclopramide passes into breast
milk; caution is advised.
Consult your doctor for
specific advice.

Infants and Children:
The dosage and use should
be determined by your
doctor. Adverse effects
are more likely to occur
in infants and children.

Special Concerns: Avoid
activities requiring alertness
for 2 hours after each dose.

OVERDOSE
Symptoms: Drowsiness,
confusion, muscle contractions, irritability, agitation.

What to Do: Call your
doctor, emergency medical
services (EMS), or the
nearest poison control
center immediately.

DRUG INTERACTIONS
Consult your doctor for specific advice if you are taking
central nervous system
depressants such as antihistamines, cold medicines,
sleep aids, or tranquilizers.

FOOD INTERACTIONS
No known food interactions.

DISEASE INTERACTIONS
Consult your doctor if you
have a history of abdominal
or stomach bleeding,
asthma, high blood pres-
sure, intestinal blockage,
Parkinson's disease,
epilepsy, or kidney or
liver disease.

Metolazone

Zaroxolyn 5 mg
(FISONS)

Additional photographs

▶ Drug Class: Thiazide-like diuretic

▶ Available in: Tablets, extended-release tablets

▶ Available OTC? No

▶ As Generic? Yes

Side Effects

SERIOUS
Skin rash, hives, intense itching, swelling of the mouth and throat, breathing difficulty, heart rhythm irregularities, lightheadedness, unusual bleeding or bruising. The powerful combination of metolazone and other diuretics may cause severe dehydration, possibly leading to kidney failure. Call your doctor immediately.

COMMON
Potassium depletion may lead to heart palpitations and weakness. Fluid depletion may lead to dizziness, especially upon arising from a sitting or lying position, as well as thirst, dry mouth, and constipation.

LESS COMMON
Decreased sexual ability, increased sensitivity to sunlight, loss of appetite, gout, increased blood sugar (a problem for diabetic patients), pancreatitis (rare).

PRINCIPAL USES
To treat conditions that cause edema (swelling of body tissues resulting from excess salt and water retention). Many patients are prescribed metolazone in conjunction with other diuretics for particularly resistant fluid retention.

HOW THE DRUG WORKS
Diuretics increase the excretion of salt and water in the urine. Metolazone acts on a part of the kidney that is not affected by loop diuretics such as furosemide or bumetanide. Metolazone and a loop diuretic, when prescribed in combination, thus have a synergistic effect.

DOSAGE
Adults: 2.5 to 10 mg, 1 or 2 times per day.

ONSET OF EFFECT
Approximately 1 hour.

DURATION OF ACTION
From 12 to 24 hours.

DIETARY ADVICE
Take it with food to avoid stomach upset.

STORAGE
Store in a tightly sealed container away from heat and direct light. Keep away from moisture and extremes in temperature.

IF YOU MISS A DOSE
Take it as soon as you remember. If it is near the time for the next dose, skip the missed dose and resume your regular dosage schedule. Do not double the next dose.

STOPPING THE DRUG
The decision to stop taking the drug should be made in consultation with your physician.

PROLONGED USE
See your doctor regularly for examinations and tests if you must take this medicine for an extended period.

PRECAUTIONS
Over 60: Adverse reactions may be more likely and more severe in older patients.

Driving and Hazardous Work: No special precautions are necessary.

Alcohol: No special precautions are necessary.

Pregnancy: Metolazone has caused birth defects in animals. Human studies have not been done. Do not take it during pregnancy unless recommended by your doctor; other diuretics are generally preferred.

Breast Feeding: Metolazone passes into breast milk; avoid or discontinue use during the first month of nursing.

Infants and Children: No unusual side effects are expected in children. The dose must be determined by a pediatrician.

Special Concerns: Metolazone is taken once a day. To prevent it from interfering with sleep, take it in the morning. If you are taking it for high blood pressure, follow the diet and weight control measures recommended by your doctor. Avoid exposure to sunlight, use a sunblock, or wear protective clothing. This medicine may cause your body to lose potassium. Follow your doctor's instructions about eating potassium-rich foods or taking a potassium supplement.

OVERDOSE
Symptoms: Fainting, lethargy, dizziness, drowsiness, gastrointestinal irritation.

What to Do: Call your doctor, emergency medical services (EMS), or the nearest poison control center immediately.

DRUG INTERACTIONS
Consult your doctor for specific advice if you are taking anticoagulants, cholestyramine, colestipol, drugs for diabetes, nonsteroidal anti-inflammatory drugs, digitalis drugs, or lithium.

FOOD INTERACTIONS
No known food interactions.

DISEASE INTERACTIONS
Caution is advised when taking metolazone. Consult your doctor if you have any of the following: diabetes, gout, lupus erythematosus, pancreatitis, heart disease, blood vessel disease, liver disease, or kidney disease.

Metoprolol

Generic 50 mg
(MYLAN)

▶ Drug Class: Beta-blocker

▶ Available in: Tablets,
extended-release tablets
(Injection is for hospital
use only.)

▶ Available OTC? No

▶ As Generic? Yes

Side Effects

SERIOUS
Shortness of breath,
wheezing; irregular or
slow heartbeat (50 beats
per minute or less);
chest pain or tightness;
swelling of the ankles,
feet, and lower legs;
mental depression. If you
experience such symp-
toms, stop taking meto-
prolol and call your
doctor immediately.

COMMON
Dizziness or lightheaded-
ness, especially when rising suddenly to a stand-
ing position; decreased
sexual ability; unusual
fatigue, weakness, or
drowsiness; insomnia.

LESS COMMON
Anxiety, irritability, nervousness; constipation;
diarrhea; dry, sore eyes;
itching; nausea or vomit-
ing; nightmares or
intensely vivid dreams;
numbness, tingling, or
other unusual sensations
in the fingers, toes, or
scalp.

PRINCIPAL USES
To treat mild to moderate
high blood pressure or
angina; to prevent or control
heartbeat irregularities (cardiac arrhythmias); to treat
congestive heart failure.
Injection is used in hospitals
for emergency treatment of
heart attack, followed by
maintenance with oral
forms.

HOW THE DRUG WORKS
Metoprolol slows the rate
and force of contraction of
the heart by blocking certain nerve impulses, thus
reducing blood pressure. By
modifying nerve impulses to
the heart, the drug also
helps to stabilize heart
rhythm.

DOSAGE
For high blood pressure or
angina— Adults: 100 to 400
mg a day in divided doses.
Extended-release tablets:
Up to 400 mg once a day.
For treatment after a heart
attack— Initial dose is 50
mg every 6 hours, followed
by a maintenance dose of
100 mg or more (up to 400
mg a day), 2 times a day for
as long as the physician recommends. For congestive
heart failure (Toprol-XL)—
The exact dose will be
determined by your doctor.
Average dose is 25 mg once
a day for 2 weeks in people
with stable heart failure
(NYHA class II) and 12.5
mg once a day in those with
more severe heart failure.
The dose may then gradu-
ally be doubled every 2
weeks to the highest dose
the patient can tolerate or
up to 200 mg a day.

ONSET OF EFFECT
Within 15 minutes.

DURATION OF ACTION
6 to 12 hours; up to 24
hours with the extended-
release tablet.

DIETARY ADVICE
Take it with food. Follow
your doctor's dietary restrictions to improve control
over high blood pressure
and heart disease.

STORAGE
Store in a tightly sealed container away from heat and
direct light.

IF YOU MISS A DOSE
Take it as soon as you
remember. However, if it is
within 4 hours of your next
dose (8 hours if using
extended-release tablet),
skip the missed dose and
resume your regular dosage
schedule. Do not double the
next dose.

STOPPING THE DRUG
This medication should not
be stopped suddenly, as this
may lead to angina and possibly a heart attack in
patients with advanced
heart disease. Slow reduction of the dose under doctor's close supervision for 2
to 3 weeks is advised.

PROLONGED USE
Lifelong therapy may be
necessary. See your doctor
regularly for examinations.

PRECAUTIONS
Over 60: Adverse reactions
may be more likely and
more severe in older
patients.

**Driving and Hazardous
Work:** Use caution until
you determine how the
medicine affects you.

Alcohol: Drink in careful
moderation if at all. Alcohol
may interact with the drug
and cause a dangerous drop
in blood pressure.

Pregnancy: Discuss with
your doctor the relative
risks and benefits of using
this drug while pregnant.

Breast Feeding: Adverse
effects in infants have not
been documented. Consult
your doctor for advice.

Infants and Children:
No special problems are
expected.

OVERDOSE
Symptoms: Unusually slow
or rapid heartbeat, severe
dizziness or fainting, poor
circulation in the hands
(bluish skin), breathing
difficulty, seizures.

What to Do: Call your
doctor, emergency medical
services (EMS), or the
nearest poison control
center immediately.

DRUG INTERACTIONS
Consult your doctor for specific advice if you are taking
amphetamines, oral antidiabetic agents, asthma med-
ication (such as amino-
phylline or theophylline),
calcium channel blockers,
clonidine; guanabenz,
halothane, immunotherapy
for allergies (allergy shots),
insulin, MAO inhibitors,
reserpine, other beta-blockers, or any over-the-counter
medicine.

FOOD INTERACTIONS
None reported.

DISEASE INTERACTIONS
Metoprolol should be used
with caution in people with
diabetes, especially insulin-
dependent diabetes, since
the drug may mask symp-
toms of hypoglycemia. Consult your doctor if you have
allergies or asthma, heart or
blood vessel disease (including congestive heart failure
and peripheral vascular
disease), hyperthyroidism,
irregular (slow) heartbeat,
myasthenia gravis, psoriasis,
respiratory problems such as
bronchitis or emphysema,
kidney or liver disease, or a
history of mental depression.

▶ Drug Class: Antibacterial/
antiprotozoal

▶ Available in: Cream, injection,
topical and vaginal gel,
tablets, extended-release
tablets

▶ Available OTC? No

▶ As Generic? Yes

Side Effects

SERIOUS
Oral and injection forms:
Pain, tingling, numbness,
or weakness in hands or
feet; seizures. Call your
doctor immediately.

COMMON
Oral and injection forms:
Diarrhea, dizziness, lightheadedness, headache,
loss of appetite, nausea,
vomiting, stomach pains
or cramps. Vaginal gel:
Vaginal itching, painful
intercourse, thick, white
vaginal discharge, irritation of sexual partner's
penis, burning urination,
more frequent urination,
redness, stinging, or itching of genital area.

LESS COMMON
Oral and injection forms:
Change in taste, dry
mouth, sharp metallic
taste in mouth. Cream
and gel: Dry skin, skin
irritation, watery eyes
with burning or stinging.
Vaginal gel: Dizziness,
lightheadedness, diar-
rhea, furry tongue, loss
of appetite, metallic taste
in the mouth, nausea,
vomiting.

PRINCIPAL USES
To treat numerous bacterial
infections, including certain
sexually transmitted dis-
eases, gynecological infections, amebiasis (amoeba
infection in the intestine
or liver), brain abscess or
meningitis, pneumonia or
other lung infections, blood
poisoning, bone and joint
infections, infections of the
internal organs (including
liver abscess and peritoni-
tis), and skin infections.

HOW THE DRUG WORKS
Metronidazole kills bacteria
and protozoa, probably by
disrupting the organism's
synthesis of DNA.

DOSAGE
The dose varies greatly
depending on many factors,
including the disorder being
treated, the patient's age,
weight, and general state of
health, and the form of
drug prescribed. Your
doctor will determine the
appropriate dosage regimen
for you.

ONSET OF EFFECT
Unknown.

DURATION OF ACTION
Unknown.

DIETARY ADVICE
Oral forms of metronidazole
can be taken with food to
minimize stomach upset.

STORAGE
Store in a tightly sealed container away from heat, moisture, and direct light. Do
not refrigerate liquid or topical forms.

IF YOU MISS A DOSE
Take it as soon as you
remember. If it is near the
time for the next dose, skip
the missed dose and
resume your regular dosage
schedule. Do not double the
next dose.

STOPPING THE DRUG
Take it as prescribed for the
full treatment period, even if
you feel better before the
scheduled end of therapy.

PROLONGED USE
If your symptoms do not
improve or become worse
after a few days, consult
your doctor.

PRECAUTIONS
Over 60: No special problems are expected.

**Driving and Hazardous
Work:** Do not drive or
engage in hazardous work
until you determine how the
medicine affects you.

Alcohol: A serious reaction, including possible
flushing, rapid heartbeat,
nausea, and vomiting, may
occur if alcohol is con-
sumed while taking this
drug. Alcohol-containing
medications (for example,
cough syrups) should also
be carefully avoided, as
they can cause the same
reaction.

Pregnancy: Metronidazole
has not caused birth defects
in animals. Use of the oral
forms during the first
trimester is not recom-
mended. Before you take
metronidazole, tell your doctor if you are pregnant or
plan to become pregnant.

Breast Feeding: Metronidazole passes into breast
milk; avoid or discontinue
use while nursing.

Infants and Children: In
children, the oral and injection forms are not expected
to cause side effects different from or more severe
than those in older persons.
There is no information on
the use of the topical forms
by children.

Special Concerns: If you
use the vaginal gel, wear
cotton panties, change daily,
and use a sanitary napkin
to prevent leakage. Avoid
using this medicine in or
near the eyes. If it does get
into your eyes, consult your
doctor.

OVERDOSE
Symptoms: No cases of
overdose have been
reported.

What to Do: Emergency
instructions not applicable.

DRUG INTERACTIONS
Consult your doctor for specific advice if you are taking
cimetidine, lithium, anticoagulants, phenytoin, or phenobarbital. If you have
taken disulfiram in the last
2 weeks, then you should
not take metronidazole.
Also tell your doctor if you
are taking any other pre-
scription or over-the-counter
medication.

FOOD INTERACTIONS
No known food interactions.

DISEASE INTERACTIONS
Consult your doctor if you
have a history of blood disease, epilepsy (or other central nervous system dis-
order), heart disease, or
liver disease.

Mexiletine Hydrochloride

BRAND NAME
Mexitil

Mexitil 200 mg
(**BOEHRINGER INGELHEIM**)

Additional photographs

▶ Drug Class: Antiarrhythmic

▶ Available in: Capsules

▶ Available OTC? No

▶ As Generic? Yes

Side Effects

SERIOUS
Chest pain, rapid or irregular heartbeat, shortness of breath, seizures, unusual bleeding or bruising, fever or chills. Call your doctor immediately.

COMMON
Dizziness or lightheadedness; nausea, vomiting, or abdominal pain; heartburn; nervousness; unsteadiness or difficulty in walking; trembling, or shaking of hands.

LESS COMMON
Confusion, blurred vision, constipation or diarrhea, headache, numbness or tingling of hands or toes, ringing in ears, skin rash, slurred speech, difficulty sleeping, unusual fatigue or weakness.

PRINCIPAL USES
To treat irregular heartbeats (cardiac arrhythmias).

HOW THE DRUG WORKS
Mexiletine slows nerve impulses in the heart and makes heart tissue less sensitive to nerve impulses, thus stabilizing heartbeat.

DOSAGE
To start, a 200 to 400 mg dose followed by 200 mg every 8 hours. The dose can be increased to 400 mg every 8 hours.

ONSET OF EFFECT
30 minutes to 2 hours.

DURATION OF ACTION
10 to 12 hours (longer in patients with liver or heart impairment).

DIETARY ADVICE
Mexiletine can be taken with food or an antacid.

STORAGE
Store in a tightly sealed container away from heat and direct light.

IF YOU MISS A DOSE
Take it as soon as you remember. If it is near the time for the next dose, skip the missed dose and resume your regular dosage schedule. Do not double the next dose.

STOPPING THE DRUG
Take it as prescribed for the full treatment period, even if you begin to feel better before the scheduled end of therapy. The decision to stop taking the drug should be made by your doctor.

PROLONGED USE
Lifelong therapy may be necessary. See your doctor regularly for examinations and diagnostic tests if long-term use is required.

PRECAUTIONS
Over 60: There is no specific information comparing use of this medicine in older patients to other age groups.

Driving and Hazardous Work: Do not drive or engage in hazardous work until you determine how the medicine affects you.

Alcohol: No special precautions are necessary.

Pregnancy: In animal studies mexiletine has caused a reduction in successful pregnancies but no birth defects. Before you take mexiletine, tell your physician if you are pregnant or plan to become pregnant.

Breast Feeding: Mexiletine passes into breast milk; you should avoid or discontinue usage while nursing.

Infants and Children: Safety and efficacy of mexiletine in children have not been established. Use and dose must be established by your doctor.

Special Concerns: Your doctor may want you to carry a card or wear a bracelet saying that you are taking mexiletine. Before you have any kind of surgery, tell the doctor or dentist in charge that you are taking this medicine.

OVERDOSE
Symptoms: Severe breathing difficulty, dizziness, drowsiness, burning sensation, nausea, change in mental state, seizures, abnormally slow heartbeat, unconsciousness.

What to Do: Call your doctor, emergency medical services (EMS), or the nearest poison control center immediately.

DRUG INTERACTIONS
Consult your doctor for specific advice if you are taking urinary alkalizers such as antacids, other antiarrhythmics, hepatic enzyme inducers, metoclopramide, theophylline, rifampin, phenytoin, or phenobarbital.

FOOD INTERACTIONS
No known food interactions.

DISEASE INTERACTIONS
Caution is advised when taking mexiletine. Consult your doctor if you have any of the following: low blood pressure, congestive heart failure, a recent heart attack, or a history of seizures. Mexiletine can cause complications in patients with liver disease, since this organ works to remove the medication from the body.

BRAND NAMES
M-Zole 3, Miconazole-7,
Monistat 3, Monistat 7,
Monistat I.V.

▶ Drug Class: Antifungal

▶ Available in: Vaginal cream
   and suppositories, injection

▶ Available OTC? Yes

▶ As Generic? Yes

Side Effects

SERIOUS
Skin rash or itching; fever
or chills; pain at site of
injection; vaginal burn-
ing, itching, discharge, or
irritation not present
prior to treatment. Call
your doctor immediately.

COMMON
No common side effects
are associated with
miconazole.

LESS COMMON
Diarrhea, nausea, vomit-
ing, constipation, dizzi-
ness, headache, redness
or flushing of skin, stomach cramps or pain, burn-
ing or irritation of sexual
partner's penis.

PRINCIPAL USES
To treat severe fungal infections, including vaginal
yeast infections.

HOW THE DRUG WORKS
Miconazole prevents fungal
organisms from producing
vital substances required for
growth and function. This
medication is effective only
for infections caused by fungal organisms. It will not
work for bacterial or viral
infections.

DOSAGE
Adults and teenagers—
Vaginal cream: At bedtime,
insert into the vagina 1
applicatorful for 7 to 14
nights. Vaginal suppositories: At bedtime, insert one
100-mg suppository into the
vagina for 7 nights, or one
200-mg or one 400-mg sup-
pository for 3 nights. Injection: 200 to 1,200 mg into a
vein 3 times a day for weeks
or months. Children ages 1
to 12— Injection: 20 to 40
mg per 2.2 lbs (1 kg) of
body weight per day, given
in 2 or 3 doses, for weeks
or months.

ONSET OF EFFECT
For cream and suppository:
Unknown. For injection:
Immediate.

DURATION OF ACTION
Unknown.

DIETARY ADVICE
No special restrictions.

STORAGE
Store in a tightly sealed
container away from heat,
moisture, and direct light.
Refrigerate suppositories.
Do not allow medication
to freeze.

IF YOU MISS A DOSE
Take it as soon as you
remember. This will help
keep a constant level of
medication in your system.
If it is near the time for the
next dose, skip the missed
dose and resume your regular dosage schedule. Do not
double the next dose.

STOPPING THE DRUG
Take as directed for the full
treatment period, even if
you begin to feel better
before the scheduled end of
therapy. Stopping prema-
turely increases the risk of
reinfection. Some fungal
infections take many
months to clear up, and
some may require continu-
ous treatment.

PROLONGED USE
Therapy with this medica-
tion may require months.
Prolonged use may increase
the risk of adverse effects.

PRECAUTIONS
Over 60: Adverse reactions
may be more likely and
more severe in older
patients.

**Driving and Hazardous
Work:** Do not drive or
engage in hazardous work
until you determine how the
medicine affects you.

Alcohol: Avoid alcohol.

Pregnancy: Adequate studies of miconazole use during pregnancy have not
been done. Consult your
doctor for advice if you are
pregnant or are planning to
become pregnant.

Breast Feeding: Miconazole passes into breast milk;
caution is advised. Consult
your doctor for advice.

Infants and Children:
Not recommended for use
by children under age 1.

Special Concerns: Sanitary napkins should be used
to prevent staining of clothing. The affected area
should be kept cool and
dry. Do not sit for a long
time in a wet bathing suit.
Avoid feminine hygiene
sprays. Wash daily with
unscented soap and dry
thoroughly with a clean
towel. Tampons should not
be used during therapy. The
patient's sexual partner
should wear a condom dur-
ing intercourse. Do not stop
using this medicine during
your menstrual period. After
urination or a bowel movement, cleanse by wiping the
area from front to back to
prevent reinfection.

OVERDOSE
Symptoms: An overdose
with miconazole is unlikely.

What to Do: Emergency
instructions not applicable.

DRUG INTERACTIONS
Tell your doctor if you are
using any other vaginal prescription or over-the-counter
medicine when using the
vaginal forms. While taking
miconazole injection, do not
take astemizole or terfenadine. Serious side effects
involving the heart may
result. Do not take medications containing alcohol,
such as cough syrups,
elixirs, and tonics. Consult
your doctor for specific
advice if you are taking
cyclosporine, phenytoin,
or warfarin.

FOOD INTERACTIONS
No known food interactions.

DISEASE INTERACTIONS
Consult your doctor if you
have a history of alcohol
abuse. Use of miconazole
can cause complications in
patients with liver or kidney
disease, since these organs
work together to remove
the medication from the
body.

Midodrine Hydrochloride

BRAND NAMES
Amatine, ProAmatine

▶ Drug Class: Alpha-adrenergic agonist

▶ Available in: Tablets

▶ Available OTC? No

▶ As Generic? Yes

Side Effects

SERIOUS
Very high blood pressure, slow heartbeat, increased dizziness, fainting. Call your doctor immediately.

COMMON
Itching, numbness, or tingling, in the extremities, goose bumps, chills, urinary difficulties.

LESS COMMON
Headache, sinus pressure, redness of face, confusion, dry mouth, nervousness, anxiety, skin rash, vision problems, dizziness, dry skin, backache, gastrointestinal distress, gas, leg cramps.

PRINCIPAL USES
To treat severe cases of orthostatic hypotension (extremely low blood pressure, causing symptoms of dizziness and faintness, especially when rising from a seated or lying position). Used when standard care, such as support stockings, fluid expansion, and lifestyle changes, is ineffective.

HOW THE DRUG WORKS
Midodrine causes constriction of the smooth muscles surrounding the blood vessels. This effect narrows the width of the blood vessels, causing blood pressure to rise, thus helping to correct low blood pressure on standing.

DOSAGE
To start, 10 mg, 3 times a day during waking hours, at intervals of 4 hours. Suggested dosage schedule is to take the medication shortly after rising, then at midday, and then late afternoon (before 6 pm). Blood pressure should be monitored while sitting and lying down at the outset of treatment for possible adjustment of doses.

ONSET OF EFFECT
Within 1 hour.

DURATION OF ACTION
From 2 to 3 hours.

DIETARY ADVICE
No special restrictions.

STORAGE
Store in a tightly sealed container away from heat, moisture, and direct light.

IF YOU MISS A DOSE
Take it as soon as you remember. If it is near the time for the next dose, skip the missed dose and resume your regular dosage schedule. Do not double the next dose.

STOPPING THE DRUG
The decision to stop taking the drug should be made in consultation with your physician.

PROLONGED USE
See your doctor regularly for measurements of blood pressure while sitting and lying down if you must take this drug for a prolonged period. Periodic tests for liver and kidney function will be done.

PRECAUTIONS
Over 60: No special problems are expected.

Driving and Hazardous Work: Do not drive or engage in hazardous work until you determine how the medicine affects you.

Alcohol: Avoid alcohol when using this medication; it may interfere with proper control of blood pressure.

Pregnancy: Adequate studies have not been done. Before taking midodrine, tell your doctor if you are pregnant or plan to become pregnant. Discuss with your doctor the relative benefits and possible risks to the unborn child when using this drug during pregnancy.

Breast Feeding: Midodrine may pass into breast milk; caution is advised. Consult your doctor for specific advice.

Infants and Children: The safety and effectiveness of midodrine in children and infants have not been established.

Special Concerns: The last dose of midodrine should be taken at least 3 hours before bedtime. Use of this drug is not recommended for patients who have persistent and excessively high systolic blood pressure.

OVERDOSE
Symptoms: Goose bumps, sensation of coldness, decreased urine output, rapid heartbeat, ringing in the ears.

What to Do: It is not known whether an overdose of midodrine is life-threatening. However, if someone takes a much larger dose than prescribed, call your doctor, emergency medical services (EMS), or the nearest poison control center immediately.

DRUG INTERACTIONS
Consult your doctor for specific advice if you are taking cardiac glycosides, phenylephrine, pseudoephedrine, beta-blockers, dihydroergotamine, fludrocortisone acetate, prazosin, terazosin, doxazosin, metformin, cimetidine, ranitidine, procainamide, triamterene, flecainide, quinidine, or any other over-the counter or prescription drug.

FOOD INTERACTIONS
No known food interactions.

DISEASE INTERACTIONS
Caution is advised when taking midodrine. Consult your doctor if you have any of the following: urinary retention problems, severe heart disease, diabetes mellitus, vision problems, glaucoma, pheochromocytoma, or thyrotoxicosis. Use of midodrine may cause complications in patients with liver or kidney disease, since these organs work together to remove the medication from the body.

Miglitol

▶ Drug Class: Antidiabetic agent

▶ Available in: Tablets

▶ Available OTC? No

▶ As Generic? No

Side Effects

SERIOUS
No serious side effects are associated with miglitol use.

COMMON
Abdominal pain, diarrhea, and flatulence.

LESS COMMON
Rash. Use in combination with sulfonylureas may cause symptoms of low blood sugar (hypoglycemia), which include sweating, tremor, anxiety, hunger, confusion, seizures, rapid heartbeat, vision changes, dizziness, headache, loss of consciousness. Hypoglycemia must be treated by ingestion of glucose (dextrose). Glucose tablets can be obtained from pharmacies over the counter. Sucrose (table sugar) and foods or drinks containing sugars or starches are ineffective because miglitol prevents their breakdown and absorption.

PRINCIPAL USES
Used as an adjunct (supplemental) therapy to dietary measures and exercise to help control blood sugar levels in patients with type 2 diabetes mellitus. May be used in combination with a sulfonylurea when diet plus either miglitol or a sulfonylurea alone do not adequately control blood sugar levels.

HOW THE DRUG WORKS
Miglitol inhibits the activity of enzymes required to break carbohydrates down into simple sugars within the intestine. This effect delays the digestion of carbohydrates and thus reduces the rise in blood sugar that typically occurs after meals.

DOSAGE
Dosage must be determined for each patient individually, based on blood glucose levels in response to the drug. The recommended starting dosage is 25 mg taken 3 times a day with the first bite of each main meal. Four to eight weeks later, dosage may be increased by your doctor to 50 mg 3 times a day. If, after 3 months, blood sugar levels are not adequately controlled, the dosage may be increased to not more than 100 mg 3 times a day, the maxiumum recommended dose.

ONSET OF EFFECT
Unknown.

DURATION OF ACTION
Unknown.

DIETARY ADVICE
This medicine should be taken with the first bite of breakfast, lunch, and dinner. Follow your doctor's advice regarding diet, weight loss, and exercise.

STORAGE
Store in a tightly sealed container away from heat, moisture, and direct light.

IF YOU MISS A DOSE
If you have finished a meal without taking the medication, skip the missed dose and resume your regular dosing schedule with the next meal. Do not double the next dose.

STOPPING THE DRUG
Do not stop taking the drug without your doctor's approval.

PROLONGED USE
Since type 2 diabetes is a chronic condition, use of miglitol will be ongoing. Blood glucose levels should be checked regularly during treatment so that the dosage may be adjusted if necessary.

PRECAUTIONS
Over 60: No special precautions required.

Driving and Hazardous Work: Miglitol should not impair your ability to perform such tasks safely.

Alcohol: Drink only in moderation when taking miglitol.

Pregnancy: Consult your doctor for advice. Insulin is usually the treatment of choice for pregnant diabetic patients.

Breast Feeding: Miglitol passes into breast milk, although it has not been shown to cause harm to nursing infants. Consult your doctor for advice.

Infants and Children: Safety and effectiveness have not been established for patients under 18 years of age. Consult your doctor for specific advice.

Special Concerns: Follow your doctor's advice about diet, exercise, and weight control. These aspects of treatment are just as essential to the proper control of diabetes as taking medications. Be sure to carry at all times some form of medical identification that indicates you have diabetes and that lists all of the drugs you are taking.

OVERDOSE
Symptoms: Increased gas, diarrhea, and stomach pain.

What to Do: These symptoms usually subside on their own within a short period of time. If not, consult your doctor for advice. Symptoms of hypoglycemia should not occur when taking miglitol alone, but may occur if a patient is also taking a sulfonylurea or insulin for diabetes.

DRUG INTERACTIONS
Consult your doctor if you are taking any of the following drugs that may interact with miglitol: digestive enzyme preparations containing amylase or pancreatin, intestinal absorbents (such as charcoal), insulin, or sulfonylureas (oral antidiabetic agents).

FOOD INTERACTIONS
Avoid foods that contain large amounts of sugar (for example, cake, cookies, candy, acidic fruits). Closely follow the diet your doctor has prescribed.

DISEASE INTERACTIONS
This drug should not be taken by patients with a history of diabetic ketoacidosis, intestinal disorders (including malabsorption or obstruction), inflammatory bowel disease (for example, Crohn's disease or ulcerative colitis), or kidney dysfunction.

▶ Drug Class: Antacid/
hyperosmotic laxative

▶ Available in: Oral suspension,
chewable tablets

▶ Available OTC? Yes

▶ As Generic? Yes

Milk of Magnesia (Magnesia; Magnesium Hydroxide)

Side Effects

SERIOUS
Dizziness or lightheadedness, continuing feeling of discomfort, irregular heartbeat, loss of appetite, mood or mental changes, muscle weakness, unusual fatigue, unusual weight loss, rectal bleeding. Call your doctor immediately.

COMMON
Nausea, diarrhea.

LESS COMMON
Increased thirst, speckling or whitish color of stools, abdominal cramps.

PRINCIPAL USES
To relieve symptoms of upset stomach; sometimes used for short-term treatment of constipation.

HOW THE DRUG WORKS
As an antacid, milk of magnesia neutralizes stomach acid. As a laxative, it attracts and retains water in the intestine, increasing intestinal movement (peristalsis) and inducing the urge to defecate.

DOSAGE
As an antacid— Adults and teenagers: 5 to 15 ml of liquid form or 650 mg to 1.3 g of tablets 3 or 4 times a day. To relieve constipation— Adults and teenagers: 2.4 to 4.8 g (30 to 60 ml) daily in 1 or more doses. Children ages 6 to 12: 1.2 to 2.4 g (15 to 30 ml) daily in 1 or more doses.

ONSET OF EFFECT
30 minutes to 3 hours.

DURATION OF ACTION
Variable.

DIETARY ADVICE
Take it 1 to 3 hours after meals or at bedtime with a full glass of water.

STORAGE
Store milk of magnesia in a tightly sealed container away from heat, moisture, and direct light.

IF YOU MISS A DOSE
Take it as soon as you remember. If it is near the time for the next dose, skip the missed dose and resume your regular dosage schedule. Do not double the next dose.

STOPPING THE DRUG
You may stop taking the drug whenever you choose.

PROLONGED USE
Do not take milk of magnesia for more than 2 weeks unless your doctor prescribes it.

PRECAUTIONS
Over 60: No special problems are expected.

Driving and Hazardous Work: This medicine should not impair your ability to perform such tasks safely.

Alcohol: Avoid alcohol.

Pregnancy: Extensive human studies have not been done. There have been reports of side effects in babies whose mothers took high doses of antacids for a long time during pregnancy. Before you take milk of magnesia, con-sult your doctor if you are pregnant or plan to become pregnant.

Breast Feeding: Milk of magnesia may pass into breast milk but has not been reported to cause problems in nursing babies. Consult your doctor for specific advice.

Infants and Children: Antacids and other magnesium-containing medications should not be given to children under age 6 unless prescribed by a doctor.

Special Concerns: Take milk of magnesia on a schedule that does not interfere with activities or sleep, as it produces watery stools in 3 to 6 hours. Remember that frequent or protracted use can lead to laxative dependence. Do not take milk of magnesia within 2 hours of taking other medications. Before swallowing, chew tablets well to allow the medicine to work more quickly and effectively.

OVERDOSE
Symptoms: Severe or protracted diarrhea, painful or difficult urination, muscle weakness, continuing loss of appetite, irregular heartbeat, difficulty breathing.

What to Do: An overdose of milk of magnesia is unlikely to be life threatening. However, if someone takes a much larger dose than prescribed, call your doctor, emergency medical services (EMS), or the nearest poison control center immediately.

DRUG INTERACTIONS
Consult your physician for specific advice if you are taking other antacids or laxatives, cellulose sodium phosphate, fluoroquinolones, isoniazid, ketoconazole, sodium polystyrene sulfonate resin, methenamine, mecamylamine, salicylates, or tetracyclines.

FOOD INTERACTIONS
None are known.

DISEASE INTERACTIONS
Do not use this medication if you have any symptoms of appendicitis or inflamed bowel such as lower abdominal or stomach pain, nausea or vomiting, cramping, soreness, or bloating. Consult your physician if you have any of the following: broken bones, colitis, hemorrhoids, intestinal blockage or bleeding, a recent colostomy or ileostomy, swelling of feet or lower legs, heart disease, toxemia of pregnancy, liver disease, or kidney disease.

Minocycline

BRAND NAMES
Dynacin, Minocin

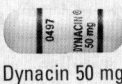

Dynacin 50 mg
(MEDICIS)

▶ Drug Class: Tetracycline antibiotic

▶ Available in: Capsules, oral suspension, tablets, powder, injection

▶ Available OTC? No

▶ As Generic? Yes

Side Effects

SERIOUS
Increased sensitivity of skin to sunlight, abdominal pain, headache, loss of appetite, severe nausea and vomiting, yellow skin, skin discoloration, changes in vision, dizziness or loss of balance, redness, soreness, or swelling at site of injection. Call your doctor immediately.

COMMON
Cramps or burning feeling in stomach, nausea, vomiting, dizziness, lightheadedness, unsteadiness, yeast infection or oral thrush (fungal infection of the mouth or throat).

LESS COMMON
Itching in the genital area; sore tongue or mouth.

PRINCIPAL USES
To treat acne or infections caused by bacteria or protozoa (single-celled parasitic organisms).

HOW THE DRUG WORKS
Minocycline kills bacteria and protozoa by inhibiting their manufacture of proteins necessary for their survival.

DOSAGE
Oral forms— Adults and teenagers: 200 mg to start, then 100 mg, 2 times a day, or 100 to 200 mg to start, then 50 mg, 4 times a day. Children age 8 and over: 1.8 mg per lb of body weight to start, then 0.9 mg per lb 2 times a day. Injection— Adults and teenagers: 200 mg to start, then 100 mg, 2 times a day. Children age 8 and over: 1.8 mg per lb to start, then 0.9 mg per lb, 2 times a day.

ONSET OF EFFECT
Immediately after injection; unknown for oral forms.

DURATION OF ACTION
Unknown.

DIETARY ADVICE
Drink extra water when taking capsules or tablets.

STORAGE
Store in a tightly sealed container away from heat, moisture, and direct light.

IF YOU MISS A DOSE
Take it as soon as you remember. If it is near the time for the next dose, skip the missed dose and resume your regular dosage schedule. Do not double the next dose.

STOPPING THE DRUG
Take as prescribed for the full treatment period, even if you begin to feel better before the scheduled end of therapy.

PROLONGED USE
If your symptoms do not improve within a few days (for infection) or a few weeks (for acne), see your doctor. Prolonged use may make you more susceptible to infections caused by microorganisms resistant to antibiotics.

PRECAUTIONS
Over 60: It is not known whether adverse reactions are more likely or more severe in older patients than in younger persons.

Driving and Hazardous Work: Do not drive or engage in hazardous work until you determine how the medicine affects you, since it may cause dizziness.

Alcohol: It is advisable to abstain from alcohol when fighting an infection.

Pregnancy: Use of minocycline during the second half of pregnancy should be avoided because it may discolor the unborn child's teeth, slow growth of teeth and bones, and cause liver problems in the mother.

Breast Feeding: Minocycline passes into breast milk and may be harmful to the nursing infant. The patient must choose between using the drug or breast feeding.

Infants and Children: This drug should not be used by children younger than 8 years old since it can cause permanent tooth staining.

Special Concerns: Oral contraceptives may not work when you take minocycline. Consult your doctor for specific advice. Before having surgery under a general anesthetic, tell the doctor or dentist in charge that you are taking

minocycline. If minocycline increases the sensitivity of your skin to the sun, take protective measures and avoid exposure to sunlight. Do not take calcium supplements, magnesium-containing laxatives, sodium bicarbonate, or iron preparations within 2 to 3 hours of taking minocycline. Women predisposed to yeast infections may need treatment with an antifungal while taking minocycline.

OVERDOSE
Symptoms: Severe nausea and vomiting, diarrhea, difficulty swallowing.

What to Do: An overdose is unlikely to be life-threatening. However, if someone takes a much larger dose than prescribed, call your doctor, emergency medical services (EMS), or the nearest poison control center immediately.

DRUG INTERACTIONS
Other drugs may interact with minocycline. Consult your doctor for specific advice if you are taking antacids, calcium supplements, cholestyramine, choline and magnesium salicylates, medicines containing iron, laxatives containing magnesium, or oral contraceptives.

FOOD INTERACTIONS
No known food interactions.

DISEASE INTERACTIONS
Consult your doctor if you have a history of kidney disease or liver disease.

Minoxidil Oral

Generic 2.5 mg
(SCHEIN/DANBURY)

▶ Drug Class: Antihypertensive

▶ Available in: Tablets

▶ Available OTC? No

▶ As Generic? Yes

Side Effects

SERIOUS
Rapid heartbeat (occasionally irregular), rapid weight gain of more than 5 pounds (2 pounds in children), chest pain, shortness of breath. Call your doctor immediately.

COMMON
Swelling of lower legs or feet; increased hair growth, usually on arms, face, and back; flushing or redness of skin.

LESS COMMON
Numbness or tingling of face, hands, or feet, skin rash and itching, breast tenderness in men and women, headache.

PRINCIPAL USES
To treat moderate to severe high blood pressure. Minoxidil is usually used after other medications have failed to achieve satisfactory results.

HOW THE DRUG WORKS
Oral minoxidil acts upon the smooth muscle tissue surrounding the arteries, causing this tissue to relax, which in turn widens the diameter of the blood vessels and thus lowers blood pressure.

DOSAGE
Adults and teenagers: 2.5 to 100 mg daily in a single dose or divided doses. Children up to 12 years of age: 200 micrograms (mcg) to 1 mg per 2.2 lbs (1 kg) of body weight daily in a single dose or divided doses.

ONSET OF EFFECT
30 minutes.

DURATION OF ACTION
2 to 5 days.

DIETARY ADVICE
Take this drug with food to minimize stomach upset. Follow a healthy diet (low-salt, low-fat, low-cholesterol) as advised by your doctor to help control blood pressure and prevent heart disease.

STORAGE
Store in a tightly sealed container away from heat and direct light.

IF YOU MISS A DOSE
Take it as soon as you remember. If it is near the time for the next dose, skip the missed dose and resume your regular dosage schedule. Do not double the next dose.

STOPPING THE DRUG
The decision to stop taking the drug should be made by your doctor. Minoxidil controls your high blood pressure but does not cure it. You may have to take this medicine for the rest of your life.

PROLONGED USE
See your doctor regularly for tests and examinations if you must take this drug for a prolonged period.

PRECAUTIONS
Over 60: Adverse reactions may be more likely and more severe in older patients. Minoxidil may reduce tolerance to cold temperatures in older patients.

Driving and Hazardous Work: The use of minoxidil should not impair your ability to perform such tasks safely.

Alcohol: No special precautions are necessary.

Pregnancy: Minoxidil has not been shown to cause birth defects in animals. Human studies have not been done, but there have been reports of unusual hair growth in newborn babies. High doses in animal studies have caused a reduced rate of pregnancy. Before you take minoxidil, tell your doctor if you are pregnant or are planning to become pregnant.

Breast Feeding: Minoxidil passes into breast milk; caution is advised. Consult your doctor for specific advice.

Infants and Children: Minoxidil is not expected to cause unusual problems in infants and children.

Special Concerns: Minoxidil commonly causes swelling due to fluid retention, so most patients need to take a diuretic with this medication. The drug also raises heart rate and therefore is often prescribed with a drug to stabilize heart rate. While taking minoxidil, weigh yourself every day. Contact your doctor immediately if you suddenly gain 5 pounds or more (2 pounds or more in children); you experience shortness of breath, especially when lying down; or your heart rate increases by 20 or more beats per minute while resting.

OVERDOSE
Symptoms: Very low blood pressure, fast heartbeat, buildup of fluid in the body.

What to Do: An overdose of minoxidil is unlikely to be life-threatening. However, if someone takes a much larger dose than prescribed, call your doctor, emergency medical services (EMS), or the nearest poison control center.

DRUG INTERACTIONS
The following drugs may interact with minoxidil. Consult your doctor for specific advice if you are taking guanethidine, nitrates, or any over-the-counter medicine for appetite control, asthma, colds, cough, hay fever, or sinus problems.

FOOD INTERACTIONS
No known food interactions.

DISEASE INTERACTIONS
Caution is advised when taking minoxidil. Consult your doctor for advice if you have any of the following: angina, heart disease, blood vessel disease, kidney disease, a recent heart attack or stroke, or pheochromocytoma.

BRAND NAME
Rogaine

- ▶ Drug Class: Hair growth stimulant

- ▶ Available in: Topical solution

- ▶ Available OTC? Yes

- ▶ As Generic? Yes

Side Effects

SERIOUS
Rapid pulse; weakness, dizziness, or lightheaded feeling; chest pain. Notify your doctor immediately. If chest pain is present, call emergency medical services (EMS).

COMMON
Burning, tingling, or mild redness of scalp at application site; mild dryness or flaking of skin; itching.

LESS COMMON
Significant irritation or allergy with redness, itching, flaking, or rash. Tingling of hands or feet; water retention (swelling of face, hands, fingers, or legs); flushing; headache. Stop the drug and notify your doctor immediately.

PRINCIPAL USES
Minoxidil topical solution is prescribed to stimulate hair growth in men and women with a specific type of baldness known as androgenetic alopecia (popularly known as male pattern baldness or female pattern baldness).

HOW THE DRUG WORKS
It is not known how minoxidil works. Although it increases the flow of blood, nutrients, and other important substances to hair follicles, other or additional poorly understood actions are believed responsible for hair growth.

DOSAGE
Adults: Apply 1 ml regardless of the size of the balding area under treatment.

ONSET OF EFFECT
At least 4 months with twice daily therapy.

DURATION OF ACTION
New hair resulting from minoxidil treatments will likely be lost 3 to 4 months following discontinuation of the medication.

DIETARY ADVICE
No special restrictions.

STORAGE
Store in a tightly sealed container away from heat and direct light. Keep away from moisture and extremes in temperature.

IF YOU MISS A DOSE
Apply it as soon as you remember. If it is near the time for the next dose, skip the missed dose and resume your regular dosage schedule. Do not double the next dose.

STOPPING THE DRUG
Use it until you are able to assess changes, if any, in hair growth and cosmetic appearance. This may take at least 4 months. If you decide to abandon efforts to achieve hair regrowth, you may stop the medication at any time.

PROLONGED USE
Ongoing therapy with this medication is required for continued results. Prolonged use may increase the risk of undesirable side effects.

PRECAUTIONS
Over 60: Adverse reactions may be more likely and more severe in older patients.

Driving and Hazardous Work: Do not drive or engage in hazardous work until you determine how the medicine affects you.

Alcohol: No special precautions are necessary.

Pregnancy: Avoid or discontinue topical minoxidil treatment if you are pregnant or trying to become pregnant. Consult your physician.

Breast Feeding: Minoxidil passes into breast milk; do not use it while nursing.

Infants and Children: Topical minoxidil is not recommended for children.

Special Concerns: Anyone with a history of allergy to minoxidil or other components of the product should not use this medication. Minoxidil has potentially serious side effects if absorbed in large amounts into the body. Persons with a history of heart disease should consult their doctor before using this product. Do not apply to irritated, blistered, bleeding, or broken skin. Do not use more than the recommended dose, and do not apply it more frequently than twice a day. Do not use hairdryers to accelerate drying of the medication.

OVERDOSE
Symptoms: Symptoms are similar to those listed under serious side effects: rapid pulse; weakness, dizziness, or a lightheaded feeling; chest pain.

What to Do: If the above symptoms occur or someone ingests the medication, call your doctor, emergency medical services (EMS), or the nearest poison control center immediately.

DRUG INTERACTIONS
Consult your doctor for specific advice if you are taking oral minoxidil, steroids, petrolatum, or acne preparations such as tretinoin. Any person using heart or blood pressure medications should discuss minoxidil use with their doctor before starting treatment.

FOOD INTERACTIONS
No known food interactions.

DISEASE INTERACTIONS
Consult your doctor if you have any disorders affecting your skin or scalp, including rashes, sunburn, or other types of skin eruption or inflammation; heart disease; or high blood pressure.

Mirtazapine

Remeron 15 mg
(ORGANON)

▶ Drug Class: Antidepressant

▶ Available in: Tablets

▶ Available OTC? No

▶ As Generic? Yes

Side Effects

SERIOUS
Mood or mental changes, confusion, breathing difficulties, increased or decreased ability to move limbs, flu-like symptoms, swelling of the lower extremities, skin rash, anxiety, agitation, extreme drowsiness, disorientation, loss of memory, rapid heartbeat. Call your doctor immediately.

COMMON
Dizziness, dry mouth, drowsiness, constipation, increased appetite, weight gain.

LESS COMMON
Muscle pains, unusual dreams, fatigue, back pain, vomiting, increased thirst, nausea, dizziness or fainting when getting up suddenly, sensitivity to touch, tremor, stomach pain, increased urination.

PRINCIPAL USES
To treat symptoms of major depression.

HOW THE DRUG WORKS
While the exact mechanism of action of mirtazapine is not known, it affects levels of brain chemicals (norepinephrine and serotonin) that are thought to be linked to mood, emotions, and mental state.

DOSAGE
To start, 15 mg once a day, at bedtime. The dose may be increased gradually by your doctor to no more than 45 mg a day.

ONSET OF EFFECT
Unknown.

DURATION OF ACTION
Unknown.

DIETARY ADVICE
No special restrictions.

STORAGE
Store in a tightly sealed container away from heat, moisture, and direct light.

IF YOU MISS A DOSE
Take it as soon as you remember. However, if it is near the time for the next day's dose, skip the missed dose and resume your regular dosage schedule. Do not double the next day's dose.

STOPPING THE DRUG
Take as prescribed for the full treatment period, even if you begin to feel better before the scheduled end of therapy. The decision to stop taking the drug should be made in consultation with your doctor.

PROLONGED USE
You should see your doctor regularly for tests and examinations if you take this medicine for a prolonged period. Prolonged use of mirtazapine can decrease the flow of saliva, which can increase the risk of cavities, periodontal disease, and other conditions.

PRECAUTIONS
Over 60: No special problems have been reported.

Driving and Hazardous Work: Exercise caution until you determine how the medicine affects you. Drowsiness or lightheadedness can occur.

Alcohol: Avoid alcohol.

Pregnancy: In animal studies, mirtazapine did not cause birth defects but was shown to cause other problems. Human studies have not been done. Before you take mirtazapine, tell your doctor if you are pregnant or plan to become pregnant.

Breast Feeding: Mirtazapine may pass into breast milk; caution is advised. Consult your doctor for advice.

Infants and Children: The safety and effectiveness of mirtazapine use by infants and children have not been established. Antidepressants increase the risk of suicidal thinking and behavior (suicidality) in children with major depression and other psychiatric disorders. Discuss with your doctor this risk versus the benefits of using this drug. Children should be observed closely for worsening of symptoms, suicidality, or unusual changes in behavior at the onset of therapy and when making changes in dosage.

Special Concerns: If dry mouth occurs, use sugarless candy or gum for relief.

OVERDOSE
Symptoms: Severe drowsiness, disorientation, loss of memory, rapid heartbeat.

What to Do: Call your doctor, emergency medical services (EMS), or the nearest poison control center immediately.

DRUG INTERACTIONS
Mirtazapine and MAO inhibitors should not be used within 14 days of each other. Very serious side effects such as myoclonus (uncontrolled muscle jerking), hyperthermia (excessive rise in body temperature), nausea, vomiting, seizures, and extreme stiffness may result. Other drugs may interact with mirtazapine; consult your doctor for specific advice if you are taking central nervous system depressants, high blood pressure medication, diazepam, or kidney medication.

FOOD INTERACTIONS
No known food interactions.

DISEASE INTERACTIONS
Caution is advised when taking mirtazapine. Consult your doctor if you have heart or blood vessel disease; phenylketonuria; or a history of seizures, drug abuse, or mental illness. Use of mirtazapine may cause complications in patients with liver or kidney disease, since these organs work together to remove the medication from the body.

Misoprostol

Cytotec 0.2 mg
(SEARLE)

▶ Drug Class: Prostaglandin

▶ Available in: Tablets

▶ Available OTC? No

▶ As Generic? No

Side Effects

SERIOUS
There are no serious side effects associated with the use of misoprostol.

COMMON
Diarrhea, mild abdominal or stomach pain.

LESS COMMON
Vaginal bleeding, constipation, cramps in lower abdomen, gas, headache, nausea and vomiting.

PRINCIPAL USES
To prevent stomach ulcers in patients taking anti-inflammatory drugs, including aspirin.

HOW THE DRUG WORKS
Ongoing therapy with anti-inflammatory drugs can irritate and damage the stomach lining, increasing the risk of ulcers. Misoprostol helps prevent ulcers and enhances the stomach's natural healing ability by increasing the production of protective mucus, as well as inhibiting the secretion of stomach acid.

DOSAGE
200 to 400 micrograms (mcg), 4 times a day, or 400 mcg, 2 times a day. The dose may be reduced to 100 mcg to prevent side effects. Treatment usually lasts 4 weeks.

ONSET OF EFFECT
30 minutes.

DURATION OF ACTION
3 hours.

DIETARY ADVICE
Misoprostol can be taken with meals to reduce the incidence of diarrhea. The last dose should be taken at bedtime.

STORAGE
Store in a tightly sealed container away from heat and direct light.

IF YOU MISS A DOSE
Take it as soon as you remember. If it is near the time for the next dose, skip the missed dose and resume your regular dosage schedule. Do not double the next dose.

STOPPING THE DRUG
Take the drug as prescribed for the full treatment period, even if you begin to feel better before the scheduled end of therapy.

PROLONGED USE
You should see your doctor regularly for tests and examinations if you take this drug for a prolonged period. You should not take misoprostol for more than 4 weeks unless directed by your doctor.

PRECAUTIONS
Over 60: Misoprostol has not caused side effects or problems in older persons different from those in younger patients.

Driving and Hazardous Work: Do not drive or engage in hazardous work until you determine how the medicine affects you.

Alcohol: Avoid alcohol.

Pregnancy: Misoprostol should not be used during pregnancy, because it may promote contractions and bleeding of the uterus and can cause miscarriage. Before you start taking misoprostol, you must have had a negative pregnancy test within the previous 2 weeks. You must start taking the drug only on the second or third day of your next menstrual period. An effective method of birth control should be used while you are taking misoprostol. If you suspect you are pregnant, stop taking the drug immediately and consult your doctor.

Breast Feeding: Misoprostol may pass into breast milk; avoid or discontinue use while nursing because it may cause diarrhea in nursing babies.

Infants and Children: Use and dosage by anyone under the age of 18 must be determined by your doctor.

OVERDOSE
Symptoms: Tremors, sleepiness, trouble breathing, abdominal pain, severe diarrhea, fever, palpitations, extremely low blood pressure, slow heartbeat.

What to Do: An overdose of misoprostol is unlikely to be life-threatening. However, if someone takes a much larger dose than prescribed, call your doctor, emergency medical services (EMS), or the nearest poison control center.

DRUG INTERACTIONS
Before you take misoprostol, inform your doctor if you are taking any other prescription or over-the-counter medicine. Antacids may be taken with misoprostol to help relieve stomach pain, unless your doctor directs otherwise. Do not take antacids that contain magnesium, since they can cause or worsen the diarrhea that sometimes accompanies misoprostol use.

FOOD INTERACTIONS
No known food interactions.

DISEASE INTERACTIONS
Caution is advised when taking misoprostol. Consult your doctor if you have a history of blood vessel disease or epilepsy.

Mitotane

Lysodren 500 mg
(BRISTOL-MYERS SQUIBB)

▶ Drug Class: Antineoplastic (anticancer) agent/antiadrenal

▶ Available in: Tablets

▶ Available OTC? No

▶ As Generic? No

Side Effects

SERIOUS
Darkening of skin, diarrhea, dizziness, drowsiness, loss of appetite, depression, severe nausea and vomiting, skin rash, unusual fatigue, blood in urine, blurred or double vision, shortness of breath, wheezing. Call your doctor immediately.

COMMON
Nausea and vomiting.

LESS COMMON
Aching muscles, dizziness or lightheadedness when rising from a sitting or lying position, fever, flushed or reddened skin, muscle twitching.

PRINCIPAL USES
To treat cancer of the adrenal cortex, the outer part of the adrenal glands, which rest on top of either kidney. The adrenal cortex produces the body's natural corticosteroid hormones.

HOW THE DRUG WORKS
Mitotane appears to suppress activity (steroid production) in the adrenal cortex. For reasons that are unknown, the drug's reduction of steroid production somehow has a destructive effect on cancer cells in the adrenal cortices, and so slows the progression of cancer in that portion of the adrenal gland.

DOSAGE
2 to 6 g daily in 3 or 4 doses. The dosage can be increased to 16 g per day; the usual range is 8 to 10 g per day.

ONSET OF EFFECT
2 to 3 days.

DURATION OF ACTION
Unknown.

DIETARY ADVICE
Can be taken with or without food, according to personal preference. To minimize side effects, the last dose is best taken after the evening meal but before bedtime.

STORAGE
Store in a tightly sealed container away from heat and direct light.

IF YOU MISS A DOSE
Take it as soon as you remember. If it is near the time for the next dose, skip the missed dose and resume your regular dosage schedule. Do not double the next dose.

STOPPING THE DRUG
The decision to stop taking the drug should be made by your doctor.

PROLONGED USE
See your doctor regularly for tests and examinations if you must take this drug for a prolonged period. Neurological assessments are recommended at regular intervals for persons who take mitotane for more than 2 years.

PRECAUTIONS
Over 60: There is no specific information about the use of mitotane in older patients.

Driving and Hazardous Work: Do not drive or engage in hazardous work until you determine how the medicine affects you.

Alcohol: Avoid alcohol.

Pregnancy: Mitotane has not been shown to cause problems during pregnancy. Consult your doctor for specific advice if you are pregnant or plan to become pregnant.

Breast Feeding: It is unknown if mitotane passes into breast milk; caution is advised. Consult your doctor for specific advice.

Infants and Children: There is no specific information about the use of mitotane in infants and children, but it is not expected to cause different side effects or problems than it does in older patients.

Special Concerns: Initial treatment with mitotane often starts in the hospital until the dose is stabilized. Your doctor may want you to carry a card saying that you are taking mitotane. Check with your doctor if

you get an infection, illness, or injury of any sort, because mitotane may weaken your body's defenses against infection and inflammation.

OVERDOSE
Symptoms: No specific ones have been reported.

What to Do: An overdose of mitotane is unlikely to be life-threatening. However, if someone takes a much larger dose than prescribed, call your doctor, emergency medical services (EMS), or the nearest poison control center immediately.

DRUG INTERACTIONS
Consult your physician for specific advice if you are taking adrenocorticoids, glucocorticoids, mineralocorticoids, corticotropin, or central nervous system depressants.

FOOD INTERACTIONS
No known food interactions.

DISEASE INTERACTIONS
Caution is advised when taking mitotane. Consult your doctor if you have any infection. Use of mitotane may cause complications in patients with liver disease, since this organ works to remove the medication from the body.

Mitoxantrone Hydrochloride

▶ Drug Class: Antineoplastic (anticancer) agent

▶ Available in: Injection

▶ Available OTC? No

▶ As Generic? No

Side Effects

SERIOUS
Fever, chills, black, tarry stools, cough or shortness of breath, blood in urine or stools, rapid or irregular heartbeat, red spots on skin, swelling of feet and lower legs, unusual bleeding or bruising, sores in mouth and on lips, stomach pain, decreased urination, seizures, blue skin or pain and redness at injection site, skin rash. Call your doctor immediately.

COMMON
Diarrhea, headache, nausea and vomiting, temporary hair loss, bluish green-colored urine.

LESS COMMON
No less-common side effects are associated with mitoxantrone.

PRINCIPAL USES
Mitoxantrone is combined with other chemotherapy agents in the initial first-line of treatment against certain kinds of leukemias. Also used to treat secondary (chronic) progressive, progressive relapsing, or worsening relapsing-remitting multiple sclerosis.

HOW THE DRUG WORKS
It is unknown precisely how mitoxantrone works, but it appears to interfere with the DNA of cancer cells, preventing them from reproducing. The drug may also affect the growth and development of other kinds of cells in the body, resulting in unpleasant side effects, particularly the suppression of bone marrow, which causes anemia and other blood problems.

DOSAGE
Mitoxantrone is administered intravenously in a hospital setting. Dosage will be determined by your doctor.

ONSET OF EFFECT
Unknown.

DURATION OF ACTION
Unknown.

DIETARY ADVICE
Maintain adequate food and fluid intake. Calorie, protein, and vitamin needs increase in patients with cancer. Good nutrition is essential to cope with the demands of chemotherapy.

STORAGE
Not applicable; the dose is administered only at a health care facility.

IF YOU MISS A DOSE
Not applicable, since medication is given by a doctor or other health professional.

STOPPING THE DRUG
The decision to stop taking the drug should be made by your doctor.

PROLONGED USE
You should see your doctor regularly for tests and examinations if you take this drug for a prolonged period.

PRECAUTIONS
Over 60: There is no specific information comparing use of mitoxantrone in older patients with use in younger persons. No special problems are expected.

Driving and Hazardous Work: The use of mitoxantrone should not impair your ability to perform such tasks safely.

Alcohol: Alcohol should be avoided while taking this medication.

Pregnancy: Mitoxantrone may cause birth defects if it is taken by either the father or the mother at the time of conception. It is best to use some kind of birth control while taking mitoxantrone. Tell your doctor immediately if you think you have become pregnant while taking mitoxantrone.

Breast Feeding: Mitoxantrone passes into breast milk; discontinue nursing before beginning treatment.

Infants and Children: There is no specific information that compares use of mitoxantrone in infants and children with use in older persons.

Special Concerns: Do not receive any immunizations without your doctor's approval while you are taking mitoxantrone. Avoid persons with infections. Be careful when using a tooth-brush, dental floss, or toothpick. Take care not to cut yourself when using sharp objects such as a razor. Avoid contact sports. Before having dental work, consult your doctor. Your doctor may want you to drink extra fluids while you are taking this drug.

OVERDOSE
Symptoms: Severe infection as a result of substantial white blood cell suppression (immune system failure).

What to Do: Contact your oncologist, who will closely monitor your blood counts and symptoms and determine the course of your treatment.

DRUG INTERACTIONS
Consult your doctor for specific advice if you are taking amphotericin B, antithyroid agents, azathioprine, chloramphenicol, colchicine, flucytosine, ganciclovir, interferon, plicamycin, zidovudine, probenecid, sulfinpyrazone, or any other cancer medication.

FOOD INTERACTIONS
No known food interactions.

DISEASE INTERACTIONS
Caution is advised when taking mitoxantrone. Consult your doctor if you have a history of any of the following: chicken pox, shingles, gout, kidney stones, heart disease, or any infection. Use of mitoxantrone may cause complications in patients with liver disease, since this organ works to remove the medication from the body.

Moexipril Hydrochloride

▶ Drug Class: Angiotensin-converting enzyme (ACE) inhibitor

▶ Available in: Tablets

▶ Available OTC? No

▶ As Generic? No

Side Effects

SERIOUS
Fever and chills, sore throat and hoarseness, sudden difficulty breathing or swallowing, swelling of the face, mouth, or extremities, impaired kidney function (ankle swelling, decreased urination), confusion, yellow discoloration of the eyes or skin (indicating liver disorder), intense itching, chest pain or palpitations, abdominal pain. Serious side effects are very rare; contact your doctor immediately.

COMMON
Dry, persistent cough.

LESS COMMON
Dizziness or fainting, skin rash, numbness or tingling in the hands, feet, or lips, unusual fatigue or muscle weakness, nausea, drowsiness, loss of taste, headache.

PRINCIPAL USES
To control high blood pressure; to treat congestive heart failure (CHF); to treat patients with left ventricular dysfunction (damage to the pumping chamber of the heart); and to minimize further kidney damage in diabetics with mild kidney disease.

HOW THE DRUG WORKS
Angiotensin-converting enzyme (ACE) inhibitors block an enzyme that produces angiotensin, a naturally occurring substance that causes blood vessels to constrict and stimulates production of the adrenal hormone, aldosterone, which promotes sodium retention in the body. As a result, ACE inhibitors relax blood vessels (causing them to widen) and reduces sodium retention, which lowers blood pressure and so decreases the workload of the heart.

DOSAGE
To start, 7.5 mg once a day. Dosage may be increased by your doctor up to 30 mg a day, given in 1 or 2 doses.

ONSET OF EFFECT
Within 1 hour.

DURATION OF ACTION
24 hours.

DIETARY ADVICE
Take it on an empty stomach, about 1 hour before mealtime. Follow your doctor's dietary advice (such as low-salt or low-cholesterol restrictions) to improve control over high blood pressure and heart disease. Avoid high-potassium foods like bananas and citrus fruits and juices, unless you are also taking medications, such as diuretics, that lower potassium levels.

STORAGE
Store in a tightly sealed container away from heat and direct light.

IF YOU MISS A DOSE
Take it as soon as you remember. If it is near the time for the next dose, skip the missed dose and resume your regular dosage schedule. Do not double the next dose.

STOPPING THE DRUG
Do not stop taking this drug abruptly, as this may cause potentially serious health problems. Dosage should be reduced gradually, according to your doctor's instructions.

PROLONGED USE
Lifelong therapy may be necessary. See your doctor for regular evaluation.

PRECAUTIONS
Over 60: Smaller doses may be recommended for older patients.

Driving and Hazardous Work: Do not drive or engage in hazardous work until you determine how the medicine affects you.

Alcohol: Consume alcohol only in moderation since it may increase the effect of the drug and cause an excessive drop in blood pressure. Consult your doctor for advice.

Pregnancy: Use of moexipril during the last 6 months of pregnancy may cause severe defects, even death, in the fetus. The drug should be discontinued if you are pregnant or plan to become pregnant.

Breast Feeding: Moexipril may pass into breast milk; caution is advised. Consult your doctor for advice.

Infants and Children: The safety and efficacy of moexipril for infants and children have not been established. Benefits must be weighed against potential risks; consult your pediatrician for advice.

OVERDOSE
Symptoms: No specific ones have been reported.

What to Do: While overdose is unlikely, call your doctor, emergency medical services (EMS), or the nearest poison control center immediately if you suspect that someone has taken a much larger dose than prescribed.

DRUG INTERACTIONS
Consult your doctor if you are taking diuretics (especially potassium-sparing diuretics), potassium supplements or drugs containing potassium (check ingredient labels), lithium, anticoagulants (such as warfarin), indomethacin or other anti-inflammatory drugs, or any over-the-counter medications (especially cold remedies and diet pills).

FOOD INTERACTIONS
Avoid low-salt milk and salt substitutes. Many of these products contain potassium. Excessive intake of tea, coffee, cola, or other drinks that could create a diuretic effect should be avoided.

DISEASE INTERACTIONS
Consult your doctor if you have systemic lupus erythematosus (SLE) or if you have had a prior allergic reaction to ACE inhibitors. Moexipril should be used with caution by patients with severe kidney disease or renal artery stenosis (narrowing of one or both of the arteries that supply blood to the kidneys).

Moexipril Hydrochloride/Hydrochlorothiazide

▶ Drug Class: Angiotensin-converting enzyme (ACE) inhibitor/diuretic

▶ Available in: Tablets

▶ Available OTC? No

▶ As Generic? No

Side Effects

SERIOUS

Fever and chills, sore throat and hoarseness, sudden difficulty breathing or swallowing, swelling of the face, mouth, or extremities, impaired kidney function (ankle swelling, decreased urination), confusion, yellow discoloration of the eyes or skin (indicating liver disorder), intense itching, chest pain or heartbeat irregularities, abdominal pain. Serious side effects are very rare; contact your doctor immediately.

COMMON

Dry, persistent cough, muscle cramps or pain, heart palpitations, dizziness (especially when rising from a sitting or lying position), dry mouth, unusual thirst, constipation.

LESS COMMON

Fainting, skin rash, numbness or tingling in the hands, feet, or lips, unusual fatigue or muscle weakness, nausea, drowsiness, loss of taste, headache, increased sensitivity to sunlight, loss of appetite, gout.

PRINCIPAL USES

To treat high blood pressure. Used in patients for whom both moexipril and hydrochlorothiazide have been prescribed.

HOW THE DRUG WORKS

This drug combines an angiotensin-converting enzyme (ACE) inhibitor (moexipril hydrochloride) and a thiazide diuretic (hydrochlorothiazide). ACE inhibitors block an enzyme that produces angiotensin, a naturally occurring substance that causes blood vessels to constrict and stimulates production of the adrenal hormone, aldosterone, which promotes sodium retention in the body. As a result, ACE inhibitors relax blood vessels (causing them to widen) and reduces sodium retention, which lowers blood pressure and so decreases the workload of the heart. Hydrochlorothiazide (HCTZ) increases sodium and water in the urine output. By reducing the overall fluid volume in the body, diuretics reduce blood volume and so reduce blood pressure.

DOSAGE

This combination medication comes in two strengths: moexipril/hydrochlorothiazide 7.5/12.5 and 15/25. The dose ranges from 7.5 to 30 mg of moexipril and 12.5 to 50 mg of hydrochlorothiazide per day. Tablets are taken either once a day or in 2 divided doses, 1 hour before meals.

ONSET OF EFFECT

Within 1 hour.

DURATION OF ACTION

Unknown.

DIETARY ADVICE

Take it on an empty stomach, about 1 hour before meals.

STORAGE

Store in a tightly sealed container away from heat, moisture, and direct light.

IF YOU MISS A DOSE

Take it as soon as you remember. If it is near the time for the next dose, skip the missed dose and resume your regular dosage schedule. Do not double the next dose.

STOPPING THE DRUG

Discontinuing this drug abruptly may cause potentially serious problems. The dosage should be reduced gradually, according to your doctor's instructions.

PROLONGED USE

See your doctor regularly for evaluation if you must take this medicine for a prolonged period. Lifelong therapy may be necessary.

PRECAUTIONS

Over 60: Adverse reactions may be more likely and more severe.

Driving and Hazardous Work: No warnings.

Alcohol: Alcohol may increase the effect of the drug and cause an excessive drop in blood pressure; drink only in moderation.

Pregnancy: Before taking this medication, tell your doctor if you are pregnant or plan to become pregnant. Use of this drug during the last 6 months of pregnancy may cause severe defects, even death, in the fetus.

Breast Feeding: Moexipril may pass into breast milk; consult your doctor for specific advice.

Infants and Children: Not recommended for use by children under 18.

Special Concerns: A rare complication is angioedema, characterized by swelling of the lips, tongue, and throat. It may be so severe as to cause obstruction of the airways, which could be fatal.

OVERDOSE

Symptoms: No cases of overdose have been reported; symptoms might include dizziness, faintness, or confusion.

What to Do: While overdose is unlikely, call your doctor, emergency medical services (EMS), or the nearest poison control center immediately if you suspect that someone has taken a much larger dose than prescribed.

DRUG INTERACTIONS

Consult your doctor for specific advice if you are taking cholestyramine, colestipol, corticosteroids, digitalis drugs, antidiabetic drugs, lithium, potassium-containing medications or supplements, or any over-the-counter drug (especially cold remedies and appetite suppressants).

FOOD INTERACTIONS

Avoid low-salt milk and salt substitutes. Many of these products contain potassium.

DISEASE INTERACTIONS

Consult your doctor if you have systemic lupus erythematosus or if you have had a prior allergic reaction to ACE inhibitors. This medication should be used with caution by patients with severe kidney disease or renal artery stenosis (narrowing of one or both of the arteries that supply blood to the kidneys). This medication can increase blood triglycerides and worsen control of blood sugar in people with diabetes.

Molindone

Moban 5 mg
(GATE)

Additional photographs

▶ Drug Class: Neuroleptic; antipsychotic

▶ Available in: Tablets, liquid concentrate

▶ Available OTC? No

▶ As Generic? No

Side Effects

SERIOUS
Restlessness, rigidity and trembling of limbs, involuntary movements of the tongue, face, mouth, or jaw, involuntary movements of the arms or legs, muscle rigidity, irregular pulse, unusually rapid heartbeat, palpitations, or other heartbeat irregularities. Call your doctor immediately.

COMMON
Drowsiness, blurred vision, palpitations, dry mouth or excessive salivation, skin rash, shaking of the hands, stiffness, stooped posture.

LESS COMMON
Increase in sexual desire, menstrual irregularities, discharge of milk from the breast, enlargement of breasts in men and women, prolonged contraction of muscles, liver abnormalities, mental depression, hyperactivity, unusual feeling of well-being (euphoria).

PRINCIPAL USES
To treat psychotic conditions (severe mental disorders characterized by distorted thoughts, perceptions, and emotions), such as schizophrenia.

HOW THE DRUG WORKS
Molindone alters the activity of certain chemicals in the central nervous system, reducing aggressiveness and hyperactivity. It also appears to produce tranquilizing and antipsychotic effects.

DOSAGE
Initial dose is 50 to 75 mg a day; can be increased to 100 mg a day after 3 or 4 days. Maintenance dose may vary from 5 to 15 mg, 3 or 4 times a day, to 10 to 25 mg, 3 or 4 times a day, or 225 mg daily in several divided doses, depending on the severity of the condition being treated. Older and debilitated patients should be started on lower doses.

ONSET OF EFFECT
Sedation may occur within minutes, but onset of antipsychotic effect may take hours to occur or may not occur until days or weeks after the beginning of therapy.

DURATION OF ACTION
24 to 36 hours.

DIETARY ADVICE
No special restrictions.

STORAGE
Store in a tightly sealed container away from heat and direct light.

IF YOU MISS A DOSE
Take it as soon as you remember. If it is near the time for the next dose, skip the missed dose and resume your regular dosage schedule. Do not double the next dose.

STOPPING THE DRUG
The decision to stop taking the drug should be made in consultation with your physician.

PROLONGED USE
Prolonged use may lead to tardive dyskinesia (involuntary movements of the jaw, lips, tongue, and, in rare cases, the arms, legs, hands, or body). Consult your doctor about the need for follow-up evaluations and tests if you must take this drug for an extended period.

PRECAUTIONS
Over 60: Adverse reactions are more likely and more severe in older patients.

Driving and Hazardous Work: Exercise caution until you determine how the medication affects you.

Alcohol: Avoid alcohol.

Pregnancy: Molindone has not been shown to cause birth defects in animals. Human studies have not been done. Before you take molindone, tell your doctor if you are pregnant or plan to become pregnant.

Breast Feeding: It is not known whether molindone passes into breast milk; caution is advised. Discuss potential risks and benefits with your doctor.

Infants and Children: Not recommended for use by children under age 12.

Special Concerns: Molindone is a newer drug very similar to phenothiazines (such as chlorpromazine and perphenazine), but does not appear to cause unexpected weight gain and is not as likely to cause tardive dyskinesia (an irreversible neurological disorder). The liquid concentrate form of molindone contains sulfite and so may cause severe allergic reactions in those who are highly sensitive to sulfites. Persons with asthma are incidentally at increased risk of sulfite sensitivity.

OVERDOSE
Symptoms: Extreme drowsiness, heartbeat irregularities, dry mouth, paradoxical restlessness or agitation, seizures, loss of consciousness.

What to Do: Call your doctor, emergency medical services (EMS), or the nearest poison control center immediately.

DRUG INTERACTIONS
Consult your doctor for advice if you are taking any drugs that depress the central nervous system, including antihistamines, antidepressants or other psychiatric medications, barbiturates, sedatives, cough medicines, decongestants, and painkillers. Be sure your doctor knows about any over-the-counter drugs you may take.

FOOD INTERACTIONS
None reported.

DISEASE INTERACTIONS
Consult your doctor for specific advice if you have any other medical condition.

Mometasone Furoate Nasal

▶ Drug Class: Nasal corticosteroid

▶ Available in: Nasal spray

▶ Available OTC? No

▶ As Generic? No

Side Effects

SERIOUS
No serious side effects are associated with mometasone.

COMMON
Headache, increased susceptibility to viral infection, sore throat, nosebleeds or bloody nasal secretions.

LESS COMMON
Cough, increased susceptibility to upper respiratory infection, menstrual irregularities, bone pain, sinus pain.

PRINCIPAL USES
To prevent and treat the symptoms of allergic rhinitis (seasonal and perennial allergies such as hay fever).

HOW THE DRUG WORKS
Respiratory corticosteroids such as mometasone primarily reduce or prevent inflammation of the lining of the airways, reduce the allergic response to inhaled allergens, and inhibit the secretion of mucus within the airways.

DOSAGE
Adults and teenagers: 2 sprays (50 micrograms [mcg] in each spray) in each nostril once a day, for a maximum daily dose of 200 mcg. To prevent the symptoms of allergic rhinitis from developing, it is recommended that patients with known seasonal allergies begin taking mometasone 2 to 4 weeks before the anticipated start of the pollen season.

ONSET OF EFFECT
From 11 hours to 2 days.

DURATION OF ACTION
Mometasone is effective as long as you continue to take the medication.

DIETARY ADVICE
Mometasone can be used without regard to diet.

STORAGE
Store in a tightly sealed container away from heat, moisture, and direct light.

IF YOU MISS A DOSE
If you miss a dose on one day, resume your regular dosage schedule the next day. Do not double the next dose.

STOPPING THE DRUG
No special instructions.

PROLONGED USE
Consult your doctor about any need for periodic physical examinations and laboratory tests.

PRECAUTIONS
Over 60: No special problems are expected.

Driving and Hazardous Work: Mometasone should not impair your ability to perform such tasks safely.

Alcohol: No special precautions are necessary.

Pregnancy: Nasal steroids have not been reported to cause birth defects if taken during pregnancy. Before using this drug, tell your doctor if you are pregnant or plan to become pregnant.

Breast Feeding: Mometasone may pass into breast milk; caution is advised. Consult your doctor for specific advice.

Infants and Children: Not recommended for use by children under age 12.

Special Concerns: Prior to your initial use of the inhaler, you must prime it by depressing the pump 10 times or until a fine mist appears. You may store the inhaler for up to 1 week without repriming. If it is unused for more than 1 week, reprime it by depressing the pump 2 times or until a fine mist appears. Avoid spraying the medication into the eyes.

OVERDOSE
Symptoms: No cases of overdose have been reported.

What to Do: An overdose with mometasone is unlikely. If someone takes a much larger dose than prescribed, call your doctor.

DRUG INTERACTIONS
Consult your doctor for advice if you are taking systemic corticosteroids, other inhaled corticosteroids, or any drugs that suppress the immune system.

FOOD INTERACTIONS
No known food interactions.

DISEASE INTERACTIONS
Consult your doctor if you have any other medical problem, particularly glaucoma, a herpes infection of the eye, a history of tuberculosis, liver disease, an underactive thyroid, or osteoporosis.

Mometasone Furoate Topical

▶ Drug Class: Antipsoriasis drug; topical corticosteroid

▶ Available in: Cream, lotion, ointment

▶ Available OTC? No

▶ As Generic? No

Side Effects

SERIOUS
No serious side effects are associated with the use of mometasone.

COMMON
Thinning of the skin may occur with prolonged use of mometasone.

LESS COMMON
Burning or discomfort when medication is applied, blisters and pus near hair follicles, unusual bleeding or easy bruising, darkening or prominence of small skin veins, numbness or tingling of affected area, or of hands and fingers, increased susceptibility to infection, cataracts.

PRINCIPAL USES
For topical therapy of skin conditions associated with itching, redness, scaling and peeling, pain, and other signs of inflammation. Topical steroids come in many strengths; your physician will prescribe mometasone, a medium strength steroid, when it is the most appropriate steroid preparation for your particular skin condition.

HOW THE DRUG WORKS
Steroids interfere with the formation of natural substances within your body that are directly responsible for the process of inflammation, which produces swelling, redness, itching, and pain.

DOSAGE
Adults: Apply to the affected areas once daily. Children: Consult your pediatrician.

ONSET OF EFFECT
Soon after application. However, recognizable changes in your condition may take several days or more to develop.

DURATION OF ACTION
Unknown.

DIETARY ADVICE
Maintain your usual food and fluid intake. Increase fluids if you have a fever or diarrhea, in hot weather, or during exercise.

STORAGE
Store in a tightly sealed container away from heat and direct light. Keep away from moisture and extremes in temperature.

IF YOU MISS A DOSE
Apply it as soon as you remember. If it is near the time for the next dose, skip the missed dose and resume your regular dosage schedule.

STOPPING THE DRUG
Apply it as prescribed for the full treatment period, even if you begin to feel better before the scheduled end of the therapy.

PROLONGED USE
Therapy with this medication may require weeks or months. Prolonged use may increase the risk of undesirable side effects (especially thinning of the skin).

PRECAUTIONS
Over 60: Adverse reactions may be more likely and more severe in older patients.

Driving and Hazardous Work: The use of topical mometasone should not impair your ability to perform such tasks safely.

Alcohol: No special precautions are necessary.

Pregnancy: Mometasone should not be used for prolonged periods by pregnant women or by women trying to become pregnant.

Breast Feeding: Mometasone may pass into breast milk; caution is advised. Consult your doctor for advice.

Infants and Children: Not recommended for prolonged use by children. Consult your pediatrician.

Special Concerns: Avoid use of this medication around the eyes. Note that mometasone is not a treatment for acne, burns, infections, or disorders of pigmentation. Do not bandage or wrap the medicated area of skin with any special dressings or coverings unless specifically told to do so by your doctor. Applying special coverings leads to increased absorption of the medication from the skin, and may increase the chance of an undesirable interaction or side effect.

OVERDOSE
Symptoms: No specific ones have been reported.

What to Do: An overdose of mometasone is unlikely to be life-threatening. However, if someone applies a much larger dose than prescribed, call your doctor, emergency medical services (EMS), or the nearest poison control center.

DRUG INTERACTIONS
None are known. Consult your doctor or pharmacist if you are concerned about a particular prescription or nonprescription drug.

FOOD INTERACTIONS
No known food interactions.

DISEASE INTERACTIONS
Consult your doctor if you have any of the following: diabetes, skin infection or skin sores and ulcers, infection at another site in your body, tuberculosis, unusual bleeding or bruising, glaucoma, or cataracts.

Montelukast

▶ Drug Class: Leukotriene receptor antagonist

▶ Available in: Tablets, chewable tablets, oral granules

▶ Available OTC? No

▶ As Generic? No

Side Effects

SERIOUS
Skin rash (indicating potentially life-threatening allergic reaction); gastroenteritis (causing loss of appetite, nausea, vomiting, stomach upset, fever, and diarrhea). Call your doctor immediately.

COMMON
Headache.

LESS COMMON
Weakness, fatigue, fever, abdominal pain, indigestion, mouth ulcers, dizziness, nasal congestion, cough, flu-like symptoms, muscle aches, bruising.

PRINCIPAL USES
To prevent and treat the symptoms of chronic asthma by preventing bronchospasm (contraction of the smooth muscle tissue surrounding the airways, which results in narrowing and obstruction of the air passages). Montelukast may be used in conjunction with other asthma treatments, such as bronchodilators. To relieve symptoms of seasonal allergies.

HOW THE DRUG WORKS
Montelukast blocks cell receptors for leukotrienes, naturally formed substances that cause inflammation and constriction of the bronchial airways. Unlike bronchodilators, which relieve the acute symptoms of an asthma attack, montelukast is prescribed to be taken regularly when no symptoms are present, to reduce the chronic inflammation of the airways that is the underlying cause of asthma. This prevents symptomatic asthma attacks.

DOSAGE
Adults and children age 15 and over: One 10-mg tablet per day. Children ages 6 to 14: One 5-mg chewable tablet per day. Children ages 2 to 5: One 4-mg chewable tablet or one packet 4-mg oral granules per day. For asthma, dose should be taken in the morning.

ONSET OF EFFECT
Unknown.

DURATION OF ACTION
Unknown.

DIETARY ADVICE
Montelukast can be taken without regard to diet.

STORAGE
Store in a tightly sealed container away from heat, moisture, and direct light.

IF YOU MISS A DOSE
If you miss a dose one day, do not double the dose the next day. Resume your regular dosage schedule.

STOPPING THE DRUG
The decision to stop taking the drug should be made in consultation with your physician.

PROLONGED USE
No special problems are expected.

PRECAUTIONS
Over 60: Adverse reactions may be more likely and more severe.

Driving and Hazardous Work: No special precautions are necessary.

Alcohol: No special precautions are necessary.

Pregnancy: Adequate human studies have not been done. Before taking montelukast, tell your doctor if you are pregnant or plan to become pregnant.

Breast Feeding: Montelukast may pass into breast milk; caution is advised. Consult your doctor for specific advice.

Infants and Children: Not recommended for use by children under age 2.

Special Concerns: Montelukast has no effect on an asthma attack that has already started. You should have a fast-acting inhaled bronchodilator on hand to treat an acute asthma attack in progress. Consult your doctor if you need to use inhaled bronchodilators more often than usual, or if you are taking more than the maximum number of inhalations in a 24-hour period. Continue to take montelukast even when you are not experiencing any symptoms, as well as during periods of worsening asthma. In rare cases, if doses of systemic corticosteroids are reduced, montelukast may cause Churg-Strauss syndrome, a tissue disorder that sometimes strikes adult asthma patients and, if untreated, can destroy organs. Early symptoms include fever, muscle aches, and weight loss. Montelukast should not be used as the sole treatment for exercise-induced bronchospasm.

OVERDOSE
Symptoms: No cases of overdose have been reported.

What to Do: An overdose with montelukast is unlikely. If someone takes a much larger dose than prescribed, call your doctor, emergency medical services (EMS), or the nearest poison control center immediately.

DRUG INTERACTIONS
Consult your doctor for specific advice if you are already taking phenobarbital or rifampin. Before you take montelukast, tell your doctor if you are allergic to any other prescription or over-the-counter medicine.

FOOD INTERACTIONS
No known food interactions.

DISEASE INTERACTIONS
If you have phenylketonuria, you should not use the chewable tablet form of montelukast, since it contains phenylalanine. Use of montelukast may cause complications in patients with severe liver disease, since this organ works to remove the medication from the body.

Morphine

M S Contin 15 mg
(PURDUE FREDERICK)

Additional photographs

▶ Drug Class: Opioid (narcotic)
analgesic

▶ Available in: Capsules,
tablets, oral solution, suppositories, injection

▶ Available OTC? No

▶ As Generic? Yes

Side Effects

SERIOUS
Serious side effects of
morphine are indistin-
guishable from those
of overdose: Confusion;
severe drowsiness,
weakness, or dizziness;
slurred speech; small,
pinpoint pupils; cold,
clammy skin; slow
breathing; seizures;
loss of consciousness.

COMMON
Dizziness or lightheaded-
ness, nausea or vomiting,
constipation, drowsiness,
itching.

LESS COMMON
Mood swings, false sense
of well-being (euphoria),
urinary retention, jerking
body movements
(myoclonus), hallucina-
tions, sweating.

PRINCIPAL USES
To relieve severe pain.

HOW THE DRUG WORKS
Opioids such as morphine
relieve pain by acting on
specific areas of the brain
and spinal cord that process
pain signals from nerves
throughout the body.

DOSAGE
Adults— Capsules, tablets,
oral solution: To start, 10 to
30 mg every 4 to 6 hours.
Dose will be adjusted for
individual needs. Extended-
release capsules or tablets:
Starting dose depends on
individual needs and will be
adjusted. Suppositories: 10
to 30 mg every 4 to 6 hours.
Injection: 5 to 20 mg into a
muscle or under the skin
every 6 hours. Children—
Dosages for all oral forms
and suppositories must be
determined by your doctor;
for injection, 0.1 to 0.2 mg
per 2.2 lbs (1 kg) of body
weight, to a maximum of 15
mg, under the skin every 4
hours.

ONSET OF EFFECT
Oral forms: Within 60 minutes. Suppositories: 20 to 60
minutes. Injection: 10 to 30
minutes.

DURATION OF ACTION
Immediate-release oral
forms: 4 to 5 hours.
Extended-release forms: 8
to 12 hours. Suppositories
and injection: 4 to 5 hours.

DIETARY ADVICE
Oral forms of morphine can
be taken with food to lessen
stomach upset. Long-acting
tablets must be swallowed
whole, without chewing.

STORAGE
Store in a tightly sealed container away from heat, moisture, and direct light. Do
not allow liquid forms to
freeze.

IF YOU MISS A DOSE
If you are taking morphine
on a fixed schedule, take it
as soon as you remember. If
it is near the time for the
next dose, skip the missed
dose and resume your regular dosage schedule. Do not
double the next dose.

STOPPING THE DRUG
The decision to stop taking
the drug should be made
in consultation with your
physician.

PROLONGED USE
See your doctor regularly
for tests and examinations if
you must take this medication for a prolonged period.
Prolonged use may lead to
physical dependence.

PRECAUTIONS
Over 60: Adverse reactions
may be more likely and
more severe in older
patients.

**Driving and Hazardous
Work:** Do not drive or
engage in hazardous work
until you determine how the
medicine affects you.

Alcohol: Avoid alcohol.

Pregnancy: Avoid use during pregnancy if possible.

Breast Feeding: Mor-
phine passes into breast
milk; caution is advised.
Consult your doctor for specific advice.

Infants and Children:
Adverse reactions may be
more likely and more
severe.

Special Concerns: If you
feel the medication is not
working adequately after a
few weeks, do not increase
the dose. Consult your doctor. Before having any
surgery, tell the doctor or
dentist in charge you are
taking morphine. Before

removing the foil wrapper
of the suppository, check if
it is firm enough to insert.
If too soft, put it in the
refrigerator for 30 minutes
or hold it momentarily
under cold water.

OVERDOSE
Symptoms: Confusion;
severe drowsiness, weak-
ness, or dizziness; slurred
speech; small, pinpoint
pupils; cold, clammy skin;
slow breathing; seizures;
loss of consciousness.

What to Do: Call your
doctor, emergency medical
services (EMS), or the
nearest poison control
center immediately.

DRUG INTERACTIONS
Consult your doctor for specific advice if you are taking
carbamazepine or other
drugs for seizures, barbiturates, sedatives, cough
medicines, decongestants,
antidepressants, other prescription pain medicine,
MAO inhibitors, naltrexone,
rifampin, or zidovudine.

FOOD INTERACTIONS
None reported.

DISEASE INTERACTIONS
Consult your physician if
you have a history of alcohol or drug abuse; emo-
tional illness; brain
disorders or head injury;
seizures; lung disease;
prostate or other problems
with urination; gallstones;
colitis; heart, kidney, liver,
or thyroid disease.

Moxifloxacin Hydrochloride

▶ Drug Class: Fluoroquinolone antibiotic

▶ Available in: Tablets

▶ Available OTC? No

▶ As Generic? No

Side Effects

SERIOUS
Serious reactions to moxifloxacin are rare and include mental confusion, nightmares, dizziness, hallucinations, anxiety, drowsiness or fainting spells, palpitations, shortness of breath, unusual swelling in the face or extremities, and loss of consciousness. Also skin burning, redness, blisters, rash, or itching on exposure to sunlight; increased risk of tendinitis or tendon rupture. Call your doctor immediately.

COMMON
Nausea, diarrhea, dizziness, headache, abdominal pain, vomiting.

LESS COMMON
Many less common side effects have been associated with moxifloxacin and may include: change in sense of taste, heartburn, weakness, insomnia, cough, dry skin, tinnitus, joint pain, dry mouth, vaginitis.

PRINCIPAL USES
To treat mild to severe bacterial infections, including acute sinusitis, community-acquired pneumonia, and acute bacterial complications due to chronic bronchitis.

HOW THE DRUG WORKS
Moxifloxacin inhibits the activity of a bacterial enzyme (gyrase) that is necessary for proper DNA formation and replication. This fights infection by preventing bacteria from reproducing.

DOSAGE
For acute sinusitis or community-acquired pneumonia: 400 mg once a day for 10 days. For acute bacterial complications due to chronic bronchitis: 400 mg once a day for 5 days.

ONSET OF EFFECT
Varies depending on the infection being treated.

DURATION OF ACTION
Unknown.

DIETARY ADVICE
Can be taken without regard to diet. Drink plenty of fluids.

STORAGE
Store in a tightly sealed container away from heat, moisture, and direct light.

IF YOU MISS A DOSE
Take it as soon as you remember. If it is near the time for the next dose, skip the missed dose and resume regular dosage schedule. Do not double next dose.

STOPPING THE DRUG
It is very important to take this drug as prescribed for the full treatment period, even if you begin to feel better before the scheduled end of therapy.

PROLONGED USE
If your symptoms do not improve or instead become worse after a few days, consult your doctor promptly. Moxifloxacin is typically taken for no more than 5 to 10 days.

PRECAUTIONS
Over 60: No special problems are expected.

Driving and Hazardous Work: Avid such activities until you determine how the medicine affects you.

Alcohol: It is advisable to abstain from alcohol when fighting an infection.

Pregnancy: In some animal tests, moxifloxacin has caused birth defects. Adequate studies in humans have not been done. It should be used during pregnancy only if potential benefits clearly justify the risks. Before you take moxifloxacin, tell your doctor if you are pregnant or plan to become pregnant.

Breast Feeding: Moxifloxacin may pass into breast milk and cause serious side effects in the nursing infant; use of the drug is discouraged when nursing.

Infants and Children: Moxifloxacin is not recommended for use by persons under the age of 18.

Special Concerns: Do not take this medicine if you are allergic to any quinolone antibiotic, such as ciprofloxacin or lomefloxacin.

OVERDOSE
Symptoms: An overdose is unlikely to occur. Possible symptoms after an excessive dose may include decreased activity, drowsiness, vomiting, diarrhea, tremors, and seizures.

What to Do: Call your doctor, emergency medical services (EMS), or the nearest poison control center immediately.

DRUG INTERACTIONS
Because moxifloxacin can affect the function of the heart, it should not be used if you are taking antiarrhythmic drugs such as amiodarone, quinidine, procainamide, or sotalol. It should be used with caution in patients taking erythromycin, antipsychotics, tricylic antidepressants, nonsteroidal anti-inflammatory drugs (NSAIDs; including ibuprofen, aspirin, and naproxen), or digoxin. Moxifloxacin should be taken at least 4 hours before or 8 hours after using ferrous sulfate (iron supplement); dietary supplements containing zinc; didanosine; sucralfate; or antacids containing aluminum salts, magnesium salts, or calcium. Also tell your doctor if you are taking any other prescription or over-the-counter drug.

FOOD INTERACTIONS
No known food interactions.

DISEASE INTERACTIONS
Moxifloxacin should not be taken by people with prolongation of the QT interval on an electrocardiogram, known heart rhythm disturbances, uncorrected hypokalemia (low blood potassium levels), or those taking antiarrhythmic drugs such as amiodarone, quinidine, procainamide, or sotalol. This drug should be used with caution in people with significant bradycardia (slow heart rate), recent myocardial ischemia, known or suspected nervous system disorders, or those who are predisposed to seizures. Use of moxifloxacin is not recommended in people with moderate or severe liver disease.

Mupirocin

▶ Drug Class: Antibiotic

▶ Available in: Ointment, cream

▶ Available OTC? No

▶ As Generic? Yes

Side Effects

SERIOUS
There are no serious side effects associated with the use of mupirocin.

COMMON
Mild stinging or burning sensation with initial application.

LESS COMMON
Persistent irritation or skin allergy with pain or discomfort (stinging or burning) at application site; itching, redness, rash, or dryness of the skin; nausea.

PRINCIPAL USES
Mupirocin is prescribed for topical therapy of certain bacteria-related skin infections. Mupirocin may be used alone or is occasionally used in combination with a second antibiotic (which is usually taken in an oral form).

HOW THE DRUG WORKS
Mupirocin works by preventing bacterial cells from manufacturing vital cell proteins and forming protective cell walls. This ultimately destroys the infecting bacterial organisms.

DOSAGE
Apply to affected skin 3 times a day. The site may be covered with a gauze dressing if desired.

ONSET OF EFFECT
Mupirocin begins antibacterial activity as soon as the ointment or cream is applied. Several days may be required, however, before its full effects become noticeable.

DURATION OF ACTION
Unknown.

DIETARY ADVICE
No special restrictions.

STORAGE
Store in a tightly sealed container away from heat and direct light. Keep away from moisture and extremes in temperature.

IF YOU MISS A DOSE
Apply it as soon as you remember. If it is near the time for the next application, skip the missed one and resume your regular dosage schedule. Do not increase the quantity of medication with the next application.

STOPPING THE DRUG
Apply as prescribed for the full treatment period, even if you begin to feel the affected area is better before the scheduled end of therapy.

PROLONGED USE
Therapy with this medication should not require more than 14 days in most cases. Prolonged use of mupirocin may increase the risk of undesirable side effects.

PRECAUTIONS
Over 60: No special precautions for older patients.

Driving and Hazardous Work: The use of mupirocin should not impair your ability to perform such tasks safely.

Alcohol: No special precautions are necessary.

Pregnancy: Mupirocin has not been evaluated in pregnant women. It is likely that mupirocin is safe for use during pregnancy in certain situations. This should be determined by your doctor.

Breast Feeding: Although not thought to be significantly absorbed into the bloodstream, if excessive amounts of mupirocin were absorbed, the drug could pass into breast milk; consult your doctor for advice.

Infants and Children: Consult your pediatrician.

Special Concerns: Mupirocin should not be used by anyone with a history of allergic reaction to mupirocin or any of the ingredients in the ointment or cream (check the label carefully). As with any other antibiotic, mupirocin is useful only against types of bacteria that are susceptible to its effects. Therefore, it is important to tell your doctor if your condition has not improved—or if it has worsened—within 3 to 5 days of starting mupirocin. The particular bacteria causing your illness may be resistant to mupirocin, and a different antibiotic may be required. Avoid using this drug near or around the eyes.

OVERDOSE
Symptoms: No cases of overdose have been reported.

What to Do: Overapplication of mupirocin is unlikely to be harmful. However, if someone swallows the medication, call your doctor, emergency medical services (EMS), or the nearest poison control center.

DRUG INTERACTIONS
No specific interactions have been reported. Consult your doctor or pharmacist if you are concerned about taking another prescription or nonprescription medication while you are using mupirocin.

FOOD INTERACTIONS
No known food interactions.

DISEASE INTERACTIONS
No disease interactions have been reported.

Muromonab-CD3

▶ Drug Class: Immunosuppressant

▶ Available in: Injection

▶ Available OTC? No

▶ As Generic? No

Side Effects

SERIOUS
Chest pain, wheezing or shortness of breath, rapid or irregular heartbeat, swelling of the face or throat. Call your doctor immediately.

COMMON
Dizziness or faintness, diarrhea, fever and chills, general feeling of illness, headache, nausea, vomiting, muscle or joint pain.

LESS COMMON
Confusion, sensitivity of eyes to light, hallucinations, itching or tingling, stiff neck, skin rash, tremor, weakness, unusual fatigue, seizures.

PRINCIPAL USES
To slow down or reduce the natural tendency of the immune system to reject organ transplants.

HOW THE DRUG WORKS
Muromonab-CD3 suppresses the immune system's reaction against foreign tissue by inhibiting activity of white blood cells, a major component of the immune system's arsenal.

DOSAGE
Adults: 5 mg injected into a vein once a day. This drug should be administered only by or under the direct supervision of your doctor. Children: The dose is determined by your doctor according to body weight.

ONSET OF EFFECT
Within minutes.

DURATION OF ACTION
One week after withdrawal of muromonab-CD3.

DIETARY ADVICE
This drug can be given without regard to meals.

STORAGE
Not applicable. Muromonab-CD3 is administered by a health care professional.

IF YOU MISS A DOSE
Contact your doctor and reschedule your appointment as soon as possible.

STOPPING THE DRUG
The decision to stop taking the drug should be made by your doctor.

PROLONGED USE
See your doctor regularly for tests and examinations if you take this drug for a prolonged period. It may cause effects such as skin cancers or lymphomas that may not occur until years after the medicine is administered.

PRECAUTIONS
Over 60: There is no information comparing use of muromonab-CD3 in older patients with use in younger persons.

Driving and Hazardous Work: Do not drive or engage in hazardous work until you determine how the medicine affects you.

Alcohol: Avoid alcohol.

Pregnancy: Studies of this medication's use during pregnancy have not been done in animals or humans. The drug may cross the placenta, but it is not known whether it harms the fetus. Before you take this drug, tell your doctor if you are pregnant or plan to become pregnant.

Breast Feeding: It is not known whether muromonab-CD3 passes into breast milk; consult your doctor for advice.

Infants and Children: Children are more likely to be dehydrated by the vomiting and diarrhea caused by muromonab-CD3.

Special Concerns: Treatment with muromonab-CD3 may increase the risk of other infections. Avoid persons who have received vaccinations recently or those with colds or other infections. If you think you are getting an infection, inform your doctor at once. Dental work should be done only with great caution during therapy. Practice dental hygiene and be cautious when using toothbrushes, toothpicks, and dental floss. Tell your doctor if you have had any allergic reaction to rodents, such as rats or mice; muromonab-CD3 is extracted from a mouse cell culture.

OVERDOSE
Symptoms: No specific ones have been reported.

What to Do: Call your doctor, emergency medical services (EMS), or the nearest poison control center immediately if you suspect an overdose.

DRUG INTERACTIONS
Consult your doctor for specific advice if you are taking azathioprine, chlorambucil, corticosteroids, cyclophosphamide, cyclosporine, cytarabine, mercaptopurine, or a live-virus vaccine.

FOOD INTERACTIONS
No known food interactions.

DISEASE INTERACTIONS
Caution is advised when taking muromonab-CD3. Consult your doctor if you have any of the following: angina, circulation problems, seizures, a history of recent heart attack, any other heart problem, kidney problems, lung problems, nervous system problems, a history of blood clots, chicken pox, shingles, or any infection.

Mycophenolate Mofetil

CellCept 250 mg
(ROCHE)

▶ Drug Class: Immunosuppressant

▶ Available in: Capsules, tablets, oral suspension

▶ Available OTC? No

▶ As Generic? No

Side Effects

SERIOUS
Anemia; chest pain; fever or chills; cough or hoarseness; pinpoint red spots on skin; pain in lower back or side; high blood pressure; painful or difficult urination; black, tarry stools; blood in urine or stools; swelling of feet or lower legs; bloody vomit; white patches on mouth, tongue, or throat; unusual bleeding or bruising; tremor. Call your doctor immediately.

COMMON
Abdominal or stomach pain, headache, nausea, vomiting, constipation or diarrhea, heartburn, weakness.

LESS COMMON
Dizziness, skin rash, insomnia, acne.

PRINCIPAL USES
To slow down or reduce the natural tendency of the immune system to reject organ transplants.

HOW THE DRUG WORKS
Mycophenolate suppresses the immune system's reaction against foreign tissue by inhibiting the activity of white blood cells, a major component of the immune system's arsenal.

DOSAGE
Adults: 1 g twice a day in combination with corticosteroids and cyclosporine. Children: Dosage and frequency will be determined by your pediatrician.

ONSET OF EFFECT
Unknown.

DURATION OF ACTION
Unknown.

DIETARY ADVICE
The medication should be taken 30 minutes before or 2 hours after meals. It can be taken with a full glass of water to lessen stomach upset.

STORAGE
Store at room temperature in a tightly sealed container away from heat, moisture, and direct light. Oral suspension may be refrigerated.

IF YOU MISS A DOSE
Take it as soon as you remember. However, if it is near the time for the next dose, skip the missed dose and resume your regular dosage schedule. Do not double the next dose.

STOPPING THE DRUG
The decision to stop taking the drug should be made by your doctor.

PROLONGED USE
You should see your doctor regularly for physical examinations and tests if you must take this drug for an extended period of time.

PRECAUTIONS
Over 60: Information on the effects of mycophenolate in older patients as compared with younger persons is not yet available.

Driving and Hazardous Work: Do not drive or engage in hazardous work until you determine how the medicine affects you.

Alcohol: Avoid alcohol.

Pregnancy: Mycophenolate has caused birth defects in animals. Human studies have not been done, but caution is advised. A pregnancy test should be taken at least 1 week before mycophenolate treatment is started, and reliable methods of contraception should be used before, during, and 6 months after discontinuation of therapy.

Breast Feeding: It is not known whether mycophenolate passes into breast milk, but caution is advised; consult your doctor for advice.

Infants and Children: The safety and efficacy of the use of mycophenolate in infants and children have not been established.

Special Concerns: Patients should avoid contact with persons who may have infections or have recently received a vaccination. They should practice frequent oral hygiene, using a soft toothbrush. The capsules should not be opened, and the powder inside and oral suspension should not be allowed to come in contact with the skin or mucous membranes. If contact occurs, the affected area should be washed thoroughly with soap and water. If the eyes are affected, they should be rinsed with plain water. Discard any unused portion of the oral suspension 60 days after reconstitution.

OVERDOSE
Symptoms: Nausea, diarrhea, vomiting, fatigue.

What to Do: Call your doctor, emergency medical services (EMS), or the nearest poison control center immediately.

DRUG INTERACTIONS
Consult your doctor for specific advice if you are taking azathioprine, chlorambucil, corticosteroids, cyclophosphamide, cyclosporine, mercaptopurine, muromonab-CD3, a live-virus vaccine, or probenecid.

FOOD INTERACTIONS
No known food interactions.

DISEASE INTERACTIONS
Caution is advised when taking mycophenolate. Consult your doctor if you have an active digestive-system disease or kidney disease.

Nabumetone

▶ Drug Class: Nonsteroidal anti-inflammatory drug (NSAID)

▶ Available in: Tablets

▶ Available OTC? No

▶ As Generic? Yes

Side Effects

SERIOUS
Shortness of breath or wheezing, with or without swelling of legs or other signs of heart failure; chest pain; peptic ulcer disease with vomiting of blood; black, tarry stools; decreasing kidney function. Call your doctor immediately.

COMMON
Nausea, vomiting, heartburn, diarrhea, constipation, headache, dizziness, sleepiness.

LESS COMMON
Ulcers or sores in mouth, depression, rashes or blistering of skin, ringing sound in the ears, unusual tingling or numbness of the hands or feet, seizures, blurred vision. Also elevated potassium levels, decreased blood counts; such problems can be detected by your doctor.

PRINCIPAL USES
To treat mild to moderate pain and inflammation caused by tendinitis, arthritis, bursitis, gout, soft tissue injuries, migraine and other vascular headaches, menstrual cramps, and other conditions. When patients fail to respond to one NSAID, another may be tried. The greatest effectiveness often requires trial and error of several different NSAIDs.

HOW THE DRUG WORKS
NSAIDs work by interfering with the formation of prostaglandins, naturally occurring substances in the body that cause inflammation and make nerves more sensitive to pain impulses. NSAIDs also have other modes of action that are less well understood.

DOSAGE
Adults: 1,000 mg once a day. It may be increased to a maximum of 2,000 mg a day. For children's dose, consult your pediatrician.

ONSET OF EFFECT
From 30 minutes to several hours or longer.

DURATION OF ACTION
Variable.

DIETARY ADVICE
Take with food; maintain your usual food and fluid intake.

STORAGE
Store in a tightly sealed container away from heat, moisture, and direct light.

IF YOU MISS A DOSE
Take it as soon as you remember. However, if it is near the time for the next dose, skip the missed dose and resume your regular dosage schedule. Do not double the next dose.

STOPPING THE DRUG
The decision to stop taking the drug should be made in consultation with your physician.

PROLONGED USE
Prolonged use can cause gastrointestinal problems, including ulceration and bleeding, kidney dysfunction, and liver inflammation. Consult your doctor about the need for medical examinations and lab studies.

PRECAUTIONS
Over 60: Because of the potentially greater consequences of gastrointestinal side effects, the dose of NSAIDs for older patients, especially those over age 70, is often cut in half.

Driving and Hazardous Work: Avoid such activities until you determine how the medicine affects you.

Alcohol: Avoid alcohol when using this medication because it increases the risk of stomach irritation.

Pregnancy: Avoid or discontinue this drug if you are pregnant or plan to become pregnant.

Breast Feeding: Nabumetone passes into breast milk; avoid use while breast feeding.

Infants and Children: May be used in exceptional circumstances; consult your doctor.

Special Concerns: Because NSAIDs can interfere with blood coagulation, this drug should be stopped at least 3 days prior to any surgery.

OVERDOSE
Symptoms: Severe nausea, vomiting, headache, confusion, seizures.

What to Do: Call your doctor, emergency medical services (EMS), or the nearest poison control center immediately.

DRUG INTERACTIONS
Do not take this drug with aspirin or any other NSAIDs without your doctor's approval. In addition, consult your doctor if you are taking antihypertensives, steroids, anticoagulants, antibiotics, itraconazole or ketoconazole, plicamycin, penicillamine, valproic acid, phenytoin, cyclosporine, digitalis drugs, lithium, methotrexate, probenecid, triamterene, or zidovudine.

FOOD INTERACTIONS
No known food interactions.

DISEASE INTERACTIONS
Consult your doctor if you have any of the following: bleeding problems, inflammation or ulcers of the stomach and intestines, diabetes mellitus, systemic lupus erythematosus (SLE, lupus), anemia, asthma, epilepsy, Parkinson's disease, kidney stones, or a history of heart disease or alcohol abuse. Use of nabumetone may cause complications in patients with liver or kidney disease, since these organs work together to remove the medication from the body.

Nadolol

Corgard 20 mg
(BRISTOL-MYERS SQUIBB)

Additional photographs

▶ Drug Class: Beta-blocker

▶ Available in: Tablets

▶ Available OTC? No

▶ As Generic? Yes

Side Effects

SERIOUS
Shortness of breath, wheezing; irregular or slow heartbeat (50 beats per minute or less); pain or feelings of tightness or pressure in the chest; swelling of the ankles, feet, and lower legs; mental depression. If you experience any such symptoms, stop taking nadolol and contact your doctor right away.

COMMON
Dizziness or lightheadedness, especially when rising suddenly to a standing position; rapid heartbeat or palpitations; decreased sexual ability; unusual fatigue, weakness, or drowsiness; insomnia.

LESS COMMON
Anxiety, irritability, nervousness; constipation; diarrhea; dry, sore eyes; itching; nausea or vomiting; nightmares or intensely vivid dreams; numbness, tingling, or other unusual sensations in the fingers, toes, or scalp.

PRINCIPAL USES
To treat mild to moderate high blood pressure and angina. It is also used to prevent or control heartbeat irregularities (cardiac arrhythmias).

HOW THE DRUG WORKS
Nadolol slows the rate and force of contraction of the heart by blocking certain nerve impulses, thus reducing blood pressure. By modifying nerve impulses to the heart, the drug also helps to stabilize heart rhythm.

DOSAGE
For high blood pressure: 40 to 320 mg, once a day. For angina: 40 to 240 mg, once a day.

ONSET OF EFFECT
Unknown.

DURATION OF ACTION
Unknown.

DIETARY ADVICE
Follow your doctor's dietary restrictions, such as a low-salt or low-cholesterol diet, to improve control over high blood pressure and heart disease. Take with a full glass of water.

STORAGE
Store in a tightly sealed container away from heat, moisture, and direct light.

IF YOU MISS A DOSE
Take it as soon as you remember. However, if it is within 8 hours of your next dose, skip the missed dose and resume your regular dosage schedule. Do not double the next dose.

STOPPING THE DRUG
This medication should not be stopped suddenly, as this may lead to angina and possibly a heart attack in patients with advanced heart disease. Slow reduction of the dose under a doctor's close supervision for 2 to 3 weeks is advised.

PROLONGED USE
Lifelong therapy may be necessary. See your doctor regularly for examinations and tests if you must take this medicine for a prolonged period.

PRECAUTIONS
Over 60: Adverse reactions may be more likely and more severe in older patients.

Driving and Hazardous Work: May impair alertness, especially in early stages of treatment. Do not drive or engage in hazardous work until you determine how the medicine affects you.

Alcohol: Drink in careful moderation if at all. Alcohol may interact with the drug and cause a dangerous drop in blood pressure.

Pregnancy: Discuss with your doctor the relative risks and benefits of using this drug while pregnant.

Breast Feeding: Trace amounts of nadolol can be found in breast milk, but adverse effects in infants have not been documented. Consult your doctor for advice.

Infants and Children: No special problems.

OVERDOSE
Symptoms: Unusually slow or rapid heartbeat, severe dizziness or fainting, poor circulation in the hands (bluish skin), breathing difficulty, seizures.

What to Do: Call your doctor, emergency medical services (EMS), or the nearest poison control center immediately.

DRUG INTERACTIONS
Consult your doctor for specific advice if you are taking amphetamines, oral antidiabetic agents, asthma medication (such as aminophylline or theophylline), calcium channel blockers, clonidine, guanabenz, halothane, immunotherapy for allergies (allergy shots), insulin, MAO inhibitors, reserpine, other beta-blockers, or any over-the-counter medicine.

FOOD INTERACTIONS
None reported.

DISEASE INTERACTIONS
Nadolol should be used with caution in people with diabetes, especially insulin-dependent diabetes, since the drug may mask symptoms of hypoglycemia. Consult your doctor for special advice if you have allergies or asthma, heart or blood vessel disease (including congestive heart failure and peripheral vascular disease), hyperthyroidism, irregular (slow) heartbeat, myasthenia gravis, psoriasis, respiratory problems such as bronchitis or emphysema, kidney or liver disease, or a history of depression.

Nafarelin Acetate

▶ Drug Class: Gonadotropin-releasing hormone

▶ Available in: Nasal spray

▶ Available OTC? Yes

▶ As Generic? No

Side Effects

SERIOUS
Vaginal bleeding between menstrual periods; longer or heavier menstrual periods; shortness of breath, chest pain, joint pain, and hives caused by an allergic reaction; bloating or tenderness of the lower abdomen; unexpected or excess flow of milk. Call your doctor immediately.

COMMON
Acne, decreased sex drive, dryness of vagina, hot flashes, pain during intercourse, decreased breast size, palpitations, oily skin, cessation of menstrual periods.

LESS COMMON
Breast pain, headache, runny nose, mental depression, mood swings, rash, weight changes.

PRINCIPAL USES
To relieve the pain and discomfort of endometriosis.

HOW THE DRUG WORKS
Nafarelin decreases the production of estrogen by the ovaries. Reduced blood estrogen levels lead to shrinking of endometrial tissue (uterine lining), which eases the painful flare-ups of endometriosis.

DOSAGE
One spray of 200 micrograms into 1 nostril in the morning and 1 spray into the other nostril in the evening, beginning on day 2, 3, or 4 of the menstrual period.

ONSET OF EFFECT
After 4 weeks.

DURATION OF ACTION
3 to 6 months.

DIETARY ADVICE
No special restrictions.

STORAGE
Store container upright away from heat and direct light.

IF YOU MISS A DOSE
Take it as soon as you remember. However, if it is near the time for the next dose, skip the missed dose and resume your regular dosage schedule. Do not double the next dose.

STOPPING THE DRUG
The decision to stop taking the drug should be made by your doctor.

PROLONGED USE
Your doctor should check your progress regularly during prolonged use.

PRECAUTIONS
Over 60: This medicine is generally not used by older patients.

Driving and Hazardous Work: The use of nafarelin should not impair your ability to perform such tasks safely.

Alcohol: Avoid alcohol.

Pregnancy: Nafarelin is not recommended during pregnancy. When taking the drug, women should use nonhormonal contraception (that is, methods other than birth control pills). If you think you are pregnant, stop taking the medicine and call your doctor immediately.

Breast Feeding: Nafarelin may pass into breast milk; caution is advised. Consult your doctor for advice.

Infants and Children: This drug is not recommended for use by children under the age of puberty.

Special Concerns: Tell your doctor if you smoke cigarettes or consume a lot of alcohol or caffeine. When using a new bottle of nafarelin spray, point the bottle away from you and pump about 7 times to prime it. Each time you use the spray, wipe the tip with a clean tissue or cloth. Every 3 or 4 days, rinse the tip with warm water and wipe the tip for about 15 seconds, then dry. To take a dose of nafarelin, first blow your nose gently. Hold your head forward a little, put the spray tip in the nostril, and aim for the back. Close the other nostril by pressing with 1 finger. After the spray, tilt your head back for a few seconds. Do not blow your nose.

OVERDOSE
Symptoms: No specific ones have been reported.

What to Do: An overdose of nafarelin is unlikely to be life-threatening. However, if someone takes a much larger dose than prescribed, call your doctor, emergency medical services (EMS), or the nearest poison control center immediately.

DRUG INTERACTIONS
Consult your doctor for specific advice if you are taking any nasal spray decongestant, adrenocorticoids, or anticonvulsant medication.

FOOD INTERACTIONS
No known food interactions.

DISEASE INTERACTIONS
Caution is advised when taking nafarelin. Consult your doctor if you have any menstrual disorder.

Nalbuphine Hydrochloride

BRAND NAME
Nubain

▶ Drug Class: Opioid (narcotic) analgesic

▶ Available in: Injection

▶ Available OTC? No

▶ As Generic? Yes

Side Effects

SERIOUS
Serious side effects of nalbuphine are indistinguishable from those of overdose: Confusion; severe drowsiness, weakness, or dizziness; slurred speech; small, pinpoint pupils; cold, clammy skin; slow breathing; seizures; loss of consciousness.

COMMON
Dizziness or lightheadedness, nausea or vomiting, constipation, drowsiness, itching.

LESS COMMON
Mood swings or false sense of well-being (euphoria), hallucinations.

PRINCIPAL USES
To relieve moderate to severe pain.

HOW THE DRUG WORKS
Opioids such as nalbuphine relieve pain by acting on specific areas of the spinal cord and brain that process pain signals from nerves throughout the body.

DOSAGE
For pain: 10 mg every 3 to 6 hours, into a vein or muscle or under the skin. Children: Dosages must be determined by your doctor.

ONSET OF EFFECT
Into a vein: 2 to 3 minutes. Into a muscle or under the skin: Within 15 minutes

DURATION OF ACTION
3 to 6 hours.

DIETARY ADVICE
This drug can be taken without regard to diet.

STORAGE
Store in a tightly sealed container away from heat, moisture, and direct light. Do not allow it to freeze.

IF YOU MISS A DOSE
If you are taking nalbuphine on a fixed schedule, take it as soon as you remember. If it is near the time for the next dose, skip the missed dose and resume your regular dosage schedule. Do not double the next dose.

STOPPING THE DRUG
The decision to stop taking the drug should be made by your doctor.

PROLONGED USE
See your doctor regularly for tests and examinations if you take this medication for a prolonged period. Prolonged use can cause mental or physical dependence.

PRECAUTIONS
Over 60: Adverse reactions may be more likely and more severe in older patients.

Driving and Hazardous Work: Do not drive or engage in hazardous work until you determine how the medicine affects you.

Alcohol: Avoid alcohol.

Pregnancy: Nalbuphine has not been shown to cause birth defects in animals. Human studies have not been done. Before you use this medication, tell your doctor if you are pregnant or plan to become pregnant. Overuse during pregnancy can cause drug dependence in the fetus.

Breast Feeding: Nalbuphine may pass into breast milk; caution is advised. Consult your doctor for advice.

Infants and Children: Adverse reactions may be more likely and more severe in children. Consult your doctor for advice.

Special Concerns: If you feel the medication is not working properly after a few weeks, do not increase the dose. Consult your doctor. Before having any surgery, tell the doctor or dentist in charge that you are taking this drug.

OVERDOSE
Symptoms: Confusion; severe drowsiness, weakness, or dizziness; slurred speech; small, pinpoint pupils; cold, clammy skin; slow breathing; seizures; loss of consciousness.

What to Do: Call your doctor, emergency medical services (EMS), or the nearest poison control center immediately.

DRUG INTERACTIONS
Consult your physician for specific advice if you are taking carbamazepine or other medicine for seizures, barbiturates, sedatives, cough medicines, decongestants, antidepressants, other prescription pain medications, MAO inhibitors, naltrexone, rifampin, or zidovudine (AZT).

FOOD INTERACTIONS
No known food interactions.

DISEASE INTERACTIONS
Consult your doctor if you have any of the following: history of alcohol or drug abuse; emotional illness; brain disorders or head injury; seizures; lung disease; prostate problems or other problems with urination; gallstones; colitis; heart, kidney, liver, or thyroid disease.

Nalidixic Acid

BRAND NAME
NegGram

▶ Drug Class: Anti-infective

▶ Available in: Suspension, tablets

▶ Available OTC? No

▶ As Generic? No

Side Effects

SERIOUS
Blurred, double, or decreased vision, change in color vision, seeing halos around lights, seizures, dark urine, hallucinations, bulging of the fontanel (soft spot) on top of an infant's head, severe headache, mood changes, pale skin, pale stools, skin rash and itching, severe stomach pain, unusual bleeding or bruising, unusual fatigue, yellow eyes or skin. Call your doctor immediately.

COMMON
Dizziness, diarrhea, drowsiness, headache, nausea or vomiting, stomach pain.

LESS COMMON
Increased sensitivity of skin to sunlight.

PRINCIPAL USES
To treat urinary tract infections (UTIs).

HOW THE DRUG WORKS
By interfering with the genetic material of bacteria, nalidixic acid prevents them from reproducing. Eventually the bacteria die out, eliminating the infection.

DOSAGE
Adults and teenagers: 1,000 mg every 6 hours for 1 to 2 weeks, then 500 mg every 6 hours for long-term use. Children 3 months to 12 years: 55 mg per 2.2 lbs (1 kg) of body weight per day in equal doses every 6 hours for 1 to 2 weeks, then 33 mg per 2.2 lbs per day for long-term use.

ONSET OF EFFECT
3 to 4 hours.

DURATION OF ACTION
Unknown.

DIETARY ADVICE
Take nalidixic acid with a full glass of water on an empty stomach, at least 1 hour before or 2 hours after eating. However, if the drug causes stomach upset, nalidixic acid may be taken with food or milk.

STORAGE
Store in a tightly sealed container away from heat and direct light.

IF YOU MISS A DOSE
Take it as soon as you remember. However, if it is near the time for the next dose, skip the missed dose and resume your regular dosage schedule. Do not double the next dose.

STOPPING THE DRUG
Take it as prescribed for the full treatment period, even if you feel better before the scheduled end of therapy.

PROLONGED USE
See your doctor for regular tests and evaluation if you must take this drug for more than 2 weeks.

PRECAUTIONS
Over 60: No special problems are expected.

Driving and Hazardous Work: Avoid such activities until you determine how the medicine affects you.

Alcohol: Drink only in strict moderation.

Pregnancy: Nalidixic acid should not be used during pregnancy because in animal tests it has been shown to cause birth defects.

Breast Feeding: Nalidixic acid passes into breast milk and causes problems in babies with glucose-6-phosphate dehydrogenase (G6PD) deficiency. Problems with other nursing children have not been reported. Consult your doctor for specific individual advice on nursing while you take this medicine.

Infants and Children: This drug is not recommended for use by infants under the age of 3 months.

Special Concerns: Avoid exposure to sunlight until you determine how this medicine affects you. Photosensitivity may last up to 3 months after the last dose. Nalidixic acid may cause false results on tests of blood sugar.

OVERDOSE
Symptoms: Lethargy, psychosis, nausea, vomiting, seizures, severe headache (caused by increased pressure within the skull).

What to Do: Call your doctor, emergency medical services (EMS), or the nearest poison control center immediately.

DRUG INTERACTIONS
Certain drugs may interact adversely with nalidixic acid. Consult your doctor for specific advice, especially if you are taking anticoagulants.

FOOD INTERACTIONS
No known food interactions.

DISEASE INTERACTIONS
Caution is advised when taking nalidixic acid. Consult your doctor if you have any of the following: hardening of the arteries in the brain, G6PD deficiency, or a seizure disorder such as epilepsy. Use of nalidixic acid may cause complications in patients with liver or kidney disease, since these organs work together to remove the medication from the body.

Naltrexone

▶ Drug Class: Opioid antagonist

▶ Available in: Tablets

▶ Available OTC? No

▶ As Generic? Yes

Side Effects

SERIOUS
Naltrexone may cause liver damage when taken in excess or by people with liver disease due to other causes. Call your doctor immediately if you develop abdominal pain lasting more than a few days, white bowel movements, dark urine, or a yellow discoloration of the eyes or skin.

COMMON
For alcoholism: Nausea, headache, dizziness, nervousness, fatigue. For narcotic addiction: Difficulty sleeping, nervousness, anxiety, abdominal pain or cramps, nausea, vomiting, decreased energy, muscle and joint pain, headache.

LESS COMMON
For alcoholism: Insomnia, vomiting, anxiety, drowsiness. For narcotic addiction: Loss of appetite, constipation, diarrhea, increased thirst, increased energy, depression, irritability, dizziness, skin rash, erectile dysfunction, chills.

PRINCIPAL USES
To aid in the treatment of narcotic and alcohol dependence, in conjunction with psychological and social counseling. Naltrexone is not effective in treating dependency on cocaine or other nonopioid drugs.

HOW THE DRUG WORKS
Naltrexone blocks the euphoric effects of opioid narcotics (such as morphine and heroin) by competitive binding to opioid receptors in the brain. While the precise mechanism of action for alcohol dependence is unclear, naltrexone has been shown to reduce alcohol craving and consumption.

DOSAGE
For alcoholism: 50 mg (1 tablet) once a day. For narcotic dependence: Treatment should not be initiated unless the patient has been opioid-free for at least 7 to 10 days. To start, 25 mg (½ tablet) for the first day. If symptoms of narcotic withdrawal do not appear, dose will be increased to 50 mg once a day. Your doctor may increase or alter the dosage and frequency if necessary.

ONSET OF EFFECT
Within 60 minutes.

DURATION OF ACTION
24 to 72 hours.

DIETARY ADVICE
Naltrexone can be taken without regard to diet.

STORAGE
Store in a tightly sealed container away from heat, moisture, and direct light.

IF YOU MISS A DOSE
What to do if you miss a dose varies by dosage schedule. If you take naltrexone once a day, take the missed dose as soon as possible. However, if you do not remember until the next day, skip the missed dose and resume your regular dosage schedule. Do not double the next dose. If your dosage schedule is different, consult your doctor for advice.

STOPPING THE DRUG
The decision to stop taking the drug should be made in consultation with your physician.

PROLONGED USE
See your doctor regularly for tests of liver function and examinations.

PRECAUTIONS
Over 60: It is not known whether naltrexone causes different or more severe side effects in older patients.

Driving and Hazardous Work: Avoid such activities until you determine how the medicine affects you.

Alcohol: Avoid alcohol.

Pregnancy: Naltrexone has been shown to cause birth defects in animals. Human studies have not been done. This medication should be given during pregnancy only if potential benefits outweigh the risks to the unborn child.

Breast Feeding: Naltrexone may pass into breast milk; caution is advised. Consult your doctor for advice on whether to discontinue nursing or discontinue the drug.

Infants and Children: The safety and effectiveness of this drug have not been established for children under the age of 18.

Special Concerns: Naltrexone will not prevent you from becoming intoxicated upon consumption of alcohol. Carry an identification card indicating you are taking naltrexone. It is of fundamental importance that patients using naltrexone abstain completely from opioid narcotics. If you have not been opioid-free for 7 to 10 days prior to taking naltrexone, it may induce symptoms of acute withdrawal. Also, the effects of naltrexone may be overcome by taking large doses of narcotics, but this poses a serious risk of a fatal narcotic overdose.

OVERDOSE
Symptoms: No cases of overdose have been reported. However, naltrexone may cause liver damage with symptoms including abdominal pain lasting more than a few days, white bowel movements, dark urine, or a yellow discoloration of the eyes or skin.

What to Do: If you suspect an overdose or if someone takes a much larger dose than prescribed, call your doctor, emergency medical services (EMS), or the nearest poison control center immediately.

DRUG INTERACTIONS
Naltrexone should not be used at the same time as narcotic pain relievers such as meperidine, morphine, and methadone. Studies with other types of medications have not be done. Consult your doctor for advice if you are taking any other prescription or over-the-counter drugs.

FOOD INTERACTIONS
No known food interactions.

DISEASE INTERACTIONS
Do not take naltrexone if you have acute hepatitis or liver failure.

Aleve 220 mg
(BAYER)

Additional photographs

▶ Drug Class: Nonsteroidal anti-inflammatory drug (NSAID)

▶ Available in: Tablets, oral suspension, gelcaps

▶ Available OTC? Yes

▶ As Generic? Yes

Side Effects

SERIOUS
Shortness of breath or wheezing, with or without swelling of legs or other signs of heart failure; chest pain; peptic ulcer disease with vomiting of blood; black, tarry stools; decreasing kidney function. Call your doctor immediately.

COMMON
Nausea, vomiting, heartburn, diarrhea, constipation, headache, dizziness, sleepiness.

LESS COMMON
Ulcers or sores in mouth, depression, rashes or blistering of skin, ringing sound in the ears, unusual tingling or numbness of the hands or feet, seizures, blurred vision. Also elevated potassium levels, decreased blood counts; such problems can be detected by your doctor.

PRINCIPAL USES
To relieve minor pain or inflammation associated with headaches, the common cold, toothache, muscle aches, backache, arthritis, gout, tendinitis, bursitis, or menstrual cramps; also, to reduce fever. When patients fail to respond to one NSAID, several others may be tried.

HOW THE DRUG WORKS
NSAIDs work by interfering with the formation of prostaglandins, naturally occurring substances in the body that cause inflammation and make nerves more sensitive to pain impulses. NSAIDs also have other modes of action that are less well understood.

DOSAGE
Adults: 440 to 1,500 mg daily. Maximum dose is 1,500 mg a day, taken in 2 to 3 evenly divided doses.

ONSET OF EFFECT
Rapid; relieves pain within 1 hour. However, it may take up to 2 weeks to suppress inflammation.

DURATION OF ACTION
Up to 12 hours.

DIETARY ADVICE
Take with food; maintain your usual food and fluid intake.

STORAGE
Store tablets in a tightly sealed container away from heat, moisture, and direct light. Store oral suspension in refrigerator, but do not freeze.

IF YOU MISS A DOSE
Take it as soon as you remember. However, if it is near the time for the next dose, skip the missed dose and resume your regular dosage schedule. Do not double the next dose.

STOPPING THE DRUG
If you are taking this drug by prescription, do not stop taking it without first consulting your doctor.

PROLONGED USE
Prolonged use can cause gastrointestinal problems, including ulceration and bleeding, kidney dysfunction, and liver inflammation. Consult your doctor about the need for medical examinations and lab studies.

PRECAUTIONS
Over 60: Because of the potentially greater consequences of gastrointestinal side effects, the dose of NSAIDs for older patients, especially those over age 70, is often cut in half.

Driving and Hazardous Work: Do not drive or engage in hazardous work until you determine how the medication affects you.

Alcohol: Avoid alcohol when taking this drug; the combination of naproxen and alcohol can be highly toxic to the liver.

Pregnancy: Avoid or discontinue this drug if you are pregnant or plan to become pregnant.

Breast Feeding: Naproxen passes into breast milk; avoid or discontinue use while nursing.

Infants and Children: Naproxen may be used in exceptional circumstances; consult your pediatrician for advice.

Special Concerns: Because NSAIDs can interfere with blood coagulation, this drug should be stopped at least 3 days prior to any surgery.

OVERDOSE
Symptoms: Severe nausea, vomiting, headache, confusion, seizures.

What to Do: Call your doctor, emergency medical services (EMS), or the nearest poison control center immediately.

DRUG INTERACTIONS
Do not take this drug with aspirin or any other NSAIDs without your doctor's approval. In addition, consult your doctor if you are taking antihypertensives, steroids, anticoagulants, antibiotics, itraconazole or ketoconazole, plicamycin, penicillamine, valproic acid, phenytoin, cyclosporine, digitalis drugs, lithium, methotrexate, probenecid, triamterene, or zidovudine.

FOOD INTERACTIONS
No known food interactions.

DISEASE INTERACTIONS
Consult your doctor if you have any of the following: bleeding problems, inflammation or ulcers of the stomach and intestines, diabetes mellitus, systemic lupus erythematosus (SLE, lupus), anemia, asthma, epilepsy, Parkinson's disease, kidney stones, or a history of heart disease or alcohol abuse. Use of naproxen may cause complications in patients with liver or kidney disease, since these organs work together to remove the medication from the body.

Naratriptan Hydrochloride

BRAND NAME
Amerge

▶ Drug Class: Antimigraine/ antiheadache drug

▶ Available in: Tablets

▶ Available OTC? No

▶ As Generic? No

Side Effects

SERIOUS
Chest pain or tightness, sudden or severe abdominal pain, shortness of breath, wheezing, heartbeat irregularities or palpitations, skin rash, hives, swelling of the eyelids, face, or lips. Seek emergency medical assistance immediately.

COMMON
Tingling, hot flashes, flushing, weakness, drowsiness or dizziness, fatigue, general feeling of illness.

LESS COMMON
There are no less-common side effects associated with the use of naratriptan.

PRINCIPAL USES
To treat severe, acute migraine headaches. Naratriptan is not intended as a migraine preventive or for use against any other kinds of pain or headache, including basilar and hemiplegic migraines. Your doctor will determine whether this medication is appropriate in your particular case.

HOW THE DRUG WORKS
The exact mechanism of action is unknown.

DOSAGE
A single tablet of 1 or 2.5 mg taken with water is generally effective. If the migraine returns or there is only partial relief, the dose may be repeated once after 4 hours, but no more than 5 mg should be taken in a 24-hour period. Since individuals may vary in response to naratriptan, your experience with the drug will determine the most appropriate initial dosage.

ONSET OF EFFECT
Within 1 to 3 hours.

DURATION OF ACTION
Up to 24 hours.

DIETARY ADVICE
The medication can be taken with or without food.

STORAGE
Store in a tightly sealed container away from heat, moisture, and direct light.

IF YOU MISS A DOSE
Not applicable, since the drug is taken only when necessary.

STOPPING THE DRUG
Consult your doctor before discontinuing naratriptan.

PROLONGED USE
No special problems are expected. However, if you are at risk for coronary artery disease (see Special Concerns), you should undergo periodic medical tests and evaluation.

PRECAUTIONS
Over 60: Naratriptan is not recommended for use in older patients.

Driving and Hazardous Work: Some people feel drowsy or dizzy during or following a migraine attack or after taking naratriptan. Avoid driving or other tasks requiring concentration if you have such symptoms.

Alcohol: No special warnings, although alcohol may trigger or exacerbate migraine headaches.

Pregnancy: Adequate human studies have not been done. Discuss with your doctor the relative risks and benefits of using naratriptan while pregnant.

Breast Feeding: Naratriptan may pass into breast milk; caution is advised. Consult your doctor for specific advice.

Infants and Children: The safety and effectiveness of naratriptan have not been established for patients under age 18. Consult your pediatrician for advice.

Special Concerns: Serious, but rare, heart-related problems may occur after naratriptan use. Anyone at risk for unrecognized coronary artery disease, such as postmenopausal women, men over age 40, or those with risk factors for coronary artery disease (hypertension, high blood cholesterol levels, obesity, diabetes, strong family history of heart disease, or cigarette smoking) should have the first dose of naratriptan administered in a doctor's office. Naratriptan should not be used by anyone with any symptoms of heart disease (chest pain or tightness, shortness of breath).

OVERDOSE
Symptoms: Increase in blood pressure resulting in lightheadedness, tension in the neck, fatigue, and loss of coordination.

What to Do: An overdose with naratriptan is unlikely. If someone takes a much larger dose than prescribed, call your doctor, emergency medical services (EMS), or the nearest poison control center immediately.

DRUG INTERACTIONS
Do not take naratriptan within 24 hours of taking almotriptan, sumatriptan, rizatriptan, zolmitriptan, ergotamine-containing medication, dihydroergotamine mesylate, or methysergide mesylate. Oral contraceptives may interact with naratriptan. Consult your doctor for specific advice.

FOOD INTERACTIONS
No known food interactions.

DISEASE INTERACTIONS
You should not take naratriptan if you have a history of angina, heart disease, stroke, uncontrolled hypertension, heartbeat irregularities, peripheral vascular disease, or severely impaired kidney or liver function.

Natamycin

▶ Drug Class: Antifungal

▶ Available in: Ophthalmic suspension

▶ Available OTC? No

▶ As Generic? No

Side Effects

SERIOUS
Eye redness, swelling or irritation not present before applying natamycin. Call your doctor as soon as possible.

COMMON
No common side effects are associated with natamycin.

LESS COMMON
No less-common side effects are associated with natamycin.

PRINCIPAL USES
To treat several types of fungal infections of the eye, including fungal blepharitis (inflammation of the eyelid), conjunctivitis (inflammation of the mucous membranes that line the inner surface of the eyelids and whites of the eyes), and keratitis (inflammation of the cornea).

HOW THE DRUG WORKS
Natamycin binds to and alters the fungal cell membrane so that vital structures inside the cell pass though the membrane and out of the cell. Without these structures, the fungal cells cannot survive.

DOSAGE
Fungal blepharitis or conjunctivitis: 1 drop every 4 to 6 hours. Fungal keratitis: 1 drop every 1 to 2 hours for the first 3 or 4 days, and 1 drop 6 to 8 times a day thereafter.

ONSET OF EFFECT
Unknown.

DURATION OF ACTION
Unknown.

DIETARY ADVICE
No special restrictions.

STORAGE
Store in a tightly sealed container away from heat, moisture, and direct light. You may store it at room temperature or in the refrigerator, but do not allow it to freeze.

IF YOU MISS A DOSE
Apply natamycin as soon as you remember and then resume your regular dosage schedule. Do not double the next dose.

STOPPING THE DRUG
Use it as prescribed for the full treatment period, even if you begin to feel better before the scheduled end of therapy.

PROLONGED USE
Therapy is generally continued for up to 14 to 21 days, depending on the type and severity of infection, or until the eye infection has been checked. However, no signs of improvement within 7 to 10 days may indicate that a microorganism not susceptible to natamycin is causing the infection; check with your doctor if symptoms do not improve within this amount of time. Your doctor should check your response to natamycin regularly, which may be as often as 3 times a week for certain eye infections.

PRECAUTIONS
Over 60: No special problems are expected.

Driving and Hazardous Work: Avoid such activities until you determine how the medicine affects your vision.

Alcohol: No special precautions are necessary.

Pregnancy: Adequate human studies have not been completed. Before taking natamycin, tell your doctor if you are pregnant or plan to become pregnant.

Breast Feeding: Natamycin may pass into breast milk; caution is advised. Consult your doctor for advice.

Infants and Children: Proper use of natamycin should be determined by your doctor.

Special Concerns: To use the eye drops, first wash your hands. Tilt your head back. Gently apply pressure to the inside corner of the eyelid and with the index finger of the same hand, pull downward on the lower eyelid to make a space. Drop the medicine into this space and close your eye. Apply gentle pressure for 1 or 2 minutes while keeping the eye closed without blinking. Then wash your hands again. Make sure the tip of the dropper does not touch your eye, finger, or any other surface. Shake the container well before each dose.

OVERDOSE
Symptoms: No specific ones have been reported.

What to Do: An overdose of natamycin is unlikely to be life-threatening. However, if someone applies a much larger dose than prescribed or accidentally ingests the medicine, call your doctor, emergency medical services (EMS), or the nearest poison control center immediately.

DRUG INTERACTIONS
None known.

FOOD INTERACTIONS
None known.

DISEASE INTERACTIONS
None known.

Nateglinide

BRAND NAME
Starlix

- ▶ Drug Class: Antidiabetic agent
- ▶ Available in: Tablets
- ▶ Available OTC? No
- ▶ As Generic? No

Side Effects

SERIOUS
Hypoglycemia (blood sugar levels that are too low), resulting in shakiness, headache, cold sweats, anxiety, and changes in mental state. Immediately ingest sugar-containing food or drink. Inform your doctor about the frequency and timing of hypoglycemic events.

COMMON
None.

LESS COMMON
Increased incidence of upper respiratory infection, flu-like symptoms, dizziness, joint pain.

PRINCIPAL USES
To help control type 2 diabetes mellitus in patients whose blood sugar cannot be adequately controlled by diet and exercise and who have not been chronically treated with other antidiabetic agents. Nateglinide may be used in conjunction with, but not substituted for, the antidiabetic agent metformin to achieve the desired results.

HOW THE DRUG WORKS
Nateglinide stimulates the pancreas to produce insulin. Increased insulin levels reduce blood glucose by promoting the transport of glucose into muscle cells and other tissues, where it is used as a source of energy. The rapid onset and short duration of nateglinide's action make it effective in controlling glucose levels after a meal.

DOSAGE
The recommended dose is 120 mg 3 times a day (with or without metformin), taken 1 to 30 minutes before meals. If you skip a meal, you should also skip the scheduled dose of nateglinide to reduce the risk of hypoglycemia.

ONSET OF EFFECT
Within 20 minutes.

DURATION OF ACTION
1 to 4 hours.

DIETARY ADVICE
Doses should be taken 1 to 30 minutes before meals. Follow your doctor's advice regarding diet, weight loss, and exercise.

STORAGE
Store in a tightly sealed container away from heat, moisture, and direct light.

IF YOU MISS A DOSE
If you miss a dose, take it just prior to the next meal. Do not double the next dose.

STOPPING THE DRUG
Do not stop taking the drug without your doctor's approval.

PROLONGED USE
Because nateglinide helps to manage diabetes but does not cure the disease, its use will be ongoing as long as your blood glucose levels are being adequately controlled.

PRECAUTIONS
Over 60: Older patients may be more susceptible to hypoglycemia, which may be more difficult to recognize in the elderly.

Driving and Hazardous Work: Do not drive or engage in hazardous work until you determine how the medication affects you.

Alcohol: Limit alcohol intake; hypoglycemia is more likely to occur after the consumption of alcohol.

Pregnancy: Nateglinide should not be used during pregnancy. Insulin is the treatment of choice for pregnant diabetic patients.

Breast Feeding: Nateglinide may pass into breast milk and should not be taken when nursing.

Infants and Children: Safety and effectiveness have not been established for young patients.

Special Concerns: Follow your doctor's advice about diet, exercise, and weight control carefully. These aspects of treatment are just as essential to the proper control of diabetes as taking the medication. Be sure to carry at all times some form of medical identification that indicates you have diabetes and that lists all of the drugs you are taking.

OVERDOSE
Symptoms: Excessive hunger, nausea, anxiety, cold sweats, drowsiness, rapid heartbeat, weakness, changes in mental state, loss of consciousness (indications of hypoglycemia). Overdose is most likely to occur when caloric intake is deficient, following or during more exercise than usual, or after consuming more than a small amount of alcohol.

What to Do: Immediately ingest sugar-containing food or drinks. Call your doctor, emergency medical services (EMS), or local hospital if symptoms persist.

DRUG INTERACTIONS
Consult your doctor if you are taking nonsteroidal anti-inflammatory drugs, (NSAIDs), salicylates, MAO inhibitor antidepressants, beta-blockers, thiazide diuretics, corticosteroids, thyroid hormone, or sympathomimetic drugs.

FOOD INTERACTIONS
A special diet is essential for proper control of blood glucose levels.

DISEASE INTERACTIONS
Do not use nateglinide if you have type 1 diabetes mellitus or diabetic ketoacidosis. Use of nateglinide may cause complications in patients with moderate-to-severe liver disease, since this organ is involved in removing the medication from the body.

Nedocromil Sodium Inhalant

BRAND NAME
Tilade

▶ Drug Class: Respiratory inhalant

▶ Available in: Inhalation aerosol

▶ Available OTC? No

▶ As Generic? No

Side Effects

SERIOUS
Increased wheezing, tightness or pain in the chest, or breathing difficulty. Call your doctor right away.

COMMON
There are no common side effects associated with nedocromil.

LESS COMMON
Cough; headache; nausea or vomiting; runny or stuffy nose; throat irritation, soreness, or difficulty swallowing; unpleasant taste.

PRINCIPAL USES
To prevent the symptoms of asthma and to prevent bronchospasm (contraction of the smooth muscle tissue surrounding the airways, which results in narrowing and obstruction of air passages). It cannot relieve an asthma attack once it has started.

HOW THE DRUG WORKS
Nedocromil prevents inflammatory cells in the lungs from releasing substances that cause asthma symptoms or bronchospasm. Unlike bronchodilators that are taken to relieve the acute symptoms of an asthma attack, nedocromil is generally prescribed to be taken on a regular basis when no symptoms are present, to reduce the chronic inflammation of the airways that underlies asthma. Nedocromil may also be used preventively just prior to exposure to certain conditions or substances (cold air, exercise, chemicals, air pollution, or allergens such as pollen or dust mites) that may trigger an acute asthma attack.

DOSAGE
For prevention of asthma symptoms, adults and teenagers: 2 puffs (3.5 to 4 mg) twice a day at regularly spaced times. To prevent bronchospasm, adults and teenagers: 2 puffs up to 30 minutes before exercise or exposure to anything that can trigger bronchospasm. Children: Consult pediatrician for proper dose.

ONSET OF EFFECT
Several days to 4 weeks.

DURATION OF ACTION
6 to 12 hours.

DIETARY ADVICE
This medicine can be taken without regard to diet.

STORAGE
Store in a tightly sealed container away from heat and direct light. Do not allow the medication to freeze. Do not puncture, break, or incinerate the aerosol canister, even if it is empty.

IF YOU MISS A DOSE
Take it as soon as you remember. If it is near the time for the next dose, skip the missed dose and resume your regular dosage schedule. Do not double the next dose.

STOPPING THE DRUG
The decision to stop taking the drug should be made by your doctor.

PROLONGED USE
You should see your doctor regularly for tests and examinations if you take this drug for a prolonged period.

PRECAUTIONS
Over 60: No special problems are expected.

Driving and Hazardous Work: The use of nedocromil should not impair your ability to perform such tasks safely.

Alcohol: No special precautions are necessary.

Pregnancy: Nedocromil has not caused birth defects in animals. Human studies have not been done. Before you take nedocromil, tell your doctor if you are pregnant or plan to become pregnant.

Breast Feeding: Nedocromil may pass into breast milk; caution is advised. Mothers who wish to breast feed while taking nedocromil should consult their doctor for advice.

Infants and Children: No special problems are expected. Use and dose must be determined by your doctor.

Special Concerns: Shake the inhaler well and test before using. Remember to clean the inhaler at least twice a week.

OVERDOSE
Symptoms: No specific ones have been reported.

What to Do: An overdose of nedocromil is unlikely to be life-threatening. However, if someone takes a much larger dose than prescribed, call your doctor, emergency medical services (EMS), or the nearest poison control center.

DRUG INTERACTIONS
Before you take nedocromil, tell your doctor if you are taking any prescription or over-the-counter medicine.

FOOD INTERACTIONS
No known food interactions.

DISEASE INTERACTIONS
No disease interactions have been reported.

Nedocromil Sodium Ophthalmic

BRAND NAME
Alocril

▶ Drug Class: Antihistamine

▶ Available in: Ophthalmic solution

▶ Available OTC? No

▶ As Generic? No

Side Effects

SERIOUS
No serious side effects are associated with nedocromil.

COMMON
Headache, temporary burning and stinging of the eye, unpleasant taste, nasal congestion.

LESS COMMON
Asthma, conjunctivitis, eye redness, increased eye sensitivity to light, runny nose.

PRINCIPAL USES
For temporary relief of itching of the eye due to allergic conjunctivitis (inflammation of the mucous membranes that line the inner surface of the eyelids and whites of the eyes).

HOW THE DRUG WORKS
Nedocromil inhibits the release and blocks the effects of histamine, a substance that causes swelling, itching, sneezing, watery eyes, hives, and other symptoms of allergic reaction.

DOSAGE
1 or 2 drops in each affected eye twice a day.

ONSET OF EFFECT
Unknown.

DURATION OF ACTION
Unknown.

DIETARY ADVICE
No special restrictions.

STORAGE
Store in a tightly sealed container away from heat, moisture, and direct light. Do not allow it to freeze.

IF YOU MISS A DOSE
Apply the next dose as needed; do not double the next dose.

STOPPING THE DRUG
This medication is to be used throughout the period of exposure (the duration of the pollen season or until the cause of the conjunctivitis is no longer present), even when symptoms are absent.

PROLONGED USE
See your doctor regularly for tests and examinations if you must take this drug for a prolonged period.

PRECAUTIONS
Over 60: No special problems are expected.

Driving and Hazardous Work: Do not drive or engage in hazardous work until you determine how the medicine affects your vision.

Alcohol: No special precautions.

Pregnancy: In animal studies, large doses of nedocromil did not cause birth defects. Human studies have not been done. Nedocromil should be used by pregnant women only if the potential benefit to the mother justifies the potential risk to the embryo or fetus. Consult your doctor for specific advice.

Breast Feeding: Nedocromil may pass into breast milk; caution is advised. Consult your doctor for advice.

Infants and Children: The safety and effectiveness of nedocromil in infants and children under the age of 3 have not been established.

Special Concerns: To use the eye drops, first wash your hands. Tilt your head back. Gently apply pressure to the inside corner of the eyelid and with the index finger of the same hand, pull downward on the lower eyelid to make a space. Drop the medicine into this space and close your eye. Apply pressure for 1 or 2 minutes while keeping the eye closed without blinking. Then wash your hands again. Make sure the tip of the dropper does not touch your eye, finger, or any other surface. If you use contact lenses, do not wear them while administering nedocromil.

OVERDOSE
Symptoms: No specific ones have been reported.

What to Do: An overdose of nedocromil is unlikely to be life-threatening. However, if someone applies a much larger dose than prescribed or accidentally ingests the medicine, call your doctor, emergency medical services (EMS), or the nearest poison control center immediately.

DRUG INTERACTIONS
Do not use with any other eye medication. Consult your doctor for specific advice.

FOOD INTERACTIONS
No known food interactions.

DISEASE INTERACTIONS
Caution is advised when taking nedocromil. Consult your doctor if you have any medical condition, especially one affecting the eyes.

Nelfinavir

BRAND NAME
Viracep

Viracept 250 mg
(AGOURON)

▶ Drug Class: Antidepressant

▶ Available in: Tablets

▶ Available OTC? No

▶ As Generic? No

Side Effects

SERIOUS
High blood sugar (diabetes) has occurred in patients taking drugs of this class, although a cause-and-effect relationship has not been established. Contact your doctor if you develop increased thirst or excessive urination.

COMMON
Diarrhea, abdominal pain, low-grade fever, nausea, gas, skin rash.

LESS COMMON
Back pain, headache, loss of appetite, gastrointestinal bleeding, mouth ulcers, vomiting, arthritis, cramps, muscle pain, anxiety, depression, dizziness, insomnia, migraine headache, seizures, drowsiness, breathing difficulty, skin problems, eye disorders, loss of sexual function.

PRINCIPAL USES
To treat HIV (human immunodeficiency virus) infection. While not a cure for HIV, this drug may suppress the replication of the virus and delay the progression of the disease.

HOW THE DRUG WORKS
Nelfinavir blocks the activity of a viral protease, an enzyme that is needed by HIV to reproduce. Blocking the protease causes HIV to make copies that cannot infect new cells.

DOSAGE
Adults: 750 mg, 3 times a day. Children: 20 to 30 mg per 2.2 lbs (1 kg) of body weight, 3 times a day. Instead of tablets, children can be given the oral powder mixed with water, milk, formula, soy milk, or a dietary supplement. Citrus or other acidic foods or juices are not recommended since they may produce a bitter taste when mixed with the medication. Other antiretroviral drugs are prescribed in combination with nelfinavir.

ONSET OF EFFECT
Initial response: Several days. Maximum therapeutic effect: 12 to 16 weeks.

DURATION OF ACTION
Unknown.

DIETARY ADVICE
Nelfinavir should be taken with a light meal or snack.

STORAGE
Store in a tightly sealed container away from heat and direct light. Once oral powder is mixed with liquid, the entire contents must be consumed to obtain the full dose. If it is not consumed immediately, the mixture must be refrigerated, up to 6 hours; taking the full dose immediately is recommended.

IF YOU MISS A DOSE
Take it as soon as you remember. If it is near the time for the next dose, skip the missed dose and resume your regular dosage schedule. Do not double the next dose.

STOPPING THE DRUG
The decision to stop taking the drug should be made in consultation with your physician.

PROLONGED USE
See your doctor regularly for tests and examinations.

PRECAUTIONS

Over 60: It is not known whether nelfinavir causes different or more severe side effects in older patients.

Driving and Hazardous Work: Avoid such activities until you determine how the medicine affects you.

Alcohol: Avoid alcohol if liver function is impaired.

Pregnancy: Nelfinavir has been shown to cause birth defects in animal studies; however, it is increasingly being used along with other drugs to treat pregnant HIV-infected women.

Breast Feeding: It is unknown whether nelfinavir passes into breast milk; however, to avoid transmitting the virus to an uninfected child, women infected with HIV should not breast feed.

Infants and Children: The safety and effectiveness of nelfinavir have not been established for children under 2 years of age.

Special Concerns: Use of nelfinavir does not eliminate the risk of passing the AIDS virus to other persons. You should take appropriate preventive measures.

OVERDOSE
Symptoms: No cases of overdose have been reported.

What to Do: An overdose of nelfinavir is unlikely to occur. Nonetheless, if you have any reason to suspect an overdose, call your doctor, emergency medical services (EMS), or the nearest poison control center.

DRUG INTERACTIONS
Nelfinavir should not be used concurrently with certain other drugs, because the combination could cause life-threatening heart abnormalities or prolonged loss of consciousness. These drugs include astemizole, midazolam, oral contraceptives, rifampin, amiodarone, quinidine, ergot derivatives (found in certain migraine medications), and triazolam. Other drugs may interact with nelfinavir, requiring some change in your drug regimen. Consult your doctor for specific advice if you are taking any other prescription or over-the-counter medication, especially anticonvulsants (carbamazepine, phenobarbital, phenytoin), indinavir, ritonavir, or rifabutin.

FOOD INTERACTIONS
Food improves the absorption of nelfinavir.

DISEASE INTERACTIONS
Consult your doctor for advice if you have any other medical condition, especially hemophilia. Use of nelfinavir can cause complications in patients with liver disease, as this organ works to remove the drug from the body.

Neomycin/Polymyxin B/Bacitracin Ophthalmic

BRAND NAMES
Ak-Spore, Neocidin,
Neosporin, Neotal,
Ocu-Spor-B, Ocusporin,
Ocutricin, Spectro-Sporin,
Triple Antibiotic

▶ Drug Class: Antibiotic
combination

▶ Available in: Ophthalmic
ointment

▶ Available OTC? No

▶ As Generic? Yes

Side Effects

SERIOUS
Itching, rash, redness,
swelling, or other eye irritation that was not present before therapy. Stop
using the medication and
call your doctor immediately.

COMMON
Blurred vision for up
to 30 minutes after
application.

LESS COMMON
There are no less-common side effects associated with ophthalmic
neomycin/polymyxin B/
bacitracin.

PRINCIPAL USES
To treat or prevent bacterial
infections of the eye.

HOW THE DRUG WORKS
Ophthalmic neomycin/
polymyxin B/bacitracin kills
bacteria by interfering with
the genetic material of bacterial cells, thus preventing
them from multiplying.

DOSAGE
Apply a thin strip of ointment every 3 to 4 hours for
7 to 10 days.

ONSET OF EFFECT
Unknown.

DURATION OF ACTION
Unknown.

DIETARY ADVICE
This medication can be
used without regard to diet.

STORAGE
Store this medication in a
tightly sealed container
away from heat, moisture,
and direct light.

IF YOU MISS A DOSE
Apply it as soon as you
remember. If it is near the
time for the next dose, skip
the missed dose and
resume your regular dosage
schedule. Do not double the
next dose.

STOPPING THE DRUG
Use this drug as prescribed
for the full treatment period,
even if you begin to feel better before the scheduled
end of therapy.

PROLONGED USE
You should see your doctor
regularly for tests and
examinations if you use this
drug for a prolonged period.

PRECAUTIONS
Over 60: No special problems are expected.

**Driving and Hazardous
Work:** Do not drive or

engage in hazardous work
until you determine how the
medicine affects your
vision.

Alcohol: No special precautions are necessary.

Pregnancy: This combination antibiotic has not been
shown to cause birth
defects or other problems
during pregnancy. Before
taking this medication, tell
your doctor if you are pregnant or plan to become
pregnant.

Breast Feeding: This
combination antibiotic has
not been shown to cause
problems in nursing babies.

Infants and Children:
There is no information
comparing the use of this
combination antibiotic in
infants and children with
use in adults.

Special Concerns: To use
the ointment, first wash
your hands. Tilt your head
back. Gently apply pressure
to the inside corner of the
eyelid and with the index
finger of the same hand,
pull downward on the lower
eyelid to make a space. Put
a short strip of ointment
(about ⅓ inch long) into
this space and close your
eye. Apply pressure for 1 or
2 minutes while keeping the
eye closed without blinking.
Then wash your hands
again. Make sure the tip
of the applicator does not
touch your eye, finger, or
any other surface. If your
symptoms do not improve
in a few days or if they
become worse, check with
your doctor. Before you use
this medication, tell your
doctor if you have had an
allergic reaction to
neomycin, polymyxin B,
bacitracin, or any related
antibiotic.

OVERDOSE
Symptoms: No specific
ones have been reported.

What to Do: An overdose
of this combination antibiotic is unlikely to be lifethreatening. If someone
accidentally ingests the
medicine, call your doctor,
emergency medical services
(EMS), or the nearest poison control center.

DRUG INTERACTIONS
Other drugs may interact
with this combination antibiotic. Consult your doctor for
specific advice if you are
taking any other prescription or over-the-counter
medication.

FOOD INTERACTIONS
No known food interactions.

DISEASE INTERACTIONS
Caution is advised when
taking this combination
antibiotic. Consult your doctor if you have any other
medical condition.

Neomycin/Polymyxin B/Bacitracin Topical

BRAND NAMES
Bactine First Aid Antibiotic, Foille, Mycitracin, Neosporin Maximum Strength Ointment, Neosporin Ointment, Topisporin

▶ Drug Class: Antibiotic combination

▶ Available in: Ointment

▶ Available OTC? Yes

▶ As Generic? Yes

Side Effects

SERIOUS
Rare, severe allergic reaction that may cause breathing difficulty or, at the extreme, total closure of the airways with potentially fatal anaphylactic shock. Contact emergency medical services (EMS) immediately. In very rare cases hearing loss may occur; if so, call your doctor immediately.

COMMON
No common side effects are associated with this medicine.

LESS COMMON
Irritation or skin allergy with burning, stinging, itching, redness, or rash. Contact your doctor as soon as possible if such side effects persist.

PRINCIPAL USES
To help prevent bacterial skin infections following minor cuts, abrasions, or burns.

HOW THE DRUG WORKS
This is a combination drug containing three distinct antibiotics that each attack and kill bacteria in a different way. Their combined, overlapping effect is capable of warding off infection by a variety of bacterial organisms.

DOSAGE
The usual treatment is to apply the ointment 2 to 5 times a day to areas of the skin that have suffered a minor injury. If you are using the prescription-strength form of the medication, follow your doctor's orders carefully; for over-the-counter forms, follow the directions.

ONSET OF EFFECT
Unknown.

DURATION OF ACTION
Unknown.

DIETARY ADVICE
This medication can be used without regard to diet.

STORAGE
Store in a tightly sealed container away from heat and direct light. Keep away from moisture and extremes in temperature.

IF YOU MISS A DOSE
Apply it as soon as you remember. However, if it is near the time for the next dose, skip the missed dose and resume your regular dosage schedule. Do not apply a double dose.

STOPPING THE DRUG
Use as prescribed for the full treatment period, even if the affected area begins to look and feel better before the scheduled end of therapy. If you stop treatment prematurely, the heartier strains of bacteria are likely to survive, reproduce, and cause a worse infection later (known as a rebound infection).

PROLONGED USE
Consult your physician if you must use this medicine for a prolonged period.

PRECAUTIONS
Over 60: No special precautions for older patients.

Driving and Hazardous Work: No special precautions are necessary.

Alcohol: No special precautions are necessary.

Pregnancy: Clinical studies of the use of this combination antibiotic during pregnancy have not been done. Consult your doctor if you become or are planning to become pregnant.

Breast Feeding: It is not known whether this combination antibiotic passes into breast milk; caution is advised. Consult your doctor for specific advice.

Infants and Children: There is no information about use of this combination antibiotic in infants and children. However, no special problems are expected.

Special Concerns: Do not use this medication if you have a history of allergic reaction to any of the active or inactive ingredients in the ointment. If you use this medicine without a prescription, do not use it to treat puncture wounds, deep wounds, serious burns, or raw areas unless you have first consulted your doctor. Do not use this medicine in the eyes. Before you apply the medication, wash the affected area with soap and water and dry thoroughly. You may cover the treated area with a gauze bandage if you desire.

OVERDOSE
Symptoms: No specific ones have been reported.

What to Do: While no cases of overdose have been reported, if someone accidentally ingests this medicine, call your doctor, emergency medical services (EMS), or the nearest poison control center.

DRUG INTERACTIONS
Do not use other topical medications with this preparation unless otherwise instructed by your doctor.

FOOD INTERACTIONS
No known food interactions.

DISEASE INTERACTIONS
No disease interactions have been reported with the use of this combination antibiotic.

Neomycin/Polymyxin B/Hydrocortisone Ophthalmic and Otic

▶ Drug Class: Antibiotic/ corticosteroid combination

▶ Available in: Ophthalmic suspension, otic solution and suspension

▶ Available OTC? No

▶ As Generic? Yes

Side Effects

SERIOUS
Itching, rash, redness, swelling, or other eye or ear irritation that was not present before therapy. Call your doctor immediately.

COMMON
No common side effects are associated with neomycin/ polymyxin B/hydrocortisone.

LESS COMMON
Burning or stinging from the eye drops. There are no less-common side effects associated with the ear preparation.

PRINCIPAL USES
To treat or prevent bacterial infections of the eye or ear and to provide relief from eye or ear irritation and discomfort.

HOW THE DRUG WORKS
Ophthalmic and otic neomycin/polymyxin B/ hydrocortisone kills bacteria by interfering with the genetic material of bacterial cells, preventing them from multiplying.

DOSAGE
Ophthalmic suspension— 1 drop every 3 to 4 hours. Otic solution and suspension, for ear canal infection— Adults: 4 drops in the ear 3 to 4 times a day. Children: 3 drops in the ear 3 to 4 times a day.

ONSET OF EFFECT
Unknown.

DURATION OF ACTION
Unknown.

DIETARY ADVICE
No special restrictions.

STORAGE
Store in a tightly sealed container away from heat, moisture, and direct light. Do not allow it to freeze.

IF YOU MISS A DOSE
Apply it as soon as you remember. However, if it is near the time for the next dose, skip the missed dose and resume your regular dosage schedule. Do not double the next dose.

STOPPING THE DRUG
Use this drug as prescribed for the full treatment period, even if you begin to feel better before the scheduled end of therapy.

PROLONGED USE
Do not use the ear medication for more than 10 days unless your doctor directs otherwise. If you use the eye medication for a prolonged period, you should see your doctor regularly for tests and examinations.

PRECAUTIONS
Over 60: No special problems are expected.

Driving and Hazardous Work: Do not drive or engage in hazardous work until you determine how the medicine affects your vision.

Alcohol: No special precautions are necessary.

Pregnancy: This medication is not likely to cause problems unless absorbed into the bloodstream; consult your doctor for advice.

Breast Feeding: This combination medication has not been shown to cause problems in nursing babies.

Infants and Children: No special precautions.

Special Concerns: To use the eye drops, first wash your hands. Tilt your head back. Gently apply pressure to the inside corner of the eyelid and with the index finger of the same hand, pull downward on the lower eyelid to make a space. Drop the medicine into this space and close your eye. Apply pressure for 1 or 2 minutes while keeping the eye closed without blinking. To use the ear drops, lie down or tilt your head so the infected ear faces up. Gently pull the earlobe up and back for adults (down and back for children) to straighten the ear canal. Drop the medicine into the ear. Keep the ear facing upward for 5 minutes (2 minutes for children) after inserting the drops to allow the medicine to reach the infection. If necessary, insert a cotton ball to prevent the medicine from leaking out. Make sure the applicator for eye or ear drops does not touch your eye, ear, finger, or any other surface. If your symptoms do not improve in a few days or if they become worse, contact your doctor.

OVERDOSE
Symptoms: No specific ones have been reported.

What to Do: An overdose of this combination medication is unlikely to be life-threatening. If a large volume enters the eye, flush with water. If a large volume enters the ear or someone accidentally ingests the medicine, call your doctor, emergency medical services (EMS), or the nearest poison control center.

DRUG INTERACTIONS
Consult your doctor for specific advice if you are taking any other prescription or over-the-counter medication.

FOOD INTERACTIONS
No known food interactions.

DISEASE INTERACTIONS
Caution is advised when taking this combination antibiotic. Consult your doctor if you have any other eye or ear infection or medical problem.

Neostigmine

▶ Drug Class: Antimyasthenic; muscle stimulant

▶ Available in: Tablets, injection

▶ Available OTC? No

▶ As Generic? Yes

Side Effects

SERIOUS
Skin rash, itching, hives, breathing difficulty, asthmatic wheezing, swelling of the tongue, lips, and throat. Call your doctor right away.

COMMON
Diarrhea, increased sweating, increased watering of mouth, nausea or vomiting, stomach pain or cramps.

LESS COMMON
Increased bronchial secretions, unusual watering of eyes, unusually constricted pupils, gas, increased urination, flushing, weakness.

PRINCIPAL USES
To provide temporary relief of the muscle weakness and fatigability associated with myasthenia gravis. It is also used sometimes to improve bladder or bowel function, particularly after surgery.

HOW THE DRUG WORKS
Neostigmine inhibits the activity of the enzyme cholinesterase, which breaks up acetylcholine, a neurotransmitter involved in muscle activity. Consequently, neostigmine increases the amount of available acetylcholine, which in turn improves muscle strength and endurance in patients with milder forms of myasthenia gravis. The drug's effect also improves the tone of the muscles controlling bladder or bowel activity.

DOSAGE
For myasthenia gravis— Adults and teenagers: Initial dose of tablets (neostigmine bromide) is 15 mg every 3 or 4 hours; maintenance dose is 150 mg every 24 hours in 1 or more doses. Injection (neostigmine methylsulfate): 500 micrograms (mcg) every few hours. Children: With tablets, 2 mg per 2.2 lbs (1 kg) of body weight per day in 6 to 8 doses; or by injection, 10 to 40 mcg per 2.2 lbs every 2 or 3 hours. For bowel and bladder conditions— Adults and teenagers: By injection, 250 to 500 mcg, as needed. Children's use and dosage must be determined by your pediatrician.

ONSET OF EFFECT
From 4 to 30 minutes for injection; 45 to 75 minutes for tablets.

DURATION OF ACTION
2 to 4 hours.

DIETARY ADVICE
Tablets should be taken with food or milk to reduce gastrointestinal upset.

STORAGE
Store in a tightly sealed container away from heat and direct light.

IF YOU MISS A DOSE
Take it as soon as you remember. If it is near the time for the next dose, skip the missed dose and resume your regular dosage schedule. Do not double the next dose.

STOPPING THE DRUG
The decision to stop taking the drug should be made by your doctor.

PROLONGED USE
You should see your doctor regularly for tests and examinations if you take this drug for a prolonged period.

PRECAUTIONS
Over 60: No special problems are expected.

Driving and Hazardous Work: Use of neostigmine should not impair your ability to perform such tasks safely.

Alcohol: No special problems are expected.

Pregnancy: Temporary muscle weakness has occurred in some babies whose mothers took neostigmine during pregnancy. Before you take neostigmine, tell your doctor if you are pregnant or plan to become pregnant.

Breast Feeding: Neostigmine is not believed to pass into breast milk. Consult your doctor for advice.

Infants and Children: No special problems are expected to occur with younger patients.

Special Concerns: Myasthenia gravis patients may be asked to keep a diary of when muscle weakness or other symptoms occur, to allow adjustment of dose size and timing.

OVERDOSE
Symptoms: Abdominal cramps, anxiety, blurred vision, clumsiness or unsteadiness, diarrhea, sweating, excessive salivation, panic attack, progressive muscle weakness leading to paralysis, muscle cramps or twitching, unusual irritability or nervousness, unusual tiredness or weakness, urgent need to urinate.

What to Do: Call your doctor, emergency medical services (EMS), or the nearest poison control center immediately.

DRUG INTERACTIONS
Consult your physician for specific advice if you are taking demecarium, echothiophate, isoflurophate, malathion, guanadrel, guanethidine, procainamide, or trimethaphan.

FOOD INTERACTIONS
No known food interactions.

DISEASE INTERACTIONS
Caution is advised when taking neostigmine. Consult your doctor if you have a history of intestinal blockage, urinary tract blockage, or a current urinary tract infection.

Nevirapine

Viramune 200 mg
(BOEHRINGER INGELHEIM)

▶ Drug Class: Antiviral

▶ Available in: Tablets

▶ Available OTC? No

▶ As Generic? No

Side Effects

SERIOUS
Severe skin rash, sometimes with peeling of skin and mucous membranes; yellowish tinge to eyes or skin (indicating liver damage); muscle or joint pain; inflammation of the tissue surrounding the eye. If such symptoms arise, call your doctor immediately.

COMMON
Mild to moderate skin rash (often with itching), abdominal pain or discomfort, diarrhea, nausea, headache.

LESS COMMON
Fever, mouth sores or ulcers, general ill feeling (malaise), inflammation of the tissue surrounding the eye, numbness, tingling, or prickling in the extremities.

PRINCIPAL USES
To treat HIV infection in combination with other drugs. While not a cure for HIV, such drugs may suppress the replication of the virus and delay the progression of the disease.

HOW THE DRUG WORKS
Nevirapine interferes with the activity of enzymes needed for the replication of DNA in viral cells, thus preventing the human immunodeficiency virus (HIV) from reproducing.

DOSAGE
To start, 200 mg once a day, for 14 days; then 200 mg, 2 times a day. Nevirapine should be given in combination with other drugs for HIV, to delay the development of resistant strains of the virus.

ONSET OF EFFECT
Unknown. With most antiretroviral drugs, an early response can be seen within the first few days of therapy, but the maximum effect may take 12 to 16 weeks.

DURATION OF ACTION
Unknown. Effects of the drug may be prolonged if nevirapine is used in combination with other effective drugs and the virus is maximally suppressed.

DIETARY ADVICE
Nevirapine can be taken with or without food. Drink plenty of fluids.

STORAGE
Store in a tightly sealed container away from heat and direct light.

IF YOU MISS A DOSE
Take it as soon as you remember. If it is near the time for the next dose, skip the missed dose and resume your regular dosage schedule. Do not double the next dose.

STOPPING THE DRUG
The decision to stop taking the drug should be made in consultation with your physician.

PROLONGED USE
See your doctor regularly for tests and examinations if you must use this medicine for a prolonged period.

PRECAUTIONS
Over 60: It is not known whether nevirapine causes different or more severe side effects in older patients than it does in younger persons.

Driving and Hazardous Work: Do not drive or engage in hazardous work until you determine how the medicine affects you.

Alcohol: Avoid alcohol if liver function is impaired.

Pregnancy: Nevirapine has been shown to cause birth defects in animals. Adequate human studies have not been done. Nevertheless, nevirapine is increasingly being used in combination with other antiretroviral drugs to treat HIV-infected women who are pregnant.

Breast Feeding: Women infected with HIV should not breast feed, to avoid transmitting the virus to an uninfected child.

Infants and Children: Safety and effectiveness of nevirapine in infants and children have not been established. Use and dose must be determined by your pediatrician.

Special Concerns: Patients who stop nevirapine therapy for more than 7 days should resume with 200 mg once a day for 7 days, then 200 mg once a day for 14 days, then 200 mg, twice a day. Patients taking nevirapine should not use oral contraceptives, but should use another method of birth control, such as condoms.

OVERDOSE
Symptoms: No cases of overdose have been reported.

What to Do: An overdose of nevirapine is unlikely to occur. Nonetheless, if you have any reason to suspect an overdose, call your doctor, emergency medical services (EMS), or the nearest poison control center.

DRUG INTERACTIONS
Consult your doctor for specific advice if you are taking cimetidine, estrogen-containing oral contraceptives, macrolide antibiotics, rifabutin, rifampin, methadone, or any other prescription or over-the-counter medication.

FOOD INTERACTIONS
No known food interactions.

DISEASE INTERACTIONS
Consult your physician if you have any other medical condition. Use of nevirapine may cause complications in patients with liver or kidney disease, since these organs work together to remove the medication from the body.

Niacin (Nicotinic Acid)

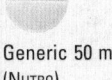

Generic 50 mg
(NUTRO)

▶ Drug Class: Antilipidemic (lipid-lowering) agent

▶ Available in: Tablets, extended-release tablets

▶ Available OTC? Yes (except Niaspan)

▶ As Generic? Yes (except Niaspan)

Side Effects

SERIOUS
Liver toxicity (more common with sustain or slow-release forms of niacin) leading to jaundice (yellow discoloration of skin and eyes) and fatigue; gastrointestinal irritation causing nausea, vomiting, and abdominal pain; peptic ulcer; increased uric acid levels leading to attacks of gout; elevated blood glucose levels.

COMMON
Itching, flushing, sweating, and dizziness, often within 20 to 40 minutes after taking niacin. These symptoms can usually be reduced or eliminated by taking an aspirin 30 minutes before the niacin. They tend to diminish or disappear after using niacin for longer periods. Slow-release and extended-release forms reduce these side effects. Nausea and vomiting may also occur.

LESS COMMON
Dry skin, headaches, eye problems.

PRINCIPAL USES
As an antilipidemic: Large doses of niacin are used to lower total and LDL cholesterol and triglyceride levels. It is the most effective drug currently available to increase HDL cholesterol levels.

HOW THE DRUG WORKS
Niacin is a vitamin required for the proper action of enzymes involved in energy metabolism. It lowers blood lipids by partially blocking the release of fatty acids from adipose (fat) tissue and reducing the liver's production of the triglyceride-carrying lipoprotein, very-low-density lipoprotein (VLDL).

DOSAGE
As an antilipidemic: 500 to 3,000 mg a day of immediate-release niacin in divided doses with meals. Initial dose is usually low and gradually increased to minimize side effects. Extended-release tablets (Niaspan): all doses are taken once a day at bedtime following a low-fat snack. Week 1: 375 mg. Week 2: 500 mg. Week 3: 750 mg. Weeks 4 to 7: 1,000 mg. After week 7, your doctor will evaluate your response to your dose. The daily dose should not be increased more than 500 mg in a 4-week period, and doses above 2,000 mg daily are not recommended.

ONSET OF EFFECT
2 to 4 weeks.

DURATION OF ACTION
As long as it is taken.

DIETARY ADVICE
Persons with elevated blood lipids should follow a diet containing no more than 30% calories from fat, with only 10% calories from saturated fat, and less than 300 mg a day of cholesterol.

STORAGE
Avoid heat and direct light.

IF YOU MISS A DOSE
Skip the missed dose and resume you regular dosage schedule. Do not double the next dose.

STOPPING THE DRUG
If you take niacin as an antilipidemic, do not stop unless so instructed by your doctor. Once niacin is stopped, lipids will increase to pretreatment levels.

PROLONGED USE
More serious side effects, such as nausea, vomiting, liver disease, and attacks of gout, are more likely with prolonged use.

PRECAUTIONS
Over 60: Possible increase in side effects and risk of developing diabetes.

Driving and Hazardous Work: No special precautions are necessary.

Alcohol: Alcohol can increase blood triglycerides in people with blood lipid abnormalities. Alcohol also increases the likelihood of flushing reactions.

Pregnancy: If taken as an antilipidemic, niacin therapy should be discontinued unless the doctor believes benefits clearly outweigh possible risks.

Breast Feeding: There is no evidence of danger to the infant from niacin as an antilipidemic, but your doctor should reconsider whether continued therapy is absolutely necessary.

Infants and Children: Safety has not been established for treatment of lipid problems.

Special Concerns: Periodic tests to assess liver function, blood glucose, and uric acid levels are needed.

OVERDOSE
Symptoms: Flushing, abdominal pain, nausea, vomiting.

What to Do: Call your doctor.

DRUG INTERACTIONS
When niacin is combined with HMG-CoA reductase inhibitors (lipid-lowering drugs known as statins), a rare complication is myositis (muscle inflammation) with muscle pain and tenderness. Severe myositis can damage kidneys and lead to kidney failure. The drugs must be stopped immediately if symptoms of myositis occur.

FOOD INTERACTIONS
Flushing may be worse when niacin is taken with hot foods or drinks.

DISEASE INTERACTIONS
Niacin should not be used by those with active liver disease or a history of gout or peptic ulcer. It should be used with caution by people with diabetes, borderline high glucose levels, or slight elevations of liver abnormalities.

Nicardipine Hydrochloride Oral

Cardene 30 mg
(SYNTEX)

▶ Drug Class: Calcium channel blocker

▶ Available in: Capsules, sustained-release capsules

▶ Available OTC? No

▶ As Generic? Yes

Side Effects

SERIOUS
Breathing difficulty, coughing, or wheezing; irregular or pounding heartbeat; chest pain; fainting. Call your doctor immediately.

COMMON
Headache, dizziness, skin flushing and feeling of warmth, swelling in the feet, ankles, or calves, palpitations.

LESS COMMON
Constipation or diarrhea, nausea, unusual fatigue and weakness, skin rash, increased urination.

PRINCIPAL USES
To prevent attacks of angina (chest pain associated with heart disease) and to control high blood pressure.

HOW THE DRUG WORKS
Nicardipine interferes with the movement of calcium into heart muscle cells and the smooth muscle cells in the walls of the arteries. This action relaxes blood vessels (causing them to widen), which lowers blood pressure, increases the blood supply to the heart, and decreases the heart's overall workload.

DOSAGE
For angina— Capsules: 20 mg, 3 times a day to start. For high blood pressure— Capsules: 20 to 40 mg, 3 times a day. Sustained-release capsules: 30 mg, 2 times a day. The dose may need to be increased.

ONSET OF EFFECT
Within 20 minutes.

DURATION OF ACTION
Capsules: 6 to 8 hours. Sustained-release capsules: Up to 12 hours.

DIETARY ADVICE
Nicardipine can be taken with or without food.

STORAGE
Store in a tightly sealed container away from heat and direct light.

IF YOU MISS A DOSE
Take it as soon as you remember. If it is near the time for the next dose, skip the missed dose and resume your regular dosage schedule. Do not double the next dose.

STOPPING THE DRUG
Do not stop taking this drug suddenly, as this may cause potentially serious health problems. If therapy is to be discontinued, dosage should be reduced gradually, according to doctor's instructions.

PROLONGED USE
You should see your doctor regularly for examinations and tests if you take this medicine for a prolonged period. Remember that this medication controls your high blood pressure but does not cure it. You may have to take nicardipine for the rest of your life.

PRECAUTIONS
Over 60: Adverse reactions may be more likely and more severe in older patients.

Driving and Hazardous Work: Do not drive or engage in hazardous work until you determine how the medicine affects you.

Alcohol: Avoid alcohol.

Pregnancy: In animal studies, large doses of nicardipine have caused birth defects. Human studies have not been done. Before you take nicardipine, tell your doctor if you are pregnant or plan to become pregnant.

Breast Feeding: Nicardipine may pass into breast milk; caution is advised. Consult your doctor for advice.

Infants and Children: Safety and effectiveness have not been determined for young patients.

Special Concerns: In addition to taking nicardipine, be sure to follow all special instructions on weight control and diet. Your doctor will tell you which specific factors are most important for you.

Check with your doctor before changing your diet.

OVERDOSE
Symptoms: Dizziness, slurred speech, nausea, vomiting, weakness, drowsiness, confusion, heart palpitations, nervousness or excitability.

What to Do: Call your doctor, emergency medical services (EMS), or the nearest poison control center immediately.

DRUG INTERACTIONS
Consult your physician for specific advice if you are taking acetazolamide, amphotericin B, corticosteroids, dichlorphenamide, diuretics, methazolamide, beta-blockers, carbamazepine, cyclosporine, procainamide, quinidine, digitalis drugs, disopyramide or the following eye medicines: betaxolol, levobunolol, metipranolol, or timolol.

FOOD INTERACTIONS
Avoid foods high in sodium.

DISEASE INTERACTIONS
Consult your doctor if you have abnormal heart rhythm or other disorders of the heart and blood vessels, mental depression, or Parkinson's disease. Use of nicardipine may cause complications in patients with liver or kidney disease, since these organs work together to remove the medication from the body.

Nicotine

Nicorette 2 mg
(HOECHST MARION ROUSSEL)

▶ Drug Class: Smoking
deterrent

▶ Available in: Chewing gum,
skin patch, nasal spray,
inhaler

▶ Available OTC? Yes

▶ As Generic? Yes

Side Effects

SERIOUS
With gum: Injury to
mouth, dental work, or
teeth. Call your dentist.
With patch: Hives, itch-
ing, skin rash, or
swelling. Call your
doctor immediately.

COMMON
Mild headache, rapid
heartbeat, increased
appetite, increased sali-
vation (with gum), sore
mouth or throat, pain in
jaw or neck, tooth prob-
lems (with gum and
inhaler), belching (with
gum), redness, burning,
or itching at site of application (with patch), stinging in the nose (with
nasal spray).

LESS COMMON
Constipation, diarrhea,
lightheadedness, dry
mouth, hiccups (with
gum), coughing (with
inhaler), hoarseness (with
gum and nasal spray),
nervousness, irritability,
loss of appetite, men-
strual pain, joint or muscle pain, stomach upset,
sweating, insomnia,
unusual dreams, runny
nose (with inhaler).

PRINCIPAL USES
To reduce nicotine with-
drawal symptoms as part of
a comprehensive smoking
cessation program.

HOW THE DRUG WORKS
It replaces the nicotine that
would otherwise be taken in
by tobacco use.

DOSAGE
Used when you have the
desire to smoke. Chewing
gum: 20 to 24 mg a day; not
to exceed 24 pieces of gum
a day. Number of sticks is
gradually reduced. Skin
patch: To start, 1 patch supplying 22 to 24 mg a day.
Dose is gradually reduced
over 2 to 5 months. Nasal
spray: 1 squirt (0.5 mg
each, for a total dose of 1
mg) in each nostril as
needed, no more than 80
times (40 mg) a day, for 3 to
6 months. Inhaler: Initially
(up to 12 weeks), 6 to 16
cartridges a day. The number of cartridges per day is
then gradually reduced over
the next 6 to 12 weeks.

ONSET OF EFFECT
30 minutes to 2 hours.

DURATION OF ACTION
3 to 6 hours.

DIETARY ADVICE
Gum should be chewed
slowly over 30 minutes.
Other forms can be used
without regard to diet.

STORAGE
Store in a tightly sealed container away from heat and
direct light.

IF YOU MISS A DOSE
If you are on a specific regimen, take a missed dose as
soon as you remember. If it
is near the time for the next
dose, skip the missed dose
and resume your regular
dosage schedule. Other-
wise, nicotine is taken as
needed.

STOPPING THE DRUG
The decision to stop taking
the drug should be made in
consultation with your doctor. Dose for the patch
should be tapered as
directed.

PROLONGED USE
Treatment should generally
not exceed 2 to 6 months. If
relapse of smoking occurs,
treatment may be repeated.

PRECAUTIONS

Over 60: Adverse reactions
are not expected to be more
severe in older patients than
in younger persons.

**Driving and Hazardous
Work:** The use of nicotine
should not impair your ability to perform such tasks
safely.

Alcohol: No special precautions are necessary.

Pregnancy: Nicotine
should not be used during
pregnancy. Before you use
nicotine, tell your doctor if
you are pregnant or plan to
become pregnant.

Breast Feeding: Nicotine
passes into breast milk; do
not use it while nursing.

Infants and Children:
Should not be used. Even
small amounts of nicotine
can cause serious problems
in infants and children.

Special Concerns: When
disposing of patches,
inhaler, or gum, be sure to
use a method that keeps
them out of the reach of
children and animals. You
should not smoke while
being treated with nicotine.
If the gum sticks to dental
work, check with your doctor or dentist. Nicotine gum
is harder to chew and stick-
ier than ordinary gum and
thus is more likely to cause
damage. Be careful to follow

directions when applying
patch and wash your hands
afterward. Do not apply a
patch in the same place for
at least a week. Do not
inhale while spraying the
nasal spray.

OVERDOSE
Symptoms: Nausea, vomiting, increased salivation,
severe abdominal or stom-
ach pain, diarrhea, severe
headache, cold sweats,
severe dizziness, hearing
and vision disturbances,
confusion, weakness,
breathing difficulty, heartbeat irregularities, seizures,
loss of consciousness.

What to Do: Call your
doctor, emergency medical
services (EMS), or the
nearest poison control
center immediately.

DRUG INTERACTIONS
Other drugs may interact
with nicotine. Consult your
doctor for specific advice
if you are taking amino-
phylline, insulin, oxtri-
phylline, propoxyphene,
or theophylline.

FOOD INTERACTIONS
No known food interactions.

DISEASE INTERACTIONS
Caution is advised when
taking nicotine. Consult
your doctor if you have a
history of diabetes, dental
problems (with gum), sinus
problems or nasal allergies
(with nasal spray), heart
or blood vessel disease,
inflamed mouth or throat
(with gum), skin allergies
(with patch), an overactive
thyroid, pheochromocy-
toma, or stomach ulcer.

Nifedipine

Generic 10 mg
(PUREPAC)

Additional photographs

▶ Drug Class: Calcium channel blocker

▶ Available in: Extended-release tablets, capsules

▶ Available OTC? No

▶ As Generic? Yes

Side Effects

SERIOUS
Breathing difficulty, coughing, or wheezing; irregular or pounding heartbeat; chest pain; fainting. Call your doctor immediately.

COMMON
Headache, dizziness, skin flushing and feeling of warmth, swelling in the feet, ankles, or calves, palpitations.

LESS COMMON
Constipation or diarrhea, nausea, unusual fatigue and weakness, skin rash, increased urination, vision problems.

PRINCIPAL USES
To treat high blood pressure and to prevent attacks of angina pectoris (chest pain associated with coronary artery disease).

HOW THE DRUG WORKS
Nifedipine interferes with the movement of calcium into heart muscle cells and the smooth muscle cells in the walls of the arteries. This action relaxes blood vessels (causing them to widen), which lowers blood pressure, increases the blood supply to the heart, and decreases the heart's overall workload.

DOSAGE
Extended-release tablets: 30 or 60 mg once a day. The doses may be increased as determined by your doctor.

ONSET OF EFFECT
Within 20 minutes.

DURATION OF ACTION
Extended-release tablets: 12 to 24 hours.

DIETARY ADVICE
Nifedipine can be taken with or without food.

STORAGE
Store in a tightly sealed container away from heat and direct light.

IF YOU MISS A DOSE
Take it as soon as you remember. If it is near the time for the next dose, skip the missed dose and resume your regular dosage schedule. Do not double the next dose.

STOPPING THE DRUG
Do not stop taking this drug suddenly, as this may cause potentially serious health problems. If therapy is to be discontinued, the dosage should be reduced gradually, according to your doctor's instructions.

PROLONGED USE
You should see your doctor regularly for examinations and tests if you take this medicine for a prolonged period. Remember that this medication controls high blood pressure but does not cure it. You may have to take nifedipine for the rest of your life.

PRECAUTIONS
Over 60: Adverse reactions may be more likely and more severe in older patients.

Driving and Hazardous Work: Do not drive or engage in hazardous work until you determine how the medicine affects you.

Alcohol: Avoid alcohol.

Pregnancy: In animal studies, large doses of nifedipine have been shown to cause birth defects. Human studies have not been done. Before you take nifedipine, tell your doctor if you are pregnant or plan to become pregnant.

Breast Feeding: Nifedipine passes into breast milk but has not been reported to cause problems; caution is advised. Consult your doctor for specific advice.

Infants and Children: While there is no specific information on the use of this medication in younger patients, the use of the capsules is not recommended.

Special Concerns: In addition to taking nifedipine, be sure to follow all special instructions on weight control and diet. Your doctor will tell you which specific factors are most important for you. Check with your doctor before changing your diet.

OVERDOSE
Symptoms: Dizziness, slurred speech, nausea, weakness, drowsiness, confusion, abnormal heartbeat.

What to Do: Call your doctor, emergency medical services (EMS), or the nearest poison control center immediately.

DRUG INTERACTIONS
Consult your physician for specific advice if you are taking acetazolamide, amphotericin B, corticosteroids, dichlorphenamide, diuretics, methazolamide, beta-blockers, carbamazepine, cyclosporine, procainamide, quinidine, digitalis drugs, disopyramide or the following eye medicines: betaxolol, levobunolol, metipranolol, or timolol.

FOOD INTERACTIONS
Avoid grapefruit juice and foods high in sodium.

DISEASE INTERACTIONS
Caution is advised when taking nifedipine. Consult your doctor if you have any of the following: abnormal heart rhythm, other disorders of the heart and blood vessels, mental depression, or Parkinson's disease. Use of nifedipine may cause complications in patients with liver or kidney disease, since these organs work together to remove the medication from the body.

Nilutamide

BRAND NAME
Nilandron

▶ Drug Class: Antiandrogen

▶ Available in: Tablets

▶ Available OTC? No

▶ As Generic? No

Side Effects

SERIOUS
Chest pain, difficulty breathing, fever, bone pain, cough, pneumonia. Call your physician immediately.

COMMON
Abdominal pain, headache, loss of appetite, decreased sex drive, nausea, constipation, difficulty of eyes adjusting to darkness, flushing or sensations of warmth.

LESS COMMON
Indigestion, flu-like symptoms, vomiting, dry skin, rash, sweating, loss of body hair, difficulty of eyes adjusting to light, color blindness.

PRINCIPAL USES
Used in conjunction with surgical castration to treat cancer of the prostate.

HOW THE DRUG WORKS
The growth of some types of prostate tumors is stimulated by the hormone testosterone. Nilutamide blocks the activity of testosterone, thus slowing or halting the growth of such tumors. Testosterone is primarily manufactured in the testicles; surgical castration thus further reduces testosterone levels in the body.

DOSAGE
Adult males: To start, 300 mg once a day for 30 days; then 150 mg once a day.

ONSET OF EFFECT
Within hours.

DURATION OF ACTION
Unknown.

DIETARY ADVICE
No special restrictions.

STORAGE
Store in a tightly sealed container away from heat, moisture, and direct light.

IF YOU MISS A DOSE
This drug is prescribed to be taken once a day. If you miss a day, skip the missed dose and resume your regular dosage schedule. Do not double the next dose.

STOPPING THE DRUG
Take it as prescribed for the full treatment period, even if you begin to feel better before the scheduled end of therapy. The decision to stop taking this drug should be made by your doctor.

PROLONGED USE
Nilutamide is not intended to be used on a long-term, ongoing basis. See your physician regularly for evaluation of your condition for the duration of therapy with this drug.

PRECAUTIONS
Over 60: The dosage may be reduced, because the medication takes longer to be eliminated from the body in older patients, but nilutamide is not otherwise expected to cause different side effects or problems in older persons than it does in younger people.

Driving and Hazardous Work: Do not drive or engage in hazardous work until you determine how the medicine affects you.

Alcohol: Avoid alcohol while using this medication.

Pregnancy: Not applicable; prostate cancer occurs only in men.

Breast Feeding: Not applicable; prostate cancer occurs only in men.

Infants and Children: Not applicable.

Special Concerns: Nilutamide treatment must start on the day of or the day after surgical castration is performed.

OVERDOSE
Symptoms: No specific ones have been reported.

What to Do: An overdose with nilutamide is unlikely to occur. If someone takes a much larger dose than prescribed, call your doctor, emergency medical services (EMS), or the nearest poison control center.

DRUG INTERACTIONS
The following drugs may interact with nilutamide. Consult your doctor for specific advice if you are taking vitamin K antagonists, phenytoin, or theophylline. Also tell your doctor if you are taking any other prescription or over-the-counter medication.

FOOD INTERACTIONS
No known food interactions.

DISEASE INTERACTIONS
Caution is advised when taking nilutamide. Consult your doctor for advice if you have severe respiratory problems or any other chronic or significant medical condition. Use of nilutamide may cause complications in patients with liver disease, since this organ works to remove the medication from the body.

Nimodipine

BRAND NAME
Nimotop

NIMOTOP

Nimotop 30 mg
(BAYER)

▶ Drug Class: Calcium channel blocker

▶ Available in: Capsules

▶ Available OTC? No

▶ As Generic? No

Side Effects

SERIOUS
Slow or irregular heartbeat, extreme dizziness, fainting, swelling of the extremities, breathing difficulty. Such side effects are rare but serious; call your doctor or emergency medical services (EMS) immediately.

COMMON
Flushing and feeling of warmth, headache.

LESS COMMON
Constipation or diarrhea, dizziness or lightheadedness, nausea, unusual fatigue.

PRINCIPAL USES
To minimize neurological damage in the aftermath of a type of stroke known as subarachnoid hemorrhage (a ruptured blood vessel that spills blood into the space between the protective layers of membranes surrounding the brain).

HOW THE DRUG WORKS
Nimodipine prevents the constriction of smooth muscle tissue that surrounds the blood vessels, especially the arteries in the brain. This helps to keep cerebral arteries open, thus maintaining blood supply to brain tissue, preventing nerve cell death, and preserving function in the areas of the brain affected by the stroke.

DOSAGE
Adults: 60 mg every 4 hours, for 21 consecutive days.

ONSET OF EFFECT
Peak effects within 1 hour.

DURATION OF ACTION
Up to 4 hours.

DIETARY ADVICE
Nimodipine can be taken with or without food.

STORAGE
Store in a tightly sealed container away from heat and direct light.

IF YOU MISS A DOSE
It is imperative to try not to miss a dose of nimodipine. However, if you do miss a dose, take it as soon as you remember. If it is near the time for the next dose, skip the missed dose and resume your regular dosage schedule. Do not double the next dose. If you miss more than one dose, contact your doctor.

STOPPING THE DRUG
Do not stop taking this drug suddenly, as this may cause potentially serious health problems. Therapy with nimodipine typically ends after 21 days, or as determined by your doctor.

PROLONGED USE
Prolonged use is not common; regular medical examinations and tests are necessary if you are required to take this medication for an extended period.

PRECAUTIONS
Over 60: Adverse reactions may be more likely and more severe in older patients.

Driving and Hazardous Work: Do not drive or engage in hazardous work until you determine how the medicine affects you.

Alcohol: Avoid alcohol.

Pregnancy: Large doses of nimodipine have been shown to cause birth defects in animals. Human studies have not been done. Before you take nimodipine, tell your doctor if you are pregnant or plan to become pregnant.

Breast Feeding: Nimodipine may pass into breast milk but has not been reported to cause problems; caution is advised. Consult your doctor for advice.

Infants and Children: While there is no specific information on use of this medication in younger patients, no special problems are expected.

Special Concerns: To be effective, it is crucial to take nimodipine at the regularly scheduled times without fail.

OVERDOSE
Symptoms: Overdose of nimodipine has not been reported. Symptoms would likely be dizziness, confusion, or fainting.

What to Do: If someone takes a much larger dose than prescribed, call your doctor, emergency medical services (EMS), or the nearest poison control center right away.

DRUG INTERACTIONS
Some drugs may interact adversely with nimodipine. Consult your doctor for specific advice if you are taking antihypertensive drugs (beta-blockers or other calcium channel blockers), cimetidine, or fentanyl.

FOOD INTERACTIONS
No known food interactions.

DISEASE INTERACTIONS
Caution is advised when taking nimodipine. Consult your doctor if you have any of the following: abnormal heart rhythm or other disorders of the heart and blood vessels, mental depression, or Parkinson's disease. Use of nimodipine may cause complications in patients with liver or kidney disease, since these organs work together to remove the medication from the body.

Nitrofurantoin

Generic 50 mg
(ZENITH)

▶ Drug Class: Anti-infective

▶ Available in: Capsules, oral suspension, tablets, extended-release capsules

▶ Available OTC? No

▶ As Generic? Yes

Side Effects

SERIOUS
Chest pain, chills, cough, fever, troubled breathing, dizziness, drowsiness, tingling or burning of face or mouth, sore throat, unusual weakness, unusual fatigue. Call your doctor immediately.

COMMON
Abdominal pain or stomach upset, diarrhea, nausea, vomiting, loss of appetite.

LESS COMMON
Dark yellow or brownish urine.

PRINCIPAL USES
To treat urinary tract infections (UTIs).

HOW THE DRUG WORKS
Nitrofurantoin interferes with bacterial metabolism and cell wall formation. Eventually the bacteria die out, bringing an end to the infection.

DOSAGE
Adults and teenagers— Capsules, oral suspension, tablets: 50 to 100 mg every 6 hours. Extended-release capsules: 100 mg every 12 hours. Children up to 12 years— Dosage must be determined by your doctor.

ONSET OF EFFECT
Within 1 hour.

DURATION OF ACTION
Capsules, oral suspension, tablets: 6 hours. Extended-release capsules: 24 hours.

DIETARY ADVICE
Nitrofurantoin should be taken with food or milk.

STORAGE
Store in a tightly sealed container away from heat and direct light. Keep the oral suspension from freezing.

IF YOU MISS A DOSE
Take it as soon as you remember. If it is near the time for the next dose, skip the missed dose and resume your regular dosage schedule. Do not double the next dose.

STOPPING THE DRUG
Take as prescribed for the full treatment period, even if you begin to feel better before the scheduled end of therapy.

PROLONGED USE
See your doctor regularly if you must take this drug for a prolonged period.

PRECAUTIONS

Over 60: Adverse reactions may be more likely and more severe in older patients.

Driving and Hazardous Work: Do not drive or engage in hazardous work until you determine how the medicine affects you.

Alcohol: Avoid alcohol.

Pregnancy: Nitrofurantoin should not be taken within several weeks of the delivery date or during labor.

Breast Feeding: Nitrofurantoin passes into breast milk; avoid use while breast feeding.

Infants and Children: Nitrofurantoin is not recommended for use by infants under 1 month old.

Special Concerns: Nitrofurantoin may cause false results in some urine sugar tests for diabetes. If your symptoms do not improve or instead become worse within a few days, check with your doctor. When taking the oral suspension, be sure to shake the container forcefully before each dose. Use a specially marked measuring spoon or other device to dispense each dose. A household teaspoon might not hold the correct amount. Tell your doctor if you have ever had an allergic reaction to nitrofurantoin or any related medicine, such as furazolidone, or if you are allergic to any other substance. When taking the extended-release capsule, swallow it whole without chewing.

OVERDOSE
Symptoms: Severe nausea, vomiting, diarrhea, loss of appetite.

What to Do: An overdose of nitrofurantoin is unlikely to be life-threatening. However, if someone takes a much larger dose than prescribed, call your doctor, emergency medical services (EMS), or the nearest poison control center.

DRUG INTERACTIONS
Consult your doctor for specific advice if you are taking acetohydroxamine, oral diabetes medicine, dapsone, furazolidone, methyldopa, procainamide, quinidine, sulfonamides, vitamin K, carbamazepine, chloroquine, cisplatin, cytarabine, vaccine for diphtheria, tetanus, and pertussis (DTP), disulfiram, ethotoin, hydroxychloroquine, lindane, lithium, mephenytoin, mexiletine, pemoline, phenytoin, pyridoxine, vincristine, probenecid, sulfinpyrazone, quinine, or any other anti-infective agent.

FOOD INTERACTIONS
No known food interactions.

DISEASE INTERACTIONS
Consult your doctor if you have any of the following: glucose-6-phosphate dehydrogenase (G6PD) deficiency, kidney disease, lung disease, or nerve damage.

Nitroglycerin

Nitrostat 0.4 mg
(PARKE-DAVIS)

▶ Drug Class: Nitrate

▶ Available in: Capsules, tablets, ointment, skin patch, aerosol

▶ Available OTC? No

▶ As Generic? Yes

Side Effects

SERIOUS
Blurred vision, severe or prolonged headache, skin rash, dry mouth. Call your doctor immediately.

COMMON
Flushing of face and neck, headache, nausea or vomiting, dizziness or lightheadedness when getting up, rapid heartbeat, restlessness.

LESS COMMON
Sore, reddened skin.

PRINCIPAL USES
To prevent or relieve attacks of angina (chest pain associated with heart disease).

HOW THE DRUG WORKS
Nitroglycerin relaxes the smooth muscle that surrounds the blood vessels and increases the supply of blood and oxygen to the heart. It also reduces the heart's workload and demand for oxygen.

DOSAGE
Ointment: 15 to 30 mg applied to skin every 6 to 8 hours. Skin patch: 1 patch applied every day, left on for 12 to 14 hours. Aerosol: 1 or 2 doses on or under the tongue at 5-minute intervals to relieve angina attack. Extended-release capsules: 2.5, 6.5, or 9 mg every 12 hours; can be taken every 8 hours. Extended-release tablets: 1.3, 2.6, or 6.5 mg every 12 hours; can be taken every 8 hours. Sublingual (under tongue) or buccal (inside the cheek) tablets: 0.15 to 0.6 mg repeated at 5-minute intervals to treat angina attack. If 3 tablets do not relieve pain, call your doctor.

ONSET OF EFFECT
Sublingual: 2 to 4 minutes. Buccal: 3 minutes. Oral: 20 to 45 minutes. Ointment and skin patch: 30 minutes.

DURATION OF ACTION
Sublingual: 30 to 60 minutes. Buccal: 5 hours. Oral: 8 to 12 hours. Ointment: 4 to 8 hours. Skin patch: Up to 24 hours.

DIETARY ADVICE
Oral forms used as a preventive should be taken 30 minutes before or 1 to 2 hours after meals.

STORAGE
Store in a tightly sealed container away from heat, moisture, and direct light.

IF YOU MISS A DOSE
Take it as soon as you remember. If it is near the time for the next dose, skip the missed dose and resume your regular dosage schedule, as prescribed. Do not double the next dose.

STOPPING THE DRUG
The decision to stop taking nitroglycerin should be made by your doctor.

PROLONGED USE
You should see your doctor regularly for examinations and tests if you take this medicine for a prolonged period.

PRECAUTIONS
Over 60: Adverse reactions may be more likely and more severe in older patients.

Driving and Hazardous Work: Do not drive or engage in hazardous work until you determine how the medicine affects you.

Alcohol: Avoid alcohol.

Pregnancy: Not recommended during pregnancy. Before taking nitroglycerin, be sure to tell your doctor if you are pregnant or plan to become pregnant.

Breast Feeding: Nitroglycerin may pass into breast milk; caution is advised. Consult your doctor for advice.

Infants and Children: No studies in infants and children have been done.

Special Concerns: Skin patch should be applied to different sites to prevent skin irritation.

OVERDOSE
Symptoms: Fast heartbeat, red and perspiring skin, headache, dizziness, palpitations, vision disturbances, nausea, vomiting, confusion, difficulty breathing.

What to Do: Call your doctor, emergency medical services (EMS), or the nearest poison control center immediately.

DRUG INTERACTIONS
Do not take nitroglycerin within 24 hours of taking sildenafil citrate. Sildenafil can enhance the action of nitrates (such as nitroglycerin), causing potentially dangerous decreases in blood pressure. Consult your doctor for specific advice if you are taking other heart medicines or drugs for hypertension.

FOOD INTERACTIONS
No known food interactions.

DISEASE INTERACTIONS
Consult your physician if you have any of the following: anemia, glaucoma, a recent head injury or stroke, a recent heart attack, or an overactive thyroid. Use of nitroglycerin may cause complications in patients with severe liver or kidney disease, since these organs work together to remove the medication from the body.

Nizatidine

Axid AR 75 mg
(WHITEHALL-ROBINS)

Additional photographs

▶ Drug Class: Histamine (H2) blocker

▶ Available in: Capsules, tablets

▶ Available OTC? Yes

▶ As Generic? Yes

Side Effects

SERIOUS
Irregular heart rhythm (palpitations), slowed heartbeat, severe blood problems, resulting in unusual bleeding, bruising, fever, chills, and increased susceptibility to infection. Call your doctor immediately.

COMMON
Headache, fatigue, drowsiness, dizziness, nausea, vomiting, abdominal pain, diarrhea, constipation.

LESS COMMON
Blurred vision, decreased sexual desire or function, swelling of breasts in males and females, temporary hair loss, hallucinations, depression, insomnia, skin rash, hives, or redness.

PRINCIPAL USES
To treat and prevent the return of ulcers of the stomach and duodenum, as well as conditions that cause increased stomach acid production (such as Zollinger-Ellison syndrome), gastroesophageal reflux (backwash of stomach acid into the esophagus, resulting in heartburn), and minor episodes of heartburn.

HOW THE DRUG WORKS
Nizatidine blocks the action of histamine (a compound produced in the body's cells), which in turn decreases the stomach's secretion of hydrochloric acid. Once stomach acid production has been decreased, the body is better able to heal itself.

DOSAGE
Adults and teenagers— To treat stomach ulcers: 300 mg once a day at bedtime, or 150 mg twice a day. To prevent the recurrence of duodenal ulcers: 150 mg once a day at bedtime. To treat gastroesophageal reflux: 150 mg, 2 times a day. To prevent minor cases of heartburn, acid indigestion, and sour stomach: 75 mg taken 30 to 60 minutes before a meal, once a day.

ONSET OF EFFECT
Within 30 minutes.

DURATION OF ACTION
Up to 12 hours.

DIETARY ADVICE
If you are taking two doses of nizatidine a day, the first dose can be taken after breakfast. Avoid foods that cause stomach irritation.

STORAGE
Store in a tightly sealed container away from heat and direct light.

IF YOU MISS A DOSE
Take it as soon as you remember. If it is near the time for the next dose, skip the missed dose and resume your regular dosage schedule. Do not double the next dose.

STOPPING THE DRUG
Take the prescription-strength form for the full treatment period, even if you begin to feel better before the scheduled end of therapy.

PROLONGED USE
Do not take the maximum daily dosage continually for more than 2 weeks unless directed by your doctor.

PRECAUTIONS

Over 60: Adverse reactions may be more likely and more severe in older patients.

Driving and Hazardous Work: Do not drive or engage in hazardous work until you determine how the medicine affects you.

Alcohol: Avoid alcohol.

Pregnancy: Risks vary, depending on patient and dosage. Consult your physician.

Breast Feeding: Nizatidine passes into breast milk and may pose harm to the child; avoid or discontinue use while nursing.

Infants and Children: Nizatidine is not recommended for young patients, although it has not been shown to cause side effects or problems different from those in adults when used for short periods of time.

Special Concerns: Avoid cigarette smoking because it may increase stomach acid secretion and thus worsen the disease. Do not take nizatidine if you have ever had an allergic reaction to a histamine H2 blocker. If stomach pain becomes worse while using the drug, be sure to tell your doctor right away.

OVERDOSE
Symptoms: No cases of overdose have been reported.

What to Do: Although an overdose is unlikely, if someone takes a much larger dose than prescribed, call your doctor, emergency medical services (EMS), or the nearest poison control center right away.

DRUG INTERACTIONS
No significant drug interactions have been identified. However, nizatidine may increase blood levels of aspirin. Consult your doctor for specific advice if you are taking aspirin.

FOOD INTERACTIONS
Tomato-based mixed vegetable juices, carbonated drinks, citrus fruits and juices, caffeine-containing beverages, and other acidic foods or liquids may irritate the stomach or interfere with the therapeutic action of nizatidine.

DISEASE INTERACTIONS
Patients with kidney disease should not use nizatidine or should use it in smaller, limited doses under careful supervision by a physician.

Norethindrone

▶ Drug Class: Progestin
(hormone)

▶ Available in: Tablets

▶ Available OTC? No

▶ As Generic? No

Side Effects

SERIOUS
Changes in menstrual
bleeding pattern, mental
depression, skin rash,
unexpected or increased
flow of breast milk. Call
your doctor immediately.

COMMON
Abdominal pain or
cramps, swollen face,
ankles, or feet, mood
changes, mild headache,
nervousness, unusual
fatigue, weight gain.

LESS COMMON
Acne, breast pain or ten-
derness, brown spots on
skin, hot flashes, loss or
gain of hair on body or
scalp, loss of sexual
desire, nausea, insomnia.

PRINCIPAL USES
To prevent pregnancy; also
used to treat menstrual disorders such as amenorrhea
(unexpected cessation of
menstrual periods) and
abnormal uterine bleeding,
and to treat endometriosis.

HOW THE DRUG WORKS
Norethindrone prevents
ovulation, probably by
inhibiting secretion of pituitary hormones that in turn
regulate menstrual and
reproductive cycles.
Norethindrone also alters
activity of uterine cells,
resulting in, among other
changes, thickening of the
cervical mucus. These
changes make it less likely
for a partner's sperm to
reach and fertilize an egg.

DOSAGE
For contraception: 0.35 mg
every day at the same time
beginning on the first day of
the menstrual period (28
days from the first day of
the last menstrual period).
For amenorrhea or abnor-
mal uterine bleeding: 2.5 to
10 mg on days 5 through 25
of the menstrual cycle. For
endometriosis: To start, 5
mg a day for 14 days. Your
doctor may gradually
increase your dose up to 15
mg a day for 6 to 9 months.
Contact your physician as
soon as your menstrual
period begins.

ONSET OF EFFECT
Unknown.

DURATION OF ACTION
Unknown.

DIETARY ADVICE
No special restrictions.

STORAGE
Store in a tightly sealed container away from heat and
direct light.

IF YOU MISS A DOSE
When you are 3 hours or
more late or miss 1 day's
dose, take the missed dose
immediately, resume your
regular dosage schedule
and use another method of
contraception for 2 days. If
you miss 2 doses, take 1
tablet immediately and use
another method of birth
control for 7 days. Do not
double the next dose. For
amenorrhea, abnormal
uterine bleeding, and
endometriosis: Take it as
soon as you remember. If it
is near the time for the next
dose, skip the missed dose
and resume your regular
dosage schedule. Do not
double the next dose.

STOPPING THE DRUG
If the medication was given
to treat amenorrhea, abnormal uterine bleeding, or
endometriosis, the decision
to stop taking it should be
made by your doctor.

PROLONGED USE
See your doctor regularly,
usually every 6 to 12
months, for examinations
and tests.

PRECAUTIONS
Over 60: No special problems are expected.

**Driving and Hazardous
Work:** The use of this drug
should not impair your ability to perform such tasks
safely.

Alcohol: No special precautions are necessary.

Pregnancy: This drug
should not be taken during
pregnancy. Problems including genital defects and
smaller-than-normal body
size have been reported in
babies born to women who
took progestins during
pregnancy.

Breast Feeding: Norethindrone passes into breast
milk but has not been
shown to cause problems in
the nursing child. Norethindrone may increase or
decrease the quality or
amount of breast milk. Low-
dose progestins are recommended for contraception
during breast feeding. Consult your doctor for advice.

Infants and Children:
Progestins can been used
for contraception by
teenagers with no unusual
adverse effects.

Special Concerns: Check
with your doctor if vaginal
bleeding continues for an
unusually long time or if
your menstrual period has
not started within 45 days
of the previous one.

OVERDOSE
Symptoms: None are
known; no cases of over-
dose have been reported.

What to Do: An overdose
with norethindrone is
unlikely to occur. Emer-
gency instructions are not
applicable.

DRUG INTERACTIONS
Other drugs may interact
with norethindrone. Consult
your doctor for specific
advice if you are taking
aminoglutethimide, carba-
mazepine, phenobarbital,
phenytoin, rifabutin, or
rifampin.

FOOD INTERACTIONS
No known food interactions.

DISEASE INTERACTIONS
Consult your doctor if you
have a history of any of the
following: breast cancer
(known or suspected), liver
disease, thrombophlebitis,
or thromboembolic disease.

Noroxin 400 mg
(MERCK)

▶ Drug Class: Fluoroquinolone antibiotic

▶ Available in: Eye drops, tablets

▶ Available OTC? No

▶ As Generic? No

Side Effects

SERIOUS
Serious reactions to norfloxacin are rare and include seizures, mental confusion, hallucinations, agitation, nightmares, depression, shortness of breath, unusual swelling in the face or extremities, and loss of consciousness. Also skin burning, redness, blisters, rash, or itching on exposure to sunlight. Call your doctor immediately.

COMMON
Increased sensitivity to sunlight (and increased risk of sunburn) for days following therapy.

LESS COMMON
Diarrhea, nausea and vomiting, stomach pain and upset, gas, headache, dizziness, restlessness, insomnia, changes in taste perception, drowsiness, itching, dry mouth, unusual body aches or pains.

PRINCIPAL USES
To treat urinary tract infections, sexually transmitted diseases, or eye infections caused by bacteria.

HOW THE DRUG WORKS
Norfloxacin inhibits the activity of a bacterial enzyme (gyrase) that is necessary for proper DNA formation and replication. This prevents bacteria cells from reproducing.

DOSAGE
For urinary tract infections: Adults: 400 mg, 2 times a day, for 3 to 21 days. For sexually transmitted diseases: 800 mg in a single one-time dose. For eye infections: 1 drop in each affected eye, 4 times a day, for 7 days.

ONSET OF EFFECT
Varies depending on the infection being treated.

DURATION OF ACTION
Unknown.

DIETARY ADVICE
Tablets should be taken on an empty stomach, 1 hour before or 2 hours after meals, with a full glass of water. Drink plenty of fluids, especially citrus juices or cranberry juice, but avoid milk and dairy derivatives.

STORAGE
Store in a tightly sealed container away from heat, moisture, and direct light.

IF YOU MISS A DOSE
Take it as soon as you remember. If it is near the time for the next dose, skip the missed dose and resume your regular dosage schedule. Do not double the next dose.

STOPPING THE DRUG
It is very important to take this drug as prescribed for the full treatment period, even if you begin to feel better before the scheduled end of therapy.

PROLONGED USE
If your symptoms do not improve or instead become worse after a few days, consult your doctor promptly.

PRECAUTIONS
Over 60: No special problems are expected.

Driving and Hazardous Work: Do not drive or engage in hazardous work until you determine how the medicine affects you.

Alcohol: It is advisable to abstain from alcohol when fighting an infection.

Pregnancy: In some animal tests, norfloxacin has caused birth defects. Adequate studies in humans have not been done. It should be used during pregnancy only if potential benefits clearly justify the risks. Before you take norfloxacin, tell your doctor if you are pregnant or plan to become pregnant.

Breast Feeding: Norfloxacin passes into breast milk and may cause serious side effects in the nursing infant; use of the drug is discouraged when nursing.

Infants and Children: Oral forms of fluoroquinolones such as norfloxacin should not be used by persons under the age of 18. Norfloxacin eye drops should not be used by children under 1 year old.

Special Concerns: If norfloxacin makes your skin or eyes more sensitive to sunlight, wear sunglasses and protective clothing, use a sunscreen with an SPF (sun protection factor) of 15 or higher, and avoid excessive exposure to the sun.

OVERDOSE
Symptoms: Nausea, headache, dizziness, vomiting, drowsiness, seizures.

What to Do: Call your doctor, emergency medical services (EMS), or the nearest poison control center immediately.

DRUG INTERACTIONS
Consult your doctor for specific advice if you are taking aminophylline, antacids, cancer drugs, cyclosporine, didanosine, iron supplements, sucralfate, theophylline, or zinc salts.

FOOD INTERACTIONS
The effects of caffeine may be magnified by this drug. Milk and dairy products can reduce blood levels of norfloxacin by as much as half.

DISEASE INTERACTIONS
Caution is advised when taking norfloxacin. Consult your doctor if you have a disorder of the central nervous system or any other medical condition. Use of norfloxacin may cause complications in patients with kidney disease, since this organ works to remove the medication from the body.

Nortriptyline Hydrochloride

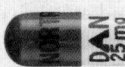

Generic 25 mg
(SCHEIN/DANBURY)

Additional photographs

▶ Drug Class: Tricyclic antidepressant

▶ Available in: Capsules, oral solution

▶ Available OTC? No

▶ As Generic? Yes

Side Effects

SERIOUS
Confusion, heartbeat irregularities, hallucinations, seizures, extreme fatigue or drowsiness, blurred or altered vision, breathing difficulty, constipation, staring and absence of facial expression, impaired concentration, difficult urination, fever, extreme and persistent restlessness, loss of coordination and balance, difficulty swallowing or speaking, dilated pupils, eye pain, fainting. Also trembling, shaking, weakness, and stiffness in the extremities; shuffling gait. Call your doctor immediately.

COMMON
Drowsiness or dizziness, headache, dry mouth or unpleasant taste, fatigue, heightened sensitivity to light, weight gain, nausea, increased appetite.

LESS COMMON
Heartburn, sleeping difficulty, diarrhea, increased or profuse sweating, vomiting.

PRINCIPAL USES
To relieve symptoms of major depression, anxiety disorders, panic disorder, or chronic pain.

HOW THE DRUG WORKS
Nortriptyline affects levels of norepinephrine, a brain chemical that is thought to be linked to mood, emotions, and mental state.

DOSAGE
Adults: 25 mg, 3 to 4 times a day; may be increased to a maximum dose of 150 mg a day. Teenagers: 25 to 50 mg a day. Children ages 6 to 12: 10 to 20 mg a day. Older adults: 25 to 100 mg a day; may be increased gradually by your doctor. Dosage is usually determined by blood level monitoring.

ONSET OF EFFECT
1 to 6 weeks.

DURATION OF ACTION
Unknown.

DIETARY ADVICE
To lessen stomach upset, take with food, unless your doctor instructs otherwise. Increase intake of fiber and fluids.

STORAGE
Store in a tightly sealed container away from heat, moisture, and direct light. Do not allow solution to freeze.

IF YOU MISS A DOSE
If you take a one-time daily bedtime dose, do not take the missed dose in the morning because it may cause drowsiness. Call your doctor for specific advice. If you take more than 1 dose a day, take it as soon as you remember. If it is near the time for the next dose, skip the missed dose and resume your regular dosage schedule. Do not double the next dose.

STOPPING THE DRUG
Take as prescribed for the full treatment period, even if you begin to feel better before the scheduled end of therapy. The decision to stop taking the drug should be made in consultation with your doctor.

PROLONGED USE
The usual course of therapy lasts 6 months to 1 year; some patients benefit from additional therapy.

PRECAUTIONS
Over 60: Adverse reactions may be more likely and more severe in older patients. A lower dose may be warranted.

Driving and Hazardous Work: Use caution when driving or engaging in hazardous work until you determine how the medication affects you. Drowsiness or lightheadedness can occur.

Alcohol: Avoid alcohol.

Pregnancy: Adequate human studies have not been done. Consult your doctor for specific advice.

Breast Feeding: Nortriptyline passes into breast milk; do not use it while nursing.

Infants and Children: Not prescribed for children under the age of 6 years. Antidepressants increase the risk of suicidal thinking and behavior (suicidality) in children with major depression and other psychiatric disorders. Discuss with your doctor this risk versus the benefits of using this drug. Children should be observed closely for worsening of symptoms, suicidality, or unusual changes in behavior at the onset of therapy and when making changes in dosage.

Special Concerns: This is a potentially dangerous drug, especially if taken in excess. Tricyclic antidepressants should not be within easy reach of suicidal patients. If dry mouth occurs, use candy or sugarless gum for relief.

OVERDOSE
Symptoms: Difficulty breathing, severe fatigue, seizures, confusion, hallucinations, dilated pupils, irregular heartbeat, fever, impaired concentration.

What to Do: Call your doctor, emergency medical services (EMS), or the nearest poison control center immediately.

DRUG INTERACTIONS
Consult your doctor for specific advice if you are taking antithyroid agents, cimetidine, clonidine, guanadrel, guanethidine, metrizamide, appetite suppressants, isoproterenol, ephedrine, epinephrine, amphetamines, phenylephrine, antipsychotic drugs, pimozide, methyldopa, metyrosine, metoclopramide, pemoline, promethazine, trimeprazine, rauwolfia alkaloids, MAO inhibitors, or any drugs that depress the central nervous system.

FOOD INTERACTIONS
No known food interactions

DISEASE INTERACTIONS
Consult your doctor if you have any of the following: a history of alcohol abuse, difficulty urinating, asthma, bipolar disorder, high blood pressure, stomach or intestinal problems, glaucoma, overactive thyroid, enlarged prostate, schizophrenia, seizures, a blood disorder, or kidney, heart, or liver disease.

Nystatin

BRAND NAMES
Mycostatin, Nilstat,
Nystex

Generic 500,000 units
(LEMMON)

▶ Drug Class: Antifungal

▶ Available in: Lozenges, oral
suspension, cream, ointment,
powder, vaginal tablets

▶ Available OTC? No

▶ As Generic? Yes

Side Effects

SERIOUS
No serious side effects
are associated with the
use of nystatin.

COMMON
No common side effects
are associated with the
use of nystatin.

LESS COMMON
Nausea, vomiting, diar-
rhea, stomach pain, skin
or vaginal irritation not
present prior to therapy.

PRINCIPAL USES
To treat fungal infections of
the skin, mouth, and vagina.

HOW THE DRUG WORKS
Nystatin prevents fungal
organisms from producing
vital substances required for
growth and function. This
medication is effective only
for infections caused by fungal organisms. It will not
work for bacterial or viral
infections.

DOSAGE
Lozenges— Adults and children age 5 and older: 1 or 2
lozenges 4 to 5 times a day
for up to 14 days. Lozenges
should be allowed to dis-
solve in the mouth, which
may take 15 to 30 minutes.
Do not swallow. Suspen-
sion— Adults and children
age 5 and older: 4 to 6 ml (1
teaspoon), 4 times a day.
Children up to 5 years: 2
ml, 4 times a day. Prema-
ture and low-birth-weight
infants: 1 ml, 4 times a day.
Follow doctor's instructions
for correct use. Cream, ointment, or powder— Adults
and children: Apply to the
affected area 2 to 3 times a
day. Vaginal tablets— Adults
and teenagers: Insert one
100,000-unit tablet into the
vagina 1 or 2 times a day
for 14 days.

ONSET OF EFFECT
Not applicable.

DURATION OF ACTION
Unknown.

DIETARY ADVICE
No special restrictions.

STORAGE
Store in a tightly sealed container away from heat, moisture, and direct light.
Lozenges should be kept in
the refrigerator, but keep
them from freezing.

IF YOU MISS A DOSE
Take it as soon as you
remember. However, if it is
near the time for the next
dose, skip the missed dose
and resume your regular
dosage schedule. Do not
double the next dose.

STOPPING THE DRUG
Take it as prescribed for the
full treatment period, even
if you begin to feel better
before the scheduled end
of therapy. The decision to
stop taking the drug should
be made by your doctor.

PROLONGED USE
Nystatin is generally prescribed for short-term therapy (1 to 3 weeks). Consult
your doctor if your condition does not improve, or
instead becomes worse,
within 1 to 2 weeks of
beginning therapy.

PRECAUTIONS
Over 60: There have been
no specific studies of the
use of nystatin in older
patients.

**Driving and Hazardous
Work:** The use of nystatin
should not impair your ability to perform such tasks
safely.

Alcohol: No special precautions are necessary.

Pregnancy: Adequate studies of use during pregnancy
have not been done. Con-
sult your doctor for specific
advice if you are pregnant
or plan to become pregnant.

Breast Feeding: Nystatin
may pass into breast milk;
caution is advised. Consult
your doctor for specific
advice.

Infants and Children:
The oral suspension should
be used for children up to 5
years of age, rather than
the lozenges. There have

been no specific studies
evaluating the use of the
other forms of nystatin in
children.

Special Concerns:
Patients with dentures may
have to soak them each
night in nystatin to kill the
fungus on the dentures. In
some cases new dentures
may be necessary.

OVERDOSE
Symptoms: Nausea, vomiting, diarrhea.

What to Do: Call your
doctor, emergency medical
services (EMS), or the
nearest poison control center immediately.

DRUG INTERACTIONS
Other drugs may interact
with nystatin. Consult your
doctor for specific advice if
you are taking any other
prescription or over-the-
counter drug.

FOOD INTERACTIONS
None known.

DISEASE INTERACTIONS
Consult your doctor for specific advice if you have any
other medical condition.

Octreotide Acetate

BRAND NAME
Sandostatin

▶ Drug Class: Hormone

▶ Available in: Injection

▶ Available OTC? No

▶ As Generic? No

Side Effects

SERIOUS
High blood sugar levels causing drowsiness, dry mouth, flushed and dry skin, fruity breath odor, increased urination, loss of appetite, severe stomach pain, nausea, or vomiting, rapid and deep breathing, unusual thirst, unusual fatigue, rapid weight loss. Low blood sugar levels causing anxiety, chills, cool and pale skin, difficulty concentrating, headache, nausea, nervousness, shakiness, sweating, unusual fatigue, weakness. Call your doctor immediately.

COMMON
Stomach or abdominal pain or discomfort; diarrhea, nausea and vomiting; pain, stinging, tingling, or burning at injection site; redness and swelling at the site of injection.

LESS COMMON
Dizziness or lightheadedness, unusual fatigue, headache, red or flushed face, swelling of feet and lower legs.

PRINCIPAL USES

To treat severe, chronic diarrhea that occurs with certain intestinal tumors (carcinoid tumors and vasoactive intestinal peptide tumors). Also used to treat acromegaly, a disease caused by the overproduction of human growth hormone during adulthood, and characterized by thick, bulky overgrowth of the bones in the hands, feet, forehead, and face.

HOW THE DRUG WORKS

Octreotide mimics the activity of the hormone somatostatin, which suppresses the release of certain chemicals that trigger diarrhea. The drug does not attack or cure intestinal cancer, but helps ease symptoms, allowing the patient to lead a more normal life. By suppressing the release of human growth hormone, octreotide slows the progression of acromegaly.

DOSAGE

For carcinoid tumor diarrhea: 100 to 600 micrograms (mcg) a day, administered subcutaneously (under the skin) in 2 to 4 doses. For vasoactive intestinal peptide tumors: 200 to 300 mcg a day in 2 to 4 doses. For acromegaly: From 50 to 300 mcg, 3 times a day. The dose is based on body weight.

ONSET OF EFFECT

Within 30 minutes.

DURATION OF ACTION

Up to 12 hours.

DIETARY ADVICE

No restrictions apply.

STORAGE

Store in a tightly sealed container away from heat and direct light. Keep away from moisture and extremes in temperature.

IF YOU MISS A DOSE

Take it as soon as you remember. If it is near the time for the next dose, skip the missed dose and resume your regular dosage schedule. Do not double the next dose.

STOPPING THE DRUG

The decision to stop taking the drug should be made by your doctor.

PROLONGED USE

You should see your doctor regularly for tests and examinations if you take this drug for a prolonged period.

PRECAUTIONS

Over 60: No special problems are expected.

Driving and Hazardous Work: Do not drive or engage in hazardous work until you determine how the medicine affects you.

Alcohol: Avoid alcohol.

Pregnancy: In animal studies, octreotide has not been shown to cause birth defects, even when given at high doses. Human studies have not been done. Consult your doctor for specific advice if you are pregnant or plan to become pregnant.

Breast Feeding: It is not known whether octreotide passes into breast milk; caution is advised. Consult your doctor for specific advice.

Infants and Children: Octreotide has not been shown to cause different side effects in infants and children than it does in other patients.

Special Concerns: Octreotide can cause either high or low blood sugar levels. Blood sugar should be monitored carefully. Follow your doctor's instructions about selecting and rotating injection sites to help prevent skin problems.

OVERDOSE

Symptoms: Very high or very low blood sugar levels.

What to Do: An overdose of octreotide is unlikely to be life-threatening. However, if someone takes a much larger dose than prescribed, call your doctor, emergency medical services (EMS), or the nearest poison control center.

DRUG INTERACTIONS

Consult your doctor for specific advice if you are taking antidiabetic agents such as glucagon or insulin, or growth hormone.

FOOD INTERACTIONS

No known food interactions.

DISEASE INTERACTIONS

Consult your physician if you have diabetes mellitus, gallbladder disease, or gallstones. Use of octreotide may cause complications in patients with kidney disease, since this organ works to remove the medication from the body.

Ofloxacin Ophthalmic

▶ Drug Class: Antibiotic

▶ Available in: Ophthalmic solution

▶ Available OTC? No

▶ As Generic? Yes

Side Effects

SERIOUS
Itching, swelling, hives, difficulty breathing. If these signs of allergy develop, stop using the drug and call your doctor immediately.

COMMON
Burning eyes.

LESS COMMON
Increased sensitivity of eyes to light; stinging, itching, tearing, redness, or drying of the eye.

PRINCIPAL USES
To treat bacterial conjunctivitis (infection of the mucous membranes that line the inner surface of the eyelids and whites of the eyes) or bacterial keratitis (infection of the cornea).

HOW THE DRUG WORKS
Ofloxacin kills bacteria by interfering with genetic material of bacterial cells, thus preventing them from multiplying.

DOSAGE
The exact dosing of ophthalmic ofloxacin varies depending on the nature of the infection and its response to treatment. Follow your doctor's instructions precisely. The following dosing example is for conjunctivitis. Adults and children 1 year of age and older: 1 drop in each eye every 2 to 4 hours, while awake, for 2 days, then 1 drop in each eye 4 times a day for up to 5 days.

ONSET OF EFFECT
Unknown.

DURATION OF ACTION
Unknown.

DIETARY ADVICE
No special restrictions.

STORAGE
Store in a tightly sealed container away from heat, moisture, and direct light. Do not refrigerate or allow it to freeze.

IF YOU MISS A DOSE
Apply it as soon as you remember. If it is near the time for the next dose, skip the missed dose and resume your regular dosage schedule. Do not double the next dose.

STOPPING THE DRUG
Use it as prescribed for the full treatment period, even if you feel better before the scheduled end of therapy.

PROLONGED USE
You should see your doctor regularly for tests and examinations if you take this drug for a prolonged period.

PRECAUTIONS
Over 60: No special problems are expected.

Driving and Hazardous Work: Do not drive or engage in hazardous work until you determine how the medicine affects your vision.

Alcohol: No special precautions are necessary.

Pregnancy: Large doses of ophthalmic ofloxacin have caused birth defects and other problems in animals. Human studies have not been done. Before you take ophthalmic ofloxacin, tell your doctor if you are pregnant or plan to become pregnant.

Breast Feeding: Ophthalmic ofloxacin may pass into breast milk; caution is advised. Consult your doctor for advice.

Infants and Children: Not recommended for use on children under age 1.

Special Concerns: To use the eye drops, first wash your hands. Tilt your head back. Gently apply pressure to the inside corner of the eyelid and with the index finger of the same hand, pull downward on the lower eyelid to make a space. Drop the medicine into this space and close your eye. Apply gentle pressure for 1 or 2 minutes while keeping the eye closed without blinking. Then wash your hands again. Make sure the tip of the dropper does not touch your eye, finger, or any other surface. If your symptoms do not improve in a few days or if they become worse, check with your doctor.

OVERDOSE
Symptoms: No specific ones have been reported.

What to Do: An overdose of ophthalmic ofloxacin is unlikely to be life-threatening. If a large volume enters the eye, flush with water. If someone accidentally ingests the medicine, call your doctor, emergency medical services (EMS), or the nearest poison control center immediately.

DRUG INTERACTIONS
Other drugs may interact with ophthalmic ofloxacin. Consult your doctor for specific advice if you are taking any other prescription or over-the-counter medication.

FOOD INTERACTIONS
No known food interactions.

DISEASE INTERACTIONS
Caution is advised when taking ophthalmic ofloxacin. Consult your physician if you have any other medical condition.

Ofloxacin Oral

Floxin 200 mg
(ORTHO)

Additional photographs

▶ Drug Class: Fluoroquinolone antibiotic

▶ Available in: Tablets

▶ Available OTC? No

▶ As Generic? Yes

Side Effects

SERIOUS
Serious reactions to ofloxacin are rare and include seizures, mental confusion, hallucinations, agitation, nightmares, depression, shortness of breath, unusual swelling in the face or extremities, and loss of consciousness. Also skin burning, redness, blisters, rash, or itching on exposure to sunlight. Call your doctor immediately.

COMMON
Increased sensitivity to sunlight (and increased risk of sunburn) for days following therapy.

LESS COMMON
Diarrhea, nausea and vomiting, stomach pain and upset, gas, headache, dizziness, restlessness, insomnia, changes in taste perception, drowsiness, itching, dry mouth, unusual body aches or pains.

PRINCIPAL USES
To treat mild to severe bacterial infections, including those of the urinary tract, lower respiratory tract (such as pneumonia), and the skin. It is also used to treat certain sexually transmitted diseases (chlamydia and gonorrhea) and prostatitis (infection and inflammation of the prostate).

HOW THE DRUG WORKS
Ofloxacin inhibits the activity of a bacterial enzyme (gyrase) that is necessary for proper DNA formation and replication. This fights infection by preventing bacteria cells from reproducing.

DOSAGE
For most infections: 200 to 400 mg, 2 times a day, for 3 to 10 days. For gonorrhea: 400 mg in a single one-time dose.

ONSET OF EFFECT
Varies depending on the infection being treated.

DURATION OF ACTION
Unknown.

DIETARY ADVICE
Take it on an empty stomach, 1 hour before or 2 hours after meals, with a full glass of water. Drink plenty of fluids.

STORAGE
Store in a tightly sealed container away from heat and direct light.

IF YOU MISS A DOSE
Take it as soon as you remember. If it is near the time for the next dose, skip the missed dose and resume your regular dosage schedule. Do not double the next dose.

STOPPING THE DRUG
Take this antibiotic as prescribed for the full treatment period, even if you begin to feel better before the scheduled end of therapy.

PROLONGED USE
See your doctor regularly for tests and examinations if you must take this medicine for a prolonged period. If your symptoms do not improve or instead get worse in a few days, consult your doctor.

PRECAUTIONS

Over 60: No special problems are expected.

Driving and Hazardous Work: Do not drive or engage in hazardous work until you determine how the medicine affects you.

Alcohol: It is advisable to abstain from alcohol when fighting an infection.

Pregnancy: In some animal tests, ofloxacin has caused birth defects. Adequate studies in humans have not been done. It should be used during pregnancy only if potential benefits clearly justify the risks. Before you take ofloxacin, tell your doctor if you are pregnant or plan to become pregnant.

Breast Feeding: Ofloxacin passes into breast milk and may cause serious side effects in the nursing infant; use of the drug is discouraged when nursing.

Infants and Children: Ofloxacin is generally not recommended for use by persons under the age of 18, as it has been shown to interfere with bone development. But ofloxacin may be used by teenagers and younger persons if no alternative treatment is available.

Special Concerns: If ofloxacin causes unusual sensitivity to sunlight, wear protective clothing, use a sunblock and try to avoid exposure to sunlight, especially between 10 am and 3 pm. Do not take any antacid 2 hours before or 2 hours after taking ofloxacin.

OVERDOSE
Symptoms: Nausea, headache, dizziness, vomiting, drowsiness, seizures.

What to Do: Call your doctor, emergency medical services (EMS), or the nearest poison control center immediately.

DRUG INTERACTIONS
Consult your doctor for specific advice if you are taking aminophylline, antacids, didanosine, iron supplements, sucralfate, or zinc salts. Also tell your doctor if you are taking any other prescription or over-the-counter drug.

FOOD INTERACTIONS
No known food interactions.

DISEASE INTERACTIONS
Consult your doctor if you have any disease of the brain or spinal cord. Use of ofloxacin may cause complications in patients with liver or kidney disease, since these organs work together to remove the medication from the body.

Ofloxacin Otic

BRAND NAME
Floxin Otic

- Drug Class: Antibiotic
- Available in: Otic solution
- Available OTC? No
- As Generic? No

Side Effects

SERIOUS
No serious side effects are associated with the use of ofloxacin.

COMMON
Bitter taste in the mouth.

LESS COMMON
Earache, itching, skin rash, dizziness or light-headedness, discomfort upon application.

PRINCIPAL USES
To treat bacterial infections of the ear canal and the middle ear.

HOW THE DRUG WORKS
Ofloxacin inhibits the activity of a bacterial enzyme (gyrase) that is necessary for proper DNA replication and repair. Inhibition of this enzyme fights infection by preventing bacteria cells from reproducing.

DOSAGE
Ear drops should be administered 2 times a day, 12 hours apart, in the affected ear for 10 days (14 days for adults with chronic middle ear infection). Adults and teenagers should receive 10 drops in the affected ear per dose. Children ages 1 to 12 should receive 5 drops in the affected ear per dose.

ONSET OF EFFECT
Unknown.

DURATION OF ACTION
Unknown.

DIETARY ADVICE
The drug can be applied without regard to diet.

STORAGE
Store in a tightly sealed container away from heat, moisture, and direct light.

IF YOU MISS A DOSE
Instill it as soon as you remember. If it is near the time for the next dose, skip the missed dose and resume your regular dosage schedule. Do not double the next dose unless your physician has instructed you to do otherwise.

STOPPING THE DRUG
Take it as prescribed for the full treatment period, even if your symptoms improve before the scheduled end of therapy.

PROLONGED USE
Ofloxacin is prescribed only for short-term use.

PRECAUTIONS
Over 60: No special problems are expected.

Driving and Hazardous Work: No special precautions are necessary.

Alcohol: No special precautions are necessary.

Pregnancy: Adequate human studies have not been done. Before taking ofloxacin, discuss with your doctor the relative risks and benefits of using this drug while pregnant.

Breast Feeding: It is not known whether ofloxacin passes into breast milk after administration to the ear; caution is advised. Consult your doctor for advice.

Infants and Children: Not recommended for use by children under 1 year of age.

Special Concerns: Gently clean any discharge from the outer ear prior to instilling the drops. Do not insert any object or swab into the ear canal. To use the ear drops, lie down or tilt your head so the infected ear faces up. For middle ear infections, the person instilling the drops should gently press the tragus (the small projection of cartilage in front of the ear canal) 4 times in a pumping motion to aid in the passage of the drops through the eardrum and into the middle ear. For ear canal infections, gently pull the earlobe up and back for adults (down and back for children) to straighten the ear canal. Drop the medicine into the ear. Keep the ear facing upward for 5 minutes after inserting the drops to allow the medicine to flow down into the ear canal and reach the infection. You may insert a cotton ball to prevent the medicine from leaking out. Make sure the applicator for the ear drops does not touch your ear, finger, or any other surface. When bathing, avoid getting the affected ear(s) wet. Avoid swimming unless your doctor has given you permission to do so.

OVERDOSE
Symptoms: An overdose with ofloxacin otic is unlikely to occur.

What to Do: If someone instills a much larger dose than prescribed or accidentally swallows ofloxacin otic, call your doctor.

DRUG INTERACTIONS
Do not take ofloxacin otic if you are allergic to ofloxacin or other fluoroquinolone antibiotics.

FOOD INTERACTIONS
None reported.

DISEASE INTERACTIONS
None reported.

Olanzapine

LILLY
4117

Zyprexa 10 mg
(LILLY)

837
Additional photographs

▶ Drug Class: Neuroleptic; antipsychotic

▶ Available in: Tablets

▶ Available OTC? No

▶ As Generic? No

Side Effects

SERIOUS
Stiffness; shuffling gait; difficulty swallowing or speaking; persistent, uncontrolled chewing, lip-smacking, or tongue movements; fever. Call your doctor immediately.

COMMON
Drowsiness, headache, dizziness, constipation, dry mouth, blurred vision, runny nose.

LESS COMMON
Stomach pain, unclear speech or stuttering, muscle tightness, faintness, increased appetite, increased cough, watering of mouth, insomnia, joint pain, nausea, sore throat, rapid heartbeat, increased thirst, urinary incontinence, vomiting, weight loss.

PRINCIPAL USES
To treat psychotic conditions (severe mental disorders characterized by distorted thoughts, perceptions, and emotions), such as schizophrenia.

HOW THE DRUG WORKS
While the exact mechanism of action of olanzapine is unknown, it appears to alter the activity of certain chemicals in the central nervous system to produce a tranquilizing and antipsychotic effect.

DOSAGE
Initial dose is 5 to 10 mg, once daily. Dose may be increased by your doctor to a maximum of 20 mg a day.

ONSET OF EFFECT
Sedation may occur within minutes, but onset of antipsychotic effect may take hours to occur or may not occur until days or weeks after the beginning of therapy.

DURATION OF ACTION
12 to 24 hours, but effects may persist for several days.

DIETARY ADVICE
No special restrictions.

STORAGE
Store in a tightly sealed container away from heat, moisture, and direct light.

IF YOU MISS A DOSE
Take it as soon as you remember. However, if it is near the time for the next dose, skip the missed dose and resume your regular dosage schedule. Do not double the next dose.

STOPPING THE DRUG
The decision to stop taking the drug should be made in consultation with your physician.

PROLONGED USE
Consult your doctor about the need for follow-up evaluations and tests if you must take this drug for an extended period. Because olanzapine is a recently released drug, its risk of inducing potentially irreversible tardive dyskinesia (involuntary movements of the jaw, lips, tongue, and body) is unknown.

PRECAUTIONS
Over 60: No special problems are expected.

Driving and Hazardous Work: Do not drive or engage in hazardous work until you determine how the medicine affects you.

Alcohol: Avoid alcohol.

Pregnancy: Large doses of olanzapine reduced fetal survival in animal tests. Before you take olanzapine, tell your doctor if you are pregnant or plan to become pregnant.

Breast Feeding: Olanzapine may pass into breast milk; avoid use while breast feeding.

Infants and Children: The safety and effectiveness of olanzapine in children under 18 have not been established.

Special Concerns: Avoid prolonged exposure to high temperatures or hot climates. Drink plenty of fluids and stay cool in the summertime. Avoid overexposure to sunlight until you determine if the drug heightens your skin's sensitivity to ultraviolet light.

OVERDOSE
Symptoms: Extreme drowsiness, slurred speech.

What to Do: Call your doctor, emergency medical services (EMS), or the nearest poison control center immediately.

DRUG INTERACTIONS
The following drugs may interact with olanzapine. Consult your doctor for specific advice if you are taking carbamazepine, omeprazole, rifampin, high blood pressure medication, or any drugs that depress the central nervous system, including antihistamines, antidepressants or other psychiatric medications, barbiturates, sedatives, cough medicines, decongestants, and painkillers. Be sure your doctor knows about any over-the-counter medication you may take.

FOOD INTERACTIONS
No known food interactions.

DISEASE INTERACTIONS
Consult your doctor if you have Parkinson's disease or any movement disorder, glaucoma, epilepsy, liver disease, or kidney disease.

Olanzapine/Fluoxetine

▶ Drug Class: Neuroleptic/SSRI antidepressant combination

▶ Available in: Capsules

▶ Available OTC? No

▶ As Generic? No

Side Effects

SERIOUS
Stroke; diabetes mellitus; persistent, uncontrolled chewing, lip-smacking, or tongue movements (tardive dyskinesia); hypotension; seizures; impaired judgment, thinking, and motor skills; difficulty swallowing; abnormal bleeding; decreased salt levels in the blood; body temperature problems; activation of mania/hypomania.

COMMON
Weight gain, drowsiness, diarrhea, dry mouth, increased appetite, feeling of weakness, swelling of the hands or feet, tremor, sore throat, trouble concentrating, body temperature problems.

LESS COMMON
Fever, hypertension, joint pain, insomnia, indigestion, ear pain.

PRINCIPAL USES
To treat depressive episodes that are associated with bipolar disorder.

HOW THE DRUG WORKS
The olanzapine/fluoxetine combination is thought to activate three chemicals in the brain (serotonin, norepinephrine, and dopamine), which results in an enhanced antidepressant effect.

DOSAGE
Adults: 1 capsule (consisting of 6 mg olanzapine and 25 mg fluoxetine) a day in the evening. If necessary, your doctor may increase the dosage to 2 capsules a day.

ONSET OF EFFECT
Sedation may occur within minutes, but onset of antidepressant effect may take days or weeks after the beginning of therapy.

DURATION OF ACTION
Unknown.

DIETARY ADVICE
No special restrictions.

STORAGE
Store in a tightly sealed container away from heat, moisture, and direct light.

IF YOU MISS A DOSE
Take it as soon as you remember. However, if it is near the time for the next dose, skip the missed dose and resume your regular dosage schedule. Do not double the next dose.

STOPPING THE DRUG
The decision to stop taking the drug should be made in consultation with your physician.

PROLONGED USE
Consult your doctor about the need for follow-up evaluations and tests if you must take this drug for an extended period.

PRECAUTIONS
Over 60: Adverse reactions may be more likely and more severe in older patients, since their metabolism is slower.

Driving and Hazardous Work: Do not drive or engage in hazardous work until you determine how the medicine affects you.

Alcohol: Avoid alcohol.

Pregnancy: This drug should be used during pregnancy only if the potential benefit justifies the potential risk to the fetus. Before you take this medicine, tell your doctor if you are pregnant or plan to become pregnant.

Breast Feeding: This drug may pass into breast milk; avoid use while breast feeding.

Infants and Children: The safety and effectiveness of this medication in children under 18 have not been established. Antidepressants used for any indication increase the risk of suicidal thinking and behavior (suicidality) in children with major depression and other psychiatric disorders. Discuss with your doctor this risk versus the benefits of using this drug. Children should be observed closely for worsening of symptoms, suicidality, or unusual changes in behavior at the onset of therapy and when making changes in dosage.

Special Concerns: Avoid prolonged exposure to high temperatures or hot climates. Drink plenty of fluids and stay cool in the summertime. Avoid overexposure to sunlight until you determine if the drug heightens your skin's sensitivity to ultraviolet light.

OVERDOSE
Symptoms: Few cases of overdose have been reported. However, symptoms may include agitation, excitement, severe nausea and vomiting, seizures, extreme drowsiness, slurred speech.

What to Do: Seek emergency medical help.

DRUG INTERACTIONS
This medication should not be used within 5 weeks of taking MAO inhibitors or thioridazine. Consult your doctor for specific advice if you are taking nortriptyline, caffeine, oral anticoagulants, central nervous system depressants, digitalis preparations, lithium, loratadine, dextromethorphan, ketorolac, buspirone, phenytoin, trazodone, tryptophan, sumatriptan, naratriptan, zolmitriptan, carbamazepine, omeprazole, rifampin, high blood pressure medication, or any drugs that depress the central nervous system, including antihistamines, antidepressants or other psychiatric medications, barbiturates, sedatives, cough medicines, decongestants, and painkillers. Be sure your doctor knows about any over-the-counter medication you may take.

FOOD INTERACTIONS
No known food interactions.

DISEASE INTERACTIONS
Consult your doctor if you have Parkinson's disease or any movement disorder, strokes or ministrokes (TIAs), glaucoma, enlarged prostate (men), epilepsy, hyper- or hypotension, paralytic ileus, liver disease, or kidney disease. Use of the medication may make diabetes or seizures worse.

Olmesartan Medoxomil

▶ Drug Class: Antihypertensive/angiotensin II antagonist

▶ Available in: Tablets

▶ Available OTC? No

▶ As Generic? No

Side Effects

SERIOUS
No serious side effects are associated with the use of olmesartan. (In clinical trials, the incidence of adverse effects was not significantly greater with the medication than with a placebo.)

COMMON
No common side effects are associated with the use of olmesartan.

LESS COMMON
Back pain, bronchitis, diarrhea, headache, blood in the urine, high blood sugar levels (diabetes), increased triglyceride levels, flu-like symptoms, runny nose, sinusitis, throat infection.

PRINCIPAL USES
To control high blood pressure. This drug appears to have the same benefits as the class of antihypertensive drugs known as ACE inhibitors, without producing the common side effect of a dry cough (experienced by as many as 30% of patients). Olmesartan may be used by itself or in conjunction with other antihypertensive medications.

HOW THE DRUG WORKS
Olmesartan blocks the effects of angiotensin II, a naturally occurring substance that causes blood vessels to narrow. Olmesartan causes the blood vessels to dilate, thereby lowering blood pressure and decreasing the workload of the heart.

DOSAGE
To start, 20 mg once a day when used as the only drug to treat hypertension. Usual maintenance dose is 20 to 40 mg daily.

ONSET OF EFFECT
Unknown.

DURATION OF ACTION
Unknown

DIETARY ADVICE
No special restrictions, unless your doctor has advised a low-sodium diet or other dietary modifications to help you control your blood pressure.

STORAGE
Store in a tightly sealed container away from heat, moisture, and direct light.

IF YOU MISS A DOSE
Take it as soon as you remember. If it is near the time for the next dose, skip the missed dose and resume your regular dosage schedule. Do not double the next dose.

STOPPING THE DRUG
Take it as prescribed for the full treatment period. The decision to stop taking the drug should be made in consultation with your physician.

PROLONGED USE
Lifelong therapy may be necessary. However, if you do change certain health habits (for example, increasing exercise or losing weight), a reduced dose may be possible under a doctor's supervision.

PRECAUTIONS
Over 60: No special problems are expected.

Driving and Hazardous Work: Do not drive or engage in hazardous work until you determine how the medicine affects you.

Alcohol: No special precautions are necessary.

Pregnancy: Olmesartan should not be used by pregnant women. Discontinue taking the drug as soon as possible when pregnancy is detected and discuss treatment alternatives with your doctor.

Breast Feeding: Olmesartan may pass into breast milk; caution is advised. Consult your doctor for specific advice.

Infants and Children: The safety and effectiveness of use in children have not been established.

Special Concerns: Olmesartan may cause excessively low blood pressure with dizziness or lightheadedness, which is most noticeable when you change position. This may lead to fainting, falls, and injury. Sit or lie down immediately if you feel dizzy or lightheaded. This side effect may be worsened by alcohol, hot weather, dehydration, salt depletion from diuretic use, fever, prolonged standing, prolonged sitting, or exercise.

OVERDOSE
Symptoms: Few cases of overdose have been reported. However, if you take a much larger dose than prescribed, you may experience fainting, dizziness, weak pulse that might be very slow or very fast.

What to Do: Call your doctor, emergency medical services (EMS), or the nearest poison control center immediately.

DRUG INTERACTIONS
No drug interactions have yet been observed with olmesartan. Consult your doctor for specific advice if you are taking any other medication, potassium supplements or potassium-sparing diuretics. Olmesartan can be taken together with diuretics or other medications for high blood pressure, if your doctor approves.

FOOD INTERACTIONS
No known food interactions.

DISEASE INTERACTIONS
Patients with liver or kidney disease are advised to exercise caution when taking olmesartan.

Olopatadine

▶ Drug Class: Antihistamine

▶ Available in: Ophthalmic solution

▶ Available OTC? No

▶ As Generic? No

Side Effects

SERIOUS
No serious side effects are associated with olopatadine.

COMMON
Headache; temporary burning and stinging of the eye.

LESS COMMON
Dry eyes, sensation of something in the eye, vomiting, swollen eyelids, itching of eyes.

PRINCIPAL USES
For temporary relief of itching of the eye due to allergic conjunctivitis (inflammation of the mucous membranes that line the inner surface of the eyelids and whites of the eyes).

HOW THE DRUG WORKS
Olopatadine inhibits the release and blocks the effects of histamine, a substance that causes swelling, itching, sneezing, watery eyes, hives, and other symptoms of allergic reaction.

DOSAGE
1 drop in each affected eye every 6 to 8 hours as needed.

ONSET OF EFFECT
Immediate.

DURATION OF ACTION
6 to 8 hours.

DIETARY ADVICE
No special restrictions.

STORAGE
Store in a tightly sealed container away from heat, moisture, and direct light. Do not allow it to freeze.

IF YOU MISS A DOSE
Apply the next dose as needed; do not double the next dose.

STOPPING THE DRUG
This medication is to be used as needed for relief of itching associated with allergic inflammation. If you are not experiencing symptoms, do not apply the medication.

PROLONGED USE
See your doctor regularly for tests and examinations if you must take this drug for a prolonged period.

PRECAUTIONS
Over 60: No special problems are expected.

Driving and Hazardous Work: Do not drive or engage in hazardous work until you determine how the medicine affects your vision.

Alcohol: Avoid alcohol.

Pregnancy: In animal studies, large doses of olopatadine did not cause birth defects. Human studies have not been done. Olopatadine should be used by pregnant women only if the potential benefit to the mother justifies the potential risk to the embryo or fetus. Consult your doctor for specific advice.

Breast Feeding: Olopatadine may pass into breast milk; caution is advised. Consult your doctor for advice.

Infants and Children: The safety and effectiveness of olopatadine in infants and children under the age of 3 have not been established.

Special Concerns: To use the eye drops, first wash your hands. Tilt your head back. Gently apply pressure to the inside corner of the eyelid and with the index finger of the same hand, pull downward on the lower eyelid to make a space. Drop the medicine into this space and close your eye. Apply pressure for 1 or 2 minutes while keeping the eye closed without blinking. Then wash your hands again. Make sure the tip of the dropper does not touch your eye, finger, or any other surface. If you use contact lenses, you should not wear them while administering olopatadine.

OVERDOSE
Symptoms: No specific ones have been reported.

What to Do: An overdose of olopatadine is unlikely to be life-threatening. However, if someone applies a much larger dose than prescribed or accidentally ingests the medicine, call your doctor, emergency medical services (EMS), or the nearest poison control center immediately.

DRUG INTERACTIONS
Other drugs may interact with olopatadine. Consult your doctor for specific advice if you are taking any other medication.

FOOD INTERACTIONS
No known food interactions.

DISEASE INTERACTIONS
Caution is advised when taking olopatadine. Consult your doctor if you have any medical condition, especially one affecting the eyes.

Olsalazine Sodium

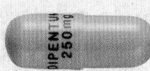

Dipentum 250 mg
(PHARMACIA)

▶ Drug Class: Gastrointestinal anti-inflammatory

▶ Available in: Capsules

▶ Available OTC? No

▶ As Generic? No

Side Effects

SERIOUS
Severe pain in the back or stomach, bloody diarrhea, rapid heartbeat, fever, nausea or vomiting, rash, abdominal swelling or stiffness, yellowish tinge to the eyes or skin (jaundice). Call your doctor immediately if such symptoms occur.

COMMON
Abdominal pain or upset; an increase in the number of loose stools; diarrhea; loss of appetite.

LESS COMMON
Joint and muscle pain, acne, depression or anxiety, dizziness, drowsiness, headache, insomnia, skin sensitivity to sunlight, bruising, bleeding in the intestinal tract causing bloody stools.

PRINCIPAL USES
The first line of drug therapy for ulcerative colitis is usually sulfasalazine, but some patients cannot take it because of intolerable side effects. Olsalazine is a chemically similar drug that can be given instead to such patients. It is generally prescribed as maintenance therapy for those who have ulcerative colitis in a state of remission (absence of recent symptom flareups).

HOW THE DRUG WORKS
The exact mechanism of action is uncertain, although it appears that olsalazine inhibits production of substances such as arachidonic acid that produce inflammation in the digestive tract.

DOSAGE
500 mg, 2 times a day.

ONSET OF EFFECT
Unknown.

DURATION OF ACTION
Unknown.

DIETARY ADVICE
Olsalazine should be taken with meals to minimize stomach upset. If stomach or intestinal problems persist, consult your doctor.

STORAGE
Store in a tightly sealed container away from heat and direct light.

IF YOU MISS A DOSE
Take it as soon as you remember, but only with meals. If it is near the time for the next dose, skip the missed dose and resume your regular dosage schedule. Do not double the next dose.

STOPPING THE DRUG
Take it as prescribed for the full treatment period, even if you begin to feel better before the end of therapy.

PROLONGED USE
You should see your doctor regularly for tests and examinations if you must take this drug for a prolonged period.

PRECAUTIONS
Over 60: Olsalazine is not expected to cause different problems in older persons than in younger patients.

Driving and Hazardous Work: Do not drive or engage in hazardous work until you determine how the medicine affects you.

Alcohol: Avoid alcohol when taking this drug.

Pregnancy: Large doses of olsalazine have been shown to cause birth defects in animals. Human studies have not been done. The drug should be used during pregnancy only if its benefits clearly outweigh the potential risks. Before you take olsalazine, be sure to tell your doctor if you are pregnant or plan to become pregnant.

Breast Feeding: Olsalazine may pass into breast milk; caution is advised. In animal studies, olsalazine has been shown to cause slowed growth and other problems during nursing. Consult your doctor for specific advice about stopping breast feeding or switching to another drug.

Infants and Children: There is no information comparing use of olsalazine in infants and children with other age groups. Use and dosage must be determined by your pediatrician.

OVERDOSE
Symptoms: No cases of overdose with olsalazine have been reported.

What to Do: While an overdose is unlikely, call your doctor, emergency medical services (EMS), or the nearest poison control center immediately if you suspect someone has taken a dose much larger than prescribed.

DRUG INTERACTIONS
Consult your doctor for advice if you are taking any other prescription or over-the-counter medication. Olsalazine should not be used by patients who have had prior allergic reactions to aspirin or other salicylate drugs.

FOOD INTERACTIONS
No known food interactions.

DISEASE INTERACTIONS
Caution is advised when taking olsalazine. Consult your doctor if you have high blood pressure or kidney disease.

Omeprazole

Prilosec 20 mg
(ASTRA MERCK)

▶ Drug Class: Antacid/proton pump inhibitor

▶ Available in: Capsules

▶ Available OTC? Yes

▶ As Generic? Yes

Side Effects

SERIOUS
No serious side effects are associated with this medication.

COMMON
Diarrhea, constipation, vomiting, headache, dizziness, stomach pain. Consult your physician if such side effects persist or interfere with daily activities.

LESS COMMON
Bloody or cloudy urine, persistent or recurring sores or ulcers in the mouth, painful or very frequent urination, sore throat, fever, unusual bruising or bleeding, unusual weakness or tiredness, muscle pain, chest pain, nausea. Consult your doctor if such symptoms occur.

PRINCIPAL USES
To treat duodenal (intestinal) ulcers, as well as conditions that cause increased stomach acid production (such as Zollinger-Ellison syndrome), erosive esophagitis (severe, chronic inflammation of the esophagus), and gastroesophageal reflux (backwash of stomach acid into the esophagus, resulting in heartburn).

HOW THE DRUG WORKS
Omeprazole blocks the action of a specific enzyme in the cells that line the stomach, thereby decreasing the production of stomach acid. Reduction of stomach acid promotes healing of ulcers.

DOSAGE
For duodenal ulcer, esophagitis, or gastroesophageal reflux: 20 mg per day. For Zollinger-Ellison syndrome or similar conditions: 60 mg per day.

ONSET OF EFFECT
Within 1 to 3 hours.

DURATION OF ACTION
At least 72 hours.

DIETARY ADVICE
Take omeprazole immediately before a meal. Capsules should be swallowed whole.

STORAGE
Store in a tightly sealed container away from heat and direct light.

IF YOU MISS A DOSE
Take it as soon as you remember. If it is near the time for the next dose, skip the missed dose and resume your regular dosage schedule. Do not double the next dose.

STOPPING THE DRUG
Take it as prescribed for the full treatment period, even if you begin to feel better before the scheduled end of therapy. The decision to stop taking the drug should be made by your doctor.

PROLONGED USE
Omeprazole should not be used indefinitely as maintenance therapy for duodenal ulcer or esophagitis; it is generally taken for a limited period of 4 to 8 weeks. Do not take it for a longer period unless instructed to do so by your doctor. See your doctor regularly for tests and examinations if you must take this drug for an extended period of time.

PRECAUTIONS
Over 60: No specific problems for older people have been reported.

Driving and Hazardous Work: Do not drive or engage in hazardous activities until you determine how the drug affects you.

Alcohol: Avoid alcohol while taking this medication, as it may aggravate your condition.

Pregnancy: In animal tests, omeprazole has not caused problems. Human tests have not been done. Before you take omeprazole, tell your doctor if you are pregnant or plan to become pregnant.

Breast Feeding: Omeprazole may pass into breast milk; caution is advised. Consult your doctor for advice.

Infants and Children: Use and dose for anyone under 18 should be determined by your doctor or pediatrician.

Special Concerns: Tell any doctor or dentist whom you see for treatment that you are taking omeprazole. Do not chew the capsules. If you have trouble swallowing them, you may open them and sprinkle the contents on applesauce or similar food. If your doctor directs, you may take an antacid along with omeprazole.

OVERDOSE
Symptoms: Blurred vision, confusion, profuse sweating, drowsiness, dry mouth, flushing of the face, headache, nausea, palpitations or unusually rapid heartbeat.

What to Do: Call your doctor, emergency medical services (EMS), or the nearest poison control center immediately.

DRUG INTERACTIONS
The following drugs may interact with omeprazole. Consult your doctor for specific advice if you are taking: ampicillin, sucralfate, iron salts or supplements, cyclosporine, diazepam, disulfiram, ketoconazole, phenytoin, or theophylline.

FOOD INTERACTIONS
No significant food interactions have been reported.

DISEASE INTERACTIONS
Caution is advised when taking omeprazole. Consult your doctor if you have liver disease, since it may increase the risk of side effects.

Ondansetron Hydrochloride

BRAND NAME
Zofran

▶ Drug Class: Antiemetic

▶ Available in: Tablets, oral solution, injection

▶ Available OTC? No

▶ As Generic? No

Side Effects

SERIOUS
Chest pain, shortness of breath, skin rash, itching or hives, troubled breathing, tightness in chest, wheezing. Call your doctor immediately.

COMMON
Constipation or diarrhea, fever, headache.

LESS COMMON
Abdominal pain, stomach cramps, dizziness or lightheadedness, dry mouth, unusual fatigue or weakness.

PRINCIPAL USES
To prevent nausea and vomiting that may occur after surgery or after treatment with anticancer medicine or radiation.

HOW THE DRUG WORKS
Ondansetron interferes with the chemical receptor sites and nerve pathways involved in the mechanisms that stimulate feelings of nausea and that induce vomiting.

DOSAGE
Tablets and oral solution— To prevent nausea and vomiting after anticancer medicine: Adults and teenagers: 8 mg or 2 teaspoons, 30 minutes before anticancer medicine is given, followed by 8 mg or 2 teaspoons, 8 hours after the first dose, then 8 mg or 2 teaspoons every 12 hours for 1 to 2 days. Children ages 4 to 12: 4 mg or 1 teaspoon, 30 minutes before anticancer medicine is given, followed by 4 mg or 1 teaspoon, 4 and 8 hours later, then 4 mg or 1 teaspoon every 8 hours for 1 to 2 days. To prevent nausea and vomiting after surgery: 16 mg or 4 teaspoons, 1 hour before anesthesia. To prevent nausea and vomiting after radiation treatment: 8 mg or 2 teaspoons, 1 to 2 hours before undergoing treatment; 8 mg or 2 teaspoons every 8 hours each day that radiation treatment is administered. Injection— To prevent nausea and vomiting after anticancer medicine: Adults: 32 mg (or 68 micrograms [mcg] per lb of body weight) into a vein over 15 minutes starting 30 minutes before an anticancer drug is given. Inject again 4 hours and then 8 hours after the initial dose. Children ages 4 to 18: 68 mcg per lb of body weight into a vein over 15 minutes starting 30 minutes before the anticancer medicine is given. To prevent nausea and vomiting after surgery: 4 mg into a vein or muscle from 30 seconds to 5 minutes before anesthesia.

ONSET OF EFFECT
Unknown.

DURATION OF ACTION
Unknown.

DIETARY ADVICE
Take the tablets with food.

STORAGE
Store in a tightly sealed container away from heat, moisture, and direct light.

IF YOU MISS A DOSE
Take it as soon as you remember. If it is near the time for the next dose, skip the missed dose and resume your regular dosage schedule. Do not double the next dose.

STOPPING THE DRUG
The decision to stop taking the drug should be made by your doctor.

PROLONGED USE
You should see your doctor regularly for tests and examinations if you take this medicine for a prolonged period.

PRECAUTIONS
Over 60: This drug has not been shown to cause different side effects or problems in older patients.

Driving and Hazardous Work: Do not drive or engage in hazardous work until you determine how the medicine affects you.

Alcohol: Avoid alcohol.

Pregnancy: Adequate human studies have not been completed. Before taking ondansetron, tell your doctor if you are pregnant or plan to become pregnant.

Breast Feeding: Ondansetron may pass into breast milk; caution is advised. Consult your doctor for advice.

Infants and Children: The dosage for children up to the age of 4 must be determined by your doctor.

OVERDOSE
Symptoms: No specific ones have been reported.

What to Do: An overdose of ondansetron is unlikely to be life-threatening. However, if someone takes a much larger dose than prescribed, call your doctor, emergency medical services (EMS), or the nearest poison control center.

DRUG INTERACTIONS
Consult your doctor for specific advice if you are taking drugs that alter liver function, such as phenobarbital or cimetidine. They may interact with ondansetron.

FOOD INTERACTIONS
No known food interactions.

DISEASE INTERACTIONS
Caution is advised when taking ondansetron. Consult your doctor if you have had recent abdominal surgery or have liver disease.

Orlistat

PRINCIPAL USES

To achieve weight loss and weight maintenance in the maintenance of obesity when used in conjunction with a reduced-calorie diet and appropriate physical activity. Orlistat is indicated for patients with an initial body mass index (BMI) of 30 or greater and in those with a BMI greater than 27 (see Special Concerns for information on BMI calculation) who also have other risk factors such as high blood pressure, high blood cholesterol, and diabetes.

HOW THE DRUG WORKS

Orlistat inhibits the activity of lipases, intestinal enzymes required for the digestion of dietary fats. Orlistat prevents the breakdown of a portion of ingested fat. The undigested fat cannot be absorbed and is excreted in the feces. Full doses of orlistat reduce the absorption of fat by about 30%.

DOSAGE

120 mg (one capsule) 3 times a day at mealtime.

ONSET OF EFFECT

Within 24 to 48 hours.

DURATION OF ACTION

48 to 72 hours.

DIETARY ADVICE

Take with liquid during or up to one hour after each main meal containing fat. Follow a balanced, reduced-calorie diet. The daily intake of fat (approximately ⅓ of the calories), carbohydrate, and protein should be spread out over the three meals. If a meal is missed or contains no fat, the dose of orlistat can be skipped. Because orlistat can also reduce the absorption of fat-soluble vitamins, a multivitamin supplement (containing vitamins A, D, and E and beta-carotene) should also

be taken once a day at least two hours before or after ingesting orlistat.

STORAGE

Store in a tightly sealed container away from heat, moisture, and direct light.

IF YOU MISS A DOSE

If you miss a dose, take it if you remember within 1 hour of eating. However, if more than 1 hour has passed, skip the missed dose and return to your regular schedule. Do not double the next dose.

STOPPING THE DRUG

The decision to stop taking the drug should be made in consultation with your physician.

PROLONGED USE

The safety and effectiveness of orlistat have not been determined beyond 2 years of use.

PRECAUTIONS

Over 60: No specific studies have been done on older patients.

Driving and Hazardous Work: No special warnings.

Alcohol: No special precautions are necessary.

Pregnancy: Adequate human studies have not been done. Before taking orlistat, tell your doctor if you are pregnant or plan to become pregnant.

Breast Feeding: It is unknown whether orlistat passes into breast milk. However, do not take the drug while nursing. Consult your doctor for advice.

Infants and Children: Safety and effectiveness have not been established for children under age 18.

Special Concerns: A medical cause for obesity (such as hypothyroidism) should be ruled out before taking orlistat. Consult your doctor or a nutritionist for information on a nutritionally-balanced, reduced-calorie diet and an exercise program. The BMI can be calculated by dividing your weight in pounds by your height in inches squared, and then multiplying by 705.

OVERDOSE

Symptoms: No cases of overdose have been reported.

What to Do: An overdose with orlistat is unlikely. If someone takes a much larger dose than prescribed, call your doctor.

DRUG INTERACTIONS

The following drugs may interact with orlistat. Consult your doctor for specific advice if you are taking: cyclosporine, statin (cholesterol-lowering) drugs, warfarin, another weight-loss medication (such as sibutramine or phentermine), or any other prescription or over-the-counter drugs.

FOOD INTERACTIONS

Orlistat reduces the absorption of fat-soluble vitamins A, D, E, and K and beta-carotene. Gastrointestinal side effects may increase following the consumption of high-fat foods or with a diet high in fat (more than 30% of the day's total calories from fat).

DISEASE INTERACTIONS

This drug should not be used if you have chronic malabsorption or gallbladder problems. Consult your doctor if you have an eating disorder (anorexia or bulimia).

Orphenadrine Citrate

BRAND NAMES
Antiflex, Banflex,
Flexoject, Mio-Rel,
Myolin, Myotrol, Norflex,
Orfro, Orphenate

▶ Drug Class: Muscle relaxant

▶ Available in: Extended-
release tablets, injection

▶ Available OTC? No

▶ As Generic? Yes

Side Effects

SERIOUS
Fainting; palpitations or
rapid heartbeat; fever;
hives and severe swelling
of face, lips, or tongue
along with shortness of
breath, chest tightness,
or wheezing (indicating a
potentially life-threatening allergic reaction); low
blood counts. Seek med-
ical help immediately.

COMMON
Dry mouth, drowsiness,
dizziness.

LESS COMMON
Inability to pass urine;
sores on lips, ulcers in
mouth; abdominal
cramps or pain; clumsi-
ness; unsteady gait; con-
fusion; constipation;
diarrhea; nervousness or
irritability; flushing or
redness of face;
headache; heartburn; hic-
cups; muscle weakness;
nausea and vomiting;
trembling; insomnia or
fitful sleep; burning, red
eyes; stuffy nose.

PRINCIPAL USES
To relieve the stiffness,
pain, and discomfort caused
by sprains and strains, muscle spasms, or other muscle
problems; sometimes used
to ease the trembling associated with Parkinson's disease. Orphenadrine may be
prescribed in conjunction
with other treatment
methods, such as physical
therapy.

HOW THE DRUG WORKS
Orphenadrine depresses
activity in the central nervous system (brain and
spinal cord), which in turn
interferes with the transmission of nerve impulses
from the spinal cord to
the muscles.

DOSAGE
Adults and teenagers—
Extended-release tablets:
100 mg, 2 times a day, in
the morning and evening.
Injection: 60 mg injected
into a muscle or vein every
12 hours as needed. Chil-
dren— Use and dosage
must be determined by
your doctor.

ONSET OF EFFECT
With tablets, 1 hour; with
injection, 5 minutes.

DURATION OF ACTION
More than 6 hours.

DIETARY ADVICE
It can be taken with or
between meals. To avoid
dry mouth, maintain ade-
quate fluid intake and suck
on ice chips if desired.

STORAGE
Store in a tightly sealed container away from heat and
direct light.

IF YOU MISS A DOSE
Take it as soon as you
remember. If it is near the
time for the next dose, skip
the missed dose and
resume your regular dosage
schedule. Do not double the
next dose.

STOPPING THE DRUG
The decision to stop taking
the drug should be made by
your doctor.

PROLONGED USE
See your doctor regularly
for tests and examinations if
you must take this drug for
a prolonged period.

PRECAUTIONS
Over 60: There is no specific information comparing
use of orphenadrine in older
patients with use in younger
persons.

**Driving and Hazardous
Work:** Avoid such activities
until you determine how the
medicine affects you.

Alcohol: Avoid alcohol
while taking this drug
because it may compound
the sedative effect and may
cause liver damage.

Pregnancy: Orphenadrine
has not been reported to
cause problems in preg-
nancy. Before you take
orphenadrine, tell your doctor if you are pregnant or
plan to become pregnant.

Breast Feeding: Orphenadrine may pass into breast
milk but has not been
reported to cause problems
in nursing babies. Consult
your doctor for advice.

Infants and Children:
There is no specific information comparing use of
orphenadrine in infants and
children with use in older
persons.

Special Concerns: If dry
mouth occurs, use sugarless
candy or gum, bits of ice, or
a saliva substitute. If dry
mouth persists for more
than 2 weeks, consult your
dentist. Do not take
orphenadrine if you are
allergic to any other skeletal
muscle relaxant. Orphen-
adrine will intensify the
effect of alcohol, sedatives,
and other central nervous
system depressants.

OVERDOSE
Symptoms: Heart rhythm
disturbances, changes in
mental state, drowsiness,
seizures, pale or clammy
skin, diminished urine output, loss of consciousness.

What to Do: Call your
doctor, emergency medical
services (EMS), or the
nearest poison control
center immediately.

DRUG INTERACTIONS
Consult your doctor for specific advice if you are taking
tricyclic antidepressants or
drugs that depress the central nervous system.

FOOD INTERACTIONS
No known food interactions.

DISEASE INTERACTIONS
Consult your doctor if you
have a history of any of the
following: disease of the
digestive tract, enlarged
prostate, rapid or irregular
heartbeat, glaucoma, myasthenia gravis, urinary tract
blockage, heart disease, or
kidney or liver disease.

Oseltamivir Phosphate

▶ Drug Class: Antiviral

▶ Available in: Capsules, oral suspension

▶ Available OTC? No

▶ As Generic? No

Side Effects

SERIOUS
No serious side effects are associated with oseltamivir.

COMMON
Nausea and vomiting.

LESS COMMON
Bronchitis, insomnia, dizziness.

PRINCIPAL USES
To treat and prevent infection from influenza type A or B. Oseltamivir can reduce the severity of symptoms and shorten the duration of flu episodes.

HOW THE DRUG WORKS
Oseltamivir is believed to interfere with the synthesis of the viral enzyme neuraminidase, which is needed in order for the virus to infect cells in the respiratory tract and elsewhere in the body. The drug affects only certain susceptible strains of the influenza type A or B viruses.

DOSAGE
For treatment— Adults and teenagers: 75 mg twice a day for 5 days. Treatment should be initiated as soon as possible, and no longer than 2 days after the onset of signs or symptoms of the flu. Children 12 and under: Consult your pediatrician. For prevention— Adults and teenagers: 75 mg once a day for 7 days. Therapy should be initiated within 2 days of exposure. For prevention during a community outbreak, 75 mg once a day for up to 6 weeks.

ONSET OF EFFECT
Unknown.

DURATION OF ACTION
Unknown.

DIETARY ADVICE
No special restrictions.

STORAGE
Store in a tightly sealed container away from heat, moisture, and direct light. Do not allow oral suspension to freeze.

IF YOU MISS A DOSE
Take it as soon as you remember. If it is near (within 2 hours) the time for the next dose, skip the missed dose and resume your regular dosage schedule. Do not double the next dose.

STOPPING THE DRUG
It is important to take oseltamivir for the full treatment period as prescribed. Do not stop taking the drug before the scheduled end of therapy even if you begin to feel better, as this may lead to a relapse.

PROLONGED USE
If your symptoms do not improve or if they become worse in a few days, consult your doctor.

PRECAUTIONS
Over 60: No special problems are expected.

Driving and Hazardous Work: Do not drive or engage in hazardous work until you determine how the medicine affects you.

Alcohol: No special precautions are necessary.

Pregnancy: Adequate studies have not been completed. Discuss with your doctor the relative risks and benefits of using this drug while pregnant.

Breast Feeding: Oseltamivir may pass into breast milk, although it is unknown if this poses any risks to the nursing infant. Consult your doctor for specific advice.

Infants and Children: The safety and effectiveness of this drug for treatment have not been established for children under the age of 1. The safety and effectiveness of this drug for prevention have not been established for children under the age of 13.

Special Concerns: This medication is not a substitute for a flu shot. Continue to receive your annual flu shot. Shake the oral suspension well before use.

OVERDOSE
Symptoms: No cases have been reported. However, nausea and vomiting are likely symptoms.

What to Do: If you have any reason to suspect an overdose, call your doctor, emergency medical services (EMS), or the nearest poison control center.

DRUG INTERACTIONS
No drug interactions have been reported.

FOOD INTERACTIONS
No known food interactions.

DISEASE INTERACTIONS
The dose of oseltamivir should be lowered in patients with significant kidney disease. Safety has not been determined in people with liver disease.

Oxacillin

▶ Drug Class: Penicillin antibiotic

▶ Available in: Capsules, oral suspension, injection

▶ Available OTC? No

▶ As Generic? Yes

Side Effects

SERIOUS
Irregular or fast breathing, fever, joint pain, lightheadedness, fainting, severely decreased urination, severe or bloody diarrhea, puffiness of face, redness of skin, shortness of breath, severe rash, hives, and itching, depression, unusual bleeding or bruising, yellow discoloration of the eyes or skin. Call your doctor immediately.

COMMON
Rash, mild diarrhea, nausea, vomiting, headache, sore tongue, sore mouth, vaginal discharge and itching, white patches in mouth.

LESS COMMON
Diminished urine output, chills, weakness, fatigue.

PRINCIPAL USES
To treat a variety of bacterial infections, especially those caused by staphylococcus bacteria. Oxacillin is effective only against infections caused by bacteria; it is ineffective against those caused by viruses, fungi, or other microorganisms.

HOW THE DRUG WORKS
Oxacillin blocks the formation of bacterial cell walls, rendering bacteria unable to multiply and spread.

DOSAGE
Oral forms— Adults and children weighing more than 88 lbs: 500 to 1,000 mg every 4 to 6 hours. Children up to 88 lbs: 5.7 to 11.4 mg per lb of body weight every 6 hours. Injection— Adults and children weighing more than 88 lbs: 250 to 1,000 mg every 4 to 6 hours. Children under 88 lbs: 5.7 to 11.4 mg per lb of body weight every 4 to 6 hours. Infants: 2.8 mg per lb of body weight every 6 hours.

ONSET OF EFFECT
Immediate after I.V. injection; unknown for other forms.

DURATION OF ACTION
Unknown.

DIETARY ADVICE
Oral doses should be given at least 1 hour before or 2 hours after meals.

STORAGE
Store in a tightly sealed container away from heat and direct light. Liquid forms can be refrigerated but not frozen.

IF YOU MISS A DOSE
Take it as soon as you remember. If it is near the time for the next dose, skip the missed dose and resume your regular dosage schedule. Do not double the next dose.

STOPPING THE DRUG
Take it as prescribed for the full treatment period, even if you begin to feel better before the scheduled end of therapy. Stopping the drug prematurely may slow your recovery or lead to a rebound infection, also known as superinfection, in which the heartier strains of bacteria survive and multiply, leading to a more serious and drug-resistant infection.

PROLONGED USE
Prolonged use of any antibiotic increases the risk of superinfection; caution is advised.

PRECAUTIONS
Over 60: Oxacillin is not expected to cause different or more severe side effects in older patients than it does in younger persons.

Driving and Hazardous Work: The use of oxacillin should not impair your ability to perform such tasks safely.

Alcohol: No special precautions are necessary.

Pregnancy: Oxacillin and other penicillins have not caused birth defects in animals. Human studies have not been done. Before you take oxacillin, tell your doctor if you are pregnant or plan to become pregnant.

Breast Feeding: Oxacillin passes into breast milk; avoid or discontinue use while nursing.

Infants and Children: No special problems are expected.

Special Concerns: Before you have any medical test, tell the doctor in charge that you are taking oxacillin. It can cause false results on some urine sugar tests for diabetics. Oral contraceptives may not be effective while you are taking oxacillin. Use other methods of contraception to avoid an unplanned pregnancy.

OVERDOSE
Symptoms: Unusual muscle excitability, agitation, confusion, hallucinations, seizures, loss of consciousness, coma.

What to Do: Call your doctor, emergency medical services (EMS), or the nearest poison control center immediately.

DRUG INTERACTIONS
Consult your physician for specific advice if you are taking aminoglycosides, ACE inhibitors, diuretics, potassium supplements or potassium-containing medications, anticoagulants or other anticlotting drugs, nonsteroidal anti-inflammatory drugs, sulfinpyrazone, cholestyramine, colestipol, oral contraceptives, methotrexate, probenecid, or rifampin.

FOOD INTERACTIONS
No known food interactions.

DISEASE INTERACTIONS
Consult your doctor if you have a history of allergies, congestive heart failure, gastrointestinal disorders (especially colitis associated with the use of antibiotics), or impaired kidney function.

Oxaprozin

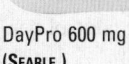

DayPro 600 mg
(SEARLE)

▶ Drug Class: Nonsteroidal anti-inflammatory drug (NSAID)

▶ Available in: Caplets

▶ Available OTC? No

▶ As Generic? Yes

Side Effects

SERIOUS
Shortness of breath or wheezing, with or without swelling of legs or other signs of heart failure; chest pain; peptic ulcer disease with vomiting of blood; black, tarry stools; decreasing kidney function. Call your doctor immediately.

COMMON
Nausea, vomiting, heartburn, diarrhea, constipation, headache, dizziness, sleepiness.

LESS COMMON
Ulcers or sores in mouth, depression, rashes or blistering of skin, ringing sound in the ears, unusual tingling or numbness of the hands or feet, seizures, blurred vision. Also elevated potassium levels, decreased blood counts; such problems can be detected by your doctor.

PRINCIPAL USES
To treat mild to moderate pain and inflammation caused by tendinitis, arthritis, bursitis, gout, soft tissue injuries, migraine and other vascular headaches, menstrual cramps, and other conditions. When patients fail to respond to one NSAID, another may be tried. The greatest effectiveness often requires trial and error of several different NSAIDs.

HOW THE DRUG WORKS
NSAIDs work by interfering with the formation of prostaglandins, naturally occurring substances in the body that cause inflammation and make nerves more sensitive to pain impulses. NSAIDs also have other modes of action that are less well understood.

DOSAGE
Adults: 1,200 mg once a day. Maximum daily dose is 1,800 mg divided into smaller amounts taken 2 or 3 times a day. Children: Consult your pediatrician.

ONSET OF EFFECT
From 30 minutes to several hours or longer.

DURATION OF ACTION
Varies.

DIETARY ADVICE
Take with food; maintain your usual food and fluid intake.

STORAGE
Store in a tightly sealed container away from heat, moisture, and direct light.

IF YOU MISS A DOSE
Take it as soon as you remember. If it is near the time for the next dose, skip the missed dose and resume your regular dosage schedule. Do not double the next dose.

STOPPING THE DRUG
The decision to stop taking the drug should be made in consultation with your physician.

PROLONGED USE
Prolonged use can cause gastrointestinal problems, including ulceration and bleeding, kidney dysfunction, and liver inflammation. Consult your doctor about the need for medical examinations and laboratory tests.

PRECAUTIONS
Over 60: Because of the potentially greater consequences of gastrointestinal side effects, the dose of NSAIDs for older patients, especially those over age 70, is often cut in half.

Driving and Hazardous Work: Avoid such activities until you determine how the medicine affects you.

Alcohol: Avoid alcohol when using this medication because it increases the risk of stomach irritation.

Pregnancy: Avoid or discontinue this drug if you are pregnant or plan to become pregnant.

Breast Feeding: Oxaprozin passes into breast milk; avoid use while nursing.

Infants and Children: May be used in exceptional circumstances; consult your doctor.

Special Concerns: Because NSAIDs can interfere with blood coagulation, this drug should be stopped at least 3 days prior to any surgery.

OVERDOSE
Symptoms: Severe nausea, vomiting, headache, confusion, seizures.

What to Do: Call your doctor, emergency medical services (EMS), or the nearest poison control center immediately.

DRUG INTERACTIONS
Do not take this drug with aspirin or any other NSAIDs without your doctor's approval. In addition, consult your doctor if you are taking antihypertensives, steroids, anticoagulants, antibiotics, itraconazole or ketoconazole, plicamycin, penicillamine, valproic acid, phenytoin, cyclosporine, digitalis drugs, lithium, methotrexate, probenecid, triamterene, or zidovudine.

FOOD INTERACTIONS
No known food interactions.

DISEASE INTERACTIONS
Consult your doctor if you have any of the following: bleeding problems, inflammation or ulcers of the stomach and intestines, diabetes mellitus, systemic lupus erythematosus (SLE, lupus), anemia, asthma, epilepsy, Parkinson's disease, kidney stones, or a history of heart disease or alcohol abuse. Use of oxaprozin may cause complications in patients with liver or kidney disease, since these organs work together to remove the medication from the body.

Oxazepam

BRAND NAME
Serax

Generic 10 mg
(PUREPAC)

▶ Drug Class: Benzodiazepine tranquilizer; antianxiety agent

▶ Available in: Capsules, tablets

▶ Available OTC? No

▶ As Generic? Yes

Side Effects

SERIOUS
Difficulty concentrating, outbursts of anger, other behavior problems, depression, hallucinations, low blood pressure (causing faintness or confusion), memory impairment, muscle weakness, skin rash or itching, sore throat, fever and chills, sores or ulcers in throat or mouth, unusual bruising or bleeding, extreme fatigue, yellowish tinge to eyes or skin. Call your doctor immediately.

COMMON
Drowsiness, loss of coordination, unsteady gait, dizziness, lightheadedness, slurred speech.

LESS COMMON
Change in sexual desire or ability, constipation, false sense of well-being, nausea and vomiting, urinary problems, unusual fatigue.

PRINCIPAL USES
To treat anxiety and panic disorder. Also used to prevent alcohol withdrawal symptoms.

HOW THE DRUG WORKS
In general, oxazepam produces mild sedation by depressing activity in the central nervous system. In particular, oxazepam appears to enhance the effect of gamma-aminobutyric acid (GABA), a natural chemical that inhibits the firing of neurons and dampens the transmission of nerve signals, thus decreasing nervous excitation.

DOSAGE
For anxiety— Adults: 10 to 30 mg, 3 or 4 times a day. Older adults: Initial dose of 10 mg, 3 times a day. The dose may be increased to a maximum of 15 mg, 4 times a day. For alcohol withdrawal symptoms— Dosage will be adjusted by your doctor on an individual basis.

ONSET OF EFFECT
30 minutes to 2 hours.

DURATION OF ACTION
8 to 12 hours.

DIETARY ADVICE
Oxazepam can be taken with food to prevent gastrointestinal upset.

STORAGE
Store in a tightly sealed container away from heat, moisture, and direct light.

IF YOU MISS A DOSE
Take it as soon as you remember. If it is near the time for the next dose, skip the missed dose and resume your regular dosage schedule. Do not double the next dose.

STOPPING THE DRUG
Discontinuing the drug abruptly may produce withdrawal symptoms. The dosage should be reduced gradually according to your doctor's instructions.

PROLONGED USE
Short-term therapy (8 weeks or less) is typical; do not take it for a longer period unless so advised by your doctor.

PRECAUTIONS
Over 60: A lower dose may be warranted.

Driving and Hazardous Work: Oxazepam can impair mental alertness and physical coordination. Adjust your activities accordingly.

Alcohol: Avoid alcohol.

Pregnancy: Use during pregnancy should be avoided if possible. Be sure to tell your doctor if you are pregnant or plan to become pregnant.

Breast Feeding: Oxazepam passes into breast milk; do not take it while nursing.

Infants and Children: Oxazepam should be used by children only under close medical supervision.

Special Concerns: Oxazepam use can lead to psychological or physical dependence. Never take more than the prescribed daily dose.

OVERDOSE
Symptoms: Extreme drowsiness, confusion, slurred speech, slow reflexes, poor coordination, staggering gait, tremor, slowed breathing, loss of consciousness.

What to Do: Call your doctor, emergency medical services (EMS), or the nearest poison control center immediately.

DRUG INTERACTIONS
Other drugs may interact with oxazepam. Consult your doctor for specific advice if you are taking any drugs that depress the central nervous system; these include antihistamines, antidepressants or other psychiatric medications, barbiturates, sedatives, cough medicines, decongestants, and painkillers. Be sure your doctor knows about any over-the-counter medication you may take.

FOOD INTERACTIONS
None known.

DISEASE INTERACTIONS
Consult your doctor if you have a history of alcohol or drug abuse, stroke or other brain disease, any chronic lung disease, hyperactivity, depression or other mental illness, myasthenia gravis, sleep apnea, epilepsy, porphyria, kidney disease, or liver disease.

Oxcarbazepine

BRAND NAME
Trileptal

▶ Drug Class: Anticonvulsant

▶ Available in: Tablets

▶ Available OTC? No

▶ As Generic? No

Side Effects

SERIOUS
No serious side effects are associated with the use of oxcarbazepine.

COMMON
Dizziness, drowsiness, fatigue, nausea, vomiting, indigestion, abdominal pain, double vision or other visual disturbances, coordination difficulties, abnormal gait, tremor.

LESS COMMON
Muscle weakness, insomnia, nervousness, speech and language difficulties, impaired hand-eye coordination, impaired concentration, acne.

PRINCIPAL USES
To control partial seizures, either alone (monotherapy) or in conjunction with other anticonvulsants, in adults with epilepsy. Oxcarbazine is also used in conjunction with other anticonvulsants in the treatment of partial seizures in children ages 4 to 16 with epilepsy.

HOW THE DRUG WORKS
The mechanism of action is unclear. It is believed that oxcarbazepine inhibits activity in certain parts of the brain and suppresses the abnormal firing of neurons that causes seizures.

DOSAGE
Adults— The drug should be taken in 2 equal doses per day. Monotherapy (use of oxcarbazepine alone): To start, 600 mg a day; dose should be increased by 300 mg a day every third day to a dose of 1,200 mg a day. Adjunctive therapy (use with other anticonvulsants): To start, 600 mg a day. If necessary, dose may be increased at weekly intervals by an additional 600 mg a day, up to 1,200 mg a day. Converting to monotherapy: This should be done in close consultation with your doctor. To start, 600 mg a day while simultaneously initiating the reduction of the other anticonvulsant. If necessary, oxcarbazepine's dose may be increased by a maximum of 600 mg a day at weekly intervals, up to 2,400 mg a day. Children ages 4 to 16— The drug should be taken in 2 equal doses per day. To start, 8 to 10 mg per 2.2 lbs (1 kg), but no more than 600 mg a day. The maintenance dose is dependent upon body weight. Your doctor will determine the appropriate dosage.

ONSET OF EFFECT
At least 2 to 3 days.

DURATION OF ACTION
Unknown.

DIETARY ADVICE
Can be taken without regard to meals.

STORAGE
Store in a tightly sealed container away from heat, moisture, and direct light.

IF YOU MISS A DOSE
Take it as soon as you remember. If it is near the time for the next dose, skip the missed dose and resume your regular dosage schedule. Do not double the next dose.

STOPPING THE DRUG
The decision to stop taking the drug should be made by your doctor. Never stop this drug abruptly because this may cause seizures. The dose is typically tapered over a period of weeks.

PROLONGED USE
This drug is often taken for prolonged periods. See your doctor for periodic checkups.

PRECAUTIONS
Over 60: Adverse reactions may be more likely and more severe.

Driving and Hazardous Work: This drug may cause drowsiness or dizziness, particularly in the first few weeks it is used. Do not drive or engage in hazardous work until you determine how the medicine affects you.

Alcohol: Avoid alcohol; it may contribute to excessive drowsiness.

Pregnancy: Oxcarbazepine has caused birth defects in animal studies. Human studies with this drug have not been done, but other anticonvulsants are known to increase the risk of birth defects. However, seizures during pregnancy can also increase the risks to the fetus. Discuss with your doctor the potential risks and benefits of using this drug during pregnancy.

Breast Feeding: Oxcarbazepine passes into breast milk. Consult your doctor for specific advice concerning the relative risks and benefits of using this drug while breast feeding.

Infants and Children: Not recommended for use by children under age 4.

Special Concerns: See your doctor for regular check-ups to detect the onset of any serious side effects. Periodic measurements of serum sodium may be required because the drug can lower sodium levels in the blood. Your doctor may advise you to carry an ID card or bracelet that says you are taking this drug. Oxcarbazepine may reduce the effectiveness of oral contraceptives; other means of contraception should be considered.

OVERDOSE
Symptoms: Few overdoses have been reported.

What to Do: If an excessive dose is taken, seek emergency medical attention immediately.

DRUG INTERACTIONS
During combination therapy, it may be necessary to lower the dose of phenytoin.

FOOD INTERACTIONS
No known food interactions.

DISEASE INTERACTIONS
A lower dose of oxcarbazepine may be needed in patients with decreased kidney function or severe liver disease.

Oxybutynin Chloride

BRAND NAMES
Ditropan, Ditropan XL

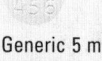

Generic 5 mg
(SIDMAK)

▶ Drug Class: Antispasmodic

▶ Available in: Syrup, tablets, extended-release tablets

▶ Available OTC? No

▶ As Generic? Yes

Side Effects

SERIOUS
Eye pain, skin rash or hives. Call your doctor immediately.

COMMON
Constipation; decreased sweating; drowsiness; dry mouth, nose, and throat.

LESS COMMON
Blurred vision, decreased sexual ability, difficulty urinating, difficulty swallowing, headache, increased sensitivity of eyes to light, nausea or vomiting, insomnia, unusual fatigue, reduced flow of breast milk.

PRINCIPAL USES
To decrease muscle spasms of the bladder and the frequent urination caused by the spasms.

HOW THE DRUG WORKS
Oxybutynin relaxes the muscle cells of the urinary tract and increases urinary bladder capacity.

DOSAGE
Syrup or tablets— Adults: 5 mg, 2 or 3 times a day. Children ages 5 to 12: 5 mg, 2 times a day. Dose may be gradually increased by your doctor to a maximum dose of 20 mg a day. Extended-release tablets— Adults: 5 mg once a day. Dose may be gradually increased by your doctor to a maximum dose of 30 mg a day.

ONSET OF EFFECT
30 to 60 minutes.

DURATION OF ACTION
6 to 10 hours. Extended-release: up to 24 hours.

DIETARY ADVICE
Take it with water on an empty stomach. It can, however, be taken with food to prevent stomach upset.

STORAGE
Store in a tightly sealed container away from heat and direct light. Keep the syrup form refrigerated, but do not allow it to freeze.

IF YOU MISS A DOSE
Take it as soon as you remember. If it is near the time for the next dose, skip the missed dose and resume your regular dosage schedule. Do not double the next dose.

STOPPING THE DRUG
The decision to stop taking the drug should be made by your doctor.

PROLONGED USE
See your doctor periodically if you must take this drug for a prolonged period.

PRECAUTIONS
Over 60: Adverse reactions may be more likely and more severe.

Driving and Hazardous Work: Avoid such activities until you determine how the medicine affects you.

Alcohol: Avoid alcohol.

Pregnancy: Oxybutynin has not been shown to cause birth defects in animals. Adequate human studies have not been done. Consult your doctor for advice.

Breast Feeding: Oxybutynin has not been reported to affect nursing infants. However, nursing may be difficult since the medication can reduce the flow of breast milk.

Infants and Children: The proper dose for children under the age of 5 has not been determined. The safety and effectiveness of the extended-release form have not been established in children under the age of 18.

Special Concerns: Wear sunglasses and avoid exposure to bright light if the drug increases your sensitivity to sunlight. Use extra care not to become overheated during warm weather or exercise, since oxybutynin may interfere with the ability to sweat, increasing the risk of heat stroke. Use sugarless gum, candy, or ice chips to relieve dryness in the mouth, nose, and throat. If dryness persists for more than 2 weeks, check with your doctor or dentist.

OVERDOSE
Symptoms: Flushing, fever, confusion, clumsiness severe drowsiness, rapid heartbeat, hallucinations, breathing difficulty, unusual nervousness, restlessness or irritability.

What to Do: An overdose of oxybutynin is unlikely to be life-threatening. However, if someone takes a much larger dose than prescribed, call your doctor, emergency medical services (EMS), or the nearest poison control center.

DRUG INTERACTIONS
Consult your doctor for specific advice if you are taking amantadine, anticholinergics, antidepressants, antidyskinetics (such as medication for Parkinson's disease or other movement disorders), antihistamines, antipsychotics, buclizine, carbamazepine, cyclizine, cyclobenzaprine, disopyramide, flavoxate, ipratropium, meclizine, methylphenidate, orphenadrine, procainamide, promethazine, quinidine, or trimeprazine.

FOOD INTERACTIONS
No known food interactions.

DISEASE INTERACTIONS
Consult your doctor if you have any of the following: severe bleeding, colitis, enlarged prostate, glaucoma, heart disease, severe and constant dryness of the mouth, hiatal hernia, high blood pressure, any intestinal or stomach problem, myasthenia gravis, toxemia of pregnancy, any problem with urination, or an overactive thyroid. Use of oxybutynin may cause complications in patients with liver or kidney disease, since these organs work together to remove the medication from the body.

Oxycodone Hydrochloride

Oxycontin 20 mg
(PURDUE)

 837

Additional photographs

▶ Drug Class: Opioid (narcotic)
analgesic

▶ Available in: Oral solution,
tablets, controlled-release
tablets

▶ Available OTC? No

▶ As Generic? Yes

Side Effects

SERIOUS
Serious side effects of
oxycodone are indistin-
guishable from those of
overdose: Confusion;
severe drowsiness,
weakness, or dizziness;
slurred speech; small,
pinpoint pupils; cold,
clammy skin; slow
breathing; seizures;
loss of consciousness.

COMMON
Dizziness or lightheaded-
ness, nausea or vomiting,
drowsiness, constipation,
itching.

LESS COMMON
Swelling in the feet,
sweating, false sense
of well-being (euphoria),
urinary retention.

PRINCIPAL USES
To relieve moderate to
severe pain.

HOW THE DRUG WORKS
Opioids such as oxycodone
relieve pain by acting on
specific areas of the spinal
cord and brain that process
pain signals from nerves
throughout the body.

DOSAGE
5 mg every 3 to 6 hours, or
10 mg, 3 to 4 times a day as
needed. Children: Dosages
must be determined by
your pediatrician. Con-
trolled-release tablets: Your
doctor will determine the
proper dosage.

ONSET OF EFFECT
10 to 15 minutes.

DURATION OF ACTION
3 to 6 hours.

DIETARY ADVICE
This medication can be
taken with food or milk to
lessen stomach upset.

STORAGE
Store in a tightly sealed container away from heat, moisture, and direct light. Do
not freeze the liquid form.

IF YOU MISS A DOSE
If you are taking oxycodone
on a fixed schedule, take it
as soon as you remember. If
it is near the time for the
next dose, skip the missed
dose and resume your regular dosage schedule. Do not
double the next dose.

STOPPING THE DRUG
The decision to stop taking
the drug should be made by
your doctor.

PROLONGED USE
You should see your doctor
regularly for tests and
examinations if you must
take this medication for an
extended period. Prolonged

use can cause physical
dependence.

PRECAUTIONS
Over 60: Adverse reactions
may be more likely and
more severe in older
patients.

**Driving and Hazardous
Work:** Do not drive or
engage in hazardous work
until you determine how
the medicine affects you.

Alcohol: Avoid alcohol.

Pregnancy: Human studies have not been done.
Before using this drug, tell
your doctor if you are pregnant or plan to become
pregnant. Overuse during
pregnancy can cause drug
dependence in the fetus.

Breast Feeding: Oxy-
codone may pass into breast
milk; caution is advised.
Consult your doctor for
specific advice.

Infants and Children:
Adverse reactions to oxy-
codone may be more likely
and more severe in chil-
dren. Consult your doctor
for specific advice.

Special Concerns: Swallow tablets whole; do not
break, crush, dissolve, or
chew them before swallow-
ing. Otherwise, the entire
12-hour dose will be
absorbed into your body all
at once, which can lead to
overdose, and possibly
death. If you feel the medication is not working properly after a few weeks, do
not increase the dose. Consult your doctor. Before having any surgery, tell the
doctor or dentist in charge
that you are taking this
drug. The controlled-release
tablets are prescribed for
use only in opioid-tolerant
patients requiring daily
doses of 160 mg or more.

OVERDOSE
Symptoms: Confusion;
severe drowsiness, weak-
ness, or dizziness; slurred
speech; small, pinpoint
pupils; cold, clammy skin;
slow breathing; seizures;
loss of consciousness.

What to Do: Call your
doctor, emergency medical
services (EMS), or the
nearest poison control
center immediately.

DRUG INTERACTIONS
Consult your doctor for specific advice if you are taking
carbamazepine or other
medicine for seizures, barbiturates, sedatives, cough
medicines, decongestants,
antidepressants, other prescription pain medications,
MAO inhibitors, naltrexone,
rifampin, or zidovudine.

FOOD INTERACTIONS
No known food interactions.

DISEASE INTERACTIONS
Consult your doctor if you
have any of the following: a
history of alcohol or drug
abuse; emotional illness;
brain disorders or head
injury; seizures; lung disease; prostate problems or
other problems with urination; gallstones; colitis;
heart, kidney, liver, or
thyroid disease.

Oxycodone/Acetaminophen

BRAND NAMES
Endocet, Percocet,
Roxicet, Roxicet 5/500,
Roxilox, Tylox

Percocet 5/325 mg
(DUPONT)

▶ Drug Class: Opioid (narcotic)
analgesic

▶ Available in: Capsules, oral
solution, tablets

▶ Available OTC? No

▶ As Generic? Yes

Side Effects

SERIOUS
Bloody, dark, or cloudy
urine; severe pain in
lower back or side; pale
or black, tarry stools; yellowish tinge to the eyes
or skin; hallucinations;
frequent urge to urinate;
painful or difficult urination; sudden decrease in
amount of urine; unusual
bleeding or bruising;
irregular heartbeat; skin
rash, hives, or itching;
unusual excitement;
swelling of face; confu-
sion; trembling or
uncontrolled muscle
movements; redness or
flushing of face. Call your
doctor immediately.

COMMON
Dizziness, lightheaded-
ness, nausea or vomiting,
drowsiness, constipation.

LESS COMMON
Allergic reaction, false
sense of well-being
(euphoria), depression,
loss of appetite, blurring
or change in vision,
headache, sweating.

PRINCIPAL USES
To relieve moderate to
severe pain when nonpre-
scription pain relievers
prove inadequate. A nar-
cotic analgesic such as oxycodone, in combination with
acetaminophen, may pro-
vide better pain relief than
either medicine used alone.
Used together, relief may be
achieved at lower doses of
the two drugs.

HOW THE DRUG WORKS
Opioids such as oxycodone
relieve pain by acting on
specific areas of the central
nervous system (brain and
spinal cord) that process
pain signals from nerves
throughout the body. Acetaminophen appears to interfere with the action of
prostaglandins, naturally
occurring substances in the
body that cause inflamma-
tion and make nerves more
sensitive to pain impulses.

DOSAGE
Adults: 1 capsule or tablet
every 4 to 6 hours, or 1 teaspoon of the oral solution
every 4 to 6 hours.

ONSET OF EFFECT
Unknown.

DURATION OF ACTION
Unknown.

DIETARY ADVICE
This medication can be
taken with food or milk to
lessen stomach irritation.

STORAGE
Store in a tightly sealed container away from heat, moisture, and direct light.

IF YOU MISS A DOSE
If you are taking the drug
on a fixed schedule, take it
as soon as you remember.
However, if it is near the
time for the next dose,
skip the missed dose and
resume your regular
dosage schedule. Do not
double the next dose.

STOPPING THE DRUG
The decision to stop taking
the drug should be made by
your doctor.

PROLONGED USE
See your doctor regularly
for examinations and laboratory tests if long-term therapy is required. Prolonged
use of narcotics can cause
physical dependence; pro-
longed use of aceta-
minophen at high doses
can cause liver damage.

PRECAUTIONS

Over 60: Adverse reactions
may be more likely and
more severe in older
patients.

**Driving and Hazardous
Work:** Do not drive or
engage in hazardous work
until you determine how the
medicine affects you.

Alcohol: Avoid alcohol.

Pregnancy: Human studies have not been done.
Before you use this drug,
tell your doctor if you are
pregnant or plan to become
pregnant. Overuse of the
medication during preg-
nancy can cause drug
dependence in the fetus.

Breast Feeding: It is not
known whether this medication passes into breast milk;
caution is advised. Consult
your doctor for advice.

Infants and Children:
Adverse reactions may be
more likely and more
severe in children.

Special Concerns: If you
feel the medication is not
working properly after a few
weeks, do not increase the
dose. Consult your doctor.

OVERDOSE
Symptoms: Severe dizziness or drowsiness; cold,
clammy skin; difficult or
slow breathing or shortness
of breath; severe confusion;
seizures; stomach cramps
or pain; diarrhea; low blood
pressure; increased sweating; constricted pupils of
eyes; nausea or vomiting;
irregular heartbeat; severe
weakness.

What to Do: Call your
doctor, emergency medical
services (EMS), or the
nearest poison control center immediately.

DRUG INTERACTIONS
Consult your doctor for specific advice if you are taking
any prescription or over-the-
counter drugs, especially
drugs with acetaminophen;
central nervous system
depressants such as antihistamines or medicine for hay
fever, allergies, or colds;
barbiturates; seizure medicine; muscle relaxants;
anesthetics; tranquilizers,
sedatives, or sleep aids.

FOOD INTERACTIONS
No known food interactions.

DISEASE INTERACTIONS
Consult your physician if
you have a head injury or
brain disease, an underactive thyroid, an enlarged
prostate, seizures, kidney
or liver disease, gallbladder
problems, a blood disorder,
or a history of alcohol or
drug abuse.

Oxycodone/Aspirin

BRAND NAMES
Endodan, Percodan,
Percodan-Demi, Roxiprin

▶ Drug Class: Opioid (narcotic)
analgesic

▶ Available in: Tablets

▶ Available OTC? No

▶ As Generic? Yes

Side Effects

SERIOUS
Serious side effects are
indistinguishable from
those of overdose. See
Overdose.

COMMON
Lightheadedness, dizzi-
ness, drowsiness, nausea
and vomiting.

LESS COMMON
Euphoric feeling,
depression, constipation,
itching.

PRINCIPAL USES
To relieve moderate to
severe pain when nonpre-
scription pain relievers fail.
A narcotic analgesic such as
oxycodone, combined with
aspirin, may provide superior pain relief than either
medicine alone, and in
lower dosages.

HOW THE DRUG WORKS
Opioids such as oxycodone
relieve pain by acting on
specific areas of the central
nervous system (brain and
spinal cord) that process
pain signals from nerves
throughout the body. Non-
steroidal anti-inflammatory
drugs (NSAIDs) such as
aspirin inhibit the release of
chemicals in the body called
prostaglandins, which play a
role in inflammation.

DOSAGE
Adults: 1 or 2 half-strength
tablets or 1 full-strength
tablet every 4 to 6 hours as
needed. Teenagers: ½ half-
strength tablet every 6 hours
as needed. Children age 6 to
12: ¼ half-strength tablet
every 6 hours as needed.

ONSET OF EFFECT
Unknown.

DURATION OF ACTION
Unknown.

DIETARY ADVICE
This drug can be taken with
food or a full glass of water
to lessen stomach irritation.

STORAGE
Store in a tightly sealed container away from heat, moisture, and direct light.

IF YOU MISS A DOSE
If you are taking the drug on
a fixed schedule, take it as
soon as you remember. However, if it is near the time for
the next dose, skip the
missed dose and resume regular dosage schedule. Do not
double the next dose.

STOPPING THE DRUG
The decision to stop the
drug should be made in consultation with your doctor.

PROLONGED USE
See your doctor regularly
for examinations and laboratory tests if long-term therapy is required.

PRECAUTIONS
Over 60: Adverse reactions
may be more likely and
more severe.

**Driving and Hazardous
Work:** Avoid such activities
until you determine how the
medicine affects you.

Alcohol: Avoid alcohol.

Pregnancy: Human studies have not been done.
Before you use this drug,
tell your doctor if you are
pregnant or plan to become
pregnant. Overuse of the
medication during preg-
nancy can cause drug
dependence in the fetus.

Breast Feeding: It is not
known whether this drug
passes into breast milk; consult your doctor for advice.

Infants and Children:
Adverse reactions may be
more likely and more
severe. This drug should
not be given to children
with a current or recent
viral infection such as
chickenpox or the flu.
Aspirin has been linked to
a rare, but potentially fatal
illness called Reye's syndrome. Consult your doctor
for more information.

Special Concerns: If you
feel the medication is not
working properly after a few
weeks, do not increase the
dose. Consult your doctor.
Prolonged use can cause
psychological and physical
dependence, whichcan lead
to abuse of the drug.

OVERDOSE
Symptoms: Loss of hearing, blood in urine, cold,
clammy skin, confusion,
seizures, diarrhea, severe
dizziness or lightheaded-
ness, severe drowsiness,
extreme excitement, ner-
vousness, or restlessness,
fever, hallucinations, severe
or ongoing headache,
increased sweating or thirst,
severe or continuing nausea
or vomiting, pinpoint pupils
of eyes, tinnitus (ringing or
buzzing in the ears), shortness of breath or breathing
difficulty, slowed heartbeat,
abdominal pain, vision problems, severe weakness.

What to Do: Call your
doctor, emergency medical
services (EMS), or the
nearest poison control
center immediately.

DRUG INTERACTIONS
Consult your doctor for specific advice if you are taking
any prescription or over-the-
counter drugs, especially
medications containing
aspirin or other NSAIDs
(such as ibuprofen, ketoprofen, or naproxen); aceta-
minophen; central nervous
system depressants such as
antihistamines or medicine
for hay fever, allergies, or
colds; barbiturates; seizure
medicine; muscle relaxants;
anesthetics; tranquilizers,
sedatives, or sleep aids.

FOOD INTERACTIONS
No known food interactions.

DISEASE INTERACTIONS
Consult your physician if
you have a head injury or
brain disease, an underactive thyroid, an enlarged
prostate, seizures, kidney
or liver disease, gallbladder
problems, asthma, diarrhea
caused by antibiotics or
poisoning, a blood disorder,
or a history of alcohol or
drug abuse.

Oxymetazoline Nasal

4-Way Long Lasting Nasal Spray, Afrin, Allerest 12-Hour Nasal Spray, Cheracol, Dristan 12-Hr Nasal Spray, Duramist Up To 12 Hours Decongestant Nasal Spray, Duration 12 Hour Nasal Spray, Neo-Synephrine 12 Hour Nasal Spray, Nostrilla Long-Acting Nasal Decongestant, NTZ Long Acting Decongestant Nose Drops, Sinarest 12 Hour Nasal Spray, Vicks Sinex Long-Acting 12-Hour Formula

▸ Drug Class: Decongestant

▸ Available in: Nasal drops, nasal spray

▸ Available OTC? Yes

▸ As Generic? Yes

Side Effects

SERIOUS
No serious side effects have been reported.

COMMON
Burning, dryness, or stinging inside the nose. An increase in nasal discharge or congestion may occur after 3 to 5 days of continuous use.

LESS COMMON
Headache, rapid or irregular heartbeat, excitability, restlessness.

PRINCIPAL USES
To relieve nasal congestion caused by allergies, colds, or sinus conditions.

HOW THE DRUG WORKS
Oxymetazoline constricts blood vessels to reduce the blood flow to swollen nasal passages and other tissues, which reduces nasal secretions and improves nasal airflow.

DOSAGE
Adults and children 6 years of age and older: 2 or 3 drops or sprays of 0.05% solution in each nostril 2 times a day, in the morning and evening. Children ages 2 to 6: 2 or 3 drops of 0.025% solution in each nostril 2 times a day, in the morning and evening.

ONSET OF EFFECT
Rapid.

DURATION OF ACTION
Unknown.

DIETARY ADVICE
Drink plenty of fluids.

STORAGE
Store in a tightly sealed container away from heat and direct light.

IF YOU MISS A DOSE
Take it as soon as you remember. If it is near the time for the next dose, skip the missed dose and resume your regular dosage schedule. Do not double the next dose.

STOPPING THE DRUG
Do not use this medicine for more than 3 days without consulting your doctor.

PROLONGED USE
Using this medicine for more than 3 days may lead to rebound congestion (more severe congestion caused by the body's adaptation to the drug).

PRECAUTIONS

Over 60: Although no studies have specifically examined the use of this drug in older patients, no special problems are expected.

Driving and Hazardous Work: Do not drive or engage in hazardous work until you determine how the medicine affects you.

Alcohol: Avoid alcohol.

Pregnancy: Oxymetazoline has not been shown to cause birth defects or other problems if taken during pregnancy.

Breast Feeding: It is not known whether oxymetazoline passes into breast milk; caution is advised. Consult your doctor for advice.

Infants and Children: This drug is not recommended for children under the age of 2.

Special Concerns: Each container of medicine should be used by only one person to avoid spread of infection. Blow your nose gently before using this medicine. To use the nose drops, tilt your head back or lie down on a bed and hang your head over the side. Keep your head tilted back for a few minutes after instilling the drops. To use the nasal spray, keep your head upright and sniff briskly while spraying. For best results, spray again in 3 to 5 minutes.

OVERDOSE
Symptoms: Rapid, irregular, or pounding heartbeat; headache or dizziness; increased sweating; nervousness; trembling; paleness; insomnia. Such symptoms are more likely to be observed in young children.

What to Do: If someone takes a much larger dose than recommended, call your doctor, emergency medical services (EMS), or the nearest poison control center immediately.

DRUG INTERACTIONS
Before you take oxymetazoline, tell your doctor if you are taking maprotiline or tricyclic antidepressants.

FOOD INTERACTIONS
No known food interactions.

DISEASE INTERACTIONS
Consult your doctor if you have a history of any of the following: high blood pressure, diabetes mellitus, heart disease, blood vessel disease, or an overactive thyroid gland.

Oxymetazoline Ophthalmic

▶ Drug Class: Ophthalmic decongestant

▶ Available in: Ophthalmic solution

▶ Available OTC? Yes

▶ As Generic? No

Side Effects

SERIOUS
No serious side effects have been reported.

COMMON
No common side effects have been reported.

LESS COMMON
Headache, rapid or irregular heartbeat, excitability, restlessness, increase in redness of the eye.

PRINCIPAL USES
To reduce redness of the eye caused by minor irritation.

HOW THE DRUG WORKS
Ophthalmic oxymetazoline reduces redness by constricting the superficial blood vessels in the whites (sclera) of the eye.

DOSAGE
Adults and children age 6 and older: 1 drop in the affected eye every 6 hours, as needed.

ONSET OF EFFECT
Rapid, within 5 minutes.

DURATION OF ACTION
About 6 hours.

DIETARY ADVICE
This medication can be used without regard to diet.

STORAGE
Store in a tightly sealed container away from heat, moisture, and direct light. Do not allow the medicine to freeze.

IF YOU MISS A DOSE
Apply it as soon as you remember. However, if it is near the time for the next dose, skip the missed dose and resume your regular dosage schedule. Do not double the next dose.

STOPPING THE DRUG
Do not use this medicine for more than 3 days without consulting your doctor.

PROLONGED USE
Consult your doctor if you intend to use this medicine for more than 3 days.

PRECAUTIONS
Over 60: Although no studies have specifically examined the use of this drug in older patients, no special problems are expected.

Driving and Hazardous Work: Do not drive or engage in hazardous work until you determine how the medicine affects you.

Alcohol: No special precautions are necessary.

Pregnancy: No problems are expected, but studies of effects in pregnancy have not been done in humans. Consult your physician.

Breast Feeding: No problems are expected, but studies of effects in breast feeding have not been done in humans. Consult your doctor.

Infants and Children: Dosage for children under the age of 6 should be determined by a pediatrician.

Special Concerns: To use the eye drops, first wash your hands. Tilt your head back. Gently apply pressure to the inside corner of the eyelid and with the index finger of the same hand, pull downward on the lower eyelid to make a space. Drop the medicine into this space and close your eye. Apply pressure for 1 or 2 minutes while keeping the eye closed without blinking. Then wash your hands again. Make sure the tip of the dropper does not touch your eye, finger, or any other surface.

OVERDOSE
Symptoms: Dizziness; headache; rapid, irregular, or pounding heartbeat; trembling; insomnia.

What to Do: Call your doctor, emergency medical services (EMS), or the nearest poison control center immediately.

DRUG INTERACTIONS
Before you take oxymetazoline, tell your doctor if you are taking maprotiline or tricyclic antidepressants.

FOOD INTERACTIONS
No known food interactions.

DISEASE INTERACTIONS
Caution is advised when taking oxymetazoline. Consult your doctor if you have a history of any of the following: high blood pressure; eye disease, infection, or injury; narrow-angle glaucoma; heart disease; blood vessel disease; or an overactive thyroid gland.

Paclitaxel Injection

BRAND NAME
Taxol

▶ Drug Class: Antineoplastic (anticancer) agent

▶ Available in: Injection

▶ Available OTC? No

▶ As Generic? No

Side Effects

SERIOUS
Black, tarry, or bloody stools; blood-tinged (pink or maroon) urine; cough or hoarseness; fever and chills; lower back or flank pain; painful, difficult urination; tiny bright red spots on skin; bleeding from gums, nose, other unusual places; easy bruising, shortness of breath. These side effects may mean that normal blood cells and special blood-clotting cells have been affected, or that normal immune cells have been affected and an infection is developing somewhere in your body. See your doctor as soon as possible if any of these side effects occur.

COMMON
Diarrhea, nausea, and vomiting; numbness, burning, or tingling in hands or feet; pain in the joints and muscles, especially in the limbs; total but temporary loss of body hair (hair begins to regrow after therapy is discontinued).

LESS COMMON
Dizziness or lightheadedness, slowed heartbeat.

PRINCIPAL USES
To treat cancers of the ovary, breast, lung, head, and neck, and to treat melanoma (a type of skin cancer that can spread to other organs). Paclitaxel is also used as secondary treatment for AIDS-related Kaposi's sarcoma.

HOW THE DRUG WORKS
Paclitaxel interferes with essential phases of cell division in cancer cells, preventing them from multiplying. The drug may also affect the health and development of other kinds of cells in the body, resulting in unpleasant side effects.

DOSAGE
135 to 175 mg per square meter of body surface, either as a 24-hour infusion or as a 3-hour infusion administered every 3 to 4 hours. AIDS-related Kaposi's sarcoma: 135 mg per square meter of body surface as a 3-hour infusion administered every 3 weeks or 100 mg per square meter of body surface as a 3-hour infusion every 2 weeks. Your oncologist will determine the proper dosage schedule.

ONSET OF EFFECT
Unknown.

DURATION OF ACTION
Unknown.

DIETARY ADVICE
Maintain adequate food and fluid intake. Calorie, protein, and vitamin needs increase in patients with cancer. Good nutrition is essential to cope with the demands of chemotherapy.

STORAGE
Not applicable; the dose is administered only at a health care facility.

IF YOU MISS A DOSE
Not applicable, since it is given by a doctor or other health care professional.

STOPPING THE DRUG
The decision to stop taking the drug should be made by your doctor.

PROLONGED USE
You should see your doctor regularly for tests and examinations if you must take this drug for a prolonged period.

PRECAUTIONS
Over 60: No special age-related problems are expected.

Driving and Hazardous Work: Do not drive or engage in hazardous work until you determine how the medicine affects you.

Alcohol: Avoid alcohol.

Pregnancy: Paclitaxel has caused fetal death and miscarriage in animals. Tell your doctor at once if you become pregnant while taking paclitaxel.

Breast Feeding: Paclitaxel may pass into breast milk; avoid or discontinue usage while nursing.

Infants and Children: There is no specific information comparing the use of paclitaxel in infants and children with its use in older persons.

Special Concerns: While taking paclitaxel, do not receive any immunizations without consulting your doctor. Avoid persons with infections. Be careful when using a toothbrush, dental floss, or toothpick. Check with your doctor before having any dental work. Do not touch your eyes or the inside of your nose unless you have just washed your hands. Be careful not to cut yourself when using sharp objects such as a razor. Avoid contact sports and other activities during which bruising could occur.

OVERDOSE
Symptoms: Excessive dosages over an extended period of time may cause weakness, fatigue, and low resistance to infections (due to anemia), numbness or tingling in the extremities (due to peripheral nerve damage), and increased inflammation of the mucous membranes.

What to Do: Notify your doctor right away if you develop such symptoms.

DRUG INTERACTIONS
Consult your doctor for specific advice if you are taking amphotericin B, antithyroid agents, azathioprine, chloramphenicol, colchicine, flucytosine, ganciclovir, ketoconazole, interferon, plicamycin, or zidovudine.

FOOD INTERACTIONS
No known food interactions.

DISEASE INTERACTIONS
Caution is advised when taking paclitaxel. Consult your doctor if you have a history of any of the following: chicken pox, shingles, heart rhythm problems, or any recent infection.

Pancrelipase

Viokase 30,000/8,000/30,000 units
(A.H. ROBINS)

▸ Drug Class: Pancreatic
enzyme

▸ Available in: Capsules,
delayed-release capsules,
powder, tablets

▸ Available OTC? No

▸ As Generic? Yes

Side Effects

SERIOUS
Serious side effects are
not likely with normal
doses. With high doses,
side effects may include
diarrhea, intestinal blockage, nausea, and stom-
ach cramps or pain. Very
high doses may cause
blood in urine, joint pain,
or swelling of feet or
lower legs. If the powder
form is accidentally
inhaled, breathing prob-
lems, tightness in the
chest, and wheezing may
occur. Call your doctor
immediately.

COMMON
No common side effects
have been reported with
the recommended
dosage.

LESS COMMON
Skin rash or hives.

PRINCIPAL USES
The pancreas secretes various substances—including
digestive enzymes, insulin,
and glucagon—that are
essential to good health.
Pancrelipase is prescribed
to replace the enzymes
needed for digestion in
patients for whom the pancreas is not functioning
properly.

HOW THE DRUG WORKS
Pancrelipase contains the
enzymes that would other-
wise be manufactured by
the pancreas to digest proteins, starches, and fats.

DOSAGE
Capsules— Adults and
teenagers: 1 to 3 capsules
before or with meals and
snacks. Children: Contents
of 1 to 3 capsules sprinkled
on food with each meal.
Delayed-release capsules—
Adults and teenagers: 1 to
2 capsules before or with
meals and snacks. Children:
1 to 2 capsules with meals.
Powder— Adults and teen-
agers: ¼ teaspoon (0.7
gram) with meals and
snacks. Children: ¼ tea-
spoon with meals. Tablets—
Adults and teenagers: 1 to 3
tablets before or with meals
and snacks. Children: 1 to 2
tablets with meals. Doses
may be altered as deter-
mined by your doctor.

ONSET OF EFFECT
Variable.

DURATION OF ACTION
Variable.

DIETARY ADVICE
Take before or with meals
and snacks as directed.

STORAGE
Store in a tightly sealed container away from heat, moisture, and direct light.

IF YOU MISS A DOSE
Take it as soon as you
remember. However, if it is
near the time for the next
dose, skip the missed dose
and resume your regular
dosage schedule. Do not
double the next dose.

STOPPING THE DRUG
The decision to stop taking
the drug should be made by
your doctor.

PROLONGED USE
You should see your doctor
regularly for tests and
examinations while taking
this medicine. Lifetime therapy with pancrelipase may
be required.

PRECAUTIONS
Over 60: No special problems are expected in older
patients.

**Driving and Hazardous
Work:** The use of this medication should not impair
your ability to perform such
tasks safely.

Alcohol: No special precautions are necessary.

Pregnancy: Animal and
human studies have not
been done. Before you take
pancrelipase, tell your doctor if you are pregnant or
plan to become pregnant.

Breast Feeding: It is not
known whether pancreli-
pase passes into breast
milk. Problems have not
been reported. Consult your
doctor for specific advice.

Infants and Children:
The dosage for children
under 6 months of age has
not been established.

Special Concerns: Be
careful not to inhale the
powder form or powder
from capsules; it may cause
stuffy nose, shortness of
breath, troubled breathing,

wheezing, or tightness in
the chest. Do not change
brands or forms of pancrelipase without consulting
your physician; different
products may work in different ways. If your physician
prescribes a personal diet
for you, be careful to
observe it.

OVERDOSE
Symptoms: Nausea or
vomiting, abdominal
cramps, diarrhea.

What to Do: Call your
doctor, emergency medical
services (EMS), or the
nearest poison control
center immediately.

DRUG INTERACTIONS
Consult your doctor for specific advice if you are taking
any prescription or over-the-
counter medication.

FOOD INTERACTIONS
No known food interactions.

DISEASE INTERACTIONS
Consult your doctor if you
have any other medical
problem, especially pancreatitis, which is sudden and
severe inflammation of the
pancreas.

Pantoprazole Sodium

▶ Drug Class: Antacid/proton pump inhibitor

▶ Available in: Delayed-release tablets

▶ Available OTC? No

▶ As Generic? No

Side Effects

SERIOUS
No serious side effects are associated with the use of pantoprazole.

COMMON
Diarrhea.

LESS COMMON
Rash, raised blood sugar levels. Many additional side effects can occur; consult your doctor if you are concerned about any adverse or unusual reactions you experience while taking this drug.

PRINCIPAL USES

For the short-term treatment of erosive esophagitis (severe, chronic inflammation or ulceration of the esophagus) associated with gastroesophageal reflux disease (GERD; backwash of stomach acid into the esophagus).

HOW THE DRUG WORKS

Pantoprazole blocks the action of a specific enzyme in the cells that line the stomach, thereby decreasing the production of stomach acid.

DOSAGE

Adults: 40 mg once a day for up to 8 weeks.

ONSET OF EFFECT

Within 1 to 3 hours.

DURATION OF ACTION

Unknown.

DIETARY ADVICE

Pantoprazole may be taken without regard to meals. Tablets should be swallowed whole.

STORAGE

Store in a tightly sealed container away from heat, moisture, and direct light.

IF YOU MISS A DOSE

Take it as soon as you remember. However, if it is near the time for the next dose, skip the missed dose and resume your regular dosage schedule. Do not double the next dose.

STOPPING THE DRUG

Take as prescribed for the full treatment period, even if your symptoms improve before the scheduled end of therapy. The decision to stop taking the drug should be made by your doctor.

PROLONGED USE

Pantoprazole should not be used indefinitely as maintenance therapy for esophagitis; it is generally taken for a limited period of up to 8 weeks. For those who have not healed within this period, an additional 8 weeks of therapy may be considered by your doctor.

PRECAUTIONS

Over 60: No special problems are expected.

Driving and Hazardous Work: No special precautions are necessary.

Alcohol: Avoid alcohol while taking this medication, as it may aggravate your condition.

Pregnancy: In animal tests, pantoprazole has not caused problems. Human tests have not been done. Before you take pantoprazole, tell your doctor if you are pregnant or plan to become pregnant.

Breast Feeding: Pantoprazole may pass into breast milk; caution is advised. Consult your doctor for advice. Discuss with your doctor the relative risks and benefits of using this drug while nursing.

Infants and Children: Safety and effectiveness have not been established for patients under age 18.

Special Concerns: Do not chew, crush, or split the tablets. If your doctor directs, you may take an antacid along with pantoprazole.

OVERDOSE

Symptoms: Few cases of overdose have been reported.

What to Do: An overdose is unlikely to be life-threatening. However, if someone takes a much larger dose than prescribed, call your doctor, emergency medical services (EMS), or the nearest poison control center immediately.

DRUG INTERACTIONS

Drug interactions are unlikely. Consult your doctor for specific advice if you are taking: ampicillin, iron salts or supplements, ketoconazole, or warfarin.

FOOD INTERACTIONS

No significant food interactions have been reported.

DISEASE INTERACTIONS

Consult your doctor if you have severe liver disease, which may increase the risk of side effects.

Papaverine Hydrochloride

Generic 150 mg
(TIME-CAP)

▶ Drug Class: Vasodilator

▶ Available in: Tablets,
extended-release capsules,
injection

▶ Available OTC? No

▶ As Generic? Yes

Side Effects

SERIOUS
Oral forms: Blurred or
double vision, drowsi-
ness, fatigue. Injection
for erectile dysfunction:
Lumps in penis, painful
or prolonged erection
(lasting more than 4
hours). Call your doctor
immediately.

COMMON
Oral forms: None. Injec-
tion for erectile dysfunction: Mild pain or burning
along the penis.

LESS COMMON
Oral forms: Dizziness,
rapid heartbeat, flushing
of face, difficult breathing. Injection: Bruising,
bleeding, or tingling at
injection site; impaired
ejaculation; dizziness.

PRINCIPAL USES
To treat problems caused
by poor blood circulation.
The injectable form of
papaverine has recently
been approved to treat erectile dysfunction (impotence)
in men.

HOW THE DRUG WORKS
Papaverine causes dilation
of blood vessels, improving
blood flow to the tissues
supplied by the affected vessels. When injected into the
penis, papaverine causes the
penile arteries to dilate,
thus promoting erection.

DOSAGE
To treat poor blood circulation (average adult dose)—
Tablets: 100 to 300 mg, 3 to
5 times a day. Extended-
release capsules: 150 mg
every 12 hours. May be
increased by your doctor to
150 mg every 8 hours, or
300 mg every 12 hours.
Injection: 30 to 120 mg into
a vein or muscle every 3
hours. (Dose for children
will be determined by pediatrician.) For erectile dysfunction— Injection: 30 mg,
self-administered at the
base of penis as needed,
just prior to sexual activity.
Patients with erectile dysfunction due to nerve
damage (as opposed to
circulatory problems) may
require lower doses. It
should not be administered
more than once per day,
more than 2 days in a row,
or more than 3 times a
week. Dose may be
increased to 60 mg a day
based on patient response.

ONSET OF EFFECT
For circulation: Rapid.
For erectile dysfunction:
Variable; usually 10 to 15
minutes.

DURATION OF ACTION
Call your doctor immedi-
ately if erection persists for
more than 4 hours.

DIETARY ADVICE
Oral forms can be taken
with meals, milk, or
antacids to minimize
stomach upset.

STORAGE
Store in a tightly sealed container away from heat, moisture, and direct light. Do
not refrigerate or freeze
injectable forms of pure
papaverine. Various mix-
tures of papaverine with
other agents may require
refrigeration.

IF YOU MISS A DOSE
Oral forms: Take the medicine as soon as you remember. If it is near the time for
the next dose, skip the
missed dose and resume
your regular dosage schedule. Do not double the next
dose. Injection: Use as
needed.

STOPPING THE DRUG
The decision to stop taking
the drug should be made in
consultation with your
physician.

PROLONGED USE
See your doctor regularly
for tests and examinations
to evaluate your condition
and make any necessary
adjustments in therapy.

PRECAUTIONS
Over 60: Oral forms may
reduce older patients' tolerance to cold temperatures.

**Driving and Hazardous
Work:** No special precautions are necessary.

Alcohol: Avoid alcohol.

Pregnancy: Adequate studies on the use of oral
papaverine during preg-
nancy have not been done;
consult your doctor for
advice.

Breast Feeding: Oral
papaverine may pass into

breast milk; caution is
advised. Consult a doctor.

Infants and Children:
Lower doses of oral
papaverine are needed; consult your pediatrician.

Special Concerns: Oral
forms: Papaverine may
cause dizziness; get up
slowly from a seated or
prone position. If you have
glaucoma, you should have
regular eye examinations. If
you have difficulty swallowing the whole capsule, you
can mix its contents with
jelly or jam and swallow the
mixture without chewing.
Avoid smoking. Injection:
Your doctor should instruct
you on how to administer
the papaverine before you
attempt to do it yourself.

OVERDOSE
Symptoms: Oral forms:
Blurred or double vision,
drowsiness, fatigue. Injection: Painful erection or
erection that persists for
more than 4 hours. This
may cause permanent dam-
age to the tissues of the
penis and may result in the
inability to achieve subsequent erections.

What to Do: Seek medical
assistance immediately.

DRUG INTERACTIONS
Consult your doctor for specific advice if you are taking
any other prescription or
over-the-counter drug.

FOOD INTERACTIONS
No known food interactions.

DISEASE INTERACTIONS
Consult your doctor if you
have had heart disease,
glaucoma, or a recent heart
attack or stroke.

Paroxetine Hydrochloride

Paxil 20 mg
(SmithKline Beecham)

▶ Drug Class: Selective serotonin reuptake inhibitor (SSRI) antidepressant

▶ Available in: Tablets, oral suspension

▶ Available OTC? No

▶ As Generic? Yes

Side Effects

SERIOUS
Muscle pain or fatigue, lightheadedness or fainting, rash, agitation or irritability, severe drowsiness, dilated pupils, severe dry mouth, rapid heartbeat, trembling, severe nausea or vomiting. Call your doctor immediately.

COMMON
Insomnia, dizziness, sexual dysfunction, unusual fatigue, loss of initiative, nausea or vomiting, constipation, difficulty urinating, headache, trembling.

LESS COMMON
Decreased sexual desire, blurred vision, increased or decreased appetite, weight gain or loss, heartbeat irregularities, change in sense of taste. Also tingling, prickling, or burning feeling.

PRINCIPAL USES
To treat symptoms of major depression, obsessive-compulsive disorder, panic disorder, social anxiety disorder, and post-traumatic stress disorder.

HOW THE DRUG WORKS
Paroxetine affects levels of serotonin, a brain chemical that is thought to be linked to mood, emotions, and mental state.

DOSAGE
Adults: To start, 20 mg once a day, usually taken in the morning; dose may be gradually increased by your doctor to 50 mg a day. Older adults: To start, 10 mg once a day; may be gradually increased by your doctor to 40 mg a day.

ONSET OF EFFECT
From 1 to 4 weeks.

DURATION OF ACTION
Unknown.

DIETARY ADVICE
This drug can be taken without regard to diet.

STORAGE
Store in a tightly sealed container away from heat, moisture, and direct light.

IF YOU MISS A DOSE
Take it as soon as you remember. If it is near the time for the next dose, skip the missed dose and resume your regular dosage schedule. Do not double the next dose.

STOPPING THE DRUG
Take as prescribed for the full treatment period even if you begin to feel better before the scheduled end of therapy. The decision to stop taking the drug should be made in consultation with your doctor. Dosage should be gradually tapered over 1 to 2 weeks.

PROLONGED USE
Usual course of therapy for depression lasts 6 months to 1 year; some patients may benefit from additional therapy.

PRECAUTIONS
Over 60: Adverse reactions may be more likely and more severe in older patients. A lower dose may be warranted.

Driving and Hazardous Work: Exercise caution until you determine how the medicine affects you.

Alcohol: Avoid alcohol.

Pregnancy: Adequate studies of paroxetine use during pregnancy have not been done. Before you take paroxetine, tell your doctor if you are pregnant or plan to become pregnant.

Breast Feeding: Paroxetine passes into breast milk; caution is advised. Consult your doctor for advice.

Infants and Children: The safety and effectiveness of the use of paroxetine in children have not been established. Antidepressants increase the risk of suicidal thinking and behavior (suicidality) in children with major depression and other psychiatric disorders. Discuss with your doctor this risk versus the benefits of using this drug. Children should be observed closely for worsening of symptoms, suicidality, or unusual changes in behavior at the onset of therapy and when making changes in dosage.

Special Concerns: Take paroxetine at least 6 hours before bedtime to prevent insomnia, unless it causes drowsiness.

OVERDOSE
Symptoms: Agitation or irritability, severe drowsiness, dizziness, coma, dilated pupils, severe dry mouth, rapid heartbeat, trembling, severe nausea and vomiting.

What to Do: Call your doctor, emergency medical services (EMS), or the nearest poison control center immediately.

DRUG INTERACTIONS
Paroxetine and MAO inhibitors should not be used within 14 days of each other. Very serious side effects such as myoclonus (uncontrolled muscle spasms), hyperthermia (excessive rise in body temperature), and extreme stiffness may result. Do not take paroxetine with thioridazine; dangerous heart rhythm irregularities may result. Tryptophan, warfarin, NSAIDs, aspirin, sumatriptan, naratriptan, rizatriptan, and zolmitriptan may also interact with paroxetine; consult your doctor for advice.

FOOD INTERACTIONS
No known food interactions.

DISEASE INTERACTIONS
Caution is advised when taking paroxetine. Consult your doctor if you have a history of alcohol or drug abuse or a seizure disorder. Use of paroxetine may cause complications in patients with liver or kidney disease, since these organs work together to remove the drug from the body.

Pemoline

Cylert 18.75 mg
(**ABBOTT**)

837

Additional photographs

▶ Drug Class: Central nervous system stimulant

▶ Available in: Tablets, chewable tablets

▶ Available OTC? No

▶ As Generic? No

Side Effects

SERIOUS
The most serious potential side effect is liver toxicity, which can cause jaundice (characterized by yellowish discoloration of the skin and eyes), nausea, vomiting, abdominal pain, fatigue, loss of appetite, and dark urine. Call your doctor immediately.

COMMON
Insomnia, loss of appetite, weight loss.

LESS COMMON
Dizziness, stomachache, drowsiness, mental depression, increased irritability, nausea, skin rash.

PRINCIPAL USES
To treat attention-deficit hyperactivity disorder (ADHD) in children and adults. Because of the risk of serious side effects, pemoline is generally not considered appropriate as first-line therapy.

HOW THE DRUG WORKS
Pemoline is thought to stimulate the release of norepinephrine, a natural hormone that promotes the transmission of nerve impulses in the central nervous system. It works by decreasing restlessness and increasing attention in adults and children who cannot concentrate for very long, are easily distracted, or are impulsive.

DOSAGE
Adults and children age 6 and older: To start, 37.5 mg every morning. Dose may be increased by your doctor in increments of 18.75 mg weekly, up to a maximum of 112.5 mg a day.

ONSET OF EFFECT
Significant benefit may not be evident until the third or fourth week of therapy.

DURATION OF ACTION
8 to 12 hours.

DIETARY ADVICE
No special restrictions.

STORAGE
Store in a tightly sealed container away from heat, moisture, and direct light.

IF YOU MISS A DOSE
Pemoline is generally prescribed for once-daily use in the morning. If you are unable to take it on a particular day, resume your regular scheduled dose the following morning.

STOPPING THE DRUG
The decision to stop taking the drug should be made in consultation with your physician.

PROLONGED USE
Liver function tests should be performed every 2 weeks after starting pemoline for as long as you remain on the medication. The drug should be discontinued if no clinical benefit is observed 3 weeks after dosage has been increased to 112.5 mg daily.

PRECAUTIONS
Over 60: No special problems are expected.

Driving and Hazardous Work: Avoid such activities until you determine how the medicine affects you.

Alcohol: Avoid alcohol.

Pregnancy: In animal studies, pemoline has been shown to cause stillbirths and decreased survival; however, it has not been shown to cause birth defects in humans. Before you take pemoline, tell your doctor if you are pregnant or plan to become pregnant, so that you may weigh the potential risks and benefits.

Breast Feeding: Pemoline may pass into breast milk; caution is advised. Consult your doctor for advice.

Infants and Children: There have been reports of slowed growth in children who have taken pemoline for long periods. Consult your doctor for advice.

Special Concerns: Your doctor should be thoroughly familiar with pemoline and should ask you to sign a patient consent form that helps spell out the risks of taking this medication. After you stop taking pemoline, you may exhibit unusual behavior and experience severe mental depression or unusual fatigue. Consult your doctor if you develop these symptoms. Pemoline can cause physical or mental dependence if taken for a long time. Signs of dependence include a strong desire to continue taking the medicine, a need to increase the dose to attain the same effect, and withdrawal symptoms when you stop taking the drug. Check with your doctor if you have such symptoms.

OVERDOSE
Symptoms: Agitation, muscle trembling or twitching, confusion, high blood pressure, seizures, false sense of well-being, rapid heartbeat, hallucinations, enlarged pupils, restlessness, vomiting, high fever with sweating, uncontrolled movements of the eyes or parts of the body, severe headache.

What to Do: Call your doctor, emergency medical services (EMS), or the nearest poison control center immediately.

DRUG INTERACTIONS
Consult your doctor for specific advice if you are taking any other prescription or over-the-counter medication.

FOOD INTERACTIONS
Avoid coffee, tea, cola, and other drinks that are high in caffeine.

DISEASE INTERACTIONS
Pemoline should not be used by patients with liver disease. Use of pemoline may cause complications in patients with kidney disease. Consult your doctor if you have Tourette's syndrome or other tic disorders.

Penbutolol Sulfate

BRAND NAME
Levatol

▶ Drug Class: Beta-blocker

▶ Available in: Tablets

▶ Available OTC? No

▶ As Generic? No

Side Effects

SERIOUS
Shortness of breath, wheezing; irregular or slow heartbeat (50 beats per minute or less); pain or feelings of tightness or pressure in the chest; swelling of the ankles, feet, and lower legs; mental depression. If you experience such symptoms, stop taking penbutolol sulfate and call your doctor immediately.

COMMON
Dizziness or lightheadedness, especially when rising suddenly to a standing position; decreased sexual ability; unusual fatigue, weakness, or drowsiness; insomnia.

LESS COMMON
Anxiety, irritability, nervousness; constipation; diarrhea; dry, sore eyes; itching; nausea; vomiting; nightmares or intensely vivid dreams; numbness, tingling, or other unusual sensations in the fingers, toes, or scalp.

PRINCIPAL USES
To treat mild to moderate high blood pressure.

HOW THE DRUG WORKS
Penbutolol sulfate slows the rate and force of contraction of the heart by blocking certain nerve impulses, thus reducing blood pressure.

DOSAGE
20 mg once a day.

ONSET OF EFFECT
Within 1 hour.

DURATION OF ACTION
Up to 24 hours.

DIETARY ADVICE
Follow your doctor's dietary restrictions, such as a low-salt or low-cholesterol diet, to improve control over high blood pressure and heart disease.

STORAGE
Store in a tightly sealed container away from heat and direct light.

IF YOU MISS A DOSE
Take the medicine as soon as you remember. If it is within 8 hours of your next dose, skip the missed dose and resume your regular schedule. Do not double the next dose.

STOPPING THE DRUG
This drug should not be stopped suddenly, as this may lead to angina and possibly a heart attack in patients with advanced heart disease. Slow reduction of the dose under your doctor's close supervision for 2 to 3 weeks is advised.

PROLONGED USE
Regular visits to your doctor are needed to evaluate the drug's ongoing, long-term effectiveness.

PRECAUTIONS

Over 60: Adverse reactions may be more likely and more severe in older patients.

Driving and Hazardous Work: Do not drive or engage in hazardous work until you determine how the medicine affects you.

Alcohol: Drink in careful moderation if at all. Alcohol may interact with the drug and cause a dangerous drop in blood pressure.

Pregnancy: Discuss with your doctor the relative risks and benefits of using this drug while pregnant.

Breast Feeding: Trace amounts of penbutolol sulfate can be found in breast milk, but adverse effects in infants have not been documented. Consult your doctor for specific advice.

Infants and Children: No special problems.

OVERDOSE
Symptoms: Unusually slow or rapid heartbeat, severe dizziness or fainting, poor circulation in the hands (bluish skin), breathing difficulty, seizures.

What to Do: Call your doctor, emergency medical services (EMS), or the nearest poison control center immediately.

DRUG INTERACTIONS
Consult your doctor for specific advice if you are taking amphetamines, oral antidiabetic agents, asthma medication (such as aminophylline or theophylline), calcium channel blockers, clonidine, guanabenz, halothane, immunotherapy for allergies (allergy shots), insulin, MAO inhibitors, reserpine, other beta-blockers, or any over-the-counter medicine.

FOOD INTERACTIONS
None reported.

DISEASE INTERACTIONS
Penbutolol sulfate should be used with caution in people with diabetes, especially insulin-dependent diabetes, since the drug may mask symptoms of hypoglycemia. Consult your doctor if you have allergies or asthma, heart or blood vessel disease (including congestive heart failure and peripheral vascular disease), hyperthyroidism, irregular (slow) heartbeat, myasthenia gravis, psoriasis, respiratory problems such as bronchitis or emphysema, kidney or liver disease, or a history of mental depression.

Penciclovir

▶ Drug Class: Antiviral

▶ Available in: Topical cream

▶ Available OTC? No

▶ As Generic? No

Side Effects

SERIOUS
No serious side effects have been reported.

COMMON
Headache, allergic reaction at site of application.

LESS COMMON
Numbness or deadening of feeling in skin at application sites, skin rash, odd taste or changes in taste perception.

PRINCIPAL USES
To treat herpes labialis infection (cold sores) of the lips and face in adults with healthy immune systems. (Other treatments are recommended for those with impaired immune function.)

HOW THE DRUG WORKS
Penciclovir interferes with the activity of enzymes needed for the replication of viral DNA in cells, thus preventing the virus from multiplying.

DOSAGE
Apply it every 2 hours during waking hours, for 4 days. Start treatment as early as possible, when the first lesions appear on the face.

ONSET OF EFFECT
Unknown.

DURATION OF ACTION
Unknown.

DIETARY ADVICE
There are no special dietary recommendations, but before eating, be sure to wash your hands thoroughly after applying penciclovir.

STORAGE
Store in a tightly sealed container away from heat and direct light.

IF YOU MISS A DOSE
Apply it as soon as you remember. If it is near the time for the next dose, skip the missed dose and resume your regular dosage schedule. Do not double the next dose.

STOPPING THE DRUG
The decision to stop using this medication should be made in consultation with your doctor.

PROLONGED USE
See your doctor regularly for tests and examinations if you must use this medicine for a prolonged period.

PRECAUTIONS
Over 60: In human tests penciclovir did not cause more side effects in older patients than it did in younger users.

Driving and Hazardous Work: The use of penciclovir should not impair your ability to perform such tasks safely.

Alcohol: No special precautions are necessary.

Pregnancy: Penciclovir has not been shown to cause birth defects in animals. Human studies have not been done. Before you take penciclovir, tell your doctor if you are pregnant or planning to become pregnant. Use this medication during pregnancy only if its benefits clearly outweigh potential risks.

Breast Feeding: In animal studies, penciclovir given orally was shown to pass into breast milk, and in fact to be present in higher concentrations than those found in the blood. While there is no information on whether penciclovir passes into human breast milk after topical application, you should consult your doctor to help you decide whether to discontinue breast feeding (if the drug is determined to be necessary to the mother) or to discontinue the drug.

Infants and Children: The safety and effectiveness of penciclovir in infants and children have not been established. This medication should be used only under close medical supervision.

Special Concerns: Be careful not to apply penciclovir to the mucous membranes of the mouth and nose. Apply it with care near the eyes, since it can cause pain and irritation if it enters them. You should not use penciclovir if you are allergic to it or to any of its chemical components.

OVERDOSE
Symptoms: No specific ones have been reported.

What to Do: An overdose of penciclovir is very unlikely to occur. However, if someone accidentally ingests a large quantity of the medicine, call your doctor, emergency medical services (EMS), or the nearest poison control center.

DRUG INTERACTIONS
Other drugs may interact with penciclovir. Consult your doctor for specific advice if you are taking any other prescription or over-the-counter medication.

FOOD INTERACTIONS
No known food interactions.

DISEASE INTERACTIONS
Consult your doctor for advice if you have any other medical condition.

Penicillamine

BRAND NAMES
Cuprimine, Depen

Cuprimine 125 mg
(MERCK)

▶ Drug Class: Chelating agent;
antirheumatic; antiurolithic

▶ Available in: Capsules,
tablets

▶ Available OTC? No

▶ As Generic? No

Side Effects

SERIOUS
Joint pain, wheezing or
tightness in chest, hives,
skin rash or itching,
cloudy or bloody urine,
shortness of breath,
unusual fatigue, sore
throat and fever, painful
or swollen glands, weight
gain, unusual bleeding.
Also white spots, sores,
or ulcers in mouth;
swollen face, feet, or
lower legs. Call your
doctor immediately.

COMMON
Diarrhea, nausea or vom-
iting, loss of taste, mild
stomach pain, loss of
appetite.

LESS COMMON
No less-common side
effects are associated
with this drug.

PRINCIPAL USES
To treat Wilson's disease
(excessive accumulation of
copper in the body tissues)
and rheumatoid arthritis,
and to prevent or treat kidney stones in patients with
excessive amounts of the
amino acid cystine in the
urine or who have a history
of recurrent cystine kidney
stones. It can also be used
to treat heavy metal (mercury, lead) poisoning.

HOW THE DRUG WORKS
Penicillamine is a chelating
(chemical binding) agent
that removes excess copper
(the underlying problem in
Wilson's disease), mercury,
and lead from the body. It is
not clear how penicillamine
improves rheumatoid arthritis, but it may suppress the
body's release of certain
chemicals that cause inflammation. Penicillamine also
binds with cystine and
eliminates it from the body;
high concentrations of
cystine can cause kidney
stone formation.

DOSAGE
For Wilson's disease—
Adults and teenagers: To
start, 250 mg, 4 times a
day; may be increased to
500 mg, 4 times a day. Children: To start, 250 mg once
a day; may be increased.
For rheumatoid arthritis—
Adults: To start, 125 to
250 mg once a day; may
be increased to 500 mg, 3
times a day. To prevent cystine kidney stones— Adults:
To start, 500 mg, 4 times a
day; may be increased to
1,000 mg, 4 times a day.
Children: To start, 3.5 mg
per lb of body weight,
4 times a day; may be
increased. To treat heavy
metal poisoning— 500 mg
to 1.5 g a day in adults for
1 to 2 months.

ONSET OF EFFECT
For Wilson's disease:
Within 1 to 3 months. For
rheumatoid arthritis: Within
2 to 3 months. For kidney
stones: Unknown.

DURATION OF ACTION
Unknown.

DIETARY ADVICE
For Wilson's disease or
rheumatoid arthritis: Take it
on an empty stomach. For
rheumatoid arthritis, take it
at least 1 hour before or
after any other food, milk,
or medicine. For prevention
or treatment of kidney
stones: Drink at least 2 full
glasses of water at bedtime
and another 2 glasses of
water during the night.

STORAGE
Store in a tightly sealed container away from heat, moisture, and direct light.

IF YOU MISS A DOSE
Take it as soon as you
remember. If you take 2 or
more doses a day and it is
near the time for the next
dose, skip the missed dose
and resume your regular
dosage schedule. If you take
1 dose a day, simply skip
the missed dose and
resume your schedule the
next day. In either case, do
not double the next dose.

STOPPING THE DRUG
Take it as prescribed for the
full treatment period.

PROLONGED USE
See your doctor regularly
for tests and examinations.

PRECAUTIONS
Over 60: Adverse reactions
may be more likely and
more severe.

**Driving and Hazardous
Work:** The use of penicillamine should not impair
your ability to engage in
such tasks safely.

Alcohol: No special precautions are necessary.

Pregnancy: Penicillamine
may cause birth defects if
taken during pregnancy.

Breast Feeding: Penicillamine may pass into breast
milk; do not use it while
nursing.

Infants and Children:
No special warnings.

Special Concerns: Do
not take any iron-containing
medication or supplement
within 2 hours of taking
penicillamine. Patients
should take 25 mg a day of
vitamin B6 during therapy,
since the drug increases
the need for this vitamin.
Patients may also take a
multivitamin, but those
with Wilson's disease must
ensure it is copper-free.

OVERDOSE
Symptoms: None known.

What to Do: If someone
takes a much larger dose
than prescribed, seek medical assistance immediately.

DRUG INTERACTIONS
Do not take gold com-
pounds or phenylbutazone
if you are taking penicillamine. Also, tell your doctor if you are taking any
other prescription or over-
the-counter medication.

FOOD INTERACTIONS
Patients with Wilson's disease should not eat foods
high in copper such as
chocolate, nuts, shellfish,
mushrooms, liver, molasses
and broccoli.

DISEASE INTERACTIONS
Consult your doctor if you
have a history of blood
problems or kidney disease.
Persons sensitive to penicillin may have allergic reactions to penicillamine.

Bicillin L-A, Crysticillin 300 AS, Pentids, Permapen, Pfizerpen

Penicillin G

▶ Drug Class: Penicillin antibiotic

▶ Available in: Capsules, oral solution, injection

▶ Available OTC? No

▶ As Generic? No

Side Effects

SERIOUS
Irregular, rapid, or labored breathing, light-headedness or sudden fainting, joint pain, fever, severe abdominal pain and cramping with watery or bloody stools, severe allergic reaction (marked by sudden swelling of the lips, tongue, face, or throat; breathing difficulty; skin rash, itching, or hives), unusual bleeding or bruising, yellowish tinge to eyes or skin. Call your doctor immediately.

COMMON
Mild rash, mild diarrhea, nausea, vomiting, headache, vaginal discharge and itching, pain or white patches in the mouth or on the tongue.

LESS COMMON
Diminished urine output, chills, weakness, fatigue.

PRINCIPAL USES
To treat a variety of bacterial infections, including those of the ear, nose, and throat, skin and soft tissues, genitourinary tract, and the respiratory tract. It is also prescribed preventively before surgery or dental work in patients at risk for endocarditis (infection of the interior lining of the heart, which may damage the heart's valves). May also be given to treat meningitis and syphilis. Penicillin G is also approved for prophylactic use following known exposure to anthrax bacteria and for treating anthrax infections.

HOW THE DRUG WORKS
Penicillin G blocks the formation of bacterial cell walls, rendering bacteria unable to multiply and spread.

DOSAGE
Oral forms— Adults and teenagers: 200,000 to 500,000 units every 4 to 6 hours. Children: 189 to 13,636 units per lb of body weight every 4 to 8 hours. Injection (benzathine form)— Adults and teenagers: 1,200,000 to 2,400,000 units in 1 dose. Children: 300,000 to 1,200,000 units in 1 dose. Injection (procaine form)— Adults and teenagers: 600,000 to 1,200,000 units once a day. Children: 22,727 units per lb of body weight once a day. Other injection forms— Adults and teenagers: 1,000,000 to 5,000,000 units injected every 4 to 6 hours. Children: 3,788 to 11,363 units per lb of body weight every 4 to 6 hours. Infants: 13,636 units per lb of body weight every 12 hours.

ONSET OF EFFECT
Immediate after intravenous injection; unknown for other forms.

DURATION OF ACTION
Unknown.

DIETARY ADVICE
Oral doses should be given at least 1 hour before or 2 hours after meals.

STORAGE
Store in a tightly sealed container away from heat and direct light. Liquid forms can be refrigerated, but not frozen.

IF YOU MISS A DOSE
Take it as soon as you remember. If it is near the time for the next dose, skip the missed dose and resume your regular dosage schedule. Do not double the next dose.

STOPPING THE DRUG
Take this drug as prescribed for the full treatment period, even if you feel better before the scheduled end of therapy.

PROLONGED USE
See your doctor regularly for tests and examinations if you must take this medicine for a prolonged period.

PRECAUTIONS
Over 60: No special problems are expected.

Driving and Hazardous Work: Use of this drug should not impair ability to perform such tasks safely.

Alcohol: No special precautions are necessary.

Pregnancy: Adequate studies of use of this drug during pregnancy have not been done; however, no problems have been reported.

Breast Feeding: Penicillin G may pass into breast milk and cause problems in the nursing infant; avoid use while nursing.

Infants and Children: No special problems are expected.

Special Concerns: Penicillin G can cause false results on some urine sugar tests for patients with diabetes. Those who are prone to asthma, hay fever, hives, or allergies may be more likely to have an allergic reaction to a penicillin antibiotic. If severe diarrhea occurs as a side effect of this drug, do not take antidiarrheal medications; call your doctor.

OVERDOSE
Symptoms: Severe nausea, vomiting, diarrhea, seizures.

What to Do: Call your doctor, emergency medical services (EMS), or the nearest poison control center immediately.

DRUG INTERACTIONS
Consult your physician for specific advice if you are taking aminoglycosides, ACE inhibitors, diuretics, potassium supplements or potassium-containing medications, anticoagulants or other anticlotting drugs, nonsteroidal anti-inflammatory drugs, sulfinpyrazone, cholestyramine, colestipol, oral contraceptives, methotrexate, probenecid, or rifampin.

FOOD INTERACTIONS
No known food interactions.

DISEASE INTERACTIONS
Consult your doctor if you have a history of allergies, asthma, bleeding disorders (such as hemophilia), congestive heart failure, cystic fibrosis, gastrointestinal disorders (especially colitis associated with the use of antibiotics), infectious mononucleosis, or impaired kidney function.

Penicillin V

Generic 500 mg
(BIOCRAFT)

Additional photographs

▸ Drug Class: Penicillin
  antibiotic

▸ Available in: Tablets, delayed-
  release tablets, liquid

▸ Available OTC? No

▸ As Generic? Yes

Side Effects

SERIOUS
Irregular, rapid, or
labored breathing, light-
headedness or sudden
fainting, joint pain, fever,
severe abdominal pain
and cramping with
watery or bloody stools,
severe allergic reaction
(marked by sudden
swelling of the lips,
tongue, face, or throat;
breathing difficulty; skin
rash, itching, or hives),
unusual bleeding or
bruising, yellowish tinge
to eyes or skin. Call your
doctor immediately.

COMMON
Mild rash, mild diarrhea,
nausea, vomiting,
headache, vaginal dis-
charge and itching, pain
or white patches in the
mouth or on the tongue.

LESS COMMON
Diminished urine output,
chills, weakness, fatigue.

PRINCIPAL USES
To treat a variety of bacterial infections, including
those of the ear, nose, and
throat, skin and soft tissues,
genitourinary tract, and the
respiratory tract. It is also
prescribed before surgery
or dental work in patients at
risk for endocarditis (infection of the lining of the
heart, which may damage
the heart's valves).

HOW THE DRUG WORKS
Penicillin V destroys susceptible bacteria by interfering with their ability to
produce cell walls as they
multiply.

DOSAGE
Adults: 500 to 2,000 mg a
day for infections; 2,000 mg
to prevent bacterial endocarditis; or as ordered by
physician. Children: 15 to
50 mg per 2.2 lbs (1 kg) of
body weight per day in
divided doses to treat infections. To prevent infection
after dental surgery, 2 g (1
g for children), 30 to 60
minutes before procedure,
then 1 g (500 mg for children) 6 hours afterward.

ONSET OF EFFECT
Unknown.

DURATION OF ACTION
Up to 6 hours.

DIETARY ADVICE
Take it on an empty stom-
ach, 1 to 2 hours before or
3 to 4 hours after a meal.

STORAGE
Store in a tightly sealed container away from heat and
direct light.

IF YOU MISS A DOSE
Take it as soon as you
remember. If it is near the
time for the next dose, skip
the missed dose and
resume your regular dosage
schedule. Do not double the
next dose.

STOPPING THE DRUG
It is very important to take
this drug as prescribed for
the full treatment period.
Stopping the drug prema-
turely may lead to serious
complications.

PROLONGED USE
Prolonged use of any antibiotic increases the risk of
superinfection (a more
severe and drug-resistant
infection); caution is
advised.

PRECAUTIONS
Over 60: No special problems are expected.

**Driving and Hazardous
Work:** The use of penicillin
should not impair your ability to perform such tasks
safely.

Alcohol: No special precautions are necessary.

Pregnancy: Adequate studies of penicillin antibiotic
use during pregnancy have
not been done; however, no
problems have been
reported.

Breast Feeding: Penicillin
V may pass into breast milk
and cause problems in the
nursing infant; avoid use
while nursing.

Infants and Children:
No special problems are
expected.

Special Concerns: Penicillin V can cause false
results on some urine sugar
tests for patients with diabetes. If severe diarrhea
occurs as a side effect of
this drug, do not take
antidiarrheal medications;
call your doctor. Oral contraceptives may not be
effective while you are taking penicillin; consider
other methods of birth control. Those who are prone
to asthma, hay fever, hives,
or allergies may be more
likely to have an allergic
reaction to a penicillin
antibiotic.

OVERDOSE
Symptoms: Severe nausea
vomiting, diarrhea, seizures

What to Do: An overdose
of penicillin is unlikely to be
life-threatening. However, if
someone takes a much
larger dose than prescribed,
call your doctor or emer-
gency medical services
(EMS) right away.

DRUG INTERACTIONS
Consult your physician for
specific advice if you are
taking aminoglycosides,
ACE inhibitors, diuretics,
potassium supplements or
potassium-containing med-
ications, anticoagulants or
other anticlotting drugs,
nonsteroidal anti-inflammatory drugs, sulfinpyrazone,
cholestyramine, colestipol,
oral contraceptives, methotrexate, probenecid, or
rifampin.

FOOD INTERACTIONS
Acidic foods or juices can
reduce the antibiotic effect.

DISEASE INTERACTIONS
Consult your doctor if you
have a history of allergies,
asthma, congestive heart
failure, gastrointestinal disorders (especially colitis
associated with the use of
antibiotics), or impaired
kidney function.

Pentamidine Isethionate

▶ Drug Class: Anti-infective; antiprotozoal

▶ Available in: Inhalation, injection

▶ Available OTC? No

▶ As Generic? Yes

Side Effects

SERIOUS
Inhalation: Chest pain or congestion, difficulty breathing or swallowing, wheezing, skin rash, burning pain, dryness or feeling of lump in throat, cough. Injection: Decreased urination, unusual bruising or bleeding due to reduced number of platelets (clotting agents) in the blood, sore throat and fever; symptoms of high blood sugar or diabetes mellitus (flushed, dry skin, drowsiness, fruity breath, increased urination and thirst, loss of appetite); symptoms of low blood sugar (nausea, headache, anxiety, cold sweats or chills, shakiness, cool, pale skin, increased appetite); signs of low blood pressure (dizziness, confusion, fatigue, blurred vision, fainting or lightheadedness); dry, red, or itchy skin; vomiting or nausea; fast or irregular pulse; abdominal pain; pain or redness at injection site. Serious side effects occur commonly; call your doctor immediately.

COMMON
Injection: Loss of appetite, diarrhea, unpleasant metallic taste, nausea and vomiting.

LESS COMMON
There are no less-common side effects.

PRINCIPAL USES
To prevent and treat Pneumocystis carinii pneumonia (PCP). This serious type of pneumonia is prevalent among AIDS patients. The inhalation form is used to attempt to prevent PCP. The injection form is used to treat PCP. It may also be used for other types of infection as determined by your doctor.

HOW THE DRUG WORKS
The exact way in which pentamidine works is unknown.

DOSAGE
To prevent PCP— Inhalation (using the Respirgard II nebulizer by Marquest), adults and children age 5 and older: 300 mg once every 4 weeks. To treat PCP— Injection: 3 to 4 mg per 2.2 lbs (1 kg) of body weight into a vein over a period of 1 to 2 hours once a day for 21 days.

ONSET OF EFFECT
Unknown.

DURATION OF ACTION
Unknown.

DIETARY ADVICE
No special restrictions.

STORAGE
Not applicable; the dose is administered only at a health care facility.

IF YOU MISS A DOSE
Be sure to receive treatment as soon as possible. Contact your doctor.

STOPPING THE DRUG
Take it as prescribed for the full treatment period. The decision to stop taking the drug should be made in consultation with your physician.

PROLONGED USE
See your doctor regularly for tests and examinations if you must take this medicine for a prolonged period.

PRECAUTIONS
Over 60: No studies have been done specifically on older patients.

Driving and Hazardous Work: Do not drive or engage in hazardous work until you determine how the medicine affects you.

Alcohol: Avoid alcohol.

Pregnancy: Adequate human studies have not been done. Before taking this drug, tell your doctor if you are currently pregnant or plan to become pregnant.

Breast Feeding: Pentamidine may pass into breast milk; avoid use while breast feeding.

Infants and Children: Adequate studies on the use of pentamidine in children younger than 4 months have not been done. Consult your doctor for more information.

Special Concerns: Do not mix the inhalation solution with any other drugs or use any other drug in the nebulizer. Injectable pentamidine can cause a sudden drop in blood pressure. Lie down while taking it. The drug may also increase the chance of infection because it can lower the number of white blood cells in your blood. Consult your doctor at once if you detect signs of an infection (fever, sore throat). Use an electric shaver rather than a razor, as pentamidine may increase the risk of uncontrolled bleeding. Consult your dentist about ways to safely clean your teeth.

OVERDOSE
Symptoms: See Serious Side Effects.

What to Do: An overdose is unlikely. However, if you suspect an overdose, call your doctor, emergency medical services (EMS), or the nearest control center immediately.

DRUG INTERACTIONS
Other drugs may interact with pentamidine. Consult your doctor if you are taking bone marrow depressants, didanosine, macrolide antibiotics, foscarnet, or any drugs that may damage the kidney. Also consult your doctor if you are undergoing radiation therapy.

FOOD INTERACTIONS
No known food interactions.

DISEASE INTERACTIONS
Consult your doctor if you have heart, kidney, or liver disease, tuberculosis, a bleeding disorder, low blood pressure, diabetes mellitus, or low blood sugar. PCP prevention by inhalation may be less effective in those with chronic obstructive pulmonary disease (emphysema).

Pentazocine

BRAND NAME
Talwin

▶ Drug Class: Opioid agonist-antagonist analgesic

▶ Available in: Injection

▶ Available OTC? No

▶ As Generic? No

Side Effects

SERIOUS
Serious side effects of pentazocine are indistinguishable from those of overdose: Confusion; severe drowsiness, weakness, or dizziness; slurred speech; small, pinpoint pupils; cold, clammy skin; slow breathing; seizures; loss of consciousness.

COMMON
Dizziness or lightheadedness, nausea or vomiting, constipation, itching.

LESS COMMON
Mood swings or false sense of well-being and euphoria; hallucinations; nightmares.

PRINCIPAL USES
To relieve moderate to severe pain.

HOW THE DRUG WORKS
Opioids such as pentazocine relieve pain by acting on areas of the brain that process pain signals from nerves throughout the body.

DOSAGE
Adults: 25 to 50 mg every 3 or 4 hours. Maximum dose is 360 mg a day. Children: The dose must be determined by your pediatrician.

ONSET OF EFFECT
Into a vein: Within 2 to 3 minutes. Into a muscle: Within 15 to 20 minutes.

DURATION OF ACTION
From 2 to 3 hours.

DIETARY ADVICE
Drink 2 to 3 quarts of fluid a day, if possible, to help prevent constipation.

STORAGE
Not applicable; the dose is administered only in a health care facility.

IF YOU MISS A DOSE
Not applicable; the dose is administered by a health care professional.

STOPPING THE DRUG
The decision to stop taking the drug should be made by your doctor.

PROLONGED USE
You should see your doctor regularly for tests and examinations if you take this medication for a prolonged period. Prolonged use can cause physical dependence.

PRECAUTIONS
Over 60: Adverse reactions may be more likely and more severe in older patients.

Driving and Hazardous Work: Do not drive or engage in hazardous work until you determine how the medicine affects you.

Alcohol: Avoid alcohol while using this medication.

Pregnancy: In animal studies, pentazocine has not been shown to cause birth defects; adequate human studies have not been done. Before using this drug, tell your doctor if you are pregnant or plan to become pregnant. Overuse during pregnancy can cause drug dependence in the fetus.

Breast Feeding: Pentazocine may pass into breast milk; caution is advised. Consult your doctor for specific advice.

Infants and Children: Adverse reactions may be more likely and more severe in children. Consult your doctor for specific advice. Not recommended for use by children under the age of 12.

Special Concerns: If you feel the medication is not working properly after a few weeks, consult your doctor about other treatment options. Before undergoing any surgical procedure (including dental surgery), be sure to tell the doctor or dentist in charge that you are taking pentazocine.

OVERDOSE
Symptoms: Confusion; severe drowsiness, weakness, or dizziness; slurred speech; small, pinpoint pupils; cold, clammy skin; slow breathing; seizures; loss of consciousness.

What to Do: Call your doctor, emergency medical services (EMS), or the nearest poison control center immediately.

DRUG INTERACTIONS
Consult your physician for specific advice if you are taking carbamazepine or other medicine for seizures, barbiturates, sedatives, cough medicines, decongestants, antidepressants, other prescription pain medications, MAO inhibitors, naltrexone, rifampin, or zidovudine (AZT).

FOOD INTERACTIONS
No known food interactions.

DISEASE INTERACTIONS
Consult your doctor if you have any of the following: a history of alcohol or drug abuse, emotional illness, brain disorders or head injury, seizures, lung disease, prostate disorders or other problems with urination, gallstones, colitis, or heart, kidney, liver, or thyroid disease.

Pentobarbital Sodium

BRAND NAME
Nembutal

▶ Drug Class: Barbiturate

▶ Available in: Capsules, elixir, injection, suppositories

▶ Available OTC? No

▶ As Generic? Yes

Side Effects

SERIOUS
Excitability, confusion, or excessive sedation to the point you cannot be awakened. Also yellowish tinge to the eyes or skin; swollen eyelids, face, or lips, wheezing, or rash (these may be signs of drug allergy); sores on lips or mouth. Call your doctor immediately.

COMMON
Clumsiness, unsteadiness, persistent drowsiness, dizziness or lightheadedness.

LESS COMMON
Anxiety or nervousness, nightmares, insomnia, constipation, feeling faint, irritability, headache, nausea or vomiting.

PRINCIPAL USES
Primarily for sedation before surgery and to control certain types of seizures. With the availability of newer sleep-inducing drugs, pentobarbital is now rarely used for short-term treatment of insomnia.

HOW THE DRUG WORKS
Barbiturates such as pentobarbital act as powerful sedatives by reducing activity in the central nervous system.

DOSAGE
Sedation before surgery—Adult oral dosage: 100 mg. Children's oral dosage: 0.9 mg to 2.7 mg per lb of body weight, usually not more than 100 mg. To control seizures— Usually given intravenously by a doctor. Pentobarbital injection (into a vein or muscle) is only done under the direction of a physician. For insomnia—Adult oral dosage: 100 mg taken at bedtime.

ONSET OF EFFECT
Within 30 minutes.

DURATION OF ACTION
1 to 4 hours for oral or rectal forms, 15 minutes for injection.

DIETARY ADVICE
Oral forms can be taken with fluid or food.

STORAGE
Store in a tightly sealed container away from heat, moisture, and direct light.

IF YOU MISS A DOSE
Take it as soon as you remember. If it is near the time for the next dose, skip the missed dose and resume your regular dosage schedule. Do not double the next dose.

STOPPING THE DRUG
The decision to stop taking the drug should be made by your doctor. There is a risk of withdrawal side effects when the drug is stopped suddenly.

PROLONGED USE
Barbiturates may be habit-forming, and prolonged use may increase the risk of dependency. Pentobarbital, as well as other barbiturates, when used for insomnia, is only prescribed on a short-term basis. It is not usually effective when used for longer than 2 weeks.

PRECAUTIONS
Over 60: Adverse reactions may be more likely and more severe in older patients and may require that smaller doses be used.

Driving and Hazardous Work: Because of sedative effects, do not drive or engage in hazardous work until you determine how the medicine affects you.

Alcohol: Avoid alcohol; its sedative effects are additive to those of the drug.

Pregnancy: Pentobarbital can cause birth defects and problems during pregnancy. Before taking pentobarbital, be sure to tell your doctor if you are pregnant or plan to become pregnant.

Breast Feeding: Pentobarbital passes into breast milk in small amounts and can cause side effects in breast-feeding infants. Consult your doctor for advice.

Infants and Children: As with older patients, infants and children are more sensitive to the effects of pentobarbital. A lower dose may be warranted.

Special Concerns: Pentobarbital may cause physical or mental dependence. Check with your doctor at once if you feel overly sedated or if you suffer withdrawal side effects when you stop the drug.

OVERDOSE
Symptoms: Severe sedation or excessive drowsiness, confusion, irritability, shortness of breath or troubled breathing, slurred speech, staggering walk, severe weakness.

What to Do: Call your doctor, emergency medical services (EMS), or the nearest poison control center immediately.

DRUG INTERACTIONS
Consult your doctor for specific advice if you are taking other seizure medicines, central nervous system depressants, warfarin (blood thinner), or oral contraceptives. Pentobarbital may make oral contraceptives less effective.

FOOD INTERACTIONS
No known food interactions.

DISEASE INTERACTIONS
Caution is advised when taking pentobarbital. Consult your doctor if you have any of the following: kidney disease, liver disease, porphyria, hyperactivity, mental depression, or a history of alcohol or drug abuse.

Pentosan Polysulfate Sodium

BRAND NAME
Elmiron

BNP 7600   BNP 7600

Elmiron 100 mg
(BAKER NORTON)

▶ Drug Class: Synthetic sulfated polysaccharide

▶ Available in: Capsules

▶ Available OTC? No

▶ As Generic? No

Side Effects

SERIOUS
Fever, unusual tiredness or fatigue, chills, itching, skin rash or hives, difficulty breathing, sore throat, unusual bleeding or bruising. Call your doctor immediately.

COMMON
No common side effects are associated with the use of pentosan.

LESS COMMON
Abdominal pain, hair loss, diarrhea, nausea, stomach distress, dizziness, rash, headache.

PRINCIPAL USES
To relieve bladder pain or discomfort caused by interstitial cystitis, an inflammatory bladder condition predominantly affecting women, marked by frequent and painful urination.

HOW THE DRUG WORKS
The exact mechanism of action is unknown, but pentosan is believed to adhere to the mucosal lining of the bladder, acting as a coating to prevent irritating substances in the urine from reaching the bladder wall.

DOSAGE
100 mg, 3 times a day.

ONSET OF EFFECT
Unknown.

DURATION OF ACTION
Unknown.

DIETARY ADVICE
Should be taken with a full glass of water on an empty stomach, at least 1 hour before or 2 hours after meals, and at least 1 hour before or after any other food, milk or milk-based product, or medication.

STORAGE
Store in a tightly sealed container away from heat, moisture, and direct light.

IF YOU MISS A DOSE
Take it as soon as you remember. If it is near the time for the next dose, skip the missed dose and resume your regular dosage schedule. Do not double the next dose.

STOPPING THE DRUG
Take it as prescribed for the full treatment period, even if you begin to feel better before the scheduled end of therapy. The decision to stop taking the drug should be made by your doctor.

PROLONGED USE
Therapy generally lasts for 3 months. You should be reassessed by your doctor at that time. If your condition has not improved and there are few side effects, your doctor may continue therapy for an additional 3 months.

PRECAUTIONS
Over 60: Adverse reactions may be more likely and more severe in older patients.

Driving and Hazardous Work: Do not drive or engage in hazardous work until you determine how the medicine affects you.

Alcohol: Avoid alcohol when taking this medication, since it may provoke further bladder irritation.

Pregnancy: Adequate studies of the use of this drug during pregnancy have not been done. Before taking pentosan, tell your doctor if you are pregnant or plan to become pregnant.

Breast Feeding: Pentosan may pass into breast milk; caution is advised. Consult your doctor for advice.

Infants and Children: The safety and effectiveness of pentosan use by patients under age 16 have not been established.

Special Concerns: This drug may increase your susceptibility to sunburn. Use measures to protect your skin from ultraviolet light until you determine how the medicine affects you.

OVERDOSE
Symptoms: An overdose of pentosan is unlikely; no cases of overdose have been reported.

What to Do: Emergency instructions not applicable.

DRUG INTERACTIONS
The following drugs may interact with pentosan. Consult your doctor for specific advice if you are taking alteplase, aspirin, warfarin or any other anticoagulant, heparin, or streptokinase.

FOOD INTERACTIONS
No known food interactions.

DISEASE INTERACTIONS
Caution is advised when taking pentosan. Consult your doctor if you have any of the following conditions: hemophilia, low platelet count or any bleeding problems, blockage or obstruction of the intestine, stomach or intestinal ulcers, polyps, liver disease, or blood vessel disease.

BRAND NAME
Trental

Trental 400 mg
(Hoechst Marion Roussel)

▶ Drug Class: Hemorheologic agent

▶ Available in: Extended-release tablets

▶ Available OTC? No

▶ As Generic? Yes

Side Effects

SERIOUS
Chest pain, heartbeat irregularities. Call your doctor or emergency medical services (EMS) immediately.

COMMON
No common side effects have been reported.

LESS COMMON
Dizziness, headache, stomach pain or upset, nausea or vomiting.

PRINCIPAL USES
To improve blood flow and reduce leg pain in patients with poor circulation.

HOW THE DRUG WORKS
It decreases the viscosity (or thickness) of blood, permitting easier red blood cell movement throughout the circulatory system.

DOSAGE
400 mg, 2 or 3 times a day.

ONSET OF EFFECT
Unknown. The full effect may take 2 to 4 weeks or longer.

DURATION OF ACTION
Unknown.

DIETARY ADVICE
Pentoxifylline should be taken with meals to lessen the risk of stomach upset. Taking an antacid may also help.

STORAGE
Store in a tightly sealed container away from heat and direct light.

IF YOU MISS A DOSE
Take a missed dose as soon as you remember. If it is near the time for the next dose, skip the missed dose and resume your regular dosage schedule, as prescribed. Do not double the next dose.

STOPPING THE DRUG
The decision to stop taking the drug should be made by your doctor. Take as prescribed for the full treatment period, even if you are feeling better before the scheduled end of therapy.

PROLONGED USE
You should see your doctor regularly for tests and physical examinations if you must take this drug for a prolonged period of time.

PRECAUTIONS
Over 60: Adverse reactions may be more likely and more severe in older patients.

Driving and Hazardous Work: Do not drive or engage in hazardous work until you determine how the medicine affects you.

Alcohol: Alcohol should be avoided while taking this medication.

Pregnancy: Pentoxifylline has not been shown to cause birth defects, but in animal studies it has caused other harmful effects. Human studies have not been done. Before you take pentoxifylline, be sure to tell your doctor if you are pregnant or plan to become pregnant.

Breast Feeding: Pentoxifylline passes into breast milk; caution is advised. Consult your doctor for specific advice.

Infants and Children: There is no specific information comparing use of pentoxifylline in infants and children with other age groups. Use and dosage must be determined by your doctor.

Special Concerns: In addition to taking pentoxifylline, you should practice such measures as weight control and exercise. Bathe your feet daily in lukewarm water, applying lanolin afterward, and wear clean cotton socks. Do not smoke cigarettes, since smoking can make your condition worse by narrowing blood vessels; indeed, tobacco of all types must be avoided. Tablets should be swallowed whole, without breaking, crushing, or chewing.

OVERDOSE
Symptoms: Flushing, very low blood pressure, nervousness, agitation, tremors, seizures, fever, agitation, loss of consciousness, very slow heartbeat. Symptoms usually appear 4 to 5 hours following an overdose.

What to Do: Discontinue the medication and call your doctor, emergency medical services (EMS), or the nearest poison control center right away.

DRUG INTERACTIONS
Consult your doctor for specific advice if you are taking anticoagulants, theophylline, drugs for hypertension, or any other prescription or over-the-counter drugs.

FOOD INTERACTIONS
No known food interactions.

DISEASE INTERACTIONS
Caution is advised when taking pentoxifylline. Consult your doctor if you have any condition in which there is a risk of bleeding, such as a recent stroke. Use of pentoxifylline may cause complications in patients with liver or kidney disease, since these organs work together to remove the medication from the body.

Pergolide Mesylate

Permax 0.05 mg
(**ATHENA**)

▶ Drug Class: Antiparkinsonism drug

▶ Available in: Tablets

▶ Available OTC? No

▶ As Generic? No

Side Effects

SERIOUS
Confusion, hallucinations, unusual or abnormal muscle movements, low blood pressure (causing dizziness, lightheadedness, fainting, or confusion) pain or burning while urinating (symptoms of a urinary tract infection).

COMMON
Dizziness or lightheadedness when standing or sitting up suddenly is particularly common when the drug is first started but usually subsides with continued use.

LESS COMMON
High blood pressure, diarrhea, dry mouth, facial swelling.

PRINCIPAL USES
Pergolide is used in conjunction with levodopa/carbidopa to treat Parkinson's disease or Parkinson-like syndromes, which can occur following injury to or infection of the nervous system, damage to the blood vessels in the brain, or exposure to certain toxins.

HOW THE DRUG WORKS
Pergolide directly stimulates receptor cells that act with the brain chemical dopamine to initiate and enhance smooth control of voluntary muscle movement.

DOSAGE
Adults: Initial dose is 0.05 mg, once a day. This is gradually increased over the course of 12 days to 0.25 mg a day. The dose can then be increased every 3 days until the ideal therapeutic response is achieved. The usual adult maintenance dose is 3 mg a day, usually given in 3 divided doses. The maximum dose is 5 mg a day. Children: This medication is generally not prescribed for children.

ONSET OF EFFECT
Unknown.

DURATION OF ACTION
Unknown.

DIETARY ADVICE
No special restrictions.

STORAGE
Store in a tightly sealed container away from heat, moisture, and direct light.

IF YOU MISS A DOSE
Take it as soon as you remember. If it is near the time for the next dose, skip the missed dose and resume your regular dosage schedule. Do not double the next dose.

STOPPING THE DRUG
Consult your doctor before stopping the drug. The dosage should be tapered gradually over the course of 7 to 14 days.

PROLONGED USE
It is not known whether long-term use of pergolide presents any special problems; study of the drug's long-term effects is very limited.

PRECAUTIONS
Over 60: No special problems are expected, but use this drug with caution.

Driving and Hazardous Work: Pergolide may cause drowsiness or confusion. Do not drive or engage in hazardous work until you determine how the medicine affects you.

Alcohol: Avoid alcohol.

Pregnancy: Adequate human studies have not been done. This drug should not be used in pregnant women.

Breast Feeding: Pergolide may inhibit the secretion of breast milk and so should not be used by nursing mothers.

Infants and Children: The safety and effectiveness of this medication for infants and children have not been established; consult your pediatrician.

Special Concerns: This drug should be used with special caution by those with any gastrointestinal disorders or any urinary difficulty, for example, problems when urinating, pain with urination, or urinary tract infection.

OVERDOSE
Symptoms: There have been very few reports of pergolide mesylate overdose. Signs and symptoms include low blood pressure and agitation.

What to Do: Call your doctor, emergency medical services (EMS), or the nearest poison control center immediately.

DRUG INTERACTIONS
Pergolide may interact with phenothiazine antipsychotic drugs such as chlorpromazine hydrochloride, thioridazine hydrochloride, or prochlorperazine. Consult your doctor for advice.

FOOD INTERACTIONS
No known food interactions.

DISEASE INTERACTIONS
Consult your doctor if you have any of the following: a gastrointestinal disorder, a urinary tract disorder, or heart disease (especially a condition associated with heart rhythm abnormalities).

Perindopril Erbumine

BRAND NAME
Aceon

▶ Drug Class: Angiotensin-converting enzyme (ACE) inhibitor

▶ Available in: Tablets

▶ Available OTC? No

▶ As Generic? No

Side Effects

SERIOUS
Fever and chills, sore throat and hoarseness, sudden difficulty breathing or swallowing, swelling of the face, mouth, or extremities, impaired kidney function (ankle swelling, decreased urination), confusion, yellow discoloration of the eyes or skin (indicating liver dysfunction), intense itching, chest pain or palpitations, abdominal pain. Serious side effects are very rare; contact your doctor immediately.

COMMON
Dry, persistent cough.

LESS COMMON
Dizziness or fainting, skin rash, numbness or tingling in the hands, feet, or lips, unusual fatigue or muscle weakness, nausea, drowsiness, loss of taste, headache.

PRINCIPAL USES
To control high blood pressure (hypertension).

HOW THE DRUG WORKS
Angiotensin-converting enzyme (ACE) inhibitors block an enzyme that produces angiotensin, a naturally occurring substance that causes blood vessels to constrict and stimulates production of the adrenal hormone, aldosterone, which promotes sodium retention in the body. As a result, ACE inhibitors relax blood vessels (causing them to widen) and reduces sodium retention, which lowers blood pressure and so decreases the workload of the heart.

DOSAGE
To start, 4 mg once a day. Doses may be increased to a maximum of 16 mg a day in 1 or 2 doses. The usual maintenance dose is 4 to 8 mg a day. Patients over the age of 65 should start with a dose of 2 mg and not take more than 8 mg a day without consulting their doctor.

ONSET OF EFFECT
Within 1 to 2 hours.

DURATION OF ACTION
Up to 24 hours.

DIETARY ADVICE
Perindopril can be taken without regard to meals. Follow your doctor's dietary advice (such as low-salt or low-cholesterol restrictions) to improve control over high blood pressure and heart disease. Avoid high-potassium foods like bananas and citrus fruits and juices, unless you are also taking medications, such as diuretics, that lower potassium levels.

STORAGE
Store in a tightly sealed container away from heat, moisture, and direct light.

IF YOU MISS A DOSE
Take it as soon as you remember. If it is near the time for the next dose, skip the missed dose and resume your regular dosage schedule. Do not double the next dose.

STOPPING THE DRUG
Do not stop taking this drug abruptly, as this may cause potentially serious health problems. Dosage should be reduced gradually, according to your doctor's instructions.

PROLONGED USE
See your doctor regularly for examinations and tests if you must take this medicine for a prolonged period. Remember that perindopril helps control high blood pressure but does not cure it. Lifelong therapy may be necessary.

PRECAUTIONS
Over 60: Some elderly patients may be more sensitive to the effects of this drug; smaller doses may be warranted.

Driving and Hazardous Work: Do not drive or engage in hazardous work until you determine how the medicine affects you.

Alcohol: Consume alcohol only in moderation since it may increase the effect of the drug and cause an excessive drop in blood pressure. Consult your doctor for advice.

Pregnancy: Use of perindopril during the last six months of pregnancy may cause severe defects, even death, in the fetus. The drug should be discontinued if you are pregnant or plan to become pregnant.

Breast Feeding: Perindopril may pass into breast milk; caution is advised. Consult your doctor for advice.

Infants and Children: Safety and effectiveness have not been established for patients under age 18.

Special Concerns: Perindopril has to be stopped if blood liver enzymes become markedly elevated.

OVERDOSE
Symptoms: Dizziness or fainting due to extremely low blood pressure.

What to Do: Few cases of overdose have been reported. However, call your doctor, emergency medical services (EMS), or the nearest poison control center immediately if you suspect that someone has taken a much larger dose than prescribed.

DRUG INTERACTIONS
Consult your doctor if you are taking diuretics (especially potassium-sparing diuretics), potassium supplements or drugs containing potassium (check ingredient labels), lithium, or gentamicin.

FOOD INTERACTIONS
Avoid low-salt milk and salt substitutes. Many of these products contain potassium.

DISEASE INTERACTIONS
Consult your doctor if you have had a prior allergic reaction to an ACE inhibitor, congestive heart failure, other types of heart disease, liver disease, or kidney failure.

Permethrin

BRAND NAMES
Elimite, Nix

▶ Drug Class: Topical antiparasitic

▶ Available in: Lotion

▶ Available OTC? Yes

▶ As Generic? Yes

Side Effects

SERIOUS
No serious side effects have been reported.

COMMON
Burning, itching, numbness, rash, redness, stinging, swelling, or tingling of scalp. In most cases such symptoms are mild and temporary; notify your doctor if they are more troublesome or if they persist.

LESS COMMON
No less-common side effects have been reported.

PRINCIPAL USES
To treat infestations of head lice.

HOW THE DRUG WORKS
Permethrin is absorbed into the bodies of lice, where it blocks nerve activity, ultimately causing paralysis and death of the lice. (The drug has no such toxic effect on humans.)

DOSAGE
For treatment of head lice (pediculus humanus capitus): After the hair has been washed with shampoo, rinsed with water, and dried with a towel, apply a sufficient amount (approximately 25 ml) of liquid. Allow it to remain on the hair for 10 minutes, then rinse off with water. Rinse thoroughly and dry with a clean towel. Use a fine-tooth comb to remove any remaining nits or nit shells. If lice are found after 7 days, repeat the treatment.

ONSET OF EFFECT
Within 10 minutes.

DURATION OF ACTION
Up to 10 days.

DIETARY ADVICE
Permethrin can be used without regard to diet.

STORAGE
Store in a tightly sealed container away from heat and direct light.

IF YOU MISS A DOSE
If a second dose is needed and you do not administer it after 7 days, do so as soon as you remember.

STOPPING THE DRUG
You need not take the second dose if no lice are found after 7 days.

PROLONGED USE
If lice recur, consult your doctor.

PRECAUTIONS
Over 60: There is no information comparing the use of permethrin in older patients with use in younger persons; no special problems are expected.

Driving and Hazardous Work: The use of permethrin should not impair your ability to perform such tasks safely.

Alcohol: No special problems are expected.

Pregnancy: In animal studies, permethrin has not caused problems or birth defects. Human studies have not been done. Before you use permethrin, tell your doctor if you are pregnant or plan to become pregnant.

Breast Feeding: Permethrin may pass into breast milk; caution is advised. Consult your doctor for advice.

Infants and Children: Use and dosage in children up to 2 years of age must be determined by your doctor.

Special Concerns: All members of your household should be examined for lice and given treatment if necessary. Any sexual partner should be examined and treated if necessary. Clothing, household linen, hairbrushes, combs, and bedding should be thoroughly cleaned by machine washing with hot water and machine drying for at least 20 minutes, using the hot cycle. Seal nonwashable items in a plastic bag for at least 2 weeks or spray them with a product designed to eliminate lice and their nits. You should not use this drug if you are hypersensitive to chrysanthemums. Treatment with permethrin may temporarily worsen the itching and other symptoms of head lice infestation.

OVERDOSE
Symptoms: No cases of overdose have been reported.

What to Do: Although overdose is unlikely, if someone accidentally ingests the drug, call your doctor, emergency medical services (EMS), or the nearest poison control center immediately.

DRUG INTERACTIONS
Before you use this medicine, tell your doctor if you are using any other prescription or over-the-counter medication that is to be applied to the scalp.

FOOD INTERACTIONS
No known food interactions.

DISEASE INTERACTIONS
Consult your doctor if you have severe inflammation of the skin.

Perphenazine

▶ Drug Class: Neuroleptic;
antipsychotic

▶ Available in: Oral solution,
tablets, injection

▶ Available OTC? No

▶ As Generic? Yes

Side Effects

SERIOUS
Rapid heartbeat, profuse
sweating, seizures, difficulty breathing, neck stiffness, swelling of the
tongue, difficulty swal-
lowing. Also a rare condition can develop called
neuroleptic malignant
syndrome, characterized
by stiffness or spasms of
the muscles, high fever,
and confusion or disori-
entation. Call your doctor
immediately.

COMMON
Nausea, reduced sweat-
ing, dry mouth, blurred
vision, drowsiness, shak-
ing of hands, stiffness,
stooped posture.

LESS COMMON
Difficult urination, men-
strual irregularities,
breast pain or swelling,
unexpected weight gain,
uncontrolled movements
of the tongue, fever,
chills, sore throat,
unusual bruising or
bleeding, heart palpita-
tions, skin rash, itching,
increased sensitivity of
the skin to sunlight.

PRINCIPAL USES
To treat psychotic condi-
tions (severe mental disorders characterized by
distorted thoughts, perceptions, and emotions), such
as schizophrenia.

HOW THE DRUG WORKS
Perphenazine blocks receptors of dopamine (a chemical that aids in the
transmission of nerve
impulses) in the central nervous system. Presumably,
this produces a tranquilizing
or antipsychotic effect.

DOSAGE
Usual adult dose: Initially,
4 to 8 mg a day. Your physician may gradually increase
the dose as needed and tolerated, not to exceed 64 mg
a day.

ONSET OF EFFECT
Sedation may occur within
minutes, but onset of
antipsychotic effect may
take hours to occur or may
not occur until days or
weeks after the beginning
of therapy.

DURATION OF ACTION
12 to 24 hours, but effects
may persist for several days.

DIETARY ADVICE
Can be taken with food or a
full glass of milk or water.

STORAGE
Store in a tightly sealed container away from heat, moisture, and direct light.

IF YOU MISS A DOSE
Take it as soon as you
remember. However, if it is
near the time for the next
dose, skip the missed dose
and resume your regular
dosage schedule. Do not
double the next dose.

STOPPING THE DRUG
The decision to stop taking
the drug should be made in
consultation with your
physician.

PROLONGED USE
Consult your doctor about
the need for follow-up evaluations and tests if you must
take this drug for an
extended period.

PRECAUTIONS
Over 60: Adverse reactions
are more likely and more
severe in older patients.

**Driving and Hazardous
Work:** Avoid such activities
until you determine how the
medicine affects you.

Alcohol: Avoid alcohol.

Pregnancy: Avoid using
perphenazine if you are
pregnant or plan to become
pregnant.

Breast Feeding: Either
avoid taking the drug if possible or refrain from breast
feeding.

Infants and Children:
Adverse reactions may be
more likely and more
severe in children.

Special Concerns: Avoid
prolonged exposure to high
temperatures or hot cli-
mates. Drink plenty of fluids
and stay cool in the sum-
mertime. Avoid overexpo-
sure to sunlight until you
determine if the drug
heightens your skin's sensitivity to ultraviolet light.

OVERDOSE
Symptoms: Extreme
drowsiness, heartbeat irregularities, dry mouth, paradoxical restlessness or
agitation, seizures, loss
of consciousness.

What to Do: Call your
doctor, emergency medical
services (EMS), or the
nearest poison control
center immediately.

DRUG INTERACTIONS
Consult your doctor for
specific advice if you are
taking amantadine, high
blood pressure medication,
bromocriptine, deferoxam-
ine, diuretics, levobunolol,
heart medication, metipranolol, nabilone, other psychiatric drugs, pentamidine,
pimozide, promethazine,
trimeprazine, a thyroid
agent, central nervous system depressants, epineph-
rine, lithium, levodopa,
methyldopa, metoclo-
pramide, metyrosine,
pemoline, a rauwolfia
alkaloid, or metrizamide.

FOOD INTERACTIONS
No known food interactions.

DISEASE INTERACTIONS
Consult your doctor if you
have Parkinson's disease or
any movement disorder,
glaucoma, epilepsy, liver
disease, or kidney disease.

Phenazopyridine Hydrochloride

BRAND NAMES
Azo-Standard, Baridium,
Eridium, Geridium,
Phenazodine, Pyridiate,
Pyridium, Urodine,
Urogesic, Viridium

Generic 100 mg
(ABLE)

▶ Drug Class: Urinary analgesic

▶ Available in: Tablets

▶ Available OTC? Yes

▶ As Generic? Yes

Side Effects

SERIOUS
Serious side effects are
rare. Call your doctor
immediately if you expe-
rience any of the follow-
ing: difficulty breathing,
swelling of the face, fingers, feet, or lower legs,
blue or purple-blue skin
color, unusual fatigue,
fever, confusion, sudden
decrease in urine output,
shortness of breath, tightness in the chest, skin
rash, yellow discoloration
of the eyes or skin,
unusual weight gain.

COMMON
Reddish orange urine.

LESS COMMON
Indigestion, dizziness,
stomach cramps or pain,
headache.

PRINCIPAL USES
For short-term relief of
symptoms caused by irritation of the urinary tract.
Such symptoms include
burning, pain, and discomfort during urination, as
well as an increased urge
to urinate with only small
amounts of urine passed on
each occasion. Irritation of
the urinary tract commonly
occurs as a result of bladder
infection; phenazopyridine
can ease symptoms but will
not cure such an infection.

HOW THE DRUG WORKS
Phenazopyridine passes
through—and has a local
anesthetic effect upon the
lining of—the urinary tract,
thus relieving the discomfort associated with infection or inflammation.

DOSAGE
Adults: 200 mg, 3 times a
day. Children: 1.8 mg per
lb of body weight, 3 times
a day.

ONSET OF EFFECT
Unknown.

DURATION OF ACTION
Unknown.

DIETARY ADVICE
This medication is best
taken with or after meals to
minimize stomach upset.

STORAGE
Store in a tightly sealed container away from heat, moisture, and direct light.

IF YOU MISS A DOSE
Take it as soon as you
remember. If it is near the
time for the next dose, skip
the missed dose and
resume your regular dosage
schedule. Do not double the
next dose.

STOPPING THE DRUG
The decision to stop taking
the drug should be made by
your doctor. If it is being

taken with an antibiotic, it
should be taken for only 2
days (6 doses).

PROLONGED USE
Phenazopyridine is intended
only for short-term use.

PRECAUTIONS
Over 60: No special problems are expected.

**Driving and Hazardous
Work:** Do not drive or
engage in hazardous work
until you determine how the
medicine affects you.

Alcohol: No special precautions are necessary.

Pregnancy: Adequate
human studies have not
been done. Before taking
phenazopyridine, tell your
doctor if you are pregnant
or plan to become pregnant.

Breast Feeding:
Phenazopyridine may pass
into breast milk; caution is
advised. Consult your doctor for advice.

Infants and Children:
No special problems are
expected.

Special Concerns:
Phenazopyridine causes
the urine to turn reddish
orange. This is harmless,
but it may stain clothing.
The drug may also cause
permanent staining or discoloration of soft contact
lenses; it is best to wear
glasses while taking the
drug. For diabetic patients,
phenazopyridine may cause
false test results with sugar
and urine ketone tests. Do
not chew the tablets; chewing may cause permanent
discoloration of teeth. Do
not use any leftover medicine for future urinary tract
infections without consulting your doctor.

OVERDOSE
Symptoms: Fatigue, paleness, shortness of breath,
heart palpitations, bloody
or cloudy urine, decreased
urine output, swelling of the
ankles and calves, lower
back or flank pain, nausea
or vomiting.

What to Do: While an
overdose is unlikely, call
your doctor, emergency
medical services (EMS), or
the nearest poison control
center immediately if symptoms of overdose occur.

DRUG INTERACTIONS
Some drugs may interact
with phenazopyridine. Consult your doctor for specific
advice if you are taking any
prescription or over-the-
counter medication.

FOOD INTERACTIONS
No known food interactions.

DISEASE INTERACTIONS
Caution is advised when
taking phenazopyridine.
Consult your doctor if you
have any of the following:
glucose-6-phosphate dehy-
drogenase deficiency
(G6PD), hepatitis, uremia,
pyelonephritis (kidney infection) during pregnancy, or
other kidney disease.

Phenelzine Sulfate

Nardil 15 mg
(PARKE-DAVIS)

▶ Drug Class: Monoamine oxidase (MAO) inhibitor antidepressant

▶ Available in: Tablets

▶ Available OTC? No

▶ As Generic? No

Side Effects

SERIOUS
Severe headache, high blood pressure, severe chest pain, dilated pupils, irregular heartbeat, sensitivity of eyes to light (photophobia), fever and sweating, nausea and vomiting, stiff neck, extreme dizziness. Call your doctor immediately.

COMMON
Blurring of vision, decreased urination, sexual dysfunction, dizziness or lightheadedness, mild headache, appetite changes including cravings for sweets, weight gain, increase in sweating, muscle twitching during sleep, restlessness, shakiness, fatigue, insomnia.

LESS COMMON
Chills, constipation, decrease in appetite, dry mouth, swelling in the lower extremities.

PRINCIPAL USES
To treat symptoms of major mental depression.

HOW THE DRUG WORKS
Phenelzine inhibits the activity of monoamine oxidase, an enzyme that renders certain brain chemicals (epinephrine, norepinephrine, and dopamine) inactive. Consequently, this drug increases the availability of these chemicals in the nervous system; this is thought to have an antidepressant effect.

DOSAGE
Adults: To start, 15 mg, 3 times a day; may be increased to 90 mg a day. Older adults: To start, 15 mg once a day; may be increased to 60 mg a day.

ONSET OF EFFECT
7 to 10 days; it may take up to 8 weeks for full effect.

DURATION OF ACTION
Up to 10 days after treatment stops.

DIETARY ADVICE
See Food Interactions.

STORAGE
Store in a tightly sealed container away from heat and direct light.

IF YOU MISS A DOSE
Take it as soon as you remember. If it is near the time for the next dose, skip the missed dose and resume your regular dosage schedule. Do not double the next dose.

STOPPING THE DRUG
The decision to stop taking the drug should be made in consultation with your physician.

PROLONGED USE
The usual course of therapy lasts 6 months to 1 year; some patients benefit from additional therapy. See your doctor regularly for tests and examinations if long-term therapy is required.

PRECAUTIONS
Over 60: Adverse reactions may be more likely and more severe in older patients.

Driving and Hazardous Work: Use caution when driving or engaging in hazardous work until you determine how the medicine affects you.

Alcohol: Avoid alcohol.

Pregnancy: Using this drug during pregnancy may increase the risk of birth defects.

Breast Feeding: Phenelzine may pass into breast milk; caution is advised. Consult your doctor for specific advice.

Infants and Children: Phenelzine is not recommended for children 16 years of age and under. Antidepressants increase the risk of suicidal thinking and behavior (suicidality) in children with major depression and other psychiatric disorders. Discuss with your doctor this risk versus the benefits of using this drug. Children should be observed closely for worsening of symptoms, suicidality, or unusual changes in behavior at the onset of therapy and when making changes in dosage.

Special Concerns: Before having any surgery, emergency treatment, or dental treatment, tell the doctor or dentist in charge that you are taking phenelzine. Your doctor may advise you to carry a card saying that you use phenelzine.

OVERDOSE
Symptoms: Profound anxiety, confusion, seizures, cold, clammy skin, severe drowsiness, irregular pulse, hallucinations, severe headache, fainting, stiff muscles, sweating, breathing difficulty.

What to Do: Seek emergency medical help.

DRUG INTERACTIONS
Consult your doctor for specific advice if you are taking or have recently taken amphetamines, blood pressure medications, diet pills, cyclobenzaprine, fluoxetine, levodopa, maprotiline, asthma medication, cold or allergy medication, meperidine, methylphenidate, another MAO inhibitor, paroxetine, sertraline, a tricyclic antidepressant, an oral diabetes drug, insulin, bupropion, buspirone, carbamazepine, any central nervous system depressant, dextromethorphan, trazodone, or tryptophan.

FOOD INTERACTIONS
Avoid foods with a high tyramine content, such as cheeses; pickled or smoked meat, poultry, or fish; processed meats; and sauerkraut. Avoid red wine or alcohol-free or reduced-alcohol beer. Do not consume beverages or foods with a high caffeine content.

DISEASE INTERACTIONS
Caution is advised when taking phenelzine. Consult your doctor if you have any of the following: a history of alcohol abuse, angina, frequent headaches, asthma, bronchitis, diabetes, epilepsy, heart disease or a recent heart attack, blood vessel disease, liver disease, Parkinson's disease, a recent stroke, kidney disease, an overactive thyroid, or pheochromocytoma.

Phenobarbital

BRAND NAMES
Barbita, Luminal, Solfoton

Generic 30 mg
(ROXANE)

▸ Drug Class: Barbiturate

▸ Available in: Capsules, elixir, tablets, injection

▸ Available OTC? No

▸ As Generic? Yes

Side Effects

SERIOUS
Excitability, confusion, or excessive sedation to the point you cannot be awakened. Also yellow discoloration of eyes or skin; swollen eyelids, face, or lips, wheezing, or rash (may be signs of drug allergy); sores on the lips or mouth. Call your doctor immediately.

COMMON
Clumsiness, unsteadiness, persistent drowsiness, dizziness or lightheadedness.

LESS COMMON
Anxiety or nervousness, nightmares, insomnia, constipation, feeling faint, irritability, headache, nausea or vomiting.

PRINCIPAL USES
Primarily used for sedation before surgery and to control certain types of seizures. With the availability of newer sleep-inducing drugs, it is now rarely used for the short-term treatment of insomnia.

HOW THE DRUG WORKS
Barbiturates such as phenobarbital act as powerful sedatives by reducing activity in the central nervous system (the brain and spinal cord).

DOSAGE
For sedation— Adult oral dose: 30 to 120 mg, 2 or 3 times a day (not to exceed 400 mg a day). Children's oral dose: 2 mg per 2.2 lbs (1 kg) of body weight, 3 times a day. For seizures— Adult oral dose: 60 to 250 mg a day. Children's oral dose: 1 to 6 mg per 2.2 lbs of body weight per day. For insomnia— Adult oral dose: 100 to 320 mg at bedtime. Dosages for injectable forms of the drug will be determined by your doctor.

ONSET OF EFFECT
About 1 hour.

DURATION OF ACTION
10 to 12 hours.

DIETARY ADVICE
Tablets may be crushed and taken with fluid or food.

STORAGE
Store in a tightly sealed container away from heat, moisture, and direct light.

IF YOU MISS A DOSE
If you are taking phenobarbital regularly, take the missed dose as soon as you remember. If it is near the time for the next dose, skip the missed dose and resume your regular dosage schedule. Do not double the next dose.

STOPPING THE DRUG
The decision to stop taking the drug should be made by your doctor. There is a risk of withdrawal side effects when the drug is stopped suddenly.

PROLONGED USE
Barbiturates may be habit-forming, and prolonged use may increase the risk of dependency. Phenobarbital, as well as other barbiturates, is used only for short-term treatment of insomnia. It is not usually effective when used for longer than 14 days.

PRECAUTIONS
Over 60: Adverse reactions may be more likely and more severe in older patients and may require that smaller doses be used.

Driving and Hazardous Work: Because of sedative effects, do not drive or engage in hazardous work until you determine how the medicine affects you.

Alcohol: Avoid alcohol; its sedative effects are additive to those of the drug.

Pregnancy: Phenobarbital can cause birth defects and problems during pregnancy. Before you take phenobarbital, tell your doctor if you are pregnant or plan to become pregnant.

Breast Feeding: Phenobarbital passes into breast milk in small amounts and can cause side effects in breast-feeding infants. Consult your doctor for advice.

Infants and Children: As with older patients, infants and children are sensitive to the effects of phenobarbital.

Special Concerns: Phenobarbital may cause physical or mental dependence.

Check with your doctor if you feel overly sedated or if you suffer withdrawal side effects when you stop taking the drug.

OVERDOSE
Symptoms: Severe sedation or excessive drowsiness, confusion, severe weakness, slurred speech, staggering walk, shortness of breath or troubled breathing.

What to Do: Call your doctor, emergency medical services (EMS), or the nearest poison control center immediately.

DRUG INTERACTIONS
Consult your doctor for specific advice if you are taking other seizure medications, central nervous system depressants, warfarin (blood thinner), or oral contraceptives. Phenobarbital may make oral contraceptives less effective.

FOOD INTERACTIONS
No known food interactions.

DISEASE INTERACTIONS
Caution is advised when taking phenobarbital. Consult your doctor if you have any of the following: kidney disease, liver disease, porphyria, anemia, hyperactivity, mental depression, or a history of alcohol or drug abuse.

Phenoxybenzamine Hydrochloride

Dibenzyline 10 mg
(SMITHKLINE BEECHAM)

▶ Drug Class: Centrally acting antihypertensive

▶ Available in: Capsules

▶ Available OTC? No

▶ As Generic? No

Side Effects

SERIOUS
In laboratory animals, high and repeated doses of phenoxybenzamine have caused tumors. Whether such effects occur in humans is unknown.

COMMON
Dizziness or lightheadedness, especially when getting up from a sitting or lying position, rapid heartbeat, constricted pupils, stuffy nose.

LESS COMMON
Drowsiness, confusion, dry mouth, headache, lack of energy, male sexual problems, unusual fatigue.

PRINCIPAL USES
To treat high blood pressure caused by pheochromocytoma, a rare type of tumor that develops inside the adrenal glands, small hormone-producing glands located atop the kidneys.

HOW THE DRUG WORKS
Phenoxybenzamine acts upon certain areas of the central nervous system (the brain and spinal cord) that regulate the activity of the heart and the smooth muscle tissue surrounding the arteries. The drug causes the blood vessels to relax and widen, which lowers blood pressure.

DOSAGE
Adults: To start, 10 mg, 2 times a day. It may be increased to 20 to 40 mg, 2 or 3 times a day. Children: To start, 0.2 mg per 2.2 lbs (1 kg) of body weight once a day. It may be increased to 0.4 to 1.2 mg per 2.2 lbs in 3 or 4 daily doses.

ONSET OF EFFECT
Several hours.

DURATION OF ACTION
3 to 4 days.

DIETARY ADVICE
Take it with milk to avoid gastrointestinal irritation. Follow a healthy diet (low-salt, low-fat, low-cholesterol) as advised by your doctor to help control blood pressure and prevent heart disease.

STORAGE
Store in a tightly sealed container away from heat and direct light.

IF YOU MISS A DOSE
Take it as soon as you remember. If it is near the time for the next dose, skip the missed dose and resume your regular dosage schedule. Do not double the next dose.

STOPPING THE DRUG
The decision to stop taking the drug should be made by your doctor.

PROLONGED USE
You should see your doctor regularly for tests and examinations if you take this drug for a prolonged period.

PRECAUTIONS
Over 60: Adverse reactions, especially dizziness and lightheadedness, may be more likely and more severe in older patients. Phenoxybenzamine may reduce tolerance to cold temperatures in older patients.

Driving and Hazardous Work: Do not drive or engage in hazardous work until you determine how the medicine affects you.

Alcohol: Alcohol should be avoided while taking this medication.

Pregnancy: Animal and human studies of phenoxybenzamine have not been done. Before you take phenoxybenzamine, tell your doctor if you are pregnant or plan to become pregnant.

Breast Feeding: It is not known if phenoxybenzamine passes into breast milk. It has not been reported to cause problems in breast-fed babies. Consult your doctor about its use while nursing.

Infants and Children: No special problems expected.

Special Concerns: Before you have any kind of dental or surgical procedure, be sure to tell the doctor or dentist in charge that you take phenoxybenzamine. If dryness of the mouth continues for more than 2 weeks, consult your doctor or dentist. Be cautious in hot weather, as well as during exercise, or if you must stand for long periods of time, since these situations may increase the chances that you will become dizzy or lightheaded.

OVERDOSE
Symptoms: Dizziness, faintness, rapid heartbeat, vomiting, lethargy, loss of consciousness.

What to Do: Call your doctor, emergency medical services (EMS), or the nearest poison control center immediately.

DRUG INTERACTIONS
Consult your doctor for specific advice if you are taking diazoxide, dopamine, guanadrel, guanethidine, epinephrine, metaraminol, methoxamine, phenylephrine, or any over-the-counter medicines for appetite control, asthma, colds, hay fever, cough, or sinus problems.

FOOD INTERACTIONS
No known food interactions.

DISEASE INTERACTIONS
Caution is advised when taking phenoxybenzamine. Consult your doctor if you have cerebrovascular insufficiency, coronary artery disease, congestive heart failure, kidney disease, or a lung infection, or if you have had a recent heart attack or stroke.

Phentermine

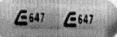

Generic 30 mg
(EON)

▶ Drug Class: Appetite suppressant

▶ Available in: Tablets, capsules

▶ Available OTC? No

▶ As Generic? Yes

Side Effects

SERIOUS
Confusion or mental depression, skin rash or hives, high blood pressure, sore throat and fever, unusual bleeding or bruising. Call your doctor immediately.

COMMON
Irritability, nervousness, restlessness, insomnia.

LESS COMMON
Blurred vision, change in sexual desire, constipation or diarrhea, difficult or painful urination, dizziness, lightheadedness, drowsiness, dry mouth, rapid heartbeat, increased urination, headache, increased sweating, nausea or vomiting, stomach cramps, unpleasant taste in the mouth.

PRINCIPAL USES
To suppress appetite in obese patients. It should be used in conjunction with a strict diet and should not be prescribed as the sole method for achieving weight loss.

HOW THE DRUG WORKS
Researchers believe that the appetite-control center for the body may be found in a part of the brain called the hypothalamus. Phentermine probably affects the transmission of nerve impulses in this area.

DOSAGE
15 to 37.5 mg once a day.

ONSET OF EFFECT
Within 1 hour.

DURATION OF ACTION
12 to 14 hours.

DIETARY ADVICE
Phentermine can be taken before breakfast or 1 to 2 hours after breakfast.

STORAGE
Store in a tightly sealed container away from heat and direct light.

IF YOU MISS A DOSE
Take it as soon as you remember. If it is near the time for the next dose, skip the missed dose and resume your regular dosage schedule. Do not double the next dose.

STOPPING THE DRUG
Take as prescribed for the full treatment period, even if you begin to observe favorable results before the scheduled end of therapy.

PROLONGED USE
Prolonged use of phentermine may result in drug tolerance or occasionally drug dependence.

PRECAUTIONS
Over 60: Adverse reactions may be more likely and more severe in older patients, especially when taken in combination with drugs that act on the central nervous system.

Driving and Hazardous Work: Do not drive or engage in hazardous work until you determine how the medicine affects you.

Alcohol: Avoid alcohol.

Pregnancy: Phentermine has not been shown to cause birth defects in humans. Before you take this drug, tell your doctor if you are pregnant or planning to become pregnant.

Breast Feeding: Phentermine may pass into breast milk; caution is advised. Consult your doctor for advice.

Infants and Children: Not recommended for use by children under age 16.

Special Concerns: After you stop taking this drug, your body may need time to adjust. Phentermine may affect blood sugar levels; consult your doctor if you have any concern. Notify your doctor if you experience mental depression, nausea or vomiting, unusual fatigue, or trembling after you stop taking phentermine. Before you have medical or dental treatment, be sure to tell your doctor or dentist that you are taking phentermine.

OVERDOSE
Symptoms: Stomach cramps, severe diarrhea, fever, hallucinations, unusual high or low blood pressure, irregular heartbeat, severe nausea or vomiting, feeling of panic, restlessness, tremor.

What to Do: An overdose of phentermine is unlikely to be life-threatening. However, if someone takes a much larger dose than recommended, call your doctor, emergency medical services (EMS), or the nearest poison control center immediately.

DRUG INTERACTIONS
The following drugs may interact with phentermine. Consult your doctor for specific advice if you are taking amantadine, amphetamines, chlophenadiol, medicine for asthma, colds, sinus problems, or allergies, methyl-phenidate, nabilone, pemoline, selective serotonin reuptake inhibitors (SSRIs), or MAO inhibitors.

FOOD INTERACTIONS
Avoid caffeine-containing beverages.

DISEASE INTERACTIONS
Caution is advised when taking phentermine. Consult your doctor if you have any of the following: a history of drug or alcohol abuse, diabetes, epilepsy, glaucoma, heart disease, blood vessel disease, high blood pressure, an overactive thyroid, or kidney disease.

Phenylephrine Hydrochloride Ophthalmic

▶ Drug Class: Adrenergic agent

▶ Available in: Ophthalmic solution

▶ Available OTC? Yes

▶ As Generic? Yes

Side Effects

SERIOUS
Dizziness; paleness; rapid, irregular, or pounding heartbeat; trembling; increased sweating. Call your doctor immediately.

COMMON
Unusually large pupils; burning, stinging, or watering of eyes; sensitivity of eyes to light; headache or brow ache.

LESS COMMON
Eye irritation not present prior to therapy.

PRINCIPAL USES
The 2.5% and 10% solutions are used to dilate the pupil of the eye (prior to eye exams or ophthalmologic procedures) and to treat certain eye conditions. The 0.12% solution is used to reduce redness of the eye caused by minor irritation.

HOW THE DRUG WORKS
Ophthalmic phenylephrine affects the muscles that control the pupils, causing them to dilate, which helps the doctor view the interior structures of the eye. The drug reduces redness by constricting the superficial blood vessels in the whites of the eye.

DOSAGE
For redness— Adults and children: 1 drop of 0.12% solution every 3 or 4 hours as needed. For certain eye conditions— Adults and teenagers: 1 drop of 2.5% or 10% solution from 1 to 3 times a day. Children: 1 drop of 2.5% solution from 1 to 3 times a day.

ONSET OF EFFECT
Rapid.

DURATION OF ACTION
From 2 to 7 hours depending on the strength of the solution.

DIETARY ADVICE
This medication can be used without regard to diet.

STORAGE
Store in a tightly sealed container away from heat, moisture, and direct light. Do not allow the medicine to freeze.

IF YOU MISS A DOSE
Apply it as soon as you remember. However, if it is near the time for the next dose, skip the missed dose and resume your regular dosage schedule. Do not double the next dose.

STOPPING THE DRUG
The decision to stop using the drug should be made by your doctor.

PROLONGED USE
You should see your doctor regularly for tests and examinations if you must use this drug for an extended period of time.

PRECAUTIONS
Over 60: No special problems are expected.

Driving and Hazardous Work: Do not drive or engage in hazardous work until you determine how the medicine affects your vision.

Alcohol: No special precautions are necessary.

Pregnancy: No problems are expected, but studies of effects in pregnancy have not been done in humans. Consult your physician.

Breast Feeding: No problems are expected, but studies of effects in breast feeding have not been done in humans. Consult your doctor.

Infants and Children: Adverse reactions may be more likely and more severe in infants and children. The 10% solution should not be used on infants. The other strengths should not be used on low-birth-weight infants.

Special Concerns: To use the eye drops, first wash your hands. Tilt your head back. Gently apply pressure to the inside corner of the eyelid and with the index finger of the same hand, pull downward on the lower eyelid to make a space. Drop the medicine into this space and close your eye. Apply pressure for 1 or 2 minutes while keeping the eye closed without blinking. Then wash your hands again. Make sure the tip of the dropper does not touch your eye, finger, or any other surface. Phenylephrine will make your eyes more sensitive to sunlight. If this occurs, wear sunglasses or avoid bright light as comfort dictates. If this effect continues for more than 12 hours after you have stopped using the medicine, consult your doctor. Ophthalmic phenylephrine is available over the counter only in the 0.12% solution. The 2.5% and 10% solutions are by doctor's prescription only.

OVERDOSE
Symptoms: Dizziness; paleness; rapid, irregular, or pounding heartbeat; trembling; profuse sweating; vomiting; coma; shock.

What to Do: Call your doctor, emergency medical services (EMS), or the nearest poison control center immediately.

DRUG INTERACTIONS
Be sure to tell your doctor if you are using any other prescription or over-the-counter medication.

FOOD INTERACTIONS
No known food interactions.

DISEASE INTERACTIONS
Consult your doctor if you have a history of heart disease, blood vessel disease, diabetes mellitus, high blood pressure, or idiopathic orthostatic hypotension (low blood pressure). This drug should not be used by those with a history of closed-angle glaucoma.

Phenylephrine Hydrochloride Systemic

▸ Drug Class: Decongestant

▸ Available in: Nasal jelly, nasal drops, nasal spray

▸ Available OTC? Yes

▸ As Generic? Yes

Side Effects

SERIOUS
No serious side effects have been reported.

COMMON
Burning, dryness, or stinging inside the nose. An increase in nasal discharge or congestion may occur after 3 to 5 days of continuous use.

LESS COMMON
Headache, rapid or irregular heartbeat, excitability, restlessness.

PRINCIPAL USES
To relieve nasal congestion caused by allergies, colds, or sinus conditions; to relieve congestion associated with ear infections.

HOW THE DRUG WORKS
Phenylephrine constricts blood vessels to reduce the blood flow to swollen nasal passages and other tissues, which reduces nasal secretions and improves nasal airflow.

DOSAGE
Adults and children 12 and over: 2 to 3 drops of 0.25% to 0.5% solution, or 1 to 2 sprays, or a small amount of jelly in each nostril every 4 hours. Children 6 to 12 years: 2 to 3 drops or 1 to 2 sprays of a 0.25% solution in each nostril every 4 hours. Children under 6 years: 2 to 3 drops of 0.125% solution every 4 hours.

ONSET OF EFFECT
Rapid.

DURATION OF ACTION
From 30 minutes to 4 hours.

DIETARY ADVICE
Drink plenty of fluids.

STORAGE
Store in a tightly sealed container away from heat and direct light.

IF YOU MISS A DOSE
Take it as soon as you remember. If it is near the time for the next dose, skip the missed dose and resume your regular dosage schedule. Do not double the next dose.

STOPPING THE DRUG
Do not use this medicine for more than 3 days without consulting your doctor.

PROLONGED USE
Using this medicine for more than 3 days may lead to rebound congestion (more severe congestion caused by the body's adaptation to the drug).

PRECAUTIONS
Over 60: Although no studies have specifically examined the use of this drug in older patients, no special problems are expected.

Driving and Hazardous Work: Do not drive or engage in hazardous work until you determine how the medicine affects you.

Alcohol: Avoid alcohol.

Pregnancy: Phenylephrine hydrochloride has not been shown to cause birth defects or other problems if taken during pregnancy.

Breast Feeding: It is not known whether phenylephrine passes into breast milk; caution is advised. Consult your doctor for specific advice.

Infants and Children: Adverse reactions may be more likely and more severe in infants and children.

Special Concerns: Each container of medicine should be used by only one person to avoid spread of infection. Blow your nose gently before using this medicine. To use the nose drops, tilt your head back or lie down on a bed and hang your head over the side. Keep your head tilted back for a few minutes after instilling the drops. To use the nasal spray, keep your head upright and sniff briskly while spraying. For best results, spray again in 3 to 5 minutes. To use the nasal jelly, first wash your hands, then place an amount of jelly about the size of a pea into each nostril and sniff it well back into the nose.

OVERDOSE
Symptoms: Rapid, irregular, or pounding heartbeat; headache or dizziness; increased sweating; nervousness; trembling; paleness; insomnia. Such symptoms are more likely to be seen in young children.

What to Do: If someone takes a much larger dose than recommended, call your doctor, emergency medical services (EMS), or the nearest poison control center immediately.

DRUG INTERACTIONS
Before you take phenylephrine, tell your doctor if you are taking any other prescription or over-the-counter drug.

FOOD INTERACTIONS
No known food interactions.

DISEASE INTERACTIONS
Consult your doctor if you have a history of any of the following: high blood pressure, diabetes mellitus, heart disease, blood vessel disease, or an overactive thyroid gland.

Dilantin 50 mg
(PARKE-DAVIS)

Additional photographs

▶ Drug Class: Anticonvulsant

▶ Available in: Prompt and
extended capsules, chewable
tablets, oral suspension

▶ Available OTC? No

▶ As Generic? Yes

Side Effects

SERIOUS
Fever, sore throat,
swollen glands, point-
like rash on the skin or
mucous membranes, blis-
tering or peeling, mouth
sores or bleeding gums,
easy bruising, pallor,
weakness, confusion, or
seizures may be a sign of
a potentially fatal blood
disorder or other compli-
cation. Call your doctor
immediately.

COMMON
Sedation, lethargy,
nervousness, dizziness,
thickened gums, exces-
sive growth of body and
facial hair. High doses
may cause abnormal
movements of the eyes,
mouth, tongue, or limbs.
Prolonged use may cause
mild nerve impairment in
the arms or legs.

LESS COMMON
Constipation, acne, mild
skin rash, incoordination.
There are numerous
additional possible side
effects; consult your doctor if you are concerned
about any adverse or
unusual reactions.

PRINCIPAL USES
To prevent or control
seizures in the treatment of
certain types of epilepsy
and other conditions.

HOW THE DRUG WORKS
Phenytoin is thought to
depress the activity of certain parts of the brain and
suppress the irregular and
uncontrolled firing of neurons that causes seizures.

DOSAGE
Adults: 200 to 500 mg a day,
as a single dose or in 2
divided doses. Children: 5
to 300 mg a day, as a single
dose or in 2 divided doses.
Some patients require
higher doses. A low dose is
used to start, then gradually
increased by your doctor.

ONSET OF EFFECT
Several hours.

DURATION OF ACTION
Maximum effect lasts for 24
hours or longer; effectiveness then gradually
decreases.

DIETARY ADVICE
Take with food to minimize
stomach upset. Tablets may
be crushed, chewed, or
swallowed whole.

STORAGE
Store in a tightly sealed container away from heat, moisture, and direct light.

IF YOU MISS A DOSE
Take it as soon as you
remember. Be especially
attentive about not missing
a dose if you are taking this
drug only once daily.

STOPPING THE DRUG
This medication should
never be stopped abruptly
because this may cause
seizures. The dose is typically tapered over a period
of weeks under the supervision of your doctor.

PROLONGED USE
This drug is often taken for
prolonged periods. See your
physician for periodic
checkups.

PRECAUTIONS
Over 60: Older patients
may require lower doses to
minimize side effects.

**Driving and Hazardous
Work:** Do not drive or
engage in hazardous work
until you determine how the
medicine affects you.

Alcohol: May contribute to
excessive drowsiness.

Pregnancy: Anticonvulsants are associated with
an increased risk of birth
defects. However, seizures
during pregnancy can also
increase the risks to the
unborn child. Discuss with
your doctor the potential
risks and benefits of using
this drug during pregnancy.
Folate supplementation is
recommended beginning
1 to 2 months before con-
ception and throughout
pregnancy.

Breast Feeding: Phenytoin passes into breast milk,
although at low levels. Consult your doctor for advice.

Infants and Children:
No special problems are
expected.

Special Concerns: The
generic version of this drug
is not recommended. Do
not change the brand of
phenytoin you are taking
without consulting your doctor. The suspension form of
phenytoin should be shaken
well before you take it. Your
doctor may advise you to
wear a medical bracelet or
carry an identification card
saying that you are taking
this medication.

OVERDOSE
Symptoms: Blurred or
double vision, difficulty
walking, severe clumsiness
or unsteadiness, severe
confusion, dizziness or
drowsiness.

What to Do: Call your
doctor, emergency medical
services (EMS), or the
nearest poison control
center immediately.

DRUG INTERACTIONS
Many other drugs may
interact with phenytoin,
including other anticonvulsants (carbamazepine, phenobarbital, primidone,
valproic acid), allopurinol,
amiodarone, anticancer
drugs, chloramphenicol,
chlorpheniramine, cimeti-
dine, diazoxide, dicumarol,
disulfiram, isoniazid, loxapine, phenylbutazone,
rifampin, sulfonamides,
trazodone, trimethoprim.

FOOD INTERACTIONS
No known food interactions.

DISEASE INTERACTIONS
Caution is advised in those
with liver or kidney disease,
since these organs work
together to remove the
medication from the body.

Pilocarpine Ophthalmic

BRAND NAMES
Adsorbocarpine,
Akarpine, Isopto Carpine,
Ocu-Carpine, Ocusert
Pilo-20, Ocusert Pilo-40,
Pilagan, Pilocar, Pilopine
HS, Piloptic, Pilostat

▶ Drug Class: Antiglaucoma agent

▶ Available in: Ophthalmic solution and gel, ocular system

▶ Available OTC? No

▶ As Generic? Yes

Side Effects

SERIOUS
Increased sweating, muscle tremors, nausea, vomiting, or diarrhea, troubled breathing or wheezing, watering of mouth, eye pain. Call your doctor immediately.

COMMON
Decreased night vision, blurred vision, change in near or far vision, eyebrow pain (usually disappears within a week).

LESS COMMON
Headache, eye irritation.

PRINCIPAL USES
To treat glaucoma and to constrict the pupil.

HOW THE DRUG WORKS
Glaucoma, a sight-threatening disorder, occurs when aqueous humor (the fluid inside the eye) cannot drain properly, causing an increase in pressure within the eyeball (intraocular pressure). This can damage the optic nerve and lead to a gradually progressive loss of vision. Pilocarpine contracts the muscles that constrict the pupil; this action appears to help open the structures that allow drainage of the aqueous humor, thereby decreasing eye pressure.

DOSAGE
Ophthalmic solution—Adults and children: Chronic glaucoma: 1 drop into the eye 1 to 4 times a day. Acute closed-angle glaucoma: 1 drop into the eye every 5 to 10 minutes for 3 to 6 doses, then 1 drop every 1 to 3 hours. Ophthalmic gel— Adults and teenagers: Once a day at bedtime. Children: Use and dosage must be determined by your doctor. Ocular system: Adults and children: 1 insert every 7 days. Infants: Use and dosage must be determined by your doctor.

ONSET OF EFFECT
10 to 60 minutes.

DURATION OF ACTION
Ophthalmic solution: 4 to 14 hours. Ophthalmic gel: Up to 24 hours; Ocular system: Up to 7 days.

DIETARY ADVICE
No special restrictions.

STORAGE
Store in a tightly sealed container away from heat, moisture, and direct light. Store the ophthalmic solution and the 3.5 g size of the ophthalmic gel at room temperature. The 5 g size of the ophthalmic gel and the ocular system should be refrigerated until used, but do not allow either to freeze.

IF YOU MISS A DOSE
Apply it as soon as you remember. If it is near the time for the next dose, skip the missed dose and resume your regular dosage schedule. Do not double the next dose.

STOPPING THE DRUG
The decision to stop using the drug should be made by your doctor.

PROLONGED USE
See your doctor regularly for tests and examinations if you take this medication for a prolonged period.

PRECAUTIONS
Over 60: No special problems are expected.

Driving and Hazardous Work: Do not drive or engage in hazardous work until you determine how the medicine affects your vision.

Alcohol: No special precautions are necessary.

Pregnancy: No specific studies in humans have been done. Consult your doctor for specific advice.

Breast Feeding: No specific studies in humans have been done. Consult your doctor for advice.

Infants and Children: No special precautions.

Special Concerns: To use the eye drops or the gel, first wash your hands. Tilt your head back. Gently apply pressure to the inside corner of the eyelid and with your index finger, pull downward on the lower eyelid to make a space. Drop the medicine or put a short strip of gel (about ½ inch long) into this space and close your eye. Apply pressure for 1 or 2 minutes while keeping the eye closed without blinking. Wash hands again. Make sure the tip of the dropper or the applicator does not touch your eye, finger, or any other surface. To use the eye insert, follow the package directions carefully. The unit should be inserted at bedtime unless your doctor instructs otherwise.

OVERDOSE
Symptoms: Sweating, nausea, vomiting, diarrhea, trouble breathing.

What to Do: An overdose of ophthalmic pilocarpine is unlikely to be life-threatening. If a large volume enters the eye, flush with water. If someone accidentally ingests the medicine, call your doctor, emergency medical services (EMS), or the nearest poison control center immediately.

DRUG INTERACTIONS
Consult your doctor for specific advice if you are taking any other prescription or over-the-counter medication.

FOOD INTERACTIONS
No known food interactions.

DISEASE INTERACTIONS
Consult your doctor if you have asthma or any other eye disease or problem. This medicine should not be used if iritis (inflammation in the eye) is present or develops.

Pilocarpine Systemic

BRAND NAME
Salagen

▶ Drug Class: Cholinergic parasympathomimetic agent

▶ Available in: Tablets

▶ Available OTC? No

▶ As Generic? No

Side Effects

SERIOUS
Serious side effects of pilocarpine are indistinguishable from those of overdose and include chest pain, heartbeat irregularities, severe or ongoing diarrhea, confusion, nausea or vomiting, headache, stomach pain or cramps, difficulty breathing, severe or persistent vision problems, severe trembling or shaking, and fatigue. Call your doctor immediately.

COMMON
Increased sweating.

LESS COMMON
Bloating or fluid retention, chills, nausea or vomiting, diarrhea, runny nose, dizziness, rapid heartbeat, headache, indigestion, frequent urination, redness of face or feeling of warmth, trembling or shaking, difficulty swallowing, excessive tearing, change in voice.

PRINCIPAL USES
To treat dryness of the mouth and throat that occurs after radiation therapy for cancer of the head and neck.

HOW THE DRUG WORKS
Pilocarpine stimulates the activity of salivary glands.

DOSAGE
Adults: 5 mg, 3 times a day. If needed, the dose may be increased to 10 mg, 3 times a day.

ONSET OF EFFECT
Unknown.

DURATION OF ACTION
Unknown.

DIETARY ADVICE
Take it with food to reduce stomach upset. Otherwise, no special restrictions.

STORAGE
Store in a tightly sealed container away from heat, moisture, and direct light.

IF YOU MISS A DOSE
Take it as soon as you remember. If it is near the time for the next dose, skip the missed dose and resume your regular dosage schedule. Do not double the next dose.

STOPPING THE DRUG
Take it as prescribed for the full treatment period, even if you begin to feel better before the scheduled end of therapy. The decision to stop taking the drug should be made by your doctor.

PROLONGED USE
See your physician and your dentist regularly for tests and examinations if you must take this drug for a prolonged period. A dry mouth condition increases the likelihood of dental cavities or other mouth problems.

PRECAUTIONS
Over 60: No special problems have been reported.

Driving and Hazardous Work: Do not drive or engage in hazardous work until you determine how the medicine affects you.

Alcohol: Moderate alcohol intake is acceptable.

Pregnancy: Adequate human studies have not been done. Before taking pilocarpine, tell your physician if you are pregnant or plan to become pregnant.

Breast Feeding: Pilocarpine may pass into breast milk; avoid or discontinue use while nursing, unless approved by your doctor.

Infants and Children: The safety and effectiveness of pilocarpine for infants and children have not been established.

Special Concerns: See your dentist regularly while taking pilocarpine. If the drug causes increased sweating, consume more fluids to prevent dehydration. Consult your doctor if you have any concerns about the proper amount of fluid intake.

OVERDOSE
Symptoms: Chest pain, heartbeat irregularities, severe or ongoing diarrhea, confusion, nausea or vomiting, severe headache, stomach pain or cramps, difficulty breathing, vision problems, severe trembling or shaking, severe fatigue.

What to Do: Call your doctor, emergency medical services (EMS), or the nearest poison control center immediately.

DRUG INTERACTIONS
Other drugs may interact with pilocarpine. Consult your doctor for specific advice if you are taking anticholinergics, antiglaucoma agents, bethanecol, cholinergics, or beta-blockers.

FOOD INTERACTIONS
No known food interactions.

DISEASE INTERACTIONS
Pilocarpine should not be used if you have uncontrolled asthma, narrow-angle closure glaucoma, acute iritis, or major heart, blood vessel, or lung disease. Consult your doctor if you have any of the following: controlled asthma, chronic bronchitis or any other breathing problem, gallbladder problems, heart or blood vessel disease, psychological disorders, detached retina, or another retinal disease.

Pindolol

Visken 10 mg
(NOVARTIS)

▶ Drug Class: Beta-blocker

▶ Available in: Tablets

▶ Available OTC? No

▶ As Generic? Yes

Side Effects

SERIOUS
Shortness of breath, wheezing; irregular or slow heartbeat (50 beats per minute or less); pain or feelings of tightness or pressure in the chest; swelling of the ankles, feet, and lower legs; mental depression. If you experience any such symptoms, stop taking pindolol and contact your doctor right away.

COMMON
Dizziness or lightheadedness, especially when rising suddenly to a standing position; decreased sexual ability; unusual fatigue, weakness, or drowsiness; insomnia.

LESS COMMON
Anxiety, irritability, nervousness; constipation; diarrhea; dry, sore eyes; itching; nausea or vomiting; nightmares or intensely vivid dreams; numbness, tingling, or other unusual sensations in the fingers, toes, or scalp.

PRINCIPAL USES
To treat mild to moderate high blood pressure.

HOW THE DRUG WORKS
Pindolol slows the rate and force of contraction of the heart by blocking certain nerve impulses, thus reducing blood pressure.

DOSAGE
Adults: 5 mg, 2 times a day. Dosage may be increased to a maximum of 30 mg, 2 times a day.

ONSET OF EFFECT
Within 1 hour.

DURATION OF ACTION
Up to 12 hours.

DIETARY ADVICE
Pindolol can be taken without regard to diet.

STORAGE
Store in a tightly sealed container away from heat and direct light.

IF YOU MISS A DOSE
Take it as soon as you remember. If it is near the time for the next dose, skip the missed dose and resume your regular dosage schedule. Do not double the next dose.

STOPPING THE DRUG
The decision to stop taking the drug should be made by your doctor. Slow reduction of the dose under doctor's close supervision for 2 to 3 weeks is advised.

PROLONGED USE
Lifelong therapy with pindolol may be necessary; prolonged use may be associated with a greater incidence of side effects. Regular monitoring and evaluation by your doctor is advised.

PRECAUTIONS
Over 60: Adverse reactions may be more likely and more severe in older patients. Resistance to cold temperatures may be decreased in older patients.

Driving and Hazardous Work: Use caution when driving or engaging in hazardous work until you determine how the medicine affects you.

Alcohol: Drink in careful moderation if at all. Alcohol may interact with the drug and cause a dangerous drop in blood pressure.

Pregnancy: Pindolol was shown to cause fetal harm in some animal studies. Before you take it, tell your doctor if you are pregnant or plan to become pregnant.

Breast Feeding: Pindolol passes into breast milk; consult your doctor about its use during nursing.

Infants and Children: The dosage must be determined by your pediatrician.

Special Concerns: Take extra care during exercise or hot weather, as taking this drug may contribute to dizziness. Check your pulse regularly while taking pindolol. If it is slower than your usual rate or less than 50 beats a minute, check with your doctor.

OVERDOSE
Symptoms: Unusually slow or rapid heartbeat, severe dizziness or fainting, poor circulation in the hands (bluish skin), breathing difficulty; seizures.

What to Do: An overdose of pindolol is unlikely to be life-threatening. However, if someone takes a much larger dose than prescribed, call your doctor, emergency medical services (EMS), or the nearest poison control center immediately.

DRUG INTERACTIONS
Consult your doctor for specific advice if you are taking allergy shots, aminophylline, caffeine, oxtriphylline, theophylline, oral antidiabetics, insulin, calcium channel blockers, clonidine, guanabenz, or MAO inhibitors.

FOOD INTERACTIONS
No known food interactions.

DISEASE INTERACTIONS
Pindolol should be used with caution in people with diabetes, especially insulin-dependent diabetes, since the drug may mask symptoms of hypoglycemia. Use of pindolol may cause complications in patients with liver or kidney disease, since these organs work together to remove the medication from the body. Also consult your doctor if you have any of the following: any allergy (including hay fever), bronchitis, emphysema, heart disease, blood vessel disease, mental depression, myasthenia gravis, psoriasis, or hyperthyroidism.

Pioglitazone Hydrochloride

▶ Drug Class: Thiazolidine-dione/antidiabetic agent

▶ Available in: Tablets

▶ Available OTC? No

▶ As Generic? No

Side Effects

SERIOUS
No serious side effects have been associated with pioglitazone.

COMMON
Upper respiratory tract infection, sore throat.

LESS COMMON
Headache, sinusitis, muscle pain, tooth disorder, edema (swelling).

PRINCIPAL USES
As a single therapeutic agent or as an adjunct (supplemental) therapy to a sulfonylurea, metformin, or insulin to control blood glucose (sugar) levels in patients with non-insulin-dependent (type 2) diabetes.

HOW THE DRUG WORKS
Pioglitazone increases the body's sensitivity and response to insulin.

DOSAGE
To start, 15 to 30 mg once a day. For people taking only pioglitazone and who do not respond adequately, the dose may be increased by a doctor to no more than 45 mg once a day. If monotherapy does not control blood glucose, combination therapy should be considered. If hypoglycemia occurs when taking pioglitazone in combination with a sulfonylurea or insulin, it may be necessary to decrease the dose of the sulfonylurea or insulin.

ONSET OF EFFECT
Within 1 week.

DURATION OF ACTION
Unknown.

DIETARY ADVICE
Pioglitazone may be taken with or without food.

STORAGE
Store in a tightly sealed container away from heat, moisture, and direct light.

IF YOU MISS A DOSE
If it is the same day, take the missed dose as soon as you remember. If you miss an entire day's dose, resume your regular dosage schedule the following day and do not double the next dose.

STOPPING THE DRUG
The decision to stop taking the drug should be made in consultation with your physician.

PROLONGED USE
See your doctor regularly for liver function tests if you take pioglitazone for an extended period.

PRECAUTIONS
Over 60: No special problems are expected.

Driving and Hazardous Work: Pioglitazone should not impair your ability to perform such tasks safely.

Alcohol: Drink only in moderation.

Pregnancy: Adequate studies of pioglitazone use during pregnancy have not been done. In general, insulin is the treatment of choice for controlling blood glucose levels during pregnancy. Pioglitazone should not be used during pregnancy unless your doctor believes the potential benefit justifies the potential risk to the fetus. Pioglitazone may stimulate ovulation in premenopausal women who have stopped ovulating. Contraception may be advised.

Breast Feeding: Pioglitazone may pass into breast milk; do not use it while nursing.

Infants and Children: Safety and effectiveness of pioglitazone have not been established in children.

Special Concerns: Another thiazolidinedione drug, troglitazone, has been associated with rare, serious, and sometimes fatal, liver-related side effects. Although no similar side effects have been reported for pioglitazone, liver function tests are recommended just prior to treatment, every two months for the first year, and periodically thereafter. If you develop unexplained symptoms of liver dysfunction, such as nausea, vomiting, abdominal pain, fatigue, loss of appetite, or dark urine, call your doctor immediately. It is important to follow your doctor's advice on diet, exercise, and other measures to help control diabetes.

OVERDOSE
Symptoms: No specific ones have been reported.

What to Do: While no cases of overdose have been reported, if someone takes a much larger dose than prescribed, call your doctor, emergency medical services (EMS), or the nearest poison control center immediately.

DRUG INTERACTIONS
No known drug interactions.

FOOD INTERACTIONS
No known food interactions.

DISEASE INTERACTIONS
Pioglitazone should not be taken by those with type 1 diabetes or for the treatment of diabetic ketoacidosis. Caution is advised if you have edema or heart failure. Consult your doctor prior to using pioglitazone if you have any type of liver abnormality.

Piperazine

▶ Drug Class: Anthelmintic

▶ Available in: Tablets

▶ Available OTC? No

▶ As Generic? Yes

Side Effects

SERIOUS
Joint pain, skin rash, fever, itching. Call your physician as soon as possible.

COMMON
No common side effects are associated with the use of piperazine.

LESS COMMON
Headache, diarrhea, stomach cramps or pain, dizziness, muscle fatigue, trembling, drowsiness, nausea or vomiting.

PRINCIPAL USES
To treat various worm infections, including ascariasis (common roundworm) and enterobiasis (pinworm), as an alternative to more standard lines of therapy. It is also used to treat partial intestinal obstruction by the common roundworm, a condition primarily occurring in children.

HOW THE DRUG WORKS
Piperazine paralyzes the worm; it is then expelled from the body in the stool.

DOSAGE
For common roundworms—Adults: 3.5 g a day for 2 days. Treatment may be repeated after a week. Children: 75 mg per 2.2 lbs (1 kg) of body weight a day for 2 days. Treatment may be repeated after 2 weeks. For pinworms— Adults and children: 65 mg per 2.2 lbs for 7 days. Treatment may be repeated after a week.

ONSET OF EFFECT
Unknown.

DURATION OF ACTION
Unknown.

DIETARY ADVICE
No special restrictions.

STORAGE
Store in a tightly sealed container away from heat, moisture, and direct light.

IF YOU MISS A DOSE
Take it as soon as possible. If it is near the time for the next dose, skip the missed dose and resume your regular dosage schedule. Do not double the next dose.

STOPPING THE DRUG
Take as prescribed for the full treatment period, even if you begin to feel better before the scheduled end of therapy.

PROLONGED USE
See your doctor regularly for tests and examinations if you take this medicine for a prolonged period.

PRECAUTIONS
Over 60: Adverse reactions may be more likely and more severe.

Driving and Hazardous Work: No special precautions are necessary.

Alcohol: No special precautions are necessary.

Pregnancy: Adequate studies of piperazine use during pregnancy have not been done. Consult your doctor for specific advice if you are pregnant or plan to become pregnant.

Breast Feeding: Piperazine may pass into breast milk; caution is advised. Consult your doctor for specific advice.

Infants and Children: Adverse reactions may be more likely and more severe in children.

Special Concerns: For pinworm infection, clothing, bedding, and towels should be washed daily. All members of the family may have to be treated to eradicate the infestation. A second treatment for all household members may be necessary after 2 or 3 weeks. All bedding and nightclothes should be washed after treatment. To prevent reinfection, you should wash the anal region daily, change your underwear and bedding every day, and wash your hands and fingernails before each meal and after bowel movements. If your symptoms do not improve after a full course of treatment, consult your doctor.

OVERDOSE
Symptoms: Muscle fatigue, seizures, difficulty breathing.

What to Do: An overdose of piperazine is unlikely to be life-threatening. However, if someone takes a much larger dose than prescribed, call your doctor, emergency medical services (EMS), or the nearest poison control center.

DRUG INTERACTIONS
Other drugs may interact with piperazine. Consult your doctor for specific advice if you are taking phenothiazines or pyrantel. Also tell your doctor if you are taking any other prescription or over-the-counter medication.

FOOD INTERACTIONS
No known food interactions.

DISEASE INTERACTIONS
Caution is advised when taking piperazine. This drug should not be used if you have a seizure disorder, especially a history of epilepsy. Use of piperazine may cause complications in patients with kidney disease, since this organ works to remove the medication from the body.

Pirbuterol Acetate

▶ Drug Class: Bronchodilator/sympathomimetic

▶ Available in: Inhalation aerosol

▶ Available OTC? No

▶ As Generic? No

Side Effects

SERIOUS
Pirbuterol may become ineffective if used too often, resulting in more-severe breathing difficulty that does not improve. Signs include persistent wheezing, coughing, or shortness of breath; confusion; bluish color to lips or fingernails; inability to speak. Other side effects include chest pain or heaviness; irregular, racing, fluttering, or pounding heartbeat; lightheadedness; fainting; severe weakness; severe headache.

COMMON
Sleeping difficulty, dry mouth, sore throat, nervousness, excitability, restlessness.

LESS COMMON
Trembling, sweating, headache, nausea or vomiting, flushing or redness to cheeks or other skin, mood changes, unusual bruising, numbness, tingling, or other change in sensation of hands and feet, loss of appetite, changes in sense of smell and taste.

PRINCIPAL USES
To dilate air passages in the lungs that have become narrowed as a result of disease or inflammation. It is used in the treatment of asthma and chronic obstructive pulmonary disease (COPD).

HOW THE DRUG WORKS
Pirbuterol widens constricted airways in the lungs by relaxing the smooth muscles that surround the bronchial passages.

DOSAGE
May be used when needed to relieve breathing difficulty. Adults and children 12 years and older, by inhalation aerosol: 1 to 2 inhalations every 4 to 6 hours. Do not exceed more than 12 inhalations per day. Infants and children less than 12 years of age: Consult your pediatrician.

ONSET OF EFFECT
Within 5 minutes.

DURATION OF ACTION
5 hours.

DIETARY ADVICE
Maintain your usual food and fluid intake.

STORAGE
Store in a tightly sealed container away from heat and direct light. Do not refrigerate inhalation solutions.

IF YOU MISS A DOSE
Skip the missed dose and resume your regular dosage schedule. Do not double the next dose.

STOPPING THE DRUG
It may not be necessary to finish the recommended course of therapy. Consult your doctor.

PROLONGED USE
Therapy may require months or years. Excessive use may result in temporary loss of effectiveness.

PRECAUTIONS
Over 60: Adverse reactions may be more likely and more severe in older patients.

Driving and Hazardous Work: Do not drive or engage in hazardous work until you determine how the medicine affects you.

Alcohol: No special precautions are necessary.

Pregnancy: Adequate studies have not been done; the benefits must be weighed against potential risks. Consult your doctor for advice.

Breast Feeding: It is not known if pirbuterol passes into breast milk. Mothers who wish to breast-feed while taking this drug should discuss the matter with their doctor.

Infants and Children: Use of the inhalation aerosol requires special coordination skills and is not recommended in young children. Dosage in children younger than 12 has not been established.

Special Concerns: Pay heed to any asthma attack or other breathing problem that does not improve after your usual nebulizer treatment or usual number of puffs. Seek help immediately if you feel your lungs are persistently constricted, if you are using more than the recommended number of treatments or puffs per day, or if you feel a recent attack is somehow different from others. Do not use with other mouthpieces or canisters.

OVERDOSE
Symptoms: Chest pain or heaviness; irregular, racing, fluttering, or pounding heartbeat; dizziness; lightheadedness; fainting; severe weakness; severe headache.

What to Do: Call your doctor, emergency medical services (EMS), or the nearest poison control center immediately.

DRUG INTERACTIONS
Consult your doctor for specific advice if you are taking a beta-blocker, ergotamine or ergotamine-like medications, antidepressants, digitalis drugs, or an MAO inhibitor.

FOOD INTERACTIONS
No known food interactions.

DISEASE INTERACTIONS
Consult your doctor if you have a history of substance abuse (especially cocaine), seizures, brain damage, heart disease, heartbeat irregularities, high blood pressure, anxiety disorders, or a thyroid condition.

Piroxicam

Generic 10 mg
(MYLAN)

Additional photographs

▶ Drug Class: Nonsteroidal anti-inflammatory drug (NSAID)

▶ Available in: Capsules

▶ Available OTC? No

▶ As Generic? Yes

Side Effects

SERIOUS
Shortness of breath or wheezing, with or without swelling of legs or other signs of heart failure; chest pain; peptic ulcer disease with vomiting of blood; black, tarry stools; decreasing kidney function. Call your doctor immediately.

COMMON
Nausea, vomiting, heartburn, diarrhea, constipation, headache, dizziness, sleepiness.

LESS COMMON
Ulcers or sores in mouth, depression, rashes or blistering of skin, ringing sound in the ears, unusual tingling or numbness of the hands or feet, seizures, blurred vision. Also elevated potassium levels, decreased blood counts; such problems can be detected by your doctor.

PRINCIPAL USES
To treat mild to moderate pain and inflammation caused by tendinitis, arthritis, bursitis, gout, soft tissue injuries, migraine and other vascular headaches, menstrual cramps, and other conditions. When patients fail to respond to one NSAID, another may be tried. The greatest effectiveness often requires trial and error of several different NSAIDs.

HOW THE DRUG WORKS
NSAIDs work by interfering with the formation of prostaglandins, naturally occurring substances in the body that cause inflammation and make nerves more sensitive to pain impulses. NSAIDs also have other modes of action that are less well understood.

DOSAGE
Adults: 20 mg once a day. The dose may be increased to 20 mg, 2 times a day. For children's dose, consult your pediatrician.

ONSET OF EFFECT
Several hours for analgesic relief; up to 2 weeks for anti-inflammatory effects.

DURATION OF ACTION
Varies.

DIETARY ADVICE
Take with food; maintain your usual food and fluid intake.

STORAGE
Store in a tightly sealed container away from heat, moisture, and direct light.

IF YOU MISS A DOSE
Take it as soon as you remember. If it is near the time for the next dose, skip the missed dose and resume your regular dosage schedule. Do not double the next dose.

STOPPING THE DRUG
The decision to stop taking the drug should be made in consultation with your physician.

PROLONGED USE
Prolonged use can cause gastrointestinal problems, including ulceration and bleeding, kidney dysfunction, and liver inflammation. Consult your doctor about the need for medical examinations and lab tests.

PRECAUTIONS

Over 60: Because of the potentially greater consequences of gastrointestinal side effects, the dose of NSAIDs for older patients, especially those over age 70, is often cut in half.

Driving and Hazardous Work: Avoid such activities until you determine how the medicine affects you.

Alcohol: Avoid alcohol when using this medication because it increases the risk of stomach irritation.

Pregnancy: Avoid or discontinue this drug if you are pregnant or plan to become pregnant.

Breast Feeding: Piroxicam passes into breast milk; avoid use while nursing.

Infants and Children: May be used in exceptional circumstances; consult your doctor.

Special Concerns: Because NSAIDs can interfere with blood coagulation, this drug should be stopped at least 3 days prior to any surgery.

OVERDOSE
Symptoms: Severe nausea, vomiting, headache, confusion, seizures.

What to Do: Call your doctor, emergency medical services (EMS), or the nearest poison control center immediately.

DRUG INTERACTIONS
Do not take this drug with aspirin or any other NSAIDs without your doctor's approval. In addition, consult your doctor if you are taking antihypertensives, steroids, anticoagulants, antibiotics, itraconazole or ketoconazole, plicamycin, penicillamine, valproic acid, phenytoin, cyclosporine, digitalis drugs, lithium, methotrexate, probenecid, triamterene, or zidovudine.

FOOD INTERACTIONS
No known food interactions.

DISEASE INTERACTIONS
Caution is advised when taking piroxicam. Consult your doctor if you have any of the following: bleeding problems, inflammation or ulcers of the stomach and intestines, diabetes mellitus, systemic lupus erythematosus (SLE, lupus), anemia, asthma, epilepsy, Parkinson's disease, kidney stones, or a history of heart disease or alcohol abuse. Use of piroxicam may cause complications in patients with liver or kidney disease, since these organs work together to remove the medication from the body.

Pneumococcal Vaccine

▶ Drug Class: Vaccine

▶ Available in: Injection

▶ Available OTC? No

▶ As Generic? No

Side Effects

SERIOUS
Serious allergic reaction involving difficulty swallowing or breathing; reddened skin, especially around the ears; itching, particularly of the hands or feet; hives; unusual and severe fatigue; swollen face, eyes, or nasal passages; and fever over 102°F. Call your doctor immediately.

COMMON
Pain, redness, swelling, or the formation of a hard lump at the site of the injection.

LESS COMMON
Fever, aches and pains in the joints or muscles, skin rash, unusual fatigue, general feeling of illness or discomfort, swollen glands.

PRINCIPAL USES
To prevent pneumococcal bacteria infections such as pneumonia, meningitis, and bacteremia (a severe bacterial blood infection).

HOW THE DRUG WORKS
Pneumococcal vaccine stimulates the body's immune system to produce its own protective antibodies against the bacteria.

DOSAGE
Adults and children age 2 and older: A single injection under the skin or into a muscle of the upper arm or midthigh.

ONSET OF EFFECT
2 to 3 weeks.

DURATION OF ACTION
5 to 10 years.

DIETARY ADVICE
No special restrictions.

STORAGE
Not applicable; the dose is administered only at a health care facility.

IF YOU MISS A DOSE
Not applicable.

STOPPING THE DRUG
Not applicable.

PROLONGED USE
Not applicable.

PRECAUTIONS
Over 60: Pneumococcal vaccine is particularly recommended for persons over the age of 50. It is not expected to cause different or more severe side effects in older persons than it does in younger people.

Driving and Hazardous Work: Do not drive or engage in hazardous work until you determine how the medicine affects you.

Alcohol: No special precautions are necessary.

Pregnancy: Studies on the effects of pneumococcal vaccine in pregnant women have not been done. However, if needed, it should be given only after the first trimester of pregnancy. It should be given only to women who have a condition that makes them more vulnerable to infection or more likely to develop serious problems from a pneumococcal infection. Before you receive pneumococcal vaccine, tell your doctor if you are pregnant or plan to become pregnant.

Breast Feeding: Pneumococcal vaccine may pass into breast milk; caution is advised. Consult your doctor for specific advice.

Infants and Children: This vaccine is not recommended for use by children under the age of 2.

Special Concerns: If you have more than one doctor, be sure they all know that you have received this vaccine. In general, only one shot of the vaccine is needed for protection. Revaccination is recommended for persons who received the pneumococcal vaccine that was distributed between 1977 and 1983 if they are at high risk for infection. A second vaccination, 3 to 5 years after the first, may be necessary for children under age 10 with nephrotic syndrome, asplenia, or sickle-cell anemia.

OVERDOSE
Symptoms: An overdose with this vaccine is unlikely.

What to Do: No cases of overdose have been reported.

DRUG INTERACTIONS
Other drugs may interact with pneumococcal vaccine. Consult your doctor for advice if you are taking any prescription or over-the-counter medication. Tell your doctor if you have had any pneumococcal vaccine in the past.

FOOD INTERACTIONS
No known food interactions.

DISEASE INTERACTIONS
Consult your doctor if you have any severe illness that is causing fever. The vaccine should be given with caution to patients receiving anticoagulant therapy. Patients who have received extensive chemotherapy or radiation treatment for Hodgkin's disease should not receive the pneumococcal vaccine.

▶ Drug Class: Antimitotic

▶ Available in: Topical gel, solution

▶ Available OTC? No

▶ As Generic? No

Side Effects

SERIOUS
No serious side effects are associated with the use of podofilox.

COMMON
Burning, inflammation, pain, itching, sores, stinging, redness at the application sites.

LESS COMMON
Local tingling, blisters, dryness, crusting, swelling, scarring, bleeding, or chafing at the application sites. Vomiting, headache, insomnia, painful intercourse.

PRINCIPAL USES
To treat external condylomata acuminata (genital and perianal warts) in adults. Genital and perianal warts are caused by the human papillomavirus (HPV).

HOW THE DRUG WORKS
The exact mechanism of action is unknown.

DOSAGE
Apply a thin layer with the supplied cotton-tipped applicator (topical solution) or with the applicator tip or finger (topical gel) to the affected area(s) 2 times a day, in the morning and evening, for 3 consecutive days. Then discontinue treatment for 4 consecutive days. This cycle of treatment may be repeated until there are no more visible warts or for a maximum of 4 cycles. Your doctor should demonstrate the proper technique prior to the initial application.

ONSET OF EFFECT
Unknown.

DURATION OF ACTION
Unknown.

DIETARY ADVICE
Podofilox can be used without regard to diet.

STORAGE
Store in a tightly sealed container away from moisture, direct light, and extremes in temperature.

IF YOU MISS A DOSE
Apply it as soon as you remember. If it is near the time for the next dose, skip the missed dose and resume your regular dosage schedule. Do not apply more than directed. It will not make the medicine work better and may increase side effects.

STOPPING THE DRUG
Apply podofilox in one-week cycles until there is no visible wart tissue or for a maximum of 4 cycles. Consult your doctor for specific advice if further treatment is needed.

PROLONGED USE
Safety and effectiveness beyond 4 weeks have not been determined. If response to therapy is incomplete after 4 one-week cycles, discontinue treatment and contact your physician.

PRECAUTIONS
Over 60: No special problems are expected.

Driving and Hazardous Work: The use of podofilox should not impair your ability to perform such tasks safely.

Alcohol: No special precautions are necessary.

Pregnancy: Adequate human studies have not been done. Before taking podofilox, discuss with your doctor the relative risks and benefits of using this drug while pregnant.

Breast Feeding: Podofilox may pass into breast milk; caution is advised. Consult your doctor for advice.

Infants and Children: The safety and effectiveness of podofilox in children under the age of 12 have not been established. Genital and perianal warts are contracted by people who are sexually active.

Special Concerns: Let the treated areas dry before allowing contact with unaffected skin. Wash your hands before and after each application. Podofilox is for external use only; do not apply to the urethra, rectum, or vagina. Do not apply the topical solution to the perianal (around the anus) area. Avoid getting podofilox into your eyes. If eye contact occurs, flush the eye at once with large quantities of water, and contact your doctor. Do not have sexual intercourse during the 3 days you are applying podofilox. Condoms may help protect new sexual partners from contracting HPV as well as other sexually transmitted diseases such as herpes and HIV. However, they are not 100% effective. If the warts reappear, contact your doctor.

OVERDOSE
Symptoms: An overdose with podofilox is unlikely.

What to Do: If someone applies a much larger dose than prescribed or accidentally ingests podofilox, call your doctor.

DRUG INTERACTIONS
None reported.

FOOD INTERACTIONS
None reported.

DISEASE INTERACTIONS
None reported.

Poliovirus Vaccine

▶ Drug Class: Vaccine

▶ Available in: Injection, oral solution

▶ Available OTC? No

▶ As Generic? Yes

Side Effects

SERIOUS

Serious allergic reaction involving difficulty swallowing or breathing; reddened skin, especially around the ears; itching, particularly of the hands or feet; hives; unusual and severe fatigue; and swollen face, eyes, or nasal passages. Call your doctor immediately.

COMMON

No common side effects are associated with the poliovirus vaccine.

LESS COMMON

Injection: Fever; soreness, rash, tenderness, or pain at injection site. There are no less-common side effects associated with the oral suspension.

PRINCIPAL USES

To prevent poliomyelitis (polio).

HOW THE DRUG WORKS

Poliovirus vaccine stimulates the body's immune system to produce its own protective antibodies against the virus that causes polio.

DOSAGE

Injection (inactivated vaccine)— All doses are given under the skin, in either the upper arm (adults) or mid-thigh (infants and children). First dose is given at initial visit. For children, this is usually at 6 to 8 weeks of age. Second dose is given 8 weeks later. Third dose is given 8 weeks to 12 months after the second dose. Fourth dose, when needed, is given 6 to 12 months after the third dose. First booster dose, for children, is usually administered upon entering school, usually between ages 4 and 6. Oral solution (live vaccine)— Follow the same dosage schedule as used for the injection form.

ONSET OF EFFECT

Within 7 to 10 days.

DURATION OF ACTION

Up to 12 years.

DIETARY ADVICE

No special restrictions.

STORAGE

Not applicable; the dose is administered only at a health care facility.

IF YOU MISS A DOSE

If your child misses a scheduled vaccination, contact your pediatrician.

STOPPING THE DRUG

The full schedule of vaccinations should be followed unless a medical problem intervenes.

PROLONGED USE

No special problems are expected.

PRECAUTIONS

Over 60: Poliovirus vaccine is not expected to cause different or more severe side effects in older patients than it does in younger persons. Inactivated poliovirus vaccine is preferred in adults.

Driving and Hazardous Work: No special precautions are necessary.

Alcohol: No special precautions are necessary.

Pregnancy: Studies on the effects of poliovirus vaccine in pregnant women have not been done. However, if needed, it should be given only to pregnant women at great risk of acquiring polio. Consult your doctor for advice.

Breast Feeding: Poliovirus vaccine has not been reported to cause problems during breast feeding. Consult your doctor for advice. If your child has taken the oral solution, refrain from breast feeding for 2 to 3 hours before and after immunization.

Infants and Children: This vaccine is not recommended for use by infants under the age of 6 weeks.

Special Concerns: Immunization with inactivated polio vaccine is recommended for any adult at risk of the disease, such as those traveling to countries where polio is not under control, those who have not had the complete series of immunizations, those who work in medical facilities or day-care centers, and those working in laboratories where poliovirus samples may be handled.

OVERDOSE

Symptoms: An overdose of poliovirus vaccine is unlikely.

What to Do: No cases of overdose have been reported.

DRUG INTERACTIONS

Consult your doctor for specific advice if you are undergoing chemotherapy for cancer or if you are taking corticosteroids.

FOOD INTERACTIONS

No known food interactions.

DISEASE INTERACTIONS

Except under special circumstances, you should not receive the poliovirus vaccine if you have ongoing diarrhea, any moderate or severe illness causing fever or vomiting, any immune deficiency condition, such as HIV, a family history of immune deficiency, or a household member with an immunodeficiency. Consult your doctor.

Polyethylene Glycol Solution (PEG)

▶ Drug Class: Stimulant
laxative

▶ Available in: Oral solution,
powder for oral solution

▶ Available OTC? No

▶ As Generic? Yes

Side Effects

SERIOUS
Skin rash. Call your doctor immediately should this occur.

COMMON
Bloating, nausea.

LESS COMMON
Stomach upset or abdominal cramps, vomiting, irritation of the anal region.

PRINCIPAL USES
To clean the colon and rectum prior to diagnostic tests or surgical procedures involving the colon.

HOW THE DRUG WORKS
Polyethylene glycol (PEG) solution induces mild diarrhea to flush solid material from the colon.

DOSAGE
Adults and teenagers: Drink 1 full glass (8 oz) of PEG rapidly every 10 minutes until at least 4 liters have been consumed. Children: 11.3 to 18.2 ml per pound of body weight per hour.

ONSET OF EFFECT
Within 1 hour.

DURATION OF ACTION
Variable.

DIETARY ADVICE
Consume no food for 4 hours before taking PEG. Afterward, drink only clear fluids like water, ginger ale, decaffeinated cola, decaffeinated tea, or broth.

STORAGE
Store in a tightly sealed container away from heat, moisture, and direct light. Refrigerate the solution but do not allow it to freeze.

IF YOU MISS A DOSE
Take it as soon as you remember. If it is near the time for the next dose, skip the missed dose and resume your regular dosage schedule. Do not double the next dose.

STOPPING THE DRUG
Continue drinking the solution until your stools are watery, clear and free of solid material. The decision to stop taking the drug should be made by your doctor.

PROLONGED USE
PEG is not intended for prolonged use.

PRECAUTIONS
Over 60: No special problems are expected in older patients.

Driving and Hazardous Work: Do not drive or engage in hazardous work until you determine how the medicine affects you.

Alcohol: Avoid alcohol.

Pregnancy: Adequate human studies have not been completed. Before taking PEG, tell your doctor if you are pregnant or plan to become pregnant.

Breast Feeding: PEG may pass into breast milk; caution is advised. Consult your doctor for specific advice.

Infants and Children: There is no specific information comparing use of PEG in children with use in other age groups. However, no special problems are expected.

Special Concerns: It will take up to 3 hours to consume the full recommended dose of PEG. The first bowel movement may start in 1 hour. Patients using the powder form of PEG should first mix the powder with water and add enough lukewarm water to reach the fill mark on the bottle. Shake well until all the ingredients are dissolved. Do not add any flavorings or other ingredients to the solution. Do not drink the solution chilled. Cases of hypothermia have been reported following ingestion of chilled solutions. Use the mixed solution within 48 hours.

OVERDOSE
Symptoms: Diarrhea, abdominal pain, bloating.

What to Do: An overdose of PEG is unlikely to occur. However, if you are concerned about the possibility of an overdose, call a doctor, emergency medical services (EMS), or the nearest poison control center.

DRUG INTERACTIONS
Any other oral medication taken within 1 hour of PEG may be flushed from the body. Consult your doctor for advice if you are taking any other medication.

FOOD INTERACTIONS
Do not consume any food for at least 4 hours before taking PEG.

DISEASE INTERACTIONS
Caution is advised when taking PEG. Consult your doctor if you have a history of any of the following: blockage or obstruction of the intestine, paralytic ileus, perforated bowel, toxic colitis, or toxic megacolon.

Polythiazide

▶ Drug Class: Thiazide diuretic

▶ Available in: Tablets

▶ Available OTC? No

▶ As Generic? No

Side Effects

SERIOUS

Skin rash, hives, intense itching, swelling of the mouth and throat, breathing difficulty, heart rhythm irregularities, lightheadedness, unusual bleeding or bruising. Call your doctor immediately.

COMMON

Fluid depletion may lead to dizziness, especially upon arising from a sitting or lying position, as well as thirst, dry mouth, and constipation.

LESS COMMON

Increased sensitivity to sunlight, loss of appetite, gout, increased blood sugar (a problem for patients with diabetes).

PRINCIPAL USES

To treat high blood pressure (hypertension); to treat conditions that cause edema (swelling of body tissues resulting from excess salt and water retention).

HOW THE DRUG WORKS

Diuretics increase the excretion of salt and water in the urine. By reducing the overall fluid volume in the body, these drugs reduce blood volume and so reduce pressure within the blood vessels.

DOSAGE

Adults: For high blood pressure, 2 to 4 mg once a day. For edema, 1 to 4 mg once a day, once every other day, or once a day for 3 to 5 days a week. Children: The dose must be determined by your doctor.

ONSET OF EFFECT

Within 2 hours.

DURATION OF ACTION

6 to 12 hours.

DIETARY ADVICE

It can be be taken with food to avoid stomach upset.

STORAGE

Store in a tightly sealed container away from heat, moisture, and direct light.

IF YOU MISS A DOSE

Take it as soon as you remember. If it is near the time for the next dose, skip the missed dose and resume your regular dosage schedule. Do not double the next dose.

STOPPING THE DRUG

The decision to stop taking the drug should be made by your doctor.

PROLONGED USE

See your doctor regularly for examinations and tests if you must take this medicine for an extended period.

PRECAUTIONS

Over 60: Adverse reactions may be more likely and more severe.

Driving and Hazardous Work: No special precautions are necessary.

Alcohol: No special precautions are necessary.

Pregnancy: This drug should not be taken during pregnancy unless recommended by your doctor. Other diuretics are generally preferred.

Breast Feeding: Because this drug passes into breast milk, avoid using it while nursing. If taking the drug is necessary, discontinue nursing.

Infants and Children: No unusual side effects are expected in children. The dose must be determined by a pediatrician.

Special Concerns: Polythiazide is usually prescribed once a day. To prevent it from interfering with sleep, take it in the morning. If you are taking this drug for high blood pressure, follow the diet and weight control measures recommended by your doctor. Avoid exposure to sunlight, use a sunblock, or wear protective clothing. This medicine may cause your body to lose potassium. Follow your doctor's instructions about eating potassium-rich foods or taking a potassium supplement.

OVERDOSE

Symptoms: Lethargy, dizziness, drowsiness, muscle weakness, cramps, heartbeat irregularities, fainting.

What to Do: Call your doctor, emergency medical services (EMS), or the nearest poison control center immediately.

DRUG INTERACTIONS

Consult your doctor for specific advice if you are taking anticoagulants, cholestyramine, colestipol, drugs for diabetes, nonsteroidal anti-inflammatory drugs, digitalis drugs, or lithium.

FOOD INTERACTIONS

Follow your doctor's advice about salt use and potassium-rich foods.

DISEASE INTERACTIONS

Caution is advised when taking polythiazide. Consult your doctor if you have any of the following: diabetes, gout, lupus erythematosus, pancreatitis, heart disease, blood vessel disease, liver disease, or kidney disease.

Potassium Chloride

K-Dur 10 750 mg
(KEY)

837

Additional photographs

▶ Drug Class: Electrolyte

▶ Available in: Liquid, soluble
granules, powder, tablets,
sustained-release capsules

▶ Available OTC? No

▶ As Generic? Yes

Side Effects

SERIOUS
Numbness or tingling in
the hands, feet, or lips;
slowed or irregular heartbeat; breathing difficulty;
unusual fatigue or weak-
ness; confusion. Stop taking the drug and consult
your doctor at once.

COMMON
Diarrhea, abdominal
discomfort, gas, nausea
and vomiting.

LESS COMMON
Black or bloody stools,
pain when swallowing.
Consult your doctor if
such symptoms persist.

PRINCIPAL USES
To restore or maintain
proper potassium levels in
the body. Potassium is an
electrolyte, a mineral that
helps maintain proper fluid
balance. It is also vital in
the transmission of nerve
impulses.

HOW THE DRUG WORKS
Potassium chloride is
absorbed in the body fluids
and taken into the cells
where it is part of a number
of metabolic actions, especially those that involve the
release of energy. It also
aids in the conduction of
nerve impulses responsible
for muscle movement and
heart contraction.

DOSAGE
20 milliequivalents (mEq) to
100 mEq daily in divided
doses. A single dose should
not exceed 20 mEq.

ONSET OF EFFECT
Unknown.

DURATION OF ACTION
Unknown.

DIETARY ADVICE
Must be taken after meals
or with food and a glass of
water or other liquid. Follow
all special dietary guidelines
as outlined by your doctor.

STORAGE
Store in a tightly sealed container away from heat and
direct light. Keep liquid
forms of potassium refrigerated, but do not allow to
freeze.

IF YOU MISS A DOSE
If you remember within 2
hours, take the missed dose
with food or liquids and
resume your regular dosage
schedule. If you remember
after 2 hours, skip the
missed dose and return
to your regular dosage
schedule. Do not double
the next dose.

STOPPING THE DRUG
Do not stop taking potas-
sium without first consulting your physician. Be
especially careful not to stop
taking potassium abruptly if
you are also taking digitalis
drugs (digoxin).

PROLONGED USE
Requires periodic testing of
blood potassium levels by
your doctor.

PRECAUTIONS
Over 60: Elderly people
may be at greater risk of
retaining too much potas-
sium owing to age-related
changes in the ability of the
kidneys to excrete it. Older
patients should have their
potassium levels checked
regularly.

**Driving and Hazardous
Work:** No special problems
are expected.

Alcohol: No special problems are expected.

Pregnancy: Potassium supplements are considered
safe during pregnancy if
used exactly as prescribed.

Breast Feeding: Potassium may pass into breast
milk. Consult your doctor
for specific advice.

Infants and Children:
Although the safety and
effectiveness of potassium
use by children have not
been established, no spe-
cific problems have been
documented.

Special Concerns:
Remember that the foods in
your diet must also be considered when calculating
your total intake of potassium. Be certain to read all
labels carefully, especially
on all products labeled "low-
sodium," such as canned
foods and some breads,
many of which contain

potassium. Do not crush
sustained-release forms.
Swallow tablets without
chewing, sucking, or crushing. Be sure the powder
form is completely dissolved
before ingesting.

OVERDOSE
Symptoms: Irregular
heartbeat; muscle weak-
ness, which may progress
to paralysis of the
diaphragm and interfere
with breathing.

What to Do: Call your
doctor, emergency medical
services (EMS), or the
nearest poison control
center immediately.

DRUG INTERACTIONS
The following drugs may
interact adversely with
potassium chloride. Consult
your doctor for advice if you
are taking digitalis drugs,
potassium-sparing diuretics,
thiazide diuretics, NSAIDs,
beta-blockers, heparin, triamterene, anticholinergics,
or ACE inhibitors.

FOOD INTERACTIONS
To prevent ingestion of too
much potassium, discuss
your diet with your doctor.
Foods high in potassium
include avocados, bananas,
broccoli, dried fruits, grapefruit, beans, meats, nuts,
spinach, low-salt milk,
squash, melon, brussels
sprouts, zucchini, frozen
orange juice, and tomatoes.

DISEASE INTERACTIONS
Consult your doctor if you
have any of the following:
intestinal obstruction, dehydration, severe diarrhea,
compression of the esophagus, delayed gastric emptying, peptic ulcer, heart
block, or a predisposition
to retaining potassium.

Pramipexole Dihydrochloride

BRAND NAME
Mirapex

▶ Drug Class: Dopamine agonist

▶ Available in: Tablets

▶ Available OTC? No

▶ As Generic? No

Side Effects

SERIOUS
Excessively low blood pressure (orthostatic hypotension), causing extreme dizziness, confusion, nausea, fainting, or blackouts, especially when rising from a seated or lying position; hallucinations; impaired control over voluntary movements (dyskinesia).

COMMON
Mild to moderate dizziness or faintness (caused by a less severe drop in blood pressure) upon standing or sitting up; drowsiness; dry mouth.

LESS COMMON
Increased sweating, vision abnormalities, joint pain, increased urine output, weakness, pneumonia, increased incidence of accidental injury, tooth disease, leg cramps.

PRINCIPAL USES
To treat the symptoms of Parkinson's disease.

HOW THE DRUG WORKS
The exact mechanism of action is unknown, but pramipexole is believed to help increase the release of certain neurological chemicals that improve control over movement.

DOSAGE
Initial dose (for first week of therapy): 0.125 mg, 3 times a day. The dose is gradually increased (usually once a week for 7 weeks) up to 1.5 mg, taken 3 times a day, for a total dose of 4.5 mg a day.

ONSET OF EFFECT
Unknown.

DURATION OF ACTION
Unknown.

DIETARY ADVICE
Pramipexole may be taken with meals, if desired, to minimize the incidence of nausea or stomach upset.

STORAGE
Store in a tightly sealed container away from heat and direct light. Keep away from moisture and extremes in temperature.

IF YOU MISS A DOSE
Take it as soon as you remember. If it is near the time for the next dose, skip the missed dose and resume your regular dosage schedule. Do not double the next dose.

STOPPING THE DRUG
The decision to stop taking the drug should be made in consultation with your doctor. Do not stop taking pramipexole suddenly; it is recommended that the dose be reduced gradually over a period of at least 1 week, according to your doctor's instructions.

PROLONGED USE
Lifetime therapy with pramipexole may be necessary; prolonged use may be associated with a greater incidence of side effects. Regular monitoring and evaluation by your doctor is advised.

PRECAUTIONS
Over 60: Adverse reactions (especially hallucinations) may be more likely and more severe in older patients. Lower doses may be advised.

Driving and Hazardous Work: Pramipexole may cause sudden and extreme drowsiness. Do not drive or engage in hazardous work until you determine how the medicine affects you.

Alcohol: Avoid alcohol.

Pregnancy: Pramipexole should not be used by pregnant women.

Breast Feeding: Pramipexole should not be taken while nursing. The patient must choose between using the drug or breast feeding.

Infants and Children: Pramipexole should not be taken by children.

Special Concerns: This drug may cause dizziness and faintness, especially when getting up out of a chair or sitting up after lying down (a condition known as postural orthostatic hypertension, characterized by temporary episodes of excessively low blood pressure). Be cautious and move slowly when arising.

OVERDOSE
Symptoms: No cases of overdose have been reported.

What to Do: An overdose of pramipexole is unlikely to occur. However, if someone takes a much larger dose than prescribed, call your doctor, emergency medical services (EMS), or the nearest poison control center right away.

DRUG INTERACTIONS
Consult your doctor for specific advice if you are taking antiulcer drugs (specifically, histamine H2 blockers such as cimetidine and ranitidine), calcium channel blockers (such as diltiazem and verapamil), potassium-sparing diuretics (such as triamterene), or other dopamine agonists (such as phenothiazines, butyrophenones, thioxanthenes, and metoclopramide).

FOOD INTERACTIONS
No known food interactions.

DISEASE INTERACTIONS
Use of pramipexole may cause complications in patients with a history of kidney disease, since this medication is eliminated from the body through the kidneys.

Pravastatin

▶ Drug Class: Antilipidemic (cholesterol-lowering agent)

▶ Available in: Tablets

▶ Available OTC? No

▶ As Generic? No

Side Effects

SERIOUS
Fever, unusual or unexplained muscle aches and tenderness. Call your doctor right away.

COMMON
Side effects occur in only 1% to 2% of patients. These include constipation or diarrhea, dizziness, gas, headache, heartburn, nausea, skin rash, stomach pain, rise in liver enzymes (detectable by your doctor).

LESS COMMON
Insomnia.

PRINCIPAL USES
To treat high cholesterol. Usually prescribed after first lines of treatment—including diet, weight loss, and exercise—fail to reduce total and low-density lipoprotein (LDL) cholesterol to acceptable levels.

HOW THE DRUG WORKS
Pravastatin blocks the action of an enzyme required for the manufacture of cholesterol, thereby interfering with its formation. By lowering the amount of cholesterol in the liver cells, pravastatin increases the formation of receptors for LDL, and thereby reduces blood levels of total and LDL cholesterol. In addition to lowering LDL cholesterol, pravastatin also modestly reduces triglyceride levels and raises HDL (the so-called "good") cholesterol.

DOSAGE
Initial dose is 40 mg once a day. The dose may be increased to a maximum of 80 mg per day. The drug is most effective when taken in the evening.

ONSET OF EFFECT
2 to 4 weeks.

DURATION OF ACTION
The effect persists for the duration of therapy.

DIETARY ADVICE
Cholesterol-lowering drugs are only one part of a total program that should include regular exercise and a healthy diet. The American Heart Association publishes a "Healthy Heart" diet, which is recommended.

STORAGE
Store in a tightly sealed container away from heat and direct light.

IF YOU MISS A DOSE
Take it as soon as you remember. Take the next scheduled dose at the proper time and resume your regular dosage schedule, as prescribed. Do not double the next dose.

STOPPING THE DRUG
The decision to stop taking the drug should be made in consultation with your doctor. Once the medication is discontinued, blood cholesterol is likely to return to original elevated levels.

PROLONGED USE
Side effects are more likely with prolonged use. As you continue with pravastatin, your doctor will periodically order blood tests to evaluate liver function.

PRECAUTIONS
Over 60: No special problems are expected.

Driving and Hazardous Work: The use of pravastatin should not impair your ability to perform such tasks safely.

Alcohol: No special precautions are necessary.

Pregnancy: Pravastatin should not be used during pregnancy or by women who plan to become pregnant in the near future.

Breast Feeding: This drug is not recommended for women who are nursing.

Infants and Children: Long-term effects of pravastatin in children have not been determined. Rarely used in young patients; consult your doctor.

Special Concerns: Important elements of treatment for high cholesterol include proper diet, weight loss, regular moderate exercise, and the avoidance of certain medications that may increase cholesterol levels. Because pravastatin has potential side effects, it is important that you maintain a recommended healthy diet and cooperate with other treatments your physician may suggest.

OVERDOSE
Symptoms: Overdose is unlikely to occur.

What to Do: Emergency instructions not applicable.

DRUG INTERACTIONS
Consult your doctor if you are taking cyclosporine, gemfibrozil, niacin, antibiotics, especially erythromycin, or medications for fungus infections. All of these drugs may increase the risk of myositis (muscle inflammation) when taken with pravastatin and may lead to kidney failure.

FOOD INTERACTIONS
No known food interactions.

DISEASE INTERACTIONS
Consult your doctor if you have any of the following problems: liver, kidney, or muscle disease, or a medical history involving organ transplant or recent surgery.

Praziquantel

Biltricide 600 mg
(BAYER)

▶ Drug Class: Anthelmintic

▶ Available in: Tablets

▶ Available OTC? No

▶ As Generic? No

Side Effects

SERIOUS
No serious side effects are associated with the use of praziquantel.

COMMON
Stomach pain or cramps, dizziness, drowsiness, bloody diarrhea, fever, nausea or vomiting, headache, increased sweating, loss of appetite, general discomfort. These symptoms are likely to occur as allergic reactions to dead worms and usually resolve on their own.

LESS COMMON
Hives, skin rash, itching.

PRINCIPAL USES
To treat trematode (fluke) infections such as clonorchiasis caused by *Clonorchis sinensis* (Chinese or Oriental liver fluke), opisthorchiasis caused by *Opisthorchis viverrini* and *O. felineus* (liver flukes), and schistosomiasis caused by *Schistosoma mekongi*, *S. japonicum*, *S. mansoni*, and *S. hematobium* (blood flukes). Praziquantel may be prescribed to treat other types of parasite-related disease as determined by your physician.

HOW THE DRUG WORKS
Praziquantel works by causing severe spasms and paralysis of the worm's muscles. The body's immune system can then better attack and expel the worm.

DOSAGE
For clonorchiasis, opisthorchiasis, and lung or intestinal fluke infection—Adults and children age 4 and older: 25 mg per 2.2 lbs (1 kg) of body weight, 3 times a day for 1 day. For schistosomiasis— Adults and children age 4 and older: 20 mg per 2.2 lbs, 2 to 3 times for 1 day. (Different doses may be prescribed in conjunction with corticosteroids to treat certain other parasite-related diseases.)

ONSET OF EFFECT
Unknown.

DURATION OF ACTION
Unknown.

DIETARY ADVICE
Praziquantel is best taken during meals with liquid. Do not chew the tablets.

STORAGE
Store in a tightly sealed container away from heat, moisture, and direct light.

IF YOU MISS A DOSE
Take it as soon as you remember. However, if it is near the time for the next dose, skip the missed dose and resume your regular dosage schedule. Do not double the next dose.

STOPPING THE DRUG
Take it as prescribed for the full treatment period.

PROLONGED USE
See your doctor regularly for tests and examinations if you must take this medicine for a prolonged period. If your condition has not improved by the end of the course of therapy, consult your doctor.

PRECAUTIONS
Over 60: Adverse reactions may be more likely and more severe in older patients.

Driving and Hazardous Work: Avoid such activities until you determine how the medicine affects you. If it does cause problems, do not drive or engage in hazardous activities the day you take praziquantel and for 24 hours after treatment.

Alcohol: No special precautions are necessary.

Pregnancy: Adequate human studies have not been done. Before taking praziquantel, tell your doctor if you are pregnant or plan to become pregnant.

Breast Feeding: Praziquantel passes into breast milk. Stop nursing the day you start therapy. Do not restart breast feeding until 72 hours after therapy is completed. All breast milk during this time should be extracted with a breast pump or squeezed out and thrown away.

Infants and Children: Use and dosage for children under age 4 must be determined by your pediatrician.

Special Concerns: Praziquantel has a bitter taste that can cause gagging or vomiting, especially if the pills are chewed. Swallow the pills whole with a small amount of liquid during meals.

OVERDOSE
Symptoms: An overdose with praziquantel is unlikely.

What to Do: An overdose with praziquantel is unlikely to be life-threatening. However, if you take a much larger dose than prescribed, take a fast-acting laxative and call your doctor.

DRUG INTERACTIONS
Consult your doctor for advice if you are taking any other prescription or over-the-counter medication, especially corticosteroids (used concurrently with praziquantel in the treatment of some parasite-related diseases), cimetidine, ketoconazole, or miconazole.

FOOD INTERACTIONS
No known food interactions.

DISEASE INTERACTIONS
Praziquantel should not be used when Taenia solium worm cysts are present in the eye. The death of the worm cysts by praziquantel may cause irreparable damage to the eyes. Caution is advised when taking praziquantel. If you have liver disease, you may be at greater risk for side effects. Consult your doctor for specific advice.

Prazosin

Generic 2 mg
(LEDERLE)

Additional photographs

▶ Drug Class: Peripherally acting antihypertensive

▶ Available in: Capsules

▶ Available OTC? No

▶ As Generic? Yes

Side Effects

SERIOUS
Dizziness or lightheadedness, especially when getting up from a sitting or lying position, fainting, loss of bladder control, pounding heartbeat, swelling of feet and lower legs, chest pain, continuing inappropriate and painful erections, shortness of breath. Call your doctor immediately.

COMMON
Drowsiness, headache, lack of energy.

LESS COMMON
Dry mouth, unusual fatigue, nervousness, nausea, frequent urge to urinate.

PRINCIPAL USES
To treat high blood pressure (hypertension).

HOW THE DRUG WORKS
Prazosin causes the blood vessels to relax and widen, which in turn lowers blood pressure.

DOSAGE
Adults: To start, 0.5 to 1 mg, 2 or 3 times a day. The dose may be increased slowly to 6 to 15 mg a day divided into 2 or 3 doses. Children: 50 to 400 micrograms (mcg) per 2.2 lbs (1 kg) of body weight divided into 2 or 3 doses.

ONSET OF EFFECT
30 to 90 minutes. The full effect may not be realized for 3 to 4 weeks.

DURATION OF ACTION
7 to 10 hours.

DIETARY ADVICE
Follow a healthy diet (low-salt, low-fat, low-cholesterol) as advised by your doctor to help control blood pressure and prevent heart disease.

STORAGE
Store in a tightly sealed container away from heat and direct light.

IF YOU MISS A DOSE
Take it as soon as you remember. If it is near the time for the next dose, skip the missed dose and resume your regular dosage schedule. Do not double the next dose.

STOPPING THE DRUG
The decision to stop taking the drug should be made by your doctor. Prazosin controls high blood pressure but does not cure it.

PROLONGED USE
Lifelong therapy may be necessary. See your doctor regularly for tests and examinations if you take this drug for a prolonged period.

PRECAUTIONS

Over 60: Adverse reactions, particularly dizziness, lightheadedness, and fainting, may be more likely and more severe in older patients. This medication may reduce tolerance to cold temperatures in older patients.

Driving and Hazardous Work: Do not drive or engage in hazardous work until you determine how the medicine affects you.

Alcohol: Avoid alcohol.

Pregnancy: In animal studies and limited human studies, prazosin has not caused birth defects. High doses in animal studies have caused reduced birth weight. Before you take prazosin, tell your doctor if you are pregnant or plan to become pregnant.

Breast Feeding: Prazosin passes into breast milk; caution is advised. Consult your doctor for advice.

Infants and Children: There is no information comparing use of prazosin by infants and children with use by older patients. Consult your doctor for specific advice.

Special Concerns: Be careful when you start using this medication or when the dose is increased, since you may be more likely to experience dizziness or lightheadedness at these times. For the same reason, as you continue to take prazosin use extra care in hot weather, as well as during exercise or if you must stand for a long time.

OVERDOSE

Symptoms: Drowsiness, slowed reflexes, extremely low blood pressure.

What to Do: An overdose of prazosin is unlikely to be life-threatening. However, if someone takes a much larger dose than prescribed, call your doctor, emergency medical services (EMS), or the nearest poison control center immediately.

DRUG INTERACTIONS
Consult your doctor for advice if you are taking nonsteroidal anti-inflammatory drugs (NSAIDs), estrogens, sympathomimetics, propranolol or other beta-blockers, or any over-the-counter drug for appetite control, asthma, colds, cough, hay fever, or sinus problems.

FOOD INTERACTIONS
No known food interactions.

DISEASE INTERACTIONS
Caution is advised when taking prazosin. Consult your doctor if you have angina, severe heart disease, or kidney disease.

Prednisolone Ophthalmic

BRAND NAMES
AK-Pred, AK-Tate, Econopred, I-Pred, Inflamase, Lite Pred, Ocu-Pred, Pred, Pred Forte, Pred Mild, Predair, Ultra Pred

▶ Drug Class: Corticosteroid

▶ Available in: Ophthalmic solution, suspension

▶ Available OTC? No

▶ As Generic? Yes

Side Effects

SERIOUS
Decreased vision or blurring of vision (from cataract); eye pain, nausea, vomiting (from increased eye pressure); pain, redness, sensitivity to bright light, discharge (from eye infection). Call your doctor immediately if you experience any of these signs or symptoms. The drug may trigger a recurrence of herpes infection of the eye; mention any previous herpes infection to your doctor.

COMMON
Increased eye pressure (especially with the topical prednisolone acetate form); this is usually reversed once the drug is stopped.

LESS COMMON
Burning, stinging, redness, or watering of eyes.

PRINCIPAL USES
To control inflammation and prevent potentially permanent damage that may result from eye problems such as conjunctivitis, herpes of the eye, and cornea injuries. It is also used to help relieve redness, irritation, and discomfort in the eye, and may be used after eye surgery to control any inflammatory response.

HOW THE DRUG WORKS
Ophthalmic prednisolone inhibits the release of natural substances that stimulate an inflammatory reaction and pain in eye tissues.

DOSAGE
Solution or suspension: 1 or 2 drops in each eye up to 16 times a day.

ONSET OF EFFECT
Unknown.

DURATION OF ACTION
Unknown.

DIETARY ADVICE
No special restrictions.

STORAGE
Store in a tightly sealed container away from heat, moisture, and direct light. Do not allow it to freeze.

IF YOU MISS A DOSE
Apply it as soon as you remember. If it is near the time for the next dose, skip the missed dose and resume your regular dosage schedule. Do not double the next dose.

STOPPING THE DRUG
It is very important to use this drug as prescribed for the full treatment period, even if symptoms improve before the scheduled end of therapy.

PROLONGED USE
You should see your doctor regularly for tests and examinations if you use this drug for a prolonged period.

PRECAUTIONS
Over 60: No special problems are expected.

Driving and Hazardous Work: Do not drive or engage in hazardous work until you determine how the medicine affects your vision.

Alcohol: No special precautions are necessary.

Pregnancy: Adequate human studies have not been done, though no birth defects have been reported. Before taking ophthalmic prednisolone, tell your doctor if you are pregnant or plan to become pregnant.

Breast Feeding: Ophthalmic prednisolone has not been reported to cause problems in nursing babies. Consult your doctor for advice.

Infants and Children: Children under 2 years of age may be especially sensitive to the effects of ophthalmic prednisolone.

Special Concerns: To use the eye drops, first wash your hands. Tilt your head back. Gently apply pressure to the inside corner of the eyelid and with the index finger of the same hand, pull downward on the lower eyelid to make a space. Drop the medicine into this space and close your eye. Apply pressure for 1 or 2 minutes while keeping the eye closed without blinking. Then wash your hands again. Make sure the tip of the dropper does not touch your eye, finger, or any other surface. If your symptoms do not improve in 5 to 7 days or if they become worse, check with your doctor. Wearing contact lenses while using this medication may increase the risk of infection. Your doctor may tell you not to wear contact lenses during and for a day or two after treatment.

OVERDOSE
Symptoms: When used topically, an overdose is very unlikely. Inadvertent oral ingestion, however, may cause fever, muscle pain, loss of appetite, dizziness, fainting, and trouble breathing.

What to Do: An overdose of this drug is unlikely to be life-threatening. However, if someone applies a much larger dose than prescribed or accidentally ingests the medicine, call your doctor, emergency medical services (EMS), or the nearest poison control center.

DRUG INTERACTIONS
Consult your doctor for specific advice if you are taking any other prescription or over-the-counter medication.

FOOD INTERACTIONS
No known food interactions.

DISEASE INTERACTIONS
Consult your doctor if you have any of the following: cataracts, diabetes, glaucoma, herpes infection of the eye, tuberculosis of the eye, or any other eye infection.

Prednisolone Systemic

BRAND NAMES
Articulose-50, Delta-Cortef, Hydeltra-T.B.A., Hydeltrasol, Key-Pred, Nor-Pred T.B.A., Pediapred, Predaject-50, Predalone 50, Predate, Predcor, Predicort-50, Prelone

▶ Drug Class: Corticosteroid

▶ Available in: Solution, syrup, tablets, injection

▶ Available OTC? No

▶ As Generic? Yes

Side Effects

SERIOUS
Vision problems, frequent urination, increased thirst, rectal bleeding, blistering skin, confusion, hallucinations, paranoia, euphoria, depression, mood swings, redness and swelling at injection site. Call your doctor immediately.

COMMON
Increased appetite, indigestion, nervousness, insomnia, greater susceptibility to infections, increased blood pressure, slowed wound healing, weight gain, easy bruising, fluid retention.

LESS COMMON
Change in skin color, dizziness, headache, increased sweating, unusual growth of body or facial hair, increased blood sugar, peptic ulcers, adrenal insufficiency, muscle weakness, cataracts, glaucoma, osteoporosis.

PRINCIPAL USES
To treat numerous conditions that involve inflammation (a response by body tissues, producing redness, warmth, swelling, and pain). Such conditions include arthritis, allergic reactions, asthma, some skin diseases, multiple sclerosis flare-ups, and other autoimmune diseases. Also prescribed to treat deficiency of natural steroid hormones.

HOW THE DRUG WORKS
This hormone mimics the effects of the body's natural corticosteroids. It depresses the synthesis, release, and activity of inflammation-producing body chemicals. It also suppresses the activity of the immune system.

DOSAGE
Oral dosage: 5 to 200 mg a day, depending on condition, in 1 or several doses. Injection: 2 to 100 mg a day injected into a muscle, joint, vein, or lesion depending on condition. Consult pediatrician for children's dose.

ONSET OF EFFECT
Within 1 hour of taking oral forms or after injection into a muscle or vein; 1 to 2 days after injection into a lesion.

DURATION OF ACTION
30 to 36 hours for tablets; 3 to 4 days for injection.

DIETARY ADVICE
It can be taken with food or milk to minimize stomach upset. Your doctor may recommend a special diet.

STORAGE
Store in a tightly sealed container away from heat, moisture, and direct light. Do not allow liquid forms to freeze.

IF YOU MISS A DOSE
If you take several doses a day and it is close to the next dose, double the next dose. If you take 1 dose a day and you do not remember until the next day, skip the missed dose and do not double the next dose.

STOPPING THE DRUG
With long-term therapy, do not stop taking the drug abruptly; the dosage should be decreased gradually.

PROLONGED USE
Long-term use may lead to cataracts, diabetes, hypertension, or osteoporosis; see your doctor for regular examinations.

PRECAUTIONS
Over 60: Adverse reactions may be more likely and more severe.

Driving and Hazardous Work: Avoid such activities until you determine how the medicine affects you.

Alcohol: May cause stomach problems; avoid it unless your physician approves occasional moderate drinking.

Pregnancy: Overuse during pregnancy can impair growth and development of the child.

Breast Feeding: Do not use this drug while nursing.

Infants and Children: Prednisolone may retard the development of bone and other tissues.

Special Concerns: This drug can lower resistance to infection. Avoid immunizations with live vaccines. Patients undergoing long-term therapy should wear a medical-alert bracelet. Call your doctor if you develop a fever.

OVERDOSE
Symptoms: Fever, muscle or joint pain, nausea, dizziness, fainting, difficulty breathing. Prolonged overuse: Moonface, obesity, unusual hair growth, acne, loss of sexual function, muscle wasting.

What to Do: Call your doctor, emergency medical services (EMS), or the nearest poison control center immediately.

DRUG INTERACTIONS
Consult your doctor for advice if you are taking aminoglutethimide, antacids, barbiturates, carbamazepine, griseofulvin, mitotane, phenylbutazone, phenytoin, primidone, rifampin, injectable amphotericin B, oral antidiabetes agents, insulin, digitalis drugs, diuretics or drugs containing potassium or sodium.

FOOD INTERACTIONS
Avoid excess sodium.

DISEASE INTERACTIONS
Consult your doctor if you have a history of bone disease, chicken pox, measles, gastrointestinal disorders, diabetes, recent serious infection, glaucoma, heart disease, hypertension, liver or kidney disorders, high blood cholesterol, thyroid problems, myasthenia gravis, or lupus.

Generic 20 mg
(SCHEIN)

Additional photographs

▸ Drug Class: Corticosteroid

▸ Available in: Oral suspension, syrup, tablets

▸ Available OTC? No

▸ As Generic? Yes

Side Effects

SERIOUS
Vision problems, frequent urination, increased thirst, rectal bleeding, blistering skin, confusion, hallucinations, paranoia, euphoria, depression, mood swings, redness and swelling at injection site. Call your doctor immediately.

COMMON
Increased appetite, indigestion, nervousness, insomnia, greater susceptibility to infections, increased blood pressure, slowed wound healing, weight gain, easy bruising, fluid retention.

LESS COMMON
Change in skin color, dizziness, headache, increased sweating, unusual growth of body or facial hair, increased blood sugar, peptic ulcers, adrenal insufficiency, muscle weakness, cataracts, glaucoma, osteoporosis.

Prednisone

PRINCIPAL USES
To treat numerous conditions that involve inflammation (a response by body tissues, producing redness, warmth, swelling, and pain). Such conditions include arthritis, allergic reactions, asthma, some skin diseases, multiple sclerosis flare-ups, and other autoimmune diseases. Also prescribed to treat deficiency of natural steroid hormones.

HOW THE DRUG WORKS
Prednisone mimics the effects of the body's natural corticosteroid hormones. It depresses the synthesis, release, and activity of inflammation-producing body chemicals. It also suppresses the activity of the immune system.

DOSAGE
Adults and teenagers— For severe inflammation or to suppress the immune system: 5 to 100 mg a day in divided doses. For multiple sclerosis: 200 mg daily for 1 week, then 80 mg every other day for 1 month. Children— Consult your pediatrician.

ONSET OF EFFECT
Variable.

DURATION OF ACTION
Variable.

DIETARY ADVICE
It can be taken with food or milk to minimize stomach upset. Your doctor may recommend a low-salt, high-potassium, high-protein diet.

STORAGE
Store in a tightly sealed container away from heat, moisture, and direct light. Do not allow liquid forms to freeze.

IF YOU MISS A DOSE
Take it as soon as you remember. If you take several doses a day and it is close to the next dose, double the next dose. If you take 1 dose a day and you do not remember until the next day, skip the missed dose and do not double the next dose.

STOPPING THE DRUG
With long-term therapy, do not stop taking the drug abruptly; the dosage should be decreased gradually.

PROLONGED USE
Long-term use may lead to cataracts, diabetes, hypertension, or osteoporosis; see your doctor for regular examinations.

PRECAUTIONS
Over 60: Adverse reactions may be more likely and more severe.

Driving and Hazardous Work: Avoid such activities until you determine how the medicine affects you.

Alcohol: May cause stomach problems; avoid it unless your physician approves occasional moderate drinking.

Pregnancy: Overuse during pregnancy can retard the child's growth and cause other developmental problems.

Breast Feeding: Do not use this drug while nursing.

Infants and Children: Prednisone may retard the growth and development of bone and other tissues.

Special Concerns: This drug can lower resistance to infection. Avoid immunizations with live vaccines. Patients undergoing long-term therapy should wear a medical-alert bracelet. Call your doctor if you develop a fever.

OVERDOSE
Symptoms: Fever, muscle or joint pain, nausea, dizziness, fainting, difficulty breathing. Prolonged overuse: Moonface, obesity, unusual hair growth, acne, loss of sexual function, muscle wasting.

What to Do: Call your doctor, emergency medical services (EMS), or the nearest poison control center immediately.

DRUG INTERACTIONS
Consult your doctor for specific advice if you are taking aminoglutethimide, antacids, barbiturates, carbamazepine, griseofulvin, mitotane, phenylbutazone, phenytoin, primidone, rifampin, injectable amphotericin B, oral antidiabetes agents, insulin, digitalis drugs, diuretics, or medications containing potassium or sodium.

FOOD INTERACTIONS
Avoid excess sodium.

DISEASE INTERACTIONS
Consult your doctor if you have a history of bone disease, chicken pox, measles, gastrointestinal disorders, diabetes, recent serious infection, glaucoma, heart disease, hypertension, liver or kidney disorders, high blood cholesterol, thyroid problems, myasthenia gravis, or lupus.

Primaquine

Generic 26.3 mg
(SANOFI WINTHROP)

▶ Drug Class: Anti-
infective/antimalarial

▶ Available in: Tablets

▶ Available OTC? No

▶ As Generic? Yes

Side Effects

SERIOUS
Discontinue taking pri-
maquine and consult
your doctor immediately
if your urine is markedly
darker than usual. Other
serious side effects
include unusual fatigue;
pain in the back, legs, or
stomach; loss of appetite;
pale skin; fever; blue
fingernails, lips, or skin;
difficulty breathing;
dizziness or lightheaded-
ness. Call your doctor
immediately.

COMMON
Stomach cramps or pain,
nausea and vomiting.

LESS COMMON
Low white blood cell
counts causing sore
throat, fever, or other
signs of infection (rare).

PRINCIPAL USES
To prevent relapses of
malaria caused by the proto-
zoans Plasmodium vivax
and Plasmodium ovale. It is
used after chloroquine treatment has been completed,
or following preventive therapy with chloroquine in people who have had heavy
exposure to these forms
of malaria.

HOW THE DRUG WORKS
Primaquine alters the DNA
and interferes with the
energy-producing biological
processes of the protozoa.

DOSAGE
Adults and teenagers: One
26.3 mg tablet (15 mg base)
once a day for 14 days; in
patients with mild G6PD
deficiency, 3 tablets (45 mg
base) weekly for 8 weeks; in
patients with severe G6PD
deficiency, 2 tablets (30 mg
base) weekly for 30 weeks.
Some strains of Plasmodium
vivax (particularly those
from Southeast Asia), may
require a higher dose of
39.4 to 52.6 mg once a day
for 14 days. Consult your
doctor. Children age 12 and
under: 0.68 mg (0.39 mg
base) per 2.2 lbs (1 kg) of
body weight once a day for
14 days.

ONSET OF EFFECT
Unknown.

DURATION OF ACTION
Unknown.

DIETARY ADVICE
Primaquine can be taken
with food or juice to minimize stomach upset. Notify
your doctor if you experience persistent stomach
upset with pain, nausea,
or vomiting.

STORAGE
Store in a tightly sealed container away from heat, moisture, and direct light.

IF YOU MISS A DOSE
Take it as soon as you
remember. However, if it is
near the time for the next
dose, skip the missed dose
and resume your regular
dosage schedule. Do not
double the next dose.

STOPPING THE DRUG
Take it as prescribed for the
full treatment period, even if
you begin to feel better
before the scheduled end of
therapy.

PROLONGED USE
See your doctor regularly
for blood tests and examinations if you must take this
medicine for a prolonged
period.

PRECAUTIONS
Over 60: Adverse reactions
may be more likely and
more severe in older
patients.

**Driving and Hazardous
Work:** Do not drive or
engage in hazardous work
until you determine how the
medicine affects you.

Alcohol: No special precautions are necessary.

Pregnancy: Primaquine
should not be used during
pregnancy. Before you take
primaquine, tell your doctor
if you are pregnant or plan
to become pregnant.

Breast Feeding: Primaquine may pass into breast
milk; caution is advised.
Consult your doctor for
advice.

Infants and Children:
Adverse reactions may be
more likely and more
severe in children.

Special Concerns: You
should not take primaquine
if you are taking or have
taken quinacrine within the
previous 3 months. If you
are of Mediterranean,
African, or East Asian
ancestry, you may be at
higher risk for side effects
due to a deficiency of the
enzyme glucose-6-phosphate
dehydrogenase (G6PD);
consult your doctor.

OVERDOSE
Symptoms: Weakness,
pale, sickly appearance,
shortness of breath, severe
abdominal cramps, vomit-
ing, heartbeat irregularities.

What to Do: Call your
doctor, emergency medical
services (EMS), or the
nearest poison control center immediately.

DRUG INTERACTIONS
Consult your physician for
specific advice if you are
taking quinacrine or any
drugs that may cause ane-
mia (such as sulfonamides
and nitrofurans) or bone
marrow suppression
(including methotrexate,
phenylbutazone, and chlo-
ramphenicol). Also, tell your
physician if you are taking
any other prescription or
over-the-counter drug.

FOOD INTERACTIONS
No known food interactions.

DISEASE INTERACTIONS
You should not take pri-
maquine if you are acutely
ill with a disease that may
reduce white blood cell
counts, such as rheumatoid
arthritis or lupus erythematosus. Consult your doctor if you have a family
history of favism or
hemolytic anemia, G6PD
deficiency, or a deficiency of
nicotinamide adenine dinu-
cleotide (NADH).

Primidone

Mysoline 250 mg
(WYETH-AYERST)

▶ Drug Class: Anticonvulsant

▶ Available in: Tablets, suspension

▶ Available OTC? No

▶ As Generic? Yes

Side Effects

SERIOUS
Fever, sore throat, swollen glands, red or purple point-like rash on the skin or mucous membranes, blistering or peeling skin lesions, mouth sores, easy bruising, paleness, weakness, confusion, lethargy, or seizures may be a sign of a potentially fatal blood reaction or other complication. Call your doctor immediately.

COMMON
Drowsiness, dizziness, loss of coordination, double vision, hyperactivity (in children).

LESS COMMON
Loss of appetite, mental or mood changes, nausea or vomiting, impotence, mild rash, lethargy followed by insomnia. There are numerous additional side effects associated with this drug; consult your doctor if you are concerned about any adverse or unusual reactions.

PRINCIPAL USES
To control certain types of seizures due to epilepsy.

HOW THE DRUG WORKS
Primidone is thought to depress the activity of certain parts of the brain and suppress the abnormal firing of neurons that causes seizures.

DOSAGE
Adults: 500 to 1,000 mg (or more) a day, in 3 or 4 divided doses. Children: 10 to 20 mg a day, in 3 or 4 divided doses. A low dose is used to start, and gradually increased.

ONSET OF EFFECT
Several hours.

DURATION OF ACTION
Maximum effectiveness:12 hours or longer; effectiveness then gradually decreases.

DIETARY ADVICE
Take with food to help avoid stomach upset.

STORAGE
Store in a tightly sealed container away from heat, moisture, and direct light. Do not freeze the liquid form.

IF YOU MISS A DOSE
Take it as soon as you remember. If it is near the time for the next dose, skip the missed dose and resume regular dosage schedule. Do not double the next dose, unless so advised by your doctor.

STOPPING THE DRUG
Never stop this drug abruptly; seizures may ensue. Your doctor will taper the dose gradually over a period of weeks to months.

PROLONGED USE
This drug is typically taken for prolonged periods. See your doctor regularly for tests and examinations.

PRECAUTIONS
Over 60: Older patients may require lower doses to minimize side effects.

Driving and Hazardous Work: This drug may cause drowsiness or dizziness. Do not drive or engage in hazardous work until you determine how it affects you.

Alcohol: May contribute to excessive drowsiness.

Pregnancy: Birth defects and bleeding problems in the mother have been reported in association with primidone use during pregnancy. Scientific studies are incomplete. However, seizures during pregnancy also increase the risks to the fetus. Discuss with your doctor the potential risks and benefits of using this drug during pregnancy. Folate supplementation is recommended beginning 1 to 2 months before conception and throughout the course of pregnancy.

Breast Feeding: Primidone passes into breast milk, although at low levels. Consult your doctor for advice.

Infants and Children: Adverse reactions may be more likely and more severe in children.

Special Concerns: The generic version of this drug is not recommended. Do not change the brand of primidone you are taking without consulting your doctor. The suspension form of primidone should be shaken well before you take it. Your doctor may want you to carry an ID card or bracelet saying that you are taking this drug.

OVERDOSE
Symptoms: Drowsiness, breathing problems, loss of consciousness.

What to Do: Call your doctor, emergency medical services (EMS), or the nearest poison control center immediately.

DRUG INTERACTIONS
Primidone may interact with other drugs, including other anticonvulsants (phenytoin, carbamazepine, clonazepam, valproic acid), benzodiazepines, caffeine, calcium channel blockers, corticosteroids, corticotropin, cyclophosphamide, cyclosporine, dacarbazine, digitoxin, disopyramide, doxycycline, general anesthetics, griseofulvin, H1 blockers, haloperidol, isoniazid, ketamine, levothyroxine, loxapine, maprotiline, metoprolol, mexiletine, phenytoin, propranolol, quinidine, theophylline, tricyclic antidepressants, vitamin D, and warfarin. May decrease the effectiveness of oral contraceptives, causing contraceptive failure.

FOOD INTERACTIONS
No known food interactions.

DISEASE INTERACTIONS
Caution is advised if you have asthma, chronic lung disease, hyperactivity (in children), kidney or liver disease, or porphyria.

Probenecid

Generic 500 mg
(SCHEIN)

▶ Drug Class: Antigout drug; adjunct to antibiotic therapy

▶ Available in: Tablets

▶ Available OTC? No

▶ As Generic? Yes

Side Effects

SERIOUS
Rapid or irregular heartbeat; puffiness or swelling around eyes; trouble breathing; tightness in chest; changes in skin color; rash, hives, or itching; bloody or cloudy urine; difficult urination; lower back or side pain; sores, ulcers, or white spots on lips or in mouth; sore throat and fever; sudden decrease in urine; swollen face, fingers, feet, or lower legs; swollen or painful glands; unusual bleeding or bruising; unusual fatigue; yellow discoloration of the eyes or skin; unusual weight gain. Call your doctor immediately.

COMMON
Headache, redness, pain or swelling in joints, loss of appetite, nausea or vomiting.

LESS COMMON
Dizziness, reddened face, frequent urge to urinate, sore gums.

PRINCIPAL USES
To treat chronic gout and gouty arthritis—specifically, to lower the uric acid level in hopes of preventing future gout attacks. Probenecid is also prescribed to enhance the action of certain antibiotics when treating infections.

HOW THE DRUG WORKS
Gout occurs when excessive amounts of uric acid build up in the blood. This leads to the formation of uric-acid-based crystals that are deposited in the joints, causing inflammation and leading to the sharp, excruciating pain of a gout attack. Probenecid promotes excretion of excess uric acid from the body and so eases or prevents gout attacks. Probenecid also slows the body's removal of antibiotics, thus increasing their levels in the blood and prolonging their duration of action.

DOSAGE
For gout— 250 mg, 2 times a day for first week, then 500 mg, 2 times a day, to maximum of 2,000 mg per day. For antibiotic therapy with penicillin— 500 mg, 4 times a day. Children ages 2 to 14: 25 mg per 2.2 lbs (1 kg) of body weight to start, then 25 mg per 2.2 lbs in 4 daily doses. To treat gonorrhea— 1 g of probenecid with or before 3.5 mg of ampicillin or 4.8 million units of injected penicillin.

ONSET OF EFFECT
To ease gout: Several months of therapy may be required before probenecid begins to prevent gout attacks. To suppress the excretion of antibiotics: 2 hours.

DURATION OF ACTION
For gout: Unknown. For enhancement of antibiotic therapy: 2 hours.

DIETARY ADVICE
It can be taken with food or antacids to reduce stomach upset. Drink 8 to 10 full glasses of water a day.

STORAGE
Store in a tightly sealed container away from heat and direct light.

IF YOU MISS A DOSE
Take it as soon as you remember. If it is near the time for the next dose, skip the missed dose and resume your regular dosage schedule. Do not double the next dose.

STOPPING THE DRUG
The decision to stop taking the drug should be made by your doctor.

PROLONGED USE
See your doctor regularly for tests and examinations if you take this drug for a prolonged period. Gout attacks may continue for a while after you start taking probenecid.

PRECAUTIONS
Over 60: No special problems are expected.

Driving and Hazardous Work: Avoid such activities until you determine how the medicine affects you.

Alcohol: Avoid alcohol.

Pregnancy: Probenecid has not been shown to cause problems during pregnancy.

Breast Feeding: Probenecid may pass into breast milk; caution is advised. Consult your doctor for advice.

Infants and Children: Not recommended for use by children under age 2.

Special Concerns: Before you have any medical tests, be sure to tell the doctor you are taking probenecid.

OVERDOSE
Symptoms: Nausea, vomiting, diarrhea, seizures.

What to Do: Call your doctor, emergency medical services (EMS), or the nearest poison control center immediately.

DRUG INTERACTIONS
Consult your doctor for specific advice if you are taking anticancer (chemotherapy) medications, aspirin or other salicylates, heparin, indomethacin, ketoprofen, methotrexate, medicine for any type of infection, nitrofurantoin, or zidovudine.

FOOD INTERACTIONS
None are likely, but a low-purine diet is recommended to reduce the risk of gout attacks. Foods high in purines include anchovies, sardines, legumes, poultry, sweetbreads, liver, kidneys, and other organ meats.

DISEASE INTERACTIONS
Caution is advised when taking probenecid. Consult your doctor if you have a blood disease, cancer, kidney disease or kidney stones, or a stomach ulcer.

Procainamide Hydrochloride

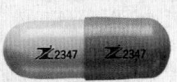

Generic 500 mg
(ZENITH)

838

Additional photographs

▸ Drug Class: Antiarrhythmic

▸ Available in: Capsules,
tablets, extended-release
tablets, injection

▸ Available OTC? No

▸ As Generic? Yes

Side Effects

SERIOUS
Fainting; rapid or irregular heartbeat (palpita-
tions); fever and chills;
joint pain or swelling;
painful breathing; skin
rash or itching; confu-
sion; sore mouth, gums,
or throat; hallucinations;
depression; unusual
bleeding or bruising;
unusual fatigue. Call
your doctor immediately.

COMMON
Diarrhea, abdominal pain,
nausea, vomiting, loss of
appetite.

LESS COMMON
Dizziness, lightheaded-
ness, weakness, dry
mouth.

PRINCIPAL USES
To treat irregular heart-
beats (cardiac arrhythmias).

HOW THE DRUG WORKS
Procainamide hydrochloride
slows nerve impulses in the
heart and reduces the sensitivity of heart tissue to certain nerve impulses, thus
stabilizing the heartbeat.

DOSAGE
Tablets and capsules—
Adults: 500 to 1,000 mg
every 4 to 6 hours. Chil-
dren: 12.5 mg per 2.2 lbs (1
kg) of body weight 4 times
a day. Extended-release
tablets— 1,000 to 2,000 mg
every 12 hours.

ONSET OF EFFECT
Oral: 60 to 90 minutes.
Injection: immediate.

DURATION OF ACTION
From 3 to 8 hours (longer
in patients with kidney disease or heart failure).

DIETARY ADVICE
Procainamide should be
taken with a glass of water
on an empty stomach 1
hour before or 2 hours after
meals.

STORAGE
Store in a tightly sealed container away from heat and
direct light.

IF YOU MISS A DOSE
Take a missed dose as soon
as you remember. If it is
near the time for the next
dose, skip the missed dose
and resume your regular
dosage schedule. Do not
double the next dose.

STOPPING THE DRUG
Take as prescribed for the
full treatment period, even if
you begin to feel better
before the scheduled end of
therapy. The decision to
stop taking the drug should
be made by your doctor.

PROLONGED USE
Lifelong therapy may be
necessary. See your doctor
regularly for examinations
and diagnostic tests if you
must take this medicine for
a prolonged period.

PRECAUTIONS
Over 60: Adverse reactions
may be more likely and
more severe in older
patients.

**Driving and Hazardous
Work:** Do not drive or
engage in hazardous work
until you determine how the
medicine affects you.

Alcohol: Avoid alcohol.

Pregnancy: Procainamide
has not been shown to
cause problems during
pregnancy. In any case, if
you are taking this drug, be
sure to tell your doctor if
you are pregnant or plan to
become pregnant.

Breast Feeding: Pro-
cainamide passes into
breast milk. Consult your
doctor for specific advice.

Infants and Children:
Procainamide has not been
shown to cause problems in
limited use in children.

Special Concerns: Your
doctor may want you to
carry a medical identification card or bracelet saying
you use procainamide.
Before having any kind of
surgical procedure or medical test, tell the doctor or
dentist in charge that you
are taking procainamide.

OVERDOSE
Symptoms: Confusion,
severe dizziness, fainting,
rapid or irregular heartbeat,
decrease in urination, nausea or vomiting.

What to Do: Call your
doctor, emergency medical
services (EMS), or the
nearest poison control
center immediately.

DRUG INTERACTIONS
Consult your doctor for specific advice if you are taking
other antiarrhythmics,
drugs for high blood pressure, antimyasthenics,
pimozide, or antihistamines.

FOOD INTERACTIONS
No known food interactions.

DISEASE INTERACTIONS
Consult your doctor if you
have any of the following:
heart block, asthma, myasthenia gravis, or systemic
lupus erythematosus. Use
of procainamide may cause
complications in patients
with liver or kidney disease,
since these organs work
together to remove the
medication from the body.

Procarbazine Hydrochloride

▶ Drug Class: Antineoplastic (anticancer) agent

▶ Available in: Capsules

▶ Available OTC? No

▶ As Generic? No

Side Effects

SERIOUS
Severe chest pain; dilated pupils; rapid or slowed heartbeat; severe headache; sensitivity of eyes to light; increased sweating; stiff neck; black, tarry stools; blood in urine or stools; bloody vomit; cough or hoarseness; fever and chills; pain in lower back or flanks; painful or difficult urination; tiny bright red spots on skin; unusual bleeding or bruising; confusion; seizures; hallucinations; absent menstrual periods; shortness of breath; thickened bronchial (lung) secretions; diarrhea; sores in mouth and on the lips; tingling or numbness of fingers or toes; incoordination or unsteady gait; yellowish tinge to eyes or skin. Such side effects may mean that normal blood cells and special blood-clotting cells have been affected, or that the immune system has been affected and an infection is developing. See your doctor immediately.

COMMON
Drowsiness, muscle or joint pain, muscle twitching, nausea or vomiting, nervousness, restlessness, nightmares, insomnia, unusual fatigue.

LESS COMMON
Constipation, darkened skin, difficulty swallowing, lightheadedness when arising, dry mouth, loss of appetite, depression, flushing of the face.

PRINCIPAL USES
To treat Hodgkin's disease (a cancer affecting the spleen and lymph nodes). Procarbazine is usually only one drug of several given in combination with other chemotherapy agents to fight cancer.

HOW THE DRUG WORKS
Procarbazine kills cancer cells by interfering with the activity of their genetic material, which prevents the cells from reproducing. The drug may also affect the growth and development of other kinds of cells in the body, resulting in unpleasant side effects. Procarbazine is also a weak inhibitor of the enzyme known as monoamine oxidase (MAO); MAO inhibitors are routinely prescribed to treat depression, although this has no impact on procarbazine's function as a cancer-fighting drug.

DOSAGE
Adults: 2 to 4 mg per 2.2 lbs (1 kg) of body weight per day for first week. Then 4 to 6 mg per 2.2 lbs per day until the blood cell count falls substantially. Then 1 to 2 mg per 2.2 lbs per day. Children: 50 mg per square meter of body surface per day for first week, then 100 mg per square meter of body surface per day until toxicity occurs, then 50 mg per square meter of body surface per day.

ONSET OF EFFECT
Unknown.

DURATION OF ACTION
Unknown.

DIETARY ADVICE
Maintain adequate food and fluid intake. Calorie, protein, and vitamin needs increase in patients with cancer. Good nutrition is essential to cope with the demands of chemotherapy. Foods high in the substance tyramine must be eliminated from the diet during therapy; see Special Concerns and Food Interactions for further information.

STORAGE
Store in a tightly sealed container away from heat and direct light. Unopened vials should be refrigerated but not allowed to freeze.

IF YOU MISS A DOSE
If you miss a dose, take it as soon as you remember. If it is near the time for the next dose, skip the missed dose and resume your regular dosage schedule. Do not double the next dose.

STOPPING THE DRUG
The decision to stop taking the drug should be made by your doctor.

PROLONGED USE
You should see your doctor regularly for tests and examinations if you take this drug for a prolonged period.

PRECAUTIONS
Over 60: Adverse reactions may be more likely and more severe in older patients.

Driving and Hazardous Work: Do not drive or engage in hazardous work until you determine how the medicine affects you.

Alcohol: Avoid alcohol.

Pregnancy: Procarbazine can cause birth defects if either the father or mother takes it. Consult your doctor for specific advice if you are pregnant or plan to become pregnant. Use of a reliable method of birth control is recommended throughout the duration of therapy with procarbazine.

Breast Feeding: Procarbazine passes into breast milk; avoid or discontinue use of this drug while breast feeding.

Infants and Children: Procarbazine is not expected to cause different problems in infants and children than it does in older persons.

Special Concerns: Like all drugs categorized as MAO inhibitors, procarbazine prevents the liver and other body tissues from neutralizing a substance called tyramine, which, in the bloodstream, causes a sudden increase in blood pressure. Therefore, foods high in tyramines must be avoided while undergoing therapy with procarbazine. Such foods include aged cheeses, processed meats, many varieties of dried or preserved foods, as well as certain kinds of liquor and wine (especially red wine). See Food Interactions for a more complete list of foods and beverages high in tyramines. While taking procarbazine, do not receive any immunizations without consulting your doctor. Avoid people with infections and those who have recently had oral polio vaccine. Be careful when using a toothbrush, dental floss, or toothpick. Check with your doctor before having any dental work done. If you are going to have surgery, tell the doctor or dentist in charge that you are taking procarbazine. Do not touch your eyes or the inside of your nose unless you have just washed your hands. Be careful not to cut yourself when using sharp objects such as a razor. Avoid contact sports and other activities during which bruising could occur.

Procarbazine Hydrochloride (continued)

OVERDOSE

Symptoms: Nausea, vomiting, diarrhea, tremors, seizures, loss of consciousness, very low blood pressure, coma.

What to Do: Call your doctor, emergency medical services (EMS), or the nearest poison control center immediately.

DRUG INTERACTIONS

Consult your doctor for specific advice if you are taking amantadine, anticholinergics, diabetes medicine, antidyskinetics, antihistamines, antipsychotics, buclizine, central nervous system depressants, cyclizine, disopyramide, flavoxate, ipratropium, meclizine, orphenadrine, oxybutynin, procainamide, promethazine, quinidine, trimeprazine, amphetamines, diet pills, dextromethorphan, levodopa, asthma or cold medicine, methyldopa, methylphenidate, narcotic pain medicine, amphotericin B, antithyroid agents, azathioprine, chloramphenicol, colchicine, flucytosine, interferon, plicamycin, zidovudine, buspirone, carbamazepine, cyclobenzaprine, maprotiline, other MAO inhibitors, antidepressants, fluoxetine, guanadrel, guanethidine, or rauwolfia alkaloids.

FOOD INTERACTIONS

Avoid tyramine-rich foods, which include aged cheeses, avocados, banana skins, bean curd, bologna and other processed lunch meats, chicken livers, chocolate, figs, canned or dried fish, pickled herring, meat extracts, pepperoni, raisins, raspberries, unpasteurized beer, Chianti, sherry, vermouth, and red wines in general. Also avoid caffeine-rich beverages or foods.

DISEASE INTERACTIONS

Caution is advised when taking procarbazine. Consult your doctor if you have a history of any of the following: alcoholism, angina, recent heart attack or stroke, chicken pox, shingles, epilepsy, frequent headaches, infection, kidney disease, liver disease, mental illness, overactive thyroid, Parkinson's disease, or pheochromocytoma.

Prochlorperazine

▶ Drug Class: Neuroleptic;
antiemetic

▶ Available in: Extended-
release capsules, syrup,
tablets, suppositories,
injection

▶ Available OTC? No

▶ As Generic? Yes

Side Effects

SERIOUS
Rapid heartbeat, profuse
sweating, seizures, difficulty breathing, neck stiffness, swelling of the
tongue, difficulty swal-
lowing. Also a rare condition can develop called
neuroleptic malignant
syndrome, characterized
by stiffness or spasms of
the muscles, high fever,
and confusion or disori-
entation. Call your doctor
immediately.

COMMON
Nausea, reduced sweat-
ing, dry mouth, blurred
vision, drowsiness, shak-
ing of hands, stiffness,
stooped posture.

LESS COMMON
Difficult urination, men-
strual irregularities,
breast pain or swelling,
unexpected weight gain,
uncontrolled movements
of the tongue, fever,
chills, sore throat,
unusual bruising or
bleeding, heart palpita-
tions, skin rash, itching,
increased sensitivity of
the skin to sunlight.

PRINCIPAL USES
To treat severe nausea and
vomiting.

HOW THE DRUG WORKS
Prochlorperazine sup-
presses activity in the trigger zones of the brain and
gastrointestinal tract that
govern the vomiting reflex.

DOSAGE
Usual adult dose: Initially,
5 to 10 mg, 3 or 4 times a
day. Injection: 10 to 20 mg
injected into a muscle every
4 to 6 hours. Your doctor
may increase the dose as
needed and tolerated.

ONSET OF EFFECT
30 to 40 minutes for oral
forms; 60 minutes for suppository; 10 to 20 minutes
after injection.

DURATION OF ACTION
3 to 4 hours; 12 hours for
extended-release capsules.

DIETARY ADVICE
Can be taken with food or a
full glass of milk or water.

STORAGE
Store in a tightly sealed container away from heat and
direct light.

IF YOU MISS A DOSE
Take it as soon as you
remember. If it is near the
time for the next dose, skip
the missed dose and
resume your regular dosage
schedule. Do not double the
next dose.

STOPPING THE DRUG
The decision to stop taking
the drug should be made by
your doctor.

PROLONGED USE
See your doctor regularly
for tests and examinations if
you must take this medicine
for a prolonged period.

PRECAUTIONS
Over 60: Adverse reactions
are more common in elderly
patients. A lower dose may
be warranted.

**Driving and Hazardous
Work:** Do not drive or
engage in hazardous work
until you determine how the
medicine affects you.

Alcohol: Avoid alcohol.

Pregnancy: Avoid using
this drug if you are pregnant or plan to become
pregnant.

Breast Feeding: Either
avoid taking the drug if possible or refrain from breast
feeding.

Infants and Children:
Adverse reactions may be
more likely and more
severe in children.

Special Concerns: Avoid
prolonged exposure to high
temperatures or hot cli-
mates while taking prochlorperazine. Drink plenty of
fluids and try to stay cool
in the summertime. Avoid
overexposure to sunlight
until you determine if the
drug heightens your skin's
sensitivity to ultraviolet radiation and increases your
risk of sunburn.

OVERDOSE
Symptoms: Extreme
drowsiness, heartbeat irregularities, dry mouth, paradoxical restlessness or
agitation, seizures, loss
of consciousness.

What to Do: Call your
doctor, emergency medical
services (EMS), or the
nearest poison control center immediately.

DRUG INTERACTIONS
Consult your doctor for specific advice if you are taking
anticholinergics, anticonvulsants, antidepressants, antihistamines, antihyperten-
sives, bupropion, central
nervous system depressants
such as barbiturates, clozapine, dronabinol, ethinamate,
fluoxetine, guanethidine,
guanfacine, lithium, methyldopa, carbamazepine,
rifampin, or trihexyphenidyl.

FOOD INTERACTIONS
None known.

DISEASE INTERACTIONS
Consult your doctor if you
have a history of alcohol
abuse, any blood disorder,
breast cancer, benign prostatic hyperplasia (BPH),
epilepsy or seizures, glaucoma, heart, lung, or blood
vessel disease, liver disease,
Parkinson's disease, peptic
ulcer, or urinary difficulty.

Procyclidine

BRAND NAME
Kemadrin

Kemadrin 5 mg
(GLAXO WELLCOME)

▶ Drug Class: Antiparkinsonism drug

▶ Available in: Tablets

▶ Available OTC? No

▶ As Generic? No

Side Effects

SERIOUS
Confusion, severe drowsiness, rapid heartbeat, hallucinations, glaucoma.

COMMON
Blurred vision; constipation; dry mouth, nose, and throat.

LESS COMMON
Dizziness and lightheadedness, loss of memory, nausea.

PRINCIPAL USES
To treat Parkinson's disease and Parkinson-like syndromes, which can occur as a result of injury to or infection of the central nervous system, damage to blood vessels in the brain, or exposure to certain toxins.

HOW THE DRUG WORKS
Procyclidine promotes the release of dopamine in the brain. Dopamine is a chemical that is necessary for both the initiation and smooth control of voluntary muscle movement.

DOSAGE
Adults: To start, 2.5 mg, 3 times a day. The dosage is increased gradually to 5 mg, 3 times a day. Children: This drug has not been extensively studied in children; consult a pediatrician.

ONSET OF EFFECT
Within 1 hour.

DURATION OF ACTION
From 6 to 12 hours.

DIETARY ADVICE
Procyclidine should be taken after meals to prevent nausea.

STORAGE
Store in a tightly sealed container away from heat, moisture, and direct light.

IF YOU MISS A DOSE
Take it as soon as you remember, unless the time for your next scheduled dose is within the next 2 hours. If so, skip the missed dose and resume your regular dosage schedule. Do not double the next dose.

STOPPING THE DRUG
The decision to stop taking the drug should be made in consultation with your doctor. The dosage should be decreased gradually.

PROLONGED USE
No special difficulties are expected with long-term use of procyclidine.

PRECAUTIONS
Over 60: Adverse reactions may be more likely and more severe in older patients. Procyclidine should be used cautiously in patients in this age group. If higher doses are needed, it is best to increase the dose very gradually.

Driving and Hazardous Work: Procyclidine can cause drowsiness or confusion. Do not drive or engage in hazardous work until you determine how it affects you.

Alcohol: Avoid alcohol; combined with the medication, alcohol is likely to cause or worsen confusion.

Pregnancy: This medication should not be used in pregnant women.

Breast Feeding: It is not known to what degree procyclidine passes into breast milk. Nursing mothers should avoid use of this medication.

Infants and Children: There is little known about the safety and effectiveness of procyclidine in infants and children. Consult your pediatrician to discuss the use of this drug in children.

Special Concerns: Procyclidine can cause or worsen glaucoma (the buildup of excessive pressure within the eye, and a leading cause of blindness). See your ophthalmologist regularly for periodic monitoring of eye pressure.

OVERDOSE
Symptoms: Clumsiness, seizures, severe mouth dryness, drowsiness, hallucinations, loss of consciousness.

What to Do: Call your doctor, emergency medical services (EMS), or the nearest poison control center immediately.

DRUG INTERACTIONS
Procyclidine may interact with many drugs, in particular drugs that depress the central nervous system (such as alcohol, barbiturates, and other sleep-inducing drugs) and MAO inhibitor antidepressants (such as phenelzine sulfate and tranylcypromine sulfate). Consult your doctor if you are taking these drugs.

FOOD INTERACTIONS
No known food interactions.

DISEASE INTERACTIONS
Caution is advised when taking procyclidine. Consult your doctor if you have any of the following: irregular heartbeat or heart rhythm abnormalities, glaucoma, intestinal obstruction, urinary retention or trouble urinating, or enlarged prostate (benign prostatic hyperplasia).

Progesterone Intrauterine System

▶ Drug Class: Progestin (hormone)

▶ Available in: Intrauterine device

▶ Available OTC? No

▶ As Generic? Yes

Side Effects

SERIOUS
Severe abdominal pain or cramping; faintness, dizziness, or sharp pain at time of IUD insertion; heavy or unexpected uterine bleeding between periods; fever; odorous discharge; unusual fatigue; any unusual uterine bleeding. Call your doctor immediately.

COMMON
No common side effects are associated with use of the progesterone IUD.

LESS COMMON
There are no less-common side effects associated with use of the progesterone IUD.

PRINCIPAL USES
As a contraceptive (birth control method).

HOW THE DRUG WORKS
Progesterone inhibits the secretion of pituitary hormones that in turn regulate menstrual and reproductive cycles; it also alters the activity of uterine cells.

DOSAGE
1 intrauterine device (IUD) is inserted into the vagina by a health professional and replaced within 12 months.

ONSET OF EFFECT
Within days.

DURATION OF ACTION
1 year.

DIETARY ADVICE
The IUD can be used without regard to diet.

STORAGE
Not applicable.

IF YOU MISS A DOSE
Not applicable; the IUD remains implanted in the body for the entire duration of use.

STOPPING THE DRUG
Consult your gynecologist if you decide you no longer wish to use the IUD.

PROLONGED USE
You should check for the IUD thread every month, especially after each menstrual period. Wash your hands thoroughly before checking. Use your middle fingers to find the thread inside the cervix. Do not pull on the thread. If you cannot find the thread, call your gynecologist.

PRECAUTIONS
Over 60: Not applicable to patients over 60.

Driving and Hazardous Work: The use of a progesterone IUD should not impair your ability to perform such tasks safely.

Alcohol: No special precautions are necessary.

Pregnancy: This IUD should not be used during pregnancy or by a woman who has had an ectopic pregnancy.

Breast Feeding: The progesterone IUD has not been shown to cause problems in nursing babies. Its use is recommended for women who require contraception while breast-feeding.

Infants and Children: Sexually active teenagers are urged to use a contraceptive method (for example, condoms) that protects them against sexually transmitted diseases; this IUD does not. Teenagers who have not given birth generally have more side effects than teenagers or adults who have. The IUD may move out of place, harming the uterus or cervix. Abdominal pain and increased menstrual bleeding are more common in teenagers than in older women.

Special Concerns: It is possible for pregnancy to occur while using the progesterone-containing IUD. Notify your doctor immediately if you feel the changes that can occur with pregnancy, such as enlarged or tender breasts, lack of menstrual period, unusual uterine bleeding, or pain and cramping in the lower abdomen. Until your doctor can see you, use another birth control method, such as condoms. If you think that the IUD has moved out of place, call your doctor immediately. If you think you are pregnant, do a home pregnancy test. Do not try to put the IUD in place inside the uterus yourself, nor try to remove it yourself.

OVERDOSE
Symptoms: Not applicable.

What to Do: Emergency instructions not applicable.

DRUG INTERACTIONS
The following drugs may interact with progesterone. Consult your doctor for specific advice if you are taking aminoglutethimide, carbamazepine, phenytoin, rifabutin, or rifampin.

FOOD INTERACTIONS
No known food interactions.

DISEASE INTERACTIONS
Caution is advised when using the progesterone IUD. Consult your doctor if you have any of the following conditions: uterine abnormalities or bleeding problems, acquired immunodeficiency syndrome (AIDS), a blood disorder, a heart defect, insulin-dependent diabetes, a recent sexually transmitted disease, abnormally slow heartbeat, or any recent surgery involving the uterus or fallopian tubes.

Progesterone Systemic and Topical

▶ Drug Class: Progestin (hormone)

▶ Available in: Injection, vaginal gel, capsules, suppositories

▶ Available OTC? No

▶ As Generic? Yes

Side Effects

SERIOUS
Changes in or cessation of menstrual bleeding; unexpected or increased flow of breast milk; mental depression; skin rash; loss of or change in speech, coordination, or vision; severe and sudden shortness of breath; severe headache. Call your doctor immediately.

COMMON
Stomach pain or cramping, swelling of face, ankles, or feet, mild headache, mood changes, unusual fatigue, weight gain, pain or irritation at site of injection.

LESS COMMON
Acne, breast pain or tenderness, hot flashes, insomnia, loss of sexual desire, loss or gain of scalp hair or body hair, brown spots on skin.

PRINCIPAL USES
To treat amenorrhea (cessation of menstruation) and abnormal uterine bleeding in the absence of structural pathology (such as uterine fibroids or uterine cancer). The vaginal gel is used as part of Assisted Reproductive Technology for infertile women with progesterone deficiency, and to promote menstruation in women with premature amenorrhea.

HOW THE DRUG WORKS
Progesterone inhibits the secretion of pituitary hormones that in turn regulate a woman's menstrual and reproductive cycles; it also alters the activity of cells in the uterine lining.

DOSAGE
Injection— For amenorrhea and abnormal uterine bleeding: 5 to 10 mg injected into a muscle daily for 6 to 10 days, or 150 mg injected into a muscle as a single dose. Your doctor may tell you to take estrogen for 2 weeks prior to receiving the injection. (Progesterone vaginal suppositories may be provided by a pharmacist in lieu of injections.) Vaginal gel— For amenorrhea: 45 mg (Crinone 4%) every other day, up to 6 doses. For progesterone supplementation: 90 mg (Crinone 8%), once a day. For progesterone replacement: 90 mg, 2 times a day. Capsules— For secondary amenorrhea: 400 mg once in the evening for 10 days.

ONSET OF EFFECT
Injection— For amenorrhea: 48 to 70 hours after the last injection. For uterine bleeding: Within 6 days. Treatment will be stopped if bleeding continues or recurs. Vaginal gel and capsules— Unknown.

DURATION OF ACTION
Unknown.

DIETARY ADVICE
Progesterone can be taken without regard to diet.

STORAGE
Store in a tightly sealed container away from heat and direct light. Do not allow gel to freeze.

IF YOU MISS A DOSE
Injection: Inject the drug as soon as you remember. However, if it is near the time for the next dose, skip the missed dose and resume your regular dosage schedule. Do not double the next dose. Vaginal gel: If you miss a dose, do not apply an excessive amount the next day. Resume regular dosage schedule. Capsules: If you miss a dose on one day, skip the missed dose and resume regular schedule. Do not double the next dose.

STOPPING THE DRUG
Consult your doctor.

PROLONGED USE
Consult your doctor about the need for periodic examinations and laboratory tests.

PRECAUTIONS
Over 60: No special problems are expected.

Driving and Hazardous Work: No special precautions are necessary.

Alcohol: No special precautions are necessary.

Pregnancy: This hormone should not be used during pregnancy. If you suspect a pregnancy, stop taking progesterone immediately and call your doctor. Before using injected progesterone, tell your doctor if you are pregnant or plan to become pregnant. The vaginal gel may be used safely as part of Assisted Reproductive Technology in progesterone-deficient women.

Breast Feeding: Progesterone passes into breast milk and may change the quality or quantity of milk. Discuss with your doctor the risks and benefits of using it while nursing.

Infants and Children: Safety and effectiveness have not been determined.

Special Concerns: You should have a Pap test at least every 6 months while receiving progesterone. Be alert for signs of excessive fluid retention in your body.

OVERDOSE
Symptoms: None.

What to Do: An overdose is unlikely to be life-threatening. However, if someone takes a much larger dose than prescribed or accidentally ingests the gel, seek emergency medical attention right away

DRUG INTERACTIONS
Consult your doctor for specific advice if you are taking aminoglutethimide, carbamazepine, phenytoin, rifabutin, or rifampin.

FOOD INTERACTIONS
Do not take the capsules if you are allergic to peanuts; they contain peanut oil.

DISEASE INTERACTIONS
Consult your doctor if you have any of the following: asthma, epilepsy, heart problems, circulation problems, migraine headaches, breast disease, bleeding problems, diabetes, high blood cholesterol, or central nervous system disorders such as depression. Use of progesterone may cause complications in patients with liver or kidney disease, since these organs work together to remove drugs and other substances from the body.

Promethazine Hydrochloride

Phenergan 25 mg
(WYETH-AYERST)

▶ Drug Class: Antihistamine

▶ Available in: Tablets, syrup, injection, suppositories

▶ Available OTC? No

▶ As Generic? Yes

Side Effects

SERIOUS
Sore throat and fever, unusual fatigue, unusual bleeding or bruising. Call your doctor immediately.

COMMON
Drowsiness, thickening of mucus.

LESS COMMON
Blurred vision; confusion; difficult or painful urination; dizziness; dry mouth, nose, or throat; increased sensitivity of skin to sunlight; faintness; increased sweating; stinging or burning of rectum (suppository form); loss of appetite; ringing or buzzing in ears; skin rash; fast heartbeat; unusual excitement or irritability.

PRINCIPAL USES
To relieve the symptoms of hay fever and other allergies, to prevent motion sickness, and to treat nausea and vomiting. Promethazine may also be used in some patients for its sedative effect.

HOW THE DRUG WORKS
Promethazine interferes with, but does not block, the release and action of histamine, a naturally occurring substance in the body that causes swelling, itching, sneezing, watery eyes, hives, and other symptoms of allergic reaction. Promethazine also has an anticholinergic effect, meaning it blocks the transmission of certain nerve impulses, which in turn relaxes the smooth muscle tissue controlling activity in the bladder, stomach, intestine, lungs, and other organ systems. This effect thereby helps to ease the symptoms of motion sickness, nausea, gastrointestinal upset, and anxiety.

DOSAGE
Tablets or syrup— For allergies: Adults and teenagers: 10 to 12.5 mg, 4 times a day before meals and at bedtime, or 25 mg at bedtime. Children 2 and older: 5 to 12.5 mg, 3 times a day, or 25 mg at bedtime. For nausea and vomiting: Adults and teenagers: 25 mg for first dose, then 10 to 25 mg every 4 to 6 hours as needed. Children 2 and older: 10 to 25 mg every 4 to 6 hours. To prevent motion sickness: Adults and teenagers: 25 mg taken 30 to 60 minutes before traveling. Children 2 and older: 10 to 25 mg, 30 to 60 minutes before traveling. For dizziness: Adults and teenagers: 25 mg, 2 times a day. Children 2 and older: 10 to 25, mg 2 times a day. As a

sedative: Adults and teenagers: 25 to 50 mg. Children 2 and older: 10 to 25 mg. Injection— For allergies: Adults and teenagers: 25 mg into a vein or muscle. Children 2 and older: 6.25 to 12.5 mg, 3 times a day into a muscle, or 25 mg at bedtime. For nausea and vomiting: Adults and teenagers: 12.5 to 25 mg every 4 hours into a vein or muscle. Children 2 and older: 12.5 to 25 mg every 4 to 6 hours into a muscle. As a sedative: Adults and teenagers: 25 to 50 mg injected into a vein or muscle. Children 2 and older: 12.5 to 25 mg into a muscle. Suppositories— For allergies: Adults and teenagers: 25 mg at first; 25 mg, 2 hours later if needed. Children 2 and older: 6.25 to 12.5 mg, 3 times a day, or 25 mg at bedtime. For nausea and vomiting: Adults and teenagers: 25 mg at first, then 12.5 to 25 mg every 4 to 6 hours if needed. Children 2 and older: 12.5 to 25 mg every 4 to 6 hours. For dizziness: Adults and teenagers: 25 mg, 2 times a day. Children 2 and older: 12.5 to 25 mg, 2 times a day. As a sedative: Adults and teenagers: 25 to 50 mg. Children 2 and older: 12.25 to 25 mg.

ONSET OF EFFECT
15 to 60 minutes orally or by suppository; 20 minutes after injection.

DURATION OF ACTION
Up to 12 hours.

DIETARY ADVICE
Take it with food or milk to lessen stomach irritation.

STORAGE
Store in a tightly sealed container away from heat and direct light at room temperature. Do not store the tablets in a place with

excessive moisture, such as the bathroom medicine cabinet. Do not allow the syrup or injection to freeze.

IF YOU MISS A DOSE
Take it as soon as you remember. If it is near the time for the next dose, skip the missed dose and resume your regular dosage schedule. Do not double the next dose.

STOPPING THE DRUG
You should take it as prescribed for the full treatment period, but you may stop taking the drug if you are feeling better before the scheduled end of therapy.

PROLONGED USE
See your doctor regularly if you take this medicine for a prolonged period. Prolonged use of this antihistamine may decrease salivary flow, which may lead to thrush (white, furry patches in the mouth caused by fungal infection), periodontal disease (disease and decay of the teeth, gums, jaw, and other supportive structures in the mouth), dental caries (cavities), and gingivitis (gum disease). Practice good oral hygiene to prevent these disorders.

PRECAUTIONS
Over 60: Adverse reactions may be more likely and more severe in older patients.

Driving and Hazardous Work: Do not drive or engage in hazardous work until you determine how the medicine affects you.

Alcohol: Avoid alcohol.

Pregnancy: Promethazine has not been shown to cause birth defects in animals. Thorough human studies have not been done. However, if the mother takes the drug within 2 weeks of delivery, the baby may have jaundice or problems with blood clotting. Before you take it, tell your doctor if you are pregnant or plan to become pregnant.

Breast Feeding: Promethazine passes into breast milk; avoid or discontinue use while nursing. The flow of breast milk may be decreased as a result of the medication.

Infants and Children: Adverse reactions, such as seizures, may be more common and more severe in infants and children. It is not recommended for children with a history of breathing difficulty while sleeping or with a family history of sudden infant death syndrome (SIDS). Children and adolescents with signs of Reye's syndrome should not take promethazine, especially by injection. Promethazine's side effects may be mistaken for symptoms of Reye's syndrome.

Special Concerns: If you have an allergy test, stop taking promethazine 4 days before the test and tell the doctor that you were taking promethazine.

OVERDOSE

Symptoms: Clumsiness; insomnia; seizures; severe dryness of mouth, nose, or throat; redness of face; hallucinations; muscle spasms; trouble breathing; jerky movements of head and face; dizziness; trembling and shaking of hands.

What to Do: Call your doctor, emergency medical services (EMS), or the nearest poison control center immediately.

DRUG INTERACTIONS

Consult your doctor for specific advice if you are taking amoxapine, antipsychotics, medications containing alcohol, barbiturates, methyldopa, metoclopramide, metyrosine, epinephrine, metrizamide, pemoline, pimozide, rauwolfia alkaloids, anticholinergics, central nervous system depressants, maprotiline, other antihistamines, tricyclic antidepressants, levodopa, or MAO inhibitors.

FOOD INTERACTIONS

No known food interactions.

DISEASE INTERACTIONS

Consult your doctor if you have any of the following: blood disease, heart or blood vessel disease, enlarged prostate, urinary tract blockage, epilepsy, glaucoma, Reye's syndrome, jaundice, or liver disease.

Propafenone

Rythmol 150 mg
(KNOLL)

▶ Drug Class: Antiarrhythmic

▶ Available in: Tablets

▶ Available OTC? No

▶ As Generic? Yes

Side Effects

SERIOUS
Fast or irregular heartbeat, chest pain, shortness of breath, swelling of feet or lower legs. Call your doctor immediately.

COMMON
Dizziness, change in taste, bitter or metallic taste.

LESS COMMON
Blurred vision, headache, constipation or diarrhea, skin rash, dry mouth, nausea or vomiting, unusual fatigue.

PRINCIPAL USES
To correct heartbeat irregularities (cardiac arrhythmias).

HOW THE DRUG WORKS
Propafenone slows the conduction of nerve impulses in the heart and reduces the sensitivity of heart tissue to specific nerve impulses, which helps to stabilize heartbeat. It also has weak beta-blocking properties.

DOSAGE
Adults: 150 mg every 8 hours. It may be increased after 3 or 4 days to 225 mg every 8 hours, or 300 mg every 12 hours, up to a maximum of 300 mg every 8 hours. The maintenance dose will be determined by careful follow-up, including ECG and blood pressure monitoring. Lower doses may be required for the elderly and those with liver or heart disease.

ONSET OF EFFECT
1 hour.

DURATION OF ACTION
8 to 12 hours.

DIETARY ADVICE
Propafenone can be taken with food to minimize stomach upset.

STORAGE
Store in a tightly sealed container away from heat, moisture, and direct light.

IF YOU MISS A DOSE
Take it as soon as you remember, unless the time for your next scheduled dose is within the next 4 hours. If so, skip the missed dose and resume your regular dosage schedule. Do not double the next dose.

STOPPING THE DRUG
The decision to stop taking the drug should be made in conjunction with your doctor.

PROLONGED USE
Lifelong therapy may be necessary. See your doctor regularly for examinations and diagnostic tests if you must take this medicine for a prolonged period.

PRECAUTIONS
Over 60: The dose may need to be reduced.

Driving and Hazardous Work: Avoid such activities until you determine how the medication affects you.

Alcohol: Avoid alcohol.

Pregnancy: Adequate studies on the use of this drug during pregnancy have not been done. Before taking propafenone, tell your doctor if you are pregnant or plan to become pregnant.

Breast Feeding: Propafenone passes into breast milk; caution is advised. Consult your doctor for advice.

Infants and Children: The safety and efficacy of propafenone in infants and children have not been established. Limited use in young patients indicates that the incidence of side effects in younger persons is the same as for older patients. Consult your pediatrician for advice.

Special Concerns: Wearing a medical bracelet or carrying an identification card saying that you take this medication is recommended. Before having any kind of surgery, tell the doctor or dentist in charge that you use this drug.

OVERDOSE
Symptoms: Dizziness or faintness, drowsiness, slow heartbeat, seizures, heart palpitations.

What to Do: Call your doctor, emergency medical services (EMS), or the nearest poison control center immediately.

DRUG INTERACTIONS
Consult your doctor for specific advice if you are taking warfarin, local anesthetics, other antiarrhythmic agents, digitalis drugs, beta-blockers, ritonavir, rifampin, cimetidine, or quinidine.

FOOD INTERACTIONS
No known food interactions.

DISEASE INTERACTIONS
Consult your doctor if you have had a recent heart attack or if you have any of the following: asthma, bronchitis, emphysema, slow heartbeat, or congestive heart failure. Use of propafenone may cause complications in patients with liver or kidney disease, since these organs work together to remove the medication from the body.

Propantheline Bromide

BRAND NAME
Pro-Banthine

54
303

Generic 15 mg
(ROXANE)

▶ Drug Class: Anticholinergic; antispasmodic

▶ Available in: Tablets

▶ Available OTC? No

▶ As Generic? Yes

Side Effects

SERIOUS
Confusion, persistent lightheadedness, dizziness, fainting, eye pain, skin rash or hives. Call your doctor immediately.

COMMON
Constipation; decreased sweating; dry mouth, nose, throat, or skin.

LESS COMMON
Blurred vision, bloated feeling, difficult urination, drowsiness, headache, sensitivity of eyes to light, memory loss, nausea or vomiting, unusual fatigue.

PRINCIPAL USES
To help treat peptic (stomach and intestinal) ulcers, usually in conjunction with other forms of therapy.

HOW THE DRUG WORKS
Propantheline inhibits nerve receptor sites that stimulate both the secretion of stomach acid and the smooth muscle activity in the digestive tract. This, in turn, promotes healing of ulcers.

DOSAGE
Adults and teenagers: 7.5 to 15 mg, 3 times a day 30 minutes before meals, and 30 mg at bedtime. The dose may be changed. Older adults: 7.5 mg, 3 times a day before meals. Children: 170 micrograms per lb of body weight 4 times a day. The dose may be changed.

ONSET OF EFFECT
Unknown.

DURATION OF ACTION
6 hours.

DIETARY ADVICE
Take it 30 minutes before meals unless your doctor advises otherwise.

STORAGE
Store in a tightly sealed container away from heat and direct light.

IF YOU MISS A DOSE
Take it as soon as you remember. If it is near the time for the next dose, skip the missed dose and resume your regular dosage schedule. Do not double the next dose.

STOPPING THE DRUG
The decision to stop taking the drug should be made by your doctor. Your doctor may reduce the dosage gradually; stopping abruptly can cause withdrawal side effects.

PROLONGED USE
See your doctor regularly for tests and examinations if you use it for a prolonged period.

PRECAUTIONS
Over 60: Adverse reactions may be more likely and more severe in older patients.

Driving and Hazardous Work: Do not drive or engage in hazardous work until you determine how the medicine affects you.

Alcohol: Avoid alcohol.

Pregnancy: Studies of propantheline in animals or humans have not been done. Before you take propantheline, tell your doctor if you are pregnant or plan to become pregnant.

Breast Feeding: Propantheline may pass into breast milk; caution is advised. Consult your doctor for advice.

Infants and Children: Use and dosage for infants and children should be determined by your doctor.

Special Concerns: Propantheline increases the risk of heat prostration; take special care not to become overheated by exercise or during hot weather.

OVERDOSE
Symptoms: Dry mouth; thirst; difficulty swallowing; muscular weakness or paralysis; restlessness; vomiting; fever; dizziness; headache; anxiety; rapid pulse and respiration; shallow breathing; abnormal heartbeat; increased need to urinate; blurred vision; flushed, hot, and dry skin; skin rash; decreased level of consciousness or loss of consciousness.

What to Do: Call your doctor, emergency medical services (EMS), or the nearest poison control center immediately.

DRUG INTERACTIONS
Consult your doctor for specific advice if you are taking antacids, diarrhea medicine containing kaolin or attapulgite, ketoconazole, other anticholinergics, tricyclic antidepressants, or potassium chloride.

FOOD INTERACTIONS
No known food interactions.

DISEASE INTERACTIONS
Caution is advised when taking propantheline. Consult your doctor if you have any of the following: bleeding problems, glaucoma, colitis, severe dryness of mouth, enlarged prostate, glaucoma, heart disease, hiatal hernia, high blood pressure, any intestinal problem, chronic lung disease, myasthenia gravis, toxemia of pregnancy, urinary difficulty, Down's syndrome, overactive thyroid, or, in children, spastic paralysis. Use of propantheline may cause complications in patients with liver or kidney disease, since these organs work together to remove the drug from the body.

Propoxyphene

BRAND NAMES
Cotanal-65, Darvon,
Darvon-N, PP-Cap

Darvon 65 mg
(LILLY)

▶ Drug Class: Opioid (narcotic) analgesic

▶ Available in: Capsules, oral suspension, tablets

▶ Available OTC? No

▶ As Generic? Yes

Side Effects

SERIOUS
Some serious side effects of propoxyphene are indistinguishable from those of overdose: Confusion; sleepiness; slurred speech; unconsciousness; small, pinpoint pupils; cold, clammy skin; slow breathing; seizures; severe drowsiness, weakness, or dizziness. Other serious side effects include dark urine, yellow discoloration of eyes or skin, and pale stools.

COMMON
Dizziness or lightheadedness, nausea or vomiting, constipation, itching.

LESS COMMON
Mood swings or false sense of well-being (euphoria), hallucinations.

PRINCIPAL USES
To relieve mild to moderate pain.

HOW THE DRUG WORKS
Opioids such as propoxyphene relieve pain by acting on specific areas of the spinal cord and brain that process pain signals from nerves throughout the body.

DOSAGE
There are two forms of propoxyphene: propoxyphene hydrochloride and propoxyphene napsylate, which is less powerful. Adults— Propoxyphene hydrochloride: 65 mg every 4 hours; no more than 390 mg a day. Propoxyphene napsylate: 100 mg every 4 hours; no more than 600 mg a day. Children— Dose will be determined by a pediatrician.

ONSET OF EFFECT
15 to 60 minutes.

DURATION OF ACTION
4 to 6 hours.

DIETARY ADVICE
It can be taken with food to lessen stomach upset.

STORAGE
Store in a tightly sealed container away from heat, moisture, and direct light. Do not freeze the liquid form.

IF YOU MISS A DOSE
If you are taking propoxyphene on a fixed schedule, take it as soon as you remember. If it is near the time for the next dose, skip the missed dose and resume your regular dosage schedule. Do not double the next dose.

STOPPING THE DRUG
The decision to stop taking the drug should be made by your doctor.

PROLONGED USE
You should see your doctor regularly for tests and examinations if you take this medication for an extended period. Prolonged use can cause nerve damage or physical dependence.

PRECAUTIONS
Over 60: Adverse reactions may be more likely and more severe in older patients.

Driving and Hazardous Work: Do not drive or engage in hazardous work until you determine how the medicine affects you.

Alcohol: Avoid alcohol.

Pregnancy: Propoxyphene has not caused birth defects in animals. Human studies have not been done. Before you use this medication, tell your doctor if you are pregnant or plan to become pregnant. Overuse during pregnancy can cause drug dependence in the fetus.

Breast Feeding: Propoxyphene passes into breast milk; caution is advised. Consult your doctor for specific advice.

Infants and Children: Adverse reactions may be more likely and more severe in children. Consult your doctor for advice.

Special Concerns: If you feel the medication is not working properly after a few weeks, do not increase the dose. Consult your doctor. Before having any surgery, tell the doctor or dentist in charge that you are taking this drug.

OVERDOSE
Symptoms: Confusion; sleepiness; slurred speech; unconsciousness; small, pinpoint pupils; cold, clammy skin; slow breathing; seizures; severe drowsiness, weakness, or dizziness.

What to Do: Call your doctor, emergency medical services (EMS), or the nearest poison control center immediately.

DRUG INTERACTIONS
Consult your doctor for specific advice if you are taking carbamazepine or other medicine for seizures, barbiturates, sedatives, cough medicines, decongestants, antidepressants, other prescription pain medications, MAO inhibitors, naltrexone, rifampin, or zidovudine.

FOOD INTERACTIONS
No known food interactions.

DISEASE INTERACTIONS
Consult your doctor if you have any of the following: a history of alcohol or drug abuse; emotional illness; brain disorders or a head injury; seizures; lung disease; prostate problems or other problems with urination; gallstones; colitis; heart, kidney, liver, or thyroid disease.

Propoxyphene/Acetaminophen

BRAND NAMES
Darvocet-N 100, Darvocet-N 50, E-Lor, Propacet 100, Wygesic

Generic 65/650 mg
(MYLAN)

▶ Drug Class: Opioid (narcotic) analgesic

▶ Available in: Tablets

▶ Available OTC? No

▶ As Generic? Yes

Side Effects

SERIOUS
Bloody, dark, or cloudy urine; severe pain in the lower back or side; pale or black, tarry stools; yellow discoloration of eyes or skin (jaundice); hallucinations; frequent urge to urinate; painful or difficult urination; sudden decrease in urine output; increased sweating; unusual bleeding or bruising; irregular heartbeat; skin rash, hives, or itching; exciteability; ringing or buzzing in the ears; pinpoint red spots on skin; sore throat and fever; confusion; trembling or uncontrolled muscle movements; redness, flushing, or swelling of the face. Call your doctor immediately.

COMMON
Dizziness, lightheadedness, constipation, nausea, vomiting, drowsiness, unusual fatigue.

LESS COMMON
Stomach pain, false sense of well-being (euphoria), depression, loss of appetite, blurred vision, nightmares or unusual dreams, dry mouth, headache, nervousness, insomnia.

PRINCIPAL USES
To relieve mild to moderate pain.

HOW THE DRUG WORKS
Opioids such as propoxyphene relieve pain by acting on specific areas of the spinal cord and brain that process pain signals from nerves throughout the body. Acetaminophen appears to interfere with the action of prostaglandins, naturally occurring substances in the body that cause inflammation and make nerves more sensitive to pain impulses.

DOSAGE
Adults: 1 or 2 tablets, depending on strength, every 4 to 6 hours. Children: Dose must be determined individually by your pediatrician.

ONSET OF EFFECT
Within 2 hours.

DURATION OF ACTION
Unknown.

DIETARY ADVICE
It can be taken with food to lessen stomach irritation.

STORAGE
Store in a tightly sealed container away from heat, moisture, and direct light.

IF YOU MISS A DOSE
If you are taking the drug on a fixed schedule, take it as soon as you remember. If it is near the time for the next dose, skip the missed dose and resume your regular dosage schedule. Do not double the next dose.

STOPPING THE DRUG
The decision to stop taking the drug should be made by your doctor.

PROLONGED USE
You should see your doctor regularly for tests and examinations if you take this medication for a prolonged period. Prolonged use can cause nerve damage as well as physical dependence.

PRECAUTIONS
Over 60: Adverse reactions may be more likely and more severe in older patients.

Driving and Hazardous Work: Do not drive or engage in hazardous work until you determine how the medicine affects you.

Alcohol: Avoid alcohol.

Pregnancy: Propoxyphene has not caused birth defects in animals. Human studies have not been done. Before you use this medication, tell your doctor if you are pregnant or plan to become pregnant. Overuse of the medication during pregnancy can cause physical dependence in the newborn.

Breast Feeding: Propoxyphene and acetaminophen pass into breast milk and may cause sedation in the nursing infant; caution is advised. Consult your doctor for advice.

Infants and Children: Adverse reactions may be more likely and more severe in children. Consult your pediatrician for advice.

Special Concerns: If you feel the medication is not working properly after a few weeks, do not increase the dose. Consult your doctor.

OVERDOSE
Symptoms: Severe dizziness or drowsiness; cold, clammy skin; difficult or slow breathing or shortness of breath; severe confusion; seizures; stomach cramps or pain; diarrhea; low blood pressure; increased sweating; constricted pupils; nausea or vomiting; irregular heartbeat; severe weakness.

What to Do: Call your doctor, emergency medical services (EMS), or the nearest poison control center immediately.

DRUG INTERACTIONS
Consult your doctor for specific advice if you are taking any prescription or over-the-counter drugs, especially other drugs containing acetaminophen, or central nervous system depressants which include: antihistamines or decongestants for hay fever, allergies, or colds; barbiturates; seizure medication; muscle relaxants; anesthetics; tranquilizers, sedatives, or sleep-inducing medications.

FOOD INTERACTIONS
No known food interactions.

DISEASE INTERACTIONS
Consult your doctor if you have a head injury or brain disease, an underactive thyroid, an enlarged prostate, seizures, kidney or liver disease, gall bladder problems, a blood disorder, or a history of alcohol or drug abuse.

Propranolol Hydrochloride

Generic 40 mg
(SCHEIN/DANBURY)

Additional photographs

▶ Drug Class: Beta-blocker

▶ Available in: Extended-release capsules, oral solution, tablets, injection

▶ Available OTC? No

▶ As Generic? Yes

Side Effects

SERIOUS
Shortness of breath, wheezing; irregular or slow heartbeat (50 beats per minute or less); pain or feelings of tightness or pressure in the chest; swelling of the ankles, feet, and lower legs; depression. Call your doctor immediately.

COMMON
Dizziness or lightheadedness, especially when rising suddenly to a standing position; decreased sexual ability; unusual fatigue, weakness, or drowsiness; insomnia.

LESS COMMON
Anxiety, irritability; constipation; diarrhea; dry eyes; itching; nausea or vomiting; nightmares or intensely vivid dreams; numbness, tingling, or prickling in the fingers, toes, or scalp.

PRINCIPAL USES
To treat angina, mild to moderate high blood pressure, irregular heartbeat (cardiac arrhythmias), hypertrophic cardiomyopathy (weakness of the heart muscle), heart attack, pheochromocytoma, tremors, and migraine headaches.

HOW THE DRUG WORKS
Propranolol blocks nerve impulses to various parts of the body, which accounts for its many effects. For example, it slows the heart's rate and force of the contraction (which helps lower blood pressure), decreases the heart's oxygen requirement (which helps prevent angina), and helps stabilize heart rhythm.

DOSAGE
Adults— For angina: 80 to 320 mg a day in 2, 3, or 4 doses. For high blood pressure: 40 mg, 2 times a day; may be increased up to 640 mg a day. For irregular heartbeat: 10 to 30 mg, 3 or 4 times a day. For cardiomyopathy: 20 to 40 mg, 3 or 4 times a day. For pheochromocytoma: 30 to 160 mg a day in divided doses. For preventing migraine headache: 20 mg, 4 times a day; may be increased to 240 mg a day. For trembling: 40 mg, 2 times a day; may be increased to 320 mg a day. Children— For high blood pressure: 0.5 mg to 4 mg per 2.2 lbs (1 kg) of body weight a day. For irregular heartbeat: 0.5 to 4 mg per 2.2 lbs of body weight a day in divided doses.

ONSET OF EFFECT
Within 30 minutes.

DURATION OF ACTION
Up to 12 hours.

DIETARY ADVICE
Mix the concentrated oral solution with water, juice, or a carbonated drink.

STORAGE
Store in a tightly sealed container away from heat and direct light.

IF YOU MISS A DOSE
Take it as soon as you remember. If it is near the time for the next dose, skip the missed dose and resume your regular dosage schedule. Do not double the next dose.

STOPPING THE DRUG
Do not stop taking this drug suddenly; the dosage must be slowly tapered under your physician's close supervision.

PROLONGED USE
Lifelong therapy with propranolol may be necessary; prolonged use may be associated with a greater incidence of side effects. Regular monitoring and evaluation by your doctor is advised.

PRECAUTIONS
Over 60: Adverse reactions may be more likely and more severe in older patients.

Driving and Hazardous Work: Do not drive or engage in hazardous work until you determine how the drug affects you.

Alcohol: Avoid alcohol.

Pregnancy: Consult your doctor to weigh the risks and benefits of using propranolol during pregnancy.

Breast Feeding: Propranolol passes into breast milk; caution is advised.

Infants and Children: Dosage will be determined by your pediatrician.

Special Concerns: Take extra care during exercise or hot weather to avoid dizziness and fainting. Check your pulse often; if it is slower than usual or less than 50 beats a minute, call your doctor.

OVERDOSE
Symptoms: Unusually slow or rapid heartbeat, severe dizziness or fainting, poor circulation in the hands (bluish skin), breathing difficulty; seizures.

What to Do: Call your doctor, emergency medical services (EMS), or the nearest poison control center immediately.

DRUG INTERACTIONS
Consult your doctor for specific advice if you are taking allergy shots, aminophylline, caffeine, oxtriphylline, theophylline, oral antidiabetics, insulin, calcium channel blockers, clonidine, guanabenz, or MAO inhibitors.

FOOD INTERACTIONS
No known food interactions.

DISEASE INTERACTIONS
Must be used with caution in people with diabetes, especially insulin-dependent diabetes, since the drug may mask symptoms of hypoglycemia. Consult your doctor if you have allergies, bronchitis, emphysema, heart or blood vessel disease (including congestive heart failure and peripheral vascular disease), mental depression, myasthenia gravis, psoriasis, hyperthyroidism, kidney disease, or liver disease.

Propranolol/Hydrochlorothiazide

Generic 40/25 mg
(PUREPAC)

▶ Drug Class: Beta-blocker/
thiazide diuretic; antihypertensive

▶ Available in: Extended-
release capsules, tablets

▶ Available OTC? No

▶ As Generic? Yes

Side Effects

SERIOUS
Slow heartbeat, difficulty
breathing, mental depres-
sion, cold hands and feet,
swelling of ankles, feet,
or lower legs. Call your
doctor immediately.

COMMON
Dizziness or lightheaded-
ness, decreased sexual
ability, drowsiness,
insomnia.

LESS COMMON
Anxiety, loss of appetite,
upset stomach, nervous-
ness or excitability, constipation or diarrhea,
increased sensitivity
of the skin to sunlight,
numbness and tingling
in the fingers and toes,
stuffy nose.

PRINCIPAL USES
To control hypertension
(high blood pressure).

HOW THE DRUG WORKS
Propranolol, a beta-blocker,
blocks nerve impulses to
various parts of the body,
which accounts for its many
effects. For example, it
reduces the heart rate and
force of the heart's contractions (which helps to lower
blood pressure), decreases
the heart's oxygen requirement (which helps prevent
angina) and helps stabilize
heart rhythm. Hydro-
chlorothiazide, a diuretic,
increases the excretion of
salt and water in the urine.
By reducing the overall
amount of fluid in the body,
diuretics reduce pressure
within the blood vessels.

DOSAGE
Adults— Extended-release
capsules: 1 capsule a day.
Tablets: 1 or 2 tablets, 2
times a day.

ONSET OF EFFECT
Unknown.

DURATION OF ACTION
Unknown.

DIETARY ADVICE
No special restrictions.

STORAGE
Store in a tightly sealed container away from heat, moisture, and direct light.

IF YOU MISS A DOSE
Take it as soon as you
remember. If it is near the
time for the next dose, skip
the missed dose and
resume your regular dosage
schedule. Do not double the
next dose.

STOPPING THE DRUG
The decision to stop taking
the drug should be made in
consultation with your
physician. Do not stop taking this drug abruptly; your
doctor will gradually
decrease your dose before
stopping completely.

PROLONGED USE
Propranolol/hydrochloroth-
iazide is used to control
high blood pressure, but it
cannot cure it. Lifelong therapy may be necessary. See
your doctor regularly for
tests and examinations if
you must take this drug for
a prolonged period of time.

PRECAUTIONS
Over 60: Adverse reactions, especially dizziness,
lightheadedness, and
reduced tolerance to cold,
may be more likely and
more severe in older
patients.

**Driving and Hazardous
Work:** Do not drive or
engage in hazardous work
until you determine how the
medicine affects you.

Alcohol: Avoid alcohol.

Pregnancy: Beta-blockers
and thiazide diuretics may
cause problems during
pregnancy. Before taking
this medication, tell your
doctor if you are pregnant
or plan to become pregnant.

Breast Feeding: This
drug passes into breast
milk; caution is advised.
Consult your doctor for specific advice.

Infants and Children:
Adequate studies of the use
of this drug by children
have not been done. No special problems are expected.
Consult your pediatrician
for advice.

Special Concerns: In
addition to taking this medicine, follow your doctor's
instructions on weight control and diet for reduction of
blood pressure. Protect
yourself from sunlight until
you determine how this
medicine affects you.

OVERDOSE
Symptoms: Slow heart-
beat, severe dizziness or
fainting, difficulty breathing,
bluish colored fingernails or
palms of hands, seizures.

What to Do: Call your
doctor, emergency medical
services (EMS), or the
nearest poison control
center immediately.

DRUG INTERACTIONS
Consult your doctor for specific advice if you are receiving allergy shots or skin
tests, or are taking oral diabetes medications, insulin,
calcium channel blockers,
digitalis drugs, clonidine,
lithium, MAO inhibitors,
xanthines, or guanabenz.

FOOD INTERACTIONS
Avoid foods high in sodium.

DISEASE INTERACTIONS
Consult your doctor if you
have any of the following:
any allergic condition,
bronchial asthma, emphy-
sema, slow heartbeat, heart
or blood vessel disease, diabetes mellitus, congestive
heart failure, kidney disease, liver disease, depression, or an overactive
thyroid (hyperthyroidism).

Propylthiouracil

Generic 50 mg
(LEDERLE)

▶ Drug Class: Antithyroid agent

▶ Available in: Tablets

▶ Available OTC? No

▶ As Generic? Yes

Side Effects

SERIOUS
Cough, continuing or severe fever or chills; hoarseness; mouth sores; pain, swelling, or redness in joints; throat infection; yellowish tinge (jaundice) in skin or eyes; general feeling of discomfort, weakness, or illness. Call your doctor immediately.

COMMON
Mild and temporary fever; rash or itching.

LESS COMMON
Backache, black and tarry stools, blood in urine or stools, shortness of breath, increased or decreased urination, swelling of feet or lower legs, swollen lymph or salivary glands, numbness or tingling of face, fingers, or toes, dizziness, nausea, stomach pain, vomiting.

PRINCIPAL USES
To treat conditions in which the thyroid gland produces too much thyroid hormone (hyperthyroidism).

HOW THE DRUG WORKS
Propylthiouracil interferes with the body's ability to use iodine in the manufacture of thyroid hormone.

DOSAGE
Adults: To start, 300 to 900 mg a day, with doses every 8 hours. Maximum dose: 1,200 mg a day. Usual maintenance dose is 50 to 600 mg a day. Children ages 6 to 10: To start, 50 to 150 mg a day in 3 doses. The dose can be adjusted later. Children ages 10 and older: 50 to 300 mg per day, in 3 doses. To treat a thyroid crisis: 400 mg or more (up to 900 mg a day) for the first day, reduced gradually over subsequent days.

ONSET OF EFFECT
5 days or more.

DURATION OF ACTION
Unknown.

DIETARY ADVICE
Take it with meals to minimize stomach upset.

STORAGE
Store in a tightly sealed container away from heat and direct light.

IF YOU MISS A DOSE
Take it as soon as you remember. If it is near the time for the next dose, skip the missed dose and resume your regular dosage schedule. Do not double the next dose.

STOPPING THE DRUG
The decision to stop taking the drug should be made by your doctor.

PROLONGED USE
No special problems are expected. It may be necessary to take this medication for several years.

PRECAUTIONS
Over 60: Adverse reactions may be more common and more severe in older patients.

Driving and Hazardous Work: The use of propylthiouracil should not impair your ability to perform such tasks safely.

Alcohol: Consult your doctor about consuming alcohol while taking this drug.

Pregnancy: Too large a dose during pregnancy may cause problems in the fetus. The prescribed dose, with careful monitoring, is not likely to cause problems.

Breast Feeding: Although propylthiouracil passes into breast milk, your doctor may allow you to continue breast feeding if the dose is kept low and the infant is checked regularly.

Infants and Children: This medicine has not been shown to cause different side effects or problems in children than it does in adults.

Special Concerns: Before undergoing any kind of medical or dental procedure, be sure to tell the doctor or dentist in charge that you are taking propylthiouracil. During and after treatment, do not receive any immunizations without your doctor's approval, and avoid persons who have recently taken oral polio vaccine.

OVERDOSE
Symptoms: Nausea, vomiting, coldness, constipation, changes in menstrual period, dry and puffy skin, headache, listlessness, muscle aches, sleepiness, swollen neck, unusual weight gain.

What to Do: An overdose of propylthiouracil is unlikely to be life-threatening. However, if someone takes a much larger dose than prescribed, call your doctor, emergency medical services (EMS), or local poison control center.

DRUG INTERACTIONS
Consult your doctor for advice if you are taking amiodarone, iodinated glycerol, potassium iodide, anticoagulants, or digitalis drugs.

FOOD INTERACTIONS
Consult your doctor about the need for a special low-iodine diet.

DISEASE INTERACTIONS
Use of propylthiouracil may cause complications in patients who have liver disease, since this organ works to remove medications from the body.

Protriptyline Hydrochloride

Side Effects

SERIOUS
Confusion, heartbeat irregularities, hallucinations, seizures, extreme fatigue or drowsiness, blurred or altered vision, breathing difficulty, constipation, staring and absence of facial expression, impaired concentration, difficult urination, fever, extreme and persistent restlessness, loss of coordination and balance, difficulty swallowing or speaking, dilated pupils, eye pain, fainting. Also trembling, shaking, weakness, and stiffness in the extremities; shuffling gait. Call your doctor immediately.

COMMON
Drowsiness or dizziness, headache, dry mouth or unpleasant taste, fatigue, heightened sensitivity to light, weight gain, increased appetite, nausea, excitability.

LESS COMMON
Heartburn or indigestion, sleeping difficulty, diarrhea, increased sweating, vomiting.

PRINCIPAL USES
To relieve symptoms of major depression.

HOW THE DRUG WORKS
Protriptyline affects levels of norepinephrine, a brain chemical that is thought to be linked to mood, emotions, and mental state.

DOSAGE
Adults: To start, 5 to 10 mg, 3 to 4 times a day; may be increased to 60 mg a day. Teenagers: To start, 5 mg, 3 times a day; may be increased gradually by your doctor. Older adults: To start, 5 mg, 3 times a day; may be increased gradually by your doctor.

ONSET OF EFFECT
1 to 6 weeks.

DURATION OF ACTION
Unknown.

DIETARY ADVICE
To lessen stomach upset, take with food, unless your doctor instructs otherwise. Increase intake of fiber and fluids.

STORAGE
Store in a tightly sealed container away from heat, moisture, and direct light.

IF YOU MISS A DOSE
If you take a one-time daily bedtime dose, do not take the missed dose in the morning because it may cause drowsiness. Call your doctor. If you take more than 1 dose a day, take it as soon as you remember. However, if it is near the time for the next dose, skip the missed dose and resume your regular dosage schedule. Do not double the next dose.

STOPPING THE DRUG
Take as prescribed for the full treatment period, even if you begin to feel better before the scheduled end of therapy. The decision to stop taking the drug should be made in consultation with your doctor.

PROLONGED USE
The usual course of therapy lasts 6 months to 1 year; some patients benefit from additional therapy.

PRECAUTIONS

Over 60: Adverse reactions may be more likely and more severe in older patients. A lower dose may be warranted.

Driving and Hazardous Work: Use caution when driving or engaging in hazardous work until you know how the medication affects you. Drowsiness or lightheadedness can occur.

Alcohol: Avoid alcohol.

Pregnancy: Adequate human studies have not been done. Consult your doctor for specific advice.

Breast Feeding: Protriptyline passes into breast milk; do not use it while nursing.

Infants and Children: This drug is not prescribed for children under age 6. Antidepressants increase the risk of suicidal thinking and behavior (suicidality) in children with major depression and other psychiatric disorders. Discuss with your doctor this risk versus the benefits of using this drug. Children should be observed closely for worsening of symptoms, suicidality, or unusual changes in behavior at the onset of therapy and when making changes in dosage.

Special Concerns: This is a potentially dangerous drug, especially if taken in excess. Tricyclic antidepressants should not be within easy reach of suicidal patients. If dry mouth occurs, use candy or sugarless gum for relief.

OVERDOSE

Symptoms: Difficulty breathing, severe fatigue, seizures, confusion, hallucinations, dilated pupils, irregular heartbeat, fever, impaired ability to concentrate.

What to Do: Call your doctor, emergency medical services (EMS), or the nearest poison control center immediately.

DRUG INTERACTIONS
Consult your doctor for specific advice if you are taking antithyroid agents, cimetidine, clonidine, guanadrel, guanethidine, metrizamide, appetite suppressants, isoproterenol, ephedrine, epinephrine, amphetamines, phenylephrine, antipsychotic drugs, pimozide, methyldopa, metyrosine, metoclopramide, pemoline, promethazine, trimeprazine, rauwolfia alkaloids, MAO inhibitors, or any drugs that depress the central nervous system.

FOOD INTERACTIONS
No known food interactions.

DISEASE INTERACTIONS
Consult your doctor if you have any of the following: a history of alcohol abuse, difficulty urinating, asthma, bipolar disorder, high blood pressure, stomach or intestinal problems, glaucoma, overactive thyroid, enlarged prostate, schizophrenia, seizures, a blood disorder, or kidney, heart, or liver disease.

Pseudoephedrine

Sudafed 12 Hour 120 mg
(GLAXO WELLCOME)

838
Additional photographs

▶ Drug Class: Decongestant/cough drug

▶ Available in: Extended-release capsules, oral solution, syrup, tablets

▶ Available OTC? Yes

▶ As Generic? Yes

Side Effects

SERIOUS
Seizures, irregular or slowed heartbeat, shortness of breath, breathing difficulty, hallucinations. Stop taking the medication and call your doctor right away.

COMMON
Nervousness, restlessness, insomnia.

LESS COMMON
Difficult or painful urination, dizziness or light-headedness, rapid or pounding heartbeat, increased sweating, nausea or vomiting, trembling, trouble breathing, paleness, weakness.

PRINCIPAL USES
To relieve nasal or sinus congestion caused by colds, sinus infection, hay fever, or other respiratory allergies.

HOW THE DRUG WORKS
Pseudoephedrine narrows and constricts blood vessels to reduce the blood flow to swollen nasal passages and other tissues, which reduces nasal secretions, shrinks swollen nasal mucous membranes, and improves airflow in nasal passages.

DOSAGE
Short-acting forms— Adults and teenagers: 60 mg every 4 to 6 hours; not more than 240 mg in 24 hours. Children 6 to 12 years of age: 30 mg every 4 to 6 hours; not more than 120 mg in 24 hours. Children 2 to 6 years of age: 15 mg every 4 hours; not more than 60 mg in 24 hours. Extended-release form— Adults and teenagers: 120 mg every 12 hours or 240 mg every 24 hours. No more than 240 mg in 24 hours.

ONSET OF EFFECT
15 to 30 minutes.

DURATION OF ACTION
3 to 4 hours for short-acting forms, 8 to 12 hours for extended-release form.

DIETARY ADVICE
Be sure to drink plenty of fluids.

STORAGE
Store in a tightly sealed container away from heat and direct light. Do not allow the liquid form to freeze.

IF YOU MISS A DOSE
Take it as soon as you remember. If it is near the time for the next dose, skip the missed dose and resume your regular dosage schedule. Do not double the next dose.

STOPPING THE DRUG
Do not take this drug longer than recommended on the label unless directed to do so by your doctor.

PROLONGED USE
Consult your doctor about taking pseudoephedrine for more than 5 to 7 days.

PRECAUTIONS
Over 60: Side effects may be more likely and more severe in elderly patients.

Driving and Hazardous Work: Avoid such activities until you determine how the medicine affects you.

Alcohol: No special precautions are necessary.

Pregnancy: Safety has not been established; it should be used only if clearly necessary. Consult your doctor for specific advice.

Breast Feeding: Pseudoephedrine passes into breast milk; avoid or discontinue use while nursing.

Infants and Children: Use of extended-release forms of pseudoephedrine is not recommended for children under the age of 12.

Special Concerns: If your symptoms do not improve within 7 days, check with your doctor. To help prevent insomnia, take the last dose at least 2 hours before your bedtime.

OVERDOSE
Symptoms: Drowsiness, sedation, profuse sweating, pale or clammy skin, low blood pressure, diminished urine output, dizziness, changes in mental state, hallucinations, seizures, loss of consciousness.

What to Do: In some cases an overdose can be fatal, especially among elderly patients. At the first sign of overdose, call your doctor, emergency medical services (EMS), or the nearest poison control center immediately.

DRUG INTERACTIONS
Consult your doctor for specific advice if you are taking beta-blockers or MAO inhibitors.

FOOD INTERACTIONS
No known food interactions.

DISEASE INTERACTIONS
Caution is advised when taking pseudoephedrine. Consult your doctor if you have any of the following: diabetes, enlarged prostate, heart disease, blood vessel disease, high blood pressure, or an overactive thyroid gland.

Pseudoephedrine/Guaifenesin

BRAND NAMES
Deconsal II, Deconsal LA,
Entex PSE

▶ Drug Class: Decongestant/
cough drug

▶ Available in: Capsules, oral
solution, syrup, tablets,
extended-release forms

▶ Available OTC? Yes

▶ As Generic? Yes

Side Effects

SERIOUS
Skin rash, hives, itching,
rapid or irregular heart-
beat, persistent head-
ache, nervousness or
restlessness, shortness of
breath or breathing difficulty, seizures, unusual
fear and anxiety. Call
your doctor or emer-
gency medical services
(EMS) right away.

COMMON
Constipation; decreased
sweating; difficult urination; dizziness or light-
headedness; drowsiness;
dry mouth, nose, or
throat; increased sensitivity of skin to sun; nausea
or vomiting; nightmares;
stomach pain; thickened
mucus; insomnia;
unusual excitement or
restlessness; unusual
tiredness or weakness.
Contact your doctor if
these symptoms persist
or interfere with your
daily activities.

LESS COMMON
There are no less-com-
mon side effects associ-
ated with this drug.

PRINCIPAL USES
To relieve nasal or sinus
congestion caused by colds,
influenza (flu), hay fever,
and other respiratory allergies. Also intended to break
up congestion in the lungs
to promote better breathing.

HOW THE DRUG WORKS
Pseudoephedrine narrows
and constricts blood vessels
to reduce the blood flow to
swollen nasal passages and
other tissues, which
reduces nasal secretions,
shrinks swollen nasal
mucous membranes, and
improves airflow. Guaifenesin purportedly breaks
up, liquefies, and loosens
mucus secretions in the
respiratory tract, making it
easier to cough up phlegm
and thus breathe easier.
(There is some debate
however as to whether
guaifenesin is actually
effective in this regard.)

DOSAGE
Take the drug as directed
to relieve symptoms.

ONSET OF EFFECT
Within 1 hour.

DURATION OF ACTION
Unknown.

DIETARY ADVICE
No special restrictions.

STORAGE
Store in a tightly sealed container away from heat and
direct light.

IF YOU MISS A DOSE
Take it as soon as you
remember. If it is near the
time for the next dose, skip
the missed dose and
resume your regular dosage
schedule. Do not double the
next dose.

STOPPING THE DRUG
The decision to stop taking
the drug should be made by
your doctor or when you
note improvement.

PROLONGED USE
Check with your doctor if
symptoms do not improve
within 5 days.

PRECAUTIONS
Over 60: Adverse reactions
may be more likely and
more severe in older
patients.

**Driving and Hazardous
Work:** Do not drive or
engage in hazardous work
until you determine how the
medicine affects you.

Alcohol: Avoid alcohol.

Pregnancy: Before taking
pseudoephedrine and
guaifenesin, tell your doctor
if you are pregnant or plan
to become pregnant.

Breast Feeding: Pseudoephedrine passes into
breast milk; avoid or discontinue use while nursing.

Infants and Children:
Check the package label or
with your doctor before giving it to infants or children.

Special Concerns: If you
have trouble sleeping, take
the last dose of pseudo-
ephedrine and guaifenesin a
few hours before bedtime.
Before having any surgery,
tell your doctor or dentist
that you are taking this
drug. Be sure your doctor
knows if you have high
blood pressure.

OVERDOSE
Symptoms: Rapid, pounding, or irregular heartbeat,
continuing and severe
headache, severe nausea or
vomiting, severe nervous-
ness or restlessness, severe
shortness of breath or troubled breathing.

What to Do: Call your
doctor, emergency medical
services (EMS), or the
nearest poison control
center immediately.

DRUG INTERACTIONS
Consult your doctor if you
are taking any prescription
or nonprescription medication. Do not take any drug
for diet or appetite control
unless you have checked
with your doctor first.

FOOD INTERACTIONS
No known food interactions.

DISEASE INTERACTIONS
Caution is advised when
taking pseudoephedrine and
guaifenesin. Consult your
doctor if you have any of
the following: anemia, gout,
hemophilia, stomach prob-
lems, brain disease, colitis,
seizures, diarrhea, gallbladder disease or gallstones,
cystic fibrosis, diabetes mellitus, any chronic lung disease, enlarged prostate,
difficult urination, glaucoma, heart or blood vessel
disease, thyroid disease, or
high blood pressure. Use
of pseudoephedrine and
guaifenesin may cause complications in persons with
liver or kidney disease,
since these organs work
together to remove the
medication from the body.

Psyllium

▶ Drug Class: Bulk-forming laxative

▶ Available in: Caramels, granules, powder

▶ Available OTC? Yes

▶ As Generic? Yes

Side Effects

SERIOUS
Difficulty breathing, intestinal blockage (resulting in severe, painful constipation), skin rash or itching, difficulty swallowing. Call your doctor immediately.

COMMON
No common side effects have been reported.

LESS COMMON
Nausea, vomiting, partial intestinal obstruction, abdominal pain or cramping.

PRINCIPAL USES
To relieve constipation. It also may be prescribed for treatment of diarrhea.

HOW THE DRUG WORKS
Psyllium is a natural soluble fiber derived from the husks of a seed grain. It absorbs liquid in the intestines and swells to form a soft, bulky stool. The increased bulk of the stool stimulates bowel activity and triggers the urge to defecate. Psyllium has also been shown in studies to improve the ratio of HDL ("good") cholesterol to LDL ("bad") cholesterol in the blood. For this reason, it is sometimes prescribed as part of a program to reduce high cholesterol levels before resorting to drug therapy.

DOSAGE
Adults: 1 to 2 rounded teaspoons or 1 packet dissolved in water, 1, 2, or 3 times a day, followed by a second glass of liquid. Children over 6: 1 level teaspoon in half a glass of water.

ONSET OF EFFECT
Usually, 12 to 24 hours. In some cases, up to 3 days.

DURATION OF ACTION
Variable.

DIETARY ADVICE
Take psyllium with a full glass of cold liquid, such as fruit juice or water, and follow with another full glass.

STORAGE
Store in a tightly sealed container away from heat, moisture, and direct light.

IF YOU MISS A DOSE
Take it as soon as you remember. If it is near the time for the next dose, skip the missed dose and resume your regular dosage schedule. Do not double the next dose.

STOPPING THE DRUG
Take it as prescribed for the full treatment period. However, you may stop taking it if you are feeling better before the scheduled end of therapy.

PROLONGED USE
Do not take psyllium for more than 1 week unless your doctor has ordered a special schedule for you.

PRECAUTIONS
Over 60: No special problems are expected.

Driving and Hazardous Work: The use of psyllium should not impair your ability to perform such tasks safely.

Alcohol: Avoid alcohol; it can irritate the gastrointestinal tract and interfere with proper digestion.

Pregnancy: Discuss with your doctor the relative risks and benefits of using psyllium while pregnant.

Breast Feeding: Psyllium may pass into breast milk; caution is advised. Consult your doctor for advice.

Infants and Children: Not recommended for use by children under age 6.

Special Concerns: You should have an adequate amount of fiber-containing food in your diet, such as cereals, fresh fruit, and vegetables. Before taking psyllium, tell your doctor if you have had any unusual or allergic reaction to laxatives. Make sure that your doctor knows if you are on any special diet. Do not take any other medicine within 2 hours of taking psyllium. Drink from 6 to 8 eight-ounce glasses of water every day.

OVERDOSE
Symptoms: Intestinal blockage.

What to Do: An overdose of psyllium is unlikely. However, if someone takes a much larger dose than prescribed, seek medical help promptly.

DRUG INTERACTIONS
Consult your doctor for advice if you are taking oral tetracyclines.

FOOD INTERACTIONS
Psyllium may interfere with the absorption of certain minerals, especially in high doses or with regular use.

DISEASE INTERACTIONS
Consult your doctor if you have any of the following: heart disease, a colostomy or ileostomy, diabetes mellitus, high blood pressure, kidney disease, rectal bleeding of unknown cause, difficulty swallowing, or any signs of appendicitis.

Pyrantel Pamoate

BRAND NAMES
Antiminth, Reese's
Pinworm Medicine

▶ Drug Class: Anthelmintic

▶ Available in: Oral suspension

▶ Available OTC? Yes

▶ As Generic? Yes

Side Effects

SERIOUS
Skin rash. Stop using the drug and call your doctor as soon as possible.

COMMON
No common side effects are associated with the use of pyrantel.

LESS COMMON
Pain or cramps in abdomen or stomach, headache, dizziness, diarrhea, drowsiness, insomnia, nausea or vomiting, loss of appetite.

PRINCIPAL USES
To treat various worm infections, including ascariasis (common roundworm) and enterobiasis or oxyuriasis (pinworm). It may be used to treat more than one worm infection at a time. It may also be used for other types of infection as determined by your doctor.

HOW THE DRUG WORKS
Pyrantel paralyzes the worm. While it is paralyzed, the worm is expelled from the body in the stool.

DOSAGE
Adults and children age 2 and older— For roundworms: 1 dose of 11 mg per 2.2 lbs (1 kg) of body weight. Maximum dose is 1,000 mg. If necessary, the dose may be repeated in 2 to 3 weeks. For pinworms: 1 dose of 11 mg per 2.2 lbs of body weight. Maximum dose is 1,000 mg. Repeat the dose in 2 to 3 weeks.

ONSET OF EFFECT
Variable.

DURATION OF ACTION
Variable.

DIETARY ADVICE
Pyrantel can be taken with fruit juice, milk, or food.

STORAGE
Store in a tightly sealed container away from heat, moisture, and direct light. Do not allow it to freeze.

IF YOU MISS A DOSE
Take a missed dose as soon as you remember.

STOPPING THE DRUG
Consult your physician.

PROLONGED USE
Pyrantel is generally prescribed for one-time use (two-time use for pinworms).

PRECAUTIONS
Over 60: Adverse reactions may be more likely and more severe in older patients.

Driving and Hazardous Work: Do not drive or engage in hazardous work until you determine how the medicine affects you.

Alcohol: No special precautions are necessary.

Pregnancy: Pyrantel is not recommended for use in pregnant women. Consult your doctor for specific advice if you are pregnant or plan to become pregnant.

Breast Feeding: Pyrantel may pass into breast milk; caution is advised. Consult your doctor for advice.

Infants and Children: Use and dosage for children under the age of 2 should be determined by your doctor. Not recommended for use by children under the age of 1.

Special Concerns: For pinworm infection, clothing, bedding, and towels should be washed daily. All members of the family may have to be treated to eradicate the infestation. A second treatment for all household members may be necessary after 2 or 3 weeks. All bedding and nightclothes should be washed after treatment. To prevent reinfection, you should wash the anal region daily, change your underwear and bedding every day, and wash your hands and fingernails before each meal and after bowel movements. Consult your doctor if your condition has not improved upon completion of therapy.

OVERDOSE
Symptoms: An overdose with pyrantel is unlikely.

What to Do: If someone takes a much larger dose than prescribed, call your doctor, emergency medical services (EMS), or the nearest poison control center right away.

DRUG INTERACTIONS
Do not take piperazine when taking pyrantel. The effectiveness of both drugs may be reduced. Consult your doctor for specific advice. Also tell your doctor if you are taking any other prescription or over-the-counter medication.

FOOD INTERACTIONS
No known food interactions.

DISEASE INTERACTIONS
Caution is advised when taking pyrantel. Consult your doctor for specific advice if you have any other medical condition.

Pyrazinamide

BRAND NAME
Pyrazinamide is available in generic form only.

Generic 500 mg
(LEDERLE)

▶ Drug Class: Anti-infective/antitubercular agent

▶ Available in: Tablets

▶ Available OTC? No

▶ As Generic? Yes

Side Effects

SERIOUS
Joint pain or swelling, especially in leg and foot joints; nausea, vomiting, weakness, fatigue, yellow discoloration of the eyes or skin (may be signs of hepatitis). Call your doctor immediately.

COMMON
Joint pain, hepatitis (see above).

LESS COMMON
Skin rash, itching, stomach upset.

PRINCIPAL USES
To treat active tuberculosis; it must be used in conjunction with other antitubercular agents such as isoniazid, streptomycin, and rifampin.

HOW THE DRUG WORKS
Pyrazinamide kills the tuberculosis bacteria.

DOSAGE
Adults: 1.5 to 2.5 g (6.8 to 13.6 mg per lb of body weight) per day. Children: 6.8 to 13.6 mg per lb once a day; not more than 2,000 mg daily. It may also be given to adults or children 2 to 3 times a week in a dose of 22.7 to 31.8 mg per lb. If the schedule is twice a week, adults should take no more than 4,000 mg per dose; if the schedule is 3 times a week, no more than 2,500 mg per dose. Children should receive not more than 2,000 mg per day, even if it is taken only 2 or 3 times a week.

ONSET OF EFFECT
Unknown.

DURATION OF ACTION
Unknown.

DIETARY ADVICE
Take it with food to minimize stomach irritation.

STORAGE
Store in a tightly sealed container away from heat, moisture, and direct light.

IF YOU MISS A DOSE
Take it as soon as you remember. This will help keep a constant level of medication in your system. If it is near the time for the next dose, skip the missed dose and resume your regular dosage schedule. Do not double the next dose.

STOPPING THE DRUG
Take it as prescribed for the full treatment period, even if you begin to feel better before the scheduled end of therapy. Treatment may continue for months or years. The decision to stop taking the drug should be made by your doctor.

PROLONGED USE
Consult your doctor about the need for periodic medical examinations and laboratory tests. If your symptoms do not improve or instead become worse in 2 to 3 weeks, consult your doctor.

PRECAUTIONS

Over 60: Adverse reactions may be more likely and more severe in older patients.

Driving and Hazardous Work: The use of pyrazinamide should not impair your ability to perform such tasks safely.

Alcohol: Avoid alcohol.

Pregnancy: Adequate human studies have not been done. Before taking pyrazinamide, tell your doctor if you are pregnant or are planning to become pregnant.

Breast Feeding: Pyrazinamide passes into breast milk; caution is advised. Consult your doctor for specific advice.

Infants and Children: Pyrazinamide has not been shown to cause different or more severe side effects in children. However, owing to the serious nature of the side effects, it should be used only under the strict supervision of your doctor. Discuss with your pediatrician the relative risks and benefits of your child's using this drug.

Special Concerns: Pyrazinamide may cause false results on urine ketone tests for diabetes. Check with your doctor before adjusting your medication dosage or diet. Patients with HIV may require a longer period of treatment.

OVERDOSE
Symptoms: Abnormal results on tests of liver function. This problem can be detected by your doctor.

What to Do: An overdose of pyrazinamide is unlikely to be life-threatening. However, if someone takes a much larger dose than prescribed, call your doctor, emergency medical services (EMS), or the nearest poison control center.

DRUG INTERACTIONS
Consult your doctor for specific advice if you are taking any other prescription or over-the-counter medication.

FOOD INTERACTIONS
No known food interactions.

DISEASE INTERACTIONS
Consult your doctor if you have a history of alcohol abuse, diabetes, or gout. The use of pyrazinamide may cause complications in patients who have liver disease, since this organ works to remove the medication from the body.

Pyrethrins/Piperonyl Butoxide

BRAND NAMES
A-200 Gel Concentrate,
A-200 Shampoo
Concentrate, Barc, Blue,
Licetrol, Pronto Lice
Killing Shampoo Kit,
Pyrinyl, R & C, Rid,
Tisit, Triple X

▶ Drug Class: Topical antiparasitic

▶ Available in: Gel, solution shampoo, topical solution

▶ Available OTC? Yes

▶ As Generic? Yes

Side Effects

SERIOUS
Skin irritation not present before use of the medicine, skin rash or infection, sudden attacks of sneezing, stuffy or runny nose, wheezing or difficulty breathing. Call your doctor immediately.

COMMON
No common side effects are associated with pyrethrins and piperonyl butoxide.

LESS COMMON
No less-common side effects are associated with pyrethrins and piperonyl butoxide.

PRINCIPAL USES
To treat head, body, and pubic lice infestations. Although this drug is available without a prescription, your doctor may have special instructions regarding its proper use.

HOW THE DRUG WORKS
Pyrethrins and piperonyl butoxide are a combination of active ingredients. The medication is absorbed into the bodies of lice, where it blocks nerve activity, ultimately causing paralysis and death of the lice. (The drug has no such toxic effect on humans.)

DOSAGE
Use 1 time, then repeat one more time in 7 to 10 days. Gel or solution: Apply enough medicine to thoroughly wet hair, scalp, or skin. Allow the medicine to remain on the affected areas for 10 minutes, then wash with warm water and soap or regular shampoo. Rinse thoroughly and dry with a clean towel. Shampoo: Apply enough medicine to wet the hair, scalp, or skin. Allow the medicine to remain on the affected areas for 10 minutes, then use a small amount of water to work shampoo more thoroughly into affected area. Rinse and dry with a clean towel. With either method, use a nit-removal comb to remove dead lice and eggs from hair.

ONSET OF EFFECT
Within 10 minutes.

DURATION OF ACTION
Up to 10 days.

DIETARY ADVICE
This medication can be used without regard to diet.

STORAGE
Store in a tightly sealed container away from heat and direct light, and away from children.

IF YOU MISS A DOSE
If you do not administer the second dose within 10 days after the initial dose, do so as soon as you remember.

STOPPING THE DRUG
Take both recommended doses, even if you are feeling better before the scheduled end of therapy.

PROLONGED USE
If lice recur, consult your doctor.

PRECAUTIONS
Over 60: No special problems are expected in older patients.

Driving and Hazardous Work: The use of pyrethrins and piperonyl butoxide should not impair your ability to perform such tasks safely.

Alcohol: No special precautions are necessary.

Pregnancy: This drug has not been shown to cause birth defects or other problems during pregnancy. Before you use pyrethrins and piperonyl butoxide, tell your doctor if you are pregnant or plan to become pregnant.

Breast Feeding: Pyrethrins and piperonyl butoxide may pass into breast milk; caution is advised. Consult your doctor for specific information.

Infants and Children: No special problems are expected in younger patients.

Special Concerns: All members of your household should be examined for lice and given treatment if necessary. Clothing, household linen, hairbrushes, combs, and bedding should be thoroughly cleaned. Furniture, rugs, and floors should be vacuumed thoroughly. Toilet seats should be scrubbed frequently. If you use this medicine for pubic lice, your sexual partner may also need to be treated. Keep this medicine away from the mouth and do not inhale it. Apply it in a well-ventilated room to help prevent inhalation. Keep the medicine away from the eyes and other mucous membranes, such as the inside of the nose or vagina.

OVERDOSE
Symptoms: If accidentally ingested, pyrethrins and piperonyl butoxide can cause nausea, vomiting, muscle paralysis, and central nervous system depression.

What to Do: Call your doctor, emergency medical services (EMS), or the nearest poison control center immediately.

DRUG INTERACTIONS
Before you use this medicine, tell your doctor if you are using any other prescription or over-the-counter medications.

FOOD INTERACTIONS
No known food interactions.

DISEASE INTERACTIONS
Consult your doctor if you have any severe inflammation of the skin.

Quazepam

Doral 7.5 mg
(WALLACE)

▶ Drug Class: Benzodiazepine tranquilizer

▶ Available in: Tablets

▶ Available OTC? No

▶ As Generic? No

Side Effects

SERIOUS
Difficulty concentrating, outbursts of anger, other behavior problems, depression, hallucinations, low blood pressure (causing faintness or confusion), memory impairment, muscle weakness, skin rash or itching, sore throat, fever and chills, sores or ulcers in throat or mouth, unusual bruising or bleeding, extreme fatigue, yellowish tinge to eyes or skin. Call your doctor immediately.

COMMON
Drowsiness, loss of coordination, unsteady gait, dizziness, lightheadedness, slurred speech.

LESS COMMON
Change in sexual desire or ability, constipation, false sense of well-being, nausea and vomiting, urinary problems, unusual fatigue.

PRINCIPAL USES
To treat insomnia.

HOW THE DRUG WORKS
In general, quazepam produces mild sedation by depressing activity in the central nervous system. In particular, quazepam appears to enhance the effect of gamma-aminobutyric acid (GABA), a natural chemical that inhibits the firing of neurons and dampens the transmission of nerve signals, thus decreasing nervous excitation.

DOSAGE
Adults: 7.5 to 15 mg in 1 dose at bedtime. Use and dose for children under the age of 18 must be determined by your doctor.

ONSET OF EFFECT
Unknown.

DURATION OF ACTION
Unknown.

DIETARY ADVICE
Quazepam should be taken 30 to 60 minutes before bedtime with a full glass of water. It can be taken with food to prevent gastrointestinal upset.

STORAGE
Store in a tightly sealed container away from heat and direct light.

IF YOU MISS A DOSE
Take it as soon as you remember, unless it is late at night. Do not take the medicine unless your schedule allows a full night's sleep.

STOPPING THE DRUG
Discontinuing the drug abruptly may produce withdrawal symptoms (sleep disruption, nervousness, irritability, diarrhea, abdominal cramps, muscle aches, memory impairment).

Dosage may need to be reduced gradually.

PROLONGED USE
Do not take quazepam for more than 8 weeks without consulting your doctor.

PRECAUTIONS
Over 60: Adverse reactions are more likely and more severe. A lower dose may be warranted.

Driving and Hazardous Work: Quazepam can impair mental alertness and physical coordination. Adjust your activities accordingly.

Alcohol: Avoid alcohol.

Pregnancy: Use during pregnancy should be avoided if possible. Be sure to tell your doctor if you are pregnant or plan to become pregnant.

Breast Feeding: Quazepam passes into breast milk; do not take it while nursing.

Infants and Children: Safety and effectiveness have not been established for children under age 18.

Special Concerns: Quazepam use can lead to psychological or physical dependence. Never take more than the prescribed daily dose. Never stop taking the drug abruptly.

OVERDOSE
Symptoms: Extreme drowsiness, confusion, slurred speech, slow reflexes, poor coordination, staggering gait, tremor, slowed breathing, loss of consciousness.

What to Do: Call your doctor, emergency medical services (EMS), or the nearest poison control center immediately.

DRUG INTERACTIONS
Other drugs may interact with quazepam. Consult your doctor for specific advice if you are taking any drugs that depress the central nervous system; these include antihistamines, antidepressants or other psychiatric medications, barbiturates, sedatives, cough medicines, decongestants, and painkillers. Be sure your doctor knows about any over-the-counter medication you may take.

FOOD INTERACTIONS
None reported.

DISEASE INTERACTIONS
Caution is advised when taking quazepam. Consult your doctor if you have a history of alcohol or drug abuse, stroke or other brain disease, any chronic lung disease, hyperactivity, depression or other mental illness, myasthenia gravis, sleep apnea, epilepsy, porphyria, kidney disease, or liver disease.

Quetiapine Fumarate

BRAND NAME
Seroquel

▶ Drug Class: Antipsychotic

▶ Available in: Tablets

▶ Available OTC? No

▶ As Generic? No

Side Effects

SERIOUS

Tardive dyskinesia (involuntary movements of the jaw, lips, and tongue), amnesia, psychosis, hallucinations, paranoia, delusions, manic episodes, suicidal impulses, catatonic reaction, stroke, shortness of breath, asthma, paralysis of one side of the body. Call your doctor immediately. Neuroleptic malignant syndrome, characterized by high fever, muscle rigidity, altered mental status, and heart rhythm abnormalities, is a potentially fatal condition.

COMMON

Drowsiness, headache, dizziness, constipation.

LESS COMMON

Dry mouth, lightheadedness when rising from a sitting or lying position (orthostatic hypotension), rapid heartbeat, indigestion, weakness, abdominal pain, skin rash, unexpected weight gain.

PRINCIPAL USES

To treat psychotic conditions (severe mental disorders characterized by distorted thoughts, perceptions, and emotions), such as schizophrenia.

HOW THE DRUG WORKS

While the exact mechanism of action of quetiapine is unknown, it appears to interfere with receptors for certain critical natural substances (neurotransmitters) in the brain to produce a tranquilizing and antipsychotic effect.

DOSAGE

Initial dose is 25 mg twice a day. On the second and third days, the dose should be increased by 25 to 50 mg, 2 to 3 times a day, if tolerated. On the fourth day, the dosage should be 300 to 400 mg a day in 2 or 3 divided doses. If needed, further adjustments in dose should occur at least 2 days apart in increments or decrements of 25 to 50 mg, 2 times a day. Clinical trials have not evaluated daily doses greater than 800 mg.

ONSET OF EFFECT

Unknown.

DURATION OF ACTION

Unknown.

DIETARY ADVICE

Quetiapine can be taken without regard to food intake.

STORAGE

Store in a tightly sealed container away from heat, moisture, and direct light.

IF YOU MISS A DOSE

Take it as soon as you remember. If it is near the time for the next dose, skip the missed dose and resume your regular dosage schedule. Do not double the next dose.

STOPPING THE DRUG

Take it as prescribed for the full treatment period. The decision to stop taking the drug should be made in consultation with your physician.

PROLONGED USE

Prolonged use may lead to a potentially irreversible condition called tardive dyskinesia (involuntary movements of the jaw, lips, and tongue). Your doctor must periodically evaluate the drug's effectiveness if it is used for an extended period. Examinations of the eyes for possible development of cataracts are recommended at the onset of treatment and at 6-month intervals during chronic treatment.

PRECAUTIONS

Over 60: Adverse reactions are more likely and more severe. A lower dose may be warranted.

Driving and Hazardous Work: The use of quetiapine may impair your ability to perform such tasks safely. Do not drive or engage in hazardous work until you determine how the medicine affects you.

Alcohol: Avoid alcohol.

Pregnancy: Adequate human studies have not been done. Discuss with your doctor the relative risks and benefits of using this drug while pregnant.

Breast Feeding: Quetiapine may pass into breast milk; avoid or discontinue breast feeding while taking this drug.

Infants and Children: Not recommended for use by children under age 18.

Special Concerns: Avoid prolonged exposure to high temperatures or hot climates. Drink plenty of fluids and stay cool in the summertime.

OVERDOSE

Symptoms: Few cases of overdose have been reported. In clinical studies, excessive doses appear to exacerbate quetiapine's known side effects.

What to Do: Call your doctor, emergency medical services (EMS), or the nearest poison control center immediately.

DRUG INTERACTIONS

Consult your doctor for specific advice if you are taking phenytoin, ketoconazole, itraconazole, fluconazole, erythromycin, antihypertensives, antiparkinsonism drugs, central nervous system depressants, or any other prescription or over-the-counter drug.

FOOD INTERACTIONS

No known food interactions.

DISEASE INTERACTIONS

Caution is advised when taking quetiapine if you have a history of liver disease, severe kidney dysfunction, symptomatic reactions to low blood pressure (dizziness, lightheadedness, or fainting, especially when rising from a sitting or lying position), heart disease, stroke, or seizures.

Quinacrine Hydrochloride

BRAND NAMES
Atabrine, Mepacrine

▶ Drug Class: Anti-infective/
antimalarial/anthelmintic

▶ Available in: Tablets

▶ Available OTC? No

▶ As Generic? No

Side Effects

SERIOUS
Hallucinations; mental or mood changes; irritability; nervousness; skin rash; reddening, itching or peeling of skin; nightmares. Call your doctor immediately.

COMMON
Yellow color of the skin and urine, stomach or abdominal cramps, loss of appetite, dizziness, headache, nausea or vomiting, diarrhea.

LESS COMMON
No less-common side effects are associated with the use of quinacrine.

PRINCIPAL USES
Used as a primary agent in the treatment of giardiasis (traveler's diarrhea), a protozoal infection of the intestinal tract, usually contracted by consuming water that is contaminated with Giardia lamblia cysts.

HOW THE DRUG WORKS
The exact way in which quinacrine works is unknown. It appears to interfere with the parasite's metabolism.

DOSAGE
Adults and teenagers: 100 mg, 3 times a day for 5 to 7 days. Children under age 12: 2 mg per 2.2 lbs (1 kg) of body weight 3 times a day, not to exceed 300 mg daily, for 5 to 7 days.

ONSET OF EFFECT
Unknown.

DURATION OF ACTION
Unknown.

DIETARY ADVICE
This medication is best taken after meals with a full glass of water, fruit juice, or tea, unless your doctor instructs otherwise. Tablets may be crushed and mixed with chocolate syrup, honey, or jam for persons who cannot stand the bitter taste or have difficulty swallowing tablets.

STORAGE
Store in a tightly sealed container away from heat, moisture, and direct light.

IF YOU MISS A DOSE
Take it as soon as you remember. If it is near the time for the next dose, skip the missed dose and resume your regular dosage schedule. Do not double the next dose.

STOPPING THE DRUG
Take it as prescribed for the full treatment period, even if you feel better before the scheduled end of therapy.

PROLONGED USE
See your doctor regularly for tests and examinations to check the medication's effectiveness. The dosage may need to be adjusted.

PRECAUTIONS
Over 60: Adverse reactions may be more likely and more severe. A lower dose may be warranted.

Driving and Hazardous Work: The use of quinacrine may impair your ability to perform such tasks safely. Exercise caution until you determine how this medication affects you.

Alcohol: Avoid all forms of alcohol, including medications such as cough syrup.

Pregnancy: Do not take quinacrine while pregnant; treatment should be delayed until after childbirth. If you are planning to become pregnant, consult your physician.

Breast Feeding: Quinacrine passes into breast milk and may be harmful to the nursing infant; caution is advised. Consult your doctor for specific advice.

Infants and Children: Adverse reactions may be more likely and more severe. Quinacrine's bitter taste may cause vomiting in children. Tablets may be crushed and mixed with chocolate syrup, honey, or jam to cover the taste. Discuss with your pediatrician the relative risks and benefits of your child using this medication.

OVERDOSE
Symptoms: Fainting, seizures, heart rhythm irregularities.

What to Do: Stop taking the drug and call your doctor, emergency medical services (EMS), or the nearest poison control center.

DRUG INTERACTIONS
Other drugs may interact with quinacrine. Do not take primaquine for up to 3 months after taking quinacrine. Also tell your doctor if you are taking any other prescription or over-the-counter medication.

FOOD INTERACTIONS
No known food interactions.

DISEASE INTERACTIONS
Consult your doctor for specific advice if you have any of the following: a history of mental illness or alcoholism, porphyria, or psoriasis. Also tell your doctor if you have any other medical condition.

Quinapril Hydrochloride

Accupril 10 mg
(PARKE-DAVIS)

838

Additional photographs

▶ Drug Class: Angiotensin-converting enzyme (ACE) inhibitor

▶ Available in: Tablets

▶ Available OTC? No

▶ As Generic? No

Side Effects

SERIOUS
Fever and chills, sore
throat and hoarseness,
sudden difficulty breath-
ing or swallowing,
swelling of the face,
mouth, or extremities,
impaired kidney function
(ankle swelling,
decreased urination),
confusion, yellow discol-
oration of the eyes or
skin (indicating liver disorder), intense itching,
chest pain or palpitations,
abdominal pain. Serious
side effects are very rare;
contact your doctor
immediately.

COMMON
Dry, persistent cough.

LESS COMMON
Dizziness or fainting, skin
rash, numbness or tin-
gling in the hands, feet,
or lips, unusual fatigue or
muscle weakness, nau-
sea, drowsiness, loss of
taste, headache.

PRINCIPAL USES
To control high blood pressure (hypertension); to treat
congestive heart failure
(CHF); to treat patients with
left ventricular dysfunction
(damage to the pumping
chamber of the heart); and
to minimize further kidney
damage in diabetics with
mild kidney disease.

HOW THE DRUG WORKS
Angiotensin-converting
enzyme (ACE) inhibitors
block an enzyme that pro-
duces angiotensin, a naturally occurring substance
that causes blood vessels to
constrict and stimulates production of the adrenal hormone, aldosterone, which
promotes sodium retention
in the body. As a result,
ACE inhibitors relax blood
vessels (causing them to
widen) and reduces sodium
retention, which lowers
blood pressure and so
decreases the workload
of the heart.

DOSAGE
10 mg once a day. Dose
may be increased to 20 to
80 mg a day, taken in 1 or 2
doses.

ONSET OF EFFECT
Within 1 hour.

DURATION OF ACTION
24 hours.

DIETARY ADVICE
Take quinapril on an empty
stomach, about 1 hour
before mealtime. Follow
your doctor's dietary advice
(such as low-salt or low-
cholesterol restrictions) to
improve control over high
blood pressure and heart
disease. Avoid high-potassium foods like bananas and
citrus fruits and juices,
unless you are also taking
drugs such as diuretics that
lower potassium levels.

STORAGE
Store in a tightly sealed container away from heat and
direct light.

IF YOU MISS A DOSE
Take it as soon as you
remember. If it is near
the time for the next dose,
skip the missed dose and
resume your regular dosage
schedule. Do not double the
next dose.

STOPPING THE DRUG
Do not stop taking this drug
abruptly, as this may cause
potentially serious health
problems. Dosage should
be reduced gradually,
according to your doctor's
instructions.

PROLONGED USE
Lifelong therapy may be
necessary. See your doctor
regularly for examinations
and tests if you must take
this drug for a prolonged
period.

PRECAUTIONS
Over 60: No special problems are expected.

**Driving and Hazardous
Work:** Avoid such activities
until you determine how the
medicine affects you.

Alcohol: Consume alcohol
only in moderation since it
may increase the effect of
the drug and cause an
excessive drop in blood
pressure. Consult your
doctor for advice.

Pregnancy: Use of
quinapril during the last 6
months of pregnancy may
cause severe defects, even
death, to the fetus. The
drug should be discontin-
ued if you are pregnant or
plan to become pregnant.

Breast Feeding: Quinapril
may pass into breast milk;
caution is advised. Consult
your doctor for advice.

Infants and Children:
The safety and efficacy of
quinapril use by infants and
children have not been
established. Benefits must
be weighed against potential
risks; consult your pediatrician for specific advice.

OVERDOSE
Symptoms: No specific
ones have been reported.

What to Do: While overdose is unlikely, call your
doctor, emergency medical
services (EMS), or the
nearest poison control
center immediately if you
suspect that someone has
taken a much larger dose
than prescribed.

DRUG INTERACTIONS
Consult your doctor if you
are taking diuretics (especially potassium-sparing
diuretics), potassium supplements or drugs containing potassium (check
ingredient labels), lithium,
anticoagulants (such as
warfarin), indomethacin or
other anti-inflammatory
drugs, or any over-the-
counter medications (especially cold remedies and
diet pills).

FOOD INTERACTIONS
Avoid low-salt milk and salt
substitutes. Many of these
products contain potassium.
Avoid consuming large
servings of high-potassium
foods like bananas and citrus fruits or juices.

DISEASE INTERACTIONS
Consult your doctor if you
have systemic lupus erythematosus (SLE) or if you
have had a prior allergic
reaction to ACE inhibitors.
Quinapril should be used
with caution by patients
with severe kidney disease
or renal artery stenosis
(narrowing of one or both
of the arteries that supply
blood to the kidneys).

Quinapril Hydrochloride/Hydrochlorothiazide

▶ Drug Class: Angiotensin-converting enzyme (ACE) inhibitor/diuretic

▶ Available in: Tablets

▶ Available OTC? No

▶ As Generic? No

Side Effects

SERIOUS
Fever and chills, sore throat and hoarseness, sudden difficulty breathing or swallowing, swelling of the face, mouth, or extremities, impaired kidney function (ankle swelling, decreased urination), confusion, yellow discoloration of the eyes or skin (indicating liver disorder), intense itching, chest pain or heartbeat irregularities, abdominal pain. Serious side effects are very rare; contact your doctor immediately.

COMMON
Dry, persistent cough, drowsiness.

LESS COMMON
Dizziness or fainting, skin rash, numbness or tingling in the hands, feet, or lips, change in color of the hands from white to blue to red (Raynaud's phenomenon) in cold weather, unusual fatigue or muscle weakness, nausea, loss of taste, headache, unusual dreams.

PRINCIPAL USES
To treat high blood pressure (hypertension). Used in patients for whom both quinapril and hydrochlorothiazide have been prescribed.

HOW THE DRUG WORKS
Angiotensin-converting enzyme (ACE) inhibitors such as quinapril block an enzyme that produces angiotensin, a naturally occurring substance that causes blood vessels to constrict and stimulates production of the adrenal hormone, aldosterone, which promotes sodium retention in the body. As a result, ACE inhibitors relax blood vessels (causing them to widen) and reduces sodium retention, which lowers blood pressure and so decreases the workload of the heart. Hydrochlorothiazide (HCTZ), a diuretic, increases sodium and water in the urine output. By reducing the overall fluid volume in the body, diuretics reduce blood volume and so reduce blood pressure.

DOSAGE
This combination medication comes in three strengths: quinapril/hydrochlorothiazide 10/12.5, 20/12.5, and 20/25. Your doctor will determine the appropriate dose.

ONSET OF EFFECT
Within 1 hour for quinapril; within 2 hours for HCTZ.

DURATION OF ACTION
24 hours for quinapril; 6 to 12 hours for HCTZ.

DIETARY ADVICE
Follow your doctor's dietary advice (such as low-salt or low-cholesterol restrictions) to improve control over high blood pressure and prevent heart disease.

STORAGE
Store in a tightly sealed container away from heat, moisture, and direct light.

IF YOU MISS A DOSE
If you do not remember until the next day, skip the missed dose and resume your regular dosage schedule. Do not double the next dose.

STOPPING THE DRUG
Discontinuing this drug abruptly may cause potentially serious problems. The dosage should be reduced gradually, according to your doctor's instructions.

PROLONGED USE
See your doctor regularly for evaluation if you must take this medicine for a prolonged period. Lifelong therapy may be necessary.

PRECAUTIONS
Over 60: Adverse reactions may be more likely and more severe.

Driving and Hazardous Work: Avoid such activities until you determine how the medicine affects you.

Alcohol: Consume alcohol only in moderation since it may increase the effect of the drug and cause an excessive drop in blood pressure. Consult your doctor for advice.

Pregnancy: Before taking this medication, tell your doctor if you are pregnant or plan to become pregnant. Use of this drug during the last 6 months of pregnancy may cause severe defects, even death, in the fetus.

Breast Feeding: Quinapril and hydrochlorothiazide may pass into breast milk; caution is advised. Consult your doctor for specific advice.

Infants and Children: Not recommended for use by children under 18.

Special Concerns: A rare complication is angioedema, characterized by swelling of the lips, tongue, and throat. It may be so severe as to cause obstruction of the airways, which could be fatal.

OVERDOSE
Symptoms: Overdose has not been reported; symptoms might include dizziness, faintness, or confusion.

What to Do: While overdose is unlikely, seek emergency medical attention immediately if you suspect that someone has taken a much larger dose than prescribed.

DRUG INTERACTIONS
Consult your doctor for specific advice if you are taking cholestyramine, colestipol, corticosteroids, digitalis drugs, antidiabetic drugs, lithium, potassium-containing medications or supplements, or any over-the-counter drug (especially cold remedies and appetite suppressants).

FOOD INTERACTIONS
Avoid low-salt milk and salt substitutes. Many of these products contain potassium.

DISEASE INTERACTIONS
Consult your doctor if you have systemic lupus erythematosus or if you have had a prior allergic reaction to ACE inhibitors. This medication should be used with caution by patients with abnormal liver function and is not recommended for those with severe kidney disease. This medication can increase blood triglycerides and worsen control of blood sugar in people with diabetes.

Quinaglute 324 mg
(BERLEX)

Additional photographs

▶ Drug Class: Antiarrhythmic

▶ Available in: Capsules, tablets, extended-release tablets

▶ Available OTC? No

▶ As Generic? Yes

Side Effects

SERIOUS
Dizziness, lightheadedness, or fainting, any change in vision, fever, severe headache, ringing or buzzing in the ears, hearing loss, skin rash or hives, shortness of breath or wheezing, rapid heartbeat, unusual bleeding or bruising, unexplained fatigue. Call your doctor immediately.

COMMON
Diarrhea, loss of appetite, bitter taste, flushing and itching skin, nausea, vomiting, stomach pain or cramps.

LESS COMMON
Mental confusion, rash.

PRINCIPAL USES
To correct irregular heartbeats (cardiac arrhythmias).

HOW THE DRUG WORKS
Quinidine slows nerve impulses in the heart and reduces the sensitivity of heart tissue to certain nerve impulses, thus stabilizing heartbeat.

DOSAGE
Capsules and tablets—Adults: 300 to 600 mg, 4 times a day. Children: 6 to 8.5 mg per 2.2 lbs (1 kg) of body weight, 5 times a day. Extended-release tablets—Adults: 300 to 660 mg every 6 to 12 hours.

ONSET OF EFFECT
Oral forms, 1 to 2 hours.

DURATION OF ACTION
6 to 8 hours.

DIETARY ADVICE
Oral forms are usually taken with a full glass of water 1 hour before or 2 hours after meals. The medication can be taken with food or milk to lessen stomach upset.

STORAGE
Store in a tightly sealed container away from heat and direct light.

IF YOU MISS A DOSE
If you miss a dose, take it as soon as you remember. If it is close to the next dose, skip the missed dose and resume your regular dosage schedule, as prescribed. Do not double the next dose.

STOPPING THE DRUG
Take as prescribed for the full treatment period, even if you begin to feel better before the scheduled end of therapy. The decision to stop taking the drug should be made by your doctor.

PROLONGED USE
Lifelong therapy may be necessary. See your doctor regularly for examinations and diagnostic tests if you must take this medicine for a prolonged period.

PRECAUTIONS
Over 60: Adverse reactions may be more likely and more severe in older patients.

Driving and Hazardous Work: Do not drive or engage in hazardous work until you determine how the medicine affects you.

Alcohol: No special precautions are required.

Pregnancy: In animal studies, quinine, a closely related drug, has caused birth defects. Tests of quinidine have not been done. Before you take quinidine, tell your doctor if you are pregnant or plan to become pregnant.

Breast Feeding: Quinidine passes into breast milk; caution is advised. Consult your doctor for specific advice.

Infants and Children: The long-acting oral dosage form is not recommended for use in children.

Special Concerns: You may have to wear dark glasses both indoors and outside if quinidine makes you sensitive to light.

OVERDOSE
Symptoms: Lethargy, confusion, headache, seizures, dizziness, vomiting, stomach pain, hearing and vision disturbances, fainting, severe weakness or fatigue, breathing difficulty, loss of consciousness.

What to Do: Call your doctor, emergency medical services (EMS), or the nearest poison control center immediately.

DRUG INTERACTIONS
Avoid diuretics if possible to prevent lowering of blood potassium levels. Consult your doctor for specific advice if you are taking digoxin, phenobarbital, phenytoin, anticoagulants, other heart medications, antacids, acetazolamide, or pimozide.

FOOD INTERACTIONS
Do not take quinidine with grapefruit juice.

DISEASE INTERACTIONS
Consult your doctor if you have any of the following: asthma, emphysema, an infection of any kind, myasthenia gravis, hyperthyroidism, or psoriasis. Use of quinidine may cause complications in patients with liver or kidney disease, since these organs work together to remove the medication from the body.

Rabeprazole Sodium

▶ Drug Class: Antacid/proton pump inhibitor

▶ Available in: Delayed-release tablets

▶ Available OTC? No

▶ As Generic? No

Side Effects

SERIOUS
No serious side effects are associated with the use of rabeprazole.

COMMON
Headache.

LESS COMMON
Weakness, fever, chills, allergic reaction, diarrhea, nausea, vomiting, abdominal pain, dry mouth, change in appetite, difficulty swallowing, muscle or joint pain. Many additional side effects can occur; consult your doctor if you are concerned about any adverse or unusual reactions you experience while taking this drug.

PRINCIPAL USES
To treat duodenal (intestinal) ulcers, as well as conditions that cause extreme increases in stomach acid production (such as Zollinger-Ellison syndrome), erosive esophagitis (severe, chronic inflammation or ulceration of the esophagus), and heartburn due to gastroesophageal reflux (backwash of stomach acid into the esophagus).

HOW THE DRUG WORKS
Rabeprazole blocks the action of a specific enzyme in the cells that line the stomach, thereby decreasing the production of stomach acid. Reduction of stomach acid promotes healing of ulcers.

DOSAGE
For duodenal ulcer, esophagitis, or gastroesophageal reflux: 20 mg a day. For Zollinger-Ellison syndrome or similar conditions: 60 to 100 mg a day, up to 60 mg twice a day.

ONSET OF EFFECT
Within 1 hour.

DURATION OF ACTION
At least 24 hours.

DIETARY ADVICE
Take rabeprazole after the morning meal. Tablets should be swallowed whole.

STORAGE
Store in a tightly sealed container away from heat, moisture, and direct light.

IF YOU MISS A DOSE
Take it as soon as you remember. However, if it is near the time for the next dose, skip the missed dose and resume your regular dosage schedule. Do not double the next dose.

STOPPING THE DRUG
Take as prescribed for the full treatment period, even if your symptoms improve before the scheduled end of therapy. The decision to stop taking the drug should be made in consultation with your doctor.

PROLONGED USE
Rabeprazole should not be used indefinitely as maintenance therapy for esophagitis; it is generally taken for a limited period of 4 to 8 weeks. For those who have not healed within this period, an additional 8 weeks of therapy may be considered by your doctor. People with duodenal ulcer generally heal within 4 weeks of therapy. Some people with Zollinger-Ellison syndrome have been treated for up to one year. See your doctor regularly for tests and examinations if you must take this drug for an extended period of time.

PRECAUTIONS
Over 60: No specific problems for older people have been reported.

Driving and Hazardous Work: Avoid such activities until you determine how the drug affects you.

Alcohol: Avoid alcohol while taking this medication, as it may aggravate your condition.

Pregnancy: In animal tests, rabeprazole has not caused problems. Human tests have not been done. Before you take rabeprazole, tell your doctor if you are pregnant or plan to become pregnant.

Breast Feeding: Rabeprazole may pass into breast milk; caution is advised. Consult your doctor for advice.

Infants and Children: Safety and effectiveness have not been established for patients under age 18.

Special Concerns: Do not chew, crush, or split the tablets. If your doctor directs, you may take an antacid along with rabeprazole.

OVERDOSE
Symptoms: Few cases of overdose have been reported.

What to Do: An overdose is unlikely to be life-threatening. However, if someone takes a much larger dose than prescribed, call your doctor, emergency medical services (EMS), or the nearest poison control center immediately.

DRUG INTERACTIONS
Consult your doctor for specific advice if you are taking ketoconazole or digoxin.

FOOD INTERACTIONS
No significant food interactions have been reported.

DISEASE INTERACTIONS
Consult your doctor if you have severe liver disease, since it may increase the risk of side effects.

Raloxifene Hydrochloride

▶ Drug Class: Selective estrogen receptor modulator (SERM)

▶ Available in: Tablets

▶ Available OTC? No

▶ As Generic? No

Side Effects

SERIOUS
No serious side effects are associated with the use of raloxifene.

COMMON
Increased incidence of infections, flu-like symptoms, hot flashes, joint pain, sinusitis, unexpected weight gain.

LESS COMMON
Leg cramps, mild chest pain, fever, migraine, indigestion, vomiting, flatulence, stomach upset, swelling of the legs and feet, muscle pain, insomnia, sore throat, increased cough, pneumonia, laryngitis, rash, sweating, yeast infection, urinary tract infection, white vaginal discharge.

PRINCIPAL USES
For the treatment and prevention of osteoporosis in postmenopausal women. Unlike estrogen, raloxifene does not stimulate overgrowth of the endometrium (the tissue lining the uterus) and thus does not increase the risk of uterine cancer.

HOW THE DRUG WORKS
Healthy bone tissue is continuously remodeled (broken down and then reformed); the minerals and other components of bone are reabsorbed by certain cells and then replaced by new bone formation. Raloxifene suppresses the activity of the cells that resorb bone; consequently, the breakdown of bone tissue occurs more slowly than the laying down of new bone. This action preserves bone density and strength.

DOSAGE
One 60 mg tablet a day.

ONSET OF EFFECT
Unknown. .

DURATION OF ACTION
Unknown.

DIETARY ADVICE
Raloxifene may be taken at any time of day without regard to meal schedule. Patients are generally advised to take calcium and vitamin D supplements to aid bone formation.

STORAGE
Store in a tightly sealed container away from heat, moisture, and direct light.

IF YOU MISS A DOSE
If you miss a dose on one day, do not double the dose the next day.

STOPPING THE DRUG
The decision to stop taking the drug should be made in consultation with your physician.

PROLONGED USE
Safety and effectiveness beyond three years of use have not been determined.

PRECAUTIONS
Over 60: No special problems are expected.

Driving and Hazardous Work: No special problems are expected.

Alcohol: Alcohol should be restricted in high-risk women because it is a risk factor for osteoporosis.

Pregnancy: Raloxifene is normally not used in premenopausal women. The drug should not be given to pregnant women.

Breast Feeding: Raloxifene should not be used by nursing mothers.

Infants and Children: Raloxifene should not be used by children.

Special Concerns: Patients taking raloxifene are encouraged to engage in regular weight-bearing exercise and should avoid cigarettes and limit alcohol, which inhibit healthy bone production. Unlike estrogen replacement therapy, raloxifene does not reduce hot flashes in postmenopausal women.

OVERDOSE
Symptoms: No cases of overdose have been reported.

What to Do: An overdose with raloxifene is unlikely. If someone takes a much larger dose than prescribed, call your doctor.

DRUG INTERACTIONS
Estrogen should not be taken concurrently with raloxifene. Since cholestyramine reduces absorption of raloxifene, the two drugs should not be taken at the same time of day. Consult your doctor if you are taking any of the following drugs that may interact with raloxifene: warfarin, clofibrate, indomethacin, naproxen, ibuprofen, diazepam, or diazoxide.

FOOD INTERACTIONS
No known food interactions.

DISEASE INTERACTIONS
You should not take raloxifene if you have a history of thromboembolic disease, including deep vein thrombosis, pulmonary embolism, and retinal vein thrombosis. Raloxifene must be used with caution by patients with impaired liver function; consult your doctor for specific advice.

Ramipril

Altace 5 mg
(HOECHST MARION ROUSSEL)

▶ Drug Class: Angiotensin-converting enzyme (ACE) inhibitor

▶ Available in: Tablets

▶ Available OTC? No

▶ As Generic? No

Side Effects

SERIOUS
Fever and chills, sore throat and hoarseness, sudden difficulty breathing or swallowing, swelling of the face, mouth, or extremities, impaired kidney function (ankle swelling, decreased urination), confusion, yellow discoloration of the eyes or skin (indicating liver disorder), intense itching, chest pain or palpitations, abdominal pain. Serious side effects are very rare; contact your doctor immediately.

COMMON
Dry, persistent cough.

LESS COMMON
Dizziness or fainting, skin rash, numbness or tingling in the hands, feet, or lips, unusual fatigue or muscle weakness, nausea, drowsiness, loss of taste, headache.

PRINCIPAL USES
To control high blood pressure (hypertension); to treat congestive heart failure; to treat patients with left ventricular dysfunction (damage to the pumping chamber of the heart); to reduce risk of heart attack, stroke, and death from cardiovascular causes; and to minimize further kidney damage in diabetics with mild kidney disease.

HOW THE DRUG WORKS
Angiotensin-converting enzyme (ACE) inhibitors block an enzyme that produces angiotensin, a naturally occurring substance that causes blood vessels to constrict and stimulates production of the adrenal hormone, aldosterone, which promotes sodium retention in the body. As a result, ACE inhibitors relax blood vessels (causing them to widen) and reduces sodium retention, which lowers blood pressure and so decreases the workload of the heart.

DOSAGE
2.5 mg to 20 mg per day, taken in 1 or 2 doses.

ONSET OF EFFECT
Within 1 to 2 hours.

DURATION OF ACTION
24 hours.

DIETARY ADVICE
Take it on an empty stomach, about 1 hour before mealtime. Follow your doctor's dietary advice (such as low-salt or low-cholesterol restrictions) to improve control over high blood pressure and heart disease. Avoid high-potassium foods like bananas and citrus fruits and juices, unless you are also taking medications, such as diuretics, that lower potassium levels.

STORAGE
Store in a tightly sealed container away from heat and direct light.

IF YOU MISS A DOSE
Take it as soon as you remember. If it is near the time for the next dose, skip the missed dose and resume your regular dosage schedule. Do not double the next dose.

STOPPING THE DRUG
Do not stop taking this drug abruptly, as this may cause potentially serious health problems. Dosage should be reduced gradually, according to your doctor's instructions.

PROLONGED USE
Lifelong therapy may be necessary. See your doctor regularly for examinations and tests if you must take this medicine for a prolonged period of time.

PRECAUTIONS
Over 60: No special problems are expected.

Driving and Hazardous Work: Do not drive or engage in hazardous work until you determine how the medicine affects you.

Alcohol: Consume alcohol only in moderation since it may increase the effect of the drug and cause an excessive drop in blood pressure. Consult your doctor for advice.

Pregnancy: Use of ramipril during the last 6 months of pregnancy may cause severe defects, even death, in the fetus. The drug should be discontinued if you are pregnant or plan to become pregnant.

Breast Feeding: Ramipril may pass into breast milk;

caution is advised. Consult your doctor for advice.

Infants and Children: Children may be especially sensitive to the effects of ramipril. Benefits must be weighed against potential risks; consult your pediatrician for advice.

OVERDOSE
Symptoms: Dizziness or fainting due to extremely low blood pressure.

What to Do: Call your doctor, emergency medical services (EMS), or the nearest poison control center immediately.

DRUG INTERACTIONS
Consult your doctor if you are taking diuretics (especially potassium-sparing diuretics), potassium supplements or drugs containing potassium (check ingredient labels), lithium, anticoagulants (such as warfarin), indomethacin or other anti-inflammatory drugs, or any over-the-counter medications (especially cold remedies and diet pills).

FOOD INTERACTIONS
Avoid low-salt milk and salt substitutes. Many of these products contain potassium. Avoid consuming large servings of high-potassium foods like bananas and citrus fruits or juices.

DISEASE INTERACTIONS
Consult your doctor if you have systemic lupus erythematosus (SLE) or if you have had a prior allergic reaction to ACE inhibitors. Ramipril should be used with caution by patients with severe kidney disease or renal artery stenosis (narrowing of one or both of the arteries that supply blood to the kidneys).

Ranitidine

Zantac 150 mg
(GLAXO WELLCOME)

Additional photographs

▶ Drug Class: Histamine (H2) blocker

▶ Available in: Capsules, tablets, injection, syrup, granules

▶ Available OTC? Yes

▶ As Generic? Yes

Side Effects

SERIOUS
Irregular heart rhythm (palpitations), slowed heartbeat, severe blood problems resulting in unusual bleeding, bruising, fever, chills, and increased susceptibility to infection. Call your doctor immediately.

COMMON
Headache, fatigue, drowsiness, dizziness, nausea, vomiting, abdominal pain, diarrhea, constipation.

LESS COMMON
Blurred vision, decreased sexual desire or function, swelling of breasts in males or females, temporary hair loss, hallucinations, depression, insomnia, skin rash, hives, or redness.

PRINCIPAL USES
To treat ulcers of the stomach and duodenum, conditions that cause increased stomach acid production (such as Zollinger-Ellison syndrome), erosive esophagitis (severe, chronic inflammation of the esophagus), and gastroesophageal reflux (backwash of stomach acid into the esophagus, resulting in heartburn).

HOW THE DRUG WORKS
Ranitidine blocks the action of histamine (a compound produced in the body's cells), which in turn decreases the stomach's secretion of hydrochloric acid. Once stomach acid production is decreased, the body is better able to heal itself.

DOSAGE
Adults— Oral dose: 150 mg, 2 times a day, in the morning and at bedtime, or 300 mg once daily before bedtime. Injection: 50 mg every 6 to 8 hours. Patients with Zollinger-Ellison syndrome may require up to 6 g per day, taken orally. For treatment of heartburn with the over-the-counter form: 75 mg, as needed, not to exceed 150 mg a day. Children— Consult your pediatrician for appropriate individual dosage.

ONSET OF EFFECT
30 to 60 minutes.

DURATION OF ACTION
Up to 13 hours.

DIETARY ADVICE
Avoid foods that cause stomach irritation.

STORAGE
Store away from heat and direct light. Keep liquid form from freezing.

IF YOU MISS A DOSE
Take it as soon as you remember. If it is near the time for the next dose, skip the missed dose and resume your regular dosage schedule. Do not double the next dose.

STOPPING THE DRUG
Take the prescription-strength medication for the full treatment period, even if you begin to feel better before the scheduled end of therapy.

PROLONGED USE
Do not take nonprescription-strength ranitidine for more than 2 weeks unless you have been otherwise instructed by your doctor.

PRECAUTIONS
Over 60: Adverse reactions may be more likely and more severe in older patients.

Driving and Hazardous Work: Do not drive or engage in hazardous work until you determine how the medicine affects you.

Alcohol: Avoid alcohol. Ranitidine may increase blood alcohol levels.

Pregnancy: Risks vary, depending on the patient and dosage. Consult your doctor.

Breast Feeding: Ranitidine passes into breast milk and may pose harm to the child; avoid or discontinue use while nursing.

Infants and Children: Ranitidine is not recommended for young patients, although it has not been shown to cause any side effects or problems different from those in adults when used for short periods of time.

Special Concerns: Avoid cigarette smoking because it may increase stomach acid secretion and thus worsen the disease. Do not take ranitidine if you have ever had an allergic reaction to a histamine (H2) blocker. If stomach pain becomes worse while using the drug, be sure to tell your doctor right away.

OVERDOSE
Symptoms: Vomiting, diarrhea, breathing problems, slurred speech, rapid heartbeat, delirium.

What to Do: Call your doctor, emergency medical services (EMS), or the nearest poison control center immediately.

DRUG INTERACTIONS
Consult your doctor for specific advice if you are taking antacids, antidepressants, aspirin, beta-blockers, caffeine, diazepam, glipizide, ketoconazole, lidocaine, phenytoin, procainamide, theophylline, or warfarin.

FOOD INTERACTIONS
Carbonated drinks, citrus fruits and juices, caffeine-containing beverages, and other acidic foods or liquids may irritate the stomach or interfere with the therapeutic action of ranitidine.

DISEASE INTERACTIONS
Patients with kidney disease should not use ranitidine or should use it in smaller, limited doses under careful supervision by a physician.

Ranitidine Bismuth Citrate

BRAND NAME
Tritec

▶ Drug Class: Antiulcer drug

▶ Available in: Tablets

▶ Available OTC? No

▶ As Generic? No

Side Effects

SERIOUS
No serious side effects have been reported.

COMMON
Diarrhea, nausea and vomiting, headache, changes in taste perception, sleep disorders, chest symptoms, skin itching.

LESS COMMON
Abdominal discomfort, tremors.

PRINCIPAL USES
To treat duodenal ulcers caused by infection with *Helicobacter pylori* bacteria. Therapy with ranitidine bismuth citrate is done in combination with the antibiotic clarithromycin.

HOW THE DRUG WORKS
Research has shown that the majority of peptic ulcers are caused by infection with a bacterium known as *Helicobacter pylori*. Clarithromycin kills bacteria; ranitidine bismuth citrate enhances clarithromycin's antibiotic effect to help eradicate *Helicobacter pylori*. Ranitidine bismuth citrate also inhibits the secretion of stomach acid, thereby facilitating the healing of ulcers.

DOSAGE
400 mg of ranitidine bismuth citrate 2 times a day for 4 weeks with 500 mg of clarithromycin, 3 times a day for the first 2 weeks. Ranitidine bismuth citrate should never be taken alone for treatment of active duodenal ulcers.

ONSET OF EFFECT
Unknown.

DURATION OF ACTION
Unknown.

DIETARY ADVICE
This drug is best taken at least 30 minutes after meals.

STORAGE
Store in a tightly sealed container away from heat and direct light.

IF YOU MISS A DOSE
Take it as soon as you remember. If it is near the time for the next dose, skip the missed dose and resume your regular dosage schedule. Do not double the next dose.

STOPPING THE DRUG
Take it as prescribed for the full treatment period, even if you begin to feel better before the scheduled end of therapy.

PROLONGED USE
This drug is not intended for prolonged use. Healing of the ulcer should occur within 4 weeks, and a second course of therapy is not warranted if the first proves ineffective.

PRECAUTIONS
Over 60: Ranitidine bismuth citrate does not cause more side effects and problems in older patients than it does in younger people.

Driving and Hazardous Work: The use of this drug should not impair your ability to perform such tasks safely.

Alcohol: Avoid alcohol.

Pregnancy: In animal studies, ranitidine bismuth citrate has not caused problems; human studies have not been done. However, ranitidine bismuth citrate taken with clarithromycin may cause problems during pregnancy. Before you take this drug combination, tell your doctor if you are pregnant or plan to become pregnant.

Breast Feeding: It is not known whether ranitidine bismuth citrate passes into breast milk; caution is advised. Consult your doctor for specific advice.

Infants and Children: The safety and effectiveness of ranitidine bismuth citrate and clarithromycin for use by infants and children have not been established.

Special Concerns: Patients whose *Helicobacter pylori* infections are not eradicated after treatment with ranitidine bismuth citrate and clarithromycin should be considered to be infected with bacteria that are resistant to clarithromycin. They should not be treated with clarithromycin again. The bismuth component of this drug may cause a temporary and harmless darkening of the tongue and the stools.

OVERDOSE
Symptoms: No specific ones have been reported.

What to Do: An overdose of ranitidine bismuth citrate is unlikely to be life-threatening. However, if someone takes a much larger dose than prescribed, call your doctor, emergency medical services (EMS), or the nearest poison control center immediately.

DRUG INTERACTIONS
Drug interactions with ranitidine bismuth citrate have not been established. Before you take the medication, tell your doctor if you are taking any prescription or over-the-counter drug.

FOOD INTERACTIONS
No known food interactions.

DISEASE INTERACTIONS
Caution is advised when taking ranitidine bismuth citrate. Tell your doctor if you have any other medical condition. Use of this drug may cause problems in patients with kidney disease, because this organ works to remove the medication from the body.

Repaglinide

▶ Drug Class: Antidiabetic agent

▶ Available in: Tablets

▶ Available OTC? No

▶ As Generic? No

Side Effects

SERIOUS
Hypoglycemia (blood sugar levels that are too low), resulting in shakiness, headache, cold sweats, anxiety, and changes in mental state. Immediately ingest sugar-containing food or drink. Inform your doctor about the frequency and timing of hypoglycemic events.

COMMON
Increased incidence of upper respiratory or sinus infection, headache, back pain, joint pain, diarrhea.

LESS COMMON
Constipation, indigestion, urinary tract infection, mild allergic reaction.

PRINCIPAL USES
Used as an adjunct (supplemental) therapy to dietary measures and exercise to help control blood sugar levels in patients with type 2 diabetes mellitus. Repaglinide is the first in a new class of oral antidiabetic drugs designed to control blood glucose levels following meals.

HOW THE DRUG WORKS
Repaglinide stimulates the pancreas to produce more insulin. Increased insulin levels reduce blood glucose by promoting the transport of glucose into muscle cells and other tissues, where it is used as a source of energy. The rapid onset and short duration of repaglinide's action make it effective in controlling glucose levels after a meal.

DOSAGE
Dosage must be determined for each patient individually, based on blood glucose levels and response to the drug. The recommended dosage range is 0.5 to 4 mg taken 15 to 30 minutes before meals. Repaglinide may be taken before meals 2, 3, or 4 times a day depending on the patient's meal pattern. The maximum recommended daily dose is 16 mg.

ONSET OF EFFECT
30 to 60 minutes.

DURATION OF ACTION
1 to 2 hours.

DIETARY ADVICE
Doses should be taken 15 to 30 minutes before meals. Follow the dietary guidelines given by your doctor.

STORAGE
Store in a tightly sealed container away from heat, moisture, and direct light.

IF YOU MISS A DOSE
If you miss a dose, take it with the next meal. Do not double the next dose.

STOPPING THE DRUG
Do not stop taking the drug without your doctor's approval.

PROLONGED USE
Prolonged use increases the risk of adverse effects. Periodic physical examinations and blood tests to monitor glucose levels are needed.

PRECAUTIONS
Over 60: Older patients may be more susceptible to adverse effects, especially hypoglycemia, which may be more difficult to recognize in the elderly.

Driving and Hazardous Work: Caution is advised until you have reached a stable dosing regimen that does not produce episodes of hypoglycemia.

Alcohol: Limit alcohol intake; hypoglycemia is more likely to occur after the consumption of alcohol.

Pregnancy: Repaglinide is not usually given during pregnancy. Insulin is the treatment of choice for pregnant diabetic patients.

Breast Feeding: Repaglinide may pass into breast milk; consult your doctor for advice if you are considering breast feeding.

Infants and Children: Safety and effectiveness have not been established for young patients.

Special Concerns: Follow your doctor's advice about diet, exercise, and weight control carefully. These aspects of treatment are just as essential to the proper control of diabetes as taking the medication. Be sure to carry at all times some form of medical identification that indicates you have diabetes and that lists all of the drugs you are taking.

OVERDOSE
Symptoms: Excessive hunger, nausea, anxiety, cold sweats, drowsiness, rapid heartbeat, weakness, changes in mental state, loss of consciousness (indications of hypoglycemia). Overdose is most likely to occur when caloric intake is deficient, following or during more exercise than usual, or after consuming more than a small amount of alcohol.

What to Do: Call your doctor or seek emergency medical help.

DRUG INTERACTIONS
Consult your doctor if you are taking antifungal agents such as ketoconazole or miconazole; also, antibiotics, rifampin, barbiturates, carbamazepine, aspirin or other NSAIDs, sulfonamides, chloramphenicol, probenecid, MAO inhibitors, beta-blockers, diuretics, corticosteroids, phenothiazines, estrogens, oral contraceptives, phenytoin, calcium channel blockers, sympathomimetics, or isoniazid. Do not take with gemfibrozil.

FOOD INTERACTIONS
A special diet is essential for proper control of blood glucose levels.

DISEASE INTERACTIONS
Do not use repaglinide if you have type 1 diabetes mellitus. Use of repaglinide may cause complications in patients with impaired liver or kidney function, since these organs are both involved in removing the medication from the body.

Resorcinol

▶ Drug Class: Acne drug

▶ Available in: Lotion, cream, stick

▶ Available OTC? Yes

▶ As Generic? Yes

Side Effects

SERIOUS
No serious side effects are associated with resorcinol during normal use (as prescribed).

COMMON
Mild redness and peeling of the skin. Such side effects tend to occur at the beginning of therapy and diminish as your body adjusts to the medication; notify your doctor if such symptoms persist or interfere with daily activities.

LESS COMMON
More-severe irritation or allergy with redness, peeling, burning, stinging, itching, or rash. Call your doctor.

PRINCIPAL USES
To treat acne and seborrheic dermatitis. Resorcinol is also infrequently used to treat eczema, psoriasis, corns, calluses, warts, and other skin conditions.

HOW THE DRUG WORKS
Resorcinol fights fungal and bacterial organisms and promotes softening, dissolution, and peeling of the skin.

DOSAGE
For acne and seborrheic dermatitis: Apply once or twice daily as recommended or as tolerated. Wash your hands thoroughly after applying resorcinol.

ONSET OF EFFECT
Unknown.

DURATION OF ACTION
Unknown.

DIETARY ADVICE
No special restrictions.

STORAGE
Store in a tightly sealed container away from heat and direct light.

IF YOU MISS A DOSE
Skip the missed application and resume your regular dosage schedule. Do not double the next dose.

STOPPING THE DRUG
If you are using resorcinol by prescription, the decision to stop using the drug should be made by your doctor. If you are using it without a prescription, you may stop using it whenever your acne clears; however, it is likely that discontinuing use of the drug will lead to a recurrence of acne.

PROLONGED USE
Do not use resorcinol for longer than prescribed.

PRECAUTIONS
Over 60: No special problems are expected.

Driving and Hazardous Work: No special precautions are necessary.

Alcohol: No special precautions are necessary.

Pregnancy: Resorcinol has not been shown to cause birth defects or other problems during pregnancy. However, it may be absorbed through the skin. Consult your doctor for specific advice if you are pregnant or plan to become pregnant.

Breast Feeding: Resorcinol may be absorbed into the body through the skin; caution is advised. Consult your doctor for advice.

Infants and Children: Resorcinol should not be used on large areas of the body of children.

Special Concerns: Anyone with a history of allergy to resorcinol or any other ingredients in the specific product should not use this medication. Resorcinol should not be used on wounds, because it may cause methemoglobinemia, a blood disorder. It should not be applied over large areas of the body, especially when used in high concentrations. Avoid contact of resorcinol with the eyes. This medication is generally not recommended for black persons, since it may significantly darken treated areas of skin. Resorcinol may darken light-colored hair.

OVERDOSE
Symptoms: If ingested, diarrhea, nausea, abdominal pain, vomiting, drowsiness, dizziness, severe or persistent headache, breathing difficulty, unusual tiredness or weakness, slow heartbeat, and profuse sweating may occur.

What to Do: In case of ingestion, call your doctor, emergency medical services (EMS), or the nearest poison control center.

DRUG INTERACTIONS
The following drugs or other products may irritate the skin and therefore should not be used with resorcinol unless recommended by your doctor: abrasive soaps or cleansers, alcohol-containing preparations (including astringents, aftershave lotions, other perfumed toiletries), any other acne agent, any preparation containing a peeling agent such as benzoyl peroxide, salicylic acid, alpha hydroxy acids, sulfur, or vitamin A, and soaps, medicated cosmetics, or other cosmetics that dry the skin.

FOOD INTERACTIONS
No known food interactions.

DISEASE INTERACTIONS
You should not use resorcinol if you have had a prior allergic reaction to it.

Rifabutin

Mycobutin 150 mg
(PHARMACIA)

▶ Drug Class: Anti-infective

▶ Available in: Capsules

▶ Available OTC? No

▶ As Generic? No

Side Effects

SERIOUS
No serious side effects are associated with the use of rifabutin.

COMMON
Reddish orange or brown discoloration of urine, saliva, phlegm, stools, sweat, skin, and tears; skin rash; nausea and vomiting; low white blood cell count.

LESS COMMON
Joint aches, eye irritation, blurred or decreased vision.

PRINCIPAL USES
A tuberculosis-like disease known as Mycobacterium avium complex (MAC) is common in people with advanced AIDS. Rifabutin is used to prevent MAC and can be used with other drugs to treat MAC infection. It is occasionally used to treat tuberculosis.

HOW THE DRUG WORKS
Rifabutin interferes with the activity of enzymes needed for the replication of RNA (ribonucleic acid) in bacterial cells, thus preventing the bacteria from reproducing.

DOSAGE
Adults and teenagers: 300 mg once a day, or 150 mg, 2 times a day.

ONSET OF EFFECT
Unknown.

DURATION OF ACTION
Unknown.

DIETARY ADVICE
Take it on an empty stomach, 1 hour before or 2 hours after meals. If nausea and vomiting develop or you are unable to swallow the pills, the contents of the capsules can be mixed with food such as applesauce.

STORAGE
Store in a tightly sealed container away from heat, moisture, and direct light.

IF YOU MISS A DOSE
Take the drug as soon as you remember. This will help keep a constant level of medication in your system. If it is near the time for the next dose, skip the missed dose and resume your regular dosage schedule. Do not double the next dose.

STOPPING THE DRUG
Take it as prescribed for the full treatment period, even if you begin to feel better before the scheduled end of therapy. Treatment may continue for months or years. The decision to stop taking the drug should be made by your doctor.

PROLONGED USE
Consult your doctor about the need for periodic medical examinations and laboratory tests. Long-term therapy is usually required.

PRECAUTIONS
Over 60: No special problems are expected.

Driving and Hazardous Work: Do not drive or engage in hazardous work until you determine how the medicine affects you.

Alcohol: Avoid alcohol.

Pregnancy: Adequate studies of rifabutin use during pregnancy have not been done. This drug should be given during pregnancy only if potential benefits clearly outweigh the risks to the unborn child. There is no evidence that the drug will reduce the risk of transmitting the virus from the mother to the fetus.

Breast Feeding: It is not known whether rifabutin passes into breast milk; caution is advised. Women who are infected with HIV should not breast feed, to avoid transmitting the virus to an uninfected child.

Infants and Children: Use and dose for infants and children must be determined by your doctor. It is not known whether rifabutin causes different or more severe side effects in infants and children than it does in older persons.

Special Concerns: Soft contact lenses may become permanently discolored. If you have been using oral contraceptives, you should use a different method of birth control while taking rifabutin.

OVERDOSE
Symptoms: An overdose with rifabutin is unlikely.

What to Do: If someone takes a much larger dose than prescribed, call your doctor, emergency medical services (EMS), or the nearest poison control center right away.

DRUG INTERACTIONS
Rifabutin should not be taken if you are also taking the protease inhibitor ritonavir, and it should be used with caution if you are taking other protease inhibitors (a class of drugs used to treat AIDS). Consult your doctor for specific advice if you are taking ketoconazole, phenytoin, prednisone, propranolol, quinidine, oral contraceptives, sulfonylureas (oral antidiabetics), warfarin, or zidovudine. Also tell your doctor if you are taking any other prescription or over-the-counter medication.

FOOD INTERACTIONS
No known food interactions.

DISEASE INTERACTIONS
Caution is advised when taking rifabutin. Consult your doctor if you have active tuberculosis (TB). If you have to take rifabutin and have active TB, you must take other medications to cure TB. Rifabutin, if used alone, may cause drug-resistant strains of the TB bacterium to thrive, resulting in a TB infection that is very hard to treat.

Rifampin

BRAND NAMES
Rifadin, Rifadin IV,
Rimactane

Rifadin 300 mg
(HOECHST MARION ROUSSEL)

▶ Drug Class: Anti-infective/
antitubercular agent

▶ Available in: Capsules,
injection

▶ Available OTC? No

▶ As Generic? Yes

Side Effects

SERIOUS
Difficulty breathing, chills,
pain in muscles and
bones, dizziness,
headache, itching, fever,
shivering, skin rash and
redness, nausea and
vomiting, diarrhea, yel-
low discoloration of the
skin or eyes. Call your
doctor immediately.

COMMON
Reddish orange or brown
discoloration of urine,
saliva, phlegm, stools,
sweat, skin, and tears;
stomach cramps.

LESS COMMON
There are no less-com-
mon side effects associ-
ated with the use of
rifampin.

PRINCIPAL USES
To treat all forms of tuberculosis (TB); must be used
in conjunction with other
antitubercular agents. Also
to prevent the spread of TB
by people who are carriers
of it but who do not have
active disease, and to treat
other bacterial infections
and persons who have been
exposed to certain types of
meningitis-causing bacteria.

HOW THE DRUG WORKS
Rifampin interferes with the
activity of enzymes needed
for the replication of RNA
(ribonucleic acid) in bacterial cells, preventing the bacteria from reproducing.

DOSAGE
To treat tuberculosis—
Adults and teenagers: 600
mg once a day. Children
ages 5 to 12: 4.5 to 9 mg per
lb of body weight once a
day (not more than 600 mg
a day). Older adults: 4.5 mg
per lb once a day. It may be
decreased to twice a week.
To prevent meningitis—
Adults and teenagers: 600
mg twice a day for 2 days.
Children 1 month to 12
years: 9 mg per lb twice a
day for 2 days, or 9 to 18
mg per lb once a day for 4
days. Newborns: 2.3 mg per
lb twice a day for 2 days.

ONSET OF EFFECT
Unknown.

DURATION OF ACTION
Unknown.

DIETARY ADVICE
Take the capsules on an
empty stomach at least 1
hour before or 2 hours after
meals. If you experience
nausea and vomiting from
taking the medication, or
you have trouble swallowing
the pills, mix the contents of
the capsules in with food
such as applesauce.

STORAGE
Store in a tightly sealed container away from heat, moisture, and direct light.

IF YOU MISS A DOSE
Take the drug as soon as
you remember. This will
help keep a constant level
of medication in your system. However, if it is near
the time for the next dose,
skip the missed dose and
resume your regular dosage
schedule. Do not double the
next dose.

STOPPING THE DRUG
Take it as prescribed for the
full treatment period, even if
you feel better before the
scheduled end of therapy.
Treatment may continue for
months or years. The decision to stop taking it should
be made by your doctor.

PROLONGED USE
Consult your doctor about
the need for periodic medical examinations and laboratory tests. If symptoms do
not improve or instead
become worse in 2 to 3
weeks, consult your doctor.

PRECAUTIONS
Over 60: No special problems are expected.

**Driving and Hazardous
Work:** Do not drive or
engage in hazardous work
until you determine how the
medicine affects you.

Alcohol: Avoid alcohol.

Pregnancy: Rifampin, in
conjunction with other antitubercular agents, can be
used to treat tuberculosis in
pregnant women. Before
you take it, tell your doctor
if you are pregnant or plan
to become pregnant.

Breast Feeding: Rifampin
passes into breast milk; caution is advised. Consult your
doctor for specific advice.

Infants and Children:
No special problems are
expected.

Special Concerns:
Rifampin can lower your
white blood cell count and
the number of platelets in
your blood, temporarily
increasing the risk of infection, slowing healing, and
making your gums more
susceptible to bleeding. Try
to delay dental work until
after therapy. Soft contact
lenses may become perma-
nently discolored. Oral
contraceptives containing
estrogen may be ineffective
during use.

OVERDOSE
Symptoms: Whole-body
itching, facial swelling,
changes in mental state,
reddish orange discol-
oration of skin, eyes, and
mouth.

What to Do: Call your
doctor, emergency medical
services (EMS), or the
nearest poison control center immediately.

DRUG INTERACTIONS
Consult your doctor for
advice if you are taking
theophylline, anticoagulants,
oral antidiabetics, azole antifungal agents, anticancer
agents, estrogens, corticosteroids, digitalis drugs,
antiarrhythmics, antitubercular agents, methadone,
phenytoin, verapamil, protease inhibitors, cyclosporine, or tacrolimus (FK506).

FOOD INTERACTIONS
No known food interactions.

DISEASE INTERACTIONS
Consult your doctor if you
have a history of alcohol
abuse. Use of rifampin may
cause complications in
patients with liver disease,
since this organ works to
remove the medication from
the body.

Rifapentine

▶ Drug Class: Anti-infective/
antitubercular agent

▶ Available in: Tablets

▶ Available OTC? No

▶ As Generic? No

Side Effects

SERIOUS
Pain or swelling in joints, fever, dizziness, headache, itching, skin rash and redness, loss of appetite, nausea, vomiting, diarrhea, yellow discoloration of the skin or eyes, dark urine. Call your doctor immediately.

COMMON
Reddish orange or brown discoloration of urine, saliva, phlegm, stools, sweat, skin, tears, and breast milk; stomach cramps.

LESS COMMON
There are no less-common side effects associated with the use of rifapentine.

PRINCIPAL USES
To treat active pulmonary tuberculosis; must be used in conjunction with other antitubercular agents (such as isoniazid, pyrazinamide, ethambutol, and streptomycin) to which the bacteria is susceptible.

HOW THE DRUG WORKS
Rifapentine interferes with the activity of enzymes needed for the formation of RNA (ribonucleic acid) in the bacteria that causes tuberculosis, preventing them from reproducing.

DOSAGE
For first 2 months of treatment: 600 mg (four 150 mg tablets) twice a week (with no more than 3 days between doses) in combination with other antitubercular agents. For the next 4 months of treatment: 600 mg once a week in conjunction with other antitubercular agents.

ONSET OF EFFECT
Unknown.

DURATION OF ACTION
Unknown.

DIETARY ADVICE
Take with liquid or food to minimize stomach irritation.

STORAGE
Store in a tightly sealed container away from heat, moisture, and direct light.

IF YOU MISS A DOSE
It is critical to take each dose to prevent the development of bacteria resistant to the drug's action. If you do miss a dose, take it as soon as you remember. This will help keep a constant level of medication in your system. However, if it is near the time for the next dose, skip the missed dose and resume regular dosage schedule. Do not double the next dose.

STOPPING THE DRUG
Take it as prescribed for the full treatment period. Treatment may continue for months or years. The decision to stop taking it should be made by your doctor.

PROLONGED USE
Tuberculosis bacteria must be tested for sensitivity to the drug (and other tuberculosis medications) before starting treatment and throughout the course of therapy. If symptoms do not improve or instead become worse in 2 to 3 weeks, consult your doctor.

PRECAUTIONS
Over 60: No special problems are expected.

Driving and Hazardous Work: No special problems are expected.

Alcohol: Avoid alcohol.

Pregnancy: Adequate studies of rifapentine use during pregnancy have not been done. This drug should be taken during pregnancy only if potential benefits clearly outweigh the risks to the unborn child.

Breast Feeding: It is not known whether rifapentine passes into breast milk; caution is advised. Consult your doctor for advice. Rifapentine may produce a redish orange or brown discoloration of body fluids, including breast milk.

Infants and Children: Safety and effectiveness for use by children under the age of 12 have not been determined.

Special Concerns: Rifapentine can lower your white blood cell count and the number of platelets in your blood, temporarily increasing the risk of infec-

tion, slowing healing, and making your gums more susceptible to bleeding. Try to delay dental work until after therapy. Soft contact lenses or dentures may become permanently discolored. Oral hormone contraceptives may be ineffective during treatment with rifapentine.

OVERDOSE
Symptoms: No overdoses have been reported.

What to Do: If someone takes a much larger dose than prescribed, seek medical attention right away.

DRUG INTERACTIONS
Rifapentine should be used with extreme caution, if at all, with protease inhibitors such as indinavir. Consult your doctor for advice if you are taking hormonal contraceptives, anticonvulsants, antiarrythmics, antibiotics, theophylline, anticoagulants, oral antidiabetic drugs, azole antifungal agents, barbiturates, benzodiazepines, beta-blockers, calcium channel blockers, clofibrate, haloperidol, estrogens and progestins, corticosteroids, digitalis drugs, other antitubercular agents, levothyroxine, narcotic analgesics, quinine, zidovudine, delavirdine, lamivudine, sildenafil citrate, tricyclic antidepressants, cyclosporine, or tacrolimus (FK506).

FOOD INTERACTIONS
No known food interactions.

DISEASE INTERACTIONS
Rifapentine should not be used if you have porphyria. Consult your doctor if you have a history of alcohol abuse. Use of rifapentine may cause complications in patients with liver disease, since this organ works to remove the medication from the body.

Riluzole

Rilutek 50 mg
(RHONE-POLENC RORER)

▶ Drug Class: Neuroprotective

▶ Available in: Tablets

▶ Available OTC? No

▶ As Generic? No

Side Effects

SERIOUS
No serious side effects are known to be associated with the use of riluzole.

COMMON
Elevated liver enzymes (detectable by your doctor); occurrence of some of the symptoms of ALS, including weakness, muscle fatigue, lack of energy, nausea, vomiting.

LESS COMMON
Dizziness, numbness or tingling around the mouth, drowsiness, loss of appetite, diarrhea.

PRINCIPAL USES
To treat amyotrophic lateral sclerosis (ALS, more commonly known as Lou Gehrig's disease). Riluzole is not a cure for the disease, but it is the first and currently only drug approved for the treatment of ALS. It can extend the life of the patient in the early stages of the disease and delay the time before a tracheostomy (surgical opening of the throat) is required to permit breathing.

HOW THE DRUG WORKS
ALS is a disease marked by degeneration of the motor nerve cells of the spinal cord, lower brain stem, and cortex, resulting in gradual loss of muscle control; the senses and mental faculties are not affected. The deterioration of the muscles governing crucial body functions—especially swallowing and breathing—eventually proves fatal. The exact way in which riluzole works is unclear, but it appears to protect nerve tissue against degenerative changes, which slows the course of ALS.

DOSAGE
Usual adult dose: 50 mg every 12 hours. It should be taken at the same time each day. Do not change the dosage on your own without consulting your doctor.

ONSET OF EFFECT
Unknown.

DURATION OF ACTION
Unknown.

DIETARY ADVICE
Riluzole works best when taken at the same time each day, with a full glass of water, at least 1 hour before or 2 hours after eating.

STORAGE
Store in a tightly sealed container away from heat, moisture, and direct light.

IF YOU MISS A DOSE
Skip the missed dose and resume your regular dosage schedule the next day. Do not double the next dose.

STOPPING THE DRUG
No special problems are expected.

PROLONGED USE
Prolonged use of riluzole is often necessary.

PRECAUTIONS
Over 60: No special problems are expected.

Driving and Hazardous Work: Do not drive or engage in hazardous work until you determine how this medication affects you.

Alcohol: Avoid alcohol.

Pregnancy: Adequate studies of the use of riluzole during pregnancy have not been done. Consult your doctor for specific advice.

Breast Feeding: It is not known if riluzole passes into breast milk, but in light of the potentially serious risks to nursing infants, it is recommended that women using this medication refrain from breast feeding.

Infants and Children: Riluzole is generally not prescribed for children; safety and effectiveness for patients in this age group have not been established.

OVERDOSE
Symptoms: No cases of overdose have been reported.

What to Do: Emergency instructions not applicable.

DRUG INTERACTIONS
Consult your doctor for specific advice if you are taking any other prescription or over-the-counter medication.

FOOD INTERACTIONS
No known food interactions.

DISEASE INTERACTIONS
No disease interactions have been reported.

Rimantadine Hydrochloride

Flumadine 100 mg
(FOREST)

▶ Drug Class: Antiviral

▶ Available in: Syrup, tablets

▶ Available OTC? No

▶ As Generic? No

Side Effects

SERIOUS
No serious side effects are associated with rimantadine.

COMMON
Nausea and vomiting, mild diarrhea.

LESS COMMON
Dizziness, trouble concentrating, nervousness, dry mouth, loss of appetite, stomach pain, unusual fatigue, insomnia.

PRINCIPAL USES
To prevent or treat influenza type A.

HOW THE DRUG WORKS
Rimantadine interferes with the activity of the virus's genetic material, blocking an essential step in the the process of viral replication. The drug affects only certain susceptible strains of the influenza type A virus.

DOSAGE
Adults and children age 10 and older: 100 mg, 2 times a day, or 200 mg once a day. Children up to age 10: 2.3 mg per lb of body weight, once a day; the dose should not exceed a total of 150 mg daily. Frail, older adults or those with impaired liver or kidney function: 100 mg once a day. The drug should be continued for about 7 days.

ONSET OF EFFECT
Unknown. For prevention of flu, take rimantadine prior to or immediately after exposure to others with influenza.

DURATION OF ACTION
Unknown.

DIETARY ADVICE
Take it on an empty stomach at least 1 hour before or 2 hours after a meal.

STORAGE
Store in a tightly sealed container away from heat and direct light. Do not allow the syrup to freeze.

IF YOU MISS A DOSE
Take it as soon as you remember. If it is near the time for the next dose, skip the missed dose and resume your regular dosage schedule. Do not double the next dose.

STOPPING THE DRUG
It is important to take rimantadine for the full treatment period as prescribed, whether for treatment or prevention of influenza. If you have the flu, do not stop taking the drug before the scheduled end of therapy even if you begin to feel better, as this may lead to a relapse.

PROLONGED USE
If your symptoms do not improve or if they become worse in a few days, you should consult your doctor. You should see your doctor regularly for tests and examinations if you take this medicine for a prolonged period.

PRECAUTIONS
Over 60: Adverse reactions may be more likely and more severe; a smaller dose is commonly prescribed.

Driving and Hazardous Work: Do not drive or engage in hazardous work until you determine how the medicine affects you.

Alcohol: Avoid alcohol.

Pregnancy: Rimantadine has been shown to cause birth defects in animals. Human studies have not been done. Before you take rimantadine, tell your physician if you are pregnant or plan to become pregnant.

Breast Feeding: Rimantadine may pass into breast milk, although it is unknown if this poses any risks to the nursing infant. Consult your doctor for specific advice.

Infants and Children: In tests, rimantadine was not demonstrated to cause unusual side effects or problems in children over 1 year of age. Tests in children under 1 year of age have not been done. Consult your pediatrician for advice.

Special Concerns: Ask your doctor about receiving an influenza vaccine (flu shot) if you have not yet had one. If you are taking the syrup form of rimantadine, use a special measuring spoon to dispense the dose accurately. If the medicine causes insomnia, take it several hours before going to bed.

OVERDOSE
Symptoms: Agitation, heart rhythm abnormalities.

What to Do: An overdose of rimantadine is unlikely to be life-threatening. However, if someone takes a much larger dose than prescribed, call your doctor, emergency medical services (EMS), or the nearest poison control center.

DRUG INTERACTIONS
Other drugs may interact with rimantadine; consult your doctor for specific advice if you are taking any other prescription or over-the-counter medication.

FOOD INTERACTIONS
No known food interactions.

DISEASE INTERACTIONS
Consult your doctor if you have a history of epilepsy or other seizures. Use of rimantadine may cause complications in patients with liver or kidney disease, since these organs work together to remove the medication from the body.

Rimexolone

▶ Drug Class: Corticosteroid

▶ Available in: Ophthalmic suspension

▶ Available OTC? No

▶ As Generic? No

Side Effects

SERIOUS
Decreased or blurred vision (from cataract); eye pain, nausea, vomiting (from increased eye pressure); pain, redness, sensitivity to bright light, discharge (from eye infection). Call your doctor immediately if you experience any of these signs or symptoms. This drug may trigger a recurrence of herpes infection of the eye; mention any previous herpes infection to your doctor.

COMMON
Increased eye pressure; this is usually reversed once the drug is stopped.

LESS COMMON
Burning, stinging, redness, or watering of eyes.

PRINCIPAL USES
To control inflammation and prevent potentially permanent damage that may result from conditions involving inflammation in the tissues of the eye. Such conditions may occur in the aftermath of eye surgery or in association with uveitis (inflammation of the uvea, the central portion of the eye).

HOW THE DRUG WORKS
Rimexolone inhibits the release of natural substances that stimulate an inflammatory reaction and pain or scarring in eye tissues.

DOSAGE
For treatment of postoperative eye inflammation: Instill 1 or 2 drops into affected eye(s) 4 times a day or as directed by your doctor. For uveitis: Instill 1 or 2 drops every hour during waking hours for the first week. The dose is then gradually tapered according to the doctor's instructions until uveitis resolves. Always shake the medicine well before using it.

ONSET OF EFFECT
Unknown.

DURATION OF ACTION
Unknown.

DIETARY ADVICE
No special restrictions.

STORAGE
Store in a tightly sealed container away from heat, moisture, and direct light. Do not allow it to freeze.

IF YOU MISS A DOSE
Apply it as soon as you remember. If it is near the time for the next dose, skip the missed dose and resume your regular dosage schedule. Do not double the next dose.

STOPPING THE DRUG
Take this drug as prescribed for the full treatment period, even if symptoms begin to improve before the scheduled end of therapy.

PROLONGED USE
See your doctor regularly for tests and examinations if you must take this drug for a prolonged period.

PRECAUTIONS
Over 60: No special problems are expected.

Driving and Hazardous Work: Do not drive or engage in hazardous work until you determine how the medicine affects your vision.

Alcohol: No special precautions are necessary.

Pregnancy: Adequate human studies have not been done; rimexolone should be used during pregnancy only if benefits clearly outweigh potential risks.

Breast Feeding: It is unknown if rimexolone passes into breast milk; caution is advised. Consult your doctor for specific advice.

Infants and Children: Safety and effectiveness have not been established for children.

Special Concerns: To use the eye drops, first wash your hands. Tilt your head back. Gently apply pressure to the inside corner of the eyelid and with the index finger of the same hand, pull downward on the lower eyelid to make a space. Drop the medicine into this space and close your eye. Apply pressure for 1 or 2 minutes while keeping the eye closed without blinking.

Then wash your hands again. Make sure the tip of the dropper does not touch your eye, finger or any other surface. If your symptoms do not improve in 5 to 7 days or if they become worse, check with your doctor. Wearing contact lenses while using this medication may increase the risk of infection. Your doctor may tell you not to wear contact lenses during treatment and for a day or two afterward.

OVERDOSE
Symptoms: When used topically, an overdose of rimexolone is very unlikely. Inadvertent oral ingestion, however, may cause fever, muscle pain, loss of appetite, dizziness, fainting, and breathing trouble.

What to Do: In case of accidental ingestion, call your doctor, emergency medical services (EMS), or the nearest poison control center right away.

DRUG INTERACTIONS
No drug interactions have been reported. Nonetheless, it is wise to consult your doctor before taking any other prescription or over-the-counter eye medication.

FOOD INTERACTIONS
No food interactions have been reported.

DISEASE INTERACTIONS
Consult your doctor if you have a history of cataracts, diabetes mellitus, glaucoma, herpes infection of the eye, fungal infection of the eye, or any other eye infection.

Risedronate Sodium

BRAND NAME
Actonel

▶ Drug Class: Bisphosphonate inhibitor of bone resorption

▶ Available in: Tablets

▶ Available OTC? No

▶ As Generic? No

Side Effects

SERIOUS
Serious side effects are rare and may include chest pain, swelling of the arms, legs, face, lips, tongue, or throat.

COMMON
Flu-like symptoms, diarrhea, abdominal pain, nausea, constipation, joint pain, headache, dizziness, skin rash.

LESS COMMON
Weakness, growth of tumors, belching, bone pain, leg cramps, muscle weakness, bronchitis, sinus infection, ringing in the ears, dry eye.

PRINCIPAL USES
To treat and prevent osteoporosis in postmenopausal women. Also used to prevent and treat steroid-induced osteoporosis in men and women who are either beginning or continuing treatment with steroids (such as prednisone) for chronic diseases. To treat Paget's disease, a disorder characterized by rapid breakdown and reformation of bone, which can lead to fragility and malformation of bones.

HOW THE DRUG WORKS
Healthy bones are continuously remodeled (broken down and then reformed); the minerals and other components of bones are reabsorbed by one set of cells (osteoclasts) and replaced by another set of cells to form new bone. Risedronate suppresses the activity of osteoclasts; consequently, the breakdown of bone tissue occurs more slowly than the laying down of new bone. As a result, bone density and strength are preserved.

DOSAGE
For treatment and prevention of osteoporosis (postmenopausal and steroid-induced): 5 mg a day or one 35-mg dose a week. For Paget's disease: 30 mg once a day for 2 months.

ONSET OF EFFECT
Unknown.

DURATION OF ACTION
Unknown.

DIETARY ADVICE
Take it with a full glass of plain water. Taking risedronate with food or beverages (including mineral water) other than plain water is likely to reduce the absorption of the drug from the intestine. Take the tablets at least 30 minutes before the first food or drink of the day (other than plain water). The drug must be taken in an upright position. Maintain adequate vitamin D and calcium intake; however, vitamin or mineral supplements should be taken no sooner than 2 hours after taking the drug.

STORAGE
Store in a tightly sealed container away from heat, moisture, and direct light.

IF YOU MISS A DOSE
If you miss a dose on one day, do not double the dose the next day. Resume your regular dosage schedule.

STOPPING THE DRUG
Take it as prescribed for the full treatment period. The decision to stop taking the drug should be made in consultation with your physician.

PROLONGED USE
For Paget's disease: Risedronate is generally prescribed for a 2-month course of therapy. A second round of treatment may be considered after this 2 month period. Consult your doctor.

PRECAUTIONS
Over 60: No special problems are expected.

Driving and Hazardous Work: Do not drive or engage in hazardous work until you determine how the medicine affects you.

Alcohol: No special precautions are necessary.

Pregnancy: Consult your doctor about whether the benefits of taking the medicine outweigh the potential risks to the unborn child.

Breast Feeding: Risedronate may pass into breast milk; caution is advised. Consult your doctor for specific advice.

Infants and Children: Safety and effectiveness have not been established for children under age 18.

Special Concerns: Remain upright for at least 30 minutes after taking this medication. If you develop symptoms of esophageal disease (such as difficulty or pain when swallowing; chest pain, specifically behind the sternum; or severe or persistent heartburn), contact your doctor before continuing risedronate.

OVERDOSE
Symptoms: No cases of overdose have been reported.

What to Do: If someone takes a much larger dose than prescribed, call your doctor, emergency medical services (EMS), or a poison control center.

DRUG INTERACTIONS
Aluminum-, calcium-, or magnesium-containing antacids, if needed, should be taken no sooner than 2 hours after taking risedronate.

FOOD INTERACTIONS
No known food interactions, although risedronate works best when taken on an empty stomach.

DISEASE INTERACTIONS
Kidney impairment or a gastrointestinal disease may increase the risk of side effects. Low blood calcium levels and vitamin D deficiency must be treated before using risedronate.

Risperdal 1 mg
(JANSSEN)

▶ Drug Class: Antipsychotic

▶ Available in: Tablets, oral solution

▶ Available OTC? No

▶ As Generic? No

Side Effects

SERIOUS
Rapid heartbeat, profuse sweating, seizures, difficulty breathing, neck stiffness, swelling of the tongue, difficulty swallowing. Also a rare condition can develop called neuroleptic malignant syndrome, characterized by stiffness or spasms of the muscles, high fever, and confusion or disorientation. Call your doctor immediately.

COMMON
Nausea, reduced perspiration, dry mouth, blurred vision, drowsiness, shaking of the hands, muscle stiffness, stooped posture.

LESS COMMON
Difficult urination, menstrual irregularities, breast pain or swelling, unexpected weight gain, uncontrolled movements of the tongue, fever, chills, sore throat, unusual bruising or bleeding, heart palpitations, skin rash, itching, increased sensitivity of the skin to sunlight.

PRINCIPAL USES
To treat psychotic conditions (severe mental disorders characterized by distorted thoughts, perceptions, and emotions), such as schizophrenia.

HOW THE DRUG WORKS
While the exact mechanism of action of risperidone is unknown, it appears to alter the activity of certain chemicals in the central nervous system to produce a tranquilizing and antipsychotic effect.

DOSAGE
Adults and teenagers— 2 to 6 mg a day in 1 or 2 divided doses. Dosage may be adjusted by your doctor, if needed, at intervals of not less than one week. Older adults— To start, 0.5 mg, 2 times a day; may be increased to 3 mg a day.

ONSET OF EFFECT
Sedation may occur within minutes, but onset of antipsychotic effect may take hours to occur or may not occur until days or weeks after the beginning of therapy.

DURATION OF ACTION
At least 12 to 24 hours, although effects may persist for several days.

DIETARY ADVICE
No special restrictions.

STORAGE
Store in a tightly sealed container away from heat, moisture, and direct light.

IF YOU MISS A DOSE
Take it as soon as you remember. However, if it is near the time for the next dose, skip the missed dose and resume your regular dosage schedule. Do not double the next dose.

STOPPING THE DRUG
The decision to stop taking the drug should be made in consultation with your physician.

PROLONGED USE
Prolonged use may lead to tardive dyskinesia (involuntary movements of the jaw, lips, tongue, and, in rare cases, the arms, legs, hands, or body). Consult your doctor about the need for follow-up evaluations and tests if you must take this drug for an extended period.

PRECAUTIONS
Over 60: Adverse reactions may be more likely and more severe in older patients.

Driving and Hazardous Work: Do not drive or engage in hazardous work until you determine how the medicine affects you.

Alcohol: Avoid alcohol.

Pregnancy: Adequate studies have not been done. Before you take risperidone, tell your doctor if you are pregnant or plan to become pregnant.

Breast Feeding: It is not known if risperidone passes into breast milk; caution is advised. Consult your doctor for specific advice.

Infants and Children: Risperidone is not commonly prescribed for patients under age 18.

Special Concerns: Avoid prolonged exposure to high temperatures or hot climates. Drink plenty of fluids and stay cool in the summertime. Avoid overexposure to sunlight until you determine if the drug heightens your skin's sensitivity to ultraviolet light.

OVERDOSE
Symptoms: Drowsiness, rapid heartbeat, low blood pressure, seizures.

What to Do: Call your doctor, emergency medical services (EMS), or the nearest poison control center immediately.

DRUG INTERACTIONS
Other drugs may interact with risperidone. Consult your doctor for advice if you are taking an antidepressant, bromocriptine, carbamazepine, clozapine, high blood pressure medication, levodopa, pergolide, or any medications that depress the central nervous system, including antihistamines, cold remedies, decongestants, and tranquilizers.

FOOD INTERACTIONS
No known food interactions.

DISEASE INTERACTIONS
Consult your doctor if you have Parkinson's disease or any movement disorder, glaucoma, epilepsy, liver disease, kidney disease, heart disease.

Ritonavir

Norvir 100 mg
(ABBOTT)

▶ Drug Class: Antiviral/protease inhibitor

▶ Available in: Capsules, oral solution

▶ Available OTC? No

▶ As Generic? No

Side Effects

SERIOUS
High blood sugar (diabetes) has occurred in patients taking drugs of this class, although a cause-and-effect relationship has not been established. Contact your doctor if you develop increased thirst or excessive urination.

COMMON
Diarrhea, abdominal pain, low-grade fever, nausea, gas, skin rash, fatigue, numbness or tingling around the mouth or in the arms and legs. Treat diarrhea with over-the-counter fiber supplements or antidiarrheal drugs. Side effects are most common during the first weeks of therapy.

LESS COMMON
Back pain, fever, headache or migraines, loss of appetite, gastrointestinal bleeding, mouth ulcers, vomiting, joint pain, muscle pain or cramps, anxiety, depression, dizziness, insomnia, seizures, drowsiness, breathing difficulty, skin problems, eye disorders, impaired sexual function.

PRINCIPAL USES
To treat HIV (human immunodeficiency virus), often in combination with other drugs. While not a cure for HIV, this drug may suppress replication of the virus and delay the progression of the disease.

HOW THE DRUG WORKS
Ritonavir blocks the activity of a viral protease, an enzyme that is needed by HIV to reproduce. Blocking the protease causes HIV to make copies that cannot infect new cells.

DOSAGE
Adults and children 12 and over: 600 mg, 2 times a day. Dose should be started lower and increased gradually, starting with 300 mg, 2 times a day for 1 to 2 days, then 400 mg, 2 times a day for 1 to 3 days, then 500 mg, 2 times a day for 1 to 8 days, then 600 mg, 2 times a day thereafter. The full dose should be reached in no later than 14 days. Lower doses (400 to 500 mg, 2 times a day) are sometimes used when ritonavir is combined with other drugs such as saquinavir. Children ages 2 to 12: 400 mg per square meter of body mass 2 times a day, not to exceed 600 mg 2 times a day. Dose should be started lower and increased gradually, starting with 250 mg per square meter and increased at 2- to 3-day intervals by 50 mg per square meter 2 times a day.

ONSET OF EFFECT
Unknown. Maximum effect may take 12 to 16 weeks.

DURATION OF ACTION
Unknown. Effects of the drug may be prolonged if it is used with other drugs and the virus is maximally suppressed.

DIETARY ADVICE
Take it with food. The solution can be mixed with chocolate milk to improve taste; take it within 1 hour after mixing.

STORAGE
Store oral solution at room temperature in a tightly sealed container. Refrigerate capsules.

IF YOU MISS A DOSE
Take it as soon as you remember. If it is near the time for the next dose, skip the missed dose and resume regular dosage schedule. Do not double the next dose.

STOPPING THE DRUG
Consult your physician.

PROLONGED USE
See your doctor regularly for tests and examinations.

PRECAUTIONS
Over 60: No special advice.

Driving and Hazardous Work: Avoid such activities until you determine how the medicine affects you.

Alcohol: Avoid alcohol if liver function is impaired.

Pregnancy: Adequate studies have not been done; consult your doctor for advice. There is no evidence the drug will reduce the risk of transmitting the virus from the mother to the fetus.

Breast Feeding: Women infected with HIV should not breast feed, to avoid transmitting the virus to an uninfected child.

Infants and Children: Not recommended for use by children under age 2.

Special Concerns: Do not switch between the capsules and solution without consulting your doctor; the

body absorbs them at different rates. Do not take ritonavir with the herbal supplement St. John's wort because it may lead to drug resistance. Taking ritonavir does not eliminate the risk of passing the AIDS virus to other persons. Take appropriate preventive measures.

OVERDOSE
Symptoms: Temporary numbness, tingling, or prickling.

What to Do: An overdose is unlikely to occur or be life-threatening. If, however, someone takes a much larger dose than prescribed, seek medical assistance right away.

DRUG INTERACTIONS
You should not take ritonavir with the following drugs because serious or life-threatening adverse effects such as heartbeat irregularities, breathing difficulties, or excessive sedation could occur: amiodarone, astemizole, bepridil, , flecainide, propafenone, quinidine, terfenadine, midazolam, triazolam, pimozide, ergotamine, or dihydroergotamine. Use of ritonavir with the cholesterol-lowering statin medications (such as simvastatin, lovastatin, atorvastatin, fluvastatin, and pravastatin) is not recommended. Consult your doctor for specific advice if you are taking any other prescription or over-the-counter medication.

FOOD INTERACTIONS
Increasing the amount of fat in the diet can help to reduce side effects.

DISEASE INTERACTIONS
Consult your doctor if you have liver disease or any other medical condition.

Rivastigmine Tartrate

BRAND NAME
Exelon

▶ Drug Class: Reversible cholinesterase inhibitor

▶ Available in: Capsules, oral solution

▶ Available OTC? No

▶ As Generic? No

Side Effects

SERIOUS
Possible gastrointestinal bleeding. No other serious side effects are associated with the use of rivastigmine.

COMMON
Significant nausea, vomiting, loss of appetite, and weight loss. Other common side effects include heartburn, weakness, dizziness, diarrhea, abdominal pain.

LESS COMMON
Increased sweating, fatigue, malaise, headache, drowsiness, tremor, flatulence, insomnia, depression, anxiety.

PRINCIPAL USES
To treat mild to moderate Alzheimer's disease.

HOW THE DRUG WORKS
The exact mechanism of action is unknown. However, rivastigmine is believed to work by inhibiting acetylcholinesterase enzymes, which reduces the breakdown of acetylcholine, a brain chemical crucial to memory. Acetylcholine deficiency is thought to result in memory loss associated with Alzheimer's disease.

DOSAGE
To start, 1.5 mg twice a day. After two weeks of treatment, your doctor may increase the dose to 3 mg twice a day. The dose may be further increased at no less than 2-week intervals to 4.5 mg twice a day and then to the maximum dose of 6 mg twice a day, if tolerated.

ONSET OF EFFECT
Unknown.

DURATION OF ACTION
Unknown.

DIETARY ADVICE
Rivastigmine should be taken with meals in the morning and evening. The oral solution may be swallowed directly from the syringe or mixed with a small glass of water, cold fruit juice, or soda.

STORAGE
Store in a tightly sealed container away from heat, moisture, and direct light. Do not freeze the oral solution.

IF YOU MISS A DOSE
Take it as soon as you remember, unless the time for your next scheduled dose is within the next 2 hours. If so, do not take the missed dose. Take your next scheduled dose at the proper time and resume your regular dosage schedule. Do not double the next dose. If therapy has been interrupted for several days or longer, consult your physician.

STOPPING THE DRUG
The decision to stop taking the drug should be made in consultation with your physician.

PROLONGED USE
No problems are expected with long-term use.

PRECAUTIONS
Over 60: No special problems are expected.

Driving and Hazardous Work: Do not drive or engage in hazardous work until you determine how the medicine affects you.

Alcohol: Avoid alcohol while using this medication.

Pregnancy: In some animal studies, large doses of rivastigmine were shown to cause problems. Before you take rivastigmine, tell your doctor if you are pregnant or plan to become pregnant.

Breast Feeding: It is not known whether rivastigmine passes into breast milk; caution is advised. Consult your doctor for specific advice.

Infants and Children: Rivastigmine is not intended for use in children.

Special Concerns: Before you have any surgery or dental or emergency treatment, tell the doctor or dentist in charge that you are taking rivastigmine. Rivastigmine will not cure Alzheimer's disease and will not stop the disease from getting worse, but it will improve cognitive ability of some patients. Caretakers should be instructed in the correct way to administer the oral solution of rivastigmine.

OVERDOSE
Symptoms: Severe nausea, vomiting, increased salivation, sweating, slow heartbeat, low blood pressure, irregular breathing, unconsciousness, increased muscle weakness, death.

What to Do: Call your doctor, emergency medical services (EMS), or the nearest poison control center immediately.

DRUG INTERACTIONS
Nonsteroidal anti-inflammatory drugs (NSAIDs) may increase the risk of peptic ulcer or gastrointestinal bleeding when taken with rivastigmine.

FOOD INTERACTIONS
No known food interactions.

DISEASE INTERACTIONS
Caution is advised when taking rivastigmine. Consult your doctor if you have any of the following: asthma, epilepsy or a history of seizures, heart problems, intestinal blockage, stomach or duodenal ulcer, liver disease, or urinary problems.

Rizatriptan Benzoate

BRAND NAMES
Maxalt, Maxalt-MLT

▶ Drug Class: Antimigraine/ antiheadache drug

▶ Available in: Tablets, orally disintegrating wafers

▶ Available OTC? No

▶ As Generic? No

Side Effects

SERIOUS
Serious side effects with rizatriptan are rare. However, rizatriptan may cause a heart attack, chest pain or tightness, sudden or severe abdominal pain, shortness of breath, wheezing, heartbeat irregularities, swelling of eyelids, face, or lips, skin rash, or hives. Seek emergency medical assistance immediately.

COMMON
Sensations of cold or warmth, dizziness, drowsiness, fatigue, hot flashes, diarrhea, vomiting, flushing, difficulty concentrating, tremor, false sense of well-being, prickling or tingling sensations.

LESS COMMON
Chills, sensitivity to heat, weakness, stiffness, muscle pain, spasms, and cramps, bone and joint pain, indigestion, increased thirst, flatulence, nervousness, insomnia, anxiety, mental depression, confusion, sore throat, nasal irritation, nose bleeds, ringing in the ears, vision difficulties, increased sweating, itching, mild rash, frequent urination.

PRINCIPAL USES
To treat severe, acute migraine headaches. Rizatriptan is not intended as a migraine preventive or for use against any other kinds of pain or headache, including basilar and hemiplegic migraines. Your doctor will determine whether this medication is appropriate in your particular case.

HOW THE DRUG WORKS
The exact mechanism of rizatriptan's action is unknown.

DOSAGE
A single dose ranging from 5 to 10 mg is generally effective. If the migraine returns or there is only partial relief, the dose may be repeated once after 2 hours, but no more than 30 mg should be taken in a 24-hour period. Since individual response to rizatriptan may vary, your doctor will determine the appropriate dosage. A general recommendation is to take one 5 mg tablet as the initial dose.

ONSET OF EFFECT
Within 2 hours.

DURATION OF ACTION
Up to 24 hours.

DIETARY ADVICE
The medication can be taken with or without food.

STORAGE
Store in a tightly sealed container away from heat, moisture, and direct light.

IF YOU MISS A DOSE
Not applicable, since the drug is taken only when necessary.

STOPPING THE DRUG
Consult your doctor before discontinuing rizatriptan.

PROLONGED USE
No special problems are expected. Patients at risk for heart disease should undergo periodic medical tests and evaluation.

PRECAUTIONS
Over 60: This drug should not be used unless the presence of coronary heart disease has been ruled out through appropriate diagnostic tests.

Driving and Hazardous Work: Some people feel drowsy or dizzy during or following a migraine attack or after taking rizatriptan. Avoid driving or other tasks requiring concentration if you have such symptoms.

Alcohol: No special warnings, although alcohol may trigger or exacerbate migraine headaches.

Pregnancy: Adequate human studies have not been done. Discuss with your doctor the relative risks and benefits of using rizatriptan while pregnant.

Breast Feeding: Rizatriptan may pass into breast milk; consult your doctor for specific advice.

Infants and Children: Safety and effectiveness have not been established for children under age 18.

Special Concerns: Serious, but rare, heart-related problems may occur after taking rizatriptan. Rizatriptan should not be used by anyone with any symptoms of coronary artery disease (chest pain or tightness, shortness of breath). Anyone at risk for unrecognized CAD—such as postmenopausal women, men over the age of 40, or those with known risk factors for heart disease (hypertension, high

blood cholesterol levels, obesity, diabetes, strong family history of heart disease, or cigarette smoking)—should have the first dose of rizatriptan administered in a doctor's office, and then only after tests show they are probably free of coronary artery disease.

OVERDOSE
Symptoms: No overdoses have been reported.

What to Do: Although overdose is unlikely, if you take a much larger dose than prescribed, call your doctor, emergency medical services (EMS), or the nearest poison control center immediately.

DRUG INTERACTIONS
Do not take rizatriptan within 24 hours of taking almotriptan, naratriptan, sumatriptan, zolmitriptan, ergotamine-containing medication, dihydroergotamine mesylate, or methysergide mesylate. Rizatriptan and MAO inhibitors such as phenelzine, tranylcypromine, procarbazine, and selegiline should not be used within 14 days of each other. Rizatriptan should be used with caution in patients taking SSRIs (selective serotonin reuptake inhibitors), which include fluoxetine, fluvoxamine, paroxetine, and sertraline.

FOOD INTERACTIONS
No known food interactions.

DISEASE INTERACTIONS
You should not take rizatriptan if you have a history of angina, heart disease, stroke, uncontrolled hypertension, heartbeat irregularities, or peripheral vascular disease. Rizatriptan should be used with caution in patients with liver disease or severely impaired kidney function.

699

Ropinirole Hydrochloride

BRAND NAME
Requip

▶ Drug Class: Antiparkinsonism drug

▶ Available in: Tablets

▶ Available OTC? No

▶ As Generic? No

Side Effects

SERIOUS
Chest pain, heart rhythm irregularities, confusion, hallucinations. Call your doctor immediately.

COMMON
Nausea, dizziness, faintness, sweating, or loss of consciousness, caused by a significant drop in blood pressure that occurs when rising from a seated or lying position (orthostatic hypotension). Also unusual drowsiness, fatigue, indigestion, vomiting, increased susceptibility to viral infection, headache, impaired ability to execute voluntary movements.

LESS COMMON
Flushing, dry mouth, increased sweating, weakness, swelling of the legs or feet, general feeling of illness, pain, decreased reflexes, abdominal pain, loss of appetite, flatulence, amnesia, impaired concentration, yawning, erectile dysfunction, bronchitis, sore throat, shortness of breath, vision abnormalities, increased incidence of accidental injury, tremor, constipation, diarrhea, joint pain, arthritis, anxiety, nervousness.

PRINCIPAL USES
To treat signs and symptoms of Parkinson's disease.

HOW THE DRUG WORKS
Ropinirole is believed to act by stimulating specific dopamine receptors in the brain, enhancing control over voluntary movements.

DOSAGE
Week 1: 0.25 mg, 3 times a day. Doses may be gradually increased on an individual basis to achieve maximal benefit with the least side effects. Week 2: 0.5 mg, 3 times a day. Week 3: 0.75 mg, 3 times a day. Week 4: 1 mg, 3 times a day. After week 4, if necessary, daily dosage may be increased by 1.5 mg per day on a weekly basis up to a dose of 9 mg a day, and then by 3 mg per day weekly to a total dose of 24 mg a day.

ONSET OF EFFECT
Unknown.

DURATION OF ACTION
Unknown.

DIETARY ADVICE
Ropinirole can be taken without regard to meals. However, taking it with food may help to reduce the risk of stomach upset.

STORAGE
Store in a tightly sealed container away from heat, moisture, and direct light.

IF YOU MISS A DOSE
Take it as soon as you remember. If it is near the time for the next dose, skip the missed dose and resume your regular dosage schedule. Do not double the next dose.

STOPPING THE DRUG
Ropinirole should be discontinued gradually over a 7-day period. The frequency of dosage should be reduced from 3 times a day to 2 times a day for 4 days. For the remaining 3 days, the frequency should be reduced to once a day before completely discontinuing the drug.

PROLONGED USE
Side effects are more likely with prolonged use.

PRECAUTIONS
Over 60: Adverse effects such as hallucinations are more likely and may be more severe in older patients. A reduced dose may be necessary.

Driving and Hazardous Work: Do not drive or engage in dangerous work until you determine how ropinirole affects you.

Alcohol: Alcohol should be avoided because this medicine increases its effects.

Pregnancy: Adequate human studies have not been done. Before taking ropinirole, tell your doctor if you are or plan to become pregnant. Discuss with your doctor the relative risks and benefits of using this drug while pregnant.

Breast Feeding: Ropinirole may pass into breast milk; caution is advised. Consult your doctor for specific advice.

Infants and Children: Ropinirole is not recommended for children under the age of 18.

Special Concerns: This drug may cause dizziness and faintness, especially when getting up out of a chair or sitting up after lying down (a condition known as postural or orthostatic hypertension, characterized by temporary episodes of excessively low blood pressure). Be cautious and move slowly when arising.

OVERDOSE
Symptoms: An overdose is unlikely to occur. Possible symptoms after an excessive dose may include mild facial paralysis or spasticity, nausea, agitation, drowsiness, sedation, orthostatic hypotension, chest pain, confusion, and vomiting.

What to Do: If someone takes a much larger dose than prescribed, call your doctor, emergency medical services (EMS), or the nearest poison control center immediately.

DRUG INTERACTIONS
Consult your doctor if you are taking any of the following drugs that may interact with ropinirole: ciprofloxacin, metoclopramide, or any sedatives, tranquilizers, or analgesics.

FOOD INTERACTIONS
None reported.

DISEASE INTERACTIONS
None reported.

Ropivacaine Hydrochloride Monohydrate

▶ Drug Class: Local anesthetic

▶ Available in: Injection

▶ Available OTC? No

▶ As Generic? No

Side Effects

SERIOUS
Dizziness, nausea, back pain, fever, headache, burning or prickling sensation, vomiting, anxiety, blurred vision, drowsiness, incoherent speech, metallic taste, numbness or tingling of mouth or lips, itching, restlessness, tremors, twitching, difficulty urinating. Call your doctor immediately.

COMMON
No common side effects have been reported.

LESS COMMON
No less-common side effects have been reported.

PRINCIPAL USES
As a local (site specific) anesthetic to help manage pain during or after surgery and during childbirth (both conventional childbirth and cesarean section).

HOW THE DRUG WORKS
Ropivacaine interferes with the ability of certain nerves to conduct electrical signals, thereby blocking the transmission of nerve impulses that carry pain messages.

DOSAGE
Dosage range and frequency vary considerably based on the reason the drug is being used and the status of the individual patient. Your doctor will determine the proper dose accordingly.

ONSET OF EFFECT
1 to 30 minutes, depending on the concentration and dose of the drug, as well as the site of administration.

DURATION OF ACTION
Depends on the concentration and dose of the drug, as well as the site of administration. Duration ranges from 30 minutes to 8 hours.

DIETARY ADVICE
No special restrictions.

STORAGE
Not applicable; this drug is administered only in a hospital setting.

IF YOU MISS A DOSE
Not applicable; your doctor will decide when to administer doses.

STOPPING THE DRUG
The decision to stop taking the drug should be made by your doctor.

PROLONGED USE
Ropivacaine is not intended for prolonged use.

PRECAUTIONS
Over 60: Adverse reactions may be more likely and more severe in older patients.

Driving and Hazardous Work: Not applicable; this drug is used only in a hospital setting.

Alcohol: Not applicable; this drug is used exclusively in a hospital setting.

Pregnancy: Ropivacaine has been shown in scientific study to cross the placenta, although sufficient studies of whether this poses harm to the fetus have not been done. Use of ropivacaine during the first phase of labor may delay or prolong the second stage by interfering with the mother's reflex urge to push or by reducing the mother's ability to push. If ropivacaine is to be used for surgical purposes (that is, other than childbirth), be sure to tell your doctor if you are pregnant or plan to become pregnant.

Breast Feeding: Ropivacaine may pass into breast milk; however, no problems have been documented. Consult your doctor for advice.

Infants and Children: Safety and efficacy of ropivacaine in children under the age of 12 have not been established.

Special Concerns: Blood pressure, heart rate, neurological status, and respiratory status should be monitored carefully during therapy.

OVERDOSE
Symptoms: Bluish lips or skin, dizziness, seizures.

What to Do: Since ropivacaine is generally used in hospital situations only, emergency procedures will be carried out by hospital personnel if an accidental overdose were to occur.

DRUG INTERACTIONS
Consult your doctor for specific advice if you are taking other local anesthetics, fluvoxamine, imipramine, theophylline, or verapamil.

FOOD INTERACTIONS
No known food interactions.

DISEASE INTERACTIONS
Caution is advised when taking ropivacaine. Consult your doctor if you have heart disease. Use of ropivacaine may cause complications in patients with liver or kidney disease, since these organs work together to remove the medication from the body.

Rosiglitazone Maleate

BRAND NAME
Avandia

▶ Drug Class: Thiazolidine-dione/antidiabetic agent

▶ Available in: Tablets

▶ Available OTC? No

▶ As Generic? No

Side Effects

SERIOUS
No serious side effects have been associated with rosiglitazone.

COMMON
Weight gain.

LESS COMMON
Upper respiratory tract infection, headache, edema (swelling).

PRINCIPAL USES
As a single therapeutic agent or as an adjunct (supplemental) therapy to metformin to control blood glucose (sugar) levels in patients with non-insulin-dependent (type 2) diabetes.

HOW THE DRUG WORKS
Rosiglitazone increases the body's sensitivity and response to its own insulin.

DOSAGE
To start, 4 mg, once a day (in the morning) or in two divided doses (in the morning and evening). Patients not responding adequately to 4 mg a day after 12 weeks may have their dose increased by their doctor to 8 mg once a day or in two divided doses.

ONSET OF EFFECT
Within 2 to 4 weeks.

DURATION OF ACTION
Unknown.

DIETARY ADVICE
Rosiglitazone may be taken with or without food.

STORAGE
Store in a tightly sealed container away from heat, moisture, and direct light.

IF YOU MISS A DOSE
Take it as soon as you remember. If it is near the time for the next dose, skip the missed dose and resume your regular dosage schedule. Do not double the next dose.

STOPPING THE DRUG
The decision to stop taking the drug should be made in consultation with your physician.

PROLONGED USE
See your doctor regularly for liver function tests if you take rosiglitazone for an extended period.

PRECAUTIONS
Over 60: No special problems are expected.

Driving and Hazardous Work: The use of rosiglitazone should not impair your ability to perform such tasks safely.

Alcohol: Drink only in moderation.

Pregnancy: Adequate studies of rosiglitazone use during pregnancy have not been done. In general, insulin is the treatment of choice for controlling blood glucose levels during pregnancy. Rosiglitazone should not be used during pregnancy unless your doctor believes the potential benefit justifies the potential risk to the fetus. Rosiglitazone may stimulate ovulation in premenopausal women who have stopped ovulating. Contraception may be advised.

Breast Feeding: Rosiglitazone may pass into breast milk; do not use it while nursing.

Infants and Children: Safety and effectiveness of rosiglitazone have not been established in children.

Special Concerns: Another thiazolidinedione drug, troglitazone, has been associated with rare, serious, and sometimes fatal, liver-related side effects. Although no similar side effects have been reported for rosiglitazone, liver function tests are recommended just prior to treatment, every two months for the first year, and periodically thereafter. If you develop unexplained symptoms of liver dysfunction, such as nausea, vomiting, abdominal pain, fatigue, loss of appetite, or dark urine, call your doctor immediately. It is important to follow your doctor's advice on diet, exercise, and other measures to help control diabetes.

OVERDOSE
Symptoms: No specific ones have been reported.

What to Do: While no cases of overdose have been reported, if someone takes a much larger dose than prescribed, call your doctor, emergency medical services (EMS), or the nearest poison control center immediately.

DRUG INTERACTIONS
No known drug interactions.

FOOD INTERACTIONS
No known food interactions.

DISEASE INTERACTIONS
Rosiglitazone should not be taken by those with type 1 diabetes or for the treatment of diabetic ketoacidosis. Caution is advised if you have edema or heart failure. Consult your doctor prior to using rosiglitazone if you have any type of liver abnormality.

Rosiglitazone Maleate/Metformin

▶ Drug Class: Antidiabetic agent combination

▶ Available in: Tablets

▶ Available OTC? No

▶ As Generic? No

Side Effects

SERIOUS
In rare cases, Avandamet may lead to lactic acidosis, a potentially life-threatening buildup of lactic acid in the blood. Symptoms include rapid, shallow breathing, unusual sleepiness or weakness, muscle pain, and abdominal distress. Avandamet occasionally causes abnormally low blood glucose levels (hypoglycemia); symptoms include blurred vision, cold sweats, confusion, anxiousness, rapid heartbeat, shakiness, and nausea. Seek medical assistance right away.

COMMON
Diarrhea, nausea, vomiting, abdominal bloating, gas, weight gain, edema (swelling), and diminished appetite. Usually such symptoms are mild and transient. Consult your doctor if the symptoms persist or increase in severity.

LESS COMMON
Unpleasant or metallic taste in mouth, upper respiratory tract infection, headache.

PRINCIPAL USES
Used to lower blood glucose (sugar) levels in patients with type 2 diabetes whose blood sugar levels are not adequately controlled by diet, exercise, rosiglitazone or metformin alone, or other oral antidiabetic agents.

HOW THE DRUG WORKS
Rosiglitazone and metformin work through different mechanisms to increase the body's sensitivity and response to its own insulin.

DOSAGE
Consult your doctor. Starting dosage is based on your current dose of rosiglitazone and/or metformin. Avandamet tablets contain 500 mg metformin and 1, 2, or 4 mg rosiglitazone. Maximum daily dosage should not exceed 8 mg rosiglitazone and 2,000 mg metformin. Avandamet is taken twice a day.

ONSET OF EFFECT
Full effect may take 4 weeks.

DURATION OF ACTION
Persists for the duration of treatment.

DIETARY ADVICE
Take with meals to reduce risk of stomach upset. Tablets must be swallowed whole, not crushed or chewed.

STORAGE
Store in a tightly sealed container away from heat, moisture, and direct light.

IF YOU MISS A DOSE
Take it with food as soon as you remember. However, if it is almost time for the next dose, skip the missed dose and resume your regular dosage schedule. Do not double the next dose.

STOPPING THE DRUG
Stop taking this drug only when your doctor advises.

PROLONGED USE
See your doctor regularly for liver function tests if you take this drug for an extended period.

PRECAUTIONS
Over 60: Because metformin is cleared by the kidneys, extra caution is warranted in thin, elderly patients with a mild decrease in renal function (not often detected by the usual tests for kidney impairment).

Driving and Hazardous Work: No special precautions are necessary.

Alcohol: Excessive amounts of alcohol can increase the effect of metformin, possibly resulting in abnormally low blood glucose levels.

Pregnancy: Do not use Avandamet during pregnancy unless your doctor believes the potential benefit justifies the potential risk to the fetus. Rosiglitazone may stimulate ovulation in premenopausal women who have stopped ovulating. Contraception may be advised. Consult your doctor if you become pregnant or plan to become pregnant.

Breast Feeding: Do not use this drug while nursing.

Infants and Children: Safety and effectiveness of this drug have not been established in children.

Special Concerns: Do not take this drug if you have previously had an allergic reaction to rosiglitazone or metformin. Liver function tests are recommended just prior to treatment, every two months for the first year, and periodically thereafter. If you develop unexplained symptoms of liver dysfunction, such as nausea, vomiting, abdominal pain, fatigue, or dark urine, call your doctor immediately.

OVERDOSE
Symptoms: Rosiglitazone: None reported. Metformin: Symptoms of lactic acidosis or hypoglycemia (see Serious Side Effects).

What to Do: Seek emergency medical assistance.

DRUG INTERACTIONS
Consult your doctor if you are taking any of the following: amiloride, calcium channel blockers, cimetidine, digoxin, furosemide, morphine, procainamide, quinidine, quinine, ranitidine, trimethoprim, triamterene, or vancomycin. Avandamet should not be used when taking insulin.

FOOD INTERACTIONS
None.

DISEASE INTERACTIONS
Do not take Avandamet if you have type 1 diabetes or to treat diabetic ketoacidosis. Caution is advised if you have edema or mild heart failure. Avandamet should not be taken by those using medications for heart failure. Consult your doctor prior to using Avandamet if you have any type of liver abnormality. Do not take Avandamet if you have any condition that requires careful control of blood glucose levels, such as severe infection; any condition contributing to abnormally low blood oxygen levels, such as congestive heart failure or emphysema; metabolic acidosis (buildup of acid in the blood); a history of alcohol abuse; or kidney or liver disease.

Rosuvastatin Calcium

Crestor

▶ Drug Class: Antilipidemic (cholesterol-lowering agent)

▶ Available in: Tablets

▶ Available OTC? No

▶ As Generic? No

Side Effects

SERIOUS
Fever, chest pain, unusual or unexplained muscle aches and tenderness. Severe muscle inflammation (myositis) can lead to kidney damage. Call your doctor right away.

COMMON
Side effects occur in only 1% to 2% of patients. These include constipation or diarrhea, dizziness or lightheadedness, bloating or gas, heartburn, nausea, allergic reaction, stomach pain, rise in liver enzymes.

LESS COMMON
Sleeping difficulty, skin rash.

PRINCIPAL USES
To treat high cholesterol. Usually prescribed after the first lines of treatment—including diet changes, weight loss, and exercise—fail to reduce to acceptable levels the amounts of total and low-density lipoprotein (LDL) cholesterol in the blood.

HOW THE DRUG WORKS
Rosuvastatin blocks the action of an enzyme required for the manufacture of cholesterol, thereby interfering with its formation. By lowering the amount of cholesterol in liver cells, rosuvastatin increases the formation of receptors for LDL, and thereby reduces blood levels of total and LDL cholesterol. In addition to lowering LDL cholesterol, rosuvastatin also reduces triglyceride levels and modestly raises HDL (the so-called "good") cholesterol.

DOSAGE
Initial dose is 10 mg a day, taken once daily. It may be increased by your doctor as needed up to a maximum dose of 40 mg per day. Unlike some other "statin" cholesterol-lowering drugs, rosuvastatin does not have to be taken in the evening to be maximally effective.

ONSET OF EFFECT
2 to 4 weeks.

DURATION OF ACTION
The effect persists for the duration of therapy.

DIETARY ADVICE
Cholesterol-lowering drugs are only one part of a total program that should include regular exercise and a healthy diet. The American Heart Association publishes a recommended "Healthy Heart" diet.

STORAGE
Store in a tightly sealed container away from heat, moisture, and direct light.

IF YOU MISS A DOSE
Take it as soon as you remember. Take your next scheduled dose at the proper time and resume your regular dosage schedule. Do not double your next dose.

STOPPING THE DRUG
The decision to stop taking the drug should be made in consultation with your doctor. Once the medication is discontinued, blood cholesterol is likely to return to original elevated levels.

PROLONGED USE
Side effects are more likely with prolonged use. Blood tests to evaluate liver function should be done before starting treatment and 12 weeks later or after an increase in dose. As you continue with rosuvastatin, your doctor will periodically order blood tests to evaluate liver function and lipid levels. Periodic tests should be done for urine proteins.

PRECAUTIONS
Over 60: No special problems are expected in older patients.

Driving and Hazardous Work: The use of rosuvastatin should not impair your ability to perform such tasks safely.

Alcohol: No special precautions are necessary.

Pregnancy: Should not be used during pregnancy or by women who plan to become pregnant in the near future.

Breast Feeding: This drug is not recommended for women who are nursing.

Infants and Children: Safety and effectiveness are not known; this drug is rarely used in children. Consult your pediatrician.

Special Concerns: Important elements of treatment for high cholesterol include proper diet, weight loss, regular moderate exercise, and avoidance of certain medications that may increase cholesterol levels. Because rosuvastatin has potential side effects, it is important that you maintain a recommended healthy diet and cooperate with other treatments your doctor may suggest.

OVERDOSE
Symptoms: An overdose of rosuvastatin is unlikely.

What to Do: Emergency instructions not applicable.

DRUG INTERACTIONS
Consult your doctor if you are taking cyclosporine, gemfibrozil, niacin, antibiotics, especially erythromycin, or medications for fungus infections. All of these drugs may increase the risk of myositis when taken with rosuvastatin and may lead to kidney failure. Do not take rosuvastatin within 2 hours of taking an antacid.

FOOD INTERACTIONS
No known food interactions.

DISEASE INTERACTIONS
Consult your doctor if you have any of the following problems: liver, kidney, or muscle disease, or a medical history involving organ transplant or recent surgery.

Salmeterol Xinafoate

▶ Drug Class: Bronchodilator/
sympathomimetic

▶ Available in: Inhalation
aerosol, inhalation powder

▶ Available OTC? No

▶ As Generic? No

Side Effects

SERIOUS
Salmeterol may become
ineffective if used too
often, resulting in more-
severe breathing diffi-
culty that does not
improve. Signs include
persistent wheezing,
coughing, or shortness of
breath; confusion; bluish
color to lips or finger-
nails; inability to speak.
Other side effects include
chest pain or heaviness;
irregular, racing, fluttering, or pounding heart-
beat; lightheadedness;
fainting; severe weak-
ness; severe headache.

COMMON
Headache, sore throat,
runny or stuffy nose.

LESS COMMON
Abdominal pain, diar-
rhea, nausea, cough,
muscle aches.

PRINCIPAL USES
Salmeterol is used to dilate
air passages in the lungs
that have become narrowed
as a result of disease or
inflammation. It is used in
the treatment of asthma and
chronic obstructive pul-
monary disease (COPD).

HOW THE DRUG WORKS
Salmeterol widens con-
stricted airways in the lungs
by relaxing the smooth
muscles that surround the
bronchial passages.

DOSAGE
This drug may be used
when needed to relieve
breathing difficulty. Adults
and children 12 years and
older— By inhalation
aerosol: Two inhalations
twice daily, approximately
12 hours apart. By inhalation powder: One inhalation
twice a day, approximately
12 hours apart.

ONSET OF EFFECT
Within 15 minutes.

DURATION OF ACTION
Up to 12 hours.

DIETARY ADVICE
Maintain your usual food
and fluid intake. Increase
fluids if you have a fever or
diarrhea, in hot weather, or
during exercise.

STORAGE
Store in a tightly sealed container away from heat, moisture, and direct light.

IF YOU MISS A DOSE
Take it as soon as you
remember. If it is near the
time for the next dose, skip
the missed dose and
resume your regular dosage
schedule. Do not double the
next dose.

STOPPING THE DRUG
The decision to stop taking
the drug should be made by
your doctor.

PROLONGED USE
It may not be necessary to
finish the recommended
course of therapy. Consult
your doctor.

PRECAUTIONS
Over 60: Adverse reactions
may be more likely and
more severe in older
patients.

**Driving and Hazardous
Work:** Do not drive or
engage in hazardous work
until you determine how the
medicine affects you.

Alcohol: No special precautions are necessary.

Pregnancy: Safety of use
during pregnancy has not
been established. Consult
your doctor.

Breast Feeding: It is not
known if salmeterol passes
into breast milk. Mothers
who wish to breast-feed
while taking this drug
should discuss the matter
with their doctor.

Infants and Children:
Use of salmeterol inhalation
aerosol is not recommended
in children younger than 12.

Special Concerns: This
medication takes 15 minutes
to work. Do not use salmeterol for acute or sudden
attacks, or for worsening
asthma. Pay heed to any
asthma attack or other
breathing difficulty that
does not improve after your
usual rescue treatment.
Seek help immediately if
you feel your lungs are persistently constricted, if you
are using more than the
recommended number of
treatments or puffs per day,
or if you feel a recent attack
is somehow different from
others. Do not wash the
device for the inhalation
powder. Keep it dry.

OVERDOSE
Symptoms: Chest pain or
heaviness; irregular, racing,
fluttering, or pounding
heartbeat; dizziness; lightheadedness; severe weak-
ness; fainting; severe
headache; muscle tremors
or shaking.

What to Do: Call your
doctor, emergency medical
services (EMS), or the
nearest poison control
center immediately.

DRUG INTERACTIONS
Consult your doctor for specific advice if you are taking
beta-blockers.

FOOD INTERACTIONS
No known food interactions.

DISEASE INTERACTIONS
Consult your doctor if you
have a history of any of the
following: heart disease or
heartbeat irregularities,
high blood pressure, anxiety disorders, or a thyroid
condition.

Salsalate

BRAND NAMES
Amigesic, Anaflex 750,
Disalcid, Marthritic,
Mono-Gesic, Salflex,
Salsitab

Generic 500 mg
(SIDMAK)

Additional photographs

▶ Drug Class: Salicylate/nonsteroidal anti-inflammatory drug (NSAID)

▶ Available in: Capsules, tablets

▶ Available OTC? No

▶ As Generic? Yes

Side Effects

SERIOUS
Hearing loss, blood in the urine, severe diarrhea, difficulty swallowing, dizziness, lightheadedness, severe drowsiness, extreme nervousness or exciteability, confusion, seizures, change in skin color, hallucinations, increased sweating and thirst, severe nausea or vomiting, shortness of breath, tightness in the chest, severe stomach pain, swollen eyelids, face, or lips, fever, bloody or black, tarry stools, severe headache, buzzing or ringing in the ears, vomiting of blood or dark material. Call your doctor immediately.

COMMON
Mild stomach or abdominal cramps, pains, or discomfort; indigestion, heartburn, nausea or vomiting; skin rash, hives, or itching.

LESS COMMON
None reported.

PRINCIPAL USES
To treat rheumatoid arthritis, osteoarthritis, and other rheumatic (joint) disorders.

HOW THE DRUG WORKS
Salsalate appears to work by interfering with the action of prostaglandins, naturally occurring substances in the body that cause inflammation and make nerves more sensitive to pain impulses.

DOSAGE
Adults and teenagers: To start, 500 to 1,000 mg, 2 or 3 times a day. The dose may be adjusted later.

ONSET OF EFFECT
Unknown.

DURATION OF ACTION
Unknown.

DIETARY ADVICE
Salsalate should be taken with food or milk, to minimize stomach upset, and a large glass of water.

STORAGE
Store in a tightly sealed container away from heat, moisture, and direct light.

IF YOU MISS A DOSE
Take it as soon as you remember. If it is near the time for the next dose, skip the missed dose and resume your regular dosage schedule. Do not double the next dose.

STOPPING THE DRUG
Take as directed for the full treatment period, even if you begin to feel better before the scheduled end of therapy.

PROLONGED USE
See your doctor regularly for tests and examinations if you must take this medicine for a prolonged period.

PRECAUTIONS
Over 60: Adverse reactions may be more likely and more severe in older patients.

Driving and Hazardous Work: Do not drive or engage in hazardous work until you determine how the medicine affects you.

Alcohol: Avoid alcohol.

Pregnancy: Adequate studies have not been done. Consult your doctor if you are pregnant or plan to become pregnant.

Breast Feeding: Salsalate passes into breast milk; caution is advised.

Infants and Children: Do not give salsalate to a child or teenager with a fever or other signs of a viral infection like the flu or chicken pox without consulting your doctor.

Special Concerns: Salsalate may cause false urine-sugar-test results for diabetics if you are taking 4 or more 500 mg doses, or 3 or more 750 mg doses, per day.

OVERDOSE
Symptoms: Confusion, dizziness, ringing or buzzing in the ears, severe drowsiness or fatigue, excitability or nervousness, rapid or heavy breathing, sweating, diarrhea, vomiting, fever, dehydration, loss of consciousness.

What to Do: Call your doctor, emergency medical services (EMS), or the nearest poison control center immediately. To prevent further absorption of salsalate, take ipecac syrup.

DRUG INTERACTIONS
Consult your doctor for advice if you are taking NSAIDs, carbonic anhydrase inhibitors, citrates, sodium bicarbonate, antacids, anticoagulants, heparin, thrombolytic agents, oral antidiabetic agents or insulin, cefamandole, cefoperazone, cefotetan, plicamycin, valproic acid, methotrexate, vancomycin, probenecid, or sulfinpyrazone.

FOOD INTERACTIONS
No known food interactions.

DISEASE INTERACTIONS
Caution is advised when taking salsalate. Consult your doctor if you have any of the following: anemia, stomach ulcer or other stomach problems, hyperthyroidism, glucose-6-phosphate dehydrogenase (G6PD) deficiency, high blood pressure, gout, heart disease, any bleeding problems, or a history of asthma or allergies. Use of this drug may cause complications in patients with liver or kidney disease, since these organs work together to remove the medication from the body.

Saquinavir

Invirase 200 mg
(ROCHE)

▶ Drug Class: Antiviral/protease inhibitor

▶ Available in: Capsules

▶ Available OTC? No

▶ As Generic? No

Side Effects

SERIOUS
High blood sugar (diabetes) has occurred in patients taking drugs of this class, although a cause-and-effect relationship has not been established. Contact your doctor if you develop increased thirst or excessive urination. Other serious side effects include: psychosis, thoughts of suicide, and lung disease.

COMMON
Burning, prickling, numbness, or tingling sensations in various parts of the body, confusion, seizures, headache, loss of muscle coordination, diarrhea, abdominal discomfort, nausea, skin rash, increased skin sensitivity to light, general weakness.

LESS COMMON
Loss of appetite, kidney stones, urinary tract bleeding, hair loss, swelling of the eyelid, nail problems, night sweats, small bump-like growths on the skin, impotence, anxiety attack, leg cramps.

PRINCIPAL USES
To treat HIV (human immunodeficiency virus) infection in combination with other drugs. While not a cure for HIV infection, saquinavir may suppress the replication of the virus and delay progression of the disease.

HOW THE DRUG WORKS
Saquinavir blocks the activity of a viral protease, an enzyme that is needed by HIV to reproduce. Blocking the protease causes HIV to make copies that cannot infect new cells.

DOSAGE
Adults and teenagers 16 and over: 600 mg, 3 times a day, in combination with other antiretroviral drugs. Higher doses (up to 1,200 mg, 3 times a day) are sometimes used. Lower doses (400 mg, 2 times a day) are used when saquinavir is combined with ritonavir, a similar drug.

ONSET OF EFFECT
Unknown. With most antiretroviral drugs, an early response can be seen within the first few days of therapy, but the maximum effect may take 12 to 16 weeks.

DURATION OF ACTION
Unknown.

DIETARY ADVICE
It should be taken within 2 hours after a full meal.

STORAGE
Capsules should be refrigerated. If brought to room temperature, store in a tightly sealed container away from heat and direct light and use within 3 months.

IF YOU MISS A DOSE
Take it as soon as you remember. However, if it is near the time for the next dose, skip the missed dose and resume your regular dosage schedule. Do not double the next dose.

STOPPING THE DRUG
The decision to stop taking the drug should be made in consultation with your physician.

PROLONGED USE
See your doctor regularly for tests and examinations.

PRECAUTIONS
Over 60: No special studies have been done on older patients.

Driving and Hazardous Work: Avoid such activities until you determine how the medicine affects you.

Alcohol: Avoid alcohol if liver function is impaired.

Pregnancy: Saquinavir has been shown to cause birth defects in animal studies. Human studies have not been done. Nevertheless, the drug is being used increasingly in combination with other antiretroviral drugs to treat pregnant HIV-infected women.

Breast Feeding: It is unknown whether saquinavir passes into breast milk; however, women infected with HIV should not breast-feed, to avoid transmitting the virus to an uninfected child.

Infants and Children: The safety and effectiveness of saquinavir in children under the age of 16 have not been established.

Special Concerns: Use of saquinavir does not eliminate the risk of passing the AIDS virus to other persons. You should take appropriate preventive measures. If saquinavir increases skin sensitivity to sunlight, wear tightly woven clothing and use sunscreen when outdoors. Do not substitute one brand of saquinavir for another without consulting your doctor. They are not equal in strength.

OVERDOSE
Symptoms: No cases of overdose have been reported.

What to Do: An overdose of saquinavir is unlikely to occur. Nonetheless, if you have any reason to suspect an overdose, call your doctor, emergency medical services (EMS), or the nearest poison control center.

DRUG INTERACTIONS
Saquinavir should not be used at the same time as triazolam, midazolam, "statins" (cholesterol-lowering drugs), ergotamine/belladonna alkaloids, or the herb St. John's wort. Consult your doctor for advice if you are taking any other medication, especially rifampin, rifabutin, nevirapine, sildenafil, tadalafil, or vardenafil. Some drugs, such as ketoconazole, delavirdine, ritonavir, and nelfinavir, are used in combination with saquinavir because they increase its blood levels and, possibly, its effectiveness.

FOOD INTERACTIONS
Fatty foods and grapefruit juice enhance the body's absorption of saquinavir. Food may reduce side effects.

DISEASE INTERACTIONS
Consult your doctor if you have any other medical condition. Use of saquinavir may cause complications in patients with liver disease, because this organ works to remove the medication from the body.

Scopolamine Ophthalmic

BRAND NAME
Isopto Hyoscine

▶ Drug Class: Eye muscle relaxant, pupil enlarger

▶ Available in: Ophthalmic solution

▶ Available OTC? No

▶ As Generic? No

Side Effects

SERIOUS
If absorbed into the bloodstream: Clumsiness or unsteadiness, flushing or redness of face, confusion or unusual behavior, hallucinations, slurred speech, fever, unusual tiredness or weakness, dizziness, rapid or irregular heartbeat, unusually dry skin, skin rash, dry mouth, swollen stomach (in infants). Seek medical assistance immediately.

COMMON
Blurred vision, increased sensitivity to light.

LESS COMMON
Eye irritation not present or not as severe as before use, swelling of eyelids.

PRINCIPAL USES
Used for eye examinations, before and after eye surgery, and to treat certain eye conditions, including uveitis (inflammation of the uvea, or the central portion of the eye) and posterior synechiae (a potentially blinding eye disorder).

HOW THE DRUG WORKS
Scopolamine relaxes the muscles that control the lens and pupil. This prevents the lens from focusing and widens the pupil to allow the doctor to view the interior structures of the eye. It immobilizes tiny structures within the eye, which prevents scarring of eye tissue and may alleviate pain somewhat.

DOSAGE
Uveitis: 1 drop up to 4 times a day for adults and children, depending on the severity of the condition and the size and weight of the patient. Posterior synechiae: 1 drop every 10 minutes for 3 doses for adults. Use in children must be determined by your pediatrician.

ONSET OF EFFECT
In less than 1 hour.

DURATION OF ACTION
Up to 1 week.

DIETARY ADVICE
No special restrictions.

STORAGE
Store in a tightly sealed container away from heat, moisture, and direct light. Keep refrigerated, but do not allow it to freeze.

IF YOU MISS A DOSE
Apply it as soon as you remember. If it is near the time for the next dose, skip the missed dose and resume your regular dosage schedule. Do not double the next dose.

STOPPING THE DRUG
Use it as prescribed for the full treatment period, even if you feel better before the scheduled end of therapy.

PROLONGED USE
Prolonged use may produce eye irritation, including redness, swelling, oozing of fluid, or skin inflammation. Call your doctor if such symptoms persist for more than 7 days.

PRECAUTIONS
Over 60: Adverse reactions may be more likely and more severe in older patients.

Driving and Hazardous Work: Do not drive or engage in hazardous work until you determine how the medicine affects your vision. Extreme caution should be observed for activities that require sharp vision for close objects (less than an arm's length away).

Alcohol: No special precautions are necessary.

Pregnancy: Adequate studies have not been done. Inform your doctor if you are pregnant or plan to become pregnant.

Breast Feeding: Use extreme caution. Ophthalmic scopolamine is absorbed systemically and passes into breast milk in small amounts. Breast-fed infants may exhibit a rapid pulse, fever, or dry skin.

Infants and Children: Infants and children with blond hair or blue eyes may be more sensitive to scopolamine ophthalmic and may have an increased risk of side effects. Use with extreme caution.

Special Concerns: To use the eye drops, first wash your hands. Tilt your head back. Gently apply pressure to the inside corner of the eyelid and with the index finger of the same hand, pull downward on the lower eyelid to make a space. Drop the medicine into this space and close your eye. Apply pressure for 1 or 2 minutes while keeping the eye closed without blinking. Wash your hands again. Make certain that the tip of the dropper does not touch your eye, finger, or any other surface.

OVERDOSE
Symptoms: Drowsiness, hallucinations, memory problems, dry mouth, dry skin, restlessness, palpitations, dizziness and disorientation, delirium.

What to Do: Call your doctor, emergency medical services (EMS), or the nearest poison control center immediately.

DRUG INTERACTIONS
If absorbed into the body, it may interact with the following: anticholinergics; certain antiglaucoma agents, such as demecarium, echothiophate, or pilocarpine; antimyasthenics; potassium citrate or supplements; or medications producing central nervous system depression, such as antiemetic agents, phenothiazines, or barbiturates.

FOOD INTERACTIONS
No known food interactions.

DISEASE INTERACTIONS
Consult your doctor for advice if you have glaucoma or another eye problem; or if a child has Down's syndrome, spastic paralysis, or brain damage.

Scopolamine Systemic

▶ Drug Class: Anticholinergic; antispasmodic

▶ Available in: Transdermal patch, injection

▶ Available OTC? No

▶ As Generic? Yes

Side Effects

SERIOUS
Confusion, lightheadedness, dizziness, skin rash or hives, fainting, eye pain. Call your doctor immediately.

COMMON
Constipation; dryness of mouth, nose, throat, or skin; decreased sweating.

LESS COMMON
Blurred vision, decreased breast milk flow, unusual fatigue, difficulty swallowing, drowsiness, false sense of well-being, headache, increased sensitivity of eyes to light, loss of memory, difficulty with urination, nausea, vomiting, bloated feeling, irritation at injection site, insomnia.

PRINCIPAL USES
To treat urinary, stomach, or intestinal cramps, or motion sickness.

HOW THE DRUG WORKS
Acetylcholine is a naturally occurring chemical in the body involved in the activity of nerves, muscles, glands, and other physiological processes. Scopolamine interferes with the action of acetylcholine, leading to a variety of effects, including the drying of secretions (saliva, perspiration), relief of intestinal muscle spasm, and changing the size of the pupils. Scopolamine may relieve nausea, vomiting, and motion sickness by acting on nerves affecting balance in the inner ear.

DOSAGE
To treat urinary problems or intestinal problems—Injection: 10 to 20 mg, 3 or 4 times a day. The dose may be changed by your doctor. To treat motion sickness—Transdermal patch: Apply a 1.5 mg patch behind the ear at least 4 to 12 hours before travel. Use of scopolamine in children is not recommended.

ONSET OF EFFECT
Injection: Within 30 minutes. Transdermal patch: Unknown.

DURATION OF ACTION
Injection: 4 hours. Transdermal patch: Up to 72 hours.

DIETARY ADVICE
No special restrictions.

STORAGE
Store in a tightly sealed container away from heat and direct light.

IF YOU MISS A DOSE
Take it as soon as you remember. However, if it is near the time for the next dose, skip the missed dose and resume your regular dosage schedule. Do not double the next dose.

STOPPING THE DRUG
The decision to stop taking the drug should be made by your doctor.

PROLONGED USE
See your doctor regularly for tests and examinations if you take this medicine for a prolonged period.

PRECAUTIONS
Over 60: Adverse reactions may be more likely and more severe.

Driving and Hazardous Work: Do not drive or engage in hazardous work until you determine how the medicine affects you.

Alcohol: Avoid alcohol.

Pregnancy: Adequate human studies have not been completed. Before taking scopolamine, tell your doctor if you are pregnant or plan to become pregnant.

Breast Feeding: Scopolamine may pass into breast milk; caution is advised. Consult your doctor for specific advice.

Infants and Children: Adverse reactions may be more common and more severe in children and infants. Consult your doctor for specific advice.

Special Concerns: Do not touch the adhesive area of the patch. Wash hands thoroughly before and after application. If patch is dislodged, place a new patch behind the other ear. Do not reapply a dislodged patch. If you use the patch for more than 72 hours, you may experience nausea, vomiting, headache, or dizziness.

OVERDOSE
Symptoms: Dry mouth, dilated pupils, delirium, disorientation, memory disturbances, dizziness, restlessness, hallucinations, drowsiness.

What to Do: Call your doctor, emergency medical services (EMS), or the nearest poison control center immediately.

DRUG INTERACTIONS
Consult your doctor for specific advice if you are taking antacids, diarrhea medicines, digoxin, ketoconazole, central nervous system depressants (such as antihistamines, sleep aids, or tranquilizers), other cholinergics, tricyclic antidepressants, potassium chloride.

FOOD INTERACTIONS
No known food interactions.

DISEASE INTERACTIONS
Caution is advised when taking scopolamine. Consult your doctor if you have a history of bleeding disorders, colitis, severe mouth dryness, enlarged prostate, fever, glaucoma, heart disease, hiatal hernia, high blood pressure, any intestinal problem, lung disease, myasthenia gravis, toxemia of pregnancy, urinary tract blockage, difficulty urinating, kidney or liver disease, or an overactive thyroid; or if a child has brain damage, Down syndrome, or spastic paralysis.

Selegiline Hydrochloride (L-Deprenyl)

Eldepryl 5 mg
(SOMERSET)

▶ Drug Class: Antiparkinsonism drug

▶ Available in: Tablets

▶ Available OTC? No

▶ As Generic? Yes

Side Effects

SERIOUS
Dizziness, low blood pressure (causing dizziness, lightheadedness, fainting, or confusion), involuntary muscle movements, heart rhythm abnormalities.

COMMON
Nausea, dry mouth.

LESS COMMON
Palpitations, drowsiness.

PRINCIPAL USES
To treat Parkinson's disease, in conjunction with levodopa/carbidopa. Also used to treat Parkinson-like syndromes, which may occur following infection of or injury to the central nervous system (brain and spinal cord), because of damage to blood vessels in the brain, or after exposure to certain toxins. Without levodopa/carbidopa, this drug has no known benefit.

HOW THE DRUG WORKS
When used with levodopa/carbidopa, selegiline allows more levodopa/carbidopa to be available for use in the body by inhibiting a nervous system enzyme called monoamine oxidase (MAO). MAO, which is found in the brain and intestinal tract, acts to break down certain chemicals that play a role in the initiation and control of muscle movement.

DOSAGE
Adults: 5 mg twice daily.
Children: This drug should not be used by children.

ONSET OF EFFECT
Approximately 1 to 2 hours.

DURATION OF ACTION
Approximately 4 hours.

DIETARY ADVICE
On rare occasions, patients taking the recommended dose of selegiline have had reactions with foods that contain tyramines. (See Food Interactions for more information.)

STORAGE
Store in a tightly sealed container away from heat, moisture, and direct light.

IF YOU MISS A DOSE
Take it as soon as you remember, unless the time for your next scheduled dose is within the next 2 hours. If so, skip the missed dose and resume your regular dosage schedule. Do not double the next dose.

STOPPING THE DRUG
Consult with your physician before stopping this drug. The dose should be tapered gradually—from 2 tablets to a single tablet for 7 days—before the drug is completely discontinued.

PROLONGED USE
Selegiline may be taken for prolonged periods. There are no known untoward effects specifically associated with long-term use.

PRECAUTIONS
Over 60: Adverse reactions may be more likely and more severe in older people. The medication should be used with caution by patients in this age group.

Driving and Hazardous Work: This drug may cause confusion or drowsiness. Do not drive or engage in hazardous work until you determine how it affects you.

Alcohol: Avoid alcohol.

Pregnancy: Adequate human studies have not been done to determine the safety of this drug during pregnancy. It should not be used by pregnant women.

Breast Feeding: The extent to which selegiline passes through breast milk is unknown. It should therefore be avoided by nursing mothers.

Infants and Children: This drug has not been tested in infants and children; safety and effectiveness have not been established. It should therefore not be used by patients in this age group.

OVERDOSE
Symptoms: Dizziness, fainting, confusion, delirium, abdominal pain.

What to Do: Call your doctor, emergency medical services (EMS), or the nearest poison control center immediately.

DRUG INTERACTIONS
Other drugs may interact with selegiline. Consult your doctor for specific advice if you are taking meperidine hydrochloride or other opioid (narcotic) analgesics, or MAO inhibitor antidepressants such as phenelzine sulfate or tranylcypromine sulfate.

FOOD INTERACTIONS
Consult your doctor before eating tyramine-rich foods, which include aged cheeses, avocados, banana skins, bean curd, bologna and other processed lunch meats, chicken livers, chocolate, figs, canned or dried fish, pickled herring, meat extracts, pepperoni, raisins, raspberries, unpasteurized beer, Chianti, sherry, vermouth, red wines in general, and caffeine-rich beverages or foods.

DISEASE INTERACTIONS
Caution is advised when taking selegiline hydrochloride. Consult your doctor if you have any of the following: a change in your mental state, significant heart disease, peptic ulcer disease, or wheezing or feelings of tightness or pressure in the chest.

Senna

Senokot 8.6 mg
(PURDUE FREDERICK)

Additional photographs

▶ Drug Class: Laxative

▶ Available in: Tablets, granules, oral solution, syrup

▶ Available OTC? Yes

▶ As Generic? Yes

Side Effects

SERIOUS
Confusion, irregular heartbeat, muscle cramps, pink to red or yellow to brown coloration of urine and stools, unusual tiredness or weakness, laxative dependence. Call your doctor immediately.

COMMON
Belching, cramping, diarrhea, nausea.

LESS COMMON
No less-common side effects have been reported.

PRINCIPAL USES
For short-term treatment of constipation.

HOW THE DRUG WORKS
Senna stimulates water and electrolyte (mineral salt) secretion in the intestine to induce defecation.

DOSAGE
Adults and teenagers: 2 tablets, or 1 teaspoon of granules, or 10 to 15 ml of syrup. Children ages 6 to 12: 1 tablet or 1/2 teaspoon of granules. The medicine should be given at bedtime.

ONSET OF EFFECT
Within 6 to 10 hours.

DURATION OF ACTION
Variable.

DIETARY ADVICE
Each dose of senna should be taken on an empty stomach with a full glass (8 oz) of water or fruit juice.

STORAGE
Store in a tightly sealed container away from heat, moisture, and direct light.

IF YOU MISS A DOSE
Take it as soon as you remember. If it is near the time for the next dose, skip the missed dose and resume your regular dosage schedule. Do not double the next dose.

STOPPING THE DRUG
Take senna as prescribed for the full treatment period. However, you may stop taking the drug if you are feeling better before the scheduled end of therapy.

PROLONGED USE
If regular bowel movement does not resume in 1 week, discontinue use of senna and consult your doctor.

PRECAUTIONS
Over 60: Adverse reactions may be more likely and more severe in older patients.

Driving and Hazardous Work: Do not drive or engage in hazardous work until you determine how the medicine affects you.

Alcohol: Avoid alcohol.

Pregnancy: Senna may cause unwanted effects during pregnancy if not used properly. Consult your doctor for specific advice.

Breast Feeding: Senna may pass into breast milk; caution is advised. Consult your doctor for advice.

Infants and Children: Senna is not recommended for use by children under the age of 6 unless it has been prescribed by a doctor.

Special Concerns: You should increase your intake of foods containing vitamin D, such as milk products, and maintain an adequate intake of foods containing folic acid, such as fresh vegetables, fruits, whole grains, and liver, while taking senna. Do not take any other medicine within 2 hours of taking senna. Senna is one of the most effective laxatives for relieving constipation caused by narcotic analgesics like morphine and codeine.

OVERDOSE
Symptoms: Sudden vomiting, nausea, diarrhea, or cramping.

What to Do: An overdose of senna is unlikely to be life-threatening. However, if someone takes a much larger dose than prescribed, call your doctor, emergency medical services (EMS), or the nearest poison control center immediately.

DRUG INTERACTIONS
Consult your doctor for specific advice if you are taking anticoagulants, digitalis drugs, ciprofloxacin, etidronate, sodium polystyrene sulfonate, or oral tetracyclines.

FOOD INTERACTIONS
No known food interactions.

DISEASE INTERACTIONS
Caution is advised when taking senna. Consult your doctor if you have a history of any of the following: appendicitis, rectal bleeding of unknown cause, colostomy, intestinal blockage, ileostomy, diabetes, heart disease, high blood pressure, kidney disease, or difficulty swallowing.

Sertraline Hydrochloride

Zoloft 50 mg
(ROERIG)

▶ Drug Class: Selective serotonin reuptake inhibitor (SSRI) antidepressant

▶ Available in: Capsules, tablets

▶ Available OTC? No

▶ As Generic? No

Side Effects

SERIOUS
Skin rash, hives, or itching; unusually fast speech, fever, extreme agitation. Call your doctor immediately.

COMMON
Insomnia, diarrhea, sexual dysfunction, decrease in appetite, weight loss, drowsiness, headache, dry mouth, stomach cramps, abdominal pain, gas, trembling, fatigue, loss of initiative.

LESS COMMON
Anxiety, agitation, increased appetite, blurred or altered vision, constipation, heartbeat irregularities, flushing, unusual feeling of warmth, vomiting.

PRINCIPAL USES
To treat symptoms of major depression, obsessive-compulsive disorder, and panic disorder.

HOW THE DRUG WORKS
Sertraline affects levels of serotonin, a brain chemical that is thought to be linked to mood, emotions, and mental state.

DOSAGE
Adults: To start, 50 mg once a day, in the morning or evening. Dose may be gradually increased by your doctor to 200 mg a day. Older adults: To start, 12.5 to 25 mg once a day. Dose may be gradually increased by your doctor to 200 mg a day. Children ages 6 to 12: To start, 25 mg once a day. Children ages 13 to 17: To start, 50 mg once a day. Dose may be gradually increased by pediatrician.

ONSET OF EFFECT
1 to 4 weeks.

DURATION OF ACTION
Unknown.

DIETARY ADVICE
No special restrictions.

STORAGE
Store in a tightly sealed container away from heat, moisture and direct light.

IF YOU MISS A DOSE
Take it as soon as you remember. If it is near the time for the next dose, skip the missed dose and resume your regular dosage schedule. Do not double the next dose.

STOPPING THE DRUG
Take it as prescribed for the full treatment period. When it is time to stop therapy, your dosage will be tapered gradually by your doctor.

PROLONGED USE
Usual course of therapy lasts 6 months to 1 year; some patients benefit from additional therapy.

PRECAUTIONS
Over 60: No special problems have been reported.

Driving and Hazardous Work: Use caution when driving or engaging in hazardous work until you determine how the medicine affects you.

Alcohol: Avoid alcohol.

Pregnancy: Adequate studies of sertraline use during pregnancy have not been done. Before you take sertraline, tell your doctor if you are currently pregnant or plan to become pregnant.

Breast Feeding: It is not known whether sertraline passes into breast milk; caution is advised. Consult your doctor for specific advice.

Infants and Children: The safety and effectiveness of the use of sertraline in children under age 6 have not been established. Antidepressants increase the risk of suicidal thinking and behavior (suicidality) in children with major depression and other psychiatric disorders. Discuss with your doctor this risk versus the benefits of using this drug. Children should be observed closely for worsening of symptoms, suicidality, or unusual changes in behavior at the onset of therapy and when making changes in dosage.

Special Concerns: Take sertraline at least 6 hours before bedtime to prevent insomnia, unless the drug causes drowsiness.

OVERDOSE
Symptoms: Sleepiness, nausea, vomiting, rapid heartbeat, anxiety, dilated pupils.

What to Do: Call your doctor, emergency medical services (EMS), or the nearest poison control center immediately.

DRUG INTERACTIONS
Sertraline and MAO inhibitors should not be used within 14 days of each other. Very serious side effects such as myoclonus (uncontrolled muscle spasms), hyperthermia (excessive rise in body temperature), and extreme stiffness may result. The following drugs may also interact with sertraline; consult your doctor for advice if you are taking cimetidine, digitoxin, warfarin, sumatriptan, naratriptan, zolmitriptan, oral antidiabetic agents (such as tolbutamide), tricyclic antidepressants, or any prescription or over-the-counter drugs that depress the central nervous system (including antihistamines, barbiturates, sedatives, cough medicines, and decongestants).

FOOD INTERACTIONS
No known food interactions.

DISEASE INTERACTIONS
Consult your doctor if you have a history of alcohol or drug abuse. Use of sertraline may cause complications in patients with liver or kidney disease, since these organs work together to remove the medication from the body.

Sibutramine Hydrochloride Monohydrate

BRAND NAME
Meridia

▶ Drug Class: Inhibitor of neurotransmitter reuptake

▶ Available in: Capsules

▶ Available OTC? No

▶ As Generic? No

Side Effects

SERIOUS
No serious side effects have yet been reported. However, if you experience symptoms such as shortness of breath or chest pain that were not present before taking the medication, call your doctor.

COMMON
Dry mouth, constipation, insomnia.

LESS COMMON
Headache, increased sweating, increased blood pressure and heart rate.

PRINCIPAL USES
To aid in the medical management of obesity in conjunction with a carefully supervised diet and exercise program. The drug is only recommended for overweight people with a body mass index (BMI) greater than 30 or greater than 27 in people with other risk factors such as diabetes or high blood pressure.

HOW THE DRUG WORKS
Sibutramine affects the appetite control center in the brain by inhibiting the reuptake of neurotransmitters like serotonin. The resulting increase in their availability suppresses appetite.

DOSAGE
To start, 10 mg once a day. Dose may be increased up to 15 mg once a day.

ONSET OF EFFECT
Significant weight changes may take several weeks or months to develop.

DURATION OF ACTION
When taking sibutramine regularly, most people lose weight within the first six months. Weight loss is maintained for the duration of therapy.

DIETARY ADVICE
Can be taken with a meal or on an empty stomach.

STORAGE
Store in a tightly sealed container away from heat, moisture, and direct light.

IF YOU MISS A DOSE
If you miss a dose one day, do not double the dose the next day. Resume your regular dosage schedule.

STOPPING THE DRUG
The decision to stop taking the drug should be made in consultation with your physician.

PROLONGED USE
The safety and effectiveness of sibutramine have not been determined beyond 2 years of use.

PRECAUTIONS
Over 60: No specific studies have been done on older patients.

Driving and Hazardous Work: Do not drive or engage in hazardous work until you determine how the medicine affects you.

Alcohol: Sibutramine may increase the sedative effects of alcohol. Consult you doctor for specific advice.

Pregnancy: Sibutramine should not be used by pregnant women. Before taking sibutramine, tell your doctor if you are pregnant or plan to become pregnant.

Breast Feeding: Sibutramine should not be used by nursing mothers.

Infants and Children: Children under the age of 16 should not use sibutramine.

Special Concerns: Although no serious adverse reactions have been reported with sibutramine (at the time of publication), other diet drugs have been associated with an increased risk of potentially grave cardiovascular and cardiopulmonary problems. If you experience any unusual or disturbing adverse effects, stop taking sibutramine and call your physician immediately.

OVERDOSE
Symptoms: No cases of overdose have been reported.

What to Do: If someone takes a much larger dose than prescribed or a child swallows the drug, call your doctor, emergency medical services (EMS), or the nearest poison control center immediately.

DRUG INTERACTIONS
You should not take sibutramine if you take MAO inhibitors, other weight loss medications, medications for depression, migraine medications, dihydroergotamine, meperidine, fentanyl, pentazocine, dextromethorphan (found in many cough medicines), lithium, or tryptophan. Sibutramine may interact with ketoconazole, erythromycin, over-the-counter cough and cold medications, allergy medicines, and decongestants. Consult your doctor for specific advice.

FOOD INTERACTIONS
No known food interactions.

DISEASE INTERACTIONS
You should not take sibutramine if you have coronary artery disease, angina, cardiac arrhythmia, history of heart attack, congestive heart failure, history of stroke, anorexia nervosa, history of seizures, or narrow angle glaucoma. Sibutramine can substantially raise blood pressure in some patients. Use of sibutramine may cause complications in patients with liver or kidney disease, since these organs work together to remove the medication from the body. Consult your doctor if you have a history of migraines, mental depression, Parkinson's disease, thyroid disorders, osteoporosis, gallbladder disease, a major eating disorder (anorexia nervosa or bulimia nervosa), or any other medical problem.

Sildenafil Citrate

▸ Drug Class: Phosphodi-
esterase type 5 inhibitor

▸ Available in: Tablets

▸ Available OTC? No

▸ As Generic? No

Side Effects

SERIOUS
Rarely, a painful or pro-
longed erection (lasting
more than 4 hours) may
occur. If erection does
not resolve on its own in
a reasonable amount of
time, seek medical help
promptly. If erection does
resolve on its own, con-
sult your doctor for spe-
cific guidelines. Serious
cardiovascular events
such as heart attack,
sudden cardiac death,
cardiac arrhythmias, cerebral hemorrhage, and
transient ischemic attack
have been reported fol-
lowing the use of silde-
nafil. However, it is
unclear whether these
events are due to the
consumption of sildenafil,
the presence of preexist-
ing cardiovascular risk
factors, to sexual activity,
or a combination of these
factors.

COMMON
Headache, flushing, indi-
gestion. Such side effects
are generally mild to
moderate and usually
short-lived.

LESS COMMON
Nasal congestion, vision
abnormalities, bloodshot
or burning eyes, diarrhea,
blood in the urine.

PRINCIPAL USES
To treat erectile dysfunction
(impotence), which may
occur in association with
atherosclerosis, vascular
disease or other circulatory
problems, diabetes, kidney
disease, hormonal abnor-
malities, neurological disease or injury, severe
depression or other psychological difficulties.

HOW THE DRUG WORKS
Sildenafil works by increasing the blood flow to the
penis necessary for establishing and maintaining an
erection. The drug accom-
plishes this by selectively
inhibiting the action of an
enzyme (phosphodiesterase
type 5) that breaks down a
substance that relaxes
smooth muscles and permits
blood flow that engorges the
columns of erectile tissue in
the penis. Unlike other treatments for erectile dysfunction, which produce
erections with or without
sexual arousal, sildenafil
allows the patient to respond
naturally to sexual stimulation. In clinical trials, over
70% of attempts at sexual
intercourse were successful
among men who took the
drug.

DOSAGE
The recommended dose for
most patients is 50 mg,
taken approximately 1 hour
before sexual activity. The
dose may be increased to
no more than 100 mg, or
may be decreased to 25 mg.
Your doctor will help to
determine the correct dose
for you. Do not take the
drug more than once in a
24-hour period.

ONSET OF EFFECT
Within 30 minutes to 4
hours.

DURATION OF ACTION
Unknown.

DIETARY ADVICE
Sildenafil can be taken without regard to meals.

STORAGE
Store in a tightly sealed container away from heat, moisture, and direct light.

IF YOU MISS A DOSE
Not applicable. Sildenafil is
taken only as needed.

STOPPING THE DRUG
Not applicable.

PROLONGED USE
Sildenafil treats but does
not cure erectile dysfunction. Patients must continue
using sildenafil to maintain
its benefit; lifelong therapy
may be warranted.

PRECAUTIONS
Over 60: No special problems are expected.

**Driving and Hazardous
Work:** This drug should
not impair your ability to
perform such tasks safely.

Alcohol: No special precautions are necessary.
However, alcohol is known
to decrease sexual function.

Pregnancy: Not applicable;
sildenafil is not approved for
use by women.

Breast Feeding: Not
applicable; sildenafil is not
approved for use by women.

Infants and Children:
Not applicable; sildenafil is
not to be used by children.

Special Concerns: Sildenafil does not offer any protection against sexually
transmitted diseases. Appropriate measures (for example, using condoms) should
be taken to ensure adequate
protection against sexually
transmitted diseases, including infection with the
human immunodeficiency

virus (HIV). Sildenafil
should be taken only by
men who have been clini-
cally evaluated for and
diagnosed with erectile
dysfunction by a doctor.

OVERDOSE
Symptoms: No cases
of overdose have been
reported.

What to Do: An overdose
with sildenafil is unlikely.
If someone takes a much
larger dose than prescribed,
call your doctor.

DRUG INTERACTIONS
Sildenafil can enhance the
action of nitrates (such as
nitroglycerin, which is used
to treat episodes of angina),
causing potentially dangerous decreases in blood pressure. Therefore, sildenafil
should not be used by
patients taking nitrates of
any kind. Use of sildenafil in
conjunction with other erectile-dysfunction medications
is not recommended. Con-
sult your doctor if you are
taking protease inhibitors
such as ritonavir and
saquinavir, which may
affect levels of sildenafil
in the blood.

FOOD INTERACTIONS
No known food interactions.

DISEASE INTERACTIONS
Caution is advised when
taking sildenafil. Consult
your doctor if you have a
history of any of the following: high or very low blood
pressure; structural deformity of the penis; a bleeding
disorder; heart attack,
stroke, or life-threatening
arrhythmia within the past
six months; heart failure;
coronary heart disease;
retinitis pigmentosa; peptic
ulcer; sickle cell anemia;
multiple myeloma; or
leukemia.

Simethicone

Mylanta Gas Relief 62.5 mg
(JOHNSON & JOHNSON/MERCK)

Additional photographs

▶ Drug Class: Antacid;
antiflatulant

▶ Available in: Tablets, chewable tablets, capsules, drops

▶ Available OTC? Yes

▶ As Generic? Yes

Side Effects

SERIOUS
No serious side effects
have been reported.

COMMON
Expulsion of excess gas
causing belching and
flatulence.

LESS COMMON
No less-common side
effects have been
reported.

PRINCIPAL USES
To relieve pain caused by
excess gas in stomach and
intestines. It may also be
employed in a clinical setting to decrease gas before
diagnostic radiography of
the stomach or intestines,
or prior to endoscopy.

HOW THE DRUG WORKS
Simethicone disperses and
prevents the formation of
gas bubbles in the gastrointestinal tract.

DOSAGE
Tablets or capsules: 60 to
125 mg, 4 times a day, after
meals and at bedtime.
Chewable tablets: 40 to 125
mg, 4 times a day after
meals and at bedtime, or
150 mg, 3 times a day after
meals. Drops: 40 to 95 mg,
4 times a day after meals
and at bedtime. The liquid
form should be taken by
mouth even if it comes in
a dropper bottle. The dose
should not exceed 500 mg
a day for all forms unless
your doctor advises otherwise. (In some cases your
doctor may wish to double
the dose.)

ONSET OF EFFECT
Immediate.

DURATION OF ACTION
Unknown.

DIETARY ADVICE
This medicine should be
taken after meals and at
bedtime for optimal results.

STORAGE
Store in a tightly sealed
container away from heat,
moisture, and direct light.
Store the liquid form at
room temperature.

IF YOU MISS A DOSE
Take it as soon as you
remember. However, if it is
near the time for the next
dose, skip the missed dose
and resume your regular
dosage schedule. Do not
double the next dose.

STOPPING THE DRUG
Take simethicone as pre-
scribed for the full treatment period. However, you
may stop taking the drug
if you are feeling better
before the scheduled
end of therapy.

PROLONGED USE
Consult your doctor if you
take simethicone for a prolonged period.

PRECAUTIONS
Over 60: There is no specific information comparing
use of simethicone in older
persons with use in younger
persons. However, no spe-
cial problems are expected.

**Driving and Hazardous
Work:** The use of simethicone should not impair
your ability to perform
such tasks safely.

Alcohol: No special problems are expected.

Pregnancy: Simethicone is
not absorbed into the body
and is not expected to cause
problems during pregnancy.

Breast Feeding: Sime-
thicone has not been
reported to cause problems
in nursing babies.

Infants and Children:
Use of simethicone for the
treatment of infant colic is
not recommended because
of limited information on its
safety in infants. Sime-
thicone should not be dispensed to children unless a
doctor instructs otherwise.

Special Concerns: If you
take the chewable tablets,
chew them thoroughly
before swallowing for more
complete and faster results.
Shake the liquid form well
before using. You should
change position frequently
and walk about to help eliminate gas. Tell your doctor if
you are on a low-sodium,
low-sugar or other special
diet. You should exercise
regularly and develop regular bowel habits. Do not
smoke before meals.

OVERDOSE
Symptoms: No specific
ones have been reported.

What to Do: An overdose
of simethicone is not life-
threatening. However, if
someone takes a much
larger dose than recom-
mended, call your doctor
or the nearest poison control center.

DRUG INTERACTIONS
None known.

FOOD INTERACTIONS
Avoid any foods that
increase gas formation.
Chew your food slowly and
thoroughly. Avoid carbon-
ated drinks.

DISEASE INTERACTIONS
None known.

Simvastatin

Zocor 10 mg
(MERCK)

Additional photographs

▶ Drug Class: Antilipidemic
(cholesterol-lowering agent)

▶ Available in: Tablets

▶ Available OTC? No

▶ As Generic? No

Side Effects

SERIOUS
Fever, unusual or unex-
plained muscle aches and
tenderness. Call
your doctor right away.

COMMON
Side effects occur in only
1% to 2% of patients.
They may include consti-
pation or diarrhea, dizziness or lightheadedness,
bloating or gas, heart-
burn, nausea, skin rash,
stomach pain, rise in liver
enzymes.

LESS COMMON
Insomnia.

PRINCIPAL USES
To treat high cholesterol.
Also used to reduce the
risk of stroke or transient
ischemic attack ("mini-
stroke") in patients with
high cholesterol and heart
disease. Usually prescribed
after first lines of treatment—including diet,
weight loss, and exercise—
fail to reduce total and low-
density lipoprotein (LDL)
cholesterol to acceptable
levels.

HOW THE DRUG WORKS
Simvastatin blocks the
action of an enzyme
required for the manufac-
ture of cholesterol, thereby
interfering with its formation. By lowering the
amount of cholesterol in the
liver cells, simvastatin
increases the formation of
receptors for LDL, and
thereby reduces blood levels of total and LDL cholesterol. In addition to
lowering LDL cholesterol,
simvastatin also modestly
reduces triglyceride levels
and raises HDL (the so-
called "good") cholesterol.

DOSAGE
Initial dose is 10 to 40 mg
once a day. It may be
increased to a maximum of
80 mg per day. Simvastatin
is most effective when
taken in the evening.

ONSET OF EFFECT
2 to 4 weeks.

DURATION OF ACTION
The effect persists for the
duration of therapy.

DIETARY ADVICE
Cholesterol-lowering drugs
are only one part of a total
program that should include
regular exercise and a
healthy diet. The American
Heart Association publishes
a "Healthy Heart" diet,
which is recommended.

STORAGE
Store in a tightly sealed container away from heat and
direct light.

IF YOU MISS A DOSE
Take it as soon as you
remember. Take your next
dose at the proper time and
resume your regular dosage
schedule. Do not double the
next dose.

STOPPING THE DRUG
The decision to stop taking
the drug should be made in
consultation with your doctor. Once the medication is
discontinued, blood cholesterol is likely to return to
original elevated levels.

PROLONGED USE
Side effects are more likely
with prolonged use. As you
continue with simvastatin,
your doctor will periodically
order blood tests to evaluate
liver function.

PRECAUTIONS
Over 60: No special problems are expected in older
patients.

**Driving and Hazardous
Work:** The use of simvastatin should not impair your
ability to perform such
tasks safely.

Alcohol: No special precautions are necessary.

Pregnancy: Should not be
used during pregnancy or
by women who plan to
become pregnant in the
near future.

Breast Feeding: This
drug is not recommended
for women who are nursing.

Infants and Children:
The long-term effects of
simvastatin in children have
not been determined. It is
rarely used in children; consult your pediatrician.

Special Concerns: Important elements of treatment
for high cholesterol include
proper diet, weight loss,
regular moderate exercise,
and the avoidance of certain
medications that may
increase cholesterol levels.
Because simvastatin has
potential side effects, it is
important that you maintain
a recommended healthy
diet and cooperate with
other treatments your
physician may suggest.

OVERDOSE
Symptoms: No specific
ones have been reported;
overdose is unlikely.

What to Do: Emergency
instructions not applicable.

DRUG INTERACTIONS
Consult your doctor if you
are taking cyclosporine,
gemfibrozil, niacin, antibiotics, especially ery-
thromycin, HIV protease
inhibitors, or medications
for fungus infections. All of
these drugs may increase
the risk of myositis (muscle
inflammation) when taken
with simvastatin and may
lead to kidney failure.

FOOD INTERACTIONS
No known food interactions.

DISEASE INTERACTIONS
Consult your doctor if you
have liver, kidney, or muscle
disease, or a medical history involving organ transplant or recent surgery.

Sodium Bicarbonate

Generic 324 mg
(CONCORD)

▸ Drug Class: Antacid

▸ Available in: Effervescent
powder, powder, tablets

▸ Available OTC? Yes

▸ As Generic? Yes

Side Effects

SERIOUS
Frequent urge to urinate,
nervousness or restless-
ness, mental or mood
changes, muscle twitch-
ing or pain, nausea or
vomiting, slow breathing,
continuing headache, loss
of appetite, swelling of
feet or lower legs,
unpleasant taste, unusual
fatigue. Call your doctor
immediately.

COMMON
No common side effects
are associated with
sodium bicarbonate.

LESS COMMON
Stomach cramps,
increased thirst.

PRINCIPAL USES
To relieve heartburn, sour
stomach, or acid indiges-
tion. It may also be pre-
scribed to treat metabolic
acidosis (excess acid
buildup in the body fluids),
to prevent urinary stones,
and as part of the treatment
of gout.

HOW THE DRUG WORKS
Sodium bicarbonate neutralizes stomach acid and
reduces the action of
pepsin, a digestive enzyme.
This provides symptomatic
relief from excess stomach
acid. Also, the bicarbonate
is a base, meaning it can
help correct the pH balance
(reduce the acidity) of
blood and urine.

DOSAGE
Effervescent powder— For
heartburn or sour stomach:
3.9 to 10 g (1 to 2 ½ teaspoons) in a glass of cold
water. Usually not more
than 19.5 g a day (5 tea-
spoons). Children ages 6 to
12: 1 to 1.9 g (¼ to ½ teaspoon) in a glass of cold
water. Powder— For heart-
burn or sour stomach: ½
teaspoon in a glass of water
every 2 hours. Dose may be
changed if needed. To make
the urine less acidic: 1 teaspoon (1.9 g) in a glass of
water every 4 hours; usually
not more than 4 teaspoons a
day. Dose may be changed
by your doctor. Tablets—
For heartburn or sour stomach: 325 mg to 2 g, 1 to 4
times a day. Children ages 6
to 12: 520 mg. Dose may be
repeated in 30 minutes. To
make the urine less acidic—
To start, 4 g; then 1 to 2 g
every 4 hours. Maximum
adult dose usually not more
than 16 g a day. Children:
23 to 230 mg per 2.2 lbs
(1 kg) of body weight a
day. Dose may be changed
if needed.

ONSET OF EFFECT
Rapid when used as an
antacid for heartburn and
sour stomach.

DURATION OF ACTION
Unknown.

DIETARY ADVICE
Sodium bicarbonate should
be taken after meals. Be
sure to account for the large
amount of sodium in this
medication if you are on a
salt-restricted diet.

STORAGE
Store in a tightly sealed container away from heat, moisture, and direct light.

IF YOU MISS A DOSE
Take it as soon as you
remember. If it is near
the time for the next dose,
skip the missed dose and
resume your regular dosage
schedule. Do not double the
next dose.

STOPPING THE DRUG
Take as directed if taking it
by prescription.

PROLONGED USE
Do not take sodium bicar-
bonate for more than 2
weeks or on a routine basis
without consulting your
physician.

PRECAUTIONS
Over 60: See Dietary
Advice.

**Driving and Hazardous
Work:** No special precautions are necessary.

Alcohol: Avoid alcohol.

Pregnancy: No problems
have been reported.

Breast Feeding: No problems have been reported.

Infants and Children:
Use and dosage for infants
and children under 6 years
of age should be deter-
mined by your doctor.

OVERDOSE
Symptoms: See Serious
Side Effects.

What to Do: An overdose
of sodium bicarbonate is
unlikely to be life-threatening. However, if someone
takes a much larger dose
than recommended, call
your doctor, emergency
medical services (EMS), or
the nearest poison control
center immediately.

DRUG INTERACTIONS
Do not take any other over-
the-counter medications
containing sodium bicarbonate such as Alka-Seltzer.
Consult your doctor for specific advice if you are taking
ketoconazole, tetracyclines,
mecamylamine, methena-
mine, urinary acidifiers,
amphetamines, anticholinergics, quinidine, citrates,
enteric-coated medications,
ephedrine, flecainide, fluoroquinolones, iron, lithium,
methotrexate, mexiletine,
sucralfate, or salicylates.

FOOD INTERACTIONS
Do not take sodium bicar-
bonate with milk or milk
products.

DISEASE INTERACTIONS
Do not take sodium bicar-
bonate if you have any sign
of appendicitis (stomach
pain, bloating, nausea, and
vomiting). If you have kidney problems, use sodium
bicarbonate only on advice
of your doctor. Consult your
doctor if you have intestinal
or rectal bleeding, edema
(swelling of the hands or
feet), heart, liver, or kidney
disease, hypertension, urination problems, or toxemia
of pregnancy.

Sodium Phosphate/Sodium Biphosphate

▶ Drug Class: Hyperosmotic laxative

▶ Available in: Oral solution, effervescent powder, enema

▶ Available OTC? Yes

▶ As Generic? Yes

Side Effects

SERIOUS
Confusion, dizziness or lightheadedness, irregular heartbeat, muscle cramps, unusual tiredness or weakness. Call your doctor immediately.

COMMON
Cramping, diarrhea, gas, increased thirst.

LESS COMMON
No less-common side effects have been reported.

PRINCIPAL USES
To treat short-term constipation or for rapid emptying of the colon prior to bowel or rectal examination.

HOW THE DRUG WORKS
This medication attracts and retains water in the intestine, increasing peristalsis (bowel activity) and the urge to defecate.

DOSAGE
Oral— Adults and teenagers: 20 to 30 ml (4 to 6 teaspoons) mixed with ½ glass cool water. Children ages 10 to 12: 10 ml (2 teaspoons). Children ages 6 to 10: 5 ml (1 teaspoon). Enema— Adults and teenagers: 118 ml (contents of 1 disposable adult enema) given rectally. Children over 2: ½ adult dose (contents of 1 disposable pediatric enema).

ONSET OF EFFECT
30 minutes to 3 hours after oral administration, 3 to 5 minutes after enema.

DURATION OF ACTION
Variable with oral use; upon evacuation with enema.

DIETARY ADVICE
Sodium phosphate/sodium biphosphate should not be used with food. The unpleasant taste that may occur when you take the medicine can be lessened by taking it with citrus fruit juice or a citrus-flavored soft drink.

STORAGE
Store in a tightly sealed container away from heat and direct light.

IF YOU MISS A DOSE
Oral forms: If you are taking this laxative on a fixed schedule, take the missed dose as soon as you remember. If it is near the time for the next dose, skip the missed dose and resume your regular dosage schedule. Do not double the next dose. Enema: Not applicable.

STOPPING THE DRUG
Take it as prescribed for the full treatment period. However, you may stop taking the drug if you feel better before the scheduled end of therapy.

PROLONGED USE
Do not use any laxative for longer than 2 weeks without consulting your doctor.

PRECAUTIONS
Over 60: Adverse reactions may be more likely and more severe in older patients.

Driving and Hazardous Work: Do not drive or engage in hazardous work until you determine how the medicine affects you.

Alcohol: Avoid alcohol.

Pregnancy: This laxative contains a large amount of sodium, which may have unwanted effects during pregnancy, such as higher blood pressure. If you have to take a laxative during pregnancy, consult your doctor for specific advice.

Breast Feeding: Sodium phosphate may pass into breast milk; caution is advised. Consult your doctor for specific advice.

Infants and Children: Do not give sodium phosphate/sodium biphosphate to children under the age of 6 without consulting your doctor.

Special Concerns: Chilling the oral form of the medication or taking it with ice or following it with citrus fruit juice or citrus-fla- vored carbonated beverages may make it more palatable. Remember that chronic use of sodium phosphate or any laxative can lead to laxative dependence. You should consume adequate amounts of bulk (fiber) in your diet, such as bran, whole-grain cereals, fruit, and vegetables. This laxative should be taken on a schedule that does not interfere with activities or sleep; it produces watery stools within 3 to 6 hours. It should not be taken within 2 hours of taking other medications.

OVERDOSE
Symptoms: Excessive bowel activity, dehydration causing low blood pressure and abnormal heartbeat, metabolic acidosis, blood chemistry abnormalities.

What to Do: An overdose of sodium phosphate/ sodium biphosphate is unlikely to be life-threatening. However, if someone takes a much larger dose than prescribed, call your doctor, emergency medical services (EMS), or the nearest poison control center immediately.

DRUG INTERACTIONS
Consult your doctor for advice if you are taking anticoagulants, digitalis drugs, ciprofloxacin, etidronate, sodium polystyrene sulfonate, or oral tetracyclines.

FOOD INTERACTIONS
No known food interactions.

DISEASE INTERACTIONS
Consult your doctor if you have a history of appendicitis, rectal bleeding of unknown cause, colostomy, intestinal blockage, ileostomy, diabetes, heart disease, high blood pressure, kidney disease, or swallowing difficulties.

Sodium Polystyrene Sulfonate

BRAND NAMES
Kayexalate, SPS

▶ Drug Class: Potassium-removing resin

▶ Available in: Powder for suspension, suspension

▶ Available OTC? No

▶ As Generic? Yes

Side Effects

SERIOUS
Severe stomach pain with nausea and vomiting (fecal impaction), heartbeat irregularities, abdominal and muscle cramps, weight gain, irritability, difficulty thinking, confusion, decreased urination, severe muscle fatigue, swelling of hands, feet, or lower legs. Call your doctor immediately.

COMMON
Loss of appetite, constipation, nausea, vomiting.

LESS COMMON
There are no less-common side effects associated with sodium polystyrene sulfonate.

PRINCIPAL USES
To treat abnormally high blood levels of potassium (hyperkalemia) caused by acute kidney failure.

HOW THE DRUG WORKS
Sodium polystyrene sulfonate is a resin that lowers potassium levels by exchanging sodium present in the medication with potassium present in the body. This process occurs within the intestines.

DOSAGE
The powder for suspension and the suspension can be taken either orally or rectally. Adults— Oral: 15 g (4 level tablespoons of powder), 1 to 4 times a day; may be increased to 40 g, 4 times a day. Rectal: 25 to 100 g as needed, given as an enema or in a dialysis bag. Children— Oral: 1 g per 2.2 lbs (1 kg) of body weight, as needed. Rectal: 1 g per 2.2 lbs, as needed, given as an enema or in a dialysis bag. Oral dosage is preferred because the drug should remain in the intestine for at least 6 hours.

ONSET OF EFFECT
Unknown.

DURATION OF ACTION
Unknown.

DIETARY ADVICE
The oral medication should not be mixed with orange juice (orange juice is high in potassium).

STORAGE
Store in a tightly sealed container away from heat, moisture, and direct light. Liquid form can be refrigerated, but do not allow it to freeze.

IF YOU MISS A DOSE
Take it as soon as you remember. However, if it is near the time for the next dose, skip the missed dose and resume your regular dosage schedule. Do not double the next dose.

STOPPING THE DRUG
The decision to stop taking the drug should be made in consultation with your physician.

PROLONGED USE
See your doctor regularly for tests and examinations if you must take this medication for a prolonged period.

PRECAUTIONS
Over 60: Side effects, especially fecal impaction, may be more likely in older patients.

Driving and Hazardous Work: Do not drive or engage in hazardous work until you determine how the medicine affects you.

Alcohol: Avoid alcohol.

Pregnancy: Adequate studies of the use of sodium polystyrene sulfonate during pregnancy have not been done. Before taking it, consult your doctor if you are pregnant or plan to become pregnant.

Breast Feeding: It is not known whether sodium polystyrene sulfonate passes into breast milk; consult your doctor for advice.

Infants and Children: No special problems are expected.

Special Concerns: If you are taking the suspension made from the powder, shake it well before using. Do not use mineral oil when administering this drug rectally. The suspension should be used within 24 hours of preparation.

OVERDOSE
Symptoms: Severe nausea, vomiting, fecal impaction, swelling of hands, feet, or lower legs, decreased urination, severe muscle fatigue, confusion.

What to Do: Call your doctor, emergency medical services (EMS), or the nearest poison control center immediately.

DRUG INTERACTIONS
The following drugs may interact with sodium polystyrene sulfonate. Consult your doctor for specific advice if you are taking antacids, digitalis drugs, laxatives, diuretics, potassium supplements, or any other prescription or over-the-counter medication.

FOOD INTERACTIONS
Orange juice can increase blood levels of potassium.

DISEASE INTERACTIONS
Caution is advised when taking sodium polystyrene sulfonate. Consult your doctor for advice if you have a history of congestive heart failure, severe high blood pressure, or severe edema (swelling of body tissues caused by fluid retention).

Somatrem

▶ Drug Class: Growth hormone

▶ Available in: Injection

▶ Available OTC? No

▶ As Generic? No

Side Effects

SERIOUS
Pain and swelling at the site of injection; pain in hip or knee (possibly causing a limp); skin rash or itching. Call your doctor right away.

COMMON
No common side effects are associated with somatrem.

LESS COMMON
No uncommon side effects are associated with somatrem.

PRINCIPAL USES
To replace growth hormone if it is not produced sufficiently by the pituitary gland.

HOW THE DRUG WORKS
Somatrem stimulates growth in the same manner as natural growth hormone.

DOSAGE
0.136 mg per lb of body weight weekly, in multiple doses as determined by your doctor.

ONSET OF EFFECT
Within 1 hour.

DURATION OF ACTION
12 to 48 hours.

DIETARY ADVICE
None.

STORAGE
Keep the liquid refrigerated, but do not allow it to freeze. Use it within 7 days.

IF YOU MISS A DOSE
Take it as soon as you remember. If it is near the time for the next dose, skip the missed dose and resume your regular dosage schedule. Do not double the next dose.

STOPPING THE DRUG
The decision to stop taking the drug should be made by your doctor.

PROLONGED USE
After 2 years of use, growth rate generally decreases. If this occurs, the patient should be checked for compliance with therapy or the presence of other medical problems or the presence of antibodies to the medicine. Prolonged use of somatrem may cause a condition known as acromegaly (overgrowth of face, hands, and feet, organ enlargement, diabetes, atherosclerosis, high blood pressure, and carpal tunnel syndrome), resulting from excess quantities of pituitary hormone.

PRECAUTIONS

Over 60: Somatrem can be used to replace deficient growth hormone levels in people of any age. Though not approved for this use, growth hormone has been administered to elderly patients to increase muscle strength. Such use can result in edema (swelling of tissues due to excess fluid retention) and high blood pressure.

Driving and Hazardous Work: The use of somatrem should not impair the ability to perform such tasks safely.

Alcohol: No special precautions are necessary.

Pregnancy: It is unknown whether somatrem causes fetal harm; the drug should be used by pregnant women only if absolutely necessary. Consult your doctor for specific advice.

Breast Feeding: It is unknown whether somatrem passes into breast milk or causes harm to a nursing infant; the drug should be used by nursing mothers only if clearly needed. Consult your doctor.

Infants and Children: Somatrem should not be given to a child whose bone ends (epiphyses) have closed, signaling the end of bone growth.

Special Concerns: If somatrem is given to adults or children with normal growth hormone production, serious unwanted effects may occur, such as diabetes, high blood pressure, atherosclerosis, and abnormal growth of bone and internal organs including the heart, kidneys, and liver. If growth with somatrem is not satisfactory, some patients may be given low doses of sex hormones to improve their response to the medication. Annual tests of bone age are recommended. Periodic tests of thyroid function should be done, since low thyroid function interferes with the response to human growth hormone. If low growth hormone production is due to a lesion in the cranium, the lesion should be monitored at frequent intervals. If somatrem is injected into muscle, the needle used for injections should be at least 1 inch long to ensure that the medicine reaches the muscle.

OVERDOSE
Symptoms: No specific ones have been reported.

What to Do: An overdose of somatrem is unlikely to be life-threatening. However, if someone receives a much larger dose than prescribed, call your doctor, emergency medical services (EMS), or local poison control center immediately.

DRUG INTERACTIONS
Consult your doctor for specific advice if you (or your child) are also taking the following drugs that may interact with somatrem: anabolic steroids, estrogens, androgens, thyroid hormones, corticosteroids, or corticotropin.

FOOD INTERACTIONS
No known food interactions.

DISEASE INTERACTIONS
Caution is advised when taking somatrem. Consult your doctor if you have low thyroid function or any malignancy (cancerous growth).

Somatropin

▶ Drug Class: Growth hormone

▶ Available in: Injection

▶ Available OTC? No

▶ As Generic? No

Side Effects

SERIOUS
Pain and swelling at the site of injection; pain in hip or knee (possibly causing a limp); skin rash or itching. Call your doctor right away.

COMMON
No common side effects are associated with somatropin.

LESS COMMON
No uncommon side effects are associated with somatropin.

PRINCIPAL USES
To replace growth hormone if it is not produced sufficiently by the pituitary gland.

HOW THE DRUG WORKS
Somatropin stimulates growth in the same manner as natural growth hormone.

DOSAGE
Adults: To start, not more than 0.006 mg per kg (2.2 lbs) of body weight given daily as an injection under the skin. The dosage may be increased by your doctor to no more than 0.025 mg per kg in patients under 35 years and 0.0125 mg per kg in patients over 35 years. Children: Up to 0.3 mg per kg weekly, divided into daily injections under the skin as determined by the doctor.

ONSET OF EFFECT
Within 1 hour.

DURATION OF ACTION
12 to 48 hours.

DIETARY ADVICE
No special restrictions.

STORAGE
Keep the liquid refrigerated, but do not allow it to freeze. Use it within 7 days.

IF YOU MISS A DOSE
Take it as soon as you remember. If it is near the time for the next dose, skip the missed dose and resume your regular dosage schedule. Do not double the next dose.

STOPPING THE DRUG
The decision to stop taking the drug should be made by your doctor.

PROLONGED USE
After 2 years of use, growth rate generally decreases. If this occurs, the patient should be checked for compliance with therapy or the presence of other medical problems or the presence of antibodies to the medicine. Prolonged use of somatropin may cause a condition known as acromegaly (overgrowth of face, hands, and feet, organ enlargement, diabetes, atherosclerosis, high blood pressure, and carpal tunnel syndrome), resulting from excess quantities of pituitary hormone.

PRECAUTIONS
Over 60: Somatropin can be used to replace deficient growth hormone levels in people of any age. Though not approved for this use, growth hormone has been administered to elderly patients to increase muscle strength. Such use can result in edema (swelling of tissues due to excess fluid retention) and high blood pressure.

Driving and Hazardous Work: The use of somatropin should not impair the ability to perform such tasks safely.

Alcohol: No special precautions are necessary.

Pregnancy: It is unknown whether somatropin causes fetal harm; the drug should be used by pregnant women only if absolutely necessary. Consult your doctor for specific advice.

Breast Feeding: It is not known whether somatropin passes into breast milk or causes harm to a nursing infant; the drug should be used by nursing mothers only if clearly needed. Consult your doctor.

Infants and Children: Somatropin should not be given to a child whose bone ends (epiphyses) have closed, signaling the end of bone growth.

Special Concerns: If somatropin is given to adults or children with normal growth hormone production, serious unwanted effects may occur, such as diabetes, high blood pressure, atherosclerosis, and abnormal growth of bone and internal organs including the heart, kidneys, and liver. If growth is not satisfactory, some patients may be given low doses of sex hormones to improve their response to somatropin. Annual tests of bone age are recommended. Periodic tests of thyroid function should be done, since low thyroid function interferes with response to human growth hormone. If low growth hormone production is due to a lesion in the cranium, the lesion should be monitored frequently. If somatropin is injected into muscle, the needle used for injections should be at least 1 inch long.

OVERDOSE
Symptoms: None.

What to Do: An overdose is unlikely to be life-threatening. However, if someone receives a much larger dose than prescribed, seek medical assistance immediately.

DRUG INTERACTIONS
Consult your doctor for specific advice if you (or your child) are also taking the following drugs that may interact with somatropin: anabolic steroids, estrogens, androgens, thyroid hormones, corticosteroids, or corticotropin.

FOOD INTERACTIONS
No known food interactions.

DISEASE INTERACTIONS
Consult your doctor if you have low thyroid function or any malignancy (cancerous growth).

Sotalol Hydrochloride

BRAND NAME
Betapace

Betapace 80 mg
(BERLEX)

▶ Drug Class: Beta-blocker; antiarrhythmic

▶ Available in: Tablets

▶ Available OTC? No

▶ As Generic? Yes

Side Effects

SERIOUS
Severe, occasionally life-threatening arrhythmias, shortness of breath, wheezing; irregular or slow heartbeat (50 beats per minute or less); pain or feelings of tightness or pressure in the chest; swelling of the ankles, feet, and lower legs; mental depression. If you experience such symptoms, stop taking sotalol and call your doctor immediately.

COMMON
Dizziness or lightheadedness, especially when rising suddenly to a standing position; rapid heartbeat or palpitations; decreased sexual ability; unusual fatigue, weakness, or drowsiness; insomnia. Notify your doctor.

LESS COMMON
Anxiety, irritability, nervousness; constipation; diarrhea; dry, sore eyes; itching; nausea or vomiting; nightmares or intensely vivid dreams; numbness, tingling, or other unusual sensations in the fingers, toes, or scalp. Call your doctor if such symptoms persist.

PRINCIPAL USES
This drug is used only to treat or prevent life-threatening heart rhythm disturbances (cardiac arrhythmias). It requires close monitoring by a physician.

HOW THE DRUG WORKS
Beta-blockers such as sotalol work by preventing—or blocking—nerve impulses from exerting an accelerating or intensifying effect on specific parts of the body, especially the blood vessels and heart. In this way, sotalol slows and stabilizes heartbeat.

DOSAGE
Adults: 80 mg, 2 times a day. The dosage may be increased to 320 mg a day in 2 or 3 divided doses.

ONSET OF EFFECT
Unknown.

DURATION OF ACTION
Up to 12 hours.

DIETARY ADVICE
Should be taken on an empty stomach, 1 hour before or 2 hours after meals.

STORAGE
Store in a tightly sealed container away from heat and direct light.

IF YOU MISS A DOSE
Take it as soon as you remember. However, if it is near the time for the next dose, skip the missed dose and resume your regular dosage schedule. Do not double the next dose.

STOPPING THE DRUG
Do not discontinue the drug abruptly, as this may cause serious health problems. Dosage must be gradually tapered in accordance with your doctor's instructions.

PROLONGED USE
Your doctor should check your progress in regular visits if you take sotalol for a prolonged period.

PRECAUTIONS
Over 60: Adverse reactions may be more likely and more severe. Resistance to cold temperatures may be decreased in older patients

Driving and Hazardous Work: Do not drive or engage in hazardous work until you determine how the medicine affects you.

Alcohol: Avoid alcohol.

Pregnancy: Before taking sotalol, tell your doctor if you are pregnant or plan to become pregnant.

Breast Feeding: Sotalol passes into breast milk; consult your doctor about its use during nursing.

Infants and Children: Dosage for infants and children must be determined by your pediatrician.

Special Concerns: To avoid dizziness and fainting, take extra care during exercise or hot weather. Check your pulse regularly while taking sotalol. If it is slower than your usual rate, or less than 50 beats per minute, check with your doctor; a slow pulse rate may indicate circulation problems.

OVERDOSE
Symptoms: Unusually slow or rapid heartbeat, confusion, severe dizziness or fainting, poor circulation in the hands (bluish skin), breathing difficulty.

What to Do: Call your doctor, emergency medical services (EMS), or the nearest poison control center immediately.

DRUG INTERACTIONS
Consult your doctor for specific advice if you are taking amphetamines, oral antidiabetic agents, asthma medication (such as aminophylline or theophylline), calcium channel blockers, clonidine, guanabenz, halothane, immunotherapy for allergies (allergy shots), insulin, MAO inhibitors, reserpine, other beta-blockers, or any over-the-counter medicine.

FOOD INTERACTIONS
No known food interactions.

DISEASE INTERACTIONS
People with the following conditions should consult their doctor before using sotalol: allergies or asthma; diabetes mellitus; heart or blood vessel disease (including congestive heart failure and peripheral vascular disease); hyperthyroidism; irregular (slow) heartbeat; a history of mental depression; myasthenia gravis; psoriasis; respiratory problems such as bronchitis or emphysema; kidney or liver disease.

Sparfloxacin

BRAND NAME
Zagam

▶ Drug Class: Fluoroquinolone antibiotic

▶ Available in: Tablets

▶ Available OTC? No

▶ As Generic? No

Side Effects

SERIOUS
Serious reactions to sparfloxacin are rare and include seizures, mental confusion, hallucinations, agitation, nightmares, depression, shortness of breath, unusual swelling in the face or extremities, and loss of consciousness. Also skin burning, redness, blisters, rash, or itching on exposure to sunlight; increased risk of tendinitis or tendon rupture. Call your doctor immediately.

COMMON
Increased sensitivity to sunlight (and increased risk of sunburn) for days following therapy.

LESS COMMON
Diarrhea, nausea and vomiting, stomach pain and upset, gas, headache, dizziness, restlessness, insomnia, changes in taste perception, drowsiness, itching, dry mouth, unusual body aches or pains.

PRINCIPAL USES
To treat pneumonia, chronic bronchitis, and other bacterial infections.

HOW THE DRUG WORKS
Sparfloxacin inhibits the activity of a bacterial enzyme (gyrase) that is necessary for proper DNA formation and replication. This fights infection by preventing bacteria cells from reproducing.

DOSAGE
Adults: To start, 400 mg in 1 dose on the first day, then take 200 mg, once a day for 9 days. For patients with kidney impairment, 400 mg to start, wait 2 days, then take 200 mg every other day for 9 days.

ONSET OF EFFECT
Varies depending on the infection being treated.

DURATION OF ACTION
Unknown.

DIETARY ADVICE
Drink plenty of fluids.

STORAGE
Store in a tightly sealed container away from heat and direct light.

IF YOU MISS A DOSE
Take it as soon as you remember. If it is near the time for the next dose, skip the missed dose and resume your regular dosage schedule. Do not double the next dose.

STOPPING THE DRUG
It is very important to take this drug as prescribed for the full treatment period, even if you begin to feel better before the scheduled end of therapy (unless you experience intolerable side effects, including increased sensitivity to sunlight, in which case, discontinue taking the drug and call your physician right away).

PROLONGED USE
See your doctor regularly for tests and examinations if you must take this medicine for a prolonged period.

PRECAUTIONS
Over 60: No special problems are expected.

Driving and Hazardous Work: Do not drive or engage in hazardous work until you determine how the medicine affects you.

Alcohol: It is advisable to abstain from alcohol when fighting an infection.

Pregnancy: In some animal tests, sparfloxacin has caused birth defects. Adequate studies in humans have not been done. It should be used during pregnancy only if the potential benefit justifies the risk. Before you take sparfloxacin, tell your doctor if you are pregnant or plan to become pregnant.

Breast Feeding: Sparfloxacin passes into breast milk and may cause serious side effects in the nursing infant; use of the drug is discouraged when nursing.

Infants and Children: Not recommended for use by persons under age 18, as it has been shown to interfere with bone development.

Special Concerns: If this drug causes increased sensitivity to sunlight, stop taking the medicine and try to avoid exposure to sunlight for the next week; also wear protective clothing and use a sunblock. Sparfloxacin should not be taken by a patient whose work makes it impossible to avoid exposure to sunlight. It is important to drink plenty of fluids while taking this antibiotic.

OVERDOSE
Symptoms: No specific ones have been reported.

What to Do: If you have any reason to suspect an overdose, call your doctor, emergency medical services (EMS), or the nearest poison control center.

DRUG INTERACTIONS
The following drugs may interact with sparfloxacin. Consult your doctor for specific advice if you are taking aminophylline, antacids, didanosine, iron supplements, sucralfate, or zinc salts. Also tell your doctor if you are taking any other prescription or over-the-counter drug.

FOOD INTERACTIONS
No known food interactions.

DISEASE INTERACTIONS
Caution is advised when taking sparfloxacin. Consult your doctor if you have any other medical condition. Use of sparfloxacin can cause complications in patients with kidney disease, since this organ works to remove the medication from the body.

Spironolactone

BRAND NAME
Aldactone

Generic 25 mg
(MYLAN)

▶ Drug Class: Potassium-
   sparing diuretic

▶ Available in: Tablets

▶ Available OTC? No

▶ As Generic? Yes

Side Effects

SERIOUS
Skin rash or itching,
shortness of breath,
cough or hoarseness,
fever or chills, pain
in lower back or side,
painful or difficult urination. Call your doctor
immediately.

COMMON
Nausea, vomiting,
diarrhea.

LESS COMMON
Dizziness, headache,
sweating, decreased sex-
ual ability, breast tenderness, breast enlargement
in men, increased hair
growth in females, irreg-
ular menstrual periods.

PRINCIPAL USES

As adjunctive (supplemen-
tary) treatment with other
diuretics to increase excretion of sodium and water in
the urine while conserving
potassium. Spironolactone
may be used on its own in
patients with liver disease
or primary hyperaldoster-
onism, a life-threatening
disorder that occurs when
the adrenal glands secrete
too much of the hormone
aldosterone.

HOW THE DRUG WORKS

Spironolactone blocks the
effect of aldosterone in the
kidneys to increase excretion of sodium and water in
the urine while conserving
potassium. In conjunction
with thiazide or loop diuretics, spironolactone reduces
the overall fluid volume in
the body, which helps to
control symptoms of liver
disease, heart disease,
and kidney disease.

DOSAGE

Adults: 100 to 400 mg a day
in 2 to 4 doses. Children: 1
to 3 mg per 2.2 lbs (1 kg) of
body weight, in 1 to 4 doses
a day.

ONSET OF EFFECT

1 to 2 days.

DURATION OF ACTION

2 to 3 days.

DIETARY ADVICE

Take it with meals to
enhance absorption.

STORAGE

Store in a tightly sealed container away from heat and
direct light.

IF YOU MISS A DOSE

Take it as soon as you
remember. If it is near
the time for the next dose,
skip the missed dose and
resume your regular dosage
schedule. Do not double the
next dose.

STOPPING THE DRUG

The decision to stop taking
the drug should be made by
your doctor.

PROLONGED USE

You should see your doctor
periodically for tests if you
take this medicine for a prolonged period.

PRECAUTIONS

Over 60: No special precautions are warranted.

**Driving and Hazardous
Work:** The use of spironolactone should not impair
your ability to perform such
tasks safely.

Alcohol: No special precautions are necessary.

Pregnancy: This drug has
not been shown to cause
birth defects in animals;
human tests have not been
done. In any case, spironolactone is not usually prescribed during pregnancy.

Breast Feeding: Spironolactone passes into breast
milk but has not been
reported to cause problems.
Consult your doctor for
advice about its use while
nursing.

Infants and Children:
No special problems are
expected in children.

OVERDOSE

Symptoms: Acute elec-
trolyte imbalance causing
central nervous system
disturbances.

What to Do: An overdose
of spironolactone is unlikely
to be life-threatening. However, if someone takes a
much larger dose than prescribed, call your doctor,
emergency medical services
(EMS), or the nearest poison control center.

DRUG INTERACTIONS

Consult your doctor for specific advice if you are taking
cyclosporine, potassium-
containing medicines or
supplements, digoxin,
or lithium. Also, since
angiotensin-converting
enzyme (ACE) inhibitors
block aldosterone produc-
tion, spironolactone is not
useful in patients taking
this type of medication.

FOOD INTERACTIONS

Avoid consuming large
servings of high-potassium
foods, which include
bananas, melons, prunes,
citrus fruits and juices (and
most fruits in general), avocados, potatoes, nuts, baked
beans, brussels sprouts, and
skim milk.

DISEASE INTERACTIONS

Caution is advised when
taking spironolactone. Consult your doctor if you have
any of the following: kidney
stones, menstrual problems,
breast enlargement, liver
disease, or kidney disease.

Spironolactone/Hydrochlorothiazide (HCTZ)

Generic 25/25 mg
(MYLAN)

▶ Drug Class: Diuretic combination

▶ Available in: Tablets

▶ Available OTC? No

▶ As Generic? Yes

Side Effects

SERIOUS
Skin rash, hives, palpitations, lightheadedness, unusual bleeding. Call your doctor immediately.

COMMON
Fluid depletion leading to dizziness, especially when rising from a sitting or lying position.

LESS COMMON
Gout, increased blood sugar levels, breast enlargement in men, decreased sexual ability, increased sensitivity of the skin to sunlight.

PRINCIPAL USES
To treat edema (swelling of body tissues resulting from excess salt and water retention) and to control high blood pressure.

HOW THE DRUG WORKS
Spironolactone, a potassium-sparing diuretic, blocks the effect of aldosterone—a hormone that regulates sodium and potassium levels in the body—in the kidneys to increase excretion of sodium and water in the urine while conserving potassium. Hydrochlorothiazide, a thiazide diuretic, increases the excretion of sodium and water in the urine. By reducing the overall fluid volume in the body, diuretics reduce pressure within the blood vessels.

DOSAGE
Adults: 1 to 4 tablets a day, usually taken as a single dose.

ONSET OF EFFECT
Within 2 hours.

DURATION OF ACTION
24 hours.

DIETARY ADVICE
Take it in the morning after breakfast.

STORAGE
Store in a tightly sealed container away from heat, moisture, and direct light.

IF YOU MISS A DOSE
Take it as soon as you remember. However, if it is near the time for the next dose, skip the missed dose and resume your regular dosage schedule. Do not double the next dose.

STOPPING THE DRUG
Take it as prescribed for the full treatment period. The decision to stop taking the drug should be made in consultation with your physician.

PROLONGED USE
See your doctor regularly for tests and examinations if you must take this medication for a prolonged period. If you are taking this medication for high blood pressure, lifelong therapy may be necessary.

PRECAUTIONS
Over 60: No special problems are expected.

Driving and Hazardous Work: The use of this drug should not impair your ability to perform such tasks safely.

Alcohol: No special precautions are necessary.

Pregnancy: This medication should not be taken during pregnancy unless recommended by your physician. Other diuretics are preferred.

Breast Feeding: Spironolactone and hydrochlorothiazide pass into breast milk; avoid or discontinue usage during the first month of breast feeding.

Infants and Children: This medication is seldom prescribed for children and infants.

Special Concerns: If you are taking this medicine to control high blood pressure, you should also follow your doctor's advice on weight control, diet, and exercise. Avoid exposure to sunlight until you determine how the medicine affects you. Spironolactone sometimes causes enlarged breasts in men and irregular menstrual periods in women.

OVERDOSE
Symptoms: Acute electrolyte imbalance causing central nervous system disturbances, fainting, lethargy, dizziness, drowsiness, confusion, gastrointestinal irritation.

What to Do: Call your doctor, emergency medical services (EMS), or the nearest poison control center immediately.

DRUG INTERACTIONS
Consult your doctor for specific advice if you are taking ACE inhibitors, cyclosporine, any potassium-containing medicines or supplements, cholestyramine, colestipol, digitalis drugs, or lithium.

FOOD INTERACTIONS
Avoid potassium-rich foods and beverages such as apple, orange, or other citrus fruit juices.

DISEASE INTERACTIONS
Consult your doctor if you have diabetes mellitus, a history of gout or kidney stones, heart or blood vessel disease, systemic lupus erythematosus, liver disease, kidney disease, or pancreatitis.

Stavudine (d4T)

BRAND NAME
Zerit

Zerit 15 mg
(BRISTOL-MYERS SQUIBB)

Additional photographs

▶ Drug Class: Antiviral

▶ Available in: Capsules

▶ Available OTC? No

▶ As Generic? No

Side Effects

SERIOUS
Burning, tingling, pain, or numbness in hands or feet. Also fever, muscle aches, joint pain, skin rash, nausea, vomiting, severe abdominal pain, unusual fatigue. Call your doctor immediately.

COMMON
No common side effects are associated with the use of stavudine.

LESS COMMON
Diarrhea, insomnia, headache, loss of appetite, general weakness and loss of energy.

PRINCIPAL USES
To treat HIV (human immunodeficiency virus) infection. While not a cure for HIV infection, this drug may suppress the replication of the virus and delay the progression of the disease.

HOW THE DRUG WORKS
Stavudine (d4T) interferes with the activity of enzymes needed for the replication of DNA in viral cells, thus preventing the virus from reproducing.

DOSAGE
Adults and teenagers weighing 132 lbs or more: 40 mg, 2 times a day. Adults and teenagers weighing up to 132 lbs: 30 mg, 2 times a day. Doses of 20 mg, 2 times a day, are sometimes used in patients with advanced HIV disease or mild peripheral neuropathy. Stavudine is usually given in combination with other antiretroviral medications.

ONSET OF EFFECT
Unknown. With most antiretroviral drugs, an early response can be seen within the first few days of therapy, but the maximum effect may take 12 to 16 weeks.

DURATION OF ACTION
Unknown. Effects of the drug may be prolonged if stavudine is used in combination with other effective drugs and the virus is maximally suppressed.

DIETARY ADVICE
Drink plenty of fluids.

STORAGE
Store in a tightly sealed container away from heat and direct light.

IF YOU MISS A DOSE
Take it as soon as you remember. However, if it is near the time for the next dose, skip the missed dose and resume your regular dosage schedule. Do not double the next dose.

STOPPING THE DRUG
The decision to stop taking the drug should be made in consultation with your physician.

PROLONGED USE
See your doctor regularly for tests and examinations if you must take this medicine for a prolonged period.

PRECAUTIONS
Over 60: No special studies have been done on older patients. A lower dose may be warranted, especially if kidney function is impaired.

Driving and Hazardous Work: Do not drive or engage in hazardous work until you determine how the medicine affects you.

Alcohol: Avoid alcohol if liver function is impaired.

Pregnancy: Stavudine has been shown to cause birth defects in animals. Human studies have not been done. Nevertheless, stavudine is increasingly being used in combination with other antiretroviral drugs to treat pregnant HIV-infected women.

Breast Feeding: It is unknown whether stavudine passes into breast milk; however, women infected with HIV should not breast-feed, to avoid transmitting the virus to an uninfected child.

Infants and Children: It is not known whether stavudine causes different or more severe side effects in infants and children than it does in older persons.

Special Concerns: Use of stavudine does not reduce the risk of passing the AIDS virus to others. Take appropriate preventive measures.

OVERDOSE
Symptoms: No cases of overdose have been reported.

What to Do: An overdose of stavudine is unlikely to occur. Nonetheless, if you have any reason to suspect an overdose, call your doctor, emergency medical services (EMS), or the nearest poison control center.

DRUG INTERACTIONS
Consult your doctor for advice if you are taking any other prescription or over-the-counter medication, especially chloramphenicol, cisplatin, dapsone, didanosine, ethambutol, ethionamide, hydralazine, isoniazid, lithium, metronidazole, nitrofurantoin, phenytoin, vincristine, or zalcitabine.

FOOD INTERACTIONS
No known food interactions.

DISEASE INTERACTIONS
Caution is advised when taking stavudine. Consult your doctor if you have pancreatitis or peripheral neuropathy. Use of stavudine may cause complications in patients with kidney or liver disease, because these organs work to remove the drug from the body.

Sucralfate

Carafate 1 g
(HOECHST MARION ROUSSEL)

▶ Drug Class: Antiulcer/
antireflux agent

▶ Available in: Oral suspension,
tablets

▶ Available OTC? No

▶ As Generic? Yes

Side Effects

SERIOUS
Drowsiness, seizures. Call
your doctor immediately.

COMMON
Constipation.

LESS COMMON
Backache, diarrhea, dizziness or lightheadedness,
dry mouth, indigestion,
nausea, stomach pain or
cramps, skin rash, hives,
or itching.

PRINCIPAL USES
To treat and prevent ulcers
of the duodenum, the first
portion of the small intestine located just after the
stomach in the digestive
tract.

HOW THE DRUG WORKS
Sucralfate coats the surface
of an ulcer, protecting the
tissue from irritation by
stomach acids, digestive
enzymes, bile salts, and
other substances that are
present in the stomach
and duodenum.

DOSAGE
Suspension— 1 g, 4 times
a day, 1 hour before each
meal and at bedtime, or 2 g,
2 times a day, upon waking
and at bedtime. Tablets—
To treat ulcer: 1 g, 4 times
a day, 1 hour before each
meal and at bedtime. To
prevent the recurrence
of duodenal ulcers: 1 g, 2
times a day on an empty
stomach.

ONSET OF EFFECT
Unknown.

DURATION OF ACTION
Up to 6 hours.

DIETARY ADVICE
This medication should be
taken without food and with
an 8 oz glass of water.

STORAGE
Store in a tightly sealed container away from heat and
direct light. Do not refrigerate the liquid form; also
keep it from freezing.

IF YOU MISS A DOSE
Take it as soon as you
remember. If it is near
the time for the next dose,
skip the missed dose and
resume your regular dosage
schedule. Do not double the
next dose.

STOPPING THE DRUG
Take the drug as prescribed
for the full treatment period,
even if you begin to feel better before the scheduled
end of therapy.

PROLONGED USE
You should see your doctor
regularly for tests and
examinations if you take
this drug for a prolonged
period.

PRECAUTIONS
Over 60: There is no specific information about the
use of sucralfate in older
persons. It is not expected
to produce side effects
different from those in
younger persons.

**Driving and Hazardous
Work:** Do not drive or
engage in hazardous work
until you determine how
the medicine affects you.

Alcohol: Avoid alcohol
while using this drug.

Pregnancy: Sucralfate has
not caused birth defects in
animals. Human studies
have not been done. Before
you use sucralfate, tell your
doctor if you are pregnant
or plan to become pregnant.

Breast Feeding: Sucralfate
may pass into breast milk
but has not been shown to
cause problems in nursing
babies. Consult your doctor
for specific advice.

Infants and Children: In
limited trials sucralfate has
not been shown to cause
problems in children. The
dose must be determined
by your pediatrician.

Special Concerns: Take
other medications at least 2
hours before or after taking
sucralfate. Do not take
antacids within 30 minutes
of taking sucralfate. Regular
exercise and intake of

dietary fiber along with
plenty of fluid can help
to prevent drug-induced
constipation.

OVERDOSE
Symptoms: No specific
ones have been reported.

What to Do: An overdose
of sucralfate is unlikely to
be life-threatening. How-
ever, if someone takes a
much larger dose than prescribed, call your doctor,
emergency medical services
(EMS), or the nearest poison control center.

DRUG INTERACTIONS
Consult your doctor for specific advice if you are taking
ciprofloxacin, digoxin, norfloxacin, ofloxacin, phenytoin, theophylline, or any
antacid or other drug that
contains aluminum. Consult
your doctor or pharmacist
for advice if you are taking
any over-the-counter drug.

FOOD INTERACTIONS
No known food interactions.

DISEASE INTERACTIONS
Caution is advised when
taking sucralfate. Consult
your doctor if you have a
history of gastrointestinal
tract obstruction or kidney
failure.

Sulfacetamide

▶ Drug Class: Anti-infective

▶ Available in: Ophthalmic solution, ointment

▶ Available OTC? No

▶ As Generic? Yes

Side Effects

SERIOUS
No serious side effects have been reported.

COMMON
Eye itching, redness, swelling, and other signs of irritation not present before use of the medicine. Stop using the medication and call your doctor.

LESS COMMON
No less-common side effects have been reported.

PRINCIPAL USES
To treat bacterial conjunctivitis (inflammation of the mucous membranes that line the inner surface of the eyelids and whites of the eyes) and other eye infections.

HOW THE DRUG WORKS
Sulfacetamide inhibits the spread of bacteria by preventing the synthesis of folic acid, which is necessary for bacterial growth and multiplication.

DOSAGE
Adults and teenagers— Solution: 1 drop, 4 to 6 times per day. Ointment: Apply 3 to 4 times per day. Infants and children— Both the use and dosage must be determined by your doctor.

ONSET OF EFFECT
Unknown.

DURATION OF ACTION
Unknown.

DIETARY ADVICE
This medication can be used without regard to diet.

STORAGE
Store in a tightly sealed container away from heat, moisture, and direct light. Do not allow it to freeze.

IF YOU MISS A DOSE
Apply it as soon as you remember. If it is near the time for the next dose, skip the missed dose and resume your regular dosage schedule. Do not double the next dose.

STOPPING THE DRUG
Use this drug as prescribed for the full treatment period, even if you begin to feel better before the scheduled end of therapy.

PROLONGED USE
You should see your doctor regularly for tests and examinations if you use this drug for a prolonged period.

PRECAUTIONS
Over 60: No special problems are expected.

Driving and Hazardous Work: The use of sulfacetamide should not impair your ability to perform such tasks safely.

Alcohol: No special precautions are necessary.

Pregnancy: Sulfacetamide has not been shown to cause problems during pregnancy. Before you take sulfacetamide, tell your doctor if you are pregnant or plan to become pregnant.

Breast Feeding: Sulfacetamide has not been reported to cause problems in nursing babies. Consult your doctor for advice.

Infants and Children: This drug is not recommended for use by infants under the age of 2 months.

Special Concerns: To use the eye drops or the ointment, first wash your hands. Tilt your head back. Gently apply pressure to the inside corner of the eyelid and with the index finger of the same hand, pull downward on the lower eyelid to make a space. Drop the medicine or put a short strip of ointment (about ⅓ inch long) into this space and close your eye. Apply pressure for 1 or 2 minutes while keeping the eye closed without blinking. Then wash your hands again. Make sure the tip of the dropper or the applicator does not touch your eye, finger, or any other surface. If your symptoms do not improve in a few days or if they become worse, check with your doctor.

OVERDOSE
Symptoms: No specific ones have been reported.

What to Do: An overdose of sulfacetamide is unlikely to be life-threatening. If a large volume enters the eye, flush with water. If someone accidentally ingests the medicine, call your doctor, emergency medical services (EMS), or the nearest poison control center.

DRUG INTERACTIONS
Other drugs may interact with sulfacetamide. Consult your doctor for specific advice if you are taking eye preparations containing silver such as silver nitrate.

FOOD INTERACTIONS
No known food interactions.

DISEASE INTERACTIONS
Caution is advised when taking sulfacetamide. Consult your doctor if you have any other medical condition.

Sulfasalazine

BRAND NAMES
Azaline, Azulfidine,
Azulfidine EN-Tabs

Azulfidine 500 mg
(PHARMACIA)

▶ Drug Class: Anti-infective/
sulfa drug; anti-inflammatory
agent

▶ Available in: Tablets, enteric-
coated tablets

▶ Available OTC? No

▶ As Generic? Yes

Side Effects

SERIOUS
Aching joints and mus-
cles; pain in back, legs
or stomach; bloody diar-
rhea; blue fingernails,
lips, or skin; chest pain;
cough; breathing diffi-
culty; swallowing diffi-
culty; fever; sore throat;
general discomfort; loss
of appetite; paleness of
skin or redness, peeling,
blistering, or loosening of
skin; unusual bleeding or
bruising; unusual fatigue;
yellow discoloration of
eyes or skin; increased
sensitivity to sunlight.
Call your physician
immediately.

COMMON
Stomach or abdominal
discomfort and cramps,
diarrhea, loss of appetite,
nausea, vomiting. Call
your doctor; these symp-
toms may be alleviated
by lowering the dosage.

LESS COMMON
No less-common side
effects have been
reported.

PRINCIPAL USES
To prevent and treat inflammatory bowel disease
(ulcerative colitis, Crohn's
disease).

HOW THE DRUG WORKS
The exact mechanism of
action is unknown. One
explanation is that it acts as
an anti-inflammatory in the
bowel. It also has antibiotic
properties that may be
important in changing the
bacteria in the bowel.

DOSAGE
Adults and teenagers: To
start, 500 to 1,000 mg, 3 or
4 times a day. The dose may
be decreased to 500 mg, 4
times a day, to reduce the
incidence of gastrointestinal
side effects. Children age 6
and over: To start, 3 to 4.55
mg per lb of body weight.

ONSET OF EFFECT
Unknown.

DURATION OF ACTION
Unknown.

DIETARY ADVICE
Take it with or immediately
following meals. Take each
dose with a full glass of
water, and consume several
additional glasses of water
during the day to reduce
the chance of side effects.

STORAGE
Store in a tightly sealed container away from heat, moisture, and direct light.

IF YOU MISS A DOSE
Take it as soon as you
remember. If it is near
the time for the next dose,
skip the missed dose and
resume your regular dosage
schedule. Do not double the
next dose.

STOPPING THE DRUG
Take it as prescribed for the
full treatment period, even if
you feel better before the
scheduled end of therapy.

PROLONGED USE
Sulfasalazine can be used
for as long as it is needed;
see your doctor for periodic
evaluation if prolonged use
is necessary.

PRECAUTIONS
Over 60: No special problems are expected.

**Driving and Hazardous
Work:** Do not drive or
engage in hazardous work
until you determine how the
medicine affects you.

Alcohol: No special precautions are necessary.

Pregnancy: Adequate studies of use during pregnancy
have not been done,
although no problems have
been reported. Consult your
doctor for specific advice.

Breast Feeding: Small
amounts of sulfasalazine
pass into breast milk; use
of this drug is not recommended while nursing,
unless benefits clearly outweigh potential risks. Consult your doctor for advice.

Infants and Children:
Not recommended for use
by children under age 2.

Special Concerns: Since
some patients experience
sensitivity to sunlight, take
preventive measures when
starting therapy: use sunscreens, wear protective
clothing, and avoid expo-
sure to the sun. Be careful
when brushing or flossing
your teeth, because sul-
fasalazine can increase the
risk of mouth infections.
The drug may also turn
skin, urine, or contact
lenses yellow.

OVERDOSE
Symptoms: Nausea, vomiting, stomach upset, blood in
urine, decreased urine volume, low back pain; in more
serious cases, extreme
drowsiness or seizures.

What to Do: Call your
doctor, emergency medical
services (EMS), or the
nearest poison control
center immediately.

DRUG INTERACTIONS
Consult your doctor for specific advice if you are taking
acetaminophen, acetohy-
droxamic acid, alfentanil,
amiodarone, aminophylline,
anabolic steroids, andro-
gens, antithyroid drugs,
anticoagulants, oral antidiabetics, caffeine, carba-
mazepine, carmustine,
chloramphenicol, chloro-
quine, oral contraceptives,
dantrolene, dapsone,
daunorubicin, disulfiram,
divalproex, estrogens, etretinate, gold salts, hydroxychloroquine, methotrexate,
mercaptopurine, methyl-
dopa, naltrexone, oral contraceptives, phenothiazine,
phenytoin, plicamycin, primaquine, procainamide,
quinidine, quinine, sulfoxone, or vitamin K.

FOOD INTERACTIONS
No known food interactions.

DISEASE INTERACTIONS
Consult your doctor if you
have anemia, another blood
problem, G6PD deficiency,
kidney disease, liver disease, intestinal or urinary
obstruction, or porphyria.

Sulfinpyrazone

BRAND NAME
Anturane

Anturane 100 mg
(Novartis)

▶ Drug Class: Antigout drug

▶ Available in: Capsules, tablets

▶ Available OTC? No

▶ As Generic? Yes

Side Effects

SERIOUS
Shortness of breath, breathing difficulty, tightness in chest, sores, ulcers, or white spots on lips or in mouth, sore throat and fever with or without chills, swollen or painful glands, unusual bleeding or bruising. Call your doctor immediately.

COMMON
Pain in lower back or side, painful or bloody urination.

LESS COMMON
Skin rash, bloody or black stools, high blood pressure, tiny bright red spots on skin, sudden decrease in urine, swelling of face, fingers, feet, or lower legs, unusual fatigue, vomiting of blood or dark material, weight gain.

PRINCIPAL USES
To treat chronic (recurring) gout or gouty arthritis by preventing attacks. (It should not be used for treating acute gout attacks in progress.)

HOW THE DRUG WORKS
Gout occurs when too much uric acid builds up in the blood. This leads to the formation of uric-acid-based crystals that are deposited in the joints, causing inflammation and leading to the sharp, excruciating pain of a gout attack. Sulfinpyrazone promotes excretion of excess uric acid from the body and so eases or prevents gout attacks. It also slows the body's removal of antibiotics, thus increasing their levels in the blood and prolonging their duration of action.

DOSAGE
200 to 400 mg a day in 2 doses to start; can be increased to as much as 800 mg a day in 2 doses.

ONSET OF EFFECT
It may take months before this medicine begins to prevent gout attacks.

DURATION OF ACTION
6 to 8 hours.

DIETARY ADVICE
Sulfinpyrazone may be taken with meals or milk to reduce stomach upset.

STORAGE
Store in a tightly sealed container away from heat and direct light.

IF YOU MISS A DOSE
Take it as soon as you remember. However, if it is near the time for the next dose, skip the missed dose and resume your regular dosage schedule. Do not double the next dose.

STOPPING THE DRUG
The decision to stop taking the drug should be made by your doctor.

PROLONGED USE
You should see your doctor regularly for tests and examinations if you take this drug for a prolonged period.

PRECAUTIONS
Over 60: No special problems are expected.

Driving and Hazardous Work: The use of this drug should not impair your ability to perform such tasks safely.

Alcohol: Avoid alcohol.

Pregnancy: Sulfinpyrazone has not been reported to cause problems during pregnancy. Before you take sulfinpyrazone, tell your doctor if you are pregnant or plan to become pregnant.

Breast Feeding: Sulfinpyrazone may pass into breast milk; caution is advised. Consult your doctor for advice.

Infants and Children: There is no specific information on the use of sulfinpyrazone in children, since it is generally prescribed only for adults.

Special Concerns: Your doctor may advise you to drink 10 to 12 full glasses of fluid every day while you take sulfinpyrazone to help prevent the formation of uric acid kidney stones. Sulfinpyrazone will not relieve a gout attack that has already started. You may also be prescribed another medicine for gout while you take this drug.

OVERDOSE
Symptoms: Nausea, vomiting, diarrhea, stomach pain, clumsiness or unsteadiness, seizures, difficulty breathing, loss of consciousness.

What to Do: Call your doctor, emergency medical services (EMS), or the nearest poison control center immediately.

DRUG INTERACTIONS
Consult your physician for specific advice if you are taking anticoagulants, carbenicillin, cefamandole, cefoperazone, cefotetan, dipyridamole, divalproex, heparin, medicine for pain or inflammation, moxalactam, pentoxifylline, plicamycin, ticarcillin, valproic acid, any cancer medicine, aspirin or other salicylates, or nitrofurantoin.

FOOD INTERACTIONS
None are likely, but a low-purine diet is recommended to reduce the risk of gout attacks. Foods high in purines include anchovies, sardines, legumes, poultry, sweetbreads, liver, kidneys, and other organ meats.

DISEASE INTERACTIONS
Consult your physician if you have any of the following: blood disease, cancer being treated by drugs or radiation, kidney stones or any other kidney disease, stomach ulcer, or any other stomach or intestinal problem.

Sulfisoxazole Ophthalmic

▶ Drug Class: Anti-infective

▶ Available in: Ophthalmic solution, ointment

▶ Available OTC? No

▶ As Generic? No

Side Effects

SERIOUS
No serious side effects have been reported.

COMMON
Eye itching, redness, swelling, and other signs of irritation not present before use of the medicine. If this occurs, stop using the medication and call your doctor.

LESS COMMON
No less-common side effects have been reported.

PRINCIPAL USES
To treat bacterial conjunctivitis (inflammation of the mucous membranes that line the inner surface of the eyelids and whites of the eyes) and other eye infections.

HOW THE DRUG WORKS
Sulfisoxazole inhibits the spread of bacteria by preventing the synthesis of folic acid, which is necessary for bacterial growth and multiplication.

DOSAGE
Solution, adults and children 2 months of age and older: 1 drop 4 times a day. Ointment, adults and children: 3 times a day and at bedtime. All forms, infants up to 2 months of age: Use and dosage must be determined by your doctor.

ONSET OF EFFECT
Unknown.

DURATION OF ACTION
Unknown.

DIETARY ADVICE
This medication can be used without regard to diet.

STORAGE
Store in a tightly sealed container away from heat, moisture, and direct light. Do not allow it to freeze.

IF YOU MISS A DOSE
Apply it as soon as you remember. If it is near the time for the next dose, skip the missed dose and resume your regular dosage schedule. Do not double the next dose.

STOPPING THE DRUG
Use this drug as prescribed for the full treatment period, even if you begin to feel better before the scheduled end of therapy.

PROLONGED USE
You should see your doctor regularly for tests and examinations if you use this drug for a prolonged period.

PRECAUTIONS
Over 60: No special problems are expected.

Driving and Hazardous Work: The use of ophthalmic sulfisoxazole solution should not impair your ability to perform such tasks safely. The use of the ointment, however, may temporarily but significantly blur vision and may interfere with your ability to drive or perform other sight-dependent tasks.

Alcohol: No special precautions are necessary.

Pregnancy: Ophthalmic sulfisoxazole has not been shown to cause problems during pregnancy. Before you take it, tell your physician if you are pregnant or plan to become pregnant.

Breast Feeding: Ophthalmic sulfisoxazole has not been reported to cause problems in nursing babies. Consult your doctor for advice.

Infants and Children: Use and dosage for infants under the age of 2 months must be determined by your doctor.

Special Concerns: To use the eye drops or the ointment, first wash your hands. Tilt your head back. Gently apply pressure to the inside corner of the eyelid and with the index finger of the same hand, pull downward on the lower eyelid to make a space. Drop the medicine or put a short strip of ointment (about ⅓ inch long) into this space and close your eye. Apply gentle pressure for 1 or 2 minutes while keeping the eye closed without blinking. Then wash your hands again. Make sure the tip of the dropper or the applicator does not touch your eye, finger, or any other surface. If your symptoms do not improve in a few days or if they become worse, check with your doctor.

OVERDOSE
Symptoms: No specific ones have been reported.

What to Do: An overdose of ophthalmic sulfisoxazole is unlikely to be life-threatening. If a large volume enters the eye, flush with water. If someone accidentally ingests the medicine, call your doctor, emergency medical services (EMS), or the nearest poison control center immediately.

DRUG INTERACTIONS
Other drugs may interact with ophthalmic sulfisoxazole. Consult your doctor for specific advice if you are taking eye preparations containing silver such as silver nitrate.

FOOD INTERACTIONS
No known food interactions.

DISEASE INTERACTIONS
Caution is advised when taking ophthalmic sulfisoxazole. Consult your doctor if you have any other medical condition.

Sulfisoxazole Systemic

BRAND NAME
Gantrisin

▶ Drug Class: Anti-infective

▶ Available in: Oral suspension, syrup, tablets

▶ Available OTC? No

▶ As Generic? Yes

Side Effects

SERIOUS
Itching, skin rash, aching joints and muscles, difficulty swallowing, pale skin or reddened, blistered, and peeling skin, sore throat and fever, unusual bleeding or bruising, unusual fatigue, yellow discoloration of the eyes or skin, pain in stomach or abdomen, bloody urine, greatly increased or decreased urine output, pain or burning while urinating, unusual thirst, lower back pain, mood or mental changes, swelling in the neck, increased sensitivity to sunlight. Call your doctor right away.

COMMON
Dizziness, diarrhea, headache, loss of appetite, nausea, vomiting, fatigue. Call your doctor. These symptoms may be alleviated by lowering the dosage.

LESS COMMON
No less-common side effects have been reported.

PRINCIPAL USES
To treat bacterial infections. It is most commonly used to treat middle ear infections or urinary tract infections. It is also used, in combination with other medications, to treat malaria.

HOW THE DRUG WORKS
Sulfisoxazole kills bacterial cells by preventing them from utilizing folic acid, a vitamin essential to cell growth and reproduction.

DOSAGE
Adults and teenagers: To start, 2,000 to 4,000 mg for first dose. Then 750 to 1,500 mg, 6 times a day, or 1,000 to 2,000 mg, 4 times a day. Children over 2 months of age: To start, 34 mg per lb of body weight. Then 11.4 mg per lb, 6 times a day, or 37.5 mg per lb, 4 times a day.

ONSET OF EFFECT
Unknown.

DURATION OF ACTION
Unknown.

DIETARY ADVICE
Take it with or immediately after meals. Each dose should be taken with a full glass of water, and several additional glasses of water should be consumed daily to decrease the chance of side effects.

STORAGE
Store in a tightly sealed container away from heat, moisture, and direct light.

IF YOU MISS A DOSE
Take it as soon as you remember. If it is near the time for the next dose, skip the missed dose and resume your regular dosage schedule. Do not double the next dose.

STOPPING THE DRUG
Take it as prescribed for the full treatment period, even if you feel better before the scheduled end of therapy.

PROLONGED USE
See your doctor regularly for tests and examinations if you take it for a prolonged period.

PRECAUTIONS
Over 60: Adverse reactions may be more likely and more severe in older patients.

Driving and Hazardous Work: Do not drive or engage in hazardous work until you determine how the medicine affects you.

Alcohol: No special precautions are necessary.

Pregnancy: Adequate human studies have not been done. Before taking sulfisoxazole, tell your doctor if you are pregnant or plan to become pregnant.

Breast Feeding: Sulfisoxazole passes into breast milk; avoid or discontinue use while nursing.

Infants and Children: Not recommended for use by infants under the age of 2 months.

Special Concerns: Since some patients experience sensitivity to sunlight, take preventive measures when starting therapy: use sunscreens, wear protective clothing, and avoid exposure to the sun. Be careful when brushing or flossing your teeth, because sulfisoxazole can increase the risk of mouth infections. If your symptoms do not improve or become worse in a few days, consult your doctor.

OVERDOSE
Symptoms: Loss of appetite, nausea, vomiting, dizziness, headache, drowsiness, loss of consciousness, blood in the urine, decreased urination, low back pain, yellow discoloration of the eyes or skin.

What to Do: Call your doctor, emergency medical services (EMS), or the nearest poison control center immediately.

DRUG INTERACTIONS
Consult your doctor for specific advice if you are taking acetaminophen, acetohydroxamic acid, amiodarone, anabolic steroids, androgens, antithyroid drugs, anticoagulants, oral antidiabetics, carbamazepine, carmustine, chloroquine, oral contraceptives, dantrolene, dapsone, daunorubicin, disulfiram, divalproex, estrogens, etretinate, gold salts, hydroxychloroquine, methenamine, methotrexate, mercaptopurine, methyldopa, naltrexone, oral contraceptives, phenothiazines, phenytoin, plicamycin, primaquine, procainamide, quinidine, quinine, sulfoxone, or vitamin K.

FOOD INTERACTIONS
No known food interactions.

DISEASE INTERACTIONS
Consult your doctor if you have anemia, another blood problem, G6PD deficiency, kidney disease, liver disease, or porphyria.

Sulfur Topical

BRAND NAMES
Cuticura Ointment, Finac, Fostex Regular Strength Medicated Cover-Up, Fostril Lotion, Lotio-Asulfa, Sulpho-Lac

▶ Drug Class: Acne drug

▶ Available in: Cream, lotion, ointment, bar soap

▶ Available OTC? Yes

▶ As Generic? Yes

Side Effects

SERIOUS
No serious side effects have been reported.

COMMON
Mild redness and peeling of skin.

LESS COMMON
Skin irritation or allergy with redness, peeling, burning, stinging, itching, or rash. Contact your doctor.

PRINCIPAL USES
To treat skin conditions including acne, seborrheic dermatitis, and scabies.

HOW THE DRUG WORKS
Topical sulfur is lethal to various strains of bacteria (which are a primary cause of acne), fungus, parasites, and other types of microorganisms. It also promotes softening, dissolution, and peeling of hard, scaly, roughened, or irregular surface skin.

DOSAGE
For acne, lotion, cream, or bar soap: Use on skin as needed. To use the soap, work up a rich lather using warm water. Wash the affected area, rinse thoroughly, apply again and rub in gently for a few minutes. Remove excess lather with a towel or tissue, without rinsing. Lotion: Apply 2 or 3 times a day. Ointment: Apply the 0.5% ointment as needed. Wash the affected area with soap and water and dry thoroughly before application. For seborrheic dermatitis: Use 1 or 2 times a day as directed on the package instructions. For scabies: Apply the 6% ointment every night for 3 nights. The ointment should be applied to the entire body from the neck down. You may bathe before each application and should bathe 24 hours after the last application.

ONSET OF EFFECT
Unknown.

DURATION OF ACTION
Unknown.

DIETARY ADVICE
Topical sulfur can be used without regard to diet.

STORAGE
Store in a tightly sealed container away from heat and direct light. Keep the cream, lotion, and ointment forms from freezing.

IF YOU MISS A DOSE
Resume your regular dosage schedule with the next application. Do not double the next dose.

STOPPING THE DRUG
If you are using sulfur by prescription, the decision to stop taking the drug should be made by your doctor. If you are using it without prescription, you may stop taking the drug when your skin has cleared; however, it is likely that the condition will recur.

PROLONGED USE
If prescribed, do not use sulfur for longer than your doctor recommends.

PRECAUTIONS
Over 60: No special precautions required.

Driving and Hazardous Work: No special precautions are necessary.

Alcohol: No special precautions are necessary.

Pregnancy: Sulfur has not been shown to cause birth defects or other problems during pregnancy. Before you use sulfur, tell your doctor if you are pregnant or plan to become pregnant.

Breast Feeding: Topical sulfur has not been reported to cause problems in nursing infants. Consult your doctor for specific advice.

Infants and Children: Use and dosage for children must be determined by your pediatrician.

Special Concerns: Anyone with a history of allergy to sulfur and other ingredients in the medication should not use this product. Keep sulfur away from the eyes. If you accidentally get some of the medicine in your eyes, flush them thoroughly with water.

OVERDOSE
Symptoms: Excessive application of topical sulfur may lead to more-severe irritation of the skin.

What to Do: If topical sulfur is accidentally ingested, call your doctor, emergency medical services (EMS), or the nearest poison control center immediately.

DRUG INTERACTIONS
Consult your doctor for specific advice if you are using abrasive soaps or cleansers, alcohol-containing preparations, any other acne agent, any preparation containing a peeling agent such as benzoyl peroxide, salicylic acid, alpha hydroxy acids, sulfur, or vitamin A, or soaps, medicated cosmetics, or other cosmetics that dry the skin. Also tell your doctor if you are using any other prescription or over-the-counter drug for a skin condition.

FOOD INTERACTIONS
No known food interactions.

DISEASE INTERACTIONS
You should not use sulfur if you have had a prior allergic reaction to it.

Sulindac

Generic 150 mg
(MYLAN)

▶ Drug Class: Nonsteroidal anti-inflammatory drug (NSAID)

▶ Available in: Tablets

▶ Available OTC? No

▶ As Generic? Yes

Side Effects

SERIOUS
Shortness of breath or wheezing, with or without swelling of legs or other signs of heart failure; chest pain; peptic ulcer disease with vomiting of blood; black, tarry stools; decreasing kidney function. Call your doctor immediately.

COMMON
Nausea, vomiting, heartburn, diarrhea, constipation, headache, dizziness, sleepiness.

LESS COMMON
Ulcers or sores in mouth, depression, rashes or blistering of skin, ringing sound in the ears, unusual tingling or numbness of the hands or feet, seizures, blurred vision. Also elevated potassium levels, decreased blood counts; such problems can be detected by your doctor.

PRINCIPAL USES
To treat mild to moderate pain and inflammation caused by tendinitis, arthritis, bursitis, gout, soft tissue injuries, migraine and other vascular headaches, menstrual cramps, and other conditions. When patients fail to respond to one NSAID, another may be tried. The greatest effectiveness often requires trial and error of several different NSAIDs.

HOW THE DRUG WORKS
NSAIDs work by interfering with the formation of prostaglandins, naturally occurring substances in the body that cause inflammation and make nerves more sensitive to pain impulses. NSAIDs also have other modes of action that are less well understood.

DOSAGE
Adults: 150 mg, 2 times a day, up to a maximum dose of 200 mg, 2 times a day. For children's dose, consult your pediatrician.

ONSET OF EFFECT
Initial effect occurs within several hours; full effect occurs in several days.

DURATION OF ACTION
Varies.

DIETARY ADVICE
Take with food; maintain your usual food and fluid intake.

STORAGE
Store in a tightly sealed container away from heat, moisture, and direct light.

IF YOU MISS A DOSE
Take it as soon as you remember. If it is near the time for the next dose, skip the missed dose and resume your regular dosage schedule. Do not double the next dose.

STOPPING THE DRUG
The decision to stop taking the drug should be made in consultation with your physician.

PROLONGED USE
Prolonged use can cause gastrointestinal problems, including ulceration and bleeding, kidney dysfunction, and liver inflammation. Consult your doctor about the need for medical examinations and laboratory tests.

PRECAUTIONS
Over 60: Because of the potentially greater consequences of gastrointestinal side effects, the dose of NSAIDs for older patients, especially those over age 70, is often cut in half.

Driving and Hazardous Work: Avoid such activities until you determine how the medicine affects you.

Alcohol: Avoid alcohol when using this medication because it increases the risk of stomach irritation.

Pregnancy: Avoid or discontinue this drug if you are pregnant or are planning to become pregnant.

Breast Feeding: Sulindac passes into breast milk; avoid use while nursing.

Infants and Children: May be used in exceptional circumstances; consult your doctor.

Special Concerns: Because NSAIDs can interfere with blood coagulation, this drug should be stopped at least 3 days prior to any surgery.

OVERDOSE
Symptoms: Severe nausea, vomiting, headache, confusion, seizures.

What to Do: Call your doctor, emergency medical services (EMS), or the nearest poison control center immediately.

DRUG INTERACTIONS
Do not take this drug with aspirin or any other NSAIDs without your doctor's approval. In addition, consult your doctor if you are taking antihypertensives, steroids, anticoagulants, antibiotics, itraconazole or ketoconazole, plicamycin, penicillamine, valproic acid, phenytoin, cyclosporine, digitalis drugs, lithium, methotrexate, probenecid, triamterene, or zidovudine.

FOOD INTERACTIONS
No known food interactions.

DISEASE INTERACTIONS
Caution is advised when taking sulindac. Consult your doctor if you have any of the following: bleeding problems, inflammation or ulcers of the stomach and intestines, diabetes mellitus, systemic lupus erythematosus (SLE, lupus), anemia, asthma, epilepsy, Parkinson's disease, kidney stones, or a history of heart disease or alcohol abuse. Use of sulindac may cause complications in patients with liver or kidney disease, since these organs work together to remove the medication from the body.

Sumatriptan Succinate

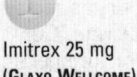

Imitrex 25 mg
(GLAXO WELLCOME)

▶ Drug Class: Antimigraine/ antiheadache drug

▶ Available in: Tablets, injection, nasal spray

▶ Available OTC? No

▶ As Generic? No

Side Effects

SERIOUS
Chest pain (mild to severe) or feeling of heaviness or pressure in the chest; wheezing or shortness of breath, and rapid, shallow, or irregular breathing; puffiness or swelling of the eyelids, face or, lips; hives; intense itching. Seek emergency medical assistance immediately.

COMMON
Pain, burning, or redness at injection site; a general feeling of warmth or heat; a feeling of numbness, tightness, or tingling; mild pain of the jaw, mouth, tongue, throat, nose, or sinuses; dizziness; drowsiness; feeling cold or weak; feeling flushed or light-headed; muscle aches, cramps, or stiffness; nausea or vomiting.

LESS COMMON
Mild chest pain; heaviness or pressure in the chest or neck; anxiety; feeling tired or ill; vision changes.

PRINCIPAL USES
To treat severe, acute migraine headaches (sumatriptan is not effective against any other kinds of pain or headache). Because of the risk of side effects, sumatriptan is generally used only when other treatments prove ineffective.

HOW THE DRUG WORKS
It appears that sumatriptan activates chemical messengers that cause blood vessels in the brain to constrict, thus lessening the effects of a migraine. The drug not only relieves the pain, but also nausea, vomiting, sensitivity to sound and light, and other symptoms associated with migraines.

DOSAGE
Tablets— A single dose of 25 to 100 mg taken with fluid is generally effective. If the headache returns or there is only partial relief, additional single doses of up to 50 mg may be given at intervals of at least 2 hours, but no more than 200 mg should be taken in a 24-hour period. Injection— Initial dose: 6 mg injection. Additional doses: Another 6 mg injection separated by at least one hour. Nasal spray— A single dose of 5, 10, or 20 mg into one nostril. A 10-mg dose may be achieved by administering a 5-mg dose in each nostril. If the headache returns or there is only partial relief, an additional single dose of up to 20 mg may be given at an interval of least 2 hours, but no more than 40 mg should be taken in a 24-hour period.

ONSET OF EFFECT
Tablets: Within 30 minutes. Injection: Within 10 to 20 minutes. Nasal spray: Within 15 to 30 minutes.

DURATION OF ACTION
Unknown, but peak effect occurs within 1 to 4 hours.

DIETARY ADVICE
The medication can be taken with or without food.

STORAGE
Keep away from heat and direct light; do not allow solution to freeze.

IF YOU MISS A DOSE
Not applicable, since the drug is taken only when necessary.

STOPPING THE DRUG
Consult your doctor before discontinuing sumatriptan.

PROLONGED USE
Consult your doctor if you have used sumatriptan for three migraine episodes and have not had relief, there is no improvement in symptoms after several weeks of use, or migraines increase in severity or frequency.

PRECAUTIONS
Over 60: Sumatriptan is not recommended for use in older patients.

Driving and Hazardous Work: Sumatriptan may cause drowsiness or dizziness. Do not drive or engage in hazardous work until you determine how the medication affects you.

Alcohol: No special warnings, although alcohol may trigger or exacerbate migraine headaches.

Pregnancy: Do not use this drug while pregnant.

Breast Feeding: Do not use this drug while nursing.

Infants and Children: Sumatriptan is not recommended for children.

Special Concerns: Rare but serious heart-related problems may occur after sumatriptan use. Anyone at risk for unrecognized coronary artery disease—such as post-menopausal women, men over age 40, or those with heart disease risk factors like high blood pressure, high cholesterol levels, obesity, cigarette smoking, diabetes, or a family history of heart disease—should have the first dose of sumatriptan administered in a doctor's office. Sumatriptan should not be used by anyone with any symptoms of active heart disease (chest pain or tightness, shortness of breath).

OVERDOSE
Symptoms: No overdoses have been reported.

What to Do: Although overdose is unlikely, if you take a much larger dose than prescribed, call your doctor, emergency medical services (EMS), or the nearest poison control center immediately.

DRUG INTERACTIONS
Do not take sumatriptan within 24 hours of taking any other migraine drug. Consult your doctor for advice if you are taking antidepressants, selective serotonin reuptake inhibitors (SSRIs), or lithium.

FOOD INTERACTIONS
See Dietary Advice.

DISEASE INTERACTIONS
You should not take sumatriptan if you have a history of coronary artery disease, especially angina, heart attack, Prinzmetal's angina, or uncontrolled high blood pressure. Sumatriptan should be used with caution in patients with liver disease or severely impaired kidney function.

Tacrine

Cognex 10 mg
(Parke-Davis)

▶ Drug Class: Psychotherapeutic; antidementia agent

▶ Available in: Capsules

▶ Available OTC? No

▶ As Generic? No

Side Effects

SERIOUS
Clumsiness or unsteadiness, severe vomiting, rapid or pounding heartbeat, slow heartbeat, seizures, elevated liver function tests (detectable by your doctor). Call your doctor right away.

COMMON
Nausea and vomiting, stomach pain or cramps, indigestion, muscle aches or pains, headache, dizziness, loss of appetite, diarrhea.

LESS COMMON
Belching, general feeling of discomfort or illness, rapid breathing, flushed skin, increased urination, increased sweating, watering of the eyes and mouth, insomnia, runny nose, swelling of the feet or lower legs.

PRINCIPAL USES
To treat mild to moderate Alzheimer's disease.

HOW THE DRUG WORKS
Tacrine prevents the breakdown of acetylcholine, a brain chemical crucial to memory. Acetylcholine deficiency is thought to result in memory loss associated with Alzheimer's disease.

DOSAGE
To start, 10 mg, 4 times a day. The dose may be increased to 40 mg, 4 times a day.

ONSET OF EFFECT
Unknown.

DURATION OF ACTION
Unknown.

DIETARY ADVICE
Best taken on an empty stomach, at least 1 hour before or 2 hours after eating. Tacrine can be taken with food to minimize stomach upset, but this will decrease the absorption and effectiveness of the drug.

STORAGE
Store in a tightly sealed container away from heat, moisture, and direct light.

IF YOU MISS A DOSE
Take it as soon as you remember, unless the time for your next scheduled dose is within the next 2 hours. If so, do not take the missed dose. Take your next scheduled dose at the proper time and resume your regular dosage schedule. Do not double the next dose.

STOPPING THE DRUG
The decision to stop taking the drug should be made in consultation with your physician.

PROLONGED USE
You should see your doctor regularly for tests and examinations if you must take this drug for a prolonged period.

PRECAUTIONS
Over 60: No special problems are expected.

Driving and Hazardous Work: Do not drive or engage in hazardous work until you determine how the medicine affects you.

Alcohol: Avoid alcohol.

Pregnancy: Adequate studies on the use of tacrine during pregnancy have not been done. Consult your doctor for specific advice.

Breast Feeding: Tacrine may pass into breast milk and be harmful to the nursing infant; do not use the drug while nursing.

Infants and Children: Tacrine is not intended for use by infants and children.

Special Concerns: Have your blood tested every other week for at least 16 weeks when you start taking tacrine, to see if it is affecting your liver. Do not smoke tobacco products while taking tacrine. Smoking will decrease the effects of tacrine.

OVERDOSE
Symptoms: Sweating and watering of mouth, seizures, increased muscle weakness, low blood pressure, severe nausea or vomiting, fast and weak pulse, large pupils, irregular breathing, slow heartbeat.

What to Do: Call your doctor, emergency medical services (EMS), or the nearest poison control center immediately.

DRUG INTERACTIONS
The following drugs may interact with tacrine. Consult your doctor for specific advice if you are taking: cimetidine, medicine for inflammation or pain, or theophylline.

FOOD INTERACTIONS
No known food interactions.

DISEASE INTERACTIONS
Caution is advised when taking tacrine. Consult your doctor if you have any of the following: asthma, epilepsy or a history of seizures, heart problems, intestinal blockage, stomach or duodenal ulcer, liver disease, Parkinson's disease, urinary problems, brain disease, or history of a head injury that involved a loss of consciousness.

Tacrolimus (FK506)

BRAND NAME
Prograf

Prograf 1 mg
(FUJISAWA)

▶ Drug Class: Immunosuppressant

▶ Available in: Capsules, injection

▶ Available OTC? No

▶ As Generic? No

Side Effects

SERIOUS
Increased bleeding, increased bruising, fluid buildup in lungs causing fever, chest pain, difficulty breathing, and cough. Call your doctor immediately.

COMMON
Headache; fever; weakness; tremor; high blood pressure causing headache and blurred vision; diarrhea; nausea; decreased urination; high blood sugar levels causing increased thirst, hunger, and urination.

LESS COMMON
Insomnia, swelling of feet or lower legs, numbness or tingling sensations, constipation, loss of appetite, abdominal pain, abdominal swelling due to fluid buildup, painful urination, back pain, electrolyte imbalance causing nausea, diarrhea, muscle weakness, and fatigue.

PRINCIPAL USES
To slow down or reduce the natural tendency of the immune system to reject liver or kidney transplants.

HOW THE DRUG WORKS
Tacrolimus suppresses the immune system's reaction against foreign tissue by inhibiting the activity of white blood cells, a major component of the immune system's arsenal.

DOSAGE
Adults— Capsules: 0.1 to 0.2 mg per 2.2 lbs (1 kg) of body weight daily in 2 divided doses every 12 hours. Injection: Dosage to be determined by your doctor. Children— 0.15 to 0.2 mg per 2.2 lbs of body weight daily in capsules on a schedule similar to that of adults.

ONSET OF EFFECT
Unknown.

DURATION OF ACTION
Unknown.

DIETARY ADVICE
The oral medication is most effective on an empty stomach; take it 30 minutes before or 2 hours after a meal. It can be taken with a full glass of water to lessen stomach upset. Do not take tacrolimus with grapefruit juice.

STORAGE
Capsules: Store in a tightly sealed container away from heat, moisture, and direct light. Injection: Not applicable; administered only at a health care facility.

IF YOU MISS A DOSE
Capsules: Take it as soon as you remember. If it is near the time for the next dose, skip the missed dose and resume your regular dosage schedule. Do not double the next dose. Injection: Not applicable; administered by health care professional.

STOPPING THE DRUG
The decision to stop taking the drug should be made by your doctor.

PROLONGED USE
See your doctor regularly for tests and examinations if you take this medication for a prolonged period.

PRECAUTIONS
Over 60: Adverse reactions may be more likely and more severe in older patients.

Driving and Hazardous Work: Do not drive or engage in hazardous work until you determine how the medicine affects you.

Alcohol: Avoid alcohol.

Pregnancy: Very high doses of tacrolimus have caused birth defects in animals. Human studies have not been done. Before you take tacrolimus, tell your doctor if you are pregnant or plan to become pregnant.

Breast Feeding: Tacrolimus passes into breast milk; discontinue breast feeding while taking the drug.

Infants and Children: No special problems have been observed, even though children may actually require higher doses than adults.

Special Concerns: In some cases, tacrolimus has been shown to cause diabetes. Consult your doctor right away if you develop symptoms of increased hunger, thirst, and urination while taking this drug.

OVERDOSE
Symptoms: No acute effects have been reported.

What to Do: Call your doctor, emergency medical services (EMS), or the nearest poison control center immediately.

DRUG INTERACTIONS
Tacrolimus should not be taken within 24 hours of receiving cyclosporine. Avoid live vaccines. Consult your doctor for specific advice if you are taking bromocriptine, cimetidine, clarithromycin, danazol, erythromycin, antifungal drugs, methylprednisolone, metoclopramide, calcium channel blockers, carbamazepine, phenobarbital, phenytoin, rifabutin, rifampin, other immunosuppressants, some vaccinations, aminoglycosides, amphotericin B, or cisplatin.

FOOD INTERACTIONS
Do not take tacrolimus with grapefruit juice.

DISEASE INTERACTIONS
Caution is advised when taking tacrolimus. Consult your doctor if you have a history of high blood pressure, heart problems, kidney disease, or liver disease.

Tadalafil

BRAND NAME
Cialis

▶ Drug Class: Phosphodi-
esterase type 5 inhibitor

▶ Available in: Tablets

▶ Available OTC? No

▶ As Generic? No

Side Effects

SERIOUS

Rarely, a painful or pro-
longed erection (lasting
more than 4 hours) may
occur. If erection does
not resolve on its own in
a reasonable amount of
time, seek medical help
promptly. If erection does
resolve on its own, con-
sult your doctor for spe-
cific guidelines. Serious
cardiovascular events
such as heart attack, sudden cardiac death, car-
diac arrhythmias, cerebral
hemorrhage, and tran-
sient ischemic attack have
been reported following
the use of similar drugs.
However, it is unclear
whether these events are
due to the consumption
of the drug, the presence
of preexisting cardiovas-
cular risk factors, sexual
activity, or a combination
of these factors.

COMMON

Headache, indigestion,
back pain, muscle aches,
flushing, stuffy or runny
nose. Such side effects
are generally mild to
moderate and usually
short-lived.

LESS COMMON

Vision abnormalities,
bloodshot or burning
eyes, diarrhea, blood in
the urine.

PRINCIPAL USES

To treat erectile dysfunction
(impotence), which may
occur in association with
atherosclerosis, vascular
disease or other circulatory
problems, diabetes, kidney
disease, hormonal abnor-
malities, neurological disease or injury, severe
depression or other psychological difficulties.

HOW THE DRUG WORKS

Tadalafil works by increasing the blood flow to the
penis necessary for establishing and maintaining an
erection. The drug accom-
plishes this by selectively
inhibiting the action of an
enzyme (phosphodiesterase
type 5) that breaks down a
substance that relaxes
smooth muscles and per-
mits blood flow that
engorges the columns of
erectile tissue in the penis.
Unlike other treatments for
erectile dysfunction, which
produce erections with or
without sexual arousal,
tadalafil allows the patient to
respond naturally to sexual
stimulation.

DOSAGE

The recommended dose for
most patients is 10 mg,
taken approximately 30 minutes to 1 hour before sexual
activity. The dose may be
increased to no more than
20 mg, or may be decreased
to 5 mg. Your doctor will
help to determine the correct dose for you. Do not
take the drug more than
once in a 24-hour period.

ONSET OF EFFECT

As soon as 30 minutes.

DURATION OF ACTION

Up to 36 hours.

DIETARY ADVICE

Tadalafil can be taken without regard to meals.

STORAGE

Store in a tightly sealed container away from heat, moisture, and direct light.

IF YOU MISS A DOSE

Not applicable. Tadalafil is
taken only as needed.

STOPPING THE DRUG

Not applicable.

PROLONGED USE

Tadalafil treats but does not
cure erectile dysfunction.
Patients must continue
using tadalafil to maintain
its benefit; lifelong therapy
may be warranted.

PRECAUTIONS

Over 60: No special problems are expected.

**Driving and Hazardous
Work:** This drug should
not impair your ability to
perform such tasks safely.

Alcohol: No special precautions are necessary.
However, alcohol is known
to decrease sexual function.

Pregnancy: Not applicable;
tadalafil is not approved for
use by women.

Breast Feeding: Not
applicable; tadalafil is not
approved for use by women.

Infants and Children:
Not applicable; tadalafil is
not to be used by children.

Special Concerns:
Tadalafil does not offer any
protection against sexually
transmitted diseases. Appropriate measures (for example, using condoms) should
be taken to ensure adequate
protection against sexually
transmitted diseases, including infection with the
human immunodeficiency
virus (HIV). Tadalafil
should be taken only by
men who have been clini-
cally evaluated for and diag-

nosed with erectile dysfunction by a doctor.

OVERDOSE

Symptoms: No cases of
overdose have been
reported.

What to Do: An overdose
with tadalafil is unlikely. If
someone takes a much
larger dose than prescribed,
call your doctor.

DRUG INTERACTIONS

Tadalafil can enhance the
action of nitrates (such as
nitroglycerin, which is used
to treat episodes of angina)
and alpha-blockers, causing
potentially dangerous
decreases in blood pres-
sure. Therefore, tadalafil
should not be used by
patients taking nitrates of
any kind or alpha-blockers
(except tamsulosin at the
0.4 mg dosage). Use of
tadalafil in conjunction with
other erectile-dysfunction
medications is not recom-
mended. Consult your doc-
tor if you are taking
protease inhibitors such as
ritonavir and saquinavir,
which may affect levels of
tadalafil in the blood.

FOOD INTERACTIONS

No known food interactions.

DISEASE INTERACTIONS

Caution is advised when
taking tadalafil. Consult
your doctor if you have a
history of any of the following: high or very low blood
pressure; structural deformity of the penis; a bleeding
disorder; heart attack,
stroke, or life-threatening
arrhythmia within the past
six months; heart failure;
coronary heart disease;
retinitis pigmentosa; peptic
ulcer; sickle cell anemia;
multiple myeloma; or
leukemia.

Tamoxifen Citrate

BRAND NAME
Nolvadex

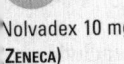

Nolvadex 10 mg
(ZENECA)

▶ Drug Class: Antiestrogen; antineoplastic (anticancer) agent

▶ Available in: Tablets

▶ Available OTC? No

▶ As Generic? Yes

Side Effects

SERIOUS
Endometrial cancer (menstrual irregularities, abnormal nonmenstrual vaginal bleeding, changes in vaginal discharge, pelvic pain or pressure); deep vein thrombosis and pulmonary embolism (pain or swelling in legs, shortness of breath, sudden chest pain, coughing up blood); cataracts (blurred vision); new breast lumps; confusion, weakness, or drowsiness; jaundice (yellowish tinge to eyes or skin). Call your doctor promptly.

COMMON
Hot flashes, weight gain.

LESS COMMON
Bone pain, headache, nausea or vomiting, skin dryness or rash, changes in menstrual period, vaginal discharge, itching in genital area of women, depression, erectile dysfunction (impotence) or decreased sexual interest in men. Other less-common side effects include high blood calcium levels and liver dysfunction; such problems can be detected by your doctor.

PRINCIPAL USES
To treat breast cancer in women and men; to help reduce the incidence of breast cancer in women at high risk.

HOW THE DRUG WORKS
Tamoxifen blocks the effects of the hormone estrogen on certain organs in the body. Because the growth of some types of breast cancer is stimulated by estrogen, tamoxifen interferes with the growth of such tumors.

DOSAGE
For treatment and prevention: 20 mg a day.

ONSET OF EFFECT
Several weeks.

DURATION OF ACTION
Several weeks.

DIETARY ADVICE
It is recommended that tamoxifen be taken after breakfast and after dinner. Swallow the tablet whole with a glass of water. Do not crush or chew.

STORAGE
Store in a tightly sealed container away from heat, moisture, and direct light.

IF YOU MISS A DOSE
Take it as soon as you remember and resume your regular dosage schedule.

STOPPING THE DRUG
The decision to stop taking the drug should be made by your doctor.

PROLONGED USE
See your doctor regularly for tests and examinations if you take this medication for a prolonged period. Tamoxifen does not prevent all breast cancers, so women taking the drug for prevention should continue to have regular breast exams and mammograms.

PRECAUTIONS
Over 60: No different side effects or problems are expected in older patients.

Driving and Hazardous Work: Use of tamoxifen should not impair your ability to perform such tasks safely.

Alcohol: No special problems are expected, but you should consult your doctor about drinking alcohol while taking tamoxifen.

Pregnancy: Tamoxifen may cause miscarriage, birth defects, fetal death, and unexpected vaginal bleeding, and so should not be taken during pregnancy. Avoid becoming pregnant for at least two months after stopping tamoxifen. A reliable birth control method other than oral contraceptives is recommended while undergoing tamoxifen therapy. Notify your physician and stop taking tamoxifen immediately if pregnancy occurs.

Breast Feeding: Tamoxifen may pass into breast milk; do not breast feed while taking the drug.

Infants and Children: Tamoxifen is not prescribed for infants and children.

Special Concerns: Women should have regular gynecological examinations while taking tamoxifen and for months or years after discontinuing it, since the medication may increase the long-term risk of uterine cancer. Tamoxifen may change or stop a woman's normal menstrual cycle; however, she may still be fertile. A reliable birth control method other than oral contraceptives (barrier method) should therefore be used while taking this drug. Tamoxifen for breast cancer risk reduction has not been studied in women under the age of 35. Risk factors for breast cancer include: early age at first menstruation, late age at first pregnancy, no pregnancies, breast cancer in a first-degree relative, history of previous breast biopsies, or high-risk changes seen on a biopsy.

OVERDOSE
Symptoms: Nausea, vomiting, irregular heartbeat, tremor, dizziness, seizures, exaggerated reflexes.

What to Do: Call your doctor, emergency medical services (EMS), or the nearest poison control center immediately.

DRUG INTERACTIONS
You should not take tamoxifen to prevent breast cancer if you are taking anticoagulants (such as warfarin). Consult your doctor for specific advice if you are taking antacids, cimetidine, famotidine, ranitidine, birth control pills.

FOOD INTERACTIONS
No known food interactions.

DISEASE INTERACTIONS
Caution is advised when taking tamoxifen. Consult your doctor if you have a medical history that includes any of the following: cataracts or other vision disturbances, high blood levels of cholesterol or triglycerides, blood clots, low white blood cell and/or platelet counts. Tamoxifen should not be taken to prevent breast cancer by women with a history of deep vein thrombosis or pulmonary embolism.

Tamsulosin Hydrochloride

BRAND NAME
Flomax

▶ Drug Class: BPH therapy agent

▶ Available in: Capsules

▶ Available OTC? No

▶ As Generic? No

Side Effects

SERIOUS
No serious side effects have been reported.

COMMON
Headache, increased susceptibility to infection, joint pain, back pain, muscle pain, dizziness, runny nose, diarrhea, abnormal ejaculation.

LESS COMMON
Mild chest pain, drowsiness, insomnia, decreased libido, sore throat, cough, sinus infection, nausea, mouth pain, vision problems. The drug may also promote orthostatic hypotension (episodes of low blood pressure most likely to occur when getting up quickly from a seated or lying position), which produces symptoms of lightheadedness, dizziness, confusion, or fainting.

PRINCIPAL USES
To treat symptoms of urinary difficulty that occur with benign prostatic hyperplasia (BPH)—a noncancerous enlargement of the prostate gland. BPH is extremely common among men over the age of 50.

HOW THE DRUG WORKS
By blocking a specific (alpha) receptor, tamsulosin relaxes muscle tissue in the prostate and the opening of the bladder. Note that tamsulosin will not shrink the prostate; symptoms may worsen and surgery may eventually be required. Unlike other alpha receptor blockers used to treat BPH, tamsulosin is not used to treat high blood pressure.

DOSAGE
0.4 mg once a day. It should be taken 30 minutes following the same meal each day. If patients fail to respond to the 0.4 mg dose after 2 to 4 weeks of therapy, they may increase the dose to 0.8 mg once a day.

ONSET OF EFFECT
Unknown.

DURATION OF ACTION
Unknown.

DIETARY ADVICE
There are no dietary restrictions. However, tamsulosin should be taken 30 minutes after the same meal every day. Do not chew, crush, or open the capsules.

STORAGE
Store in a tightly sealed container away from heat, moisture, and direct light.

IF YOU MISS A DOSE
If therapy is discontinued or interrupted for several days at either the 0.4 mg dose or the 0.8 mg dose, therapy should be started again with the 0.4 mg once daily dose.

STOPPING THE DRUG
Take tamsulosin as prescribed for the full treatment period.

PROLONGED USE
If you take this drug for a prolonged period, see your doctor regularly so that changes in prostate size can be monitored.

PRECAUTIONS
Over 60: No special problems are expected.

Driving and Hazardous Work: Tamsulosin may impair mental functioning, causing drowsiness, lightheadedness, or dizziness, especially when you take the medication for the first time. Caution is advised; for 24 hours after the initial dose, avoid driving or other activities requiring mental alertness. Effects should diminish after several doses.

Alcohol: May increase effects of dizziness or fainting; drink in moderation.

Pregnancy: Tamsulosin is not indicated for use by women.

Breast Feeding: Tamsulosin is not indicated for use by women.

Infants and Children: Tamsulosin is not indicated for use by children.

Special Concerns: The first dose is likely to cause dizziness or lightheadedness. Take the drug at night and get out of bed slowly the next day. Be cautious while exercising and during hot weather. Tell your primary care physician if you are planning to have surgery requiring general anesthesia, including dental surgery. Do not chew, crush, or open the capsules.

OVERDOSE
Symptoms: An overdose i[s] unlikely to occur. Possible symptoms after an excessive dose may include severe headache or orthostatic hypotension (see Les[s] Common Side Effects).

What to Do: If someone takes a much larger dose than prescribed, keep the patient lying down and call your doctor, emergency medical services (EMS), or the nearest poison control center immediately.

DRUG INTERACTIONS
Tamsulosin should not be used in conjunction with other BPH therapy agents. Consult your doctor if you are taking either cimetidine or warfarin, which may interact with tamsulosin.

FOOD INTERACTIONS
None reported.

DISEASE INTERACTIONS
None reported.

Tazarotene

Tazorac

▶ Drug Class: Retinoid

▶ Available in: Topical gel

▶ Available OTC? No

▶ As Generic? No

Side Effects

SERIOUS
No serious side effects are associated with the use of tazarotene.

COMMON
Common side effects are limited to the skin. When used for psoriasis: Itching, redness, burning, stinging, worsening of psoriasis, irritation, skin pain. When used for acne: Peeling, burning, stinging, dry skin, redness, itching.

LESS COMMON
When used for psoriasis: Skin rash, peeling or scaling, increased risk of dermatitis caused by external irritants, skin inflammation, cracking, bleeding, dry skin. When used for acne: Skin pain, irritation, cracking, swelling of treated area, skin discoloration.

PRINCIPAL USES
To treat psoriasis. Tazarotene is also used to treat mild to moderate acne.

HOW THE DRUG WORKS
The exact way in which tazarotene works is unknown. It appears to establish a more normal pattern of growth and shedding of skin cells.

DOSAGE
For psoriasis: Apply to the affected area once a day, in the evening, using enough to cover the lesion with a thin film. Be sure the area is clean and dry before applying. For acne: Apply once a day in the evening. First gently wash and dry your face, then spread a thin film on the area of skin where acne appears. Avoid applying tazarotene near the eyes, eyelids, and mouth.

ONSET OF EFFECT
1 to 4 weeks.

DURATION OF ACTION
Unknown.

DIETARY ADVICE
Tazarotene can be used without regard to diet.

STORAGE
Store in a tightly sealed container away from heat, moisture, and direct light.

IF YOU MISS A DOSE
If you fail to apply the medication on one day, return to your regular schedule the next day; do not apply an extra amount in an attempt to compensate for the missed dose.

STOPPING THE DRUG
In the treatment of psoriasis, you should apply it for the full treatment period as prescribed by your doctor. For acne, apply the drug for up to 12 weeks as directed by your doctor.

PROLONGED USE
Side effects are more likely with prolonged use.

PRECAUTIONS
Over 60: No special problems are expected.

Driving and Hazardous Work: The use of tazarotene should not impair your ability to perform such tasks safely.

Alcohol: No special precautions are necessary.

Pregnancy: Tazarotene should not be used if you are pregnant or plan to become pregnant. Adequate birth-control methods should be practiced when tazarotene is used in women of child-bearing age.

Breast Feeding: Tazarotene may pass into breast milk; caution is advised. Consult your doctor for specific advice.

Infants and Children: Not recommended for use by children under age 12.

Special Concerns: If tazarotene comes in contact with your eyes, flush your eyes with large amounts of cool water. If eye irritation persists, contact your doctor. Wash your hands after applying the medication. Do not cover the treated area with tight-fitting clothing or bandages. If the drug causes increased sensitivity to sunlight, wear protective clothing, use a sunblock, and try to avoid exposure to direct sunlight. Avoid sunlamps completely. Caution is advised for all patients with fair skin or who are particularly sensitive to sunlight. Weather extremes such as wind or cold may be more irritating to the skin while you use this drug. When tazarotene is used to treat psoriasis, avoid applying it to normal-appearing areas of skin.

OVERDOSE
Symptoms: Excessive use of tazarotene may lead to skin redness, peeling, or discomfort.

What to Do: An overdose is unlikely to occur. If someone accidentally ingests tazarotene, call your doctor.

DRUG INTERACTIONS
Consult your doctor for advice if you are taking any of the following drugs that may interact with tazarotene: vitamin A supplements; other skin medications, creams, or lotions; drugs that increase your sensitivity to sunlight (such as thiazide diuretics, tetracyclines, fluoroquinolone antibiotics, phenothiazines, or sulfonamides); or products such as astringents or medicated soaps that dry the skin.

FOOD INTERACTIONS
No known food interactions.

DISEASE INTERACTIONS
You should not use tazarotene if you have eczema or other chronic skin diseases, or a recent sunburn.

Tegaserod Maleate

BRAND NAME
Zelnorm

▶ Drug Class: Selective 5-HT4 (serotonin) receptor agonist

▶ Available in: Tablets

▶ Available OTC? No

▶ As Generic? No

Side Effects

SERIOUS
Diarrhea with cramping, abdominal pain, or dizziness. Call your doctor immediately.

COMMON
Headache, diarrhea.

LESS COMMON
Nausea, flatulence, migraine, back pain.

PRINCIPAL USES
On a short-term basis, to treat irritable bowel syndrome (IBS) in women whose primary symptom is constipation. The safety and effectiveness of tegaserod in men have not been established.

HOW THE DRUG WORKS
By enhancing the action of serotonin, tegaserod stimulates the bowel motility (peristalsis), which increases the movement of stools through the bowels, and also inhibits colorectal sensitivity, decreasing the pain and discomfort of IBS.

DOSAGE
Dose ranges from 2 to 6 mg twice a day before meals for 4 to 6 weeks. Therapy may be continued an additional 4 to 6 weeks for patients who respond to therapy.

ONSET OF EFFECT
Unknown.

DURATION OF ACTION
Unknown.

DIETARY ADVICE
Tegaserod should be taken before meals.

STORAGE
Store in a tightly sealed container away from heat, moisture, and direct light.

IF YOU MISS A DOSE
If you miss a dose, skip the missed dose and resume your regular dosage schedule. Do not double the next dose.

STOPPING THE DRUG
Take it as prescribed for the full treatment period. The decision to stop taking the drug should be made in consultation with your physician.

PROLONGED USE
Therapy typically lasts 4 to 6 weeks. If therapy is tolerated, your doctor may prescribe an additional 4 to 6 weeks of tegaserod.

PRECAUTIONS
Over 60: No special problems are expected.

Driving and Hazardous Work: No special problems are expected.

Alcohol: No special restrictions are necessary.

Pregnancy: Tell your doctor if you are pregnant or plan to become pregnant. Tegaserod is not recommended for use by pregnant women.

Breast Feeding: Tegaserod may pass into breast milk; caution is advised. Consult your doctor for advice on whether to discontinue nursing or discontinue the drug.

Infants and Children: Safety and effectiveness have not been established for patients under age 18.

OVERDOSE
Symptoms: No cases of overdose have been reported. Symptoms from an excessive dose of tegaserod may include headache and diarrhea.

What to Do: Call your doctor, emergency medical services (EMS), or the nearest poison control center immediately if you suspect that someone has taken a much larger dose than prescribed.

DRUG INTERACTIONS
No drug interactions have been reported.

FOOD INTERACTIONS
No known food interactions.

DISEASE INTERACTIONS
Do not take tegaserod if you now have diarrhea (or have diarrhea often), severe kidney or liver disease, ever had bowel obstruction, gallbladder disease, or abdominal adhesions causing pain and/or intestinal blockage.

Telmisartan

- Drug Class: Antihypertensive/ angiotensin II antagonist

- Available in: Tablets

- Available OTC? No

- As Generic? No

Side Effects

SERIOUS
No serious side effects are associated with the use of telmisartan. (In clinical trials, the incidence of adverse effects was not significantly greater with the medication than with a placebo.)

COMMON
No common side effects are associated with the use of telmisartan.

LESS COMMON
Headache, dizziness, back pain, upper respiratory tract infection, sore throat, and nasal congestion.

PRINCIPAL USES
To control high blood pressure. This drug appears to have the same benefits as the class of antihypertensive drugs known as ACE inhibitors, without producing the common side effect (experienced by as many as 30% of patients) of a dry cough. Telmisartan may be used by itself or in conjunction with other antihypertensive medications.

HOW THE DRUG WORKS
Telmisartan blocks the effects of angiotensin II, a naturally occurring substance that causes blood vessels to narrow. Telmisartan causes the blood vessels to dilate, thereby lowering blood pressure and decreasing the workload of the heart.

DOSAGE
To start, 40 mg once a day when used as the only drug to treat hypertension. Usual maintenance dose is 20 to 80 mg daily.

ONSET OF EFFECT
Within 2 weeks.

DURATION OF ACTION
Up to 24 hours.

DIETARY ADVICE
No special restrictions, unless your doctor has advised a low-sodium diet or other dietary modifications to help you control your blood pressure.

STORAGE
Store in a tightly sealed container away from heat, moisture, and direct light.

IF YOU MISS A DOSE
Take it as soon as you remember. If it is near the time for the next dose, skip the missed dose and resume your regular dosage schedule. Do not double the next dose.

STOPPING THE DRUG
Take it as prescribed for the full treatment period. The decision to stop taking the drug should be made in consultation with your physician.

PROLONGED USE
Lifelong therapy may be necessary. However, if you do change certain health habits (for example, increasing exercise or losing weight), a reduced dose may be possible under a doctor's supervision.

PRECAUTIONS
Over 60: No special problems are expected.

Driving and Hazardous Work: Do not drive or engage in hazardous work until you determine how the medicine affects you.

Alcohol: No special precautions are necessary.

Pregnancy: Telmisartan should not be used by pregnant women. Discontinue taking the drug as soon as possible when pregnancy is detected and discuss treatment alternatives with your doctor.

Breast Feeding: Telmisartan may pass into breast milk; caution is advised. Consult your doctor for advice.

Infants and Children: The safety and effectiveness of use in children have not been established.

Special Concerns: Telmisartan may cause excessively low blood pressure with dizziness or lightheadedness, which is most noticeable when you change position. This may lead to fainting, falls, and injury. Sit or lie down immediately if you feel dizzy or light-headed. This side effect may be worsened by alcohol, hot weather, dehydration, salt depletion from diuretic use, fever, prolonged standing, prolonged sitting, or exercise.

OVERDOSE
Symptoms: Few cases of overdose have been reported. However, if you take a much larger dose than prescribed, you may experience fainting, dizziness, weak pulse that might be very slow or very fast.

What to Do: Call your doctor, emergency medical services (EMS), or the nearest poison control center immediately.

DRUG INTERACTIONS
No clinically significant drug interactions have yet been observed with telmisartan. Consult your doctor for specific advice if you are taking digoxin or any other medication, especially other drugs for high blood pressure. Telmisartan can be taken together with diuretics or other medications for high blood pressure, if your doctor approves.

FOOD INTERACTIONS
No known food interactions.

DISEASE INTERACTIONS
Patients with moderate to severe liver or kidney disease are advised to exercise caution when taking telmisartan.

Temazepam

Generic 15 mg
(PUREPAC)

▶ Drug Class: Benzodiazepine tranquilizer

▶ Available in: Capsules, tablets

▶ Available OTC? No

▶ As Generic? Yes

Side Effects

SERIOUS
Difficulty concentrating, outbursts of anger, other behavior problems, depression, convulsions, hallucinations, low blood pressure (causing faintness or confusion), memory impairment, muscle weakness, skin rash or itching, sore throat, fever and chills, sores or ulcers in throat or mouth, unusual bruising or bleeding, extreme fatigue, yellowish tinge to eyes or skin. Call your doctor immediately.

COMMON
Loss of coordination, unsteady gait, dizziness, lightheadedness, drowsiness, slurred speech.

LESS COMMON
Stomach cramps or pain, vision disturbances, change in sexual desire or ability, constipation or diarrhea, dry mouth or watering mouth, false sense of well-being, rapid or pounding heartbeat, headache, muscle spasms, nausea and vomiting, urinary problems, trembling.

PRINCIPAL USES
To treat insomnia.

HOW THE DRUG WORKS
In general, temazepam produces mild sedation by depressing activity in the central nervous system. In particular, temazepam appears to enhance the effect of gamma-aminobutyric acid (GABA), a natural chemical that inhibits the firing of neurons and dampens the transmission of nerve signals, thus decreasing nervous excitation.

DOSAGE
Adults: 15 mg, taken at bedtime. Older adults: To start, 7.5 mg, taken at bedtime. The dose may be increased. Use and dose for children under 18 must be determined by your doctor.

ONSET OF EFFECT
Unknown.

DURATION OF ACTION
Unknown. It may take more than 2 hours.

DIETARY ADVICE
Take it 30 minutes before bedtime with a full glass of water. Temazepam can be taken with food to prevent gastrointestinal upset.

STORAGE
Store in a tightly sealed container away from heat and direct light.

IF YOU MISS A DOSE
Take it as soon as you remember, unless it is late at night. Do not take the medicine unless your schedule allows a full night's sleep.

STOPPING THE DRUG
Discontinuing the drug abruptly may produce withdrawal symptoms (sleep disruption, nervousness, irritability, diarrhea, abdominal cramps, muscle aches,

memory impairment). The dosage should be reduced gradually according to your doctor's instructions.

PROLONGED USE
This medication may slowly lose its effectiveness, and adverse reactions are more likely to occur with prolonged use. You should see your doctor for periodic evaluation if you must take it for an extended time.

PRECAUTIONS
Over 60: Adverse reactions may be more likely and more severe. A lower dose may be warranted.

Driving and Hazardous Work: Do not drive or engage in hazardous work until you determine how the medicine affects you.

Alcohol: Avoid alcohol.

Pregnancy: Use during pregnancy should be avoided if possible. Be sure to tell your doctor if you are pregnant or plan to become pregnant.

Breast Feeding: Temazepam passes into breast milk; do not take it while nursing.

Infants and Children: Safety and effectiveness have not been established for children under age 18.

Special Concerns: Temazepam use can lead to psychological or physical dependence if the drug is not taken in strict accordance with your doctor's instructions. Never take more than the prescribed daily dose.

OVERDOSE
Symptoms: Extreme drowsiness, confusion, slurred speech, slow reflexes, poor coordination,

staggering gait, tremor, slowed breathing, loss of consciousness.

What to Do: Call your doctor, emergency medical services (EMS), or the nearest poison control center immediately.

DRUG INTERACTIONS
Consult your physician for advice if you are taking any drugs that depress the central nervous system; these include antihistamines, antidepressants or other psychiatric medications, barbiturates, sedatives, cough medicines, decongestants, and painkillers. Be sure your doctor knows about any over-the-counter medication you may take.

FOOD INTERACTIONS
None reported.

DISEASE INTERACTIONS
Consult your doctor if you have a history of alcohol or drug abuse, stroke or other brain disease, any chronic lung disease, glaucoma, hyperactivity, depression or other mental illness, myasthenia gravis, sleep apnea, epilepsy, porphyria, kidney disease, or liver disease.

Terazosin

BRAND NAME
Hytrin

Hytrin 1 mg
(**ABBOTT**)

▶ Drug Class: Antihypertensive;
BPH therapy agent

▶ Available in: Tablets,
capsules

▶ Available OTC? No

▶ As Generic? Yes

Side Effects

SERIOUS
No serious side effects
have been reported.

COMMON
Dizziness.

LESS COMMON
Chest pain; lightheaded-
ness or fainting, espe-
cially when getting up
quickly from a seated
or lying position. Such
symptoms are typically
more common when you
first take the medication,
and generally diminish
over time. These symp-
toms tend to recur when
the dosage is increased.
Take it at bedtime to minimize such problems.

PRINCIPAL USES
To lower and control high
blood pressure (hyperten-
sion). It is also used to treat
symptoms of urinary difficulty that occur with benign
prostatic hyperplasia (BPH).

HOW THE DRUG WORKS
Terazosin helps to control
hypertension by relaxing
blood vessels and permit-
ting them to expand,
decreasing blood pressure
in the process. When used
for BPH, it helps relax the
muscles in the prostate
gland and the opening of
the bladder, improving the
passage of urine.

DOSAGE
For high blood pressure:
Initially, 1 mg taken at bedtime, then 1 to 5 mg once
daily. For children, the dose
and frequency must be
determined by your pedia-
trician. For BPH: Initially,
1 mg taken at bedtime, then
5 to 10 mg once daily.

ONSET OF EFFECT
Within 15 minutes, with
peak blood pressure effect
within 2 to 3 hours. When
the drug is used to treat urinary difficulty associated
with BPH, the full effect
may not be seen for 4 to 6
weeks.

DURATION OF ACTION
24 hours.

DIETARY ADVICE
Terazosin can be taken
before, with, or after meals.

STORAGE
Store in a tightly sealed container away from heat, moisture, and direct light.

IF YOU MISS A DOSE
Take it as soon as possible
the same day. If it is the
next day, skip the missed
dose. Do not double the
dose. Resume your regular
dosage schedule.

STOPPING THE DRUG
Do not discontinue taking
the medication suddenly,
even if you start to experience unpleasant side
effects. Consult your physician. If terazosin is discontinued for several days, you
may need to start therapy
over, using the initial dosing
regimen.

PROLONGED USE
When taking the medication
for hypertension, blood
pressure measurement is
recommended at regular
intervals.

PRECAUTIONS
Over 60: Older persons
are generally more sensitive
to terazosin and more likely
to experience adverse side
effects, especially when getting up from a lying or
seated position. Rise slowly
to minimize symptoms.

**Driving and Hazardous
Work:** Terazosin may
impair mental ability, causing drowsiness, lightheadedness, or dizziness, especially
when you take the medica-
tion for the first time. Caution is advised; for 24 hours
after the initial dose, avoid
driving or other activities
requiring mental alertness.
Effects should diminish
after several doses.

Alcohol: May increase
effects of dizziness or fainting; drink in strict moderation, if at all.

Pregnancy: Well-controlled
studies have not been done.
Consult your physician if
you are pregnant or plan to
become pregnant.

Breast Feeding: It is not
known whether terazosin
passes into breast milk.
Consult your physician
for specific advice.

Infants and Children:
Adequate studies of tera-
zosin use in this age group
have not been performed.
Discuss the risks and benefits with your pediatrician.

Special Concerns: Be
sure to notify your doctor if
you are taking nonprescription medications for asthma,
colds, cough, allergy, or
appetite suppression. These
drugs can increase blood
pressure and cause other
complications if they are
taken with terazosin.

OVERDOSE
Symptoms: Extremely low
blood pressure (hypoten-
sion), with accompanying
fatigue, weakness, head-
ache, palpitations, fainting,
or dizziness.

What to Do: Call your
doctor, emergency medical
services (EMS), or the
nearest poison control
center immediately.

DRUG INTERACTIONS
Several drugs may interact
with terazosin, including
anti-inflammatory medica-
tions, especially indomethacin, which can cause fluid
and sodium retention, and
estrogen, which can reduce
the antihypertensive effects
of the drug. Consult your
doctor.

FOOD INTERACTIONS
None are expected.

DISEASE INTERACTIONS
Consult your physician if
you have kidney disease,
severe heart disease, or
chest pain caused by
angina. Terazosin may
aggravate these conditions.

Terbinafine Hydrochloride

BRAND NAME
Lamisil

- ▶ Drug Class: Antifungal
- ▶ Available in: Tablets, topical cream
- ▶ Available OTC? Yes
- ▶ As Generic? No

Side Effects

SERIOUS
Serious side effects with terbinafine are rare. However, terbinafine tablets may cause liver dysfunction; severe skin reactions such as Stevens-Johnson syndrome (a serious inflammatory disease affecting children and young adults, characterized by high fever, boils, ulceration of the mucous membranes, pneumonia, joint pain); severe blood disorders, potentially resulting in increased susceptibility to infection, uncontrolled bleeding or other problems; or severe allergic reactions. Seek emergency medical assistance immediately.

COMMON
Headache, diarrhea, rash, abdominal pain, indigestion, nausea.

LESS COMMON
Tablets may cause flatulence, itching, skin eruptions, loss of taste, weakness, fatigue, vomiting, joint and muscle pain, or hair loss. Terbinafine cream may cause redness, itching, burning, blistering, swelling, oozing, or other signs of skin irritation not present before using the drug.

PRINCIPAL USES
The tablets are used only to treat fungal infections of the fingernails and toenails (tinea unguium). The cream is used to treat fungal infections of the skin, such as tinea corporis (ringworm), tinea cruris (jock itch), and tinea pedis (athlete's foot).

HOW THE DRUG WORKS
Terbinafine inhibits an enzyme essential for the production of substances vital for the reproduction and survival of some types of fungal organisms.

DOSAGE
Tablets: 250 mg once a day for 6 weeks for fingernail fungus; 250 mg once a day for 12 weeks for toenail fungus. Cream: Apply a thin film of medicine to the affected area 1 to 2 times a day for ringworm or jock itch; 2 times a day for athlete's foot. Apply the cream for at least 1 week, but no longer than 4 weeks.

ONSET OF EFFECT
Tablets: The optimal effect is seen several months after the completion of treatment. Cream: Unknown.

DURATION OF ACTION
Unknown.

DIETARY ADVICE
Terbinafine can be taken or applied without regard to meals.

STORAGE
Store in a tightly sealed container away from heat, moisture, and direct light. Do not allow the cream to freeze.

IF YOU MISS A DOSE
It is important to not miss any doses. Take or apply as soon as you remember. If you do not remember until the next day, skip the missed dose and resume your regular dosage schedule. Do not double the next dose or use excessive amounts of the cream.

STOPPING THE DRUG
Take terbinafine tablets as prescribed for the full treatment period.

PROLONGED USE
Side effects are more likely to occur with prolonged use. Tests of liver function are recommended if the tablets are used for longer than 6 weeks.

PRECAUTIONS
Over 60: No special problems are expected.

Driving and Hazardous Work: This drug should not impair your ability to perform such tasks safely.

Alcohol: No special precautions are necessary.

Pregnancy: Adequate human studies have not been done. Terbinafine tablets are not recommended for pregnant women.

Breast Feeding: Terbinafine passes into breast milk; avoid or discontinue use of the tablets while nursing.

Infants and Children: Terbinafine is not recommended for children under the age of 18.

Special Concerns: Wash your hands before and after applying the cream. Avoid allowing topical terbinafine to come into contact with the eyes, nose, and mouth. If using terbinafine for ringworm, wear loose-fitting, well-ventilated clothing and avoid excess heat and humidity. It is also recommended to use a bland, absorbent powder like talcum once or twice a day after the cream has been applied and absorbed by the skin. If using the medication for jock itch, do not wear underwear that is tight or made from synthetic materials; wear loose-fitting cotton underwear. If using terbinafine for athlete's foot, dry your feet carefully after bathing and wear clean cotton socks with sandals or well-ventilated shoes. Before applying the medication, wash the affected area with soap and warm water and dry thoroughly.

OVERDOSE
Symptoms: Tablets: nausea, vomiting, abdominal pain, dizziness, rash, frequent urination, and headache.

What to Do: Call your doctor as soon as possible.

DRUG INTERACTIONS
Consult your doctor if you are taking the following drugs that may interact with terbinafine: rifampin, cimetidine, tricyclic antidepressants, selective serotonin reuptake inhibitors (SSRIs), beta blockers, MAO inhibitors, or any other prescription or over-the-counter preparation that is to be applied to the same area of skin as terbinafine cream.

FOOD INTERACTIONS
No known food interactions.

DISEASE INTERACTIONS
Use of terbinafine tablets may cause complications in patients with liver or kidney disease, since these organs work together to remove the medication from the body. Consult your doctor if you have a history of alcohol abuse (a potential cause of liver disease).

Terbutaline Sulfate

Brethine 5 mg
(**NOVARTIS**)

Additional photographs

▶ Drug Class: Bronchodilator/ sympathomimetic

▶ Available in: Inhalation aerosol, tablets

▶ Available OTC? No

▶ As Generic? Yes

Side Effects

SERIOUS
Inhaled form: May become ineffective if used too often, resulting in more-severe breathing difficulty that does not improve. Signs include persistent wheezing, coughing, or shortness of breath; confusion; bluish color to lips or fingernails; inability to speak. Ingested form: Chest pain or heaviness; irregular, racing, fluttering, or pounding heartbeat; lightheadedness; fainting; severe weakness; severe headache.

COMMON
Insomnia, dry mouth, sore throat, anxiety, nervousness, restlessness.

LESS COMMON
Trembling, sweating, headache, nausea or vomiting, flushing or redness to cheeks or other skin surfaces, muscle aches, cramps, or twitching, unpleasant or unusual taste in the mouth.

PRINCIPAL USES
Terbutaline is used to dilate air passages in the lungs that have become narrowed as a result of disease or inflammation. It is used in the treatment of asthma and chronic obstructive pulmonary disease (COPD).

HOW THE DRUG WORKS
Terbutaline widens constricted airways in the lungs by relaxing the smooth muscles that surround bronchial passages.

DOSAGE
Use when needed to relieve breathing difficulty. Inhalation aerosol— Adults and children age 12 and older: 1 to 2 in-halations every 4 to 6 hours. Wait 1 minute between first and second inhalations. In-fants and children under 12 years of age: Not recommen-ded. Tablets— Adults and children age 12 and older: 2.5 to 5 mg taken 3 times a day, ideally at 6-hour intervals. Children under 12 years of age: Consult a pediatrician.

ONSET OF EFFECT
Inhalation: Within 5 minutes. Oral: 1 to 2 hours.

DURATION OF ACTION
3 to 6 hours for the inhalation; up to 8 hours for tablets.

DIETARY ADVICE
Maintain your usual food and fluid intake.

STORAGE
Store in a tightly sealed container away from heat and direct light. Do not refrigerate inhalation solutions.

IF YOU MISS A DOSE
Skip the missed dose and resume your regular dosage schedule. Do not double the next dose.

STOPPING THE DRUG
It may not be necessary to finish the recommended course of therapy. Consult your doctor.

PROLONGED USE
Therapy with this medication may require months or years. Excessive use may result in temporary loss of the drug's effectiveness.

PRECAUTIONS
Over 60: Adverse reactions may be more likely and more severe.

Driving and Hazardous Work: Avoid such activities until you determine how the medicine affects you.

Alcohol: No special precautions are necessary.

Pregnancy: Adequate studies have not been done; the benefits must be weighed against potential risks. Consult your doctor for advice.

Breast Feeding: It is not known if terbutaline passes into breast milk. Mothers who wish to breast-feed while taking this drug should discuss the matter with their doctor.

Infants and Children: Use of the inhalation aerosol is not recommended in children younger than 12.

Special Concerns: Pay heed to any asthma attack or other breathing problem that does not improve after your usual nebulizer treatment or usual number of puffs. Seek help immediately if you feel your lungs are persistently constricted, if you are using more than the recommended number of treatments or puffs per day, or if you feel a recent attack is somehow different from others.

OVERDOSE
Symptoms: Chest pain or heaviness; irregular, racing, fluttering, or pounding heartbeat; dizziness or light-headedness; fainting; severe weakness; severe headache.

What to Do: Call your doctor, emergency medical services (EMS), or the nearest poison control center immediately.

DRUG INTERACTIONS
Consult your doctor for specific advice if you are taking a beta-blocker, ergotamine or ergotamine-like medications, antidepressants, digitalis drugs, or an MAO inhibitor.

FOOD INTERACTIONS
No known food interactions.

DISEASE INTERACTIONS
Consult your doctor if you have a history of substance abuse (especially cocaine), seizures, brain damage, heart disease, heartbeat irregularities, high blood pressure, anxiety disorders, or a thyroid condition.

Terconazole

▶ Drug Class: Antifungal

▶ Available in: Cream, suppositories

▶ Available OTC? No

▶ As Generic? Yes

Side Effects

SERIOUS
Vaginal burning, itching, discharge, or irritation not present prior to treatment. Call your doctor immediately.

COMMON
No common side effects have been reported.

LESS COMMON
Headache, stomach cramps or pain, irritation or burning of sexual partner's penis.

PRINCIPAL USES
To treat candidiasis, a fungal infection of the vagina.

HOW THE DRUG WORKS
Terconazole prevents fungal organisms from producing vital substances required for growth and function. This drug is effective only for infections caused by fungal organisms. It will not work for bacterial or viral infections.

DOSAGE
Cream— 0.4% cream: 20 mg (1 applicator) inserted in the vagina at bedtime for 7 nights. 0.8% cream: 40 mg (1 applicator) inserted in the vagina at bedtime for 3 nights. Suppositories— 80 mg (1 suppository) inserted in the vagina at bedtime for 3 nights. Wash your hands before and after insertion or application.

ONSET OF EFFECT
Unknown.

DURATION OF ACTION
Unknown.

DIETARY ADVICE
Terconazole can be taken without regard to diet.

STORAGE
Store in a tightly sealed container away from heat, moisture, and direct light. Do not refrigerate or freeze.

IF YOU MISS A DOSE
Take it as soon as you remember. However, if it is near the time for the next dose, skip the missed dose and resume your regular dosage schedule. Do not double the next dose.

STOPPING THE DRUG
Take it as prescribed for the full treatment period, even if you begin to feel better before the scheduled end of therapy.

PROLONGED USE
If your symptoms do not improve after a few days, or if they become worse, consult your doctor.

PRECAUTIONS
Over 60: Adverse reactions may be more likely and more severe in older patients.

Driving and Hazardous Work: The use of terconazole should not impair your ability to perform such tasks safely.

Alcohol: No special precautions are necessary.

Pregnancy: Studies on the use of terconazole during the first 3 months (trimester) of pregnancy have not been done. No adverse effects from using terconazole during the second or third trimesters have been reported.

Breast Feeding: Terconazole may pass into breast milk; caution is advised. Consult your doctor for advice.

Infants and Children: Studies of the use of terconazole in infants and children have not been done.

Special Concerns: Sanitary napkins should be used to prevent staining of clothing. The affected area should be kept cool and dry. The patient should wear loose-fitting cotton clothing and freshly laundered cotton underwear or pantyhose with a cotton crotch. Avoid underwear made from nonventilating materials. Do not sit for a long time in a wet bathing suit. Avoid feminine hygiene sprays. Wash daily with unscented soap and dry thoroughly with a clean towel. Tampons should not be used during therapy. The patient's sexual partner should wear a condom during intercourse and should consult a doctor if penile redness, itching, or discomfort occur. Do not stop using this medicine during your menstrual period. After urination or a bowel movement, cleanse by wiping the area from front to back to prevent reinfection.

OVERDOSE
Symptoms: An overdose with terconazole is unlikely.

What to Do: Emergency instructions not applicable.

DRUG INTERACTIONS
Other drugs may interact with terconazole. Consult your doctor for specific advice if you are taking any other prescription or over-the-counter medication.

FOOD INTERACTIONS
No known food interactions.

DISEASE INTERACTIONS
Consult your doctor for advice if you have any other medical condition.

Teriparatide

▶ Drug Class: Bone formation agent

▶ Available in: Injection

▶ Available OTC? No

▶ As Generic? No

Side Effects

SERIOUS
No serious side effects are associated with the use of teriparatide. However, contact your health care provider if you have continuing nausea, vomiting, constipation, low energy, or muscle weakness. These may be signs there is too much calcium in your blood.

COMMON
Dizziness, leg cramps.

LESS COMMON
Muscle pain, fatigue, nausea, indigestion, depression.

PRINCIPAL USES
To treat osteoporosis in postmenopausal women and in men who have had osteoporotic fractures or who are at high risk for fractures.

HOW THE DRUG WORKS
Teriparatide, which is the same as the active part of a natural hormone called parathyroid hormone or "PTH," stimulates new bone formation, which leads to increased bone mineral density and bone strength and results in decreased fracture risk.

DOSAGE
20 mcg subcutaneous (under the skin) injection once a day. It must not be administered intramuscularly or intravenously. Rotate the site of injections from abdomen to thighs. After injection, do not massage the site of the injection. Watch for signs of bruising or bleeding at injection sites.

ONSET OF EFFECT
Unknown.

DURATION OF ACTION
Unknown.

DIETARY ADVICE
Teriparatide may be taken at any time of day without regard to meal schedule. Patients are generally advised to take calcium and vitamin D supplements to aid bone formation.

STORAGE
Store in the refrigerator but do not allow it to freeze.

IF YOU MISS A DOSE
If you miss a dose on one day, do not double the dose the next day. Resume your regular dosage schedule.

STOPPING THE DRUG
Take it as prescribed for the full treatment period. The decision to stop taking the drug should be made in consultation with your physician.

PROLONGED USE
Teriparatide is generally prescribed for no longer than a 2-year course of therapy.

PRECAUTIONS
Over 60: No special problems are expected.

Driving and Hazardous Work: Do not drive or engage in hazardous work until you determine how the medicine affects you.

Alcohol: No special precautions are necessary.

Pregnancy: Teriparatide is normally not used in premenopausal women. The drug should not be given to pregnant women.

Breast Feeding: Teriparatide should not be used by nursing mothers.

Infants and Children: Teriparatide should not be used by children.

Special Concerns: Patients taking teriparatide are encouraged to engage in regular weight-bearing exercise and should avoid cigarettes and limit alcohol, which inhibit healthy bone production.

OVERDOSE
Symptoms: No cases of overdose have been reported.

What to Do: An overdose with teriparatide is unlikely. If someone takes a much larger dose than prescribed, call your doctor.

DRUG INTERACTIONS
No drug interactions have been reported.

FOOD INTERACTIONS
No known food interactions.

DISEASE INTERACTIONS
Do not take teriparatide if you have a history of Paget's disease, a history of radiation therapy to the bone, a history of primary bone cancer or metastases, unexplained elevations in alkaline phosphatase, or pre-existing hypercalcemia.

BRAND NAME
Teslac

Teslac 50 mg
(BRISTOL-MYERS SQUIBB)

▶ Drug Class: Antineoplastic (anticancer) agent

▶ Available in: Tablets

▶ Available OTC? No

▶ As Generic? No

Side Effects

SERIOUS
No serious side effects have been reported.

COMMON
No common side effects have been reported.

LESS COMMON
Skin rash; increased blood pressure; numbness or tingling of fingers, toes, or face; diarrhea; loss of appetite; nausea or vomiting; pain or swelling in feet or lower legs; swelling or redness of the tongue; hair loss; aching and swelling of arms and legs; high blood calcium levels causing confusion, increased thirst, and constipation.

PRINCIPAL USES
To treat some cases of advanced breast cancer in either postmenopausal women or premenopausal women in whom ovarian function has been terminated. It is not recommended for treatment of breast cancer in men.

HOW THE DRUG WORKS
Testolactone is chemically similar to the hormone testosterone. The mechanism by which testolactone inhibits breast cancer growth is unclear. The growth of some types of breast cancer is stimulated by the hormone estrogen; testolactone is thought to interfere with the synthesis of estrogen and thus slow the growth of such types of breast cancer.

DOSAGE
The dosage should be 250 mg, 4 times a day, for at least 3 months.

ONSET OF EFFECT
6 to 12 weeks.

DURATION OF ACTION
Unknown.

DIETARY ADVICE
Testolactone can be taken with or between meals. Be sure to get plenty of fluids.

STORAGE
Store in a tightly sealed container away from heat and direct light.

IF YOU MISS A DOSE
Take it as soon as you remember. If it is close to the next dose, skip the missed dose and resume your regular dosage schedule. Do not double the next dose. If you miss more than 1 dose, consult your doctor.

STOPPING THE DRUG
The decision to stop taking the drug should be made by your doctor.

PROLONGED USE
You should see your doctor regularly for tests and examinations if you must take this drug for a prolonged period.

PRECAUTIONS
Over 60: There is no specific information comparing the use of testolactone in the elderly with use in other age groups. However, no special problems or side effects are expected in older patients.

Driving and Hazardous Work: The use of testolactone should not impair your ability to perform such tasks safely.

Alcohol: Avoid alcohol.

Pregnancy: Large doses of testolactone have been shown to cause birth defects and other problems in animal studies. Human studies have not been done. Before you take testolactone, tell your doctor if you are pregnant or plan to become pregnant. If you become pregnant while taking testolactone, tell your doctor immediately.

Breast Feeding: Testolactone may pass into breast milk; caution is advised. Consult your doctor for advice.

Infants and Children: Safety and effectiveness of testolactone in infants and children have not been determined.

Special Concerns: If you vomit shortly after taking a dose of testolactone, check with your doctor to learn whether you should take the dose again or wait for the next dose. Testolactone may cause an excess buildup of calcium in the body, which can produce unwanted or even dangerous side effects. Therefore, drink large amounts of fluids while taking testolactone to rid your body of excess calcium. Your doctor may want to check blood calcium levels regularly while you take testolactone.

OVERDOSE
Symptoms: No specific ones have been reported.

What to Do: An overdose of testolactone is unlikely to be life-threatening. However, if someone takes a much larger dose than prescribed, call your doctor, emergency medical services (EMS), or the nearest poison control center.

DRUG INTERACTIONS
Consult your doctor for specific advice if you are taking anticoagulants such as warfarin. Testolactone may boost the anticlotting effect of such drugs, leading to uncontrolled internal or external bleeding.

FOOD INTERACTIONS
No known food interactions.

DISEASE INTERACTIONS
Caution is advised when taking testolactone. Consult your doctor if you have a medical history that includes heart or kidney disease.

Testosterone

▶ Drug Class: Male hormone (androgen)

▶ Available in: Injection, skin patch, gel

▶ Available OTC? No

▶ As Generic? Yes

Side Effects

SERIOUS
In men: Prolonged, possibly painful erection (which may cause permanent damage to the tissues of the penis and result in the inability to achieve further erections), frequent head-ache, increased thirst, increased urination, nausea or vomiting, swollen feet or legs, unusual bleeding, unusual fatigue, rapid weight gain, hives, significant changes in emotions. Call your doctor immediately. In women: Enlarged clitoris, deepening of voice, male-pattern baldness. Such side effects are rare; call your doctor immediately if any occur.

COMMON
In men: Enlarged, sore breasts, frequent erections, acne, frequent urination. The skin patch may cause itching. In women: Acne, decreased breast size, excessive hair growth, irregular menstrual periods.

LESS COMMON
No less-common minor side effects are associated with testosterone.

PRINCIPAL USES
To replace the hormone when the body does not produce enough; to stimulate puberty in boys with delayed onset of puberty; to increase libido in women (prescribed in combination with estrogen; brand name: Estratest).

HOW THE DRUG WORKS
Testosterone supplementation replaces the natural testosterone normally produced by the body.

DOSAGE
For hormone replacement in men: 100 mg weekly intramuscular injection or 200 mg injection every 2 weeks. Gel: To start, apply the contents of one 5G package in the morning to clean, dry skin on the shoulders, upper arms, or abdomen. Do not apply to the genitals. For delayed puberty in boys: Up to 100 mg injection once a month for 4 to 6 months. For all purposes— Scrotal patch: One new patch applied to scrotal skin in the morning. Nonscrotal patch: 2 to 3 patches a day applied to skin on the arm, back, or upper buttocks.

ONSET OF EFFECT
Blood levels of testosterone peak 5 to 12 hours with the skin patch and in 24 hours with intramuscular injection. Some long-term effects such as improved sexual function may occur after a few weeks of therapy. Other effects (such as those affecting body composition and maturation) may take months to years.

DURATION OF ACTION
Unknown.

DIETARY ADVICE
Testosterone can be taken without regard to diet.

STORAGE
Store skin patch and gel in a tightly sealed container away from heat and direct light.

IF YOU MISS A DOSE
Take it as soon as you remember. If it is near the time for the next dose, skip the missed dose and resume your regular dosage schedule. Do not double the next dose.

STOPPING THE DRUG
The decision to stop taking the drug should be made by your doctor.

PROLONGED USE
You should see your doctor regularly if you are required to use this hormone for a prolonged period.

PRECAUTIONS
Over 60: Increased risk of causing dormant prostate cancer to grow in men. Repeated examinations should be done, using a blood test for prostate specific antigen (PSA) and a digital rectal examination by your doctor.

Driving and Hazardous Work: Do not drive or engage in hazardous work until you determine how the medicine affects you.

Alcohol: Moderate alcohol consumption is acceptable while taking this drug.

Pregnancy: Testosterone should not be taken during pregnancy.

Breast Feeding: Testosterone passes into breast milk and may be harmful; do not use it while breast feeding.

Infants and Children: Not recommended for use by children under the age of puberty.

Special Concerns: The scrotal skin patch should be applied to a shaved area of the scrotum. Men who have experienced skin irritation using a nonscrotal patch can apply triamcinolone cream (0.1%) prior to placement.

OVERDOSE
Symptoms: No specific ones have been reported.

What to Do: An overdose of testosterone is unlikely to be life-threatening. However, if someone takes a much larger dose than prescribed, call your doctor.

DRUG INTERACTIONS
Consult your doctor if you are taking anabolic steroids, anticoagulants (blood thinners, such as warfarin), or an oral contraceptive.

FOOD INTERACTIONS
No known food interactions.

DISEASE INTERACTIONS
Consult your doctor if you have a history of breast cancer (men or women), prostate cancer, diabetes, edema (swelling due to fluid retention), kidney disease, liver disease, enlarged prostate, or cardiovascular disease.

Tetanus Toxoid

BRAND NAMES
Tetanus Toxoid Adsorbed,
Tetanus Toxoid Fluid

▶ Drug Class: Vaccine

▶ Available in: Injection

▶ Available OTC? No

▶ As Generic? No

Side Effects

SERIOUS
Serious allergic reaction involving difficulty swallowing or breathing; reddened skin, especially around the ears; itching, particularly of the hands or feet; hives; unusual and severe fatigue; and swollen face, eyes, or nasal passages. Call your doctor immediately.

COMMON
Hard lump or redness at site of injection.

LESS COMMON
Fever, chills, unusual fatigue, irritability. Also skin rash, pain, itching, swelling, or tenderness at site of injection.

PRINCIPAL USES
To prevent, but not to treat, tetanus (lockjaw).

HOW THE DRUG WORKS
Tetanus toxoid stimulates the body's immune system to produce protective antibodies against tetanus.

DOSAGE
Depending on the type of vaccine being administered, injections are given in the upper arm or midthigh, either into a muscle or under the skin. For adults, children, and infants 6 weeks of age and older: An initial dose at first visit, a second dose 8 weeks later. Depending on the vaccine being used, a third dose may be given 8 weeks after the second dose, and a fourth dose 6 to 12 months later (usually at 15 to 18 months of age in infants). Booster shots should be administered every 10 years. If you sustain a wound that is unclean or difficult to clean, you may need an emergency booster injection if more than 5 years have elapsed since your last booster shot.

ONSET OF EFFECT
Most patients develop immunity following the second dose.

DURATION OF ACTION
Up to 10 years.

DIETARY ADVICE
It may be administered without regard to diet.

STORAGE
Not applicable; the immunizations are administered only at a health care facility.

IF YOU MISS A DOSE
If you miss a scheduled vaccination, contact your doctor to reschedule it.

STOPPING THE DRUG
Follow the full immunization schedule unless a medical problem arises that rules out receiving a vaccination.

PROLONGED USE
No special problems are expected.

PRECAUTIONS
Over 60: Tetanus toxoid should not cause different or more severe side effects in older patients than in younger persons. Vaccine may be slightly less effective. Two-thirds of all tetanus cases in the past few years have been in people age 50 and older.

Driving and Hazardous Work: The administration of tetanus toxoid should not impair your ability to perform such tasks safely.

Alcohol: No special precautions are necessary.

Pregnancy: Adequate studies have not been done. However, if the mother is immune to tetanus, tetanus antibodies from the mother can protect the child from tetanus infection at birth.

Breast Feeding: Tetanus toxoid has not been shown to cause problems during breast feeding.

Infants and Children: Not recommended for use by children less than 6 weeks old.

Special Concerns: Regardless of immunization status, dirty wounds should always be properly cleaned and treated.

OVERDOSE
Symptoms: No specific ones have been reported.

What to Do: If any unexplained symptoms arise after receiving an immunization, call your doctor, emergency medical services (EMS), or the nearest poison control center.

DRUG INTERACTIONS
Other drugs may interact with tetanus toxoid. Consult your doctor for specific advice if you are taking any prescription or over-the-counter medication.

FOOD INTERACTIONS
No known food interactions.

DISEASE INTERACTIONS
Consult your doctor if you have had a severe reaction or a high fever following a previous injection; or if you have pneumonia, bronchitis, or another illness affecting the lungs; any severe illness that is causing fever; or neurological disorders or a history of seizures.

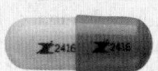

Generic 250 mg
(ZENITH)

▶ Drug Class: Tetracycline antibiotic

▶ Available in: Capsules, tablets, liquid, topical forms, ophthalmic forms, injection

▶ Available OTC? No

▶ As Generic? Yes

Side Effects

SERIOUS
Increased frequency of urination, increased thirst, unusual fatigue, discoloration of skin and mucous membranes. Call your doctor immediately.

COMMON
Stomach cramps and discomfort, diarrhea, nausea, vomiting, increased sensitivity of skin to sunlight, itching in genital or rectal area, sore mouth or tongue, dizziness, lightheadedness, or unsteadiness.

LESS COMMON
No less-common side effects have been reported.

PRINCIPAL USES
To treat infections caused by bacteria or protozoa (tiny single-celled organisms); also, to treat acne.

HOW THE DRUG WORKS
Tetracycline kills bacteria and protozoa by inhibiting the manufacture of specific proteins needed by the organisms to survive.

DOSAGE
Oral forms (capsules, tablets, liquid), for bacterial and protozoal infections: 500 to 2,000 mg,1 to 4 times a day, as determined by your doctor. Topical forms (cream, topical ointment, topical solution), for acne or skin infections: Apply 1 or 2 times a day to affected areas. Ophthalmic forms (ophthalmic ointment, ophthalmic solution) for eye infections: Apply once every 2 to 12 hours as determined by your doctor.

ONSET OF EFFECT
Unknown.

DURATION OF ACTION
Unknown.

DIETARY ADVICE
Oral forms are best taken on an empty stomach with a full glass of water.

STORAGE
Store in a tightly sealed container away from heat and direct light. Refrigerate liquid forms but do not freeze.

IF YOU MISS A DOSE
Take it as soon as you remember. If it is near the time for the next dose, skip the missed dose and resume your regular dosage schedule. Do not double the next dose.

STOPPING THE DRUG
Take this antibiotic as prescribed for the full treatment period, even if you begin to feel better before the scheduled end of therapy.

PROLONGED USE
May increase susceptibility to infections by microorganisms resistant to antibiotics.

PRECAUTIONS
Over 60: It is not known whether tetracycline causes different or more severe adverse reactions in older patients than it does in younger persons.

Driving and Hazardous Work: Do not drive or engage in hazardous work until you determine how the medicine affects you.

Alcohol: It is advisable to abstain from alcohol when fighting an infection.

Pregnancy: Tetracycline should not be used during pregnancy.

Breast Feeding: Tetracycline passes into breast milk and may be harmful to the nursing infant. The patient must choose between using the drug or breast feeding.

Infants and Children: Tetracycline should be used by children younger than 8 years of age only if other antibiotics are unlikely to be effective, since it can cause permanent tooth staining.

Special Concerns: If tetracycline causes increased sensitivity of your skin to sunlight, wear protective clothing, use a sunscreen with an SPF (sun protection factor) of 15 or higher, and try to avoid direct exposure to sunlight, especially between 10 am and 3 pm. Before having surgery, tell the doctor or dentist in charge that you are taking tetracycline. If you use makeup, it is best to apply only water-based cosmetics and to keep the amount to a minimum during tetracycline therapy for the skin. Tetracycline can reduce the effectiveness of oral contraceptives. You should use a different method of birth control while taking this antibiotic. Absorption of tetracycline may be altered if you take antacids.

OVERDOSE
Symptoms: Severe nausea, vomiting, diarrhea, difficulty swallowing.

What to Do: An overdose is unlikely to be life-threatening. However, if someone takes a much larger dose than prescribed, call your doctor, emergency medical services (EMS), or the nearest poison control center immediately.

DRUG INTERACTIONS
Consult your physician for specific advice if you are taking antacids, calcium supplements, cholestyramine, choline and magnesium salicylates, medicines containing iron, laxatives containing magnesium, or oral contraceptives.

FOOD INTERACTIONS
Avoid dairy products while taking tetracycline.

DISEASE INTERACTIONS
Consult your doctor if you have a history of kidney disease or liver disease.

Theophylline

Slo-Bid 50 mg
(RHONE-POULENC RORER)

Additional photographs

▶ Drug Class: Bronchodilator/
xanthine

▶ Available in: Tablets, capsules, extended release
forms, elixir, syrup, oral
solution

▶ Available OTC? No

▶ As Generic? Yes

Side Effects

SERIOUS
Vomiting, trembling, con-
fusion, rapid, irregular, or
pounding pulse, chest
pain, dizziness, convul-
sions, skin rashes.

COMMON
Restlessness, insomnia,
loss of appetite, nervousness, irritability, nausea.

LESS COMMON
Heartburn, diarrhea.

PRINCIPAL USES
Theophylline is used to
reduce the frequency and
severity of breathing problems in people with asthma,
emphysema, bronchitis, and
other lung disorders.

HOW THE DRUG WORKS
An asthma attack occurs
when the smooth muscles
in the bronchial passages of
the lungs go into a spasm
(bronchospasm). Theo-
phylline relaxes these muscles, helping to widen the
constricted airways and
restore normal breathing.

DOSAGE
Adults not currently taking
any theophylline medica-
tions: Your physician will
prescribe a "loading dose,"
which is based on your
weight and taken only once.
This is followed by a daily
maintenance dose, usually
300 to 600 mg per day,
taken in 1 or 2 doses.
Patients given extended-
release capsules: After the
loading dose, take one-half
of the total daily dose at
12-hour intervals, unless
otherwise directed by your
doctor. Adults currently taking theophylline: Dose is
determined by blood level
of theophylline. Children:
Consult a pediatrician.

ONSET OF EFFECT
Variable.

DURATION OF ACTION
Variable.

DIETARY ADVICE
Avoid large amounts of caffeine-containing foods or
beverages, including colas.
Otherwise, maintain your
usual food and fluid intake.

STORAGE
Store in a tightly sealed container away from heat and
direct light. Keep away from
moisture and extremes in
temperature.

IF YOU MISS A DOSE
Take it as soon as you
remember. If it is near
the time for the next dose,
skip the missed dose and
resume your regular dosage
schedule. Do not double the
next dose.

STOPPING THE DRUG
The decision to stop taking
the drug should be made by
your doctor.

PROLONGED USE
Therapy with this medica-
tion may require months or
years.

PRECAUTIONS
Over 60: Adverse reactions
may be more likely and
more severe in older
patients.

**Driving and Hazardous
Work:** Do not drive or
engage in hazardous work
until you determine how the
medicine affects you.

Alcohol: Avoid alcohol.

Pregnancy: Discuss the
relative risks with your doctor. Generally, this drug
should be used only if necessary and if a substitute
cannot be prescribed.

Breast Feeding: Theo-
phylline passes into breast
milk and may be toxic to
nursing infants; avoid or discontinue use while breast
feeding.

Infants and Children:
Theophylline has been used
in children of all ages. Consult your pediatrician for
specific dosages. Theo-
phylline elixir contains alcohol and should not be used
by children.

Special Concerns: You
will need periodic blood
tests to determine theo-
phylline levels. Do not
switch between different

brands of theophylline, and
especially do not switch
between extended-release
forms and other forms without notifying your doctor.
Inform your doctor if you
have stopped smoking;
tobacco affects the level of
theophylline in the blood.

OVERDOSE
Symptoms: Abdominal
pain; disorientation, extreme
anxiety, or unusual behavior; bloody vomiting; twitching, trembling, or shaking;
seizures; rapid, pounding, or
irregular heartbeat; lightheadedness, dizziness, or
fainting.

What to Do: Call your
doctor, emergency medical
services (EMS), or the
nearest poison control center immediately.

DRUG INTERACTIONS
Consult your doctor for specific advice if you are taking
beta-blockers, cimetidine,
ciprofloxacin, clarithro-
mycin, enoxacin, erythro-
mycin, fluvoxamine,
mexiletine, pentoxifylline,
propranolol, tacrine, thiabendazole, ticlopidine,
troleandomycin; moricizine,
phenytoin, or rifampin.

FOOD INTERACTIONS
Your doctor may suggest
that you restrict caffeine
intake.

DISEASE INTERACTIONS
Consult your doctor if you
have a history of convul-
sions, heart failure, liver disease, or underactive thyroid.

Thiabendazole

Mintezol 500 mg
(MERCK)

▶ Drug Class: Anthelmintic

▶ Available in: Oral suspension, chewable tablets

▶ Available OTC? No

▶ As Generic? No

Side Effects

SERIOUS
Severe nausea and vomiting, confusion, skin rash or itching, severe diarrhea, hallucinations, delirium, disorientation, loss of appetite, irritability, tingling or numbness of hands or feet, decreased pulse or blood pressure. Call your physician immediately.

COMMON
Dry eyes or mouth, dizziness, drowsiness, buzzing or ringing in ears, headache, asparagus-like odor from urine.

LESS COMMON
Elevated liver enzymes, temporary decrease in white blood cell count (these effects are detectable by your doctor); fever, flushing of the face, swelling.

PRINCIPAL USES
To treat infections caused by worms, primarily strongyloidiasis (threadworms). It may also be used to treat cutaneous larva migrans (creeping eruption), trichinosis, and visceral larva migrans, although less toxic drugs are available.

HOW THE DRUG WORKS
The exact way in which thiabendazole works is unknown. It appears to interfere with the metabolic or energy-producing processes of worms, including the uptake of glucose (sugar).

DOSAGE
Adults and children: 25 mg per 2.2 lbs (1 kg) of body weight twice a day (up to a maximum of 3,000 mg per day) for 2 to 5 days. Consult your doctor for specific dose. The oral suspension can be used topically for cutaneous larva migrans.

ONSET OF EFFECT
Unknown.

DURATION OF ACTION
Unknown.

DIETARY ADVICE
Take it after meals to reduce stomach upset and some of the common side effects.

STORAGE
Store in a tightly sealed container away from heat, moisture, and direct light. Keep the oral suspension from freezing.

IF YOU MISS A DOSE
Take it as soon as you remember. If it is near the time for the next dose, skip the missed dose and resume your regular dosage schedule. Do not double the next dose.

STOPPING THE DRUG
Take it as prescribed for the full treatment period, even if you feel better before the scheduled end of therapy.

PROLONGED USE
Thiabendazole is generally prescribed for short-term therapy (2 to 5 days). If your condition shows no signs of improvement or worsens within this time, consult your doctor. Another treatment regimen may be prescribed.

PRECAUTIONS
Over 60: Adverse reactions may be more likely and more severe in older patients.

Driving and Hazardous Work: Do not drive or engage in hazardous work while undergoing treatment.

Alcohol: No special precautions are necessary.

Pregnancy: Do not take thiabendazole while pregnant. Consult your doctor for advice if you are pregnant or plan to become pregnant.

Breast Feeding: Thiabendazole may pass into breast milk. Breast feeding may need to be discontinued while you take the drug. Consult your doctor for advice.

Infants and Children: Use and dosage for infants weighing less than 30 pounds should be determined by your doctor.

Special Concerns: To prevent reinfection with trichinosis, all pork, pork-containing products, and game meat should be cooked until the center is no longer pink. To prevent reinfection with cutaneous larva migrans or visceral larva migrans, keep your dogs or cats away from beaches and bathing areas, deworm them regularly, and keep children's sandboxes covered when not in use. Note that approximately half of all patients who take thiabendazole experience at least one side effect.

OVERDOSE
Symptoms: Sporadic vision disturbances, changes in mental state.

What to Do: An overdose of thiabendazole is unlikely to be life-threatening. However, if someone takes a much larger dose than prescribed, call your doctor, emergency medical services (EMS), or the nearest poison control center.

DRUG INTERACTIONS
Consult your doctor for specific advice if you are taking theophylline. Also tell your doctor if you are taking any other prescription or over-the-counter medicine. If you have trichinosis, your doctor may also prescribe a corticosteroid to help reduce inflammation from the pork worm larvae; it is important to take the corticosteroid and thiabendazole together.

FOOD INTERACTIONS
No known food interactions.

DISEASE INTERACTIONS
Use of thiabendazole may cause complications in patients with liver disease, since this organ removes the drug from the body.

Generic 40 mg
(GLAXO WELLCOME)

▶ Drug Class: Antimetabolite;
antineoplastic (anticancer)
agent

▶ Available in: Tablets

▶ Available OTC? No

▶ As Generic? Yes

Side Effects

SERIOUS
Black, tarry, or bloody
stools; blood-tinged (pink
or maroon) urine; cough
or hoarseness; fever and
chills; lower back or flank
pain; painful, difficult urination; tiny bright red
spots on skin; bleeding
from gums, nose, or
other unusual places;
easy bruising, shortness
of breath. These side
effects may mean that
normal blood cells and
special blood-clotting
cells have been affected,
or that normal immune
cells have been affected
and an infection is developing somewhere in your
body. See your doctor
immediately if any of
these occur. Some of
these side effects may
occur after you stop tak-
ing thioguanine; notify
your doctor if they do.

COMMON
No common side effects
have been reported.

LESS COMMON
Diarrhea, loss of appetite,
nausea and vomiting,
skin rash or itching.

PRINCIPAL USES
To treat some forms of
leukemia.

HOW THE DRUG WORKS
It kills cancer cells by interfering with the activity of
their genetic material,
which prevents the cells
from reproducing. It may
also affect the growth and
development of other cells
in the body, resulting in
unpleasant side effects.

DOSAGE
2 mg per 2.2 lbs (1 kg) of
body weight per day, usu-
ally in 1 dose. The dose can
be increased to 3 mg per
2.2 lbs per day if there is
no response after 3 weeks.

ONSET OF EFFECT
Unknown.

DURATION OF ACTION
Unknown.

DIETARY ADVICE
Maintain adequate food and
fluid intake. Calorie, protein,
and vitamin needs increase
in patients with cancer.
Good nutrition is essential
to cope with chemotherapy.

STORAGE
Store in a tightly sealed container away from heat and
direct light.

IF YOU MISS A DOSE
If you miss a dose, skip
the missed dose and
resume your regular dosage
schedule. Do not double the
next dose.

STOPPING THE DRUG
The decision to stop taking
thioguanine should be made
in consultation with your
doctor.

PROLONGED USE
You should see your doctor
regularly for tests and
examinations if you take
this drug for a prolonged
period.

PRECAUTIONS
Over 60: No special problems are expected.

**Driving and Hazardous
Work:** Do not drive or
engage in hazardous work
until you determine how the
medicine affects you.

Alcohol: Consult your doctor about drinking alcohol
while taking this drug.

Pregnancy: Thioguanine
can cause birth defects if
either the father or mother
takes it. It is best to use
some kind of birth control
while taking thioguanine.
Consult your doctor for specific advice if you are pregnant or plan to become
pregnant.

Breast Feeding: Thioguanine may pass into breast
milk; avoid or discontinue
use while nursing.

Infants and Children:
No special problems are
expected.

Special Concerns: While
taking thioguanine, do not
receive any immunizations
without consulting your doctor. Avoid people with infections and those who have
recently had oral polio vaccine. Be careful when using
a toothbrush, dental floss,
or toothpick. Check with
your doctor before having
any dental work done. If
you are going to have
surgery, tell the doctor or
dentist in charge that you
are taking thioguanine. Do
not touch your eyes or the
inside of your nose unless
you have just washed your
hands. Be careful not to cut
yourself when using sharp
objects such as a razor.
Avoid contact sports and
other activities where bruising could occur. If you
vomit shortly after taking a
dose of thioguanine, consult

your doctor about taking
the dose again.

OVERDOSE
Symptoms: Nausea, vomiting, general malaise, high
blood pressure.

What to Do: Call your
doctor, emergency medical
services (EMS), or the
nearest poison control
center immediately.

DRUG INTERACTIONS
Consult your doctor for specific advice if you are taking
antithyroid agents, azathioprine, chloramphenicol,
colchicine, flucytosine, interferon, plicamycin, zidovudine, probenecid, or
sulfinpyrazone.

FOOD INTERACTIONS
No known food interactions.

DISEASE INTERACTIONS
Caution is advised when
taking thioguanine. Consult
your doctor if you have any
of the following: chicken
pox, shingles, gout, kidney
stones, kidney disease, liver
disease, or any infection.

Generic 100 mg
(CREIGHTON)

Additional photographs

▶ Drug Class: Neuroleptic;
antipsychotic

▶ Available in: Oral solution,
oral suspension, tablets

▶ Available OTC? No

▶ As Generic? Yes

Side Effects

SERIOUS
Rapid heartbeat, profuse
sweating, seizures, difficulty breathing, neck stiffness, swelling of the
tongue, difficulty swal-
lowing. Also a rare condition can develop called
neuroleptic malignant
syndrome, characterized
by stiffness or spasms of
the muscles, high fever,
and confusion or disori-
entation. Call your doctor
immediately.

COMMON
Dizziness or faintness,
drowsiness, constipation,
decreased sweating, dry
mouth, nasal congestion,
shaking or trembling of
the hands, stiffness,
stooped posture.

LESS COMMON
Menstrual irregularities,
sexual dysfunction,
unusual milk secretion,
breast pain or swelling,
unexpected weight gain,
difficult urination.

PRINCIPAL USES
To treat moderate to severe
psychiatric conditions
including schizophrenia,
manic states, and drug-
induced psychosis. It is
also used to treat extreme
behavior problems in children (including infantile
autism), to ease the symptoms of Tourette's syn-
drome, and to reduce
nausea and vomiting
associated with chemo-
therapy for cancer.

HOW THE DRUG WORKS
Thioridazine blocks receptors of dopamine (a chemical that aids in the transmission of nerve impulses)
in the central nervous system. Presumably, this produces a tranquilizing and
antipsychotic effect.

DOSAGE
Adults: Initially, 25 to 100
mg, 3 times a day. Your doctor may increase the dose
as needed and tolerated, not
to exceed 800 mg a day.

ONSET OF EFFECT
Sedation may occur within
minutes, but onset of
antipsychotic effect may
take hours to occur or may
not occur until days or
weeks after the beginning
of therapy.

DURATION OF ACTION
12 to 24 hours, but effects
may persist for several days.

DIETARY ADVICE
Should be taken with food
and a full glass of water.

STORAGE
Store in a tightly sealed container away from heat and
direct light. Do not allow
liquid forms to freeze.

IF YOU MISS A DOSE
Take it as soon as you
remember. If it is near the
time for the next dose, skip
the missed dose and

resume your regular dosage
schedule. Do not double the
next dose.

STOPPING THE DRUG
The decision to stop taking
the drug should be made in
consultation with your doctor. Gradual reduction of
doses may be required if
you have taken this medication for an extended period.

PROLONGED USE
See your doctor regularly
for tests and examinations if
you must take this medicine
for a prolonged period.

PRECAUTIONS
Over 60: Adverse reactions
are more likely and more
severe in older patients.

**Driving and Hazardous
Work:** Do not drive or
engage in hazardous work
until you learn how this
medication affects you.

Alcohol: Avoid alcohol.

Pregnancy: Avoid using
thioridazine if you are pregnant or plan to become
pregnant.

Breast Feeding: Either
avoid taking the drug if possible or refrain from breast
feeding.

Infants and Children:
Adverse reactions may be
more likely and more
severe in children.

Special Concerns: Avoid
prolonged exposure to high
temperatures or hot cli-
mates. Drink plenty of fluids
and stay cool in the sum-
mertime. Avoid overexpo-
sure to sunlight until you
determine if the drug
heightens your skin's sensitivity to ultraviolet light.

OVERDOSE
Symptoms: Extreme
drowsiness or paradoxical

restlessness or agitation,
heart rhythm irregularities
or palpitations, dry mouth,
seizures, stiffness or
impaired muscle control,
loss of consciousness.

What to Do: Call your
doctor, emergency medical
services (EMS), or the
nearest poison control
center immediately.

DRUG INTERACTIONS
Thioridazine should not be
used within 5 weeks of taking fluoxetine. Consult your
doctor for specific advice if
you are taking anticholinergics, anticonvulsants, antidepressants, antihistamines,
antihypertensives, bupro-
pion, central nervous system depressants such as
barbiturates, clozapine,
dronabinol, ethinamate,
guanethidine, guanfacine,
lithium, methyldopa, carbamazepine, rifampin, or trihexyphenidyl.

FOOD INTERACTIONS
No known food interactions.

DISEASE INTERACTIONS
Consult your doctor if you
have Parkinson's disease or
any movement disorder,
glaucoma, epilepsy, liver
disease, or kidney disease.

Generic 1 mg
(MYLAN)

839

Additional photographs

▶ Drug Class: Neuroleptic; antipsychotic

▶ Available in: Capsules, solution, injection

▶ Available OTC? No

▶ As Generic? Yes

Side Effects

SERIOUS
Rapid heartbeat, profuse sweating, seizures, difficulty breathing, neck stiffness, swelling of the tongue, difficulty swallowing. Also a rare condition can develop called neuroleptic malignant syndrome, characterized by stiffness or spasms of the muscles, high fever, and confusion or disorientation. Call your doctor immediately.

COMMON
Nausea, reduced perspiration, dry mouth, blurred vision, drowsiness, shaking of the hands, muscle stiffness, stooped posture.

LESS COMMON
Difficult urination, menstrual irregularities, breast pain or swelling, unexpected weight gain, uncontrolled movements of the tongue, fever, chills, sore throat, unusual bruising or bleeding, heart palpitations, skin rash, itching, increased sensitivity of the skin to sunlight.

PRINCIPAL USES
To treat psychotic conditions (severe mental disorders characterized by distorted thoughts, perceptions, and emotions), such as schizophrenia.

HOW THE DRUG WORKS
Thiothixene blocks receptors of dopamine (a chemical that allows the transmission of nerve impulses) in the central nervous system. Presumably, this produces a tranquilizing or antipsychotic effect.

DOSAGE
Oral forms: Initial dose is 2 mg, 3 times a day, or 5 mg, 2 times a day. The dose may be increased up to 60 mg a day. Injection: 4 mg injected into a muscle, 2 to 4 times a day. The dose may be increased up to 30 mg a day.

ONSET OF EFFECT
Sedation may occur within minutes, but onset of antipsychotic effect may take hours to occur or may not occur until days or weeks after the beginning of therapy.

DURATION OF ACTION
12 to 24 hours, but effects may persist for several days.

DIETARY ADVICE
This drug may be taken without regard to diet.

STORAGE
Store in a tightly sealed container away from heat and direct light. Do not allow liquid forms to freeze.

IF YOU MISS A DOSE
Take it as soon as you remember. However, if it is within 2 hours of the next dose, skip the missed dose and resume your regular dosage schedule. Do not double the next dose.

STOPPING THE DRUG
The decision to stop taking the drug should be made in consultation with your physician.

PROLONGED USE
Prolonged use may lead to tardive dyskinesia (involuntary movements of the jaw, lips, tongue, and, in rare cases, the arms, legs, hands, or body). Consult your doctor about the need for follow-up evaluations and tests if you must take this drug for an extended period.

PRECAUTIONS
Over 60: Adverse reactions are more likely and more severe in older patients.

Driving and Hazardous Work: Do not drive or engage in hazardous work until you determine how the medicine affects you.

Alcohol: Avoid alcohol.

Pregnancy: Adequate studies have not been done. Before you take thiothixene, tell your doctor if you are pregnant or plan to become pregnant.

Breast Feeding: It is unknown if thiothixene passes into breast milk; consult your doctor for advice.

Infants and Children: Thiothixene is not commonly prescribed for patients under age 12.

Special Concerns: Avoid prolonged exposure to high temperatures or hot climates. Drink plenty of fluids and stay cool in the summertime. Avoid overexposure to sunlight until you determine if the drug heightens your skin's sensitivity to ultraviolet light.

OVERDOSE
Symptoms: Severe breathing difficulty, severe dizziness, extreme fatigue or sedation, muscle spasms, stiffness, or twitching, constricted pupils, unusual excitability.

What to Do: Call your doctor, emergency medical services (EMS), or the nearest poison control center immediately.

DRUG INTERACTIONS
Other drugs may interact with thiothixene. Consult your doctor for specific advice if you are taking anticholinergics, anticonvulsants, antidepressants, antihistamines, antihypertensives, bupropion, central nervous system depressants such as barbiturates, clozapine, dronabinol, ethinamate, fluoxetine, guanethidine, guanfacine, lithium, methyldopa, carbamazepine, rifampin, or trihexyphenidyl.

FOOD INTERACTIONS
No known food interactions.

DISEASE INTERACTIONS
Consult your doctor if you have Parkinson's disease or any movement disorder, glaucoma, epilepsy, liver disease, or kidney disease.

Tiagabine Hydrochloride

BRAND NAME
Gabitril

▶ Drug Class: Anticonvulsant

▶ Available in: Tablets

▶ Available OTC? No

▶ As Generic? No

Side Effects

SERIOUS
No serious side effects are associated with the use of tiagabine.

COMMON
Dizziness, fatigue, lack of energy, drowsiness, nausea, nervousness, irritability, tremor.

LESS COMMON
Abdominal pain, diarrhea, vomiting, general pain, increased appetite, mouth sores, joint aches, insomnia, speech difficulties, clumsiness or incoordination, difficulty concentrating, amnesia, mental depression, emotional instability, hostility or agitation, confusion, abnormal eye movements, sore throat, numbness, prickling or tingling sensations, rash, flu-like symptoms.

PRINCIPAL USES
Used in combination with one or more anticonvulsant drugs to control partial seizures (those which begin with an abnormal burst of electrical activity in a small portion of the brain).

HOW THE DRUG WORKS
Although its precise mechanism of action is unknown, tiagabine is thought to increase the activity of an inhibiting neurotransmitter that depresses brain activity and suppresses the abnormal firing of neurons that causes seizures.

DOSAGE
Teenagers: For the first week, 4 mg once a day. At the beginning of the second week, the total daily dose may be increased by 4 mg. The total daily dose may be further adjusted by 4 to 8 mg on a weekly basis, up to 32 mg a day in 2 to 4 divided doses. Adults: For the first week, 4 mg once a day. The total daily dose may be further adjusted by 4 to 8 mg on a weekly basis, up to 56 mg a day in 2 to 4 divided doses.

ONSET OF EFFECT
Unknown.

DURATION OF ACTION
Unknown.

DIETARY ADVICE
Tiagabine should be taken with meals.

STORAGE
Store in a tightly sealed container away from heat, moisture, and direct light.

IF YOU MISS A DOSE
Take it as soon as you remember. If it is near the time for the next dose, skip the missed dose and resume your regular dosage schedule. Do not double the next dose.

STOPPING THE DRUG
The decision to stop taking the drug should be made by your doctor. Never stop this drug abruptly because this may cause seizures. The dose is typically tapered over a period of weeks.

PROLONGED USE
Side effects are more likely with prolonged use.

PRECAUTIONS
Over 60: Adverse reactions may be more likely and more severe.

Driving and Hazardous Work: Do not drive or engage in hazardous work until you determine how the medicine affects you.

Alcohol: May contribute to excessive drowsiness.

Pregnancy: Adequate human studies have not been done. Before taking tiagabine, tell your doctor if you are or are planning to become pregnant. Discuss with your doctor the relative risks and benefits of using this drug while pregnant.

Breast Feeding: Tiagabine may pass into breast milk; caution is advised. Consult your doctor for specific advice.

Infants and Children: Not recommended for use by children under age 12.

Special Concerns: Your doctor may want you to wear a medical alert bracelet or carry an identification card saying that you are taking this drug.

OVERDOSE
Symptoms: Few cases of overdose have been reported. In clinical trials, the most common symptoms following overdose have been drowsiness, agitation, confusion, speech problems, hostility, mental depression, weakness, and muscle spasms.

What to Do: Call your doctor, emergency medical services (EMS), or the nearest poison control center immediately.

DRUG INTERACTIONS
There are no significant drug interactions.

FOOD INTERACTIONS
No known food interactions.

DISEASE INTERACTIONS
A lower dose or longer dosing intervals may be warranted in patients with impaired liver function.

Ticlopidine Hydrochloride

BRAND NAME
Ticlid

Ticlid 250 mg
(ROCHE)

▶ Drug Class: Antiplatelet drug

▶ Available in: Tablets

▶ Available OTC? No

▶ As Generic? Yes

Side Effects

SERIOUS
Bleeding that is difficult to stop, bruising, increased susceptibility to infection, sores, ulcers or white spots in the mouth, severe abdominal or stomach pain, back pain, peeling or loosening of the skin or lips or mucous membranes, bloody or tarry stools, blood in urine, coughing up blood, dizziness, fever or chills, severe headache, loss of coordination, pinpoint red spots on skin, thickened or scaly skin, difficulty speaking, unusually heavy menstrual flow, vomiting of blood or dark material. Call your doctor immediately.

COMMON
Skin rash, mild stomach pain, diarrhea, indigestion, nausea.

LESS COMMON
Gas or bloating, dizziness, vomiting.

PRINCIPAL USES
To reduce the chance of stroke in patients who have had a stroke or have high risk factors for stroke. While beneficial in this regard, ticlopidine is potentially a very dangerous medication prescribed only when all other therapeutic measures have failed.

HOW THE DRUG WORKS
Blood clots are a primary cause of stroke and heart attack. Ticlopidine prevents platelets from clumping clumping together to form blood clots, thus reducing the risk of stroke.

DOSAGE
250 mg, 2 times a day.

ONSET OF EFFECT
Within 2 days.

DURATION OF ACTION
1 to 2 weeks.

DIETARY ADVICE
Should be taken with food.

STORAGE
Store in a tightly sealed container away from heat and direct light.

IF YOU MISS A DOSE
Take it as soon as you remember. If it is near the time for the next dose, skip the missed dose and resume your regular dosage schedule. Do not double the next dose.

STOPPING THE DRUG
The decision to stop taking the drug should be made by your doctor.

PROLONGED USE
You should see your doctor regularly for blood cell counts and physical examinations if you must take this medication for a prolonged period.

PRECAUTIONS
Over 60: No special problems are expected.

Driving and Hazardous Work: Do not drive or engage in hazardous work until you determine how the medicine affects you.

Alcohol: Avoid alcohol.

Pregnancy: In animal studies, ticlopidine has caused harmful effects; human studies have not been done. Before you take ticlopidine, be sure to tell your doctor if you are currently pregnant or plan to become pregnant.

Breast Feeding: It is not known whether ticlopidine passes into breast milk; caution is advised. Consult your doctor for specific advice.

Infants and Children: There are no studies of ticlopidine use in children.

Special Concerns: Be sure to tell all of your doctors, dentists, and pharmacists that you are taking ticlopidine. You may have to stop taking the drug 10 days to 2 weeks before an operation or dental work. Ticlopidine can cause serious bleeding, especially after an injury. Ask your doctor whether there are activities you should avoid while taking this drug. Frequent blood tests, every 1 or 2 weeks, should be done during the first 6 months of ticlopidine therapy.

OVERDOSE
Symptoms: Uncontrolled bleeding, fever, infection.

What to Do: Discontinue the medication and call your doctor, emergency medical services (EMS), or the nearest poison control center right away.

DRUG INTERACTIONS
Consult your doctor for specific advice if you are taking anticoagulants, carbenicillin, dipyridamole, divalproex, heparin, medicine for pain or inflammation, pentoxifylline, plicamycin, sulfinpyrazone, ticarcillin, or valproic acid.

FOOD INTERACTIONS
No known food interactions.

DISEASE INTERACTIONS
Caution is advised when taking ticlopidine. Consult your doctor if you have a history of any of the following: a blood clotting problem, severe liver disease, stomach ulcers, any blood disease, or severe kidney disease.

Tiludronate Disodium

BRAND NAME
Skelid

▶ Drug Class: Bisphosphonate inhibitor of bone resorption

▶ Available in: Tablets

▶ Available OTC? No

▶ As Generic? No

Side Effects

SERIOUS
No serious side effects are associated with the use of tiludronate.

COMMON
Diarrhea, nausea, stomach upset, indigestion.

LESS COMMON
Mild chest pain, swelling of the ankles, numbness, rash, vomiting, flatulence, increased susceptibility to infection, runny nose, sinus infection, cataract, conjunctivitis, glaucoma, dental problems.

PRINCIPAL USES
To treat Paget's disease, a disorder characterized by rapid breakdown and reformation of bone, which can lead to fragility and malformation of bones. Treatment is indicated if serum alkaline phosphatase (as measured in blood tests) is at least two times normal, or if the patient has symptoms or is at risk for complications.

HOW THE DRUG WORKS
Healthy bones are continuously remodeled (broken down and then reformed); the minerals and other components of bones are reabsorbed by one set of cells (osteoclasts) and replaced by another set of cells to form new bone. Tiludronate suppresses the activity of osteoclasts; consequently, the breakdown of bone tissue occurs more slowly than the laying down of new bone. As a result, bone density and strength are preserved.

DOSAGE
400 mg, once a day for 3 months.

ONSET OF EFFECT
Unknown.

DURATION OF ACTION
Unknown.

DIETARY ADVICE
Take it with a full glass of plain water. Taking tiludronate with food or beverages (including mineral water) other than plain water is likely to reduce the absorption of the drug from the intestine. Take the tablets at least 2 hours before or after eating. Maintain adequate vitamin D and calcium intake; however, vitamin or mineral supplements should also be taken at least 2 hours before or after taking the drug.

STORAGE
Store in a tightly sealed container away from heat, moisture, and direct light. Do not remove tablets from the foil strips until they are to be used.

IF YOU MISS A DOSE
If you miss a dose on one day, do not double the dose the next day. Resume your regular dosage schedule.

STOPPING THE DRUG
Take it as prescribed for the full treatment period. The decision to stop taking the drug should be made in consultation with your physician.

PROLONGED USE
Tiludronate is generally prescribed for a 3-month course of therapy. Adequate studies on the safety and effectiveness of tiludronate beyond this period of time have not been done.

PRECAUTIONS
Over 60: No special problems are expected.

Driving and Hazardous Work: The use of tiludronate should not impair your ability to perform such tasks safely.

Alcohol: No special precautions are necessary.

Pregnancy: Adequate human studies have not been done. Discuss with your doctor the relative risks and benefits of using this drug while pregnant.

Breast Feeding: Tiludronate may pass into breast milk; caution is advised. Consult your doctor for specific advice.

Infants and Children: Not recommended for use by children under age 18.

OVERDOSE
Symptoms: No cases of overdose have been reported.

What to Do: An overdose with tiludronate is unlikely. If someone takes a much larger dose than prescribed, call your doctor.

DRUG INTERACTIONS
Calcium supplements, aspirin, and indomethacin should not be taken within 2 hours before or after taking tiludronate. Aluminum- or magnesium-containing antacids, if needed, should be taken at least 2 hours after taking tiludronate.

FOOD INTERACTIONS
No known food interactions, although tiludronate works best when taken on an empty stomach.

DISEASE INTERACTIONS
Patients with severe kidney disease should not take tiludronate.

Timolol Maleate Ophthalmic

▶ Drug Class: Antiglaucoma drug; ophthalmic beta-blocker

▶ Available in: Ophthalmic solution

▶ Available OTC? No

▶ As Generic? No

Side Effects

SERIOUS
Palpitations; trouble breathing; dizziness and weakness caused by low blood pressure. Call your doctor right away.

COMMON
Stinging or irritation of the eye when drops are applied; tearing.

LESS COMMON
Decreased night vision; eyebrow pain; crusted eyelashes; dry eyes; increased sensitivity of eyes to light; redness, stinging, burning, watering, or other irritation of the eye; droopy eyelid; eye inflammation.

PRINCIPAL USES
To treat glaucoma.

HOW THE DRUG WORKS
Glaucoma, a sight-threatening disorder, occurs when aqueous humor (the fluid inside the eye) cannot drain properly, causing an increase in pressure within the eyeball (intraocular pressure). This can damage the optic nerve and lead to a gradually progressive loss of vision. Timolol decreases the production of aqueous humor, thereby reducing intraocular pressure.

DOSAGE
Adults and older children: 1 drop 1 or 2 times a day. Younger children and infants: Use and dosage must be determined by your doctor.

ONSET OF EFFECT
Within 30 minutes.

DURATION OF ACTION
12 to 24 hours.

DIETARY ADVICE
This medication can be used without regard to diet.

STORAGE
Store in a tightly sealed container away from heat, moisture, and direct light. Do not allow it to freeze.

IF YOU MISS A DOSE
Apply it as soon as you remember. If it is near the time for the next dose, skip the missed dose and resume your regular dosage schedule. Do not double the next dose.

STOPPING THE DRUG
The decision to stop using the drug should be made by your doctor.

PROLONGED USE
You should see your doctor regularly for tests and examinations as part of glaucoma follow up if you take this drug for a prolonged period.

PRECAUTIONS
Over 60: Adverse reactions may be more likely and more severe in older patients.

Driving and Hazardous Work: Do not drive or engage in hazardous work until you determine how the medicine affects your vision.

Alcohol: Use alcohol with caution.

Pregnancy: Timolol has not caused birth defects in animals. Human studies have not been completed. Before you take timolol, tell your doctor if you are pregnant or plan to become pregnant.

Breast Feeding: Timolol may pass into breast milk; caution is advised. Consult your doctor for advice.

Infants and Children: Adverse reactions may be more likely and more severe in infants.

Special Concerns: To use the eye drops, first wash your hands. Tilt your head back. Gently apply pressure to the inside corner of the eyelid and with the index finger of the same hand, pull downward on the lower eyelid to make a space. Drop the medicine into this space and close your eye. Apply pressure for 1 or 2 minutes while keeping the eye closed without blinking. Then wash your hands again. Make sure the tip of the dropper does not touch your eye, finger, or any other surface. Timolol may make your eyes more sensitive to bright light. If this occurs, wear sunglasses or avoid bright light as necessary. Before you have any surgery, dental treatment, or emergency treatment, tell the doctor or dentist in charge that you are using timolol.

OVERDOSE
Symptoms: Nervousness, chest pain, irregular or pounding heartbeat, hallucinations, wheezing, mental confusion.

What to Do: If a large volume enters the eye, flush with water. If someone accidentally ingests the medicine, call your doctor, emergency medical services (EMS), or the nearest poison control center.

DRUG INTERACTIONS
It is not recommended to use two ophthalmic beta-blockers at the same time. Special caution is warranted in people taking antidiabetic drugs, as timolol may mask symptoms of low blood sugar. Consult your doctor for specific advice if you are taking any other prescription or over-the-counter medication.

FOOD INTERACTIONS
No known food interactions.

DISEASE INTERACTIONS
Caution is advised when taking timolol. Consult your doctor if you have any of the following: asthma, emphysema or another lung disease, low blood sugar, heart disease, blood vessel disease, or an overactive thyroid. In diabetes, timolol can affect blood sugar levels or mask symptoms of low blood sugar.

Timolol Maleate Oral

Generic 5 mg
(GENEVA)

▶ Drug Class: Beta-blocker

▶ Available in: Tablets

▶ Available OTC? No

▶ As Generic? Yes

Side Effects

SERIOUS
Shortness of breath, wheezing; irregular or slow heartbeat (50 beats per minute or less); pain or feelings of tightness or pressure in the chest; swelling of the ankles, feet, and lower legs; mental depression. If you experience any such symptoms, stop taking timolol and contact your doctor right away.

COMMON
Dizziness or lightheadedness, especially when rising suddenly to a standing position; decreased sexual ability; unusual fatigue, weakness, or drowsiness; insomnia.

LESS COMMON
Anxiety, irritability, nervousness; constipation; diarrhea; dry, sore eyes; itching; nausea or vomiting; nightmares or intensely vivid dreams; numbness, tingling, or other unusual sensations in the fingers, toes, or scalp.

PRINCIPAL USES
To treat high blood pressure; to prevent recurrence of and lower mortality from heart attack; to prevent migraine headaches.

HOW THE DRUG WORKS
Beta-blockers such as timolol work by preventing—or blocking—nerve impulses from exerting an accelerating or intensifying effect on specific parts of the body, especially blood vessels and the heart. This slows the heart and widens the vessels, thus lowering blood pressure. By relaxing blood vessels in the brain, timolol also helps prevent migraines.

DOSAGE
For high blood pressure: 10 mg, 2 times a day; may be increased to a maximum of 60 mg per day. After heart attack: 10 mg, 2 times a day. Migraine headache prevention: 10 mg, 2 times a day; may be increased to 30 mg per day.

ONSET OF EFFECT
Within 15 to 30 minutes.

DURATION OF ACTION
Up to 12 hours.

DIETARY ADVICE
Timolol can be taken with meals to minimize the risk of stomach upset.

STORAGE
Store in a tightly sealed container away from heat and direct light.

IF YOU MISS A DOSE
Take it as soon as you remember. If it is near the time for the next dose, skip the missed dose and resume your regular dosage schedule. Do not double the next dose.

STOPPING THE DRUG
Do not discontinue the drug suddenly, as this may cause serious health problems. The dosage must be gradually tapered in accordance with your physician's instructions.

PROLONGED USE
Lifelong therapy with timolol may be necessary. Visit your doctor regularly if you take it for a prolonged period.

PRECAUTIONS
Over 60: Adverse reactions may be more likely and more severe. Resistance to cold temperatures may be decreased in older patients.

Driving and Hazardous Work: Do not drive or engage in hazardous work until you determine how the medicine affects you.

Alcohol: Avoid alcohol.

Pregnancy: Discuss with your doctor the relative risks and benefits of using this drug while pregnant.

Breast Feeding: Timolol passes into breast milk; consult your doctor about its use while nursing.

Infants and Children: The dosage must be determined by your pediatrician.

Special Concerns: Take extra care during exercise or hot weather to avoid dizziness and fainting. Check your pulse regularly while taking timolol. If it is slower than your usual rate or less than 50 beats a minute, check with your doctor.

OVERDOSE
Symptoms: Unusually slow or rapid heartbeat, severe dizziness or fainting, poor circulation in the hands (bluish skin), breathing difficulty, seizures.

What to Do: Call your doctor, emergency medical services (EMS), or the nearest poison control center immediately.

DRUG INTERACTIONS
Consult your doctor for specific advice if you are taking amphetamines, oral antidiabetic agents, asthma medication (such as aminophylline or theophylline), calcium channel blockers, clonidine, guanabenz, halothane, immunotherapy for allergies (allergy shots), insulin, MAO inhibitors, reserpine, other beta-blockers, or any over-the-counter medicine.

FOOD INTERACTIONS
No known food interactions.

DISEASE INTERACTIONS
Timolol should be used with caution in people with diabetes, especially insulin-dependent diabetes, since the drug may mask symptoms of hypoglycemia. People with the following conditions should consult their doctor before using timolol: allergies or asthma, heart or blood vessel disease (including congestive heart failure and peripheral vascular disease), hyperthyroidism, irregular (slow) heartbeat, myasthenia gravis, psoriasis, respiratory problems such as bronchitis or emphysema, kidney or liver disease, or a history of mental depression.

Tioconazole

▶ Drug Class: Antifungal

▶ Available in: Vaginal ointment

▶ Available OTC? Yes

▶ As Generic? Yes

Side Effects

SERIOUS
Vaginal itching, burning, discharge, or irritation not present prior to treatment. Call your doctor as soon as possible.

COMMON
No common side effects have been reported.

LESS COMMON
Headache, stomach cramps or pain, irritation or burning of sexual partner's penis.

PRINCIPAL USES
To treat fungal (yeast) infections of the vagina.

HOW THE DRUG WORKS
Tioconazole prevents the growth and function of some fungal organisms by interfering with the production of substances needed to preserve the cell membrane. This drug is effective only for infections caused by fungal organisms. It will not work for bacterial or viral infections.

DOSAGE
A single 300 mg (1 applicatorful) dose of ointment, inserted with an applicator into the vagina at bedtime.

ONSET OF EFFECT
Some relief may be felt within 1 day. Complete relief of symptoms generally occurs within 7 days.

DURATION OF ACTION
Unknown.

DIETARY ADVICE
Tioconazole may be used without regard to diet.

STORAGE
Store in a tightly sealed container away from heat, moisture, and direct light. Do not allow it to freeze.

IF YOU MISS A DOSE
Not applicable. Tioconazole is usually effective with a single, one-time use.

STOPPING THE DRUG
Tioconazole is generally used on a one-time basis. If needed, a second dose may be applied 1 to 2 weeks following the first dose.

PROLONGED USE
Tioconazole is for short-term use only.

PRECAUTIONS
Over 60: No special problems are expected.

Driving and Hazardous Work: This drug should not impair your ability to perform such tasks safely.

Alcohol: No special precautions are necessary.

Pregnancy: Adequate studies on the use of tioconazole during pregnancy have not been done; however, there are no reports of adverse effects while using it. Consult your doctor.

Breast Feeding: No problems are expected. Consult your doctor before using this medicine while nursing.

Infants and Children: No studies have been done on the use of tioconazole in children. Consult your pediatrician for specific advice.

Special Concerns: Tioconazole may be used with oral contraceptives and antibiotic therapy. Sanitary napkins should be used to prevent staining of clothing. The affected area should be kept cool and dry. The patient should wear loose-fitting cotton clothing and freshly laundered cotton underwear or pantyhose with a cotton crotch. Avoid underwear made from non-ventilating materials. Do not sit for a long time in a wet bathing suit. Avoid feminine hygiene sprays. Wash daily with unscented soap and dry thoroughly with a clean towel. Tampons should not be used during therapy. Do not have sex for 3 days after treatment and wait an additional 3 days before relying upon a condom or diaphragm, since the medication may weaken latex. After this time, the patient's sexual partner should wear a condom during intercourse and should consult a doctor if penile redness, itching, or discomfort occurs. You may use this medicine during your menstrual period. After urination or a bowel movement, cleanse by wiping the area from front to back to prevent reinfection.

OVERDOSE
Symptoms: An overdose with tioconazole is unlikely.

What to Do: If someone should swallow a large amount of the medicine, call your doctor.

DRUG INTERACTIONS
Tell your doctor if you are using any other vaginal prescription or over-the-counter medication.

FOOD INTERACTIONS
No food interactions have been reported.

DISEASE INTERACTIONS
No disease interactions have been reported.

Tizanidine Hydrochloride

BRAND NAME
Zanaflex

▶ Drug Class: Muscle relaxant

▶ Available in: Tablets

▶ Available OTC? No

▶ As Generic? Yes

Side Effects

SERIOUS
Liver damage causing nausea, vomiting, loss of appetite, and yellowish tinge to eyes and skin (jaundice). Call your doctor immediately.

COMMON
Drowsiness, dry mouth, dizziness, slowed heartbeat, very low blood pressure causing lightheadedness when arising from a sitting or lying position.

LESS COMMON
Infection, constipation, rapid heartbeat, vomiting, speech problems, blurred vision, frequent urination, flu syndrome, nervousness, movement difficulties, inflamed mucous membranes, nasal inflammation.

PRINCIPAL USES
To relieve the muscle spasticity and cramping associated with multiple sclerosis and spinal cord injury.

HOW THE DRUG WORKS
Tizanidine is a short-acting drug that temporarily inhibits nerve activity that causes spasticity. Because of the risk of side effects, it should be taken only at times of the day when reduced spasticity is most important.

DOSAGE
Initial dose is 4 mg, every 6 to 8 hours. This may be increased as needed in 2 to 4 mg increments to 8 mg every 6 to 8 hours (not exceeding 3 doses in 24 hours), until a satisfactory therapeutic effect is achieved. Maximum dose is 36 mg a day.

ONSET OF EFFECT
Within 1 hour.

DURATION OF ACTION
Up to 6 hours.

DIETARY ADVICE
It can be taken with or between meals. Dry mouth is a common complaint with such drugs; maintain adequate fluid intake and suck on ice chips if desired.

STORAGE
Store in a tightly sealed container away from heat and direct light.

IF YOU MISS A DOSE
Take it as soon as you remember. If it is near the time for the next dose, skip the missed dose and resume your regular dosage schedule. Do not double the next dose.

STOPPING THE DRUG
The decision to stop taking the drug should be made by your doctor.

PROLONGED USE
You should see your doctor regularly for tests and examinations if you must take this drug for a prolonged period.

PRECAUTIONS
Over 60: Adverse reactions may be more likely and more severe in older patients.

Driving and Hazardous Work: Do not drive or engage in hazardous work until you determine how the medicine affects you.

Alcohol: Avoid alcohol.

Pregnancy: In some animal studies, large doses of tizanidine have been shown to cause problems. Human studies have not been done. This drug should be used during pregnancy only if clearly needed. Consult your doctor for advice.

Breast Feeding: Tizanidine may pass into breast milk; caution is advised. Consult your doctor for advice.

Infants and Children: There is no specific information about the use of tizanidine in infants and children.

Special Concerns: Tizanidine is a newly introduced medication, and it is possible that side effects not found in early studies may occur with widespread use. Patients should be alert for the signs of significantly lowered blood pressure (dizziness, faintness, disorientation). In clinical trials of tizanidine, a small number of patients experienced hallucinations that continued after treatment was stopped. Dose-related eye damage (retinal degeneration and corneal opacities) was detected in some animal studies but has not been seen in human clinical trials.

OVERDOSE
Symptoms: Loss of consciousness and respiratory depression have been noted thus far in limited experience with the drug. Other symptoms may occur.

What to Do: If apparent overdose occurs, call your doctor, emergency medical services (EMS), or the nearest poison control center immediately.

DRUG INTERACTIONS
Consult your doctor for specific advice if you are taking oral contraceptives or any other prescription or over-the-counter medication, especially those that produce sedation as a side effect, such as benzodiazepine tranquilizers and baclofen, or medications that are used for lowering high blood pressure.

FOOD INTERACTIONS
No known food interactions.

DISEASE INTERACTIONS
Caution is advised when taking tizanidine. Consult your doctor if you have any other medical condition. Tizanidine may cause complications in patients with kidney disease, since the kidneys are involved in the removal of the drug from the body.

Tobramycin

- ▶ Drug Class: Aminoglycoside antibiotic

- ▶ Available in: Injection, ophthalmic solution and ointment, inhalation

- ▶ Available OTC? No

- ▶ As Generic? Yes

Side Effects

SERIOUS
Loss of balance, dizziness; ringing, buzzing, or feeling of fullness in the ears, any loss of hearing; increased thirst, greatly decreased or increased amount of urine or frequency of urination, loss of appetite, nausea or vomiting; muscle twitching or seizures; skin rash, itching, redness, or swelling (especially around the eye or eyelid) not present prior to treatment. Call your doctor immediately.

COMMON
Ophthalmic ointment: Temporary blurred vision immediately following administration.

LESS COMMON
Ophthalmic forms: Stinging or burning of the eyes.

PRINCIPAL USES
To treat a variety of bacterial infections including those of the bones and joints, central nervous system, the abdominal cavity, eyes, lungs, skin and soft tissue, urinary tract, and the blood. Tobramycin is also used in the management of lung infections in patients with cystic fibrosis.

HOW THE DRUG WORKS
Tobramycin interferes with bacteria's genetic material—specifically its RNA, which is necessary in the manufacture of proteins. Without the ability to manufacture protein, the bacteria cannot survive.

DOSAGE
Standard dose for most infections— Injection: Dosage depends on the weight of the patient and the infection being treated. Mild eye infections— Adults and teenagers: 1 drop of solution in the affected eye every 4 hours or a thin strip of ointment applied every 8 to 12 hours. Severe eye infections— Apply the solution or ointment every 3 to 4 hours until improvement occurs, then adjust the frequency of doses as directed by your doctor. Lung infections in those with cystic fibrosis— Injection: Initially, 10 mg per 2.2 lbs (1 kg) of body weight a day in 4 divided doses. Inhalation: 300 mg (1 single-use ampule) 2 times a day for 28 days. Stop therapy for 28 days, and then resume therapy for the next 28 days. Inhalations should be taken as close to 12 hours apart as possible and not less than 6 hours apart.

ONSET OF EFFECT
Variable.

DURATION OF ACTION
Variable.

DIETARY ADVICE
Drink plenty of fluids.

STORAGE
Store in a tightly sealed container away from heat and direct light. Refrigerate the inhalation form.

IF YOU MISS A DOSE
Take it as soon as you remember. If it is near the time (within 6 hours for the inhalation) for the next dose, skip the missed dose and resume your regular dosage schedule. Do not double the next dose.

STOPPING THE DRUG
Take as prescribed for the full treatment period, even if your symptoms subside.

PROLONGED USE
Periodic kidney function tests may be needed. Consult your doctor if your condition does not improve after 7 days, or 1 to 3 days for eye infections.

PRECAUTIONS
Over 60: Adverse reactions may be more likely and more severe.

Driving and Hazardous Work: Avoid such activities until you determine how the medicine affects you.

Alcohol: Avoid alcohol.

Pregnancy: Discuss with your doctor the relative risks and benefits of using this drug while pregnant. Some studies show that injectable tobramycin may cause damage to the infant's hearing, sense of balance, and kidneys. However, this medication may be necessary for the mother.

Breast Feeding: Tobramycin may pass into breast milk; caution is advised. Consult your doctor for advice.

Infants and Children: Tobramycin may be used by infants and children with proper doses.

Special Concerns: To use the eye drops or the ointment, first wash your hands. Tilt your head back. Gently apply pressure to the inside corner of the eyelid and with the index finger of the same hand, pull downward on the lower eyelid to make a space. Drop the medicine or put a short strip of ointment (about ⅓ inch long) into this space and close your eye. Apply pressure for 1 or 2 minutes while keeping the eye closed. Wash hands again. Make sure the tip of the dropper or applicator does not touch your eye, finger, or any other surface.

OVERDOSE
Symptoms: Injection: Decreased urine output, blood in the urine, swelling of the ankles or other body parts, impaired muscle control, severe breathing difficulty. Ophthalmic forms: Eye pain and redness, increased tear production, swelling and itching of the eyes or eyelids. Inhalation: None reported.

What to Do: Seek medical attention immediately.

DRUG INTERACTIONS
Consult your doctor for specific advice if you are taking any other aminoglycoside, capreomycin, methoxyflurane, polymyxins, cyclosporine, dornase alfa, or vancomycin.

FOOD INTERACTIONS
No known food interactions.

DISEASE INTERACTIONS
Consult your doctor for specific advice if you have loss of hearing or balance, kidney disease, Parkinson's disease, or myasthenia gravis.

Tocainide Hydrochloride

BRAND NAME
Tonocard

Tonocard 400 mg
(ASTRA MERCK)

▶ Drug Class: Antiarrhythmic

▶ Available in: Tablets

▶ Available OTC? No

▶ As Generic? No

Side Effects

SERIOUS
Fainting; rapid or irregular heartbeats (palpitations); trembling or shaking; severe rash, blisters, peeling or scaling of skin; cough or shortness of breath; fever or chills; unusually slow heartbeat; mouth sores; unusual bleeding or bruising, loss of appetite, unusual anxiety; jaundice (yellowish tinge to skin or whites of eyes); profuse sweating. Call your doctor immediately.

COMMON
Dizziness or lightheadedness, loss of appetite, nausea.

LESS COMMON
Mental confusion, blurred vision, headache, anxiety or irritability, skin rash, sweating, vomiting, numbness or tingling of fingers and toes.

PRINCIPAL USES
To correct irregular heartbeats (cardiac arrhythmias). This drug is used only to treat severe, life-threatening heart rhythm disorders, since it has been shown to cause serious adverse side effects in some patients.

HOW THE DRUG WORKS
Tocainide slows nerve impulses in the heart and reduces the sensitivity of heart tissue to certain nerve impulses, thus stabilizing heartbeat.

DOSAGE
To start, 400 mg every 8 hours. The dose may be increased to 600 mg, 3 times a day. It is best to take doses at equally spaced intervals. Early adverse effects may be decreased by administering the medication in smaller, more frequent doses.

ONSET OF EFFECT
Within 2 hours.

DURATION OF ACTION
Approximately 8 to 11 hours.

DIETARY ADVICE
Tocainide can be taken with food or milk to avoid gastrointestinal upset.

STORAGE
Store in a tightly sealed container in a dry place away from heat and direct light.

IF YOU MISS A DOSE
Take it as soon as you remember. However, if it is near the time for the next dose, skip the missed dose and resume your regular dosage schedule. Do not double the next dose.

STOPPING THE DRUG
Take tocainide as prescribed for the full treatment period, even if you begin to feel better before the scheduled end of therapy. The decision to stop taking the drug should be made by your doctor.

PROLONGED USE
Lifelong therapy may be necessary. See your doctor regularly for examinations and diagnostic tests if you must take this medicine for a prolonged period.

PRECAUTIONS
Over 60: Adverse reactions may be more likely and more severe in older patients.

Driving and Hazardous Work: Avoid such activities until you determine how the medicine affects you.

Alcohol: Avoid alcohol.

Pregnancy: Animal studies have shown that high doses of tocainide can cause fetal deaths. No defects or other problems have been found in humans. Before you take tocainide, tell your doctor if you are pregnant or plan to become pregnant.

Breast Feeding: Tocainide may pass into breast milk; caution is advised. Consult your doctor for advice.

Infants and Children: Studies of tocainide in infants and children have not been done. Use and dose must be determined by your pediatrician.

Special Concerns: Before having any kind of surgery, tell the doctor or dentist in charge that you are taking tocainide. Your doctor may require weekly blood tests for the first 3 weeks of treatment and frequently after that. Tell your doctor if you have any unusual allergic reaction to tocainide or to an anesthetic.

OVERDOSE
Symptoms: Tremors, seizures, heartbeat irregularities, nausea, vomiting, weakness, cardiac arrest.

What to Do: Call your doctor, emergency medical services (EMS), or the nearest poison control center immediately.

DRUG INTERACTIONS
Consult your doctor for specific advice if you are taking rifampin, beta-blockers, or any other prescription or over-the-counter medication.

FOOD INTERACTIONS
No known food interactions.

DISEASE INTERACTIONS
Caution is advised when taking tocainide. Avoid this medication if you have congestive heart failure. Use of tocainide may cause complications in patients with liver or kidney disease, since these organs work together to remove the medication from the body.

Tolazamide

Generic 100 mg
(ZENITH)

▶ Drug Class: Antidiabetic agent/sulfonylurea

▶ Available in: Tablets

▶ Available OTC? No

▶ As Generic? Yes

Side Effects

SERIOUS
Convulsions, fainting, low blood sugar causing anxious feeling, blurred vision, cold sweats, confusion, drowsiness, excessive hunger, rapid heartbeat, headache, nausea, nervousness, restless sleep, shortness of breath, unusual weight gain, unusual bleeding or bruising. Call your doctor at once. Other serious but less common side effects include bone marrow suppression, hemolytic anemia, and elevation of liver-associated enzymes; these problems can be detected by your doctor.

COMMON
Changes in taste, constipation or diarrhea, more frequent urination, headache, heartburn, increased or decreased appetite, nausea, stomach pain or fullness, vomiting.

LESS COMMON
Increased sensitivity of skin to the sun.

PRINCIPAL USES
To help control blood sugar in patients with non-insulin-dependent (type 2) diabetes.

HOW THE DRUG WORKS
Tolazamide stimulates insulin release from the pancreas and reduces glucose output by the liver.

DOSAGE
Adults: 100 to 250 mg once a day to start. It can be increased to 1,000 mg per day. If more than 500 mg per day, tablets are usually taken in 2 doses. Children: The dose must be determined by your doctor.

ONSET OF EFFECT
Within 4 to 6 hours.

DURATION OF ACTION
12 to 24 hours.

DIETARY ADVICE
If 1 dose daily, take it before breakfast. If 2 doses, take one before breakfast and one before dinner.

STORAGE
Store in a tightly sealed container away from heat and direct light.

IF YOU MISS A DOSE
Take it as soon as you remember. If it is near the time for the next dose, skip the missed dose and resume your regular dosage schedule. Do not double the next dose.

STOPPING THE DRUG
The decision to stop taking the drug should be made by your doctor.

PROLONGED USE
At some point, tolazamide may stop working effectively and your blood sugar may go up. Consult your doctor about the need for periodic examinations and blood tests.

PRECAUTIONS

Over 60: Adverse reactions may be more likely and more severe in older patients.

Driving and Hazardous Work: Do not drive or engage in hazardous work until you determine how the medicine affects you.

Alcohol: Alcohol should be avoided while taking this medication.

Pregnancy: Before you take tolazamide, tell your doctor if you are pregnant or plan to become pregnant. This medicine is rarely used during pregnancy (insulin is the treatment of choice for pregnant diabetic women).

Breast Feeding: Tolbutamide may pass into breast milk; caution is advised. Consult your doctor for advice.

Infants and Children: Non-insulin-dependent (type 2) diabetes is rare in infants and children.

Special Concerns: Be sure to carry a card or medical ID bracelet saying that you have this type of diabetes. Follow your prescribed diet closely. Consult your doctor about exercises you should do. Be sure you take your daily dose of tolazamide even when you become ill. You may have to be switched temporarily to insulin. Test your blood sugar level at least every 4 hours when you are ill. Keep some source of quick-acting sugar readily available to handle episodes of low blood sugar.

OVERDOSE
Symptoms: Tingling of lips and tongue, lethargy, confusion, nausea, nervousness, sweating, tremors, hunger, convulsions, loss of consciousness. (Most symptoms of overdose are due to serious hypoglycemia.)

What to Do: Call your doctor, emergency medical services (EMS), or the nearest poison control center immediately.

DRUG INTERACTIONS
Consult your doctor if you are taking anticoagulants, antifungal agents, aspirin, chloramphenicol, cimetidine, ciprofloxacin, quinidine, ranitidine, asparaginase, corticosteroids, lithium, asthma medicine, allergy medicine, beta-blockers, cyclosporine, guanethidine, MAO inhibitors, octreotide, pentamidine, or anticonvulsants.

FOOD INTERACTIONS
Be careful to follow the low-sugar diet prescribed for you by your doctor.

DISEASE INTERACTIONS
Consult your physician if you have any of the following: diarrhea, heart disease, hyperthyroidism, or underactive adrenal or pituitary gland. Use of tolazamide may cause complications in patients with liver or kidney disease, since these organs work together to remove the medication from the body.

Tolbutamide

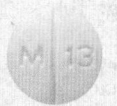

Generic 500 mg
(MYLAN)

▶ Drug Class: Antidiabetic
agent/sulfonylurea

▶ Available in: Tablets

▶ Available OTC? No

▶ As Generic? Yes

Side Effects

SERIOUS
Seizures, fainting, low blood sugar causing anxious feeling, blurred vision, cold sweats, confusion, drowsiness, excessive hunger, fast heartbeat, headache, nausea, nervousness, restless sleep, shortness of breath, unusual weight gain, unusual bleeding or bruising. Call your doctor at once. Other serious but less common side effects include bone marrow suppression, hemolytic anemia, and elevation of liver-associated enzymes; these problems can be detected by your doctor.

COMMON
Changes in taste, constipation or diarrhea, more frequent urination, headache, heartburn, increased or decreased appetite, nausea, stomach pain or fullness, vomiting.

LESS COMMON
Increased sensitivity of skin to the sun.

PRINCIPAL USES
To help control blood sugar in patients with non-insulin-dependent (type 2) diabetes.

HOW THE DRUG WORKS
Tolbutamide stimulates insulin release from the pancreas and reduces glucose output by the liver.

DOSAGE
Adults: 1,000 to 2,000 mg per day to start, in 2 divided doses. It can be increased to 3,000 mg (3 g) a day, although little additional benefit is derived from more than 2 g a day. Children: The dose must be set by a pediatrician.

ONSET OF EFFECT
Within 1 hour.

DURATION OF ACTION
6 to 12 hours.

DIETARY ADVICE
Tolbutamide should be taken 30 minutes before the morning and evening meals.

STORAGE
Store in a tightly sealed container away from heat and direct light.

IF YOU MISS A DOSE
Take it as soon as you remember. If it is near the time for the next dose, skip the missed dose and resume your regular dosage schedule. Do not double the next dose.

STOPPING THE DRUG
The decision to stop taking the drug should be made by your doctor.

PROLONGED USE
At some point, tolbutamide may stop working effectively and your blood sugar may rise unexpectedly. Consult your doctor about the need for periodic examinations and blood tests.

PRECAUTIONS

Over 60: Adverse reactions may be more likely and more severe in older patients.

Driving and Hazardous Work: Do not drive or engage in hazardous work until you determine how the medicine affects you.

Alcohol: Avoid alcohol.

Pregnancy: Before you take tolbutamide, tell your doctor if you are pregnant or plan to become pregnant. This medicine is rarely used during pregnancy.

Breast Feeding: Tolbutamide may pass into breast milk; caution is advised. Consult your doctor for specific advice.

Infants and Children: The safety and effectiveness have not been established for young patients.

Special Concerns: Be sure to carry a card or medical ID bracelet saying that you have this type of diabetes. Follow your prescribed diet closely. Consult your doctor about exercises you should do. Be sure you take your daily dose of tolbutamide even when you become ill. You may have to be switched temporarily to insulin. Test your blood sugar level at least every 4 hours when you are ill.

OVERDOSE

Symptoms: Tingling of lips and tongue, lethargy, confusion, nausea, nervousness, sweating, tremors, hunger, convulsions, loss of consciousness. (Most symptoms of overdose are due to serious hypoglycemia.)

What to Do: Call your doctor, emergency medical services (EMS), or the nearest poison control center immediately.

DRUG INTERACTIONS
Consult your doctor if you are taking anticoagulants, antifungal agents, aspirin, chloramphenicol, cimetidine, ciprofloxacin, quinidine, ranitidine, antiseizure medication, asparaginase, corticosteroids, lithium, asthma medicine, allergy medicine, beta-blockers, cyclosporine, guanethidine, MAO inhibitors, octreotide, or pentamidine.

FOOD INTERACTIONS
Be careful to follow the low-sugar diet as prescribed.

DISEASE INTERACTIONS
Caution is advised when taking tolbutamide. Consult your doctor if you have any of the following: diarrhea, heart disease, overactive thyroid, or underactive adrenal or pituitary gland. Use of tolbutamide may cause complications in patients who have liver or kidney disease, since these organs work together to remove the medication from the body.

Tolcapone

▶ Drug Class: Antiparkinsonism drug/COMT inhibitor

▶ Available in: Tablets

▶ Available OTC? No

▶ As Generic? No

Side Effects

SERIOUS
Liver damage is a significant serious side effect. Symptoms include persistent nausea, fatigue, lethargy, loss of appetite, yellow discoloration of the skin and eyes (jaundice), dark urine, itchiness, and abdominal pain on the right side. Call your doctor immediately. Dizziness, lightheadedness, or fainting, especially when rising from a sitting or lying position, owing to a sudden drop in blood pressure (orthostatic hypotension). Such symptoms, in addition to nausea, are more common at the beginning of therapy.

COMMON
Impaired ability to execute voluntary movements, nausea, sleep difficulties, quirky involuntary muscle movements that contort the body, excessive dreaming, loss of appetite, muscle cramps, drowsiness, diarrhea, confusion, headaches, hallucinations, vomiting.

LESS COMMON
Constipation, increased susceptibility to upper respiratory tract infection, increased incidence of falling, increased sweating, dry mouth, abdominal pain, discolored urine.

PRINCIPAL USES
To treat Parkinson's disease in conjunction with standard levodopa/carbidopa therapy. It should only be used by patients who are experiencing symptom fluctuations and are not responding satisfactorily or those who are inappropriate candidates for other adjunctive therapies.

HOW THE DRUG WORKS
When used with levodopa/carbidopa, tolcapone sustains higher levels of levodopa in the blood. Tolcapone is believed to increase blood levels of levodopa by blocking the action of catechol-O-methyltransferase (COMT), one of the enzymes responsible for breaking down levodopa, before it reaches its receptors in the brain. Levodopa raises the amount of dopamine available in the brain; dopamine plays an essential role in smooth movement of muscles and is deficient in patients with Parkinson's disease.

DOSAGE
Initial dose: 100 mg, 3 times a day in conjunction with levodopa/carbidopa. The first dose of the day should be taken together with levodopa/carbidopa and the remaining doses should be taken 6 and 12 hours later. The dose can be increased to 200 mg 3 times a day if the anticipated increase in benefit is justified. Tolcapone may be taken with either the immediate or the sustained-release forms of levodopa/carbidopa. Many patients may need to reduce their daily dose of levodopa.

ONSET OF EFFECT
Unknown.

DURATION OF ACTION
Unknown.

DIETARY ADVICE
Tolcapone can be taken without regard to meals.

STORAGE
Store in a tightly sealed container away from heat, moisture, and direct light.

IF YOU MISS A DOSE
Take it as soon as you remember. If it is near the time for the next dose, skip the missed dose and resume your regular dosage schedule. Do not double the next dose.

STOPPING THE DRUG
Take it as prescribed for the full treatment period. The decision to stop taking the drug should be made in consultation with your physician.

PROLONGED USE
Liver function tests are strongly recommended just prior to treatment, every 2 weeks for the first year of therapy, every 4 weeks for the next 6 months, and then every 8 weeks thereafter if you must take this medicine for a prolonged period.

PRECAUTIONS
Over 60: Adverse reactions may be more likely and more severe in older patients.

Driving and Hazardous Work: Do not drive or engage in hazardous work until you determine how the medicine affects you.

Alcohol: Avoid alcohol.

Pregnancy: Adequate human studies have not been done. Before taking tolcapone, tell your doctor if you are or are planning to become pregnant. Discuss with your doctor the relative risks and benefits of using this drug while pregnant.

Breast Feeding: Tolcapone may pass into breast milk; caution is advised. Consult your doctor for specific advice.

Infants and Children: Not applicable. No potential use for tolcapone has been identified in children.

Special Concerns: If tolcapone does does not provide significant benefit within three weeks of the initiation of treatment, therapy should be discontinued. Your doctor should be thoroughly familiar with tolcapone and should ask you to sign a patient consent form that helps spell out the risks of taking this medication.

OVERDOSE
Symptoms: An overdose with tolcapone is unlikely. However, nausea, vomiting, and dizziness or fainting may occur with an excessive dose.

What to Do: If someone takes a much larger dose than prescribed, seek medical attention immediately.

DRUG INTERACTIONS
Consult your doctor for specific advice if you are taking any of the following drugs, which may interact with tolcapone: desipramine, MAO inhibitor antidepressants (such as phenelzine sulfate or tranylcypromine sulfate, but not selegiline), or antihypertensive drugs.

FOOD INTERACTIONS
No known food interactions.

DISEASE INTERACTIONS
Do not use tolcapone if you have liver disease or have had a prior reaction to tolcapone. Caution is advised for patients with low blood pressure or severe kidney dysfunction.

Tolmetin Sodium

Generic 600 mg
(PUREPAC)

▶ Drug Class: Nonsteroidal anti-inflammatory drug (NSAID)

▶ Available in: Tablets, capsules

▶ Available OTC? No

▶ As Generic? Yes

Side Effects

SERIOUS
Shortness of breath or wheezing, with or without swelling of legs or other signs of heart failure; chest pain; peptic ulcer disease with vomiting of blood; black, tarry stools; decreasing kidney function. Call your doctor immediately.

COMMON
Nausea, vomiting, heartburn, diarrhea, constipation, headache, dizziness, sleepiness.

LESS COMMON
Ulcers or sores in mouth, depression, rashes or blistering of skin, ringing sound in the ears, unusual tingling or numbness of the hands or feet, seizures, blurred vision. Also elevated potassium levels, decreased blood counts; such problems can be detected by your doctor.

PRINCIPAL USES
To treat mild to moderate pain and inflammation caused by tendinitis, arthritis, bursitis, gout, soft tissue injuries, migraine and other vascular headaches, menstrual cramps, and other conditions. When patients fail to respond to one NSAID, another may be tried. The greatest effectiveness often requires trial and error of several different NSAIDs.

HOW THE DRUG WORKS
NSAIDs work by interfering with the formation of prostaglandins, naturally occurring substances in the body that cause inflammation and make nerves more sensitive to pain impulses. NSAIDs also have other modes of action that are less well understood.

DOSAGE
Adults: 400 mg, 3 times a day. Maximum dose is 1,800 mg a day. Children: Consult your pediatrician.

ONSET OF EFFECT
From 30 minutes to several hours or longer.

DURATION OF ACTION
Varies.

DIETARY ADVICE
Take with food; maintain your usual food and fluid intake.

STORAGE
Store in a tightly sealed container away from heat, moisture, and direct light.

IF YOU MISS A DOSE
Take it as soon as you remember. If it is near the time for the next dose, skip the missed dose and resume your regular dosage schedule. Do not double the next dose.

STOPPING THE DRUG
The decision to stop taking the drug should be made in consultation with your physician.

PROLONGED USE
Prolonged use can cause gastrointestinal problems, including ulceration and bleeding, kidney dysfunction, and liver inflammation. Consult your doctor about the need for medical examinations and laboratory tests.

PRECAUTIONS
Over 60: Because of the potentially greater consequences of gastrointestinal side effects, the dose of NSAIDs for older patients, especially those over age 70, is often cut in half.

Driving and Hazardous Work: Avoid such activities until you determine how the medicine affects you.

Alcohol: Avoid alcohol when using this medication because it increases the risk of stomach irritation.

Pregnancy: Avoid or discontinue this drug if you are pregnant or are planning to become pregnant.

Breast Feeding: Tolmetin passes into breast milk; avoid use while nursing.

Infants and Children: May be used in exceptional circumstances; consult your doctor.

Special Concerns: Because NSAIDs can interfere with blood coagulation, this drug should be stopped at least 3 days prior to any surgery.

OVERDOSE
Symptoms: Severe nausea, vomiting, headache, confusion, seizures.

What to Do: Call your doctor, emergency medical services (EMS), or the nearest poison control center immediately.

DRUG INTERACTIONS
Do not take this drug with aspirin or any other NSAIDs without your doctor's approval. In addition, consult your doctor if you are taking antihypertensives, steroids, anticoagulants, antibiotics, itraconazole or ketoconazole, plicamycin, penicillamine, valproic acid, phenytoin, cyclosporine, digitalis drugs, lithium, methotrexate, probenecid, triamterene, or zidovudine.

FOOD INTERACTIONS
No known food interactions.

DISEASE INTERACTIONS
Consult your doctor if you have any of the following: bleeding problems, inflammation or ulcers of the stomach and intestines, diabetes mellitus, systemic lupus erythematosus (SLE, lupus), anemia, asthma, epilepsy, Parkinson's disease, kidney stones, or a history of heart disease or alcohol abuse. Use of tolmetin may cause complications in patients with liver or kidney disease, since these organs work together to remove the medication from the body.

BRAND NAMES
Aftate, Genaspore, NP-27, Tinactin, Ting, Zeasorb-AF

▶ Drug Class: Topical antifungal

▶ Available in: Cream, gel, powder, solution

▶ Available OTC? Yes

▶ As Generic? Yes

Side Effects

SERIOUS
Skin irritation that was not present before use of tolnaftate. Call your doctor immediately.

COMMON
No common side effects have been reported.

LESS COMMON
No less-common side effects have been reported.

PRINCIPAL USES
To treat a variety of fungal infections of the skin, including tinea corporis (ringworm), tinea cruris (jock itch), and tinea pedis (athlete's foot).

HOW THE DRUG WORKS
Tolnaftate prevents fungi from manufacturing vital substances required for growth and function. This medication is effective only for infections caused by ringworm fungal organisms. It will not work for bacterial or viral infections.

DOSAGE
Apply to the affected area 2 times a day. All forms should be used immediately after the affected area is washed and dried. Wash your hands before and after application.

ONSET OF EFFECT
Unknown.

DURATION OF ACTION
Unknown.

DIETARY ADVICE
No special restrictions.

STORAGE
Store in a tightly sealed container away from heat, moisture, and direct light.

IF YOU MISS A DOSE
Apply it as soon as you remember. If it is near the time for the next dose, skip the missed dose and resume your regular dosage schedule. Do not double the next dose.

STOPPING THE DRUG
Use of tolnaftate should continue for 2 weeks beyond the time that symptoms disappear. This helps to ensure eradication of the fungus.

PROLONGED USE
You should consult your doctor if symptoms do not improve within 10 days of beginning therapy.

PRECAUTIONS
Over 60: No special problems are expected.

Driving and Hazardous Work: The use of tolnaftate should not impair your ability to perform such tasks safely.

Alcohol: No special precautions are necessary.

Pregnancy: Tolnaftate has not been shown in studies to cause problems when used during pregnancy.

Breast Feeding: Tolnaftate may pass into breast milk, but no problems have been reported. Consult your doctor for specific advice.

Infants and Children: Tolnaftate should be used by children under the age of 2 years only under a doctor's close supervision.

Special Concerns: Do not allow tolnaftate to come into contact with your eyes. If your skin condition does not improve or instead gets worse after 10 days of treatment, consult your doctor. Tolnaftate should not be used alone to treat fungal infections of the hair or nails; your doctor will prescribe an additional medication. If you are using tolnaftate for an infection of the feet, be sure to wear well-fitting and well-ventilated shoes and to change your shoes and socks every day. Do not cover the treated area of skin with bandages unless your doctor instructs you to do so.

OVERDOSE
Symptoms: None are known; no cases of overdose have been reported.

What to Do: An overdose of tolnaftate is unlikely to occur. However, if someone accidentally ingests some of the medication, call your doctor, emergency medical services (EMS), or the nearest poison control center immediately.

DRUG INTERACTIONS
Some drugs may interact adversely with tolnaftate. Consult your doctor for specific advice if you are taking any other prescription or over-the-counter medication that is applied to the same area of skin being treated by tolnaftate.

FOOD INTERACTIONS
No known food interactions.

DISEASE INTERACTIONS
Caution is advised when taking tolnaftate. Consult your doctor for specific advice if you have a history of any other skin condition.

Tolterodine Tartrate

▶ Drug Class: Anticholinergic

▶ Available in: Tablets

▶ Available OTC? No

▶ As Generic? No

Side Effects

SERIOUS
Chest pain. Consult your doctor immediately.

COMMON
Headache, constipation, indigestion, dry eye, dry mouth.

LESS COMMON
Numbness, tingling or prickling sensation, abdominal pain, flatulence, nausea or vomiting, bronchitis, cough, dry skin, nervousness, drowsiness, blurred vision.

PRINCIPAL USES
To treat overactive bladder with symptoms of urinary frequency, urgency, or urge incontinence.

HOW THE DRUG WORKS
Tolterodine decreases the urge to urinate by blocking nerve receptors that trigger contractions of the bladder.

DOSAGE
Adults: 2 mg, twice a day. Dose may be lowered by your doctor to 1 mg, twice a day, depending upon response to the medication. Adults with impaired liver function: no more than 1 mg, twice a day.

ONSET OF EFFECT
Unknown.

DURATION OF ACTION
Unknown.

DIETARY ADVICE
Tolterodine can be taken without regard to diet.

STORAGE
Store in a tightly sealed container away from heat, moisture, and direct light.

IF YOU MISS A DOSE
Take it as soon as you remember. If it is near the time for the next dose, skip the missed dose and resume your regular dosage schedule. Do not double the next dose.

STOPPING THE DRUG
The decision to stop taking the drug should be made in consultation with your physician.

PROLONGED USE
See your doctor periodically if you must take this drug for a prolonged period.

PRECAUTIONS
Over 60: No special problems are expected.

Driving and Hazardous Work: The use of tolterodine should not impair your ability to perform such tasks safely.

Alcohol: No special problems are expected.

Pregnancy: No human studies have been done. Before taking tolterodine, tell your doctor if you are pregnant or plan to become pregnant.

Breast Feeding: Tolterodine may pass into breast milk; avoid use while nursing. Consult your doctor for specific advice.

Infants and Children: Not recommended for use by children under the age of 18.

OVERDOSE
Symptoms: Drowsiness, mental confusion, dizziness, loss of coordination, dry mouth.

What to Do: Few cases of overdose have been reported. However, if someone takes a much larger dose than prescribed, call your doctor, emergency medical services (EMS), or the nearest poison control center immediately.

DRUG INTERACTIONS
The following drugs may interact with tolterodine. Consult your doctor for specific advice if you are taking fluoxetine, macrolide antibiotics, or antifungal drugs.

FOOD INTERACTIONS
No known food interactions.

DISEASE INTERACTIONS
You should not take tolterodine if you have: urinary retention, gastric retention, or uncontrolled narrow-angle glaucoma. Tolterodine should be used with caution in patients with liver or kidney disease, since these organs work together to remove the medication from the body.

Topiramate

Topamax 100 mg
(McNEIL)

839

Additional photographs

▶ Drug Class: Anticonvulsant

▶ Available in: Tablets, capsules

▶ Available OTC? No

▶ As Generic? No

Side Effects

SERIOUS
Intense pain in the kidney area may be a sign of kidney stones, which occur with greater frequency in those taking topiramate. Blurred vision, pain around the eyes. Seek immediate medical attention.

COMMON
Drowsiness, fatigue, dizziness, anxiety, loss of coordination, unusual eye movements, tingling sensations, confusion, speech problems, depression, poor concentration or attention, mood changes, memory impairment, poor appetite, weight loss, tremor.

LESS COMMON
Back pain, nausea and vomiting, indigestion, dry mouth, abdominal pain, constipation, muscle aches, hearing difficulty, menstrual irregularities, sinus infections, double vision. Consult your doctor if you are concerned about any other adverse or unusual reactions you experience while taking this drug.

PRINCIPAL USES
To help control certain types of seizures in the treatment of epilepsy and other disorders. It is often used in conjunction with other anticonvulsant drugs after they have failed to be effective on their own.

HOW THE DRUG WORKS
Topiramate appears to block the uncontrolled firing of neurons that causes seizures, but its precise mechanism of action is unknown.

DOSAGE
Adults: 100 to 400 mg a day, in 2 divided doses. Some patients require higher doses. Initially, a low dose is prescribed; it may then be gradually increased by your doctor. Children ages 2 to 16: 5 to 9 mg per 2.2 lbs (1 kg) a day, in 2 divided doses. As with adults, dosage may be adjusted by a doctor on an individual basis.

ONSET OF EFFECT
Several hours.

DURATION OF ACTION
Maximum effectiveness lasts 24 hours or longer; effectiveness then gradually decreases.

DIETARY ADVICE
Take it with food or milk to minimize stomach upset. Because of their bitter taste, tablets should be swallowed whole, without breaking, crushing, or chewing. Capsules may be swallowed whole or opened and the contents sprinkled on a small amount (one teaspoon) of soft food to make the drug more palatable. It should be swallowed immediately, without chewing.

STORAGE
Store in a tightly sealed container away from heat, moisture, and direct light.

IF YOU MISS A DOSE
Take it as soon as you remember. If it is near the time for the next dose, skip the missed dose and resume your regular dosage schedule. Do not double the next dose unless so advised by your doctor.

STOPPING THE DRUG
Never stop this drug abruptly, because seizures may ensue. The dose is typically tapered over a period of weeks to months under your doctor's supervision.

PROLONGED USE
This drug may be taken on a long-term basis. See your doctor regularly for tests.

PRECAUTIONS
Over 60: Older patients may require lower doses to minimize side effects.

Driving and Hazardous Work: Avoid such activities until you determine how this medication affects you.

Alcohol: May contribute to excessive drowsiness.

Pregnancy: Topiramate has caused birth defects in animal studies. Human studies with this drug have not been done, but other anticonvulsants are known to increase the risk of birth defects. However, seizures during pregnancy can also increase the risks to the fetus. Discuss with your doctor the potential risks and benefits of using this drug during pregnancy. Folate supplementation is advised starting 1 to 2 months before conception and throughout pregnancy.

Breast Feeding: Topiramate may pass into breast milk, although at low levels. Consult your doctor for advice.

Infants and Children: Special caution is advised in children. Use of the drug in children has been limited.

Special Concerns: Because this drug may predispose to the formation of kidney stones, you should drink plenty of fluids while taking it. Your doctor may suggest that you carry an ID card or bracelet saying that you are taking this medication.

OVERDOSE
Symptoms: No specific symptoms of overdose have been reported.

What to Do: Call your doctor, emergency medical services (EMS), or the nearest poison control center immediately.

DRUG INTERACTIONS
Topiramate interacts with a number of other drugs, including other anticonvulsants (carbamazepine, phenytoin, valproic acid); carbonic anhydrase inhibitors, such as acetazolamide or dichlorphenamide; and digoxin. This drug can interfere with oral contraceptives, leading to contraceptive failure.

FOOD INTERACTIONS
No known food interactions.

DISEASE INTERACTIONS
Special caution is advised if you have liver disease or kidney disease, including a history of kidney stones or hemodialysis.

Toremifene Citrate

BRAND NAME
Fareston

▶ Drug Class: Antiestrogen; antineoplastic (anticancer) agent

▶ Available in: Tablets

▶ Available OTC? No

▶ As Generic? No

Side Effects

SERIOUS
Vaginal bleeding, cataracts or other eye problems.

COMMON
Hot flashes, sweating, nausea, vaginal discharge, dizziness.

LESS COMMON
Swelling in the extremities, vomiting.

PRINCIPAL USES
To treat metastatic breast cancer in postmenopausal women.

HOW THE DRUG WORKS
Toremifene blocks the effects of the hormone estrogen by interfering with the binding of estrogen to its receptors on estrogen-sensitive cells. The growth of some breast tumors is stimulated by estrogens; toremifene may therefore slow the growth of such tumors.

DOSAGE
60 mg once a day.

ONSET OF EFFECT
Unknown.

DURATION OF ACTION
Unknown.

DIETARY ADVICE
Toremifene can be taken without regard to meals. Maintain adequate food and fluid intake, since calorie, protein, and vitamin needs increase in patients with cancer.

STORAGE
Store in a tightly sealed container away from heat, moisture, and direct light.

IF YOU MISS A DOSE
Toremifene is prescribed for once-daily use only. If you are unable to take the medication on a particular day, simply resume your regular dosage schedule the following day. Do not double the next dose.

STOPPING THE DRUG
You may need to remain on this medication for an extended period, and you should take toremifene exactly as prescribed throughout the course of treatment. The decision to stop taking the drug should be made in consultation with your physician. Do not stop taking toremifene on your own.

PROLONGED USE
There is no standard duration of therapy with toremifene, although you can expect to remain on it for at least several weeks in order to determine if it is effective. Your doctor will decide whether your response to the drug is satisfactory or not, and will recommend continuation or discontinuation of therapy.

PRECAUTIONS
Over 60: No special problems are expected.

Driving and Hazardous Work: The use of toremifene should not impair your ability to perform such tasks safely.

Alcohol: No special precautions are necessary.

Pregnancy: Toremifene must not be used in pregnant women. Although toremifene is not generally prescribed for premenopausal women, it is important that patients be sure they are not pregnant before starting treatment with this drug.

Breast Feeding: Use of this drug is not recommended while nursing; the benefits must clearly outweigh potential risks. Consult your doctor for advice.

Infants and Children: Use of toremifene is not approved for infants and children.

Special Concerns: Patients with cancer are very often weakened by their illness, by poor nutrition, and by the effects of chemotherapy, radiation, and surgery. Such patients are more likely to experience undesirable side effects of a medication. In addition, these side effects may be more pronounced. Follow all medication directions carefully. Some women with metastases to bone may develop musculoskeletal pain and elevated levels of blood calcium during the first week of treatment.

OVERDOSE
Symptoms: No cases of overdose have been reported.

What to Do: An overdose is unlikely; however, if you have any reason to suspect that one has occurred, call emergency medical services (EMS) to receive evaluation and treatment in the closest emergency facility.

DRUG INTERACTIONS
Consult your doctor for specific advice if you are taking thiazide diuretics or warfarin, which may interact with toremifene.

FOOD INTERACTIONS
No known food interactions.

DISEASE INTERACTIONS
Toremifene should not be used in women with a history of thromboembolic disease. Long-term treatment is not generally advised in women with preexisting endometrial hyperplasia.

Torsemide

Demadex 10 mg
(BOEHRINGER MANNHEIM)

839

Additional photographs

▶ Drug Class: Loop diuretic

▶ Available in: Tablets, injection

▶ Available OTC? No

▶ As Generic? No

Side Effects

SERIOUS
Skin rash, hives, intense itching, swelling of the mouth and throat, breathing difficulty, heart rhythm irregularities, lightheadedness, unusual bleeding or bruising, black or tarry stools. Call your doctor immediately.

COMMON
Muscle cramps or pain. Potassium depletion may lead to heart palpitations and weakness. Fluid depletion may lead to dizziness, especially upon arising from a sitting or lying position, as well as thirst, dry mouth, and constipation.

LESS COMMON
Buzzing or ringing in ears, loss of hearing (particularly after intravenous treatment or with very high doses), diarrhea, loss of appetite, gout, increased blood sugar (a problem for diabetic patients).

PRINCIPAL USES
To reduce fluid (salt and water) accumulation that leads to edema (swelling of body tissues) and breathlessness in patients with heart disease, liver disease, and kidney disease. Torsemide is also sometimes prescribed to help control high blood pressure.

HOW THE DRUG WORKS
Loop diuretics work on a specific portion of the kidney (the loop of Henle) to increase the excretion of water and sodium (and other salts) in the urine.

DOSAGE
For high blood pressure— Tablets: 5 to 10 mg once a day. The dose may be increased as determined by your doctor. For eliminating excess body water (edema)— Tablets: 5 to 60 mg once a day. Injection: 5 to 20 mg, injected once a day. The dose may be increased.

ONSET OF EFFECT
For injection, 10 minutes; for tablets, 1 hour.

DURATION OF ACTION
6 to 8 hours.

DIETARY ADVICE
Take it with or after meals to reduce stomach irritation.

STORAGE
Store in a tightly sealed container away from heat and direct light.

IF YOU MISS A DOSE
Take it as soon as you remember. If it is near the time for the next dose, skip the missed dose and resume your regular dosage schedule. Do not double the next dose.

STOPPING THE DRUG
The decision to stop taking the drug should be made by your doctor.

PROLONGED USE
See your doctor regularly if you must take this medicine for a prolonged period.

PRECAUTIONS
Over 60: No special precautions are warranted.

Driving and Hazardous Work: The use of this drug should not impair your ability to perform such tasks safely.

Alcohol: No special precautions are necessary.

Pregnancy: Human studies have not been done. Consult your doctor about taking torsemide during pregnancy.

Breast Feeding: Torsemide may pass into breast milk; caution is advised. Consult your doctor for advice.

Infants and Children: There is no specific information on the use of torsemide in infants and children. Use and dose must be determined by a pediatrician.

Special Concerns: If you take torsemide for high blood pressure, follow your doctor's advice on diet and weight control. This medicine may cause your body to lose potassium. Consult your doctor about eating potassium-rich foods or taking a supplement.

OVERDOSE
Symptoms: Dehydration, palpitations or heartbeat irregularities, weakness, dizziness, confusion, vomiting, cramps, loss of consciousness.

What to Do: Call your doctor, emergency medical services (EMS), or the nearest poison control center immediately.

DRUG INTERACTIONS
Consult your doctor for specific advice if you are taking any ACE inhibitor, antibiotics, amphotericin B, carmustine, cisplatin, corticosteroids, corticotropin, cyclosporine, deferoxamine, dichlorphenamide, digitalis drugs, lithium, methazolamide, methotrexate, penicillamine, gold salts, pentamidine, streptozocin, tiopronin, or vitamin B_{12}.

FOOD INTERACTIONS
No known food interactions.

DISEASE INTERACTIONS
Caution is advised when taking torsemide. Consult your doctor for advice if you have diabetes, gout, or a hearing problem, or have had a recent heart attack.

Tramadol Hydrochloride

Ultram 50 mg
(McNEIL)

▶ Drug Class: Analgesic

▶ Available in: Tablets

▶ Available OTC? No

▶ As Generic? Yes

Side Effects

SERIOUS
Blurred vision, difficulty urinating, frequent urge to urinate, blisters under the skin, change in walking balance, dizziness or lightheadedness when getting up, fainting, fast heartbeat, memory loss, hallucinations, shortness of breath. Also numbness, tingling, pain, or weakness in hands or feet; redness, swelling, and itching of skin; trembling and shaking of hands or feet; trouble performing routine tasks. Call your doctor immediately.

COMMON
Dizziness, vertigo, headache, drowsiness, nausea, vomiting, constipation.

LESS COMMON
Weakness, lack of energy, anxiety, confusion, euphoria, nervousness, insomnia, visual disturbances, stomach upset, dry mouth, diarrhea, abdominal pain, loss of appetite, gas, menopausal symptoms, sweating, muscle spasm, rash.

PRINCIPAL USES
To help manage moderate to somewhat severe pain, such as that which occurs following joint surgery and certain gynecological procedures (for example, cesarean section).

HOW THE DRUG WORKS
Tramadol acts on the central nervous system to block the transmission of pain signals. It works similarly to narcotic analgesics, and while not a narcotic, it can be habit-forming, leading to mental and physical drug dependence.

DOSAGE
1 or 2 tablets (50 mg each) every 6 hours as needed. For severe pain, your doctor may prescribe 2 tablets for the first dose.

ONSET OF EFFECT
Usually within 1 hour, with a peak effect at 2 hours.

DURATION OF ACTION
6 to 7 hours.

DIETARY ADVICE
Tramadol can be taken with or without food.

STORAGE
Store in a tightly sealed container away from heat and direct light.

IF YOU MISS A DOSE
Take it as soon as you remember. However, if it is near the time for the next dose, skip the missed dose and resume your regular dosage schedule. Do not double the next dose.

STOPPING THE DRUG
The decision to stop taking the drug should be made by your doctor.

PROLONGED USE
You should see your doctor regularly for tests and examinations if you must take this drug for a prolonged period of time.

PRECAUTIONS
Over 60: Tramadol stays longer in the body of older patients than younger ones; your doctor may adjust the dose accordingly.

Driving and Hazardous Work: Do not drive or engage in hazardous work until you determine how the medicine affects you.

Alcohol: Do not consume alcohol while taking this medication since it may compound the drug's sedative effect on the central nervous system.

Pregnancy: Tramadol has caused birth defects and other problems in animals. Human studies have not been done. Before you take tramadol, tell your doctor if you are pregnant or are planning to become pregnant.

Breast Feeding: Tramadol passes into breast milk; avoid or discontinue use while nursing.

Infants and Children: Safety and effectiveness have not been established for the use of tramadol in children under 16 years old.

Special Concerns: Before undergoing any kind of surgery, including dental surgery, be sure your doctor or dentist knows that you are taking tramadol.

OVERDOSE
Symptoms: Breathing difficulty, seizures, vomiting.

What to Do: Call your doctor, emergency medical services (EMS), or the nearest poison control center immediately.

DRUG INTERACTIONS
Consult your doctor for specific advice if you are taking carbamazepine, anesthetics, MAO inhibitors, or any drugs known to depress the central nervous system, including antihistamines, sedatives, tranquilizers, sleeping pills, other prescription pain medicines, barbiturates, medications for seizures, or muscle relaxants.

FOOD INTERACTIONS
No known food interactions.

DISEASE INTERACTIONS
Caution is advised when taking tramadol. Consult your doctor if you have severe abdominal or stomach conditions, or a history of alcohol abuse, drug abuse, head injury, or seizure disorders. Use of tramadol may cause complications in patients with liver or kidney disease, since these organs work together to remove the medication from the body.

Trandolapril

Mavic 1 mg
(KNOLL)

▶ Drug Class: Angiotensin-converting enzyme (ACE) inhibitor

▶ Available in: Tablet

▶ Available OTC? No

▶ As Generic? No

Side Effects

SERIOUS
Fever and chills, sore throat and hoarseness, sudden difficulty breathing or swallowing, swelling of the face, mouth, or extremities, impaired kidney function (ankle swelling, decreased urination), confusion, yellow discoloration of the eyes or skin (indicating liver disorder), intense itching, chest pain or palpitations, abdominal pain. Serious side effects are very rare; contact your doctor immediately.

COMMON
Dry, persistent cough.

LESS COMMON
Dizziness or fainting, skin rash, numbness or tingling in the hands, feet, or lips, unusual fatigue or muscle weakness, nausea, drowsiness, loss of taste, headache.

PRINCIPAL USES
To control high blood pressure; to treat congestive heart failure; to treat patients with left ventricular dysfunction (damage to the pumping chamber of the heart); and to minimize further kidney damage in diabetics with mild kidney disease.

HOW THE DRUG WORKS
Angiotensin-converting enzyme (ACE) inhibitors block an enzyme that produces angiotensin, a naturally occurring substance that causes blood vessels to constrict and stimulates production of the adrenal hormone, aldosterone, which promotes sodium retention in the body. As a result, ACE inhibitors relax blood vessels (causing them to widen) and reduces sodium retention, which lowers blood pressure and so decreases the workload of the heart.

DOSAGE
To start, 1 mg once a day, except black patients, who should start with 2 mg once a day. Doses may be increased to a maximum of 8 mg a day in 1 or 2 doses.

ONSET OF EFFECT
Within 4 hours.

DURATION OF ACTION
Up to 24 hours.

DIETARY ADVICE
Take it on an empty stomach, about 1 hour before mealtime. Follow your doctor's dietary advice (such as low-salt or low-cholesterol restrictions) to improve control over high blood pressure and heart disease. Avoid high-potassium foods like bananas and citrus fruits and juices, unless you are also taking medications, such as diuretics, that lower potassium levels.

STORAGE
Store in a tightly sealed container away from heat, moisture, and direct light.

IF YOU MISS A DOSE
Take it as soon as you remember. If it is near the time for the next dose, skip the missed dose and resume your regular dosage schedule. Do not double the next dose.

STOPPING THE DRUG
Do not stop taking this drug abruptly, as this may cause potentially serious health problems. Dosage should be reduced gradually, according to your doctor's instructions.

PROLONGED USE
See your doctor regularly for examinations and tests if you must take this medicine for a prolonged period. Remember that trandolapril helps control high blood pressure but does not cure it. Lifelong therapy may be necessary.

PRECAUTIONS
Over 60: Some elderly patients may be more sensitive to the effects of this drug; smaller doses may be warranted.

Driving and Hazardous Work: Exercise caution until you determine how the medicine affects you.

Alcohol: Consume alcohol only in moderation since it may increase the effect of the drug and cause an excessive drop in blood pressure. Consult your doctor for advice.

Pregnancy: Not recommended, especially during the last 2 trimesters (final 6 months) of pregnancy. If you become pregnant, notify your doctor as soon as possible.

Breast Feeding: Trace amounts of trandolapril can be found in breast milk; however, adverse effects in infants have not been documented. Consult your doctor for advice.

Infants and Children: The safety and effectiveness of trandolapril in children 18 and under have not been established.

OVERDOSE
Symptoms: No specific ones have been reported.

What to Do: While overdose is unlikely, call your doctor, emergency medical services (EMS), or the nearest poison control center immediately if you suspect that someone has taken a much larger dose than prescribed.

DRUG INTERACTIONS
Consult your doctor if you are taking diuretics (especially potassium-sparing diuretics), potassium supplements or drugs containing potassium, lithium, anticoagulants, anti-inflammatory drugs, any over-the-counter drugs (especially cold remedies and diet pills).

FOOD INTERACTIONS
Avoid low-salt milk and salt substitutes. Many of these products contain potassium.

DISEASE INTERACTIONS
Consult your doctor if you have systemic lupus erythematosus (SLE) or if you have had a prior allergic reaction to ACE inhibitors. Trandolapril should be used with caution by patients with severe kidney disease or renal artery stenosis (narrowing of one or both of the arteries that supply blood to the kidneys).

Trandolapril/Verapamil Hydrochloride

BRAND NAME
Tarka

▶ Drug Class: ACE inhibitor/ calcium channel blocker combination

▶ Available in: Tablets

▶ Available OTC? No

▶ As Generic? No

Side Effects

SERIOUS
Serious side effects are very rare; they include fever and chills, sore throat and hoarseness, sudden difficulty breathing or swallowing, swelling of the face, mouth, or extremities, worsening kidney function (ankle swelling, decreased urination), confusion, jaundice (yellowish tinge to eyes or skin, indicating liver problems), intense itching, chest pain or heart palpitations, abdominal pain, irregular or slow heartbeats, low blood pressure (causing dizziness or faintness). Call your doctor immediately.

COMMON
Mild swelling of arms and legs (edema), fatigue, mild headache, dizziness, constipation, cough, flushed skin.

LESS COMMON
Fainting, dry mouth, diarrhea, gas, nausea, vomiting, rectal pain, gout, neck pain, joint swelling, nervousness, insomnia, drowsiness, skin rash, increased eye pressure, impotence, hot flashes.

PRINCIPAL USES
To control high blood pressure (hypertension).

HOW THE DRUG WORKS
Angiotensin-converting enzyme (ACE) inhibitors such as trandolapril block an enzyme that produces angiotensin, a naturally occurring substance that causes blood vessels to constrict and stimulates production of the adrenal hormone, aldosterone, which promotes sodium retention in the body. As a result, ACE inhibitors relax blood vessels (causing them to widen) and reduces sodium retention. Verapamil, a calcium channel blocker, interferes with the movement of calcium into heart muscle cells and the smooth muscle cells in the walls of the arteries. As a result of the combined action of trandolapril and verapamil, blood vessels relax (causing them to widen), which lowers blood pressure and thereby decreases the workload of the heart.

DOSAGE
From 1 to 4 mg of trandolapril and 120 to 480 micrograms (mcg) of verapamil per day. Tablets containing both active ingredients are taken either once a day or in 2 divided doses.

ONSET OF EFFECT
Within 15 hours.

DURATION OF ACTION
Unknown.

DIETARY ADVICE
Best taken without food. Can be taken with grapefruit juice.

STORAGE
Store in a tightly sealed container away from heat, moisture, and direct light.

IF YOU MISS A DOSE
Take it as soon as you remember. If it is near the time for the next dose, skip the missed dose and resume your regular dosage schedule. Do not double the next dose.

STOPPING THE DRUG
The decision to stop taking the drug should be made by your doctor.

PROLONGED USE
See your doctor periodically for tests and examinations if you must take this medication for a prolonged period.

PRECAUTIONS
Over 60: No special problems are expected.

Driving and Hazardous Work: Avoid such activities until you determine how the medicine affects you.

Alcohol: Consume alcohol only in moderation since it may increase the effect of the drug and cause an excessive drop in blood pressure.

Pregnancy: This drug should not be used during pregnancy and is especially dangerous to the unborn child during the final 6 months (second and third trimesters). Consult your doctor if you are pregnant or plan to become pregnant.

Breast Feeding: Trandolapril with verapamil passes into breast milk; avoid use while nursing or discontinue breast feeding.

Infants and Children: The safety and effectiveness of trandolapril with verapamil use by children have not been established.

Special Concerns: Trandolapril with verapamil is not recommended as the first line of therapy when high blood pressure is diagnosed. It may be prescribed after other medications have proved unsatisfactory. Before you undergo surgery, tell the doctor or dentist in charge that you are taking this drug.

OVERDOSE
Symptoms: No cases of overdose have been reported. Symptoms might include extreme dizziness, fainting, or confusion.

What to Do: If someone takes a much larger dose than prescribed, seek medical assistance right away.

DRUG INTERACTIONS
Consult your physician for specific advice if you are taking digitalis drugs, lithium, cimetidine, beta-blockers, antiarrhythmic drugs (such as disopyramide, flecainide, and quinidine), anticonvulsants, cyclosporine, or theophylline.

FOOD INTERACTIONS
No known food interactions.

DISEASE INTERACTIONS
Consult your doctor if you have congestive heart failure (CHF), heart rhythm irregularities (cardiac arrhythmia), or any other medical condition. This drug should be used with caution by patients with severe kidney disease or renal artery stenosis (narrowing of one or both of the arteries that supply blood to the kidneys).

BRAND NAME
Parnate

Parnate 10 mg
(SMITHKLINE BEECHAM)

▶ Drug Class: Monoamine oxidase (MAO) inhibitor antidepressant

▶ Available in: Tablets

▶ Available OTC? No

▶ As Generic? No

Side Effects

SERIOUS
Severe chest pain, dilated pupils, irregular heartbeat, sensitivity of eyes to light, sweating or fever, nausea and vomiting, stiff neck, extreme dizziness. Call your doctor immediately.

COMMON
Blurring of vision, decreased urination, sexual dysfunction, mild dizziness or lightheadedness, mild headache, appetite changes including cravings for sweets, weight gain, increase in sweating, muscle twitching during sleep, restlessness, shakiness, fatigue, insomnia.

LESS COMMON
Chills, constipation, decrease in appetite, dry mouth.

PRINCIPAL USES
To treat symptoms of major mental depression.

HOW THE DRUG WORKS
Tranylcypromine inhibits the activity of monoamine oxidase, an enzyme that renders certain brain chemicals (epinephrine, norepinephrine, and dopamine) inactive. Consequently, this drug increases the availability of these chemicals in the nervous system; this is thought to have an antidepressant effect.

DOSAGE
Adults: To start, 10 mg, 3 times a day; this may be increased to 60 mg a day. Older adults: To start, 10 mg, 2 times a day; this may be increased to 40 mg a day.

ONSET OF EFFECT
48 hours; it may take up to 3 weeks for full effect.

DURATION OF ACTION
Up to 10 days after stopping treatment.

DIETARY ADVICE
See Food Interactions.

STORAGE
Store in a tightly sealed container away from heat, moisture, and direct light.

IF YOU MISS A DOSE
Take it as soon as you remember. However, if it is near the time for the next dose, skip the missed dose and resume your regular dosage schedule. Do not double the next dose.

STOPPING THE DRUG
Take it as prescribed for the full treatment period. The decision to stop taking the drug should be made in consultation with your physician.

PROLONGED USE
The usual course of therapy lasts 6 months to 1 year; some patients benefit from additional therapy.

PRECAUTIONS
Over 60: Adverse reactions may be more likely and more severe in older patients. A lower dose may be warranted.

Driving and Hazardous Work: Use caution until you determine how the medicine affects you.

Alcohol: Avoid alcohol.

Pregnancy: Use during pregnancy may increase the risk of birth defects.

Breast Feeding: Tranylcypromine may pass into breast milk; caution is advised. Consult your doctor for specific advice.

Infants and Children: This drug is not recommended for children age 16 and under. Antidepressants increase the risk of suicidal thinking and behavior (suicidality) in children with major depression and other psychiatric disorders. Discuss with your doctor this risk versus the benefits of using this drug. Use this drug only under close medical supervision.

Special Concerns: Before having any surgery, emergency treatment, or dental treatment, tell the doctor or dentist in charge that you are taking tranylcypromine. Your doctor may advise you to carry a card saying that you use tranylcypromine.

OVERDOSE
Symptoms: Profound anxiety, confusion, seizures, cold, clammy skin, severe drowsiness, irregular pulse, hallucinations, severe headache, fainting, stiff muscles, sweating, breathing difficulty.

What to Do: Seek medical attention immediately.

DRUG INTERACTIONS
Consult your doctor for specific advice if you are taking or have recently taken amphetamines, blood pressure medications, diet pills, cyclobenzaprine, fluoxetine, levodopa, maprotiline, asthma medication, cold or allergy medication, meperidine, methylphenidate, another MAO inhibitor, paroxetine, sertraline, a tricyclic antidepressant, an oral diabetes drug, insulin, bupropion, buspirone, carbamazepine, a central nervous system depressant, dextromethorphan, trazodone, or tryptophan.

FOOD INTERACTIONS
Do not eat foods with a high tyramine content, such as cheeses; yeast or meat extracts; pickled or smoked meat, poultry, or fish; processed meats like bologna, salami, and pepperoni; and sauerkraut. Do not drink alcohol-free or reduced-alcohol beer and wine. Do not drink beverages or eat food with a high caffeine content, such as coffee and chocolate.

DISEASE INTERACTIONS
Consult your physician if you have any of the following: a history of alcohol abuse, angina, frequent headaches, asthma, bronchitis, diabetes mellitus, epilepsy, heart disease or a recent heart attack, blood vessel disease, liver disease, Parkinson's disease, a recent stroke, kidney disease, an overactive thyroid, or pheochromocytoma.

Trazodone

Generic 50 mg
(PUREPAC)

▶ Drug Class: Antidepressant

▶ Available in: Tablets

▶ Available OTC? No

▶ As Generic? Yes

Side Effects

SERIOUS
Muscle twitching, confusion. Call your doctor immediately.

COMMON
Drowsiness, dry mouth, dizziness, lightheadedness, unpleasant taste in mouth, nausea and vomiting, headache.

LESS COMMON
Blurred vision, muscle pains, diarrhea, constipation, unusual fatigue.

PRINCIPAL USES
To treat symptoms of major depression. It may be taken with selective serotonin reuptake inhibitor (SSRI) antidepressants such as fluoxetine, sertraline, and paroxetine when these drugs cause insomnia.

HOW THE DRUG WORKS
Trazodone helps to balance levels of serotonin, a brain chemical that is profoundly linked to mood, emotions, and mental state.

DOSAGE
Adults: To start, 50 mg, 3 times a day, or 75 mg, 2 times a day, or 100 mg at bedtime. The dose may be gradually increased by your doctor to 400 mg a day. Older adults: To start, 25 mg, 3 times a day, or 50 mg at bedtime. The dose may be increased by your doctor.

ONSET OF EFFECT
1 to 4 weeks.

DURATION OF ACTION
Unknown.

DIETARY ADVICE
It can be taken with a meal or light snack to reduce the chance of dizziness and to increase the absorption of the drug by the body.

STORAGE
Store in a tightly sealed container away from heat, moisture, and direct light.

IF YOU MISS A DOSE
Take it as soon as you remember, unless the time for your next scheduled dose is within the next 4 hours. If so, do not take the missed dose. Take your next scheduled dose at the proper time and resume your regular dosage schedule. Do not double the next dose.

STOPPING THE DRUG
Take as prescribed for the full treatment period, even if you begin to feel better before the scheduled end of therapy. The decision to stop taking the drug should be made in consultation with your doctor.

PROLONGED USE
The usual course of therapy lasts for 6 months to 1 year; some patients benefit from additional therapy beyond that period.

PRECAUTIONS
Over 60: Adverse reactions may be more likely and more severe in older patients. Lower doses may be needed.

Driving and Hazardous Work: Use caution when driving or engaging in hazardous work until you determine how the medicine affects you. Drowsiness may occur.

Alcohol: Avoid alcohol.

Pregnancy: Adequate studies of trazodone use during pregnancy have not been done. Before you take trazodone, tell your doctor if you are pregnant or plan to become pregnant.

Breast Feeding: Trazodone passes into breast milk; caution is advised. Consult your doctor for specific advice.

Infants and Children: The safety and effectiveness of trazodone use by infants and children have not been established. Antidepressants increase the risk of suicidal thinking and behavior (suicidality) in children with major depression and other psychiatric disorders. Discuss with your doctor this risk versus the benefits of using this drug. Children

should be observed closely for worsening of symptoms, suicidality, or unusual changes in behavior at the onset of therapy and when making changes in dosage.

OVERDOSE
Symptoms: Severe nausea and vomiting, loss of coordination, drowsiness.

What to Do: Call your doctor, emergency medical services (EMS), or the nearest poison control center immediately.

DRUG INTERACTIONS
The following drugs may interact with trazodone. Consult your doctor for specific advice if you are taking high blood pressure medication, central nervous system depressants (including cold and allergy drugs, narcotic pain relievers, and muscle relaxants), fluoxetine, or tricyclic antidepressants.

FOOD INTERACTIONS
No known food interactions.

DISEASE INTERACTIONS
Caution is advised when taking trazodone. Consult your doctor if you have a history of alcohol abuse or any heart condition. Use of trazodone may cause complications in patients with liver or kidney disease, since these organs work together to remove the medication from the body.

Tretinoin

BRAND NAMES
Avita, Renova, Retin-A,
Retinoic Acid

- Drug Class: Acne drug
- Available in: Cream, gel, liquid
- Available OTC? No
- As Generic? Yes

Side Effects

SERIOUS
No serious side effects are associated with regular applications of tretinoin when used as directed.

COMMON
Mild redness and peeling, or excessive dryness, at the site of application.

LESS COMMON
Irritation or allergy with severe redness, swelling, blistering, pain, rash, or crusting at sites of application; changes in pigment (either lightening or darkening of skin color). These problems generally improve when the medication is stopped or reduced in dosage or frequency of application. Consult your doctor.

PRINCIPAL USES
Tretinoin is used to treat mild to moderate acne.

HOW THE DRUG WORKS
Although the exact mechanism of action is unknown, tretinoin appears to affect skin cells so that they are shed in a more normal fashion, therefore "unplugging" blackheads and whiteheads (comedones), the initial changes in acne formation.

DOSAGE
Adults: Apply once daily at bedtime.

ONSET OF EFFECT
Variable, usually within 2 to 6 weeks after starting therapy.

DURATION OF ACTION
The effect of tretinoin typically persists for as long as the drug is being used.

DIETARY ADVICE
No special restrictions.

STORAGE
Store in a tightly sealed container away from heat and direct light. Keep away from moisture and extremes in temperature. The gel form of this medication is flammable; keep away from heat and open flame.

IF YOU MISS A DOSE
This drug is applied once every 24 hours, at night. If you miss a day, resume your regular dosage schedule the next day. There is no need to apply extra medication with the next dose to compensate for the missed dose.

STOPPING THE DRUG
Use as prescribed for the full treatment period, even if you show signs of improvement before the scheduled end of therapy.

PROLONGED USE
Therapy with this medication is frequently prolonged.

PRECAUTIONS
Over 60: No special problems are expected.

Driving and Hazardous Work: No special precautions are necessary.

Alcohol: No special precautions are necessary.

Pregnancy: Avoid or discontinue tretinoin if you are pregnant or trying to become pregnant.

Breast Feeding: Tretinoin may pass into breast milk; caution is advised. Consult your doctor for advice.

Infants and Children: Not recommended for use on children.

Special Concerns: Persons with a history of allergy to tretinoin or any other ingredients in the medication should not use the product. Do not apply large amounts of tretinoin to your skin in expectation of better or faster results. This will only lead to unnecessary irritation of affected skin and surrounding areas. Sunburned skin is more susceptible to irritation from tretinoin, and application should be avoided. Avoid excessive exposure to sunlight or use of sunlamps. Keep this medication away from your eyes, mouth, and nostrils. Severe irritation and redness may result. Do not apply tretinoin to inflamed skin. If your skin becomes reddened and painful while using tretinoin, discontinue use of the medication and call your doctor. If you are using cosmetics, gently cleanse skin to be treated before applying the medication.

OVERDOSE
Symptoms: Excessive application of tretinoin may lead to severe irritation of the skin.

What to Do: If tretinoin is ingested, call your doctor, emergency medical services (EMS), or the nearest poison control center.

DRUG INTERACTIONS
Consult your doctor for specific advice if you are taking other acne medications that are applied to the same area of skin, including prescription and nonprescription treatments containing sulfur, resorcinol, alpha hydroxy acids, or salicylic acid; medicated soaps, abrasives, cleansers, or cosmetics; topical preparations with a high concentration of alcohol, astringents, extract of lime, or spices; and medications used for a drying effect.

FOOD INTERACTIONS
No known food interactions.

DISEASE INTERACTIONS
Caution is advised when using tretinoin. Consult your doctor if you have eczema.

Triamcinolone Inhalant and Nasal

▶ Drug Class: Respiratory corticosteroid

▶ Available in: Nasal spray, oral inhalation

▶ Available OTC? No

▶ As Generic? No

Side Effects

SERIOUS
No serious side effects have been reported.

COMMON
Oral inhalation: Sore throat, white patches in mouth or throat, hoarseness. Nasal spray: Nosebleeds or bloody nasal secretions, nasal burning or irritation, sore throat.

LESS COMMON
Eye pain, watering eyes, gradual decrease of vision, stomach pain and digestive disturbances.

PRINCIPAL USES
Oral inhalation: To treat bronchial asthma. Nasal spray: To treat allergic rhinitis (seasonal or perennial allergies such as hay fever), and to prevent recurrence of nasal polyps after surgical removal.

HOW THE DRUG WORKS
Respiratory corticosteroids such as triamcinolone primarily reduce or prevent inflammation of the lining of the airways (the underlying cause of asthma), reduce the allergic response to inhaled allergens, and inhibit the secretion of mucus within the airways.

DOSAGE
Adults and children ages 12 and older— Oral inhalation: 2 inhalations of 100 mcg each, 3 or 4 times a day. Maximum dose is 16 inhalations a day. In some patients maintenance can be achieved when the total daily dose is given 2 times a day. Nasal spray: 2 sprays (55 micrograms [mcg] each) in each nostril once a day. It can be increased to 440 mcg per day in 1 or up to 4 doses. After relief is achieved, it can be decreased to as little as 1 spray (55 mcg) in each nostril once a day.

ONSET OF EFFECT
Usually within 1 week; it may take 3 weeks for the full effect to occur.

DURATION OF ACTION
Several days.

DIETARY ADVICE
No special restrictions.

STORAGE
Store in a tightly sealed container away from heat and direct light.

IF YOU MISS A DOSE
Take it as soon as you remember. However, if it is near the time for the next dose, skip the missed dose and resume your regular dosage schedule. Do not double the next dose.

STOPPING THE DRUG
The decision to stop taking the drug should be made in consultation with your physician.

PROLONGED USE
Consult your doctor about the need for regular periodic medical tests and examinations if you must take this drug for a prolonged period.

PRECAUTIONS
Over 60: No special problems are expected with older patients.

Driving and Hazardous Work: The use of triamcinolone should not impair your ability to perform such tasks safely.

Alcohol: No special precautions are necessary.

Pregnancy: Inhaled or nasal steroids have not been reported to cause birth defects if taken during pregnancy. Before using such drugs, tell your doctor if you are or are planning to become pregnant.

Breast Feeding: Triamcinolone may pass into breast milk; caution is advised. Consult your doctor for advice.

Infants and Children: No special problems are expected in children, but the lowest possible dose should be used.

Special Concerns: Inhaled steroids will not help an asthma attack in progress. Inhaled steroids can lower resistance to yeast infections of the mouth, throat, or voice box. To prevent yeast infections, gargle or rinse your mouth with water after each use; do not swallow the water. Know how to use the spray properly; read and follow the directions that come with the device. Before you have surgery, tell the doctor or dentist that you are using a steroid.

OVERDOSE
Symptoms: No specific ones have been reported.

What to Do: Call your doctor, emergency medical services (EMS), or the nearest poison control center if you have any reason to suspect an overdose.

DRUG INTERACTIONS
Consult your physician for advice if you are taking systemic corticosteroids, other inhaled corticosteroids, or any drugs that suppress the immune system.

FOOD INTERACTIONS
No known food interactions.

DISEASE INTERACTIONS
Consult your physician if you have any of the following: nasal septal ulcers, ocular herpes simplex, or any fungal, bacterial, or systemic viral infection. If you are exposed to chicken pox or measles, tell your doctor at once.

Triamcinolone Systemic

- Drug Class: Corticosteroid
- Available in: Syrup, tablets, injection
- Available OTC? No
- As Generic? Yes

Side Effects

SERIOUS
Vision problems, frequent urination, increased thirst, rectal bleeding, blistering skin, confusion, hallucinations, paranoia, euphoria, depression, mood swings, redness and swelling at injection site. Call your doctor immediately.

COMMON
Increased appetite, indigestion, nervousness, insomnia, greater susceptibility to infections, increased blood pressure, slowed wound healing, weight gain, easy bruising, fluid retention.

LESS COMMON
Change in skin color, dizziness, headache, increased sweating, unusual growth of body or facial hair, increased blood sugar, peptic ulcers, adrenal insufficiency, muscle weakness, cataracts, glaucoma, osteoporosis.

PRINCIPAL USES
To treat numerous conditions that involve inflammation (a response by body tissues, producing redness, warmth, swelling, and pain). Such conditions include arthritis, allergic reactions, asthma, some skin diseases, multiple sclerosis flare-ups, and other autoimmune diseases. Also prescribed to treat deficiency of natural steroid hormones.

HOW THE DRUG WORKS
This hormone mimics the effects of the body's natural corticosteroids. It depresses the synthesis, release, and activity of inflammation-producing body chemicals. It also suppresses the activity of the immune system.

DOSAGE
Adults and teenagers: 4 to 60 mg a day in 1 or several doses. Children's doses depend on size and body weight and should be determined by your doctor.

ONSET OF EFFECT
Variable.

DURATION OF ACTION
Variable.

DIETARY ADVICE
It can be taken with food or milk to minimize stomach upset. Your doctor may recommend a special diet.

STORAGE
Store in a tightly sealed container away from heat, moisture, and direct light. Do not freeze the liquid form.

IF YOU MISS A DOSE
If you take several doses a day and it is close to the next dose, double the next dose. If you take 1 dose a day and you do not remember until the next day, skip the missed dose and do not double the next dose.

STOPPING THE DRUG
The decision to stop taking the drug should be made by your doctor.

PROLONGED USE
Long-term use may lead to cataracts, diabetes, hypertension, or osteoporosis; see your physician for regular visits.

PRECAUTIONS
Over 60: Adverse reactions may be more likely and more severe in older patients.

Driving and Hazardous Work: Avoid such activities until you determine how the medicine affects you.

Alcohol: May cause stomach problems; avoid it unless your physician approves occasional moderate drinking.

Pregnancy: Overuse during pregnancy can impair growth and development of the child.

Breast Feeding: Do not use this drug while nursing.

Infants and Children: Triamcinolone may retard the development of bone and other tissues.

Special Concerns: This drug can lower your resistance to infection. Avoid immunizations with live vaccines. Patients undergoing long-term therapy should wear a medical-alert bracelet. Call your doctor right away if you develop a fever.

OVERDOSE
Symptoms: Fever, muscle or joint pain, nausea, dizziness, fainting, difficulty breathing. Prolonged overuse: Moonface, obesity, unusual hair growth, acne, loss of sexual function, muscle wasting.

What to Do: Call your doctor, emergency medical services (EMS), or the nearest poison control center immediately.

DRUG INTERACTIONS
Consult your doctor for specific advice if you are taking aminoglutethimide, antacids, barbiturates, carbamazepine, griseofulvin, mitotane, phenylbutazone, phenytoin, primidone, rifampin, injectable amphotericin B, oral antidiabetes agents, insulin, digitalis drugs, diuretics, or medications containing potassium or sodium.

FOOD INTERACTIONS
Avoid excess sodium.

DISEASE INTERACTIONS
Consult your doctor if you have a history of bone disease, chicken pox, measles, gastrointestinal disorders, diabetes, recent serious infection, glaucoma, heart disease, hypertension, liver or kidney disorders, high blood cholesterol, thyroid problems, myasthenia gravis, or lupus.

Triamcinolone Topical

BRAND NAMES
Aristocort, Delta-Tritex, Flutex, Kenac, Kenalog, Kenalog in Orabase, Kenonel, Oracort, Oralone, Triacet, Triaderm, Trianide

▶ Drug Class: Topical corticosteroid

▶ Available in: Cream, lotion, ointment, aerosol, dental paste

▶ Available OTC? No

▶ As Generic? Yes

Side Effects

SERIOUS
Serious side effects from the use of topical triamcinolone are very rare.

COMMON
Burning, itching, irritation, redness, dryness, acne, stinging and cracking of skin, and numbness or tingling in the extremities have been reported in 0.5% to 1% of patients, although the risk is increased when the medication is used with bandages or other occlusive dressings.

LESS COMMON
Blistering and pus near hair follicles, unusual bleeding or easy bruising, darkening or prominence of small surface veins, increased susceptibility to infection.

PRINCIPAL USES
To treat rashes and inflammation of the skin. It is also used for treatment of inflammatory conditions within the mouth.

HOW THE DRUG WORKS
Topical triamcinolone appears to interfere with the formation of natural substances within the body that are directly responsible for the process of inflammation, which produces swelling, redness, and pain.

DOSAGE
Cream (0.025%, 0.1%, and 0.5% strength)— Adults: Apply 2 to 3 times daily. Children: 1 to 2 times daily (0.025%); once daily for all others (0.1% and 0.5%). Lotion (0.025% and 0.1% strength)— Adults: Apply 2 to 4 times daily. Children: 1 to 2 times daily (0.025%); once daily for all others (0.1%). Ointment (0.025%, 0.1%, and 0.5% strength)— Adults: Apply 2 to 4 times daily. Children: 1 to 2 times daily (0.025%); once daily for all others (0.1% and 0.5%). Aerosol (0.015% strength)— Adults: Apply 3 or 4 times daily. Children: 1 or 2 times daily. Dental paste (0.1% strength)— Adults: Apply to affected areas of the mouth 2 to 3 times daily after meals and at bedtime. Children: Consult a pediatrician.

ONSET OF EFFECT
Soon after application. However, recognizable changes in your condition may take several days or more to develop.

DURATION OF ACTION
Unknown.

DIETARY ADVICE
No special restrictions.

STORAGE
Store in a tightly sealed container away from heat and direct light.

IF YOU MISS A DOSE
Apply it as soon as you remember. If it is near the time for the next dose, skip the missed dose and resume your regular dosage schedule.

STOPPING THE DRUG
Take as prescribed for the full treatment period, even if you begin to feel better before the scheduled end of therapy.

PROLONGED USE
Avoid prolonged use, particularly near the eyes, on the face, genital, or rectal areas, or in the folds of the skin.

PRECAUTIONS
Over 60: Side effects may be more likely and more severe in elderly patients.

Driving and Hazardous Work: No special precautions are necessary.

Alcohol: No special precautions are necessary.

Pregnancy: This drug should not be used for prolonged periods by pregnant women or by women trying to become pregnant.

Breast Feeding: Although problems have not been documented, caution is advised. Do not apply to breasts prior to nursing. Consult your doctor for specific advice.

Infants and Children: This medication should not be used for more than 2 weeks in children and adolescents, unless otherwise directed by your doctor. Do not use tight-fitting diapers or plastic pants on children when treating skin irritation in the diaper area.

Special Concerns: Wash your hands thoroughly after application. Do not wrap the treated area with bandages or tight-fitting clothing unless otherwise instructed by your doctor.

OVERDOSE
Symptoms: None known.

What to Do: An overdose of a topical corticosteroid is unlikely to be life-threatening. However, in case of accidental ingestion or an apparent overdose, call your doctor, emergency medical services (EMS), or the nearest poison control center right away.

DRUG INTERACTIONS
Do not mix topical triamcinolone with other products, especially alcohol-containing preparations (which include colognes, aftershave, and many moisturizer lotions), since this may cause dryness and irritation, or increase the risk of an allergic reaction.

FOOD INTERACTIONS
Potassium supplements may decrease this drug's effects. Avoid foods high in sodium.

DISEASE INTERACTIONS
Caution is advised when taking this drug. Consult your doctor if you have any of the following: cataracts; diabetes mellitus; glaucoma; infection, sores, or ulcerations of the skin; infection at another site in your body; tuberculosis.

Triamterene

Dyrenium 50 mg
(SmithKline Beecham)

▶ Drug Class: Potassium-sparing diuretic

▶ Available in: Capsules

▶ Available OTC? No

▶ As Generic? No

Side Effects

SERIOUS
Skin rash, hives, light-
headedness, unusual
bleeding. Call your doc-
tor immediately.

COMMON
No common side effects
have been reported.

LESS COMMON
Dizziness, nausea, vomit-
ing, stomach cramps,
diarrhea, headache,
increased sensitivity
of skin to sunlight.

PRINCIPAL USES
Used as an adjunctive, supplementary treatment with
other diuretics to conserve
potassium while promoting
the excretion of sodium and
water. In conjunction with
thiazide or loop diuretics,
triamterene reduces the
overall fluid volume in the
body and so helps to control
symptoms of heart disease,
kidney disease, and liver
disease.

HOW THE DRUG WORKS
Triamterene promotes the
excretion of sodium and
excess water by altering
kidney enzymes that control
urine production. Unlike
most other types of diuretics, triamterene promotes
fluid and salt loss but does
not deplete normal levels of
potassium.

DOSAGE
Adults: 25 to 100 mg a day.
Dose may be increased to
no more than 300 mg a day.
Children: 0.9 to 1.82 mg per
lb of body weight, once a
day or once every other
day. Dose may be increased.

ONSET OF EFFECT
Within 2 to 4 hours.

DURATION OF ACTION
From 7 to 9 hours.

DIETARY ADVICE
Triamterene should be
taken after meals, though it
can be taken with food or a
full glass of milk to minimize the risk of stomach
upset.

STORAGE
Store in a tightly sealed container away from heat, moisture, and direct light.

IF YOU MISS A DOSE
Take it as soon as you
remember. However, if it is
near the time for the next
dose, skip the missed dose
and resume your regular
dosage schedule. Do not
double the next dose.

STOPPING THE DRUG
The decision to stop taking
the drug should be made by
your doctor.

PROLONGED USE
See your doctor regularly
for tests and examinations if
you must take this drug for
a prolonged period.

PRECAUTIONS
Over 60: Adverse reactions
may be more likely and
more severe in older
patients. In particular, signs
of excess potassium levels
are more likely to occur in
older patients.

**Driving and Hazardous
Work:** The use of triam-
terene should not impair
your ability to perform
such tasks safely.

Alcohol: No special precautions are necessary.

Pregnancy: Adequate
human studies have not
been done. Before taking
triamterene, tell your doctor
if you are pregnant or plan
to become pregnant.

Breast Feeding: Triamterene passes into breast
milk; caution is advised.
Consult your doctor for
specific advice.

Infants and Children:
No special problems are
expected.

Special Concerns: Avoid
exposure to the sun until
you determine how the
medicine affects you.
Before having any kind of
surgery, tell the doctor or
dentist in charge that you
are taking triamterene.

OVERDOSE
Symptoms: Dizziness or
faintness, nausea, vomiting,
confusion, heartbeat irregularities, nervousness, numbness or tingling in hands,
feet, or lips, weak or heavy
legs, unusual fatigue or
tiredness.

What to Do: Call your
doctor, emergency medical
services (EMS), or the
nearest poison control
center immediately.

DRUG INTERACTIONS
Other drugs may interact
with triamterene. Consult
your doctor for specific
advice if you are taking
ACE inhibitors, cyclo-
sporine, potassium-containing medicines or supple-
ments, digoxin, or lithium.

FOOD INTERACTIONS
Avoid foods and beverages
high in potassium, such as
some salt substitutes,
bananas, and citrus juices.

DISEASE INTERACTIONS
Consult your doctor if you
have a history of gout or
kidney stones. Use of triamterene may cause complications in patients with liver
or kidney disease, since
these organs work together
to remove the medication
from the body.

Triazolam

Generic 0.125 mg
(GENEVA)

▶ Drug Class: Benzodiazepine tranquilizer

▶ Available in: Tablets

▶ Available OTC? No

▶ As Generic? Yes

Side Effects

SERIOUS
Difficulty concentrating, outbursts of anger, other behavior problems, depression, convulsions, hallucinations, low blood pressure (causing faintness or confusion), memory impairment, muscle weakness, skin rash or itching, sore throat, fever and chills, sores or ulcers in throat or mouth, unusual bruising or bleeding, extreme fatigue, yellowish tinge to eyes or skin. Call your doctor immediately.

COMMON
Loss of coordination, unsteady gait, dizziness, lightheadedness, drowsiness, slurred speech.

LESS COMMON
Stomach cramps or pain, vision disturbances, change in sexual desire or ability, constipation or diarrhea, dry mouth or watering mouth, false sense of well-being, rapid or pounding heartbeat, headache, muscle spasms, nausea and vomiting, urinary problems, trembling, unusual fatigue.

PRINCIPAL USES
To treat insomnia.

HOW THE DRUG WORKS
In general, triazolam produces mild sedation by depressing activity in the central nervous system (brain and spinal cord). In particular, triazolam appears to enhance the effect of gamma-aminobutyric acid (GABA), a natural chemical that inhibits the firing of neurons and dampens the transmission of nerve signals, thus decreasing nervous excitation.

DOSAGE
Adults: 0.125 to 0.250 mg at bedtime. Use and dose for children under 18 must be determined by your doctor.

ONSET OF EFFECT
Unknown.

DURATION OF ACTION
Unknown.

DIETARY ADVICE
Take with a full glass of water. Can be taken with food to lessen stomach upset.

STORAGE
Store in a tightly sealed container away from heat and direct light.

IF YOU MISS A DOSE
Take it as soon as you remember, unless it is late at night. Do not take the medicine unless your schedule allows a full night's sleep.

STOPPING THE DRUG
Stopping the drug abruptly may produce withdrawal symptoms (sleep disruption, nervousness, irritability, diarrhea, abdominal cramps, muscle aches, memory impairment). Dose should be reduced gradually according to your doctor's instructions.

PROLONGED USE
Triazolam may slowly lose its effectiveness, and adverse reactions are more likely to occur with prolonged use. You should see your doctor for periodic evaluation if you must take it for an extended time.

PRECAUTIONS
Over 60: Adverse reactions may be more likely and more severe. A lower dose may be warranted.

Driving and Hazardous Work: Triazolam can impair mental alertness and physical coordination. Adjust your activities accordingly.

Alcohol: Avoid alcohol.

Pregnancy: Use during pregnancy should be avoided if possible. Be sure to tell your doctor if you are pregnant or plan to become pregnant.

Breast Feeding: Triazolam passes into breast milk; do not take it while nursing.

Infants and Children: Safety and effectiveness have not been established for children under age 18.

Special Concerns: Triazolam use can lead to psychological or physical dependence if it is not taken in strict accordance with your doctor's instructions. Never take more than the prescribed daily dose.

OVERDOSE
Symptoms: Extreme drowsiness, confusion, slurred speech, slow reflexes, poor coordination, staggering gait, tremor, slowed breathing, loss of consciousness.

What to Do: Call your doctor, emergency medical services (EMS), or the nearest poison control center immediately.

DRUG INTERACTIONS
Other drugs may interact with triazolam. Consult your doctor for specific advice if you are taking any drugs that depress the central nervous system; these include antihistamines, antidepressants or other psychiatric medications, barbiturates, sedatives, cough medicines, decongestants, and painkillers. Be sure your physician knows about any over-the-counter medication you may take.

FOOD INTERACTIONS
None reported.

DISEASE INTERACTIONS
Caution is advised when taking triazolam. Consult your doctor if you have a history of alcohol or drug abuse, stroke or other brain disease, any chronic lung disease, glaucoma, hyperactivity, depression or other mental illness, myasthenia gravis, sleep apnea, epilepsy, porphyria, kidney disease, or liver disease.

Trifluoperazine Hydrochloride

Generic 10 mg
(GENEVA)

840

Additional photographs

▶ Drug Class: Neuroleptic; antipsychotic

▶ Available in: Oral solution, tablets, injection

▶ Available OTC? No

▶ As Generic? Yes

Side Effects

SERIOUS
Rapid heartbeat, profuse sweating, seizures, difficulty breathing, neck stiffness, swelling of the tongue, difficulty swallowing. Also a rare condition can develop called neuroleptic malignant syndrome, characterized by stiffness or spasms of the muscles, high fever, and confusion or disorientation. Call your doctor immediately.

COMMON
Nausea, reduced perspiration, dry mouth, blurred vision, drowsiness, shaking of the hands, muscle stiffness, stooped posture.

LESS COMMON
Difficult urination, menstrual irregularities, breast pain or swelling, unexpected weight gain, uncontrolled movements of the tongue, fever, chills, sore throat, unusual bruising or bleeding, heart palpitations, skin rash, itching, increased sensitivity of the skin to sunlight.

PRINCIPAL USES
To treat psychotic conditions (severe mental disorders characterized by distorted thoughts, perceptions, and emotions), such as schizophrenia.

HOW THE DRUG WORKS
Trifluoperazine appears to block receptors of dopamine (a chemical that aids in the transmission of nerve impulses) in the central nervous system. Presumably, this produces a tranquilizing and antipsychotic effect.

DOSAGE
Usual adult dose: Initially, 2 to 5 mg, 2 times a day. Your doctor may increase the dose if necessary (and if side effects are tolerated) up to a maximum of 40 mg a day.

ONSET OF EFFECT
Sedation may occur within minutes, but onset of antipsychotic effect may take hours to occur or may not occur until days or weeks after the beginning of therapy.

DURATION OF ACTION
12 to 24 hours, but effects may persist for several days.

DIETARY ADVICE
Can be taken with food or a full glass of milk or water.

STORAGE
Store in a tightly sealed container away from heat and direct light.

IF YOU MISS A DOSE
Take it as soon as you remember. However, if it is near the time for the next dose, skip the missed dose and resume your regular dosage schedule. Do not double the next dose.

STOPPING THE DRUG
The decision to stop taking the drug should be made in consultation with your doctor. Gradual reduction of doses may be required if you have taken this medication for an extended period.

PROLONGED USE
Prolonged use may lead to tardive dyskinesia (involuntary movements of the jaw, lips, tongue, and, in rare cases, the arms, legs, hands, or body). Consult your doctor about the need for follow-up evaluations and tests if you must take this drug for an extended period.

PRECAUTIONS
Over 60: Adverse reactions are more common in elderly patients. A lower dose may be warranted.

Driving and Hazardous Work: Do not drive or engage in hazardous work until you determine how the medicine affects you.

Alcohol: Avoid alcohol.

Pregnancy: Avoid using this drug during pregnancy.

Breast Feeding: Either avoid taking the drug if possible or refrain from breast feeding.

Infants and Children: Adverse reactions may be more likely and more severe in children.

Special Concerns: Avoid prolonged exposure to high temperatures or hot climates. Drink plenty of fluids and stay cool in the summertime. Also, avoid overexposure to sunlight until you determine if the drug heightens your skin's sensitivity to ultraviolet light.

OVERDOSE
Symptoms: Extreme drowsiness or paradoxical restlessness or agitation, heart rhythm irregularities or palpitations, dry mouth, seizures, stiffness or impaired mental control, loss of consciousness.

What to Do: Call your doctor, emergency medical services (EMS), or the nearest poison control center immediately.

DRUG INTERACTIONS
Consult your physician for specific advice if you are taking amantadine, high blood pressure medication, bromocriptine, deferoxamine, diuretics, levobunolol, heart medication, metipranolol, nabilone, other psychiatric drugs, pentamidine, pimozide, promethazine, trimeprazine, a thyroid agent, central nervous system depressants, epinephrine, lithium, levodopa, methyldopa, metoclopramide, metyrosine, pemoline, a rauwolfia alkaloid, or metrizamide.

FOOD INTERACTIONS
No known food interactions.

DISEASE INTERACTIONS
Consult your doctor if you have Parkinson's disease or any movement disorder, glaucoma, epilepsy, liver disease, or kidney disease.

Trihexyphenidyl Hydrochloride

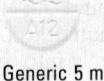
Side Effects

SERIOUS
Confusion, hallucinations,
blurred vision, glaucoma.
Call your doctor at once.

COMMON
Dry mouth, nausea.

LESS COMMON
Difficult urination.

PRINCIPAL USES

To treat Parkinson's disease
and the Parkinson-like
symptoms induced by cer-
tain central nervous system
drugs. Such symptoms
include slowed movement,
stiffness and muscle rigidity, tremor, and loss of balance. Trihexyphenidyl is
also used to treat Parkinson-
like syndromes that can
occur as a result of injury
to or infection of the central
nervous system, damage
to blood vessels in the
brain, or exposure to
certain toxins.

HOW THE DRUG WORKS

The exact mechanism of
action of trihexyphenidyl is
unknown, although it is
thought to increase the
availability of dopamine, a
brain chemical that is critical in the initiation and
smooth control of voluntary
muscle movement.

DOSAGE

Adults: To start, 2 mg, 3
times a day. The dose is
gradually increased until
the desired therapeutic
response is achieved. The
usual maximum mainte-
nance dose is 5 mg, 3 times
a day. Once a maintenance
dosage is established, your
physician may switch you to
sustained-release capsules
(sequels), which can be
taken less frequently (once
or twice a day). Children:
The dosage for children has
not been established; consult your pediatrician for
advice.

ONSET OF EFFECT

Usually within 1 hour.

DURATION OF ACTION

The effect may last for at
least 24 hours.

DIETARY ADVICE

No special restrictions.

STORAGE

Store in a tightly sealed container away from heat, moisture, and direct light.

IF YOU MISS A DOSE

Take it as soon as you
remember, unless the time
for your next scheduled
dose is within the next 2
hours. If so, skip the missed
dose and resume your regular dosage schedule. Do not
double the next dose.

STOPPING THE DRUG

The decision to stop taking
the drug should be made in
consultation with your doctor. The dosage is typically
tapered gradually over the
course of 7 days.

PROLONGED USE

The prolonged use of tri-
hexyphenidyl may cause
glaucoma (elevated pres-
sure within the eye, and a
leading cause of blindness)
or increase its severity.
Arrange for regular check-
ups with your eye doctor to
have your eye pressure
monitored.

PRECAUTIONS

Over 60: Adverse reactions
may be more likely and
more severe in older
patients. Lower doses
may be needed.

**Driving and Hazardous
Work:** Do not drive or
engage in hazardous work
until you determine how the
medicine affects you.

Alcohol: Avoid alcohol.

Pregnancy: This drug
should not be used by pregnant women.

Breast Feeding: Tri-
hexyphenidyl passes into
breast milk; this drug
should not be used by
nursing mothers.

Infants and Children:
Very low doses may be
used by children; consult
your pediatrician. The drug
is not recommended for use
by children under age 10.

Special Concerns: Your
eye doctor should regularly
monitor your intraocular
pressure to check for glaucoma. Consult your doctor
to determine the best
schedule for regular
physical examinations.

OVERDOSE

Symptoms: Clumsiness,
confusion, delirium, inability
to urinate, seizures.

What to Do: Call your
doctor, emergency medical
services (EMS), or the
nearest poison control
center immediately.

DRUG INTERACTIONS

Consult your doctor for specific advice if you are taking
any of the following: other
drugs for Parkinson's disease (such as levodopa),
medications that depress
the central nervous system
(such as alcohol, barbiturates, or other sleep-inducing drugs), or MAO
inhibitor antidepressants
(such as phenelzine sulfate
or tranylcypromine sulfate).

FOOD INTERACTIONS

No known food interactions.

DISEASE INTERACTIONS

Caution is advised when
taking trihexyphenidyl. Consult your doctor for specific
advice if you have glau-
coma, prostate disease, or
enlarged prostate (benign
prostatic hyperplasia).

Trimethobenzamide Hydrochloride

BRAND NAMES
Arrestin, Benzacot, Bio-Gan, Stemetic, T-Gen, Tebamide, Tegamide, Ticon, Tigan, Tiject-20, Triban, Tribenzagan

▶ Drug Class: Antiemetic

▶ Available in: Capsules, injection, suppositories

▶ Available OTC? No

▶ As Generic? Yes

Side Effects

SERIOUS
Seizures, yellow discoloration of the eyes and skin, skin rash, body spasms, convulsions, mental depression, shakiness or tremors, sore throat and fever, unusual fatigue, severe or continuing vomiting. Call your doctor immediately.

COMMON
Drowsiness.

LESS COMMON
Dizziness, lightheadedness, muscle cramps, fainting, blurred vision, diarrhea, headache.

PRINCIPAL USES
To treat nausea, vomiting, and motion sickness.

HOW THE DRUG WORKS
Trimethobenzamide acts on the brain center that controls vomiting.

DOSAGE
Capsules— Adults and children 12 years and older: 250 mg, 3 or 4 times a day, as needed. Children weighing 30 to 90 lbs: 6.8 mg per lb of body weight, not to exceed 200 mg, 3 or 4 times a day. Injection— Adults and children 12 years and older: 200 mg into a muscle, 3 or 4 times a day. Suppositories— Adults and children 12 years and older: 200 mg, 3 or 4 times a day. Children 30 to 90 lbs: 1/2 to 1 suppository (100 to 200 mg), 3 or 4 times a day. Children under 30 lbs: 1/2 suppository (100 mg), 3 or 4 times a day.

ONSET OF EFFECT
Capsules: 10 to 20 minutes. Injection: 15 to 35 minutes. Suppositories: Variable.

DURATION OF ACTION
Capsules: 3 to 4 hours. Injection: 2 to 3 hours. Suppositories: Variable.

DIETARY ADVICE
Capsules can be opened and the contents mixed with food if so desired.

STORAGE
Store in a tightly sealed container away from heat, moisture, and direct light. Suppositories should be refrigerated.

IF YOU MISS A DOSE
Take it as soon as you remember. If it is near the time for the next dose, skip the missed dose and resume your regular dosage schedule. Do not double the next dose.

STOPPING THE DRUG
The decision to stop taking the drug should be made by your doctor.

PROLONGED USE
See your doctor regularly for tests and examinations if you take trimethobenzamide for a prolonged period. Using more than the recommended dosage or taking it more often than directed can increase the possibility of side effects.

PRECAUTIONS
Over 60: No special problems are expected.

Driving and Hazardous Work: Do not drive or engage in hazardous work until you determine how the medicine affects you.

Alcohol: Avoid alcohol.

Pregnancy: Adequate human studies have not been completed. Before taking trimethobenzamide, tell your doctor if you are pregnant or plan to become pregnant.

Breast Feeding: Trimethobenzamide may pass into breast milk; caution is advised. Consult your doctor for advice.

Infants and Children: Trimethobenzamide should be used in infants and children only under the direction of your doctor. Some side effects may be more severe in children. Do not use the injectable form in children. Do not use the suppository form in either premature or newborn infants.

Special Concerns: When used for motion sickness, trimethobenzamide should be taken 30 minutes before exposure to motion. If the suppository is too soft to insert, chill it with running water or refrigerate it for 30 minutes. To reduce irritation and pain around the area of the injection, inject the medicine deeply into the outer area of the buttocks.

OVERDOSE
Symptoms: Seizures, unconsciousness.

What to Do: Call your doctor, emergency medical services (EMS), or the nearest poison control center immediately.

DRUG INTERACTIONS
Consult your doctor for specific advice if you are taking aspirin, phenobarbital, tricyclic antidepressants, or other central nervous system depressants such as tranquilizers, sleeping pills, or cold and allergy drugs.

FOOD INTERACTIONS
No known food interactions.

DISEASE INTERACTIONS
Caution is advised when taking trimethobenzamide. Consult your doctor if you have a high fever, severe vomiting, dehydration, or an intestinal infection, or if a child has Reye's syndrome.

Trimethoprim/Sulfamethoxazole

BRAND NAMES
Bactrim, Cotrim, Septra,
Sulfamethoprim, Uro-D/S,
Uroplus

Generic 160/800 mg
(SCHEIN/DANBURY)

▶ Drug Class: Anti-infective

▶ Available in: Tablets, injection

▶ Available OTC? No

▶ As Generic? Yes

Side Effects

SERIOUS
Skin rash, sore throat,
fever, joint pain, short-
ness of breath, pale skin,
reddish spots on skin,
unusual bleeding or
bruising. Call your
doctor immediately.

COMMON
Nausea, vomiting, loss of
appetite, allergic skin
reactions, itching, hives.

LESS COMMON
Abdominal pain, diar-
rhea, seizures, dizzi-
ness, ringing in ears,
headache, hallucinations,
depression, unusual sen-
sitivity to sunlight.

PRINCIPAL USES
To treat urinary tract infections, ear infections, chronic
bronchitis, Pneumocystis
carinii pneumonia (a lung
infection commonly seen in
patients with compromised
immune systems), traveler's
diarrhea, and other types of
diarrheal disease.

HOW THE DRUG WORKS
This medication is a combination of two active ingredients. Both trimethoprim and
sulfamethoxazole kill or
inhibit growth of bacteria by
disrupting their ability to
make necessary proteins.

DOSAGE
For common bacterial infections— Adults: The usual
dose is 1 double strength
(DS) tablet 2 times a day.
Duration of therapy
depends on the type of
infection and will be determined by your doctor. For
alternative dosages and for
treatment of children, consult your pediatrician, as
dosages can vary considerably depending on age,
weight, and kidney function.

ONSET OF EFFECT
Unknown.

DURATION OF ACTION
Unknown.

DIETARY ADVICE
Tablets should be taken
with a full glass of water
and can be taken with food
to lessen stomach upset.

STORAGE
Store in a tightly sealed container away from heat and
direct light.

IF YOU MISS A DOSE
Take it as soon as you
remember. However, if it is
near the time for the next
dose, skip the missed dose
and resume your regular
dosage schedule. Do not
double the next dose.

STOPPING THE DRUG
Take the drug as prescribed
for the full treatment period,
even if you begin to feel better before the scheduled
end of therapy.

PROLONGED USE
See your doctor regularly
for tests and examinations if
you must take this medicine
for a prolonged period.

PRECAUTIONS
Over 60: Adverse reactions
may be more likely and
more severe in older
patients.

**Driving and Hazardous
Work:** Do not drive or
engage in hazardous work
until you determine how the
medicine affects you.

Alcohol: No special problems are expected, although
it is generally advisable to
abstain from alcohol when
fighting an infection.

Pregnancy: Trimethoprim
with sulfamethoxazole has
caused birth defects in animals. Human studies have
not been done. It should be
used during pregnancy only
if the benefits clearly outweigh the possible risks.
Before you take this med-
ication, tell your doctor if
you are pregnant or plan
to become pregnant.

Breast Feeding:
Trimethoprim with sul-
famethoxazole passes into
breast milk; avoid or discontinue use while nursing.

Infants and Children:
This medication is not recommended for use by chil-
dren under the age of 2
months.

Special Concerns: Since
some patients experience
increased sensitivity to sunlight, take preventive measures: use sunscreens, wear
protective clothing, and
avoid exposure to the sun.
Patients with acquired
immunodeficiency syn-
drome (AIDS) may have
a higher incidence of side
effects, especially rash.
Nonetheless, trimethoprim
with sulfamethoxazole
remains valuable for treating a number of problems
associated with this disease.

OVERDOSE
Symptoms: Loss of
appetite, nausea, vomiting,
dizziness, headache, drowsiness, depression, confusion,
altered mental status, fever,
blood in urine, yellow skin
or eyes.

What to Do: Call your
doctor, emergency medical
services (EMS), or the
nearest poison control
center immediately.

DRUG INTERACTIONS
The following drugs may
interact with trimethoprim
with sulfamethoxazole. Consult your doctor for specific
advice if you are taking
cyclosporine, methotrexate,
phenytoin, procainamide,
sulfonylureas, or warfarin.

FOOD INTERACTIONS
No known food interactions.

DISEASE INTERACTIONS
Use of sulfamethoxazole
may cause complications in
patients with liver or kidney
disease, since these organs
work together to remove
the medication from the
body. This drug can also
cause complications in
patients with certain types
of anemia. Consult your
doctor for specific advice if
you have any other medical
condition.

Triprolidine Hydrochloride

BRAND NAMES
Actidil, Myidil

▶ Drug Class: Antihistamine

▶ Available in: Syrup

▶ Available OTC? Yes

▶ As Generic? Yes

Side Effects

SERIOUS
Sore throat and fever, unusual tiredness or weakness, unusual bleeding or bruising. Call your doctor immediately.

COMMON
Drowsiness, thickening of mucus.

LESS COMMON
Blurred vision; rapid heartbeat; skin rash; stomach upset; nervousness; increased sensitivity of skin to sunlight; confusion; difficult or painful urination; dizziness; dry mouth, nose, or throat; loss of appetite; nightmares; ringing or buzzing in ears; restlessness; irritability.

PRINCIPAL USES
To relieve symptoms of hay fever and other allergies.

HOW THE DRUG WORKS
Triprolidine blocks the effects of histamine, a naturally occurring substance that causes swelling, itching, sneezing, watery eyes, hives, and other symptoms of allergic reaction.

DOSAGE
Adults and children age 12 and over: 2.5 mg every 4 to 6 hours. The maximum dose is 10 mg per day. Children ages 6 to 12: 1.25 mg (1 teaspoon) every 4 to 6 hours. The maximum dose is 5 mg per day. Children ages 4 to 6: 0.938 mg (¾ teaspoon) every 4 to 6 hours. The maximum dose is 3.744 mg per day. Children ages 2 to 4: 0.625 mg (½ teaspoon) every 4 to 6 hours. The maximum dose is 2.5 mg per day. Children ages 4 months to 2 years: 0.313 mg (¼ teaspoon) every 4 to 6 hours. The maximum dose is 1.25 mg per day.

ONSET OF EFFECT
15 to 60 minutes.

DURATION OF ACTION
4 to 6 hours.

DIETARY ADVICE
This drug should be taken with food or milk to reduce stomach upset.

STORAGE
Store in a tightly sealed container away from heat and direct light. Do not allow the drug to freeze.

IF YOU MISS A DOSE
Take it as soon as you remember. If it is near the time for the next dose, skip the missed dose and resume your regular dosage schedule. Do not double the next dose.

STOPPING THE DRUG
The decision to stop taking the drug should be made by your doctor.

PROLONGED USE
Tolerance, or decreased responsiveness to the drug, usually does not develop with prolonged use. If it does, consult your doctor.

PRECAUTIONS
Over 60: Adverse reactions may be more likely and more severe in older patients.

Driving and Hazardous Work: Do not drive or engage in hazardous work until you determine how the medicine affects you.

Alcohol: Avoid alcohol.

Pregnancy: Before you take triprolidine, tell your doctor if you are pregnant or plan to become pregnant.

Breast Feeding: Triprolidine passes into breast milk; avoid or discontinue use while nursing. Flow of breast milk may be reduced.

Infants and Children: Adverse effects may be more likely and more severe in children.

Special Concerns: Stop taking triprolidine 4 days before you have an allergy skin test. Drink water frequently or use ice chips, sugarless candy, or sugarless gum if dry mouth occurs. Coffee or tea may reduce the common side effect of drowsiness.

OVERDOSE
Symptoms: Central nervous system depression or, paradoxically, nervous system stimulation; very low blood pressure; breathing difficulty; seizures; loss of consciousness; severe dryness of the mouth, nose, or throat.

What to Do: Call your doctor, emergency medical services (EMS), or the nearest poison control center immediately.

DRUG INTERACTIONS
Consult your doctor for specific advice if you are taking anticholinergics, clarithromycin, erythromycin, itraconazole, ketoconazole, bepridil, disopyramide, maprotiline, phenothiazines, pimozide, procainamide, quinidine, tricyclic antidepressants, central nervous system depressants, MAO inhibitors, or quinine.

FOOD INTERACTIONS
No known food interactions.

DISEASE INTERACTIONS
Caution is advised when taking triprolidine. Consult your doctor if you have an enlarged prostate, urinary tract blockage, difficult urination, or glaucoma. Use of triprolidine may cause complications in patients with liver disease, since this organ works to remove the medication from the body.

Trovafloxacin

▶ Drug Class: Antibiotic

▶ Available in: Tablets, injection

▶ Available OTC? No

▶ As Generic? No

Side Effects

SERIOUS
Serious reactions are rare. The most serious potential side effect is liver toxicity, which can cause jaundice (character- ized by yellowish discol- oration of the skin and eyes), nausea, vomiting, abdominal pain, fatigue, loss of appetite, and dark urine. Liver failure has led to a small number of deaths and liver trans- plants. Other serious side effects may include chest pain, heart rhythm irregu- larities, diarrhea, anaphy- laxis (a severe allergic reaction marked by sud- den swelling of the lips, tongue, face, or throat; breathing difficulty; skin rash, itching, or hives), seizures, and confusion or other mental distur- bances such as restless- ness, nightmares, and insomnia. Call your doc- tor immediately.

COMMON
Dizziness, lightheaded- ness, nausea, headache.

LESS COMMON
Vomiting, abdominal pain, yeast infection (females), itching, increased sensitivity to sunlight.

PRINCIPAL USES
To treat a number of seri- ous bacterial infections such as pneumonia, gynecologi- cal infections, and compli- cated skin infections, especially when acquired in a hospital or nursing home. Your doctor will determine if this drug is appropriate for your condition.

HOW THE DRUG WORKS
Trovafloxacin inhibits the activity of two bacterial enzymes, including DNA gyrase, that are necessary for proper DNA formation and replication. This fights infection by preventing bac- teria cells from reproducing.

DOSAGE
The dosage varies, depend- ing on the site and type of infection. Daily doses of the tablets range from 100 to 200 mg for periods of 3 to 14 days. Your doctor will determine the correct dosage for your specific condition. Intravenous doses, when necessary, are administered by a health care professional.

ONSET OF EFFECT
Unknown.

DURATION OF ACTION
Unknown.

DIETARY ADVICE
Trovafloxacin can be taken without regard to meals.

STORAGE
Tablets: Store in a tightly sealed container away from heat, moisture, and direct light. Injection: Not applica- ble; injectable dose is administered only at a health care facility.

IF YOU MISS A DOSE
Tablet: Take it as soon as you remember. If you miss the dose one day, resume your regular dosage sched- ule. Do not double the next dose. Injection: Consult your doctor.

STOPPING THE DRUG
Take it as prescribed for the full treatment period, even if you begin to feel better before the scheduled end of therapy. The decision to stop taking the drug should be made by your doctor.

PROLONGED USE
Trovafloxacin is generally prescribed only for short- term use and should not be used for more than14 days.

PRECAUTIONS
Over 60: No special prob- lems are expected.

Driving and Hazardous Work: Do not drive or engage in hazardous work until you determine how the medicine affects you.

Alcohol: It is advisable to abstain from alcohol when fighting an infection.

Pregnancy: Adequate human studies have not been done. Before taking trovafloxacin, discuss with your doctor the relative risks and benefits of using this drug while pregnant.

Breast Feeding: Trovafloxacin passes into breast milk; extreme cau- tion is advised. Consult your doctor for specific advice.

Infants and Children: Not recommended for use by children under the age of 18 years.

Special Concerns: Take trovafloxacin with food or at bedtime to reduce the likelihood of dizziness. If trovafloxacin causes height- ened sensitivity to sunlight, stop taking the drug and try to avoid exposure to sun- light for the next 5 days; also wear protective cloth- ing and use a sunblock.

OVERDOSE
Symptoms: An overdose with trovafloxacin is unlikely to occur.

What to Do: If someone takes a much larger dose than prescribed, call your doctor, emergency medical services (EMS), or the nearest poison control center immediately.

DRUG INTERACTIONS
Trovafloxacin should be taken at least 2 hours before or after taking certain antacids, sucralfate, citric acid buffered with sodium citrate, or vitamin or mineral supplements containing iron.

FOOD INTERACTIONS
No known food interactions.

DISEASE INTERACTIONS
Trovafloxacin should not be used at all in patients with liver disease or those who have had an allergic reac- tion to quinolone antibiotics in the past. The drug should be used with caution in those with a history of seizures or any nervous system disorders that may increase the risk of seizures. Be sure to inform your doctor if you have any other medical condition.

Undecylenic Acid

BRAND NAMES
Caldesene Medicated
Powder, Cruex Antifungal,
Decylenes Powder,
Desenex Antifungal,
Gordochom Solution

▶ Drug Class: Topical antifungal

▶ Available in: Aerosol foam,
aerosol powder, cream, ointment, powder, solution

▶ Available OTC? Yes

▶ As Generic? Yes

Side Effects

SERIOUS
No serious side effects
have been reported.

COMMON
No common side effects
have been reported.

LESS COMMON
Skin irritation that was
not present before use of
this medicine. Call your
doctor promptly.

PRINCIPAL USES
To treat fungal infections of
the skin. (Note: Unde-
cylenic acid has generally
been replaced by newer and
more effective topical antifungal medications; how-
ever, your physician may
find it worthwhile to prescribe undecylenic acid
under certain circum-
stances—for example, if you
have a history of allergic
reaction to other antifungal
preparations.)

HOW THE DRUG WORKS
Undecylenic acid prevents
the growth and reproduc-
tion of fungus cells.

DOSAGE
Aerosol foam, aerosol powder, ointment, powder, or
solution: Apply to the
affected area of the skin 2
times a day. The aerosol
powder and aerosol spray
form of the medicine should
be sprayed on the affected
area from a distance of 4 to
6 inches. The powder may
also be sprayed in socks
and shoes. If the powder is
used on the feet, sprinkle it
between the toes, on the
feet, and in shoes and
socks. Cream: Apply to the
affected area of the skin as
often as necessary.

ONSET OF EFFECT
Unknown.

DURATION OF ACTION
Unknown.

DIETARY ADVICE
No special restrictions.

STORAGE
Store in a tightly sealed container away from heat and
direct light. Keep aerosol,
cream, ointment, and liquid
solution forms of unde-
cylenic acid from freezing.
Do not puncture, rupture,
or incinerate the aerosol
container.

IF YOU MISS A DOSE
Apply a missed dose as
soon as you remember. If
it is close to the next dose,
skip the missed dose and
resume your regular dosage
schedule. Do not apply a
double dose.

STOPPING THE DRUG
Take as prescribed for the
full treatment period, even
if you begin to feel better
before the scheduled end
of therapy. Discontinuing
the drug prematurely may
result in an even worse fungal infection later (known as
rebound infection). In general, keep using this medication for two weeks after
burning, itching, and other
symptoms have cleared up.

PROLONGED USE
If your skin problem does
not improve or becomes
worse after 4 weeks of treatment, consult your doctor.

PRECAUTIONS
Over 60: There is no specific information comparing
use of undecylenic acid in
older persons with use in
other age groups.

**Driving and Hazardous
Work:** No special precautions are necessary.

Alcohol: No special precautions are necessary.

Pregnancy: Undecylenic
acid has not been shown to
cause birth defects or other
problems in humans.

Breast Feeding: Unde-
cylenic acid may pass into
breast milk; caution is
advised. Consult your
doctor for advice.

Infants and Children:
Not recommended for use
on children under age 2.

Special Concerns: Keep
this medicine away from the

eyes, nose, and mouth. To
help prevent reinfection,
the powder or spray form
of undecylenic acid may
be used every day after
bathing and careful drying.
Do not use on pus-produc-
ing sores or on badly broken skin.

OVERDOSE
Symptoms: No specific
ones have been reported.

What to Do: An overdose
of undecylenic acid is
unlikely. However, if someone accidentally ingests the
drug, call your doctor,
emergency medical services
(EMS), or the nearest poison control center.

DRUG INTERACTIONS
Consult your doctor for specific advice if you are taking
any other topical prescription or over-the-counter
medication that is to be
applied to the same area
of the skin.

FOOD INTERACTIONS
No known food interactions.

DISEASE INTERACTIONS
Caution is advised when
taking undecylenic acid.
Consult your doctor if you
have any other medical condition that affects the skin.

Uracil Mustard

BRAND NAME
Uracil mustard is available in generic form only.

▶ Drug Class: Alkylating agent

▶ Available in: Capsules

▶ Available OTC? No

▶ As Generic? Yes

Side Effects

SERIOUS
Black, tarry, or bloody stools; blood in urine; fever and chills; cough or hoarseness; pain in lower back or side; difficult or painful urination; red spots on skin; unusual bleeding or bruising; joint pain; sores on lips or in mouth; swollen feet or lower legs; yellow tinge to eyes or skin (jaundice). Call your doctor immediately. Some of these side effects may recur after you stop taking uracil mustard. Consult your doctor if they do.

COMMON
Diarrhea; nausea or vomiting; temporary hair loss.

LESS COMMON
Darkening of the skin, irritability, depression, nervousness, skin rash and itching.

PRINCIPAL USES
To treat leukemia, Hodgkin's disease and other lymphomas (a type of cancer affecting the lymphatic system), polycythemia vera (a blood disease characterized by the overproduction of some types of blood cells), and mycosis fungoides (a rare type of skin cancer that affects the lymphatic system).

HOW THE DRUG WORKS
Uracil mustard kills cancer cells by interfering with the activity of their genetic material, thus preventing the cells from reproducing. The drug may also affect the growth and development of healthy cells in the body, resulting in unpleasant side effects.

DOSAGE
Initial weekly dose of 0.15 mg per 2.2 lbs (1 kg) of body weight for at least 4 weeks to provide an adequate trial period. Dosage and duration of treatment can then be altered to meet the needs of individual patients.

ONSET OF EFFECT
Unknown.

DURATION OF ACTION
Unknown.

DIETARY ADVICE
Best taken at bedtime to minimize stomach upset.

STORAGE
Store in a tightly sealed container away from heat and direct light.

IF YOU MISS A DOSE
Take it as soon as you remember. If it is near the time for the next dose, skip the missed dose and resume your regular dosage schedule. Do not double the next dose.

STOPPING THE DRUG
The decision to stop taking the drug should be made by your doctor.

PROLONGED USE
You should see your doctor regularly for tests and examinations if you must take this medication for a prolonged period of time.

PRECAUTIONS
Over 60: No special problems are expected.

Driving and Hazardous Work: The use of this medication should not impair your ability to perform such tasks safely.

Alcohol: Avoid alcohol.

Pregnancy: Uracil mustard can cause birth defects if taken by either the father or the mother. Persons of childbearing years should take steps to prevent pregnancy when taking it.

Breast Feeding: Not recommended during therapy.

Infants and Children: Although there is no specific information about the use of uracil mustard in infants and children, it is not expected to cause different side effects than it does in adults.

Special Concerns: Do not receive any immunizations without your doctor's approval while taking uracil mustard. Avoid persons who have recently had oral polio vaccine and those with any infection. Check with your doctor before having any dental work done. Consult your doctor or dentist about appropriate ways to clean your teeth to avoid injury. Be careful not to cut yourself when using sharp objects such as a safety razor or nail cutters. Avoid activities and contact sports where bruising or injury could occur. If you vomit shortly after taking a dose of uracil mustard, check with your doctor. You may be told to take the dose again. After completing a different regimen of chemotherapy or radiation, a period of 2 to 3 weeks is recommended before starting uracil mustard because of the risk of bone marrow damage.

OVERDOSE
Symptoms: Vomiting, severe nausea, severe diarrhea, unusual weakness, hemorrhaging.

What to Do: Call your doctor, emergency medical services (EMS), or the nearest poison control center immediately.

DRUG INTERACTIONS
Consult your doctor for advice if you are taking amphotericin B, antithyroid agents, azathioprine, chloramphenicol, colchicine, flucytosine, interferon, plicamycin, probenecid, sulfinpyrazone, or zidovudine. Also consult your doctor if you are taking any over-the-counter drugs.

FOOD INTERACTIONS
None are known.

DISEASE INTERACTIONS
Caution is advised when taking uracil mustard. Consult your doctor if you have any of the following: chicken pox, shingles, any infection, gout, kidney disease, or liver disease.

Ursodiol

Actigall 300 mg
(SUMMIT)

▶ Drug Class: Antigallstone agent

▶ Available in: Capsules, tablets

▶ Available OTC? No

▶ As Generic? Yes

Side Effects

SERIOUS
No serious side effects have been reported.

COMMON
No common side effects have been reported.

LESS COMMON
Diarrhea.

PRINCIPAL USES
To treat gallstones as an alternative to surgical removal of the gallbladder (cholecystectomy). Ursodiol works only when gallstones are composed entirely of cholesterol, and works best when the gallstones are small.

HOW THE DRUG WORKS
Ursodiol is a natural bile acid that safely dissolves cholesterol gallstones over a period of months or years. The time required to dissolve a stone is proportional to the stone's size. Multiple stones usually dissolve more easily than a single large stone.

DOSAGE
Adults and teenagers: 3.6 to 4.5 mg per lb of body weight a day, divided into 2 or 3 equal doses.

ONSET OF EFFECT
Variable. It may take 6 months to 2 years for gallstones to dissolve.

DURATION OF ACTION
For as long as the medication is taken.

DIETARY ADVICE
Ursodiol should be taken with or immediately after meals.

STORAGE
Store in a tightly sealed container away from heat, moisture, and direct light.

IF YOU MISS A DOSE
Take as soon as you remember or double the next dose.

STOPPING THE DRUG
Take it as prescribed for the full treatment period.

PROLONGED USE
You should see your doctor regularly for tests and examinations if you take this medicine for a prolonged period. Liver function tests (AST and ALT) should be done periodically. Ultrasound imaging should be done every 6 months for the first year of therapy to monitor the response to ursodiol. It may take 6 months to 2 years to dissolve gallstones, depending on their size and composition. Ursodiol treatment is not likely to be effective if gallstones are not partially dissolved after 12 months of therapy. Ursodiol should be continued for at least 3 months after the gallstones have dissolved.

PRECAUTIONS
Over 60: No special precautions are needed.

Driving and Hazardous Work: The use of ursodiol should not impair your ability to perform such tasks safely.

Alcohol: No special precautions are necessary.

Pregnancy: Adequate human studies have not been done. Before taking ursodiol, tell your doctor if you are or are planning to become pregnant.

Breast Feeding: It is not known whether ursodiol passes into breast milk; caution is advised. Consult your doctor for specific advice.

Infants and Children: Ursodiol is not expected to cause different or more severe side effects in children than it does in older persons.

Special Concerns: If you experience severe pain in the abdomen or stomach, particularly on the upper right side, or nausea and vomiting, call your doctor immediately. These symptoms may indicate the presence of other medical problems or that your gallbladder condition requires immediate care. Gallstones recur after 5 years in about half of those patients whose stones were successfully dissolved by ursodiol.

OVERDOSE
Symptoms: An overdose with ursodiol is unlikely.

What to Do: If someone takes a much larger dose than prescribed, call your doctor, emergency medical services (EMS), or the nearest poison control center right away.

DRUG INTERACTIONS
Other drugs may interact with ursodiol. Cholestyramine, colestipol, and antacids that contain aluminum can prevent the absorption of ursodiol from the intestine. Estrogen and oral contraceptives may interfere with the action of this medication.

FOOD INTERACTIONS
No known food interactions.

DISEASE INTERACTIONS
Ursodiol treatment is usually inappropriate when complications of gallstone disease, such as obstruction of the bile duct, cholecystitis (inflammation of the gallbladder) or pancreatitis (inflammation of the pancreas) are present. These conditions may require gallbladder surgery, because benefits from ursodiol would take too long to achieve.

Valacyclovir Hydrochloride

Valtrex 500 mg
(GLAXO WELLCOME)

▶ Drug Class: Antiviral

▶ Available in: Tablets

▶ Available OTC? No

▶ As Generic? No

Side Effects

SERIOUS
A rare but serious bleeding disorder marked by symptoms such as bruising, pinpoint red spots on the skin, and blood in the urine has been reported in a few patients with severely weakened immune systems.

COMMON
Headache, nausea.

LESS COMMON
Constipation or diarrhea, loss of appetite, dizziness, stomach pain, vomiting, unusual fatigue.

PRINCIPAL USES
To treat the symptoms of shingles (herpes zoster). Also used for the treatment and suppression of genital herpes.

HOW THE DRUG WORKS
Valacyclovir is converted in the body to acyclovir, which interferes with the activity of enzymes needed for the replication of viral DNA in cells, thus preventing the virus from multiplying. Although it cannot cure herpes infections, it can relieve symptoms and speed the healing of herpes lesions. It may also reduce the duration of any lingering pain (postherpetic neuralgia).

DOSAGE
For shingles: Adults: 1 gram (g), 3 times a day for 7 days. To treat initial episodes of genital herpes: 1 g, 2 times a day for 10 days. To treat recurrent genital herpes: 500 mg, 2 times a day for 5 days. For suppression of chronic recurrent genital herpes: 1 g, once a day. In patients with a history of 9 or fewer recurrences per year: 500 mg, once a day.

ONSET OF EFFECT
Within 30 minutes.

DURATION OF ACTION
Unknown.

DIETARY ADVICE
No special restrictions.

STORAGE
Store in a tightly sealed container away from heat, moisture, and direct light.

IF YOU MISS A DOSE
Take it as soon as you remember. If it is near the time for the next dose, skip the missed dose and resume your regular dosage schedule. Do not double the next dose.

STOPPING THE DRUG
The decision to stop taking the drug should be made with your doctor.

PROLONGED USE
Usual course of therapy lasts 7 to 10 days. If for any reason you must take the drug for a longer period, see your doctor for regular tests and examinations.

PRECAUTIONS
Over 60: No special problems are expected, although a smaller dose may be warranted for those with a history of impaired renal (kidney) function.

Driving and Hazardous Work: Exercise caution until you determine how the medication affects you.

Alcohol: No special precautions are necessary.

Pregnancy: Human studies of valacyclovir in pregnancy have not been done, but birth defects or other problems have not been reported. Before you take valacyclovir, tell your doctor if you are pregnant or plan to become pregnant.

Breast Feeding: Valacyclovir may pass into breast milk, although it is unknown if this poses any risks to the nursing infant; no problems have been reported. Consult your doctor for specific advice.

Infants and Children: The safety and effectiveness of this drug in children have not been established.

Special Concerns: Keep the body areas affected by shingles or herpes clean and dry, and wear comfortable, loose-fitting clothes to avoid irritation. Start taking valacyclovir as soon as possible after the symptoms

appear, ideally within 72 hours. Do not take valacyclovir if you have ever had an allergic reaction to antiviral drugs.

OVERDOSE
Symptoms: No cases of overdose of valacyclovir have been reported. If an overdose were to occur, symptoms would likely be those of acute kidney failure, which include blood in the urine, passing only small amounts of.urine, swelling of the ankles, hands, face, or other areas, shortness of breath, itching, fever, and flank pain.

What to Do: Seek medical assistance right away.

DRUG INTERACTIONS
Consult your doctor for specific advice if you are taking any other prescription or over-the-counter medication, especially cimetidine or probenecid. These drugs slow the kidney's removal of valacyclovir, increasing the possibility of adverse side effects.

FOOD INTERACTIONS
No known food interactions.

DISEASE INTERACTIONS
Caution is advised when taking valacyclovir. Use of valacyclovir may cause complications in patients with kidney disease, since this organ works to remove the medication from the body. Consult your doctor if you have a weakened immune system; for example, if you are infected with the human immunodeficiency virus (HIV), or are taking immunosuppressant drugs to prevent organ rejection following a kidney or bone marrow transplant. Use of valacyclovir by patients with weakened immune systems can cause extreme side effects that may be fatal.

797

Valdecoxib

▶ Drug Class: Nonsteroidal anti-inflammatory drug (NSAID)/COX-2 inhibitor

▶ Available in: Tablets

▶ Available OTC? No

▶ As Generic? No

Side Effects

SERIOUS
Serious, potentially fatal skin reactions, including toxic epidermal necrolysis, Stevens-Johnson syndrome, and erythemia multiforme. Stop taking the drug and call your doctor at the first appearance of skin rash, mucosal lesions (such as sores inside the mouth), or any other sign of hypersensitivity. Stomach ulcers. Black, tarry stools may signal stomach bleeding. Symptoms of liver disease (nausea, fatigue, lethargy, itching, yellowish discoloration of the eyes or skin, fluid retention). Call your doctor immediately.

COMMON
Indigestion, diarrhea, and mild abdominal pain.

LESS COMMON
Flatulence, mild swelling, sore throat, and upper respiratory tract infection.

PRINCIPAL USES
To relieve the pain, inflammation, and stiffness of osteoarthritis and rheumatoid arthritis. To relieve menstrual pain. Because valdecoxib may be associated with an increased risk of stroke and heart attack, use of this drug may be limited to patients who cannot take other pain medications or who have a history of gastrointestinal bleeding.

HOW THE DRUG WORKS
By inhibiting the activity of the enzyme cyclooxygenase-2 (COX-2), valdecoxib reduces the synthesis of prostaglandins that play a role in causing arthritis pain and inflammation. It does not inhibit the activity of COX-1, the enzyme involved in the synthesis of prostaglandins that help protect against stomach ulcers.

DOSAGE
For arthritis: 10 mg once a day. For menstrual pain: 20 mg twice a day.

ONSET OF EFFECT
Unknown.

DURATION OF ACTION
Unknown.

DIETARY ADVICE
Valdecoxib may be taken with or without food.

STORAGE
Store in a tightly sealed container away from heat, moisture, and direct light.

IF YOU MISS A DOSE
Take it as soon as you remember. If it is near the time for the next dose, skip the missed dose and resume your regular dosage schedule. Do not double the next dose.

STOPPING THE DRUG
The decision to stop taking valdecoxib should be made in consultation with your doctor.

PROLONGED USE
The risk of gastrointestinal side effects may be increased with extended use.

PRECAUTIONS
Over 60: No special problems are expected.

Driving and Hazardous Work: No special problems are expected.

Alcohol: Avoid alcohol when using this medication because it increases the risk of stomach irritation.

Pregnancy: Discuss with your doctor the relative risks and benefits of using this drug while pregnant. Do not use valdecoxib during the last trimester.

Breast Feeding: Valdecoxib may pass into breast milk; caution is advised. Consult your doctor for advice on whether to discontinue nursing or discontinue the drug.

Infants and Children: The safety and effectiveness of this drug have not been established for children under the age of 18.

Special Concerns: The risk of cardiovascular events may be increased in patients taking valdecoxib. Discuss these risks with your doctor before using this drug.

OVERDOSE
Symptoms: No cases of overdose have been reported. Symptoms may include lethargy, drowsiness, nausea, vomiting, abdominal pain, black, tarry stools, breathing difficulty, and coma.

What to Do: If you suspect an overdose or if someone takes a much larger dose than prescribed, call your doctor, emergency medical services (EMS), or the nearest poison control center immediately.

DRUG INTERACTIONS
Do not take this drug with aspirin or any other NSAIDs without your doctor's approval. In addition, consult your doctor if you are taking ACE inhibitors, hydralazine, furosemide, dextromethorphan, lithium, warfarin, fluconazole, or ketoconazole.

FOOD INTERACTIONS
No known food interactions.

DISEASE INTERACTIONS
Do not take valdecoxib immediately following coronary artery bypass graft (CABG) surgery. Valdecoxib should not be taken by people who have experienced asthma, hives, or allergic-type reactions after taking aspirin or other NSAIDs or by those with hypersensitivity to sulfonamides. Consult your doctor if you have any of the following: bleeding problems, inflammation or ulcers of the stomach and intestines, asthma, high blood pressure, or heart failure. Use of valdecoxib may cause complications in patients with liver or kidney disease, since these organs both work to remove the medication from the body.

Valproic Acid (Valproate; Divalproex Sodium)

Depakote 500 mg
(ABBOTT)

840

Additional photographs

▶ Drug Class: Anticonvulsant

▶ Available in: Capsules, syrup

▶ Available OTC? No

▶ As Generic? Yes

Side Effects

SERIOUS
Severe abdominal pain and vomiting, muscle weakness and lethargy, yellow discoloration of the skin or eyes, facial swelling, abnormal bleeding or bruising, or seizures may be a sign of liver failure or other potentially fatal complications. Call your doctor immediately.

COMMON
Nausea and vomiting, heartburn, diarrhea, cramps, loss of appetite and weight loss, increased appetite and weight gain, hair loss, tremor, dizziness, clumsiness or unsteadiness, confusion, sedation.

LESS COMMON
Drowsiness, restlessness, constipation, unusual excitability, skin rash, headache, blurred or double vision, irritability or other changes in mental state. There are numerous additional side effects; consult your doctor if you are concerned about any adverse or unusual reactions.

PRINCIPAL USES
To control certain types of seizures in the treatment of epilepsy and other disorders. Also used to treat acute mania in the treatment of bipolar disorder.

HOW THE DRUG WORKS
Valproic acid is thought to depress the activity of certain parts of the brain and suppress the abnormal firing of neurons that causes seizures.

DOSAGE
Adults and children: 7 to 27 mg per lb of body weight, in 3 or 4 divided doses. Higher doses may be required. A low dose is used to start; it may be gradually increased by your doctor to achieve maximum therapeutic benefit with a minimum of side effects.

ONSET OF EFFECT
Within several hours.

DURATION OF ACTION
Maximum effect lasts for 12 hours or longer. Effectiveness then gradually decreases.

DIETARY ADVICE
Take it with food to minimize stomach upset. The syrup can be taken with liquids, but avoid carbonated beverages because the combination can irritate the mouth and throat.

STORAGE
Store in a tightly sealed container away from heat, moisture, and direct light. Do not allow the syrup to freeze.

IF YOU MISS A DOSE
Take it as soon as you remember. If it is almost time for the next dose, skip the missed dose and resume your regular dosage schedule. Do not double the next dose without doctor's approval.

STOPPING THE DRUG
Abruptly stopping this drug may cause seizures. Your doctor will taper the dose over a period of weeks.

PROLONGED USE
See your doctor regularly for tests if you must take this drug for a prolonged period.

PRECAUTIONS
Over 60: Older patients may require lower doses to minimize side effects.

Driving and Hazardous Work: This drug may cause drowsiness or dizziness. Do not drive or engage in hazardous work until you determine how it affects you.

Alcohol: May contribute to excessive drowsiness.

Pregnancy: Valproic acid is associated with an increased risk of birth defects when taken during pregnancy. However, seizures during pregnancy can also increase the risks to the fetus. Discuss with your doctor the potential risks and benefits of using this drug during pregnancy. Folate supplementation is recommended starting 1 to 2 months before conception and throughout pregnancy.

Breast Feeding: Valproic acid passes into breast milk, although at low levels. Consult your doctor for specific advice before nursing.

Infants and Children: Adverse reactions may be more likely and more severe in children.

Special Concerns: The generic version of this drug is not recommended. Your doctor may advise you to wear a medical bracelet or carry an identification card saying that you are taking this drug.

OVERDOSE
Symptoms: Restlessness, sleepiness, hallucinations, trembling arms and hands, loss of consciousness.

What to Do: Call your doctor, emergency medical services (EMS), or the nearest poison control center immediately.

DRUG INTERACTIONS
Valproic acid can interact with many drugs, including other anticonvulsants (carbamazepine, clonazepam, ethosuximide, felbamate, lamotrigine, phenobarbital, phenytoin, primidone), antacids, aspirin and other NSAIDs, barbiturates, cholestyramine, haloperidol, heparin, isoniazid, loxapine, MAO inhibitors, maprotiline, phenobarbital, tricyclic antidepressants, and warfarin.

FOOD INTERACTIONS
No known food interactions.

DISEASE INTERACTIONS
Special caution is advised if you have a history of blood disease, brain disease, or kidney or liver disease.

Valsartan

- ▶ Drug Class: Antihypertensive/ angiotensin II antagonist
- ▶ Available in: Capsules
- ▶ Available OTC? No
- ▶ As Generic? No

Side Effects

SERIOUS
No serious side effects have been reported.

COMMON
No common side effects have been reported.

LESS COMMON
Headache, dizziness, upper respiratory infection, cough, diarrhea, rhinitis, sinusitis, nausea, viral infection, abdominal pain, fatigue, edema, joint pains, heart palpitations, skin rash, constipation, dry mouth, gas, anxiety, insomnia, erectile dysfunction (impotence) in men.

PRINCIPAL USES
To control high blood pressure. This drug appears to have the same benefits as the class of antihypertensive drugs known as ACE inhibitors, without producing the common side effect (experienced by as many as 30% of patients) of a dry cough. Valsartan may be used by itself or in conjunction with other antihypertensive medications.

HOW THE DRUG WORKS
Valsartan blocks the effects of angiotensin II, a naturally occurring substance that causes blood vessels to narrow. Valsartan causes the blood vessels to dilate, thereby lowering blood pressure and decreasing the workload of the heart.

DOSAGE
To start, 80 mg once a day. It may be increased by your doctor to a maximum dose of 320 mg per day.

ONSET OF EFFECT
Within 2 to 4 weeks.

DURATION OF ACTION
Unknown.

DIETARY ADVICE
Follow a healthy diet (low-salt, low-fat, low-cholesterol) as advised by your doctor to help control blood pressure and prevent heart disease.

STORAGE
Store in a tightly sealed container away from heat, moisture, and direct light.

IF YOU MISS A DOSE
Take it as soon as you remember. If it is near the time for the next dose, skip the missed dose and resume your regular dosage schedule. Do not double the next dose.

STOPPING THE DRUG
Take it as prescribed for the full treatment period. The decision to stop taking the drug should be made in consultation with your physician.

PROLONGED USE
Lifelong therapy may be necessary. However, if you do change certain health habits (for example, increasing exercise or losing weight), a reduced dose may be possible under a doctor's supervision.

PRECAUTIONS
Over 60: No special problems are expected.

Driving and Hazardous Work: Do not drive or engage in hazardous work until you determine how the medicine affects you.

Alcohol: No special precautions are necessary.

Pregnancy: In certain ways valsartan is similar to a class of drugs that have caused damage to the unborn child when taken in the second or third trimester of pregnancy. Because safer, more effective medications can lower blood pressure during pregnancy, and because adequate studies on the use of valsartan during pregnancy have not been done, women who are pregnant or planning to become pregnant should not take it.

Breast Feeding: Valsartan may pass into breast milk; caution is advised. Consult your doctor for advice.

Infants and Children: The safety and effectiveness of use in children have not been established.

Special Concerns: Valsartan may cause dizziness or lightheadedness, which is most noticeable when you change position. This may lead to fainting, falls, and injury. Sit or lie down immediately if you feel dizzy or lightheaded. This side effect may be worsened by alcohol, hot weather, dehydration, fever, prolonged standing, prolonged sitting, or exercise.

OVERDOSE
Symptoms: Fainting, dizziness, weak pulse that might be very slow or very fast, nausea, vomiting, confusion, chest pain.

What to Do: An overdose of valsartan is unlikely to be life-threatening. However, if someone takes a much larger dose than prescribed, call your doctor, emergency medical services (EMS), or the nearest poison control center immediately.

DRUG INTERACTIONS
No drug interactions have yet been observed with valsartan. Consult your doctor for specific advice if you are taking any other medication, including other drugs for high blood pressure. Valsartan can be taken together with diuretics or other medications for high blood pressure, if your doctor approves.

FOOD INTERACTIONS
No known food interactions.

DISEASE INTERACTIONS
Caution is advised when taking valsartan. Use of valsartan may cause complications in patients with liver or kidney disease, since these organs work together to remove the medication from the body.

Valsartan/Hydrochlorothiazide

▶ Drug Class: Antihypertensive/ angiotensin II antagonist; thiazide diuretic

▶ Available in: Tablets

▶ Available OTC? No

▶ As Generic? No

Side Effects

SERIOUS
No serious side effects have been reported.

COMMON
Dizziness, fatigue.

LESS COMMON
Viral infection, sore throat, coughing, diarrhea.

PRINCIPAL USES

To control high blood pressure (hypertension). Valsartan appears to have the same benefits as the class of antihypertensive drugs known as ACE inhibitors, without producing the common side effect (experienced by as many as 30% of patients) of a dry cough. This drug combination is not used as initial treatment for hypertension.

HOW THE DRUG WORKS

This drug combines an angiotensin II antagonist (valsartan) and a thiazide diuretic (hydrochlorothiazide). Valsartan blocks the effects of angiotensin II, a naturally occurring substance that causes blood vessels to narrow. Valsartan causes the blood vessels to dilate, thereby lowering blood pressure and decreasing the workload of the heart. Hydrochlorothiazide (HCTZ) increases the excretion of salt and water in the urine. By reducing the overall fluid volume in the body, it decreases blood volume and so reduces pressure within the blood vessels.

DOSAGE

To start, 1 tablet containing 80 mg valsartan and 12.5 mg HCTZ once a day. The dose may be increased by your doctor to a maximum of 4 of these tablets or 2 tablets containing 160 mg valsartan and 12.5 mg HCTZ once a day.

ONSET OF EFFECT

Valsartan component: 2 to 4 weeks. HCTZ component: 2 to 4 hours.

DURATION OF ACTION

Valsartan component: Unknown. HCTZ component: 6 to 12 hours.

DIETARY ADVICE

It can be be taken with food to avoid stomach upset.

STORAGE

Store in a tightly sealed container away from heat, moisture, and direct light.

IF YOU MISS A DOSE

If you miss a dose on one day, do not double the dose the next day.

STOPPING THE DRUG

The decision to stop taking it should be made in consultation with your doctor.

PROLONGED USE

Lifelong therapy may be necessary.

PRECAUTIONS

Over 60: No special problems are expected.

Driving and Hazardous Work: Exercise caution until you determine how the medicine affects you.

Alcohol: No special precautions are necessary.

Pregnancy: Because safer, more effective medications can lower blood pressure during pregnancy, and because adequate studies have not been done on the use of this drug during pregnancy, women who are pregnant or planning to become pregnant should not take this medication unless recommended by your doctor.

Breast Feeding: Because of the potential for side effects on the infant, discuss with your doctor the relative risks and benefits of using this drug while nursing.

Infants and Children: The safety and effectiveness of use in children have not been established.

Special Concerns: The drug may cause dizziness or lightheadedness, which is most noticeable when you change position. This may lead to fainting, falls, and injury. Sit or lie down immediately if you feel dizzy or lightheaded. This side effect may be worsened by alcohol, hot weather, dehydration, fever, prolonged standing or sitting, or exercise. This medicine may cause your body to lose potassium. However, do not eat potassium-rich foods, salt substitutes, or take a potassium supplement without consulting your doctor.

OVERDOSE

Symptoms: Few cases of overdose have been reported. Symptoms may include: fainting, lethargy, dizziness, drowsiness, weak pulse that might be very slow or very fast, nausea, vomiting, confusion, chest pain.

What to Do: Call your doctor, emergency medical services (EMS), or the nearest poison control center immediately.

DRUG INTERACTIONS

Consult your doctor for specific advice if you are taking anticoagulants, cholestyramine, colestipol, drugs for diabetes, nonsteroidal anti-inflammatory drugs, digitalis drugs, or lithium.

FOOD INTERACTIONS

No known food interactions.

DISEASE INTERACTIONS

Consult your doctor if you have any of the following: diabetes, gout, systemic lupus erythematosus (SLE), pancreatitis, heart disease, blood vessel disease. This medication should be used with caution in patients with moderate to severe liver or kidney disease.

Vancomycin

BRAND NAMES
Lyphocin, Vancocin,
Vancoled

Vancocin 125 mg
(LILLY)

▶ Drug Class: Antibiotic

▶ Available in: Capsules, oral
solution, injection

▶ Available OTC? No

▶ As Generic? Yes

Side Effects

SERIOUS
Skin rash (with oral
forms), change in the
frequency or amount
of urination, breathing
difficulty, drowsiness,
unusual thirst, loss of
appetite, weakness,
hearing loss, ringing or
buzzing in ears, chills
or fever, fast heartbeat,
fainting, nausea or vomiting, itching, redness of
face, neck, upper back,
and arms, tingling,
unpleasant taste. Call
your doctor immediately.

COMMON
Bitter or unpleasant taste,
mouth irritation.

LESS COMMON
There are no less-com-
mon side effects associ-
ated with the use of
vancomycin.

PRINCIPAL USES
To treat severe bacterial
infections such as colitis
(infection and inflammation
of the colon); also used
prior to surgical or dental
procedures to prevent heart
valve infection in susceptible patients (for example,
those with a history of
rheumatic fever or heart
valve replacement) who
are allergic to penicillin.

HOW THE DRUG WORKS
Vancomycin kills and
inhibits the growth of bacteria by interrupting their formation of cell walls.

DOSAGE
To treat bacterial infec-
tions— Oral forms: Adults
and teenagers: 125 to 500
mg, 4 times a day for 5 to
10 days. Children: 4.5 mg
per lb of body weight (up to
125 mg), 4 times a day for 5
to 10 days. Injection: Adults
and teenagers: 1,000 mg
twice a day or 500 mg, 4
times a day. Children: 4.5
mg per lb, 4 times a day or
9.1 mg per lb, 2 times a day.
Infants over 1 week: 6.8 mg
per lb to start, then 4.5 mg
per lb, 3 times a day. Newborns up to 1 week: 6.8 mg
per lb to start, then 4.5 mg
per lb, 2 times a day. To
prevent heart valve infection— Injection: Adults and
teenagers: 1,000 mg 1 hour
before surgery or dental
work, then 1,000 mg, 8
hours later. Children: 9.1
mg per lb of body weight 1
hour before surgery or dental work, then 9.1 mg per lb,
8 hours later.

ONSET OF EFFECT
Unknown.

DURATION OF ACTION
Unknown.

DIETARY ADVICE
No special restrictions.

STORAGE
Store the medicine in a
tightly sealed container
away from heat, moisture,
and direct light. Refrigerate
any liquid form but do not
allow it to freeze.

IF YOU MISS A DOSE
Take it as soon as you
remember. If it is near the
time for the next dose, skip
the missed dose and
resume your regular dosage
schedule. Do not double the
next dose.

STOPPING THE DRUG
Take it as prescribed for the
full treatment period, even
if you feel better before the
scheduled end of therapy.

PROLONGED USE
If your symptoms do not
improve or instead become
worse after a few days, consult your doctor.

PRECAUTIONS
Over 60: Adverse reactions
may be more likely and
more severe in older
patients.

**Driving and Hazardous
Work:** No special precautions are necessary.

Alcohol: No special problems are expected, although
it is generally advisable to
avoid alcohol when recovering from an infection.

Pregnancy: Adequate studies of the use of vancomycin
during pregnancy have not
been done, although no
problems are expected.
Before using vancomycin,
consult your doctor if you
are pregnant or plan to
become pregnant.

Breast Feeding: Vancomycin passes into breast
milk; caution is advised.
Consult your doctor for
specific advice.

Infants and Children:
Consult your pediatrician
about the relative risks and
benefits of using vanco-
mycin for children.

Special Concerns: If you
take vancomycin for diar-
rhea caused by other antibiotics, do not take any other
diarrhea medicine without
consulting your doctor.

OVERDOSE
Symptoms: Hearing loss,
ringing in ears, dizziness.

What to Do: Call your
doctor, emergency medical
services (EMS), or the
nearest poison control
center immediately.

DRUG INTERACTIONS
Other drugs may interact
with vancomycin. Consult
your doctor for specific
advice if you are taking
cholestyramine, colestipol
(with oral forms of van-
comycin), aminoglycosides,
amphotericin B, bacitracin,
bumetanide, capreomycin,
cisplatin, cyclosporine,
ethacrynic acid, furosemide,
paromomycin, polymixins,
or streptozocin.

FOOD INTERACTIONS
No known food interactions.

DISEASE INTERACTIONS
Consult your doctor if you
have a history of kidney disease, inflammatory bowel
disease, or hearing loss.

Vardenafil Hydrochloride

▶ Drug Class: Phosphodi-esterase type 5 inhibitor

▶ Available in: Tablets

▶ Available OTC? No

▶ As Generic? No

Side Effects

SERIOUS

Rarely, a painful or prolonged erection (lasting more than 4 hours) may occur. If erection does not resolve on its own in a reasonable amount of time, seek medical help promptly. If erection does resolve on its own, consult your doctor for specific guidelines. Serious cardiovascular events such as heart attack, sudden cardiac death, cardiac arrhythmias, cerebral hemorrhage, and transient ischemic attack have been reported following the use of similar drugs. However, it is unclear whether these events are due to the consumption of the drug, the presence of preexisting cardiovascular risk factors, sexual activity, or a combination of these factors.

COMMON

Headache, indigestion, dizziness, flushing, stuffy or runny nose. Such side effects are generally mild to moderate and usually short-lived.

LESS COMMON

Vision abnormalities, bloodshot or burning eyes, diarrhea, blood in the urine.

PRINCIPAL USES

To treat erectile dysfunction (impotence), which may occur in association with atherosclerosis, vascular disease or other circulatory problems, diabetes, kidney disease, hormonal abnormalities, neurological disease or injury, severe depression or other psychological difficulties.

HOW THE DRUG WORKS

Vardenafil works by increasing the blood flow to the penis necessary for establishing and maintaining an erection. The drug accomplishes this by selectively inhibiting the action of an enzyme (phosphodiesterase type 5) that breaks down a substance that relaxes smooth muscles and permits blood flow that engorges the columns of erectile tissue in the penis. Unlike other treatments for erectile dysfunction, which produce erections with or without sexual arousal, vardenafil allows the patient to respond naturally to sexual stimulation.

DOSAGE

The recommended dose for most patients is 10 mg, taken approximately 1 hour before sexual activity. The dose may be increased to no more than 20 mg, or may be decreased to 5 mg. Your doctor will help to determine the correct dose for you. Do not take the drug more than once in a 24-hour period.

ONSET OF EFFECT

Within 30 minutes to 2 hours.

DURATION OF ACTION

Unknown.

DIETARY ADVICE

Vardenafil can be taken without regard to meals.

STORAGE

Store in a tightly sealed container away from heat, moisture, and direct light.

IF YOU MISS A DOSE

Not applicable. Vardenafil is taken only as needed.

STOPPING THE DRUG

Not applicable.

PROLONGED USE

Vardenafil treats but does not cure erectile dysfunction. Patients must continue using vardenafil to maintain its benefit; lifelong therapy may be warranted.

PRECAUTIONS

Over 60: No special problems are expected.

Driving and Hazardous Work: This drug should not impair your ability to perform such tasks safely.

Alcohol: No special precautions are necessary. However, alcohol is known to decrease sexual function.

Pregnancy: Not applicable; vardenafil is not approved for use by women.

Breast Feeding: Not applicable; vardenafil is not approved for use by women.

Infants and Children: Not applicable; vardenafil is not to be used by children.

Special Concerns: Vardenafil does not offer any protection against sexually transmitted diseases. Appropriate measures (for example, using condoms) should be taken to ensure adequate protection against sexually transmitted diseases, including infection with the human immunodeficiency virus (HIV). Vardenafil should be taken only by men who have been clinically evaluated for and diagnosed with erectile dysfunction by a doctor.

OVERDOSE

Symptoms: No cases of overdose have been reported.

What to Do: An overdose with vardenafil is unlikely. If someone takes a much larger dose than prescribed, call your doctor.

DRUG INTERACTIONS

Vardenafil can enhance the action of nitrates (such as nitroglycerin, which is used to treat episodes of angina) and alpha-blockers, causing potentially dangerous decreases in blood pressure. Therefore, vardenafil should not be used by patients taking nitrates of any kind or alpha-blockers. Use of vardenafil in conjunction with other erectile-dysfunction medications is not recommended. Consult your doctor if you are taking protease inhibitors such as ritonavir and saquinavir, which may affect levels of vardenafil in the blood.

FOOD INTERACTIONS

No known food interactions.

DISEASE INTERACTIONS

Caution is advised when taking vardenafil. Consult your doctor if you have a history of any of the following: high or very low blood pressure; structural deformity of the penis; a bleeding disorder; heart attack, stroke, or life-threatening arrhythmia within the past six months; heart failure; coronary heart disease; retinitis pigmentosa; peptic ulcer; sickle cell anemia; multiple myeloma; or leukemia.

Vasopressin (8-Arginine-Vasopressin)

▸ Drug Class: Antidiuretic hormone

▸ Available in: Injection, nasal spray

▸ Available OTC? No

▸ As Generic? No

Side Effects

SERIOUS
Allergic response characterized by wheezing, rash, hives, itching, swelling of face, lips, hands, or feet, closing of throat, breathing difficulty, and slow or irregular pulse; drowsiness; water intoxication causing listlessness, headache, confusion, weight gain, seizures, loss of consciousness. Call your doctor immediately.

COMMON
No common side effects have been reported.

LESS COMMON
Tremor, dizziness, chest pain, abdominal cramps, nausea, vomiting, diarrhea, inability to urinate, pale skin around mouth, profuse or unusual sweating, uterine cramps. Such symptoms are generally associated only with excessively large doses.

PRINCIPAL USES
To treat diabetes insipidus, a relatively rare disorder characterized by excessive loss of water in the urine, potentially leading to dehydration. Vasopressin is generally prescribed for short-term use only and has largely been replaced by a long-lasting analog known as DDAVP (desmopressin acetate).

HOW THE DRUG WORKS
Vasopressin is a hormone involved in kidney function. It helps the kidneys to reabsorb water from urine before it is excreted, thereby maintaining proper fluid and electrolyte balance in the body.

DOSAGE
Subcutaneous (under the skin) injection— Adults: 5 to 10 units, 2 or 3 times a day. Children: 2.5 to 10 units, 3 or 4 times a day. Nasal spray— Adults or children: Spray into nostril as directed by your doctor.

ONSET OF EFFECT
Within 1 hour.

DURATION OF ACTION
From 6 to 8 hours.

DIETARY ADVICE
It can be taken with or between meals. Take it with 1 or 2 glasses of water to prevent nausea, skin whitening, and abdominal cramps.

STORAGE
Store in a tightly sealed container away from heat and direct light.

IF YOU MISS A DOSE
Take it as soon as you remember. If it is near the time for the next dose, skip the missed dose and resume your regular dosage schedule. Do not double the next dose.

STOPPING THE DRUG
The decision to stop taking the drug should be made by your doctor.

PROLONGED USE
No apparent problems are associated with prolonged use of vasopressin.

PRECAUTIONS
Over 60: Adverse reactions may be more likely and more severe in older patients.

Driving and Hazardous Work: Do not drive or engage in hazardous work until you determine how the medicine affects you.

Alcohol: Drink alcohol only in moderation.

Pregnancy: Vasopressin has not been shown to cause birth defects or other problems in humans. Animal and human studies have not been done. Before you take the drug, tell your doctor if you are pregnant or are planning to become pregnant.

Breast Feeding: Vasopressin has not been shown to cause problems in nursing babies. Consult your doctor about its use if you are breast feeding.

Infants and Children: Adverse reactions may be more likely and more severe in children under the age of 18.

Special Concerns: Electrocardiograms and laboratory tests of fluid status should be done periodically while you take vasopressin. Tell your doctor if you are allergic to any preservative or dye. Vasopressin may worsen the effect of migraine headaches.

OVERDOSE
Symptoms: Drowsiness, listlessness, headache, confusion, inability to urinate, unexpected weight gain or fluid retention.

What to Do: An overdose of vasopressin is unlikely to be life-threatening, but it can cause excessive retention of water (water intoxication) and spasm of the blood vessels. If someone takes a much larger dose than prescribed, call your doctor, emergency medical services (EMS), or poison control center immediately.

DRUG INTERACTIONS
Consult your physician for specific advice if you are taking carbamazepine, chlorpropamide, demeclocycline, ethanol, fludrocortisone, heparin, lithium, norepinephrine, or tricyclic antidepressants.

FOOD INTERACTIONS
No known food interactions.

DISEASE INTERACTIONS
Consult your doctor if you have a history of any of the following: seizures, migraine headaches, asthma, heart disease, blood vessel disease, heart failure, or kidney disease.

Venlafaxine

Effexor 37.5 mg
(WYETH-AYERST)

▶ Drug Class: Antidepressant

▶ Available in: Tablets, extended-release capsules

▶ Available OTC? No

▶ As Generic? No

Side Effects

SERIOUS
Headache, changes in or blurred vision, decreased sexual ability or desire, difficulty urinating, itching, skin rash, chest pain, heartbeat irregularities, changes in moods or mental state, extreme drowsiness or fatigue. Call your physician immediately.

COMMON
Fatigue, dizziness or drowsiness, anxiety, dry mouth, changed sense of taste, loss of appetite, nausea, vomiting, chills, diarrhea, constipation, prickly sensation of skin, heartburn, increased sweating, runny nose, stomach gas or pain, insomnia, unusual dreams, weight loss.

LESS COMMON
Frequent yawning, twitching.

PRINCIPAL USES
To treat symptoms of major depression and generalized anxiety disorder (GAD).

HOW THE DRUG WORKS
Venlafaxine helps to balance levels of serotonin and norepinephrine, brain chemicals that are profoundly linked to mood, emotions, and mental state.

DOSAGE
Tablets: Adults: To start, 75 mg a day in 2 or 3 divided doses. The dose may be gradually increased by your doctor to 375 mg a day. Extended-release capsules: To start, 75 mg, once a day. The dose may be increased by up to 75 mg at a time at intervals of not less than 4 days, up to a maximum dose of 225 mg a day.

ONSET OF EFFECT
2 weeks or more.

DURATION OF ACTION
Unknown.

DIETARY ADVICE
Venlafaxine should be taken with meals.

STORAGE
Store in a tightly sealed container away from heat, moisture, and direct light.

IF YOU MISS A DOSE
Tablets: Take it as soon as you remember, unless the time for your next scheduled dose is within the next 2 hours. If so, skip the missed dose, take the next scheduled dose, and resume your regular schedule. Do not double the next dose. Extended-release capsules: If you miss a dose on one day, do not double the dose the next day.

STOPPING THE DRUG
Take this medication as prescribed for the full treatment period, even if you begin to feel better before the scheduled end of therapy.

PROLONGED USE
See your doctor regularly for tests and examinations if you must take this medicine for a prolonged period.

PRECAUTIONS
Over 60: No special problems are expected.

Driving and Hazardous Work: Do not drive or engage in hazardous work until you determine how the medicine affects you.

Alcohol: Avoid alcohol.

Pregnancy: Adequate studies of venlafaxine use during pregnancy have not been done. Before you take venlafaxine, tell your doctor if you are pregnant or plan to become pregnant.

Breast Feeding: It is not known whether venlafaxine passes into breast milk; caution is advised. Consult your doctor for specific advice.

Infants and Children: The safety and effectiveness of venlafaxine use by infants and children have not been established. Antidepressants increase the risk of suicidal thinking and behavior (suicidality) in children with major depression and other psychiatric disorders. Discuss with your doctor this risk versus the benefits of using this drug. Children should be observed closely for worsening of symptoms, suicidality, or unusual changes in behavior at the onset of therapy and when making changes in dosage.

Special Concerns: Venlafaxine can cause an elevation in blood pressure. Therefore, blood pressure should be monitored regularly, especially in the first several months of therapy.

OVERDOSE
Symptoms: Extreme drowsiness or fatigue.

What to Do: Call your doctor, emergency medical services (EMS), or the nearest poison control center immediately.

DRUG INTERACTIONS
Venlafaxine and MAO inhibitors should not be used within 14 days of each other. Serious side effects such as myoclonus (uncontrolled muscle spasms), hyperthermia (excessive rise in body temperature), and extreme stiffness may result. Consult your doctor for specific advice if you are taking any other prescription or over-the-counter medication.

FOOD INTERACTIONS
No known food interactions.

DISEASE INTERACTIONS
Consult your physician if you have a history of any of the following: high or low blood pressure, alcohol or drug abuse, heart disease, or seizures. Use of venlafaxine may cause complications in patients with liver or kidney disease, since these organs work together to remove the medication from the body.

Verapamil Hydrochloride

Isoptin SR 120 mg
(KNOLL)

Additional photographs

▸ Drug Class: Calcium channel blocker

▸ Available in: Extended-release capsules, tablets, injection

▸ Available OTC? No

▸ As Generic? Yes

Side Effects

SERIOUS
Breathing difficulty, coughing, or wheezing; irregular or pounding heartbeat; chest pain; extreme dizziness; fainting. Call your doctor immediately.

COMMON
Headache, dizziness, constipation, flushing and a feeling of warmth, swelling in the feet, ankles, or calves, heart palpitations.

LESS COMMON
Diarrhea, nausea, unusual fatigue and weakness, skin rash, increased urination, ringing in the ears.

PRINCIPAL USES
To treat high blood pressure, angina pectoris (chest pain associated with heart disease), and heartbeat irregularities (cardiac arrhythmias).

HOW THE DRUG WORKS
Verapamil interferes with the movement of calcium into heart muscle cells and the smooth muscle cells in the walls of the arteries. This action relaxes blood vessels (causing them to widen), which lowers blood pressure, increases the blood supply to the heart, and decreases the heart's overall workload.

DOSAGE
Adults: 40 to 160 mg, 3 times a day. Your doctor may increase dose as necessary, up to a maximum of 480 mg per day. Extended-release capsules: 200 to 480 mg once a day. Extended-release tablets: 120 mg once a day to 240 mg every 12 hours. Children: Dose is determined by a pediatrician.

ONSET OF EFFECT
Oral forms: 1 to 2 hours. Injection: 1 to 5 minutes.

DURATION OF ACTION
Extended-release capsules: 24 hours. Tablets: 8 to 10 hours. Injection: 1 to 6 hours.

DIETARY ADVICE
Take oral forms with food.

STORAGE
Store in a tightly sealed container away from heat and direct light.

IF YOU MISS A DOSE
Take it as soon as you remember. If it is near the time for the next dose, skip the missed dose and resume your regular dosage schedule. Do not double the next dose.

STOPPING THE DRUG
Do not stop taking this drug suddenly, as this may cause potentially serious health problems. If therapy is to be discontinued, dosage should be reduced gradually, according to doctor's instructions.

PROLONGED USE
Lifetime therapy with verapamil may be necessary; regular medical exams and tests are important in such cases.

PRECAUTIONS

Over 60: Adverse reactions may be more likely and more severe in older patients.

Driving and Hazardous Work: Do not drive or engage in hazardous work until you determine how the medicine affects you.

Alcohol: Avoid alcohol.

Pregnancy: Large doses of verapamil have been shown to cause birth defects in animals; human studies have not been done. Before you take verapamil, tell your doctor if you are pregnant or plan to become pregnant.

Breast Feeding: Verapamil passes into breast milk but has not been reported to cause problems; caution is advised. Consult your doctor for advice.

Infants and Children: Oral doses for children 1 to 15 years old must be determined by your pediatrician.

Special Concerns: In addition to taking verapamil, be sure to follow all special instructions on weight control and diet. Your doctor will tell you which specific factors are most important for you. Check with your doctor before making changes in your diet. Extended-release forms should not be crushed or chewed.

OVERDOSE
Symptoms: Extremely slow heartbeat and heart palpitations; dizziness or fainting (due to excessively low blood pressure).

What to Do: Call your doctor, emergency medical services (EMS), or the nearest poison control center immediately.

DRUG INTERACTIONS
Consult your physician for specific advice if you are taking acetazolamide, amphotericin B, corticosteroids, dichlorphenamide, diuretics, methazolamide, beta-blockers, carbamazepine, cyclosporine, lithium, procainamide, quinidine, digitalis, disopyramide or the following eye medicines: betaxolol, levobunolol, metipranolol, or timolol.

FOOD INTERACTIONS
Avoid foods high in sodium.

DISEASE INTERACTIONS
Caution is advised when taking verapamil. Consult your doctor if you have any of the following: abnormal heart rhythm or other disorders of the heart and blood vessels, mental depression, or Parkinson's disease. Verapamil may cause complications in patients with liver or kidney disease, since these organs work together to remove the medication from the body.

Vitamin A (Retinol)

BRAND NAMES
Alphalin, Aquasol A, Del-Vi-A, Solaneed, Vi-Dom-A

Aquasol A 25,000 IU
(ASTRA)

▶ Drug Class: Vitamin

▶ Available in: Capsules, oral solution, tablets

▶ Available OTC? Yes

▶ As Generic? Yes

Side Effects

SERIOUS
No serious side effects occur with recommended doses of vitamin A (see Overdose).

COMMON
No common side effects occur with recommended doses of vitamin A.

LESS COMMON
No less-common side effects occur with recommended doses of vitamin A.

PRINCIPAL USES
To treat vitamin A deficiency. Most Americans get sufficient amounts of vitamin A from their diet. Most vitamin A is obtained from the conversion of dietary beta-carotene to vitamin A in the intestine. Foods rich in beta-carotene include yellow-orange fruits and vegetables; dark-green leafy vegetables such as spinach and lettuce; liver; and fortified milk and margarine. Supplementation may be necessary with certain medical conditions such as long-term chronic illness, liver disorders, intestinal malabsorption associated with chronic diarrhea or pancreatic disease, and surgical removal of the stomach. Vitamin A deficiency can cause night blindness, dry eyes, eye infections, and skin problems.

HOW THE DRUG WORKS
Vitamin A plays an essential role in night vision and proper growth and maintenance of the skin, bones, and reproductive organs.

DOSAGE
For severe vitamin A deficiency: 100,000 International Units (IU) daily for 3 days, followed by 25,000 to 50,000 IU daily for 2 weeks, then 10,000 to 20,000 IU daily for 2 months. To prevent vitamin deficiency, recommended dietary allowances (RDAs)— Adults: 3,330 IU daily for men, 2,665 IU daily for women. Children ages 7 to 10: 2,330 IU daily. Children ages 4 to 6: 1,665 IU daily. Children ages 1 to 3: 1,330 IU daily. Infants: 1,250 IU daily.

ONSET OF EFFECT
Unknown.

DURATION OF ACTION
Unknown.

DIETARY ADVICE
Absorption of vitamin A requires some fat in the diet.

STORAGE
Store in a tightly sealed container away from heat, moisture, and direct light.

IF YOU MISS A DOSE
Take it as soon as you remember.

STOPPING THE DRUG
If you are taking vitamin A because of a deficiency, take it as prescribed for the full treatment period.

PROLONGED USE
Prolonged use of high doses may cause serious toxicity (see Overdose).

PRECAUTIONS
Over 60: Adverse reactions associated with high-dose, long-term use may be more likely and more severe in older patients.

Driving and Hazardous Work: The use of recommended doses of vitamin A should not impair your ability to perform such tasks safely.

Alcohol: No special precautions are necessary.

Pregnancy: Adequate vitamin A intake is essential during pregnancy. However, vitamin A overdose (more than 6,000 IU daily) can cause birth defects or slow or reduce growth in the fetus.

Breast Feeding: Vitamin A passes into breast milk; caution is advised. Ingesting too much vitamin A during breast feeding can be harmful to the nursing infant.

Infants and Children: Children are more sensitive to side effects from high doses of vitamin A.

Special Concerns: Vitamin A can be highly toxic (see Overdose) when taken in high doses. Take only as directed.

OVERDOSE
Symptoms: Acute overdose: Bleeding from gums, sore mouth, confusion or unusual excitement, diarrhea, drowsiness or dizziness, double vision, severe headache, irritability, peeling skin, especially on lips and palms, severe vomiting. Chronic overdose (with prolonged overuse): Drying or cracking of skin or lips, bone or joint pain, fever, general feeling of discomfort, increased sensitivity of skin to sunlight, increased urination, loss of appetite, hair loss, stomach pain, unusual fatigue, yellow-orange patches on soles of feet, palms of hands, or skin around the nose and lips.

What to Do: For an acute overdose, call your doctor, emergency medical services (EMS), or the nearest poison control center immediately. For symptoms of chronic overdose, contact your doctor.

DRUG INTERACTIONS
Consult your doctor for specific advice if you are taking etretinate or isotretinoin.

FOOD INTERACTIONS
No known food interactions.

DISEASE INTERACTIONS
Consult your doctor if you have a history of alcohol abuse, liver disease, or kidney disease.

Vitamin B$_6$ (Pyridoxine)

▶ Drug Class: Dietary supplement

▶ Available in: Tablets

▶ Available OTC? Yes

▶ As Generic? Yes

Side Effects

SERIOUS
When taken for several months, high doses of vitamin B6 (2 to 6 grams daily) may cause reversible nerve damage; symptoms include numbness, tingling, or prickling in the feet, loss of manual dexterity, and unsteady gait.

COMMON
No common side effects are associated with recommended doses.

LESS COMMON
No less-common side effects are associated with recommended doses.

PRINCIPAL USES
To treat or prevent vitamin B$_6$ deficiency, which can cause anemia, dermatitis, nervous system problems, and painful cracking at the outer sides of the mouth. Deficiency does not occur in healthy people eating a well-balanced diet. However, several genetic abnormalities may lead to a requirement for higher doses of vitamin B$_6$ than can be obtained from the diet. Supplements may also be necessary in people with alcoholism, an overactive thyroid, or intestinal diseases associated with nutritional malabsorption.

HOW THE DRUG WORKS
Vitamin B$_6$ is used to manufacture a substance required for the proper action of enzymes involved in the metabolism of carbohydrates, fats, and proteins.

DOSAGE
Recommended dietary allowances (RDAs) for vitamin B$_6$ are 0.1 to 0.5 mg from birth to age 3; 0.6 mg from age 4 to 8; 1.0 mg from age 9 to 13; 1.3 mg in adolescent and adult males; and 1.2 to 1.3 mg in adolescent and adult females. For men over 51: 1.7 mg; For women over 51: 1.5 mg. For vitamin B6 deficiency or an inherited abnormality causing increased vitamin B$_6$ requirements, consult your doctor.

ONSET OF EFFECT
Unknown.

DURATION OF ACTION
As long as the vitamin is taken.

DIETARY ADVICE
Eat a well-balanced diet. Foods rich in vitamin B$_6$ include egg yolks, meats, bananas, and whole grain cereals.

STORAGE
Store in a cool, dry place.

IF YOU MISS A DOSE
Take the next regularly scheduled dose.

STOPPING THE DRUG
If the vitamin was prescribed for a deficiency, consult your doctor before stopping.

PROLONGED USE
No problems are expected with recommended doses of vitamin B$_6$.

PRECAUTIONS
Over 60: No special problems are expected with recommended doses.

Driving and Hazardous Work: No special precautions are necessary.

Alcohol: Alcoholism can lead to a vitamin B$_6$ deficiency. Conversely, those who are being treated for vitamin B$_6$ deficiency should abstain from alcohol.

Pregnancy: Vitamin B$_6$ requirements increase during pregnancy to 1.9 mg per day. Very large doses may cause vitamin B$_6$ dependency in the newborn child.

Breast Feeding: Vitamin B$_6$ requirements increase during breast feeding to 2.0 mg per day.

Infants and Children: No problems are expected with recommended doses.

OVERDOSE
Symptoms: Overdose is extremely rare. Two cases that caused central nervous system toxicity (see Serious Side Effects) have been reported.

What to Do: Although an overdose is highly unlikely to occur, call your doctor right away if you have any reason to suspect that one has occurred.

DRUG INTERACTIONS
Vitamin B$_6$ is used in the treatment of toxicity associated with the drugs cycloserine and isoniazid. Other drugs that may increase the daily requirement for vitamin B$_6$ include ethionamide, hydralazine, penicillamine, immunosuppressants, and estrogen.

FOOD INTERACTIONS
No food interactions have been reported.

DISEASE INTERACTIONS
No disease interactions have been reported.

Vitamin B$_{12}$ (Cyanocobalamin)

▶ Drug Class: Dietary supplement

▶ Available in: Tablets, extended-release tablets, injection, nasal gel

▶ Available OTC? Yes

▶ As Generic? Yes

Side Effects

SERIOUS
Breathing difficulty, fever, hives, rash, swelling of face, mouth, lips, throat, or tongue. These may be signs of a rare but potentially serious allergic reaction. Seek medical assistance immediately.

COMMON
No common side effects have been reported with recommended doses.

LESS COMMON
Mild allergic reaction, diarrhea, itching.

PRINCIPAL USES
Cyanocobalamin is a synthetic form of vitamin B$_{12}$, prescribed to correct vitamin B$_{12}$ deficiency and to remedy the associated medical conditions (anemia and nerve damage) that may result from such a deficiency. B$_{12}$ deficiency can occur for a number of reasons, including a diet lacking in animal protein, pernicious anemia, intestinal malabsorption, surgical removal of portions of the stomach or small intestine, the effects of certain drugs (including colchicine, neomycin, and PAS), or because an individual is unable to keep up with an increase in the daily requirements of the vitamin (as occurs during pregnancy or during periods of great physical stress).

HOW THE DRUG WORKS
Vitamin B$_{12}$ is essential for the proper production of blood platelets and red and white blood cells, the manufacture of vital substances needed for cell function, and the metabolism of nutrients necessary for cell growth.

DOSAGE
Recommended dietary allowances (RDAs)— Adults and teenagers: 2.4 micrograms (mcg). Pregnant or breast-feeding women: 2.6 to 2.8 mcg. Children ages 9 to 13: 1.8 mcg. Children ages 4 to 8: 1.2 mcg. From birth to 3 years of age: 0.4 to 0.9 mcg. (Extended-release tablets are not recommended for children.) To treat severe vitamin B$_{12}$ deficiency— The dose will be determined by your doctor based on individual criteria. Patients with pernicious anemia or loss of intestinal function require the injection form of vitamin B$_{12}$. As an alternative to the injection, patients may use the nasal gel with a dose of 500 mcg, once a week.

ONSET OF EFFECT
Immediate.

DURATION OF ACTION
For as long as the supplement is taken.

DIETARY ADVICE
Eat a healthy, well-balanced diet. Foods rich in vitamin B$_{12}$ include animal protein (such as beef, lamb, and veal), clams and oysters, liver, fish, milk, and egg yolks.

STORAGE
Store in a tightly sealed container away from heat, moisture, and direct light.

IF YOU MISS A DOSE
Take the next regularly scheduled dose.

STOPPING THE DRUG
If the vitamin was prescribed for a deficiency, consult your doctor before stopping.

PROLONGED USE
Therapy may require weeks or months. Lifelong therapy is necessary for pernicious anemia or following certain types of gastrointestinal surgery. No problems are expected with prolonged use when the vitamin is taken as directed.

PRECAUTIONS
Over 60: No special problems are expected with recommended doses.

Driving and Hazardous Work: No special precautions are necessary.

Alcohol: Alcoholism can lead to pancreatic insufficiency and vitamin B$_{12}$ malabsorption.

Pregnancy: Vitamin B$_{12}$ requirements increase during pregnancy to 2.6 mcg daily.

Breast Feeding: Vitamin B$_{12}$ requirements increase during breast feeding to 2.8 mcg per day.

Infants and Children: No problems are expected with recommended doses.

Special Concerns: Vitamin B$_{12}$ deficiency is unlikely to occur in healthy people who are able to consume a normal, balanced diet. However, nutritional supplements should be considered for those who are ill or weakened by radiation therapy, chemotherapy, or any other condition that interferes with normal food and fluid intake. Also, healthy adults over age 51 should aim to meet their vitamin B$_{12}$ requirements with the use of B$_{12}$-fortified foods (such as fortified ready-to-eat cereal) or supplements.

OVERDOSE
Symptoms: Overdose is extremely rare.

What to Do: Although an overdose is highly unlikely, call your doctor right away if you have any reason to suspect that one has occurred.

DRUG INTERACTIONS
Consult your doctor for specific advice if you are taking analgesics, antibiotics, colchicine, folic acid, or other vitamin supplements.

FOOD INTERACTIONS
No known food interactions.

DISEASE INTERACTIONS
Consult your doctor if you have Leber's disease (a very rare eye disease).

Vitamin C (Ascorbic Acid)

Generic 500 mg
(NUTRO)

Additional photographs

▶ Drug Class: Dietary
  supplement

▶ Available in: Tablets,
  capsules

▶ Available OTC? Yes

▶ As Generic? Yes

Side Effects

SERIOUS
Occasionally, kidney
stones may develop
(especially with doses
greater than 1 g per day
over a prolonged period
of time), causing back,
side, or flank pain.

COMMON
No common side effects
are associated with rec-
ommended doses.

LESS COMMON
High doses may cause
diarrhea, flushing and
redness of the skin, nau-
sea and vomiting, or
headache.

PRINCIPAL USES
To prevent or treat vitamin
C deficiency, which causes
scurvy, a disorder characterized by bleeding into the
skin, swollen and bleeding
gums, poor wound healing,
muscle weakness, and
fatigue. Deficiency does not
occur in healthy people eating a well-balanced diet. Vitamin C requirements may
be increased in those with
AIDS, alcoholism, overac-
tive thyroid, chronic infection, and intestinal diseases
associated with nutritional
malabsorption.

HOW THE DRUG WORKS
Vitamin C is required for
the body's synthesis of col-
lagen (tissue that constitutes the tendons, liga-
ments, and other inelastic
fibers), for the metabolism
of a variety of body sub-
stances, and to maintain
structural and functional
integrity of cell walls and
small blood vessels.

DOSAGE
Recommended dietary
allowances (RDAs) for vitamin C are as follows: 40 to
50 mg from birth to 1 year
of age; 15 to 25 mg from
age 1 to 8; 45 to 75 mg for
boys from age 9 to 18; 45 to
65 mg for girls from age 9
to 18; 90 mg for adult men;
75 mg for adult women;
smokers require an addi-
tional 35 mg daily.

ONSET OF EFFECT
Unknown.

DURATION OF ACTION
As long as it is taken.

DIETARY ADVICE
Eat a well-balanced diet to
avoid vitamin C deficiency.
Foods rich in vitamin C
include citrus fruits and
juices, green vegetables,
and tomatoes.

STORAGE
Store in tightly sealed container away from heat, moisture, and direct light.

IF YOU MISS A DOSE
No problems are expected.
Take the next dose at
the regularly scheduled
time and do not double the
next dose.

STOPPING THE DRUG
If vitamin C is taken for a
deficiency or because of a
disorder associated with a
need for a higher intake of
the vitamin, consult your
doctor before stopping.

PROLONGED USE
No problems are expected
with prolonged use.

PRECAUTIONS
Over 60: No special problems are expected.

**Driving and Hazardous
Work:** No special precautions are necessary.

Alcohol: Alcoholism may
lead to vitamin C deficiency.

Pregnancy: Vitamin C
requirements increase during pregnancy to 85 mg per
day. Very large doses during pregnancy may harm
the fetus.

Breast Feeding: Vitamin
C requirements increase
during breast feeding to 120
mg per day. Vitamin C does
enter breast milk, but so far
no problems have been
reported from taking the
recommended amounts of
the vitamin.

Infants and Children:
No problems are associated
with recommended doses.

Special Concerns: Use of
large doses of vitamin C is
commonplace for the pre-
vention of colds, cancer, and
other disorders. However,

studies have shown that
blood levels of the vitamin
do not increase further
when vitamin C doses
exceed 250 to 500 mg per
day. High doses of vitamin
C may cause kidney stones
in people with a prior history of the disorder or
those with kidney disease
treated with hemodialysis.

OVERDOSE
Symptoms: No specific
ones have been reported.

What to Do: Emergency
instructions not applicable.

DRUG INTERACTIONS
None reported with recom-
mended doses.

FOOD INTERACTIONS
No known food interactions.
However, it is worth noting
that vitamin C can improve
the body's absorption of
iron, specifically nonheme
iron (the type of iron found
in foods derived from plant
sources).

DISEASE INTERACTIONS
None reported.

Drisdol 50,000 IU
(SANOFI WINTHROP)

▶ Drug Class: Dietary supplement

▶ Available in: Capsules, oral solution, tablets

▶ Available OTC? Yes

▶ As Generic? Yes

Side Effects

SERIOUS
Serious side effects are associated with excessively high doses (see Overdose).

COMMON
No common side effects are expected with recommended doses.

LESS COMMON
No less-common side effects are expected with recommended doses.

PRINCIPAL USES
Vitamin D is necessary for good health, and especially to maintain strong, healthy bones. It is derived from dietary sources, plus the body manufactures its own vitamin D upon exposure to sunlight. Vitamin D deficiency is thus rare among Americans, but some people—notably, those who are bedridden, have poor or highly restricted (vegan or macrobiotic) diets, or who cannot get adequate nutrition due to intestinal malabsorption—require supplementation. Supplements may also be prescribed for people with chronically low blood levels of calcium, and for alcoholics, dark-skinned people (who manufacture smaller amounts of vitamin D on their own), pregnant women, and nursing infants who get inadequate exposure to sunlight. Vitamin D supplements are also often recommended to increase calcium absorption and prevent osteoporosis in post-menopausal women.

HOW THE DRUG WORKS
Vitamin D promotes the absorption of calcium from the intestine and the utilization of calcium and phosphorus in the body. This ensures that levels of these minerals are high enough to support the constant breakdown and rebuilding of bone tissue, and to supply cells with the calcium needed to perform essential functions.

DOSAGE
Adequate intakes—Teenagers and adults up to age 50: 200 international units (IU). Adults age 51 to 70: 400 IU. Adults over age 70: 600 IU. Infants and children up to age 12: 200 IU. Pregnant or breast-feeding women: 200 IU. Vitamin D supplementation for defi-ciency or other medical condition— Same as above or higher, as determined by your doctor.

ONSET OF EFFECT
Within 12 to 24 hours; maximum effect: 10 to 14 days.

DURATION OF ACTION
As long as vitamin is taken.

DIETARY ADVICE
The best sources of vitamin D are fish and vitamin D fortified milk.

STORAGE
Store in a tightly sealed container away from heat and direct light.

IF YOU MISS A DOSE
When vitamin D is used as a dietary supplement, no problems are expected if you miss a dose. When it is prescribed to treat a specific medical condition, take the missed dose as soon as you remember. If it is near the time for the next dose, skip the missed dose and resume your regular dosage schedule. Do not double the next dose.

STOPPING THE DRUG
Do not stop taking the supplement without first consulting your doctor.

PROLONGED USE
Your doctor will take periodic blood tests to check levels of calcium and phosphorus if you are taking vitamin D for the treatment of low blood calcium levels.

PRECAUTIONS
Over 60: No special problems are expected.

Driving and Hazardous Work: No special precautions are necessary.

Alcohol: No special precautions are necessary.

Pregnancy: No problems are expected with recommended dose.

Breast Feeding: Trace amounts pass into breast milk; however, no problems have been reported.

Infants and Children: Infants who get little exposure to the sun and are totally breast-fed, especially those with dark-skinned mothers, may require vitamin D supplementation. Problems have not been reported with recommended amounts; however, prolonged excess doses may stunt a child's growth.

OVERDOSE
Symptoms: Early symptoms: Constipation (especially in children), diarrhea, dry mouth, increased thirst and frequency of urination, persistent headache, loss of appetite, metallic taste, nausea and vomiting, unusual fatigue. Advanced symptoms: Bone and muscle pain, irregular heartbeat, persistent itching, extreme drowsiness, mental changes. Severe vitamin D toxicity may be fatal.

What to Do: See your doctor at once.

DRUG INTERACTIONS
Consult your doctor if you are taking calcium-containing preparations, magnesium-containing antacids, or thiazide diuretics.

FOOD INTERACTIONS
No known food interactions.

DISEASE INTERACTIONS
Consult your doctor if you have high blood levels of calcium (hypercalcemia), a history of heart or blood vessel disease, pancreatitis, or impaired kidney function.

Vitamin E (Tocopherol)

BRAND NAMES
Amino-Opti-E, Aquesol E,
E-1000 IU Softgels, E-200
IU Softgels, E-Complex-
600, E-Vitamin Succinate,
Liqui-E, Pheryl-E, Vita Plus
E

Generic 400 IU
(GOLD CAPS)

▶ Drug Class: Dietary
supplement

▶ Available in: Capsules

▶ Available OTC? Yes

▶ As Generic? Yes

Side Effects

SERIOUS
No serious side effects
are associated with rec-
ommended doses.

COMMON
No common side effects
are associated with rec-
ommended doses.

LESS COMMON
Large doses (greater than
400 IU per day) have
been associated with
diarrhea, nausea,
headache, blurred vision,
dizziness, and fatigue.
Doses greater than 800
IU per day have been
reported to increase the
danger of bleeding, espe-
cially in people deficient
in vitamin K.

PRINCIPAL USES
For the prevention and
treatment of vitamin E deficiency. Vitamin E deficiency
is extremely rare and does
not occur in healthy individuals eating a well-balanced
diet. However, a deficiency
of vitamin E can result from
any disorder that causes
poor absorption of fat from
the intestine. Vitamin E is
an antioxidant that is often
prescribed to prevent the
oxidation of low-density
lipoprotein in an effort to
prevent atherosclerosis
(buildup of fatty plaques
within the arteries), the
underlying cause of coro-
nary heart disease. The
value of vitamin E supplements for this purpose is
unproven.

HOW THE DRUG WORKS
Although considered an
essential vitamin, the exact
function of vitamin E
remains unknown. It does
help to prevent oxidation of
the fatty acids present in
the membranes of all cells
(that is, it has antioxidant
properties).

DOSAGE
Vitamin E requirements are
small, ranging from 6 international units (IU) at birth
to 28 IU in breast-feeding
women. Recommended
dietary allowance (RDA) for
adults is 22 IU. Large doses
(100 IU) are given when
deficiency results from
intestinal malabsorption.
The usual doses prescribed
for protection against coronary heart disease range
from 400 to 800 IU per day.

ONSET OF EFFECT
Unknown.

DURATION OF ACTION
Unknown.

DIETARY ADVICE
Eat a well-balanced diet.
Foods rich in vitamin E
include vegetable oils,
whole grains, and leafy
green vegetables. Cooking
and storage may cause significant losses of vitamin E.

STORAGE
Store in a tightly sealed container away from heat, moisture, and direct light.

IF YOU MISS A DOSE
No problems are expected.
Take the next dose at
the regularly scheduled
time and do not double the
next dose.

STOPPING THE DRUG
If prescribed for a defi-
ciency, do not stop taking
vitamin E without consulting your doctor first. There
is no evidence that stopping
vitamin E when it is taken
to prevent coronary heart
disease is harmful.

PROLONGED USE
No problems are associated
with prolonged use.

PRECAUTIONS
Over 60: No problems are
expected at recommended
doses.

**Driving and Hazardous
Work:** No special precautions are necessary.

Alcohol: No special precautions are necessary.

Pregnancy: No problems
are expected with recom-
mended doses.

Breast Feeding: Vitamin
E enters breast milk, but
no problems have been
reported with recom-
mended doses.

Infants and Children:
No problems have been
documented at recom-
mended doses.

OVERDOSE
Symptoms: No cases of vitamin E overdose have been
reported.

What to Do: Emergency
instructions not applicable.

DRUG INTERACTIONS
Consumption of large doses
of vitamin E in combination
with anticoagulants (such
as warfarin) might lead to
uncontrolled bleeding.

FOOD INTERACTIONS
Absorption of vitamin E
from the intestine requires
the consumption of some
dietary fat.

DISEASE INTERACTIONS
No disease interactions
have been reported.

Vitamin K (Phytonadione; Menadiol)

Side Effects

SERIOUS
Menadiol has been asso-
ciated with anemia and
jaundice (yellow discol-
oration of the eyes and
skin) in some newborns
because their liver func-
tion is still poorly developed. Unless high doses
are used, the risk is less
with phytonadione.

COMMON
No common side effects
are associated with rec-
ommended doses.

LESS COMMON
Flushing of the face,
reactions at injection site.

PRINCIPAL USES
Vitamin K is used to pre-
vent or treat bleeding disorders resulting from reduced
formation of proteins
needed for blood coagula-
tion. The need may be due
either to vitamin K defi-
ciency or impairment of its
function by anticoagulant
drugs such as warfarin, salicylates, and some antibi-
otics. Vitamin K does not
overcome the anticoagulant
effects of heparin. Because
vitamin K is normally made
by bacteria in the intestine,
dietary deficiency is rare.
Bile salts are needed for
absorption of vitamin K
from the intestine, so
absorption may be poor
when obstruction of the bile
ducts prevents entry of bile
salts into the intestine. In
newborns, the American
Academy of Pediatrics recommends administration of
phytonadione at birth to
prevent bleeding disorders
that can occur because adequate amounts of vitamin K
may fail to cross the placenta from the mother to
the fetus, and newborns
have no bacteria in their
intestines at birth. In people
receiving all nutrition by
injection for long periods,
intramuscular injections of
vitamin K are needed.

HOW THE DRUG WORKS
Vitamin K is necessary
before a number of blood
coagulation factors can
become active in preventing
or stopping bleeding.

DOSAGE
Oral doses— Menadiol
sodium phosphate: Adults:
For obstruction of bile duct:
5 mg a day. For problems
related to use of antibacteri-
als or salicylates: 5 to 10 mg
a day. Children: 5 mg a day.
Phytonadione: Adults: 2.5 to
10 mg (but up to 25 mg) if
needed; can be repeated
after 12 to 48 hours. Injections— Menadiol sodium
phosphate: Adults: 5 to 15
mg once or twice a day.
Children: 5 to 10 mg once
or twice a day. Phytona-
dione: Adolescents and
adults: 2.5 to 25 mg; can be
repeated if necessary. Children: 5 to 10 mg. Infants: 1
to 2 mg. During long-term
total parenteral (intra-
venous) nutrition: Adults: 5
to 10 mg a week. Children:
2 to 5 mg a week.

ONSET OF EFFECT
Oral phytonadione: 6 to 12
hours. Injected phytona-
dione: 1 to 2 hours. Injected
menadiol sodium phos-
phate: 8 to 24 hours.

DURATION OF ACTION
12 to 24 hours.

DIETARY ADVICE
No interactions. The best
dietary sources of vitamin K
are leafy green vegetables,
meats, and dairy products.

STORAGE
Store in a cool dry place
away from light. Avoid
allowing injectable forms to
freeze.

IF YOU MISS A DOSE
Take as soon as remem-
bered unless close to next
dose. Do not double the
next dose.

STOPPING THE DRUG
Do not stop taking vitamin
K unless instructed to do so
by your doctor.

PROLONGED USE
Prolonged use is uncom-
mon; no problems are
expected at recommended
doses.

PRECAUTIONS
Over 60: No information is
available on the effects of
age on vitamin K doses.

**Driving and Hazardous
Work:** No special precautions are necessary.

Alcohol: No special precautions are necessary.

Pregnancy: No information is available.

Breast Feeding: No problems have been reported.

Infants and Children:
Caution is required with vitamin K injections in new-
borns because of the risk of
anemia and liver toxicity.

Special Concerns: The
smallest effective dose
should be given to over-
come bleeding due to an
overdose of anticoagulant.
Too large a dose may delay
the subsequent action of the
anticoagulant. Laboratory
tests of clotting function
(prothrombin time) are
needed to determine the
proper dose of vitamin K.

OVERDOSE
Symptoms: No specific
ones have been reported.

What to Do: Emergency
instructions not applicable.

DRUG INTERACTIONS
Antacids, antibiotics, and
sucralfate can decrease vitamin K absorption. Vitamin
K can interfere with the
action of drugs like salicylates and anticoagulants.
Other drugs may interact
with vitamin K; consult your
doctor if you are taking any
prescription or over-the-
counter drug.

FOOD INTERACTIONS
None reported.

DISEASE INTERACTIONS
Caution is advised in people
with liver disease.

Warfarin

Coumadin 2 mg
(**DUPONT**)

Additional photographs

▶ Drug Class: Anticoagulant

▶ Available in: Tablets, injection

▶ Available OTC? No

▶ As Generic? Yes

Side Effects

SERIOUS
Allergic reaction (marked by wheezing, breathing difficulty, hives, or swelling of lips, tongue, and throat); bleeding into skin and soft tissue; abnormal bleeding from nose, gastrointestinal tract, urinary tract, or uterus; severe infection; excessive or unexpected menstrual bleeding; black vomit; bruises or purple marks on skin. Consult your doctor immediately.

COMMON
No common side effects have been reported.

LESS COMMON
Loss of appetite, unusual weight loss, nausea, vomiting, skin rash, diarrhea, cramping.

PRINCIPAL USES
To prevent blood clot formation in patients suffering from heart, lung, and blood vessel disorders that could lead to heart attack, stroke, or other problems.

HOW THE DRUG WORKS
Warfarin blocks the action of vitamin K, a compound necessary for blood clotting.

DOSAGE
Adults: To start, 10 to 15 mg daily, taken once a day. Long-term, usually 2 to 10 mg per day, taken once a day. Children: The dose must be determined by a pediatrician. It should be taken at the same time every day.

ONSET OF EFFECT
36 to 48 hours.

DURATION OF ACTION
24 to 96 hours.

DIETARY ADVICE
Warfarin can be taken with liquid or food.

STORAGE
Store in a tightly sealed container away from heat and direct light.

IF YOU MISS A DOSE
If you miss a dose, take it as soon as you remember, unless it is almost time for the next dose. In that case, skip the missed dose and go back to your regular schedule. Do not double the next dose.

STOPPING THE DRUG
Take it as prescribed for the full treatment period, even if you begin to feel better before the scheduled end of therapy. The decision to stop taking the drug should be made by your doctor.

PROLONGED USE
Regular tests of prothrombin time (a simple test that measures the time it takes for one stage of blood coagulation to occur) are needed when taking this drug. Your doctor may also take stool and urine samples periodically to check for the presence of blood.

PRECAUTIONS
Over 60: Adverse reactions may be more likely and more severe in older patients.

Driving and Hazardous Work: Avoid if you have blurred vision or feel dizzy. Avoid activities that could cause injury.

Alcohol: Use with caution. Alcohol can increase or decrease the effect of warfarin. Usually, consume no more than one drink a day.

Pregnancy: Warfarin may cause birth defects. Do not use during pregnancy.

Breast Feeding: Warfarin passes into breast milk. Do not use while nursing.

Infants and Children: Not recommended for children under 18.

OVERDOSE
Symptoms: Bleeding gums, uncontrolled nosebleeds, blood in the urine or stools.

What to Do: Discontinue the medication and call your doctor, emergency medical services (EMS), or the nearest poison control center right away.

DRUG INTERACTIONS
Consult your doctor for specific advice if you are taking steroid drugs, acetaminophen, allopurinol, aminogluthemide, antibiotics, antiarrhythmic heart drugs, androgens, antacids, antifungal drugs, antihistamines, aspirin, antidiabetic drugs, disulfiram, a non-steroidal anti-inflammatory drug (NSAID), barbiturates, benzodiazepine tranquilizers, calcium supplements, chloramphenicol, or any cholesterol-lowering drugs.

FOOD INTERACTIONS
Avoid green, leafy vegetables and other foods that are rich in vitamin K (liver, broccoli, cauliflower, kale, spinach, and cabbage). Intake of too much vitamin K can override the anticlotting effect of warfarin and render the drug useless. Conversely, certain substances can interfere with the absorption of vitamin K so much that normal, healthy clotting (necessary for wounds to heal) is impaired. Megadoses of vitamin E can do this, as can fish oil supplements and foods high in omega-3 fatty acids. These substances can enhance the effect of anticlotting drugs so much that a tendency to hemorrhage may result.

DISEASE INTERACTIONS
Consult your doctor about taking warfarin if you have high blood pressure, diabetes, serious liver or kidney disease, or a severe allergy.

Generic 5.4 mg
(MIKART)

▶ Drug Class: Alpha-adrenergic blocking agent

▶ Available in: Tablets

▶ Available OTC? Yes

▶ As Generic? Yes

Side Effects

SERIOUS
Rapid heartbeat; increased blood pressure, possibly causing symptoms such as persistent headaches or ringing in the ears. Call your doctor immediately.

COMMON
No common side effects have been reported.

LESS COMMON
Headache, dizziness, irritability, nervousness, restlessness, flushing of skin, shakiness, increased sweating.

PRINCIPAL USES
To aid in the treatment of male erectile dysfunction (impotence).

HOW THE DRUG WORKS
The exact way in which yohimbine works has not been determined. It is believed to block certain chemical receptors that cause constriction of blood vessels. In doing so, yohimbine theoretically improves blood flow into (and inhibits blood flow out of) the spongy columns of tissue in the penis involved in the mechanics of erection. Yohimbine may also have a mild stimulant effect and may promote the release of brain chemicals that control mood, relaxation, and sex drive, among other functions.

DOSAGE
Adult males: 5.4 mg, 3 times a day.

ONSET OF EFFECT
Within 2 to 3 weeks in most cases.

DURATION OF ACTION
Unknown.

DIETARY ADVICE
No special restrictions.

STORAGE
Store in a tightly sealed container away from heat, moisture, and direct light. Do not refrigerate medication or allow it to freeze.

IF YOU MISS A DOSE
Take it as soon as you remember. If it is near the time for the next dose, skip the missed dose and resume your regular dosage schedule. Do not double the next dose.

STOPPING THE DRUG
The decision to stop taking the drug should be made in consultation with your physician.

PROLONGED USE
See your doctor regularly for tests and examinations if you take this drug for a prolonged period of time.

PRECAUTIONS
Over 60: No special problems are expected.

Driving and Hazardous Work: Do not drive or engage in hazardous work until you determine how the medicine affects you.

Alcohol: No special restrictions; however, excess alcohol consumption may impair sexual function.

Pregnancy: Yohimbine is generally not prescribed for women and should not be used during pregnancy.

Breast Feeding: Not applicable to female patients.

Infants and Children: Not applicable to children.

Special Concerns: This drug should be used only by men who have been diagnosed with and are being medically treated for erectile dysfunction.

OVERDOSE
Symptoms: Agitation, restlessness, dizziness, heart palpitations.

What to Do: An overdose with yohimbine is unlikely. However, if someone takes a much larger dose than prescribed, call your doctor, emergency medical services (EMS), or the nearest poison control center.

DRUG INTERACTIONS
Consult your doctor for specific advice if you are taking antidepressants (especially MAO inhibitors) or any other mood-modifying medications, including selective serotonin reuptake inhibitors (SSRIs), such as fluoxetine. Before you take yohimbine, tell your doctor if you are taking any other prescription or over-the-counter drugs, especially cold remedies or weight-loss aids.

FOOD INTERACTIONS
Since yohimbine is a mild MAO inhibitor, it should not be taken with any food or drink containing tyramines, including cheese, chocolate, beer, aged meats, and nuts, and particularly not with the amino acids tyrosine or phenylalanine. A dangerous rise in blood pressure may result.

DISEASE INTERACTIONS
Caution is advised when taking yohimbine. Consult your doctor if you have a history of angina pectoris, mental depression or any other psychiatric illness, heart disease, high blood pressure, or impaired kidney function. Use of yohimbine may cause complications in patients with liver disease, since this organ works to remove the medication from the body.

Zafirlukast

Accolate 20 mg
(ZENECA)

▶ Drug Class: Leukotriene receptor antagonist

▶ Available in: Tablets

▶ Available OTC? No

▶ As Generic? No

Side Effects

SERIOUS
Burning or prickling sensation, skin rash. A rare side effect with high doses is liver dysfunction (symptoms include: abdominal pain, nausea, fatigue, lethargy, itching, yellow discoloration of the eyes or skin, and flu-like symptoms). Call your doctor immediately.

COMMON
Headache.

LESS COMMON
Weakness, abdominal pain, back pain, diarrhea, dizziness, mouth ulcers, nausea, vomiting.

PRINCIPAL USES
To prevent the symptoms of asthma on a maintenance basis and to prevent bronchospasm (contraction of the smooth muscle tissue surrounding the airways, which results in narrowing and obstruction of the air passages). Zafirlukast may be used in conjunction with other asthma treatments, such as bronchodilators.

HOW THE DRUG WORKS
Zafirlukast blocks cell receptors for leukotrienes, chemicals that cause inflammation and constriction of the bronchial airways. Unlike bronchodilators, which relieve the acute symptoms of an asthma attack, zafirlukast is prescribed to be taken regularly when no symptoms are present, to reduce the chronic inflammation of the airways that underlies asthma. This prevents symptomatic asthma attacks.

DOSAGE
Adults and teenagers: 20 mg twice a day. Children ages 7 to 11: 10 mg twice a day. Doses are usually taken in the morning and evening, on an empty stomach (at least 1 hour before or 2 hours after eating).

ONSET OF EFFECT
Within 1 week.

DURATION OF ACTION
Unknown.

DIETARY ADVICE
Zafirlukast should be taken 1 hour before or 2 hours after meals. Taking it with a high-fat or high-protein meal reduces its availability in the body by 40%.

STORAGE
Store in a tightly sealed container away from heat and direct light.

IF YOU MISS A DOSE
Take it as soon as you remember. If it is near the time for the next dose, skip the missed dose and resume your regular dosage schedule. Do not double the next dose.

STOPPING THE DRUG
The decision to stop taking the drug should be made by your doctor.

PROLONGED USE
No problems are expected. It is important to take zafirlukast every day, even during symptom-free periods.

PRECAUTIONS
Over 60: In clinical trials, mild or moderate infections, primarily of the respiratory tract, occurred more often than expected in older patients. The rate of infection was proportional to the dose of zafirlukast taken. Other adverse reactions were no more likely or more severe in older patients than in younger persons.

Driving and Hazardous Work: Do not drive or engage in hazardous work until you determine how the medication affects you.

Alcohol: No special precautions are necessary.

Pregnancy: In some animal studies, zafirlukast caused birth defects and other problems. Human studies have not been done. Before you take zafirlukast, tell your doctor if you are pregnant or plan to become pregnant.

Breast Feeding: Zafirlukast passes into breast milk; do not use it while nursing.

Infants and Children: The safety and effectiveness of zafirlukast in children under the age of 7 have not been established.

Special Concerns: Zafirlukast has no effect on an asthma attack already in progress. In very rare cases, the drug may cause Churg-Strauss syndrome, a tissue disorder that strikes adult asthma patients and, if untreated, can destroy organs. Early symptoms include fever, muscle aches, and weight loss.

OVERDOSE
Symptoms: None.

What to Do: Call your doctor if you suspect an overdose.

DRUG INTERACTIONS
Consult your doctor for specific advice if you are taking aspirin, carbamazepine, cyclosporine, felodipine, isradipine, nicardipine, nifedipine, nimodipine, phenytoin, tolbutamide, erythromycin, terfenadine, theophylline, or warfarin. Patients who are taking warfarin or any other anticoagulant should have their prothrombin time monitored closely, and appropriate changes made in the anticoagulant dosage, when they start taking zafirlukast. Before you take zafirlukast, tell your doctor if you are allergic to any prescription or over-the-counter medicine.

FOOD INTERACTIONS
No known food interactions.

DISEASE INTERACTIONS
Consult your doctor if you have any other medical condition. Use of zafirlukast can cause complications in patients with liver disease, since this organ works to remove the medication from the body.

Zalcitabine (Dideoxycytidine; ddC)

BRAND NAME

HIVID

HIVID 0.375 mg
(ROCHE)

▶ Drug Class: Antiviral

▶ Available in: Tablets

▶ Available OTC? No

▶ As Generic? No

Side Effects

SERIOUS
Burning, tingling, pain, or numbness in hands or feet, fever, muscle pain, joint pain, skin rash, ulcers in mouth and throat, nausea, vomiting, fever, sore throat, yellow discoloration of eyes or skin. Call your doctor immediately.

COMMON
No common side effects are associated with the use of zalcitabine.

LESS COMMON
Diarrhea, headache.

PRINCIPAL USES
To treat HIV (human immunodeficiency virus) infection, usually in combination with other antiretroviral drugs. While not a cure for HIV, such medications may suppress the replication of the virus and delay the progression of the disease.

HOW THE DRUG WORKS
Zalcitabine (ddC) interferes with the activity of enzymes needed for the replication of DNA in viral cells, thus preventing the virus from reproducing.

DOSAGE
Adults and teenagers: 0.75 mg, 3 times a day in combination with other antiretroviral drugs. Children: Dose must be determined by your pediatrician.

ONSET OF EFFECT
Unknown. With most antiretroviral drugs, an early response can be seen within the first few days of therapy, but the maximum effect may take 12 to 16 weeks.

DURATION OF ACTION
Unknown. Effects of the drug may be prolonged if zalcitabine is used in combination with other effective drugs and the virus is maximally suppressed.

DIETARY ADVICE
No special restrictions.

STORAGE
Store in a tightly sealed container away from heat and direct light.

IF YOU MISS A DOSE
Take it as soon as you remember. If it is near the time for the next dose, skip the missed dose and resume your regular dosage schedule. Do not double the next dose.

STOPPING THE DRUG
The decision to stop taking the drug should be made in consultation with your physician.

PROLONGED USE
See your doctor regularly for tests and examinations if you must take this medicine for a prolonged period.

PRECAUTIONS
Over 60: No special studies have been done on older patients. A lower dose may be warranted, especially if kidney function is impaired.

Driving and Hazardous Work: Do not drive or engage in hazardous work until you determine how the medicine affects you.

Alcohol: Avoid alcohol if liver function is impaired.

Pregnancy: Zalcitabine has been shown to cause birth defects in animals. Human studies have not been done. Nevertheless, zalcitabine is increasingly being used in combination with other antiretroviral drugs to treat pregnant HIV-infected women.

Breast Feeding: It is unknown whether zalcitabine passes into breast milk; however, women infected with HIV should not breast feed, to avoid transmitting the virus to an uninfected child.

Infants and Children: It is not known whether zalcitabine causes different or more severe side effects in children than it does in older persons. Use it for young patients only under close medical supervision.

Special Concerns: Use of zalcitabine does not reduce the risk of passing HIV to other persons. Take appropriate preventive measures.

OVERDOSE
Symptoms: Rash; fever; numbness, tingling, or prickling sensation in the arms and legs.

What to Do: An overdose of zalcitabine is unlikely to occur. Nonetheless, if you have any reason to suspect an overdose, call your doctor, emergency medical services (EMS), or the nearest poison control center.

DRUG INTERACTIONS
Consult your doctor for specific advice if you are taking asparaginase, azathioprine, estrogens, furosemide, methyldopa, pentamidine, sulfonamides, sulindac, tetracyclines, thiazide diuretics, valproic acid, injected aminoglycosides, amphotericin B, foscarnet, antacids, chloramphenicol, cisplatin, dapsone, didanosine, ethambutol, ethionamide, hydralazine, isoniazid, lithium, metronidazole, nitrous oxide, phenytoin, stavudine, vincristine, cimetidine, probenecid, or nitrofurantoin.

FOOD INTERACTIONS
No known food interactions.

DISEASE INTERACTIONS
Consult your doctor if you have a history of pancreatitis, peripheral neuropathy, or high levels of cholesterol or triglycerides in the blood. Use of zalcitabine may cause complications in patients who have kidney or liver disease, because these organs work to remove the medication from the body.

Zaleplon

▶ Drug Class: Sedative/hypnotic

▶ Available in: Capsules

▶ Available OTC? No

▶ As Generic? No

Side Effects

SERIOUS
Hallucinations, abnormal thoughts or behavior, confusion or disorientation, unsteadiness, dizziness, lightheadedness, unusual nervousness, agitation, difficulty breathing. Call your doctor immediately.

COMMON
Daytime drowsiness, general pain or discomfort, memory problems, headache.

LESS COMMON
Abdominal pain, weakness, fever.

PRINCIPAL USES
For the short-term treatment of insomnia.

HOW THE DRUG WORKS
By depressing activity in the central nervous system (the brain and spinal cord), zaleplon causes drowsiness and mild sedation. Because the drug is metabolized quickly compared with similar medications, zaleplon is associated with a lower incidence of side effects such as daytime drowsiness.

DOSAGE
The appropriate dosage will be determined by your doctor. The recommended dosage for adults: 10 mg. Debilitated patients and people over 60: 5 mg. Zaleplon should only be taken at bedtime or after the patient has gone to bed and has difficulty falling asleep.

ONSET OF EFFECT
Within 1 hour.

DURATION OF ACTION
About 4 hours.

DIETARY ADVICE
Do not take following a high-fat, heavy meal. The absorption of zaleplon may be slowed and reduce the drug's effectiveness.

STORAGE
Store in a tightly sealed container away from heat, moisture, and direct light.

IF YOU MISS A DOSE
If the medication was not taken at bedtime and you are unable to fall asleep, the drug may be used unless it is within 4 hours of when you need to be awake.

STOPPING THE DRUG
The decision to stop taking the drug should be made in consultation with your doctor.

PROLONGED USE
Zaleplon is usually prescribed only for short-term therapy (lasting several days or up to 4 weeks). See your doctor for periodic evaluation if you must take this drug for a longer time. Persistent insomnia may be a sign of an underlying medical problem.

PRECAUTIONS
Over 60: Adverse reactions may be more likely in older patients. Smaller doses usually are prescribed.

Driving and Hazardous Work: Avoid such activities until you determine how this medication affects you.

Alcohol: Avoid alcohol.

Pregnancy: In large doses zaleplon has been shown to slow the progress of fetal development in animals. Human studies have not been done. Zaleplon is not recommended for use by pregnant women. Before you take zaleplon, be sure to tell your doctor if you are pregnant or plan to become pregnant.

Breast Feeding: Zaleplon passes into breast milk, but its effect on the nursing infant is unknown. Women who are nursing should not take this medication.

Infants and Children: Safety and effectiveness have not been established for patients under age 18.

Special Concerns: When you stop taking zaleplon, you may have trouble falling asleep for the first few nights.

OVERDOSE
Symptoms: Severe drowsiness, breathing difficulty, severe clumsiness or unsteadiness, severe dizziness, severe nausea and vomiting, slow heartbeat, vision problems.

What to Do: Call your doctor, emergency medical services (EMS), or the nearest poison control center immediately.

DRUG INTERACTIONS
Other drugs may interact with zaleplon. Consult your doctor for specific advice if you are taking rifampin, phenytoin, carbamazepine, phenobarbital or other drugs that depress the central nervous system; these include antihistamines, other psychiatric medications, barbiturates, sedatives, cough medicines, decongestants, and painkillers. Be sure your doctor knows about any over-the-counter medication you may take.

FOOD INTERACTIONS
No known food interactions.

DISEASE INTERACTIONS
Caution is advised when taking zaleplon. Consult your doctor if you have a history of alcohol abuse or drug dependence, chronic respiratory disease (including asthma, bronchitis, or emphysema), mental depression, or sleep apnea. Use of zaleplon may cause complications in patients with liver disease, since this organ works to remove the medication from the body.

Zanamivir

▶ Drug Class: Antiviral

▶ Available in: Inhalant

▶ Available OTC? No

▶ As Generic? No

Side Effects

SERIOUS
No serious side effects are associated with zanamivir.

COMMON
There are no common side effects associated with zanamivir.

LESS COMMON
Dizziness.

PRINCIPAL USES
To treat influenza type A or B. Zanamivir can reduce the severity of symptoms and shorten the duration of flu episodes.

HOW THE DRUG WORKS
Zanamivir is believed to interfere with the synthesis of the viral enzyme neuraminidase, which is needed in order for the virus to infect cells in the respiratory tract and elsewhere in the body. The drug affects only certain susceptible strains of the influenza type A or B viruses.

DOSAGE
Adults and teenagers: 2 inhalations (one 5-mg blister per inhalation) every 12 hours for 5 days. On the first day of treatment, however, 2 doses should be taken whenever possible provided there is at least 2 hours between doses. On subsequent days, follow the above dosage schedule. Treatment should be initiated within 2 days after the onset of signs or symptoms of the flu.

ONSET OF EFFECT
Unknown.

DURATION OF ACTION
Unknown.

DIETARY ADVICE
No special restrictions.

STORAGE
Store in a tightly sealed container away from heat and direct light.

IF YOU MISS A DOSE
Take it as soon as you remember. If it is near the time for the next dose, skip the missed dose and resume your regular dosage schedule. Do not double the next dose.

STOPPING THE DRUG
It is important to take zanamivir for the full treatment period as prescribed. Do not stop taking the drug before the scheduled end of therapy even if you begin to feel better, as this may lead to a relapse.

PROLONGED USE
If your symptoms do not improve or if they become worse in a few days, you should consult your doctor.

PRECAUTIONS
Over 60: No special problems are expected.

Driving and Hazardous Work: Do not drive or engage in hazardous work until you determine how the medicine affects you.

Alcohol: No special precautions are necessary.

Pregnancy: Adequate studies have not been completed. Discuss with your doctor the relative risks and benefits of using this drug while pregnant.

Breast Feeding: Zanamivir may pass into breast milk, although it is unknown if this poses any risks to the nursing infant. Consult your doctor for specific advice.

Infants and Children: Zanamivir is not recommended for children under the age of 12.

Special Concerns: Zanamivir should be administered using the Diskhaler device. See your doctor for instructions and a demonstration of the proper use of this device.

OVERDOSE
Symptoms: No specific ones have been reported.

What to Do: If you have any reason to suspect an overdose, call your doctor, emergency medical services (EMS), or the nearest poison control center.

DRUG INTERACTIONS
No known drug interactions.

FOOD INTERACTIONS
No known food interactions.

DISEASE INTERACTIONS
Consult your doctor if you have any respiratory illness, such as chronic obstructive pulmonary disease or asthma.

Zidovudine (AZT)

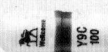
Side Effects

SERIOUS
Anemia (low red blood cell count) causing paleness, fatigue, or shortness of breath; fever. If such symptoms occur, call your doctor right away.

COMMON
Headaches, nausea, muscle aches, insomnia, mood swings, stomach upset, loss of appetite.

LESS COMMON
Bands of discoloration on the fingernails; hepatitis (liver inflammation, which may cause yellowish discoloration of skin and eyes).

PRINCIPAL USES
To treat HIV infection in combination with other drugs and to prevent passage of the virus from pregnant women to their babies. While not a cure for HIV, this drug may suppress the replication of the virus and delay the progression of the disease. Also used to treat HIV-related dementia and HIV-related thrombocytopenia (low platelet count).

HOW THE DRUG WORKS
Zidovudine (AZT) interferes with the activity of enzymes needed for the replication of DNA in viral cells, thus preventing the human immunodeficiency virus (HIV) from reproducing.

DOSAGE
For HIV infection— Adults and teenagers: Capsules: 200 mg, 3 times a day, or 300 mg, 2 times a day. Injection (given until oral dose can be taken): Adults and teenagers: 0.9 mg per lb of body weight injected slowly into a vein every 4 hours (6 times a day). To prevent the transmission of HIV to newborns— For pregnant women: Capsules: 100 mg, 5 times a day from 14th week of pregnancy to delivery. Injection: 0.9 mg per lb of body weight for first hour of delivery, followed by 0.45 mg per lb until baby is delivered. For newborns: Syrup: 0.9 mg per lb of body weight starting within 12 hours of birth and continuing for 6 weeks. Higher doses (up to 1,200 mg per day) are sometimes use to treat HIV-related dementia or thrombocytopenia.

ONSET OF EFFECT
Unknown. With most antiretroviral drugs, an early response can be seen within the first few days of therapy, but the maximum effect may take 12 to 16 weeks.

DURATION OF ACTION
Unknown. Effects of the drug may be prolonged if zidovudine is used in combination with other effective drugs and the virus is maximally suppressed.

DIETARY ADVICE
Take with food to minimize side effects.

STORAGE
Store in a tightly sealed container away from heat and direct light.

IF YOU MISS A DOSE
Take it as soon as you remember. If it is near the time for the next dose, skip the missed dose and resume your regular dosage schedule. Do not double the next dose.

STOPPING THE DRUG
The decision to stop taking the drug should be made in consultation with your physician.

PROLONGED USE
See your doctor regularly for tests and examinations as long as you take this medication.

PRECAUTIONS
Over 60: No special studies have been done on older patients. A lower dose may be warranted, especially if kidney function is impaired.

Driving and Hazardous Work: Do not drive or engage in hazardous work until you determine how the medicine affects you.

Alcohol: Avoid alcohol if liver function is impaired.

Pregnancy: Zidovudine can decrease the risk of passing the AIDS virus to the unborn child; in animal studies it has not caused birth defects.

Breast Feeding: Women who are infected with HIV should not breast feed, to avoid transmitting the virus to an uninfected child.

Infants and Children: Use and dose in infants and children must be established by your doctor.

Special Concerns: Use of zidovudine does not eliminate the risk of passing HIV to other persons. You should take appropriate preventive measures.

OVERDOSE
Symptoms: Sudden nausea and vomiting; headache, dizziness, or drowsiness.

What to Do: Seek medical assistance right away.

DRUG INTERACTIONS
Consult your doctor for specific advice if you are taking amphotericin B (by injection), anticancer agents, thyroid drugs, azathioprine, chloramphenicol, colchicine, cyclophosphamide, flucytosine, ganciclovir, interferon, mercaptopurine, methotrexate, plicamycin, clarithromycin, or probenecid. Also consult your doctor for specific advice if you are taking any other prescription or over-the-counter medication.

FOOD INTERACTIONS
Zidovudine may be better tolerated if taken with food.

DISEASE INTERACTIONS
Caution is advised when taking zidovudine. Consult your doctor if you have anemia or another blood problem or liver disease.

Zileuton

BRAND NAME
Zyflo

▶ Drug Class: Selective 5-lipoxygenase inhibitor

▶ Available in: Tablets

▶ Available OTC? No

▶ As Generic? No

Side Effects

SERIOUS
Liver problems causing nausea, fatigue, lethargy, skin rash or itching, yellow discoloration of the eyes or skin, flu-like symptoms, urine that is darker than normal. Call your doctor immediately.

COMMON
Headache, general pain, abdominal pain, nausea, indigestion, muscle soreness, weakness.

LESS COMMON
Joint pain, chest pain, inflammation of the tissues surrounding the eye (conjunctivitis), constipation, dizziness, fever, gas, insomnia or sleepiness, neck pain, nervousness, urinary tract infection, vomiting.

PRINCIPAL USES
To prevent and treat chronic asthma. Zileuton will not relieve a chronic asthma attack once it has started.

HOW THE DRUG WORKS
Zileuton blocks the activity of a specific enzyme needed in the manufacture of certain substances known as leukotrienes, which are known to contribute to allergic and inflammatory reactions, and appear to play a role in the development of inflammatory diseases including asthma and rheumatoid arthritis.

DOSAGE
Adults and teenagers: 600 mg, 4 times a day.

ONSET OF EFFECT
Within 1 to 2 hours. Several days or weeks may be required for the full effect in preventing asthma attacks.

DURATION OF ACTION
Unknown.

DIETARY ADVICE
Zileuton can be taken with meals and at bedtime, without regard to diet.

STORAGE
Store in a tightly sealed container away from heat, moisture, and direct light.

IF YOU MISS A DOSE
Take it as soon as you remember. If it is near the time for the next dose, skip the missed dose and resume your regular dosage schedule. Do not double the next dose.

STOPPING THE DRUG
Take it as prescribed for the full treatment period, even if you feel better before the scheduled end of therapy.

PROLONGED USE
See your doctor regularly for examinations and tests, especially of liver function, if you must take zileuton for a prolonged period.

PRECAUTIONS
Over 60: No special problems are expected.

Driving and Hazardous Work: Do not drive or engage in hazardous work until you determine how the medicine affects you.

Alcohol: Avoid alcohol.

Pregnancy: Adequate studies have not been done. Before taking zileuton, tell your doctor if you are pregnant or plan to become pregnant, and discuss the relative risks and benefits of using this drug.

Breast Feeding: Zileuton may pass into breast milk and be harmful to the nursing infant; avoid or discontinue using the drug while nursing or discontinue breast feeding.

Infants and Children: The safety and effectiveness of zileuton for children under the age of 12 have not been determined.

Special Concerns: Liver function should be tested before you start taking zileuton. While taking the drug, you should continue to take any other asthma medications that your doctor has prescribed. Tell your doctor if your use of short-acting bronchodilators increases when you start taking zileuton. It may indicate a worsening of your asthma that may require a change in dosage.

OVERDOSE
Symptoms: None are known; no cases of overdose have been reported.

What to Do: An overdose is unlikely to occur. However, if someone takes a much larger dose than prescribed, call your doctor, emergency medical services (EMS), or the nearest poison control center.

DRUG INTERACTIONS
Other drugs may interact with zileuton. Consult your doctor for specific advice if you are taking warfarin, propranolol, terfenadine, theophylline, calcium channel blockers, cyclosporine, and astemizole. Before you start taking zileuton, tell your doctor if you regularly take any other prescription or over-the-counter medication.

FOOD INTERACTIONS
No known food interactions.

DISEASE INTERACTIONS
Caution is advised when taking zileuton. Consult your doctor if you have hepatitis or jaundice. Use of zileuton may cause complications in patients with liver disease, since this organ works to remove the medication from the body.

Zinc Oxide

▶ Drug Class: Sunscreen

▶ Available in: Cream, ointment

▶ Available OTC? Yes

▶ As Generic? Yes

Side Effects

SERIOUS
Acne, folliculitis (burning, pain, inflammation, and itching in hairy regions of the skin; pus in hair follicles), and skin rash may occur with zinc oxide and other physical sunscreens that block the pores. Notify your doctor if you experience such side effects.

COMMON
No common side effects have been reported.

LESS COMMON
No less-common side effects have been reported.

PRINCIPAL USES
To prevent sunburn.

HOW THE DRUG WORKS
Zinc oxide blocks ultraviolet radiation in sunlight from reaching the skin.

DOSAGE
Apply as needed before exposure to sunlight. A sunscreen should be applied uniformly to all exposed skin surfaces, including the lips.

ONSET OF EFFECT
Immediate.

DURATION OF ACTION
Keeps working until removed or worn off from perspiration or swimming.

DIETARY ADVICE
Zinc oxide can be used without regard to diet.

STORAGE
Store in a tightly sealed container away from heat and direct light.

IF YOU MISS A DOSE
If you forget to apply zinc oxide before exposure to sunlight, apply as soon as you remember.

STOPPING THE DRUG
No special warnings.

PROLONGED USE
No problems are expected.

PRECAUTIONS
Over 60: Studies suggest that frequent use of sunscreens like zinc oxide may increase the risk of vitamin D deficiency, which may promote osteoporosis or bone fractures later in life. Oral vitamin D supplements and consumption of foods rich in vitamin D may be recommended.

Driving and Hazardous Work: The use of zinc oxide should not impair your ability to perform such tasks safely.

Alcohol: No special precautions are necessary.

Pregnancy: No problems have been reported.

Breast Feeding: No problems have been reported.

Infants and Children: Zinc oxide should not be used on children (especially infants under 6 months of age) who have shown signs of allergic skin reaction (hypersensitivity). Otherwise, it is safe for use in children. To prevent accidental ingestion, do not allow small children to apply sunscreens themselves. In general, children should be kept out of the sun during peak daylight hours (from 10 am to 2 pm) and physically protected from direct sun exposure with clothing and other physical barriers (such as a beach umbrella). Infants over 6 months of age should be protected by a sunscreen with an SPF (sun protection factor) of 15 or higher. Older children should regularly use a sunscreen with an SPF of 15 or higher to protect against excess and repeated exposure to solar ultraviolet radiation, which can lead to skin cancer and other skin damage later in life.

Special Concerns: Zinc oxide sunscreen should be applied liberally before exposure to sunlight and reapplied every 1 to 2 hours, especially after swimming or heavy perspiration and after eating and drinking. Contact of zinc oxide with the eyes should be avoided. If skin rash or irritation develops, consult your doctor. Keep sun exposure to a minimum during peak daylight hours (10 am to 2 pm), when the sun's rays are strongest. Extra precautions should be taken around reflective surfaces such as sand, water, and concrete.

OVERDOSE
Symptoms: No specific ones have been reported.

What to Do: Not applicable. However, if someone accidentally ingests zinc oxide, call a doctor, emergency medical services (EMS), or the nearest poison control center.

DRUG INTERACTIONS
Consult your doctor for specific advice if you are using any other topical medications or skin preparations.

FOOD INTERACTIONS
No known food interactions.

DISEASE INTERACTIONS
Consult your doctor for advice if you have a history of any of the following: dermatitis (skin inflammation), herpes labialis (herpes simplex of the mouth and face), lichen planus (a rare non-malignant skin condition causing chronic itching and a distinctive skin eruption), systemic lupus erythematosus (lupus), photosensitivity (heightened sensitivity to sunlight), phytophotodermatitis (dermatitis caused by contact with certain plants followed by exposure to sunlight), polymorphous light eruption (skin lesions occurring after exposure to sunlight), or xeroderma pigmentosum (a rare genetic disorder causing extreme sensitivity to ultraviolet light, skin lesions including malignancies, and serious eye problems).

Zinc Sulfate Ophthalmic

▶ Drug Class: Ophthalmic
astringent/analgesic

▶ Available in: Ophthalmic
solution

▶ Available OTC? Yes

▶ As Generic? Yes

Side Effects

SERIOUS
No serious side effects
have been reported.

COMMON
Overuse of this drug may
cause increased eye irri-
tation and redness.

LESS COMMON
No less-common side
effects have been
reported.

PRINCIPAL USES
For the temporary relief
of discomfort and redness
from minor eye irritation. It
is prescribed in combination
with other drugs such as
phenylephrine, naphazoline,
and tetrahydrozoline.

HOW THE DRUG WORKS
The mineral zinc is an integral component in the
proper functioning of several important enzymes
involved in wound healing
and the general mainte-
nance and proper hydration
of certain body tissues. Zinc
sulfate ophthalmic solution
has a mild astringent effect
(that is, it causes tissues to
contract when applied topically), which can help to
shrink the tiny blood vessels in the whites of the eye
(sclera) and so relieve redness and irritation.

DOSAGE
Instill 1 to 2 drops in the
affected eye(s) up to 4
times a day.

ONSET OF EFFECT
Rapid.

DURATION OF ACTION
Up to several hours.

DIETARY ADVICE
No special restrictions.

STORAGE
Store in a tightly sealed container away from heat and
direct light. Do not allow
the solution to freeze.

IF YOU MISS A DOSE
Instill the missed dose as
soon as possible unless it is
near the time for the next
dose. In that case, skip the
missed dose and go back to
your regular schedule. Do
not double the next dose.

STOPPING THE DRUG
You may stop applying this
drug, or resume using it
after discontinuing, as comfort dictates. No complications are expected.

PROLONGED USE
Eye drops containing zinc
sulfate should generally not
be used for self-medication
for more than 3 days. If
relief is not achieved in this
time, or if redness and irritation persist or worsen, discontinue using it and
contact your doctor or ophthalmologist right away.

PRECAUTIONS
Over 60: No special problems are expected.

**Driving and Hazardous
Work:** The use of this medication should not affect
your ability to perform such
tasks safely.

Alcohol: No special precautions are necessary.

Pregnancy: No problems
are expected; however, if
you are pregnant or plan to
become pregnant and you
have any concerns about
the safe use of this or any
other medication, consult
your doctor.

Breast Feeding: Adequate
studies on the use of ophthalmic zinc sulfate during
breast feeding have not
been done; however, no
adverse consequences have
been reported. Consult your
doctor for specific advice.

Infants and Children:
No specific information is
available on the use of this
medication by children.

Special Concerns: Contact your ophthalmologist or
general practitioner right
away if you experience eye
pain, changes in vision, or if
eye irritation persists for
more than 72 hours. To use
the eye drops, first wash
your hands. Tilt your head
back. Gently apply pressure
to the inside corner of the
lower eyelid and with the
index finger of the same
hand, pull downward on
the eyelid to make a space.
Drop the medicine into this
space and close your eye.
Apply pressure for 1 or 2
minutes while keeping the
eye closed without blinking.
Then wash your hands
again. Make sure that the
tip of the dropper does not
touch your eye, finger, or
any other surface.

OVERDOSE
Symptoms: No cases of
overdose have been
reported.

What to Do: An overdose
is unlikely to occur; in case
of accidental ingestion, call
your doctor, emergency
medical services (EMS), or
the nearest poison control
center right away.

DRUG INTERACTIONS
No drug interactions have
been reported, although
phenylephrine, naphazoline,
and tetrahydrozoline (other
medications prescribed in
combination with zinc sulfate ophthalmic solution)
may adversely affect the
action of certain glaucoma
drops. Consult your doctor
first before taking any other
prescription or over-the-
counter eye medications.

FOOD INTERACTIONS
No known food interactions.

DISEASE INTERACTIONS
If you have glaucoma, do
not use this medication
without consulting your doctor first. It is not an over-
the-counter substitute for
antibiotic or anti-inflammatory drops. Consult your
doctor for specific advice if
you have any other eye disorders or a history of allergic reaction to any other
ophthalmic preparations.

Zinc Sulfate Systemic

Generic 220 mg
(Upsher-Smith)

▶ Drug Class: Dietary
supplement

▶ Available in: Capsules,
tablets, extended-release
tablets, injection

▶ Available OTC? Yes

▶ As Generic? Yes

Side Effects

SERIOUS
Side effects are rare and
occur only with large
doses. Zinc itself may
cause indigestion, heart-
burn, and nausea from
irritation of the stomach.
By interfering with the
absorption of copper, zinc
may interfere with the
production of white and
red blood cells, leading
to infections, sores, or
ulcers in the mouth or
throat, and weakness due
to anemia. Call your doc-
tor if such symptoms
occur.

COMMON
No common side effects
have been reported.

LESS COMMON
No less-common side
effects have been
reported.

PRINCIPAL USES
To prevent or treat zinc deficiency. Zinc deficiency does
not occur in healthy people
who eat a proper, balanced
diet. Conditions associated
with zinc deficiency include
alcoholism, eating disor-
ders, and intestinal problems that result from
malabsorption.

HOW THE DRUG WORKS
Zinc is essential to numerous physiological processes,
including the function of
many enzymes in the body.
Deficiency may lead to poor
night vision, slow healing of
wounds, poor sexual development and function in
males, poor appetite (perhaps owing to a decrease
in the sense of taste and
smell), a reduced ability to
ward off infections, diarrhea, dermatitis, and, in
children, retarded growth.

DOSAGE
Recommended daily allow-
ances are as follows: 5 to 10
mg a day for children from
birth to age 3; 10 mg a day
for children ages 4 to 10; 15
mg a day for adolescent and
adult males; 12 mg a day
for adolescent and adult
females; 15 mg a day for
pregnant women; and 16 to
19 mg a day for breast-feeding women.

ONSET OF EFFECT
Unknown.

DURATION OF ACTION
Unknown.

DIETARY ADVICE
Most effective if taken 1
hour before or 2 hours after
meals. It can be taken with
food if stomach upset
occurs.

STORAGE
Store in a tightly sealed container away from heat, moisture, and direct light.

IF YOU MISS A DOSE
No cause for concern.

STOPPING THE DRUG
If you are taking zinc sulfate
by prescription, the decision
to stop should be made by
your doctor.

PROLONGED USE
You should see your doctor
regularly for tests and
examinations if you take
zinc sulfate for a prolonged
period.

PRECAUTIONS
Over 60: Zinc deficiency
is more likely to occur in
older persons; no special
problems are expected from
zinc supplementation.

**Driving and Hazardous
Work:** The use of zinc sulfate should not impair your
ability to perform such
tasks safely.

Alcohol: Excessive alcohol
intake can increase the likelihood of zinc deficiency.

Pregnancy: There are no
known problems with rec-
ommended doses, but tak-
ing large amounts of zinc
during pregnancy may be
harmful to the fetus.

Breast Feeding: No problems have been reported
with recommended doses.

Infants and Children:
Problems have not been
reported in infants and children receiving the recom-
mended daily intake of zinc
sulfate.

Special Concerns:
Injectable zinc sulfate
should be given under the
supervision of a health care
professional. Zinc is found
in peas, beans, seafood such
as oysters and herring, and
in lean red meats. It is also
found in whole grains, but
consuming large amounts of

whole grains can decrease
the amount of zinc absorbed
from the intestine. Be aware
that food stored in uncoated
tin cans may have less zinc
available for absorption.

OVERDOSE
Symptoms: Chest pain,
vomiting, yellowish tinge to
eyes or skin, dehydration,
shortness of breath, restlessness, profuse sweating,
dizziness.

What to Do: Call your
doctor, emergency medical
services (EMS), or the
nearest poison control
center immediately.

DRUG INTERACTIONS
Consult your doctor for specific advice if you are taking
copper supplements or oral
tetracyclines.

FOOD INTERACTIONS
Some foods can interfere
with absorption of zinc sulfate into your body. Avoid
taking zinc sulfate within 2
hours of eating bran, whole-
wheat breads and cereals,
and other fiber-rich foods,
or phosphorus-containing
foods such as milk and
poultry.

DISEASE INTERACTIONS
Consult your doctor if you
have a copper deficiency or
any other medical condition.
Zinc supplements make a
copper deficiency worse.

Ziprasidone Mesylate

▶ Drug Class: Antipsychotic

▶ Available in: Capsules, injection

▶ Available OTC? No

▶ As Generic? No

Side Effects

SERIOUS
Tardive dyskinesia (involuntary movements of the jaw, lips, and tongue), amnesia, psychosis, hallucinations, paranoia, delusions, manic episodes, suicidal impulses, catatonic reaction, stroke, heart arrhythmia, shortness of breath, asthma, paralysis of one side of the body. Call your doctor immediately. Neuroleptic malignant syndrome, characterized by high fever, muscle rigidity, altered mental status, and heart rhythm abnormalities, is a potentially fatal condition.

COMMON
Drowsiness, nausea, stomach upset, constipation, dizziness, restlessness, diarrhea, rash, cough, runny nose, abnormal muscle movements, including tremor, shuffling, and uncontrolled involuntary movements.

LESS COMMON
Lightheadedness when rising from a sitting or lying position (orthostatic hypotension), loss of appetite, dry mouth, muscle pain, abnormal vision.

PRINCIPAL USES
To treat schizophrenia and symptoms of bipolar (manic-depressive) disorder.

HOW THE DRUG WORKS
While the exact mechanism of action of ziprasidone is unknown, it appears to alter the activity of certain chemicals in the central nervous system to produce a tranquilizing and antipsychotic effect.

DOSAGE
Capsules: To start, 20 mg twice a day with food. Your doctor may increase the dose if necessary (and if side effects are tolerated) up to a maximum of 80 mg twice a day. Injection: Typically administered by a health care professional.

ONSET OF EFFECT
Unknown.

DURATION OF ACTION
Unknown.

DIETARY ADVICE
Take it with meals in order to reduce stomach upset.

STORAGE
Store in a tightly sealed container away from heat, moisture, and direct light.

IF YOU MISS A DOSE
Take it as soon as you remember. If it is near the time for the next dose, skip the missed dose and resume your regular dosage schedule. Do not double the next dose.

STOPPING THE DRUG
Take it as prescribed for the full treatment period. The decision to stop taking the drug should be made in consultation with your physician.

PROLONGED USE
Prolonged use may lead to tardive dyskinesia (involuntary movements of the jaw, lips, tongue, and, in rare cases, the arms, legs, hands, or body). Consult your doctor about the need for follow-up evaluations and tests if you must take this drug for an extended period.

PRECAUTIONS
Over 60: Adverse reactions are more likely and more severe. A lower dose may be warranted.

Driving and Hazardous Work: The use of ziprasidone may impair your ability to perform such tasks safely. Do not drive or engage in hazardous work until you determine how the medicine affects you.

Alcohol: Avoid alcohol.

Pregnancy: Adequate human studies have not been done. Discuss with your doctor the relative risks and benefits of using this drug while pregnant.

Breast Feeding: Ziprasidone may pass into breast milk; avoid or discontinue breast feeding while taking this drug.

Infants and Children: The safety and effectiveness of loxapine in children have not been established.

Special Concerns: Avoid prolonged exposure to high temperatures or hot climates. Drink plenty of fluids and stay cool in hot weather.

OVERDOSE
Symptoms: Few cases of overdose have been reported. In clinical studies, excessive doses appear to result in extreme drowsiness, slurring of speech, and heartbeat irregularities.

What to Do: Call your doctor, emergency medical services (EMS), or the nearest poison control center immediately.

DRUG INTERACTIONS
Other drugs may interact with ziprasidone. You should not take ziprasidone if you are taking dofetilide, sotalol, quinidine, other Class Ia and III anti-arrhythmics, mesoridazine, thioridazine, chlorpromazine, droperidol, pimozide, sparfloxacin, gatifloxacin, moxifloxacin, halofantrine, mefloquine, pentamidine, arsenic trioxide, levomethadyl acetate, dolasetron mesylate, probucol or tacrolimus. Consult your doctor for specific advice if you are taking any other prescription or over-the-counter drug or natural/herbal remedies.

FOOD INTERACTIONS
No known food interactions.

DISEASE INTERACTIONS
Consult your doctor if you have a history of heart disease, fainting or dizziness, or liver dysfunction.

Zolmitriptan

▶ Drug Class: Antimigraine/antiheadache drug

▶ Available in: Tablets

▶ Available OTC? No

▶ As Generic? No

Side Effects

SERIOUS
Serious side effects with zolmitriptan are rare. However, zolmitriptan may cause a heart attack, chest pain or tightness, sudden or severe abdominal pain, shortness of breath, wheezing, heartbeat irregularities, swelling of eyelids, face, or lips, skin rash, or hives. Seek emergency medical assistance immediately.

COMMON
Hot flashes or chills, numbness, prickling or tingling sensations, dry mouth, dizziness, drowsiness, weakness.

LESS COMMON
Indigestion, nausea, muscle ache.

PRINCIPAL USES
To treat severe, acute migraine headaches. Zolmitriptan is not intended as a migraine preventive or for use against any other kinds of pain or headache, including basilar and hemiplegic migraines. Your doctor will determine whether this medication is appropriate in your particular case.

HOW THE DRUG WORKS
The exact mechanism of zolmitriptan's action is unknown.

DOSAGE
A single dose ranging from half of a 2.5 mg tablet to one 5 mg tablet is generally effective. If the migraine returns or there is only partial relief, the dose may be repeated once after 2 hours, but no more than 10 mg should be taken in a 24-hour period. Since individual response to zolmitriptan may vary, your doctor will determine the appropriate dosage. A general recommendation is to take one 2.5 mg tablet as the initial dose.

ONSET OF EFFECT
Within 2 hours.

DURATION OF ACTION
Up to 24 hours.

DIETARY ADVICE
The medication can be taken with or without food.

STORAGE
Store in a tightly sealed container away from heat, moisture, and direct light.

IF YOU MISS A DOSE
Not applicable, since the drug is taken only when necessary.

STOPPING THE DRUG
Consult your doctor before discontinuing zolmitriptan.

PROLONGED USE
No special problems are expected. Patients at risk for heart disease should undergo periodic medical tests and evaluation.

PRECAUTIONS
Over 60: Zolmitriptan is not recommended for use in older patients.

Driving and Hazardous Work: Do not drive or engage in dangerous work until you determine how the medication affects you.

Alcohol: No special warnings, although alcohol may trigger or exacerbate migraine headaches.

Pregnancy: Do not use zolmitriptan without first consulting your doctor if you are pregnant or suspect you might be pregnant.

Breast Feeding: Zolmitriptan may pass into breast milk; consult your doctor for specific advice.

Infants and Children: The safety and effectiveness of zolmitriptan in patients under age 18 have not been established.

Special Concerns: Serious, but rare, heart-related problems may occur after using zolmitriptan. Anyone at risk for unrecognized coronary artery disease—such as postmenopausal women, men over the age of 40, or those with known risk factors for heart disease (hypertension, high blood cholesterol levels, obesity, diabetes, strong family history of heart disease, or cigarette smoking)—should have the first dose of zolmitriptan administered in a doctor's office. Zolmitriptan should not be used by anyone with any symptoms of active heart disease (chest pain or tightness, shortness of breath).

OVERDOSE
Symptoms: Increase in blood pressure resulting in lightheadedness, tension in the neck, fatigue, and loss of coordination.

What to Do: An overdose with zolmitriptan is unlikely. If someone takes a much larger dose than prescribed, call your doctor, emergency medical services (EMS), or the nearest poison control center immediately.

DRUG INTERACTIONS
Do not take zolmitriptan within 24 hours of taking almotriptan, naratriptan, sumatriptan, rizatriptan, ergotamine-containing medication, dihydroergotamine mesylate, or methysergide mesylate. Zolmitriptan and MAO inhibitors such as phenelzine, tranylcypromine, procarbazine, and selegiline should not be used within 14 days of each other. Zolmitriptan should be used with caution in patients taking SSRIs (selective serotonin reuptake inhibitors), which include fluoxetine, fluvoxamine, paroxetine, and sertraline.

FOOD INTERACTIONS
See Dietary Advice.

DISEASE INTERACTIONS
You should not take zolmitriptan if you have a history of angina, heart disease, stroke, uncontrolled hypertension, heartbeat irregularities, or peripheral vascular disease. Zolmitriptan should be used with caution in patients with liver disease or severely impaired kidney function.

Zolpidem Tartrate

Ambien 5 mg
(SEARLE)

▶ Drug Class: Sedative/hypnotic

▶ Available in: Tablets

▶ Available OTC? No

▶ As Generic? No

Side Effects

SERIOUS
Hallucinations, abnormal thoughts or behavior, confusion or disorientation, unsteadiness, dizziness, lightheadedness, unusual nervousness, agitation, difficulty breathing. Call your doctor immediately.

COMMON
Daytime drowsiness, diarrhea, general pain or discomfort, memory problems, nausea, bizarre or unusually vivid dreams, vomiting.

LESS COMMON
Stomach discomfort, agitation, feelings of panic, convulsions, muscle cramps, nausea, vomiting, unusual fatigue, uncontrolled weeping, worsening of emotional problems, vision problems, dry mouth.

PRINCIPAL USES
For the short-term treatment of insomnia.

HOW THE DRUG WORKS
Zolpidem depresses activity in the central nervous system (the brain and spinal cord), which causes drowsiness and mild sedation.

DOSAGE
Adults: 10 mg at bedtime. Patients over 60: 5 mg at bedtime.

ONSET OF EFFECT
Within minutes.

DURATION OF ACTION
2 to 4 hours.

DIETARY ADVICE
Zolpidem may be taken without regard to diet, although it generally works faster on an empty stomach.

STORAGE
Store in a tightly sealed container away from heat and direct light.

IF YOU MISS A DOSE
Take it as soon as you remember unless it is late at night. Do not take the drug unless your schedule permits 7 or 8 hours of sleep.

STOPPING THE DRUG
The decision to stop taking the drug should be made in consultation with your doctor. Discontinuing the drug abruptly may produce withdrawal symptoms (sleep disruption, nervousness, irritability, diarrhea, abdominal cramps, muscle aches, memory impairment). The dosage should be reduced gradually according to your doctor's instructions.

PROLONGED USE
Zolpidem is usually prescribed only for short-term therapy (lasting several days or up to 2 weeks). See your doctor for periodic evaluation if you must take this drug for a longer time. Persistent insomnia may be a sign of an underlying medical problem.

PRECAUTIONS
Over 60: Adverse reactions may be more likely and more severe in older patients. Smaller doses usually are prescribed.

Driving and Hazardous Work: Zolpidem may impair mental alertness and physical coordination. Adjust your activities accordingly.

Alcohol: Avoid alcohol.

Pregnancy: In large doses zolpidem has been shown to slow the progress of fetal development in animals. Human studies have not been done. Before you take zolpidem, be sure to tell your doctor if you are pregnant or plan to become pregnant.

Breast Feeding: Zolpidem passes into breast milk, but its effect on the nursing infant is unknown. Consult your doctor for advice.

Infants and Children: Safety and effectiveness have not been established for patients under age 18.

Special Concerns: When you stop taking zolpidem, you may have trouble falling asleep for the first few nights.

OVERDOSE
Symptoms: Severe drowsiness, breathing difficulty, severe clumsiness or unsteadiness, severe dizziness, severe nausea and vomiting, slow heartbeat, vision problems.

What to Do: Call your doctor, emergency medical services (EMS), or the nearest poison control center immediately.

DRUG INTERACTIONS
Other drugs may interact with zolpidem. Consult your doctor for specific advice if you are taking tricyclic antidepressants (such as amitriptyline, clomipramine, doxepin, or nortriptyline) or other drugs that depress the central nervous system; these include antihistamines, other psychiatric medications, barbiturates, sedatives, cough medicines, decongestants, and painkillers. Be sure your doctor knows about any over-the-counter medication you may take.

FOOD INTERACTIONS
No known food interactions.

DISEASE INTERACTIONS
Caution is advised when taking zolpidem. Consult your doctor if you have a history of alcohol abuse or drug dependence, chronic respiratory disease (including asthma, bronchitis, or emphysema), mental depression, or sleep apnea. Use of zolpidem may cause complications in patients with liver or kidney disease, since these organs work together to remove the medication from the body.

The following pages contain additional examples of many of the pills described in the individual drug profiles throughout the book. They are organized alphabetically by generic name (consult index for brand names).

Please note that the physical appearance of a particular drug may vary considerably from one manufacturer to another, or from one dosage strength to another even when made by the same manufacturer. Each picture that appears here (and elsewhere in the book) represents but one dosage strength of one brand of a drug made by one manufacturer. If the pill you take looks different from the one you see in the photograph, do not be alarmed. However, if you have any doubts, concerns, or questions whatsoever about the medication you take, consult your doctor or pharmacist.

Acetaminophen
80 mg
Panadol Children's
SMITHKLINE BEECHAM

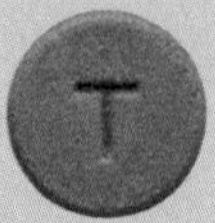

Acetaminophen
160 mg
Tempra Quicklets Junior Strength
BRISTOL-MYERS SQUIBB

Acetaminophen
80 mg
Tylenol Children's
MCNEIL

Acetaminophen
80 mg
Tylenol Children's
MCNEIL

Acetaminophen
650 mg
Tylenol Extended Relief
MCNEIL

Acetaminophen
500 mg
Tylenol Extra Strength
MCNEIL

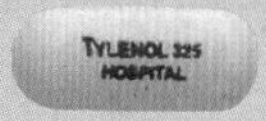

Acetaminophen
325 mg
Tylenol Hospital
MCNEIL

Acetaminophen
160 mg
Tylenol Junior Strength
MCNEIL

Acetaminophen/Codeine
300/15 mg
Generic
GOLDLINE

Acetaminophen/Codeine
300/30 mg
Generic
GOLDLINE

Acetazolamide
250 mg
Diamox
STORZ

Allopurinol
100 mg
Generic
SCHEIN/DANBURY

Amitriptyline Hydrochloride
10 mg
Generic
SIDMAK

Amitriptyline Hydrochloride
25 mg
Generic
MYLAN

Amlodipine
5 mg
Norvasc
PFIZER

Amoxicillin
500 mg
Generic
BIOCRAFT

Ampicillin
250 mg
Generic
BIOCRAFT

Aspirin
81 mg
Ascriptin Adult Low Strength
NOVARTIS

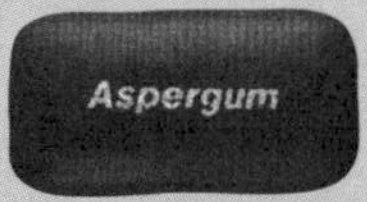

Aspirin
227 mg
Aspergum
SCHERING-PLOUGH

Aspirin
325 mg
Bayer
BAYER

Aspirin
325 mg
Bayer
BAYER

Aspirin
81 mg
Bayer Adult Low Strength
BAYER

Aspirin
81 mg
Bayer Children's
BAYER

Aspirin
500 mg
Bayer Extra Strength
BAYER

Aspirin
325 mg
Bufferin
BRISTOL-MYERS SQUIBB

Aspirin
81 mg
Bufferin Low Dose
BRISTOL-MYERS SQUIBB

Aspirin
162 mg
Halfprin
KRAMER

Aspirin
81 mg
St. Joseph Adult Chewable
SCHERING-PLOUGH

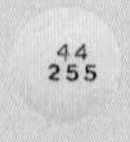

Aspirin
81 mg
Generic
LNK

Aspirin
325 mg
Generic
TIME-CAP

Aspirin (Enteric Coated)
81 mg
Ecotrin
SMITHKLINE BEECHAM

Aspirin (Enteric Coated)
500 mg
Ecotrin Maximum Strength
SMITHKLINE BEECHAM

Atenolol
25 mg
Generic
LEDERLE

Atenolol
50 mg
Generic
GENEVA

Benztropine Mesylate
0.5 mg
Generic
PAR

Benztropine Mesylate
1 mg
Generic
PAR

Bisacodyl
5 mg
Dulcolax
BOEHRINGER INGELHEIM

Bisacodyl
5 mg
Generic
PADDOCK

Bismuth Subsalicylate
262 mg
Pepto-Bismol
PROCTER & GAMBLE

Caffeine
200 mg
Nōdōz
BRISTOL-MYERS SQUIBB

Calcium 500 mg **Os-Cal 500** SMITHKLINE BEECHAM	Calcium Acetate 667 mg **Phoslo** BRAINTREE	Calcium Carbonate 1.25 g **Generic** ROXANE	Captopril 12.5 mg **Generic** APOTHECON
Captopril 25 mg **Generic** APOTHECON	Carbamazepine 100 mg **Tegretol** BASEL	Cephalexin 500 mg **Generic** BIOCRAFT	Chlorpheniramine Maleate 4 mg **Chlor-Trimeton Allergy 4 Hour** SCHERING-PLOUGH
Chlorpheniramine Maleate 4 mg **Generic** ADVANCE	Chlorthalidone 25 mg **Generic** MYLAN	Cimetidine 200 mg **Tagamet HB** SMITHKLINE BEECHAM	Ciprofloxacin 250 mg **Cipro** BAYER
Ciprofloxacin 500 mg **Cipro** BAYER	Clarithromycin 250 mg **Biaxin** ABBOTT	Clomipramine Hydrochloride 25 mg **Anafranil** NOVARTIS	Clonidine Hydrochloride 0.1 mg **Generic** MYLAN
Codeine 30 mg **Generic** ROXANE	Codeine 60 mg **Generic** ROXANE	Cortisone 5 mg **Generic** UPJOHN	Cortisone Acetate 5 mg **Generic** UPJOHN

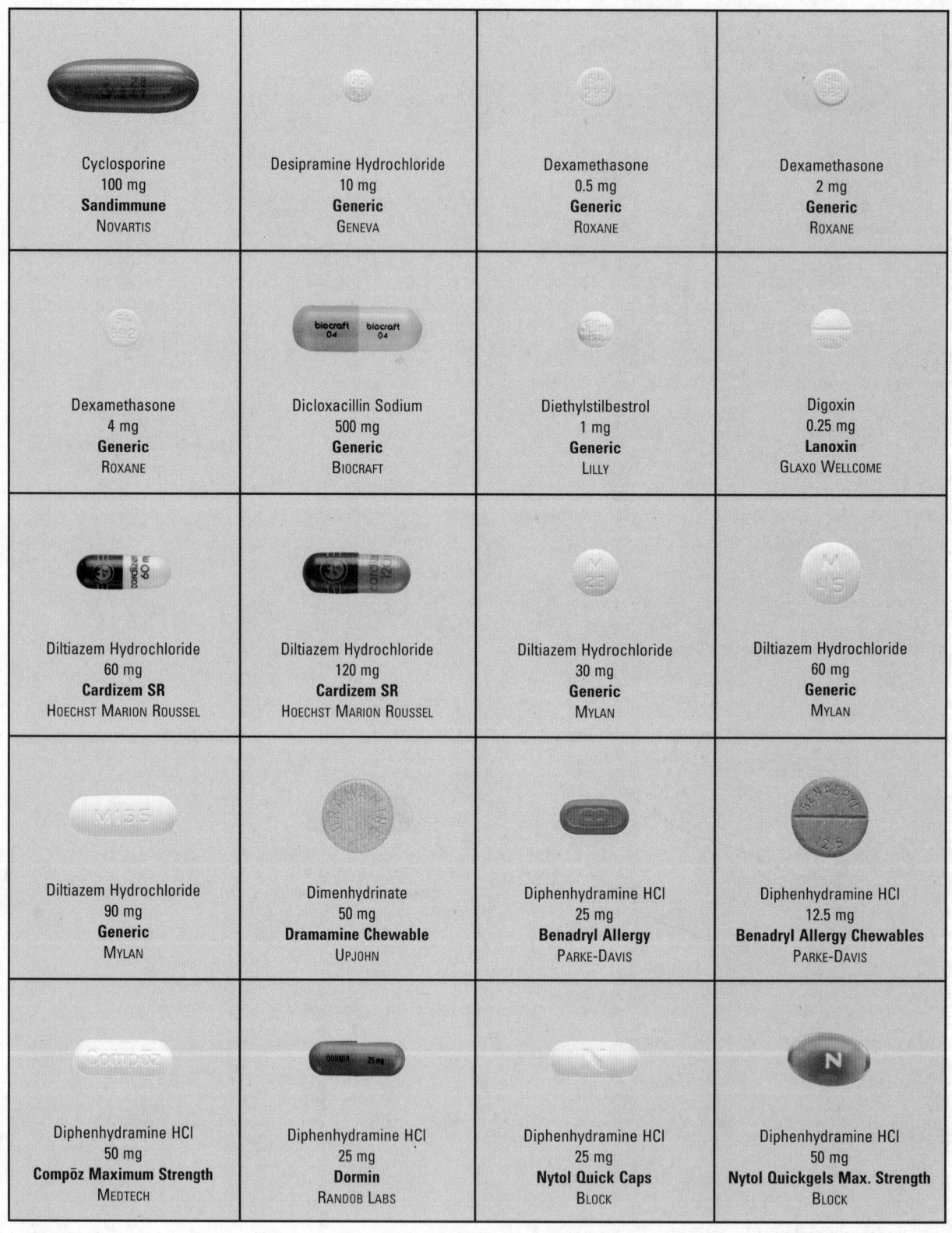

Cyclosporine
100 mg
Sandimmune
NOVARTIS

Desipramine Hydrochloride
10 mg
Generic
GENEVA

Dexamethasone
0.5 mg
Generic
ROXANE

Dexamethasone
2 mg
Generic
ROXANE

Dexamethasone
4 mg
Generic
ROXANE

Dicloxacillin Sodium
500 mg
Generic
BIOCRAFT

Diethylstilbestrol
1 mg
Generic
LILLY

Digoxin
0.25 mg
Lanoxin
GLAXO WELLCOME

Diltiazem Hydrochloride
60 mg
Cardizem SR
HOECHST MARION ROUSSEL

Diltiazem Hydrochloride
120 mg
Cardizem SR
HOECHST MARION ROUSSEL

Diltiazem Hydrochloride
30 mg
Generic
MYLAN

Diltiazem Hydrochloride
60 mg
Generic
MYLAN

Diltiazem Hydrochloride
90 mg
Generic
MYLAN

Dimenhydrinate
50 mg
Dramamine Chewable
UPJOHN

Diphenhydramine HCl
25 mg
Benadryl Allergy
PARKE-DAVIS

Diphenhydramine HCl
12.5 mg
Benadryl Allergy Chewables
PARKE-DAVIS

Diphenhydramine HCl
50 mg
Compōz Maximum Strength
MEDTECH

Diphenhydramine HCl
25 mg
Dormin
RANDOB LABS

Diphenhydramine HCl
25 mg
Nytol Quick Caps
BLOCK

Diphenhydramine HCl
50 mg
Nytol Quickgels Max. Strength
BLOCK

Diphenhydramine HCl 50 mg **Sleepinal Maximum Strength** THOMPSON MEDICAL	Diphenhydramine HCl 50 mg **Sleepinal Softgels Max. Strength** THOMPSON MEDICAL	Diphenhydramine HCl 25 mg **Sominex** SMITHKLINE BEECHAM	Diphenhydramine HCl 50 mg **Unisom SleepGels** PFIZER
Diphenhydramine HCl 25 mg **Generic** PUREPAC	Diphenhydramine HCl 50 mg **Generic** BARR	Dipyridamole 25 mg **Generic** BARR	Docusate 240 mg **Surfak** UPJOHN
Docusate 100 mg **Generic** SCHERER	Doxepin Hydrochloride 50 mg **Generic** MYLAN	Doxycycline 500 mg **Generic** ZENITH	Enalapril Maleate 5 mg **Vasotec** MERCK
Erythromycin 250 mg **Erythrocin** ABBOTT	Estrogen, Conjugated 0.3 mg **Premarin** WYETH-AYERST	Estrogen, Conjugated 0.625 mg **Premarin** WYETH-AYERST	Ethchlorvynol 200 mg **Placidyl** ABBOTT
Famotidine 10 mg **Mylanta AR** MERCK	Famotidine 10 mg **Pepcid AC** MERCK	Ferrous Gluconate 320 mg **Fergon** BAYER	Ferrous Sulfate 200 mg **Feosol** SMITHKLINE BEECHAM

Ferrous Sulfate 324 mg **Generic** CHASE	Fluconazole 100 mg **Diflucan** ROERIG	Fluphenazine 1 mg **Generic** GENEVA	Fluphenazine 2.5 mg **Generic** GENEVA
Fluphenazine 5 mg **Generic** GENEVA	Fluvoxamine Maleate 50 mg **Luvox** SOLVAY	Fosinopril 20 mg **Monopril** BRISTOL-MYERS SQUIBB	Furosemide 40 mg **Generic** ROXANE
Glyburide 5 mg **Generic** GENEVA	Haloperidol 1 mg **Generic** GENEVA	Haloperidol 2 mg **Generic** GENEVA	Haloperidol 10 mg **Generic** GENEVA
Hydralazine Hydrochloride 25 mg **Generic** LEDERLE	Hydralazine Hydrochloride 50 mg **Generic** LEDERLE	Hydroxyzine Hydrochloride 10 mg **Generic** SCHEIN/DANBURY	Ibuprofen 200 mg **Advil Gel Caplets** WHITEHALL
Ibuprofen 100 mg **Advil Junior Strength** WHITEHALL-ROBINS	Ibuprofen 50 mg **Motrin Children's** MCNEIL	Ibuprofen 200 mg **Motrin IB** PHARMACIA & UPJOHN	Ibuprofen 200 mg **Motrin IB** PHARMACIA & UPJOHN

Ibuprofen 100 mg **Motrin Junior Strength** McNeil	Ibuprofen 200 mg **Nuprin** Bristol-Myers Squibb	Ibuprofen 400 mg **Generic** Schein	Ibuprofen 600 mg **Generic** Schein
Imipramine 10 mg **Generic** Biocraft	Imipramine 50 mg **Generic** Biocraft	Isoniazid 300 mg **Generic** Barr	Isosorbide Dinitrate 40 mg **Sorbitrate** Zeneca
Isosorbide Dinitrate 5 mg **Generic** Geneva	Isosorbide Dinitrate 10 mg **Generic** Geneva	Ketoprofen 12.5 mg **Actron** Bayer	Ketoprofen 12.5 mg **Orudis KT** Whitehall-Robins
Ketoprofen 25 mg **Generic** Lederle	Labetalol Hydrochloride 100 mg **Trandate** Glaxo Wellcome	Labetalol Hydrochloride 300 mg **Trandate** Glaxo Wellcome	Lamotrigine 25 mg **Lamictal** Glaxo Wellcome
Lansoprazole 15 mg **Prevacid** TAP	Leucovorin Calcium 5 mg **Wellcovorin** Glaxo Wellcome	Levodopa/Carbidopa 100/10 mg **Generic** Lemmon	Levodopa/Carbidopa 100/25 mg **Generic** Lemmon

Levodopa/Carbidopa 250/25 mg **Generic** LEMMON	Levothyroxine Sodium 0.3 mg **Levothroid** FOREST	Levothyroxine Sodium 0.025 mg **Levoxyl** DANIELS	Levothyroxine Sodium 0.05 mg **Levoxyl** DANIELS
Levothyroxine Sodium 0.15 mg **Levoxyl** DANIELS	Levothyroxine Sodium 0.2 mg **Levoxyl** DANIELS	Lisinopril 10 mg **Zestril** ZENECA	Lisinopril 20 mg **Zestril** ZENECA
Loperamide Hydrochloride 2 mg **Imodium A-D** MCNEIL	Loxapine 5 mg **Generic** WATSON	Meclizine 25 mg **Bonine** PFIZER	Medroxyprogesterone 2.5 mg **Cycrin** ESI
Megestrol Acetate 40 mg **Generic** PAR	Methyldopa 500 mg **Generic** LEDERLE	Methylphenidate 10 mg **Generic** MD PHARM	Methylprednisolone 4 mg **Medrol** UPJOHN
Metolazone 2.5 mg **Zaroxolyn** FISONS	Mexiletine Hydrochloride 150 mg **Mexitil** BOEHRINGER INGELHEIM	Molindone 25 mg **Moban** GATE	Morphine 30 mg **M S Contin** PURDUE FREDERICK

Morphine 60 mg **M S Contin** PURDUE FREDERICK	Morphine 100 mg **M S Contin** PURDUE FREDERICK	Nadolol 40 mg **Generic** MYLAN	Naproxen 250 mg **Generic** MYLAN
[DISCONTINUED] Nefazodone Hydrochloride 100 mg **Serzone** BRISTOL-MYERS SQUIBB	[DISCONTINUED] Nefazodone Hydrochloride 150 mg **Serzone** BRISTOL-MYERS SQUIBB	Nifedipine 60 mg **Adalat CC** BAYER	Nizatidine 150 mg **Axid** LILLY
Nortriptyline Hydrochloride 10 mg **Generic** SCHEIN/DANBURY	Ofloxacin 400 mg **Floxin** ORTHO	Olanzapine 5 mg **Zyprexa** LILLY	Oxycodone Hydrochloride 10 mg **Oxycontin** PURDUE
Pemoline 37.5 mg **Cylert** ABBOTT	Penicillin V 250 mg **Generic** BIOCRAFT	Perphenazine 4 mg **Generic** GENEVA	Phenytoin 100 mg **Dilantin** PARKE-DAVIS
Piroxicam 20 mg **Generic** NOVOPHARM	Potassium Chloride 1,500 mg **K-Dur 20** KEY	Prazosin 1 mg **Generic** LEDERLE	Prazosin 5 mg **Generic** LEDERLE

Prednisone 1 mg **Generic** ROXANE	Prednisone 5 mg **Generic** SCHEIN	Prednisone 10 mg **Generic** SCHEIN	Prednisone 50 mg **Generic** ROXANE
Procainamide Hydrochloride 500 mg **Procanbid** PARKE-DAVIS	Procainamide Hydrochloride 1,000 mg **Procanbid** PARKE-DAVIS	Procainamide Hydrochloride 375 mg **Generic** SCHEIN/DANBURY	Propranolol Hydrochloride 10 mg **Generic** SCHEIN/DANBURY
Propranolol Hydrochloride 20 mg **Generic** SCHEIN/DANBURY	Propranolol Hydrochloride 80 mg **Generic** WATSON	Pseudoephedrine 240 mg **Efidac 24 Once Daily** NOVARTIS	Pseudoephedrine 30 mg **Sudafed** GLAXO WELLCOME
Pseudoephedrine 30 mg **Generic** ROXANE	Quinapril Hydrochloride 5 mg **Accupril** PARKE-DAVIS	Quinapril Hydrochloride 20 mg **Accupril** PARKE-DAVIS	Quinidine 300 mg **Generic** SCHEIN
Ranitidine 75 mg **Zantac 75** GLAXO WELLCOME	Salsalate 500 mg **Salsitab** UPSHER-SMITH	Salsalate 750 mg **Generic** SIDMAK	Senna 17 mg **SenokotXTRA** PURDUE FREDERICK

Simethicone
125 mg
Alka-Seltzer Liquid Gelcaps
BAYER

Simethicone
125 mg
Gas-X Extra Strength
NOVARTIS

Simethicone
150 mg
Maalox Anti-Gas Extra Strength
NOVARTIS

Simethicone
95 mg
Phazyme
BLOCK

Simethicone
125 mg
Phazyme Maximum Strength
BLOCK

Simethicone
80 mg
Generic
GOLDLINE

Simvastatin
5 mg
Zocor
MERCK

Stavudine
20 mg
Zerit
BRISTOL-MYERS SQUIBB

Terbutaline Sulfate
2.5 mg
Brethine
NOVARTIS

Theophylline
100 mg
Slo-Bid
RHONE-POULENC RORER

Theophylline
200 mg
Theo-Dur
KEY

Theophylline
300 mg
Theo-Dur
KEY

Theophylline
450 mg
Theo-Dur
KEY

Thioridazine Hydrochloride
25 mg
Generic
CREIGHTON

Thioridazine Hydrochloride
50 mg
Generic
CREIGHTON

Thiothixene
5 mg
Generic
GENEVA

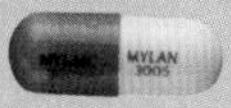

Thiothixene
5 mg
Generic
MYLAN

Thiothixene
10 mg
Generic
MYLAN

Topiramate
25 mg
Topamax
McNEIL

Torsemide
5 mg
Demadex
BOEHRINGER MANNHEIM

Trifluoperazine Hydrochloride 1 mg **Generic** GENEVA	Trifluoperazine Hydrochloride 2 mg **Generic** GENEVA	Trifluoperazine Hydrochloride 5 mg **Generic** GENEVA	Valproic Acid 250 mg **Depakene** ABBOTT
Valproic Acid 250 mg **Depakote** ABBOTT	Verapamil Hydrochloride 180 mg **Isoptin SR** KNOLL	Verapamil Hydrochloride 240 mg **Isoptin SR** KNOLL	Verapamil Hydrochloride 80 mg **Generic** GENEVA
Verapamil Hydrochloride 120 mg **Generic** SCHEIN/DANBURY	Vitamin B1 100 mg **Generic** NUTRO	Vitamin B6 (Pyridoxine) 50 mg **Generic** NUTRO	Vitamin C 250 mg **Generic** NUTRO
Warfarin 2.5 mg **Coumadin** DUPONT	Warfarin 5 mg **Coumadin** DUPONT	Warfarin 10 mg **Coumadin** DUPONT	

A Guide to
Dietary Supplements

A Guide to
Dietary Supplements

DIETARY SUPPLEMENTS: AN OVERVIEW

As the use of medications increases, more people than ever are also using a constantly expanding variety of dietary supplements to prevent, treat, or manage a range of health problems.

As defined by the U. S. Food and Drug Administration (FDA), dietary supplements encompass not only vitamins and minerals, but also herbs and other plant-derived substances ("botanicals"), various enzymes, amino acids, and even some human hormones.

Available without a prescription, these products are now sold in supermarkets, drug stores, and specialty stores, through catalogs, and on many Internet sites. They have become enormously popular, with users numbering in the millions. In a recently published study based on data from the National Health and Nutrition Examination Survey, 52 percent of adults reported having taken a dietary supplement in the previous month. Supplements are also big business. Though growth has slowed somewhat since the mid-1990s, the supplement industry sells an estimated $18 billion worth of products a year, of which more than $4 billion is spent on herbal supplements.

Supplements, and particularly herbs, are among the therapies considered part of complementary and alternative medicine, or CAM. Like other CAM practices, such as acupuncture or massage therapy, supplements may be used alone or in addition to conventional mainstream medicine. The following overview explains the key differences between dietary supplements and conventional medications, and sorts through the dilemmas and confusions facing the consumer interested in using supplements. As a further guide, starting on page 848, there are individual profiles of 10 of the most popular supplements marketed in the United States. The profiles summarize and assess the principal claims made for each supplement and offer precautions and guidelines concerning their use.

THE BASIC PROBLEM: A LACK OF RELIABLE EVIDENCE

Despite the widespread use of dietary supplements, surprisingly few places provide consumers with reliable, authoritative information on their effectiveness and safety. The need for supplements of vitamins and certain minerals to help prevent or treat diseases resulting from nutritional deficiencies is well established. Those uses—for which doses are based on the government's Recommended Dietary Allowances (RDAs)—are covered in the main section of this book. But most other benefits claimed for dietary supplements—benefits that range from curing colds to preventing heart disease—are largely unproven.

As interest in supplements has increased, so has scientific scrutiny of their therapeutic potential and safety. Some supplements, perhaps many of them, may prove to have real therapeutic value. However, most of the research on supplements, especially on herbs, has had limitations. Much "evidence" is anecdotal; clinical studies are often small, short-term, and poorly designed; negative results may be underreported; and effects of long-term use of supplements are lacking.

Even in Germany, where a government-approved body of experts known as Commission E has systematically reviewed the evidence on some 300 herbs over the past three decades, the scientific basis for the Commission E recommendations has not been made public. Only recently have researchers begun to undertake the kind of well-designed clinical trials that are routinely required to assess the safety and efficacy of conventional medications. Some supplements show promise. To date, however, there is simply a lack of definitive evidence for or against the effectiveness of most products that are within easy reach of the American consumer.

Perhaps the greatest misconception many people have about dietary supplements, and herbal preparations in particular, is that they are safe because they are derived from a natural source. This assumption is not necessarily true. Many herbs do have physiological effects; some effects are mild, but others are severe and dangerous, just like the effects from certain drugs. In fact, many drugs are "natural" in the sense that they originally came from plants. And just like drugs, different herbs can interact with one another, or with conventional medications, in ways that can have serious consequences.

The difference is that a drug, in order to be marketed, must undergo clinical studies to determine its effectiveness, safety, possible interactions with other substances, and appropriate dosages; then the FDA must review these data and authorize the drug's use before it can be put on the market. Supplements do not have to undergo testing or approval by the FDA. No authoritative body oversees the effectiveness and safety of supplements or their manufacture.

In addition, American physicians generally receive little or no training concerning the use of herbal medicines or other types of dietary supplements. In a number of Western European countries, medical students are routinely taught about medicinal herbs, and physicians commonly prescribe herbal preparations for a wide range of ailments. For example, the herb St. John's wort is widely prescribed to treat depression by doctors in Germany, where it outsells Prozac, the world's best-selling antidepressant medication, by a substantial margin. Herbal products in Europe must also conform to manufacturing standards, and studies examining supplements in European countries typically use standardized products containing consistent amounts of active ingredients—qualities that are not assured in the United States.

WHY CLAIMS CAN'T BE TRUSTED

In many ways, American consumers are on their own when it comes to using supplements—and the primary reason for this is government legislation. With the Dietary Supplement Health and Education Act (DSHEA) of 1994, Congress essentially removed dietary supplements from regulatory control by the FDA. Provided the label for a supplement makes no claims about the product's effectiveness against specific diseases, it is exempt from the normally rigorous testing the FDA requires to establish the safety and efficacy of drugs and food additives. So although labels can state dosages and make health-related claims that give them an air of authority, such information is not based on the kind of data that drug manufacturers must submit to the FDA in order to get a medication approved. Indeed, supplement manufacturers can make claims about a product without any scientific evidence to support them.

In 2000 the FDA published a ruling that defines the types of claims supplement manufacturers can make on product labels. This ruling prohibits the label from stating that a supplement can prevent, treat, or cure a specific disease—unless such a claim has passed an FDA review for efficacy. A few dietary supplements have met this condition: labels for calcium supplements, for example, can state that they help prevent osteoporosis; likewise, labels for folic acid supplements can claim that they help prevent birth defects. But these are exceptions. In practical terms, supplement labels cannot state, for example, that they prevent cardiovascular disease or treat depression.

However, manufacturers are permitted to make claims about how their supplements affect the "structure or function" of the body. This is where language can become misleading, since such claims may imply that a product can help treat a health problem. The label on a bottle of St. John's wort, for example, cannot claim to "treat depression." But it can state that the supplement "helps improve mood"—leaving open the question as to whether it can actually help someone who is depressed.

The FDA had initially hoped to limit such claims, but some consumer groups, and virtually all supplement manufacturers, expressed concern that government interference might take popular supplements off the market. Under considerable pressure, the agency reconsidered and ultimately relaxed the proposed restrictions. Any product that promises structure/function benefits must also display a disclaimer stating that the claim has not been approved by the FDA, nor is the product intended to "diagnose, treat, cure, or prevent any disease." But the disclaimer can appear in small type and may be overlooked by—or fail to impress—many consumers.

As a result, it's often impossible for consumers to distinguish between claims that may be reasonable and ones that have little if any validity. Consumers are often left with no more knowledge about the judicious use of supplements than their marketers deign to offer. To complicate matters, many supplements contain two or more ingredients whose individual and combined effects are anybody's guess.

As if all this weren't sufficiently confusing to consumers, the limited restrictions the FDA imposes on the labeling of supplements don't apply to their marketing. As a result, ads for supplements in magazines, catalogs, or on the Internet often claim unlikely benefits. To date, the Federal Trade Commission (FTC), which regulates advertising claims, has taken enforcement actions against a number of manufacturers making demonstrably false or misleading claims. For example, the FTC recently brought charges against several companies promoting St. John's wort as a safe and effective treatment for HIV/AIDS. Not only is the herb unproven as a treatment, but also it poses a risk of adverse interactions with prescription medications commonly used for treating the disease. Unfortunately, given its limited resources, the FTC can only monitor and challenge a fraction of the dizzying number of claims made in the promotional materials used to sell supplements.

NO GUARANTEES OF PURITY

The deregulation of supplements also means that the government does nothing to ensure that they meet quality standards. Because the purity and consistency of products is left up to the manufacturer, consumers can't be sure that a product contains what the label states. This is less of an issue with vitamin and mineral supplements, which are relatively simple to standardize. Herbal supplements are another matter. The amount of active chemical ingredients can vary considerably among different batches of the same plant. In addition, manufacturers do not isolate the active ingredients. Instead, many products contain all the components or compounds contained in the plant. In most cases, the active ingredient, if any, is unknown, and the product contains many other chemicals that occur naturally in the plant.

Tests conducted by independent laboratories in recent years have shown that the ingredients contained in different brands of an herbal supplement, such as St. John's wort or saw palmetto, can vary widely. In one study assessing the content of 24 ginseng products, a third of the products contained no ginseng components at all. A study of 880 brands of the top herbs, published in the *Archives of Internal Medicine* in 2003, found that fewer than half the products contained the recommended amount of the ingredients. Both *Consumer Reports* and ConsumerLab.com have also tested various herbal supplements and found that a product's ingredients can be considerably different from those stated on the label. The haphazardness of manufacturing standards also means that statements about dosages—which experts don't agree on to begin with—are all the more questionable.

Recent FDA regulations at least require that the labels for all supplements begin to carry a "Supplement Facts" panel that lists all the ingredients in a product and clearly identifies the name and address of the manufacturer or distributor. Still, this ruling doesn't mean that the bottle contains what is on the label. And even if it does, there remains the fundamental problem any consumer faces in choosing a supplement: despite cleverly-worded and scientific-sounding claims, no clear evidence exists that the vast majority of herbs and other products have any benefit at all.

THE ISSUE OF SAFETY

Although few supplements have proven efficacy, and few data support their use, most appear to be fairly safe when taken as directed. Thus, they may not help, but they probably won't hurt.

However, there are notable exceptions. An Associated Press analysis of FDA records revealed more than 2,600 reports of adverse reactions, including 101 deaths, associated with dietary supplements between 1993 and 1998. Since millions of people use supplements, these numbers are relatively low (perhaps due, in part, to spotty reporting); yet such calamities are still tragic, all the more so because they are avoidable. Unfortunately, the safety of a supplement, like its efficacy, does not have to be demonstrated before a product is marketed—in contrast to drugs. And once a supplement is in the

Checklist for Supplement Users

Because dietary supplements are largely unregulated, keep these points in mind if you decide to try a supplement, especially an herbal product:

▶ **Don't rely on any type of supplement to self-treat a serious health problem.** Be sure to consult your doctor for a proper diagnosis and for treatment recommendations.

▶ **Communicate with your doctor.** Report all of your symptoms and tell your doctor about any supplements you are taking. Some of them might produce adverse effects when combined with drugs prescribed for you.

▶ **Don't stop conventional treatment.** You should never discontinue or alter the dosage of a prescribed medication without first consulting your doctor.

▶ **Buy established brands from reputable vendors.** This step is no guarantee of purity in a product, but at least major manufacturers and distributors have the financial resources to establish quality control procedures; they also have reputations to protect.

▶ **Check the label.** Be sure supplements are carefully labeled (some manufacturers list potential drug interactions) and contain standardized extracts, if possible. ("Standardized" means that each capsule or tablet contains a uniform amount of a certain compound.) Beware of extravagant claims, "quick-fix" promises, and terms such as "clinically proven," "guaranteed potency," "naturally occurring," or "maximum absorption." Such terms have no standard definition; they are simply advertising jargon.

▶ **Look for products with the USP notation.** The United States Pharmacopeia (USP), an independent non-profit organization that sets standards of potency and purity for conventional medications, has established comparable standards for vitamins, minerals, and, most recently, some herbs. Compliance with USP standards is up to the manufacturer, but the presence of "USP" on a product from a nationally-known manufacturer means it is likely that the standards have been met. (The absence of "USP," however, does not mean that a product has failed to meet the standards—and standards have yet to be established for many herbal supplements.)

▶ **Be conservative with supplement dosages.** Dosages have not been scientifically established for most supplements,. Nor can you be sure that a product's contents matches what's on the label—so you may be risking an overdose if you start off taking the highest dosage. If a range is given, begin with the lowest dose.

▶ **Most supplements, especially herbs, shouldn't be used on a long-term basis.** There is little or no evidence to indicate how long you should take most supplements before you begin to experience a benefit. If you take an herbal product or some other type of supplement for a specific health problem, and you experience no benefit after several weeks, stop taking it. (Vitamins and mineral supplements are less likely to cause problems when taken in appropriate doses for long periods. The precautions that do apply are spelled out in the vitamin and mineral profiles in the main section of this book.)

▶ **Watch for side effects.** Many people think herbal products are safe, but herbs and other supplements can produce serious side effects. Be alert to unusual signs or symptoms that occur after you've begun taking a supplement. If any develop, stop taking the supplement and call your doctor or other health-care provider.

▶ **Avoid herbs if you are pregnant or breastfeeding.** The consequences simply haven't been established. Also, don't give supplements to children (other than multi-vitamin/mineral supplements) without first talking to your doctor.

▶ **Before surgery, inform your doctor.** As many as 70 percent of patients using herbs don't tell their doctors during exams before surgery. It's crucial not to withhold such information. The American Society of Anesthesiologists suggests stopping supplements at least two to three weeks before a surgical procedure.

Note: If you suffer a serious harmful effect or illness that you think is related to supplement use, you should contact MedWatch to report it. Only in this way can information about the adverse effects of dietary supplements be centrally obtained and circulated. Your doctor can also file a report. Call MedWatch at 800 332-1088 or go to their Web site at www.fda.gov/medwatch.

marketplace, no process is in place to track the occurrence of adverse reactions. The FDA keeps track of a drug's adverse side effects through reports filed by physicians, and can act promptly to take a drug off the market or restrict its use. The FDA can't rely on such reports for supplements, which are sold over-the-counter and can't be overseen by physicians. Moreover, as stipulated by the DSHEA legislation, the FDA has to prove that a product is unsafe before it can be removed from the market.

Consequently, in the past few years, the FDA has issued only a handful of warnings about supplements. Probably the strongest statements have been directed at the diet supplement ephedrine (also called ephedra and ma huang) and the steroid-like drug andostenedione (marketed as an athletic performance enhancer). The FDA has warned the public to avoid products containing either of these substances. Ephedra has been linked to deaths, heart attacks and strokes; andostenedione has been linked to hormonal problems such as testicular atrophy, impotence, and breast enlargement in men, and deepening of the voice and increased facial hair in women. The agency has also warned that kava can cause severe liver damage, and that St. John's wort can interact with other drugs to make them less effective. In addition, the FDA publicized a warning by the California Department of Health Services not to take PC-SPES, a so-called "herbal supplement" promoted to treat prostate cancer that was found to be tainted with prescription drugs, including diethylstilbestrol (DES).

A recent issue of the British medical journal *The Lancet* featured a review of all Medline database reports of adverse effects from dietary supplements that occurred between 1966 and 1998. (Medline is the National Library of Medicine's premier bibliographic database containing citations from over 4,000 biomedical journals.) Among the key observations in the article: many herbal products are mislabeled (a different and sometimes toxic plant may have been used instead of the one specified on the label, often as a result of poor translation from, say, Chinese to English); thousands of imported herbal products also contain potent added pharmaceutical agents (including caffeine, acetaminophen, anti-inflammatory drugs, diuretics, and

steroids); and about 10 percent of herbal products from Asia are contaminated with dangerous heavy metals, such as lead, arsenic, and mercury.

In a survey of 260 Chinese herbal medicines sold over-the-counter in California, investigators in the California Department of Health Services found that 32 percent of the products contained undeclared pharmaceutical agents or heavy metals.

MIXING SUPPLEMENTS AND MEDICATIONS

In addition to adverse effects caused by supplements themselves, there is a potential for even greater harm when supplements, particularly herbs, are used along with conventional medications because of possible interactions that may enhance, reduce, or eliminate the effects of a particular medication in ways that are largely unknown. Such interactions are critical for medications with a narrow therapeutic range—those drugs that require precise dosages in order to be effective without being toxic (see chart, page 847).

One of the most serious herb-drug-related complications occurs when warfarin—an anticoagulant with a narrow dosage range that is often prescribed to prevent blood clots in people with atrial fibrillation (a heart rhythm disturbance)—is taken with ginkgo (said to improve memory) or garlic tablets or powders (said to improve glucose, cholesterol, and blood pressure control). Either combination can prompt internal bleeding that may trigger a stroke.

Similarly, herb-drug interactions are more likely for medications that typically require "fine tuning" adjustments of dosages to determine the most effective dose for a particular individual. One example of such a drug is the antiparkinsonian medication levodopa (Dopar and Larodopa). In a survey of 200 patients with Parkinson's disease, Johns Hopkins researchers found that about a quarter used a vitamin or herb supplement and most did not inform their physicians when they started to take the supplement.

The risk of problems also rises when supplements and drugs are taken for the same purpose, presumably because they may share similar actions or address similar underlying causes. For example, St. John's wort, marketed primarily for depression, can increase the side effects of selective serotonin reuptake inhibitors (SSRIs), the most commonly prescribed type of antidepressant medication. Confusion, allergic reactions, stomach upset, headache, and restlessness may result.

Potential supplement-drug problems are a special concern when a patient's health is compromised due to chronic medical problems (especially kidney or liver impairment), frailty, poor nutrition, or surgery. A study reported in *The Journal of the American Medical Association (JAMA)* found that eight commonly used herbs can cause complications in the period immediately following surgery. The problems include an increased risk of stroke, excessive bleeding, hypoglycemia (low blood glucose), allergic reactions, or the sedative effects of anesthesia. Some of the most popular herbs—including ginkgo, garlic, and St. John's wort—are among the offenders.

WHAT YOU CAN DO

The federal government is currently funding research into dietary supplements, but definitive results may be a long way off. In the meantime, our recommendation is: Proceed with caution.

The best way to avoid dangerous reactions from dietary supplements is to let your doctor and pharmacist know of any products you are taking or intend to take. Increasingly, pharmacists and physicians are more knowledgeable about how drugs interact with each other and with other substances.

Yet patients are often their own worst enemy. Two landmark studies showed that 40 to 70 percent of the millions of people using nontraditional remedies do not tell their doctors about it. They may fear chastisement for straying from orthodoxy or harbor the common misconception that "natural" remedies are somehow harmless, especially since they are available without a prescription.

Good communication is essential for reducing potential problems and may prevent a disaster. It's

---

An Overview of Herb-Drug Interactions

Herb-drug interactions are more likely when using	Selected examples:
Drugs with a narrow therapeutic range	• Warfarin, taken for atrial fibrillation • Digoxin, taken for congestive heart failure • Theophylline, taken for asthma • Lithium, taken for bipolar disorder (manic depression) • Phenytoin, an anti-seizure medication
Drug that typically require trial and error to find the right dose	• Levothyroxine, taken for an underactive thyroid • Levodopa, an antiparkinson drug
Drugs and herbs that may have similar actions or be used for the same purpose	• St. John's wort with SSRIs for depression • Saw palmetto with finasteride or terazosin for an enlarged prostate • Ginkgo or garlic with low-dose aspirin to discourage blood clots • Soy (a non-herbal plant product that contains estrogen) with hormone replacement therapy
Herbs around the time of surgery	• Ginkgo, garlic, St. John's wort, echinacea, Panax ginseng, ephedra, Kava, and valerian

especially important whenever you are starting a new medication or having elective surgery. Also see "Checklist for Supplement Users" (page 845) for advice on choosing and using supplements.

PROFILES OF POPULAR SUPPLEMENTS

The following pages contain information and guidelines on ten best-selling dietary supplements used for medicinal purposes. Most of them are herbs, but others, such as fish oil and coenzyme Q-10, are created from natural compounds. The supplements profiled in this section have been selected primarily because they are among the most commonly used. They are also among the best-studied: some, though not all, have shown promise for treating or alleviating specific conditions.

Each profile covers the use (or uses) the supplement is commonly promoted for; the evidence for its effectiveness; its safety, including known and potential interactions with conventional medications; and any special considerations you should be aware of if you decide to try the supplement.

Keep in mind that the FDA has not reviewed these supplements either for efficacy or safety. Also, the potency and purity of any products you buy are left up to manufacturers; there is no assurance that the capsules or pills in a bottle contain what is on the label. Active ingredients can vary from brand to brand and you may not be taking the same preparation that has been used in a research study—or even by a friend who recommended the supplement to you.

In compiling the profiles, we have drawn on a number of sources containing evidence-based information on dietary supplements. One especially useful general source is the *Professional's Handbook of Complementary and Alternative Medicines* (third edition) by C. W. Fetrow, PharmD and Juan R. Avila, PharmD (Lippincott Williams & Wilkins, 2003)—a comprehensive reference for which the authors reviewed hundreds of journal articles. Other helpful sources include the following:

- **National Center for Complementary and Alternative Medicine**
  Telephone: 888-644-6226
  Website: www.nccam.nih.gov

- **United States Pharmacopeia (USP)**
  Telephone: 800-822-8772
  Website: www.usp.org

- **Quackwatch**
  Website: www.quackwatch.org

Coenzyme Q-10

WHAT IS IT?

Coenzyme Q-10, also known as CoQ10, mitoquinone, ubidecarenone, and ubiquinone, is an antioxidant that is found naturally in the body, and in small amounts in meat and seafood. The supplement is marketed primarily as a treatment for heart failure and coronary heart disease. It is also purported to be useful for treating high blood pressure, angina, arrhythmias, Bell's palsy, deafness, diabetes, heart problems caused by certain chemotherapy agents, immunodeficiency, mitral valve prolapse, and gum disease.

COMMON FORMS

Available as a tablet, capsule, and liquid, and as a topical preparation for treatment of gum disease. In addition, an intravenous/intramuscular form has been used for heart protection during heart bypass surgery.

HOW IT WORKS

Coenzyme Q-10 is an antioxidant that destroys free radicals, protecting cell membranes from oxidative damage. This includes protecting heart muscle from damage caused by interruptions in blood flow, as occurs in heart attacks. In addition, it is essential for production of adenosine triphosphate (ATP), a major source of energy for cellular reactions.

RESEARCH AND EVIDENCE

Because people with heart failure are deficient in coenzyme Q10, researchers hoped that coenzyme Q10 supplementation might be an effective treatment for heart failure. Unfortunately, controlled trials in people have produced mixed results, and insufficient evidence exists for this use.

Coenzyme Q10 did produce promising results in

a preliminary study of 144 people who had suffered a recent heart attack. The study found that people randomized to take 120 mg per day of coenzyme Q10 for 4 weeks had fewer heart problems such as angina and arrhythmias compared with those who took a placebo. Larger studies are needed to confirm these results.

In one 12-week trial in people with hypertension, taking 60 mg of coenzyme Q10 twice a day reduced systolic blood pressure.

Trials have found that combinations of coenzyme Q10 and vitamin E do not reduce levels of low-density lipoprotein (LDL) cholesterol. Coenzyme Q10 is also ineffective for reducing fatigue.

POSSIBLE SIDE EFFECTS

Damage to heart during intense exercise, and gastrointestinal problems such as loss of appetite, diarrhea, abdominal pain, and mild nausea.

POTENTIAL DRUG INTERACTIONS

Coenzyme Q10 may make warfarin less effective. Oral antidiabetic agents such as metformin (Glucophage) may lessen the effects of coenzyme Q10 supplements.

SPECIAL CONSIDERATIONS

- Coenzyme Q10 need not be taken with the cholesterol drugs called statins , as some alternative remedy practitioners suggest. Although statins may deplete blood levels of coenzyme Q10, tissue levels appear to remain normal. It is also unclear whether a decline in blood levels of coenzyme Q10 is harmful or whether taking supplements to replace it is beneficial.
- People with heart disease should not attempt to self-medicate with coenzyme Q10. If your doctor recommends coenzyme Q10, typical doses are 100 to 600 mg for heart failure (2 mg per kilogram of body weight), 120 mg a day for 4 weeks after a heart attack, and 75 to 360 mg a day for high blood pressure.
- Do not perform intense exercise during therapy with coenzyme Q10 because damage to heart muscle may occur. Some studies have suggested that coenzyme Q10 shortens the time it takes for heart muscle to become fatigued.
- People with heart failure should always report changes in their condition to their doctor.

Echinacea

Latin name: Echinacea purpurea, e. pallida, and others

WHAT IS IT?

Extracts of echinacea, a plant that is part of the daisy family, have been used as herbal medicines for centuries. Nine varieties of echinacea grow in the United States, and three of them—the most common being Echinacea purpurea—are used in dietary supplements. The principal claim made for the supplements is that they strengthen the immune system and can thereby ward off infections, particularly colds and flu. As part of its immune-boosting effect, echinacea is also claimed to be effective for speeding up the healing of burns, cuts, wounds, and inflammations of the skin.

COMMON FORMS

Available as capsules, tablets, and in other forms that include juices, lozenges, teas, and tinctures.

HOW IT WORKS

The herb is pharmacologically complex, containing at least 15 different compounds. Although several classes of compounds appear to stimulate immune system activity, no single component has been identified as the "active ingredient" responsible for the benefits attributed to echinacea.

RESEARCH AND EVIDENCE

Echinacea has been extensively studied, with mixed results. In some studies examining its effect on treating the common cold—probably the most popular use of the herb—echinacea seemed to have no effect; in others, it appeared to reduce the severity or duration of symptoms. Moreover, in most studies finding that echinacea stimulated the immune system, the herbal extract was injected, a form of administration that is not available in the United States. As a strategy for preventing colds, the evidence is even less persuasive: studies show little difference between echinacea and a placebo. A recent review found insufficient evidence to recommend echinacea for either the treatment or prevention of upper respiratory infections.

POSSIBLE SIDE EFFECTS

Side effects in healthy people have seldom been

reported. But any preparations containing echinacea may have an adverse effect on people with severe illnesses, including autoimmune diseases, HIV infection, leukemia, multiple sclerosis, or tuberculosis.

POTENTIAL DRUG INTERACTIONS
No significant interactions have been reported.

SPECIAL CONSIDERATIONS
• If you decide to try echinacea for preventing or treating a cold or bout of flu, it's unknown which variety of echinacea is most effective or what is the proper dosage. Also, more than most other herbs, the concentration of active ingredients can vary significantly in different preparations depending on the variety of echinacea, the part of the plant used, growing conditions, and how the ingredients were extracted.
• Commercial echinacea preparations are often diluted with inactive ingredients. Be sure to check the label. Many tinctures contain significant amounts of alcohol and may not be appropriate for children or for adults who should avoid alcohol.
• Anyone who is infected with HIV, has an autoimmune disease, or has another serious illness should avoid using echinacea.
• Pregnant or breastfeeding women should not use echinacea; the effects are unknown.
• Any therapeutic effects of echinacea are usually evident within 10 to 14 days. If an illness you are treating has not improved within that time, be sure to see your doctor. And do not, in any case, use echinacea for more than 8 weeks.

Fish Oil

WHAT IS IT?
Fish is a healthy food; the American Heart Association (AHA) recommends that people without heart disease eat at least two servings a week and that people with heart disease eat about one serving per day. For people with heart disease who don't wish to eat fish every day, the AHA suggests that people consider taking a daily fish oil supplement after consulting a physician. The principal claim for fish oil, which is rich in polyunsaturated fatty acids called omega-3 fatty acids, is that it reduces the risk of sudden death and death from other causes in people with heart disease. Fish oil also can reduce elevated triglycerides (lipids, or fats, found in the blood), and is purported to treat high blood pressure and rheumatoid arthritis.

COMMON FORMS
Available in capsules and in a more highly-concentrated liquid form.

HOW IT WORKS
Fish oil contains the omega-3 fatty acids eicosapentaenoic acid (EPA) and docasahexaenoic acid (DHA). In the body, EPA and DHA get converted to hormone-like substances called eicosanoids that have anti-inflammatory, antiarrhythmic, and vasodilatory properties. They also lower triglyceride levels in the blood, probably by blocking the synthesis of very-low-density lipoprotein and triglycerides in the liver.

RESEARCH AND EVIDENCE
Fish oil has a proven effect on the heart. One large Italian study of people with heart disease found that after three and a half years, people who received 850 mg a day of omega-3 fatty acids had a 45 percent reduction in sudden death and a 20 percent reduction in death from all causes.

Some evidence shows that fish oil supplements can reduce blood triglyceride levels. One review article found that 4 g per day of omega-3 fatty acids reduced blood triglycerides by 25 to 30 percent in people with elevated triglyceride levels. Fish oil also appears to have a modest effect on blood pressure in people with hypertension: a meta-analysis of 31 trials found that 5.6 g per day of fish oil reduced blood pressure by 3.4/2.0 mm Hg.

Finally, some evidence exists for the use of fish oil in rheumatoid arthritis. Several small studies have found that taking at least 3 g per day of fish oil can reduce morning stiffness and the number of tender, swollen joints in people with rheumatoid arthritis.

POSSIBLE SIDE EFFECTS
The most common side effects of fish oil are a fishy aftertaste and gastrointestinal symptoms such as

nausea, bloating, and belching. Higher doses are associated with more pronounced side effects.

POTENTIAL DRUG INTERACTIONS

Although fish oil prolongs bleeding time, there are no documented cases of bleeding problems, even when taken in high doses and combined with anticoagulant medications such as warfarin (Coumadin). Nevertheless, people taking anticoagulants should avoid high doses of fish oils.

SPECIAL CONSIDERATIONS

- If you wish to start taking fish oil, consult your doctor. Don't stop taking your regular medications for heart disease, high blood pressure, high blood triglycerides, or arthritis without your doctor's okay.
- The American Heart Association (AHA) recommends that people with heart disease get about 1 g per day of EPA plus DHA. Although the AHA recommends oily fish as the best source of these fatty acids, it states that people can meet that goal by using supplements as long as they consult with a physician.
- The AHA recommends that people who need to lower their triglyceride levels get 2 to 4 g a day of EPA plus DHA in supplement form.
- Fish oil capsules generally contain 180 mg of EPA and 120 mg of DHA per 1 g. Fish oil liquid concentrate generally contains 1 to 3 g of EPA plus DHA per teaspoon.
- In addition to standard fish oil from salmon or herring, fish oil is available as cod liver oil and omega-3 fatty acid concentrate.

Garlic

Latin name: *Allium sativum*

WHAT IS IT?

A member of the onion family, garlic has been used for thousands of years as a medicinal plant, and today garlic supplements are extremely popular as well as extensively researched. Promoters of the supplements make countless claims for garlic's benefits: it is marketed for treating everything from headaches to infections to cancer. Probably the chief claim made for garlic, however, is that it can reduce the risk of heart disease by lowering blood cholesterol levels. Hundreds of garlic studies have investigated these and other claims during the past ten years. Despite the studies and much advertising promoting garlic's curative powers, there is no clear evidence that garlic supplements have any health benefit.

COMMON FORMS

Most commonly available as tablets of compressed powder made from dried garlic bulbs. Also sold as fresh bulbs, freeze-dried powder, fresh extract, and oil.

HOW IT WORKS

Garlic contains more than 23 constituents, but alliin and allicin are often cited as the key active ingredients. Allicin is an unstable sulfurous compound that is formed from alliin by enzymes when the clove is chewed, crushed, or ground; allicin gives garlic its strong odor. Allicin then breaks down into other sulfur-containing compounds. However, alliin and allicin are not present in all garlic supplements, so if they are indeed the active ingredients, more may be available in raw garlic or powdered forms of garlic. The problem is, some other compound might be beneficial—or not. No one knows.

RESEARCH AND EVIDENCE

With regard to the claims for garlic's cholesterol-lowering effect, a few clinical trials have shown a modest benefit. But these studies—like most studies on claims for garlic—have been small, poorly designed (many with no control group), and use different forms of garlic, so their results are questionable.

Two well-designed controlled studies concluded that garlic had no effect on cholesterol levels. Both studies—one published in the *Archives of Internal Medicine*, the other in the *Journal of the American Medical Association*—involved subjects with elevated cholesterol and compared the results of taking garlic supplements against a placebo over 12 weeks. Each study used a different form of garlic—an oil and a powder tablet—but neither form reduced cholesterol levels. By contrast, a review article published in 2001 concluded that garlic does have a small effect on total cholesterol—but that the effect disappeared after 6 months of treatment.

POSSIBLE SIDE EFFECTS

No serious adverse reactions have been reported from taking garlic supplements. The most common side effects have been heartburn, upset stomach, and irritation of the mouth and throat, especially from high doses.

POTENTIAL DRUG INTERACTIONS

There may be a risk of bleeding if garlic supplements are taken with anticoagulant medications such as warfarin (Coumadin).

SPECIAL CONSIDERATIONS

- Although garlic appears to be safe, there is no evidence for relying on it to lower blood cholesterol levels—or to treat any other health problem, for that matter. Indeed, it's far from clear that garlic in any form has any significant pharmacological effect. And if there is some benefit from using garlic, it's not known how long you would have to eat garlic or take supplements to obtain the benefit.
- If you still want to try garlic supplements, the standard dose in studies documenting their effect on lipid levels has been 600 to 900 mg per day in pill form or 5 to 8 mg of garlic oil (equivalent to half a clove to a clove of raw garlic).
- If you take a prescription medication, talk to your doctor before using garlic in high doses or over the long term. Avoid taking garlic supplements if you are on an anticoagulant medication.

Ginkgo biloba

Latin name: *Ginkgo biloba*

WHAT IS IT?

Supplements of ginkgo biloba are among the most widely used herbal remedies in the world. The supplements are made from a leaf extract of the ginkgo tree, a primitive native of China that dates back some 230 million years and now grows in many other countries. In Germany and France, standardized ginkgo extracts are among the most commonly prescribed remedies for circulatory and neurological problems. But in the United States, the herb is most actively promoted as a "memory booster" that can help sharpen mental focus in healthy people as well as slow or prevent "normal" memory loss—claims that have no evidence to support them.

COMMON FORMS

Standardized ginkgo biloba extract (called GBE) is available in capsules and tablets, and also in tinctures, powders, liquids, sprays, and even "nutrition bars." In Asia, seeds of the ginkgo biloba tree are used medicinally, but can cause severe allergic reactions, and so should be avoided.

HOW IT WORKS

Ginkgo extracts contain a variety of active ingredients, including flavonoids and terpenoids, that act in concert to induce antioxidant and anti-inflammatory effects. These properties could account for its supposed benefits to the brain. Some studies show that it may relax blood vessels, increase blood flow, reduce clotting, and reduce the abnormalities that afflict the brain in those with dementia.

RESEARCH AND EVIDENCE

Most studies on ginkgo biloba have been small and poorly designed. The first American trial to rigorously examine the herb, published in the *Journal of the American Medical Association (JAMA)* in 1997, found that cognitive performance and social functioning were more likely to stabilize or improve in ginkgo-takers than in those taking a placebo. Subjects were evaluated over the course of a year. The results indicate that ginkgo can aid some people with dementia; however, even though side effects were minimal, one third of the 309 subjects dropped out of the study, suggesting that many experienced no benefit. In an updated analysis of the trial published in 2002, the researchers concluded that ginkgo improved cognitive and social functioning in some people with mild cognitive impairment, but only slowed down decline in people with more severe dementia.

Most medical experts are not ready to fully embrace ginkgo for treating dementia. And there was no indication at all in the *JAMA* study, or in any other controlled studies, that ginkgo can enhance mental alertness or help prevent the type of normal memory loss (such as having trouble recalling names or locating familiar objects) that almost everyone experiences with age. Although ginkgo has also been investigated as a remedy for other disorders, further research is needed to confirm its effectiveness.

POSSIBLE SIDE EFFECTS

In studies, side effects have been minor and include headache, diarrhea, flatulence, nausea, and allergic skin reactions. No serious adverse effects have been reported in human trials using ginkgo biloba extract.

POTENTIAL DRUG INTERACTIONS

Because ginkgo interferes with blood clotting, it may interact with medications often referred to as "blood-thinners," such as aspirin and warfarin (Coumadin), and increase the risk of internal bleeding.

SPECIAL CONSIDERATIONS

- People with Alzheimer's disease or other forms of dementia will gain more from prescription drugs such as galantamine (Reminyl), rivastigmine (Exelon), donepezil (Aricept), and memantine (Namenda), which have been extensively studied and are approved by the FDA, than from taking ginkgo biloba.
- If you decide to try ginkgo, dosages are uncertain. Most trials have used 120 to 160 milligrams a day, divided into three doses, and a four-to-six-week course of treatment has been necessary to determine effectiveness. But because of the lack of government regulation, brands of ginkgo in the United States undoubtedly vary as to their purity and the potency of their active ingredients.
- Talk to your doctor before taking ginkgo if you take any medications regularly. This is especially important if you are taking any type of blood-thinning medication. Also call your doctor if, while taking ginkgo, you experience any signs of bleeding, easy bruising, or any other possible side effects.
- If you are undergoing elective surgery, it's very important to tell your doctor beforehand that you are using ginkgo biloba. Stop taking ginkgo at least one week before surgery or if you are undergoing an endoscopy.
- Pregnant or breastfeeding women should avoid taking ginkgo. Also, do not give ginkgo in any form to children.

Ginseng (Panax)

Latin name: *Panax ginseng, Panax quinquefolius,* and others

WHAT IS IT?

Ginseng has been part of Chinese medicine for thousands of years, and it is now one of the most popular—and most hyped—herbal supplements in Western countries. The herb has many health claims associated with it; the most common are that it boosts energy, reduces emotional stress, and enhances sexual potency. Long-term use of ginseng as a "tonic" is reputed to improve well-being, particularly in older people suffering from degenerative diseases.

Ginseng supplements are made from the dried root of several different species. *Panax ginseng,* also called Asian ginseng, is extensively cultivated in China, Japan, and Korea, while a closely-related species, *Panax quinquefolius,* commonly known as American or Western ginseng, is grown in the United States.

A third plant, Siberian ginseng (*Eleutherococcus senticosys*), is from the same family, but contains different chemical components that set it apart from the other ginsengs.

COMMON FORMS

Both Asian and Western ginseng are available as extracts in capsule form or in an alcohol base, as teas, and in powders made from the root. Ginseng has also been added to creams, juices, "nutrition bars," and other dietary supplements. The root can also be bought in bulk.

HOW IT WORKS

The active ingredients in Asian ginseng are called ginsenosides, also known as panaxosides. At least 12 major ginsenosides have been isolated. They occur only in very small amounts, so are difficult to purify and standardize. Different ginsenosides appear to have varied, even opposing, pharmacological actions, ranging from analgesic and depressant effects that are "calming" to effects that stimulate the central nervous system. Like many herbs, ginseng is complex, containing numerous other compounds that include volatile oils, vitamins, minerals, plant hormones, sugar, and fats.

Only a few of the specific ingredients have been linked to a particular effect.

RESEARCH AND EVIDENCE

Most studies on ginseng have been small and poorly designed, and so are inconclusive. In addition, preparations of ginseng used in different studies have varied considerably. In a handful of studies that measured ginseng's effect on cognitive function, the herb appeared to have some benefit compared to a placebo, but the effect could hardly be called significant.

One of the few controlled studies on ginseng, published in 2001 in the *Journal of the American Dietetic Association*, found that chronic ginseng supplementation was no more effective than a sugar pill in reducing stress or improving mood in healthy young adults. An earlier study published in the same journal, which assessed ginseng's effect on physical endurance in a group of healthy, active young men who were not elite athletes, found that taking ginseng daily over an eight-week period did not improve aerobic exercise performance.

Some preliminary evidence suggests that ginseng may help people with diabetes. In a small study published in *Diabetes Care*, patients with type 2 diabetes who took ginseng decreased their fasting blood glucose by about 10 percent over a two-month period. More research is needed to determine whether ginseng is useful in the treatment of diabetes.

POSSIBLE SIDE EFFECTS

Adverse reactions, which tend to be associated with high doses or prolonged use of ginseng, include headache, insomnia, nervousness, nausea, diarrhea, chest pain, palpitations, and skin rashes.

POTENTIAL DRUG INTERACTIONS

Ginseng may intensify the effect of drugs used to treat diabetes, including insulin. The herb can also interact adversely with MAO inhibitors prescribed to treat depression.

SPECIAL CONSIDERATIONS

- Despite its popularity, there is little evidence to support benefits from ginseng. Better studies are needed to understand its chemistry, identify its most promising uses, and ascertain its potential for adverse effects.
- Dosages vary, usually ranging from 200 to 600 mg of ginseng extract taken daily. The purity of commercial ginsengs is a problem, however. Surveys indicate that products vary widely in their active ingredients, and some contain no ginseng ingredients at all.
- If you decide to try ginseng, be sure to check with your doctor first if you have any medical problems. People with diabetes should be especially cautious about initiating any therapy with ginseng. No one should use the herb for a prolonged period.
- Anyone taking prescription medications for depression should avoid ginseng.
- Pregnant or breastfeeding women should not use ginseng.
- At the first sign of any unusual symptoms (see Possible Side Effects), you should stop taking ginseng.

Glucosamine and Chondroitin

WHAT IS IT?

Glucosamine and chondroitin sulfate are substances naturally present in the body. Glucosamine is believed to help rebuild damaged cartilage and promote production of hyaluronic acid, a lubricating component of the synovial fluid within joints. Chondroitin sulfate is a glycosaminoglycan—an important component of cartilage.

Both substances are marketed as dietary supplements for halting the gradual deterioration of joint cartilage that characterizes osteoarthritis (OA). The loss of glycosaminoglycans may contribute to the breakdown of cartilage, which helps absorb the shock of body movements and provide the joints with strength and elasticity. The release of cartilage-degrading enzymes by certain cells in the joint, known as chondrocytes, also contributes to the deterioration, which may be repaired by chondroitin sulfate.

While existing medications for OA, such as non-steroidal anti-inflammatory drugs (NSAIDs) and COX-2 inhibitors, treat the symptoms of OA, they don't halt or reverse joint deterioration. Taking supplements of glucosamine and chondroitin, either alone or in combination, may target the underlying defect in OA and relieve symptoms in some people.

COMMON FORMS

Available as capsules and tablets. Various forms of glucosamine are used in supplements, but the one most commonly used in clinical studies is glucosamine sulfate, synthetically manufactured from glycosamine. Glucosamine and chondroitin sulfate are prepared from extracts obtained from animal tissue—glucosamine from shellfish, chondroitin sulfate from the cartilage of cattle tracheas.

Most glucosamine/chondroitin products sold in the United States contain both substances. Products containing glucosamine sulfate alone are also commonly available; only a few brands containing chondroitin alone are on the market, possibly because chondroitin costs manufacturers about four times as much as glucosamine.

HOW THEY WORK

How these compounds may work to treat OA isn't known, but it's thought that glucosamine stimulates the formation of new glycosaminoglycans. Chondroitin might inhibit the production of cartilage-destroying enzymes and be useful for the production of new cartilage that helps the body repair damaged joints.

RESEARCH AND EVIDENCE

The initial evidence for glucosamine came from small, preliminary European and Asian studies. (The supplements have been used in Europe for more than 10 years.) Additional clinical research is now emerging that appears to support early results. A recent review in the *Journal of the American Medical Association* evaluated the results of 15 trials— 6 with glucosamine, 9 with chondroitin—on the effect of the two supplements on OA of the knee. Overall the studies support the notion that the supplements are safe and mildly to moderately effective. But the review authors noted problems in the studies: short treatment periods, small sample sizes, and possible publication bias (where only positive results get published) because many of the trials were sponsored by supplement manufacturers.

A more persuasive randomized, double-blind study, reported in *The Lancet* in 2001, followed 212 patients with mild-to-moderate OA of the knee over a three-year period. Those who took 1,500 mg of glucosamine sulfate daily had significantly less pain and disability than those taking a placebo. X-rays indicated that the glucosamine group also showed less deterioration of the knee joint. In addition, a meta-analysis published in the *Archives of Internal Medicine* in 2003 concluded that both agents were effective at relieving pain, although it was unclear whether they could repair damaged cartilage.

Studies have generally focused on subjects with moderate arthritis. It's not known whether the supplements have any effect on severe OA, and no studies have shown that the supplements offer any benefit for other types of arthritis.

The comparative effectiveness and safety of glucosamine and chondroitin has not been determined in a carefully designed clinical trial. In what should be a pivotal study, the National Institutes of Health is conducting research that will compare the two supplements alone, in combination, and to a placebo. This long-term clinical trial, which is being carried out at thirteen research centers nationwide, is expected to be completed in 2005.

POSSIBLE SIDE EFFECTS

Reported side effects of glucosamine include abdominal discomfort, diarrhea, nausea, headache, drowsiness, skin rash.

Chondroitin may carry a risk of internal bleeding—it has some structural similarity to the anticoagulant heparin—but there have been no reports of this adverse effect in humans.

Some reports suggest that glucosamine, even in low doses, can have adverse effects on blood sugar levels by interfering with the production of insulin by beta cells of the pancreas. However, it isn't known whether glucosamine might harm people with diabetes. In the *Lancet* study cited above, glucosamine produced no major adverse effects, nor did it affect blood glucose levels.

POTENTIAL DRUG INTERACTIONS

Chondroitin may enhance the effect of anticoagulant medications such as heparin or warfarin.

SPECIAL CONSIDERATIONS.

• If you have OA, talk to your doctor before using

glucosamine or chondroitin—particularly if you have diabetes, a bleeding disorder, or are taking anticoagulant medication.

- The long-term effectiveness and safety of these supplements have not been studied. Before beginning to use them, you may want to wait for the results from the long-term study sponsored by the National Institutes of Health.
- If you choose to take glucosamine and/or chondroitin, it's important not to stop taking proven treatments, such as NSAIDs or COX-2 inhibitors, without first consulting your doctor.
- Keep in mind that the supplements are not regulated. Look for products that clearly label how much of each ingredient is present. Suggested daily doses are 1,500 mg of glucosamine and 1,200 mg of chondroitin.
- Glucosamine-only products are much less expensive than those containing chondroitin alone or a mixture of the two. Also, perhaps because chondroitin is more expensive to manufacture, some combination products may contain less chondroitin than their labels claim. Consumer-Labs.com, which tests dietary supplements for potency and purity, found that 6 of 13 combination products and two chondroitin-only products contained lower levels of chondroitin than stated on the labels.
- Women who are pregnant or breastfeeding should avoid these supplements.

Saw Palmetto

Latin name: Serenoa repens, Serenoa serrulata, and other species

WHAT IS IT?
Saw palmetto is an herbal extract derived from the dried berries of the dwarf palm tree. As a supplement, it has long been a popular remedy for genitourinary problems. In some European countries, saw palmetto has become a standard treatment for symptoms of benign prostatic hyperplasia (BPH), and is gaining popularity in the United States as an alternative to finasteride (Proscar) and other medications generally recommended as the first line treatments for symptoms of BPH.

By law, saw palmetto cannot be labeled as a treatment for BPH in the United States; labels on supplement products typically claim that the herb supports or improves "prostate health."

COMMON FORMS
Available as capsules, liquid extract, tablets, teas, and dried berries.

HOW IT WORKS
Saw palmetto contains certain phytosterols—substances that seem to curb prostate cell growth. The action of the herb may be similar to that of finasteride and other medications that are standard treatment options for BPH.

One component, beta-sitosterols, may inhibit the activity of male hormones within the prostate by blocking androgen receptors and by preventing the conversion of testosterone into the more active form dihydrotestosterone—a process believed to be important in BPH. Saw palmetto also exhibits some anti-inflammatory properties. A recent study of an herbal blend containing saw palmetto suggested that the herb may decrease the percentage of epithelial cells in the transition zone (the part of the prostate most affected by BPH).

RESEARCH AND EVIDENCE
Evidence is sparse but growing. A review of 18 controlled trials involving nearly 3,000 men published in the *Journal of the American Medical Association* found a 28 percent greater improvement in overall urinary symptoms, which included more urgent and/or frequent urination and nighttime urination (nocturia), among men with BPH taking saw palmetto than those taking a placebo. In addition, peak urine flow increased by 24 percent, compared with placebo. In some studies comparing saw palmetto to finasteride, saw palmetto was just as effective in improving urinary tract symptoms and peak urine flow, and had fewer adverse effects. Even though some of the studies were short in duration or small or had other shortcomings, the reviewers thought they were worthy of notice.

A recent monograph published by the United States Pharmacopeia (USP)—the nonprofit organization that helps set quality standards for drugs—carefully reviewed the data from 10 controlled trials considered sufficiently large and well-designed to allow a scientific assessment. The reviewers concluded that there is "evidence of moderate scientific quality" that saw palmetto is more effective than a placebo in relieving symptoms of BPH. However, the reviewers suggested that more studies are needed to determine saw palmetto's effect in different age groups and whether it has any significant interactions with conventional drugs.

POSSIBLE SIDE EFFECTS

Side effects are generally mild and may include headache, a rise in blood pressure, abdominal pain, diarrhea, constipation, nausea, urine retention, and erectile dysfunction.

POTENTIAL DRUG INTERACTIONS

None have been reported.

SPECIAL CONSIDERATIONS

- Saw palmetto appears to be safe and modestly effective in treating mild to moderate symptoms of BPH. If you choose to try it, be sure to see your doctor first. Don't self-diagnose BPH; your symptoms may be caused by a more serious condition that requires another treatment.
- Choose a product containing standardized amounts of *Serenoa repens*. This extract has been studied most extensively, appears to be well tolerated, has demonstrated greater efficacy than a placebo, and matched the effectiveness of finasteride in several trials.
- In most clinical trials, the dosage for treating symptoms of BPH is 320 mg per day taken in two doses of 160 mg. Take saw palmetto with food to minimize any gastrointestinal discomfort.
- If saw palmetto is going to work, symptoms usually begin improving within a month. Stop taking the supplements if you experience no improvement after a month.
- There has been some concern that saw palmetto can affect the results of PSA testing, the screening test for prostate cancer. Recent reports have shown no effect of saw palmetto on PSA results, but you should inform your doctor if you are taking saw palmetto and are scheduled for a PSA test.

St. John's wort

Latin name: Hypericum perforatum

WHAT IS IT?

St. John's wort is a common, shrub-like flowering plant in the family *Hypericaceae* that was probably named by early Christians in honor of John the Baptist. The plant is native to Europe, but now grows in many parts of the world. St. John's wort bears bright yellow flowers that, when dried, have been used for centuries in teas as folk remedies for nervous disorders that include anxiety, insomnia, and upset stomach. As a liquid tincture, it has been applied to wounds, bruises, bites, stings, and other skin traumas to combat infection and inflammation.

In recent years, the herb has become popular for treating mild to moderate depression. In Germany, where St. John's wort is regularly prescribed by physicians as an antidepressant, it outsells Prozac, the world's best-selling antidepressant medication, by a substantial margin. St. John's wort is viewed as a milder alternative to conventional antidepressant medications, which can cause undesirable side effects, including reduced sexual function.

COMMON FORMS

Available as capsules, sublingual capsules, oils, teas, and tinctures as well as the dried plant.

HOW IT WORKS

Scientists haven't determined exactly how St. John's wort produces antidepressant effects, but one or more of its active components—at least ten have a pharmacological action—may increase levels of serotonin, a brain chemical that elevates mood.

RESEARCH AND EVIDENCE

St. John's has been studied much more extensively than most other herbal remedies, and it does appear to have some antidepressant qualities. In 15 trials that compared extracts of St. John's wort to a placebo, St. John's wort was two times more effective than placebo in treating mild to moderate depressive symptoms. In eight other trials, St. John's wort was found to be as effective as a tricyclic antidepressant such as imipramine.

Only a few side effects were associated with St. Johns wort in these trials, and the herb consistently produced fewer side effects than the conventional medications.

However, these studies were small, poorly designed, or otherwise flawed: for example, the duration of treatment was brief (typically four to eight weeks), different formulations of St. John's wort were used, and in some cases high doses of the herb were compared to low doses of standard antidepressants.

In one large, well-designed study published in the *Journal of the American Medical Association*, St. John's wort was not significantly more effective than a placebo in treating people with severe depression when used over an eight-week period. But there has never been evidence that the herb could alleviate major depression, and it isn't generally recommended for that purpose.

Questions of effectiveness and safety may be cleared up at the completion of a large trial sponsored by the National Institutes of Health, which will compare St. John's wort to prescription antidepressants.

POSSIBLE SIDE EFFECTS

The most common side effects reported in studies have been gastrointestinal symptoms, allergic reactions, headaches, and fatigue. Other noted side effects include dizziness, sleep disturbances, and dry mouth. St. John's wort also increases sun sensitivity, making sunburn more likely.

POTENTIAL DRUG INTERACTIONS

An increasing number of interactions with standard medications have been reported. St. John's wort can reduce blood levels of indinavir (Crixivan), a common HIV medication, and it may interact with other HIV drugs to reduce their effectiveness. It also lowers blood concentrations of the heart drug digoxin and cyclosporine (Sandimmune), a drug that helps prevent organ transplant rejection. And it may reduce the effectiveness of oral contraceptives in preventing pregnancy.

Combining prescription antidepressants with St. John's wort may cause dizziness, confusion, anxiety, and headaches—symptoms that may be more severe in older people. The supplement can also intensify or prolong the effect of some anesthetic agents used during surgery.

Overall, physicians suspect that St. John's wort can interfere with a range of medications, including those prescribed to treat mood disorders, heart disease, seizures, and some cancers.

SPECIAL CONSIDERATIONS

- For people with mild depression, there is probably no harm in trying St. John's wort. But be alert to signs of major depression, such as withdrawal from everyday activities, changes in sleeping and eating habits, and thoughts of suicide. Consult a physician if you experience any of these symptoms.
- Do not combine the supplement with any antidepressant drugs, especially MAO inhibitors, or any of the other medications noted above. Also, do not stop taking a prescribed antidepressant and substitute St. John's wort without talking to your doctor.
- Allow three weeks for St. John's wort to take effect. A dose used in many studies is 300 mg of standardized extract (standardized to 0.3 percent hypericin) taken three times a day. Consult your doctor if the depression persists.
- Avoid consuming large quantities of foods containing the natural chemical tyramine, which may adversely intensify the effect of St. John's wort. Tyramine-rich foods include red wine, meat, aged cheese, and fava beans. Also avoid alcohol and the use of over-the-counter cold and flu medications.
- Photosensitivity has been reported with very high doses of St. John's wort in humans. If you are very sensitive to the sun, avoid too much sun exposure, especially if you are taking other photosensitizing drugs (such as the antibiotic tetracycline). Discontinue the supplement if a rash or other symptoms occur.
- Before any major surgery, make sure your anesthesiologist is aware you are taking St. John's wort.
- The safety of taking St. John's wort during pregnancy has not been studied. Women who are pregnant or breastfeeding should avoid using the supplement.

Valerian

Latin name: Valeriana officinalis

WHAT IS IT?

Valerian, also known as heliotrope, was used as a medicinal plant in ancient Rome and is probably named after a Roman province. Today the dried roots of the plant are widely promoted in various forms for use as a mild sedative and sleep aid. Valerian is also touted for reducing daytime restlessness and tension. There are more than 200 species of the plant family Valeriana, but *V. officinalis* is the one usually cultivated for use in herbal products. Extracts of valerian are also used as flavorings in foods and beverages.

COMMON FORMS

Available as standardized capsules and tablets, as well as tinctures and teas containing the crude dried herb. The latter are less likely to produce an effect than the standardized pills.

HOW IT WORKS

The herb contains a number of active ingredients, including volatile oils, alkaloids, flavonoids, and amino acids, but it isn't clear which components may produce a sedative effect. It's possible that some compound in valerian may act on the brain in a similar manner to prescription sedatives and tranquilizers such as Valium, but to a milder degree and without the side effects of prescription sleeping pills or their potential for causing dependency.

RESEARCH AND EVIDENCE

Commission E, the agency that officially evaluates herbal remedies in Germany, regards valerian as safe and effective for treating insomnia. But in a recent review of placebo-controlled trials of valerian, published in *Sleep Medicine*, researchers found the studies were small, had various design flaws, and reported inconsistent findings—positive results in some studies, while others found no difference between valerian and a placebo. The evidence for using valerian to treat insomnia, they concluded, was "inconclusive." The U.S. Pharmacopeia drew a similar conclusion when it reviewed the scientific literature and found insufficient evidence to recommend the use of valerian as a short-term treatment for insomnia. Better planned, well-controlled studies are needed to assess whether the herb really is effective.

POSSIBLE SIDE EFFECTS

Headaches, dizziness, and nausea are among the reported side effects, but they are mainly associated with long-term use lasting weeks. High doses have been reported to cause cardiac dysfunction and depression of the central nervous system.

POTENTIAL DRUG INTERACTIONS

Although interactions of valerian with other medications haven't been established, taking the herb with barbiturates, benzodiazepines, or other sleep-inducing medications that affect the central nervous system could intensify sedating effects.

SPECIAL CONSIDERATIONS

- If you have severe or persistent insomnia, you should get medical advice; the insomnia may be caused by an underlying medical problem.
- If you try valerian, avoid products that contain alcohol. Start with a low dose: 450 mg of extract taken before bedtime was sufficient in some studies. Don't use the herb for more than two weeks. If your insomnia persists, see your doctor.
- Avoid using valerian in combination with alcohol, tranquilizers, or barbiturates. It also shouldn't be used when driving or in other situations when you need to be alert.
- Women who are pregnant or breastfeeding should avoid using valerian.

GENERAL INDEX

The index lists all of the drugs and dietary supplements, including herbal preparations, profiled in this book. Each profile is organized under a generic name, which is shown in capital letters (for example, IBUPROFEN). The brand names under which drugs are marketed are shown in lower-case letters (for example, Advil or Motrin).

You can look up drugs used in treating specific disorders in the Disorder Index that begins on page 17. For information on using drugs safely, see pages 8-15. For an overview of dietary supplements, including precautionary guidelines and information on common herb-drug interactions, see pages 842-847.

A

B

G

O

PHYSICIANS

Physician	Specialty	Address	Telephone

DIAGNOSTIC TESTS

Date	Physician	Test	Results

PHYSICIANS

Physician	Specialty	Address	Telephone

DIAGNOSTIC TESTS

Date	Physician	Test	Results

MEDICATIONS

Medication	Condition	Dose	Date Begun	Date Stopped

MEDICATIONS

Medication	Condition	Dose	Date Begun	Date Stopped

Meilleurs souhaits
pour une bonne année
et un joyeux noël
à Cathy
de Ta mère

THE CHURCH / A PICTORIAL HISTORY

the church

A PICTORIAL HISTORY

by EDWARD RICE

FARRAR, STRAUS & CUDAHY / NEW YORK

Published simultaneously in Canada by Ambassador Books, Ltd., Toronto.
Manufactured in the United States of America.

contents

THE CHURCH / A PICTORIAL HISTORY

THE EARLY

The awesome moment when Christ looked upon Peter and called him "the rock upon which I found my Church" led to a radical transformation of human history. Within a short time the entire Roman Empire was to be permeated with the new, earth-shaking doctrine of the Redemption. Christianity spread across the Western world with the power of an exploding sun, quickening Jew and pagan alike. At the time of the Ascension, perhaps 500 men and women believed in Christ. When Peter, pulsating with the fires of the Holy Spirit, spoke to the crowds of foreign Jews who had come to Jerusalem from all over the empire for Pentecost, he converted 3,000, who went home bearing the word of the New Dispensation. Rome, even before Peter's arrival, Ephesus, Alexandria, Corinth, Carthage, Damascus, Antioch—almost all of the cities of the empire had small, vocal Christian communities. When Jerusalem, with the astonishing number of 15,000 Christians among its 50,000 inhabitants, was destroyed by Titus in 70 A.D., the Diaspora sent fresh waves of Christians throughout the world. By 313, when toleration was proclaimed, there were an estimated 6,000,000 Christians in the empire's 50,000,000 inhabitants and nearly 1,000 episcopal sees.

But though Christianity was a universal movement, it was not a mass one, engulfing whole cities, villages or races in a wave of religious enthusiasm. The

The Christians' central act of worship was the Eucharistic banquet, as in this second-century fresco. Circular letters from the Apostles were read and everyone received a portion of the consecrated bread and wine

CHRISTIANS

way of the Christian was hard, demanded sacrifices, and required intelligence and fortitude, unlike the pagan cults which appealed to wildly sensual or emotional appetites. The acceptance of Christianity was an individual choice; Origen, writing in the third century, said, "It is not with us as with the Jewish people or the Egyptians, that we should be one single stock, but on the contrary, the Christians gather together individuals from different peoples."

Christian selflessness was in radical opposition to Roman hedonism and brutality: the result was a constant state of warfare. By an almost diabolical perspicacity, the Romans recognized that the Christians ("A mischievous sect," Suetonius called them) were as great a menace as the shaggy barbarians who swarmed around the edges of the empire. The Romans, who tolerated all other sects within the empire—sun worshipers, the Egyptian cult of Isis, astrologers—made the extermination of Christianity a matter of policy. When the state did not order a persecution, the local governors or private citizens were likely to engage in their own campaigns against the Christians. What is remarkable is that Christianity survived and "won" by a literal following of Christ's teachings: its passive resistance and sometimes eager acceptance of death showed that love, not violence, was the greater power.

The Roman empire

The Roman world presented an outward appearance of orderliness and efficiency, springing from an ingrained virtue of strict discipline. However fierce the Romans' inner nature, which showed itself in the cruelties of the arenas, terrible civil wars such as the world has not experienced again, and the ruthless treatment of conquered enemies, the Romans' feeling for law and order was deeper. Their sense of orderliness and efficiency gave a realistic, factual and efficient cast to the Empire, which was manifested in their great engineering triumphs, and put the heavy imprint of the Romans everywhere, from the Irish Sea to the banks of the Euphrates River. The empire was linked together by a triumph of engineering: the long, durable stone roads, monuments to human effort and science which pierced hostile forests, traversed mountain ranges and crossed sun-baked deserts. On these roads messengers sped with imperial documents, troops moved to meet the threat of rebellious generals or marauding barbarians, and resourceful merchants transported wine and food for the maw of the populace. And there were other triumphs of engineering skill: vast waterworks which quenched the thirst of the cities; the civic and sports amphitheatres designed to divert the people from their problems; the omnipresent contemporary architecture, a vulgarization of classic Greek ideals; the triumphal arches of the victorious generals; the bustling ports. These were marks of a vast, homogenized empire that filled the borders of the Western world. Within this area was a system of order that was not merely superficial: the Romans imposed on the petty tribes and kingdoms they conquered a sense of belonging to a larger scheme of things, all bound to an absolute impersonal authority. The Roman conception of law was magnificent: Rome spread the idea that within her boundaries a man must be assumed innocent until proven guilty. But within this display of material success, justice and democracy, was an appalling disintegration. The imperial court was a center of intrigue, graft and perversion: the ruthless, vain emperors were often a schizophrenic combination of good intentions and evil acts, who might reform the law courts, distribute food and money to the needy and at the same time torture friends to death and seize the estates of their heirs, engage in wasteful military campaigns and offer obscene sacrifices to the gods. It was no wonder that Christianity had an appeal not only to the oppressed but to the more honest nobility.

Engineering projects of great skill and daring, like Spain's great Tarragona aqueduct, were part of Rome's amazing system of public works. Baths, gymnasia, libraries and lecture halls were all provided by the empire for her citizens; and corn, oil, wine, bacon and money were given to the needy.

Roman troops (here shown in battle in a second-century Greek painting) extended the empire across most of the known world. The Romans built their empire upon the Greek system of city-states welded together by Alexander the Great and his successors, who spread Hellenistic civilization throughout the Mediterranean, the Black Sea and Asia Minor. Though the empire was Latin politically, it was culturally Hellenic, and most people knew Greek.

From the beginning St. Peter, here seen in the act of preaching, was considered the head of the new community. He settled in Rome and was martyred there. The early Christians always looked to his successor as the head of the Church.

The Christians' world

"See how these Christians love each other," said a pagan quoted by the brilliant third-century apologist, Tertullian. Love, of God, of man, was the keynote of the early Christian community; coupled with it was a joyful spirit of renunciation of material goods in favor of the grace-filled and more meaningful things of God. Outwardly the Christian resembled his pagan neighbor, but his probity and disinterestedness bore witness to a further calling. By his baptism, he made a firm commitment to another City ("Christians are made, not born," said Tertullian); "There are two roads," stated the Didache, a second-century manual of Christian worship, "the road to life and the road to death." The Christian chose the road to life, even at the risk of martyrdom, and with a complete commitment centered in its visible manifestations: on the rule of love expressed in the weekly celebration of the Eucharistic banquet and in systematic relief to the unfortunate.

The Christian was often a proletarian—a slave or a servant—but large numbers were members of the upper classes, dissatisfied with the corrupt life of the provincial courts; some converts were soldiers, active though often short-lived, who chose to join in martyrdom those they were ordered to execute. The first converts were Jews; but after the dispute over missionary goals was settled in a forthright statement by Peter at the Council of Jerusalem in favor of proselytizing Jew and Gentile on an equal basis, the Church spread rapidly, cutting unconditionally across racial, social and economic lines. Since most of the early converts were Greek-speaking, urban Jews, they converted others who understood Greek, and Christianity was strongest in the cities.

The Christian community was organized around the bishop, aided by his deacons and small groups of lay people, the *continentes* and the virgins who, for the love for Christ, bound themselves to a life of perpetual continency. The widows, in a like spirit, made a perpetual consecration of their state; occupied with little but the service of God, they were the recognized agents for the vast charitable

A portrait of an upper class Christian family group from the fourth century.

services which were the primitive Church's leading activity.

In romantic retrospect, the age of the primitive Church seems one of unusual saintliness. But not all of its members were saints. The Church fought a difficult battle in the care of souls and was not always successful. Some of its leading, most brilliant members, men like Origen, Tertullian and Hippolytus, went into heresy. The Epistles are not only messages of instruction and confirmation for those firm in the Faith, but of chastisement for the lukewarm and the sinner; the problems of indifference and fear were great, and the Church had also to contend with the attractions of secular society. Clear theological concepts and a precise idea of Christian teaching had yet to be developed. Consequently, there were endless heresies and schisms, whose echoes are still felt today. Pastoral methods had to be perfected, and in the beginning the insufficiency of regular church buildings, or the complete lack of them, and the dangers of meeting were obstacles to steady growth. Persecution did not, as often believed, quicken the growth of the Church but affected it adversely. Yet the Church did grow, in size and sanctity, forging, painfully at times, the meaning of Christian life and worship.

Today little more than deserted ruins remain at Corinth, one of the great centers of early Christianity and the object of special concern on the part of St. Paul, whose Epistles to its faithful are among the most important documents of the early Church. The picture above shows the abandoned Temple of Apollo, a famous pagan shrine.

14

An early bishop

Thascius Cyprian, bishop of Carthage, stands as a more-than-typical example of the early Christian. A prominent teacher, orator and lawyer of Carthage, born a pagan in 200 A.D., Cyprian was converted in middle age and was ordained a priest soon afterwards. In 248 he was designated bishop of Carthage, but refused; popular demand made him accept the office. The Decian persecutions began a year later, and Cyprian went into hiding, an act criticized by the Christians of both Africa and Rome; however, he issued a steady stream of brilliantly worded exhortations on the faith from his refuge. Afterwards he became involved in a series of disputes, taking the side of Rome against various schismatics, heretics and anti-popes. He was next engaged in a battle over the treatment of Christians who had weakened under persecution; the general feeling was to cut them off from the Church; Cyprian believed that they needed the strength gained from the Body and Blood of the Lord. In 257 he was arrested; at the trial Cyprian made a resounding statement of his beliefs. "I am a Christian and a bishop," he said. "I know no other gods but the one and true God who made heaven and earth, the sea and all that is in them. This God we Christians serve; to Him we pray day and night, for ourselves and for all men and for the safety of the emperors themselves." Tried again in 258, he was ordered to sacrifice to the gods and refused. "Do what is required of you," he told the judges, "there is no room for reflection on so clear a matter." He was immediately beheaded.

The last pope to be martyred was St. Marcellinus. Under torture he weakened and sacrificed to the pagan gods; upon reasserting his belief in Christ, he was beheaded.

The papacy

Though for much of the first three centuries the popes lived as hunted men, it was through popes that the Church heard the voice of Christ. From the beginning St. Peter acted and spoke with authority; after his death the questions that could not be settled locally by bishops were frequently referred to his successors. In the second century St. Irenaeus, in a phrase which summarizes the beliefs of other Christian spokesmen, said of the Church of Rome: "With this Church all other Churches must be in agreement because of its special pre-eminence." St. Cyprian was equally forthright: "There is one God, and one Christ and but one episcopal chair, originally founded on Peter, by the Lord's authority. There cannot be set up another altar or another priesthood." The acceptance of Peter's chair brought with it the likelihood of Peter's fate: only a few popes escaped martyrdom. Yet they guided the growing Church with the hand of authority, some gently, others firmly or even harshly, solving the increasing problems of doctrine, discipline and organization. The importance of the papacy was obvious to Rome's emperors, who reasoned that a Church without a pope might die, and there were several periods when the emperors were able to delay papal elections. During the terrible persecutions of the early fourth century, the papacy, in the person of Pope Marcellinus, underwent its greatest trials. The papacy was then vacant for four years. Finally, in 313, the conquering Emperor Constantine was able to guarantee freedom of worship to Pope Melchiades.

A Greek miniature shows St. Cyprian before his baptism. He is surrounded by equipment used in magic, and idols of pagan gods. The fact that such utensils were known shows that the old religion of the Empire had not died out and that paganism was still being practiced.

A popular Eucharistic symbol, a fish and loaves of bread, is repeated many times in the catacombs. (The letters of the word FISH, in Greek, stand for the phrase, "Jesus Christ, Son of God, Savior.")

The liturgy and the sacraments

Through the Church Christ instituted a sacramental system for all of mankind. For the first time most human activities could be sanctified; the sacraments gave a previously unknown stability to life: the marriage bond, for example, was hallowed in a manner unknown to pagans; and so eventful was baptism that a catechumen often needed years of preparation before being received as a Christian.

The Mass developed from the uniting of two separate actions: a Jewish service of prayer growing out of the rites of the Synagogue, and the celebration of the Eucharist, according to the teaching of Christ. The primitive Christians held their worship not on the Sabbath, which was a Jewish feast, but on Sunday, the day on which Christ rose and which was the beginning of the new week; at first the Eucharistic banquet was celebrated in private homes in a supper-room (the *cenaculum*); houses were soon set aside, or chapels built, for worship, and though many of these were destroyed in the persecutions, new ones appeared in the years of peace.

Though the Liturgy took several hours to celebrate, it was observed with the greatest simplicity—vestments, candles, incense, bells, organs and melodic singing are all developments of later centuries. Worship was conducted in the language of the people: in Syriac, Coptic, Aramaic, and especially in Greek, which was the common tongue of the Empire. When Latin replaced Greek as the vernacular, it was used in the Liturgy, since it was an early principle of the Church to hold its services in a tongue the people knew.

The Christian Church introduced a new concept of marriage and
family life, the bond being entered into, as St. Ignatius wrote,
"with the sanction of the bishop." The Christian ideals were
premarital chastity, monogamy and marital fidelity. The
pagan crime of abortion or of abandoning an unwanted child
in the countryside was forbidden and punished as murder. The
illustration is a decoration from a glass bowl and shows a young
Christian couple joining hands in the bonds of matrimony. The
inscription says, "May you live in God."

Documents of the early Church

● *In 1875 a Greek scholar discovered an early medieval copy of a second-century manuscript in the Jerusalem Monastery of the Holy Sepulchre in Constantinople. This was the* DIDACHE, *a manual on morals and church practice which throws some light on customs of the primitive Church. Following is an excerpt dealing with baptism and the celebration of the Eucharist. The references to false prophets apparently concern the Christian Gnostics, a heretical sect particularly prevalent at the time.*

. . . Concerning baptism, baptize in this way . . . baptize in the name of the Father and of the Son and of the Holy Ghost, in living water. But if you have not living water, baptize into other water; and, if thou canst not in cold, in warm. . . pour water thrice on the head in the name, etc. . . . Before the baptism let the baptizer and the baptized fast, and others if they can. And order the baptized to fast one or two days before. . . .

Concerning the Eucharist, give thanks in this way. First for the cup: "We give thanks to thee, our Father, for the holy vine of David thy servant, which thou madest known to us through thy servant Jesus. To thee be the glory for ever." And for the broken bread: "We give thanks to thee, our Father, for the life and knowledge, which thou madest known to us through thy servant Jesus. To thee be the glory forever. As this broken bread was scattered upon the hills, and was gathered together and made one, so let thy Church be gathered together

into thy kingdom from the ends of the earth; for thine is the glory and the power through Christ Jesus for ever."

Let none eat or drink of your Eucharist, save such as are baptized into the name of the Lord. For concerning this the Lord hath said: "Give not that which is holy to the dogs."

And after ye are filled, give thanks thus: "We give thee thanks, Holy Father, for thy holy name, which thou hast made to tabernacle in our hearts, and for the knowledge, faith and immortality which thou hast made known to us through thy servant (*or* Son) Jesus. To thee be glory forever. Thou, Lord Almighty, didst create all things for thy name's sake, and gavest food and drink to men for their enjoyment, that they might give thee thanks; and to us thou didst grant spiritual food and drink and life eternal, through thy servant (*or* Son). Above all we thank thee that thou art mighty. To thee be glory for ever. Remember, Lord, thy Church, to deliver her from all evil and to make her perfect in thy love, and to gather from the four winds her that is sanctified into thy kingdom which thou didst prepare for her; for thine is the power and glory for ever. Let grace come, and let this world pass away. Hosanna to the God of David. If any is holy, let him come: if any is not holy, let him repent. *Maranatha.* Amen."

But allow the prophets to give thanks as much as they will.

Whoever then shall come and teach you all the aforesaid, receive him. But if the teacher himself turn and teach another doctrine to destroy this, do not listen to him; but if it be to the increase of righteouness and of the knowledge of the Lord, receive him as the Lord. Now, as concerning the apostles and prophets, according to the teaching of the Gospel, so do ye; and let every apostle that cometh to you be received as the Lord; and he shall stay but one day, and, if need be the next day also; but if he stay three days he is a false prophet. When the apostle goeth forth, let him take nothing but bread, [to suffice] till he reach his lodging; if he ask money he is a false prophet. Ye shall not try or judge any prophet speaking in spirit. For "Every sin shall be forgiven, but this sin shall not be forgiven." But not everyone that speaketh in spirit is a prophet, but only if he have the ways of the Lord. Therefore by their ways shall be known the false prophet and the prophet. Every prophet that appointeth a table in spirit eats not thereof; otherwise he is a false prophet. Every prophet that teacheth the truth, if he doeth not the things that he teacheth, is a false prophet. Every prophet approved as true, that doeth something for the worldly mystery of the Church, but teacheth not to do what he himself doeth,

shall not be judged of you; for he hath his judgment with God. For even so did also the prophets of old. But whosoever shall say in spirit, "Give me money, or other things," ye shall not listen to him; but if he bid you give for others that are in need, let no man judge him.

. . . Let everyone that "cometh in the name of the Lord" be received; then, when ye have proved him, ye shall know, for ye can know the right hand from the left. If he that cometh be a passer-by, give him all the help ye can; but he shall not stay, except, if there be need, two or three days. If he wish to abide with you, being a craftsman, let him work and eat. If he have no craft, use your common sense to provide that he may live with you as a Christian, without idleness. If he be unwilling so to do, he is a "Christmonger." Beware of such.

But every true prophet that willeth to abide with you is "worthy of his food." In like manner a true teacher is also, like the laborer, "worthy of his food." Therefore thou shalt take and give to the prophets every firstfruit of the produce of the winepress and the threshing floor, of oxen and sheep. For the prophets are your high priests.

If ye have no prophet, give them to the poor. If thou art making a batch of bread, take the first-fruit and give according to the commandment. In like manner when thou openest a jar of wine or oil, take the firstfruit and give it to the prophets. And of money and rainment and any other possession take the firstfruit, as may seem good to thee, and give it according to the commandment.

On the Lord's day assemble and break bread and give thanks, having first confessed your sins, that your sacrifice may be pure. If any have a dispute with his fellow, let him not come to the assembly till they be reconciled, that your sacrifice be not polluted. For this is the sacrifice spoken of by the Lord: "In every place and at every time offer to me a pure sacrifice; for I am a great king, said the Lord, and my name is wonderful among the Gentiles."

. . . Elect therefore for yourselves bishops and deacons worthy of the Lord, men that are gentle and not covetous, true men and approved; for they also minister to you the ministry of the prophets and teachers. Therefore despise them not; for these are they that are honored of you with the prophets and teachers. . . .

● *Further light on Eucharistic practices in the primitive Church comes from this passage in the* FIRST APOLOGY *of St. Justin Martyr (c. 100-c. 165), a Samarian convert to Christianity.*

After thus washing him who has been persuaded and has given his assent, we bring him to those that are called the brethren, where they are assembled, to offer prayers in common, both for ourselves and for him who has been illuminated and for all men everywhere, with all our hearts, that as we have learned the truth, so we may also be counted worthy to be found good citizens and guardians of

the commandments, that we may be saved with an eternal salvation.

We salute one another with a kiss when we have ended the prayers. Then is brought to the president of the brethren bread and a cup of water and wine. And he takes them and offers up praise and glory to the Father of all things, through the name of his Son and of the Holy Ghost, and gives thanks at length that we are deemed worthy of these things at his hand. When he has completed the prayers and thankgiving all the people present assent by saying, Amen. Amen in the Hebrew tongue signifies "So be it." When the president has given thanks and all the people have assented, those who are called deacons with us give to those present a portion of the Eucharistic bread and wine and water, and carry it away to those that are absent.

This food is called with us the Eucharist, and of it none is allowed to partake but he that believes that our teachings are true, and has been washed with the washing for the remission of sins and unto regeneration, and who so lives as Christ directed. For we do not receive them as ordinary food or ordinary drink; but as by the word of God, Jesus Christ our Savior took flesh and blood for our salvation, so also, we are taught, the food blessed by the prayer of the word which we received from him, by which, through its transformation, our blood and flesh is nourished, this food is the flesh and blood of Jesus who was made flesh. For the Apostles in the memoirs made by them, which are called Gospels, have thus narrated that the command was given; that Jesus took bread, gave thanks, and said: "This do ye in remembrance of me; this is my body." And he took the cup likewise and said, "This is my blood," and gave it to them alone. This very thing the evil demons imitated in the mysteries of Mithras, and commanded to be done. For, as you know, or can discover, bread and a cup of water are set out in the rites of initiation with the repetition of certain words.

Now we always thereafter remind one another of these things; and those that have the means assist them that are in need; and we visit one another continually. And at all our meals we bless the maker of all things through his son Jesus Christ and through the Holy Ghost. And on the day which is called the day of the sun there is an assembly of all who live in the towns or in the country; and the memoirs of the Apostles or the writings of the prophets are read, as long as time permits. Then the reader ceases, and the president speaks, admonishing us and exhorting us to imitate these excellent examples. Then we arise all together and offer prayers; and, as we said before, when we have concluded our prayers, bread is brought, and wine and water, and the president in like manner offers up prayers and thanksgivings with all his might; and the people assent with Amen; and there is the distribution and partaking by all of the Eucharistic elements, and to them that are not present they are sent by the hand of the deacons. And they that are prosperous and wish to do so give what they will, each after his choice. What is collected is deposited with the president, who gives aid to the orphans and widows and such as are in want by reason of sickness or other cause; and to those also that are in prison, and to strangers from abroad, in fact to all that are in need he is a protector.

We hold our common assembly on the day of the sun, because it is the first day, on which God put to flight darkness and chaos and made the world, and on the same day Jesus Christ our Savior rose from the dead; for on the day before that of Saturn they crucified him; and on the day after Saturn's day, the day of the sun, he appeared to his Apostles and disciples and taught them these things we hand on to you . . .

A funeral meal chamber in a Roman catacomb includes a seat or CATHEDRA *which was reserved in memory of the deceased, who was held to share in the meal.*

The catacombs

Despite common belief today, the early Christians did not celebrate the Eucharist underground in the catacombs, which were merely burial chambers and rooms where the funeral meal was held. These vast, gloomy cemeteries date from the first three centuries and are still in existence, though there are no more than half a dozen traces of ecclesiastical buildings earlier than Constantine's Edict of Toleration (313). Today's knowledge of church life from this period is too frequently based on what is known of the catacombs in Rome and other cities, and gives a distorted picture of how early Christians worshipped.

An inscription from a *mensa,* or tombstone in the form of a table, from North Africa, tells us how the funeral meals were celebrated (the first and last letters of each line, in the original Latin, form the words, "The children, to their dearest mother"). The inscription reads:

TO THE MEMORY OF AELIA SECUNDULA

We have already spent much on mother Secundula's tomb:
Now we have decided, at the spot where she rests,
To place a stone funeral table
Where, from henceforth, being gathered together,
We shall often remember all that she did for us.
When the food is set out, the cups are filled and
*   the cushions*
Arranged round about, we, to heal the wound that
*   pains our hearts,*
Shall talk, late in the evening, eagerly and with praise
Of our worthy mother—and the good old lady will sleep.
Yes, she who once fed us is now done with food for ever.
*   She lived 72 years.*
*   260 Provincial era.*
*   Erected by Statulenia Julia.*

The persecutions

Although Christians died for their beliefs before the reign of Nero, it is Nero who is generally regarded as the author of state-sponsored persecutions. To produce public scapegoats for the burning of Rome, he advised his courts to consider Christians notorious criminals. This judicial precedent made Christianity a crime, but the strict Roman legal tradition that a criminal had to be publicly accused before the state could proceed made it possible for the Christians to live, work and conduct schools openly. Trajan's rescript, allowing sacrifice to the Roman gods as grounds for acquittal, resulted in the terrible tortures suffered by Christians: it was in an attempt to force them to acquit themselves, for legal, not religious motives, that torture—unusual for the Roman penal system—was employed. Many provincial governors tried to avoid passing death sentences and judges took it as a personal defeat if they could not persuade Christians to recant. An enraged proconsul in Asia once shouted, "You scoundrels, if you really want to die, jump off a cliff or hang yourselves."

Until the third century, persecution took the form of individual criminal procedures, and was by no means full-scale massacre, but in 202, when Septimus Severus made baptism a criminal act, the police, previously forbidden to interfere, began to seek out Christians, initiating a century of mass martyrdoms, confiscation of Church property and harassment. Totally unprepared for danger on such a scale, many Christians recanted, giving sacrifice to the pagan gods or buying certificates that they had. However, there were many thousands of martyrdoms, very few of which were joyfully sought. Hundreds of thousands of other Christians endured a total suspension of civil rights, submitting to imprisonment, torture, exile, flight, confiscation of property and ostracism from the community.

On this spot—the floor of the Colosseum—thousands of indomitable Christians are believed to have died, either as unwilling gladiators or in the jaws of wild beasts. The Colosseum was built by the labor of Jewish captives after the revolt of 70 A.D. A cross now marks the mass shrine of the Christian martyrs.

A relic of the age of persecution is this Egyptian BRANDEA, a cloth which was placed on the stone slab covering the tomb of a martyred Christian.

The Diocletian persecutions of 305 took the life of St. Alban, the first Briton to be martyred. Alban, a pagan, sheltered a fugitive priest and was converted and baptized. When soldiers searched his house for the priest, Alban disguised himself in the priest's cloak and was killed. (The priest was later captured and stoned to death.) The picture portrays Alban's death; his soul, in the form of a tiny bird, flies off to heaven, while the executioner's eyes drop from his head.

Constantine brings peace

In 306, while the Christians were attempting to recover from their losses under Diocletian, the empire was ravaged by generals fighting for the throne. Constantius Chlorus, Emperor of the West, had died in England in July; the troops soon afterwards elected his eighteen-year-old son, Constantine, emperor, but Constantine prudently informed the other claimants that he had no desire for the honor. While Constantine battled the Franks, the military situation grew steadily worse; the other generals kept the empire in turmoil. Suddenly, in the spring of 312, Constantine, now 24, crossed the Alps to challenge Maxentius, who controlled Italy. This move was to have fruitful consequences for both empire and Church. Constantine won battle after battle, and with only 20,000 men pushed towards Rome and Maxentius's powerful army of 100,000 troops. The night before the attack, Constantine had a mysterious experience. Though a pagan, he had a heavenly vision—he related later—and heard the command to conquer in the sign of Christ; he ordered his men to carry the XP (or *chi rho*) on their shields, though most of them were also pagans. The armies met at the Tiber, and Maxentius suffered a complete defeat. Directly after his victory Constantine granted tolerance to the Christians, and the next year, confirmed it with the famous Edict of Milan.

Constantine's actions were pregnant with implications for centuries to come. By waging the first war in the name of Christ, he had set aside Christianity's Christ-given injunction to reject violence as a means of combatting force; his mysteriously-awarded insight into the beliefs of the "unpatriotic" Christian minority put him in opposition to the powerful and influential pagan section of the populace—an act of sheer madness by political standards; he soon made Christianity the favored religion. Despite his concern for the Church, Constantine remained merely a catechumen until death, though he was a generous and intelligent patron, and a careful guardian of Christianity's most precious beliefs.

A primitive Greek manuscript shows Constantine's dream of the CHI RHO, *his defeat of Maxentius and his enthronement.*

BYZANTIUM

In 324 A.D. Constantine, now secure as Rome's ruler, strode around a jutting promontory on the eastern tip of Europe and with a spear marked out the fortifications of a new city. This city, an expansion of a thousand-year-old Greek town called Byzantion, was to replace Rome as the center of the empire; the city itself would be a monument to his taste and imagination. During the previous thirteen years, Constantine had destroyed all possible claimants to the throne and had consolidated the empire, previously ruled by combinations of co-emperors and Caesars or governors. Among his victims were relatives and former friends, as well as hereditary enemies; the dead included his first wife, Fausta, and his own son, his sister and her husband Licinius, Constantine's former companion in arms, and their son; thousands of men had also died in the civil wars. Constantine ranged across Europe and Asia, eliminating rivals, particularly those who had a birthright to the throne. His victory over Maxentius was achieved, so Constantine later told the Christian historian Eusebius (who may have been gullible), because it was fought in the sign of Christ. However, since the XP also stood for the pagan sun god Chronos and was, as well, considered a lucky sign, Constantine, no matter what feelings he may have had later about Christianity, was obviously playing to both pagans and Christians. His victory did lead to decrees allowing tolerance of Christian worship, and the Christians, a minority of some six to ten million in an empire of fifty million population, soon received further recognition by Constantine; by the end of the century, their faith was accepted as the state religion.

The creation of Byzantium was not the continuation of Caesarian Rome but rather marked a transition into a whole new empire, a culture and a civilization greater than anything before or since in the West. It lasted more than 1,100 years, was the bulwark of the Western world against both barbarians and Moslems, was the first Christian state and the greatest, was the breeding ground of some of the Church's worst heresies and of much of her highest spirituality, and yet is just beginning to be rediscovered.

EDENTE CLEMENTE X PONT OPT MAX

Constantine (here portrayed in a fragment of a colossal statue in Rome) was the son of a Roman general and a Bythinian barmaid; his mother later became famous as the finder of the Holy Cross and is commemorated as St. Helena. Constantine, a brilliant leader of great foresight, ingenuity and sensitivity, ranks with Julius Caesar as a military leader and a politician. What gave a new dimension to his traditional and almost ritualistic acts in removing his opposition in his drive for power was that he operated with a special tolerance for Christians, whose patron he became, although he himself was not a true believer and it was not until his last hours that he was converted—by an heretical bishop.

Life in the city of Byzantium revolved around the Hippodrome where (as shown in this drawing from a plaque), the emperor presided at horse races, wild beast hunts and athletic and cultural events. The Hippodrome was also a political arena: here the names of new emperors were presented to the people by ministers of state and the senate. Spectators usually supported one of two competing factions, the Blues or the Greens, originally city militia. Each faction had its own athletes and entertainers, and was involved in politics. The Blues, farmers and landowners, were conservative and supported the Church. The Greens, largely artisans and merchants, were usually radical and often inclined to heretical faiths. However, when the great sixth-century emperor Justinian raised taxes and started building ships for a war against the Vandals and the Goths, Blues and Greens led a revolt from the Hippodrome. The crowds elected a new emperor, and Justinian was forced to order his general, Belisarius, to charge the Hippodrome and restore order; 30,000 were reported killed

Seventeen miles of fortifications protected Byzantium; her towers reached sixty feet into the sky, and one gate was gold.

Constantine's New Rome

In fifty years the new city of Byzantium—or Constantinople as it was soon called—became the greatest in the empire, replacing Rome itself, which was slowly dying of age and inertia. The city stood between two bodies of water, a small channel called the Bosphorus (or ox-ford) and the Golden Horn, a magnificent anchorage seven miles long that emptied into it. On one side the Bosphorus led through the Sea of Marmora into the Hellespont and Aegean, on the other into the Black Sea, dotted with Greek colonies and on whose shores were great grain fields that supplied the empire.

New Rome (Constantine's name for the city) took five-and-a-half years to complete. It was dedicated in May, 330, not at first to the Holy Trinity and the Mother of God as was later believed, but to the Emperor himself, statues of whom were everywhere to be seen. Constantine filled the city with the plunder of the empire: ancient cities, temples, shrines and civic buildings were looted to provide furnishings and decorations. "Constantinople is dedicated, while almost all other cities are denuded," complained St. Jerome.

Later emperors kept adding to the city and improving its walls. Aqueducts brought water into vast cisterns, and an ingenious sewerage system emptied into the sea. Its 700,000 inhabitants—Greeks, Armenians, Goths, Huns, Egyptians and dozens of other peoples—lived in fourteen different districts. In the central square, the Augusteum, news bulletins were posted for the information of the people: NEW LAND GRANT TO VETERANS; MONK OF THE SYRIAN DESERT: ACCUSES OUR CLERGY OF FEASTING WHILE LAZARUS WAITS; COMET SEEN: WHAT DOES IT PORTEND? MASTERS OF SCIENCE UNABLE TO DECIDE; AUDIENCE WITH NUBIAN KING: WEIRD ETIQUETTE OF JUNGLE COURT—these are some that have survived.

The only disadvantage was the climate: throughout winter and spring an incessant north wind blew across the Black Sea from the frozen steppes. Hot, sultry summers followed, and the extremes of climate seemed to reflect the rising and falling fortunes of the city and the empire it controlled.

The rude life of the Byzantine peasant is portrayed in an ivory panel. Though the court became more and more luxurious, conditions hardly changed for the peasant over the course of the centuries.

Byzantium today (now called Istanbul), seen from across the Bosphorus.

Constantine's mother, Flavia Julia Helena, was a formidable woman and a great saint. Her origins are obscure: she was born in a small Balkan town (she is often claimed, incorrectly, by the British as the daughter of King Coel), and some sources say she was a barmaid. Nevertheless, she became a concubine of the great Roman general, Constantius Chlorus, and bore him a son. Her husband became Caesar and left Helena to marry the stepdaughter of the Emperor Maximian. Though his parents were now separated, young Constantine remained faithful to his mother, and she was his friend and advisor as long as she lived. Shortly after Constantine proclaimed toleration of Christianity, Helena, 63, was

converted, becoming such "a devout servant of God . . . that one might believe her to have been a disciple of the Savior of mankind from her very childhood." She inspired the ordinary people by her constant attendance at church, had new churches built throughout the empire, and gave crown funds for the support of the indigent. But she is most renowned for her visit to the Holy Land in 324 A.D. to give thanks to God at the sacred places. Golgotha and the Holy Sepulchre had been covered with a shrine to Venus which was removed. Later chronicles credit Helena with the finding of the three crosses at the site of the excavations. This mosaic shows her with Constantine.

An illumination from an old Greek manuscript shows Arians setting fire to a Catholic church. The Arian heresy continued for about four centuries (it has since survived in other forms), and was strong even in Constantinople itself; in Byzantium religious questions were often affected by politics or by the whims of the wives or mothers of the emperors.

Church, state and heresy

In recognizing Christianity, Constantine found that he inherited not only the blessings of its nascent organization and the probity and charity of its adherents, but its conflicts too. Within Christianity there were a variety of beliefs, especially about the relationship between the humanity and the divinity of Christ. One of the most virulent of heretically divergent views was that of an Alexandrian priest named Arius; his thesis, roughly summarized, was this: if the Son is begotten of the Father there was a time when the Son did not exist; consequently the Son is not from eternity and is not God. This view, which attacked Christianity at its very roots, spread from Alexandria and was popular both in the East and among the barbarians of the West. Several important bishops subscribed to it, and Arianism reached the point where a synod of 100 Egyptian and Lybian bishops was called at Alexandria in 318 to discuss it; the heresy was condemned and its adherents excommunicated in a circular letter of great severity.

However the Arians refused to submit to the authority of the synod and the dispute reached such intensity that in 325 Constantine, though not yet a Christian, intervened and called a council at Nicea, a small city in Asia Minor, near the capital. It was presided over by Hosius, the bishop of Cordoba in Spain; Pope Sylvester I sent two priests from Rome and altogether one fourth of the episcopate, some 300 bishops (largely from the East), attended. A formula of belief used in the baptismal rite was accepted as the basis for a definition of the faith similar to the so-called "Apostles' Creed," but with the insertion of the words "consubstantial with the Father." All but two of the Arian bishops subscribed (these two and Arius himself were excommunicated) and the Council went on to deal with other problems. This first ecumenical council set a pattern for latter councils and was of great historical importance. Constantine's intervention in the sessions established a personal devotion on the part of many Eastern bishops to the throne. Through its decisions the council showed that there was a core of belief and of discipline subscribed to by most Christians. Yet the effects of Arianism were still to be felt. Many bishops were displeased with the Greek word *homoousios* (consubstantial), feeling either that it was too precise or not precise enough. The Arians also fought among themselves, and one faction offered the term *homoiousios* (of like substance), as a compromise; however, the addition of the letter *iota* left the term still contrary to orthodox doctrine. Arianism remained strong and its adherents were powerful even in the imperial court; they were able to bring about the banishment of St. Athanasius of Alexandria, one of the Nicene leaders.

Besides the frequent and innumerable synods there was a series of general councils in which major problems were discussed and settled. So powerful was the voice of the Eastern emperor that the first eight ecumenical councils were called by him; the emperor often treated the pope like a court official, and several popes or their legates suffered humiliating experiences when summoned to New Rome to hear the emperor expound his own theological innovations. This domination of the Church by the throne (known as "Caesaropapism") prevailed mainly in the East and the growing strength and interest of the emperors, as well as their erratic beliefs, frequently set Byzantium against the papacy. The constant theological controversies kept the Eastern churches in turmoil, and resulted in the early losses of large areas to orthodox Christianity. Armenia, Georgia, Egypt, Chaldea (and southern India), Persia and parts of Syria were among those that cut themselves off from Constantinople and thus from Rome.

Theodosius the Great convoked the Council of Constantinople in 381 in order to secure ecclesiastical conformity in the East. It was attended by 150 Eastern Catholic bishops and 36 heterodox bishops. No Latins were present, nor was the pope represented. However, the Council was later established as ecumenical by the Council of Chalcedon (451) and by several popes. In this illumination Theodosius is seated in the upper right and is marked by a nimbus; the open Gospel rests upon the throne. At the lower left the Pneumatomachian heretic Macedonius, who taught that the Holy Ghost was but a ministering spirit, sits alone. The Council condemned Macedonius as well as other heretics and formulated Catholic belief in the Holy Ghost as being consubstantial with the Father and the Son. It also established the patriarch of Constantinople as second in honor to the pope, an action resented by the sees of Antioch and Alexandria.

大秦景教流行中國碑

An early witness to the wide dissemination of Nestorian Christian beliefs is the Singan Fu stone, also known as the Nestorian stone. Cut in 781 (and rediscovered in 1625 by Westerners), the monument testifies to the work of a Nestorian missionary. The inscription, in Chinese and Syriac, contains an allusive statement of Christian doctrines and gives an account of the fortunes of Christianity in China before 780.

The Nestorian heresy

One of the most troublesome heresies to afflict the Church was Nestorianism, the doctrine that there are two separate Persons in the Incarnate Christ, one divine, the other human (the orthodox teaching is that Christ was a Single Person, at once God and man). The false teaching came from Nestorius, a Syrian-born, fifth-century patriarch of Constantinople who had obtained the throne because he was a forthright supporter of orthodoxy. However, Nestorius soon became embroiled in a discussion of the Theotokos, a term long used by theologians of the highest orthodoxy and popular because it expressed the growing devotion to the Virgin as the Mother of God. The false teachings of Nestorius were anathematized by Pope Saint Celestine in 430 and by the council of Ephesus in 431. Nestorius was banished and his books condemned, but his doctrines remained and were particularly popular in the East, where missionaries from a portion of the Church which refused to accept the anathema carried them as far as Persia and Iran.

*The page above, showing the Four Evangelists, is from a Persian
Nestorian* DIATESSARON, *a story of the life of Christ complied
by rearranging the four Gospels.*

Theodosius the Great

The last great absolute ruler to govern both halves of the empire was Theodosius, a completely orthodox Christian (and strongly anti-Arian) who abolished the government budget for most of the pagan religious services and began the codification of Roman law; the *Codex Theodosianus*, which included some of the emperor's own laws, marked the official end of paganism and the definite Christianization of public life. Arianism and other heresies became legal offenses. Theodosius tore down the statues of the pagan gods: in the East by force, since paganism was strong; in the West, the pagan temples were closed and turned into museums.

Theodosius is best known today for his conflict with St. Ambrose, bishop of Milan, then the Western capital of the empire. The people of Thessalonica had revolted, and, urged on by his court advisors, Theodosius had his troops slaughter the people indiscriminately while watching a performance in the public amphitheatre; 7,000 were killed. When the emperor came to Milan, Ambrose refused him the sacraments until he had done penance. "Did not David also sin?" asked Theodosius. Ambrose answered, "Whom you have imitated in sinning, imitate also in doing penance." "Theodosius," wrote St. Augustine in *The City of God*, "did penance in such a way that the people, who were praying for him, wept more to see the emperor's majesty so humbly prostrated than they had feared his wrath after their transgression." The whole world heard of this act of penance, which has always been the symbol of the moral courage of a Christian ruler, while Ambrose's act marks the courage of a bishop to his calling, no matter how dangerous it might be. "This and other good works, too many to mention here, Theodosius took with him from out of the mist that veils human existence," concluded Augustine. "The reward of these works is eternal bliss which God grants only to the truly pious."

The Emperor Theodosius the Great sits enthroned portrayed in the iconographic position later to be used in Byzantine portraits of Christ. The Emperor is robed in the purple chlamys, wears a jeweled crown on his head which is encircled by a halo; the halo was originally used in the symbolism of the pagan Greek gods and demi-gods, later of the Roman emperors and was finally transferred to portraits of Christ and the saints. Originally the color was blue, but by the fifth century gold was being used

The state ruled by Christ

Reverenced like a diety, the basileus was usually portrayed with Christ, the Virgin or a saint.
This is the Emperor Constantine IX Monomachus and the Empress Zoë paying homage to Christ, the all-powerful king.

The Constitution of the Byzantine state was the Gospel, and according to the custom of the centuries following Justinian, the ruler was Christ himself. The normal term for emperor was "basileus"—in Byzantium it meant a king who is vicar of Christ. The emperor dressed as Christ, with the jeweled richness of the *kyrios* of an ikon; during important imperial conferences and ecumenical meetings the open Gospel book sat upon a throne next to that of the emperor's. Laws were promulgated in the name of Christ the Master. On Easter Sunday the basileus might appear swathed in white bands, his face as pale as death and surrounded by twelve followers. At meals the basileus often re-enacted the Last Supper, breaking and blessing bread before twelve tables of twelve noblemen each. Yet this imitation of Christ was often an unconscious, blasphemous parody: since a meal was a religious ceremony a servant who dropped a plate could be decapitated, and the spectators blinded, if they should admit having seen such a sacrilege. The poverty of Christ was lost in the magnificence of the imperial palaces: twenty thousand servants were hardly too many for the basileus, and these were dressed in clothes so sacred that they could not be worn on the street. The palace itself resembled a gigantic golden jewel, beset with rare stones, marbles and pearls and decorated with silks and damasks and the finest works of art, including golden trees operated by clockwork. The emperor's mere glance made things sacred, and what he gazed upon could not be shown to the outside world. Yet, this exalted position might be open to anyone, and many emperors had come from the lowest ranks: Leo I was a butcher, Justin a swineherd, his nephew Justinian a ragged farmhand, Phocas a centurion, Leo II an odd-job man, Michael III a servant, Romanus Lecapenus a petty officer in the navy. The empress was usually selected by delegates of the royal family: the prime stipulations were that she be beautiful and intelligent. Consequently some strange and exotic creatures wore the imperial purple, among them, an animal-trainer, a cook, and a memorable succession of peasants, farm girls and courtesans.

Since Byzantium was established as the Lord's own city, the ordinary man spoke with intimate knowledge of His Master. The intricacies of the Trinity, the natures of Christ and the Mother of God were common topics. St. Gregory of Nyssa wrote in amazement in the fourth century: "Everywhere, in humble homes, in the streets, in the market place, at street corners, one finds people talking about the most unexpected subjects. If I ask for my bill the reply is a comment about the virgin birth; if I ask the price of bread, I am told that the Father is greater than the Son; when I ask whether my bath is ready, I am told that the Son was created from nothing." Such was the atmosphere in which the Byzantine lived.

When an emperor was chosen, he was lifted up on a shield and acclaimed by the people (as was David in this Greek illumination). Dynastic rule in Byzantium was very insecure; there was much intrigue and bloodshed within ruling families, and outsiders were often able to seize control of the throne.

The Church fathers

Under the beneficent eye of Constantine and his successors Christianity flourished. New churches were constructed, the contemplative life developed; art, music and architecture broke free of the restraints of the first three centuries; monasteries and convents sprang up; in the deserts of Egypt, Syria and Lybia the eremitical life was so abundant that its founders complained regularly of crowded conditions. In the cities and towns the Christian bishop replaced the old Roman magistrate as the local leader, and from his hands came the food and money which earlier had been distributed by the state. The papacy grew wealthy from generous gifts of money, jewels and land: it held domains not only around Rome but in southern Italy, Sicily and even abroad. Equally significant was the growth of Christian thought, manifested by a group of Latin and Greek fathers, who took the rough stones of primitive Christianity and hewed them into a heavenly temple. In

the West, Augustine, Ambrose and Jerome are the most famous; in the East, Basil, Gregory of Nyssa and Gregory Nazianzen (called the three Cappadocians), John Chrysostom and Athanasius; others of lesser fame are Cyril of Jerusalem, Didymus the Blind (a layman), Macarius the Great, Ephraem the Syrian, Mesrob of Armenia, John Climacus, Maximus the Theologian and John of Damascus. The Byzantine church was also active in missionary work; the conversion of the Slavic lands was due largely to Sts. Cyril and Methodius.

The life of a patriarch

One of the four Greek Fathers, Saint John Chrysostom (his surname means "Golden Mouth," a tribute to his eloquence), was born in Antioch in 347, the son of a general, and was educated as a lawyer by the finest masters in the empire; as a youth he achieved fame as an orator. Baptized at twenty according to the custom of the age, he studied at a school for monks; at thirty he went to the Syrian mountains to live as a hermit, but after seven years, poor health forced him to return to Antioch. Here he was ordained deacon and then priest, and was assigned by his bishop to preach at Antioch. The city then had a Christian population of 100,000; John preached almost every day to the people, and often several times a day. His fame reached Constantinople and the emperor persuaded him to come there as patriarch. He accepted immediately, cut down the patriarchal expenses, giving the money to the poor and the sick; he reformed the clergy, he founded convents, expanded the Church's missionary activities, preached frequent reception of the Holy Eucharist, and spoke out against the immorality of the capital. However, he was mild and compassionate toward sinners, saying, "If you have fallen a second time, or even a thousand times into sin, come to me and you shall be healed."

But his popularity and forthrightness plunged him unwillingly into the intrigues that plagued both the imperial court and the Church. The Empress Eudoxia, whom he had called "Jezebel," and archbishop Theophilus of Alexandria conspired to bring about his deposition. A cabal of his enemies persuaded the emperor to banish him. The people rioted, and the dispute went on for months. After Theophilus obtained confirmation of the deposition by appeal to canons of an Arian council, the emperor tried to force John out with soldiers; troops swept through the city's churches on Holy Saturday and many people were killed. Pope Innocent and the Western emperor tried to convene a new council to discuss John's case, but his enemies were able to prevent it. Finally, after Pentecost, the emperor ordered John's exile, and he was escorted to Armenia, the border of the Christian world. Meanwhile Innocent and the Western emperor sent five bishops to Constantinople to intervene for John; the delegation was imprisoned. After an exhausting trip through strange land in especially hot weather, John, now sixty and in ill health, begged for a rest. However he was forced to continue. Though his attendants then tried to aid him, he weakened and died on the feast of the Holy Cross, September 14, 407. His last words were, "Glory be to God for all things."

The relics of John Chrysostom are honored by the Emperor Theodosius II (whose father had banished the saint) as they are brought back to Constantinople in 438 to be enshrined in the church of the Apostles, seen in the background.

A desert father

St. Anthony of Egypt came from a simple Christian home. He was born in 251 into a family of landholders in Coma, a village in the Nile valley, about a hundred miles from the Egyptian Delta. He lived a pious, liturgical life, observing the Coptic feasts and fasts with love and understanding. His parents died when he was about eighteen or twenty, leaving him with a younger sister to care for. Six months later a crisis changed his life. He was at Mass, meditating upon the calling of the Apostles, who had given up all to follow their Redeemer, when in the reading of the Gospel he received an answer to his thoughts, "If thou wilt be perfect," (Christ told the rich man) "go, sell what thou hast, and give to the poor, and thou shalt have treasure in heaven; and come, follow me." Anthony went home, put his affairs in order, and gave his abundant fields to the village and his possessions to the poor, keeping only a small amount of money for his sister (he later persuaded her to surrender even this portion and enter a convent). Then, in the manner of the ascetics of his day, he took up residence in a hut outside the village to train himself in the strictest abstinence and self-denial and to build the interior fortifications which would soon be under siege.

But Anthony was not, as critics have charged, an escapist; he was engaged in a search for the Truth in its purest, clearest form, and it was only by freeing himself of earthly attachments that he could attain his goal. As he progressed in the spiritual life, he sought out neighboring ascetics to learn from each his own special virtue. Anthony's growing sanctity (he was called Theophilus, the God-lover, by his friends) earned him the hatred of the Devil. Appearing in a multitude of forms, Satan began his attacks.

Anthony was in his twenties when they began. His comparative youthfulness gives the struggle a special poignancy. At first he was overwhelmed with temptations. Solicitude for his sister and his kinsfolk, the love of money, lust and greed, the hard life which he had already lived, fear of the future—these made up the storm that whirled through his burning mind "like a cloud of dust." Taking advantage of Anthony's youthful, vigorous

masculinity, the Devil aroused in him erotic and maddening thoughts, and at length appeared to him in the form of a woman. But Anthony resisted. The Devil retired temporarily and Anthony took advantage of the lull to strengthen his spiritual defenses. He began to spend entire nights in prayer. He followed a strict fast, living on a single meal of bread, salt and water taken after sunset; sometimes he ate nothing at all for several days. He slept on a mat, and often on the bare ground.

Then the Devil renewed his attacks. "O my Lord!" cried Anthony, "this I entreat Thee: let not Thy love be blotted out from my mind. By Thy grace I am innocent before Thee." Eventually the battle abated, and Anthony, preparing for further struggles which he knew would come, took up residence in a tomb some distance from the village. Here he was scourged by demons; a friend found him almost dead upon the ground. Anthony was carried to the village church and stretched out for burial. The villagers crowded around in the death watch, but at midnight Anthony arose and returned to the tomb to continue the battle. Battered and bruised, too weak to stand, he threw himself upon the ground to pray. After a while, he shouted at his adversary: "Here I am. I am not going to run away from your blows, for even if you beat me again, nothing can separate me from the love of Christ." And he chanted the psalm, "*Si consistant adversum me castra non timebit cor meum.*"

The struggle began again. St. Athanasius, Anthony's friend and biographer, says the onslaught commenced with "demons taking the forms of different beasts and reptiles. The place was one mass of spectral lions, scorpions and wolves. . . . The noise of the demon animals was hideous and their rage terrible. Scourged and goaded by the demons, Anthony's pain grew even greater. He lay groaning in body, but watchful and fearless of soul."

Anthony tried to divert the attacks by joking gaily with the demons, but the torment continued and he felt he was waging the battle unaided. Then—"looking upwards he saw the roof [of the tomb] open and a ray of light shine through it. The demons vanished in a flash, his bodily anguish ceased and his dwelling was whole again." But Anthony thought he had been alone in the struggle. He drew a deep breath and demanded of his Savior: "Where were you? Why were you not there sooner to lighten my torment?" But as Anthony learned, it is in our loneliest struggles that the Lord is sometimes closest: "I was here, Anthony, waiting and watching your struggle. Because you have endured and conquered I will always be

your helper and I will make your name renowned throughout the world."

Satan had been defied. Anthony decided to withdraw from the habitations of men and retire into absolute silence. On a mountain east of the Nile he found an abandoned fort. Here he spent the next twenty years of his life without seeing a human face. Twice a year bread was thrown over the wall to him.

His was an age whose thirst for God seemed insatiable: there were as many monks in the desert as there were laymen in the cities of the East, and the wilderness was filled with men abandoning all in order to transcend the human state and attain union with God. Anthony's fort was one of the goals of the desert pilgrims, but he refused to see his would-be disciples. A number of them established themselves in the nearby caves. Finally (it was the year 305), so great was their demand for Anthony's guidance that they forcibly breached the door of the fort and Anthony came forth, radiant, utterly tranquil, neither wasted from fasting and battling demons nor fat from lack of exercise. His soul shone from its great depths.

Anthony became the spiritual leader of the monks in the surrounding community, some 6,000 according to contemporary accounts, directing them solely by his word and example. A rule based on his letters and his precepts was eventually compiled, and there are still monasteries in the East which claim to adhere to it. (Anthony is known as the father of Christian monasticism and is listed in the Roman calendar—his feast is celebrated on January 17—as "abbot.") After five years, he withdrew again into the wilderness, to spend the last 45 years of his life in the desert between the Nile and the Red Sea. At the risk of his life he twice traveled to Alexandria, once to appear in court to give spiritual strength to the Christian martyrs in the persecutions of 311, and again in 350 to preach against the Arian heresy. According to St. Jerome he made one other trip, the journey which resulted in his famous meeting with St. Paul the Hermit, another of the great Egyptian desert fathers. Anthony was ninety at the time, and thinking he had been the first to dwell in the desert, was tempted to vainglory over the honor. But in a vision he saw a greater solitary than himself, and he set out across the desert to find Paul. A she-wolf led him to the cave. Paul heard Anthony approach and bolted the door. After hours of pleading, Anthony finally gained admittance by crying, "If thou receivest beasts, why dost thou turn away men? If I prevail not here, I shall die before thy door."

The hermits embraced each other. Paul questioned his visitor about the world: "Behold him whom thou has sought with so much labor, a shaggy white head and limbs worn with age. Behold thou lookest on a man who is soon to be dust. Yet because love endureth all things, tell me, I pray thee, how fares the human race? Have new roofs risen in ancient cities? Whose empire it is that now sways the world? Do any still survive, snared in the error of demons?"

A crow brought them food (each day for sixty years the crow had carried half a loaf of bread to Paul; on this day he set a whole loaf before the two men). "Behold," Paul remarked, "God has sent us our dinner: God the merciful, God the compassionate." They sat down by a cool spring and gave thanks to their Creator and Benefactor.

At the age of 105, in the year 356, Anthony knew that his life was at an end. He told his two most trusted disciples that in order to forestall undue reverence for his remains the location of his grave was to be kept a secret: "Hide my body under the earth . . . and tell no man where you lay me: and there shall I rest until the resurrection of the dead, when I shall receive again this body without corruption." He gave brief instructions as to the disposition of his few possessions, then stretched out his legs. His brothers began to cry out to him. Anthony's face "was now full of joy unspeakable at the meeting of those who had come for him, and it resembled that of a man when he sees a friend whose friendship gives him great pleasure. So the blessed man held his peace and died, and was gathered to his fathers."

Vast colonies of hermits settled in the deserts of the Middle East. These are the remains of the old community in the valley of Goreme in Cappadocia (now part of Turkey). The first Christian settlers here were refugees from the persecutions, who founded villages among the rock masses. Later, hermits, anchorites and monks arrived and carved cells out of the solid rock At the height of Goreme's fame, 40,000 monks lived here, having cut whole monasteries into the rocks; the upper levels contained churches and chapels, highly decorated in the Byzantine style.

Monasticism, which originated in Egypt, was introduced into the West, primarily in Gaul and Italy, in the fourth century. The monks followed the Eastern models, particularly those of Pachomius and Basil. Great austerity was the keynote. The first major change came with St. Benedict in the sixth century. About the year 500 A.D., Benedict, wearied of the licentious society of Rome, withdrew to a cave of Subiaco to live as a hermit. His saintliness and the sanity of his way of life attracted others and he eventually founded twelve monasteries with twelve monks each. In 525, he moved to Monte Casino where he drew up his famous rule. This was the first detailed legislation suited for European needs, and it superceded all other rules in Europe: from the eighth to the twelfth centuries, Benedictine monasticism was supreme in the West. These are sixth century monks.

*The ancient Benedictine monastery of Monte Cassino
was seriously damaged during World War II by Allied bombers
because the high command believed—incorrectly—that
the Germans were using it for an observation post.
These are statues rescued from the rubble.*

Situated in a gorge on the slopes of Mt. Sinai, St. Catherine's
monastery was founded by the Emperor Justinian in the sixth century.
According to tradition Justinian had a church built on Mt.
Sinai for the hermits who had previously lived among the
rocks and caves. The monastery was eventually fortified
to protect it against the Moslems. Once a famous shrine for
pilgrims, from both Latin and Orthodox Churches, it
gradually fell into oblivion, and today only a handful of
monks live in its crumbling ruins.

Isolated from the world for centuries, St.
Catherine's is a storehouse of religious and
artistic treasures of incredible richness.
Its great works were untouched by the
ikonoclastic controversy, and the dread
hand of the professional restorer has never
molested its mosaics and frescoes. This is a
seventh-century encaustic ikon of St. Peter,
holding the keys to heaven and a cross.

An irascible saint

Saint Jerome—Hieronymous Eusebius was his Latin name—was born about 340 A.D. (some accounts say 347) on the upper Adriatic in a Dalmatian town later so completely destroyed by barbarians that today we do not know its precise location. He was the son of wealthy Christian parents who sent him to Rome at the age of twelve to study.

Jerome was a desert-toughened, witty and intelligent man who through some freak of physiognomy seemed ancient and wizened almost from the moment of birth. From the time he took up the life of a hermit he is shown to us hoary and wrinkled; yet he was only in his twenties, and he had before him almost 55 years of active and public life. There has probably been no recluse less retiring, no saint more irascible, no peacemaker who enjoyed an opponent's discomfiture more than Jerome.

Like his contemporary, Augustine, Jerome spent a profligate youth "among bands of girls," the memory of whom haunted him in the desert. But in Rome he was drawn to other things besides girls: his newly conceived passions were for the Greek and Latin classics, the enthusiasm of Christians and the mystical atmosphere of the catacombs. His parents had never bothered to have him baptized, so Jerome was not received into the Church until the age of twenty. After a wandering scholar's tour of Italy, France and Germany, he returned to Dalmatia to join a group of friends who had set up a monastic colony inspired by Saint Athanasius's accounts of the Egyptian desert fathers. But he hated his native land. Dalmatia, Jerome wrote later, "is prey to barbarism; in it men's only god is their belly; they live only for the present and the richer a man is the holier he is held to be." Of the local clergy he remarked, "to use a well-worn proverb, the dish has a cover worthy of it, for Lupicinus [the bishop] is their priest. What I mean is that an unstable pilot steers a leaking ship, that the blind is leading the blind straight to the pit." The group lasted until 373, when for some unknown reason it dissolved in "a monstrous tearing asunder," and Jerome, now thirty-three, began wandering again.

After some months spent studying the classics in Alexandria and Antioch, he settled down in the fierce and violent desert of Chalcis, southwest of Antioch. Jerome had been moved to do this by a dream in which God had accused him of being a Ciceronian rather than a Christian; he resolved then to spend the rest of his life as a hermit; he wanted to become a saint. He saw the vast solitude and terrible harshness of the desert "bright with the flowers of Christ . . . gladdened with God's special presence . . . lovelier to me than any city." But like Saint Anthony of Egypt, he was attacked by fierce and painful temptations, and his mind surged with salacious thoughts. "How often," he recollected later, "did I fancy myself among the pleasures of Rome. I used to sit alone because I was filled with bitterness. Sackcloth disfigured my unshapely limbs and my skin was black from neglect, like an Ethiopian's. . . . Now, although in my fear of hell I had consigned myself to this prison where I had no companions but scorpions and wild beasts, I often found myself among the dances of maidens. My face was pale and my body chilled from fasting, yet my mind was burning with desire and the fires of lust kept bubbling up before me when my flesh was as good as dead. Helpless, I cast myself at the feet of Jesus, I watered them with my tears, I wiped them with my hair; and then I subdued my rebellious body with weeks of abstinence."

To tame the turbulence of his passion, he prayed and fasted, spending long hours without sleep until his "bare bones crashed against the ground" from weariness. To distract himself from his desires and as a penance he began the study of Hebrew, "a language of hissing and broken-winded sounds," which he learned from a fellow anchorite, a converted rabbi. But Jerome was the most unhermit-like of desert fathers: he had brought with him an extensive library, and was continually buying and begging other volumes from friends. At Chalcis he wrote a series of lives of the fathers which are still read.

Since he was a man of repute in the desert, he was drawn into theological and political disputes much against his will. When the partisans of the four claimants to the episcopal throne of Antioch clamored for his support, Jerome answered, "Anyone who is united with Peter's chair, he is my man." He wrote to Rome for a decision. He waited a year for an answer, received none, and wrote again to Pope Saint Damasus, who still did not reply. By 379 Jerome had become physically exhausted, disillusioned and tired of the endless disputes. "I am forced to cry out against the inhumanity of this country," he said. "Better to live among wild beasts than among such Christians."

And so he left the desert. At Antioch the bishop persuaded Jerome to take Holy Orders. It was a curious step, to which Jerome reluctantly agreed on condition that he might remain a monk. (It is probable that he never exercised his priestly rights, even though the Middle Ages represented him as a cardinal.) Then Jerome spent almost two years in Constantinople, where the representatives of the pope were impressed by his talents and persuaded him to go to Rome. There he was befriended by Damasus and on the basis of his desert writings was asked to make a new Latin translation of the Bible to replace the multitude of inferior and inaccurate versions then in use.

As the pope's protégé Jerome was immediately drawn into the intrigues of Rome. Damasus was a reforming pope and therefore unpopular. An antipope had been raised against him; Damasus was accused of adultery, but the Emperor Gratian exonerated him, as did a Roman synod of bishops who in turn excommunicated his accusers; numerous other attempts to depose him were equally unsuccessful. The anti-Damasus factions attacked Jerome because there had gathered about him a group of ascetic upper-class women who formed a sort of convent, the first of its kind in Rome. These women, among them Saint Paula and her daughters Blesilla, Paulina and Eustochium, all knew Greek and were learning Hebrew, and they helped Jerome with his translation of the New Testament. The defense of them and of himself involved him in a battle with the clergy. "There are some," he wrote in a letter which was recopied and distributed to the general public, "who enter the clerical state only to gain a freer hand with the ladies. Their hair is done up in the latest style, their fingers glisten with rings and stones, and to keep the wet ground from soiling their tender soles, they mince about on their toes." Of one priest he wrote, "Chastity and fasting alike are distasteful to him. What he likes is a savory breakfast—say, off a plump young crane."

In 384 Damasus died, and Jerome's career was finished. He was accused of an affair with Paula. He had been mentioned as a possible pope, but another man was elected. The new pope told him to leave Rome, and he did. "The whole city was in uprising against me," he said dramatically. "Men who used to kiss my hands were secretly biting me with viper's teeth . . ."

After some further wandering, Jerome settled down in Bethlehem, next to the cave in which the Christ Child was born. There he established a monastery which included a school, a hospice and a convent for Paula and Eustochium, who had followed with Jerome's brother and some other friends. Again he was criticized for this friendship with Paula, Eustochium and the other women, a criticism that was to persist even as late as the Middle Ages with references to them being often deleted from Jerome's dedications, and Jerome himself portrayed as a surly and solitary figure, accompanied only by his faithful (though nonexistent) lion.

In Bethlehem Jerome settled down—for the rest of his life as it turned out—to complete the heroic work for which he is best remembered, the Vulgate Bible. His New Testament was not exactly popular. Augustine had complained that his translation was too far from the current Greek version; Jerome replied that if Augustine didn't like the new version he didn't have to read it.

In Bethlehem he spent the first few years in revising his earlier translation of the Psalms and in writing homilies and commentaries of various kinds. From 390 on, he gave more attention to the translation of the Old Testament from the Hebrew. His women assistants gathered all available copies in all languages and checked them against each other. Jerome spent his own days in running the monastery, taking care of visitors, dictating letters to a corps of secretaries (he was a prolific, colloquial and witty correspondent), and handing out advice to anyone who wanted it. Then at night he turned to the commentaries and translation.

Retranslating the Bible presented enormous problems. The Sacred Scriptures had been some 1,400 years in the compiling, and there were hundreds of versions in dozens of languages, with errors on every page due to the inaccuracy of "copyists more asleep than awake," all of it undermined by "the blundering alterations of confident but ignorant critics." The Church was wracked with arguments over the unfolding doctrine: there were endless battles over the nature of Christ and over hundreds of other points, some basic to the essential dogma of Christianity, some of importance primarily to theologians. "If we are to pin our faith on Latin texts," said Saint Jerome, "our opponents ask us which; for there are as many forms of texts as there are copies. If on the other hand, we are to learn the truth from a comparison of many, why not go back to the original Greek and correct the mistakes?"

He examined everything he could get his hands on. He had access to numerous Greek and other manuscripts which even then were considered ancient and are now lost. But most of what he looked at was useless—"dull in perception, frivolous in expression, sleepy in sense—rubbish." He had to trace the Old Testament from Greek back to Hebrew, and when he found that the book of Daniel was written in Chaldaic, he learned Chaldaic. The ancient Jews had selected one copy of the Bible as the standard version and had destroyed variations, but passages remained that still caused trouble. Of the Hebrew version of the book of Job, Jerome said: "An indirectness and slipperiness attaches to the whole book even in the Hebrew. And it is tricked out with figures of speech, and while it says one thing, it does another; just as if you close your hand on an eel, the more you squeeze it, the sooner it escapes." He had been told it was a waste of time to translate from the Hebrew, but he later boasted that, "Our version is more intelligible for it has not turned sour by being poured three times over into different casks."

His aim was to produce a universal Bible. "A version made for the use of the Church, even though it may possess a literary charm, ought to disguise and avoid that as far as possible in order that it may not speak to the idle schools and few disciples of the philosophers, but may address itself rather to the human race."

The Bible was the greatest work of his life, his ultimate passion. "Ignorance of scriptures is ignorance of Christ," he said. "Never let the Bible out of your hands. What other life can there be without knowledge of the Bible wherein Christ, the life of them that believe, is set before us?" When the Old Testament was finished in 405, he turned back to his homilies and commentaries, and though the world seemed beyond the possibility of change, to giving out advice. Some of it is surprisingly gentle. To a parent inquiring about the education of a daughter he wrote, "Get her a set of letters made of boxwood or ivory . . . let her play with these so that they may teach her something." To a young girl who wanted to be an ascetic: "I am not the one to lay down the law about extreme fasting or abnormal abstinence from food . . ."

His last ten years were spent in a state of near-mourning. For in 410 Rome had fallen before Alaric's brutal onslaught. Jerome's friends had been killed or imprisoned, and the values men lived by were under siege. "While the barbarians are spread throughout our lands, all is uncertain," he had written earlier. It was only with horror "that the mind can contemplate the calamity of our age." When, close to eighty, he died on September 30, 420 A.D., all seemed lost. Yet Pope Benedict could say of him, "Such was his love of Holy Scripture that he ceased not from writing or dictating till his hand stiffened in death, and his voice was silent forever."

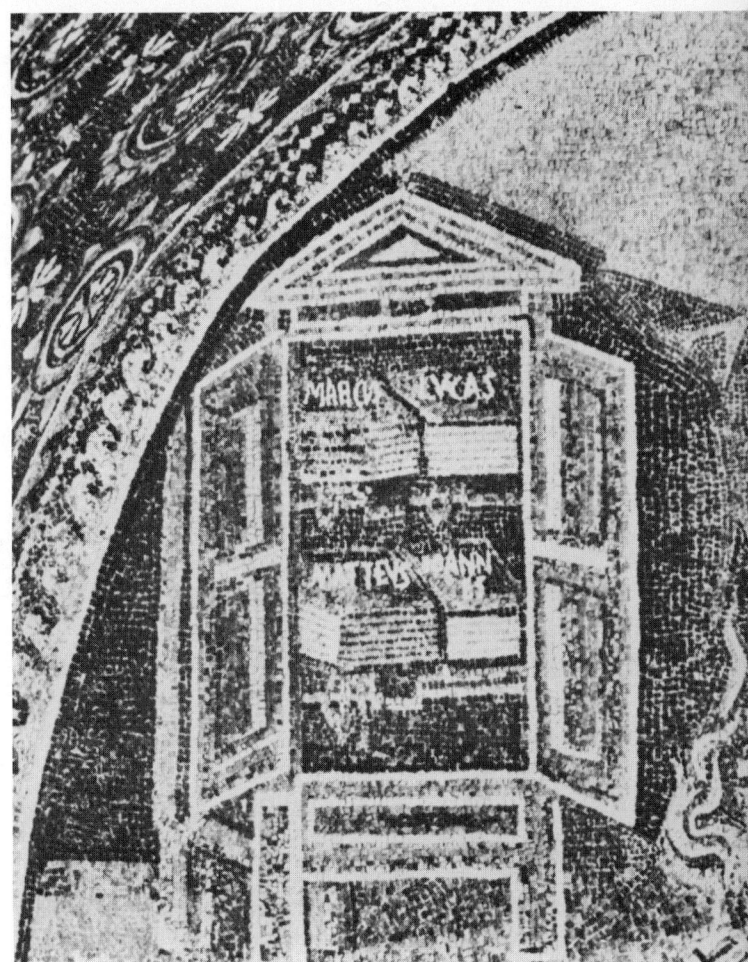

Early in St. Jerome's time the books of the four Evangelists were kept in a cupboard known as the ARMARIUM, *which stood in the sacristy of a basilica. The manuscripts were originally written in scroll form and were carried about in a leather pouch. By the beginning of the fifth century scribes were writing on flat sheets and binding the codices together in books*

ΛΑΒωΝΠΙΤΙΗ͡ΡΙΟΝΕΥΧΑΡΙCΤΗCΑCΕΛωΚΕΝΑΥΤΟΙC
Α ΤΥ ΙΟΥΥΦΙΕΙCΙΟΤΙΛΙΤΦΑΜΟΥ

MⲰⲨⲞⲎC   ΛΛΛ   ΛΛΛ   CΟΛΟΜⲰΝ
                                                 ΛΤΛ

The reception of Holy Communion was at first frequent, but declined with the mass conversions of the fourth century, when many nominal Christians came into the Church. The communicants approached the priest in a single file and accepted the Sacred Host in the palm of the right hand, then received the Chalice. After the Liturgy, those who had not communicated were given the EULOGIA or blessed bread.

Worship and the sacraments

During the fourth century the liturgy became more elaborate in its celebration. Such a tool as the ordinary knife, used for cutting the sacred bread for consecration, evolved into a liturgical lance. This is sixth century Byzantine.

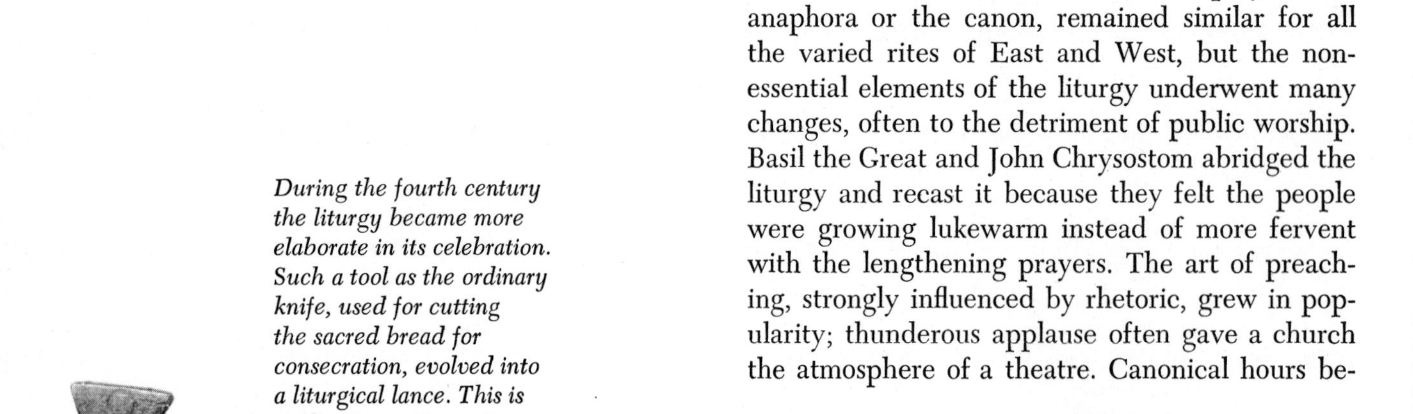

When Christianity was given toleration by Constantine and officially recognized as the state religion by Theodosius the Great in 380, the Church was free to develop her liturgy on a grand scale and give proper observance to the sacramental life. The essential Eucharistic prayers, the anaphora or the canon, remained similar for all the varied rites of East and West, but the non-essential elements of the liturgy underwent many changes, often to the detriment of public worship. Basil the Great and John Chrysostom abridged the liturgy and recast it because they felt the people were growing lukewarm instead of more fervent with the lengthening prayers. The art of preaching, strongly influenced by rhetoric, grew in popularity; thunderous applause often gave a church the atmosphere of a theatre. Canonical hours be-

ΤωΝ ΑΡΤωΝ ΕΥΧΑΡΙCΤΗCΑC ΕΔωΚΕΝ ΤΟΙC
ΜΑΘΗΤΑΙC ΤΟΥΤΟ ΕCΤΙΝ ΤΟ CωΜΑ ΜΟΥ

ΔΑΔ   MWCHC   ΑΔΑ   ΗCΑΙΑC

came popular, with morning services and vespers
attended by the laity even on weekdays. In the
fourth and fifth centuries special Christological
feasts were added to the observances of Sunday,
among them Epiphany, Christmas and the Ascension; Byzantium, with its great devotion to the
Blessed Virgin, introduced a number of Marian
feasts—the Annunciation, the Assumption and the
Divine Maternity of the Blessed Virgin.

Confession of sins and reconciliation with the
Church after penance were public; however, at
first, the sacrament was rarely administered—Christians being assumed to have turned their backs on
sin completely with baptism. Over the centuries,
confession became more frequent, the severe early
penances were mitigated and confession became
private. Clerical celibacy developed into a controversial subject in East and West. Married men
could be ordained and there were special ceremonies for blessing a cleric's wife as deaconess.

*The Eucharist was often set aside in a special
box, originally of wood but later of precious
metal or ivory (this is from sixth-century Egypt
and shows the three Marys visiting the Sepulchre).
The use of the pyx as a container for bringing
the Host to the sick was later made mandatory
to end the practice of carrying It in a corporal
hung from the priest's neck or between the pages
of a book.*

Baptism by triple immersion (left) was the common form of administering
the sacrament. It was usually conferred in a special chapel
near the parish church (at first solely by the bishop), during
the vigils of Easter or Pentecost or the Epiphany. The recipient
underwent a strict preparatory fast, confessed his sins and
renounced the devil. After the ceremony he partook of a symbolic
meal of milk and honey. Most of the baptised were adults who
had served a rigorous catechumenate; infant baptism became more
common after the fifth century. Before that, adults often delayed baptism
for fear of the responsibilities it entailed, until death was imminent.
Normally baptism took place in a large basin or pool in
the center of the floor of the baptistry (above). The
recipients of the sacrament chastely donned their
baptismal robes in little curtained compartments ringing
the basin. After infant baptism became general, the baptismal
font in its present form was adopted and the sacrament
administered in the church.

The decline of the West

While the city of Byzantium was growing in wealth, the empire was experiencing a time of troubles, particularly in the West. The barbarian nations which had menaced Rome since the late second century burst out in an explosion of pillage in the fourth. Jutes, Angles and Saxons invaded Britain, wiping out the Roman colony; the Vandals, who became a symbol of destruction, swept across Europe, into Spain and Africa, and pushed eastward to invade Italy by sea. Franks in Gaul, Visigoths in Spain, Ostrogoths in Italy and the Balkans plundered the empire. At the same time there was a universal decline in population. From a high of 80,000,000 inhabitants in the late second century the population fell to less than half that number by the sixth. Cities shrank, towns and villages were abandoned; the buildings of Imperial Rome rotted and collapsed; weeds grew in the ruins; aqueducts damaged by barbarians were never repaired because there was no one to do the work. The army disintegrated; commerce barely moved on the neglected roads; landowners could not pay the increasing taxes and deserted their farms. Most tragic was the city of Rome. Her population dropped from 1,000,000 inhabitants to 50,000. Cattle grazed in the public gardens, the famous defensive wall crumbled into ruins; the drainage system fell into disrepair, allowing malarial swamps to spread close to the city.

The Ostrogoths, under Theodoric, established their capital at Ravenna. Most of the German nations were Arians, having been first Christianized by Uffila, the Gothic bishop converted by an Arian patriarch of Constantinople. Although he imprisoned Pope John I and executed the famous philosopher Boethius, Theodoric was normally tolerant of the Italian Christians under his rule. The Gothic chiefs above are represented as the Three Magi in a mosaic at Ravenna.

Throughout the Empire the great Graeco-Roman inheritance fell to pieces before the ravages of time and the onslaught of barbarians. These are the ruins of a temple in Sicily.

TIETQUARETRISTISINCEDO ·IUUENTUT
DUMADELICITMEINIMICUS

THE
DARK
AGES

As the fourth century opened, there was but one power in the world, and that was Rome. Despite barbarian migrations and generals' revolts, a sort of Victorian optimism prevailed among cultured men. A few years later, having acted on the fateful decision to move its capital to Byzantium, on the edge of Europe facing Asia Minor, Rome was sharing its place with two other powers, the Church and the German barbarians; a third, Islam, was around the corner. A new world was being born, but the birth was bloody, and men saw only chaos and despair.

Wrecking monuments and buildings, murdering civil servants, terrifying farmers and tradesmen, the Germans inflicted such a heavy paralysis upon the West that the seven centuries following the removal of the seat of government to Byzantium are known as the Dark Ages.

MEAM. IAREUULTUSMEIETDSMS

The period was one of unimaginable disaster, brightened by a few, enduring flashes of light that came from a handful of great men—two popes, Leo and Gregory, the emperors Justinian and Charlemagne—and from the courageous activities of the missionaries who travelled among iron-age savages to preach the word of Christ. The constant marauding of wandering Germanic nations, along with Huns, Avars, Moslems and others, shattered the empire but the outcome was the building of a whole new civilization based on a fusion of German vitality and the Christian faith. The process took a long time. Estranged politically and economically from New Rome, the Church was forced to rely upon the barbarians. The result was a shift of power from Byzantium to the West, and the start of modern Europe.

The Dark Ages present an almost unrelieved portrait of warfare and desolation. This illustration from the ninth-century Utrecht Psalter shows a typical battle scene: mounted warriors (probably Saxons) are attacking a fortified town. The manuscript was made at a monastery near Rheims by northern artists; its drawings, executed in a forceful, near-violent, manner are almost cartoons; however they had a strong effect on later medieval art.

A mounted German warrior is portrayed on a barbarian plaque from c. 700 A.D. The natural fighting ability of the Germans led them to serve as troops under the Romans, once they were civilized, and then as the empire's generals.

The migrating nations

The torrents of Germanic tribes that filled the vacuum created by the failure of Rome to keep order were the last waves of mass migrations of Indo-European peoples who had been sweeping back and forth across the Asiatic heartland and into Europe for several thousands of years. Their early history is lost in the fierce mists of time, but they left traces of their migrations behind them as they pushed into almost every corner of the Asiatic-European land mass—India, Persia, Asia Minor, the Balkan, Italian, Scandinavian and Spanish peninsulas, leap-frogging to the Mediterranean and Atlantic islands and to northern Africa. (The Philistines, who invaded Asia Minor by way of Crete, were part of these migrations; their champion, Goliath, who died by David's stone, was a tall blond giant who spoke a language cognate to primitive German.) After leaving most of the West in ruins, they began to settle down in the fourth and fifth centuries. Tribes such as the Lombards, Burgundians and the Franks settled in lands that still bear their names. Under a leader named Clovis, the scattered tribes of Franks were united into a single kingdom and were baptized by St. Remy, archbishop of Rheims, in 496. The Catholic bishops became the leaders of a new order.

Numerically the Germans were small, comprising some five percent of the population. Barbarians married Roman women, and the Germans became Romanized with notable rapidity. The crude barbarian religion, culture and customs, along with racial distinctions, began to disappear. Whatever virtues the barbarians had brought with them were soon corrupted. Gregory of Tours reports on almost every page of his history of the Franks the grossest moral decay: drunkenness, debauchery, cupidity, murder, abominable acts of cruelty. Women encouraged their lovers to murder their husbands; brother betrayed brother, and sons their parents. Gold—often supplied from Byzantium to keep the barbarians divided—bought all but the most saintly men; corruption infected the clergy. By the fifth century invasions had ended, but for generations Western Europe suffered a series of petty wars, in which unending dynastic struggles heightened the terror of the times.

In the fourth century the Goths received a Bible in their own language, translated by Uffila, a Cappadocian bishop who had converted them. Uffila omitted the Books of Kings, feeling that their deeds would have an unfortunate effect upon such a warring people as the Goths. Unfortunately, Uffila was an Arian in his beliefs, and for several centuries the Gothic peoples retained an Arian form of Christianity. This is a page from the Uffila Bible.

Mohamet, the last of the prophets according to Islamic belief, was born in Mecca in 570 A.D., at the time a prosperous center of trade between Southern Arabia and the Mediterranean countries. The prophet himself was engaged in the caravan trade, but at the age of forty he received the call to proclaim the worship of Allah, the One God, against the common polytheistic beliefs and idol worship of his fellow Arabs. His preaching made little progress for the first ten years, but gradually all of Arabia accepted his doctrines and began to proclaim them throughout the Mediterranean and Eastern world at the point of a sword. The term "Islam" denotes a surrender to God; the adherents of the faith are "Muslems," or believers. Here we see Mohamet preaching his farewell sermon.

The Moslem challenge

Early in the seventh century the Arabian mystic, Mohamet, began preaching a new religion centered on the oneness of God. His followers multiplied rapidly and by his death in 632 they were sufficiently numerous to undertake the conquest of the world. They proved to be more formidable enemies to the Church than others it had been facing. Where the barbarians came naïvely and were assimilated and Christianized, the Moslems rode through the world bearing a dynamic new teaching which annihilated Christianity wherever it went and substituted a belief—"There is but one God and Mohamet is his prophet"—which demanded equal loyalty.

Enervated by luxury and blinded by palace rivalries, the Byzantine empire was an easy prey. Many of its subjects held heretical doctrines which gave way to the similar but stronger discipline of Mohamet. With Asia Minor and northern Africa completely under the spell of Mohamet's beliefs (Islam still has its faithful today in almost every country where it was first imposed), the Arabs now dared to invade Europe. In 711 a force of 7,000 Berber warriors crossed the straits of Gibraltar and launched into the conquest of the West. For a century and a half see-saw battles raged around the Mediterranean; the Arabs pushed into Gaul, their new converts now doing the bulk of the fighting, and plundered it at will. The famous battle in which Charles Martel halted the Moslems was in actuality only a skirmish: Arab marauders continued to raid Provence until thrust back by a Frankish drive in 759 which culminated in the taking of Barcelona.

A Christian vanquishes a Moor in a tenth-century Italian mosaic.
The Moslems made greatest progress in the lands where Christianity
had attained heretical forms; in Spain, Sicily, Italy and Byzantium
Christians died for their beliefs rather than join the Moslems, who
were unable to achieve a complete victory over the West. Meanwhile,
Islam spread across Asia into India and Indonesia. Today it has
some 350,000,000 members and is again gaining converts, especially
in East and West Africa.

The unity of the Western Church was tightened due to the work of St. Boniface (here shown preaching and suffering martyrdom in Frisia in 753) who began a reform of the Frankish Church. A great diplomat and evangelist, Boniface helped strengthen papal supremacy beyond the Alps, founded monasteries, and lent episcopal authority to the new Frankish kingdom by anointing Pepin the Mayor of the palace of the ineffectual Merovingian dynasty, a once-great family that had grown weak during several centuries of settled life.

Two great popes

Even though freed by Constantine of the persecutions of pagan Rome, the popes of liberated Christendom found themselves at the mercy of an imperial court which fluctuated between a smothering with kindness and a killing with neglect or bullying. The quiet strength of the Church and the loyalty it received from the people were temptations to Constantinople. The "most Christian" emperors constantly sought to make the papacy a servile instrument of the government, and rarely hesitated to depose, jail or exile popes.

Two great, sainted popes, Leo and Gregory, stand out in a progression of colorless men who held the papal chair. Both were noted for their diplomatic and administrative talents, their resounding teachings and their protection of the Church against spiritual and physical harm.

Though secular history remembers Leo mainly for his courageous confrontation of Attila the Hun and his ravaging hordes of warriors in 452—Leo was the sole guardian of an abandoned city—his greatest, most enduring efforts were in other fields: his outspoken defense of the Church in the spirit-

ual and political realm (his denouncement of the "robber council" of Ephesus called by Emperor Theodosius II clarified both the teaching of the Church on the nature of Christ and the primacy of the papacy); his sermons, some of which still guide the faithful through the Roman Breviary.

Gregory's life bears striking parallels to Leo's. A great scholar and a spokesman for the Church, consecrated in an age of increasing savagery, lawlessness and ignorance, Gregory had a profound effect upon Christendom, and his life and work redirected it into channels that were more spiritual and more humane. His hand was felt in innumerable fields, from the tightening of ecclesiastical discipline to the strengthening of the papacy, the aid of the poor and the sick and the diversion of barbarian attacks.

Despite the treatment of the emperors and the mediocrity of some of its inhabitants, the See of Peter grew as a center of world-wide importance; it enjoyed undisputed authority everywhere, and what learning existed survived almost solely due to the Church; the monastic life flourished from Monte Casino to Iona, and Benedictine and Irish missionary monks penetrated lands where the empire was only a dim name.

Though he had twice refused the honor of the papal chair, a crowd of Romans forced Gregory to his consecration, despite his protests. A member of a patrician family of Rome, Gregory knew the horrors of his times. He had experienced barbarian attacks; as a child he had been one of 500 survivors of a siege, and had lived on grass and nettles during it. At thirty, he held office as prefect of the city; ordained one of the Seven Deacons of Rome, he then served as delegate for Pope Peleagius II to the court at Byzantium; in 585 he retired to a life of contemplation. The fortunate act of the mob catapulted into office one of the greatest figures of Western civilization.

Ireland received Christianity as early as the fourth century, apparently through the work of missionaries from Britain. When St. Patrick arrived on the island in 432 there was already a small group of Christians awaiting him. The saint further reorganized the Church there. After the dissolution of the Roman Empire, Ireland was forced to develop her Church life alone, which she did with such vitality that, despite their isolation, the Irish monasteries were centers of learning and the Irish monks went to the mainland as missionaries: the most famous were St. Columba, who evangelized Scotland in 563, and St. Columbanus, who arrived on the continent in 590. County Kerry's 1,400-year-old tiny Gallarus Oratory, built of unmortared stone, is characteristic of the early Christian architecture of Ireland.

One of the curiosities of Irish Christianity
was the unique role of the bishop. Because of
the odd structure of Irish feudalism, the heads
of land-owning communities (such as abbots
and abbesses and even laymen) often
exercised authority over the bishops, who
were consecrated in great numbers though
they did not possess dioceses. Many of them
took to the road. The stone figure of Lough
Erne shows a traveling bishop, holding his
crook in one hand and a bell in the other.

A fine example of the work of Irish monasteries is the Book of Kells
from County Meath. A highly ornamented commentary on the Gospels, it is the most beautiful specimen of Irish
handwriting now extant; it was once thought to belong to St. Columba, but it actually dates from the eighth century.

The age of Justinian

Of the many rulers of New Rome who followed Constantine, only Justinian shared his world view of empire and Church. A Balkan peasant who succeeded his uncle to the throne in 527 by a high-handed coup d'etat, Justinian, then 45, effected as great a transformation in New Rome as Constantine had upon pagan Rome. He engineered vast reforms and, during his own reign at least, restored it almost to its Caesarian dimensions. His interests covered nearly the entire scope of human activity: one of his first acts was a complete revision of Roman law along Christian and humanistic lines; he built new churches of startling design in many parts of the empire, employing the most imaginative architects. In the reconstruction of Hagia Sophia (the church had been burned in riots against Justinian's war on the Western barbarians), his architects evolved a plan for a cathedral greater than anything ever attempted before. It called for a vast dome 160 feet above the flooring, suspended upon partially concealed arches; the stresses upon the stonework were tremendous, and Justinian had his chemists develop a new, stronger cement.

Theodora, the actress daughter of a Hippodrome bear keeper, led a wild youth. Deserted by a lover at Alexandria, she became a Christian and amended her ways. This portrait of her at Ravenna was made shortly before she died of cancer of the throat in 548.

The famed mosaic of Justinian and his retinue at San Vitale in Ravenna, one of the several churches built by the emperor after the defeat of the Goths in 540, has the candidness of a snapshot. Justinian (in the nimbus) is accompanied by his chief of staff, Count Belisarius (on his right), Julianus Argentarius, the architect of the Ravenna churches, and Maximian, the archbishop of the city, whom the emperor hoped to make primate of Italy during the detention of Pope Vigilius.

At the same time, he did everything at top speed. The tremendously complex scheme of the *Corpus Juris Civilis* was done in a year; the detailed plans for Hagia Sophia, demanding previously untried engineering concepts, two months; the cathedral was finished in five years by 200 foremen bossing 10,000 workers. His other great extant architectural masterpieces, the churches at Ravenna, were built in only five years.

The success of his reign was due largely to two people upon whom he depended: his great, imaginative, and courageous general, the lank, bearded Count Belisarius; and the empress Theodora, a former actress and courtesan from Egypt, who helped him greatly, but whose heretical religious views—she believed with the Monophysites that Christ was not truly man—eventually permeated his otherwise orthodox beliefs.

His military and political actions were daring, though sometimes desperate. He was able to recover the West from the barbarians, who had been lopping off sections of it for the previous two hundred years, leaving Byzantium little more than Asia Minor, the Balkans and Egypt. In 533 Justinian's generals, the most famous of whom was Belisarius, sailed into waters which had not seen a

Chemical warfare was one of many innovations developed by Justinian's researchers. Here a Byzantine ship uses a flame thrower—known as "Greek fire"—against an enemy.

Hagia Sophia is the greatest of all of Justinian's many famous churches. It was turned into a mosque by the Turks and is now a museum.

Byzantine ship for a century, and during the next two decades smashed the Vandals and the Goths —both nations were Arian and Justinian saw his wars as religious rather than purely military—extending the empire to the Atlantic. At Ravenna, the Ostrogothic capital, Justinian—after expelling the Arians—established an orthodox bishop. With the West again Roman, and Catholic, Belisarius was sent to the East to halt the Persians. Other generals carried the empire to the mountains of Armenia.

But while restoring the physical dimensions of the empire, Justinian came near to destroying its religious unity. An uncompromising ascetic, he lived and worked in a bare room, ate bread and herbs from earthenware dishes captured from the Huns, and when other officials participated in elaborate religious ceremonies, he would go quietly to a smaller church to render thanks. His position shifted from one of strict orthodoxy and repression of heretics to one of compromise. He spent his declining days attempting to work out a middle way between Catholicism and the conflicting heresies. Like Constantine, Justinian believed that God Himself had ordained him for the holy cause of directing Church as well as empire: he was the "Basileus," a king who is vicar of Christ—a title that was applied to succeeding rulers.

After the capture of Ravenna in 540, Justinian attempted to subvert the authority of the papacy and to transfer it to Ravenna. In 545, the weak and sickly Pope Vigilius was spirited away from his see and finally brought to New Rome in 547; about the same time, the metropolitan of Milan, the second most important see in Italy, was also kidnapped, leaving Justinian's hand-picked bishop of Ravenna the spiritual ruler of Italy and the West. For seven years Vigilius languished in New Rome, under pressure to accede to certain involved and near-heretical rulings of Justinian's. When Vigilius finally submitted in 554, the churches of the West threatened schism rather than follow the pope into a heresy imposed by the throne. After Justinian's death in 565, the empire rapidly lost its recent conquests, and the churches of East and West resumed their mutual suspicion of each other.

The beautiful, ornate Church of the Holy Apostles, standing on the fourth of Byzantium's seven hills, was one of the most famous creations of the age of Justinian. It was cruciform and had five cupolas. During the Latin occupation of Constantinople the church was allowed to deteriorate; during the Turkish conquest it was destroyed entirely by Mohammed II and a mosque was built on its site.

The "Christian Topography" of Cosmas Indicopleustes (Cosmas the Indian Voyager) reports the development of the Byzantines' exploration, as well as their interest in the rest of the world. Cosmas was a sixth-century Greek born in Alexandria; he traveled not only the Mediterranean but also the Red Sea, the Persian Gulf, and possibly even into India, and gathered information about the lands of the Far East. The work is a curious mixture of direct, accurate observation and reporting—it gives a good picture of the extent of Christianity in the time, plus unrealistic speculation of the kind that delighted men in the past (according to Cosmas, the world is a rectangle corresponding in form to the Tabernacle of the Old Testament). The page above, from the manuscript in the Vatican, shows Christ, the Virgin, and several saints.

The destruction of Ephesus was a mark of the failing powers of Byzantium. One of the first great centers of Christendom in Asia Minor (second only to Antioch), it was the ruler of 36 suffragan sees and the scene of the councils of 431 and 449. The city was raided by Arabs in the seventh and eighth centuries and destroyed in the eleventh by the Seljuk Turks. Rebuilt by the Byzantines, crusaders and Turks fought over it; Ephesus was finally destroyed in the fifteenth century.

Arab armies added further troubles to the hard-pressed Byzantines. Fired by the newly revealed faith given Mohammed they swept across Africa to penetrate Spain, engulfed the Holy Land and Syria and pushed into Byzantium from the East.

The challenge to Byzantium

In the eighth century a political change intensified the growing schism between Byzantium and the West when a Frankish ruler named Pepin incorporated several smaller kingdoms into one and was anointed by St. Boniface with the approval of Pope Zachary. This was the culmination of increasing alliances between the Holy See and the barbarian kings, and was a further step in the estrangement of the churches of Constantinople and Rome. Pepin proceeded to Italy with his troops, defeated the Lombards and gave Ravenna and part of Umbria to the Pope. Half a century later Pepin's son Charlemagne was anointed as emperor by Pope Leo III in Rome. Charles unified most of Europe, and thus ended forever Byzantium's political and religious influence in the West. From then on Byzantium stood alone, and though her fortunes were to rise and fall many times, the trend was always downward.

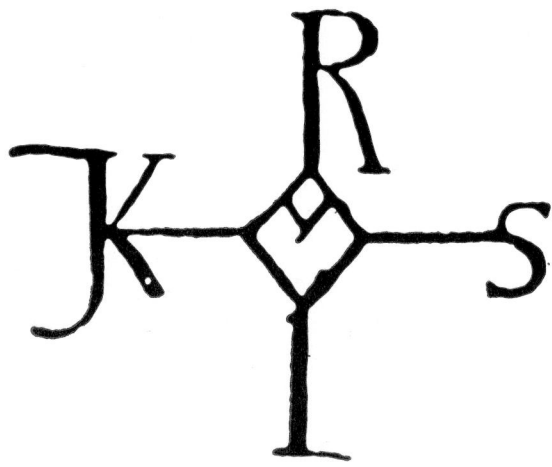

Charles's monogram (the letters form the word KAROLUS*): although the emperor himself was barely literate he was obsessed with learning and established schools for his nobles. He also ordered the standardization of cursive handwriting (the minuscule) for documents, state papers and books throughout his empire.*

charles the great

Though the barbarians had been invading the Empire for nearly a millennium, they had never presented a united front. Their attacks had been in the nature of raids, and none of their leaders had the vision and the talent to unite all the Germans into a powerful force with which to challenge Rome. But the events which would realize this threat were quietly developing among the Franks. In 751 a Frankish Mayor, Charles Martel's son Pepin the Short, who ruled in place of the powerless Merovingian king, took the bold step of asking Pope Zachary if the man who held the power should not indeed be king. Zachary agreed. Anointed by St. Boniface in Biblical fashion, Pepin was king "by the grace of God"; a holy imprint had been placed upon the dynasty of Pepin and the kingly office of Francia. Pepin was now God's vice regent, with public duties to God and the Church for the people committed to his care. This anointing with the holy oils, an act hitherto the unique prerogative of the Roman emperor, thus threw the papacy into close alliance with the Catholic Franks. On Pepin's death, his two sons, Carloman and Charles, appeared to be locked in a dynastic struggle. Carloman died suddenly; Charles, 29, was free to rule in his own way.

Charles, the hero of two nations today, France (as Charlemagne) and Germany (as Karl der Grosse),

was the one man who had the imagination, the talent and the nerveless ambition to pull together the chaotic Germanic dukedoms and kingdoms and make them into a European empire.

Physically, he was perfect for his role. In an age of disease and malnourishment, when men were barely more than five feet tall and rarely lived beyond their twenties because of plague and famine, Charles stood above six feet and enjoyed perfect health for most of his 72 years. He bore a deep and abiding love for his Church; as a child he had been anointed a patrician of Rome by Pope Zachary and to him the spreading of the faith was a divinely commissioned and integral part of his policy of conquest. He imported the best scholars, among them the famous Alcuin of York, to teach the children of his nobles, and underwrote missions to other peoples—yet he presents a hard case for Christianity. Where the Word failed, he resorted to the sword, and the backsliding Saxon tribes needed the presence of Charles's soldiers to keep them Christian. The moral tone of his court belied his strongest profession of Christianity: he divorced at least one wife, married three others, kept concubines, and six of his fourteen children were illegitimate. Devoted to all of his children, he would not let his daughters marry.

A statuette of Charles the Great made shortly after his death shows him as he probably looked. He wears the heavy mustache of the German warrior but is beardless and is dressed in simple clothes—the Arabs' hold on the Mediterranean kept the luxurious fabrics of the East from Western Europe.

The new Europe

In 776 Charles accompanied missionaries into Saxony to convert the fierce tribes there, but after he departed to fight the Moors in Spain the Saxons, led by Witikind, revolted and expelled the missionaries. Charles returned and defeated the Saxons in battle; he decreed that all of them had to accept baptism under pain of death and should also pay tithes to the Church. This edict resulted in a further Saxon revolt in 778; soldiers and civilians alike were slain and the monastery at Fulda was burned.

The fierce, war-loving Saxons (seen here in a drawing from the Utrecht Psalter) were the last heathen and independent tribe of inner Germany. Their favorite occupation was raiding their neighbors. Their incorporation into Francia was the most hard-fought of all of Charles's wars and took up 32 years. Firmly attached to their ancestral paganism they resisted conversion; after several Saxon revolts Charles deported part of the population and replaced it with his own people.

Five years later, in reprisal, Charles killed over 4,000 Saxon prisoners at Verden. Witikind bowed before the superior force of the Christian king, and was baptized, Charles acting as godfather. Alcuin pointed out that the results of his policy would be unsatisfactory, as indeed they proved to be in later centuries. But the Saxon campaign was only the beginning of Charles's efforts to extend both Christianity and Frankish rule. On an appeal by Pope Leo III for aid, Charles crossed the Alps and reduced the Lombards to submission. He arrived in Rome at a particularly crucial time for Leo. The Byzantine throne, on which the papacy was still dependent, was occupied by a woman, and the relations with the empire were as tense as ever. Leo had also just suffered a near-fatal beating from Roman nobles. Charles's arrival offered him the support he needed, and in an act of mutual advantage, Leo boldly made the decision to ignore political ties with Byzantium and anoint Charles as Emperor of Europe. The anointing on Christmas Day, 800, under the Byzantine ceremony, earned Charles the duty of protecting the Church and of extending the faith, of lending his powers to the protection of its culture, and to discipline and reform of the clergy.

Charles pushed his rule eastward across what is now Germany, extending his borders to the edge of the Slavic lands. In 812, the Byzantine emperor, Michael, recognizing a *de facto* division of the empire, ceded Venice and Dalmatia to Charles.

In government Charles developed and systematized the administrative machinery of his predecessors; he left conquered peoples in possession of their own laws, which he codified when possible—and issued many capitularies, or legislative and administrative decrees. He was also concerned with the welfare of the poor and the prevention of abuses. He held a general assembly yearly, and conferred periodically with his administrators in distant territories; he also called religious councils to settle theological controversies. In all, there was little that did not attract his attention, and later generations enlarged the heroic dimensions of his life into a legend of mythic, almost-god-like proportions which entertained Europe until the Renaissance.

A drawing of a mosaic (now destroyed), made during Charles's lifetime, shows him with Pope Leo III before St. Peter. Leo's anointing of Charles has provoked endless dispute. Charles told his biographer, Einhard the Dwarfling, "If I had known what Leo meant to do I would never have set foot in this church, even on this holy day!" However, other sources say Charles readily agreed to the anointing. Until 812 the Byzantines continued to claim the West, and the emperors of both halves of Christendom were no longer co-rulers but rivals. Leo's act also signified that the papacy was now strong enough to bestow or withhold the crown as it chose.

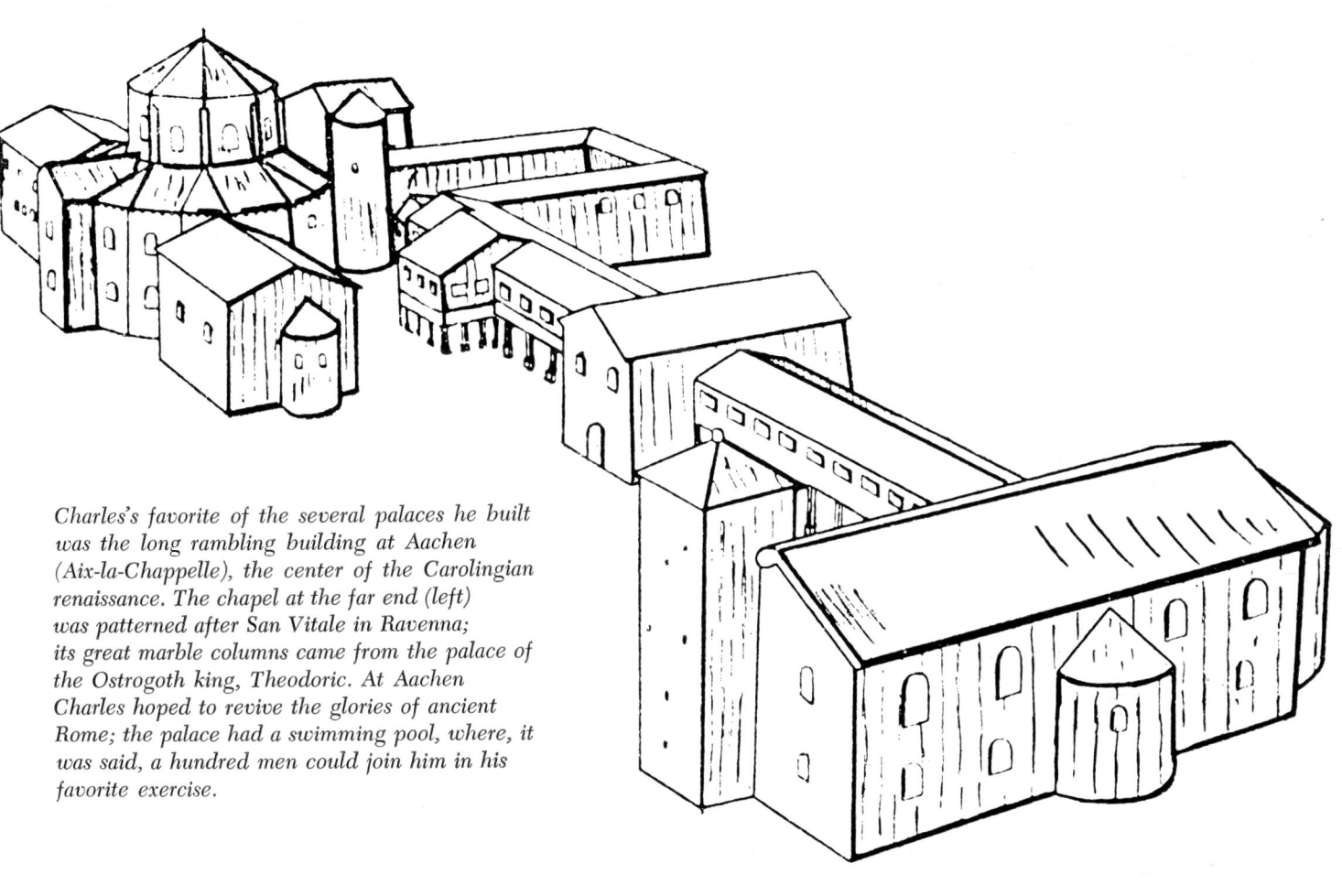

Charles's favorite of the several palaces he built
was the long rambling building at Aachen
(Aix-la-Chappelle), the center of the Carolingian
renaissance. The chapel at the far end (left)
was patterned after San Vitale in Ravenna;
its great marble columns came from the palace of
the Ostrogoth king, Theodoric. At Aachen
Charles hoped to revive the glories of ancient
Rome; the palace had a swimming pool, where, it
was said, a hundred men could join him in his
favorite exercise.

One of the few standing monuments to Charles is the
palace chapel at Aachen, where he is buried. The rest
of the palace has been destroyed but the chapel is now
a part of Aachen cathedral, which has been built
around it. The great stone throne in the center was
used for centuries for the crowning of German kings.
Charles soon developed into a legendary hero: the
anti-pope, Paschal III, canonized him, and an office
was composed for his feast.

MAVRVS ALBINVS SCSMAR TINVS

*The great scholar Alcuin, attached to Charles's court, guides
Rabanus Maurus, later archbishop of Mainz, to the episcopal
throne of St. Martin, the fourth-century bishop of Tours.
Other scholars of the period were the Venerable Bede; Daniel
of Winchester, a West Saxon; Paul the Deacon, a
Lombard nobleman; and the Irish monk, St. Ferghal
(Vergilius), bishop of Salzburg, an astronomer and
theologian who taught that the world was round.*

...Haec scribo uobis ut sciatis qn'm uita habeatis aeterna quicreditis innomine filiidi ecbaec e fiduciaqua'

The look of the text of the Bible was important to the Carolingians. Alcuin developed a new style of writing, the miniscule. Radically departing from the popular uncial script, the miniscule was soon in use throughout Europe and is, indirectly, the model for today's printers' typefaces. Also from Alcuin's workshops came a series of splendid Gospel books, written in gold upon purple or white vellum and adorned with designs derived from Anglo-Celtic manuscripts.

The first scholastics

Born in England about 735, Alcuin was educated at the cathedral school of York by a disciple of the great English scholar, the Venerable Bede; Alcuin soon became the outstanding scholar of his era. Returning from a visit to Rome, he met Charles and was invited to set up a school to combat the overwhelming illiteracy of the times; Charles himself was enthusiastic about educational projects; he felt that popular education would solidify the empire-building on which he was engaged. For fifteen years, until his death in 804, Alcuin was the moving spirit of the Carolingian renaissance. One of his first steps was the establishment of a primary school at the palace; this led to schools of the seven liberal arts, the *"trivium"* and *"quadrivium"* which were the basis of later medieval education. Gifted students were then expected to continue with studies in Scripture and the writings of Fathers.

Decrees were issued in the name of the emperor commanding that all clerics, regular and secular alike, upon penalty of suspension, be able to read and write, and possess a sufficiently broad knowledge for the intelligent performance of duties. A scheme, imperfectly realized, for universal education was also projected, by which the children of even the most obscure peasants were to receive free education at a primary school conducted by the village priest.

Meanwhile Alcuin traveled about Europe to study and search out classical texts. Though scholars from many lands were attracted to his side, his own work was hardly great or even original. He was a teacher rather than a thinker, but his vigorous treatises against the Spanish bishop Felix of Urgel stemmed the heresy of adoptionism, which held that Christ was born of man and became Son of God by adoption when He was baptized in the Jordan.

Intimately connected with his scholarly and liturgical efforts was his work on the Bible. The available texts in France stemmed largely from Irish or Spanish sources; both families of texts were seriously corrupt due to the gross errors of ignorant copyists, and the emperor was concerned over the state of Holy Scripture. Charles forbade the Bible to be copied by inexperienced scribes, and Alcuin was directed to prepare an authentic text. At Tours, a great school of scholars and copyists, working largely with texts imported from York, prepared a correct edition of the Vulgate, which was presented amid much ceremony to the emperor on Christmas day of 801.

Meanwhile, biblical research continued at other centers. At Orleans, Theodulf, a bishop of Visigoth ancestry, was also at work on a restoration of the Vulgate, and on the shores of Lake Constance, in the monastery of St. Gall, which had earlier been colonized by Irish monks, there was intense textual research along the lines of the best Celtic manuscripts.

Vigorous work on the Bible, in research, decoration and the preservation of the texts, continued during the ninth century, but the decline of the house of Charlemagne was reflected in the decay of Vulgate text, the accuracy and purity of which had so intrigued the emperor. The errors of copyists undid the labors of scholars, and when the Norsemen broke into the schools of Tours, the true text of Jerome's Vulgate was dispatched into a second period of gloom and decay.

Alcuin initiated a reform of the Frankish liturgy, fusing the Roman with older Gallican rites. At the time priests celebrated Mass as often as they wished—Pope Leo III is said to have offered as many as seven Masses on a single feast day. However, the reception of Holy Communion was infrequent, sometimes as little as two or three times a year, even among the devout. By the eighth century the use of small, round discs of unleavened bread for the Host, instead of the loaves of the primitive Church, was common.

Typical of the various rites was the Mozarab practiced in Spain in the areas under Arab influence. member of the family of Gallican rites, it was prolix a oratorical, and differs in form from the Roman Ma which eventually became the dominant form of the litur throughout Europe. Constant attempts at suppressi the Mozarabic rite finally succeeded; today it is observe and indifferently at that—only in the cathedral and s parish churches of Toledo. This is a page from tenth-century Mozarabic miss

quo idem se suscipi perpetua-
lis praedixit oraculis. Euouae. Qui

OFFM IN DIEM
SCI [illegible] APLI

Confessio——nem et
decorem induisti a——
mictum lumen sicut vesti-
mentum——————o. ij

Confessio——et speci-
e in conspectu——sanctitas
et magnificentia in sanc-
tificatione eius. SNO

Confitebor tibi domine in toto
corde meo narrabo mirabilia tua

Charles the Bald, grandson of Charles the Great, received what roughly corresponds to modern France in dividing the empire with his brothers. He was unable to control the powerful ambitious nobles under him, and their power grew, setting the basis for the coming of feudalism. Charles was as weak as any of his grandfather's other heirs, and the slighting appellations these kings have received—names like Lewis the Pious, Charles the Fat, Lewis the Blind, Louis II the Stammerer and Charles the Simple—show how they were regarded. The illustration is from the Lothair Gospels.

The dissolution of the Empire

In 814 Charles the Great died. His son, Louis the Pious, was crowned by Pope Stephen V two years later and ruled until 840. Truly religious and strongly influenced by his bishops and successive wives, Louis lacked his father's unique, tremendous personality; the empire, with its diverse, untamed peoples, its poor communications, its impassable forests, marshes and mountain ranges, was impossible for him to administer. After Louis's death, his three sons engaged in a devastating civil war over the throne, but exhausted by the struggle, compromised by dividing the empire into three sections. The East (later Germany) went to Louis the German; the West (later France) to Charles the Bald, and the Middle Kingdom, a sort of buffer state which stretched from the North Sea past Rome, to Lothair, who also gained the imperial title. From that moment the vast domains of Charles the Great began to disintegrate. The remainder of the century was taken up with contests for power between the various descendants of Louis the Pious, in which the papacy, anxious to save the empire and to gain help against the Moslems, became increasingly involved. One by one the great accomplishments inherited from ancient Rome, Byzantium and the Carolingian revival disappeared under frightful conditions. The Middle Kingdom fell apart. The Moslems ravaged Italy, and in Spain turned the churches into mosques; Roman, Lombard and French adventurers despoiled each other's lands. The one institution that stood out as solid and enduring was the Church; her bishops attained unique importance and many were of great saintliness. Her monasteries were centers of refuge for the helpless and islands of learning. But the papacy reached the darkest age of its history. An accepted tale, illustrating the barbarism of the century, relates that Pope Stephen VII disinterred the corpse of Formosus, his predecessor, held a trial over it and cast it into the Tiber. Stephen was soon afterwards strangled in prison. Civil war reigned among rival claimants to the papal throne. Looking back upon the events of the century a bishop at a synod in Rheims in 991 commented: "A pope who possesses no charity, but is merely swollen with knowledge would be anti-Christ. But if he has neither charity nor knowledge, he stands as an idol in the temple of God. How are we to obtain guidance from a stone block?" But ahead, under the saintly Ottonian kings of Germany and the Hildebrand popes, lay the glories of the Middle Ages.

The Vikings helped force the disintegration of the Carolingian Empire. The boldest and most skillful seafarers of all Europe, whose desire was to gain everlasting fame by a hero's death in battle, the Norsemen burst forth in an explosion of pillage in the ninth century. The notoriety of their cruelty was paralyzing —a child might be tossed on their spears. They raided the shores of England and Ireland —"great sea-cast floods of foreigners"—and then swept over France and circled Spain to raid the Mediterranean. At first the Franks bought them off with huge ransoms, but finally surrendered part of the coast in exchange for protection against later raiders. The thickly settled Normans adopted the language and faith of their new country and immediately became a dynamic force in Europe.

In 726 Leo III the Isaurian, the Byzantine emperor, for
reasons still not clear, ordered the removal of all images of
angels and saints from the churches; a few years later,
images of Christ and the Blessed Virgin. The imperial
decrees, enforced with the gravest harshness, were greeted
with an uproar on the part of the faithful, led by the
monks. The pope, bishops, and theologians all denounced
the emperor's policy of ikonoclasm; Leo's police killed
many clergy and laity who were defending the sacred
images. The controversy continued into the ninth century
before it was successfully resolved in favor of the
ikonodules, but in the meanwhile thousands of sacred
images, mainly ikons, were destroyed. The illumination
above shows Leo ordering the destruction of an ikon,
while St. Germanus, patriarch of Constantinople,
protests in vain.

Far to the north of Byzantium the Slavic tribes were expanding into the great plains above the Byzantine colonies on the northern shores of the Black Sea. The Slavs were soon dominated by fierce Scandinavian warriors, the Rus, who in the tenth century established a loosely organized state, centered around Kiev, and even pushed as far south as Constantinople, where they were repelled with Greek fire. But the Rus found a greater prize in Byzantium than mere gold and jewels: Princess Olga, whose late husband had unsuccessfully stormed Constantinople, made a long pilgrimage there in 954 and was baptized. Her grandson, the warrior prince Vladimir, a polygamous heathen who gained the throne of Kiev by murdering his brothers, also fell under the influence of Byzantium's rich culture. Vladimir saw Christianity as the backbone of civilization. He dismissed his flock of wives and was baptized along with his unwilling nobles. The effect was far-reaching. The vast domains of Russia became part of the Christian East, and priests, architects, ikon painters, writers and musicians flowed north to make an indelible imprint upon a people who would someday reach from the Baltic to the Pacific. Here we see Vladimir's envoys appearing before Constantine IX of Byzantium and returning home to announce that the prince could be received as a Christian.

The ancient crown of the Holy Roman emperors.

THE HOLY ROMAN EMPIRE

"Warned by the prophecy of Holy Writ," wrote Ralph Glaber, a crabbed cleric who died at the monastery of Cluny in 1044, "we see clearer than daylight that in the process of the Last Days, as love waxed cold and iniquity abounded among mankind, perilous times were at hand for men's souls." This was an age when men almost constantly expected the Millennium—the end of the world. Though later ages were to over-estimate the importance of chiliastic fears, many men sensitive to the signs of the times, and misreading the Gospels and the book of Revelation, firmly believed that the corruption, sin and natural catastrophes of their particular century meant the coming of the anti-Christ, followed by a golden age during which the Savior himself would appear. To the medieval man, the foreshadowings of com-

ing calamity were manifold: Vesuvius had erupted with a great loss of life; fires had destroyed many cities throughout France and Italy (even the beams of St. Peter's had been partly burned), a plague caused by a poisonous mould generated in spoiled rye flour had swept the continent; and a five-year famine so fierce that men not only ate the carcasses of wild beasts and snakes but were also driven to kill their children for food.

What was happening in Christendom was even worse: covetousness, corruption and incontinence among the clergy; manslaughter, heresy and sins of the most frightful kinds among the nobles and peasantry. The great empire of Charles the Great in the ninth century had been corrupted and now died at the hands of his unworthy heirs. Vassals became stronger than their feudal lords and

Otto the Great, founder of the Holy Roman Empire, dedicates Marburg Cathedral to Christ. Like Constantine and Charles the Great, Otto was a generous patron of the Church, furthering her ideals, culture and civilizing mission.

a state of civil war was general. The Church, too, was deeply affected by the disorders of the age. Through the custom of lay investiture, episcopal seats and even the papacy were given to the sons and friends of the powerful. It was mainly in the monasteries that Christendom was able to withstand the sins of the century. The dreaded year 1000 passed with no sign of the anti-Christ, then a physical and spiritual renewal developed, commencing with a rebuilding of churches. "Every nation of Christendom vied with the other as to which should worship in the seemliest buildings," wrote Glaber of the post-millennial epoch. "It was as though the world had shaken herself and cast off her old age, and were clothing herself everywhere in a white garment of new churches."

A secular revival of the previous century which halted the frightful deterioration of the ruling classes had begun under the influence of a dynastic line of forceful Saxon dukes, beginning with Henry the Fowler. His son Otto established a new, great state known later as the Holy Roman Empire. Otto, born in 912, was a devout and saintly child, surrounded by the influences of sanctity. His mother, Mathilda, his brother, Bruno, archbishop of Cologne, and many of his numerous descendants are honored as saints; yet Otto's own devotion to the Church and his inborn piety were tempered by a strong appreciation of political realities.

A descendant of the fierce Saxon warriors on whom Charles the Great forced Christianity in a relentless 32-year campaign in the ninth century, and precocious in both secular and spiritual worlds, Otto was early conscious of his powers: he had a shrewd genius for understanding people, and for organization and diplomacy. His ascent to the Saxon throne came at a time of extreme danger to the Germanic dukedoms. On the West they were harassed by the Vikings, on the East by a new enemy, the Magyars, a cruel Asiatic race which threatened to wipe out the remnants of civilization in a brutal sweep to the Atlantic coast. The Vikings eventually turned their attention to the islands of Britain, and the Magyars were halted temporarily by Henry the Fowler, who turned the prestige of his victory into a political coup and brought together four of the German duchies into a confederation. Otto, at 24, stepped into the Saxon throne as a full-fledged king, bearing in his nimble mind a plan to rebuild the empire of Charles the Great. Feared more than loved, he achieved by force his ambition to be the actual ruler of Germany and not merely the most powerful of her dukes. When he was crowned in Aachen, in 936, on the throne of

Charles the Great, the four dukes of Lotharingia, Franconia, Swabia and Bavaria, now his vassals, acted as his personal attendants at the coronation feast. The sacred oil bestowed on his forehead by the archbishop of Mainz confirmed him as the Lord's Anointed, and gave him a mission to fulfill for which he had been prepared since childhood. With fire and sword Otto now began to extend his domains and spread the word of Christ through Europe; the duchies, despite a constant cross-current of changing loyalties and rebellions among his vassals, were further unified; the invading barbarians were exterminated, and missionaries, moving eastward to convert the forest tribes, were protected by his soldiers. But no man could be emperor of the west unless crowned by the pope. Italy was being ravaged by civil wars, and Otto easily effected its conquest; he took as his second wife the beautiful widowed Italian queen Adelaide, who had asked for aid against her enemies.

Otto did not obtain complete control of Italy for several years but finally, in order to attain the honors of a Charles the Great, he moved to have himself anointed by the dissolute young John XII; the pope was only too glad to perform the rite in exchange for protection against his enemies in Italy. After this solemn occasion emperor and pope quarreled—John had discovered that Otto was not an ally but his lord, and Otto had him driven from Rome. A synod of bishops obedient to Otto chose a layman as Pope Leo VIII. Upon John's death, the Romans elected a pope of irreproachable character, Benedict V. Otto invaded Rome, imprisoned the new pope and reinstated Leo.

The intrigues in Italy kept Otto busy for six years. An endless shifting of loyalties, the buying and selling of positions, the bribes and other scandals that involved both dukes and bishops, as well as the complicated struggles over the papal throne are impossible to summarize. But Otto's epoch-making reign, during which opposition to his policies was ruthlessly crushed, bishops installed as vassals, and the papacy made an accessory to his ambitions, still produced some good effects on the continent. The anarchy of the tenth century was halted, the barbarians subdued and a strong state, running from the North Sea to the Mediterranean, provided a groundwork for reviving Western civilization after its near-collapse. But most of all, the excesses against the Church made it clear that a major reform had to be undertaken. Some of Otto's successors began to realize that fact, and a few saintly men now began to work in earnest to bring new order into the affairs of the Church.

The young Emperor Otto III receives the homage of the four great peoples under his rule. This illumination shows strong Byzantine influence.

The growth of the empire

In 972, the year before his death, Otto the Great arranged a marriage between his son, Otto II, and the Byzantine princess Theophano, thereby establishing in the German court, at least, strong cultural ties with the East. Young Otto inherited his father's quarrels and at least some of his talents as a warrior. Emperor at 25, he crushed the Danes and the Bohemians, broke a rebellious Bavaria into three duchies, but got himself embroiled in an inconclusive war in France; he then suffered a disastrous defeat at the hands of the Arabs in southern Italy, escaping with his life only by swimming from the battlefield to a nearby Byzantine ship. Conscious of his position as emperor more strongly than of king of Germany alone, in 983 he forced the German nobles to accept his three-year-old son Otto III as their ruler. Immediately after this, Otto II died prematurely at 28. The new emperor was too young to rule. Amid the plots and counterplots that accompanied the throne, his uncle, the duke of Bavaria, tried to depose him, but his mother, Theophano, and later his grandmother, Adelaide, took over as regents until he attained his majority.

Otto III, as a part time ascetic, a military and political genius whose talents never developed, was given to pilgrimages and grand plans for reform of the Church and expanding the empire. Like his father and grandfather, he could not keep his hands off the papacy. His first pope, a cousin, was turned out by the Roman mob; his second choice was his own tutor, the brilliant French scholar Gerbert who reigned as Sylvester II; this was a fortunate choice, for Sylvester, a man of extensive knowledge, also had a deep understanding of the office and was the only pope of the tenth century of any distinction: an able theologian, mathematician and scientist, his learning became legendary. But Otto was popular with almost no one. Affected by his position as the scion of both eastern and western imperial houses, he established his palace in Rome, wore Byzantine costume and introduced Greek titles and ceremonies into his court. At 22, he was expelled from his palace by the Italian nobles; he died while trying to regain Rome, leaving no heir to the throne, which passed to his cousin, Henry II. What Otto III only dreamed of, Henry tried to make a reality. He subdued the rebellious German duchies, and worked steadily for Church reform, although his heavy hand antagonized both clergy and bishops. Henry left no children and the throne passed to Conrad II, a man of the world, who proceeded to undo Henry's work; Conrad saw Church reform as a menace to the proper ordering of society, and threw in his hand with the great worldly prelates, opposing the influence of Cluny. He also tried to divert the secular power of the clergy by promoting serfs to the civil service. He suppressed civil revolts in France and Italy and brought most of Europe within the empire. A thrifty ruler, he encouraged commercial enterprises. Under his son, Henry III, the empire reached its greatest power and solidity, extending its eastern borders to the boundaries it held (as Austria and Hungary) until 1919. But Henry's primary interest was in religious matters and he thought of himself as priest-king, supporting the Cluniac reforms; in 1043, setting himself as the model of the Christian ruler, he proclaimed that he was forgiving his personal enemies and giving up all thought of vengeance, urging his nobles to do likewise, a suggestion that no duke took seriously. Three years later he set aside three contestants to the papacy and caused the election of a reform-minded German who reigned as Clement II. The three succeeding popes—all appointed by Henry—were also excellent men and convinced Clunians who brought to the papacy some of its early influence and prestige. But this new papacy was achieved only at a cost of violating its most sacred principles. Did not the emperor, no matter how honorable his motives might be, still select the occupant of Peter's chair? A battle was shaping up over the question. The opponents were already present: a brilliant cardinal, Hildebrand, and the emperor's six-year-old son, Henry IV. The emperor suddenly died at 39, leaving Henry IV, a mere child, to become the anvil on which papal freedom was to be painfully hammered out.

The feudal system

The most striking institution in the structure of medieval Europe was that of feudalism, an unwieldy, complicated and often confused web of relationships between the great and the small, tying together princes, warriors, bishops and priests into an expanding pyramid, the base of which rested on the serf, a helpless peasant bound to land he must work but could never own. The soil belonged to the king; he, however, did not exploit it, but conferred it as benefices (or fiefs) on his vassals, in return for services, primarily in war. The medieval ruler then was less an official than a landlord whose public guise was that of warrior-aristocrat, holding his lands because of services to some more powerful man.

The growth of feudalism began under the Carolingian kings, Charles Martel, Pepin the Short and Charles the Great, who developed a system of personal loyalty to a chief which the Franks had brought from the forests of Germany. This system was combined with that of the old benefice, a custom whereby the Frankish church, which held a third of the lands of the state, granted land for a fixed term in order to have it cultivated. The kings were soon giving Church lands to their warriors, as well as those taken by conquest.

Though benefices were granted on a limited basis, rulers found that it was extremely difficult to deprive an ascendant warrior of his benefice, and so it would pass on to his sons. The Church was drawn into the whirlpool of feudalism: bishops, abbots and priests became the vassals of great or lesser princes. The feudal lord who built a church would give it as a benefice to a priest, who then became his vassal; the number of proprietary churches (as they were called) soon surpassed those free of feudal relationship. Dioceses and monasteries followed a similar pattern.

Though the abuses and inequalities of feudalism were manifest, feudalism made its own contribution to medieval culture, and became a fundamental element of political life in western Europe. Its inherent negation of a central ruler inhibited the development of absolutist government and of nationalism, and indirectly prepared the foundations for the modern concept of democratic government. Feudalism colored the entire fabric of medieval life: its ethical codes, its concept of love and marriage, of honor and duty, of music, art and literature, of religion and life, and in its support of the creative person, scholar and thinker—poet, artist, musician—it underwrote the cultural flowering of the Middle Ages.

The monastery of Cluny as it looked before being destroyed during the French Revolution.

Cluny fights for reform

The drive to purify and free Church and papacy came first from the great monastery of Cluny, founded in 910 by William the Pious, Duke of Aquitaine. By the middle of the century it was second only to Rome in ecclesiastical importance. Cluny's abbot ranked as a sovereign, with complete control of an immense domain, the right to mint money and to wage war. Under him were 10,000 monks, housed in 400 dependencies throughout Europe. But these statistics, which make Cluny seem a mere ecclesiastical state, conceal her true importance as the starting place of the great monastic impulse that surged through the Middle Ages. Cluny's vitality came from the fact that she was subject to no secular nor spiritual lord but the pope himself: unlike the proprietary monasteries Cluny was founded solely for work and prayer; the emancipation of the entire Church to these high ends was a major point of Cluny's program. The abuses Cluny was fighting seemed almost impossible to eradicate. Under the feudal custom of lay investiture, noblemen often established their younger sons as bishops; these men, unfit for the office, married, or kept concubines, and passed their sees to their children. A vacant see would be sold to the highest bidder; bribery and violence,

the selling of ordinations, were common; episcopal sees had even been given to women. Monastic life was equally corrupt: abbots married, and kept their families at the monasteries: their monks followed the practice. An honest bishop risked his life in trying to initiate reforms—the saintly Erluin, abbot of the great monastery of Lobbes, was blinded and his tongue cut out by rebellious monks who objected to his reforms. The Holy See, too, fell under the system. John XII, son of king Alberic of Italy, was one of the worst examples of feudal interference. Appointed to the papacy at sixteen, he had no idea of the obligations of his office, kept mistresses, used the Church's treasury for his debauchery, consecrated children as bishops, toasted the devil at Lateran banquets, and finally was murdered at the age of 27. None of the twenty-five popes of his century was canonized, and the age itself was rare in saints of any kind, most of them being a few outstanding bishops, missionaries, or members of the nobility, such as some of the Ottonian family, Olga of Russia and Stephen of Hungary. But it was from Cluny that saintliness radiated: seven of her first eight abbots, ruling over an amazingly long period of two and a half centuries, are honored as saints; during this time the papacy experienced fifty-two popes, few of them men of character.

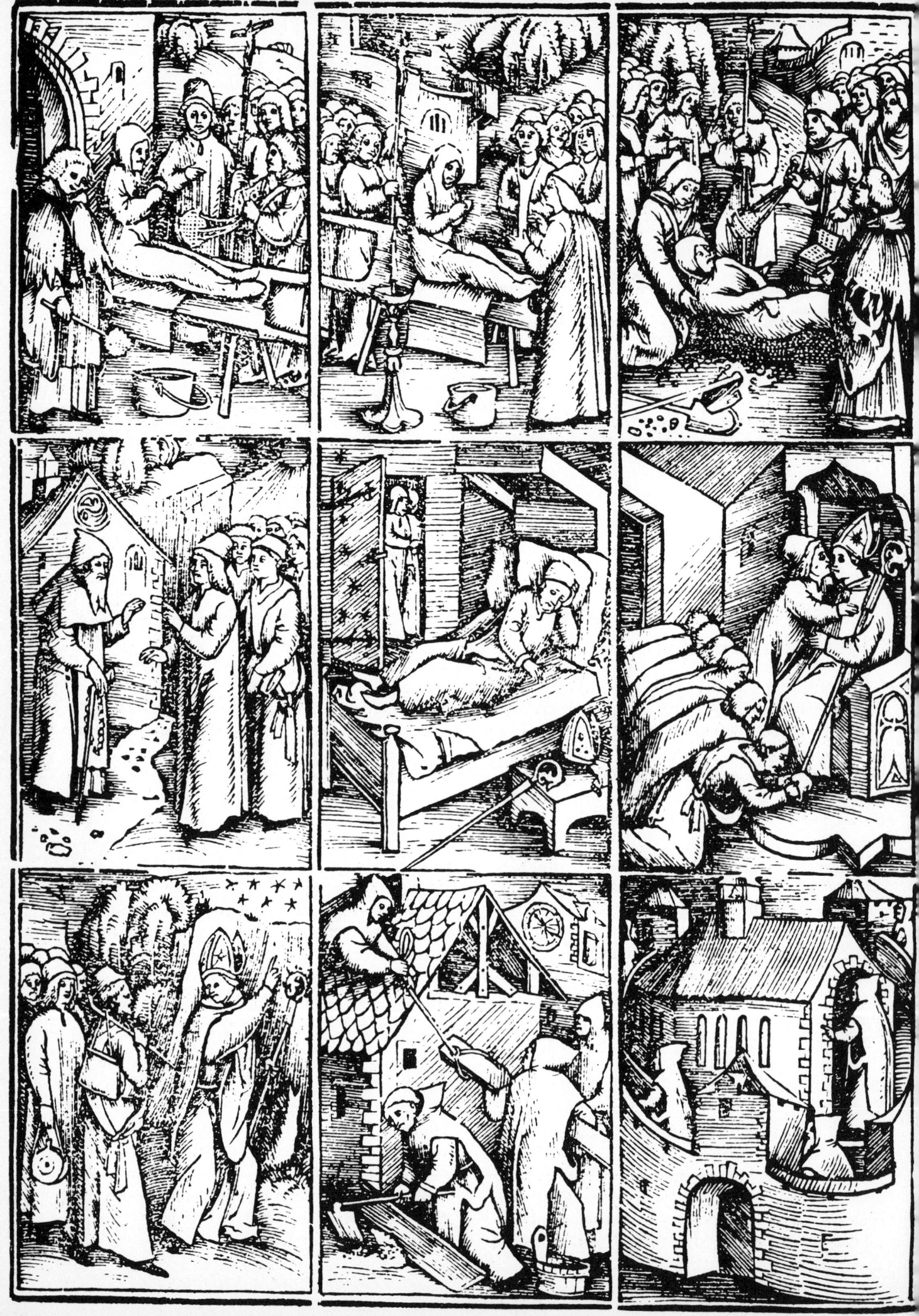

An important role in the spiritual revival of the century was played by the Carthusians, a strict contemplative order whose aim was to revive the early monastic ideal of solitary adoration of God, and to combine with it certain communal features which would give it stability and provide for each monk the strengthening example of others. This sequence shows the founding of the Carthusians by St. Bruno. Supposedly turned towards monasticism after seeing a Parisian doctor raised three times from the dead (top panels), St. Bruno placed himself temporarily under the direction of the noted hermit St. Robert (far left). Later St. Hugh, to whom God had shown St. Bruno and his companions in a dream in the form of stars (center), confirmed the men in their vows and led them to a remote site in the French Alps, to found the first charterhouse (below), the Grand Chartreuse. At the peak of the Order's success, there were 206 charterhouses throughout Europe, with thousands of monks (priest-hermits), lay brothers and nuns.

Gregory VII faces Henry IV

Within a few months of his accession to the papal throne in 1073, the 53-year-old peasant's son, Hildebrand, as Gregory VII, denounced the prime abuses of his day—simony and incontinence among the clergy, and lay investiture. With most of Europe opposing him, including a great number of bishops, most of the priests of France, Italy and Germany, plus many of its princes, Gregory calmly proceeded to purify the Church and to free it of secular control. Secretary to one pope, and chief counselor to five others, Gregory had, except for a period of monastic retreat (according to tradition, at Cluny), spent most of his life at Rome dealing with temporal problems of the Church.

He had an extraordinary ability as an administrator, and under his skillful direction, Church properties which had been diverted to Roman nobles and to the Normans in Italy, were regained. He was also largely responsible in obtaining the celebrated decree of election by which the power of choosing the pope was vested in the College of Cardinals. For over twenty years he had been the most prominent and capable figure in the Church and on the death of Pope Alexander II in April, 1073, during the funeral rites in the Lateran basilica, the crowd of clergy and people suddenly cried out, "Let Hildebrand be pope!" Gregory protested, but he was the man of the hour, accepting the honor "with fear and trembling"; thus the See of Peter received one of its greatest men. The problems before him were appalling. He said later, "The Eastern Church has fallen away from the Faith and is now assailed on every side by infidels. Wherever I turn my eyes—to the west, to the north, to the south—I find everywhere bishops who have obtained their offices in an irregular way, whose lives and conversations are strangely at variance with their sacred calling; who go through their duties not for the love of Christ but from motives of worldly gain. There are no longer princes who set

Gregory VII was the first churchman who had the courage to anathematize an emperor, and—as a man of extreme courage—went beyond this purely ecclesiastical penalty to pronounce—with complete success—the deposition of Henry IV from the throne.

God's honor before their selfish ends, or who allow justice to stand in the way of their ambition." His enemies were formidable. Philip I, king of France, has been called "the most discreditable [ruler] the annals of France have known"; Henry IV of Germany was a greedy young tyrant, and the best was the cruel and ruthless William the Conqueror, king of England. Gregory could not trust his bishops to carry out his plans for reform, since many of them were appointed by the princes and their vassals, and he received help from few people; the men on whom he relied were nearly all monks. William accepted some of Gregory's decrees, and the French cooperated grudgingly, many of the bishops being deposed during a long struggle. But it was Henry IV, half of Gregory's age, who became his fiercest enemy, in a great contest of wills in which the course of the battle fell first to one man and then the other.

Henry was completely opposed to the Gregorian reforms. He aroused the clergy of Germany and northern Italy and the anti-papal Roman nobles. At midnight Mass at Christmas Gregory was kidnapped and held for a few hours until the people of Rome effected his release. A synod of German bishops denounced him, some of the northern Italian bishops refused him obedience, and Henry announced that Gregory was an usurper whom he was going to replace. The next day, with special solemnity, Gregory excommunicated the emperor, releasing his subjects from their allegiance to him.

The result shattered Germany: though the bishops and clergy sided with Henry, the nobles, who wished to get rid of Henry, met in October, 1076, and agreed that he should forfeit his crown unless he received absolution from Gregory within a year. Henry finally surrendered to expediency. With his wife and child and a single servant, he crossed the Alps in the dead of a severe winter, to come up with the pope at the castle of Canossa, in northern Italy. What happened next is one of the most famous incidents in history. Henry, dressed as a

Henry IV, who inherited the empire when he was six, came into his majority at fifteen, the customary age in Frankish law. When a boy, he had been married to Bertha of Savoy but now tried to repudiate her; his marriage was saved by St. Peter Damian, the papal legate sent to enforce the new reforms. Bertha became a deeply religious wife; she accompanied her husband when he made his humiliating submission to Gregory at Canossa.

REX ROGAT ABBATEM. MATHILDIM SUPPLICAT ATQ:

Henry, after agonizing debate with himself,
kneels in St. Nicholas Chapel at
Canossa to beg Hugh, abbot of Cluny, and the Countess
Matilda to intercede for him with Gregory.

penitent in a rough shirt, stood barefoot in the snow and ice for three days outside the castle gates, begging admission. Inside, Gregory, apparently, was debating with himself as to Henry's sincerity, but finally, without actual proof of any bad faith on Henry's part, was forced to receive him and give him absolution.

Events proved that Henry was hardly serious about his submission. Facing a battle with his nobles, who had elected Rudolph of Swabia as anti-king, Germany was plunged into civil war; the anti-king was reluctantly supported by Gregory, but Rudolph was killed in battle and then Henry, having made his own pope, Clement III, marched on Rome. A deadly siege ensued, but the papal forces held out for two years before Henry was able to break his way into the city. Gregory took refuge in the Castle Sant'Angelo from which he was rescued by a group of Norman adventurers. The Normans, among whom was the famous Godfrey de Bouillon, soon to be one of the leaders of the First Crusade, sacked the city. Humiliated by his allies and bearing the wrath of the Romans, Gregory retired to Monte Cassino, and then went to his birthplace, Salerno. Worn by his labors and having no friends but the Normans, he died on May 25, 1085, expressing forgiveness to all his enemies and raising all the excommunications except that of Henry and the anti-pope. "I have loved righteousness and hated iniquity," said Gregory in his last moments, "and that is why I die in exile."

Norman adventurers, ambitious and cruel, pushed themselves into the complex struggles that were taking place in Italy. Invited in 1016 to serve as mercenaries in Apulia and Salerno, they soon seized all of Southern Italy and Sicily, establishing kingdoms by murder and pillage, taking on Byzantine, Moslem, Holy Roman and papal armies. Originally merciless and godless brigands who feared no one, they eventually accepted a modicum of Christianity from the lands of their invasion. The great Roger II of Sicily, seen in a mosaic from a church in Palermo (above), crowned by the hand of Christ, kept a harem, used Moslem mercenaries in his army and defied both Eastern and Western emperors and the pope as well.

While Henry IV and his anti-pope, Clement III, occupy the Lateran Palace, a soldier drives Gregory, the true pope, into the street. Henry avoided battle with the Normans who came to help Gregory; in three days of uncontrolled pillaging the Pope's allies brought final devastation to much of the marble Rome of antiquity. The Normans took Gregory with them when they retreated. His feast was proclaimed in 1728.

105

The new king, Henry V, was a cunning and heartless man, but he had the ambition of maintaining the empire. At the head of a powerful army, before which all opposition dispersed, Henry V approached Rome in February, 1112, and arrested Pope Paschal II and the cardinals. To obtain his release, Paschal offered an idealistic compromise: he would anoint Henry emperor and give up the fiefs and secular jurisdictions of the papacy if Henry would in turn renounce lay investiture. Henry agreed. The announcement of the proposal led to riots in Rome. Churchmen saw their wealth suddenly written away, and noblemen saw their rights of investiture dismissed. The usual civil wars, arrests, election of anti-popes, excommunications ensued, and empire and papacy were both in chaos. What happened a few years later was a sudden conclusion to the terrible struggles of the previous decades. In 1119 Henry and Pope Calixtus II entered into negotiations, finally agreeing, in 1122, to a compromise solution to end the investiture controversy: the emperors were to renounce the right to invest bishops or abbots, but they retained the right to prevent the election of any not to their liking. Neither side granted much, but at last the lines of authority were more clearly defined. From then on, in theory at least, the nobles were the collaborators and not the ruling powers of the Church in her mission to the world.

The quarrel is settled

Gregory's death left Henry, the prime enemy of papal reform, the seeming victor. Yet the mastery of the papacy over the Church was being vindicated and the reform movement steadily gained ground. The program of the reformers—clerical celibacy and the prohibition of simony—was being accepted as law, and the distinction between separation of the clergy and the laity was being sharpened.

On the temporal scene, Henry appeared to hold control. His anti-pope was in the Lateran palace. The new orthodox pope was Victor II, the abbot of Monte Cassino, who died shortly after his election, to be succeeded by Urban II, former abbot of Cluny.

Clement may have held physical possession of the papal lands, but Rome was wherever the true pope might be. During Urban's years of exile the papacy was never more powerful, due to the enthusiastic veneration and the devotion of the faithful, capturing a love that the emperor never held. Wandering about Europe, Urban, in 1095, called forth the tremendous response of a crusade to save the sacred places of the Holy Land. Henry fell into the background, troubled by treason and rebellion, while the other princes of Europe, for the first time united by a common cause, set forth to liberate Jerusalem. The vicissitudes of fortune soon engaged Henry in civil wars with his sons Conrad and then Henry V, during which he died in exile at Liege in 1106.

Pope Calixtus II, holding the Concordat of Worms with Henry V, walks over anti-pope Mauritius Burdinus.

Murder in the cathedral

In England a struggle between Church and state culminated in the famous murder of Thomas à Becket, archbishop of Canterbury. In his early years Thomas was an archdeacon; he lived pompously and was an intimate friend of the English king, Henry II. The excesses of his living and actions—though a cleric he even engaged in war—caused much criticism. When Henry pressed for his friend's appointment as archbishop of Canterbury, the leading see of England, Thomas at first demurred, but was finally persuaded to accept; he was ordained a priest and anointed bishop. A radical change took place in his life. He abandoned his profligate ways, wore a hair shirt, fasted and prayed. He also found himself in a conflict with Henry over certain privileges the king demanded of the Church. Henry's demands increased; when Thomas stiffened his resistance, the king called a council of barons and bishops to depose him. Thomas fled to France, and even there was pursued by the king's wrath. But seven years later, in 1170, a reconciliation was affected and Thomas returned to his homeland. The conflict suddenly came to a head again. Thomas refused to absolve certain disobedient bishops, tools of the king, unless they renewed their obedience to the pope. Henry, in a high rage at hearing this, made some remarks which were interpreted by four of his knights as a rebuke for allowing Thomas to live any longer. The knights set off for Canterbury, arriving as Thomas was about to celebrate Vespers. There was a violent argument, at the end of which the four attacked the archbishop, beating him to his knees with blows from their swords. "For the name of Jesus and in defence of the Church I am willing to die," murmured Thomas and fell forward on his face. The murderers struck again, spilling the archbishop's brains on the pavement, then fled. The body lay for a long time in the transept before anyone dared touch it.

Universal anger was aroused by the crime, and the news spread throughout Europe. Henry did penance for his part, at first shutting himself up for forty days of lamentation and fasting. Thomas was almost immediately canonized, his story becoming one of the best known of all saints' and his name being venerated as far away as Armenia.

Henry's knights strike down Thomas at Canterbury. Only the archbishop's friend, the English monk Edward Grim, remained with him; the other clerics fled at the approach of the assassins.

ιοαμεροσ. καὶ ὁ μαρκελλαει

ππο δρομίασα γομένησ· Αρλαμίδοασ· καὶ τᾶσ ὑπασ
τοῦ φαρουαρίουμηνὸσ τῆσ ϛα ἰνζ ΚΑ ΠΕ ΛΥΕ τὴν θεσ
ναῖ τοῦ θρόνου. επι χαλλὸ κηρουλαριοσ· κατὰ τὴν ἡμεα
φαμοτρό φοσαῦτὸμ α ἀτα νε ε πι μου νὴν Ββ ύε ιοσ·

ἐξορία μ κηρουλ πα
φανοτρό φ

πη νθσαυρίομένου, ἐμ τῇ τοῦ ἀλ θ ίου μεω ῇ· καὶ πέμ ψασ
μεμον ἐι κοσ καὶ πὲν τε · μαὶ οὐ δὲ δ λ γ δβ α τ αντ ἰνζ· ἐκ
ἐν ὡ χαρίσ ω πὲμ μαρν κατου· ἐω ομένησ φαντ νῆ τιὸ
ιπὸ ω χεῖν κρα τῶν λόγοσ τὸ δαὶ τοῦ τούτου· ἐ κο τὸ νῆ
τοῦ αῖ τοῦ μ λύ νησ α τοσ α πὸ λυ νόκε ι·

The tragic year of 1054

In 1054—after Michael Cerularius, patriarch of Constantinople, had denounced the pope, made an attack on Latin-rite customs, closed Latin churches in the city, and refused to meet with the pope's legates to mediate the quarrel, these legates—two cardinals and an archbishop—solemnly marched through the crowds assembled for the Divine Liturgy in Hagia Sophia, and walked into the sanctuary to place a papal bull of excommunication upon the high altar. Only Cerularius and his two aids were excommunicated; the ban was never extended to the peoples of the Eastern churches who remain, in theory, under the protection of the See of Peter. But the move, which some historians believe ill-considered, resulted in the hardening of schismatic tendencies and the eventual loss of practically the entire East.

The background of the schism was complicated, and many of the causes have now been buried in history. But Constantinople, which had given many saints to the Church, and had been the seat of four ecumenical councils and many lesser councils, had as well been the breeding ground for wild and extravagant ideas about the nature of Our Lord (nineteen patriarchs had been open heretics), and in fact had been out of communion with Rome for over 250 years since the death of Constantine in 337. Despite this, the main cause of the break was the ambition and ill will of Cerularius, who had been forced into the priesthood in order to avert his political machinations; the

suicide of his brother brought about his real conversion to the priesthood, but the religious life did not stifle his ambitions, and when his best friend Monachamus, with whom he had once plotted the overthrow of the emperor, ascended to the throne of Constantinople through a fortuitous marriage, Cerularius saw his future secured. Monachamus was installed as Constantine IX, and a short while later—in 1034—was able to make Cerularius the Patriarch of Constantinople.

The new patriarch of the second most important church in Christendom belonged to the extreme wing of the anti-papal party; from later events it was apparent that his intentions were to break with the pope upon the proper excuse. In 1053, in a letter from one of his metropolitans to a bishop in Apulia but meant for "all the bishops of the Franks and for the most venerable pope," he denounced three customs of the Latin Church—celibacy of the clergy, fasting on Saturdays and the use of azyme (unleavened) bread. His next move was to close, without provocation, all the Latin churches in Constantinople, including that of the papal legate.

Leo tried to pacify Cerularius, pointing out that Rome was not trying to impose Latin customs on the East, and emphasizing that he never tried to change the customs of Byzantine monasteries and churches in the West. At the same time he wrote a friendly letter to the emperor, who in turn accepted the pope's delegates with understanding

Michael Cerularius, the quarrelsome
patriarch of Constantinople, is
arrested in his palace, the
Phanar, and goes into exile.

109

and a great display of good will towards the West.

The papal legates spent several weeks in discussion with the emperor and various high clergy. There was a great amount of sympathy for the Roman side, and possibly the situation would have been resolved satisfactorily but for Cerularius. He refused to meet the papal legates, accused them of being "insolent, boastful, rash, arrogant and stupid," and then struck the pope's name from the diptychs of Hagia Sophia, thus declaring an open schism. This led to the drawing up of the bull of excommunication by the papal legates. Despite the ban against Cerularius, the legates bore with them the good will of the emperor when they left on the Tuesday following the fateful day. On Friday Cerularius excommunicated the pope and the whole of the Latin Church. John of Antioch gently reproached him for his conduct.

But the harm was done, and Cerularius gained the support of the common people. He became the most powerful man in Constantinople, terrorized Constantine, and when the emperor died, locked up his successor in a monastery, and installed a puppet emperor, Isaac I. Despite his priestly office, Cerularius ran the state like a dictator. "Losing all shame," said Psellus, Constantine's secretary of state, "he joined royalty and priesthood in himself; in his hand he held the cross while imperial laws came from his mouth."

Isaac however revolted when Cerularius tried to have himself crowned emperor. Psellus turned against the patriarch, and denounced him in a trial. Cerularius was accused of treason, paganism and magic; he was called "impious, tyrannical, murderous, sacrilegious, unworthy." The sentence was banishment to an island on the Hellespont, but on the way, Cerularius was shipwrecked, and he died as the result of injuries and overexposure. As soon as Cerularius was dead, Isaac reversed his position. He had the body brought back to Constantinople, and Psellus preached a panegyric describing the patriarch as "the best, the wisest and the most misunderstood of men." The date was 1058, four years after the break with Rome. But in those four years Cerularius had been able to destroy a century and a half of peaceable relations and good will between the East and the West, to divide Christendom, to bring out of communion with Christ's vicar many millions of people of Byzantium who had shared a common faith, common doctrine, common beliefs, and to plant the seeds of mutual distrust and suspicion, which, despite the efforts of popes and patriarchs, of men of good will on both sides, have, except for the return to Rome of less than ten million souls, lasted to this day.

Though separated from the See of Peter because it followed the patriarch of Byzantium rather than the pope, the Russian Orthodox Church showed great vitality. St. Sergius of Radonezh, venerated by both Catholics and Orthodox, was one of the holiest men to spring from the deep roots of Eastern spirituality. Sergius dressed in rags and shared his food with wild animals; nevertheless his reputation for wisdom and sanctity led him to be consulted by the leaders of Church and state; it was primarily at his suggestion that Prince Dimitri of Moscow revolted against the Tartars and broke their power in Russia. Here we see Sergius directing the construction of his monastery; from it grew numerous foundations, all dedicated to the Most Holy Trinity.

Without its ties to the West, the Orthodox Church continued at a slower, more sedate pace with little development in either theology or organization. Nevertheless, its monasteries have been centers of great piety and devotion and both clergy and laity have shown a profound mysticism and a deep love of Our Lord and the saints, and particularly of the Blessed Virgin. These are fourteenth century nuns in a convent at Constantinople the life of the religious has hardly changed since that time

A new kind of saint

Boris and Gleb were two of the fourteen sons of the grand duke St. Vladimir. One hot July day in 1015, shortly after Vladimir's death, Boris, leading his troops home from a fruitless campaign against the Pechnegs, a savage nomadic tribe, was approached by a messenger who warned him that his eldest brother Svyatapulk was determined to have him killed on his return to Kiev. Boris's men immediately drew up in battle formation, but the prince dissuaded them from the idea of armed resistance against Svyatapulk and ordered his troops to proceed home peacefully. "It is not right for me," he said, "to raise my hand against an elder brother who now stands in the place of my father." He would prefer, in imitation of Christ, to be an innocent victim of man than to shed the blood of his brothers in flesh and in God. "It is better for me to die," he said, "than to be the occasion of death to many."

After his men had left, Boris pitched his tent upon the banks of the river Al'ta; only a servant remained with him. Wrapping himself up in animal skins, he lay down to sleep. But, turning his mind to the holy men of the past who had been killed by their relatives, he rose to his knees to pass the night in prayer. Meditating upon the emptiness of all earthly things, except "good deeds and true love and right religion," he was sad to realize that he would soon leave "the marvellous light" of day and his "good and beautiful body," and that his beautiful young wife would presently be a widow. He then chanted the psalms of matins and when finished, gazed upon an ikon of Christ, praying, "Help me now to endure my passion. For I accept it not from those who were my enemies, but from the hand of my brother. Hold it not against him as a sin, O Lord!"

Toward dawn of July 24th the assassins sent by Svyatapulk entered Boris's tent and fell upon him with the ferocity of wild animals. The faithful servant attempted to protect his master, but was killed; the murderers then beheaded him to remove his golden collar. After the first blows of the assassins' spears Boris begged for a few moments of life in order to pray; then, as meekly as a lamb, he offered himself as a victim, saying, "Hurry, brother, do the job and may peace be with you."

With Boris dead, Svyatapulk now turned his attention to Gleb. Near Smolensk, the duke's men found Gleb travelling down the Dnieper; they boarded the boat and threatened his cook, persuading him that he must kill his master. As the assassins approached, Gleb was terrified and threw himself down upon his knees, promising to be their slave if only they would spare him. As a proven warrior he might have resisted, but he would not, and when he realized that his pleas were useless, he resigned himself to death. "I am in your hands and the hands of my brother, your prince," he said to the assassins. "I am being slain; I know not what for; but thou, Lord, knowest. And I know, O my Lord, that thou didst say to thine apostles that for thy name's sake hands would be laid on them and they would be betrayed by kinsmen and friends, and that brother would bring death to brother." While Gleb was praying, the cook crept up behind him and slit his throat.

Five years later another brother, known as Yaroslav the Wise, was able to place the incorrupt bodies of the murdered princes in the church of St. Basil at Novgorod. The tomb immediately became a shrine for pilgrims, and the same year, because of the popular devotion to the brothers, they were canonized by the Church. But the family feud did not stop there. Yaroslav now led an armed rebellion against the duke; in two fearful battles he defeated Svyatapulk.

Here a question must be asked: the two young princes had led good lives and died heroically, and yet, why were they canonized? The metropolitan of Kiev, a Greek missionary bishop, at first resisted the popular demand for canonization; the brothers were not ascetics nor teachers nor even martyrs in the traditional sense, but were the victims of an all-too-common dynastic feud; they could not be placed among any of the categories of saints. Their canonization, the first of the young church in Russia, posed a real problem but it signified the recognition of another form of sanctity. The Russians call Boris and Gleb *strastoterptsy*, that is, "men having undergone a passion"—innocent men unwilling to die but who had yet repudiated violence and quietly accepted suffering and death in the unresisting spirit of Christ. Though the brothers had offered a passive resistance by tears and supplication in order to remain alive in the pleasurable world, they were content at the end to accept death as a gift sent from God. Their last thoughts, according to their biographers, were that every disciple of Christ is to suffer in this world and that all suffering, voluntary or not, is endured in the name of Christ. Such a spirit triumphed over the brothers' natural human weaknesses by a humble and gentle vision of Christ offering Himself for the salvation of man as an innocent victim: a characteristically Christian concept and one that deeply informed the Russian soul in the centuries to come.

Knights Templars leave their fortress to fight the Moslems. This fresco in a Templars' chapel in France was painted in honor of a crusader's victory over the enemy in Syria in 1163. The Templars wear a burnous under their helmets and the Cross

the CRUSADES

The great wave of Christian fervor that swept across Europe in the eleventh century not only resulted in a revival of learning, the building of the cathedrals and the freeing of the Church from control by the nobles, but in the crusades as well. Urban II, the vigorous, shrewd, French-born pope who so forcefully opposed Henry IV, the violent ruler of the Holy Roman Empire, was also the pope who initiated a crusade to free the sacred places of the Holy Land from Moslem control.

Though a pope without a see—Rome was occupied by an antipope supported by Henry's soldiers—Urban was one of the most popular of medieval pontiffs (practically all of the bishops and Henry's second wife and son supported Urban) and even when wandering about Europe he gave the papacy a new prestige. His influence quickly overshadowed that of the emperor. In 1095 at

...on their tunics. The Knights Templars played a great role in the defense of the Latin States, but their rivalry with the other military orders and worldly interests contrary to the Statutes written down by St. Bernard, led unfairly to their suppression.

Clermont, in his native France, Urban called a council of bishops and nobles to discuss the conflict with the emperor. It was at the height of the lay investiture quarrel. For nine days, bishops, abbots and the pope talked about church reform and the troublesome Henry. On the tenth, Urban arose and broached a new and apparently unrelated subject: the Holy Sepulchre of Jerusalem. The most sacred of all places of the world, it was held by Moslems; Christian pilgrims visited it at the risk of their lives. Was Jerusalem to remain in the hands of the infidel, Urban asked. The reply was not an answer but a command: "Men of God, men chosen and blessed among all, combine your forces! Take the road to the Holy Sepulchre assured of the imperishable glory that awaits you in God's kingdom. Let each one deny himself and take the Cross!" The crusades had begun.

The crusades begin

Urban's plan for a crusade was one that had been discussed for years, but no one had given it shape. His proposal was motivated by several considerations. One was a series of unrelated military offensives by the poorer states of Europe against the exposed Islamic outposts of Spain and Sicily. More important were the increasing reports of atrocities against Christian pilgrims to the Holy Land. In the past, after the initial attack against the West, the Moslems had been extremely tolerant of the pilgrims, but now a new force had appeared in the Middle East—the Seljuk Turks, a dynamic young people who swept up Armenia and Asia Minor, lopped off sections of the Byzantine empire, and scorned the other Islamic nations for their friendly relations with the Christians. The Turkish threat had particularly worried Alexius Comnenus, basileus of Byzantium, who was having increasing difficulty holding even his sea coasts against the enemy. Though the churches of Byzantium had been out of communion with the Holy See since 1054, Alexius had no choice but to ask help of the Pope himself. In 1094 a delegation from Alexius approached Urban suggesting a holy war against Islam, and hinting at re-union of the churches.

The nobles at Clermont enthusiastically took up Urban's call with the slogan: "God wills it so!" The cross, painted on the right shoulder of the knight's tunic, was immediately adopted as the symbol of the coming campaign. By evening there was no more red paint nor red cloth available: men had the cross tattooed on their right shoulders; some were even branded with a hot iron. The movement spread across Europe, fanned by monastic preachers. To all those who took the cross, the Church granted a special blessing, as well as plenary indulgences, suspension and even cancellation of debts and protection of family and property during the knight's absence.

Of all the crusades that occupied Europe for the next two centuries, this was the greatest and perhaps the best justified. It was essentially one great feudal war, in which the Western nobility acted as a body under the inspiration of the pope—the emperor, Henry IV, was ignored, as were the kings. Its warriors came largely from France, England, the low lands and Norman Italy—the countries in which the feudal system was most advanced. It was an expedition of knights, not of the masses; its fighting forces numbered some tens of thousands.

Pope Urban calls for a crusade. The crowd at Clermont has been estimated at 100,000 clergy and lay people.

The First Crusade

In 1095, in four armies, taking four different routes, the crusaders set out to meet at Constantinople, the rallying point. But while the knights were making their careful preparations, a people's crusade had impetuously set off the attack on the Saracens, fanned into action by a hairy prophet named Peter the Hermit. Thousands of lay folk, with wives and children, on foot or in carts pulled by their oxen shod like horses, set out across Europe in four divisions; one was commanded by Peter; another, consisting of just eight impoverished knights, by an adventurer named Walter the Penniless; a third division came from Italy, while a fourth, which began by massacring the Jews of the Rhineland and Bohemia, was annihilated in Hungary. Of each town, the People's Crusade asked: "Is that Jerusalem?" and most of them were pillaged to provide food for the crusaders. Belgrade was sacked and the People's Crusade arrived in Constantinople. The Greeks ferried them across to Asia Minor, where the peasants fell upon the Turks, who ferociously massacred them, almost to the last man.

As professional soldiers, the knights made careful preparations. Four columns set out, each following a different route, with Constantinople as their goal. The most famous of the crusaders was Godfrey de Bouillon, a man of spotless character and splendid physique, who had made the unfortunate mistake of once siding with Henry IV and of participating in the sack of Rome in 1084. As the crusaders arrived in Byzantium the Greeks put spies out to watch them and checked their foraging expeditions with light cavalry. "Persons of intelligence could feel they were witnessing a strange occurrence," wrote Anna Comnena, the daughter of the basileus. "Each army was proceeded by an unspeakable number of locusts, and all who saw them realized them as forerunners of the frankish armies." The four divisions joined forces in August, 1097, outside the walls of Constantinople, an event which now made Alexis realize what a power he had invited into his weak kingdom. It took until the following spring before he could ferry them across to Asia Minor, where the crusaders, in a bold assault, fell upon Nicea and freed it from the Turks, only to find that this ancient Christian citadel was almost bare of booty. Disappointed by their meager winnings, the crusaders made a forced march across the bare plains of Anatolia (now today's Turkey) towards the Holy Land. Enervated by heavy iron armor, marching in unbelievable heat, and weakened from lack of provisions, they almost were wiped out by a surprise attack by the Turks. But the battle turned in the favor of the Franks, and they massacred the enemy, capturing an enormous quantity of booty. This event foreshadowed the crusaders' military superiority over the Turks for the next century, but ahead lay the frightful obstacles of the desert north of the Holy Land, studded with saltpans and marshes. The leaders argued among each other, and some left the main body of the army to look for booty. Ahead lay a wearying eight-month siege of Antioch, in which the crusaders were sickened by plague and malnutrition. The campaign dragged out: the crusaders fought among each other; the Byzantines, frightened by the power of the Franks, made a secret pact with the Egyptians; the Franks replaced the Greek bishops with Latin-rite clergy. At last June 15, 1099, after a five-week siege, the crusaders prepared to hurl themselves upon the walls of Jerusalem. The crusaders occupied the same positions as the Romans had under Titus in 70 A.D. Siege towers poured heavy stones into the city, which was defended by a Moslem force from Egypt. With Godfrey at their head, the crusaders, in imitation of Josuah's siege of Jericho, walked barefoot around the city. Then the attack began; bridges were thrown from the towers to the city walls and the crusaders dropped upon the Turks in a hideous slaughter of which the Franks were afterwards ashamed, butchering nearly all of the enemy. Even the Mosque of Omar, which was believed to stand upon the site of the altar of Solomon's temple, was covered with blood. The Jews were shut into the synagogue, which was set afire. At dusk the conquerors, barefooted and now washed of blood and calmed of their insane fury, climbed the Via Dolorosa, "sighing and weeping, through the Holy Place of the city where Jesus Christ the Savior of the world had trodden corporeally, then gently kissed the spots on which His feet had stood."

*The crusaders make the final
assault upon Jerusalem. They are
using a wheeled siege tower and a
catapult. During the siege they
occupied the same positions as the
Romans had in their attack
on the city in 70 A.D.*

The first Latin king of Jerusalem was Godfrey the Bouillon. Tall, big-chested and a model of Christian piety, he was a prototype of the legendary Christian knight. His famous strength is exemplified in the panel showing him decapitating an obstreperous camel with a single blow.

The Latin Kingdom

Pope Urban died before the taking of Jerusalem could be reported back to him. Godfrey de Bouillon was chosen head of the new Latin Kingdom of Jerusalem; he quickly annihilated a Moslem relief force sent up from Egypt. A year later Godfrey was dead, being succeeded by his brother Baldwin. A capable military leader, though a schemer and opportunist, Baldwin captured most of the coast. Other kingdoms and seigniories were founded, among them Edessa, Antioch, Tripoli, Galilee and Lesser Armenia, all established along feudal lines. Recruits from Europe arrived to bolster the new states, but operations were handicapped by lack of funds. The Franks controlled the sea, the coast and a few key cities, but their rule rarely extended very far inland: Asia Minor was still held by the Moslems, who constantly harassed them. Along with the Moslems the Franks had to face another enemy, their own selves: they soon went oriental; Godfrey lived like a monk, but Baldwin wore a golden bernous, sat cross-legged upon a carpet to receive his prostrated subjects. Oriental ideas of luxury and morality infected many of the crusaders, knights and clergy alike.

To help hold the East, a unique institution known as the Military Order was formed, the most famous units being the Hospitalars and the Templars. As knights bound by oaths of poverty, charity and obedience they were true monks, but as the orders became more powerful they fought with each other and defied their rulers. The Latin kingdom survived nearly two hundred years, initially strong, but soon tottering and ineffectual, always inadequately supplied, undermanned, constantly at war not only with the Moslems but even with the Byzantines and their own European allies.

The imposing Krak des Chevaliers, built in 1099,
is one of the many surviving crusaders' buildings in the
Holy Land. Though it possessed cisterns, mills and
armories and could support 2,000 men-at-arms, it fell
easily before a Moslem siege in 1271.

The Moslems defend Tyre against the Franks. The city was taken in 1124 by troops under Baldwin II, who extended Crusader rule of the Middle East to its farthest dimensions.

A Moslem counter-attack

At first the initiative in the Middle East lay with the crusaders. They had constant trouble with the Greeks (who resented the westerners' practice of replacing Byzantine clergy with Latins) and the Greeks were blamed for all that went wrong. Byzantium's policy was obviously to keep the Franks weak: she never took part in any crusade, never supported the Franks, failed to put full weight against the Turks even when the opportunity arose; what was worse she often negotiated with the enemy for her own purposes. A Latin chronicler, Odo of Deuil, found that the Greeks were "despicable, arrogant and violent," and said they had "degenerated entirely into women, putting aside all manly vigor, both of words and of spirit. They believe that anything done for the holy [Byzantine] empire cannot be considered perjury." But with the Moslems the situation was different; when not actively engaged against them the crusaders grew to admire their enemy, respecting their courage and chivalry. The Moslems, for their part, had little respect for the Franks. An Arab named Usāmah wrote of the crusaders: "Mysterious are the works of the Creator, the author of all things! When one comes to recount cases regarding the Franks, he cannot but glorify Allah (exalted is he!) and sanctify him, for he sees them as animals possessing the virtues of courage and fighting, but nothing else; just as animals have only the virtues of strength and carrying loads."

Soon the Latin states found themselves involved in a major war. In 1143 the enemy regained the entire Christian territory north of the Kingdom of Jerusalem, including Edessa, then an important city beyond the Euphrates River. The Holy Land was in danger. Pope Eugenius III made a special appeal but could arouse no other recruits than King Louis VII of France and Conrad II of Germany. Then St. Bernard spoke up to challenge the Christian world: "Do not betray your king! What do I say? Do not betray the King of Heaven for whose sake your own sovereign embarks upon so arduous a journey!" Unlike the first crusade, which was strongly organized under a united leadership, the second was inadequately prepared. The two kings took separate routes instead of pooling their resources: from the start the expedition was doomed. The Greeks were unusually troublesome and were suspected (justly) of dealing with the enemy; despite a few early victories the entire campaign developed into a progression of defeats. Bad luck and irremediable errors were partly responsible. An unbelievably stupid decision was made not to attack the real enemy at Aleppo and Damascus but to turn the campaign against the emir of Damascus, the one Moslem who had steadily collaborated with the Franks. The complexities of Near Eastern politics were too much for the two rival kings, who, after taking Damascus, gave up the campaign and embarked for home, blaming everyone from the Greeks to St. Bernard for their failure. The Moslems, plagued like the Latin states by the quarrels of rival leaders, were suddenly pulled together by the arrival of a brilliant statesman and military leader named Saladin, an empire builder of the stature of Alexander the Great, Caesar and Charlemagne. A man of outstanding integrity, so remarkable a leader was Saladin that he became the personal friend of Richard the Lion-Hearted and his character was so esteemed in the Middle Ages that Dante puts him in that special part of Hell—the circle of the Righteous Pagans—where the souls are gathered whose single sorrow it is not to have known Jesus. Saladin united discordant Moslem states into one and turned his attention to freeing the Middle East of the Franks. Before long he had recaptured Jerusalem from the Latins: the Holy City was again a Moslem citadel.

THE FLOWERING OF THE MIDDLE AGES

Of all the memorable phenomena of life in the Middle Ages, no two stand out more strongly than the Gothic cathedral and the crusades—the one the symbol of a creative, intelligent and highly imaginative drive towards the supernatural, the other its active form, the self-sacrificing desire to gain a touch of sanctity by rescuing the sacred places of the Holy Land from the infidels (not without a bit of booty along the way). By the twelfth century, barbarism had disappeared and the Europe of the new age was in a golden flowering never before experienced. It was an amazing period in the history of mankind: though man's physical condition was hardly better than before—primitive housing conditions, dirt, superstition and ignorance left man prey to plague, famine, witchcraft and exploitation by rapacious warlords—a corner of the world containing a mere 30,000,000 Christians produced a civilization whose art, literature, architecture, mystical and theological speculation have never been surpassed. Along with its intellectual and spiritual developments, the twelfth century gave birth to great practical innovations: the growth of new cities, the beginnings of modern agriculture and commerce and the revival of the monasteries.

Symbolic of the flowering of medieval life in the twelfth century is Chartres cathedral. This is the central bay of the north or royal portal. Dominating the composition is Christ enthroned, judging mankind. Around Him are symbols of the four evangelists. In the archings appear the elders of the Apocalypse, and below, the twelve apostles, grouped three by three. This portal was executed between 1140 and 1160 and is probably the greatest remaining example of Gothic sculpture.

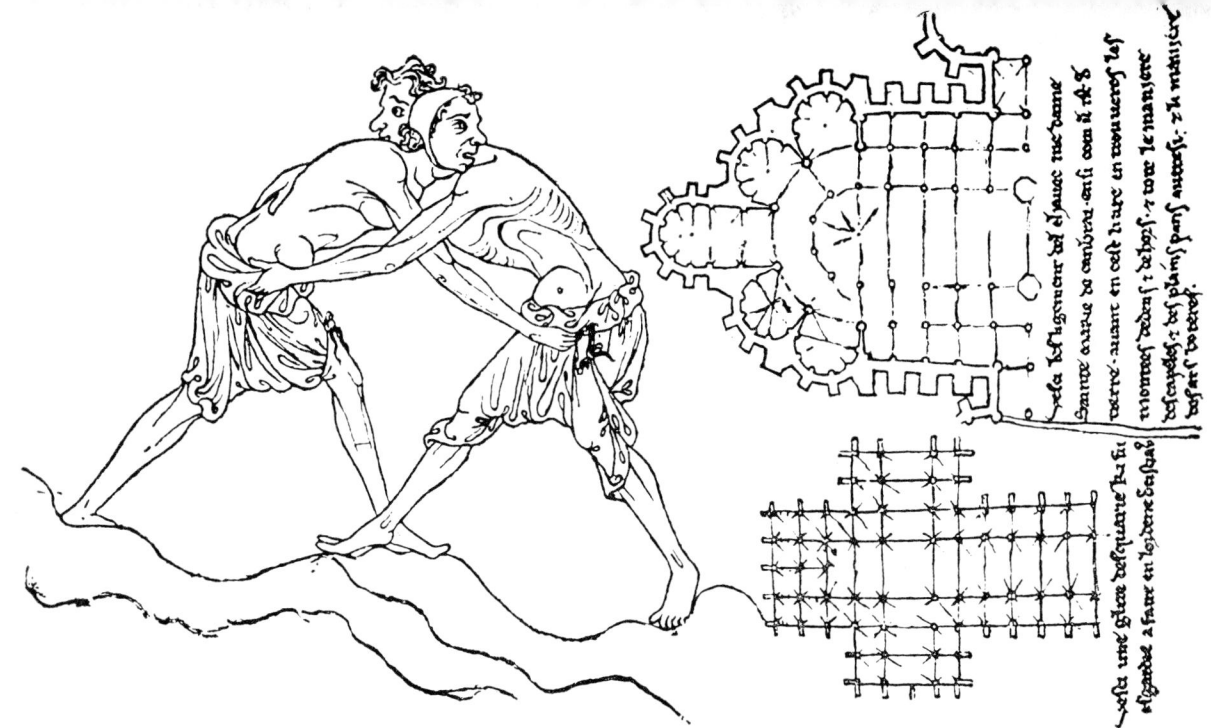

ptud est presbiteriam beate marie uacelleusis
ecclie ordinis cistercii

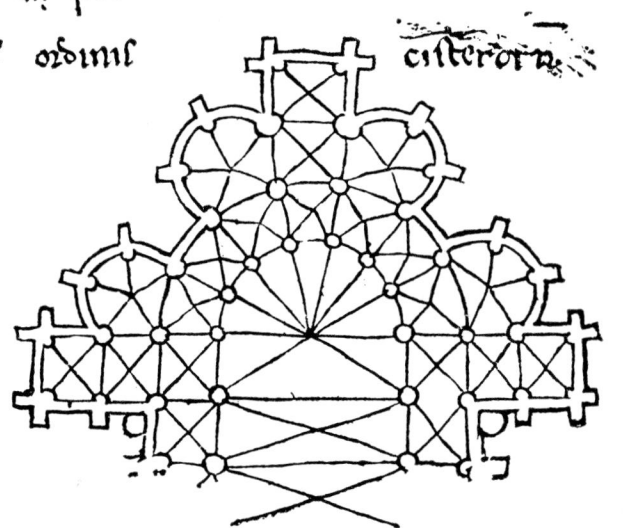

Ce est un image deu si cum il est cheus.

A twelfth-century manuscript illumination (from the Guthlac roll) depicts monks building an English church.

The gothic cathedral

The "gothic" cathedrals which arose in the twelfth century in France represent an entirely new approach to building: in the past the building was a massive walled enclosure: the aim of the gothic builder was an open skeleton of stone, supporting stone vaulting; each member of the building fulfilled a calculated and indispensable function, both structurally and artistically. The builders discovered principles of elasticity and equilibrium, thrust and counterthrust, which enabled them to achieve greater height and lightness. The pointed arch helped decrease the lateral pressure caused by the immense weight of wall and roof and gave even more flexibility in building. Extraordinary lightness of appearance was the result and the builders composed effects steadily increasing in audacity, though not without some failures—in 1284 part of the cathedral at Amiens collapsed because the vaulting was so delicate, and the piers had to be doubled. English builders were equally enterprising and other countries, mainly Germany, Spain and Italy, drew upon France's inspired achievements.

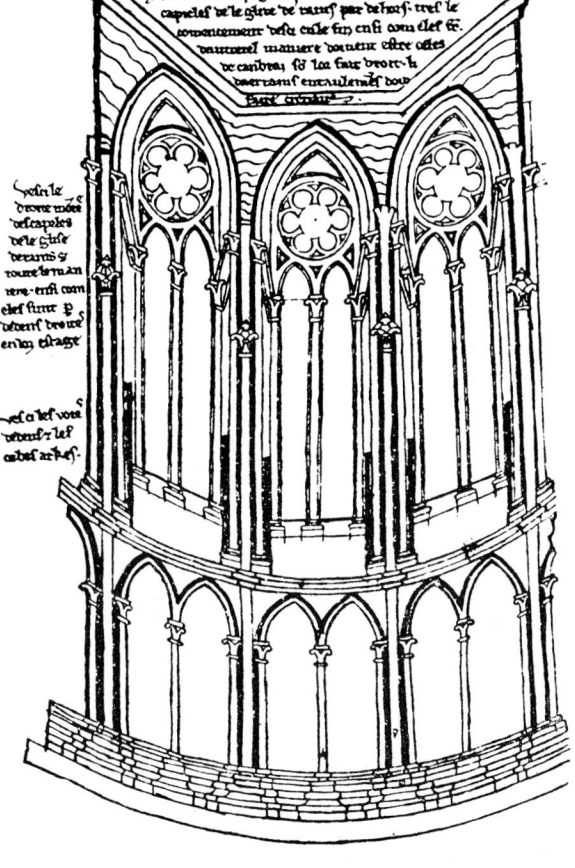

Sketches from the notebook of Villard de Honnecourt, prepared about 1235, describe in detail the construction of cathedrals. An architect, Villard was also skilled in geometry, masonry, carpentry and drawing. His notebook includes a disciple and a late Cistercian floor plan.

127

Perhaps more than any other French cathedral, that of Chartres approaches perfection. The upward sweep of her towers, her fine proportions, the magnificence of her decorations (right), evoke a spirit of Christian joy. The term "gothic" was applied during the Renaissance to such architecture as a symbol of barbarism.

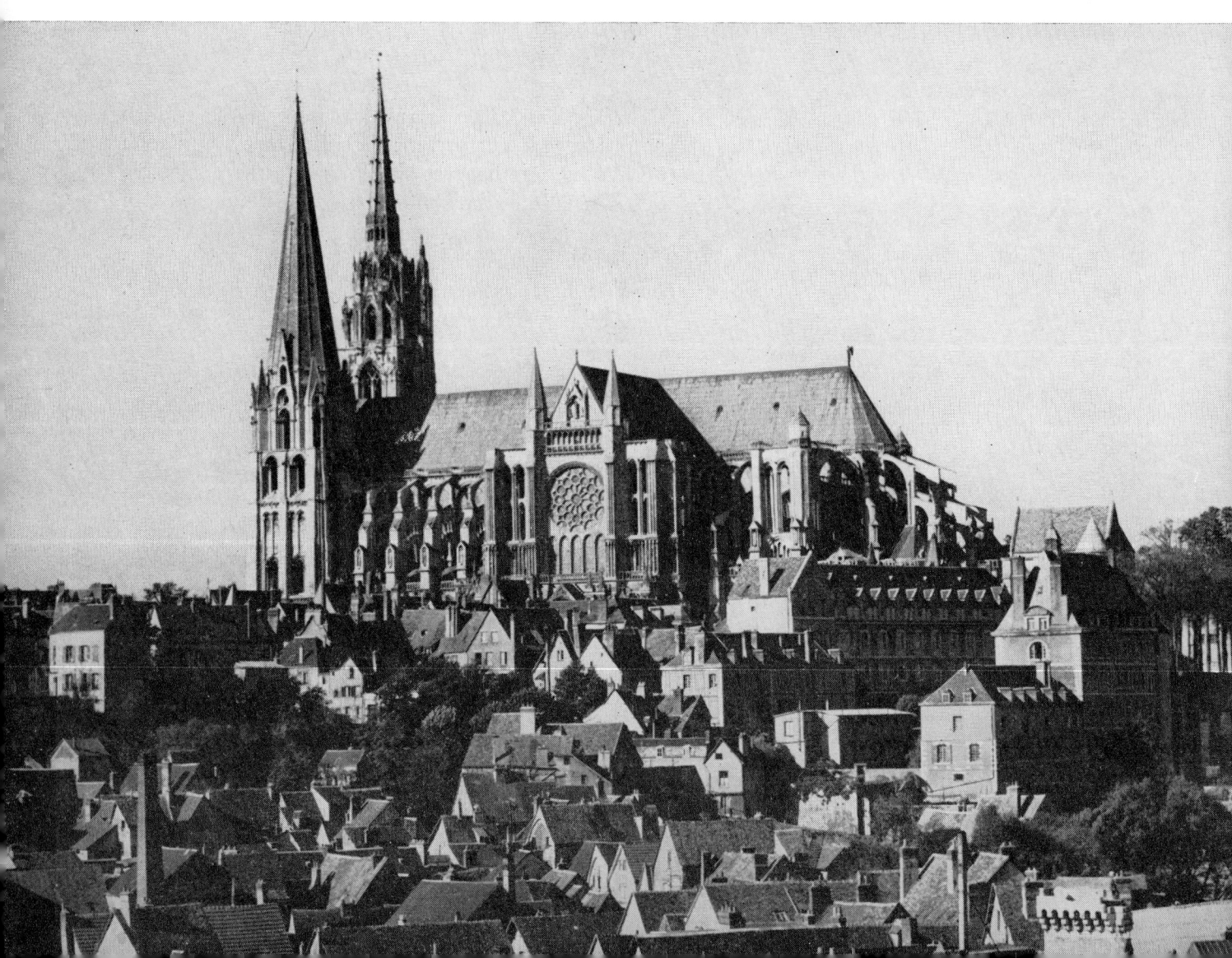

The building of Chartres

One of the most famous of all cathedrals is Chartres. Since the fourth century the town was an episcopal see and parts of the original church building are still to be seen within the present cathedral. The church was several times rebuilt because of fires, but a final one on Friday, June 10, 1194, left it a crumbling mass of stones. Dedication to the Blessed Virgin was widespread in France, and, as old chronicles have poetically told us, the people of France were determined to give her a place of refuge, therefore the cathedral must be rebuilt. As far away as Normandy people left their homes to come to Chartres.

The migration to Chartres was spontaneous and continuing. Roads were crowded with pilgrims, both men and women, dragging along huge tree trunks and great beams. Even cripples and the sick were brought along; their role was to pray while others worked.

A city of tents sprung up around Chartres; the huge crowds of men and women and children of all social conditions—knights, ladies, peasants, clerics, tradesmen—all submitted willingly to a self-imposed discipline, setting aside rank and calling.

The commune was self-organized. The workers elected their own leaders, who in turn were responsible to monk supervisors. Monastery cellarmen took charge of the commissaries and the supply of raw materials. All was under the direction of the now anonymous genius who designed the new cathedral and supervised its building. Throughout the entire project ran a spirit of sacrifice and penance, but perhaps the greatest motivation of all was the honor of working on the new cathedral. So sacred was the enterprise that no one dared touch materials thus dedicated to the Virgin unless he had first been shriven and had reconciled himself with his enemies. Impenitent workers were expelled from the community.

The work progressed rapidly and the cathedral, embodying the latest architectural and artistic concepts, was dedicated in 1260.

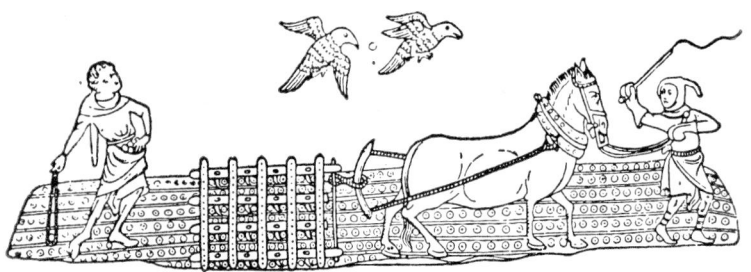

The horse collar, an important discovery, brought about a change in agriculture in the twelfth century; it enabled the horse to pull a bigger plow and also heavier wagons. Other innovations that aided economic progress were the rudder, developed in northern Europe, and from the East, the windmill, the paper-mill and the compass.

A typical small fortified city (with JONGLEURS leading a parade through its gate) is centered around its parish church. Outside the walls, merchants would set up stalls, which soon became permanent, and the old town would be swallowed by its FAUBOURGS. European commerce benefited from the "Truce of God," a few days in each week during which Christians were forbidden under pain of excommunication to fight each other; a sudden boom in population also stimulated commercial activity.

The city emerges

The West was basically an agricultural society when the Middle Ages began. Only in Asia Minor was there any significant commercial activity. From such great seaports as Constantinople textiles and foodstuffs were carried by Syrian ships into the West, to be sold by Levantine merchants. But until the tenth century, the European city, as a center of commercial activity, did not exist; the town was merely a fortified administrative stronghold; its key figure was usually the bishop whose person combined both spiritual and temporal rule. The episcopal city had little importance except as a center of ecclesiastical activity and was largely composed of those dependent on the Church for a livelihood—the clerics of the cathedral, monks, students, and the servants and artisans who were needed for the proper functioning of the religious institution. Peasants appeared in town only on market day. All this soon changed.

In the tenth century a revival of trade commenced. Merchants began setting up markets in the *forisburgus* (or *faubourg*)—the outer enclosure of a fortified place: a bridge-head, a point commanding a pass through a forest or between hills or the gate of a monastery or castle. Small shopkeepers, weavers and artisans in turn were attracted to the *forisburgus* and a middle class began to emerge. The city just grew, haphazardly and unplanned.

By the twelfth century, its development was in full swing, and great centers of commerce like Venice, Milan, Florence, Siena, Marseilles, Barcelona, Ghent, Bruges, Ypres and the Hanseatic towns of northern Germany became so important that they were able to establish themselves as separate states.

Serfdom was the lot of the common people of Europe. The serf was bound to work on land not his own—the manor—in a halfway state between freedom and slavery. Numerous customs and laws gave him a measure of protection, but his life was hard and short. The spread of a money economy broke down the manorial system and helped destroy serfdom.

The University of Paris was one of the outstanding schools of higher learning in the Middle Ages. A manuscript illumination shows a special meeting of the faculty. The standing men hold scepters containing relics. Instruction was oral: the master read from the text and made comments from glosses written on the margins of the books. The word UNIVERSITAS had nothing whatever to do with the supposed idea of universal knowledge. It was a common word in classical Latin for a guild or corporation; the University of Bologna, for example, was a guild of students; Paris, a guild of masters.

The first universities

The expansion of Europe's horizons gave twelfth century man both the incentive and the leisure time for study. Though learning, especially on the higher levels, was limited to a small percentage of the population, there were still thousands of poor young men who were ready to endure any hardship in order to acquire it. And education was hard—there were few texts; many students, too poor to buy paper on which to write notes, were forced to rely on memory; many schools and even universities lacked benches; the students either stood or squatted upon straw-covered floors. Schools arose everywhere, and at the Third Lateran Council (1179), the Church ruled that every cathedral church should support a master to instruct ecclesiastical students, giving his services without charge to indigent scholars. The medieval university established the custom of licensed masters, formal examinations and degrees.

St. Anselm, St. Bernard, Ivo of Chartres, Peter Lombard and St. Peter Damian are some of the noted scholars of the century, but the most famous and the most influential, aside from St. Bernard, was the brilliant, unfortunate Peter Abelard. In 1100, at the age of 21, he went to Paris to study at the school of Notre Dame. Abelard soon became Master but then, forced out in 1112, established his own school outside the walls of the city. His fame as a dialectician attracted great numbers of students, and he is usually regarded as the founder of the later University of Paris. This part of his career was cut short by his notorious affair with Heloïse, niece of Fulbert, canon of Notre Dame. St. Bernard complained of Abelard's rationalistic tendencies, and actively opposed his teachings; after his condemnation at the Council of Soissons in 1121, Abelard retired to Troyes where he built a hermitage. But so great was his fame and the respect that scholars still had for him that pupils hunted him out and, as he said in his *Historia Calamitatum*, "Instead of spacious houses, they built themselves little tents; in place of delicate food they ate only herbs and rough country bread; for beds they gathered straw and stubble. . . . As for myself, my scholars, of their own accord, provided me with all necessities, so that no household care might detract me from my studies." He died in 1142, the last of the men who were in effect self-contained universities.

The seal of St. Bernard

The first Cistercians

The great monastic system of Cluny, springing out of the tenth century, had helped forge a new look in the Church, giving both the spiritual sources for reform and the physical means—the men and the quiet strength that even the wildest nobleman could respect. But Cluny's power brought about its own decline. Its monks in their 2,000 monasteries adopted the very things its founders had rejected—soft furs on their robes, luxurious foods and plenty of them, and servants and manual laborers to do the unpleasant jobs. The monasteries were decorated with costly works of art, gilded statues, mosaics; worst of all, they had buried worship in a maze of processions and unnecessary and endless liturgical innovations which were so onerous that the monks were often drowsy with fatigue.

During the eleventh century several saintly men set about a reform of the monastic life. Many of them were in effect exiles—few Clunians really wanted a reform of their way of life, though many of them spoke feelingly about the need—and the reformers, St. Stephen of Grandmont, St. Bruno, St. Robert of Molesme, St. Romuald, were shunted from house to house. Each of them, however, was responsible for the initiation of a major order, each one of which was to have a deep effect upon the medieval Church. Perhaps the most important of the new centers was that founded by St. Robert of Molesme. A monk at fifteen, he was involved in attempts at reforming or founding nearly one

hundred monasteries. A final attempt at Molesme seemed successful, but a dispute with his monks drove Robert out in 1198 to found still another house at Citeaux, in a swamp in Burgundy where, as at Molesme, Robert introduced the primitive Benedictine rule in its powerful simplicity. Eighteen months later, the Molesme monks begged for Robert to return; he did, and under him Molesme became an important Benedictine center. Citeaux continued nobly for a while, then began to fail. It might have disappeared entirely but for St. Bernard.

Bernard was five years old when Pope Urban began preaching the first Crusade. His childhood ambition was to take part in Europe's attempt to free the Holy Land from the Moslems. He was one of seven children (of whom four others have been beatified). All were well educated and Bernard's five brothers were trained as knights; because of ill health, Bernard could not serve as a warrior against the Moslems: instead he was sent to study at a college of canons. In his early teens he had a dream of the newly born Christ in the stable at Bethlehem; this was an event that changed his whole life, and from then on his thoughts were directed to contemplation of the life of our Lord.

Handsome and witty, affable, good-tempered, Bernard attracted all who knew him, but after a brief show of worldliness, he grew more serious. At 22, he became interested in Citeaux, and in a remarkable instance of his influence on others, so affected four of his brothers and a number of his other kinsmen—31 in all—that they went with him into Citeaux. The group arrived at Eastertide, 1112. The English-born abbot, St. Stephen, welcomed them: the monastery had not had a vocation in several years and was close to failure. Bernard's sole purpose was to immerse himself in prayer and to die to the memory of men, but three years later he was sent out with twelve monks to found a new house. The site for it was in a lonely forest called the Valley of Wormwood. Though they were aided by the local bishop and his people, the monks were so poor that they sometimes lived on beech leaves for want of vegetables; at best their bread was of coarse barley. The strain of this harsh life apparently began to tell on Bernard: he became overly rigorous and severe; his monks became so discouraged that it looked as if the monastery might fail. But Bernard recognized his fault, imposed a strict silence upon himself and provided more regular meals, though the food was still simple and coarse. Eventually the monastery gained so great a reputation for holiness that it numbered 130 monks and gave birth to a number of other houses. The fame of the monastery led to the changing of its name to Clairvaux, or illustrious valley.

When William of Champeaux arrived at Clairvaux to consecrate Bernard as abbot, he was horrified to find how weak the young monk had grown through vigils and fasting and he ordered him to take a year of rest. Bernard was moved from his cell and placed in a hut outside the monastery, where he was fed health-giving herbs and special foods. The treatment brought about his complete recovery.

Cluny was dying, but the Cistercians to whom Bernard had brought such great vitality were long to stand as an example of the monastic life at its finest and purest. Young men came to Citeaux by the hundreds. Monks were sent out to found new houses in France, the Netherlands, Germany and England. By the end of the twelfth century, the Cistercians had 530 abbeys. Part of their popularity was due to their enthusiastic emphasis on the love of God and of Jesus Christ, and the cheerful practice of extreme austerities. The Cistercians restored farming as a chief occupation of monks and became leaders in the development of new agricultural techniques in Europe. (The English Cistercians, for example, were an important factor in the growth of their country's wool culture.)

They were also pledged to teach the ignorant and aid the poor (in one case, the monastery in Westphalia killed its cattle and pawned its chalices and books in order to provide for starving peasants). Each monastery had a house for the reception of the poor and an infirmary for the sick.

Bernard became famous throughout Europe, not only as a scholar but as a preacher and a miracle worker. His great sanctity and vitality involved him in both Church and state: though he reproved the Knights Templar for worldliness, he drafted a rule for them; he aided Pope Innocent II, who was driven from Rome by the Normans of Sicily, and was advisor and friend to a number of other popes. Eugenius III, who was a former Cistercian and a friend of Bernard's, enlisted his aid in preaching the second Crusade in 1145 in order to help the Latin kingdoms of Palestine. Speaking in numerous French and German cities, Bernard aroused intense enthusiasm. (During the same year he also spoke against the Albigensians, though with only passing success.) But the second crusade was a complete failure, due largely to rivalry among the crusaders and their own ineptitude; the stragglers who returned blamed Bernard for the frightful disaster of war in the Holy Land.

One of Bernard's most famous encounters was with Abelard, whose book explaining the doctrine of the Trinity on rational grounds had been burned after being condemned at Soissons. When, despite this condemnation, Abelard continued an active life as a teacher, Bernard denounced him publicly; to clear himself, Abelard demanded a duel of words at the Council of Sens held in 1140. The meeting took place, but so fierce was Bernard in his attack on Abelard's doctrines that Abelard walked out of the assembly.

Never robust, and often ill, Bernard suffered a great loss of strength in 1153. He was then 63. His last public act was typical of his generous personality. The people of Metz had been attacked by the Duke of Lorraine and were about to make a counter attack in revenge. The archbishop of Trier journeyed to Clairvaux to ask Bernard to intervene. Though he was seriously ill, Bernard made the long trip and prevailed upon both sides to set aside their arms and sign a treaty he had drawn up. Back at Clairvaux his health failed completely. On August 20 he died.

Citeaux today. When St. Bernard arrived here, the monastery bordered upon destitution. The Cistercians were influential for nearly two centuries, but then declined in numbers and fervor. A revival came in France in the seventeenth century with the reform at La Trappe, and recently again in America.

The swamps of Citeaux (from CISTELS, *or reeds) were reclaimed by Robert of Molesme and his monks. Throughout Europe, the Cistercians turned the wilderness into farmland and revolutionized agricultural techniques. Their* INSTITUTA *forbade the exploitation of serfs; neither were they allowed to live off parishes or other benefices. They supported themselves by their own labors, from their farms, herds and flocks, vineyards, orchards, forests, quarries and fishponds.*

Church and state in conflict

Despite its drive toward spiritual perfection the century was never to be free of the age-old conflict between the spiritual and temporal. Though the Church and empire had come to a working agreement in 1122 at Worms, the conflict kept arising with each new shift of political power.

After the Concordat of Worms, the popes possessed the dominant influence in every quarter of Western Christendom. But they were not free of the opposition of the emperor and the nobles, nor of that from politically-minded prelates. Three hours after Innocent III was elected, a group of dissident cardinals elected an anti-pope; the legitimate pope was embroiled in a battle with his enemies that continued through most of the thirteen years of his rule. Lucius II was mortally wounded in a battle with rebellious Romans; Blessed Eugenius III, a Cistercian abbot elected pope in 1145, for a while shared a dual rule of Rome with an annually elected senate; despite his troubles, Eugenius continued the reforms of the Church, deposing disobedient bishops in England and Germany, sending missionaries to Scandinavia, working with St. Bernard and Peter Lombard on the Church's intellectual revival and with Gratian on the codifying of its canons. The troubled peace between papacy and nobles came to a climax in the middle of the century when William of Sicily seized part of the papal territory and also 5,000 pounds' weight of gold which the Greek emperor Manuel I had sent to Pope Adrian IV. The pope was forced to recognize William's seizure of the papal lands; as a result he antagonized Frederick Barbarossa, who thought he had prior claim.

Frederick moved against the papacy with all the resources at his command. When Adrian died, his agents tried to install Frederick's own pope, who was "elected" by a group of four cardinals. But the other 23 cardinals chose instead Alexander III, a former professor of canon law at the University of Bologna. The emperor called the rival claimants to appear before his throne, but Alexander refused and excommunicated Frederick, releasing his subjects from their obedience to him. The schism lasted seventeen years, ending only when the emperor suffered a humiliating defeat at the battle of Legnano—his crack troops were routed by the Lombard towns of northern Italy, the first time the feudal horsemen were bested by foot soldiers in a major battle. For a while, at least, the defeat of Frederick meant the collapse of the strongest foe the papacy was to face for some time.

Frederick Barbarossa (or Red Beard) the Holy Roman Emperor, attempted to restore Germany to the great position it held before Henry IV, but was in constant conflict with the papacy. Though he experienced a humiliating defeat by the armies of Pope Alexander III, Frederick was a good enough Christian to be shocked by Saladin's victories in the Holy Land and to place himself under Pope Clement III for the Third Crusade. He scored some of his greatest victories against the Moslems with only 2,000 men. Frederick is seen here in the guise of a reliquary for relics of St. John the Evangelist.

The crusades are resumed

By 1188 Europe realized that it could no longer fake its way through a campaign in the Holy Land with half-hearted measures. Pope Clement III immediately ordered a tax on all revenues, including benefices, and asked the three most powerful rulers of Europe to take the Cross. They were Frederick Barbarossa of Germany, Philip Augustus of France and Henry II of England (who was succeeded by his son Richard the Lion-Hearted). Frederick seized the initiative from all, aligning himself with the pope in this venture and the other two kings joined the crusade partly to protect their own interests.

After careful preparation (this was the most skillfully planned of all crusades), Frederick advanced rapidly into Greece, occupying a number of cities with his troops, and sending allies to fight against Byzantium which, as usual, had been too friendly with the enemy. Crossing into Asia Minor, Frederick rolled up a string of victories as Saladin retreated, destroying each city and village behind him. But disaster now hit the Germans. "It might have been written," said an Arab named Ibn-al-Athis, "that Syria and Egypt no longer belong to Islam, had not Allah deigned to show clemency towards his faithful servants by causing the German king to perish." While bathing in an icy stream Frederick suffered a stroke and died. A blow to the West, it was a fortunate event for the Moslems.

Philip Augustus and Richard, who had spent the winter scheming against each other, now joined forces to take Acre, after which Philip announced that he had fulfilled his vow and returned home to France. Richard, a hardy and brave warrior, but an indifferent leader and detested by many of the crusaders, attempted to carry on. Though he hated the enemy (he once had 3,000 Moslem captives put to death), his personal friendship with Saladin enabled him to gain a treaty promising free access by the Christians to the Holy Places. Like the other crusades, this, too, ended inconclusively and in a short time the situation was as bad as ever before.

Frederick Barbarossa, shown here in a contemporary portrait with his two sons, Duke Frederick of Swabia and King Henry VI, was so typical a Germanic emperor that he seems more fictional than true. A handsome, impressive red-haired, well educated, courageous figure of great personal magnetism, he hated being thwarted and had a tremendous opinion of his powers and his rights.

His vassals pushed back both heathen Slavs and the Danes, colonizing their lands with Germans, and extending German power across the shore of the Baltic. The rest of his empire he either bought, married into, confiscated or took by force. His church policy was simple: to put into every empty bishopric one of his own candidates and to regard papal power as a threat to his own. Against the nobles his policy was similar: he tried to break up the great fiefs, creating a Germany of small principalities, bishoprics and free cities.

But in the English Pope, Adrian IV, Frederick met a will as hard as his own. The Pope needed Frederick's help against the Normans. Frederick wanted the Pope to anoint him Emperor. The Pope refused until Frederick, after bitter expostulations going on a day and a half, consented to hold his bridle and stirrup, thus bowing before the papacy.

Albigensians and Waldensians

During the twelfth century the discipline of the Church was tightened considerably. As a result of the lawless ages of the period after Charles the Great, three great ecumenical councils were held at the Lateran during the twelfth century; the first, in 1123, endorsed the Concordat of Worms, in which the agreement between Church and state limiting the areas of lay investiture was drawn up. The next council (1139) was convoked to eliminate the traces of schism resulting from the efforts of an anti-pope, Anacletus; his supporters were excommunicated; other results were disciplinary canons for the improvement of clerical morals, the prohibition of usury, jousts, marriage of blood relatives and hereditary claims to Church office or Church property. The following ecumenical council (1179) was primarily concerned with ending the seventeen-year schism caused by the excommunication of Frederick Barbarossa; it also promulgated decrees for the reformation of the clergy. One of its main concerns was to stop the spread of heresy by two sects, the Albigensians and the Waldensians, whom it condemned.

These two sects were powerful enemies of the Church, and were becoming increasingly dangerous as the century ended. The Albigensians, a group in southern France and northern Italy, technically were not Christians at all, but Provençal inheritors of the dualistic system of Manichaeism. Though St. Bernard and other Cistercians preached against them, they continued to grow in strength. They seized Church property by force, drove bishops and Catholic clergy from their sees and churches. Equally menacing were the Waldensians, led by Peter Waldo; a well-to-do merchant of Lyons, he initiated a reform movement toward evangelical poverty. The Waldensians led austere lives and had a reputation for personal sanctity; denouncing wealthy clergy, they insisted upon personal effort and renunciation as more efficacious than the reception of the sacraments; as pacifists they denounced all wars. When their activities became extreme, they were forbidden to preach in public. They continued, nevertheless, and in 1184 were condemned as heretics by Pope Lucius III. In the end the Waldensians were led to deny the authority of the Church and taught that every just man could absolve, consecrate and preach the Gospel without sacramental ordination.

The valleys and mountains of northern Italy, near Turin, became a refuge for the Waldensians after their banning in the twelfth century. (This is one of their villages today.) The Waldensians established themselves as a separate religious body and attempted to proselytize among Catholics. Throughout the Middle Ages, their efforts led to the burnings and massacres of their members; in the sixteenth century they established contact with the Reformation; but continually at war with the Italian state, they did not receive political and religious freedom until 1848.

the "greatest" of centuries

The thirteenth century was marked by rapid and profound changes in medieval society on many levels. The papacy, under Innocent III, reached the peak of its temporal glory (though it was inevitably embroiled in quarrels with the secular powers). The feudal lord by this time had attained the height of his power, and on the continent of Europe was likely to hold many of the rights of sovereignty: minting money, holding court, setting up markets, levying tolls on bridges and roads. But at the same time, he was being challenged by new concepts in government: those particularly of the empire and the ascendant papacy; Saint Louis IX in France and later Edward I in England strengthened the power of the central government; on the economic level the holding of money, mostly in the hands of merchant princes, was becoming more important than the possession of land. New movements grew in the Church: the orders founded by St. Francis of Assisi and St. Dominic; new intellectual currents were developed by the schoolmen, among them, St. Thomas Aquinas; a renascence was under way in the arts and sciences, a new intellectual curiosity stimulated in part by contact made with the Oriental world both through the crusades and the Arabs of Spain.

A simple but important shift took place in economic terms: a sounder financial base for Europe (with the reminting of gold coins), the appearance of banking (developed by branches of the Knights Templar who transferred credits from one chapter to another on behalf of merchant princes); along with these economic changes came a geographical-political development: the growth of the city states. The thirteenth century was an exciting time for men of all classes and with its concern with learning, the arts and the human spirit it stands as the greatest of medieval centuries.

Typical of the new typ
of man to develop in the hig
Middle Ages was Frederick II. Though ruler c
the Holy Roman Empire, he was b
character and influence
Sicilian Norman; high
irreligious, he was accused
declaring that Christ, Moses an
Mohammed were all imposters. H
had the doubtful honor of havin
his excommunication the primar
subject of discussion at th
Council of Lyons. He
seen here with a favorite falcor

Innocent III

In the history of the papacy, Innocent III stands as a gigantic figure. Elected pope in 1198 at the age of 37, his nomination had been a surprise, although he encountered little opposition. He seems to have assumed the papal throne with a well-thought out, if extreme, theory of ecclesiastical power. Spiritual matters, he reasoned, take pre-eminence over the corporal; the Church's rule is spiritual, the monarch's merely material, and so, he concluded, the king must in all matters, be subject to the pope; any idea of limitation to the Church's authority was foreign to Innocent's thinking. Once elected, he set out immediately to establish his ideal of the pope as both political and ecclesiastical ruler of the world. From that time on, he was never inactive in political matters.

His first step in the establishment of his position was to acknowledge young Frederick II as King of Sicily, in exchange for the return of certain ecclesiastical privileges on the part of the king's mother, Constance. Frederick later became the pope's ward, and was nurtured for the imperial throne by Innocent, who was having difficulty with the series of imperial claimants early in the

century. In 1211 Innocent excommunicated the emperor, Otto IV, and dictated the election of Frederick in his place.

Innocent wielded an equally firm hand in other countries. When King John of England challenged his nomination of Stephen Cardinal Langton as Archbishop of Canterbury, the pope put England under interdict, excommunicated John and then formally deposed him. The barons and the people supported the pope and John had to submit, receiving England as a fief in return (subsequently the pope supported John when Langton and the barons forced him to accept the Magna Carta, declaring it null because the king signed it unwillingly). Equally active in other countries, Innocent initiated the Fourth Crusade (whose members disappointed him cruelly by attacking two Christian states, Zara and Constantinople), and later the European crusade against the Albigensians (where again he was forced, but in vain, to object to the misbehavior of Simon de Montfort's knights); he also supported the Teutonic knights in their push along the Baltic. He provided the impetus to St. Dominic's missions and gave the first approbation to the preaching order of St. Francis of Assisi. His greatest triumph was the Fourth Lateran Council, the most important synod of the Middle Ages.

The Fourth Lateran Council, held in 1215, commonly known as the "Great Council," brought together some 1,400 leading ecclesiastics to discuss pressing problems. Seventy canons on Church government and discipline were ratified, and important doctrinal subjects were discussed (the term "transubstantiation" was used here for the first time), as well as relations between the Greek and Latin churches; the doctrines of the Albigensians, Waldensians and other heretics were condemned; the secrecy of confession was formally initiated.

Innocent III as he looked during his lifetime.

The Council of Lyons was called in 1245 by Innocent IV to deal with what he called "the five wounds of the Church—the bad lives of the clergy and the faithful, the danger of the Saracens, the Greek schism, the invasion of Hungary by the Mongols and the quarrel with Frederick II.

A dictatorial emperor

No two medieval rulers so typify the extremes of their age as do Frederick II, the Holy Roman Emperor, and St. Louis IX, King of France. One was the epitome of cynicism and corruption (accompanied by an admirable mind and a keen interest in worldly things); the other was a simple man, naïve, courageous and devoted to the Church and the papacy.

"Of faith in God he had none," wrote a contemporary chronicler—a Franciscan named Salimbene—about Frederick. "He was crafty, wily, avaricious, lustful, malicious, wrathful; and yet a gallant man at times, when he would show his kindness or courtesy; full of solace, jocund, delightful, fertile in devices. He knew to read, and sing, and to make songs and music. He was a comely man, and well-formed, but of middle stature. . . . He knew to speak with many and varied tongues, and, to be brief, if he had been rightly Catholic, and had loved God and His Church, he would have had few emperors his equals in the world."

But Frederick had little interest in the Church except to further his own interests. It was expected of the medieval ruler that he embark on a crusade to fight for the Holy Land, but Frederick saw no gain for himself in such a luckless adventure and was excommunicated on three different occasions for his behavior in the crusades. His eventual landing in the East was a peaceable and a bloodless one. From birth Frederick was involved in struggle, against kinsmen and relatives, against the Church, against the nobles, against the free city states of Italy. At one point—in 1241—he captured the General Council on its way to Rome. But the other side of his cruel character showed the talents that might have made for real greatness. He was keenly interested in science (his treatise on hawking, *De Arte Venandi cum Avibus*, was also a study of anatomy and the life of birds and was the first such in modern ornithology), medicine, mathematics, astronomy and astrology. However, these were studies he pursued with more zest than human compassion. He had a man entombed in a barrel to prove somehow that the soul did not survive death; and on occasion, he used living men for medical experiments.

In the secular field his most important work was the creation of the first modern state. There was nothing feudal in his administration of Sicily, his favorite domain. He developed the idea of a strong state supported by an efficient system of taxation and produced an economical regime, encouraging commerce into Egypt, Morocco and Spain. Agriculture and industry flourished under his rule. A natural dictator, he believed in a firm restriction of civil liberties, strong governmental control of trade, and terrorization by a ruthlessly dehumanized police force.

A falcon, the king of birds, from the court of Frederick II, ruler of the Holy Roman Empire, is symbolic of his position in medieval society. Like the falcon which despises all other birds, Frederick looked down on the common lot of men; he used the bird as his symbol everywhere.

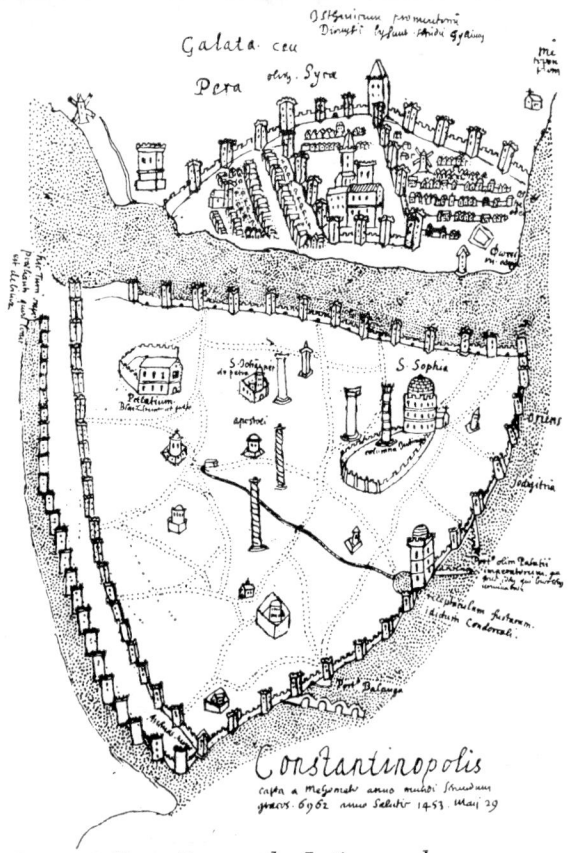

Byzantium as the Latins saw her.

The Crusaders take the wrong city

It was now the role of Pope Innocent III to persuade a reluctant Christendom to throw itself into the quicksands of the Middle East. Denouncing Europe's selfish rulers as men "less willing to suffer for Christ than was Christ for them," and her clergy as men who refused to give our Lord a glass of water when He asked for it, Innocent was finally able to whip together an acceptable crusading army. But the Holy Land was still far away; an overland route was ruled out and the Venetians, whose fleet had been increasing greatly because of the new trade with the Middle East, offered their ships for the price of half of the territory to be conquered plus a down payment of 85,000 gold marks. Only part of the money was delivered so the Venetians marooned the crusaders on an island, keeping them there until they had exacted a promise of helping settle a private affair, the destruction of Zara, the Venetians' rival city on the Adriatic.

Innocent was outraged when he heard of the sacking of Zara: "Instead of winning back the Holy Land you have thirsted for the blood of your brethren," he said. "Satan, the arch-deceiver, has seduced you." And he excommunicated the leaders.

When Innocent finally lifted the excommunication, it was with the warning, "Please God, your repentance is sincere; may He prevent a repetition of your sin!" But the expedition went on its way to Constantinople, another of Venice's rivals. A Latin chronicler wrote that when the crusaders saw the mighty prize before them, "no man there was of such hardihood but that his flesh trembled." On July 27, 1203, Constantinople was taken, its basileus fleeing, and a puppet government was established.

The next year a riot by the citizens, who hated the crusaders, gave a pretext for a complete, three-day sacking of Constantinople, in which even the churches were desecrated. Loot from the city and the empire itself decorated all of Europe: Venice's famed bronze horses, which stand before St. Mark's, were taken from Constantinople's Hippodrome. The pope wrote angrily, "These soldiers of Christ who should have turned their swords against the infidel have steeped them in Christian blood. They spared neither religion nor age nor sex. They openly committed adultery, fornication, incest. . . . They stripped the altars of silver, violated the sanctuaries, carried off ikons, crosses and relics."

With a single blow the crusaders had removed the one power that protected the Bosphorus from the enemy. Instead of marching to free the Holy Land they set up a Latin Kingdom of Byzantium, while the Greek nobles took refuge in Asia Minor. Troops that should have gone into the Holy Land were diverted into Latin Byzantium, an empire whose ways were soon to be hopelessly muddled and degenerate. The quick material successes gained from plunder were cancelled by the political and religious losses that ensued. Latin-rite clergy drove out the Greeks and since then, except for small minorities, the Eastern churches have remained out of communion with the West, and among them the name Frank is one of opprobrium.

For nine hundred years the St. Mark's horses stood in the Hippodrome in Constantinople before being stolen by a Crusader named Enrico Dandolo, doge of Venice, who placed them over the central door of his city's basilica. Originally they were cast in Corinth, Greece about 200 B.C. and most likely formed a group with a chariot. Nero took them from Greece in 68 A.D. and brought them to Rome to adorn his triumphal arch on Capitoline Hill. In looting the Empire in 330 for suitable ornamentation for New Rome, Constantine brought the group to his capital. In 1797 Napoleon stole them to place atop the Arc du Carrousel in Paris. After his exile, they were returned to Venice.

St. Louis lands at Damietta in an attempt at breaking Moslem power. The landing was successful, but the Crusaders lacked the will to capitalize upon their victory.

St. Louis leads the Crusades

Next, two children's crusades were expected to achieve by innocence what grown men failed by brute force, but these two ended disastrously; a sixth crusade, under the impious emperor, Frederick II, brought only temporary success. Finally there appeared the one man who brought to the scene all the old fervor, sanctity, integrity and spirit of the very first attempt to free the Holy Land. He was Louis IX of France, one of the Church's greatest saints. Almost alone of all the nobles to be persuaded to undertake still another venture into the Holy Land, St. Louis bore the true crusader's enthusiasm. Before he departed he made a pilgrimage to the abbeys of his country, barefoot and carrying the traditional pilgrim's staff and scrip. After a wearying voyage across the Mediterranean, St. Louis and his fleet appeared before Damietta, a city east of Cairo, capturing it easily. But Louis failed to follow up his victory. Weeks later, when the campaign did get moving again, the crusaders were unable to penetrate the fierce maze of swamps and canals around Damietta. The army was demoralized and enervated by typhus and scurvy. Louis fell sick, his men were routed by the Turks, and he was captured while lying feverish on a pallet in a mud hut. Most of the army was slaughtered; ransomed at an exorbitant price, Louis went to the Latin Kingdom and was installed as its ruler. Though he passed four years there, he refused to beg permission of the Moslems to visit Jerusalem and so he never saw the Holy Places. Finally he returned home to plan another crusade.

Louis IX "had the face of an angel, and mien full of grace," wrote Salimbene. "The King was spare and slender, somewhat lean and of a proper height. He came [on foot] to our church, not in regal pomp, but in a pilgrim's habit, with the staff and the scrip of his pilgrimage hanging at his neck, which was an excellent adornment for the shoulders of a king . . . his blood brethren, who were three counts . . . followed him in the same humble guise. In truth, he might rather be called a monk in devotion of heart, than a knight in weapons of war."

A somewhat fanciful map of the Mediterranean, prepared for the cause of St. Louis, shows his campaigns against the Moslems. In the bottom left he is seen dying at Tunis.

The last crusade

Now another figure appeared on the scene to confuse the drama that already entangled Frank, Greek and Moslem—the Mongol. A small warlike tribe that sprung unknown out of central Asia, the Mongols (misnamed the Tartars by Europeans) without warning swept across China to the Pacific under the great Genghis Khan, and suddenly found themselves rulers of half the world. Having subdued Asia (while the crusaders were looting Byzantium), they turned westward in a wild orgy of murder, kill-ing men, women and children alike and visiting their cruelties even on cats and dogs.

Large parts of the Moslem world fell before one Mongol force: another drove into Russia. From the backs of their stocky horses they hunted down Chinese, Persians, Russians and Hungarians as other men hunted wild game. Reaching the Volga, the Mongols were temporarily delayed by the death of the Khan, but his two sons resumed the campaign and rushed on towards Vienna.

Yet with all their cruelty there was one curious fact about the Mongols:

many of them were nominally Christians, members of tribes converted by Nestorian missionaries who had wandered East. Though heretics, the Nestorian Mongols were properly baptized, and where Moslems were annihilated by them, Christians were often spared. There were factions among both Mongol and Western war-lords who thought it possible to unite in a common effort against Islam. St. Louis himself sent several emissaries to the Mongols with inconclusive results. By 1258 a Mongol army had taken Bagdad and overrun Mesopotamia. Their generalissimo, a Nestorian Christian, persuaded Franks and Armenians to join forces with him, and it looked as if Jerusalem would be liberated in a "yellow crusade." However, the Latin barons at Tyre refused the alliance, preferring to deal with a new dynasty in Egypt, the Mamelukes, who, once an agreement was effected, turned on Christians and Mongols alike, driving the latter back into Persia. Only a new crusade—the eighth—could save Jerusalem for the West.

But this last crusade, lead by St. Louis, foolishly headed for North Africa instead of the Holy Land, landing at Tunis, whose ruler, it was erroneously believed, was open to conversion. The crusaders' advance was easily thwarted by Berber horsemen. The frightful heat sapped the crusaders' strength, an epidemic broke out, and Louis fell ill, weakening slowly. On August 25, 1270, after speaking out in a clear voice the beginning of the 42nd Psalm, he died.

As far as history is concerned, St. Louis was the last crusader. The situation in the East deteriorated steadily. The Mongols sent mission after mission to the heads of Europe, to Edward I, Gregory X and the Council of Lyons in 1274, asking for a joint attack on the Moslems. Aided by a few Armenian and Syrian Christians, the Mongols attacked the Mamelukes but failed. The Mamelukes calmly mopped up each surviving Christian outpost, ending with an appalling massacre at Tyre in 1291 in which 20,000 defenders were overwhelmed by 100,000 Moslems. The crusades were over.

Masters of half the world, the Mongols swept down on Asia Minor and Europe, shooting Russians, Turks and Hungarians from horseback like animals. Their threat to the West ended when all their forces went home to select a new khan. They never returned.

The rite of ordination received special attention in the thirteenth century. Saints Bonaventure, Albert the Great, Aquinas and Duns Scotus all wrote about the sacrament at length. Here a bishop and ordinand are shown during the rite as practiced in the Middle Ages.

The liturgy

Under Innocent there were also some changes in the Mass: the *Judica* psalm, the *Confiteor* (said twice in turn, as today) and then an absolution with versicle and prayers including *Aufer a nobis* were inserted by Innocent in the Missal of the Roman Curia and later they were made obligatory; until the twelfth century they had been said by priest on the way to the altar. During the same period, the kissing of the altar at Mass was a frequent action, though the custom of having all the clergy (and even the people) kiss the Gospel book was dying out. The thirteenth century saw a great devotion to the Holy Eucharist, which was then being held up for the faithful to see after the consecration, but the practice of receiving communion was becoming rare—St. Louis, who attended at least one mass a day, communicated only six times a year; the Lateran Council of 1215 sanctioned the minimum of a single annual communion at Eastertide.

The Divine Office as well as the Mass underwent a series of minor changes and additions in the thirteenth century, partly through the initiative of Pope Innocent. By his time the Office included the feasts of over 150 saints, and the list of required prayers was constantly growing. Innocent edited the Office and published it in a single book called the Breviary. In 1241 the Franciscans revised it and eventually the private recitation of the canonical hours was required of monks when they were unable to recite the office in choir. A number of liturgical hymns which are still popular date from this time: the *Pange Lingua* and *Adore Te* of St. Thomas Aquinas; the *Stabat Mater* and *Dies Irae* written by Franciscan friars; the *Jesu Dulcis Memoria*, *Alma Redemptoris Mater* and the *Salve Regina*.

Ticking off their arguments on his fingers, St. Dominic preaches to the Albigenses. In the foreground black-and-white dogs (representing the Dominicans) rescue sheep from the wolves.

St. Dominic

Like many of the outstanding ecclesiastical figures of his age, St. Dominic was born of noble parents. A Castilian, he had tried to ransom captives held by the Moors by selling himself into slavery. In 1203, when Dominic was about 23, he went to Rome with his bishop to ask permission to evangelize the Tartars; instead Innocent III sent him to France to preach to the Albigenses. With a rule of absolute poverty, Dominic and his companions wandered about Languedoc, preaching wherever they could. They were the first Catholic missionaries to achieve any success with the Albigenses. In 1208 a full-scale crusade against the Albigenses, the first against any Christian country, was proclaimed; the crusaders soon lost sight of their original intention; southern France was a worthwhile prize, but the fighting was bloody and dragged on for years; finally, in 1229, by the Peace of Paris, Toulouse fell to St. Louis IX. Meanwhile Dominic's efforts increased; in 1216 he received a house and church for his followers, who now numbered sixteen. Pope Honorious III approved his plans for a new order, which had the novel vocation of study and preaching; working closely with the newly founded Friars Minor, the Order of Preachers spread all over Europe, attracting some of the most brilliant intellects to their ranks and founding houses in almost every Christian country. In 1233 Pope Gregory IX commissioned the Dominicans to investigate the secret practices of the Albigenses, who were still active; this was the beginning of the Inquisition.

Dominic and Francis meet in Rome at the home of Cardinal Ugolino. They approached Ugolino together to ask him not to look for candidates for bishoprics from among their brethren.

St. Clare introduced a rule for women far stricter than any previously employed.

St. Francis

The conversion of a well-to-do young Italian named John Bernadone (nick-named Francesco, the Frenchman) was to have immeasurable effects not only upon the thirteenth century but on all those that followed. Francis was on his way to take part in one of the endless struggles that ravaged Italy, and seeing a poverty-stricken gentleman gave him his own magnificent armor and clothing. Subsequently Francis had several visions, in one of which he was urged "to serve the master, not the man." He began to turn away from his former profligate life and to meditate upon the Gospel. Riding one day near Assisi he met a leper covered with running sores. The young man dismounted and as the leper reached out for alms, Francis kissed his hand. He began to visit the sick. Self-renunciation and devotion to the sick and poor were his guide: a deeper conversion came later and his true vocation was revealed to him in the words of Jesus in Matt. 10, 7–10: he began preaching the Gospel, and living by its word, in utter poverty, bare-footed and preaching repentance "with words that were like fire, penetrating the heart." Others of his time followed the same ideal, but Francis brought an originality and a more profound conviction to his faith.

Francis's extraordinary personality and his radically new approach to Christ drew followers by the hundreds. One of them was St. Clare, who founded an austere order for women based on the ideals of Francis. His order approved by Innocent III, Francis continued to preach with extraordinary success, traveling as far as the Holy Land; however, he was called back to cope with dissension within the order. At a great assembly near Assisi, Francis resigned from active leadership, feeling that his followers had become too unwieldy for him to manage. His original rule of austerity and poverty was later mitigated, and out of his ideals came three orders of varying strictness, the Friars Minor, the Friars Minor Conventual, and the Friars Minor Capuchins. In 1224 Francis received the stigmata, dying in 1226; two years later he was canonized.

Cimabue's portrait of St. Francis the church of San Francesco at As

The schoolmen

The political, social and economic ferment of the period, heavily affected by contact with the Byzantine and Arabic worlds, had its parallel in the intellectual life. A new kind of scholar, the schoolman, was coming into being, a man who brought the clear light of his intellect to bear on the problems of God, man and the universe in a way that had never been done before. At the same time popular arts were beginning to mature, and the vernacular slowly took its place as a means of literary expression. New insights in art, with great innovations in the use of plastic space, color, light and form developed in the hands of Duccio, Cimabue, and particularly of Giotto (though his main work was to come in the next century); in literature, Dante began writing a vernacular literature with *Vita Nuova*.

But perhaps the greatest intellectual achievement of the age was the extraordinary system known as scholasticism, the fusion of philosophy with theology. The men who developed scholasticism were largely Dominicans and Franciscans; the first included Albert the Great and Thomas Aquinas, the second, Robert Grosseteste, St. Bonaventure, Alexander of Hales, Roger Bacon, Raymond Lully and Duns Scotus. Unafraid to look into the truth no matter where it might be found, they looted not only the classical Greeks but their contemporaries among the Mohammedans and Jews: these sources contributed to the great edifice of medieval Christian thought, of which St. Thomas was the chief architect. His two chief works were *Summa Contra Gentiles* and *Summa Theologica;* the latter became the favorite textbook in Catholic schools and still forms the core of Catholic philosophical studies.

St. Thomas lectured both at the University of Paris and at the papal school for outstanding scholars which accompanied the pope in his travels. In the bottom panel of this picture the devil is trying—hopelessly—to subvert the saint's clearminded attack on philosophical problems. Thomas died on the way to attend the Council of Lyons.

Young Dominicans are among the students learning theology from another member of the order at the University of Paris. By 1223 there were 120 Dominicans at the University.

VERE HIC
EST LVMĒ
ECCLESIE

HIC ADINVENI
OMNEM VIĀ DISCIPLINE

St. Thomas took such a deep approach to philosophy and theology that he was often misunderstood by his contemporaries, who could not grasp the subtleties of his mind, and there was some opposition to his thinking. However, during his lifetime, a gathering of doctors of the Church, in the Council of Anagni in 1256 (above) under Pope Alexander IV, vindicated his teachings. After his death further opposition arose and several propositions drawn from his works were condemned by different authorities; for a time the Franciscan Order forbade its members to study his works. However, four years after Thomas's death, the General Chapter of the Dominicans officially imposed his teachings on the Order, and in 1323 he was canonized by John XXII.

Silıgo

The harshness of life

Life for the thirteenth-century peasant was as hard as ever in the past, but an increasing number of his fellows were in the process of freeing themselves of the land and becoming established in the cities. A middle class of tradesmen, skilled craftsmen and merchants was growing up. With the feudal lords enmeshed in the crusades, the towns began to prosper. Craft guilds came into existence, replacing the merchant guilds. The new guilds set high standards of work, fixed ceiling prices, forbade unethical practices such as cornering the market, provided a simple kind of social insurance in the form of death benefits and care for widows and orphans. New materials flooded Europe: to the wool trade that had been developed by the Cistercians in the previous century were added cotton, muslin and damask. Better techniques of navigation and the development of new instruments resulted in larger ships, more daring voyages and greater cargoes.

Not many benefits from all this filtered down to the peasant at first. He lived a simple life, hardly better than the animals he cared for, ate crude food and was freed from his monotonous existence only by the frequency of the feast days that filled the church calendar.

The poor had little for sustenance but peas, beans, cereal; grains in bread and porridge with weak beer to drink, and sometimes cheese and eggs; there was little meat except for an occasional fowl or hare.

The rich had a better table. Beef, mutton and pork, chickens and geese, and wild game were their regular fare, meat was either boiled or roasted and served directly on skewers; chunks were cut off and eaten with the fingers. In the autumn animals were killed and salted down; little was known about preservation; spices that would disguise the taste of rotted meat were valued. For all classes there were few vegetables and many that would be considered edible today were then classed as herbs and roots which only the starving would eat.

For the upper classes food was served in appetizing ways, and considering the times, with a great deal of imagination. A monastic dinner given Saint Louis and his entourage (which included a cardinal, an archbishop and other ecclesiastical and civil dignitaries) included "first, cherries, then most excellent white bread; and choice wine, worthy of the King's royal state, placed in abundance before us; and, after the wont of the French, many invited even the unwilling and compelled them to drink. After that we had fresh beans boiled in milk, fishes and crabs, eel-pasties, rice cooked with milk of almonds and cinnamon powder, eels baked with most excellent sauce, tarts and cheeses, and all the fruits of the season in abundance and comely array."

Drawings from a medieval manuscript illustrate the principle of credit: payment passing from one group to another through a middleman. The bottom panel depicts a common right of the road: a traveller may cut as much grain for his horse as he can reach standing in one place.

The work-day for the land-bound was long and arduous. The Italian peasants shown here are beating rye with flails. Rye, the medieval world believed, was "good for reducing humors, but it occasions color and melancholia. This can be remedied by mixing wheat with it."

Along with the universities, the monasteries were great centers of learning. At the Benedictine monastery of Tavara in Spain monks are shown in the scriptorium working with compasses on mathematical problems. At the left other monks are about to ring the bells for the Divine Office.

The pilgrimage was one of the most popular of all medieval devotions. Many pilgrims made the long trip to the Holy Land, where they were likely also to visit St. Catherine's monastery on Mount Sinai. Others journeyed to Rome or to Santiago de Compostela in Spain. But even local pilgrimages were popular, such as the one to Canterbury. Here exhausted pilgrimages sprawl on the ground before the shrine of our Lady of Ratisbonne.

Three witches are burned at the stake (to the dismay of the devil flying overhead), while in the background a fourth is beheaded.

The prevalence of witches

Witches and wizards people the medieval scene, a vertical invasion of evil which added to the precariousness of life. The malevolent presence of the other world was not only sensed but it became a tangible reality. Rural areas particularly had their old crones who were known to deal with the devil and were thought to lay spells. Many of the people accused of witchcraft or anti-Christian practices were actually the pagan descendants of older cultures which had never been converted and held on tenaciously to pre-Christian religions passed from family to family. Though this vertical paganism was most common in rural areas and among the poor, there were also cases of witchcraft among the well-to-do.

Certain features in common marked European witchcraft. One was the worship of a horned deity, a practice also observed in ancient Mesopotamia, India, Crete, Greece, Egypt and Rome. This feature of the Old Religion was widespread. In the seventh century, in an England in theory fully Christianized, Theodore of Canterbury was forced to denounce anyone "who goes about as a stag or a bull [that is, by wearing a mask] . . . [for] those who transform themselves into the appearance of a wild animal, penance for three years because this is devilish." Three centuries later King Edgar sadly discovered that the Old Religion was more common than the Faith, and

urged fervent instruction of the young. But the cult tenaciously held on, being particularly powerful, despite official proscription, during the Middle Ages. Dozens of witches were tried and burned, yet they continued to worship.

The witches were normally organized in covens of thirteen, with a horned leader in charge to whom homage was paid in meetings on the witches' Sabbath. Ritual meals were partaken, and often hallucinations were induced with the aid of plants like belladonna or certain mushrooms. (A flying sensation often resulted, leading to the myth of the witches' broom.) The witches were commonly recluses who kept animal companions and employed herbs and charms; they were likely to be called upon by the local Christian peasantry as healers or for divination of the future: the overt use of such practices, however, was punishable by the stake.

Official attitudes towards the witch changed over the centuries. Charlemagne forbade the persecution of witches, as did many early bishops; Gregory VII ruled against the killing of old women for supposed crimes, such as causing storms or epidemics. But by the fourteenth century witches were being hunted down by the Inquisition, not without a few mistakes (the case of Joan of Arc is a striking example). The Protestant Reformers, especially in England, were deeply concerned with the extirpation of witchcraft, and it is to them that the greatest persecutions must be attributed.

The right of sanctuary was a privilege often used in the Middle Ages. By seeking refuge in a church, where he had to touch a certain object, either the altar (in early times) or, as in the abbey at Hexham, England, the frith or sanctuary stool, a criminal would be free from arrest or pursuit by enemies. At Durham the petitioner, once he had placed both hands on the knocker (above) was admitted to the cathedral by the monks for thirty-seven days, at the end of which time he could either take his chances in escaping or devote the remainder of his life to the service of the Church. In most cases, however, a criminal was given forty days in which to take an oath of abjuration and be escorted to a seaport to go into exile; otherwise he might be forcibly extricated. (The privilege was not extended to sacrilege or high treason.) At the Reformation the right of sanctuary was curtailed and was finally abolished.

The plight of the Jews

The Jews occupied a special position in medieval life. Both protected and abused, they alternated between freedom and despair. They had been fairly free from persecution during the growth of the new nations in the Dark Ages, but by the time of the crusades their status had changed, and in the first crusade one army of knights tuned up for war in the Holy Land by slaughtering the Jews along their route to Byzantium.

The Jews were denied ownership of land and barred from most occupations except petty trading and money lending, a trade in theory forbidden to Christians, although the prohibition was soon ignored by the new class of merchant princes. The Jews segregated themselves into separate streets and areas, at first voluntarily, but later by order; the custom became a civil law and the ghettoes were surrounded by a wall; the inhabitants had to be inside by a certain hour at night or suffer penalties. The Jews were often unjustly charged by popular rumor with imaginary crimes, among them the ritual murder of children and the desecration of the sacred Host. At Fulda, 34 Jews, who confessed after torture, were murdered on these charges. Frederick II had the trial investigated, found the charges untrue and forbade a repetition, but similar incidents persisted for centuries. In 1247 the Jews of France and Germany begged Innocent IV to defend them against a like accusation; the pope branded the charge false, as did many other popes in later years. The Jewish problem was constantly before the Church: over a hundred letters of the popes and fifty decrees of local and general councils mention the Jews; the bull extending protection to them was renewed five times but with little success.

King John of England was one of the worst offenders, restricting Jews to 25 towns so they could be easily registered and taxed, and forbidding them to leave England since they were a valuable source of income. A few years later their privilege of lending money was restricted, thus depriving them of one of their principal means of support. Destitute, the Jews were finally expelled in 1290, their presence in England being illegal for four hundred years. A short while later, they were expelled from France, Spain and Portugal, many of them fleeing to Poland, where, in 1264, the generous ruler of Poland, Boleslaus the Pious, had opened his lands to Jewish refugees, giving them privileges they were to hold for five centuries.

German Jews of the thirteenth century, like those of most European countries, wore a distinctive dress.

The Inquisition began in 1233 under Gregory IX when the Pope appointed a tribunal of members of the mendicant order —chiefly Dominicans and Franciscans—to rout out heresy and bring about a return to the true Faith. In the past the discovery and punishment of heretics had usually been initiated by the princes or by an aroused public. Originally a means to insure a fair trial for the accused and to keep him from abuse by secular powers, the Inquisition drifted into progressively harsher methods. At first an obstinate heretic was punished by imprisonment: but soon the use of torture was also introduced, and unrepentant heretics were turned over to the secular arm for execution. The scene at the right shows the various stages of a trial before the Inquisition (presided over by St. Dominic), ending with a Dominican attempting to console three despondent heretics awaiting their turn at the stake.

The Polos initiate an age of exploration

In 1271 a group of Venetian merchants, the Polos, set off on a trading expedition into the Far East, taking with them two Dominicans as missionaries who were to go to the court of Kublai Khan. The older Polos, Niccolo and his uncle, Maffeo had already traveled in this area and were friends of the Khan, who had expressed an interest in Christianity and asked the Pope to send him a hundred learned men to expound both Christianity and the seven arts. Young Marco became a favorite of the Khan's, and served him on business in China and India and even ruled the city of Hankow. After seventeen years in the East, the Polos started home, and returned to Venice in time for Marco to join the Venetian forces fighting Genoa; he was taken prisoner and, in captivity, dictated an account of his travels to a fellow prisoner. Polo was still wonderstruck at the splendors of what he had observed and experienced; though he was at times overly credulous, the book is largely factual and has been of great value to historians, for several centuries being the most reliable guide to many parts of the Far East.

The Polos set off from Venice on their daring expedition into the Far East.

Boniface proclaims the first Holy Year. In the following centuries the Holy Year was held every fifty years and then every thirty-three.

The first Holy Year

As the year 1299 drew to a close, a vast crowd assembled in St. Peter's Basilica for Christmas eve Vespers. A large number of the worshippers were pilgrims from other countries, attracted by a rumor that various indulgences could be obtained during the coming year by all who visited the tombs of Peter and Paul. After Christmas the number of pilgrims increased, many bearing different versions of what indulgences were to be obtained and under what conditions. The tombs of the saints were besieged, and the streets of Rome were so crowded that it was almost impossible to walk through them.

Finally the pope, Boniface VIII, questioned an old man of 107 who was being carried in the arms of his sons to see the handkerchief of St. Veronica. "I remember," said the pilgrim, "that at the beginning of the last century my father, who was a laborer, came to Rome and stayed here as long as his means lasted, in order to gain the indulgence. He told me not to forget to come at the beginning of the next century, if I should live so long." Two other centenarians and a number of elderly pilgrims confirmed the report. Though no written document in support of the belief could be discovered, it was apparent that from oral testimony the people had expected special blessings in the opening years of the new century. Unwilling that his people should be deprived of what they had tried so hard and at such great inconvenience to obtain, Boniface proclaimed a Holy Year, the first officially on record.

Pope Boniface VIII as he looked during the Holy Year

an age of chaos

Few centuries have seen such change as did the fourteenth. Midway through it a devastating plague, the Black Death, which was to recur every decade or two for years to come, swept across Europe, bringing in its wake a vast disruption of the social fabric: Church, state, city and countryside were affected; people died by the tens of thousands. The plague's one beneficial result was a

gradual bettering of the peasantry's conditions, often by way of rebellion, and a rejection of traditional doctrines. At the same time, the Church was rent by a deep cleavage that put Europe into opposing camps with rival popes in Rome and Avignon, and shook the wavering faith of millions. Plague and schism helped lead to the Reformation, whose rumblings had been heard for generations.

The Conquest of Death—carrying away good and evil alike—is illustrated in a manuscript which draws its inspiration from the continual recurrence of the plague in the late Middle Ages.

The Black Death

In 1349, a German chronicler named Jacob von Königshofen sadly took up his pen and began a record of the frightful events that had taken place that year. "There occurred," wrote Jacob, "the greatest epidemic that ever happened. Death went from one end of the earth to the other, on that side and this side of the sea, and it was greater among the Saracens than among the Christians. In some lands everyone died so that no one was left. Ships were also found on the sea laden with wares; the crew had all died and no one guided the ship. The bishop of Marseilles and priests and monks and more than half of all the people there died with them. In other kingdoms and cities so many people perished that it would be horrible to describe. The pope at Avignon stopped all sessions of court, locked himself in a room, allowed no one to approach him and had a fire burning before him all the time. [This measure was apparently intended as a kind of disinfectant.] And from what this epidemic came, all wise teachers and physicians could only say that it was God's will. And as the plague was now here, so was it in other places, and lasted more than a whole year. This epidemic also came to Strasbourg in the summer of the above-mentioned year, and it is estimated that about 16,000 people died."

The plague had started in Constantinople, where thousands of people began to experience swellings of the lymph glands in the groin and armpits. Each case was marked by a high fever, collapse of the victim and, invariably, death. This was the West's introduction to the disastrous bubonic epidemic known as the Black Death (from the dark color of the body after death). It soon swept Europe, destroying almost all before it: the death toll has been estimated as high as three quarters of the population. The highly contagious disease was carried by rat fleas that had become infected from biting diseased rats; it had apparently been brought to the capital of Byzantium from the Crimean grain port of Kaffa.

The disease spread rapidly across the Mediterranean, reaching Provence by 1348 and England by 1349. Following the trade routes, it crossed Germany and Scandinavia and invaded Poland from the west. The results were cataclysmic: every level of society—social, economic and political—was affected and there was no escape. The entire fabric was altered. The nobles died as quickly as the peasants; towns were emptied; without teachers or pupils, schools decayed. Communications and trade came to a halt. The number of religious declined. Since the peasantry was reduced to half, their labor was soon hired at a premium. To halt inflation, the English crown passed the Statute of Laborers in 1351, freezing wages at the pre-plague level, a law everyone tried to by-pass. But the result was the arousing of the people and the increase of tension between rich and poor. About one third of Europe's population was carried off during the first three years of the plague. What was worse, it continued to return almost every ten years, thus halting the continuous increase of population of the past. Population figures remained almost stagnant for generations. In Germany, accompanying the panic, there was an outburst of pogroms against the Jews, who were accused of causing the plague. Many of their communities were destroyed while the remnant fled to the East. Systematic attempts were made to check the epidemic; quarantines were established, those infected were isolated in hospitals, and special doctors and health commissioners appointed, but little improvement resulted; frequent wars and long sieges had too seriously interfered with sanitation, and had accelerated the communication of disease. All across Europe came a lowering of standards: instead of a heightened piety caused by the fear of death, men became less honorable, more debased and callous.

he plague kept coming back. In this
teenth-century painting a priest
ads the burial service over
ague victims, while in heaven
. Sebastian intercedes for them.

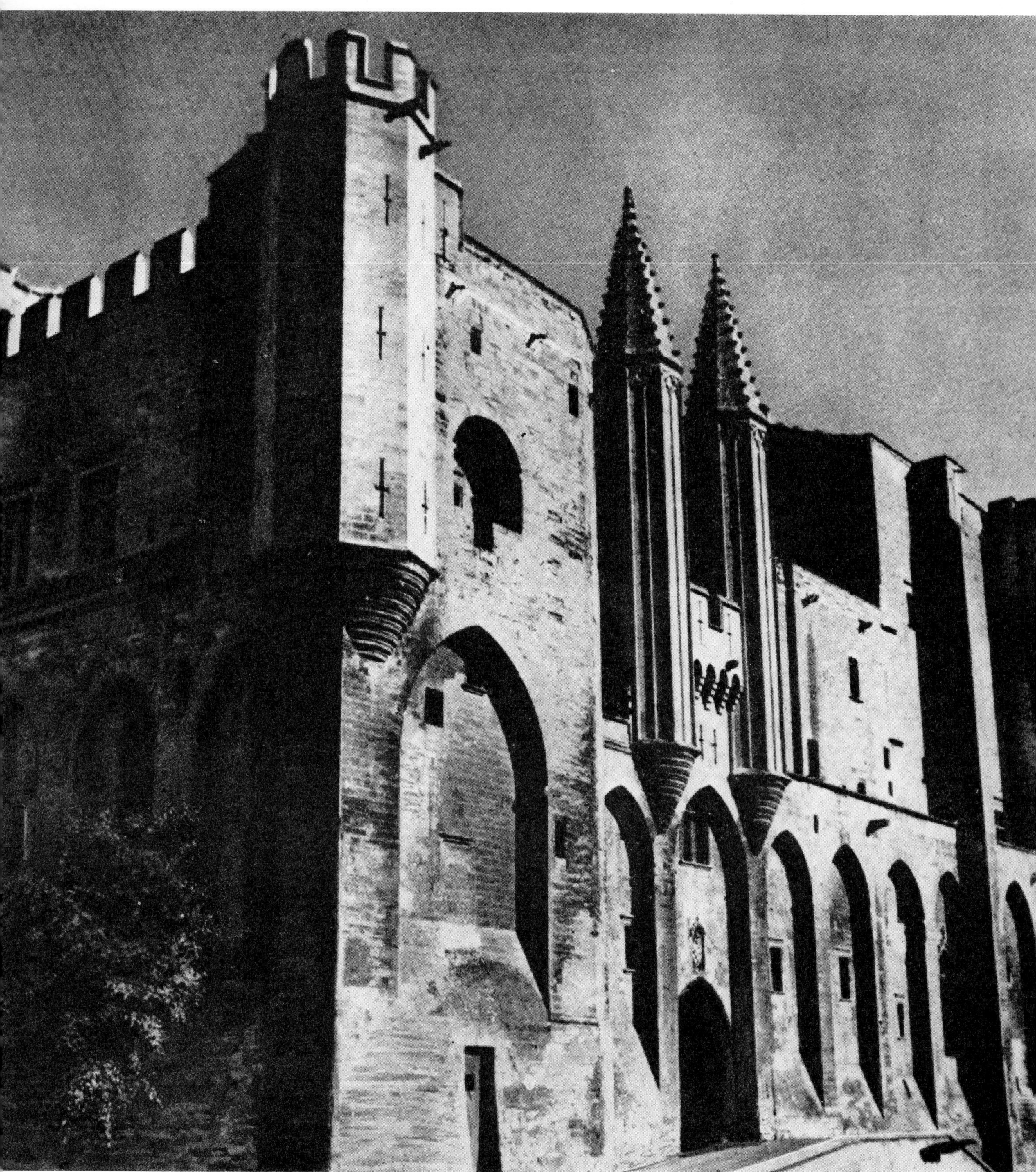

*Once an Albigensian center, Avignon became the residence of
the popes from 1309 until 1377 in their "Babylonian captivity," a
phrase used metaphorically by the humanist and poet, Petrarch, who
grew up near the city. The papal residences were not finally owned
by the Holy See until 1348. After the ending of the schism, two
anti-popes, Clement VII and Benedict XIII, returned to Avignon
to live.*

The Great Schism

The great schism of Avignon divided the Church for a period of 35 years and helped to plant the seeds of the Reformation. There was no question of faith or practice involved; the schism was entirely a matter of people and politics, incited by men's vanity and the interests of princes. Avignon, a commercial city in southern France, was so attractive that Pope Urban V (1367-70) chose to move the papal court there from Rome. When his successor, Gregory XI (the last French pope), was elected, he attempted—under the urging of Sts. Brigid of Sweden and Catherine of Siena—to re-establish his court at Rome, and circumstances almost prevented him from doing so. Avignon had strong support and the Italians were inhospitable: civil war was ravaging the land: yet Gregory finally succeeded in moving his court back to Rome. It was the events after his death that led to the Great Schism.

The Romans feared the return of the papal court to Avignon, and the mob demanded a Roman, or at least an Italian, pope. On April 8, 1378, the sixteen cardinals present elected Urban VI. The new pope began to act offensively and it is considered that he may have been insane. The cardinals slipped out of Rome and declared unanimously that Urban's election was null, being done in fear of the mob. A few weeks later, they elected Robert of Geneva as Clement VII. The next year Clement fled Italy for Avignon, surrounded by the former Roman court. There were thus two popes and two lines of successors, each drawing allegiance from parts of Europe.

The situation was one of constant annoyance to the more responsible members of the Church: the group most eager to end the schism was centered around the University of Paris. They urged the calling of a general council (this led to the development of the conciliar theory: that popes are subject to such councils). In 1409 Europe's leading ecclesiastics met at Pisa to try to solve the situation.

However, the council at Pisa served only to complicate the situation further. Summoned by members of the College of Cardinals of the two rival papal lines, Gregory XII in Rome and Benedict XIII at Avignon, the plan was to depose both and elect a new one. The Council—uncanonical because most of the cardinals involved owed their creation to a pope holding office illegally—declared both popes heretical and schismatic and elected Alexander V, thereby complicating the schism with a third claimant. Alexander's successor, the

Elected pope at the Council of Constance in 1417, Martin V rides to his coronation with the Holy Roman Emperor Sigismund holding his bridle.

anti-pope John XXIII (a title to be taken again by Angelo Roncalli in 1958), gained the allegiance from his rivals of much of Europe. In 1414 John reluctantly convened the Council of Constance, some of whose sessions are recognized as the sixteenth ecumenical council. Reform of Christian life and the extirpation of heresy was among its aims. Its 45 sessions lasted from November, 1414 to April, 1418, and were dominated by French theologians. Instead of an assembly of bishops moved by the Holy Spirit to speak, it was organized as a convention of nations (Germans, Italians, French and English, and later the Spanish), each with one vote. The reforms it voted were minor in view of the problems facing the Christian world. But it did resolve the question of Avignon.

Gregory XII, the Roman pope, resigned and John and Benedict, both of whom refused to step down, were deposed. Martin V was elected by the council, which had the support of Europe, and the schism was at an end. The main effects of the disastrous years of schism were to delay the major reforms that were an admitted need of the Church and to strengthen the conciliar theory. Most Catholic historians are agreed that the Roman line was the canonical one.

Dante stands before the walls of Florence, holding LA COMMEDIA *in his hand. At the left, devils drive the souls of the damned into Hell. In the rear, other souls work out their salvation on the hill of Purgatory. An angel marks the heads of newcomers with the sins to be expiated, while others reach the summit of the hill and the earthly paradise symbolized by Adam and Eve.*

Dante Alighieri

One of the few favorable events of the century was the continuing development of arts and letters, which were beginning to draw upon the classical age of Greece and Rome, though without completely understanding it. Perhaps the most typical of his time was Dante Alighieri, whose *Commedia* has been called "the one truly universal poem in European literature."

Dante was born in Florence in 1265, and spent his early life in public affairs. Upon the rising of the Black Guelphs, Dante, a White Guelph, was fined and banished, spending the rest of his life wandering through Italy. A vigorous opponent of the abuses of his time, he strongly denounced ecclesiastical corruption, and in *La Commedia* (1307-1320) pictured famous and infamous men suffering in Hell. In the *Monarchia* he taught that the civil authority of the emperor is derived from God and therefore is exercised independently of the pope. (Under his theory—the treatise was publicly burned in Bologna by the papal legate— Charlemagne received no new rights from Pope Leo III.) By using the Florentine dialect instead of Provençal, he gave Italy its national language in works that are still read today: *La Vita Nuova* (a prose narrative with inserted lyrics telling of his love for Beatrice Portinari, whom he first saw in 1274), *La Commedia, Convivio* (an allegorical encyclopedic work) and various lyrics. He also wrote, in Latin, treatises on the Italian vernacular and the monarch, as well as epistles and eclogues.

John XXII (portrayed with St. Thomas Aquinas and St. Louis of Toulouse) was undoubtedly the most important pope of the fourteenth century. The son of a cobbler, he was a great ruler, though often reckless and lacking self control; however, he was considerate toward his enemies. He was a notable intellectual, and founded university chairs of Hebrew, Arabic and Chaldean. He was also an outstanding poet. His bull, DOCTA SANCTORUM, *is the first important papal statement on church music.*

Joan of Arc

In 1426 a young peasant girl named Joan (the French know her as Jeanne la Pucelle) began experiencing a series of supernatural manifestations —angelic voices—which eventually unfolded to her the surprising mission—appalling to her—that she was to come to the rescue of her country. France was torn by civil war: Burgundy and Orleans were fighting over the throne, and the English, who had invaded the country a few years before, were vigorously and successfully supporting Burgundy. The situation looked hopeless to the frivolous Charles VII of Orleans, commonly known as the Dauphin. The voices of the saints spoke more insistently to Joan; after two years of hearing them, Joan, only sixteen, went to one of Charles's generals; he sent her home, but the voices persuaded her to return. Finally she was passed on to the Dauphin. Charles was convinced of her mission, though most of his court opposed her. Joan was examined by a panel of theologians, who found nothing wrong with her and cautiously advised Charles to make prudent use of her services. At last Joan, wearing white armor, was permitted to lead a force against the English besieging Orleans, and after a hard fight she forced the enemy to abandon the siege.

Further victories fell to Joan and her troops. She pressed for the coronation of the Dauphin at Rheims, and it was achieved. But this was the most that the voices had promised her. She was now dogged by military failures, largely as the result of Charles's lack of support. Disaster came on May 23, 1430, when she was captured during a sortie against the Burgundians. The Duke of Burgundy held her prisoner until late in the fall, then sold her to the English for the equivalent of about $65,000 in today's money. Charles made no attempt to save her, either by ransom or by force.

Instead of a summary execution, the British insisted on the farce of a trial, ostensibly for heresy and witchcraft but actually to discredit Charles and his clergy. A venal group of French clergy in English pay conducted the inquiry. Alone and without counsel Joan defended herself with amazing skill, only to be condemned to the secular arm for refusing to retract her story of divine aid. However, for a brief time she did recant—her reasons seem unclear today—and she was returned to prison. Immediately she regained her strength of mind and spirit. The judges condemned her as a relapsed heretic, and on May 29, 1431, Joan, barely nineteen, was burned at the stake.

The only known true-life portrait of Joan. Her case was later reopened; in 1456 she was completely rehabilitated.

Upon Joan's request a Dominican friar holds a cross before her eyes. Her last words were: "Jesus! Jesus!" Her ashes were scattered into the Seine. An English witness cried, "We are lost; we have burned a saint!"

The conditions of the peasantry, steadily growing
worse since the beginning of the century, resulted
in revolts in many countries. In France in 1357,
the peasants—the Jacques—driven by poverty, rose
against the nobles. The Jacquerie had no leaders,
no plan of attack and soon the "black, stunted and
poorly armed villeins" (as Froissart called them)
were being hunted down like animals by the French
lords (above).

John Ball, the heretic priest (on horseback), and Wat Tyler, leader of the revolt, join armies in the peasants' rebellion of 1381.

The peasants revolt

Near the end of the 1300's, 100,000 English peasants revolted under the leadership of an obscure roofer named Wat the Tyler. Their wages frozen for thirty years by the Statute of Laborers, and excited by the imposition of a higher poll tax, as well as by John Wyclif's subversive theories and the harangues of an excommunicated priest named John Ball, they began by murdering Archbishop Sudbury of Canterbury. Then, joined by an ever-increasing mob, Tyler led the rebels on to London. The king, Richard II, avoided a meeting; the mob sacked the city and finally Richard was forced, at Mile End, to promise to abolish not only serfdom, but all feudal service, all market monopolies, and all restrictions on buying and selling. He also promised pardon to the rebels. But Tyler, not yet satisfied, had several government officials executed in the Tower of London. Disorder continued throughout the city as he met again with the king to present new demands. During the talks the derogatory remark of a bystander caused Tyler to draw his dagger. In the scuffle that followed, Wat Tyler was mortally wounded by Wentworth, the Mayor of London, and died. Richard, with a great show of courage, cowed the mob and held it at bay until Wentworth could arrive with more reinforcements; the rebels broke and the revolt, which had raged all over England, was speedily put down with extreme cruelty. Richard, free again, revoked the Mile End Concessions.

179

Twenty years after his death, Wyclif's bones are exhumed, burned and thrown into the river. Public sympathy was with Wyclif during his life and he died peacefully in his own parish. It was only later that the crown turned against his doctrines.

The Reformation begins

The Bohemian priest John Hus was heavily influenced by Wyclif and translated many of his works into Czech. Hus's own teachings were soon denounced in Rome. Czech national feelings entered the scene, also complicated by opposing allegiances to the Roman and Avignon popes. Eventually Hus was excommunicated by the anti-pope John XXIII. Given a safe conduct to the Council of Constance, Hus was arrested and eventually tried. He died bravely at the stake on July 6, 1415 (left), becoming a national hero. But the schism he introduced among his people persisted, and his doctrines were among the most powerful to affect the course of the Reformation.

John Wyclif, by birth a Yorkshireman, as much as any man gave impetus to the Reformation. His Bible, translated from the Vulgate, was the first full version in English, and was a major accomplishment. His theories, which he propounded with vigor and clarity, summarized beliefs which had been undermining the orthodox doctrines of Christians for centuries. In short, Wyclif taught that Christ is man's only overlord and that power should depend on a state of grace; he insisted on the authority of the Scriptures alone and the right of all to have access to them; the poverty of the clergy was another of his teachings. He attacked transubstantiation, and said that the sacraments of the Church are not a prerequisite to grace. Such teachings, which attracted people by the thousands, led to his condemnation as a heretic in 1380 and again in 1382. Wyclif's influence spread to the continent, affecting the Bohemian John Hus and through Hus on Luther.

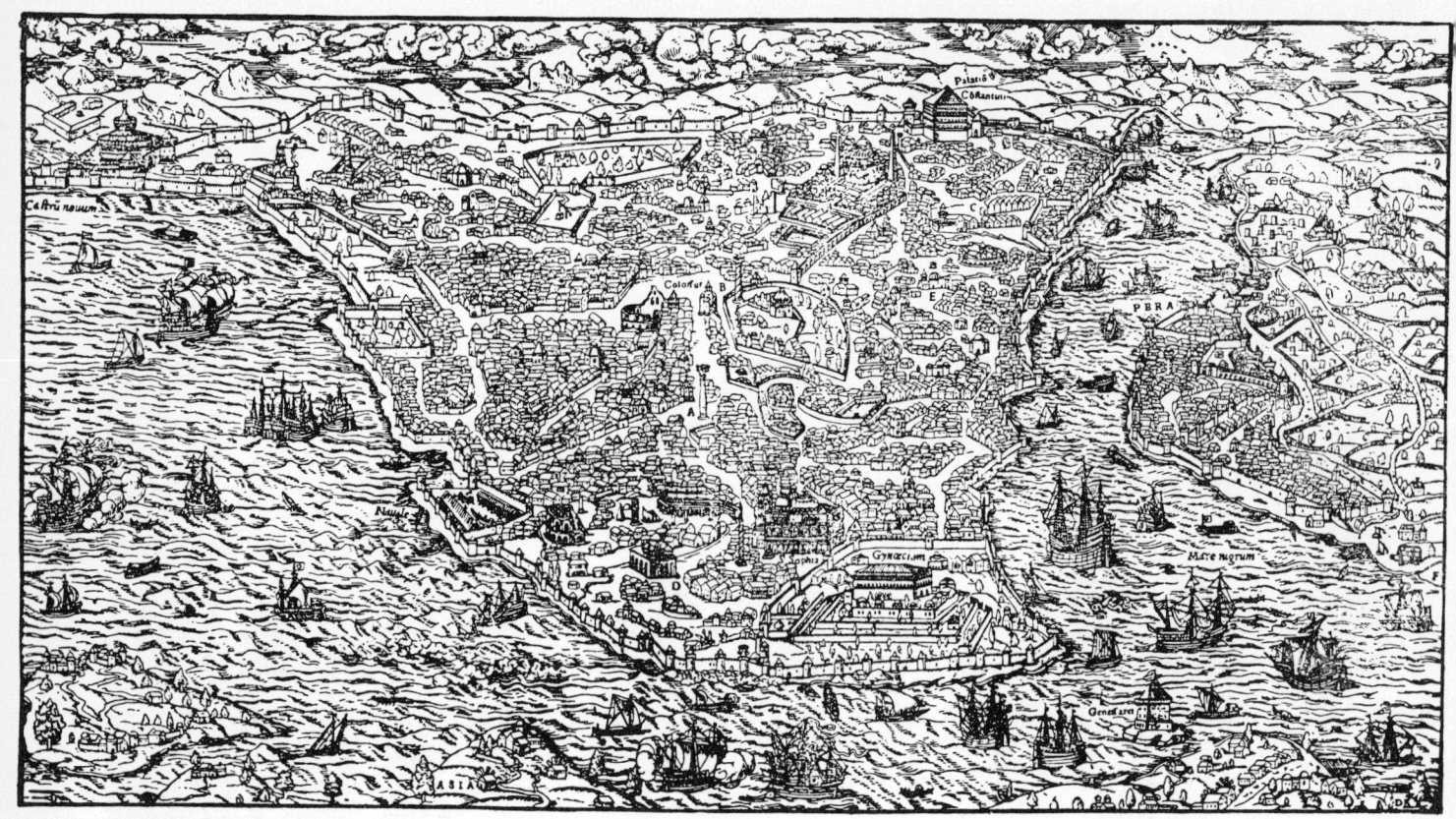

A European map of Constantinople shows the battleground. The Turks attacked the land wall (top) and along the Bosphorus (left). Frustrated by the boom which crossed the mouth of the Golden Horn and thus protected the third wall, the enemy moved his ships overland behind neutral Pera (right) and into the bay.

THE FALL OF BYZANTIUM

On the morning of April 5, 1453, a frightful roaring was heard in Constantinople. The Turks were approaching. Thousands upon thousands of them —200,000 in all—were moving into position along the land wall with a great fanfare of shouts and war cries, accompanied by the terrible blasts of their harsh trumpets and heavy drums. And most frightening of all were the Janissaries, an elite corps composed of Christians captured as children who, for half a century, had given the Turkish army its supremacy in battle. The leader of this deadly host was 23-year-old Sultan Mohamet II. After the midday prayers to Mecca, Mohamet formally announced the siege; at the same time his fleet appeared—it was composed of 500 ships containing another 200,000 Turks and allies.

Thus, on one side were 400,000 skilled soldiers. On the other? Eight thousand, with fifteen ships.

The situation seemed hopeless. Five of the eight thousand were Greeks, many of them monks, the remainder were soldiers of fortune and pirates who had rushed to aid Christendom's Eastern outpost. Constantinople's defenses were commanded by a skilled soldier, a Genoese nobleman named John Giustiniani; her fifteen ships were larger and heavier than the Turks' and she had a chain boom which stretched across the entrance to the Golden Horn; she also had magnificent fortifications which through the centuries had frustrated numerous barbarian attacks.

The battle commenced with a salvo from the greatest gun in the world; it had been pulled by 200 oxen and was escorted by 10,000 soldiers; its barrel was three feet in diameter and expelled a projectile weighing 1,500 pounds; it had been designed by a Christian turn-coat from Byzantium. For a week the gun fired point blank into the city's walls. After each blast women and children rushed forth to repair the walls but they were crumbling and the moat was filling in.

At last, early on the 18th, the Turks hurled themselves upon the walls, attacking with violent cries which could be heard twelve miles away in Asia Minor. Giustiniani and 700 Genoese soldiers of fortune threw them back in four hours of hand to hand fighting. At dawn the Christians went

to Hagia Sophia to give thanks. The Turks now turned to a naval assault; three hundred ships, spewing fire arrows, dashed at the boom. The Byzantine fleet, which had the advantage of higher decks, hurled back a steady shower of stones, javelins, lances and darts; the enemy withdrew. That night the Turks rolled up an enormous siege tower which hurled gigantic rocks, crushing an opening in the wall. The enemy poured into the gap; the defenders hurled them back again, while women and children repaired the wall; the mighty siege tower caught fire and was reduced to ashes. Then Mohamet ordered his engineers to construct a gun capable of destroying the Christian fleet. One was built and its projectile broke a ship in two; the others moved out of range, and the Turks were again frustrated.

The battle went on. From their towers the Byzantines saw four ships on the horizon; they were Christian allies; the Turks attacked them in a moment of calm, and for hours the Christians fought off their attackers with fire, stones, and lances before they gained the safety of the boom. Then, at night, in an incredible feat of engineering, Mohamet moved his ships overland and into the Golden Horn. This left three miles of the eastern wall open to attack; a bitter battle between Greeks and Turks in the bay was inconclusive. Day after day, the attacks continued, each of which the garrison repelled. Turkish engineers began a tunnel under the wall; when the sound of their digging was discovered, they were a quarter of a mile into the city. Directed by a German named John Grant, the garrison dug its own tunnel into the Turks' and wiped out the enemy. New tunnels were crushed; the enemy was burned alive by Greek fire, Byzantium's notorious secret weapon which consumed men in a sheet of flame; new siege towers were overthrown. The siege went on, while the garrison grew smaller and hungrier. On May 27th the Turks wavered and the Sultan considered ending the siege, only to be persuaded to a final assault.

For three days the Greeks watched the enemy regroup his forces; the garrison mended its pitiful defenses, and through the city went long processions chanting the *Kyrie eleison*. The walls were blessed with the holy ikons, which had always protected the city in the past. On May 28th the entire population—Greeks and Italians, Orthodox and Catholic, Emperor Constantine XI and his soldiers, the clergy, merchants and the poor—gathered around Hagia Sophia for the night office.

On the plain before the city, the Sultan gave the order to attack. It was one o'clock in the morning. Inside the walls, Constantine rode among the defenders, giving them his blessing. Fifty thousand Turks made a concerted drive at the walls, while Giustiniani and the 700 Genoese hurled oil and rocks upon them. The enemy recoiled, and the Sultan's Janissaries drove the attackers again into the battle with whips. After two hours the enemy force was decimated. A second force of 50,000 was hurled at the walls and was repelled in three hours of hand to hand combat. At the same time Turkish ships were bombarding the sea walls, probing for weak spots.

No city could have withstood the final assault. Bowmen, archers and musketeers methodically opened fire on the walls, keeping the garrison under cover. The Janissaries, who had not yet fought, moved in safety to the base of the fortifications and threw up ladders. At the same time horrible blasts of horns, fifes, drums, cymbals and cries of "Allah" pierced the steady roar of cannons and small arms. Inside the city the church bells tolled slowly. The Janissaries threw themselves over the walls at Giustiniani. There was furious hand to hand fighting, and the Janissaries appeared to weaken. Was Constantinople to be saved? But a dreadful tragedy occurred. A squad of Janissaries had poured through a gate that had been carelessly left unlocked. The defenders fell into panic, yet rallied and expelled the enemy. But it was too late. Others of the garrison had seen the Turkish banners flying within the walls and had assumed the city had fallen. Then another disaster occurred. Giustiniani was killed by an enemy pikeman. The garrison fled in disorder, and the enemy raced forward. Constantine dismounted from his horse, plunged into the combat and was killed. The Turks reached the heart of the city.

A Christian renegade, who was serving with the Sultan, wrote, "Nothing will ever equal the horror of this harrowing and terrible spectacle. The enraged Turkish soldiers gave no quarter. When they had massacred and there was no longer any resistance, they roamed through the town stealing, pillaging, raping, taking captive men, women, children, old men, young men, monks, priests. All the most sacred places were violated and broken to get out the holy treasures." At Hagia Sophia the Turks paraded about in priests' robes and stabled their horses and women in the sanctuary. Mohamet seized Constantine's teen-age daughters for his harem and killed the young prince. And then, when the slaughter and pillage had ceased, the Sultan walked through the ruined streets, looking at the wreckage. Tears came to his eyes. "What a town this was!" he exclaimed. "And we have allowed it to be destroyed."

Turkish power was not checked until the great naval battle off Lepanto, Greece, in 1571, when a force of over 200 ships from the Christian powers, mainly Spanish, Venetian, and papal, decisively defeated the Moslems. In this picture by Veronese, Venice's patron saints intercede with the Virgin on behalf of the Christian fleet, while the black shadows of anathema fall upon the enemy, and an angel (at the right) hurls burning arrows. Some 15,000 of the Turks were killed or captured and 10,000 Christian galley slaves liberated. A victory would have made the Turks supreme in the Mediterranean.

A procession around Venice's Great Piazza on the Feast of Corpus Christi was painted by Gentile Bellini in 1496.

"God Himself will intervene"

On the surface the smooth tenor of life continued in growing richness and complexity. Arts and the secular culture flourished, and the exterior aspects of the Church grew in magnificence. Great processions, like the one pictured here for the Feast of Corpus Christi in Venice near the end of the fifteenth century were popular manifestations of men's devotion to God. In times of crisis the people paraded daily, imploring heaven to intercede; often they went barefoot and fasting, "weeping piteously, with many tears, in great devotion." But behind the scenes life became more corrupt. In Venice, where men could so proudly proclaim their love of God, the city fathers could, behind closed doors, vote to order the murder of

the duke of Padua (it was to be done by poison, administered by the archbishop of Trebizond; the city fathers shaved the price for the task from 180 ducats, Trebizon's requested fee, to a mere 50). Venice usually kept an official poisoner; attempts were made at poisoning the Holy Roman emperor, popes, kings, sultans, bishops and a host of minor personages; the Venetians even waged germ warfare (with vials of bubonic plague) against hostile troops. But Venice was hardly alone in underhanded deeds. In every city there were plots and counter-plots, assassinations (the Duke of Gandia, eldest son of Pope Alexander VI, was mysteriously murdered and his body dumped into the Tiber one night); there were also continual wars of unbridled violence (when papal troops sacked Florence in 1512 in three weeks of unlimited pillage, women killed their daughters and committed sui-

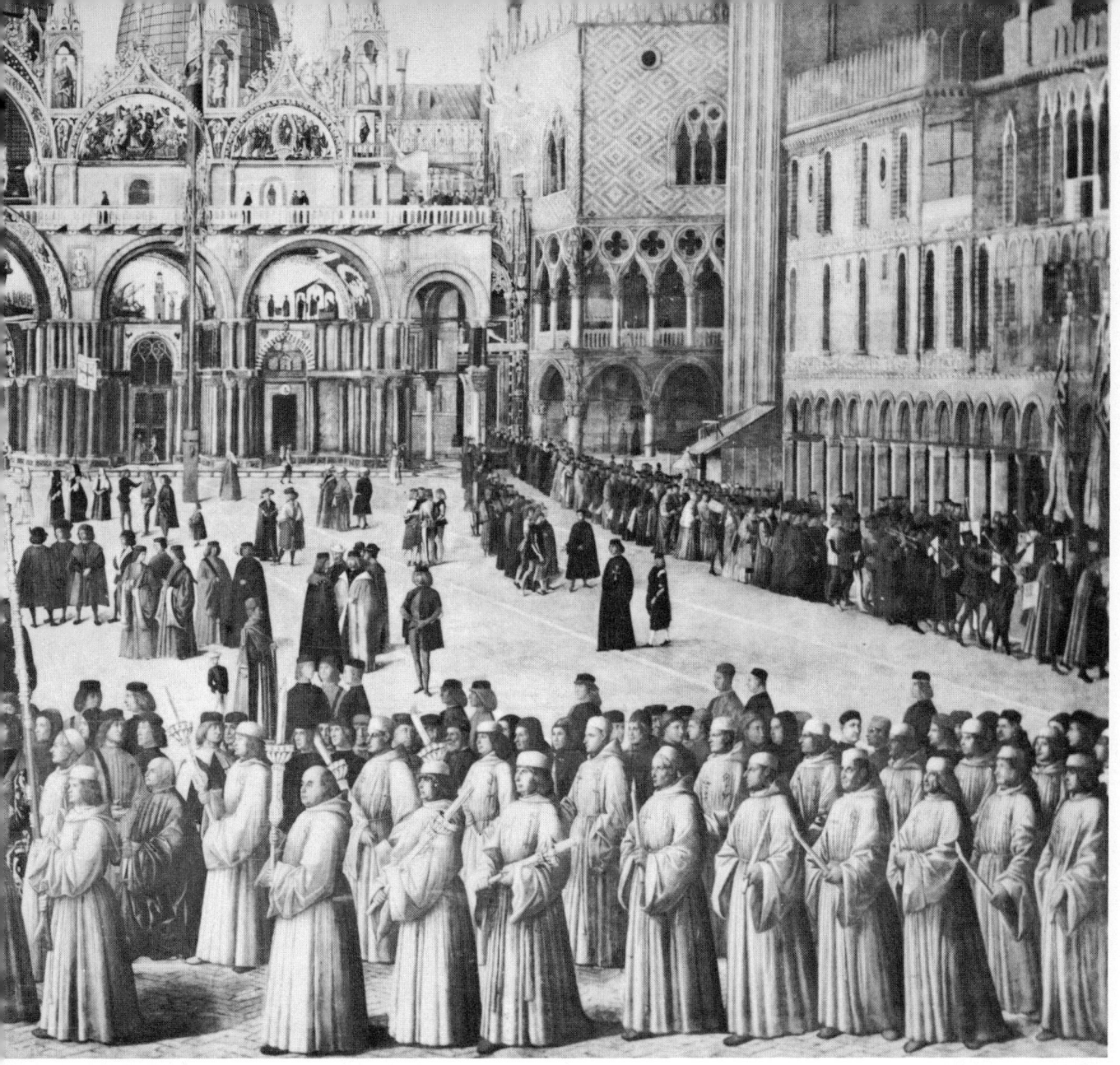

cide to avoid being violated). Perhaps the most dastardly act of an unending series of outrages was the attempt in 1478 on Lorenzo and Giuliano dei Medici, the two young heads of the great banking family. Known as the Pazzi conspiracy, it involved young Cardinal Riaro, a grand nephew of Pope Sixtus IV, an archbishop, two priests and some professional murderers. After an abortive attempt to poison the brothers, it was decided to stab them to death at High Mass at the cathedral of Florence. (One of the professionals squeamishly refused to participate in a murder in church.) A sword thrust split Giuliano's skull as he knelt before the high altar; Lorenzo, attacked by the two priests, was merely wounded and got away without serious harm. The plot collapsed and most of the conspirators were violently executed by the

populace. Riaro escaped; in 1517 he was implicated in a plot to poison Pope Leo X.

But while public figures with powerful friends were likely to go unpunished, more thoughtful men saw a final dreadful day of retribution. Of Leo X, pope during the days of Martin Luther's fateful outbreak (Leo was infamous for appointing 41 cardinals largely for personal or political motives, being richly rewarded for doing so), a perceptive layman, the humanist Pico della Mirandola, wrote, "If Leo leaves crimes unpunished any longer, God Himself will intervene." And the great English bishop, St. John Fisher, commented that, "If the pope will not reform the Curia, God will find means to do it." A collective Judas was at work within the Church, and no one seemed able to halt the impending disaster.

187

The mighty secular spirit of the Renaissance, the vital, splendid concern with art and letters, reached right into the papal court—indeed the popes themselves were the leading patrons of scholars, artists and poets. The rediscovery of classical forms, including the works of Homer, Plato and Aristotle, and Horace, Cicero and Ovid, the finding of buried Roman statuary, the arrival of learned refugees from Byzantium—all contributed to the reaction against the barbarousness of earlier times (for which the phrase "The Dark Ages" was coined). Raphael's painting of a pope surrounded by cherubs and a classical nymph is indicative of the almost pagan frame of mind into which even the Church was sinking.

The worldliness of Christians did not go unchallenged. Toward the end of the fifteenth century the Dominican friar Girolomo Savanarola (right) achieved great fame in Florence by denouncing the immorality of both clergy and laity and preaching repentance. He prophesied on the future, sometimes with startling accuracy. His success brought him to the attention of the notorious Pope Alexander VI (left), who demanded that Savanarola come to Rome for investigation; the monk refused; Alexander forbade him to preach further, a command ignored by Savanarola, who was then excommunicated. His position deteriorated rapidly after that, and, in 1498, he was hanged in the Florence market place, venerated by some as a saint, despised by others as a fanatic.

The appointment of relatives was a common practice of Renaissance popes. Here Pius II, the Sienese Aeneas Piccolomini, places the cardinal's hat on a favorite nephew. "Those who surrounded [Pius] were almost all Sienese, and of these Sienese, the majority were Piccolomini," said one commentator.

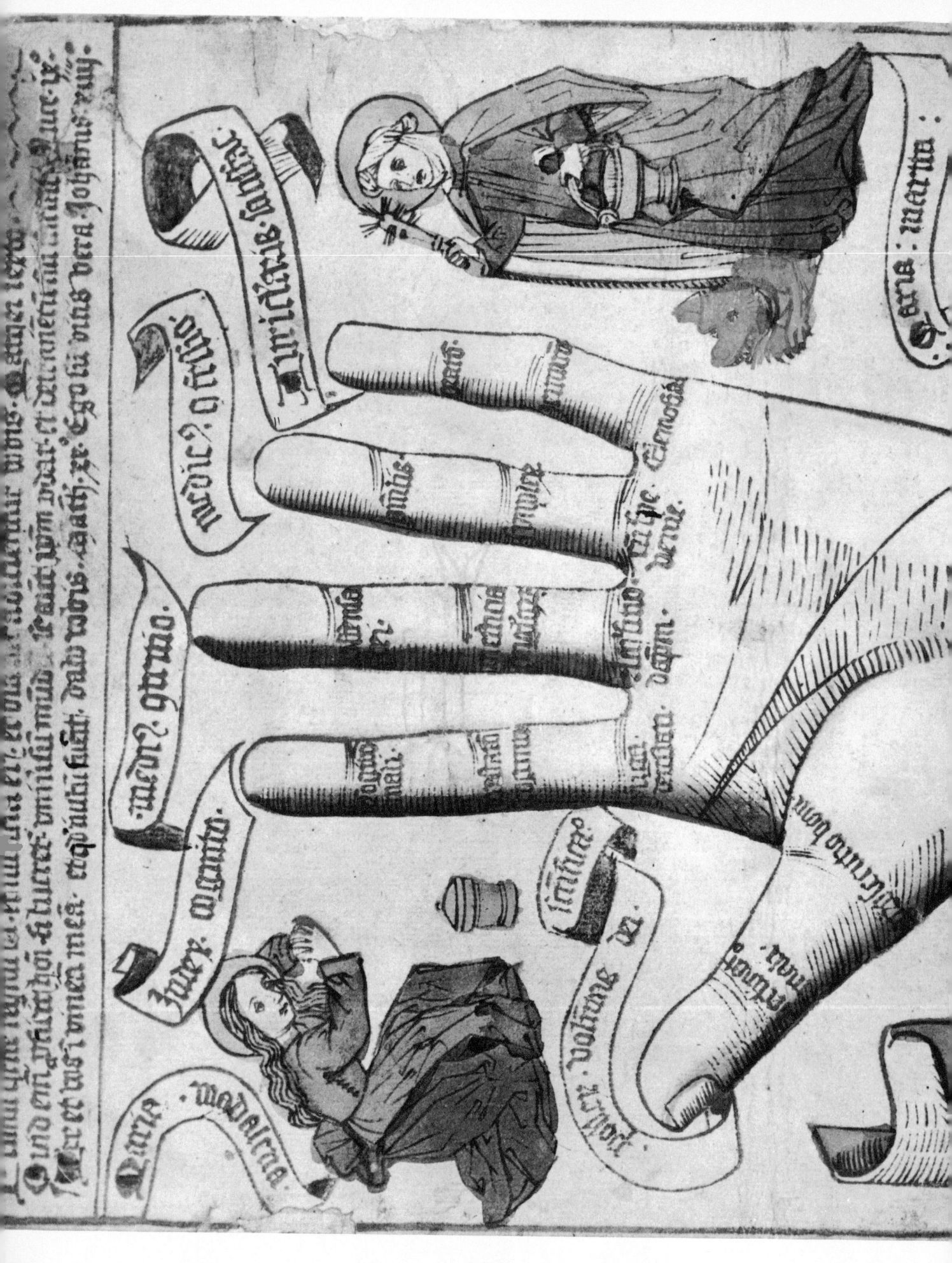

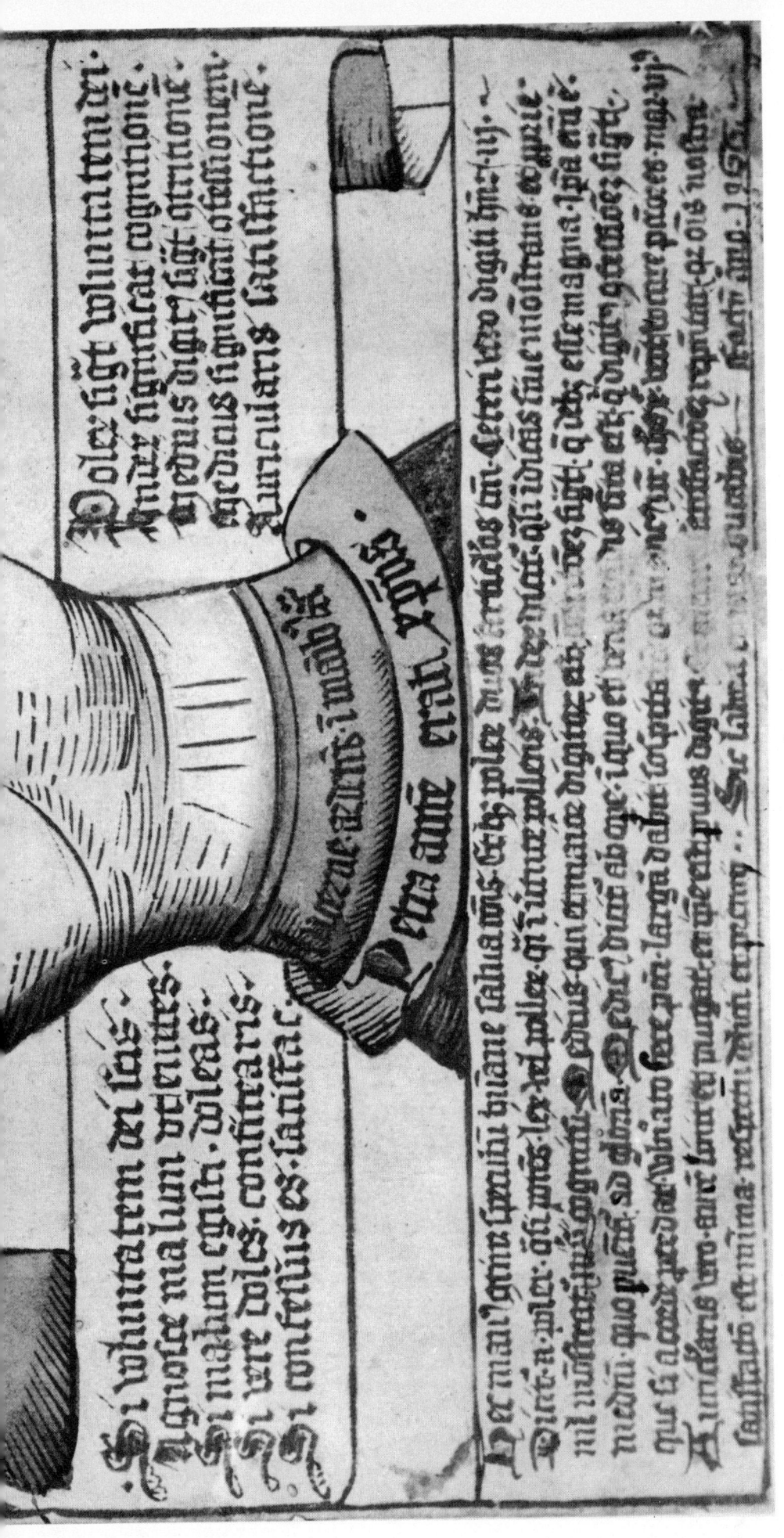

"The Hand with the Mirror of Salvation"

In the fifteenth century few outside the clergy had adequate educations. Simple devotional prints aided the layman in his spiritual life. Their use was widespread, and on occasion they were employed by poorer members of the priesthood, themselves often only partially educated. The giant hand above was printed in Suabia in 1466 as a guide to the examination of conscience. Mary Magdalen, identified by her ointment jar, kneels above the thumb as the symbol of the repentant sinner. Facing her is Mary Martha with a dragon (a symbol of evil) which she subjugated with holy water. For those who could read, two short verses

by the wrist explained the symbolism of the five fingers and told what must be done to achieve a good confession:

Si voluntatem dei scis	When thou knowest the will of the Lord
Agnosce malum ut euites	Then own the faults in order to avoid them
Si malum egisti, doleas	When thou hast done evil then repent of it
Si vere doles, confitearis	When thou verily repentest then confess it
Si confessus es, satisfac	When thou hast confessed then do penance
Polex significat voluntatem dei	The thumb signifies God's will
Index significat cognitionem	The forefinger signifies the examination
Medius digitus significat contricionem	The middle-finger signifies the repentance
Medicus significat confessionem	The ring-finger signifies the confession
Auricularis satisfactionem	The ear-finger signifes the satisfaction

The first printed books

Gutenberg's remarkable discovery of movable type helped revolutionize society and contribute to the end of the Middle Ages. Printing also freed education and learning from the control of the clerical world. With the advent of the mass-produced book and pamphlet, it was now possible—in theory at least—for every man to learn to read.

Gutenberg was born in Mainz in 1396 and was trained as a goldsmith. By 1448 he was experimenting with movable type cast in separate letters. He became involved in financial difficulties, losing most of his property, but was able to produce a complete Bible in 1456. Known as the Mazarin Bible (after the name of one of its owners, Cardinal Mazarin), it was probably the first book printed in Europe, and was an extremely beautiful work. It was issued in two volumes, each page printed in two columns, with 42 lines per column. Forty copies are known to have survived (of which only two are absolutely complete). In his old age Gutenberg was pensioned by the archbishop of Mainz and continued to work until his 98th year.

The art of printing spread rapidly. Many printers learned their craft at Mainz where Gutenberg had established his shop. Next to the Bible, psalters and books about Mary were popular. The illustrations for such books were carved in wood and were used over and over again with a frequency disconcerting to the historian.

The fault of the Gutenberg Bible was that it was printed from the current manuscript versions, which contained errors due to the mistakes of copyists over the centuries (there was some work on the text during the following century, but an authoritative edition did not appear until Sixtus V in 1585). In Gutenberg's time the best manuscripts were as yet unknown to scholars or were unavailable; the result is that the texts of the sixteenth and seventeenth centuries were full of inaccuracies, although they did not affect the fundamentals of the faith.

An early print shop.

The first illustrated book to be printed in Italy (at Rome, in 1467) was the MEDITATIONES *of Johannes de Turrecremata. This page shows the Assumption.*

Irmiſſime credimus domine iheſu q̃ tu qui de honorandis
parentibus legem hominibus tradidiſti·glorioſã matrẽ tuã
i eius aſſũptione ita oĩmoda ĩ corpore ⁊ aĩa illuſtraueris gloria·
⁊ honore ſublimaueris·ut nulla mortalis lingua ualeat exprimer̃
Quis eni cogitare ſufficiat q̃ honorabiliter hodie regina mũdi p̃
ceſſerit·quãto deuotionis affectu·tota in eius occurſu celeſtiũ legi
onũ ̃pdierit multitudo·quãtis ad thronũ glorie canticis ſit deduc
ta·q̃ placido uultu·q̃ ſerena facie q̃ diuinis ampleribus a filio ſit
ſuſcepta ⁊ ſup omnẽ creaturã exaltata Glorificemus ergo uirginẽ
quã hodie padiſus excepit gaudẽs·quã angeli cũ laudibus p̃ſecũt
quã ap̃lo̅z chorus uenerat̃·quã martires cãdidati beatificãt·quã
ſanctorũ cõfeſſorũ incolatus cõcelebrat numerus·cui hodie ſanc
torũ uirginũ cũ ſuis palmis iuictricibus exultans occurrit exerci
tus·quoniã hec ẽ p̃ quã ois maledictio ſoluta eſt·⁊ celeſtis bene=
dictio in totũ uenit mundũ·Clama ergo fidelis aĩa O maria ſtella
maris·dignitate ſingularis·in ſupremo ſita poli·nos cõmẽda tue
̃pli·ut tecum letemur in gloria·

Continental reformation leaders are seen clustered around their protector, John Frederick the Magnanimous, elector of Saxony, in this detail from a painting by Lucas Cranach the Elder. At the left: Luther and John Oecolampadius, a Swiss who promoted Luther's views; at the right foreground: Huldreich Zwingli and Phillip Melanchthon. John Frederick's family sheltered Luther at Wartburg castle after he refused to recant his heretical propositions.

THE GREAT REVOLT

The Great Schism signaled the end of the pope as an important figure on the stage of history. The other great personage of the medieval scene, the Holy Roman emperor, had also disappeared as a significant power. The states themselves were now attaining greater autonomy in both political and religious affairs: Europe was undergoing a metamorphosis, new nations were on the threshold of birth, and old powers were gaining freedom from imperial ties. The pope could no longer force the submission of a disobedient emperor, nor of the national kings. The papacy was still dominant within the Church, but the Church was taking a new form. Having lost its temporal influence in Europe, it became increasingly concerned with religion alone. And yet there were forces abroad

which were to challenge it even in that sphere.

In 1537—a generation too late, it might be said —Pope Paul received a memorial from a group of cardinals and other prelates he had appointed to look into the evils afflicting the Church. The Commission, in a report of startling frankness, listed 28, beginning with misuse of ecclesiastical wealth and going on to abuses within the Curia and others throughout the Church. Substantially the same things had been pointed out, though in gentle terms, since the beginning of the century but the damage had been done. Christendom had been in a highly unstable and inflammatory condition for decades: there was ecclesiastical misconduct, maladministration on all levels of Church society, heavy taxes imposed by the Church, an often il-

literate or uninstructed clergy. Heightening the tensions within the Church was widespread anti-clerical propaganda (effective because it was often based on known fact), a decline of Catholic teaching, a conviction that the Scriptures could be individually interpreted, and a spread of humanistic ideas. The discovery of new lands in the Western hemisphere and new routes to the East, with the invitation of wealth beyond the farthest dreams for the adventurous and their financiers, had also wrought a change in the social fabric.

The age was ready to rebel, and it did. The first skirmish centered around the German priest-monk Martin Luther, whose tentative challenge of a common abuse turned into a full-scale rebellion.

JOHANNES TECELIUS PIRNENSIS
Dominicanus, Nundinator Romani Pontificis, anno
1517. à μεγαλαυδεω Luthero territus & in fugam versus,
uti talis ejus effigies visitur in templo Pirnensi.

O ihr Deutschen mercket mich recht,
    Des heiligen Vaters Bapstes Knecht
Bin Ich, vnd bring euch ihr allein
    Zehn tausent vnd neun hundert tausent,
Gnad vnd Ablaß von einer Sünd,
    Vor euch, ewer Eltern, Weib vnd Kind,
Sol ein jeder gewehret sein,
    So viel ihr legt ins Kästelein,
So bald der Gülden im Becken klingt,
    Im hun die Seel in Himmel springt.

The fiery Dominican John Tetzel (here seen in a satiric woodcut selling indulgences) was the spark that unwittingly ignited Luther's revolt against the Church. In 1516 the indulgence had been issued to help the rebuilding of St. Peter's in Rome. Tetzel was assigned to preach in Germany, but the extravagance of his claims was causing scandal. The indulgence was not permitted in Saxony and Tetzel was forbidden to preach there. When Tetzel arrived in a small German town on all Hallows' Eve in 1517 to preach sermons recommending indulgences, Martin Luther, attached to the Augustinian monastery in nearby Wittenberg, nailed a document containing 95 theses, some of which attacked the validity of indulgences, to the door of the castle church. The challenge to a disputation was an ordinary custom among scholars, but Luther's aroused such excitement that he felt it important to send letters by way of explanation to two bishops. Tetzel replied to Luther with two counter-theses defending the Catholic position, but the controversy soon involved most of Europe.

Luther's challenge to the Church

At the end of the fifteenth century there were nearly 7,000 courtesans in Rome, hardly an edifying scene for the pilgrim to report at home. Popes, cardinals and the higher clergy appeared in public with their mistresses, acknowledged their illegitimate children and even enriched them with the proceeds from their benefices. Many of the higher clergy were completely worldly, and it was through the patronage of cardinals, bishops and popes that the humanistic revival succeeded. The state of the lower clergy was hardly better.

It is against this scene that Luther's protest and final revolt must be measured. The son of a miner in Saxony, he distinguished himself in school and planned to become a lawyer. However, in 1642 a fear of the afterlife incurred witnessing a friend's death led him to drop his career and become an Augustinian monk. But he failed to find peace as a cleric in the monastery, though in 1508 he achieved some relaxation of the fears that hounded him through being assigned by the general of his order to a chair in theology at the University of Wittenberg. It was there that his thinking culminated in the famous theses against the sale of indulgences and led to the shattering of the Christian world.

Luther's protest was acclaimed by many and understood by few. It was a popular revolt, yet the real ideas that sparked it were above the heads of most of Luther's followers. Luther's fundamental concern—to simplify a very complex issue—was whether and in what way he could be absolutely certain about his eternal salvation. A misinterpretation of basic Catholic teaching on hope, confused with his personal conviction of the fulfillment of this hope, led him to believe that man could not earn a claim to salvation by deeds (or lack of them), but by faith alone. Abuses in the Church and the supersitions of the people about indulgences only helped confirm Luther's thinking. What attracted the ordinary people were the attacks upon the clergy high and low, the denunciation of the traffic in holy things, the deriding of the sacraments, the hope of political and economic freedom from the control of the no-

bles and the chance to read the Bible (which had been so long kept from them except when doled out in fragments by the clergy). For their part, the nobles saw an end to Rome's interference in their affairs and the opportunity for spoils from the secularization of ecclesiastical estates. A great revolt was underway, and the curious thing is that, aside from some specialized attacks on Luther's doctrines, the Church did almost nothing to combat it. In general, neither princes nor people came to the aid of the Church, and in its turn, the Church was apathetic in seeking the help of the nobles or in influencing the common people. By the time an awakening came, half of Europe had turned against the Church.

Luther was serious and pessimistic ("All we do is in vain, even in the best life," he once said). He was a brilliant orator but unscrupulous in argument, and as a writer had a fine command of language.

Luther, hat in hand, appears before Charles V at the imperial diet at Worms. For two days he and the papal delegates sparred in Latin over his theses, at the end of which he refused to recant. Then he went into hiding to avoid assassination.

Attempts to end the revolt

At the Diet of Worms, on April 18, 1521, Luther appeared before Charles V, the Holy Roman Emperor, to defend his doctrines. The papal delegate had already appeared and stated his case against Luther. However Luther refused to recant, concluding his answer, according to popular belief, with the words, *"Hie stehe ich. Ich kann nicht anders. Gott helff mir. Amen."* The next month his teachings were formally condemned in the Edict of Worms. However, the German princes entered the dispute, turning a religious quarrel into a grave political issue. Five years later, at the Diet of Speyer, they demanded both the prohibition of the Mass and the suppression of religious orders. A compromise decree tried to hold matters to the status quo (Europe was being invaded by the Turks and an attempt at preventing internal dissension was being made), but some princes went ahead with their innovations. In 1529, again at Speyer, the Emperor decreed the freedom of Catholic worship everywhere, and called for an end to the innovations, but the pro-Luther princes objected, gaining for themselves the title of "Protestants."

Charles V, the Holy Roman emperor, assumed
his throne at the age of nineteen, just at the
outbreak of the Lutheran rebellion. He soon became
the most powerful man in Europe, his sovereignty
extending not only to the empire, but to
Burgundy, the Netherlands, the kingdom of Naples,
Spain and the Spanish colonies in America. His
most constant problem was the rise of Protestantism
and the revolt of the Lutheran princes. Though
Charles achieved some successes, the Protestant
nobles finally forced him out of Germany; at
Augsburg in 1555 he was forced to accept the
principle of "CUIUS REGIO, EIUS RELIGIO." To avoid
the further conflict implied by this rule within
his own lands, Charles abdicated the next
year; he died in a Spanish monastery in 1558

1526

VIVENTIS·POTVIT·DVRERIVS·ORA·PHILIPPI
MENTEM·NON·POTVIT·PINGERE·DOCTA
MANVS

Luther's disciple and greatest ally was Philipp Melanchthon, who was professor of Greek at Wittenberg. Melanchthon recast
Luther's doctrines in more organized and rational form, and drew up the first coherent presentation of reformist beliefs.
A student of the Bible, he translated some of the texts and wrote commentaries, breaking new ground for biblical studies,
treating the New Testament like the classics and calling for their understanding in the light of both history and archeology.
He was the leading figure at the Diet of Augsburg in 1530, where a Confession presented the Lutheran doctrines in 21
articles and called for remedies to the abuses as seen by Luther and his followers. Durer's study of Melanchthon shows
him as he looked in early days of the revolt.

200

Armed with farm implements, peasants slaughter nobles.

The German peasants revolt

A side effect of Luther's revolt was an uprising of the peasants, the *bauern*. In Germany the status of the peasant had increasingly deteriorated since the Middle Ages, and a form of serfdom was being re-established, in which all the rights the people had gained earlier were being abrogated. With the first success of the Reformation the peasants took a further step: they attacked the nobles who were oppressing them. In 1524 riots broke out; the revolt spread from Luxemburg to Bohemia, in some places gaining the support of the urban populations. The next year the peasants, aided by a number of knights and apostate priests, presented a charter called the Twelve Articles which demanded not only religious but social liberty, and the end of abuses and restoration of ordinary rights. Luther professed agreement with the Articles but soon advocated a ruthless extermination of the rebels when the violence got out of hand. Peasant bands burned castles and monasteries. The nobles were forced to agree to the conditions of the Articles. A chiliastic spirit seized the rebels under the fanatic teachings of the brilliant Anabaptist, Thomas Münzer, who preached the coming of a world of love and justice, to be achieved, however, by the massacre of the unrighteous. Suddenly the Protestant nobles' resistance stiffened. In the battle of Frankenhausen, on May 15th, 1526, the peasant bands were cut to pieces. The knights pitilessly revenged themselves upon the poor, imposing a heavier yoke than ever before.

FRANCISCVS·VON·SICKINGEN

ALLEIN·GOT·DI·ER·LIEB
DEN·GEMEINE·NVCZ·BESCH
IRM·DI·GERECHTIKEI
I H

The German knight, Franz von Sickingen, was typical of the many nobles who threw in their lot with Luther, not only because of religious beliefs but because they saw a chance for personal gain. Von Sickingen was a leader of bands of LANDSKNECHTE, *who pretended to help the weak and oppressed but usually took the chance of plunder and murder. Though he was Imperial Councilor to Charles V, von Sickingen took up the cause of the reformers, opening his castles to them as places of refuge; by his support he hoped to seize power from the princes of the Church and enrich himself and his knights. In 1522 he led a campaign against the Archbishop of Trier, but was repulsed. The archbishop, aided by other princes, pursued von Sickingen and cornered him at Landstuhl. In the defence the knight was mortally wounded, surrendering before death.*

Das Alte Testament deutsch.

M. Luther.

Wittemberg.

The first part of Luther's famous translation of the Bible
appeared in 1522. However, contrary to popular belief,
Luther's was not the first vernacular version in German:
nineteen full Bibles, plus Psalters and other books,
appeared starting in 1466. In the hands of the reformers
the Bible became a weapon by which to reach the common
people. The Church on its side feared the advisability of
letting uneducated or partly educated people read the
Scriptures without the accompaniment of oral commentaries
and instruction. Luther's Bible has stood to this day as
the great German translation.

A Cranach woodcut shows Luther and Hus administering Communion under both Species, a popular move of the
Reformers. However, the various leaders did not agree over the nature of the Eucharist, and for many Protestants the
celebration eventually became little more than a memorial rite.

The revolt reaches Switzerland

In Switzerland the attack on the Church equalled that in Germany. Huldreich Zwingli was a year younger than Luther and paralleled his efforts in the revolt. A Swiss priest, he took up Luther's doctrines with the support of local authorities. Both clergy and laymen were in a deplorable state and the new teaching was popularly accepted. Indulgences, a prime target of the reformers, were abolished, as were the Mass and the sacraments of Penance and Extreme Unction. Altars, sacred vessels and holy pictures, and relics of the saints were destroyed. Like Luther, Zwingli advocated the end of clerical celibacy and eventually married. The state took over Church property. Switzerland, like Germany, fell into two hostile groups. In Zurich and Basle, Catholic monasteries were closed. Catholics were expelled from the Great Council. In 1529 the Catholic cantons came together in a pact of mutual self defense and war broke out with the Protestants, in the course of which, in 1531, Zwingli was killed.

Meanwhile, another reformer had also appeared on the scene in Switzerland. He was a French-born lawyer, John Calvin, who found Switzerland more congenial to his strict doctrines. He made Geneva his headquarters, and from there, through a theological academy whose pupils proselytized most of Europe, led the reform of Christian worship and doctrine. Industrious and skillful, a prolific correspondent, and sermon writer (some 2,300 of his manuscripts are still extant), he had a far-reaching effect upon Europe. He published catechisms in Latin and French, composed a new liturgy (introducing the congregational singing of the Psalter) and organized a theocracy. Severe penalties brought conformity to his ideas, and several non-believers, particularly other Protestants, were executed.

Nevertheless, Calvin's harsh doctrines were eagerly accepted by people who a generation before had been morally lax, and they spread across Europe. His chief teaching, one which was to do irreparable harm for centuries to come, was the irrevocable predestination of man, either to salvation or to damnation. The Huguenots of France, the Presbyterians of Scotland, the English Puritans and all their descendants were among the leading inheritors of the Calvinistic doctrines.

Zwingli, who at first had agreed with Luther's doctrines, soon went radically beyond him on many points, particularly in his view of the Eucharist, where he denied any presence of Christ at all.

An early portrait of John Calvin.

*The block print and the printing press were valuable weapons in the religious wars between Catholic and Protestant.
Here a set of woodcuts by Cranach are used to attack the Church. At the top, Cranach contrasts the difference between
Christ's washing of his apostles' feet and the pope's having his foot kissed; at the bottom, Christ drives money changers
from the temple while the pope is seen taking gold and silver for the sale of indulgences.*

206

LUTHER   PABST   CALVINUS

A Catholic attack on the reformers shows the pope holding his ears against the noisy squabble as Luther pulls Calvin's beard (Calvin had called the German "a minister of Satan"). Below: A cartoon shows Luther and his wife, the 26-year-old Katharina von Bora, a former nun, and their child; on Luther's back are some of his followers; in the barrow his chief lieutenants and Bibles; and in his hand a tiara signifying that he has set himself up as pope of the new church

In this family sketch by Holbein, More is the central figure. Brilliant and self-disciplined, he rose rapidly in his profession of the law and at 26 was elected to Parliament. A trusted friend of the King's, More represented Henry on the most difficult missions. As a humanistic scholar, More was interested in the revival of Greek and Latin culture. His

UTOPIA *pictures an ideal state where all is ordered for the best of mankind as a whole and from which evils such as poverty have been abolished.*

The Reformation in England

An Italian who visited England in 1500 wrote of the people: "They all attend Mass every day and say many *Paternosters* in public. The women carry long rosaries in their hands and any who can read take the Office of Our Lady and with some companion recite it in church verse by verse, in a low voice, after the manner of Churchmen. On Sunday they always hear Mass in their parish church and give liberal alms." This testimony to the faith of the English was corroborated by others. Yet within two generations, on the whim of a profligate English king, the Church to which these people belonged was to be destroyed, the lands and buildings expropriated and hundreds of its members executed or imprisoned. As on the continent, the fault lay not with the common people but with their leaders, the men of good family who saw the Church less as a vocation than a means to a profitable living. St. John Fisher, one of the first to fall before the English Reformation, said of the English bishops, "The fort is betrayed even of them which should have defended it."

The Reformation in England did not at first involve questions of doctrine. Henry VIII's spirited attack on Luther won the thirty-year-old king, in 1521, the title of "Defender of the Faith" from Pope Leo X. (Henry had said, "the whole Church is not only subject to Christ, but, for Christ's sake, to Christ's only vicar, the Pope of Rome.") The primary goal of the English reformers was the wealth of the Church; doctrinal changes came later, after Henry, led into opposition with the papacy as the result of his attempt to annul his marriage to Catherine of Aragon in favor of Anne Boleyn, began his piece-meal dissolution of the Church. Henry had been attracted to Anne (then only fourteen) when she came to his court from France in 1521. Six years later he initiated proceedings to dissolve his marriage to Catherine. By 1532 Anne was openly the king's mistress; the next year she became pregnant and they were married. This union was unpopular among the people and brought the outright opposition of Sir Thomas More, Henry's Lord Chancellor. Unwilling to support the adulterous marriage, More resigned (an act that cost him almost all his fortune) and went into retirement. Henry, in a complete reversal of his earlier insistence on the primacy of the Pope, sought recognition himself for himself as titular head of the Church in England, and gained the assent of all but one of the bishops—John Fisher—all but one of the lay officials—Thomas More—and of all the secular and religious clergy except for a Brigittine prior, a group of Carthusians, and two or three isolated, courageous others. Fisher, More and the monks went to the scaffold within a few weeks of each other. More's dying words summarized the conflict when he said, "I die the King's good servant, but God's first."

Once estranged from Rome and common Christian morality, Henry could not stop. Tired of Anne, he had her beheaded on charges of adultery in 1536 and ten days after the execution married Jane Seymour, the third of his six wives. In repeated steps he dissolved the last ties with Rome, suppressed the monasteries (their wealth went to the Crown and its friends), and established a national church. A Catholic uprising, the Pilgrimage of Grace, was ruthlessly crushed, though Henry still considered himself Catholic; his attempts to prove it included the burning of a Protestant woman for heretical ideas on the Eucharist. But Protestant ideas were not to be held down: after Henry's death in 1547 Protestantism became the official doctrine of England and every effort was made to exterminate all traces of Catholicism.

Henry's successor, his son Edward VI by Jane Seymour, was only ten when he attained the throne. The real force in England, the Calvinistically-inclined Privy Council, brought about the revolution in doctrines that was to give the English church its special character. The changes paralleled those on the Continent: attacks on the Mass, the liturgy and the Bible in the vernacular, Communion under both species, the recognition of clerical marriages, a gradual undermining of traditional Catholic teachings, and the confirmation of authority in a national church. Mass was forbidden, and there were severe penalties, including death, for non-attendance at services of the national church. English Catholics fled to the Continent (particularly to Douai, where in Elizabeth's time, a seminary was established and an English translation of the Bible begun); an underground was established to smuggle priests and laymen back into the country and thus to keep the rudiments of the Faith. But the weight of the state was too great: by oppressive legislation, faked plots, rigged trials, lying propaganda, and the execution of priests and laity, the state managed to bring Catholicism to a point of near-extinction and keep it there for almost two hundred years. At the same time its own Protestantism gradually declined into an insipid form of Christianity.

Edmund Campion is typical of the brave men who worked in the Catholic underground to bring the Faith to his people. Born in 1540 a member of the national church (in which he was ordained a deacon), young Campion became increasingly pro-Catholic while abroad. He was received into the Church at 21, and joined the Jesuits. After ordination he worked in Bohemia, returning to England in 1580 in the first Jesuit mission. Great success greeted his efforts, but he was arrested the following year. Offered his life if he would return to the national church, he refused, was put to the rack, and after experiencing great torture, died on December 1, 1581.

The illegitimate daughter of Henry VIII and Anne Boleyn, Queen Elizabeth, who herself lacked religious conviction, sought a mean between the Catholicism of the people and the Calvinism of the ruling classes. However she was more and more drawn into Protestantism and was eventually excommunicated by Pius V. Under her rule the persecution of Catholics increased. The defeat of the Spanish Armada by her admirals in 1588 removed English fears of domination by a Catholic power and brought about a creative, energetic nationalism which resulted in a flowering of literature and music and England's expansion into the world. It was during Elizabeth's reign that England became the foremost Protestant power of Europe

The headsman's axe ends the unhappy career of Mary Queen of Scots. A dynamic, stormy personality, though devoutly religious in later life, Mary was constantly charged, often unfairly, with involvement in plots and counter-plots. She was also accused, with how much justification no one knows, of conspiring with Bothwell (whom she later married) in the murder of her second husband, Henry Stuart.

The unlucky queen

In Scotland, John Knox inflamed nobles and people against the Church. Civil war ravaged the country: the Scottish primate, Cardinal Beaton, was assassinated; Knox led Protestants to seize the castle of St. Andrew, while English troops crossed the border to meet and defeat Scottish Catholics in the battle of Pinkie in 1547. The young queen, Mary Stuart, was sent to France, where, in 1558, only sixteen, she married the Dauphin, later known as King Francis II.

In vain Catholic leaders tried to correct the serious abuses which affected the Church in their country, but it was too late. The Protestant movement was too powerfully entrenched, and new outbreaks were soon to happen. In 1557, a group of nobles, under the name of the "Lords of the Congregation," swore to promote the new doctrines, demanding toleration for their form of worship. The government refused and the next year Knox was at the head of mobs attacking churches and monasteries. Civil war followed, the French aiding the Catholics, the English the Protestants. By 1560, the rebels were strong enough to force a pact which led to the establishing of Protestantism as the state religion. As in England Mass was prohibited under pain of death. The considerable fortunes of the Church were expropriated, its properties going to certain of the rebels.

Despite the triumph of her enemies, the unhappy Mary, Queen of Scots, now nineteen, returned to her homeland. Francis II had died, and Mary married first Henry Stuart, Lord Darnley, who was murdered a few years later (1567), then the Earl of Bothwell. But English intrigues and a rising of the Scottish nobles brought her abdication and imprisonment; she escaped, fled unwisely to seek refuge with her cousin, Queen Elizabeth, a mistake which she was to repent at leisure during nineteen hard years in English prisons. Attempts by Catholics to free her always ended in disaster, and finally, to insure her exclusion from the throne in case Elizabeth should die, she was cruelly murdered. Meanwhile, a determined policy enforced by law and by murder, made the doctrines of Calvinism victorious in Scotland. Only in a few isolated areas, mainly the highlands and the outlying islands, did Catholicism survive.

John Knox inflames th[e]
Scottish leaders against the Church

212

The Council of Trent

The first major Catholic attempt to meet and discuss the Protestant revolt took place in 1545 when, after almost ten years of delays caused by the hostility of princes or the indifference of certain bishops, and the general unsettled political conditions, Pope Paul III was able to bring together a small group of prelates at Trent, within imperial territory.

The meeting was the Church's nineteenth ecumenical council. It spanned eighteen years (and the reigns of five popes) and was often interrupted, but it gradually gained widespread support, brought about reforms in innumerable areas and touched off at least a partial revitalization of Catholic life. Special conferences of theologians and canonists prepared material for the bishops to discuss and evaluate: out of 25 sessions came decrees on the Holy Eucharist, and other sacraments, and an elaborate series of reform decrees. An early decision of the council was to discuss dogma and disciplinary reform concurrently. Consequently over the years the equal validity of Scriptures and tradition was asserted; the sacraments (particularly the Eucharist and Baptism) were carefully defined; the Lutheran, Calvinist and Zwinglian doctrines on the Eucharist were considered at length but were repudiated in favor of that of transubstantiation; and it was affirmed that to receive the Body and Blood of Christ it is not necessary to communicate under both Species.

Vast changes in the discipline of the Church struck at the roots of the abuses that had encouraged the reformers. Many bishops were deprived of benefices and other privileges; in the papal territories dissolute clergy were arrested, some going to the galleys or prison; monasteries were reformed, and honest bishops and clergy dispatched to take over notorious trouble spots. The orders (particularly the Jesuits), played a vital role in the reforms. What could not be accomplished by the council was assigned to the Pope to complete: thus a revision of the Vulgate, the founding of the Congregation of the Index, the publication of a catechism and a revision of the Breviary followed from the council. The work of the council touched all areas of Catholic life, and affects Catholics even today; yet one of its major goals was never accomplished: when it opened in 1545 there were hopes that a significant portion of the Protestants

could be reconciled to the Church, but during the nearly two decades of the council Protestant tendencies hardened, and by 1563, when Pius IV dissolved the council, Europe (and the New World) was still split into two hostile factions. The Protestant initiative was to continue for a century more before it too would be besieged by the forces of a secular enlightenment.

Titian's painting of the Council of Trent
shows mitred bishops in session.

Seriously wounded in battle in 1521, the Spanish knight Ignatius of Loyola studied the lives of the saints during a long convalescence, and was converted to a life dedicated solely to the service of God. After a trip to the Holy Land (where he had hoped to preach to the Moslems), he and six companions, all newly ordained priests, went to Rome to place themselves at the disposal of Pope Paul III. The zeal, learning and courage of the new community, the Society of Jesus (nicknamed "Jesuits"), involved its members in difficulties with jealous fellow Catholics, but at the same time threw them into the heart of the Counter-Reformation. They became one of the most valued instruments for aiding the renewal and reformation of the Church. Though they subordinated the individual to the Society and the Church, some of the greatest figures of the Counter-Reformation were Jesuits, among them not only Ignatius (whose death mask is seen here) but Francis Xavier, Francis Borgia, Peter Canisius, Aloysius Gonzaga and Robert Bellarmine, all of them canonized.

All across Europe and the New World the battle for men's souls was waged with violence. This illustration from a broadsheet shows the fate of William Gardiner, an English merchant and a Protestant, who was strung up over a fire by an angry mob in Portugal. When his feet had been consumed by the flames, his "tormentors asked hym whether he did not yet repent hym." Gardiner answered, "The truth remayneth always one and lyke unto it selfe." He was dropped into the flames.

St. Teresa, of Avila.

The Spanish mystic, Teresa of Avila, brought a reform in the extremely lax monastic life of Spain, thereby effecting the life of the religious in other countries. Professed at twenty, St. Teresa underwent a series of mystical experiences—interior conversations, mystical marriage and the piercing of her heart by God's love—of great intensity. She received excellent spiritual direction, but her superiors and the other nuns constantly derided her and censured her. "It seems to be," she wrote, "there is no reason why I should live but only to suffer, and accordingly this is the thing which I beg with most affection of God. Sometimes I say to Him with my whole heart: Lord, either to die or to suffer; I beg no other thing for myself." Eventually, after 25 years in the relaxed and near-corrupt atmosphere of a typical convent, she endeavored to begin a foundation that would return to the primitive Carmelite rule. Almost universal opposition greeted her, but finally, in 1562, she was able to open St. Joseph's monastery for women. The opposition continued, but some seventeen new convents based on the strict observance were found by St. Teresa. These influenced the reform of other houses, almost always against opposition, and led to a strengthening of the interior life of the Church. Here we see Spanish Carmelites living much as they did under St. Teresa, austere and strict, but at the same time able to experience the joy of living which the saint insisted was so much a part of life.

An allegory of religious strife in the Netherlands,
which were occupied by Spain, is Pieter Breugel's
"The Massacre of the Innocents," in which,
under the guise of the Biblical account, the artist
shows Spanish Catholic soldiers slaughtering
Dutch Protestant children. Despite his alleged
sympathy for the Protestants, Breugel was also
patronized by Catholic prelates. The religious
warfare continued in every country: in Italy 4,000
Waldensians were killed or sent into exile by
Catholic troops; in Brazil Huguenots captured fifty
Catholic missionaries arriving by ship and
executed them. The height of the cruelties imposed
by Christians upon each other came with the great
St. Bartholomew's Day massacres (right), when
Catherine de Medici, queen-mother of France,
attempted to crush the Protestants in her country.
Some 10,000 Huguenots were put to death in
Paris and other French cities.

Even though they were besieged on all sides, the princes of
the Church found time to give a final fillip to the
Renaissance. Their continuing interest in the arts produced
the baroque period, an age of grandiosity and
richness in art, architecture, literature and music. The
movement began in the late sixteenth century with such works
as Lorenzo Bernini's masterful columns in St. Peter's Square
and the music of Palestrina, and reached its height throughout
Europe in the following century (declining into the fanciful
rococo manner). Baroque spread even to South America, where
it dominated art and architecture. This is the baroque
Wies-Kirche in Bavaria.

Giovanni Pierluigi da Palestrina presents a Mass to Pope Julius III (Julius was a famous patron of the arts and a protector of Michaelangelo). Palestrina's music conformed to the requirements stipulated by the Council of Trent, re-orienting church music which had become extremely secular, to proper religious modes. His cool, objective polyphony—102 Masses and hundreds of motets and other liturgical compositions—captured in essence the most sober and conservative aspects of the Counter-Reformation; Palestrina also revised the Chant and purged it of "barbarisms, obscurities, contrarieties, and superfluities" which they contained (so Gregory XIII wrote) "as the result of the clumsiness or negligence or even wickedness of the composers, scribes and printers."

Columbus's fortunate discovery of the New World and its rapid exploration and colonization by two countries destined to remain Catholic—Portugal and Spain— eventually brought the Church vast numbers of new members, either by conversions or as the children of immigrants. At the same time as the expansion into the Americas, missionaries were pushing into the East, where they also made converts in remarkable numbers. In both East and West the Jesuits were particularly active. St. Francis Xavier, one of the original seven members of the Society, went to Goa, on the invitation of King John III of Portugal, then on to India, the Indies, Ceylon, China and Japan. Despite the most rigorous journeys (Francis was subject to seasickness) and the shortness of the period in which he worked (he died at the age of 46), he is credited, perhaps optimistically, with over 700,000 conversions. The Italian Jesuit, Roberto di Nobili, preached in India, where he adopted the native way of life (a method of evangelization his superiors forced him to discontinue until he received the backing of the Holy See), bringing to the Church some 100,000 souls. Another Italian Jes-

A woodcut entitled "The Arrival of the South Savages" shows a missionary welcoming traders to Japan. The church founded there by St. Francis experienced terrible persecution.

St. Francis Xavier as the Japanese saw him.

THE MISSIONS

uit, the famous Matteo Ricci, was equally successful in China. Like di Nobili, he was an astute student of native culture, and attempted to adapt Chinese ways to Christianity rather than supplant it, an aim that was eventually denied by the Holy See.

In the New World, Franciscans, Dominicans, Augustinians, secular clergy and later the Jesuits arrived by the hundreds in the wake of the Spanish and Portuguese conquistadores. The Indians, often leaderless because of the conquistadores' practice of destroying the Indian chiefs, were usually responsive converts, but soon a conflict broke out between Cross and Crown: while the Church saw the Indians as souls to be saved, the Crown regarded them as bodies to be worked in plantations and mines. The Indians often failed to distinguish among the whites, and there were mutinies and assassinations throughout the colonial territories. The main support for the Indian cause came from the Dominican bishop, Bartolomé de Las Casas, who was outstanding in his efforts to obtain justice for his charges. De Las Casas and others brought about extensive legislation on their behalf, thus preserving most of them from death from overwork or the kind of policies practiced by the Anglo-Saxons in the North, who systematically exterminated the natives as they pushed westward.

A curious picture made of cloth shows a Jesuit missionary in Chinese robes.

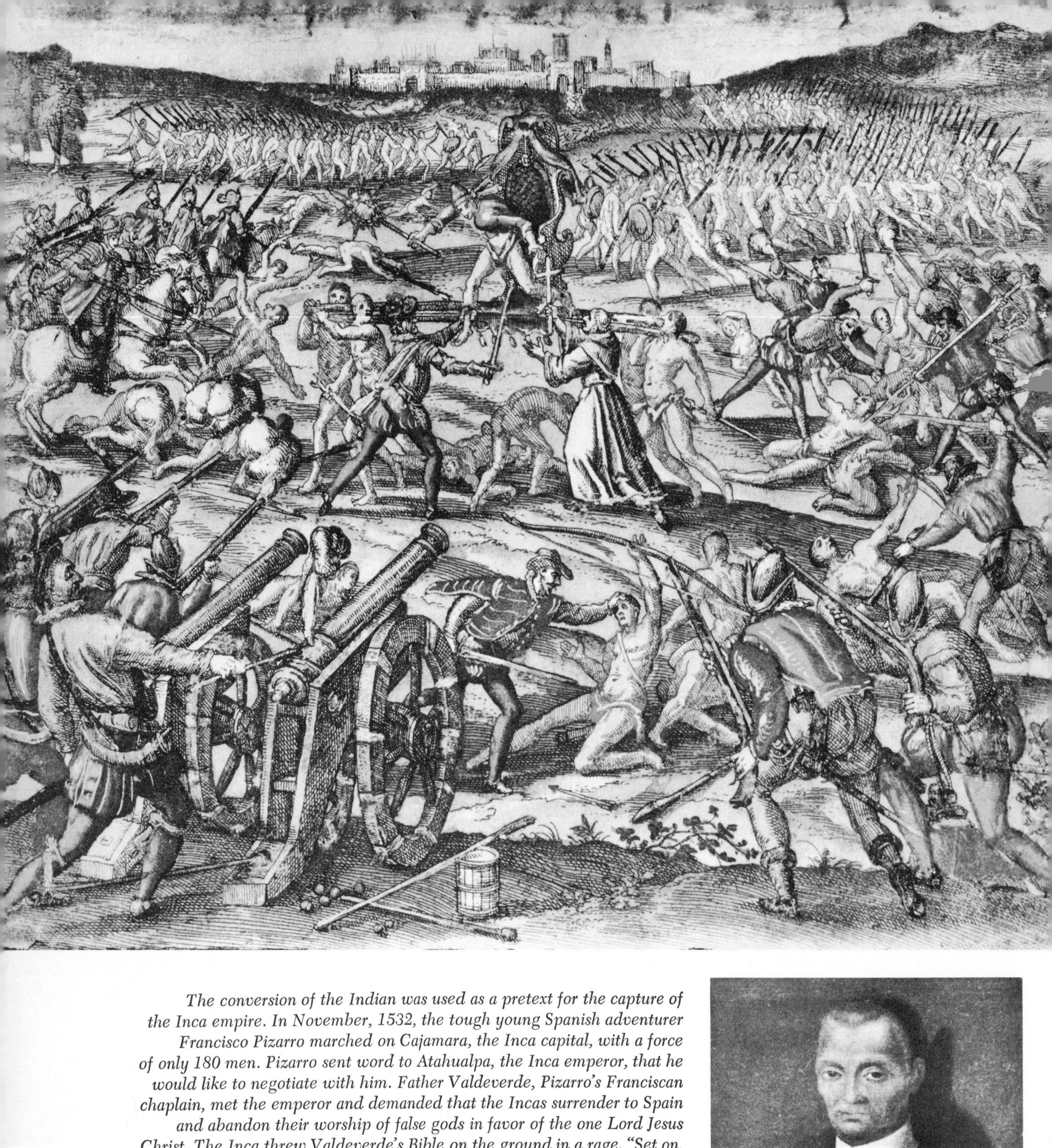

The conversion of the Indian was used as a pretext for the capture of the Inca empire. In November, 1532, the tough young Spanish adventurer Francisco Pizarro marched on Cajamara, the Inca capital, with a force of only 180 men. Pizarro sent word to Atahualpa, the Inca emperor, that he would like to negotiate with him. Father Valdeverde, Pizarro's Franciscan chaplain, met the emperor and demanded that the Incas surrender to Spain and abandon their worship of false gods in favor of the one Lord Jesus Christ. The Inca threw Valdeverde's Bible on the ground in a rage. "Set on, at once, I absolve you!" cried Valdeverde to the Spaniards. They turned their full fire power on the Incas (above) and slaughtered 4,000, the leaders of Inca society. A short while later Pizarro offered Atahualpa his life if he would become a Christian. The emperor accepted and was baptized. Immediately the Spaniards strangled him. Missionaries from Spain arrived a few years later to convert the people through gentler means. One of the notable members of the new Church was Blessed Martin de Porres (right), a mulatto born only 47 years after the conquest of Peru. His father was a Spanish nobleman, his mother a freed slave. With great humility he dedicated his life to aiding the poor of Lima as a Third Order Dominican.

A saintly Indian convert was Kateri Tekakwitha, a Mohawk whose cause is now being promoted.

Catherine Tegahkouita Iroquoise...

French explorations, by Jacques Cartier, Samuel de Champlain, and later by Father Jacques Marquette, Louis Jolliet and René Robert, Sieur de la Salle, brought the Church into contact with North American Indians. Some tribes were friendly and accepted conversion; others showed great hostility and there were a number of martyrs among the French missionaries. Perhaps the most intrepid of the explorers was la Salle, who roamed the American Midwest and descended the Mississippi in search of a route to China. (Here la Salle and his men erect a cross at the confluence of the Arkansas and Mississippi rivers.) At the Gulf of Mexico, wrote a priest in the party, "we discovered the open sea, so that on the ninth of April, 1682, with all possible solemnity, we performed the ceremony of planting the cross and raising the arms of France. After we had chanted hymns . . . the Sieur de la Salle, in the name of his Majesty [King Louis XIV], took possession of that river, of all the rivers that enter it, and of all the country watered by them." This land, Louisiana, settled by French and Spanish and their baptized slaves, was for centuries a Catholic enclave in the future United States

A crucial point in Latin American history was the defeat
of the Dutch in Brazil by a Spanish-Portuguese force
early in the seventeenth century, which thereby gained
control of the continent for Catholic powers.
Here, while the wounded are being treated, the victorious
general, Don Fradique de Toledo, exhibits a picture
symbolic of the battle: Philip IV of Spain receiving
a laurel wreath from his friend and prime minister, the
Conde-Duque de Olivares; behind Philip Victory tramples
the bodies of the Protestant enemy. The recapture of
Bahia on May 1, 1625 broke Dutch power in Latin
America and opened up two centuries of prestige and
prosperity for the city as the capital of Brazil. A
Dutch victory would have dealt a disastrous blow to
Catholic hopes in South America.

A melancholy colonial
Brazilian Christ is typical
of the intense aspects of
Latin American Catholicism,
which, influenced by the
abysmal social conditions
of the continent, emphasizes
the suffering and sorrow
of Christ and the saints.

The vitality and zeal of Japan's Christians—and the unfortunate rivalry for souls among the various missionary orders—brought large scale persecutions in the seventeenth century. All priests were either executed or banished, and nearly a million of the laity were beheaded or crucified (as in this scene). A small group managed to escape to isolated islands off Nagasaki, where, without priests, they managed to retain a vestige of Christianity. These hidden Christians (below) were discovered when Japan opened its doors to the West in the mid-nineteenth century. About half returned to the Church, but the remainder, their Christianity mixed with pagan customs and suspicious of outsiders, refused to accept the "new" form of Christianity. These men are carrying a relic box in a procession at their version of the Easter festival.

Since they were the most powerful arm of the Church—and sometimes it seemed like the only one—in her struggle for existenc in the new currents of the world, the Jesuits were soon targets for attack by enemies outside the Church (and even within it). They were expelled over and over again from many countries of Europe—from France (above, where they are seen on their w to be exiled to Rome in 1764) and from Portugal, Spain and Naples. Their enemies within the Church were so powerful that in 1773 Pope Clement XIV decreed the ecclesiastical dissolution of the Society. Retaining some rights in the German-speaking lands and Russia, they were at last fully restored in 1814.

AFTER THE REFORMATION

Seriously hurt by Luther's revolt, the Church fell into a slow decline. Protestantism, with a firm hold on Europe, still could not keep itself from splintering, while, increasingly free of the need to defer to basic Christian principles, a new type of man came into being. Throughout most of Europe peace reigned; soon the battlefields were to fall quiet. Around the world vast new areas were being opened to exploitation; new peoples were to find that the white man, having freed himself of feudalism, was to impose it—in a new, more brutal form—upon Asians, Africans and Indians through his merchant companies; daring merchant adventurers were building economic empires which could resourcefully chal-

lenge the numerous nations and petty states of Europe. Greatest of these traders were the frugal, ambitious Dutch, whose country, the Netherlands, was the first modern state to be governed by businessmen. Their economic achievements were admired all over Europe. "The merchants and tradesmen," wrote the English ambassador to the Netherlands in 1668, "are of mighty industry. Never has any country traded so much and consumed so little. They buy infinitely, but 'tis to sell again. . . They furnish infinite luxury which they never practice, and traffic in pleasures which they never taste; their common riches lie in every man's spending less than he has coming in." The Dutch were abused for their

Born shortly after the closing of the Council of Trent, Francis de Sales grew up in an atmosphere of religious struggle. Assigned to Geneva (where he eventually became bishop), he found himself in the heart of the conflict between Protestants and Catholics, in battles waged with words as well as weapons. Francis developed the art of pamphleteering— innumerable tracts came from his pen, a catechism and two great works: INTRODUCTION TO THE DEVOUT LIFE *and* TREATISE OF THE LOVE OF GOD; *he also preached regularly, was famed as a confessor and spiritual director, and aided St. Jane Frances de Chantal in founding the Visitandine nuns, one of several new communities which were to help bring about a religious revival in France.*

Half a century after de Sales, St. John Baptist de la Salle revitalized education by his work with children of the poor and of the artisan class. A member of a noble family from Reims, de la Salle founded a new congregation to aid the helpless and to inlucate better religious principles among teachers. His group, though hampered by internecine battles, became known as the Institute of the Brothers of the Christian Schools; its use of the vernacular in teaching and its new methods eventually affected all education and set a pattern for modern education in the West.

success by other nations, but their new-found wealth and skill in business were the secret ideal of many, both Protestant and Catholic. In Protestantism the rising bourgeoisie could find both a motivating force and rationale for their way of life. There was now no need to confess usury, for example, and the doctrines that Calvin had left behind easily led one to the conclusion that the wealthy man was also the most God-fearing.

But it was not only in the field of commerce and business that post-Reformation man was alert. With the proliferation of reading matter, education became possible for many. Science began to develop rapidly. Harvey's discovery of the circulation of the blood was a major step in the development of medicine; Newton's mathematical investigations destroyed the imperfect world of Aristotle and laid the basis of a mathematical view of mankind; Tycho Brahe's observatory made possible the calm exploration of the solar system—to name but a few important advances. In other fields Descartes, Francis Bacon, and later John Locke worked to make popular a rationalistic and pragmatic approach to religious, scientific, social, and economic issues. The restrictions of the Middle Ages disappeared under the attacks of new ways of thought. Freedom, reason and humanitarianism were the catch-words of the day.

And what of the Church in this age? Her tragic plight was enlivened only by rare saints and the fervent faith of her ignored people, a submerged mass who, the new philosophers proclaimed, would soon be freed of their superstition by the great advance of progress. Those of the ruling classes who took an interest were more likely to express their Catholicism in aberrations, like the well-to-do Parisians who adopted the heresy of Jansenism. For the Enlightened Man, the Church was merely the barbaric remnant of another age. In many areas she was being systematically oppressed. In others, she was embarrassed by the antics of the Catholic sovereigns. Her missions were in trouble. And worse than oppression was the fact that thinking men, having rejected Catholicism, were now opposed to Christianity in any form. Christ Himself was being denied. A Bach cantata of 1723 includes the line, "Belial invades the House of God, since even Christian folk from Christ are turning." The wonderful world of the Enlightenment had become a second Dark Age for the Church.

Voltaire, one of the most brilliant minds of his age, saw the Church as a threat to the progress of mankind, and brought the full powers of his devastating and cynical wit against her.

The plump Dutch burghers, rich in the fruits of their new markets, took a complacent view of religion and never let it, as in other countries, interfere with their own progress.

An allegory on the twelve-year truce between Catholic Spain
and the Protestant Netherlands is shown in "The Fishers for
Souls," painted in 1614 by a Dutch (Flemish) artist named
Adriaen Pietersz de Venne. In it both sides are competing
for converts in the Netherlands. On the left bank of the
river stand the Protestant princes James I of England and
Maurice of Holland. On the right are the Catholic Archduke
Albert of Austria and his wife Isabella. In the center are
boats of Protestant divines and Catholic monks (one with the
pope) fishing for the souls of the faithful.

The end of the religious wars between Catholics and Protestants is symbolized in this painting of the Peace of Munster, in which the Dutch gained religious and political freedom from Spain; the Peace also marked the end of the power of the Holy Roman Empire, which fell into a number of states. Here the Dutch Prince Frederick Henry puts away his sword (upper right) while angels exchange his helmet for a wreath of olive leaves; at the same time his son receives an olive branch from an angel of peace (left). The signing of the treaties, known as the Peace of Westphalia, in 1648 ended the era of religious warfare, and the first European-wide attempt at toleration was achieved. Out of the Peace, France emerged as the dominant nation in Europe.

Though religious strife had abated on the continent it continued in England.
A victim of the English persecutions was the well-born Irish bishop, Oliver Plunkett.
After serving in Rome as representative of the Irish bishops, he returned to his homeland,
where he worked hard to raise the standards of education and to halt immorality among
the Irish. While Plunkett was in Ireland, the British began persecutions of his people
in 1673. Six years later, as a result of the fury engendered by the Titus Oates plot,
he was arrested, tried and condemned, and finally executed in 1681. His head is now
in Drogheda, Ireland, where it is venerated in the Blessed Oliver Plunkett chapel.

Although Pascal was allied through most of his life to the heretical Jansenists of Port Royal, his writings, particularly the PENSÉES, have taken their place among the classics of the Western world and have far more than sectarian validity. "We know the truth," wrote Pascal, "not only by the reason, but by the heart. The heart has its reasons which the reason does not know."

The Jansenistic heresy was a matter of great public concern in France and in the Church. This cartoon hopefully shows Jansenists denounced by pope and king alike, acknowledging their errors and renouncing the hidden taint of Calvinism in their doctrines.

The Jansenists

Near the middle of the seventeenth century a new heresy arose in the French church and with serious consequences. The rigorous and pessimistic beliefs known as Jansenism, based on the works of a Belgian bishop named Cornelius Jansen, were highly attractive to many among the dissolute Parisian society. In essence Jansenism taught that without special grace from God the observance of His commandments is impossible; God's grace was an irresistible upward pull, given only to a few at His pleasure, and could be withdrawn. The Jesuits, who leaped into the battle, pointed out that every man is granted sufficient grace for life, and that it is up to him to respond. Pope Innocent X's bull condemning the Jansenist position was ignored as not accurately representing their views. The heresy continued to grow, especially since the Jansenists had as their ally a most formidable friend, Blaise Pascal, whose *Provincial Letters* in support of the Jansenists were an outstanding success, and gave the impression that only the Jansenists possessed truth, justice and the true faith. Using his great skill and often quoting out of context, Pascal mercilessly ridiculed the Jesuits. The *Letters* were condemned and are on the Index, but it must be said that the Jesuits handled their side of the controversy poorly. Jansenism gradually died out, either as the result of persecution in France or indifference; it survived longest in Holland where, as the Old Catholic Church, it still claims a small number of adherents.

The beggar saint

By the end of the eighteenth century, among thinking men, God was considered dead or at least was relegated to an inactive role in the affairs of man. The supreme force was an absolute faith in enlightened reason, progress and the coming perfectibility of human society. Nevertheless, in 1770 a young French peasant named Benedict Joseph Labre walked out of a Trappist monastery and set forth to search Him out in the farthest corners of Europe. Three times dismissed from monasteries, several times more refused admittance, Benedict bore the stigma of the religiously unstable.

His final choice was to be a homeless wanderer, to ask for nothing except eternal life, and to live in such a way that the hard boards and simple fare of the Trappist would be unimagined luxury. With no possessions except the rags on his back and a few holy books, refusing to ask alms, too weak to accept the few jobs he was offered, Benedict passed fifteen years as a holy tramp. So dirty that the ordinary person was unable to go near him, he was abused and physically assaulted by the beggars he met in the road or in the slums; though a frequent communicant, he was suspected of being a Jansenist by one priest, and a Huguenot by another. A touring American minister, examining Catholicism as he would Mohammedanism, wrote so mockingly of Benedict, whom he came across in Rome, that his Protestant friends accused him of having exceeded the bounds of good taste. Even a sympathetic Catholic biographer, a bishop, called him "the great unwashed."

Upon leaving the Trappists Benedict began to wander about Europe, visiting the sacred shrines of Christendom. He turned up during the next seven years in France, Germany, Italy, Spain and Switzerland, a gaunt, shy wanderer who remarked once that "it was God who told me to undertake the journey I am now making." Oblivious of wind and rain, he went everywhere on foot, spending whole days in constant prayer. His clothes fell off his back, he gave his few possessions to those even poorer, he rarely begged for food but picked up fruit peels and rotten vegetables from garbage heaps. In Moulins he was suspected of theft and thrown out of the church; in Gascony he was arrested for assaulting a man he had in fact been aiding. But though he was despised by most, there were a surprising number who saw the saint beneath the rags. Church-goers, on their way to confession, looked at him and had a rare insight into their own sins, which they were able to confess properly for the first time. People asked for advice and phrases such as "You must be patient," or "You must trust in God"—which would have seemed banal from the bourgeois—brought consolation. The beatification proceedings revealed that Benedict had several times cured the sick and had miraculously multiplied a few crusts of bread for twelve scoffing beggars he had gathered together to feed on Holy Thursday (his only explanation was that he had a generous benefactor who gave him all he wanted).

Benedict's lodging was most often the bare ground, at best a doorway or a shed. There were also periods when he was taken in by sympathetic farm families or was given a bed in a monastery. But he never sought to better his condition. "A poor man," said Benedict, "must be satisfied with what he finds; the ground is good enough." After each prolonged contact with people, fearful of some tie that might threaten his eternal seeking after God, he would set off again, abandoning even the slight comforts of a storeroom or attic in favor of his life of destitution. "The poor don't carry money on their journeys," he said. "The poor have scraps of bread, not loaves. The poor should not be well dressed. The poor must mortify themselves and overcome their flesh just like everyone else." After seven years on the road he finally took the road of the apostles, to settle in Rome.

"There are more beggars in Rome than anywhere else," wrote a French traveler of the late 1770's. Another one said of the beggars that "they are an unbearable vermin to other citizens and a shame to the state." It was among these people that Benedict chose to pass his life. By 1777 he settled permanently in Rome, leaving it only for an annual visit to the shrine of Loreto. His home was in one of the arcades of the Colosseum, which earlier in the century had been dedicated by Pope Benedict XIV to the memory of the Christian martyrs. His favorite sleeping place was on a heap of straw and dried ferns, under the fifth station of the Colosseum's Via Crucis, in which Simon of Cyrene takes up the Cross of Our Lord. In the middle of the night Benedict came forth to pray in expiation of the sins of mankind. In the morning he faced one of the most dreadful experiences of his day: when he left the Colosseum to attend early Mass at the Church of the Madonna dei Monti, he was often abused violently and even attacked by the beggars, whom he occasionally reproached for their blasphemy; he was sometimes stoned by beggar children.

At Madonna dei Monti he spent hours in prayer. One cold, dark, winter's morning a parishioner, Maria Poeti, saw him kneeling on the stone floor of the church, cleansed of all dirt and luminously surrounded with light like the Christ of the Transfiguration. At San Ignacio a worshipper ran to inform the sacristan that Benedict was raised off the floor while praying; "The saint is in ecstasy," said the sacristan calmly and continued sweeping the steps.

In Holy Week of 1783 Benedict was so weak from his fasts and the rigors of his life that he could not make his usual pilgrimage to Loreto to celebrate Easter. Each day seemed to bring him closer to the Passion of Christ. On Palm Sunday one of the women who gave him food saw him slowly walking to the church of Santa Croce, so feeble that he seemed likely to fall at every step. On Monday he was seen by a priest, a Father Balducci, in San Ignacio, a poor heap of rags coughing his lungs out; Balducci said he had never said Mass so fervently before in his life. "I prayed that God would purify my soul more and more," he testified later, "that I might become worthy to give Communion to this poor man whom I felt to be a saint." On Tuesday Benedict was seen in the church of Saint Praxedes, in front of the Column of the Flagellation, so worn out he could hardly speak. On Wednesday he went to Madonna dei Monti to hear the Passion read; here

were friends of his—small shopkeepers, gardeners, workers—who had fed him and had tried to care for him. His friends began to whisper, "Benedict will die at the same time as Christ. He will fall at the *exspiravit*." But, by a heroic effort, Benedict pulled himself to his feet. However, a few minutes later he collapsed on the steps of the church. The crowd gathered around him; a neighbor brought him brandy. Zaccarelli the butcher came by and with the help of his son carried Benedict home. "Why take on such a burden?" asked a priest. Zaccarelli tried without success to feed Benedict. A Father Piccilli who like Benedict but suspected him of Jansenism rushed over to convert him to the true Church. The day passed quickly, with Benedict in a coma. In the evening he died, and the word passed quickly through the neighborhood.

And then a strange thing happened. His confessor and first biographer, a Father Montini, wrote, "Scarcely had this poor follower of Christ breathed his last when all at once the little children from the houses hard by filled the whole street with their noise, crying out with one accord 'The saint is dead, the saint is dead.'—but presently there were not only young children who published the sanctity of Benedict; all Rome soon joined in their cries, repeating the self-same words: 'A saint is dead.' . . . Great numbers of persons who have been eminent for their holiness and famous for their miracles, have ended the days of their mortal life in this city; but the death of none of them ever excited so rapid and lively an emotion in the midst of the people as the death of this poor beggar. This stirred a kind of universal commotion; for in the streets scarcely anything could be heard but these few words: 'There is a saint dead in Rome. Where is the house in which he had died?'"

Hardly was Benedict dead than the pastors of two churches were contending for his body; finally the honor of possessing his remains was given to the Madonna dei Monti, which he had frequented most, and on the afternoon of Easter Sunday his body was buried in the church near the altar. Benedict was only thirty-five.

Benedict Joseph's home in Rome was th
ruins of the Colosseum, seen here swarmin
with beggars in a contemporary sketc

THE AGE OF REVOLUTIONS

The liberating ideas of the Enlightenment had brought Europe to the verge of revolution. The growth of the middle classes, the development of capitalism, the expansion of trade were often achieved by the continued exploitation of the urban proletariat and the peasants, many of whom still lived under feudal conditions. At the same time the tendency of the monarchs to make their rule absolute added to the tensions upon Europe's social structure. Discontent was widespread, old institutions were under attack, and new ideas, which ran counter to those of the Church and to traditional social ideals were infecting all classes.

The first major outbreak came in France. Here the direct cause of the Revolution was the chaotic state of public finance. The government was on the verge of bankruptcy, partly because of its aid to the American revolutionists. In 1789, for the first time in over a century and a half, a meeting of the States-General was called. The three Estates: the First, the clergy; the Second, the nobility; and the Third, the commons, presented their grievances. It was apparent that drastic political and social reforms were needed. The curés of the First Estate pointed out the great disparity between the wealth of some of the bishops and the poverty of the parish priests; at the same time there was a decline in both the secular and particularly the religious clergy. (It was curious that the curés were looking not to the pope but to the French king, Louis XVI, for reform.) The Third Estate soon dominated the scene, proclaiming its interests to be identical with those of the nation. The king yielded and recognized its leaders as the National Assembly, though he then ordered his troops to surround Paris. This led to a popular uprising and the storming of the Bastille. Violence spread through-out the country. The government, afraid of bloodshed, held back its troops, while the peasants burned chateaux and terrorized their landlords. Then in one startling move, the clergy and the nobles who were members of the Assembly relinquished their privileges, and in a single day the entire feudal structure of France came officially to an end. The strength of the mob increased; the king and queen were confined to their quarters. The rights of the crown were curtailed by the Assembly, which also, in several stages, diminished the privileges of the Church: her lands were nationalized, religious orders were suppressed, and the clergy and bishops, sharply reduced in number, were called upon to support the Civil Constitution of the Clergy. But only four of the bishops and about a third of the curés agreed under oath to support it. Rioting broke out across France in favor of one faction or the other. Only the Constitutional Clergy could legally perform marriages, baptisms and burials (although the non-swearing priests were allowed to say Mass but not distribute Communion). Many of the wealthy bishops went into exile abroad along with the emigré nobility. By the end of 1792 the Paris Commune was in full control; the following January Louis XVI was executed and the Reign of Terror broke out. Its excesses finally ended in 1795 with the establishment of the Directory. Stability, in the person of Napoleon, was soon to replace disorder. The old France was ended. The new bourgeois and capitalist classes came to dominance; the revolutionary, nationalistic, anti-religious ideas of the Commune were to spread throughout Europe. In the coming years, the Church was to be stripped of her secular power, leaving her to concentrate all her energies in the spiritual sphere.

The fish women march on Versailles. The women of the French Revolution were bloodthirstier than the men in demanding the heads of the aristocracy.

An exalted view of Napoleon in this nineteenth-century engraving shows him as a warrior-saint.

Napoleon takes on the Church

The end of the eighteenth century saw the Church suffering new losses in the long descent that had begun with the Protestant revolt. The French Revolution had not only reduced the Church as an active force in French life, but had at the same time shaken the prestige of the papacy. The Church was also harassed in neighboring Belgium and in the Rhineland. The ancient Catholic country of Poland was controlled by powers hostile to the Church, and in Catholic Austria she was at the mercy of the whims of the emperor; Spain and Portugal had anti-clerical governments, and in England and Ireland the movement for Catholic emancipation had been rejected by King George III.

As the nineteenth century loomed large on the horizon the brilliant young French general, Napoleon Bonaparte, was overrunning both the northern and southern provinces of the papal states and dictating terms to the aging Pope Pius VI at Tolentino. An uprising in Rome, inspired by French revolutionary ideas, gave the French the excuse for occupying the city and in February, 1798, Pius, eighty years old, was kidnapped. The Austrians made an attempt to rescue him, so the French dragged the ailing pontiff through the Alps in the dead of winter; he finally died during the summer of 1799 in a fortress at Valence.

Since Rome was occupied, the conclave to elect a successor was held at Venice, where 35 penniless members of the Sacred College met under the protection of Francis II, the Hapsburg Holy Roman emperor, who hoped to achieve the selection of a pope congenial to his wishes. However, the choice of a simple Benedictine, the bishop of Imola, who took the name of Pius VII, was an affront to the emperor; he refused permission for the coronation ceremonies in St. Mark's cathedral in Venice; in turn, the new pope demanded the return of the northern papal states, which Francis had taken from the French.

Meanwhile, the young Napoleon was on the way to making himself a new Charlemagne. He saw that the Church, despite its sufferings, still held the allegiance of millions of the French and of other Europeans. Would she make a better ally than enemy? The answer was obvious, and Napoleon set about to undo—on his own terms—the harm wrought by the French Revolution. Later he commented cynically: "My political method is to govern men as the majority of them want to be governed. That, I think, is the way to recognize the sovereignty of the people. It was by making myself a Catholic that I won the war in the Vendée, by making myself a Moslem that I established myself in Egypt, by making myself an Ultramontane that I gained men's souls in Italy. If I were governing a people of the Jewish race, I would rebuild the temple of Solomon." In northern Italy he spoke firmly to the anti-clericals who had seized Milan: "Leave your priests free to say their Mass; the people is sovereign; if it wants its religion, respect its will."

Coincidental with the effort by Napoleon, the new pope reached the Holy City, having made most of the journey by boat. He found to his pleasure, on his arrival, the first of Napoleon's overtures. But the general's friendship could be gained only by vast concessions and these the pope would not make. Accepting the great material losses in France, the pope still insisted on the Church's spiritual freedom. A year was consumed in working out a Concordat satisfactory to both sides (it has since served as a model for similar agreements between the Church and various nations). A second agreement was signed in Italy and provisional ones were made with the German states.

Napoleon reads off the terms
of the Concordat to Pius VII.

A fight for independence

By the spring of 1804 Napoleon had done so much for France that it was fitting for the Senate to decree him Emperor of the French, a title that extended as well to Belgians, Dutch, Rhinelanders and North Italians. Napoleon saw that, like Charlemagne's, his title—hardly acceptable to the Austrian Emperor, the Russian Tzar and the kings of various other lands—would be more effective if blessed by the pope. He invited the pope to Paris.

For three months the pope and his chief counselor, Cardinal Consalvi, debated the question. The anointing of the French emperor would be an affront to the other Catholic monarchs and a tacit acceptance of certain conitions that still plagued the Church in France. But at last the decision was made that the favorable advantages would be greater than the risk, and Pius and his entourage began the difficult trip to Paris, amid the acclaim of Napoleon's subjects, passing, as the pope remarked, among a people on its knees. After the coronation Napoleon also had himself anointed king of Italy in a ceremony in Milan.

The peace between pope and emperor was only temporary. Except for the central area around Rome, Napoleon controlled both the southern and northern papal states. He was at war with England and asked that the pope prevent England, a Protestant power, from using the few papal harbors still open. The pope refused, saying *he* was not at war with the English; at the same time he asked for the return of his lands. In reply the emperor reminded the pope of how other emperors had treated other obstinate popes. Pius persisted in his demands and Napoleon ordered the occupation of Rome by his forces. In May of 1809 he formally incorporated the whole of the papal states into his Empire. A month later the pope was forced to barricade himself into the Quirinal, issuing a bull which excommunicated anyone who attacked the Holy See. But it was to no purpose. The French forced their way into the pope's apartments and arrested him. Ill of dysentery, with no baggage and no money, he was packed into a locked coach and shunted about Italy and France for 42 days. Finally Pius was shut up in the archbishop's palace at Savona, where to prevent him from continuing his work, the French even deprived him of writing materials. Pius refused to surrender to Napoleon's demands; for two years the Emperor denounced the "imbecilic old man." In the end it was Napoleon, shattered by his disaster in Russia, who went into exile while Pius, having maintained his determination to preserve the spiritual independence of the papacy, returned to Rome triumphant.

A tense scene takes place between Pius VII and Napoleon, who has brought the pope to Fontainebleau to discuss relations between the Church and the Empire. Napoleon later issued a distorted version of the talks as a new concordat; the pope said he had been betrayed and "defiled." After this the emperor refused Pius all visitors, even a server for Mass.

t his coronation Napoleon places the crown upon his own head
e had refused to accept it from the hand of the pope, since
would have meant that he was subservient to the spiritual
ower); however he did allow the Pope to anoint him. Pius also
rced the regularization of Napoleon's marriage to Josephine,
hich had first been performed only in a civil ceremony.

The Roman mob attacks Pio Nono in 1848 in his palace, the Quirinal, forcing him to flee.

Pio Nono was elected pope in 1846 and ruled until 1878, the longest pontificate in history; his reign exceeded the 25 years traditionally ascribed to St. Peter. Pio Nono began the tradition of general audiences for Catholic and non-Catholic visitors to Rome; he also encouraged the bishops' AD LIMINA visits.

The end of the papal states

Pio Nono, as Pius IX was affectionately known by the world, took over his pontificate with a strong sympathy for Europe's liberal movements. He began his reign by repudiating the oppressive measures of his predecessor, Gregory XVI, in the papal states, granting an amnesty to political prisoners and exiles and expressing his approval with the Risorgimento, the Italian nationalist movement; he allowed greater freedom of the press and gave the city of Rome her own elective government. He also took practical steps by introducing gaslight to the streets of Rome and planning railways through the papal territories.

Then a dilemma arose for Pio Nono. The Italian Nationalists asked him for support in their drive to free Lombardy and Venetia from Austria, one of the papacy's most fervent supporters. The Pope refused. The Roman mob turned on Pio Nono, and besieged him in the Quirinal palace. Unable to carry out his duties, the Pope fled to Naples, disguised as a parish priest. The city of Rome was taken over by the revolutionary leaders, Mazzini and Garibaldi, and a republic was established. However, it did not survive very long. The French intervened and the pope was restored to Rome.

The papacy at bay

The nationalist movement was too fervent for even a pope to control. It was apparent that it was only a matter of time before the papacy would be stripped of its lands. The most powerful of the Italian rulers, young King Victor Emmanuel II, and his skillful premier, Cavour, began undercover machinations with the French which would dispossess the papacy. A series of steps by the alliance reduced Austrian power in northern Italy; with this friend lost, the pope was at the mercy of Victor Emmanuel, whose allies took over the papal states. A short while later all of Italy was formally incorporated into Victor Emmanuel's empire; the city of Rome itself, protected by the French, being all that was left to the pope. Then, in 1870, when the French were forced to withdraw their troops for the Franco-Prussian War, Rome, too, fell to the king. Pio Nono protested in vain. Victor Emmanuel moved into the Quirinal. Now deprived of virtually all temporal sovereignty, the pope became the prisoner of the Vatican.

But though his reign suffered disastrously in the political realm, Pio Nono achieved striking spiritual and ecclesiastical successes. One was his definition of the doctrine of the Immaculate Conception, in the bull, *Ineffabilis Deus*, issued on December 8, 1854. It stated that "from the first moment of her conception the Blessed Virgin Mary was, by the singular grace and privilege of Almighty God, and in view of the merits of Jesus Christ, Savior of mankind, kept free from all stain of original sin."

Ten years later his controversial Syllabus of Errors, a set of eighty theses, came as a broad attack on trends of the modern world which Pius found alarming. Actually a rough document—the pope called it "raw meat needing to be cooked"—it was a summary of his earlier pronouncements on a number of subjects and then dealing with specific instances demanding correction. But Catholics and non-Catholics joined in the uproar that greeted the Syllabus. (One historian remarked that "the majority of Catholics were stupefied.") Besides its condemnation of such doctrines as pantheism, naturalism, absolute rationalism, the Syllabus also took a harsh view of many things that modern Catholics were accustomed to, such as, in the United States, a free press and separation of Church and state. Prolonged discussion eventually brought some understanding of the pope's position, but acceptance of the Syllabus in full was never quite achieved.

Four years after Pio Nono defined the dogma of the Immaculate Conception, a young French peasant girl, the fourteen-year-old daughter of a miller, Bernadette Soubirous, who had spent her life in extreme poverty, experienced a series of eighteen apparitions of the Blessed Virgin in a grotto at Lourdes. The Virgin manifested herself to Bernadette as the "Immaculate Conception." After a period of harassment, Bernadette entered a convent to spend her life. Meanwhile Lourdes became, next to Rome itself, the most popular of all contemporary Christian shrines.

The Vatican Council began with long discussions of the chief errors of the age—rationalism, materialism, pantheism and kindred subjects. Dogma, ecclesiastical discipline, religious orders and relations with the Oriental Church were also on the agenda. But the main topic was that of papal infallibility. In Germany, Austria and Switzerland there were groups of the faithful who would not accept the decree of the Council; they organized themselves as the Old Catholics, who allied themselves with the Jansenist Old Catholic Church of Holland and eventually with the Church of England.

The Vatican Council

The most striking achievement of Pio Nono's reign was the Vatican Council of 1870, where papal infallibility was defined. The Council was attended by 800 Church dignitaries, some of them quite poor. (Pio Nono commented: "I don't know if the pope will emerge from this Council fallible or infallible. But he certainly will be bankrupt.") Although a number of important subjects were on the agenda, the issue of infallibility occupied most attention. Opinion was varied: a majority favored some kind of definition; the minority—140 bishops—either agreed with the majority but felt that the time was not ripe for a definition, or that the pope's infallibility was linked to the infallibility of the Church and so did not need defining. The debate took several months, and at times it became acrimonious. Finally the issue was defined, to the disappointment of extremists in both camps, that the pope is infallible only when speaking "*ex cathedra*, that is, when exercising the office of pastor and teacher of all Christians, he defines with his supreme apostolic authority a doctrine concerning faith or morals to be held by the universal Church." All but two of the dissident bishops left Rome during the vote; eventually all of them accepted the judgment of the Council.

Pio Nono also saw the Church attacked in the newly unified nation of Germany, a powerful force as a result of her defeat of two "Catholic" countries, Austria in 1866 and France in 1870. Otto von Bismark, the chancellor (left), saw the faith of Catholics as a threat to national unity. His "Kulturkampf" was a series of repressive movements to control the Church through legislation. Leading Protestants called for an energetic sequel of the Reformation. The Jesuits were expelled and some other religious orders were dissolved. Several Catholic bishops and dozens of priests were imprisoned. Others went into exile. However Bismark had underestimated the strength of Catholicism in Germany. Passive resistance by Catholics eventually led him to believe a concordat was a better solution. He also saw the Church as an ally against the rising strength of the Socialists. Peace was made with the new pope, Leo XIII, in 1878. The Kulturkampf had the effect of strengthening the faith of German Catholics and helped create a religious revival.

A rare newsreel scene captures Leo XIII out for a ride in the Vatican gardens.

A NEW GOLDEN AGE

A papal diplomat, Leo XIII, while a secular priest, served in the leading cities of Europe, becoming acquainted with modern social conditions. Succeeding Pio Nono in 1878, it was obvious that his pontificate was to usher in a new age in the Church. England's Cardinal Manning had said: "A new task is before us. The Church has no longer to deal with parliaments and princes, but with the masses and the people." This was to be Leo's preoccupation. His first encyclical outlined his intention to reconcile the Church with contemporary civilization. Having achieved peace with Bismarck, he turned to other nations, establishing an apostolic delegation in Washington and opening up contacts with Japan and Russia. A significant event was the visit of King Edward VII of England to the Vatican. But with Catholic countries he was less fortunate: both Italy and France continued and even increased their hostility to the papacy.

The Bible, the Greek and Protestant churches, Marian devotion, the rosary, the missions (he encouraged the formation of a native clergy), were some of Leo's special interests. His great encyclical, *Rerum Novarum* issued in 1891, is perhaps his best-known work: it defines traditional Catholic teaching on labor, the role of both employer and employee, and the concepts of profit and ownership in the light of the conditions imposed by the industrial revolution: the encyclical lays down minimum standards for a just wage (enough to support the wage-earner and his family "in reasonable and frugal comfort"), and upholds the right of the worker to unionize. This document, remarkable at the time, was denounced by many, Catholics of course included, as being revolutionary and subversive, but it stands now, as when written, as a most important statement on social justice, and has had widespread influence.

Born of a poor family in northern Italy, Pius X, then Giuseppe Sarto, rose to be cardinal of Venice in 1893. Ten years later he was elected pope. In contrast to Leo, Pius X aimed to be a religious rather than a political pope, though he was inevitably drawn into conflicts with the anti-clerical governments of France and Portugal. Like Leo, Pius was profoundly concerned with the problems of social justice. He laid down the principles of Catholic Action and denounced all tendencies within and without the Church which he saw as a danger to society. One of his most important achievements was the codification of canon law. He also reformed the Breviary and encouraged a revival of Gregorian chant in the liturgy. In 1905 he recommended daily Communion, and thus gave a deep reinforcement to the inner life of the people. He was canonized in 1954.

Benedict XV worked unceasingly to help end World War I.

Popes of peace

Benedict XV, who succeeded Pius X, came to power in a divided Europe. Elected shortly after the outbreak of World War I, his constant preoccupation was peace. His repeated efforts at negotiation were spurned by the governments on either side. Yet Benedict continued to work for peace both openly and in secret. At the same time he showed unending concern for its victims: the prisoners, their children, the people starving behind the lines on either side; he also negotiated the exchange of the wounded and strongly denounced atrocities and reprisals. The one great voice for peace was Benedict's, yet most were deaf to it. Had his efforts succeeded, the world might have been spared the appearance of a new secular power, Russian communism, whose violence and virulence towards religion surpassed any attacks of the past. Benedict died in 1922, leaving behind him a world still torn by civil turmoil.

Peace was naturally the primary concern of the new pope, Pius XI, who saw the people of many countries subject if not to outright oppression, at least to subtle psychological debasement and to paralyzing legal restrictions. The totalitarian and anti-religious character of the new Russia was soon to be paralleled in the governments of Italy and Germany. Although a concordat with Mussolini in 1929 recognized for the first time since 1870 the sovereignty of the pope and also restored long-absent rights, such as the privilege of nominating

bishops in Italy, two years later, in 1931, it became obvious that Il Duce had no real intention of respecting the Church, and Pius, in his powerful *Non Abbiamo Bisogno*, made it clear that no Catholic could remain an active Fascist. However, for years many Italian Catholics tried to bridge the two points of view. The concordat with Hitler proved to be even less successful. Though the attack on the Church was secondary to the persecution of the Jews, Hitler began a slow campaign of attrition which, during the war resulted in the wholesale arrests of hundreds of priests from Germany and the conquered territories, and their imprisonment in some of the most notorious of his concentration camps, particularly Dachau, where over 1,000 died. Before the war, however, in 1937, Pius had denounced the whole Nazi conception of life as utterly anti-Christian in his forceful encyclical *Mit Brennender Sorge*. Its results, however, were not spectacular: many German Catholics still supported Hitler.

Pius' reign was dominated by the theme of restoring "all things in Christ," symbolic of this was his institution of the Feast of Christ the King. He also issued a number of encyclicals and other documents on current problems, the best known of which is his reaffirmation, in *Quadregesimo Anno*, of Leo XIII's *Rerum Novarum*. He died a few months before the coming of a new world war, which was to present his successor with even graver problems.

The greatest problem facing Pius XI was the rise of the totalitarian states.

The most powerful foe of the Church in centuries, communism, established in Russia in 1917, directly attempted to crush not only Catholicism but all forms of religion (the Russian soldiers above are removing ikons from an Orthodox seminary in Moscow during the persecutions of 1930). Pius XI and later Pius XII strongly denounced this atheistic communism, to which the lives of millions and the faith of more were being sacrificed, not only in Russia but in its satellite countries. After World War II, the Church found herself opposed by the communists in many areas outside the Iron Curtain.

The troubled age of Pius XII

Pius XII—Eugenio Pacelli—was a Roman-born member of a highly respected, aristocratic family which had traditionally supported the popes in their struggles with the secular powers. His grandfather had founded the *L'Osservatore Romano* and was an official in the papal states. From early childhood he held the priesthood as his single goal. Lean, dedicated, selfless and intellectual, he rose through the minor ranks of the Church to become a papal diplomat. His first major assignment came when, newly consecrated an archbishop, he was made nuncio to Bavaria and carried to the Kaiser a plan which Pope Benedict hoped would bring an end to the war. Like others to the same purpose, it was rejected.

Still nuncio, Archbishop Pacelli spent twelve years in Germany where, as dean of the diplomatic corps, he exercised considerable influence. He left Germany in 1929 to be made cardinal by Pius XI. The next year he was appointed the Vatican's secretary of state, a post which enabled him to visit both Americas. Pius's whole training, his background, his association with two popes dedicated to peace, his inheritance of the tradition in which the ordinary man was of special concern, his interest in recent work in the field of the liturgy—all directed him into one of the most fruitful and energetic pontificates of history. Although he was constantly rebuffed on the political scene—the Allies of World War II paid little more attention to his continued efforts to achieve peace than did Germany and Italy—he achieved great successes in the spiritual realm, issuing a steady stream of encyclicals, letters and speeches by which he attempted to guide not only his own people but all of mankind to peace and the exercise of charity. Pius was willing to grant an audience to almost any earnest group of pilgrims: cyclists, midwives, bee-keepers, doctors, American basketball players—people of every race or religion; and for each he had at least a brief and appropriate homily. Active in almost every field that concerned the Church, Pius inaugurated liturgical reforms (among them that of Holy Week), fostered closer relations with the Eastern Catholic churches, strengthened the hierarchy with the creation of cardinals from other continents, encouraged the organization of native hierarchies in the mission areas, and worked unceasingly through various Church organizations to help the oppressed of all nations. Despite repeated bouts with ill health in his last years, his death at the age of 78 came as a shock to mankind.

The world that Pius XII left at his death was not the world he had inherited. There were marked and profound changes in all areas, not only politically, but socially and intellectually. Although there were greater political restrictions than ever in many countries, especially those that were dominated by either the Russians or the Chinese communists, Catholics gained new freedom and respect in many other lands. In the Scandanavian countries there was a relaxation of restrictions on the Catholic orders and the development of a small but important group of converts. In England (where many leading intellectuals joined the Church) and in the United States there were marked numbers of adult baptisms, In Africa and parts of free Asia there were also tens of thousands of converts, despite the shortage of missionaries. But in the great traditional Catholic continent of South America the Church faced not only the hostility of some states but a general apathy owing to the serious lack of indigenous vocations, the scarcity of missionaries and the extreme conservatism of the hierarchy and well-to-do laity in approaching social problems.

This loss of the proletariat was also observed in other traditionally Catholic countries, notably France, Spain and Italy. An attempt in France at forming a new kind of parish by specially trained clergy, the Worker Priests, who lived among the poor instead of in rectories, was short-lived and controversial. Another French effort has been far more successful: the Little Brothers of Jesus, small groups of priests and brothers formed after a rule drawn up by Père Charles de Foucauld (who lived among the Tuaregs of the Sahara). Their object is to spend a life of prayer among the most miserable of the proletariat, not to make conversions but to bear witness to the hidden life of Christ at Nazareth. The ancient, strict orders, the Trappists, Carthusians, and Camaldolese are all undergoing a revival at present. The excellent opportunities for education are giving large numbers of the laity, especially in the western countries, a theological and spiritual training which even priests of past centuries often lacked. And widespread interest in the liturgy and sacraments (and the spread of vernacular usage), plus extended work on the serious question of ecumenical unity (paralleled by a similar interest in the non-Catholic Christian world) gives a far distant hope for the common solution of the problems that have disrupted Christendom.

A poignant moment in the reign of Pius XII was his proclamation on November 1, 1950, of the dogma of the Assumption of the Virgin

Pope John XXIII

One of a family of poor farmers in northern Italy, Pope John XXIII—Angelo Roncalli—brought a touch of informality to the Vatican. Though unknown to most Americans, he was popular in Europe, where he had served the Church with distinction in a number of posts, among them as apostolic delegate to Bulgaria and Turkey and as nuncio to France during the difficult period of reconstruction. When he left France in 1953 to assume the post of patriarch of Venice, Edouard Herriot, the Radical leader, remarked, "If all priests were like Nuncio Roncalli, there would be no anticlericals left!" As pope, John broke with tradition in many ways. With extreme candor and friendliness he went out into the streets of Rome to make personal contact with his flock, visiting prisons, orphanages and hospitals. Three of his initial moves, each of which will have a far-ranging effect on the Church, are a reform of the administration of the Vatican state and the Roman Curia; an expansion and rejuvenation of the College of Cardinals, and a summons for an ecumenical council. The council in particular is expected to bring about reforms within the Church and the most serious effort to date to reach the estranged members of Christendom: the Protestants and, primarily, the Orthodox. Like his immediate predecessors John is first of all concerned with peace. As he proclaimed on the day of his election: "There is a very great difference between peace and slavery. True peace is tranquillity in freedom."

John XXIII ignored recent custom to go out among his flock. Here a highly emotional scene greets him as he visits poor Romans in a hospital ward.

The author is indebted to Robert Lax, who edited the manuscript, to Father H. A. Reinhold, who read certain parts of the text, to Miss Pauline Holman, who typed the text, and his wife, Margery, who did the final proof-reading. The author is also indebted to the pictorial source listed below (and regrets the omission of any credits that might have been overlooked).

Dr. Edgar Alexander, 175; Alinari, 26, 185, 186, 187, 250; American Heritage, 266 top, 267 bottom. Biblioteca Apostolica Vaticana, 141; Biblioteca Nacional, Madrid, 75 bottom, 93, 108; Bibliothèque Nationale, Paris, 24, 32, 39, 40-41, 158; BIPS, 138, British Information Service 163; British Museum, 179. Yvonne Chevalier, 218 bottom, 219. Czechoslovakian Information Center, 180. D. Van Nostrand and Co., 157. French Government Cultural Services and Tourist Office, 62, 63, 90, 101, 124, 125, 128, 129, 133, 135. Fitzwilliam Museum, Cambridge, 88. Graymoor News Service, 22 top. Hanover House, 189 top. International News Photos, 14, 261; Irish Tourist Office, 70, 72-73, 239; Italian State Tourist Office, 147. Jesuit Mission Bureau, 210. P. E. Schramm, *Die Deutschen Kaiser und Könige in Bildern*, 81, 83, 86, 97, 103, 104, 139; Sheed and Ward, 242; Spanish Tourist Agency, 11. Three Lions, 46; Toledo Museum of Art, 194-5 (detail); *The Torch*, 226 bottom; Turkish Information Center, 28 right, center, 79 top. University Library, Jena, 105; University Library, Uppsala, 65. Vatican Library, 78; Von Matt, 216. Walters Museum of Art, 170; Wide World, 263.